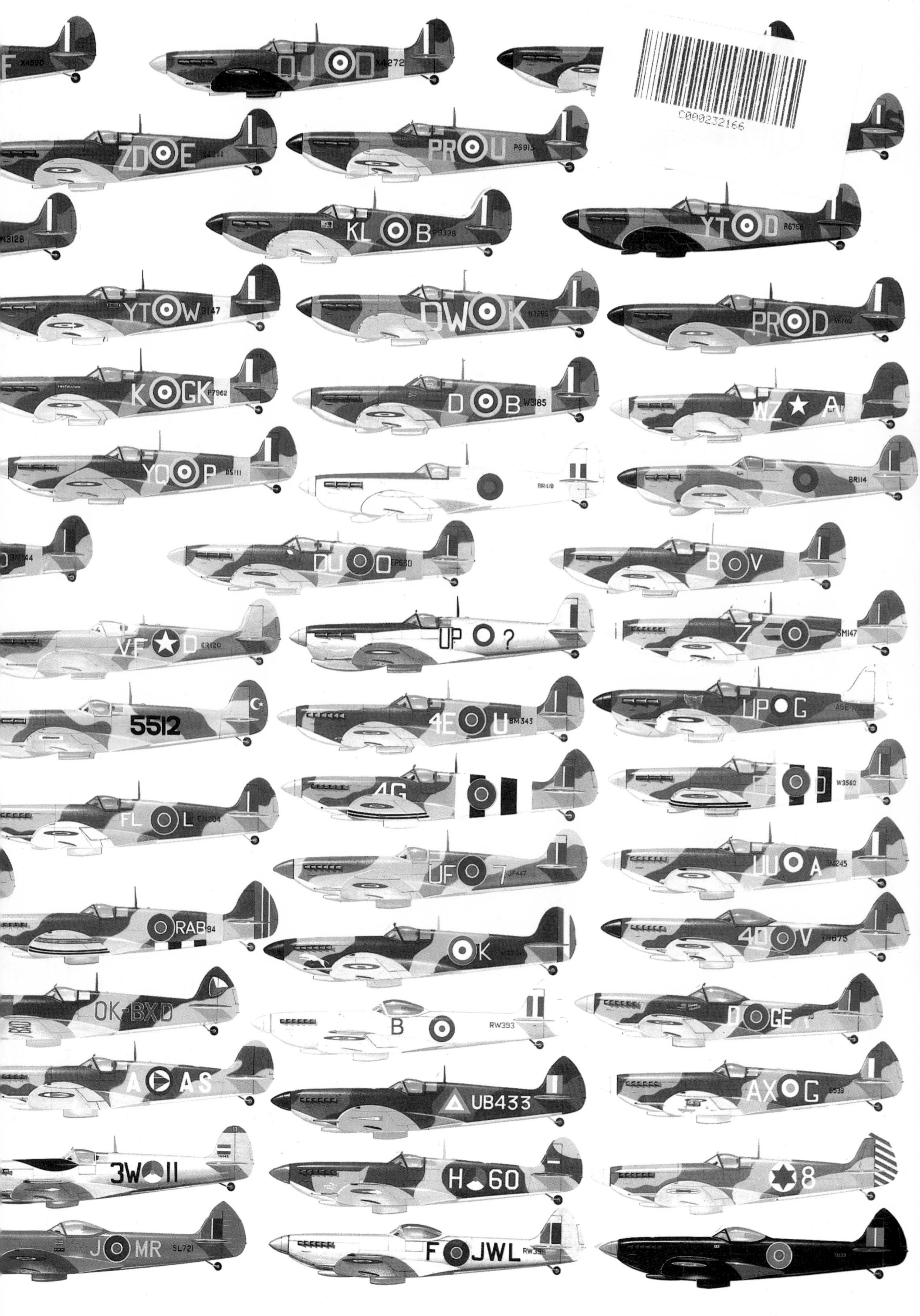
X4590
QJ D
X4272
ZD E
PR U
KL B
YT D
YT W
DW K
PR D
K GK
P7962
D B
W3185
WZ A
YQ P
BR114
DU O
B V
VF D
ER120
UP ?
Z
5512
4E U
BM343
UP G
4G
FL L
EN204
W3560
UF 7
JF447
UU A
RAB
4D V
K
OK-BXD
B
RW393
D GE
A AS
UB433
AX G
3W 11
H 60
8
J MR
SL721
F JWL
RW396

SPITFIRE

THE HISTORY

Eric B. Morgan
and
Edward Shacklady

GUILD PUBLISHING LONDON

Acknowledgements

THE INITIAL spark to the eventual production of Spitfire: The History was struck by Eric Morgan and as the flames grew amateur and professional historians were attracted like moths to a light. They were numerous, too numerous to list in this small space and if we, the authors, have omitted to include a name rest assured that it is remembered with gratitude.

As George Orwell might have said, some contributors were more equal than others and into this category must be included Brian Kervall and Denis Goode of the library at R.A.E. Farnborough. The former was like a ferret in his efforts to root out and digress at length on the thousand and one items linked to the Spitfire. Mention a date or fact hidden in the mist of time and Brian produced an answer. Some of these cannot be published for they are still sensitive, but the majority were nuggets to be treasured. Denis Goode, Chief Librarian, Farnborough, made available the facilities of his library and files of data. He may have trodden on a few toes but the recipients' pain will be forgotten when they recall their contribution to these pages. Freddy Jones discussed, over many cups of tea, his connection with the Spitfire as an accident investigator and there is little doubt that this contribution to the Spitfire as an aeroplane was real.

The library staff of British Aerospace were extremely patient and no doubt heaved a sigh of relief when the last piece of paper had been examined, allowing them to return to their daily duties. The staff at Vickers House, in London, made available the photographic files as did their contemporaries at 'The Aeroplane' and 'Flight'. R.A.E. Boscombe Down contributed in no

This edition published 1988 by Guild Publishing by arrangement with Key Publishing Ltd, P.O. Box 100, Stamford, Lincolnshire, PE9 1XQ, England.

CN 6918

Printed in Great Britain by William Clowes Ltd, Beccles, Suffolk.

SPITFIRE THE HISTORY

mean measure and the computer and its accolytes as at the Public Records Office in Kew were made to work extremely hard in finding, making available records and retrieving them without complaint.

Mike Evans, tucked away at Rolls-Royce, Derby, was sought out and he responded magnificently, as did his colleagues. It is unfortunate that there is not enough space in this book to include the mass of the material gathered on the Spitfire and Merlin/Griffon engines. Perhaps that is a book in itself? Hawker Dynamics at Hatfield opened their files and many historic items were discovered and recorded.

The Spitfire must have been the most photographed fighter ever judging by the record number of illustrations we received. Ted Hooton, RAF Museum, Imperial War Museum, FAA Museum, Michael Gurney, Norman Parker, Freddy Underwood all generously contributed and there were a large number of prints which were anonymous in that they had been passed from hand to hand until the original source could not be traced. If any source is able to identify its work we will be pleased to make the name known eventually.

The RAF Museum in its infancy in 1967 had 50,000 Spitfire drawings "dumped" on them to save them being burned by British Aircraft Corporation at Weybridge, and the help and cooperation is gratefully recorded.

The majority of drawings appearing in these pages were made available from official sources, the Air Ministry giving their authority to use any of the drawings out of the Spitfire Air Publications which saved a lot of work instead of looking for a particular one in the above mentioned 50,000. J.H. (Harry) Robinson was most generous and helpful, making available free use of his line drawings.

Richard Ward produced the end papers and the coloured profiles and we are grateful to him for the hard work he faced with a repetitive view in different guise. We hope he recovers from the ordeal.

Alan Clifton for the microfilms of the Supermarine Technical Reports.

The Air Historical Branch for their assistance when this book was in its infancy 1950-1960.

Jeffrey Quill for additional information in some particular cases, and his foreword.

Norman Parker for his dissertation on the dispersal units.

Derby Childerhouse and staff of British Aerospace Weybridge Photographic Department.

Finally, to all the contributors of fact, photograph, drawing and other information we offer our thanks. Your contribution was welcomed for with it we were able to fill in a large number of gaps in this history. We are not able to record your name but you will recognise where that information made the history recognisable.

Eric Morgan, Horsell, 1986
Edward Shacklady, Sunningdale, 1986

262
261

SPITFIRE THE HISTORY

SEAFIRE

APPENDICES

Left: Spitfires in final assembly at Eastleigh.

Foreword

Synonymous with the Spitfire, Jeffrey Quill played a major part in testing of the prototype during 1936/37 and later, as Chief Test Pilot for Supermarine, was responsible for development flying throughout the aircraft's long career. In more modern times he has been a director of both Sepecat and Panavia, concerned with the Jaguar and Tornado programmes respectively. Now retired, he is president of the Spitfire Society.

THIS is an exceptionally well documented book. Eric Morgan and Edward Shacklady have undoubtedly had access to a unique collection of Supermarine company records, including much correspondence to and from official sources at relevant times during the design and development stages of this much developed aircraft.

They have made full use of the material at their disposal to produce what must be as definitive a history of the Spitfire as is ever likely to be written.

A book so lavishly documented from many original sources poses in itself a problem for the reviewer or a writer of forewords insofar that it is virtually impossible to check such a wealth of detailed information.

Many of the illustrations are unique. It would be possible to criticise the book on the grounds that sometimes it tends to get bogged down under its own weight of detail and perhaps misses some of the broader interpretations. However, the authors are to be congratulated on a most comprehensive and detailed history of the Spitfire.

It is there for those who care to study it. It is not a book for light reading, but will be an essential on the shelves of serious aviation historians, and anyone who wishes to study and be well informed about this remarkable aircraft which was by any standards a great national achievement.

Jeffrey Quill

"IT WILL NOT BE CALLED SPITFIRE"

"Achtung Shrew". The young German aviator's voice rang through the intercom of a Heinkel He111 high over England in that fateful summer of 1940. Seconds later the graceful shape of one of Fighter Command's new interceptors curved into the attack. Fiction? Yes, but it could have been fact, for the name Shrew was one of many suggested for the Supermarine Type 300 fighter before the Air Ministry agreed to adopt the name chosen by Sir Robert McLean, chairman of Vickers (Aviation) Ltd. Sir Robert had demanded that the name of the company's new fighter should suggest something venomous, and because of the sibilant it had to begin with the letter 'S'. His choice was Spitfire* but, as related later in this chapter, the Air Ministry was cool towards the chosen name and not until the prototype F 37/34 had made its maiden flight several years later was Sir Robert's choice agreed to.

Although minor this was not the only decision to affect what was arguably the most successful fighter of World War Two. Many decisions, some more significant than a simple change of name, decided its future. At one time serious consideration was given to cancelling the entire Spitfire programme, with Supermarine building a Gloster design under licence as the first order for 310 Mk I versions was beyond the production capacity of the Southampton factory which, up to the receipt of that first order, had never built more than 25 aircraft to a single contract. Also, the graceful curves of wings and fuselage delayed production as it was difficult to manufacture them to the close tolerances demanded. Fortunately for Britain all design and production problems were resolved by the Supermarine team and a total in excess of 22,500 airframes was eventually constructed.

The Spitfire started life as a gulled winged, fixed undercarriage, four gun, single seat day and night fighter in 1934 and it was to pass through a number of major design changes before its final metamorphosis into the unmistakable shape that is still remembered decades after it took to the air in 1936. It all began in the last months of 1931 when the Air Ministry published Specification F7/30** see Appendix III, page 597 on 1 October, just 18 days after Supermarine's S.6B floatplane (S1595) had won the Schneider Trophy outright for England.

The Specification was a bold move in a plan to provide the Royal Air Force with a modern, front line interceptor which was, in the Air Ministry's edict—"To be on par with any Air Force's equipment by the year 1940". The significance of the pronouncement was to be fully appreciated during the Battle of Britain. The Specification called for a maximum speed of 195mph, reasonable landing speed, good visibility for the pilot by day and night, and an armament of four .303in machine guns (much heavier than contemporary fighters then in service). It also stipulated that the aircraft be constructed entirely of metal, this being in keeping with the Air Ministry's decision, taken in April 1928, to accept all-metal aircraft only for the Royal Air Force.

A copy of the Specification arrived at the Supermarine Woolston factory on 5 November and for R. J. Mitchell, Chief Designer, it was a challenge as it was the company's first venture for ten years into the design of a single seat fighter. Work started immediately and one hundred and six days later, on 20 February 1932, the Supermarine Type 224 design tender arrived at the Air Ministry's offices in Kingsway, London, along with rival designs from Blackburn (F3), Gloster (SS.37 Gladiator), Hawker (PV3) and Westland (PV4), plus a further three from other companies. Of these three were chosen—Blackburn, Westland and Supermarine—and awarded a contract. A letter accompanying the Specification called for (according to Supermarine) (1) a conventional and (2) novel design, the company to choose. Supermarine never revealed which they submitted.

The Air Ministry was pleased with the industry's efforts to F 7/30 for in the report assessing the qualities of the submissions the DACS stated—"This specification has brought out more originality and more serious attempts to meet the operational requirements, in addition to technical needs, than any other preceeding specification and you will see that some of the estimated performances are surprisingly high. None of the Pushers submitted was good enough for selection. You will notice, however, that both the Supermarine and Westland companies show landing speeds in excess of that stipulated. I do not think we should pass this (i) because of the specification (ii) because high stalling speed not only affects night flying adversely but also manoeuvrability (iii) because as time goes on the weights of aeroplanes grow and the landing speeds go up. Fortunately, by increasing slightly the wing area and sacrificing some of the speed we can obtain the required landing speed and I strongly recommend that we should insist upon this at this stage, otherwise we are liable to have day fighting aeroplanes only.

"The order of merit of the best five designs is considered to be—

(1)	Supermarine monoplane	re-rated Kestrel S
(2)	Blackburn Biplane	"
(3)	Parnall Biplane	" shaft extension
(4)	Westland Biplane	" "
(5)	Boulton & Paul monoplane	two Napier S

There are three questions of policy to consider—The best four designs are based on the re-rated Kestrel S which gives 535bhp @ 13,500ft and 2500rpm. This engine is being developed by Rolls and we expect to have it running about September.

"In the two best designs the pilot's view could be improved by using an inverted engine. This engine is being considered by Rolls but no design has been produced, and I think it too early to start designing aircraft for it. I am rather sorry we are not choosing the Boulton & Paul twin because of its retractable undercarriage and its Napier engines. But it does have some undesirable external wiring and would not be a handy fighter. ASMR gives the types of experimental aircraft he proposes to select to meet the four gun, single seat fighter specification, together with his reasons. The comparative table of performance against specification requirements is as follows—

Type	Specification Requirements	Supermarine Monoplane	Blackburn Monoplane
Speed at 15,000ft(mph)	195	244	212
Time to climb to 15,000ft (mins)	8½	7.36	8.32
Landing speed (mph)	60	65	59
	Parnall Biplane	Westland Biplane	Boulton & Paul T E Monoplane
Speed at 15,000ft(mph)	208	204	211.5
Time to climb to 15,000ft (mins)	7.89	7.98	8.7
Landing speed (mph)	59	64	59

"The Supermarine, which has by far the highest performance, is a low wing, cantilever monoplane reminiscent of the Schneider Trophy machines. The view would be much improved on the Blackburn and Supermarine had the inverted engine been ready and it is regretted that when producing the new engine (Goshawk) Rolls-Royce continued with an upright type. I am advised that the inverted type may eventually prove to be necessary if steam cooling is to be successful. I think we ought to press on with development of the inverted engine, so that it can be adopted in later models of these fighters". Rolls-Royce was later to propose an inverted PV12 for the Type 300 Spitfire prototype, but it too was rejected.

Although the DCAS thought well of the submissions to Specification F7/30 he was to be replaced soon after contracts has been awarded, and his replacement was quick to voice dissatisfaction over the Fury replacement—"My predecessor initiated investigation for a Fury replacement and I wish to raise the question whether we require a replacement at all. It could be used as (a) an interceptor fighter (b) a specialised zone fighter.

"As regards (a) the Fury was introduced to test out the principle of employing aircraft of the highest possible performance from advanced aerodromes to intercept enemy aircraft. The system was a failure because it was found that on the inward journey of the enemy a stern chase was ineffectual unless they were seen from the aerodrome. Allowing four

* *The name Shrike was also considered for the prototype F 7/30*

** *see Appendix III, page 597*

minutes under the existing warning system for the Fury to take off, it would have to reach a speed of 270mph in order to successfully intercept. The chances of intercepting an enemy aircraft on the return journey are a matter of luck because of the large area to protect. It has now been agreed that in war the interceptor squadrons are to be stationed in the advanced zone,* and I think that (a) therefore does not arise.

"As regards (b) the number of classes of fighters has risen from two to three owing to the introduction of the two-seat fighter. It is desirable to return to two classes only. I think that a Fury replacement as a third class of zone fighter can only be justified if its rate of climb over that of the day and night fighter is such that its chances of interception are appreciably greater.

"We now have information of predicted performance, and I must ask you to read minutes 8 and 9 which raise the important question of whether a higher octane fuel can be employed with the new engines. The octane value is, in effect, the anti-detonation quality, and as this is raised so can the degree of boost and power output be increased. In order to get comparable figures for predicted performance for the Fury and Bulldog replacement I have assumed that agreement will be given to the introduction of the more efficient fuel. Consultation with technical experts allowed me to produce a table of comparative predicted performances. This is based on the assumption that the Supermarine aircraft now being built will be successful. If it is unsuccessful, or if the high quality fuel is not utilised, all predictions will be optimistic.

	All day fighters except for Bulldog replacement			
	4-gun Bulldog replacement	4-gun Fury replacement	6-gun Fury replacement	8-gun Fury replacement
Max speed @ 15,000ft(mph)	240	265	261	256
Climb to 20,000ft(mins)	8.2	7.8	8.2	8.6
Service ceiling (feet)	38,000	37,500	36,500	35,400
Landing speed (mph)	60	66	66	66
Endurance @ normal rpm(hrs)	2.5	1.7	1.7	1.7

"In effect the Fury replacement is a redesigned Bulldog replacement, the increase in speed and climb being obtained at the expense of endurance and by a reduced area with consequent loss of ceiling and increased landing speed. It will be noted that if the Air Staff proposed requirement of six guns in the Fury replacement is maintained there is no gain in climb. I do not think the improvement in speed alone counterbalances the disadvantages of having a third type of fighter which would be confined to day flying only and one which would have a high landing speed. Before making a decision to proceed with the Fury replacement you may wish to consult ADGB to ask if it would be practicable to make an additional one or two guns as an alternative load to part of the night flying equipment of the Bulldog replacement when it is put into production".

The reply to this argument was soon forthcoming—"The minute argues that because the performance of the single seat day and night fighter and single seat day fighter are verging so closely, there is no justification for the continuation of three separate types of fighter. We need only consider that day phase and take it for granted that if an enemy finds our defence by day is weak, he will be quick to profit by this".

Mitchell and his team had considered numerous studies before selecting three—two with straight, cantilevered wing and one with a cranked wing. All were tested as models in the wind tunnel at Vickers' Weybridge works and results showed the gull wing design to be appreciably better than the other two. The Rolls-Royce Goshawk (a modified Kestrel evaporatively cooled) was selected as the engine for it promised to provide the power necessary to meet the Supermarine Specification for a maximum speed of 249mph. Comparative figures for the three designs were—

Model	1	2	3
Wing	cranked	straight	straight
Condenser	internal	honeycomb	honeycomb
Weight(lbs)	3975	3975	4175
Max speed(mph) @16,000ft	249	243	231
Max rate of climb(ft min)	2650	2560	2260
Time to 15,000ft (mins)	6.6	6.9	7.95
Service ceiling(ft)	43,500	42,000	37,000

The service (and absolute) ceiling of 44,800ft was remarkably high in view of the need for an efficient face mask and oxygen

General arrangements of Type 224 designs as tested by Mitchell in the Vickers, Weybridge, wind tunnel.

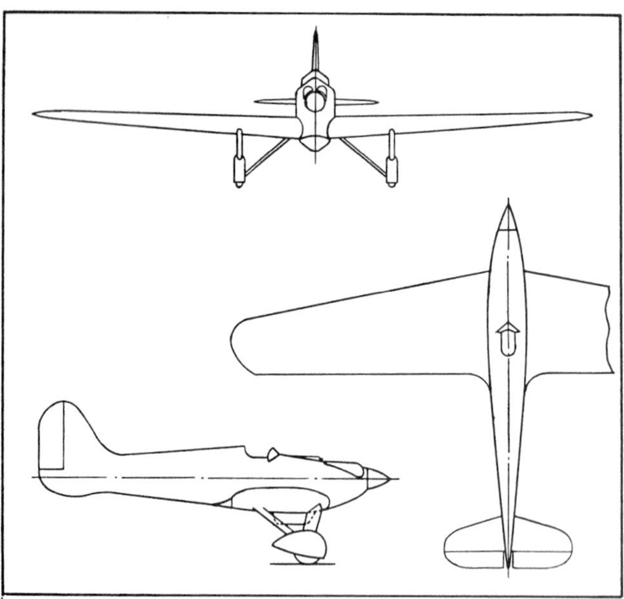

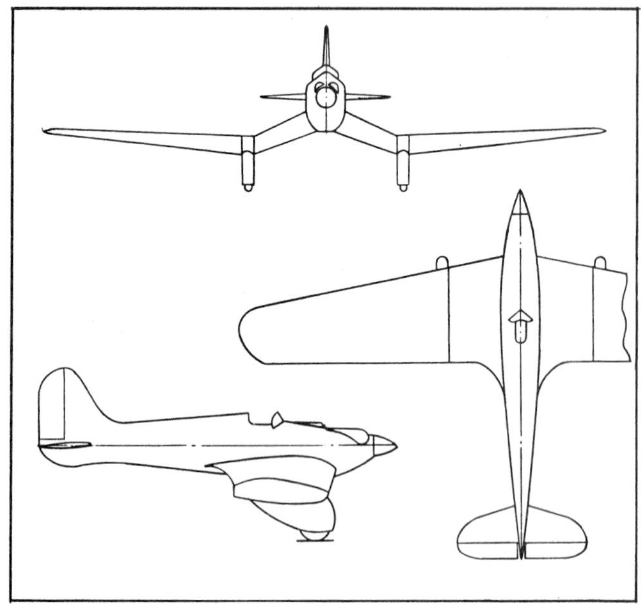

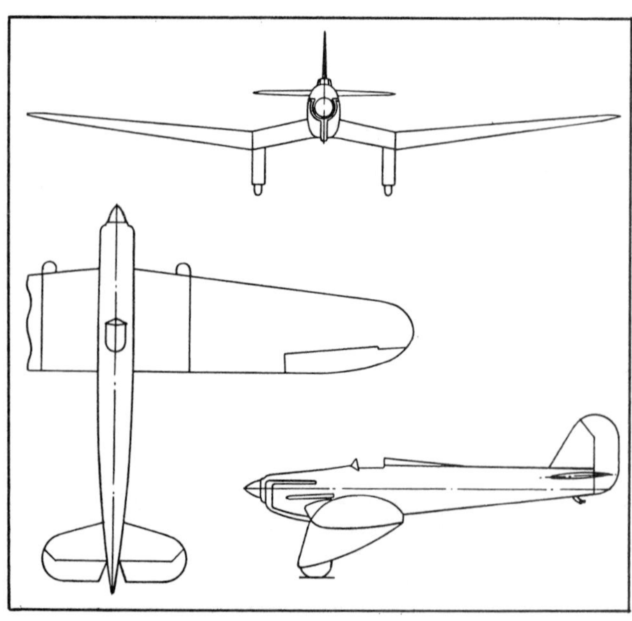

* *not specified*

Wind tunnel models of the Type 178/224.

supply, coupled with an open cockpit.

The complete submission to the Air Ministry for the Supermarine Type 224 (Supermarine Specification No 404) read as follows—

SUPERMARINE SINGLE SEATER MONOPLANE-DAY AND NIGHT FIGHTER A.M SPECN F7/30

ROLLS-ROYCE 'KESTREL' S (INCREASED RATING) ENGINE

Summary of Chief Points in the design.

This aircraft has been designed to fulfil the duties of a Single Seater Day and Night Fighter in accordance with the requirements laid down in the Air Ministry Specification F 7/30. It is a single engine all metal monoplane fitted with the Rolls-Royce 'Kestrel' (increased rating) engine. Although different in type from existing fighter aircraft, it cannot be considered very experimental. It embodies the experience gained by the Supermarine firm in the construction of high speed monoplanes,* and other monoplane types of varying characteristics.

In order to reduce chassis height the wing is bent and this feature greatly improves the pilot's view. The engine is evaporatively cooled, the system incorporating a leading edge condenser. The wing is of single spar type with metal covered leading edge giving torsional stiffness and forming the compartment for the leading edge condenser. This principle of wing construction and cooling system were developed for the Supermarine Six Engine Flying Boat and the results of the experimental work carried out justify the inclusion of these features in the present design. The main characteristics of the aircraft are—

(1) A good performance attained by the inclusion of leading edge evaporative cooling and a Rolls-Royce 'Kestrel' (increased rating) S engine in a clean monoplane design.

(2) An excellent view for fighting, formation work, or landing, due to the 'bent' low wing and small fuselage.

(3) A robust, easily detachable chassis of wide track and a low CG which render the aircraft particularly suitable for night or emergency landings.

(4) Simplicity of construction lending itself to rapid production and easy maintenance.

Artist's impression of the Type 178.

SUMMARY OF PERFORMANCE

All up Weight 3975lbs

	Required by Specn: F7/30	Estimated from Wind tunnel tests
Speed at 15,000ft (mph)	195	245.5
Alighting speed (mph)	60	60
Service ceiling (feet)	28,000	43,500
Time to 15,000ft (mins)	8.5	6.6

AERODYNAMIC AND FLYING QUALITIES

Every effort has been made to keep this aircraft clean. Wind tunnel tests have been carried out on a preliminary model and

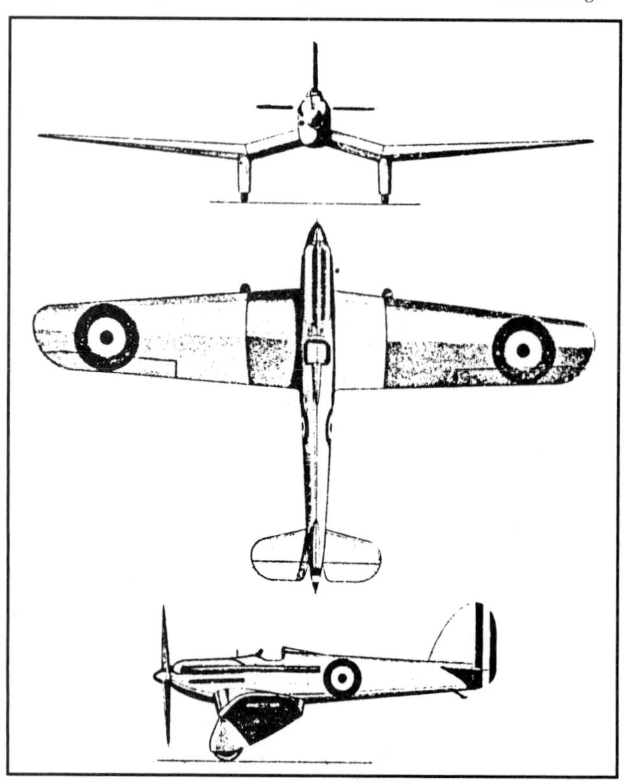

The Type 178 as originally submitted to Specification F 7/30. Supermarine Type No.178 was applied to all miscellaneous drawings

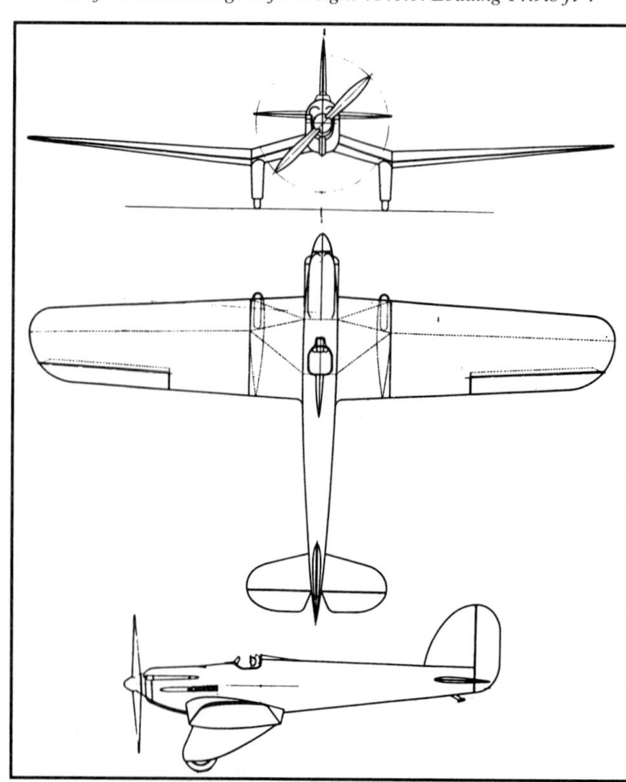

The Type No.224 was given to the first design of the proposed submission to Air Ministry Specification F 7/30 with Kestrel S engine. Span 46ft, chord 7.8ft, area (including fuselage) 300.7ft², aspect ratio 7, section NACA 0018, sweep 1.5°, ailerons 25ft², movement e/w 30°, dihedral 4°. Length 29ft 9in. Height (standing) 8ft 6in. Tailplane (overall) 34.6ft², elevators 12.48ft², movement e/w 30°. Fin and rudder 25.2², rudder 11.6², movement e/w 30°. Propeller diameter 10ft 6in, pitch 12.98ft. Undercarriage 10ft. Weight 4140lb. Loading 14.9lb ft².

* see Appendix VIII, page 619.

indicate that chassis drag and interference are appreciably reduced by bending the wing and reducing the chassis height. As this feature also improves the pilot's view and at the same time provides a natural drain for the wing condensers with very little complication, it has been adopted.

A wing of similar form to the present design was tested for the Six Engine Monoplane Boat in the Duplex Tunnel at the National Physical Laboratory, and gave a maximum L/D of 22.8. It was of RAF 34 basic section and has been modified to suit this design. Special precautions have been taken to reduce the possibility of tail buffetting or loss of longitudinal control near the stall. For this reason the section is modified from the chassis inwards until at the root it is symmetrical, and at a reduced incidence. In addition the sides of the fuselage are flat and fillets are used so that all re-entrant angles are avoided. Finally, the rear portion of the fuselage is of monocoque construction thus ensuring a rigid mounting for the tail unit. It is pointed out that the Vickers Interceptor has a similar disposition of the tail in relation to the root chord, and since being fitted with a monocoque fuselage has proved perfectly satisfactory, both as to control at slow speed and lack of buffetting.* There is, therefore, every reason to anticipate that the present design will prove free from trouble in these respects. The centre of gravity is located well forward at approximately .22 of the chord to make the aircraft sufficiently stable, while adequate control volumes are provided to confer rapidity of manoeuvre.

The wind tunnel tests of the preliminary model showed a 'Rudder' Power; of 13 at 22° incidence against 10 required by A.D Memo No 131. Since this test the effective rudder has been increased so that the rudder control is very powerful indeed. The tail plane is adjustable in flight. The ailerons are of the Frise balance type which give a minimum yawing effect when operated. All control surfaces are mass balanced. The wing is designed to give adequate control and stability below the stall without the aid of slats. To achieve this it has been given wash out so that the tips retain their lift when the centre portion of the wing commences to stall. In this way control is retained until the aircraft is completely stalled. If considered essential slats can be fitted. A further safety feature is that the speed change between best climbing and stalling speeds is very great, due to aerodynamic cleanness, so that there is little danger of accidental stalling, e.g should the engine cut out in climb the risk of stalling is greatly reduced.

On the wind tunnel model the dihedral angle of the outer portions of the wing was adjustable, and tests were carried out to determine the correct angle for the outer portions to provide suitable lateral stability for an aircraft of this type.

NIGHT OR EMERGENCY LANDING

The aircraft is very well adapted for emergency or night landing purposes. The air brake facilitates a steep angle of descent while the low CG and wide wheel track minimise the possibility of overturning even when it is necessary to use the full power of the wheel brakes either to pull up or swing the aircraft. It is anticipated that the wing will prove to have high maximum lift when landing owing to the close proximity to the ground. If in spite of these advantages the aircraft should overturn, it will rest upon the fin and engine. The bulkhead behind the pilot is specially strengthened to take the shock after the fin has buckled and the fuselage panels on each side of the pilot's shoulders are hinged in order to make it possible for the pilot to crawl out whilst the aircraft is still inverted. These panels also facilitate a quick exit when a parachute descent is necessary.

VIEW

Specification F 7/30 draws attention to the necessity for a good fighting view such as the low wing monoplane provides. For this reason the fuselage had been kept as fine a possible forward, and in conjunction with 'bent' wing permits an extremely good view downwards and forwards on each side. It should be noted that in the tail down position the pilot without moving his head from the centre, can see the ground approximately 70 feet in front of the wheels. With the fuselage horizontal the pilot can see the ground 60 feet ahead over the centre line of the aircraft with the seat in normal position. It is contended that the view provided is exceptional, whether for fighting, formation flying, or landing.

EQUIPMENT AND ARMAMENT

The pilot's seat is adjustable vertically and is arranged to take a seat type parachute. The flying controls embody the split stick type of control column for ailerons and elevator in order to obtain fullest control without restricting the freedom of movement of the pilot. A pivoted rudder bar and a handwheel for adjusting the incidence of the tailplane are used, the rudder pedals being adjustable to suit pilots of different heights. Palmer wheel brakes are fitted, capable of independent operation for steering and also provided with a control for locking the brakes in the 'on' position.

Cockpit heating is provided for by allowing a supply of warm air controlled by the pilot to enter near the pilot's feet. The heating is obtained from the leading edge condenser so that no possible danger can arise from leakage.

The armament consists of either 4 Vickers guns, or 2 Vickers guns and 2 Lewis guns. Two Vickers guns are mounted in the cockpit with link and empty case chutes emptying through the fuselage fairings on either side. The two guns are controlled through C.C gear by a thumb lever in the centre of the control column spade grip, and the ammunition boxes have a capacity of 600 rounds each. The remaining two guns are located in the chassis fairing and may be either Vickers type, or Lewis type with 400 round drums. These guns are outside the propeller disc and do not, therefore, require C.C gear.

They are controlled by a second thumb lever in the spade grip. It is considered that the chassis guns will be kept sufficiently warm by the adjacent hotwell of the evaporative cooling system. Attention has been paid to the provision of a rigid mounting whilst allowing the necessary adjustment in order that the lines of fire may be altered to converge at any given range. Provision is made for the installation of a ring and bead sight on the centre line of the aircraft and a standard reflector sight. The pilot is provided with a signal pistol and 8 cartridges mounted in a readily accessible position.

The 4 × 20lb bombs are carried in the wing behind the spar. They are half sunk in the wing in order to reduce resistance to a minimum while allowing their release in a steep dive. The electrical equipment provides for lighting, wing tip flares, etc, the power supply being derived from an engine driven generator. The wireless equipment is carried behind the pilot and is operated by remote control. The fixed aerial runs from the box rib at the inner end of the aileron to the top of the fin post. The oxygen supply is carried below the seat. Accessibility of the equipment is ensured by the arrangement of the cowling in detachable panels.

STRUCTURE (a) WING

The wing of this aircraft achieves a high degree of aerodynamic efficiency with a simple robust construction. It is designed to have great stiffness both flexural and torsional and to comply with Specification requirements for strength. The constructional principles are the same as those developed for the wing of the Six Engine Monoplane Flying Boat for which a great deal of test work had been completed. It will, therefore, be possible to produce the proposed design with a minimum of delay for experimental work.

The wing is a full cantilever with each side built in two sections—an inner section which attaches to the fuselage and has anhedral and an outer portion which has dihedral. The chassis is attached at the joint between the two sections.

The spar construction has been arranged with the specific object of permitting the use of M.G.7 alloy* should the tests which are being carried out confirm the suitability of this material. Alternatively, Duralumin can be used without any alteration of form, and the weight estimate is based upon this material. The spar flanges consist of a number of strips connected by angles to a single sheet web with pressed vertical corrugations.

The wing forward of the spar in the case of the outer sections is covered with corrugated sheet riveted to spar flanges, leading edge, and ribs. The resultant D section box is an extremely rigid structure and forms at the same time the steam cooling chamber. In the case of the inner sections an oil tank and cooler replaces the condenser immediately adjacent to the fuselage, and a rigid diagonal bracing member is provided which contributes greatly to the torsional stiffness of the wing, and provides a support for the petrol tank. The trailing portion of the wing consists throughout of normal type ribs with channel section flanges and tubular bracing, the covering being fabric.

The prevention of wing flutter is aimed at firstly by mass balancing the ailerons, which it is believed has so far never failed as a remedy; secondly, the construction adopted with its high orders of stiffness in flexure and torsion, and its forward axes of inertia flexure, conforms more nearly to the recommendations of R. & M. 1177 than any known alternative of construction.

** This illustrates the cooperation between Mitchell and R. K. Pierson, Designer at Weybridge.*

** Mitchell's reference to M. G. 7 is most interesting and its use for fabrication of F7/30 was mentioned at the first meeting of the Aviation Design Committee, held at Weybridge on Monday 11 January 1932. During discussions on the various aircraft and projects under consideration Mitchell proposed approaching the Air Ministry to obtain permis-*

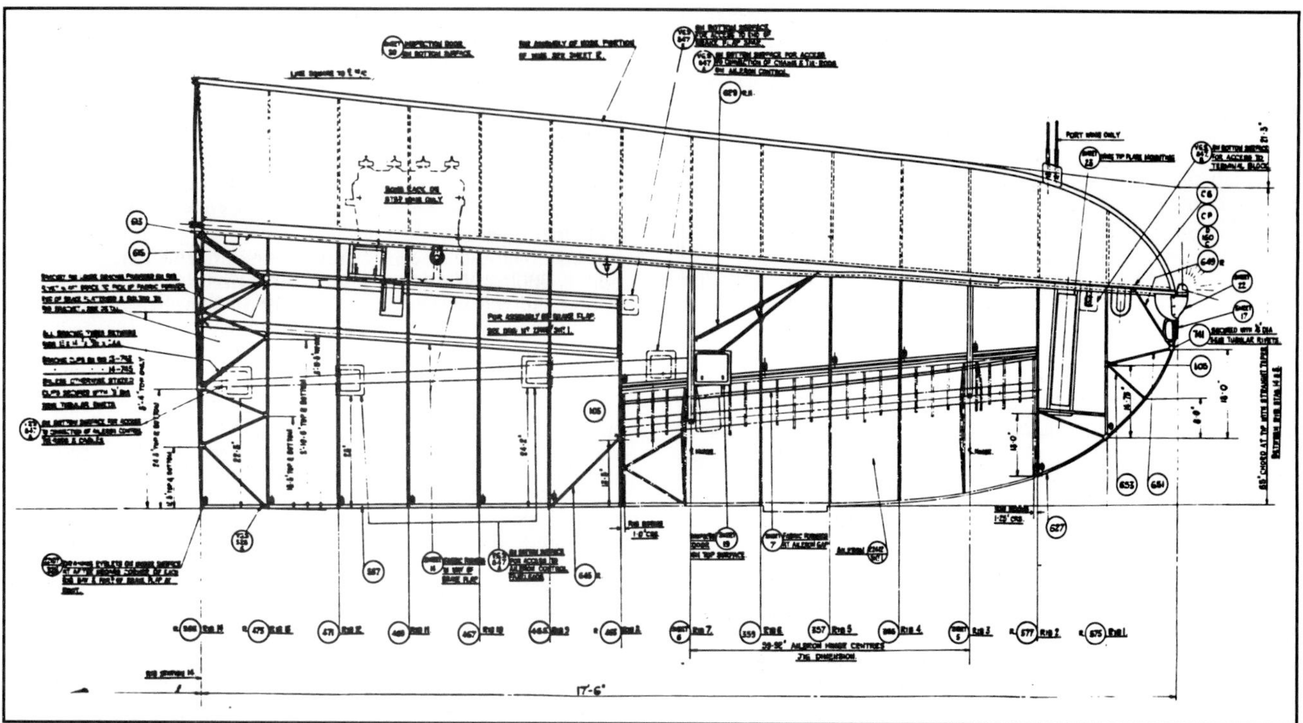

Wing construction. Dihedral 6.5°, incidence -2° at root twisting to -½° at tip. These angles were eventually adopted for the Type 300.

The weight estimate of 530lbs for this wing is based on careful analysis and calculation of the sizes of members, and is considered to be a conservative figure.**

(b) FUSELAGE

The fuselage is constructed in three sections. The forward section extends from the nose to the after end of the pilot's cockpit. It is a braced structure built up of steel tubes and covered with detachable panels. The second section extends to the front spar of the tailplane and is of monocoque construction. This type of construction has been found to be the most satisfactory for providing a rigid mounting for the tail unit and for the prevention of tail flutter. The aftermost portion of the fuselage consists of a braced section carrying the tail skid. Thus in the event of tail skid failure the monocoque portion of the fuselage will not be damaged and the affected portion can quickly be replaced. At the same time the tail trimming gear, controls, etc, are rendered immediately accessible by removing panels.

(c) TAIL UNIT

The tail surfaces are of a cantilever type. The elevator and rudder are statically balanced in order to minimise the risk of tail flutter. The fin and tailplane are not built integral with the fuselage and are easily replaceable in the event of damage.

(d) CHASSIS

The chassis is of the fixed type but its resistance has been considerably reduced by dispensing with the usual strut and wire bracing. It incorporates a Standard Vickers Oleo leg and is attached to the wing at four points and the connection at the top of the Oleo leg. It is, therefore, very easily replaceable in the event of damage. The wheels are fitted with knock-out axles and the removal of the nose fairings allows the wheel to be run out

Section view of engine mount. The long chord exhaust pipe was eventually shortened.

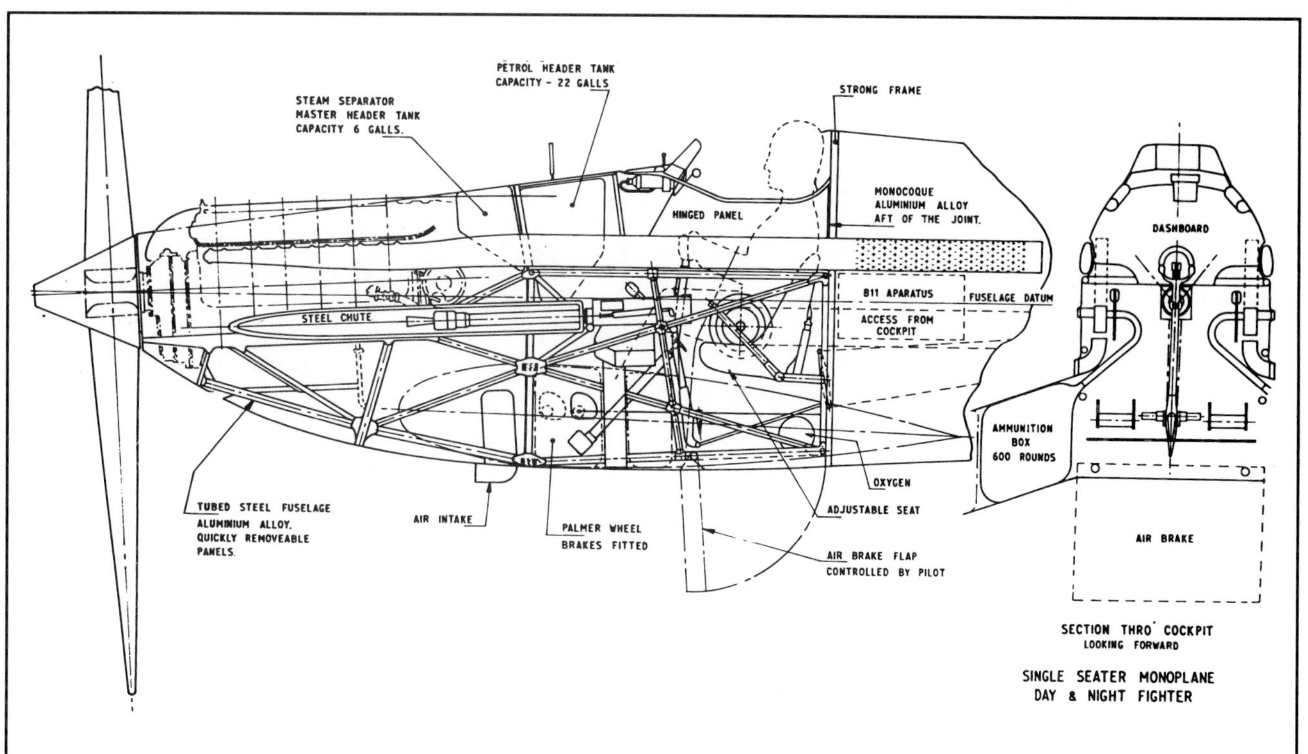

sion to plate (affix the outside skin) one Southampton flying boat with the metal for trial purposes. He said the materials had been in use in Germany for many months and technical reports suggested it could no longer be regarded as experimental.

*** During the ninth meeting of the committee the question arose of how wing loading, stalling speed and efficiency of wing section would affect manoeuvrability. The chairman (McLean) said that the trimming flap was becoming common procedure in aircraft, and if the company could get a patent on such a system with a differential movement it would be worth*

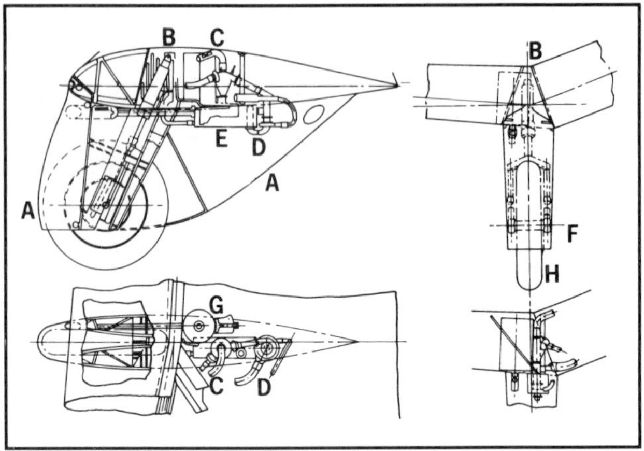

Details of undercarriage: (A) detachable front and rear fairings (B) oleo leg (C) steam separator (D) turbine and pump (E) hotwell (F) knock-out axle (G) machine gun (H) 600x80 tyre.

forwards. The wheel is mounted in a fork which slides between the two built up forks attached to the wing.

Although the wing design is suited to the incorporation of a retractable chassis, it is preferred to regard this as a probable future development rather than add such an experimental feature at this stage to an aircraft otherwise straightforward in design.

POWER PLANT (a) ENGINE

The engine is a Rolls Royce 'Kestrel' S (increased rating) developing a normal output of 535 bhp at 2500rpm at 13,000ft.

(b) PETROL SYSTEM

The petrol supply is 92 gallons—sufficient for ½ hour at full throttle at sea level and 2 hours full throttle at 15,000ft. It is carried in three tanks—a gravity tank of 22 gallons situated in the top of the fuselage and two wing tanks, each of 35 gallons capacity situated in the wing roots. The gravity fuel supply is sufficient for 40 minutes flight at rated boost and normal rpm. The wing fuel is lifted from the wing tanks to the gravity tanks by engine driven pumps, the overflow being returned to the wing tanks. The pilot is provided with a flow indicator in the overflow pipes. It should be noted that this system is similar to that used with complete success on the S.5 and S.6 aircraft, but the suction lift from the wing tank to the header tank is approximately halved in the Fighter Aircraft.

(c) OIL SYSTEM

The oil tank forms the leading edge of the wing at the root and incorporates a surface cooler with a bypass valve which short circuits the cooler until it has been cleared of cold oil. In order to heat the oil for quick take-off from cold the tank is divided so that only a small part of the oil comes into circulation at first. In addition hot water from the separator is circulated through a coil in the tank and also through a heater which jackets the oil supply to the engine. The heating water can be shut off as soon as the oil is warm. If preferred an electric immersion heater can be fitted.

Oil system diagram, capacity 5gals.

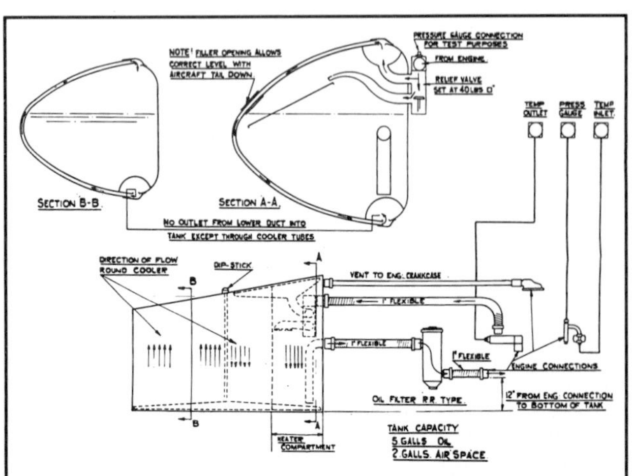

while. Pierson (Chief Designer Vickers) was asked to look into the matter. Some progress was made with this flap for at the next meeting McLean asked Mitchell if he would look into Mr Wallis's (Assistant Designer Vickers) new differential flap in connection with its possible use in the new day and night fighter under construction at Southampton.

(d) COOLING SYSTEM

An evaporative cooling system is fitted. The steam separator is mounted directly behind the engine outlets and the steam is led thence to the leading edge of the wing. The steam chamber is formed by the spar and metal covered leading edge. The condensate drains to a hotwell at the lowest part of the wing and is returned to the header tank by two turbine driven pumps, the turbines being driven by the steam supply from the engine. Alternatively, the engine hotwell pump can be used. If preferred a normal type of honeycomb condenser can be fitted under the fuselage, the increase in weight of the aircraft being approximately 200lbs. Wind tunnel tests show that the increased weight and resistance results in a sacrifice of 12mph top speed and 300ft min climb.

(e) ENGINE ACCESSORIES, ETC.

Provision is made for the installation of the RAE Mark II starter and for the attachment of a compressor type engine starter. A wooden airscrew is supplied but provided that suitable types are available a metal airscrew can be fitted. An

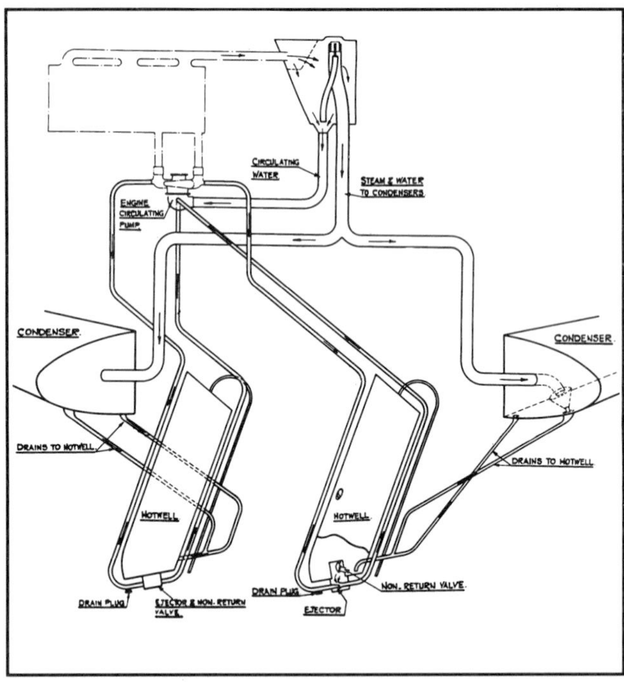

Goshawk engine evaporative cooling system. Distribution of coolant in system was – cylinder block 2¾gals, header tank 2½, hotwells 4; total 9¼gals.

Construction of leading edge. Lower view shows spar construction.

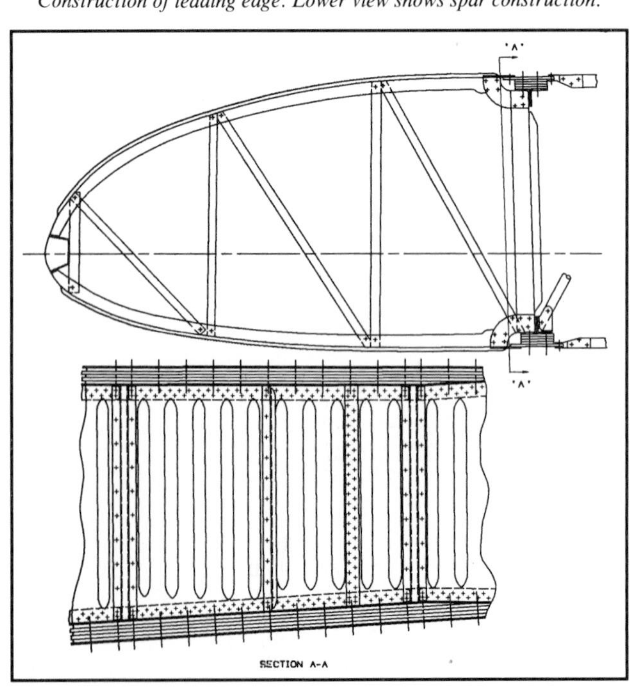

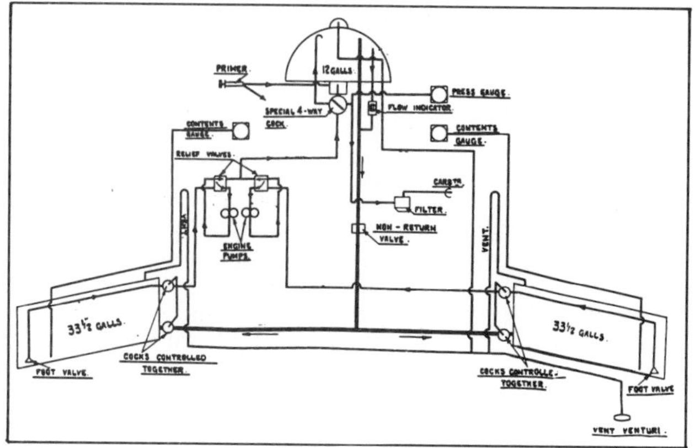

Petrol system diagram – fuselage tank 12gals, plus 33½ in each wing.

exhaust manifold is fitted, with tail pipes to provide adequate silencing and flame damping.

SUITABILITY FOR RAPID AND EASY PRODUCTION IN QUANTITY

This question has received careful consideration throughout the design. The braced part of the fuselage is very simply constructed of steel tubes connected by plate gussetts, while the monocoque portion consists of panels curved in one plane only, thus eliminating hand forming. The wing construction is very straightforward indeed. Once the necessary jigs are made the majority of parts can be produced very economically. As soon as any quantity are built a monoplane, provided it is of simple design, scores over a biplane on account of the absence of complicated wiring lugs and strut attachments which require accurate positioning.

MAINTENANCE, ACCESSIBILITY, TRANSPORT AND STORAGE

For ordinary routine service maintenance many advantages are apparent. For example, rigging is eliminated. The petrol and oil tanks are very accessible and quickly removable. Greasers are grouped as far as possible. All cowling and fuselage covering forward of the pilot's seat is arranged in large and easily detachable panels. The removal of this cowling lays bare the whole of the engine installation and the fuselage equipment. The engine can be lifted straight out after breaking the usual connections. There are no obstructions in the monocoque portion of the fuselage which is thus easily inspected. The tail portion has removable panels to facilitate inspection and repair of the tail skid and tail controls. The controls themselves are straight lengths of cable and should, therefore, need no attention apart from taking up stretch, etc. To enable the inside of the leading edge condenser to be inspected, handholes are provided at suitable intervals in the covering.

The whole design had been evolved with the possibility in view of using M.G. 7 alloy. The use of this material, combined with stainless steel where necessary and efficiently insulated, would render the aircraft practically non-corrosive. For transport, storage, or replacement of damaged parts, the aircraft can be divided into convenient units. Thus the fuselage consists of three portions while each wing is readily disconnected from the fuselage and each chassis component from the wing. At the cost of a certain amount of added complication and weight, a further detachable joint can be incorporated in each wing at the chassis attachment if desired. In the event of damage, therefore, any part of the aircraft is easily replaced, while the simplicity of construction facilitates field repairs to minor damage.

MAIN DIMENSIONS, WEIGHTS AND PARTICULARS

(1) Main dimensions. Span 44ft 0in, length overall 27ft 9in, height (on ground) 8ft 6in, root chord 7ft 6in, wing area (inc fuselage) 264 sq ft. Area of tailplane and elevator 28.7 sq ft, area of fin and rudder 22.80sq ft. Track of chassis 11ft 1in. Diameter of propeller 10ft 6in.

(2) Weight summary. Empty 2545 lbs, military load 660lbs, petrol 710lbs, oil 60lbs, total 3975lbs. Wing loading 15lbs sq ft. Power loading (on rated power) 7.43lbs/bhp.

(3) Engine data. The data assumed for the Rolls-Royce 'Kestrel' S engine has been taken from a folder issued by Messrs Rolls-Royce dated 12-1-32. Rated altitude 13,500ft, rated boost pressure-½lbs sq in, normal rpm 2500 - not to be exceeded on climb. max rpm 3000, bhp on climb at rated altitude 535bhp to 3,500ft, max bhp at rated boost pressure 600 bhp at 16,000ft, gear ratio .55:1, weight complete 950lbs.

Fuel consumption. Specific consumption at operational height .52 pts/bhp/hr. consumption for ½hr at rated boost & normal rpm @ sea level 15 gals. Oil consumption 8pts/hr. It is stated that the above figures have received tentative approval of R. D. E. Air Ministry.

Predicted Performances. The performances for the final aircraft from the wind tunnel tests are (all up weight 3,975lbs):

Standard height (ft)	Level speed (mph)	rate of climb (ft min)	Time to height (mins)
0	195	2500	1.96
4500	210	2090	5.75
13500	241	2650	6.75
16000	249	2350	8.58
20000	246	1945	11.41
25000	242	1490	15.31
30000	236	1075	21.00
35000	229	680	

The new Supermarine project was a sophisticated design and many of its unique features were to be utilised in aeroplanes which followed years later. It was accepted by the Air Ministry, along with the Westland PV4 and Blackburn F3, and a Contract 189222/32 to the value of £8,400.13s.0d was received by the company on 2 August 1932 for a single prototype. Almost at the same time the serial number—K2890—and schedule arrived and progress stage payments were—ailerons and tail unit 20% of total, fuselage structure 20%, undercarriage made, engine and instruments fitted 25%, aircraft painted 15%, after delivery and acceptance 20%.

During the second meeting of the Design Committee, attended by Mitchell, Barnes Wallis and 'Mutt' Summers, Mitchell mentioned wheel brakes for the F 7/30 which Pierson, also present, suggested should be of the Palmer steerable type. Sir Robert McLean (in the chair) wanted to know if the condenser system could be tested as it had been specified for the prototype. It was agreed that if the design submission was approved by the Air Ministry the system "could probably be tried out then, but as there were no previous results to go upon it could not be said definitely whether or not the system would be a success". It was then proposed that a mock-up be built and McLean agreed for work to begin immediately and an estimate of costings prepared.

At the third meeting, held 3 March 1932, Mitchell again referred to the condenser system saying he was going to conduct ground tests on a sample piece of spar. The alloy M.G.7 was again examined and it was agreed that a complete Southampton hull be constructed using the material. Barnes Wallis, however, thought that provided proper shop methods were observed there was little danger of corrosion in duralumin. McLean, although agreeing that the Southampton hull be built of M.G.7, expressed the view that reports on the metal were not encouraging. Wallis agreed, and said although he was hopeful of the results of trials he did not think it was ready for commercial use. The trials, apparently, proved negative for no further mention was made of the alloy and the prototype F 7/30 was structured from duralumin.**

During the sixth meeting (16-6-32) McLean told Mitchell to prepare a model of the new fighter for trials in the Weybridge wind tunnel. Mitchell asked if it would be possible for the air flow behind the wings to be traced to find where the 'burbling' started.

At the next meeting at Weybridge, in a reply to McLean, Mitchell said he had not received from the Air Ministry the modifications they had promised to send him concerning F 7/30. McLean asked the Committee Secretary (General W. B. Caddell) to enquire into the matter. Caddell's action resulted in a letter from F. E. Cowlin (Air Ministry) who wrote to Mitchell on 13 July and said—"I understand you are worried about the F7/30 because you are not clear as to whether certain

***An informal meeting to discuss the new alloy was next held at Southampton on 3 February with Pierson and Wallis of Vickers, and Black of Supermarine, present. Dr Aitchinson of J. Booth represented the metal fraternity. Dr Aitchinson said there was no evidence of any intercrystalline corrosion but the alloy was reduced in strength by heating to 100°C. He also said that by over hardening by rolling, then tempering back to 125°C, the metal would meet the specification figures. Cold working could produce problems and a major draw back was that material and labour costs were much higher than those of duralumin. It was considered that the time was not right for switching over to the new alloy.*

A twenty day corrosion test in sea water was also carried out, and comparisons with Alclad and Duralmin revealed that M. G. 7 was affected to a greater extent than the other two metals. Of the three Alclad was far superior in many areas.

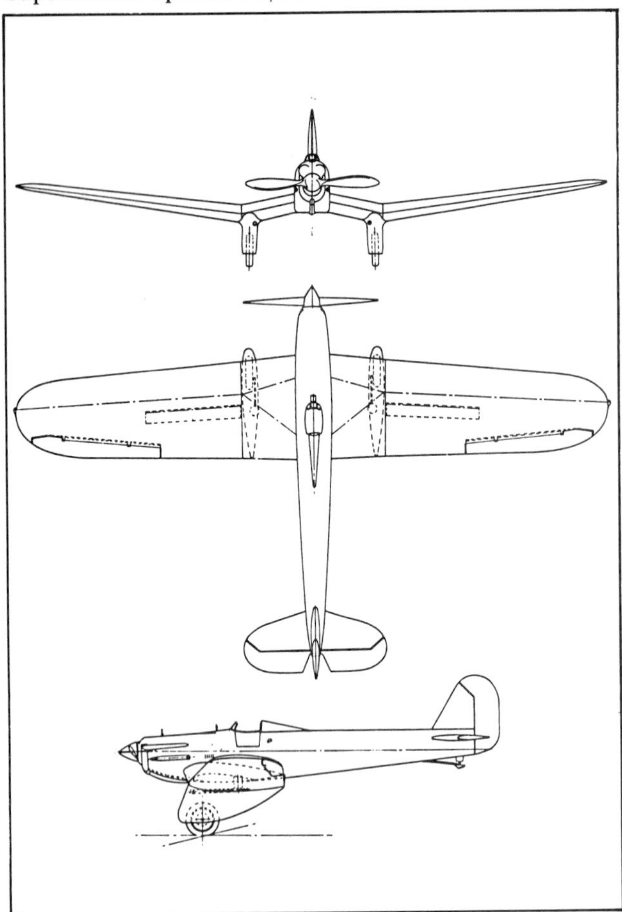

First revision of Type 224, 20 February 1933 illustrates the great changes made to the design. All particulars as original design except for tailplane area 30.6² (excluding elevators), rudder area 25.2ft², weight 4,950lb, loading 17.85lb ft².

unspecified alterations are to be considered before the mock-up is constructed. I have enquired into this and find that the items you list were standard equipment not likely to affect the mock-up. You are quite safe to go ahead and construct the mock-up".

A revised design was issued by Supermarine on 14 July because the Air Ministry considered that the wing loading of 15lb sq ft was too high. Mitchell increased the aircraft's overall size by 12% at the Air Ministry's request, whilst retaining the original shape. The following table compares both original and revised aircraft and it shows that wing loading was reduced to just over 13lb sq ft.

	Original	Revised
Span (ft/in)	44.0	46.0
Length (ft/in)	27.9	29.9
Height (on ground ft/in)	8.6	8.6
Root chord	7.6	7.10
Wing area (inc fuselage) (sq ft)	264	300.7
Tailplane & elevator area (sq ft)	28.7	34.6
Elevator (sq ft)		12.48
Fin & rudder area (sq ft)	22.33	25.2
Rudder (sq ft)		11.6
Aileron area (total)	25.80	32
Chassis track (ft/in)	11.1	10.1
Propeller diameter (ft/in)	10.6	10.6
Cooling area (sq ft)	163	165
Weight (lbs)	3975	4020
Wing loading (lb sq ft)	15	13.41
Power loading (lbs bhp)	7.43	7.51
Aspect ratio		7

But, maximum speed was reduced by 5mph and the design cancelled. On 1 September a third, modified design was considered in an attempt to reduce what was again thought to be a high wing loading. This design was to utilise the Bristol Hydra engine and comparative figures are shown above right.

At a meeting with Mr Ellor of Rolls-Royce on 19 October various matters concerning the engine installation were discussed and it was agreed that the area of 154 sq ft available for steam cooling was adequate for English summer conditions. It was also agreed that the best position for reserve water was the wing root sump and six gallons considered adequate. The

	Present design	Similar to present design	Aircraft as tendered	Wind tunnel figures quoted in tender
Engine	Kestrel	Hydra	Kestrel	Kestrel
Span (ft in)	46	55	44	44
Length (ft in)	29.9	31	27.9	27.9
Wing area (sq ft)	280	388	245	244
Auw (lbs)	4020	5585	3875	3975
Propeller (all 10ft 6in dia)	2-blade	3-blade	2-blade	2-blade
Max speed(mph) @ 15,000ft	140	215	245.5	245.5
Rate of climb @ 10,000ft (ft/min)	2080	2050	2200	2600
Wing loading (lb sq ft)	14.35	14.35	15.6	16.3
Power loading (lb max hp)	6.7	6.56	6.45	6.63

This design, too, was abandoned.

system was to be filled from the header tank and distribution was (on ground) engine 4¾gals, header tank 2½gals, wing sumps 4½gals. Steaming in flight, engine 3½gals, header tank 2gals, wing sumps 5½gals. Total water carried 11gals, reserve 6gals. Provision was to be made for inverted flight and both header tank and wing sumps were to be modified using the 'unspillable inkwell' principle. Warning devices indicating water level and escaping steam from wing tip vents were to be fitted, and it was also agreed that two hot well pumps were necessary. The bottom of the Goshawk crankcase was to be finned to increase heat dissipation. the nose ring of the engine was to heat air entering louvres for cooling the crankcase, and the short stub exhausts were to be modified as it was thought they would result in the pipes burning out.

By November 1932 detail design was well advanced and minor changes incorporated, including a lengthened and widened cockpit, steam cooling confined to the outer wing sections, these being of RAF 34 aerofoil changing to NACA 0018 at the fuselage. RAE Farnborough was conducting spinning trials of models in addition to free flight tests of two, 1/24th scale models. Fin and rudder sizes were tested and the tailplane

Various fin and rudder designs were tested in the Farnborough wind tunnel, December 1932. Top 13.2ft², (rudder 11.1), middle 8.7 (7.4), bottom 9.75 (9.9).

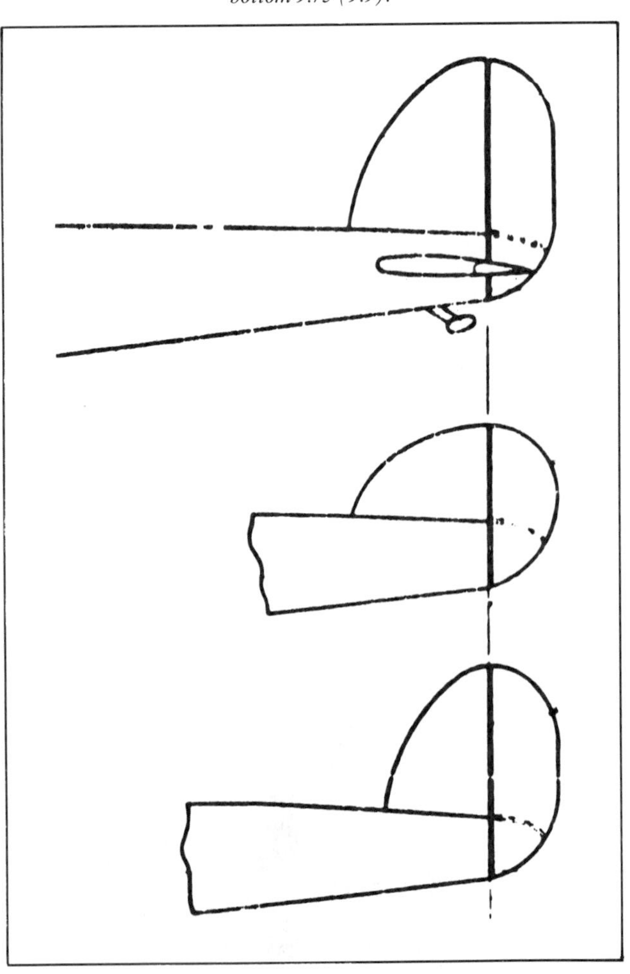

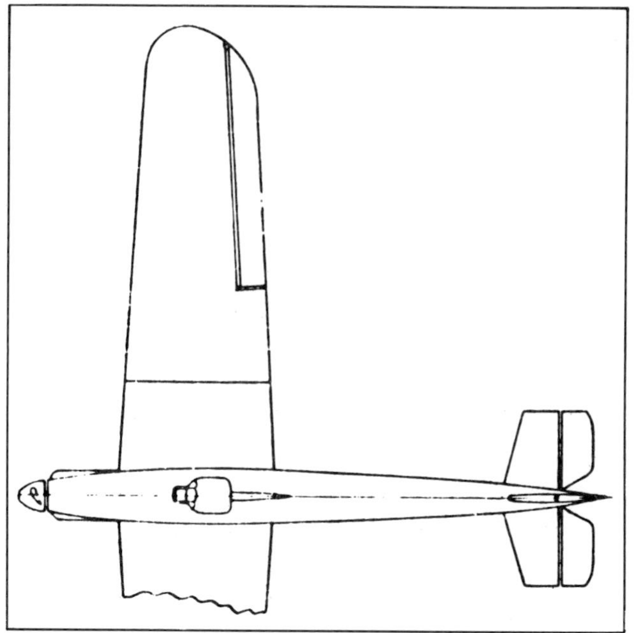

Following spinning tests at Farnborough the tailplane of K2890 was cropped at the tips. A model was then tested in the wind tunnel, July 1935.

position varied, but under no circumstances could a flat spin be induced. The complete wing, when built, was to be tested in a specially built rig by RAE.

Progress with the mock-up was slow and Cowlin wrote to Mitchell on 30 December expressing concern, and to ask for the return of a mock-up Goshawk engine to enable other manufacturers to use it for their designs. Mitchell wanted to retain this mock-up in order that bearer design could be completed. The Air Staff's private opinion at that time was that Supermarine were designing the F 7/30 around the Goshawk.

Wind tunnel tests at Vickers, Weybridge, on 1/16th scale models were urgently required as the design of the prototype was being held up pending results. Weathercock stability tests were asked for on the original fin and rudder, and on a smaller version, with engine on and off. Also needed was determination of the outer wing dihedral for lateral stability, plus the consequences of using a smaller size of outer wing panels. As a result of these tests the wing was swept back at the tip to 26.5in from the original sweep of 14.5in, and dihedral increased from 4° to 6½° at tip. The inner portion's anhedral was also increased.

By March 1933 Mitchell was not entirely satisfied with the new design and a series of investigations was initiated to ascertain the effect of wing loading and high altitude performance. For comparison he used the F 7/30, a smaller monoplane and two biplanes and an analysis of the results showed that for every pound per square foot increase in wing loading an aircraft's ceiling dropped by an average of 600 feet for monoplanes and 700 for biplanes. General conclusions were for high altitude performance a low wing loading was of more advantage than small size of aircraft; a monoplane of normal aspect ratio will have a better altitude performance than the normal biplane. High wing loading may lead to successful high altitude performance if the aspect ratio is high enough, and there appeared to be an optimum wing loading for maximum speed. The table below lists the conclusions.

Machine	14M	22M	13.6B	22B
Span (ft)	46	36	34 (upper)	26 (upper)
Area (sq ft)	295	180	283	166
Auw (lb)	4149	3960	3840	3650
Aspect ratio	7.2	7.2	4.5 (effective)	4.5 (effective)
Power loading (lb hp)	6.46	6.2	6	5.7
Max speed (mph @ 15,000ft)	239	247	232	227
Landing (mph)	60	75.3	60	76.2
Ceiling (ft absolute)	38,800	34,100	34,700	28,800

Monoplane (M). The ceilings were calculated for two versions of the F 7/30, viz-14M wing loading (14lb sq ft) of the actual machine; 22M with increased wing loading (22lb sq ft).

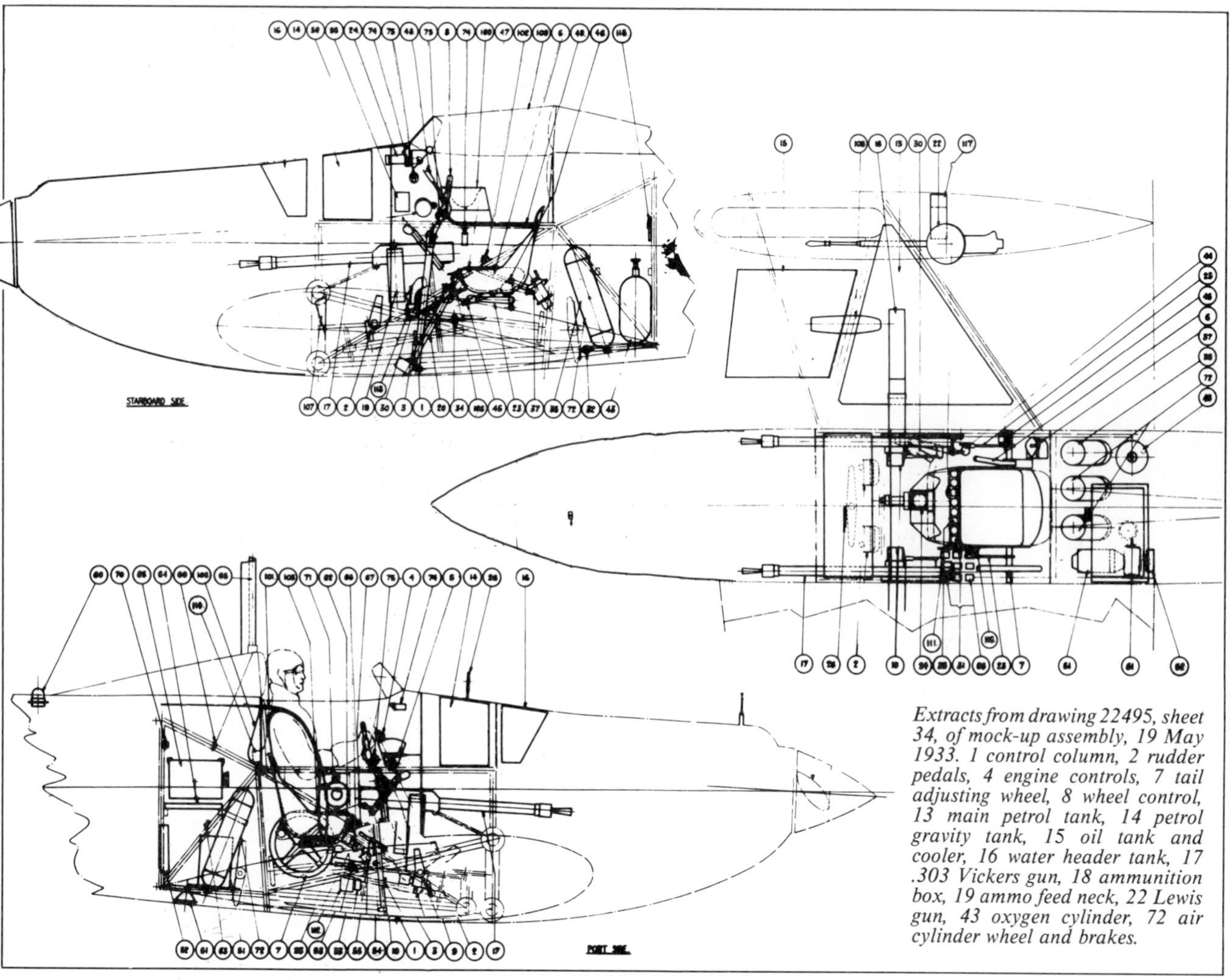

Extracts from drawing 22495, sheet 34, of mock-up assembly, 19 May 1933. 1 control column, 2 rudder pedals, 4 engine controls, 7 tail adjusting wheel, 8 wheel control, 13 main petrol tank, 14 petrol gravity tank, 15 oil tank and cooler, 16 water header tank, 17 .303 Vickers gun, 18 ammunition box, 19 ammo feed neck, 22 Lewis gun, 43 oxygen cylinder, 72 air cylinder wheel and brakes.

Biplane (B). The ceilings were calculated for two versions of the F 7/30 Biplane (Specn No 405), viz- 13.6B with wing loading of Specn No 405 (13.6lb sq ft); 22B with increased wing loading (22lb sq ft).

The mock-up conference took place at Woolston on 20 April with Mitchell, Joseph Smith (Supermarine Deputy Designer), RAF and RAE personnel in attendance and production of the prototype approved. By 6 November the finalised design was 95% complete, construction of components 75%, main assembly 50%; but Supermarine was still waiting for an embodiment loan of the Goshawk. Doubts about delivery of this engine had been expressed by Rolls-Royce in July 1932 because of the many unexpected problems that had arisen during development, and when the prototype aeroplane was fully assembled at the end of November 1933 it had still not appeared. There was an exchange of letters and telephone calls and it was not until 8 December that the engine was finally installed. Rolls-Royce had reported to the Air Ministry on 13 November that the fully supercharged Goshawk engine on type test had failed after 65 of its 100 hour run, and during a second run had broke down at 93 hours. Also, the F 7/30 engine had been held up for minor modifications to the valve guides and Rolls had promised the Air Ministry, and it is assumed Supermarine, that the engine would be delivered on 15 November.

The aeroplane at this time was still known as F 7/30 Type 224 and, as already mentioned, Sir Robert McLean wanted to call it Spitfire. On 20 December General Cadell wrote to H. Grinstead of the Air Ministry as follows—"Dear Grinstead, confirming my telephone conversation this morning, would you kindly reserve the name 'Spitfire' for our day and night fighter now being built at Southampton". Grinstead's reply was unexpected for he wrote—"Until accepted for supply to the RAF it is requested that you will continue to refer to this aircraft by the title Supermarine F 7/30". When the prototype was finally taken on charge at Farnborough many months later the Air Ministry form containing its service history did carry the name Spitfire so the name was, apparently, adopted.

The following day (21 December) it was decided to fit hinged flaps to the underside of each outer portion of the wing extending from the inner end of the aileron to the wing joint.

After all modifications were completed the prototype was ready for its first flight and weighing on 10 February 1934. It had a tare weight of 3422lb (wooden propeller) and 3468 (metal). Take off weights were 4743 and 4798 respectively. Of this the typical load was 94gals petrol at 724lb; five gals oil at 45lb. Final dimensions were, wing span 45ft 10in, overall length 29ft 10in, height (tail down) 8ft 6in, wing area 295 sq ft. An attempt was made after weighing to fly the aeroplane from Eastleigh but it had to be abandoned when cooling water was ejected into the wing condensers and hot wells*. The maiden flight took place on 20 February and lasted for ten minutes.

K2890, prototype Type 224, F 7/30, at Supermarine, Woolston, works on completion. The four vertical rods on the wing are temperature guages connected to the steam condensers (Shenstone).

A second flight was made almost immediately after the aircraft had landed. It had taken 20 months to construct the F 7/30 prototype and its builders were not convinced it would meet Air Ministry requirements. E. H. Mansbridge, the aerodynamicist said later—"We were too cautious. Choosing the thick section wing was a mistake when we could have used a modified, thinner section as used on the S.5 floatplane". On 2 May Mitchell proposed a number of modifications under

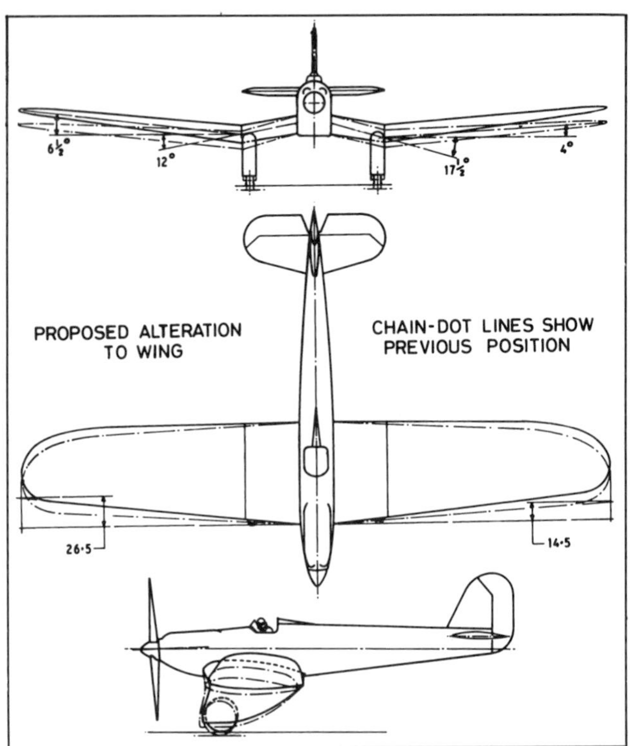

After the flight of K2890 Mitchell proposed drastic modifications, including an increase in wing sweep back plus an increase in outer wing dihedral and inner wing anhedral.

Supermarine Spec 421, and two days later the prototype was dismantled and the modifications incorporated. Increased length and new design ailerons (30in to 10 feet); the outer wing spar had to be strengthened and additional wing ribs. Other changes proposed were alterations to the cooling system as the prototype could not fly inverted, plus a new method of returning water from the hot wells to the header tank. Four new propellers of varying pitch diameter ratios; three designs of exhaust systems; silencing and flame damping; two additional shapes of wing root fillets; mods to tailplane to vary degree of stability; covering of wing leading edge with a smooth skin; split, trailing edge flaps, and a completely enclosed cockpit. Mitchell said the total cost of all these modifications would be approximately £3,000, but if Supermarine had to bear all the risk of the prototype during further trials, this cost might be increased.

A second, more powerful Goshawk was installed as F 7/30 had attained only a speed of 230mph against the predicted 245. This engine was producing 600bhp at 11,500ft and even with new propellers to permit maximum revs performance was still disappointing. One unforeseen problem was the finely corrugated leading edge skin, designed to dissipate engine heat via steam through the evaporative system and unable to deal efficiently with heat exchange. The leading edge back to the spar at .33 of the chord was the main cooling condenser made of steel and when hot it expanded causing the wing to curve in a slight arc. This produced extra drag and also resulted in the ailerons tightening up in flight. The proposed cost of covering the leading edge with a smooth skin was considered prohibitive.

At the second weighing at Eastleigh on 24 June subsequent

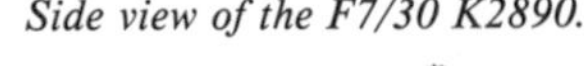
Side view of the F7/30 K2890.

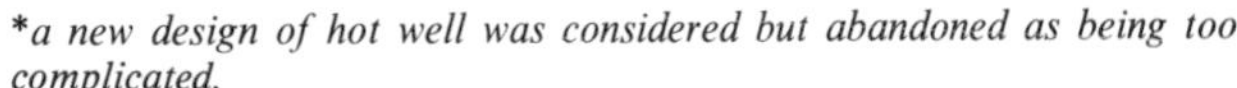
**a new design of hot well was considered but abandoned as being too complicated.*

Head on and rear views of the prototype. Original photographs show the corrugated leading edges clearly. Note span of ailerons.

to the new modifications, tare had risen to 3623lbs (with metal propeller), with auw at 4945 and the aircraft was ready in time to appear at the RAF pageant at Hendon on 30 June, bearing its serial number K2890 and a large, black number 2 on the fuselage. By now Mitchell had realised that further improvement in performance was almost unattainable and had started to re-think the basic design. During the period of trials with the prototype Mr Ellor and Dorey of Rolls-Royce had spoken to him about his views on inverted engines (R-R were in the early stages of designing the PV12 engine) and Mitchell had thought the mounting would improve the forward view of single seat fighters. He went on to say there would be trouble with the exhaust. His views, and those of other designers, were to have a profound effect on the ultimate design of the new engine.

Checking angles at Southampton (Shenstone).

Wing-fuselage junction on prototype lacked fillet originally (Shenstone).

Details of fin and rudder.

Supermarine Spitfire F7/30

On 27 July 1934 Supermarine wrote to the Air Ministry in the following terms—"We have the honour to refer to the proposal by our Mr Mitchell to modify our day and night fighter K2890 with the view to improving performance and enclose for your consideration our Specification and drawing. The estimate of time for the necessary modifications is six months. (a) a new set of wings (b) retractable undercarriage (c) combined oil tank and cooler under engine (d) new petrol tanks in wings (e) new propeller (f) new tailplane and rudder (g) mods to fin (h) flight trials up to a duration of eight hours. Total cost of modification is £7000". It was a remarkable effort by Mitchell and Supermarine for they had offered to produce a practically new design, with the exception of the fuselage, and all for the sum of £7000.

But the Air Ministry would not agree to this major change; they wanted the original F 7/30, and in a letter to Supermarine dated 3 September rejected the proposal but did not slam the door completely. The letter said—"The department does not agree with the extensive modifications and require that the K2890 be delivered as soon as possible. I am to request that you inform the Air Ministry what would be the cost and time of delivery of the new aeroplane. I am to add that this request must not be taken as indicative of any intention of the department to order such an aeroplane". Supermarine's estimate of costs and delivery time seem to have been overlooked.

Two months later the Air Ministry again wrote asking for details of an alternative proposal for F 7/30 utilizing the Napier Dagger, in line, air cooled engine which was developing 700hp, together with a quotation and estimated date of delivery. At a board meeting on 6 November the Supermarine directors decided that a Dagger engined aeroplane would have a lower performance (20mph slower) than that of the current machine and agreed to decline the proposal, but not before Verney (DTD) had previously telephoned McLean informing him that he (Verney) did not want the Dagger and Supermarine was to use either the Goshawk, or the forthcoming Rolls-Royce PV12. The assumption that the PV12 was to be considered for the F 7/30 was first mentioned in Supermarine Report TD 1232 dated 13 October that year, and it also stated that with the same gear ratio as the Goshawk a one foot larger diameter propeller would be required. It also considered (a) a two pitch propeller which would allow increased rpm, and (b) a three blade unit.

Rejection of the Napier engine might be considered surprising, for although a major redesign of the cowling and engine mounts would have been required the savings in weight and deletion of the complicated steam cooling system, necessary for the Goshawk, would have increased the prototype's performance, particularly as the Dagger was promised by its makers to produce 800hp in the near future. However, it must be remembered that Supermarine and Rolls-Royce had established a rapport over the years with provision of the engines for the winning Schneider Trophy floatplanes, and that both companies were negotiating for a fully supercharged Goshawk and the new PV12.

Maker's trials continued with the prototype which took part in comparative trials with the other two prototypes from Westland and Gloster at Martlesham Heath. A production contract was awarded to Gloster Aircraft for their SS.37 Gladiator. Many well known pilots flew F7/30, including George Pickering, who managed to land it safely after the engine cut out on two occasions, and Flt. Lts. Atcherley and White, the latter to be killed in the prototype Type 300 Spitfire in 1939. All work on K2890 was cancelled on 9 January 1935 but test flights were continued as part of the programme to produce its successor—K5054. Engine cooling still proved to be troublesome and inverted flying prohibited because of loss of water. McLean wrote to Air Marshall Dowding (CinC Fighter Command) requesting permission to deliver the aircraft to an RAF Station in February, but this was denied.

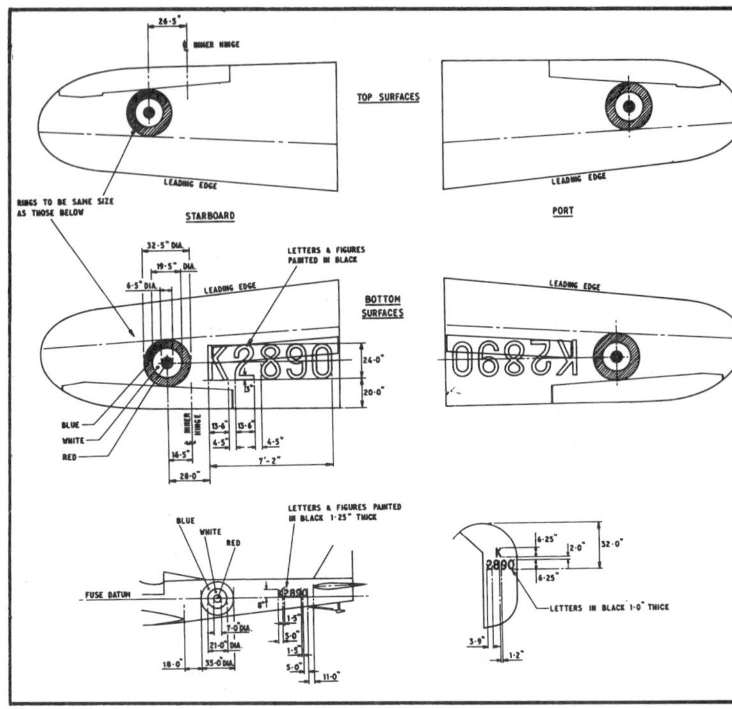

Original sketch of national markings for K2890. Wing roundel width 36.5in, fuselage 35in, wing serial 24in tall, stroke thickness 3in, fuselage serial 9in tall, fin 6.25in.

By the following July K2890 had changed shape once more, particularly the tailplane which had been clipped at the tips. A model was tested in the Farnborough wind tunnel, followed by further tests at Weybridge. In addition three models of different configurations were tested. It was also proposed to introduce an underslung radiator, but this altered the air flow so drastically it had to be abandoned. Numerous wind tunnel tests were carried out to decide the shape of the windscreen during April by using the complete mock-up of the fuselage mounted in the tunnel. A total of 44 tests were made using six different shapes.

In an obviously prompted letter to Mitchell, Joseph 'Mutt' Summers, Chief Test Pilot, Vickers, wrote on 3 May 1935—"I flew the Spitfire twice on 7 February 1935 and am of the opinion that it is airworthy for the purpose of tests at RAE". As a result Verney accepted delivery of K2890 on 3 July and it was taken on charge at Farnborough on the 24th. On 2 December that year Major Buchanan wrote to Verney saying—"Her

May 1934 rear view of K2890 after modification following first flights. The ailerons are much wider in span and slimmer in chord. Rigging board can be seen on wing.

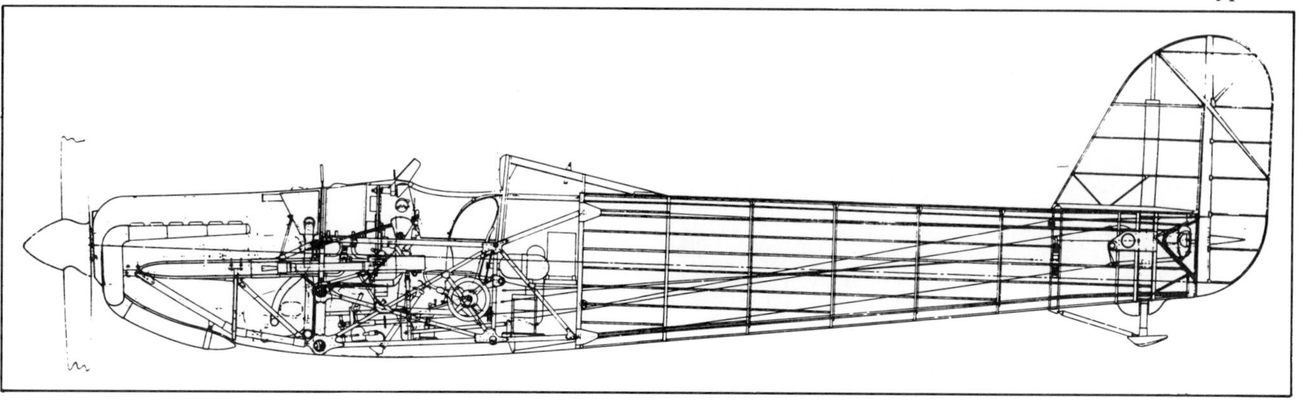

Side elevation of Type 224 fuselage in its final form.

Prototype at Southampton, complete with fuselage number 2, before making its debut at the RAF Pageant at Hendon, 30 June 1934.

Perhaps the only flying view of K2890, seen here over Hendon.

Artist's impression of the Type 224 as illustrated in the Vickers/ Supermarine sales brochure of 1934. Note the straight wing and lack of inner section anhedral.

Engine cowling of K2890 following modifications to the exhaust system. Note also the extended oil cooler inlet on leading edge (Shenstone).

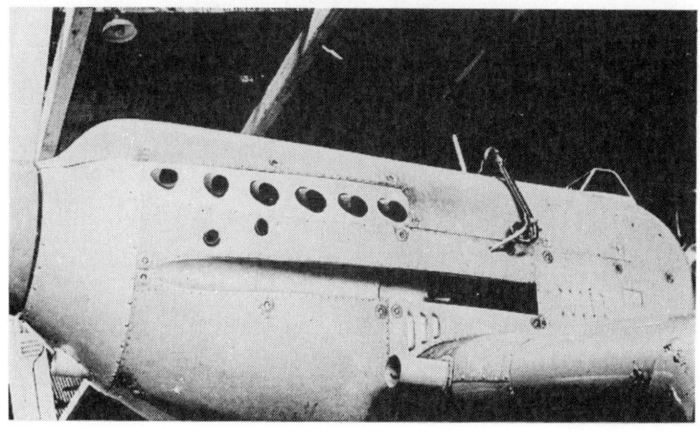

Date of this photograph is unknown and it shows K2890 with a large wing fillet, similar to that installed on a later date to the Type 300 Spitfire. A metal plate covers the display number 2 and wool streamers can be seen on the wing. Experiments with these took place in February 1935. The alteration to the wing fillets might have been influenced by a visit to Eastleigh on 9 October 1934 by Eric Bonar, pilot of 'Irish Swoop', a single seat aeroplane which had been entered for the MacRobertson Australian Air Race. Bonar talked to Mitchell about the tail buffetting experienced by F 7/30 during landing approaches and supplied him with wing tunnel figures of the Bellanca 28-70's wing fillet design. Mitchell did design and install large fillets to the F7/30 after its initial flight programme.

performance is not such to be of interest in face of up to date performances". He went on to say he did not propose to pursue development any further. The aircraft was finally transferred to Martlesham Heath on 25 May 1937 where it stayed, inactive, until final transfer to Orfordness in June as obsolete to requirements and for use as a gunnery target. It was an ignoble end to an advanced concept which, had it been fitted with the Rolls-Royce PV12, might have been an outstanding success.

Static thrust tests were required for the prototype F 7/30 and wool streamers were located on the underside of the fuselage and, later, the fuselage and inner wing section in order to study air flow.

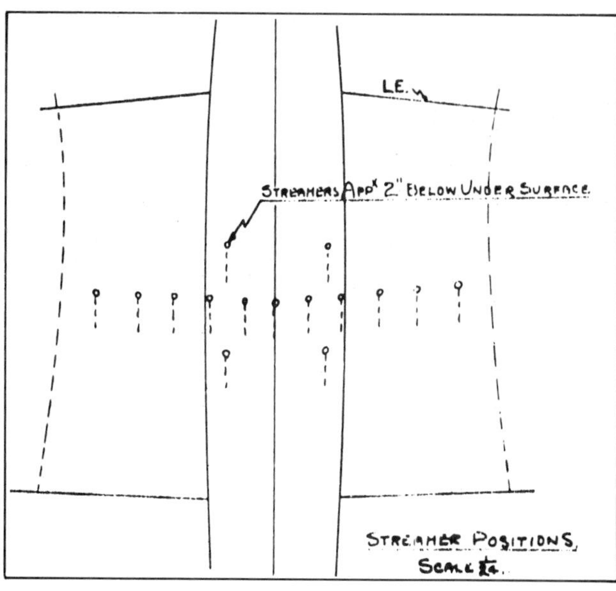

K2890 after further modification and start of additional trials (Shenstone).

Although the original contract for F 7/30 was valued at £8,500, the total spent by the Air Ministry and Supermarine was well in excess of this. First recorded expenditure was £218 as of 20 April and a further £190 up to June 1932, when Supermarine were unofficially informed that a prototype order would be forthcoming. On 2 November £425 had been committed and by 11 July 1933 the company admitted that the prototype was running behind schedule but the preliminary tests of cooling and structure were satisfactory, with drawings being issued to the shops. An extension of six months had been applied for, and granted, and by 1 November the prototype was 45% complete and £3,822 had been accounted for. By 31 December the figures were—costs £10,923.17s.6d, written off £4,000, valuation £6,923.17s.6d. Expenditure up to the first flight was said to be £17,093 with the contract price now quoted at £9,293. The final figures of December 1934 were—materials £2,819, labour £6,329, factory charges (overhead) £9,491—total £18,639. Add profit and loss charges (35% of wages) £2,215.

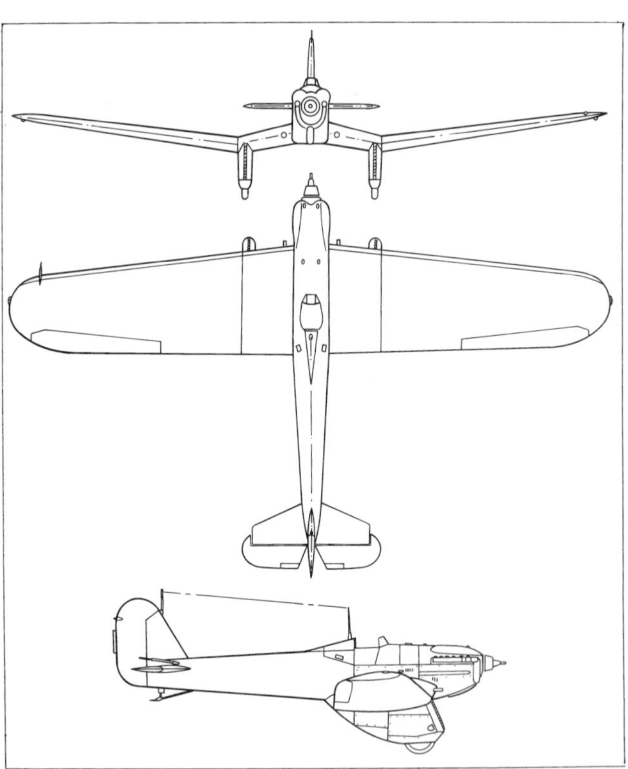

General arrangement of F 7/30 during the final series of trials.

Gross total £20,854. A final £30 was spent in January and £20 in February 1935. It had been an expensive first attempt at the military fighter by Supermarine, but one that was to eventually reap huge dividends.

A little known facet of the Type 224's history is the consideration given by Supermarine to enter K2890 as a contender for the MacRobertson Air Race from England to Australia in 1934. Sir MacPherson Robertson announced the details of the race in March 1933, and the Supermarine Report No 870 of 21 November contained the following details of cruising speed at rated power—Goshawk 205mph; with Griffon I 250mph; range at maximum cruising 1330 miles. The Griffon engine was a development of the Rolls-Royce 'R' which powered the winning S.6B floatplane in the last Schneider Trophy race, and the name was continued for the well known engines which were used for the later Spitfire marks. The idea for entering K2890 had to be abandoned for the Air Ministry would not countenance a secret prototype fighter being used for "commercial gain".

K2890 at Farnborough, 10 June 1937. Guns have been removed and it was finally seconded for use as a target to Orfordness.

PHOENIX FROM ASHES

Spirits were low at Eastleigh after K2890's first flight, but 'Mutt' Summers was boosting morale by spreading the idea of producing a private venture fighter. His enthusiasm was infectious for both McLean and Mitchell proposed a number of ideas for such an aeroplane. It has been supposed, and suggested, by many sources that the Spitfire was a private venture design which was eventually adopted by the Air Ministry and, indeed, Sir Robert McLean was to endorse this in letters to various newspapers during 1957. He said he felt the Air Ministry's approach to the single seat fighter was not conducive to the very basis of fighter efficiency, speed and aggressiveness.

He also felt that Mitchell and Wallis would do much better by devoting their qualities not to the official F7/30 Specification but to a real 'killer fighter', which was eventually to become the Spitfire. After discussion with the Air Ministry, Sir Robert and A F Sidgreaves, Chairman of Rolls-Royce, decided the two companies should together finance the building of such an aircraft. Sir Robert said that the Air Ministry was informed of this decision and were told that under no circumstances would any technical member of the Ministry be consulted or allowed to interfere with the designer.

It has not been possible to verify these claims, as records are not available, but from 22 February 1934, when Mitchell started revising the F7/30 design, until 28 December, when the Air Ministry accepted the revised scheme and issued Specification F37/34, the many projects by Supermarine of the design were a private venture risk by the company. The Air Ministry was at all times kept fully informed of development and progress of the original F7/30 design up to the prototype Spitfire, K5054.

Preliminary steps for a redesign started on 1 May 1934 when two alternatives were considered. 1, Freeze the original design but aim to reduce weight by 177lb, ie, 3.7% of the structure. However, there was no appreciable increase in performance. 2, Clean-up the design and use a reduced area (258ft^2) wing with a higher lift section (NACA 2412) and configuration. 2, was approved on 2 May and by the 3rd the drawing office had started work.

By July 1934 Mitchell's early thoughts on an improved F7/30 design were specified in Supermarine Report No 1151, which incorporated a number of proposals set out in the Air Ministry Draft Specification for F5/34*, a copy of which had been forwarded to the company. This Draft was a requirement from the DTD for an eight gun Fury replacement dated 27 February 1933, which called for an aeroplane similar in design to the F7/30. A Goshawk engine rated for 84 octane fuel was to provide 690hp at 3000rpm (plus 3lb boost at 15,000ft), a maximum speed of 286mph and landing of 66, and a ceiling of 35,400ft. Airframe weight was 1365lb, engine plus fuel tanks 1414lb, fuel (80gal) and oil 655lb, military load 700lb. Total 4134lb. Permission was also granted for development of a new engine.

Squadron Leader Sorley was one of the great exponents of the eight gun fighter for it had been accepted in the early thirties that due to higher, monoplane bomber speeds a fighter pilot would be able to hold his gunsight on target for about two seconds. In that brief moment eight guns, under the best possible circumstances, would deliver 256 rounds to the target. It seemed reasonable, therefore, that the (then) large armament was a necessary requirement. Air Marshall Ludlow-Hewitt, DCAS, also asked for eight guns.

But there were many who were just as enthusiastic in their opposition to the idea. Air Marshall Brooke-Popham, CinC ADGB, wrote to Ludlow-Hewitt—"I think eight guns is going a bit too far and we should be content with four. With eight guns you are going to get a lot of leading edge resistance. Also, I think, based on experience, this aircraft should be issued to squadrons in 1941. The retractable undercarriage should be designed to act as an airbrake". R W Oxland had the same reservations for he also wrote to Ludlow-Hewitt—"The installation of eight guns in this fighter (F5/34) is an entirely new departure and it is probable that the designer will experience considerable difficulty when he comes to incorporate this requirement; therefore, it is of the utmost importance that we should ask only for essentials".

The Supermarine Report 1151 did not include the requirement for additional guns and read as follows:

Introduction. In order to improve performance of the above machine (SS Fighter F7/30) it is proposed to reduce overall drag to a minimum. To this end the wing area is to be reduced using a higher lift section with split trailing edge flaps so that landing speed is not increased. It is proposed to retract the chassis completely and this report discusses the important points in these connexion.

Basic data. The new wing is in one piece per side and is similar to the existing outer wing; the main spar is arranged to bolt direct to the existing main fuselage fittings and drag loads are taken by a single strut attached to the top spar flange a few feet from the fuselage and the existing rear fuselage fitting. The following components are also to be mounted in the new wing on each side in such positions that the overall structure and chassis efficiency is a maximum – (1) one 41 gal tank (2) one receptacle for 600 rounds of SAA for the fuselage Vickers guns (3) one Vickers gun with 400 rounds of SAA.

General considerations. Owing to the great height of the chassis in comparison with the wing chord, it is impossible to fold the wheels straight back without large projections; in fact the only place where the wheels will fit satisfactorily is in a position close to the thicker part of the wing. This means the wheels must fold up sideways.

The method of arrangements falls, broadly, into four categories—(1) Fuel tank close to fuselage, chassis outside tank folding outwards; (2) Fuel tank as (1) chassis outside tank folding inwards; (3) Chassis close to fuselage folding outwards, fuel tank outside chassis; (4) Chassis as (3) folding inwards, fuel tank outside chassis. The chief difference between these methods is that (1) and (2) the fuel is inboard and (3) and (4) it is outboard. This means the rolling moment of inertia for the

Revised F7/30 as submitted with Supermarine Specifications 425, drawing 30000, sheet 1. The four Vickers guns located in engine cowling and wing roots, fired through the propeller disk. The undercarriage retracted outwards with the fuel tanks (41 gals each) outside the main wheels. This was to arrangement (3) in Mitchell's Report 1151 of July 1934. Wing span 39ft 4in, area (C/L) 255ft², nett including ailerons 233ft², ailerons 19ft². Fin 5.9ft², rudder 8.7ft². Tailplane 15ft², elevators 11.6ft². oil five gals. Cooling surface 7ft².

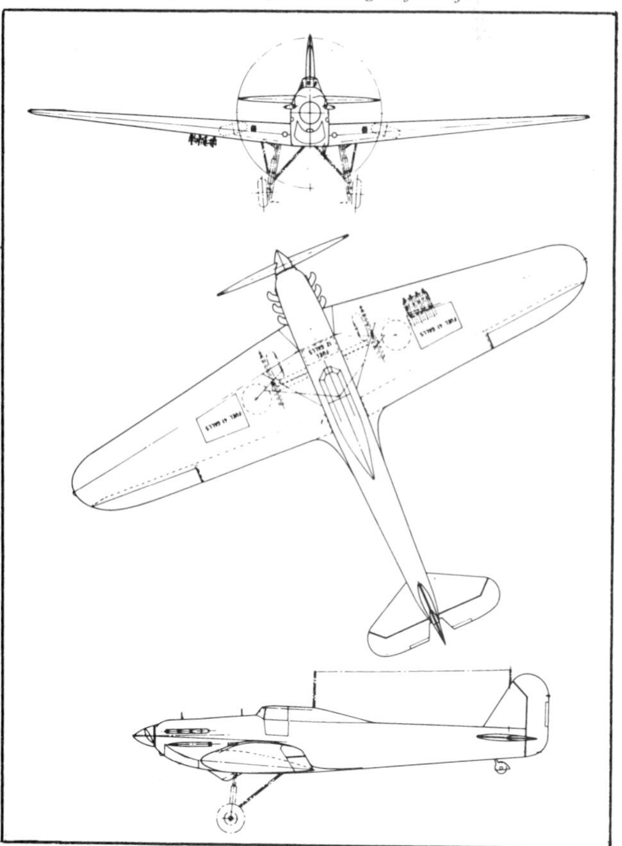

* *see Appendix III, page 601*

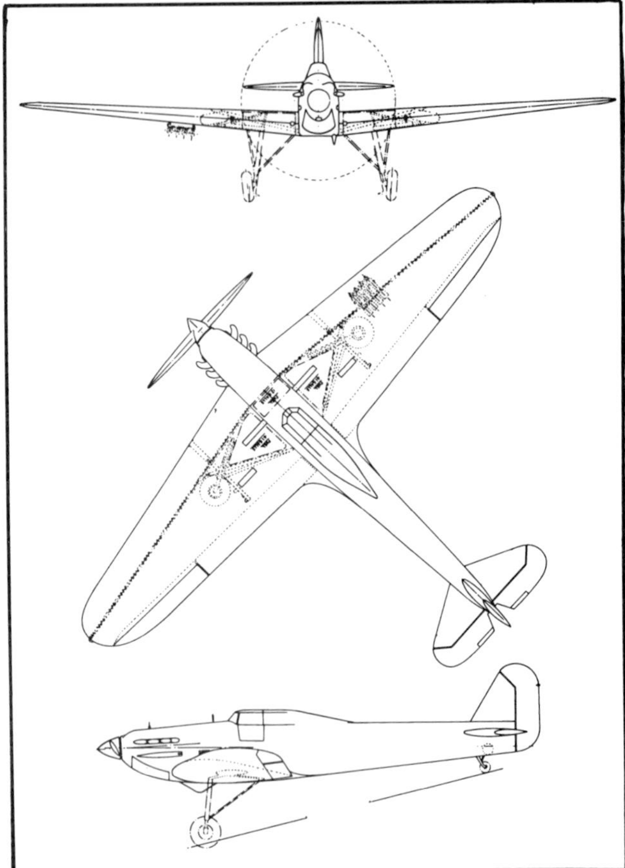

Minor modifications appeared on the second design submission to 425A, drawing 30000, sheet 2. Fuel tanks were relocated close to the fuselage with the undercarriage legs folding outwards and the front and rear of the fuel tanks as to arrangement (1) in 1151. The main oleos were attached to the wing structure further away from the fuselage, and the auxiliary strut to the wing root instead of the C/L. Wheel track was now 9ft 4in and wing guns relocated to fire outside the propeller disk. Tailwheel retracted and engine exhaust stubs faced forwards. Main angles of wing, +2° at root twisting to –½° at tip. Dihedral 4½°; tailplane –1°; engine –3°.

complete machine changes by 40%. This believed to have little or no effect on the manoeuvrability of the aircraft. (A flight test is now being arranged on the existing machine (F7/30) in this connexion). Outboard fuel reduces wing stress and fire risk. Comparing the schemes (1) and (2), if the wheels fold inwards as in (2) the track will be too big so that (1) is the only possible choice. Also, with outboard fuel, chassis folding inwards as (4) the top part of the rear stay must be attached to a weak part of the wing. This means weight increase due to strengthening. It is also difficult to fit in the fuselage gun ammunition. If the chassis folds outwards as in (3) there is ample room for chassis and gun controls and the chassis is attached to the stoutest parts of the existing structure, which means little, or no, local stiffening. It is considered, therefore, that the outward folding chassis for the outboard fuel scheme is the better of the two methods.

Mitchell's views on chassis retracting methods of the period are interesting, for when the Spitfire finally evolved fuel tanks had been repositioned in the fuselage ahead of the pilot, but the chassis still retracted outwards. The report went on to consider manual and power retracting systems and recommended retraction by electric motor. It stated—"It will be appreciated that there is no room, or time, for a fighter pilot to haul up manually a retractable chassis". Pilots of early Spitfire Mk Is were only too aware of this.

On 16 July 1934 Michell's proposals for a revised F7/30 – Supermarine Type 300 – were ready for submission to the Air Ministry in Supermarine Specification No 425. It read:

SUPERMARINE DAY AND NIGHT FIGHTER TO AIR MINISTRY SPECIFICATION F7/30 PROPOSED MODIFICATIONS

Arrangement. It is proposed to modify the existing aeroplane by building a new pair of wings incorporating a retractable chassis. The new wings are of reduced area, the present inner sections of negative dihedral being dispensed with. Split trailing edge flaps are provided to increase the lift and thus retain the same landing speed. The proposed arrangement is shown on the drawing attached.

Construction. The elimination of the downward sloping wing roots results in the view for the pilot being slightly worse, but not to a serious extent. On the other hand construction is greatly simplified by making each wing in one piece. Other features which simplify construction are the substitution of a lattice for a web plate, enabling the riveting of the nose to be more easily carried out, and the provision of smooth in place of corrugated covering.

Weight and Performance. It is estimated that the proposed modifications will result in a saving of 250lb weight and an improvement in top speed of 30mph, the climb remaining practically unaltered. The following figures, giving the comparison between the existing and modified aeroplane, are estimated. Performance tests so far carried out are incomplete, but present indications are the estimates are reasonably correct.

	Specn F7/30	Present machine cleaned up	New wing and retractable chassis
Weight	—	4950lb	4700lb
Max speed	195mph	235mph	265mph
Time to 15,000ft	8½min	8min	8¼min
Span	—	45ft 10in	39ft 4in
Length	—	29ft 10in	29ft 4in
Wing area (gross)	—	295 sq ft	255 sq ft
Wing loading	—	16.8 lb/sq ft	15.4 lb/sq ft
Power loading	—	8.25lb/bhp	7.84lb/bhp

The curious point about Specification 425 is that the accompanying drawing showed a design with an entirely new fuselage and enclosed cockpit. The only recognisable features it had in common with the prototype F7/30 was the engine cowling, fin and rudder. This was corrected, however, by a supplementary Specification No 425A dated 26 July 1934. It was practically identical to No 425 but at the end of the first paragraph it stated—"The existing aircraft is shown on drawing No 22400 and the proposed arrangement on drawing 30000, sheet 2".

The new design still included a Goshawk II engine with evaporative cooling and a hot-well incorporated into the lower

Final design to 425 before the elliptical wing Type 300 appeared on Sheet 11 on 24 September 1934. The fuselage had been fined down to blend into the rudder post. Wings were equi-tapered and the four guns relocated to fire outside the propeller disk (500rpg). The thin, NACA Series 220 section wing had eight small bombs faired into the under surface, while the fuel tanks had been transferred to the fuselage just ahead of the cockpit. The u/c, width of track 6ft 0in, retracted outwards.

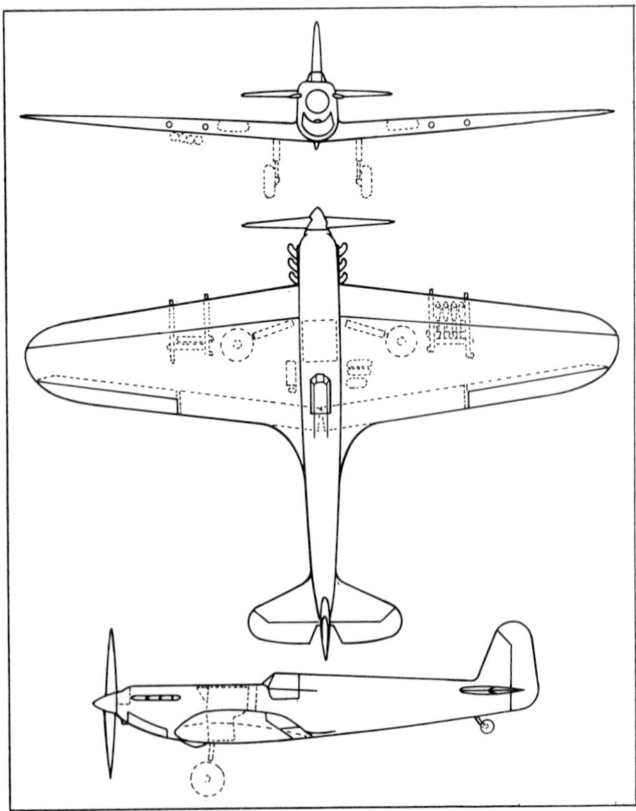

cowling lines. The undercarriage retracted outwards with 82 gallons of fuel in tanks (41gal in each wing) inboard of the undercarriage (scheme (3) as proposed by Mitchell in Supermarine Report No 1151). There was provision for the carriage of eight small bombs under the wings.

An update of the design appeared on 24 September with the issue of a drawing based upon the machine illustrated in Specification 425. As our drawing shows it was a handsome design powered by the Goshawk II enclosed in a long, smooth cowling; an enclosed cockpit faired into the rear fuselage which, in turn, tapered into the fin. The undercarriage still retracted outwards with the four Vickers machine guns located outboard of it. On the wing under surface eight small bombs, four per wing, were to be installed between each pair of machine guns. Ammunition totalled 2000 rounds.

The wing was now equi-tapered on leading and trailing edges and fuel was to be stored in the fuselage ahead of the pilot. Neither of the two designs were acceptable to the Air Ministry but their promise was such that the revised Specification F37/34* was issued to Supermarine on 28 December 1934 and it covered the design and construction of an experimental SS day and night fighter. Before all this took place, however, three almost totally unconnected events happened which were to result in the final development of the prototype F37/34 Supermarine Type 300.

GENESIS OF THE MERLIN

First was a decision in the early months of 1932 by Rolls-Royce to develop an almost exact scale up of the Kestrel engine with an 1649 in^3 displacement instead of the existing 1295 in^3, and it was expected to yield about 750bhp. Rolls-Royce had originally proposed, in agreement with the Air Ministry, an inverted installation in order to provide improved visibility to pilots, plus other sound technical reasons. However, the airframe manufacturers of the time were, in general, totally opposed to the idea when the mock-up engine was revealed to them at the end of that same year. It appeared that an inverted installation involved too many awkward design problems. The new engine was, therefore, revised for upright installation.

The new design, the PV12, was initially financed by Rolls-Royce and it differed from the Kestrel, apart from its size, in two areas. The cylinder block and upper half of the crankcase was a single casting with a separate head. Its cooling system was a modified steam evaporative design based upon the Goshawk. Difficulties with the latter had caused Rolls-Royce to experiment with a composite system utilising both radiator and condensers. A finished mock-up of more than 11,000 working parts was manufactured from hard woods to prove the design.

Detailed design of the PV12 started in early 1933 and first drawings were ready for the shop floor by April. The Air Ministry was fully informed of development and its interest was intense, but there were no public funds available and early development expenses were borne by Rolls-Royce. The first two engines were ready for trials in October, and by that time funding development had changed for a contract had been signed with the Air Ministry and government money was available. In the event only the first two engines can be regarded as private venture.

Early running of the two engines had led to strengthening of the block casting and the reduction gearing was partially redesigned. The first unit passed its Type test in July 1934 at an International Rating of 790hp at 12,000ft, the same month Mitchell had submitted his proposal for a revised F7/30 to the Air Ministry. At the same time work had commenced on a new version of the engine with a different cylinder head. It was hoped to shorten flame travel and produce higher turbulence in the air/petrol mix. On, or about, Thursday 10 January 1935 the new engine had been named Merlin and two examples of the 'B' version were ready for testing by the following February. The Merlin now produced 950bhp up to 11,000ft and production eventually commenced under the designation of Merlin I. Small changes in construction resulted in the Merlin C and the first two examples were tested in April, flying trials being undertaken in Hawker Hart I K3036.

The composite cooling proved troublesome and after a few hours' flight time it was decided to adopt pure ethylene glycol as the coolant. Glycol had been used by the American Army for a number of years and Rolls-Royce had experimented with it in the Schneider Trophy S.5 floatplane. At that time its use had to be abandoned because, like all similar anti-freeze material, it tended to leak through every gasket and joint. The Air Ministry had authorised the investigation of glycol cooling on 27 November 1931. Before that date official policy was to concentrate efforts on evaporative cooling. American engines using glycol had many leakage problems with their material named 'Prestone'.

Bench tests of the Merlin B revealed faults and a Merlin C failed its first civil 50-hour non-stop running trials in May 1935; the Merlin E also failed its 100-hour test in March 1936. An emergency solution to the many problems was a decision to scale up the Kestrel head to fit the Merlin and to make the head

Side and front views of the original wooden mock-up of the proposed inverted Rolls-Royce PV12 engine. Rolls-Royce dropped the design after aircraft designers opted for an upright installation.

Hawker Audax prototype K1438 with a supercharged Goshawk engine installed for trials in July 1936.

* *see Appendix II, page 601*

and cylinder block in one piece. Designs of the Merlin G with all modifications incorporated were issued in May 1936.

The first Merlin engine to enter full-scale production was the F, an improved version of the E, and as the Merlin I first examples were delivered in July 1936. Production ceased after 180 had been built, and all were used for the Fairey Battle single engined light bomber. The Merlin II, production version of the G, followed and the first engines were delivered in August 1937. In January 1934 work had started on a two-speed drive for the supercharger of the Kestrel and one year later the Merlin two-speed version was being developed. The first two-speed Merlin was produced in September 1937 and it entered production as the Merlin X. Except for minor details the X was virtually the Merlin II.

Just before the outbreak of World War Two an important change was introduced to the Merlin. A pressurised cooling system containing 70% water and 30% glycol had proved superior to pure glycol at atmospheric pressure, and it was not so prone to seepage through joints. Also, a reduced cylinder head temperature meant longer engine life. The system was introduced to all Merlins after the II and X. Glycol was expensive and in servicing manuals issued by the Air Ministry to the RAF, air frame and engine fitters were instructed—"to save at all costs the glycol coolant".

SPITFIRE WING-EARLY STEPS

The second event to affect the eventual Spitfire design came about after a visit to America by two Supermarine employees from the design and engineering departments. B S Shenstone and T Westbrook were to assess the value of American aviation techniques and in a report dated May 1934 Shenstone summarised their findings, two paragraphs of which are relevant to the design of the F37/34 wing.—"The care taken to keep the leading edge true and smooth is shown to be worthwhile by recent NACA tests. No corrugated leading edges are used, nor are they considered advisable". The report went on—"Biplanes appear to have a wing thickness of about 12% and the new NACA sections, especially series 22 and 24, are coming into wide use. Inset hinge balances of about 10-15% are often used on elevators and rudders and the slotted aileron with hinge at or near the bottom surfaces are usually long and narrow. NACA now say that their favourable results on wide ailerons were misleading and that narrow ones are better".

THE COLT BROWNING GUN

The third event arose out of a conference held at the Air Ministry on 19 July 1934, during which the Senior Technical Officer of Ballistics, Captain F W Hill, showed a committee results of extensive trials made by the A&AEE at Martlesham Heath with multiple machine gun arrangements. Charts were displayed of fields of fire, ratios of firing and target results. In his summing up Captain Hill advised the committee that in the brief time a target would be in an attacking aircraft's sights, eight guns firing at not less than 1000 rounds per minute were necessary if that target was to be destroyed.

As already mentioned one of the major exponents of the eight gun fighter was Squadron Leader (later Air Marshall) R G Sorley of the Air Ministry's Operational Requirements Branch. He had given much thought to the problem of improved bomber technology in the early thirties and his opinions crystallised into the need for a multiple gun (minimum eight) monoplane fighter. The choice at that time lay between the .303 and .5 inch machine gun and the new 20mm Hispano cannon, the latter favoured by the French. The cannon was new and temperamental, while the.303 gun had been under test for some considerable time and appeared to offer the best possibilities for rate of fire.

With the aid of Major H S V Thompson, Sorley had obtained an obsolete airframe and had it set up on the range at Shoeburyness. Eight Colt Browning guns firing .303 ammunition were mounted at a distance of 400 yards from the target, and in a series of bursts with solid and explosive shells had reduced it to so much scrap. Following further extensive tests at Martlesham Heath of various other machine guns—Darne, Kireleji, Masden, Vickers and Colt – the last named was found to be the superior weapon. It had a high rate of fire (1200rpm) and was reasonably reliable. Sorley's thoughts concerning the Supermarine F37/34 design as an eight gun fighter are worth recording. On 9 August an extract from the minutes of an Air Ministry Staff meeting quotes him as saying—"It is difficult to express any opinion of the gun installation until something more definite is known about the monoplane design, and that if steam cooling is adopted it would add to the difficulty".

In September 1934 Major Thompson and C H Keith, both of the Air ministry, went to America and called at the Colt Automatic Weapon Corporation, Hartford, Connecticut, to negotiate a licence from Colt to build the Browning in England. It was granted and a number of British companies were invited to submit tenders for manufacture of the gun, which differed from the American model in that it had to be adapted to fire .303 calibre rimmed ammunition. By a strange oversight one of the largest weapon manufacturers, Birmingham Small Arms, was not sent a copy of the specification and when the error was discovered they were provided with a set of blueprints. In June 1935 they were asked to quote for the production of 1050 guns at the rate of 50 per week. James Leek, of BSA, at a meeting in the Air Ministry some time after the quote was recieved, expressed an opinion that a rate of 2000, not 50, guns per week would be necessary if the United Kingdom was ever to be called upon to meet the threat of Germany's military preparations. He had recently visited that country and obtained first hand knowledge of events taking place. Also, he had a shrewd idea of the true figures of military aircraft production. His advice was ignored, but he was later to be completely vindicated when his prediction that 2000 guns per week were necessary when that total was required, and ordered, in June 1940.

Squadron Leader Sorley had helped draw up Specification F37/34 based upon the Supermarine Specification No 425/A and the events mentioned were already catching up and overtaking the design.

On 23 November E W Hives (Director of Engineering Policy), Lappin, Ellor and Parkin of Rolls-Royce, visited Supermarine to discuss the Type 300's engine. The most suitable type to use was considered in conjunction with variable pitch propellers and for comparison a Goshawk with two speed blower and VP propeller (weight 1326lb) and the PV12 with fixed pitch propeller (weight 1250lb) were selected. The latter arrangement gave an extra 130hp for take off, 190 more climb and an extra 200 at top speed than the Goshawk arrangement. A further disadvantage of the Goshawk scheme was that the VP propeller gave the engine a harder time. While gain in climb and top speed for the PV12 was apparent it was not certain if take off with the fixed pitch propeller would be satisfactory. Mr Hives said that, if considered advantageous, power could be increased considerably for take off by over riding the boost control so that the engine behaved as a straight engine. By this method 1000hp would be available at take off, but whether the extra engine power with a fixed pitch provided extra thrust was debatable. It was decided to check this by static thrust tests of the prototype F7/30 (see page 13) using increased boost pressures up to approximately 7 lb/in^2. It was also agreed, subject to confirmation provided by the test, that the engine to be utilised should be the PV12 with a fixed pitch propeller. Rolls-Royce promised to have one engine available for use at Woolston six months before delivery of the prototype aircraft to the Air Ministry, even though the engine had not been satisfactorily type tested for glycol.

The 'Short' PV12 with rearranged auxiliaries would not be ready in time for installation in the Type 300 and it was considered necessary for the 'Long' engine to be used instead. The question of cooling was also discussed and Rolls-Royce engineers pressed for experiments on the F7/30 in order to try to reproduce conditions that had led to failure in static tests. In a marginal note Mitchell agreed to this as and when F7/30 became available. Rolls did admit that several instances of defective circulation had occurred. The table below is of preliminary estimates on the existing F7/30 and the F37/34 with four engine types.

	Aircraft			
	Existing design		New design	
Engine	Goshawk	re-rated Goshawk	present PV12	high powered PV12
HP dissipated	220	202	220	242
HP to be dissipated	299	333	388	510
Excess water evaporated	79	131	168	268
per minute (lb)	3.36	5.59	7.15	11.4
Total per climb (lb)	30	50	57	74
Excess over existing m/c	—	20	27	44

Hives went on to explain that in spite of this the company was satisfied with the engine when evaporatively cooled, but was not in the same position to claim the same when it was glycol cooled. It was noted that the Supermarine leading edge condenser provided about half the cooling necessary for the PV12 during climb and that additional cooling in some form would be required. Mr Ellor estimated that a water radiator of approximately 1 sq ft (in the slip stream) would be sufficient and be required only for climb, not at maximum or cruising speed. For glycol cooling an estimated 1.7 sq ft unit would suffice.

The 14th Paris Aero Show opened during November 1934 and Shenstone submitted notes of his visit to the design office. He mentioned, in particular, the Heinkel 70 calling it the most outstanding exhibit and considered it to be—"one of the most efficient (aerodynamically) aeroplanes in the world". He also commented favourably on the Gallay radiator, quoting the manufacturer's claim that it saved 17% in weight and drag over the standard British type.

The Air Ministry was by now showing a great interest in the Type 300 powered by the PV12 and on 5 December, Mitchell, Major Payne and Alan Clifton of Supermarine went along to the Kingsway office to discuss the improved D.N Fighter. Supermarine's proposals, including Drawing 30000, Sheet 13, were outlined and this drawing was of the greatest significance for, without doubt, it illustrated for the first time the Type 300 with an elliptical wing and the change from the straight taper wing as illustrated on Drawing 30000, Sheet 11 (page 16). The precise date of Mitchell's decision to use the elliptical wing in preference to the straight taper is not known, but it occurred during the second or third week of November 1934. The changes to the design of the Type 300 between the issue of Sheet 11 of 11 September 1934 and first flight of the prototype F37/34 on 5 March 1936 were numerous, and the events influencing them are examined below in chronological order.

THE ELLIPTICAL WING

Supermarine Drawing 30000, Sheet 11, was a redrawn Sheet 10 and it revealed minor modifications. But the most significant changes must have appeared on Sheet 12, details of which are unknown, but it is assumed that it illustrated the intermediate stage between the straight taper and the ellipse. This assumption is strengthened by Mr R J Fenner, who was employed in the Supermarine design office at the time of the Type 300 development. Mr Fenner recalls that—"During my nine years in the Supermarine drawing office my main efforts were spent in the Control Section working with C Blazdal on a number of aircraft contracts. When Alf Faddy joined the design team in 1933 (I think) we formed the 'three Fs' with Bill Fear and did most of the work on the original Spitfire with the Goshawk steam cooled engine and the 'W' wing. This aircraft was built to the Ministry Specification F7/30 and it had a gull wing with straight taper leading and trailing edges, the former helping with the steam cooling. The aircraft was not a success and Mitchell decided the concept was wrong and issued guidance and instructions to the Stress and Drawing offices to produce something more effective and agressive.

"In conjunction with H Holmes, Ernie Mansbridge, Alan Clifton and 'the three Fs' a number of different designs were produced—all as F7/30 development aircraft. Drawing Sheet 11 was actually drawn by Faddy who, with me and Bill Fear (all three sitting in a row) did all the general arrangement drawings while the other two supplied the various schemes for the different parts of the aircraft, under direct supervision from RJM, of course, along with various members of the Stress office. We also had considerable advice from Beverley Shenstone on his return from the USA.

"Alf Faddy, who was our Section Leader, would have persuaded RJM to go for the elliptical type wing since this gave greater depth for the retracted landing gear and the outer ammunition boxes. I was responsible for the initial schemes for the eight gun armament and the depth of the wing was critical as the requirement called for a satisfactory amount of ammunition per box without extending the box too far out along the span. As it was the 'goose neck' feeds to the inner pairs of Browning guns over the top of the outer pairs was quite difficult enough. The performance of high speed being the criterion, it was essential to maintain a low t/c ratio for the wing section and to keep the armament as close inboard as possible. The compromise was the elliptical wing. I remember well the mild consternation when told the six gun version, which I had already schemed, was to be increased to an eight gun installation*.

"When we came to the final version with the Merlin engine RJM had fixed the smaller wing area, lower thickness/chord ratio and the optimum single spar position and I had the job of producing the lay-out to meet his proposals, plus the basic design of landing gear retraction; mounting of the jack in the wing; the locking mechanism and coolant radiator. The hand pump and jack for the manual/hydraulic retraction mechanism was designed by a stressman named R Kember.

"The planform of the wing was, originally, perfectly elliptical and then bent forward along its major axis until the optimum spar position was straight. I remember clearly making several drawings of alternative planform and RJM, in his rounds of the drawing boards, selecting the scheme as described except for minor changes to the wing tips. I also had the pleasure of submitting to RJM several designs of retracting landing gear and the cantilever pintle finally selected was favoured although T Westbrook, as manager, complained bitterly about the fine drawing limits in the angles to ensure backward reaction into the wing with only the slightest blister to the skin. When it was proved correct he was big enough to come and compliment the design office".

The drawing below is a representation of how this redesigned aeroplane might have appeared with a wing formed from two half ellipses, a swept back main spar, four guns and eight bombs and an undercarriage that retracted first to the rear and twisting to accomodate the wheel into the wing.

The elliptical wing emerges: Drawing 30000, Sheet 11.

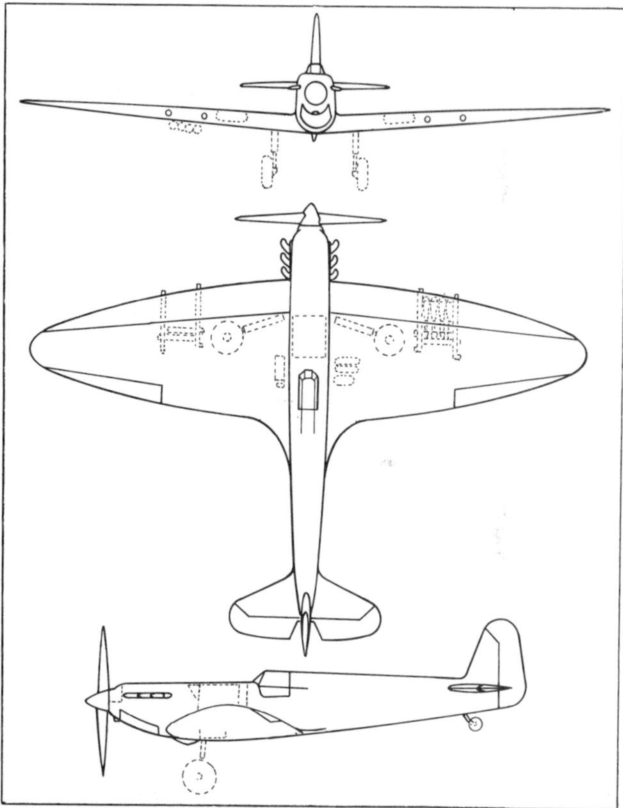

A second Supermarine employee, who was also working in the design office at the same period, confirms this event. Mr E J Davis told the authors—"The wing shape was decided before final detail design started in the drawing office and the key was the wing spar, which was not swept back. The original kinked spar of F7/30 would have made the wing joints almost impossible to make (bending the booms for dihedral was bad enough). Also, the line of the spar web was the datum for setting up the twist as each rib had a different incidence. Manufacture would have been most difficult if the spar was not at right angles to the ribs. Although the final wing shape was not a true ellipse it was evolved from one. The spar, positioned at 25% chord, together with the thick nose skin, provided all the bending and torsional strength of the wing, but in a true ellipse it would have curved backwards from the root to tip."

A third ex-Supermarine employee is able, by proxy, to contribute towards this story. Mr Davis also revealed that he had worked with R S Dickson on the Type 300 and he states—"As further proof I have photocopies of some of the early calculations made in May 1934 on the F7/30, Type 224 development by R S Dickson, a young engineer who made the project drawings for Allan Clifton and Ernie Mansbridge. At

**This must have occurred after Sorley visited Supermarine on 26 April 1935.*

that time the amended design had a Goshawk steam cooled engine and a straight tapered wing. Dickson told me—"The wing at this stage had no kink in it, as the F7/30, and was straight tapered, but later the final, elliptical shape was shown on my drawing. This was condemned as not producable in quantity, but the eight gun installation appeared about this time (F5/34) from the Air Ministry and it was not found possible to get the outer guns in a straight taper but easier in an ellipse. So the elliptical wing prevailed".

When Mitchell and his team went to the Air Ministry on 5 December 1934 the Sheet 13 drawing was similar to that reproduced below and, as this drawing illustrates the aeroplane had a distorted ellipse wing, with the main spar at right angles to the fuselage, a T-shaped exhaust, cooling louvres and an evaporative cooling system in the wing leading edge.

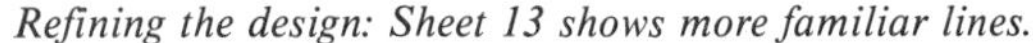

Refining the design: Sheet 13 shows more familiar lines.

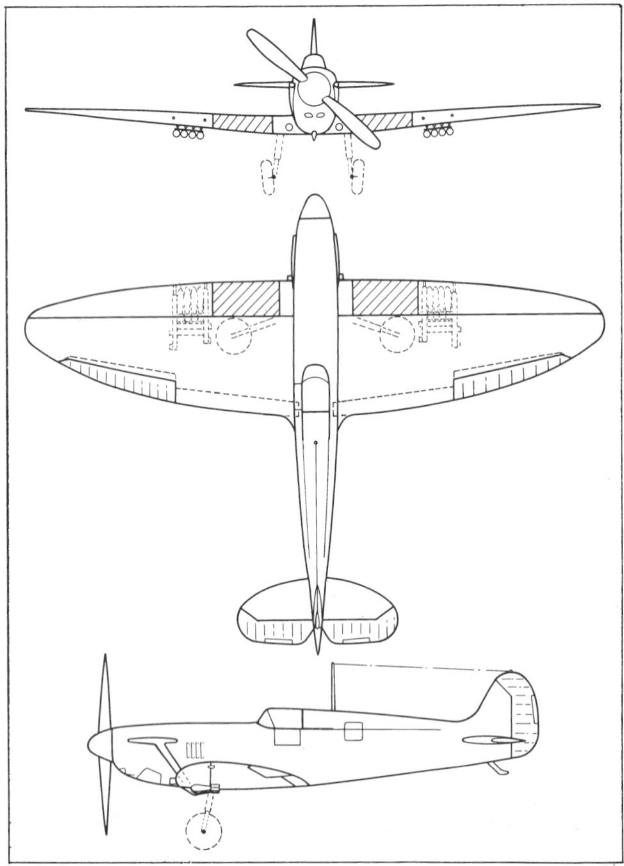

It is difficult to understand why Mitchell decided to adopt the new wing shape for it posed many problems, the main one being difficulty of manufacture. One reason for using it may have been his response to the final issue of Specification F5/34, which Supermarine received on 16 November 1934, and which called for an eight gun armament. What, then, were the advantages of an elliptical wing shape? An aerodynamicist has calculated that to arrive at an accurate total weight, each rib, spar, etc, must have been investigated and the whole assessed for aerodynamic performance. After all this effort by the drawing office it was estimated that the aerodynamic performance difference between the straight taper and elliptical wing was less than one per cent at high speeds.

What is clear is that Mitchell had used the shape before when he specified it for the six engined flying boat of July 1929, designed to Air Ministry Specification 20/28 issued in January 1929. The high speed wing section was adopted following B Shenstone's visit to America in 1934, when he returned with details of the NACA 2200 Series of aerofoils, and it was a logical move to combine these two desirable features. Mitchell had, apparently, resurrected his elliptical wing, combined it with the NACA aerofoil, retained the main spar arrangement of the flying boat, together with the wing incidence and dihedral of the revised, straight taper winged F7/30 to produce the new wing. That the wing was a success can be judged by the fact that both Vickers and Supermarine were to use the planform for a number of subsequent designs which are illustrated in this chapter.

Supermarine six engined flying boat project showing the elliptical wing.

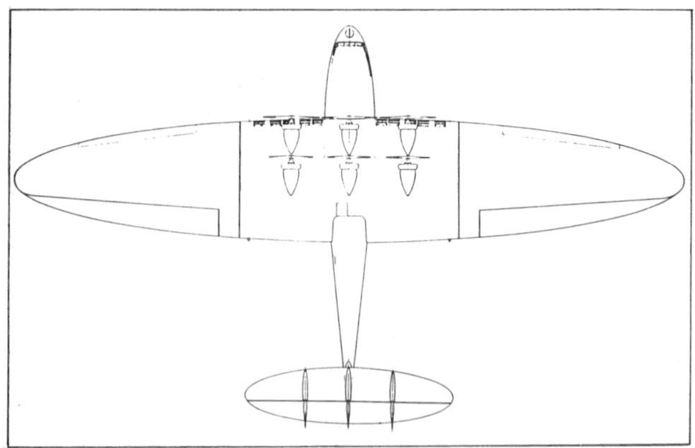

On 28 December 1934 the revised design of F7/30 was accepted by the Air Ministry and Specification F37/34 written around Supermarine Drawing 30000 Sheet 13. This Specification asked for only four guns and an evaporative cooling system using wing condensers in association with an auxiliary radiator for, as Rolls-Royce had estimated, this system was necessary if Supermarine wanted to avoid the provision of additional cooling water in wing tanks.

Reverting back to the 5 December Air Ministry meeting, all present agreed that the PV12 engine would be used for the prototype and one example would be ready for use six months before the delivery date of the completed aeroplane. The engine was providing a normal power output of just 790hp at 12,000 feet and it had not been satisfactorily tested for glycol cooling. Major Buchanan, Air Ministry, ruled that work could proceed with the evaporative system and an auxiliary radiator, but no mention was made regarding the positioning of this radiator. Due to the loss of performance with the stub exhausts a manifold was to be fitted. Buchanan also approved of the four gun arrangement and did ask if a tailwheel could be fitted in place of a skid.

Supermarine proposed deletion of a mock-up but Buchanan decided one was necessary. The programme of design and construction was not to be delayed by waiting for opinions expressed at mock-up conferences and the mock-up was to be used for positioning of detail equipment. But, if items were not available at a particular time the equivalent amount of space would be reserved. Pilot's view was discussed, with particular reference to rearward sighting as the cockpit faired into the rear fuselage. It was decided to wait until the mock-up was complete and to improve the view by fitting transparent material in the aft fairing. A contract to the value of £10,000 for a prototype aeroplane was agreed upon.

Despite Mitchell's comments in Specification 425 concerning powered undercarriage retraction it was proposed to adopt a manual, hydraulic system for the Type 300. A modified hand pump from the Supermarine Seagull with handle length reduced from 18 to ten inches was suggested after an engine driven pump was considered, then dismissed. A quote from Report 1362 states—"There will be but comparatively little work for the pilot to do in using the hand pump to raise or lower the wheels. Furthermore, the proposed pump may not be reliable for some time, and in any case will be continuously taking power from the engine". It was a retrograde step that was to be corrected in the future.

The formal signing of Air Ministry Contract 361140/34 for a prototype to Specification F37/34 took place on 3 January 1935 and detail design began in earnest. For a period of twelve months the redesign of the original F7/30 had been a private venture by Supermarine.

At a meeting between Rolls-Royce and Supermarine on the same day consideration was given to improving take off performance of the prototype. The suggestion was the adoption of two-speed engine gears and controllable pitch propellers,

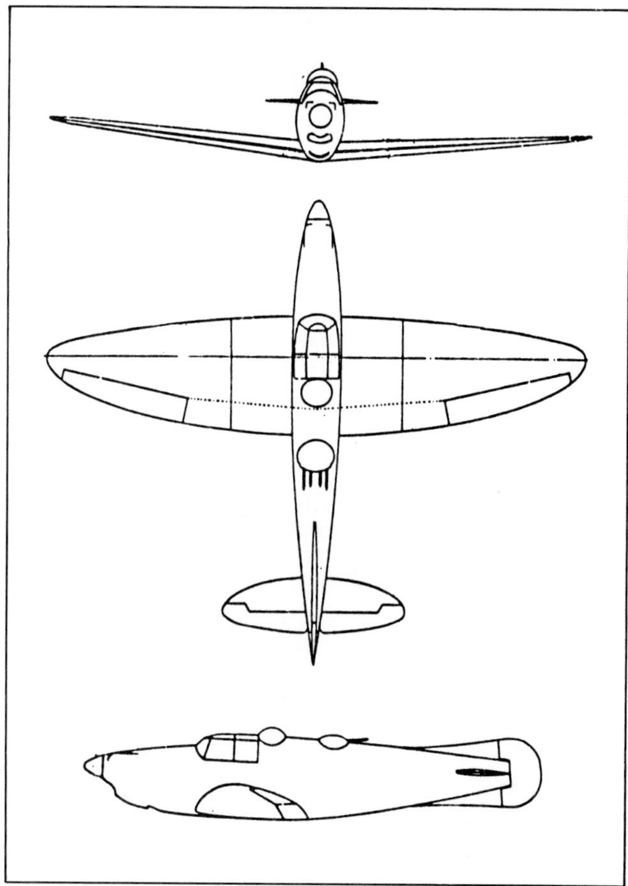

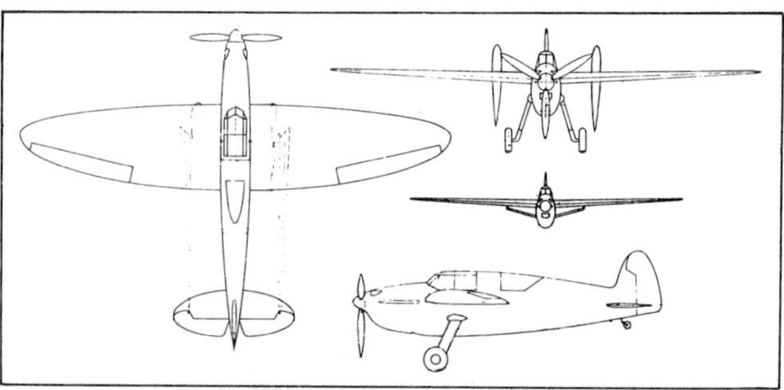

Supermarine had used the elliptical wing shape before, as can be seen by the six engined flying boat (Specification 20/28 of August 1929). It then appeared on the Vickers 037/34 dive bomber of 7 April 1936. The Vickers two-seat day and night fighter of 1936 to F9/35 had a similar wing. The flying boat was to be later redesigned and the wing shape altered. It resembled the straight tapered wing of the interim F7/30.

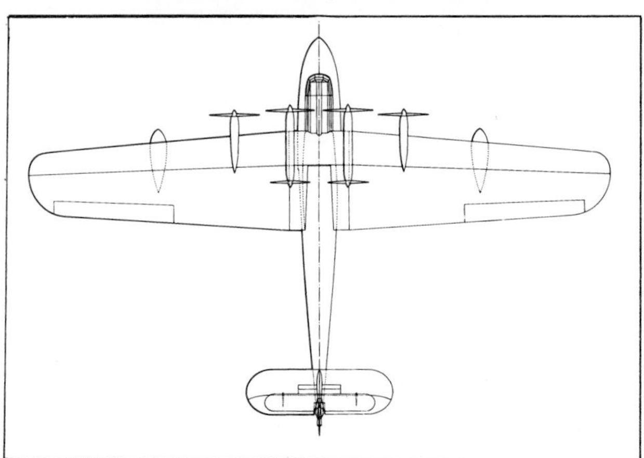

plus means to increase engine power. The two-speed gears found some favour for it would result in a smaller weight increase than the CP propeller. Rolls-Royce said, however, although a two-speed gear had been satisfactorily fitted to an Eagle engine with little weight increase they were not in favour of its application to the PV12. Their reasoning was that the type of gearing used made adaptation more difficult; at best it was a compromise, particularly in view of the tendency towards higher speeds. They were developing a CP propeller which they hoped would save a lot of weight and—"Supermarine was the only company, at present, interested in the two-speed gear, and once the CP propeller was under way they did not think interest would be shown in the gears". The Supermarine team observed that the impression was that Rolls-Royce would not be prepared to commit themselves to producing the two-speed gear. Estimates as to how long design and testing would take varied between one and two years. Rolls-Royce were convinced that suitable CP propellers would be ready in time for the prototype, but as Supermarine was uncertain of the situation Mr Ellor was to go to America and visit the Hamilton company to obtain the latest information on the subject. It was revealed that Rolls-Royce had actually placed an order for a CP propeller and it was due for delivery in six months. The 'Long' engine could be fitted with a fixed or CP propeller, but on the future 'Short'* engine the CP hub would be regarded as standard.

Mr Ross, Supermarine, visited Derby six days later to discuss re-rating the PV12 and had, tentatively, agreed figures for the fully supercharged engine, now known as the Merlin. The test engine was the Merlin BS and those to be delivered to Supermarine for the prototype Type 300 were to be similar but have electric starting and be called OS. The 'Short' engine was the Merlin DS, the bore of which was to be increased by 10% for future development. All engines were designed for VP propellers, which were not to be used on initial aircraft. Rolls-Royce had received particulars of the Hamilton blade and were in process of negotiation with de Havilland for it was thought that three blades would be sufficient to absorb the Merlin power output. Provisional data for both engine types was – Power. Rated 950bhp at 2600rpm at 11,000 feet. Maximum 1045bhp at 3000rpm at 15,000 feet. Weight 1225lb. Fuel consumption .525 pints at two thirds power at normal rpm at 15,000 feet. Sea level .550 pints at 852bhp at normal rpm.

By 14 January the auxiliary radiator had been added to the design as the drawing below illustrates, but the actual location

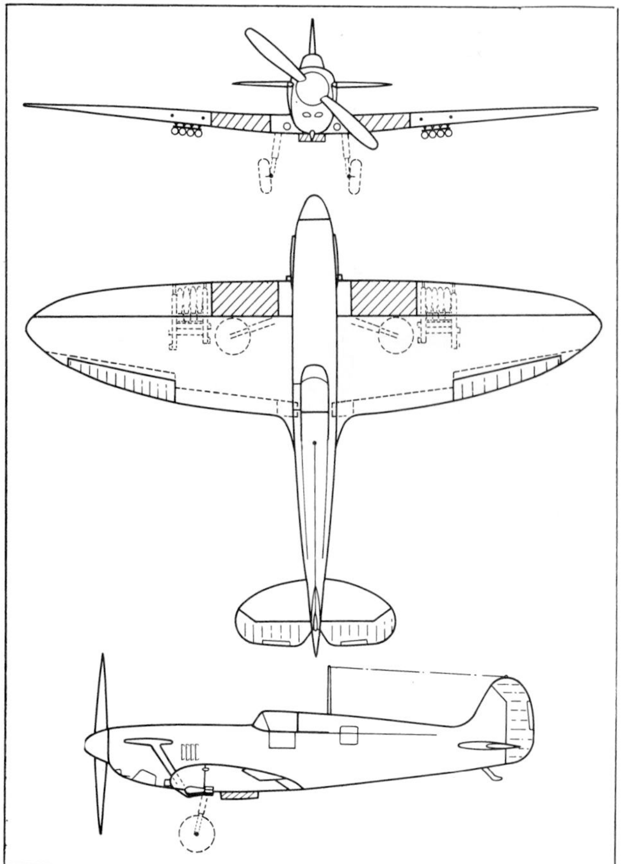

**Length of piston stroke.*

has never been satisfactorily explained. Two versions of the location have been disclosed to the authors, the first being from Mr Frank Parry, another ex-Supermarine employee, who recalls—"Seeing a drawing which showed the small radiator underneath the wing centre section, just on the vertical datum point". But R J Fenner is just as emphatic as to its position for he states—"Now as far as the radiator was concerned in this six gun version it was always inboard of the landing gear under the port wing—half buried in the wing.** It was because of this and the optimum positioning of the Browning guns and their ammunition boxes that the landing gear had to be retracted outwards". Both are interesting observations and information concerning either location has never come to light.

Tests of two propellers were investigated at Eastleigh on F7/30 with .477 gear ratio and maximum thrust obtained was 1,345lb at 2,460rpm. The next day, 14 March, comparisons were made of the proposed Supermarine and RAE radiators. For the same cooling the first had 5.6 times the drag of the latter and core area was virtually identical. Speed and ceiling were not affected by both types and there was only 17 seconds difference in climb to 15,000 feet, with the RAE radiator providing the best results. Figures for a Gallay radiator obtained four days later revealed it could cope with 41 gallons of coolant a minute with a section of 3in x 440mm and 170gal/min with a section 12in x 440mm as compared to less than half the coolant dealt with by a normal radiator.

On 19 March Mr Henry of Rolls-Royce arrived at Supermarine for further discussion on Merlin cooling for the problems of draining on the prototype design had made the use of two hot wells necessary. A two stage pump, then not developed for the Merlin, could be fitted to the Goshawk, but the result would be a pressure of $40lb/in^2$ to the ejector pump with the water at boiling point. A single stage pump for the Merlin would be available and work efficiently provided the water did not reach boiling point, so an efficient radiator was vital. A test unit, designed and constructed by the Serck Radiator Company, was to be installed in a test rig of the complete cooling system which Rolls-Royce would supervise.

Cooling of the Kestrel engine had been researched by Rolls-Royce on a Hawker Hart (K2969) and it had the advantage of permitting use of a partially submerged radiator and avoidance of a large cooling system which was fully employed only at peak load conditions in higher temperatures. Tests with the Hart were to examine the possibility of glycol as a cooling medium as an alternative to composite cooling. Glycol had a boiling point of 197° and freezing of -12°c, so it was possible to reduce frontal area of the Hart installation from 2.886 sq ft for the water cooled to 1.8 sq ft for the glycol. Partially submerging it in the fuselage reduced frontal area to 0.71 sq ft, but maximum speed was reduced by 7.5mph at 15,000 feet. Rolls-Royce in their report under 'Future Developments' wrote—"We anticipate that an appreciable reduction in the size of coolant pipes could be employed with glycol; also in the size of the header tank as it is not asked to deal with steam. The amount of reserve carried could also be less as loss through evaporation and occasional boiling does not occur as with water". This, to any designer, would be of prime importance especially where weight was concerned. Mitchell received a copy of the Rolls-Royce report on 3 December 1934.

It was decided to examine the effects of a similar radiator on the speed of F37/34 with the assumption that it would have an area of 2.4 sq ft and be partially submerged in the wing,* the cowling having an entry of 1 sq ft. Speed reduction was an estimated 24mph from a maximum of 310 at 15,000 feet. However, further RAE tests showed that by careful cowling this loss could be reduced to that of the Hart test bed.

At a meeting (15 April) with Mitchell, Pierson, Smith and Larsson (Vickers) the proposed four gun installation was discussed. Drawings were inspected and a sketch handed to Larsson showing one gun in the wing section and the two port guns and magazine in plan, together with a half plan of the aircraft showing positioning of the guns in relation to the airframe. The Dunlop pneumatic firing system was specified and approved by the Air Ministry who had agreed that reloading in the air was unnecessary (if not impossible). Larsson appeared nonplussed and said Vickers had designed an electrical firing system for the Vickers gun and intended to proceed with its adaptation for the Colt Browning. The Supermarine team was firm about its committment to the Dunlop system and said the Vickers plan would not be used as the preferred system was not only satisfactory but lighter.

April 26, 1935, was of particular significance to the final design of F37/34 for Squadron Leader Sorley went to the Supermarine Woolston factory and was shown the nearly completed mock-up, and Mitchell mentioned he had received a

Close up, and general view, of the F 7/30 wooden mock-up hanging in the rafters of the Supermarine works at Hythe. Note the T-shaped exhaust pipe as shown on Drawing Sheet 13 (original), which established that at the time of the mock-up a composite cooling arrangement of leading edge condensers and a small, ventral radiator was to be used to cool the PV12 engine.

***Mr Fenner did correct his statement at a later date saying he was, possibly, mistaken about the radiator's position, but is firm in his assertion that at this time six guns had been selected as main armament.*

* *This was the first time a wing mounted radiator was considered for the F37/34.*

copy of the Air Staff's requirements for a day and might fighter to specification F10/35* the previous day. Sorley and Mitchell discussed the requirements, in particular paragraph 3 which read—"Not less than six guns, but 8 guns are desirable. These should be located outside the airscrew disc. Re-loading in the air is not required". Sorley, as already mentioned, had devoted a great deal of time promoting the eight gun fighter and it was only natural that the possibility of adapting the prototype's wing to accept this weight of armament should be discussed. Mitchell then assured Sorley he was confident that four additional guns could be accomodated in the design, but it did mean that the bomb load would have to be deleted and fuel capacity reduced to 66 gallons in an effort to reduce weight. Sorley left Woolston in a buoyant mood and on return to his office wrote a letter to the DTD, and the relevant extracts concerning F37/34 are reproduced below.

"On Friday, 26 April 1935, I saw at Supermarine a mock-up of a fighter which they are building to Specification F37/34. This was the one got out by AMRD to cover the redesign of the Supermarine F7/30. According to the 37/34 Specification it is to comply with the requirement of the F7/30 Specification subject to certain concessions. As designed it has every feature required by our latest Specification 10/35 with the following differences—

	37/34	10/35
(i) Guns	4 in wings	6 or 8 in wings
(ii) Bombs	4 × 20lb	nil
(iii)	94 gals = $\frac{1}{2}$hr max + 2hr @ normal rpm	66gals = $\frac{1}{4}$hr max + 1hr @ normal rpm

"Mitchell received the Air Staff's requirements for the 10/35 while I was there and is naturally desirious of bringing the aircraft now building into line with this specification. He says he can include four additional guns without trouble or delay. (ii) and (iii) are, of course, deletions he would welcome. The savings in fuel amounts to 273 lb (Mitchell's estimate is 59 gals), thus there is a big saving in weight (180 lb) even after additional four guns. Hawkers also have a similar aircraft under construction to a similar sort of specification (F36/34), the mock-up of which we have seen. I suggest that we should likewise relate the requirements of this one to the 10/35". Sorley then discussed the various reasons for not producing the Gloster Gladiator.

"I then suggest we should now speculate the cost of jigs and tools for both the Hawker and Supermarine aircraft while the prototypes are being completed. The risk of a dead loss is to my mind small since both designers have been notable for their first time successes. We could then select either, or both, for production to commence immediately we have satisfied ourselves on their flying capabilities. If by some mischance they both should fail then we shall still have the Gloster F7/30 to fall back on.

"I am aware that this is an unorthodox method but with the political situation as it is and the possibility of increased expansion close upon us we should take steps to produce the latest design in the shortest possible time. It may be said that action to tool-up for these two aircraft would be unfair to other firms tendering for the 10/35 Specification. I suggest that the situation no longer allows of tender feelings for others, and we require the best aircraft we can get at the appropriate moment". OR 1/5/35.

Sorley's letter was endorsed by the DCAS who added a hand written appendix—"I have discussed the above with Sorley and fully agree. I feel it is an opportunity that we should take advantage of without delay. I suggest that the firms be asked to press on with the work at the greatest possible speed even if it means additional cost to the Air Ministry in order to cover the extra cost of working continous shifts".

Air Commodore Verney (DTD) was as swift in his reaction to Sorley's letter as was the latter's speed in submitting it, for his reply was dated 4 May. He wrote—"As a matter of principle I am against asking firms to make alterations on prototypes once the decision to place an order has been given, and I have had my design conference with the designer. But I realise that there are special circumstances which may make the case of these monoplanes exceptions to the rule. As regards the Supermarine F37/34, I agree that there should be no great difficulty in adding four additional guns. Deleting the bombs would be a help, but I should not be in favour of reducing the tankage, as this could be done in production models if required; it is always much easier to decrease than increase, and experience shows that as the engine power goes up we often wish to add extra tankage. Nor need the aeroplane be flown with full tanks.

"The Hawker monoplane has provision for 107 gallons of petrol. Here again, we could delete the bombs, but I should not be in favour of adding more guns to the wings, which are already nearly constructed. At present, there are two interrupter guns in the fuselage, and two wing guns. We may find some difficulty in making the interrupter guns work satisfactorily with the 3-bladed VP airscrew which they propose to use, and in any future model Hawkers would prefer to have only wing guns. What could be done, if desired, would be to design and build a new set of wings with eight guns in them, so as to have them in reserve, but nothing, in my opinion, should be allowed to delay the construction and flying test of this aeroplane. We must realise that we have very little experience of monoplanes of this type, and difficulties in developing them are certain to be faced. I should be very opposed to holding back on the Gloster F7/30 with Perseus engine, and feel that we should press forward as quickly as possible as a reserve.

"The question as to how much should be risked to save a delay in putting either or both these two monoplanes in production, if they should prove satisfactory, is a matter of policy rather beyond me. It should be realised that if the design and construction of jigs, etc, were begun now there would be the serious alterations, and possibly wholesale scrapping, if changes had to be made. I would rather say that directly the aeroplanes have flown, and we know the best or worst, as the case may be, that then would be the time for a production gamble if the circumstances necessitated".

Verney's letter is a textbook example of how the more experienced officer handles the younger man's enthusiasm without detracting from the merits of his suggestions.In dealing with the question of reducing fuel tankage the DTD suggests the F37/34 prototype could conduct its trials with half empty tanks. Sorley's paragraph 9 urges risk with the Hawker and Supermarine monoplanes, but still recommends insurance in the form of the Gloster aircraft, a point with which Verney agreed.

The matter did not rest there, however, for Mitchell also responded to Sorley's suggestions, putting his thoughts on an eight gun wing in a report dated 7 May, the day on which the mock-up aeroplane was completed. Mitchell wrote—"Summary of changes to the Colt-Browning installation in Supermarine Day and Night Fighter to Specification F37/34 since Mr Larsson's visit on 15 April. Drawing No 30062 indicates these changes viz (1) the complete installation is now to be for eight guns instead of four (2) the elevation of the guns had been raised to be parallel with the horizontal datum of the aircraft and has been increased + 2.3/4 degrees from that shown on the drawing handed to Mr Larsson (3) the magazine volume per gun has been reduced from 500 rounds to 300 (4) the guns have been replaced to suit the eight gun arrangement. In addition all guns, when aligned on their normal axes, will converge to a point 400 yards ahead of the axis of the aircraft".

A report of the performance data of F37/34 with its revised armament was telephoned to the Air Ministry on 9 May, so urgent was the need to obtain official approval. Because of the additional four guns the Merlin FS was used and it was estimated to provide a maximum speed of 365 mph at 15,000 feet. In spite of the enormous amount of design effort needed to convert the wings to take the extra guns Mitchell was confident that he, and his team, could still fulfil the Air Ministry's demands and have a prototype ready for the agreed delivery date. The major problem with the revised armament was the need to keep the gun breech blocks and ammunition containers in the same area as the aircraft's vertical datum, so that when ammunition was expended fore and aft trim would not be too greatly disturbed. The elliptical wing shape was ideal for this.

Mr Dorey, of Rolls-Royce, arrived at Woolston on 9 May 1935 to continue discussions on the various properties of radiators and the engine composite cooling system. He produced a number of drawings and agreed that if necessary extra cooling water could be carried in the wings as a reserve if required. On glycol cooling Dorey stated that the radiator area required would be two square feet, with an air intake area of 0.6 sq ft. He also confirmed that a mock-up of the latest Merlin would shortly be delivered.

Verney then wrote to the Air Ministry on 21 May and his letter makes clear his thoughts on the current situation."The Air Staff's requirements for this Specification (F10/35) were circulated to the firms on 25 April and its specification is in draft. In view of the probable decision (not yet notified to me) that F36/34 Hawker and F37/34 Supermarine fighters are to be

See Appendix III, page 602

converted to this specification, by ordering new wings for the Hawker, and altering the Supermarine which is still in the design stage, is it a matter for careful consideration whether the issue of this specification should still be made?

"In addition to the Hawker and Supermarine fighters, we have the Single-Seater 8-gun fighters to Specification F5/34 on order from Bristol and Gloster, and there are at least three PVs of the type. It does seem, however, that our requirements in 8-gun fighters should be met, even allowing for the inevitable delays which may occur. I suggest, therefore that the Air Staff might consider three alternatives- (a) to let F10/35 continue (b) to withdraw it for a time (c) to recast it making demands for an even more advanced design. I favour course (c). I suggest that our advanced design might take the form of a 'No-allowance fighter'. We have completed a long programme of development work with the COW and Vickers guns, with uniformly satisfactory results. It seems a great pity that all this valuable work should be read and then put away without any real interest to translate it into practical results.

"As I understand it the view of the Air Staff is that the fighter's opportunities will be so fleeting that nothing but the maximum rate of fire in a minimum time is worth having. While agreeing with this, I feel sure that the trend of weapon development must be to increase the range of attack, the 'long-bow' versus the 'cross-bow'. My suggestion is for a single-seater fighter with eight guns in the no allowance position either in the wings or fuselage, plus the COW gun in the fuselage. Such a fighter could attack from the rear at a range of 100 to 500 yards using its COW gun. When the range had closed sufficiently the machine guns will be used. Utilising the apparatus we have under development for traversing wing guns, it might be feasible to vary their elevation".

So, F10/35 was dead (it was later brought into line with F37/35) as the Supermarine prototype embraced all the Specification's requirements, except for one specific area. In F9/35 paragraph (3) called for "Some or all of the guns mounted to permit a degree of elevation and traverse with some form of control from the pilot's seat". The original proposal was initiated on 8 January 1935 and the basic idea was that a fighter could approach a flight of enemy aircraft from the rear, at a fairly wide angle, and bring its guns to bear. A Hendy Heck, K8853, was converted for trials with two Browning guns in each wing, each gun having the muzzle pivoting in an adjustable bush.

The Hendy Heck 2C wing revealing installation of the lateral and vertical swivelling mounts for the Browning guns.

The scheme was put forward by Wing Commander Keith and based on a proposal by Frazer-Nash. Verney asked for the scheme to be included in F10/35 with particular reference to the Supermarine prototype. During trials with the Hendy Heck all guns were pre-set on the ground to 6.25, 12.50 or 18.75 degrees and they could be centralised in flight by the pilot. The Heck went to Northolt for flying trials and then to Boscombe Down for gunnery tests. It arrived at Boscombe in April 1937 and was later transferred to Martlesham Heath, where the reflector sight was installed. The weight penalties were enormous and to make the installation more practical it was suggested that lateral movements be deleted in favour of vertical only, so that fighters could attack the undersides of enemy aircraft*. Summing up the system on 1 July 1937 Dowding wrote—"I would recommend, therefore, that energy be no longer devoted to the devising of laterally adjustable guns. If, however, we consider the question of vertical adjustment certain advantages become apparent". The scheme was abandoned two weeks later on 16 July.

**The method of attack was adoped by German night fighters against British bombers during World War II.*

Verney wrote to the Air Ministry once more on 28 May 1935 and in a letter to the Director of Contracts, B E Holloway, said – "Dowding has agreed to Air Staff proposals that this aeroplane (F37/34) should be brought into line with the F10/35 proposals. This involves the design and manufacture of a new set of wings to take eight Vickers Mk V or Browning guns with 300 rounds of ammunition per gun. Could you please ask the firm to quote for the above in addition to the contract, but at the same time inform them it is not desired that any alterations should be made to the aeroplane at the present state of manufacture as it is of the utmost importance that it should be completed as quickly as possible. It is desired that the design and manufacture of new wings should proceed at the same time so that conversion could be made at a later stage of the flying trials". Verney also wrote to Supermarine at the same time and informed them that the wings for F37/34 were to be altered to incorporate the eight gun requirement of the F10/35, and also suggested he would be content for the prototype to make its first flight with the original four gun arrangement.

The Director of Contracts also wrote to Supermarine on 21 June as follows – "Gentlemen, Type F10/35. With reference to the department's letter of 25 April 1935, I am directed to inform you that action in connection with the preparation of the specification of the above type of aeroplane is suspended for the time being and that consideration is being given to the issue of requirements for a different type of fighter in substitution therefore".

The three, apparently unconnected, events mentioned in this chapter had merged to produce the graceful prototype. There was, however, a fourth which was to improve engine cooling, reduce drag and make the aeroplane easily recognisable at almost any single angle when seen in the air- the Meredith radiator, of which more, later.

On 26 June the name Spitfire appeared for the first time on the Supermarine reports and it was without Air Ministry knowledge. On 27 July a general arrangement drawing of the aircraft appeared and was similar to that reproduced on page

During spinning trials of a model of F 37/34 at Farnborough a number of fuselage lengths, tailplane sizes, fin and rudder shapes and positions were tested and the table below lists them. The RAE considered that the original Type 300 design was unsatisfactory owing to a short fuselage, small fin and rudder and low set tailplane. The tail unit was redesigned for the model and the fuselage lengthened by nine inches. The tailplane was also raised by seven inches. These changes did improve performance, much of which was lost when the VP propeller was installed.

Expmnt	*fuselage*	*tailplane*	*rudder*	*propeller*
1-3	*original*	*original*	*original*	*wood*
4-9	,,	,,	*large*	,,
10-21	,,	*raised 12"*	*large*	,,
22-30	*9" longer*	*raised 9"*	*inter-mediate*	,,
31-35	*9" longer*	*raised 9"*	*original*	,,
36-45	*9" longer*	*raised 7"*	*original*	,,
46-52	*9" longer*	*raised 7"*	*original*	,,

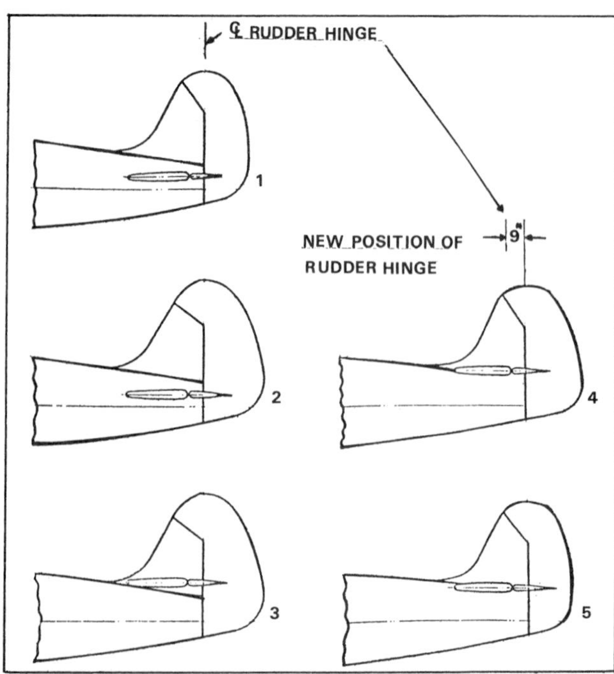

74. It contained the aircraft's weight and other data- weight 3050lb; gross wing area (inc, fuselage) 242 sq ft; nett area 220 sq ft; wing loading 20.85lb/sq ft (on gross area); span 37.08 feet; aspect ratio 5.68; dihedral 6°; wing section NACA Series 2200; form of wings elliptical taper plan form, and 13.2 to 6.6% taper thickness.

In August 1935 RAE Farnborough issued a report on spinning tests of an F37/34 model and it was a mixture of praise and criticism. The report began by describing the aircraft and how it differed from the F7/30 previously tested, It then stated—"In common with other modern, low-wing monoplanes the wing loading is high (22.3lb/sq ft). Past experience coupled with theory leads to the conclusion that such a design is fundamentally bad from a spinning point of view and requires a really good tail unit if trouble is to be avoided. The original design submitted had a rather short fuselage, small fin and rudder and low tailplane. The flatter type of spin no longer occurred and recovery was possible in about four seconds at 15,000 feet. The firm (Supermarine) were unwilling to raise the tailplane and have so large a rudder so a compromise design was submitted having the fuselage nine inches longer, the tail raised nine inches and an intermediate sized rudder. The rudder was finally reduced to the original size and the tailplane height reduced to seven inches below the original.

"The final design was given the normal routine tests at an equivilant height of 11,000 feet. No flat spin was found and recovery with full opposite controls was satisfactory. Further tests were subsequently made to investigate the effect of adding a Glycol radiator and a variable pitch airscrew". With regard to the latter Verney had asked for a VP unit in a letter to Supermarine the previous May, and he said—"In view of the uncertainty as to take off of the aeroplane, I wish to have a VP airscrew ordered for it. Could you please quote for this as an addition to the contract?". The report's conclusions were that the original design, in spite of a deep, elliptic, cross section fuselage, was unsatisfactory. The final design with improved tail unit and wooden propeller was satisfactory. With a VP propeller it was only just satisfactory and it was recommended that initial spinning trials be made with a wooden propeller.

THE MEREDITH RADIATOR

In June 1934 an RAE report on the cooling of aircraft engines, with special reference to Ethylene Glycol radiators enclosed in ducts, had been published. Its author was F. W. Meredith, and his conclusions were that the employment of the principle of low velocity cooling avoided the necessity for an increasing expenditure with increasing speed, provided the exit conditions of the radiator were adjusted to suit the speed. Further, the combined effects of compressibility and heat transfer from the radiator could reduce the power consumption to nil if the size of the radiator was adequate. Also, by use of the exhaust heat an appreciable thrust could be expected from the presence of the cooling stream. Finally, attention was drawn to the importance of the momentum of engine exhaust gases for a high speed aeroplane. A ducted radiator and carefully designed exhaust ducts could provide additional thrust and, therefore, speed*.

It was over one year later when Meredith's proposals were incorporated into the Type 300's cooling system and took place on 11 September 1935 when Meredith, Major Stewart, Dr Roxbee Cox and other Supermarine personnel met to discuss the glycol radiator.—

(1) Examination of Type 300 in light of the latest theories regarding drag. Mr Meredith expressed the opinion that the glycol radiator system as proposed would cost us about 15% of engine HP, i.e about 15mph in drag at top speed. He thought it might be improved considerably by tunnel testing a model. He explained his reasons for believing that our radiator position was not good, the chief point being that air should be taken from the nose of the wing or body where the pressure is normally atmospheric, instead of from a point further aft where it may well be less than atmospheric. In latter case the process of building up the necessary pressure to push the air through the radiator requires careful fairing, and a length of cowling which depends upon the pressure difference, as there is a certain pressure gradient. i.e change of pressure per unit length, which cannot be exceeded without causing a breakaway of flow and hence unwanted drag. Mr Meredith was of the strong opinion we should get a standing eddy in our radiator cowling mouth unless we fitted vanes, and/or vented the opening. He also suggested we fair off the oil and ejector cooler openings more smoothly than shown on the mock-up and the best place for the louvres would be as indicated in sketch, which is higher than the position now being considered and less likely to disturb the flow over the fillet.

As a result of this meeting the Meredith radiator scheme was adopted for the F37/34, the T-shaped exhaust pipes deleted and flush ports fitted, the engine louvres moved into a higher position to the rear and the oil cooler inlets moved to the rear on the engine cowling, as per the Meredith sketch (page 26) and the drawing below. Also, the wing mounted evaporative units were removed, but their original positions can be clearly seen in

Models of the Meredith radiator scheme were tested at Farnborough for comparison with alternative Supermarine designs during 1936. Meredith-based cowls are shown on the left.

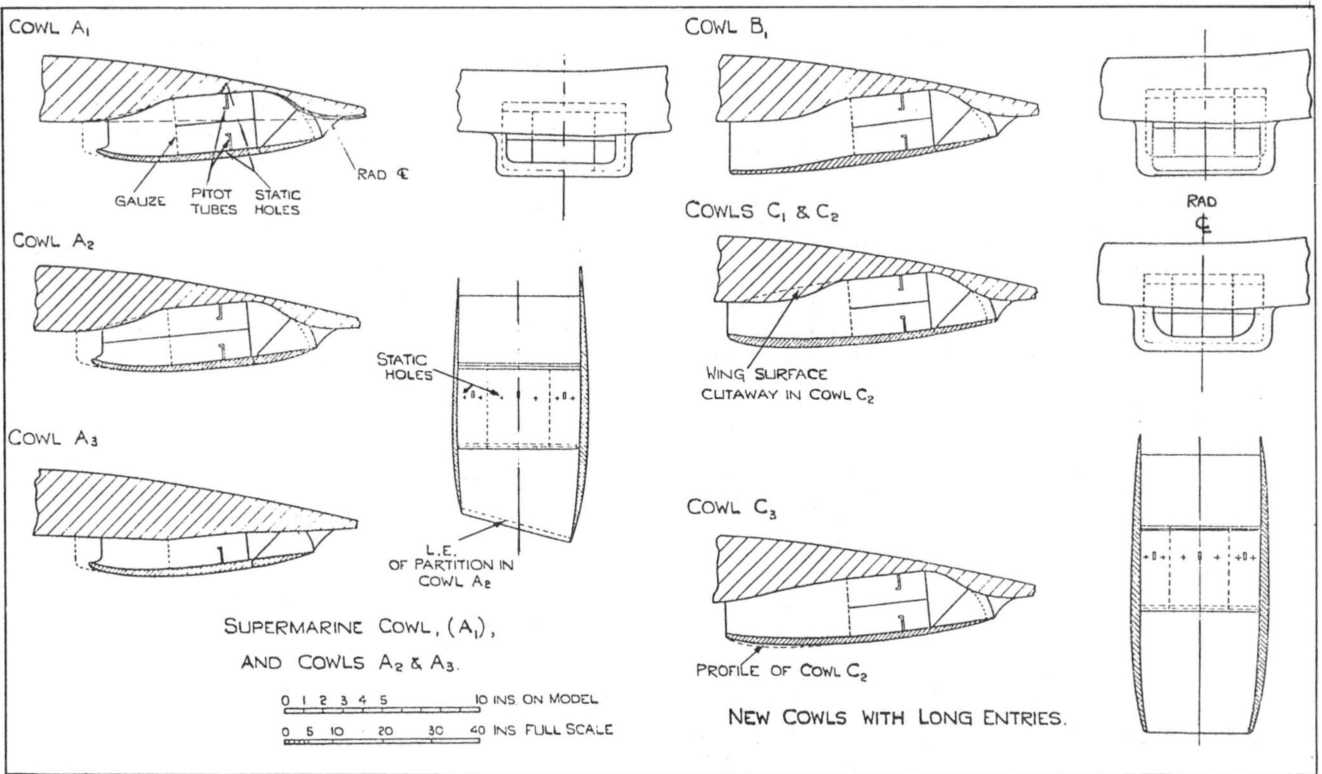

**RAE tests on the ducted radiator proved it had low drag and Mr E. J Davis recalls that he and his colleagues were of the opinion that the thrust of warm air from the radiator balanced the drag. It was, he said, in effect a rudimentary jet engine*

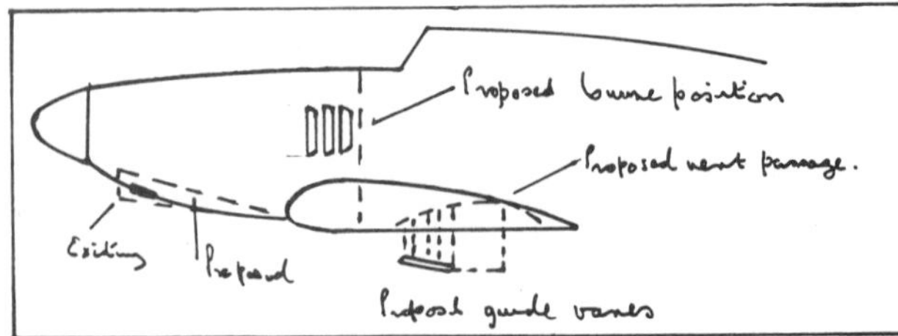

An accurate copy of the sketch Meredith made on the bottom of Supermarine Report TD 1635 of 11 September 1935. He also proposed a new engine cowling louvre position, re-positioning of the carburetter air intake and the guide vanes inside his radiator cowl.

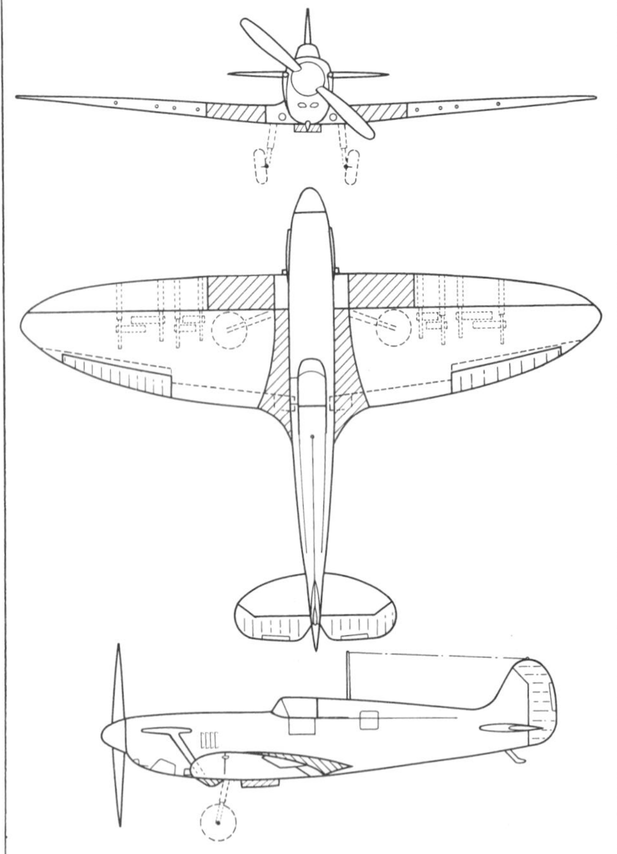

F 37/34 after Supermarine had adapted the wings to accept an eight gun armament, bringing the design into line with F 10/35. Another change had also taken place for on 8 April the large, wing root/fuselage fillets were added.

the head-on photograph of the prototype taken before its first flight. A series of trials with the radiator cowl were conducted on a ¼ scale model in the Farnborough wind tunnel, with the radiator located under the starboard wing, and they demonstrated that it was satisfactory.

Major Stewart then raised the subject of higher speed aeroplanes and said the RAE, after investigation, thought a fighter with a 1000hp engine, 28lb/sq ft wing loading and low drag flaps could reach 380mph. He thought 360mph was fairly certain and wanted Supermarine's opinion before submitting the idea to the Air Ministry for inclusion in a new fighter specification. Supermarine thought 380mph would be very difficult to obtain from the conditions stated.

Verney was to visit Supermarine on 26 November and in his notes he wrote—"The fuselage is nearly completed and the engine installed. The wings have been plated and some parts of the undercarriage still have to be finished. I liked the design of the undercarriage very much, also the flush riveting of the surface of the fuselage and wings. The glycol radiator is in the starboard wing,** with controlled outlet cooling. Tubular honeycomb oil coolers are set forward under the engine. As far as I can see it cannot be flying this year, but it should be in early January. It is in many ways of much more advanced design than the Hawker, and should be a great deal lighter". The oil cooler was to be relocated under the port wing sometime during December and this was the reason why the first flight took place three months later than Verney had estimated.

A comparison of drag of F37/34 with a glycol radiator and Merlin with a radial air cooled engine of equal power revealed a maximum speed of 340mph at 18,000 feet for the former and 329 for the latter. In December Mr Hartshorn of RAE went to Supermarine for further discussions on drag and thought that the radiator as then installed was close to the best possible. Dissipation was satisfactory and drag minimal. Drag gains possible were still low, but by placing the radiator further out towards the wing tip; making the cross section more square, a gain of 100ft/sec could be achieved. But, by locating the radiator forward and slightly below the engine cowling the gain would be greater. If speed of air through the radiator could be further increased a much smaller radiator could be utilised. A series of trials of the new radiator cowling were conducted on a ¼ scale model in the Farnborough wind tunnel, with the new, and smaller, radiator still located under the wing, and they demonstrated that cooling and drag would be as good as the Meredith scheme. Mitchell was to use the nose radiator position of his Type 312 proposal for a four-cannon Spitfire variant, details of which appear on page 41.

Before the first flight of K2890 Mitchell was considering fitting a retractable undercarriage. On 17 October 1933 the Supermarine Aviation Works (Vickers) Ltd., had applied for a provisional patent numbered 2807/33 under their name and that of R. S. Dickson, who had also contributed to the deign of F7/30. This unit rotated through 90° before stowage in the wing, as mentioned by R. J. Fenner. Mitchell wanted this unit for the Type 300 and Fenner was to adapt it for the aircraft. For this the unit had to retract sideways and the main leg was mounted on the canted pintle bolted to the main spar. It was canted in two planes at such angles that a straight pull by a single hydraulic jack gave the desired result. It was an elegant solution to a difficult problem.

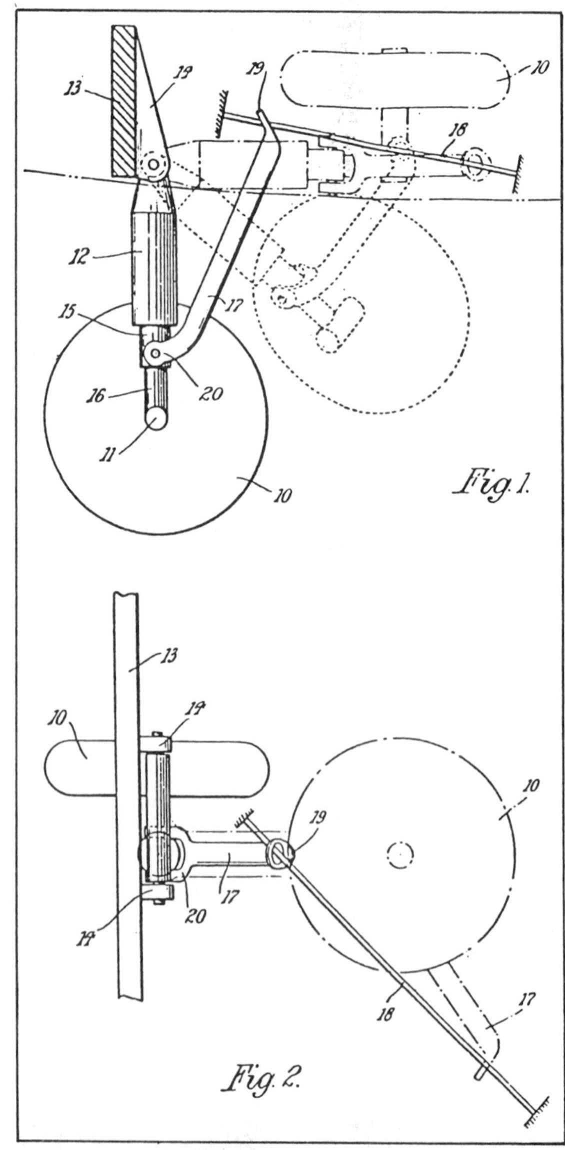

***The final radiator position was on record for the first time and it differed from Fenner's disclosure that it was, originally, in the port wing.*

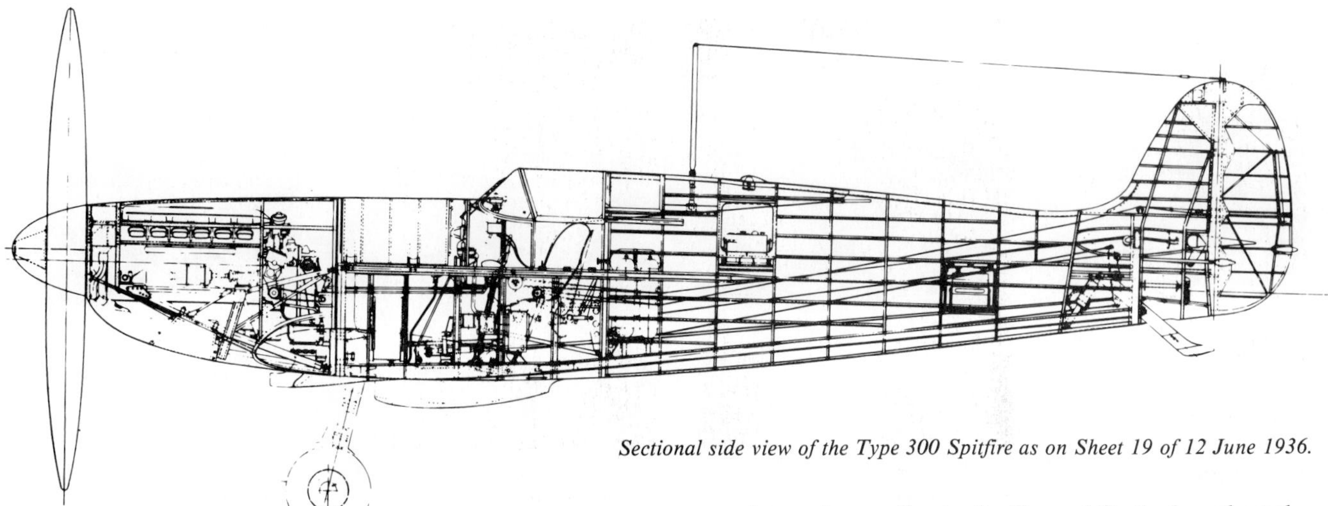

Sectional side view of the Type 300 Spitfire as on Sheet 19 of 12 June 1936.

Through the remaining weeks of 1935 the prototype took shape; security was tight and it was under constant guard. Personnel were searched and secrecy at times carried to absurd lengths. An apprentice had, supposedly, thrown a piece of metal into a waste bin and was immediatley hauled up in front of the works manager because of the possibility of a security leak. During tea and lunch breaks the prototype was covered with a large tarpaulin.

Tests were conducted on transparent material for the cockpit and samples included the German Plexiglass and French Rhodoid. The German material was superior to any other form of acetate sheet for transparency and weight, but was highly inflammable and brittle. Rhodoid was considered to be the more suitable.

The results of all tests and trials produced a large number of modifications to the prototype airframe and as late as December 1935 the position of the oil coolers was still under consideration. In the first few weeks of January 1936 it was complete and according to the General Particulars sheet the new fighter, now serialled K5054, weighed 3979 lb tare; auw 5250; length 29ft 11in; height (tail down) 8ft $2\frac{1}{2}$in. Engine one Rolls-Royce Merlin 'C'. It was weighed with an AID inspector present on 24 February 1936.

On the morning of 5 March 1936 'Mutt' Summers climbed into the cockpit of the unpainted aircraft at Eastleigh aerodrome for the maiden flight. The prototype took off into a 35° cross wind and the months of design, experiments, second thoughts and doubts were about to be resolved. K5054 seemed to drift into the air, its undercarriage locked firmly into the down position looked flimsy without the fairings in position, and within minutes all present knew that their faith in the project was justified. Several days later (25 March) George Pickering, Supermarine test pilot, flew the new aeroplane, to be followed the next day by Jeffrey Quill* who was to practically live with it, and its successors, for many years to come. After Quill had landed the ASI was calibrated from 40 to 160mph in divisions of 2mph and from 160 to 400 in divisions of 10mph. Initial Service flights were made by Sammy Roath but Quill was responsible for the majority of tests. After the first sequence of level speeds on 27 March, Mitchell confessed to being "Very disappointed with the results, which were a lot slower than I had hoped for". Quill continued with the tests using various types of propeller design and managed to reach a true air speed

Half model of prototype mounted in the Farnborough wind tunnel in November 1935. By this time the Meredith radiator scheme had been adopted.

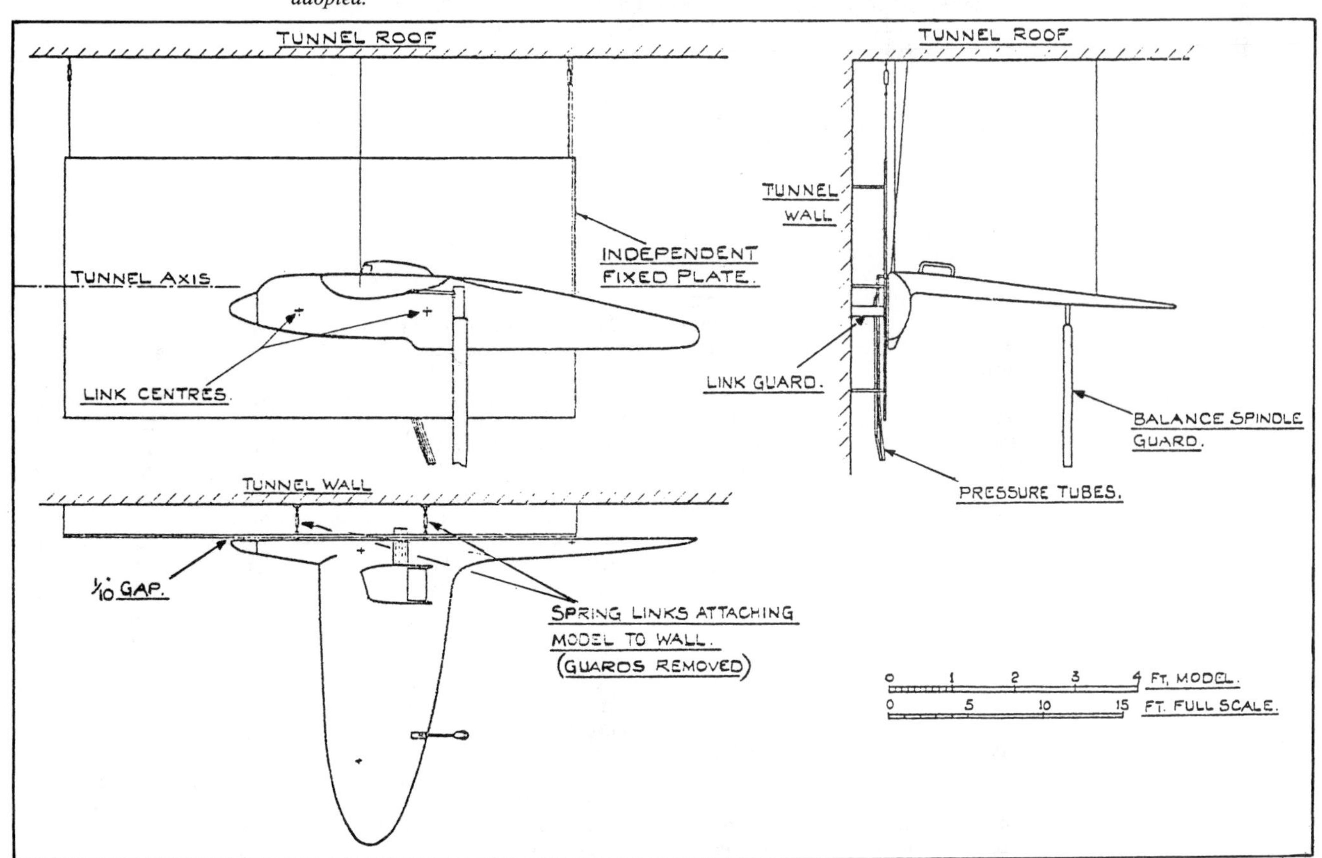

**Jeffrey Quill told the authors that K5054 made the important first flight with a special propeller designed to deliver maximum revs. It was replaced by a normal pitch one for the second flight.*

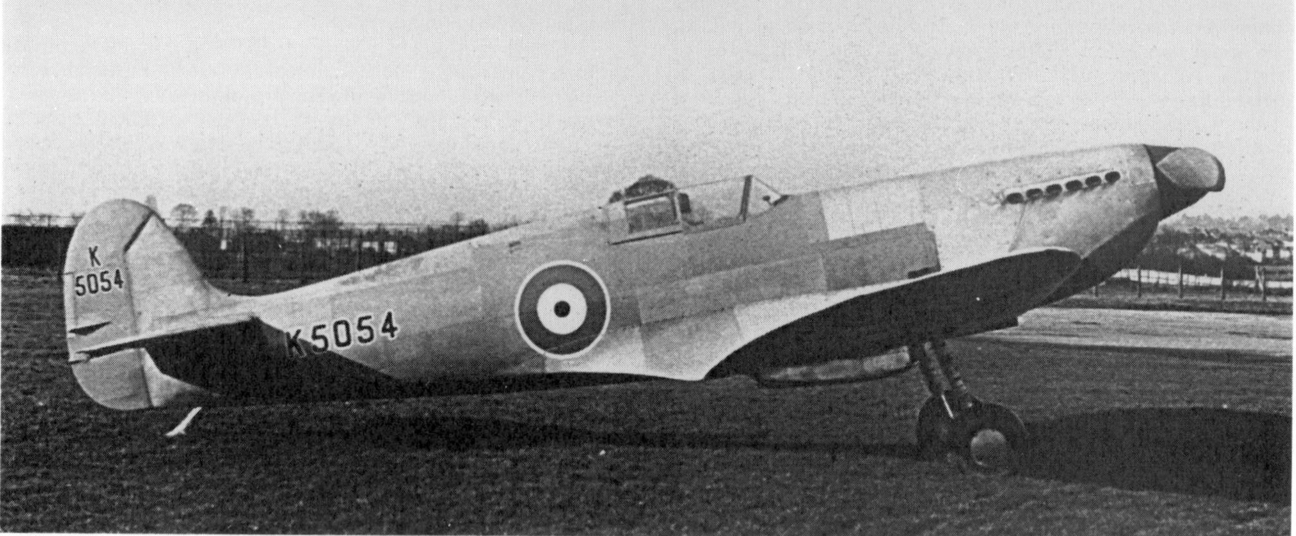

of 349mph at about 18,000 feet before sending the prototype to Martlesham Heath for official trials. Mitchell told Quill he had hoped for a maximum speed of 350mph, but was satisfied with 349.

The Air Ministry Certificate of Design was issued on 6 March and K5054 was still known as the Type 300, no name being specified. In an attempt to correct this omission an official of Supermarine wrote to the Air Ministry on 10 March saying- "We refer to our conversation of this morning with A. E. Slater. Would you be good enough to reserve the name 'Spitfire' for our fighter to Specn: F 7/30 (modified)". Slater replied- "It has been noted for consideration when, and if, an order is placed for this aircraft". On 10 June a second letter arrived at

Prototype F37/34 on roll-out. Points to note are the joint lines of the engine cowling panels and original rudder horn. Head on view clearly reveals the location of the leading edge condensers which were not fitted. E Mansbridge, who was associated with F37/34, recalls that the component parts of the evaporative system were constructed but never installed.

During initial flights of the prototype comments were made on the method of take-off. At times the nose of K5054 was not aimed straight into wind but 35° across it. Jeffrey Quill explained why – "The blade angles of the fixed wooden props were designed to produce 3000rpm @ max level speed at full throttle @ 18000 feet. This meant they had to be much too coarse for take-off and only gave about 1900rpm static at full throttle. This produced high torque reaction, but torque reaction on its own only has the effect of causing the aircraft to roll, or lean, about its lateral axis. The tendency to swing is produced by the effect of the rotating slip stream on the rear fuselage and has to be corrected by rudder. If the throttle was opened carefully and the tail kept down initially, the aircraft could be kept straight and it was not necessary to 'aim off'. Although it was quite possible to take off straight with the wooden props, they were, on the whole, better suited to grass airfields than runways." A number of propellers were tested on K5054 – (i) special for first take-off (ii) designed for top speed conditions using blade widths greater than normal to improve take-off (iii) designed for max speed (iv) designed for use during demonstrations (v) four blade prop. A Hamilton 3-blade VP propeller reduced take-off run at same a.u.w. to about ⅔rds that with wooden. Weight increased by 325lbs (including tail ballast) and handling qualities not as good as wooden prop. The Fairey Reed metal was slower at max speed than the wooden prop and gave worser take-off. A new two-blade propeller was selected as being the most satisfactory for production a/c. The de Havilland 3-blade, 2 pitch was superior to the new two-blade type.

Supermarine stating that the name was now approved for the F 7/30 (F 37/34 modified).

On 19 March K5054 was taken into the Woolston works for minor modifications, including sealing of all joints in the engine cowling with tape as an interim measure until a new cowling complete with airtight seals could be made and installed. There were oil leaks through the bottom surface of the wing as well as the rear of the spinner, and for the latter a disc had to be fitted. The underwing surfaces were causing drag problems due to the bad fit of the many doors (total 18) caused by installing them before fitting the seals. It was decided that when the fuselage was returned once more to the works to have the new cowling fitted, the aircraft would be turned upside down and all access doors be remade. A temporary measure was to tape round the edges.

By now the wheel fairings had been installed and K5054 painted. An expert from a dope manufacturers was brought in to do the job and he advised all rivet indentations and joints be filled and the airframe painted with a high quality gloss paint. The engine air intake was redesigned and shortened and the ailerons, which had twisted, straightened, as were the wing tips. No specific tests had been made on the wing root fillets so a series of trials was carried out by Supermarine, during which a film of dark oil was released at the wing leading edge when the aircraft was travelling at high speed. The direction of flow of the oil provided a fairly accurate indication of air flow over the fillets.

Modifications completed, K5054 was flown to Martlesham Heath by George Pickering on 26 March and during April many high speed flights were made. In one dive it reached a speed of 430mph indicated. It has been claimed that the aircraft was then delivered to Farnborough, in a dismantled condition, in the back of a Tate and Lyle lorry but there is no evidence to confirm this. The rudder horn was modified in early May and the aircraft had its final weighing on the 10th. Empty it was 4,180lbs, tare 4,240 with an auw of 5,439lb.

First public appearance of K5054 was before an invited audience of about 300 people from the aircraft industry and the press, who were taken to Eastleigh by special train to view the prototype and other Vicker's types on show on 18 June. Piloted by Quill the aircraft's debut was abruptly curtailed by a broken oil connection, but Quill made a perfect landing. Its second appearance in public was on the afternoon of Saturday, 27 June at the RAF Pageant at Hendon. In the official programme it was listed as 'new aircraft No 2' and spectators saw it, and the equally new Hawker Hurricane, as they performed as a pair, K5054 being flown by Flt-Lt. J. H. Edwardes-Jones, RAF. Three days later the last public demonstration was made at the Society of British Aircraft Constructors' display at Hatfield. 'Mutt' Summers was the pilot and the press was almost lyrical in its praise of the new machine.

K5054 was depatched to Farnborough for spinning trials and an official of Supermarine went along to supervise installation of the anti-spin parachute. First thought was to cut a hole in the rear fuselage immediately aft of the cockpit, but this was vetoed as the company wanted to avoid yet another door in the airframe. Next proposal was to pack the 'chute into a box on top of the fuselage near the foot of the aerial mast holding it in position with a canvas band strapped around the body. Eventually the parachute was stowed in a box just ahead of the fin and screwed into position. The aircraft was weighed once more, following modifications, at Eastleigh on 27 November and had a tare weight of 4498 and an auw of 5663lb.

Now named Spitfire the aircraft arrived at Martlesham

After its first flight K5054 was returned to the flight shed for painting. The grey, high gloss metal finish is apparent. A new rudder was also fitted. (Shenstone).

Heath for full handling trials on 23 February 1937. Auw was now 5321lb and a true air speed ranging from 330mph at 10,000ft, to 349 at 16,800 was recorded. At 30,000 speed had dropped to 324. Time to height of 20,000ft was 8min 12sec at 1,770ft/min. At sea level the rate of climb was 2,400ft/min. This performance vindicated Mitchell's speed of 349mph, and time to 15,000ft of 6.25mins was far in excess of the 265mph and 8.25mins demanded in the Air Ministry Specification. Many changes were now being made to the aeroplane, the Merlin C engine being replaced by the F, which produced 1,045hp, a reflector sight installed plus a dimmer screen on front of the windscreen, a parachute guard on the fin, new exhaust dampers and a tailwheel, two types of which- all metal and a Dunlop rubber with twin wheels- had been tested. One interesting Supermarine report dated 30 September recorded – "Flight Instructions 42. Remove engine driven chassis system and re-fit standard system", this suggesting that the original hand operated type had at some time been extensively modified.

The diary of Quill's test flight programme with the Spitfire is worth noting – "20 December 1936, de Havilland VP airscrew fitted. 5 January 1937, flight to test effect of round headed rivets on speed. Seven flights were made and in order to test the effect fully the machine was covered with split peas to represent rivets in the position which they would be on the production machine".

By 31 January flight tests for the following had been carried out by the makers – spinning, modified elevator gearing, new-type tail trimming, opening and closing of cabin top, modifications to chassis warning horn, effect of gun installation on handling, reflector sight panel in windscreens, installation of Merlin F, 5½in oil cooler (axial flow), 5½in oil cooler (cross flow), airscrew 3001100 (two blade), airscrew 3001200 (four blade), airscrew 3001300 (four Blade modified), VP airscrew (six pitch settings). tailwheel (metal), tailwheel (rubber), modified air intake, electrical generator cooling tests, exhaust manifolds, W/T mast and aerial and effect of dummy rivet heads. The last test resulted in a speed reduction of 22mph. The tests recorded above necessitated 50 flights totalling 26hrs 33mins flying time. Total flying time by now was 95hrs 50mins, of which 46hrs 2mins was by Supermarine pilots, the remainder by Martlesham personnel.

On 22 March the Spitfire was making flight tests to ascertain the effectiveness of modified elevator controls to overcome buffeting. During a high 'G' turn Flt Lt J. F. McKenna noticed that the engine showed symptoms of oil starvation and he quickly made a wheels-up landing. The official report tells the whole story –

"Spitfire K5054 forced landing at 11.15 hours on 22 March 1937, near Sutton on the Woodbridge-Bawdsey road. Alterations had been made to the gearing of the elevator

Mechanics run up the Merlin of K5054 before the press demonstration on 18 June 1936. Other views show Quill taxying away from the aircraft display park to take off. Minutes later he had to force land because of a broken oil feed pipe.

Prototype returns to the flight shed after its engine seized at the press fly past.

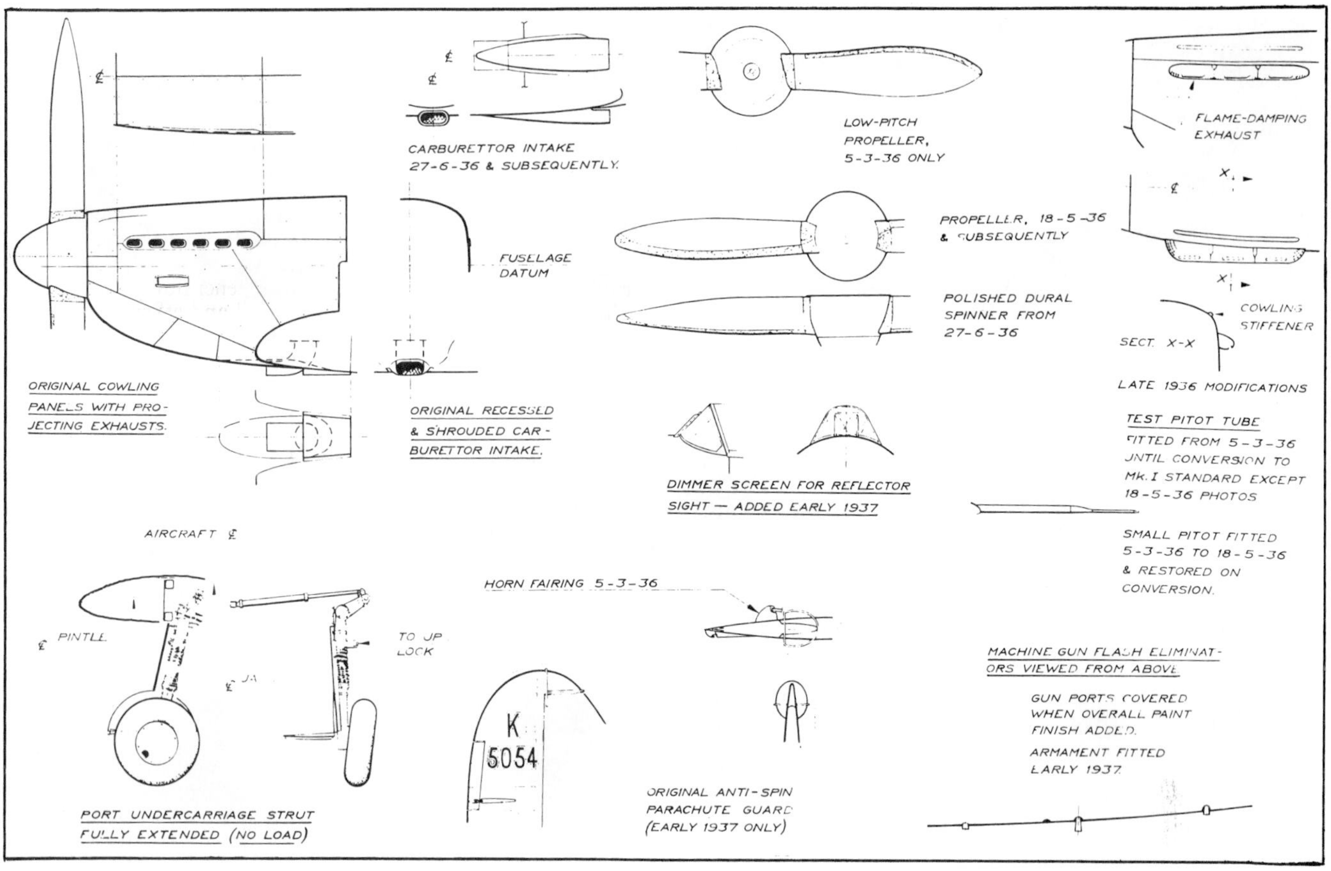

Sketch showing modifications made to K5054 after the first flight.

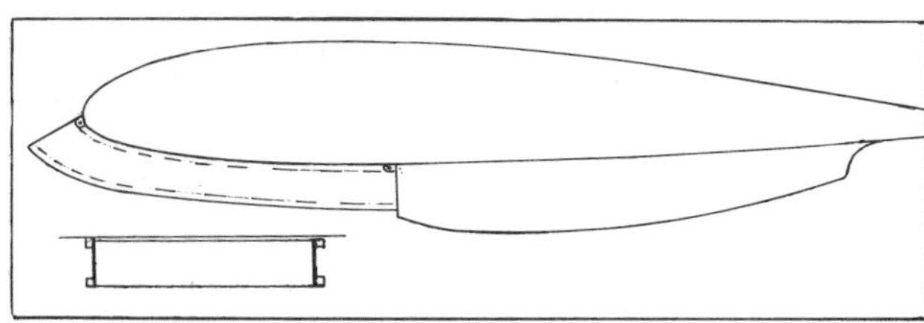

Cooling duct designed to direct cold air into the wing radiator during ground running tests of the Merlin engine. It was made of plywood and could be placed into position in seconds. A fine water spray injected into the duct at 0.3gals/min stabilised engine temperature at 103°C.

One of the more unusual trials with K5054 was the application of split peas to the airframe to represent 'snap' head rivets. The aircraft was first flown with a pea over virtually every rivet position. They were then removed from the leading edges, and tailplane, back to the front spar. All the transverse rivet lines, wings and fuselage, were next removed (Shenstone).

control. The pilot had carried out several loops with progressively increasing accelerations up to 4G. A dive had been carried out up to about 350mph, and also a series of tight turns with accelerations up to 4G. When checked all thermometers and gauges were normal as the coolant temperatures were low.

Later, the pilot noticed that his oil pressure was low and he throttled back to 1600rpm, with the intention of returning to Martlesham. The oil pressure fell rapidly to 0, there was a loud noise in the engine, which became very rough, and a little later another noise in the engine. Eventually the pilot decided to land and switched off the engine, which immediately stopped with the propeller horizontal.

"The pilot selected a heath on the Woodbridge-Bawdsey road for the landing. As there were ditches and banks on the heath, the surface of which was broken, he did not lower the undercarriage but lowered flaps fully. The tail wheel touched first and its track could be followed on the ground for about a hundred yards. Thereafter the body came into contact and a progressively deepening furrow could be seen for a further fifty yards. The air intake chutes of the radiator and oil cooler apparently acted as skids. The aeroplane came to rest without turning over and without injury to the pilot. At the end of the

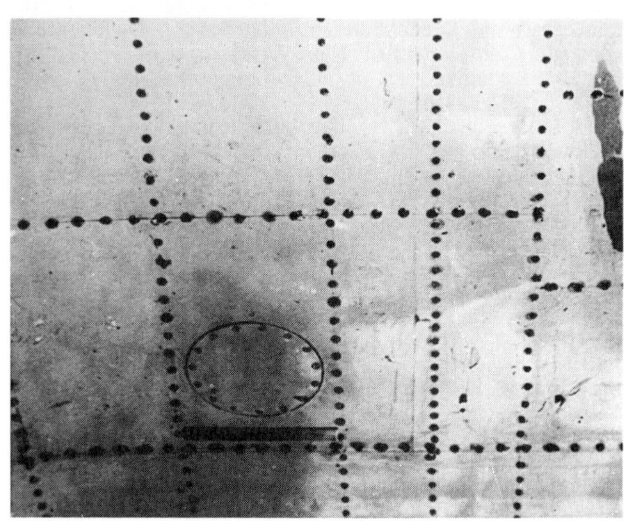

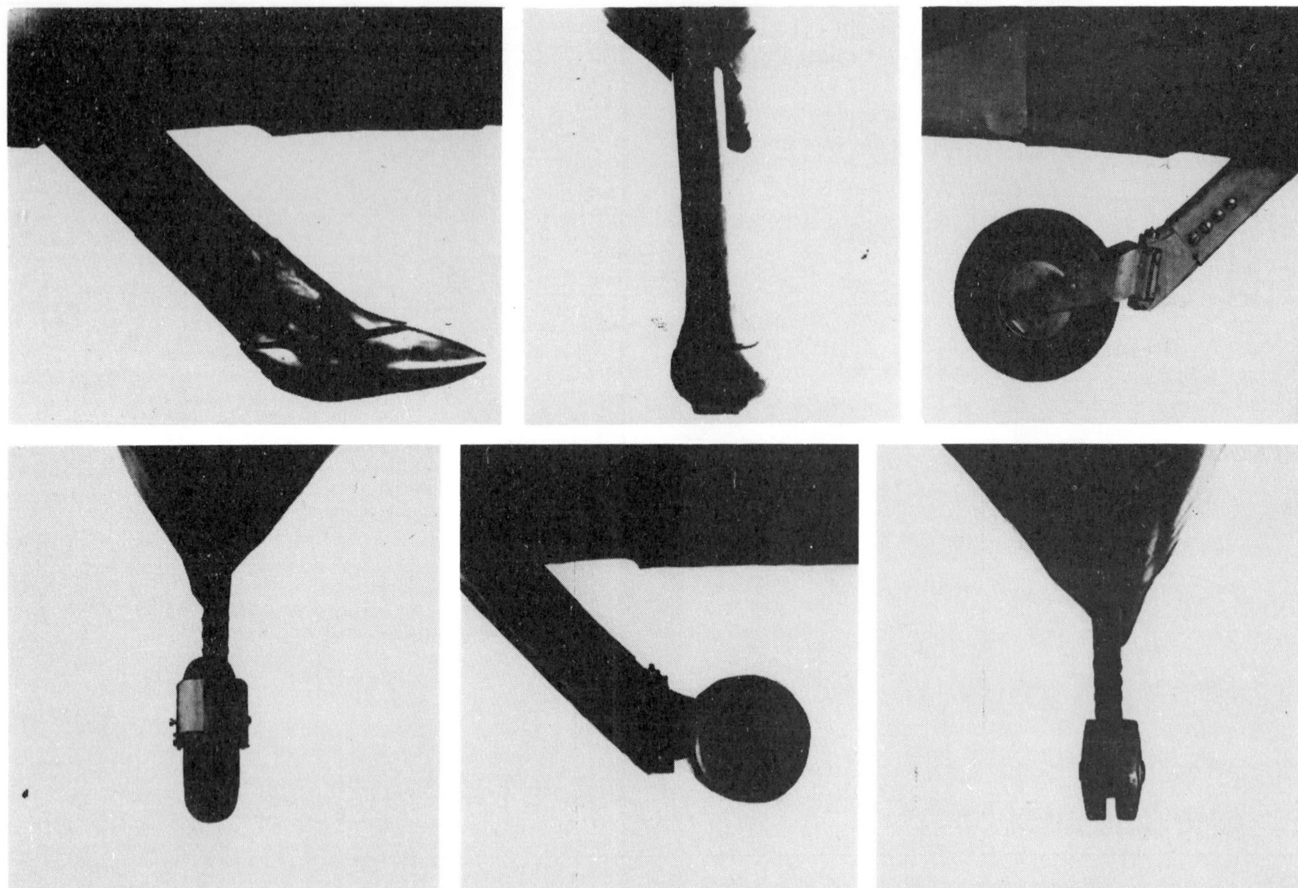

After the first series of trials the original metal tail skid was replaced by a fixed and swivelling units. First was a twin wheel, metal Dunlop, 8 January 1937. Next a single, rubber tyred, swivelling model, which was to be later standardised.

run the pilot states that the aeroplane tilted forward through about 30 degrees. His wisdom in keeping the undercarriage up was apparent because the aeroplane came to rest within twenty yards of a three foot bank and ten yards of a deep hole. The pilot states that the deceleration was not severe except during the last few yards of the run.

"The intake of the radiator and oil cooler were badly torn, but the oil cooler was undamaged and the radiator appeared to be sound except for slight superficial damage to the casing.

"There is a wrinkle in the bulkhead in front of the main spar, but unless there is further damage to it (which seems unlikely) this is of no consequence. The engine bearer was badly dented, presumably by a connecting rod coming through the crankcase, but in all other respects the airframe appeared to be airworthy. It was lifted by crane and the undercarriage lowered in a perfectly normal manner.

"The airframe, however, was despatched to Supermarine for detailed examination. Four holes were found in the crankcase, and it could be seen that several big ends and connecting rods had failed. There was evidence of considerable heat and a complete lack of oil. The engine was despatched to Rolls-Royce.

"Assuming that the gallery pipe in the engine is neither broken or obstructed, it appears likely that the cause in the failure of the oil supply may be in the effect of acceleration forces in the oil system".

The Merlin's oil system was modified to prevent a re-occurence of oil starvation, and in a report on the condition of K5054, issued several days before the accident took place, mention is made that during flights and ground running the engine showed no signs of overheating.

It was at this point of the Spitfire's history that its designer R. J. Mitchell died on Friday 11 June 1937 after a long illness at the age of 42. Reginald Joseph Mitchell joined Supermarine in 1916 when he was 21 years old as personal assistant to Hubert Scott Paine, and in 1918 he became assistant to Mr. Leach, the works manager. Hargreaves, chief designer, left Supermarine in 1919 and Mitchell was appointed chief designer and in 1920, aged 25, he took over as chief engineer. Mitchell was appointed a director of the company in 1927 and retained the positions of director and chief designer when the company was absorbed by Vickers-Armstrong the following year. In 1933 he contracted cancer which failed to respond to treatment and died as the Spitfire was entering large scale production.

Joseph Smith, his assistant, was chosen to fill the vacant position Mitchell had left. Smith began his career as an

First forced landing of K5054 resulting in damage was on heathland next to the Woodbridge-Bawdsey road. A caption writer at that time had written on the rear of the photograph, "The Supermarine Spitfire prototype was deliberately crashed to ascertain the strength of the airframe".

R J Mitchell, left, seated with his wife, at the Schneider Cup Dinner, held at the South Western Hotel, Southampton, on 7 October 1931, after the final victory for the S Type racers.

Joseph Smith became Chief Designer at Supermarine following Mitchell's death. He was to be responsible for development of the Spitfire up to, and including, the Spiteful.

Captain Joseph 'Mutt' Summers, Chief Test Pilot, Vickers, was the first pilot to fly the Spitfire.

Summers was followed by George Pickering, left, and Jeffrey Quill, both Supermarine pilots.

apprentice to the Austin Motor Company and worked for a period in their aviation department. He joined Supermarine in 1921 and such was his ability that Mitchell made him chief draughtsman five years later at the age of 28 years. Smith was involved with the Spitfire programme from the first design and specifications stages of the F7/30, and he was responsible for the translation of Mitchell's designs into the finished product. This training was invaluable and after Mitchell's death he was able to continue development of the original Type 300 Spitfire from the early marks to the final development, the Spiteful. Under Smith's leadership the design team were producing three, or more, Spitfire types every year throughout the war.

In September 1937 the prototype Spitfire was extensively modified to bring it up to Mk I production standard. It was now powered by a Merlin II with stub exhaust manifolds, these being rejected in favour of the ejector type following tests on a Kestrel engine fitted into the Rolls-Royce test-bed Heinkel 70. With the new exhausts maximum speed at 20,000 feet was raised from 334 to 347mph. The folding wheel covers were removed and the high gloss paint finish gave way to the Air Ministry dark green and earth day fighter camouflage scheme. The Merlin II gave the Spitfire the following performance – a duration of 1.63hrs at 305mph at 15,000 feet for a still air range of 495 miles. At 1800rpm and a speed of 192mph duration was 4.05hrs, range 775 miles at 15,000 feet. When weighed at Eastleigh on 11 September tare was 5034lb and auw 5566.

On 23 October it returned to Martlesham Heath for further trials and was taken on charge by the Royal Air Force from that date. It was then shuttled to Eastleigh on 29 December for gun heating equipment, returning once more to Martlesham on 12 May 1938 for full armament trials. A Type GD 5 Barr and Stroud reflector sight was installed in front of the pilot's seat and it made use of the flat centre panel of the Triplex windscreen as the reflecting screen. A G22 camera gun was mounted on the starboard wing over the number two gun position, its shutter being released by pneumatic control and re-set by Bowden cable. It all worked perfectly on the ground but not in flight and Martlesham recommended that the problem be investigated by the RAE and the controls so positioned that a straight pull could be obtained. Hand control did not work and the problem was finally overcome when the camera gun was installed in the wing root, with automatic operation by the guns firing. A number of production Spitfires still had the cumbersome wing mounted camera when serving as trials aircraft with No 19 Squadron.

A series of night flying trials was initiated in March 1938 to measure the amount of glare from the engine exhaust and on the 15th Sergeant Wareham, the pilot, had made two successful landings. During the third he overshot the runway and ran the Spitfire into soft ground, tipping it on to the nose, breaking the propeller and damaging the engine cowling. Following repairs the trials were continued and on the night of 24 March disaster struck again as the aircraft touched down heavily, bounced for nearly 100 yards until the port wing tip touched the ground.

The aircraft ground looped and the port undercarriage leg was forced up into the wing. A total of 400 landings had been made and on the last the oleos were found to have travelled the complete length in compression. It was thought that fatigue had caused the accident.

The aircraft was again taken to Eastleigh on 13 April and was not finally cleared for flying until 12 October, when it returned to Martlesham for gun heating trials up to 30,000 feet. Gun heating was by means of two 3½ inch ducts fitted into the rear of the radiator and passing into the wing just ahead of the main spar. Despite the fitting of bulkheads to direct hot air from the radiator to the guns only the inner guns received warmth. Bulkheads were then installed to box in both inboard and outboard guns separately; the ducting extended to the outer guns space and the heating problem was solved.

During trials a full load of ammunition was carried and the guns fired at heights of between 27,000 and 30,000 feet. Originally an experimental heater was fitted to one gun but had to be removed due to a short circuit. After initial trials the Mk I guns were replaced by Mk II and at the conclusion of the first set of trials the starboard wing guns were pronounced satisfactory.

On 24 November a G.42 cine camera gun was installed in the port wing root and was controlled by a pneumatic unit attached to the gun firing button. The time taken to reload and harmonise the camera was 1hr 35mins.

K5054 was finally transferred to Farnborough for further trials on 7 November and an examination of the control tower flight log shows that it worked hard, being used at times for pilot training. On 4 September 1939, one day after England had declared war on Germany, it took off at 14.45hrs and landed 45 minutes later to be written off in an accident that killed the pilot, Flt Lt G. S. White. The official accident report is very concise on what took place:–

"The accident occurred at 15.30hrs during a landing run after an experimental flight. The aeroplane was observed to make a normal approach and touch down; the tail then began to lift slowly until the airscrew touched the ground. The aeroplane was then moving at a comparatively slow speed, the tail rose sharply and the aeroplane turned over onto its back. The pilot, Flt Lt G. S. White suffered injuries which subsequently proved fatal.

"After the accident a preliminary examination revealed that the wheels were free, there was no binding of the brakes; the undercarriage was locked down and the indicator signalled down. The elevator trim tab was set .62ins down and the cockpit ventilator was fully open. The Sutton harness was locked back and the pilot's seat fully raised.

"The fuselage bulkheads forward of the W/T compartment, the cockpit hood and windscreen, the tail unit and airscrew were damaged beyond repair. The wireless mast was telescoped into the fuselage until the base of the mast jammed against the top of the forward flare chute.

"Subsequent examination of the structure showed the anchorage cable of the Sutton harness passes through two guides on the under surface of the wireless mast bearer. When the mast was forced into the fuselage it carried the cable attachment to it and shortened its effective length. This had the effect of pulling the pilot back into the seat, probably violently with sufficient force to distort the seat back. The strong point at the head rest had partly collapsed under side load due to failure of the longitudinal member fitted to carry that load. This allowed the head rest to move forward, and the pilot's injuries were consistent with this movement combined with the jerk on the Sutton harness".

As a result of this incident a modification was made to the cable run of the Sutton harness to the anchorage in the rear fuselage and it was immediately applied to Spitfire K9787, then at Farnborough for wireless trials. The cables were run over the wireless mast support brackets.

The report does *not* specify what made K5054 tip on to its nose and overturn, but the authors did talk to a member of RAE who was at Farnborough at the time of the accident, and he said that what took place was White, on landing, had loosened the restraint straps of his Sutton harness. The long anchorage straps in the rear fuselage had dropped, fouling the elevator cables. The elevator was forced into the down position, with the result that the Spitfire overturned.

The damaged airframe was declared obsolete the following month and had completed 151.30 flying hours. The remains were stored at Farnborough for several years but before final destruction it was used in the early months of 1940 as a mock-up fuselage for the installation of the early PR Spitfire cameras.

K5054 in the 'New Types' aircraft park at Hendon in summer 1936.

In flight view shows the classic lines of K5054.

On 25 January 1936 the following report was issued to all design and production departments connected with the Spitfire and other aircraft.

REPORT No. T.D. 1766.
Type Records.
Revised System of Numbering

The numbering of Type Record Reports is to be brought in line with the System used for the numbering of Drawings. If the Type Number of a machine is 300, the Type Record will be designated;

R-300 meaning, 'Record of Type 300'. The reports con-

K5054 with guns installed and new exhaust stubs fitted.

tained therein on various components take the standard component number, eg.

R-30021 heads report on strength of Fin and Rudder. As some of the component groups used in Type Record work are not quite the same as in the drawing work, the most important numbers to be used are given here. Numbers not given may be taken from standard component list.

It is usual when a major modification to an aircraft is made such as a new engine type, the machine number is altered for the parts involved, which automatically gives a number for the covering type record. If however a change in the type number is not made when such a major modification is made or when a machine goes into production and new type record is required, the original number with a suffix A, B, etc. will be used, as for instance –

R-300A and R-30021A which means the first major alteration in Type 300, the type number on the drawings being unchanged.

The above instructions refer to all Type Records commenced after the date of Issue of this memorandum.

A study of the table below indicates when the four additional machine guns altered the weight of the prototype. On 14 January 1935 weight of the F37/34 prototype's wing was estimated as being 630lb; three months ater it had risen to 650 after the four extra guns were added and bomb fittings removed. Under the second section of the table headed Load Carried these two dates show that petrol weight was 724 and 455lb respectively and that the military load (30-4-45) had risen to 603lb with 8-guns.

Number for Type Record	Component of Group
00	General Arrangements
01	Wings
09	Ailerons
14	Wing Tip Floats
15	External Wing Bracing
17	Tailplane and Elevator
21	Fin and Rudder
25	Tail Bracing
26	Tail Skid and Water Rudder
27	Hull and Fuselage
33	Flying Controls
35	Seating and Flooring
37	Engine Mounting
39	Engine Installation
43	Airscrew
45	Petrol System
50	Land and Launching Chassis
57	Bomb Gear
64	Equipment and Instruments
66	Tail Adjusting Gear
70	Slinging and Jacking
75	Float Chassis
84	Test Specimens
·99	Trial Flights
100	Miscellaneous

	11/34	14/1/35	8/4/35	30/4/35	9/8/35	15/10/35	8/1/36	13/2/36	27/2/36	2/6/36*	1/12/36	5/1/37	17/3/37	8/11/37
A. Structure:														104+
Wing	630	630	650	650	680	680	704	722+	722+	762	771	771	771	771
Engine Cowling	40	40	40	40	60	60	60	60	86	86	86	86	86	86
Engine Mounting	50	50	55	55	58	58	58	58	58	58	58	58	58	58
Front Fuselage	244	255	228	228	250*	250*	355*	365+		390	398	398	398	398
Rear Fuselage	244	255	100	100	100	100	355*	365+	365+	390	398	398	398	398
Tail Plane & Elevator	54	60	60	60	60	60	60	60	69	49	49	49	49	49
Fin & Rudder	25	30	30	30	30	30	30	30	30	28	28	28	28	28
Tail Skid	20	20	20	20	20	20	20	22+	22+	22+	22	22	22	27
Wheels & Brakes	58	58	64	64	64	64	64	80+	80+	80+	80	80	80	80
Chassis & Retracting gear	160	160	200	200	200	185	185	185	185	192	194	194	194	194
Controls	80	80	80	80	85	85	85	91+	91+	91+	91	91	91	82
Accommodation	23	23	23	23	23	23	23	23	23	23	24	24	24	25
Total Structure (lb)	1384	1406	1550	1550	1630	1615	1644	1696	1696	1781	1801	1801	1801	1902
B. Power Plant:														
Hub						36	36	36	36	36	36	36	36	36
Engine	1150	1225	1225	1225	1225	1284	1284	1284	1284	1284	1412	1412	1412	1361
Airscrew & Spinner	85	85	105	105	140	122	122	122	122	96	96	96	96	96
Exhaust	77	65	45	45	35	35	35	16+	16+	16+	41	31	31	31
Acc. & Piping	70	70	53	53	20	20	20	56+	56+	61	61	61	61	61
Radiator	–	70	70	70	75	98	98	98	98	98	98	98	98	98
Cooling System (less rad)	60	60	70	82	56	56	56	56	56	56	56	56	56	56
Cooling Water	160	116	116	116	142	142	142	142	142	142	142	142	142	151
Petrol Tanks	65	65	65	60	52	52	52	52	52	52	52	52	52	52
Oil Tank & Cooler	60	60	60	48	45	47	47	47	47	47	47	47	47	47
Total Power Plant (lb)	1727	1816	1809	1804	1790	1892	1892	1909	1909	1888	2041	2031	2031	1989
C. Load Carried:														
Pilot & Parachute	200	200	200	200	200	200	200	200	200	200	200	200	200	200
Military Load (Fixed)	508	508	470	603	611	625	625	625	620	620	620	620	620	244/459*
Petrol (94 galls)	724	724	724	455+	455+	455+	455+	578+	578+	578+	578	578	578	578
Oil (7 galls)	63	63	63	54*	54*	54*	54*	59+	59+	50	50	50	50	50
Total Load (lb)	1495	1495	1457	1312	1320	1334	1334	1462	1457+	1448	1448	1448	1448	1531
Total Weight:														
Structure	1384	1414	1550	1550	1635	1615	1644	1696	1696	1781	1801	1801	1801	1902
Power Plant	1727	1815	1809	1804	1790	1892	1892	1909	1909	1888	2041	2031	2031	1989
Load Carried	1495	1495	1457	1312	1320	1334	1334	1462	1457	1448	1448	1448	1448	1531
Sundries not acc. for	284	284	284	284	285	284	285	283	188*	200	373	383	204	150
Total Weight: (lb)	4890	5008	5100	4950	5030	5125	5155	5350	5250	5317	5663	5663	5484	5572
Area (gross) (sq. ft.)	242	242	242	242	242	242	242	242	242	242	242	242	242	242
W/A	20.3	20.7	21.1	20.5	20.8	21.5	21.3	22.1	21.7	22.0	23.4	23.4	23.4	23.0
KL for 60 m.p.h.	1.1	1.12	1.145	1.11	1.13	1.15	1.15	1.2	1.18	1.19	1.27	1.27	1.27	–
C.G. below fuselage datum	6.25	7.1	7.6	7.95	7.9	7.87	7.87	8.16	7.02	7.75	7.75	7.75	7.75	7.72
behind F.S. datum	6.3	5.8	5.5	5.65	5.6	5.21	5.21	5.75	7.6	9.68	8.06	8.06	8.06	7.38
on equiv. chord.	–	–	.312	.313	.313	.309	.309	.314	.34	.36	.34	.34	.34	.334
Chassis angle	–	–	18°	18°	18°	17½°	17½°	18°	19.75°	22°	20°	20°	20°	19.75°

30/4/35 +59 galls *6 galls
9/8/35 etc 250* (including fillet)
13/2/36 +Alterations 578+ = 75 galls 59+ = 6½ galls
27/2/36 188* Includes 86lbs finishing allowance
2/6/36 *Based on Martlesham weighing
1/12/36 Weights based on Supermarine weighing 27.11.36
17/3/37 104lb = ballast in nose and mounting. Weights based on Martlesham weight 26.10.37
8/11/37 244/459* = 244 Military load fixed, 459 removable

After repairs K5054 was camouflaged in standard RAF day fighter colours and brought up to Mk I standards. An anti-spin parachute fitting is seen just ahead of the fin. The venturi (4 inch) for airdriven instruments was installed on the starboard fuselage.

Of interest to this Spitfire history was the activities of the Messerschmitt Company of Germany, in particular those connected with the **Bf109 fighter.** On 27 May 1938 Shenstone went to visit the German company and an edited report of this visit follows – "I was received by Messerschmitt at his works, but was not allowed to see inside the factory, the interview being held in his office overlooking the works and aerodrome. Following is a summary of the conversation as far as it concerned aeroplanes.

"Type 109, single seat, single engine fighter. The design started in the summer of 1934 and the first production machines were coming out in the spring of 1936. The prototype was fitted with the Kestrel engine and the first production **machines with Jumo 210s. Since the Daimler Benz engine (940 at 13,000ft) came out they have been equipped with that engine. Production was started before the machine was developed at all and great difficulties were encountered getting the bugs out. For instance, the armament had not been decided before going into production.**

"The straight tapered wing is quite thin, being 14% thick at the root and 9% thick at the tip. There is no twist, as slots are used. The chassis is operated by compressed air from an engine **pump. CPF factor is about 12, but even so, some have been broken in pulling out of a TV dive. Such dives (no speed limit)** have to be carried out. Apart from actual breakages, wings have been bent in a pull out, but the machine safely landed. VDM,VP propellers (both 3 and 2 bladed) are used on production machines. The effect of flying with no radiator was to increase the speed from about 340 to 349½mph.

"The Type 109 is not yet available for sale in foreign countries. Although Messerschmitt has used slotted flaps to date, he has recently tried split flaps and found them very satisfactory. The report in the "Aeroplane" that Messerschmitt **is using a venetian blind-type of flap is not true, as he stated that** such a flap would be far too complex, and he had no intention of trying it.

"The record breaking aeroplane was quite standard except for some detail cleaning-up such as sealing the slots closed. Messerschmitt stated that the record could now be improved but no steps would be taken to do it until we (or somebody else) had taken a shot at it. He was unable to discuss the published speed of 440mph for his newest type. In like manner I was not able to reply to him when he asked by how much we expected to break the present record.

"All BFW aircraft are completely flush riveted. Heinkel explosive riveting has not yet been used. Messerschmitt uses a great deal of shot welding in light alloys and is using more all the time. It is very cheap and quick. Messerschmitt has not yet

***Although the Heinkel He 70 monoplane did not contribute to the** final shape of the Spitfire, the numerous experiments carried out with it by Roll-Royce on cooling and exhaust systems helped in the development of **radiator design and coolants and exhaust manifolds. G-ADZF was** delivered to Rolls-Royce, Hucknall, on 27 March 1936 with a Kestrel V engine, water cooled and this was changed at once for a Kestrel XVI. The German oil cooler was also replaced, the new type being a honeycomb type manufactured by John Marston Ltd. The original propeller installation was considered to be dangerous and the Airscrew Company of Weybridge were asked to supply a replacement.*

Initial trials were on the radiator which had been designed for dealing with a water cooled engine, whereas the Kestrel XVI was glycol cooled. The new Watts propeller was slightly better that the original, but take off performance showed no improvement, indeed, under full load it, too, was considered dangerous. A Hamilton three blade VP propeller was then tested. It had a 11ft diameter and two pitch settings - 35½° coarse, 26° fine. All round performance was greatly improved. A summary of results showed that with a Kestrel V engine 30% of power developed was wasted in overcoming radiator drag when the latter was fully exposed to the airstream. Improvements made to the radiator cowl (Kestrel XVI) showed a great improvement, with the redesigned cowl providing a much higher speed to the outgoing air. A new, cantilever engine mounting enabling the whole to be removed as one unit was installed.

*The next series of trials on the exhaust manifolds with five types **under test. (1) Stub pipes based on early production Spitfire installations.** (2) Streamlined blisters based on production Spitfire units. (3) Ejector which fed exhaust gases directly into the line of flight. Five sizes of ejector nozzles were considered with the 3" the best all round.*

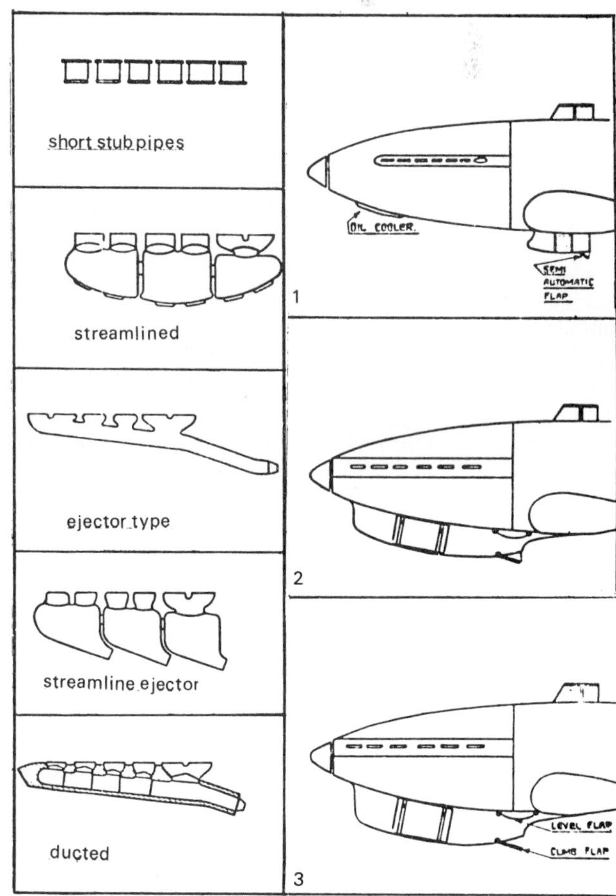

seriously considered the tricycle chassis, and his wing loadings are all of the order of 25lb/sq ft. Type records are not sent to the Air Ministry, but technical men visit the aircraft firms and check over the calculations and assumptions. I forgot to ask whether they were a nuisance.

"Messerschmitt admitted that he himself paid a great deal of attention to weight estimates and to simplification of design, as he considered them both of such fundamental importance that his personal action was necessary. The design department is in three parts, project, general design including all stressing, and drawing. The project office carries schemes right through until the geometry at least of all major elements is fixed. Thus relatively complete schemes are handed over to the drawing office. The design staff occupies a building (three storeys) about twice as big as the Supermarine office building, i.e the design staff would be of the order of five times as large.

"The BFW factory comprises 7 units scattered around the aerodrome, each part complete in itself, including canteen, so that dislocation due to a direct bomb hit would be a minimum. A guess of the number of workers employed is 5–6000.

"The main five-storey building just completed is very imposing. The interior finish, hardware and furniture makes the Supermarine building look really cheap. There is also no attempt to crowd people, and the entrance, halls and stairs are broad and spacious. Marble is used extensively for hall and stairs and there is no plaster and paint as on our stairs, where damage is easily done and where dirt collects. The office furniture has been obviously designed specially and unobtrusive filing cabinets were a feature. No expense has been spared to make the conditions of work pleasant and efficient. It is now general in Germany to pay great attention to the working conditions, and such an interest here could easily improve our conditions immensely".

Shenstone did have a most observant eye and his report reveals that he was impressed with the Messerschmitt works. Money was, obviously, no object for the German government had no opposition to curb its ambitions.

Night flying trials with a modified, anti-dazzle exhaust manifold were undertaken. During these trials the second accident occurred.

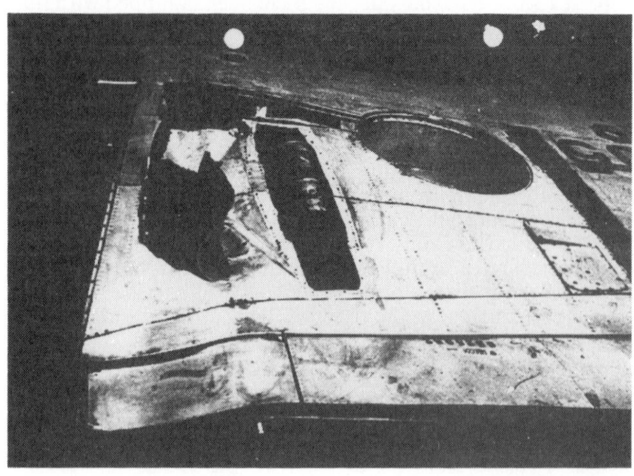
On 24 March K5054 made a heavy landing at night, bounced several times before ground looping and driving the port undercarriage leg through the wing.

The demise of the Spitfire prototype was at Farnborough on 4 September 1939. After nosing over on to its back the fuselage remained intact but the cockpit was crushed. Note how the radio mast has broken away from the main structure.

LEADING PARTICULARS

Spitfire prototype K5054. Air Ministry Specification F 37/34. Supermarine Type 300.

Wing. Span 37ft 8in, area (gross) 242 sq ft, nett (main outer planes) 220 sq ft, chord (outer planes) 6.38ft, (centre section) 8.33 ft, mean aerodynamic 7.08 ft, section NACA Series, root 2213, tip 2205, incidence + 2° at root to $-\frac{1}{2}$° at tip, dihedral 6°. Ailerons (Frise), area 18.9 sq ft, span 6.83 ft, movement up 25°, down 19°, droop 0°. Flaps (split) area 15.8 sq ft, span 8.17 ft, movement down 57°.

Fuselage. Length 29ft 11in, height (tail down) 8ft 2½in, tip of prop tail down 12ft 8in, prop clearance take off 7.15in.

Tailplane Span 10ft 5in, area 18.2 sq ft, total with elevators 31.46 sq ft, chord 3.90ft, incidence 0° root to $-\frac{1}{2}$° tip. Elevators. Span 10ft 5in, area 13.26 sq ft, movement up and down 28°, tab area 1.74 sq ft, movement up 10°, down 15°.

Fin. Area 4.61 sq ft, incidence to fuselage 0°, rudder area 8.23 sq ft, tab area .38 sq ft, total area 12.75 sq ft. Rudder movement port 28°, starboard 29.5°, tab to port 13°, to starboard 6°.

Undercarriage track 5ft 8½in. Tailskid fitted.

Weights. Tare 5,034lb, auw 5,200lb, wing loading 21.5lb sq ft.

Engine. Merlin II 990bhp normal @ 12,000ft, 1,050 maximum @ 16,000ft. RPM 2,600 @ 12,250ft 6¼lb boost, maximum 3,000 @ 16,000ft. Power loading lb/bhp 5.25. Electric starting. Propeller 10.67 ft, diameter, pitch 24.5 ft, gear ratio .477:1, coolant 100% Ethylene Glycol, 13½ gallons.

COSTS OF THE PROTOTYPE SPITFIRE

		1935													1936				
		Jan	Feb	Mar	Apr	May	19June	31Aug	Sep	Oct	Nov	Dec	Jan	Feb	5March	Mar	Apr	May	June
Material	£	7	9	13	117	277	180	764	439	299	423	922	63	198	First	194	338	125	824
Labour	£	18	20	26	88	317	378	987	311	270	349	589	488	530	flight	378	221	261	37
Factory Charges	£	28	30	39	131	476	568	1480	466	404	523	883	733	795		568	332	391	55
Total	£	53	59	78	336	1,070	1,126	3,231	1,216	973	1,295	2,394	1,284	1,523		1,140	891	777	916
Overall Total	£	53	112	190	526	1,596	2,722	5,953	7,169	8,142	9,437	11,831	13,115	14,638	15,000	15,778	16,669	17,446	18,362
Profit & Loss	£	6	7	9	31	111	132	346	109	94	122	206	171	185		132	77	91	13
Total	£	59	125	212	579	1,760	3,018	6,595	7,920	8,987	10,404	13,004	14,459	16,167		17,439	18,407	19,275	20,204

Original contract price of £10,000 of 1 December, 1934 under AM 361140/34. Profit and loss charges were taken as 35% of wages or labour as quoted above. Overall total (excluding profit and loss) up to 31 August 1937 was £20,738.

Last record is at 30 october 1937 when the AM contract figure had risen to £12,478, expenditure to date £20,738 and estimated total to complete £27, making a total expenditure of £20,765. Up to this date £8,280 had been claimed from the AM.

Rolls-Royce had already agreed to pay £7,500 before 25 June 1935 and this was paid to Supermarine. Total overall costs, up to the first flight in brackets. Material (£3,711) £5,192, Labour (£4,371) £5,268, Factory Charges (£6,556) £7,902, Profit and Loss (£1,529) £1,842.

NOTE – These are Supermarine figures and do NOT include embodiment loan items issued by the Air Ministry, such as the engine and most of the instuments. Thus, of the total expenditure of £20,765, £7,500 was paid by Rolls-Royce, £12,478 by the Air Ministry, and the profit of approx £2,000 by Supermarine turned into a deficit of £787. So it can be said that Supermarine built the prototype Spitfire for only £787.

"VARIATION OF THE THEME"

Even before the prototype F37/34 had flown the Air Ministry was beginning to toy with the idea of its eventual replacement, and in early 1935 was considering that an observer might have to be carried in the aeroplane—'So as to provide an additional pair of eyes for searching". It was firmly in the tradition of the two seat observation aeroplane of World War One. While you are carrying a passenger you may as well give him more to do than just scan the sky. So might have run the Air Staff's thoughts for on 20 May 1935 the DTD, Verney, issued specification F9/35 for a two seat fighter. The Specification demanded that maximum speed be 20mph in excess of contemporary bombers at 15,000ft, have a movable battery of at least four machine guns, a maximum speed of not less than 290mph at 15,000ft, a ceiling of 30,000ft, endurance $\frac{1}{4}$hr maximum power at sea level plus $1\frac{1}{2}$ hrs at 15,000ft, two hrs cruise at 15,000ft plus $\frac{1}{4}$hr maximum speed at 15,000ft. Provision to be made for 8x20lb bombs and 400rpg ammunition. Supermarine submitted their Specification No 438 on 16 August. The references on the copy were RJM and BMS (Mitchell and Shenstone).

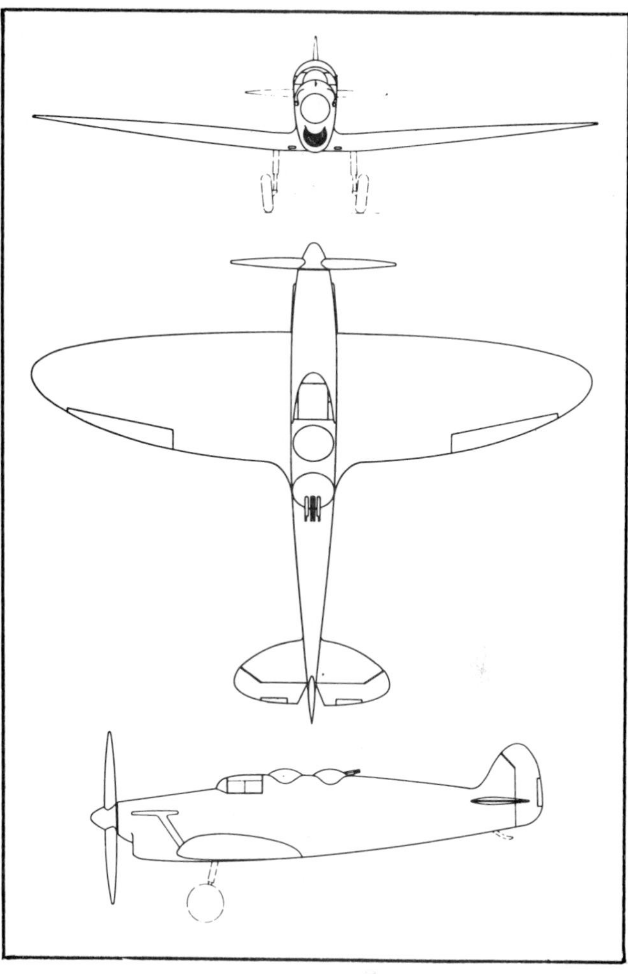

General arrangement of the Supermarine Type 305 to Air Ministry Specifications F 9/35. The first submission had four .303 Colt Browning machine guns in a remote turret with the gunner seated under a closely streamlined perspex dome. Engine air intake was located under the nose, behind the propeller.

SUPERMARINE TWO SEATER DAY AND NIGHT FIGHTER
A.M. SPECIFICATION F9/35
ROLLS-ROYCE MERLIN S ENGINE

Summary of chief points in the design.

This aeroplane, designed to meet the requirements of Air Ministry Specification F9/35, is a low wing monoplane equipped with a Rolls-Royce Merlin engine, glycol cooled. It is a development of the Supermarine monoplane fighters to A.M Specifications F7/30 and F37/34, and is almost identical with the latter machine. Modifications to the fuselage are of course necessary to convert from the single seater to the two seater arrangement, but the wings, engine installation, tail unit and retractable chassis reamain substantially unaltered. It is therefore considered that the new machine can be designed and constructed in a very short time, and is very unlikely to develop unexpected troubles. The chief points to be noted are as follows:-

(1) Performance: Other things being equal, the single engined aeroplane necessarily has less drag than the twin engined type, and the most efficient aeroplanes in existence are therefore single engined. More particularly is this the case where small high powered aeroplanes such as fighters are concerned because the engines are too large to fair neatly into the small wing. The single engined type has therefore been chosen for the present design.

(2) The most powerful liquid cooled engine available (the Rolls Royce Merlin) has been chosen. Although air cooled engines have been greatly improved where drag is concerned by the introduction of low drag cowling, it is considered that the liquid cooled engine using glycol still has considerably less drag than current air cooled types of similar horse power.

(3) Great attention has been paid to reducing parasite drag. To this end the chassis retracts completely, and fuselage, wing and tailplane are entirely covered with smooth flush riveted metal sheet. The excrescences caused by pilot's cockpit, gunner's station, and the gun turret have been reduced to the minimum consistent with the necessity to preserve adequate fields of view and fire.

(4) Armament: The requirements of the Specification for a movable battery of four machine guns are met by a straightforward scheme which adds a minimum of drag and weight, permits close cooperation between pilot and gunner, and provides an excellent view both for searching and firing.

(5) Construction: Experience with high speed Schneider Trophy seaplanes, combined with a large amount of research into single spar wing construction in connection of a robust and efficient structure comprising monocoque fuselage and single spar cantilever wing, largely metal covered.This type of construction, applied to the Supermarine F7/30 fighter, has required no modification in service, and has therefore been utilised for the Supermarine F37/34 fighter now building.

The proposed two seater fighter to Specification F9/35 is structurally almost identical with the latter machine; it utilises the same retracting chassis, and a very similar engine installation. It is therefore claimed that the possibility of trouble in service will be minimised by the use of a structure which will have been already tried out.

Detailed description

Wing. The cantilever wing consists of a single light alloy spar situated near the point of maximum thickness. To this spar is attached the torsion resisting leading edge box and the trailing ribs. The wing is completely covered with flat alloy sheet and is flush riveted in order to reduce the skin drag to a minimum. There are $2\frac{1}{2}°$ of washout on both wings. Air brakes and landing flaps are of the split type extending from the ailerons to the wing roots, and are operated by compressed air. They are designed to close automatically at higher speeds, thus relieving the wing of large loads. The wing is so designed that a suitable landing light may be installed without added drag. Existing deicing equipment can be used. Our experience on our F7/30 monoplanes has shown us that such a twisted wing has a very good behaviour at the stall, and that slots are not at all necessary. For this reason we consider that on this design also slots are unnecessary for good manoeuvrability at low airspeeds.

Fuselage. The main fuselage is of semi monocoque construction and also flush riveted. Only the engine mounting is of tubular construction with detachable cowling to facilitate maintenance. The top of the main fuselage is cut away for the gun unit described below. The wing and fuselage are blended together in the most favourable aerodynamic manner in order to prevent tail buffeting or other results of premature local stalling.

Accommodation of crew. The pilot's and the gunner's cockpits are closed in with transparent screens. The roof of the gunner's cockpit can be opened up and formed into a windscreen in order that he may stand up and make observations while awaiting the enemy. There is also a sliding side panel on each side which gives the gunner the good view in all directions which is so essential before using the sight to train the guns on the objective. If the pilot requires a position higher than normal for landing or for any special purpose the cockpit cover may be opened, thus enabling the seat to be raised further without the pilot touching the roof, resulting in a much improved view. The cockpits will be heated by oil radiators or by the exhaust in an indirect manner. Various methods are under investigation and a suitable system will be developed.

Chassis. The completely retracting chassis is of simple form, there being but one strut per wheel, which results in the minimum retardation of take off due to extra drag. The chassis folds upwards and outwards into a position behind the spar. The operating gear is hydraulic and closely follows our successful Seagull type.

Tail. Both the fin and the tailplane are built into the fuselage but so arranged that replacement of these units when damaged is relatively easy. Tail trimming is by elevator trailing edge flap. Fin and tailplane are metal covered, but the elevator and rudder and also the ailerons are fabric covered. There are trimming tabs on the rudder and one aileron adjustable on the ground.

Power Plant. The engine, a Rolls-Royce Merlin with glycol cooling, is accessibly mounted in a steel tube frame. A honeycomb radiator combining oil and engine cooling sections is slung beneath the engine and the cowling has been carefully designed to give good cooling with minimum drag. The radiator is designed for English Summer conditions, with provision for fitting a larger radiator for tropical use. The special low drag exhaust system developed for the F37/34 fighter is used, having an extension pipe which is flush with the side of the fuselage and emits the exhaust gases below the wing, thus greatly facilitating night landings.

Airscrew. A variable pitch constant rpm type of airscrew will be fitted. In the weight estimated the 3 blader duralumin Hamilton type has been assumed, but if a more suitable type becomes available it will be used.

Fuel and oil systems. The fuel tanks are in the leading edge of the wing, one each side of the fuselage in convenient positions for refuelling. In flight the fuel is pumped directly to the engine and the required auxiliary pump is supplied. The engine may be fed from either or both tanks. The total fuel carried is 80 gallons. The oil tank is situated just aft of the engine under the top cowling and forward of the fireproof bulkhead. As stated above oil cooling is by means of a honeycomb combined with the main radiator. The oil carried is 7 gallons.

Armament. The unit of four Browning machine guns and operating gear is installed in the aircraft as a single removable item. The gunner sits closely behind the pilot on a rotatable but non tilting parachute seat with built in footrest, and controls the guns which are attached to a double ring aft of the gunner. The rotating and elevating motions of the guns required for aiming are effected electro-mechanically by the gunner when using his prismatic telescopic sight. The gun ring and gunner's seat rotate in unison, but only the guns and sights are tilted, the gunner always remaining in an upright position.

The actual mechanism is briefly as follows—The two rings around the guns, to the upper one of which the guns are actually fixed, are duplicated around the gunner. The rings are geared together in two independent pairs, each pair being driven by a motor. If both motors are operated together the upper and lower pairs rotate as one and the guns are rotated only. The lower ring has a rack machined on it which meshes with a gear attached to the gun mounting on the upper ring. If the upper and lower rings rotate at different speeds in different directions this gear is operated by the rack and elevates or depresses the guns. The control is by handle switches and rheostats so that the guns may be moved backward or forward or elevated and depressed at varying speeds. The motion suggested is a back and forward motion of the handles for tilting the guns and a twist for the rotation of the turret. The field of fire covers the whole upper hemispheres except for the local limitation of the airscrew disc and fin in the fore and aft direction. It is hoped that the bombs will be placed inside the wing with an ejecting mechanism, now under development, so that they may be thrown clear of the aircraft when released in a dive. If this is not available in time at least the bomb rack attachments will be dragless.

General. The aeroplane will be designed to meet all detailed requirements of Specification F9/35 not referred to in the foregoing description.

Main particulars and dimensions	
Dimensions	37ft 0in
Length	30ft 6in
Wing area	242 sq ft
Airscrew diameter	11ft 0in
Wheel track	6ft 1in
Estimated weights (lbs)	
Structure	2030
Power plant	2040
Load	900
Fuel and Oil	680
Total auw	5650

Engine data:

Type. Rolls-Royce Merlin fully supercharged, glycol cooled. Normal rating 950bhp at 2,600 rpm at 11,000ft 5lb/sq in boost

Maximum rating 1,000bhp @ 3,000rpm @ 15,000ft. 5lb sq in boost. Maximum cruising rpm 2600.

Estimated performance. Maximum speed @ 15,000ft 315mph

Service ceiling 30,000ft

Take off run 275yds.

There were many interesting features in the design, not least being the engine cooling arrangements. By the time the design study was submitted to the Air Ministry Supermarine were fully aware of the Meredith radiator scheme which was installed in the underwing surface of the Spitfire, but despite this the under fuselage nose scheme was chosen. Also, the Merlin ejector exhaust manifolds were discarded in favour of the original Spitfire scheme in the shape of a large, staggered T flush to the cowling sides and exhausting under the wing root. Fuel tanks in the wing leading edge were to be later utilised in the photo reconnaissance Spitfires.

The proposed gun turret and its position was an inspired

The second Supermarine submission featured four Lewis guns in a remote turret and the gunners position now had fully glazed side panels. The air intake was modified and both designs featured the T-shaped engine exhaust pipes as originally specified for the prototype F37/34.

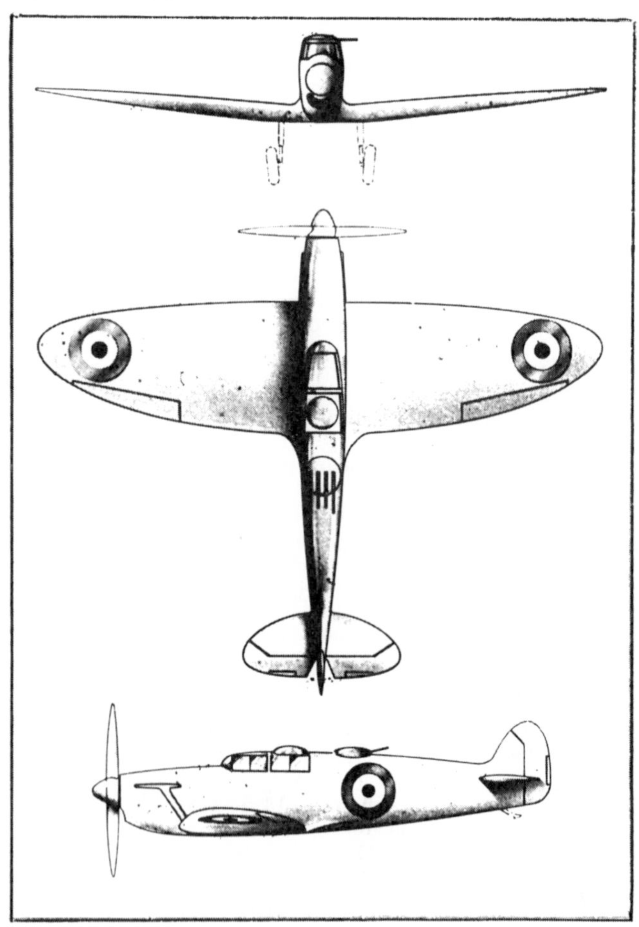

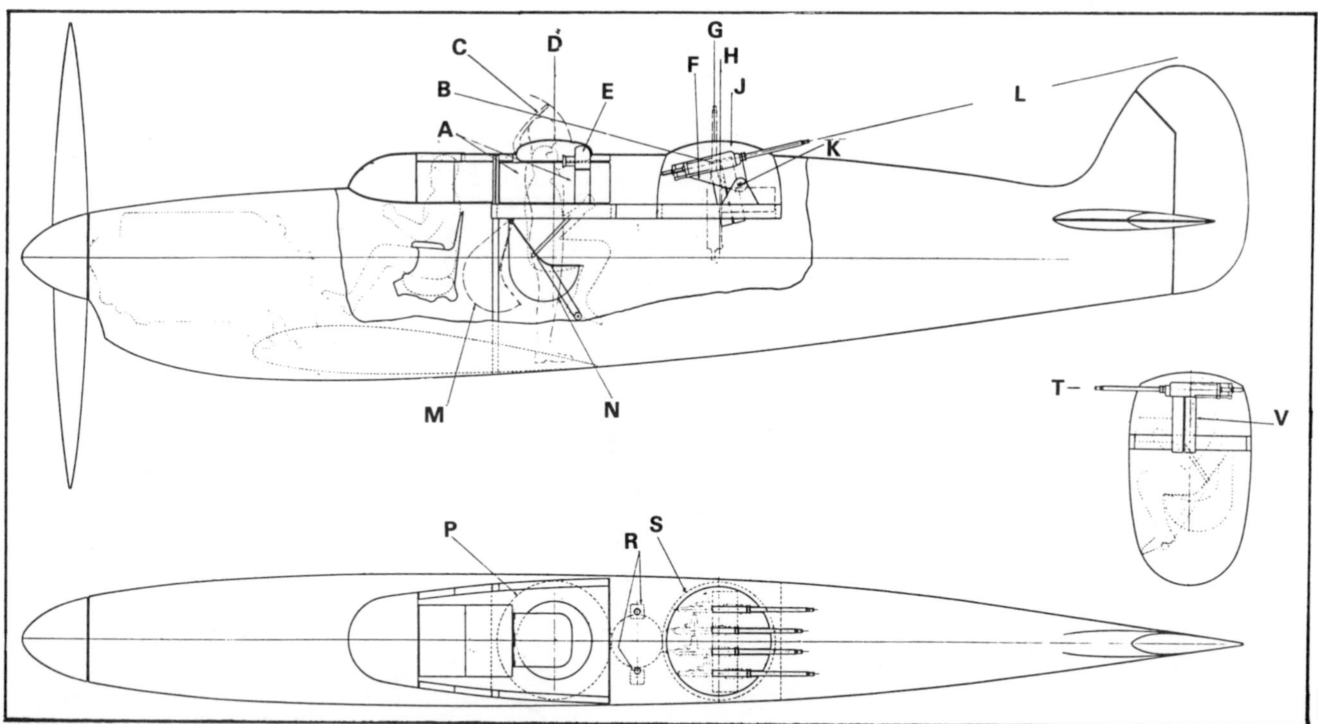

The Supermarine Type 305 with four .303 Brownings as to the original design submission. The gunner's seat swung forward to clear the gunner in standing position, and when sitting his feet rested on a fixed step. The glazed side panels slid to the rear leaving an opening, and the guns were sighted via a prismatic telescope attachment and reflector. As the gunner traversed his guns electric motors drove the turret round.

A Sliding glass panels, B line of fire at maximum depression, C non-rotatable transparent screen with hinged portion to protect gunner from slipstream, D axis of gunner's rotation, E prismatic sight with telescope attachment and tilting reflector, F gun mounting, G direction of fire at maximum elevation, H axis of gun turret, J rotating turret housing 4 × .303 Brownings, K axis for elevating guns, L direction of fire at maximum depression, M seat swings to clear gunner in standing position, N rotating seat geared to rotating turret, P ring supporting gunner's seat, R electric motors driving elevating and traversing mechanism of geared rings carrying gun-mounting, seat and sights, S mounting ring for gun turret, T direction of fire at maximum depression crosswind, V ammunition boxes. It was intended to install guns and controls as a self-contained detachable unit.

design, but during a visit to Nash and Thompson, specialists in turret design and manufacture, on 26 March 1936, Beverley Shenstone was told by the company that they thought the mounting would not be rigid enough. Also, Nash and Thompson thought the gunner should not be separated from his guns. A second design was submitted to the Air Ministry and this featured a revised cockpit for both occupants, four Lewis instead of Browning guns, but with the guns still in a remote turret. Vickers-Armstrong also submitted a similar aeroplane to the F9/35 Specification (see page 21). Contracts for the two-seat turret fighter were awarded to Hawker Aircraft for their Hotspur and to Boulton & Paul for the Defiant. The latter entered production. Sir Robert McLean wrote to Pierson on 14 August before the design was submitted to the Air Ministry and said he had talked with Dowding, who had advised McLean that work should continue with the Warwick bomber and the two-seat fighter abandoned.

The second, and final design, to make use of the basic F37/34 layout and technology was the Supermarine Type 312 submitted to A M Specification F37/35. It was basically the Spitfire airframe with a number of major modifications, the most obvious being adoption of four, wing mounted Oerlikon cannon and the installation of an underside, nose, engine air intake in place of the Meredith wing radiator. Supermarine Specification No 481 dated 28 March 1936 outlined the proposal for a 20mm cannon fighter as follows:–

SUPERMARINE SINGLE SEATER DAY AND NIGHT FIGHTER
A. M. SPECIFICATION F 37/35
SINGLE ENGINE

The Supermarine experimental F37/34 monoplane on which contractor's flight trials are almost complete, has shown itself to be a very satisfactory aeroplane without vices and of high performance. This aeroplane can be adapted to meet the requirements of AM Specification F37/35 by modification of the wings to accomodate 4-20mm calibre cannon. The fuselage, engine installation, tail unit and retracting chassis remain unaltered. Alternatively, should a production order be placed for the F37/34 the provision of an alternative set of wings would enable one of the production machines to fulfil Specification F37/35.

The requirements of the specification for a battery of 4-20mm calibre cannon are met by wing installations of Oerlikon Type FF cannon well outside the airscrew disc. The Oerlikon Type G cannon may be used if it is found suitable for a wing installation. This installation adds a minimum of drag. Except for the outer parts of the barrels, they are completely housed in the wings, if hopper-type ammunition boxes are provided. If these are not available, a slight excresence on the bottom surface of each wing will be necessary to fair in the ammunition drums. So far as wing construction is concerned, this is unaltered except in respect of the mountings for the guns.

Main particulars

Estimated Performance	
Maximum speed at 15,000ft	355mph
Time for climb to 20,000ft	9.5min
Service ceiling	31,000ft
Dimensions	
Wing span	37ft 0in
Length	29ft 11in
Wing area	242 sq ft
Estimated weights (based on existing F 37/34)	
Structure	2046lb
Power plant	2174
Load	510
Total auw	5800lb

Engine Data:

Type. Rolls-Royce Merlin S fully supercharged glycol cooled

Normal rating 950hp @ 2,600rpm @ 11,000ft, 4½lb sq in boost

Maximum rating 1,010hp @ 3,000rpm @ 15,000ft, 4½lb boost

Maximum cruising rpm 2,600.

Mitchell's association with alternative armament other than the .303 Browning had a long history, and it is obvious that as a result of this Joseph Smith was able to meet the Air Ministry requirements for a two-cannon Spitfire in 1939. A Vickers design calculation of 10 January 1935 investigated the

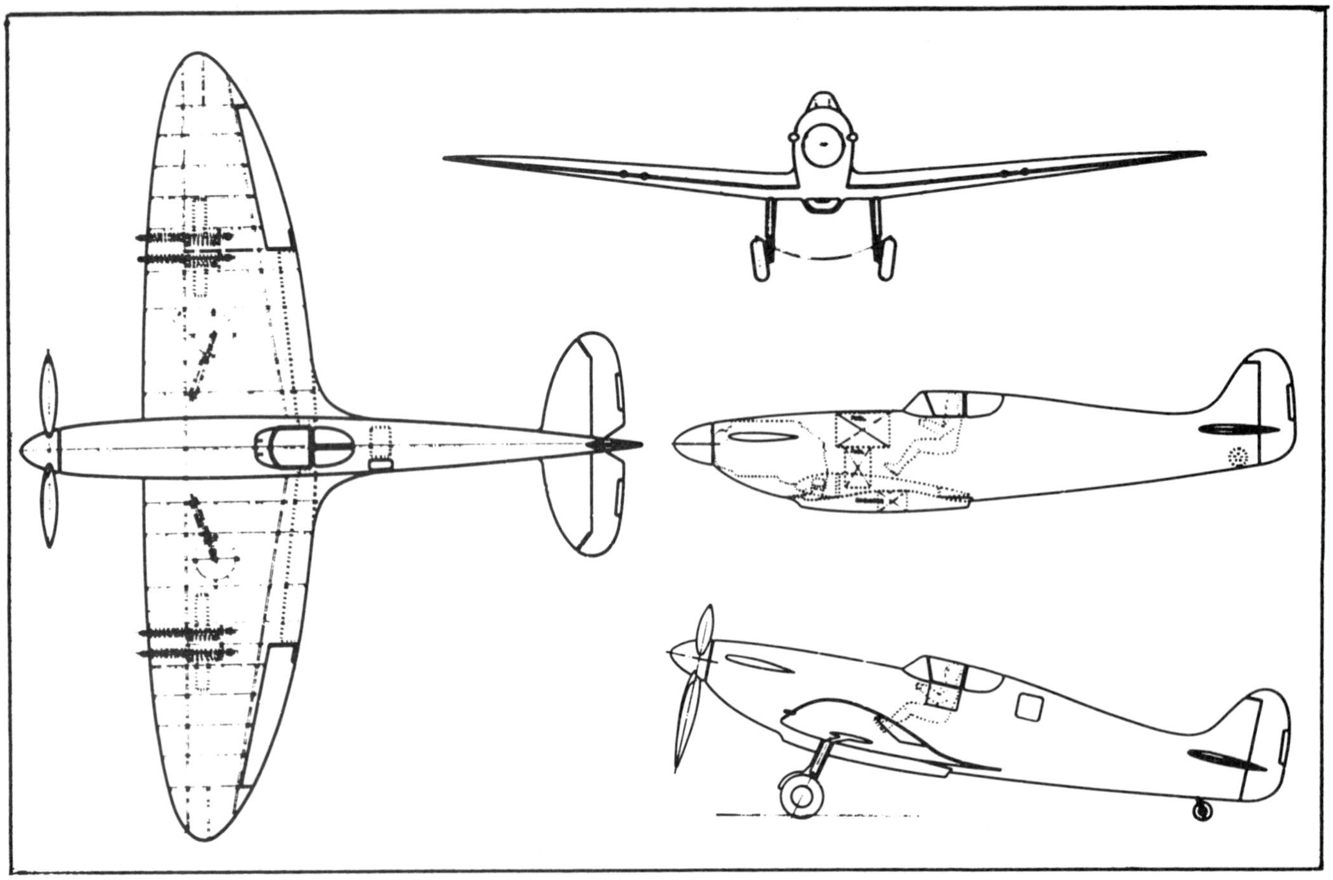

Above: Mitchell's final single seat fighter design was the Type 312 to Air Ministry F37/35. The basic design was similar to the Type 300 F37/34 but it was to be armed with four Oerlikon or Hispano 20mm cannon buried in the wings. This armament was located to fire outside the propeller disc, while the Merlin engine was to be cooled via the ventral radiator. This arrangement, it is thought, is similar to that drawn on Drawing 30000 Sheet 13 as presented to the Air Ministry on 5 December 1934 for F37/34.

Below: The Oerlikon could also be mounted in a pod under an aircraft's wing as on the Polish PZL parasol fighter. Sydney Camm installed two Oerlikons in a similar fashion under the wings of a Hawker Hurricane (L1750), and this fighter did operate for a period as a trials aircraft during the Battle of Britain. Mitchell discarded this application for his cannon fighter.

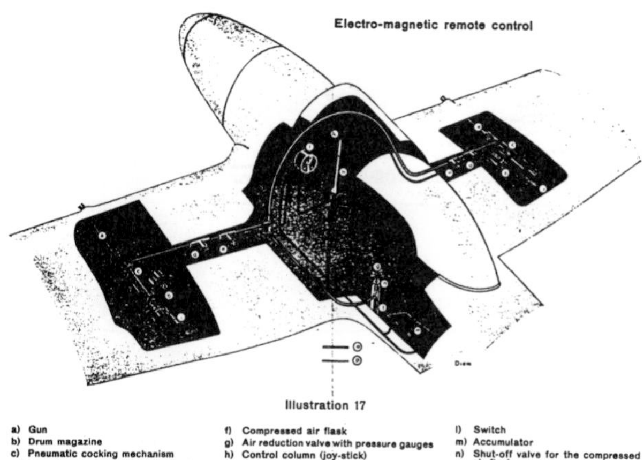

Illustration 17

a) Gun
b) Drum magazine
c) Pneumatic cocking mechanism
d) Valve for pneumatic cocking device
e) Stop cock for cocking device
f) Compressed air flask
g) Air reduction valve with pressure gauges
h) Control column (joy-stick)
i) Electric trigger control
k) Push-button for electric trigger control
l) Switch
m) Accumulator
n) Shut-off valve for the compressed air flask
o) Compressed air pipes
p) Wiring

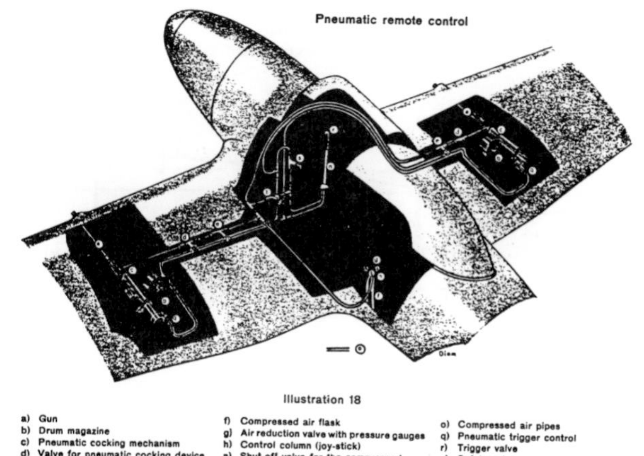

Illustration 18

a) Gun
b) Drum magazine
c) Pneumatic cocking mechanism
d) Valve for pneumatic cocking device
e) Stop cock for cocking device
f) Compressed air flask
g) Air reduction valve with pressure gauges
h) Control column (joy-stick)
n) Shut-off valve for the compressed air flask
o) Compressed air pipes
q) Pneumatic trigger control
r) Trigger valve
s) Safety valve
t) Shut-off cock for trigger and safety control

A typical twin cannon installation for electro-magnetic remote control. Facing is a pneumatically controlled installation.

The 20mm Oerlikon FF cannon which could have been mounted sideways in the wing of the Supermarine Type 312.

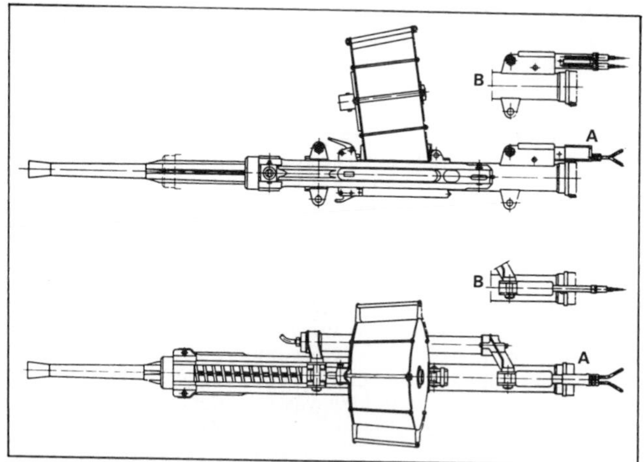

Views of the Oerlikon FF cannon showing side and normal mounting. (A) firing and safety operated pneumatically (B) by Bowden cable.

Single-seat fighter, the PZL P-XXIV, with FF wing arrangement.

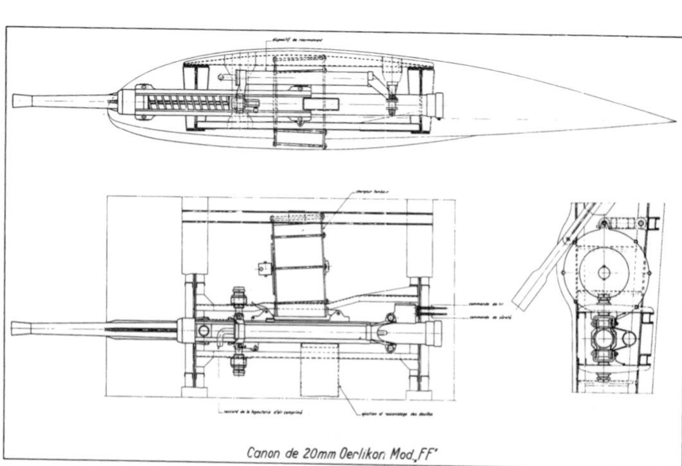

Mitchell wanted to bury his cannon in the Spitfire wing and, as already mentioned, Oerlikon had supplied drawings of such a mounting. A second proposal showed the cannon mounted on its side with a small blister covering it on the wing under surface. Yet another proposal was for the cannon in an upright position with the magazine contained within the wing structure and the gun hung under the wing and covered by a larger blister fairing.

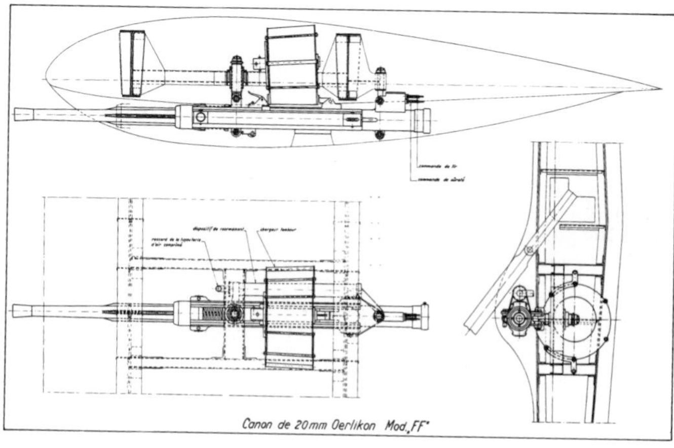

The Air Ministry asked Joseph Smith in 1939 to consider mounting the 20mm Hispano cannon under the Spitfire wing. Oerlikon had supplied drawings for a similar mounting for their guns to Mitchell in 1937. The magazine was contained in the wing structure but the gun was mounted clear of the under surface and covered by a blister fairing.

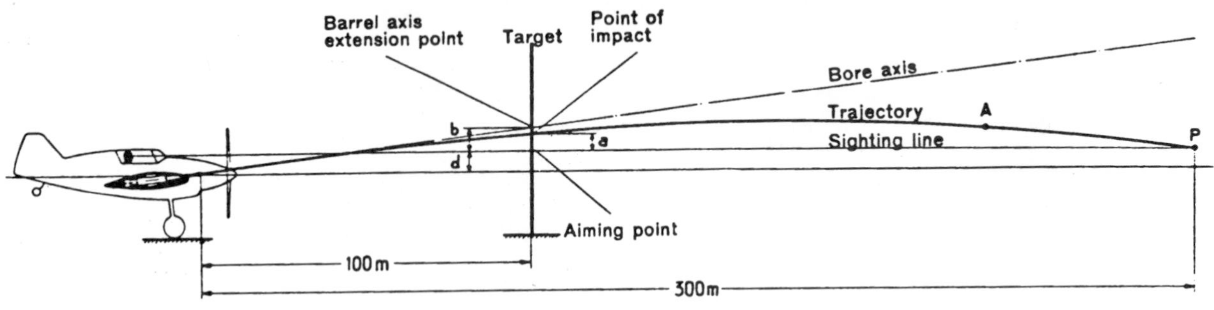

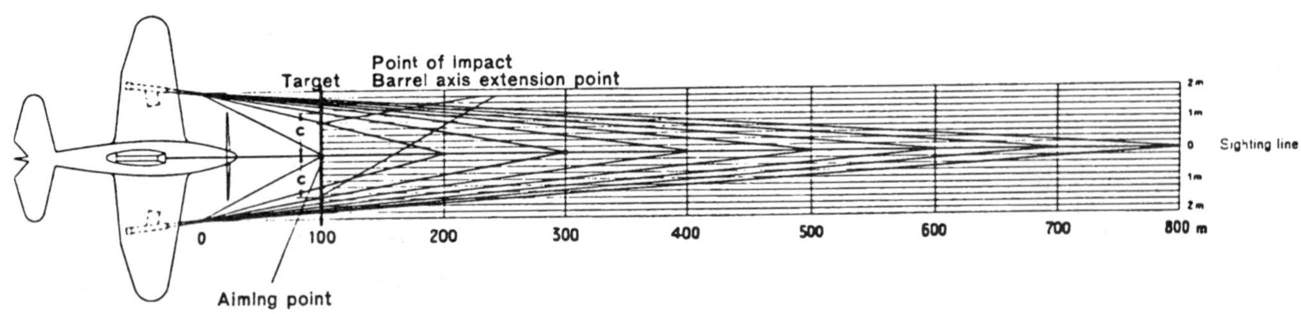

Diagrammatic views of gun settings and relevant converging points of Oerlikon cannon in a single seat fighter.

Vickers 12.7mm or 25.4mm machine gun firing through the propeller disc of the new PV12 engine. In a letter from H R Kilner to Brig. General W B Caddell of 2 January 1936 Kilner wrote — "Unless the gun (25.4mm) is restricted to firing at elevation only, I do not think that it is possible to meet the requirement laid down in the last paragraph of your letter". Investigation was then switched to the 20mm Hispano Suiza cannon with a muzzle velocity of 1,000m/s. The gun was belt fed and fired at the rate of 600rpm with a recoil of 500lb.

Drawings of the Vickers 'S' and 25.4mm guns were sent to R. K. Pierson on 5 February 1936, and by 24 April Mitchell had finished his proposals for the Type 312 with four 20mm Oerlikon cannon. The following October he received details of the 23mm Hispano cannon and in December he had all the necessary information on the 23mm Madsen gun.

Mitchell's approach to the Air Ministry Specification F 37/35 for a four-cannon, single seat fighter must have been influenced by the Oerlikon Company, for as early as 1932 the company had finalised design of the cannon for installation in an aircraft's wing or over the engine. Mitchell's interest was in the wing-mounted version and Oerlikon provided details of their "FF" type. Cocking was accomplished by compressed air and the gun came with 45, 60, 75 or 100 rounds in drums. The gun could be mounted by means of four upper and lower fixing lugs in the upright, inverted or on its side positions. Firing and safety mechanism were on the control column.

Ammunition came in eleven different types which are worth recording:– 1) Blank; 2) non-hardened steel bullet; 3) light tracing cartridge; 4) Cartridges with armour piercing shell (a) armour piercing without explosive charge (b) AP with light tracing charge (c) AP with fire charge (incendiary) which is set on fire and makes the shell burst when piercing, armour plate (d) AP and burst inside the target; 5) Cartridge with explosive fire shell. On impact the fire charge is dispersed and ignites inflammable materials. It was an early type of napalm; 7) Cartridge light tracing explosive shell; 8) Cartridge with high explosive shell. Highly sensitive contact fuse and powerful explosive effect; 9) Cartridge with high explosive light tracing shell and sensitive contact fuse; 10) cartridge with high explosive shells with light and with contact and time fuse. It was an amazing mixture and ideal for the Type 312.

Mitchell's association with the Spitfire came to an end with this design for he became fully occupied with the Supermarine B12/36 four engined bomber, and until his death in June 1937 his only interest in the fighter was to observe the early flight tests of the prototype.

PRODUCTION AND PROBLEMS

Before the prototype Spitfire had completed its official handling trials at Martlesham Heath the Air Staff was convinced of its future potential, and to speed production and entry into squadron service Specification F16/36* was drawn up and issued to cover development and series production of the Type 300 Mk I. The Specification reached Supermarine on 28 July 1936 and was followed immediately by an initial order for 300 examples, plus an additional ten airframes for experiment and development. The signator of both documents was Air Commodore R. H. Verney, the DTD, and the contract was worth £1,860,000 plus £136,400 for spares.

The first production order was back dated to 3 June 1936 under Contract B.527113/36. Supermarine had never before received such a large order; the Woolston factory was not equipped for mass production on the scale envisaged, and the workforce was only 500. Subcontracting was the obvious answer and Supermarine wanted to employ other aircraft manufacturers to produce the detail parts while they would handle all major assemblies and final assembly of the airframe. But the Air Ministry thought otherwise and Supermarine was directed to subcontract a large proportion of the major assemblies, such as tailplane, wings, etc, with final assembly taking place in two, large, modern hangars which had been erected at Eastleigh Aerodrome, situated just outside Southampton.

The main companies involved in producing large assemblies in the early days of production were – Aero Engines Ltd (ailerons and elevators), J Samuel White and Co (fuselage frames), Singer Motors Ltd (engine mountings), Folland Aircraft Ltd (tailplane and rudder), General Aircraft Ltd (wings), Pobjoy Motors Ltd (wings), General Electric Co (wing tips), The Pressed Steel Co (wing leading edge), G Beaton and Son Ltd (wing ribs) and Westland Aircraft Ltd (wing ribs).

In theory subcontracting should have solved the production dilemma; in practice it was almost disaster for the elliptical wing raised many, major problems as it was something totally new to the industry and its manufacture demanded that new techniques had to be learned. Production proper had begun in March 1936 and by the end of the year only six fuselages were complete, and they were awaiting wings. Four sets had been delivered but wing flutter in the prototype Spitfire meant that to raise the flutter threshold some internal redesign was necessary, with the result that the spar web was moved from the front face of the spar boom to the rear. Also, the leading edge covering metal had to be increased in gauge from 16 to 14 and from 18 to 16 at the wing tip. The effect was an increase in torsional stiffness of about 40% with a weight penalty of 20 lb. The RAE thought that with the modifications production wings would be free of flutter up to 480 ASI.

An Air Ministry official visited the Supermarine works in early 1937 and saw a number of fuselages, fully equipped, awaiting delivery of wings. There followed an exchange of letters between Supermarine and the Air Ministry about the long delay in wing deliveries. Supermarine stated – "Alterations in design and inaccuracies in drawings were no more than usual in the initial stages of production development of a new design, but it was inevitable that their effect would be more evident when the production development was carried out by a subcontractor not in direct contact with the drawing office. General Aircraft have informed us that drawing alterations and corrections for the Spitfire were not more numerous or serious in effect than they have experienced with any similar subcontracts from other Air Ministry contractors.

"No serious delay in production has resulted from delay in the supply of parts made by the Supermarine works. Delays have occurred in the supply to General Aircraft of parts made by other subcontractors. Also, delays have occurred in the supply of materials ordered by us for delivery to General Aircraft and the causes of these delays were outside our direct control and not due to any want of attention by the Supermarine works.

"The decision that the Spitfire components should be subcontracted was made by the Air Ministry and the selection of the subcontractors was controlled by the DAP. It is not equitable that we, or our subcontractors, should be held responsible for the difficulties consequent on this policy".

The Air Ministry's response was immediate and to the point – "The firm's (General Aircraft) methods of production of main planes have been investigated by representatives of this department and the delay in supply of requisite parts is due to the default of your Supermarine works". Attached to the letter was a detailed diary of events connected with wing production at General Aircraft and it showed that after receipt of an order from Supermarine for 100 sets of wings, the first set of wings was not delivered until 12 months later. The intervening period was taken up with promises of supply of drawings and parts which were either inaccurate or not forthcoming at the specified date.

It was then proposed that General Aircraft should concentrate on the production of one wing with Pobjoy Motors producing the other wing. Supermarine had to make arrangements to build wings at Woolston, but this only aggravated production of fuselages resulting in late delivery dates for them. The proposed contract date for delivery of the final Spitfire Mk I was deferred to August 1939, and at one time such was the delay in production it was suggested that the Spitfire programme be abandoned and Supermarine should build production models of another company's design under licence. A second plan put forward by the Air Ministry was for Supermarine to complete production of the 310 Mk I Spitfires, after which the company would produce the Bristol Beaufighter under licence.

These proposals came as a shock to Supermarine, but there was sound reasoning behind them for the 'L' Expansion Scheme proposed by the Air Ministry called for the production of 12,000 aircraft, including the second generation of monoplane fighters – the Hawker Tornado and Typhoon, and the Westland Whirlwind – to succeed the Spitfire and Hurricane. Any delay with the production and delivery of the last two types would mean accelerating the newer designs with the subsequent production problems. Also, the Air Council had forecast a front line loss of up to 500 fighters per month if the air war had to be carried to the enemy, and Schemes F and L had been designed to replenish these losses. Therefore, there could be no permitted delay in Spitfire production.

The managements of Supermarine and Vickers were able to finally convince the Air Ministry that as their (and their subcontractors) work force, most of it new and inexperienced, became used to new methods of manufacture the production problems would, eventually, solve themselves. Convinced by the arguments the Air Ministry placed a second order for 200 Mk I Spitfires on 24 March 1938, and the two orders (to the same contract) covered the K, L and N prefix serials. The official Supermarine submission to the Air Ministry of the same date contained the following details.

Particular care had to be taken with protective finishing, as an all metal airframe brought with it corrosion problems. An Air Ministry order for 19 May 1937 specified protective and camouflage schemes for all new aeroplanes. All aluminium parts to be protected by ADM 324, steel parts by ADM 323, aluminium parts other than those constructed of Alclad to be anodised, contact surfaces to be treated with chromac jointing pastes (Duralac) and assembled wet, organic protectives to be applied in accordance with DTD 902. All components and parts to be finally protected with one coat of yellow chromate to DTD 260, followed by a finishing coat pigmented with aluminium to DTD 260 unless otherwise stated. So, every Spitfire before camouflage and delivery had to be painted aluminium overall, Cockpit interior to be finished in grey green cellulose enamel to DTD 63 with the aircraft exterior in camouflage finish in accordance with the official drawing. Fabric to be treated with Cellon scheme X.

The Air Ministry was not completely satisfied with the spin recovery of the Spitfire, and at a meeting on 17 January 1938, chaired by Air Cdr. Verney, Supermarine persuaded those in attendance that no modifications be made to production aircraft apart from the addition of an anti-spin parachute. For the Air Ministry Verney said that based upon model tests at Farnborough production aircraft could not be passed for spinning even with a tail parachute. Supermarine then pointed out that Jeffrey Quill had made sixteen successful spins of eight turns in the prototype. After more discussion the DTD agreed to accept the Supermarine proposal and that the first 20 production models should be fitted with the tail parachute and undergo further spinning trials. He, DTD, would be satisfied with recovery at 15,000 ft.

When the first production Mk 1 Spitfire, K9787, was

see Appendix III, page 602

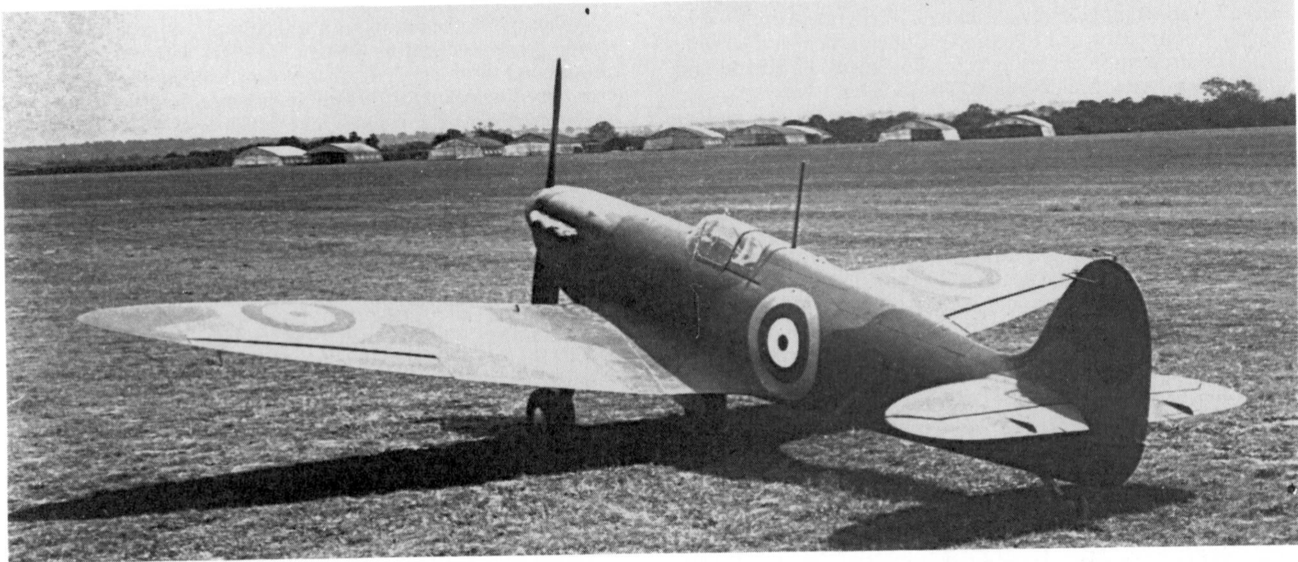

Round the clock views of the first production Spitfire Mk I K9787. It was used for extensive maker's trials and numerous experiments, which resulted in modifications adopted on later production models. K9787 was to be converted to one of the original PRU aeroplanes and in this role was lost on operations on 30 June 1941.

completed at the beginning of May 1938 an anti-spin parachute was duly fitted and the aircraft made its first flight from Eastleigh, piloted by Quill, on 14th of the same month. The second aircraft, K9788, followed shortly afterwards and both were retained for makers' trials. The former was then delivered to Martlesham Heath on 27 July for handling trials; the latter had gone to Rolls-Royce, Hucknall, ten days previously for engine trials. The first weighing of K9787 had taken place at Eastleigh on 8 May with main wheels on an Avery ground platform and tail wheel suspended from a Denison weigher. Tare 4,341 lb.typical service load 495, pilot and parachute 200, fuel (petrol @ 7.5 lb/gal) 630 and oil 6 gals @ 9 lb/gal). Total weight 5,720 lb.

Wing production was again flagging and in a bid to improve the situation it was suggested that a plywood covering of the wing aft of the main spar in place of duralumin would speed up deliveries. The metal skin weighed 100 lbs, with the plywood estimated at 93. However, strength and stiffness comparison revealed that with a 2mm plywood skin torsional stiffness was reduced by 8%. The final recommendation was to simplify construction in other areas; one was to manufacture a composite rib of wood reinforced with metal. Other areas of activity which affected production was the introduction of modifications and weight increases. The proposed switch from a two blade, wooden propeller to a three blade, two pitch metal unit increased the auw by 130 lbs, but take off run was decreased from 330 to 245 yards; time to 15,000ft increased by one minute and to 20,000 by 1.8. Installation of the Merlin III engine also increased weight to a total of 5930 lb. During a test flight of K5054 (the prototype) on 14 May 1936, a top inner wing door on the upper surface for servicing the wheel oleos was lost in a TV dive at 380 IAS and the port undercarriage door tore away striking, and damaging, the underside of the fuselage. Quill, the pilot, said that the TAS was 465mph. New support brackets for the door had to be designed and incorporated.

As part of the programme for improving performance a model Spitfire was tested in the compressed air tunnel at the National Physical Laboratory, this model being fitted with two radiator sizes, different styles of cockpit hood, plus a normal and reduced span wing. Results showed that any modification to these standard items would have little, or no, effect on drag. **Two days before the first flight of K 9787 de Havilland's** had revealed details of the Hamilton 'Hydromatic' propeller, then being used by a number of American airlines. This

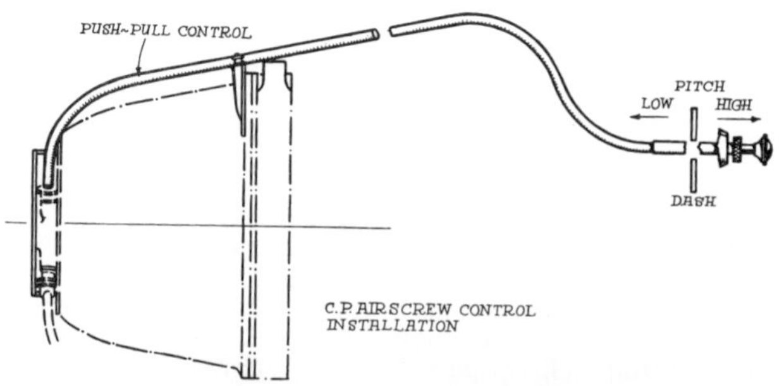

Schematic of the basic control system for the de Havilland two pitch propeller. For take off in fine pitch the knob was pulled; for normal forward speed it was pushed home.

propeller provided for a 35° pitch change for the constant speed operation with a 45° change to the feathering position, the latter taking approximately five seconds to accomplish. It was nearly 40 lbs heavier than the unit usually fitted but this penalty was outweighed by the advantages it conferred. A 'Hydromatic' was flight tested on K9787 the following September and de Havilland's speculated that multi-blade propellers would soon become standard and all high speed aircraft would have a two speed gear.

GUN SIGHTING

The early production Spitfires were fitted with a ring and bead sight, but provision had been made for a reflector unit as this was of immense value to a pilot when attacking an enemy aeroplane. Many sights had been considered by the Air Ministry and by May 1938 two were through the prototype stage — the Georz GJ 1 and GJ 3, first specified for the Westland F37/35. Other, similar, sights awaiting Air Ministry trials and approval were the Barr and Stroud GM 2, a third sight by Georz, and the Collimateur Clair, Ross prismatic, Alkan ring and bead. All were tested at Farnborough and by AFDU by July 1938, with the GM 2 proving to be the better sight. During the following trials of the GM 2 a number of pilots on No 111 Squadron said they actually preferred the older ring and bead to any other sight and suggested a compromise of deleting the actual ring as reflected on the windscreen and replacing it with an engraved ring on the flat windscreen panel. The Air Ministry thought this opinion was due to natural conservatism. Not so, replied the pilots; as the reflector sight throws an illuminated image on the windscreen why not have a permanent one engraved on the glass?

There was yet another sighting system submitted by Aldis

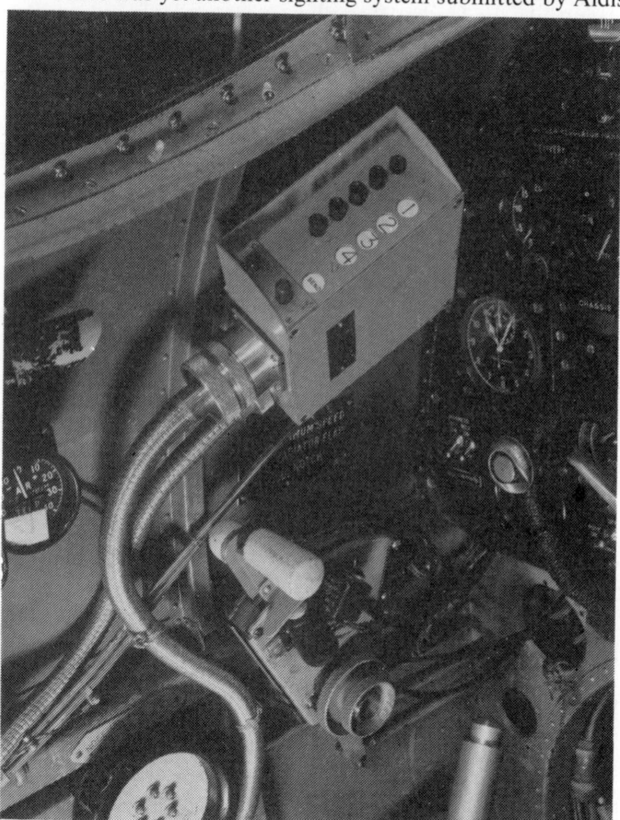

Cockpit control for pitch settings (see page 52).

for a combination of prismatic and ring and bead, but it was rejected for part of the sight protruded through the windscreen. The contract for the development and production of a reflector sight was finally awarded to Barr and Stroud for their GM 2 reflector on 12 July 1938 under contract No.579006/36/C.CI (9). Squadron Leader Gillan carried out initial trials of early production models. The GM 2 Mk II was ordered into production on 19 July 1939 with the GJ Mk III on 23 August the same year.

With reflector sight in position and switched on the pilot

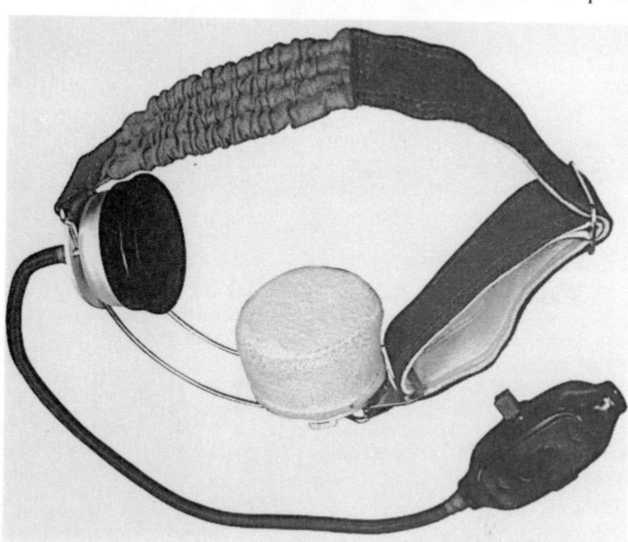

The Langryaphone was an early attempt by the RAF to combine the pilot's oxygen mask with a radio telephone. Two models were tested, the X1 and X2 and the model is wearing the latter. Note the on/off switch attached to its flex. Also illustrated is the channel selection box with four selector buttons, send and receive switches of a later model of an early TR radio as installed and tested in an early production Spitfire Mk I. Trials of all equipment began in 1937 and ended in the summer of 1938.

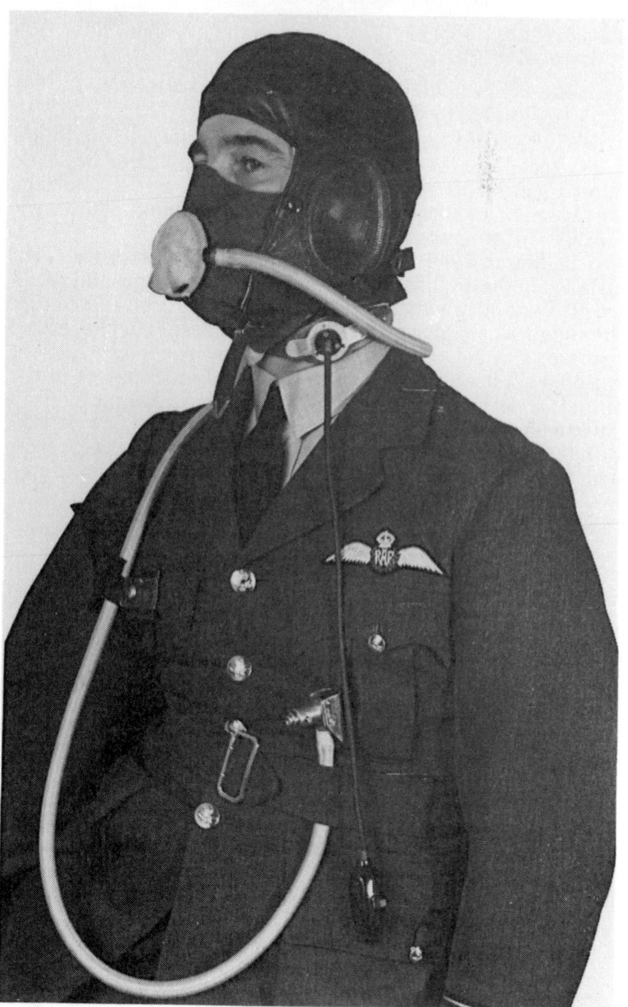

One of the many trial installations applied to K9787 was a series of exhaust manifolds. Illustrated is (above) an ejector type and (below) streamlined unit with special exits for damping glare for night flying.

saw a white dot surrounded by a ring reflected on to his windscreen. The lower graticule control ring had to be set to approximately the span of an enemy aircraft, but with use the average pilot soon learned to use the sight without adjusting it for different wing span aircraft.

In March 1940 K9830 was flown with a prismatic sight installed in the modified starboard windscreen panel and it had the effect of obstructing the pilot's view. It was considered that the sight was an improvement on the standard reflector model because (1) it could be stowed away below eye level when not required (2) it was not illuminated and so independent of the aircraft's electrical system and (3) it had an opaque graticle pattern incorporated. However, Quill, who test flew K9830 with the prismatic sight, thought that to replace a reflector sight with a prismatic was a retrograde step. Quill — "The reflector was in full production with deliveries totalling 1800 units per month, whereas prismatic production was subject to an initial order for 100. The only faults applicable to the reflector were (1) obstruction to forward view (2) its complete dependence upon filament lamps and (3) it imposed stringent optical requirements on the bullet-proof windscreen".

Quill then discussed the periscopic sight, also installed in K9830, and said he was not impressed with its performance. A Spitfire, Hurricane and Fulmar were all tested with the sight, and a P.1 sight was fitted with a gyroscope for automatic correction for relative speeds of hunter and target. A second, much smaller, version was installed in a Spitfire in July 1940 and, after trials at Boscombe Down, Elliot Bros Ltd were given the contract to develop the automatic, or gyro, gun sight. 2,000 units were ordered and allotted to the fixed gun fighters of the period, and in view of the need for secrecy the new sight was referred to as the 'No 6 Mechanism'.

In June 1938 it was proposed to install Lorenze Blind Landing equipment in production Spitfires, this increasing the auw to 5824 lbs with a two blade propeller and 5880 with a three blade. To compensate for CoG movement the former would have an extra 187 lb of ballast in the nose, while the latter would need 5 lb. In the event the problem was resolved when all Spitfires were converted to the three blade propeller. Armour plate was to add a further 78 lb.

Air Ministry Certification of Design for the Spitfire was approved on 13 July 1938 and the first production machine to reach the RAF was K9789, which arrived at No 19 Squadron on 4 August to begin intensive flying trials. It was returned to Supermarine several weeks later for stripping down and detailed examination. The first Spitfire to enter RAF service was K9792 when it reached the Central Flying Establishment, Cranwell, on 30 July for evaluation by instructors.

No 19 Squadron completed 300 hours flying time within a short period and the small number of obvious defects were dealt with, one being the notorious undercarriage pump lever. In the design of K5054 it will be remembered that powered retraction of the undercarriage was originally specified but later changed to manual. As a result of this pilots tended to develop 'Spitfire knuckle', a painful complaint caused by the clenched fist striking against the cockpit side when working the long handle. During this operation the Spitfire could be seen to wobble erratically until the undercarriage was fully up or down. Mercifully, powered retraction was rapidly introduced and skinned knuckles were the rarity.

Throughout the summer and autumn of 1938 production increased slowly with No.19 Squadron receiving one aeroplane per week and it was not until the end of the year that the last of sixteen aircraft (K9811) was delivered on 11 November. Meanwhile, the Merlin III was becoming available and the first Spitfire to have one installed was the 194th production K9980, delivered to No. 611 Squadron on 19 May 1939. The engine was pressure cooled with a mixture of 70% distilled water and 30% glycol, a mix that was not to vary in all future models until later in the war when mains water replaced the expensive distilled. Starting was by means of the Coffman cartridge system. Airframe weight had risen again to 6082 lb.

Deliveries were still behind schedule and actual number of aircraft delivered to the RAF at the end of December 1938 was 49. A further 18 were delivered in January 1939, 27 in February, 13 in March. The Munich crisis of 1938 had made production of fighter aircraft crucial for, as everyone was aware, war was a matter of months away and the Air Staff wanted production accelerated. 'Peace in our Time' was all very well, but a piece of paper would not keep the bombers away and an apprehensive British public looked for reassurance to the Royal Air Force

K9789, third production Mk I, at Eastleigh aerodrome. Used mainly as a trials aircraft it eventually became maintenance airframe 3594M in 1944.

Gun installation trials were conducted with K9788, the second production Mk I, in August 1938. The aircraft lacked any type of heating and trials were restricted to lower altitudes. Illustrated is the rear mounting of the outboard port gun above and below the wing surface. Gun and ammunition bays were covered by 22 panels secured with 150 turn buttons. Re-arming was accomplished in 30 minutes by four ground crew.

Right: K9791 was used for many trial installations, including twin 70 gallon overload fuel tanks on the wings. It had a Merlin XII engine and Coffman starter, plus a larger nose oil tank for use in its final role as a PRU aircraft. At this time it still carried the aluminium, black and white under surface camouflage scheme and had a constant speed de Havilland propeller. The date was 24 January 1940, the period when Sholto-Douglas wrote to Supermarine – "Of a requirement for the Spitfire to have a range of 1,500 miles to cope with re-inforcement plans for the Middle East, and the aircraft to have room for 214 gallons of fuel". With the 70 gal wing tanks and full fuel load, combat range was estimated at 1,224 miles with maximum speed reduced by 5mph. Auw was 7,310lbs at take off, and with all armament and ammunition removed 6,950.

and its ability to defend the homelands against the horror of air raids as portrayed in the newsreels of the Spanish Civil War.

Action had been initiated, however, for during the previous April a contract for 1,000 Spitfire Mk Is was promised to the Nuffield Organisation, designers and builders of the Morris motor car, but Nuffield was required to build and operate a shadow factory. The site chosen was Castle Bromwich, near Birmingham, and one year later the contract was placed. It was for the Spitfire Mk II, and this will be discussed in chapter five.

PRODUCTION, FUTURE UNCERTAINTIES

But the overall situation was still uncertain as the minutes of an Air Ministry meeting of the period noted that the Air Staff had been considering aircraft orders to be placed — "With certain firms whose existing orders will run out in early 1940. The firms of immediate importance are Supermarine and de Havilland. This minute will deal only with Supermarine. Supermarine will run out of their order for Spitfires in February or March 1940, and since it will be impossible to get a new aircraft into production at Supermarine before September 1940 there is certain to be a six months gap we will have to fill".

As a result of Munich further contracts had been placed with the company, the first being No. B980383/39 for 200 aircraft bearing the prefix P serials. This was the contract which the above minute was discussing. The minute continued – "In order to bridge the gap with as few machines as possible, Supermarine will be told later on to reduce the amount of sub contracting and to get their men on to a single shift so that

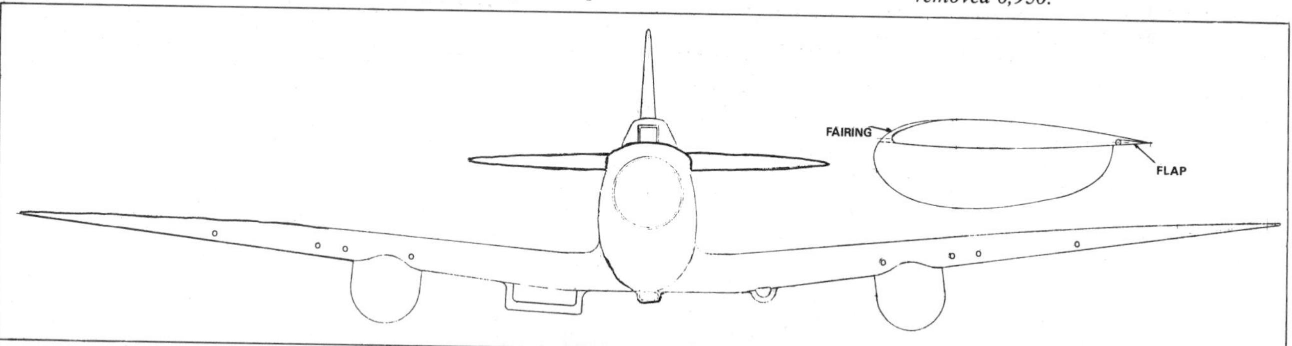

70 gallon overload tanks were fitted in mock-up form on K9791. They were located between the inner and inside middle guns. This installation was to be tested by No 602 Squadron Spitfires in June 1940. A letter relating to a long range fuel tank for the Spitfire was received at HG Fighter Command on 3 June 1940. It read – "As a result of investigations by the Air Ministry, it has been decided to manufacture 100 wing tanks of 29 gallons capacity. This will provide just over 200 miles additional range at most economical speed. The tanks will be self sealing and Supermarine estimate that the tank should not result in a loss of more than 3 miles per hour at maximum speed. The first tank will be available by about the middle of June and you will decide which squadrons will be fitted with the tank". Dowding replied on 17 June— "Arrangements are being made to fit No 602 Squadron with the long range tanks in the first instance. The installation however, cannot be fitted in conjunction with the Hispano cannon Spitfire, and owing to the extensive nature of the modification it is necessary to confine the fitting of Hispano guns to new production aircraft and the present intention is to produce 30 aircraft of this type. The tank can be fitted to standard Spitfires retrospectively".

although Supermarine production is likely towards the end of the present contract to exceed 48 aircraft per month it is hoped that we can reduce the gap in production to 30 aircraft a month.

"Vickers are pressing for a more generous release of Spitfires for foreign orders , and it does seem that, provided no releases are made until October, we could go some way to meet them this year and could release aircraft for foreign orders freely after the Spring of next year, when the Castle Bromwich factory will be coming into production. It is suggested that the following releases might be made to whet the foreign appetites: 2 in October 1939, 4 November, 6 December, 8 January 1940, 8 February and 8 March, and after March the whole of the firm's production except that required to replace releases from Air Ministry contracts in the period from October 1939 to March 1940. As regards past foreign sales we are prepared to order a further 100 Spitfires, to include 30 in replacement of foreign orders. A total number of 300 will probably be needed to fill the gap, so that they would be able to sell abroad (should we concur) about 230".

The minute, signed by R. Saundby, provides a clear insight into the Air Ministry's revised views on Supermarine's capabilities of handling large scale Spitfire production. Consideration does not appear to have been given to the international situation, in particular to Germany's armed resurgence. The minute continued in the same vein – "The engine position, however, will be difficult since Merlin IIIs are required for foreign orders and they will not be available when Rolls-Royce have turned over to the Merlin X and XII. I should propose, therefore, that the 200-250 Spitfires to be delivered to the Royal Air Force from the Supermarine works from November 1939 to March 1940 should be delivered *without engines*,* Merlin X being fitted in due course. This would leave all the Merlin IIIs available in this period for foreign orders". Saundby obviously thought that the foreign air forces needed to re-arm with the latest equipment before the RAF.

That the Air Ministry still had doubts about Supermarine becomes clearer as is evident by the minutes' continuation – "The type of aircraft that could be put into production at Supermarine after the end of their contract would be the Beaufighter, the new Gloster Fighter or the Westland Lysander and Whirlwind. It is not certain yet whether the two former aircraft are suitable (owing to size) for the Supermarine works, and I take it that the output of the Westland fighter from the Westland-Nuffield-John Brown Group will be sufficient to meet our needs of Westland aircraft. We cannot decide on the type at present, but I should like to know if we should consider the Gloster or whether we should concentrate all our energies on the Beaufighter".

Production of the Spitfire by Supermarine after the initial contracts were completed now looked extremely doubtful, and the position was made more gloomy at another meeting on 11 July 1939, just two months before the outbreak of war. Saundby again signed the minutes – "Yesterday the Supply Committee considered the future programme of work at the Supermarine and Gloster factories. The Committee came to the following decisions, pending your approval (i) the Supermarine works to have an order for 450 additional Spitfires (this was to Contract No.B19713/39, placed on 9 August, and bearing the R prefix serials) to cover the gap between the end of the present

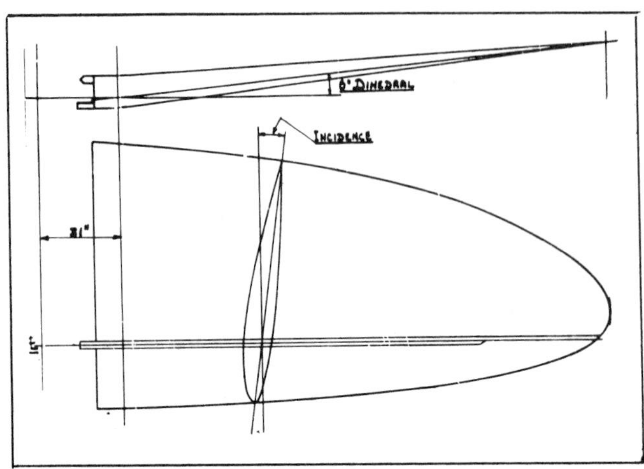

Main structure of Mk I wing (starbd) shows wheel bay, aileron control runs and armament location. Elevation shows wing datum to C/L of aircraft. The fabric gun port patches measured 8 x 8in approximately. Small view shows wing angle and incidence to fuselage.

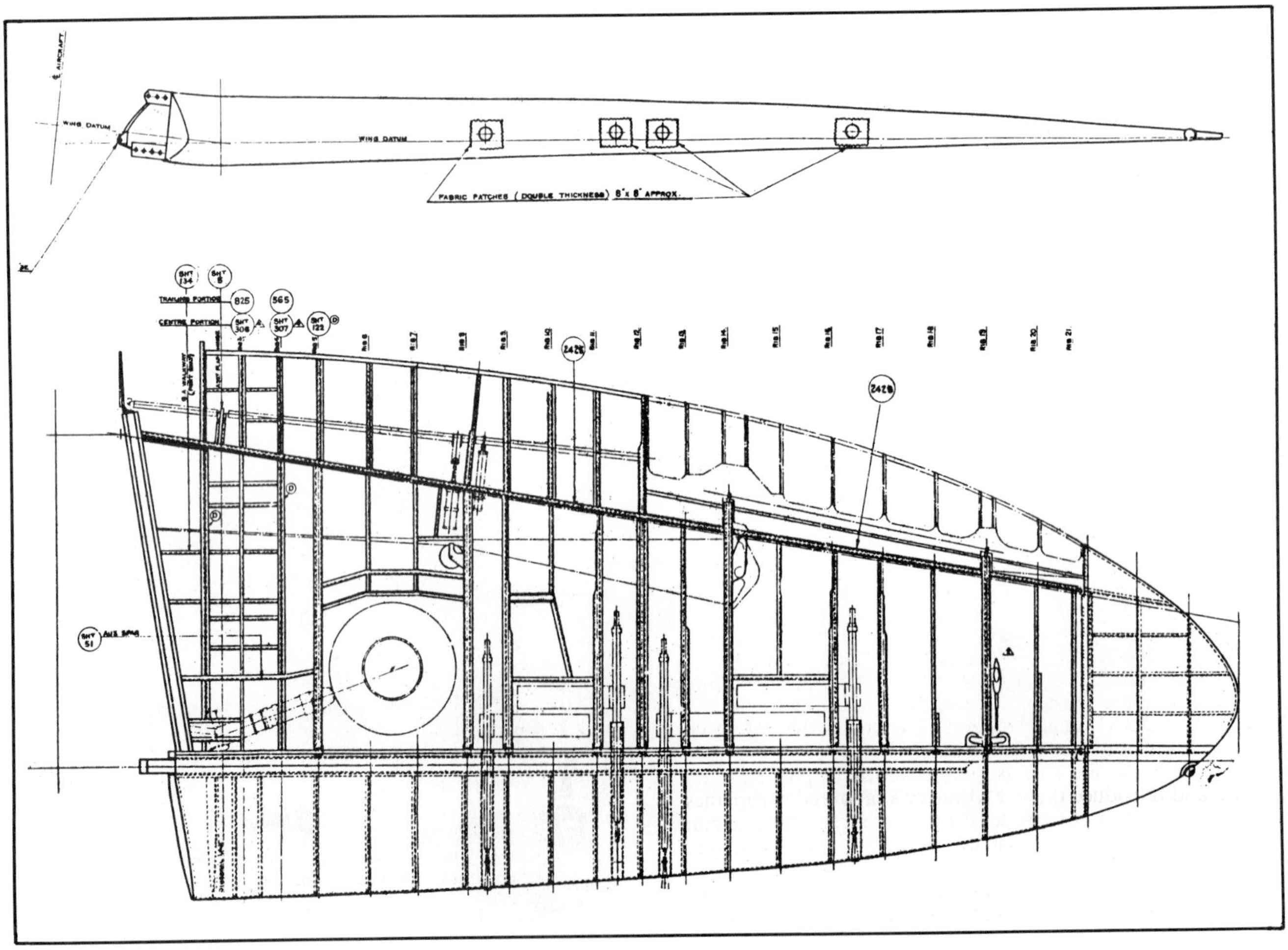

* *Author's italics*

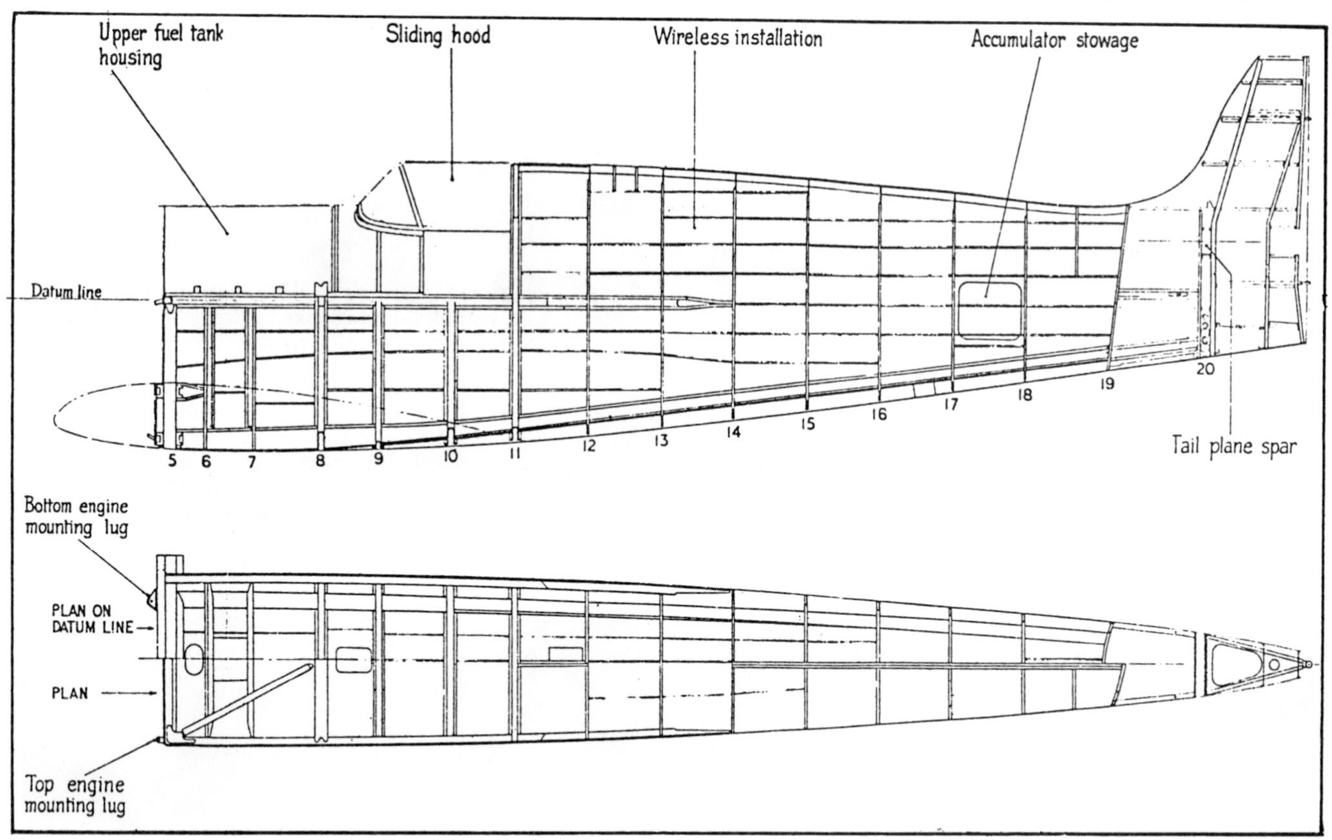

Basic layout of the Mk I fuselage showing equipment locations.

contracts for Spitfires and the earliest date at which production could begin on any new type. They should be given an order for the Beaufighter to follow on after this extended Spitfire contract. (ii) The Gloster factory to build the Camm fighter (Tornado), and to get it into production as soon as possible. An order of 1,000 divided between Hawkers and Glosters is proposed. (iii) Both these decisions to be conditional on the satisfactory performance of the Beaufighter and the Camm Fighter. The Beaufighter is due to fly in two weeks' time and the Camm fighter in four or five weeks. (iv) Supermarine and Gloster to be allowed to *sell Spitfires and Hurricanes abroad** after the expiry of their present contracts in order to avoid working short time during the gap.

"With regard to paragraph 1(i), there is really no practicable alternative. The only possible alternative would be the Westland Whirlwind, and there are two arguments against this – (i) it could not be brought into production as soon as the Beaufighter and we would, therefore, have to order more Spitfires to bridge the gap, and (ii) the Whirlwind is not as good a production job as the Beaufighter and the difficulties and consequent risk of dealy would therefore be greater".

The Spitfire was in danger of being eliminated from the re-armament programme despite the fact that it was in full scale production, and the alternatives had yet to make their first flight. They were unproven and yet, apparently, preferred. There had to be a reason and it can be found in the additions to the minutes of the same meeting, which read as follows – "With regard to paragraph 1(ii), the possible alternatives were the Camm fighter, the Beaufighter and the Whirlwind. the arguments in favour of taking the Camm fighter are as follows – (i) we can get it into production more quickly than the other two and so reduce the gap, (ii) the Camm fighter has the best estimated performance of all fighters under development, (iii) the Hawker-Gloster Group would be building an aircraft to their design on which they are very keen and we can, therefore, rely on their doing their best to push on with it and make it a success, (iv) DGRD considers that the Camm is the 'safest bet' of the fighters now under development."

However, despite all this manoeuvering to phase out the Spitfire and introduce the Air Ministry's favoured aeroplanes, its future was assured because of the stubborness of one man who was nothing to do with Supermarine. The minutes tell it all – "One effect of these decisions would be to reduce the proportion of Whirlwinds in our future fighter force. 400 have been ordered from the Westland-John Brown Group, and it is intended to order 600 more from Nuffield. As Nuffield now insists on producing the whole of the original 1,000 Spitfires ordered, the Nuffield Whirlwind order has been squeezed out. I recommend that you should accept this, as we have grave doubts about the qualities of the Whirlwind. Any delay in the approval of these decisions would increase further the gaps which would have to be filled by increased orders for the Spitfire". It is interesting to note that just a few months later, November 1939, the Air Ministry agreed with Supermarine that

**Author's italics.*

K9791 took part in propeller trials with the Mk II Spitfire and is seen here with the Rotol constant speed unit with Schwartz blades on 14 December 1939. Leading edge location of the cannon barrel mock-up is still clearly visible.

the company would be able to produce a total of 1200 Griffon engined Spitfires, the Mk IV, as against a promise of 550 Beaufighters for the same period.

A third order to Contract B.19713/39 for a further 500 Spitfires was placed; Westland Aircraft also received an order (Contract No. B.124305/40) for a further 300 Mk Is with the AR prefix serials. In the event only 50 of the latter were delivered as Mk Is, the remainder being built as Mk Vs.

The first Spitfire order was completed by the second week of August 1939 and at the outbreak of war on 3 September, less than one month later, eight squadrons were fully equipped with a total of 307 machines – Nos 19, 41, 54, 65, 66, 72 and 611. Nos 603 and 609 were in process of conversion. Several types of propeller had been tested to improve performance as the original two blade, fixed pitch unit, had been designed to provide maximum advantage at the specified operating height. But it did have faults, in particular at take off. The de Havilland three blade type was an improvement having two settings – fine for take off and coarse for top performance. It worked well until the pilot forgot to select fine pitch, and during take-off in coarse the Spitfire was unable to get airborne as the propeller was moving the aircraft forward too slowly. The cockpit control for the two pitch settings is illustrated on page 47. It was a simple mechanism, but it did need the pilot's cooperation. De Havilland's were asked on 5 April if it was possible to convert the propeller to a constant speed unit, as this type was in widespread use on multi engined types, but the company was not happy with the proposal and suggested adoption of the 'Hydromatic' C.S. unit.

Other design changes included a bullet proof windscreen and the installation of 6mm armour on the rear engine bulkhead and behind the pilot's seat. The original Spitfire windscreen was moulded, clear plastic and offered no protection whatsoever. Dowding had been presented with the practicality of an armoured glass unit and had ordered its production for the Spitfire and Hurricane in November 1936. He is quoted as saying – "If the Chicago gangster can have bullet proof glass in his limousine, my pilots deserve to have it in front of them when in battle". A weight saving device was the introduction of a plastic pilot seat which was eminently suitable until subjected to sudden loads and tended to fracture.

Production, however, was the be all and end all and after pressure from the Air Ministry Supermarine felt obliged to write to the Under Secretary of State for Air informing him why delays kept occurring in the promised output programme. In November 1939 a promise was made to deliver at least 50 aircraft per month rising to 70 per month by the following October. The letter of 7 February 1940 goes on to state that Supermarine were then to make arrangements for the delivery of a minimum of 100 aircraft per month. Supermarine had agreed to the revised figures and estimated the target would be reached in twelve months. But they had to change their plans, they claimed, because the Air Ministry was to blame. The reasons were summarised under four headings: (1) An Air Ministry letter of 8 November 1939 instructed the company to *reduce* output of finished aircraft by 20% in order to give a larger output of spares. This was a reduction of ten aircraft from a total of fifty. (2) Shortage of embodiment loan equipment. The deficiencies in deliveries of many items was the limiting factor in Spitfire production and the position showed no signs of improvement. (3) Shortage of light alloy extrusions, supplies of which had fallen behind requirements and (4) Shortage of light alloy stampings, also less than required. The letter also claimed that even with the loan of materials from Castle Bromwich the situation would be little changed and in addition no overtime had been worked on the final assembly line at Eastleigh since the previous December. The programme had to be revised and a fresh estimate of 96 aircraft per month by January 1941 was promised. By then, the letter continued, Griffon Spitfires would be coming into production and would result, again, in a temporary reduction in output.

The Air Ministry was also aware that war produces casualties and also that it would not concern only the United Kingdom but her Allies and Dominions overseas. The Spitfire and Hurricane* were natural re-inforcement fighters and a large transport aircraft to ferry main planes and other larger assemblies by air to repair crews and the MUs was needed. Two types were specified – one for the UK to carry spares to aircraft that had forced landed or had been shot down away from base, plus a second for (in particular) the Middle East and other parts of the globe. At one time it was proposed to adopt the Harrow, or even the Wellesley, for the overseas transport, while the

Spitfire cockpit photographed at Farnborough in April 1940. It is thought to be K9791 and the interesting items are the two control boxes for the Type 35 F52 35 inch telephoto lens cameras.

Early production Spitfire cockpit shows the clear plastic windscreen which lacks armoured glass, and the ring and bead sight.

**Originally it was the intention of the Air Ministry not to send the Spitfire overseas, and as late as January 1939 Supermarine was instructed not to cater for overseas equipment in the design.*

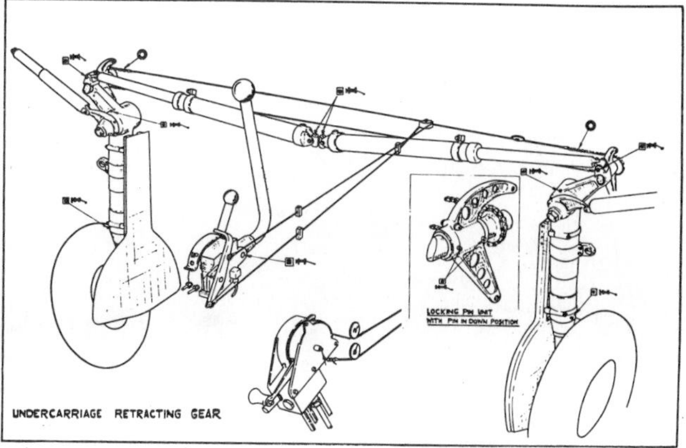

The Spitfire undercarriage retracting arrangement altered little between the Mk I and Mk 24. The handpump operated version soon gave way to the hydraulic unit (inset). Second view shows the undercarriage in plan and elevation, plus location of mechanical indicator on the upper wing surface.

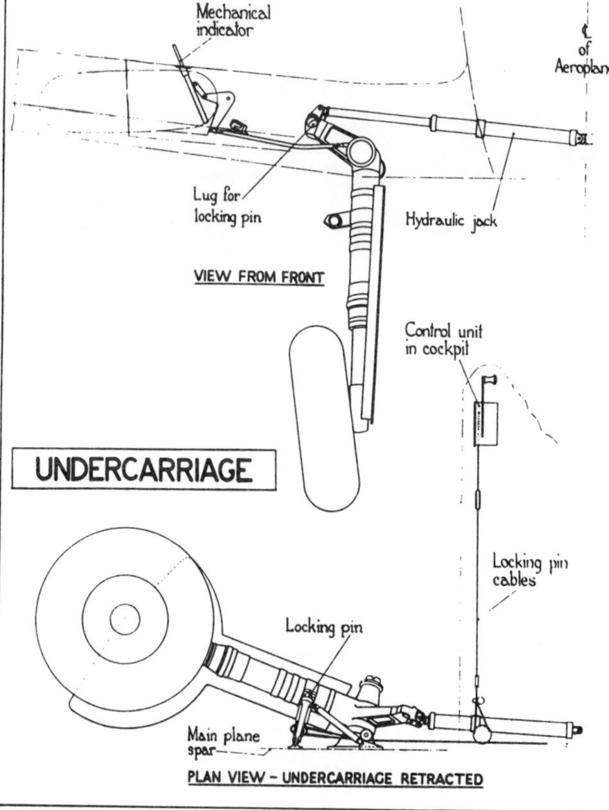

answer to the UK problem was development of the 'Queen Mary' road transport.

Spitfires destroyed their first enemy aircraft on 16 October 1939 when fighters of Nos. 602 and 603 Squadrons shot down two Heinkel He 111s over the Firth of Forth in Scotland. On 28 October Spitfires of the same two squadrons shot down another He 111, which crashed near the village of Himbie in the Lammermuir Hills. A considerable number of Spitfires were destroyed in the Battle of France, and over Dunkirk, and the squadrons were withdrawn to England to await the forthcoming Battle of Britain, as promised by Winston Churchill in his 'blood and sweat' speech.

THE SWITCH TO CONSTANT SPEED PROPELLERS

It was evident from the analysed reports of engagements with the German Luftwaffe that the Spitfire needed additional urge and it was forthcoming from two sources. Despite the de Havilland claim that converting the two pitch propellers, then installed on most of the RAF fighters, to constant speed units would be difficult because the pitch changing unit was unsuitable for interceptors, they responded magnificently when an engineer officer of the RAF telephoned Hatfield on 9 June 1940 to ask whether a propeller on one of his Spitfires could be converted to constant speeding "without a lot of paper work and fuss". The reply was it could, easily, and the DH Propeller Division sent their test pilot with an engineer to explain that the work involved could be accomplished, but if the company was eventually called upon to make conversions in quantity paper work would be inevitable, for they would have to be given authority to divert materials and labour from the contracts upon which they were fully engaged.

Despite this proviso the company at once manufactured the parts and pipe lines (one set) needed for the trial conversion. Four days later a number of hand picked de Havilland propeller engineers completed the conversion by working all night. Dowding was able to write to the Under Secretary for Air on 17 June and report that one Spitfire of No 65 Squadron had been modified and had made comparative flights with a second Spitfire fitted with the Rotol CS unit. There was little difference in performance and Dowding asked for permission to convert

First Spitfire to be fitted with the Type 5/20 unit was K9783, seen here at Martlesham Heath in July 1939.

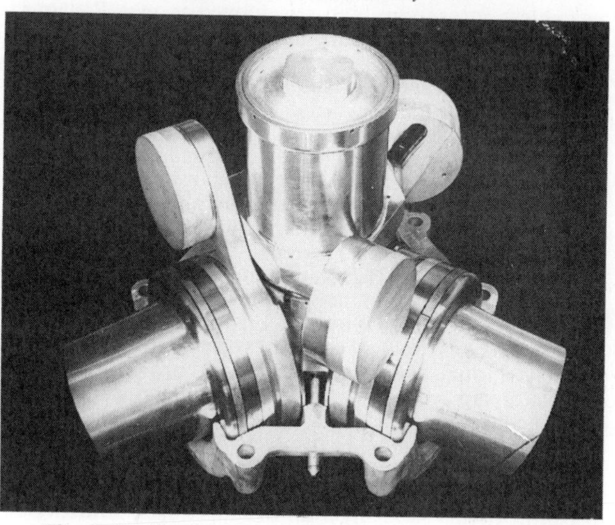

The de Havilland 'bracket' type, two pitch propeller installed on early production Spitfires. Pitch was changed by the pilot pulling a toggle mounted in his cockpit. The counter weights moved along a prescribed distance in the slots in the 'bracket'. Some Mk Is had the Type 5/20 for the Merlin II engine, and later aircraft the Type 5/21 for the Merlin III. All Spitfires were converted to the 5/29 and 5/30 constant speed units in June/July 1940.

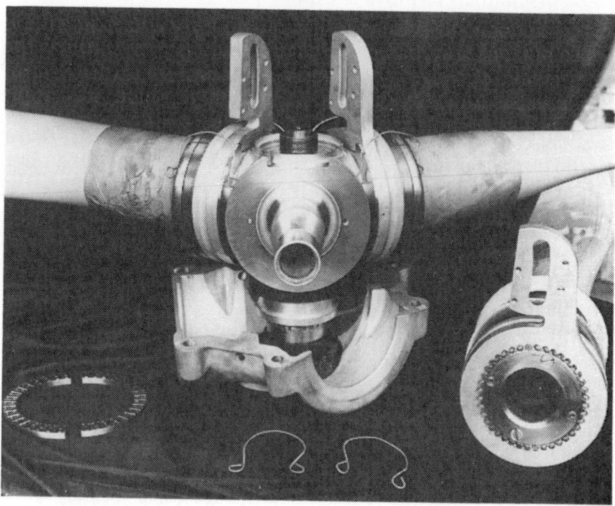

The de Havilland Hydromatic propeller was basically similar to the bracket-type but had a pitch range of 35° instead of 20° of the latter. For single engined aircraft the feathering pump was deleted. Oil from the constant speed unit turned the blades from fine to coarse pitch with the change back being made with the aid of the centrifugal twisting moment of the blades backed by oil at engine pressure. The constant speed unit was set for a given rpm and as the latter increased oil supplied by the CS unit pushed a piston forwards. A cam turned the blades to a coarser pitch.

Parade of Mk I Spitfires at Hornchurch on 8 June 1939. All have de Havilland two pitch propellers; normal day fighter camouflage scheme of Dark Earth and Green with aluminium under surfaces. K9910 heads the right hand section; K9912 the left. Cards hung under the aircraft read – "serviceable aircraft". 9910 was destroyed in the Battle of Britain (No 65 Sqdn) on 9 September 1940, and 9912 was used as a test bed for the Merlin III engine.

his fighters retrospectively. It was granted at once. Previous to this MAP had instructed Supermarine to fit the Rotol constant speed unit to ten Spitfires after first replacing the original Merlin IIIs with a specially modified engine.

On 20 June de Havilland test pilot E. Lane-Burslem reported that he, too, had flown the converted Spitfire, as had Squadron Leader Cooke, CO of No 65 Squadron and a number of his pilots. They estimated there was more than 7,000 feet of increase in ceiling, improved manoeuvrability at height, reduced take-off run and increased rate of climb. On Saturday 22 June 1940 de Havilland were verbally instructed to convert in the field all Spitfires, Hurricanes and Defiants, with priority over other contracts, and the Spitfires had to be converted first. The Senior Technical Officers of Fighter Command reported that conversions would begin at twelve Spitfire stations on Tuesday, 25 June and the company would provide twelve men capable of supervising one station each. It was estimated the time to convert an entire squadron would be ten days and all Spitfire squadrons would be completed by 20 July.

De Havilland had put in hand the production of 500 conversion sets, without a formal contract, and they would be delivering twenty sets daily from 24 June. Supermarine were to be supplied with twenty sets per week from 25 June for each aircraft fresh off the production line. After completing the squadrons all aircraft in MUs were converted. The conversion was fairly simple – a small shaft drive connected it to the engine; four external engine oil pipes and a complete cockpit control unit. Propeller blades did not have to be changed, but each had to be dismantled to move the index pins so as to give full pitch range and shift the range several degrees towards the coarse limit. Rolls-Royce, snowed under with heavy demands for its engines, could not produce the quill shafts for driving the CS units, or the engine oil pipes and de Havilland had to produce them at their Gipsy engine plant.

Starting on Monday 24 June de Havilland engineers drove to the twelve Spitfire stations, each carrying six conversion sets. On arrival the engineers asked for a picked crew of fitters who had to watch the de Havilland man convert an aircraft, instructing the RAF fitters at the same time. A second aircraft was then converted by the RAF crew with the engineers' help, and a third aircraft was completed with him supporting only. He then proceeded to the next station. By 16 August every Spitfire and Hurricane had been converted, including those in store. The problem of conversion had been fairly straightforward; the paper work after the event proving to be the bone of contention, even until March 1943 when the Air Ministry was still asking for proof that the work had been done. During the conversion period a de Havilland clerk was overheard saying to a colleague – "We shall probably never be paid for this work", to which his colleague replied – "If it isn't done we may never live to be paid for anything".

The change to de Havilland constant speed propellers had a decided effect on Spitfire performance for the unit's efficiency was estimated to be 91%. The Rotol Mk III VP CS propeller was claimed to be better than this. Propeller efficiency was important for every 1% gained was equal to 1 to ⅓rd mph at

Engine installation (Merlin II) of early production Mk Is and wooden, fixed pitch propeller. Header tank for the cooling system is just visible behind the spinner.

K9912 in mint condition before delivery to an MU and No 65 Squadron. It was damaged on operation during the Dunkirk evacuation and after the repair was used as a test bed for the Merlin III and de Havilland propellers.

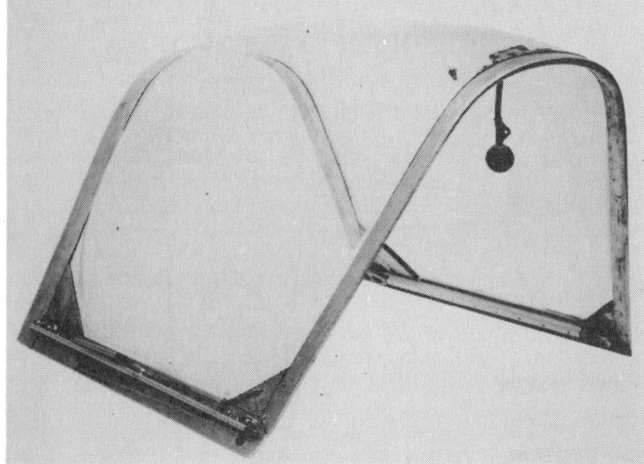

Red rubber ball hood pull, part of the Martin Baker hood jettison system.

height. An example is the original two blade, fixed pitch with an efficiency of 83%.

100 OCTANE FUEL

The second source of additional performance came via America and was 100 octane fuel, developed when chemists were endeavouring to increase the anti-knock (pre-ignition) qualities of petrol. They had worked in a close relationship with Anglo-American Oil and their progress was such that in 1939 Secony-Vacuum Oil (now Mobil) was producing it at their Jersey plant. It was extremely expensive, but despite the high cost the US Army Air Corps was using it in its aircraft in late 1939.

The Royal Air Force first got involved with 100 octane fuel in the summer of 1935, when on 29 July it was decided that 95 or 100 octane would be in general aviation use in two or three years time. The decision was the result of a visit to America the previous month by D. R. Pye of the Air Ministry. A copy of his long, and detailed report was sent to Pierson of Vickers-Armstrongs and contained the facts concerning 100 octane fuel, petrol injection and knock ratings of aviation fuels.

Samples of both 95 and 100 octane fuel were received from America, and the Asiatic Petroleum Company offered 90 octane in quantity in 1936 at the rate of 15M gallons per annum. Shell Mex and Anglo American offered the same quantities the following month. By 2 November 1937 three RAF squadrons were using 100 octane in their aircraft, and a minute from the Air Ministry stated—"Deliveries under existing commitments will be, say, 17,000 tons (5.3M gallons) a year from March 1938 (from Trinidad) and 72,000 tons (22.4M gallons) a year from March 1939 from all sources".

A meeting was held in the AMDP's room on 16 March 1939 to consider the question of when the 100 octane fuel should be introduced into general use for all RAF aircraft, and what squadrons, number and type, were to be supplied. The decision taken was initial delivery to sixteen fighter and two, twin-engined bomber squadrons by September 1940, the change over resulting in the consumption of approximately 10,000 tons (3.1M gallons) per annum. A reserve of 800,000 tons (250M gallons) was to be built up also. On 100 octane the Merlin II engine produced 1,030hp @ 16,250ft (42.6" manifold pressure) and 1,160hp @ 9,000ft (54.3" mp). There was no

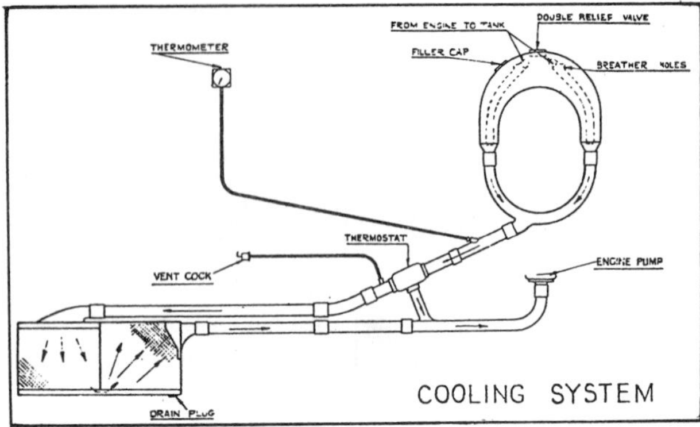

Basic cooling system of the Mk I and Mk II was to remain virtually unchanged until the introduction of the inter-cooled Merlins and the Griffon.

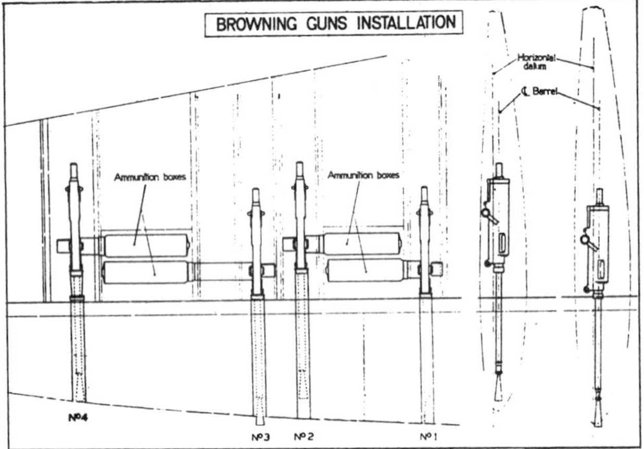

The eight .303 Browning gun 'A' wing was standard on the majority of the early production Mk Is.

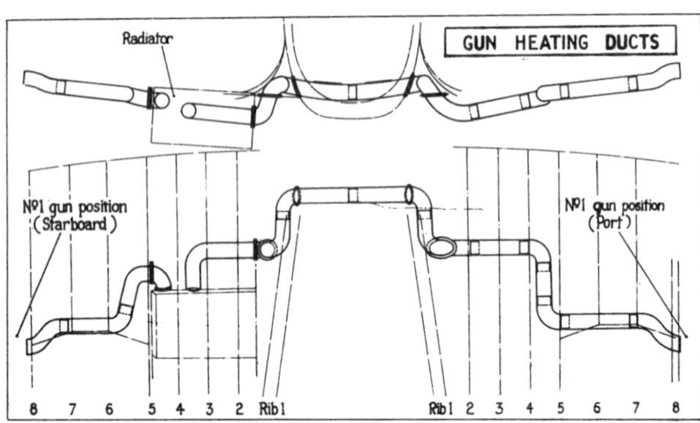

Heating the Spitfire guns posed enormous problems and this arrangement for the Mk I and Mk II utilised heated air extracted from the starboard wing radiator. The port wing guns suffered because of the long piping run from the starboard wing. To overcome this the radiator air was supplemented by extracting heat from the engine exhaust stubs by means of a small bore pipe running through the stubs. See illustrations on pages 139 and 267 for a typical installation.

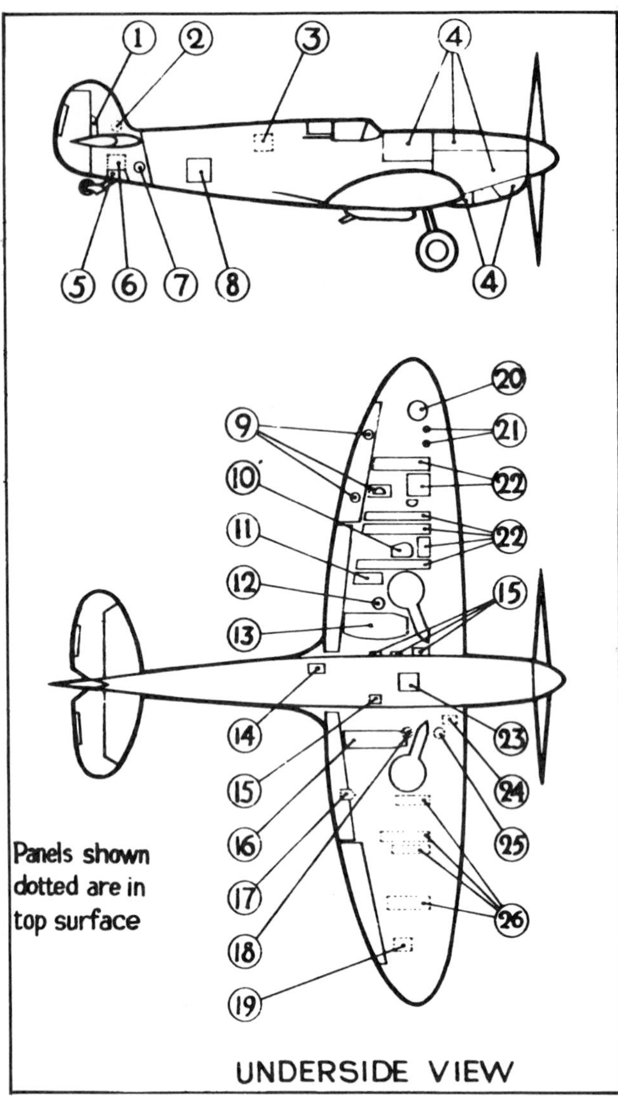

Access doors and inspection panels of the Mk I and Mk II (underside view). 1 rudder tab control pulleys, 2 handhole port only, 3 wireless compartment port only, 4 engine cowling panels, 5 tailwheel, 6 electrical connections port only, 7 tailwheel shock absorber strut, 8 accumulator stowage, 9 aileron hinges and control lever, 10 landing lamps 11 flap operating cylinder, 12 radiator mounting, 13 radiator fairing, 14 pneumatic system charging valve, 15 pipe connections inside fairing, 16 oil cooler fairing, 17 flap operating gear, 18 handhole starboard only, 19 pressure head, 20 handhole, 21 mooring rope, 22 Browning guns and ammunition boxes, 23 fuel drain cock, 24 coolant vent cock, 25 electrical connections, 26 Browning guns.

difference in weight per gallon (7.2 lb) between 87 and 100 octane fuel.

First trials of the fuel in a Spitfire took place at Rolls-Royce, Hucknall, on 24 September 1939 when K9788, fitted with a Merlin RM3S (XII)* suitably modified to burn the fuel made its first flights. Take off run was decreased by 30 yards and performance improved at all altitudes. When weighed at Eastleigh on the previous 30 June K9788, with Rotol Jablo propeller and tail parachute, had a tare weight of 4710 lb and an auw of 6048. A second Mk I, X4181, was used for similar tests and it was noted that the conversion from 87 to 100 octane fuel burning cost £53 5s. 0d. per aircraft. Initially all 100 octane had to be shipped from America and large numbers of tankers carrying the fuel were sunk by German submarines, but eventually it was refined at Abadan, Persia, and the supply situation eased. The combination of a CS propeller and 100 octane fuel put the British fighters on par with the Luftwaffe. There appeared an enigmatic Supermarine report on 16 February 1938 which mentioned a Spitfire Mk I Production Bi-fuel installation. This was a method devised by Rolls-Royce to increase the power of combat engines, initiated during 1938. Experiments using water injection on a Merlin II Special (No 2409) were started with the intention of installing it in the RAE trials Hurricane, L1717, and to absorb the additional power one of the de Havilland High Speed Spitfire propellers was to be fitted. The RAE called water injection an 'anti-detonant' and the following table indicates the benefits obtained from it:

Engine speed 3000rpm at ground level

Boost 16/in²	fuel (octane)	bhp	approx life (hours)
$6\frac{1}{4}$	87	1030	100
12	100	1320	10 (20 with stronger blocks)
with water injection			
$18\frac{1}{2}$	110	1450	$2\frac{1}{2}$ full throttle
25	SR24	2150	15mins (F.T)

Cooling the intake air was accomplished by evaporating a fine spray of water which was introduced into the main intake. The liquid evaporated quickly, thus increasing the mass flow of air and postponing the onset of fuel detonation and permitting

For use with 100 octane Rolls-Royce modified the Merlin III calling it the Merlin X, and it failed during its 100 hour type test on April 4 1938. 94 hours, including four at maximum take off power of 1250hp @ 3000rpm + 12 lb boost were completed.

Well known, but nevertheless superb view, of K9795 of No 19 Squadron. Fuselage roundels are Type A I 35in diameter and wing A I 56in diameter with yellow outer rings. This Spitfire fought in the Battle of Britain before conversion to maintenance airframe 4867M. In accordance with Dowding's request it had an anti-spin parachute and fin guard.

K9822 was the 37th production Mk I and was delivered to No 66 Squadron in December 1938. It crash landed one month later at Duxford and was downgraded to 1357M as a maintenance airframe.

Factory fresh K9845 having its compass swung at Eastleigh on 1 January 1939 prior to delivery to No 41 Squadron. After a wheels up landing at Catterick in June the same year it was struck off charge and converted to maintenance airframe 1479M.

K9814 sets off for the Paris Aero Show on 14 November 1938 with Jeffrey Quill at the controls. Below, the aircraft can be seen mounted on a pylon in the static display pavilion.

operation at high boost pressures and cylinder temperatures. The programme was discontinued and relegated to 'B' priority.

There was a momentary panic during the Battle of Britain when the following Signal was sent from the Air Ministry to all fighter stations—'Examine immediately all upper wing surfaces above, and in the vicinity of, wheel well for cracks". Reason for the Signal was the collapse of a Spitfire's wing as it came into land. It had not been damaged in any way and was approaching the airfield in a normal manner. Investigations by the Accident Branch at Farnborough discovered fatigue cracks and the ultimate antidote was skin strengthening, but as an interim measure two wing fences were fitted to some aircraft. In order to verify strength of the Spitfire wing, tests were called for and two damaged port wings were taken from service in for repair. One failed under test at 12.3G at C_L max and 6,200lb weight; the second at 13G, corresponding to pull out at 800 mph and 6,200lb.

During the intensive fighting of the period August/September 1940 the urgent need arose for a jettisonable cockpit canopy for the Spitfire in order to improve the pilot's chances of escape when the aircraft had to be abandoned. Martin Baker Ltd. were asked to design the mechanism, plus a scheme capable of easy retrospective fit by service personnel under field conditions. The scheme evolved employed unlocking pins actuated by cables, operated by the pilot pulling a small, red rubber ball mounted on the hood arch. This operation released the hood, freeing it to be taken away by the slipstream. The prototype was air tested by Wing Commander D. O. Findlay at speeds up to 500mph and the scheme became standard on all Spitfires. The retro-fit took seven man hours.

THE SPITFIRE Mk 1B

Fighter equipment of the Royal Air Force and the Luftwaffe during the Battle of Britain consisted of the Spitfire and Hurricane, and Bf109 and 110, the former pair with a battery of eight .303 Browning machine guns; the latter with a mixture of machine guns and cannon. The weight of cannon fire was devastating when a direct hit was achieved, and although the Air Ministry was aware that the British fighter armament was effective an improved, and heavier type, was needed for Luftwaffe aircraft were being equipped with heavier armour plate and this nullified, to some extent, the effect of concentrated machine gun strikes. Fighter Command was not at all disappointed with early results during the opening days of the Battle of Britain, and when offered the Hispano 20mm cannon was agreeable only if 60rpg could be guaranteed in drums. A second proposal was for four cannon with 150rpg or 6 × .5in machine guns.

In his original paper on the eight gun fighter Sqdn. Ldr. Sorley had not overlooked the heavier calibre gun for he had written: "The choice lay between the .303 gun, the .5in and a new 20mm Hispano-Suiza cannon, which was of great attraction to the French and other Continental countries. The .5in gun was newly developed and very heavy and was, in fact, a small cannon, and the Hispano was 'supersensitive' to rigidity of mounting and was difficult to mount in aeroplane wings".

Progress had been made with the wing mounted cannon as can be witnessed by Mitchell's submission of the Supermarine Type 305* with four Oerlikon cannon in the wings to Air Ministry Specification F37/35 in April 1936, full details of which appear in chapter three. Also, Supermarine were always aware of the possibilities of the cannon as can be seen by Beverley Shenstone's report of the Paris Air Show in November 1936. Among other things he was looking for was examples of cannon armed aircraft. Part of his report relates: "One went to the exhibition hoping to see several types of cannon gun installation. Herein one was very disappointed. Where cannon guns were indicated in French machines they were mock ups,

**In this submission reference was made to: "If production order for the Type 300 F37/34 is forthcoming, one set of wings can be fitted with four cannon guns to speed construction of a prototype to Specification F37/35".*

When Joseph Smith was asked by the Air Ministry to convert a Spitfire to accept the Hispano 20mm cannon in underwing containers, he counter proposed an internal wing installation with upper and lower wing fairings to accommodate the ammunition drums. Mock ups of the fairings and gun barrels were fitted to K9791.

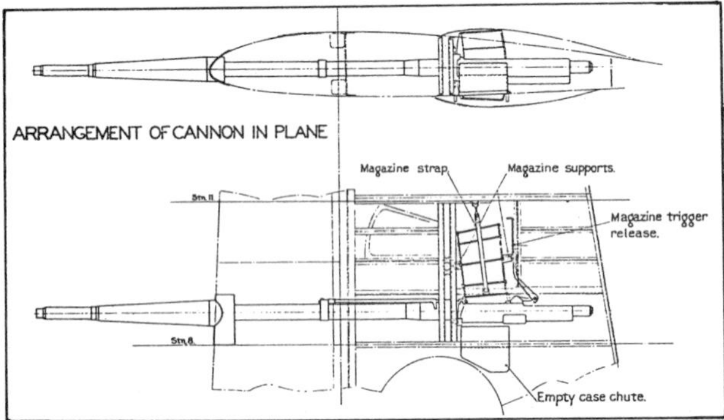

A small number of Mk Is were modified to have two Hispano cannons installed in the wings. As it was only a T.1 (trial installation) it soon gave way to the 'B' wing. This had two × 20mm cannon and four × .303 Browning machine guns as standard armament.

L1007, Merlin III, was the first Spitfire to be fitted with the twin 20mm Hispano cannon installation and Brownings removed. It had a rear view hood, unarmoured windscreen and ring and bead sight. Table (below) reveals it was marginally slower than K9783 and 9797 with eight Browning guns. Handling trials were complete at Martlesham Heath on 20 July 1939.

Spitfire	K9787	K9783	L1007
Engine	Merlin II	Merlin II	Merlin III
Propeller	2 blade wood fixed pitch	3 blade DH 2 pitch	3 blade DH Type 5/21 bracket
Time to 20,000ft(min)	9.4	11.4	10.7
Speed @ 18,500ft (mph)	363	367	364
Ceiling (feet)	31,900	34,400	34,500
HP @ 12,250ft	966	998	953
Weight (lbs)	–	5935	5925

and very rough ones too. The installations were crude in the extreme, and one cannot think that they represented serious proposals. Wing installations seem to have died a natural death and the fuselage installation, either in or below, has taken its place. This change has, of course, been made possible by the use of twin engined machines".

Previous to Shenstone's Paris trip a Mr. Orleans of Aero Engines Ltd, had visited Supermarine on 30 March to discuss installation problems associated with the Hispano 20mm cannon in the Spitfire, and he produced a drawing (S.K.1218) showing attachments points and other particulars. The gun was entering production in France following trials with it mounted above an aircraft's engine. No wing installation had been attempted. The maximum recoil force was 1100 lbs, and a 60 round cylindrical magazine had been developed and was also available in smaller sizes with fewer rounds. Hispano was of the opinion that a belt feed was not possible. The cannon, mounted on the engine, was held at four points and these positions could, with adjustment, be used for a wing installation. Recoil was absorbed by the front attachment and transmitted to the wing structure via a spring, the stored energy in the spring being expended in an adjacent dash pot.

The complete gun moved through a travel of 20mm when fired with the magazine remaining stationary relative to the structure. It would also function on its side and rate of fire, which could be pre-set, was between 520 and 720 rpm. Mr Orleans left Supermarine with the size of the wing section under consideration and a request for further information regarding mounting.

Dowding was not impressed with the Hispano cannon for on 25 June 1938 he wrote to Sholto-Douglas at the Air Ministry saying he did not want nine squadrons of Defiants. He then commented: "There has been a lot of talk about the efficiency of the 20mm cannon and I have seen no proof that this gun will give decisive results. We ought to have carried out the most careful experiments to prove its value before we adopt it. If this was not done I shall wake up in a year's time and be told I am committed to have 15 squadrons of something with a 20mm cannon; whereas I can tell you now I do not want any and so perhaps save a large sum of money. I also want to be in the picture about the new single seat fighters".

Trials had taken place place at Shoeburyness on, among other obsolete airframes, the F7/30 prototype K2890. Poor results were obtained with cannon shells exploding on contact with the outside skin with little effect to internal structure. Dowding thought that if cannon were to be specified for the Spitfire he would rather have a larger gun with a heavier missile and slower rate of fire, whereby one direct hit would destroy the target. He said: "Therefore, we should make a bold jump and start trials with a 37mm cannon". But this was contrary to the

Photographs of converted, twin cannon Mk Is are rare and this view shows X4272 and R6908 (cannon) with X4561 (standard IA) of No 92 Squadron in the winter of 1940.

current thinking of Sorley and Buchanan, who favoured the eight gun fighter.

Following upon the visit to Supermarine by Mr. Orleans, W. M. Hingston, of DTD, arrived at Woolston on 4 August 1938 with details of the Hispano cannon tests, during which it had functioned correctly in (a) an upright position, (b) raked up at 42° from vertical and (c) inverted. It failed on its side, but as the magazine was unsupported it was thought it would perform correctly with the magazine when supported in the test rig at Boulton and Paul. Tests were also made on the effect of blast on wing leading edges. It was considered practicable to replace the drum feed by an assisted belt, or hopper, to facilitate housing in the thin wing, but no work had been done on this.

Despite Dowding's objections a letter arrived at Supermarine, addressed to Joseph Smith, on 20 December 1938, and he was instructed to prepare a scheme for a Spitfire to be equipped with one Hispano cannon under each wing, and also to produce drawings and a mock up*. Smith informed the Air Ministry that he was totally opposed to having exposed cannon under the wings and that he could design an installation which would mean fitting them on their sides in the wing with small blisters on the upper and lower wing surfaces. Pierson followed up Smith's suggestions on 9 January 1939 with a plan for four cannon in the wings, and the Air Ministry's reply on the 24th of the month was that two were sufficient at the moment. Smith and Pierson had obviously resurrected the Type 305 fighter for both had included features of this design.

The fifth production Spitfire Mk I—K9791—was used as the mock-up trials aircraft and despite the need for a belt feed the 60-round drum was specified. This resulted, as forecast by Smith, in a blister above and below the wings to accommodate the magazine. In order to speed trials and not wait for official approval of the mock up, work had proceeded with the installation of two Hispano cannon in Spitfire L1007. Vickers wrote to the Air Ministry on 19 January requesting delivery of the embodiment loan of guns and ammunition, but not until the end of March were they delivered. Weighing and C.G. determination took place at Eastleigh on 16 June and the aircraft had a tare of 4,589lb, and auw of 5,916.

First trials by Vickers took place the same month against a barrage balloon target and the following month, accompanied by Hurricane L1750 fitted with two cannon mounted under the wings, L1007 arrived at Martlesham Heath for further tests.

The Spitfire went next to AFDU at Northolt for service trials, which revealed that the gun was unreliable at low temperatures and heating would have to be provided. Early in January 1940 the aircraft was transferred to Drem for squadron trials and on the 13th, piloted by P.O. Proudman, it attacked and shot down a Heinkel 111 at 20,000 feet. Forty one rounds were expended before the guns jammed. L1007 was then transferred to Dishforth on 15 March, where it was found the deflector plates for the ejector chutes were partially to blame for gun stoppages. Squadron Leader J. G. Munro was to design a pair of successful replacements.

Dowding had, by now, accepted the idea of the cannon armed Spitfire and Supermarine was awarded a contract (980385/39) to select and convert 30 Spitfires to take the cannon wing. Lord Beaverbrook, then in complete control of aircraft production, was most impressed by the cannon Spitfire and in his impetuous manner authorised the production of 30 pairs of cannon wings, giving this order the utmost priority. Of the 30 Spitfires ordered 24 had been delivered by 16 August.

The second Spitfire to be converted to cannon armament was P9504, a MkI, and it was ready for squadron use by 4 April 1940. The first cannon Spitfire to reach an RAF squadron was R6261, going to No.19 in June for trials, and it was followed within days by R6770 and 6776. On 1 July the Air Ministry informed the CO of No.19 Squadron that the squadron was to be completely re-equipped with the cannon Spitfire, but when they were delivered they stayed on for only a few days at any one time, being rapidly returned to No.6 MU at Brize Norton for examination. The new Spitfires were not a great success for combat reports showed clearly the frustration of pilots who, having moved in for a kill, found the guns had jammed solid after a few rounds had been fired. Also, the aerolasticity of the wing made it twist slightly in tight manoeuvres causing the ammunition drum to come into contact with the skin and jam. It did seem pointless to scramble a number of cannon Spitfires

Arrangement of the fuselage fuel tanks of the Mk I and Mk II.

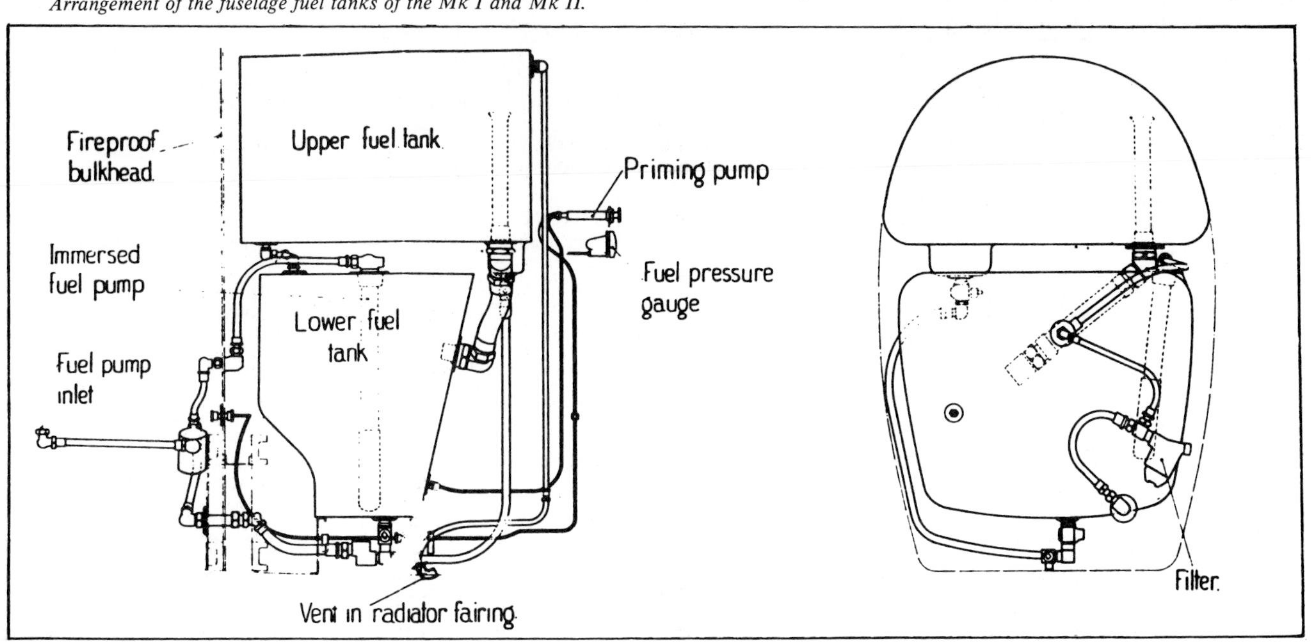

* *The Oerlikon cannon was installed in this manner on the PZL -XXIV. See chapter three, page 43, for details.*

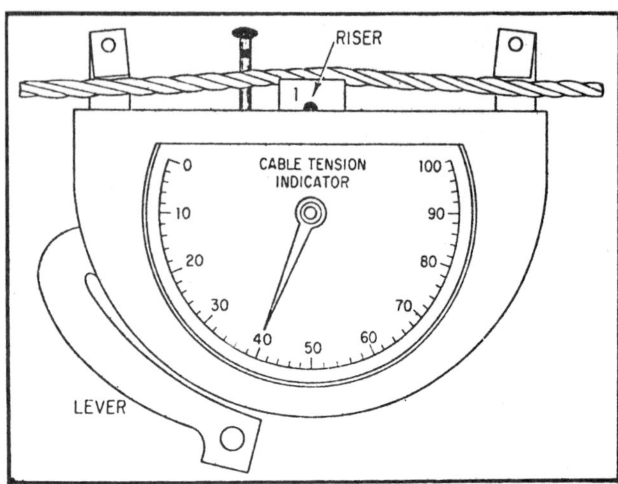

The Tensometer, or Tensiometer, was used by the Spitfire ground crew to ensure that control cables to ailerons, elevator and rudder were set to the correct tension after every flight. This was necessary for when the early production Spitfires were left standing outside at night, a temperature drop could result in cable slackening and as a result the ailerons, in particular, drooped and did become unharmonised. In the Leading Particulars for the early Spitfires it will be noted that aileron droop was specified as nil, whereas the same information for later models specified the droop as $\frac{3}{8}$in. Tightening cable runs was a vital chore for ground crew. The American Tensometer was of a different design but the working principle the same.

only to have stoppages at the vital moment. Dowding was blunt about the situation for in a letter to the Air Ministry on 15 July he wrote: "Two cannon Spitfire unreliable". The converted Mk Is carried the prefix designation CIG which, presumably, stood for cannon wing.

What was needed was a stop gap, a British compromise, and it appeared in the shape of a mixed armament Spitfire. P9504 was still at Manby with the new cannons installed but, what was fortuitous, it still had four of the original Browning

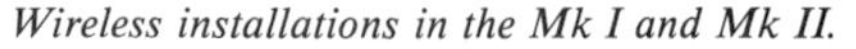

Wireless installations in the Mk I and Mk II.

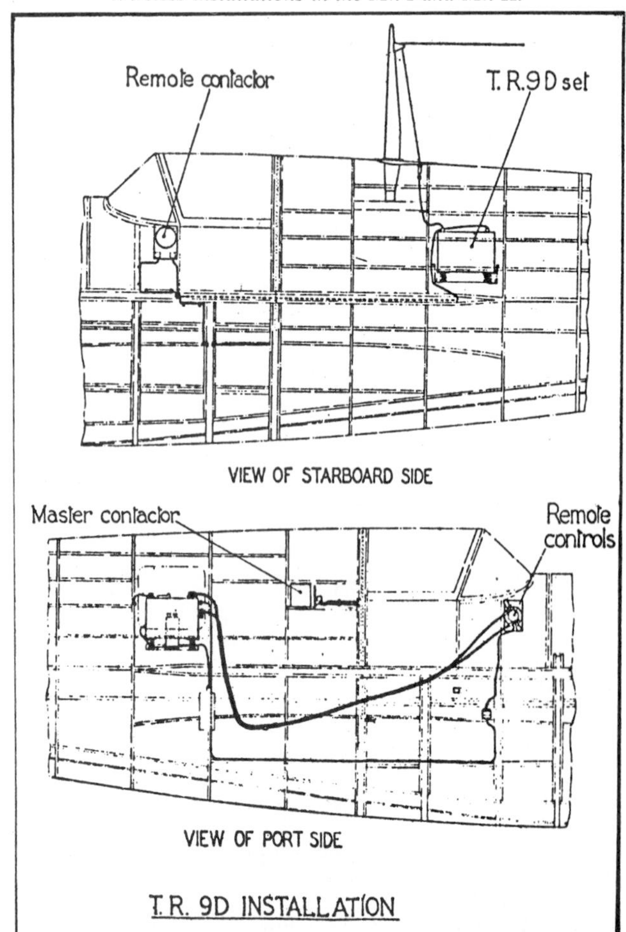

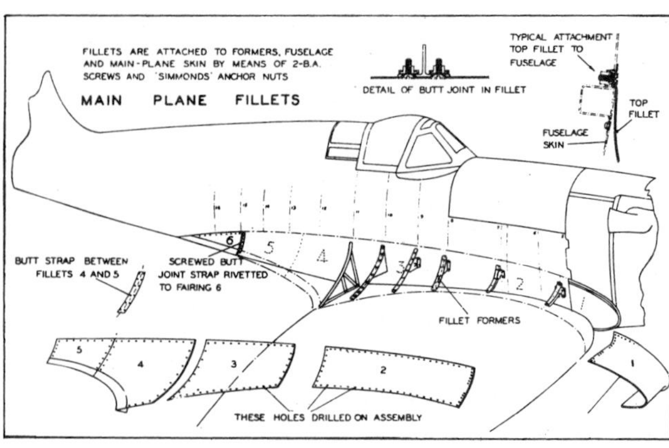

Main plane/fuselage fillets were standard on all marks of the Spitfire up to the F Mk 21.

machine gun mountings in the wings. It was used to test a trial installation of two Hispano cannon and four Browning guns, which proved to be a great success, and within days a second Spitfire—X4257—had a wing, built from scratch, with the new armament and service trials began on 20 August. Five days later R6761, 6770, 6889, 6904 and 6919 were withdrawn from No.19 Squadron and modified to the same standards. They were soon followed by R6776 and 6833. All these R-serialled Spitfires carried the suffix CIG after the digits on the Supermarine works dockets, and X4257, together with a number of X-serialled Spitfires, had the suffix CMG which, presumably, indicated cannon/machine gun.

P9504 and R6770, together with X4257, were despatched to Boscombe Down for trials with the new armament, R6770 having modified spars because the cannons were still jamming in tight turns. R6904 was returned to Eastleigh for modifications to its cartridge ejection chutes. The cannon wing was now known as the 'B' and with it the Spitfire's tare weight was increased to 4893 lb and at take off 6385. The four cannon wing was given some consideration at that time but was turned down until the twin cannon aircraft was proven in service. Production of the Mk IB Spitfire was agreed with Supermarine, who

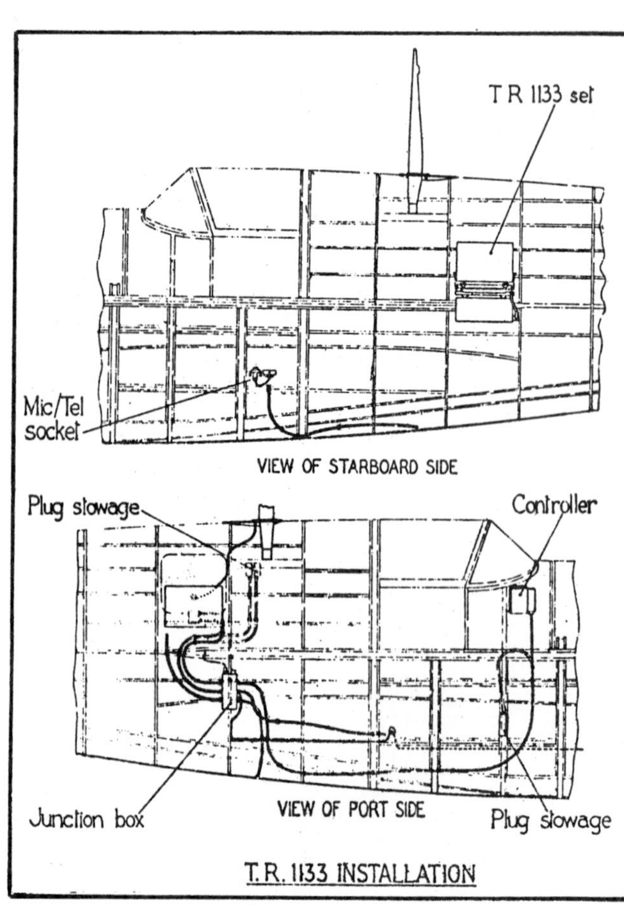

X4257 is considered to be the prototype 'B' wing Spitfire and was finally converted to Mk VB standards with a Merlin 45 engine.

guaranteed delivery of ten aircraft in October rising to 20 a month by November, plus the delivery of the first four cannon variant powered by a Merlin XX engine by the end of September. By this time, however, the urgency for the cannon installation had diminished for the German daylight raids were faltering.

The first modified IB to go into action was R6889, which had rejoined No.19 Squadron on 3 October, and it was not an outstanding success. It was under-powered and even with the promised Merlin III engine had to be flown at maximum power to keep up with the Browning gun aircraft. The majority of converted Spitfires were never given an official designation and most of them had to be converted to Mk VB standards with Merlin 45 at a later date. All Browning gun Spitfires were to be retrospectively designated Mk IA and the few cannon, and mixed armament aircraft, Mk IB. There were no true Mk IBs built on the production line. The actual cost of converting a set of 'A' wings to accept the Hispano gun armament was £379 16s. To convert a set of wings to the full 'B' wing standards was £640 11s.

The British version of the Hispano cannon was jointly developed with the French Air Ministry at the Chatelerault Arsenal until the fall of France in May 1940. Development was then transferred to the RAF Section of the Royal Small Arms Factory at Enfield. Series production was undertaken by four factories, one of which was the British Manufacturing and Research Co., a manufacturing subsidiary of Hispano Suiza.

ALTERNATIVE GUNS

Before leaving this history of the early cannon Spitfires mention must be made of other armament specified and tested during, and before, the same period. As long ago as July 1937 the Air Fighting Committee of the Air Ministry was considering a replacement of the .303 Browning machine gun and had issued a Memorandum on the 7th of that month for an ultra high speed gun capable of firing 2000rpm. The Memorandum called for trials with eight of the guns firing explosive ammunition and storage space for 4800 rounds. Full scale trials took place on 14 December 1937 with the Hungarian Gebauer gun and the effect was likened to a "welder's torch held against a stressed skin aircraft". The new gun was intended to replace the Browning five years in the future. There were problems, of course, for increased rate of fire resulted in attendant barrel wear* and increased weight. The suggestion was to drop the ultra high speed gun and concentrate on a gun with a higher muzzle velocity, which would provide an increased lethal range, but the additional velocity entailed a larger powder charge and cartridge. A compromise in the shape of an armour piercing .276in was suggested.

The Air Ministry took out insurance by asking for designs of two new .303in guns in March 1938 as Browning replacements—the ultra-high-speed and the high muzzle velocity. A Blenheim airframe (K7154) was used for firing trials of the high velocity weapon on 9 December but penetration of vital, internal parts was insufficient. Blenheim K7041 was also used for the same weapon trials with better results when the gun was fired towards the target's stern.

The Masden gun was also considered for the Spitfire as a replacement for the .303in Browning. This gun was the standard infantry model modified for remote, automatic control when installed in an aeroplane. The calibre was either 6.5, 8 or 11.35mm and the rate of fire increased from 450rpm to 1000 and 1200, and for this the special recoil spring had to be reinforced. The gun was belt fed and the rounds held together by steel links, this making the task of collecting the empty belt easy when compared to the standard gun belt. A 23mm Masden cannon was also considered and this, too, was belt fed with rounds connected with steel links, and it had a rate of fire of 400rpm. The Hispano company also produced a 23mm cannon, while Vickers had their .5in automatic gun, a 25.4mm, 37 and 40mm cannon. The first had a rate of fire of 450 to 650rpm; the second 100 and the last two 200. The table below lists details of the various guns available for the Spitfire during the design/prototype stage.

	Vickers 12.7mm	Hispano 20mm	Hispano 23mm	Vickers 25.4	Vickers 37mm	American Armament Co 37mm	COW 37mm	Oerlikon model FF 20mm
Total weight (lb)	52.5	83.5	88.5	280	600	235	198	55
Length (ins)	51.3	89	97	102	—	—	—	52.8
Muzzle velocity (fs)	2550	2885	—	3000	2300	1250	2000	1970
Pull of recoil (lbs)	614	881	—	950	3790	1000	2000	231
Shell weight (lb)	.08	.55	.695	.551	1.25	1.1	1.5	—
Weight of shells per min (max lbs)	52	384	—	55	250	110	180	—
Horizontal range (yds)	4000	—	—	—	—	4375	—	—
Type of feed	belt	drum	drum	drum	belt	hopper	hopper	drum
Rounds	—	60	60	30	—	5	5	75

Another new weapon to come to the Air Ministry's attention was the American .5in Colt, examples of which arrived in England in June 1940. Drawings were ready the following month and trial installations commenced, and by the following August Supermarine were proceeding with a trial installation of six of the new guns, plus a second installation of six .5in and two 20mm Hispano cannons (with 120rpg), this being specified for the proposed Spitfire Mk III. In the meantime the two 20mm cannon and four .303 Browning machine gun installation had been accepted and eventually developed into the 'B' wing with the result that the Colt installations were put on a low priority on 9 December 1940 and the .5in machine gun eventually adopted several years later for the Spitfire Mk IX.

Before closing this chapter on Spitfire armament mention must be made of the work both BSA and Vickers completed on a version of the .5in Colt using a shaped charge. It proved difficult to produce and was eventually abandoned. Also, the

**Barrel life of the .5in machine gun was said to be 7,000-8,000 rounds.*

Air Ministry had listened to Dowding's idea for a larger weapon for the Spitfire and on 23 April 1940 gave approval for the development of a 13.2mm weapon based upon the French Hotchkiss gun, the new weapon being specified for the first Griffon engined Spitfire, the Mk IV. Supermarine also prepared a design study for a Spitfire armed with this gun with a Merlin engine as the Type 345.

THE PERISCOPIC GUN SIGHT

The Spitfire as a gun platform was entirely satisfactory, but attempts were always being made to improve it. One of the drawbacks of the Supermarine fighter in gun sighting was the long engine cowling, synonymous with the in-line cooled Merlin, which did deprive the pilot of his view over the nose while taxying, during take-off and a few moments during dog fighting. In the summer of 1941 the British Purchasing Commission in Washington, America, received details of the USAAF's use of a periscopic mirror sight, which was an additional fitment to the normal sight. First example of this new method of sighting was installed in the Curtiss P-40 fighter, and it was claimed to increase view over the nose by as much as 4 to 7%.

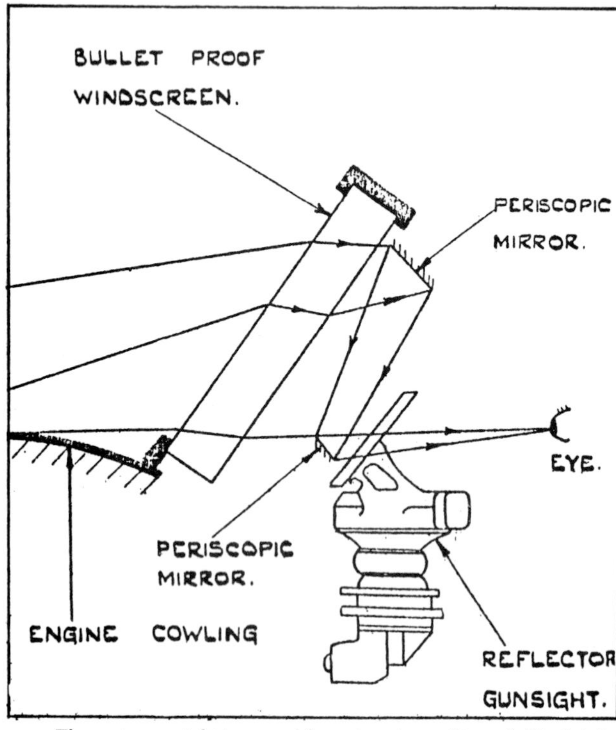

The periscope sight imported from America and installed in Spitfire K9830. The method of harmonising the sight with the normal reflector unit was to, first, harmonise the latter in the normal manner and make a line with a chinograph pencil along the axis of symetry of each mirror. Place a circular cardboard disc over the top lens of the reflector sight (⅛in hole in disc centre) and adjust the mirrors so that the pencil lines were con-incident as were the horizontal straight edges of the mirrors. Remove pencil lines from mirrors. The periscope sight had been examined by the RAF in 1935 but was abandoned because a binocular arrangement was thought to be essential for sighting.

The Air Staff were interested and a set of parts was shipped over to England, arriving in September 1941. The complete sight was installed in a Hawker Typhoon, then at prototype stage, and in the hands of the professional test pilots it did live up to its promise. Farnborough was then involved in the testing and development of the installation and a number of companies were invited to build prototypes. As the Spitfire was, with the Hurricane, the RAF's front line fighter eight sets of sights were ordered for trials and Spitfire K9830 was chosen as the test vehicle. The sight was installed vertically in front of the pilot and consisted of a series of mirrors installed in the windscreen in such a way as to reflect a view over the nose of that grey area where the normal pilot could not see unless he performed some very gymnastic movements. The mirrors focused an image on to the normal reflector sight, which then reflected the complete image on to the flat windscreen in the normal manner.

The first production model was ordered as the Mk III and an order for 300 units was placed. It was made of plastic and deliveries began in Winter 1941 at the rate of 40 per week. Samples were tested at Boscombe Down on Blenheim V5958 and a modified version was manufactured for the Stirling and Lancaster heavy bombers. A Mk II reflector sight was finally adapted to take the periscopic sight mirrors in June 1942. Reports claimed that the new tests were continued with a number of Typhoons, Mustangs and a Blackburn Firebrand naval torpedo fighter.

Coincidently a second sight with the same basic ideas had been submitted to the Air Ministry by a Lt. B. Rabineau of the Free French Navy, but his was for rear view sighting. He supplied a mock-up for installation in blisters in the normal fighter cockpit hood and claimed his device allowed the pilot to aim at an aircraft attacking from the rear either from above or below. It was, he said, demonstrated by trials held in France before the capitulation and films and reports were available. Field of view was 90° either side of the fuselage and armament was to be a fixed cannon. He did not specify where the cannon was to be installed in the single seat fighter.

Rabineau's letter was dated 8 May 1942 and the initial response from the Air Ministry was rejection as the RAF and RAE had been working on a similar device some 19 months earlier. There were second thoughts, however, and Rabineau was invited to visit Duxford to study the American periscopic sight in Spitfire K9830 as it was hoped his sight could be adapted for forward gunnery. The trials did not come up to expectation for the Air Ministry had demanded a 4° downward view and it was not possible to achieve this figure. Rabineau's sight was them modified and installed in a Typhoon, but there are no records of these trials. It is possible that the RP sight could have had a similar fitment.

Extremely rare photograph showing an early periscopic sight fitment in the windscreen of a North American Mustang. This fitting was to be tested on Spitfire Mk I K9830.

LIGHT, NIGHT FIGHTERS

At the beginning of Winter 1940, with the Battle of Britain over, the British War Cabinet was concerned about the increasing attacks by the Luftwaffe and the apparent lack of success of British night fighters. Professor Lindemann put a proposal to Winston Churchill for a hunter/killer team of Spitfires, one of which would have four 4in training flares of approximately ½million candle power installed at the wing tips, with ignition controlled by the pilot from the cockpit.

The scheme proposed was that after being directed to the

The hunter/killer Spitfire wing tip flares were tested on an underwing mounting of this Douglas Havoc I AX926 at the RAE in October 1940.

vicinity of an enemy aircraft the flares were ignited on the hunter aircraft, thus illuminating the enemy and enabling the killer aircraft to shoot the intruder down. Churchill sent a note to the Ministry of Aircraft Production on 18 September — "Let precise order be given for an experiment with chemical searchlights without delay". He was, it will be remembered, a man of instant decision.

The flares were to be towed behind the wing trailing edge and first trials were made with Blenheim P4899 with a Whitley bomber as the target. On the night of 23 September 1940 both aircraft took off at 20.30hrs and the Blenheim duly ignited its flares, only to be attacked by a passing enemy bomber but, luckily, the British aeroplane was only slightly damaged. There was too much glare as the flares were streamed at distances ranging from 500 to 1000ft behind the Blenheim. Flare shields were then fitted and trials switched to a Douglas DB-7 Havoc, with the flares attached to the fuselage wing root with surrounding areas painted white. Our photograph shows the installation.

The system, originally produced for night interception and reconnaissance of enemy shipping, was adjudged a success but the CinC Fighter Command, Dowding, wanted more trials, especially with the single seat fighters before he would allow hunter/killer teams to be formed. Hurricanes played a major part in these trials, but pilots did not like it, preferring the current system of vectoring. Code name for the new system was Cyclamen and on 30 October 1940 it was tried once again, this time with infra-red gun sights.

THE HIGH SPEED SPITFIRE

The high speed aeroplane was not a new innovation to Supermarine, in fact it was among world leaders of the state of the art. Spitfire development had made full use of the technology that had produced the S series of floatplanes which eventually won the Schneider Trophy for England, and thoughts of a new record breaking aeroplane built by the company were given fresh impetus during the 4th International Flying Meeting, held at Zurich, Switzerland from 23 July to 1 August 1937. Messerschmitt's Bf109 fighter, heavily modified, won the Circuit of the Alps and the German's claimed, with some justification, that they possessed the world's fastest fighter. The challenge could not be ignored and at the instigation of the DTD, Air Comdre R. H. Verney, Supermarine initiated plans to prepare a Spitfire for an attempt on the World's Air Speed Record. Smith, Clifton, Pierson and Quill were consulted and as a result Specification F35/35 was issued for a high speed aeroplane capable of being converted to a single-seat fighter if the need arose.

A Contract was raised (B817241/38) for the design and completion of one prototype to Supermarine Type 323, and to save time and money a Mk I airframe was taken off the Woolston production line for adaptation. The allocated RAF serial K9834 was not to be used. First meeting of the Supermarine team took place at Eastleigh on 7 September 1937 to consider the problems associated with the attempt. E. H. Mansbridge chaired the meeting, the minutes of which read —

Summary. It is estimated that the Spitfire without serious modification could attain a speed of between 375 and 400 mph under World's Record Conditions. (1) Engine Output. It is understood that using special fuel the Merlin should develop 1850/1900 bhp at 3000 rpm on the bench at sea level. Allowing for forward intake effect this becomes approximately 2100 bhp. With this, it is estimated that the maximum level speed of the Spitfire would be 373 mph. This assumes no unforeseen drag or compressibility effects occur and is based on the Martlesham level speed of 349 mph at 16,000ft with a Merlin C engine developing 1000 hp for the prototype aircraft. On 7 August a modified Merlin II was running at Rolls-Royce producing 1536 hp. Fuel was a mix of petrol, Benzol and Methanol, with lead added for anti-knock.

(2) Possible increases. The above figure does not include allowance for use of a four bladed airscrew, which has shown an increase of 4-5 mph on the standard engine and is suitable for use under the proposed record conditions. Use of momentum type exhaust system, about to be tested. Improved windscreen shape. Effect of diving. In the case of the S.6B it was estimated that on the two speed record attempts this effect was responsible for 7 and 17.5 mph increase respectively. Improved shape of cowling.

(3) Modifications to aircraft. The following list of work is required to prepare the aircraft for an attempt (excluding that in changing the engine, if necessary). Make and fit new windscreen, remove tailwheel and fit skid, remove W/T aerial and fittings, fill in cartridge ejection slots, make and fit new air intake, fit new oil coolers and ducts, make and fit a larger, or a smaller auxiliary oil tank if consumption is greatly increased, polish wings, make and fit new nose cowling. The question of wing area was raised and it was agreed that the easiest way of reducing area would be to use a standard wing from the fuselage out to the wheel housing, leaving the chassis and glycol cooling system untouched. A new wing tip would be designed It was estimated that maximum speed could be increased by 10-15 mph by such a reduction. The basic design assumptions were listed in Supermarine Report 2468 — Overall length 29.92ft, height (less prop. tail down) 8.19ft, propeller diameters (a) fixed pitch four blade 9.75ft and 10ft. Datum Lines 3in below and parallel to thrust line, ℄ of centre section spar booms. Track 5.71ft. Wing Section NACA 2200 series. Platform elliptical wing of Spitfire I reduced in span. Thickness 13.2% at root to 8.8% at tip. Incidence. Root +2° to fuselage datum. Tip +.18° to fuselage datum. Aspect ratio 4.90. Aerodynamic mean chord 7.22ft. Geometric mean chord 6.85ft. Centre line chord 8.33ft. Span, 33.67ft. Area outside fuselage 209 sq ft. Gross area 231 sq ft. Dihedral 6°. Control surfaces. Aileron, Span 6.40ft. Area 9.12 sq ft. Mean chord 1.43ft. Balance area 5.02 sq ft. Elevator and rudder. As Spitfire I. Stressing assumptions. Weight 5500 lbs (VP prop). Weight of wing 806 lbs. Normal top speed at SL 348 mph (510 fps). Stalling speed (flaps up) 82 mph (120 fps).

A Rolls-Royce team, under the direction of Mr. Lovesey and Parkin, were to develop a racing version of the Merlin II,

The Speed Spitfire, K9834, was a handsome machine in its livery of blue and silver. The first three views were taken at Eastleigh and are followed by two of the aircraft being prepared for flight. Front, side and rear views are normal publicity photos that clearly reveal the different propeller. K9834 was displayed at the 1939 Brussels Aero Show with the de Havilland metal propeller in place (note the faired roots), while the final views are of N17 with a Merlin 45 and converted to PRU standards while serving with Coastal Command. It was struck off charge in 1946. Photos G Tuttle, N Wheeler et al.

and when they met the Supermarine people at Eastleigh on 10 September fuel and cooling systems were considered. Estimated fuel consumption was .7 pints per bhp/hr compared with .855 for the S.6B engine. On this basis it was estimated that 83 gallons would suffice and a normal Spitfire production tank of 84 gallons capacity would be adequate. The worst oil consumption recorded was 88 pints/hr and on this pessimistic figure it was considered a total of $5\frac{1}{2}$ gallons would be needed. The production tank held 5.8 gallons, more than enough. Oil cooling was considered the problem and trials were necessary to assess heat dissipation requirements. At this time bench runs of the Merlin II Special returned a hp of 1,710 @ 3,000rpm with the engine running at full throttle for 20 mins. Four engines had been allocated for the attempt, two for the actual record runs and two for tests, all to be water cooled.

On 9 November Pierson, Clifton, Mansbridge and Joseph Smith of Vickers/Supermarine met the Rolls-Royce team once again. Rolls said that the first engine would be ready in a few weeks time and it would provide 1,995hp for a forward speed of 375 mph. It was agreed that the cooling systems and propeller should be tested on the prototype aeroplane as soon as possible with the maximum temperature set at 120°. The actual engine for the record attempt would provide 2,000/2,100bhp @ 3,200 rpm (3,400 in a dive) and the 100 octane fuel would have the lead content increased by 10%. The special fuel consisted of 20% straight-run petrol, 60% benzol, 20% methanol and 3.3cc lead per U.S. gallon.

The first, full meeting of the record attempt team took place at the Air Ministry on 25 November. Present was Grp Capt Orlebar, of the RAF's High Speed Flight and it was agreed that two aircraft should be prepared — K9834 for the actual attempt, the second held in reserve. In the event the back up aeroplane was neither modified or needed. On 29th of the month Martlesham Heath produced figures of flying tests of K5054 fitted with a Merlin C, two blade propeller, stub exhausts and a polished finish. Maximum speed @ 16,000ft was 348mph @ 985hp. This report took into account a bad windscreen shape and projection of a number of access doors.

At an Air Ministry conference four days later Rolls said that a standard engine providing 2,000hp could be ready in six weeks and that a special engine of 2,100hp would require some development and be ready in 12 weeks. The special engine was selected. It ran at $27\frac{1}{2}$ lbs boost, had special fuel and hot plugs. The engine was started and warmed up until immediately before take-off, when soft plugs were removed and the hard fitted. The DTD decided that K5054 could be used for comparison trials, but a normal production Spitfire (Supermarine to select) was to replace it as soon as possible. It was also decided to place a firm order for six engines, six propellers and two racing aeroplanes.

All test flying was to take place from Eastleigh aerodrome, with the record attempt run over the old Schneider Trophy Solent Speed Course, RAE pilots and personnel checking the course and equipment beforehand. The next conference was held on 13 December and all agreed that five runs of ten miles each at an average of 380 mph on full throttle at eight minutes would be necessary. RAE stated that a Fairey Reed propeller would need a spinner of approximately three feet diameter because of bad blade roots and perhaps a Hamilton with blade root fairings would be the better unit. Efficiency of the former was .90 to give a maximum speed of 405 mph, while the latter was .860, 388 mph. This assumed the engine over revving in the

General arrangement of the 'Speed Spitfire'.

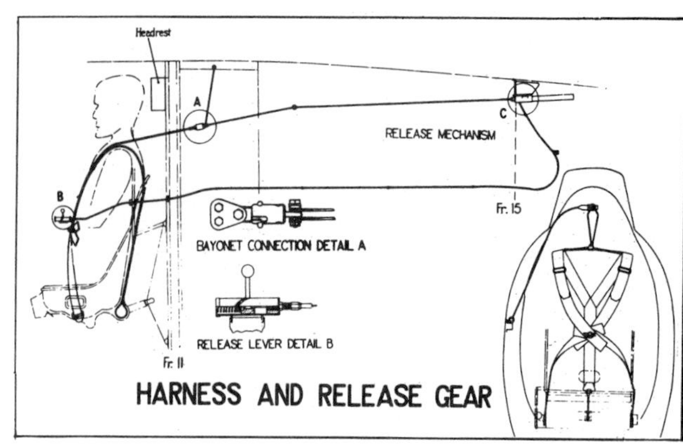

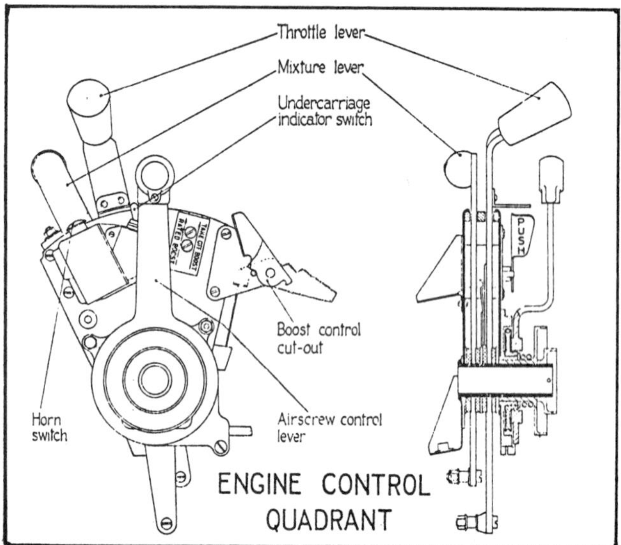

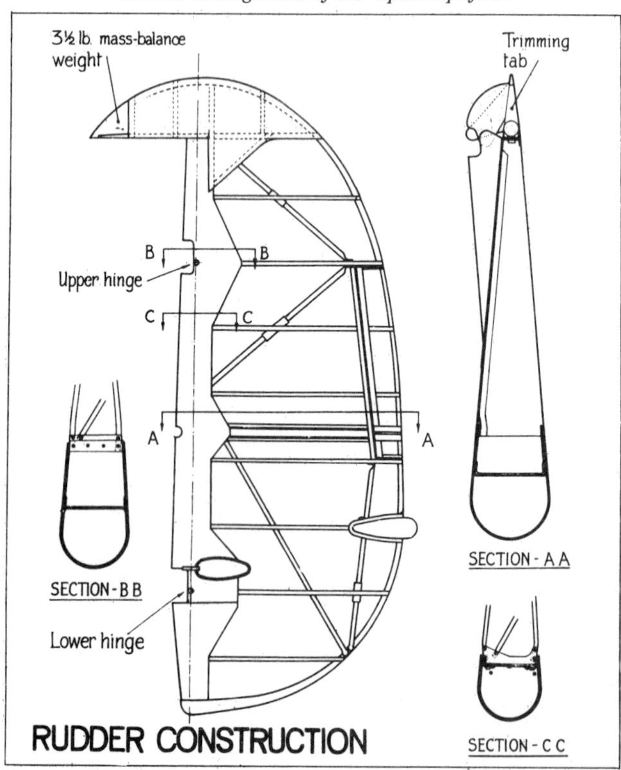

run up to the dive, dropping to normal revs during the record run.

On 11 November previous to this conference the Me113R (Bf109 V-130) had raised the World's Air Speed Record to 379.39 mph, and in view of this yardstick and the estimated speed of the Speed Spitfire the Air Ministry and Supermarine felt confident of success when their attempt was made. By 12 May 1938 work on the prototype aircraft seemed to have slowed down for at a meeting at de Havilland's Stag Lane factory the propeller situation was still under consideration. Three were being manufactured; they were of variable pitch with a synthetic resin fairing around the blade roots extending 12 inches up the blades. The shape was considered to be poor and the adhesive qualities of the fairing questioned. Two of the propellers were modified to have metal fairings attached to the spinner. These propellers were expected to provide a maximum speed of 422 mph with the aircraft in a Shellac finish, and slightly faster with a smooth finish. Sixteen coats of high gloss paint, rubbed down between coats to obtain the fine finish, were completed by experts from Rolls-Royce Motor Company.

On 20 June the first Special engine had been cleared for normal water cooling and a flight engine promised for the middle of July. A total coolant loss system engine was awaiting the enlarged header tank.

Squadron Leaders Purvis and Heycock attended the next meeting on 13 December and it was agreed to fly the Spitfire over the nine mile railway speed course between Farnborough and Basingstoke using hand timing. Two days later Quill flew level speed trials with the de Havilland propeller installed, and these continued until 6 March when K9834 went back to Eastleigh for the total loss cooling system to be installed. The upper fuel tank was removed and a replacement glycol tank/cum condenser fitted. Quill took the modified aircraft out after completion of modifications and as he taxied to begin his take off a steam pipe burst, filling the cockpit with steam. During another flight by Purvis the engine cut out but the pilot gained a little height and managed to coax the aircraft back to base.

N17 was weighed at Eastleigh on 15 March 1940 in the following condition — 62 gallons water tank fitted in place of the normal header tank and radiator; wooden four blade propeller; 37 gallons fuel; four gallons oil; cooling system full (67 gals); no wireless or tail ballast. Tare weight 4,520lb; take off 5,229. With one tail ballast weight (as flown) 5,246lb. Wing loading 23lb sq/ft. Engine, Merlin II Special 2,100hp @ 3,200rpm @ SL: boost + 28lb. Fuel – mix of petrol, methanol, benzol, plus lead. Consumption 3.12 galls per min. Propellers — Watts four blade wood, fixed pitch of 10ft diameter, 9ft 9in dia or, Hamilton (de Havilland) three blade two pitch metal of 10ft 9in diameter.

The Speed Spitfire appeared at the 2nd International Salon of Aeronautics held at Brussels in July, and by then doubts about performance were being expressed. Sir Wilfred Freeman, Air Member for Development and Production, said that although the immediate purpose of the project was research the record attempt could be made if he was assured that the aircraft could attain 450mph. Test flights had shown that this was not possible and, reluctantly, the project was abandoned.

The prototype aeroplane, which had been flying in B condition markings as N17, was transferred to the RAF and delivered to PDU at Heston on 24 November 1940. Much of the special equipment was removed, a Merlin XII installed and PR Mk III camera equipment fitted. The aircraft still retained its blue and silver colour scheme and was test flown on a number of occasions by the chief test pilot of General Aircraft. It then went to PRU Benson to become the personal aircraft of Air Comdre. J.N. Bootham, who flew it over the Normandy beach head on D-Day, 4 June 1944. It was finally struck off charge by Coastal Command as Cat E on 14 June 1946.

OFFICIAL REPORTS ON Mk I

These reports are of official trials/experiments from all sources and are in chronological order.

Martlesham Heath, 18 August 1938, K9788. Gun installation. This differed from that in the prototype in that the guns had a new type of rear mounting. A special thin spanner was necessary for gun adjustment. Gun bays and ammunition boxes were covered by a total of 22 panels held in place by 150 turn buttons. (The Hurricane has two panels and 32 buttons).

Martlesham Heath, 23 September 1938. K9788. Pyrotechnics. Two launching tubes for the 4in training flares are fitted in tandem behind the cockpit. They are set at an angle of 44° to the datum line, the centre line of the tube being inclined backwards. The flares are retained in the tubes by flap doors which are part of the fuselage, the doors being operated by a ring and wire cable installed on the pilot's left hand side. During trials three flares were released at 230mph and failed to clear the tubes until the aircraft was zoomed. As the flare dropped and protruded from the tube the slipstream held it against the rear of the tube. A spring was fitted to each tube lid and when the flap was open it forced the flare out.

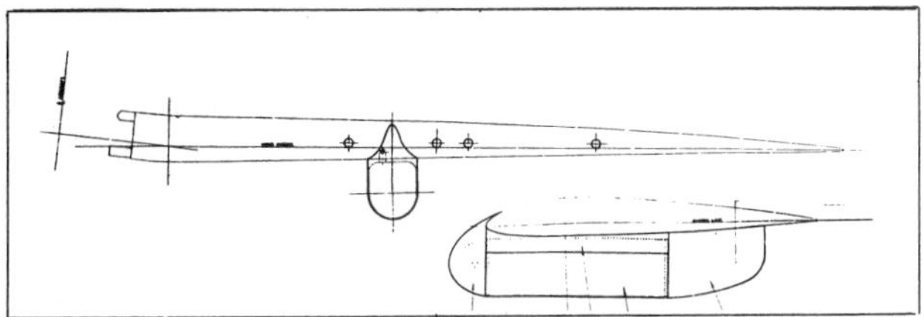

G.A of 30 gallon wing tank.

N3171 before and after installation of bullet proof windscreen, 14 February 1940. This Spitfire was eventually used for the compilation of pilot's notes.

Martlesham Heath, 8 October 1938. K9793. Wireless trials. First trial abandoned due to vibration to T.R. 9b. The Spitfire crate was changed for a Gauntlet type and trials progressed satisfactorily.

Martlesham Heath, 19 October 1938. K9787. Spinning and Diving trials. Typical Service load 5784lbs CoG 7.8ins aft of datum. Spinning behaviour satisfactory. Diving, aircraft reached speeds of 450mph. Engine cut in and out, hood impossible to move, poor manoeuvrability, all faults at high dive speeds. Night flying. Streamline exhausts slightly superior to ejector type, but considerable flame from both types in level flight and cruising speed. Manifolds not acceptable for night flying in present condition. Cockpit lighting satisfactory. Landing lights satisfactory. Take off. Flare path of at least 800 yards necessary. Taxying. Aeroplane tends to reach limiting coolant temperature very quickly. Ground running of engine should be limited.

Martlesham Heath, 27 October 1938. K9793. Electrical trials. Satisfactory.

Martlesham Heath, 6 January 1939. K9787. Merlin II performance trials. Speed trials with guns fitted flash elimina-

P9565 at Boscombe Down on 2 May 1940 with 30 gallon overload fuel tank on port wing. Pilots found that when the tank was full and they banked with the tank on the inside of the turn, the Spitfire tended to tighten the turn as a consequence of the additional load and area. The Supermarine Type No 343 was applied to any Mk I fitted with the wing tank. After use as a trials aircraft P9565 was first converted to Mk VA standards and later to the PR Mk VII Type G. It was refurbished in 1944 and eventually sold to Turkey.

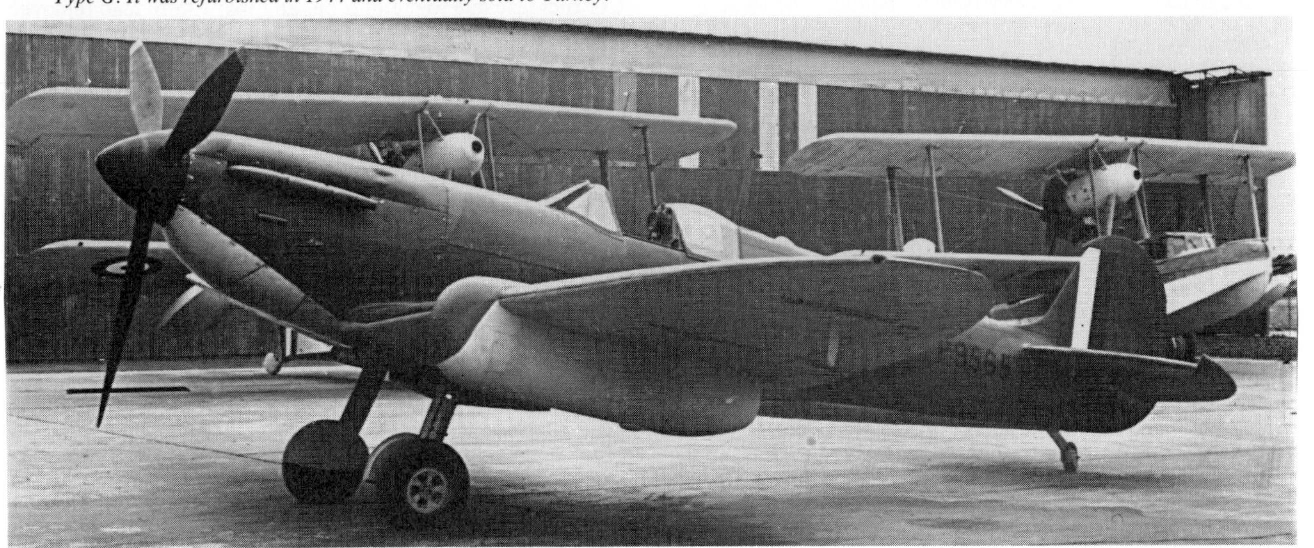

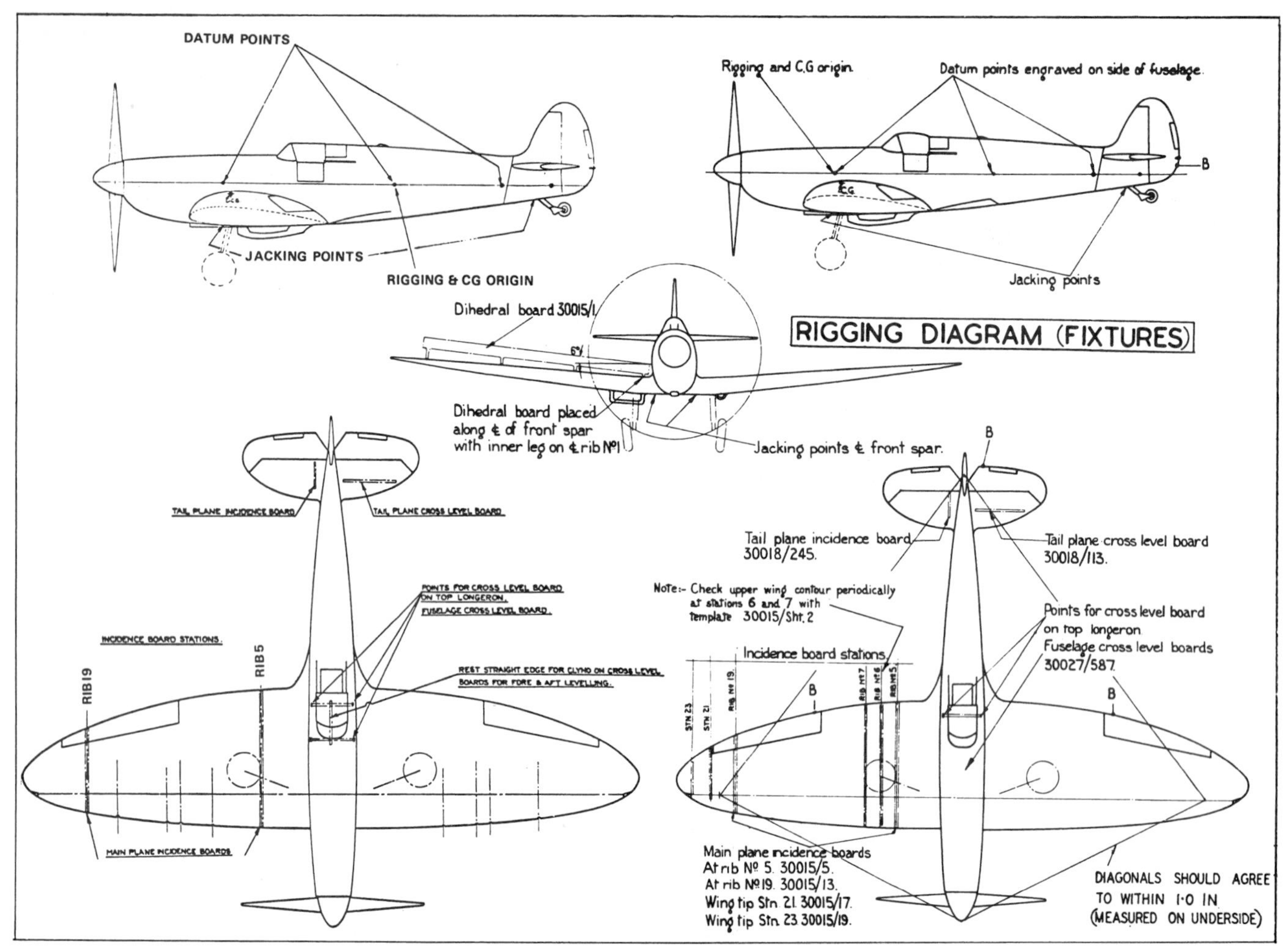

Rigging diagram fixtures on the Mk I and Mk II. Locations for fittings were indicated as blue spots on the aircraft's surfaces. Rigging of the Spitfire did not differ much from the early production F Mk IAs to the final production model. However, there were minor alterations as can be seen by the side view of the early aircraft (left) and the late Mk Is, IIAs and F VA. Plan view of the early Mk Is (left) is different to the late models, the Mk IIA and VA.

tors. No speed differences. Comparison with prototype K5054

	K5054	K9787
Max. cruising @ 15,000ft	311	318
Maximum speed	349 @ 16,800	362 @ 18,500
Time to 15,000	5.7 mins.	6.5
Time to 30,000	17.0	22.4
Service ceiling	35,400	31,900
Weight	5332	5819

Martlesham Heath, 15 May 1939. K7987,9788,9783. Operational trials. Is A/C weatherproof (yes), are pegging down and anchorage facilities satisfactory (yes), minimum time to swing compass (30mins), minimum refuelling time (4 to 11 mins depending on inlet pipe size), re-arming minimum time (30mins-4 armourers), remove and replace guns (remove 40, replace 30 mins-4 armourers), is ammunition stowing satisfactory (too many panels), are flying instruments positioned and lit satisfactory (yes), minimum size of aerodrome, grass (wooden prop T/O 420yds, land 380, two pitch prop T/O 320, land 235), max speed @ 1,000ft (295mph), 10,000 (292), 15,000 (288), 20,000 (276), 30,000 (202), economical cruise speed @ 15,000ft (198mph), fuel consumption (29.1gal/hr), oil (3/4gal/hr), is pilot's view satisfactory by day and night (yes), dive limitation (450 ASI), are navigational facilities satisfactory (yes), can A/C be readily abandoned (clearance with parachute limited and in high speed flight might be difficult). Exit would be easier from port side-door being fitted – Hood tends to stick at 250mph plus. Hood has to be fully back to allow opening of side door). No station keeping lights fitted. Gun sights (satisfactory), oxygen arrangements (satisfactory).

Martlesham Heath, 15 June 1939. K9787. Fixed pitch wooden propeller. Fuel consumption, handling & diving trials. Fuel consumption satisfactory. Handling satisfactory. Range of landing flaps increased to 90°.

Martlesham Heath, 29 June 1939. K9793. Merlin II. Tests of different ailerons. The force required to operate ailerons on prototype was not heavy, even at high speeds, but on production A/C it is stated that ailerons become almost immovable in a dive. Ailerons tested (1) standard production (2) flush strung as on K5054 (3) flush strung as above but with half the rib spacing. Results, with No. 2 light and effective from stall up to 340mph, control progressively heavier with speed increase. With No. 3 as per No. 2. With a smooth surface less force is required to move ailerons.

Martlesham Heath, 3 July 1939. K9793. Test of BTH type magneto. Performance of A/C are same as when fitted with standard magneto.

Martlesham Heath, 12 July 1939. K9793. Short performance with 2 pitch metal propeller. The most suitable fine pitch is 32½° at 42in radius. Spinning satisfactory with less turns required for recovery than with fixed pitch prop. Weight and CG Increase due to metal prop. 262 lbs; 135 lb lead removed from engine bearers, 40 lb installed in rear fuselage. Take off and climb satisfactory.

Martlesham Heath, 20 July 1939. L1007. Merlin III, handling and performance with two 20mm cannon fitted. Handling in normal, stall, aerobatics and dives normal and unaltered by cannon installation. Maximum level speed about 3mph less than machine gun aircraft. A.U.W. similar to standard Spitfire 5925 lb. Also flown at 7250 lb auw with 1200 lbs of lead weights in the wings.

Martlesham Heath, 19 March 1940. N3171. Merlin III, Rotol C/S propeller comparative performance trials with 2 pitch propellers. Flying characteristics not greatly changed with Rotol.

Boscombe Down, December 1939 to 13 January 1940. K9944. Comparative ailerons tests with Curtiss H-55 and Gloster F.5/34. Aileron control on H-55 and F.5/34 superior to Spitfire, but Spitfire pilot could easily break off combat owing to his superior speed.

Boscombe Down, 18 October 1940. X4268. Merlin III. Tests of brake flaps. Flaps were strengthened for tests for speeds up to 390mph. Flaps would not go fully down at 280mph plus. When lowered A/C rose vertically by about 150

K9804, 23rd production aircraft, failed to return from Dunkirk 28 May 1940 while operating with No.616 Squadron.

P9386 (No 19 Squadron) in typical early war period markings. It crashed in East Lothian on 5 May 1944.

R6923 of No.92 (East India) Squadron, one of the original converted twin cannon Mk Is after subsequent conversion to Mk VB standards with a Merlin 45. It was to be shot down by a Bf109 on 22 June 1941.

Diagrams of undercarriage retracting systems. Left, hand pump, manual on early aircraft. Right, engine driven.

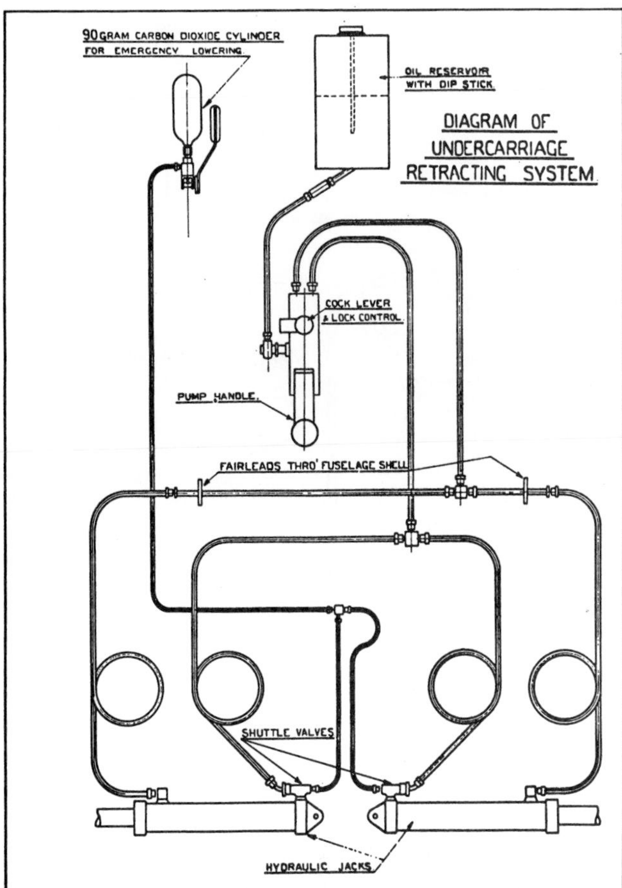

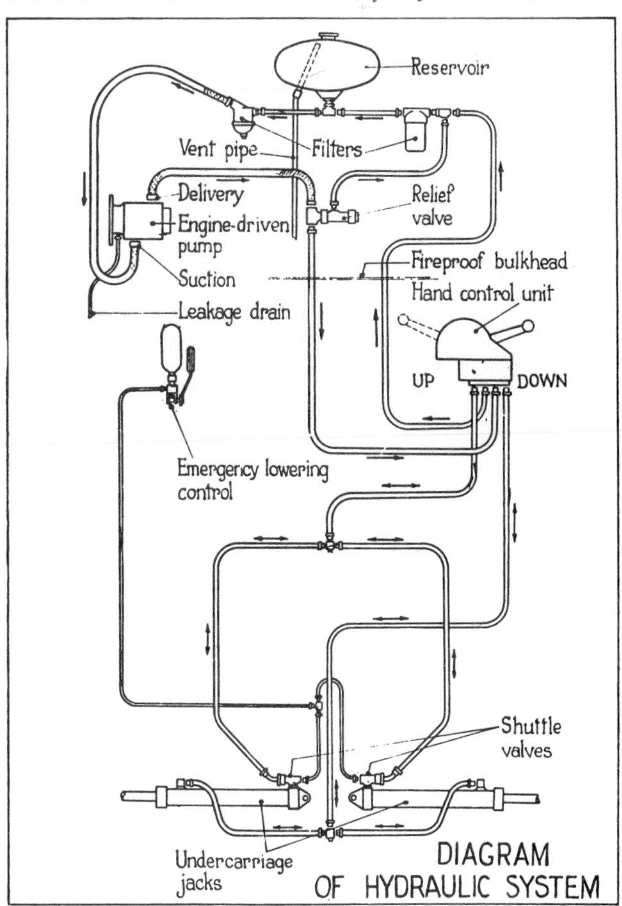

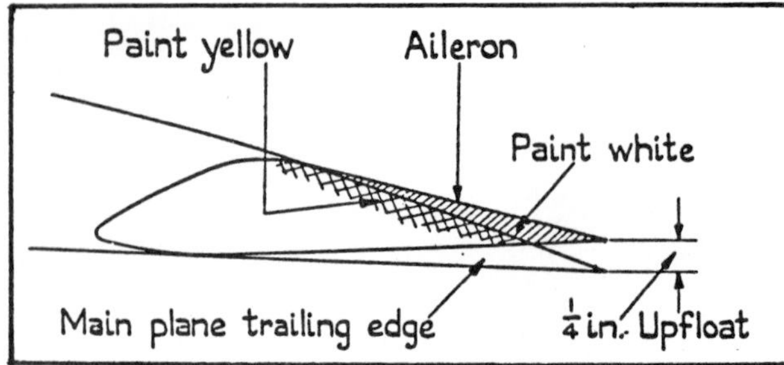

To assist the Spitfire pilot to assess the amount of aileron upfloat the upper part of the inner ends was painted white, this allowing for a ¼in upfloat, close to the maximum specified. Under the white section there appeared a yellow segment, and as the aileron rose higher to its allowable maximum the pilot could be made aware of the situation when the second colour started to appear, allowing him to take the appropriate action.

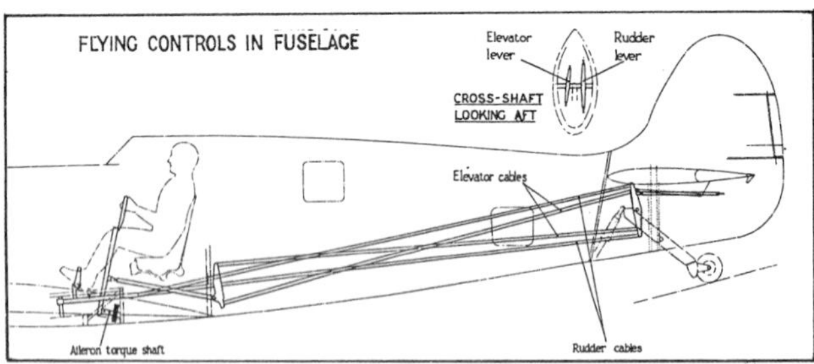

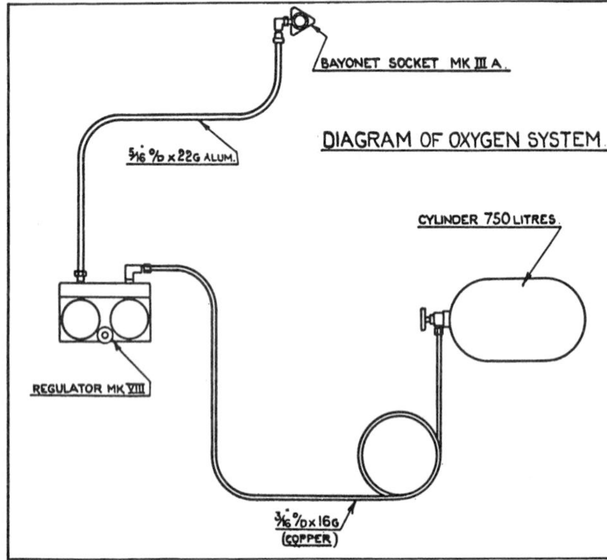

feet, they took about 15 seconds to fully retract. Flaps could not be used as air brake during combat.

Boscombe Down, 18 October 1940. X4268. Tests of automatic radiator shutter. Shutter fitted with thermostatic control which worked satisfactorily.

Boscombe Down, 31 October 1940. P9565. Brief performance and handling trials with 30 gallon overload fuel tank on port wing. Tank was 87½in long, 25¼in deep and projected 10½in below wing, and 12¾in in front of wing. Additional weight totalled 440lb. Control column held well over to right to keep aircraft level and as acceleration builds it is moved back to centre. During climb and level flight a little right aileron required. Stall similar to standard Spitfire but if control column pulled right back the port wing drops rapidly and aircraft goes into spiral dive. In dive ailerons heavy at 350mph.

Boscombe Down, 19 February 1941. X4257 and R6770. Merlin III 2 × 20mm cannon and 4 × .303 machine guns (Mk IB). Brief performance and handling trials. In earlier tests the cannons failed to fire during tight turns. R6770 has modified spars to overcome jamming. Aircraft handled satisfactorily.

Boscombe Down, 1 March 1941. K9788. Merlin XLV(45) (modified to F Mk V). Brief performance and cooling trials. Maximum speed 369mph @ 19,600ft, maximum rate of climb 3,460ft min at 14,400ft. Time to 20,000 6.2mins. Service ceiling approximately 38,000ft. Water radiator and oil cooler suitable for English Summer conditions.

Boscombe Down, 12 March 1941. N3053. Merlin R.M.5.S. (modified to F Mk V). Brief performance trials. Merlin 45 with modified blower. Satisfactory.

Boscombe Down, 28 April 1941. N3053. Brief performance trials with Rotol four blade propeller. Maximum rate of climb 3,190ft/min @ 18,000ft. Time to 20,000 6.6 mins. Service ceiling 40,500. Maximum speed 369mph @ 23,000ft. Ceiling increased **by 1,200ft, maximum rate of climb increased by 210ft/min. Time** to 39,000ft reduced by 4.3min. Speed increased by 10mph @ 37,000ft.

Boscombe Down, 29 April 1941. X4922. Merlin 45 (modi-fied to F Mk V). Brief performance trials. De Havilland propeller pitch settings increased to 34° fine and 54° coarse. Maximum speed @ 20,800ft 375mph. Propeller satisfactory. Recommended that settings be applied to production F Mk V Spitfire.

Supermarine, Eastleigh, 16 June 1941. R6718. Merlin III. Aircraft fitted with experimental slotted flaps for use on F Mk **IV Spitfire. Weighing and CG loadings. Tare 4,786lb, auw 6,169 take off 6,426. 110 modifications incorporated.**

Vickers-Armstrongs Ltd B. A. Dept Note. August 1941. **X4268. Flight measurements of wing internal pressure. Guns** and ammunition boxes removed. Tests made in straight flight at speeds from 80 to 440mph. Pressure measured at points fore and aft of main spar in each wing.

Boscombe Down, 15 October 1941. X4922. Merlin 46, F Mk VA. Cooling trials. Aircraft fitted with tropical conversion set. Coolant radiator and oil cooler within requirements for tropical temperatures.

Boscombe Down, X4922. Cooling and performance trials with tropical mods and 90 gallon external mock up fuel tank. **Auw 7,420lb. Maximum level speed 356mph @ 21,600ft. Rate of climb 2,050ft/min @ 16,000. Service ceiling (estimated)** 35,500.

Boscombe Down, X4922. Performance trials with tropical mods. Auw 6440 lb, maximum speed 363mph @ 20,800 ft, **maximum rate of climb 2,680ft/min @ 14,600. Service ceiling** (100ft min) 38,500ft.

Boscombe Down, 9 December 1941. X4782. Variation of longitudinal stability with altitude. Pronounced deterioration in stability as altitude increased.

De Havilland Aircraft Co, 28 May 1942. Flight tests of

Oil system.

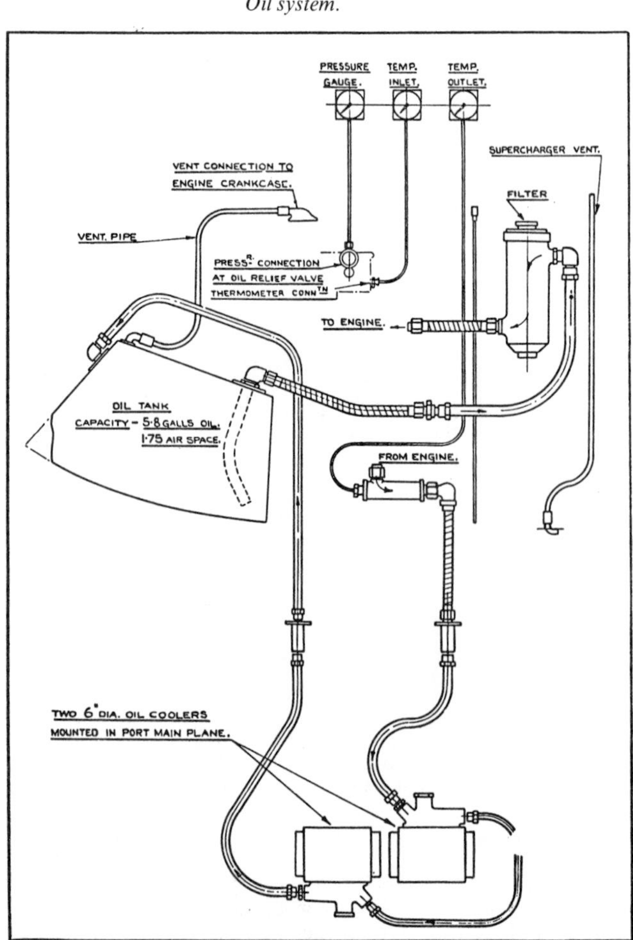

A young Jeffrey Quill (left) hands over a Mk I to its service pilot.

Gas warning panel on this Spitfire is diamond shaped and coloured yellow.

airbrake propeller on Spitfire Mk I. Tests originally carried out on de Havilland DH.93 Don with special propeller which would go into zero pitch for use as an airbrake intended primarily for use in dive bombing. The hydromatic propeller can be developed as an airbrake for dive bombing and fighting. Peak decelerations of at least 6G can be obtained in level flight with aircraft control satisfactory. When fitted with brake propeller aircraft structure must be designed to absorb increased fore and aft loads. Twenty hours of tests conducted with Spitfire, including 75 pitch change cycles – normal to braking pitch to normal. The rapid deceleration tended to throw the pilot (Flt Lt Hartnoll, test pilot DeH.) forward onto the stick and gave the impression that the Spitfire was "about to fall out of the sky". Mock battle with a Fairey Battle bomber with record of events by cine camera installed on Spitfire took place.

Supermarine, Eastleigh, 7 July 1942. X4922. Merlin 46, Level speed performance on combat rating. Operating at 16 lb sq/in boost maximum speed @ 15,600ft increased by 29mph.

Boscombe Down, 2 August 1942. X4266 Merlin III, BM559 (Mk VB) Merlin 45. Investigation into handling and stability characteristics with special reference to pull out from dives and steep turns. Tests made with and without $6\frac{1}{2}$ lb inertia weight in elevator system.

Farnborough, March 1943. High speed wind tunnel tests on Spitfire Mk I. Serial unknown.

Boscombe Down, May 1943. X4782. Use of Spitfire as a tug for Hotspur glider. Fighter squadrons wanted gliders as "luggage carriers" when moving to advanced bases. A Spitfire squadron with twelve Hotspurs could move sufficient ground personnel and equipment (excluding petrol) in one trip to set up an advanced base. The use of a twin Spitfire tow for a fully loaded Horsa was also considered for six Horsas had a greater capacity than 12 Hotspurs. Range estimated at 700 miles. Range of Spitfire with 170 gallon overload fuel tank and fully loaded Hotspur estimated at 900 miles. Code name "Hasty Hitch". Towing yoke fitted to the tailwheel axle and electrical wiring inside fuselage for operating the cartridge operated tow rope release. Test tows with Hotspurs BV112 and BT903. Tow speeds between 130 to 160 mph.

Boscombe Down, 22 January 1940. Investigation of estimating Positional Error (Spitfire) from generalised curves.

MODIFICATIONS INTRODUCED TO SPITFIRE MK I AND DATES

215 Delete flap position indicator 20-3-40; 216 Introduce plastic instrument panel 25-4-40; 222 Strengthen rear fuselage 25-4-40; 223 Introduce Linatex covered lower fuel tank 25-4-40; 229 Alter identification marks 21-5-40; 233 Introduce 30 gallon wing tank 21-5-40; 247 Armour glycol tank 6-6-40; 259 Replace gun covers with fabric patches 3-7-40; 260 Replace 4 × .303 M/Gs with 2 × 20mm cannon 3-7-40; 263 Modify chassis for use on Spitfire Mk III 28-2-40; 265 Introduce wooden rudder 27-7-40; 273 Fit self sealing to lower fuel tank 27-7-40; 283 Fit Spitfire Mk III windscreen & hood 27-7-40; 286 Introduce wooden elevators 3-11-41; 298 Modify camouflage to DTD circular 83 19-9-40; 315 Fit fireproof bulkhead behind pilot 20-11-40; 318 Fit elektron lower fuel tank 20-11-40; 319 Introduce metal covered elevators 20-11-40; 324 Fit hood jettison gear 20-11-40; 329 Introduce prismatic gun sight (cancelled) 16-9-41; 331 Introduce Merlin 45 15-1-41; 333 Delete mirror (A&B) camouflage scheme 26-4-41; 334 Strengthen tail plane spar 15-1-41; 338 Strengthen empennage attachment 15-1-41; 352 Introduce inertia weight elevator 10-7-41; 359 Cancel station keeping lights 22-8-41; 372 Fit vertical stiffeners between fuselage frames 15 & 19 19-5-41; 381 Mk IB only. Fit new type gun firing button 19-5-41; 388 Modify camouflage scheme to

P9450 of No 64 Squadron, lost on operations 5 December 1940. This view shows the aircraft on its pre-delivery flight. A second view on page 131 is the same photograph after a Supermarine artist had painted in four cannon guns as specified for the forthcoming Mk III Spitfire.

A Mk V Spitfire, now coded AA963, on display at an air force base in America. Wheels have been removed.

X4922 'H&H' at Boscombe Down 21 December 1941 for trials with a 90 gallon slipper overload fuel tank. The mock-up fitment can be seen installed behind the huge tropical air filter. The aircraft was converted to a Mk VA.

AR213, Westland built, survived the war and was once with the Shuttleworth Trust as G-AIST. Four blade propeller is non-standard for a Mk I. It is now owned by the estate of the late Hon Patrick Lindsay.

DTD No 183 14-7-41; 422 Introduce $\frac{1}{4}$ inch droop of metal covered ailerons 15-10-41; 425 Provide for conversion to PRU D type 29-8-41; 426 Revise camouflage colour scheme (replace earth & green) 10-11-41.

MODIFICATIONS INCORPORATED INTO ORIGINAL DESIGN AND DATES

60 Fit wheel on ball runner for easy movement of sliding hood 16-1-39; 62 Replace DeH 2 pitch prop with Rotol C/S Feb-39; 65 Introduce height and airspeed computer Mk II 6-2-39; 69 Delete G.22 cine camera 24-1-40; 76 Introduce DeH C/S prop 3-7-40; 89 G.42B & G.45 cine camera 2-6-39; 99 Provide defrosting of bullet proof W/S 11-7-39; 105 Introduce Gallay type radiator 17-7-39; 109 Modify u/c warning horn to operate at lower speed 27-7-39; 113 Stiffen wing ribs 10 & 11 18-8-39; 114 Strengthen radiator fairing 18-8-39; 116 Improve anchorage of pilot's harness 19-9-39; 125 Bring national markings & serials into line with S.I.S.4 and delete a/c numbers from wings 5-9-39; 133 Fit exhaust shield to stop glare 29-12-39; 135 Introduce station keeping lights 20-3-40; 140 Fit rear armour 19-10-39; 141 Provide waterproof engine cover 19-10-39; 153 Provide I.F.F. 10-11-39; 155 Strengthen pilot's rear bulkhead 10-11-39; 156 Strengthen fin for somersault landing 10-11-39; 159 Revise aircraft cover's camouflage scheme 12-1-40; 160 Improve wing skinning 5-12-39; 176 Introduce spot welded engine cowling 9-1-40; 183 Cancel introduction of blind landing equipment 9-1-40; 189 Introduce plastic pilot's seat 14-2-40; 195 Strengthen wing flaps 14-2-40; 201 Change roundels from blue & red rings to blue, white and red rings 9-1-40; 455 Stiffen wing skin at wheel wells 19-11-41; 461 To fit ballon type hood 21-8-42; 472 Introduce VHF blind approach equipment 21-10-41; 479 Fit DeH Hydromatic prop 30-12-41.

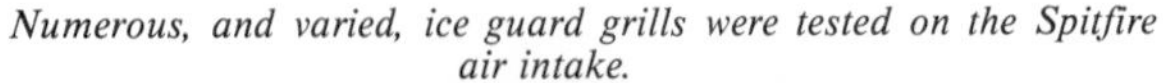

Numerous, and varied, ice guard grills were tested on the Spitfire air intake.

Rear fuselage (from an aircraft with partial serial X4-43) under test at Farnborough, October 1941.

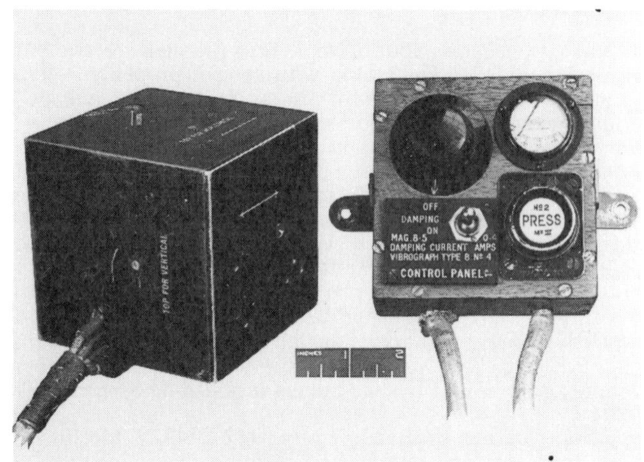

Standard pre-war vibrograph.

Pecking, or bogging, happened to a large number of Spitfires on take off or landing. If the unit was metal the propeller could be repaired and the de Havilland company was to repair, and return, hundreds of propellers.

Aircraft – 16/36/Spitfire I/Day and Night Fighter/Production
Engine – Rolls-Royce Merlin II

Dimensions and General Particulars

General Air Ministry Serial Nos	K9787-K9999 & L1000-L1096
Firm's Serial No	300
Overall length	29.98ft
Overall height, standing	8.19ft (tail down less airscrew)
Overall span	37.08ft
Airscrew diameter	10.67ft (2 blader)
Datum lines	3in below and parallel to thrust line 0 of C/S spars and perpendicular to thrust line
Wheel track	5.71ft
Wing Aerofoil section	NACA 2200 Series
Planform	Elliptical
Thickness	13.2% at root, 6% at tip
Incidence	Root $+2°$ to fuselage datum, tip $-\frac{1}{2}°$ to fuselage datum
Dihedral	6°
Aspect ratio	5.68
Aerodynamic mean chord	7.08ft
Geometric mean chord	6.53ft
Chord at centre line	8.33ft
Area outside fuselage	220 sq ft
Gross wing area	242 sq ft

Control surfaces	Span ft	Mean chord ft	Balance area	Surface area sq ft
Lateral	6.83	1.39	2.63	9.45
Total lateral			5.26	16.90
Longitudinal				
Fixed tailplane				18.2
Elevator and tabs	10.5	1.075	1.20	13.26
Elevator tab	1.74	.22	–	.38 × 2
Total Longitudinal			2.40	31.40
Directional				
Fixed fin				4.61
Rudder inc tab	5.33	1.47	.38	8.23
Rudder tab	1.61	.22	–	.35
Total directional				12.84
Brake flap	8.17	.968		7.80 × 2

Control movements & Settings

Aileron	20° up 25° down at L.E
Elevator	30° up 25° down
Rudder	30° both ways
Elevator tabs	15° both ways
Rudder tab	8° both ways
Fixed tailplane setting	0° to fuselage datum
Fin setting	0° to centre line of fuselage
Flap movement*	85°
Engine	Rolls-Royce Merlin II fully supercharged
Normal BHP	990 at 12000ft
Normal RPM	2600 at 12000ft
Maximum BHP	1060 at 17000ft
Maximum RPM	3000 at 17000ft
Static thrust	1275 lb two blade wooden airscrew
Static torque	4160 lbs ft
Ground clearance	At airscrew tip 7.25in Thrust line horizontal and aircraft standing

**Note, flap movement had been increased from 57° down on the prototype to 85° on production aircraft. This movement was to remain unaltered on all future production Spitfire/Seafires, except on the F24 and Seafire Mk 47.*

Spitfire F Mk IA. Late production models.

Wing. Planform elliptical; section NACA 2200 Series; incidence° root +2, tip $-\frac{1}{2}$; dihedral° 6; thickness% root 13.2, tip 6; aspect ratio 5.68; area sq ft nett 220, gross 242; chord (geometric) 6.3, (ma) 7.01 Ailerons. Area sq ft 18.9; chord 5.54; movement° up 26, down 19, droop $\frac{3}{8}$in. Flaps. Area sq ft 15.6, movement° down 85. Wing loading lb/sq ft 36.0. Power loading lb/hp 5.54. Wing span decreased by $3\frac{1}{2}$in when Air Ministry decided that wing tips should be detachable. New tips were less pointed.

Tailplane. Area sq ft 31.46; Chord (ma) 4.0; incidence° root 0, tip $\pm\frac{1}{2}$; dihedral° 0. Elevators. Area sq ft 13.26; movement° up 28, down 23. Tab. Area sq ft 0.38, movement° up 20 down 7. Fin. Area sq ft 4.61. Rudder. Area sq ft 8.23; movement° each way 28. Tab. Area 0.35; movement° each way 12.

Undercarriage. Wheels Dunlop AH2061; Tyres Dunlop 7-50-10. Oleo pressure lb/sq in 355; Tailwheel fixed castoring. Wheel Dunlop AH2184; tyre Dunlop Ecta 3-00-4. Oleo pressure 214.

Spitfire F Mk 1 general arrangement.

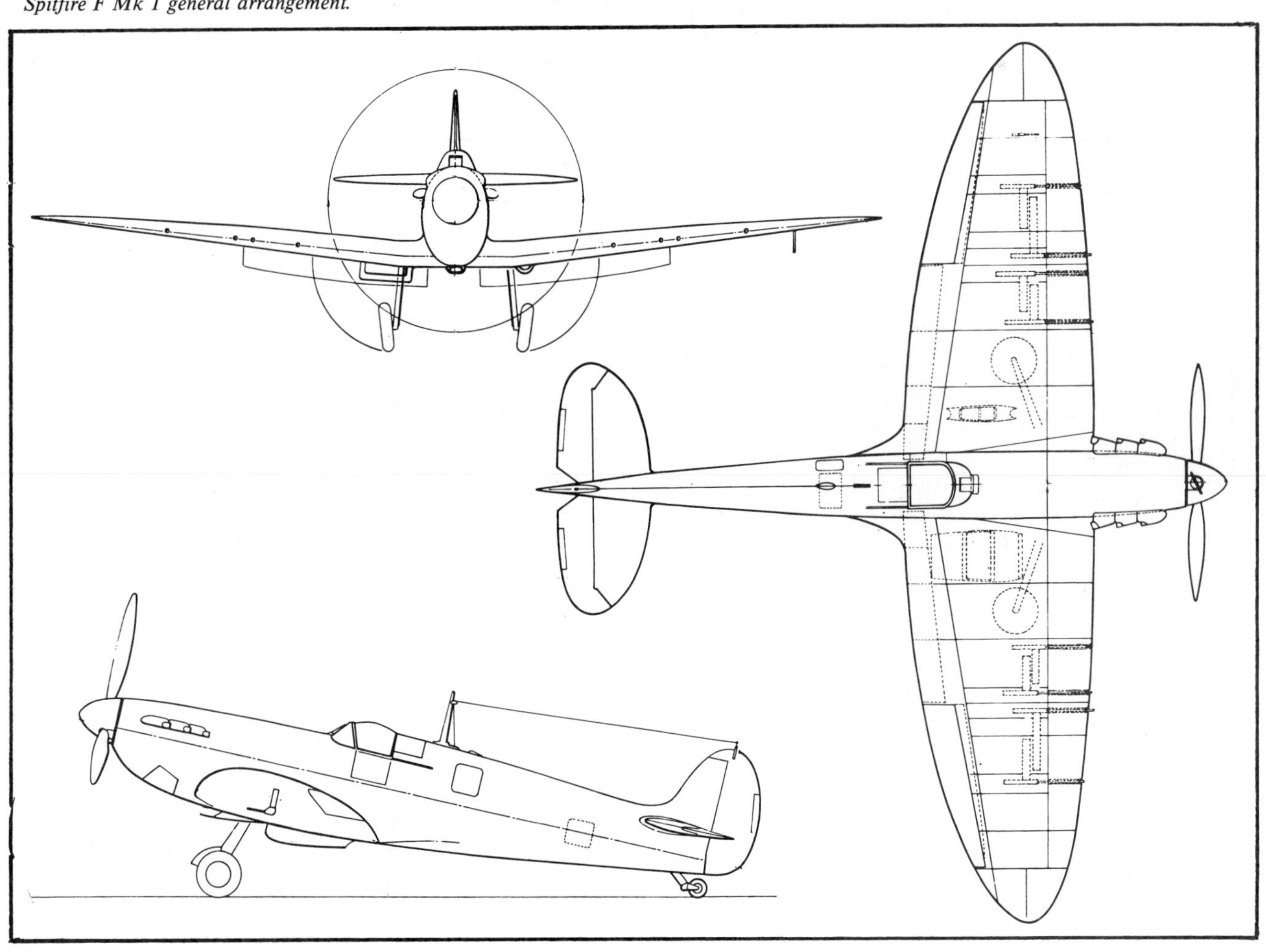

Engine/s. Merlin RMII 12 cylinder V supercharged speed. electric starter. 990hp @ 12,000ft, 1060 @ 17,000. Recc rpm, take off 3000 (boost $+6\frac{1}{4}$lb), climb 2600 ($+6\frac{1}{4}$), cruise 2600 ($4\frac{1}{2}$), max combat or emer 3000 ($+6\frac{1}{4}$lb) 5mins max. Fuel consumption 29.1 gal/hr. 12 volt system.

Propeller/s. first 50 a/c Weybridge 2-blade, fixed pitch 20° (24ft 6in), mahogony right hand tractor. Diameter 10ft 8in. Small number a/c with de Havilland 3-blade, 2-pitch 20°, fine pitch 30° Bracket Type 5/20 metal. Diameter 10ft 9in. Some early a/c also retrofitted. Tip clearance at take off 7.25in.

Coolant. 100% Ethylene Glycol. In engine 4.25 gals, radiator 4.25, header tank 1.5, piping 3.5, total 13.5.

Fuel. DTD 230 87 octane. Capacity (fuselage) upper 48 gals, lower 37, total 85.

Oil. Y/Y. 5.8 gals under engine.

Armour. Some a/c 73lb.

Armament. 8 × .303 Colt Browning Mk II machine guns, 300rpg (A wing). de Wilde tracer rounds incorporated. Gunsight GM.2 reflector. Small number a/c with ring and bead sight retrofitted with reflector.

Cine camera. G.22 in starbd wing root. Small number a/c with wing mounted (uppersurface).

Radio. TR.9B.

Performance. Max speed 295mph @ 2,000ft, 328 @ 10,000, 362 @ 18,500, 315 @ 30,000. Time to climb 1000ft 1min, 10,000 4min 18sec, 18,500 8min 25sec, 30,000 22min 25sec. Rate of **climb (ft min) 2,195 (2,000ft), 2,490 (10,000), 1,700 (18,500), 325** (30,000). Service ceiling 31,900ft (100ft min). Take off run 420yds, landing 380. Take off speed (normal) 86mph. Max dive 450mph.

Weights. Tare 4,341lb, take off (2-blade prop) 5,875 (3-blade) 6,200.

Spitfire F Mk IA. Late production models.

Wing. Planform elliptical; section NACA 2200 Series; incidence° root +2, tip $-\frac{1}{2}$; dihedral° 6; thickness% root 13.2, tip 6; aspect ratio 5.68; area sq ft nett 220, gross 242; chord (geometric) 6.3, (ma) 7.01 Ailerons. Area sq ft 18.9; chord 5.54; movement° up 26, down 19, droop $\frac{3}{8}$in. Flaps. Area sq ft 15.6, movement° down 85. Wing loading lb/sq ft 36.0. Power loading **5.54 lb/hp. Wing span decreased by 3½in when Air Ministry decided that wing tips should be detachable. New tips were less pointed.**

Tailplane. Area sq ft 31.46; Chord (ma) 4.0; incidence° root 0, tip $\pm\frac{1}{2}$; dihedral° 0. Elevators. Area sq ft 13.26; movement° up 28, down 23. Tab. Area sq ft 0.38, movement° up 20 down 7. Fin. Area sq ft 4.61. Rudder. Area sq ft 8.23; movement° each way 28. Tab. Area 0.35; movement° each way 12.

Undercarriage. Wheels Dunlop AH2061; Tyres Dunlop 7-50-10. Oleo pressure lb/sq in 355; Tailwheel fixed castoring. Wheel Dunlop AH2184; tyre Dunlop Ecta 3-00-4. Oleo pressure 214.

Engine/s. Merlin RMIII, electric starter.

Propeller/s. de Havilland 3-blade, 2-pitch, metal Bracket Type 5/21 (some a/c Merlin II 5/20); or 5/29 constant speed (CS); or 5/30. Small number a/c with Rotol 3-blade, 2-pitch, Jablo. Propeller clearance at take off 7.25in.

Coolant. 70% water, 30% Glycol (some a/c 100% Glycol). engine 4.25, radiator 4.25, piping 3.5, header tank 1.5, total 13.5 gals.

Fuel. 100 octane. Capacity (fuselage) upper 48 gals, lower 37, total 85.

Oil. 5.8 gals under engine.

Armour. 73lb including 2in thick glass windscreen and $\frac{1}{4}$in stainless steel behind pilot seat.

Armament. A wing. Some a/c modified to 2×20mm Hispano cannon, 60rpg in drums. Gunsight GM.2 reflector.

Cine camera. G.42B in port wing root.

Radio. TR1133, some a/c TR.9B.

Performance. Max speed 363mph @ 18,500ft, cruise 210 @ 20,000. Rate of climb 2,530 ft min; time to 20,000ft 9.4mins; 30,000 22.4mins. Ceiling 31,900ft. Range 575; combat 395. Stall **@ 6,250lb flaps and u/c up 73mph; down 74, landing 85. Speed** for max range @ min rpm @ 14,000ft 160mph. Max dive 450mph.

Hydraulic system via engine driven pump. Pneumatic system via engine driven compressor feeding two storage cylinders holding air @ 300 lb sq in.

EVERYBODY WANTS THE SPITFIRE

From the moment K5054 took to the air on its maiden flight in March 1936, the majority of contemporary interceptors throughout the world became obsolete. It represented a great leap forward in technology and if other Air Forces wanted a fighter to match its potential the governments concerned would have to spend a great deal of money to finance design and development of a similar aircraft, or purchase the expertise in the form of completed airframes. Although France had its own aircraft industry its products were not as advanced as its British counterparts and the French Air Ministry wanted to buy Spitfires. As a principal partner in any European war the French would have priority for British weapons, but a large number of other countries also wanted the Spitfire, and were asking for technical data and delivery dates; the Air Ministry had to call upon the Foreign Office for advice. It would have been irresponsible to allow the sale of such an advanced aeroplane to all comers. On 17 November 1938 the Foreign Office wrote to the Chief of the Air Staff listing the preferred countries in order of priority, with France heading that list.

Country	date of quote	number of a/c	priority/ allotment
France	25-4-38	3-plus	1
Belgium	28-9-38	15-45	2
Estonia	29-7-38	12	3
Turkey	–	30 + 30	4
Roumania	29-3-38	10	5
Portugal	16-2-38	15	6
Switzerland	–	15	7
Yugoslavia	25-2-38	12	8
Holland	29-7-38	18-36	9
Greece	23-9-38	12 + 12/24	10
Bulgaria	30-6-38	12	11
Iran	–	24	12
Lithuania	2-3-39	12	–

For all foreign enquiries Supermarine allotted Specification 456, beginning with the suffix A and updated to E by April **1940. Details of 456 are listed right:**

Class. Single Seater Day and Night Fighter

Type. Single engined monoplane with retractable undercarriage

Power Plant. Rolls-Royce Merlin II engine Rated 990 bhp at 2600 rpm at 12250 ft (1002 Cv at 3740m); Maximum 1030 bhp at 3000rpm at 16250 ft (1043 Cv at 4950 m).

Airscrew. 2 blade wooden

Construction. All metal with metal covering except on moving control surfaces which are fabric covered. Wings, Single spar with metal covered leading edge forming torsion box. Fuselage, Monocoque construction

Equipment. 8 Browning guns with 300 rpg; Wireless; Electrical equipment; Night flying equipment; Forced landing flares; Blind flying instruments

Main Dimensions and Particulars

Span 36ft 10in (11.25m); Length overall (thrust line horizontal) 30ft (9.15m); Wing area (gross) 242sq ft (22.5sq m).

Tankage. Fuel 84 gal (381 litres); Oil 6gal (27 litres).

Design Load Factors, C.P. Forward 10.0; C.P. Aft 7.5; Terminal Dive 2.0.

Weight Distribution. The following are the approximate weights bare and fully loaded for the production aircraft together with a typical distribution of the useful load.

Weight bare 4409 lb (2000 kg); Armour 73 lb (33 kg); Fixed equipment 270 lb (122 kg); Tare 4752 lb (2155 kg); Removable equipment 449 lb (204 kg); Pilot and parachute 200 lb (91 kg); Fuel (84 gal) 630 lb (286 kg); Oil (6 gal) 54 lb (24 kg); Weight fully loaded 6058 lb (2760 kg).

Wing loading. 25.1 lb sq ft (122.5 kg sq m).

Performance. The following performances are based on official trials. Max speed 362 mph at 18500 ft (581 kph at 5640 m).

Engine conditions not exceeding 3000 rpm or $6\frac{1}{4}$ lb boost. Climb, Time to 15000 ft (4580 m) 8 mins; Service Ceiling (at which rate of climb is 30.3 m min 30000 ft (9150 m); Max landing run 400 yds (365 m); Max take-off run 360 yds (330 m).

Tolerances. The above performances can be guaranteed within the following tolerances under the conditions quoted below.

Speed −3%; Climb +10%; Service Ceiling −6%.

Conditions for test. Aeroplane to be tested and results corrected in accordance with British practice by the Contractor at Eastleigh Aerodrome, Southampton. Engine and airscrew to be in accordance with description in Specification 456E. Aircraft weight not exceeding 6085 lb (2760 kg).

An examination of records relating to overseas orders reveals that the first enquiry appears to have come from Yugoslavia as part of a blanket order for the Blenheim, Spitfire, Battle and Hind, and the dispatch from Belgrade was dated 28 January 1937. It asked for 30 Hurricanes, or Spitfires, and in an Air Ministry reply of 26 April the Yugoslavs were informed that the delivery situation was confused. They replied with an amended order reduced to 12 Blenheims and Hurricanes (plus a request for a licence to build). Also, Colonel Stanoyevitch of the Yugoslav Air Force in London, visited the DCAS the same month and asked by what date could four of his pilots be allowed to fly the Spitfire; would Supermarine be empowered to release details of performance before a licence could be negotiated; by what date could Yugoslavia have a Spitfire? Supermarine were authorised to let the Colonel have certain performance details.

In the meantime an enquiry had been received from Lithuania (12 March) for 14 Spitfires, but it was never allotted a priority number, and as the Air Ministry never did confirm this order it eventually lapsed. Sir Robert McClean said that in the absence of a reliable delivery date forecast it was not possible to deal with the enquiry, and it would depend entirely on at least 150 Spitfires being delivered to the Royal Air Force. Japan asked for one example, while Egypt asked for various quotes for the delivery of either 18 Spitfires or Hurricanes.

The French order had arisen after an approach had been made to the Curtiss Aircraft Company of America in early 1938 about the possibility of purchasing a single seat fighter for immediate delivery. As a result of this Curtiss promised to deliver 100 fighters between November and December of that year, and at the same time a Major Jullerot, of the French Air Force, was endeavouring to interest his superiors in purchasing the Spitfire. He had an interview with the French Secretary of State for Aviation and was informed that the Minister was very much in favour of the idea, if Supermarine could supply 100 complete Spitfires before the end of Spring 1939. Also he was interested in obtaining a manufacturing licence.

Major Jullerot had to inform the Minister that this was virtually impossible for the Supermarine company was committed to deliver the first order of 300 Spitfires solely to the RAF. The French Air Force then asked that they be allowed to send two of their pilots to England in order to test fly the Spitfire; this was agreed and the event took place in September 1938. The French then enquired through their London Embassy if the Air Ministry would give them three Spitfires before the end of the year, but were told that they would receive one machine only as other countries, namely Belgium, had to be thought of as well.

The French were, by now, very anxious to get hold of Spitfires and when the Speed Spitfire was exhibited at the Brussels Air Show asked if they could – "purchase examples of the shortened wing Spitfire". They also asked the Air Ministry about the possibility of deliveries of – "a few squadrons of Spitfires, possibly the proposed Mk II variant or the 'clipped wing' type". They suggested the setting up of depots in France for holding Spitfire spares and engines and for the repair of RAF machines, but nothing came of this proposal. It is interesting to note that the total cost of one Spitfire delivered to France, complete with spare Merlin III, was £16,436.0s.0d.

By August 1938 Switzerland, Yugoslavia, Belgium and Holland were all awaiting permission to licence buld, and a quotation for 15 Spitfires had been received from Turkey. A price of £13,000 per complete Spitfire was quoted by Supermarine and accepted. By 19 January 1939 the Turkish government was getting restless over delivery dates and had placed a revised order for 60 aircraft consisting of 15 complete airframes, plus 45 sets of components, and a further request for the granting of a licence to build. The Air Ministry took the decision to release 60 complete aircraft for delivery as follows – five each in April and May 1939; 10 in June, July, August, September and October. The Turkish Spitfires were to be formed into four squadrons, with three flights to each squadron. Sixteen spare engines were also ordered and this was considered abnormally high by Rolls-Royce, but it was pointed out that the Turkish Air Force did not have the same service facilities as the RAF.

Colt 7.9mm machine guns were specified as the Turks were producing this calibre ammunition in their factories, but Supermarine pointed out that the Colt armament would have resulted in a slightly modified Spitfire wing and the Turks accepted the normal .303in gun. At a later stage the Turks suggested that their machine be converted to accept a cannon armament. They also asked for a supply of tropical air filters and spares equal to one third of the aircraft supplied.

Spitfire F Mk Is, Type 336, of the Portuguese Air Force with Merlin III engines. They were sent to Lisbon on SS Rugeley on 9 August 1943.

In January 1938 Latvia had forwarded an enquiry on delivery times, but nothing further came of this, and Yugoslavia asked for a firm delivery date for its order of twelve aircraft and permission to build 30 under licence. Bulgaria wanted to purchase five examples, an order that was to be increased to 12 later that same year, but the Air Ministry deferred a decision on this until April 1939.

Holland wanted to buy a single Spitfire and licence-build 40, and Greece entered the market with an order for 12 aircraft in November. This was to be increased by a firm order for 24 aircraft on 22 March 1939 and the price quoted by Supermarine for each Spitfire (including packing and delivery) was £9,335.0s.0d. One example was to be flight tested at Martlesham Heath by a British test pilot, and the remainder by Supermarine staff. Payment terms were 35% of the total value of the Contract to be paid within 20 days of signature; 50% of the value of each Spitfire after completion and tests at Supermarine works; and 15% of the value of each aircraft within one year of acceptance at the Supermarine works. The last named sum was to bear an interest rate of 3% per annum added to the final payment.

The Greek Air Force wanted the normal eight Browning gun armament changed to four .303 guns and two 13.2mm (350 rpg) guns, plus the British made R/T replaced by a German Telefunken 274d. The Contract was signed in June 1939 and the sum of £28,185 deposited with Supermarine. But the contract was cancelled the following October, despite a promise of the delivery of 12 aircraft by December and the remaining 12 in early 1940.

A group of Estonian Air Force officers arrived at the Supermarine works on 5 July 1938, and made a second visit on the 27th to watch demonstration flights. Convinced of the Spitfire's performance the Estonians made an advance payment on 12 aircraft to Order No. C.186/39. The Air Ministry approved the order and a firm contract was received from Estonia on 2 March 1939.

War was close now and enquiries poured into Supermarine. By May 1939 China wanted to buy the Spitfire, as did Finland, and Norway asked for quotes. Switzerland increased its order from 15 to 30 or 40 aircraft with delivery scheduled for 1940, but they wanted three aircraft before the end of 1939. The original Latvian enquiry had suddenly firmed into an order for 12 aircraft on 24 May 1939, and Iceland said they were interested in purchasing a *second hand* Spitfire for instructional purposes. They had to be advised that nothing suitable was available. Greece now asked for additional Merlin II engines to be added to their order and Sweden wanted to place an order (12 May) for an immediate delivery of 12 Spitfires. Greece then wanted to double its latest order, but withdrew it later.

A party of Yugoslavian pilots arrived in England in the first week in September 1939 and they were advised by the Air Ministry that they, and the Belgium and Turkish pilots already in the country, would be allowed to fly a Spitfire (with all secret equipment removed). The Spitfire allocated was K9791, the trials aircraft used for many experiments including the wing cannon mock-up and overload fuel tanks. The week beginning 12 September was selected for trials to commence with the Belgians allocated the first day, followed by the Yugoslavs on the 13th, French the 15th, followed by, in turn, the Dutch, Swiss, Rumanians, Turks and Greeks. In the event only the first two teams flew the Spitfire and all expressed satisfaction with its performance. The Belgians preferred the French Renard, even though its maximum speed was considerably lower than the Spitfire (310 to 380 mph), and the Yugoslavs were not happy with the fixed pitch propeller and asked that a constant speed unit be made available as the take off run was too long.

The French team did eventually fly the Spitfire, and the Turks flew on 26th and 27th of the month, with the Swiss taking their turn on the 29th. The latter claimed that handling qualities were good but gliding and landing characteristics inferior to the Bf109, which they had flown previously. Nevertheless, the Swiss did place an order for three aircraft, this being increased to 15 plus the opportunity to licence-build at a later date, but Supermarine had to cancel the order because of the war situation. Iran had placed an order for 24 Spitfires in November 1938 but never followed up their enquiry and it had to be cancelled.

Portugal placed an order for 15 aircraft on 23 February 1939 accompanied by an advanced payment and a number were delivered during the war years. Turkey also received two Spitfires of their order and they were delivered via S.D.F. Christchurch in June 1940 as the Type 341 (serials P9566 and 9567) but the Spitfires, apparently, turned up in the Middle East in late 1942 bearing the markings HK854 and HK856*. All other Spitfire orders were cancelled but one Spitfire, apart from the Turkish pair, was delivered to France. The Turkish Spitfires were delivered in the first week of June 1940 and each cost £11,700. £226 was charged for the erection of each aircraft in Turkey**.

HK854, Mk I, photographed in the Middle East in late 1942. It is thought to be ex-P9566 or 9567 and was supplied to the Turkish Air Force originally.

HK856 was photographed by (then) Flying Officer Neville Duke at No. 1 M E Training School, El Ballah, in April 1942. This Spitfire is also thought to be either P9566 or P9567.

The French Air Force Spitfire Mk I delivered during late 1939. Legend ahead of fuselage roundel reads – FW8.

The French Spitfire was the 251st production aircraft of the L-serial batch, and it flew for the first time on 25 May 1939. It was painted in standard RAF day fighter camouflage, but carried the French tricolour roundels and rudder markings. Quill flew it for performance trials on 26 and 27 June and conducted level speed comparison tests with a Hurricane on 5 July. It was flown to France on 18 July bearing B-series marks and was later coded 01. It had a three-blade, two-pitch, de Havilland metal bracket propeller and during tests by the French Air Force attained speeds of 363 mph. The log book for the spare Merlin III engine was handed over on 16 October. According to reports it was burnt by the French authorities in Orleans to prevent it falling into German hands, but it did seem to have escaped this fate for our photograph (above) shows the dilapidated airframe later in the war.

* *Impressment serials (HK811-HL539).*
***Remainder of order cancelled.*

SERIAL NUMBERS

The following serial number list of Spitfire Mk Is (and subsequent Marks) contains a short Service history of all constructed. Where available the serial number is followed by the manufacturers' airframe number; the location where it was built; first flight date, pilot's initials, name (if any), first MU and squadrons. Major incidents then follow and the history ends with the SOC date.

When shipped overseas the boat's name is in italics and the destination named. To help follow the histories more easily a facsimile of Air Ministry Form 78 is reproduced. Note should also be made of the contents of a typical Spitfire history, see below, as should Appendix X which contains a list of abbreviations used in this book. All contracts and orders appear in **Appendix V, page 604.**

Every Royal Air Force aeroplane had **A. M.** Form 78 allotted which contained details of its service life. Reproduced here is one side of the form for a typical Spitfire. The Type is followed by its serial number and contractor. **The M.A.P. contract** number is in the top right hand corner. Engine type was normally followed by the number, but large numbers of cards did not contain this information. R6710 was a Mk I which does not appear on any of the initial Spitfire batches cards, and not until the Air Ministry straightened out the Mk number and role additions did this information appear. This particular Spitfire was taken on charge at No 9 Maintenance Unit on 3 June 1940 from Supermarine, **Eastleigh,** and was checked and the specialised equipment installed. It reached the MU on 9 June. It then went to No 54 Squadron on 12 June. It was apparently damaged shortly after arrival for it was at Air Service Training Hamble on 26 July and allocated **to 12 MU on 30th,** reaching this unit on 2 August. It was then transferred to **No 6 MU before** reaching No 266 Squadron on the 19th. No 72 Squadron took it on charge on 6 September 1940 and it was damaged **by a Bf109 on** the 11th. As Category 3 (extensive damage) it went to Scottish **Aviation Ltd (4 MU)** on 21 September and spent several months under repair before allocation **to No 12 MU on** 3 January 1941. Taken on charge at 12 MU on 26 February it remained in store until transfer to No 61 Operational Training Unit on 4 July. It was slightly damaged by the trainee pilots for it had to be Repaired on Site by Vickers on 14 October under the authority of the Civilian Repair Organisation. It was returned to 61 OTU on 1 November; was declared Cat B during a major inspection on 12 October 1942 and sent to Scottish Aviation Ltd by CRO the same month and Repaired in (the) Works. On 21 November it was awaiting collection and was at 45 MU on the 24th. On 12 July 1943 it was at No 17 Service Flying Training School and just over a year later (28 October 1944) was stored at No 33 MU.

The reverse of Form 78 normally continued with the aircraft's history and in a separate section listed the various incidents, such as the event of 11 September 1940 when it was damaged in combat. There was a separate section which had number of hours flown. **R6710 was presumed to be struck off** charge on 21 June 1947. The aircraft had not been lost, but may well have been despatched overseas and used by an Allied Air Force, which did not report its demise.

In order that the maximum number of histories be published in this book they have of necessity been contracted. But, most of the squadrons **the** aircraft served with do appear, as do major events and final demise. An excellent example is a Mk I X4501. The manufacturer's number was 1627 and it made its first flight from High Post Aerodrome. It was loaned to Heston Aircraft Ltd and then converted to PR Mk III Type C standards. It went to No 1 PRU (Benson), suffered an engine failure and made a wheels up landing at Fair Isle. It was Category E (badly damaged) and struck off charge. Scottish Aviation Ltd repaired it and converted the airframe to PR Mk VI Type F, installing a Merlin 45 engine. It went to 8 Operational Training Unit, was damaged - category B and struck off charge one more. Total flying hours 262 hours 50 mins.

AIRCRAFT — A.M. Form 78

Contract No. 19713/39

Type SPITFIRE — R.A.F. No. R6710 — Contractor SUPERMARINE

Type of Engine MERLIN III — Engine Nos.

	(1)	(2)	(3)	(4)	(5)	(6)	(7)	(8)	(9)
Taken on Charge of	9MU	54 SQN	A.S.T. 4MU.	12MU	6M.U	266 SQN	72 SQN	S.A.L 4MU	12MU
Date taken on Charge	9.6.40	12.6.40	26.7.40	2.8.40	16.8.40	19.8.40	6.9.40	21.9.40	26.2.41
Authority	1623A	1623D	1623D	1632D	1623A	1623A	1623D	CAT B	1623A

	(10)	(11)	(12)	(13)	(14)	(15)	(16)	(17)	(18)
Taken on Charge of	61 OTU	ROS VICKERS	61 OTU	M.I CAT B	R.I.W S.A.L	AW/CN	45 MU	17 SFTS	33 MU
Date taken on Charge	4.7.41	14.10.41	1.11.41	12.10.42	27.10.42	21.11.42	24.11.42	12.7.43	28.10.44
Authority	1623D	CRO	CRO	1623A	CRO	CRO	1632D	15/7 63	21/10 78

Date	Unit to whom allotted	Authority	Date	Unit to whom allotted	Authority
3-6-40	9MU	10086			
30-7-40	12MU	10958			
3-1-41	12 MU	14134			

Facsimile of Air Ministry Form 78.

Supermarine Aviation (Vickers) Ltd
Contract No B527113/36

First Order for 310 Spitfire Mk I dated 3 June 1936. Built at Woolston as Mk I variants between May 1938 and September 1939. K9787 to 9999; L1000 to 1096. Total built 308. Under Air Ministry Expansion Scheme 'F' 300 Mk Is were ordered for the RAF with a further 10 for allocation to AMDP for trials and development. From 1938 serial batches were issued as blocks with unused black-out numbers between each block. The first 74 aircraft (to K9960) had Rolls-Royce Merlin II engines, the remainder having Merlin III. The first 77 (to K9963) had a mahogany, two blade, fixed pitch propeller and all were retrofitted with constant speed, three blade de Havilland propellers. The remainder had three blade, two speed de Havilland propellers, also replaced in June 1940 with the constant speed unit. Deliveries started with K9787 on 17 July 1938 (to Rolls-Royce, Hucknall, for Merlin engine trials). The first 49 aircraft were costed at £8,783 each; the next 26 £5,696; next 31 £5,768.10s.

These prices were for Supermarine construction and do not include embodiment loan items such as; engine, instruments, etc.

K9787 1 FF 14-5-38 JKQ Mkrs trls. Farn May to June 38, M Hth 18-8 gun instal 23-9 pyro 8-10 wire trls 19-10 spin & dive trls 27-10 elect trls 6-1-39 perf trls. Vickers 13-4 for incor of ods. Farn 26-4 to replace K9852 as radio trls a/c 15-5 oper trls @ M Hth with K9788 & 9793. 15-6 M Hth fuel cons trls, hand & dvng. Trls with 30 different types of fixed pitch props; cock hood funct trls which demo the canopy was difficult to open @ 350mph. Suggested remedy – a 2nd entry/exit door in fus as emergcy. Super for instal Mer III & Rotol C/S 3-blade Jablo prop. AMDP Gloster A/C 23-10, FIE shed Farn mods. Con PRIII Type C @ BMU 11-7-40 Comp trls with N3297 (proto Mk III) & fitt 7lb sliding int wt on elev cont. PRU 1-6-41 FTR ops 30-6 FH363.50

K9788 2 BDn 19-7-38 R-R H 27-7 2 days invest Merlin II high cool temps when grd run. M Hth 18-8 gun instal, maint & firing trls 23-9 pyro with 2 x 4in dia tubes for flares behind pilot in fus. Speed course trls Farn (straight 9 mile rail line between Farn & Basingstoke used as rough & ready timing run). M Hth 15-5-39 trls with K9787 & 9793. R.R. 30-6 Mer XII (RM-3S) instal. VA 16-12 repairs B DN 21-12-40 for RM-5S eng trls 1-3-41 perf & cool trls 1 CRU Oxfd 30-4. Cat B retired from active duty. Con to Mk VA *Taran* to Port Sudan (with K9876 & L1000) 29-1-43 ME 24-2 SOC 27-7-44

K9789 3 19S Dux 4-8-38 intns serv trls 4MU VA stripped for detailed exam MMO rep 11-9-39 9MU 10-1-40 65S 27-2 8MU 5-7 PRU 11-7 FACA 1-8 57 OTU 28-11 FAAC 13-1-41 WAL 33MU 19-5 61 OTU 22-11 FACB 7-4-42 ROS 45MU 14-12 to 359M 14-12-44 2SoTT SOC

K9790 19S 11-8-38 intns serv trls VA stripped for detailed exam 6-5-39 9MU 18-12 AMDP VA 24-1-40 two months trls with ails 8MU 13-6-40 7OTU 7-7 cd/ldg Haw CE 15-7 SOC 22-7

K9791 5 AMDP reserve a/c for K9787 BDn 5-10-38 Super 18-10 for use as trls and mods A/C. Can m/up on wings. Trls with 3-blade, 2-speed DH prop Dec '38 M Hth gun firing and assoc trls. DeH trls with C/S prop. Trls a/c for 2 x 70gal, o/ld fuel tanks under wings. fltt Merelin XII PDU Ben 4-6-40 FTR ops 17-8 FH126

K9792 6 originally allot AMDP no requirement 19S 29-7-38 CFS Cranwell 30-7 19S 16-8 cd Dux 3-11 SOC 31-11 to Ins A/F Grp Ass 2SoTT FH41.35

K9793 7 AMDP M Hth 9-9-38 gnrl eqip elect syst & wire trls. Trls DeH 3-blade metal prop; Wt difference was an added 282lb. 135lb lead removed from eng bearers and 62lb, instal in rear fus. Super 7-12 M Hth 15-5 oper trls with K9787 & 9788 29-6 trls with various types of ails. Short t/o perf to det minm run. 3-7 trls with two types of magnetos Farn 8-7 cont of ails trls with N3171. Serious lack of response in fast, tight turns M Hth 12-7 short perf trls with 2-pitch metal prop Farn trls to det ignition interference with radio. Trls instal of snow guard on air intake. 8MU 1-9-40 19S 1-9 92S B HII 1-9 s/dn by Bf109 nr Dung 16-10hr 11-9 P/O Hargraves kld SOC 5-10 FH164 50

K9794 8 19S Dux 18-8-38 cd/ld Dlg 10-1-39 CE SOC 18-4 FH36.35

K9795 9 19S Dux 27-9-38 64S 18-4-40 s/dn by AA fire Dover ld Hawk 13-7 49MU 15-7 49MU 15-7 GAL 603S 29-9 222S 14-10 e/fd cd Terling 16.30hr P/O Edridge safe C2 15-10 SOC 12-1-41 58 OTU 26-2 to 4867 M6SoTT 1-1-42

K9796 10 19S 3-10-38 SOC 29-8-39 AST for Grp Ass 21-11 cancel rep 8MU 13-6-40 AMDP Farn 11-7 flown by ETPS pilots was actively engaged with Luft during BoB while primarily trls a/c one pilot was 'Roly' Falk, later test pilot of Avro's Vulcan delta wing jet bomber. July '40 to May '41 ext ails trls. Fitt spcl, thin blade prop resulting in speed loss of 4mph. BDn July '41 gun sight trls. M Hth 39MU 16-6-42 8MU 17-12 41Grp 31-3-44 SOC 30-4-45 FH149.00

K9797 11 19S 7-10-38 e/fd while acting as target a/c for cine gun practise f/ld Acton Sgt Unwin safe CE 9-3-39 Practise Flt Strad (non fly) 11-5 SOC 8-6 FH88-55

K9798 13 FF GP 30-7-38 19S 17-9 w/u ldg Dxfd 18-4-39 SOC 20-5 to 149M 1AAS 6SoTT 29-6-42 FH168.30

K9799 14 19S 17-10-38 FACB 9-7-40 GAL 15-7 222S 31-8 C2 ops 2-9 1CRU 58 OTU 2-1-41 FACB 2-1 Air Taxis Ltd 53 OTU 1 TEU 26-2-44 ASTEx 12-8 SOC 18-8

K9800 16 19S 21-10-38 AST 18-3-40 5 OTU 14-7 7 OTU 21-8 FAC2 16-11 2GAS Manby 18-3-41 to 3277M 10SoTT 26-11 SOC 18-7-42 CE 13-5-44

K9801 18 19S 14-10-38 1CRU 28-5-40 7 OTU 14-9 FAC 2 28-10 58 OTU 3-1-41 61 OTU 14-10 AST CB 6-1-42 53 OTU 14-7 FAAC 6-2-43 AEAF Heston 31-12 53 OTU 19-5-44 39MU 4-8 SOC 18-1-45

K9802 20 66S Dxfd 31-10-38 w/u ldg Dxfd dbr 25-4-39 SOC 17-5 FH93.35

K9803 66S 28-10-38 616S 30-10-39 19S 3-5-40 603S 13-9 dam by Bf109 nr Ashford Kent Sgt Baile safe C2 18-9 45MU 23-2-41 HAL 30-3 AW 8-11-61 OTU 19-3-43 FACB 8-1-44 OTU 21-5 33 MU 13-8 SOC 21-6-47

K9804 23 66S 23-10-38 616S 20-10-39 dam night ldg at base May '40 FTR 28-5 FH234.45

K9805 25 66S 18-11-38 41S 27-5-39 64S 19-4-40 CAC ops 23-11 53 OTU 16-7-41 FAAC 25-2-42 SAL 1-9 58 OTU 24-3-43 9MU 14-2-44 RNDA 17-3 33MU 10-8 SOC Apl '45

K9806 27 66S 18-11-38 w/u ldg Dxfd 18-7-39 SOC 25-8 to 1638M 1SoTT 25-8 RTP 26-5-44

K9807 12 FF GP 10-10-38 19S 11-10 616S 7-8-40 C2 ops 15-8 603S 29-9 s/d by Bf109 P/O Morton aban a/c 5-10

K9808 15 19S 18-10-38 cd f/ld Egmere Norfolk 28-11 to 123M 2 SoTT 22-1-39

K9809 17 1S Dxfd 25-10-38 dvdi/grd on t/o 1½ miles from base 29-2-40 CE SOC 15-3

K9810 19 66S 31-10-38 Farn 17-4-39 19S 616s 15-11 i/sea 12 miles SE off Hornsea 21-2-40

K9811 21 19S 5-11-38 cd f/ld Clare Suffolk 24-1-40 54MU 2-2 SOC 6-2

K9812 22 66S 28-10-38 e/fd cd into wood nr Royston Cambs 16-2-39 to 1382M Csf d 31-3 FH26.55

K9813 24 66S 8-11-38 41S 1-6-39 64S 11-8 FTR ops Dunk 31-5-40

K9814 26 FF GP 6-2-38 alloc 66S 28-10 cancel 6MU Brize Norton in spc 1 fin and flown to Paris Aero Show via Croydon 14-11 demo at French airfields after show 6MU 9-2-39 5 OTU 28-5-40 cd ADn 3-6- CB 1CRU SOC 19-6

K9815 28 66S 23-11-38 41S 8-3-39 19S 23-1-40 609S 13-7 cd/ld Piddlehinton Dorset 26-7 SOC 1-8 FH286.15

K9816 30 66S 23-11-38 cd/ld Dxfd 1-12 SOC 24-1-39 scr

K9817 31 66S 29-11-38 616S 17-11-39 FAC 2 7-8-40 PRU 20-9 SAL 6-10 58 OTU 13-1-41 FACB 21-3-53 OTU 17-7-58 OTU 3-2-43 OTU 3-2-43 FACB 26-2 SAL RNAS 23-5 ret to RAF 13-4-45

K9818 32 FF GP 28-11-38 66S 28-11 616S 30-10-39 dam op 1-6-40 610S 27-8 cd Ainmouth F/O Bacon kld 30-9

K9819 33 FF GP 29-11-38 66S 29-11 616S 8-11-39 s/dn nr Calais Sgt Wareing POW 25-8

K9820 34 19S 1-12-38 cd/ld Dxfd 16-1-39 to 1361M 22-3

1SoTT SOC 13-2-43 FH253.30

K9821 36 FF GP 2-12-38 19S 5-12 air coll with K9854 f/ld Newn Hth 6-10-39 FAC 29-5-40 54MU AST FACE 2-7-40 47OTU 14-11 SOC 20-7-41

K9822 37 66S 6-12-38 cd/ld Dxfd 6-1-39 to 1357M Csfd 3-5 FH8.35

K9823 38 66S 10-12-38 Farn July '40 57 OTU 31-10 43Grp 9-4-41 53 OTU 17-7 P&PSM 16-4-42 RNAS 13-5-43

K9824 39 First with Mer III FF GP 6-12-38 19S 9-12 5 OTU 4-6-40 7 OTU 30-10 FACB 28-3-41 57 OTU 7-6 FA del flt CB 4-9 CGS 15-10 Stn Flt StA 13-6-42 air coll with N3266 cd CE 19-11-43

K9825 40 FF GP 9-12-38 19S Dxfd 19-12 609S 13-7-40 FACA 14-7 1CRU 30-7 7 OTU 25-9 FAAC 15-4-41 AST con to FVA M45 12-7 332S 31-1-42 164S 3-5 FACA 4-6 602S 10-9 34S 7-7-43 61 OTU 1-8 Stn Flt North 13-8 52 OTU 22-8 1695Flt 9-9-44 FAAC 24-1-45 SOC Sept '45

K9826 41 19S 12-12-38 2FTS 30-12-39 616S dam night ldg May '40 222S 2-7 s/dn a/c aban nr Barham Kent P/O Edridge inj 30-8

K9827 43 66S 18-12-38 616S 17-11-39 s/dn nr Dung 26-5-40 dam by Bf109 Sgt Copeland inj f/ld 26-8 COAL 3-9

K9828 43 66S 18-12-38 616S 19-11-39 FA 22-5-40 72S 7-10 58 OTU 9-3-41 57 OTU 17-7 AST 21-3-43 222MU 8-8 Port 14-8

K9829 44 FF GP 20-12-38 66S 22-12 616S 15-11-39 dam ops Sgt Ridley safe 1-8-40 7 OTU 26-9 FA 31-10 37MU to 3200M 3SoTT 20-3-41

K9830 70 Mer XII FF GP 15-12-38 AMDP Super 21-1-39 BDn 13-6-41 armour plate trls inst AFDU 30-10 CRD RAF Horn 14-3-42 trls periscopic gun sight and gun heat AFDU 27-5 52 OTU 10-9 3501SU 16-2-42 58 OTU 5-10 1TEU 17-6-44 recat E 14-8 SOC First Mk 1 con to Mk II see page 62 for further details

K9831 45 FF GP 20-12-38 41S 30-12 w/u ldg Catt 30-1-39 to 1362M 22-3 SOC 17-8 FH 19.30

K9832 FF GP 41S 30-12-38 64S 9-3-40 FTR Dunk 29-5

K9833 47 FF GP 29-12-38 41S 3-1-39 602S 20-1-40 603S 5-7 602S 4-8 FAC2 28-8 58 OTU 2-1-41 cd f/ldg Dunblane Perths CE 18-4 to 2574M

K9834 35 MXII trans to AMDP Super Contract B817241/38 for con to High Speed spitfire FF 10-11-38 as N-17 PDU Heston 24-11-40 con to PRIII Type C FACB 27-8-42 HAL 31-8 PRU 4-9 CC 14-6-46 CE SOC 21-3 see page 64 for further details

K9835 48 41S 3-1-39 MMOx 26-2-40 57 OTU 17-6 e/fld cd Llandrillo Denbs 10-2-41 58 OTU FACE 16-6-43 1TEU 26-2-44 SOC 22-8

K9836 49 FF 1-1-39 41S 5-1 19S 23-1-40 FTR i/sea ops 1-6 FH298.00

K9837 50 41S 5-1-39 w/u ldg Catt 8-6 SOC 17-8 to 1628M 2AAS RAF Weeton 17-8 RTP 31-5-44

K9838 51 FF GP 6-1-39 41S 11-1 struct fail in div Eryholme Yorks 16-3 SOC FH21.25

K9839 52 41S 11-1-39 602S 23-1-40 Farn June '40 AST 25-8 602S 29-8 dam Do17 P/O Aries safe 7-9 58 OTU 23-3-41 SOC 7-1-42 to 2868M 10-1-6SS

K9840 53 FF 11-1-39 41S 13-1 64S 2-5-40 FA 26-5 266S 19-8 72S 25-8 dam ops 2-9 152S 23-9 57 OTU 24-1-41 FACE dbf 2-3-46

K9841 54FF GP 11-1-39 66S 13-1 19S 29-4 AST 21-11 611S 6-6-40 609S 18-7 dam op 12-8 AST 12-8 609S 18-8 616S 25-8 72S 2-9 dam ops f/ld Etchingham Surrey P/O Males safe 10-9 SOC AST cancel 26-9 SOC 8-4-41

K9842 55 FF GP 8-1-39 41S 16-1 cd in night ldg Catt 23-5 SOC 14-6 FH97.15

K9843 74 FF 12-1-39 41S 4-2 AST 10-12 54S SOC 18-7-42 to 3229M

K9844 56 FF GP 12-1-39 41S 16-1 64S 11-3-40 lost cont a/c aban cd nr Chu Fen 25-3 SOC 5-4

K9845 57 FF 13-1-39 41S 17-1 w/u ldg Catt 3-4 SOC 15-5 to 1479M 15-6 FH42.25

K9846 58 FF GP 13-1-39 41S 22-1 616S 17-9 cd night t/o Catt dbf 6-11 F/O Overall kld SOC 21-11 63/4/134

K9847 59 FF GP 15-1-39 41S 22-1 64S 11-3-40 AST 4-5 72S 2-9 e/fld f/ld Halstead 8-10 AST 12-10 57 OTU 21-2-41 Farn 8-4 Ins A/F 23-6-43

K9848 60 FF GP 19-1-39 41S 26-1 e/fld cd f/ldg Nr Catt 20-4 SOC 17-5 FH23-35

K9849 62 FF GP 19-1-39 41S 26-1 cd on t/o Catt 14-9 SOC FH 132.10

K9850 63 FF 20-1-39 41S 26-1 FAC2 6-2-40 266S 17-8 FA 18-8 58 OTU 29-12 53 OTU 17-7-41 FACE 28-3-43

K9851 64 FF 20-1-39 19S 27-1 Farn Mar '39 AST 30-4-40 7 OTU 13-7 19S 3-9 7 OTU 10-9 FAC2 10-12 10SoTT 1-8-41 CE 23-9-44 FH401.25

K9852 65 FF 24-1-39 AMDP Farn 31-1 radio trls and pilot trng Super 25-4 R/T instn & trls. ETPS Farn 26-6-40 VHF aerial trls for R3002 Oct '40 snow guard instn & eng trls 610S 15-10 fought numerous airfield defensive actions during Farn trls. BDn 25-10 FA AST 53 OTU 6-5-41 FA cd nr Tang 7-6 SOC

K9853 66 FF 26-1-39 19S 31-1 Farn Feb '39 hand trls GAL 15-7-40 dam ops Sept '40 SOC 15-1-41

K9854 71 FF 26-1-39 alloc 66S 31-12-38 trans Farn Mar '39 trls 19S 4-5 air coll with K9821 f/ld Newm Hth 6-10 SOC 14-10 RTP

K9855 68FF GP 27-1-39 41S 4-2 o/s ldg Catt to 1646M 1AAS Manby 4-11 SOC 6-11

K9856 69 FF GP 28-1-39 41S 15-2 fire in flight cd/ld Catt 27-4 SOC 9-5 FH20.50

K9857 73FF GP 1-2-39 19S 11-5 w/u ldg Dxfd 20-5 7 OTU 7-7-40 FAC2 5-9 57 OTU 19-12 FAAC 16-4-41 1CRU 1-8 8 OTU 24-5-42 FAAC 11-6 8 OTU 25-7 e/fld fire in flight a/c aban i/sea pilot rescued by ASR off Fraser 11-11

K9858 75 FF 4-2-39 19S 24-4 cd on t/o H St F 31-3-40 SOC 9-4

K9859 76 FF GP 4-2-39 19S 24-4 strk fence on app Dxfd 9-5 to 1825M

K9860 78 FF GP 9-2-39 74S 14-2 cd/ld South 9-11 SOC 18-1-40 FH74.20

K9861 79 FF GP 9-2-39 74S 13-2 std dvdi/grd Grays Thurrock Essex Sgt Gower kld 30-8

K9862 80 FF GP 9-2-39 74S 13-2 1CRU 20-5-46 64S 19-8 57 OTU 3-2-41 AST 5-3 57 OTU 24-7 53 OTU 22-8-42 air coll with K9850 cd Pontravel Farm Glam 28-3-43

K9863 81 FF GP 9-2-39 74S 13-2 dam ops P/O Freeborn safe 10-7-40 57 OTU 8-5-41 air coll with X4164 cd nr Sealand 26-1-42

K9864 82 FF GP 11-2-39 74S 15-2 266S 29-12 S/dn f/ld nr Faversham Kent P/O Soden inj 16-8-40 57 OTU air coll with R6769 cd River Dee nr Flint Scotland 8-5-42

K9865 83 FF 11-2-39 74S 16-2 u/c clpse ldg Horn 3-3 AST 7 OTU 21-7-4- 67 OTU 31-12-41 FACA 7-5-42 SOC 7-5

K9866 84 FF 13-2-39 74S 14-2 cd 3-3 to 1428M 6SoTT 14-4 53 OTU SOC 26-8-44 FH136.30

K9867 85 FF 14-2-39 74S 18-2 AMDP 11-1-40 FRT 23-5

K9868 86 FF 15-2-39 74S 15-2 cl/ldg Cherbourg France 21-11 21 Dept 5-12 SOC 9-2-40

K9869 87 FF 15-2-39 74S 2-2 AST 14-5-40 e/fld on t/o del flt to 6MU 13-7 i/sea off Hamble C3

K9846, Merlin II, stands outside final erection hangar at Eastleigh. This aircraft was one of the first production units to have gun heating.

K9849 before serial number was applied. Allocated to No 62 Squadron.

K9842 and 9791 (background) at Eastleigh.

K9870 88 FF GP 17-2-39 74S 17-2 dam ops 8-8-40 72S 7-10 s/dn by Bf109 nr Deal a/c aban P/O Pool inj 11-10

K9871 89 FF GP 17-2-39 74S 21-2 dam ops f/ld P/O Szezesny safe 13-8-40 57 OTU 19-12 MMOx 30-4-41 con to FVA M45 3-6 53 OTU 15-7 AST 24-8 303S 5-12 81S 12-2-42 S&H 18-10 51 OTU 27-5-43 53 OTU cd on t/o Ouston CE 21-12 SOC 1-1-44 recat 6-1 39MU 1-5 SOC 15-10-45

K9872 90FF 19-2-39 74S 23-2 w/u ldg Horn 24-3 SOC to 1450M 24-4 RAF StA FH7.55

K9873 91 FF 21-2-39 74S 23-2 AST 12-11 7 OTU 22-9040 FAAC 5-10 58 OTU 4-2-41 53 OTU 3-1-42 hvy ldg Lland o/t CE 20-4 76MU 1-10 *Taran* Port Sudan 29-1-43 ME 28-2 FA cd 10 miles E Bilbeis Egypt C3 13-1-44

K9874 92 FF GP 22-2-39 74S 27-2 AST 7-5-40 7OTU 17-8 19S 3-9 7 OTU 10-9 FAC2 4-10 GAL 29-10 Ins A/F at 57 OTU 21-2-41 SOC 23-6-43

K9875 93 FF GP 23-2-39 74S 27-2 FTR Dunk 27-5-40

K9876 94 FF 23-2-39 74S 1-3 AST 18-10 5 OTU 4-6-40 7OTU 13-8 FAC2 14-8 610S 15-10 602S 14-12 57OTU 4-2-41 GAL 12-5 P&PSM 27-4-42 new eng con to FVI BDn July '42 dvng trls 45SLG 24-8 76MU 3-10 *TAran* Port Sudan 29-1-43 ME 31-3 to 4384M

K9877 95 FF GP 24-2-39 54S 1-3 152S 18-2-40 o/s ldg o/t Ack 16-3 SOC 11-4

K9878 96 FF GP 24-2-39 74S 1-3 222S 4-9-40 AST 26-11 CGS 4-2-41 58 OTU 14-3 FAAC 23-3 61 OTU 15-5-43 RNAS 25-5 SOC 30-12-4

K9879 97 FF GP 1-3-39 74S 4-3 MMOx 11-9 PRU Ben 11-7-40 cd Lt Cmdr Kingdon kld after oxygen starvation dvdi/grd ne Crew Som CE 1-8 SOC 1-8

K9880 98 FF 27-2-39 54S 2-3 152S 2-1-40 s/dn Bf109 P/O Posener miss 20-7

K9881 99 FF 28-2-39 54S 2-3 w/u ldg at Base May '39 152S 4-1-40 dam ops 16-2 602S 24-3 Dam e/a 16-8 AST 4-9 4SoTT 15-3-41 53 OTU took off in coarse pitch strk P7840 Llandow CE 1-4-42 SOC 18-7 to 3215M RNDA 25-5

K9882 100 FF GP 2-3-39 54S 17-2 152S 2-1-40 s/dn off IoW Sgt Christie kld 26-9

K9883 144 FF 2-3-39 54S 24-4-39 152S 3-1-40 CB ops 20-7 1CRU 58 OTU 28-3-41 FAAC 4-6-43 1TEU 1-3-44 Royal Navy Milmeed 22-3

K9884 101 FF GP 3-3-39 54S 10-3 152 3-1-40 o/s ldg cd Ack 19-6 SOC 24-6

K9885 102 FF GP 9-3939 54S 13-3 152S 16-1-40 f/ld cd nr Nottingham 16-1 SOC 1-5

K9886 103 FF GP 6-3-39 54S 8-3 cd circling beacon at night nr Basildon, Essex 8-11 SOC 14-12

K9887 104 FF 7-3-39 54S 10-3 AST 9-11 bboc 9MU 26-3-40 5 OTU 4-6 WAL 7-7 58 OTU 12-3-41 SAL 14-6 52 OTU 1-1 57 OTU 1-11 FACE 24-2-43 SAL 10-11 53 OTU 9-5-44 TEU 14-6 SOC 21-6-47 rtp

K9888 60 FF 19-1-39 66S 30-1 41S 4-5 hit high grd Appleby, Cumb 18-7 Sgt Mitchell kld

K9889 77FF 4-2-39 6MU 9-2 5 OTU 28-5-40 7 OTU 10-9 SAL 27-9 AST 23-5-41 57 OTU 5-8 61 OTU 27-11-43

K9890 67 FF GP 28-1-39 41S 4-2 294S 4-6-40 602S 13-7 41S 21-7 603S 20-9 C2 23-9 AST out of fuel ld nr Hooton Park in River Mersey 1-2-41

K9891 72 FF 31-1-39 6MU 7-2 66S 24-4 ASTH 20-11 5 OTU 4-6-40 FA 19-6 WA 58 OTU 2-2-41 SAL 11-3 53 OTU 9-12 coll with P7840 on t/o Lland CE 1-4-42 SOC 13-4

K9892 105 FF 8-3-39 54S 13-3 602S 29-11 ldg acc Drem P/O Moody safe 2-8-40 610S 15-10 602S 14-12 57 OTU 4-2-41 descended through cloud with X4167 hit hill Ruabon Denbs dbf CE 3-7 SOC 15-7

K9893 106 FF 7-3-39 54S 13-3 152S 16-1-4- e/fld cd in fd/ldg Broughton Lincs CE 16-1 SOC 3-2

K9894 107 FF 9-3-39 54S 13-3 152S 2-1-40 GAL 58 OTU 1-1-41 57 OTU hit hill in cloud Ruabon Nr Wrexham 3-7 CGS 9-7 DeH 18-8-42 57 OTU 13-6-43 RAF Medical Rehabilitation Loughborough 26-4-44 to 4868M SOC 29-8-46

K9895 108 FF 10-3-39 CFS 15-3 hand trls AST 18-12 64S 14-80-40 57 OTU 3-2-41 61OTU u/c clpse ldg Slnd 12-5 57 OTU FACE ttl wrck 20-7 SOC 6-8

K9896 169 FF 10-3-39 54S 15-3 Farn March '39 152S 3-1-40 u/s ldg Catt 6-6 CE SOC 16-6

K9897 110 FF GP 13-3-39 54S 15-3 u/s ldg strk obs Horn 4-7 SOC 15-8 rtp

K9898 109 FF GP 14-3-39 54S 17-3 152S 4-1-40 SOC 2-5

K9899 111 FF 13-3-39 54S 17-3 152S 15-2-40 602S 24-3 dam ops 23-7 57 OTU 7-11 AST 24-5-41 53 OTU 24-8 o/s ldg Lland CB 15-10 SOC 18-10

K9900 112 FF GP 15-3-39 54S 21-3 SOC 12-12 bboc 152S 2-1-40 57 OTU 1-2-41 FAAC 27-3 AST 21-6 53 OTU 3-9 RNAS Yeov as trner 7-9 SOC 30-12-44

K9901 113 FF 16-3-39 54S 20-3 152S 16-1-40 s/dn by Bf109 25-7 1CRU 28-7 FH262.30

K9902 114 FF 17-3-39 54S 22-3 152S 1-3-40 SOC 20-5

K9903 115 FF 17-3-39 65S 21-3 dam ops 28-5-40 64S 3-9 cd nr Tern 6-9 SOC 7-10

K9904 116 FF 19-3-39 65S 22-3 FAC 2 23-9-40 53 OTU 21-7-41 cd in f/ldg Cwmffrwd Carn 3-9 SOC 9-9

K9905 117 FF GP 19-3-39 5S 24-3 Farn Nov '39 s/dn in Dover area by Bf109 Flt Sgt Phillips kld dbf 8-8-40 SOC 14-8

K9906 FF 21-3-39 65S 24-3 64S 17-4-40 FA 23-5 7 OTU 11-10 ASTH 18-10-41 con to PRIII Type C 1PRU Ben 26-2-42 FACE 18-3 8(c)OTU 17-6 SAL 29-11 RNDA 22-5-43 SOC 22-5

K9907 119 FF GP 23-3-39 65S FTR over Channel 8-7-40 S/Ldr Cooke kld

K9908 120 FF 21-3-39 65S 24-3 AMDP R-RH 16-1-40 FA 29-5 AST dam ops 26-8 610S 27-8 HAL 11-9 7 OTU 13-10 u/c clpse during maint CAC Dec '40 SOC 1-6-41

K9909 121 FF 23-3-39 65S 25-3 s/dn by Bf109 nr Dover Sgt Keymer kld 22-8-40 SOC 8-10

K9910 122 FF 23-3-39 65S 28-3 cd/ld May '39 602S 6-3-40 cd/ld des after comb P/O Webb inj 9-9

K9911 123 FF GP 24-3-39 65S 28-3 s/dn by Bf109 Dover dbf Sgt Kirton kld 8-8

K9912 130 FF GP 25-3-39 65S 4-4 dam ops 26-5-4 SOC 14-8 test bed for Mer III and DeH 3-blade, 2-speed prop

K9913 124 FF GP 25-3-39 65S 28-3 cd t/o Horn 27-7 to 1632M 5SoTT 12-8 SOC 15-3-44

K9914 125 FF GP 26-3-39 65S 1-4 AST 9-1-40 66S 4-6 eng fire cd/ld Colt 8-7 to 1632M SOC 21-8

K9915 126 FF GP 27-3-39 65S 30-3 AST 24-5-40 65S 30-5 FTR ops P/O Pyman kld 16-8

K9916 127 FF GP 28-3-39 65S 1-4 603S 14-12 FTR on patrol F/O Peel assumed dead 17-7-40

K9917 128 FF GP 28-3-39 65S 1-4 cd Ald 5-12 SOC 3-1-40

K9918 129 FF 30-3-39 65S 1-4 4MU 31-5-40 611S 4-6 4MU 6-6 7 OTU 21-8 FAC2 31-8 34S 3-9 1 CRU 7-9 CB 24MU 14-11 53 OTU 8-4-41 61 OTU 11-7 SOC 30-9

K9919 131 FF GP 31-3-39 65S 4-4 night cd Horn 9-8 4MU 4-12 SOC rtp

K9920 132 FF 1-4-39 65S 12-4 e/fld cd Nth Foreland, Kent CE 22-5-40 SOC 27-5

K9921 133 FF 2-4-39 65S 12-4 FA 28-5 54MU 31-5-40 7 OTU 16-8 FA 25-9 FA 28-12 to 2457M SOC 18-1-41

K9922 134 FF 3-4-39 72S 11-4 cd Ack CE 27-8-40 43MU 30-8 SOC 3-9

K9923 143 FF 3-4-39 72S 21-4 w/u ldg Chu Fen 13-7 rtp

K9924 135 FF GP 4-4-39 72S 11-4 AST 6MU 15-11-40 58 OTU 28-12 12MU 1-1-41 58 OTU 2-2 CB 21-5-42 33MU 22-9-43 53 OTU 24-10 CAC 3-2-44 CE SOC 11-8

K9925 136 FF GP 4-4-39 72S 11-4 std on app Wools 26-5-40 SOC 14-6

K9926 137 FF 6-4-39 72S 14-4 603S CE SOC 31-5-40

K9927 138 FF 11-4-39 74S 14-4 w/u ldg Chu Fen 19-7 SOC 28-8

K9928 151 FF GP 11-4-39 72S 21-4 74S 10-5-40 strk by lightning cd nr Margate dbf Sgt White kld 8-7 49MU 8-7 SOC 31-7

K9929 139 FF GP 12-4-39 72S 14-4 dam ops 3-8-40 WAL 27-9 8MU 17-10 7 OTU 24-10 34 MU 19-12 52 OTU 31-1-41 FACB 17-6 AST recat E1 24-7-42

K9930 140 FF 12-3-39 54S 15-4 152S 23-2-40 AST 10-9 53 OTU 7-9-41 a/c aban jammed cont cd nr Cowbridge, Glam 11-9

K9931 141 FF 13-4-39 74S 18-4 AST 8-5-40 610S 7-7 dam ops cd dbf P/O Gardiner inj 25-8

K9932 142 FF GP 14-4-39 74S 19-4 54MU 12-5-40 e/fld cd f/ldg Canvey Island Essex 4-5 SOC 13-5

K9933 145 FF 15-4-39 72S 17-4 602S 23-11 AST 25-1-40 7 OTU 13-7 SAL 27-9 OTU 2-1-41 53 OTU 17-7 strk by P9368 Lland CE 14-12-42 recat B 57 OTU 28-7-43 SOC 6-3-45

K9934 146 FF 15-4-39 72S 18-4 2 SoTT 4-9 AST 30-11 5 OTU 4-6-40 7 OTU 30-8 FAC2 22-9 58 OTU 31-12 to 3083M 1 SoTT 16-5-42

K9935 147 FF FP 16-4-39 72S 19-4 dam by Bf109 over Channel F/Sgt Steere safe 5-10 58 OTU 9-3-41 stld dvd i/grd Ackl 14-4 SAL 18-4 SOC 30-4

K9936 148 FF GP 18-4-39 72S 21-4 FAC2 2-7-40 58 OTU 2-1-41 57 OTU 30-7 52 OTU 23-8 57 OTU 1-11 52 OTU 9-7-42 57 OTU 29-8-43 85GCS 10-5-44

K9937 149 FF 17-4-39 72S 19-4 cd/ld Chu Fen 30-6 SOC 21-7 rtp

K9938 150 FF GP 18-4-39 72S 21-4 s/dn a/c aban cd nr Herne Bay dbf Sgt Norfolk safe 2-9-40

K9939 152 FF 19-4-39 72S 21-4 AST 18-12 222S 31-8 s/dn by Bf 109 cd Northam P/O Edridge kld 30-10 (Edridge was s/dn 3 times in BoB)

K9940 153 FF 19-4-39 72S 24-4 FAC2 6-10-40 58 OTU 1-1-41 CGS 9-7 FAAC 27-12 53 OTU 27-11-43 FAAC 21-2-44 42 OTU 12-8 SOC 20-12

K9941 154 FF GP 21-4-39 72S 24-4 cd Hooton Roberts Yorks 21-8

K9942 155 FF GP 21-4-39 72S 24-4 FA 5-6-4- 7 OTU 17-8 57 OTU 17-8 FACB 6-2-42 53 OTU 10-4-43 RNDA 17-3-44 to 52MU for museum 28-8-44 RAF Museum Hendon as SD-V 8383M flown by F/O JB Nicholson VC extant 1984

K9943 156 FF GP 21-4-39 72S 24-4 MMOx 9-7 7 OTU 17-6-40 AST 22-11 to 3229M 13-3-41 5SoTT

K9944 157 FF 22-4-39 66S 27-4 Spcl Flt North 19-10 snow guard and eng trls 27-2-40 VHF radio trls Apl '40 comp ails trls with Curtiss H-75 Hawk and Gloster F.5/34 Hawk superior to Spit in dive attack and dogfight but Spit could break off comb due to higher speed 609S 4-6 54S 8-6 19S 17-6 66S 18-7 s/dn 5-9 F/Lt Christie inj SOC 11-11 FArn Aprl '41 trls with double trail edge flaps perforated with holes, later slots. Spoiler was fitt to tailplane. Trls with fabric ails which tended to reverse at high Mach numbers in dive . Lost effectiveness at 400mph. FH237.25

K9945 158 first a/c to have desig F.Mk.IA FF 22-44-39 66S 27-4 616S 15-11 AST 2-2-40 7 OTU 21-7 Farn Sept '40 FAC2 24-10 57 OTU 19-12 CGS 11-10 41 1 CRU 28-7-42 58 OTU 26-1-43 FACE 1-6 SOC 30-6

K9946 159 FF 24-4-39 66S 28-4 616S 17-11 e/fld cd f/ldg nr Catfoss 5-3-40 Farn Aug '40 SOC 16-8

K9947 160 FF GP 25-4-39 66S 28-4 616S 14-11 AST 2-6-40 610S 10-8 s/dn Sgt Gardner f/ld Wye 14-8 222S 23-9 58 OTU 9-2-41 CGS 9-7 222S cd f/ldg nr King's Lynn Norfolk CE 13-4-42 ASTH SOC

K9948 161 FF 26-4-39 66S 28-4 74S 2-5 616S 11-11 FTR ops 1-6-40 FH 244.50

K9949 162 FF 26-4-39 66S 28-4 hit obst night ldg Dxfd 1-6 FH26.50

K99450 163 FF 27-4-39 66S 2-5 616S 8-11 611S 3-6-40 GAL 7-6 dam ldg Sgt Burt safe 22-7 64S 29-9 fire in flight a/c aban over Turnbridge Wells Kent 28-11

K9951 164 FF GP 28-4-39 74S 2-5 92S 12-9-40 SAL 1-10 53 OTU 17-7 FAAC 28-1-42 53 OTU coll with P8249 ldg lland CE 27-5

K9952 165 FF GP 28-4-39 74S 2-5 FTR Dunk 24-5-40

K9953 166 FF 28-4-39 74S 2-5 92S 12-4-40 Farn June '40 pilot A. G. 'Sailor' Malan 7 OTU 1-11 FAAC 4-3-41 AST 10-3 57 OTU 16-6-42 air coll with R6883 cd nr Eshott CE 7-10-43

K9954 167 FF 1-5-39 54S 5-5 152S 27-12 dam ops 5-8-40 SOC 20-8

K9955 168 FF 1-5-39 54S 5-5 602S 8-11 dam ops f/ld 4-9-40 AST to 3267M 10SOTT SOC 18-9-44

K9956 170 FF 1-5-39 65S 6-5 603S 4-12 o/t in cd/ld Drem 17-4-40 AST SOC 13-5

K9957 171 FF 2-5-39 65S 6-5 74S 6-12 FTR Dunk 21-5

K9958 172 FF 2-5-39 73S 8-5 WAL 9-9-40 64S 2-10 53 OTU 16-7-41 cd/ld Llandow 9-9 ASTEx 15-9

K9959 173 FF 4-5-39 72S 8-5 1 CRU 26-8-40 1 PRU 9-10 e/fd cd F/ld Long Marston Herts 22-1-41

K9960 174 FF 3-5-39 10MU 6-5 610S 2-10 222S 17-6-40 610S 23-7 FA 17-8 72S 5-9 hit obst while taxy Croydon 7-9 a/c aban cd Orlestone Sgt Bell-Walker safe 14-9

All Spitfires from K9961 fitted DeH 3-blade 2-speed prop

K9961 178 FF 8-5-39 602S 10-5 AST 29-2-40 7 OTU 21-7 58 OTU -1-41 CGS 9-7 cd f/ldg Tern CAC 15-5-42 recat B recat E 26-5 FH297.55

K9962 175 FF 4-5-39 602S 8-5 AST 4-3-40 222S 3-9 s/dn by Bf109 cd West M Kent Sgt Ramshaw kld 4-9

K9963 176 FF 4-5-39 602S 8-5 AST 27-11 611S 4-6 234S 1-9 603S 6-9 C3 ops 5-10 SOC

K9964 179 FF 8-5-39 602S 10-5 1CRU 21-5-40 64S 14-8 s/dn nr Calais P/O Roberts safe POW 15-8

K9965 177 FF 5-5-39 602S 10-5 cd nr Glasgow on trnng flight 8-9 SOC 3-10

K9966 180 FF 8-5-39 602S 12-5 u/c clpse on t/o Abbots 8-7 SOC 15-8 rtp

K9967 181 FF 8-5-39 602s 10-5 w/u ldg MMOx 30-5 7 OTU 17-6-40 19S 3-9 7 OTU 10-9 cd/ldg Haw 14-9 C3 SOC 23-9

K9968 182 FF 9-5-39 602S 12-5 66S cd Dxfd 6-9 pilot kld SOC rtp

K9969 183 FF GP 10-5-39 602S 18-5 dam ops nr Southampton F/O Fergusson cd after striking HT cables CAC 18-8-40 1416Flt Hendon 3-4-41 140S 3-4 HAL 18-7-42 RN Arb 4-9 SOC 26-1-45

K9970 184 FF 10-5-39 602S 12-5 611S 4-6-40 w/u ldg Digby P/O Lund safe 28-7 1CRU3-8 610S 9-9 602S 14-12 e/fld Cd f/ldg nr West Kilbride CE 6-1-41 SOC 17-1

K9971 185 GP 11-5-39 602S 18-5 o/s ldg Chu Fen 18-7 SOC rtp

K9972 188 FF 11-5-39 602S 16-5 MMOx 23-9 7 OTU 22-7-40 FACB 28-8 57 OTU cd f/ld Rhyl N Wales dbf 25-4 SOC 10-5

K9973 189 FF GP 12-5-39 602S 16-5 MMOx 30-11 SOC 10-11-42

K9974 186 FF GP 12-5-39 602S 15-5 o/s ldg strk L1079 C3 26-11 SOC 16-1-40

K9975 187 FF 15-5-39 602S 18-5 AST 11-2-40 610S 14-9 222S 23-9 GAL 1-10 58 OTU 13-1-41 FAAC 4-2 57 OTU 29-5-42 dvd i/grd nr Slnd 29-5 CE

K9976 190 FF 15-5-39 602S 18-5 AST 14-11 5 OTU 4-6-40 7 OTU 21-8 FAC2 6-9 AST 25-2-41 53 OTU 21-7 spun i/grd nr Hemingstone Suffolk 11-9 SOC 18-9

K9977 191 FF 16-5-39 602S 18-5 lost wing during aerob cd Haddington E Lothian 30-12 Sgt Bailey kld SOC 11-2-40

K9978 192 FF 16-5-39 602S 18-5 out of fuel cd nr Dunbar E Lothian 2-3-40 SOC 13-5

K9979 197 FF 16-5-39 602S 22-5 ASTH 14-11 7 OTU 22-9 40 FAO cd B 25-9 52 OTU 31-10-41 CB ops 25-4-42 GAL 12-7 31SLG 12-12 52 OTU 3-6-43 58 OTU 21-6 FAAC 12-9-43 2CTW 20-10 1TEU 26-2-44 cd 25-5 SAL 12-8 CE 28-8

K9980 193 MIII 1st with MIII eng FF 16-5-39 611S 19-5 152S 15-2-40 FAC3 21-7 SOC 22-10 FH182.10

K9981 194 MIII FF 17-5-39 611S 19-5 AST 5-3-40 611S 4-6 7OTU 21-8 cd f/ldg River Dee nr Flint 12-9 SOC 3-10

K9982 195 MIII FF 17-5-39 611S 20-5 152S 9-20-40 s/dn off IoW 16.40hrs F/O Deanesley aban a/c inj 26-9 SOC

K9983 196 MIII FF 18-5-39 611S 20-5 616S 9-2-40 AST 17-5 7 OTU 16-8 FAC2 15-11 58 OTU 26-3-41 to 3275M 10SoTT 18-12-42 CE 3-8-44

K9984 198 MIII FF GP 19-5-39 611S 22-5 616S 9-2-40 FA 27-4 7 OTU 21-7 FAC2 21-9 SOC 3-10

K9985 199 MIII FF GP 19-5-39 611S 22-5 flew i/grd nr Wattisham 2-9 P/O Leech kld SOC FH54.30

K9986 200 MIII FF GP 20-5-39 66S 22-5 cd at night Dxfd 6-9 SOC 18-9

K9987 201 MIII FF 22-5-39 66S 23-5 cd/ld Dxfd 31-9 SOC FH53.90

K9988 202 MIII FF GP 23-5-39 66S 23-5 616S 14-11 CE SOC 16-3-40

K9989 203 MIII FF GP 23-5-39 66S 10-9 611S 9-2-40 FA 8-6 72S B Hill 9-9 coll with X4544 during scramble 09.35hrs P/O Sutton kld 5-10

K9990 204 MIII FF GP 23-5-39 66S 10-9 61S 30-11 52S s/dn by AA fire from British Convoy a/c aban off IoW 18-7-40 FH149.15

K9991 205 MIII FF GP 24-5-39 415S 8-9 64S 17-4-40 s/dn by Bf109 08.30hrs P/O Donahue safe C2 5-8 ASTH 57 OTU 1-11 t/o in coarse pitch Slnd hit bank CE 13-3-41 61 OTU 30-8 GAL 8-9 Port 18-9-43

K9992 206 MIII FF 24-5-39 74S 28-9 s/dn Dunk 31-5-40

K9993 207 MIII FF 24-5-39 66S 30-9 19S 30-11 FA 13-6-40 GAL 19-6 41S 10-9 222S 13-9 s/dn by Bf109 11.50 hrs P/O Assheton aban a/c Malden Surren 20-9

K9994 208 MIII FF 25-5-39 74S 28-9 ASTH 1-12 7 OTU 18-6 FA 5-7 AST 65S 20-10 57 OTU 28-11 f/ld Prestatyn N Wales 8-6-41 SOC E Oct '41

K9995 209 MIII FF 26-5-39 504S 2-11 603S 6-11 C2 ops 19-7-40 1CRU 602S 19-8 65S 27-8 FA 27-8 COAL 57 OTU hit grd fly low off Dee Estuary 8-6 ROS 57 OTU 6-9 FACE ttl wrk 21-9 SOC 14-10

K9996 210 MIII FF GP 31-5-39 504S 2-11 603S 6-11 AST 15-11 266S 17-8-40 616S 7-9 57 OTU 4-4-41 FACB 26-3 cd on t/o Haw e/fld CE 30-7 SOC 9-8

K9997 211 MIII FF 1-6-39 504S 2-11 603S 6-11 AST 6-1-40 FACB 17-4 609S 4-6 dam e/a 12-8 7 OTU 5-10 SAL 22-4-41 53 OTU 17-7 ROS 20-9 cd CE 24-1-42

K9998 212 MIII FF 1-6-39 504S 2-11 603S 6-11 AST 24-2-40 92S 2-7 7 OTU 1-11 WAL 4-11 7 OTU 4-11 57 OTU FACB 16-8-41 cd/ld Haw 26-8 1CRU to 2822M 6 SoTT 27-12 SOC 4-12

K9999 213 MIII FF 1-6-39 10MU 5-6 611S 18-9 152S 15-2-40 s/dn by Ju88 off IoW 12-8

L-series all F Mk IA Merlin III unless otherwise indicated

L1000 214 FF 2-6-39 10MU 7-6 610S 2-10 s/dn by AA fire nr Hawk 10-7-40 GAL 7 OTU 15-9 AST 22-2-41 140S 1-7 1CRU 6-7 82MU 7-11-42 *Taran* Port Sudan 29-1-43

L1001 215 FF 2-6-39 10MU 7-6 610S 3-10 74S 28-5-40 616S 28-9 FAC2 5-10 57 OTU 4-1-41 3 SofGR 25-4-42 8 OTU 24-5 FACB 19-9 LMS 21-9 57 OTU 25-4-43 SAL 14-8-44 SOC 16-8

L1002 216 FF 5-6-39 10MU 7-6 602S C2 ops 10-9-40 602S 24-9 dam night ladg 27-9 58 OTU 29-1-41 coll with Miles Master nr Grangemouth dbf 10-3 SOC 21-3

L1003 217 FF 5-6-39 10MU 7-6 610S 7-10 FTR ops 27-5-40 FH114.10

L1004 218 FF 5-6-39 10MU 7-6 602S GAL 12-9 58 OTU 13-1-41 SAL 2-6 con to F VA M45 57 OTU 6-8-41 FACB 26-8 ASTH 5-9 HAL 4-8-42 inst cameras and accessories VA 10-12 con to PRXIII 2nd proto Hal 16-2-43 mods BDn March '43 Mer 32 wts and CG load, cool trls with trop mods. Climb and level speed and dvng trls. HAL 14-5-43 VSM 15-5 con to Sea MkIII proto RNDA 3-3-44 HAL 23-5-44 SOC 28-3-45

L1005 219 FF 7-6-39 10MU 12-6 602S 24-9 C2 ops 18-8-40 57 OTU 23-10 AST 13-4-41 SOC 9-12

L1006 220 FF 6-6-39 10MU 12-6 610S 2-10 FTR ops 29-5-40 SOC June '40

L1007 233 FF 15-6-39 AMDP 21-6 2 × 20mm can inst VA BDn 21-6 hand and perf trls 603S AFDU Oct'39 65S 5-11 609S 18-4-40 as proto Mk IB 72S Drem s/dn Heinkel over Scotland January 1940 SOC E 28-5 See page 58 for details.

L1008 221 FF 7-6-39 10MU 14-6 610S 2-10 AST 28-12 609S 8-6-40 FArn June '40 pilot F/Lt J. Dundas. F/ld nr Glastonbury. Sgt Hughes-Rees sfe 25-9 C2 AST to 3242M 6 SoTT 11-3-41

L1009 222 FF 7-6-39 10MU 14-6 610S 3-10 92S 18-10 C2 ops 14-8-40 7 OTU 1-11 57 OTU 1-11 e/fld u/s in f/ld Slnd 2-5-41 53 OTU 18-8-41 FACB 26-8 AST SOC Oct '41

L1010 223 FF 8-6-39 10MU 13-6 610S 3-10 222S 26-6-40 202S glycol leak Sgt Johnson aban a/c 07.30hrs 3-9

L1011 224 FF 9-6-39 10MU 12-6 610S 4-10 dam ops 29-5-40 266S 17-8 41S 17-9 222S 18-9 AST 5-11 to 3236M 6SoTT 27-3-41 CE SOC 25-11-44

L1012 225 FF 10-6-39 5MU 13-6 616S 7-11 o/s runway C2 30-8-40 AST 5-9 57 OTU 15-11 AST 4-12 5SoTT 11-3-41 FACB 6-5-42 dam ops 28-8 SOC 30-9 to 3223M 5SoTT 24-1-44 rtp

L1013 226 FF 12-6-39 5MU 14-6 164S 610S 3-10 dam ops 1-6-40 SOC FH153.55

L1014 227 FF 12-6-39 5MU 14-6 610S 4-10 FAAC 16-4-40 MMOx 92S 14-9 7OTU 1-11 58 OTU 7-6-41 53 OTU 14-9 spun out of cloud cd Skirrid Abergavenny CE 8-3-42

L1015 228 FF 13-6-39 5MU 16-6 610S 4-10 AST 15-1-40 5 OTU 7-7 to 3253M 7SoTT 26-3-41 SOC 22-5-44

L1016 229 FF 14-6-39 6MU 16-6 610S 4-10 FTR 27-5 SOC 1-7 FH185.15

L1017 230 FF 15-6-39 5MU 19-6 610S 4-10 AST 31-5-40 603S 1-9 AST 6-9 7 OTU 28-9 FAC2 10-10 AST to 3206M 4SoTT 11-3-41 CE 23-9-44

L1018 231 FF 14-6-39 602S 17-6 FAC2 28-1-40 5 OTU 13-7 19S 3-9 7 OTU 10-9 SAL 25-9 58 OTU 4-1-41 FAAC 17-3 SOC 28-5

L1019 232 FF 15-6-39 602S 24-6 s/dn by Ju87 nr Portsmouth 14.37hrs Sgt Whall safe 18-8 SOC 29-10 FH209.40

L1020 234 FF 16-6-39 20MU 20-6 603S 15-9 CE ops 6-9-40 SOC 21-9

L1021 235 FF 16-6-39 20MU 26-6 603S 15-9 s/dn f/ld nr Lympne P/O Hillary safe 29-8-40 57 OTU 4-4-43 57 OTU 18-11 CE SOC 6-3-45

L1022 236 FF 19-6-39 20MU 26-6 603S 15-9 SOC April'40

L1023 237 FF 17-6-39 20MU 26-6 603S 15-9 std cd in finals Turn 7-10 ttl wrk SOC

L1024 238 FF 17-6-39 20MU 26-6 603S 15-9 dam ops 1-9-40 57 OTU 23-10 FACC 9-5-41 52 OTU 16-5-42 AEAF Com Flt 20-1-44 SOC 2-6-47

L1025 239 FF 20-6-39 20MU 26-6 603S 15-9 u/c jam after hvy touch & go ldg a/c aban CE 26-4-40 SOC 6-5

L1026 240 FF 20-6-39 20MU 20-6 603S 15-9 lost in fog flew i/grd Slains Aberdeen 19-3-40

L1027 241 FF 22-6-39 20MU 29-6 19S 8-10 602S 21-12 s/dn by Bf110 16.14hrs P/O Rose inj 11-9-40 53 OTU 17-7-41 stld cd/ld Lland CE 28-9 SOC 4-10

L1028 242 FF 21-6-39 66S 26-6 616S 11-11 ASTH 2-2-40 7 OTU 16-8 FAAC 6-2-41 AST con to FVA M45 145S 26-11 134S 20-12 133S 28-12 134S 31-12 133S 2-1-42 58MU 16-1 FACB WAL 16-1 VSM 24-10-42 fuel system mods wing stiff 52 OTU 11-9-43 FLS 2-2-44 57 OTU 8-9 FACB 21-4-45 recat E SOC 22-4

L1029 243 FF 22-6-39 19S 29-6 64S 25-7-40 s/sdn by bf109 over Kent 08.40hrs Sgt Isaaca kld 5-8

L1030 244 FF 23-6-39 19S 3-7 w/u ldg Dxfd 8-6-40 64S 14-9 57 OTU 3-2-41 AST 3-4 57 OTU 20-7 1CRU 8-10 SOC 4-12

L1031 245 FF 23-6-39 19S 29-6-39 19S dam ops 26-5-40 222S 3-9 58 OTU 5-2-41 FACB 10-2 AST con to FVA M45 57 OTU 28-7 ASTEx 6-8 322S 7-2-42 164S 22-4 strk P7498 on grd Skae 14-8 61 OTU 21-6-43 FACB 8-7 1CRU 15-7 FACE SOC 25-1-45

L1032 246 FF 26-6-39 19S 29-6 dam ops 19-6-40 SOC E 24-6 FH195

L1033 247 FF 26-6-39 611S 1-7 64S 19-3-40 cd night ldg Ken CE 19-5

L1034 248 FF 28-6-39 611S 30-6 616S 19-2-40 57 OTU 4-1-41 FA bt CE 12-3 FH383

L1035 249 FF 27-6-39 611S 30-6 64S 19-3-40 s/dn by Bf109 off Kent coast 18.00hrs S/Lt Dawson-Paul died later 25-7 FH191.10

L1036 250 FF 28-6-39 611S 30-6 616 9-2-40 i/sea after combat Ju88 no fuel 10.40hrs Sgt Iveson rescued 16-9

251 French Air Force 0-1 FF 25-5-39 del date 18-7 flown under B Condition marks as N.21. See page 76 for further details

L1037 252 FF 29-5-39 611S 4-7-39 64S 29-2-40 FAC 27-7 610S B H 11 s/dn by Bf109 cd Fyfield P/O Merrick inj 24-8 610S 30-8 FAC3 30-9 SOC E 7-10

L1038 253 FF 29-6-39 611S 4-7 64S 29-2-40 in f/ldg Hawk after comb Bf109 over South Coast Sgt Mann inj C2 16-8 53 OTU 23-7-41 FACC 29-12 AST recat E 20-5-42

L1039 254 FF 29-6-39 611S 4-7 64S 29-2-40 s/dn by Bf109 nr Dover P/O Kennard-Davis aban a/c & died of wounds dbf 8-8 SOC 17-8

L1040 255 FF 30-6-39 602S 10-7 dam by Bf109 nr Dunge Sgt Elcombe safe 31-8 cd Bognor racecourse after patrol Sgt Elcombe safe 10-9 C/E

L1041 256 FF 30-6-39 41S 6-7 54S 29-5-40 66S 21-6 GAL 8-8 222S 2-10 58 OTU 5-2-41 SAL 23-6 53 OTU 27-8 FACE cd/ld 28-9 SOC 9-10

L1042 257 FF 3-7-39 41S 6-7 54S 29-5-40 19S 19-6 54S 26-7 7 OTU 25-9 FACE 11-2-41 57 OTU 29-7 cd in snow storm Hill Farm Pilton Cheshire dbf 7-12 SOC 12-12

L1043 258 FF 3-7-39 19MU 7-7 610S 6-12 266S 18-6 7 OTU 9-9 57 OTU FAC2 24-9 SOC 18-8-41

L1044 259 FF 4-7-39 19MU 7-7 610S 3-10 s/dn New Romney ops P/O Smith aban a/c safe 12-8-40

L1045 260 FF GP 5-7-39 610S 3-10 dam by bf109 8-8-40 ASTH 14-8 9FPP downwind ldg o/s Squires Gate o/t 29-12 CE SOC 8-1-41

L1046 261 FF GP 5-7-39 603S 20-9 FTR ops P/O Macdonald miss 28-2-40

L1047 262 FF GP 5-7-39 603S 18-9 L1059 ld on L1047 whilst it was taxy at Grange pilot kld 1-10 SOC

L1048 263 FF 7-7-39 19MU 11-7 603S 18-9 FA 13-6-40 152S 28-9 609S 28-9 152S 3-10 cd/ld nr Torquay 3-10 DGRD VA 20-12 RAF North 23-12 to 3248M 7SoTT 14-3-41 SL Tng Com 4-5-44 rtp 18-5

L1049 264 FF 6-7-39 19MU 11-7 603S 18-9 dam ops 18-7-40 602S 23-9 57 OTU 24-10 FAC2 16-12 cd/ld Speke to 3876M 1SoTT 26-3-41 ASTH 22-7-44 CE 38

L1050 265 FF GP 7-9-39 9MU 12-7 603S 19-9 FA cd Balerno Midlothian CE 12-6-40 SOC 19-6

L1051 266 FF GP 7-7-39 9MU 12-7 611S 9-9 i/sea nr East Dudgeon light-ship after comb 31-3-40

L1052 267 FF GP 10-7-39 9MU 13-7 611S 9-9 64S 17-4-40 FTR ops 29-5

L1053 268 FF 11-7-39 9MU 13-7 611S 9-9 64S 19-3-40 FTR ops 1-6

L1054 269 FF 11-7-39 9MU 17-7 611S 9-9 152S 15-2-40 FAC2 7-8 58 OTU 28-12 53 OTU 15-9-41 i/sea off Llantwitmajor Glam 25-9

L1055 270 FF 12-7-39 9MU 17-7 66S 22-9 616S 15-11 AST 6-4-40 64S 2-7 C2 ops 18-7 ROS dam by Ju88 off Dover S/Ldr McDonnell safe 25-7 HAL 2-10 1PRU Benson 9-10 cd on t/o in coarse pitch CE 5-3-41 SOC 10-3

L1056 271 FF 13-7-39 72S 24-7 SAL 8-1-40 C3 ops 31-2 57 OTU 16-8 72S s/dn by bf110 f/ld Sgt Pocock inj 1-9 57 OTU 6-9-41 VA 22-11 45SLG 21-5-42 57 OTU 2-7 FACE coll with P8342 20-6-43 RNDA 23-1-44

L1057 272 FF GP 13-7-39 603S 16-9 SAL 22-9-40 SOC 5-4-41 to 2644M 12SoTT 13-7-42 SOC 12-4-45

L1058 273 FF 14-7-39 27MU 22-7 603S 6-9 FTR ops 1-6-40 SOC 8-6

L1059 274 FF 14-7-39 27MU 22-7 603S 16-9 cd on to L1047 whilst ldg Grange 1-10 AST 30-11 266S 4-6-40 strk building ldg Wittering C2 Sgt Eade safe 9-8 1CRU 17-10 58 OTU 29-1-41 dvdi/grd Slamannan Stirling dbf 14-2 SOC 21-2

L1060 275 FF 15-7-39 609S 6-9 o/s ldg strk L1082 & bowser 21-11 AST 3-12 7 OTU 27-7-40 SOC 7-9

L1061 276 FF 15-7-39 27MU 22-7 603S 16-9 e/fld cd/ld Prestwick 13-1-40 ASTH 7 OTU 26-10 1CRU 21-4 53 OTU 23-7 AST 29-9-42 con to F.VA M45 9-2-43 61 OTU 8-5 CE 30-6-44

L1062 277 FF 17-7-39 7MU 27-7 603S 16-9 610S 30-9 FTR ops 29-5-40 FH 97.40

L1063 278 FF 18-7-39 27MU 22-7 609S 6-9 AST 12-6-40 5 OTU 21-7 FAC3 dbf 10-8 SOC 15-8

L1064 279 FF 19-7-39 27MU 25-7 609S 6-9 u/c jam a/c aban cd Crook of Alves Moray 7-1-40 SOC 16-1

L1065 280 FF 20-7-39 27MU 25-7 609S 6-9 7 OTU 5-11-40 FACB 28-8-41 SAL 4-9 53 OTU 2-6-42 57 OTU 6-5-44 to Ins AF 25-6-47

L1066 281 FF 21-7-39 36MU for packing & despatch to Poland diverted when Germany overran country. To Turkey as Type 341 19-8 deleted from original RAF contract. Sent to docks 19-8

L1067 282 FF 20-7-39 27MU 26-7 603S 16-9 s/dn by bf110s S/Ldr Denholm aban a/c safe 30-8-40

L1068 284 FF 24-7-39 27MU 31-7 609S 6-9 FA 25-5-40 MMOx 64S 14-8 dam by AA fire P/O Simpson inj C2 16-8 AST to 3259M 8SoTT 14-3-41 11SoTT 10-5-42

L1069 s283 FF 21-7-39 27MU 25-7 609S 3-9 FTR after comb over Portland F/Lt Barran died 11-7-40

L1070 285 FF 24-7-39 27MU 26-7 603S 16-9 C2 ops 1-9-40 57 OTU 25-10 FAAC 23-7-41 GAL 7-10 SOC 29-12

L1071 286 FF 26-7-39 27MU 31-7 609S 6-9 NMOx 29-3-40 5 OTU 7-7 FAC2 9-9 58 OTU 14-1-41 FACC 22-11 ROS recat E 28-4-43

L1072 287 FF 27-7-39 54S 14-8 152S 27-12 s/dn by bf110 nr Portsmouth Sgt Reddington kld 30-9-40

L1073 288 FF 9-8-39 41S 15-8 64S 2-5-40 FAAC 21-4 SAL 24-9 53 OTU 8-4-41 AST 4-9 SOC 1-9-43

L1074 292 24MU 18-8-39 610S 5-10 43Grp 28-12 SOC CE 29-12

L1075 289 FF 10-8-39 24MU 14-8 610S 5-10 603S 17-10 FTR ops 9-7

L1076 290 FF 11-8-39 24MU 14-8 610S 5-10 AST 7-7-40 603S 1-9 s/dn by Bf109 F/Lt MacDonald kld 28-9

L1077 291 FF GP 12-8-39 72S 15-8 FA 2-6-40 92S 28-8 s/dn by Bf109 P/O Saunders inj 9-9

L1078 293 FF 15-8-39 72S 17-8 cd/ld Ack C3 6-8-40 SOC 14-8

L1079 294 FF GP 16-8-39 602S 18-8 stk by K9974 Drem w/o 16-11 SOC 12-1-40

L1080 297 FFGP 16-8-39 611S 23-8 coll with K9974 ldg at Drem 26-11 92S 3-6-40 FAC2 19-8 1PRU Benson 2-10 C2 ops 2-11 57 OTU 7-8-41 FACB 11-11 St Flt Atcham 13-6-42 53 OTU 7-8 FACB 8-8 SOC 18-8

L1081 295 FF 17-8-39 609S 19-8 FTR 31-5-40

L1082 296 FF 17-8-39 609S 19-8 dam by L1060 Drem 21-11 609S s/dn by Bf110 nr Ryde IoW P/O Mamedoff safe 24-8-40 58 OTU 29-1-41 57OTU 30-7 FA ttl wrk 22-8 SOC 2-9

L1083 298 FF 19-8-39 609S 29-8 54S 8-6-40 66S 21-6 Farn 13-7 72S 23-7 222S 4-12 72S 5-2-41 FACB 12-3 58OTU 21-8 FTR 11-11

L1084 299FF GP 22-8-39 609S 29-8 74S 9-5-40 FTR over France 27-5

L1085 300 FF GP 22-8-39 609S 29-8 1CRU 27-5-40 SOC CE 19-6 FH178.35

L1086 301 FF 22-8-9 609S 29-8 cd Great Oakley on ops CE 30-5-40 SOC 7-6

L1087 302 FF GP 23-8-39 609S 27-8 FTR ops 31-5-40

L1088 303 FF 24-8-39 609S 29-8-39 MMOx 18-9 610S dam by L1074 16-10 266S 4-6-40 FAC2 18-8 57 OTU 23-10 FA dbf 17-6 SOC 22-6

L1089 304 FF 25-8-39 20MU 29-8- 19-S -10 74S 12-12 222S 4-9-40 dam ops 15-10 AST 22-10 to 3178M 2SoTT 20-3-44 SOC 16-2-45

L1090 305 FF 24-8-39 36MU Sealand 29-8 shipped to USAAC Wright Field Dayton Ohio. Trans to No 1 Testing Centre RCAF Canada May '40. Ret to UK 1-8-40 to 3201M 14SoTT 13-5-44 CE 4-9

L1091 306 FF 30-8-39 20MU 4-9 65-S 16-9 u/s hit fence CE SOC 26-4-40

L1092 307 FF 31-8-39 20MU 4-9 72S 16-9 C2 ops 1-9-40 to 3230M 9SoTT 14-4-41 SOC 30-9-42

L1093 308 FF 30-8-39 41S 2-9 54S 29-5-40 SOC16-7

L1094 309 FF 2-9-39 65S 6-9 dam ops 8-8-40 dam by Bf109 22-8 610S 27-10 dvd i/grd on ops Cd Edlingham Northumb C3 4-11 AST SOC 12-11

L1095 310 FF 4-9-39 alloc 609S 6-9 AMDP Farn 12-6-40 replacement trls a/c for K9944. Fairoaks, for medical research trls 20-6 609S FTR ops aban over Portland P/O Mitchell miss i/sea 11-7

L1096 311 FF GP 5-9-39 609S 7-9 AST 7-11-40 58 OTU 28-12 FACB 7-3-41 53 OTU 17-7 RNDA 4-9-42 con to F.VA M45 RNAS Yeov as train

Of a total of 96 aircraft constructed, over 50% were damaged by enemy action, 40 were involved in accidents.

Second order for 200 Spitfire Mk I dated September 1938. Built as Mk I variants between September 1939 and January 1940. Total built 199. N-series all F.Mk IA Merlin III unless otherwise indicated. Deliveries stated 8th September 1939. N3023 to N3072, 3091 to 3130 3160 to 3203, 3221 to 3250, 3264 to 3296, 3298 to 3299.

N3023 312 FF 6-9-39 609S 8-9 s/dn over Weymouth Bay by Bf109 P/O Buchanan kld 27-7-40 FH 219.05

N3024 313 FF 7-9-39 609S 11-9 FTR ops 14-8 F/O McD Goodwin miss

N3025 314 FF 8-9-39 609S 11-9 u/s ldg Drem 19-3-40 SOC E 13-5

N3026 315 FF 9-9-39 72S 11-9 603S 21-2-40 cd/ld Montrose S/Ldr Montrose safe 23-7 303S 10-9-41 61 OTU 2-10 ROS 28-11 52 OTU 9-6-42 dvd i/grd nr Nailsworth Glos dbf SOC E 8-11 F/S Booth kid.

N3028 317 FF 11-9-39 9MU 15-9 66S 28-9 FTR Dunk 2-6-40

N3029 318 FF GP 13-9-39 9MU 15-9 66S 28-9 s/dn by Bf109 P/O Mathers safe C2 5-9-40 cd/ld nr Graves Sgt Willcocks safe C3 14-9 SOC 1-10 12MU 5-3-41 FA 24-4-42 76MU 15-10 *Pet Mear* 18-11 lost at sea 8-1-43 FH 247.10

N3030 319 FF 13-9-39 9MU 7-10 19S 3-10 54S 10-1-40 FTR ops 27-5

N3031 320 FF 14-9-39 9MU 18-9 66S 30-11 cd Wilbraham Cambs CE 14-12 SOC 18-12

N3032 321 FF GP 14-9-39 9MU 18-9 66S 27-9 s/dn by Bf109 C2 4-9-40 92S 19-9 dam by Bf109 nr Dover f/ld Mans P/O Sherrington safe 21-9 GAL 12-10 Farn Feb'41 to 3184M 2SoTT 20-3 SOC 28-9-46

N3033 322 FF 18-9-39 19MU 21-9 66S 10-10 FTR Dunk 2-6-40

N3034 323 FF 18-9-39 19MU 21-9 66S 30-9 MMOx 29-3-40 7 OTU FAC2 9-8 7SoTT 14-3-41 CE 11-9-44

N3035 324 FF 16-9-39 19MU 18-9 66S 10-10 dam ops 29-9-40 57 OTU 30-7-41 FAAC 4-8-42 58 OTU 16-1-43 remains found at Craighorn Alva Clackmannan CE 14-8 SOC 30-9

N3036 325 FF 18-9-39 19MU 21-9 66S 10-10 54MU 16-1-40 SOC E 29-1

N3037 326 FF GP 20-9-39 19MU 21-9 66S 10-10 FA 28-5-40 7 OTU 27-7 FAC2 23-11 SAL 5-12 53 OTU 17-7 FACE 17-12 SOC 29-12

N3038 327 FF 20-9-39 24MU 22-9 41S 27-9 s/dn by Bf109 nr Dover F/O Gamblen kld 29-7-40

N3039 328 FF 20-9-39 24MU 22-9 257S 21-5-40 7 OTU 17-6 19S 3-9 152S 26-9 s/dn f/ld WDn P/O Akroyd(died 8-10) 7-10

N3040 329 FF 21-9-39 RAF Dxfd 22-9 19S 30-11 VAEA 2-1-40 RAF Dxfd 11-1 service trls of fairings to cut exhaust glare at night 19S 15-3 92S 22-7 s/dn in transit by Ju88 nr Tonbridge a/c aban F/Lt Stanford Tuck safe CE 18-8

N3041 330 FF 22-9-39 8MU 27-9 66S 9-11 i/sea on ops 24-7-40 FH 187.56

N3042 331 FF 23-9-39 8MU 27-9 66S 9-11 cd off Orford 29-7-40 SOC 7-8

N3043 332 FF GP 24-9-39 8MU 27-9 66S 5-11 s/dn P/O Allen safe 5-9-40 AST 8-9 66S 24-9 s/dn Bf109 cd Rochester Kent Sgt Ward kld 8-10

N3044 333 FF GP 25-9-39 8MU 27-9 66S 5-11 FAAC 16-4-40 f/ld nr Billericay F/Lt Dunworth inj 4-9 65S 6-11 145S 19-1-41 118S 8-3 FACB 10-5 61 OTU 21-8 9MU 30-11-44

N3045 334 FF GP 26-9-39 8MU 27-9 66S 5-11 AST 16-2-40 7 OTU 21-7 61 OTU 4-7-41 57 OTU 17-6-42 53 OTU 26-7-43 FAAC 21-12 RNDA 12-6-44 SOC E 14-10

N3046 339 FF 27-9-39 8MU 30-9 66S 18-11 AST 2-5-40 7 OTU 22-7 19S 10-9 1CRU 13-9 222S 31-10 57 OTU 10-5-41 out of fuel cd/ld S l nd 17-5 SOC Oct'41

N3047 335 FF GP 27-9-39 8MU 30-9 66S 30-10 FTR ops 2-6-40

N3048 336 FF 27-9-39 8MU 30-9 66S 5-11 s/dn by Bf109 Sgt Smith aban a/c(died 6-9) 4-9-40

N3049 337 FF GP 28-9-39 8MU 30-9 66S 30-10 s/dn by Bf109 over Cowden Kent P/O Corbett aban a/c safe

N3050 338 FF GP 28-9-39 8MU 30-9 611S 1-3-40 AST 2-6 7 OTU 16-7 cd f/ld nr Chester dbf 29-10 SOC 11-11

N3051 340 FF GP 29-9-39 8MU 2-10 611S 1-3-40 7 OTU 21-8 FAC2 16-10 57 OTU ROS 15-8-41 61 OTU 31-1-43 FAAC 26-2-43 57 OTU 13-6 SOC 20-6-47

N3052 341 FF GP 30-9-39 8MU 2-10 611S 1-3-40 GAL 18-5 7 OTU 21-8 61 OTU 28-6-41 FACB 13-5-42 57 OTU 4-3-43 cd f/ld Red House Farm Northumb 16-6-44

N3053 342 FF GP 1-10-39 24MU 5-10 611S 25-1-40 AMDP Farn 11-6 eng & flame damping on exhaust manifolds. Fought numerous defence actions during BoB while trls a/c. R-RH 18-9 RAF Digby 2-11 R-RH 16-1-41 con to F.VA M45 & TR1133, FF as FVA 13-2 DGRD BDn 1-3 comp trls with P7661(VA); AB488 (F VC with low boost eng); X4922 (F VA Trop) and X4942 (prot FV1). 12-3 brief perf trls. R-R 15-4 dev trls. BDn 28-4 brief perf trls with 4-blade Rotol prop. Cd/ldg 15-3-42 ASTEx CE. Repaired 9-4 recat E SOC 12-9

N3054 343 FF 2-10-39 24MU 5-10 611S 25-1-40 AST 2-6 fitt TR1133 57 OTU 14-7 7 OTU 13-8 57 OTU 30-7-41 FACB 21-11 ASTEx recat E SOC 8-12

N3055 344 FF 3-10-39 fitt TR1133 24MU 5-10 611S 25-1-40 FTR ops 2-6

N3056 345 FF GP 2-10-39 24MU 5-10 611S 25-1-40 dam on ops 2-6 603S 20-7 s/dn by Bf109 nr Maids Sgt Stokoe aban a/c inj 2-9 FH 151.25

N3057 346 FF 3-10-39 24MU 4-10 611S 25-1-40 dam by signal flare while taxy Digby 30-5 234S 29-8 58 OTU 23-3-41 234S u/s ldg Grange CE 31-7 SOC 9-8

N3058 347 FF 4-10-39 24MU 7-10 611S 25-1-40 dam on ops 2-6 610S 26-8 dam C2 24-9 111S 3-5-41 58 OTU 30-5 52 OTU 17-7-42 53 OTU 16-2-43 61 OTU 17-1-44 SOC 6-3-45

N3059 348 FF 5-10-39 27MU 7-10 611S 25-1-40 41S 27-8 s/dn by Bf110 over Thames Estuary Sgt Hewitt safe 11-9 64S 15-12 58 OTU 29-3-41 AST 4-4 con to F.VA M45 8 OTU 8-6-43 FA FTR 10-11

N3060 349 FF 4-10-39 27MU 7-10 611S 25-1-40 66S 28-8 s/dn by Bf109 F/O King aban a/c 5-9 FH 158.00

N3061 350 FF 6-10-39 27MU 10-10 611S 15-2-40 234S 29-8 s/dn off Weymouth Bay P/O Horton aban a/c inj 6-9 FH 194.25

N3062 351 FF 6-10-39 27MU 10-10 611S 15-2-40 FAC2 22-7 57 OTU i/sea off Caernarvon 28-7-41

N3063 353 FF 7-10-39 27MU 10-10 611S 15-2-40 a/c aban on night flight cd Kilvington Notts. 27-4-40

N3064 352 FF GP 5-10-39 27MU 10-10 611S 15-2-40 FTR ops 2-6 FH 77.30

N3065 354 FF GP 8-10-39 611S 16-3-40 Farn June'40 7 OTU 22-8 FAAC 19-1-41 52 OTU a/c aban cd Longhope on Main Glos CE 2-6-42

N3066 355 FF 9-10-39 9MU 11-10 611S 16-3-40 616S 29-8 out of fuel f/ld Broughton C2 Sgt Ivey safe 18-10 616S 26-2-41 65S 26-2 308S 13-4 403S 27-5 57 OTU 26-7 FACE 2-11 SOC 15-11

N3067 356 FF 9-10-39 9MU 12-10 611S 16-3-40 7 OTU 22-8 o/s ldg Haw 18-10 to 2303M 29-10

N3068 357 FF 10-10-39 611S 16-3-40 602S 31-8 72S 6-9 s/dn by Bf109 nr Sevenoaks F/O Davies-Cooke kld C3 27-9 FH 73.00

N3069 358 FF 10-10-39 6MU 12-10 PDU HAL con to PRIII Farn 20-10 for hand trls FA 1-8-40 SOC Aug'40

N3070 359 FF 11-10-39 6MU 16-10 54S 18-11 611S 16-12 616S 27-8-40 72S 2-9 s/dn by Bf109 nr Maids P/O Elliott aban a/c safe 6-9

N3071 360 FF 11-10-39 27MU 12-10 BDn 25-10 comp trls with K9793. PDU HAL con to PRII(2xF.24 vert cameras, one per wing, pale green Camotint overall). Farn for trls. 212(PR)S May'40 first PR Spit on ops, sortie to Aachen, Germany 18-11-39 from Lille, France. Housed in hangar 'Special Survey Flight', second sortie 20-11

N3072 361 FF GP 12-10-39 6MU 12-10 54S 18-11 611S 18-12 7 OTU 23-8-40 FAC2 13-11 AST to 3258M 11SoTT 8-5-42

N3091 362 FF 12-10-39 6MU 16-10 P&P 3-1-40 74S s/dn over Kent F/Lt Brezezina aban a/c safe 13-8 FH 153.35

N3092 363 FF GP 13-10-39 6MU 16-10 266S 19-1-40 FTR Dunk 2-6 FH 97.30

N3093 364 FF 13-10-39 6MU 16-10 616S 8-1-40 72S 2-9 s/dn by Bf109 over Tunbridge Wells dbf Sgt Gray kld 5-9

N3094 365 FF 14-10-39 8MU 19-10 266S 12-2-40 FA 13-4 72S 2-9 dam ops C2 14-9 57 OTU 23-8-41 53 OTU 26-3-43 SOC 2-6-47

N3095 366 FF 14-10-39 8MU 19-10 266S 12-2-40 s/dn nr Addisham Canterbury P/O Bowen kld 16-8

N3096 367 FF 16-10-39 8MU 23-11-39 54S 1-3-40 FTR 25-5

N3097 368 FF 16-10-39 8MU 19-10-39 54S 17-12 1CRU 14-3-40 54S 19-6 s/dn by Bf109 i/sea off Dover Sgt Lawrence safe 15-8

N3098 369 FF 17-10-39 8MU 17-10 611S 21-1-40 41S 21-1 s/dn f/ld Standford le Hope Sgt Carr-Lewty safe 5-9 61 OTU 28-6-41 FACB 24-7 AST con to F.VA M45

N3099 370 FF 17-10-39 8MU 19-10 611S 21-1-40 41S 21-1 FA 13-7 603S 29-9 266S 17-10 111S 8-4-41 58 OTU 29-5 FACE dbf 10-8 SOC

N3100 371 FF GP 18-10-39 9MU 19-10 41S 19-3-40 C23 ops 21-7 603S 18-9 266S 17-10 111S 8-4-41 58 OTU 29-5 air coll with P9545 cd nr Abernethy Perth 21-4-42 RNAS 19-5-43 dbr SOC 26-1-45

N3101 372 FF 18-10-39 9MU 19-10 65S 2-4-40 234S 17-2-41 FTR 2-3

N3102 381 FF 24-10-39 9MU 29-10-39 41S 19-3-40 CE SOC 23-4

N3103 373 FF 19-10-39 9MU 23-10 54S 10-12 FTR ops 25-5

N3104 374 FF 19-10-39 9MU 23-10 54S 10-12 strk disp bay ldg Horn CE 9-1-40 SOC 29-1-43

N3105 375 FF 20-10-39 9MU 23-10 603S 11-4-40 s/dn cd P/O Benson kld C3 28-8

N3106 376 FF 20-10-39 24MU 23-10 222S 10-3-40 66S 10-3 AST 1-6 5 OTU 14-7 FAC2 11-8 AST 92S 15-10 C3 ops dbf 10-11 SOC 18-12 FH 198.10

N3107 377 FF 21-10-39 24MU 25-10 41S 22-3-40 FTR ops 1-6

N3108 378 FF GP 21-10-39 41S 22-3-40 FA 14-5 AST 64S 24-10 303S 22-1-41 dam ops 25-2 AST 25-2 DGRD Farn 17-4 gunnery & ails trls cd during trls 22-6 AST SOC 2-7

N3109 379 FF 23-10-39 24MU 25-10 602S 24-12 603S 5-10 s/dn by Bf109 nr Godmersham Park F/O Matthews kld 7-10 FH 195.30

N3110 380 FF GP 23-10-39 24MU 25-10 54S 14-12 1CRU 13-3-40 54S 20-8 des by bombs on t/o pilot safe 31-8 SOC 10-9

N3111 382 FF GP 24-10-39 54S 13-12 AST 10-7-40 PRU Heston 23-8 con to PRII Type C Farn April '41 for camera tls HAL 11-6 con to PRV PRU Benson 21-6 R-RH M45 instal 27-7 FACB 21-4-42 543S 30-9 cd Worlington Devon dbf 27-2-43. Was named "The Brest Express" and con to FVA

N3112 383 FF GP 24-10-39 27MU 27-10 41S 1-3-40 s/dn by Bf109 C2 29-7 616S f/ld Broughton Sgt Ivey safe C2 18-11 AST 25-11

N3113 384 FF GP 25-10-39 27MU 28-10 41S 1-3-40 cd/ld 29-7 ASTH 1-8 609S 10-8 C2 ops 30-9 72S 11-10 92S 11-10 dam ops 20-10 61 OTU 1-7-41 Hal 25-8 con to PRIV 61 OTU 30-8 Northolt 8-4-42 HAL 30-6 M46 instal con to PRVIII Type G 8 OTU 27-3-43 SOC 27-3-45

N3114 385 FF 25-10-39 27MU 28-10 41S 3-3-40 s/dn by He111 3-4-40 SOC 1-5

N3115 386 FF GP 26-10-39 27MU 28-10 41S 3-3-40 cd f/ld on ops nr Purfleet 29-5 AST SOC E 12-6

N3116 387 FF GP 26-10-39 27MU 28-10 No 2 Camera Unit HAL 4-2-40 con to PRIII Type C. Farn April '40 212(PR)S May '40 sortie along French coast 5-6 FA 15-8 SOC 26-8 FH 182.00

N3117 390 FF 27-10-39 27MU 28-10 No 2 Camera Unit HAL 4-2-40 con to PRIII Type C Farn trls April '40 dm ops 9-12 GAL con to PRV M45 instal PRU Ben 20-6-41 SOC E 9-12

N3118 388 FF 27-10-39 266S dam ldg Witt S/Ldr Spencer safe 14-9 41S 17-9 s/dn by Bf109 nr dover Sgt McAdam aban a/c 24-9

N3119 389 FF 28-10-39 6MU 3-11-39 HQ Horn 4-1-40 602S 14-3 AST 22-8 222S 12-9 s/dn by Bf109 12.05hrs Battle P/O Davies kld 30-10 AST SOC 5-11 cancel 16-2-41 53 OTU 5-6-42

N3120 391 FF 29-10-39 6MU 3-11 266S 20-1-40 broke up in test flight to alt Pilot Gleed thrown out cd 14-40hrs Littleport Cambs. 18-2 SOC 22-2

N3121 392 FF 30-10-39 6MU 3-11 66S 11-1-40 s/dn by Bf109 C3 4-9 FA C2 11-10 AST 53 OTU 6-5-41 P&P 27-3-42 con to F VA M45 53 OTU 1-9 349S 6-7-43 61 OTU 1-8 Stn Flt North 13-8 strk by BM120 Ast Dn CE 19-8 SOC 27-8

N3122 393 FF 31-1-39 6MU 3-11 54S 17-12 AST 6-6-40 FA 31-8 303S 22-1-41 58 OTU 31-12 1 TEU 10-7-44 SOC rtp 1-8

N3123 394 FF 31-10-39 41S 18-2-40 FA CB 3-9 AST 57 OTU 9-8-41 cd during acrob Kinnerton Cheshire 11-8 SOC 18-8

N3124 395 FF 1-11-39 8MU 4-11 54S 21-12 AST 23-4-40 616S dam by Bf109 nr Dover 08.05hrs Sgt Gardner inj 12-8 610S 11-9 FAC2 13-10 DeH SAL 11-3-41 con to F.VA M45 53 OTU 17-7 FAAC 3-4-42 SOC 14-6-45

N3125 396 FF GP 1-11-39 8MU 4-11 266S 12-2-40 AST 6-5 92S 21-10 53 OTU 5-3-41 cd f/ld Chessington Surrey dbf CE 13-6 SOC 19-6 FH201-40

N3126 397 FF GP 1-11-39 8MU 4-11 41S 21-1-40 AST 20-9 SOC E 7-10

N3127 398 FF GP 2-11-39 8MU 4-11 266S 15-2-40 FA 18-8 AST 22-8 65S 18-10 145S 16-1-41 118S 3-3 66S 9-4 501S 24-4 53 OTU 14-5 61 OTU 1-7 AST 12-12 57 OTU 30-9-42 FACB 18-2-43 LMS 53 OTU 31-7 9MU 4-8-44

N3128 399 FF 2-11-39 9MU 9-11 65S 2-4-40 cd on t/o S/Ldr Sawyer kld. 2-8 AW 2-8

N3129 400 FF 3-11-39 9MU 9-11 65S 2-4-40 s/dn Bf109 20.50hrs nr Folkestone pilot miss 7-7

N3130 401 FF 3-11-39 9MU 9-11 54S 10-12 AST 17-1-40 616S 31-5 dvd i/grd after t/o Roch, Essex CE 4-6 SOC 7-6

N3160 402 FF 4-11-39 9MU 9-11 54S 10-12 f/ld nr Dartford Kent 15.20hrs on ops P/O Edsall safe CB 12-8 GAL 234S 14-2-41 58 OTU 27-3 WAL 15-1-42 to 3088M 2SoTT 18-7 SOC 16-2-45

N3161 403 FF 6-11-39 9MU 9-11 65S D 3-4-40 FAC2 15-1- AST 61 OTU 18-8-41 65S FA cd f/ld nr Hemel Hempstead 6-11 tl wrk SOC 13-11

N3162 404 FF GP 6-11-39 24MU 12-11 41S 24-12 HAL 13-9-40 FACB 30-4-41 57 OTU 10-5 GAL 1PRU Ben 22-9-42 8 OTU 17-12 FACB 18-1-43 ROS RNAS 12-5-43 CAC ROS 6-6 SOC 13-10-44

N3163 405 FF GP 7-11-39 24MU 10-11 41S 24-12 65S 8-8-40 AST 9-12 57 OTU 1-8-41 runway coll with X4896 CB 4-6-43 53 OTU 26-10 e/fld cd/ldg Hibald CE 10-3-44

N3164 FF GP 7-11-39 24MU 10-11 602S 4-12 AST 13-3 7 OTU 16-7 FAC2 24-9 SAL 53 OTU 7-5-41 ROS 11-9

N3165 407 FF 7-11-39 24MU 10-11 602S 27-12 dam ops 27-5-40 AST SOC E 14-6

N3166 408 FF GP 8-11-39 602S 53 OTU o/s ldg Lland 25-9-41

N3167 409 FF GP 8-11-39 27MU 10-11 92S dam ops 23-5-40 night ldg acc Pembrey Sgt Baraclough safe 26-7 AST SOC E 1-9

N3168 410 FF 9-11-39 27MU 13-11 266S 15-2-40 s/dn by Bf109 19.00hrs Teston Maidstone P/O Cale kld C3 15-8

N3169 411 FF GP 9-11-39 27MU 13-11 266S 15-2-40 dam ops 2-6 AST 222S 31-8 65S 7-11 57 OTU 10-5-41 HAL 22-5 to 2843M 5SoTT 13-12 SOC 18-12

N3170 411 FF GP 9-11-39 27MU 13-11 266S 15-2-40 strk tractor taxy P/O Ashton safe 18-7 1CRU 610S 9-9 66S 18-9 dam by Bf109 f/ld. Sgt Wright safe 28-9 GAL 308S 18-5-41 for defence of Austin Works 131S u/c clpse on ldg CB 9-9

N3171 413 FF 10-11-39 27MU 13-11 AMDP 16-11 BDn 19-3-40 comp perf trls (Rotol C/S prop) with K9793 (2-blade fixed pitch) CFS 24-2 for compilation of pilot's notes. ECFS Hullav 13-6-42 SOC 18-8-45

N3172 414 FF 11-11-39 6MU 15-11 54S 12-12 1CRU 5-6-40 7 OTU 14-9 SAL 5-6-41 82MU 6-10-42 *Pet Mear* 8-11 lost at sea 8-1-43

N3173 415 FF 13-11-39 6MU 15-11 54S 9-3-40 AST 2-9 152S 20-9 s/dn cd 11-50hrs nr Woolv Sgt Holland kld. C3 25-9

N3174 417 FF GP 13-11-39 6MU 15-11 54S 12-12 SAL 7-6-40 222S 19-11 53 OTU 16-3-41 u/c cllpse ldg Farn. 22-6 53 OTU 27-8

N3175 418 FF 14-11-39 6MU 15-11 266S 19-1-40 s/dn nr Portsmouth 12-18hrs f/ld Bembridge IoW dbf P/O Williams safe 12-8 SOC 20-8

N3176 419 FF 14-11-39 6MU 20-11 54S 12-12 AST 17-4-40 152S 15-10 dam ops 10-11 AST 58 OTU 23-3-41 SOC 19-12

N3177 420 FF 15-11-39 8MU 20-11 610S 28-3-40 FTR ops 29-5 FH73.10

N3178 421 FF 15-11-39 8MU 20-11 266S 15-2-40 dam e/a 13-8 dam by bombs 07.18hrs Eastchurch C2 28-8 AST 66S 15-10 64S 27-11 C2 ops 29-11 1CRU 58 OTU 25-8-41 cd f/ld 15-9 AST

N3179 422 FF GP 15-11-39 8MU 20-11 266S hit trees ldg at Witt CE 3-5-40 SOC 9-5

N3180 416 FF 13-11-39 8MU 20-11 74S 16-1-40 covering a/c with P9389 for Miles Master picking up S/Ldr White. Pilot F/lt Deere s/dn Bf109 23-5 54S FTR ops 28-5 FH124/10

N3181 423 FF 16-11-39 8MU 4-12 266S 15-2-40 dam e/a 15-8 1CRU 3-9 61 OTU 4-7-41 e/fld a/c aban nr Hanwell, Middx dbf 10-8

N3182 424 FF 17-11-39 9MU 20-11 66S 2-4-40 s/dn by He111 off East Coast 18.35hrs P/O Studd aban a/c i/sea drowned 19-8

N3183 425 FF GP 18-11-39 9MU 25-11 54S 10-12 s/dn by Bf109 nr Dover 19.15hrs 9-7-40 P/O Evershed miss

N3184 445 FF 18-11-39 9MU 4-12 54S 22-1-40 e/fld a/c aban off Clacton P/O Kemp rescued by destroyer 21-7

N3185 426 FF 21-11-39 9MU 25-11 54S 10-12 hit grd nr Brentwood CE 15-5

N3186 427 FF 21-11-39 2 Camera Unit PDU HAL 22-1-40 o/s ldg during trls at Heston hit beacon 3-3 ASTH 8-4 SOC 13-5

N3187 428 FF 21-11-39 24MU 15-11 54S 16-12 FTR ops 18-5-40

N3188 429 FF 22-11-39 24MU 25-11 54S 21-12 i/sea 25-5-40 SOC 1-6 FH 94-55

N3189 430 FF 22-11-39 24MU 11-11 266S 11-3-40 s/dn by He111 nr Deal Sgt Hawley missing 15-8

N3190 431 FF 23-11-39 24MU 4-12 602S 3-5-40 dam ops a/c aban over Pentland Hills Midlothian 26-6

N3191 432 FF 23-11-39 24MU 2-12 234S 22-3-40 lost wings in dive cd nr Truro cornwall CE 16-1-41 AST 14-2 SOC 23-4

N3192 433 FF 24-11-39 27MU 2-12 92S 20-3-40 54S dam ops f/ld Sizewell nr Orford Sgt Collett inj 24-7 SOC 31-7

N3193 434 FF 24-11-39 27MU 2-12 92S 30-3-40 s/dn by Bf109 nr Graves P/O Mittram inj 18-9 CE

N3194 435 FF 25-11-39 27MU 2-12 92S 30-3-40 FTR ops 23-5 FH 46.50

N3195 436 FF 25-11-39 27MU 2-12 1AAS Manby 6-3-40 w/u ldg after e/fld on t/o 7-4 CE SOC 23-4

N3196 437 FF 27-11-39 27MU 2-1-40 41S 14-4 ASTH 5-5 603S 3-9 s/dn by Bf109 f/ld P/O Stapleton safe 7-9 AST 57 OTU 7-8-41 dvd i/grd Shotley Bridge Northumb CE 9-4-43 SOC 25-4

N3197 438 FF 27-11-39 8MU 2-12 266S 15-2-40 FTR ops 5-6 FH 71.00

N3198 439 FF 28-11-39 8MU 2-12 19S 19-4-40 602S 6-8 s/dn by Bf109 nr Tunbridge Wells P/O Moody kld 7-9 SAL 19-9 53 OTU cd f/ld Lland 15-9-41 SOC 28-9

N3199 440 FF 28-11-39 8MU 2-12 19S 19-4-40 7 OTU 7-8 19S 3-9 57 OTU 31-7-41 to 3167M July '42

N3200 441 FF 29-11-39 8MU 2-12 19S 19-4-40 FTR ops 27-5

N3201 443 FF 29-11-39 8MU 2-12 610S 28-3-40 s/dn F/O Keighley aban a/c inj 20-7

N3202 444 FF 30-11-39 8MU 2-12 609S 16-4-40 FTR ops 31-5

N3203 445 FF 28-11-39 8MU 2-12 609S 25-4-40 dam ops CB 17-7 222S 31-8 s/dn by Bf109 nr Roch P/O Whitbread kld 20-9

N3221 446 FF 2-12-39 20MU 13-12 72S 1-4-40 C2 ops 22-8 SAL 609S 28-9 57 OTU 30-2-41 FACB 6-1-42 WAL 53 OTU 22-7 CE 6-2-43

N3222 447 FF 3-12-39 20MU 12-12 609S 25-4-40 FTR 1-6

N3223 448 FF 3-12-39 8MU 13-12 609S 25-4-40 u/c jam F/O Nowierski aban a/c cd nr M Wall 5-10

N3224 449 FF 3-12-39 9MU 12-12 66S 2-4-40 spun i/grd after fighter affil with Blenheim nr Kilbolton Hunts 24-4 SOC 30-4 FH 21.00

N3225 450 FF 5-12-39 9MU 12-12 66S 4-4-40 AST 9-9 41S 18-9 dam by Bf109 nr Dung F/O Lovell safe 5-10 611S 24-10 152S 17-1-41 58 OTU 23-3 SAL 26-6 61 OTU 27-11-42 FACE 25-7-43 SOC

N3226 451 FF 4-12-39 9MU 12-12 602S 7-4-40 s/dn by Bf109 nr Dorchester Sgt Sprague aban a/c 25-8

N3227 452 FF 5-12-39 9MU 12-12 602S 7-4-40 AST 24-8 602S s/dn by Bf109 over Hailsham Sussex Sgt Whipps aban a/c safe 6-9

N3228 453 FF 6-12-39 9MU 12-12 602S 7-4-40 72S 13-10 GAL 18-10 53 OTU 30-8-41 FAAC 7-9 3SoTT 31-12-42 61 OTU 16-2-43 57 OTU 13-6-43 cd out of cont nr Long Horsley Northumb 18-11 SOC 19-11-43

N3229 454 FF 7-12-39 9MU 12-12 dam ops 25-3-40 603S 11-4 C2 ops 23-7 72S 2-9 C2 ops 4-9 92S 3-11 C3 ops 17-11 AST 308S 18-5-41 for defence of VA Works cd/ldg ADwn 5-12 52 OTU 12-11-44 FACB 5-12 SOC 6-12

N3230 455 FF 6-12-39 9MU 13-12 64S 13-5-40 C2 ops 15-8 AST 53 OTU 8-5-41 cd dbf CE 9-7 SOC 15-7

N3231 456 FF 7-12-39 9MU 13-12 234S 28-3-40 C2 ops 12-7 64S 21-7 dam ops 25-7 AST 31-7 609S 28-9 s/dn nr Sutton Waldron P/O Staples aban a/c inj 7-10

N3232 457 FF 9-12-39 9MU 13-12 222S 9-3-40 FTR Dunk 1-6 FH 107.35

N3233 463 FF 10-12-39 9MU 2-1-40 222S 9-3 s/dn by Bf109 cd/ld Eastchurch F/Lt Robinson inj 31-8 HAL 123S 25-6-41 58 OTU 25-9 57 OTU 29-8-43 SOC 28-4-45

N3234 458 FF 9-12-39 24MU 21-12 19S 5-4-40 41S 20-7 cd t/o Mans CB 5-8 AST SOC 28-8 FH 108.55

N3235 459 FF GP 10-12-39 24MU 21-12 257S 24-5-40 7 OTU 21-7 dvdi/grd nr Holywell Flint dbf 21-10 SOC 29-10

N3236 460 FF 11-12-39 24MU 21-12 602S 3-5-40 FA 5-6 122S 2-6-41 FACB 13-9 WAL SOC 4-12 to 2826M

N3237 461 FF 13-12-39 24MU 21-12 19S 6-4-40 FTR 27-5 FH 41.00

N3238 462 FF 12-12-39 24MU 21-1-40 19S 5-4 7 OTU 11-8 19S 10-9 609S 28-9 s/dn by Bf109 over Yeovil Sgt Feary aban a/c kld 7-10

N3239 467 FF 13-12-39 24MU 21-12 234S 16-3-40 Farn June '40 s/dn cd IoW P/O Zurakowski (later Gloster test pilot) safe 24-8 SOC 1-10

N3240 468 FF 14-12-39 24MU 21-12 266S 11-3-40 s/dn Nr Deal S/Lt Greenshields miss 16-8 FH 79.00

N3241 464 FF 14-12-39 24MU 2-1-40 234S 22-3 AST 2-9 con to PRV Type C 15-9 HAL 30-4-41 1PRU 18-9 R-R 3-10 con to FVA M45 instal HAL 27-5-42 con to PRVII Type G 1PRU 2-6-42 542S 10-12 8 OTU 10-5-43 FAAC 12-5

N3242 465 FF 14-12-39 24MU 2-1-40 234S 22-3 C2 ops 16-9 602S 13-9 C2 ops 28-11 AST con to FVA M45 603S i/sea 9-12-41

N3243 466 FF 15-12-39 24MU 2-1-40 234S 22-3 74S 10-5 FTR Dunk 24-5

N3244 469 FF 16-12-39 24MU 29-12 266S 16-2-40 FAC2 18-7 603S 21-9 s/dn by Bf109 i/sea off Folkestone P/O Cardell kld 27-9

N3245 470 FF 18-12-39 27MU 29-12 266S 16-2-40 C2 ops 15-8 26S 29-8 57 OTU 25-10 FA cd CAC 3-3-41 SOC 6-5

N3246 471 FF 18-12-39 27MU 29-12 266S 16-2-40 AST 13-5 222S 31-10 cd in bad visibility 6-3-41 AST 457S 28-7 53 OTU 20-10 FAAC 28-3-42 58 OTU 23-7 DeH 24-11 RNAS 19-5-43

N3247 472 FF 19-12-39 27MU 29-12 266S 16-2-40 AST 2-5 64S 7-10 FACB 25-10 53 OTU 2-5 ASTEx 1-6 53 OTU 17-9 strk parked P9512 Lland 12-4-42 ROS FACE 8-11 SOC 13-12

N3248 473 FF 19-12-39 27MU 29-12 92S 20-3-40 s/dn by Bf109 nr Dover Sgt Eyles miss 20-9 FH 172.45

N3249 474 FF GP 21-12-39 27MU 29-12 92S 20-3-40 C2 ops cd/ld Bibury 31-8 602S 10-11 FTR 14-2-41

N3250 475 FF GP 21-12-39 92S 20-3-40 7 OTU 16-7 FAAC 1-3-41 e/fld cd f/ld Tattenhall nr Chester 9-4 SOC 18-4

N3264 476 FF 22-12-39 27MU 2-1-40 41S cd/ld after comb Bf109 Mans 29-7 GAL 610S 13-10 C3 ops 29-10

N3265 477 FF 22-12-39 27MU 19-1-40 92S 4-4 AST 4-5 7 OTU 16-7 19S 10-9 e/fld f/ld P/O Hradil safe C2 18-9 SAL 602S 24-1-41 61 20-4 57 OTU 1-9-42 58 OTU 9-3-43 57 OTU 16-4-44 SOC 22-4-45

N3266 478 FF 29-12-39 27MU 2-1-40 92S 20-3-40 41S 14-8 dam ops 7-9 dam by Bf109 P/O Chalder safe 17-9 SAL 123S 9-3-41 58 OTU 25-9 57 OTU 30-3-43 air coll with K9824 cd nr Long Whitton Northum CE 19-11

N3267 480 FF 29-12-39 9MU 16-1-40 603S 11-4 C2 ops F/O Boulter inj 29-8 41S 19-9 s/dn by Do17 nr Folkestone P/O Adams aban a/c 7-10

N3268 479 FF GP 29-12-39 9MU 10-1-40 603S 11-4 Farn June '40 92S 13-8 dam by Do17 off St Gowans Head f/ld F/Lt Stanford Tuck inj 25-8 COAL SOC 21-9

N3269 481 FF 29-12-39 9MU 10-1-40 616S 9-4 AST 19-6 7 OTU 16-8 FAC2 18-9 SAL 131S 15-7-41 o/s ldg Tern CAC 11-9 ROS 57 OTU 11-10 FACE dbf 23-11

N3270 482 FF 1-1-40 9MU 10-1 616S 10-4 1CRU 1-6 5 OTU 20-7 FAC2 7-8 GAL 609S 11-12 66S 24-2-41 602S 7-3 61 OTU 20-4 ASTH 29-10 con to FVA M45 521S 3-5-42 8 OTU 28-3-43 NEA SOC E 29-5-46

N3271 483 FF 2-1-40 9MU 10-1 616S spun i/grd nr Beverley Yorks Sgt Walsh kld C3 4-8 SOC 12-8

N3272 484 FF 3-1-40 9MU 16-1 64S 13-5 FTR ops 29-5 FH 9.00

N3273 485 FF 3-1-40 9MU 16-1 64S 13-5 AST 2-7 5 OTU 14-7 7 OTU 31-8 609S 5-10 57 OTU 21-6-41 FACE 3-8-42 57 OTU dvd i/grd nr Whitchurch Shrops 25-7-43

N3274 486 FF 3-1-40 9MU 16-1 610S 23-4 FTR ops 31-5 FH 24.75

N3275 487 FF GP 3-1-40 9MU 22-1 616S 25-5 s/dn by Bf109 F/O St Aubin inj C3 26-8

N3276 488 FF 5-1-40 24MU 16-1 245S 8-4 dam ops 21-5 AST 234S AST con to PRIV 234S 8-9 58 OTU 28-3-41 57 OTU 16-6-42 st ld cd in River Dee nr Hawar CE 10-8 SOC 18-8

N3277 490 FF 5-1-40 24MU 16-1 234S 15-4 reported shot nr IoW. Was dam and f/ld in Cherbourg France 15-8 P/O Hardy PoW a/c had Daimler Benz eng fitt

N3278 489 FF 5-1-40 24MU 16-1 234S 15-4 e/fld f/ld nr Liskeard Cornwall C3 Sgt Szlagowski safe 8-8 SOC 17-8 1CRU 6-9 Farn Oct '40 122S 8-7-41 57 OTU 4-10 82MU 9-10-42 *Pet Mear* 18-12 lost at sea 8-1-43

N3279 491 FF GP 5-1-40 24MU 16-1 234S 15-4 C2 ops 6-9 AST 53 OTU 25-8 FACE 29-9

N3280 492 FF GP 9-1-40 24MU 16-1 234S 25-4 609S 5-9 C2 ops 25-9 AST 41S 20-10 611S 24-10 485S 15-3-41 57 OTU 29-4 52 OTU 16-5-42 BDn 24-3-43

N3281 493 FF 9-1-40 24MU 19-1 234S 16-3 AST 23-4 5 OTU 14-7 7 OTU 21-8 FAC2 21-9 GAL 61 OTU 4-7-41 AST 24-7 con to FVA M45 RNDA Yeov as train 10-9-42

N3282 494 FF 9-1-40 24MU 16-1 234S 15-4 FA 27-5 AST 602S 19-8 dam by Do17 Sgt Whall inj 9-9 602S s/dn by Bf110 over Sussex Coast Sgt Sprague kld 11-9

N3283 498 FF GP 10-1-40 24MU 22-1 234S 25-4 ASTH 30-5 92S s/dn by Bf109 nr Graves P/O Bartley safe 18-9 SAL 53 OTU 17-7-41 FAAC 18-12 AST 76MU 28-9-42 *C of Evans* 9-10 Port Sudan 23-12 ME 31-12 SOC 27-7-44

N3284 495 FF GP 11-1-40 27MU 16-1 610S 14-5 AST 7-9 65S 15-12 145S 19-1-41 118S 8-3 FAAC 16-4 122S 27-5 131S 2-9 FACB 10-9 ROS 131S 20-9 53 OTU 24-3-42 strk AD315 while taxy 16-8 52 OTU broke up in flight cd Thatcham Berks dbf CE 15-9

N3285 502 FF 16-1-40 27MU 24-1 92S 20-3 1CRU 4-8 66S dam by Bf109 P/O Bodie safe 5-10 dam by Bf109 P/O Bodie safe 13-10 AST 64S 16-12 303S 22-1-41 58 OTU 29-3 1PRU Bens 25-9-42 57 OTU 28-4-43 SOC E 17-8-44

N3286 496 FF 11-1-40 27MU 16-1 Farn July '40 7 OTU 23-7 19S 3-9 92S 22-10 s/dn by Do17 nr Brighton Sgt Ellis safe 10-11 AST 132S 11-7-41 broke up in flight Grimondgarth Aberdeen CE 15-8 SOC 20-8 Farn Jan '42

N3287 497 FF 12-1-40 27MU 19-1 92S 3-3 lost on night patrol a/c aban P/O Wade cd nr Exeter 27/28-7 SOC 2-8

N3288 499FF 13-1-40 27MU 19-1 603S 31-5 dam ldg Dyce P/O Kilroy safe 26-7 AST dam ops 1-9 609S 18-9 C2 ops 26-9 AST 65S 20-10 145S 23-1-41 178S 8-3 FAAC 20-3 123S 11-10 58 OTU 6-11 61 OTU 13-8-42 WAL 8-1-43 to 3545M 12SoTT 3-2 SOC 5-5-45

N3289 501 FF 15-1-40 27MU 19-1 610S 14-5 FTR ops 29-5 FH 24.50

N3290 503 FF 16-1-40 27MU 24-1 92S 20-3 FTR ops 3-6 FH 95.45

N3291 500 FF 15-1-40 27MU 19-1 92S 20-3 cd f/ldg Edenbridge Kent 25-3 SOC E 29-3

N3292 504 FF 16-1-40 234S 15-3 dam ops 23-3 AST 29-7 54S 1-11 dam ops 10-11 AST stld on t/o cd Catt 7-12 AST 57 OTU 2-6-41 AST 23-7 con to FVA M45 145S 26-11 134S 19-12 133S 28-12 421S 12-4-42 601S 12-4 421S 21-5 P&P 9-6 RNAS Yeov 8-9 FAAC 3-4-43 ROS

N3293 505 FF 17-1-40 9MU 22-1 222S 9-3 64S 17-4 C2 ops 28-10 AST 124S 27-8-41 340S 20-10 52 OTU 12-11 58 OTU 11-2-42 CFS 2-5-43 17SFTS 25-8-43 SOC 6-8-45

N3294 506 FF 18-1-40 9MU 22-1 222S 9-3 FA cd nr Withernsea Yorks Sgt Lewis kld 4-7 SOC 12-7

N3295 507 FF 18-1-40 9MU 22-1 222S 9-3 FTR Dunk 31-5 FH 48.55

N3296 del as fus only to CBAF as pattern a/c 24-1-40 counted as cro until SOC authorised 8-6

N3297 Ff 20-9-41 deleted from contract and con to proto F Mk III.

N3298 Details as N3296.

N3299 Details as N3296.

Supermarine Aviation (Vickers) Ltd.

Contract No. B980383/39.

Order for 200 Spitfire Mk I dated 20 April 1939. Built as Mk Is between January and August 1940. P9551 and 9552 transferred to contract No. S.B.2415/C.23A for conversion to PR Mk III prototypes in August 1940. P9553 to 9567 deleted from contract in June 1940 for export to Turkey.
Order cancelled and aircraft completed for the RAF. P9568 to 9584 deleted from contract and intended for export to Portugal. Not built. P9566 and 9567 were never taken on charge by the RAF. P9305 to 9339; 9360 to 9399; 9420 to 9469; 9490 to 9519; 9540 to 9550 and 9553 to 9567. P-series all F Mk IA Merlin III unless otherwise indicated.

P9305 509 FF 19-1-40 24MU 24-1 19S 5-4 FTR 27-5

P9306 508 FF 19-1-40 24MU 24-1 74S 6-7 s/dn bf 109E, dam 109E and 2 bf 110S P/O PCF Stevenson 54MU 17-7-41 131S 7-41 52 OTU 10-41 61 OTU Cat B WA 4-5-43 Extant Chicago Museum of Science & Industry, USA

P9307 510 FF GP 19-1-40 PDU 2 HAL 11-2 con to PRIII Type C Farn for tls 1PRU Benson 25-5 dam e/a 19-9 FTR ops 10-4-41 FH 119.05 (originally for Turk)

P9308 511 FF GP 22-1-40 PDU 2 HAL 11-2 con to PRIII Type C. VEA for mods (additional fuel tanks in wings, range 2,000 miles wing became Type 353 'D'). PDU 1-4 First PR op against Emden, Germany 5-4 by F/Lt Le Mesurier. FTR ops P/O Coleman miss 19-5 (originally for Turk).

P9309 512 FF 22-1-40 PDU 2 HAL 9-2 con to PRIII Type C. Tls Farn May, dam ops 10-11 AST mod to PRVI 309S 18-5-41 defence of VA factory 52 OTU 21-11 lost wing in flight cd nr Yatesbury 10-5-42 (originally for Turk).

P9310 513 FF 23-1-40 PDU 2 HAL 11-2 con to PRIII Type C PDU 19-5 PRU Wick 1-7 HAL 8-12 mod to PRVI Type F 8 OTU 27-7-42 M45 instal FAAC 31-7 ROS 8 OTU 4-8 FTR train flt 2-10 FH 682.40 (originally for Turk).

P9311 514 FF 24-1-40 27MU 12-2 249S 22-5 610S 14-9 602S 17-12 61 OTU 20-4-41 HAL 9-4-42 *Taran* Port Sudan 29-1-43 ME 28-2 strk Kittyhawk AK727 on t/o Abu Suier CE 22-10

P9312 515 FF 25-1-40 10MU 14-2 266S 16-5 s/dn nr Canterbury F/Lt Bazley aban a/c 16-8

P9313 517 FF 25-1-40 10MU 14-2 PDU HAL 21-3 con to PRIII Type C PDU 19-5 PRU St Eval 1-7 dam e/a 19-9 FTR ops 9-11 (originally for Turk).

P9314 516 FF GP 25-1-40 10MU 14-2 41S 14-4 FTR ops 22-6

P9315 518 FF 26-1-40 10MU 14-2 Farn 6-5 25MU PDU 28-5 HAL 3-7 con to PRIII Type C cd/ldg Bens C2 5-11 3PRU Oak 7-2-41 FTR ops 23-2 (originally for Turk)

P9316 519 FF 29-1-40 27MU 10-2 92S 20-3 AST 1-7 66S s/dn by Bf109 over Kent a/c aban CE 4-9 P/O Appleford inj

P9317 520 FF 29-1-40 9MU 10-2 222S 9-3 FTR ops 1-6 FH86.10

P9318 521 FF 29-1-40 FF GP 8-2 9MU 10-2 222S 9-3 dam Bf109 C2 29-10 Sgt Burgess safe 58MU OTU SOC 15-4-45

P9319 522 FF 1-2-40 9MU 10-2 234S 15-3 FA C2 3-10 AST 11-10 39MU S Farm dis 129S 16-7-41 HAL 7-10 to 3143M H Ercall 2-7-42

P9320 523 FF 1-2-40 9MU 10-2 234S 15-3 58 OTU 23-3-41 FAAC 8-6 FTR train flt 31-10

P9321 524 FF 1-2-40 9MU 10-2 234S 15-3 74S 11-5 f/ld in Calais/Marck France 24-5

P9322 525 FF 2-2-40 9MU 10-2 609S 8-6 dam by Bf110 25-8 AST 61 OTU 16-8 broke up in flight nr Llanishen Cardiff 15-9-42

P9323 526 FF 6MU 13-2 222S 16-3 s/dn Isle of Sheppey Sgt Spears aban a/c 31-8

P9324 527 FF 3-2-40 6MU 13-2 222S 21-3 41S 13-9 s/dn by Bf109 nr Graves P/O Langley k/d 15-9 SOC 2-10

P9325 528 FF 3-2-40 6MU 13-2 222S 16-3 s/dn f/ld Eastchurch Sgt Baxter safe 30-8 HAL 122S 25-7-41 FAAC 12-2-42 RNAS 4-7-43 CE 15-10-44

P9326 529 FF 5-2-40 6MU 13-2 222S 16-3 1CRU 2-5 54S 1-9 57 OTU 1-2-41 FAAC 7-4 SAL 52 OTU 26-11 53 OTU 9-8-42 spun i/grd Narnby Lincs CE 16-5-43 SOC 26-5

P9327 530 FF 5-2-40 10MU 13-2 152S 3-5 Farn June'40 C2 ops 25-7 AST 7 OTU dvd i/grd nr Abergole Denbigh abt 12-10 SOC 19-10

P9328 531 FF 6-2-40 10MU 13-2 602S 20-5 222S 21-5 s/dn by Bf109 9-9 GAL 12-9 PDU HAL 8-3-42 con to PRV Type G M46 140S 11-6 140S TAF 31-3-43 FAAC 16-10 SOC E 14-8-45

P9329 532 FF 7-2-40 10MU 14-2 257S 24-5 7 OTU 17-6 C2 12-10 SOC 22-11 bboc 65S 29-11 AST 11-12 61 OTU 11-8-42 flew into hill with X4852 Chu Str Salop CE 20-1-43 SOC 24-1 FH359.20

P9330 533 FF 7-2-40 10MU 14-2 257S 21-5 610S 13-7 dam by Bf109 nr Dover 12-8 AST 610S 7-10 o/t ldg Hooton Park 7-11 AST SOC 22-11

P9331 534 FF 9-2-40 24MU 29-2 212S 7-4 Pres lost over Dunk SOC June'40. Later found to have been captured intact by German Army

P9332 535 FF 8-2-40 27MU 5-3 249S 20-5 7 OTU 17-6 FA C2 12-10 AST 61 OTU 30-6-41 53 OTU 18-8-42 to 3595M 5SoTT 2-3-43 CE 23-9-44

P9333 536 FF 9-2-40 27MU 1-3 266S 16-5 s/dn over Portsmouth P/O Ashton k/d 12-8 SOC 1-9 FH78

P9334 537 FF 9-2-40 27MU 1-3 41S 1-6 C2 ops 28-7 GAL 122S 11-6-41 ROS 24-9 57 OTU 31-12 FACB 28-6-42 AST 76MU 22-9 *City of Ev* P Sudan 23-12 ME 31-12 SOC 27-7-44

P9335 538 FF 12-2-40 27MU 1-3 249S 20-5 7 OTU 22-7 FAC2 20-8 1CRU 41S 11-10 611S 24-10 dam ops CA 12-12 57 OTU 16-6-41 61 OTU 2-9 57 OTU 16-6-42 FACB 17-2-43 DeH 12-11

P9336 539 FF 13-2-40 27MU 1-3 249S 20-5 74S 11-7 s/dn by Bf109 nr Dover Sgt Mould aban a/c 28-7 AW SOC 4-8

P9337 540 FF 12-2-40 6MU 25-2 222S 25-3 s/dn by Bf109 Ashford Kent dbf P/O Davies inj 31-8 SOC 18-9

P9338 541 FF 12-2-40 6MU 2-3 72S 6-6 cd nr Folkes believed s/dn P/O Case kld 12-10 SOC 17-11

P9339 542 FF 13-2-40 6MU 25-2 222S 16-3 SOC June 40 FH92.05

P9360 543 FF 14-2-40 6MU 25-2 222S 16-3 des on ops 31-8 SOC 19-9

P9361 544 FF 14-2-40 6MU 25-2 222S 16-3 FA ops 11-5 MMO 7 OTU 13-8 58 OTU 8-9-41 SAL 8-12-42 57 OTU 14-4-43 FACB 3-6 SOC 6-3-45

P9362 545 FF GP 15-2-40 6MU 25-3 222S 21-3 SAL 19-8 66S 15-10 57 OTU 1-11 WAL new eng 30-5-41 1PRU 10-4-42 SOC 6-1-45

P9363 547 FF 15-2-40 9MU 24-2 234S 15-3 C3 ops 15-8 AST to 3371M 1SoTT 13-10-42

P9364 546 FF 15-2-40 9MU 24-2 222S 11-3 FTR ops 27-9 Sgt Scott missing

P9365 548 FF 17-2-40 9MU 24-2 234S 15-3 cd night ldg St Eval Sgt Thompson inj 31-7 SOC FH210.50

P9366 549 FF 19-2-40 9MU 2-3 234S 27-3 des night ldg St Eval P/O Horton safe 6-8 SOC 20-8

P9367 550 FF 19-2-40 9MU 24-2 92S 6-3 54S 12-6 57 OTU 1-2-41 ASTH 6-8 con to FVA M45 316S 5-12 306S 12-12 81S 18-2-42 165S 12-4 167S 27-5 ATA 21-3-44 SOC 6-6-45

P9368 551 FF 19-2-40 9MU 24-2 92S 6-3 616S 26-8 72S 2-9 dam by Bf109 nr Graves P/O Lloyd inj 18-9 SAL 111S 3-5-41 132S 17-7 FAAC 31-7 52 OTU 9-1-42 53 OTU 17-6 52 OTU 1-9-43 RNDA 14-6-44

P9369 552 FF 20-2-40 9MU 6-3 54S 17-4 dam e/fld cd Capel Surrey Sgt Squier inj 8-8 CE

P9370 553 FF 20-2-40 9MU 1-3 92S 11-3 FTR ops 23-5 FH64.20

P9371 554 FF GP 21-2-40 9MU 1-3 92S 6-3 s/dn by bf109 cd/ld P/O Pattison inj 23-9 SAL 132S 22-7-41 58 OTU 15-6-42 FAAC 2-6-43 ROS coll with R7144 nr Cuithmuir Angus 18-12 AST 1-6-45

P9372 555 FF 22-2-40 9MU 1-3 92S 6-3 dam ops 24-5 des by bf109 P/O Watling aban a/c safe 9-9 FH99.35

P9373 556 FF GP 22-2-40 9MU 1-3 92S 6-3 FTR 23-5 FH25

P9374 557 FF 23-2-40 9MU 2-3 92S 6-3 FTR ops 24-5 FH32.05

P9375 558 FF 23-2-40 6MU 1-3 222S 15-3 C3 ops 30-8 AST 53 OTU 18-3-41 a/c aban nr Gat 4-6 FH345.05

P9376 559 FF GP 24-2-40 6MU 1-3 222S 15-3 dam ops 29-5 ASTH 2-6 72S 3-9 dam by Bf109 nr Maids AST 57 OTU 1-8-41 52 OTU 17-5-42 FACB 7-3-43 53 OTU 13-6-43 to 4606M 6SoTT 11-3-44 CE 4-12

P9377 560 FF 26-2-40 6MU 1-3 222S 15-3 FTR ops 1-6 FH63.35

P9378 561 FF 26-2-40 6MU 1-3 222S 15-3 s/dn nr Roch P/O Carpenter aban a/c 4-9

P9379 562 FF 27-2-40 27MU 27-3 54S 11-5 74S 26-5 s/dn by Bf109 nr Folke P/O Gunn kld 31-7 SOC 31-8 FH88.35

P9380 563 FF GP 27-2-40 27MU 2-3 249S 20-5 65S 11-7 74S 12-7 dam ops 8-8 GAL 23-9 222S 31-10 53 OTU 16-3-41 FACB 27-3 HAL o/s ldg u/c retracted to stop a/c Hibald 8-3-44 CE

P9381 565 FF 28-2-40 27MU 5-3 249S 20-5 602S 13-7 s/dn nr Dorchester dbf F/O Coverley aban a/c 25-8

P9382 564 FF 28-2-40 27MU 2-3 1PRU Ben 7-5 Farn fuel syst trls CE ops 25-7 SOC 31-10 FH113

P9383 566 FF 29-2-40 27MU 2-3 616S 6-6 Farn trls FA C2 26-7 SAL 53 OTU 6-5-41 cd Colwinston Glam CE ttl wrk 9-7 SOC 14-7

P9384 567 FF 29-2-40 27MU 5-3-40 HAL 1PRU 5-5 con to PRIII Type C Farn fuel syst trls 1PRU 19-7 FTR on flt to Wick 19-10 FH120 (originally for Turk)

P9385 568 FF 1-3-40 27MU 6-3 2PDU HAL 1-4 con to PRIII Type C dam e/bombs Ben 27-2-41 HAL M45 instal in wts tests 18-5 8 OTU 26-8-42 FACB 25-10 HAL 12-11 con to PRVI Type F 8 OTU 29-3-43 (originally for Turk)

P9386 569 FF 1-3-40 AMDP Airspeed trls with company test pilots 6-3 38MU 11-5 257S 18-5 19S 3-9 152S 26-9 58 OTU 23-3-41 SAL 12-9 52 OTU 17-11 57 OTU 29-8-43 dvd i/grd East Lothian CE 5-5-44

P9387 570 FF GP 4-3-40 9MU 9-3 54S 25-4 s/dn by Bf109 nr Dover P/O Turley-George safe 25-7 GAL 122S 11-6-41 FA CE 22-6 SAL MXII instal 53 OTU 23-9 FACB 4-12 AST recat E 20-5-42

P9388 571 FF GP 3-3-40 9MU 7-3 54S 19-4 FTR ops 25-5 FH17.35

P9389 572 FF GP 5-3-40 9MU 9-3 54S 19-4 s/dn cd Kingsdown nr Dover by Bf109 P/O Stewart aban a/c safe 24-8 SOC 6-9

P9390 573 FF 4-3-40 9MU 9-3 54S 25-4 dam by Bf109 over Deal C3 2-7 SOC 19-7 to 2111M 22-10

P9391 574 FF 5-3-40 9MU 9-3 238S 20-5 19S 3-9 152S 26-9 C3 ops pilot thrown out cd nr Dorchester 11-10 SOC 28-10

P9392 575 FF 6-3-40 24MU 9-3 212S 7-4 FTR ops 19-6

P9393 576 FF GP 7-3-40 24MU 8-3 74S 3-6 s/dn by Bf109 off Dover i/sea P/O Stevenson aban a/c 11-8 FH84.45 7555M

P9394 577 FF 7-3-40 24MU 11-3 212S 7-4 R-RH June'40 603S 30-8 41S 13-9 dam by Bf109 nr Horn C2 30-9 Platts GarageC2 57 OTU 23-12-41 ops 30-9 P&P 27-3-42 new eng 52 OTU 15-7 53 OTU 13-12-43 SOC 16-8-44

P9395 578 FF 8-3-40 24MU 11-3 257S 2-6 FAC3 11-10 SOC 18-10

P9396 579 FF GP 13-3-40 24MU 27-3 212S 7-4 FAC2 20-7 AST 1PRU 14-11 FTR ops 10-4-41 FH129.35 (originally for Turk)

P9397 585 FF 15-3-40 6MU 20-3 222S 4-6 C2 ops 15-10 GAL 57 OTU 12-6-41 con to FVA M45 25-9-41 130S 21-10 134S 31-12 FAAC 23-3-42 421S 11-4-43 RNAS Yeov 8-9

P9398 580 FF 13-3-40 6MU 20-3 64S 18-5 74S 26-5 54S air coll with Bf109 F/Lt Deere f/ld Mans 9-7 s/dn by Bf109 into Folkes Harbour Sgt Eley kld 31-7 FH72.20

P9399 581 FF GP 14-3-40 6MU 20-3 64S 18-5 74S 26-5 dam f/ld Lympne P/O Cobden safe 10-7 SOC 15-7 to 2137M 22-10

P9420 582 FF 15-3-40 6MU 20-3 222S 4-6 C3 ops 26-6 SOC 2-7

P9421 583 FF GP 16-3-40 6MU 20-3 64S 18-5 s/dn by Bf109 off Dover F/O Jeffrey kld 25-7 SOC FH82.15

P9422 584 FF 15-3-40 27MU21-3 7 OTU 23-7 19S 3-9 s/dn by Bf109 nr Horn S/Ldr Pinkham kld 5-9 SOC

P9423 586 FF 16-3-40 27MU 27-3 249S 20-5 602S 13-7 s/dn by Ju88 nr Westh dbf 19-8 SOC 6-9

P9424 587 FF19-3-40 27MU 27-3 249S 20-5 266S 19-8 72S 25-8 C3 ops 31-8 SAL 123S 25-6-41 58 OTU 25-9 FACE 23-12

P9425 588 FF 19-3-40 27MU 27-3 Farn 9-4 trls trans to Fairoaks aerodrome Surrey for medical research trls. CFS 31-12 hand trls dam on train flt 12-4 1 TEU 26-2-44 SOC 20-11

P9426 589 FF 19-3-40 27MU 28-3 HAL 2PDU 1-4 con to PRIII Type C Farn 10-4 trls dam e/a 19-9 t/o with fitter on tail dam on ldg 21-11 949649 AC1 Rhodes H(Flt/Mech) Pilot P/O R Dyrgallo both inj HAL SOC 5-12

P9427 590 FF GP 19-3-40 8MU 28-3 609S 25-4 C2 ops 25-5 MMOx 74S 21-8 41S 13-9 152S 2-10 FTR ops 28-11 (originally for Turk)

P9428 591 FF GP 21-3-40 8MU 28-3 41S 13-5 believed air coll R6635 S/Ldr Wood kld 5-9 SOC 13-9

P9429 592 FF GP 20-3-40 8MU 28-3 41S 13-5 dam by Bf109 nr Dover cd/ld Mans F/O Lovell inj 28-7 ASTH 74S 9-10 41S 12-10 611S 24-10 303S 12-9-41 306S 6-10 57 OTU 10-1-42 FAAC 16-5 58 OTU 16-3-43 cd on t/o Gran CE 29-6

P9430 593 FF 21-3-40 8MU 28-3 41S 13-5 s/dn at Rayleigh Sgt McAdam safe C3 7-9 SOC 1-10 FH120.05

P9431 594 FF GP 21-3-40 8MU 30-3 66S 11-5 19S 3-9 cd/ld after combat Bf109 Sgt Roden inj 15-9 CE

P9432 595 FF GP 27-3-40 8MU 30-3 66S 11-5 dam ops 31-5 AST 152S 18-7 C2 ops 21-9 AST Stn Flt Ken 24-11 C2 ops 24-11 WAL 222MU 27-9 *Taran* 24-1-42 P Sudan 29-1-43 ME 31-3 std cd on app Aqir C3 2-8

P9433 596 FF GP 27-3-40 8MU 30-3 92S 22-5 Farn June '40 C2 ops 5-7 WAL 610S 9-8 s/dn by Bf110 over Mayfield Sgt Manton kld 29-8 AST 131S 11-9-41 52 OTU 26-10 50 OTU 9-5-42 FACB 12-3-43 SAL RNAS 27-5 CE 13-10-44

P9434 597 FF GP 28-3-40 8MU 30-3 92S 23-5 s/dn in transit Stanford Tuck safe 13-7 1CRU 222S 22-9 dam by Bf109 nr Battle P/O Carpenter safe C2 30-10 AST 57 OTU 28-7-41 spun into grd Picton Cheshire 6-12 SOC 16-12

P9435 598 FF 28-3-40 6MU 30-3 65S 23-5 FTR ops 28-5

P9436 599 FF 28-3-40 6MU 1-4 65S 11-5 C2 ops 5-8 AST 57 OTU e/fld f/ld o/t Caerwys racecourse Flint CE 10-7-41 SOC 21-7 FH138.20

P9437 600 FF GP 30-3-40 6MU 1-4 65S 11-5 FTR ops 26-5

P9438 601 FF 29-3-40 6MU 1-4 72S 12-5 dam by Bf109 nr Dung F/Lt Smith aban a/c cd New Romney C3 31-8 9

P9439 602 FF GP 30-3-40 6MU 1-4 72S 11-5 FAC2 26-6 SAL 72S 2-9 602S 14-12 61 OTU 6-7-41 e/fld w/u ldg o/t Stevenage Herts C3 21-11 SOC 27-11

P9440 603 FF GP 30-3-40 6MU 1-4 152S 11-5 dam by Bf109 P/O Baynes safe C2 18-7 AST 603S 3-9 dam ops 15-10 AST 61 OTU 28-6-41 19S 7-9 331S 17-11 61 OTU 29-10-42 39MU NEA 21-11-44 SOC 3-5-45

P9441 604 FF 1-4-40 6MU 5-4 74S 12-5 s/dn over e/tr 24-5-40

P9442 605 FF 31-3-40 6MU 2-4 152S 11-5 602S 61 OTU 4-8-41 GAL 30-9 recat E SOC 29-12

P9443 606 FF 1-4-40 6MU 5-4 222S 4-6 s/dn des in cd/ld nr Sittingbourne F/Lt Matheson inj 3-8

P9444 607 FF 2-4-40 Farn 23-5 cont syst trls 6MU 23-5 72S 4-6 airframe overstrained in dive after P/O Elliot passed out through lack of oxygen C3 cd/ld 3-7 1CRU Ros 19-8 58 OTU CATB 5-5-4 72S markings Extant Science Mus London

P9445 608 FF GP 2-4-40 8MU 5-4 92S 23-5 50 OTU 20-7 53 OTU i/sea off Southendown Glam 5-10-41

P9446 609 FF GP 3-4-40 8MU 5-4 54S 1-6 dam ops Sgt Mould ldg Mans safe 10-7 GAL 602S dam by Ju88 nr Beachy Head P/O Hart safe 12-10 234S 8-11 FACB 8-2-41 AST 52 OTU 16-5-42 eng fire a/c aban cd nr ADn CE 6-2-43

P9447 610 FF 3-4-40 8MU 5-4 64S 2-6 Farn June '40 41S 17-9 s/dn by Bf109 nr West Kingsdown P/O Lecky aban a/c kld 11-10

P9448 611 FF GP 4-4-40 ETPS Farn 11-4 aero-medical, photographic and neg G trls. To RAF for service neg G trls 72S 4-6 dam by Bf109 f/ld F/O Thompson inj CE 1-9 AST con to FVA M45 Farn aero-medical trls with emphasis on effect of black out in high G manoeuvres 530TU 24-6-41 81S ran off runway ldg stk obst Ouston CE 7-2-42

P9449 612 FF 4-4-40 8MU 8-4 64S 2-6 FTR ops over France 5-7

P9450 613 FF GP 5-4-40 8MU 8-4 64S 2-6 dam by Bf109 nr Rouen France

P9451 614 FF 5-4-40 8MU 8-4 610S 2-6 dam by Bf109 cd/ld Sandwich P/O Gardiner inj 25-8 GAL C3 ops 11-12 SOC 27-12

P9452 615 FF 5-4-40 8MU 8-4 610S 2-6 Farn July '40 FTR ops 18-7 P/O Litchfield missing

P9453 616 FF 6-4-40 8MU 10-4 HAL 22-4 con to PR IV Type C 212S France. E Flt PRU for exp flts with F/Lt Longbottom and Dr Hislop July '40 FTR ops 14-9 FF22.20

P9454 617 FF 6-4-40 8MU 8-4 92S 4-6 e/fld f/ld in bog nr Cardiff P/O Bartley safe 5-7 1CRU 65S 26-8 s/dn over Tilehurst Sussex a/c aban dbf 1-12

P9455 618 FF 7-4-40 9MU 10-4 54S 19-4 FTR ops 24-5 FH21.15

P9456 619 FF GP 6-4-40 9MU 12-4 152S 25-4 believed s/dn by Ju88 off St Catherines Point 12-8 F/Lt Withall mising

P9457 620 FF GP 8-4-40 8-4-40 9MU 11-4 72S 3-5 Farn June '40 s/dn by Bf109 nr Dung P/O Wilcox kld 31-8

P9458 621 FF GP 8-4-40 9MU 11-4 72S 3-5 s/dn by Bf109 over Kent P/O Pigg kld 2-9

P94559 622 FF 9-4-40 9MU 11-4 603S 6-5 dam by Bf109 f/ld F/Lt Rushmer inj 29-8 COAL 53 OTU 3-9-41 air coll with X4823 i/sea off Nash Point Glam 29-10

P9460 623 FF GP 9-4-40 9MU 11-4 72S 4-5 61 OTU 1-7-41 FAAC 11-8-42 to 3593M 6SoTT 2-3-43 CE 4-12-44

P9461 624 FF 10-4-40 9MU 12-4 602S 3-6 dam on ops cd in night ldg Drem C2 1-8-40 SAL SOC 6-9

P9462 624 FF 10-4-40 9MU 12-4 5 OTU 6-6 FAC2 17-8 1CRU 41S 3-1 92S 14-11 53 OTU 25-3-41 SOC Oct '41

P9463 626 FF 10-4-40 9MU 12-4 602S 3-6 dam e/a Tang C2 16-8 AST 152S 8-9 s/dn on ops nr Portsmouth Sgt Silver kld CE 25-9

P9464 627 FF GP 11-4-40 9MU 12-4 238S 20-5 92S 20-8 s/dn by Bf109 East London P/O Edwards kld 11-9 SOC 3-10 FH52.15

P9465 628 FF GP 11-4-40 24MU 15-4 74S 3-6 dam ops cd/ld Mans PO Stevenson safe 8-7 1CRU 7 OTU 16-8 54S 27-9 C2 ops 30-9 SAL 58 OTU 26-2-41 131S 23-8 CAC 18-9 ASTH SOC 19-12

P9466 629 FF 11-4-40 24MU 13-4 234S 18-5 s/dn by Bf109 SE London S/Ldr O'Brien kld 7-9 SOC 23-9

P9467 630 FF 12-4-40 24MU 15-4 609S 4-6 C2 ops 12-7 1CRU 603S s/dn ops 7-9 Sgt Sarre aban a/c inj

P9468 631 FF 12-4-40 24MU 15-4 249S 20-5 234S 20-5 w/u ldg St Eval Sgt Harker safe C2 10-8 1CRU 57 OTU 10-5-41 53 OTU 27-11 a/c aban nr Widercombe Devon CE 15-8-42

P9469 633 FF GP 13-4-40 24MU 17-4 602S 20-5 222S 21-5 s/dn over Hawkhurst P/O Broadhurst kld 7-10 a/c dug up in Aug 71 on Kent/Sussex border by Robertsbridge Aviation Society

P9490 632 FF 12-4-40 24MU 15-4 7 OTU 24-7 FAC2 24-12 AST H St Fm dis 5-4-41 61 OTU 12-11 53 OTU 17-7-42 SFTS 12-7-43 dvd i/grd nr Desborough CE 10-1-44 SOC 1-2-44 FH564.10

P9491 634 FF 13-4-40 24MU 17-4 249S 20-5 234S 20-5 C2 ops 4-7 AST 602S 19-8 234S 13-11 dam ops 2-1-41 58 OTU 27-3 53 OTU 17-7 flew into high grd nr Tonpentre Glam CE 3-1-42

P9492 635 FF GP 14-4-40 24MU 17-4 74S 3-6 222S 15-9 s/dn by Bf109 cd Denham Sgt Hutchinson inj C3 30-9

P9493 636 FF 15-4-40 24MU 17-4 249S 20-4 234S 20-5 cd Porthdown Cornwall P/O Gout kld C3 25-7 SOC FH71.15

P9494 637 FF 15-4-40 24MU 17-4 249S 20-5 234S 20-5 dam by Bf109 nr Portsmouth f/ld Sgt Boddington inj C2 26-8 HAL St Fm dis 9-4-41 57 OTU 10-1-42 air coll with X4270 nr Haw CE 14-3

P9495 638 FF 16-4-40 8MU 610 2-6 dam by Bf109 nr Dover C3 12-8 SOC 24-8

P9496 639 FF GP 16-4-40 8MU 18-4 610S 2-6 a/c aban over Hawk dbf 26-8

P9497 640 FF 12-4-40 8MU 20-4 5 OTU 3-5 7 OTU 13-8 C3 ops 31-8 SAL 58 OTU 4-7-41 spun into grd nr Bannockburn Stirling dbf CE 2-10 SOC 9-10

P9498 641 FF 17-4-40 8MU 20-4 610S 7-6 hit tractor during scramble t/o Graves cd CE 29-6 SOC 6-7

P9499 642 FF GP 17-4-40 8MU 20-4 OTU 3-5 603S 6-9 266S 30-10 111S 3-4-41 FAAC 28-4-41 58 OTU 16-6 spun i/grdc Bannockburn 2-10 52 OTU 23-11 61 OTU 30-1-43 cd f/ldg Rednal CB 5-8

P9500 643 FF 18-4-40 8MU 20-4 5 OTU 3-5 FA 28-5 AST 41S 6-9 s/dn by Bf109 C2 20-9 SAL air coll with AR240 w/u ldg nr Cowbridge Glam 15-3-42

P9501 644 FF 18-4-40 8MU 20-4 5 OTU 3-5 7 OTU 13-8 129S 14-8-41 58 OTU 4-9 52 OTU 7-2-42 58 OTU 21-6-43 CE 18-8-44

P9502 645 FF 19-4-40 8MU 23-4 610S 2-6 dvdi/grd Titsey Park Sgt Ireland k/d C3 12-7

P9503 646 FF 19-4-40 AMDP DeH prop trls 26-4 9MU 5-6 257MU 7-6 610S 11-7- C2 ops 31-7 GAL 609S 26-9 C3 ops p/o Baillon a/c aban nr Upaven 27-10 SOC 1-11

P9504 666 FIB first prod a/c with 2 × 20mm can and 4 × .303 m/gs FF 30-4-40 1AAS 8-5 FA dam 23-5 SOC 4-10 to 2728M 30-9-41 SOC 3-6-45

P9505 647 FF 20-4-40 12MU 25-4 249S 18-5 222S 6-7 C2 ops 31-8 234S 21-10 266S 21-10 DGRD BDn 29-12 seven days requirement for check on metal ails. 111S 3-4-41 58 OTU 11-9 HAL 16-5-42 con to PRVII Type G M46 140S TAF 19-2-43 SOC 27-2-45

P9506 648 FF 20-4-40 12MU 25-4 249S 20-5 FA ops 25-5 AW 54S 1-9 cd f/ld S Ellerton 10-2-41 SAL SOC E 28-2

P9507 649 FF 21-4-40 12MU 25-4 19-5 64S 3-7 s/dn by Bf109 5-7 s/dn by Bf109 f/ld Hailsham F/O Taylor inj 17-7 to 2119M 22-10

P9508 651 FF 21-4-40 12MU 3-5-40 249S 19-5 234S 19-8 FAC2 1-11 AST 123S 15-8-41 215MU 28-9-42 *Pet Mer* 8-11 lost at sea 8-1-43

P9509 650 FF 23-4-40 12MU 25-4 19S 18-9 152S 26-9 58 OTU 23-3-41 53 OTU 6-1-42 e/fd w/u ldg nr Llan CE 2-4 SOC 9-4

P9510 652 FF 23-4-40 12MU 4-5 249S 20-5 602S 13-7 C2 ops 30-9 P/O Hart safe 61 OTU 20-4-41 52 OTU 30 10 FACB 13-3-43 175FTS 16-7 SOC 8-3-45

P9511 653 FF 23-4-40 12MU 4-5 249S 19-5 610S 25-8 s/dn by Bf109 nr Deal P/O Cox kld 28-8

P9512 654 FF GP 23-4-40 12MU 4-5 249S 20-5 610S 7-7 C2 ops 14-7 AST C3 ops 27-9 41S e/fld cd/ld nr Romford Sgt McAdam safe CE 12-10 SOC 21-10

P9513 655 FF 23-4-40 12MU 4-5 249S 19-5 92S 7-7 s/dn by Bf109 f/ld Hawk P/O Wade safe 15-9 152S 21-10 452S 8-5-41 313S 21-5 61 OTU 14-8 53 OTU 11-1-42 strk by N3247 while parked CE 12-4 SOC 14-4

P9514 656 FF 24-4-40 24MU 29-4 5 OTU 10-5 hit wall on t/o ADn CE 21-5 SOC

P9515 657 FF GP 25-4-40 24MU 29-4 5 OTU 10-5 o/s ldg hit wall ADn CB 26-5 AW 6MU 21-7 602 27-8 dam by Bf109 at Mayfield P/O Lyall safe 30-10 610S 14-12 53 OTU 2-3-41 DeH 15-4-42 new eng 52 OTU 7-7 58 OTU 21-6 1TEU26-2-44

P9516 658 Ambonia FF GP 25-4-40 24MU 29-4 5 OTU 11-5 FA ops 22-5 65S 12-7 C2 ops 3-8 222S 20-11 f/ld o/t New Romney Kent 14-1-41 1CRU 132S 17-7 flew i/grd Tilley Maud Farm Northaven ttl wrk 29-11 SOC 30-11-44

P9517 659 FF 26-4-40 24MU 29-4-40 5 OTU 11-5 cd f/ld nr Leominster Hereford CE 20-5 SOC

P9518 661 FF GP 27-4-40 24MU 7-5 5 OTU 23-5 FAC3 7-8 GAL HAL 7-1-42 contract loan con to PRVII Type G 1PRU 4-5 CB ops 10-8-42 HAL 8 OTU 27-2-43 e/fld f/ld nr Fraser CE 16-12

P9519 662 FF 27-4-40 24MU 7-5 7 OTU 17-6 FAC2 18-7 1CRU 234S 10-9 66S 18-9 C2 ops 27-9 1CRU 64S 22-12 303S 10-2-41 FACB 2-3 1CRU 1CRU 412S 9-7 58 OTU dam 14-2-42 GAL CE 12-7-44

P9540 644 FF 30-4-40 38MU 7-5 257S 19-5 GAL 22-8 61 OTU 4-7 AST 4-9 con to FVA M45 121S 26-4-42 164S 20-5 602S 10-9 61 OTU 10-8-43 52 OTU 22-8 1 TEU 1906-44

P9541 665 FF GP 30-4-40 38MU 6-5 257S 18-5 57 OTU 21-7 hvy ldg Sealand C2 17-12 AST 52 OTU 17-7-42 eng fire in h/a dive a/c aban cd Highcombe Cemetery Bath 8-4-43 SOC

P9542 667 FF 30-4-40 38MU 6-5 257S 18-5 7 OTU 17-6 FA 20-6 222S 7-9 C2 on ops 14-9 AST 92S 24-10 C2 ops 1-12 GAL 308S 18-5-41 for defence of Austin works 52 OTU FACB 8-12 58 OTU 21-7-42 33MU 27-8-44

P9543 668 FF GP 1-5-40 38MU 6-5 252S 18-5 7 OTU 22-7 FAC2 24-9 152S 26-9 58 OTU 23-3-41 3 SGR w/u ldg Squires Gate 21-3-42

P9544 670 FF 2-5-40 38MU 6-5 257S 18-5 1 OTU 17-6 FAC2 6-7 GAL 92S 12-9 C2 ops cd/ld Lewes Racecourse P/O Wade safe 27-9 GAL 222MU 11-9-43 *Tellas Forca de Tarsmaga* 7-10-43 Port 16-10

P9545 672 FF 5-5-40 38MU 7-5 257S 18-5 610S 11-7 dam by Bf109 nr Dover C2 12-8 AST 64S 29-9 FAC2 10-10 SAL 58 OTU 26-2-41 132S 12-8 air coll with N3100 nr Abernethy Perth CE 21-4-42

P9546 673 FF 5-5-40 38MU 6-5 257S 18-5 19S 3-9 457S 14-8-41 58 OTU 22-10 52 OTU 7-2-42 struct fail in flt cd nr Dymuck Station Glos 12-2-42

P9547 674 FF 5-5-40 8MU 8-5 54S 4-6 74S 4-6 s/dn by Bf109 nr Dover P/O Young kld 28-7 SOC 31-8 FH80.35

P9548 676 FF 4-5-40 8MU 9-5 92S 4-6 a/c aban cd/ld Martlesham P/O Hargreaves safe C3 27-8 SOC 11-9

P9549 677 FF 4-5-40 8MU 8-5 54S 4-6 FA 25-7 GAL 53 OTU 25-10 flew into hill nr Trebanog ttl wrk 21-11-41 SOC 28-11

P9550 678 FF GP 6-5-40 8MU 2PDU HAL 20-5 con to PRIII Type C 1PRU 27-4-41/PRU Wick 1-7 C2 ops cd/ld Bexhill 27-12 AST HAL 31-1 mods to PRV 1PRU 17-4 R-R M45 instal 7-8 1401Flt 1-9 HAL 9-9 FTR ops 7-11 (originally for Turk)

P9551 1162 The Bowser PRIII Type D proto CRD contract SB 2415/C23A not on contract 980356/39 FF 15-9-40 HAL 18-9 Malta 27-1-41 FTR ops 2-2

P9552 1473 initial details as 9551 HAL 22-2-41 2PRU 26-2 FTR ops 10-5 FH87.400

P9553 738 FF 29-5-40 6MU 10-6 603S 8-9 s/dn over Thames Estuary by Bf109 P/O Dexter aban a/c inj dbf 2-10 (originally for Turk)

P9554 739 FF 29-5-40 6MU 10-6 64S 14-8 s/dn by a Bf109 at Waldron Sussex S/Ldr MacDonnell aban a/c 16-8 FH17 (originally for Turk)

P9555 740 FF 31-5-40 6MU 11-6 65S 16-8 303S 22-1-41 58 OTU 20-3 air coll cd nr Airdrie Lanarks CE 26-4-42 (originally for Turk)

P9556 776 FF 12-6-40 6MU 13-6 64S 16-8 f/ld Rotherfield Sussex into ditch 21-12 53 OTU 30-8-41 ASTH 17-10 con to FVA M45 RNDA 4-9-42 RNAS 7-1-44

P9557 780 FF 13-6-40 6MU 14-6 64S 16-8 FAAC 18-8 SAL 57 OTU 9-8-41 222MU 9-11-42 *Algarab* 11-3-43 P Sudan 12-3 ME 31-3 SOC 27-7-44

P9558 693 FF GP 20-6-40 9MU 25-6 54S 1-9 e/fld a/c aban nr Catt 25-10 (originally for Turk)

P9559 694 FF 20-6-40 9MU 20-6 54S 1-9 5 OTU 3-2-41 FAAC 27-4 air coll with Spit cd Kimmel Park Bodelwydd An Flint dbf 2-11 SOC 15-11

P9560 701 FF GP 21-6-40 9MU 25-6 54S 1-9 dvd into grd nr Bolton on Swale Kent P/O Sanders kld C3 7-9 (originally for Turk)

P9561 685 FF GP 26-6-40 8MU 26-6 PRU 19-8 con to PRIII Type C PRU Benson FTR ops 16-2-41 FH101.20 (originally for Turk)

P9562 675 FF GP 28-6-40 8MU 29-6 65S 18-8 FACB 13-1-41 AST CGS 13-3 DeH 16-4-42 new eng 52 OTU 15-7 air coll with P7834 SOC 6-3-45 (originally for Turk)

P9563 671 FF 2-5-40 8MU 4-7 64S 19-8 cd Hartington Sgt Lloyd safe C3 5-9 SAL 53 OTU 15-7-41 con to FVA M45 2-8-41 332S 27-1-42 164S 10-5 FACE 23-8 SOC 31-8

P9564 669 FA 11-3-40 8MU 5-7 64S 19-8 FA cd C3 Sgt Laws safe 30-9 SOC 7-10 (originally for Turk)

P9565 702 FF 16-5 -40 AMDP BDn as Type 343 30-8 trls with 30 gal o/ld tank under port wng. Trls with DeH prop. Service trls with No. 66, 118 and 152S. AMDP VA 29-9 Spcl Duty Flt Christchurch 15-10 con to FVA M45 13-3-41 59 OTU 2-10 HAL 30-4-42 con to PRVIII Type G 1PRU 16-7 542S 30-9 8 OTU 5-5-43 CE 25-2-44 SOC 25-8 sold to Turk

P9566 660 FF 27-4-40 SDF Christchurch N22 marks. Sold to Turk as Type 341

P9567 663 FF 27-4-40 details as 9566 N23 marks. Sold Turk.

P9568 to 9584, 17 a/c cancelled.

Contract No.B19713/39

First order for 450 Spitfire Mk 1 dated 9 August 1939. Built as Mk I and Mk VA/VB between April 1940 and April 1941. Serial allocation in the 'R' range was halted at R7022 in July 1940 and 'X' series applied from X4009 to 4997 (see page 89 and 95). The 'R' series continued again from R7023 to 7350 from January to April 1941. The following serials apply to Mk I variants built to this first order. R6595 to 6644; 6683 to 6722; 6751 to 6780; 6799 to 6818; 6829 to 6840; 6879 to 6928; 6957 to 6996; 7015 to 7028; 7057 to 7074; 7114 to 7163; 7192 to 7206; 7211, 7212, 7214 to 7216; 7250 to 7252; 7257. Total built 348. First delivery 29-4-40 All F Mk IA Merlin III unless otherwise indicated (Contract Price £4,250 each)

R6595 679 FF 7-5-40 8MU 9-5 PDU 28-5-40 VEA 4-6 PDU 28-7 FTR ops 26-8

R6596 686 FF 7-5-40 8Mu 12-5 92S 4-6 C2 ops 9-9 AST C3 ops 30-9 HAL 131S 17-7-41 52 OTU 22-10 DeH 9-10 57 OTU 11-5-43 FACB 17-3-44 SOC 1-4 FH1148.05

R6597 687 FF 7-5-40 8MU 12-5 92S 4-6 dam night ldg Pembrey Sgt Fokes safe C2 22-7 41S 29-9 152S 5-11 C3 ops 28-11 SOC 20-12

R6598 680 FF GP 7-5-40 8MU 9-5 28-5 con to PRIII Type C PRU ben FTR ops 22-2-41 FH207-35

R6599 681 FF 8-5-40 9MU 11-5 238S 20-5 7 OTU 15-6 FACB 2-7 SAL 8-7 610S 11-9 FAC3 12-10 SOC 25-10

R6600 682 FF 8-5-40 238S 20-5 FA 31-5 AST 602S 19-8 FAC2 6-9 dam ldg 15-9 SAL 152S 13-11 58 OTU 4-6-41 57 OTU 2-8-43 e/fld hit trees and lost wngs in f/ldg nr Warkworth N'Land CE 22-12-43

R6601 683 FF GP 9-5-40 9MU 11-5 238S 20-5 602S 20-8 610S 14-12 CAC ops 5-2-41 57 OTU 12-6 o/s ldg Haw cd Two Mills nr Ledsham Cheshire dbf 10-7 SOC 11-7

R6602 685 FF 10-5-40 9MU 13-5 238S 20-5 65S 11-8 PRU 20-11 CB opos 19-1-41 53 OTU 16-7 AST con to FVA M45 30-8 North 9-5-42 2USA 52nd Ftr Grp 4-8 FAAC 9-8 S&H 61 OTU 20-3-44 FACE 6-5 rtp 27-5

R6603 689 FF 10-5-40 9MU 14-5 238S 20-5 74S 10-8 66S 13-9 s/dn by Bf109 nr Graves Sgt Corfe inj CE 18-9 SOC 3-10

R6604 688 FF GP 10-5-40 9MU 13-5 238S 20-5 41S 1-8 s/dn nr Dover Sgt Darling safe 24-9 1CRU 54S 4-1-41 41S 22-2 452S 30-4 313S 22-5 FAAC 5-4 FACB 30-6 61 OTU 8-11 CB 12-10-42 RNDA 11-5-43 RNAS 9-7

R6605 690 FF GP 13-5-40 9MU 14-5 238S 19-5 41S 30-8 s/dn by Bf109 S/Ldr Lister aban a/c inj 14-9

R6606 691 FF 13-5-40 9MU 15-5 238S 19-5 FACB 10-6 AST 74S 1-9 C3 ops 15-9 61 OTU 1-7-41 53 OTU 23-6-42 58 OTU 28-1-43 flew into high grd West Cairn Hill Midlothian CE 17-2-43 SOC FH296.30

R6607 692 FF 14-5-40 9MU 16-5 238S 19-5 7 OTU 15-6 FAC2 2-7 WAL 152S 27-9 cd nr Dorchester Sgt Shepperd k/d 18-10

R6608 695 FF 15-5-40 9MU 16-5 238S 19-5 152S 21-7 dam over Portland P/O Inness inj C2 13-8 AST 152S 8-10 58 OTU 23-4-41 610S 9-10 FACB 11-10 SOC 17-10

R6609 696 FF GP 15-5-40 12MU 17-5 65S 1-6 s/dn by Bf109 nr Folkes 7-7 FTR

R6610 697 FF 16-5-40 238S 18-5 8MU 16-7 65S 4-8 41S 9-9 dam by Bf109 C2 17-9 SAL 1416 Flt 14-9-41 FTR ops 24-11

R6611 698 FF 16-5-40 12MU 3-5 238S 18-5 41S 30-7 FAC2 3-9 616S 1-1-41 65S 26-2 308S 6-4 403S 27-5 FAAC 2-7 61 OTU 30-7 dvd into grd Waterbury Oxen dbf 16-9 SOC 2-10

R6612 FF 17-5-40 12MU 18-5 238S 18-5 41S 30-7 dam in combat C2 15-9 AST 610S 7-11 602S 14-12 52 OTU 4-2-41 FACB 27-3 GAL 412S 9-7 dam e/ac CAC 11-8 53 OTU 23-6 fire after e/fld f/ld nr Llan CE 13-2-42

R6613 700 FF GP 18-5-40 12MU 3-5 238S 18-5 92S 20-8 s/dn by Bf109 E London F/Lt Paterson safe CE 11-9 SOC 3-10

R6614 703 18-5-40 12MU 21-5 19S 31-5 e/a 31-5 AST 152S 26-7 s/dn i/sea by Bf109 P/O Jones aban a/c & drowned 11-8 FH12.15

R6615 704 FF 18-5-40 12MU 21-5 65S 1-6 s/dn by Bf109 nr Folkes FTR7-7

R6616 705 FF 19-5-40 12MU 24-5 92S 31-5 C2 ops P/O Hill safe 16-9 ops air coll X4038 F/O Drummond kld aban a/c10-10 FH44-45

R6617 706 FF GP 20-5-40 12MU 21-5 65S 1-6 dbf ops 1-8 SOC 13-8

R6618 707 FF 20-5-40 12MU 24-5 65S 1-6 dbf 16-8

R6619 708 FF 21-5-40 12MU 24-5 65S 1-6 603S 10-9 41S 10-9 dam by Bf109 nr Horn C2 28-9 SAL 111S 3-5-41 FACE 8-5 SOC 22-5

R6620 709 FF 21-5-40 12MU 24-5 65S 1-6 C2 ops 23-8 GAL 152S 11-12 58 OTU 23-3-41 SAL 26-5 con to FVA M45 58 OTU 23-8 P&P 2-3-43 RNAS 24-7 SOC 23-11-44

R6621 710 FF 22-5-40 12MU 24-5 FA del flt AST 610S 24-7 dam ops P/O Keighley inj 20-7 dam by Bf109 nr Dover C2 12-8 AST 234S 5-10 C2 ops 9-10 AST 61 OTU 1-7-41 CGS 25-1-42 53 OTU 9-7 strk P7827 ldg Llan CAC 2-5-43 ROS 39MU NEA 11-7-44 SOC 8-3-45

R6622 711 FF 21-5-40 12MU 26-5 92S 31-5 s/dn by Bf109 Sgt Oldfield kld 27-9 SOC 9-10

R6623 712 FF GP 22-5-40 12MU 26-5 19S 4-6 64S 5-8 41S 28-2 452S 24-4 313S 23-8 ASTH 26-8 con to FVA M45 303S 5-12 81S 12-2-42 FAAC 31-3 ROS 165S 12-4 45S 15-7 coll with EN848 on ldg CB 28-7 S&H 61 OTU 10-5-43 FACE 22-4-44 rtp 27-5

R6624 713 FF 23-5-40 12MU 26-5 92S 31-5 s/dn by Bf109 Sgt McGowan aban a/c safe CE 14-9

R6625 714 FF GP 23-5-40 12MU 26-5 19S 31-5 Oxygen failed cd Orsett Sussex Sgt Marek kld 14-9

R6626 FF GP 23-5-40 12MU 25-5 603S 20-7 266S 20-10 111S 11-4-41 CAC ops 16-4 58 OTU 17-6 SAL 4-6-42 PRU Ben 24-9 222MU 10-8-43 *Emp Rhod* 14-8 Port 29-8

R6627 716 FF 24-5-40 12MU 25-5 19S 31-5 C2 ops 2-8 234S 8-9 FAC2 8-9 HAL 11-9 602S 24-1-41 124S 22-7-41 52 OTU 12-11 1TEU 22-3-44 CE 18-8

R6628 717 FF GP 24-5-40 12MU 28-5 202S 8-6 s/dn cd Bishopsbourne Sgt Johnson kld 31-8 SOC 11-9

R6629 718 FF 24-5-40 24MU 27-5 610S 31-5 C2 ops 31-8 1CRU 313S 4-7 58 OTU 5-9-41 FAAC 23-7-42 ROS 57-OTU 4-3-43 RNDA 15-1-44

R6630 719 FF 24-5-40 24MU 27-5 610S 31-5 s/dn by Bf109 off Calais Sgt Neville kld 11-8

R6631 720 FF GP 25-5-40 24MU 21-5 FA 31-5 609S 16-8 FTR ops 28-11 FH93.10

R6632 721 FF 25-5-40 24MU 28-5 616S 31-5 dam nr Dung f/ld P/O Walker inj C226-8 COAL 130S 7-9-41 132S 12-9 52 OTU 28-10 FACB 19-7-42 stn flt 12 Grp 7-11 SOC 26-4-45

R6633 722 FF 26-5-40 12MU 28-5 616S 1-6 s/dn by Bf109 nr Dung P/O Marples inj 26-8

R6634 723 FF 26-5-40 24M 30-5 609S 4-6-40 i/sea ops a/c aban 18-7

R6635 724 FF GP 26-5-40 24MU 30-5 Farn June'40 41S 5-6 air coll P9428 over Kent F/Lt Webster kld

R6636 725 FF 27-5-40 24MU 30-5 609S 4-6 s/dn by Ju88 f/ld Studland Beach F/O Edge safe C2 18-7 SOC 26-7 to 2139M 2SoTT 19-8-42 409S ATC 15-11-43

R6637 726 FF 27-5-40 24MU 30-5 609S 4-6 FTR ops F/O Drummond-Hay 9-7-40

R6638 727 FF GP 27-5-40 24MU 30-5 611S 6-6 dam ops 20-6 WAL 222S 8-9 s/dn by Bf109 f/ld P/O Assheton safe C2 11-9 123S 30-5-41 58 OTU 2-10 e/fld lost wng ldg nr Ladybank Fife CE 29-7-42 SOC 4-8

R6639 728 FF 28-5-40 38MU 31-5 64S 26-7 dam by Bf109 Sgt Mann safe C2 9-8 AST 53 OTU 25-8-41 FACB 10-9 GAL SOC 29-12

R6640 729 FF 28-5-40 38MU 31-5 5 OTU 5-6 FAC3 1-7 SOC 6-7

R6641 730 FF GP 28-5-40 38MU 31-5 610S 13-8 C2 opd 24-8 AST SOC 18-4-45

R6642 731 FF GP 29-5-40 38MU 31-5 92S 26-9 FTR after comb Bf109 Sgt Parker kld 15-10 FH20.20

R6643 732 FF 29-5-40 38MU 31-5 64S 26-7 dam by Ju87 over St Margarets Bay f/ld Sgt Binham safe C3 29-7 AST 152S 23-9 58 OTU

R6644 733 EA FF 30--5--40 DEL 31-5 23-3-41 FA FTR 10-4-41

R6683 736 FF 30-5-40 64S Lecon 26-7 dam ldg Catf Sgt Goodwin safe 22-9 64S i/sea Sgt Vinyard kld 6-10 FH124

R6684 734 FF GP 30-5-40 38MU 31-5 5 OTU 5-6 FA 1-7 WAL 222S 19-12 53 OTU 30-3-41 AST 18-6 con to FII MXII 64S 14-8 611S 12-11 52 OTU 23-3-42 FACB 30-5 1CRU 57-OTU 14-9 53 OTU 18-7-43 5(P)AFU 4-11-44 ASTH 15-5-45

R6685 742 FF GP 3-6-40 38MU 7-6 222S 6-9 132S 14-9 R-R 19-10 FA CE dbf 18-9-41 SOC 7-10

R6686 735 FF GP 31-5-40 38MU 31-5 610S 19-8 s/dn cd nr Eastbury Sgt Arnfield inj FAC3 24-8 SAL 57 OTU 30-7-41 FAC3 9-4-42 SOC 12-4

R6687 737 FF 1-6-40 6MU 3-6 Farn June'40 19S 7-6 7 OTU 7-8 57 OTU 6-12-41 e/fld cd/ld nr Esh CE 24-5-44

R6688 741 FF 1-6-40 6MU 3-6 19S 7-6 cd dbf C3 Sgt Birch kld 13-7 SOC 20-7

R6689 743 FF GP 2-6-40 6MU 3-6 66S 7-6 FAC2 11-8 66S s/dn by Bf109 a/c aban 4-9 P/O Cooke inj FH39.35

R6690 744 FF 3-6-40 6MU 5-6 609S 7-6 s/dn by Bf110 over S London P/O Daunt kld 15-9 SOC 18-9

R6691 745 FF 3-6-40 6MU 5-6 609S 7-6 C2 ops 25-9 AST 616S 10-11 602S 2-5-41 58 OTU 12-6 air coll with AR246 Letham Moor Stirling CE 18-3-43 SOC 31-3 FH672. 10

R6992 746 FF 3-6-40 6MU 5-6 609S 7-6 SOC E 2-9

R6693 747 FF GP 4-6-40 6MU 5-6 610S 7-6 cd burnt Sgt Smith kld 25-7

R6694 748 FF 5-6-40 6MU 5-6 610S 7-6 e/a C2 18-8 1CRU 485S 30-2-41 Fairey Av 19-5 52 OTU 20-11 42 OTU 31-1-44 SOC 18-12

R6695 749 FF 4-6-40 6MU 5-6 610S 7-6 s/dn dbf 22-8 Sgt Corfe safe

R6696 750 FF GP 5-6-40 Farn June'40 615S 7-6 night fly acc

R6697 751 FF 5-6--40 8MU 7-6 64S C2 ops 4-8 AST 41S 6-9 485S 30-3-41 FAAC 17-4 HAL to 2842M 5SoTT 3-12 SOC 18-12

R6698 752 FF 6-6-40 8MU 7-6 616S 9-6 cd/ld after t/o acc C2 P/O Casson safe 11-8 GAL 61 OTU 16-8 57 OTU 1-4-43 e/fld w/u ldg Eshott CE 9-6

R6699 753 FF 4-6-40 8MU 5-6 609S 7-6 C2 ops 25-9 AST 54S 26-1-41 41S 22-2 313S 18-6 61 OTU 14-8 FAC3 24-12 SOC 7-2-42

R6700 754 FF GP 5-6-40 8MU 7-6 64S 8-6 303S 22-1-41 CB ops 14-2 AST R-R 13-10 M61 instal FF with new eng 6-1-42 VAWD 6-1 trls SOC E 10-8 FH10.40

R6701 755 FF GP 6-6-40 8MU 7-6 616S 9-6 s/dn by Bf109 nr Dung

R6702 756 FF 7-6-40 8MU 7-6 616S 9-6 FAC2 11-8 GAL 41S 19-9 222S 20-9 s/dn by Bf109 Wennington F/O Smith inj C3 27-9 AST SOC 6-10

R6703 759 FF 7-6-40 8MU 10-6 92S 7-7 s/dn by Ju88 over Solent a/c exploded on ldg P/O Wade safe 19-8 SOC 20-9

R6704 757 FF 7-6-40 8MU 7-6 616S 9-6 72S 2-9 s/dn by Bf109 Sgt Bell-Walker inj C2 18-9 SAL 124S 9-5-41 58 OTU 6-11 RNAS Yeov 5-9-42 FACE 1-5-44

R6705 758 FF GP 7-6-40 8MU 7-6 54S 10-6 s/dn by Bf109 C3 9-7 P/O Garton kld

R6706 760 FF 7-6-40 8MU 10-6 74S 12-7 dam by Bf109 28-7 609S 26-9 66S 24-2-41 57 OTU 7-4 RNAS Don 26-2-42 P&P 28-2 53 OTU 14-1-43 ails fail cd Bell Cemetery Barrow on Humber 22-8

R6707 761 FF GP 8-6-40 9MU 9-6 54S 12-6 s/dn by Bf109 nr Dover F/Lt Way FTR 25-7

R6708 762 FF 8-6-40 9MU 9-6 54S 12-6 s/dn by Bf109 off Deal Sgt Collett kld 22-8 SOC 29-8

R6709 763 FF 8-6-40 9MU 9-6 54S 12-6 41S 22-2 452S 9-4 313S 16-6 FTR 26-6

R6710 764 FF GP 9-6-40 54S 12-6 dam by Bf109 24-7 AST 26-7 266S 19-8 72S 6-9 dam by Bf109 P/O Douthwaite inj C3 11-9 SAL 61 OTU 4-7-41 17SFTS 12-7-43

R6711 765 FF 9-6-40 9MU 10-6 54S 12-6 C3 ops 7-7 SOC 1207

R6712 766 FF GP 10-6-40 9MU 11-6 65S 10-7 FAC2 18-10 AST 53 OTU 6-5-41 FACE 11-5 SOC 24-5

R6713 767 Mk IB FF 10-6-40 9MU 11-6 65S 10-7 FTR after comb over Kent 18-8 parts of a/c dug up from Kent Marsh in 1971. F/O Gruszka buried Northwood Cemetery

R6714 768 FF 11-6-40 9MU 11-6 65S 10-7 cd nr Gateside Sgt Pearson kld 16-10

R6715 769 FF GP 11-6-40 9MU 11-6 66S 11-7 s/dn by Do17 i/sea off Norfolk P/O Pickering safe 30-8 FH 27.20

R6716 770 FF 11-6-40 9MU 14-6 74S 10-8 66S 12-9 DeH 24-11 129S 22-6-41 61 OTU 26-8 53 OTU 17-6-42 RNAS 14-9-43 dbr SOC

R6717 771 FF 11-6-40 12MU 13-6 603S 29-6 cd Inkhorn Aberdeen Sgt Arber kld C3 2-8

R6718 772 FF 12-6-40 12MU 13-6 AMDP Farn 7-7 trls of slotted flaps & ails for use on DP845 proto Mk XII. Trls continued with K9944 April '41. CGS 11-7 Farn 13-9 VAWD 25-9 AST 23-1-41 DGRD VA 21-5 wts & CG load GAL 9-5-42 52 OTU 28-8 140S 31-1-43 SOC 6-3-45

R6719 773 FF 12-6-40 12MU 13-6 222S 10-7 s/dn by Bf109 nr Rainham Sgt Hutchinson safe C2 30-8 1CRU 132S 11-7-41 RNAS 16-7-43 61 OTU 7-9 ASTH 5-5-45

R6720 774 FF GP 12-6-40 12MU 13-6 222S 10-7 s/dn f/ld nr Bekesbourne Kent P/O Assheton safe 30-8 COAL 3-9 8MU 22-12 con to FVA M45 22-12 130S 21-10-41 134S 25-12 133S 25-12 166S 6-11-42 288S 15-1-43 FAAC 31-1 ROS to 5425M 4-7-50

R6721 775 FF 12-6-40 12MU 13-6 603S 14-7 92S 24-9 f/ld Effingham Sgt Kingaby safe 27-10 FH 67.20

R6722 1650 FF 10-5-41 Arkwright fitt floats as Type 342. See page 380 for details. 39MU 10-5-41 54S 1-6 dam by Bf109 C2 25-6 AST 124S 17-11 81S 17-12 164S 12-4-42 167S 27-5 GAL 1-8 con to FVA M45 RNAS Stret 801S 9-9 884S LoS Oct '42 ret to RAF 30-1-45

R6751 777 FF 13-6-40 12MU 14-6 603S 14-7 s/dn C3 28-8 F/Lt Cunningham miss FH 21.30

R6752 778 FF 13-6-40 12MU 14-6 cd on del flt to 603S P/O Manlove safe 20-7 603S w/u ldg Horn after after comb P/O Haig safe 2-9 1CRU 266S 17-10 C2 ops 15-11 72S 27-3-41 57 OTU 2-5 58 OTU 23-8 61 OTU 17-6-42 57 OTU 8-8-43 CAC 22-10

R6753 779 FF 13-6-40 12MU 14-6 603S 14-7 s/dn Bf109 which badly dam R6753 F/O Pickney aban a/c inj bf 29-8

R6754 784 FF GP 12-6-40 12MU 18-6 603S 20-7 66S 24-9 57 OU 1-11 FA 11-11 to 2419M

R6755 785 FF 14-6-40 24MU 19-6 603S 5-7 dam by He111 f/ld Old Meldrum P/O Kilroy safe 18-7 SAL 41S 20-9 s/dn by Bf109 W Mall F/Lt Ryder aban a/c dbf 27-9

R6756 781 FF 14-6-40 24MU 15-6 41S 30-7 s/dn by Bf109 nr Dover dbf F/O Scott kld 8-9

R6757 782 FF GP 15-6-40 24MU 15-6 74S 29-7 s/dn by Bf110 off Clacton P/O Cobden kld 11-8 SOC 31-8 FH 18.05

R6758 783 FF 14-6-40 24MU 15-6 616S 18-8 s/dn by Bf109 nr Dunge dbf Sgt Ridley kld 26-8

R6759 786 FF GP 15-6-40 24MU 17-6 74S 30-7 C2 ops 13-8 AST 611S 8-11 57 OTU 15-4-41 AST 25-7 con to FVA M45 41S 26-11 81S 17-2-42 165S 10-4 167S 10-4 RNDA Yeov 6-9 CE 20-12-47

R6760 787 FF GP 15-6-40 24MU 17-6 92S 3-8 cd B Hill After combat Bf109 Sgt Bowen-Morris safe 27-9 1CRU 234S 23-11 R-RH con to FVB M45 58 OTU 28-3-41 dvdi/grd Strathallan Camp nr Auchterarder 20-10 SOC 24-10

R6761 788 FF 18-6-40 24MU 19-6 6MU B Norton 21-6 cann wing fitt 19S 27-6 1CRU further mods 26-8 R-RH 21-4-41 con to FVA M45 92S 3-5-41 FTR ops 23-6 SOC 30-6 FH 151.35

R6762 789 FF GP 16-6-40 6MU B Norton 17-6 cann wing fitt 7 OTU 21-7 first cann Spitfire to RAF 19S 27-6 266S e/a C2 18-8 AST 222S 31-10 FAC2 16-11 AST 53 OTU 23-6-41 57 OTU 27-4-43 CE 12-4-44

R6763 790 FF 18-6-40 24MU 19-6 152S 22-7 FAC2 14-10 64S 6-12 303S 6-2-41 58 OTU 29-3 FAAC 7-2-42 53 OTU 19-11-43 SOC E 16-8-44

R6764 791 FF GP 17-6-40 24MU 17-6 152S 22-7 234S 25-10 FAC3 7-11 SOC 4-12

R6765 792 FF 17-6-40 6MU 19-6 610S 13-7 f/ld 8-8 GAL 12-8 41S 17-10 611S 24-11 485S 15-3-41 61 OTU 4-7 FACE ttl wrk 20-10 SOC 28-10

R6766 793 FF 17-6-40 6MU 20-6 65S 13-7 cd Eastry P/O Gregory aban a/c too low kld 13-8

R6767 794 FF 18-6-40 6Mu 19-6 64S 18-7 C2 ops 23-7 AST 92S 13-9 s/dn by Bf109 nr Maidstone F/Sgt Sydney kld 27-9

R6768 795 FF 19-6-40 6MU 20-6 266S 21-7 s/dn nr Deal dbf S/Ldr Wilkinson kld 16-8

R6769 796 FF 19-6-40 6MU 19-6 609S 31-7 C2 night ldg acc 2-9 AST 64S 11-12 FACB 22-2-41 AST 57 OTU air coll with K9864 CB 18-6-42 ASTH 61 OTU 2-2-43 cd low fly Hatton Hill Farm Hatton Cheshire 3-10

R6770 (CIG) 797 F.IB FF 20-6-40 6MU 23-6 cann wing fitt 19S 27-6 CE ops 22-8 1CRU BDn 7-10 with 2 × 20mm cann & 4 × .303 m/gs, mod spars. Perf & hand trls in comp with X4257. 92S 8-3-41 R-RH 30-3 con to FV M45 dam by Bf109 C2 14-6 1CRU MMOx 74S 5-12 CB ops 11-12 AST con to FIX M61 FF as IX 6-1-42 VAWD 20-3 310S 4-6 CA ops 16-6 306S 10-7-43

R6771 798 FF GP 19-6-40 6MU 20-6 74S 13-7 C2 ops 21-7 GAL 66S 8-9 92S 2-10 C3 ops 19-10 GAL 131S 23-8-41 134S 20-9 52 OTU 26-10 58 OTU 7-3-43 FAAC 12-7

R6772 799 FF GP 19-6-40 6MU 20-6 74S 13-7 222S 15-9 cd after comb Bf109 Sgt Hutchinson aban a/c inj 18-9 CE

R6773 800 FF GP 20-6-40 6MU 20-6 74S 13-7 222S 15-9 e/fd f/ld Latchingdon Derby Sgt Davis safe C3 26-10 HAL 303S 18-4-41 SOC 19-12

R6774 801 FF 20-6-40 6MU 23-6 AMDP Hatfield 26-6 Farn Oct'40 to 3597 3SoTT 2-3-43

R6775 802 FF 20-6-40 8MU 22-6 65S 12-7 54S 7-2-41 41S 22-2 hit steam roller on t/o 1-4 AST 58 OTU 9-3-43 CE rtp 15-8-44

R6776 (CIE) 807 FF 22-6-40 6MU 25-6 cann wing fitt 19S 27-6 BDn 4-9 VA 5-9 AFDU Dxfd 11-1-41 R-RH 10-2 con to FVB M45 AFDU Dxfd 21-2 92S 3-3 e/fd cd/ld 19-3 AST 316S 12-10 306S 12-12 e/a CAC 1-5-42 recat E WAL SOC 12-5 FH 234.00

R6777 803 FF 21-6-40 8MU 22-6 65S 12-7 C2 ops 30-7 GAL 616S 20-8 72S 2-9 92S 3-11 145S 4-2-41 AFDU 6-3 152S 13-3 Stn Flt H 10-4 57 OTU 4-8 61 OTU 3-1-42 FAC3 8-7

R6778 804 FF GP 21-6-40 8MU 22-6 19S 1-8 616S 4-8 dam by Do17 over Kenley C3 P/O Casson safe 1-9 SOC 8-9

R6779 805 FF 21-6-40 8MU 24-6 74S 12-7 C2 ops 28-7 AST 66S 10-9 s/dn by Bf109 cd P/O Corbett kld 8-10

R6780 806 FF GP 21-6-40 8MU 24-6 74S 12-7 602S 13-9 C2 ops 19-11 AST 152S 14-2-41 58 OTU 23-3 FA dbf 4-9 SOC 11-9

R6799 836 FF GP30-6-40 8MU 2-7 65S 12-7 t/o acc Horn dbf 2-8 SOC 10-8

R6800 837 FF GP 1-7-40 8MU 8-7 66S 26-7 s/dn by Bf109 P/O Reilly kld dbf 17-10 FH 19.45

R6801 (CIG) 848 FF GP 3-7-40 8MU 4-7 152S 26-7 609S 14-8 152S 13-10 AST 27-7-41 con to FVA M45 332S 24-1-42 164S 7-4 FACB 29-7 SAL 10-8 61 OTU 2-8-43 air coll with P7986 CE 3-10

R6802 865 FF 9-7-40 8MU 9-7 610S 7-8 s/dn by Bf109 nr Dung F/Lt Warner miss 16-8

R6803 882 FF GP 12-7-40 8MU 13-7 65S 8-8 53 OTU 6-5-41 FACE 10-10 SOC 13-10

R6804 808 FF GP 22-6-40 6MU 24-6 PDU HAL con to PRIII Type C 25-6 FACE 5-5-41 1PRU 6-6 FTR 27-7

R6805 809 FF GP 22-6-40 6MU 24-6 PDU HAL con to PRIII Type C C2 ops 16-9 SAL HAL 2-2-41 PRU Bens 9-4 FTR ops 3-5 FH 114.35

R6806 810 FF GP 23-6-40 6MU 24-6 610S 28-6 C3 ops 2-9 GAL 132S 12-7-41 52 OTU 24-8 strk R7114 ldg A Dwn CA 12-4-42 58 OTU 2-7-43 SOC 23-3-45

R6807 811 FF 23-6-40 6MU 25-6 610S 13-7 cd Skid House Tatsfield Sgt Watson-Parker kld 13-7

R6808 812 FF GP 24-6-40 6MU 25-6 603S 28-7 FAC3 1-9 SOC 11-9

R6809 (CIG) 813 FF GP 26-6-40 6MU 28-6 cann wing fitt 19S 5-7 222S 20-9 R-RH 11-1-41 con to FVB M45M AFDU Dxfd 22-2 91S 10-4 302S 17-11 CE ops 21-4-42 ASTEx P&PSM 11-10 fuel syst mods 222S 26-2-43 64S 31-3 118S 25-9 350S 13-4-44 CGS 3-10 SOC 4-9-45

R6810 814 FF GP 24-6-40 6MU 25-6 152S 21-7 s/dn off Portland P/O Hogg miss 25-8 FH 50.50

R6811 815 FF GP 24-6-40 6MU 29-6 152S 21-7 s/dn by Bf109 f/ld nr Bestwall Sgt Robinson safe a/c dbf 8-8

R6812 816 FF GP 25-6-40 8MU 26-6 54S 12-7 s/dn by Bf109 nr Foreness dbf P/O Allen kld 24-7 SOC 30-7

R6813 817 FF 25-6-40 8MU 26-6 AST 7-7 64S 1-9 C2 ops 5-12 AST 61 OTU 12-11 FACB 18-11 ASTEx 57 OTU 3-7-42 air coll with R7067 nr Morpeth CE 7-7-43 SOC 11-7

R6814 818 FF GP 25-6-40 8MU 26-6 54S 12-7 e/fd a/c aban over Lodeming dbf 24-10 SOC 31-10

R6815 819 FF 25-6-40 8MU 26-6 54S 12-7 f/ld Lympne after combat Bf109 P/O Kemp inj AST 122S 9-8-41 53 OTU 12-10 e/fld w/u ldg Penterey nr Chepstow dbf 4-6-42

R6816 820 FF GP 26-6-40 8MU 26-6 54S 12-7 s/dn by Bf109 off Dover P/O Finnie kld 25-7 SOC 8-8

R6817 821 FF GP 26-6-40 RNAS S'ton 27-6 8MU 14-11 R-RH con to FVA M45 8-5-41 521S 14-8-42 e/fld cd/ld CE 11-11 SOC 30-11

R6818 822 FF 26-6-40 8MU 28-6 65S 26-7 Farn July '40 to 2481M 3SoTT 14-6-44 SOC 27-8

R6829 823 FF GP 27-6-40 9MU 28-4 152S 10-8 dam C2 by Ju88 off The Needles P/O Beaumont safe 22-8 AST 57 OTU 11-8-41 FACE 13-2-42

R6830 824 FF 27-6-40 9MU 28-6 4FPP e/fld f/ld Stapleford Abbot Essex on del flt to 74S C3 13-8 SOC 23-8

R6831 825 FF GP 27-6-40 9MU 18-6 152S 19-8 s/dn i/sea by He111 W of Portland P/O Beaumont aban a/c 27-8

R6832 826 FF 27-6-40 9MU 29-6 54S 19-8 s/dn by Bf109 F/Lt Deere aban a/c 28-8 FH 16.40

R6833 (CIG) 827 FF GP 28-6-40 6MU 29-6 cann wing fitt 19S 1-7 Farn 4-9 trls of VHF Type TR1133 VA 5-9 AFDU North 21-10 92S 12-11 R-RH 16-2-41 con to FVB M45 92S 26-2 CAC ops 15-4 AST 312S 6-12 cd nr Aberystwyth CE 24-1-42 SOC June '42

R6834 828 FF 28-6-40 9MU 29-6 602S 19-8 s/dn by Bf109 over Hailsham C2 6-9 AST 54S 19-2-41 57 OTU 11-5 cd on Snowdonia dbf 26-5 SOC 11-6

R6835 829 FF GP 28-6-40 12MU 1-7 603S 14-7 C2 ops 31-8 1CRU 11-9 457S 22-6-41 53 OTU 20-10 St Flt Atcham 13-6-42 FAAC 24-6 61 OTU 14-8 RNAS 17-5-43

R6836 830 FF 28-6-40 12MU 6-7 266S 24-10 FAC2 5-11 GAL 61 OTU 30-6-41 FACE dbf 22-8 SOC 29-8

R6837 831 FF 30-6-40 12MU 1-7 222S 1-9 C2 ops 4-9 AST 65S 14-10 FAC2 18-10 145S 7-2-41 118S 8-3 66S 9-3 501S 27-4 61 OTU 4-8 39MU dis St. Frm 8-4-42 57 OTU 16-4-44 SOC 9-2-45

R6838 832 FF GP 29-6-40 24MU 30-6 FAC2 30-7 AST 92S 19-9 s/dn Bf109 cd nr High Halstow F/Lt Kingcome aban a/c inj 15-10 FH44.50

R6839 834 FF 30-6-40 24MU 30-6 74S 29-7 602S FTR ops Sgt Elcome miss 26-10

R6840 833 FF GP 29-6-40 74S 29-7 222S 15-9 dam by Bf109 cd Horn P/O Edsall safe C2 20-9 SAL CGS 13-3-41 76MU 6-10-42 *Tarantia* Port Sudan 29-1-43 ME 31-3 SOC 27-7-44

R6879 835 FF 29-6-40 24MU 2-7 con to PRIII Type C 1PRU 13-9 FA FTR 13-8 FH14

R6880 838 FF 1-7-40 24MU 4-7 4FPP strk balloon cable over Brockworth cd on del flt to 152S 13-8 SOC 23-8

R6881 839 FF 1-7-40 24MU 3-7 266S 13-8 72S 6-9 s/dn by Bf109 nr Canterbury P/O Laindsay safe 20-9 57 OTU 2-5-41 FACB 1-2-43 SAL RNAS 12-5-43 FAAC 21-6-43 SOC 21-6-45

R6882* 840 FF 1-7-40 6MU B Norton 28-6 cann wing fitt 7 OTU 3-9 AFDU Dxfd 11-1-41 R-RH 10-2 to FVB M45 92S 9-3 609S 30-8 FACE 10-1-42 SOC 17-1

R6883 841 FF 2-7-40 57 OTU air coll with K9953 7-10-43

R6884 842 FF GP 2-7-40 8MU 28-6 65S 12-7 s/dn ops 24-8

R6885 843 FF GP 2-7-40 8MU 4-7 41S 30-7 s/dn nr Benfleet F/O Lovell aban a/c 5-9

R6886 844 FF GP 2-7-40 8MU 3-7 65S 18-8 C2 ops 3-11 SAL 122S 3-6-41 FACB 23-10 SAL 3SoGR 27-2-42 8 OTU 24-5 e/fld a/c aban 5-11

R6887 845 FF GP 2-7-40 8MU 4-7 41S 30-7 dam by

* *Designation CMG applied. Thought to have indicated cannon and m/guns fitted.*

Bf109 over Kent C3 P/O Mackenzie safe 17-9 485S 15-3-41 57 OTU 15-3 air coll with Tiger Moth 4-6 AST Ex 12-6 con to FVA M45 41S 4-11 81S 15-12 165S 27-4-42 167S 27-5 RNDA 31-8 RNAS St Merryn cd nr St. Merryn pilot kld 27-6-43

R6888* 846 FF 3-7-40 8MU 5-7 cann wing fitt 19S 11-7 AFDU Northolt 28-11 92S 4-2-41 strk obst on t/o CE 10-2-41 HAL con to LFVB M45M 302S 12-9 P&PSM 12-10 fuel syst mods. 302S strk BL547 after ldg CB 20-12 HAL VASM 24-4-43 mods 308S 18-8 FAAC 28-8 9MU 16-11

R6889* 847 FIB FF 3-7-40 8MU 4-7 cann wing fitt 19SD 11-7 VA 25-8 first Mk. I to have 'B' wing (2 cann & 4 m/gs) Merlin XII. 152S 27-9 19S 5-10 Flt Lt lawson s/dn Bf109 5-11. First kill by Spit with 'B' wing. FAC2 22-12 MMOx con to FVB interim stage M45 and parts supplied by R-R. First flight in new config 13-2-41 R-RH 13-2 M46 instal 1-4 used for gen devl of rad and oil cool and props. BDN July '42 for trls. M32 instal. returned to MMOx 9-12 con back to normal FV 5-2-43 7RS 2-4 71MU 16-8-44 CE 29-8

R6890 849 FF 4-7-40 8MU 8-7 cann wing fitt 19S 11-7 R-RH 8-2-41 M45 instal 92S 8-3 dam by Bf109 15-5 92S dam by Bf109 12-6 AST 616S 22-7 403S 12-9 CAC 13-3-42 ROS 121S 13-4 FACB 20-5 GAL con to FVA M46 P&PSM 12-10 guns removed fuel syst mods 316S 21-1-43 306S 16-3 FAAC 3-8 ROS 312S 4-12 444S 27-2-44 53OTU 27-6 FAAC 25-8 ROS PAL 4-10-45 SOC 13-10

R6891 850 FF 4-7-40 8MU 4-7 610S 13-8 dam in ldg acc C2 18-8 FAC3 19-11 SOC 26-11

R6892 850 FF 4-7-40 6MU 4-7 54S 25-6 41S 22-2-41 425S 8-5 57 OTU 21-10 FACE 20-2-42 SOC 21-2

R6893 852 FF 4-7-40 6MU 6-7 54S 9-7 41S 1-3-41 e/fld on t/o strk obs CE 21-3 SOC 27-3

R6894| 858 FF 5-7-40 PDU HAL con to PRIII Type C. Farn 6-7 trls 1 PRU 3-8 FTR ops 8-10

R6895 853 FF 5-7-40 6MU 5-7 54S 9-7 FAC2 2-8 dam by bombs on t/o C3 31-8 SOC 6-9 AST 17-9 58 OTU 21-8-41 FACB 30-8 SAL 61 OTU 14-8-42 RNDA 15-1-44 SOC 6-3-45

R6896 854 FF 5-7-40 6MU 7-7 234S C2 ops 16-8 234S FTR ops P/O Kane pow 23-9 FH66.30

R6897* 855 FF 5-7-40 6MU 7-7 cann wing fitt 19S 11-7 FAC2 26-8 1CRU R-RH 11-1-41 con to FVB M45 AFDU Dxfd 23-2 92S 3-3 e/fld cd/ld 19-3 AST 234S 14-9 FACB 19-11 ASTEx 310S 20-6-42 332S 3-8 P&PSM 19-8 mods 411S 20-11 air coll with AB847 Alby Lincs 28-1-43 SOC

R6898 860 FF GP 5-7-40 6MU 7-7 54S 13-7 41S 12-3-41 452S 18-4 313S 24-5 61 OTU 16-8 FACE 8-12 SOC 12-12

R6899 856 FF GP 6-7-40 6MU 7-7 54S 13-7 FACE 3-2-41 SOC 10-2 FH220.45

R6900 859 FF GP 6-7-40 ANMP Farn 6-7 con to PRIII Type C fuel syst trls. 1PRU 17-9 dam by bombs 19-9 R-RH 27-3-41 M45 instal 1PRU 17-4 CB HAL 11-1-42 con to PRIV 8 OTU 30-7 CB 25-1-43 FACB 4-10 HAL SOC 15-3-45

R6901 857 FF 6-7-40 6MU 7-7 54S 13-7 FTR ops P/O Krepsi miss 7-9

R6902 861 FF 8-7-40 PDU HAL 9-7 con to PRIV Type F PRU St Eval July '40 R-RH 10-3-41 M45 instal HAL 26-4 DGRD Farn 22-5 camera trls 3PRU Oakington 7-6 1PRUV21-7 PDU HAL 13-10 con to PRVI FAAC 26-7-42 SOC 22-3-45

R6903 862 FF GP 8-7-40 9MU 8-7 AMDP Farn 8-7 PDU HAL 9-8 con to PRIII Type C Farn for trls FACB 5-1-41 HAL 3PRU May '41 FTR ops 21-7

R6904* 863 FF 8-7-40 6MU 10-7 cann wing fitt 19S 13-7 VA 25-8 con to FVB AFDU North 27-9 19S 30-10 service trls 92S 22-1-41 R-RH 16-2 M45 instal AST 25-7 615S 24-9 65S 6-10 121S 9-1-42 FAAC 2-6 306S 18-6 FTR ops 22-8

R6905 864 FF 8-7-40 HAL PDU 9-7 con to PRIV PRU St Eval HAL 3-6-41 con to FV parts supplied by R-R M45 fitt 1PRU 9-8 1401Flt 11-8 521S 4-8-42 80 OTU 11-4-43 con to PRVI Type F SOC 22-3-45

R6906 866 FF 9-7-40 PDU 13-7 HAL 13-7 con to PRIII Type C 1PRU Ben 13-7 ops 17-1-41

R6907 867 FF 9-7-40 152S 10-8 dam ops 29-11 SOC 16-1-41

R6908* 868 FF GP 9-7-40 R-RH con to FV M45 92S 28-2-41 dam by Bf109 9-5

R6909 869 FF 9-7-40 152S 19-8 s/dn by Do 17 i/sea Sgt Barker kld 4-9 SOC 8-9 cancel CB con to PRIII Type C 6-1-41 con to PRVI Type F July 1941

R6910 885 FF GP 9-7-40 9MU 13-7 152S 10-8 C2 ops 15-8 1CRU 65S 21-10 145S 2-2-41 118S 4-3 FACB 14-3 AST HAL 27-7 con to PRIV(X) M45 1PRU 28-8 HAL 10-11 con to PRVII Type G 140S 2-142 SOC 22-4-45

R6911* 870 FF GP 10-7-40 6MU 11-7 can wng fitt 19S 14-7 7 OTU 10-9 FAC2 14-9 AST 18-10 SOC 21-9 cancel R-RH con to FVB 52 OTU 8-11-41 Wal 8-5 215MU 19-9 *Pet Mer* 8-11 lost at sea 8-1-43

R6912* 871 FF 10-7-40 6MU 11-7 can wng fitt 19S 14-7 dam by Bf109 cd/ld C3 P/O Aeberhardt kld 31-8 SOC 1-9 FH43.40

R6913 872 FF 10-7-40 6MU 11-7 54S 23-7 AST 26-8 8-11 58 OTU 27-3-41 SAL 26-6 con to FVA M45 52 OTU 16-6-43 North 22-8

R6914 873 FF 10-7-40 6MU 11-7 54S 25-7 dam by Bf109 f/ld Lympne P/O Turley-George inj C2 12-8 AST 611S 2-12 485S 30-3-41 123S 13-6 53 OTU 13-1-42 FACB 16-7 WAL 61 OTU 3-2-43 to 4525M 2SoTT 7-2-44

R6915 874 FF GP 11-7-40 6MU 11-7 609S 21-7 dam by He111 f/ld WW 7-9 dam by He111 f/ld W 30-9 dam by Bf109 f/ld F/O Dundas inj 7-10 602S Jan '41 61 OTU July SOC 21-6-47 extant Imp War Mus London. 57 sorties flown in BoB by 13 pilots. Shot down four e/ac plus 6 dam

R6916 875 FF 11-7-40 6MU 11-7 72S 22-7 FAC2 11-8 GAL 222S 2-11 61 OTU 1-7-41 FACB 6-11 SOC 25-11 recat B AST 16-1-42 82MU 1-12 *Algarab* 31-12 P Sudan 12-3-43 ME 31-3 SOC 27-7-44

R6917* 876 FF GP 11-7-40 6MU 11-7 can wng fitt 19S 14-7 7 OTU 3-9 FAC2 21-9 SAL MMO 12-12 con to FVB M45 parts supplied by R-RH 11-4-41 74S 16-5 609S 14-8 122S SOC 27-11 o/t on ldg CE 10-3-42 SOC 27-3

R6918 877 FF GP 11-7-40 6MU 12-7 can wng fitt 610S 28-7 s/dn by Bf109 off Calais FTR F/Sgt Tanner kld 11-8

R6919* 878 FF 11-7-40 6MU can wng fitt 19S 14-7 MMO 6-8 mods & con to FVB AFDU North 21-10 19S 8-11 service trls 92S 22-1-41 R-RH 16-2 M45 instal 316S 3-5-42 41S 31-8 e/fld cd/ld nr Penrhos CE 26-10

R6920 879 FF GP 12-7-40 6MU 12-7 266S 28-7 e/a C2 18-8 AST 266S 20-10 cd Swinderley 10-1-41 SAL 58 OTU 4-7 215MU 8-11-42 *Castilian* Port 12-12

R6921 880 FF 12-7-40 6MU 13-7 611S 22-7 7 OTU 23-8 3-9 AST 131S 27-8-41 52 OTU FACE 23-11 SOC 9-12

R6922 881 FF 12-7-40 6MU 13-7 609S 15-8 FAC2 15-9 AST 92S 15-10 cd nr Smarden Sgt Alton kld 19-10

R6923* 883 FF 12-7-40 6MU 16-7 can wgn fitt 19S 22-7 7 OTU 3-9 R-RH 7-4-41 con to FVB M45 92S 26-11 s/dn i/sea by Bf109 a/c aban 22-6-41

R6924* 893 FF 15-7-40 6MU 16-7 can wng fitt 19S 19-7 7 OTU 3-9 AST 8-9 con to FMk II MXII AFDU North 28-11 92S 22-1-41 lost in fog cd pilot kld C3 7-2 AST SOC 18-2 cancel 504S 5-11 58 OTU 8-3-42 53 OTU 23-9 hit steamroller o/s Fairwood Common 26-1-43

R6925 884 FF GP 13-7-40 12MU 16-7 266S 19-8 66S 6-9 s/dn P/O Mathers aban a/c 18-9

R6926 888 FF 13-7-40 12MU 16-7 22MU 9-8 616S 11-8 s/dn F/O Dundas aban a/c 22-8

R6927 886 48MU 14-7-40 266S 19-8 66S 6-9 57 OTU 1-11 FACB 1-3-41 MMO 61 OTU 30-6 SOC 29-12

R6928 887 FF GP 13-7-40 12MU 14-7 72S 15-8 e/act dbf 31-8 SOC 23-9

R6957 889 FF GP 14-7-40 12MU 16-7 234S 17-8 57 OTU 15-4-41 ASTEx 30-8 con to FVA M45 332S 7-2-42 164S 12-4 602S 10-9 349S 6-7-43 61 OTU 1-8 FAAC 16-5-44 SOC 27-9-45

R6958* 890 FF 15-7-40 6MU 16-7 can wng fitt 19S 30-7 s/dn by Bf109 nr NWld F/O Brinsden aban a/c 31-8 FH32.20

R6959 891 FF 14-7-40 12MU 16-7 234S 19-8 132S 22-7-41 52 OTU 18-11 FACB 14-5-43 58 OTU 3-10 CE 18-8-44

R6960* 892 FF GP 15-7-40 6MU 16-7 R-RH 5-2 con to FVB M45 AFDU Dux 28-2 92S 26-3 91S 29-3 R-R 8-4 91S dam CAC ops 15-5 GAL 234S 25-7-42 316S 12-12 306s 4-4-43 FACB 26-5 DeH 453S 12-10 57 OTU 6-12-44 CE 16-12

R6961 894 FF 15-7-40 12MU 18-7 609S 13-8 61 OTU 1-7-41 53 OTU 4-6-42 SOC 6-3-45

R6962 895 FF GP 15-7-40 48MU 17-7 54S 28-7 74S 2-8 s/dn by Bf110 off Clacton P/O Smith kld 11-8 SOC 31-8 FH10.25

R6963 899 FF 16-7-40 24MU 16-7 616S 13-8 FAC2 3-9 AST 65S 16-4-41 57 OTU 22-10 61 OTU 12-8-42 str X4426 taxy CAC 5-3-43 ROS SOC 27-8-44

R6964 896 FF 16-7-40 24MU 16-7 152S 13-8 58 OTU 26-2-41 SAL 13-8 con to FVA M45 HAL 28-4-42 con to PRVII Type G PRU Ben 30-8 FTR ops 7-12 FH253.55

R6965 897 FF GP 16-7-40 24MU 17-7 92S 611S 30-7 602S 31-8 610S 14-12 53 OTU 3-5-41 FAAC 5-1-42 ROS 61 OTU 30-1-43 con to ASR (IIC) 278(ASR) 12-4-44 SOC 5-3-45

R6966 898 FF 16-7-40 24MU 17-7 616S 13-8 s/dn by Bf109 Sgt Westmoreland missing 25-8

R6967 900 FF 16-7-40 24MU 17-7 234S 30-7 s/dn by Bf109 nr Southampton P/O Dewhurst aban a/c 16-8

R6968 901 FF GP 16-7-40 24MU 17-7 152S 14-8 C2 ops 15-8 1CRU 152S 30-9 58 OTU 25-3-41 SAL 14-6 con to PRIII Type C 1PRU 13-3-42 8 OTU 19-6 f/ld Clunie Glen nr Braemar CE 60-9 SAL 58 OTU cd Marsham Kent CE 25-2-43

R6969 902 FF 17-7-40 37MU 19-7 54S 17-8 dam by Bf109 f/ld Mans C2 P/O Shand inj 25-8 1CRU 602S 24-12 122S 11-6-41 53 OTU 12-11 cd Aberthan cement works Glam dbf 7-12 SOC 11-12

R6970 903 FF 17-7-40 37MU 18-7 610S 19-8 C2 ops 26-8 HAL 52 OTU 16-11-41 FACB 24-4-42 RNAS Yeov 11-12

R6971 904 FF 17-7-40 37MU 18-7 610S 19-8 72S s/dn nr Hartfield a/c aban P/O Males safe dbf 4-9 SOC 23-9

R6972 905 FF GP 17-7 37MU 18-7 64S 23-8 58 OTU 15-3-41 57 OTU 24-7 MMO 21-3-42 new eng 1PRU 10-4 53 OTU 16-7 FACE 10-1-43 AST RNAS 2-7 FACB 1-8

R6973 906 FF 17-7-40 37MU 18-7 54S 17-8 57 OTU 1-2-41 SOC 20-9 to 2683M 1SoTT rtp 11-5-44

R6974 907 FF GP 17-7-40 37MU 19-7 54S 17-8 124S 7-5-41 e/fld i/sea off Duncansby Head Caithness 18-7 SOC 6-9

R6975 908 FF GP 18-7-40 6MU 19-7 64S 24-7 303S 22-1-41 58 OTU 29-3 131S 18-7 52 OTU 28-10 61 OTU 19-3-43 FAAC 8-6 ROS SOC 9-2-45

R6976 909 FF GP 18-7-40 6MU 19-7 610S 24-7 GAL 3-11 53 OTU 25-6-41 61 OTU 4-5-43 OTU 7-6-44 SOC 25-5-45

R6977 910 FF GP 18-7-40 6MU 19-7 609S 22-7 64S 6-12 303S 10-2-41 FACB 24-2 AST 412S 9-3 58 OTU 3-8 RNAS 26-5-43 CE 13-10-44

R6978 911 FF GP 18-7-40 6MU 19-7 611S 24-7 65S 31-8 FTR ops 12-12

R6979 912 FF 18-7-40 6MU 19-7 609S 22-7 FACB 26-9 66S 24-2-41 501S 26-4 61 OTU 1-7 ASTE 2-11 SOC 6-3-45

R6980 918 FF GP 19-7-40 6MU 616S 27-7 65S 26-2-41 61 OTU 4-8 e/fld w/u ldg nr Rednal 14-7-42

R6981 913 FF GP 19-7-40 6MU 20-7 72S 24-7 54S 9-8 s/dn F/Lt Deere aban a/c inj 15-8

R6982 914 FF GP 19-7-40 6MU 20-7 54S 25-6 74S 2-8 65S 6-8 FTR ops 12-12

R6983 921 FF GP 19-7-40 6MU 21-7 74S 27-7 dam by Bf109 nr Folkes ld Mans F/Lt Kelly safe 31-7 GAL 234S 27-9 58 OTU 28-3-41 hit high grd Ben Gengie Hill Alloa 26-9 SOC 12-10

R6984 915 FF GP 19-7-40 6MU 20-7 54S 2-8 616S 28-9 65S 26-2-41 403S 28-5 61 OTU 5-8 e/fld a/c aban cd Heathrow Middx 8-9 SOC 13-9

R6985 919 FF 19-7-40 6MU 21-7 234S 25-7 s/dn P/O Parker POW 15-8

R6986 919 FF 20-7-40 6MU 20-7 609S 28-7 611S 24-11 485S 14-3 131S 18-7 1PRU 18-2-42 8 OTU 19-6 FAAC 26-6 ROS HAL 7-9 53 OTU 26-5-44 AST 27-2-45 for rtp SOC 6-3-45

R6987 917 FF GP 20-7-80 8MU 23-7 65S 11-8 u/s ldg strk house 26-11 SAL 132S 17-7-41 FACB 19-9 ROS 215MU 23-9-42 *City of Lan* 7-9-43 Port 20-11

R6988 920 FF GP 20-7-40 8MU 21-7 234S 8-8 s/dn nr Swanage P/O Hight kld 15-8 AST SOC 2-9

R6989 923 FF GP 20-7-40 8MU 21-7 603S 8-8 s/dn C2 F/O Ritchie inj 28-8 COAL 61 OTU 2-9-41 FACB 1-12 ROS 57 OTU 28-7 e/fld cd nr Holywell Flints CE 15-8-42

R6990 923 FF GP 21-7-40 8MU 21-7 64S 26-7 C2 ops 31-7 64S s/dn nr Dung P/O Andrear missing 15-8

R6991 924 FF 21-7-40 8MU 22-7 64S 6-8 dam by Bf109 P/O Andrear ret to Ken C2 11-8 Rollasons 266S 17-8 19S 12-9 dam by Bf109 Sub Lt Blake safe C2 15-9 SAL 58 OTU 16-2-41 61 OTU 16-6-42 FACE dbf 26-6-42

R6992 925 222-7-40 8MU 22-7 64S 6-8 dam by Bf109 Sgt Mann safe C2 9-8 GAL 53 OTU 25-6-41 FACB 2-1-42 WAL 1402 Flt 28-4 CE ops 20-9 SOC 21-9 FH54.05

R6993 926 FF 22-7-40 8MU 22-7 610S 26-7 602S 14-12 303S 18-7-41 FAAC 25-7 61 OTU 15-8-42 RNAS 19-5-43 CAC 26-11-43 ROS

R6994 944 FF 22-7-40 8MU 29-7 152S 18-8 s/dn by Bf109 off Portland FTR 25-8 P/O Wildblood miss FH6.45

R6995 927 FF GP 22-7-40 8MU 26-7 64S 29-7 C2 ops 9-8 SOC 28-8

R6996 928 FF 23-7-40 8MU 24-7 610S 19-8 64S 12-10 303S 2-2-41 58 OTU 29-3 e/a CB 21-11 SAL 53 OTU 23-3-43 RDNA 15-1-44

R7015 929 FF GP 23-7-40 8MU 24-7 54S 4-8 s/dn C3 15-8 cd Hythe Sgt Klozinsky inj

R7016 930 FF GP 23-7-40 8MU 24-7 152S 18-8 ops P/O Beaumont missing 23-9

R7017 931 FF GP 32-7-40 24MU 24-7 54S 28-7 234S 9-9 C2 ops 9-11 AST 39MU St Fm dis 8-4-41 53 OTU 30-6 FACE 1-9 SOC 7-9

R7018 932 FF GP 24-7-40 12MU 25-7 615S 9-8 s/dn by Bf109 C3 26-8 ASTH 1-9 57 OTU 3-6-411 FAAC 21-6 ROS SOC 2-9

R7019 933 FF 23-7-40 12MU 25-7 54S 28-7 C2 ops 15-8 AST SOC 27-9

R7020 934 FF 24-7-40 12MU 25-7 609S 13-8 FAC2

R6915 on display in the Imperial War Museum, London.

13-8 13-8 1CRU 603S 6-10 266S 17-10 FACB 11-2-41 AST con to PRIII Type C 8 OTU 24-5-42 FAAC 1-9 ROS 57 OTU 3-7-43 hit H/T cables o/t in f/ld nr Netherwitton N'land 14-3-44

R7021 935 FF GP 24-7-40 12MU 25-7 54S 28-7 s/dn Bf109 cd West Malling a/c aban Sgt Sarre safe 30-8

R7022 936 FF 24-7-40 12MU 25-7 266S 19-8 72S 6-9 s/dn by Bf110 Sgt White safe 7-9 AST 53 OTU 25-6041 322S 7-2-42 164S 16-4 602S 10-9 P&PSM 22-10 con to FVA M45 349S 6-7-43 FAAC 5-8 61 OTU 11-9 CE 16-3-44 SOC FH490.25

The allocation of R prefix serials was halted with R7022 in July'40. The next Spitfire on the production line bore the serial X4011, manufacturer's number 937. The prefix X serial Mk Is ended with X4997, manufacturer's number 1415, at end of Jan'41 and the R series started again with R7023 below. A letter from MAC of 22 March 1940 ordered this change of production and specified that the Merlin X be installed in these aircraft serialled from R7023 to R7350 W3109 to W3970 so as to bring them up to Mk III standards. However events overtook this instruction and from R7258 on the Merlin 45 was installed thus converting them to F Mk V standards.

R7023 1416 FF 28-1-41 8MU 1-2 DGRD VA 1-2 61 OTU 23-10 RNDA 7-9-42

R7024 1421 FF 28-1-41 6MU 1-2 66S 28-2 57 OTU 31-3 FACE 20-10-42

R7025 1417 FF 29-1-41 6MU 1-2 611S 16-2 485S 15-3 123S 13-6 SAL 7-8-42 *Pet Mer* 8-11 lost at sea 8-1-43

R7026 1418 FF 29-1-41 6MU 1-2 303S 28-2 58 OTU 29-4 FACB 18-11-42 SAL 52 OTU 25-5-43 1TEU 1-3-44 57 OTU 16-4

R7027 1422 FF 28-1-41 8MU 15-2 123S 19-8 215MU 2-10-42 *City of Lan* 7-1-43 Port 20-1

R7028 1423 Sunderland FF 30-1-41 6MU 3-2 DGRD Farn 18-3 1416Flt 12-4 DGRD 21-4 SAL 15-7 con to FV M45 140S 18-12 HAL PDU 5-1-42 con to PRVII Type G 140S 17-1 FACB 17-4 HAL 10-7-43

R7057 1424 Caithness FF 31-1-41 53 OTU 3-2 flew into high grd nr Glyn-Neath Glam 12-8-41

R7058 1425 R J Mitchell FF 31-1-41 6MU 3-2 308S 14-5 403S 28-5 57 OTU 26-7 FAAC 18-11 to 2877M 6SoTT 18-12 SOC 23-12

R7059 1426 Southampton I FF 1-2-41 6MU 7-2 HAL 14-3 con to PRVII Type G 1PRU 1-5 8 OTU 19-6-42 FAAC 3-7 HAL 8 OTU 13-2-43 e/fld fire, cd Newton Farm Laurencekirk Kincardine 25-6 CE

R7060 1427 Southampton II FF 1-2-41 9MU 4-2 313S 1-6 61 OTU 16-8 FACB 8-9 1CRU con to FVA 332S 20-3-42 164S 15-4 FAAC 22-5 61 OTU 28-7 ASTE 27-2-44 9MU 18-12

R7061 1428 Edglets FF 3-2-41 9MU 4-2 485S 20-4 52 OTU 18-11 flew into hill France Lynch ADn 18-12 SOC 27-12

R7062 1429 The Brit FF 3-2-41 9MU 6-2 308S 10-5 403S 28-5 57 OTU 26-10 FA SOC 21-12

R7063 1430 DSG Worth Valley FF GP 3-2-41 9MU 4-2 61 OTU 1-7 CAC 17-2-42 ASTH 57 OTU 24-4-43 FACE 11-10

R7064 1431 Mercury FF 5-2-41 9MU 6-2 44S 5-7 52 OTU 23-11 struct dam in spin cd nr ADn CE 25-3-42 SOC 3-4

R7065 14322 Chelmsford FF GP 5-2-41 24MU 6-2 403S 10-6 61 OTU 408 57 OTU 2-1-42 FAAC 3-3-43 ROS coll with Beaufort W6540 Wingate's Moor NF'land CE 19-6-44

R7066 1433 Galleywood FF GP 5-2-41 24MU 7-2 403S 10-6 61 OTU 30-7 FACE 19-8 AST SOC 22-8

Wreckage of R7033, converted to PR IV, following crash 5 October 1941.

R7067 1434 Hastings FF GP 6-2-41 24MU 7-2 303S 9-8 306S 6-10 308S 11-12 57 OTU 31-12-42 air coll with R6813 Blagdon Hall nr Morpeth CE 7-7-43 SAL 53 OTU 6-1-44 CE 11-8

R7068 1435 Worthing FF 6-2-41 24MU 13-2 403S 10-6 52 OTU 21-7 FACB 25-11 SOC 10-12

R7069 1436 Jason FF 6-2-41 12MU 15-2 72S 30-3 111S 26-4 58 OTU 29-5 61-OTU 10-10 FACB 22-9-42 AST SOC 6-3-45

R7070 1437 Pegasus FF 7-2-41 6MU 11-2 PDU HAL 31-3 con to PRIII Type C PRU Ben 11-4 FTR ops 25-5 FH53.40

R7071 1438 Perseus FF 7-2-41 12MU 15-2 602S 28-4 61 OTU 28-7 FAAC 30-4-42 ROS 222MU 31-8 *Ocean Vol* 14-9 Port 26-9

R7072 1439 Sunderland I FF GP 7-2-41 12MU 26-2 124S 7-5 FACB 12-10 SAL 53 OTU 13-1-42 CB 28-3 ASTEx 215MU 19-9 *Pet Mer* 8-11 lost at sea 8-1-43

R7073 1441 Sunderland II FF GP 8-2-41 12MU 15-2 123S 23-5 58 OTU 25-9 FACE 17-4-42

R7074 1442 Sunderland III FF GP 8-2-41 12MU 15-2 124S 7-5 i/sea off Dunnet Head Caithness 27-7

R7114 1440 Sunderland IV FF 8-2-41 6MU 9-2 1PRU 10-3 HAL 19-5 52 OTU 8-11 strk by R6806 CE SOC 12-4-42

R7115 1443 FF 10-2-41 6MU 13-2 122S 11-6 dvdi/grd nr Gandale Camp ttl wrk 19-9 SOC 26-9

R7116 1444 St Austell & District FF GP 10-2-41 6MU 13-2 HAL 14-3 140S 26-4 AST 10-12 con to FVA M45 140S 24-12 HAL 17-1-42 con to PRVII Type G 140S 20-1 FTR ops 9-11

R7117 1445 FF GP 10-2-41 6MU 13-2 FAC3 14-3 1CRU 313S 1-6 57 OTU 27-8 FAAC 30-3-42 ROS CE 9-8-44

R7118 1443 FF 10-2-41 8MU 21-2 HAL 24-5 AFDU Dux 17-7 61 OTU 17-4-42 CB 27-4-44 39MU NEA 6-11 to 4519M 15-3-45 SOC

R7119 1446 FF GP 11-2-41 8MU 15-2 132S 9-7 52 OTU 24-4 FACB 9-12 AST RNAS Yeov 9-9-42

R7120 1447 FF GP 12-2-41 8MU 14-2 con to FV DGRD Farn 31-3 exp h/a Mer 61 instal Stab trls in June. Mk IX supercharger fitt to M61, pressure cabin; FF 25-8 exhaustive trls commenced. CRD BDn 17-9 con to FVI stab trls. Still with Mk 1 wngs and used for comp trls at all alt with X4942, second proto FVI. CRD Farn 10-11 CRD HAL 2-9-42 Malcolms WW 31-12 'Lobelle' blister, sliding hood instal for press cabin. ETPS Farn trls of GGI R/T at h/a (40,000ft) with X4942. Comp trls with AB528 with 3 and 4 blade props, to 3566M 11SoTT 7-3-43 CE SOC 20-1-45

R7121 1448 FF 11-2-41 8MU 14-2 DGRD Farn 3-7

R7121, a trials Spitfire, spent most of its active life at Farnborough. It is shown here in April 1942 undergoing trials with metal ailerons.

R7058, named in honour of the designer. It ended its days at Hednesford as 2877M.

air-to-air homing trls. RAF and ETPS pilots discovered that a number of German aircraft were operating equip which distorted the homing beam. A number of RAF a/c were lost due to this distortion. FIE shed 17-11 trls with Oboe f/ld Esh 19-5 SOC 26-5

R7122 1449 Erimus Middlesborough FF GP 13-2-41 8MU 14-2 DGRD Farn 31-3 123S 1-6 FACE 9-7 SOC 16-7

R7123 1450 Caput Inter Nibila FF 13-2-41 8MU 14-2 132S 9-7 FACE 3-8 SAL 215MU 2-10 *City of Lan* 7-1-43 Port 20-1

R7124 1451 FF 13-2-41 8MU 15-2 132S 9-7 53 OTU 14-2-42 cd into River Severn nr Newham CE 24-4

R7125 1454 Gateshead FF 15-2-41 9MU 21-2 123S 22-6 61 OTU 11-10 FAAC 28-6-42 ROS RNAS 19-5-43 CB 16-6 SOC 30-12-44

R7126 1452 Villae de Poole FF GP 14-2-41 9MU 16-2 conv to FV 411S 22-6 57 OTU 14-8 cd Parkgate Rd Chester ttl wrk 7-12

R7127 1455 Turris Jehova Fortissmo ETS Nomen FF 14-2-41 9MU 19-2 411S 7-7 AST 15-3 con to FVA M45 54S 18-9 332S 17-1-42 164S 24-4 FACA 4-6 602S 10-9 P&PSM 10-10 fuel syst mods 61 OTU 18-7-43 air coll with X4173 12-8 CE SOC 30-9 FH 311.10

R7128 1456 Hawick Terribus Newcastle Under Lyme FF GP 15-2-41 9MU 20-2 con to PRIII 1PRU 25-6 3SoGR 13-2-42 o/s ldg Squires Gate hit obst CE 22-4 ASTE SOC 23-4

R7129 1457 Secundus du Busque Rectus FF 14-2-41 9MU 19-2 308S 13-5 403S 28-5 52 OTU 21-7 61 OTU 5-8 FACE dbf 21-8 SOC 27-8

R7130 1460 Swansea FF 17-2-41 12MU 21-2 124S 7-5 FACB 29-8 SAL con to PRIII Type C M45 HAL 10-3-42 con to PRVII Type G 140S TAF 11-6 FAAC 21-3-43 ROS 140S 14-7 SOC 6-3-45

R7131 1458 Presentation FF GP 15-2-41 12MU 21-2 124S 7-5 340S 20-10 52 OTU 31-10 e/fld w/u ldg CE 22-11 ASTH 1PRU 28-2-42 FACE 12-7 SAL Ben 30-9 AST 19-5-45

R7132 1461 Industria FF 17-2-41 12MU 21-2 124S 7-5 123S 31-12 58 OTU 7-1-42 FACB 9-7 SAL 18-5 con to FVA(T) 801S Sept '42 222MU 8-10 *Taran* Nov '42 P Sudan 29-1-43 ME 28-2 SOC 1-3-44

R7133 1459 FF GP 15-2-41 12MU 7-3 129S 22-6 FACE dbf 10-8 SOC 20-8

R7134 1462 Swansea Wales 1st Flight FF GP 16-2-41 12MU 25-2 124S 7-5 52 OTU 3-11 FACB 10-4-42 ASTE 61 OTU 22-2-43 FACB 8-3 P&PSM 16-3

R7135 1463 The Dauntless FF 18-2-41 12MU 21-2 124S 7-5 52 OTU 3-11 cd Oldbury Sands River Severn CE 8-2-42

R7136 1464 Tra-Mor-Tramerion Merioneth FF GP 18-2-41 12MU 5-3 124S 7-5 340S 20-10 52 OTU 9-12 FACB 15-4-42 1CRU RNAS Yeov 5-9 ASTH 7-11 SOC 23-11-44

R7137 1465 FF GP 19-2-41 12MU 25-2 129S 22-6 CB ops 2-9 SOC 22-9

R7138 1466 FF 19-2-41 12MU 25-2 122S 11-6 57 OTU 4-10 FAAC 31-3-42 ROS strk X4611 ldg CB 2-5 ASTH burst tyre ldg Esh tip onto nose CB 19-10-43 recat E 9-11

R7139 1477 Walsall II FF 19-2-41 6MU 25-2 con to FVA M45 HAL con to PRIV 14-3 1416Flt 7-5 140S 31-10 HAL 15-12 con to PRVII Type G 1PRU 22-2-42 543S 30-9 FAAC 17-5-43 HAL 8 OTU 21-8 SOC 6-3-45

R7140 1467 FF GP 20-2-41 6MU 20-2 308S 14-5 403S 28-5 FACB 3-6 AST 57 OTU 1-8 SOC 15-1-42

R7141 1468 FF 20-2-41 6MU 22-2 501S 11-5 AST 31-5 factory defence Baginton 2-9 61 OTU 21-3-43 FAAC 25-6 ROS 39MU NEA 6-11-44 SOC 22-3-45

R7142 1469 FF 21-2-41 6MU 22-2 DGRD Farn 18-3 trls R-RH 7-9 con to FVA M45 1PRU Ben 27-9 con to PRIV CE SOC 16-12

R7143 1470 Walsall I FF 20-2-41 6MU 20-2 DGRD Farn 18-1 1416Flt 2-4 HAL 2-4 con to PRIV R-RH 7-9 con to FVA 140S 3-10 FACB 10-3-42 1CRU 6MU 1-6 con to PRVII Type G Ben 29-10 47MU 12-12 arma removed *Man Prog* 16-1-43 Canada 10-2

R7144 1471 FF 20-2-41 8MU 21-2 132S 9-7 52 OTU 3-11 FAAC 16-6-42 58 OTU 21-6 2TEU air coll with P9371 nr Cuthmuir Angus CE 18-12-42 SOC 6-1-44 FH927.50

R7145 1488 BB & GI Railway II FF 28-2-41 8MU 4-3 132S 9-7 Squires Gate PRU Tan Flt 11-4-42 8 OTU 24-5 FAAC 15-6 SAL RNDA 4-9 RNAS 17-12-43

R7146 1472 FF 21-2-41 8MU 23-2 1PRU 16-5 HAL 3-1-42 con to PRIII Type C 1PRU 5-1 3SoGR 9-1 8 OTU 29-5 FA 24-7 222MU 8-8-43 *Emp Rhod* 14-8 Port 11-9

R7147 1475 FF GP 22-2-41 8MU 23-2 con to PRIII Type C 1PRU 22-5 FACB 22-6 1CRU 4SA BC Bovington 14-8-42 recat E 16-8-44

R7148 1476 FF GP 23-2-41 8MU 26-2 WAL as pattern a/c 27-5 131S 16-8 52 OTU 26-10 CE 26-2-42 WAL 8-3 recat E dbf 6-4 SOC

R7149 1478 FF GP 24-2-41 9MU 17-2 122S 30-6 57 OTU 4-10 FACB 14-5-43 58 OTU 27-7 e/fld cd/ldg Leuch CE 24-9

R7150 1479 FF GP 24-2-41 9MU 26-2 308S 10-5 403S 28-5 61 OTU 4-8 FA dbf 22-8 SOC 27-8

R7151 1480 Victor McLagen Seattle FF GP 25-2-41 123S 18-6 58 OTU 10-8 FACB 24-11 SAL 19-12 CE 9-3-44

R7152 1481 FF 24-2-41 9MU 26-2-41 123S 22-6 58 OTU 2-10 flew into hill nr Penicuik Midlothian 5-10 SOC 1-10 cancel SAL 61 OTU 16-6-42 76MU 10-10 *Taran* Nov '42 P Sudan 29-1-43 ME 28-2 SOC 1-3-44

R7153 1482 FF 25-2-41 9MU 27-2 411S 22-6 129S 6-8 58 OTU 15-9 for Gosport War Weapons SAL 13-8-44 CE 18-8

R7154 1483 Accrington Church Oswaldtwistle FF 26-2-41 12 MU 1-3 124S 7-5 f/ldg 30-9 SOC 30-3-42

R7155 1484 Kukuyu Embu FF 26-2-41

R7156 1485 BB & C I II Railway I FF 28-2-41 12MU 1-3 124S 7-5 FACE 27-8 SOC 3-9

R7157 1486 Southern Belle FF 27-2-41 12MU 1-3 124S 7-5 52 OTU 3-11 FACE 26-9-42

R7158 1489 Cheshire FF GP 28-2-41 6MU 6-2 92S 23-3 R-RH 15-4 con to FVB M45 315S 31-8 402S 14-3-42 312S 4-5 129S 17-4-43 316S 15-5 416S 22-5 421S 23-5 1CRU 28-6 M55 instal 340S 1-12 57 OTU 12-10-44 recat E 28-5-45 SOC 1-6

R7159 1487 Kamba Meru FF GP 28-2-41 24MU 3-3 411S 23-6 53 OTU 22-7 ASTEx 12-11 215MU 30-9-42 *Castalian* 27-11 Port 12-12

R7160 1490 Smyc Brighton and Hove FF GP 2-3-41 452S 13-5 313S 31-5 61 OTU 16-8 57 OTU 31-12 FAAC 11-5-42 MMO RNAS 5-9

R7161 1503 EA Mombasa FF 6-3-41 92S 8-4 con to FVB M45 VSM 30-3-43 fuel syst mods wing stiff

R7162 1491 Toby FF 1-3-41 24MU 3-3 411S 22-6 FACB 21-7 AST 303S 12-9 306S 6-10 61 OTU 15-10 FAAC 19-2-42 ROS 53 OTU 14-4-43 CE 11-8-44

R7163 1492 Bridgwater FF GP 2-3-41 452S 24-4 313S 20-5 FACE ttl wrk 27-5 SOC 5-6

R7192 1506 Peterborough & District FF 8-3-41 9MU 12-3 92S 23-3 111S 25-8 GAL 5-10 111S 6-1-42 FACE 14-3 SOC 31-3

R7193 1493 Silver Snipe FF 2-3-41 37MU 4-3 313S 4-7 57 OTU 27-8 FAAC 24-12 ROS RNDA Yeov 10-9-42 RCAF Canada July '43. 36 in telephoto camera instal Ret to UK 30-12-44

R7194 1494 Bristol Civil Defence FF GP 3-3-41 37MU 5-3 129S 24-6 ASTE con to FVA M45 145S 23-11 136S 19-12 133S 25-12 134S 30-12 601S 2-1-42 FAAC 6-5 ROS 421S 24-5 VSM 24-9 fuel syst mods wng stiff 61 OTU night ldg o/t Mountford Bridge 15-4-44

R7195 1508 Holmwood I FF 10-3-41 6MU 12-3 92S 23-3 R-RH 7-4 con to FVB M45M 129S 17-4-42 CB ops 18-8 ROS 66S 19-2-43 VSM 24-5 fuel syst wng stiff & elev mods, Mk III IFF 501S 28-10 CAC ops 15-12 ROS

R7196 1495 Holmwood II FF 4-3-41 38MU 5-3 412S 7-7 145S 21-11 134S 19-12 133S 23-12 601S 14-4-42 1CRU 22-5 con to FVA M45 2USA 5-8 FAAC 9-8 ROS HAL 14-8 61 OTU 4-2-44

R7197 1496 Stainbridge & District FF 4-3-41 38MU 5-3 66S 15-4 CB ops 15-4 AST 501S 11-5 412S 12-7 HAL 10-3-42 con to PRVII Type G 1PRU 23-6 140S TAF 24-1-43 SOC 27-2-45

R7198 1497 Sherwood Forrester FF 4-3-41 38MU 5-3 412S 7-7 1PRU 1-4-42 as train HAL 29-4 con to PR IV M45 8 OTU 31-7 flew into hill Isle of Skye 19-6-43

R7199 1498 Woolton FF GP 6-3-41 24S 11-7 510S 31-12-42 FAAC 7-1-44 ROS 510S 8-9 CE 10-12

R7200 1502 Frome District FF 6-3-41 45MU 8-3 124S 7-5 340S 23-10 52 OTU 1-11 FACB 2-7-42 SAL RNAS 4-7-43

R7201 1499 Lest We Forget FF GP 6-3-41 45MU 8-3 123S 29-5 58 OTU 2-10 FAAC 28-4-42 ROS FACE 7-7 LMS 7-7 ASTH 3-5-45

R7202 1500 Preston & District FF 8-3-41 45MU 8-3 122S 2-6 53 OTU 12-10 cd Wilton Farm Lland CE 15-12 SOC 15-12 cancel AST 57 OTU 27-6-42 flew into high grd Durdon Hill Rothbury 3-2-43

R7203 1501 Preston & District II FF 7-3-41 45MU 8-3 123S 30-5 58 OTU 1-10 57 OTU 16-5-43 CE 17-8-44

R7204 1504 London Stock Exchange FF GP 8-3-41 45MU 9-3 123S 3-6 ldg acc Drem with P7747 C2 19-6 58 OTU 2-8 46MU 16-8-42 *Pet Mer* 8-11 lost at sea 8-1-43

R7205 1507 Provident FF 8-3-41 37MU 9-3 452S 13-5 313S 10-6 ASTE 1-9 con to FVA M45 1401Flt 13-5-42 521S 27-9 HAL 7-12 61 OTU 10-6-43 ATA WW 17-8-44 CAC 5-10 SOC 10-7-45

R7206 1505 City of Liverpool II FF 8-3-41 37MU 9-3 131S 29-7 52 OTU 12-12 e/a CB 6-2-42 AST recat E 20-5

R7211 1511 Spirit of Leek FF 11-3-41 37MU 15-3 HAL 15-5 con to FVA M45 33MU 16-10 con to PRIV 28-10 1PRU 10-12 HAL FACB 31-12 con to PRVII 1PRU 13-3-42 541S 30-9 TDU Gosport 9-6-43 SOC 15-3-45

R7212 1512 Puck FF 12-3-41 37MU 13-3 132S 10-7 52 OTU 23-11 CAC 16-12 SOC 19-12

R7214 1515 Batley FF 13-3-41 8MU 18-3 132S 9-7 SAL 12-10 RNAS 20-2-42 for instruction maint personnel reallotted RAF 8-3 222MU 2-10 *Taran* 23-11 P Sudan 29-1-43 ME 28-2 SOC 27-7-44

R7215 1517 Stockport FF 14-3-41 8MU 18-3 132S 9-7 FAAC 11-7 ROS 52 OTU 3-11 215MU 25-9-42 *Pet Mer* 8-11 lost at sea 8-1-43

R7216 1518 Woolwich FF 15-3-41 8MU 18-3 132S 9-7 58 OTU 8-12 FACB 21-3-42 SAL recat E 16-5

R7250 1532 CHA FF GP 18-3-41 37MU 23-3 132S 12-7 52 OTU 3-11 FACB 18-3-42 DeH 22-3 recat E 8-6

R7251 1533 CHA FF 18-3-41 24MU 23-3 411S 22-6 FACB 3-7 WAL Platts Garage 11-8 P&PSM 27-4-42 new eng Com Flt Cole 10-10 SOC 27-9-45

R7252 1550 CHA FF GP 27-3-41 24MU 31-3 411S 22-6 53 OTU 28-7 FAAC 3-2-42 ROS 53 OTU 14-2 AST 24-6 RNAS 16-7-43 61 OTU 7-9 RNDA 12-6-44

R7257 1571 CHA FF 5-4-41 24MU 7-4 411S 22-6 57 OTU 28-7 eng fire f/ldg hit tree Alston St Crewe CE 29-5-42

Third order for 500 Spitfire Mk I dated 9 June 1940. Built as Mk I, VA and VB between July 1940 and January 1941. The following serials apply to Mk I variants built to this third order; X4009-4038, 4051-4070, 4101-4110, 4159-4188, 4231-4280, 4317-4356, 4381-4390, 4409-4428, 4471-4505, 4538-4562, 4585-4624, 4641-4662, 4671-4685, 4708-4722, 4765-4789, 4815-4859, 4896-4945 and 4988-4997. All Mk I Merlin III unless otherwise indicated.

X4009 945 FF 24-7-40 37MU 28-7 234S 19-8 s/dn by Bf109 SE London F/Lt Hughes kld 7-9 SOC 30-9 FH28.25

X4010 946 FF 24-7-40 37MU 28-7 234S 18-8 66S 18-9 C2 ops 23-9 GAL 412S 9-7-41 53 OTU 9-9 ASTH 7-12 140S 3-4-42 FAAC 12-5 180S 26-5 FAAC 2-4-43 53 OTU 11-4-44 FAAC 9-8 SOC 27-9-45

X4011 937 FF 24-7-40 37MU 26-7 610S 27-8 s/dn cd/ldg Gat Sgt Baker safe FAC3 29-8

X4012 938 FF 25-7-40 37MU 26-7 152S 26-8 602S 13-10 C2 ops 15-11 GAL 61 OTU 3-7-41 SOC 1-12 con to synthetic train as 3307M 5-12

X4013 950 FF 25-7-40 37MU 30-7 610S 27-8 s/dn by Bf109 over Tunbridge Wells P/O Winter kld 5-9 SOC 18-9

X4014 939 FF 25-7-40 37MU 26-7 610S 27-8 DGRD BDn 5-5-41 124S 29-8 340S 20-10 52 OTU 2-11 215MU 19-9 *Pet Mer* 8-11 lost at sea 8-1-43

X4015 940 FF 25-7-40 6MU 26-7 611S 30-7 65S 31-8 FAC2 7-10 SAL C2 ops 17-2-41 53 OTU 2-5 FACE ttl wrck 15-6 SOC 20-6

X4016 941 FF GP 25-7-40 6MU 27-7 234S 11-8 s/dn by Bf109 off IoW F/O Connor aban a/c 16-8

X4017 942 FF GP 25-7-40 6MU 27-7 152S 9-8 41S 5-10 611S 24-10 485S 15-3-41 61 OTU 25-6 FAAC 26-6-43 ROS RNAS Hens 19-7-44 CE 23-9

X4018 943 FF 26-7-40 6MU 27-7 64S 9-8 s/dn by Bf109 P/O Donahue aban a/c dbf 12-8

X4019 947 FF GP 26-7-40 6MU 28-7 54S 1-8 dam e/a P/O Campbell safe 24-8 603S 7-10 266S 17-10 111S 11-4 58 OTU 29-5 CBAF 24-12 82MU 6-11-42 *Pet Mer* 8-11 lost at sea 8-1-43

X4020 947 FF 26-7-40 46MU 28-7 66S 31-7 AST 13-10 152S 10-11 58 OTU 23-3-41 SOC 14-4-45

X4021 949 FF 26-7-40 46MU 28-7 54S 1-8 41S 2-8 s/dn f/ldg F/O Wallens inj CE 5-9 1CRU 266S 24-11 w/u ldg Cranwell CB 10-1-41 111S 3-4 58 OTU 29-5 AST 26-7 con to FVA M45 603S 29-9 130S 22-11 81S 17-2-42 165S 12-4 167S 27-5 HAL 23-9 con to PRVII Type G HAL 29-4-43 con to PRXIII M32 VSM 29-4 fuel syst mods wing stiff RNDA 3-3-44

X4022 951 FF 26-7-40 6MU 28-7 54S 1-8 74S 2-8 coll with X4027 Sgt Skinner aban a/c safe 30-8

X4023 952 FF 26-7-40 8MU 28-7 234S 11-8 dam by Bf109 nr Portsmouth w/u ldg M Wallop P/O Horton safe 26-8 AST 152S 6-11 58 OTU 23-3-41 457S 20-9 53 OTU 20-10 FAAC 5-7-42 SOC 8-3-45

X4024 953 FF 27-7-40 8MU 29-7 74S 14-8 222S 4-9 C2 ops 14-9 AST 72S 11-10 92S 11-10 FAC2 14-11 AST 53 OTU 24-6-41 coll with X4607 Treharris Glam dbf CE 7-7 SOC 15-7

X4025 954 FF 27-7-40 8MU 30-7 152S 18-8 o/s ldg o/t 23-11 AST CB ops 23-2-41 AST 61 OTU 3-7 FACE 29-7 SOC 18-8

X4026 955 FF 27-7-40 8MU 30-7 64S 19-8 cd 16-11 AST 616S 1-1-41 65S 26-2 308S 4-4 403S 29-5 131S 9-9 52 OTU 22-10 e/fld w/u ldg nr Pers dbf 15-11 SOC 22-11

X4027 956 FF GP 28-7-40 8MU 30-7 74S 14-8 FAC2 coll with X4022 P/O Churches safe 30-8 234S 11-11 i/sea ops off Newquay pilot missing 16-11 SOC 1-12

X4028 957 FF 28-7-40 8MU 29-7 610S 19-8 602S 14-12 61 OTU 20-4 6MU 13-9 con to FVA 54S 18-9 FA ttl wrk SOC 24-1-41

X4029 958 FF 28-7-40 8MU 31-7 PRU 3-8 dam by en bombs 19-9 FTR ops 31-3-41

X4030 959 FF 28-7-40 8MU 31-7 602S 11-8 266S 12-8 C2 ops 16-8 AST 616S 1-1-41 65S 26-2 308S 16-4 403S 27-5 57 OTU 25-10 FACB 7-10-42 GAL RNAS 19-7-43 SOC 20-12-44

X4031 960 FF GP 29-7-40 12MU 31-7 64S 17-8 GAL 54S 13-11 C2 ops 24-11 41S 22-2 452S 19-4 313S 28-5 61 OTU 16-8 FAAC 22-8 FACE 25-2-42

X4032 961 FF 29-7-40 12MU 1-8 64S 17-8 FTR ops Sgt Dyke missing 27-9 FH39.20

X4033 962 FF 29-7-40 12MU 31-7 266S 19-8 61S 7-9 65S 26-2-41 308S 10-4 403S 27-5 131S 16-7 to 2685M 6SoTT 22-10 SOC 20-9

X4034 963 FF GP 30-7-40 12MU 11-8 72S 11-8 s/dn by Bf109 F/O Sheen aban a/c inj 5-9

X4035 964 FF 12MU 31-7 234S 17-8 s/dn nr Buxted Sussex C3 6-9 AST SOC 30-9 FH10.40

X4036 965 FF GP 30-7-40 12MU 31-7 234S 17-8 C2 ops 11-10 AST 66S 13-4-41 e/a CB 16-4 AST 52 OTU 20-11 FACE 24-2-42

X4037 966 FF 30-7-40 39MU 1-8 92S 21-8 s/dn by Bf109 NWld P/O Bryson kld dbf 24-9 SOC 30-9

X4038 967 FF 30-7-40 39MU 1-8 92S 21-8 air coll with Spit cd nr Brighton C3 10-10 P/O Williams kld FH86.35

X4051 968 FF 30-7-40 39MU 1-8 92S 21-8 dam f/ld BH11 Sgt Mann inj 4-9 AST 610S 23-2-41 53 OTU 3-3 457S 14-8 58 OTU 26-10 FACB 7-11-42 SAL e/fd f/ld nr Bedford CE 20-7-44 SOC

X4052 990 FF 5-8-40 39MU 7-8 66S 21-8 s/dn by Bf109 f/ld F/Lt Christie inj C2 4-9 AST 41S 19-9 FTR ops F/O O'Neill kld 11-10

X4053 969 FF 31-7-40 39MU 2-8 54S 23-8 s/dn by Bf109 S/Ldr Finlay aban a/c 28-8 (41S air coll with X4554 F/O O'Neill kld 11-10 suspect wrong a/c) SOC

X4054 970 FF 31-7-40 39MU 3-8 54S 23-8 s/dn by Hurricane nr Mans Sgt Gibbons aban a/c dbf 31-8

X4055 971 FF GP 31-7-40 39MU 1-8 616S 30-8 C2 ops 5-11 FACE 8-1-41 SOC 20-1 FH110.35

X4056 972 FF GP 31-7-40 39MU 2-8 616S 30-8 FAC3 8-11 SOC 11-11

X417? Mk V with A type wing.

X4057 973 FF GP 31-7-40 39MU 1-8 222S 1-9 s/dn by Bf109 nr Dover Sgt Chipping aban a/c dbf 5-9 SOC 21-9

X4058 974 FF 1-8-40 39MU 2-8 222S 1-9 129S 22-6-41 58 OTU 12-9 FAAC 5-5-42 C2 ops 9-9 52 OTU 23-5-43 CE 18-8-44

X4059 975 FF GP 2-8-40 6MU 3-8 65S 9-8 19S dam ops f/dn C2 F/O Haines safe 11-9 SAL 58 OTU 10-5-41 FAAC 28-2 SAL 52 OTU 7-2-42 FACE dbf 15-10

X4060 976 FF 1-8-40 6MU 2-8 64S 9-8 74S 9-10 41S 12-10 611S 30-12 485S 14-3-41 123S 13-6 61 OTU 11-10 FACE 6-11 SOC 15-11

X4061 977 FF 1-8-40 6MU 3-8 74S 9-8 266S 18-8 des on grd Mans 18-8 SOC 28-8 FH8

X4062 978 FF 1-8-40 6MU 2-8 R-RH 5-2-41 con to FVA M45 AFDU Dux 21-2 92S 3-3 FTR ops 11-4 SOC 12-4

X4063 979 FF GP 2-8-40 6MU 3-8 266S 13-8 C3 ops 16-8 AST 72S 9-9 s/dn by Bf109 nr Graves P/O Brown safe dbf 23-9 SOC 12-10

X4064 980 FF 2-8-40 6MU 3-8 610S 11-8 57 OTU 4-2-41 131S 17-7 ASTH 24-8 con to FVA M45 AFDU 13-10 Farn July'42 air cleaner trls 61 OTU 15-5-43 FAAC 12-7 1TEU 21-6-44

X4065 981 FF 2-8-40 8MU 4-9 610S 12-8 57 OTU 3-6-41 303S 17-7 dvd i/sea nr Prestatyn N Wales 11-8 SOC

X4066 982 FF 8MU 4-8 266S 16-8 des on grd Mans 18-8 SOC 28-8 FH5

X4067 983 FF 3-8-40 8MU 4-8 64S 11-8 610S s/dn by Bf109 nr Dover P/O Gray inj 24-8 222S 23-9 53 OTU 27-5-41 AST 27-6 con to FII MXII 130S 26-8 134S 5-1-42 53 OTU 12-2-42 air coll with P7822 nr St A CE 15-2

X4068 984 FF GP 3-8-40 8MU 4-8 74S 12-8 41S 13-9 FAC2 15-10 AST 61 OTU 28-6-41 Farn 12-3-42 gunnery trls, to ETPS for air-to-air homing 58 OTU 18-7 FAAC 18-2-43 1TEU 26-2-44 a/c aban cd nr Tealing CE 26-3-44

X4069 985 FF 3-8-40 8MU 4-8 74S 14-8 92S 12-9 dam on ops f/ld P/O Wright inj 30-9 AST SOC 17-10

X4070 986 FF 3-8-40 8MU 4-8 610S 12-8 19S 10-9 s/dn off French Coast Sgt Potter pow 15-9

X4101 987 FF 4-8-40 8MU 6-8 74S 14-8 41S 13-9 s/dn by Bf109 f/ld Lympne P/O Bennions safe 20-9 SAL 72S 8-12 485S 11-5-41 61 OTU 25-6 131S 17-7 ASTE 29-8 SOC 29-12

X4102 988 FF 4-8-40 8MU 6-8 610S 13-8 s/dn cd/ld nr Shepherdswell P/O Gray inj ops 24-8

X4103 989 FF GP 5-8-40 8MU 6-8 610S 13-8 66S 7-10 57 OTU FAC2 6-11 HAL 131S 17-7-41 4SoTT 18-10 SOC 20-9 to 2684M 3-2-42 rtp 18-5-44

X4104 991 FF GP 6-8-40 8MU 7-8 609S 16-8 dam Bf110 F/Lt Howell safe 24-8 602S 12-9 610S 14-12 53 OTU 3-3-41 FACB 25-5 WAL MMO new eng 21-3-42 222MU 15-11 *Algarab* 18-12 P Sudan 12-3-43 SOC 27-7-44

X4105 992 FF 5-8-40 8MU 6-8 610S 13-8 C2 ops 2-9 GAL 222S 17-1-41 53 OTU 23-6 61OTU 2-9 FACB 1-11 SOC 9-11

X4106 993 FF 6-8-40 6MU 7-8 92S 8-3 MMO 2-5 con to FVB M45 parts from R-R 92S 12-5 FAAC 13-9 401S 26-10 154S 1-3-42 66S 24-3-43 234S 19-4 312S 29-6 VSM 5-11 fuel syst mods 443S 25-2-44 288S 24-5-45 Sold J Dale 8-1-48

X4107 994 FF GP 6-8-40 8MU 8-8 609S 16-8 air coll with Bf110 nr Weybridge P/O Miller kld C3 27-9

X4108 995 FF GP 7-8-40 8MU 9-8 54S 16-8 124S 7-5-41 dbf 3-9 SOC 12-10

X4109 996 FF 7-8-40 9MU 8-8 72S 13-8 a/c aban F/O Sheen safe ops 1-9 SOC 28-9

X4110 997 FF 7-8-40 9MU 9-8 602S 16-8 s/dn by Bf109 over Solent F/Lt Urie aban a/c inj 18-8 COAL SOC 5-10

X4159 998 FF 8-8-40 6MU 10-8 can wng fitt 19S 1-9 7 OTU 3-9 FA 13-9 oxygen failure cd Tatton Hall, Cheshire, Sgt Edgar kld

X4160 999 FF 7-8-40 9MU 10-8 602S 16-8 air coll with Spit P/O Ritchie ret to Westh 23-8 s/dn by Ju88 nr Seaford Sgt Whall kld 7-10

X4161 1000 FF 8-8-40 9MU 9-8 602S 16-8 s/dn by bf 109 nr Portsmouth P/O Moddy safe C2 18-8 COAL 2-9 308S 11-5-41 403S 28-5 FACB 3-6 DeH new eng 21-3-42 52 OTU 11-7 FACB 24-7-43 ROS 58 OTU 14-9 SOC 30-8-45

X4162 1001 FF 8-8-40 9MU 9-8 602S 16-8 FAC2 23-11 124S 7-5-41 340S 20-10 52 OTU 21-10 FACB 24-1-42 ASTH HAL 15-6 con to PRVII M45 8 OTU 4-2-43

X4163 1002 FF 8-8-40 9MU 9-8 54S 13-8 41S 22-2-41 452S 24-4 313S 1-6 53 OTU 20-10 FACB 5-12 WAL 57 OTU 16-4-44 SOC 24-5-45

X4164 1003 FF 8-8-40 9MU 10-8 152S 19-8 603S 20-8 266S 13-10 ldg acc Sgt Ody safe 17-10 111S 11-11 58 OTU 28-5-41 SAL 111S air coll with K9863 nr Slnd CE 26-1-42

X4165 1004 FF 9-8-40 24MU 10-8 609S 16-8 66S 15-4-41 501S 27-4 61 OTU 1-7 FAAC 16-5-43 ROS RNDA 15-1-44 SOC 30-12

X4166 1005 FF GP 9-8-40 24MU 10-8 610S 15-8 FAC2 12-10 AST SOC 22-10 cancel 61 OTU 2-9-41 SOC 7-11 to 2827M

X4167 1006 FF GP 9-8-40 24MU 10-9 74S 16-9 72S 1-12 57 OTU 2-5-41 flew into hill with K9892 Ruabon Denbighs 3-7 SOC 15-7

X4168 1008 FF 9-8-40 24MU 10-8 610S 15-8 222S s/dn nr Hurst Green Sussex 7-9 SOC 11-9

X4169 1010 FF 10-8-40 24MU 11-8 602S 15-8 152S 13-9 C2 ops 24-9 AST 602S 29-10 52 OTU 10-5-41 FA dbf 7-8 SOC 18-8

X4170 1011 FF GP 10-8-40 24MU 12-9 266S 17-9 19S 17-9 dam ops f/dn Eastchurch P/O Lawson safe 18-9 66S 29-9 s/dn by Bf109 over Tunbridge Wells P/O Oxspring aban a/c 25-10 FH45.35

X4171 1009 FF 10-8-40 24MU 11-8 152S 15-8 58 OTU 23-3-41 CAC 2-6 SAL 132S 12-8 o/t ldg Peterhead CE 1-11 SOC

X4172 1012 FF GP 10-8-40 24MU 12-8 266S 17-8 616S 7-9 65S 26-2-41 308S 4-4 FA 4-5 AST 130S 26-10 CAC 12-11 VA 133S 26-2-42 601S 11-4 FAAC 5-5 421S 24-5 RNDA 1-9 AST 10-10 hook fitt RNAS Mach 17-10

X4173 1013 FF GP 11-8-40 24MU 12-8 266S 17-8 19S 13-9 609S 28-9 66S 24-2-41 57 OTU 14-3 AST 24-7 con to FVA M45 145S 23-11 134S 20-12 164S 9-5-42 602S 10-9 61 OTU 6-6-43 air coll with R7127 CAC 12-9 ROS cd Prestatyn Range Flints CE 19-5-44

X4174 1014 FF 11-8-40 24MU 13-8 266S 17-8 616S 7-9 65S 26-2-41 308S 16-4 303S 21-7 306S 6-10 57 OTU 10-1-42 53 OTU 11-8-43

X4175 1015 FF GP 11-8-40 24MU 13-8 266S 17-8 66S 6-9 57 OTU 31-10 FA 13-3-41 AST 412S 9-7 FA ttl wrk 2-8 SOC 8-8

X4176 1016 FF 11-8-40

X4177 1017 FF 12-8-40 24MU 13-8 152S 23-9 s/dn cd nr Frome Som S/Ldr Devitt safe C2 25-9 AST 54S 26-1-41 41S 22-2 452S 18-4 303S 19-7 306S 6-10 61 OTU 15-11 1TEU 1-3-44 SOC 6-3-45

X4178 1018 FF 12-8-40 24MU 13-8 266S 17-8 41S 25-9 dam Bf109 F/O Boyle safe 17-19 dam C2 7-10 FTR ops Sgt Lloyd kld 15-10

X4179 1019 FF GP 12-9-40 24MU 15-8 266S 18-8 19S 13-9 609S 27-9 66S 24-2-41 57 OTU 14-3 FA 8-5 MMO 131S 24-8 140S 3-4-42 FAAC 8-1-43 ROS 57 OTU 9-6 e/fld on t/o w/u ldg o/t Eshott CE 24-10-43

X4180 1020 FF 12-8-40 48MU 13-8 61S 26-8 FAC2 27-8 61 OTU 28-6-41 1 CRU 20-8 con to FVA M45 121S 7-12 403S 31-12 133S 6-2-42 2 USA 6-6 FAAC 10-1-43 61 OTU 28-2-44 CE 12-8

X4181 1021 FF GP 14-8-40 12MU 17-8 used for 100 octane fuel tests 616S 26-8 s/dn by Bf109 nr Graves F/Lt Gillam aban a/c C3 2-9 SOC 8-9 cancel 61 OTU o/t ldg Rednal 31-10-42

X4182 1022 FF GP 13-8-40 12MU 14-8 234S 19-8 dam by Bf110 nr Haslemere Sgt Olenski safe 4-9 234S cd nr Colan Newquay P/O McKay aban a/c inj CE 25-9

X4183 1023 FF GP 13-8-40 12MU 14-8 234S 19-8 s/dn nr Northian Sussex Sgt Hornby aban a/c inj

X4184 1024 FF 13-8-40 12MU 15-8 616S 26-8 65S 26-2-41 308S 4-4 58 OTU 21-8 FTR 14-9-43

X4185 1025 FF GP 13-8-40 12MU 12-8 603S 1-9 s/dn by Bf110 over Thames Estuary P/O Stewart-Clarke aban a/c inj 3-9

X4186 1026 FF 14-8-40 12MU 16-8 616S 26-8 C2 ops 133-11 AST 57 OTU 10-1-42 61 OTU 30-6 air coll with AR252 cd Slnd Flints CE 14-8

X4187 1027 FF 14-8-40 12MU 15-8 602S 21-8 s/dn by Bf109 P/O MacLean inj C2 26-8 AST 58 OTU 15-9-41 17SFTS 4-9-43 SOC 8-3-45

X4188 1028 FF GP 14-8-40 12MU 15-8 602S 21-8 s/dn by Bf109 Sgt Babbage aban a/c i/sea 26-8 FH4.50

X4231 (CMG)** 1007 FF GP 7-8-40 12MU 9-8 19S 10-8 s/dn by Bf109 nr N Weald F/O Coward aban a/c 31-8 FH23.55

X4232 1029 FF GP 16-8-40 8MU 17-8 65S 21-8 C2 ops 31-10 145S 21-1-41 118S 4-3 53 OTU 27-8 FACE 5-2-42

X4233 1030 FF 14-8-40 8MU 16-8 65S 21-8 C3 ops ttl wrk 26-11 SOC 23-12

X4234 1031 FF GP 15-8-40 8MU 16-8 609S 24-8 dam combat P/O Staples safe 27-9 AST 66S 13-10 57OTU 1-11 FACB 27-6-42 ROS wng fail in spin cd Alsager Cheshire CE 25-9

X4235 1032 FF 8MU 16-8 54S 25-8 dam t/o 31-8 C3 ops 11-9 SOC 19-9 cancel 19-9 111S 3-5-41 58 OTU 29-5 SOC 30-12-44

X4236 1035 FF 16-8-40 8MU 18-8 54S 25-8 dam by bombs on t/o Horn C3 31-8 SOC 10-9 to 2358M

X4237 1033 FF GP 16-8-40 8MU 17-8 19S 10-9 s/dn by Bf109 nr Canterbury Sgt Cox inj C3 27-9

X4238 1036 FF GP 17-8-40 8MU 19-8 54S 25-8 41S 22-2-41 AST 2-3 con to FVA M45 61 OTU 30-6 130S 5-11 332S 13-2-42 164S 12-4 strk by R7220 ldg Skae CE 4-5 SOC 25-5 FH252.25 Recat B 16-8 61 OTU 9-5-43 1TEU 21-6-44

X4239 1038 FF 17-8-40 8MU 18-8 610S 20-8 s/dn by Bf109 nr Folkes cd Hawk Sgt Cork safe 22-8 602S 17-12 72S 11-2-41 303S 19-7 306S 6-10 57 OTU 10-1-42 flew into Cynbowydd Snowdonia FTR 5-4

X4240 1039 FF 17-8-40 37MU 19-8 610S 7-10 602S 14-12 FACB 10-2-41 SAL 58 OTU 7-7 52 OTU 7-2-42 FACB 1-3 AST recat E 20-5

X4241 1040 FF 18-8-40 37MU 20-8 610S 30-8 C3 ops 2-9 AST 234S 4-2-41 58 OTU 28-3 flew into high grd Maddie Moss nr Alloa 10-6-43 SOC 30-6 FH959.40

X4242 1041 FF 18-8-40 37MU 20-8 54S 3-9 41S 22-2-41 452S 19-4 313S 21-5 61 OTU 16-8 20-12 con to PRIII Ben 26-3-42 for use Comdg General 215MU 20-10 *Pet Mer* 8-11 lost at sea 8-1-43

X4243 1042 FF 19-8-40 37MU 20-8 245S 8-9 234S 9-9 C2 ops 25-12 AST 132S 12-7-41 CE dbf 19-7 SAL SOC 31-7 FH39

X4244 1043 FF 19-8-40 37MU 20-8 245S 8-9 234S 9-9 58 OTU 28-3-41 52 OTU 12-11-41 FACB 15-4-42 ASTH RNAS Yeov 9-9 RNAS 13-12-43 SOC 30-12-44

X4245 1044 FF 19-8-40 37MU 21-8 610S 7-10 602S 14-12 FA i/sea 26-4-41 SOC 3-5 FH 190.45

X4246 1045 FF 19-8-40 38MU 20-8 152S 28-8 FAC2 9-9 222S 7-11 53 OTU 17-3-41 FAAC 24-8

X4247 1046 FF 20-8-40 38MU 21-8 152S 28-8 129S 22-6-41 e/fld std ldg Cherry Burton Yorks CE 9-7 SAL SOC 14-7

X4248 1047 FF 20-8-40 38MU 21-8 616S 28-8 s/dn by Bf109 West Mall F/O Bell kld C3 30-8 SOC 14-10

X4249 1048 FF 20-8-40 38MU 20-8 222S 3-9 s/dn by Bf109 Aveley Essex Sgt Johnson aban a/c 14-9

X4250 1049 FF 20-8-40 38MU 21-8 603S 30-8 dam by Bf109 f/ld Horn S/Ldr Denholm safe 7-9 FAC2 27-9 f/ld

** *CMG Cannon, machine gun wing.*

Folkestone beach P/O Dexter safe

X4251 1050 FF 20-8-40 6MU 20-8 234S 22-8 58 OTU 27-3-41 411S 25-7 129S 8-8 58 OTU 15-9-41 hit high grd nr Peebles dbf 3-10 SOC 8-11

X4252 1051 FF 20-8-40 6MU 21-8 266S 24-8 72S 6-9 C3 ops 16-1-41 SOC 27-7

X4253 1052 FF 21-8-40 6MU 21-8 266S 24-8 C2 ops 6-9 41S 5-10 611S 24-10 485S 14-3-41 123S 13-6 58 OTU 5-1-42 3AGS 28-7 RNDA 1-9

X4254 1053 FF 21-8-40 6MU 22-8 266S 24-8 72S 6-9 (s/dn by Bf110 over Thames Estuary F/O Elsdon inj C3 7-9 suspect) HAL SOC 19-9 cancel 266S 1-11 111S 23-4-41 58 OTU 29-5 cd nr Brackford Aucherarder CE 5-9 SOC 13-9

X4255 1054 FF 21-8-40 6MU 21-8 266S 24-8 66S s/dn by Bf109 Hawk P/O Allan inj C2 11-10 AST 53 OTU 25-6-41 e/fld o/s f/ld CE 15-6-42

X4256 1055 FF 21-8-40 6MU 22-8 602S 24-8 s/dn by Bf109 F/O Coverley kld 7-9 SOC 1-10 FH15.50

X4257*. 10371037 FIB FF 17-8-40 6MU 20-8 first Spit with 'B' wng Type 340. AMDP EA 30-8 Farn 3-9 BDn 20-10 1CRU new eng 8MU 15-11 AFDU Dux 11-1-41 R-RH 10-2 M45 fitt redesig FVB 92S 16-21-41 service trls e/fld cd Maids 19-3 AST 411S 8-11 BDn Jan '42 R/T function trls at h/a with R7120 (FVI) 242S 25-9 VSM 5-4-43 fuel syst mods wng stiff 118S 2-7 64S 25-9 power loss f/ld hit obst nr Lodiswell S Devon CE SOC 3-7-44

X4258 1056 FF 21-8-40 6MU 22-8 152S 16-9 FAAC 15-11 AST 66S 27-2-41 501S 27-4 53 OTU 14-5 AST 22-9 con to FVA M45 CRD Farn Jan'42 gunnery. Sutton harness & recovery trls. Nov. trls with HF/VHF 'Relay' homing device and R/T fighters. Dec. fitt 'Monica IFF'. Feb'43 dvng & alt trls. Mar. weather trls. BDn March for cool trls. WDn and WW mods. Artificial horizon; neg 'G' and weather trials. Farn June/July. trls a/c for 'Monica' with Ju88 fitt 'Flensburg' and other devices. Back-up a/c for JL227 (see page). Target a/c for h/a trls with Mosquito DZ725 equip with 'Monica IA'. DTD Aug. Jan to March 1944. Fighter affil into bomber stream with Lancaster ED630 fitt with 'Monica'. Escort a/c for Ju88 and bf109. Trls with Wellington HZ202 and HZ579 fitt ASO 'Eureka/Babe' and Harvard FE788 with spcl VHF. Fw190 fitt FUG R16Z took part in trls. CE 20-11-44

X4259 1057 FF 22-8-40 12MU 24-8 603S 1-9 266S 17-10 FAC2 5-11 SOC12-1-41

X4260 1058 FF 22-8-40 12MU 23-8 603S 1-9 s/dn over France P/O Caister pow 6-9 SOC 2-11 FH9.55

X4261 1059 FF 22-8-40 12MU 24-8 603S 1-9 s/dn by Bf109 F/Lt Rushmer kld 5-9 SOC 1-12 FH8.60

X4262 1069 FF 23-8-40 12MU 27-8 72S 2-9 dbf ops 3-9 SOC 23-9

X4263 1061 FF 23-8-40 38MU 24-8 603S 30-8 e/td t/ld Sgt Sarre safe C2 4-9, AST 602S 21-10 610S 14-12 53 OTU 3-3-41 dvdi/sea off Llan SOC 26-8

X4264 1062 FF 23-8-40 38MU 25-8 222S 3-9 s/dn by Bf110 f/ldg Detling Sgt Hutchinson inj 14-9 603S 14-10 266S cd Strad P/O Williams kld 21-10 SOC 25-10 FH17.40

X4266 1064 FF 24-8-40 37MU 25-8 66S 5-9 FAC2 HAL 602S 24-11 610S 14-12 53 OTU 3-3-41 FAAC 23-3 HAL CRD BDn 11-4-42 hand, stab, recovery from dive and steep turns. Comp trls with BM559. 222MU 19-8 57 OTU 20-8 air coll with AR222 cd Warkworth N'land CE 17-3-43

X4267 1065 FF 24-8-40 37MU 25-8 19S 21-9 7 OTU 5-10 FAC2 14-11 GAL 123S 25-6-41 58 OTU 1-10 82MU 13-9-42 *Pet Mer* 8-11 lost at sea 8-1-43

X4268 1066 FF 24-8-40 AMDP VA 24-8 Farn Sept aile trls. pilot J Quill. Farn July '41 flight measurements of wng internal pressure for invest into struct fail of Spit wngs Ret VAWDn for contin of trls. ASTH for flaps mods. CRD BDn 8-9-41 M45 instal. Strengthened flaps tested as air brakes. 18-10 trls with thermostatically-operated rad shutter ROS VA 8-10 CRD DeH 23-11 39MU 18-2-42 3SoGR 10-3 C Flt PRU e/fld w/u ldg nr Weeton Lancs CE 21-4-42 SOC 30-4-42.

X4269 1067 FF 24-8-40 6MU 25-8 602S 27-8 s/dn by Bf109 Mayfield P/O Gage safe C2 30-10 GAL 58 OTU 10-5-41 35GR 3-4-42 AST 4-7 RNDA 7-9 *Pet Mer* 8-11 lost at sea 8-1-43

X4270 1068 FF 24-8-40 6MU 25-8 602S 27-8 57 OTU 9-8-41 air coll with P9494 nr Haw CB 14-3-42 WAL RNDA 1-9 FACC 20-4-43 RNAS 14-7

X4271 1070 FF 25-8-40 6MU 27-8 603S 30-8 s/dn by Bf109 cd Wanstead P/O Gilroy aban a/c 31-8 FH3.50

X4272 1071 FF 25-8-40 6MU 9-9 can wng fitt 92S 7 OTU R-RH con to FVB M45 92S 21-3-41 222S VSM 14-7-43 fuel syst mods wng stiff bomb carr

X4273 1072 FF 26-8-40 6MU 27-8 603S 30-8 s/dn by Bf109 nr Ilford Essex F/O Waterson kld 31-8

X4274 1073 FF 26-8-40 6MU 27-8 603S 30-8 266S 17-10 FACE dbf 19-1-41 SOC 27-1 cancel AST 25-2 57 OTU 3-6 215MU 29-10-42 *Taran* 20-11 P Sudan 27-1-43 ME 28-2 SOC 27-7-44

X4275 1074 Ff 26-8-40 6MU 29-8 222S 31-8 dam by Bf109 nr Graves cd in flames Rochford Sgt Baxter kld 14-9

X4276 1075 FF 27-8-40 6MU 27-8 54S 29-8 FA 28-12 SOC 4-1-41

X4277 1076 FF 27-8-40 6MU 28-8 603S 30-8 s/dn in flames off N Foreland P/O Hilary (author 'The Last Enemy') aban a/c severly inj 3-9 FH7.45

X4278 1077 FF 27-8-40 6MU 28-8 222S 31-8 s/dn by Bf109 ChuSt F/O Cutts kld 4-9

X4279 1078 FF 29-8-40 6MU 29-8 can wng fitt 19S 9-9 7 OTU 10-9 72S 24-10 R-RH 6-2-41 con to FVB M45 AFDU Dux 28-2 92S 14-3 C2 ops 24-3 616S 23-7 129S 13-12 41S 3-3-42 cd/ld on beach West End Pwllheli CE 1-2-43

X4280 1079 FF 28-8-40 6MU 29-8 222S 31-8 C2 2-9 65S 30-12 61 OTU 2-9-41 AST 16-10-42 con to FVA M45 670bs Grp USA 25-3-43 ATA 186 12-3-44 SAL 18-12

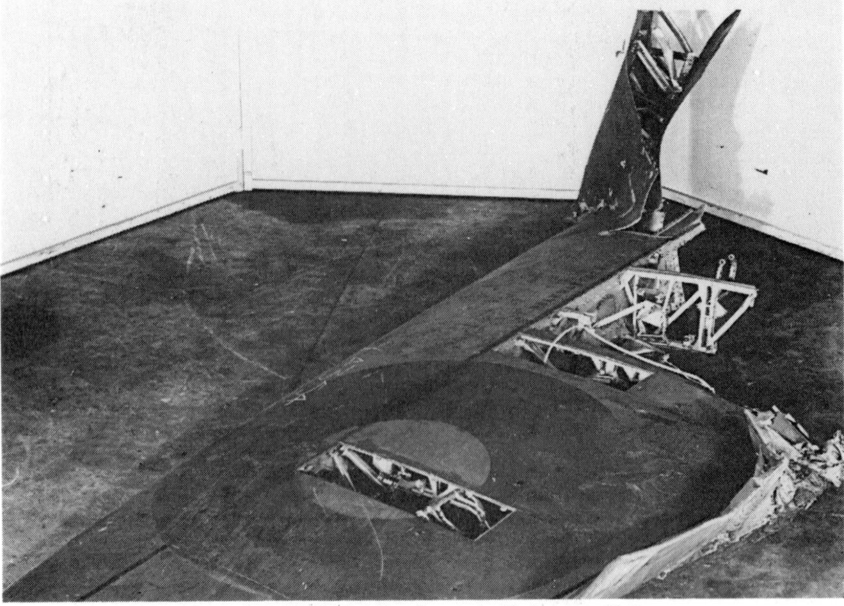

Remains of X4354 at Farnborough, 30 January 1942.

X4317 1081 FF 28-8-40 8MU 29-8 54S 3-9 FAC2 7-9 41S 23-9 611S 24-10 485S 14-3-41 52 OTU 21-7 58 OTU 4-9 o/s f/ld nr Alnwick N'land CE 25-9 SOC 2-10

X4318 1082 FF 28-8-40 8MU 29-8 54S 2-9 FAC3 6-9 SAL 111S 3-5-41 58 OTU 24-5 flew into Graigs Head Carnbo Kinross dbf 1-7 SOC 13-7

X4319 1083 FF 29-8-40 8MU 30-8 54S 4-9 41S 22-2-41 452S 18-4 403S 7-6 52 OTU 21-7 245 8-3-42 510S 31-12 SOC 1-12-44

X4320 1084 FF 29-8-40 8MU 30-8-40 66S 5-9 FTR ops F/Lt Gillies kld 4-10 FH45.15

X4321 1085 FF 29-8-40 8MU 30-8 66S 5-9 dam by Bf109 over Norfolk f/ld P/O Bodie safe C3 7-9 HAL SOC 12-9 cancel 64S 19-12 303S 28-2-41 58 OTU 20-3 strk water cd Incailloch Island Loch Lomond CE 14-6-42

X4322 1086 FF 29-8-40 8MU 31-8 66S 5-9 dam by Bf109 nr Burwash Sussex f/ld P/O Watkinson safe C3 28-9 SOC 8-10

X4323 1087 FF 29-8-40 9MU 31-8 603S 3-9 s/dn Bf109 cd Fennington P/O Howes kld 18-9

X4324 1088 FF 30-8-40 9MU 31-8 603S 3-9 s/dn by Bf109 over Kent P/O Pease kld 15-9 SOC 21-9

X4325 1089 FF 30-8-40 9MU 31-8 41S 6-9 s/dn by Bf110 over Thames Estuary P/O Langley aban a/c safe 11-9

X4326 1090 FF 30-8-40 9MU 31-8 66S 5-9 dam by Bf109 P/O Heron ret to Gaves safe 7-10 AST 61 OTU 3-7-41 8 OTU 11-9-42 cd nr Fort William CE 16-5-43 SOC 1-6 FH462.40

X4327 1091 FF 30-8-40 9MU 2-9 603S 5-9 s/dn by Bf109 nr Ashford P/O Robbins inj 14-9 SOC 31-9

X4328 1092 FF 30-8-40 24MU 31-8 616S 7-9 s/dn by Bf109 C3 27-9 GAL SOC 3-2-41

X4329 1094 FF 31-8-40 8MU 2-9 616S 7-9 65S 26-2-41 308S 13-4 403S 21-5 61 OTU 11-8 e/fld hit tree in f/ld nr Ellesmere Salop CE 16-6-42

X4330 1095 FF 31-8-40 58 OTU 616S cd/ld base Sgt Hogg safe 14-10

X4331 1096 FF 31-8-40 24MU 1-9 19S 15-9 609S 28-9 66S 24-2-41 57 OTU 7-4 MMOx 10-7 con to FVA M45 306S 3-10 610S 18-11 133S 17-1-42 601S 9-4 RNSA 11-9-42 for use as train

X4332 1034 FF 16-8-40 PDU HAL 17-8 con to PRIII Type C PRU 31-8 FTR 17-10 FH11.15

X4333 1060 FF 22-8-40 PDU HAL 22-8 con to PRIII Type C 1PRU Ben 31-8 R-RH 29-4-41 con to FVA M45 1PRU 14-5 e/fld f/ld strk house 22-9 HAL 7-10 con to PRVII 354S 12-4-42 8 OTU 6-8 std ldg i/sea nr Fraser CE 22-1-42 SOC 23-1 FH44-.05

X4334 1080 FF 27-8-40 FArn 27-8 camera trls PDU HAL 21-10 con to PRIII R-R 22-12 con to FVA M45. Fuel cons trls FF 13-1-41 PRU Ben 6-2 dam ops 21-4 HAL con to PRV 8 OTU 19-6-42 FACB 5-12 HAL CE 10-2-44

X4335 1093 FF 31-8-40 PDU HAL 31-8 con to PRIII R-RH 10-3-41 M45 con to FVA 1PRU 27-3 HAL 31-5 con to PRIV 1PRU 19-7 SOC 23-12 7SoTT 8-12 PRU Ben CAC ops 17-4-42 8 OTU 19-6 542S 29-11 FACB 24-2-43 HAL SOC 22-3-45

X4336 1098 FF 2-9-40 24MU 3-9 19S 13 9 FAC2 25-9 GAL 610S 19-12 602S 4-1-41 61 OTU 20-4-41 131S 13-7 OTU 59 OTU 3-9 RNDA 7-9-42 as train

X4337 1097 FF 2-9-40 8MU 3-9 72S 7-9 dam C2 by Bf109 18-9 AST 65S 21-12 145S 31-1-41 118S 8-3 53 OTU 27-8 9-9-42

X4338 1099 FF 2-9-40 8MU 4-9 41S 7-9 122S 11-6-41 123S 14-7 61 OTU 17-9 FACB 20-5-42 DeH complete overhaul 53 OTU 29-6-43 SOC E 7-5-46

X4339 1100 FF 2-9-40 8MU 4-9 66S 7-9 s/dn by He 111 f/ld C2 P/O Cruickshanks safe 11-9 SAL 57 OTU 3-6-41 306S 6-10 215MU 21-10-42 *Bar For* 9-11 Port 21-11

X4340 1101 FF 3-9-40 8MU 5-9 72S 9-9 s/dn by Bf109 nr Sevenoaks P/O Males kld 27-9

X4341 1102 FF 3-9-40 8MU 8-9 222S 7-9 C2 ops 16-12 AST 53 OTu 8-5-43

X4342** 1103 FF 3-9-40 8MU 5-9 6MU 9-9 can wng fitt 19S 9-9 7 OTU 10-9 R-RH 11-1-41 con to FVB M45 AFDU 24-2 92S 13-3 R-RH 15-4 dam by Bf109 14-6 AST 316S 15-10 154S 13-6-42 121S 18-7 CAC ops 22-7 340S 13-9 131S 27-10 FTR ops 18-11

X4343 1104 FF 3-9-40 9MU 4-9 41S 6-9 dam Bf110s P/O Bennions inj 11-9 HAL 53 OTU 6-5-41 as 2635 SOC 22-7

X4344 1105 FF 3-9-40 9MU 5-9 41S 6-9 dam by Bf109 nr Dung ld Horn C2 F/O Lovell safe 30-9 GAL 303S 22-2-41 58 OTU 10-3 61 OTU 8-11 53 OTU 3-1-42 215MU 26-9 *Taran* 8-11 P Sudan 29-1-43 ME 31-3 SOC 1-2-44

X4345 1106 FF 4-9-40 9MU 5-9 41S 6-9 s/dn by Bf109 nr Sittingbourne P/O Aldous aban a/c 28-9 SOC 10-10

X4346 1107 FF 4-9-40 9MU 5-9 41S 6-9 AST 20-9 234S 12-10 61 OTU 3-7-41 53 OTU 31-12

X4347 1108 FF 4-9-40 9MU 7-9 603S 8-9 266S 17-10 FA dbf 8-3-41 SOC 17-3

X4348 1109 FF 5-9-40 9MU 7-9 603S 8-9 266S 17-10 111S 8-4-41 58 OTU 29-5-41 FACB 30-7 ROS FACE SOC 1-9

X4349 1110 FF 5-9-40 9MU 6-9 603S 8-9 C3ops 23-9 SOC 2-10

X4350 1111 FF 5-9-40 1PRU 15-9 FTR ops 16-12

X4351 1112 FF 5-9-40 24MU 7-9 19S 13-9 e/a C2 22-9 bombed SOC

X4352 1113 FF 5-9-40 24MU 7-9 19S 13-9 s/dn by Bf109 over Kent P/O Burgoyne kld 27-9 SOC31-10

X4353 1114 FF 6-9-40 24MU 7-9 19S 13-9 7 OTU 5-10 65S 28-11 145S 16-1-41 118S 8-3 66S 9-4 501S 27-4 1 CRU 17-6 con to FVA M45 603S 5-11 145S 18-11 134S 20-12 FTR ops 16-3

X4354 1115 FF 6-9-40 24MU 7-9 234S RAF Baginton for defence B&P 2-6-41 Farn AUG'41 52 OTU 5-12 port wng broke off in dive cd Stratton St Margaret Swindon dbf 7-12 SOC 18-12

X4355 1116 FF 6-9-40 6MU 7-9 234S 10-9 dam by Ju88 f/ld nr Porthleven P/O Mortimer-Rose safe 26-10 AST HAL 14-5-41 to 2844M 7SoTT 14-5 SOC 18-12

X4356 1118 FF 6-9-40 92S 23-9 s/dn by Bf109 nr Graves C2 Sgt Ellis safe 24-9 AST 226S 4-2-41 111S 3-4 58 OTU 29-5 215MU 26-9-42 *Taran* 8-11 P Sudan 3-2-43 ME 28-2 SOC 27-7-44

X4381 1122 FF 6-9-40 6MU 10-9 152S 13-9 501S 5-11 53 OTU 7-7-41 stbd wng broke off after high speed dive out of cloud Tonpentre nr Pontypridd dbf CE 16.30hr 6-8 SOC 21-8 Farn 30-1-42

X4382 1119 FF 6-9-40 6MU 7-9 602S 10-9 610S 14-12 53 OTU 3-3-41 412S 19-7 58 OTU 7-8 SAL 23-1-42 RNAS Arb 4-9 SOC 26-1-45

X4383 1117 FF 7-9-40 AMDP Farn 8-9 con to PRIII 1PRU 14-12 3PRU 17-12 R-RH 6-5-41 M45 instal 8 OTU 9-6-42 ASTH 11-10 con to PRV dam hydraulics (brakes, flaps) cd boundary wall CB 10-5-43 recat E 26-5

X4384 1134 FF 11-9-40 PDU HAL 12-9 con to PRV 3PRU 7-4-41 dam by bombs 27-4 R-RH 9-7 M45 instal PRU Ben 19-7 HAL 24-9 con fo PRVII Type C 1PRU 27-2-42 8 OTU 19-6 strk P8321 Detling CB 19-7 HAL M46 instal SOC 27-2-45

X4385 1142 FF 13-9-40 PDU HAL 14-9 con to PRIII Type C 3PRU Bomb Comm 23-11 f/ld Oak 9-1-41 DGRD Farn 28-3 camera trls R-RH 4-5 con to PRV M45 instal 1PRU 21-7 FTR ops 22-9

X4386 1142 FF 13-9-40 PDU HAL 20-9con to PRIII 3PRU Bom Com 24-11 first sortie 27-11 FTR recce Bremen 12-1-41 F/Lt Marshall pow FH42.50

X4387 1120 FF 7-9-40 MU 9-8 234S 10-9 FAC2 19-11 MMO 306S 6-10-41 52 OTU 3-1-42 CE 8-9-43 42 OTU 3-5-44 SOC 17-9-45

X4388 1121 FF 7-9-40 8MU 8-9 616S 13-9 452S 30-4-

X4381 with No 501 Squadron, June 1941, with Sgts Thomas and Marsden. It lost its starboard wing in a dive on 6 August that year.

41 303S 3-6 313S 11-6 61 OTU 16-8 57 OTU 31-12 cd Connahs Quay Flints CE 27-2-42

X4389 1123 FF 8-9-40 8MU 9-9 602S 12-9 610S 14-12 53 OTU 3-3-41 61 OTU 1-7 AST 26-7 con to FV M45 603S 29-9 FTR ops 13-10

X4390 1124 FF 8-9-40 8MU 9-9 602S 12-9 610S 14-12 53 OTU 3-3-41 FA 21-3 HAL 412S 19-7 58 OTU 3-8 17SFTS 7-5-43 SOC dbr 23-1-45

X4409 1125 FF 9-9-40 24MU 10-9 41S 12-9 s/dn by Bf109 Stelling Minnies P/O Baker safe 17-9 41S s/dn by Bf109 Sittingbourne P/O Chalder aban a/c 28-9

X4410 1126 FF 9-9-40 24MU 10-9 72S 17-9 s/dn by Bf109 nr Ashford Kent P/O Holland aban a/c kld 20-9

X4411 1127 FF 9-9-40 6MU 10-9 602S 13-9 FAC2 8-11 HAL con to PRV Type G 57 OTU 3-6-41 306S 6-10 61 OTU 12-10 HAL 30-6-42 con to PRVI Type G 8MU 26-8 con to PRVII 3SIG 2-10 SOC CE 28-2-43

X4412 1128 FF 10-9-40 6MU 11-9 602S 13-9 92S 11-10 C2 ops 20-10 145S 22-1-41 118S 18-2 66S 94 e/a 13-4 AST 61 OTU 2-10 CGS 28-3-42 RNAS Arb 1-9 SOC 26-1-45

X4413 1129 FF 10-9-40 6MU 12-9 72S 14-9 57 OTU 2-5-41 132S 9-8 52 OTU 28-10 58 OTU 6-9-43 1TEU 26-2-44 57 OTU 16-4 SOC 9-2-45

X4414 1130 FF 10-9-40 6MU 11-9 602S 13-9 s/dn by Bf109 nr Mayfield P/O Gage safe C2 27-9 GAL 52 OTU 26-10-41 57 OTU 25-4-43 e/fld and fire f/ld Esh CE 28-11

X4415 1131 FF 11-9-40 6MU 12-9 603S 14-9 FA C2 23-9 SAL 53 OTU 9-5-41 FAAC 12-9 ASTM SOC Oct'41

X4416 1132 FF 11-9-40 9MU 11-9 72S 13-9 222S 17-10 61 OTU 17-7-41 53 OTU 27-7-42 FAAC 10-7-43 ROS SOC MAL CE 16-8-44

X4417 1133 FF 11-9-40 9MU 13-9 92S 17-9 s/dn by Bf109 nr Dover dbf P/O Hill kld 20-9 SOC 3-10 FH7.15

X4418 1135 ff 11-9-40 9MU 13-9 92S 17-9 SOC 9-11

X4419 1136 FF 11-9-40 9MU 14-9 72S 16-9 92S 20-10 CAC ops 8-4-41 61 OTU 13-8 215S MU 8-11-42 *Pet Mer* 8-11 lost at sea 8-1-43

X4420 1137 FF 12-9-40 8MU 13-9 66S 15-9 e/ac C3 dbf 10-11 SOC 1-12 FH47.20

X4421 1138 FF 12-9-40 8MU 13-9 66S 16-9 57 OTU 21-10 steep dive from low cloud, violent pull out, high speed stall, spun, wng fail Pilot thrown clear but kld 15.15hr cd Northrop Flints 27-3-41 SOC cancel Farn 8-4 AST 13-5 rebuilt as FVA M45 164S 29-4-42 FACE 18-8 (Rebuild suspect).

X4422 1144 FF 12-9-40 8MU 13-9 92S 18-9 s/dn by Bf109 nr Maids F/Lt Paterson kld 27-9 SOC 10-10

X4423 1139 FF 12-9-40 8MU 13-9 54S 19-9 FAC3 8-11 SOC 17-11

X4424 1140 FF 13-9-40 8MU 13-9 19S 18-9 129S 22-6-41 GAL 14-8 61 OTU 20-11 57 OTU 10-1-42 FACE 5-3-43 WAL recat E

X4425 1141 FF 13-9-40 8MU 14-9 19S 18-9 92S 57 OTU 8-3-41 CAC ops 2-7 61 OTU 20-11 Farm Jan'42 FAce 4-4-43

X4426 1148 FF 13-9-40 8MU 17-9 41S 19-9 reputed s/dn by Bf109 Sitingbourne F/O Boyle kld 28-9 SOC 7-10 cancel 61 OTU strk R6963 taxy Rednal CE 5-3-43

X4427 1142 FF 13-9-40 8MU 14-9 92S 19-9 dam by Bf109 nr Swanley S/Ldr Lister inj C2 24-9 HAL 129S 22-6-41 53 OTU 1-6-42 air coll with X4996 Llan CE 25-6-

X4428 1145 FF 14-9-40 MU 15-9 234S 18-9 FTR after com Ju88 16-1-41 FH58.20

X4471 1146 FF 14-9-40 6MU 16-9 609S 18-9 66S 24-2-41 308S 7-4 57 OTU 22-6-42 FACE 1-2-43 52 OTU 28-5-43 57 OTU 29-8 SOC 13-4-45

X4472 1147 FF 14-9-40 6MU 16-9 609S 18-9 C2 ops 8-10 41S 22-6-41 53 OTU 22-7 RNDA 23-1-44 ret RAF 12-5-45

X4473 1149 FF 16-9-40 6MU 17-9 19S 20-9 66S 29-9 s/dn by Bf109 P/O Kendall kld C2 5-10 AST 457S 22-6-41 58 OTU 5-1 42 FACE 14-7-43 SOC 20-4-45

X4474 1150 FF 16-9-40 6MU 17-9 19S 20-9 7 OTU 5-10 602S 22-10 610S 14-12 53 OTU 3-3-41 ASTH 11-4-42 to 3598M 6SoTT 2-3-43 Allot RDAF cancel 22-9-47

X4475 1151 FF 16-9-40 6MU 18-9 19S 20-9 7 OTU 5-10 SOC 25-4-41

X4476** 1152 FF 17-9-40 39MU 18-9 R-RH 6-2-41 con to FVA M45 92S 8-3 dam by Bf109 21-6 FTR ops 3-7

X4477 1153 FF 17-9-40 39MU 18-9 616S 26-9 65S 26-2-41 308S 13-4 DeH 16-4-42 new eng 53 OTU 33-7 fire during cleaning dbf 25-11

X4478 1154 FF 17-9-40 9MU 19-9 72S 20-9 66S 13-9 92S 53 OTU 21-5-41 SAL 8-10 RNDA 23-2-42 for con to Sea Mk IA not suitable DAM 61 OTU e/fld cd/ld nr West Felton Salop 26-7

X4479 1155 FF 17-9-40 9MU 19-9 66S 23-9 COAL 2-10 s/dn by Bf109 f/ld Burham C2 S/Ldr Leigh safe 13-10 AST 129S 22-6-41 52 OTU 25-8-42 FACB 13-9 recat E

X4480 1156 FF 9MU 19-9 72S 20-9 92S 22-9 s/dn by Bf109 cd Penhurst C2 P/O Mansell-Lewis safe 25-10 145S 22-1-41 CB ops 22-2 MMO 53 OTU 6-5 61 OTU 15-10 FAAC 21-7-42 ASTH SOC 17-4-43

X4481 1157 FF 18-9-40 9MU 19-9 72S 20-9 C3 ops 5-10 AST 64SS 24-11 303S 2-2-41 58 OTU 29-3 FAAC 11-6 SAL 53 OTU 21-4-43 RNDA 21-3-44 57 OTU 29-5 FACB recat E SOC 24-7

X4482** 1158 FF 19-9-40 39MU 11-9 MMO 21-9 RAF Baginton for Defence B&P 2-6-41 52 OTU 5-12 57 OTU 17-6-42 FACB 8-7-43 recat E

X4483 1159 FF GP 19-9-40 9MU 19-9 72S 23-9 485S 29-4-41 61 OTU 25-6 FACE ttl wrk 10-9 SOC 17-9

X4484 1160 FF 19-9-40 9MU 19-9 92S 24-9 Farn Mar'41 61 OTU 15-10 FACB 13-6-42 ROS to 4524M 2SoTT 5-2-44 SOC 23-9-47

X4485 1161 FF GP 19-9-40 9MU 19-9 92S 24-9 C2 ops 5-11 129S 22-6-41 FAAC 15-6-42 VSM 21-10 fuel syst mods, wng stiff con to FVA M45 349S 1-7-43 61 OTU 1-8

X4486 1163 FF GP 19-9-40 8MU 20-9 72S 24-9 122S FACB 5-6-41 WAL 61 OTU 27-10 57 OTU 10-1 42 e/fld Molt Denbigh CE 11-5-43 SOC 31-5 FH827.50

X4487 1164 FF 19-940 8MU 20-9 72S 24-9 92S 24-9 C3 ops 1-11 AST 602S 3-1-41 58 OTU 4-7 1PRU 10-1-42 con to PRV 8 OTU 19-6 hit high grd Clen Clova Angus CE dbf 10-11 SOC 20-11

X4488 1165 FF 20-9-40 8MU 21-9 72S 24-9 C2 ops 2-10 GAL 411S 22-6-41 57 OTU 10-8 58 OTU 25-7-42 AST 23-11 con to FVA M45 61 OTU 15-6-43

X4489 1166 FF 20-9-40 8MU 21-9 603S 24-9 C2 ops 5-10 122S 8-7-41 76MU 22-9-42 *C o Evans* 21-10 P Sudan 23-12 ME 31-1-42 SOC 27-7-44

X4490 1167 FF GP 20-9-40 8MU 21-9 603S 24-9 266S 17-10 111S 23-4-41 58 OTU 30-5 57 OTU 1-8 AST 21-12 con to PRIII 1PRU 7-3-42 8 OTU 17-6 MSFU Speke 23-4-42 53 OTU 27-2-43 strk by X4659 waiting t/o Hilbald CAC 10-8-44 recat E

X4421 went into a high speed stall after recovering from a dive on 27 March 1941. Both wings failed but the pilot was thrown clear.

X4474 served with the RAF in the last weeks of the Battle of Britain and is seen here in the colours of No.19 Squadron. It was converted to maintenance airframe 3598M in 1943.

X4491 1168 FF 20-9-40 Farn 20-9 trls con to PRV 10-11 DTD R-RH 27-3-41 con to FVA M45 1PRU 17-4 FTR ops 20-8

X4492 1296 EA FF 14-9-40 Farn 17-9 PDU HAL con to PRIV (W) R-RH 18-4-41 con to FVA M45 1PRU 29-4 8MU 15-11 con to PRVII BDn con to proto FVI M47, extended wng tips. known as exp a/c 152 to ROC. Trls with 3 & 4 blade props. 140S 12-2-42 47MU 5-12 *Man Prog* 16-1-43 Rockcliffe Canada 17-2. 36in telephoto camera. Trls July '43. Used to photo total eclipse of sun 9-7-45 F24 oblique instal to sight upwards. Pilot F/Lt Percival

X4493 1361 EA 1PRU 27-9-40 6MU 24-11 PDU HAL 21-12 con to PRIV 3PRU 2-2-41 Farn Mar-Aprl 1941 trls F.8 40in camera R-RM 1-7 M45 instal 1PRU 21-7 FTR ops 27-8

X4494 1373 EA PDU HAL 28-12-40 con to PRIV 3PRU 26-2-41 R-RH 4-4 M45 instal 3PRU 16-5 1PRU 31-7 FACB 5-12 HAL 21-12 con to PRVI Type F 8 OTU 31-7-42 FA FTR 23-4-43

X4495 1383 EA Farn F1E 4-4-41 PDU HAL con to PRIII Type C ETPS Farn 10-3 1PRU 18-3 FTR ops 3-5 FH44.50

X4496 1393 EA PDU HAL 12-1-41 con to PRIII Type C DGRD Farn trls & dev 1PRU 26-2 FTR ops 9-6 FH167.25

X4497 1534 HPA PDU 12-1-41 HAL 24-3 con to PRIII Type C 1PRU 26-4 R-RH 14-5 instal Ben 25-5 FTR ops 20-8

X4498 1553 HPA PDU HAL 29-3-41 con to PRIII Type C DGRD Farn 27-5 3PRU 17-6 1PRU 21-7 HAL con to PRVI Type F M45 8 OTU 13-9-42 e/fld pilot fail to clear a/c cd nr Dornie Inverness CE 19-1-43 FH326.05

X4499 1596 HPA DGRD Farn 19-4-41 1PRU 16-6 HAL 3-7 con to PRIV M45 Farn July '41 1PRU 1-8 140S 12-2-42 542S 2-11 8 OTU 11-3-43 FA 4-5 HAL con to PRVI M55 TTC Hq 21-12-44 10 ATS 10-1-46 SOC 4-9-47

X4500 161 7 HPA DGRD Farn 28-4-41 R/T fighter trls ETPS. con to PRV Type C M45 2-7 1PRU 10-7 FTR ops 1-9

X4501 1627 HPA on loan to HAL 4-2-41 con to PRIII Type C 28-4 1PRU 1-6 e/fld w/u ldg Fair Isle CE 12-7 SOC 23-8 SAL 3SoGR 4-5-42 con to PRVI Type F M45 8 OTU 24-5 FACB 22-1-43 SOC FH262.50

X4502 1632 HEA contract loan HAL 4-2-41 con to PRV Type C 3-5 1PRU 29-6 CB ops 4-9 HAL 1PRU 13-9 HAL con to PRVI Type F 1PRU 18-11 140 Army Coop S 22-4-42 FA FTR 2-6-43 FH177.45

X4503 1644 HEA DGRD Farn 8-5-41 HAL 30-9 con to PRV Type C M45 1PRU 3-10 FTR ops 16-3-42

X4504 1655 HEA DGRD Farn 16-3-41 HAL 17-5 con to PRV Type C M45 1PRU Ben 8-7 e/fld f/ld CE Nordelph Norfolk 11-7 SOC 31-7

X4505 1687 HEA on loan HAL 16-3-41 con to PRV Type C 20-5 1PRU 12-9 FAAC 26-1-42 HAL con to PRVI Type F M45 8 OTU 26-7 dvd i/grd Cotes Farm 31-5-43 FH200.10

X4538 1693 HEA on loan HAL 16-3-41 con to PRV Type C M45 DGRD Farn 22-5 intns trls 1PRU 19-8 FACB 25-14 SOC 15-1-42

X4539 1169 FF 21-9-40 24MU 21-9 609S 29-9 66S 24-2-41 57 OTU 31-3 306S 6-10 61 OTU 15-10 SOC 17-4-45

X4540 1172 FF 21-9-40 24MU 22-9 FAC2 AST 61 OTU 28-6-41 FACE total wreck 20-10 SOC 26-10

X4541 1170 FF GP 21-9-40 24MU 21-9 602S 2-10 dam by Ju88 nr Beachy Head Sgt Babbage safe 12-10 AST SOC FH6.50

X4542 1171 FF 21-9-40 24MU 21-9 602S 2-10 s/dn by Bf109 Mayfield Sgt Smith inj 30-10 last Spit s/dn in BoB SOC 13-11

X4543 1173 FF 22-9-40 24MU 22-9 66S 2-10 dam by Bf109 Sgt Wright safe 5-10 s/dn by Bf109 f/ld Horn Sgt Cook safe 13-10 SOC 11-11

X4544 1174 FF 22-9-40 39MU 23-9 72S 27-9 coll K9989 during scramble Sgt Staples safe 5-10 123S 15-5-41 61 OTU 14-10 cd Sheffield Green Guildford ttl wrk 19-10 Sgt Law kld

X4545 1175 FF 22-9-40 39MU 23-9 41S 28-9 strk parked a/c during scramble Sgt Norwell safe 2-10 SOC 8-10

X4546 1176 FF GP 23-9-40 39MU 23-9 222S 29-9 53 OTU 30-3-41 FACE 27-4 SOC 6-5

X4547 1177 FF 23-9-40 39MU 24-9 41S 2-10 611S 24-10 C2 ops 22-11 FTR after com Bf109 5-2-41

X4548 1178 FF 23-9-40 39MU 25-9 222S 29-9 dam ops cd Lenham out of fuel P/O Edsall inj 27-10 SOC 5-11

X4549 1179 FF 23-9-40 39MU 25-9 FAC3 2-10 SOC 8-10

X4550 1180 FF 24-9-40 8MU 25-9 152S 27-9 C3 ops 2-10 e/fld f/ld Whitcombe Dorset 11-11 SOC 18-11

X4551 1181 FF GP 24-9-40 8MU 25-9 92S 28-9 72S 28-9 C2 ops 7-10 306S 6-10 53 OTU 16-7-42 e/fld w/u ldg Kinl CE 11-7-43 RNDA 12-6-44

X4552 1182 FF 24-9-40 8MU 26-9 92S 28-9 s/dn by Do17 nr Brighton Sgt Ellis safe C3 10-10 AST 61 OTU 28-6-41 cd Boroughfield Nr Reading ttl wrk 10-9 SOC 23-9

X4553 1183 FF 24-9-40 8MU 26-9 92S 28-9 SOC 23-10

X4554 1184 FF 25-9-40 8MU 26-9 41S 28-9 air coll with Spitfire Sgt Carter aban a/c C3 11-10

X4555 1185 FF 25-9-40 6MU 26-9 92S 28-9 C2 ops 1-11 GAL 132S 16-2-41 HAL 29-4-42 conv to PRIV M45 1PRU Ben 15-11 con to PRVII Type G 47MU 3-1-43 *Tom Couston* 10-3 RCAF Canada 4-4 36in telephoto instal for trls

X4556 1186 FF GP 25-9-40 6MU 26-9 92S 29-9 145S 22-1-41 118S 4-3 604S 31-12 52 OTU 9-3-42 58 OTU 21-6-43 57 OTU 26-11 SOC 16-8-44

X4557 1187 FF 25-9-40 6MU 26-9 92S 29-9 Farn Oct '40 C2 ops 1-11 ASTH 152S 5-12 610S 19-12 SAL 10-4-41 132S 12-8 w/u ldg Peterhead CAC 31-8 SAL 58 OTU 5-1-42 FACE SOC 9-9

X4558 1188 FF GP 26-9-40 6MU 27-9 41S 29-9 C2 by Bf109 w/u ldg Horn S/Ld Finlay safe 9-10 611S 14-10 129S 22-6-41 57 OTU 13-12 53 OTU 17-6-42 FAAC 11-11 P&PSM SOC 28-9-44

X4559 1189 FF GP 26-9-40 6MU 28-9 41S 29-9 s/dn by Bf109 over Horsham P/O Bennions aban a/c 1-10

X4560 1190 FF 27-9-40 6MU 28-9 609S 2-10 C2 ops 8-11 GAL 123S 14-7-41 FACE dbf SOC 5-9

X4561 1194 FF 27-9-40 92S Dec '40 Farn Apl '41

X4562 1191 FF GP 27-9-40 12MU 29-9 66S 9-10 s/dn by Bf109 nr Canterbury P/O Pickering inj dbf 11-10 FH4.00

X4585 1193 FF GP 28-9-40 12MU 30-9 65S 11-10 C2 ops 15-10 45S 23-1-41 FACE 10-2 SOC 17-2 FH32.55

X4586 1195 FF 29-9-40 39MU 30-9 609S 8-10 FTR ops 28-11 FH37.55

X4587 1196 FF 30-9-40 39MU 1-10 609S 8-10 66S 24-2-41 53 OTU 24-6 FACB 30-4-42 510S 21-11 CE 24-11-44

X4588 1197 FF 30-9-40 39MU 2-10 609S 8-10 FAC3 2-12 AST 129S 22-6-41 53 OTU 29-9 flew into mountain Brecon CE 23-5-42

X4589 1192 FF 28-9-40 39MU 29-9 41S 7-10 611S 24-10 485S 15-3-41 123S 16-7 215MU 21-10-42 *Bar For* 7-11 Port 21-11

X4590 1198 FF GP 30-9-40 609S Oct '40 dam 25-10 66S 24-2-41 to 8384M extant Battle of Britain Museum, Hendon

X4591 1199 FF GP 1-10-40 39MU 3-10 92S 11-10 s/dn by Bf109 nr Postling Herts P/O Pattinson kld dbf 12-10 SOC 24-10 FH4.45

X4592 1200 St George FF 1-10-40 8MU 2-10 41S 8-10 611S 25-10 FTR ops 25-2

X4593 1201 Kerala FF GP 1-10-40 8MU 2-10 603S 8-10 266S 17-10 FAC3 ttl wrk 22-11 SOC 1-12 FH85.05

X4594 1202 Andhradesa FF 1-10-40 8MU 2-10 603S 8-10 266S 17-10 FTR after com Ju88 8-3-41 FH183.40

X4595 1203 Tomiland FF 2-10-40 8MU 5-10 72S 9-10 57 OTU 2-5-41 FACE 17-3-44

X4596 1204 FF 2-10-40 6MU 5-10 72S 8-10 123S 15-5-41 HAL 14-2-42 con to PRIV Type G M45 140S 25-4 dam ops 4-6 HAL con to PRVII Type G & M45 to FVA 66S 8-1-43 542S 10-1 8 OTU 17-4 HAL 17-6 SOC 22-3-45

X4597 1205 FF 2-10-40 6MU 5-10 acc PSO 9-10 SOC 14-1-40

X4598 1206 FF GP 3-10-40 6MU 5-10 66S 8-10 609S 29-10 AST 2-2-41 53 OTU 26-9 std spun cd nr St Nicholas Cardiff 4-10 SOC 12-10

X4599 1207 Plymouth & Southsea I FF 3-10-40 6MU 6-10 66S 8-10 FBC2 20-10 57 OTU 6-11 FAC2 AST 234S 4-2-41 58 OTU 7-5 SAL 20-6 1PRU 9-3 HAL 13-4-42 con to PRV 1PRU 18-4 HAL 6-8 con to PRVII Type G M45 8 OTU 6-8 FTR ops believed into Channel 5-1-43 FH312

X4600 1208 Portsmouth & Southsea II FF 3-10-40 9MU 7-10 72S 13-10 57 OTU 2-5-41 FA FTR 16-6

X4601 1209 Argonaut FF 3-10-40 9MU 7-10 72S 13-10 485S 24-4-41 61 OTU 1-6 53 OTU 26-9 FACE 8-9-42

X4602 1210 Bahamas I FF 4-10-40 9MU 7-10 72S 13-10 485S 15-5-41 61 OTU 25-6 FACB 27-1-42 53 OTU 14-4-43 1TEU 10-7-44

X4603 1212 FF 4-10-40 9MU 9-10 602S 13-10 610S 14-12 53 OTU 3-3-41 std on ldg Heston CE 18-3 GAL to 2558M SOC 31-3 FH82.15

X4604 1211 Ceylon II FF 4-10-40 38MU 7-10 41S 14-10 611S 24-10 FAC2 28-10 57 OTU 24-5-41 FACB 29-5-42 MMO RNAS Arb 5-9

X4605 1212 Ceylon III FF 4-10-40 38MU 8-10 92S 17-10 e/a C2 10-11 AST 61 OTU 30-12 57 OTU 16-12-41 air coll with AR212 f/ld CAC 16-3-42. Spun i/grd Flintshire CE 10-10

X4606 1214 Ceylon V FF 5-10-40 38MU 7-10 92S 16-10 145S 22-1-41 118S 27-3 66S 9-4 501S 27-4 53 OTU 24-5 2USAS 1-9-42 AST 27-7-43 con to FVA M45 61 OTU air coll with P7906 Lightwood Farm Salop CE SOC 8-8-44 FH510.15

X4607 1215 FF 5-10-40 38MU 8-10 92S 17-10 53 OTU 26-3-41 air coll with X4024 nr Treharris Glam dbf 7-7 SOC 15-7

X4608 1216 FF 6-10-40 37MU 8-10 234S 30-10 58 OTU 23-3-41 131S 16-7 52 OTU 23-11-41 FA 5-1-42 SOC 17-1

X4609 1217 FF 7-10-40 37MU 10-10 41S 17-10 611S 24-10 485S 14-3-41 CE ops 5-5 SOC 12-5

X4610 1218 FF 7-10-40 37MU 10-10 222S 17-10 53 OTU 18-3-41 HAL 25-3 DGRD BDn 8-5 Fairey Av 31-12 57 OTU 3-9-42 SFTS 12-7-43 FAAC 31-8 recat E

X4611 1219 FF GP 7-10-40 6MU 8-10 64S 27-11 303S 10-2-41 58 OTU 20-3 57 OTU 27-7 strk by R7138 ldg Haw CE 2-5-42 AST RNAS 30-7-43

X4612 1220 FF GP 9-10-40 6MU 10-10 66S 15-10 FAC2 15-10 AST 53 OTU 25-6-41 e/fld cd CE 18-3-42

X4613 1233 FF 13-10-40 6MU 13-10 603S 17-10 266S 24-10 CE ops 2-3-41 SOC 20-3

X4614 1221 FF GP 10-10-40 6MU 11-10 66S 15-10 92S 13-11 53 OTU 13-3-41 501S 17-6 58 OTU 4-7-42 flew into high grd with AR254 & P8276 Kingseal Hill Kincardine CE 16-1-43

X4615 1222 FF 12-10-40 24MU 15-10 616S 26-10 602S 14-12 61 OTU 30-6-41 121S 13-12 332S 17-1-42 164S 17-4 FACB 1-6 SAL con to FVA M45 HAL 10-9 con to PRXIII M32 VSM 25-1-43 fuel syst mods wng stiff 6MU 10-4-43 RNDA 3-3-44

X4590 is extant at Hendon, England.

X4620 was initially named "Falkland Island VII" and later became a PR VII.

X4616 1223 FF 13-10-40 24MU 15-10 92S 24-10 53 OTU 13-3-41 FAAC 18-3-42 WAL 52 OTU 22-7 17SFTS 12-7-43 39MU NEA 23-11

X4617 1224 FF 15-10-40 24MU 16-10 616S 26-10 65S 26-2-41 308S 6-4 FAAC 8-5 DeH 30-4-43 222MU 4-9 *Fort El* 12-9 Port 9-10

X4618 FF GP 16-10-40 24MU 21-10 92S 2-11 53 OTU 13-3-41 FACE 27-4 SOC 10-5

X4619 1227 FF 18-10-40 8MU 20-10 C2 ops 23-11 58 OTU 10-5-41 82MU 1-10-42 *Taran* 8-11 P Sudan 29-1-43 ME 28-2 SOC 27-7-44

X4620 1229 Falkland Island VII FF 19-10-40 8MU 22-10 611S 5-11 cd on t/o 22-1-41 485S 14-3 123S 13-6 CRD HAL 31-10-42 trl instal Con to PRVII M45 8 OTU 4-2-43 FACE 4-2 HAL 14-8-44 FACE 25-8

X4621 1232 Martin Evans Bevan FF 19-10-40 8MU 22-10 72S 2-11 485S 27-4-41 61 OTU 1-6 MMO 20-7 con to FVA M45 61 OTU 25-2-42 fail to recover from dive Ridgley Cheshire CE 14-11 SOC 23-11

X4622 1225 Falkland Islands FF 16-10-40 con to F MkIIA MXII

X4623 1226 Scillonia FF 17-10-40 9MU 21-10 610S 1-11 61 OTU 23-11-41 FACE 10-3-43 SOC 9-2-45

X4624 1230 FF 18-10-40 9MU 21-10 54S 1-11 FAC2 5-11 GAL 52 OTU 20-11-4153 OTU 17-6-43 39 MU NEA 6-11-44 SOC 9-3-45

X4641 1234 FF 21-10-40 6MU 24-10 609S 11-11 66S 24-2-41 501S 27-4 53 OTU 17-6 to 3466M 8SoTT 25-12-42

X4642 1231 FF 19-10-40 6MU 20-10 609S 27-10 66S 24-2-41 57 OTU 7-4 306S 6-10 61 OTU 7-4 306S 6-10 61 OTU 15-10 disin in air Brynegiws Denbig 5-8-42 SOC 19-8

X4643 1235 FF 221-10-40 6MU 23-10 72S 26-10 485S 7-5-41 61 OTU 1-6ASTE 13-3-42 RNAS 9-9 CE 13-10-44

X4644 1236 Sarkar I Tirhut FF GP 21-10-40 8MU 22-10 611S 22-10 403S 22-6-41 52 OTU 24-7 61 OTU 24-7 fire in flight CE 10-7-42

X4645 1237 FF21-10-40 8MU 24-10 1 PRU 14-11 FAC2 17-11 118S 13-3-41 66S 9-4 e/fd f/ld 15-4 501S 26-4 53 OTU 17-6 HAL 8-3-42 con to PRIV 140 S TAF 2-5 HAL 11-2-44 con to PRVII M45 CE 7-9

X4646 1238 FF 22-10-40 8MU 10 266S 16-11 111S 8-4-41 i/sea ops 14-4 SOC 17-4

X4647 1239 FF GP 22-10-40 8MU24-12 64S 20-11 303S 22-1-41 58 OTU flew into mountain on f/f Ben Ledi Perths FTR 10-3

X4648 1240 FF GP 24-10-40 24MU 25-10 610S 7-11 602S 14-12 61 OTU 30-6-41 53 OTU 20-2-43 RNDA 15-1-44 CE 9-8

X4649 1241 FF 23-10-40 24MU 25-10 610S 7-11 FA ttle wrk 11-12 SOC 27-12

X4650 1242 FF 23-10-40 24MU 25-10 54S 14-11 FA PSO 28-12 SOC 4-1-41

X4651 1243 FF GP 24-10-40 37MU 25-10 54S 7-2-41 41S 22-2 452S 19-4 313S 1-6 61 OTU 16-8 SOC 29-12

X4652 1244 FF 24-10-40 37MU 25-10 54S 4-4-41 41S 22-2 452S 19-4 313S 5-9 57 OTU 16-6 RNAS 7-8-43 ASTH 31-3-44

X4653 FF 24-10-40 37MU 25-10 41S 28-2-41 452S 19-4 313S 1-6 57 OTU 27-8 hit sea off Rhyl ttl wrk 20-9 SOC 27-9

X4654 1246 FF GP 25-10-40 9MU 26-10 222S 10-11 53 OTU 30-3-41 FACE 23-4 WAL DeH 16-4-42 new eng 57 OTU 18-6 53 OTU 13-6-43 ASTH 5-5-45

X4655 1249 FF GP 25-10-40 9MU 27-10 65S 5-12 145S 19-1-41 Soc 29-2 FH32.40

X4656 1247 FF 25-10-40 9MU 27-10 92S 10-11 C2 ops 7-12 AST 61 OTU 28-6-41 53 OTU 31 12

X4657 1250 FF GP 27-10-40 6MU 28-10 60DGDR 1-12 66S 24-2-41 57 OTU 7-4 61 OTU 20-11 FACB 27-6-42 AST RNAS 5-9

X4658 1251 FF 26-10-40 6MU 28-10 602S 1-11 C2 ops 11-12 SOC 30-12

X4659 1248 FF GP 26-10-40 6MU 26-10 602S 1-11 610S 17-12 cd/ldg on beach Pevensey 53 OTU 31-3-43 52 OTU 21-6-42 53 OTU 31-3-43 strk by X4490 on runway CAC 17-6-44 recat E 23-6

X4660 1252 FF 28-10-40 6MU 1-11 609S 1-12 66S 24-2-41 57 OTU 7-4 ASTH 22-10 con to FVA M45 HAL 28-7-42 con to PRXIII M32 Farm 31-12 trls Relay Homing, VHF BA & TR1143, plus repositioned amplifier HAL 18-3--434 VSM 8-4 mods RNDA Hens 1-3-44

X4661 1259 FF 31-10-40 9MU 8-11 602S 9-12 610S 14-12 53 OTU 10-4-41 HAL 12-5 to 2845M 7SoTT 4-12 SOC 18-12

X4662 1260 FF 1-11-40 9MU 8-11 485S 15-3-41 61 OTU 25-6 131S 17-7 pull out steep dive stbd wng broke away cd dbf pilot kld 12.07hr N Alleron 27-7 SOC 1-8

X4671 1253 FF 28-10-40 6MU 1-11 602S 29-11 610S 14-12 53 OTU 3-3-41 61 OTU 1-7 FACB 29-8 ASTE con to FVA M45. M32 instal during 1943

X4672 1254 FF GP 29-10-40 6MU 1-11 1PRU Ben 27-8-41 R-RH 12-8 con to FVA M45 1PRU 27-8 HAL 3-10 con to PRVII Type G 541S 30-9-42 8 OTU 15-7-43 SOC 14-3-45

X4673 1255 FF GP 30-11-40 8MU 1-11 602S 17-11 610S 14-12 ASTH 15-2-41 Farn Sep'41 ail trls ASTH 23-10 recat E SOC

X4674 1256 FF 30-10-40 8MU 1-11 1PRU 14-11 FACA 21-12 AST 403S 29-6-41 52 OTU 21-7 61 OTU 30-7 58 OTU 6-4-43 SOC 30-4-45

X4675 1257 FF 31-10-40 9MU 2-11 65S 5-12 145S 16-1-41 118S 27-3 122S 20-5 FAAC 17-9 AST

X4676 1261 FF 31-10-40 9MU 5-11 222S 22-2-41 53 OTU 20-3 HAL 4-4 to 2847M 7SoTT 3-12

X4677 1258 FF 31-10-40 9MU 2-11 602S 12-12 610S 14-12 53 OTU 5-3-41 RNDA 4-9-42 58 OTU 30-1-43 CE 18-8-44

X4678 1262 FF GP 1-11-40 12MU 4-11 610S 23-11 std o/t ldg Wools CE 3-12 SOC

X4679 1263 FF 1-11-40 12MU 4-11 601S 22-11 602S 14-12 122S 11-6-41 53 OTU 30-9 e/fld cd/ldg Rhoose 3-4-42 AST SOC

X4680 1264 FF 2-11-40 12MU 5-10 72S 17-1-41 CB ops 9-4 SAL 123S 3-6 steep dive & pull out from cloud, wngs & tailplane broke off. Fus hit grd Kirknewton pilot kld 1600hrs 15-6 SOC 1-7 FH77.50 Farn acc invest 20-8-41

X4681 1266 FF 1-11-40 24MU 5-11 610S 14-11 602S 14-12 FTR ops 24-5

X4682 1265 FF 2-11-40 24MU 6-11 152S 14-11 58 OTU 23-3 SAL 24-4 strk by P8605 while taxy CE 12-11 SOC 20-11

X4683 1267 FFm 3-11-40 24MU 6-11 54S 28-11 Farn Dec'40 41S 22-2-41 452S 19-4 313S 16-6 57 OTU 27-8 53 OTU 20-2-43 AST 13-5-45

X4684 1275 FF GP 4-11-40 38MU 10-11 234S 18-11 58 OTU 27-3-41 1TEU 8-3-44 CE 15-4-45

X4685 1273 FF GP 4-11-40 38MU 10-11 234S 18-11 58 OTU 28-3-41 124S 19-7 340S 20-10 52 OTU 2-11 FACE 5-9-42 SOC 17-9

X4708 1268 FF 5-11-40 cd before delivery not replaced SOC 5-11

X4709 1269 FF 5-11-40 12MU 7-11 602S 3-1-41 SAL 29-5 con to FVA M45 131S 18-7 CE ops 21-8 ASTH 131S 17-11 134S 25-12 164S 25-6-42 602S 10-9 82Grp USA SOC 18-9-45

X4710 1270 FF GP 5-11-40 12MU 6-11 129S 16-8-41 58 OTU 15-10 61 OTU 17-6-42 RNDA 17-3-44 SOC 23-1-45

X4711 1271 FF 5-11-40 24MU 7-11 54S 19-11 hit tree nr Richmond Yorks ttl wrk 17-2 SOC 28-2

X4712 1274 FF GP 6-11-40 24MU 11-11 con to PRIII 1PRU 21-11 3PRU 9-1-41 DGRD Farn 28-2 3PRU 29-3 sortie Hamburg ldg Farn FTR ops 9-4 FH99.50

X4713 1272 FF 6-11-40 24MU 7-11 411S 22-6-41 57 OTU 14-8 FA FTR 16-11 SOC 18-12

X4714 1276 FF GP 7-11-40 37MU 10-11 313S 4-7-41 61 OTU 16-8 57 OTU 10-1-42 76MU 26-9 *C o Evans* 21-10 P Sudan 23-12 ME 31-2 SOC 27-7-44

X4715 1277 FF GP 8-11-40 37MU 11-11 58 OTU 4-1-41 122S 2-6 57 OTU 11-10 1PRU 21-4-42 3SoGR 17-5 8 OTU 24-5 i/sea off Troup Head Banffs 30-6

X4716 1278 FF GP 8-11-40 37MU 10-11 266S 14-2-41 111S 11-4 58 OTU 29-5 215MU 16-9-42 *Castalian* 27-11 Port 12-12

X4717 1279 FF 8-11-40 38MU 10-11 57 OTU 7-8-41 to Sea FIB RNAS 12-5-44 CE 9-8

X4718 1280 FF GP 8-11-40 9MU 16-11 54S 26-1-41 41S 22-2 452S 24-4 52 OTU 28-7 124S 31-7 340S 10-10 58 OTU 2-7-43 to 4437M 14SoTT 6-12 CE 11-9-44

X4719 1281 FF GP 9-11-40 9MU 19-11 92S 15-2-41 53 OTU 8-3 FACE ttl wrk 2-6 SOC 10-6

X4720 1282 FF 9-11-40 39MU 14-11 66S 15-4-41 501S 24-4 53 OTU 24-5 e/fld w/u ldg o/t Porthcawl Glam CE 25-7 SOC 1-8

X4721 1283 FF 9-11-40 39MU 13-11 53 OTU 25-6-41 5USA 22-8-42 61 OTU 27-3-44 SOC 8-5-46

X4722 1285 FF GP 10-11-40 39MU 13-11 S Farm dis 53 OTU 25-6-41 dvd i/grd Port Talbot CE 27-12

X4765 1286 FF GP 10-11-40 6MU 13-11 610S 6-2-41 53 OTU 3-3 5MU dis 11-8 ASTE 23-9 P&P SM 27-4-42 *Pet Mer* 8-11 lost at sea 8-1-43

X4766 1287 FF 11-11-40 6MU 14-11 308S 14-5-41 403S 28-5 52 OTU 21-7 61 OTU 30-7 72S 26-11 81S 15-12 165S 4-5-42 GAL 24-6 con to FVA M45 HAL 22-8 con to PRVII Type G HAL 11-6-43 con to PRXIII VSM 22-7 fuel syst mods wng stiff 400S 25-12 83GSU 15-6-44 SOC 27-2-45

X4767 1289 FF GP 13-11-40 6MU 13-11 222S 3-2-41 53 OTU 16-3 61 OTU 26-7 P&P SM 15-9-42 *C o Evans* 21-10 P Sudan 23-12 ME 31-12 SOC 1-1-47

X4768 1290 FF GP 12-11-40 6MU 14-11 610S 6-2-41 53 OTU 3-3 58 OTU 1-7-42 53 OTU 8-4-43 dvd i/grd Moortown South Kelsey Lincs CE 19-5-43

X4769 1291 FF GP 13-11-40 8MU 14-11 602S 21-11 53 OTU 3-3-41 SOC 30-7

X4770 1292 FF GP 13-11-40 8MU 14-11 64S 27-11 302S 22-1-41 58 OTU 20-3 52 OTU FACB 18-3-42 215MU 25-9 *Pet Mer* 8-11 lost at sea 8-1-43

X4771 1293 FF 13-11-40 8MU 14-11 152S 27-11 58 OTU 23-3-41 53 OTU 20-2-43 o/s ldg Hibald o/t CE 5-3-44

X4772 1294 FF 13-11-40 8MU 14-11 152S 1-12 53 OTU 24-6-41 spun i/grd Caerphilly Common Glam CE 7-11 SOC 12-11

X4773 1295 FF GP 14-11-40 9MU 16-11 609S 9-1-41 57 OTU 12-6 131S 31-12 52 OTU 24-4-42 53 OTU 16-2-43 dvd i/grd nr Cardiff CE 27-3-43 SOC 27-3

X4774 1297 FF 14-11-40 9MU 16-11 54S 26-1-41 41S 22-2 CE ops 3-3 AST 57 OTU 27-7 58 OTU 22-7-42 53 OTU 11-5-43 SOC 30-4-45

X4775 1302 FF 14-11-40 9MU 19-11 2S 15-2-41 53 OTU 3-3 5SoTT 5-12 SOC 18-12

X4776 1298 FF GP 14-11-40 5MU 16-11 DGRD 22-2-41 AST 24-6 con to FII MXII 313S 8-10 306S 7-11 308S 11-12 315S 1-4-42 61 OTU 28-5 2GTW 12-10-43 FLS Mlfld 30-6-44 SOC 26-1-45

X4777 1299 FF 14-11-40 5MU 16-11 152S 2-12 58 OTU 23-3-41 FA dbf CE 1-8 SOC 9-8

X4778 1300 FF GP 15-11-40 5MU 16-11 60DGDN 1-12 66S 24-2-41 111S 10-4 58 OTU 28-5 w/u ldg nr Gran CE 22-4-42 SOC 26-4

X4779 1303 FF GP 16-11-40 6MU 21-11 92S 5-12 53 OTU 13-3-41 FACE 25-3 57 OTU 27-7 to 3144M 7-7-42

X4780 1301 FF GP 16-11-40 6MU 13-11 cd del flt 24-11 AST 92S 22-4-41 61 OTU 13-8 ASTH 2-2-42 RNAS 7-9 76MU 6-10 *Taran* 8-11 P Sudan 29-1-43 ME 28-2 SOC 27-7-44

X4781 1304 FF GP 17-11-40 9MU 19-11 92S 15-2-41 53 OTU 3-3 u/s f/ld Llan ttl wrk 16-10 SOC 22-10

X4782 1305 FF GP 17-11-40 9MU DGRD BDn 24-11 endurance trls and variation of longitudinal stab with alt CRD Farn 11-10-41 fitt 'Hasty Hitch' two lugs on tailwheel for towing GAL Hotspur. Speeds of 130 & 160 mph achieved. 1942, flexi-tank trls with 29gal fuel tank of moulded plywood with collapsible, plastic inner skin to establish if inner membrane would prevent build-up of petrol fumes in empty tank and so avoid risk of fire. Target a/c with Wellington X9674 fitt Monica I. Airfield defence 19-8 R/T fighters & hand trls 3-9, trls ended 22-10-42. ETPS Jan'43 for attitude indicator trls in connection with glider towing. Can wing & weather trls. March'43, artificial horizon & gyro gunsight trls, instrument fly Towed Hotspur PT303 to Hatfield; max range with glider 900 miles. Fresh trls with flexi-tank at Brooklands. F/ldg Tonbridge Kent 22-6-43. Modified, target a/c for Defiant AA354 fitt Maxson turret & gyro gunsight. Monica IIC trls. Cool trls, dinghy dropping for use in ASR duties. Double tow of Airspeed Horsa with Spit FV NH403; max range 700 miles. RNDA 24-2-44 CE 9-8

X4783 1306 FF 18-11-40 9MU 21-11 92S 15-2-41 53 OTU 25-3 132S 27-7 58 OTU 24-11 46MU 9-9-42

X4784 1307 FF 18-11-40 9MU 20-11 1PRU 13-4-41 HAL 17-4 con to PRV AST 8-12 con to FVA M45 140S 23-12 HAL 17-1-42 con to PRVII Type G FA FTR 14-4

X4785 1308 FF 19-11-40 9MU 22-11 222S 22-2-41 53 OTU 30-3 FACB 4-5 HAL 1416FU 19-8 CGS 28-4-42 215MU 26-9 *Taran* 8-11 P Sudan 27-1-43 ME 28-2 SOC 27-7

X4786 9MU 22-11-40 5MU 24-2-41 1PRU 13-4 FACB 15-9 HAL con to PRVII Type G M45 1PRU Ben 3-1-42 VSM 9-4 con to FVA 543S 30-9 8 OTU 7-8-43 HAL 9-3-44 SOC 27-2-45

X4787 1309 FF 1309 FF GP 20-11-40 37MU 24-11 57 OTU 28-5-41 FACB 2-12 1TEU 13-4-44 SOC 27-2-45

X4788 1310 FF 20-11-40 37MU 23-11 129S 22-6-41 61OTU 19-9 GAL 7-10 58 OTU 4-7-42 53 OTU 24-4-43 RNDA 14-3-44 CE 9-8

X4789 1313 FF GP 20-11-40 37MU 25-11 57 OTU 28-5-41 132S 12-9 e/fld w/u ldg Newborough CB 17-9-52 OTU 15-9-42 58 OTU 29-8-43 1TEU 1-3-44 ASTH 13-8 CE 18-8

X4815 1314 FF 23-11-40 6MU 25-11 AFDU 8-2-41 61 OTU 17-4-42 FACB 19-8 AST SOC 26-1-45

X4816 1311 FF 21-11-40 6MU 24-11 AFDU Dux 7-2-41 61 OTU 21-5-42 RNAS 7-8-43

X4817 1312 FF 22-11-40 6MU 24-11 611S 27-12 27-12 485S 14-3-41 457S 21-7 58 OTU 22-10 1 PRU 3SGR 1-3-42 222MU 18-3 *Pet Mer* 8-11 lost at sea 8-1-43

X4818 FF GP 24-11-40 6MU 26-11 457S 22-6-41 53 OTU 20-2-43 RNAS 1-6 53 OTU s/dn by second Spit when guns inadvertently fired. cd River Humber nr Goole 14-7

X4819 1315 FF 23-11-40 6MU 25-11 92S 5-12 53 OTU 5-3-41 PDU HAL & Farn June '41 RNDA 14-6-44

X4820 1316 FF 23-11-40 8MU 26-11 65S 30-12 145S 4-2-41 118S 3-3 FAAC 26-3 AST CB 13-1-43 57 OTU 6-5 61

X4942 never entered RAF service. It was built as a Mk I and converted to Mk VA standards with Merlin 45 in November 1941. A Merlin 46 was then installed and it eventually became the prototype high altitude Mk VI with a Merlin 47 engine, and is seen as such in this view. It had wide span wings (see below), a pressure cabin and a four blade propeller. Note test equipment on windscreen. It was known to the Royal Observer Corps as aircraft 152 and finally became maintenance airframe 4264M.

OTU 9-10 SOC 25-5

X4821 1317 8MU 27-11-40 61 OTU 28-6-41 AST 27-7 con to FVA M45 130S 21-10 134S 25-12 421S 13-4-42 5USA 22-8 349S 3-7-43 61 OTU 10-9 FACE 6-5-44

X4822 1318 FF GP 26-11-40 8MU 27-11 145S 14-2-41 118S 8-3 FACE ttl wrk 6-4 SOC 13-4 FH47.30

X4823 1319 8MU 27-11-40 145S 14-2-41 118S 3-3 66s 9-4 501S 26-4 53 OTU 25-5 air coll with P9459 i/sea off Nash Point Glam 29-10

X4824 1320 8MU 3-12-40 457S 22-6-41 58 OTU 26-10 FAAC 26-11 SAL 57 OTU 25-11-43

X4825 FF GP 29-11-40 9MU 5-12 452S 19-4-41 FACE 3-5 SOC 10-5 FM20.35

X4826 1322 9MU 29-11-40 118S 30-3-41 FACE dbf 6-4 SOC 13-4 FM9.10

X4827 1323 FF GP 27-11-40 9MU 28-11 411S 22-6-41 53 OTU 23-7 P&PSM 4-11 61 OTU 26-6-42 57 OTU 7-12 RNAS 14-6-43 ret to RAF 30-12-44

X4828 1324 9MU 29-11-40 485S 19-4-41 61 OTU 1-6 303s 17-7 306s 6-10 308S 11-12 57 OTU 2-1-42 GAL overhaul 19-11 52 OTU 15-5-43 1TEU 8-3-44 ASTH 8-3 CE 15-4-45

X4829 1325 FF GP 29-11-40 12MU 5-12 602S 26-2-41 52 OTU 18-7 61 OTU 4-8 FACB 10-4-42 82MU 2-10 *Pet Mer* 8-11 lost at sea 8-1-43

X4830 1326 12MU 2-12-40 129S 22-6-41 53 OTU 29-9 FAAC 29-3-42 ASTH 76MU 25-9 *C o Evans* 2-10 P Sudan 23-12 ME 31-12 SOC 27-7-44

X4831 1327 FF GP 29-11-40 12MU 29-11 129S 22-6-41 61 OTU 26-8 3SoGR 8-1-42 FAAC 3-6 ROS 61 OTU e/fld t/o strk fence Rednall CB 2-1-43 WAL

X4832 1328 FF GP 28-11-40 12MU 7-12 1PRU Ben 25-3-41 on to PRV 1PRU 29-11 8 OTU 24-5-42 SAL 7-7-44 CE 29-8

X4833 1329 FF GP 30-11-40 24MU 5-12 266S 12-1-41 111S 23-4 53 OTU 29-5 61 OTU 23-6-43 53 OTU 20-8 SOC 6-3-45

X4834 1331 FF 2-12-40 24MU 4-12 266S 12-1-41 111S 8-4 58 OTU 24-5 129S 16-8 61 OTU 16-6-42 FACB 11-2-43 WAL 53 OTU 27-11 CE 11-8-44

X4835 1332 FF 3-12-40 24MU 4-12 452S 12-5-41 313S 22-5-41 61 OTU 14-8 FACE 26-8 ASTE SOC 9-9

X4836 1333 FF 37MU-7-12 57 OTU 28-5-41 303S 18-7 hit tractor ldg Speke dbf 4-8 SOC 9-8

X4837 1334 FF GP 4-12-40 37MU 7-12 57 OTU 28-5-41 131S 13-7 61 OTU 23-10 GAL 9-4-42 82MU 18-10 *Pet Mer* 8-11 lost at sea 8-1-43

X4838 1335 FF 4-12-40 37MU 7-12 122S 14-6-41 57 OTU 11-10 FACB 17-3-42

X4839 1336 FF GP 5-12-40 39MU 7-12 HAL 15-6-42 con to PRVIII Type G M45 3SIG 13-9 8 OTU 4-2-43 FTR believed i/sea 22-5 FH145.45

X4840 1337 FF 6-12-40 39MU 7-12 FACB del flt 23-1-41 AST 457S 22-6 58 OTU 22-10 FACE 23-9-42

X4841 1338 FF 6-12-40 8MU 8-12 64S 16-12 FAC2 AST 303S 1-3-41 58 OTU 15-3 SOC 16-12

X4842 1339 FF GP 7-12-40 8MU 8-12 457S 22-6-41 58 OTU 22-10 FAAC 19-5-43 1TEU 17-3-44 CE 18-8

X4843 1340 FF GP 8-12-40 8MU 10-12 57 OTU 27-7-41 hit mountain Snowdonia FTR 26-9

X4844 1341 FF GP 10-12-40 8MU 11-12 457S 22-6-41 53 OTU 19-10 CB ops 16-4-42 ROS RNDA 16-1-44 57 OTU 6-5-44 SOC 18-4-45

X4845 1342 FF 9-12-40 8MU 12-12 457S 22-6-41 FACB 15-9 SAL 61 OTU 9-8-42 CRD Deff 22-3-43 SOC 20-5-45

X4846 1343 FF 10-12-40 61 OTU 28-6-41 AST 19-9 RNAS Mach 1-9-42 AST 31-10 con to FVA M45 plus other mods. LoS 11-12 FAAC 14-5-43 SOC 22-4-45

X4847 1346 9MU 16-12-40 92S 15-2-41 53 OTU 3-3 HAL 4-5 to 2846M 7SoTT 3-12 SOC 18-12

X4848 1344 FF 11-12-40 9MU 13-12 412S 14-7-41 FAAC 17-7 ROS 58 OTU 12-9 222MU 20-1-42 *Taran* 8-11 P Sudan 29-1-43

X4849 1345 FF 15-12-40 9MU 13-12 411S 22-6-41 53 OTU 23-7 std cd Sutton nr Barry Glam ttl wrk 21-11 SOC 29-11

X4850 1347 FF GP 12-12-40 9MU 16-12 411S 22-6-41 57 OTU 10-8 FA ttl wrk 23-11 SOC

X4851 1349 FF 13-12-40 9MU 16-12 412S 19-7-41 58 OTU 14-8 FACE 16-12 SOC

X4852 1348 FF 13-12-40 9MU 16-12 411S 22-6-41 61 OTU 2-10 137S 24-1-42 FACB 20-7 61 OTU flew into hill nr Chu Str CE 20-1-43 SOC 24-1 FH381.10

X4853 1350 FF 14-12-40 39MU Star Fm dis 5-1-41 131S 11-9 137S 25-1-42 Manston 8-8-43 SOC 9-2-45

X4854 1351 FF 14-12-40 53 OTU i/sea nr Dunraven Castle. Thought struct fail of stbd wing 2-1-43

X4855 1352 FF 15-12-40 12MU 16-12 129S 22-6-41 71 OTU 9-7 61 OTU 10-8 FACB 21-7-42 SAL 45MU 8-10 *Castalian* 27-11 Port 12-12

X4856 1353 FF GP 16-12-40 12MU 23-12 403S 14-7-41 52 OTU 24-7 61 OTU 7-8 53 OTU 15-3-44 CE 14-8

X4857 1354 FF 16-12-40 12MU 21-12 72S 1-2-41 57 OTU 2-5 3-6S 6-10 53 OTU 20-6-42 FAAC 14-4-43 222MU 3-8 *Emp Rhod* 14-8 Port 29-8

X4858 1355 FF 17-12-40 12MU 21-12 129S 22-6-41 58 OTU 9-9 e/fld f/ld nr Rinflats Stirling CE 30-7-42 SOC 4-8

X4859 1356 FF GP 18-12-40 12MU 21-12 308S 13-4-41 129S 5-8 58 OTU 15-9 spun i/grd Polmont N'land CE 24-11

X4896 1357 FF 18-12-40 24MU 22-12 118S 31-3-41 66S 9-4 501S 27-4 53 OTU 24-5 AST 39MU dis S Fm 16-4-42 57 OTU 30-7 strk N3163 on runway Esh CE 4-6-43

X4897 1358 FF 19-12-40 24MU 22-12 66S 9-4-41 e/a 16-4 AST 53 OTU 30-9-42 FAAC 16-12 SOC 13-4-45

X4898 1359 FF 19-12-40 24MU 22-12 Stn Flt Turn 1-6-41 FACE 16-8 SOC 31-8

X4899 1360 FF GP 19-12-40 24MU 26-12 Stn Flt Turn 1-6-41 Farn June '41 57 OTU 4-10 FACB 13-12 58 OTU 11-7-42 1TEU 26-2-44 SOC 6-3-45

X4900 1362 FF 23-12-40 38MU 27-12 53 OTU 22-6-41 CE 9-6-42 AST RNAS 5-9 ASTH 23-10 hook fitt RNAS 10-11

X4901 1363 FF GP 21-12-40 38MU 27-12 58 OTU 22-6-41 AST 6-9

X4902 1364 FF 21-12-40 38MU 27-12 66S 27-2-41 57 OTU 7-4 AST 6-9 con to FVA M45 81S 23-12 165S 12-4-42 167S 27-5 RNDA 31-8 SOC 15-2-45

X4903 1365 FF GP 22-12-40 6MU 24-12 485S 2-3-41 e/fld w/u ldg Buckton Yorks CE 9-5 SAL SOC 19-5

X4904 1366 FF GP 23-12-40 6MU 28-12 152S 3-2-41 58 OTU 23-3 hit high grd Ochill Hills Perths 17-10 SOC 28-10

X4905 1367 FF 23-12-40 6MU 24-12 457S 22-6-41 58 OTU 9-12 FACE 17-4-42 SAL

X4906 1368 Ff GP 26-12-40 6MU 28-12 457S 24-6-41 53 OTU 23-10 FAAC 16-5-42 attached Farn 1-6-42

X4907 1369 Macclesfield FF 23-12-40 6MU 28-12 HAL 4-5-41 14-S 15-7 HAL 24-1-42 con to PRVII Type G M45 140S 17-1 CE ops 17-3 SOC 31-3

X4908 1370 Southern Railway Invicta FF 27-12-40 8MU 4-1-41 457S 22-6 130S 2-11 81S 16-2-42 165S 12-4 5USA 22-8 P&PSM 6-1-43 con to FVA M45 61 OTU 15-6-43 FACB 18-7 AST SOC 6-6-45

X4909 1371 Kensington II FF 28-12-40 8MU 30-12 222S 14-3-41 53 OTU 18-3 61 OTU 1-8 53 OTU 24-2-42 39MU NEA 25-11-44

X4910 1372 Kensington I FF 8MU 123S 1-6-41 FACE 5-9 SOC 11-9

X4911 1375 Bournemouth FF GP 29-12-40 8MU 2-1-41 457S 22-6 58 OTU 26-10 FACE 16-3-42

X4912 1374 Sutton Coldfield FF 29-12-40 8MU 4-1-41 457S 22-6 53 OTU 23-10 FACB 14-6-42 57 OTU 27-4-43 cd Middlepart Farm N'land 10-7

X4913 1376 Flying Scotsman FF GP 31-12-40 9MU 3-1-41 411S 22-6 53 OTU 22-7 FTR on train flt 3-11 wreck found Pen-Y-Fan Brecons 21-7-42

X4914 1377 FF 30-12-40 9MU 2-1-41 411S 22-6 57 OTU 30-7 AST 16-12 58 OTU 12-7-42 air coll with P7978 cd CE 17-6-4 SOC 30-6 FH820.50

X4915 1378 City of Hull II FF 30-12-40 9MU 2-1-41 54S 22-2 452S 19-4 403S 7-6 52 OTU 21-7 61 OTU 30-7 to 2824M 6SoTT Feb '42 SOC 4-12

X4916 1379 City of Hull I FF 1-1-41 9MU 3-1 485S 13-4 CB ops 26-4 131S 2-9 u/c clpse ldg Tern 12-9 SOC 4-12 to 2825M 6SoTT Feb '42

X4917 1380 MXII Greenock FF 2-1-41 9MU 5-1 66S 15-4 CB ops 22-4 AST SOC 30-4 cancel 123S 14-7 57 OTU 4-8 61 OTU 19-9 P&PSM 13-5-42 52 OTU 6-5-43 57 OTU 29-8 CE 14-8-44

X4918 1382 West Bromwich FF 3-1-41 12MU 4-1 123S 22-5 FA FTR 31-7 FH93.20

X4919 1381 Blackburn I FF 2-1-41 12MU 4-1 72S 2-3 FAR Deff 23-5-42 FACE 26-2-43 SOC 31-5 FH165.35

X4920 1384 Victor FF 5-1-41 12MU 9-1 72S 3-3 61 OTU 8-11 215MU 23-9-42 *C o Lan* 7-11-42 Port 20-1-43

X4921 1385 Nix Over Six Primus FF GP 6-4-41 12MU 12-1 72S 22-3 57 OTU 2-5 306S 6-10 61 OTU 14-10 FACB 9-6-42 ASTE RNAS 5-7-43 to 4750M 28-3-44

X4922 1386 M45 H&H FF GP 7-1-41 DGRD FArn 1-2 con to FVA proto M46 instal ASTH DGRD BDn 11-3 comp spin trls with X4942 and N3053. Fitt Vokes Multi-Vee air filter, cool trls. DGRD VAWD 17-4 CRD BDn 7-10 CRD VWD trls with trop rad and oil cool and wooden m/up of fus 90 gall external o/ld tank VAWD 7-7-42 level speed tests with curved w/s and whip aerials plus 16lb eng boost AST BDn perf trls with trop mods 8MU 20-5-43 349S 6-7 61 OTU 1-8 52 OTU 22-8 CE SOC 17-11-44

X4923 1387 Nix Over Six Secundus FF 7-1-41 24MU 11-1 57 OTU 28-5 411S 22-6 129S 8-8 61 OTU 26-8 71 OTU 26-8 FACE 4-12 SOC 24-12

X4924 1388 Sir Harry and Lady Oaks FF GP 8-1-41 24MU 11-1 403S 2-7 Farn July '41 52 OTU 24-7 61 OTU 30-7 SOC 26-8

X4925 1388 Sir Harry and Lady Oaks II FF GP 8-1-41 24MU 11-1 411S 22-6 129S 8-8 53 OTU 29-9 SOC 13-4-45

X4926 1390 FF 10-1-41 24MU 12-1 FACB del flt AST 13-2 66S 23-4 501S 24-4 MMO 21-3-42 new eng 1PRU

10-4 57 OTU 20-8 e/fld f/ld Stn Farm Chester CE 27-10

X4927 1394 FF 11-1-41 24MU 17-1 FACB del flt AST 28-2 53 OTU 31-7-42 RNDA 23-1-44 ret RAF 3-1-45

X4928 1391 FF GP 9-1-41 37MU 13-1 452S 13-5 123S 21-6 58 OTU 1-8 i/sea 12-9

X4929 1392 FF 11-1-41 37MU 13-1 57 OTU 28-5 131S 17-7 52 OTU 22-10 222MU 22-9-42 *Taran* 8-11 P Sudan 29-1-43 ME 28-2 FAC3 22-9

X4930 1397 FF 13-1-41 37MU 19-1 129S 24-6 MMO 27-7 conv to FVA M45 122S 16-11 134S 28-12 601S 10-4-42 61 OTU 21-5-43 air coll withMosquito HJ881 cd Shrewsbury CE 31-5-43

X4931 1395 FF 13-1-41 45MU 16-1 111S 3-5 FA 8-5 1406 Met Flt Wick 9-5-42 61 OTU 9-6-43 ASTE 5-3-44 con to FVA M45

X4932 1396 FF GP 13-1-41 45MU 16-1 124S 7-5 340S 20-10 52 OTU 31-10 FACE 6-2-42

X4933 1401 FF 16-1-41 6MU 1-2 telecommunications 3-7 RAF Deff 23-5-42 to 3596M 5SoTT

X4934 1398 FF 14-1-41 6MU 19-1 222S 3-2 53 OTU 18-3 SOC 30-6 to 2627M at 53 OTU

X4935 1399 FF 16-1-41 6MU 1-2 122S 11-6 53 OTU 12-10 FAAC 19-4-42 WAL SOC 22-3-45

X4936 1402 In Memory of R J Mitchell FF 17-1-41 6MU 1-2 457S 23-6 58 OTU 22-10 FACB 26-11-42 SAL 5 FTS Cranwell 12-7-43 RNDA 15-1-44

X4937 1403 FF 17-1-41 6MU 1-2 65S 6-3 308S 13-4 403S 28-5 AST con to FVA M45 FACE 3-6 RNDA Yeov 1-9-42 ASt 11-4-43

X4938 1400 FF GP 17-1-41 6MU 1-2 457S 23-6 53 OTU 20-10 61 OTU 19-3-43 57 OTU 254-44 FAAC 20-6-44 SOC 8-9

X4939 1405 FF 21-1-41 6MU 2-2 FA 12-2 on del flt AST 53 OTU 23-6 FACE 29-9 SOC 19-12

X4940 1404 FF 18-1-41 6MU 1-2 118S 13-3 66S 9-4 501S 27-4 53 OTU 23-6 FACB SOC 20-12

X4941 1474 EA Swansea Wales First Flight FF 19-2-41 12MU 26-2 313S 10-6 61 OTU 16-8 ASTE 4-9 con to FVA M45 302S 31-1-42 164S 24-4-42 dam AC in f/ld 22-8 602S 18-9 61 OTU 29-5-43 Spun i/grd nr Shrewsbury CE 29-6

X4942 HA 12MU 14-1-41 CRD VA 26-6 CRD B Dn 15-9 CRD VA 5-11 con to FVA M45 M46 instal Dec '41. BDn March '42 comp trls at h/a with R7120, X4258 & AB528. Cool and perf trls with trop mods. Wooden m/up of 90-gal o/ld tank fitt VAHP 20-10-42 invest into pilot's seat. Con to proto FVI M47 with pressure cabin, whip aerial. Trls at high alt with 3 & 4 blade Rotols, FIA wngs with extended tips, plain ails with balanced and geared tabs, increased horn balance. Farn May '43 after mods by Super. Comp trls with N3053 and X49222. Known to ROC as exp a/c No.152 R-RH 27-9-43 mods to TT standard to 4264M 1SoTT 20-11

X4943 1406 FF 20-1-41 6MU 2-2 234S 26-2 58 OTU 7-5 SAL 20-6 con to PRIII Type C 1PRU 9-3-42 215MU 25-9 *Pet Mer* 8-1 lost at sea 8-1-43

X4944 1410 FF 24-1-41 6MU 1-2 HAL 4-5 con to PRVI 1PRU Ben 27-5 8 OTU 19-6-42 e/fld w/u ldg Fraser CE 3-8-43

X4945 1406 FF GP 22-1-41 6MU 2-2 303S 26-2 58 OTU 10-3 222MU 30-9-42 *Taran* Nov '42 P Sudan 29-1-43 ME 28-2

X4988 1407 FF GP 22-1-41 39MU 29-1 53 OTU 25-6 cd Marcross Glam CE 10-7 SOC 22-7

X4989 1408 FF 22-1-41 39MU 28-1 66S 15-4 501S 27-4 53 OTU 23-6 ASTM 1-8 con to FVA M45 RNAS Mach 1-9-42 AST 31-10 mods LoS 29-1-43

X4990 1409 FF 23-1-41 39MU 29-1 501S 10-5 53 OTU coll with X4993 Llan CE SOC 17-4-42

X4991 1411 FF 24-1-41 6MU 1-2 609S 22-2 66S 24-2 58 OTU 20-6 flew i/grd nr Winchurch 4-11 57 OTU 7-4-42 SOC 9-7 to 2631M

X4992 1420 FF 29-1-41 con to FVA(T) 66S FACE 20-6 SOC 29-6

X4993 1412 FF 24-1-41 6MU 1-2 611S 14-2 FAC2 12-2 457S 22-6 53 OTU 20-10 coll with X4990 Llan CE SOC 17-4-42

X4994 1516 The Derby Ram FF 13-3-41 38MU 18-3 24S 11-7 57 OTU 1-11-43 SOC 18-4-45

X4995 1413 FF 25-1-41 6MU 1-2 66S 1-3 cd on t/o 3-3 Farn Mar '41 111S 10-4 58 OTU 28-1-43 e/fld w/u ldg nr Gran CE 14-7 FH409.35

X4996 1414 FF 27-1-41 6MU 1-2 457S 24-6 Farn Apl '42 53 OTU 23-10 air coll with X4427 Llan CA 25-6-42 AST

X4997 1415 FF 27-1-41 6MU 1-2 266S 14-2 111S 8-4 58 OTU 29-5 ASTH 26-6 con to FVA M45 130S 2-11 134S 31-12 601S 7-4-42 GAL 26-5 hook fitt RNAS Mach 4-9 LoS 20-11

(R-prefix serials restarted at 1416, R7023)

Westland Aircraft Ltd.
Contract No. B124305/40

First order for 300 Spitfire Mk I dated August 1940. Built as Mk 1/VB/VC between July 1941 and September. The following serials apply to the Mk I variants built to this first order. In the event only 50 Mk Is were constructed, the remainder as Mk V variants. AR212 to AR261 built only. Merlin III unless otherwise indicated.

AR212 6MU 18-7-41 57 OTU 9-8 27 OTU 27-9 air coll with X4605 cd Chester CE 16-3-42 SOC

AR213 FIB 12MU 24-7-41 57 OTU 31-7 FAAC 19-4-43 SOC 30-8-45 sold Grp Cpt Wheeler 10-3-47 Shuttleworth Trust as G-AIST 25-10 sold P Lindsay 1974 extant

AR214 12MU 7-8-41 132S 11-8 FACE 18-9 SOC 30-9

AR215 12MU 19-4-41 132S 28-8 58 OTU 5-1-42

Mk I AR238 served with No.52 OTU.

AR216 12MU 14-8-41 123S 24-8 61 OTU 19-9 ASTE SOC 10-10

AR217 12MU 26-8-41 124S 31-8 52 OTU 12-11 cd on f/f dbf 7-12 SOC 19-12

AR218 5MU 30-8-41 131S 17-9 ASTE 4-10 SOC 29-12

AR219 5MU 1-9-41 131S 17-9 FACB 8-9-42 SAL 58 OTU 9-11 1TEU 26-2-44 CE 18-8

AR220 5MU 9-9-41 132S 21-9 52 OTU 22-1 o/s ldg o/t ADn CE 10-11-42 SOC 16-11 recat B 57 OTU 27-4-43 SOC 30-12-44

AR221 5MU 9-9-41 61 OTU 2-10 Heston 16-2-42 52 OTU 7-5-43 flew into hill Long Mynd Salop 11-6-43

AR222 33MU 15-9-41 53 OTU 26-9 57 OTU air coll with X4266 cd Warkworth N'land Ce 17-3-43

AR223 33MU 15-9-41 53 OTU 26-9 58 OTU 26-1-43 1TEU 26-2-44 SOC CE 16-8

AR224 33MU 20-9-41 61 OTU 9-10 FAAC 6-8-42 57 OTU 17-7-43

AR225 38MU 26-9-41 52 OTU 3-11 FACB 28-6-42 WAL 61 OTU 1--5-43 53 OTU 20-3-44 SOC 17-4-44

AR226 38MU 26-9-41 52 OTU 8-11 FACE SOC 25-11

AR227 38MU 26-9-41 52 OTU 3-11 FACE dbf 14-12-42 SOC

AR228 38MU 29-9-41 53 OTU 2--12-42 SOC 8-3-45

AR229 M45 5MU 3-10-41 61 OTU 23-10 53 OTU 17-4-4257 OTU 15-7-43 e/fld cd/ld nr Esh CE 29-12

AR230 5MU 13-10-41 61 OTU 23-10 FACE ttl wrk 6-11 SOC 10-11

AR231 5MU 13-10-41 61 OTU 23-10 39MU 29-5-43 con to FVA M45 FAAC 17-8 CE 15-12

AR232 5MU 13-10-41 52 OTU 11-11 FACB 30-1-42 GAL 308S 5-7 140S 28-7-43 RNDA 16-1-44 525 RR Merton 1-11 349S 7-12 SOC 9-2-45

AR233 6MU 17-10-41 61 OTU 23-10 SOC 23-11 allot 61 OTU as Ins A/F

AR234 6MU 20-10-41 MAL 28-10 con to PRVII Type G M45 140S 13-3-42 FTR ops 3-6

AR235 6MU 20-10-41 MAL 28-10 con to PRVII Type G M45 1PRU 10-2-42 543S 30-9 8 OTU 6-6-43 SOC 28-6-45

AR236 8MU 27-10-41 52 OTU 3-11 RNAS 14-5-43 SOC 22-11-44

AR237 8MU 27-10-41 52 OTU 8-11 FACE 30-4-42 53 OTU 17-4-43 DeH 4-11

AR238 8MU 27-10-41 52 OTU 3-11 FACB 8-1-42 GAL RNDA Yeov 9-9 SOC 26-1-45

AR239 5MU 3-11-41 52 OTU 27-11 FACB 1-2-42 WAL HAL 18-5 con to PRVII Type G M45 140S 22-11 cd on low-level photography CE 3-1-43 FH121.10

AR240 5MU 4-11-41 52 OTU 27-11 air coll with P9500 15-3-42 std cd/ldg CE Ast D 2-1-43 SOC 25-1

AR241 5MU 6-11-41 1PRU 30-11 con to PRIII Type C 3SoGR 9-1-42 8 OTU e/fld i/sea Fraserburgh Bay SOC 11-6

AR242 33MU 10-11-41 HAL 30-11 con to PRVII Type G M45 1PRU 5-4-42 FACB 19-5 HAL 542S 30-10 8 OTU 17-4-43 dvd i/sea nr Colliston Aberdn 19-11 FH280.45

AR243 33MU 10-11-41 61 OTU 7-12 e/fld w/u ldg Esher Surrey 27-1-42 HAL

AR244 33MU 15-11-41 HAL 27-11 con to PRVII Type G M45 1PRU 13-2-42 140S 12-1-43 cd Mount Bron t/o 12-2 FH62.00

AR245 33MU 15-11-41 HAL 24-11 con to PRVII Type G M45 1PRU 30-1-42 FTR ops 27-3

AR246 5MU 18-11-41 57 OTU 6-12 FACB 13-2-42 ASTH 58 OTU 19-7 air coll with R6691 Letham Moor Stirlings CE 18-3-43 SAL

AR247 5MU 26-11-41 53 OTU 2-1-42 AST 11-2-43 RNAS 19-5 SOC 20-12-44

AR248 5MU 25-11-41 61 OTU 9-1-42 FACB 31-5 recat E 14-9

AR249 6MU 11-12-41 53 OTU 2-4-42 CE 15-3

AR250 6MU25-11-41 57 OTU 15-12 FACB 29-1-44 SOC 9-2-45

AR251 6MU 26-11-41 57 OTU 13-12 61 OTU 2-2-43 FACB 15-3 GAL SAL 27-4-44 SOC 12-4-45

AR252 6MU 26-11-41 57 OTU 12-12 air coll with X4186 CE 14-8-42

AR253 12MU 8-12-41 CRD TFU 28-12 FAAC 22-6-42 53 OTU 9-5-44 SOC 27-9-45

AR254 12MU 8-12-41 58 OTU 19-12 flew into high grd with P8276 & X4614 Kingseat Hill Kincardine 16-1-43 SOC FH585.30

AR255 12MU 13-12-41 53 OTU 6-1-42 FACE 30-10

AR256 12MU 8-12-41 58 OTU 5-1-42 RNDA Arb 9-9-42 FAAC 7-1-43 SOC 26-1-45

AR257 12MU 13-12-41 HAL 7-1-41 HAL 7-1-42 con to PRVII Type G M45 1PRU 4-3 painted Pink Camotint 541S 30-9 8 OTU 29-5-43 sank into soft grd taxy Aldergrove 27-6 recat E

AR258 37MU 16-12-41 57 OTU 18-12 HAL 17-1-42 con to PRVII Type G M45 140S 25-3 8 OTU 1-3-43 SOC 27-8-45

AR259 37MU 16-12-41 1PRU 19-2-42 con to PRIII Type C 8 OTU 19-6 Ben 29-10 Heston MR 29-1-44 SOC 27-2-45

AR260 37MU 17-12-41 HAL 26-1-42 con to PRVII Type G M45 1PRU 20-5 542S 29-9 CRD Gosport 30-5-43 Rotol Props Ltd 11-10 12-4-44 SOC 6-3-45

AR261 37MU 5-1-42 HAL 15-2 con to PRVII Type G M45 1PRU 5-5 542S 30-9 FACB 24-11 ROS 8 OTU 17-4-43 Stn Fm Dis 31-3-45

To RNAS; K9817, 9823, 9878, 9881, 9883, 9900, 9906, 9942, 9969, L1004, L1056, 1096, N3045, 3100, 3162, 3281, P9368, 9397,9433, 9556, R6620, 6629,6704, 6706,6716, 6719, 6722, 6759, 6881, 6887, 6895, 6970, 6972, 6977, 6993, 7119, 7136, 7145, 7160, 7193, 7200, 7252, X4017, 4021, 4165, 4172, 4244, 4253, 4270, 4331, 4336, 4337, 4382, 4412, 4478, 4604, 4643, 4648, 4652, 4657, 4660, 4710, 4780, 4782, 4788, 4816, 4818,4819, 4827, 4844, 4846, 4900, 4902, 4921, 4937, 4989, 4997, AR232, 236, 238.

Converted to Seafire F IA X4717.

Converted to Seafire F IB X4478.

Converted to floatplane R6722.

Converted to PR III K9787, 9834, 9906, N3069, 3071, 3111, 3116, 3117, P9307-9310, 9313, 9315, 9384 ,9385, 9426, 9453, 9550, 9551, 9561, R6598, 6804, 6805, 6879, 6894, 6900, 6903, 6906, 6909, 6968, 7020, 7070, 7128, 7130, 7146, 7147, X4242, 4332-4335, 4385, 4386, 4490, 4495-4498, 4501, 4712, AR241, 259.

Converted to PR IV N3113, 3276, P9505, R6902, 6905, 6910, 7139, 7142, 7143, 7211, X4492-4494, 4499, 4555, 4596, 4645.

Converted to PR V N3241, P9328, X4384, 4411, 4487, 4491, 4500, 4502-4505, 4599, 4784, 4832.

Converted to PR VII N3113, P9318, 9365, R6964, 7028, 7059, 7116, 7130, 7143, 7197, 7211, X4021, 4162, 4333, 4384, 4596, 4599, 4620, 4645, 4672, 4766, 4784, 4786, 4839, AR234, 235, 239, 242, 244, 245, 257, 258, 260, 261.

Converted to PR XIII L1004, X4021, 4615, 4660, 4766.

Converted to F V K9788, 9825, 9871, L1004, 1028, 1031, 1061, 1096, N3053, N3059,3098, 3121, 3124, 3242 3270, 3281, 3292, P9367, 9397, 9448, 9540, 9556, 9563, 9565, R6602, 6620 6623 6720, 6722, 6759-6761, 6770, 6776, 6801, 6809, 6817, 6833, 6882, 6887-6890, 6897, 6904, 6908, 6911, 6913, 6917, 6919, 6923, 6957, 6960, 6964, 7022, 7028, 7060, 7116, 7120, 7126-7127,7132, 7139, 7142-7143, 7158, 7161, 7194-7196, 7205, 7211, X4021, 4028, 4062, 4064, 4106, 4173, 4180, 4238, 4257-4258, 4272, 4279-4280, 4331, 4331, 4342, 4353, 4839, 4421, 4476, 4485, 4488, 4492 4606, 4615, 4621, 4671-4672, 4709, 4766, 4786, 4821, 4846, 4902, 4907-4908, 4922, 4930-4931, 4937, 4941-4942, 4989, 4997, AR231.

Converted to F VI; K9876, R7120, X4492, X4942.

Converted to F IX; R6770.

Shipped to USA; L1090.

Shipped to Canada; R7143, 7193, X4492, 4555.

Shipped to Middle East; K9788, 9876, 9873, L1000, N3283, P9311, 9334, 9432, 9551, 9557, R6840, 6916, 7132, 7152, 7214, X4274, 4344, 4356, 4489, 4619, 4714, 4767, 4780, 4785, 4830, 4848, 4929, 4945.

Lost at sea on SS Peter Mearsk 8.1.43. N3029, 3278, P9508, R6911, 7025, 7072, 7204, 7215, X4014, 4019, 4242, 4267, 4269, 4419, 4765, 4770 4817, 4820, 4837, 4943.

To Portugal; K9828, 9991, P9544, R6920, 6987, 7027, 7146, 7159, X4339, 4589, 4855, 4857, 4920.

To Turkey; L1066, P9565-9567, R7123.

Maintenance airframes. K9789(3594) K9795(4867) K9798(1494) K9800(3277) K9808(1238) K9812(1382) K9820(1361) K9822(1357) K9829(3200) K9831(1362) K9837(2868) K9837(1628) K9843(3229) K9845(1479) K9855(1646) K9859(1825) K9872(1450) K9876(4384) K9881(3215) K9894(4868) K9913(1632) K9921(2457) K9934(3083) K9942(8383) K9943(3229) K9955(3276) K9983(3275) K9998(2822)

L1008(3242) L1011(3236) L1012(3223) L1015(3252) L1017(3206) L1048(3248) L1057(2644) L1068(3259) L1089(3178) L1090(3201) L1092(3230) N3032(3184) N3072(3258) N3160(3088) N3169(2843) N3199(3167)

P9319(3143) P9330(3595) P9363(3371) P9376(4606) P9390(2111) P9460(3593) P9504(2728) P9507(2119) R6697(2842) R6720(5425) R6774(3597) R7058(2877) R7120(3566)

X4012(3307) X4033(2685) X4103(2684) X4355(2844) X4381(3546) X4474(3598) X4484(4524) X4603(2558) X4641(3466) X4661(2845) X4676(2847) X4718(4437) X4779(3144) X4915(2824) X4916(2825) X4921(4750) X4934(2627) X4942(4264) X4991(2631)

Spitfire F.I into service before 1 July, 1940.

K series. 9787, 9789, 9792, 9794-9829, 9831-9833, 9835-9851 and 9853-9999.

L series. 1000-1006, 1008-1066, 1068-1089 and 1091-1096.

N series. 3023-3072, 3092-3116, 3119-3129, 3160-3170, 3172-3203, 3221-3250, 3264-3270, 3272-3285 and 3287-3295.

P series. 9305, 9308, 9311-9312, 9314, 9316-9339, 9360-9383, 9386-9399, 9420-9421, 9423-9424, 9427-9459, 9491-9496, 9498-9508, 9510-9513, 9515-9519 and 9540-9549.

R series. 6596-6597, 6599-6620, 6622-6625, 6627-6630, 6632-6639, 6684, 6687-6702, 6704-6705, 6707, 6709-6711, 6717, 6761, 6770, 6776, 6806 and 6982.

Destroyed before 1 July, 1940. K9810, 9832, 9941 and 9948-9949. L1003, 1016, 1033, 1051 and 1084. N3107, 3185, 3237 and 3243. P9314 and 9441.

Struck off charge before 1 July, 1940.
K9792, 9794, 9796-9798, 9802, 9806, 9809, 9811, 9813-9814, 9816, 9831, 9836-9838, 9842, 9844-9846, 9848-9849, 9854-9856, 9858, 9860-9861, 9867-9868, 9872, 9875, 9877, 9884-9888, 9893, 9896-9898, 9900, 9902, 9917, 9919-9920, 9923, 9925-9927, 9932, 9937, 9952, 9956-9957, 9965-9966, 9968, 9971, 9974, 9977-9978, 9985-9988 and 9992. L1006-1007, 1013, 1022, 1025-1026, 1032, 1046-1047, 1052-1053, 1058, 1062, 1064, 1074, 1079, 1081, 1085-1087 and 1091. N3025, 3027-3028, 3030-3031, 3033, 3036, 3047, 3055, 3063-3064, 3092, 3096, 3102-3103, 3114, 3120, 3165, 3179-3180, 3186-3188, 3194-3195, 3197, 3200, 3202, 3222, 3224, 3232, 3272, 3274, 3289-3291 and 3295. P9305, 9308, 9317, 9321, 9331, 9339-9370, 9372, 9374, 9377-9388, 9392, 9435, 9455, 9504, 9514 and 9517.

Converted to F.II K9788, K9830, R6684, R6924, X4067, X4622 and X4776.

Converted to ASR.II(c) R6965.

Converted to 'Cannon' wing. R6761-6762, R6770, R6776, R6809, R6833, R6882, R6888-6890, R6897, R6904, R6911-6912, R6917-6919, R6923-6924, R6958, X4106, X4272, X4279, X4159 and X4342.

New Designs For 1936

It has been said by many critics that the Air Ministry as a whole were ultra cautious and not aware of the technological advances of aviation in the 1930s. For instance, the F7/30 prototypes were deemed failures because the Air Ministry insisted that the Rolls-Royce Goshawk engine be used as the powerplant. This is patently untrue as can be ascertained by the section regarding the engine for F7/30, which appears in the complete Specification on page 597.

The Air Ministry was aware of events in the world of aviation, so much so that in September 1935, even before the prototype Spitfire had flown, they were looking into the future by issuing a proposal for a number of high speed fighter designs based upon a 1000 hp engine. Maximum speed was envisaged as 408mph @ 15,000ft, auw 4982lb, wing span 31ft 6in, wing area 166.1 sq ft, length 27ft 0in, stall speed 77mph, climb to 20,000ft 6mins, ceiling 39,000ft. They were to follow the Spitfire and Hurricane into service and relate as close as possible to Specifications F5/34 and F9/35. For both the Oerlikon cannon was specified.

The designs were to follow the Spitfire and Hurricane into production and prototypes were to cost approximately £10,000 and could be constructed of either metal or wood, so wide was the specification. The Air Ministry was "very conscious of the need for such an aeroplane and designs submitted had to be based upon R.A.E. proposals". Our two drawings show the basics of two types of high speed aeroplanes issued by the DTD in July and September 1935. The first is an unorthodox single seat fighter with twin booms and engines somewhat reminiscent of the Lockheed Lightning. The pilot was seated in the top part of the port boom/wing junction, again similar to that of the Twin Mustang arrangement of 1945. The second sketch is an orthodox single seat fighter with 1000hp engine, four .303 Browning machine guns firing outside the propeller disc. The undercarriage retracted outwards and fuel was stored in the wings adjacent to the fuselage. The biplane design was issued after the monoplane.

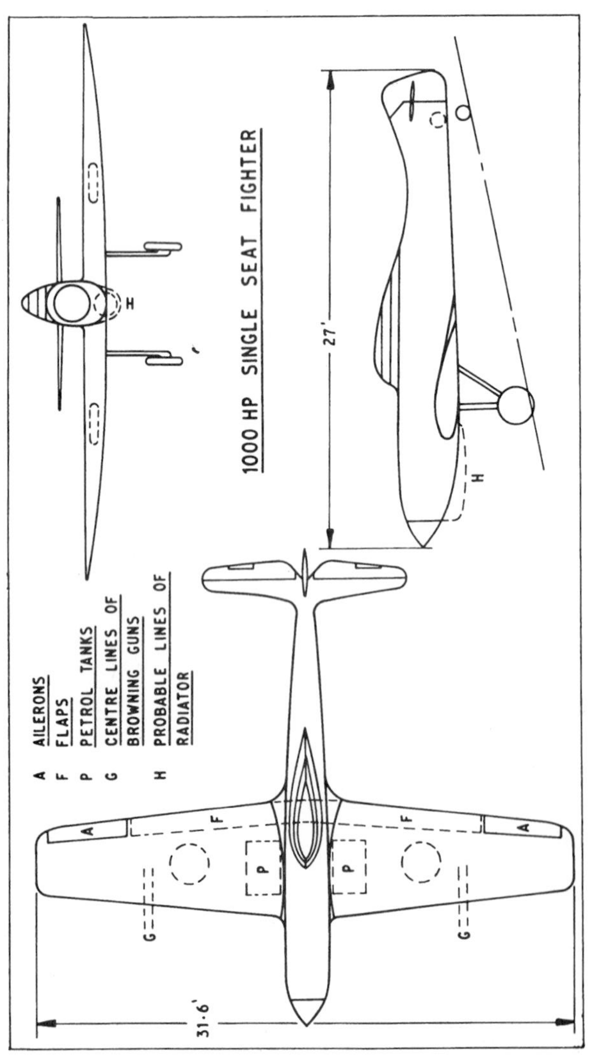

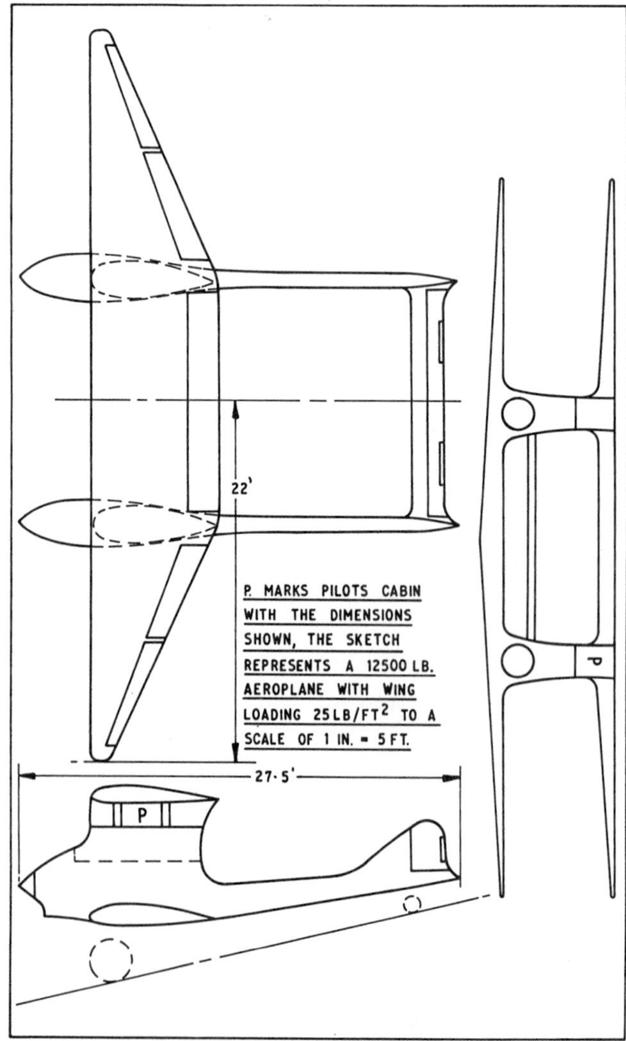

"NUFFIELD'S SPITFIRES"

During the early days of producing the Spitfire in quantity it was glaringly obvious that the numbers required would not be readily available, even with the system of sub-contracting as arranged by Supermarine. What was needed was a production line system similar to that used by the motorcar industry, and such a system was totally new to the aircraft industry as it was then. There were a number of British industrialists capable of setting up and managing such a system, and one in particular who had the flair necessary to carry it through.

He was Lord Nuffield, or William Morris, pioneer of the inexpensive, mass produced motorcar for the British market. He was approached by the Air Ministry and the first meeting between him and the Air Staff took place on 25 May 1938 in order to decide where the new 'Shadow Factory', as it was to be called, was to be located. There were political as well as production problems to be overcome for in the 1930s unemployment was rife and every member of Parliament wanted Government Contracts to go to his area of influence. Liverpool was a depressed area and the Government of the day insisted that the new Spitfire factory be built there.

Nuffield, however, had other plans. Although he appreciated the human problem of unemployment in the Liverpool area he pointed out that in the time needed to train the large numbers of workers to the standard demanded, production would suffer and the shortage of Spitfires would not be alleviated. Nuffield said the site for the new factory should be Birmingham for that was where the skilled labour force existed. After long negotiations it was agreed that the factory should be erected on a site at Castle Bromwich, Birmingham, and the Corporation sold a projected housing area to the Air Ministry, who also bought an adjoining piece of land from the Dunlop Company*. The site was 1,414 acres and it cost £1,000 per acre.

In the House of Commons Sir Kingsley Wood, the Air Minister, made a statement saying he had approached Nuffield to build and run the new factory, and the latter had agreed to accept the commission for a nil salary. The sum of £5,000 was deposited into the new company's account by the Air Ministry and work began on 12 July 1938. When finished and totally equipped the factory had cost over £4 million and the estimated production was 60 aircraft per week for a total of 1,050,000 man hours. Nuffield, in his search for engineering and managerial talent, poached C.T. Skipper from the Daimler Company to run Castle Bromwich, and Daimler complained to MAP saying that they would not be able to meet their production commitments because of the loss of one of their most senior executives. But MAP would not, or could not, comment.

The first contract to be placed with Castle Bromwich Aircraft Factory (CBAF) was No. B981687/39 for 1000 Mk IIA Spitfires dated 12 April 1939 in the serial range P7280 to 8799. The first aircraft (P7280) was delivered to Boscombe Down on 27 June 1940, while the second had preceded it to No. 6 MU on the 17th of the month for equipment installation before delivery to No. 612 Squadron on 27 August. The differences between the early Mk I and new Spitfire were minor and apart from the Merlin XII engine running on 100 octane fuel they consisted of a Coffman cartridge starter instead of the original electric start of the Merlin II, and a small fairing on the port side engine cowling housing the new starter. In the air they were identical and the designation was just a means to identify the aircraft as CBAF-built when ordering spares. A small number of Mk IIs had two station keeping lamps mounted on each side of the fuselage near the wing fuselage junction. They were intended as an aid to night formation flying and illuminated the upper wing surface, but the installation was soon dropped. The Merlin was pressure cooled with a mixture of 70% water and 30% glycol, this mix being originally tested in the Mk I K9788. The cannon armed version of the Mk II, the IIB, was ordered on 13 February 1940.

CHOICE OF PROPELLER

In May 1939, at a meeting held at Eastleigh with representatives of the Air Ministry, Rolls-Royce, Rotol Airscrews and Supermarine present, the choice of propeller for the new Merlin and Mk II airframe was under consideration. As a result of trials of the prototype Mk II (actually the converted Mk I K9791) the speed had been raised from 330mph to 370 with a Rotol CS propeller. With the de Havilland two-pitch unit (this could also be operated as a CS unit) an extra 5mph was available. K9791 had been ballasted to full load after the armament had been removed and a whole series of trials with various propellers initiated.

1) Rotol with Scharz blades 10ft 6in dia 170mm bearings. Max speed at 18,500ft 363mph. Photo 1, page 117.

2) Fixed pitch wood Type 3001700. Max speed at 18,500ft 363mph.

3) Rotol, Scharz blades, 10ft 6in dia 150mm bearings. Max speed at 17,500ft 346mph. Photo 2. Improvement due to reduction in root diameter and close fitting spinner.

4) Rotol with magnesium blades RA 611 10ft 6in dia 150mm bearings. Max speed at 18,500ft 369mph. Photo 3.

5) Propeller 4, pointed spinner. Max speed at 18,500ft 365mph. Photo 4.

6) Rotol, Schwarz blades 10ft 2in dia 150mm bearings. Max speed at 17,500ft 362mph. Photo 5. Scope for improvement.

7) Rotol, magnesium blades RA 621 10ft 6in dia 150mm bearings. Max speed at 18,000ft 366mph. Photo 6.

8) Propeller 8, pointed spinner. Max speed at 18,000ft 364mph. Photo 7.

9) de Havilland 2 pitch 10ft 9in dia 114mm bearings × 126mm. Max speed at 19,000ft 375mph. Standard for Merlin II. Photo 8.

10) Rotol, Supermarine Jablo blades 10ft 4in dia 150mm bearings. Max speed at 18,500ft 366mph.

11) Rotol, magnesium blades RA 630 10ft 6in dia 150mm bearings. Max speed at 18,500ft 366mph.

12) Rotol, magnesium blades RA 640 10ft 9in dia 150mm

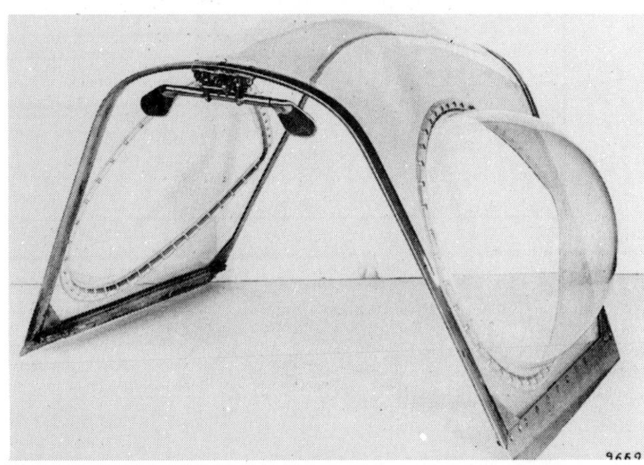

The experimental blister hood installed on P7280 was a modification of Cotton's hood and was to be adapted for use on the early PR Mk IIIs and IVs. It was also suggested for use on the periscope sight Spitfire, K9830, for use with the scheme on the rearward sighting of guns.

Design of inertia weight arm and its location in the elevator system of P7280. The $3\frac{1}{2}$lb weight was adjustable in a forward and back direction.

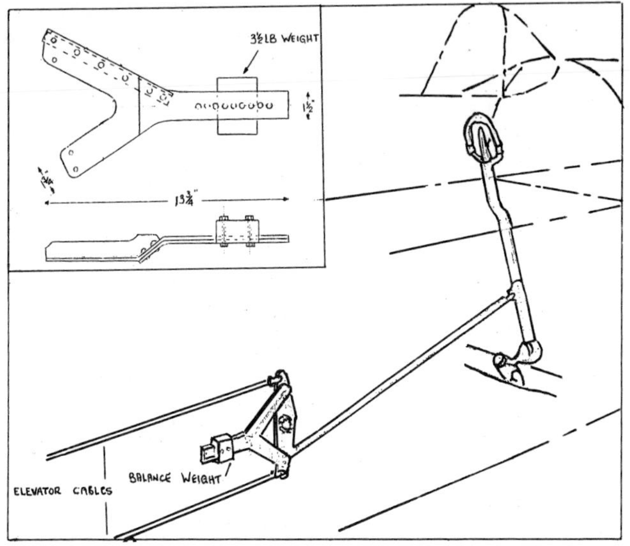

Rootes Securities were awarded a 'Shadow Factory' producing Blenheims and later Halifaxes at Speke, Liverpool, in due course.

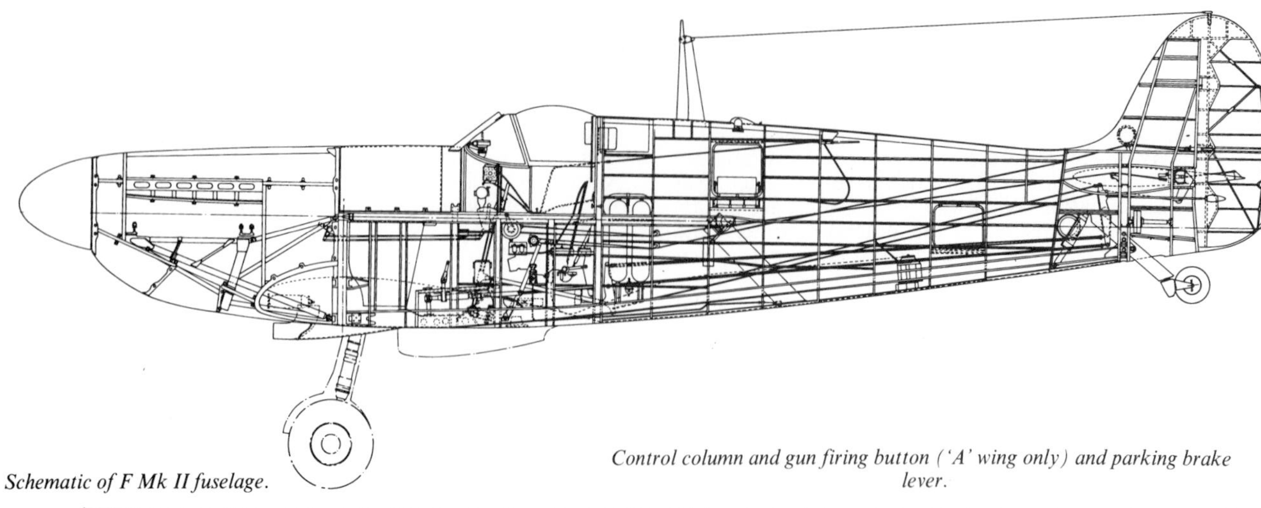

Schematic of F Mk II fuselage.

Control column and gun firing button ('A' wing only) and parking brake lever.

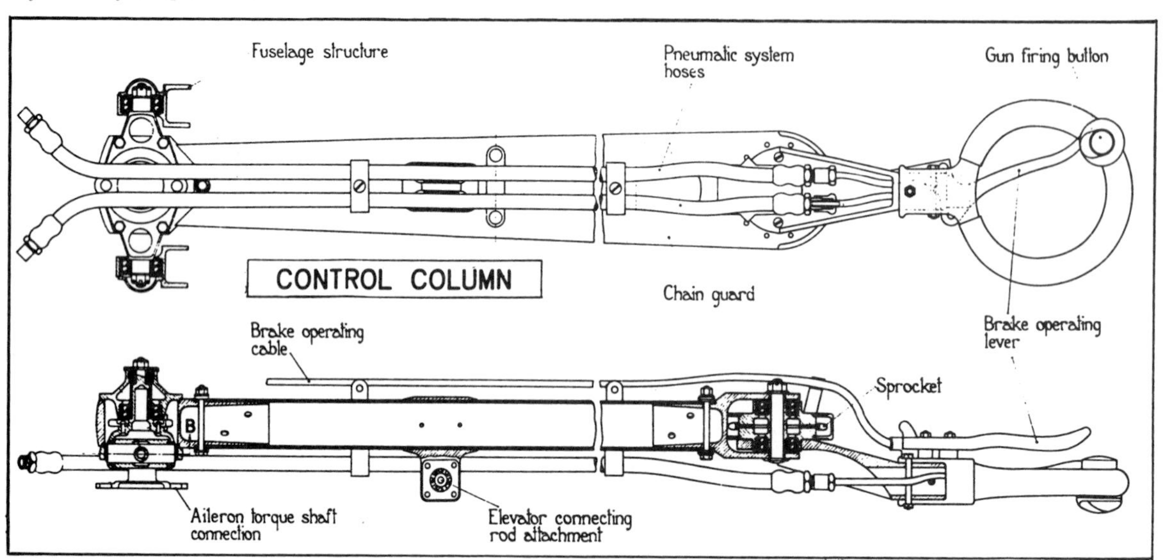

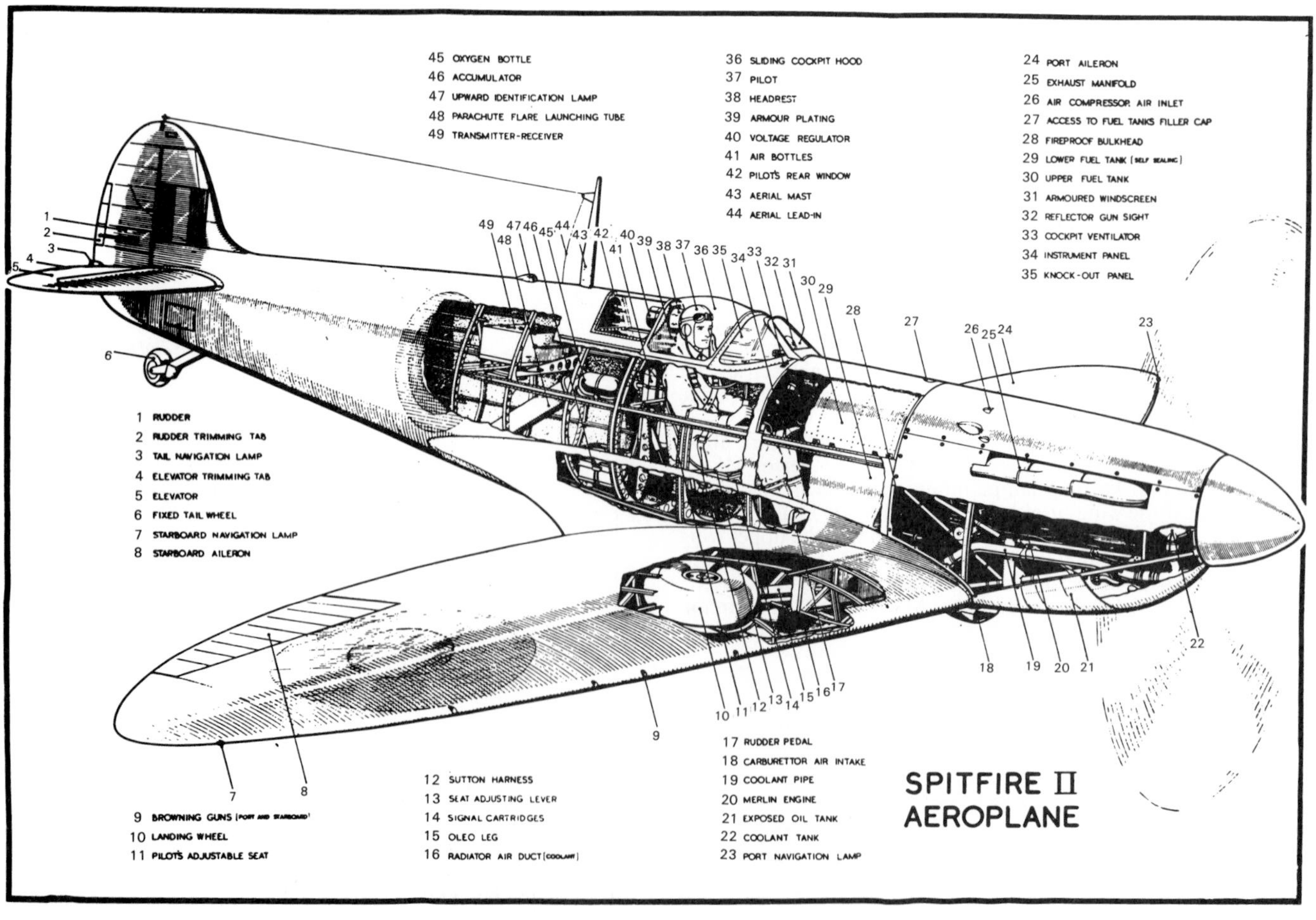

Fuselage structure
Pneumatic system hoses
Gun firing button
CONTROL COLUMN
Chain guard
Brake operating cable
Brake operating lever
Sprocket
B
Aileron torque shaft connection
Elevator connecting rod attachment

45 OXYGEN BOTTLE
46 ACCUMULATOR
47 UPWARD IDENTIFICATION LAMP
48 PARACHUTE FLARE LAUNCHING TUBE
49 TRANSMITTER-RECEIVER
36 SLIDING COCKPIT HOOD
37 PILOT
38 HEADREST
39 ARMOUR PLATING
40 VOLTAGE REGULATOR
41 AIR BOTTLES
42 PILOT'S REAR WINDOW
43 AERIAL MAST
44 AERIAL LEAD-IN
24 PORT AILERON
25 EXHAUST MANIFOLD
26 AIR COMPRESSOR AIR INLET
27 ACCESS TO FUEL TANKS FILLER CAP
28 FIREPROOF BULKHEAD
29 LOWER FUEL TANK (SELF SEALING)
30 UPPER FUEL TANK
31 ARMOURED WINDSCREEN
32 REFLECTOR GUN SIGHT
33 COCKPIT VENTILATOR
34 INSTRUMENT PANEL
35 KNOCK-OUT PANEL
1 RUDDER
2 RUDDER TRIMMING TAB
3 TAIL NAVIGATION LAMP
4 ELEVATOR TRIMMING TAB
5 ELEVATOR
6 FIXED TAIL WHEEL
7 STARBOARD NAVIGATION LAMP
8 STARBOARD AILERON
9 BROWNING GUNS (PORT AND STARBOARD)
10 LANDING WHEEL
11 PILOT'S ADJUSTABLE SEAT
12 SUTTON HARNESS
13 SEAT ADJUSTING LEVER
14 SIGNAL CARTRIDGES
15 OLEO LEG
16 RADIATOR AIR DUCT (COOLANT)
17 RUDDER PEDAL
18 CARBURETTOR AIR INTAKE
19 COOLANT PIPE
20 MERLIN ENGINE
21 EXPOSED OIL TANK
22 COOLANT TANK
23 PORT NAVIGATION LAMP
SPITFIRE II
AEROPLANE

P7290 of No.611 Squadron based at Digby 14 August 1940. Note the various modifications, including the fish tail exhaust manifolds; the ice guard on carburetter air intake and hook just aft of the tailwheel. This hook was, supposedly, for use as a towing device.

P7490 (LZ-Z of No.66 Squadron) was named 'City of Coventry'. It was to be converted later to ASR (IIC) standards and eventually sold to John Dale as scrap. Note the tiny, wing tip roundels.

P7508, F Mk IIA, before delivery to No.41 Squadron in October 1940. It was struck off charge in August 1944.

bearings. Max speed at 18,500ft 370mph.

13) Rotol, Supermarine Jablo blades, faired roots 10ft 3in dia. Max speed at 18,500ft 363mph.

Supermarine agreed to design and construct a fixed pitch, four blade Jablo for trials and Mr Collins, Air Ministry, said that the best propeller for the Spitfire II appeared to be the Rotol CS with magnesium blades. As a result of further trials in November 1939 the following results were obtained:

Blade	(1) Alt (2) Max speed	Speed at Altitude feet/mph 16000	12000	8000	4000	2000	SL
DH2 pitch	18000	365	348	331	313	304	296
Merlin II	376.5						
Rotol mag	18000	362	343	324	304.5	295	285
RA 640	372						
Rotol mag	18000	362	346	330	314	306	298
RA 611	370.5						
Rotol mag	18000	361	346	331	315	308	300
RA 621	369						
Rotol mag	18000	358	340	321	303	294	285
RA 630	367						
Rotol Jablo	18000	359	344	229	314	307	299
3001800	366						
Rotol Schwarz	17000	358	344	330	316	309	302
RA 654 150mm Rt	364						
10ft 2in dia							
3001700 wood	17000	360	347	334	320	314	307
fixed pitch	365.5						
Rotol Jablo	17400	358	344	330	316	308	301
3001900	363						
3001700 wood	18000	355	341	326	312	305	298
fixed pitch	362						
Merlin II							
Rotol Schwarz	17400	347	333	319	304	297	290
150mm Rt	352						
10ft 6in dia							

K9788 was then tested with three different propellers with the Merlin XII at different boost:

Propeller	Boost 7 lb	9 lb	12 lb
Rotol mag: mph	366.5	369.5	372.5
feet	18,900	16,700	13,450
Heine Jablo	363	366	368.5
	19,700	17,200	13,700
de Havilland	363.5	366	368.5
	19,650	17,200	13,900

Engine failure occurred with the Heine propeller in April 1940 and a Merlin RM 4S engine was installed and the trials continued. The speed at full throttle at 20,000 feet was 383mph with a Rotol RA640 (10ft 9in dia) and a RA630 (10ft 6in). One result of these trials was that MAP instructed de Havilland to produce metal blades and not to use magnesium, and Rotol was to concentrate on wood and Jablo blades.

An analysis of the Spitfire Mk I performance with the Merlin III and of the Mk I with the Merlin XII indicated that maximum speed of the latter should have been 380mph but, as the table above shows, it fell short of this figure. In March 1941 K9791 was fitted with the Merlin XII and it, too, was tested with the propellers mentioned in the table. The speed range was found to be between 343 and 361mph at 16,800 feet. The problem was passed to Boscombe Down and trials were conducted with a Mk II, P7661, with a four blade Rotol and a three blade de Havilland propeller. The latter had a thinner section blade and trials revealed that the speed of the Rotol propeller decreased as engine speed increased from 2856 to 3000rpm. Rate of climb was unaltered. Speed of the de Havilland unit increased with engine rpm and the rate of climb showed some improvement. It was thought that the compressibility losses with the Rotol increased more rapidly as the engine rpm increased, due to the larger diameter propeller. Also, the Rotol was designed to use a gear ratio of .42 and was actually using a .477. Further trials were carried out but the results never published.

The Mk II took part in the Battle of Britain when the first example, P7282, arrived at No. 61 Squadron on 22 August 1940. When the last, P7564, was delivered a total of 195 had been accepted for service with the RAF before the end of October. The MUs had taken delivery of the initial batches of Mk IIs on 17 June. This Mk of Spitfire was used extensively when Fighter Command began mounting sorties against mainland Europe during the Winter of 1941/42. In January 1941 a mixture of Mk I and II Spitfires of No. 66 Squadron took off from Biggin Hill and crossed the Channel, making landfall at a

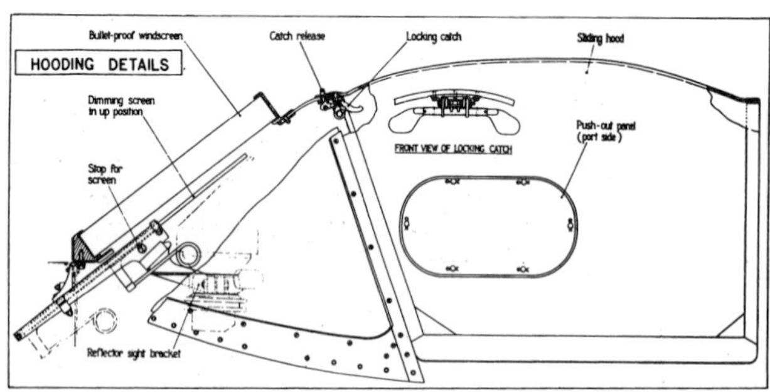

Details of windscreen and hood with bullet-proof screen fitted to all later production Mk I and IIs.

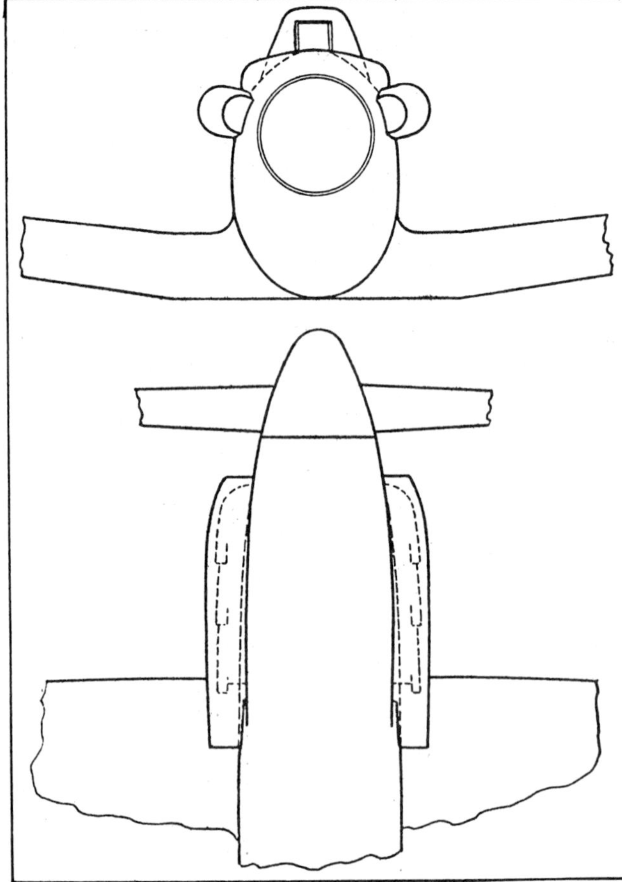

Exhaust screens as installed on P8791.

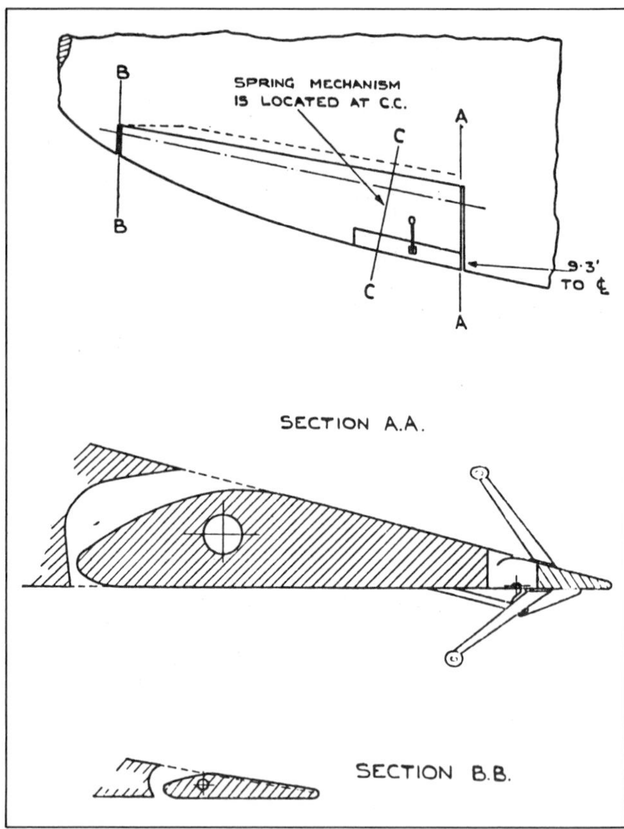

A spring tab installation was designed and built for the Spitfire fabric-covered aileron by de Havilland Aircraft and tested at Farnborough. Drawings show aileron and tab, plan and section.

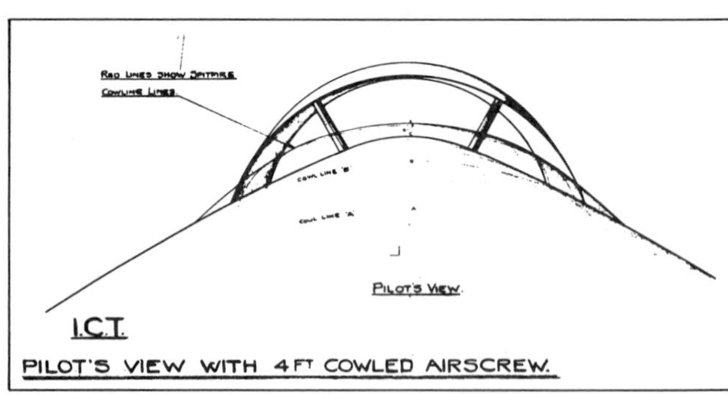

One of the more interesting proposals for the Spitfire was a Mk II adapted for a four foot diameter, cowled propeller assembly, together with an Internal Combustion Turbine engine. The drawings, below and above, show the engine installation and pilot's forward view.

P7661 with trial exhaust flame dampers fitted at Boscombe Down in July 1941. It was to be converted to F Mk VA standards with a Merlin 47 engine modified for fuel injection.

P7613 approaches to land with flaps fully extended. It was struck of charge in June 1945.

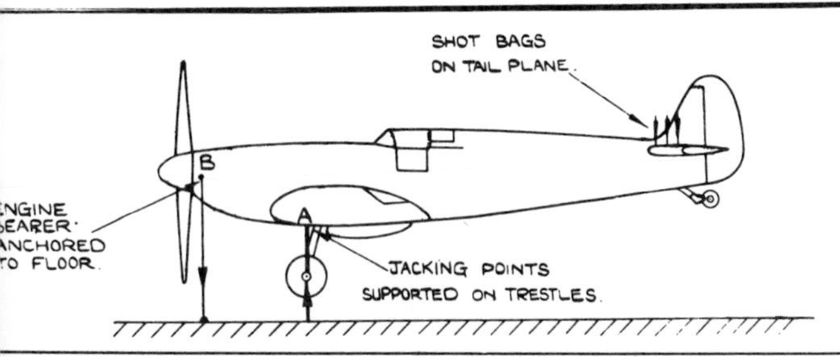

Position of recording cameras, mirrors and 'Festoon' lamps as installed on P7521 for tail deflecting tests. View above shows the static rig.

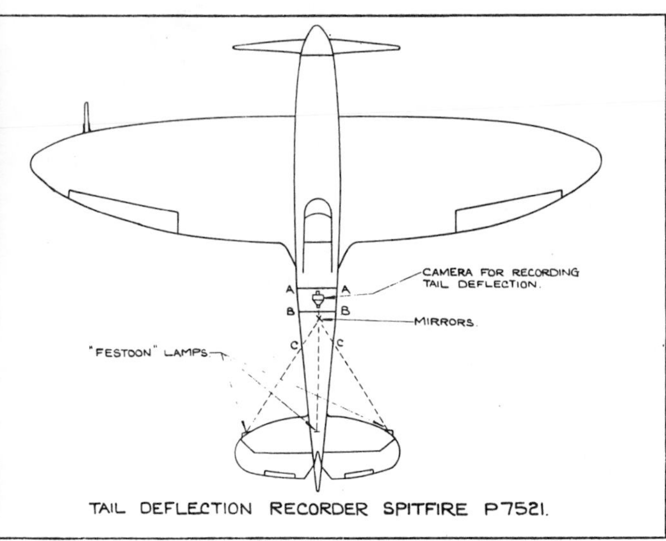

Installation of Desynn transmitter in the wing of P7521 during aileron hinge movement trials. Below: Close-up of distortion unit and the transmitters.

General arrangement drawing of apparatus for measuring surface distortion of fabric and metal covered ailerons as installed on P7521. The Spitfire aileron problem was never fully resolved despite many trial installations.

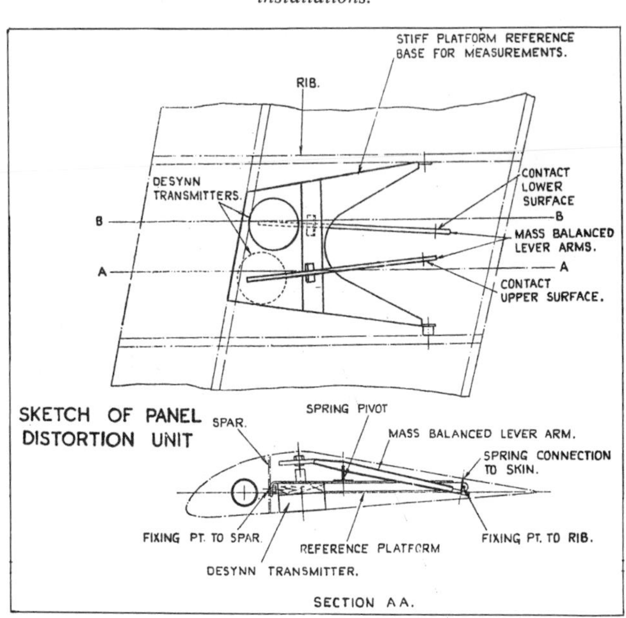

P7665 of No.65 East India Squadron, January 1941. It was shot down by a Bf109 the following month.

point near Dieppe. Flying low across France the fighters reached a position north of Paris before turning back for home, shooting at targets of opportunity on the return flight. All aircraft had landed safely at 5.15pm, just after dusk, and in doing so completed the first offensive, daylight sortie by Fighter Command since the days of Dunkirk, some six months previously.

A minor incident that could have had severe repercussions was when No. 6 MU reported they had found six Spitfires with incorrectly assembled fuel cocks. When the sight lever indicated fuel was on the cock was actually off. A search of all Mk IIs revealed 14 aircraft with the fault. They were P8143, 8144, 8146, 8148, 8160, 8161, 8163, 8199, 8201, 8202, 8204, 8206, 8243 and 8246.

During 1942 an official modification of the Mk IIA/B for Air-Sea Rescue duties was designated Type 375 Spitfire Mk IIC. In this instance, however, the 'C' suffix did not refer to wing armament but was to distinguish it from the fighter versions. Although essentially a non-combatant aircraft the IIC retained its armament and, in addition, was fitted with a small rack for two rescue marker smoke bombs under the port wing root inboard of the oil cooler. The two flare chutes in the rear fuselage were adapted to take two canisters containing a small dinghy in one and food in the other. Both were attached to a small parachute and the whole was known as the 'Sea Rescue Type E (Spitfire)'. When the role prefixes were introduced in late 1942 the designation was changed to ASR Mk II. P7734, converted May 1944, was weighed at High Post with a tare of 5036 lb and an auw of 6478.

ASR Spitfires were issued to Nos. 276 and 277 (ASR) Squadrons and pooled for their own use and for issue to other ASR squadrons Nos. 275, 278 to 282 inclusive, as and when required. The principal user of the ASR IIC was, undoubtedly, No. 277 based at Hawkinge, Kent.

Before closing this chapter on the Spitfire Mk II mention must be made of two aircraft about which little is known, but which were of great interest. One was (supposedly) used for ground testing the Rolls-Royce PI-26, two-stroke, 2300hp diesel engine in late 1941. This engine was a 12-cylinder V, liquid cooled unit with an exhaust system incorporating a ducted fan, and was claimed to be an adaptation of the supercharged Condor III engine (see page 107). Status of the engine remains a mystery but it is on record the Spitfire Mk

P7420 Of No. 19 Squadron refuelling with 100 octane. Note Coffman starter fairing on engine cowling. Weight of the new starting system was 86lb, but with deletion of tail ballast to compensate the actual increase in auw was 58lb. This Spitfire flew into a tree near Boxford, Sussex, on 15 November 1940, killing the pilot, Sergeant Roden.

II P7674 was delivered to Rolls-Royce on loan in 1941 after modifications by Scottish Aviation Ltd., following upon repairs to the aircraft after a flying accident. Unfortunately, the Contract and Shipping Office records at Rolls-Royce do not list this Spitfire and there is little, or no, information to be had on the engine installation. All that is known does suggest that such an exercise did take place and P7674 was the airframe utilised, and that the engine had been running on the bench for long periods by 1943.

The second mystery Spitfire Mk II is reported to have been fitted with a fixed, spatted undercarriage similar to that used on the Miles M 20 fighter prototype. It was an unofficial modification by a squadron to a Cat 3 damaged airframe, and the resultant aircraft was probably used to sharpen up the taxiing techniques of unseasoned pilots.

After all Spitfire IIs had been withdrawn from front line fighter squadrons, with No. 111 probably the last to use it up to August 1942, they continued to be used as trainers with derated Merlins at various UK based establishments such as the Operation Training Units (OTUs). The Air Fighting and Development Unit (AFDU) used over 40 Mk IIs from February 1944 onwards to form 'circuses' in air fighting techniques. Six such circuses, each with six Mk IIs, were attached to Nos. 1, 3, 4, 5, 6 and 8 Groups of Bomber Command, plus two smaller flights of three Mk IIs affiliated to No.2 Group of the 2nd Tactical Air Force (TAF) and to Coastal Command.

Production of the Spitfire Mk II was confined to Castle Bromwich and the first 750 aircraft were built with the normal 'A' wing with 8 × .303 Browning guns. The final 170 Mk IIs had the 'B' wing with 4 × 20mm cannon and 4 × .303 machine guns as a new system of belt feed had been perfected for the Hispano guns. Subsequently a number of Mk IIAs were retrospectively converted to Mk IIB standards. Operational use of the Mk I had resulted in the incorporation of armour protection for the pilot and engine in the form of 60 lb of plating; an externally mounted, bullet proof windscreen; the lower fuel tank covered with self sealing material and a constant speed propeller. The armour for the engine was in the form of thicker gauge metal on top and sides of the cowling. All these refinements, in addition to the Merlin XII, were built into the Mk II.

A small number of Spitfire Mk Is were converted to Mk II standards, including K9830 which was used as a Mk I for trials with the periscopic gun sight. It was converted to Mk II by Supermarine in March 1940 and with the Merlin XII engine and 79 modifications was weighed at Eastleigh on 5 April. Auw was 6,183lb, tare 4,864.

P7856 of No.65 Squadron with a group of Sergeant pilots. It collided in the air with Spitfire P8144 and crashed on 7 May 1943.

P8137 'Sarum and South Wilts Spitfire' which was lost on operations on 10 July 1941 while serving with No.234 Squadron.

Alex Henshaw, Supermarine test pilot.

Aerial view of the vast Castle Bromwich Aero Factory (CBAF).

OFFICIAL REPORTS ON Mk II

Boscombe Down, 27 September 1940. P7280. Merlin XII, Rotol CS propeller. Comparative performance trials. The first Nuffield built Spitfire was tested against a standard Mk I. The handling and flying characteristics were similar to the Mk I but it was less stable in the climb. Ceiling was increased as was climb.

Boscombe Down, 15 January 1941. P7280. Addenda to performance trials. Landing run during first trials was longer than expected. Fresh brake drums and linings were fitted. Run shortened by 40 yards.

Boscombe Down, 16 January 1941. P7280. Tests with 'Blistered' hood. Sliding hood had side blisters (see photo, page 97) and trials were to establish if these had any effect on maximum speed. The modified hood was strongly recommended for service use.

Boscombe Down, 16 January 1941. P7280. Diving tests with inertia device fitted. Brief tests carried out with 7lb weight in the elevator control system, first tried on the prototype Spitfire Mk III. Initial tests revealed that control column became heavy, particularly during steep turns and the weight was reduced to 3½lbs. When the weight was at the middle of the arm the aeroplane was pleasant on the elevators during steep turns at low speeds. For any given ASI the acceleration on recovery from dives was considerably reduced when the inertia device was fitted.

Boscombe Down, 18 January 1941. P7525. Complaints by No. 66 Squadron over the handling qualities included a diving speed restricted to 320mph in spite of full forward trim; flew left wing low and aileron snatch. Tailplane trailing edges were swept up spoiling air flow over rudder and elevators. The edges were dressed down and lengths of standard size trimming cord doped to the upper and lower starboard aileron trailing edge were removed and a single 10in length doped to the upper trailing edge of the port aileron. The modifications restored handling qualities to normal.

Boscombe Down, 26 April 1941. P7661. High altitude Development flight. Performance with 10ft 9in diameter 3-blade Rotol metal propeller. With the 4-blade Rotol Jablo the speed decreased as the engine speed increased from 2,050rpm to

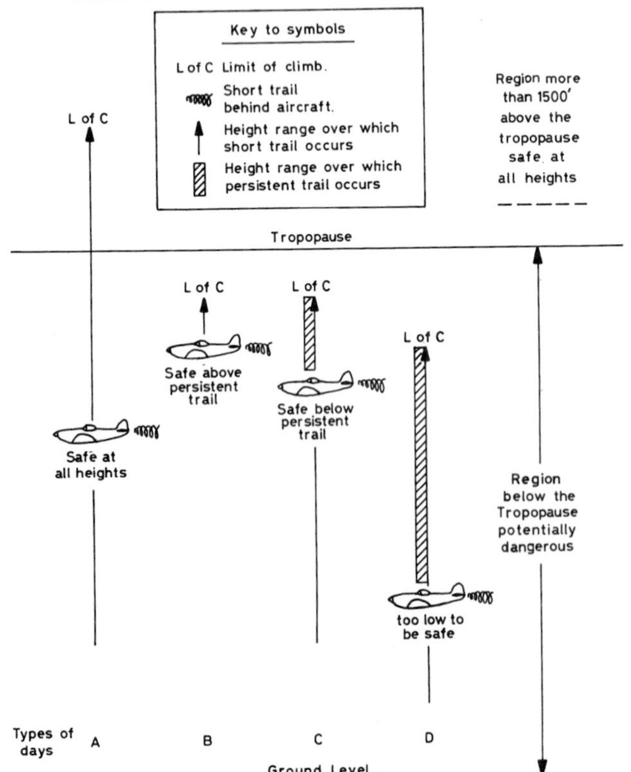

P8021 was used for high altitude research connected with the formation of vapour trails from condensing exhaust, with particular emphasis for the photo reconnaissance Spitfires. It is seen here at Boscombe Down in January 1941 when fitted with the Merlin 47 engine. Note the sensor on the wing undersurface and similar fitment on upper surface. They were electrical and capillary thermometers. The vapour trail streaming from P8021 was forming at 30,000ft and PR aircraft pilots were provided with a special, rear facing mirrors in order to sight the trails and take action to stop them. This Spitfire was one of the few fitted with the two station keeping lamps mounted each side of the fuselage just above the wing root. The lamp circuit was linked to the tail navigation lamp so that when the station lamps were used the tail lamp automatically dimmed. the graph (left) shows the area in which vapour trials would be formed.

3,000, while rate of climb was unaltered. With the 3-blade propeller rate of climb and speed increased with rpm. Probable explanation was that compressibility losses with the Jablo increases more rapidly as the rpm rises.

Boscombe Down, 28 May 1941. P9830. Gun heating trials (8 machine guns). Temperature in the port gun bay was improved by utilising hot air drawn from round the exhaust stubs in addition to that drawn from behind the radiator. The standard system of leading hot air from the radiator through ducts to the gun bays was insufficient, in particular the port guns as the heat had to travel from the starboard wing. The new system was recommended for service use.

Boscombe Down, August 1941. P8021. Formation of condensation trails at high altitude of such importance to operational flying that it warranted special investigation. Sqdn Ldr Longbottom was the pilot and he took it up to 40,000ft on numerous occasions. The region above the tropopause was considered the safest area for flying for it produced short condensation trails. Below this the area was considered dangerous, particularly to bombers over Germany, as the trails were long and persistent.

Boscombe Down, August 1941. P7661. Effect of triple ejector flame damper exhausts on speed, which was unaffected by the installation. See photo page 101.

Boscombe Down, 16 September 1941. P8036. Brief performance and handling trials with an extra wing fuel tank. Tank identical to that fitted to P9565, Mk I (see page 67). With metal covered ailerons it was pleasant to fly.

Aero Note. November 1941. Effect of oxygen boosting on Spitfire performance. Oxygen (liquid) was fed into mouth of air intake (as per photos on page 107) from tank in wing. Gain in hp was 75 and oxygen lasted for five minutes.

Farnborough, June 1942. P7251. Failures of Spitfire tailplanes had occurred in high speed dives and tests were required to investigate cause. During tests a new mainplane had to be fitted. To measure tailplane deflection in dives special recording instruments and a camera were installed as shown in the accompanying drawing. *Two pull outs were made at 300mph and one at 400. In all dives the downward deflection of the starboard tailplane tip was considerably greater than that of the port. This tended to twist the fuselage, but the effect would disappear when full left rudder was applied and nearly doubled with full right rudder. The terminal velocity of the Spitfire was about 560 TAS and corresponded to a Mach number of about .79. Static tests were made by jacking up the aircraft on trestles, anchoring the nose via the engine bearer to the floor, and then loading bags of lead shot on the tailplane. The fuselage mounted camera used in flight trials recorded results.

Farnborough, August 1942. P8781. Addendum to note on speed reduction due to exhaust screens. The fish-tail exhaust flame dampers reduced maximum speed by 9-12mph, according to trials by Rolls-Royce at Hucknall. The Farnborough tests confirmed these results and also showed that speed loss rose with altitude. At 2000ft there was no loss, 5000ft 4mph and at 20,000 8mph. With screens removed exhaust thrust increased speeds by 6mph at 2,000ft, to 21mph at 20,000ft. Drawing shows shape of screens. See page 100.

Farnborough, August 1942. P8441. Flight tests of spring tab ailerons. The spring tab for the fabric covered aileron was designed by de Havilland Aircraft. Pilot's impressions were that lateral control felt normal, except that ailerons were much lighter at high speeds. The rapid hardening up of control with increase of speed which was a feature of fabric covered ailerons no longer occurred. Drawing depicts spring tab design and location on ailerons. See page 100.

Farnborough, September 1942. Spitfire Mk II aileron tests

Line up of new production F Mk IIBs. P8339 'Madura' (NEI) was converted to F Mk VB standards, Merlin 45, and lost on operations on 21 September 1942.

P8448 'Counter Attack' is delivered to No.152 Squadron by ATA pilot. Unusual is the 70 gallon underwing fuel tank.

P8327 'Java' of Netherlands East Indies (purchase scheme). An F Mk IIB, it was lost over France on 24 July 1942.

* *see page 101.*

Rare photograph showing two F Mk IIAs with 70 gallon under wing fuel tanks.

in the 24ft wind tunnel. Investigation to study effect on aileron characteristics of changes in shape and position similar to those which arose during manufacture and assembly of ailerons. Conclusions – both hinge moments and pressures over aileron nose were sensitive to small changes of nose shape. Bending the upper shroud upwards tends towards overbalance of the up going aileron, but made the interconnected pair of ailerons heavier. Adding turbulence wires to bring laminar transition point to 10c helped.

Boscombe Down, 24 October 1942. P7661. Performance and fuel consumption tests with Bendix Stromberg Injection carburettor (converted to F Mk VA standards). Merlin 47 engine (Special). Fuel consumption was much greater at all heights up to 20,000ft. Over this height the Stromberg improved and it was superior at 39,000ft.

Boscombe Down, 23 November 1942. P7661. Fuel system and handling tests with Bendix Stromberg. Fuel system adequate for all conditions encountered in temperate or tropical zones, provided the immersed fuel pump in the lower tank was in operation.

Farnborough, February 1943, P7521. Flight measurements of the hinge movements on single ailerons. Part I, port aileron. Measurements were made over the speed range from 150-400mph.

Farnborough, 3 March 1943. P7521. Aileron tests in the 24ft tunnel on eleven Spitfire ailerons, including P7521 and P8441.

Boscombe Down, March 1943. P7884. Handling tests with de Havilland airbrake propeller. This aircraft was fitted with a modified version of the braking propeller installed on Spitfire Mk I. Before tests could begin the high pressure oil pump failed and the aircraft had to be returned to de Havilland for rectification. During tests the blades turned rapidly from normal fine pitch to the braking position to prevent engine speed rising too high. The coffman starter was replaced by the engine driven high pressure VSG oil pump, control of which was situated in the cockpit. Application of the brake was recommended by de Havilland at 2600rpm ASI 200mph. Close throttle and move brake control lever to 'brake'. The result was a pause of about three seconds when engine speed rose to 3300rpm and fell away rapidly to tickover. Initial deceleration was very large and then fell away as the rpm dropped. For the return to normal flight the throttle still had to be in the closed position. Brake lever moved to 'inbrake' and after rpm had passed their peak open throttle gradually and return brake lever to constant speed. Time taken was 15 to 20 seconds. The conclusions of the report were that the braking effect prevented a pilot keeping his gun sight on a target, but the system was to be developed for the dive bombing role and to reduce landing run of bombers.

Boscombe Down, 25 June 1943. P8397. Note on carbon monoxide contamination tests. Tests showed contamination exceeded the ground acceptance limit but not flight during climb and cruising conditions.

Boscombe Down, September 1943. P8194. Tests of landing brake propeller. Excellent results when propeller used during landing, especially when flaps had failed.

Farnborough, April 1945. P7521. Flight measurements of

P8088, F Mk IIA, 'The Borough of Lambeth', No.118 Squadron, Ibsley, Hants, May 1941. Mascot under cockpit was 'Capt. Reilly-Ffoul' of Daily Mirror fame. The aircraft dived into the ground at Prees, Salop, on 23 September 1944.

P7973, F Mk IIA, was converted to VA standards. It was flown by Sqn Ldr 'Bluey' Truscott, RAAF, and presented to Australia in 1944.

Jeffery Quill demonstrates P8136 on 4 April 1941. The Spitfire was officially named 'Aldershot', and unoffically as 'The Cat' by its pilots.

The Condor II supercharged engine was said to have been converted into the Rolls-Royce P1-26 diesel engine and fitted into Spitfire P7674.

hinge moment and surface distortion on fabric and metal covered ailerons. Results were recorded by a Desynn micro-transmitter installed in the wing. See page 101.

MODIFICATIONS TO SPITFIRE Mk II

367 fit Mk III oil cooler 11-4-41; 420 Provide extra heating for machine guns 9-8-41; 510 Pressurise fixed fuel tanks 13-1-42; 517 Provide collectors for links of .303 guns 2-12-42; 531 fit extra deflector armour to pilot's seat 16-12-41.

F Mk IIA, IIB, IIC

Wing. Planform elliptical; section NACA 2200 Series; incidence° root +2, tip $-\frac{1}{2}$; dihedral° 6; thickness % root 13.2, tip 6; aspect ratio 5.68; area sq ft nett 220, gross 242; chord (geo) 6.38, (ma) 7.01. Ailerons. Area sq ft 18.9; chord (ma) movement° up 26, down 19; droop $\frac{3}{8}$in. Flaps. Area sq ft 15.6, movement° down 85. Wing loading lb/sq ft 35.0; power loading lb/hp 5.34.

Tailplane. Area Sq ft 31.46; chord (ma) 4.0; incidence° root 0, top $\pm\frac{1}{2}$; dihedral° 0. Elevators. Area sq ft 13.26; movement° up 28, down 23. Tab. Area 0.38, movement° up 30, down 30. Fin. Area sq ft 4.61. Rudder. Area sq ft 8.23, movement° each way 28. Tab. Area 0.35, movement° each way 12.

Undercarriage. Wheels Dunlop AH2061; tyres Dunlop 7-50-0. Oleo pressure lb/sq in 355; Tailwheel fixed castoring. Wheel Dunlop AH2184; tyre Ecta 3-00-4.

Engine/s. Merlin RM XII, one speed. Coffman cartridge starter. 1,050hp @ 13,000ft; 1,175 @ take-off. Recc rpm @ take off to 1,000ft or 3 mins 3,000 (boost + 12lb); climb 2,850 (+9) 30 mins max; cruise normal mix 2,650 (+ 7); weak mix 2,650 (+ 3¾); max emer or combat 3,000 (+ 9) 5 mins; min rpm 2,270 (+ 12); max dive 3,600 (+ 9) 20 secs. Fuel consumption climb 93.5 gal/hr @ 13,000ft, all out level speed @ 3,000rpm @ 14,000ft 98; max cruise normal mix @ 13,000ft 77.5; weak mix ditto 55.6. Small number a/c fitted Merlin 45, and Merlin III.

Propeller/s (Merlin III and XII). Rotol 3-blade CS variable pitch (VP) RX5/1 magnesium pitch range 35° fine pitch 30° 15′ or; RX5/3 3-b CS VP Jablo pitch range 35°, fine pitch 30° 15′ or; RX5/14 3-b CS VP Jablo pitch range 35° fine pitch 29° 57′ or; RS5/24 (Merlin 45). All 10ft 3in diameter; or de Havilland 3-b CS VP Bracket Type 5/39A dural pitch range 20° fine pitch 32°; diameter 10ft 9in.

Coolant. 100% Glycol. In main system 13.5gals.

Fuel. 100 octane. Capacity (fuselage) upper 49gals, lower 37, total 85. Plus 40gal o/ld tank.

Oil. 58gals under engine.

Press photograph of Spitfire ASR (IIC) (cannon armed), dropping a dinghy to the airman in the water after locating him by means of the smoke bomb.

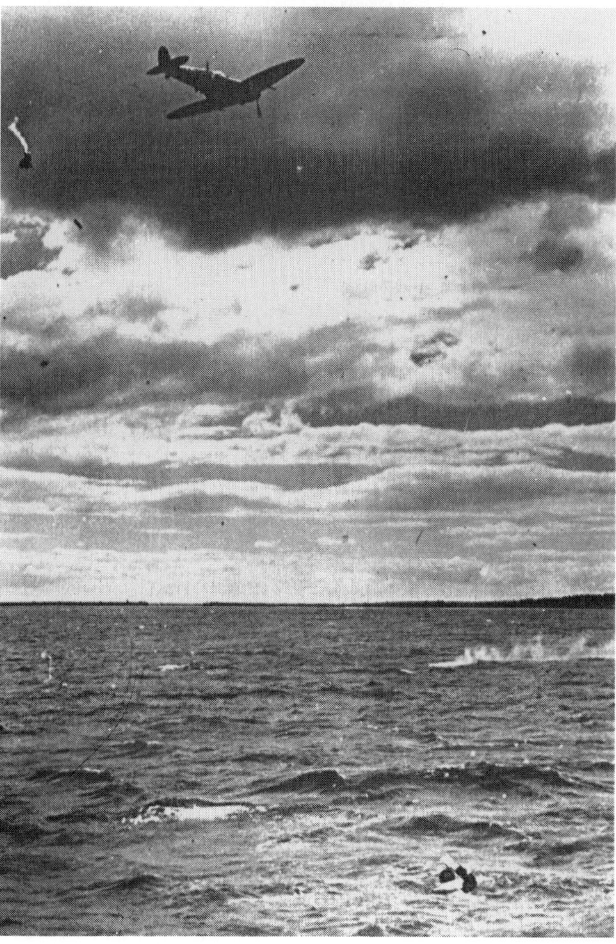

A Mk II Spitfire was used for liquid oxygen, LOX, trials as a boost to engine power. LOX is pumped into the Spitfire at Farnborough in January 1942. The air intake has a pipe from the LOX tank feeding into the opening. The bulge just behind the oleo houses the LOX tank.

Armour. 73lb.
Armament. A wing (Mk II Star guns) or; F Mk IIB 2 × 20mm Hispano cannon 60rpg and 4 × .303 Browning m/gs 300rpg (B wing). Gunsight. GM.2 reflector.

Cine camera. G42B in port wing.
Radio. TR.9D or TR.1133 plus (IFF) R3002.
Performance. Max speed @ rated altitude 370mph, 290 @ SL, 294 @ 2,000ft, 306 @ 5,000. Initial climb rate 2,600ft min, 2,925 @ 2,000, 2,955 @ 5,000. Time to 5,000ft 1 min 42 secs. Rate of climb 2,995 @ 10,000, 2,715 @ 20,000, 995 @ 30,000. Combat radius for sweeps over Channel limited to 70-80 miles inland France from South coast UK. Take off run 230yds, landing 350, landing speed 67mph.

Weights. Tare 4,783lb, take off 6,275.

F Mk IIC

Merlin XX engine.

SERIAL NUMBERS

Vickers-Armstrongs (Castle Bromwich) Ltd.

Contract No. B981687/39/C.23(C).

First order for 1,000 Spitfire Mk II dated 12 April 1939. Built as Mk IIA/IIB/VA/VB between June 1940 and July 1941. The following serials apply to Mk II variants built to this first order. P7280-7329, 7350-7389, 7420-7449, 7490-7509, 7520-7569, 7590-7629, 7661-7699, 7730-7759, 7770-7789, 7810-7859, 7880-7929, 7960-7999, 8010-8049, 8070-8099, 8130-8149, 8160-8209, 8230-8279, 8310-8439, 8360-8399, 8420-8449, 8460-8479, 8500-8531, 8533-8536, 8540-8541, 8543-8549, 8562-8563, 8565-8577, 8579-8580, 8582-8584, 8586-8599, 8601-8602, 8605, 8608,8641-8679, 8690-8698, 8701-8702, 8704-8706 and 8725-8729. The official Air Ministry form listed a number of F Mk IIBs as having been converted from F Mk IAs. All F Mk IIA Merlin XII unless otherwise indicated.

P7280 Morris First Spitfire by Nuffield Organ. AMDP BDn 27-6-40 dvng trls with 7 lb int wt on elev cont syst, hand trls AST 25-10 DTD BDn 29-10 403S 17-7-41 457S 4-10 61 OTU 5-1-42 FACB 29-4 61 OTU 2-7-43 trls with blister hood Oct'43 comp trls with N3171 (Mk 1) cd Crickheath Farm nr Oswestry CE 15-9-44

P7281 Morris 6MU 17-6-40 612S 27-8 611S 27-8 41S 24-10 54S 22-2-41 616S 10-7 417S 26-1-42 15 OTU 15-2 57 OTU 30-7 CB 22-4-43 SOC 23-1-44

P7282 Morris 6MU 26-6-40 611S 22-8 41S 24-10 s/dn by bf109 P/O Draper inj C3 30-10 SOC 14-11

P7283 Morris 8MU 1-7-40 611S 26-8 41S 24-10 C2 ops 17-11 54S 12-2-41 234S 3-7 152S 28-10 8FTS 13-6-43 10 AGS 17-4-45 FTR ops 17-5-45 SOC 18-6

P7284 Morris 8MU 7-7-40 611S 26-8 41S 24-10 C2 ops 26-10 54S 22-2-41 308S 14-7 610S 11-9 3 Dl Flt cd/ldg Valley Aerodrome CE 24-11 SOC 5-12

P7285 Morris 8MU 1-7-40 266S 5-9 603S 7-10 FTR ops 8-10 F/O Kirkwood missing

P7286 Morris 9MU 13-7-40 152S 17-7 603S 17-10 s/dn by bf109 P/O Maxwell 27-10 AST BDn 16-1-41 trls with Rotol c/s prop Morris rad and int wt 234S 12-5 VA3-7 66S 31-7 152S 3-9 CAC ops 16-9 ASTE SOC 10-11

P7287 Morris 9MU 13-7-40 266S 6-9 603S 17-10 65S 29-6-41 122S 31-9 FACE 24-10 ASTM con to FVA M45 28-1-42 2USA 6-8 COAL 17-3-44 for con

P7288 Morris 9MU 15-7-40 266S 6-9 603S 29-10 FACB 10-1-41 111S 24-5 610S 8-9 340S 28-11 58 OTU 30-4-42 to 4409M 14SoTT 30-11-43

P7289 First Spit built at CBAF under Vickers management. 6MU 17-7-40 266S 6-9 603S 20-10 19S 7-9-41 33S 30-10 331S 20-2-42 CGS 8-12 wing strk grd cd Redhouse Farm nr Long Sutton Lincs 9-9-43 SOC 30-9 FH422.80

P7290 12MU 19-7-40 611S 14-8 dam by Do215 F/O Watkins safe 21-8 AST 421Flt 22-11 f/ldg Arlington after escort Wellington across Channel 15-1-41 AST AFDU Dux 23-3-42 53 OTU 24-12 RNAS 4-8-43

P7291 12MU 20-7-40 611S 14-8 FAC2 8-10 SAL 64S 2-3-41 des on grd by e/a 20-5 SOC 26-5

P7292 12MU 21-7-40 611S 14-8 dam e/a 21-8 74S 11-10 66S 30-11 609S 24-2-41 FTR after com Bf109 4-6 FH112.35

P7293 37MU 20-7-40 616S 26-2-41 130S 27-8 131S 21-12 53 OTU 2-3-43 form coll with P7826 cd CE nr Blyton Lincs 16-11

P7294 37MU 21-6-40 266S 6-9 603S 24-10 41S 6-4-41 145S 28-7 417S 8-1-42 266S 6-9 52 OTU 24-10 53 OTU 26-9-43 o/s ldg hit wall Kin L CB 26-6-44 CE 16-8

P7295 37MU 25-7-40 266S 6-9 603S 17-10 65S 12-8-41 61 OTU 31-10-42 hit mountain Cadair Bronwen Denbighs CE 14-12

P7296 37MU 25-7-40 266S 6-9 f/ld Little Bytham Sgt Goodwin safe 4-10 34S 14-3-41 64S 30-6 504S 29-11 57 OTU 27-3-42 SOC 8-3-45

P7297 37MU 27-7-40 266S 6-9 603S 17-10 602S 6-7-41 41S 6-8 33MU 18-11-41 con to FV M45 350S 17-12 North Stn Flt 23-3-42 61 OTU 2-6-44 SOC 21-11

P7298 6MU 30-6-40 611S 21-8 s/dn by Bf109 nr Croydon Sgt Sheppherd kld 11-9

P7299 6MU 30-6-40 612S 27-8 41S 25-10 54S 22-2-41 234S 3-7 19S 21-8 8MU 15-11 con to FV 66S 10-2-42 strk by P7304 while parked Porth CE 26-2

P7300 6MU 1-7-40 611S 21-8 41S 24-10 54S 22-2-41 s/dn by bf109 nr Maids dbf 3-3

P7301 6MU 1-7-40 611S 21-8 41S 7-11 e/fld cd Horn 19-11 19S 3-3-41 CRD BDn 8-8-41 HAL 8-3-42 F24 oblique camera for h/a Met photo BDn for trls 1687Flt 7-10-44

P7302 24MU 3-7-40 611S 14-8 41S 5-11 s/dn by Bf109 a/c aban dbf 20-2-41

P7303 24MU 26-7-40 611S 14-8 dam nr Downham Mrkt P/O Lund safe 21-8 dam by Bf110 W London C2 15-9 66S 5-10 C2 ops 11-10

P7304 24MU 28-7-40 611S 14-8 dam by Do17 nr Downham Mrkt P/O Brown safe 21-8 152S 5-3-41 166S 29-7 234S 12-8 66S 21-8 strk P7299 on grd Porth CB 61 OTU 24--43 strck air wall fly low 1-2 coll with P7444 cd nr High Ercall CE pilot kld 22-8

P7305 24MU 28-7-40 611S 14-8 dam ldg after comb Do17 over Mablethorpe Sgt Darling safe 21-8 AST 611S 23-8 strk obst ldg Dux P/O Lund safe 17-9 303S 5-3-41 609S 6-4 s/dn by Bf109 pilot kld ttl wrk 9-5 SOC FH75.35

P7306 24MU 28-7-40 74S 10-9 s/dn by Bf109 over Chatham ttl wrk 27-11 SOC 31-12 FH60.10

P7307 24MU 30-7-40 266S 7-10 603S 20-10 C2 ops 26-10 WAL 421Flt 30-12 65S 19-4-41 308S 21-7 154S 23-11 61 OTU 8-3-42 air coll with BM140 cd Hayes Middx CE 15-3 SOC 1-9 FH117.15

P7308 24MU 30-7-40 74S 10-9 54S 22-5-41 308S 12-6 71S 20-8 CB ops 27-8 ASTE con to FVA M45 1-9 133S 1-4-42 421S 16-4 164S 17-5 602S 10-9 61 OTU 21-7-43

P7309 24MU 3-8-40 260S 5-9 603S 17-10 s/dn over Brede Sussex 25-10 SOC 11-11

P7310 24MU 1-8-40 266S 6-9 74S 10-9 CAC ops 10-1-41 609S 15-5 41S 18-6 145S 28-7 417S 30-11 53 OTU 15-2-42 1TEU 17-7 SOC 16-8-44

P7311 24MU 1-8-40 266S 6-9 603S 17-10 FAC3 17-12 SOC 27-12

P7312 24MU 2-8-40 74S 12-9 FTR ops 2-11

P7313 24MU 2-8-40 266S 5-9 s/dn by Bf109 over Billericay P/O Roach aban a/c 11-9 First Mk II des in BoB

P7314 12MU 4-8-40 611S 14-8 dam by Do17 nr Mablethorpe Sgt Burt safe 21-8 41S 24-10 C2 ops 8-11 GAL 611S 28-2-41 308S 26-5 into Channel 5-7-42

P7315 12MU 6-8-40 266S 19-9 603S 17-10 FACB 17-12 AST 41S 8-5-41 145S 28-7 417S 5-12 53 OTU 22-2-43 MEA 6-11-44

P7316 12MU 6-8-40 74S 15-9 CAC ops 7-5-41 41S 14-6 145S 28-7 CB ops 17-9 19S 10-9 9MU 28-1-42 con to FV RNAS 884 Unit Mach 1-9 for use as train SOC 20-2-45

P7317 12MU 6-8-40 421Flt 1-11 66S 7-11 C2 ops 14-11 AST 234S 13-3-41 air coll over Channel with P7779 13-5 SOC FH87.35

P7318 48MU 8-8-40 19S 27-9 CE comb o/s ldg hit dis pen 12-1-41 AST 1401Flt 12-9 53 OTU 13-1-43 FACB on loan Ellisons Perry Barr B'ham 20-1-44 SOC 1-3-45

P7319 12MU 9-8-40 424Flt 3-11 C3 ops 11-11 AST 152S 22-4-41 CB ops 20-6 130S 27-8 AST 53 OTU 6-5-42 fire in flt a/c aban StA 24-9

P7320 9MU 10-8-40 611S f/ld nr Henlow Sgt Sheppherd safe 9-9 HAL 41S 30-3-41 CAC ops 3-4 145S 28-7 417S 5-12 53 OTU 15-4-42 CGS 14-12-43 SOC 2-11-44

P7350 was sold as scrap after the war to John Dale Co Ltd, who donated it the RAF. It was used in the Battle of Britain film and is extant as ZH of No.226 (Rhodesia) Squadron.

P7321 9MU 11-8-40 611S 21-8 s/dn by Bf109 f/ld nr Ken Sgt Levenson safe C2 11-9 HAL 65S 20-4-41 GAL 16-8 con to ASR(IIC) 277S 15-1-43 CE ops 2809 AST 16-8-44

P7322 9MU 11-8-40 611S 21-8 41S s/dn by Bf109 pilot aban a/c FTR 20-2-41

P7323 9MU 11-8-40 611S 21-8 s/dn by Do17 nr Kidderminster f/ld Crooksey Green Sgt Pattison kld 11-10 SOC 1-11

P7324 8MU 16-8-40 266S 5-9 603S 17-10 111S 25-5-41 AST 23-8 con to FVA M45 81S 4-1-42 165S 12-4 167S 29-5 521Met S 16-8 61 OTU 18-5-44 Recat E 22-8

P7325 9MU 14-8-40 266S 6-9 603S 17-10 C3 ops 25-10 GAL 41S 30-3-41 145S 28-7 19s 21-9 331S 6-11 FACB 16-11 SAL con to ASR(IIC) 57 OTU 22-6-43 277S 31-12 CE 25-7-44

P7326 8MU 15-8-40 611S 2-10 FTR ops 10-12 FH15.00

P7327 8MU 15-8-40 266S 5-9 603S 17-10 C2 ops 28-10 616S 19-5-41 FTR ops 25-6 FH113.55

P7328 8MU 16-8-40 603S 17-10 FAC2 24-10 ASTE 74S 11-3-41 FTR ops 27-3 FH88.55

P7329 8MU 17-8-40 74S 13-9 FTR after air coll with P7373 8-10 FH60.10

P7350 TOC 6MU 13-8-40 266S 603S 17-10 FACB 616S 10-4-41 SAL 5-8 CGS 27-4-42 FACB 4-2-43 AST sold J Dale Donated RAF Colerne. Used in BoB film G-AWIJ. Extant with BBMF, Coningsby.

P7351 6MU 16-8-40 421Flt 30-10 AST 25-2-41 91S 28-2 CB on test flight 7-3 91S i/sea ops 20-4

P7352 6MU 16-8-40 74S 13-9 234S 19-6-41 64S 30-6 403S 19-7 54S 4-8 131S 29-9 57 OTU 25-1-42 broke up after dive from 23,000ft cd nr Brunton CE 19-4-43

P7353 6MU 212-9-40 74S 212-10 41S 18-6-41 154S 14-8 417S 30-11 52 OTU 17-3-42 e/fld w/u ldg Brockhampton CB 15-7 WAL recat E 28-7

P7354 6MU 22-8-40 612S 27-8 611S 27-9 41S 24-10 510S 22-2-41 501S 9-8 504S 26-10 58 OTU 15-2-42 FACB 21-3 CGS 24-4-44 SOC 2-11-44

P7355 6MU 22-8-40 74S 13-9 C3 ops 20-10 ASTE 611S 21-2-41 dam by Bf109 15-4 AST w/u ldg C2 3-5 402S 14-7 403S 14-10 61 OTU 2-1-42 strk Oxford L9703 ldg Tatenhill CE 1-4-44 SOC 21-4 FH831.00

P7356 6MU 23-8-40 74S 14-9 611S 21-9 Stn Flt North 31-12-41 OTU 9-1-42 e/fld a/c aban cd nr Stafford 2-10-43

P7357 6MU 23-8-40 19S 26-9 FACB 24-2-41 GAL 331S 24-11 58 OTU 17-4-42 53 OTU 26-10-43 SOC 26-4-45 FH126.00

P7358 6MU 24-8-40 421Flt 2-12 C2 ops 27-12 AST 19S 15-3-41 504S 25-11 58 OTU 15-2-42 SAL 18-7 FAAC 30-7-43 FLS Mlfld 30-6-44

P7359 6MU 27-8-40 603S 7-11 64S 13-8-41 66S 3-9 19S 6-9 331S 2-11 58 OTU 4-5-42 FAAC 26-10 SAL 23-3-43 con to ASR(IIC) 377S 4-5 ASTE Recat B 28-5-44

P7360 8MU 26-8-40 74S 10-9 s/dn Bf109 F/O Ricalton kld C3 17-10 SOC 31-10

P7361 8MU 26-8-40 74S 10-9 C2 ops 8-11 610S 24-2-41 130S 19-6 FACB 3-8 306S 18-8 308S 11-12 315S 1-4-42 61 OTU 19-5 CB 31-5 57 OTU 3-12-44

P7362 8MU 29-8-40 74S 10-9 s/dn i/sea Sgt Ayers aban a/c kld 23-9 FH68.25

P7363 8MU 28-8-40 74S 10-9 C2 ops 14-12 AST 66S 6-7-41 std low alt cd nr Gull Rock Porth CE 20-3-42 SOC 31-3

P7364 8MU 29-8-40 74S 13-9 s/dn by Bf109 P/O Spurdie aban a/c 22-10 SOC 31-1-41 FH42.15

P7365 8MU 30-8-40 266S 6-9 603S 17-10 s/dn by Bf109 P/O Dewey kld 27-10

P7366 8MU 1-9-40 74S 10-9 FACE 5-3-41 AST 19S 4-9 331S 30-10 58 OTU 5-8-42 61 OTU 22-10 FACB 17-2-43 1 CRU con to ASR(IIC) 276S 5-5 SOC 25-7-44

P7367 8MU 1-9-40 74S 12-9 41S 18-6-41 145S 28-7 19S 10-9 CAC ops 14-9 53 OTU 17-1-42 FACE 14-8-44

P7368 8MU 1-9-40 74S 12-9 74S 10-9 C2 ops 27-10 GAL 611S 28-2-41 hit fence ldg Horn 13-3 AST 403S 14-7 54S 4-8 403S 25-8 457S 27-9 57 OTU 12-2-42 FACB 2-6 AFDU 21-12 dvd i/grd Hardwicke Cambs 2-2-44

P7369 8MU 1-9-40 611S 19-9 ldg acc Tern P/O Sutton safe C2 28-9 AST SOC 7-10

P7370 8MU 5-9-40 74S 10-9 s/dn by Bf109 over Maids Sgt Kirk aban a/c died later 20-10 SOC 31-10

P7371 8MU -6-9-40 611S 14-9 41S 24-10 54S 22-2-41 FTR on sweep 10-3

P7372 Hyderabad 8MU 6-9-40 19S 26-9 R-RH 19-12 121S 22-10-41 340S 11-11 53 OTU 20-4-42 FACB 16-5 air coll with P8193 nr Pontypool Glam CE 9-11 SOC 22-11

P7373 8MU 8-9-40 74S 13-9 FTR thought air coll with P7329 8-10

P7374 8MU 11-9-40 611S 29-9 485S SOC 30-11-44

P7375 8MU 11-9-40 611S 29-9 41S 24-10 s/dn by Bf109 nr Canterbury Sgt Garvey kld C3 30-10 SOC 12-11

P7376 8MU 8-9-40 611S 14-9 FAC2 1-10 SAL 72S 23-4-41 74S 9-7 350S 18-12 FACB 26-3-42 ASTH con to ASR(IIC) 277S 21-12 ASTH 23-5-44 39MU NEA 21-11 SOC 2-6-45

P7377 8MU 8-9-40 19S 29-9 C2 ops 8-11 HAL 91S 13-3-41 CB ops 22-4 19S 9-8 64S 22-11 58 OTU 17-4-42 SOC 20-8-45

P7378 12MU 9-9-40 421Flt 1-11 CAC ops 2-3-41 AST 91S 29-3 501S 12-5 ASTH 350S 17-12 58 OTU 13-2-42 53 OTU 31-1-43 coll with P8641 during emerg ldg Lland CE 4-4-43

P7379 12MU 10-9-40 19S 27-9 f/ld Roch Sgt McGregor safe 29-10 19S FTR after comb with Bf109 27-6-41

P7380 12MU 11-9-40 19S 26-9 234S 28-8-41 ASTH 9-10 52 OTU 12-5-42 61 OTU 24-2-43 e/fld cd f/ld Aldersey Cheshire CE SOC 18-7-43

P7381 12MU 12-9-40 19S 26-9 e/a C2 30-10 GAL 11-11 74S 13-4-41 FTR after comb Bf109 19-4 FH88.55

P7382 12MU 119-40 421Flt 3-11 501S 27-5-41 58 OTU DeH 27-7-42 FLS Mlfld 30-6-44 CFE SOC 26-3-45

P7383 12MU 13-9-40 421Flt 11-11 C2 ops 13-11 CRU 54S 17-3-41 FTR after comb 20-4

P7384 38MU 12-9-40 64S 16-11 19S 7-9-41 331S 6-11 58 OTU 17-4-42 CGS 18-12 tyre burst on t/o o/t CE 25-4-44

P7385 38MU 14-9-40 74S 24-10 C3 ops 29-10 GAL 303S 15-4-41 64S 7-8 611S 12-11 52 OTU 16-2-42 Digby 26-8-43 SOC 9-2-45

P7386 38MU 14-9-40 74S 24-10 s/dn nr Sandwich Kent a/c aban 14-11

P7387 39MU 14-9-40 603S 28-10 coll He111 both des Sgt Plant kld 21-11

P7388 39MU 14-9-40 603S 28-10 111S 24-5-41 123S 22-11 331S 5-2-42 58 OTU 17-4 CGS 2-9-44 5PAFU 5-1-45 SOC 28-6

P7389 39MU 15-9-40 603S 28-10 64S 24-7-41 611S 12-11 340S 28-12 53 OTU 17-4-42 CGS 8-12 HAL 22-2-44

P7420 6MU 16-9-40 19S 26-9 flew i/tree nr Boxford Sussex Sgt Roden kld 15-11 SOC 23-11 FH44.40

P7421 6MU 16-9-40 19S 26-9 f/ld after sweep 25-2-41 131S 11-10 57 OTU 4-5-42 CGS 9-12 CE 12-9-44

P7422 6MU 16-9-40 19S 26-9 AST 27-6-41 234S 24-8 ASTM 25-10 SOC 18-11

P7423 6MU 16-9-40 19S 26-9 s/dn by Bf109 at Chelmsford S/Lt Blake kld 29-10 SOC 31-10

P7424 6MU 16-9-40 66S 28-10 C3 ops 29-11 GAL 610S 5-4-41 130S 19-6 spun i/grd Rosemergy Morvah Cornwall dbf pilot kld 3-7 SOC 8-7.

P7425 6MU 19-9-40 19S 26-9 a/c aban cd Albury Herts CE 31-7-41 SOC

P7426 9MU 21-9-40 74S 24-9 s/dn by Bf109 over Maids Sgt Hilken inj aban a/c 20-10

P7427 9MU 19-9-40 19S 26-9 C2 ops 8-11 AST CAC ops 6-5-41 58 OTU 15-4-43 loss of cont a/c aban cd nr Dunfermline Fife CE 17-2-44 SOC 1-3 FH416.50

P7428 9MU 20-9-40 19S 26-9 C2 ops 8-11 74S 23-3-41 CAC 31-3 SOC 17-5 FH92.34

P7429 9MU 20-9-40 19S 26-9 FACE 24-3-41 SOC 25-3

P7430 9MU 21-9-40 19S 26-9 1CRU 23-6-41 71S 10-8 401S 12-9 154S 27-11 61 OTU cd f/ld nr Mostyn Flints CE 29-1-43 SOC

P7431 9MU 23-9-40 74S 11-10 s/dn by Bf109 P/O John kld 22-10 SOC 10-11

P7432 8MU 23-9-40 19S 26-9 FAC3 28-9 recat 2 610S 25-4-41 501S 6-8 504S 26-10 58 OTU 13-2-42 LMS 25-8-42 FLS 30-6-44 CE 17-8

P7433 8MU 23-9-40 66S 22-10 C2 ops 1CRU 19S 15-3-41 501S 24-5 504S 24-10 58 OTU 13-2-42 e/fld f/ld Aberuthven Perths 22-6

P7434 8MU 23-9-40 19S 26-9 308S 3-7-41 315S 21-7 610S 11-9 340S 28-1-42 OTU 7-4-42 MM 31-7 39MU NEA 21-11-44 SOC 1-6-48

P7435 8MU 23-9-40 19S 26-9 FAC2 28-10 WAL 65S 13-1-41 616S 20-2 a/c aban nr Hove FTR ops 25-6 FH158.00

P7436 37MU 25-9-40 603S 27-10 609S 15-5-41 FTR ops 21-5 FH39.15

P7437 37MU 25-9-40 66S 29-10 des on grd 20-5 ASTE 27-5 SOC 1-12

P7438 37MU 2-10-40 FA del flt SAL 245S 22-2-41 403S 6-9 457S 29-9 57 OTU 25-1-42 53 OTU strk by EP114 KinL CE 15-10-44

P7439 37MU 29-9-40 603S 25-10 s/dn by Bf109 F/O Goldsmith kld CE 27-10 SOC 14-11

P7440 8MU 29-9-40 66S 23-10 609S 24-2-41 FAAC 13-3 118S 6-6 501S 13-7 152S 31-7 HAL 26-9 CGS 15-8 1CRU 22-5-43 SFTS 14-9 SOC 18-6-45

P7441 8MU 30-9-40 66S 5-10 s/dn nr Ashford Kent C3 12-10 SOC 22-10 FH15.00

P7442 8MU 30-9-40 611S 13-10 145S 22-3-41 403S 22-7 54S 4-8 403S 25-8 154S 22-11 61 OTU 8-3-42 53 OTU 27-9 e/fld cd/ldg Water End Farm Coleby Glos 12-12 SOC 23-12

P7443 8MU 1-10-40 616S 12-10 41S 24-10 54S 24-2-41 FTR after comb Bf109 26-2 FH98.05

P7444 8MU 29-9-40 66S 5-10 dam ops 15-10 GAL 485S 2-7-41 312S 22-10 416S 22-12 61 OTU 2-4-42 air coll with P7304 lnd Rednal CAC 22-8-43 CGS 4-5-44 SOC 2-11

P7445 Amangabad 8MU 30-9-40 66S 5-10 dam ops 20-10 64S 16-1-41 HAL 29-4 457S i/sea off IoM 29-11 SOC 9-12

P7446 Guwbunga 8MU 29-9-40 66S 5-10 ldg acc West Mall Sgt Corbin safe 30-10 AST 222S 13-3-41 308S 28-6 130S 26-8 133S 25-10 134S 21-12 61 OTU 9-7-42 58 OTU 11-3-43 39MU NEA 21-11-44 SOC 22-3-45

P7447 8MU 29-940 66S 5-10 C2 ops 28-12 118S 12-4-41 AST 15-4 con to FVA M45 616S 25-6 412S 5-8 2USA S 1-8-42 5USA S 23-8 338S 8-11 349S 24-6-43 61 OTU 1-8 SOC 19-7-45

P7448 9MU 29-9-40 611S 11-10 f/ld Capel Surrey 7-12 AST 65S 30-3-41 comb bf109 cd/ldg Horn CB 15-4 234S 14-6 501S 12-7 152S 3-8 FACB 27-942 WAL 7-10 57 OTU a/c aban cd Alwick N'land CE 12-7

P7449 Bidar 9MU 2-10-40 603S 24-10 dam ops P/O Rafter kld 29-11 57 OTU 25-1-42 CAC 24-3

P7490 City of Coventry I 9MU 2-10-40 66S 24-10 609S 24-2-41 65S 29-8 122S 30-9 154S 5-12 SAL 24-1-42 con to ASR(IIC) 277S 9-1-43 SOC 2-6-44 sold J Dale

P7491 City of Coventry II 9MU 3-10-40 66S 24-10 air coll with P7492 over Edenbridge Kent 28-11 AST SOC 17-12 FH 20.05

P7492 City of Coventry III 9MU 2-10-40 66S 24-10 air coll with P7491 over Edenbridge Kent 28-11 C3 28-11 SOC 16-12 FH34.45

P7493 9MU 2-10-40 66S 24-10 e/a C2 10-11 1CRU 145S 22-2-41 air coll with P7737 over Tang dbf pilot kld 21-5 SOC 28-5 FH80.35

P7494 38MU 2-10-40 74S 23-10 cd/ldg C2 27-10 AST 611S 21-2-41 308S 1-6 610S 11-9 123S 31-12 CGS 1-4-42 53 OTU 23-6-43 SHAEF Com S 29-3-45 SOC 15-5

P7495 no record SOC 19-11-40

P7496 38MU 5-10-40 603S 25-10 dam e/a 8-11 64S 13-8-41 CGS 27-4-42 FAAC 24-6-42 SOC 24-6-44 FH822.00

P7497 12MU 7-10-40 66S 5-11 421Flt 24-11 SOC 9-1-41

P7498 12MU 7-10-40 421Flt 2-11 C2 ops 1-12 GAL 610S 21-3-41 510S 1-8 FACB 11-9 WAL conv to FVA M45 164S strk by L1031 on grd Skae CE 14-8-42 SOC 21-8

P7499 12MU 7-10-40 421Flt 2-11 C3 ops 27-11 SOC 15-1-41

P7500 6MU 7-10-40 66S 1-11 C2 ops 14-11 1CRU 19-11 64S 25-2-41 308S 3-7 FTR ops 17-7

P7501 6MU 7-10-40 74S 29-10 C2 ops 1-11 GAL 610S 26-2-41 cd after comb CE 8-3 AST 19S 9-8 234S 29-9 306S 13-10 308S 11-12 61 OTU 21-3-43 FAAC 27-12 ROS Vic 24-3-44

P7502 6MU 10-10-40 74S 29-10 602S 11-6-41 MMO 20-7 313S 26-8 457S 23-11 cd Vonby Farn IoM CE 5-12 SOC 12-12

P7503 6MU 10-10-40 421Flt 30-10 611S 19-3-41 308S 25-5 315S 16-7 306S 15-10 Stn Flt North 7-6-42 7PAFU 6-11-44 1CGS 18-2-445 strk bowser Pembrey CE 11-4 SOC 18-4

P7504 8MU 11-10-40 66S 21-10 dam by Bf109 14-2-41 AST 74S 9-7 53 OTU 19-5-42 air coll with P8592 nr Crowbridge Glam CE 5-7

P7505 8MU 10-10-40 66S 21-10 e/a C2 12-11 AST 91S 14-2-41 118S 6-5 403S 31-7 54S 4-8 AST 2-9 con to FVB M45 54S 1-5-42 133S 10-3 601S 10-4 164S 20-5 602S 10-9 P&PSM 21-10 fuel syst mods HAL 25-1-43 con to PRXIII M32 4S 30-12 SOC 28-3-45

P7506 8MU 14-10-40 74S 24-10 s/dn by Bf109 off Dung CE 12-3-41 SOC 22-3 FH91.15

P7507 9MU 11-10-40 41S 26-10 hit balloon cable cd nr Dagenham C3 1-11 SOC 11-11

P7508 9MU 16-10-40 41S 27-10 FACE 19-11 GAL 54S 22-2-41 234S 28-8 131S 3-10 61 OTU 6-1-42 SOC 5-8-44

P7509 9MU 12-10-40 603S 29-10 dam ops 5-11 AST 19S 17-1-41 234S 21-8 350S 18-12 52 OTU 24-3-42 cd into River Severn CE 23-7

P7520 6MU 13-10-40 66S 21-10 FTR after comb Bf109 11-2-41 FH43.40

P7521 6MU 13-10-40 66S 21-10 WAL 15-11 MHth for hand trls.Issued to 66S whose pilots complained of low left wing fly attitudes 14-2-41 609S 24-2 dam by bf109 24-4 AST CRD Farn 30-8 ails and rate of roll tests. Jan'42 tail deflection load hood lost during one trl. Flight measurements of ails hinge movements. Langley Mar'43 repeat ails trls. Total loss of stab on May 11 f/ld AST 24-5-44 7PAFU19-11 1AGS 18-2-45 10AGS 9-5 SOC 18-6

P7522 6MU 13-10-40 66S 21-10 R-RH 8-1-41 66S dam by Bf109 14-2 65S 4-4 Farn Aug '41 trls with F52 camera instal Loss of cont wngs broke off in dive ttl wrk nr Binbrook Lincs 13-9 SOC 30-9

P7523 6MU 16-10-40 74S 29-10 FTR ops 1-11 FH5.00

P7524 6MU 16-10-40 66S 28-1-42 CGS 30-9 e/fld f/ld o/t Holbeach Range Lincs 9-6-43 SOC 2-11-44 FH661.00

P7525 8MU 16-10-40 66S 30-10 GAL w/u ldg Croydon 29-11 SOC 10-1-41 BDn 18-1 hand and dive recovery trls

P7526 8MU 15-10-40 74S 24-10 s/dn by Bf109 Sgt Scott kld dbf 27-10 SOC 10-1-41

P7527 8MU 15-10-40 74S 24-10 AST 22-3-41 308S 27-7 57 OTU 22-10-42 13 OTU 17-6-44 SOC 13-10-44

P7528 8MU 15-10-40 603S 27-10 111S 25-5-41 FTR over France 19-8

P7529 8MU 15-10-40 603S 27-10 111S 25-5-41 403S 3-9 457S 4-10 57 OTU 24-5-42 FACB 3-12 WAL cd/ldg CB Esh 11-12 react E 24-12

P7530 37MU 15-10-40 65S 29-6-41 ASTH 1-9 CGS air coll with Wellington P9228 nr Laken CE 13-9 SOC 30-9

P7531 27MU 25-10-40 Farn tail deflection with various loads in dives 421Flt 8-11 91S 14-2-41 i/sea off Ramsgate 24-4 SOC 1-5

P7532 27MU 25-10-40 19S con to FVA M45 81S

P7533 15-10-40 66S 57 OTU a/c aban cd Parkside Birkenhead 14-10-42

P7534 37MU 15-10-40 421Flt 10-11 CE SOC 6-12

P7535 38MU 21-10-40 dvd i/grd after t/o Dux 22-2-41 SOC ME 17-3

P7536 38MU 21-10-40 74S 4-11 C2 ops 11-11 AST 611S 23-2-41 308S 25-5 FTR over France 2-7-42

P7537 38MU 21-10-40 74S 4-11 CE ops ttl wrk 7-5-41 AST SOC 28-5

P7538 6MU 24-10-40 66S 29-10 609S 24-2-41 dam C2 by Bf109 29-4 306S 12-8 303S 6-10 308S 11-12 315S 1-4-42 53 OTU 20-4 57 OTU 24-3-43 u/s w/u ldg strk fence Esh 14-8-44 CE 16-8

P7539 6MU 21-10-40 66S 24-10 s/dn by Bf109 Tunbridge Wells P/O Mathers kld 27-10 SOC 11-11

P7540 6MU 20-10-40 66S 29-10 609S 24-2-41 266S 14-6 312S 6-7 cd into Loch Doon Ayrs CE 25-10 SOC 2-11 FH21.25 wreck at Dumfries & Galloway Museum 1983

P7541 6MU 24-10-40 66S 29-10 dam by Bf109 14-2-41 SOC 1-3

P7542 8MU 21-10-40 74S 28-10 609S 11-3-41 616S 21-6 CB 18-7

P7543 8MU 21-10-40 603S 234S 52 OTU cd nr Babdown Farm CE 17-10-42

P7544 8MU 24-10-40 41S 5-11 WAL 30-11 266S 31-3-41 dam CB by Bf109 15-4 19S 27-7 1CRU 13-8 313S 8-10 417S 25-11 strk by P7983 while parked Charmy Dn CB 2-1-42 WAL SOC CE 4-4

P7522, a Farnborough trials Spitfire, lost both wings in a dive. These views show the wrecked wings and an accident inspector's view of the break up lines. It was being used for F 52 camera trials.

P7445 8MU 21-10-40 19S 2-11 C3 ops 5-11 SOC 23-11 FH3.35

P7546 8MU 24-10-40 603S 22-11 C2 ops 12-1-41 1CRU 21-1 303S 4-3 CB ops 20-4 No 1 Flt 7-9 dvdi/grd E Wretham CE 26-2-42 SOC

P7547 9MU 24-10-40 19S 1-11 FTR ops 21-7-41

P7548 9MU 24-10-40 41S 1-11 CB ops 1-1-41 AST 152S 3-3 234S 29-8 131S 24-9 57 OTU ADGB Com North 6-5-44 SOC 1-4-45

P7549 9MU 24-10-40 603S 57 OTU air coll with P7598 cd High Kinnoton Flint CE 16-7-42

P7550 9MU 25-10-40 603S 5-11 cd CE Grantshouse Berwicks 31-12 SOC 9-1-41

P7551 45MU 25-10-40 72S 14-5-41 74S 9-7 CE ops 26-11 SOC 29-11

P7552 45MU 1-11-40 flew i/grd in bad weather Nigg Ray Aberds Ce 17-1-41 SOC 27-1

P7553 45MU 1-11-40 611S 24-2-41 308S 26-5 74S 9-8 416S 23-12 58 OTU 1-9-42 53 OTU 26-7-43 f/ld cd nr KinL CB 22-4-44

P7554 39MU 29-10-40 234S 8-3-41 610S 7-9 61 OTU 11-12 58 OTU 23-7-42 FACE 27-5-44

P7555 39MU 29-10-40 64S 14-1-41 FTR after comb Bf109 13-3 SOC 30-3 FH42.45

P7556 39MU 29-10-40 222S 9-3-41 501S 7-6 30S 20-7 spun i/grd ops Porth CE 14-8 SOC 20-8

P7557 8MU 27-10-40 74S 8-11 C2 ops 14-11 AST 54S 3-4-41 152S 9-7 306S FACB 23-12 52 OTU 14-7-42 53 OTU 8-3-43 FACB 22-9 57 OTU 20-4-44 SOC 8-3-45

P7558 8MU 29-10-40 41S 10-11 1CRU 4-1-41 64S 19-5 74S 7-11 61 OTU 9-1-42 58 OTU 13-10 SAL 23-3-43 SFTS 10-7 SOC 20-12-44

P7559 8MU 29-10-40 74S 8-11 cd/ld after comb Eastbourne CB 24-2-41 AST 1-3 des by e/a on grd whilst under rep 20-5 SOC 26-5

P7560 38MU 25-10-40 19S 8-11 131S 1-10-41 cd Dale Mead Farm nr Marpur Hill Derbys a/c aban CE 22-11 SOC 5-12

P7561 38MU 25-10-40 74S 4-11 cd/ld Detling after comb Bf109 ttl wrk 10-1-41 SOC 18-1

P7562 38MU 28-10-40 64S 16-1-41 cd C3 6-3 AST 54S 18-5 452S 15-6 FTR ops 11-6

P7563 9MU 8-11-40 91S 22-2 501S 24-5-41 135S 28-10 134S 31-12 53 OTU 13-2-42 e/fld f/ld nr Llanwit Glam CB 30-5

P7564 9MU 29-10-40 603S 11-12 111S 25-5-41 CAC ops 27-6 401S 12-9 570 OTU 5-5-42 e/fld cd/ld Beeches Farm nr Maw CE 21-8

P7565 9MU 2-11-40 91S 14-1-41 cd after comb ttl wrk CE 4-4 SOC 13-4

P7566 9MU 2-11-40 19S 10-11 C2 ops 28-11 SAL 603S 31-5-41 485S 9-6 121S 19-10 340S 11-12 58 OTU 12-4-42 FLS 30-6-44 CE 13-8

P7567 12MU 1-11-40 303S 4-3-41 dam by Bf109 13-4 452S 18-5 312S 10-10 RAF Stn Ayr 29-12 57 OTU 24-5-42 SFTS 20-10-43 PAFU 23-11-44 SOC 11-5-45

P7568 12MU 9-11-40 66S 17-11 64S FTR after comb Bf109 11-2-41 FH36.10

P7569 12MU 2-11-40 234S 27-3-41 FTR ops 17-6 FH113.10

P7590 12MU 1-11-40 41S 16-11 CB ops 10-1-41 1CRU 19-1 303S 4-3 452S 4-6 FTR ops 9-8

P7591 12MU 1-11-40 74S 17-11 41S 5-6-41 313S 21-8 AFDU 25-4-42 e/fld f/ld strk pole nr Sessay Stn Yorks CE 27-1-44

P7592 12MU 1-11-40 C2 ops 27-12 AST 23-3-41 308S 27-7 123S 16-9 53 OTU 19-7-42 FACB 6-8 SAL RAF North 22-8-43

P7593 12MU 1-11-40 421Flt 17-11 4FPP dvdi/grd 12.30hr after stbd wng & tailplane broke away Sgt White kld nr Leek Cheshire CE 17-11

P7594 12MU 1-11-40 266S 28-3-41 485S 28-3 4FPP hit high grd on del flt Kirkbridge West M 28-3 FTR ops 7-8 SOC 12-8

P7595 12MU 1-11-40 610S 25-2-41 130S 27-6 411S 27-7 121S 19-10 340S 23-11 53 OTU 25-4-42 CRD VA 2-12-44 CE 27-12

P7596 12MU 1-11-40 610S 25-2-41 FTR ops 5-3

P7597 12MU 1-11-40 603S 17-11 FACE 16-2-41 SOC 28-2 FH65.30

P7598 37MU 8-11-40 421Flt 29-12 e/a CB 8-2-41 GAL 609S 16-5 111S 16-6 131S 19-10 57 OTU 25-1-42 air coll with P7649 cd High Kinnoton Flints CE 16-7

P7599 37MU 1-11-40 234S 14-3-41 501S 25-7 504S 26-10 58 OTU 13-2-42 FAAC 10-1-44 SOC 26-1-45

P7600 37MU 9-11-40 66S 26-11 609S 24-2-41 cd/ld WestM 13-5 SOC

P7601 37MU 9-11-40 421Flt 29-12 602S 29-5-41 313S 13-8 154S 7-2-42 61 OTU 8-3-42 57 OTU 15-10-43 SOC 30-12-44

P7602 37MU 9-11-40 66S 26-11 dam by Bf109 14-2-41 609S 24-2 dam C2 by bf109 f/ld Dover 16-5 313S 21-8 417S 25-11 53 OTU 15-2-42 57 OTU 1-7-43 39MU NEA 23-11-44 SOC 1-6-45

P7603 37MU 9-11-40 145S 23-2-41 FACB 28-4 266S 5-7 411S 1-8 121S 21-10 340S 23-11 CGS 28-4-42 5PAFU 2-10 SFTS 13-6-43 SOC 28-6-45

P7604 38MU 8-11-40 421Flt 5-12 64S 14-3-41 f/ld C2 15-3 SAL 64S 17-10 611S 12-11 52 OTU 16-2-42 CGS 27-4-44 SOC 2-11

P7605 38MU 8-11-40 64S 16-1-41 145S 16-3 485S 1-6 610S 5-10 52 OTU 28-1-42 9MU 2-12 con to ASR(IIC) 277S 16-1-43 ASTM 16-5-44

P7606 38MU 8-11-40 611S 21-1-41 1CRU 12-5 12-5 SOC 12-5 cancel 315S 14-7 308S 14-7 CE ops 29-8

P7607 38MU 8-11-40 611S 21-2-41 f/ld after Channel recce 13-5 66S 9-7 130S 17-7 52 OTU 20-2-43 dvdi/grd nr Gilfach Goch Glam CE 23-4-43

P7608 45MU 12-11-40 603S 3-2-41 111S 25-5 FACB 27-5-42 57 OTU 22-6-43 61 OTU 14-3-44 air coll with P8079 cd Marsbrook Salop CE 27-4

P7609 45MU 12-11-40 611S 25-2-41 dam C2 by Bf109 15-4 64S 15-8 61 OTU 27-6-42 f/ld cd Bagley Marsh Salop 1-2-43 recat E 21-7

P7610 6MU 9-11-40 41S 19-11 54S 22-2-41 cd i/hangar 3-4 71S 10-8 401S 19-9 302S 13-10 417S 4-1-42 58 OTU 6-5 CAC ops 11-7-43 ROS cd/ldg Bal Br CE 24-9

P7611 6MU 9-11-40 421Flt 11-12 266S 26-3-41 457S 27-9 61 OTU 22-12 u/c clpse taxy Rednal CB 17-7-44 ASTE recat SOC 16-8

P7612 6MU 15-11-40 41S 3-1-41 54S 22-4 234S 3-7 231S 6-9 152S 5-12 57 OTU 8-5-42 SOC 30-12-44

P7613 6MU 9-11-40 610S 10-3-41 308S 14-7 315S 16-7 610S 11-9 350S 19-12 Mand S Mull 12-3-43 FAAC 23-10 LMS Barasssie 28-6-44 5PAFU 5-12 SOC 28-6-45

P7614 9MU 5-11-40 74S 1-12 AST 21-3-41 SOC 30-4 FH48.20

P7615 9MU 1-11-40 91S 3-2-41 e/a CAC 8-2 AST 91S 16-4 CAC ops dbf 26-4 AST SOC 9-5

P7616 9MU 5-11-40 91S 14-1-41 609S 23-5 616S 20-6 234S 4-7 19S 13-9 331S 26-11 58 OTU 7-4-42 61 OTU 30-9 276S 28-4-43 FAAC 21-10 ASTM 23-5-44 recat E 25-7

P7617 9MU 5-11-40 19S 22-11 a/c aban cd Claxton Norfork 21-3-41

P7618 41S 54S 19S s/dn f/ld 12-1-41 74S FTR ops 24-2

P7619 24MU 8-11-40 41S 1-12 19S 1-12 234S 21-8-41 1CRU 25-9 con to FVA M45 1402Flt 23-9-42 61 OTU 7-9-43 FACB 3-10 ATA WW 13-5-44 PAL 14-9-45 SOC 21-9

P7620 6MU 11-11-40 19S 19-11 234S 21-8-41 350S 26-1-42 52 OTU 26-3 58 OTU 31-12 e/fld w/u ldg Beechhall Farm nr Stirling 21-7-43 CE SOC FH770.35

P7621 37MU 13-11-40 145S 21-2-41 609S 23-5 485S 1-6 152S 13-6 65S 24-8 122S 1-10 131S 14-10 1CRU 6-11 CGS 20-2-42 SOC 2-11-44 FH965.00

P7622 37MU 10-11-40 FACB 15-1-41 AST 616S 21-12 66S 24-3 118S 19-4 403S 19-4 403S 19-7 54S 408 122S 17-9 154S 8-12 61 OTU 3-3-42 dvdi/grd nr Bettisfield Salop CE dbf 14-6

P7623 37MU 9-11-40 74S 11-12 602S 11-6-41 412S 22-7 61 OTU 15-12 58 OTU 6-3-43 SOC 23-11-44

P7624 37MU 11-11-40 41S 19-11 46S 11-10 145S 29-10 cd during aero nr Catt CE 4-11 SOC 9-11

P7625 Guildford I 38MU 11-11-40 66S 20-11 609S 24-2-41 1CRU 5-9 331S 6-1-42 54S 15-2 58 OTU 1-9 57 OTU 27-3-43 FACE 26-4-44

P7626 38MU 14-11-40 64S 16-1-41 f/ld nr Shepherds Well C2 2-2 AST 452S 17-7 485S 28-7 65S 18-8 122S 30-9 154S 5-12 57 OTU 9-4-43 SOC 8-5-46

P7627 38MU 14-11-40 91S 15-2-41 501S 17-5 133S 28-10 61 OTU 19-4-43 CB 31-5 5PAFU 23-11-44 SOC 28-6-45

P7628 45MU 13-11-40 511S 28-2-41 308S 26-5 HAL 29-6 504S 20-11 dam ops CB 7-12 S&H 16-12 CGS 6-12-42 39MU 9-2-43 con to ASR(IIC) 277S 19-4 CB ops 18-10 AST CGS 6-5-44 CE 2-11

P7629 45MU 13-11-40 611S 2-3-41 308S 26-5 AST 15-7 con to FV M45 4S 52PGP S&H 7-8 61 OTU 21-6-43 FAAC 3-2-44

P7661 6MU 14-11-40 DGRD BDn 2-1-41 effect of triple ejector flame damper exhaust on speed. Fitt Hurricane Rotol Jablo prop for Merlin XX. Slight deterioration in climb at H/A improved ceiling T/O improved. Farn July'41 perf trls of same, plus fuel syst trls. R-RH 8-1-42 trls wilth Rotol metal and Jablo four blade props. M47 instal with R-R version of Bendix-Stromberg Su carb with fuel injection. BDn 24-10 perf and fuel cons tests with same. 23-11 continuation of tests with trop eng intake FACB 20-12-43 61 OTU 27-3-44 FAAC 31-3 ROS HAL 28-7 recat E. Con to FVA standard, probably when M47 instal

P7662 6MU 15-11-40 65S 2-2-41 616S 26-2 CE ops 10-3 SOC 21-3 FH32.40

P7663 6MU 16-11-40 64S 28-2-41 std ldg South C3 8-3 1CRU 19-3 234S 19-6 130S 21-7 152S 25-8 CAC 17-4-42 53 OTU 26-9 AST 30-3-43 u/s ldg Hibald CB 15-1-44 CE ops 208

P7664 6MU 19-11-40 421Flt 1-12 501S 24-5-41 FACE 1-8 SOC 9-8

P7665 6MU 16-11-40 65S 12-1-41 FTR after comb bf109 5-2

P7666 Observer Corps 8MU 15-11-40 41S 21-11 54S FB-2 22-2-41 s/dn by Bf109 a/c aban 20-4

P7667 8MU 15-11-40 74S 5-12 65S 29-8-41 122S 10-10 131S 14-10 61 OTU 5-1-42 53 OTU 8-11-43 e/fld f/ld nr Faldingworth CB 15-4-44 recat E 27-8

P7668 8MU 16-11-40 66S 29-11 609S 26-2-41 FACB 30-3 GAL 19S 28-6 133S 18-11 134S 31-12 58 OTU 13-10-42 CGS 30-4-44 SOC 1-6-45

P7669 8MU 23-11-40 66S 30-11 609S 11-2-41 FTR after comb Bf109 29-4 FH105.15

P7670 8MU 21-11-40 66S 29-11 dam by Bf109 cd Mans 15-2-41 AST 111S 26-6 SAL 25-12 SOC 2-11-44 FH682.00

P7671 8MU 21-11-40 66S 30-11 FAAC 14-3-41 152S 13-6 610S 7-9 cd Winfield Farm nr Driffield Yorks CE 27-10 SOC 30-10

P7672 9MU 20-11-40 91S 14-1-41 CAC ops 21-1 AST 501S 12-6 306S 15-10 2USA 1-8-43 5USA 22-8 FAAC 11-2-44 61 OTU 18-3 FACB 7-4 ASTE 14-4

P7673 9MU 11-10-40 310S 9-11 416S 5-10 1CRU 18-12 con to ASR(IIC) Alp'42 277S 14-1-43 FAAC 31-3-44 7PAFU 6-11 1AGS 18-2-45 10AGS SOC 20-6

P7674 9MU 20-11-40 91S 14-1-41 FACB17-1 1CRU 8-3 602S 28-5 FACB 6-6 485S 28-7 SAL 31-12 detatched to R-RH 26-6-42 for instal of R-R exp two-stroke diesel eng (PI-26) no further knowledge 61 OTU 26-7 58 OTU 10-11-43

P7675 9MU 7-11-40 91S 14-1-41 CB ops 25-2 AST 4-3 308S 15-7 315S 16-7 266S 2-9 123S 20-9 58 OTU 8-5-42 cd Thornhill Stirlings taking evasive action against 'jumper' CE 16-5

P7676 9MU 22-11-40 91S 14-1-41 CB ops 26-2 MMOx 266S 5-7 123S 30-9 52 OTU 30-6-42 cd into River Severn CE 11-9

P7677 9MU 23-11-40 91S 14-1-31 502S 17-5 CGS 28-11-42 air coll with Wellington N2865 cd nr Huntingdon CE 10-4-43 SOC FH331.55

P7678 12MU 24-11-40 64S 16-1-41 FAAC 17-5 SAL CGS 20-2-42 dvdi/grd nr Wisbech, Cambs CE9-4-43 FH510-15

P7679 12MU 22-11-40 610S 25-2-41 130S 27-6 411S 27-7 i/sea ops 13-10 SOC

P7680 12MU 22-11-40 19S 26-3-41 152S 2-7 132S 21-8 FTR ops 24-10

P7681 12MU 22-11-40 222S 20-3-41 501S 23-6 53 OTU 20-2-43 FAAC 23-2-44 1CRU 7-3-44 HQ TTCF 24-6 FAAC 8-7 SOC 8-3-45

P7682 12MU 22-11-40 222S 13-3-41 452S 27-5 FTR ops 9-8 SOC 10-8

P7683 Londonderry 12MU 24-11-40 603S 22-12 111S 24-5-41 123S 25-11 58 OTU 12-3-42 53 OTU 24-9 58 OTU 7-7-43 air coll with P8387 cd Hammering Mere Farm CE 19-8 SOC 31-8 FH744.05

P7684 Belfast 24MU 23-11-40 610S 26-2-41 FTR ops 15-4

P7685 Marlandie 24MU 24-11-40 610S 26-2 flew i/hill in bad weather nr Westdean SussexCE 22-3 SOC 31-3

P7686 24MU 24-11-40 19S 1-12 603S 6-12 FAC2 21-12 AST 152S 3-3-41 266S 5-7 1CRU 9-9 conv to FVA M45 2USA 22-5-42 332S 8-11 61 OTU 7-12-44 SOC 19-7-45

P78687 24MU 24-11-40 41S 6-4-41 145S 28-7 417S 5-12 53 OTU 19-2-42 61 OTU 14-8 53 OTU 29-6-44 SOC 23-11

P7688 24MU 24-11-40 41S 5-4-41 403S 10-9 131S 1-10 61 OTU 5-1-42 57 OTU 15-8 ADGB 21-4-44 CE SOC 26-12-45

P7689 24MU 29-11-40 41S 9-2-41 54S 22-2 a/e aban cd nr Maids CE 12-3-SOC 22-3

P7690 38MU 26-11-40 64S 16-1-41 f/ld nr Edinburgh C2 2-2 AST 65S 30-3 504S 12-12 58 OTU 15-2-42 DeH 26-7 AFDU 12-12 1687DDF 5-3-44

P7691 38MU 29-11-40 609S 24-2-41 CB ops 26-2 AST 56S 18-5 66S 18-5 130S 20-7 152S 15-8 FTR nr Rotterdam Holland 28-8 FH99.10

P7692 38MU 27-11-40 74S 1-2-41 CB ops 11-2 485S 21-6 CAC ops 24-7 CAC ops 24-7 603S 29-9 315S 24-11 81S 22-12 164S 26-6-42 602S 10-9 82Grp USA 12-11 61 OTU 1-6-43 flew into target Prestatyn Bridge Flints CE 26-7

P7693 38MU 26-11-40 91S 15-2-41 C3 ops 12-3 AST 19S 24-7 FTR ops 12-8

P7694 38MU 26-11-40 65S 2-2-41 616S 26-2 411S 1-9 53 OTU 26-2-42 FAAC 9-4 FAAC 5-6 ROS 39MU NEA 1-10 1-10-44 ASTH 3-5-45

P7695 38MU 29-11-40 64S 16-1-41 131S 3-11 61 OTU 5-1-42 FACB 16-10 SAL 1TEU 17-6-44 5(P)AFU 6-11 e/fld on app hit obst short of runway Tern CE 5-4-45 SOC 18-6

P7696 FIIB 45MU 28-11-40 611S 26-2-41 308S 26-5 234S 27-9 457S 27-9 57 OTU 10-1-42 FACB 31-3-43 SAL 5(P) AFU 23-11-44 cd on ldg Tern CB 16-3-45 recat E SOC 7-4

P7697 Zanzibar I 45MU 4-12-40 222S 14-3-41 485S 31-5 CB ops 20-6 AST 65S 12-8 FTR ops 21-8 SOC 5-9

P7698 Zanzibar II 45MU 29-11-40 611S 28-2-41 308S 26-5 416S 22-12 58 OTU 4-5-42 FACE 3-9-43 recat B 11-9 57 OTU 2-6-44

P7699 Zanzibar III 45MU 28-11-40 SAL 29-11 222S 14-3-41 s/dn by enemy intruder night of 3/4-5 pilot kld dbf SOC 13-5

P7730 Pemba I 6MU 2-12-40 65S 8-2-41 616S 26-2 FTR ops 21-6 FH161.25

P7731 Pemba II 6MU 2-12-40 421Flt 3-1-41 501S 24-5 FTR ops 6-8 FH181.25

P7732 Rowley Regis 6MU 7-12-40 65S 12-1-41 616S 26-2 1CRU 21-5 19S 7-9 331S 8-11 FACE 11-4-42 SOC 5-6 SAL 21-2-43 con to FV M45 58 OTU 13-3 6MU 31-12 con to ASR(IIC) 276S 18-1-44 Farn 23-11 air cleaner trls EA and Hamble for hand trls Feb to June '45 SOC 5-6

P7733 Guildford II 6MU 4-12-40 65S 12-1-41 FTR after comb Bf109 5-2

P7734 Gillingham 6MU 4-12-40 66S 14-2-41 609S 24-2 dam C2 by Bf109 8-5 1CRU 9-5 dam ops 21-5 71S 10-8 504S 3-11 58 OTU 15-2-42 FACB 18-3 SAL 31-3 con to ASR(IIC) May '44 277S 18-12 HAL 20-6-44 SOC 18-8

P7735 Fairwarp 6MU 21-12-40 421Flt 3-1-41 91S des on grd Hawk by Bf109 4-2 SOC 10-2

P7736 Cambridgeshire 8MU 7-12-40 65S 12-1-41 616S 26-2 FTR ops 24-4 FH70.53

P7737 Cambrdigeshire Workshop 8MU 5-12-40 610S 17-12 FAC2 19-12 AST 145S 28-3-41 air coll with P7493 over Tang pilot kld 21-5 SOC 29-5 FH42.50

P7738 City of Nottingham 8MU 2-12-40 41S 12-12 54S 22-2-41 dam C1 by AA fire 17-4 AST 71S 12-8 401S 12-9 316S 13-10 306S 12-12 52 OTU 23-2-42 ADGB CS e/fld w/u ldg New House Farm Denham Middx CE 5-9-44

P7739 Eric 8MU 8-12-40 41S 24-12 54S f/ld West M 25-2-41 AST 56S 18-5 66S 18-5 152S 29-10 154S 9-12 58 OTU 7-6-42 57 OTU 23-12 CGS 20-9-43 CE 2-11-44

P7740 Bankline 8MU 5-12-40 74S 28-12 hit wind sock ldg Mans 21-4-41 AST 29-4

P7741 Fashion Flyer 8MU 7-12-40 74S 28-12 FTR after comb Bf109 2-2-41 FH8.50

P7742 N.E.M. 9MU 7-12-40 603S 17-5-41 111S 24-5 145S 29-9 61 OTU 11-12 53 OTU 23-9-42 61 OTU 20-3-44 SOC 20-11

P7743 Brentwood 9MU 7-12-40 66S 21-3-41 118S 9-4 403S 23-7 54S 4-8 457S 28-10 61 OTU 21-12 cd f/ld Llandevemmy Wales CB 13-2-42 AST recat E 20-5

P7744 Bow Street Home Guard 9MU 7-12-40 66S 18-3-41 118S 9-4 403S 19-7 54S 4-8 122S 15-9 74S 22-11 350S 4-1-42 57 OTU 15-5 61 OTU 2-2-43 57 OTU 26-6 FACB 22-7 SOC 28-4-45

P7745 HRH The Nawab of Bahawalpur 9MU 7-12-40 66S 18-3-41 118S 9-4 313S 1-10 306S 6-11 308S 11-12 1CRU 18-1-42 58 OTU 27-7 FLS 30-6-44

P7746 City of Bradford I 9MU 7-12-40 303S 4-3-41 403S 14-7 54S 4-8 403S 25-8 131S 2-10 cd in snowstorm The Wrekin Salop CE pilot kld 4-12 SOC 30-12

P7747 City of Bradford II 12MU 8-12-40 64S 16-1-41 ldg coll with R7204 Drem 19-6 SAL 417S 28-1-42 53 OTU 19-2 head on coll with Master DL559 Llan CE 14-1-43 recat B AST 19-2 CB 23-1-44

P7748 City of Bradford III 12MU 7-12-40 64S 16-1-41 out of fuel f/ld Faversham C2 2-2 AST CE ops 15-4 recat B 66S 11-5 130S 21-7 152S 10-10 58 OTU 13-10-42 coll with Lysanders P1620 & P1665 on t/o Bal Br CE 31-5-43

P7749 CB City of Bradford IV 12MU 8-12-40 603S 22-12 111S 24-5-41 306S 28-10 cd in circuit bad weather nr S Gate dbf CE 5-12 SOC 13-12

P7750 CB City of Bradford V 12MU 7-12-40 603S 31-12 111S 24-5-41 air coll with P7848 cd CE 23-7 SOC 1-8

P7751 CB City of Bradford VI 12MU 7-12-40 64S 16-1-41 dam C2 comb with Ju88 9-2 C3 ops cd Hawk 14-2 AST 72S 14-5 74S 9-7 u/s ldg hit pillbox Ack CE 9-9 SOC 15-9

P7752 CB The Warden of London 12MU 9-12-40 65S 14-1-41 C2 comb Ju88 19-1 GAL 610S 26-2 FTR ops 5-3

P7753 CB Pampero I 24MU 11-12-40 65S 14-1-41 606S 26-2 CE ops 5-5 SOC 13-5 FH93.25

P7754 CB Pampero II 24MU 9-12-40 65S 13-1-41 616S 26-2 19S 4-9 331S 2-11 CGS 24-2-42 53 OTU 13-1-43 SOC 25-9-44

P7755 CB Pampero III 24MU 9-12-40 610S 26-2-41 130S 27-6 41S 22-7 FTR on train flt presume i/sea off Grimsby 29-7 SOC 20-8

P7756 CB Pampero IV 37MU 10-12-40 54S 13-3-41 403S 14-7 457S 27-9 PIGTW CGS 25-2-42 CE 19-11-44

P7757 Sayles 37MU 10-12-40 234S 14-3-41 66S 9-7 AST 15-9 con to FV M45 61 OTU 15-1-43 spun off turning climb on t/o Mount Br cd i/coppice CE 12-2-43 SOC 23-2 FH289.55

P7758 37MU 10-12-40 145S 21-2-41 485S 1-6 cd during aero Lecon dbf CD 18-6 SOC 23-6

P7759 37MU 10-12-40 65S 15-1-41 616S 26-2 24S 11-7 412S 21-7 310S 21-10 231S 28-12 dvd i/sea off Brough Head Orkneys 16-3-42

P7770 37MU 8-12-40 64S 6-2-41 611S 12-11 58 OTU 25-7-42 eng fire on start after refuelling CE 14-8 SOC

P7771 37MU 10-12-40 616S 18-3-41 1CRU 26-6 19S 30-7 FTR ops 6-8

P7772 37MU 11-12-40 64S 2-2-41 611S 12-11 52 OTU 23-2-42 FAAC 29-3 DeH 28-3 Mar Cam 10-10-45 SOC 17-10

P7773 37MU 10-12-40 145S 21-2-41 485S 1-6 FTR ops 16-7 SOC 31-7

P7774 38MU 10-12-40 611S 21-12 FTR after comb bf109 28-4-41

P7775 38MU 15-12-40 610S 26-2-41 64S 1-8 611S 12-11 CB ops 29-1-42 SAL 13-2 con to ASR(IIC) 277S 29-12 1696 Flt 3-10-44 39MU NEA 7-12

P7776 38MU 15-12-40 611S 21-2-41 strk Hurricane ldg 16-5 71S 10-8 403S 4-9 459S 29-9 FACB 16-10 58 OTU 5-6-42 air coll with P8679 nr Dunfermline Fife CD 5-6

P7777 38MU 2-1-41 610S 26-2 412S 21-7 316S 21-10 416S 5-12 61 OTU 20-3-43 FACB 13-8 1CRU 19-8 SOC 30-12-44

P7778 39MU 3-1-41 64S 14-1 FTR after sweep 23-2 FH21.00

P7779 39MU 11-12-40 234S 8-2-41 air coll with P7317 over Channel 13-5 FH70.15

P7780 39MU 22-12-40 222S 9-3-41 steep dive from cloud disin in air pilot kld 15.07hr nr Southborough Norfolk 3-4 SOC 13-4

P7781 39MU 22-12-40 64S 14-1-41 417S 10-1-42 53 OTU 15-2-43 i/sea off St Donats Glam 21-5

P7782 45MU 12-12-40 74S 23-3-41 602S 11-6 412S 22-8 310S 21-10 416S 16-2-42 53 OTU 30-7 CGS 23-4-44 SOC 20-4-45

P7783 45MU 16-12-40 91S 18-3-41 CE ops 4-4 SOC 14-4

P7784 45MU 16-12-40 64S 23-3-41 FTR ops 9-4 FH35.20

P7785 45MU 19-12-40 609S 23-2-41 s/dn by Bf109 Hawk pilot kld 27-3 SOC 1-4

P7786 12MU 16-12-40 303S 4-3-41 452S 21-5 313S 14-8 331S 30-10 58 OTU 28-3-42 RNAS 7-8 FAAC 13-10 SOC 23-11-44

P7787 12MU 16-12-40 234S 14-3-41 66S 8-7 FTR ops 12-8

P7788 12MU 16-12-40 222S 13-3-41 485S 31-5 FTR ops 12-8

P7789 12MU 16-12-40 303S 4-3-41 452S 18-5 FACB 23-7-42 S&H con to FVA M45 52 OTU 3-9-43 61 OTU 4-2-44 PAL 25-9-45 SOC 27-9

P7810 9MU 4-2-41 152S 4-3 130S 26-8 350S 31-1-42 Stn Flt North 23-3 SOC 20-12-44

P7811 6MU 24-12-40 64S 16-2-41 cd/ldg CB 13-3 AST 452S 14-7 121S 22-10 340S 11-11 SOC 23-12

P7812 6MU 21-12-40 65S 8-2-41 616S 26-2 i/sea ops 21-4 SOC 2-5 FH70.40

P7813 6MU 21-12-40 19S 21-2-41 s/dn by Bf109 27-6 SOC 30-6

P7814 8MU 16-12-40 65S 12-1-41 616S 26-2 457S 30-9 57 OTU 2-4-42 FACB 19-8-43 61 OTU 18-3-44 PAL 2-10-45

P7815 Wilfrun 8MU 24-12-40 65S 1-2-41 CB ops 17-2 VA 27-2 616S 24-6 CE ops cd f/ld nr Bacton Norfolk 26-6 SOC 4-7 FH7.35

P7816 8MU 16-12-40 41S 6-2-41 54S 22-2 cd nr Ashford Kent 24-2 SOC 1-3

P7817 8MU 16-12-40 611S 24-2-41 FA 15-2 SOC 19-3

P7818 9MU 20-12-40 41S 24-2-41 54S 25-2 CAC ops 30-3 AST 602S 15-7 71S 6-8 403S 4-9 457S 29-9 FACB 23-10 SAL 29-10 12MU 14-1-42 con to ASR(IIC) CGS 24-2 277S 30-1-43 CB 19-9 CE 8-11

P7819 9MU 20-12-40 303S 4-3-41 s/dn by Bf109 16-4 SOC 1-5

P7820 Parganus 9MU 30-12-40 91S 14-1-41 222S 7-5 485S 31-5 64S 20-8 416S 19-12 FACB 19-3-42 SAL 57 OTU 10-10 CB 27-7-43 53 OTU 10-11 air coll with Wellington BJ819 cd Sturton Lincs CE 22-5-44 2MPRD 29-5

P7821 9MU 3-1-41 303S 4-3 CB ops cd/ldg Hawk 10-3 AST 152S 20-6 66S 16-7 i/sea ops 20-8 SOC 28-8

P7822 12MU 31-12-40 145S 22-2-41 485S 1-6 19S 25-9 331S 30-10 58 OTU 4-4-42 53 OTU 9-1-43 air coll with X4067 i/sea nr St A 15-2 SOC 9-3

P7823 Down 12MU 24-12-40 504S 6-11-41 152S 31-12 dvd i/grd nr Lurgan Co Down CB 7-1-42

P7824 12MU 23-12-40 603S 22-2-41 CB ops 16-5 111S 24-5 s/dn over France 19-8 SOC 20-8

P7825 12MU 28-12-40 145S 24-2-41 403S 15-7 cd nr Csfd Salop dbf 30-7 SOC 5-8

P7826 Sind I 24MU 4-1-41 65S 6-4 122S 30-9 74S 4-10 350S 28-11 52 OTU 24-4-42 53 OTU air coll with P7293 CE KinL 16-11

P7827 Sind II 24MU 1-1-41 65S 14-1 616S 26-2 Farn Apl '41 AST 616S 28-6 411S 17-7 74S 4-10 121S 19-10 340S 23-11 53 OTU 7-4-42 strk by R6621 while parked CE 2-5-43

P7828 Antrim 24MU 30-12-40 65S 13-1-41 616S 26-2 FACB 7-7 GAL 19-8 121S 22-10 340S 23-11 58 OTU 5-6-42 coll with P8660 on t/o CE Bal Br 24-2-43 SOC 31-3

P7829 24MU 1-1-41 65S 13-1 616S 26-2 412S 12-8 340S 12-2-42 53 OTU 27-3 dvd i/grd nr St A CE 22-11

P7830 Sind IV 6MU 1-2-41 66S 16-2 609S 24-2 dam by Bf109 19-3 66S 8-7 152S 30-4-42 57 OTU 10-10 83MU 27-1-45 SOC 5-3

P7831 6MU 24-12-40 145S 22-2-41 CB ops 16-3 485S 16-6 FTR ops 24-7

P7832 Enniskillen 6MU 1-1-41 FACB 12-1 1CRU 72S 23-4 74S 9-7 610S 8-9 340S 28-11 61 OTU 28-9-42 52 OTU 7-5-43 FACB 28-7 SAL Gosport 23-5-44 5PAFU 6-11-44 SOC 28-6-45

P7833 Portadown 6MU 1-1-41 54S 5-4 FTR ops 20-4 SOC 30-5

P7834 Mid Ulster 6MU 9-1-41 66S 16-2 609S 24-2 CB ops 28-5 AST 313S 2-10 417S 25-11 52 OTU 11-5-42 air coll with P9562 cd nr Bear Inn Cirencester CE 10-9

P7835 Ballymena 6MU 9-1-41 66S 16-2 609S 24-2 118S 6-6 308S 9-7 315S 22-7 FTR ops 24-7

P7836 Sind V 8MU 5-1-41 65S 14-2 610S 26-2 52 OTU 6-5-42 FACB 19-8 ASTE 23-8 con to ASR(IIC) 277S 20-3-43 57 OTU 27-3 air coll with P8071 w/u ldg nr Boul CB 19-7 DeH SOC 26-1-45

P7837 Sind III 8MU 12-1-41 616S 10-3 FAAC 11-5 310S 21-10 std cd nr Dyce wrk 19-11

P7838 Fermanagh 8MU 5-1-41 611S 21-2 o/t on t/o Oak Devon 22-2 AST 602S 4-7 122S 19-9 FACB 20-11 1CRU 21-2-42 9MU 11-4 con to ASR(IIC) 277S 21-12 AEAF Com Flt 28-4-45 SOC 5-6

P7839 City of Derby 8MU 1-1-41 74S 5-3 CB ops 28-4 1CRU 10-5 308S 9-7 315S 22-7 610S 11-9 cd ttl wrk nr Bewholme 3-10

P7840 Mountains O Mourne 8MU 9-1-41 64S 14-2 340S 10-12 53 OTU strk by K9891 Llan CAC 1-4-42 ASTE CGS 25-9 CE 2-11-44 (according to Air Min records this a/c was built by Eng Elec & powered by two Pegasus XVIII eng!)

P7841 Larne 8MU 3-1-41 65S 2-2 616S 26-2 FA dbf CE 5-3 SOC 12-3 FH24.50

P7842 Bangor 9MU 3-1-41 66S 18-3 48S 9-4 cd f/ld nr Ibsley CB 3-5 152S 9-6 SOC 25-6

P7843 Aldergrove 9MU 3-1-41 66S 18-3 118S 9-4 152S 9-6 306S 31-10 66S 7-11 air coll with P8430 off The Lizard 24-1-42 SOC 31-1

P7844 |Newfoundland I 9MU 9-1-41 152S 4-3 68S 30-8 CB 5-1-42 Farn 18-2 air cleaner trls. Trail edge & vibrograph trls. Fitt vacuum pump for pressure cabin trls. Oct '42 hand Feb '43 CO tests. Sept '43 escort for Fw190 during Monica & Benito trls (see JL227). 39MU NEA 27-11-44 SOC 8-3-45

P7845 Newfoundland II 9MU 3-1-41 54S 30-3 308S 12-6 FTR over France 8-7-42

P7846 Newfoundland III 9MU 3-1-41 616S 8-3 AST 20-6 con to FV M45 54S 18-9 FTR ops 3-10

P7847 9MU 2-2-41 222S 10-3 lost cont a/c disin tail unit broke away first. Pilot kld cd dbf 12.30hrs Salhouse nr Wrexham Norfolk 24-3

P7848 12MU 5-1-41 603S 3-2 air coll with P7750 cd dbf CD 23-7 SOC 31-7

P7849 Armagh 12Mu 9-1-41 19S con to FV M45 to USAAC 18-11-42

P7850 12MU 9-1-41 610S 5-4 1CRU 17-5 266S 26-7 CB ops 8-8 123S 18-9 58 OTU 7-6-42 CB 10-10-43 CGS 16-5-44 SOC 20-11 FH731.00

P7851 12MU 9-1-41 603S 17-5 111S 24-5 74S 12-10 CGS 27-4-42 FAAC 20-9 HAL 25-2-44 7SFTS 5-1-45 1AGS 18-2 10AGS 4-5 SOC 21-5

P7852 12MU 1-2-41 222S 9-3 452S 27-5 129S 26-8 610S 26-8 61 OTU 18-12 Ftr Affil Circus 23-5-44 5PAFU 6-11-44 SOC 28-6-45 FH222.50

P7853 24MU 5-1-41 222S SOC 28-6-45

P7854 24MU 5-1-41 74S 1-3 spun i/grd during slow roll over Mans after comb dbf CD 10-4 SOC 21-4 FH71.30

P7855 East India 24MU 4-1-41 65S 6-4 FACB 15-4 308S 3-7 315S 21-7 130S 26-7 CRD Rotol 13-10 AFDU 28-4-42 61 OTU 24-1-43 air coll with P7889 during exercise cd / Shrawardine Salop CAC 27-7 ROS SHAEF Com S 3-5-45 SOC 12-12

P7856 38MU 2-2-41 65S 57 OTU air coll with P8144 cd Shillbottle N'land 7-5-43

P7857 38MU 2-2-41 222S 9-3 2FPP e/fld hit house f/ld Willsbridge nr Bristol 8-3-42 SOC 7-4

P7858 38MU 4-1-41 303S 5-3 452S 22-5 313S 18-8 611S 26-11 340S 28-12 FAAC 15-2-57 OTU 15-5 FACB 28-6 GAL con to ASR(IIC) 277S 24-1-43

P7859 38MU 4-1-41 303S 4-3 s/dn by Bf109 FTR 20-4

P7880 6MU 12-1-41 610S 10-3 130S 21-6 411S 27-7 FAAC 7-9 306S 19-10 GAL 30-10 rtp 1-4-42

P7881 6MU 12-1-41 66S 15-2 609S 24-2 strk by taxy Master Dyce 27-4 616S 21-6 FTR ops 24-7

P7882 6MU 2-2-41 152S 3-3 130S 3-3 134S 31-12 312S 2-8-42 ECFS 2-8-53 OTU 8-7-43 u/s ldg Hibald CE 15-5-44

P7883 Grahams Heath 6MU 1-2-41 152S 5-3 611S 14-3 308S 26-5 19S 15-8 CAC on f/f/ 21-8 234S 21-8 152S 7-9 74S 28-9 61 OTU 5-5-42 53 OTU 2-2-43 flew i/hill nr Chapel-en-le-Frith Derbys CE 10-12

P7884 6MU 1-2-41 66S 23-4 501S 12-7 ASTEx 21-7 152S 6-12 North Detach 19-5-42 DeH 6-7 BDn 16-5-43 trls with DeH reversible pitch prop. Normal hydromatic type with operating cams reversed to enable cam travel to turn blades to negative incidence instead of feathering. The blades acted as an air brake. During trls the blades were reversed at 200mph and initial deceleration was ¾G. The time from braked to normal position was considerable;- about 15-20 secs. 57 OTU 27-11 air coll with BL697 CE30-9-44

P7885 6MU 1-2-41 FACB 7-2 AST 66S 19-5 152S 7-9 52 OTU 21-10-42 53 OTU 25-10-43 CE 30-12-44

P7886 8MU 12-1-41 611S 23-2 FAAC 13-3 308S 1-6 19S 4-9 331S 2-11 58 OTU 17-4-42 CB 9-6 GAL AFDU 16-2-43 FACA 10-3 ROS 1695BDF 5-3-44

P7887 Sind VI 8MU 30-1-41 66S 6-4 118S 9-4 19S 21-8 std on t/o dbf CE 4-9 SOC 9-9

P7888 8MU 12-1-41 CE ops 10-2 AST recat B 308S 9-7 FTR ops 12-7-42

P7889 8MU 2-2-41 234S 17-3 66S 5-7 19S 3-9 52 OTU 5-7-42 FACB 10-9 SAL con to ASR(IIC) 277S 24-1-43 61 OTU 22-2 air coll with P7855 Haw Salop CB 27-7 recat E 11-8 SOC 31-8 FH298.50

P7890 8MU 14-2-41 19S 3-3 FAAC 3-3 FTR ops 21-7

P7891 8MU 2-2-41 234S 13-3 41S 16-7 145S 28-7 CGS 23-242 1 CRU 23-1-43 61 OTU 8-4 6MU 7-9-44 SOC 22-4-45

P7892 9MU 1-2-41 266S 29-3 123S 15-9 AST 5-1-42 58 OTU 5-8 RNAS 7-8-43

P7893 9MU 2-2-41 152S 5-3 308S 8-7 401S 11-9 316S 13-10 133S 18-11 57 OTU 10-1-42 FACB 14-8 AST 21-8-61 OTU 24-2-43 ASTH 22-5-44 SOC 30-10

P7894 9MU 2-2-41 FACB 7-2 AST 65S 5-4 122S 5-10 52 OTU 28-1-42 cd f/ld Kee 15-2 recat ESOC 24-2-44

P7895 9MU 2-2-41 65S 20-4 72S 20-4 74S 9-7 57 OTU 19-2-42 AST 21-3-43 7PAFU 31-12 7SFTS cd on t/o Peterborough CB 8-3-45 recat E SOC 27-3

P7896 9MU 2-2-41 64S 15-3 340S 17-2-42 61 OTU 6-10 cd/ldg Rednall CB 27-3-43 recat E 20-4

P7897 9MU 2-2-41 152S 5-3 CB ops 10-6 WAL 310S 18-11 416S 28-8 61 OTU 26-2-42 eng fire cd f/ld Pudleston Herts 4-1-44

P7898 12MU 2-2-41 234S 8-3-41 66S 5-7 152S 29-10 57 OTU 5-7-42 FACB 10-4-44 ROS SOC 26-1-45

P7899 39MU 3-2-41 222S 9-3 308S 7-6 123S 16-9 57 OTU 12-5-42 e/fld f/ld West Kirby Cheshire CE 15-6 AST 61 OTU 15-1-43 SFTS 1-9 FAAC 9-10 ROS 5PAFU 1-12-44 SOC 28-6-45

P7900 12MU 2-2-41 266S 11-2 130S 28-6 350S 29-1-42 Stn Flt North 23-3 FACB 3-6 57 OTU 26-9-50 OTU 17-5-43 CB 19-7 RAF Heston 6-11 39MU NEA 21-11-44 SOC 7-5-45

P7901 12MU 1-2-41 266S 11-3 s/dn by Bf109 cd/ldg CB 15-4 AST 152S 9-7 s/dn by British convoy off Cromer Norfolk i/sea pilot kld 27-10 SOC 29-10

P7902 39MU 4-2-41 152S 3-3 501S 12-7 66S 31-7 ASTH 3-3-42 61 OTU 25-7 57 OTU 11-4-43 air coll with Hurricane AG111 of 59 OTU cd nr Wooler N'hants CE 5-5 SOC 15-5

P7903 39MU 4-2-41 152S 3-3 FACB 20-6 WAL 53 OTU 10-11-42 FACB 21-2-43 AST 3-3 e/fld w/u ldg Beckwell Farm Framcote Glos CE 20-6

P7904 39MU 8-2-41 152S 5-3 130S 26-7 FTR ops over Ijmuiden Holland 21-8 FH32.00

P7905 39MU 2-2-41 152S 3-3 FACB 22-6 AST 403S 7-9 457S 29-9 cd/ldg Andreas CAC 31-12 recat E 20-5-42

P7906 39MU 4-2-41 152S 3-3 501S 12-7 AST 2-8 con to FVA M45 603S 2-11 164S 27-6-42 6-3S 10-9 6th Ftr Wng Atcham 24-11 61 OTU 29-9-43 air coll with X4606 eng fire a/c aban cd Lightwood Farm Salop 8-8-44

P7907 37MU 24-2-41 222S 6-4 616S 23-6 234S 2-7 19S 21-8 152S 27-10 flew i/water Loch Foyle FTR 15-2-42

P7908 37MU 2-2-41 145S 23-2 CAC ops 28-3 485S 1-6 401S 9-9 154S 10-12 58 OTU 29-5-42 2TEU 2-12-43 13Grp Com Flt 14-7-44 SOC 25-5-45

P7909 37MU 22-2-41 222S 13-3 266S 14-7 FACB 14-9 SAL con to FVA M45 RNDA 4-9-42 SOC 6-2-45

P7910 City of Birmingham I 9MU 4-2-41 152S 4-3 41S 25-6 145S 28-7 340s 23-11 53 OTU 26-3-42 coll with Master DL556 of 20 OTU ADn CE 13-1-43

P7911 City of Birmingham II 9MU 4-2-41 66S 18-3 118S 9-4 403S 19-7 54S 4-8 403S 25-8 122S 2-10 154S 10-12 58 OTU 3-5-42 277S 3-5-43 flaps rtracted on touchdown Shoreham strk wall CE 28-2-44 recat 57 OTU 19-7 SOC 9-3-45

P7912 City of Birmingham III 9MU 4-2-41 64S 25-2 FACB 6-3 AST 19S 24-7 234S 21-8 131S 12-10 61 OTU 6-1-42 AFDU 12-12 1687BDF 5-3-44 ASTE 25-7 SOC 16-8

P7913 City of Birmingham IV 9MU 3-2-41 66S 4-3 118S 9-4 CGS 25-2-42 eng fire a/c aban cd Middle Drove Norfolk CE 8-6-43 SOC 30-6 FH413.50

P7914 6MU 11-2-41 610S 1-3 130S 3-7 411S 21-7 52 OTU 8-11-42 RAF North 22-8-43 1ORS 24-11 as 4366M CE 1-4-45

P7915 6MU 11-2-41 610S 10-3 130S 27-7 411S 23-9 121S 19-10 340S 27-11 53 OTU 5-4-42 e/fld f/ld nr Usk Monmouth CB 17-6 recat E AST 24-7 con to ASR (IIC) 277S 10-1-43 53 OTU 14-1 39MU NEA 5-11-44 SOC 7-11 FH897.00

P7916 6MU 1-2-41 145S 22-2 485S 1-6 CAC ops 26-6 130S 26-8 133S 17-11 134S 31-12 57 OTU 3-3-42 52 OTU 28-6 FACB 21-9 ROS FLS 30-6-44 SOC 26-1-45

P7917 6MU 1-2-41 64S 25-2 cd C2 6-3 AST 609S 18-5 f/ld 21-5 1CRU 403S 14-7 54S 4-8 457S 29-9 58 OTU 28-7-42 CE ops 13-1-43 SAL 25-8 con to ASR (IIC) 277S 14-1-44 SOC 16-8

P7918 Northampton 8MU 1-2-41 54S 24-2 412S 23-7 310 21-10 416S 19-12 LMS 18-3-42 12MU 21-11 con to AST (IIC) 277S 29-1-43 57 OTU 1-2 52 OTU 27-5 air coll with Mustang AG489 of 20MU cdnr Brincombe Stn Glas dbf Ce 4-7

P7919 Bacoo 8MU 1-2-41 611S 23-2 308S 25-5 315S 16-7 123S 16-9 AFDU 21-2-43 1690Flt 5-3-44 CE 22-11

P7920 The Red Rose 8MU 2-2-41 54S 24-2 43Grp DA 26-4 con to FVA M45 332S 28-1-42 24S 4-4 53 OTU FACE 11-5-43 52 OTU 22-8 6- OTU 4-2-44 cd/ldg Rednall CB 22-9 CE 28-11

P7921 Every Ready 8MU 5-2-41 19S 3-3 FACB 4-7 ASTH AFDU 26-4-42 61 OTU 13-2-43 air coll with P8429 ldg safe CB 8-4 39MU 1-10-44 SOC 25-1-45

P7922 Man of Metal 12MU 1-3-41 234S 9-3 s/dn by bf109 a/c aban i/sea 19-5 FM110.30

P7923 Venture I 12MU 1-2-41 610S 25-2 130S 3-7 411S 27-7 1CRU 31-10 CGS 27-11-42 FAAC 11-7-44 ROS FAAC 17-9 ROS CE 9-11

P7924 Venture II 12MU 1-2-41 145S 22-2 FAAC 16-3 AST 19S 28-6 AST 8-8 SOC 15-8

P7925 Weston Super Mare 12MU 28-2-41 234S 15-3 152S 5-7 66S 17-12 58 OTU 25-7-42 LMS 26-01 Stn flt North 21-9-43 39MU NEA 4-1-45

P7926 Hereward The Wake 24MU 1-2-41 610S 26-2 130S 31-6 411S 27-7 121S 21-10 340S 11-11 FACB 2-6-42 MMOx 6-6 CFS 9-8 FAAC 4-3-43 ROS

P7927 24MU 1-2-41 FACE 28-2 AST 152S 18-5 130S 25-8 133S 8-11 134S 31-12 52 OTU 21-5-42 53 OTU 6-9-43 61 OTU 16-4-44 SOC 20-12

P7928 Devon 24MU 1-2-41 74S 28-2 s/dn by Bf109 CAC pilot kld 12-3 74S 30-4 FTR ops 6-5 SOC 14-5 FH78.15

P7929 The Transport Men-Ace 24MU 1-2-41 HQ SFP e/fld w/u ldg Beeston Farm Tern 28-2 222S 30-3 19S 18-9 331S 2-11 58 OTU 4-5-42 FACB 19-3-43 LMS 25-3 53 OTU 24-9 SOC 30-12-44

P7960 9MU 4-2-41 6FPP u/s ldg strk house CE 9-2 SOC 17-2

P7961 37MU 7-2-41 145S 23-2 e/c CB 16-3 AST 34MU 26-11 HAL 14-3-43 FTR Com Com S Heston SOC 6-3-45

P7962 Inspiration 9MU 4-2-41 303S 12-3 s/dn by bf109 a/c aban 9-5 SOC 9-5

P7963 9MU 4-2-41 54S 28-2 19S 15-6 331S 8-11 58 OTU 4-4-42 61 OTU 11-7 cd into farmhouse on t/o Houghton Farm Rednal CE 8-9 SOC 10-9

P7964 City of Exeter Devon Sod 45MU 1-2-41 610S 27-3 130S 19-6 411S 22-7 AST 29-7 con to FVA M45 145S 2-12 134S 20-12 133S 28-12 FACB 27-1-42 1 CRU RNAS Stret 4-9-42 ret to RAF 27-1-45 to 5262M 9-3 516S ATC

P7965 45MU 5-2-41 72S 24-4 74S 9-7 FACB 17-9 ASTH con to FVA M45 2 USA 6-8-42 5 USA 22-8 332S 8-11 ROS 24-3-43 9MU 6-11-44 SOC 19-7-45

P7966 Manxman 45MU 24-2-41 616S 23-3 412S 5-8 154S 9-1-42 61 OTU 3-3 HAL 11-3 52 OTU 3-10 dvd i/building Quedgeley MU Glos CE 15-10

P7967 45 MU 24-2-41 41S 5-4 u/c dam on t/o Catt a/c aban 5-6 SOC 11-6

P7968 45MU 1-2-41 42S 25-4 74S 9-7 610S 7-9 61 OTU 5-1-42 52 OTU 28-1 e/fld w/u ldg nr Nympsfield Glos CE 30-5-42

P7969 Pride of the Isle 24MU 1-2-41 65S 20-4 122S 30-9 154S 8-12 AFDU 23-3-42 CGS 7-2-44 39MU 1-11 CE 29-11

P7970 24MU 1-2-41 CB ops 8-4 1CRU 16-5 485S 10-7 FTR ops 12-8

P7971 MIII 24MU 2-2-41 266S 20-4 19S 7-5 low app hit trees nr Colt CE 12-10 SOC 15-10

P7972 1-2-41 610S 26-2 130S 19-6 dvd i/grd St Just Cornwall dbf pilot kld 3-7 SOC 8-7 FH98.15

P7973 6MU 4-2-41 452S hit obst in sweep over France FD ldg Predannack CE 28-9 313S Aust for Canberra Museum 23-2-45 Extant, Aust War Memorial

P7974 6MU 4-2-41 145S 22-2 485S 1-6 266S 19-8 53 OTU 10-5-42 FACB 6-8 AST CGS 17-11 w/u ldg Cottingham nr Hull CB 3-4-44 recat E 14-4

P7975 6MU 4-2-41 145S 22-2 485S 1-6 i/sea ops 23-6 SOC

P7976 6MU 7-2-41 54S 26-2 111S 2-6 74S 2-11 350S 38-11 52 OTU 24-4-42 FACB 3-11 HAL 61 OTU 13-8-43 SOC 23-11-44

P7977 6MU 5-2-41 145S 18-3 485S 1-6 FTR ops 19-8

P7978 6MU 1-2-41 64S 25-2 411S 2-9 CB 22-1-42 58 OTU 28-7 air coll with X4914 cd nr Alloa Clackmannan CE 17-6-43 SOC 30-6 FH565.50

P7979 9MU 4-2-41 54S 6-3 602s 15-6 545S 21-8 411S 29-09 121S 27-10 340S 23-11 CB 17-12 CB ops 7-2-42 SAL 61 OTU 21-3-43 dvd i/grd Berriew nr Welshpool Montgom CE 5-2-44 SOC 1-3 FH517.35

P7980 9MU 4-2-41 54S 6-3 485S 1-6 616S 24-6 CB ops 19-3 FTR ops 3-7 FH32.05

P7981 9MU 9-2-41 41S 30-3 145S 28-7 f/ld cd Burneston Yorks dbf CE 10-8 SOC 18-8

P7982 9MU 4-2-41 64S 25-2 46S 19-12 416S skid i/snowbank Peterhead CAC 6-2-42 strk by Stirling N6086 on grd CE 7-2

P7983 Leylands Leeds City 9MU 6-2-41 154S 14-8 145S 4-11 417S 30-11 strk P7544 on grd Charmy down 2-1-42 53 OTU 19-2 FAAC 7-8-43 SOC 8-3-45

P7984 12MU 7-2-41 222S 13-3 616S 23-6 234S 2-7 e/fld i/sea off Exmouth 25-7 SOC 31-7

P7985 12MU 5-2-41 234S 13-3 412S 5-8 121S 21-10 340S 5-1-42 53 OTU 27-2 dvd i/grd bad weather Digby CE 15-6-43

P7986 12MU 5-2-41 145S 24-2 485S 1-6 ASTH 28-8 con to FVA M45 1401Flt 3-5-42 521S 1208 CB ops 19-12 AST 349S 13-7-43 61 OTU 1-8 air coll with R6801 cd Leicester CE 3-10

P7987 12MU 10-2-41 234S 13-03 comb Bf109 cd/ld 19-5 AST 71S 10-8 401S 19-9 317S 13-10 133S 10-11 310S 25-11 134S 31-12 57 OTU 24-6-42 ASTH 30-6 FAAC 10-1-44 39MU NEA 21-11 SOC 3-5-45

P7988 12MU 5-2-41 152S 5-3 111S 24-7 131S 31-12 61 OTU 5-1-42 CB 31-5 CRU 4-6 FACB 22-8 57 OTU 14-9 FAAC 21-5-43 53 OTU 20-10 FAAC 24-11 FTL charge 1-10-44 PAL 4-10-45 SOC 9-10

P7989 37MU 7-2-41 303S 3-3 154S 14-8 310S 9-11 410S 14-12 FACB 15-3-42 LMS 23-3 53 OTU 2-9 FACB 25-7 ASTM 4-8 SOC 5-3-46 bboc 5-3

P7990 37MU 10-2-41 222S 13-3 501S 21-6 FAAC 23-6 ROS 5-4S 26-10 57 OTU 12-2-42 FACE 11-4 ASTH 11-4

P7991 37MU 5-2-41 111S 25-4 501S 13-7 234S 31-7 19S 21-8 66S 17-9 cd on app St Mer CE 12-1-42 SOC 31-1

P7992 9MU 4-2-41 66S 21-3 58 OTU 13-10-42 u/s ldg Bal Br CE 27-10

P7993 38MU 24-2-41 234S 13-3 66S 5-7 234S 11-8 CAC ops 13-1-42 ROS 58 OTU 23-11 SAL 17-3-43 33MU 5-10-44 PAL 6-10 SOC 12-10-45

P7994 38MU 5-2-41 64S 15-3 133S 22-11 134S 31-12 53 OTU o/t ldg Lland CE 15-2-42 GAL con to ASR (IIC) 277S 9-2-43 FTR ops 25-11

P7995 38MU 22-2-41 64S 15-3 66S 9-7 234S 14-7 FTR ops 28-8

P7996 38MU 22-2-41 152S 19-3 501S 1607 152S 3-8 66S 1-12 53 OTU 13-8-42 FAAC 5-11-43 ROS SOC 8-3-45

P7997 39MU 7-2-41 152S 5-3 501S 12-7 152S 29-7 cd/ldg Fowl CB 30-8 AST recat E 20-5-42

P7998 9MU 14-2-41 66S 18-3 118S 9-4 458S 9-11 452S 23-3-42 57 OTU 2-4 61 OTU 21-3-43 53 OTU 28-6 FAAC 11-12 recat 28-12 39MU 3-1-45

P7999 39MU 14-2-41 152S 5-3 501S 14-7 130S 31-7 66S 25-8 313S 1-10 66S 6-11 swerved on t/o Porth cd CE 18-3-42 SOC 31-3

P8010 33MU 4-2-41 266S 26-3 123S 20-9 FAAC 31-1-42 SAL CGS 9-12 e/fld f/ld Pendona Sands nr Kings Lynn Norfolk CB 6-3-43

P8011 9MU 15-2-41 234S 29-3 AST 3-4 SOC CE 2-5

P8012 33MU 7-2-41 66S 23-4 65S 30-6 AST 14-7 412S 18-2-42 53 OTU 29-6-44 CE 14-8

P8013 33MU 5-2-41 65S 4-4 GAL 27-8 39MU 17-4-42 57 OTU 5-5 276S 14-9-43 AST CB 28-5-44 recat E 25-7

P8014 33MU 7-2-41 26-S 26-3 dam C2 by Bf109 15-4 AW 65S 16-8 122S 10-10 154S 25-11 61 OTU 13-3-42 53 OTU 19-9 1CRU 5-3-43 RAF Cole 11-5-44 FAAC 13-6 ROS SOC 25-8-45

P8015 33MU 28-2-41 234S 2-7 FTR ops 10-7 FH15.50

P8016 6MU 23-2-41 74S 20-2 loss of cont a/c aban cd nr Sutton Surrey CE 4-3

P8017 9MU 14-2-41 19S 29-3 403S 17-8 457S 29-9 452S 23-3-42 57 OTU 8-4 FACB 25-6 ROS e/fld i/sea nr Boul CE 5-1-44

P8018MU 11-2-41 74S 26-2 FAAC 7-5 145S 13-8 417S 5-12 CB 31-12 CGS 6-12-42 SOC 2-11-44 FH720.00

P8019 6MU 7-2-41 610S 10-3 130S 19-6 FA FTR 19-8

P8020 39MU 10-2-41 41S 30-3 145S 28-7 610S 11-9 350S 31-12 CB 1-2-42 ASTE 11-2 53 OTU 1-9 39MU 26-8-43 con to AST (IIC) 277S 14-9 CB 26-6-44 recat E SOC 16-8

P8021 6MU 11-2-41 DGRD BDn 20-2 eng trls DGRD R-RH 29-6 M47 intal. BDn 26-7 h/a dev trls. See page 104/5 for details. Farn/HAL 11-2-43 mods 9MU 17-4 CGS 28-6 SOC 2-11-44 FH701.00

P8022 12MU 12-2-41 266S 28-3 485S 28-6 306S 17-8 303S 6-10 308S 16-12 FACB 3-1-42 ASTH con to ASR(IIC) 277S 22-12 FAAC 6-12-43 1CRU 12-12 5PAFU 12-11-44 10AGS 12-5-45 SOC 18-6

P8023 6MU 11-2-41 66S 17-2 609S 24-2 54S 7-5 602S 15-6 65S 23-8 122S 1-10 154S 8-12 58 OTU 5-5-42 FAAC 1-8 ROS CB 24-10-43 recat E 9-11

P8024 12MU 3-3-41 FAAC 16-3 39MU 6-7 111S 24-7 130S 1-9 61 OTU 5-1-42 FAAC 25-2 ROS WAL 11-2-43 recat E 2-3

P8025 12MU 15-2-41 145S 24-2 485S 1-6 485S 1-6 CAC ops 23-6 306S 17-8 61 OTU 18-3-42 P&PSM 13-5 OTU 24-6 SOC 23-11-44

P8026 12MU 10-2-41 HAL 8-4 234S 17-5 501S 13-7 19S 27-8 152S 27-10 FACB 15-12 ROS burst tyre on t/o tip onto nose CE Eglinton 9-4-42 S&M

P8027 12MU 14-2-41 610S 25-2 FTR ops 5-3

P8028 72MU 28-2-41 222S 13-3 FACE 27-3 SOC 7-4

P8029 12MU 14-2-41 303S 3-3 s/dn by enemy AA fire FTR 12-4

P8030 24MU 28-2-41 72S 6-5 74S 9-7 310S 21-10 416S 5-12 61 OTU 12-5-42 8MU 17-11 con to ASR(IIC) 277S 11-2-43 CAC ops 14-2-44 1CRU 21-4 SOC 30-10

P8031 24MU 28-2-41 64S 15-3 485S 2-7 SAG Ken 4-7 71s 10-8 308S 2-10 3-6S 6-10 308S 11-12 52 OTU 7-2-42 FACB 2-7 SAL PAFU 11-11-44 SOC 11-5-45

P8032 24MU 21-2-41 152S 18-3 501S 16-7 234S 7-8 19S 21-8 66S 26-11 CE ops 30-1-42 ASTH con to ASR(IIC) 277S 2-2-43 SOC 8-1-46

P8033 24MU 21-2-41 145S 13-3 CB ops 6-5 71S 10-8 74S 16-9 350S 12-12 CGS 21-8-42 FAAC 4-10 SOC 2-11-44

P8034 24MU 12-3-41 266S 20-4 i/sea off Dover 4-6 SOC 1-7 FH49.00

P8035 45MU 28-6-41 64S 28-7 611S 12-11 52 OTU 17-3-42 FACB 16-5 61 OTU 20-8 AFDU 16-1-43 1695Flt 5-3-44 FAAC 14-4 7 PAFU 5-11 SOC 29-6-45

P8036 38MU 23-2-41 234S 13-3 AST con to FVA M45 501S 12-7 152S 11-8 BDn 16-9 trls with additional fuel tank under wing. It was trans to BDn after service complaints of poor perf and hand. Test pilots reported a/c satisfactory in all respects 1402Flt 15-9-42 HQ ATA 18-4-44 FACB 22-6 SOC 16-8

P8037 38MU 23-2-41 234S 13-3 501S 12-7 130S 3-8 152S 21-9 61 OTU 13-8-42 CGS 15-5-43 e/fld w/u ldg nr Kings Lynn CE 19-6 recat B 30-6

P8038 38MU 23-2-41 302S 13-3 452S 18-5 313S 16-8 ASTE 23-8 con to FVB M45 332S 16-5-42 USA 26-8 611S 26-7-43 PAL 27-9-45 SOC 29-9-45

P8039 Hereward The Wake 38MU 23-2-41 303S 4-3 comb with Bf109 FTR 16-4

P8040 Venture II 38MU 23-2-41 303S 5-3 cd/ldg Hawk 10-3 CAC 452S 4-6 313S 16-8 350S 17-12 57 OTU 27-3-42 f/ld cd Picton Cheshire CE 26-10

P8041 Country of Northampton 38MU 25--2-41 303S 5-3 452S 19-5 FACB 4-7 1CRU 14-7 403S 11-10 154S 25-11 CE 20-5-42

P8042 45MU 23-2-41 72S 24-4 74S 9-7 53 OTU 23-5-42 FAAC 12-6-44 CGS 14-7 SOC 2-11

P8043 45MU 23-2-41 41S 5-4 504S 2-11 cd on t/o Kirkistown CAC 30-1-42 S&M recat E 28-5

P8044 First Canadian Division 45MU 23-2-41 41S 7-4 145S 28-7 dvd i/grd Kirby Moorside Yorks dbf 28-10 SOC 30-10 FH523.25

P8045 City of Worcester I 45MU 23-2-41 72S 9-7 spun i/grd Ouston N'land dbf CE 2-8 SOC 18-8

P8046 City of Worcester II 39MU 23-2-41 74S 11-3 234S FTR ops 26-8

P8047 The Malverns 39MU 23-2-41 74S 11-3 6-2S 11-6 313S 13-8 417S 3-1-42 61 OTU 9-5 FACB 20-5 P&PSM 3-6 AFDU 12-12 3502SU 22-3-44 CE 11-10

P8048 Kidderminster Bewdley and Stourport 39MU 23-2-41 64S 15-3 CGS 27-4-42 FAAC 25-7 ROS u/c torn off on t/o Sutton Bridge CB 1-5-43 recat e 38MU 20-5-44 North Com S 4-1-45

P8049 39MU 1-3-41 41S 30-3 dvd i/grd nr Richmond Yorks CE 2-4 SOC 7-4

P8070 38MU 28-2-41 145S 18-3 616S 18-6 FTR ops 9-7

P8071 38MU 28-2-41 145S 18-3 313S 14-9 417S 25-11 53 OTU 18-6-42 FAAC 23-8 ROS 57 OTU 1-3-43 air coll with P7836 i/sea off Boul 10-7

P8072 38MU 28-2-41 66S 8-7 130S 21-7 152S 14-1-42 FACB 31-1 S&M 53 OTU 23-9 AST 30-3-43 con to ASR(IIC) 277S 21-7 61 OTU 1-4-44 SOC 26-1-45

P8073 37MU 24-2-41 303S 3-3 452S 18-5 313S 18-8 52 OTU 16-5-42 FAAC 15-6 AST 53 OTU 8-10 CB 1-6-43 CRU 15-6 58 OTU 1-48 LMS 22-7-44 SOC 16-8

P8074 Garfield Weston I 37MU 24-2-41 222S 13-3 dam by Ju88 4-4 501S 2-6 133S 28-10 f/ld Maladerack Eire dbr 30-11 SOC

P8075 Garfield Weston II 24MU 22-2-41 91S 21-3 222S 11-5 501S 7-6 504S 21-10 58 OTU 29-1-42 FACB 23-6 SAL 61 OTU 27-12 FAAC 13-4-43 2TEU 15-12 SOC 8-3-45

P8076 24MU 22-2-41 152S 18-3 130S 2-7 411S 27-7 340S 11-11 o/s ldg hit disp bay Drem CE 28-12 SOC 31-12

P8077 24MU 6-3-41 152S 21-5 501S 16-7 234S 31-7 FAAC 9-8 19S 21-8 66S 7-9 152S 10-10 spun i/grd nr Eglington CE 24-3-42

P8078 Garfield Weston III 37MU 24-2-41 222S 13-3 308S 27-7 306S 8-8 dam ops 16-8 SAL 58 OTU 8-5-42 e/fld wng torn off in f/ldg nr Milnathort Kinross CE 20-7

P8079 37MU 24-2-41 303S 3-3 dam by Bf109 13-4 8MU 5-7 DGRD FArn 12-7 LOX inject trls to boost eng at ha. FAAC 17-5-42 39MU 15-10 con to ASR(IIC) 277S 2-2-43 61 OTU 9-10 air coll with P7608 cd Marshbrook salop CE 27-4-44

P8080 Horwich 37MU 10-3-41 602S 1-7 71S 10-8 401S 9-9 61 OTU 501042 57 OTU 28-11 cd High House Farm Alnwick CE 1-3-43

P8081 Garfield Weston IV 37MU 28-2-41 222S 13-3 452S 27-5 312S 20-10 FACB 17-11 SAL 58 OTU 1-7-42 o/t ldg Bal Br CE 18-5-43 SOC 28-5 recat B 1-6 53 OTU 26-10 7PAFU 6-11-44 1AGS 18-2-45 SOC 21-5

P8082 Skysweeper 45MU 15-3-41 41S 7-4 122S 30-9 154S 25-11 FACB 512 WAL 52 OTU 12-5-42 38MU 14-4-43 con to ASR(IIC) 276S 13-7 CE 25-7-44

P8083 Garfield Western V 38MU 25-2-41 152S 19-3 234S 15-7 66S 28-9 152S 23-3-42 CB 21-5 45MU 19-6 con to FV M45 AFDU 10-2-43 FAAC 23-1-44 1687BTD 22-3

P8084 Garfield Western VI 9MU 1-3-41 64S 11-4 flew i/grd nr Kirknewton aerodrome dbf 1-11 SOC 8-11

P8085 Garfield Weston VII 38MU 26-2-41 303S 13-3 452S 27-5 cd nr Conisholme Yorks CE5-7 SOC 11-7

P8086 39MU 1-3-41 66S 21-2 118S 9-4 412S 27-7 1CRU 23-10 con to FVA M45 2 USA S 22-8-42 116S 4-11 61 OTU 18-5-43 1402 Met Flt 2-7 8 OTU CB 14-3-44 SOC 18-9-45

P8087 39MU 1-3-41 65S 4-4 308S 7-7 306S 8-8 303S 6-10 CGS 22-8-42 FACB 25-9 6MU 5-9-44 SOC 18-5-54

P8088 Borough of Lambeth 39MU 1-3-41 66S 21-3 118S 9-4 152S 9-7 19S 23-8 61 OTU 21-9-42 FAAC 19-5-43 recat B CGS 1-8 MAL 22-2-44 OTU 1-7 dvd/grd Prees Salop CE 23-9

P8089 Miners of Durham I 39MU 1-3-41 66S 21-3 185S 9-4 313S 2-10 306S 2-10 306S 6-11 308S 11-12 350S 8-2-42 58 OTU 16-8 e/fd cd Bal Br CE 23-12

P8090 Ideal 39MU 1-3-41 66S 21-3 118S 9-4 403S 27-7 54S 4-8 457S 27-9 CGS 23-2-42 FACB 1-8 ASTH AFDU 8-11 FAAC 10-11 ROS 11SoTT 28-10-43 CE 20-1-45

P8091 Miners of Durham II 24MU 8-3-41 72S 6-5 74S 9-7 350S 3-12 1CRU 25-5-42 AFDU 8-11 1690BDF 5-3-44 7PAFU 2-12 FAAC 7-1-45 recat E 11-1 SOC 18-1 to 4936M

P8092 Elland 37MU 10-3-41 266S 23-6 123S 29-9 52 OTU 13-6-42 FACB 21-11 AST AFDU 26-2-43 FAAC 13-7 ROS to 52MU for Museum purposes 20-9-44

P8093 Halifax II 37MU 10-3-41 266S 26-3 123S 30-9 CB 7-1-42 ASTH 52 OTU 6-5 std ldg ADn CE 26-6

P8094 On the Target 24MU 8-3-41 609S 30-3 WAL 308S 27-7 FTR over France 7-8

P8095 Halifax III 39MU 11-3-41 65S 30-3 coll with Bf109 in comb CB 26-6 AST con to FVA M45 39MU 16-4-42 5USA S 22-8 322S 8-11 61 OTU 9-6-43 hit tree in fog Staffs CE 16-4-44

P8096 Corn Exchange 8MU 21-3-41 FACB 12-4 GAL 266S 5-7 123S 18-9 CGS 26-4-42 AST 7-2-43 con to ASR(IIC) 277S 9-4 53 OTU 12-2-44 SOC 6-11-45

P8097 9MU 23-3-41 152S 21-4 66S 130S 17-7 123S 4-11 66S 17-12 FAAC 7-2-42 61 OTU 9-7 FACB 30-1-43 CRD CGS 25-5 61 OTU 18-3-44 CE 14-8

P8098 Enfield Spitfire 9MU 9-3-41 609S 30-5 f/ld 21-5 GAL 130S 24-8 hit disp hut on aerodrome beat-up Porth 11-10 SOC 17-10

P8099 8MU 31-3-41 303S 22-4 452S 18-5 313S 14-8 WAL 25-10 39MU 27-6-42 con to FVA M45 2USA S 4-8 82Gp USA 18-11 HAL 11-3-43 CRD Farn Dec'43 neg G trls CB 1-2-44 61 OTU 2-6 CE 6-11

P8130 Luton I 8MU 6-4-41 303S 22-4 452S 4-6 FACE ttl wrk 11-6 SOC 16-6

P8131 Luton II 8MU 15-5-41 66S 6-7 CGS 23-2-42 f/ld Marholm Northants CB 23-3 recat E ASTM 1-4 61 OTU 21-9 1CRU 5-2-43 con to ASR(IIC) 276S 30-4 1AGS 18-2-45 1OAGS 4-5 SOC 18-6

P8132 33MU 28-2-41 65S 4-4 122S 27-9 145S 3-10 417S 5-12 52 OTU 14-1-43 3501SU 22-9 FAAC Farn 12-9-44 ROS North Com S 26-10 SOC 8-3-45

P8133 37MU 13-3-41 266S 26-3 121S 19-10 340S 23-11 53 OTU 20-4-42 spun into grd nr Llanbirt Glam CE 25-4

P8134 con from FI to FIIB DRGD BDn 12-3-41 9MU 14-5 58 OTU 14-8-42 53 OTU 21-6-43 1CRU ROS 24-3-44 SOC 14-12-45

P8135 con from FI to FIIB 6MU 14-3-41 66S 22-4 CAC ops 5-5 145S 20-6 306S 8-7 308S 14-7 308S 8-8 222S 14-8 64S 29-8 611S 12-11 57OTU 16-1-43 FAAC 8-2-44 SOC 30-12

P8136 Aldershot (unofficial name The Cat) 8MU 30-3-41 FAAC 30-3 65S 14-5 340S 22-11 58 OTU 12-4-42 SAL 11-5 strk HT cables Kirkcaldy Fife Sgt Given safe CB 1-7-43 LMS 7-7 CGS 6-5-44 SOC 2-11-44

P8137 Sarum and South Wales 33MU 18-5-41 234S 2-7 FTR ops 10-7

P8138 The Norfolk Farmer 8MU 15-5-41 234S 25-5 66S 10-7 52 OTU 28-6-42 61 OTU 7-11 5PAFU 6-11-44 FAAC 7-4-45 ROS SOC 25-6

P8139 Robert Peel 8MU 11-5-41 56S 18-5 66S 18-5 130S 21-7 57 OTU 9-10 13 OTU 29-1-44 tipp onto nose on t/o Bicester CAC 10-6 SOC 16-8

P8140 Nuflier 10MU 16-3-41 74S 3-4 R-RH 29-4 61S 12-5 308S 25-5 CB ops 12-7 SOC 26-7

P8141 Rugby and District 24MU 8-3-41 222S 30-3 501S 13-6 504S 26-10 dam ops 9-12 S&H 9-12 61 OTU 24-10-42 CB ops 9-1-43 57 OTU 15-10 39MU NEA 21-11-44 SOC 8-3-45

P8142 Southport I 24MU 8-3-41 266S 20-4 dam by Bf109 27-6 AST 71S 12-8 303S 2-10 306S 6-10 308S 11-12 CAC 26-1-42 61 OTU 26-3 CAC 12-6-44 SOC 16-8

P8143 Southport II 10MU 16-3-41 91S 6-4 501S 23-5 hit balloon cable nr Weston Super Mare dbf 10-6 SOC 15-6 FH95.55

P8144 24MU 6-3-41 222S 30-3 74S 8-8 350S 18-12 61 OTU 28-3-42 57 OTU 5-8 air coll with P7856 cd Shibottle N'Land CE 7-5-43 SOC 13-5

P8145 Mabel 38MU 11-3-41 616S 10-7 412S 5-8 310S 21-10 416S 14-3-42 61 OTU 23-4 FACB 5-6 57 OTU 12-10-43

P8146 Covent Garden 45MU 15-2-41 72S 24-4 74S 9-7 350S 15-12 57 OTU 24-5-42 CB 23-6-43 HQ TTC Com Flt 14-12

P8147 City of Norwich 24MU 8-3-41 65S 29-4 WAL 29-8 308S 11-12 350S 4-2-42 52 OTU 29-5 5PAFU 25-9 57 OTU 11-9-43 CGS 7-2-44 SOC 30-11-44

P8148 45MU 15-3-41 72S 3-5 452S 7-7 610S 29-8 522 OTU 11-2-42 FAAC 9-5 air coll with P8278 a/c aban over Weston Super Mare 12-7

P8149 Lewis & Harris Fighter 24MU 6-3-41 72S 6-5 74S 9-7 350S 12-12 North Stn Flt 23-3-42 SOC 1-4-45

P8160 P.J. 33MU 8-3-41 65S 29-6 FTR ops 21-8

P8161 Leylands Leeds City 9MU 9-3-41 603S hit high grd Colne Lancs 14-5 SOC 28-5

P8162 DS&G North Valley 37MU 10-3-41 41S 5-6 1CRU 14-9 416S 31-12 CB ops 31-1-42 ROS 61 OTU 23-4 CGS 10-10 FAAC 24-10 SOC 2-11-44

P8163 33MU 13-3-41 41S 6-4 53 OTU flew i/high grd nr Northallerton Yorks CE 1-6 SOC 10-6

P8164 39MU 12-3-41 65S 20-4 72S 20-4 FACB 29-4 19S 9-8 234S 21-8 131S 12-10 57 OTU 8-3-42 1CRU 17-7 45MU 15-10-44 SOC 31-12

P8165 6MU 16-3-41 65S 30-3 WAL 27-8 504S 2-11 57 12-2-42 CGS 17-6-43 CE 2-11-44

P8166 45MU 15-3-41 72S 3-5 64S 20-8 19S 4-9 cd Langham aeordrome ttl wrk 5-9 SOC 9-9

P8167 Assam I Lakhimpur 37MU 13-3-41 266S 26-3 ASTE 27-8 con to FVA M45 FACB 9-11 610S 30-11 133S 19-1-42 601S 7-4 164S 16-5 602S 10-9 61 OTU 25-10-44 CE 15-12

P8168 Assam II Lakhimpur 33MU 13-3-41 41S 6-4 145S 29-10 417S 5-12 53 OTU 19-2-42 FACA 12-4 ASTH 5PAFU 2-10 5FTS 31-7-43 7PAFU 11-11-44 cd/ldg Peterborough FAAC 6-5-45 recat E SOC 30-5

P8169 Assam II Lakhimpur 9MU 9-3-41 71S 12-8 401S 19-9 64S 4-10 611S 12-11 52 OTU 23-3-42 hit water in form cd nr Lyndney Glos CE 14-5

P8170 Assam IV Lakhimpur 37MU 10-3-41 266S 26-3 cd/ld 8-4 dam by bf109 23-6 HAL 452S 14-7 610S 29-8 61 OTU 12-12 57 OTU 27-3-43 61 OTU 1-4-44 SAL 26-7 recat E 16-8

P8171 9MU 13-3-41 41S 30-3 145S 30-7 19S 10-9 FACB 17-11 ASTE 31-12 61 OTU 16-10-42 CB 4-11 FACB 27-3-43 SAL recat E SOC 16-8-44

P8172 By Dand 33MU 17-3-41 610S 19-4 130S 27-6 411S 22-7 i/sea ops 27-9

P8173 45MU 14-3-41 266S 26-3 FTR ops 3-7 FH143.00

P8174 Baltic Exchange 39MU 12-3-41 65S 20-4 72S 20-4 122S 30-9 74S 4-10 350S 18-12 FACB 21-5-42 AST FACB 29-4 52 OTU 28-9 7PAFU 12-11-44 1OAGS 2-4-45 SOC 21-5

P8175 Baltic Exchange II 33MU 13-3-41 66S 24-4 HAL 111S 11-8 403S 3-9 457S 23-9 57 OTU 14-2-42 f/ld cd nr Huxley Cheshire CB 25-7 recat E 31-7

P8176 North Borneo I 39MU 12-3-41 66S 21-3 1CRU 15-4 71S 10-8 131S 3-10 53 OTU 14--5-42 CGS 19-9-43 FAAC 24-8-44 ROS 5-9

P8177 North Borneo II 38MU 11-3-41 65S 30-3 122S 20-9 154S 25-11 1690BDT Flt 29-4-44CAC ops 14-5 CE 22-11

P8178 Castle Queen 38MU 11-3-41 54S 27-4 FTR ops 7-5

P8179 Montague Bee 38MU 11-3-41 65S 31-3 dam by Bf109 f/ld Hawk 15-4 WAL 308S 27-7 401S 11-9 61 OTU 5-5-42 FAAC 17-5 DeH 2-9 con to ASR(IIC) 277S 31-1-43 FLS 13-3 12Grp 4-6-44 SOC 14-6-45

P8180 St Vincent 6MU 16-3-41 65S 30-3 122S 10-10 131S 14-10 57 OTU 25-1-42 FAAC 12-12 ROS 1690BDT Flt 13-7-44 5PAFU 2-11 SOC 10-7-45

P8181 Tasmania 39MU 12-3-41 65S 5-4 64S 14-10 611S 12-11 61 OTU 12-5-42 std cd Cherry Orchard Farm Haw dbf CE 10-7

P8182 Tasmania II 8MU 13-3-41 66S 6-4 118S 9-4 152S 1-6 a/c aban nr Totnes Devon 15-6

P8183 Tamania III 8MU 13-3-41 74S 12-4 602S 11-6 71S 6-8 306S 15-11 308S 11-12 port wng fail i/sea nr Lytham Pier Lancs 21-12 SOC 29-12

P8184 Transkeinan Territories I 8MU 13-3-41 66S 21-3 118S 9-4 74S 20-9 u/c jam a/c aban i/sea off Llan 10-10 SOC

P8185 Transkeinan Territories II 8MU 13-3-41 266S 29-3 FTR after comb Bf109 27-6 FH49.00

P8186 8MU 13-3-41 64S 3-4 145S 3-10 417S 30-11 53 OTU 19-2-42 1CRU 17-7 58 OTU 31-12 SOC 22-4-45

P8187 45MU 14-3-41 266S 26-3 123S 20-9 58 OTU 10-3-42 dvdi/sea of Menteith nr Aberfoyle Perths CE 3-6-43 SOC 30-6 FH531.40

P8188 45MU 14-3-41 266S 26-3 FTR after comb bf109 27-6 FH132.00

P8189 FI con to FIIB 6MU 14-3-41 66S 22-4 303S 28-5 Farn June'41 306S 28-7 655S 15-9 616S 6-10 132S 21-10 52 OTU 10-4-42 AFDU 24-1-44 39MU 8-9 SOC dbr 25-1-45

P8190 45MU 14-3-41 266S 29-3 123S 15-9 331S 20-1-42 58 OTU 4-4-43 FACE fire in flight a/c aban cd Norman Law Fire dbf CE 11-9

P8191 45MU 14-3-41 41S 7-4 401S 7-4 401S 9-9 317S 13-10 133S 14-11 134S 31-12 53 OTU 11-2-42 61 OTU 13-1-43 FAAC 8-3 CGS 2-9 FACB 14-7 LMS 25-7 recat E SOC 16-8-45

P8192 45MU 15-3-41 72S 24-4 145S 30-7 417S 28-2-42 53 OTU 7-12 57 OTU 27-11-43 e/fd a/c aban cd nr Shilbottle N'Land 4-9-44 SOC

P81933 La Rosalinda 39MU 17-3-41 66S 9-5 313S 16-9 306S 6-11 53 OTU 8-3-42 air coll with P7372 9-11 ROS 57 OTU 23-7-43 hit tree fly low nr Billingham N'Land CE 26-4-44 2MPRD 6-5

P8194 Gold Crest I 10MU 16-3-41 91S 9-4 234S 3-5 66S 14-7 152S 14-1-42 57 OTU 7-8 DeH 8-4-43 prop mod to turn to minus 25° for use as ldg brake. BDn 14-9 trls with mod prop. Reduced ldg run from 465 to 270 yds. FACB 28-1-44 recat E 20-3

P8195 10MU 16-3-41 655S 30-3 FACB 26-6 AST con to FVA M45 130S 30-10 134S 25-12 133S 28-12 421S 17-4-42 FAAC 25-4 GAL M46 instal P&PSM 14-10 fuel syst mods 61 OTU 29-5-43 air coll with JP8505 cd Bomere Heath Salop CAC 12-6 ROS FAAC 21-3-44

P8196 10MU 16-3-41 91S 6-4 501S 16-6 133S 28-10 134S 31-12 57 OTU 31-3-42 FAAC 13-1-43 ROS CRD VA 27-4-45 cd during t/o on exper tail wheel trls CE 12-6 SOC 23-6

P8197 6MU 16-3-41 65S 30-3 122S 2-10 74S 4-10 61 OTU 2-4-42 HAL 15-4 57 OTU cd just after t/o nr Boul 22-11

P8198 6MU 16-3-41 54S 28-3 AST 14-5 111S 2-6 FTR ops 9-8

P8199 6MU 16-3-41 74S 3-4 HAL CB 3-9 331S 26-11 58 OTU 4-4-42 FAAC 13-10 ROS CGS 23-6-43 FAAC 21-9 ROS CE 12-9-44

P8200 Winged Victory 45MU 19-3-41 72S 24-4 74S 9-7 350S 8-12 FAAC 30-12 ROS 52 OTU 11-10-42 FACE 11-10 AST SOC 26-1-45

P8201 45MU 19-3-41 41S 5-4 FAAC 1-5 145S 28-7 417S 5-12 58 OTU 6-5-42 SAL 9-8-43 53 OTU 29-6-44 SOC 8-3-45

P8202 FI con to FII 6MU 16-3-41 66S 22-4 303S 28-5 616S 28-10 504S 25-11 52 OTU 20-11-42 FACB 17-5-43 CE 29-9

P8203 6MU 25-3-41 266S 3-4 123S 20-9 FACA 31-10 SAL 45MU con to ASR (IIC) 277S 29-12 CE ops 24-6-43 recat B 1-7 57 OTU 8-11 5PAFU 6-12-44 u/s ldg Tern CE 24-5-45 SOC 21-7

P8204 8MU 21-3-41 118S 12-4 130S 17-7 19S 27-8 66S 7-9 FAAC 16-2-42 ROS 152S 25-3 AFDU 9-2-43 1695BDF FLT 5-3-44 SOC 14-12

P8205 6MU 17-3-41 66S 22-4 303S 28-5 s/dn by Bf109 Tonbridge CB 4-6 AST 9-6

P8206 45MU 19-3-41 41S 5-4 306S 19-10 308S 11-12 air coll with P7745 Woodvale CE 9-1-42

P8207 FI con to FIIB 12MU 28-3-41 72S 23-4 74S 9-7 122S 4-10 132S 8-12 52 OTU 8-4-42 air coll with P8208 cd River Severn Monmouth CE 26-1-43 AST 39MU 1-10-44 SOC 25-1-45

P8208 12MU 26-3-41 303S 12-5 1CACF 24-12 FAAC 2-1-42 1CRU 52 OTU 9-10 air coll with P8207 during gunnery pract cd River Severn CE 26-1-43 SOC 3-2

P8209 Kerr 9MU 23-3-41 152S 22-4 501S 30-7 504S 26-10 FACB S&H 18-2-42 58 OTU 3-4-43 SOC 9-3-45

P8230 FI con to FIIB MXX 24MU 29-3-41 501S 13-5 145S FTR after comb Bf109 18-6 report safe 1CACU 10-1-42 FACB 21-12 AST TAF 19-6-43 AFDU 23-10 1687BDF Flt FAAC 13-4-44

P8231 45MU 19-3-41 72S 24-4 FTR after comb Bf109 i/sea Farne Island 29-4 FH10.30

P8232 24MU 29-2-41 222S 22-5 308S 26-8 655S 15-9 616S 6-10 FACB 17-10 GAL 1CAEU 9-5-42 33MU 29-12 con to ASR(IIC) 276S 14-5-43 s/dn i/Channel by Fw190 31-8 FH260.30

P8233 8MU 21-3-41 118S 12-4 403S 19-7 54S 4-8 403S 25-8 131S 15-10 61S 5-1-42 52 OTU hit tree nr Kee CE 25-6-43

P8234 FI con to FIIB 24MU 29-3-41 222S 21-5 308S 26-8 132S 12-10 61 OTU 5-5-42 FACB 29-6 SAL AFDU 7-10 FACB 11-8 SAL 13Gp Com Flt 20-12-43 SOC 12-4-45

P8235 9MU 23-3-41 65S 19-4 61 OTU 14-12 52 OTU 11-2-42 FACB 28-2 ASTH 58 OTU 25-10-43 2TEU 24-3-44 53 OTU 26-4 CB 17-9 recat E 26-9

P8236 9MU 23-4-41 266S 17-4 CE ops 21-6 GAL 30-6 con to FVA M45 1402 Met Flt 15-6-42 CAC ops 11-9 ROS SOC 17-4-45

P8237 39MU 2-5-41 118S 6-5 603S 16-5 152S 30-7 1CRU 14-9 con to FVA M45 RNAS 4-9 61 OTU 21-7-43 hit high grd Rhos-Fach Farm Oswestry CE 9-12-43 FH189.35

P8238 Borneo (NEI) 45MU 19-3-41 72S 26-4 74S 9-7 417S 10-1-42 53 OTU 15-2 hit trees fly low nr Skirlough Yorks CE 5-5-44

P8239 8MU 26-3-41 64S 8-4 603S 16-5 111S 25-5 130S 1-9 ASTEx 11-10 con to FVA M45 53 OTU 8-5-42 FAAC 8-2-43 ROS fld strk pole Wenvoe Glam CE 31-3

P8240 9MU 29-3-41 152S 26-4 SOC CE 21-5

P8241 8MU 21-3-41 609S 12-4 C2 by Bf109 f/ld Dover 17-5 AST 19S 9-8 350S 13-1-42 57 OTU 27-3 FAAC 2-3-43 ROS FACB 10-4-44 LMS 5PAFU 7-11 SOC 28-6-45

P8242 FIIB 24MU 30-3-41 501S 13-6 306S 9-7 308S 14-7 132S 12-10 61 OTU 4-6-42 coll with P8345 on t/o Mount Br CE 14-6

P8243 33MU 24-3-41 66S 24-4 130S 21-7 19S 27-8 FTR ops 29-8

P8244 FII 24MU 30-3-41 222S 22-5 FTR ops 19-8

P8245 9MU 23-3-41 611S 17-4 struct fail cd Dengie Flats pilot kld CE 18-5 Farn Jan'42 for acc research

P8246 39MU 25-3-41 66S 23-4 501S 13-7 152S 30-7 ASTM 15-8 con to FVA M45 121S 26-4-42 RNAS Yeov 7-9-43

P8245 at Farnborough, April 1942, after structural failure in the air.

P8247 FIIB 37MU 31-3-41 306S 28-6 303S 13-7 FA FTR SOC 23-7

P8248 33MU 25-3-41 66S 24-4 report miss ops 5-5 safe 64S 7-8 611S 12-11 52 OTU 16-2-42 5PAFU 27-1-43 FAAC 27-2 SFTS 13-6-43 9PAFU 1-12-44 1OAGS 17-4-45 FAASC 1-6 recat E SOC 13-6

P8249 33MU 24-4-41 91S 29-4 501S 24-5 133S 28-10 134S 31-12 53 OTU 26-2-42 air coll with P8366 Minehead CA 8-4 coll with K9951 in app 27-5

P8250 33MU 24-3-41 145S 10-5 234S 14-7 412S 5-8 310S 21-10 CGS 20-2-42 FACB 30-5 ROS 45MU 10-9-44 SOC dbr 28-1-45

P8251 33MU 24-3-41 66S 24-4 130S 18-8 19S 27-8 152S 15-9 154S 17-3-42 57 OTU 21-11 FAAC 6-11-43 ROS cd/ld Boul CB 10-3-44 recat E SOC FH691.05

P8252 FIIB 12MU 31-3-41 72S 23-4 74S 23-7 122S 4-10 CB 16-2-42 SAL 550S 23-11 AFDU 27-11 FAAC 2-2-44 RSO 1BDF 4-3 CE 14-8

P8253 39MU 25-3-41 66S 27-4 152S 5-7 154S 18-12 SAL CB 9-3-42 45MU 2-5 con to ASR(IIC) 276S 13-1-43 FAAC 5-5 ROS ASTH 23-5-44 SOC 25-7

P8254 The Transpitfire 37MU 1-4-41 145S 14-6 FTR ops 18-6 FH5.55

P8255 39MU 25-3-41 66S 23-4 CB 19-8 AST FTR ops 29-8

P8256 33MU 25-3-41 91S 29-4 501S14-6 133S 28-10 134S 31-12 57 OTU 8-4-42 FACB 24-10 recat E SOC 30-10-44

P8257 FI con to FIIB 12MU 13-3-41 72S 23-4 74S 9-7 122S 4-10 132S 4-12 FAAC 9-3-42 LMS AFDU 9-1-43 cd Dunnet Head Caithness 22-2 Stn Flt Gosport 7-3-44 5PAFU 9-11 cd/ld Tern 14-3-45 recat E SOC 10-11

P8258 33MU 25-3-41 66S 24-4 C2 taxy coll 17-6 266S 16-8 133S 25-11 134S 31-12 57 OTU 3-3-42 LMS CB 7-12 58 OTU 11-10-43 2CTW 20-10 FLS 30-6-44 SOC 8-3-45

P8259 53MU 25-3-41 74S 12-5 602S 1-6 313S 13-8 FACB 22-10 ASTH 3-11 con to FVA M45 1406Flt 14-6-42 spun i/grd Dunnet Head Caithness 23-2-43

P8260 39MU 25-3-41 66S 8-5 234S 14-7 152S 8-11 SAL 6-5-42 CB 13-5 AFDU 8-11 FAAC 10-10-43 ROS 1AGS 18-2-45 SOC 21-5

P8261 33MU 25-3-41 74S 12-5 122S 1-10 154S 25-11 61 OTU 8-3-42 GAL 33MU con to ASR(IIC) 277S 29-12 3501SU 14-5-44 SOC 11-5-45

P8262 12MU 31-3-41 303S 14-5 43GpDA 16-6 con to FVA M45 1CACU 27-6-42 TAF 19-6-43 AFDU 23-10 FAAC 11-2-44 ROS

P8263 33MU 25-3-41 610S 19-4 130S 19-6 411S 22-7

P8264 9MU 29-3-41 609S 1-5 dam by Bf109 8-5 452S 20-6 AST 23-8 131S 27-11 FACB 5-1-42 ROS 61 OTU 17-3 FACB 12-4 ECFS 9-8 SOC 30-12-44

P8265 FIIB hit lorry on t/o 23-5-41 37MU 1-6 61S 27-6 1CACU 18-4-42 FAAC 20-6 ROS GAL 28-8 con to ASR(IIC) 276S 29-12 FAAC 11-2-43 ASTH recat E 25-7-44

P8266 8MU 30-3-41 609S 16-4 616S 20-6 234S 2-7 FAAC 26-7 AST 152S 6-11 FTR 10-1-42

P8267 8MU 30-3-41 54S 21-4 111S 2-6 last flew with 111S 30-8 Sqdn converting to FV Sgt Fowler (4 Del Flt) was del a/c from 4MU Haw to 133S Eglington on 16-12 lost f/ld in Eire Interned and repatriated in 1943 S&H 20-7-43 61 OTU 25-2-44 cd Bradley nr Wrexham CE 15-5

P8268 8MU 30-3-41 54S 26-4 FACB 23-5 111S 3-6 610S 8-9 340S 28-11 61 OTU 10-8-42 air coll with Wellington BK186 cd nr Little Stretton Salop pilot kld 14-5-43 SOC 26-5 FH636.25

P8269 9MU 4-4-41 65S 24-4 air coll with Hurricane cd dbf nr Grantham 3-5 SOC 13-5 FH17.10

P8270 9MU 4-4-41 609S 1-5 Farn June'41 152S 21-6 130S 21-7 19S 31-8 66S 7-9 FTR ops 25-9 FH159.45

P8271 9MU 4-4-41 609S 1-5 616S 22-6 501S 12-7 130S 26-7 66S 30-8 CAC 23-4-42 WAL 10-6 con to ASR(IIC) 277S 7-1-43 53 OTU 14-1 57 OTU 31-10 SOC 16-10-44

P8272 9MU 4-4-41 616S 26-4 AST 22-6 FTR ops 25-6 FH63.15

P8273 33MU 9-4-41 DGRD BDn 6-6 cd nr Over Wallop ttl wrk 3-7 SOC 11-7

P8274 6MU 10-4-41 74S 2-5 313S 28-7 ASTE 11-9 33MU 2-7 con to ASR(IIC) 53 OTU 7-7-42 277S 11-1-43 FAAC 31-3 ROS FACB 8-4 DeH 15-4-44 5PAFU 14-11 SOC 18-6-45

P8275 6MU 10-4-41 74S 23-4 602S 11-6 313S 13-8 312S 6-11 CB ops 5-12 416S 31-12 83MU Salvage Unit 1-4-42 58 OTU 27-7 hit tree low fly Thornhill Stirling CE 14-11 SOC 24-11

P8276 8MU 7-4-41 74S 22-4 616S 3-7 411S 17-7 121S 2-10 340S 11-11 58 OTU 5-5-42 flew into high grd with AR254 & X4614 Dollar Bank Farm Kincardine CE 16-1-43 SOC FH420.45

P8277 9MU 29-3-41 64S 26-4 66S 3-9 19S 6-9 o/s ldg Matlaske CB 5-9 SOC 9-9

P8278 Enfield Spitfire 9MU 29-3-41 152S 26-4 501S 13-7 66S 31-7 FA 10-9 GAL 52 OTU 14-5-42 air coll with P8148 over Weston Super Mare 12-7 ROS FAAC 18-9-43 53 OTU 28-4-44 SOC 8-3-45

P8279 8MU 7-4-41 66S 24-4 dam ldg acc 2-6 130S 26-8 CGS 23-2-42 FAAC 1-12 ROS 57 OTU 8-11-43

P8310 37MU 1-4-41 145S 14-6 FTR over France 14-8

P8311 37MU 31-2-41 308S 28-6 FTR over France 29-8

P8312 FIIB 24MU 1-4-41 501S 13-5 52 OTU 8-10-42 5SFTS 23-8-43 air coll with Dakota a/c aban cd nr Navenby Lincs dbf 27-10 FH202.20

P8313 FIIB 24MU 1-4-41 145S 11-5 306S 9-7 308S 14-7 FTR over France 22-7-42

P8314 FIIB 24MU 2-4-41 501S 13-5 145S FTR after comb Bf109 26-6 FH35.45

P8315 FIIB 24MU 1-4-41 FACE 7-4 SOC 21-4 FH1.00

P8316 FIIB 24MU 1-4-41 222S 22-5 64S 29-8 54S 17-2-42 CB 24-5 CGS 23-11 cd/ld Catf 9-8 CB recat E SOC 18-8

P8317 FI con to FIIB 24MU 2-4-41 145S 12-5 306S 9-7 308S 14-7 132S 20-9 53 OTU 14-4-42 CB 23-12 1CACU 15-5-45 TAF 19-6 AFDU 32-10 FAAC 2-3-44 SOC 21-11

P8318 FIIB 24MU 2-4-41 145S 12-5 308S 14-7 FTR ops 22-7

P8319 FI con to FIIB 24MU 2-4-41 145S 12-5 306S 9-7 308S 14-7 132S 15-10 61 OTU 23-4-42 FAAC 22-5 FAAC 31-5-43 CGS 10-9-44 CE 2-11

P8320 FIIB 24MU 1-4-41 222S 21-5 16-11 AFDU 16-11-42 FACB 20-12 ROS e/fd o/s ldg o/t CE Kirmington 5-2-44

P8321 FIIB 24MU 2-4-41 222S 26-5 dam by bf109 26-4 GAL CACU 12-12 strk by X4384 parked Detling CB 14-7-42 AST 1CRU 22-7 E 30-7

P8322 FI con to FIIB 12MU 9-4-41 72S 23-4 74S 9-7 CB ops 19-8 122S 4-10 132S 4-12 57 OTU8-4-42 FACB 16-11 SAL con to ASR(IIC) 31-3-43 61 OTU 1-4-44 SOC 27-9-45

P8323 FIIB 45MU 8-4-41 145S 12-5 a/c aban nr Worthing CE 4-6 FH14.50

P8324 45MU 8-4-41 145S 12-5 306S 9-7 CE ops 27-8 AST 154S 27-2-42 313S 8-6 GAL 25-7 con to FVA M45 P&PSM 15-10 fuel syst mods wng stiff guns removed further mods 30-3-43 122S 15-7 FAAC 12-8 HAL 277S 10-2-44 o/s ldg Hawk strk AA862 CB 5-3-44 5APFU 14-7-45 SOC CE 19-7-46

P8325 FIIB 12MU 14-4-41 303S 12-5 65S 15-9 416S 1-4-42 61 OTU 18-5 FACB 20-6 SAL 1CACU 28-10 ops 14-1-43 1CRU 22-1 con to ASR(IIC) 275S 5-5 ASTE 22-5-44 recat E SOC 16-8

P8326 FIIB 45MU 10-4-41 145S 12-5 306S 9-7 308S 14-7 FTR over France 19-8

P8327 FIIB Java (NEI) 45MU 10-4-41 145S 12-5 FTR over France 24-7-42

P8329 F Mk 11B 'Sumbawa' of NE1, served only with No.303 Squadron.

P8328 FIIB 45MU 10-4-41 145S 10-5 FTR after comb Bf109 18-6 FH24.55

P8329 FIIB Sumbawa (NEI) 12MU 14-4-41 303S 13-5 CB ops 2-7 SOC 9-7

P8330 FIIB Batavia (NEI) 12MU 14-4-41 303S 12-5 air coll with Bf109 cd Mans CE 23-6 SOC 3-7

P8331 FIIB Sumatra (NEI) 12MU 14-4-41 303S 13-5 FTR ops 27-6

P8332 FIIB Baron (Soebang NEI) 45MU 29-4-41 222S 21-5 ASTH 27-8 82MU 7-12 *Man Es* 13-4-42 RCAF Rockliffe Montral Ins A/F A166 extant Ontario National Museum Science & Technology Ottawa

P8333 FIIB Banda (NEI) 12MU 20-4-41 303S 14-5 SAL 17-7 124S 7-11 54S 18-11 CB 9-3-42 SAL 1CACU 28-10 flew i/grd Church Hunton Kent CE 9-11 SOC 22-11

P8334 FIIB 12MU 14-4-41 303S 1-5 FTR 23-7

P8335 FIIB Semarang (NEI) 12MU 14-4-41 303S 14-5 s/dn i/sea by Bf109 a/c aban 28-6

P8336 FI con to FIIB Flores (NEI) 12MU 20-4-41 303S 14-5 FA 8-4-42 57 OTU 5-7 1CRU 25-3-43 M45 instal 53 OTU 21-6 FACB 18-10 CGS 9-3-44 cd f/ld Catf CAC 25-9 recat E 29-9

P8337 45MU 23-4-41 222S 21-5 132S 9-12 53 OTU 18-4-42 FAAC 30-9 ROS 58 OTU 4-10-43 2CTW 12-10 61 OTU 20-4-44 f/ld cd Cheshire CB 3-6 recat E 26-8

P8338 FI con to FIIB Bandoeng (NEI) 12MU 20-4-41 303S 13-5 312S 18-11 52 OTU FAAC 7-5-42 SOC 8-3-45

P8339 Madura (NEI) FIIB 45MU 24-4-41 145S 12-5 dam by Bf109 C2 21-6 AST con to FVB M45 121S 15-3-42 P&PSM 23-6 mods FTR ops 21-9

P8340 FIIB Balikpapan (NEI) 45MU 12-4-41 FACB 8-5 WAL 124S 20-10 54S 18-11 FIW 8-4-42 52 OTU 15-5 cd CAC 21-6 ROS HAL 20-2-43 61 OTU 30-9 dam u/c on first ldg 2nd ldg w/u CB Rednal 27-4-44 recat E 25-8

P8341 FI con to FIIB Lumbok (NEI) 45MU 23-4-41 145S 15-5 dam by Bf109 21-6 306S 9-7 308S 14-7 132S 17-9 61 OTU 14-1-43 FACB 29-1 AST 1CACU 7-5 TAF 19-6 53 OTU 23-10

P8342 FI con to FIIB Ceram (NEI) 45MU 25-4-41 145S 12-5 306S 13-7 dam on sweep 29-8 ASTE 4-9 57 OTU 31-3-43 strk L1056 taxy Esh CAC 20-6 ROS 61 OTU 5-7-44 SOC 25-4-46

P8343 Medan (NEI) FI con to FIIB 45MU 24-4-41 222S 20-5 AST 15-7 132S 11-11 57 OTU 10-4-42 FACB 23-8

P8344 Orkney FI con to FIIB 45MU 26-4-41 145S 15-5 266S 7-9 65S 25-9 616S 6-10 54S 5-12 57 OTU 8-10-42 broke port u/c on t/o CE Esh 6-5-43 recat 45MU 16-10-44 SOC

P8345 FIIB 45MU 6-5-41 222S 21-5 64S 27-8 611S 12-11 CB 1CRU 20-1-42 61 OTU 9-6 coll with P8242 t/o Mount Br CAC 14-6 ROS f/ld cd CB 26-3-43 recat E SOC 5-4

P8346 FIIB Ossett and Horbury 37MU 26-4-41 303S 19-6 FTR after comb Bf109 28-6

P8347 FI con to FIIB Richmond Jubilee 45MU 26-4-41 222S 20-5 266S 3-9 65S 25-9 616S 6-10 500S 25-11 312S 7-12 SAL 12-1-42 9MU 23-10-44

P8348 British and Friends ex Japan 222S 416S 52 OTU con to FV SOC 25-9-45

P8349 Sucka Boemi (NEI) 8MU 21-4-41 66S 26-4 130S 26-8 53 OTU 5-2-42 1CRU 3-5-44 61 OTU 14-6 SOC 27-9-45

P8360 6MU 10-4-41 303S 18-4 7-8 457S 29-2 452S 23-3-42 57 OTU 10-4 air coll with P8362 nr Esh CE 27-2-43

P8361 Krakatao (NEI) 6MU 10-4-41 303S 18-4 452S 4-6 FTR ops 9-8 SOC 10-9

P8362 8MU 9-4-41 66S 5-7 air coll with P8360 nr Esh 27-2-43 57 OTU 30-7

P8363 Banka (NEI) 6MU 13-4-41 74S 2-5 CE on ops 16-5 SOC 27-5 FH32.05

P8364 Surinam (NEI) 6MU 13-4-41 74S 2-5 CE on ops 6-5 SOC 14-5 FH5.15

P8365 Rotterdam (NEI) 6MU 18-4-41 54S 8-5 64S 15-6 610S 27-7 611S 12-11 52 OTU 23-2-42 FAAC 16-9 ROS 57 OTU 28-3-43 FACB 17-8 29-12-44

P8366 Palembang (NEI) 8MU 20-4-41 66S 24-4 1CRU 22-5 19S 31-7 133S 18-11 53 OTU 26-2-42 air coll with P8249 cd Cat Park Minehead CE 8-4 ASTE 9-4

P8367 Bali (NEI) 8MU 20-4-41 616S 1-5 485S 14-7 313S 17-9 306S 6-11 308s 11-12 FAAC 7-1-42 ROS 53 OTU 8-3 FACE 26-5 AST OTU 16-10-43 f/ld cd nr KinL CB 5-1-44 recat E 7-2

P8368 Sibayak (NEI) 38MU21-4-41 118S 13-5 e/a dbf CE 30-6 SOC 5-7 FH71.25

P8369 Toba (NEI) 8MU 20-4-41 609S 14-5 616S 21-6 310S 21-10 416S 28-11 CB 26-2-42 LMS 61 OTU 20-9 CAC 22-1-44 recat E 9-11

P8370 Oldham 38MU 23-4-41 66S 6-5 130S 17-7 SOC 27-8 FH177.00

P8371 Palembang-Oeloe (NEI) 8MU 20-4-41 601S 14-5 130S 21-6 452S 21-7 411S 30-7 131S 12-1-42 57 OTU 14-2 CB 27-7-43 53 OTU 11-10 dbr SOC 25-1-45

P8372 FI con to FIIB 45MU 26-4-41 145S 15-5 306S 9-7 308S 14-7 CB ops 27-7 GAL 1CACU 15-4 FAAC 3-5 FACB 22-9 ROS dam CAC ops 17-10 ROS TAF 19-6-43 53 OTU 23-10 SOC 23-11-44

P8373 6MU 27-4-41 74S 8-5 403S 24-7 54S 4-8 53 OTU 14-5-42 FACB 9-3-43 AST RNAS Yeov 22-7 57 OTU 14-8

P8374 FIIB Dulvercombe 37MU 29-4-41 610S 14-6 FTR ops 10-7

P8375 Celebes (NEI) 9MU 25-4-41 602S 28-5 71S 6-8 FACB 10-9 MMO 13-9 con to ASR(IIC) 277S 20-12-42 53 OTU 28-1-44 PAL 6-10-45 SOC CE 9-10

P8376 Bedoeki (NEI) 38MU 26-4-41 118S 13-5 cd dbf CE 30-6

P8377 Siwabong (NEI) 38MU 22-4-41 118S 13-5 403S 19-7 54S 4-8 403S 25-8 122S 17-9 350S 2-12 74S 4-12 52 OTU 24-3-42 spun i/grd Stow on the Wold CE 10-8 SOC 18-8

P8378 Sourabaya (NEI) 38MU 23-4-41 152S 26-5 u/s ldg Swanton Morley hit bowser CB 21-10 ASTE 29-11 recat E 10-5-42

P8379 Oldham and Leeds 9MU 25-4-41 452S 24-6 313S 14-8 312S 8-11 416S 22-12 o/t ldg Peterhead CB 11-1-42 SAL CGS 23-12 SOC 2-11-44 FH77.00

P8380 Black Velvet 9MU 30-4-41 74S 9-5 403S 24-7 54S 4-8 403S 25-8 457S 27-9 hit lorry at base CE 1-12 ASTE 31-12 53 OTU 15-6-42 flew i/grd bad visibility Cymmer Wales CE 15-8 SOC 21-8

P8381 Stroud and District 9MU 1-5-41 609S 18-12 425S 20-6 Farn June '41 129S 26-8 61 OTU 18-12 52 OTU 11-2-42 cd app Babdown Farm dbf CE 14-10

P8382 Crawn Crete 12MU 27-4-41 303S 14-5 65S 6-10 54S 8-12 CB 19-3-42 SAL AFDU 8-11 downwind t/o strk obst CE 20-5-43 Dux

P8383 FIIB City of Bradford VII 12MU 29-4-41 222S 22-5 308S 26-8 FTR over France 4-9 FH117.15

P8384 Fei Yue (NEI) 9MU 24-4-41 611S 6-5 308S 25-5 FACB 30-6 AST 19S 7-9 a/c aban cd Manor Farm nr Swanton Morley dbf CE 2-11 SOC 4-11

P8385 FI con to FIIB Impregnable 12MU 27-4-41 303S 12-5 306S 13-7 65S 6-10 133S 18-11 134S 31-12 AFDU 8-11-42 FAAC 28-11 ROS hit van taxy CB 28-1-43 61 OTU 26-3-44 SOC 21-11

P8386 6MU 29-4-41 616S 11-5 AST 24-6 FTR ops 9-7

P8387 Barty 9MU 30-4-41 611S 9-5 308S 25-5 315S 16-7 266S 2-9 123S 20-9 58 OTU 29-7-42 air coll P7683 cd Hammering Mere Farm CE 19-8 SOC 31-8 FH872.30

P8388 6MU 29-4-41 74S 8-5 152S 28-7 12 OTU 12-5-42 58 OTU 1-7 FAAC 3-1-44 ROS 1690Flt 28-9 FAAC 10-11 recat E 1-12

P8389 FI con to FIIB Metalbox 37MU 11-5-41 610S 10-6 130S 27-6 616S 19-7 315S 27-6 HAL 12-8 61 OTU 9-10-42 FACB 20-12 AST 61 OTU 9-4-43 FAAC 12-8 ROS

P8390 Bostonian 37MU 16-5 303S 19-6 122S 4-10 132S 4-12 416S 14-1-42 61 OTU 23-4 CB 12-10 SAL 57 OTUY 1-4-43 FACE 5-7

P8391 39MU 16-7-41 412S 23-7 310S 21-10 416S 28-12 61 OTU 6-4-42 FAAC 5-3-43 ROS recat E SOC 16-8-44

P8392 Magnet 9MU 30-4-41 616S 9-5 FACE 2-6 recat B AST 71S 10-8 410S 12-9 57 OTU 24-5-42 FACB 16-6-43 CGS 19-2-44 SOC 30-11

P8393 Garfield Weston VI 33MU 6-5-41 234S 25-5 308S 17-8 401S 11-9 302S 13-10 133S 18-11 134S 31-12 i/sea off Rathin Island FTR 6-1-42

P8394 Gibraltar 9MU 30-4-41 74S 9-5 152S 6-7 S&H 10-3-42 58 OTU 14-11 FACE 29-1-43 cd Gate Hill nr Stirling SOC FH345.35

P8395 Spirit of Crewe 33MU 18-4-41 234S 3-7 FTR ops 17-7 SOC 31-7

P8396 Bermuda II 9MU 2-5-41 74S 9-5 602S 11-6 71S 10-8 401S 19-9 308S 17-12 306S 20-12 53 OTU 7-2-42 FACB 26-2 ROS air coll with X4067 St Hilary Glam CE 16-1-43

P8397 Cheshunt and Waltham 5MU 22-5-41 616S 6-7 310S 21-10 416S 25-11 58 OTU 22-5-42 Farn 2-6-43 carb monox contam tests. On grd with hood open limit exceeded acceptable in flt LMS 21-7-44 recat E 16-8

P8398 Cheeping Wycombe 37MU 11-5-41 610S 2-6 CACF 12-12 FAAC 13-2-42 ASTM AFDU 12-12 CB 27-1-43 58 Otu 9-11 61 OTU 30-4-44 CE 14-8

P8399 Benone 24MU 11-5-41 616S 24-5 610S 25-5 FTR ops 28-6

P8420 8MU 7-4-41 66S 24-4 130S 25-8 ASTE 2-11 52 OTU 8-6-42 RAF North 22-8-43

P8421 R&S 6MU 11-4-41 74S 24-4 AST 8-7 1CRU 29-10 57 OTU 29-11-42 CAC 16-4-43 dbr SOC 1-6-45

P8422 R&S 6MU 11-4-41 609S 24-4 266S 14-6 123S 22-9 66S 11-1-42 416S 11-2 61 OTU 6-4 CB 28-8 58 OTU 20-3-43 FACB 29-7 ROS 1TEU 17-6-44 5PAFU 7-11 SOC 28-6-45

P8423 6MU 13-4-41 74S 2-5 602S 11-6 71S 10-8 401S 19-9 64S 15-10 130S 16-10 133S 25-11 134S 31-12 53 OTU 19-1-42 FACB 28-5 52 OTU 3-9 FACB 22-4-43 FLS 30-6-44 CE 16-8

P8424 9MU 24-4-41 65S 1-5 122S 30-9 154S 18-11 CB 20-2-42 SAL 58 OTU 5-5 FLS 30-6-44 SOC 8-3-45

P8425 Spirit of Crewe 9MU 24-4-41 611S 6-5 308S 26-5 403S 19-7 54S 4-8 403S 25-8 457S 29-9 CGS 23-2-42 HAL 22-2-44 61 OTU 7-11

P8426 6MU 27-4-41 54S 8-5 602S 15-6 313S 13-8 61 OTU 6-1-42 CB 28-2 ASTH 52 OTU 8-6 FACB 5-9 GAL 58 OTU 26-1-43

P8427 9MU 1-5-41 64S 16-5 611S 12-11 52 OTU 16-2-42 FACB 10-1-44 SOC 25-4-46

P8428 9MU 1-5-41 603S 14-5 111S 25-5 s/dn over France FTR 19-8

P8429 Frimley and Camberley 33MU 5-5-41 609S 24-5 152S 21-6 130S 25-8 61 OTU 5-1-42 air coll with P7921 cd nr Mount Br CE 8-4-43 FH452.50

P8430 9MU 10-5-41 609S 25-5 616S 2-11 234S 1-7 66S 2-11 air coll with P7843 NW of The Lizard CE 24-1-42 SOC 31-1

P8348 'British and Friends ex Japan', an F Mk IIB converted to F Mk VB standards later in its career.

P8431 33MU 31-5-41 1406Flt 13-9 FAAC 23-5-42 recat B 12MU 8-11 con to ASR(IIC) 277S 14-1-43 57 OTU 1-2

P8432 33MU 16-5-41 234S 3-7 19S 21-8 66S 7-9 AST 11-12 cd del flt to 39MU 25-1-42 AST 57 OTU 31-3-43 CB 28-7 SAL con to ASR(IIC) 277S 31-12 RAF Com Flt Heston 11-2-44 FAAC 8-5 CE 4-1-45

P8433 8MU 16-5-41 152S 7-7 61 OTU 28-9-42 CB 30-1-43 P&PSM 8-2 FAAC 14-10 ROS 52 OTU 23-11 SOC 30-12-44

P8434 38MU 31-5-41 616S 28-6 cd on app nr Bognor Regis dbf CE 21-7 SOC 26-7 FH37.45

P8435 Marvi 8MU 16-5-41 234S 25-5 66S 9-7 FTR ops 20-8 FH123.30

P8436 Marvi 9MU 8-5-41 602S 3-6 71S 6-8 401S 9-9 FACB 12-9 WAL 39MU 8-4-42 RAF Bovington con to FVA M45 15-5-43 67TH OG 30-8 1CRU 1-7-44 SOC 12-10-45

P8437 39MU 22-5-41 266S 29-6 123S 20-9 58 OTU 11-3-42 52 OTU 14-7 CB 23-6-43 SAL CGS 7-9 CE 2-11-44

P8438 Cardiff 33MU 18-4-41 616S 28-6 AST con to FVA M45 145S 24-11 134S 20-12 133S 29-12 air coll with P8595 cd Epworth Lincs 2-4-42 SOC 3-4

P8439 Crosby 33MU 18-4-41 234S 2-7 91S 21-8 FTR ops 28-8 SOC 31-8

P8440 Crosby 33MU 31-5-41 1402Flt 12-9 AFDU 14-12-42 air coll with P8468 over base w/u ldg CAC 13-2-43 ROS 1690BDF 5-3-44 CE 22-11

P8441 39MU 4-6-41 DeH spring tab ails filt CRD Farn 15-7 trls with spring tab plus cord on trial edge of same. (see page 100 for details). Comp trls with Bf110, Aug '42 trls' with OBoe and Gee (Cat and Mouse) equip G suffix applied to serial. Further trls with sliding int wt on ele syst for det CG under various conditions. 39MU 8-11 con to ASR(IIC) 277S 28-1-43 61 OTU 26-1-44 SOC 30-12

P8442 33MU 31-5-41 234S 2-7 19S 21-8 66S 9-1-42 152S 26-3-42 FAAC 27-3 ROS 61 OTU 22-8 CB 16-4-43 57 OTU 22-6 FAAC 11-7 ROS FACB 16-9 ROS SOC 30-12-44

P8443 Molukken (NEI) 6MU 10-6-41 66S 8-7 FACE 19-11 SOC 29-3-42 cancel 37MU 7-4 57 OTU 24-5 LMS 61 OTU 31-1-44 ails jam a/c aban cd nr Baschurch Salop 2-6-44

P8444 MES (NEI) 8MU 12-6-41 152S 9-7 131S 22-11 FACB 9-12 AST 52 OTU 30-6-42 CGS 28-6-43 SAL 7-4-44

P8445 India Telegraph 9MU 15-6-41 303S 19-7 122S 17-11 ASTH con to FVB M45 131S 14-4-42 cd/ld Merston CB 19-5 recat E SOC 25-5

P8446 38MU 11-6-41 152S 28-7 FTR over Holland (Antwerp) 12-8

P8447 FI con to FIIB 37MU 18-6-41 308S 15-9 616S 6-10 133S 18-11 134S 31-12 53 OTU 7-6-42 hit tree Gowley Farm Llancarfan Glam CAC 9-2-43

P8448 Counter Attack 8MU 13-6-41 152S 6-7 FACB Nov'41 f/ld cd Eglington CE 15-2-42

P8449 38MU 11-6-41 234S 4-7 91S 21-8 1CRU 30-8 i/sea 29-8 SOC 30-8

P8460 9MU 31-5-41 19S 25-6 dam by Bf109 f/ld 27-6 AST 74S 11-9 dvd i/sea off Fairbourne Merioneth 30-11 SOC 12-12

P8461 Kalahari 24MU 18-6-41 303S 30-6 FTR ops 23-7 FH50.55

P8462 39MU 22-6-41 303S 11-7 FTR ops 15-8 FH49.20

P8463 Canadian Scot Fort William 24MU 19-6-41 303S 30-6 FTR ops 2-7

P8464 FI con to FIIB 24MU 26-6-41 610S 12-7 315S 30-7 266S 9-9 FACB 28-9 124S 8-10 54S 18-11 CB SAL 8-12 1CACU 17-11-42 CAC ops 5-12 TAF 19-6-43 FAAC 9-8 ROS 61 OTU 23-10 FAAC 14-1-44 ROS SOC 20-12-44

P8465 F.E.F. FIIB 39MU 20-6-41 303S 7-7 f/ld hit poles Richmond Park Surrey CE 23-7 SOC 30-8

P8466 FIIB 37MU 18-6-41 306S 25-7 FTR ops 12-8

P8467 FI conv to FIIB 37MU 18-6-41 118S 17-7 132S 22-11 57 OTU 10-4-42 CAC 16-11 ROS e/fd f/ld W Thurston N'land CB 8-3-43

P8468 12MU 15-6-41 64S 2-7 611S 12-11 MM CB 6-1-42 61 OTU 9-5 FACB 25-7 ASTH 52 OTU 11-10 CB 6-11 air coll with P8440 over aerodrome Newm CE 15-2-43 SOC 28-2 FH380.30

P8469 FI con to FIIB 12MU 15-6-41 111S 30-6 130S 1-9 BDn 17-11 arma removed trls with rear view tear drop cockpit hood 133S 17-11 57 OTU 10-1-42 FAAC 12-8 FAAC 18-11 SOC 12-12-44

P8470 FIIB 12MU 15-6-41 485S 30-6 FTR ops 8-7 SOC 31-7

P8471 Pudukalai Nagaratha 24MU 27-6-41 266S 28-6-41 266S 28-6 hit hangar on t/o Colly Weston dbf CE 31-8 SOC 1-9

P8472 45MU 24-6-41 602S 7-7 412S 22-7 310S 21-10 416S 25-11 FAAC 19-12 ROS SAL 21-3-42 61 OTU 25-6 e/fd w/u ldg Ellesmere Salop CE 2-9

P8473 FIIB 24MU 29-6-41 306S 24-7 FTR 15-8 FH37.10

P8474 FIIB 38MU 1-7-41 222S 12-7 FTR ops 18-7

P8475 37MU 7-7-41 145S 1-8 FACB 17-9 ASTH 308S 17-12 61 OTU 14-2-43 FACB 15-5 39MU 19-10-44 SOC 8-3-45

P8476 FI con to FIIB 12MU 6-7-41 306S 23-7 CACF 12-12 FAAC 19-2-42 ROS 1CACU 1-8 CAC ops 12-1-43 ROS TAF 19-6 AFDU 23-10 1690BDF 5-3-44

P8477 24MU 23-7-41 65S 12-8 122S 30-9 154S 25-11 61 OTU 8-3-42 1CRU 13-5 CGS 11-8 CE 11-9-44

P8478 45MU 30-6-41 602S 17-7 FTR ops 21-7

P8479 British Glues & Chemicals Ltd Emblem 37MU 7-7-41 74S 10-8 61 OTU 9-1-42 FAAC 1-4 ROS FACB 29-6 SAL 6-7 con to ASR(IIC) 277S 9-1-43 FAAC 23-4 61 OTU 27-5-44 CE 14-8

P8500 39MU 20-6-41 616S 4-7 FTR ops 6-7

P8501 FI con to FIIB North West Frontier V 24MU 14-6-41 306S 24-7 65S 18-9 616S 11-10 53 OTU 29-8-43 CAC 4-3-44 1CRU 18-3 CGS 10-9 SOC 2-11 FH512.00

P8502 FIIB The Heart of England I 24MU 14-6-41 303S 27-6 FTR ops 8-7

P8503 FI con to FIIB Skyscraper 12MU 2-5-41 222S 20-5 FAAC 14-8 315S 27-8 266S 7-9 124S 16-9 54S 18-11 FACB 11-12 SAL 550S 31-10-42 AFDU 12-11 1690BDF 5-3-44 FAAC 17-11 recat E 14-12

P8504 FIIB Bermuda IV 37MU 16-5-41 610S 6-6 FTR ops 8-7

P8505 FIIB J.G. 12MU 2-5-41 222S 21-5 266S 4-9 616S 6-10 54S 9-12 61 OTU 26-1-43 air coll with P8195 cd Bomere Heath Salop CE 12-6 SOC 21-6 FH392.40

P8506 FIIB Faversham 37MU 11-5-41 610S 6-6 616S19-7 315S 26-7 FTR ops 5-8

P8507 FIIB Bermuda I 12MU 2-5-41 303S 27-5 FTR ops 17-6

P8508 39MU 22-5-41 501S 2-6 417S 5-12 53 OTU 15-2-42 i/sea off Porthcawl Glam CE 10-9

P8509 FIIB The Old Lady 45MU 5-5-41 266S 3-9 9MU 8-12 con to ASR(IIC) 277S 21-12-42 FAAC 1-4-43 ROS 61 OTU 1-4-44 air coll cd nr Rednal CE 7-4

P8510 North West Frontier I 6MU 7-6-41 501S 12-7 152S 31-7 61 OTU 15-8-42 SAL 15-7-43 39MU 6-12-44 CE 28-12

P8511 FIIB 12MU 2-6-41 188S 22-6 CAC 24-7 i/sea ops 1-9 SOC 8-10

P8512 38MU 12-6-41 152S FTR ops 24-7

P8513 Hecla 8MU 13-6-41 66S 5-7 CGS 24-2-42 FAAC 30-8-44 ROS 7PAFU 29-12 10AGS 2-4-45 SOC 21-5

P8514 33MU 26-5-41 1406Flt 8-9 53 OTU 29-8-43 5PAFU 23-11-44 SOC 28-6-45

P8515 North West Frontier III 6MU 12-6-41 266S 25-6 123S 29-9 61 OTU 3-8-42 CAC 11-3-44 ROS SOC 27-9-45

P8516 FIIB Amboina (NEI) 45MU 11-6-41 118S 26-6 CAC 24-7 hit hill in cloud nr Overmoigne Dorset dbf CE 4-8 SOC 15-8

P8517 Bechuana 24MU 18-6-41 222S 4-7 AST 13-8 con to FVB M45 315S 13-12 FTR ops 29-7-42

P8518 FI con to FIIB Nabha III 24MU 10-6-41 303S 25-6 306S 14-7 132S 15-10 FAAC 30-12 SAL 58 OTU 6-6-42 FAAC 23-7 SAL 1 CACU 8-4-43 TAF 19-6 61 OTU 23-10 SOC dbr 26-1-45

P8519 FIIB 45MU 29-5-41 306S 30-6 308S 14-7 FTR over France 17-7 FH18.55

P8520 FIIB The Mendip Spitfire 12MU 8-5-41 610S 27-5 FTR ops 10-7

P8521 FIIB Sulhamstead 12MU 6-5-41 610S 21-6 124S 25-11 54S 2-12 LMS ASTH 3-1-43 con to ASR(IIC) 276S 16-5 ASTH 28-5-44 recat E 25-6 SOC 25-7

P8522 FI con to FIIB Melton Mobray & District 24MU 12-5-41 303S 19-6 65S 15-9 616S 6-10 611S 23-11 1CACF 21-4-42 FACB 16-7 ROS TAF 19-6-43 61 OTU 23-10 SOC dbr 26-1-45

P8523 FIIB Bansi 12MU 13-5-41 610S 22-5 FTR ops 10-7

P8524 FIIB 24MU 22-4-41 303S 19-6 FTR ops 16-8 FH104.05

P8525 Leigh 5MU 26-5-41 308S 26-6 FTR over France 2-7 FH13.25

P8526 FIIB Breadbury and Romily 12MU 8-5-41 610S 3-6 306S 9-8 CB ops 19-8 SOC 25-8

P8527 FIIB Mauritius II 37MU 18-4-41 610S 6-6 616S 19-7 315S 27-7 266S 7-9 124S 21-9 54S 18-11 53 OTU 5-6-42 dvd i/grd nr Pontypool Road Glam CE 24-8

P8528 Township of Shipley 5MU 26-5-41 308S 26-6 315S 17-7 R-RH 20-8 130S 8-10 134S 31-12 57 OTU 31-12-42 hit H/T cables cd nr Wheldon Bridge N'land CE 9-4-43

P8529 FIIB Borough of Colwyn Bay 45MU 22-5-41 118S 23-6 132S 14-10 CAC 13-3-42 LMS 58 OTU 16-1-43 cd Airdrie Mains Farm nr Slamannan Stirling 8-4 SOC FH217.40

P8530 FIIB The Clan 24MU 23-4-41 145S 2-6 124S 31-10 54S 18-11 61 OTU 30-6-42 air coll with P8628 cd Bowmer Heath Salop CE 10-9 SOC

P8531 FIIB Who's Afeared 24MU 22-4-41 Stn Flt North 1-6 1CACU 18-3-42 std cd Camer Farm Graves Kent CE 23-6

P8533 FIIB 45MU 6-5-41 610S 29-5 CBAF 9-7 222S 18-8 145S 30-8 154S 8-12 132S 11-3-42 53 OTU 14-4

P8534 FIIB Hunter 24MU 22-4-41 610S 11-6 616S 3-11 1CAEF 3-3-42 FAAC 25-3 ROS 58 OTU 8-7-43 61 OTU 29-4-44 ASTH 18-5 recat E 25-7

P8535 FI con to FIIB 45MU 28-5-41 118S 29-6 124S 26-9 54S 18-11 58 OTU 4-4-42 61 OTU 18-4-44 FAAC 28-4 ROS SOC 26-12

P8536 FIIB Boron 37MU 19-4-41 145S 19-6 FTR ops 2-7 FH35.45

P8540 FIIB 39MU 26-6-41 315S 2-8 132S 20-11 52 OTU 8-4-42 13Gp C Flt 26-8-43 FAAC 3-12 ROS SAL 25-7-44 recat E SOC 16-8

P8541 FIIB 24MU 26-6-41 64S 21-7 222S 21-7 FTR ops 12-8

P8543 FIIB Assam VI 9MU 15-6-41 308S 19-7 132S 20-9 3SoGR 10-3-42 1CACF 3-4 57 OTU 28-3 CAC 27-8 recat E 3-9

P8544 FIIB Heart of England III 14-6-41 74S 5-7 i/Channel ops 17-7

P8545 FIIB Indian Telegraph II 24MU 29-6-41 610S 12-7 616S 19-7 315S 27-7 WAL 23-8 con to FVB M45 72S 30-4-42 350S 20-5 CB ops 22-6 AST P&PSM 23-2-43 mods 3501SU 19-7 FTR 23-8

P8546 12MU 23-6-41 403S 18-7 54S 4-8 403S 25-8 131S std cd f/ld Tryddyn nr Wrexham 23-10 SOC 2-11

P8547 FIIB Indian Posts 9MU 15-6-41 308S 19-7 132S 17-9 51 OTU 10-4-43 57 OTU 2-7 FAAC 23-7 SAL 58 OTU 8-11 e/fd wrk in f/ldg Sleadale Clackmannan 23-12 SOC 1-1-44 FH517.45

P8548 FIIB Assam V 24MU 14-6-41 64S 21-7 222S 21-7 145S 30-8 1CRU 22-11 1CACU 20-7-42 FAAC 26-9 air coll with AD388 nr Sittingbourne Kent dbf CE 14-4

P8549 FIIB 39MU 20-6-41 303S 3-7 350S 2-6-42 FACE 18-7 ROS 401S 7-12 402S 16-1-43 416S 23-5 DeH con to FVB M45 341S 26-12 FLS 23-2-44 bomb exploded in flight over Gofinch Ranges N'land ttl wrk 9-3 FH357.20

P8562 FI con to FIIB Stur-Gar 37MU 26-5-41 610S 6-6 AFDU 8-12-42 FAAC 8-3-43 ROS 1687BDF 5-3-44

P8563 City of Leicester I 5MU 26-5-41 RAF North 4-7 315 S14-7 308S 14-7 ASTH con to FVA M45 51S 3-1-42 hit high grd nr Stanhope Durham 27-3 SOC 28-3

P8565 FI con to FIIB City of Leicester II 45MU 31-5-41 118S 30-6 124S 3-10 54S 18-11 FACB 23-2-42 con to ASR(IIC) 276S 3-12 ASTE 7-5-44 PAFU 9-11

P8566 38MU 29-5-41 266S 30-6 des ops 3-7 SOC 9-7 FH4.30

P8567 FII Picture Post 37MU 26-5-41 303S 24-6 65S 15-9 616S 6-10 611S 23-11 CAC 20-2-42 SAL LMS 61 OTU efd lost wngs f/ldg ne Myddle Salop 15-12 ROS 58 OTU 26-2-43 57 18-2-44 e/fd f/ld nr Esh CAC 9-9 SOC 9-9

P8568 FI con to FIIB City of Stoke on Trent I 12MU 25-5-41 118S 22-6 e/fd f/ld o/t nr Heathfield Kent 14-7 132S 12-10 53 OTU 7-5-42 61 OTU 27-5-44 SOC 23-11

P8569 FIIB 45Mu 31-5-41 118S 23-6 124S 26-9 54S 18-11 61 OTU 25-7-42 FACE 30-1-43 SOC FH363.50

P8570 FI con to FIIB 38MU 3-7-41 CAC 18-7 65S 2-10 616S 6-10 312S 25-11 417S 11-1-42 58 OTU 7-6 FAAC 15-11 ROS 53 OTU 14-4-43 SOC 11-9-44

P8571 39MU 22-6-41 412S 23-7 310S 6-12 416S 14-12 58 OTU 18-5-42 FLS 30-6-44 SOC E 20-3-45

P8572 45MU 27-6-41 602S 17-7 hit grd recovering from dive nr Ongar Essex CE 9-8 SOC 19-8

P8573 12MU 6-7-41 308S 26-7 FTR over France 7-8

P8574 45MU 30-6-41 602S 17-7 313S 16-8 52 OTU 4-4-42 hit H/T cable Slimbridge Glos CE 7-3-43

P8575 FI con to FIIB 24MU 26-6-41 222S 4-7 145S 30-8 154S 8-12 FACB 7-1-42 AST 53 OTU FAAC 8-7-44 ROS SOC 24-5-45

P8576 FIIB City of Bundaberg & District 24MU 17-6-41 308S 24-7 65S 15-9 616S 6-10 504S 25-11 a/c aban i/Irish Sea nr IoM 4-2-42

P8577 45MU 30-6-41 111S 17-7 403S 3-9 610S 7-9 61 OTU 5-1-42 e/fd w/u ldg Houghton Salop CE 12-7

P8579 FI con to FIIB 39MU 20-6-41 303S 54S 15-2-42 FACB 12-3 SAL 61 OTU 18-5-44 CE 30-9

P8580 FIIB City of Stoke on Trent II 12MU 25-5-41 118S 22-6 315S 17-8 118S 9-9 132S 15-10 cd/ld Skae CE 24-2-42 SOC 8-5

P8582 12MU 1-6-41 610S 1-7 616S 19-7 315S 26-7 118S 12-9 132S 2-11 58 OTU 6-6-42 FAAC 18-12 ROS dvdi/sea of Dunbar E Lothian 5 5-43 SOC 28-5 FH329.55

P8583 39MU 31-5-41 234S 6-7 19S 21-8 66S 7-9 CGS 22-2-42 air coll with Hampden P2067 nr Crowland Lincs CE 31-8

P8584 FIIB Nabha II 45MU 10-6-41 118S 26-6 124S 26-9 54S 18-11 FACB 20-2-42 SAL con to ASR(IIC) 276S 10-5-43 ASTE CB 22-5-44 recat E SOC 16-8

P8586 38MU 29-5-41 616S 16-7 412S 5-8 FACEdbf 31-8 SOC 7-9

P8587 FIIB 12MU 5-6-41 303S 3-7 306S 13-7 132S 29-10 o/s ldg Peterhead hit obst CE 14-1-41 recat B 57OTU 20-10 FACB 14-1-43 VAO flew i/high grd Cheviot Hills N'land CE 25-3-43

P8588 FIIB Scawfell 37MU 26-5-41 610S 6-6 616S 19-7 315S 2-8 118S 12-9 132S 14-10 e/fd cd/ld Pitluarg Aberdeen CE 21-10 SOC 6-11

P8589 FIIB Makassar 5MU 8-6-41 118S 30-6 65S 25-9 616S 6-10 ASTH 7-11 con to FVB M45 FAAC 28-7-42 ROC 121S 13-8 CE dbf 19-8 SOC 25-8

P8590 FIIB 12MU 7-6-41 306S 1-7 308S 14-7 FTR over France 22-7-42 FH29-55

P8591 FI con to FIIB 12MU 2-6-41 222S 26-6 132S 21-11 52 OTU 9-4-42 FACB 28-4 CGS 14-8 FACB 25-6-43

P8592 FIIB 38MU 4-7-41 222S 12-7 132S 27-11 53 OTU 20-5-42 air coll with P7504 cd nr Cowbridge Glam CE 5-7 1CRU 7-7 recat E 16-7

P8593 FIIB 12MU 1-6-41 222S 6-8 64S 29-8 611S 12-11 54S 13-2-42 58 OTU 27-8 FAAC 15-8-43 SAL CGS 12-6-44 f/ld cd nr Beverley Yorks CB 25-6 recat E 1-7

P8594 9MU 31-5-41 41S 25-6 145S 28-7 ASTE 27-9 57 OTU 5-5-42 FAAC 8-5 CGS 23-6-43 SOC 5-7-45

P8595 Middelberg (NEI) 6MU 7-6-41 66S 8-7 CB Ops 24-8 ASTE con to FVA M45 133S 1-4-42 air coll with P8438 cd nr Epworth Lancs CE 3-4 SOC

P8596 Riouw (NEI) 24MU 10-6-41 303S 25-6 FTR ops 2-7

P8597 Katwijk (NEI) 6MU 10-6-41 266S 25-6 123S 18-9 FACB 20-12 SAL 61 OTU 8-4-42 CB 31-7 AST CGS 9-11 CE 14-11

P8598 38MU 11-6-41 485S 3-7 313S 22-8 FAAC 28-2-41 ROS 58 OTU 14-4 CB 30-5 53 OTU 20-9 FAAC 17-1-44 SOC 11-9

P8599 37MU 19-6-41 64S 14-8 FACE dbf 27-7 SOC 30-9

P8601 FIIB Delhi 12MU 14-6-41 74S 26-7 FA ttl wrk 17-9 SOC 21-9

P8602 FIIB Malang (NEI) 45MU 10-6-41 118S 30-6 132S 15-10 132S 8-4-42 57 OTU 8-4 e/fd f/ld nr Lowick N'land CE 6-11-43

P8605 39MU 20-6-41 452S 17-7 71S 3-8 61 OTU CB ASTE 16-4-42 58 OTU 15-10 strk X4682 ldg CE 12-11 SOC 20-11

P8608 38MU 12-6-41 266S 4-7 123S 16-9 61 OTU air coll with P8539 cd Bomere Heath Salop CAC 10-9-42 52 OTU 29-1-43 SOC 20-12-44

P8641 FIIB North West Surrey 37MU 26-4-41 303S 7-6 s/dn by bf109 cd/ld 17-6 MMO 25-6 53 OTU 8-10-42 coll with P7378 on t/o Llan; P7378 on emer ldg CE 4-4-43

P8642 Courageous 12MU 27-4-41 303S 16-6 HAL 22-6 145S 1-10 ASTE 19-11 53 OTU 3-10-42 58 OTU 27-9-43 61OTU 20-4-44 CE 14-8

P8643 FI con to FIIB Margaret Helen 12MU 29-4-41 222S 21-5 CB ops 24-6 AST 266S 3-9 1 CACU 17-7-42 CB ops 29-1-43 WAL 33MU 5-9 FACE 12-11 recat 61 OTU 30-3-44 SOC 11-9

P8644 FIIB Huntley Cock of the North 12MU 29-4-41 222S 21-5 315S 27-8 266S 9-9 124S 8-10 54S 18-10 58 OTU 6-6-42 stbd wng struct fail cd nr Bogside Stn Clackmannan CE 18-6

P8645 FIIB Gaumont British 12MU 29-4-41 222S 20-5 o/s ldg dam 24-6 AST con to FVB M45 452S 14-10 i/sea ops 8-11 F/Lt Dunston aban a/c off N.Forland

P8646 FIIB Rochdale and District II 6MU 29-4-41 616S 8-5 331S 15-1-42 58 OTU 4-4 5PAFU 2-10 FAAC 18-11 ROS SFTS 4-6-43 CE ttl wrk 4-11-44

P8647 FIIB Ariel 37MU 4-5-41 145S 19-6 306S 9-7 308S 14-7 65S 15-9 616S 6-10 312S 25-11 132S 31-12 61 OTU 27-6-42 SAL 25-7-43 cd/ld Esh CB 5-2-44 recat E 1-3

P8648 FI con to FIIB 45MU 6-5-41-m FA on f/f to 610S 29-5 SAL 315S 12-8 266S 6-9 124S 8-10 54S 18-11 58 OTU 4-4-42 61 OTU 6-3-43 FACE 19-8 SOC 31-8 recat B CGS 3-4-44 SOC 2-11 FH688.45

P8649 FI con to FIIB Bermuda III 45MU 6-5-41 222S 21-5 308S 26-8 65S 15-9 616S 6-10 132S 21-10 FACB 27-11 SAL 58 OTU 8-6-42 61 OTU 26-3-44 SOC 28-9

P8650 FIIB Defendamas 24MU 11-5-41 616S 24-5 610S 25-5 CBAF 9-7 118S 7-8 132S 14-10 416S 20-2-42 61 OTU 30-6 DeH 2-9 e/fd cd nr Queensferry Flints CE 30-3-43 SOC 31-3 recat B 2TEU hit trees Angus CE 29-12 FH305.05

P8651 St Helens 33MU 26-5-41 616S 28-FTR ops 5-7

P8652 33MU 6-5-41 WAL 8-5 308S 28-7 401S 11-9 610S 17-10 350S 31-12 53 OTU 6-9-43 FAAC 19-2-44 ROS 7PAFU 6-11 1AGS 10-2-45 SOC 29-7

P8653 FIIB 37MU 11-5-41 54S 16-2-42 AFDU 18-4 FACB 19-11 SAL 57 OTU 24-3-43 t/o in coarse pitch cd o/t CE Esh 1-2-44

P8654 Flint 33MU 6-5-41 609S 24-5 s/dn by Bf109 pilot kld dbf 11-6 SOC 21-6

P8655 FIIB Bewtonia 24MU 11-5-41 145S 28-5 306S 13-7 308S 14-7 124S 20-10 54S 18-11 61OTU 24-4-42 FAAC 24-6 ROS 1CRU 19-1-43 CE 26-1-44

P8656 MXX Nippy 39MU 23-5-41 234S 4-7 e/fd w/u ldg West Knighton Dorset CE 14-7 SOC 23-7 FH17.00

P8657 The City of Leicester Flight III 38MU 29-5-41 152S 20-6 130S 2114-7 411S 27-7 340S 27-4 CB ops 17-2-42 SAL 58 OTU 26-11 FACB 15-12 61 OTU 14-4-42 6RS as 4431M 5-12 CE 1-4-45

P8658 FIIB Borough of Morley 24MU 11-5-41 616S 25-5 cont jam f/ld cd Heathfield Kent 14-7 SOC 22-7

P8659 39MU 31-5-41 234S 4-7 19S 2-8 152S 10-10 GAL B 27-6 61 OTU 30-1-43 ASTM 14-5-44 1AGS 18-2-45 10AGS 29-5 SOC 31-5

P8660 FI con to FIIB Buxton 37MU 14-5-41 610S 2-6 118S 9-8 124S 8-10 54S 18-11 58 OTU 4-4-42 coll with P7828 on t/o Bal Br CB 24-2-43 SAL CGS 26-7 FAAC 10-12 ROS strk by P7524 while parked Catf 26-9-44 recat E 29-9

P8661 LTR Fighter 5MU 23-5-41 Robin Sites 22-6 308S 3-7 315S 17-7 610S 11-9 123S 15-9 3Del Flt cd nre Llanfair Anglesey on f/f to 350S CE dbf 24-11 SOC 6-12

P8662 FI con to FIIB First City of London Textiles 45MU 18-5-41 61 OTU 9-3-42 1CACU 12-10 TAF 19-6-43 53 OTU 23-10 SOC 8-3-45

P8663 38MU 29-5-41 616S 28-6 411S 12-8 FAAC 8-9 SAL CGS 20-2-42 FAAC 20-12 ROS 61 OTU 25-7-44 39MU NEA 29-3-45

P8664 39MU 18-5-41 501S 21-10 58 OTU 28-2-43 air coll with Whitley V LA847 cd in Spey Bay pilot kld CE 14-6-43 SOC 30-6 FH335.15

P8665 FIIB Bingley(UDC) 12MU 18-4-41 610S 27-5 616S 19-7 315S 26-7 266S 9-9 65S 25-9 616S 6-10 133S 18-11 134S 31-12 1CRU 17-1-42 61 OTU 9-10 FACB 10-3-43 ROS lost cont cd Gellifor Denbighs CE 26-1-44 SOC 1-3 FH618.40

P8666 FIIB Cuba 37MU 18-4-41 610S 2-6 616S 19-7 315S 26-7 266s 6-9 65S 25-9 616S 610 504S 25-11 f/ld cd nr Kirkistown 14-1-42 S&H 17-1

P8667 9MU 31-5-41 19S 26-6 313S 1-10 417S 25-11 61 OTU 17-3-42 GAL 33MU 22-11 con to ASR(IIC) 276S 29-12 e/fd t/o cd Fairwood Common nr Blyton Lincs CE 7-11-43 SOC 1-12 FH334.25

P8668 39MU 31-5-41 234S 7-8 FTR ops 27-8

P8669 FIIB Cornwall 12MU 25-5-41 303S 1-7 ROS VA 4-8

P8670 FIIB 2nd City of London Textiles 24MU 22-4-41 610S 11-6 616S 19-7 315S 2-8 f/ld cd nr Wattisham CE 9-8 AST

P8671 FIIB Cambourne-Redruth 45MU 19-5-41 118S 30-6 132S 14-10 57 OTU 10-4-42 e/fd f/ld on Goswick Sands N'land CE 28-4-43

P8672 FIIB Cardiff II 37MU 26-5-41 303S 16-6 FTR after comb bf109 25-6

P8673 FI con to FIIB 45MU 22-5-41 118S 22-6 FAAC 24-8 ROS 154S 10-12 132S 11-3-42 52 OTU 12-4 53 OTU 24-6-43 SOC 20-11-44

P8674 Afrikaander 39MU 7-6-41 412S 23-7 310S 21-10 416S 5-12 FAAC 26-2-42 ROS 58 OTU 27-4 33MU 21-9 con to ASR(IIC) 276S 29-12 i/sea ops nr Sept Isles France 8-6-43 FH289.20

P8675 FI con to FIIB Cliftonian 45MU 31-5-41 118S 29-6 124S 27-9 FACB 1-11 SOC 9-11 SAL AFDU 17-11-42 cd/ld Dalton CAC 1-10-43 recat E SOC 14-12

P8676 FIIB Ceredigian II 37MU 26-5-41 145S 19-6 306S 9-7 308S 14-7 dvd into grd CE dbf nr Ruislip Middx 9-8 SOC 19-8

P8677 FI con to FIIB 45MU 22-5-41 118S 29-6 124S 27-7 54S 18-11 61 OTU 19-6-42 FACB 19-9-43 ROS CE 29-7-44

P8678 9MU 31-5-41 452S 10-7 129S 26-8 610S 26-8 flew i/grd nr Scarborough Yorks dbf 4-10 SOC 10-10

P8679 9MU 31-5-41 19S 29-6 1CRU 1-8 504S 3-11 58 OTU 13-2 air coll with P7776 cd Dunfermline Fife CE 5-6-42

P8690 FIIB Caernarvonshire 12MU 25-5-41 610S 3-6 616S 19-7 FTR ops 21-7

P8691 FI con to FIIB Ceredigian I 12MU 23-5-41 72S 9-7 416S 14-1-42 FAAC 9-3 ROS 58 OTU 31-12 1CACU 22-3-43 TAFD 19-6 61 OTU SOC dbr 26-1-45

P8692 FIIB Crisps 12MU 25-5-41 222S 26-6 53 OTU 8-10-42 FTR 5-11

P8693 FIIB Grebbeberg 45MU 11-6-41 118S 30-6 124S 3-10 FACB 15-10 SAL 61 OTU 30-6-42 FAAC 26-12 ROS FACB 8-2-43 ASTE 19-2 58 OTU 4-7 strk house in low level mock attack Kirriemuir Angus CE 18-10 SOC 31-10 FH529.35

P8694 FIIB 12MU 31-5-41 306S 1-7 308S 14-7 65S 15-9 616S 6-10 22-11 58 OTU 8-6-42 hit grd fly low Dripmoss West Haugh Stirling CE 2-7-43 SOC 9-7 FH639.25

P8695 North West Frontier IV 8MU 12-6-41 152S 6-7 611S 31-12 AFDU 24-3-42 1687BDF 5-3-44 FAAC 30-9 ROS SOC 20-8-45

P8696 FIIB Dilawar 12MU 14-6-41 610S 1-7 616S 19-7 315S 30-7 FTR ops 9-8

P8697 FIIB 12MU 7-6-41 118S 23-6 124S 27-9 54S 18-11 std in circuit cd Castletown CE 28-1-42 SOC 1-2

P8698 39MU 20-6-41 308S 3-7 FTR over France 17-7-42 FH20.55

P8701 FIIB 39MU 22-7-41 303S 4-7 65S 18-9 616S 6-10 FTR ops 18-11-42 FH81.50

P8702 24MU 22-4-41 71S 12-8 401S 9-9 74S 20-10 350S 28-11 CE 9-1-42 SOC 22-1

P8704 24MU 22-4-41 64S 14-8 611S 12-11 52 OTU 16-2-42 FACB 5-4 1CRU 11-4 53 OTU 16-9 FAAC 3-9-43 ECFS 1-7-44 5PAFU 4-12 SOC 28-6-45

P8705 FI con to FIIB 38MU 6-7-41 118S 5-8 124S 26-9 54S 18-11 58 OTU 4-4-42 FAAC 21-9-43 61 OTU 9-5-44 SOC CE 9-10 PAL 6-10-45

P8706 37MU 29-6-41 19S 6-8 234S 21-8 FAAC 26-8 ASTH 5-9 con to FVA M45 72S 26-11 332S 13-2-42 164S 23-4 std app Skae CE 8-7 SAL SOC FH172.30

P8725 FIIB 38MU 5-7-41 222S 12-7 CAC ops 18-7 ASTE 11-8 con to FVB M45 302S 25-4-42 spun i/grd Fairmile Henley on Thames 29-5 SOC 5-6

P8726 37MU 1-7-41 403S 16-7 54S 25-8 FTR ops 27-8 SOC 28-8

P8727 24MU 18-7-41 FAAC 23-7 SAL PIGTW 25-2-42 AST 5-2-43 con to FV M45 con to ASR(IIC) 276S 13-7 ASTE CB ops 20-5-44 SOC sold L Branson Kings Langley 24-7-46 G-AHZI cd Kastrup Airport Denmark 15-4-47

P8728 12MU 25-7-41 222s 29-7 145S 30-8 e/fd t/o cd nr Catt CE 19-10 SOC 26-10

P8729 37MU 25-7 19S 6-9 331S 8-11 e/fd w/u ldg Cleat Farm Kirkwall 10-1-42 SOC 8-2

A total of 170 F IIBs were produced, plus a number of F IIAs converted to IIB standards. These were recorded as being F I con to F IIB, the assumption being an F I fuselage married to the B wing.

Converted to ASR(IIC). P7321 7325 7359 7366 7490 7605 7628 7673 7732 7734 7775 7818 7836 7858 7889 7915 7917 7918 7994 8020 8022 8030 8032 8072 8079 8082 8096 8131 8179 8203 8232 8253 8261 8265 8271 8274 8322 8325 8375 8341 8441 8479 8509 8521 8565 8584 8667 8674 8727

Converted to FVA/B P7287 7297 7299 7316 7324 7447 7498 7505 7352 7619 7629 7661 7686 7732 7757 7789 7846 7849 7906 7909 7920 7964 7965 7986 8036 8038 8083 8086 8095 8099 8167 8195 8237 8239 8346 8259 8262 8324 8339 8348 8436 8438 8445 8517 8545 8549 8563 8589 8595 8645 8706 8725

To Royal Navy P7316 7786 7892 7909 7964 8237 8246 8373

To Middle East P7315

Maintainence and Ins. airframes. P7288(4409) 7964(5262) 8090(4256) 8091(4936)

To USAAF P7849

1 2 3 4

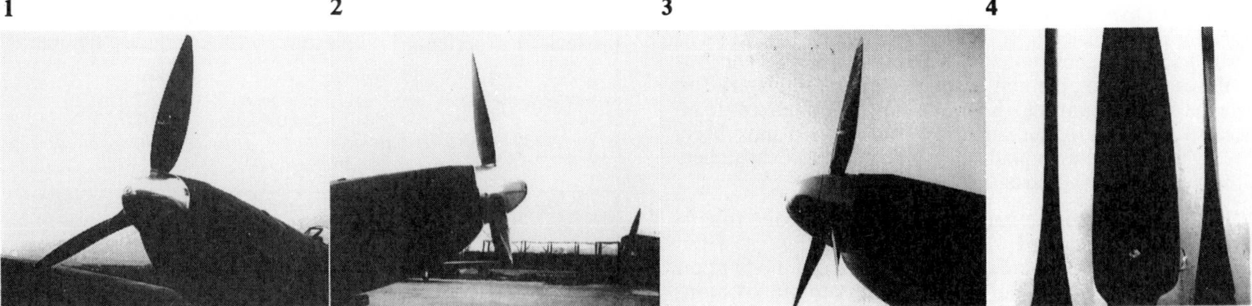

K9791 was used for a whole series of trials with varius propellers. See page 97 for full details and decode of numbers.

5 6 7 8

SPITFIRES IN THE BATTLE OF BRITAIN

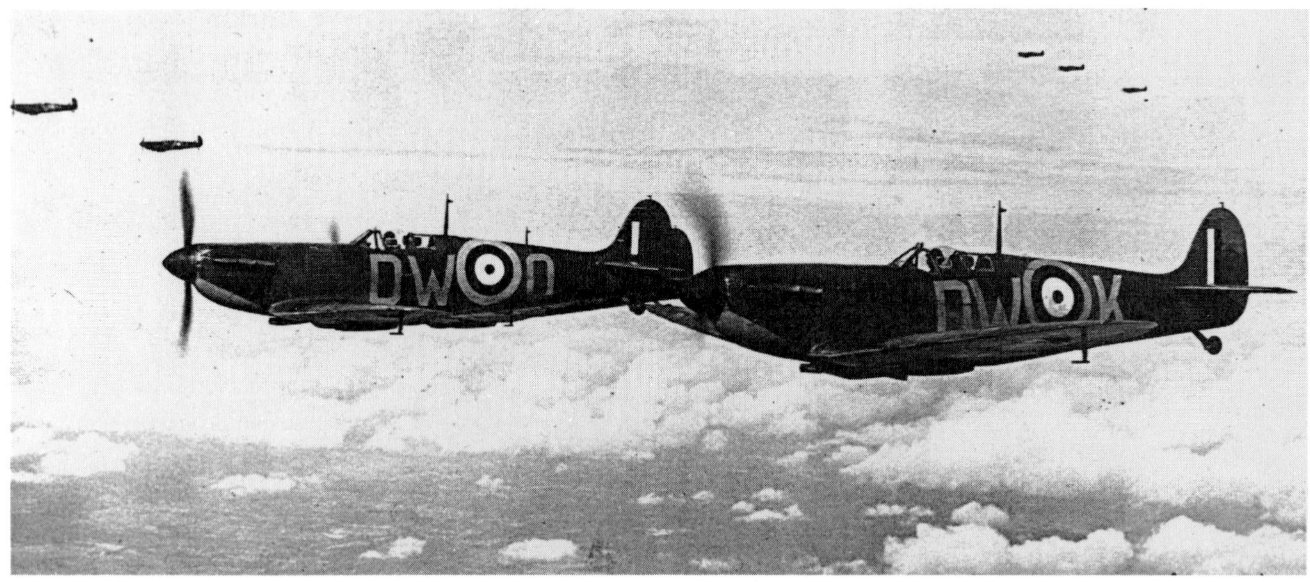
N3029 (DW-K) during the BoB. It was shot down by a Bf109 on 5 September 1940 and crash landed near Gravesend, Kent. It was repaired by Air Service Training, Hamble, and sent overseas for the Middle East, only to be lost when transport Peter Mearsk was torpedoed and sunk.

On 1 July 1940 Fighter Command stood ready awaiting the expected onslaught by the German Luftwaffe. Churchill had sounded the warning; Hitler declared the subjugation of England; Goering predicted the destruction of the Royal Air Force. The British people might have been forgiven, when swamped with the tide of rhetoric, for thinking that preparations for the forthcoming Battle of Britain had been hastily cobbled together after the retreat from Dunkirk. But this was not so for such an event had been examined by the Air Staff and a defence system built up through the late 20s and 30s. Dowding was one of the plan's architects which considered every possibility from the loss of mainland France and having to continue a war from British bases, to the defeat of England and continuation of the fight from across the Atlantic in Canada.

The first possibility was now a fact, the second could happen, and Dowding's letter to the War Cabinet concerning despatch of British fighters to go to the aid of the French forces is too well known to repeat in these pages. But what is not known is that Dowding had actually anticipated such an event as is evidenced by his letter of 16 September 1939, just 13 days after war had been declared on Germany. It read – "The Air Council's estimate for the number of squadrons necessary for the defence of this country (UK) was 52 and although aware of the necessity to send fighter squadrons to France, I have been repeatedly told that these squadrons would never be despatched until the safety of the home base had been assured.

"I learned with consternation that four Hurricane squadrons were to be despatched to France within ten days of the declaration of war and before any attack had been made upon this country. In addition I had received orders to put six more squadrons on a mobile basis by January 1940, and although I have received assurances that these would never be withdrawn from the defence unless this could be done with safety, I know how much reliance to place upon such assurances. My next shock was to discover that the Air Ministry contemplated reduction of my remaining fighter squadrons from 36 to 27. This is a grim prospect – the number is exactly half that laid down by the Air Council as necessary for the defence of this country.

"It is clear, therefore, that the despatch of four field force squadrons has opened a tap through which will run the entire Hurricane force, and that the Hurricane squadrons will become a diminished force doomed to extinction by February 1940".

The necessity for preserving the Spitfire squadrons now becomes crystal clear and Dowding was determined not to part with one of them for he knew he would need every aeroplane to fight off an air attack on England should France fall.

Churchill was still on the fringe of politics at this period and his comments are not available, but not every member of the Establishment was against Dowding's ideas as is made clear by the thoughts of Sir Archibald Sinclair, the Minister of Air. He had written to Dowding as early as 26 May 1938 saying that during forthcoming talks with the French Government Mission no encouragement should be given to members of the Mission – "Should the attempt to create the impression that the impending staff conversations include discussion of war plans and amount virtually to a defensive alliance between our two countries". He went on to say that in particular no reference was to be made to (a) RDF (radio direction finding) (b) Fighter Command Organisation (d) Policy for use of RDF (e) Cathode ray direction finding (RADAR) (f) explosive ammunition (g) aircraft and engine production (h) reserves of above (i) aircraft, engines and armament on the secret list. Was this normal prudence by a cabinet minister to keep secrets from an Ally, or was it the more, deep-seated feelings of mistrust that had existed between the two countries for many years?

After Dowding's second well-known letter, and Churchill's action in preventing additional British fighters being sent to France, there never was a serious, long term shortage of aircraft for Fighter Command. The most pressing problem was the lack of experienced pilots to man the machines. Churchill,

X4330 of No.92 Squadron lands with its companion after an interception.

determined to be involved in every aspect of the war, wrote a series of letters to Sinclair about pilot shortage, letters that began with Sinclair signing his "Archie" and ending several months later with his full title of Secretary of State for Air. Winston could be very pedantic and wearing.

Churchill's first letter, dated 3 June 1940, said – "He was aware that 7,000 pilots for whom there were no aircraft had to be re-mustered, and all of whom had done many more flying hours than those of German pilots. How then was the shortage explained".

Sinclair replied – "The 7,000 pilots were peace time entries for the RAFVR and this had not been in existence long enough to produce trained pilots. It was not correct to say they had been re-mustered but they had to wait a long time before they could be absorbed by the training machine. The present shortage of pilots was due to wastage owing to the intensive warfare of the past three weeks in France and Dunkirk; formation of new squadrons from 21-26 pilots per squadron; bad weather affecting training made a total of 550 pilots. Also, personnel had to be supplied for the creation of the Dominion Training Scheme. We do hope to tap other sources of trained pilots – Poles, Norwegians, Belgiums, and we hope to obtain some Americans by launching an appeal in America and perhaps the Admiralty can help. The total deficiency in Fighter Command in May 1940 was 448 pilots."

At the beginning of July Sinclair informed Churchill that 1,058 fighter pilots were available, but Churchill was not convinced. On 9 August with the Battle of Britain approaching its peak he instructed Sinclair – "To comb out all squadrons in all branches to obtain more pilots". Sinclair did initiate several schemes but by the time the pilots were available the great urgency was over and Churchill turned his mind to other matters of the moment.

A large number of RAF fighters were lost in France during the retreat to the Channel ports and Dowding then wrote his dramatic second letter in which he said that the loss of additional fighters in the defence of France could ultimately lead to the defeat of England. Churchill listened, and acted, and as a result among the fighter squadrons standing ready on 1 July 1940 were nineteen equipped with Mitchell's Spitfire.

After the victorious conclusion of the campaign against France on 25 June 1940 it was the intention of the German General Staff to force a swift defeat on England by landing on the mainland. The operations which followed this decision met with greater difficulties than on the Continent because of the problems associated with transporting an army across the English Channel. England was protected by the Royal Navy and was able to supplement, and even to re-inforce, her power from overseas and as a sea power could only be defeated at sea.

German naval forces were inadequate due mainly to the failure to rebuild its Fleet after the defeat of World War I. In these circumstances the German High Command had decided to attack the British mainland and to do this it was necessary to achieve air superiority by crushing the Royal Air Force. At the time of Dunkirk there were those who thought this could be accomplished, but historical hindsight has revealed that it was a task almost beyond the capability of the German forces as they existed at that time.

The Luftwaffe strength committed to the task of overwhelming the Royal Air Force was divided into three, major sections — in Norway and Denmark, Luftflotte 5 with Fliegerkorps X; in Holland, Belgium and Northern France, Luftflotte 2 with Fliegerkorps I and II, the 9th Fliegerdivision, Jagdfuhrer 2 and the Night fighter Division; in other parts of France, Luftflotte 3 with Fliegerkorps IV, V and VIII, and Jagdfuhrer 3.

According to the order dated 2 August 1940, preparation for the campaign was to be completed by 5 August in order that from the following day Luftflotten 2 and 3 could deal a strong initial blow. The attack order was code named 'Eagle Day'.

The first German troops were scheduled to land in England four weeks after the beginning of the air war and according to the plans for this oepration (code name 'Sealion') the 6th and 9th German Armies were to cross to various positions on the south and south east coast of England, with the main attack falling on the area between Dover and the Isle of Wight. To carry out the preliminary air operations, Reichmarshall Goering had assigned Luftflotten 2 and 3 the task of gaining air superiority over southern England by destroying the Royal Air Force, in particular fighters, in the air

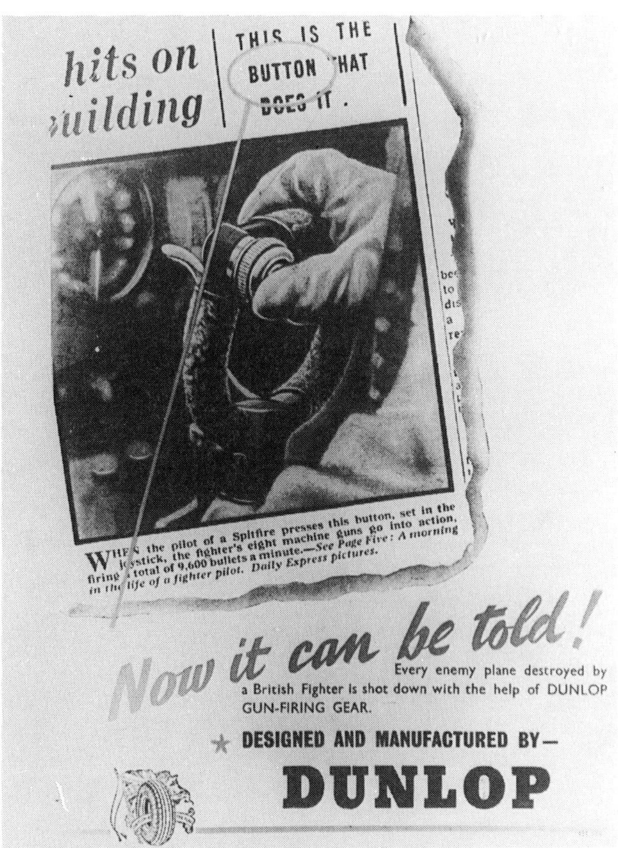

The propaganda war enhanced the Spitfire legend as this contemporary (1940) Dunlop advertisement reveals. (Dunlop).

The Dunlop spade grip and firing button of the Spitfire joystick. (Dunlop).

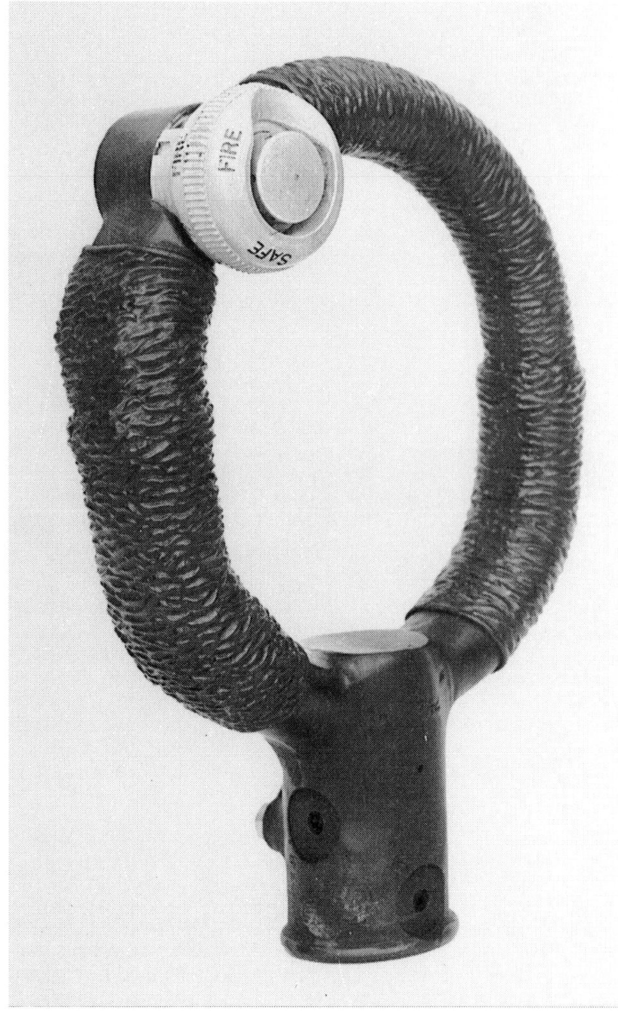

X4178 (EB-K) was lost on operations while serving with No.41 Squadron in the final days of the Battle.

YT-F of No.65 Squadron, pilot officer David Glaser. Note anti-glare shield on cowling. (Glaser).

and on the ground; airfield bases and supply installations, particularly those of night fighter formations.

Luftflotte 5 was to begin its attack on the RAF and the aircraft industry in the Newcastle area on the afternoon of 'Eagle Day' plus one. The German Command thought it possible to defeat Fighter Command in the forward areas of southern England in just four days, after which the air offensive was to be moved north over a line running from Kings Lynn to Leicester.

Bad weather and other factors delayed 'Eagle Day' by seven days and in anticipation of an improvement 'Eagle Day' was set for 13 August. RAF Pilots in southern England had been fighting off Luftwaffe attacks and were unaware that the main battle had yet to begin. The first large scale attacks extended to about 30 airfields and a number of industrial installations, and up to the 17th 44 airfields had been attacked with eleven severely damaged*.

The air war grew in intensity and by 7 September London was attacked for the first time and the RAF hard pressed, but because of the determined defence operation "Sealion" had to be postponed and eventually abandoned. RAF aircraft losses are listed in the following pages; German sources claim that in the same period the total Luftwaffe losses, including those not directly associated with the BoB, were 2,071 for the period July to October. The last Spitfire to be destroyed in the Battle of Britain was Mk I X4542.

The conflict was to last 18 weeks or 116 days, and during this period 326 were destroyed, 589 damaged and 76 struck off charge. But 808 entered service and this total includes Spitfires having been repaired and returned to active service. The following records have been taken to cover the period 1 July to 31 October 1940. From the German viewpoint the aerial attack on England was initiated in the German Operations Order dated 2 July, which stated that attacks would start the following day. The British view is that the attacks began on 10 July and ended 31 October (Ministry of Defence). So to cover all aspects the four month period has been selected.

Many Spitfires were damaged as Category I, but most of these were repaired on site (ROS) by the squadrons so that no record is found of these incidents on the Aircraft Record Card (Form 78) from which this listing is compiled. Abbreviations used:- I.S. (Into service), Dam (Damaged). Des (Destroyed). The first Spitfire to be destroyed was K9928 of No 74 Squadron on 3 July. Hitler finally cancelled "Operation Sealion" and England was never again attacked in strength by the Lufwaffe by day. The 'Few' had won their victory and passed into history.

A group of No.74 Squadron Spitfire Mk Is coming into land.

* *Eastchurch, Gosport, Lee on Solent, Lympne, Manston, Tangmere, Hawkinge, Portsmouth, Rochester, Driffield and Martlesham Heath. Twelve more were badly mauled; Andover, Benson, Biggin Hill, Cardiff P.M., Detling, Kenley, Netheravon, Odiham, Redhill, Gravesend, Maidstone and Sealand. Twenty-one had slight damage; Abingdon, Boscombe Down, Farnborough, Hullavington, Old Sarum, Blandford, Bristol-Whitchurch, Canterbury, Filton, Halton, Hamble, Middle Wallop, Reading-Hodley, Wilmington, Worthy Down, Yeovil, Kinloss, Linton on Ouse, Montrose, Penrhos and Wick. Not all were RAF stations, and included supply stores, flying schools and bomber stations.*

July 1 I.S P9310, P9550. Dam R6640, R6684.
July 2 I.S K9998, L1055, Dam P9390, R6590, R6599, R6607. SOC P9420.
July 3 Des K9928.
July 4 Dam P9491. Des N3294.
July 5 I.S R6809. Dam K9994, P9433, P9450, P9454, P9507. Des P9449.
July 6 Dam P9444, P9544, SOC P9498, R6640.
July 7 I.S K9857, K9931, L1071, P9513, R6703. Dam K9910, L1080. Des N3129, R6609, R6615, R6711.
July 8 Dam K9914, L1001, P9465, R6806. Des K9907, R6634.
July 9 I.S R6893, R6895, R6905. Dam K9799, R6637. Des L1075, N3183, R6637, R6705.
July 10 I.S R6712, R6713, R6714, R6719, R6720. Dam K9863, P9399, P9446.
July 11 I.S K9879, R6715, R6889, R6890, R6897. Des L1069, L1095.
July 12 I.S P9516, R6706, R6775, R6777, R6779, R6780, R6799, R6812, R6814, R6815, R6816, R6884. Dam N3231, P9467. Des P9502.
July 13 I.S K9890, K9933, L1018, P9381, R6765, R6766, R6771, R6772, R6773, R6807, R6898, R6899, R6901, R6906. Dam K9795, N3099, P9434. Des K9869, R6688.
July 14 I.S K9800, N3054, N3106, N3273, N3281, R6271, R6835, R6911, R6912, R6917, R6919. Dam K9825, P9512.
July 15 Dam K9790, N3060, N3245, P9434. SOC P9399.
July 16 I.S N3034, N3050, N3164, N3250, N3265. Dam L1000. SOC. L1093.
July 17 I.S P7286 (II), P9375. Dam K9942, N3203, P9507. Des K9916.
July 18 I.S K9841, P9432, R6767. Dam L1049, L1055, N3170, N3240, N3244, P9440, P9519, R6636, R6755, R6765. Des K9990, P9452.
July 19 I.S P9384, R6924. Dam K9825, K9995, P9324, R6770.
July 20 I.S N3056, N3234, N3270, P9445, R6626, R6752, R6754. Dam K9821, K9883, K9936, R6621, R6752. Des K9880.
July 21 I.S K9865, K9945, K9961, K9984, N3234, R6768, R6810, R6811. Dam K9980, N3100, P9499, R6771. Des N3184. SOC K9869.
July 22 I.S K9972, N3046, P9335, R6763, R6764, R6916, R6921, R6923, R6977, R6979. Dam K9950, N3062, P9334, R6597. SOC P9507.
July 23 I.S L1083, N3286, P9422. Dam K9899, N3026, R6767.
July 24 I.S P9490, R6621, R6975, R6976, R6978, R6981. Dam R6976. Des N3041, N3192, R6812.
July 25 I.S R6914, R6984, R6985. Dam K9901, L1055, N3288, P9327, P9382, P9387, P9549. Des L1035, P9421, P9493, R6707, R6816.
July 26 I.S R6614, R6643, R6683, R6800, R6801, R6818, R6990. Dam K9815, N3118, N3167, N3288, P9383. Des N3201.
July 27 I.S L1060, N3037, P9372, R6775, R6980, R6983. Dam K9982, L1037, P9396. Des N3023, N3287.
July 28 I.S R6808, R6918, R6920, R6962, R6986, R7017, R7019, R7021. Dam K9970, P9334, P9336, P9429, R6627, R6779. Des P9547.
July 29 I.S R6757, R6839, R6840, R6995. Dam L1083, N3112, N3264, R6643. Des N3038, N3042.
July 30 I.S R6756, R6759, R6885, R6887, R6958, R6965, R6967, X4015. Dam R6714, R6777, R6838.
July 31 I.S R6769, X4020. Dam P9503, R6983, R6990, R9817. Des P9365, P9379, P9398, R6693. SOC K9901, K9928, R6693.

Aug 1 I.S R6778, X4019, X4021, X4022. Dam K9789, K9829, K9892, N3069, P9461. Des K9879, R6617. SOC K9815.
Aug 2 Dam K9892, R6627, R6717, R6895. Des N3128, R6717, R6799.
Aug 3 I.S R6760, R6894, X4029. Dam K9929, P9516.
Aug 4 I.S R6610, R7015. Dam R6697. Des N3271. SOC P9336.
Aug 5 Dam K9891, K9954, N3234. Des L1029.
Aug 6 I.S N3198, R6992. Dam K9991. Des L1078, P9366.
Aug 7 I.S K9807, N3199, N3270, R6802. Dam K9817, L1054, N3270, P9518. Des R6696.
Aug 8 I.S R6627, R6803, R6988, R6989. Dam K9870, K9894, L1094, N3278, P9380, P9436, R6995. Des K9905, K9911, L1039, R6811.
Aug 9 I.S P9433, R7018, X4017, X4018, X4059, X4060, X4061. Dam L1059, N3034, R6639, R6992. Des P9369.
Aug 10 I.S K9947, N3113, R6716, R6907, R6910, X4231. Dam P9468, R6901. Des L1063.
Aug 11 I.S R6926, R6987, X4016, X4023, X4030, X4034, X4064, X4067. Dam N3106, R6689, R6698, R6702, R6908, R6916, R6991. Des L1037, P9393, R6614, R6630, R6757, R6916, R6918, R6962.
Aug 12 I.S X4065, X4068, X4070. Dam L1045, N3124, N3160, P9330, P9495, P9545, R6621, R6815, R6914. Des K9999, L1044, N3175, P9333, P9456, X4018.
Aug 13 I.S N3268, P9361, P9497, R6641, R6879, R6881, R6891, R6961, R6963, R6964, R6966, R7020, X4063, X4102, X4103, X4105, X4109, X4163. Dam K9871, R6608, R6759, R6830, R7020. Des N3091, R6880.
Aug 14 I.S K9895, K9964, L1068, P7290 (II), P7291, P7292, P7302, P7303, P7304, P7305, P7314, P9554, R6801, R6968, X4024, X4027, X4069, X4101. Dam K9876, K9947, L1009. Des N3024. SOC. K9912, L1078.
Aug 15 I.S K9997, R6769, R6922, R6928, X4166, X4168, X4169, X4171. Dam K9807, N3097, N3116, N3230, N3245, P9363, R6910, R6968, R7019. Des K9964, N3168, N3189, N3277, R6981, R6988, R6990, R7015.
Aug 16 I.S K9921, K9983, L1028, L1056, N3269, P9465, P9555, P9556, P9557, R6631, X4066, X4104, X4107, X4108, X4110, X4160, X4161, X4165, X4167. Dam K9864, L1038, N3242, P9463, R6896, R6985, X4030, X4063. Des K9915, N3095, N3240, P9312, P9554, R6618, R6768, R6802, R6967, R6985, X4016. SOC. K9946, N3095, P9369.
Aug 17 I.S K9850, K9874, K9996, L1011, R6957, R6969, R6973, R6974, R6991, X4031, X4032, X4035, X4036, X4170, X4172, X4173, X4174, X4175. Dam K9959, K9960, P9307, P9462. Des K9791.
Aug 18 I.S K9841, P9562, R6758, R6886, R6994, R7016, X4010, X4025, X4179. Dam K9969, L1005, L1088, N3127, P9557, R6694, R6762, R6891, R6920, X4110. Des L1019, N3040, R6713.
Aug 19 I.S K9840, K9862, K9904, K9995, N3282, P9491, P9561, P9563, R6600, R6686, R6710, R6831, R6832, R6834, R6909, R6925, R6927, R6959, R6970, R6971, R6996, R7022, X4009, X4026, X4028, X4033, X4164, X4182, X4183. Dam L1080, R6913, X4026. Des N3182, R6703.
Aug 20 I.S N3110, R6777, X4239. Dam P9335. SOC K9954, P9366.
Aug 21 I.S K9918, L1063, P7298, P7300 (II), P7301, P7321, P7322, P7323, P9427, X4037, X4038, X4051, X4052, X4187, X4188, X4232, X4233. Dam P7290, P7303, P7304, P7305, P7314 (All IIs).
Aug 22 I.S X4251. Dam K9997, N3221, P9492, R6770, R6829, X4239. Des K9909, R6695, R6708. SOC N3097.

Aug 23 I.S N3058, N3072, X4053, X4054. Dam K9833, K9933, R6620, X4032, X4160, X4177. Des R6926. SOC. R6830.
Aug 24 I.S X4234, X4252, X4253, X4254, X4255, X4256. Dam K9975, L1037, L1082, R6641, R6686, R6884, X4067. Des N3239, P9389, X4102. SOC P9495.
Aug 25 I.S K9840, P9511, X4235, X4236, X4238. Dam N3268, P9322, P9451, R6969. Des K9819, K9931, N3226, P9381, R6810, R6966, R6994.
Aug 26 I.S N3227, P7283 (II), P7284, P9368, P9454, X4012, X4180, X4181, X4184, X4186. Dam K9827, K9908, K9947, P9494, R6632, R6897, R6970, R7018, X4011, X4023, X4187. Des N3275, P9496, R6595, R6633, R6701, R6758, X4188, SOC N3116, X4263.
Aug 27 I.S K9818, L1060, P7281 (II), P7299, P7354, P9515, R6961, X4011, X4013, X4014, X4269, X4270. Dam K9922, K9995, X4180. Des P9548, R6831. SOC R6818.
Aug 28 I.S L1077, X4246, X4247, X4248. Dam K9833, K9972, R6989, X4053. Des N3105, P9511, P9547, R6832, R6751. SOC N3234, R6766, R6995, X4061, X4066.
Aug 29 I.S N3057, X4276. Dam L1021, N3267, P9433, P9459, P9555, R6691, X4011. Des R6753.
Aug 30 I.S K9824, K9934, P9394, X4055, X4056, X4241, X4250, X4264, X4271, X4273, X4274, X4277. Dam L1012, P9325, P9375, R6719, R6720, X4020, X4027. Des K9826, L1067, P9443, R6628, R6715, R7021, X4022, X4248. SOC R6985.
Aug 31 I.S K9799, K9939, N3169, X4275, X4278, X4280, X4332. Dam K9918, L1040, N3122, N3233, N3249, P9424, P9438, P9497, P9505, R6629, R6835, R6895, X4236. Des N3110, P9323, P9337, P9360, P9457, R6628, R6912, R6928, R6958, X4054, X4231.
Sept 1 I.S L1017, L1076, P9326, P9506, P9558, P9559, P9560, R6606, R6813, R6814, R6837, X4057, X4058, X4159, X4185, X4259, X4260, X4261. Dam L1024, L1056, L1070, L1092, N3266, N3288, P9328, P9448, R6778. Des R6808, X4109, X4271, X4273. SOC N3167.
Sept 2 I.S K9847, N3094, N3229, P9376, P9439, X4262, X4318. Dam K9799, K9840, R6752, R6769, R6806, X4105, X4181, X4241, X4280. Des K9938, N3056, P9458. SOC R6692.
Sept 3 I.S K9903, K9962, L1031, N3196, P9440, R6882, X4242, X4249, X4265, X4317, X4323, X4324. Dam N3123, R6611, R6921, R6963, X4317. Des L1010, X4185, X4262, X4277. SOC K9922.
Sept 4 I.S X4319. Dam K9955, N3032, N3121, N3229, R6837, X4051, X4052, X4182, X4263. Des K9962, N3048, P9316, P9378, R6689, R6971, X4278.
Sept 5 I.S K9960, P7285 (II), P7309, P7313, P7324, P7327, X4266, X4320, X4321, X4322, X4326, X4327. Dam K9857, K9944, N3029, N3043, N3044, N3060, N3098, P9563, X4021. Des N3093, P9422, P9428, R6635, R6885, X4013, X4034, X4057, X4261, X4264.
Sept 6 I.S P7287, P7288, P7289, P7294, P7295, P7296, P7297, P7310, P7311, P7325, P7365, P7365, P9500, R6685, R6692, X4325, X4343, X4344, X4345, X4346. Dam K9903, K9976, L1020, N3279, P9376, R6600, R6834, X4035, X4253, X4318. Des L1020, N3061, N3070, N3227, P9304, P9423, X4183, X4260. SOC P9461.
Sept 7 I.S P9542, X4328, X4329, X4337, X4338, X4339, X4341. Dam K9839, K9960, N3196, N3198, R6612, R7022, X4250, X4254, X4263, X4321, X4343. Des P9430, P9466, P9467, P9560, X4009, X4168, X4256. SOC L1060.
Sept 8 I.S. N3276, P9463, R6627, R6638, R6771, R7017, X4243, X4244, X4347, X4348,

X4349. Dam R6627. SOC R6778.
Sept 9 I.S K9970, K9989, N3170, X4063, X4340. Dam K9910, L1071, N3282, P7320, P9328, R6596, R6986, X4246. Des L1077, N3049, P9372, R6901, X4260.
Sept 10 I.S K9889, K9993, L1018, N3238, P7306, P7308, P7360, P7361, P7362, P7363, P7366, P7368, P7370, P9519, R6619, R6779, X4237, X4355. Dam K9841, L1002, L1040, X4011, X4270. SOC X4236.
Sept 11 I.S N3124, R6599. Dam K9824, L1027, N3059, P7321, P9513, R6638, R6710, X4059, X4235, X4339. Des K9793, N3282, P7298, P7313, P9464, R6613, X4325.
Sept 12 I.S N3119, P7312, P7367, P9544, X4389, X4390, X4409. Dam K9981, P7310, X4254. SOC P9438.
Sept 13 I.S N3242, P7329, P7352, P7355, P7373, R6767, X4351, X4352, X4353, X4381, X4388, X4411, X4412, X4414, X4416. Dam X4159, X4422. Des R6879.
Sept 14 I.S K9801, L1014, L1030, N3172, P7356, P7371, P7376, X4067, X4413, X4415. Dam K9801, K9967, N3094, P9542, R6911, X4024, X4265. Des K9960, P9453, R6605, R6624, R6625, X4249, X4275.
Sept 15 I.S L1000, P7316, P9492, R6773, X4331, X4420. Dam N3198, P7303, R6600, R6606, R6612, R6991, X4017. Des P9324, P9431, R6690, X4070, X4324.
Sept 16 I.S X4258, X4419, X4421. Dam R6616, R6805, R6922. Des L1036.
Sept 17 I.S P9447, R6900, X4410, X4417, X4418. Dam P7305, R6610, R6887, R6996, X4178, X4409.
Sept 18 I.S N3100, N3170, N3225, N3288, P9509, X4354, X4422, X4424, X4425, X4428, X4471, X4472. Dam K9803, L1018, N3265, N3269, N3283, P9368, P9439, R6704, X4170, X4337. Des N3193, R6603, R6925, X4327.
Sept 19 I.S N3032, P7315, P7369, R6702, R6838, X4052, X4279, X4423, X4426, X4427. Dam L1073, L1093, P9307, P9313, P9426, R6900, X4029.
Sept 20 I.S N3173, R6755, R6809, X4473, X4474, X4475, X4478, X4480, X4481. Dam N3026, P9332, P9500, P9510, R6840, R6881, X4101, X4266. Des K9993, N3203, N3248, X4410, X4417. SOC P9496.
Sept 21 I.S N3244, X4267. Dam K9984, N3032, N3281, P9432, R6917. SOC N3268.
Sept 22 I.S K9873, K9979, P9434. Dam K9934, P9550, R6683, X4351, X4482. SOC X4351.
Sept 23 I.S L1049, R6643, X4177, X4356, X4479, X4483. Dam K9890, K9904, K9975, P9371, X4010, X4317, X4415, X4540. Des P7362, R6896, R7016, X4063, X4349. SOC K9967, X4159.
Sept 24 I.S N3043, P7426, R6721, R6754, X4484, X4485, X4486, X4486, X4488, X4489, X4490. Dam L1043, N3058, N3164, N3166, P9309, P9543, R6604, X4169, X4356, X4427. Des N3118, X4037.
Sept 25 I.S K9921, K9979, L1008, N3280, R6691, R6699, X4177, X4336. Des N3173, P9463, X4182.
Sept 26 I.S K9829, P7357, P7372, P7380, P7381, P7420, P7421, P7422, P7423, P7425, P7428, P7429, P7430, P7432, P7435, R6642, R6706, X4477. Dam N3288. Des K9882, K9982.
Sept 27 I.S P7318, P7379, R6607, R6889, X4544, X4550, Dam L1002, P9512, P9515, P9519, P9544, R6702, R6760, R6884, X4234, X4250, X4414. Des N3068, N3244, P9364, R6622, R6767, X4032, X4107, X4237, X4328, X4340, X4352, X4422. SOC P7019, X4323.
Sept 28 I.S K9865, L1048, N3221, N3231, X4545, X4551, X4552, X4553, X4554, X4555. Dam N3045, N3170, P7432, P7369, P9394, P9558, R6619, X4322. Des L1076, R6755, X4345, X4409, X4426. SOC N3198.
Sept 29 I.S K9795, K9807, N3099, P7375, P9545, R6597, X4539, X4546, X4548, X4556, X4557, X4558, X4559. Dam N3035, P7440.
Sept 30 I.S L1059. Dam K9943, N3113, P9465, R6596, X4069, X4344. Des K9818, L1072. SOC K9910, P9492, X4035.
Oct 1 Dam P7376. Des R6756, X4559.
Oct 2 I.S K9958, L1041, L1080, P7326, R6771, X4541, X4543, X4547, X4560. Dam K9958, P7438, R6972, X4488, X4550. Des P9553, X4545, X4549.
Oct 3 I.S P9462. Dam L1048. SOC K9981, K9984.
Oct 4 Dam K9874, P7296. Des X4320.
Oct 5 I.S N3109, P7441, P7444, P7445, P7446, P7447, X4017. Dam K9873, K9935, K9963, L1001, N3225, P7361, P9490, X4473, X4481, X4489, X4543, X4544. Des K9807, K9989, N3223. SOC R6772, X4110.
Oct 6 I.S R7020. Dam K9940, P9327, P9497. Des R6683. SOC R6702.
Oct 7 I.S K9828, K9870, N3247, P7307, X4019, X4103, X4240, X4245, X4589. Dam X4011, X4015, X4326, X4551. Des L1059, N3039, N3109, N3238, N3267, P9469, X4160. SOC K9903, N3126, P7369, X4237.
Oct 8 I.S X4586, X4587, X4588, X4592, X4593, X4594, X4596, X4598, X4599. Dam K9847, K9825, N3043, P7291, X4472. Des N3231, P7285, P7329, P7373, R6779, R6894. SOC X4250, X4322.
Oct 9 I.S K9959, P9429, X4060, X4562, X4595. Dam X4558. Des X4597.
Oct 10 Dam L1017, P7524, P9516, P9545, R6995, X4239, X4552. Des X4038.
Oct 11 I.S K9906, N3113, P7431, P7448, P9335, X4024, X4036, X4412, X4585, X4591. Dam P9391, P9395, R6616, X4036, X4255, X4337. Des K9870, P7303, P7323, P9391, P9447, X4052, X4053, X4554, X4562. SOC K9963, X4053.
Oct 12 I.S P7443. Dam P9329, P9332, P9392, P9446, P9512, X4166, X4541. Des P7441, P9327, R6599, X4591.
Oct 13 I.S N3228, N3264, P7442, R6801, X4012, X4600, X4601, X4602, X4603. Dam N3124, N3285, X4479. Des X4543.
Oct 14 I.S R6837, X4265, X4604. Dam R6763, X4330. SOC N3043.
Oct 15 I.S K9852, K9876, K9892, N3106, N3176, N3178, P9362, R6922, X4612, X4614. Dam K9795, L1089, N3161, P7444, P9397, P9440, X4068, X4585, X4612. Des R6642, R6838, X4178.
Oct 16 I.S X4606. Dam N3051, R6714.
Oct 17 I.S P7328, R6752, R6765, X4416, X4605, X4610, X4613. Dam X4164. Des P7360, R6800, X4332. SOC X4069.
Oct 18 I.S N3127. Dam N3054, N3066, N3067, P9562, R6607, R6712, R6837, R6983. SOC P9395.
Oct 19 Dam R6771. Des P9384, R6922. SOC N3039.
Oct 20 I.S N3280, N3288. Dam N3113, P7352, P7355, P9308, X4412, X4599. Des P7370, P7426.
Oct 21 I.S N3125, P7353, P7504, P7505 P7520, P7521, P7522, P7524, P9505, P9513. Dam P7504. Des N3235, X4265. SOC P9512.
Oct 22 I.S N3286, P7433. Des P7364, P7431. SOC K9980.
Oct 23 I.S L1005, L1024, L1088, P7440, P7494. Dam P9433, X4175. SOC R6714, X4541, X4553.
Oct 24 I.S K9929, N3108, P7385, P7386, P7449, P7490, P7491, P7492, P7493, P7506, P7526, P7527, P7539, P9542, R6836, X4609. Dam K9874, K9945, P7328, P9490. Des R6814.
Oct 25 I.S L1070, P7325, P7439, P7496, R6764. Dam K9852, K9970, P7325, X4480, X4590. Des P7309, P9558, X4170.
Oct 26 I.S L1061, P7507, X4615, X4617, X4643. Dam P7284, P7307, R6773, R6979, X4355. Des R6839.
Oct 27 I.S L1094, P7436, P7508, P7528, P7529. Dam N3264, P7286, P7368, P7494, P9503, R6721. Des P7365, P7439, P7526, P7539, X4548. SOC R6800.
Oct 28 I.S P7387, P7388, P7389, P7424, P7542. Dam K9801, N3293, P7327, P7435, X4604.
Oct 29 I.S P7437, P7501, P7502, P7509, P7523, P7538, P7540, P7541. Dam N3050, P7379, P7385, R6687, X4333. Des N3050, P7423. SOC L1019.
Oct 30 I.S P7351, P7503, P7525, X4608. Dam N3119, P7381, P7446, P9434, P9515,X4269. Des K9939, P7282, P7375, X4542.
Oct 31 I.S N3246. Dam K9829,P7446, X4232. SOC P9382, R6616.

THE 'AEROLITE' SPITFIRE

During the second half of 1940 it was considered by MAP that owing to the loss of access to the French-controlled bauxite deposits, there could come a time when the supply of sheet aluminium might affect aircraft production. In the event this shortage never occurred but as an insurance against such a happening it was decided to explore the viability of substituting plastic materials for metals. There were a number of companies in existence specialising in plastics and among them was a small unit based at Duxford named Aero Research Ltd, whose managing director was Norman A De Bruyne.

The company was founded in 1934 and its declared aim was to carry out industrial research of all kinds, but chiefly to develop synthetic resins into materials for use in aircraft structures. At about that period de Havilland Aircraft's propeller division was exploring the possibilities of using reinforced plastics in variable pitch propellers, and in cooperation with the Bakelite Company they were investigating the properties of cotton cord re-inforcement (as used in motor car tyres) impregnated with a solution of phenol formaldehyde resin.

De Bruyne, too, was researching the same area for re-inforced plastic was approximately half as dense as aluminium alloy and the centrifugal forces at the root end of a propeller were correspondingly reduced. De Bruyne had purchased four, second hand hydraulic presses from George Cohen and Co, and installed them in the company's factory at Duxford to produce a platen large enough to press a re-inforced stepped Bakelite blank, which could then be machined to the correct shape in the same manner as a wooden blade. But he was unable to produce a uniformly cured block of material because of its considerable thickness, and the project was dropped. He was still interested in producing a stronger, re-inforced material for aircraft construction and at the suggestion of a Mr Gordon, an undergraduate at Trinity College, he tried flax as the re-inforcement. This produced a strong material which was called Gordon Aerolite. It had a specific gravity of one half of that of duralumin.

With crossed re-inforcement a sheet material could be produced with approximately equal strength and stiffness along, and across, the grain as in plywood. The RAE reported – "It is considered that this material is the most promising organic sheet material yet produced for stressed skin aircraft covering, and it appears probable that, if available in quantity, it could be used directly to replace duralumin sheet in existing designs".

The major problem was to get the flax fibres to lay parallel to one another and de Bruyne used a machine originally designed for making material for felt hats. This machine was made to de Bruyne's order in Germany and he had to go in person to place the order, walking from Freiburg, rucksack on back, to Waldshut on the edge of the Black Forest. The Air Ministry, now showing an interest in the material, had made funds available through the good offices of a Mr Pye, who was at Trinity with de Bruyne and was then Director of Scientific Research in the Ministry. Gordon Aerolite was manufactured by coating untwisted fibres of flax with phenolic resin and making it up into six inch wide bands, these being placed side by side to make sheets of the required width. They were then laid over each other at right angles to the required thickness and subjected to pressure. Aerolite was dark brown which faded on exposure to normal atmospheric conditions without affecting the material's mechanical properties.

The first application of Aerolite to aircraft structures was this cruciform tail unit on test at Farnborough in March 1941.

There were other companies exploring the same area and Beverley Shenstone, of Supermarine, visited one called Ebenestos on 5 July 1940. He was impressed by a process for producing re-inforced plastic extrusions and sections as a continuous moulding. Like Aerolite, layers of fabric were impregnated and made in a short mould which was moved slowly forwards. Such was Air Ministry interest in the process that Mr Grinstead and N. E. Rowe of MAP were appointed as consultants to the company to advise on the material's application to the aircraft industry. A third company – Deekay Corporation – worked with felt re-inforced moulded synthetic resin and laminated woods.

The de Bruyne Gordon Aerolite was considered to have the greatest possibilities as a substitute for flat panels and a contract was placed with Aero Research for the design and production of a main wing spar for the Bristol Blenheim. During tests at Farnborough it failed at 80% load. A second contract was awarded to the company for the production of 30 Miles Magister trainer tailplanes, and at the same time de Bruyne was asked if he could produce a Spitfire fuselage in Aerolite. This was on 7 January 1940, and one year later, February 1941, the Air Ministry placed a contract No. 1164/SAS/C.38(B) for the development and production of a single fuselage at an agreed price of £5,500. Dr J.E. Gordon (now Professor, Dept of Engineering, Reading University) of Farnborough recalls that all the fuselage components, apart from a number of stress bearing members such as wing pick-up points, were manufactured from Aerolite and it was almost a "Chinese copy" of the metal airframes."

The Spitfire fuselage under construction at Duxford, 1 January 1942. The number of rivets used to pin the panels to formers was almost double that of the metal airframe.

There were many problems, mainly due to the size of sheet material. The machine producing the strips could, as already mentioned, only manage fairly narrow strips initially, and this led to almost twice the number of rivets being used to hold the plating to the framework. Also, solid rivets were useless as they tended to split the plating and eventually 'pop' rivets had to be used. The fuselage skin was made up of continuous, unbroken planks running the complete length of the airframe, and each end was moulded to include a joggle so that when joined the outer surface was flush. Engine attachment fittings were taken from a crashed Spitfire, bolted to mild steel plates and attached to the ends of Aerolite longerons with piano wire nails or pins.

There was no intention to mass produce a plastic Spitfire, but interest was considerable and a second order was placed for another prototype after the first was completed on 2 April 1941. Work began on the second airframe on 28 May but by this time de Bruyne was quarrelling with MAP and the Air Ministry. He was under capitalised and had frequently to ask for funds to

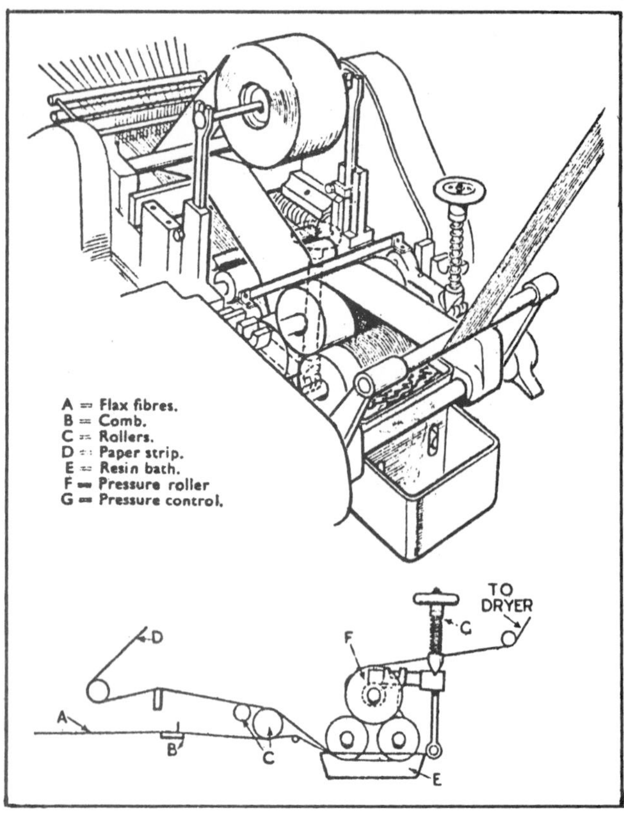

The special machine for manufacturing Aerolite.

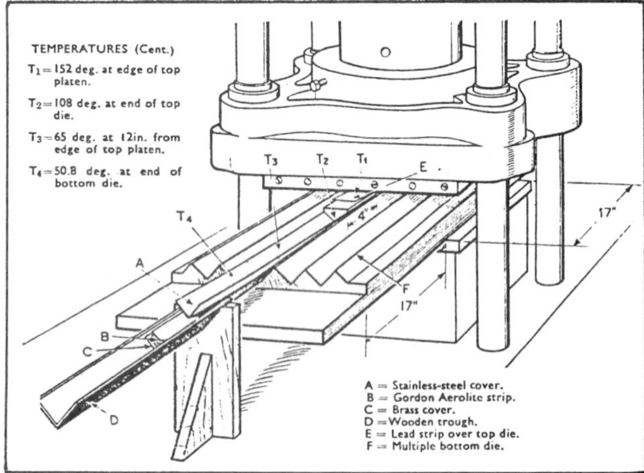
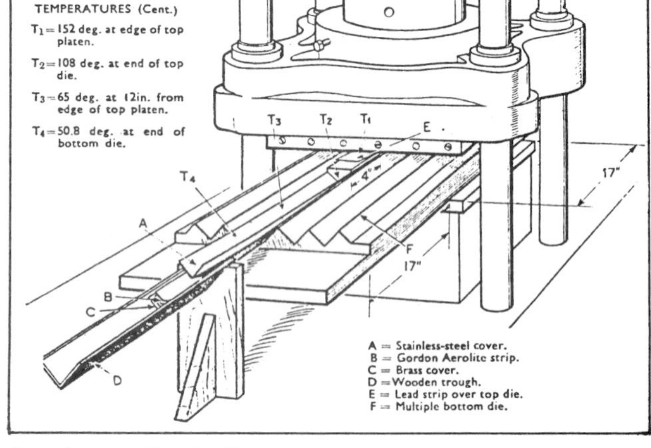

Press for extruding Aerolite.

Aerolite skin panels were joggled along one edge to provide a flush joint with a second, similar, panel.

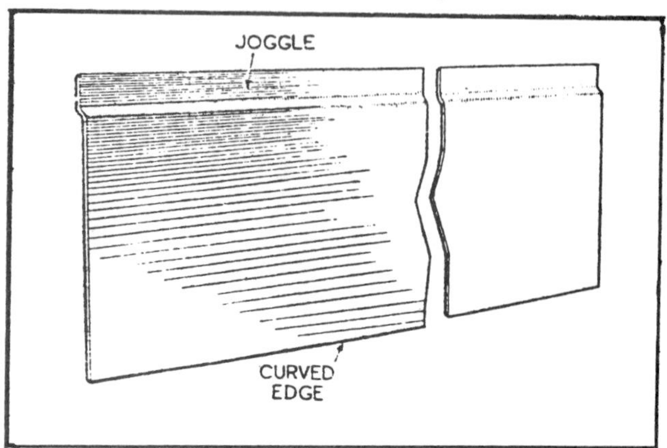

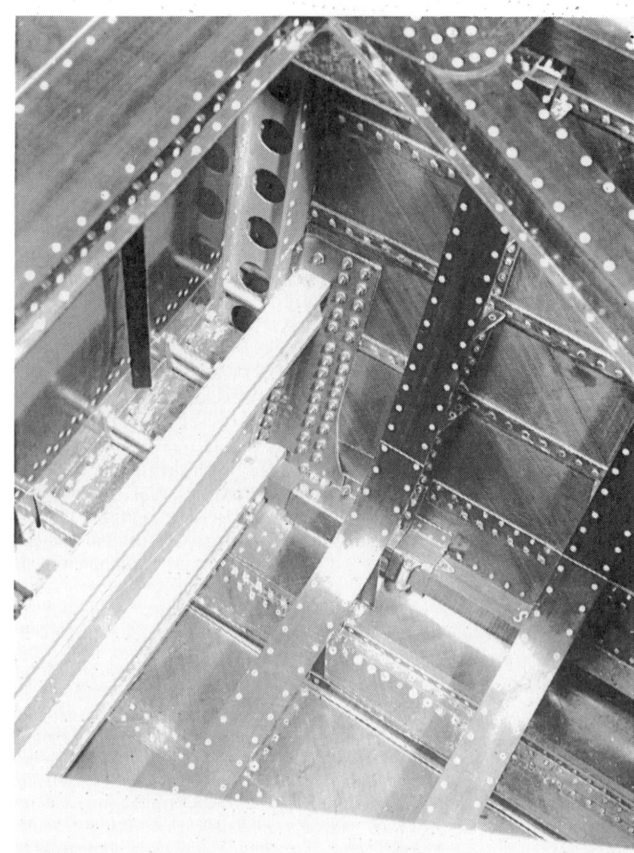

Details of the fuselage interior showing some of the metal components. Cross grain of the Aerolite is just visible.

Sections of the second plastic fuselage were sent to Farnborough and tested to destruction. The plating cracked under load at the wireless stowage position.

maintain his work force for payment from MAP was extremely slow. At this time most of the company's contracts were with the Air Ministry who were of the opinion that the proper function of the company was research, under their direction. De Bruyne resisted this attitude arguing that with controlled expansion research, production of specialised glues, moulded components and even complete aircraft could be accomplished.

An exchange of correspondence revealed how far apart de Bruyne and the Air Ministry were in their approach to the problems and, inevitably, he asked to be released from the various contracts with the second fuselage still partially finished. The Air Ministry agreed to this and withdrew all their equipment and the company went on to sub-contract the construction of Airspeed Oxford and Short Stirling sub assemblies.

De Bruyne's work was not wasted, however, for the work on specialised glues led to the development of the adhesives used by the aircraft industry for attaching metal to metal. A number of Beaufighters serving in the Middle and Far East theatres had wings with Aerolite panels installed aft of the main spar. It did tend to split along the rivet lines but was eminently suitable for tropical conditions. Bristol Aircraft adapted the material to construct copies of the German V.1 flying bomb and the Americans built a complete Harvard trainer using a similar material.

The two plastic Spitfire fuselages were transferred to Farnborough along with other equipment and used for numerous trials. An RAE Farnborough report of October 1945 contains full details of how the plastic fuselage acted during long term weathering tests. It reads – "In the early days of the war there was a shortage of light alloys for use in aircraft structures. The problem of substituting organic materials for these alloys was extensively studied at the RAE Chemical Research Lab, and elsewhere. Many different types of high strength materials were examined and it was found that plastics based on high strength cellulose fibres were the most promising. One, made by impregnating parallel bands of these fibres with phenolic resin and then curing the mass under heat and pressure, was already marketed under the name 'Gordon Aerolite'. It had excellent mechanical properties and was developed by Messrs Aero Research.

"Further, it was becoming apparent that conventional types of construction using combined metals and plastics were unsatisfactory. Several aircraft had been fitted with the rear wing surfaces covered with paper and fabric base plastic sheet securely riveted to the metal framework. Although no specific complaint was received from the service, examination showed severe buckling of the panels. Sheets attached in a dry condition buckled at high moisture contents. If attached when wet the stresses developed in shrinkage caused failure at the attachment points.

"It was decided that more conclusive results could be obtained with a structure made almost entirely of plastics. A Spitfire fuselage made from 'Gordon Aerolite' by Aero Research of Duxford, Cambridge, which had been strength tested by the Structural and Mechanical Engineering Dept, RAE, was chosen as the subject for a large scale, long term, weathering test at Farnborough.

"During two years and eight months the fuselage was completely exposed to the weather and was untouched except when it was inverted to clear it of water and rubbish. The conditions experienced were very varied. At one time the specimen was completely buried in snow, while temperature variations of −12C to 37C were recorded. During July 1945 test pieces were cut from the fuselage skin panels, box section frames and indirectional longerons. After conditioning for 14 days to 75% R.H. the moisture content of the specimens being 7.1%, the test pieces were broken in tension at a rate of loading of approximately 4,000 lb per sq in per minute.

"Although the surface finish of panels had been dulled there was no appreciable change in the general appearance of the fuselage. The riveting showed no change and there was no fungoid growth. The metal attachments were badly rusted, but the plastic beneath unaffected. No panels or stringers showed signs of buckling or failure at the attachment points. There was reduction of the mechanical properties of 'Aerolite' and this was thought to be the inherent sensitivity to moisture of the cellulose fibre."

In April 1941 Aero Research had manufactured a rear plastic fuselage based upon that of the Miles Magister for test purposes for investigation into the possibilities of using the material for construction of similar units. The specimen was tested at Farnborough and the report's conclusions were that it had sufficient strength to be used for small, training aircraft. The method of attaching the skin to stringers by wood screws was deemed unacceptable, and normal riveting was suggested as an alternative.

Although Aero Research was no longer associated with the development of plastic structures it was successful with synthetic glues and one of them – 'Ardux' – was under test by Supermarine in April 1942. Today it would have been known as an impact adhesive for when under test all those years ago the report by Supermarine describes how it was applied; – "It is applied to the surfaces to be joined, and then left for a few minutes until it became tacky. The surfaces are then clamped together and heated to 155° for six minutes. The results obtained indicate that the cement will give joints in synthetic resin which are stronger than the actual material joined." The Aero Research company also developed 'Redux'.

Research with plastics produced, among other things, the plastic pilot's seat, the first of which appeared in the latter part of 1939. One was tested in Spitfire Mk IIA (R7986) and it failed under load.

In 1946 RAE Farnborough were still producing test specimens of plastic structures, including a wing with a honeycomb interior. The material eventually appeared as 'Durestos' and sections of the Spiteful wing were produced using this material and used for tests. The delta wings of the Fairey E.10/47 were made from Durestos as an experiment in March 1952.

The Aerolite Spitfire fuselage before and after 2½ years weathering in the open.

The second Aerolite fuselage during CPB tests, Farnborough, August 1942.

SUPERIORITY SPITFIRE

As mentioned in chapter four there was at one period of time uncertainty about the future of the Spitfire, and this uncertainty was eventually resolved. Its effects upon Spitfire development can be ascertained by the following extracts from a letter written by Alan Clifton in March 1939 when he was commenting on continuation of production at Southampton. He wrote, "The whole of the new Itchen Shed is now in occupation, and by the end of the month there will be no Walrus machines left in the main works. The increased floor space will enable us to make more rapid progress with the construction of the first four-engined bomber, and will also facilitate Spitfire production, though the limiting factor in this respect will continue to be the supply of wings. Here also, the floor space will enable us to accelerate the supply of wings from our own jigs.

"Improved Spitfire. I attach a specification of an Improved Spitfire which you will note provides for 2 × 20mm Cannon Guns and is calculated to give a top speed of 400mph at 21,000 feet. This has been prepared in the hope that it may assist us to obtain further production orders for Supermarine to follow on the present contracts, a matter about which I am most concerned.

"I understand there are at the present time 35 Fighter Squadrons at home and four abroad. The present programme is seven Spitfire Squadrons for the RAF and one or two more for the Auxiliary RAF. This programme is liable to alteration. The final number of Spitfire Squadrons cannot be estimated as only the Air Council know the number of machines to be allocated to reserve, and this cannot be disclosed. Our own orders total 710, which will all be delivered in about a year from now, and Nuffield will then be starting regular deliveries of his contract for 1,000 off. It may, of course, at a later date be intended to increase the number of Fighter Squadrons, but even so there may be a reluctance to place further orders for Spitfires, and by the end of June we shall be wanting them if we are to maintain continuous production.

"If we obtain an order for the twin-engined fighter armed with one 40mm Gun, which we discussed with Sir Wilfred Freeman and which is now in the hands of the Air Staff, this would be suitable for production at Southampton, but no production orders can be expected until about the end of 1940 at the earliest. I, therefore, propose to submit the specification of the Improved Spitfire to Sir Wilfred Freeman and ask for one machine from the present contract to be allocated for modification on the lines suggested. We might have this flying in about three months from the date of instructions to proceed".

Joseph Smith, recently appointed Chief Designer of Vickers-Supermarine, had remarked that the Spitfire would see us (England) through the forthcoming war for he knew the design was capable of much development and that his main efforts would be devoted to this. At the same time the Air Ministry was formulating plans for an aeroplane to eventually replace the Spitfire, but did want enough Spitfires to cover the development period for such an aircraft. After receipt of Clifton's specification for an Improved Spitfire it was decided that with the additional advantage of advances in Merlin engine development, a second generation Spitfire could provide an aircraft to bridge the gap and as a result a specification for a Superiority Spitfire was drawn up and a Contract, number No.B23634/39, awarded to Supermarine for a single prototype. To avoid a lengthy development period of building a new airframe from scratch the Air Ministry agreed to the Supermarine proposal to take a Mk I airframe off the normal production line and modify it to the required specification. Unfortunately Supermarine's estimate of having the new Spitfire ready for initial flight trials in three months from ITP was over optimistic.

N3297 of the third serial batch was taken from the line at Woolston and developed into the Type 330 Spitfire Mk III, a design that showed remarkable promise, but which was never to be built in quantity. It was to incorporate many of the features and modifications thought desirable on the early Mk I following on its introduction into RAF service. The major change was the adoption of the Rolls-Royce Merlin RM 2SM (Mk XX) engine developing 1,390hp, an additional 300hp over that of the Merlin I and II. Other improvements to the airframe included a strengthened fuselage and engine mounting, a retractable tailwheel, an internal bullet-proof windscreen, additional armour plating and a strengthened undercarriage which had its legs raked forward by two inches at the axle. This was an (unsuccessful) attempt to cure a basic Spitfire fault, that of tipping on to its nose in rough airfield conditions. Wheel cover flaps, similar to those fitted to the prototype Spitfire, K5054, were installed, and the wings had a 3.5ft section removed from each tip to improve rate of roll, total area being reduced to 220 sq ft.

Supermarine Specification No 462 of 20 February 1939 outlined proposals for the 'Improved Spitfire'. "This specification outlines improvements to the production Spitfire to give a greatly increased performance without interfering with the rate of production.

Improved Performance. (a) below 10,000ft the maximum speed is increased by 30mph (b) at 21,000ft the maximum speed is increased to 400mph (c) the take off run is reduced by 40% compared with the production machine with fixed pitch propeller (d) the time to 15,000ft is reduced from 6.5mins to 4.5. It is proposed to fit the aircraft with two 20mm Hispano cannon. If desired the wings can be equipped to take as alternatives two cannons or four Browning guns."

In a meeting held at Southampton, and attended by Joseph Smith, Clifton and Mr Serby of ADRDL, the former was informed of the requirements for the new Spitfire's armament. They were (a) first priority to a trial installation of two 20mm Hispano cannon mounted right way up with belt feed plus four .303 Brownings (b) second priority was a four cannon installation and (c) third priority to a six .5in Colt Browning gun installation. The target date for the installation of (a) was put at no later than December but – "Production Mk Is with twin cannon would be produced at the rate of twenty per month". Joseph Smith did enquire if there would be any objection in adapting all three installations in such a manner that alternatives of cannon and machine guns could be installed. The Supermarine Specifications continued –

"The improvements in performance are analysed in Appendix II* to the Specification. The main alterations are given below and it should be noted that of these the reinforced fuselage, reduced wing area, larger radiator and oil cooler have already been incorporated and flown in the High Speed Development Spitfire.

Engine. The engine is changed from Merlin II to Merlin RM 2SM ie. 100 octane engine with 2-speed blower. This necessi-

Two types of experimental radiators were also tested for the Mk III and the differences are apparent in these photographs. Note the wing has the wheel wells faired over.

** Appendix II compared the Mk IIIs' performance with that of the Mk I.*

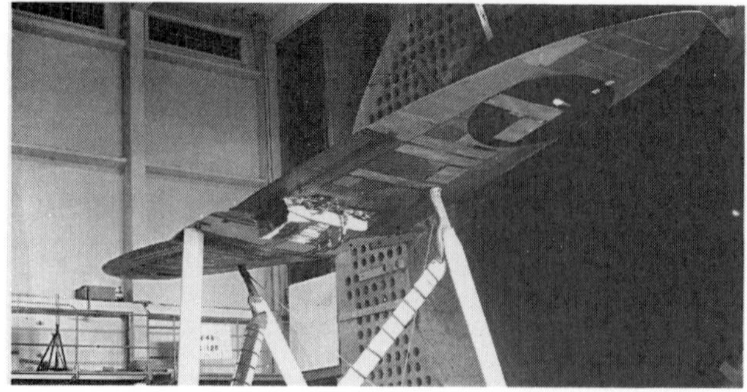

To test airflow around the Mk III radiator it was installed on a pair of Mk I wings and this photograph shows the wings mounted in the Farnborough wind tunnel on 2 November 1940. The radiator was again tested in a similar manner when fitted to the wings of W3237, the second Mk III prototype. An air by-pass was installed above the radiator to improve flow and the lip of this is just visible

The Mk III cockpit was also tested in the Farnborough wind tunnel on a facsimile fuselage. It was mounted in the inverted position.

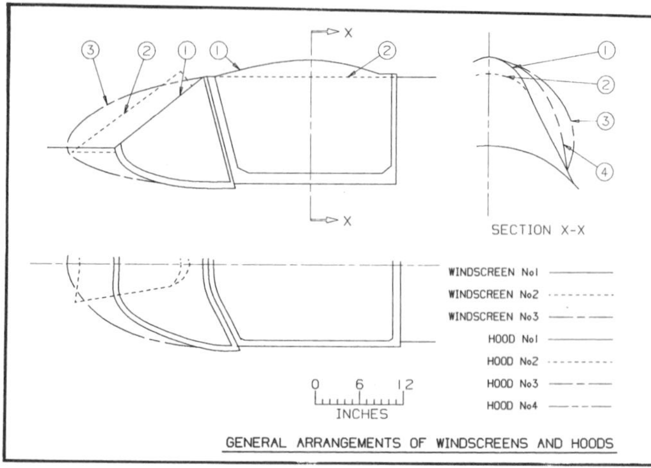

tates slight reinforcing of the fuselage and modifications to the engine mounting and cowling. This engine has been chosen because it gives substantial improvements to rate of climb and speed at lower altitudes, as well as in maximum speed at high altitudes.

Cooling System. The new engine necessitates a larger radiator and advantage is taken of this to improve aerodynamic efficiency of the installation. It is not proposed to interfere with the mounting or piping systems. The increased oil cooling requirements are met by a change of cooler and cowl to attach to the standard mounting and piping.

Wing surface. The wing area is slightly reduced without interfering with the main structural members, except at the tip where the area is removed.

Detail improvements. These include aerodynamic improvements to wheel fairings and cooling ducts, and retraction of the tailwheel. Fuel tanks. In order to retain the same duration with the more powerful engine, additional fuel tankage of 15 gallons is provided. Tyre size. Tyres are now available and can be accomodated on the aircraft to cater for increased operational load without increase of tyre pressure. Strength of structure. The standard Spitfire meets specification requirements for strength at an auw of 6,200 lb with no concessions. The estimated weight of the Improved Spitfire is 6,350 lb, an increase of 2¼% only, and to retain full standard factors, if required, only a few minor modifications are necessary".

Main particulars and performance. Span 33ft 8in; length 30ft 4in; wing area (gross) 231 sq ft; engine Rolls-Royce Merlin RM 2SM; airscrew constant speed fixed pitch. Tare weight 4,926; typical service load 608; fuel 750; oil 58. Totals 6,350. Performance . Max speed @ 21,000ft 400mph; @ 5,000 340; 10,000 360; 15,000 369. Take off distance 250yds. Climb to 15,000ft 4.5mins; to 20,000ft 6.4. Service ceiling 38,000ft.

Sir Wilfred Freeman was extremely anxious to get the new Spitfire into squadron service, and he also wanted the armament to be the 20mm Hispano cannon only. On 21 April 1939 Major H. R. Kilner, of Vickers, had a meeting at the Air Ministry with Sir Wilfred, and among other things discussed was the second generation Spitfire. Freeman wanted development of the fighter to be pushed ahead with all possible speed, and in order to introduce it into service quickly suggested that the final 200 Mk Is off the production lines should be brought up to 'Superiority Spitfire' standards. (A letter of 22 March 1940, from MAP to Supermarine, instructed the company to halt application of the 'R' prefix serials to the Spitfire Mk I and to switch to the 'X' prefix. The serial range R7023 to R7257 (98 a/c) and W3109 to W3970 (102 a/c) were to be applied to the first batch of Spitfire Mk IIIs). Sir Wilfred also discussed the question of Vickers manufacturing a belt feed for the Hispano cannon so as to provide the new Spitfire with two guns, each with 150rpg, and said that the aircraft would be a winner.

One of the first official meetings connected with the now designated Mk III was held at Rolls-Royce, Hucknall, on 31 August 1939, with Ellor and Dorey (R-R) and Smith and Mansbridge (Super) present. The first RM 2SM engine was promised for the end of September for installation in N3297, but owing to development problems it was doubtful if production engines would be ready in time and the Merlin X might have to be used for the first batch of Mk IIIs off the line. The first engine was to have electric starting and modified exhaust manifolds.

The RM 2SM engine extended fully supercharged altitude to 25,000 feet as compared to the 16,500 feet of the Merlin II, and preliminary figures issued by Rolls-Royce in December predicted a speed of 399mph @ 19,500ft (16 lb boost), and 394 (11 lb) at 21,500. To obtain additional height it was proposed to cool the 'charge' with Methanol; fit a higher speed blower and/or a two stage supercharger to the engine.

The propeller presented a number of problems as it was still of a fixed pitch type, and during a meeting between Rotol and Supermarine a Mr Brierley, of Rotols, practically accused Supermarine of misleading his company over blade design. Supermarine denied the allegation and said their only objective was to obtain the best propellers for the Spitfire. At a further meeting with a Dr Young, of the Weybridge Company, he, too, expressed concern over the proposed Mk III propeller. He said the original order had been switched from the Spitfire Mk II to the Mk III, and his company could not proceed with the order for the blades until the design had been finalised. And if the order was not placed soon the company would be forced to reduce staff owing to the lack of immediate orders.

Young was also concerned about receiving drawings for the propeller for the prototype aircraft and not production machines, and launched into a lengthy discussion about materials supplied for the propellers. His company had been using spruce with the grain running straight across the section, but owing to curvature of the core some degree of end grain at the sides of the junction caused the fairing to crumble during shaping. He thought the spruce should have a curved grain.

Four new propellers were available for the Spitfire Mk III – Rotol 3-blade dural of 10ft 9in diameter; Rotol 4-blade dural of 10ft 9in diameter; uncropped de Havilland Spitfire Mk I dural of 11ft 0in diameter; and a Rotol Jablo of 10ft 9in diameter. Rotols estimated that their propellers weighed approximately 320 lbs with spinner and Supermarine expressed some doubts about tip losses. Rotols then suggested a similar unit with wider blades, but with an additional weight of 35 lbs. Supermarine agreed to test all units. Mr Gillmore, of de Havillands, thought that the .477 reduction gear was a better proposition with their propeller than the .42 and recommended that narrow blades be used. Rotols said they were testing a VDM propeller which was not adapted for constant speed but the pitch was variable in flight. They proposed cropping and reshaping the blades to assess performance.

Despite propeller and other delays in equipment supply,

N3297, first prototype Mk III, with original shorter span wings disliked by Dowding.

the prototype Mk III N3297 was ready for weighing and CG determination at Eastleigh on 14 March 1940. It had a tare of 5,127lb and an auw of 6,572. The de Havilland propeller was fitted and the finish was quoted as being – "an egg-shell paint". It made its first flight the following day and to avoid confusion by the RAF and Royal Observer Corps it was to be known as Experimental Aircraft Type 101. It was delivered to No 11 Group Fighter Command and initial flights with the Group on 18 July confirmed the manufacturer's trials, showing great improvement over the Mk I. A report of the service trials were forwarded to Air Marshall Dowding on 30 July, a report which Dowding forwarded to the Air Ministry on 4 August accompanied by a covering letter – "I have the honour to forward... herewith a report on trials with the Spitfire Mk III carried out in accordance with your signal A300 dated 22/6. There appear to be two serious disadvantages in an otherwise excellent aircraft.

(a) The landing run is dangerously long, and probably prohibitive for night flying and (b) the square ends to the wings will make the Spitfire still more difficult to differentiate from the Bf109, a matter in which mistakes have already been made. May a pair of ordinary wings please be fitted to the Spitfire III so that it may be ascertained what reduction in the landing run is thereby obtained. I feel that the present Spitfire is already wing-loaded to the maximum extent compatible with efficiency and, if extra weight is to be added the wing surface ought to be increased rather than reduced".

Back came the Air Ministry's reply on 2 September – "I am directed to refer to your letter dealing with the above (Spitfire Mk III) subject and to inform you that calculations are now being made to determine the effect on performance and weight of fitting the Mk I Spitfire wing on to the Spitfire III. The prototype Spitfire III is now having its radiator fitted and when tests of this radiator have been completed at the A&AEE (Boscombe Down) the Mk I wings will be fitted in order that your Command may carry out further tests".*

The prototype had its second weighing and the tare had dropped to 5,069 lb but the gross raised to 6,623. It had a Merlin XX engine driving a Rotol CS propeller. The fuel tanks held 98 gallons and 76 lb ballast was carried. It was despatched to Boscombe Down later in September for trials, which were so promising that the following letter arrived at Vickers House, in Westminster, London, on 24 October 1940 – "In connection with my letter of today's date I am directed by the Ministry of Aircraft Production to inform you that it has been decided to place an order with you for 1,000 Spitfire Aeroplanes (for manufacture at the Castle Bromwich Aeroplane Factory) additional to the 1,500 Spitfire aeroplanes ordered under instruction number B.981687/39/36/a, dated 12 April 1939. Formal instructions will be issued at an early date bearing the reference number B.981687/39C.36(a) which should be used in all correspondence relating to this new order. The serial numbers allotted to the additional 1,000 aeroplanes are – Spitfire III (Merlin XX – 8 Browning guns). BL231-267, BL285-304, BL311-356, BL365-391, BL403-450, BL461-500, BL509-551, BL562-600, BL613-647, BL655-699, BL707-736, BL748-789, BL801-833, BL846-864, BL887-909, BL918-941, BL956-998, BM113-162, BM176-211, BM227-274, BM289-329, BM343-386, BM399-430, BM447-493, BM508-543, BM556-596, BM624-653. A second letter of the same date ordered (among two orders for the A and B wing Spitfire Mk I) a further 120 Mk IIIs armed with four cannon and Merlin XX engine, in the serial ranges BS573-618, BS634-659, BS677-724. The instructions concerning modification of the 200 Mk Is to Mk IIIs, of 22 March 1940, were cancelled.

N3297 arrived once again at Boscombe Down on 14 February 1941** for radiator suitability and oil cooling tests which showed that while oil cooling was adequate and the radiator suitable on the climb, the latter was not good enough for level flight. Turning performance at heights from 20,000 to 35,000 feet showed rapid deterioration in manoeuvrability and this was accentuated by the high wing loading even with engine power increased to maintain a constant ceiling. The aircraft was returned to Supermarine on 3 March and delivered to Rolls-Royce, Hucknall, for installation of the Merlin 60 and 61 to become the prototype F Mk IX, details of which appear in chapter 18.

Despite many reports to the contrary there was more than one Mk III prototype for in early 1941, just before N3297 was seconded to Hucknall for conversion to the Mk IX prototype, W3237, one of a batch of Mk V airframes, was converted at Eastleigh to Mk III standards by strengthening of the fuselage, installation of a Merlin XX, a Rotol CS propeller and an anti-spin parachute. This conversion was confirmed in a letter of 17 October to Supermarine. This letter referred to a previous note of over one year previous and dated 20 May 1940. It read – "Conversion of a second Spitfire I aeroplane to a Mk III. W3237 has been selected for the conversion at a cost to be agreed, less the sum of £4,037 already paid under contract

***Trials with a Spitfire II (P8194) fitted with a reversible-pitch de Havilland propeller did prove that landing runs could be considerably shortened.*

*****At almost the same moment in time the new Mk V Spitfire was also at* *Boscombe Down undergoing trials. On 6 March Air Chief Marshall Sir Charles Portal, at a meeting of the Joint Development and Production Committee, decided that the Spitfire V was to be produced and the Mk III abandoned.*

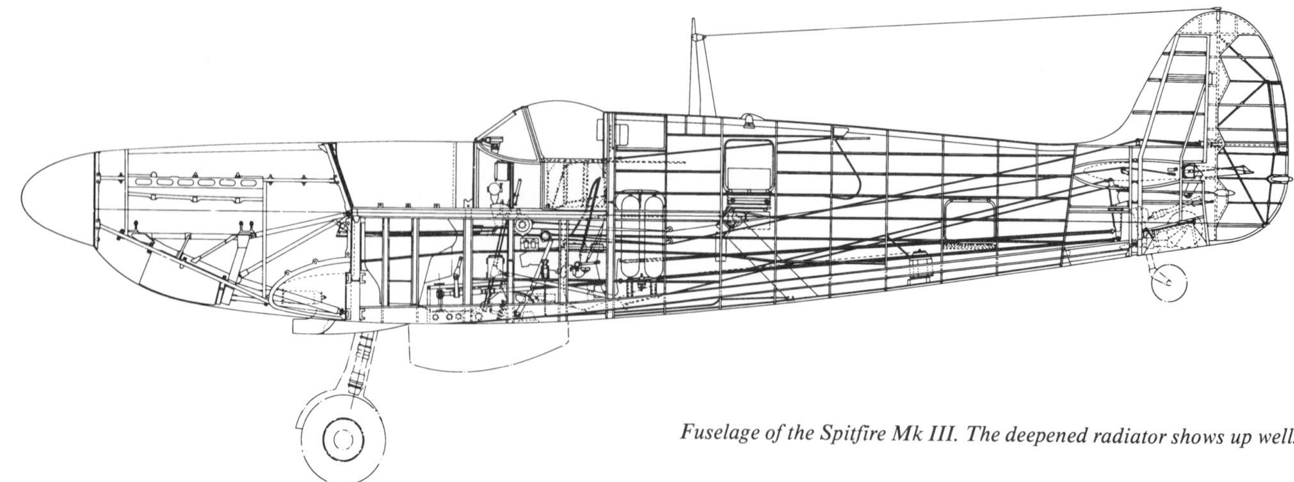

Fuselage of the Spitfire Mk III. The deepened radiator shows up well.

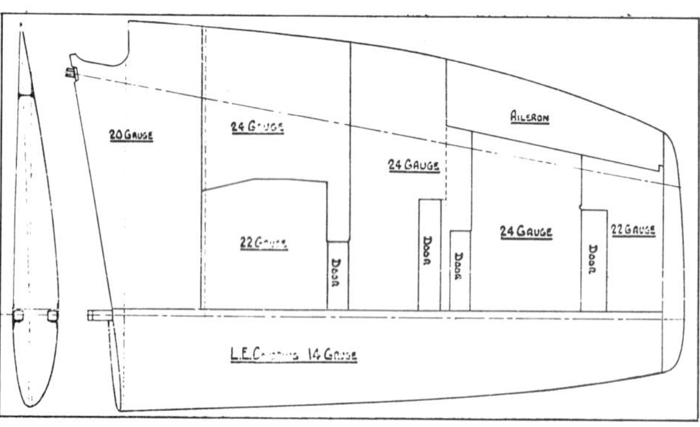

Supermarine drawing of the original Mk III wing showing skin guage.

B.19713/39C.23(c)". It was weighed at Eastleigh for the first time on 4 June 1941 and the Supermarine Technical Report (No 3106) states it was the 2nd Prototype Spitfire Mk III W3237. **Tare weight of 5,229 lb, auw with A wing (6,831, auw B wing 7,020, and with the new C wing (4 x 20mm cannon) 7,455 lb. It is** obvious that although it was a Mk III prototype it was also an interim step between that Mk and the forthcoming Mk VC with universal wing. After weighing it made its first flight late in the afternoon of the same day and was shipped to Boscombe Down some weeks later for various trials.

Returned to Eastleigh it was also used for trials with extended wing tips for installation on the PR Mk VI, one of the many, early conversions of the Mk V airframes for photo-reconnaissance duties. By the time W3237 was ready for trials

N3297 fitted with normal span wings as requested by Dowding. Note black painted area around exhaust stubs and lack of cowling to radiator.

events had overtaken it and the Mk III Superiority Spitfire programme dropped in favour of the Mk V, and so it was used mainly for experiments, the first of which took place on 29 April 1942. By this time Admiralty interest in the Spitfire as a sea-borne fighter was growing and trials were needed to test its deck landing and take off performance. The Spitfire's flaps had two positions – up and down – and what was needed was a flap with intermediate settings. The modification of such a system to the existing flaps would have meant a major redesign of the wings and to avoid such a change W3237 was used with the flaps fixed in four positions, 0°, 9°, 18° and 30°. All up weight was 7,050 lb and with Quill as the pilot the aircraft was taken off at least four times for each flap position. The runs averaged 254 yards for 0°; 238 9°; 243 18° and 251 30°.

The results of the tests showed that 9° of flaps produced the shortest take off run, but it was thought that for higher wind speeds, such as those over a carrier deck, a larger flap angle would be necessary and the 18° setting was chosen as the intermediate. To ensure that the flaps were at the correct angle a set of four wooden blocks were made and installed at the inner and outer ends of the flaps and were held in position for take off by the force exerted by the flap return spring. On reaching a safe height and speed of approximately 160mph the flaps had to be fully lowered in order that the blocks could fall away. Only some of the Seafires used this system and a number of them were at Farnborough for RATOG trials in conjunction with the blocks. The aircraft were MB367, NX958, MA125, MB138, MB306, MB307 and NF487.

W3237 was then used for roll performance tests by Supermarine on 15 October in three conditions (a) normal wing, no guns or ammunition (b) wing tips removed and wooden fairings fitted (c) as (b) but with 4 × 20mm cannon, 4 × .303 machine guns and a full load of ammunition; auw was 7,550 lb. Ailerons were rigged for standard droop of ⅜ in for condition a and b and with ⅜ in upfloat for c. Removal of wing tips resulted in an improvement in roll and an increase of speed at sea level of 3mph. The operational ceiling was reduced by 1,600 feet.

To determine control circuit operating loads for the purpose of designing an inertia device in the tab control circuit unit for limiting normal accelerations during pull out from a dive, W3237 was sent to Worthy Down on 15 May for modification and trials. During trials it was loaded to 7,000 lb auw and flown with a 7 lb weight in the elevator system. The same series of tests were then made on Spitfire F Mk VI AB176 with a pressure cabin and Merlin 47 engine. During the last few years of its life W3237 was used extensively for trials and in September 1944 was fitted with a pilot static comb and automatic observer.

W3237, the second prototype Mk III, with 18° setting wooden blocks installed between the wing and flaps. The blocks were marked with the legends 'outboard and inboard'.

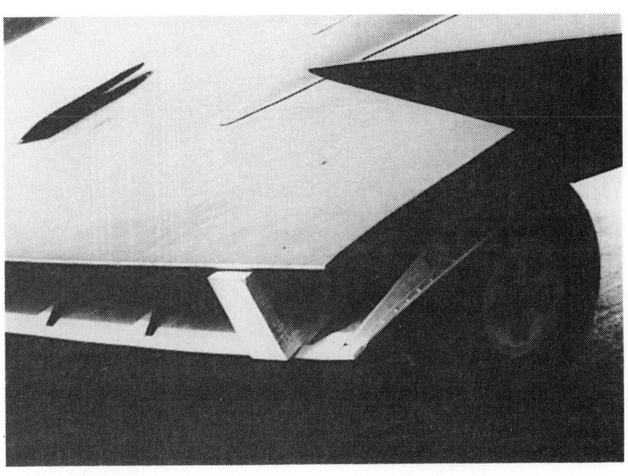

It was proposed at one time to develop a floatplane version of the Mk III as Middle East Command was calling for such a fighter for use in Malta. A series of trials on models was conducted at Farnborough in the large wind tunnel and full details of this variant will be found in chapter 19.

The radiator of the Mk III was of different design to that of the Mk I and tests of it were conducted in the Farnborough tunnel. For these tests the wings of W3237 were joined to a dummy centre section and mounted in an inverted position as shown in our photograph.* The Spitfire Mk III was an interesting type but it never entered full scale production despite its obvious advantages over current production aircraft. The combination of a modified Merlin XX and Mk I airframe was rushed into RAF service to combat the high flying Bf109F. This compromise aeroplane was such a success that the Air Ministry decided to order it into full scale production and the 'Improved Spitfire' was abandoned. The German bombing of the Supermarine factories at Southampton also affected the Mk III development programme for the first set of strengthened wings was destroyed during the first raid of September 1940, together with the majority of production drawings. The Air Ministry had issued three Mark numbers for future production aircraft – Mk IIIA, Merlin XX and eight Browning guns; Mk IIIB, Merlin XX and 2 × 20mm cannon and 4 × .303 machine guns; Mk IIIC, Merlin XX and four 20mm cannon. A Mk IIID was contemplated and the D suffix indicated an armament of 12 Brownings.

* *see page 128*

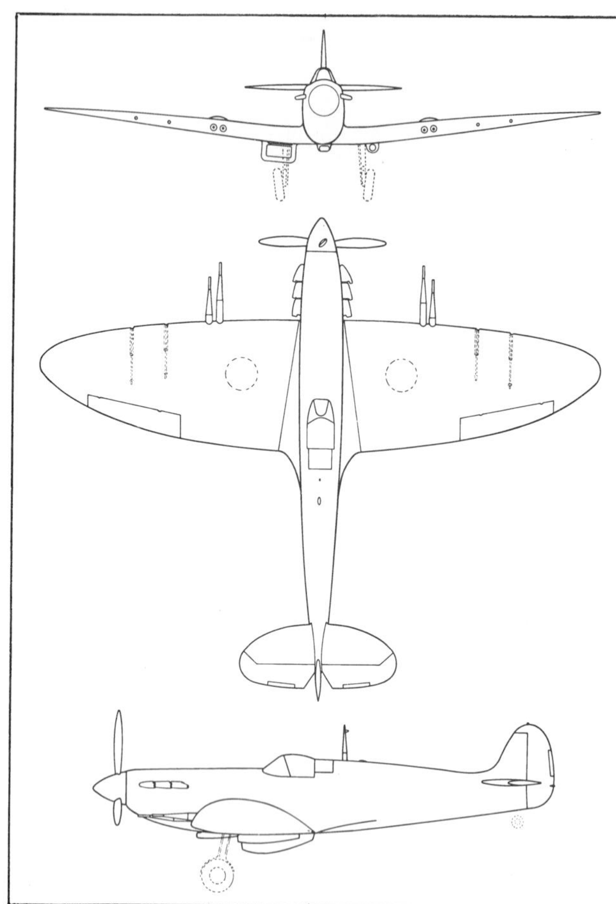

General arrangement of the Spitfire Mk III with four 20mm Hispano cannon inboard and four .303 Colt Browning machine guns outboard. Compare with mock up photograph of Mk I P9450 right.

Wing. Planform elliptical; section NACA 2200 Series; incidence° root +2, tip $-\frac{1}{2}$; dihedral° 6; thickness % 13.2, tip 6; aspect ratio 4.21; area sq ft nett 198, gross 220; chord (geo) 6.38, (ma) 7.23. Ailerons. Area sq ft 16.40; span 5.42ft; chord (ma) 1.15; movement° up 26, down 19, droop $\frac{3}{8}$in. Flaps. Area sq ft 15.6, span 8.16ft; movement° down 85.

Tailplane. Area 31.46; chord (ma) 4.0; incidence° root 0, tip $\pm\frac{1}{2}$; dihedral° 0. Elevators. Area sq ft 13.26; movement° up 28, down 23. Tab. Area 0.38; span 1.61ft, movement° up and down 13.5. Fin. Area sq ft 4.61. Rudder. Area sq ft 8.23, movement° each way 28. Tab. Area 0.34, movement° each way 12.

Undercarriage. Wheel Dunlop AH2061; tyres Dunlop 7-50-0. Oleo pressure sq in 355; Tailwheel retractable, castoring. Wheel Dunlop AH2184; tyre Dunlop Ecta 3-00-4. Oleo pressure 214;

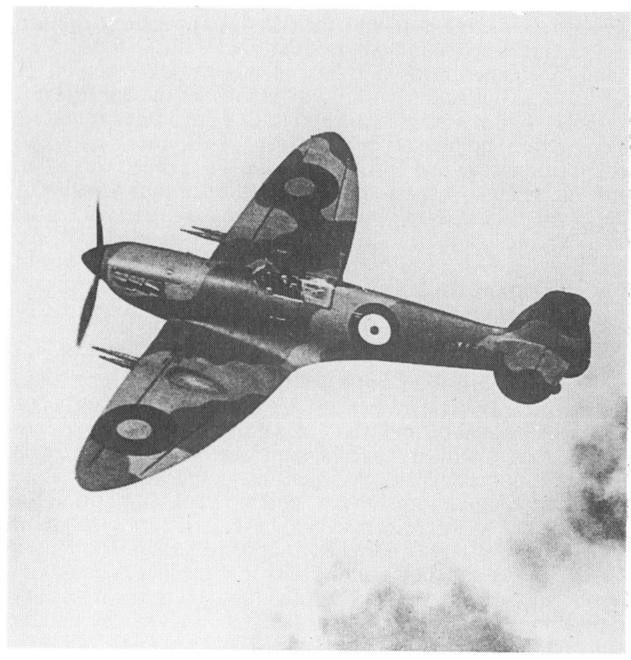

This photograph of P9450, a Mk I, was modified by an artist to illustrate the four cannon armament of the Mk III.

Engine/s. Merlin RM 2SM X. Electric starter. 1,265hp @ 9,500ft, 1,145 @ 16,750.
Fuel consumption (max) 101gal/hr

Merlin RM 3SM XX. Electric starting. 1,280hp @ 3,000rpm.

Merlin 61
Propeller/s. Supermarine 3-blade CS VP Jablo. Diameter 10ft 9in.

Coolant. 70% water, 30% Glycol. 16.5gals in system.

Fuel. 100 octane. Capacity (fuselage) upper 53gals, lower 46.5, total 99.5.

Oil. 6.8gals. Consumption 1.75 to 2.5gal/hr.

Armour

Armament. A and B wing or 4 × 20mm Hispano cannon and 4 × .303 Browning m/gs.

Cine camera.

Radio. TR1133.

Performance. (Merlin X) Max speed 340mph @ 5,000ft; 360 @ 10,000; 369 @ 15,000; 400 @ 21,000. Max dive 450. Take off run 250yds. Climb to 15,000ft 4.5mins, 20,000 6.4. Service ceiling 38,000. Stall flaps and u/c up 93. Landing run 600yds.

A NEW SPITFIRE

By the late 1930s the Rolls-Royce Merlin series of engines was recognised by the aircraft industry as a technological triumph and eminently suitable for the aircraft then in production and at early design stage. Continuous experiments and trials with the Merlin resulted in Rolls-Royce deciding that to produce more power a larger volume unit would be necessary, even though the two stage, supercharged Merlin was on the test bench and would be capable of several years development. A larger engine would be required but, ideally, it had to be dimensionally similar to the Merlin.

Such an engine was in existence – the Griffon – which was a detuned Type R used to power later models of the Schneider Trophy floatplanes built by Supermarine. Before the Merlin was in the project stage Rolls-Royce, Supermarine and the Air Ministry were in agreement that the Kestrel had just about reached the end of its development capability and it was decided to type test a modified Type R engine.* It was bench running during 1932 and the photograph reproduced below shows the modified unit at Rolls-Royce undergoing a two hour endurance run. The placard above the test stand reads – "Griffon Aero Engine. 2 hours endurance test, 12 cylinder supercharged, bore 6.0, stroke 6.6. Normal rpm 2,400, max rpm, 2,750. Rated output 1,000bhp @ sea level. Supercharger gear ratio 2.42:1. Evaporatively cooled installation. Weight 1,600 lb." The interesting fact about the unit was the intention to cool it in the same manner as the modified Kestrel unit, the Goshawk, specified for the Type 224 F7/30.

The whole affair seems to have been in keeping with the Air Ministry's search at that period for the 1,000hp engined fighter, details of which can be found in chapter four. The 37 litre Griffon was far too large for aircraft of the period but the Kestrel would eventually be too small, and as history has shown the Merlin emerged as the natural replacement.

Interest in the Griffon quickened again in 1938 when the Royal Navy approached Rolls-Royce and asked if a larger 'Merlin type' engine could be produced. Rolls-Royce suggested the Griffon I and by 1939 a developed version of the Type R racing engine was on the test bench and it was known as the RR-37 V12. Air Ministry interest was minimal as the Merlin suited its requirements for the foreseeable future. Supermarine was also informed of the development for its increased power output over the current Merlin III for a minimal increase in weight made it an attractive proposition for a developed Spitfire.

The first Griffon (Type R) engine on the test bench at Roll-Royce in 1932. A thrust monitoring unit can just be seen in front of the engine.

The first intimation that the Griffon II might be considered for the Spitfire was on 8 November 1939 when N. E. Rowe, of MAP, said that although the Griffon would provide additional power it was necessary to carry 100 lb of ballast in the tail to counteract the additional forward weight. In view of this it was decided on 19 November not to devote any more time to Griffon potential and to concentrate on the forthcoming Spitfire Mk III powered by the Merlin XX. However, there was a swift change of opinion for barely three weeks later permission was given to Supermarine to explore the advantages of adapting the Griffon for installation in a Spitfire airframe, and as a result Supermarine was able to issue their Specification No. 466 on 4 December. It is reproduced below.

**A variant of the Griffon was specified as the power unit for a variant of the F7/30 prototype to be entered in the MacRobertson England to Australia air race of 1934.*

SPITFIRE WITH ROLLS-ROYCE GRIFFON ENGINE

This specification outlines the main characteristics of the Spitfire with Griffon engine. With a maximum speed of over 420mph and climb to 15,000 feet in 4½ mins. there is a substantial increase in performance. Endurance is also increased by half an hour to F18/37 standards. Modifications to the airframe currently in production are few and comprise a new engine mounting, alteration to the wings to accommodate larger tyres, higher lift wing flaps and additional fuel tankage. A modified oleo leg provides shock absorbing capacity and improved braking. The airframe is altered in minor detail and existing jigs and plant can be used for construction. The necessary strengthening to maintain present factors is achieved by substitution of stronger alloys. A survey of the material position had indicated that this is possible. A brief description follows –

(1) Improved performance. The estimated maximum speed is 423mph at 18,500ft compared with 367 for the standard Spitfire with Merlin II engine; 366 at 5,000; 384 at 10,000; 402 at 15,000. Take off run 245 yards. Climb to 15,000ft 4½mins; to 20,000 6.6. Service ceiling 36,000 feet.

(2) Engine and installation. The engine is the Rolls-Royce Griffon and the mounting and cowling have been redesigned to accomodate this engine. The standard bulkhead and attachment points as used with the Merlin are retained.

(3) Cooling systems. The cooling systems are similar to those of the standard Spitfire but the radiator and oil cooler area are increased.

(4) Petrol system. Fuel tankage is increased to 130 gallons by the provision of an additional tank in the wing. This is sufficient for ¼ hour at maximum take off power, plus two hours patrol at economical cruising speed at 15,000 feet, plus ¼ hour at full throttle level flight.

(5) Fuselage. Apart from slight stiffening necessary to cater for the increased power of the engine, the fuselage is as the standard Spitfire.

(6) Main planes. Major part is unaltered except for changes in material in order to give the same strength at the increased all up weight. The wheel housing is increased to accommodate a larger tyre; fuel tanks are provided in the leading edge and flaps of greater span are fitted.

(7) Tail unit. Is the same as the Spitfire Mk III.

(8) Undercarriage. Standard wheels are replaced by Dunlop 8.50 × 10.0 which carry the increased load at a tyre pressure of 49 lb sq/in. The wheel position has been moved forward to give improved braking. The oleo legs have greater travel and improved shock absorbing capacity. The tailwheel is retractable as on the Mk III.

(9) Armament. The aircraft can be supplied with provision for eight Browning guns, or two cannon, as in the Mk I.

Tests have already been carried out on a standard Spitfire I at Eastleigh Aerodrome at an all up weight of 7,200 lb*. This is 400 lb heavier than the weight of the Griffon Spitfire in its landing condition i.e with ammunition and fuel expended. Compared with the Spitfire thus tested the Griffon version will have the further advantage of higher lift flaps, larger wheels and improved braking.

At a conference held on 13 December 1939 Sir Wilfred Freeman asked that the possibility of fitting an armament of greater calibre to the Griffon Spitfire should be looked into, and as a result two alternatives to the A and B wing were proposed. (1) 4 × 20mm cannon with 120rpg in power driven magazines or (2) 6 × 5in or 13.2mm Browning guns with 250rpg, belt fed. Proposal (2) was an update of the Supermarine Type 345, a Mk I Spitfire development, and the French Spitfire N.21 was at one time scheduled to be armed with either the 13.2 mm Hotchkiss or the Masden gun. Compared with eight Brownings either of the above installations resulted in an increase in weight of approximately 475 lb. Performance estimates were revised in accordance with type of armament specified.

The cooling systems of the new Spitfire were tested in a

**Thought to be L1007*

standard Mk I wing in the Farnborough wind tunnel on 9 January 1940. Comparative speed estimates with the Hawker Tornado and Typhoon designs showed that the Griffon Spitfire would be 10mph faster, and the Air Ministry announced plans to introduce the new type into service by the end of 1941 under the designation of Mk IV.

On 27 February Supermarine produced Specification No. 468 which was to supersede No. 466. It read – The information given in Specification No. 466 is brought up to date in accordance with the latest data and present requirements for fighters.

(1) Performance. A speed of over 430mph at 23,500ft and service ceiling of 38,500ft is estimated for the aeroplane in its initial form. Full consideration has been given to the possibilities of development. The Griffon engine will be subject to the same development as the Merlin with regard to intercoolers and two stage blowers and will, therefore, yield a proportionate increase in power on the same basis as the Merlin, both in regard to performance and increased altitude. On this assumption the Spitfire with Griffon engine should attain the following performances. Max speed 470mph at 35,000ft. Operational ceiling (climb 500fpm) 43,500. Service ceiling (climb 100fpm) 46,300. Compared with a new type of aeroplane the modifications to the airframe at present in production are not extensive.

(2) Engine and installation. The engine mounting and cowling have been redesigned to accommodate the Griffon engine. The existing bulkhead and attachment points are retained. The cooling systems are very similar to the present type, with the same size of oil cooler and a larger radiator.

(3) Fuselage. Some strengthening of the fuselage to take the increased engine loads is necessary. The fuel tanks, pilot's cockpit, controls, installation of service equipment, tail unit and retracting tailwheel, all remain identical with the Spitfire III.

(4) Main planes. As a result of careful investigation and test the main spar, and its attachments including the leading edge covering, requires only minor modification. The wheel housing is altered to accommodate a longer chassis and larger tyre. Provision for six cannons necessitate some modification to ribs in the neighbourhood of the armament. A new slotted flap was proposed for this aeroplane in order to increase lift. This is about to be tested on a Spitfire I (R6718). Recent experience with fighters, however, indicates that at the moderate wing loading of the Griffon Spitfire (32 lb sq/ft) the landing run with existing split flap will be quite acceptable. It is probable therefore that the flap and aileron will remain unaltered. A wing tip which increases the span has been designed with the object of obtaining the highest possible ceiling, and this will be used for high altitude work. It is interchangeable with the standard wing tip.

(5) Fuel tankage. By the provision of Mareng bags in the wing leading edge which supplement the standard tanks in the fuselage, the fuel capacity is increased to 130 gallons.

(6) Undercarriage. The wheel sizes proposed as alternatives are Palmer 8¼ x 10 (pressure @ 8,000 lb auw 50 lb sq in), Dunlop 8 × 10¼ (57 lb sq in). The wheel position has been moved forward to give improved braking. The oleo shock absorbers are of the same basic type as the present Spitfire but are longer to provide ground clearance for an 11ft 0in propeller.

(7) Armament. Pending a decision on the type of armament required the prototypes are designed to accomodate six cannons with 120rpg. Experience and investigations have indicated the practicability of other armament arrangements but for production reasons an early decision on this question is essential.

(8) Strength. The airframe has an adequate reserve of strength to cater for subsequent development.

(9) Pressure cabin. Work is being proceeded with to provide the Spitfire with a pressure cabin. This is applicable to the Griffon Spitfire and is in fact a necessity at the very high altitudes of which the machine is capable.

Particulars and performance figures had to be adjusted for the modified airframe – Wing Span 40ft 6in, area 250 sq ft. Weights. 2 x 20mm cannon @ 4 x .303 m/gs. (A) tare 6,010 lbs, auw 7,895. With 4 x 20mm cannon (B), tare 6,010, auw 8,095. Wing loading 31.5 lb sq ft and 32.4 respectively. Maximum speed 433 mph @ 23,500ft, 374 @ 5,000, 388 @ 15,000, 429 @ 25,000. Take off run (A) 275yds (B) 285. Time to 15,000ft (A) 5.3min (B) 5.5., to 30,000 (A) 13.3., (B) 13.9. Rate of climb @ 30,000ft (A) 1,185 ft min, (B) 1,100. Operational ceiling (A) 100ft min 38,500ft, (B) 37,900. Landing distance (full load) (A) 575 yds, (B) 595. Engine. Rolls-Royce Griffon RG 2SM. Take off (M blower) 1,640hp International bhp (M blower) 1,550 @ 3,500ft. (S blower) 1,430 @ 16,000. Propeller Rotol four blade constant speed 11ft 0in diameter.

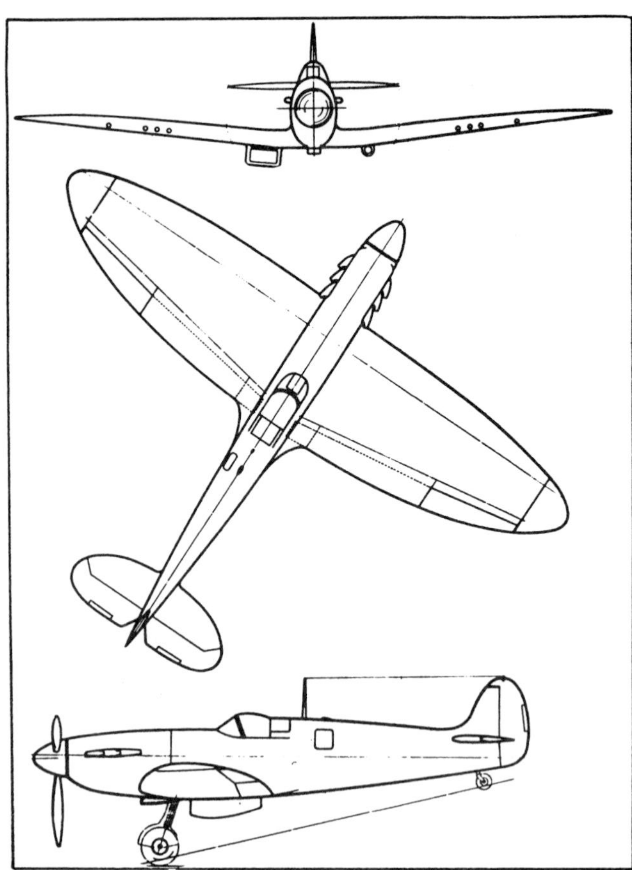

Drawing of the prototype Griffon Spitfire which utilised a Mk I airframe modified to accept the new engine. It was known as the Type 337. Note the armament location well out to the wing tips.

Speed estimates have been based upon the actual performance of the Mk I with the following improvements – (a) bypass duct over the radiator assumed to give drag reduction of 21 lb @ 100ft/sec, (b) tailwheel retracted assumed to give a drag reduction of same. It has now been established the Spitfire intake has an efficiency of 98% and the increase in supercharger heights of 1,250ft due to change of forward speed from 365 to 420mph may be expected. The Griffon engine is, however, rated at 15,000ft instead of 16,250ft of the Merlin. The full throttle height of the Griffon will be 18,500ft and the bhp 1,485.

Specification 466, however, did not contain the full facts for the Spitfire airframe had a frontal area of 7.5 sq ft and much modification was necessary to accomodate the Griffon, and then only after various engine accessories had been moved to produce a frontal area of 7.9 sq ft. On the question of suitable materials Supermarine staff members visited Reynolds Tubes, Northern Aluminium, English Steel Corp, and Firth and John Brown Ltd, and there were a number of provisos that had to be accepted by Supermarine before all the companies concerned would agree on the possibility of material supply.

Flight trials of the prototype Griffon engines, installed in a Hawker Henley (L3414), commenced in 1940 and were adjudged to be promising. Sidney Camm, chief designer Hawker Aircraft, was now showing an interest in the Griffon for the Hurricane and he eventually produced the following comparison between a Spitfire and Hurricane powered by the engine in an attempt to stretch the service life of the Hawker machine –

	Griffon Hurricane	Griffon Spitfire
Max speed @ 18,500ft	425mph	411
Endurance (cruise)	2 hours	1.75

Supermarine had by this time completed a great deal of work on the Griffon Spitfire but had yet to receive a firm indication from the Air Ministry on whether an ITP was to be issued. A letter to MAP on 12 November 1940 read – "We have been working on an advanced version of the Spitfire with a Griffon engine. This we call the Mk IV. We discussed this in

January last with Sir Wilfred Freeman and he gave verbal instructions to proceed with two prototypes. Work is proceeding but we have no contract".

There was no immediate action by the Air Ministry but in February 1941 they issued Specification **F4/41**, which was written around the Griffon Spitfire. It was history repeating itself in much the same manner as with the original **F7/30** design of 1934/35 when Sorley wrote **F37/34** around the revised design. The new Specification stated – "**Air Ministry F4/41** which is to be a derivation of the Spitfire using as far as possible parts already in production. Maximum speed not less than 410mph. Performance ¼ hour @ maximum power, plus 3½ hours cruising at 20,000ft, plus ¼ hour maximum speed level flight @ 20,000ft; reinforcing ¼ hour @ maximum speed, plus 1,500 miles cruising @ 20,000ft. Ceiling not less than 39,000ft. Armament 6 × 20mm cannon; or 2 × 20mm cannon and 8 × .303 machine guns; or 12 × .303 machine guns".

The new slotted flap was flight tested on Mk I R6718 and also on K9944, but trials with both aircraft indicated that the moderate wing loading of the prototype Mk IV (32 lb sq/ft) enabled it to have an acceptable landing run with the normal Spitfire flaps as fitted on the Mk I.

A letter of 3 April 1941 from MAP to Supermarine reminded the company – "Of the requirement to introduce the Spitfire Mk IV (Griffon) as early as possible. I am to request that you will adjust your commitments in respect of materials and sub contract orders to the revised requirements". On 17 April Joseph Smith told MAP that he was proceeding with the Mk IV development with the six cannon armament, and he was also producing a conversion kit with 2 × 20mm cannon and 4 × .303 machine guns. He promised first deliveries of ten aircraft per month by March 1942, rising to 100 by the following August. An unusual proposal was substitution of the Griffon by the Merlin RM 6SM 60, but this was rejected. Smith then said he was going to develop a universal wing for the Mk IV with – (1) 6 × 20mm cannon (2) 4 × 20mm cannon and 4 × .303 machine guns (3) 12 × .303 machine guns. This was noted and consideration given to development of a second type of universal wing which would delete the .303 guns and only include the six cannon armament or 2 × 20mm cannon and 4 × .5in machine guns. The .5in guns would have necessitated considerable redesign revisions and were not considered to be valid.

Sir Henry Tizard had expressed doubts about the wisdom of upsetting normal Merlin Spitfire production in favour of a complete swing over to the Griffon powered aircraft, and had raised the matter at a meeting held on 20 April 1941. An answer to his doubts from the CinC, Fighter Command, arrived on his desk nine days later. – "We do wish to go ahead with production of the Spitfire Mk IV on the lines already agreed last February, when we said that Mk IV production should take over as early as possible in 1942 all Spitfire capacity, except that which is required for the pressure cabin aircraft. It is agreed we are heading for specialisation in fighters and this is inevitable. Specialisation must be between the pressurised and non-pressurised fighter. In other words, the dividing line must come on the limit of altitude which can be tolerated by the human body unassisted by artificial pressure. Let us put this line at 35,000 feet.

"Below this there can be no specialisation and our aim must be to provide all aircraft (non-pressurised) with a performance to make them reasonable for fighting machines up to 35,000 feet. Another class of fighter for employment up to, say, 25,000 feet, would place quite intolerable operational limitations on fighter operations and could not be accepted as a policy. Owing to the march of events the present service ceiling of the Typhoon and Tornado is inadequate and must be improved.

"The Spitfire V and IV approach our requirements much more closely and are, indeed, the only non-pressurised fighters existing or projected which do so. If the Whittle proves successful then it will go far to solve our problem in both classes of fighter. But, until it has been proved it would be quite wrong for us to relax our efforts in any other type of fighter. Therefore, your suggestion that the Whittle in its present state can be allowed to influence the question of whether or not we go ahead with the Spitfire IV cannot be accepted. Although the Mk II has merged into the Mk V we must anticipate it being outclassed by 1942 when nothing below a maximum speed of 400mph will be much good to us. It is here that the introduction of the Spitfire Mk IV will be invaluable". It was a well considered judgement, but as events turned out the Fw190 appeared before sufficient progress had been made with the Spitfire/Griffon combination and it, too, was dropped in favour of the compromise Merlin 61 Spitfire, the Mk IX.

The contract for two prototype aircraft, DP845 and DP851, was placed at last with Supermarine on 26 May 1941, three days after Specification **F4/41** was officially issued to the company. No mock-up was specified and DP845 flew for the first time on 27 November, with DP851 following the next month.

A meeting held at the Air Ministry on 8 June referred to the Mk IV as follows – "The Spitfire IV with the Griffon engine would represent a very definite advance over the Spitfire V in the unpressurised class of day fighter. The operational ceiling (i.e. 500 ft/min) with 4 × 20mm guns in position would be of the order of 35,500 feet, and its climb to height and speed at lower altitudes represent a marked improvement over the Spitfire V. The existing programme for the introduction of the Spitfire IV with the Griffon engine should, therefore, stand; the date of change over to be determined by the Production Division. Every endeavour should be made to increase performance of the Griffon II in its present intrinsic form. In the layout of the Spitfire V airframe the possibility of a two-speed, two-stage Griffon must be kept in mind and every step taken towards facilitating change over of design at a future date". Mr Elliot reported that the normal Spitfire wing jigs would not be seriously altered and Joseph Smith said alterations to production tooling would affect 25 to 30% of tools.

On 23 August Supermarine had received a contract, No. 981687/39/C.23(c), for the production of 750 Spitfire Mk IV to be manufactured at the CBAF factory and the following serial numbers were allocated – ER206-229, ER245-283, ER299-345, ER461-510, ER524-571, ER583-626, ER634-679, ER695-744, ER758-791, ER815-834, ER846-894, ER913-948, ER960-998, ES105-154, ES168-214, ES227-264, ES276-318, ES335-369. The first production aircraft was scheduled for delivery in December but Sholto-Douglas, CinC Fighter Command, was still unhappy over the proposed armament and proposed (1) 12 × .303 Brownings (2) 2 × 20mm Hispano and 6 × .303 Brownings and (3) 4 × 20mm Hispano but, as was pointed out, the planned, additional wing fuel tanks precluded items (1) and (2). Rolls-Royce representatives had visited Supermarine on 9 July and told the company that bench running of the Griffon was proceeding well and the first engine would arrive at Hursley Park on the 19th. Supermarine was to decide which version of the Griffon would be used on the second prototype, DP851, and following production aircraft. Ten engines were promised by March 1942, rising to 100 per month by the following August.

On 5 September a scheme was prepared for the split flap to be fitted to DP851 and on the 9th it was proposed to install Youngman brake flaps. To test the effect of all types of flaps on the Spitfire Mk IV tests were started with a slotted version on the 11th in a specially built test rig. Apart from a certain amount of jarring which occurred when the engine was started, lowering or raising the flaps caused no major problems.

At a meeting to discuss production of the Mk IV it was decided to alter a number of wing ribs and gun extension tubes, and to fit the split flaps to both prototypes and delete the slotted version. The leading edge fuel tanks were to be similar to those specified for the Spitfire Mk III, and a test wing incorporating all these modifications was to be installed on a Spitfire Mk V to determine the effects of bullet strikes on flexible wing tanks. SME, Farnborough, conducted tests which showed that the tank's self sealing properties could cope with normal damage with low fuel losses. On 14 October Joseph Smith told MAP that in order to save time a mock up of the new aeroplane would be deleted. Other points covered were – manufacturing a tropical conversion kit; delaying installation of ultra-violet cockpit lighting until available in 12 volt form; installation of air brakes after trials had been completed at Boscombe Down and design of a higher velocity undercarriage. On 12 November the decision was taken to abandon development of the Griffon Hurricane and build additional Spitfire Mk IVs.

The first prototype, DP845, made its maiden flight from Worthy Down on 27 November 1941 with Jeffrey Quill at the controls. He flew it for 15 minutes. The results of trials of R6618, the Mk I fitted with the NACA type slotted flaps, were available on 6 February 1942 an in order to compare performance with the standard split flap a Mk VB, R7337, and a Mk I, R7023, were flown on similar trials. The pilot's reports on R6718 read – "Handling trials have been carried out by Quill, Pickering, Wedgewood and Bartley with the slotted flap

DP845, prototype F Mk IV with original Mk I fuselage, slotted flaps and Griffon engine.

Spitfire and R7023, both aircraft being loaded to normal Mk I service load. The pilots found little difference in the touching down speed with the two aircraft and it is their opinion that the slotted flaps do not have any appreciable effect on the actual landing speed".

Certain points were noted, however, which all pilots liked – (1) at 43° flap setting the aircraft approached in a more nose down attitude, giving a far better view during the approach, (2) the aircraft was steadier, both fore and aft and laterally on the approach glide, (3) the elevator control was less sensitive on glide than it was with the split type flap, and the stick could be pulled fully back for landing. Generally, it was considered that the slotted flaps had the advantage in handling characteristics on the glide, but produced no reduction in landing speed. With regard to the handling trials with the slotted flaps at three different angles (43, 35 and 32°) there was no appreciable difference in the landing speeds at the varying angles. The effect of reducing the angle, however, was to flatten the approach path and to give an increasing nose up attitude as the angle was reduced. The slotted flaps terminated at the fuselage junction and the normal split flap was retained, being linked to the slotted flap so that both deflected to the same angle.

At a meeting at MAP on 27 March 1942, attended by Smith and Clifton, the Griffon Spitfire was now being referred to as the Mk 20, this being in line with the new Air Ministry issue of the Spitfire Mk numbers. It was stated that provision for the Griffon 61 engine was to be made right from the start of F 20 production, and that a longer engine mounting be designed and provision made for a radiator on the port as well as on the starboard win. A pressure cabin would not be required and new type ailerons fitted on all production aircraft. Wooden ailerons were tested but rejected. Estimated weights of the Mk 20 prototype were – empty 5,897 lb, tare 6,439, auw 9,150. This was later increased to 9,300, and with a gross wing area of 248.5 sq ft and loading was 37.4 lb/sq ft.

DP845 was eventually to become the prototype Mk XII and DP851 continued to be used for the Spitfire Mk 20 and 20 Series trials. With a Griffon IIB engine DP845 carried out performance and cooling tests – maximum level speed (MS gear) 383mph at 5,600 feet, FS gear 409 at 18,600ft. It had a 10ft 9in diameter Rotol propeller with four dural blades; a mock up windscreen with curved front panel; B wing armament. All tests were concluded on 24 September.

Introduction of the Griffon engine into the Spitfire airframe transformed the fighter's handling and flying characteristics. Not only did the engine rotate in an opposite direction to the Merlin, the increased power caused considerable torque which led to the redesign of the rudder and, later, the entire tail unit. But it was a promising design for on 20 July 1942 DP845, as the prototype F Mk XII, was flown to test its capabilities against the Fw190 and Typhoon before an audience of senior RAF personnel, including Sholto-Douglas, at Farnborough. It was expected that the Fw190 would lead the trio home, followed by the Typhoon and Spitfire. Jeffrey Quill, who was flying the Mk XII writes – "We approached Odiham from the west in careful line abreast at easy cruising power and on a heading for Farnborough. I was flying to the starboard of the Fw190 and Seth-Smith to port at 1,000 feet. On a signal from Wilson we all opened our throttles and went hell for leather for the line at Farnborough. I won comfortably, the Typhoon was second and the Fw190 last. In fairness, Wilson had problems with his engine and had to reduce power towards the finish, but the Spitfire XII would have beaten him anyway".

The prototype Mk IV fitted with a mock-up, six-cannon installation.

DP845 went to Boscombe Down on 10 September 1942 for trials and ended its active life at No. 1 MPRD, Cowley in 1946. The F Mk IV/20 contract was cancelled and the serial numbers switched to the Mk V. DP851 was converted later into the prototype Mk 21. Supermarine predicted that the Griffon Spitfire could be developed to reach a maximum speed of 470mph at 35,000 feet, and have a service ceiling of 46,300 feet. Although the various Griffon powered Spitfires were excellent aeroplanes they were never built in the same quantities as the Merlin powered variants.

DP845 with six mock-up cannon installed.

F Mk IV.

Wing. Planform elliptical; section NACA 2200 Series; incidence° root +2, tip −½; dihedral 6°; thickness% root 13.2, tip 6; aspect ratio 5.68; area nett 220, gross 242; chord(geo) 6.38, (ma) 7.01 Ailerons. Area 18.9; chord; movement° up 26, down 19; droop ⅜ in. Flaps. Area 15.6; movement° down 85. Wing loading 36.0; loading 5.45.

Tailplane. Area 31.46; chord(ma) 4.0; incidence° root 0, tip ±½; dihedral 0. Elevators. Area 13.26; movement° up 28, down 23. Tab area 0.38; span 1.6ft; movement° up 13.5, down 13.5; chord .22 Fin. Area 4.61. Rudder. Area 8,23; movement° 28 each way. Tab area 0.35; movement° 12 each way.

Undercarriage. Wheels Dunlop AH2061; tyres Dunlop 8.50 × 10; oleo pressure 355; Tailwheel retractable castoring. Wheel Dunlop AH2184. Tyre Dunlop Ecta 3-00-4; oleo pressure 214;

The proposed redesigned Griffon Spitfire with 6 × 20mm cannon, extended wing and other refinements. Note also the large, rectangular gun blisters on the wing upper surfaces.

Engine/s. Griffon RG 2SM IIB 1,445hp @ 15,000ft.

Propeller/s. Rotol 4-blade XH5/4D-RG SS CS 2-pitch, 4-blade wooden or Dural 10ft 9in or 11ftn 0in diameter.

Coolant.

Fuel. Fuselage (upper) 55 gals, lower 45.5, wing 2 × 17¼. Total 130 gals.

Coolant.

Oil. 7.5gals.

Armour. 245 lb.

Armament. Alternatives proposed. See text.

Radio. TR1133.

Cine Camera.

Gunsight

Performance. Max speed 433mph, @ 23,500ft 374 @ 5,000, 388 @ 25,000. Climb to 15,000ft 4.5min, 20,000 6.6. Service ceiling 36,000ft. Take off run 245 yds, landing (full load) 622, empty 512. With CP 470mph @ 35,000ft. Service ceiling 46,300ft; operational ceiling 43,500. Climb 500fpm. With 2-speed Griffon Max speed @ SL (MS) 354mph, 383 @ 5,600, 378 @ 10,000 (FS), 409 @ 18,600, 391 @ 15,000, 397 @ 25,000.

Weights. A wing tare 5,985, take off 7,870; B wing tare 5,597, take off 7,310, with 4 x 20mm cannon, take off 9,300. With 6 x 20mm cannon, tare 6,439, take off 9,150.

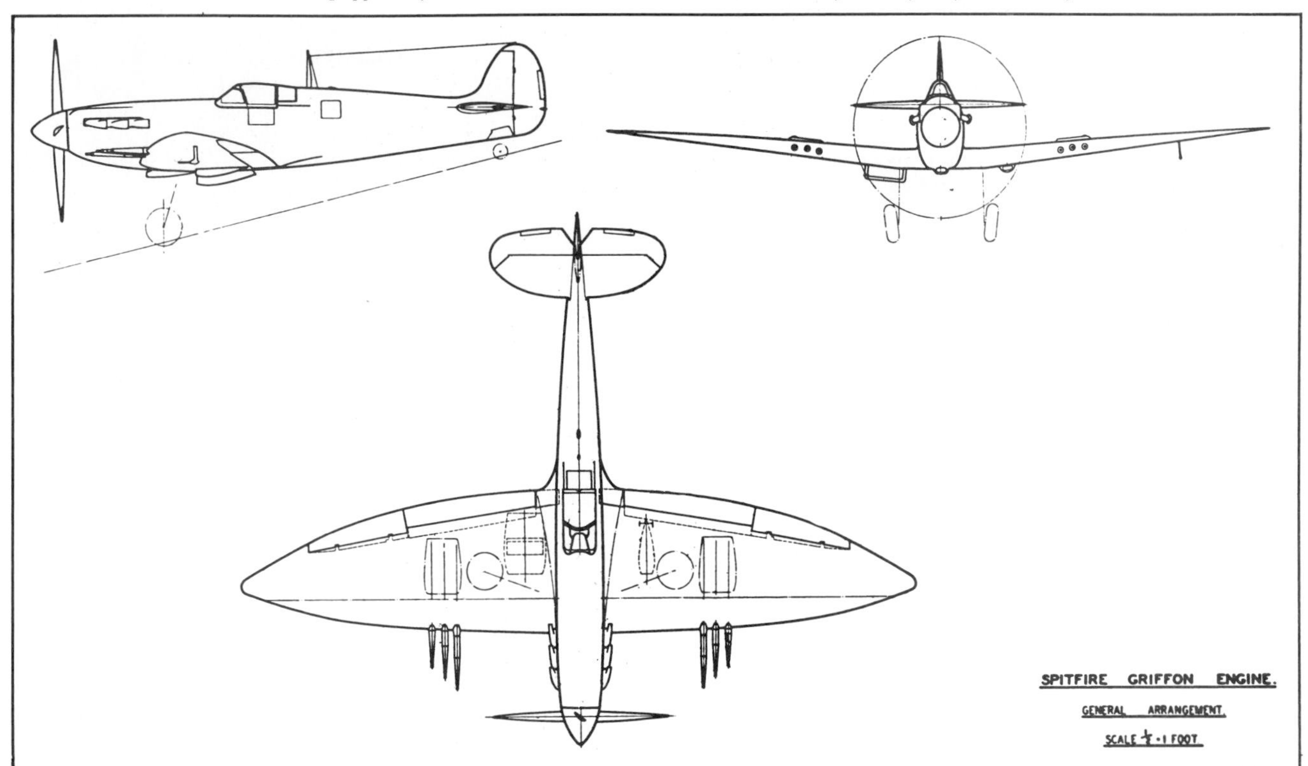

"A TEMPORARY EXPEDIENT"

The most widely used and, generally accepted to be most successful, variant of the Spitfire was the F Mk V. It was produced in large numbers and in four major versions, but despite its pedigree it was not designed and built as the logical development of its immediate predecessor, the F Mk II, and emerged eventually as an amalgam of a modified version of the Merlin XX engine and the F Mk III airframe. The latter was cancelled after the Air Ministry's decision to order the Mk V in quantity.

Had it not been for a change in Luftwaffe tactics in the closing months of 1940 the Mk V might never have been produced and the Mk III would have been the natural replacement of the Spitfires that had fought the Battle of Britain. During the critical months of July and October the Royal Air Force had fought off mass, daily attacks on the United Kingdom until the original German impetus faltered, then dwindled, at the end of October. In the following November the Luftwaffe began sending over Southern England small batches of the new Bf109F, which was flying higher and faster than those previously encountered. The Hurricane could not fly and fight the 109F above 20,000ft, and the Spitfire I and II lost much of the advantage they had over the earlier marks of Messerschmitt's fighter.

Verney, DTD, and a Mr Vessy, visited Group Captain Beardsworth at Fighter Command HQ on 15 November to discuss the general problem of high altitude flying, with particular reference to the improvement of performance of fighters and bombers. Intelligence reports compared the performance of British and enemy aircraft at heights above 30,000 feet, and Beardsworth said that any increase in performance was likely to accrue from extending the wings of the Spitfire. Verney pointed out that any such extension would have to be accompanied by overall wing strengthening. It was then generally agreed that the desirable increase in performance at height was mainly a function of the engine, and in particular of improved supercharging. The possibility of German aircraft having an advantage through the use of direct fuel injection engines was noted, and it was agreed that the possibilities of exhaust driven blowers should be investigated. American experience on this should be obtained.

Verney commented – " . . . One combat report suggested that the new Bf109 could get to 38,000 feet, when the Spitfire laboured to reach 36,500. Further, the adverse effects of rapid rates of climb such as that which the Whittle would provide should be examined, and the problem of providing oxygen pressure at height by some form of iron lung should also be looked at. Some German aircraft were reaching speeds of between 240 and 300 mph at high altitude and something had to be done to overcome this disadvantage".

During the Spring and Summer of 1940 Rolls-Royce was experimenting with a modified Merlin equipped with a two-stage supercharger, and this engine was eventually produced in small batches as the Merlin XX for installation in the production Spitfire Mk III. On Christmas Eve 1940 a meeting of RAE staff members, Supermarine employees and a number of Fighter Command's senior pilots, gathered at Boscombe Down to discuss the situation. Once again it was acknowledged that the Spitfire was being outmanoeuvred at heights above 25,000 feet. The replacement fighter, the Mk III, was not ready.

The Merlin XX engine would have provided power for a Spitfire to fight off the 109F, but it was a fairly complex engine, more difficult to produce than previous Merlins. It had a low-altitude blower and this feature was hindering large scale production. Rolls-Royce suggested that the pertinent blower be deleted in order to produce an engine with the necessary high-altitude performance. The final result was the emergence of the Merlin RM 5S or Mk 45, which was to increase the Spitfire's ceiling by 2,000 feet. Mr Hives, for Rolls-Royce, said he could provide at least 300 of the modified Merlins by 1 March and a further 200 by 1 April. He also stated that this would not affect Merlin XX production. Sholto-Douglas, also present, said – "We will have to reserve the entire production of the new engine for the Spitfire as this will be a priceless asset in the struggle for air superiority over the south-east corner of England".

The Air Ministry wanted swift action and Rolls-Royce said they could convert the production Merlin III to the new specification and as a result 500 conversions were ordered. Also, until production of the Merlin 45 proper got under way, and a modified Spitfire airframe was developed to take the engine, a large number of Spitfire Mk Is were to have the converted Merlin IIIs installed at the CROs. While waiting for the converted Spitfires to appear, high altitude trials were needed to assess performance. It was decided to send N3053, from Digby, where it was undergoing service trials, to Rolls-Royce, Hucknall, and it arrived there in early January 1941.

One of the modified Merlin XXs was installed and N3053 transferred to Boscombe Down on 13 February for trials. It was soon joined by X4334, a Mk I, which had flown with the new engine on 13 January. K9788, also at Boscombe, was also fitted with the new engine on 26 December 1940. Figures detailing performance were produced and the table overleaf lists the increases in speed and height. Note that an increase of wing span would have added a further 1,500 feet to the service ceiling.

Two views of R7347 at Wright Field, Dayton, Ohio, USA, in the summer of 1941. It was one of a number of Allied fighters under test by the USAAF.

Merlin 45, left, Merlin XX, right.

Change of performance @ 30,000 feet

Nature of change	Service ceiling ft	Max level speed	R/c max	Rate of climb mph 200	250	300
Merlin XII to XX both @ 6000 lb	+4300	+33	+355 ft/min	+210	+370	+685
Change of weight 6000 to 5700 lb Merlin XII	+1300	+2	+140	+140	+140	+120
Increase wing span from 37 ft (6000 lb) to 42.55 ft (6300)	+1500	−0.5	+40	+55	+25	+5

During performance and handling trials with the new engine one major fault did emerge. It was damaged on several occasions by over revving due to oil freezing in the de Havilland constant speed propeller unit. This fault was also to affect the Mk V in squadron use, and to cure the fault at Boscombe the experimental trio had blade pitch coarsened by 4° to prevent excessive rpm, particularly in a dive. Maximum speed was increased to 369mph @ 19,600ft, and rate of climb to 3,469ft/min @ 14,400 ft. Time to 20,000 ft was 6.2min. The estimated service ceiling was 38,000 ft, more than sufficient to meet the German high fliers.

K9788 was badly damaged during trials and the Air Ministry ordered additional conversions of the Mk I Spitfire, a contract for 46 aeroplanes being placed with Rolls-Royce. The engine company could not convert the Merlin XX for these 46 airframes as they did not have enough engines and the modified Merlin III was fitted. To differentiate between the modified Merlin III and the normal production unit, the former was designated Merlin 45. Both engine and Mk I airframe conversions were regarded by the Air Ministry as – "A temporary expedient" until production examples of the Spitfire Mk III became available. It was also planned to convert several hundred Spitfire IIs to the new standard, but this plan was abandoned.

N3053 was next fitted with a second version of the modified Merlin XX (this was later named the Merlin 46) and it was tested with the three blade, constant speed, de Havilland propeller. Total weight was now 6,170lb. Climbs to height and measurements of speed at height ranging from 15,000 to 37,000 feet were made revealing a maximum climb rate of 2,930ft min at 18,000 feet; time to 20,000 feet 7 min; service ceiling 39,300 feet and maximum speed at 23,000 feet was 368 mph. A four blade Rotol propeller was then installed and with this the maximum rate of climb increased to 3,190ft min; time to 20,000 feet 6.6 min; service ceiling 40,500 feet. On 13 March X4922, another Merlin XX conversion, arrived at Boscombe Down complete with armament and weighing 6,450lb. It was used for trials of a standard, completely equipped aeroplane.

It was obvious from trial reports that the converted Spitfire Mk I with the modified engine was an unqualified success and the Air Ministry wanted to have a production machine in service in large numbers as quickly as possible. Supermarine could not produce the projected Mk III Spitfire in the time specified by the Air Ministry and a compromise had to be reached. It was decided that the Merlin 45 would be married to a strengthened Mk I airframe, a larger radiator installed and the resulting Spitfire be called the F Mk V. The contract for 1,500 Mk III Spitfires was cancelled and the serials re-allocated to the new Mk V. This decision was the outcome of a meeting held on 6 March when Air Chief Marshall Sir Charles Portal decided that the Mk V be produced in quantity instead of the

Mk III. He said – "If the type is a success the Air Staff will want as many as can be produced". The next variant was to be the modified airframe with the Merlin 46 installed, plus a pressure cabin (similar to that on the Mk VI), to be followed by the same airframe fitted with a two stage blower Merlin.

At the same period of time the problem of designating the various versions of the Spitfire was beginning to cause complications, especially when re-ordering replacement parts, and the Air Ministry issued a list of Mk numbers with the result that the eight Browning gun Mk V became known as the Spitfire Mk VA, the order for which was placed with Castle Bromwich in March 1941. Most of the initial Mk I conversions were made to the Mk IBs and the Air Ministry had to revise its contracts for the VA, eventually taking delivery of only 100 examples.

The Rolls-Royce conversions were rushed into service, as they were urgently needed, and the aeroplane was soon in trouble, the first hint of which was a message to the Air Staff from the DOR dated 23 March 1941. It said – "You will remember that the proper oil cooler for the Merlin 45 Spitfire, i.e, the same type as used on the Spitfire Mk III, was not

W3119, F Mk VA, was at Wright Field with R7347 and was later transferred to NACA at Langley Field the same year. It was used for experimental exhaust system trials.

W3134 went to Boscombe Down in September 1941 for flame damping trials of triple exhausts fitted with intensifier tubes for gun heating to augment the radiator heating system. It crashed at South Marston in November 1943.

available when the first batch of 23 Spitfires were converted at Hucknall. We realised that oil cooling would probably be a little inadequate and we have had the following signal from Fighter Command – 'From Headquarters Fighter Command. Spitfire oil coolers evidence from 92 Squadron, Biggin Hill, gives excessively high oil temperatures above 150°C and low oil pressure below 45 lb per sq in at high altitudes. Request immediate consideration of Mk II oil coolers retrospectively'. It is clear we should make the change as soon as possible. If you agree can you please arrange for Fighter Command to be instructed to return their machines in suitable sized batches".

It was a setback of plans to equip the RAF with the new fighter and the Air Ministry was not in the mood to withdraw it from the service en masse, for the reply to the signal was cautious – "Your signal Spitfire V coolers. In order that improved oil coolers may be fitted request arrangements to be made for aircraft to be delivered to Hucknall in batches of three". A request for a promised trial installation of cabin heaters was ignored. An engineering officer from No II Group went to Biggin Hill to examine three Spitfires, R6897, R6776, X4257, and his report was revealing for the real problem was the de Havilland constant speed unit of the propeller.

His report stated – "That after climbing to 36,000 feet X4257 was subjected to intense cold and in these conditions it was not possible to control engine speed by use of the constant speed unit, and engine speeds in excess of 3,800 rpm were recorded. X4257 took off at 2,750 rpm to 30,000 feet, where the revs were increased to 3,000rpm and the climb continued to 36,000 feet. After 30 minutes at this height propeller control was not possible and engine speeds rose to 3,250 rpm. Control was moved to full coarse position and the aircraft dived to 28,000 feet. The Spitfire was then climbed again to engage an enemy aircraft but rpm decreased to 2,400. Moved control to 3,200 rpm, and at approximately 33,300ft engaged enemy and afterwards lost consciousness due to defect in the oxygen system. Recovered and noted that engine speed was such that the indicator had gone beyond its full travel. After recovering normal flight, engine failed to respond and oil pressure gauge registered zero".

The aircraft crashed near Maidstone, Kent, and first arrivals on the scene 30 minutes afterwards saw a coating of ice covering the spinner and blades up to 18 inches from the boss. The next report concerned R6776, whose pilot dived through a formation of enemy aircraft and had to close the throttle as the engine was running badly at high speed. Airspeed was noted as 400mph. This aircraft also crashed and ice was also found on the spinner and propeller boss. All the evidence pointed to freezing of the de Havilland propeller and pending modifications pilots were warned to exercise it at height. As an interim measure heavier counter weights for the unit were installed. A number of Rotol propellers were diverted from the Hurricane production lines until sufficient numbers became available for the Spitfire.

The letter from MAP to Supermarine concerning the switch from Spitfire Mk VAs to VBs arrived on 3 March, and it also stated that a 'Universal Wing' with the Chatellerault ammunition feed and a modified undercarriage was to be introduced on to the production lines not later than the 520th airframe.

Rolls-Royce were asked by the Air Ministry to provide 100 M45 engines, specials, and to fit them in a Special Duty batch of Mk V production aircraft beginning in June. "They will be used for high altitude operations without a pressure cabin until the Merlin RM4SM engine is available."

On 26 May 1941 a letter from Fighter Command arrived at the Air Ministry and it concerned a meeting held the previous March between MAP and Operational Training Unit Commanders. Attending this particular meeting was Lord Beaverbrook, who said that the meeting was called to discuss the fact that the OTUs 'broke' too many aeroplanes. In fact, during the previous eleven months 40 Spitfires had landed with their wheels in the up position. Despite every effort to eliminate these accidents the problem was still unsolved and as a result a startling proposal was put forward for consideration. The proposal was that OTU aircraft should have some form of a detachable skid fitted to the under surface wing root position in such a manner that if the Spitfire, and indeed the Hurricane, did make a wheels up landing the aircraft would be supported on an even keel and so lessen the damage. A drawing of that skid showed it to be a clumsy affair. Nothing much seems to have happened to the proposal and it was cancelled on 14 October the same year.

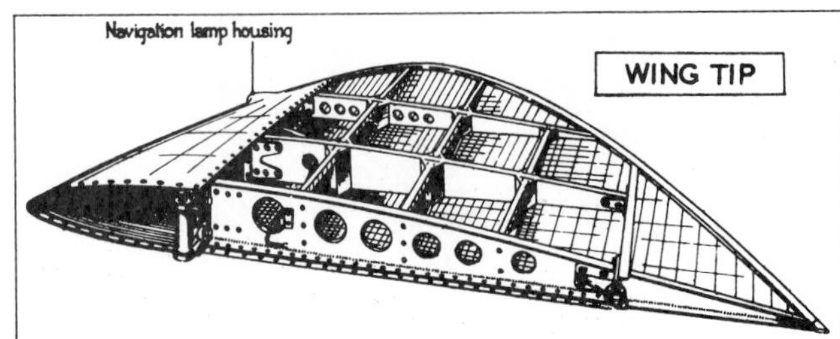

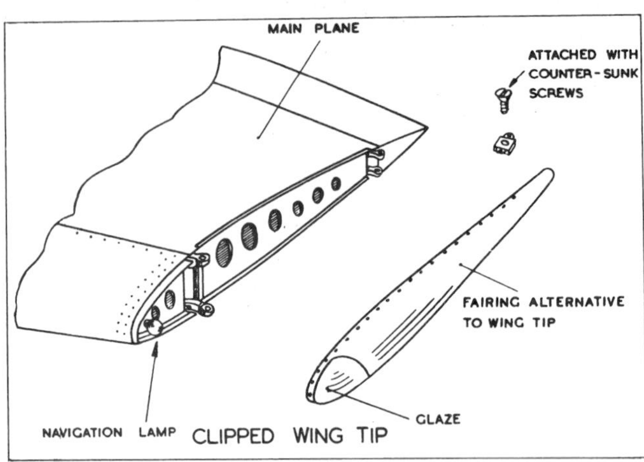

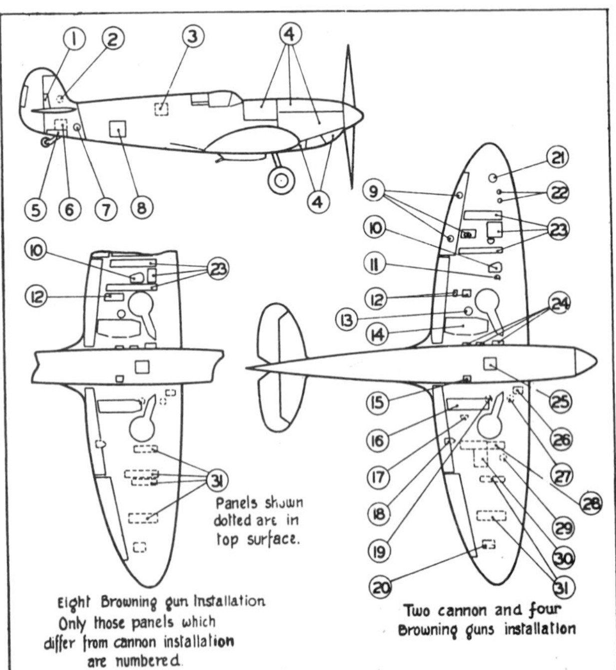

Access doors and inspection panels F VA and VB, underside views. 1 rudder tab control pulleys, 2 handhole (port only), 3 wireless compartment (port only), 4 engine cowling panels, 5 tailwheel, 6 electrical connections (port only) 7 tail wheel strut, 8/11 access door to rear fuselage, 9 ailerons hinges and control lever, 10 landing lamps, 12 flap operating cylinder, 13 radiator mounting, 14 radiator fairing, 15/24 pipe connection inside fillet, 16 oil cooler fairing, 17 access door aileron pulleys, 18 flap operating gear, 19 handhole (strbd only), 20 pressure head, 21 handhole, 22 mooring rope, 23 Browning guns and ammo, 25 fuel drain cock, 26 coolant vent cock, 27 electrical connections, 28 cannon, 29 landing lamp connections, 30 cannon magazine, 31 Browning guns.

During the Spring and Summer of 1941 many converted Mk I/Vs were delivered to Nos. 41, 54, 64, 91 and 92 Squadrons and they were able to meet the Bf109 threat with confidence. The new variant was officially revealed publicly in May, and by then production of the true Mk V was in full flow. Such was the rate of deliveries from the factories that the Supermarine and Vickers test pilots were overworked in their attempts to clear the aeroplanes for transfer to the RAF. A story making the rounds at that time hinted at the problem, and it was alleged that in order to clear the backlog a large number of Mk Vs were flight tested by securing the aircraft by the wing to a central pole by wire. The engine was started and the pilotless Spitfire flew round the pole as the propeller torque pushed the aircraft

W3373, LR VB, Merlin 45M. After four years with the RAF it was SOC in September 1945.

Right and Below: 'Manchester Air Cadet' Mk VC, four Hispano. Serial AA873. Boscombe Down January 1943 before conversion to F Mk IX standards (Merlin 61) one month later. Eventually transferred to de Havilland Co. for contra-prop trials.

W3759 moments after roll out at Castle Bromwich. Evident are the rubber cannon nozzle protectors. SOC October 1945.

away from it. It was a lovely, ridiculous story that was totally untrue. By late summer the Mk V was being phased into general RAF service and it became the spearhead of the Fighter Command air offensive into Europe. By the following December forty-four squadrons were equipped with the new fighter.

The question of a correct propeller for the Mk V continued to demand attention, and although the Rotol with Jablo blades was an improvement over the de Havilland metal type performance was below estimated values. Trials with N3053 did show some improvement when flown with a number of four blade units, and X4922 went to Boscombe Down for trials with a Rotol metal propeller of 10ft 6in diameter and modified gearing. It was 100 lb heavier than the de Havilland and tail ballast had to be carried to compensate for the forward shift in CoG. However, this metal Rotol provided an increase in speed of 5mph above 20,000ft and the service ceiling was raised to 39,600ft. A report dated 11 June 1941 stated that in addition to this improvement the take-off run was shortened, and when flown with the spinner removed there was no sign of freezing at 39,750ft.

Comparison of results

	standard 3 blade de Hav	Dural 4 blade	Jablo 4 blade
Auw (lbs)	6450	6550	6450
Max level speed	372	371	365
(mph) @ (feet)	23,000	23,000	23,000
@ 35,000 ft	327	330	317
@ 10,000 ft	323	323	320
Service ceiling @ 3000rpm	39,600	41,200	40,500
Operational ceiling (500 ft/min @ 3000rpm)	36,500	37,600	36,300
Max rate climb ft min	2600 @ 18,000	2550 @ 18,000	2650 @ 18,000
@35,000ft	700	800	800
Time to 35,000ft changing to 3000rpm @ 20,000ft (min)	19.5	19.05	18.5

Despite the improvements the Air Ministry was reluctant to specify the Rotol as standard equipment for the Mk V as there was some doubt about supplies of metal blades. Because of this quantity production could not be assured for at least twelve months, and the Rotol propellers were needed more urgently for the high altitude Spitfires then coming into service. Comparative tests were then made with X4922 with a Merlin 45 and N3053 (Merlin 46) and the results were as follows –

		Merlin 45	Merlin 46	Merlin 46 v 45
Max level speed	@ mph	380	370	– 10
	@ feet	20,500	23,000	
Level speed	@10,000ft (mph)	341	327	– 14
	@ 30,000ft (mph)	354	353	– 1
Service ceiling (ft) @ 3000rpm		37,750	39,200	+ 1400
Operational ceiling (500ft/min)		34,900	36,300	+ 1400
Max rate climb	(ft min)	3100	2700	– 400
	@ feet	14,500	18,000	
Rate of climb ft min	@ 10,000	2980	2580	– 400
	@ 30,000	1170	1380	+ 210
Time to 30,000ft changing to 3000rpm @ 20,00ft (min)		13.2	13.0	– 0.2

There was also concern over the delay in the introduction of metal ailerons, which increased manoeuvrability at high speeds. Seven months after the decision was taken to install them to all Mk Vs, Spitfires were still being delivered with the original style fabric units. Sholto-Douglas, CinC Fighter Command, wrote to the Air Ministry on 18 June and said – "The fitting of metal ailerons instead of fabric was requested last November and I am informed that only now are they being fitted to aircraft on the production line. A large number of Spitfires need to have them retrospectively fitted and I am told that Supermarines are only able to carry out this action at the rate of 10 sets per week". When the USAAF began operating Spitfires they replaced the fabric ailerons with plywood covered sets.

But, the more serious problem was pilot protection against fire from the bottom fuel tank. Sholto-Douglas said that the tank could not have a self sealing covering owing to insufficient clearance between it and the fuselage skin. A metal bulkhead had been designed for installation between the tank and cockpit for this, it was suggested, would allow the pilot sufficient time to vacate the aircraft in the event of fire. This modification took months to reach production aircraft and retrofitting was necessary. Working parties had to go on a 24-hour shift system to clear the backlog and each Spitfire took 40 man-hours to modify. Information from Supermarine had promised that the

AA876 in which Supermarine Test Pilot George Pickering crashed after reaching a speed of 520mph in a dive. The accompanying drawings which Mr 'Freddie' Jones of Accident Research, Farnborough, generously made available show how the Spitfire broke up in the air. Pickering was seriously injured and never flew again.

AA937, LF VB, Boscombe Down, November 1942. Trials with normal and clipped wings. Table below compares performance.

	Clipped wings	*Normal wings*
Max rate of climb at 15,200ft	*2670 ft/min*	*2840 ft/min*
Time to 10,000ft	*3.9mins*	*3.7mins*
Time to 20,000ft	*7.9mins*	*7.4mins*
Time to 30,000ft	*15.0mins*	*13.6mins*
Service ceiling	*36,200ft*	*38,000ft*
Estimated absolute ceiling	*37,000ft*	*38,800ft*
Max speed at 17,000ft	*343mph*	*342mph*
Max speed at 19,600ft F/T height	*353mph*	*353mph*
Max speed at 25,000ft	*342mph*	*346mph*

modifications were about to be incorporated on to the production line, and many more promises made about retrospective modifications but, as Sholto-Douglas complained—"Time slips by and very little seems to happen". He then wrote directly to Supermarine urging them to keep to their timetable.

At a meeting at Boscombe Down on 30 June it was decided that all F Mk Vs should have an inertia weight installed in the elevator control system, 6½lbs for the VB and 3½ for the VA. It was claimed that no dangerous condition would arise should any squadron omit to change the weights when a Mk VA was modified to VB standards, and vice versa. The installation of the weights did not find favour with every squadron, in particular those in No. 11 Group. Hornchurch: "All pilots are beginning to complain"; Biggin Hill: "Condemned for making Spitfire difficult to land and reducing manoeuvrability"; Kenley: "Did not notice the effect of the weight, but opinion of the Spitfire in general was low"; Tangmere: "Do not care for

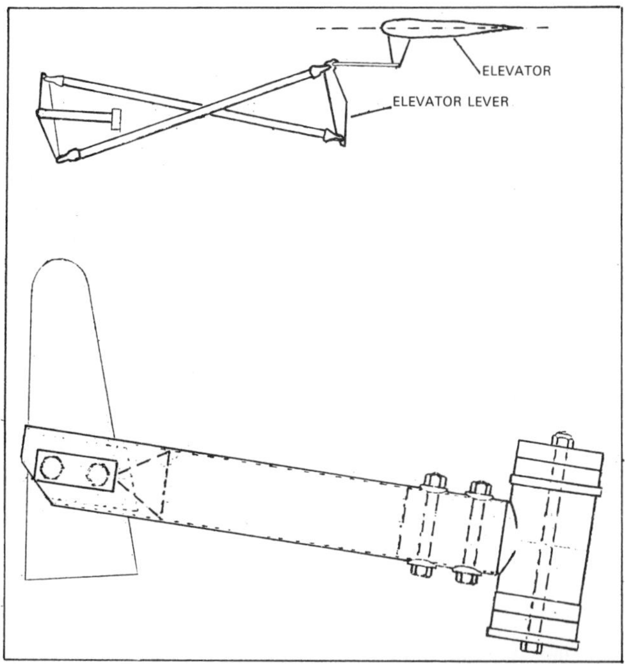

Bob weight, 6½lb, fitted on to elevator control system of W3134 when at Boscombe Down for trials in September 1941.

the device but will give it a fair trial". After trials at RAE it was decided that the 6½lb weight MUST be fitted to the Mks F VI, PR IV, VI and VII, Seafire Mks I and II; no weights for the Mks I, II and V, provided that with the Browning wing the rear oxygen cylinder was removed, and with the cannon wing the oxygen cylinder, signal discharger and IFF radio be deleted.

In order to determine the degree of protection against strikes by enemy gun fire an all Elektron fuel tank, covered with ¼ in rubber Sorbo, was subjected to an attack with .303 armour piercing ammunition at a range of 30 yards. Although the tank stood up to the test fairly well it had lost most of its rigidity and was showing signs of collapse.

The weighing and CoG determination of the early production Mk VB took place at Eastleigh and the aircraft, P8603, had a tare weight of 4,840lb, service load 711, fuel 665, oil 50, pilot and parachute 200, making a gross total of 6,406lb for take off.

Although the Mk V was a much superior aircraft to the Mk I pilots were not making the most of it, and a signal from Wing Commander, Hornchurch, of 15 July, listed the essentials if the Spitfire was to cope with the Bf109:

"(1) it is essential that fighter aircraft should attain their maximum speed at the greatest possible height, but a comparatively small increase in ceiling would not justify any substantial reduction of speed at medium heights. It is, therefore, considered that the superiority in speed at medium heights is more important that superiority in ceiling with a consequent sacrifice in speed.

AB197, built as a VC and converted to the second prototype Mk IX, Merlin 60, 26 February 1942. It was transferred to Boscombe Down for extensive gun heating trials, including a number with a RAE DC experimental unit.

"(2) diving attacks are always the most effective as the element of surprise is achieved, but turning radius and quick initial acceleration are equally important. At all heights a Spitfire can turn inside a Bf109, but the 109 appears to have quicker initial acceleration in a dive and also in climbing. The greatest disadvantage in this respect is the cutting out of the Merlin engine on application of negative G. The diving attack is probably of greater importance as it cannot easily be evaded, whereas it is usually comparatively easy to avoid a circling attack.

"(3) light ailerons at high speed are absolutely essential. This is one of the greatest advantages of Spitfire over the Bf109. It is impossible to bring guns to bear on an aircraft which is diving fast and aileron turning at the same time. Quick turns either level or diving are a sure method of evasion against a less manoeuvrable aircraft.

"(4) reserve of power and manoeuvrability are the foremost requirements for efficient fighting at great heights. The superiority in this respect of the Bf109, particularly the Bf109F, must, to a large extent, be due to its light weight. At present the Spitfire V has insufficient reserves of power to stay in combat with the Bf109 at 35,000 feet. The latter definitely has greater speed at that height on the level, climb or dive."

The Mk V did need additional power and something needed to be done about the float carburettor, the former being overcome by the installation of more powerful Merlins; the latter by fitting of the 'Shilling' orifice into the carburettor, initially, and the adoption of a modified Bendix Stromberg carburettor later. On 12 May MAP issued a notice to the efffect that all new production Merlin 46 and 47 engines would be fitted with the Rolls-Royce negative G carburettor. Also, the 46 was to be given a new mark number.

Development was always a constant factor and at times it was not always to the Spitfire's advantage. The weighing and CoG determination of R7337 on 17 July revealed how modifications could result in large weight increases. Nearly 160 alterations and mods had resulted in a tare weight of 4,932lb and a gross of 6,513. P8063 had nearly 180 modifications incorporated and when weighed several days later had a tare of 5,008lb and a gross of 6,574. Engine power remained the same in both instances.

AA581 was the first production VB to be fitted with the Merlin 46 and was weighed at Eastleigh on 16 October 1941. Tare weight 4,977lb with the CoG 2.37 inch aft of the vertical datum, auw 6,564, CoG 8.12 inch aft of datum. Number of modifications incorporated 191.

Type Record for the 331/1 Production Mk VB was issued on 17 December 1942 and the Certificate of Design on 28 January 1943. The former stated: "This Type Record covers the Spitfire I production with the above engines (R-R Merlin 45 or 46) and with wings adapted to take two cannons and four Browning machine guns, thus converting the aircraft to Spitfire F Mk VB production. Normal auw 6,700lb and maximum level speed 384mph at 18,250 feet. Addendum No. I covered the VB

First production Mk VC was AA878 'Manchester Merchant Trader'. To Boscombe Down, July 1942, for trials with Universal Wing. At the time it had four × 20mm Hispano cannon installed.

AB488, VC, Merlin 61, Boscombe Down, March to April 1943, for variation of power to height trials. Guns and ammunition were removed and a Cambridge-type, electrical thermometer installed in the carburetter a/c air intake. Second view (right) shows it with Merlin 46.

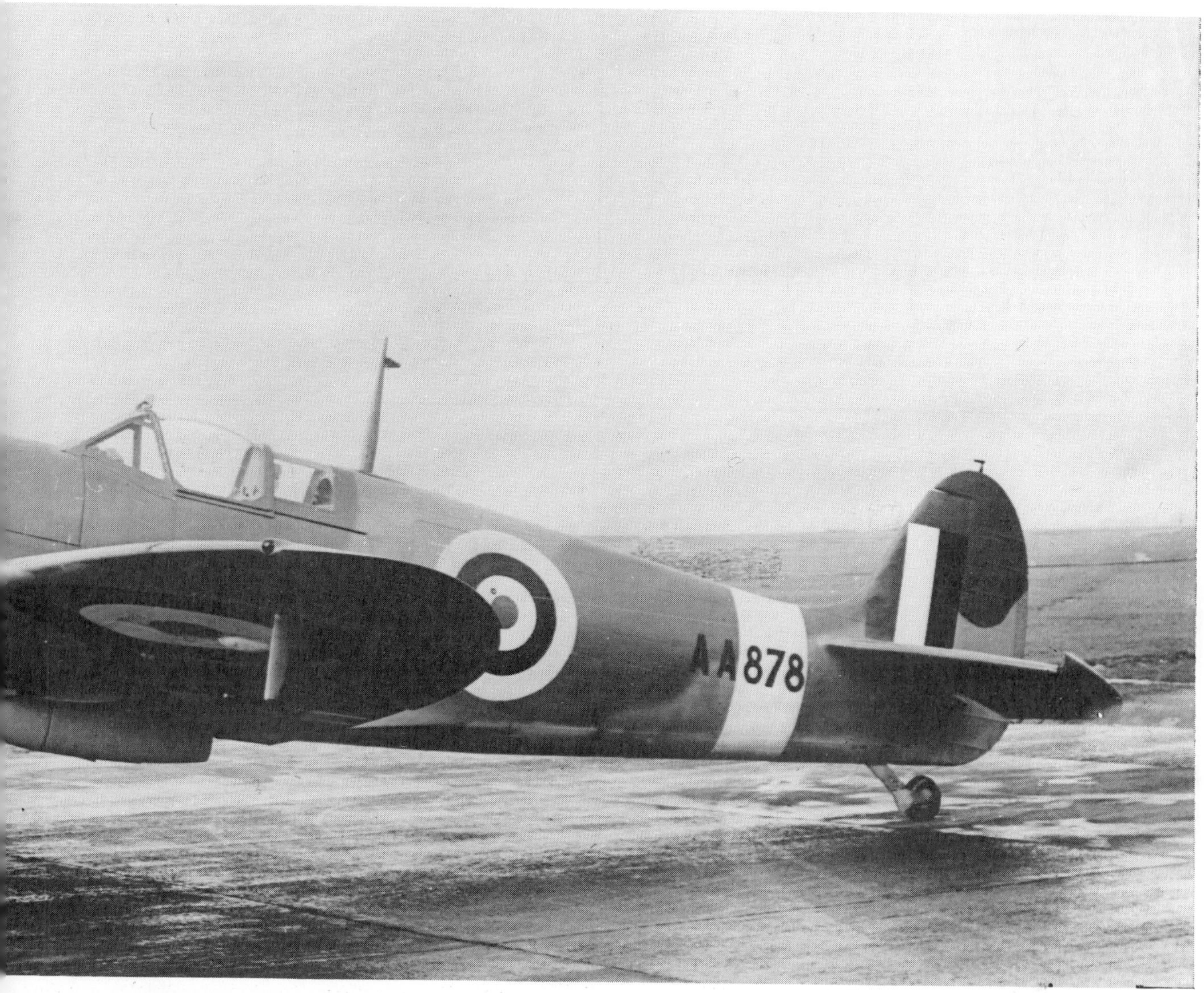

with the Merlin 45 and 46 boosted from 9 to 16lb for emergency use.

The American Air force had large numbers of Mk Vs seconded to them and its pilots needed, as did the RAF's, to be informed of its best points. A Memorandum issued on 9 February 1942 was clear about meeting the Luftwaffe on not quite equal terms: "At the present stage of the war the enemy is equipped with the Fw190 and to avoid casualties our aircraft must fly as fast as possible in the combat zone. Wings must fly at the most economical rpm when they are flying under the enemy RDF screens, but is essential as soon as they are liable to be detected they must open up to maximum power for formation flying. The acceleration of the Spitfire is relatively poor. It is therefore dangerous to cruise at plus 2 boost and 1,900 rpm when the Hun is about, because the time taken to accelerating to maximum speed will allow him to draw quickly into firing range. It is fully realised that the speed of formations depends on the ability of the worst pilots to keep up. This is only a question of training and practice. At present 5lb boost and 2,650 rpm are the maximum settings known to be successfully used by a Wing. Spitfires are now modified to give plus 16 emergency boost. It must be impressed on pilots that this gives a great increase of speed under 21,500 feet and 18,250 feet for the Merlin 46 and 45 respectively, and that if used for combat only there is no chance of engine failure.

SAFETY FAST—OR PRUNE'S GUIDE FOR LIVING

"Don't loiter. When you can't keep up don't blame your leader; pull your finger out and cut the corners.

"Low revs and high boost will bring you safely back to roost.

"Don't wait until you see the Hun before you decide to get a

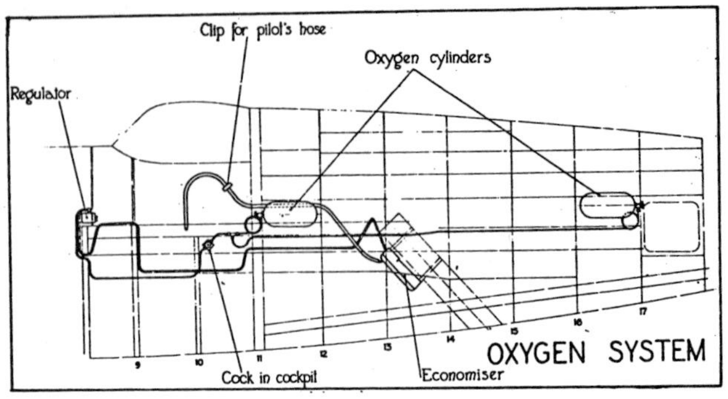
Clip for pilot's hose
Oxygen cylinders
Regulator
Cock in cockpit
Economiser
OXYGEN SYSTEM

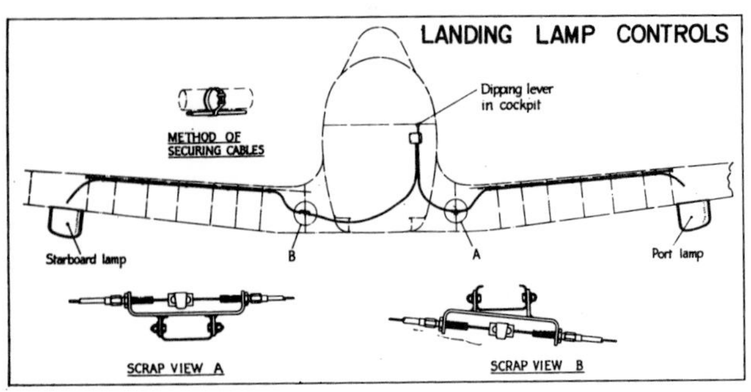
LANDING LAMP CONTROLS
METHOD OF SECURING CABLES
Dipping lever in cockpit
Starboard lamp
B
A
Port lamp
SCRAP VIEW A
SCRAP VIEW B

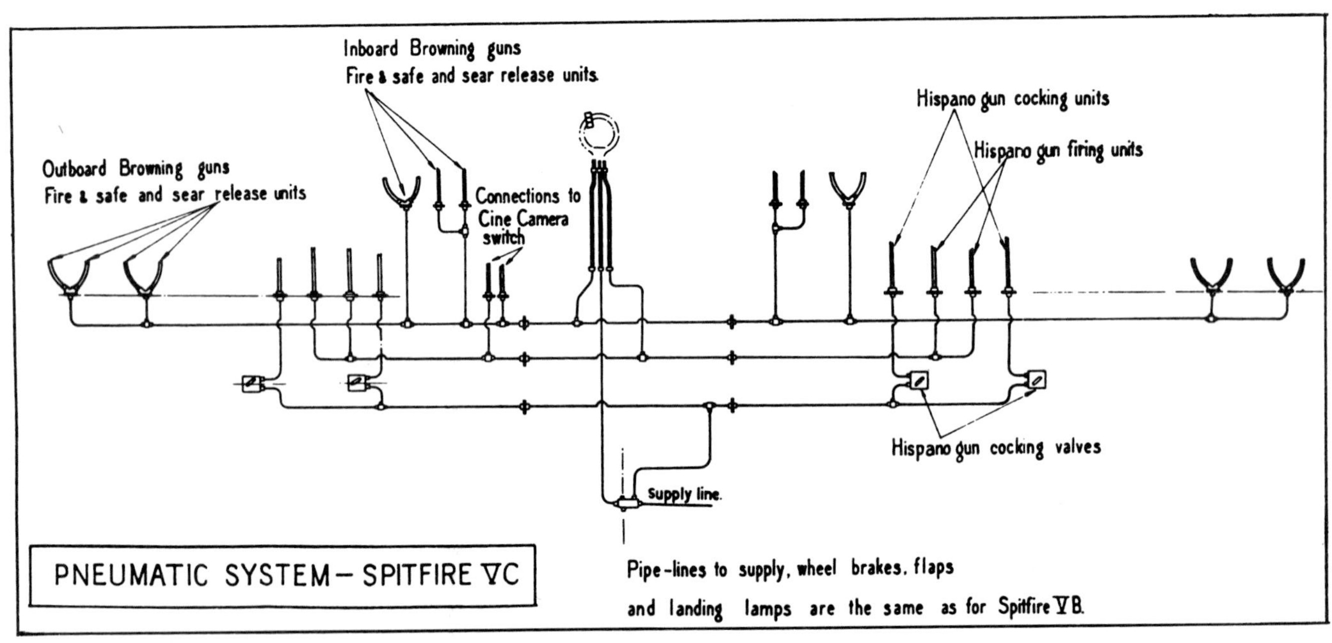
Inboard Browning guns
Fire & safe and sear release units.
Outboard Browning guns
Fire & safe and sear release units
Connections to Cine Camera switch
Hispano gun cocking units
Hispano gun firing units
Hispano gun cocking valves
Supply line.
PNEUMATIC SYSTEM – SPITFIRE VC
Pipe-lines to supply, wheel brakes, flaps and landing lamps are the same as for Spitfire VB.

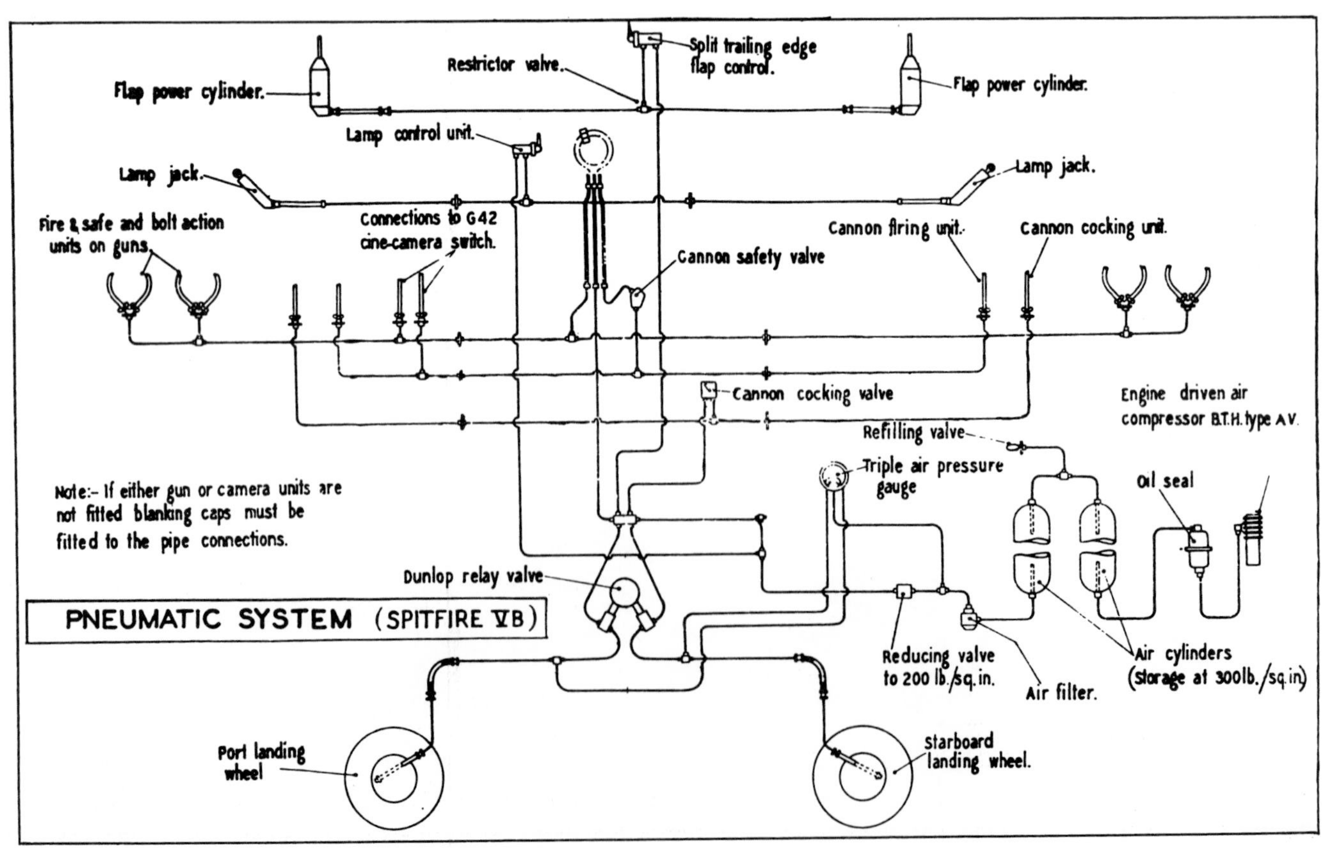
Flap power cylinder.
Restrictor valve.
Split trailing edge flap control.
Flap power cylinder.
Lamp control unit.
Lamp jack.
Lamp jack.
Fire & safe and bolt action units on guns.
Connections to G42 cine-camera switch.
Cannon firing unit.
Cannon cocking unit.
Cannon safety valve
Cannon cocking valve
Engine driven air compressor B.T.H. type A.V.
Refilling valve
Triple air pressure gauge
Oil seal
Note:- If either gun or camera units are not fitted blanking caps must be fitted to the pipe connections.
Dunlop relay valve
PNEUMATIC SYSTEM (SPITFIRE VB)
Reducing valve to 200 lb./sq.in.
Air filter.
Air cylinders (Storage at 300lb./sq.in)
Port landing wheel
Starboard landing wheel.

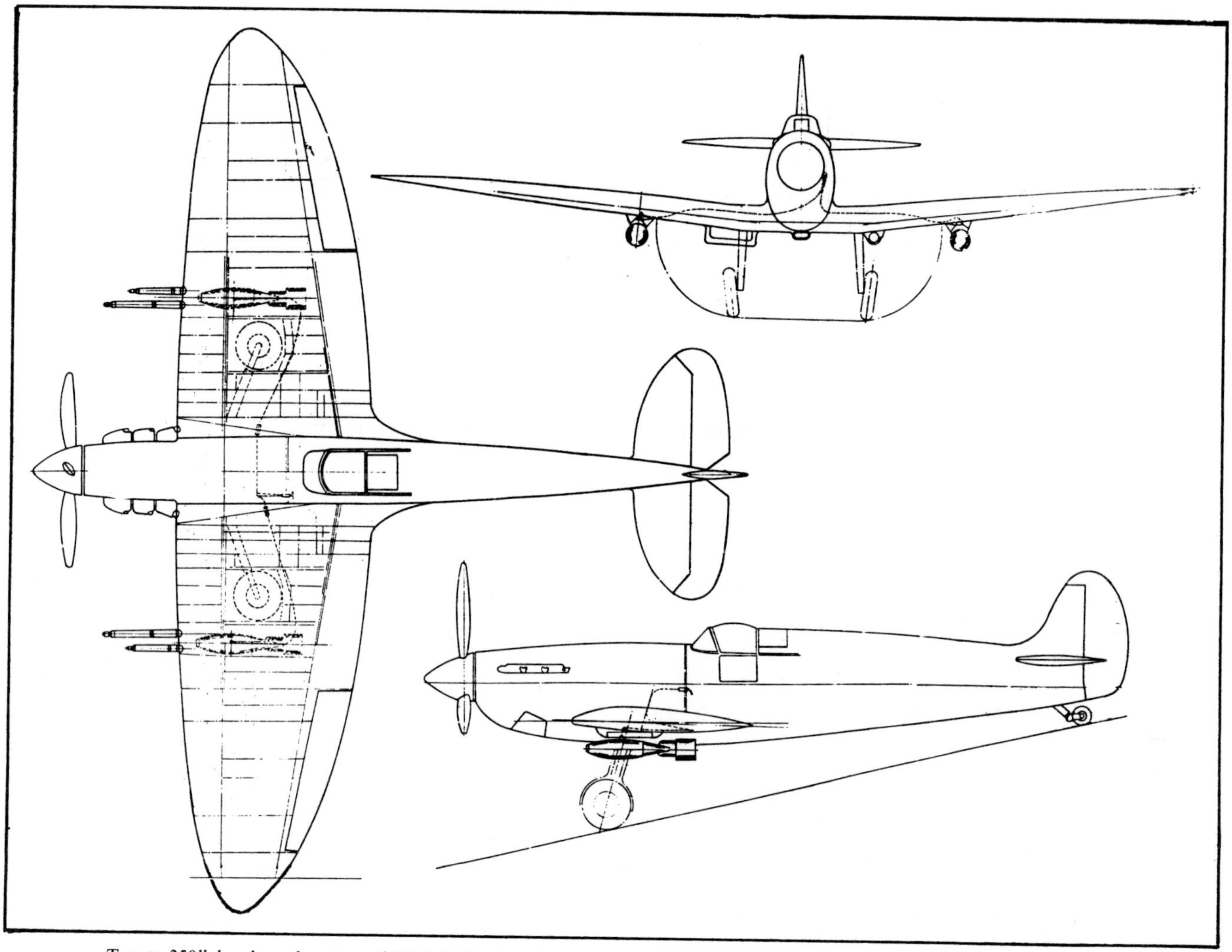

Two × 250lb bombs under wings of F Mk V. Bombs released in sequence of milli-seconds between launch by lever in cockpit.

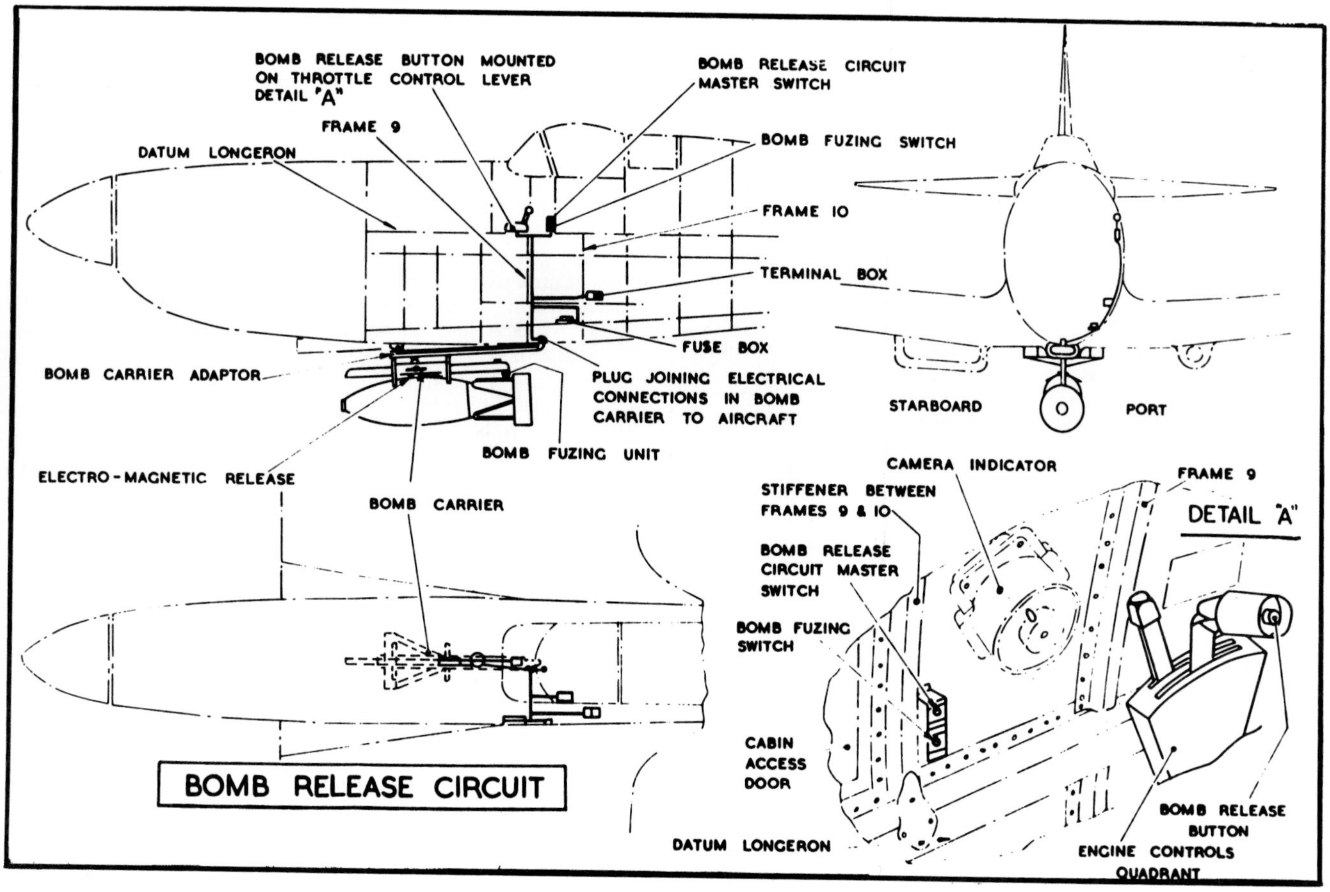

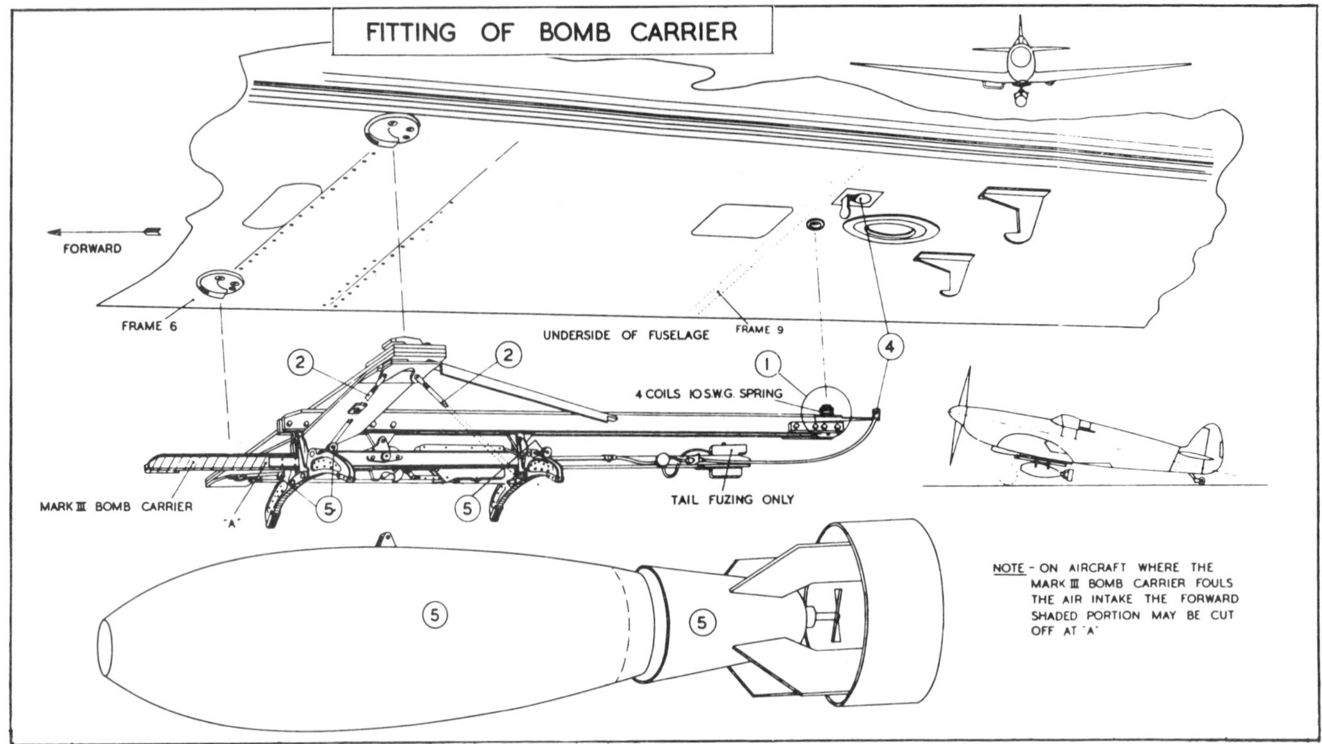

Fitting of bomb carrier. 1 With spring fitting over rear attachment fitting, offer up carrier in a similar manner to the fitting of a drop tank. 2 ensure that tension in tie-rods is slackened. 3 check master and fusing switches in the cockpit and see that they are in the 'off' position. 4 connect electrical 5-point plug to adapter in the bottom of the fuslage. 5 fit bomb minus fins to carrier and adjust crutches. 6 tension tie-rods and add fin to bomb. Note- removal of carrier is the reverse process, but it is essential to see that the tension on tie-rods is released. System also applies to the Seafire F Mk XV.

move on. When you are liable to meet the enemy fly always at the maximum cruising speed.

"If you want to live on the other side you must move fast, but equally if you want to come back again you must save petrol."

Advice was for free and woe betide the pilot who ignored it. There were the amusing moments, however, to all this advice and one piece of information had been seized upon by pilots and amended in the 'press on' tradition. It came under the heading of 'Forced landing': "The principles for forced landing this aeroplane are the same for any other type. Maintain ample speed, select a landing ground and decide whether the undercarriage is to be used. If in doubt land with the undercarriage up". The pilots' amendment to this was: "and don't forget to add 10 miles an hour for the wife and kids".

The advice about saving petrol was valid and it was always appreciated by the Air Ministry that the original Spitfire Specification had been written around a short range, home defence interceptor. Because of the loss of French bases in 1940 the Spitfire, in order to carry the fight back across the Channel, had to fly considerable distances and it could not live up to its true potential when used in the offensive role. During the early sweeps over France the roles of the British and German pilots were reversed with a vengeance, for the Bf109 was operating at its most effective, rising to meet the Mk V when the latter was almost at its maximum combat range. To stretch the range more fuel was needed and Verney's comments to Sorley about fuel capacity were fully justified. It could only be carried in jettisonable fuel tanks as internal tankage was static.

Initial trials with overload tanks had taken place as early as 1939 when K9791 was equipped with 30 gallon tanks under each wing. subsequent trials with this modification were established a year later and the final outcome was the 'slipper' fuselage tank of various sizes, ranging from 30 gallons of fuel to 170, the latter for ferry flights only. The slipper tanks fitted flush to the underside of the fuselage, behind the air intake and between the wheels.

The smaller tanks were for combat and escort duties and not for reinforcement and the map* shows the Spitfire's range for both types. Trials aircraft for the large ferry tank was BR202, which was seconded to Boulton & Paul Aircraft in early 1942. Under sub Contract B.6833 the company designed and installed a huge ferry tank capable of carrying 170 gallons of fuel. When used all guns and ammunition had to be stripped from the aircraft and the pilot had to fly the aeroplane practically straight and level. He was able to jettison the tank if in trouble but it was not recommended. The first trials took place on 4 May 1942 and with 400 gallons of fuel aboard tyre pressures had to be raised to 60lbs sq in. No noticeable difference was found from the normal Spitfire when taxying and ground manoeuvring was simple.

Take-off was straightforward with acceleration noticeably slower and run much longer. Climb at 170mph was stable and level flight showed that at 155mph with rudder free the aircraft was unstable. At 170mph the aircraft was stable with rudder free and it handled well in gentle turns. Gliding with flaps and undercarriage up at speeds less than 140mph produced marked juddering; steep gliding turns were forbidden. Stall was fairly normal at 93mph. Approach with elevator trim right back was normal and on landing at 95mph the tendency to float disappeared and the aircraft settled firmly. Jettison trials were carried out with a Halifax as escort and during initial flights the tanks would not leave the Spitfire. The next series of trials were more successful and the tank left the aircraft with only a slight judder to tell the pilot of the event.

To extend range even further it was decided to modify BR202 by installing a 29 gallon tank in the rear fuselage. Two types of tank were tried, a normal light alloy and a Mareng bag. The new tank meant that the water tank, oxygen bottle and R3002 wireless had to be relocated. Official approval and Certificate of Design were issued on 7 July 1942.

With the 170 gallon tank maximum weight of the Mk V rose to 8,400lb and its first real test came just after the installation trials had been completed. Operation 'Quarter', the reinforcement of Malta, required that a number of Spitfires be flown direct from England. Sixteen Spitfires were made ready and they were stripped of all extraneous equipment (which would be refitted on arrival). The route was England to Gibraltar, and the average time taken for this first leg was 5½ hours. The Spitfires were then transferred to an aircraft carrier, which rendezvoused with a Blenheim flown out from Malta for the last part of the flight to the island. On another occasion a further 15 Spitfires (AB262, 264, 329-332, 334-338, 341, 343, 344 and 346) were shipped aboard the *Cape Hawk* to Gibraltar, transferred to *HMS Eagle* and flown off to meet the navigating Blenheim when within 500 miles of Malta. Deck take off weight, full tanks, was 7,420lb; flap setting 25°; 3,000rpm plus 12lb boost; take off run 650 feet.

The leg to Gibraltar was causing problems as difficulties were experienced with the fuel system and a representative of Supermarine was sent to Gibraltar to sort things out. Two batches of Spitfires were involved and after arriving at Gibral-

* *see page 150.*

BR202, LF VC Merlin 46, used for fuel consumption and drop tank trials. It was converted to carry the 170 gallon ferry tank by Boulton and Paul and was sent to Boscombe Down in August 1942 to start trials. It had a larger oil tank and a 29 gallon rear fuselage fuel tank, and the trials included fitting a fairing at the front of the tank to reduce drag. Table right lists endurance and ranges.

Condition	*Height* ft	*Mean weight* lb	*ASI* mph	*RPM*	*Boost* lb/sq in	*Air miles per gallon*
With tank	*15,000*	*7,200*	*170*	*1950*	*Full throttle*	*5.35*
	24,000	*7,250*	*170*	*2450*	*Full throttle*	*4.95*
Without tank	*15,000*	*5,950*	*150*	*1600*	*−4*	*8.18*
	24,000	*6,000*	*150*	*1850*	*−4*	*7.52*

Fuel capacities

Main tank	*85 gallons*
Overload tank	*170*
Total	*225*

Maximum still air ranges

	15,000 feet	24,000 feet
Distance covered on climb	*30 air miles*	*55 air miles*
Distance covered cruising with tank	*910*	*840*
Distance covered cruising without tank	*510*	
Total range	*1,450*	*1,300*

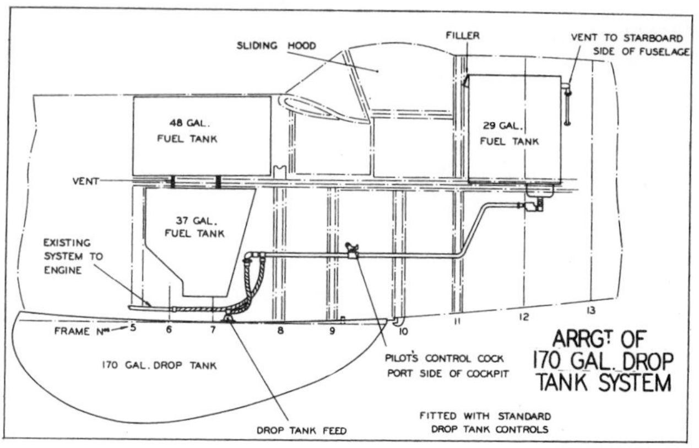

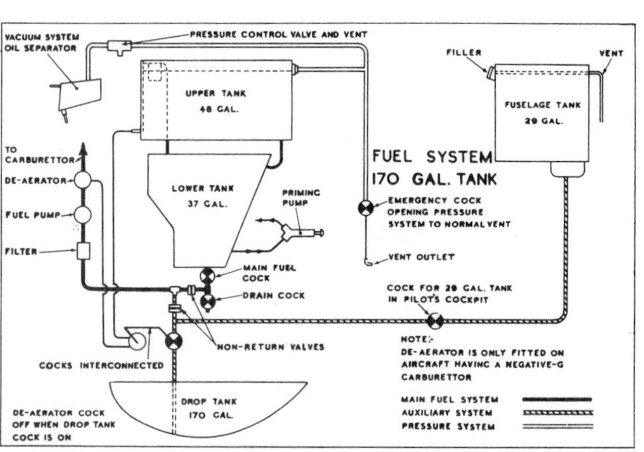

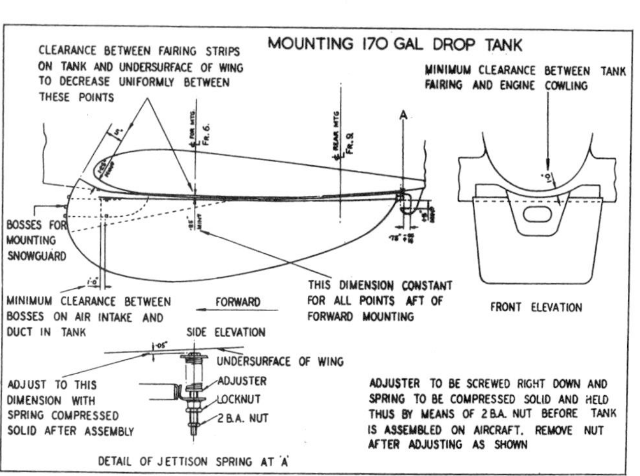

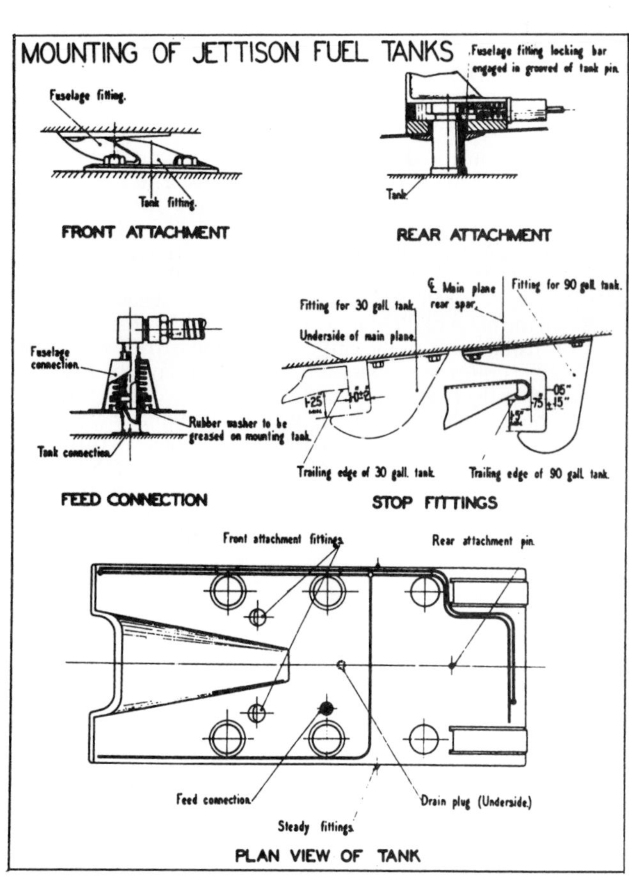

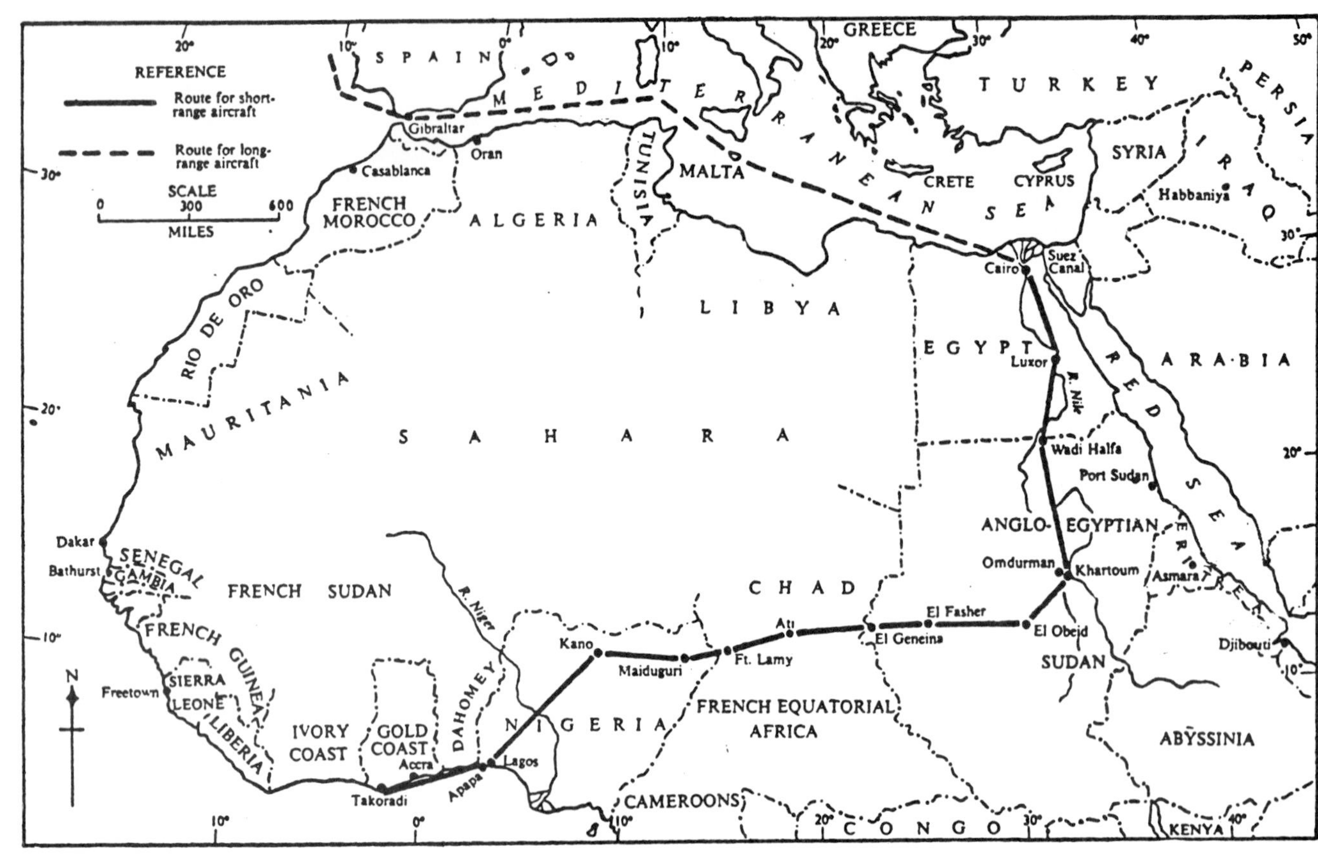

Aircraft ferry routes to the Middle East, 1941. Dotted line is of long range route (surface and air); solid line short range. Ship to Takoradi and then ferry flight. Some Spitfires were landed at Casablanca, French Morroco.

tar in crates the Supermarine rep spent most of his time overseeing assembly of the aircraft on the carrier deck. A number of overload tanks had been damaged, particularly the sumps, but after all repairs were completed the first attempt to ferry the Spitfires to Malta was made on 22 February 1942. The Fleet had put to sea before engine runs had been made with the overload tanks and when the moment arrived for the take off only three aircraft were serviceable. Frantic efforts to improve this total resulted in another two machines being readied after five hours work. The operation was postponed and the Fleet returned to Gibraltar. An urgent signal was sent to Supermarine requesting more technical help and it arrived at Gibraltar aboard a Catalina on 5 March.

Work commenced immediately and by midnight of the 5th 12 Spitfires had made successful engine runs. The Fleet sailed again the next day and succesfully delivered the first batch mentioned above. The carrier returned to Gibraltar on 10 March and the second batch of Spitfires were readied. They were AB461, 263, 340, 333, 348, 343, 347, 419, 458, 560, 418, 420; BP844, 845, 850, 856 and 849. The Fleet sailed again for Malta on the night of 20 March. The method of transferring the Spitfires from crates in the cargo ship to the carrier was fairly simple. The crates were unloaded on to the quay, the fuselage jacked up on the front trestle and wings attached, temporarily, by four bolts each side. The u/c was lowered and the Spitfire swung on board the carrier by the ship's crane. Two further days were spent in final assembly. To increase the Spitfire's range on the flight from the carrier to Malta the gap between the overload tank and fuselage was faired over resulting in an increase of speed of 9mph and range by 33 miles.

Spitfire Overload Tanks

Table shows relative merits of various types of overload tanks.

Capacity (gals)	Description	Drag at 100ft/sec at SL
30	Blister type	6.70lb
45	Blister type	7.00lb
90	Blister type	8.80lb
170	Blister type	35.0lb
45	Torpedo type	2.80lb
170	Torpedo type	8.60lb

Spitfire and Seafire blister drop tanks

Tank (gals)	constructor	material	designer
30	Vickers	tinned steel	Vickers
30	Essex Aero	welded elektron	Vickers

Maximum long range bomber escort shown as shaded area — UK-Berlin. Ferry range, full overload tanks. Solid line UK to Casablanca, Gibraltar and Hapmat.

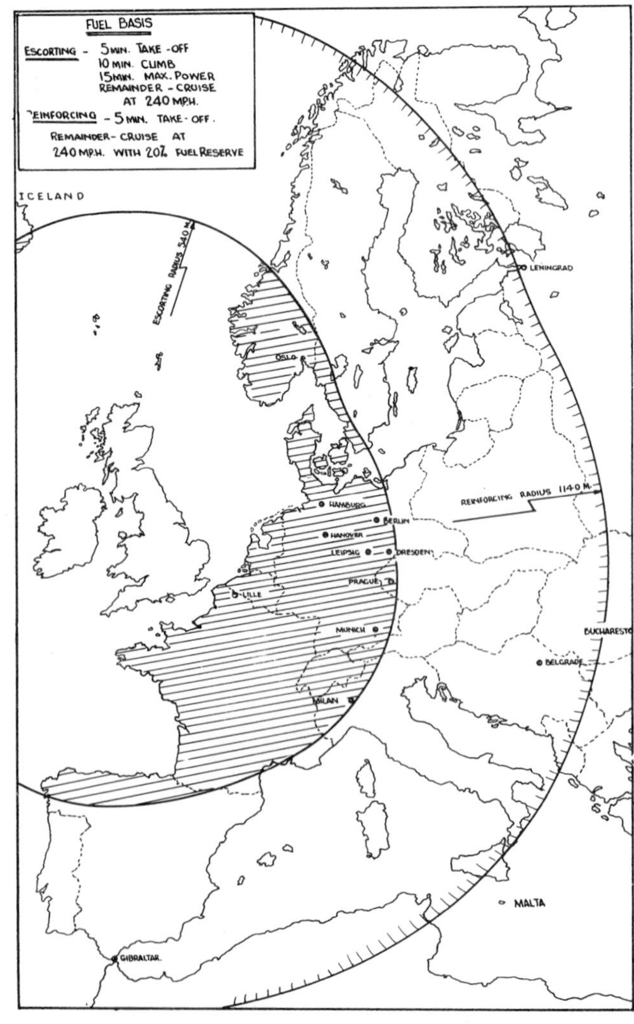

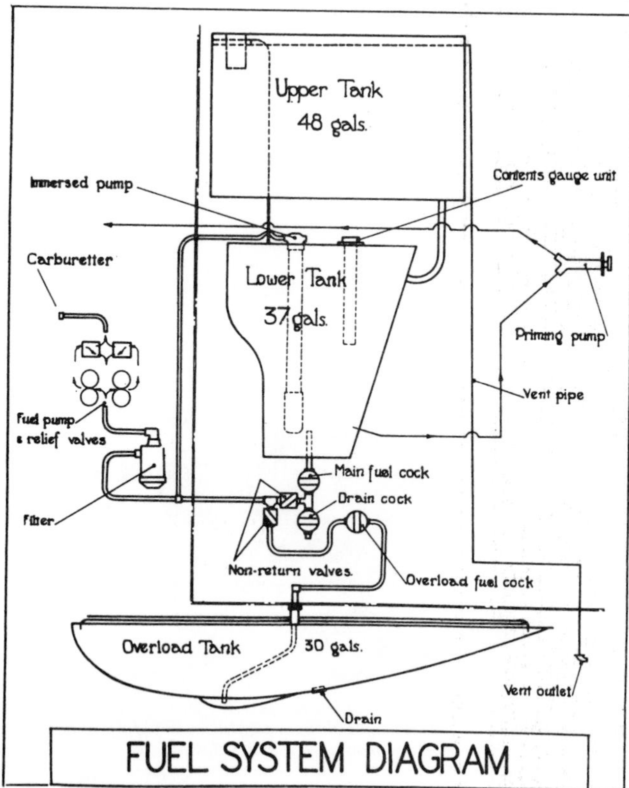

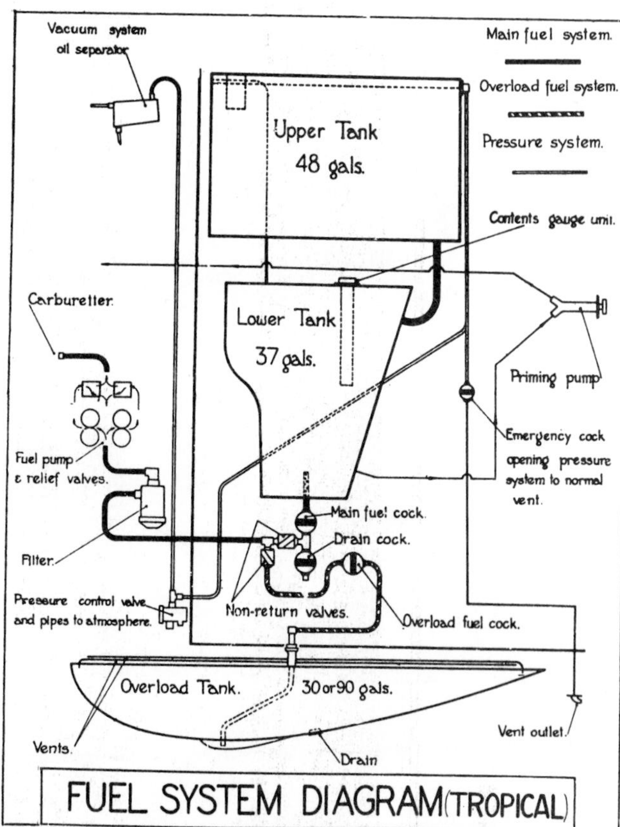

30	Vulcanised Fibre	vulcanised fibre	Vickers
30	Smith Meters	tinned steel	RAE
30	Southern Aircraft	3-ply	RAE
30	Stanley Smith	3-ply	RAE
30	Saro Laminated Wood	laminated wood	RAE
45	Vickers	tinned steel	Vickers
45	Stanley Smith	3-ply	RAE
90	Vickers	tinned steel	Vickers
90	Saro Laminated Wood	laminated wood	RAE
90	Auto Metalcraft	laminated wood	RAE
90	Stanley Smith	3-ply	RAE
90	Vulcanised Fibre	vulcanised fibre	Vickers
170	Boulton & Paul	welded steel	B&P

To determine the suitability of a number of the above tanks for use on a Spitfire using a catapult, or assisted take off, the 90 gallon laminated wood type was tested at Farnborough to ascertain if the tank attachments would absorb forward accelerations of 7G. The tank was filled with paraffin and the results showed the internal plywood structure had distorted under load and the rear support bracket had torn.

A 200 gallon overload tank was proposed for the Spitfire but was to be dropped in favour of the 170 gallon type. The former produced much more drag and the additional fuel did not equal the range obtained with the smaller tank. The C-in-C, Ceylon, said: "One of the sharpest lessons learned in recent operations against Japan is the vital need for equipping our fighters with the extra fuel tanks, those that may be jettisoned when battle is joined. The Japs employ this device with great success and fighters so equipped would enable us to provide fighter cover for our ships and as escorts for our bombers."

THE MK VC

The Spitfire Mk VC was the next major variant of the basic Mk V airframe and the most obvious modification was adoption of the universal wing, which enabled the type to be fitted with alternative armaments of—the A wing, B wing and the C wing (4 × 20mm Hispano cannon.) Test bed for the universal wing was W3227 and deliveries were scheduled to begin in October 1941 as the Supermarine Type 349. Engine was specified as the Merlin 45 or 46. The second production VC, AA874, was weighed at Eastleigh on 24 October 1941 and with a Merlin 45 engine the tare weight of the A, B and C wings were (A) 5,048lb, CoG 2.31in, auw 6,499 CoG 10.9; (B) as (A) but auw 6,737, CoG 7.63in; (C) as (A) but auw 6,969, CoG 7.65in. The weights specified were for normal ammunition loadings, but with a proposed increase to 650rpg for the Brownings an increase of 20lb per gun was registered, and an increase of 150rpg for the Hispanos raised the weight per gun by 19lb.

A comparison between two VCs, AA873 (Merlin 45) and AB488 (Merlin 46) revealed that the former was the better aircraft, but both were sightly inferior in performance to X4922 and N3053, converted from Mk Is. One of the reasons for performance reduction was attributed to both Spitfires being fitted with the C wing. Trials with R7207 in a similar configuration had shown that the drag from the wing blisters and cannon muzzles reduced maximum speed in level flight by 5mph. The table below is a comparison of results.

	AA873	AB488	AB488 v AA873	M46 v M45
Max level speed mph	374	358	-16	-12
@ feet	19,000	21,000		
level speed @ 10,000ft	336	315	-21	-16
Service ceiling @ 3000rpm (ft)	38,000	38,000	0	+950
Operational ceiling 500ft/min @ 3000rpm (ft)	35,100	35,100	0	+950
Max rate of climb (ft/min)	3180	2670	-510	-450
@ feet	13,400	17,100		
Rate of climb @ 10,000ft (ft/min)	3180	2670	-510	-450
Rate of climb @ 30,000ft (ft/min)	1210	1210	0	+150
Time to 30,000ft changing to 3000rpm @ 20,000 (min)	12.7	13.6	+0.9	+0.2

The Mk VC served mainly in overseas theatres, particularly the Middle East, and the first production models were ready for delivery by late 1941. By then the desert war was developing rapidly following upon General Wavell's impressive victory over Italian forces. Erwin Rommel arrived in the Middle East with the Afrika Korps and so began the seesaw of the many advances and retreats by both sides across the bleak landscape. The Royal Air Force had to be reinforced to combat the Luftwaffe, and the Bf109 in particular. The new Mk V was the obvious aircraft but in its Northern Europe guise it could not cope with the severe conditions to be found in the desert air war. The fine grit thrown up by taxying, take-off and landing filtered into the finely balanced Merlins, with the result that their active life between overhaul was considerably reduced.

The problem of sand penetration had been anticipated, however, for X4922 had been modified by the addition of a Vokes tropical air filter fitted over the carburetter air intake, and the Spitfire was to undergo extensive trials at Boscombe Down. The new filter was a cumbersome affair that reduced maximum level air speed considerably, but it was adjudged successful if only because there was no alternative to it and it became standard equipment for all aircraft operating under desert conditions. The majority of VCs were fitted with the Vokes and a large number of VBs were retrofitted. With the new filter the latter aircraft bore the Supermarine Type number 352, and with the new modification, plus a desert survival kit, the tare weight rose to 6,566lb and an auw of 6,800. When kitted out for long range ferrying (B&P 170gal tank), armament deleted and the rear 29 gal fuselage tank full, tare weight rose to

Battered VB, Malta, February 1942, fitted with twin 44gal. Hawker Hurricane ferry tanks under fuselage. The special frame was a local modification.

AB320, VA, was converted to the prototype LR VB(T) tropical Spitfire. It was at Boscombe Down from February to March 1942 for fuel systems trials with a 90 gal. ferry drop tank. Table below relates to weights.

Tare Weight	*5,176 lb*
Service load	*976*
Fuel Normal 84 gals @7.2 lb/gal	*605*
Fuel Jettisonable Tank. 90 gal @ 7.2 lb/gal	*648*
Oil 8.5 gals @ 9.0 lb/gal	*77*
Flying weight	*7,482 lb*

F VB, sans guns and carrying additional and external fuel, plus enlarged oil tank, runs up for take off from Gibraltar to Malta.

AB344, VB(T), ferried to Gibraltar in February 1942. Note long range tank. It was loaded on to HMS Eagle *and delivered to Malta.*

6,689lb and auw 8,000. With a 90 gal slipper fuselage tank auw was reduced to 7,600lb.

To convert a standard VA or VB for tropical operations no less than 26 major modifications were necessary, including deletion of two bottom engine cowling panels, replacement of the standard oil tank with a larger unit, replacement of the air intake fairing, installation of fixed fittings for three types of overload tanks and application of a desert camouflage scheme. Proofing trials of the tropical intake took place during January 1942 and because the new intake tended to work loose during a series of dives, production models had to be strengthened. A trial contract for 50 Spitfires was placed on 3 February and the serials were AB262-264, AB320-349, AB418-420, AB451, AB500, AB502, BP844-853. Comparative results for the temperate and tropical radiator are listed below.

	Temperate rad	Tropical rad	Temperate v Tropical rad
Max level speed (mph)	379	374	+5
@ feet	22,000	22,000	—
Level speed (mph)			
@ 5000ft	309	302	+7
10,000	328.5	321.5	+7
15,000	349	343	+6
20,000	370.5	364.5	+6
25,000	375.5	371.5	+4
30,000	365	358	+7

An Air Staff requirement dated 13 August 1941 had called for a range of not less than 1,000 miles for a tropical Spitfire and this resulted in a demand for an additional 90 gallons of fuel ca-

Below: Route flown by Spitfires from HMS Eagle to Malta.

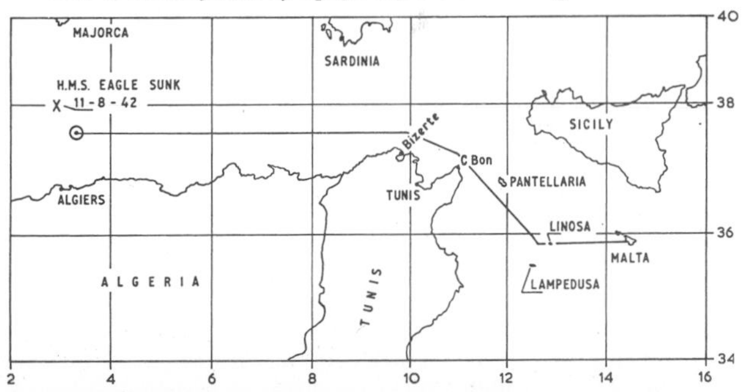

F VB(T) taking off from HMS Eagle *and heading for Malta, 7 March 1942.*

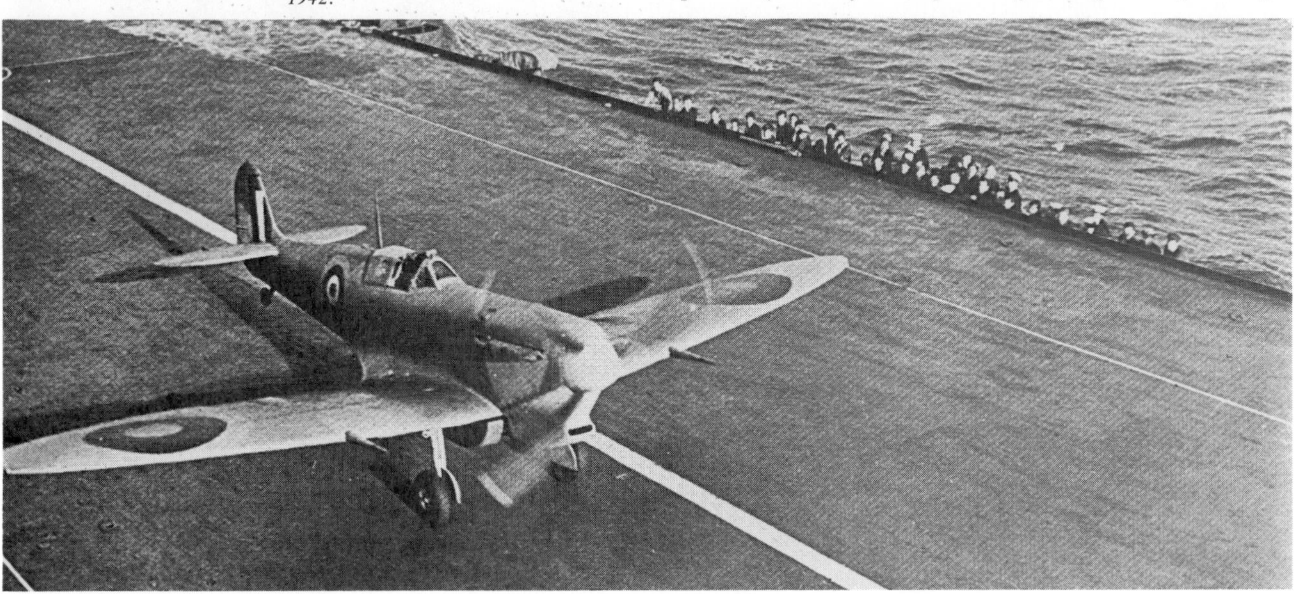

pacity. Trials were needed and AB320 was fitted with a large, overload slipper tank under the fuselage. Cruising at 1,800rpm at 15,000ft at a speed of 170 ASI, the Spitfire had an endurance of 2hr 30min at 6.4mpg. When the tank was jettisoned air speed rose to 200mph without any increase in engine revolutions. The table below lists fuel consumption, mpg and miles covered.

	Petrol (gals)	Mpg	Air miles
fuel for take off, etc	5	—	—
fuel for climb (WM)	15	—	45
cruise on o/ld tank	90	6.4	575
cruise on main tank	60	6.9	415
residue	4	—	—
totals	174		—1035

Sholto-Douglas regarded the overload, jettisonable tank as an interim solution for an extended range Spitfire, arguing that the tanks seriously affected performance, and his ultimate requirement was for an additional 30 gallons of fuel to be accommodated inside the wing: "If this additional tankage presents grave difficulties in production, I would be willing to accept an extra 10 gallons in each wing as a 'Pis Aller' (a last resource)". Type Record 352/1 covered the Mk VB adapted for tropical operations with the Merlin 45 or 46. Maximum speed (TV) was 450mph and cruising 265 at 20,500 feet. All up weights were 30 gallon overload tank 7,100lb; 90 gallon tank 7,600. Certificate of Design was issued on 8 January 1943 and Addendum No. 3 covered the VB with a 170 gallon tank, plus a 29 gallon rear fuselage tank, increased fuel capacity and armament deleted. Auw stood at 8,000lb. It was also planned to fit an additional 30 gallon internal fuel tank in the wings of the Mk VC, but the complications of the universal wing resulted in this scheme being abandoned.

The tropicalised VC was the Type 352/6 which had a tare weight of 6,986lb and related to the C wing with four cannon. Internal equipment resulted in an auw of 7,300; with a 30gal overload tank 7,600; with 90gal 8,100 and with 170gal and rear fuselage fuel tank 9,100. JK161, a production VC(T), built at Castle Bromwich, was weighed at Worthy Down on 20 January 1943 with a Merlin 46 engine and Rotol Jablo propeller. It had a total of 229 modifications and in the tare condition weighed 5,107lb. Normal take off weight raised this to 6,851; with 30 gal overload tank 7,142; 90gal tank 7,641. A Westland production aircraft, EF647, was also weighed at Worthy Down on 12 April and it differed from the other machine by having a Merlin 50 engine, plus 242 modifications. Tare was 5,095 and normal auw 6,767, to which had to be added the overload tank weights.

Nos. 145 and 92 Squadrons were despatched to the Middle East with their Mk VC(T)s on 18 December 1941 in convoy WS16 and the total number of aircraft despatched was 50. A reinforcement of 10 Spitfires per month was allocated to replace wastage beginning February 1942, increasing to 70 per month. They were to be off-loaded at Port Sudan and then flown to units. The first 50 aircraft were packed in cases, but it was realised that as deliveries accelerated this would not be possible. To accommodate additional numbers the outer wing panels and wheels were removed and stowed separately, and the fuselages stacked with their oleos in the down position and axles resting on wooden blocks. Needless to state a number were damaged in rough seas.

Russia was most interested in obtaining models of the VC and a request was made in March 1942 for the shipment of six whole fighter squadrons, together with 160 flying personnel and 700 ground staff, from the Middle East to Basrah on convoy WS18, leaving on 15 April and arriving at the end of June. Sir Charles Portal, in a letter to Churchill about this request, said – "However, the Spitfire situation is such that spares are short and the aircraft completely untried in the rough and ready conditions to be expected in South Russia. The six squadrons might be out of action in a matter of weeks and could we, therefore, send Kittyhawks or Hurricanes. Whatever we decide it will weaken the Middle East situation substantially. Four squadrons of Spitfires were being sent to the Middle East in next WS convoy". Sir Alan Brooke said – "It would be wrong to send fighters to Russia when we were so short of them in the Middle East and India, and at the present time there was only one squadron fully equipped with Spitfires in the area".

However, the decision was taken to provide Russia with the Spitfires and six complete squadrons and 1,900 RAF personnel named the 'Invective Force' set sail on four ships in June to be used for the defence of the Archangel and Murmansk area. Churchill had warned Stalin, by telegram, that the Germans were assembling forces to invade Russia through Norway and Finland that same month and that the RAF and Russian Air Force would have to fight side by side to contain the threat. However, it all came to nothing for the fighters, due to arrive on 4 August, never reached their destination as they were diverted by a signal of 20 July. A number of Spitfires (Mk Vs) for Russia had the prefix HF to the serial numbers. Some of these Mk Vs turned up in the Middle East.

AB910, the Spitfire on which WAAF Margaret Horton was taken aloft hanging on to the tail unit. The aircraft survived the war, was registered G-AISU, and is extant. Cockpit details shown below.

The large Vokes tropical intake was not liked by the services and it was not long before unofficial modifications began to appear, the most successful designed and installed by that most resourceful team at No 103 MU Aboukir. They trimmed the filter back to a much smaller unit, one that was more efficient and drag reducing. It was named the Aboukir filter and the Vokes Aero-Vee, fitted to the Mk IX Spitfire, was based upon this local modification. Supermarine were quick to appreciate the lower drag of the modified intake and they tested a number of hand-built units on two VCs and a Seafire Mk II. The tests comprised speed runs with the normal temperate intake, the normal tropical and the Aboukir. The VCs were EF541 and JK940 and the Seafire NM977, the former with Merlin 45s and de Havilland Hydromatic propellers, the latter with Merlin 46 and Rotol Jablo. The new type of cowling was infinitely better of the three tested and there was a weight

EP498, at Hapmat, March 1943, prior to delivery to the Soviet Union.

reduction of 20lb. Another bonus was that with the filter element removed the Aboukir could be used as a normal temperate intake.

MIDDLE EAST MODS

The Spit-bomber, a sub variant of the Mk VC, was introduced by Keith Park when he was C-in-C, Malta. In a note to the Air Ministry, dated December 1942, urging production of conversion kits for the Spitfire, he wrote – "The reason I introduced the Spit-bomber was that the enemy was ignoring our fighter sweeps over his aerodromes in the south of Sicily. I used Hurricane bombers at first and the enemy reacted by sending up his fighters to intercept. As a result of flying trials we found that the fitting of 2 × 250 lb bombs to the Spitfire slightly increased the take off run, and slowed down the rate of climb by about 10%. There was practically no difference in the speed at level flight, and in the dive the speed was increased owing to the higher wing loading.

"We designed the bomb gear so that there was no loss of performance when the bombs were dropped. Unlike the Hurricane bomb gear, our Spitfire throws away all external fittings with the exception of a steel rib which protrudes less than one inch from the wing. Our practice is for 50% of a Spitfire sweep to carry bombs with stick extension and to approach the target at about 20,000 feet. The aircraft do a stall turn over the target diving at an angle of about 74 degrees, and release the bombs at between 7 and 12,000 feet, depending on the intensity of heavy flak". The scheme was code named 'Malta' and in addition to the wing bombs a fuselage mounted 500 lb bomb was tested. Take off weight with 2 × 250 lb wing and a 500 lb fuselage bomb (B wing) was 7,800 lb. With the D wing it was 8,200lb.

Another successful Middle East modification, again by No 103 MU, was the high altitude VC developed to meet the high flying Junkers Ju86P twin engined, photo-reconnaissance aircraft. Allied naval movements from Egyptian bases, so vital to the defence of the Middle East, were being monitored by a team of four Ju86s and there was little the RAF could do when the German aircraft flew over at heights of 37,000 ft plus. Normal operation ceiling of the VC was approximately 36,000 ft, but at that height it had to be an exceptional aeroplane and was, normally, an unstable gun platform. The staff of No 103 MU, practically built their own high altitude fighter by taking a new VC (BP985) that had arrived at the depot on 4 May 1942 and stripping it of all unnecessary weight.

It was not feasible to increase the supercharger gear ratio so it was decided to raise the compression ratio of the Merlin 46 by as much as possible. The cylinder block was modified by hand as were the liners. A four blade de Havilland 45/1 Hydromatic propeller was installed, plus an Aboukir filter which incorporated the $9\frac{1}{2}$ gallon oil tank. All armoured plate was removed together with the Hispano cannon installation

AD236 with BL625 and others in line up at Hapmat before delivery to Russia. March 1943.

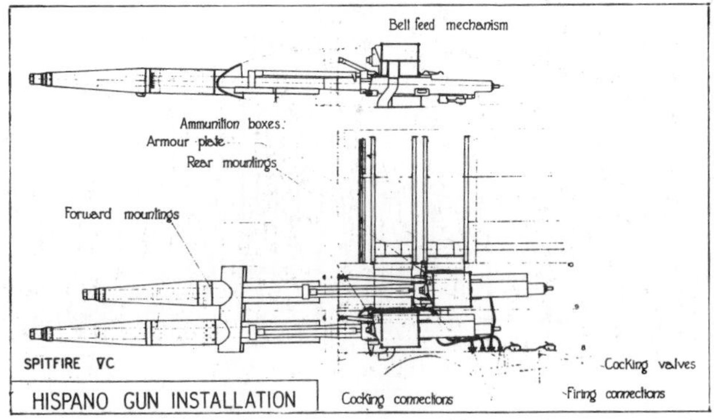

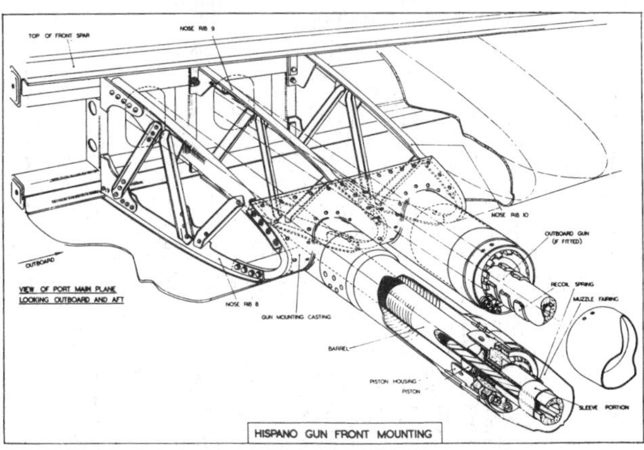

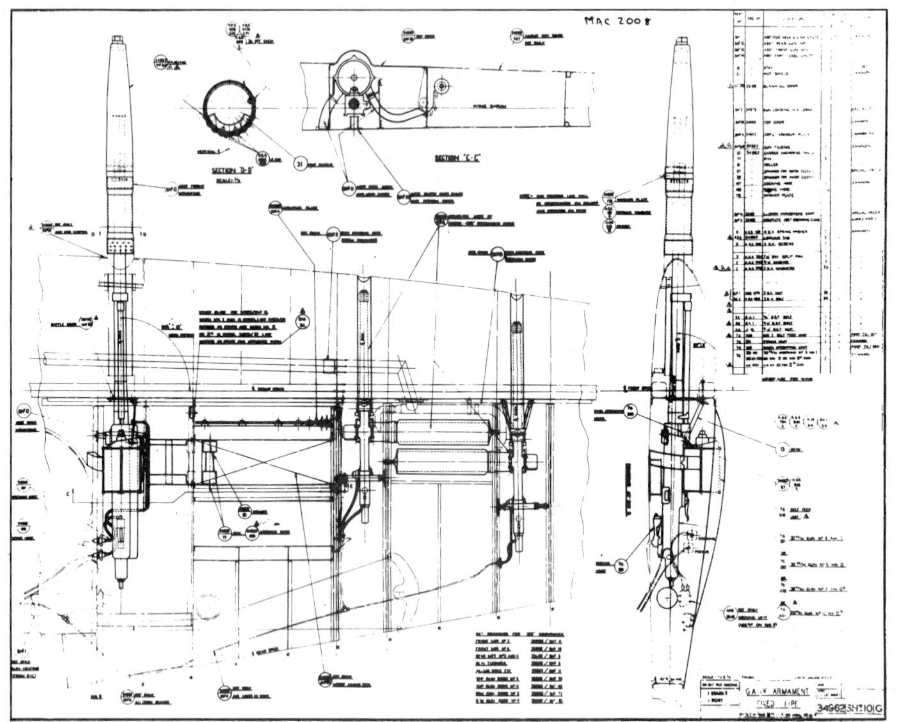

Diagram of 'B' wing armament with belt fed Hispanos.

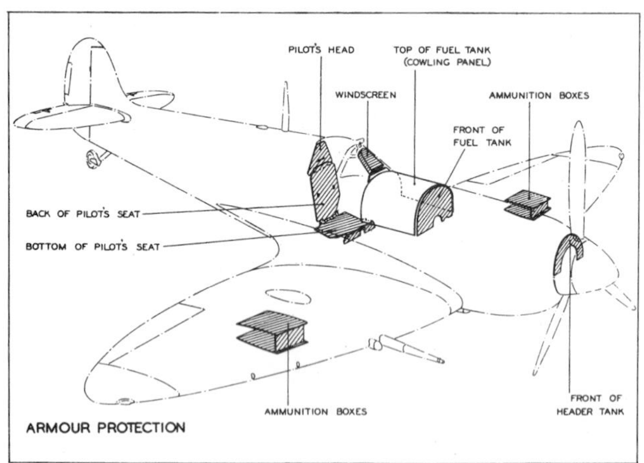

AB186 was used for trials at Boscombe Down with an enlarged elevator horn balance in October 1942. Six months later an experimental Westland-designed elevator with convex surfaces was under trial.

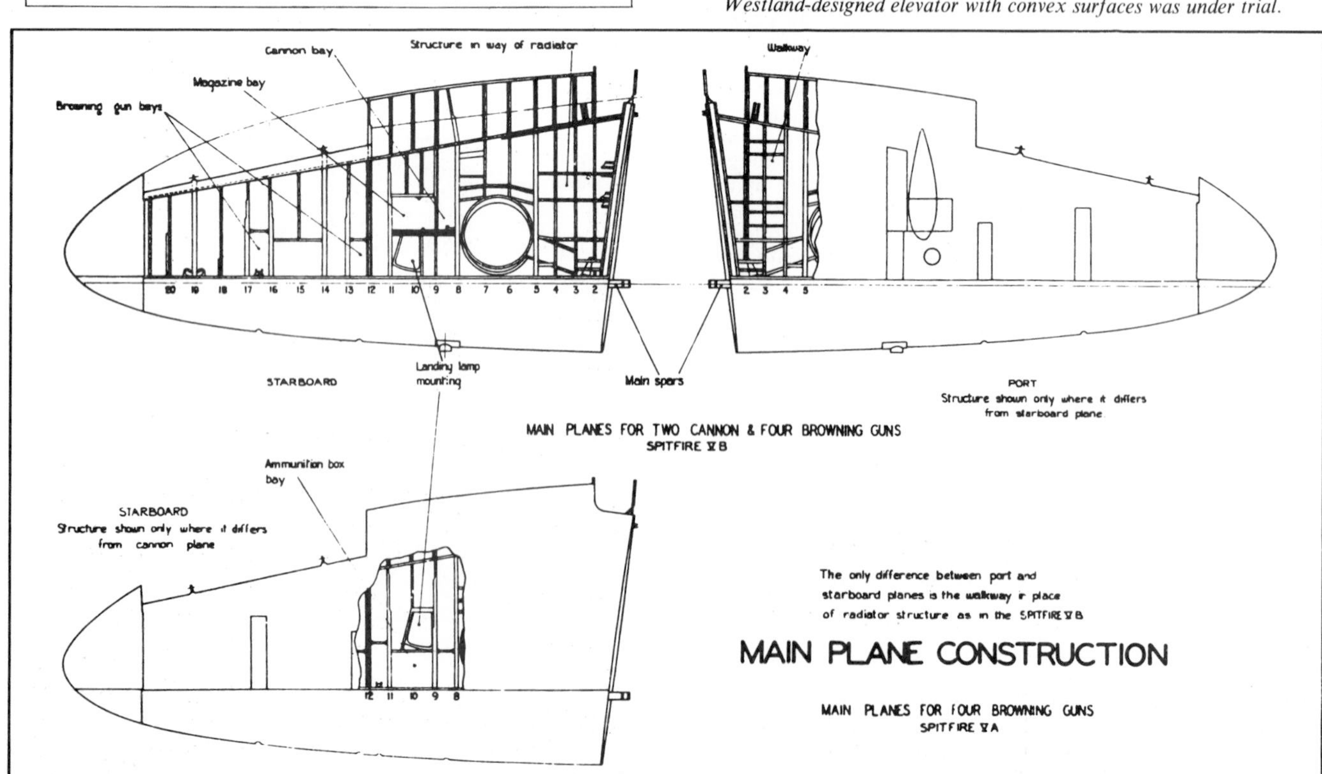

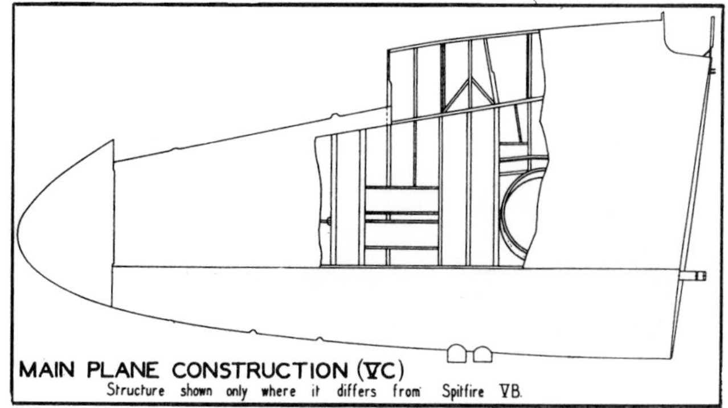

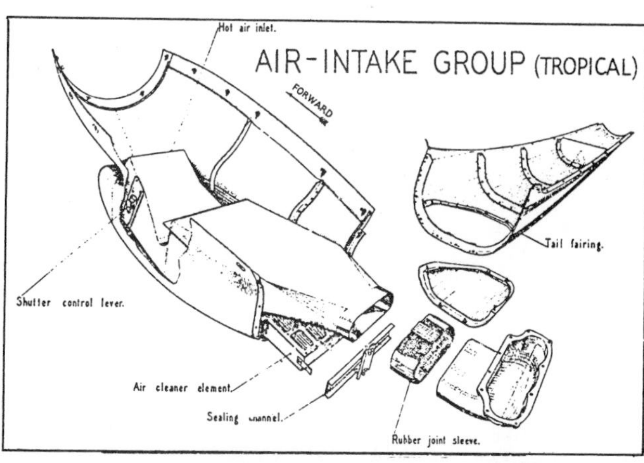

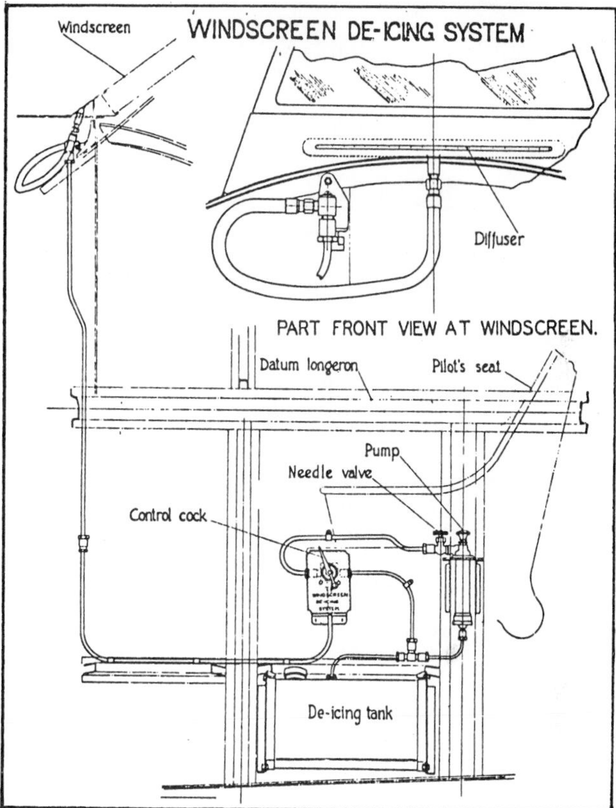

leaving just the two inner .303 Browning machine guns. Finally, extended wing tips of local manufacture were added.

A second contract for the Mk VC was placed with Supermarine on 12 May 1942 and it called for 426 aircraft in the serial range MB761 to MC403 and stated – "A proportion of these additional aeroplanes will probably be fitted with Merlin 61 engines". This contract was followed 16 days later with a third order to Castle Bromwich for 2,190 VCs and an accompanying letter said – "A proportion will be required to be completed as F Mk IXs. Serial range MH298-428".

THE CLIPPED WING VB

Prototype for the clipped wing Spitfire VB can be considered to be W3248 and this variant was developed for low altitude duties, appearing in all war theatres. In the Middle East local modifications resulted in wooden tip fairings with more rounded profile than those fitted in England. In the fighter reconnaissance (FR) role several Spitfires, including EP878, were fitted with an oblique camera behind the cockpit. All skin joints were taped over and other blemishes removed and the whole aircraft highly polished. Engine supercharger blades were also cropped in an effort to increase speed. Several FR VBs were operated by No 40 Squadron of the SAAF during the fighting and chase of the Afrika Korps after the Second Battle of El Alamein in November 1942.

Production of the Mk V continued until the latter half of 1943, with Castle Bromwich building their last example- MH646- in August, and Westland the following October when they rolled out EF753. These models were very different from the original Mk Vs by having metal covered ailerons, an inertia weight on the elevator control system, modified horn balance to elevator. Engines included the Merlin 45, 46, 50, 50A, 50M, 55, and 56.

An interesting Mk VB was EN830 of No 131 Squadron which, whilst flying over France in a sweep on a dull November day, was intercepted and made a forced landing in a practically undamaged state. It was repaired and painted in standard Luftwaffe fighter splinter camouflage of dark and light green upper surfaces and blue under surfaces. It was coded CJ+ZY and seconded to Daimler Benz for the installation of an 1,475hp DB605A engine. Armament was recovered and many minor modifications carried out. An example was the carburetter air intake installed on the port side of the engine cowling.

During trials the Mk V was no match for the Bf109G as the following figures demonstrate, but it is interesting to note that its climb rate to 19,000ft was far better than that of the German aircraft. It must be borne in mind, however, that the Spitfire's armament would have added 600lbs dead weight.

	SPITFIRE (AUW 6550)	Me109G (AUW 6054)
Max speed s/l	300 mph	316
Max speed @ 22,000ft	379 mph	385
Rate of climb to 19,000ft	3,540 f/min	2,520

Report No 3478, issued by Supermarine in August 1942, concerned the Spitfire VC with a Griffon engine. Details of structure, power plant (Griffon IIB) and military load carried were forwarded to the C-in-C Fighter Command Leigh Mallory. The proposed variant was to have a normal B wing, additional armour plating and an auw of 7,300lb.

THE AILERON PROBLEM

When Mitchell finalised design of the Spitfire wing there were a lot of unknowns about its efficiency and strength, and the effect of aileron movement at high speed could not be fully appreciated as wind tunnel facilities were practically non-existent and experiments on the actions of flying controls had to be conducted on full scale aircraft. Through its early production and service life the Spitfire had trouble with aileron control and in an attempt to resolve the problem a meeting was held at MAP, Millbank, London, on 22 July 1942. Squadron Leader Raynhan of the Accidents Branch said that the most significant fact emerging from recent Spitfire accidents was that no change in the type of failure had been brought about by the introduction of the inertia device or by moving forward the CoG. This, he thought, pointed to aileron instability. Also, there had been evidence of ailerons flying right up at a very early stage of the accident in certain instances, and failures of the aileron circuit which could not be explained by the wing coming off. Further, there was definite evidence of pilots who, during tests for upfloat, had observed the rate of upfloat on reaching certain speeds went up suddenly and disproportionately to the increase in speed. The instability was not necessarily any form of oscillation or flutter, but more in the nature of divergence.

Mr Perrring, for the RAE, said that the accident rate per hour appeared to be fairly constant and thought a number of accidents were due to mishandling. Stiffness of the aileron circuit depended on the initial tension in the cables, and these were set by aid of the tensometer. The normal cable was 15cwt

S/Ldr M Rook of No 43 Squadron, NW Africa, April 1943.

size and a simple method of increasing stiffness would be an increase in size to 25cwt.

Full scale tests in the Farnborough 25ft wind tunnel had failed to divulge any large unstable hinge moments, except when absurdly maladjusted. It was found necessary to drop the aileron by ¾in in relation to the wing in order to obtain aileron instability. However, the tests had also shown that the upfloating hinge moment might vary by 100% on nominally similar ailerons, and this explained the difficulties in matching ailerons on any given Spitfire.

Mr Perring, continuing, said he had been struck by the frequency of the mention of fuselage frame No 19. Out of 36 accidents the tail unit had come off in the air in 24 and the pilot had been thrown out in 15. The tail unit usually came off at frame 19. It was suggested that failure would seem to be associated with lack of strength of attachment of the skin rather than in the attachment bolts. The Type Record had cleared the attachment strength, but owing to concentration of stress due to the discontinuous stringers, the local rivet stress might be doubled. There was a good joint in the lower longerons, but the joint formed between two stringers on the fuselage sides was thought to be poor.

Wing Commander Mayes was not satisfied with the proposed safety mods - inertia weights, aileron droop, aileron reflexing and circuit stiffening. These, he thought, were making the Spitfire more dangerous on operations by worsening the controls. He stated the result of the mods might save the inexperienced pilots at the expense of experienced pilots on operation.

Dr Roxbee-Cox, discussing the inertia device, said what was needed was an instrument which exerted control progressively with speed increase, and it might be possible to devise such an instrument by linking up with the pitot head. Theoretically, however, all such inertia devices were unsound in that they could be 'cheated'. The RAE agreed to investigate the effects of varying the initial tension in the ailerons circuit, the change in elastic stretch under lead and the change in elastic stiffness with wing deflection.

At a further meeting at MAP which Clifton, Summers and Smith attended, it was decided that waffling of ailerons should be applied immediately to one squadron of Spitfires at Kenley. This was a means to reduce aileron up-float. Conditions aimed for were a ⅜in droop initially and mean uplift zero at 450mph. One Polish squadron had fitted 8 inch aileron tabs.

In August 1942 Spitfire R7267 (F Mk V) was used by Supermarine to determine the effects of variations in rigging and form of ailerons on stability. The aircraft was dived to speeds up to 400mph with ailerons rigged to zero droop and with them rigged to ½in negative droop. The following October a Mk VA, X4922, was used as a trials aircraft by Supermarine for high speed dives, with and without an inertia weight on the elevator circuit, to test the effect of aileron droop.

DIVE BRAKES

A lot of thought and design time was expended on

BM181, VB, of the 67th Reconnaissance Group, 8th Air Force, Membury, July 1943.

providing air brakes for the Spitfire and many experiments resulted in data which produced no solution to the problem of slowing down the aeroplanes at critical moments. Supermarine Report 3316 outlined the general requirements for split trailing edge air brakes stressing assumptions. The brakes were to be suitable for losing speed rapidly before a tight turn, reducing speed in a dive, reducing speed after a pull-out from a fast dive down to the engaging speed. Two conditions were to be investigated of 325 and 500mph.

In September 1941 a Spitfire was fitted with Youngman brake flaps and it was noted that use of the flaps up to 450mph had no serious effects on the tail plane and fuselage. The strength of the wing in torsion and normal bending was satisfactory and with the flaps the current speed restriction was raised from 250 to 300mph. Heston Aircraft Limited proposed a variation on the theme with their brake flap which involved the use of 12 air cylinders to operate them as compared with the two in use. The lever operating the lower half of the split flap cut away a portion of the upper-flap spar and this was considered to be a bad feature of the design. By May 1942 the Heston flap prototype was ready for installation on a Spitfire VC. The flap control in the cockpit had three positions:– off, on and neutral. The air bottles had a working pressure of 300 lbs sq in, which was to be raised to 450 lbs. The Spitfire wing had to be extensively modified to accept the Hendon brake flap and a considerable number of rib straps to strengthen the wing were recommended. The fuselage was strengthened at frame 10.

Spitfire VC BR372 was ready for flight tests in November 1942 and the initial limiting/landing speed for operation was kept to that of a normal Mk VC – 160mph. With wing and centre section flaps in operation the limiting dive speed was 325mph, with wing flaps only 375. Modifications to strengthen the flaps resulted in 375mph all flaps, 425 wing flaps only.

TOWING VERSUS TANKS

Reinforcement plans for transferring fighters to overseas theatres of war included the use of long range, jettisoning fuel tanks; normal surface transport and air towing by means of tug aircraft. The latter was examined in close detail for it allowed a fighter to be air towed to its destination fully equipped with guns and ammunition, whereas the fighter ferried with the large overload tanks often had to have its equipment installed when the destination was reached. The first trials with a towed fighter took place in June 1942 when Flight Refuelling adapted a Whitley bomber for use as a tug by installing towing bridles to each wing, the bridles being connected to the tow line which was fitted with a grapnel hook at one end and was streamed under the bomber's fuselage. The fighter flew under the tug, picked up the line with a weighted hook and reeled it in to a locking device situated just ahead of the cockpit.

Hurricane Z2905 was used for the early trials but difficulties arose due to the fabric covering. To extend the re-inforcement range this aircraft was equipped for ultra-long range by means of two additional 97 gallon overload tanks with a resultant auw of 9,150 lb. The decision was taken to modify a Spitfire to enable the trials to continue and a Mk V, BF274, was chosen. The single line fitting was retained and two Malcolm No 4 towing hooks were installed, one in each wing leading edge. The wings had to be stiffened to cope with the additional loads. Four towing proposals were tested – (1) off the ground with engine off (2) ditto with engine running (3) take off with tow line attached and (4) air to air pick up as described above.

Work on the Spitfire started on 31 August 1942 with the Whitley replaced by a Wellington Mk III. The tow rope was wound around the rear turret and supported on six tubes, with the plug end inserted into a Malcolm No 6 release. The Spitfire was towed (single tow) by means of the release hooks in the wing and to enhance lateral stability an enlarged rudder was fitted. Before a flight the bridle on the Spitfire was placed on the runway and attached to the tow rope and both aircraft then took off. When the Spitfire pilot wanted to release the tow he first put the propeller into fine pitch and as it windmilled he would fire the engine. The tow rope was then released. In an emergency the tow was jettisoned by means of an electrically fired cartridge.

Jeffrey Quill took part in the Spitfire trials and on one occasion the tow rope broke and he had to land with a dead stick. There were many proposals considered for this method of re-inforcement, including towing three fighters at one time with a Wellington. The centre machine had the cockpit attachment, while the aircraft to port and starboard were towed with the line attached to a point on the wing by the cannons.

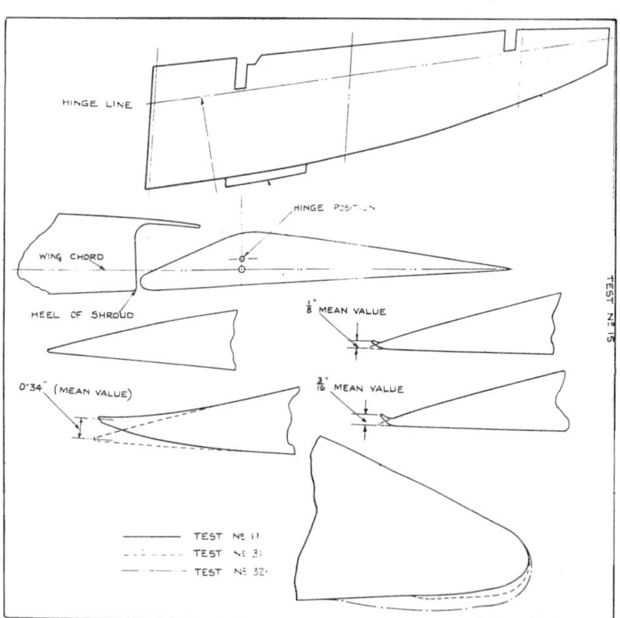

The amount of aileron reflex was tested at Farnborough on many occasions and this drawing illustrates the numerous trailing edge shaped and modified nose profiles. A large metal tab was fitted for one trial.

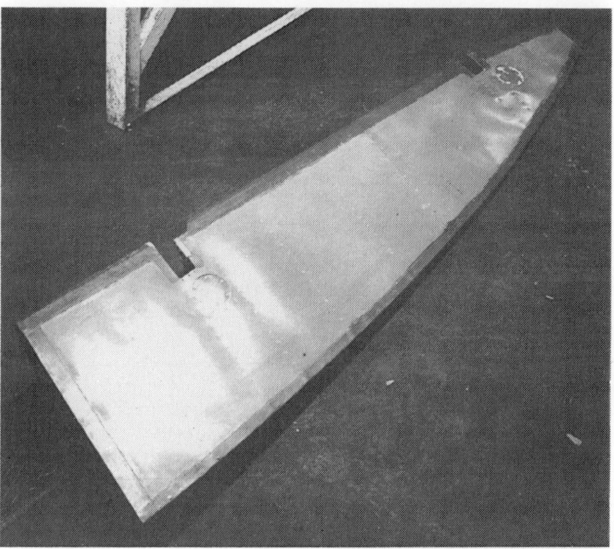

Metal aileron for Mk V under test at Farnborough. Fabric on all edges.

Another scheme was to mount a Spitfire on the back of a Whitley rather like the German 'Mistel' concept. The problems were enormous, not the least being that the fighter had to be carried without the propeller and if the carrier malfunctioned both aircraft had to be abandoned. Dr Walker, of RAE Farnborough, proposed that two fighters could be ferried in this manner on one carrier.

A third scheme was for fighters to help convoy defence in mid-Atlantic with a tug (Whitley, Wellington) towing the fighter to the designated area and releasing it to loiter for two hours. A second fighter relieved the original, which picked up the carrier tow line and was returned to base. There was a scheme for towing fighters on long distance bombing raids, the bomber acting as a carrier. The fighter was released when the bomber came under attack and the former had to make its way back to base after dealing with the enemy aircraft. Contract No SB.22 was raised to cater for the towed fighter, but it still came to nothing as the long range tank provided the necessary range. The contract was cancelled on 15 September 1943 but not before Barnes Wallis, of Vickers, had asked Alan Cobham, managing Director of Flight Refuelling, if he could convert a Lancaster to tow two Mosquito bombers, each carrying two 'Highball' bouncing bombs.

Originally consideration was given to the fighter picking up the tug's tow rope in flight as this would allow the former to be contacted in its operational area and towed back to base

Various types of overload tanks were tested on the Spitfire Mk V including slipper and torpedo. Some underwent trials at Farnborough, as did the 200 gallon version (bottom right).

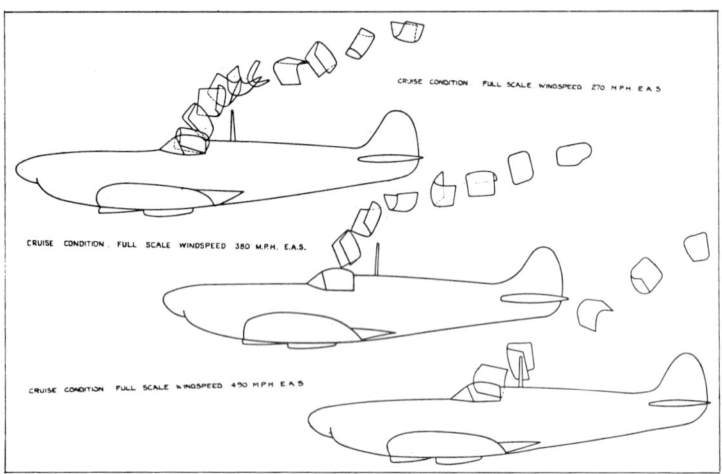

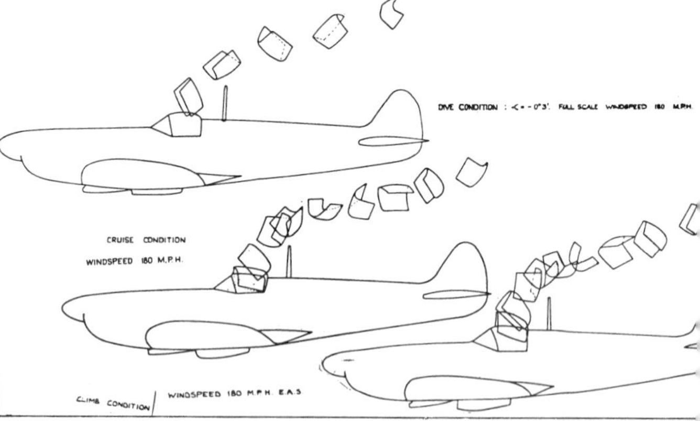

Hood jetison test in Farnborough wind tunnel. Various airspeeds and hood trajectories are illustrated.

after completing its operations and, possibly, low on fuel. But changing operational demands resulted in cancellation of this project and the ground take off scheme adopted. Towing, two fighters at one time by means of the tow ropes being attached to the side of the fuselage was also given serious consideration, but fears that the rope could foul the fighter's propeller also resulted in this scheme being abandoned. In early trials the fighter's propeller was allowed to turn slowly but the engine oiled up. Stopping the propeller presented two problems (a) unless the propeller was feathered the drag was enormous and (b) in cold weather the engine was difficult to start just on accumulator power. In a number of tests the Spitfire was in the wash of the tug and nearly uncontrollable and it had to take off well to one side. The original steel cables were soon abandoned in favour of a hemp rope as this had sufficient stretch to absorb the shock which occurred when the fighter took up the tow. Each loop of the rope around the rear of the tug was tied with a light cord to ensure that the loops paid off consecutively.

By June 1943 plans for operation 'Overlord' were well advanced and consideration given to the transportation of Fighter Command, its ground crews and stores, to Normandy by carrying them in gliders towed by operational fighters. "There appears to be no good reason why all marks of Spitfires with fixed tailwheels should not be able to tow gliders. Twelve Hotspurs could move sufficient ground crew and equipment to set up an advanced base. Provision must be made for communication between the fighter tug and glider via the tow rope. We do need to have trials, but can we have them speeded up for when a problem, such as this, is put to A&AEE it normally disappears for three months unless it is graded first priority. The Spitfire/Hotspur combination must be quickly cleared for towing at about 150 mph as soon as possible. Also, can we make this applicable to the Marks I, II, V, IX, XII and XIV. The US Ninth Air Force is very interested in this scheme so please order 100 sets of towing gear for trials and a further order for 340 sets for the TAF". Air Ministry signal.

Trials got underway quickly with No 401 Squadron operating with eight Hotspur gliders. The scheme was also tested on the Typhoon and Mustang fighters. The scheme made fighter squadrons semi-independent of air and motor transportation and during one trial operation six Spitfires and Hotspurs moved an entire squadron over a distance of 100 miles with great success. In another operation the Mk Vs acted as tugs and were escorted by Mk IXs. Flight preparation normally took about two hours.

Personnel and stores for a typical operation were – an adjutant, Sgt Fitter, MO and five spare pilots. Personal kit for all personnel of 120 lb per man, medical stores and publications, one complete re-arming for each fighter consisting of 488 rounds 20mm cannon, plus two belt feeds; 1,400 rounds .303 per aircraft. Overall weight per squadron 5 tons 1 cwt. When base was occupied the rest of the squadron flew in on normal transport. Max. permissable weight of Spitfire 6,800lb; glider 3,600; still air range 200 miles @ 168mph.

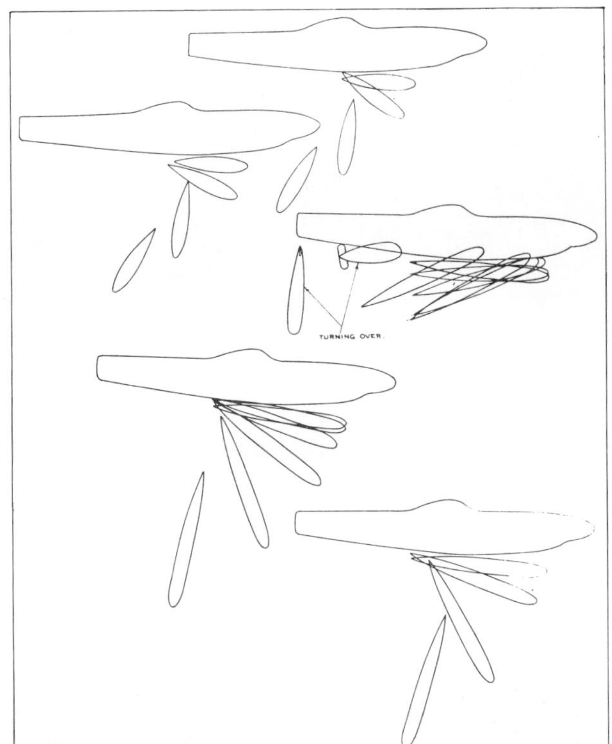

Drop tanks trials at Farnborough. Top to bottom- 45gal. airship reversed fitting of attachments; 45gal. airship new rear fitting; 170gal. torpedo with tailplane; 170gal. with reversed fittings; 170gal. new rear fittings. The 170gal. with tailplane was prone to damage underside of fuselage when leaving aircraft. Speed 140 feet per sec.

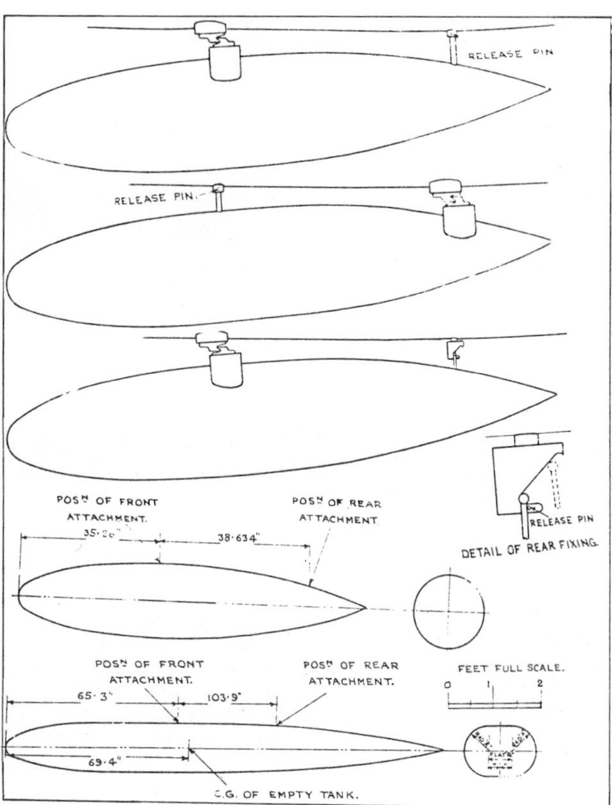

Methods of attachment of overload tanks to Spitfire fuselage studied at Farnborough. Top to bottom- normal fitting; normal fitting reversed; new rear fitting.

ACCIDENTS

No aeroplane can escape the rough and tumble of service life, particularly in war time, and there were numerous incidents when the Spitfire came to grief because of mishandling by the pilots who flew it. The incidents recorded below are indicative of what could happen and some of the cures recommended.

"A visit was paid to Farnborough on 16 September 1941 to obtain particulars of cracks and rivet failures in the skin over the wheel well on Spitfires. A number of defects on the plating over wheel wells have also been reported. These occur after upwards of 100 hours flying and take the form of circumferential cracks between the rivets connecting the plating to the vertical wheel well. The cracks have the appearance of fatigue, which suggests the presence of vibration. But the pulling out of rivets seems to confirm estimates which show that this panel and its attachments are highly stressed under the local pressures.

"In connection with this failure one of the above panels has now been removed after a break up in the air. On inspection it was found to have about 2in of dishing. The Accidents Dept say that the rivet holes in the plate show that it failed under normal load before the main spar. It is significant that the panel did not fail at the vertical wall attachment rivets, which indicates that the cracks and rivet failures discussed would not have had serious consequences.

"One PRU aeroplane had severe 'oil-canning' of one wheel well plate. On the same wing the rivets, in a number of rows, were connected by a continuous scratch. This is thought to be caused by the dolly (anvil) in rivetting, and while not serious in itself would encourage the formation of cracks if occurring at a troublesome point, for example, at the wheel wells".

Visit to Hornchurch 30 September 1941. "Buckling of the top skins in the leading edge and behind the main spar have occurred on a small number of Spitfires. These are due to discontinuity of stringers and are not of serious consequence. When sizes of buckles are excessive they should be dressed out and rivets replaced. It will be necessary to return the wings to repair units for this purpose.

"Two of the Spitfires had been subjected to violent manoeuvres and although the root pins were not appreciably bent, the buckles indicate the wings had been subjected to considerable loading. The buckles behind the main spar are not detrimental to strength and only seem to occur on VB wings."

"Aircraft AB200 was inadvertently subjected to high loading in flight by a squadron leader, and it was found that the wings had been damaged. They were removed and sent to Eastleigh for examination. There was pronounced chordwise wrinkle in aft skin between outboard side of wheel well and rib, running out at corner of gun door. Wheel well panels and stiffeners have appearance of having been subjected to heavy upwards loading. The covering and stiffeners have further been damaged by hammering to accommodate wheel and by use of this area as a walkway. Wing attachment bolts not bent or damaged are being used on the aircraft to attach new wings. The wings are being sent to AST for repair."

"Spitfire AA912 examined at No 1 CRU for suspected tailplane failure. May 1942. Squadron Leader Craxston said that in the course of a dive to 465mph violent oscillation of the elevator occurred while pulling out gently. The oscillation was of high frequency and violent enough to throw him about the cockpit and he thought that a tail surface was coming away. He closed the throttle and eased the machine out even more gently, whereupon the oscillations ceased and he was able to make a normal landing. The oscillations lasted a few seconds and he had kept the Spitfire fully trimmed into the dive. There was no abnormal tendency for the elevator control to take charge in coming out of the dive.

"On external examination the starboard tail plane appeared to have partially failed while the port appeared normal. The trim tabs and control circuit was quite normal. An examination of main planes and ailerons revealed no defects. An inertia device was fitted. When the tail unit was removed it was found that the tail plane spars were of the non-reinforced type. It had been removed from Spitfire X4916 and fitted to AA912. The starboard front spar had failed under down load at the first lightening hole, the lower flange and both webs below the hole being buckled and completely fractured. The port front spar had also failed under download at the first lightening hole in exactly the same manner. No 1 CRU have been instructed to fit the modified tailplane".

Tangmere 31 May 1942. "During an interception flight in very bad weather in the Winchester area the pilot of this Spitfire VB was leader of two aircraft. His aircraft was badly damaged in an engagement but he was able to note that the other Spitfire went into a high speed dive. Ground witnesses saw wreckage coming through clouds consisting of fuselage only, both wings being off. The fuselage caught fire after impact and was almost

No details of this experimental fitting are available but it was used for the air towing of Spitfires behind Wellington bombers as a means of reinforcing Malta.

destroyed. The pilot who returned to base thought the other pilot lost control.

"The port wing had broken off at the root bolts and the leading edge rivet seam was sheared from one foot outside the cannon to the outer m/g, indicating high torsion due to aileron flutter. Practically all the structure aft of the spars was broken away. The aileron lever rivets were sheared on the starboard wing. On the port wing, part of the lever comprising the two arms was broken off from its attachment flange and pulled through by the cables to rib 12, where it jammed. Both rear cables are thought to have broken first, ie. those holding the ailerons down.

"The starboard tailplane is thought to have broken upwards, shearing the bolts. The tail end had torn away at the rear joint rivets but was intact. It is considered that structural failure was due to excessive normal loading, produced by an uncontrolled pull out at high speed".

Hampnet, near Tangmere, 1 July 1942. "Spitfire BL513 has been reported by Accidents Branch to have developed signs of strain in the fuselage. It had waves and buckles at frames 14 and 19 and a small bulge in the vertical plating of the aft

Proposal by Flight Refuelling Ltd., to tow Spitfire behind multi-engined tugs. Fighter could be solo towed by means of double line, or two aircraft towed by one tug with the line attached to the 20mm cannon leading edge mounting. Illustrated opposite are 'A' single tow, 'B' twin tow fitments for the cables.

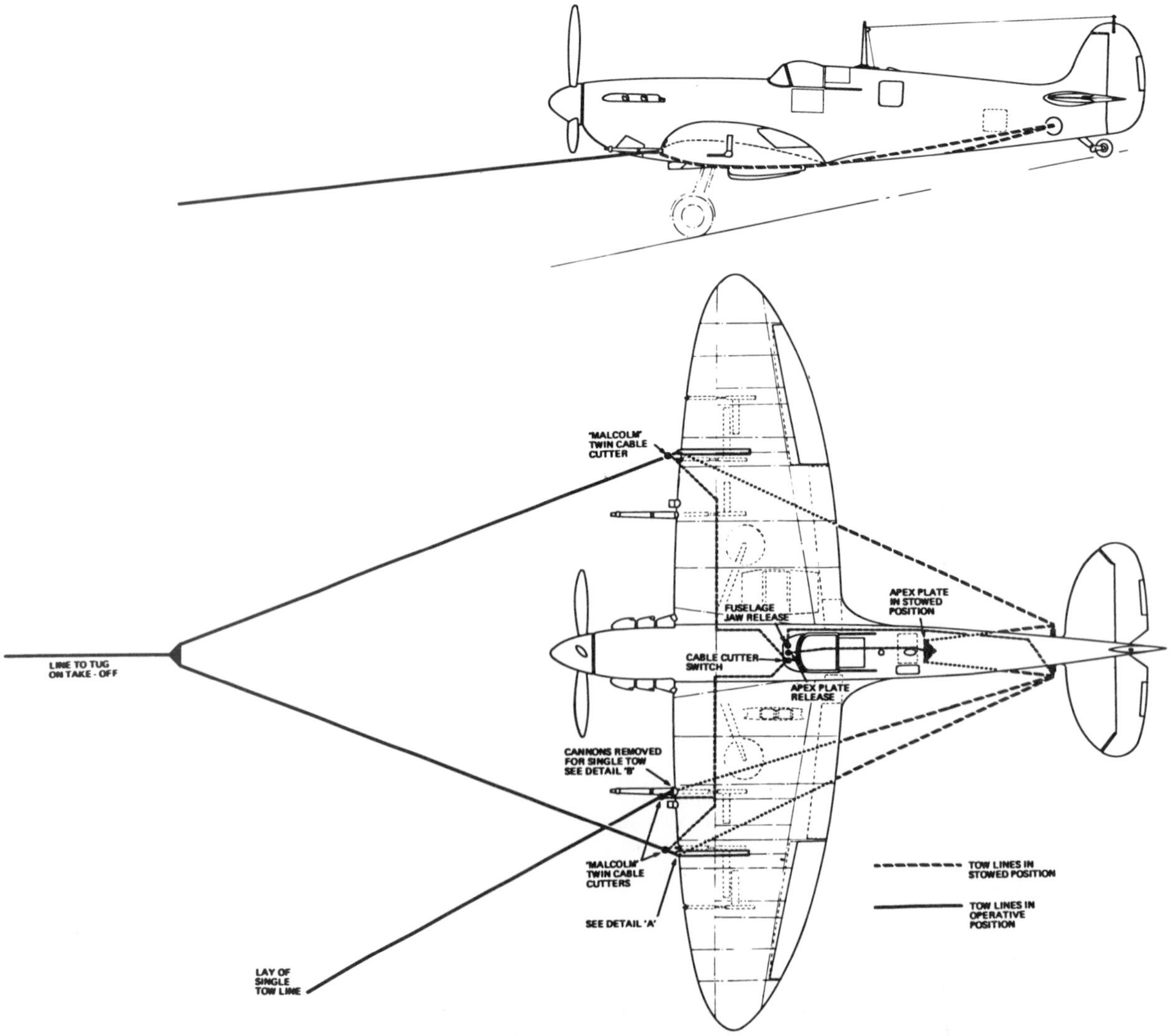

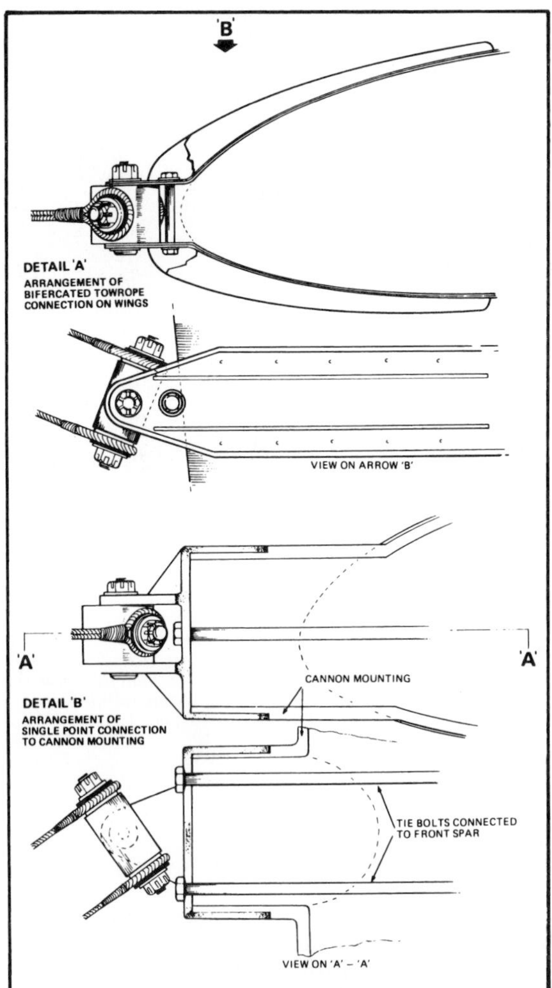

portion of the wing root fillet. Upon removal of the tail wheel fairing the leg was found to be bent to port. Damage was diagnosed as the result of heavy landings. The aircraft had been used for target towing on the flight prior to discovery of the damage and had lost its drogue by fracturing the tow line. A specimen of the line failed at a load of 400 lbs".

Spitfire VB EP335 at Charmy Down, 20 April 1943. "The aircraft was damaged during combat exercises and during pull out of a high speed dive the pilot blacked out, but made a normal landing. The pilot said the aircraft came out of the dive suddenly of its own accord, thereby causing him to blackout. The wings and centre section were buckled and the tail plane damaged".

One disturbing factor emerged after the VB had been in service for some time. There occurred a number of totally unexplainable accidents in which Spitfires dived into the ground for no apparent reason. The Accidents Branch investigated and eventually issued the following statement – "It had been found that firing the VB's cannons damages, in some ways, or dislocates the oxygen regulating apparatus so that thereafter the rate of supply cannot be varied". Another factor considered was the run of the oxygen piping, thought to be unneccessarily long. The statement said – "The greater the length of piping the more chance there was of a stoppage of supply due to a collection of condensation freezing, with the result that the pilot would black out. This investigation was most thorough and the recommendations saved the lives of many pilots.

The Accidents Branch was also very active in rooting out defects on the Spitfire production lines. The problems were enormous due to the dispersal scheme and the need to adhere rigidly to specified standards. In November 1942 a manufacturing errors list was prepared and it resulted in a tightening up of quality control. Rivets attaching aileron control sprockets at the base of the pilot's control column were, normally, of stainless steel, but on numerous occasions duralumin rivets were used; rivetting of the leading edges of wings were repaired with aluminium instead of Alclad; rivetting of the leading edge was also completed with non-standard rivets with the result that some heads stood proud of the surface by as much as 1/32nd of an inch. Apart from the effect on wing strength they also caused loss of performance. The list ended with these words – "An essential part of the organisation for ensuring structual strength of aeroplanes is the arrangement whereby careful inspection is carried out at every stage from raw material right through to the finished product. As a result of non-function the structural safety of the Spitfire in certain cases is being most seriously affected".

The Spitfire F Mk V was declared obsolete for all RAF purposes in September 1945, and in March 1948 the remaining VBs and VCs in storage were scrapped.

OFFICIAL REPORTS ON Mk V

Official Reports on Mk V trials aircraft, and experiments, in chronological order.

Boscombe Down, 18 June 1941. W3134. Brief performance trails. Auw 6,525lbs. Maximum speed 371mph @ 20,100ft. Maximum rate of climb 3,250 ft/min @ 15,200ft. Time to 20,000ft 6.4mins. Service ceiling 37,500ft.

Farnborough July 1941. Investigation of optimum position of dive brakes on Spitfire. Main dive brake flaps mounted on spar of underwing surface. Spoiler fitted to tailplane, operated pneumatically on the same system as main brake flaps, to correct change of trim. The Youngman dive brake was required to produce a deceleration of 1g at 400mph. Flap operated by means of bellows attached to rear of flap which had

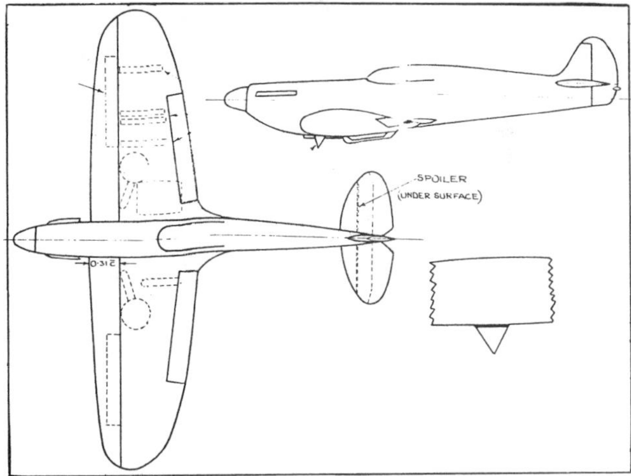

A dive brake flap was tested on a Spitfire in summer 1941 which operated in conjunction with a tailplane spoiler. The air brake was mounted on the under wing spar and opened pneumatically by means of bellows attached to the rear face of the flap.

Diagram of proposed skid for minimising damage to OTU Spitfires in a wheels up landing following Beaverbrook's complaint. May 1941, Hawarden.

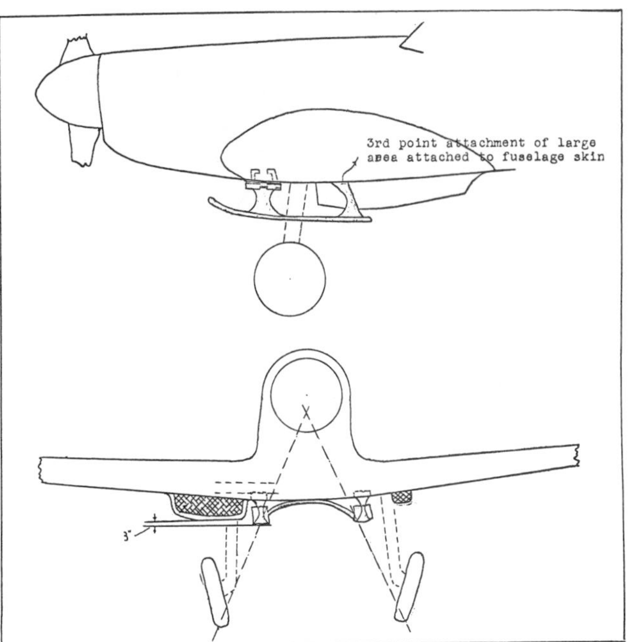

a maximum setting of 60°. Drawing of model shows positions of brake flaps and tailplane spoiler.

Boscombe Down, July 1941. W3134. Merlin 45 and 46. Comparative tests of two engines. Results were:

	M45	M46
Max rate of climb (ft/min)	2750 @ 13,000ft	2740 @ 15,200ft
Time to 20,000ft (mins)	7.8	7.6
30,000	15.9	14.5
35,000	27.5	21.9
Estimated service ceiling (ft)	36,250	38,100
absolute ceiling	37,400	39,000
Maximum speed (mph)	353 (18,000ft)	352 (20,200ft)

Boscombe Down, 2 September 1941. W3134 and P8781. Merlin 45 Low fuel pressure tests. Investigation into alleged loss of performance attributed to low fuel pressure. Fuel was pre-heated by electric immersion unit before take off to 43-45°C. Effect of heating fuel lowered height to where pressure started to drop, which was beneficial to performance.

Boscombe Down, September 1941. W3134. Flame damping tests with triple ejector exhaust fitted intensifier tube. Tests to ascertain if intensifier tube (for gun heating) attained higher temperature than rest of exhaust system.

Boscombe Down, October 1941. W3134. Trials with inertia weight in elevator control system. Requirement to find suitable weight and lever arm. 6½ lb weight proved to be most acceptable and was recommended for all Mk Vs. Drawing shows type of **arm and weight fitted. See page 143.**

Boscombe Down, October 1941. R7337. Gun heating trials. Exhaust muff type of heater satisfactory on the triple exhaust system.

Farnborough, December 1941. Brake flap tests showed large effects on lift and trim and the use of double split flaps was investigated in the wind tunnel. Drawing of model shows movement of flaps. The flaps were perforated for subsequent trials and it was proposed cutting vertical and horizontal slots in them for testing effect on tail buffetting.

Farnborough, December 1941. Additional tests of brake flaps on wings and body. Drawing shows position of flaps, the wing fittings opened to 30°, the fuselage to 30, 45 and 60°. Wing flaps gave a small nose up change of trim and when used with the body flap this trim increased. Buffetting occurred when wing flaps were opened to 60°.

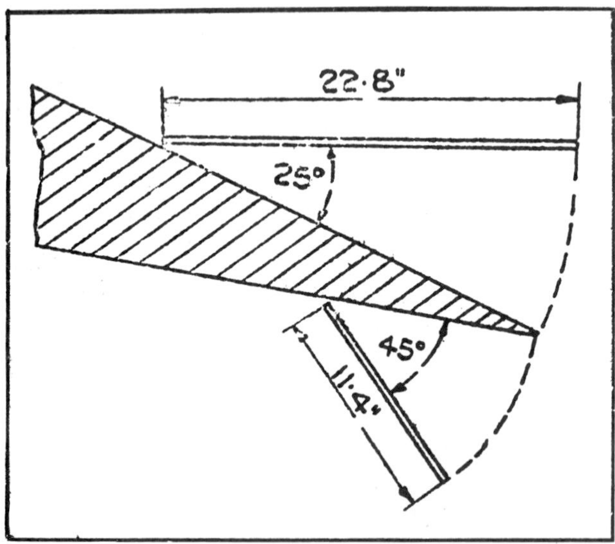

Trials continued in December 1941 with a short span Mk V equipped with the split flap air brake with an up and down movement of 30°. By doubling the chord of the upper portion of the flap and altering movement to 25° up and 45° down deceleration was improved. The tailplane was kept clear of any disturbed airflow and there were no appreciable changes of lift or trim. The flaps were next perforated with no alteration in performance.

Boscombe Down, July 1941 to January 1942. W3134. Analysis of cooling results. Thirty-three performance climbs were made with W3134 over a period of six months to obtain cooling data.

Boscombe Down, February 1942. AA873. Weights and loading data. Spitfire with Universal wing. Details (a) 8 × .303 Brownings, (b) 2 × 20mm cannon and 4 × .303 Brownings and (c) 4 × 20mm cannon.

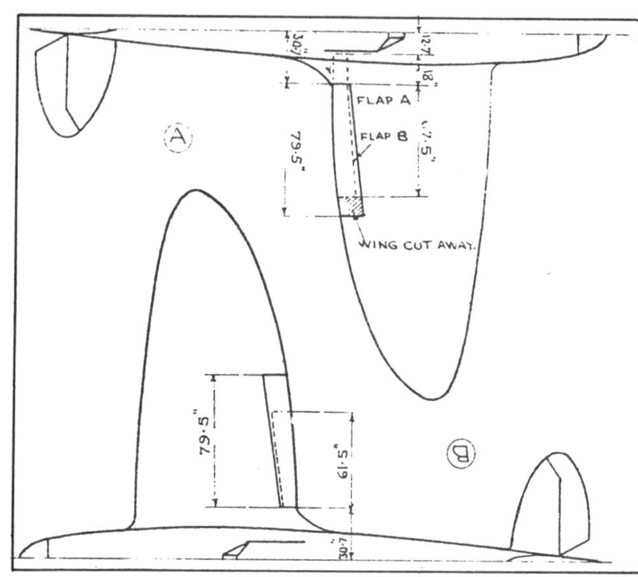

Tunnel tests of air brakes failed to reveal that under certain conditions the flap would give additional lift, together with a nose down attitude. Two new types of flap were tested to cure this condition. Opening angles (flap 'A') made no difference, but reducing the area lengthwise (flap 'B') by 18 inches, or by 12 inches plus the addition of a small flap on the centre section undersurface, it was greatly improved.

	(a)	(b)	(c)
Tare (lbs)	5003	5033	5033
Service load	904	1032	1264
Fuel	605	605	605
Oil	52	52	52
Take off	6564	6722	6954

Weights based on de Havilland propeller. When Rotol used weight reduced by 35 lb.

Boscombe Down. W3134. Analysis of performance at varying air temperatures. During the same period (July 1941 to **January 1942) data on performance at varying temperatures was collected in addition to that for cooling.**

Boscombe Down, January 1942. W3322. Tests of pressure fuel system, Merlin 45. Fuel tanks pressurised by admitting exhaust air from the Pesco vacuum pump to tanks. Conclusions were system would perform satisfactory only when initial temperature was less than 35°C. Over this and engine would cut out due to over richness. Trials installation by Rolls-Royce, similar to that fitted to Hurricane.

Boscombe Down, January 1942. W3228. Aerobatic han-dling trials with Rolls-Royce diaphragm type carburetter. This carburetter was considered to transform the Mk V into a much better fighting machine as any manoeuvre could be made without loss of power.

Boscombe Down, January 1942. W3228. Further trials and short performance with diaphragm carburetter. Large diameter jets fitted and de-aerator for fuel. No change in performance reported.

Boscombe Down, February 1942. AA875. Gun heating trials 'B' wing. Heating for cannon satisfactory but for machine guns it was below minimum requirements. Large size extractors recommended.

Boscombe Down, March 1942. AB320 (Merlin 45) and BP866 (Merlin 46). Tests of fuel system with 90 gallon external overload tank. Tests of fuel functioning of a tropicalised Spitfire VB with 90 gal. overload tank required. Fuel system satisfactory; tank jettison caused problems for pilot who was always unaware of tank leaving aircraft.

Boscombe Down, April 1942. W3322. Effect of balloon hood on speed. Results showed no measurable difference in speed due to balloon hood. It was satisfactory up to speed of 460mph in a dive, and had no noticeable effect on handling.

Boscombe Down, April 1942. AB488. F Mk VC Merlin 46. Brief performance tests. Aircraft allotted for research work on the effects of ignition advance and varying mixture strengths at high altitude. Performance considered poor.

Boscombe Down, April 1942. AB320. F Mk VB(T). Position error, performance with and without 90 gallon tank. A fully tropicalised Spitfire. Performance results

	Without tank	With tank
Weight (lbs)	6695	7485
Max rate of climb (ft/min)	2660 @ 14,000ft	2145 @ 14,000
Service ceiling	36,300ft	34,500

W3322 'Hendon Griffon' during trials at Boscombe Down to determine the effects of a balloon hood on performance in April 1942. Windscreen de-icer fitment at base of screen. It was to become 5584. (Triplex).

Time to 20,000ft	8 mins	10
Max speed @ 17,400ft	354mph	337.5

Boscombe Down, May 1942. AB320. Weights and loading data, with 90 gallon overload tank. Tare (lbs) 5,176, service load 976, fuel (84 gals) 605, overload tank 648, oil 77. Take off 7,482.

Boscombe Down, May 1942. AB488. F Mk VC Merlin 46. Mk II N I.F.F. tests. The aeroplane was easily followed throughout the test flights.

Boscombe Down, May 1942. AB320. Fuel consumption trials, with and without overload fuel tank. Conditions for optimum range:

Condition	Heigth(ft)	ASI mph	rpm	air miles per gal
With overload tank in use	20,000	170	2000	6.93
	6,000	170	1850	5.98
Without o/ld tank	20,000	180	1850	6.65
	6,000	180	1850	6.65
With o/ld tank fitted but empty	20,000	150	1900	7.51
	6,000	170	1850	6.43

Maximum ranges and endurance were estimated from the fuel comsumption results for conditions quoted in second table.

Condition	Height(ft)	Range–air miles Max	Range–air miles Practical	Endurance–hrs Max	Endurance–hrs Practical
O/ld tank used first jettison when empty	20,000	1235	1060	5.55	4.95
	6,000	1030	890	5.7	5.2
O/ld tank used first retained when empty	20,000	1130	985	5.05	4.6
	6,000	1010	875	5.65	5.1
No o/ld tank used	20,000	600	425	2.8	2.2
	6,000	490	350	2.85	2.3

Take off weights with o/ld tank full 7485 lb, o/ld fitted but empty 6835, without o/ld tank 6695.

Boscombe Down, May 1942. AB320. Take off trials with 90 gallon overload tank. Take off run 413 yards into 7.2 mph wind. Technique same as with normal Spitfire but weight increase noticeable.

Boscombe Down, May 1942. AB213. Further tests of split flaps as brake flaps. Landing flaps strengthened for use as air brakes and operated by compressed air from reservoir charged by engine compressor. Similar flaps tested previously on Mk I X4268, but modified. Tests included diving aircraft to speeds above 400 mph and extending flaps, which worked evenly and retracted more rapidly.

Boscombe Down, 7 June 1942. W3322. Longitudinal stability with experimental fittings in elevator control system. Four variations of system tested (1) standard system (2) plus inertia weight (3) control cables as tight as possible (4) with frictional device at elevator cross shaft. Two engines, Merlin 45 and 46 used.

Boscombe Down, July 1942. BR202. F Mk VC. Merlin 46. Fuel consumption tests and range flights. Aircraft fitted 170 gallon overload tank and engine with locked mixture control.

Condition	Height(ft)	Weight(lbs)	ASI mph	rpm	air miles per gal
With tank	15,000	7200	170	1950	5.35
	24,000	7250	170	2450	4.95
Without tank	15,000	5950	150	1600	8.18
	24,000	6000	150	1850	7.52

Maximum still air range @ 15,000ft 1450 miles. New tank was tested which had fairing at its forward end to cover gap between tank and fuselage, plus an extension at rear end into fuselage. An overload tank to carry 200 gallons was being developed at the same time.

Boscombe Down, August 1942. BR288. F Mk VC Merlin 46. Spin trials with 30 gallon jettisonable tank. Aircraft fitted tropical air intake. Exhibited a pitching motion during spins.

Boscombe Down, August 1942. BM589. VB Merlin 45. Handling and stability with special reference to pull out from dives and tight turns. Aircraft had Rotol propeller and was tested with, and without, 6½ lb inertia weight in elevator circuit. Pilots did not, apparently, like the inertia weight and it was suggested that this be fitted only on Spitfires with Rotol propeller.

Boscombe Down, August 1942. AA875. Further gun heating tests on Spitfire VB. Heating for Browning guns was improved by either moving the hot air exit to the rear of the gun compartment or by closing up the exit. The cannon gun temperature was above the minimum requirement. It was recommended that the gun compartments be isolated from cold air in the wing and the extractors be eliminated to reduce drag.

Farnborough, July 1942. Effect of oxygen boosting on performance of Spitfire V and VII. The use of LOX can increase engine power by 100 to 200hp and maintain it for several minutes. Could the extra power be employed efficiently by a propeller designed for normal engine power, and if not, what modifications were necessary? The Mk V with Merlin 45 had a de Havilland 3-blade, 10.75ft diameter propeller, the Mk VII was similar but with four blades. The Mk V experiment produced the best results with an hp increase of 165 at maximum speed at 20,000ft, while the Mk VII produced 105hp increase at 25,000ft.

Farnborough, July 1942. Aileron comparison of Spitfire and Mustang. The Mustang aileron area was 13.54 sq ft as compared with 18.9 of the Spitfire, with the former having 0° droop and the latter 1.5°. At speeds of 150mph and over the Mustang aileron was more effective. Also, the Mustang wing was stiffer and the large losses in effectiveness of the Spitfire ailerons was due to wing twist.

Boscombe Down, August 1942. AA878. Gun heating tests F Mk VC. Merlin Heating system of Universal wing on the Mk VC did not comply with Air Ministry requirements.

Boscombe Down, August 1942. BR202. F Mk VC Merlin 46. Fuel consumption and range tests with 170 gallon overload tank and 29 gallon internal tank behind pilot. Range at 15,00ft still air was 1,625 miles and at 3,000ft 1,610. Ranges were obtained by using overload tank for climb and initial part of level flight. Tank then jettisoned and flight continued using the rear fuselage tank first, followed by the main tank. Basic propeller pitch was 45°. If finer pitch used ranges were decreased. Auw at take off 7,835lbs with a total fuel load of 284 gallons. Distance covered on climb to level speed height 65 miles, on 170 gallon tank 715, on rear fuselage tank 200 and on main tank 570. Total 1,550. Take off run was 580 yards.

Farnborough, July 1942. Tests of flame damping screens for Spitfire. Wind tunnel tests showed a decrease in exhaust thrust of an average value of 1.2 lb at 100 ft sec. The results did not account for the large loss in top speed measured in preliminary flight tests.

Farnborough, August 1942. P8791. Note on speed reduction due to exhaust screens. Maximum loss of speed with screens was 8 mph @ 20,000ft.

Boscombe Down, July to October 1942. AA878. Effect on performance of armament and wings. Climb and level speeds performance tests were made on AA878 with (A) VC universal wing and VB armament (B) ditto with VC armament and (C) with VB wing and associated armament. All tests made at a take off weight of 6,965 lbs.

Climb performance

	VC (2 × 20mm & 4 × .303 guns)	VC (4 × 20mm guns)	VB (as VC(A))
Max rate of climb (ft/min)	2650 @ 14,900	2380 @ 14,900	2670 @ 14,900
Time to 10,000ft (mins)	3.8	4.25	3.8
20,000	7.9	8.85	7.85
30,000	14.8	17.15	14.35

Enclosed exhaust flame dampers on test, Farnborough, September 1942.

This highly specialised set of flame dampers were developed at Farnborough in October 1942.

Third type of flame dampers, Farnborough August 1943.

Service ceiling (100ft min)	37,200	36,100	38,200
All out level flight Max speed (mph)	359.5 @ 19,900	353 @ 19,900	355.5 @ 19,900

Farnborough, August 1942. Flight investigations of short period longitudinal oscillations with free elevator.

Farnborough, September 1942. Effect of body on wing bending moment. Wing tunnel tests on wing. Model featured modified ellipse with outer portion straightened.

Farnborough, September 1942. Aileron tests in 24ft tunnel. Hinge moment and pressure over nose of aileron were sensitive to small changes of nose shape. Peculiar aileron characteristics had been cited as possible cause of a number of Spitfire accidents. A model wing, made in three sections, conformed in plan and section to the Spitfire wing outboard, while the central portion was of rectangular plan form.

Boscombe Down, 17 September 1942. BP654. Carbon monoxide contamination after firing guns. Results were negative contamination.

Farnborough, October 1942. W3310. Effect of improving surface finish on speed. During minor modifications to surface and external details in progress on Spitfire EN946 (changes of paintwork and panel fit) it was thought desirable to obtain a Spitfire in a poor external condition. A Mk VB EN310 was chosen. The leading edge yellow strip had been painted by hand and ran in spanwise ripples, while the general paintwork revealed that several coats had been applied at various times and large areas were extremely rough. In addition flaking had occurred. Panel fit was poor as was the engine cowling, which had several fasteners missing. All paint was stripped off the airframe and detachable panels joggled back into shape. Rivets and small gaps and cracks were filled in and the whole surface rubbed down until a smooth surface was obtained. The standard camouflage scheme was applied. Comparative results showed that before new paint scheme a speed of 281 mph was attained at 1,000ft with engine rpm of 2,800. After repainting the speed at same height (and rpm) was 292.5.

Boscombe Down, 16 November 1942. AB186. Tests with modified elevator horn balance. Aircraft fitted with Rotol propeller but no inertia weight which had previously resulted in poorer stability characteristics than a Spitfire with de Havilland unit. With the original elevator the aircraft handled worse than with the modified unit.

Farnborough, 23 November 1942. Wind tunnel tests on cleaned up wing. The wing was off a crashed Spitfire and in poor condition. The paint was cleaned off the front half of the wing and a deep ridge along the spar line filled with putty. By closing the aileron gap with a fairing over the upper surface sectional drag was reduced by about 10%. The aeroplane was considered to be considerably over-cambered but a modification to the nose of the aerofoil can reduce this.

Boscombe Down, September to October 1942. BR288 and BR351. F Mk VC Merlin 46. Ammunition temperature tests with modified heating system for Browning guns. Hot air for guns supplied by intensifier tubes (1½in) running through engine exhausts. Heating, too high before modifications, was reduced by new fitments.

Boscombe Down, 2 October to 11 December 1942. W3322. Performance with Rolls-Royce SU fuel injection pump. Merlin 46. Climb and level speed were above average. Table, below, lists comparisons with other Spitfires.

Comparative performance of Spitfire V (Merlin 46) and Spitfire VI (Merlin 47)
Climb results at 2850 rpm except ceiling (3000 rpm)
Level results at 300 rpm

Aircraft	Take off Wt lb	FT Ht on climb ft	Maximum rate of climb (ft/min)	Service ceiling (100ft/min) ft	FT Ht level speed (+9 boost) ft	Top speed mph	Remarks
Mk VB W 3322	6516	18,000	2740	39,400	22,500	368	SU Injection pump 3-blade DH prop
Mk VA P 7661	5960	17,300	2880	40,100	21,600	356	Stromberg carburettor 3-blade Rotol prop
Mk VA N 3053	6710	18,000	2980	39,500	22,600	368	Prototype engine AVT 40 carburettor 3-blade DH prop
Mk VC AB 488	6720	17,100	2500	37,000	21,000	360	Low boost 3-blade DH prop
Mk VA X 4922	7420	16,000	2050	35,000	21,600	356	Tropical modifications 3-blade DH prop
Mk VI R 7120	6530	18,000	2740	38,000	–	–	Pressure cabin 3-blade DH prop Mk IA wings
Mk VIB BR 309	6250	16,700	2575	38,200	21,000	352	Pressure cabin Extended wings 4-blade metal prop negative g carb
Mk VIB AB 200	6740	17,100	2610	39,000	22,000	356	Pressure cabin Extended wings 4-blade Jablo prop
Mk VI X 4942	6550	17,600	2640	39,000	22,000	365	Pressure cabin 3-blade DH prop Mk IA wings extended
Mk VB W 3134	6380	15,200	2740	38,100	20,200	352	Engine below average 3-blade DH prop

Boscombe Down, November 1942. R7306. F Mk VA Merlin 45. Tests of modified constant speed unit with de Havilland propeller. Several instances of severe over speeding of DH Hydromatic props had occurred, and one of the measures taken was the fitting of a 400 lb sq in relief valve spring in the CS unit. The new modification did not completely cure over speeding.

Boscombe Down, 27 September to 15 October 1942. BR288. Cooling trials at combat rating with tropical modifications.

Boscombe Down, 7 November 1942. AA937. Performance with normal and clipped wings. Tests carried out to investigate performance caused by removing wing tips and replacing them with small wooden fairings. Span was reduced to 35ft 6in, and area to 231 sq ft.

	Clipped wing	Normal
Max rate of climb		
@ 15,200 ft (ft min)		
Time to 10,000 ft (mins)	2670	2840
20,000	3.9	3.7
30,000	7.9	7.4
Service ceiling	15.0	13.6
Estimated absolute ceiling	36,200ft	38,000
Max speed @ 17,000 ft (mph)	37,000	38,800
@ 19,600	343	342
@ 25,000	353	353
	342	346

Boscombe Down, 11 October 1942. W3322. Fuel consumption and handling with Rolls-Royce S.U. injection pump. Carburation qualities of pump satisfactory at all engine conditions.

South Farnborough, December 1942. Development of drop tanks. Thirty gallon, 90 gallon and 170 were produced in metal, fibre and wood with a 220 gallon under consideration. An auxiliary fuselage tank of 29 gallons consisting of a flexible lining in wooden tank also under development, this known as a 'Flexi-tank'.

Flexi-tanks as flight tested at Farnborough November 1941.

Boscombe Down, 24 December 1942. AB186. Tests with elevator with convex surfaces. Designed by Westland Aircraft to cure tendency to tighten up during dive recoveries and tight turns. Satisfactory for these two conditions, but pilots complained of lack of feel when flaps lowered.

Vickers-Armstrongs, Weybridge, 7 December 1942. Tailwheels on Mk VB and VC were designed for load of 525 lbs and tyre pressures of 67 lb sq in recommended. Fighter Command found that a pressure of 35 lb sq in was satisfactory, and recommended that it be adopted. S.M.E. Farnborough, were alarmed by this pressure reduction until reassured that the lower tyre (and oleo) resulted in fewer rear fuselage failures due to heavy landings.

NACA report, 15 January 1943. R7347. Stalling characteristics of Mk VA.

NACA report, 15 January 1943. R7347. Measurements of flying qualities. Langley Field, Virginia. Conclusions – satisfactory.

Boscombe Down, 2 February 1943. W3322. Fuel system tests with Rolls-Royce S.U. injection pump. Satisfactory for temperate conditions in U.K. In tropical conditions engine cutting may occur at 20,000ft. To cure this it was necessary to install either a fuel cooler or immersed fuel pump.

Boscombe Down, 16 February 1943. W3322. Flight tests of effect of wind gradient on rate of climb.

Boscombe Down, March to April 1943. AB488. Variation of power with height of a Merlin 46. All guns, ammunition and certain armour removed, take off weight 6,160 lb.

Farnborough, April 1943. Aileron tests in wind tunnel Part II.

Boscombe Down, April 1943, W3228. Merlin 50M. Climb and level speed performance Merlin 50M with cropped supercharger impeller. Impeller cropped to diameter of 9.5in. Maximum boost was 18 lb sq in instead of normal 16 lb. Results inconclusive.

Boscombe Down, May 1943. AB191. Handling tests of push rod aileron circuit. Ailerons set with no droop. Handling similar to normal Spitfire with cables under tension, but with more positive feel in control. Up float of $\frac{3}{8}$in reduced by one third.

Boscombe Down, 8 May 1943. AB167. Intensive flying trials with Merlin 45M. Merlin with cropped impeller and 18 lb sq in boost tested in AB167 and W3228. Tests abandoned due to internal coolant leak in engine which was returned to Rolls-Royce. Forced landing due to lack of fuel pressure.

Boscombe Down, 3 June 1943. AB488. Determination of propeller power coefficients.

Farnborough, July 1943. Further tests of Spitfire air brake in wind tunnel. During initial tests with the split flaps a nose down moment of about $1\frac{1}{2}$ of elevator occurred when the brake flap was extended. To cure this 18in was cut off the outboard end of the lower flap.

Boscombe Down, 12 July 1943. BL304. F Mk VB Merlin 45. Comparative level speed tests with curved and normal windscreens. The modified screen had a curved, transparent panel forward of the existing bullet proof item. Fairings were also added to the front and top of the hood and windscreen frame to conform to the new shape forward. Results –

	Curved screen	Normal
Max speed @ 16,000 ft	339mph	338
19,200	351mph	349
24,000	342mph	340

Field of view remained unaltered

Farnborough, July 1943. EN946. Comparison of four production Spitfires. Four Spitfires were sent to RAE for an examination of finish and measurement of performance. EN946 and EF644 were Mk VBs (Merlin 45 and 50 respectively) and JL 227 and EN498 (Merlin 63) were Mk IXs. The IXs were in better condition than the Vs. An attempt was made to switch the top engine cowling from EN498 to JL227, but the fit was bad. EN946 had a good paint finish, while EF644 was poor. The IXs were thought to be fairly good. General fitting of panels was good, but interchangeability bad.

Boscombe down, 14 July 1943. W3322. Performance trials with normal AVT.40 carburettor. Speeds tests were made to compare with results obtained with the same aircraft with S.U. fuel injection pump. The S.U. pump increased performance.

Boscombe Down, 25 July 1943. BL712. LF Mk VB Merlin 45M. Handling tests of alleged rogue aircraft. The Spitfire was from No. 602 Squadron, which complained the aircraft was unstable about the lateral axis and it flicked out of turns. The camera gun was badly fitted and this was corrected, and the wing tips then removed. Conclusions reached were the aircraft was normal.

Boscombe Down, 31 July 1943, AB167. F Mk VC Merlin 45M. Comparative suitability trials of all-copper baked radiator, type QED and normal Mk V radiator. The suitability of the all-copper fitting was from 0 to 3% higher than that of the normal radiator.

Boscombe Down, 3 August 1943. AB197. Merlin 61 (converted to Mk IX). Tests of RAE experimental DC gun heaters on Browning machine guns. The normal gun heating system was not providing sufficient hot air. The RAE electric heaters were originally intended for bomber turret guns and they fitted over the breech blocks. The tests proved the heaters unsuccessful.

Farnborough, September 1943. EF731. This aircraft was sent to RAE from Westland Aircraft as representative of a recent production machine. The finish was of exceptionally

AB197 was used for gun heating trials. Illustrated is an RAE experimental DC electrical heater installed in August 1943. Second view shows the heater fitted to a Browning. The device was not successful.

high quality. Maximum speed with the Merlin 55M was 368mph @ 9,600ft.

Boscombe Down, 2 October 1943. EF731. Merlin 55M. Comparative climb and level speed performance with a normal and armoured Rotol propeller. Some Rotol props were being supplied with the Jablo blades having an armoured leading edge, which consisted of a mild steel sheath 40.5in long with a reinforcing wire (30.5in long) welded to it. Results –

	Normal prop	Armoured
Max rate of climb (ft/min)	2870	2730
Rate of climb @ 10,000ft	2860	2420
20,000	1620	1490
30,000	620	570
Service ceiling (100ft/min)(ft)	34,100	33,800
Max speed (mph)	363 @ 7400ft	358 @ 7200

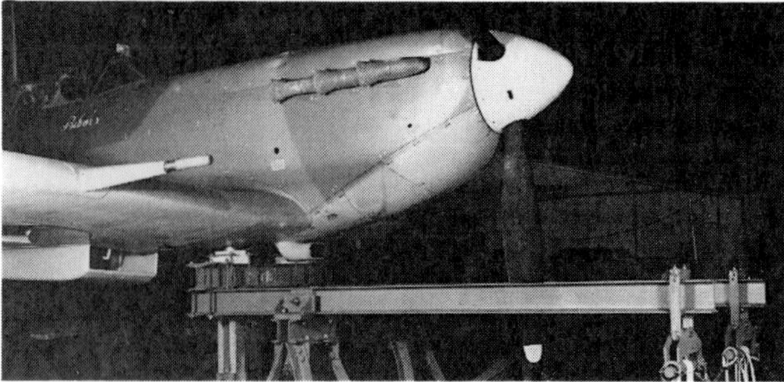

'Bihar V' on test, Farnborough, November 1941, for LOX engine boost trials.

Boscombe Down, 24 November 1943. JL165. Merlin 66 (converted to F IX). Trials at + 25lb sq in boost* with Rotol 4-blade propeller.

This Spitfire used 150 octane fuel and results were compared with Spitfire BS543. 18 lb boost.

Condition	radiators	JL165	BS543
Max rate of climb			
MS gear (ft/min)	open	4200	4700
In FS gear	open	3500	3850
Max level speed			
MS gear (mph)	shut	364	384
In FS gear	shut	388	407

With 25 lb boost the figures for JL165 were FS gear climb rad shut 5100, MS gear max speed 374mph, FS gear 409. Fuel consumption increased by 24%.

Boscombe Down, December 1943. JL165. Cooling trials at combat rating of 25 lb boost. Cooling of installation was within limitations under all conditions of flight.

Farnborough, December 1943. Dropping tests of two auxiliary tanks. Difficulties had been encountered in dropping the 45 gallon 'airship' and 170 gallon 'torpedo' overload tanks from the Spitfire. Forward of the CG of the tanks there were two struts on the top of which a wedge shaped bracket slid into a similar bracket on the aircraft's fuselage. The rear of the tank was steadied by a peg which fitted into a hole in the fuselage. Aerodynamic pitching moment about the front struts prevented the rear peg dropping out of the fuselage making it impossible for the tanks to be dropped. Drawings show the fittings. New rear fittings cured the fault. See page 161.

Boscombe Down, 28 December 1943. BM257. LF VB Merlin 45M. Tests of alleged rogue aircraft. Aircraft belonged to No 118 Squadron who reported it as flying left wing low. The tendency to fly in the condition reported was due to a mismatched pair of ailerons. A new set were fitted and the aircraft returned to No 118 as 'cured'.

Farnborough, December 1943. Obtaining clear view from

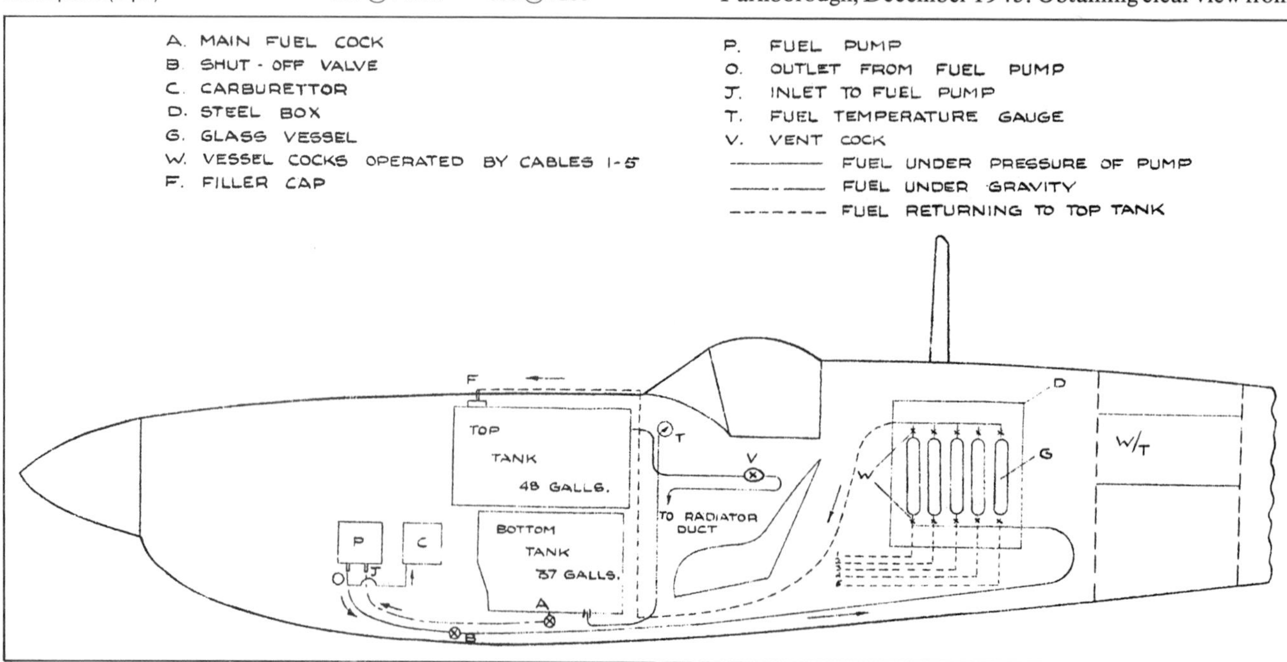

Tests were required in 1943 to confirm laboratory tests that air dissolved in fuel had an effect on the problem of vapour locks in fuel systems. A VB, W3322, was equipped with a petrol tight steel box containing five glass vessels through which fuel from the engine pump was passed and then returned to the main fuel tank. The amount of disolved air increased with altitude. W3322 has a Merlin 46 with normal AVT 40 carburetter.

Location of systems parts- A main fuel cock, B shut of valve, C carburetter, D steel box, F filler cap, G glass vessels, J inlet to fuel pump, O outlet fuel pump, P fuel pump, T temperature guage, V vent cock, W vessel cocks operated by cables 1 to 5. Solid line is fuel under pressure of pump. Broken line shows fuel pumped into base of glass vessels and returned to top main tank.

*'Basta'.

Spitfire W3248. During trials the aircraft was stored in the open for a period of eight weeks and used for aerodrome defence, escort duties and sundry flights. To prevent pilot touching clear panels with his hands on entry or exit small walkways were fitted on both wings, a handgrip fitted on port side of fuselage, mirror support extended and strengthened for use as hand grip, knob fitted on balloon hood so it could be operated without hand gripping perspex. To protect perspex from being scratched or soiled by cockpit covers when stored in open a soft flannelette cover was placed under the normal covers, a canvas bag on the pilot's seat to store flannelette cover in the aircraft.

Boscombe Down, 10 February 1944. AA973. LF LR Mk V. Tests of alleged rogue aircraft. No 3037 Echelon Hawkinge, complained of excessive aileron upfloat and a tendency to skid. The port aileron was positioned higher relative to the wing than the starboard and the shrouds distorted. It was recommended that the vertical position of the hinges checked and shrouds rectified. If still ineffective the port wing to be changed.

Boscombe Down, 8 March 1944. W3322. Flight tests to determine air solubility in fuel. Tests required to confirm in flight laboratory trials of the amount of air dissolved in fuel as this had a bearing on the problem of vapour locks in fuel systems. RAE provided the Spitfire, fuel installation and pilot, while the Thornton Laboratory made the analysis of the fuel **sample obtained in flight. Drawings show RAE installation.***

Farnborough, May 1944. Jettison tests of Spitfire hood in wind tunnel. Tests to see if behaviour of the jettisoned hood was sensitive to incidence, windspeed and CG position. Behaviour was almost independent of incidence, was slightly better at higher windspeeds and very sensitive to CG change. On release the hood should first rise rapidly with a small backward rate of rotation. Too high a rate destroyed lift and the hood drifted towards the fin in a dangerous manner. The tests proved that the rotation rate could be effectively altered by shifting the **hood's CG. Drawings on page 160 show various CG positions.**

Aeronautical Research Committee, 5 June 1944. Analysis of flight tests held at Boscombe Down of Spitfire VC propeller AB488.

Boscombe Down, June 1944. MA648. Merlin 66 (converted to Mk IX). Fuel consumption trials with Rolls-Royce Mk II S.U. injection pump. Satisfactory under all conditions.

BR372 was fitted with a double, trailing edge brake flap from May 1943 to February 1944, in response to a demand from service pilots who found they were overshooting their targets. The standard flap was modified into two parts, with the upper opening to 25°, the lower 43° up and down respectively for the decelerating manoeuvre. The lower flap was used independently for landing. By the time trials were completed the Spitfire Mk VII's strengthened flaps made the modified units obsolete.

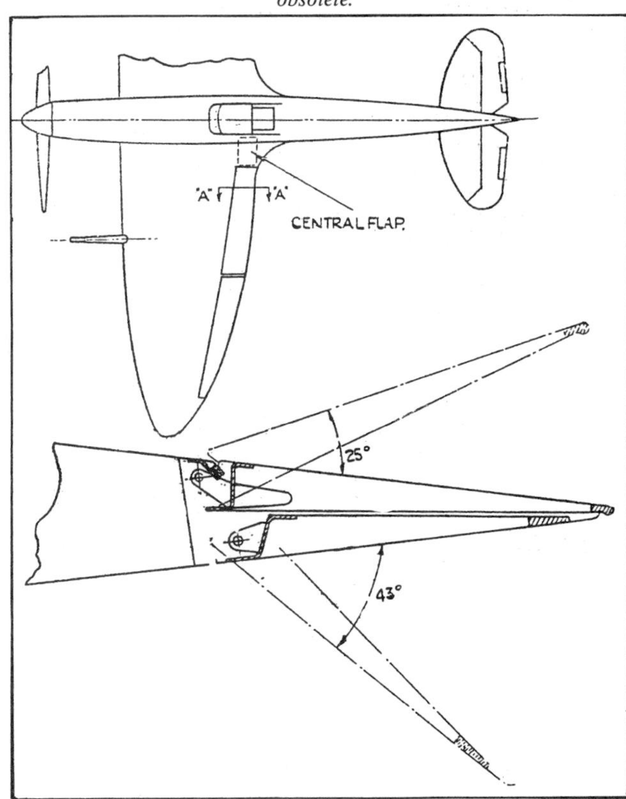

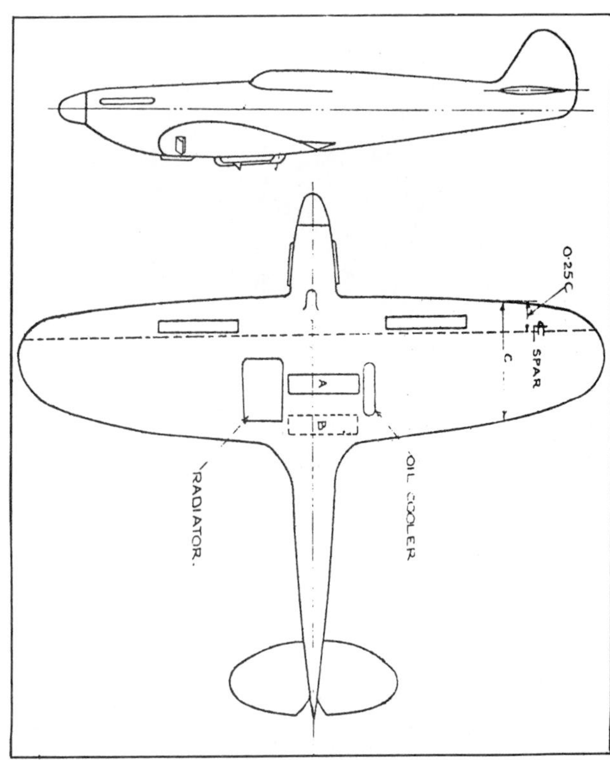

In an attempt to slow the Spitfire when in a dive from overshooting, a pair of spoilers, plus a large dive brake installed in two positions as shown by the broken and solid oblongs on the under wing surface, produced variable results. The spoilers were fitted to the wing spar position.

A variety of carburetter air intakes were on test at Farnborough in June 1941.

* *see facing page.*

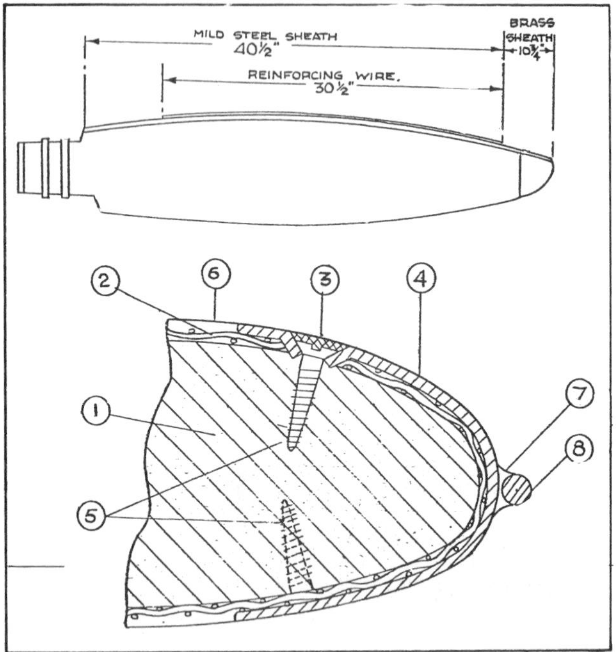

An armoured leading edge Rotol propeller was installed on VC EF731 in October 1943 for prototype trials of production Jablo blades incorporating the modification. It reduced maximum rate of climb by 140 ft min and speed by 5mph. 1 Jablo timber, 2 gauze, 3 solder, 4 outer steel sheath, 5 screws, 6 Jablo enamel, 7 weld, 8 reinforcing wire.

Farnborough, August 1944. BR372. Tests of double trailing edge brake flaps. The flaps produced a peak deceleration of .5G at 400mph, but if the engine was throttled simultaneously the deceleration increased to .6G Change of trim and lift did not cause any difficulty and pilots reported that a target could be kept in sight when operating the brake flaps.

Supermarine, 30 June 1942. R6700 and AB196. Prototype Mk IXs Merlin 61. Dives to determine variation of drag with Mach number.

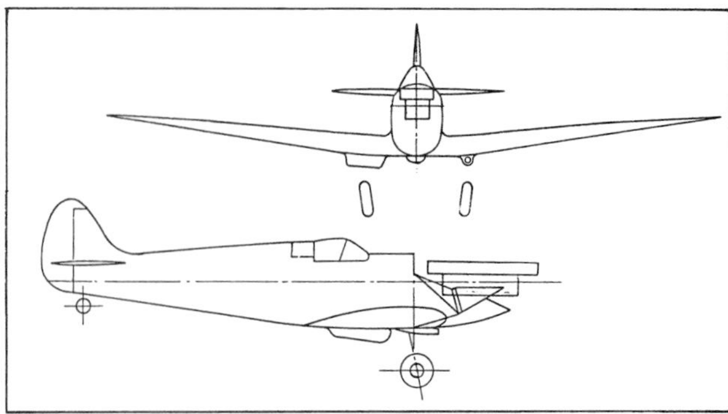

BR138 was tested for resonance with a vibrograph when experimentally fitted with a mock-up Merlin 60 engine at Farnborough. The trials were then compared with similar tests of a prototype Mk IX with Merlin 61 fitted.

Supermarine, 23 July 1942. Investigation of reducing wing area of Spitfire by 25%, from 242 sq ft to 180. Gains would be **rate of climb up to 20,000ft. Increase in maximum speed of** about 10mph, lighter ailerons and elvators by about 35%, an increase in maximum rate of roll by about 25%. Losses — Reduced ceiling and flatter angle of climb, reduction in speed imposed by compressibility on wing, about 20mph @ 36,000ft unless some method of thinning the wing without blisters could be found, an increase in time to turn of about 10%, an increase in minimum of turn. Conclusions reached were a small **reduction in wing area was worthwhile, two positions of flaps** at take off were likely to show a gain on angle of climb.

Supermarine, 27 August 1942. BR351. Mk VD (Trop). Comparative flight trials with Merlin 46 engine and de Havilland bracket type and hydromatic propeller. With hydromatic the maximum level speed increased by 2 mph, but @ 30,000ft it fell by 3 mph. Rate of climb and ceiling unaltered. Both props had a diameter of 10ft 9in.

Supermarine, 14 October 1942. Tests on wing with leading edge tank. A Mk VA wing was modified to include a leading edge fuel tank representative of that to be installed on the F Mk VIII. The starboard wing failed under test before the port, but this was thought to be that the radiator might have made a difference and also the wing had been in sea water for some time after the donor aircraft crashed.

Supermarine, 14 October 1942. Cracks had appeared in the wooden rudder of a number of operational Spitfires. It was considered that considerable internal stresses were produced when bending the plywood around the nose and the screw holes then produced cracks. The cure suggested was replacement of the ply nose by a wood block.

Supermarine 21 October 1942. Investigation into alternative pilot's seats. The existing seat could be improved by incorporating armour into it. The conclusions reached were that the present design was more than adequate and difficult to improve on.

Supermarine, 20 November 1942. X4922. Level speed performance on combat rating. Engine was Merlin 46 with 16 lb sq in boost. With this the level speed at 15,600ft increased by 29mph.

Tailwheel fitting as used on Mk Vs for 'Hasty Hitch' glider towing experiments.

MODIFICATIONS TO F MK V

362 Introduce Universal wing 24-3-41; 370 fit larger inertia weight, elevator 29-8-41; 372 fit vertical stiffeners between frame 15 & 19 19-5-41; 380 provide for electrically heated gloves & boots 22-6-41; 385 TR 1143 replace TR 1133 radio 22-6-41; 386 replace chassis locking cables with rods 22-6-41; 387 modify camouflage scheme to DTD circular 183 14-7-41; 399 fit Heywood compressor 22-6-41; 411 provide for tropicalisation 9-4-41; 420 VB only additional exhaust Brownings heating 9-8-41; 422 introduce $\frac{1}{4}$in elevator droop 29-8-41; 425 provide conversion to PRU D Type 29-8-41; 426 revise camouflage scheme (colour) 10-11-41; 431 delete clearview panel in hood 10-9-41; 436 introduce 30 gallon drop tank 29-8-41; 437 introduce 90 gallon drop tank 29-8-41; 439 introduce Merlin 46 10-9-41; 440 fit class matrix radiator Merlin 46 only 10-9-41; 446 introduce letter 'P' on fuselage for prototype a/c 10-11-41; 455 stiffen wheel well top skin 10-10-41; 460 fit $1\frac{1}{4}$lb incendiary bomb 21-10-41; 461 fit balloon hood (retrofit all marks) 21-10-41; 468 fit Martin Baker hood jettison gear 18-11-41; 472 introduce A 1271 VHF blind approach equipment (retrofit all marks) 4-11-41; 479 introduce de Hav Hydromatic prop (retrofit all marks) 30-12-41; 507 strengthen wheel axle (VB & VC only) 27-1-42; 510 pressurised fixed fuel tanks (retrofit all marks) 13-1-42; 511 instal neg 'G' carburetter (retrofit all marks) 2-12-41; 517 trial installation of .303 link collectors 2-12-42 (cancelled); 531 fit additional armour under pilot's seat 16-12-41; 560 make VA fuselage interchangeable with VB & VC wings 10-3-42; 565 introduce gyro gun sight 24-4-42; 566 introduce LOX (trial installation) by Heston A/C 24-2-42; 574 delete height and airspeed computer (all marks) 10-3-42; 598 redesign run of exhaust gun heating pipes 14-4-42; 603 stiffen wheel fairings 14-4-42; 622 amend camouflage to amendment 3 DTD circular 144 14-7-42; 623 delete landing lamps 5-5-42; 646 amend camouflage to amendment 4 16-7-42; 647 fit tropical oil tank as standard 19-5-42; 650 strengthen engine mount on Merlin 45,46,47 3-6-42; 657 fit 170 gallon tank and 14.5 gal oil tank Mk VC only 16-6-42; 662 delete pilot's headrest (all marks) 16-6-42; 664 redesign rudder pedals on pressure cabin a/c (V,VI,IX,PR IV) 30-6-42; 678 delete tail ballast VB & VC only 14-7-42; 683 standardised armament ('B' wing) VC & Mk IX 11-8-42; 696 delete signal discharger 11-8-42; 697 introduce improved paint scheme using DTD 517 type S (retrofit all marks) 9-3-43; 729 introduce rear fuselage 29 gal tank for ferrying VC only 22-9-42; 736 strengthen rear fuselage @ frame 19 22-9-42; 743 introduce Westland convex elevator (not VB (T) 20-10-42; 749 introduce cannon fairing for Hispano Mk II (retrofit) all cannon wings. Production before TI cleared 6-10-42; 787 delete painting fuselage interior (all marks) 13-9-43; 788 introduce clipped wings (all marks) 17-11-42; 801 introduce R 3067 (radio) Mk III IFF (retrofit) 12-1-43; 803 strengthen rear fuselage (all marks) 1-12-42; 804 introduce Merlin 50 for production a/c and replacement 1-12-42; 805 introduce Merlin 50A for production a/c and replacement 1-12-42; 806 introduce Merlin 56 for production and replacement VC only 1-12-42; 814 trial installation mock up torpedo 50 gal o/ld tank 15-12-42; 820 remove outboard cannon 15-12-42; 824 amend tailplane incidence from ± 20′ to ± 10′ 15-2-43; 848 introduce flush rivetting fuselage (all marks) 12-1-43; 856 stiffen rear fuselage (all marks) 9-3-43; 911 introduce new air cleaners 23-2-43; 919 introduce whip aerial (all marks) 9-3-43; 928 delete dimming screen (all marks) 4-5-43; 931 delete u-c indicator rods in wings 4-5-43; 934 introduce interim bomb carrying scheme 17-3-43; 951 introduce bomb carrying all marks except VI, VII & IX 6-4-43; 962 introduce 50 gal torpedo tank 12-11-43; 966 introduce multi ejector exhausts VB(T) only 20-4-43; 969 introduce Merlin 45M (special) VB(T) only 20-4-43; 972 oleo fairings (all marks) 4-5-43; 987 introduce 2 additional downward ident. lights, red & green 18-5-43; 993 trial installation 60gal drop tank (no further action) 15-6-43; 1006 introduce Merlin 50M 15-6-43; 1007 introduce Merlin 55M 15-6-43; 1012 introduce Merlin 55 15-6-43; 1013 strengthen M engine mounts 12-8-43; 1024 delete rudder pedal straps (all marks) 29-6-43; 1099 introduce 45gal o/ld tank (all marks) 19-10-43; 1111 strengthen stern post 19-10-43; 1117 strengthen pilot's seat 19-10-43; 1126 delete u/c warning horn (all marks) 2-11-43; 1128 delete neg G carburetter (all marks) 2-11-43; 1231 modify 90gal o/ld tank for use on any mark 2-5-44; 1239 introduce RP installation 25-1-44; 1287 introduce exhaust shields (all marks) 21-3-44; 1363 strengthen cannon fairings (all marks). Cancelled 30-5-44; 1377 introduce Mk VII bottom fuel tank all rear view a/c 27-6-44; 1668 trial installation pressurised drop tanks 10-7-45; 1691 alter position of roundels & reintroduce serials under wings (all marks) 10-7-45.

VB (YO-X), 401 Squadron RCAF.

AB-serialled VB(T) with Aboukir filter.

JK- (R-OB) SAAF, VC(E) with fuselage bomb.

Group of LF VBs with Aboukir filters in the Middle East. It was while flying AB502, nearest camera, that Air Commodore Gleed was killed on 16 April 1943.

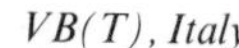

VB(T), Italy

Line of various Spitfires at the Westland Ilchester factory undergoing repair. W3841, AD313, AD380 and AD411 went back into service only to be destroyed in various sweeps over France in 1942.

Supermarine Spitfire F Mk VA/B/C/VB(T)

F Mk VA, VB, VC, LF Mk VA, VB and VC

Basic data as for normal span a/c. Wing. Planform elliptical; section NACA 2200 Series; incidence° root +2, tip $-\frac{1}{2}$; dihedral° 6; thickness% root 13.2, tip 6; aspect ratio 5.68; area nett 220, gross 242; chord(geo) 6.38, (ma) 7.01. Ailerons. Area 18.9; chord; movement° up 26, down 19; droop $\frac{3}{8}$in. Flaps. Area 15.6; movement° down 85. Wing loading 36.0; power loading. Clipped wing variants – LF VA, B and C. Wing area 231 sq ft;

Tailplane. Area 31.46; chord(ma) 4.0; incidence° root 0, tip $\pm\frac{1}{2}$; dihedral° 0. Elevators. Area 13.26; movement° up 28, down 23. Tab area 0.38; movement° up 20, down 7. Fin area 4.61. Rudder. Area 8.23; movement° each way 28 . Tab area 0.35; movement° port 18, starbd 6.

Undercarriage. Wheels VA, B, C Dunlop AH2061; tyres VA Dunlop IJ 12, 13 or 17, VB same, VB(T) IJ13 or 17, VC same, VC(T) same. Oleo pressures VA 240, VB 455, VB(T) same, VC 365 or 440 (max load), VC(T) 380 or 465 (FO). Tyre pressures VA 51, VB 55, VB(T) same, VC same, VC(T) 57. Tailwheel, Fixed castoring. Wheel Dunlop AD 2184/IX. Tyre VA Dunlop TA 11, 12 or 14, VB same, VB(T) same, VC TA 12 or 14, VC(T) same. Tyre pressures. VA 36, VB 43, VB(T) same, VC 51, VC(T) same. Oleo pressures. VA 215, VB 230, VB(T) same, VC 255, VC(T) same.

Engine/s. Merlin RM 45 VA, B and C; 45M LF VA, B and C; 45N and 46 VA, B and C; 46N and 50 VA, B and C; 50A VA, B and C; 50M LF VA, B and C, 55 VC; 55M LF VA, B and C; 56C VC.

Take of power

boost	hp	boost	hp	altitude(ft)
+12	1185	+16	1470	9250
12	1230	18	1585	2750
12	1100	16	1415	14,000

Propeller/s. de Havilland Type 5/29A Hydromatic 3-blade CS VP Dural pitch range 20° fine pitch 34° or, DH Type 5/39 ditto coarse pitch 54° or, DH 45/1 Hydromatic ditto pitch range 35° fine pitch 25° or, DH 45/4 ditto. All with diameter of 10ft 9in. Or, Rotol RX5/10 3-blade Jablo CS VP pitch range 35° fine pitch 30° and/or 29° 57', coarse pitch 64° 57', diameter 10ft 3in or, RX5/14 ditto or; RS5/24 ditto both with diameter of 10ft 9in. Ground clearance at take off – VB 1.3in, VC .95in with max deflection of tyres and oleos, datum (horizontal).

Coolant. 70% distilled water, 30% Glycol.

Fuel. 100 octane.

Capacity. Fuselage (upper) 48 gals, lower 37. Total 85. Plus 30, 90 and 170 gal o/ld tanks. Rear fus tank (ferry only) 29 gals. Totals 115, 175 or 234 gals.

Oil. 5.8 gals under engine; 8.5 later a/c, 14.4 in enlarged tank for ferry.

Armament. VA A wing Browning Mk II Star 350rpg; VB B wing 60rpg and 350; VC universal wing (plus) 4 × 20mm Hispano Mk I or II cannon 120rpg plus normal A and B wing. Plus provision for 2 × 250 or 1 × 500 lb bombs.

Gunsight. GM2 reflector.

Radio. TR 1133, TR 1143, ARI 5000, TR 9D.

Armour. 73 lb.

Cine camera. G42B or G45 port wing.

Weights (lbs). VA tare 4,981, take off 6,416, max permissible 6,700; VB tare 5,065, take off 6,622, max permissible 6,700; VC (B wing) tare 5,081, take off 6,785 max permissible 7,300; VC(C) wing tare 5,081, take off 7,016.5, max permissible 7,300; VA(Temp) DH Hydromatic 4,981; VA(T) ditto 5,036; VA(Temp) DH Bracket 4,990; VA(T) ditto 5,045; VA(Temp) Rotol 4,951; VA(T) ditto 5,006; VB(Temp) DH Hydromatic 5,024; VB(T) ditto 5,079; VB(Temp) DH Bracket 5,053; VB(T) ditto 5,088.5; VB(Temp) Rotol 4,994.5; VB(T) ditto 5,049.5. All weights tare. VC(Temp) DH Hydromatic 5,081.5; VC(T) ditto 5,136.5; VC(Temp) DG Bracket 5,090.5; VC(T) ditto 5,145.5; VC(Temp) Rotol 5,051.5; VC(T) ditto 5,106.5.

Performance. Max speed 331 mph @ 10,000ft; 351 mph @ 15,000ft; 359 mph @ 25,000ft; 370 mph @ 19,500ft; Max dive 450. Stall flaps and u/c up 71 down 68. Rate of climb 2,600 ft min. Ceiling 32,800ft. Range 395 miles. Initial climb 4,740 ft min; 3,240 ft min @ 5,000ft; 3,250ft min @ 15,000ft; 11,750ft min @ 39,000ft. Service ceiling 36,500. Max range with o/ld tank 1,135.

Limiting operational conditions: –

Take off up to 1000ft or 3mins	max rpm 3000, min rpm	@ max boost (+12) 2270
Climb (30 mins period)	max rpm 2850	max boost (+9)
Max cruise, mix normal	max rpm 2650	max boost (+7)
Max cruise, mix weak	max rpm 2650	max boost (+3$\frac{3}{4}$)
All out level (5 mins)	max rpm 3000	max boost (+9)
Max dive (20 secs)	momentary max rpm 3600	max boost (+9)

Maximum fuel consumptions (altitude stated).

Climb 2850rpm	93.5 gal hr	@13,000ft	
All out level 3000rpm	98	14,500	
Max cruise, normal mix	77.5	13,000	@2650rpm
Max cruise, weak mix	55.5	18,000	2650rpm

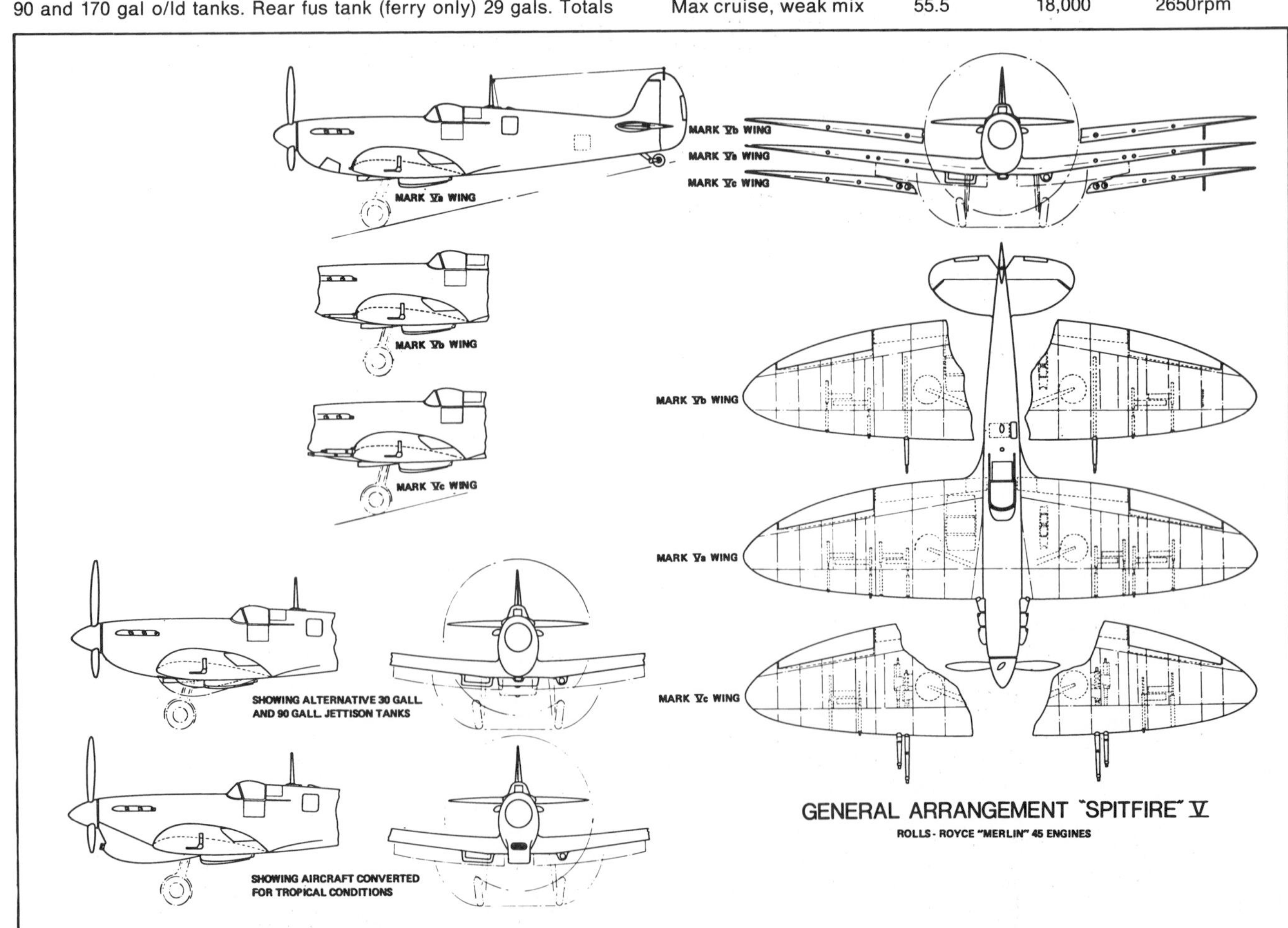

SERIAL NUMBERS

Supermarine Aviation (Vickers) Ltd. Contract No. B19713/39.

First Order for 450 Spitfire F Mk I dated 9 August 1939. Built as Mks IA and VA, VB between April 1940 and April 1941. Serials below apply to Mk V variants built to this order:–
R7029-7044 7055 7056 7207-7210 7213 7217-7231 7253-7256 7258-7279 7290-7309 7333-7350.

Second Order for 450 Spitfire F Mk I dated 22 March 1940. Built as Mks VA, VB between April and October 1941. W3109-3138 3168-3187 3207-3216 3226-3265 3305-3334 3364-3383 3403-3412 3422-3461 3501-3530 3560-3579 3599-3608 3618-3657 3697-3726 3756-3775 3795-3804 3814-3853 3893-3902 3931-3970.

Third Order for 500 Spitfire F Mk I dated 9 June 1940. Ordered as Mk I was constructed as Mk V between July 1940 to January 1941 Serials below apply to F Mk Vs built to this order.
X4663-4670

Fourth Order for 500 Spitfire F Mk I dated 19 July 1940. Built as PR Mk IV, F VB,VC, F VI between August 1941 and February 1942. Serials below apply to Mk V variants built to this order.
AA718-767 833-882 902-946 963-982 AB133-152 167-175 177-199 201-210 212-216 240-284 320-349 363-382 401-420 450-469 487-497 499-502 504 505 507-512 514 515 517-522 524-526 531 532 535 536.

Fifth Order for 1100 Spitfire F Mk I dated 24 October 1940. Built as PR Mk IV, F VB,VC F VI, F VII, F IX between February and November 1942. 202 deleted from contract– BR683-721 745-772 799-831 849-877 890-935 950-976. Serials below apply to Mk.V variants built to this order. BP844-878 950-993 BR106-143 160 161 163 165 166 168 169 170 173 175-177 179 180 182-185 187 188 190 192 194-196 198 199 201-204 226-242 244-246 248 249 251 253 254 256 282-285 288 290-296 299-301 303 304 306 308 311-313 315-317 320-325 327 328 344-393 459-499 515-549 562 564-566 568 570 572-574 576 580 582-584 586 589 591 621-640 BS158 160-166 168 169 171 173-175 178 181 182 184 186-188 190 191 193 197 199 201 218-226 230-238 271-291 293 295 298 300 305 335-354 530-559.

Seventh Order for 500 Spitfire F Mk VC dated 23 August 1941. Built as PR Mk IV, F VI, F VII, F IX, PR XI F XII between November 1942 and August 1943. Sixty deleted from contract—EN686-695 710-759. Serials below apply **to Mk VCs built to this order.**
EN112-121 239-258 351-370 515-534 551-583 628-637.

Vickers Armstrong (Castle Bromwich). Contract No.B981687/39

First Order for 1000 Spitfire F Mk II dated 12 April 1939. Built as Mks IIA, IIB, VA, VB between June 1940 and July 1941. Serials below apply to Mk V variants built to this order.
P8532 8537-8539 8542 8560 8561 8564 8578 8571 8585 8600 8603 8604 8606 8607 8609 8640 8699 8700 8703 8707-8724 8740-8759 8780-8799.

Second Order for 500 Spitfire F Mk I dated 22 June 1944. Built as Mk VB between July and November 1941.
AB779-828 841-875 892-941 960-994 AD111-140 176-210 225-274 288-332 348-397 411-430 449-478 498-517 535-584

Third Order for 1000 Spitfire F Mk III dated 24 October 1940. Built as Mk VB between November 1941 and May 1942. BL231-267 285-304 311-356 365-391 403-450 461-500 509-551 562-600 613-647 655-699 707-736 748-789 801-833 846-864 887-909 918-941 956-998 BM113-162 176-211 227-274 289-392 343-386 399-430 447-493 508-543 556-597 624-653.

Fourth Order for 904 Spitfire F Mk V dated 23 August 1941. Built as VB and VC between April and August 1942. EN887 not allotted—error for EP887. EN763-800 821-867 888-932 944-981 EP107-152 164-213 226-260 275-316 327-366 380-417 431-473 485-523 536-579 594-624 636-669 682-729 747-795 812-847 869-915 951-990 ER114-146 159-200.

Fifth Order for 750 Spitfire F Mk IV dated August 1941. Bilt as Mk VB, VC between August and December 1942. ER206-229 245-283 299-345 461-510 524-571 583-626 634-679 695-744 758-791 804-834 846-894 913-948 960-998 ES105-154 168-214 227-264 276-318 335-369.

Sixth Order for 989 Spitfire F Mk VB dated 1 January 1942. Built as Mk VC and Mk IX between December 1942 and April 1943. Serials below apply to VCs built to this order.

JG713-752 769-810 835-852 864-899 912-960 JK101-145 159-195 214-236 249-285 303-346 359-394 396-408 425-472 506-551 600-610 612-620 637-640 642-649 651-678 705-742 756-769 771-795 803-842 860-880 885-892 922-950 967-979 981-992 JL104-133 139 140 159-176 181-188 208-225 231-251 301-338 346-374 378-382 385-395.

Seventh Order for 300 Spitfire F Mk VC dated March 1942. Order cancelled in 1943.

Eighth Order for 680 spitfire F Mk VC dated May 1942. Built as Mk VC and IX between March and June 1943. Serials below apply to F VCs built to this order. LZ807-815 817-830 834 835 844-848 862-887 926-946 969-988 MA261-266 279-298 328-368 383-397 643-657 670-682 684-686 688 689 691 692 694-704 850-853 855-859 861-863 877 880-883 885-906.

Ninth Order for 2190 Spitfire F Mk VC dated 28 May 1942. Built as Mk VC, IX, XVI between July 1943 and May 1944. Serials below apply to VC built to this order.
MH298-311 564-568 581-596 600 605 637-646 750-755.

Westland Aircraft Ltd. Contract No.B124305/40.

First order for 300 Spitfire F MkI dated August 1940. Built as Mk I, VB, VC between July 1941 and September 1942. Serials below apply to Mk V variants built tothis order.
AR274-298 318-347 362-406 422-471 488-532 546-570 592-621

Second Order for 200 Spitfire F Mk **V dated September 1941. Built as Mk** VC between September 1942 and February 1943.
EE600-644 657-690 713-753 766-811 834-867.

Third Order for 185 Spitfire F Mk V dated October 1941. Built as Mk VC between February and November 1943. EF526-570 584-616 629-656 671-710 715-753.

The Spitfire F Mk V was produced in large numbers and many versions, and was used as a trials and experimental aircraft. Many were converted to other Marks and the following list chronicles a short history of every Mk V constructed. Such a list can never be 100% complete as the most meticulous records contain errors. With the pressures of war and the passage of time these errors were never corrected. Also a number of Air Ministry forms containing these details have been mislaid. However, all Spitfire histories have been checked and are as accurate as interpretation of official and company records allow. Check Appendix Seventeen for abbreviations.

All F Mk VB with Merlin M45 engine unless otherwise indicated.

P8532 The Harry Livingston 6MU 2-6-41 92S 21-6 FTR ops 26-6

P8537 6MU 2-6-41 92S 26-6 AST 16-7 313S 2-11 CB ops 28-3-42 AST 2-4 hook fitt 4-9 RNAS LoS as hooked Spit 18-9 WAL 23-12 RNAS Mach 31-3-43 ROS 16-4

P8538 The George Parbury 6MU 2-6-41 1FPP o/s BHll hit barracks on del flt to 92S CE 26-6 ASTH 28-6 SOC 3-7

P8539 6MU 2-6-41 611S 8-7 CB ops 10-7 SOC 10-7 BBOC 61 OTU air coll P8608 (F II) cd Bomere Hth Salop CE 10-9-42

P8542 Violette 33MU 15-6-41 61OS 7-7 FTR ops 13-10

P8560 6MU 2-6-41 74S 19-6 72S 29-7 ASTH 14-8 FTR ops 23-9

P8561 Kalahari 6MU 2-6-41 611S 25-6 GAL 11-7 132S 29-4-42 308S 30-5 CB ops 26-6 FAAC 30-8 ROS AST 18-12 402S 26-4 43 19S 5-5 65S 30-6 130s 15-8 CB ops 5-9 26S 8-4-44 FTR ops 23-6

P8564 6MU 2-6-41 609S 23-6 WAL 28-6 FACB 21-8 317S 19-10 ASTE 2-11 317S 4-11 CE ops 7-3-42

P8578 39MU 20-6-41 74S 3-7 ASTE 18-7 SOC 14-7

P8581 6MU 2-6-41 611S 8-7 FTR ops 14-7 F/O Dexter missing

P8585 Teling Tinggi (NEI) 6MU 10-6-41 74S 22-6 609S 10-9 603S 15-11 FA CB 28-1-42 SAL 5 USA S 7-8 FAAC 20-8 ROS S&H 4-9 VSM 15-1-43 fuel syst mods 118S 22-7 64S 25-9 FACB 5-3-44 ROS LMS 25-6 17SFTS 15-10 5 PAFU 14-7-45 f/ld cd nr Manby CB 24-1-46 recat E SOC 31-1

P8600 Lady Linlithgow 9MU 14-6-41 74S 5-7 FTR ops 10-7 FH 4.25

P8603 Nabha I 33MU 15-6-41 611S 29-6 AST 11-7 39MU Star FM dis 10-10 611S 7-11 603S 11-11 lost over en tr 8-12

P8604 Jamshedpur Golmuri III 33MU 15-6-41 74S 5-7 FTR ops 10-7 FH 11.05

P8606 Delhi II 8MU 14-6-41 609S 8-7 CB ops 27-8 ASTH 316S 26-1-42 FTR ops 4-4 FH 102.45

P8607 Palembang Oeloe II 9MU 11-6-41 611S 7-7 64S 14-11 124S 14-5-42 41S 25-7 dvd i/grnd nr Weston Patrick Hants dbf CE 20-8 SOC

P8609 Heart of England II 33MU 15-6-41 74S 5-7 72S 27-7 i/sea ops 27-8

P8640 6MU 2-6-41 609S 26-6 92S 16-9 610S 15-11 1CRU 26-3-42 308S 12-9 CB ops 8-11 VSM 13-5-43 fuel syst mods 416S 7-7 ROS 20-7 186S 10-2-44 130S 18-4 ROS 23-5 SAL 8-6 I AGS 4-5-45 PAL 4-9 SOC 10-9

P8699 39MU 29-6-41 609S 6-7 111S 3-8-42 FTR ops 19-8

P8700 M45M 12MU 27-6-41 54S 10-7 ASTH 6-8 92S 20-9 86MU 1-12 72S 7-12 FC CAC 27-1-42 ROS 154S 16-3 313S 8-6 66S 4-7-43 310S 19-7 303S 3-10 505S 25-12 129S 26-1-44 VSM 23-3 fuel syst 'Basta' mods AST 7-5 577S 7-6-45 to 5517 28-7 StA

P8703 37MU 18-7-41 452S 11-8 FTR ops 8-9

P8707 39MU 29-6-41 616S 7-7 610S 19-7 CB ops 17-9 ASTE 331S 18-6-42 CB ops 29-6 LMS VSM 13-6-43 fuel syst mods S type ptfin MkII IFF ROS 3-12 COAL RNDA 21-2-44 hook fitt RNAS Hens as hook Spit 11-5

P8708 8MU 5-7-41 266S 13-8 FACB 17-3-42 ICRU 111S 24-6 312S 31-12 COAL 26-6 con to Seafire Mk IB 39MU 30-8 RNAS Hens 9-11

P8709 M45M 39MU St Frn dis 6-7-41 WAL 26-9 on loan as pattern a/c AGME 5-1-42 CRD BDn 17-1 VSM 31-8-43 fuel syst mods Type S pt fin Mk III IFF bomb racks 234S 10-1-44 AST 30-5 144AF 31-5 CB ops 4-8 ROS AGME 22-12 3505SU 7-6-45 587S 14-6 ASTH 10-10 DBR SOC 25-10

P8710 39MU 29-6-41 616S 7-7 610S 19-7 129S 31-12 e/fld cd nr Brighton CE 10-4-42 ASTH 23-4

P8711 37MU 20-7-41 452S 10-8 CE ops 18-2 42 SOC 28-2

P8712 8MU 3-7-41 145S 17-7 FTR ops 23-7

P8713 45MU 19-7-41 72S 27-7 FTR ops 29-8

P8714 South of Warrington 45MU 17-7-41 234S 16-9 FTR ops 15-10

P8715 Wulfrun 39MU St Fm dis 6-7-41 19S 8-12 416S 10-2-43 411S 3-3 CE ops 14-4 FH 323.0

P8716 33MU 27-7-41 452S 4-8 FA CAC 7-9 CE SOC 16-9

P8717 33MU 27-7-41 452S 4-8 6-2S FTR ops 19-8

P8718 38MU 25-7-41 602S 2-8 ROS 1-11 485S 7-12 o/s ldg Ken strk W3578 CAC 11-1-42 AST VSM 13-5-43 mods 504S 1-9 313S 22-9 315S 1-2-44 AST 3-6 FAF 19-1-45 GC 2/18

P8719 9MU 20-7-41 602S 31-7 FTR ops 7-8-42 SOC

P8720 6MU 22-7-41 6-3S 27-7 332S P&PSM 22-6-42 501S 2-12 e/fd f/ld Cloughley golf Course Co Down Ireland dbf CE 26-2-43

P8721 6MU 22-7-41 610S 1-8 FTR ops 21-8

P8722 45MU 23-7-42 602S 6-8 CE ops 2-1-42 SOC 5-1

P8723 33MU 27-7-41 602S 10-8 i/sea ops 25-1-42 SOC

P8724 45MU 25-7-41 602S 2-8 FA CE 4-4-42

P8740 37MU 18-6-41 54S 7-7 403S 4-8 FTR ops 21-8 FH 63-25

P8741 Bhabnagar 33MU 15-6-41 74S 5-7 501S 15-10 AST 14-5-42 5USA 5-9 501S 15-2-43 air coll with BL688 cd Portaferry Co. Down Ireland CE 12-4

P8742 Ada 12MU 1-7-41 610S 10-7 air coll with W3333 ldg Westh CB 7-9 ICRU DeH 27-4-42 HAL 31-5 403S 20-8 ROS 21-11 416S 3-6-43 t/o wrong runway strk wall Perr CE 7-7

P8743 37MU 29-6-41 611S 17-7 64S 14-11 ROS 13-12 AST 30-3-42 w/u ldg South 24-3 ASTE Recat E 20-5

P8744 Wonkers 12MU 23-6-41 54S 7-7 AST 19-7 403S 4-8 ASTH 26-8 72S 21-11 WAL 11-1-42 152S 4-8 VSM 11-5-43 fuel syst mods 165S 5 8 FTR ops 6-1-44

P8745 37MU 29-6-41 609S 28-7 FTR ops 16-8 SOC FH19.0

P8746 12MU 1-7-41 611S 12-7 64S 14-11 308S 10-7-42 air coll with W3774 cd Stockwell Potato Fm Yorks CE 14-5-43 FH 525.45

P8747 39MU 23-6-41 92S 5-7 CE ops 21-8 ASTH St Flt Cole 18-2-42 AST 26-6-43 453S 27-8 341S 3-11 52 OTU 25-1-44 FLS Mf ld 2-2-44 3501SU 11-5 63S 7-6 CE ops 8-6

P8748 M45M 39MU 29-6-41 615S 7-7 610S 19-7 FACB 29-1-42 GAL 7-2 602S 28-8 164S 11-9 341S 3-2-43 316S 27-2 340S 23-3 3501SU 28-9 VSM 24-3-44 fuel syst 'Basta' mods hit trees nr Luton CE 17-6

P8749 12MU 1-7-41 72S 9-7 610S 11-7 i/sea off Scarborough Yorks 16-3-42

P8750 12MU 27-6-41 72S 9-7 SAL 1-8 ROS 15-12 401S 2-4-42 FTR 1-5 SOC

P8751 12MU 23-6-41 72S 10-7 CB ops 19-7 SAL 29-7 VSM 17-4-43 fuel syst mods wng stiff 3501SU 8-7 CAC ops 9-9 ROS 186S 10-2-44 FTR train flt 14-3 FH 205.0

P8752 37MU 29-6-41 610S 11-7 FTR ops 21-9 SOC BBOC Farn May '43 buffetting and catapult trls

P8753 LR LF VB 37MU 30-6-41 609S 23-7 ICRU 9-9 305S 10-7-42 FACB 27-7 WAL 7-8 VSM 8-2-43 mods 118S 14-3 Farn 1-7 rogue a/c buffetting from badly fitt cowling 316S 15-12 63S 1-5-44 61 OTU 10-5-45 SOC 22-6

P8754 VA 12MU 27-6-41 54S 7-7 FTR ops 11-7 FH 5.45

P8755 33MU 29-6-41 616S 25-7 610S 25-7 65S 6-10 129S 31-12 252S 11-2-42 GAL 27-8 222MU 18-11 *Marhagas* 19-12 USSR 17-4-43

P8756 12MU 1-7-41 611S 14-7 FTR ops 7-8

P8757 39MU 6-7-41 72S 14-7 CB ops 15-11 ASTH 154S 13-6-42 air coll with BM453 Horn CE 2-6 AST SOC 20-7

P8758 LR LF VB 12MU 1-7-41 GAL 6-11 133S 14-6-42 306S 16-5-43 316S 1-10 316S 25-12 63S 27-4-44 FAAC 5-7 ROS CAC ops 5-9 ROS 1665HCU 7-3-45 SOC CE 12-12

P8759 8MU 3-7-41 145S 14-7 41S 28-7 FACB 18-2-42 AST FACB del flt Cole 2-7 P&PSM 26-8 fuel syst mods 421S 11-10 FAAC 4-10 ROS 403S 25-1-43

P8780 8MU 5-7-41 611S 11-7 ICRU 17-8 222S 15-12 FTR ops 30-4-42

P8781 39MU 29-6-41 616S 7-7 610S 19-7 BDn 2-8 low press fuel syst trls Farn Nov. Flame damping exhaust trls; shroud reduced speed by 9-12 mph as it reduced thrust from stubs. Comp trls with W3134 fitt Mer 45. 1-4-42 VHF push-to-seak radio trls of 'Laryngophone'. direct speech throat mike also tested. Oct '41 SP oil tank pressure trls andGAL flame dampers. Mar '43 fuel tank explosion trls in conjunction with flexi-tank on X4782. As tanks emptied nitrogen was pumped in to prevent fire or explosion of petrol vapour. An attempt was also made to duct exhaust gases into fuel tanks to achieve same result; trls inconclusive. June '43 nitrous oxide instead of LOX injected into Mer to increase sprint speeds. Large increase in power output for limited period. Trans to BDn; ret Farn July, used as escort for Ju88 taking part in Flensburg/Monica* trls together with JL227. Addition trls with Wellingtons HZ202 and HZ579 fitt Eureka-Babs aids. HAL 8-1-44 mods/RAF Davidstone Moor 7-2 247 Grp 22-3 Stn Flt Lagens 2-1-45 269S 30-8 CE SOC 28-3-46

P8782 M46 8MU 5-7-41 145S 14-7 41S 28-7 GAL 10-11 308S 18-4-42 CB ops 3-5 VSM 21-11 fuel syst mods, wng stiff 3501SU 4-8-43 504S 11-8 313S 4-12 118S 2-6-44 611S 3-10 Pers 24-3-45 FAF 9-9

P8783 38MU 6-7-41 72S 12-7 401S 31-12 VSM 15-9-42 fuel syst mods 82MU 31-10 *Bar Inch* USSR 24-3-43

P8784 38MU 6-7-41 92S 24-7 ROS 603S 12-9 CAC 27-10 ROS 332S 22-4-42 403S 16-7-42 e/fd w/u ldg Leeming CE 22-8 AST 25-11 VSM 4-3-43 fuel syst mods wng stiff Mk.III IFF bomb carr HAL 28-4 con to PR XIII M32 39MU 4-6 RNDA 3-3-44

P8785 37MU 19-7-41 ROS 4-8 266S 26-9 154S 12-3-42 CB 22-4 VSM 3-9 Fuel syst mods 602S 17-7-43 504S 10-10 head on coll BL887 cd nr Hatton Aberdeen CE 28-12 FH 392.45

P8786 37MU 19-7-41 485S 9-8 CB ops 2-9 ROS 603S 17-11 There is doubt about the fate of this a/c

P8787 45MU 17-7-41 152S 25-6-42 VSM 7-8-43 Mk III IFF bomb carr 402S 27-4-44 SAL 25-7 1656CU 30-11 R&S refurb to Port 22-8-47

P8788 37MU 7-7-41 152S 25-6-42 VSM 7-8-43 Mk III IFF bomb carr 402S 27-4-44 SAL 25-7 1656CU 30-11 R&S refurb to Port 22-8-47

P8789 Borough of Wanstead & Woodford 9MU 20-7-41 CBAF 21-8 118S 15-9 ROS 65S 7-11 i/sea ops CE 1-6-42

P8790 38MU 6-7-41 602S 2-8 FTR ops 21-9-43

P8791 M45M 39MU 24-7-41 6002S 30-7 AST 14-12 411S 30-6-42 242S 25-9 133S 29-9 336S 1-10 AST 12-11 131S 15-4-43 310S 30-6 313S 29-7 3501SU 24-9 MM 17-44-44 M55M instal 290S 10-1-45 R&S refurb to Port 12-11-47

P8792 6MU 22-7-41 54S 27-7 403S 4-8 ROS 403S 20-9 54S 29-10 124S 18-11 e/fd w/u ldg o/td nr BHll CE 3-4-42 ASTH 8-4

P8793 39MU 24-3-41 602S 30-7 FTR ops 16-8

P8794 39MU Sl Fm dis 21-7-41 121S 4-11 ROS 26-11 FA FTR 4-5-42 FH194.45

P8795 39MU 6-7-41 610S 25-7 129S 31-12 FTR ops 30-4-42 FH219.25

P8796 33MU 27-7-41 603S 22-8 i/sea off Newburgh Aberdeen 19-12

P8797 South of Warrington 45MU 17-7-41 54S 22-8 124S 17-11 FTR ops 13-3-42

P8798 38MU 6-7-41 611S 28-7 ICRU 20-9 2USA S 22-8-42 ASTE 21-10 61 OTU 26-9 43 FACB 15-5-44 AST 25-5 PAL 25-9-45 SOC 27-9

P8799 9MU 21-7-41 602S 30-7-41 R-RH 1-9 602S 6-10 118S 23-4-42 234S 14-6 GAL 16-10 81S 7-4-43 41S 23-4 501S 7-7 CAC ops 26-7 ROS 129S 31-1-44 63S 11-6 e/fd hit trees in fd/ldg Crays Hill Essex CE 13-11

R7029 1688 HEA FF 21-5-41 HAL 22-5-41 con to PRIV Type C Ben 14-7 FAAC 27-7 HAL CE SOC 28-4-42 FH 154.52

R7030 1694 HEA FF 22-5-41 Farn 24-5-41 HAL 30-5 con to PRIV Type D Ben 30-10 ROS 26-1-42 FAAC 20-2 8 OTU 20-6 HAL 14-1-43 6MU 6-3 HAL 13-3 ASTE 3-7-44

R7031 1714 HEA HAL 30-5-41 con to PRIII Type C Ben 24-7 GAC 9-9 M46 instal HAL 10-9 mods to PRIV Type d 39MU Star Fn dis 16-4-42 8 OTU 1-8 PRU Fraser CB ops 21-8 HAL 30-8 CE 4-5-43 SAL 10-1-44 S Fm 31-3-45

R7032 1715 HEA Farn 31-5-41 as PRIII Type C Ben 1-8 FAB 27-8-42 HAL 31-8 mods to PRIV Ben 3-9-8 OTU 18-1-43 FAAC 15-3 ROS 6MU 9-2-44 con to PRVI Type F SOC 6-3-45

R7033 1738 HEA HAL 8-6-41 con to PRIII Type C Ben 7-8 loss of cont in storm at h/a pilot thrown clear at 1000ft landed safe ttl wrk 5-10 remains to Farn for acc invest Jan '42

R7034 1755 HEA Farn 7-6-41 con to PRIII Type C later to PRV Spcl FACB 2-4-42 h/a trls 4-8 ETPS 19-11 air homing trls Trans to BDu Apl '43 eng change to Sunbeam Talbot ret Farn same month for cool trls and drag reduction mods. To Peterborough June for chemistry application trls. Left UK 12-6-43 for Gib, temperature rating tests. Flew around ME. Gib-Maison Blanc; Tripoli-Cairo; Tripoli-Malta; Algiers-Gib A/c had jett o/ld tanks. Main purpose was validity of trop filters and various cool. Landed Farn 15-7. Flexi tank trls in Aug. Tanks fitt later to Blenheim and Mosquito a/c. Ret Farn as comm a/c. Recco trls with Spit Mk IX 19-1-44. Trls TR1196 radio from June. From June R7034 was used as Farn hack. ACR trls with Firebrand EK670 20-11-46. VHF and SBA trls. To RAF film unit Hucknall. Photo sessions with Lancaster FM201. This a/c spent practically all its service life at RAE and A&AEE and was still on charge in 1954, quote from official records.

R7035 1838 HEA Ben 9-7-41 con to PRIV Type D 23-12 PRU Leuch 19-2

*R7036 1856 HEA HAL 7-7-41 Con to PRIV Type C. 1 PRU Ben 8-7-42 FTR ops 18-3

R7037 1901 HEA HAL 7-7-41 con to PRIV FF 16-7-41 to PRV Ben 2-8 HAL 15-10 Ben 16-12 FTR ops 3-6-42 FH257.55

R7038 1922 HEA HAL 7-7-41 con to PRIV FF 19-7-41 Ben 9-8 HAL 19-12 mods to PRVI Type F FACB 2-1-42 FTR ops 16-9 FH109.45

R7039 1943 HEA HAL 7-7-41 con to PRIV FF 2-8-41 to PRV Farn Aug for trls Ben 18-8 FTR ops 10-9

R7040 1944 HEA 7-7-41 con to PRIV FF 2-8-41 Ben 12-8 FTR ops 2-12

R7041 1945 HEA FF GP 16-8-41 as PRIV HAL Ben 17-8 FACB 30-3-42 HAL 6-4 541S 1-10 FTR ops 12-1-43 FH128.15

R7042 1946 HEA FF 3-8-41 as PRIV HAL 17-8 Ben 19-8 541S 30-9-42 cd nr Turweston Bucks b CE 16-2-43 FG254.25

R7043 1971 HEA HAL 7-7-41 con to PRIV FF 9-8 Ben 21-8 FTR ops 30-9

R7044 1972 HEA HAL 7-7-41 con to PRIV FF 13-8 22-8 PRU Wick 16-2-42 CB ops 27-4 HAL Ben 541S 12-11 FTR ops 13-1-43

R7055 1996 HEA FF 24-8-41 as PRIV Hen 26-8 HAL 7-7 Ben 28-8 Gib 15-4-42 CE SOC 26-4 FH130.40

R7056 1997 HEA FF 24-8-41 as PRIV Hen HAL 7-7 Ben 28-8 CE ops 12-4-42 SOC FH72.30

R7207 1509 EA Preston & District FF 10-3-41 39 MU 16-3 DeH 6-7 Farn 1-1-42 dvng tests for vibration WDn 17-3 ROS 9-4 RNDA Yeov 18-9

R7208 1513 VA City of Liverpool III FF 12-3-41 39MU 15-3 611S 13-5 SOC 11-7

R7209 1510 VA EA FF 12-3-41 City of Liverpool I 39MU 15-3 611S 13-5 FTR ops 22-6

R7210 1514 VA EA FF 4-3-41 City of Liverpool IV 39MU 19-3 Star Fm dis 145S 30-6 41S 28-7 FTR ops 12-8

R7213 1531 VA EA FF 22-3-41 33MU 23-3 611S 6-6 145S 3-7 41S 28-7 e/fd i/sea nr Bognor Regis 23-11

R7217 1519 VA EA FF GP 15-3-41 Onward (Fleetwood) 39MU 19-3 611S 13-5 C2 ldg coll with R7255 6-6 ASTH 41S 11-8 FTR ops 18-8 FH10.50

R7218 1520 VA EA FF Vetustas Dignitatem-Generat Retford & District 17-3-41 38MU 21-3 611S 18-5 92S C2 by Bf109 16-6 145S 6-7 FTR ops 8-7 FH62.55

R7219 1521 FF 16-3-41 Mosque Lahore Nihil 8MU 21-3 92S 26-3 R-RH 15-4 dam by Bf109 9-5 dam by Bf109 28-5 AST 17-6 74S 5-7 SOC 30-7

R7220 1522 VA Bournemouth II Crest FF 18-3-41 38MU 21-3 54S 26-5 FAAC 26-5 403S 4-8 CB ops 26-10 74S 8-1-42 332S 27-1 164S 15-4-42 strk X4238 ldg at Skae CAC 4-5 ROS 602S 10-9 82GRP USAAF 8-11 DeH 14-2-43 349S 7-7 58 OTU 12-8 FAAC 29-7 ROS to 5586M FAF 3-4-46

R7221 1525 VA FF GP 19-3-41 39MU 26-3 603S 25-5 FTR ops 27-7

R7222 1526 VA CA FF 20-3-41 33MU 23-3 54S 25-5 AST 28-6 FTR ops 5-7

R7223 1523 VA EA FF 9-3-41 38MU 21-3 64S 16-5 603S 16-5 41S 19-8 i/sea ops 27-8

R7224 1524 EA FF 20-3-41 8MU 21-3 91S 29-6 ASTE 22-6 609S 22-10 603S 15-11 416S 31-5-42 FACB 3-6-42 SAL 9-6 93S 28-8 FAAC 11-9 AST 306S 19-3-43 302S 3-10 to 4406M 5SoTT 3-12 Camonering 11-7-45 SOC 26-11-46

R7225 1524 VA FF GP 21-3-41 33MU 23-3 54S 25-5 CE ops 12-7 SOC FH62.05

R7226 1528 VA EA FF 21-3-41 33MU 23-3 64S 14-5 603S 16-5 flew i/Aucterhouse Hill, Angus 1-1-42 SOC 9-1

R7227 1529 EA FF 21-3-41 VA 33MU 23-3 64S 13-5 603S 16-5 FTR ops 23-7

R7228 1530 EA FF 22-3-41 6MU 23-3 74S 16-5 72S 29-7 FACB 26-8 SOC 2-9

R7229 1535 VA EA BRC Stafford I FF 25-3-41 38MU 27-3 64S 16-5 603S 16-5 ROS 2-10 315S 24-11 81S 22-12 165S 10-4-42 167S 27-5 GAL 24-6 HAL 20-8 mods to V VA 61 OTU 23-10 FAAC 29-2-44 AST 61 CTU CE 10-1-45 SOC 19-1

R7230 1536 VA EA Brenda FF 26-3-41 39MU 29-3 611S 15-5 HAL 27-6 602S 25-11 FAAC 15-12 ROS AST 30-1-42 recat E 20-5

R7231 1541 VA EA Grimsby II FF 27-3-41 39MU 29-3 611S 13-5 taxy coll with R7306 C3 26-6 MM 332S 11-2-42 164S 8-4 FA SAL 7-5 RNDA Stret 7-9 ROS 9-9 AST 5-3-43 RNAS 25-5

R7253 1551 VA CHA FF GP 29-3-41 39MU 31-3 611S 13-5 dam by Bf109 23-6 145S 3-7 cd during seach for cd a/c, Shripney Sussex ttl wrk 21-7

R7254 1552 VA CHA FF GP 29-3-41 39MU 3-4 611S 13-5 C2 by bf109 4-6 AST 25-6 GAL 17-7 41S 15-10 81S 11-2-42 FACE 20-5 SOC FH159.25

R7255 1563 VA CHA FF GP 3-4-41 39MU 6-4 611S 15-5 strk R7217 while ldg 6-6 145S 6-7 41S 28-7 SOC 1-9 FH99.25

R7256 1570 VA CHA FF 5-4-41 38MU 8-4 54S 25-5 403S 4-8 AST 13-8 54S 25-8 AFDU 16-9 130S 21-10 R-RH 9-3-42 601S 7-4 2 USA 3-8 5 USA 22-8 FAAC 29-12 ROS 61 OTU 14-1-44

R7258 1577 VA CHA FF GP 9-4-41 33MU 12-4 54S 25-5 AST 4-7 ICRU 14-8 41S 30-9 dbf ops 13-10

R7259 1579 VA CHA FF 10-4-41 33MU 12-4 54S 25-5 FTR after comb bf109 25-6 FH28.20

R7260 1542 VA EA Bristol Air Raid Warden FF 27-3-41 38MU 30-3 54S 19-6 403S 4-8 i/sea ops 7-8 FH14.20

R7261 1540 EA Bolsover I FF 26-3-41 38MU 30-3 2 USAS 12-7 FACB 2-9 S&H 14-9-62 OTU 14-10-43 DeH 18-2-44 PAL 12-9-45

R7262 1537 EA Bromley FF GP 22-3-41 132S 331S VSM 1943 fuel syst mods

R7263 1543 VA BRC Stafford II FF GP 27-3-41 39MU 29-3 611S 16-5 145S 3-7 FTR ops 8-7 FH70.50

R7264 1554 VA EA Brycheiniog FF 31-3-41 38MU 4-4 54S 25-5 FTR ops 14-7 FG63.40

R7265 1538 Grimsby I FF GP 25-3-41 6MU 29-3 91S 2-5 CE ops 13-6 AST 17-6 72S 30-9 e/fd t/o Graves 5-12 WAL 313S 25-7 42 403S 23-8 FACE 24-8 SOC 24-9 FH179.0

R7266 1545 VA EA Jamshed Pur Gulmari II FF 29-3-41 38MU 30-3 54S 26-5 FAAC 26-5 403S 4-8 FTR ops 9-8 FH63.25

R7267 1547 VA Bromley & District FF GP 28-3-41 38 MU 31-3 54S 26-5 dam ops 26-8 AST GAL 1-9 332S 7-2-42 164S 21-4 f/ld nr aerodrome Dounby Yorks CE 15-6 SOC 28-6 FH166.30

R7268 1557 VA The Swan FF 2-4-41 38MU 4-4 54S 25-5 FTR ops 23-7 FH45.45

R7269 1548 VA JamshedPur Gulmari I FF GP 29-3-41 38MU 31-3 54S 25-4 FTR ops 9-7 FH45.45

R7270 1558 VA Nae Bother FF 2-4-41 38MU 4-4 603S 26-6 SOC 30-6 FH19.15

R7271 1549 VA EA Beverley District FF 29-3-41 39MU 30-3 611S 15-5 145S 3-7 41S 28-7 ROS 26-11 65S 27-12 133S 17-1-42 FA CB 26-2 ASTH 8-3 RNAS 884S Yeov 9-9 ROS 24-10 SOC 29-4-45

R7272 1559 VA EA FF 2-4-41 38MU 4-4 64S 16-5 603S 16-5 FTR after comb Bf109 P/O Newman missing 26-6 FH 35.40

R7273 1560 VA EA Bombay Gymkhana I FF GP 3-4-41 38MU 4-4 54S 19-6 i/sea ops 27-8 FH83.15

R7274 1564 VA EA West Riding FF GP 4-4-41

*Monica was airborne radar installed in British bombers to warn of approach of enemy aircraft. Flensburg homed in on the emissions.

As an aid to RATOG take off Farnborough developed a thrust absorbing head rest in March 1944.

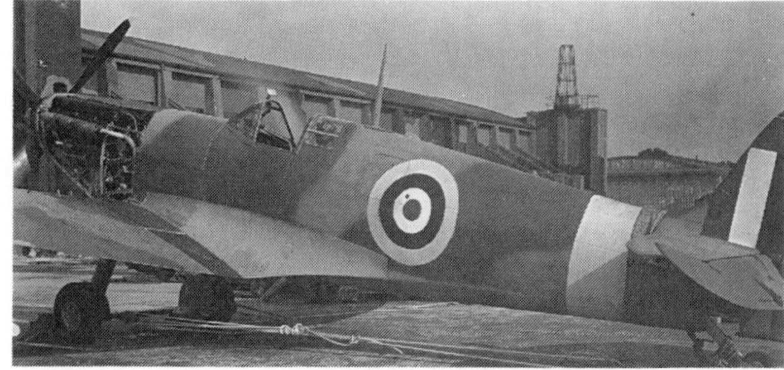

Thrust measurements on experimental VC with four blade propeller. Cine camera in cockpit, no tail ballast. Note gun heating ducts in head on view.

Rearming USAAF Spitfires, Sicily 1943, Note the 'ready' round in magazine.

King George V inspects VBs of Fighter Command. Censor has deleted background.

39MU 6-4 611S 13-4 145S 22-7 41S 28-7 FTR ops 12-8

R7275 1569 VA EA Bombay Gymkhana II FF 5-4-41 33MU 12-4 54S 25-5 i/sea after comb Bf109 4-6 FH15.50

R7276 1539 EA Bolsover II FF 26-3-41 6MU 29-3 91S 2-5 i/sea SOC 9-9

R7277 1565 EA Foremost FF 4-4-41 39MU 6-4 611S 15-5 FTR ops 8-7 Sgt Feely missing

R7278 1544 EA Birkenhead FF 28-3-41 6MU 29-3 74S 16-5 FTR after comb Bf109 17-6 FH23.30

R7279 1566 EA VA Kings Messenger FF GP 5-4-41 38MU 6-4 54S 25-5 403S 4-8 FTR ops 21-8 FH118.55

R7290 1546 MXII Donningtonian FF 29-3-41 8MU 30-3 91S 4-5 FTR ops 1-10

R7291 1567 VA EA Trustworthy FF 5-4-41 39MU 6-4 611S 15-5 145S 6-6 41S 28-7 FTR ops 18-8

R7292 1555 EA Newbury I FF 31-3-41 9MU 4-4 71S 26-8 CE ops 1-10 FACE 27-3-42 AST H 308 USA 20-4 91S 11-10 CAC ops 14-10 ROS 1 CRU 21-3-43 VSM 2-7 fuel syst mods Mk III IFF wng stiff 306S 27-10-43 FAAC 27-5-44 ROS 345S 3-7 recat E SOC 8-12 coll with AB254 ldg Hawk CB 2-11-43

R7293 1573 VA EA Sans Touche FF 8-4-41 38MU 10-4 64S 16-5 611S FTR ops 3-7 Sgt McHugh missing

R7294 1556 EA Derrick FF 1-4-41 9MU 3-4 91S e/a dbf 5-5 SOC 17-5

R7295 1574 VA EA The Pastures FF GP 8-4-41 38MU 10-4 54S 26-5 dam by Bf109 a/c aban i/sea 16-6 FH26.0

R7296 1561 EA Newbury II FF 3-4-41 9MU 3-4 91S 4-5 AST 9-5 611S 2-11 64S 14-11 317S 22-5-42 Rollason 13-8 HAL 11-8 41S 1-10 flew into hill with BL518 and BM573 Tarren Hendre Merioneth 22-10

R7297 1575 VA EA Ideal FF GP 5-4-41 38MU 11-4 54S 26-5 cd 17-6 AST 41S 16-8 ASTH 22-8 81S 15-12 165S 27-4-42 FAAC 7-5 SAL 5 USA 9-7 HQ 12FC USA 16-9 61 OTU 2-6-44 SOC 19-3-45

R7298 1562 Rotherham and District FF 3-4-41 9MU 5-4 610S 10-7 ASTH 14-8 72S 28-10 ASTE 5-12 309 USA 22-8-42 FACB 11-11 1CRU 131S 18-3-43 310S 30-6 313S 27-7 FAAC 27-8 ROS VSM 5-11 fuel syst mods 1TEU 16-6-44 61 OTU 28-9 FACE 9-11

R7299 1576 VA EA Aitch-Aitch FF 9-4-41 33MU 12-4 64S 13-5 603S 16-5 dbf ops 8-7 SOC 10-7 FH74.50

R7300 1584 VA CHA FF 11-4-41 33MU 12-4 64S 14-5 603S 16-5 FTR ops 21-8 FH24.0

R7301 1594 VA CHA FF GP 16-4 H1 33MU 20-4 54S 25-5 403S 4-8 54S 25-8 CB ops 17-9 WAL 24-9 42S 28-3-42 RNDA Yeov 1-9

R7302 1595 VA CHA FF GP 19-4-41 33MU 20-4 54S 26-5 124S 17-11 81S 17-12 165S 11-4-42 165S 24-8 602S 10-9 14 Gp Com Flt 24-9 FAAC 19-8-43 ROS 520TU 2-6-44

R7303 1599 VA CHA FF 19-4-41 33MU 23-4 54S FTR ops 22-7

R7304 1610 VA CHA FF 23-4-41 39MU 25-4 611S 15-5 dam by Bf109 4-6 145S 6-7 41S 28-7 SOC 1-9 FH95.50

R7305 1611 VA CHA FF 24-4-41 5MU 27-4 54S 8-6 603S 9-6 1CRU 4-10 RNDA Yeov 4-9-42 AST 20-9 LoS 21-9

R7306 1618 VA CHA FF 26-4-41 5MU 29-4 611S 10-6 taxy coll with R7231 26-6 145S 6-7 AST 28-7 DeH 24-4-42 Hydromatic prop with 400lb psi relief spring valve SME Farn BDn 27-10 trls with DeH prop, mod to be tested on service a/c FACA 11-5-43 DeH 52 OTU 14-7 ROS SOC 29-11-45

R7307 1626 VA CHA FF GP 29-4-41 5MU 3-5 611S 10-6 41S 28-6 145S 3-7 FTR ops 3-8 FH117.45

R7308 1630 VA CHA FF GP 29-4-41 5MU 3-5 54S 18-6 cd on test flt C2 20-6 AST 124S 17-11 81S 10-1-42 165S 27-4 167S 27-5 HAL 23-7 con to PRVII Type G 8 OTU 14-2-43 HAL 30-6 con to PRXIII M32 instal VSM fuel syst mods wng stiff 400S 25-12-43 ROS 22-2-44 83GSU 15-6 SOC 28-3-45

R7309 1634 VA CHA FF 2-5-41 39MU 4-5 611S 15-5 145S 3-7 FTR ops 9-7

R7333 1579 VA EA The Kirby I FF GP 11-4-41 33MU 12-4 64S 14-5 603S 16-5 hvy ldg C2 19-6 ROS 603S FTR over e/tr 8-12

R7334 1568 EA Perfect FF 5-4-41 9MU 6-4 92S 21-7 501S 17-9 ROS 8-11 118S 8-1-42 FAAC 28-3-42 ROS dvdi gnd Fordingbridge Hants CE 13-6 SOC 19-6 FH111.45

R7335 1583 VA EA The Kirby II FF 11-4-41 33MU 12-4 64S 13-5 603S 16-5 1CRU 4-9 401S 27-11 332S 17-1-42 164S 18-4 SAL 3-8 HAL 4-9 con to PRVII Type G 8 OTU 9-2-43 HAL 24-3 con to PRXIII VSM 23.4 M32 fuel syst mods RNDA 3-3-44

R7336 1572 EA Hominis Vis FF 7-4-41 8MU 8-4 91S 4-5 HAL 10-8 41S 2-10 401S 7-1 42 CB ops 25-42 ROS 131S 28-8 VSM mods 17-9 610S 27-1-43 340S 4-4 coll with Martlett FN266 ldg app Ayr CE 28-5

R7337 1580 Ajax Ff 8-4-41 DGRDVA 12-4 M Hth BDn 7-7 gun htng trls (2 × 20mm can 4 × 303mgs) 1¾in tubes through stub exhausts. Hot air through ducts along lead edge wing to exhaust between Brownings. Hot rad air ducted on to 20mm gun breeches. FACB 24-7 ASTE 452S 12-11 602S 8-3-42 41S 25-3 FAAC 5-5 131S 13-5 CE 15-7

R7338 1582 EA Papyrus FF 11-4-41 8MU 12-4 91S 4-5 dam w/u CE ops 17-5 ldg Hawk 10-5

R7339 1586 VA EA Mah Tal FF GP 12-4-41 33MU 12-4 64S 14-5 603S 16-5 FTR ops 4-7 FH68.40

R7340 1581 VA Nab FF 10-4-41 8MU 12-4 91S 4-5 FTR ops 1-7

R7341 1589 VA EA FF 16-4-41 38MU 20-4 603S 17-7 e/fd i/sea off N Foreland 23-7 SOC 31-7

R7342 1593 VA EA FF 16-4-41 38MU 23-4 e/fd cd/ld Hatfield 13-5 54S 1-8 403S 4-8 SOC 1-9 FH16.50

R7343 1587 VA EA Hexham and District FF 13-4-41 38MU 20-4 611S 15-5 AST 2-6 54S 29-6 403S 11-8 124S 17-11 ROS 28-11 134S 18-12 133S 28-12 1CRU 11-3-42 FAAC 7-8 ROS S&H 22-12 61 OTU 25-7-43 FACE 13-5-44 scr rtp 29-5

R7344 1585 EA FF 12-4-41 8MU 12-4 91S 28-4 WAL 11-4-42 308S 14-7 FTR ops 19-8

R7345 1585 VA FF 17-4-41 38MU 24-4 64S 16-5 603S 16-5 s/dn by Bf109 cd/ldg Goodwin Sands 21-6 SOC 22-6 FH36.50

R7346 1588 EA FF 13-4-41 8MU 92S 21-4 FTR ops 18-8 FH109.05

R7347 1598 EA FF 18-4-41 39MU 47MU 25-4 To Wright Field Dayton Ohio USA summer 1941

R7348 1591 EA FF 19-4-41 8MU 20-4 91S 29-4 AST 15-5 457S 11-12 452S 23-3-42 FACB 11-6 AST VSM 22-3 mods 165S 17-8 303S 10-10 315S f/ld Heston CE 3-2-44 FH314.45

R7349 1592 VA EA FF GP 19-4-41 38MU 20-4 611S 13-5 FTR after comb Bf109 24-6 F/Lt Buys missing

R7350 1603 VA EA FF 21-4-41 39MU 24-4 145S 8-7 41S 28-7 ROS 31-10 41S 31-10 71S 4-11 603S 8-11 332S 25-2-42 12 Grp Com Flt 15-3 61 OTU 12-2-44 SOC 12-10

W3109 1639 VA CHA FF 3-5-41 39MU 8-5 54S 8-6 403S 4-8 54S 25-8 i/sea ops 3-10 FH68.40

W3110 1645 VA CHA FF GP 8-5-41 38MU 10-5 64S 16-5 603S 16-5 t/ld 23-6 HAL 26-6 FAAC 30-12 ROS SAL 18-3-42 2 USA 3-8 ASTH 10-8-43 61 OTU 25-2-44 SOC 12-10

W3111 1646 VA CHA FF GP 8-5-41 38MU 11-5 64S 16-5 603S 16-5 PRU Ben FTR after comb Bf109 7-6 P/O Burleigh missing

W3112 1620 VA CHA FF 28-4-41 5MU 28-4 603S 27-6 81S 14-1-42 165S 12-4 167S 27-5 GAL 24-6 VSM 26-9 fuel syst mods wng stiff HAL 13-10 con to PRXIII M32 BDn 2-2-44 M46 instal for trls FAAC ROS 20-3

W3113 1663 VA CHA FF GP 13-5-41 33MU 16-5 603S 27-6 ASTH 8-8 315S 24-11 HAL 18-12 ROS 10-2-42 165S 9-5-42 FACB 12-5 ROS R Navy 4-9 116S 31-10 52 OTU 6-9-43 CE 3-10-44

W3114 1667 VA CHA FF GP 13-5-41 54S 29-6 403S 4-8 GAL 20-8 332S 31-1-42 164S 16-4 602S 10-9 82 Grp USA 8-11 DeH 20-3-43 61 OTU 4-10 SOC 30-9-44

W3115 1676 CHA FF 16-5-41 8MU 18-5 609S 28-5 SOC 8-7 FH38.55

W3116 1654 CHA FF GP 10-5-41 6MU 11-5 609S 27-5 CE ops 22-6 SOC 1-7

W3117 1675 CHA FF GP 16-5-41 8MU 18-5 609S 28-5 SAL 13-8 123S 27-12 167S 16-4-42 165S 27-5 65S 23-9 FACE 14-10 SAL 24-10 340S 7-6-43 eng fire and fail w/u ldg nr Fortune CE 22-6-43

W3118 1678 VA CHA Fiji III FF 17-5-41 33MU 18-5 603S 25-6 452S 24-11 332S 17-1-42 164S 12-4 FAAC 15-5 ROS SAL 5-11 288S 31-12 1CRU 22-6-43 61 OTU 24-10 FAAC 6-3-44 ROS

W3119 1606 VA EA FF 22-4-41 39MU 25-4 to Wright Field Dayton Ohio USA July '41 NACA Langley Field Dec '41 spcl eng manifold fitt

W3120 1590 EA FF 18-4-41 8MU 20-4 74S 29-4 dam by bf109 27-6 92S dbf ops 31-8 SOC 9-9

W3121 1608 VA EA FF 23-4-41 39MU 24-4 603S 22-6 FTR ops 24-6 P/O McKelvie missing FH6.0

W3122 1600 EA FF 19-4-41 8MU 22-4 91S 29-4 Heston 8-12 ASTH 24-2-42 IIIS 3-5 Dux 31-12 to 3457m 10 SoTT 12-1-43

W3123 1612VA EA FF GP 24-4-41 5MU 26-4 64S 16-5 603S 16-5 AST 24-6 603S FTR 21-10

W3124 1602 EA FF 20-4-41 8MU 22-4 92S 29-4 1CRU 18-5 222S 24-8 FTR ops 4-9

W3125 1605 EA FF 22-4-41 6MU 23-4 91S 2-5 CB ops 27-11 ASTH 5-12 332S 8-6-42 P&PSM mods 13-8

W3126 1604 EA FF 21-4-41 23-4 91S 2-5 i/sea ops 16-6

W3127 1607 EA FF GP 22-4-41 6MU 23-4 74S 16-5 AST 8-7 401S 27-9 WAL 5-11 340S 9-3-42 CE ops 1-8 AST 9-8 453S 2-1-43 222S 31-3 167S 19-5 3501 SU 27-5 WAL 19-1-44 CGS 8-10 SOC 11-12-46 to 5537M

W3128 1609 FF 23-4-41 6MU 24-4 192S 11-5 dam by bf109 14-6 ASTE 23-8 266S 22-11 610S 27-4-42 93S 17-7 SAL 3-9-43 VSM 30-3 mods 416S 30-6 130S 18-4-44 air coll with AB208 off IoW CB 16-6 AST 1696 Bd flt 21-11 R&S refurb to Port 11-9-47

W3129 1613 EA FF GP 24-4-41 8MU 26-4 91S 6-5 ROS 13-11 DeH 1-5-42 FAAC 5-9 5 USA 8-9 VSM 28-2-43 fuel syst mods 402S 20-8 FAAC 15-4-44 ROS 402S 13-5 527S 15-7 dvd into grd Essex CE 8-8

W3130 1614 VA EA FF 25-4-41 5MU 27-4 64S 16-5 603S 16-5 52 OTU 31-12 HQ 81Grp Com Flt 1-6-42 116S 14-10 238S 1-1-43 FAAC 14-5 recat E SOC 18-4-45

W3131 1619 EA FF 25-4-41 8MU 28-4 91S 8-5 AST 20-5 401S 27-9 FTR ops 12-2-42

W3132 1615 EA FF 26-4-41 8MU 26-4 91S 8-5 CE ops 8-2-42

W3133 1616 EA Cawnpore I FF 26-4-41 8MU 26-4 91S 9-5 MM 10-7 ASTH 9-4-42 65S 28-6 USA 22-8 332S 8-11 FACB recat E 19-2-43

W3134 1622 EA FF 28-4-41 8MU 10-4 BDn 18-6 brief perf trls (371mph @ 20100ft time to 20000ft 6.4min) 2-9 low fuel press tests with P8781 fuel heated before t/o. Farn 24-11 exhaust flame dampers on stubs with intensifier tubes. Trls with and without snow grd. Int wt on elev cont syst at BDn Mk Vs with Univ wng had to have standard wt to cater for change of arma Aug '42 comp tests with Mer 45 and 46. Latter better at height. Perf trls at varying air temps. Cool trls over six months. VSM 29-8-43 mods cd during test prog 24-11 AST 78MU 6-6-45 SOC dbr 28-6-45

W3135 1624 EA FF 29-4-41 8MU 4-5 91S 10-12 HAL 10-4-42 ASTH 16-4 VSM 21-10 fuel syst mods wng stiff HAL 29-12 con to PRXIII M32 Ben 5-4-43 541S 25-4 HAL 14-9 39MU NEA 25-1-45 SOC 26-2

W3126 1623 VA EA FF GP 29-4-41 5MU 4-5 R S North 17-6 603S 4-7 MM 10-7 54S 10-10 124S 17-11 81S 10-1-42 154S 12-4 167S 27-5 RNDA 6-9 AST 21-9 hook fitt RNAS LoS on loan as hook Spit 20-11 WAL 6-6-43

W3137 1631 EA Brum 128 FF GP 2-5-41 8MU 4-5 91S 10-5 CB ops 7-7 92S 19-9 FTR ops 2-10

W3138 1628 EA Cawnpore I FF GP 30-4-41 5MU 4-5 603S 27-6 dam by Bf109 30-6 1CRU 4-10 164S 29-4-42 602S 10-9 82Grp USA 11-11 ROS 17-11 CAC ops 22-10-43 ROS MAL 3-8-44 SOC 17-8

W3168 1629 Cawnpore II FF 30-4-41 8MU 4-5 74S 18-5 92S 7-8 ROS 22-11 72S 24-10 133S 15-6-42 65S 23-9 FACB 22-12 LMS 66S 7-10-43 340S 15-11 239S 16-2-44 68S 22-3-44 68S 22-3 26S 2-5 1TEU 17-8 ASTH 7-12-45

W3169 1625 VA FF 29-4-41 EA 5MU 4-5 North 28-5 54S 7-6 f/ld Mans 19-6 FTR ops 9-7 FH48.10

W3170 1635 EA Hen FF 2-5-41 9MU 5-5 74S 16-5 72S 27-7

W3171 1636 EA Huddersfield I FF 3-5-41 9MU 6-5 AST 16-7 71S 30-10 CB ops 25-4-42 CBAF CE 4-4

W3172 1637 EA Huddersfield IIFF 2-5-41 9MU 6-5 74S 16-5 i/sea 7-7

W3173 1638 EA Barnwell FF 3-5-41 9MU 5-4 609S 31-5 AFDU 31-10 DeH 20-3-43 VSM 28-7 mods 3501SU 28-11 129S 4-2-44 530TU 5-9 e/fd after t/o o/l ldg KinL CE 27-9

W3174 1649 EA Oswald Finney I FF 9-5-41 6MU 10-5 74S 16-5 cd Hawk after comb Bf109 16-6 AST 24-6 SOC 22-9

W3175 1601 HPA FF 12-4-41 6MU 24-4 91S 4-5 ROS dam ops 24-2-42 ASTE recat E 20-5

W3176 1621 HPA FF 26-4-41 6MU 11-5 74S 18-5 FA FTR 16-7

W3177 1652 HPA FF GP 9-5-41 6MU 11-5 74S 23-5 CB ops 21-6 GAL 313S 21-10 412S 16-4-42

W3178 1651 CHA FF 9-5-41 6MU 10-4 74S 23-5 AST 8-7 401S 27-9 CE ops 11-2-42

W3179 1668 HPA FF 14-5-41 8MU 30-4 609S 28-5 s/dn by Bf10922-6 1CRU 92S 2-9 FTR ops 20-9

W3180 1677 M45M HPA FF 17-5-41 9MU 16-5 609S 31-8 1CRU 7-9 VSM 22-3-43 fuel syst mods wng stiff 131S 8-7 310S 24-9 FACB 7-3 44 DeH R&S refurb to Port 17-7-47

W3181 1681 City of Leeds I FF 19-5-41 6MU 17-5 92S 11-6 CAC ops 28-6 72S 9-7 FTR after comb Bf109 19-7

W3182 1685 EA City of Leeds II FF 20-5-41 6MU 17-5 92S 11-6 FTR ops 4-9

W3183 1696 HPA FF 23-5-41 9MU 25-5 92S 26-6 FTR ops 11-7

W3184 1712 VA CHA FF 29-5-41 38MU 30-5 603S 26-6 FTR ops 24-7

W3185 1653 VA EA Lord Lloyd I FF 10-5-41 39MU 11-5 145S 30-6 AST 22-7 145S 22-7 41S 28-7 616S 28-7 AST 29-7 air coll with Bf109 over France Sdn Ldr Bader pow 7-8

W3186 1658 EA Oswald Finney II FF 12-5-41 6MU 13-5 74S 23-5 i/sea 9-6 FH 7.30

W3187 1657 EA Lord Lloyd II FF 10-5-41 6MU 13-5 609S 27-5 i/sea 31-7 FH87.50

W3207 1659 LF VB Abbotts Haugh Falkirk Bairn FF GP 12-5-41 6MU 13-5 609S 27-5 MM 27-6 222S 16-9 FAAC 15-7-42 AST VSM 21-10 fuel syst mods M55M instal 317S 24-1-43 413S 29-6 126S 10-8 133S 17-2-44 132S 7-3 504S 15-3 310S 15-7 61 OTU 28-6-45 hit truck taxy Kee tip on to nose AC 20-9 recat E 23-10

W3208 1661 EA Eastbourne FF 13-5-41 8MU 14-5 74S 18-5 FTR ops 6-7

W3209 1660 M45M LF VB EA Edmonton-London-Alberta FF 13-5-41 6MU 13-5 609S 27-5 AST 22-6 452S 20-8 ROS 1-11 302S 3-11 FACB 9-1-42 411S 20-8 242S 25-9 133S 29-9 336S 1-10 AST 25-3-43 VSM 30-6 fuel syst mods wng stiff S Type pt MkIII IFF bomb carr 130S 25-1-44 222S 16-2 322S 17-3 350S 11-5 CB ops 12-6 1AGS 21-2-45 SOC 17-9-46

W3210 1662 EA Malta FF 13-5-41 8MU 14-5 74S 18-5 FTR ops 27-6

W3211 1664 EA Norman Merrett FF 14-5-41 8MU 16-5 609S 28-5 dbf after comb Bf109 18-6 SOC 24-6 FH28.35

W3212 1665 EA Ghawdex FF GP 14-5-41 8MU 16-5 74S 18-5 AST 10-8 92S 17-9 417S 6-2-42 FACB 10-2 ROS ASTH 17-2-43 con to Seafire IB-NX883

W3213 1666 VA EA Cecil McKay FF 14-5-41 33MU 16-5 603S 25-6 SAL 19-8 2USA 7-8-42 FACB 22-11 61 OTU 18-4-44 FAAC 24-6 ROS

W3214 1669 EA Metal Trade Australia FF 14-5-41 24MU 13-5 ASTH 28-6 350S 22-3-42 FAAC 1-6 ROS FTR ops 10-8

W3215 1670 EA Marksman FF 15-5-41 6MU 16-5 609S 1-6 AST 1-7 411S 2-10 FTR ops 24-3-42

W3216 1671 VA EA Maidenhead and District FF GP 16-5-41 33MU 17-5 54S 26-6 dbf ops 27-7 SOC FH34.30

W3226 1705 HPA FF GP 27-5-41 9MU 29-5 611S 29-6 AST 18-7 603S 11-8 FAAC 3-3-42 ROS 332S 17-4 133S 3-5 167S 19-5 165S 27-5 SAL 13-7 421S 2-10 412S 3-2-43 602S 19-4 416S 26-9 e/fd a/c aban over Channel 22-10

W3227 1713 EA FF GP 27-5-41 9MU 28-5 611S 29-6 ROS 5-8 611S 20-8 CE ops 21-10 SOC 22-10

W3228 1721 HPA FF 27-5-41 R-RH 27-6 Mer RM3S (MXII) and RM6S (M56) trls and gen dev of M45, 46, 50, 55. BDn 16-9 initial trls R-RH 20-10 BDn 17011 aero hand trls with R-R diaphragm type carb. R-RH 15-12 MR5S (M50) instal. BDn 10-1-42 trls with mods to diaphragm carb. Mer 45M (M50 Spcl) with 'cropped' supercharger impeller (9.5in). Trls with same. Eng then trans to AB167 (VC) for similar trls. R-RH for new rad. AST 21-7-43 130S 6-7-44 53 OTU 10-8 VA 4-6 527S 17-5-45 to 5939M 5 SoTT 18-4-46 SOC 10-2-47

W3229 1729 HPA FF 31-5-41 9MU 7-6 72S 8-7 HAL 7-8 306S 3-9 303S 6-10 CAC 17-2-42 AST 4USA 12-8 RNDA 23-2-44 COAL 30-4 RNAS Yeov 22-7 Ret to RAF 12-6-45 to 5572M FAF 16-3-46

W3230 1724 CHA FF 30-5-41 9MU 1-6 611S 28-6 MM 7-7 308S 11-9 HAL 3-10 316S 13-12 FAAC 15-1-42 ROS 129S 19-8 602S 29-11 66S 19-2-43 234S 19-4 312S 29-6 RNDA 23-2-44 loan Admiralty as train

W3231 1736 M45 MHPS FF GP 4-6-41 6MU 7-6 91S 8-7 CB ops 17012 ASTH 331S 23-7-42 SAL 25-10 308S 20-5-

Above: Women played a large part in the history of the Spitfire. A good proportion of the personnel at the production centres and with the Civilian Repair Depots were female. The work of women ferry pilots in the ATA is well known. Below: Diagramatic representation of filter installations, with data from trials aircraft.

INTAKE TYPE	SEAFIRE NM977			SPITFIRE V. JK940			SPITFIRE V. EF541		
	V. MAX. BELOW F.T.H	F.T.H.	V. MAX. AT F.T.H.	V. MAX. BELOW F.T.H.	F.T.H.	V. MAX. AT F.T.H.	V. MAX. BELOW F.T.H.	F.T.H.	V. MAX. AT F.T.H.
OLD TROPICAL (FILTER)	302 mph AT SEA LEVEL 338·5 mph AT 10,000'	14,600'	355 mph	312 mph AT SEA LEVEL 355·5 mph AT 10,000'	10,200'	357 mph	305·5 mph AT SEA LEVEL 347 mph AT 10,000'	11,100'	351·5 mph
NEW TROPICAL (FILTER)				312 mph AT SEA LEVEL 355·5 mph AT 10,000'	10,700'	358·5 mph	304 mph AT SEA LEVEL 344·5 mph AT 10,000'	11,000'	348 5 mph
TEMPERATE	302 mph AT SEA LEVEL 338·5 mph AT 10,000'	15,900'	361 mph	316 mph AT SEA LEVEL 360 mph AT 10,000'	10,700'	383 mph	308 mph AT SEA LEVEL 348 mph AT 10,000'	11,200'	354 mph
'ABOUKIR' (FILTER, SHUTTER)				305 mph AT SEA LEVEL 348 mph AT 10,000'	11,500'	354 mph			

43 234S 22-8 VSM 25-1-44 fuel syst mods DeH 3-6 1687 Flt 5-12 FAAC 19-7-45 recat E SOC 27-7

W3232 1720 EA FF 30-5-41 6MU 2-6 74S 24-6 FTR ops 13-7

W3233 1728 EA FF 31-5-41 6MU 2-6 92S 603S 7-8 FTR ops 27-9

W3234 1743 CHA FF GP 6-6-41 8MU 9-6 92S 26-6 1CRU 12-7 123S 20-2-42 167S 10-4 165S 27-5 FACB 5-8 SAL VSM 14-5-43 fuel syst mods wng stiff target tow hook 315S 2-7 611S 11-7 CAC ops 2-10 AST 64S 12-10 65S 3-5-44 278S 13-10 SOC 27-9-45

W3235 1749 HPA FF GP 7-6-41 6MU 12-6 91S 29-6 FACB 18-3-42 AST 341S 12-3-43 RNDA 16-1-44 RNAS Hens as train 11-3

W3236 1672 EA Llanelly FF 16-5-41 6MU 17-5 609S 1-6 CAC ops 17-9 ROS AST 29-10 310S 25-2-42 130S 28-2 ASTE 30-4 307S USA 22-8 350S 12-9 CE ops 21-9 SOC 27-9

W3237 1735 CHA FF 4-6-41 See main text.

W3238 1673 EA The London Butcher FF 17-5-41 6MU 17-5 609S 27-5 Farn July FACB 16-9 92S 8-10 ROS FACE 9-11 SOC 1-12

W3239 1674 EA BoB FF 17-5-41 6MU 17-5 609S 27-5 i/sea ops 8-7

W3240 1679 EA City of Leeds II FF 17-5-41 609S 28-5 ASTH 12-8 121S 4-11 cd Ipswich 8-1-42 SOC 13-1

W3241 1680 EA L.E.P. FF GP 19-5-41 8MU 21-5 609S 28-5 i/sea ops 19-8 FH15.50

W3242 1683 EA Crispin of Leicester FF 20-5-41 8MU 22-5 611S 22-6 Cl by AA fire 30-6 25-8 ASTH 12-9 gun fail e/fd convoy patrol a/c aban i/sea nr Harwich 9-12

W3243 1684 EA The Falkirk Bairn FF 20-5-41 8MU 26-5 611S 22-6 AST 28-7 ROS 3-8 315S 12-12 GAL 21-2-42 167S 17-7 CE ops 19-9 SOC 25-9

W3244 1686 EA Devon Squadron FF 20-5-41 5MU 3-10 122S 16-11 242S 23-4-42 FA FTR 5-5

W3245 1722 EA Lincoln Imp 30-5-41 8MU 6-6 92S 24-6 CB ops 3-8 ROS 222S 17-10 FACB 24-3-42 HAL 4USA 4-8 332S 8-11 416S 10-3-43 41S 23-3 ROS 20-4 501S 19-7 485S 14-11 SAL 4-3-44 1655Flt 15-10 ASTH 4-9-45 SOC

W3246 1689 EA Devon Squadron FF GP 21-5-41 9MU 18-5 611S 22-6 FTR ops 23-7 F/O Sutton pow

W3247 1680 EA City of Hull III FF 19-5-41 9MU 18-5 611S 22-6 FTR ops 26-8

W3248 1691 M46 EA Letchworth FF GP 23-5-41 9MU 18-5 611S 22-6 AST 6-7 64S 14-11 MM 9-1-42 mods First clipped wng Spit re-desig LF VB Farn 14-4 acc invest with BL770. June external mirror drag trls. Aug G-suffix serial, lifted 30-9 after f/ldg on 19-9. Dec '42 cockpit sight parameter trls & clear view w/s. Jan '43 ails trls. HAL Sep/Oct cockpit misting trls at alt. Farn Feb '44 trls with new type cockpit panels. Comp trls with 'Spider Crab'* latter flown by John Cunningham, Michael Daunt, 'Sailor' Malan. ETPA 10-5. Metro Com Sqdn 3-9 refurb to Port 17-10-47

W3249 1698 EA Baltic Exchange III FF 23-5-41 9MU 26-6 CB ops 17-7 AST 312S 10-12 222S 5-9-42 602S 23-12 129S 22-1-43 66S 19-2 312S 29-6 12 Gp Flt 5-10-43 402S 10-5-44 HAL 3-6 287S 2-12 FAAC 5-2-45 ROS Mar Cam 15-11 SOC

W3250 1699 EA FF Central Provinces and Berar II 23-5-41 9MU 18-5 91S 26-2 WAL 27-8 74S 28-11 1CRU 13-10-42 222S 3-4-43 167S 24-5 303S 25-3-44 402S 30-5 CAC on ops 8-6 527S 17-5-45 to 5938M 12 SoTT 27-4-46 RNeAF 25-11

W3251 1700 EA Central Provinces and Berar I FF GP 24-5-41 6MU 18-5 74S 12-6 FTR after comb Bf109 17-6 FH11.10

W3252 1701 EA Central Provinces and Berar III FF 24-5-41 6MU 18-5 74S FTR after comb Bf109 27-6

W3253 1703 EA Central Provinces and Berar IV FF GP 24-5-41 9MU 25-5 92S 26-2 ASDT 212-7 222S 16-9 1CRU 8-12 VSM 24-10-42 fuel syst mods 602S 9-1-43 129S 19-2 234S 12-5 312S 29-6 317S 4-10 52 OTY 5-5-44 VSM 20-1-44 mods FLS Mlfld 2-2 AST 10-5 AGS 2-11 SOC 29-8-46

W3254 1704 EA Central Provinces and Berar V FF GP 26-5-41 9MU 25-5 609S FTR ops 9-9

W3255 1706 EA FF 26-5-41 9MU 1-6 611S 30-6 SOC 21-7

W3256 1707 EA FF 26-5-41 9MU 28-5 72S 8-7 FTR ops 23-7

W3257 1708 EA FF GP 27-5-41 9MU 28-5 611S 8-7 FTR ops 31-7

W3258 1709 EA FF 27-5-41 9MU 30-5 74S 30-6 FTR ops 4-7

W3259 1710 EA FF 28-5-41 9MU 28-5 74S 30-6 FTR ops 2-7

W3260 1716 EA FF 28-5-41 9MU 16-6 611S 30-6

W3261 1717 EA FF 29-5-41 9MU 1-6 611S 29-6 GAL 6-8 122S 15-11 FACB 20-2-42 242S 26-2 FAAC 7-7 ROS 222S 30-8 FACB 2-11 SAL 350S 3-4-43 FAAC 3-9 ROS VSM 22-12 fuel syst mods 1652CU 3-5-44 26S 26-4 AST 3-6 SOC 29-11-45

W3262 1718 M45M LF LR VB EA FF 29-5-41 6MU 2-6 91S 8-7 CAC ops 11-7 ROS GAL 6-2-42 307S 14-7 350S 12-9 AST 20-10 VSM 13-3-43 mods 9-10 303S 6-3-44 SAL 19-7 17SFTS 12-1-45 CE 5-7-46 SOC

W3263 1719 EA FF 30-5-41 6MU 2-6 74S 22-6 FTR ops 2-7

W3264 1730 EA FF 31-5-41 6MU 2-6 92S 23-6 CB ops 25-6 ASTE 2-7 5 USA 6-8-42 332 Ser S 3-12 345S 26-6-44 strk obst nosed over CE 30-7

W3265 1725 EA FF 31-5-41 6MU 18-5 92S 17-6 i/sea ops 8-7

**'Spider Crab' was Farn code call sign for the prototype DeH Vampire jet fighter not the original, proposed name.*

W3305 1727 FF 31-5-41 6MU 6-6 91S 19-6 FACB 17-7 AST 74S 30-11 FACB 29-3-42 S&H VSM 2-6-43 fuel syst mods wng stiff ASTE 24-8 186S 8-2-44 611S 18-5 350S 17-6 57 OTU 23-7 GACB 17-3-45 recat E SOC 27-3

W3306 1748 EA FF 406-41 6MU 11-6 74S 19-6 GAL 29-6 316S 16-11 ROS 17-11 306S 12-12 312S 29-12 FACB 4-5-42 WAL 12-5

W3307 1731 EA FF 4-6-41 8MU 6-6 609S 24-6 FTR ops 21-7

W3308 1732 EA Raj Pipla FF 4-6-41 6MU 6-6 92S 17-6 MM1-7 266S 13-9 FTR 1-1-42

W3309 1733 The Wiltshire I EA FF 4-6-41 6MU 7-6 611S 25-6 AT 15-7 FAAC 28-8-42 307S 16-9 VSM 9-3-43 fuel syst mods 312S 25-5 234S 4-7 504S 30-6 313S 22-9 118S 2-6-44 CAC 11-8 SAL 313S 22-9 118S 2-6-44 41 OTU 18-3-45 Mar Cam 6-12 SOC 4-2-46

W3310 1970 M45M LF LR VB EA FF GP 5-6-41 6MU 31-5 AST 10-6 111S 24-8 Farn 14-9-42 pt removed a/c waxed and polished for trls Speed gain of 12½ mph 132S 18-2-44 504S 15-3 345S 31-5 FAAC 3-8 ROS 245S 26-8 57 OTU 15-9

W3311 1737 EA FF 5-6-41 611S FTR 6-7 Sgt Smith pow

W3312 1740 EA Moonraker FF 6-6-41 6MU 8-6 92S 20-6 609S 26-9 124S 13-11 CA ops 27-4-42 65S 2-5 CE ops 3-9

W3313 1741 M45M EA Nike FF 6-6-41 8MU 8-6 509S 29-6 1CRU 39MU Star Fm dis 23-8 266S 13-9 FAAC 26-3 42 ROS 154S 28-3 FAAC 26-5 SAL 308S 27-6 401S 5-12 402S 12-12 416S 23-3-43 501S 28-6 DeH 26-10 26S 2-4-44 ASTH 6-9 SOC 5-9-45

W3314 1744 EA Hosiery Flight Leicester FF 7-6-41 8MU 8-6 92S 30-6 CB ops 12-10 ASTH 30-10 131S 3-4-42 243S 3-7 ROS 30-9 65S 31-12 130S 31-3-43 349S 19-7 SAL 7-11 26S 10-4-44 air coll with AA850 and BL 638 cd Old Alresford Hants CE 19-8

W3315 1745 EA Stockton Thornaby Bellingham & Tees FF 7-6-41 8MU 8-6 609S 29-6 f/ld Graves 21-9 ASDT SOC 27-9

W3316 1750 EA City of Salford FF 7-6-41 8MU 11-6 72S 29-6 FTR ops 24-7

W3317 1751 Newport Hundreds and Wolverton Urban District FF 7-6-41 8MU 11-6 74S 29-6 FTR ops 7-7

W3318 1753 EA Jewellery Watch & Allied Trades FF GP 10-6-41 9MU 12-6 611S 29-6 dam ops 16-8 403S 20-9 ROS AFDU 12-10 610S 17-11 411S 25-9-42 to 3405M 10 SoTT 17-10-42

W3319 1754 EA Winchester & District FF 10-6-41 9MU 12-6 92S 12-7 FTR ops 27-8

W3320 1756 EA The Darlington Spitfire FF GP 11-6-41 9MU 12-6 92S 12-7 ASTH 11-11 545S 1-3-42 FACB 19-4 ROS VSM 14-3-43 fuel syst mods wng stiff 118S 8-7 64S 25-9 611S 10-7-44 234S 5-10 FACB 28-10 63S 4-11

W3321 1757 EA Elacardo The Thistle FF 11-6-41 9MU 12-6 74S 5-7 72S ROS 19-8 FAAC 25-3-42 ROS VSM 18-6 mods 124S 29-6 FAAC 2-7 ROS ASTH 29-8 602S 3-1-43 129S 22-1 66S 19-2 FTR off Noup Head Orkneys 12-3 FH229.40

W3322 1765 EA Hendon Griffin FF 12-6-41 9MU 14-6 DGRD VA 27-6 R-R 12-8 pressure fuel syst install BDn 3-9 guns removed trls with new fule syst. Apl '42 trls of Triplex designed balloon hood. No effect on perf June '42 trls with M45 and 46 when fitt with (1) int wt elev cross shaft. Trls to determine best syst for the Spit H/A MkVI. All devices did not affect perf 1-10 Perf trls with R-R SU fuel injection pump feeding fuel into supercharger intake. Perf above average. 11-10 Fuel cons and hand tests with SU pump. Eng used less fuel above 30000ft 1-2-43 Fuel syst tests with SU pump. Valid for temperate zones. Engine surging and cut -out in tropical conditions. 14-7 Fitt normal ATV40 carb for comp trls with SU pump. Lower perf with ATV40. 19-9 comp fuel cons with P7661 (IIA), N3053 (VA with M61) AB488 (VC low boost eng) X4922 (VAT). 8-3-44 Trls to determine air solubility in fuel. See drawing for instal. Thorton Lab analysed results. A/c trans to RAF Houston Pk and flown from there as base aerodrome AST 9-5-41 OTU 14-9 to 5584M FAF 16-3-46

W3323 1764 EA The New Forest FF 12-6-41 6MU 14-6 54S 23-6 dam comb Bf109 25-6 SOC 1-7 BBOC 129S air coll with P8742 a/c aban cd in Chichester Harbour 7-9 FH2.25

W3324 1766 Newcastle on Tyne II FF GP 3-6-41 6MU 14-6 92S 8-7 GAL 14-8 403S 5-5-42 FA FTR 2-6-43 FH205.50

W3325 1772 CHA Newcastle on Tyne I FF 14-6-41 6MU 14-6 611S 25-6 s/dn P/O Johnston missing 9-7

W3326 1776 EA Mesopotamia FF 14-6-41 8MU 8-7 92S 8-7 FTR ops 19-7

W3327 1777 EA Horsham and District FF 14-6-41 6MU 16-6 611S 25-6 CE ops 21-10 SOC 22-10

W3328 1779 EA The Flying Fox FF 16-6-41 6MU 19-6 611S 25-6 AST 14-7 315S 27-9 CB ops 6-1-42 VSM 11-6 fuel syst mods 4USA 12-8 332S 8-11 VSM 25-5-43 M50M cropped supercharger eng instal RNAS 20-2-44 COAL 12-5 LoS 24-4-45 to 5571M FAF 16-3-46

W3329 1778 Spirit of Uruguay FF 14-6-41 6MU 15-6 611S FTR 21-7 nr Lille Sgt Grainger missing

W3330 1781 EA Vectis FF GP 17-6-41 92S 8-7 ASTH 26-8 611S 11-2-42 242S 4-6 222S 11-8 WAL 15-10 65S 31-12 130S 31-3-43 349S 1-8 VSM 5-11 fuel syst mods 278S 18-4-44 ROS 11-6 275S 4-8 SOC 20-2-45

W3331 1796 The King Rufus FF GP 21-6-41 8MU 28-6 92S 1-7 FTR ops 6-7 FH7.15

W3332 1800 EA Hendon Griffon FF 18-6-41 8MU 28-5 AST 20-6 54S 24-7 403S 4-8 124S 17-11 CAC ops 13-3-42 ROS FTR 25-5

W3333 1785 EA Hendon Pegasus FF 18-6-41 8MU 20-6 610S 22-8 i/sea 7-9

W3334 1789 EA Progress I FF GP 20-6-41 8MU 21-6 616S 22-7 FTR ops 27-9

W3364 1681 VA CHA FF 19-5-41 39MU 18-5 603S 22-6 f/ld 24-6 AST 29-6 602S 25-11 81S 16-12 2USA 5-8-42 DeH 27-2-43 52 OTU 2-12

W3365 1695 VA CHA FF 20-5-41 6MU 25-5 609S 13-6 Farn July ROS 19-8 dbf 2-9 SOC 10-9

W3366 1692 VA CHA FF GP 21-5-41 39MU 18-5 145S 30-6 FTR ops 6-7 FH2.55

W3367 1697 CHA FF GP 20-5-41 6MU 25-5 74S 12-6 72S 29-7 FTR ops 7-11

W3368 1702 CHA FF 24-5-41 6MU 25-5 609S 23-6 ASTH 8-9 71S 24-5-42 CB ops 24-7 GAL 165S 11-6-43 122S 18-7 15-8 VSM 25-1-44 fuel syst mods SOC 26-2-45

W3369 1711 VA CHA FF 29-5-41 38MU 29-5 603S 26-6 FTR ops 22-7

W3370 1723 CHA FF GP 30-5-41 8MU 1-6 609S cd del flt 23-6 611S 31-12 616S 28-1-42 307S USA 20-4-42 350S 12-9 411S 20-12 402S 25-3-43 19S 26-4-43 COAL 9-11 RNAS LoS 28-2-44

W3371 1726 CHA FF 30-5-41 8MU 7-6 609S 25-6 ROS 9-10 266S 30-10 AST 22-11 65S 24-7-42 317S 4-9 303S 7-11 HAL 62-43 VSM 4-6 con to Seafire IB-PA119

W3372 1734 CHA FF 4-6-41 8MU 7-6 609S 25-6 CAC ops 21-7 SAL 167S 30-6 610S 14-10 131S 25-1-43 SAL 13-4 ASTH 221S con to Seafire IB-NX980

W3373 1739 M45M LF LR VB CHA FF 5-6-41 8MU 9-6 609S 25-6 SAL 25-7 154S 26-6-42 AST 17-7 315S 5-9 AST 3-7-43 349S 8-10 303S 6-3-44 FAAC 20-5 ROS SAL 19-7 51 OTU 24-9 SOC 10-9-45

W3374 1742 CHA FF 7-7-41 8MU 8-6 145S 7-7 28-7 AST 29-8 FA ttl wrk 16-9 SOC 27-9

W3375 1747 CHA FF 7-6-41 8MU 9-6 92S 8-7 610S 15-11 315S 17-7-42 FAAC 30-9 AST 29-7-43 453S 22-1-44 602S 20-2 118S 13-3 64S 11-6 53 OTU 17-7 burst tyre t/o o/t KinL 4-3-45

W3376 1759 CHA FF GP 11-6-41 33MU 14-6 610S 7-7 FTR ops 21-7

W3377 1760 CHA FF GP 11-6-41 33MU 14-6 TFU 24-8 AST 25-3-44 26S 24-12 41 OTU 25-1-45 58 OTU 22-3

W3378 1761 CHA M45M FF GP 11-6-41 33MU 14-6 145S 18-11 134S 19-12 133S 28-12 CB ops 5-2-42 ASTH recat E 20-5

W3379 1768 VA M45M CHA FF GP 13-6-41 33MU 14-6 AST 10-7 609S 17-9 CAC ops 14-4-42 R-R 30-4 AST 17-5 41S 2-9 610S 12-3-43 FACB 4-4 SAL 131S 17-6 310S 30-6 313S 29-7 350S 9-10 FACB 20-10 ROS 501S

W3380 1774 CHA FF 13-6-41 33MU 21-6 74S 6-7 72S 27-7 ASTH 29-8 412S 26-1-42 FAAC 25-2 ROS 38MU 7-11 M46 instal 167S 8-3-43 308S 7-5 401S 7-8 303S 25-3-44 53 OTY 2-9 PAL 10-9 45 SOC 14-9

W3381 1773 CHA FF 14-6-41 33MU 15-6 92S 10-7 FTR ops 24-7

W3382 1782 CHA FF 17-6-41 33MU 21-6 610S 7-7 602S 8-12 FTR ops 9-3-42

W3383 1787 CHA FF 19-6-41 33MU 21-6 41S 28-7 ASTH 3-2-43 CE 11-5

W3403 1746 EA The Dog Fighter FF GP 7-6-41 6MU 11-6 92S 9-7 SOC 11-7

W3404 1762 EA FF 7-6-41 6MU 12-6 609S 8-7 ROS 54S 17-3-42 167S 31-5 610S 14-10 131S 25-1-43 AST 3-3 VSM 2-6 VSM fuel syst mods wng stiff 308S 20-7 CE ops 16-8 SOC 31-8 FH353.25

W3405 1752 Monmouth Chepstow & Forest of Dene Spitfire FF 7-6-41 6MU 11-6 91S 19-6 GAL 26-5-42 4USA 6-8 332S 8-11 DeH 20-6-44 41 OTU 10-2-45 FAAC 20-3 ROS 58 OTU 19-4 SOC 3-11-46

W3406 1769 HPA FF GP 13-6-41 5MU 15-6 485S 10-8 ROS 24-10 425S 22-11 72S 13-2-42 FTR ops 25-4 FH92.05

W3407 1770 HPA FF GP 13-6-41 5MU 15-6 602S 18-8 485S 28-10 FAAC 12-1-42 ROS 81S 5-4 317S 1-5 122S 19-5-43 313S 18-8 DeH 16-6-44 CGS 13-10 SOC 25-10-45

W3408 1758 EA Mr & Mrs Albert Ehrman FF 11-6-41 9MU 13-6 72S 8-7 FTR ops 28-8

W3409 1763 EA The Peruvian Oil Fields FF GP 12-6-41 9MU 13-6 74S 30-6 92S 7-8 FTR ops 21-8

W3410 1767 EA Lancastrian Ff 14-6-41 9MU 15-6 92S 5-7 AST 16-7 316S 11-10 306S 12-12 CB ops 7-5-42

W3411 1771 HPA FF 14-6-41 5MU 15-6 74S 6-7 SOC 17-7

W3412 1775 RA Rhodesian Pioneer FF 14-6-41 24MU 16-6 74S 22-6 222S 26-8 FAAC 1-1-42 ROS 131S 10-5 FAAC 8-6 ROS AST 12-9 VSM 212-10 fuel syst mods wng stiff 504S 14-3-43 AST 11-4 165S 4-7 308S 10-10 SAL 1-12-44 8 OTU 10-3-45 SOC 25-10

W3422 1798 EA FF GP 21-6-41 24MU 23-6 91S 20-7 Heston 8-9 91S 10-9 FTR ops 1-10

W3423 1799 EA M45M FF GP 20-6-41 24MU 23-6 609S 20-7 AST 20-9 603S 21-12 2USA 31-7-42 26S 2-4-44 FAAC 8-9 ROS 41 OTU 21-1-45 to 5383M 5 SoTT 13-7-45 SOC 29-11

W3424 1802 EA FF 21-6-41 24MU 23-6 616S 22-7 WAL 18-8 317S 1-11 CAC ops 3-5-42 SOC E 29-5

W3425 1803 EA FF 21-6-41 24MU 23-6 452S w/u ldg u/c jam Metal Swarf found in hydraulic system 20-8 5-8 dam by bf109 7-10 ROS 129S 11-10 CB ops 18-12 WAL 232S 9-5-42 4USA 5-8 VSM 24-9 fuel syst mods 401S 6-12 91S 9-12 FTR 24-3-43

W3426 1804 EA FF 22-6-41 24MU 25-6 452S 4-8 AST 16-8 403S 12-9 CAC ops 12-4-42 AST 602S 27-8 164S 9-1-43 341S 22-2 340S 23-2 34S 13-2-44 DeH 28-7 FAF 9-4-45

W3427 1805 FF 22-6-41 38MU 25-6 610S 19-7 CE ops 23-7 AST 307S USA 13-7-42 FACA 18-8 303S 11-9 VSM 24-10 fuel syst mods wng stiff 315S 6-6-43 hit high grd in form with AR338 & BL469 Clady Corner Co Antrim Ireland CE 11-9 SOC 28-9

W3428 1807 EA LF LR VB M45M FF GP 23-6-41 38MU 26-6 616S 22-7 65S 6-10 131S 4-5-42 FAAC 6-6 AST

No 303 Squadron (Polish), Kirton on Lindsey, August 1942.

Yugoslav Air Force VB(T).

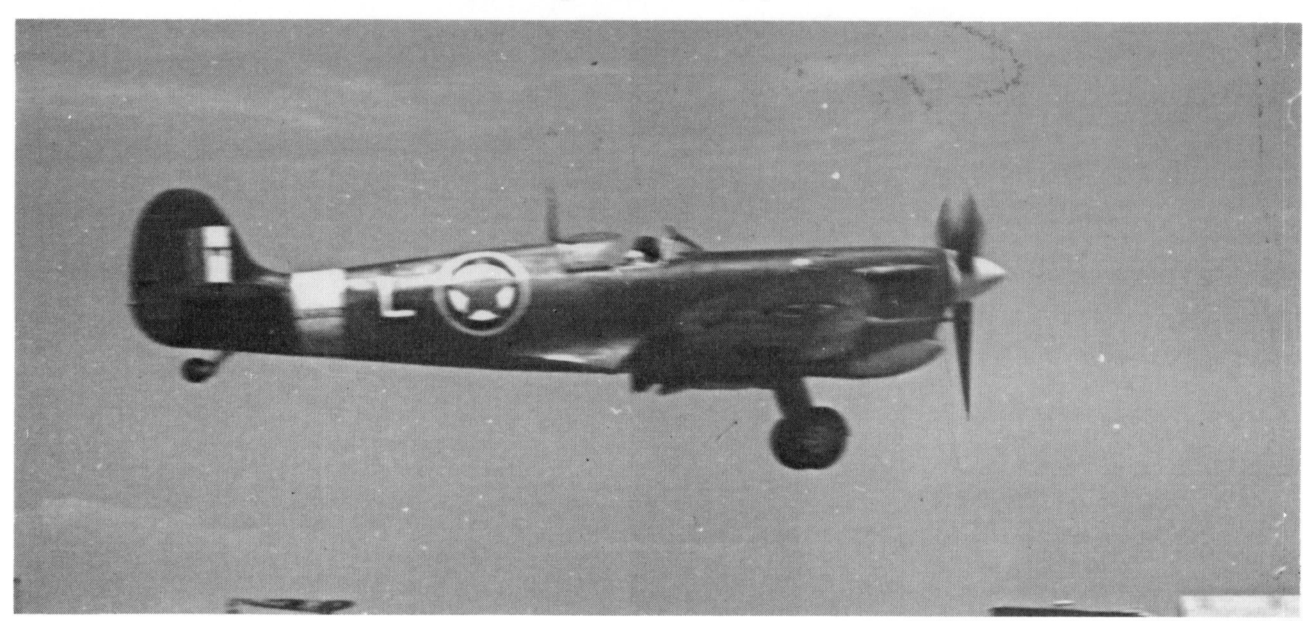

316S 30-1-43 306S16-3 302S 3-10 sal 18-10 602S 1-3-44 118S 13-3 FAAC 11-4 ROS

W3429 1808 EA FF 24-6-41 38MU 26-6 72S 20-7 222S 15-2-42 CB ops 10-6 VSM 15-9 fuel syst mods 118S 2-3-43 FTR ops 10-4

W3430 1809 EA President Roosevelt FF 25-6-41 38MU 26-6 72S 20-7 222S 14-5-42 FACB 23-9 SAL 6-6-43 222MU 29-9-43 *Emp Ort* 6-10-43 Port 19-10

W3431 1828 Kaapstad III FF 30-6-41 38MU 1-7 72S 24-7 ROS 3-10 403S 31-12 FAAC 30-3-42 ROS WAL 5USA 6-8 6MU 11-11-43 M55M instal VSM 23-2-44 fuel syst mods wng stiff Mk III IFF S Type pt bomb carr CGS 3-10 R&R refurb to Port 22-9-47

W3432 1810 EA Cordell Hull FF 25-6-41 38MU 26-6 616S 22-7 65S 6-10 FAAC 31-12 ROS 130S 27-8-42 402S 22-4-43 19S 26-4 65S 4-7 130S 15-8 VSM 5-10 'Basta' mods 303S 20-2-44 VSM 24-3 fuel syst mods 277S 17-6 SOC 10-5-46

W3433 1815 EA Progress II FF 26-6-41 38 MU 28-6 616S 22-7 ASTH 23-8 FTR ops 23-9

W3434 1817 EA Aberdare and Mountain Ash FF 27-6-41 45MU 29-6 610S 22-7 FTR ops 21-8

W3435 1816 EA FF 27-6-41 45MU 30-6-41 616S 9-7 610S 19-7 129S 31-12 SOC CE 28-2-42

W3436 1820 EA Midland Banker FF 28-6-41 45MU 3-7 54S 11-7 403S 4-8 124S 17-11 FTR SOC 24-4-42

W3437 1821 Kaapstad II EA FF GP 28-6-41 45MU 27-6 54S 11-7 AST 27-7 611S 12-2-42 242S 2-6 222S 11-8 SAL 16-10 64S 31-3-43 FAAC 1-5 ROS COAL 7-2-44 for con RNAS Hens 20-4 ROS 14-5

W3438 1826 EA Kaapstad I FF 28-6-41 45MU 4-7 54S 11-7 403S 4-8 SOC 22-8

W3439 1827 M45M EA Kaapstad IV FF 26-6-41 6MU 27-6 92S 10-7 19S 25-2-42 FACB 25-6-42 401S 12-3-43 416S 3-6 19S 7-6 322S 20-7 FACB 24-8 SOC 31-8 recat B AST USAAF 7-5-44 FAAC 21-8ROS 1687 BDTF 4-4-45 o/s at Binbrook onto nose CAC 1-7-46 Recat E 9-7 SOC

W3440 1829 EA Trengganu FF 1-7-41 6MU 2-7 72S 10-7 ROS 18-10 401S 8-12 93S 6-9-42 VSM 18-2-43 fuel syst mods wng stiff 308S 19-7 FA FTR 22-9

W3441 1830 EA Alloway FF GP 1-7-41 6MU 27-6 72S 10-7 417S 24-4-42 243S 6-6 FAAC 4-8 ROS 131S 21-11 FACB 4-12 317S 26-3-43 form coll with W3950 cd nr Slough Bucks CE 7-6

W3442 1834 Progress II (trans from W3433) FF GP 2-7-41 6MU 3-7 611S 14-7 FTR ops 27-9

W3443 1835 EA M45M Cape Town I FF GP 3-7-41 6MU 27-6 609S 8-7 GAL 8-8 VSM 16-2-43 fuel syst mods wng stiff 416S 4-9 FACB 3-10 63S 8-4-44 26S 11-6

W3444 1836 EA New Yorklin FF GP 3-7-41 5MU 27-6 92S 10-7 FACE 15-11 SOC 16-11

W3445 1837 EA Cape Town II FF 3-7-41 5MU 5-7 611S 10-7 GAL 12-9 312S 8-12 VSM 12-8-42 mods HAL 26-8 91S 26-8 e/a CB 11-5-43 fuel syst mods wng stiff 317S 23-7 312S 3-3-44 41 OTU 25-1-45 58 OTU 22-3 SOC 17-7-45 to 5393M

W3446 1845 EA Jennifer FF 4-7-41 5MU 8-7 54S 20-7 403S 4-8 AST 29-8 81S 20-4-42 72-S 1-5 350S 20-5 cd on return convoy patrol Norwich CE 14-6 SOC 15-6

W3447 1842 EA Cape Town IV FF 4-7-41 8MU 5-7 145S 14-7 41-7 41S 28-7 FTR ops 14-8 FH37.50

W3448 1848 EA Cape Town III FF GP 5-7-41 8MU 6-7 222S 24-8 ROS 27-12 CE ops 25-1-42

W3449 1851 EA Borough of Ashton Under Lyme FF GP 5-7-41 8MU 8-7 610S 22-8 FACE 5-10 SOC 10-10

W3450 1852 Dunottar Castle FF 5-7-41 8MU 9-7 111S 25-8 ROS 12-10 129S 11-10 41S 3-3-42 FTR ops 12-4-43 FH143.10

W3451 1853 EA Progress III FF 5-7-41 8MU 6-7 111S 25-8 i/sea ops 4-9

W3452 1854 Midnight Sun FF 5-7-41 9MU 11-7 401S 1-10 burnt ops 27-10 SOC 31-10 FH25.0

W3453 1855 County Borough of Reading FF 7-7-41 9MU 14-7 54S 22-7 403S 4-8 ASTH 23-8 54S 2-9 ASTH 11-9 124S 17-11 FAAC 24-7-42 ROS 165S 28-8 CE 19-9-42 FH135.05

W3454 1856 EA Heston and Isleworth FF GP 9-6-41 485S 7-8 ASTE 23-9 611S 11-2-42 243S 2-6 222S 11-8 SAL 19-8 VSM 27-3-43 fuel syst mods wng stiff 402S 11-7 FAAC 7-10-44 ROS SOC 25-10-45

W3455 1861 EA Smethwick FF 10-7-41 9MU 11-7 610S 25-7 FTR ops 21-8

W3456 1863 EA Watford FF 11-7-41 9MU 14-7 616S 22-7 ASTH 8-9 65S 6-10 AST 14-12 302S 12-9-42 308S 13-9 FACE 29-10 AST 11-11-43 VSM 14-4- fuel syst mods wng stiff 308S e/fd app Heston cd CE 10-11

W3457 1862 EA Cynon Valley FF 10-7-41 12MU 13-7 616S 23-7 65S 6-20 AST 23-12 340S 9-3-42 FAAC 13-7 ROS 41S 16-8 FACB 27-8 WAL M46 instal 501S 4-4-43 FACB 11-9 COAL 4-2-44 hook fitt RNAS Hens 28-3 SOC 28-3-45

W3458 1864 EA Mirfield FF 11-7-41 12MU 16-7 616S 23-7 FTR ops 9-8

W3459 1872 EA Cape Town V FF 12-7-41 12MU 16-7 92S 27-7 FTR ops 2-10

W3460 1871 EA Cape Town VI FF 12-7-41 12MU 16-7 616S 24-7 i/sea ops 21-9

W3461 1874 EA Kaapstad V FF 12-6-41 45MU 16-7 65S 22-7 FTR ops 27-4-42

W3501 1793 HPA FF 21-6-41 45MU 20-6 616S 19-7 SOC 10-10 FACE 5-10

W3502 1780 EA Wolds and Buckrose FF 17-6-41 45MU 17-6 616S 10-7 403S 4-8 54S 25-8 603S 26-9 332S 8-6-42 VSM 7-9 mods FTR SOC 10-10

W3503 1784 HPA FF 17-6-41 45MU 22-6 616S 10-7 610S 19-7 FTR ops 27-8

W3504 1791 HPA FF 20-6-41 616S 10-7 610S 19-6 FTR ops 21-8

W3505 1786 VC Hendon Endeavour FF 18-6-41 45MU 22-6 485S 10-8 Heston 30-8 109 Obs S USA 22-8-42 air coll with W3797 cd Chetwynd Salop CE 11-2-43

W3506 1797 EA Hendon Lamb FF 21-6-41 37MU 24-6 306S 6-7 303S 3-10 HAL 9-4-42 FTR ops 12-4

W3507 1795 HPA FF GP 21-6-41 37MU 28-6 315S 30-8 ASTH 14-2-42 317S 5-9 FACB 7-4-43 VSM 28-6 fuel syst mods Mk III IFF bomb carr 316S 18-12 FAAC 31-12 ROS 129S 4-3-44 61 OTU 28-9 sold J Dale 8-7-48

W3508 1793 CHA FF 21-6-41 37MU 24-6 452S 20-8 ROS 10-9 FTR ops 18-9

W3509 1806 HPA FF 21-6-41 37MU 24-6 71S 26-8 FTR ops 17-9

W3510 1801 CHA FF 21-6-41 37MU 25-6 HAL 4-10 308S 6-10 316S 13-12 FAAC 22-6-42 ROS 316S 14-8-FTR ops 26-11 FH87.50

W3511 1811 HPA FF 25-6-41 12MU 26-6 72S 27-7 ROS 16-10 FTR ops 8-11

W3512 1814 CHA FF GP 26-6-41 12MU 28-6 452S 5-8 FTR ops 18-9

W3513 1819 HPA FF 27-6-41 12MU 30-6 72S 31-7 ROS 23-8 54S 10-10 315S 23-10 124S 13-12 316S 23-12 CE ops 13-2-42 SOC 23-2

W3514 1823 CHA FF 28-6-41 12MU 30-6 616S 24-7 FTR ops 14-8

W3515 1825 HPA FF GP 27-6-41 12MU 3-7 615S 15-7 FTR ops 21-10

W3516 1788 EA FF 19-6-41 9MU 21-6 72S 27-7 FTR ops 19-9

W3517 1790 CHA FF GP 19-6-41 9MU 22-6 616S 22-7 FTR ops 22-9

W3518 1792 CHA FF GP 20-6-41 9MU 23-6-41 611S 22-7 ROS 29-9 65S 6-10 ASTH 30-10 145S 17-12 FACB 4-4-42 ROS 350S 5-4 FAAC 13-4 ROS 129S 5-5 2USA 22-8 SAL 28-1-43 M55M instal 302S 21-4 118S 10-10 132S 25-1-44 VSM 20-3 fuel syst mods 'Basta' mods ASTE 18-8 R&S refurb to Port 14-7-47

W3519 1794 CHA M55MA FF GP 21-6-41 9MU 22-6 616S 22-7 65S 6-10 WAL 8-5-42 340S 26-3-43 VSM 28-11 fuel syst mods AST 14-5-44 CGS 3-10 R&S refurb to Port 22-8-47

W3520 1812 CHA FF GP 25-6-41 9MU 27-6 452S 11-8 FTR ops 12-10

W3521 1813 FF GP 26-6-41 38MU 27-6 616S 22-7 65S 6-10 ROS 18-5-42 DeH 6-6 93S 2609 402S 16-4-43 FACE 14-5 AST F1S Mlfld 11-2-44 350S 17-6 57 OTU 23-7 coll with EE715 ldg Esh CB 25-8 LMS 61 OTU 16-3-45 CE 24-5

W3522 1823 FF GP 28-6-41 38MU 30-6 611S 28-7 R-R mods 64S 14-11 154S 10-5-42 FACB 10-6 WAL RNAS Stret 4-9 ASTH 18-9 hook fitd RNAS LoS 8-10

W3523 1818 CHA FF GP 27-6-41 38MU 30-6 611S 28-7 SOC 27-8

W3524 1833 CHA FF 2-7-41 38MU 6-7 308S 5-9 FTR ops 17-9 FH17.40

W3525 1824 CHA FF GP29-6-41 37MU 2-7 616S 23-7 ROS 26-9 145S 18-11 350S 7-2-42 eng cut coll with W3626 ldg Atcham CE 17-2 SOC 28-2

W3526 1839 CHA FF 3-7-41 24MU 5-7 452S 5-9 145S 31-12 602S 1-3-42 CE ops 13-3 SOC 31-3

W3527 1840 CHA FF 3-7-41 24MU 5-7 485S 7-8 FTR ops 27-8

W3528 1846 M45M FF 4-7-41 24MU 7-7 485S 30-8 118S 10-4-42 VSM 24-8 fuel syst mods 93S 30-9 317S 24-1-43 FAAC 11-4 ROS 611S 20-5 306S 20-6 316S 6-12 222S 1-1-44 FAAC 14-1-44 ROS VSM 20-4 mods 277S 10-6 SOC CE 22-4-45

W3529 1847 CHA Caithness FF 5-7 41 24MU 7-7 452S 5-8 FACA 21-2-42 129S 8-3 131S 22-10 VSM 18-11 fuel syst mods wng stiff 610S 27-1-43 310S 30-6 313S 24-7 402S 4-12 SAL 13-6-44 57OTU 4-10 577S 14-6-45 SOC 25-10

W3530 1857 CHA FF GP 7-7-41 24MU 11-7 485S 30-8 cd into hill nr Lavant CE26-9 SOC 5-10 to 4871M

W3560 1831 HPA FF GP 1-7-41 33MU 3-7 616S 6-10 SOC 11-11

W3561 1832 HPA FF GP 2-7-41 33MU 3-7 313S 26-10 130S 17-12 FTR ops 19-8-42 FH118.20

W3562 1841 HPA FF GP 3-7-41 33MU 5-7 92S 12-7 SOC 15-7

W3563 1843 HPA FF 4-7-41 24MU 5-7 611S 14-7 64S 14-11 222S 2-5-42 FTR 27-5

W3564 1849 HPA FF GP 5-7-41 24MU 9-7 145S 17-7 41S 28-7 AST 27-8 403S 28-1-42 CE ops 2-6-42 FH231.40

W3565 1850 HPA FF 3-7-41 24MU 9-7 145S 17-7 41S 28-7 CE ops 12-2-42

W3566 1858 HPA FF GP 8-7-41 24MU 11-7 AFDU 17-7 e/fd f/ld nr Coningsby 1-10 SOC 9-10

W3567 1859 HPA FF 9-7-41 24MU 11-7 611S 28-7 FTR ops SOC 16-8

W3568 1865 HPA FF 11-7-41 12MU 12-7-41 92S 27-7 FTR ops SOC 8-8

W3569 1866 HPA LF LR VB M45M FF 11-7-41 12MU 12-7 603S 25-7 611S 25-8 SAL 25-10 416S 7-3-42 FAAC25-3 ROS 602S 15-7 164S 11-9 341S 3-2-43 340S 23-3 coll with BM133 Athelstone Ford E Lothian CA 6-4-43 316S 1-12 FACE 21-3-44

W3570 1870 HPA FF GP 12-7-41 12MU 15-7 222S 22-8 411S 16-10 ROS 4-11 CB ops 8-1-42 CE SOC 3-2

W3571 1876 HPA FF 14-741 12MU 17-7 452S 5-8 ROS 30-9 AST 19-5-42

W3572 1877 HPA FF 15-7-41 12MU 17-7 452S 5-8 ROS 20-2 AST H 14-5 222S 31-12 64S 31-3-43 i/sea after mock attack on bomber nr Lady Isle of Clyde CE 29-4

W3573 1887 HPA FF 16-7-41 12MU 20-7 54S 24-7 403S 4-8 FTR ops 19-8 SOC 20-8

W3574 1888 HPA FF 17-7-41 33MU 20-7 609S 1-8 downwind ldg N Wld cd 16-10 65S 23-9 Farn for acc invest 453S 11-10 222S 31-3-43 167S 19-5 SAL 5-8 310S 24-9 416S 16-11 186S 10-2-44 ROS 12-5 PAL 27-9-45 SOC 29-9

W3575 1889 HPA FF GP 19-7-41 33MU 20-7 222S 7-9 AST 29-12 417S 4-4-42 242S 21-4 FAAC 19-6 243S 19-8 FAAC 30-9 ROS SAL 8-1-43 VSM 3-3 fuel syst mods wng stiff 310S 21-5 131S 2-7 ASTE 4-8 443S 27-2-44 SAL 20-3 530TU 2-9 e/fd f/ld Ce 4-1-45

W3576 1890 HPA FF GP 19-7-41 33MU 20-7 92S 21-8 FTR ops 26-8

W3577 1904 FF 30-7-41 33MU 1-8 484S 7-8 FTR ops 27-3-42

W5388 1905 FF 30-7-41 33MU 1-8 485S 7-8 FACE 31-1-42 SOC

W3579 1906 FF GP 31-7-41 33MU 1-8 485S 7-8 HAL 23-10 FA FTR 31-10

W3599 1867 CHA FF GP 11-7-41 33MU 14-7 92S 22-8 610S 16-11 HAL 7-12 133S 14-6-42 91S 15-6 CAC ops 23-6 AST 234S 16-9 FACE 12-12 SOC 16-12

W3600 1868 CHA FF 112-7-41 33MU 14-7 452S 24-8 FTR ops 16-9

W3601 1873 CHA FF 12-7-41 37MU 19-7 41S 26-9 401S 28-9 CE ops 27-10 SOC 31-10 FH16.30

W3602 1869 CHA FF 12-7-41 37MU 14-7 131S 10-13 FACB 23-3-42 ROS 93S 23-7 308S 13-12 315S 26-12 AST 7-4-43 FACB 20-5 VSM 6-7 fuel syst mods wng stiff S Type pt bomb carr COAL 7-11 RNAS LoS 8-2-44

W3603 1880 CHA FF 17-7-41 37MU 19-7 609S 2-8 AST 12-8 401S 28-10 CB ops 13-2-42 610S 8-6 111S 16-7 FTR ops 25-7

W3604 1893 CHA M 45M FF 19-7-41 37MU 20-7 403S 12-9 610S 16-11 65S 25-5-42 303S 22-8-42 VSM 22-8 mods 65S 31-8 315S 6-6-43 340S 28-9 485S 11-11 VSM 20-3-44 fuel syst mods AST 9-5 570TU 6-10 Sold J Dale

W3605 1894 CHA FF 19-7-41 37MU 20-7 452S 20-8 118S 3-3-42 AST 10-3 SAL 13-6 242S 29-7 222S 11-8 VSM 19-4-43 fuel syst mods wng stiff 302S 2-7 501S 8-11 SOC 25-4-46

W3606 1895 CHA M45 FF 19-7-41 39MU 20-7 222S 24-8 CB ops 25-3-42 VSM 31-8 fuel syst mods 91S 28-12 CAC ops 26-12 62S 10-6-43 602S 16-6 CAC ops 4-9 501S 31-3-44 FAAC 3-4 ROS 287S 17-1-45 SOC 8-9

W3607 1900 CHA FF GP 29-7-41 39MU 1-8 S Frm dis 41S 30-8 ASTH 3-10 FACE 8-5-42 SOC

W3608 1908 M45M FF 31-7-41 39MU 1-8 S Frm dis 41S 1-9 412S 9-10-43 CGS 1-10-44 1AGS 28-11 SOC 19-8-46

W3618 1909 FF 31-7-41 39MU 27-6 Star Fm dis 72S 30-8 315S 1-9 HAL 23-9 AST 12-6-42 RNAS Stret 4-9 ASTH 3-10 hook fitt RNAS LoS 28-10

W3619 1914 FF 1-8-41 39MU 5-8 Star Fm dis 15S 29-8 315S 29-8 307 USA 12-9-42 350S 23-9 401S 7-12 VSM 16-9 mods 64S eng fire cd/ld Langley Sussex 11-8-43 DeH ARF 2-12-43 315S 24-5-44 HAL 12-7 FAF CG 2/18

W3620 1915 FF GP 2-8-41 45MU 20-8 54S 22-8 FTR ops 4-9

W3621 1916 EA FF GP 2-8-41 39MU 13-7 609S 7-8 DeH 31-5-42 VSM 21-10 fuel syst mods wng stiff M46 instal 504S 29-3-43 416S 11-6 FACB 27-3 DeH 350S 28-3-44 610TU 16-9 flew i/grd after t/o Mont Br CE 19-10 SOC

W3622 1924EA FF GP 5-8-41 39MU 9-8 602S 14-8 FTR ops 20-9

W3623 1931 EA FF 7-8-41 39MU 9-8 602S 16-8 FTR ops 12-10 FH31.20

W3624 1932 EA LF VB FF 8-8-41 39MU 9-8 603S 16-8 ASTH 1-9 72S 2-1-42 ROS 23-1 504S 8-7 501S 19-10 S&H 19-3-43 VSM 21-5 fuel syst mods wng stiff 131S 4-7 602S 27-2-44 118S 13-3 616S 3-10 SOC 10-4-45

W3625 1936 CHA FF 8-8-41 39MU 10-8 609S 14-8 CE ops 27-9 SOC 30-9

W6326 1941 CHA FF GP 9-8-41 39MU 10-8 41S 14-8 501S 7-10 ROS 18-10 145S 29-1-42 350S 10-2 coll with W3525 ldg Atcham 17-2 FTR ops 1-6

W3627 1954 CHA FF 13-8-41 39MU 16-8 71S 27-8 FACE ttl wrk 15-11 SOC 23-11

W3628 1883 EA Oman FF GP 14-7-41 6MU 20-7 603S 24-7 ASTH 11-11 cd on del flt 17-12 ASTH 611S 9-2-42 315S 13-4 flew i/hill 20m from Preston Yorks 16-7 SOC 25-7

W3629 1875 EA FF 12-7-41 6MU 16-7 616S 22-7 65S 6-10 FTR ops 11-11

W3630 1884 EA LF LR VB M45M Kuwait FF 14-7-41 6Mu 20-7 54S 27-7 403S 4-8 72S 20-10 124S 17-11 ROS 28-11 308S 26-7-42 CAC ops 5-9-42 WAL VSM 9-3-43 fuel syst mods wng stiff 610S 4-7 AST 3-5-44 CGS 24-2-45 sold J Dale

W3631 1878 EA FF 15-7-41 6MU 17-7 603S 24-7 332S 18-5 42 DeH 31-5 MM 26-7 VSM 6-10 fuel syst mods wng stiff 130S 17-3-43 65S 31-3-43 CE ops 19-9 SOC 28-9 FH500.10

W3632 1885 EA Bahrein FF 15-7-41 6MU 21-7 603S 24-7 54S 20-9 124S 17-1 5 USA 6-8-42 109 Obs S 28-2-43 VSM 12-3-43 mods 341S 16-6 3409 FFS 26-7 1TEU 3-6-44 57 OTU 17-8 FAAC 18-10 SOC 29-11-45

W3633 1879 EA FF GP 16-7-41 8MU 17-7 616S 22-7 65S 6-10 SOC 1-11

W3634 1886 EA March Brown FF 16-7-41 8MU 20-7 145S 28-7 41S 28-7 332S 12-6-42 CAC ops 21-7 ROS VSM 18-8 mods AST 13-11 312S 31-12 VSM 3-4-43 fuel syst mods wng stiff 402S 6-6 cd Leith Hill Surrey CE 19-10

W3635 1881 EA Joseph Snooka FF 17-7-41 8MU 19-7 145S 24-7 41S 28-7 AST 12-11 FTR ops 7-8-42

W3636 1882 EA FF GP 17-7-41 8MU 19-7 145S 24-7 41S 28-7 CAC ops 25-7-42 ROS 334 USA 26-10 CE 27-11

W3637 1896 EA FF 19-7-41 8MU 30-7 610S 22-8 ASTH 30-9 302S 30-1 42 FACB 8-4 WAL SOC CE 29-4

W3638 1891 EA M45M FF 19-7-41 9MU 20-7 602S 25-3-42 P&P SM 6-6 411S 8-1-43 402S 25-3 19S 2-4 65S 30-6 26S 22-5-44 FAAC 18-12 recat E SOC 1-1-45

W3639 1897 EA FF 19-7-41 9MU 8-7 411S 2-10 ASTE 6-8 CE SOC 16-12

W3640 1892 EA M45M FF 19-7-41 9MU 20-7 602S 1-8 485S 21-11 308S 1-4-42 AST 65S 12-3-43 130S 31-3 349S 19-7 VSM 17-11 fuel syst mods 277S 44-3-44 AST 2-6 53 OTU

VB(T), 5512, and OK.14 (below right) of the Turkish Air Force.

VB(T)s, Sicily 1943.

XR-K. 334th Pursuit Squadron USAAF.

LF Mk V, No.315 (Polish) Squadron.

VB(T) on the lift in HMS Furious during operation 'Bellows'.

5-1-45 o/s ldg cd Hibald CE 20-2 SOC 21-2

W3641 1898 EA F 19-7-41 9MU 20-7 602S 31-7 610S 16-11 AST 20-12 M45M instal FAAC 22-2-42 421S 7-6 SAL 25-8 331S 2-4-43 349S 1-8 VSM 17-11 fuel syst mods 277S 25-3-44 290S 11-1-45 FAAC 3-9 R&S rfurb to Port 25-8-47

W3642 1902 EA FF GP 28-7-41 9MU 30-7 602S 10-8 FTR ops 17-9

W3643 1903 FF GP 29-7-41 6MU 1-8-41 485S i/sea ops 29-8

W3644 2116 EA FF 27-7-41 6MU 16-7 AST 1-8 19S 16-4-42 FTR ops 23-6 FH76.50

W3645 1907 Joseph Smooha FF 31-7-41 6MU 3-8 485S 15-8 CB ops 18-12 ASTH 121S 30-4-42 FTR ops 31-5

W3646 1919 EA FF GP 2-8-41 6MU 5-8 452S 16-8 GAL 21-9 145S 22-11 350S 11-2-42 VSM 29-7 mods FAAC 26-8 ROS FACB 18-11 DeH COAL 31-5-43 con to Sea IB-NX965 cancel later COAL 11 8 RNDA 19-1-44

W3647 1910 FF 1-8-41 6MU 2-8 611S 9-8 ASTE 14-9 603S 22-10 322S 15-4-42 FAAC 23-6 ROS 421S 21-11 412S 3-2-43 HAL 10-3 VSM 15-8 mods 277S 4-3 CAC ops 10-11 SOC 17-2-45

W3648 1918 EA Wisbech FF 2-8-41 6MU 3-8 609S 9-8 72S 20-8 FACB 4-1-42 AST VSM 8-9 fuel syst mods wng stiff Mk III IFF bomb carr 222MU 18-12 *Emp Corn* 3-1-44 Port 17-2

W3649 1913 Shepley FF 1-8-41 6MU 5-8 602S 16-8 303S 28-10 485S 24-12 lost over channel 28-3-42

W3650 1920 EA FF 2-8-41 6MU 3-8 611S 9-8 403S 12-9 ROS 20-9 71S 9-3-42 CB ops 27-4 SOC CE 30-4

W3651 1921 EA Carbine FF 2-8-41 6MU 2-8 609S 9-8 FTR ops 23-8 FH27.45

W3652 1923 EA Blue Charm FF 5-8-41 6MU 8-8 485S 15-8 HAL 26-9 416S 3-6-43 118S 7-6 FACB 15-6 SAL 129S 25-1-44 FACE 8-3 LMS CGS 15-10 SOC 25-10-45

W3653 1925 EA Doncaster FF 6-8-41 6MU 7-8 403S 11-8 54S 25-8 i/sea ops 17-9 FH46.45

W3654 1926 EA March Brown FF GP 6-8-41 8MU 7-8 616S 16-8 129S 5-10 65S 31-10 41S 6-1-42 FTR ops 12-4 FH202.30

W3655 1930 EA Silver Grey FF 7-8-41 8MU 7-8 616S 16-8 i/sea ops 27-9

W3656 1934 EA Afric Scot FF GP 7-8-41 8MU 10-8 92S 16-8 AST 23-8 122S 22-11 FAAC 28-2-42 ROS 167S 12-4 FACB 14-8 WAL VSM 9-3-43 fuel syst mods wng stiff 118S 27-5 64S 25-9-43 CA ops 12-6-44 ASTH 1668CU 29-11 to 5842M 12SoTT 6-3-46

W3657 1937 EA Pendel FF 8-8-41 8MU 10-8 92S 16-8 GAL 7-10 308S 12-9 42 CE ops 2-2-43 FH219.25

W3697 1899 EA FF 19-7-41 45MU 2-8 243S 23-9 ROS 26-11 65S 31-12 GAL 7-8-42 VSM 20-11 fuel syst mod wng stiff 313S 4-4-43 66S 4-7 FAAC 13-8 ROS 165S 13-9 308S 1-10 FACE 18-11 DeH

W3698 1982 HPA FF 20-8-41 45MU 22-8 315S 30-8 FTR ops 23-11

W3699 1983 HPA FF GP 20-8-41 45MU 22-8 308S 9-9 ROS 5-11 316S 13-12 CB ops 11-1-42 SOC 14-1

W3700 1987 HPA FF 45MU 11-7 cd on del flt to 131S 9-1-42 e/fd strk tree in f/ldg nr Criccieth N Wales CE 18-4 ASTE SOC 26-4

W3701 1988 HPA FF 22-8-41 45MU 26-8 306S 4-9 FTR ops 17-9 FH14.30

W3702 1989 HPA FF 22-8-41 45MU 25-8 308S 10-9 HAL 22-9 302S 9-12 FAAC 12-1-43 ROS VSM 28-6-43 fuel syst mods wng stiff S Type pt Mk III IFF bomb carr 501S 24-10 510S CE ops 12-7-44

W3703 2002 HPA FF 26-8-41 37MU 27-8 501S 19-9 FACE 5-2-42 ROS 111S 18-3 FTR 18-5

W3704 2003 HPA FF 27-8-41 37MU 28-8 72S 19-9 FTR ops 25-10

W3705 2019 HPA FF 27-8-41 37MU 28-8 609S 22-10 FAAC 27-3-42 HAL 313S 28-7 340S 1-8 FTR over e/tr 5-9 FH177.10

W3706 2020 HPA FF 28-8-41 37MU 1-9 118S 16-9 FTR ops 15-11

W3707 1955 CHA LF LR VB FF 13-8-41 8MU 16-8 609S 21-8 AST 3-9 74S 23-11 FACB 18-3-42 S&H M55M instal 93S 6-10 VSM 25-2-43 fuel syst mods wng stiff 610S 15-5 CAC ops 8-10 ROS 316S 29-11 AST 21-4-44 42 OTU 27-9 FAAC 18-10 ROS to 5931M 12SofTT 27-4-46

W3708 1957 CHA FF GP 14-8-41 9MU 16-8 71S 27-8 dam ops 17-4-42 ASTH SOC CE 18-4

W3709 1962 CHA FF 16-8-41 9MU 18-8 92S 28-8 ASTH 23-9 602S 29-1-42 71S 3-4 FACE 6-8 SOC 21-8

W3710 1963 CHA FF GP 16-8-41 9MU 18-8 92S 28-8 SOC 4-10

W3711 1964 CHA FF 16-8-41 9MU 18-8 603S 30-8 CB ops 4-9 ASTE FTR over e/tr 7-12

W3712 1911 FF 31-7-41 9MU 6-8 403S 20-8 54S 25-8 FTR ops 31-8 FH12.25

W3713 1913 M45M FF 1-8-41 12MU 6-8 41S 11-8 ROS 17-3-42 5 USA 5-9 317S 4-2-43 HAL 17-5 VSM 23-7 fuel syst mods Mk III IFF 316S 22-11 63S 1-5-44 FACA 8-7 ROS 57OTU 1-2-5 strk tree night t/o w/u ldg Boul CE 2-3 SAL 15-3

W3714 1917 EA FF 2-8-41 12MU 6-8 610S 10-8 129S 31-12 CB ops 27-4-42 ROS 610S 19-5 Hatfield on del flt to GAL 26-5 AST CE 31-5

W3715 1927 EA FF 6-8-41 12MU 10-8 111S 18-8 SOC 1-9

W3716 1928 EA FF 7-8-41 12MU 10-8 111S 19-8 FTR ops 21-7-42

W3717 1929 EA FF 7-8-41 12MU 10-8 111S 19-8 WAL 19-10 308S 9-12 316S 13-12 FACB 3-5-42 CE SOC 8-5

W3718 1935 HPA FF 8-8-41 37MU 11-8 306S 3-9 303S 6-10 316S 9-1-42 4USA 6-8 66S 12-10-43 340S 15-11 239S 16-2-44 26S 22-3 278S 27-9 530TU 22-2-45 std on app Hibald cd CE 26-4-45

W3719 1942 HPA FF 9-8-41 37MU 11-8 41S 1-9 ROS 2-11 WAL 8-6-42 RNAS Stret 6-9 VSM 28-4-43 fuel syst mods wing stff 35-1SU 8-8 FTR ops 22-8 FH266.50

W3720 1951 HPA FF GP 12-8-41 37MU 14-8 222S 2-9-41 ROS 7-11 403S 24-2-42 i/sea ops 27-2

W3721 1952 HPA FF GP 13-8-41 37MU 14-8 266S 26-9 SOC Feb'44 BBOC 62 OTU 8-2-45 SOC 14-6

W3722 1953 HPA FF GP 13-8-41 37MU 24-8 452S 7-9 ROS 25-9 501S 12 10 ASTH 11-11 118S 26-4-42 FTR ops 9-5 FH49.35

W3723 1961 HPA FF GP 14-8-41 38MU 19-8 222S 24-8 FTR ops 27-8

W3725 1967 HPA FF 16-8-41 38MU 19-8 602S 28-8 FTR ops 21-9

W3726 1968 HPA FF 16-8-41 38MU 19-8 602S 22-8 222S 24-8 FTR ops 8-3-42

W3756 1938 John Stephens FF GP 8-8-41 38MU 11-8 602S 28-8 ROS 25-9 R-Rmods 15-11 118S 11-5-42 GAL 27-6 RNAS 885S LoS 10-9 hook fitt SAL 19-3-44 Hens 31-5

W3757 1933 Bruce Stevens EA FF GP 9-8-41 45MU 11-8 111S 21-8 FTRm ops 21-9

W3758 1939 EA FF GP 9-8-41 45MU 12-8 54S 22-8 124S 8-11 FTR ops 27-4-42 FH239.50

W3759 1940 EA FF 9-8-41 45MU 10-8-41 ASTH 15-8 129S 2-11 CB ops 7-9-42 AST 316S 24-1-43 306S 16-3 FAAC 21-9 350S 26-3-44 53 OTU 12-10 PAL 2-10-45 SOC 5-10

W3760 1947 EA FF 11-8-41 DTD VA 15-8 floats instal Wts and CG WDn 1-11-42 Tare 5851 lb, AUW 7418, land 6717. CRD MAEE Helensburgh 11-11 Super 31-12 perf trls at AUW with M45 at +9lb. boost 2-3-43 52MU 27-9 *Pen Cast* 6-10 ME 30 10 SOC28-14-44 (see page 381)

W3761 1948 EA Blue Nose FF 12-8-41 37MU 15-8 315S 31-8 71S 29-4-42 FTR ops 19-8-42

W3762 1949 EA Junagarth FF 12-8-41 37MU 15-8 92S 10-9 FTR ops 2-10

W3763 1950 EA Thane of Fife FF 13-8-41 37MU 15-8 71S 10-9 FTR ops 12-9

W3764 1956 EA Fun of the Fair FF GP 14-8-41 37MU 17-8 306S 7-9 HAL 17-9 303S 6-10 315S 15-3-42 FACB 16-6 to 3386M 11SoTT 21-9-53 RTP 14-10

W3765 1958 M45M Roller Spitfire FF 14-8-41 37MU 19-8 306S 7-9 HAL 16-9 303S 18-9 FACB 13-3-42 302S 29-12 308S 25-6-43 132S 27-7 CAC ops 27-9 SAL 9-11 345S 3-4-44 57 OTU 17-6 FAAC 9-2-45

W3766 1959 EA Wandsworth (Putney Roehampton and Southfields) FF 14-8-41 8MU 18-8 609S 22-8 GAL 9-10 312S 29-1-42 AST 5-7 5USA 7-9 222S 21-1-43 64S 31-3 228S 25-9 SAL 19-10 61 OTU 2-8-44 SOC 11-5-45

W3767 1960 EA Wandsworth (Streatham and Central Divisions) FF 14-8-41 8MU 18-8 609S 22-8 FTR ops 17-9

W3768 1969 EA Higham Ferrers-Irthlingborough FF GP 16-8-41 CRD DeH Airscrews 23-8 501S 15-9 AST 14-6-42 93S 9-7 VSM 1-5-43 fuel syst mods wng stiff 504S 27-8 313S 22-9 441S 27-2-44 SAL 20-3 350S 26-6 57 OTU 23-7 FACB 12-12 SOC 18-12

W3769 1956 EA Western India States FF GP 16-8-41 8MU 18-8 222S 30-8 131S 10-5-42 AST 30-5 RNAS Stret 5-9 ASTH 10-9 hook fitt 27-9 SAL 4-3-44

W3770 1973EA FF GP 18-8-41 8MU 19-8 41S 22-8 FTR ops 10-4-42 FH140.30

W3771 1974 EA M45M FF 18-8-41 9MU 18-8 72S 30-8 ASTH 9-9 610S 30-11 CB ops 10-3-42 SAL 41S 8-11 303S 14-3-43 315S 6-6 19S 26-6 602S 10-7 345S 10-4-44 FTR ops 10-7

W3772 1975 EA Moray FF GP 19-8-41 9MU 22-8 54S 7-9 FTR ops 12-9 FH9.00

W3773 1976 EA Leyland FF 19-8-41 9MU 20-8 111S 30-8 306S 2-7-42 FTR ops 20-9

W3774 1980 EA Samson FF GP 19-8-41 9MU 22-8 485S 2-9 124S 3-5 42 FAAC 20-6 ROS 306S 2-7 VSM 26-8 mods 308S 22-11 air coll with P8746 cd Stockwell Potato Fm Yorks CE 14-5-43 FH394.15

W3775 1981 EA Rushdens Hell for Leather FF GP 20-8-41 CRD VA 23-8 Farn 3-3-42 VHF BA LR ASV radio trls ETPS 28-4 radio clearance trls RNAS Stret 7-9 AST 24-9 hook fitt LoS 11-10

W3795 1977 CHA FF GP 19-8-41 33MU 21-8 222S 29-8 FAAC 27-1-42 ROS 303S 11-9 to 3655M 9-4-43 at 6th Army Ftr Wng

W3796 1978 CHA FF 19-8-41 33MU 21-8 41S 29-8 ROS 4-9 145S 18-11 350S 7-2-42 FACB 20-3 ASTH RNAS LoS 5-9 ASTH 18-9 hook fitt

W3797 1979 CHA FF GP 20-8-41 33MU 21-8 91S 29-8 CAC ops 10-1-42 5USA 6-8 air coll with W3505 cd Chetwynd Salop CE 14-2-43

W3798 1990 CHA FF 22-8-41 33MU 25-8 308S 9-9 HAL 28-10 316S 13-12 AST 4-6-42 129S 19-8 66S 19-2-43 234S 19-4 CA ops 3-5 ROS 312S 29-6 to 4263M 30-10 CE 28-1-45

W3799 1992 CHA FF 22-8-41 33MU 27-8 54S 7-9 124S 18-11 FACE 19-2-42 SOC 4-3

W3800 1991 CHA FF 22-8-41 39MU 25-8 129S 7-9 AST 24-9 CE ops SOC 12-2-42

W3801 1995 CHA FF 23-8-41 39MU 27-8 71S 2-9 s/dn over France 7-9

W3802 2004 CHA FF 25-8-41 39MU 29-8 611S 10-9 64S 14-11 FTR 28-3

W3803 2009 CHA FF 25-8-41 39MU 29-8 129S 7-9 154S 12-2-42 FAAC 8-3 ROS 8-6 FACB 15-9 AST VSM 9-6-43 fuel syst mods wng stiff Mk III IFF bomb carr 222MU 5-13 *Drurunone* 9-1-44 Port 28-1

W3804 2010 CHA FF 26-8-41 39MU 29-8 611S 10-9 154S 12-2-42 121S 26-3 FTR ops 26-4 FH53.40

W3814 1984 EA Popocatepetl FF 21-8-41 8MU 22-8 111S 25-8 FAAC 3-2-42 ROS CE ops 19-8

W3815 1985 EA Sierre Leone II FF 22-8-41 8MU 24-8 611S 29-8 64S 14-11 GAL 21-3-42 FAC 5-4-42 ROS 4USA 7-6 332S 8-11 FAAC 2-12 LMS 58 OTU 23-3-45 SOC to 5388M 17-7

W3816 1986 The Shopmate FF GP 22-8-41 8MU 24-8 611S 29-8 FTR ops 20-9

W3817 1993 Wellingborough FF 23-8-41 8MU 27-8 92S 1-9 417S 6-2-42 242S 18-4 243S 6-6 SAL 4-7 501S 9-11 FAAC 24-3-44 DeH recat E BBOC 25-8 17SFTS 7-10 FACB 9-8-45 SOC 18-9

W3818 1994 EA FF 23-8-41 8MU 25-8 611S 29-8 64S 14-11 316S 20-4-42 308S 29-4 DeH 25-5 222MU 25-10 *Narhagus* 19-12 17-3-43

W3819 2001 EA FF 25-8-41 9MU 27-8 71S 10-9 SOC CE 18-4-42

W3820 2006 EA The Rhonda FF 26-8-41 9MU 27-8 308S 9-9 316S 13-12 CE ops 20-2-42 310S strk by MA228 parked NWld CB 28-10-44 SOC

W3821 2007 Pemba III FFGP 26-8-41 9MU 27-8 452S 11-9 CAC 17-1-42 SOC 25-1

W3822 2008 EA Zanzibar IV FF 26-8-41 9MU 28-8 403S 12-9 std off turn into wind cd M Hth CE 14-10 ROS SOC cancel 12-11 129S 19-8-42 602S 29-11 129S 22-1-43 66S 19-2 234S 19-4 312S 29-6 AST 25-4-44 1688 Bd Flt 29-9 SOC 27-6-46

W3823 2011 Holt I FF 26-8-41 9MU 29-8 403 12-9 SAL 6-11 402S 29-4-42 412S 8-5 131S 24-5 VSM 9-6-43 fuel syst mods wng stiff 302S 2-8 CAC ops 18-8 ROS 315S 9-10 64S 10-6-44 CB ops 24-6 AST 1AGS 5-12-44 SOC 13-9-46

W3824 2012 EA Holt II FF 27-8-41 24MU 29-8-41 129S 11-9 FTR ops 27-9

W3825 2013 EA Holt III FF GP 28-8-41 24MU 29-8 308S 4-9 ROS 5-11 316S 13-12 CB ops 29-3-42 ASTE 2USA 7-8 65S 2-3-43 130S 31-3 349S 19-7 SAL 27-10 AST 14-11-44 CE SOC 8-1-45

W3826 2014 Holt IV FF 28-8-41 24MU 29-8 308S 9-9 FACB 1709 AST 122S 15-11 CB ops 23-4-42 recat E

W3827 2015 Holt V FF 29-8-41 24MU 29-8 316S 17-10 FACE 26-3 42 SOC

W3828 2016 Holt VI FF GP 29-8-41 24MU 30-8 266S 13-9 154S 8-3-42 ASTH 6-5 309S 30-7 340S 12-3-43 LMS 666S 11-10 340S 15-11 FACA 26-11 ROS 350S CB ops 27-6-44 DeH 1AGS 10-3-45 e/td w/u ldg on beach Grange over Sands Lancs CE 14-12-45 SOC 9-1-46

W3829 2017 M45M Holt VII FF 29-8-41 37MU 30-8 611S 27-9 64S 14-11 152S 20-2-42 313S 8-6 222S 1-8 242S 11-8-43 331S 1-10 VSM 16-10 fuel syst mods 350S 20-11 CAC ops 19-9-43 ROS ECFS 11-11 SOC scr 16-11-47

W3830 2023 EA Holt VIII FF 30-8-41 37MU 3-9 234S 1-10 FTR ops 2-11

W3831 2024 EA Holt IX FF 30-8-41 37MU 31-8 302S 11-10 FAAC 11-3-42 ROS 316S 5-4 FACB 27-7 AST VSM 3-3-43 fuel syst mods wing stiff HAL 3-5 con to PRXIII M32 RNDA 3-3-44

W3832 2032 EA Holt X FF GP 1-9-41 37MU 6-9 118S 16-9 cd on del flt CE 11-2-42 SOC 23-2

W3833 2035 EA Holt XI FF 2-9-41 37MU 7-9 603S 27-12 FAAC 22-2-42 ROS 332S 29-4 WAL 17-6 FTR ops 24-7

W3834 2033 EA Holt XII FF 2-9-41 38MU 5-9 266S 13-9 154S 23-2-42 FAAC 12-4 ASTE M45M instal 5USA 6-8 421S 10-3-43 416S 23-5 401S 1-6 126S 10-8 HAL 12-11 1659 CU 5-1-45 SOC 17-9

W3835 2034 EA Holt XIIA FF 3-9-41 38MU 5-9-41 234S 13-9 WAL 14-6-42 VSM 29-8 52 OTU 29-1-44 2TEU 17-6

W3836 2036 EA Holt XIV M45M FF 3-9-41 38MU 7-9 266S 13-9 243S 23-7-42 FACA 4-10 ROS 65S 2-3-43 130S 31-3 349S 1-8 SAL 27-10 26S 3-4-44 41 OTU 8-3-45 58 OTU 22-3

W3837 2040 EA Evening Telegraph FF GP 4-9-41 38MU 7-9 266S 13-9 312S 7-6-42 243S 2-9 SAL 19-11 66S 12-5-43 312S 29-6 FAAC 26-8 ROS 504S 6-10 67 Grp USAAF 6-1-44 AST 10-3 53 OTU 5-9 SOC 22-5-45

W3838 2045 EA Valparaiso FF 5-9-41 38MU 7-9 611S 15-9 FTR ops 22-10

W3839 2046 Kettering District FF GP 5-9-41 45MU 7-9 611S 2-10 64S 14-11 AST 14-3-42 403S 20-8 air coll with BM346 cd Stubb House Yorks CE 17-2-43 FH297.30

W3840 2055 EA John Peels Hunter FF GP 6-9-41 45MU 7-9 501S 16-9 FTR ops 25-4-42

W3841 2051 EA FF 6-9-41 45MU 7-9 501S 16-9 WAL 20-1-42 72S 14-4 121S 29-5 FTR 16-6 FH163.20

W3842 2057 EA St Kitts Nevis I FF 8-9-41 45MU 12-9 501S 16-9 71S 19-9 ROS 11-10 FTR ops 4-6-42 FH214.45

W3843 2058 EA St Kitts Nevis II FF 8-9-41 45MU 12-9 501S 26-9 ROS 13-11 41S 14-5-42 412S 10-10 421S 31-1-43 504S 3-5 317S 17-5 350S 20-5 345S 7-4-44 CE ops 6-6

W3844 2060 EA County of Montgomery FF 9-9-41 8MU 11-9 234S 14-9 ROS 1-10 302S 21-10 CE ops 27-1-42 SOC 2-2

W3845 2064 EA John Mackintosh FF 10-9-41 8MU 11-9 501S 17-9 ASTH 16-10 FTR ops 9-5-42 FH204.50

W3846 2065 EA FF 10-9-41 8MU 11-9 501S 17-9 dam ops 11-7-42 RNAS Stret 1-9 CBAF 10-11 hook fitt RNAS Yeov 26-1-43

W3847 2066 EA Travancore I FF 10-9-41 8MU 11-9 111S 22-9 WAL 7-10 SOC 2-11

W3848 2070 M45M Travancore II FF 11-9-41 8MU 11-9 111S 22-9 FAAC 29-5-42 41S 22-8 122S 14-3-43 222S 19-5 67 Recc Grp 2-11 HAL 16-6-44 1661 CU 29 11 SOC 27-12-45

W3849 2071 EA FF 11-9-41 9MU 13-9 118S 18-9 SOC 8-10

W3850 2072 EA Westmorland I FF 11-9-41 9MU 13-9 609S 20-9 CE ops 21-10 SOC 1-11 FH23.40

W3851 2073 EA Nyasland I FF 12-9-41 12MU 13-9 130S 28-10 CE ops 27-5-42 SOC 3-6-45

W3852 2080 EA Usco-Vereeni-Ging FF 13-9-41 12MU 14-9 41S 26-9 FTR 12-4-42 FH161.50

W3853 2083 EA Nyasland II FF 13-9-41 12MU 14-9 602S 30-9 HAL 10-11 411S 26-3-42 AST 18-9 VSM 28-2-43 fuel syst mods wing stiff 313S 28-6 66S 4-7 FACE 19-9

W3893 2084 EA Nyasland IV FF 13-9-41 129S 26-9 AST 28-10 302S 29-7-42 e/td cdld nr Finningley CE 26-10 65S 12-3-42 130S 31-3 349S 19-7 VSM 5-11 fuel syst mods CAC ops 23-4-44 278S 21-7 151RU 9-3-45

W3894 2085 EA Nyasland III FF 13-9-41 12MU 14-9 501S 26-9 FTR ops 25-4-42

W3895 2090 EA Nyasland V FF GP 15-9-41 33MU 17-9 92S 22-9 417S 7-2-42 242S 28-3 VSM 3-2-43 fuel syst mods wing stiff 504S 2-9 313S 22-9 CE ops 24-9

W3896 2092 EA Nyasland VI FF GP 16-9-41 33MU 21-8 315S 26-9 FTR ops 23-11

W3897 2093 EA Nyasland VII FF 16-9-41 33MU 21-8 602S 25-9 FTR ops 23-10 FH13.50

W3898 2097 EA LF LR VB M45M FF 17-9-41 35MU 19-9 602S 25-9 19S 2-4-42 ASTH 11-8 VSM 12-5-43 mods 350S 4-10 322S 11-1-44 CGS 7-10 1AGS 28-11 SOC 29-9-45

W3899 2098 EA LF LR VB M45M FF GP 17-9 41 33MU 19-9 401S 28-9 P&P 4-11 154S 1-7-42 121S 18-7 CAC ops 21-7 ROS 335 USA 1-10 VSM 9-6-43 fuel syst elev & rud mods wing stiff 350S 9-10 FAAC 6-1-44 ROS 322S 1-2-44 AST 30-5-44 FAF 19-1-45

W3900 2101 EA FF 18-9-41 45MU 24-9 411S 9-10 ROS 6-11 412S 26-11 CAC ops 16-4-42 FA dbf CE 24-9

W3901 2102 EA FF 18-9-41 37MU 25-9 316S 17-10 306S 12-12 P&P 12-8 mods 306S 24-8 AST 15-9 VSM 21-10 duel syst mods 118S 22-3-43 FTR ops 21-6

W3902 2108 EA M45M FF 19-9-41 37MU 26-9 302S 12-10 VSM 28-8-42 mods 132S 28-6-43 1696 Flt 21-11-44 R&S refurb to Port 30-12-47

W3931 2021 HPA FF 30-8-41 45MU 1-9 234S 26-9 FACB 16-5-42 AST 4USA S 5-8 VSM 11-7-43 fuel syst elev & rud mods wing stiff S Type Pt Mk III IFF bomb carr 501S 23-10 CA ops 9-4-44 ROS FAF 19-1-46 GC 2/18

W3932 2022 HPA LF VB FF GP 29-8-41 45MU 1-9 308S 10-9 316S 13-12 FACB 28-12 ROS M50M instal 317S 4-4-43 412S 29-6 303S 3-12 SAL 1-1-44 M55M instal 567S high app hvy ldg Hawk CE 16-6-45 SOC 3-7

W3933 2028 HPA FF 30-8-41 45MU 1-9 266S 13-9 154S 12-2-42 DeH 5-5 RNAS LoS 6-9 ASTH 18-9 hook fitt

W3934 2029 HPA FF GP 30-8-41 45MU 1-9 234S 13-10 FTR ops 11-11

W3935 2041 HPA FF GP 2-9-41 45MU 7-9 234S 18-9 AST 18-4-42 VSM 11-6 fuel syst mods 41S 22-8 316S 15-3-43 306S 16-3 DeH 18-7 341S 15-11 coll with BM317 taxy Perr dbf CE 5-1-44 FH562.55

W3936 2042 HPA FF GP 4-9-41 234S

W3937 2043 HPA FF GP 4-9-41 9MU 7-9 ROS 13-12 234S 22-12 air coll on patrol ld Porth CAC 3-6-42 SOC 5 6 ROS 303S 10-12 315S CAC ops 12-6-43 ROS fast ldg o/s Bally o/td CE 9-9

W3938 2047 HPA FF GP 5-9-41 9MU 7-9 403S 12-9 131S 3-4-42 AST 30-5 RNAS 885S LoS 5-9 AST 10-9 hook fit

W3939 2048 HPA FF GP 5-9-41 9MU 7-9 501S 17-9 59S 19-5-42 AST 11-6-42 5USA S 12-8-42 341S 5-3-43 340S 23-3 FAAC 26-8 ROS RNDA 20-2-44 COAL 25-4 mods Yeov 24-7 sold J Dale

W3940 2059 HPA FF 5-9-41 33MU 10-9 308S 13-9 FTR ops 27-9 FH6.55

W3941 2063 HPA FF 9-8-41 33MU 10-9 308S 13-9 e/td w/u ldg nr North CE 18-12 SOC 22-12 AST 15-1-42 401S 16-7 416S 3-6-43 129S 12-6 453S 17-7350S 23-7 SAL 28-7 COAL 12-11 hook fitt RNDA 14-2-44

W3942 2078 HPA FF GP 10-9-41 43MU 13-9 71S 19-9 111S 5-6-42 4USA 13-9-42 CE ops 30-5-43

W3943 2079 HPA FF GP 10-9-41 33MU 13-9 118S CE ops 13-3-42 SOC

W3944 2076 HPA FF 12-9-41 33MU 13-9 315S 22-9 FTR ops 8-11

W3945 2082 HPA FF GP 12-9-41 45MU 15-9 317S 15-10 316S 18-11 306S 12-12 FTR 30-12 FH34.20

W3946 2088 HPA FF GP 13-9-41 45MU 15-9 501S 23-9 152S 3-5-42 421S 20-11 412S 3-2-43 602S 15-5 416S 15-12 186S 13-2-44 130S 18-4 CE 22-6 M46 and M45M instal during service career

W3947 2089 HPA FF GP 13-9-41 45MU 15-9 611S 17-10 64S 14-11 310S 18-4-42 FTR ops 4-5 FH255.30

W3948 2099 HPA M45M FF 17-9-41 45MU 26-9-41 303S 29-4-42 FACB 27-7 ROS 340S 28-9-43 FACA 15-10 ROS 278S 23-5-44 276S 22-2-45 SOC 29-11

W3949 2100 HPA FF 17-9-41 8MU 26-9 412S 7-10 e/fd cd/ld nr GAL Middx CE 10-6-42 AST SOC 22-6

W3950 2104 HPA LF LR VB M45M FF 18-9-41 8MU 26-9 452S 1-10 457S 22-3-42 303S 13-4 AST 14-8 VSM 11-10 fuel syst mods 317S 6-4-43 form coll with W3441 nr Slough Berks 7-6 H 350S 5-10 FAAC 21-10 ROS 322S 11-1-44 1696 Bd Flt 21-11-44 R&S refurn to Port w/o R&S 30-10-47

W3951 2105 HPA FF 18-9-41 8MU 26-9 411S 2-10 FAAC 11-12 ROS 402S 29-1-42 19S 26-4-43 FAAC 3-5 ROS 602S 16-6 AS 28-6 82MU 26-9 C o Lan Port 9-11

W3952 2126 HPA FF 24-9-41 8MU 29-9 412S 7-10 R-R 22-10 mods. FTR ops 8-11

W3953 2127 HPA FF 25-9-41 37MU 29-9 401S 1-11 FACB 10-1-42 FAAC 3-9 ROS 302S 18-9 VSM 30-6-43 fuel sys, elev & rud mods wing stiff Mk III IFF bomb carr COAL 8-11 hook fitt RNAS Hens 9-4-44

W3954 2128 HPA LF LR M45M FF 25-9-41 37MU 29-9 130S 8-11 FAAC 16-2-42 ROS 302S 10-4 CAC ops 7-9 132S 28-6-43 118S 10-10 504S 15-3-44 recat E 12-4

W3955 2133 HPA FF 26-9-41 37MU 29-9 401S 19-10 FTR ops 27-10 FH11.20

W3956 2138 HPA FF 27-9-41 38MU 29-9 602S 14-10 CE ops 3-3-42 SOC 9-3

W3957 2142 FF 29-9-41 38MU 1-10 71S 20-10 GAL 6-6-42 129S 19-8 602S 29-11 66S 19-2-43 234S 12-5 312S 29-6 118S 13-3-44 611S 3-10 FAF 29-1-45 GC 2/18

W3958 2155 HPA Ff 30-9-41 38MU 1-10 412S 12-10 FACE 23-7-42

W3959 2156 HPA FF 30-9-41 38MU 9-10 412S 12-10 FTR ops 8-11

W3960 2158 HPA FF GP 2-10-41 38MU 3-10 302S 11-10 CAC ops 19-9-42 ROS 67Grp 25-2-43 341S 16-1-44 52 OTU 6-2 402S 17-6 SOC 27-9-45

W3961 2159 HPA FF GP 2-10-41 38MU 3-10 316S 11-10 306S 12-12 FACB 16-4-42 WAL 222S 24-10 64S 31-3-43 FACE 11-8 SOC 31-8 FH388.15

W3962 2168 HPA FF 6-10-41 38MU 14-10 312S 23-10 WAL 25-12 FACB 31-12 recat SOC 6-4-42

W3963 2169 HPA FF GP 6-10-41 38MU 14-10 71S 22-10 FACE dbf 16-11

W3964 2173 HPA FF 7-10-41 38MU 14-10 401S 22-10 CE ops 27-10 SOC 31-10 FH7.00

W3965 2179 HPA FF GP 9-10-41 38MU 14-10 313S 26-10 154S 26-2-42 FAAC 18-6 412S 2-9 VSM 5-9 fuel syst mods 421S 31-1-43 AST 21-2 610S 9-4 485S 24-4 122S 25-4 222S 19-5 530TU 15-2-45 PAL 9-10

W3966 2184 HPA FF 10-10-41 38MU 14-10 19S 23-10 65S 2-1-42 CAC ops 18-4 SOC 23-4 AST 3-9 FTR ops 16-4 FH200.40

W3967 2191 HPA FF 14-10-41 39MU 17-10 234S 22-10 FAAC 26-2-42 ROS

W3968 2189 HPA FF 11-10-41 39MU 13-10 317S 19-10 flew i/high grd nr Princetown Dartmoor CE 29-11 SOC 18-12

W3969 2192 FF GP 14-10-41 39MU 17-10 313S 26-10 152S 24-4-42 cd into Lough Foyle NI 7-5

W3970 2199 HPA LF LR VB M45M FF GP 16-10-41 39MU 20-10 317S 26-10 FAAC 22-12 AST 41S 27-10-42 302S 14-3-43 322S 24-1-44 350S 13-3 57 OTU 23-7 SOC 14-6-45

X4663 1633 EA VA FF GP 3-5-41 39MU 4-5 603S 22-6 FTR ops 5-8

X4664 1656 EA F.A.N.Y FF 5-5-41 6MU 12-5 609S 1-6 AST 22-6 FTR ops 4-7

X4665 1642 EA VA Earl Shilton FF 6-5-41 38MU 9-5 64S 16-5 603S 16-5 SOC 6-10-43

X4666 1641 EA Kaffraria I FF GP 7-5-41 9MU 8-5 609S 31-5 dam ops 31-7 ROS 401S 10-1-42 CE ops 28-2-42

X4667 1640 VA Huddersfield III FF 5-5-41 5MU 7-5 611S 1-6 145S 6-7 CE 7-7 SOC 23-7

X4668 1645 Burbage FF GP 8-5 8MU 9-5 74S 18-5 FTR after comb bf109 27-6

X4669 1647 EA VA Kaffraria II FF GP 9-5-41 38MU 11-5 64S 16-5 603S 21-5 81S 7-1-42 165S 12-4 FAAC 4-5 ROS 167S 28-5 5 USA 22-8 cd Kings Nordley Salop 27-3-43

X4670 1648 EA The Bright Ventura FF GP 9-5-41 6MU 9-5 74S 16-5 AST 20-6 111S 20-8 CE 11-5-42 DeH SOC 13-5

AA718 2025 CHA LF M45M FF GP 30-8-41 39MU 31-8 266S 13-9 R-R 25-10 mods 616S 31-1-42 FAAC 28-3 ROS VSM 26-8 fuel syst mods 41S 10-11 402S 29-7-43 313S 27-8 504S 15-12 129S 26-1-44 VSM 20-3 mods AST 7-5 FAF 9-1-45 GC 2/18

AA719 2030 CHA FF 29-8-41 5MU 8-9 306S 19-9 303S 3-10 616S 26-4 VSM fuel system mods 131S 10-10 FTR ops 11-11

AA720 2026 CHA FF GP 30-8-41 266S 13-9 154S 12-3-42 WAL 11-4 121S 18-6 335S 1-10 AST 27-3-43 VSM 29-6 fuel syst & rud mods wng stiff S Type pt Mk III IFF 416S 9-11 186S 13-2-44 FAAC 23-3 350S 22-5-44 CE ops 10-6

AA721 2027 CHA FF 30-8-41 39MU 31-8 129S FTR ops 13-10

AA722 2037 CHA FF 3-9-41 5MU 7-9 234S 13-9 ASTH 20-11 FTR ops 5-12

AA723 2038 CHA FF 4-9-41 12MU 7-9 230S 14-9 SOC 5-12

AA724 2039 CHA FF 4-9-41 12MU 7-9 401S 27-9 118S 2-1-42 WAL 19-4 FACE SOC 12-5 FH46.50

AA725 2049 CHA FF 5-9-41 12MU 7-9 234S 14-9 f/ld nr Bodmin Cornwall with AA726 BL241 BL669 CAC 15-3-42 118S 10-5 132S 12-7 CB ops 15-12 CE 4-1-43

AA726 2050 CHA FF 5-9-41 12MU 8-9 234S 14-9 f/ld nr Bodmin CE 15-3-42

AA727 2054 CHA FF 6-9-41 12MU 11-9 234S 20-9 FTR 12-2-42

AA728 2056 CHA M45M FF 6-9-41 12MU 11-9 234S 19-8 CAC ops 3-4-42 ROS 412S 19-7-43 126S 10-8 303S 3-12 SAL 11-1-44 USAAF 8-5-44 R&S refurb to Port 6-5-47

AA729 2061 CHA M45M FF GP 9-9-41 12MU 11-9 118S 18-9 FAAC 1-6-42 ROS 122S 5-4-43 222S 19-5 349S 19-8 67Grp Membury 20-12 DeH 20-6-44 290S 17-1-45 R&S refurb to Port 6-5-47

AA730 2062 CHA Heather FF GP 9-9-41 12MU 11-9 118S 24-9 HAL 10-11 306S 3-5 FACB 4-8 VSM 16-2-43 fuel syst mods wng stiff 132S 30-5 302S 28-6 306S 3-10 CAC ops 4-12 MAL RNDA 5-3-44 COAL mods 12-5

AA731 2067 CHA FF 10-9-41 8MU 12-9 91S 19-9 FTR ops 17-4-42

AA732 2068 CHA FF 10-9-41 8MU 12-9 485S 19-9 609S 20-4-42 121S 1-6 FAAC 9-6 ROS CA ops 21-2 FTR 21-9

AA733 2069 CHA FF 10-9-41 124S 132S

AA734 2081 CHA FF 12-9-41 9MU 14-9 616S 25-9 65S 6-10 FACE 27-3-42 SOC 30-4

AA735 2086 CHA FF GP 13-9-41 9MU 14-9 308S 18-9 316S 13-12 FACB 25-11-42 SAL 66S 23-3-43 234S 12-5 312S 29-6 317S 4-10 52 OTU 5-10 FLS 2-2-44 VSM 10-4 fuel syst mods AST 3-6 61 OTU 9-12 FACB 18-4-45 recat E SOC 7-5

AA736 2087 CHA FF 13-9-41 9MU 14-9 306S 20-9 303S 6-10 FACB 26-1-42 GAL 403S 2-6 FACB 8-6 AST SOC 14-9

AA737 2095 CHA FF GP 16-9-41 9MU 18-9 610S 25-9 65S 6-10 ASTH 23-10 CE SOC 13-12

AA738 2096 CHA LF LR FF GP 17-9-41 9MU 18-9 401S 1-10 ROS 16-10 154S 24-2-42 313S 8-6 403S 21-8 FAAC 9-3-43 ROS 401S 5-4 416S 3-6 504S 11-6 165S 1-7 340S 5-9 402S 30-3-44 53 OTU 20-7 SOC 18-5-45

AA739 2103 CHA FF 18-9-41 39MU 25-9 411S 2-10 WAL 13-11 123S 29-12 167S 17-4-42 165S 27-7 FA 8-9 AST 65S 23-9 VSM 23-4-43 fuel syst mods HAL 28-5 Con to PRXIII M32 RNDA 1-3-44

AA740 2106 CHA FF 19-9-41 39MU 25-9 118S 3-10 FACE 11-2-42 SOC 27-2

AA741 2107 CHA FF GP 19-9-41 39MU 25-9 118S 3-10 FACE 2-2-43 SOC 28-3

AA742 2112 CHA FF 20-9-41 39MU 25-9 118S 6-10 501S 24-8-42 504S 22-10 FAAC 22-11 ROS 421S 7-12 64S 24-12 453S 2-4-43 DeH 17-7 39MU 15-11 RNDA 16-1-44

AA743 2121 CHA FF GP 23-9-41 39MU 26-9 234S 3-10 ASTH 29-10 M46 instal 340S 1-3-42 FAAC 23-6 ROS 234S 31-7 AST 8-12 64S 9-6-43 118S 9-10 VSM 7-11 fuel syst mods 501S cd t/o Hawk CE 2-4-44

AA744 2114 M46 FF GP 20-9-41 33MU 25-9 118S 11-10 MM 27-4-42 M45M instal VSM 1-10 mods 317S 4-2-43 412S 29-6 126S 10-8 602S 26-2-44 118S 13-3 313S 21-7 FACB 29-8 LMS 57 OTU 30-3-45

AA745 2122 CHA FF 24-9-41 33MU 27-9 92S 10-10 417S 6-2-42 242S 6-5 243S 6-6 SAL 28-8 VSM 26-2-43 fuel syst mods wng stiff 504S 31-8 313S 22-9 312S 5-1-44 58 OTU 2-4-44 SOC 19-6-46

AA746 2129 CHA FF 25-9-41 33MU 28-9 65S 14-12 CAC ops 18-12 AST 234S 6-6-42 WAL 8-12 VSM 15-3-43 fuel syst mods wng stiff 412S 17-5 FTR ops 7-6

AA747 2130 CHA FF GP 25-9-41 33MU 28-9 302S 11-10 CE ops 26-1-42 SOC 2-2

AA748 2134 CHA FF 26-9-41 33MU 28-9 412S 8-12 FAAC 14-3-42 ROS e/fd on t/o o/t ldg MHth CE 8-5

AA749 2135 CHA FF 27-9-41 6MU 28-9 72S 3-10 FTR ops 8-12

AA750 2141 CHA FF 29-4-41 6MU 1-10 316S 11-10 star wng det in flt cd Fulham London 22-10 306S 12-12 FACB 28-3-42 AST SOC CE 5-42 recat B 5USA 10-9 ASTH con to Sea IB-NX946 16-5-43 (this history is, obviously, inaccurate and a good example of incorrect records)

AA751 2152 CHA LF LR VB M45M FF 30-9-41 92S 6-10 ROS 26-11 154S 24-2-42 313S 8-6 303S 4-8 SAL 14-8 42SLG 23-9 VSM 8-4-43 fuel syst mods wng stiff 308S 14-7 349S 29-10 222S 6-3-44 303S 17-4-44 SAL 19-7 1669CU 29-11 FAF 3-3-46

AA752 2153 CHA Josenka FF GP 30-9-41 6MU 1-10 302S 13-10 AST 13-1-42 118S 9-3 129S 8-6 Farn 14-6 G suffix serial neg G trls. Trls with Oboe and Gee (cat and mouse) equip 402S 11-7 121S 24-9 335 USA 1-10 i/sea ops 21-11 FH198.20

AA753 2154 CHA LF LR VB FF GP 30-9-41 92S 6-10 AST 8-1-42 403S 2-6 2USA 22-8 VSM 2-6-43 fuel syst mods wng stiff 402S 2-9 FAAC 26-11 ROS 129S 16-2-44 DeH 10-7 1687 Bd Flt 30-11 R&S refurb to Port 18-4-47

AA754 2161 CHA FF 3-10-41 no record

AA755 2163 FF 5-10-41 8MU 10-10 129S 14-10 CAC ops 26-3-42 ASTH FACB 27-4 ASTH recat E VSM 20-2-43 fuel syst mods wng stiff 504S 15-7 CE ops 25-7 FH186.0

AA756 2172 CHA M45M FF 7-10-41 8MU 317S 19-10 FA 31-1-42 AST SOC 9-2 sched rtp cancel M55MA instal 5 USA 7-9 132S 20-9 122S 21-5-43 234S 15-8 CAC ops 19-8 ASTE 64S 27-4-44 R&S refurb to Port 14-1-48

AA757 2175 CHA FF 8-10-47 8MU 12-10 313S 21-10 FAAC 28-2-42 ROS 609S 6-4 312S 31-5 CB ops 23-6 AST 412S 9-2-43 602S 19-4 CE 25-5

AA758 2178 CHA Bazyli Kuick FF 9-10-41 8MU 12-10 317S 19-10 HAL 4-4-42 317S 7-6 164S 20-12 341S 21-2-43 340S 23-3 COAL 9-3-44 mods RNAS Hens 23-5

AA759 2186 CHA FF 11-10-41 71S 15-10 FACE 22-10 SOC 12-11 Farn Jan '42

AA760 2183 CHA FF 10-10-41 8MU 13-10 65S 15-10 CAC ops 14-4-42 SOC E

AA761 2187 CHA FF 11-10-41 8MU 13-10 54S 15-10 124S 17-11

AA762 2188 CHA FF 11-10-41 8MU 13-10-41 317S 19-10 AST 9-3-42 SOC 2-4 HAL mr 12-5 VSM 8-8 mods CB ops 11-9 AST recat E 5-10

AA763 2198 CHA FF 15-10-41 33MU 18-10 65S 22-10 FACE 21-11-42 SOC

AA764 2201 CHA FF 17-10-41 33MU 19-10 19S 23-10 AST 4-8-42 USAAF 22-12 CE 5-9-43

AA765 2205 CHA Hyderabad FF 18-10-41 6MU 20-10 313S 24-10 152S 24-4-42 VSM 1-3-43 fuel syst mods wng stiff 308S 8-9 349S 29-10 57 OTU 5-9-44 FAAC 11-12 ROS SOC 5-6-45

AA766 2206 CHA M45M FF 17-10-41 6MU 20-10 609S 29-10 154S 5-6-42 65S 23-9 FACA 1-11 SAL 118S 6-3-43 412S 9-9 303S 3-12-43 DeH 16-1-44 130S 6-7 FAAC 5-4-45 ROS SOC 25-4-46

AA767 2209 CHA FF 19-10-41 6MU 25-10 317S 2-11 e/fd f/ld Exeter aerodrome CE 17-11 SOC 27-11

AA833 2109 EA FF 19-9-41 24MU 24-9-41 411S 6-10 AFDU Dux 9-11 service trls elev int wt Gun heat 411S fast ldg strk hangar Horn CB 8-1-42 ASTE 167S 22-9 610S 14-10 131S 25-1-43 310S 30-6 FACB 10-8 345S 3-4-44 CAC ops 22-6 410RSU 13-7 CE 11-9

AA834 2110 EA FF 20-9-41 24MU 24-9 403S 3-10 FAAC ROS 29-12 FTR ops 27-4-43

AA835 2111 EA FF 20-9-41 24MU 24-9 403S 3-10 FACB 15-1-42 MM 4-4 368S FTR ops 24-6

AA836 2117 EA LF VB M45M FF 22-9-41 24MU 24-9 411S 11-10 132S 1-9-42 CAC ops 6-12 ROS 91S 25-1-43 122S 12-5 AST 7-7 130S 27-1-44 222S 16-2 276S 11-7 FRU 14-9 SOC 27-9-45

AA837 2118 EA FF 22-9-41 24MU 26-9 501S 12-10 FA FTR 4-11

AA838 2119 EA FF 23-9-41 12MU 24-9 91S 4-10 GAL 31-10 152S 25-5-42 swung on t/o strk obst CE 7-6 SOC 8-6

AA839 2120 EA M45M FF 23-9-41 12MU 27-9 411S 3-10 303S 14-8-42 CB ops 20-3-43 P&P SM 28-3 mods 66S 11-10 340S 15-11 CE ops 5-12-43 AST 611S 26-5-44 53 OTU 6-8 to 5348M 5 SoTT SOC 29-11

AA840 2123 EA FF 24-9-41 12MU 27-9 411S 2-10 FTR ops 8-12

AA841 2125 EA FF 25-9-41 12MU 28-9-41 412S 9-10 72S 14-4-42 121S 24-5 FACB 2-7 ROS CA ops 19-8 335 USA 1-10 121S u/c clpse on ldg CB 2-7 SOC 20-1-43

AA842 2124 EA FF 25-9-41 12MU 27-9 457S 8-12 134S 11-2-42 FACB 6-6 SAL M46 instal 131S 3-2-43 CAC ops 22-6 LMS 315S 19-11 FAAC 27-12 ROS 53 OTU 17-7-44 SOC 18-5-45

AA843 2131 EA FF 26-9-41 12MU 29-9 412S 31-12 FAAC 30-1-42 ROS 350S 24-2 93S 9-8 610S 16-11 131S 25-1-43 310S 30-6 313S 29-7 strk hill cd Wormshill Kent CE 12-9

AA844 2132 EA FF 26-9-41 8MU 28-9 411S 2-10 air coll with AB265 i/sea 28-2-42 SOC 3-3

AA845 2136 EA FF 27-9-41 8MU 28-9 91S 2-10 CE ops 16-4-42

AA846 2137 EA FF 27-9-41 38MU 29-9-41 302S 15-10 FACB 21-3-42 AST 130S 30-9 421S 15-11 412S 3-2-43 602S 19-4 ASTH 4-8 341S 15-11 329S 23-2-44 63S 13-3 275S 25-5 SOC 20-2-45

AA847 2139 EA FF 29-9-41 38MU 3-10 316S 12-10 306S 12-12 e/a CB 17-4-42 ASTEx 306S 16-3-43 FAAC 23-7 ROS 401S 24-9 345S FTR ops 10-7-44

AA848 2140 EA LF LR M45M FF 29-9-41 38MU 1-10 302S 11-10 VSM 13-6-42 316S 29-6 VSM 13-9-43 mods 132S 23-2-44 504S 14-5 63S 31-5 41 OTU 1-2-45 58 OTU 23-4 SOC to 5387M 17-7

AA849 2149 EA M46 FF GP 30-9-41 38MU 1-10 VSM 23-10 mods 54S 30-10 124S 18-11 452S 3-3-42 CE ops 9-3

AA850 2150 EA M45M FF 30-9-41 58MU 1-10 302S 13-10 VSM 31-8-42 mods FAAC 9-4-43 ROS 302S 27-4 132S 28-6 26S 3-4-44 air coll with W3314 ld Old Alresford Hants CE 22-7

AA851 2164 EA M46 FF 5-10-41 609S 7-11 124S 18-11 401S 25-11 452S 1-3-42 CB ops 14-3 457S 22-3 SOC CE 9-5 Super 31-12

AA852 2151 EA FF 30-9-41 39MU 1-10 92S 4-10 417S 6-2-42 242S 18-4 Farn June '42 243S 16-6 FACE 20-7 SOC 27-7

AA853 2157 EA LF LR VB M45M FF GP 1-10-41 39MU 7-10 302S 13-10 FAAC 28-1-42 VSM 22-8 mods FACB 15-5-43 LMS 501S 9-11 350S 31-2 322S 11-1-44 air coll with AR498 i/sea CE 30-4

AA854 2162 EA FF 4-10-41 39MU 7-10 302S 14-10 FA FTR 8-8

AA855 2165 EA FF 5-10-41 39MU 7-10 71S 17-10 FTR ops 27-10

AA856 2170 EA FF 7-10-41 39MU 10-10 302S 14-10 CAC ops 17-4-42 ROS FA FTR 8-9

AA857 2171 EA FF 7-10-41 39MU 10-10 71S 17-10 629S 5-1-42 350S 1-5 i/sea ops CE 9-5

AA858 2174 EA FF 8-10-41 33MU 11-10 316S 17-10 306S 12-12 FAAC 26-2-42 e/a 3-5 ASTEx 309S 31-7 302S 12-9 VSM 7-3-43 fuel syst mods wng stiff 611S 29-8 SOC 6-4-44

AA859 2177 EA FF 9-10-41 33MU 11-10 316S 16-10 306S 12-12 CE ops f/ld nr Prawle Devon 16-3-42 SOC

AA860 2180 EA M45M FF 10-10-41 33MU 11-10 316S 17-10 306S 12-12 FAAC 14-4-42 317S 4-5 CB ops 3-6 AST 67th Obs Grp 18-2-43 303S 16-4-44 57 OTU 2-8 SOC 5-2-45

AA861 2182 EA 10-10-41 39MU 14-10 302S strk obst ldg Harrow CE 21-4-42 SOC

AA862 2211 EA Blackburn II FF GP 21-10-41 39MU 22-10 HAL 6-11 403S 8-6-42 FACB 14-7 SAL VSM 25-8-43 fuel syst & elev mods wng stiff S Type pt Mk III IFF bomb carr 501S 18-1-44 strk by P8324 ldg Hawk CE 5-3-45 AST 290S 10-8-45 R&S refurb to Port 28-4-47

AA863 2181 EA FF GP 10-10-41 39MU 11-10 118S 22-10 FTR 29-1-42

AA864 2190 EA Dirty Girty Vancouver 10-10-41 39MU 15-10 72S 19-10 FTR ops 8-12

AA865 2193 EA Eustace FF GP 13-10-41 39MU 17-10 313S 26-10 FTR ops 10-4-42

AA866 2194 EA Manchester Weatherproof FF 14-10-41 6MU 15-10 401S 23-10 CAC ops 28-12 ROS ASTH RNAS 884S LoS 3-9-42 AST 10-9 hook fitt

AA867 2196 EA FF 15-10-41 6MU 17-10 72S 22-10 FAAC 14-1-42 ROS 222S 14-3 FTR ops 9-4

AA868 2197 EA FF 15-10-41 6MU 17-10 19S 23-10 412S 24-12 CE ops 6-8-42 SOC 11-8

AA869 2202 EA FF GP 17-10-41 6MU 20-10 313S 24-10 FTR ops 18-3-42

AA870 2465 EA FF 4-1-42 6MU 30-1 VSM fuel syst and elev mods wng stiff Mk III IFF bomb carr C&C 20-2 *SS441* 20-3 ME 1-8 SOC 27-10-44

AA871 2214 EA Royal Tunbridge Wells FF GP 22-10-41 9MU 25-10 121S 5-11 SOC 27-12

AA872 2204 EA FF GP 18-10-41 6MU 20-10 316S 26-10 306S 12-12 FACE 9-1-42 AST RNAS 885S LoS 5-9 AST 10-9 hook fitt

AA873 2222 EA VC Manchester Air Cadet FF GP 25-10-41 first prod with C wng (4 × 20mm can) Farn Nov '41 wts and CG load BDn 11-12 ordnance trls. CRD R-RH 14-2-42 con to F Mk IX M61 instal BDn 19-2 gun heat trls. With univ wng a/c could be flown with three load CG. See data on page 141 for details. R-R 29-3 64S AFDU Horn 2-6 service trls R-RH 13-7 M63 instal Rotol Stav 15-4-43 M63 trls with various props. On contract loan to R-R 8-5 M66 instal gen dev. DeH Airscrews 1-1-45 contra props instal. W/o scr 29-1

AA874 2220 EA VC Manchester Scholar FF GP 24-10-41 8MU 26-10 VSM 11-11 mods CFS 17-12 ASTEx 19-4 FAAC 24-7 ROS 306S 8-8 Hull Hand Sq 14-9 VSM 15-6-43 fuel syst & rud mods Super 8-9 131S 27-9 312S 11-10 315S 6-12 61 OTU 13-8-44

AA875 2226 EA Manchester Killer FF 26-10-41 Mart Hth gun heat comb rating, perf trls. BDn 28-10 continuation of gun heat trls. Flow of hot air too fast due to extractor exit for Brownings. Deflector plates deleted cured problem. CRD VA 8-12. BDn 25-4-42 continuation of gun heat trls. Extractors deleted. VSM 19-4-43 fuel syst mods wng stiff 302S 27-8 306S 3-10 12FU 7-1-45 1 OADU 17-1-45 FAF 19-1 GC 2/18

AA876 2223 EA FF GP 25-10-41 during test flight 6-2-42 George Pickering reached a speed of 520mph in a dive. The a/c distin (details on page 142). He was severely inj and never flew again. SOC before delivery, not to be replaced. Airframe to Farn 9-4-42 for acc invest.

AA877 2227 EA Manchester Chairman FF 26-10-41 8MU 26-10 317S 12-11 332S 3-8-42 VSM 28-8 mods M46 instal 334 USA 22-11 AST 25-3-43 131S 3-7 CAC on ops 12-7 ROS 501S 6-1-44 1 TEU 13-8-44 FAAC 2-3-45 ROS 61 OTU 29-3-45 SOC 17-5

AA878 2248 EA VC Manchester Merchant Trader. 1st prod VC. FF 31-10-41 CRD VA 31-10 required for one month for gun testing. BDn 1-4-42 climb, level speed trls at comb rating with (1) VC with univ wing (2 × 20mm & 4 × .303 guns); (2) VC (4 × 20mm); (3) VB. Gun heat trls FAAC 15-10 ROS CRD VA 24-10 wing insufficiently stressed for firing of four can simultaneously. 411S 4-6-43 341S 17-10 453S 27-10 o/s ldg Sumburgh tip onto nose CB LMS 1TEU 17-8-44 SOC 25-10-45

AA879 2230 EA Manchester Civil Service Defender FF 27-10-41 33MU 29-10 616S 8-11 AST 13-1-42 118S 26-4 CB ops 9-5 recat E SOC 9-5 FH67.45

AA880 2231 EA Manchester Smithfield Market FF 27-10-41 33MU 29-10 121S 15-11 GAL 8-7-42 93S 26-9 65S 3-12 FACB 1-4-43 SAL 402S 26-6-43 air coll with AB897 CE 21-2-44

AA881 2232 EA Manchester Corporation Transport FF 28-10-41 33MU 29-10 71S 6-11 FACB 13-6-42 VSM 24-10 fuel syst mods 313S 4-4-43 66S 4-7 340S 15-11 FAAC 1-12 ROS AST 595S 18-12 R&S refurb to Port 3-1-48

AA882 2233 EA Borough of Wanstead & Woodford FF 28-10-41 33MU 29-10 303S 4-11 FACB 24-6-42 AST DeH 17-6-44 41 OTU 22-2-45 631S 21-6-45 SOC 30-8

AA902 2215 CHA FF 22-10-41 33MU 25-10 41S 30-10 CE 23-5-42 SOC 31-8

AA903 2216 CHA FF 22-10-41 33MU 25-10-41 121S 3-11 AST 31-5-42 2USA 3-8 FACE 11-8 SOC 19-8

AA904 2224 CHA FF 25-10-41 38MU 27-10 121S 2-11 GAL 16-6-42 RNAS LoS 5-9 AST 18-9 hook fitt Hens 25-4-44

AA905 2225 CHA FF 25-10-41 38MU 27-10-41 19S 3-11 610S 17-11 AST 26-1-42 RNAS 1-9 AST hook fitt LoS 17-10

AA906 2229 CHA FF 27-10-41 38MU 1-11 74S 25-11 o/s Bally cd CE 25-2-42 SOC 4-3

AA907 2237 CHA FF 28-10-41 38MU 30-10 91S 9-11 HAL 16-12 91S e/fd i/sea off Margate 12-3-42

AA908 2238 CHA FF 29-10-41 38MU 1-11 303S 16-12 GAL 11-6-42 AST 7-7 76MU 31-10 *C o Lil* 8-12 USSR 16-2-43

AA909 2251 CHA FF 31-10-41 38MU 3-11 152S 9-11 313S 23-3-42 VSM 28-4-43 fuel syst mods wng stiff 302S 28-8 FTR ops 8-9 FH362.15

AA910 2252 CHA LF LR VB M45M FF 31-10-41 39MU 2-11 501S 11 11 FACA 8-1-42 ROS 130S 4-5 AST 17-11 412S 4-2-43 602S 19-4 350S 7-10 322S 11-1-44 CAC ops 22-3 ROS 57 OTU 23-7 SOC 1-6-45

AA911 2253 CHA FF 31-10-41 39MU 2-11 92S 22-11 417S 6-2-42 242S 17-4 312S 31-12 66S 10-4-43 234S 12-5 317S 4-10 52 OTU 5-10 FLS Mlfld 2-2-44 SAL 7-4 M46 Instal 12FU 13-1-45 FAF 22-1

AA912 2254 CHA FF 2254 CHA FF 31-10-41 39MU 2-11 412S 11-11 FACB 5-3-42 AST VSM 19-2-43 fuel syst mods wng stiff 308S 27-8 FTR ops 23-9

AA913 2255 CHA FF 31-10-41 6MU 2-11 72S 12-11 FACB 24-12 303S 8-4-42 VSM 2-9 mods 302S 23-12 CB ops 29-3-43 HAL VSM 6-8 fuel syst mods Mk III IFF bomb carr RNDA 26-3-44 hook fid SOC 3-5-45

AA914 2256 CHA FF 31-10-41 6MU 2-4 72S 12-11 VSM fuel syst mods Mk III IFF bomb carr CAC 27-3-42 FACE SOC

AA915 2260 CHA FF 1-11-41 6MU 3-11 72S 12-11 145S 15-11 350S 7-2-42 306S 3-5 64S 31-7 411S 4-2-43 402S 2503 19S 22-4 65S 30-6 130S 15-8 DeH 29-2-44 53 OTU 11-8 527S 17-5-45 RWE WAtton 18-4-46 sold scr 3-9-47

AA916 2263 CHA FF 3-11-41 6MU 15-11 39MU 23-11 145S 17-12 53 OTU FAAC 5-2-45 ROS recat E SOC 25-5

AA917 2266 CHA FF 4-11-41 6MU 27-11 504S 6-1-42 501S 19-10 FTR ops 11-7-43 FH365.40

AA918 2274 CHA M45M FF 7-11-41 33MU 18-11 313S 29-1-42 412S 16-4 2USA 22-8 VSM 4-3-43 fuel syst mods 322S 7-7 FACB 6-1 ROS 222S 1-1-44 VSM 15-3 'Basta' mods 83GSU 22-2-45 2nd TAF 5-7 BAFO Com Wng 19-7 3BRU Ce 12-9

AA919 2275 CHA FF 7-11-41 33MU 22-11 316S 8-12 306S 12-12 FTR ops 14-4-42 FH62.25

AA920 2276 CHA M45M FF 8-11-41 33MU 18-11 72S 30-11 CAC ops 28-2-42 ROS 124S 26-3 71S 31-8 334 USA 1-10 CAC ops 16-11 AST 222S 4-4-43 167S 19-5-43 VSM 15-3-44 fuel syst 'Basta' mods 1S 8-4-44 FAAC 13-4 ROS 402S 5-6 57 OTU 20-7 FACE 18-4-45 SOC 28-4

Shown in its element is this Mk VB.

AA921 2285 CHA FF 11-11-41 33MU 18-11 129S 5-12 CE ops 13-2-42 SOC 28-2

AA922 2200 HPA VB(O) M46 17-10-41 9MU 20-10 121S 1-11 CAC ops 18-3-42 ROs 403S 6-4 FAAC 2-4-43 ROS 3-6S 19-8 118S 25-12 61 OTU FAAC 12-5-45 recat E SOC 19-6

AA923 2210 HPA FF GP 20-10-41 9MU 24-10 616S 8-11 CE ops 6-1-42 SOC 31-1

AA924 2228 HPA FF 27-10-41 9MU 501S 7-11 FACB 1-4-42 ROS 72S 26-4 306S 18-5 133S 29-9 336S 1-10 air coll with Mosquito HJ643 cd nr Atcham Ce 8-8-43

AA925 2212 HPA FF 21-10-41 38MU 24-10 401S 28-10 FTR ops 8-11

AA926 2217 HPA FF GP 23-10-41 38MU 24-10 401S 28-10 FAAC 11-5-42 CE 18-8 SOC FH235.10

AA927 2218 HPA FF 23-10-41 38MU 29-10 19S 3-11 AST 5-7-42 222S 2-9 64S 31-3-43 SOC 17-10-45 to 3779M

AA928 2235 HPA FF 28-10-41 38MU 30-10 452S 9-11 CAC ops 29-03-42 ROS 411S 31-5 FACB 5-8 VSM 4-4-43 fuel syst mods wng stiff 302S 24-8 FTR ops 8-9 FH231.05

AA929 2236 HPA FF 28-10-41 39MU 2-11 316S 12-11 3-6S 12-12 FAAC 25-4-42 ROS 315S CA ops 14-8 317S 5-9 412S 29-6-43 303S 3-12 405RSU 13-7-44 63S 4-10 58 OTU 22-3-45 to 5382M 13-7 SOC 5SoTT 29-11

AA930 2239 HPA FF M45M FF 29-10-41 39MU 30-10 122S 22-11 3-6S 30-4-42 VSM 30-9 fuel syst mods wng stiff 412S 22-4-43 317S 28-6 312S 4-10 277S 17-5-44 SAL 29-7 41 OTU 27-3-45 61 OTU 10-5 603S 21-6 SOC 19-9

AA931 2240 HPA FF M45M FF 29-10-41 6MU 30-10 41S 6-11 FAAC 24-2-42 GAL 19S 24-6 131S 6-9 610S 27-1-43 350S 27-3 316S 5-10 322S 25-11 222S 1-1-44 VSM 23-3-44 fuel syst 'Basta' mods 278S 27-9 53 OTU 22-2-45 FAAC ROS 41 OTU 24-5 SOC 4-7-50

AA932 2246 HPA FF 30-10-41 6MU 2-11 616S 7-11 FAAC 23-8-42 41S 23-8 ASTH con to Sea IB-PA108 VSM 12-3-43 mods and trls

AA933 2257 HEA FF 31-10-41 6MU 7-11 145S 22-11 FACB 1-2-42 350S 10-2 234S 26-9 303S 10-12 FAAC 29-3-43 504S 31-8 313S 22-9 144AF 25-2-44 442S 27-3 VA 28-3 61 OTU 25-6 dvd i/grd nr Wrexham Ce 18-11-44

AA934 2258 HEA FF 31-10-41 6MU 7-11 145S 22-11 350s 11-2-42 CB ops 30-4

AA935 2245 HPA FF 30-10-41 6MU 2-11 452S 12-11 457S 22-3-42 303S 15-4 FACB 7-6 AST VSM 11-3-43 fuel syst mods wng stiff 308S 24-8 FTR ops 23-9 FH262.50

AA936 2247 HPA M45M FF 30-10-41 9MU 2-11 616S 9-11 FACB 27-1-42 VSM 11-6 fuel syst mods 331S 20-8 453S 12-10 222S 31-3-43 167S 19-5 234S 8-1-44 CE ops 6-6

AA937 2269 HPA LF FF 5-11-41 33MU 18-11 64S 5-12 Farn 7-11-42 BDn Nov '42 perf trls with normal and clip wngs. AFDU 1943

AA938 2264 HPA FF 3-11-41 234S 23-11 FACE 18-4-42 SOC 24-4

AA939 2272 HPA FF 6-11-41 38MU 15-11 74S 25-11 232S 8-4-42 FACB 7-5 recat E 15-5

AA940 2273 HPA FF 7-11-41 38MU 15-11 303S 5-12 HAL 13-4-42 FTR ops 27-4

AA941 2289 HPA FF 12-11-41 38MU 20-11 317S 3-12 CE ops 18-12 SOC 27-12

AA942 2280 HPA FF 8-11-41 38MU 15-11 602S 5-12 610S 30-3-42 CE ops 18-4 SOC FH86.0

AA943 2290 HPA FF 12-11-41 39MU 18-11 315S 26-11 317S 5-9-42 412S 29-6-43 M55 instal 61 OTU 28-9-44 FACB 2-4-45 recat E SOC 29-4

AA944 2295 HPA M45M FF 15-11-41 5MU 18-11 234S 8-12 421S 10-6 FAAC 6-7 ROS AST 21-7 41S 7-11 122S 14-3-43 222S 19-5 349S 19-08 26S 12-4-44 CAC ops 7-6 ROS 41 OTU 25-1-45 58 OTU 23-3 FACB 11-5

AA945 2296 HPA FF 15-11-41 5MU 22-11 72S 11-12 306S 22-8-42 FACB 1-10 ROS P&PSM 10-12 350S 12-4-43 504S 20-12 129S 26-1-44 SAL 8-2 501S 27-4 345S 15-8 61 OTU 28-9 SOC 30-7-45

AA946 2309 HPA FF 18-11-41 5MU 22-11 234SS 8-12 FAAC 27-12 ROS CAC ops 21-7-42 ROS 130S 15-8 VSM 13-3-43 fuel syst mods wng stiff 222MU 3-10 *Bar For* 16-10 Port 9-11

AA963 2277 EA FF 8-11-41 9MU 12-11 47MU 21-2-42 spcl committment *Evanger* America Feb '42 exhibited Chicago May stayed in USA

AA964 2241 Dirty Girty FF 29-10-41 118S 7-11 CAC ops 2-2-42 ROS 111S 16-3 HAL 19-11 67th Obs S USAAF 17-5-43 RNDA 21-4-44 hook fitt Hens 2-5

AA965 2242 EA Eustace FF30-10-41 9MU 1-11 616S 9-11 HAL 24-4-42 609S 26-4 616S 28-4 243S 13-7 ASTH 4-10 VSM 27-3-43 fuel syst mods wng stiff 504S 1-7 165S 1-7 CAC ops 16-9 ROS 66S 23-10 340S 15-11 52 OTU 6-2-44 FLS 22-2 o/t fld Lowick N'land CE 2-6

AA966 2243 EA FF 30-10-41 9MU 1-11 616S 15-11 FACB 26-1-42 VSM 11-6 fuel syst mods 4 USA 12-8 332S 8-11 VSM 6-6-43 elev & Rud mods RNDA 26-2-44

AA967 2249 EA Indian Telegraphs FF 31-10-41 24MU 1-11 403S 22-11 M55M instal CB ops 24-2-42 308S 30-7 132S 19-8-43 26S 28-4-44 350S 7-5 501S 8-7 616S 1-2-45 GAL 25-5 M45M instal 151GU 2-8 R&S refurb to Port 28-10-47

AA968 2278 EA LR VC Bombay & Baroda Central Railway FF 8-11-41 24MU 12-11 WAL 1-6-42 M46 instal VSM fuel syst mods 21-6-43 further mods M61 instal 505S CAC ops 4-5 ROS 165S 8-7 AST 4-8 M46 instal 308S 1-10 FTR 13-12

AA969 2250 EA FF 31-10-41 24MU 1-11 54S 2-4-42 167S 31-5 610S 14-10 131S 25-1-43 310S 30-6 313S 29-7 USAAF 22-11 SAL 12-4-44 57 OTU 13-8 577S 14-6-45 to 5596M FAF 23-3-46

AA970 2262 EA FF French Hope FF 31-10-41 24 MU 3-11 312S 30-11 DeH 1-9-42 341S 9-3-43 cd nr Gifford East Lithian struct fail CE 13-3

AA971 2261 EA FF 1-11-41 39MU 3-11 122S 22-11 242S 23-4-42 FAAC 31-5 SAL cd f/f CAC 23-7 SAL RNDA 4-9 AST hook fitt 7-1-43 RNAS 6-8

AA972 2265 EA FF 4-11-41 39MU 6-11 122S 22-11 FACE 15-3-42 ASTH 130S 27-8 VSM 21-5-43 fuel syst mods wng stiff 118S 2-7 64S 25-9 611S 10-7-44 53 OTU 6-8 FACE 30-8

AA973 2267 EA M45M Bihar V FF 5-11-41 CRD Farn 6-11 LOX eng boost trls 39MU 15-12 401S 4-1-42 133S 3-8 306S 22-8 316S 1-10 DeH 5-4-43 122S FAAC 4-7 ROS 234S 15-8 CAC ops 19-8 HAL 23-8 for con 501S 24-11 BDn 10-2-44 'Rogue aircraft' ails made a/c skid at speeds in excess of 230 mph

AA974 2268 EA FF 5-11-41 39MU 6-11 74S 25-11 232S 8-4-42 ASt 8-12 66S 19-4-43 313 4-7 HAL 11-7 FAAC 23-7 COAL for con 24-12 RNAS Hens 11-4-44

AA975 2279 EA The Boy David FF 8-11-41 24 MU 12-11 610S 22-3-42 FAAC 4-5 recat E

AA976 2291 LF VC Grand Hotel Manchester FF 12-11-41 24MU 27-11 91S 14-3-32 VSM 9-6-43 fuel syst elev & rud mods Mk III IFF S type pt bomb carr 130S 25-1-44 222S 16-1 322S 7-3 CAC ops ROS SOC 10-1-46 M45M and M46 instal during service career

AA977 2301 EA VC FF 5-11-41 24MU 7-12 WAL 27-6-42 M46 instal VSM 27-7-43 fuel syst elev & rud mods Mk III IFF 340S 6-12 FLS 28-2-44 FACB 19-8 HAL 81 OTU 5-5-45 R&S 4-10-46

AA978 2283 EA A N Kenion II FF 10-11-41 24MU 12-11 350S 23-2-42 CAC ops 29-5 ROS cd on f/f 6-9 AST VSM 8-10 M46 instal fuel syst mods 452S 5-7-43 275S 30-4-44 CAC ops 8-4 ROS recat E SOC 26-3-45

AA979 2284 EA Yaounda FF 11-11-41 24MU 12-11 129S 15-12 FACB 30-12 AST 403S 2-4-42 VSM 9-3-43 fuel syst mods wng stiff 610S 25-9 602S 4-3-44 18S 13-3 SAL 26-9 M55MA instal 290S 15-3-45 R&S refurb to Port 17-7-47

AA980 2302 EA Kaapstad VI VC FF 15-11-41 5MU 27-11 WAL 2-6-42 M46 instal R-RH 22-4 M61 instal VSM 26-1-43 fuel syst mods 402S 16-5 CE ops 4-6

AA981 2292 Kolhapur IF 14-11-41 20MU 22-11 234S 8-12 CAC ops 5-4-42 ROS WAL 30-4 SOC 9-5

AA982 2307 EA City of Liverpool FF 17-11-41 8MU 22-11 457S 16-12 452S 23-3-42 93S 4-6 AST 11-11 65S 12-3-43 130S 31-3 349S 19-7 67Grp USAAF 6-1-44 SAL 12-4 527S 18-8 RWE Watton 18-4-46 sold H Bath 27-10-49

AB133 2286 CHA FF 11-11-41 38 MU 20-11 65S 27-11 CAC ops 1-6-42 AST 602S 1-9 164S 11-9 341S 1-2-43 340S 23-3 222MU 24-10 *Dromore* 9-1-44 Port 28-1

AB134 2287 CHA FF 12-11-41 38 MU 20-11 74S 25-11 232S 8-4-42 CAC 15-4

AB135 2288 CHA FF 12-11-41 38 MU 21-11 317S 7-12 CB ops 7-3-42 WAL 504S 14-9 FACE 27-9 FH20.20 S&H 15-10 recat E 19-10

AB136 2293 CHA FF 14-11-41 38MU 20-11 *SS441* 20-3-42 Malta 1-7 145S dam ops 21-9 FTR ops ops 18-3-43

AB137 2305 CHA FF 15-11-41 38MU 27-11 131S 11-12 CAC ops 4-4-42 ROS mr CE 24/4

AB138 2294 CHA FF 15-11-41 33MU 18-11 457S 5-12 452S 23-3-42 93S 4-6 FAAC 17-9 VSM 24-3-43 fuel syst elev & Rud mods Mk III IFF bomb carr 316S 22-11 63S 1-5-44 AST 9-6 61S 21-6-45 FAAC 2-8 recat E SOC 16-8

AB139 2231 CHA VC FF 23-11-41 33MU 30-11 WAL 5-5-42 M46 instal VSM 13-6 fuel syst mods. MacLaren, Heston 1-6-43 mods HAL 28-10-44 CGS 23-3-45 to 5589M FAF 16-8-46

A58-104 and-173 of RAAF.

White-tailed Mk Vs in SEAC markings. Note long-range tanks.

AB140 2311 CHA FF 19-11-41 33MU 25-11 457S 16-12 452S 23-3-42 93S 4-6 SAL 9-8 VSM 3-4-43 fuel syst mods wng stiff 66S 25-7 340S 15-11 239S 16-2-44 63S 13-3 AST 14-3 57 OTU 6-2-45 595S 21-6 to 5590M FAF 16-3-46

AB141 2312 CHA M45M FF 20-11-41 39MU 23-11 504S 4-1-42 S&H 9-4 401S 12-3-43 CA ops recat E 350S 9-10 322S 11-1-44 FAAC 28-2-44 ROS 26S 10-6 FACE 19-9

AB142 2313 CHA FF 20-11-41 6MU 27-11 457S 16-12 452S 3-1-42 93S 4-6 FACA 12-6 ROS 131S 16-2-43 310S 310S 3-7 313S 31-7 52OTU 31-1-44 FLS Mlfld 10-2-44 57 OTU 12-10 SOC 29-11-45

AB143 2317 HPA LR VB FF 20-11-43 39MU 25-11 123S 10-1-42 167S 10-4 165S 27-5 FACB 4-6 SAL VSM 14-5-43 fuel syst mods wng stiff 118S 29-6 64S 25-9 CE ops 26-7-44

AB144 2310 HPA FF 19-11-41 39MU 25-11 603S 11-12 332S 8-4-42 FAAC 21-5 222S 2-9 air coll with AR274 cd Dreghorn Ayrs CE 8-1-43 FH266.40

AB145 2322 HPA FF 21-11-41 37MU 27-11 82MU 20-2-42 *SS437* 11-3- Malta 1-7 206S FA 20-4

AB146 2323 HPA FF 22-11-41 37MU 27-11 82MU 20-2-42 *SS437* 11-3 Malta 1-7 206S SOC 27/9

AB147 2324 HPA FF 22-11-41 37MU 26-11 82MU 27-2-42 Tak 15-3 Malta 1-7 CE SOC 13-9-45

AB148 2334 HPA FF 25-11-41 6MU 27-11 457S 16-12 93S 4-6-42 FACB 26-7 AST 416S 24-1-43 aban cd Cuckfield Sussex 16-3

AB149 2344 HPA FF 27-11-41 6MU 9-12 505S 4-1-42 e/fd t/o w/u ldg nr Kirkistown CB 7-6 S&H SOC 12-6 FH88.00

AB150 2345 HPA FF 27-11-41 6MU 5-12 72S 16-12 VA mr 18-4-42 FTR ops 29-5 FH37.20

AB151 2353 HPA FF 29-11-41 8MU 8-12 AST 15-12 611S 11-2-42 305S 7-5 e/fd f/ld nr Ossington Notts CE 1-8 SAL recat E 8-9

AB152 2359 HPA FF 30-11-41 8MU 8-12 124S 16-12 FAAC 25-4-42 VA 124S 5-5 CE 28-5 AST SOC 6-6 FH118.20

AB167 2306 EA Kolhapur II FF 15-11-41 37MU 24-11 122S 15-3-42 FACB 18-5 ROS BDn trls with all-copper, baked QED & normal rad. Former marginally superior for trop operation. BDn 8-5-43 arrived with M50 instal to begin 100 hr intns fly to test the cropped supercharger impeller. These trls had started with the eng in W3228, and 14hr 10min had been completed before the Merlin was trans to AB167. After another 62hr 55mins the eng was con to M45M standards by removal ofneg G carb and fuel de-aerator. f/ld during trls due to fuel starvation. FAAC 4-2-44 R-RH 23-2 AST 7-3 63S 12-12 151RU 1-2-45 2nd TAF C Sq 3-5-45 2GSU 7-6 R&S 30-8-46

AB168 2363 EA FF 30-11-41 37MU 7-12 82MU 27-2-42 *SS437* 12/3 Malta 1-7 NAASC 1-11-43 ME 28-4-45 SOC 29-8-46

AB169 2303 EA VC weather trls ROS 10-11 AFDU 27-12 FAAC 24-5-44 ROS AST 19-11 63S 14-12 8 OTU 13-2-45 SOC 29-11

AB170 2556 EA VC FF 4-2-42 39MU 11-2 91S 13-3 dam ops 15-4-42 ROS dam by Spits o/t ldg 23-5 AST M46 instal VSM 28-3-43 fuel syst mods 610S 6-7 611S 3-8 DeH 17-4-44 CGS 9-10 Mar Cam 8-11-45 SOC

AB171 2314 EA FF 20-11-41 39MU 23-11 457S 11-12 452S 23-3-42 FACE 7-5 AST SOC FH117.50

AB172 2308 EA FF 18-11-41 39MU 23-11 312S 1-12 struct fail at h/a Pilot thrown clear cd Otterton Devon CE 29-6-42 SOC 9-7

AB173 2315 EA FF 20-11-41 39MU 23-11 145S 9-1-42 350S 10-2 FTR ops 1-6

AB174 2319 EA VC FF 21-11-41 8MU 27-11 303S 15-3-42 FAAC 4-9 AST VSM 6-7-43 fuel syst elev & rud mods Mk III IFF 313S 21-10 144AF 25-2-44 442S 27-2 56 OTU 30-3 1TEU 9-5 spun i/grd nr Farnell Angus 9-5

AB175 2316 EA FF 20-11-41 8MU 22-11 457S 9-12 452S 23-3-42 93S 4-6 SAL 28-8 VSM 28-2-43 fuel syst mods wng stiff 308S 18-8 349S 29-10 FTR ops 11-2-44

AB177 2384 EA ISP FF 7-12-41 39MU 9-12 123S 5-1-42 167S 16-4 t/o in coarse pitch Scorton cd CE 14-5 SOC 19-5

AB178 2332 EA FF 23-11-41 39MU 25-11 AFDU 16-12 130S 2-7-42 FACB 2-9 AST VA 15-6-43 fuel syst mods 317S 26-8 312S 4-10 313S 25-10 144AF 25-2-44 441S 27-2 56 OTU 30-3 FACB recat E SOC 15-2-45

AB179 2327 EA FF 22-11-41 39MU 25-11 501S 5-12 e/td o/r w/u ldg nr Worth Matravers Dorset CE 25-4-42 ASTE SOC 1-5

AB180 2328 EA LF LR M45M FF 22-11-41 39MU 25-11 308S 9-12 316S 13-12 FAAC 5-1-42 VSM 18-6 mods 306S 27-3-43 FAAC 11-6 AST 350S 9-10 322S 1-2-44 277S 2-9 SOC 17-2-45

AB181 2339 EA One From Avro FF 26-11-41 39MU 5-12 411S 10-12 165S 12-4-42 312S 19-9 FAAC 24-9 ROS Farn June '42 tail buffetting trls AST 11-5-43 con to Sea IB-NX943

AB182 2340 EA VC FF 27-11-41 33MU 30-11 306S 19-3-42 Farn June '42 hand trls FTR ops 14-6 FH13-20

AB183 2335 EA M45M FF 25-11-41 33MU 30-11 411S 11-12 CB ops 24-3-42 303S 29-7 CB ops 25-8 HAL 350S 25-8 43 FAAC 25-11 ROS 501S 30-3-44 234S 30-4 CB ops 14-6 AST Sold H Bath 27-10-49

AB184 2346 EA M45M Cameroon Francais FF 28-11-41 33MU 30-11 603S 11-12 332S 18-4-42 CA ops 10-8 ASTH 501S 29-1-43 DeH 14-11 26S 26-6-44 595S 18-1-45 SOC 6-9

AB185 2336 EA Kolhapur III FF 25-11-41 602S 7-12 ROS 22-2-42 457S 2-4 FAAC 23-5 ROS 402S 10-7 350S 28-8 485S 18-9 19S 1-7-43 411S 28-8 FACE 21-5-44

AB186 2343 EA M45M FF 27-11-41 Crd VA 1-12 BDn 6-10-42 trls with enlarged elev horn balance mod improved hand. M46 instal 7-3-43 trls of Westland convex elev surfaces. Good in high speed dives and turns, lack of response at lower particularly when flaps lowered. ASTE 23-3 M50M instal BDn Apl '43 speed trls with new eng. VSM 3-7 mods 501S 25-12 CAC ops 22-2-44 ROS FAAC 23-3 ROS 61 OTU 13-8 631S 21-6-45 SOC 17-9

AB187 2347 EA FF 29-11-41 129S 6-12 452S 1-3-42 FTR ops 29-3

AB188 2348 EA VC Forestry Commission FF 29-11-41 609S 11-12 FACE 22-1-42 SOC

AB189 2355 EA FF 30-11-41 33MU 5-12 C&C 22-2-42 ME 1-7-43 Malta CE 13-9-45 SOC

AB190 2364 EA FF 30-11-41 6MU 5-12 145S 17-12 ROS 25-1-42 616S 14-2 o/s night ldg Witt CB 3-4 AST RNAS LoS 5-9 AST 18-9 hook fitt RNAS Mach 10-10

AB191 2365 EA VC FF 1-12-41 6MU 5-12 FACB 19-12 AST WAL 26-5-42 M46 instal VSM fuel syst mods CRD Farn 21-9 ails trls AFDU 1-8-43 BDn Mar '43 ails cables replaced by push/pull rods and cord fitt on top surface of port ails trls revealed improved positive feel less up-float on ails andmore response at all attitudes. 82MU 28-9 *Emp Orto* 6-10 Port 19-10

AB192 2366 EA Oganilil FF 1-12-41 6MU 5-12 129S 26-12 CB ops 26-3-42 306S 4-7 HAL 22-8 36S 29-9 336S USA to 4462M 7SoTT 6-5-44

AB193 2368 EA FF 3-12-41 6MU 5-12 504S 6-1-42 FACB 29-9 SAL VSM 20-4-43 mods 129S 1-7 453S 17-7 341S 3-11 52 OTU 25-1-44 FLS 2-2 S&H 7-10 FCC North 22-2-45 to 5443M StA 9-8

AB194 2369 EA FF 3-12-41 6MU 5-12 72S 16-12 FAAC 9-1-42 ROS 111S 28-2 FAAC 15-7 ROS 232S 15-8 SAL 18-11 VSM 28-3-43 fuel syst mods wing stiff 402S 11-6 FAAC 9-8 ROS 64S 26-10 HAL 6-7-44 FACB 1687 Flt hit vehicle taxy 6-4-46 recat E SOC 24-4

AB195 2387 EA CWS Defiant FF 10-12-41 6MU 12-12 452S 28-12 FACE 4-1-42 i/sea SOC 24-1

AB196 2392 EA VC FF 11-12-41 CRD Contract R-RH 15-12-41 con to F Mk IX proto Merlin 61. F/F as Mk IX 27-3-42 WDn 27-4 R-R 20-6 Farn 3-7-43 eng/airframe resonance trls with mock-up eng. Also M61 driving flywheel. comp tests with BR138. Both a/c had vibbrograph sessions. HAL 303S 21-7 AST 28-7 308S 16-11 80S FAAC 29-5-44 AST CE 10-7

AB197 2377 EA VC FF 5-12-41 CRD Contract R-RH 7-12 con to 2nd protoMer 60. F/F as Mk IX 26-2-42. BDn 14-5 M61 instal as FIXC. Wt and CG load with 5 × 17.5lb ballast wts on bar nr tail wheel. Tare 5749lb t/o 7445lb Maint trls. There were problems with tyre failures and movement of oleo legs whch had problems absorbing ldg loads. After 186 land the u/c would not fully retract in flight as the port leg rake had moved forward 1¼in. Super pointed out that prod models would have different layout. A series of gun heat trls started on 23-12, the first to compare syst of Mks VII and IX with Brownings heated via intensifier exhaust tubes and can via eng coolant rad. Heat insufficient. Second tests 12-6-43, heat tests with arma as for Mk VIII. Syst heat via twin eng rads. The four can did not get enough heat. Third tests 3-8 with RAE exprl DC heat. See illustration page 168. Fourth tests 6-7-44 Continuation of RAE CD heat showed no advantage overnormal syst. Fifth, and final tests 12-7. Spcl manifolds fitt wing rads. WDn 14-0 SAL SOC 25-4-45

AB198 2393 EA Central provinces & Berar IV FF 11-12-41 5MU 12-12 134S 17-1-42 81S 4-4 452S 5-5 93S 4-6 303S 10-6 AST 5-12 VSM 8-3-43 fuel syst mods wng stiff 412S 18-6 317S 28-6 312S 4-10 306S 4-2-44 AST 18-5 1652CU 29-11 e/fd on t/o w/u ldg CB 2-5-45 recat C SOC 14-5

AB199 2391 EA Mesopatamia FF 11-12-41 5MU 16-12 71S 2-2-42 dam ops 19-8 VSM 6-10 fuel syst mods 129S 12-3-43 453S 17-7 341S 3-11 AST 11-11 VSM 20-11 M46 instal USAAF 9-5-44 31St Trans Grp 9-7 11FU 4-1-45 1 OADU 8-1 FAF 19-1 GC 2/18

AB201 2398 EA Dorothy of Great Britain and the Empire FF 13-12-41 5MU 15-12 65S 4-1-42 FACB 3-4 222S 28-8 64S 31-3043 FACA 23-5 COAL for con 8-12 RNDA 22-3-44 SOC 27-9-45

AB202 2407 EA VC Tudokkattai Nagarathars FF 18-12-41 8MU 24-12 S HQ N Wld 14-3-42 GAL 12-9 M46 instal VA 29-5-43 322S 22-7 308S 30-7 349S 29-10 CB ops 25-1-44 DeH 57 OTU 12-2-45 567S 7-6 to 5597M 23-8 FAF 26-3-46

AB203 2399 EA M45M FF 13-12-41 8MU 15-12 123S 29-12 167S 17-4-42 165S 29-5 65S 23-9 232S 2-10 SAL 11-12 VSM 19-4-43 fuel syst mods wng stiff 416S 24-6 CB ops 21-9 132S 12-2-44 504S 15-3 310S 15-7 strk EP 485 while ldg Haw CB 8-9 AST 290S 1-2-45 R&s refurb tp Port

AB204 2408 EA VC FF 18-12-41 8MU 24-12 130S 13-3-42 CA ops 19-8 P&P SM 19-10 M46 instal fuel syst mods 308S FACB 22-10-43 442S 7-3-44 26S 25-3 SAL 3-6 CGS 3-10 SOC 27-12-45

AB205 2400 EA FF 13-12-41 CRD VA 13-12 778S 24-1-42 AST con to Sea IB. Farn 14-1-43 catapult trls. Replacement for AB986 March land flaps at different settings for t/o Apl, clear vision cockpit trls WDn. Farn Jan '44 positional error. June braking tail parachute designed and instal by fabric shop. Emrgcy release gear assembled and instal in F.1.E sheds. Initially complete fail as first three models burst on streaming at 120 mph. The 7ft dia model fitt with new fus attachment and strengthened panels. Streamed on 25 & 50ft cables & attached to rear star fus. During trls a/c yawed violently to port. Scheme aband as unsuitable as deck land aid. Used in trls with a Fairey Barracuda to explore effects of carrier wind wake on a/c ldg. Trls on *Pret Cast*. The Seafire completed many successful ldg but Barracuda fared badly. A hydrofoil was attached to Seafire's arrester hook as a means of keeping tail down in the event of ditching.

AB206 2409 EA Bihar VI FF 18-12-41 8MU 2-1-42 121S 8-1 CE ops 8-3 SOC 28-3

AB207 2410 EA Bihar VII FF 18-12-41 33MU 2-1-42 C&C 8-1 *SS441* 20-3 FTR ops 25-10

AB208 2415 EA VC Lancastria Avenger I FF 20-12-41 33MU 2-1-42 M61 instal WAL 5-5 M46 instal P&P SM 14-6 fuel syst elev & rud mods Mk III IFF S type pt FACA 21-7 VSM 19-2-44 M45M instal 'Basta' mods bomb cart 6MU 20-4 130S 22-5 air coll with W3128 i/sea nr IoW 16-6

AB209 2417 EA Lancastria Avenger IV FF 20-12-41 9MU 6-1-42 611S 31-1 LMS 22-2 131S 26-4 AST 22-8 FACA 30-8 132S 22-12 411S 15-5-43 ROS 27-7 126 AF 10-8 341S 17-10 602S 25-1-44 FAAC 5-2-44 ROS AST 7-5 CGS 2-10 MFS 25-10-45 SOC 28-10

AB210 2416 EA LR VC Lancastria Avenger V FF 20-12-41 9MU 24-12 WAL 5-5-42 M46 instal VSM 15-6 fuel syst mods 29-1-43 M45M instal plus mods 315S 1-7 611S 6-7 AST 2-5-44 CGS 9-10 FACB 16-4-45 recat E SOC 23-4

AB212 2421 EA VC Lancastria Avenger III FF 22-12-41 9MU 24-12 WAL 5-5-42 M46 instal 66S 4-6 310S 26-7 306S 7-10 FAAC 19-1-44 53 OTU 2-9 616S 16-3-45 PAL 4-9 SOC 10-9

AB213 2422 EA M45M Lancastria Avenger II FF 22-12-41 CRD VA 22-12-41 9MU 24-12 BDn 23-4-42 trls of split flaps as brake flaps. Valve in cockpit ensured flaps lowered together. Operational up to 280mph. CRD WD 9-7 VSM 23-11 fuel syst mods wng stiff 129S 15-5-43 453S 17-7 strk BL968 ldg Bradwell Bay CAC ROS COAL 8-12 hook fitt RNDA 14-3-44 Hens 28-3

AB214 2435 EA VC FF 27-12-41 9MU 30-4-42 WAL 3-6 M46 instal VSM 30-7 fuel syst & rud mods Mk III IFF FLS Mlfld 11-2-44 57 OTU 14-9 FAAC SOC 25-10-45 M61 was instal during service career

AB215 2423 EA FF 22-12-41 24MU 2-1-42 315S 4-5 317S 5-9 412S 29-6-43 313S 4-7 126S 10-8 RNDA 21-2-44 COAL 30-4 83GSU 6-7 WDn 13-7

AB216 2437 EA VC FF 28-12-41 24MU 2-1-42 91S 15-3 CB ops 2-6-43 GAL VSM 30-3 fuel syst mods Mal WW 25-5 instal of tail-wheel tow attachment. CRD A&AEE Sherburn in Elmet 9-8 Farn 16-9 form trls with JK940 towing Hotspur BT903. continued trls with JK940 as twin in double tow of Hotspur. Oct weather trls and mechanic release of Hotspur BT901 during double tow with JK940. Duplication of trls with Horsa LG927. Horsa was then towed by Beaufighter fitt with Monica III to test emmissions. AB216 formated on Beaufighter to assess possibility of twin tow. 61 OTU 8-9 B Hill for service trls as Hotspur tug. RAF code name for exp was 'Hasty-Hitch'. Trls were to assess validity of towing Hotspur carrying ground crew and equip to forward airfields during advance through France. Eng fire in flight w/u ldg dbf nr Sleap Salop 2-2-45 SOC 9-2

AB240 2320 CHA M45M FF 21-11-41 39MU 23-11 504S 28-12 SAL 18-2-42 215S 4-5 167S 12-7 swg off runay on t/o o/t CB 24-10 CE 1-11 SAL 26S 6-4-44 CE ops 13-6

AB241 2321 CHA FF 21-11-41 6MU 27-11 315S 10-12 317S 5-9-42 AST 11-4-43 VSM 4-7 fuel syst mods Mk III IFF S type pt 341S 24-12-43 FLS 3-4-44 2TEU 17-6 61 OTU 28-9 AST 5-6-45 SOC 30-7

AB242 2329 CHA FF 22-11-41 6MU 27-11 131S 10-12 strk water tower Llanb CE 10-3-42

AB243 2330 CHA FF 22-11-41 39MU 25-11 457S 9-12 452S 23-3-42 FAAC 16-4 SOC CE FH 31.0

AB244 2333 CHA FF 25-11-41 8MU 30-11 457S 9-12 452S 23-3-42 air coll with BL251 CE SOC 8-5-42

AB245 2337 CHA FF 26-11-41 8MU 30-11 457S 9-12 FAAC 24-3-42 ROS 452S 16-4 93S 4-6 DeH 17-10 303S 4-4-43 315S 6-6 19S 26-6 hit grd NE of Ballymena Co Antrim Ce 22-8

AB246 2338 CHA FF 26-11-41 8MU 30-11 616S 8-2-42 tyre burst on t/o u/c clpse Witt CE 2-6 AST SOC 13-6

AB247 2349 CHA FF 29-11-41 39MU 5-12 315S 12-12 mr CE 9-4-42

AB248 2350 CHA FF 29-11-41 39MU 5-12 91S 14-3-42 315S 13-5 CB ops 13-5 SOC CE 23-5

AB249 2351 CHA FF 29-11-41 39MU 5-12 145S 17-12 1PRU e/td os badly dam 25-3-42 412S 14-4 FAAC 18-5 ROS 132S 19-9 167S 3-10 610S 14-10 131S 25-1-43 310S 30-6 313S 29-7 FACB 6-8 SAL 315S 4-3-44 41 OTU 20-1-45 58 OTU 22-3 t/o in coarse pitch cd/ldg Tedmore Salop CE 15-5 SOC 17-5

AB250 2352 CHA FF 29-11-41 38MU 7-12 308S 28-1-42 FACE 19-5 SOC 21-5

AB251 2356 CHA FF 30-11-41 38MU 7-12 501S 6-1-42 FTR ops 23/4

AB252 2362 CHA FF 30-11-41 38MU 26-2-42 Tak 15-3 Malta 145S 1-7 NAASC 31-10-43 ME 26-1-45 SOC 29-8-46

AB253 2367 CHA FF 1-12-41 38MU 7-12 C&C 20-2-42 *SS441* 20-3 ASTH 10-5 ME FAC3 1METS 26-1-43

AB254 2381 CHA VC FF 6-12-41 38MU 13-12 R-R 22-4-42 M61 instal WAL 27-5 M46 instal VSM 26-2-43 fuel syst mods 341S FAAC 19-4 504S 1-5 165S 8-7 308S 10-10 coll with R7292 on ldg CE Hawk 2-11

AB255 2371 CHA FF 4-12-41 39MU 8-12 411S 11-1-42 FAAC 28-1 ROS 129S 20-2 ASTH CE17-4

AB256 2376 CHA Contract 4336(c)23C FF 5-12-41 39MU 8-12 GA CAC 9-12 67th Obs Grp 9-2-43 222MU 4-1-44 CRD WAL 17-5 mods to Prof Hill's designs. Holes in upper & lower tailplane surfaces latter connected to servo cylinder in rear fus Second version servo assist elev fitt late 1945 for boundary layer exp. Sold scp Thompson & Taylor

AB257 2380 CHA FF 6-12-41 39MU 8-12 310S 29-12 CB ops 3-2-42 ASTH 4USA 9-8 FACE 10-9

AB258 2382 CHA FF 6-12-41 39MU 8-12 72S 28-12 Farn for press cabin trls FTR ops 4-4-42 FH54.55

AB259 2385 CHA FF 7-12-41 39MU 12-12 123S 6-1-42 167S 15-4 165S 27-5 65S 23-9 CAC ops 102-43 ROS 610S 19-2 350S 27-3 316S 5-10 234S 27-11 VSM 25-1-44 fuel syst mods SAL 14-4 1 AGS 3-2-45 PAL 8-9 SOC 13-9

AB260 2527 FF 25-1-42 8MU 28-1 118S 8-3 452S 28-2

457S 22-3 611S 30-5 72S 4-8 504S 21-6-43 165S 1-7 FTR ops 31-7 FH250.50

AB261 2530 M46 FF 26-1-42 8MU 15-2 AST con to Sea IB-MB337 6-3

AB262 2510 CHA VBT FF 24-1-42 8MU 30-1 C&C 3-2 *C Hawk* 7-3 flown off Eagle to Malta dam in Kalafram workshop SOC 11-4

AB263 2511 VBT FF 24-1-42 8MU 4-2 C&C 10-2 *Queen V* 2-3 Malta 1-4 SOC 6-5

AB264 2519 CHA FF 24-1-42 30-1 C&C 3-2 *C Hawk* 15-2 Malta 7-3 C2 ops 3-5-43 NWA USAAF 1-10 ME 31-8-44

AB265 2354 HPA FF 29-11-41 39MU 5-12 411S 10-12 FAAC 17-12 ROS air coll with AA844 Mans CB 28-2 WAL M46 instal 222S 11-3-43 64S 31-3 118S 28-8 AST 9-5-44 CGS 5-10 nto 5541M StA 4-8-45 recat E 7-7-48

AB266 2361 HPA FF 30-11-41 39MU 8-12 616S 15-12 CBAF 6-1-42 FACE 1-5 SOC FH139.0

AB267 2370 HPA FF 3-12-41 33MU 5-12 134S 13-4-42 81S 4-4 412S 18-5 strk by BM121 in night ldg CE 11-6 SOC AST 18-6

AB268 2372 HPA FF 5-12-41 33MU 8-12 411S 9-1 FTR ops 24-3

AB269 2373 HPA FF 5-12-41 33MU 8-12 603S 9-1-42 332S 8-4 FTR ops 19-8

AB270 2378 HPA FF 6-12 41 33MU8-12 134S 13-1-42 152S 20-5 coll with AD359 ldg at Eglington CE 27-7 SOC 5-8

AB271 2383 HPA LF VB M45M FF 6-12-41 33MU 13-12 123S 28-12 167S 15-4 165S 27-5 133S 29-9 336S 1-10 FACB 16-11 AST VSM 8-5-43 fuel syst mods wng stiff 416S FAAC 2-7 ROS 130S 11-2-44 222S 16-2 322S 17-3 303 17-4 CE ops 23-6

AB272 2388 HPAFF 10-12-41 33MU 13-12 123S 29-12 CE ops 13-2-42 167S 15-4 165S 27-5 65S 23-9 91S 31-12 303S 1-5-43 315S 6-6-43 19S 26-6 FAAC 15-5-44 130S 6-7 303S 23-11 41 OTU 19-4-45 SOC 19-6

AB273 2389 HPA FF 10-12-41 33MU 13-12 308S 28-1-42 FACE 9-2 AST VSM 19-10 fuel syst mods COAL 26-6-43 hook fitt RNDA 18-1-44

AB274 2390 HPA FF 11-12-41 33MU 13-12 312S 31-1-42 317S 17-8 315S 9-9 VSM 30-9 fuel syst mods AST 1-12 411S 4-2-43 402S 25-3 19S 26-4 65S dam ops 13-6 306S u/c clpse on t/o hit three USAAF a/c 26-11

AB275 2396 HPA M45M FF 12-12-41 33MU 15-12 164S 9-1-42 81S 5-4 41S 3-5 FAAC 31-5 ROS VSM 9-9 mods 308S 31-12 FAAC 26-3-43 501S 27-8 DeH 14-11 402S 28-6-44 CAC ops 6-7 ROS 53 OTU 14-10 631S 21-6-45 SOC 17-9

AB276 2397 HPA M45M FF 13-12-44 33MU 15-12 313S 13-1-42 91S 8-6 VSM 18-6 fuel syst mods wng stiff CAC ops 19-12 AST 610S 30-6-43 CAC ops 9-9 350S 10-4-44 57 OTU 15-7 595S 21-6-45 SOC 6-5-49

AB277 2403 HPA FF 16-12-41 33MU 2-1-42 C&C 8-2 *SS441* 20-3 SOC 23-9

AB278 2404 HPA FF 17-12-41 24MU 23-12 316S 5-6-42 311S 19-3-43 306S 27-3 ROS 3-10 to 4467M 5SoTT 3-12

AB279 2411 HPA M45M FF 19-12-41 24MU 24-12 222S 5-3-42 FAAC 21-7 ROS 332S 14-9 CAC ops 1-11 ROS 91S 10-11 65S 1-5-43 308S 17-5 501S 27-8 HAL 26-10 234S 30-4-44 57 OTU 5-10 SOC CE 1-11-46

AB280 2412 HPA FF 20-12-41 8MU 2-1-42 124S 9-1 FACE 19-4-43 SOC

AB281 2413 HPA FF 20-12-41 8MU 2-1-42 411S 8-1 FTR ops 24-3

AB282 2414 HPA FF 20-12-41 8MU 5-1-42 611S 7-2 CAC ops 13-3 ROS 242S 2-6 SAL 27-10 VSM 26-4-43 fuel syst mods wng stiff 131S 3-7 e/fd f/ld nr Redhill Surrey CE 8-9

AB283 2425 HPA FF 23-12-41 8MU 24-12 72S 2-1-42 FACB 10-2 ASTH 411S 19-5 FACE 14-12 FH256.05

AB284 2444 HPA LR VB FF 29-12-41 8MU 2-1-42 91S 9-1 CB ops 24-3 ASTH 41S 23-8 VSM 9-3-43 mods 611S 1-7 CAC ops 17-8 ROS 416S 5-9 FTR ops26-11 FH186.00

AB320 24188 CHA VBT FF 13-12-41 CRD VA con to prot trop VB.BDn 25-2-42 comp trop trls with BP866 (VBT) Trls of fuel syst with 90gal o/ld tank, including jet Tank left a/c cleanly but pilot was unaware of event. Recommended that red light in cockpit be fit Second trls May'42. Positional error and perf with and without o/ld tank. Third trls 10-5-42 wt and CG load with o/ld tank tare 5175lb. T/o 7482lb. Fourth trls fuel cons with and without o.ld tank. Sixth trls. T/o with and without o/ld tank 215MU 19-7-42 *Emp Puma* 17-8 Tak 23-7 ME 1-12 SOC after com 27-4-43

AB321 2419 CHA VBT FF 15-12-41 6MU 1-1-42 C&C 10-1 *Conak* 8-3 Tak ME 9-5 RHAF 25-4-46

AB322 2406 VBT FF 18-12-41 6MU 1-1-42 C&C 12-1 *Laysian* 25-2 Tak ME 9-6 FTR ops 29-6

AB323 2432 CHA VBT FF 26-12-41 6MU 1-1-32 *Cape Hawk* 10-1 ME 9-6 SOC 1-10

AB324 2420 CHA VBT FF 18-12-41 6MU 1-1-42 C&C 10-1 ME 3-5 RHAF 25-4-46

AB325 2424 CHA VBT FF 22-12-41 6MU 1-1-42 C&C 10-1 *Conak* 8-3 Tak ME 10-6 FACB25-7 SOC CE 6-8

AB326 2431 CHA VBT FF 26-12-41 C&C 10-1 *Laysian* 25-2 Tak ME 9-5 FTR ops 23-6

AB327 2436 CHA VBT FF 27-12-41 6MU 10-1-42 C&C 26-1 *Queen V* 2-3 ME 601S 21-4 s/dn F/O Home inj 22-7

AB328 2433 CHGA VBT FF 27-12-41 6MU 10-1-42 C&C 26-1 *Conak* 8-3 Tak ME 5-11 f/f NAAF 1-11-43 SE 12-12-44

AB329 2439 CHA VBT FF 28-12-41 6MU 10-1-41 C&C 26-1 *Cape Hawk* Gib 15-2 fl/o *Eagle* to Malta 7-3 SOC 6-5

AB330 2443 CHGA VBT FF 29-12-41 8MU 4-1-42 C&C 26-1 *Cape Hawk* Gib 15-2 fl/o *Eagle* to Malta 7-3 FACE SOC 11-3

AB331 2449 CHA VBT FF 30-12-41 8MU 4-1-42 C&C 26-1 GIB 1502 fl/o *Eagle* to Malta 7-3 SOC 31-3 FH15.35

AB332 2452 VBT FF 31-12-41 8MU 6-1-42 C&C 29-1 *Cape Hawk* GIB 15-2 fl/o *Eagle* to Malta 7-3 FTR 18-10

AB333 2455 VBT FF 2-1-42 8MU 4-1 C&C 29-1 *Cape Hawk* ME 1-4 Malta SOC May'42 FH10.50

AB334 2462 VBT FF 3-1-41 8MU 4-1 C&C 26-1 *Cape Hawk* GIB 15-2 fl/o *Eagle* to Malta 7-3 FTR ops 18-3 FH19.15

AB335 2466 VBT Stockbridge FF 5-1-41 8MU 11-1 C&C 2-2 *Cape Hawk* Gib 15-2 fl/o *Eagle* to Malta 7-3 126S 2-4 missing 2-4 Flt 2-10

AB336 2471 CHA VBT FF 7-1-42 8MU 11-1 C&C 31-1 *Cape Hawk* Gib 15-2 fl/o *Eagle* to Malta 7-3 des on grd SOC 18-4 FH15.20

AB337 2472 VBT FF 7-1-42 8MU 11-1 C&C 31-1 *Cape Hawk* Gib 15-2 fl/o *Eagle* to Malta 7-3 CE ops SOC 30-3 FH15.55

AB338 2478 VBT FF 8-1-41 8MU 26-1 C&C 2-2 *Cape Hawk* Gib 15-2 fl/o *Eagle* to Malta 249S 7-3 SOC 7-4 FH.4.40

AB339 2479 VBT FF 8-1-42 8MU 2-2 C&C 4-2 *Conak* 25-2 Tak ME 22-5

AB340 2487 VBT FF 10-1-42 6MU 4-2 C&C 10-2 *Queen V* 2-3 Malta 7-4 CE ops 6-5 SOC 8-5 FH17.45

AB341 2488 VBT FF 10-1-42 6MU 29-1 C&C 2-2 *Cape Hawk* Gib 15-2 fl/o *Eagle* to Malta 7-3 des on grd SOC 28-4 FH19.15

AB342 2489 VBT FF 10-1-42 6MU 4-2 C&C 10-2 *Queen V* 2-3 Malta CB ops CE ops 15-4 SOC FH10

AB343 2495 VBT FF 14-1-42 6MU 30-1 C&C 2-2 *Cape Hawk* Gib 15-2 fl/o *Eagle* to Malta 7-3 CE ops 10-3 SOC 19-3 FH7.45

AB344 2503 CHA VBT FF 17-1-42 6MU 30-1 C&C 2-2 *Cape Hawk* Gib 15-2 fl/o *Eagle* to Malta 7-3 Wk shops Kalafrana des on grd 18-4 FH14.20

AB345 2504 VBT FF 17-42 8MU 4-2 C&C 10-2 *Conak* 8-3 Tak 9-5 ME 14-5 FACB 30-5 NAASC 31-10-43 Turk 28-9-44

AB346 2516 VBT FF 24-1-42 8MU 2-2 C&C 4-2 *Cape Hawk* Gib 15-2 fl/o *Eagle* to Malta 249S 7-3 CE ops SOC 9-4 FH23.25

AB347 2517 VTB FF 24-1-42 8MU 4-2 C&C 10-2 Malta 1-4 des on grd 12-4 SOC FH9.45

AB348 2518 VBT FF 24-1-42 8MU 4-2 C&C 10-2 *Queen V* 2-3 Malta des on grd SOC 28-4

AB349 2509 VBT FF 24-1-42 8MU 4-2 C&C 10-2 *Conak* 8-3 Tak 9-5 ME 13-6 145S FACB 19-6 FTR ops 3-9

AB363 2429 FF 23-12-41 5MU 29-12 316S 31-12 134S 13-1-42 i/sea ops 21-4

AB36452430 EA LF LR VB M45M FF 26-12-41 5MU 29-12 403S 11-1-42 FAAC 3-4 131S 25-5 340S 25-1-43 331S 26-3 AST 4-5-43 611S 20-5 306S 8-6 CAC ops 15-9 ROS P&P SM 20-10 132S 22-2-44 504S 15-3 310S 15-7 41 OTU 4-9 FAAC 9-12 SOC 13-6-45

AB365 2440 EA FF 29-12-41 5MU 5-1-42 310S FAAC 12-4-42 R-RH 22-4 M61 instal WAL 17-6 con to VC M46 instal VSM 2-3-43 fuel syst mods 313S 7-6 66S 4-7 FAAC 25-9 AST 303S 26-6-44 ADGB Com Sq North 28-9 SOC 29-11-45

AB366 2434 EA FF 27-12-41 5MU 29-12 134S 12-1-42 81S 23-4 242S 4-5 243S 4-6 232S 9-10 VSM 3-3-43 fuel syst mods wng stiff 611S 13-8 o/s ldg strk obst Westh CE 16-8 SOC 27-8

AB367 2441 EA VC FF 29-12-41 5MU 5-1-42 R-RH 22-4 M61 instal WAL 26-5 M46 VSM 6-3-43 fuel syst mods 308S 27-8 FACE 5-10

AB368 2442 EA VC FF 29-12-41 9MU 4-1-42 122S 17-3 FACA 15-6 GAL VSM 4-6-43 fuel syst elev & rud mods Mk III IFF 310S 18-10 441S 27-2-44 61 OTU 13-8 287S 7-6-45 SOC 27-12

AB369 2448 EA FF 30-12-41 9MU 4-1-42 611S 31-1 242S 2-6 CE ops 5-12

AB370 2451 FF 31-12-41 9MU 4-1-42 416S 25-3 602S 15-7 CB ops 18-8 ROS VSM 18-4-43 fuel syst mods wng stiff 610S 30-6 flew i/grd nr Kingbridge Devon CE 8-8 SOC 31-8

AB371 2454 VC FF 1-1-42 9MU 4-1 R-RH 22-4 M61 instal WAL 8-6 M46 instal VSM 1-3-43 fuel syst mods 402S 11-5 CE ops 31-5

AB372 2453 VC FF 1-1-42 9MU 4-1 R-RH 22-4 M61 instal WAL 26-5 M46 instal VSM 26-1-43 fuel syst mods 412S 17-5 317S 28-6 312S 4-10 CE ops 25-10 FH229.50

AB373 2463 VC FF 3-1-42 33MU 9-1 C&C 8-1 *SS437* 23-3 ME 1-7 FA SOC 19-7

AB374 2467 VC M46 FF 6-1-42 33MU 9-1 152S 18-2 501S 1-5 CAC ops 5-10 GAL 302S 24-8 306S 3-10 FACE 26-11 ROS 15-12

AB375 2464 FF 3-1-42 33MU 9-1 124S 10-2 FTR 24-4 FH68.40

AB376 2474 VBT FF 8-1-42 33MU 9-1 39MU for tropicalisation 13-2 AST con to Sea IB-MB336 6-3 BDn 10-6 radio trls

AB377 2477 VC FF 8-1-42 33MU 27-1 R-RH 22-4 for M61 cancel WAL 5-5 M64 instal 47MU 21-6 *Emp Tern* 1-7 Malta 1-8 FTR ops 21-10

AB378 2473 FF 7-1-42 39MU 9-1 41S 8-2 ROS 1-5 VSM 18-6 mods 332S dam ops 31-7 AST 91S 22-10 FTR ops 2-11

AB379 2484 FF 10-1-42 39MU 11-1 AST 9-6 con to Sea IB-MB342

AB380 2475 VC FF 8-1-42 39MU 9-1 91S 13-3 St Flt North 23-10 FACB 18-8-43 AST 350S 21-6-44 FACE 20-4-45 SOC 24-4

AB381 2483 VC FF 9-1-42 39MU 11-1 152S 19-2 501S 1-5 FTR ops 4-6 FH52.15

AB382 2485 FF 10-1-42 39MU 11-1 611S 9-2 242S 2-6 e/a CB 12-8 LMS VSM 21-5-43 fuel syst mods 453S 21-7 DeH 5-8 441S 27-2-44 56 OTU 30-3 288S 24-5-45 SOC 22-11

AB401 2445 VBT FF 29-12-41 6MU 10-1-42 65S 7-3 FTR ops 27-4

AB402 2456 FFF 2-1-42 6MU 5-1 501S 14-5 FTR ops 19-8

AB403 2457 VBT FF 2-1-42 6MU 10-1 FAAC 14-5 ROS 501S 6-7 118S 13-7 strk by EP120 on grd CE 16-7 SOC AST recat 26-7 64S 25-9-43 AST 28-6-44 1666CU 20-11 SOC 7-9-45

AB404 2456 FF 2-1-42 6MU 5-1 AST con to Sea IB-MB350 26-4

AB405 2461 FF 3-1-42 6MU 10-1 AST con to Sea IB-MB351 20-6

AB406 2468 FF 38MU 11-1 AST con to Sea IB-MB352

AB407 2476 FF 8-1-42 39MU Star Fam dis 15-2 AST con to Sea IB-MB353 11-6

AB408 2482 FF 9-1-42 38MU 11-1 AST conv to Sea IB-MB335

AB409 2490 FF 10-1-41 5MU 25-1 39MU Star Fam dis 25-1 AST con to Sea IB-Mb343 30-4

AB410 2494 FF 13-1-41 5MU 25-1 AST con to Sea IB-MB333 9-3

AB411 2491 FF 11-1-41 5MU 25-1 C&C 25-1*SS437* 22-3 ME 145S 1-7 FTR ops

AB412 2493 FF 13-1-42 5MU 25-1 C&C 8-2 *SS437* 22-3 ME 1-7 FACB 20-8 SOC 8-12

AB413 2512 FF 5MU 13-2 con to Sea IB-MB334 6-3

AB414 2513 FF 24-1-42 5MU 13-2 39MU Star Fam dis AST con to Sea IB-MB341 30-4

AB415 2502 FF 17-1-42 5MU 25-1 AST con to Sea IB-MB338 26-4

AB416 2523 FF 25-1-42 AST con to Seafire IB-MB332

AB417 2560 VC Spcl M46 FF 4-2-42 5MU 13-2 66S 8-3 AST 15-5 u/c fail to lock on ldg CE 5-8 SOC 13-8

AB418 2532 VBT Spcl M46 FF 27-1-42 6MU 11-2 C&C 18-2 *Queen V* 3-3 Malta 1-4 des on grd 4-4 SOC FH6.35

AB419 2533 VBT FF 27-1-42 6MU 10-2 C&C 18-2 *Queen V* 3-3 Malta 28-4 des on grd SOC FH15.20

AB420 2534 VBT FF 27-1-42 6MU 10-2 C&C 19-2 *Queen V* 3-3 Malta 1-4 des on grd 3-4 SOC 6-4

AB450 3284 EA FF 22-8-42 CRD R-R Contract con to proto F VII Mer 61 Aug'42 BDn for trls R-RH 10-9 prop reduction gear change supercharger mods RAF Sp Flt North 16-9 original day ftr camouflage painted over PR blue upper/deep sky (No.2 pattern) under surfaces. BDn Oct'42 carb mono cockpit contam trls cool trls with new reduction gear R-R fitt of tail parachute and fin guard 124S 25-1-43 BDn 13-2 CE 14-6-44

AB451 2548 VTB FF 31-1-42 6MU 14-2 501S 6-5 FA CB 27-8 AST 340S 15-12-43 52 OTU 602044 FLS Mlfld 11-2 SOC CE 6-3-45

AB452 2549 VC Special M46 FF 31-1-42 6MU 14-2 501S 6-5 FA GB 27-8 AST 340S 15-12-43 52 OTU 6-2-44 FLS Mlfld 11-2 SOC CE 6-3-45

AB453 2571 HPA VC Kenya Daisy FF 10-2-42 33MU 12-2 66S 12-4 FAAC 19-4 ROS WAL 11-2-43 610S 17-5 std cd Wesden Beacon Ivybridge Devon dbf 2-10 FH427-05

AB454 2550 VBT FF 31-1-42 33MU 10-2 C&C 18-2 *Queen V* 3-3 Malta 1-4 des on grd 6-4FH17.45

AB455 2578 HPA FF 11-2-42 BDn 21-2 66S 12-4 CE ops 24-7 SOC 31-7 BDn 22-10 to 423M 1SoTT

AB456 2579 HPA VC FF 11-2-42 6MU 14-2 R-R 24-4 con to F IX *Emp Cra* 19-1 Gib 13-2 FAF 29-2-44 SOC 18-10-45

AB457 2772 VC M64 6MU cd del flt ASTH 24-2-42 FF 3-4 6MU 3-4 R-R 25-4 con to F IX M61 331S 10-1-43 AST mods 19-2 Farn LOX eng Boost trls

AB458 2615 HPA VC M46 FF 24-2-42 6MU R-R 25-4 con to F IX M61 *Llanb* 11-3-43 Gib 24-3 NWA 30-4 SOC 18-3-45

AB459 2585 HPA VC M46 FF 12-2-42 6MU 14-2 R-R 25-4 con to F IX M61 Malta 1-7-43 FTR ops 4-7

AB460 2586 HPA VC Spcl M46 FF 12-2-42 6MU 14-2 R-R 25-4 con to F IX 401S 21-11 air coll with BR630 cd Swanage Bank Hospital

AB461 2591 Hea VC M46 FF 14-2-42 8MU 17-2 660S 8-3-42 CE ops 30-7-42 SOC

AB462 2592 Hea VC M46 FF 14-2-42 8MU 17-2 66S 8-3 FACE 25-3 SOC 4-4 AST 6-5

AB463 2599 HPA FF 19-2-42 8MU 24-2 con to VCT M46 23-3 FAAC 17-4 P&P SM 14-6 76MU 9-12 *Hamble VII* 30-12 GIB 18-1-43 NWA 28-2 SOC 30-4

AB464 2603 HPA VC M46 FF 21-2-42 8MU 28-2 con to VCT 22-3 *H Farm* 26-5 Malta 1-7 SOC 22-7

AB465 2626 HPA VC M46 FF 28-2-42 8MU 28-2 con to VCT 22-3 82MU 20-5 *H Farm* 26-5 Malta 1-7 CE ops 6-1-43 FH129.10

AB467 2619 HPA VC M46 FF 27-2-42 9MU 28-2 Farn 6-5 neg G trls 504S 19-10 313S 21-10 130S 7-11 310S 1-12 167S 5-5-43 132S 19-5 19S 25-5 315S 26-6 611S 6-7 AST 19-5-44 1662CU 21-11 R&S 14-1-47 sold J Dale

AB468 2620 HPA VCT M46 FF 27-2-42 6MU 8-3 C&C 4-5 *Alderamin* 4-5 Tak 23-6 ME 29-6 145S CE ops 5-9 SOC

AB469 2627 HPA VCT M46 FF 28-2-42 6MU 15-3 82MU 23-3 *Emp Hth* 4-4 Tak Malta 186S 8-6 CE ops 14-7 SOC 15-7 FH52.00

AB487 2486 FF 10-1-42 9MU 31-1 Crd HAL 18-2 eng mods FArn 16-5 LOX eng boost trls. PDU HAL 27-5 M55M instal Farn 27-6 AFDU Dux 10-7 service trls PRU Ben 9-8 FArn 3-9 65S 31-12 130S 31-3-43 3501SU 15-11 186S 14-2-44 FAAC 26-5 ROS ASTE R&S refurb to Port 22-4-47

AB488 2492 VC FF 12-1-42 9MU 25-1 M46 instal arma removed BDn h/a trls with mod cowling and exhaust manifold. May, strengthened split flaps used as air brakes operated bay compressed air cylinder charged by eng compressor in fus. Trlsf with Mk IIN IFF M45 re-fitt for trls of power co-efficients and prop blade angles. To 4257M 1SoTT 22-10-43

AB489 2498 VC The Harrow Bulldog FF 16-1-42 9MU 28-1 66S 15-3-42 CAC ops ROS 129S 19-2-43 DeH 402S 18-6 FTR ops 23-6-44

AB490 255 M46 FF 31-1-42 9MU 17-2 64S 11-4 AST 2-7 154S 19-7 ASTH 9-10 485S 1-3-43 CB ops 21-4 DeH 165S 7-9-43 308S 10-10 FAAC 2-12 133AF 31-5-44 LMS 6-7-44 53 OTU 30-11 SOC 5-9-45

AB491 2496 VC FF 15-1-42 9MU 17-1 501S 6-5 FTR ops 17-9 FH105.05

AB492 2505 FF 15-1-42 39MU dis St Frm 13-2 AST con to Sea IB-MB354 30-4

AB493 2497 VC FF 15-1-42 39MU 24-1 66S 22-2 1CRU 1-10 M46 instal 411S 22-12 501S 29-1-43 e/fd a/c aban i/Irish Sea 23-3 FH265.05

AB494 2506 VBT FF 15-1-42 39MU Star Frm dis 11-2 con to Sea IB-MB355 M46 30-4

AB495 2499 VC FF 16-1-42 39MU 24-1 452S 12-3 457S 25-3 FAAC 24-4 recat E WAL SOC FH35.40 M46 instal during service

AB496 2500 VC FF 17-1-42 39MU 24-1 66S8-3 FACE 25-3 SOC 3-4

AB497 2501 VC FF 17-1-42 9MU 25-1 501S 5-5-42 FTR ops 20-6 FH43.30

AB499 2507 VCT M46 FF 24-1-42 CRD R-RH 11-2 after design and instal of press cabin by VA Mer 61 press cabin and accessories. Redesg Mk VII Spcl FF as mod a/c 26-1-43. BDn 14-3 flame exhaust damping trls with close fitt shrouds. Not sufficient for opnl requirements. R-RH Mer 71 instal providing 404mph @ 27,000ft 371 @ 40,000 and 302 @s/l 2GSU 28-6-43 To 424M 6SoTT 24-10

AB500 2522 VBT M46 FF 25-1-42 6MU 11-2 C&C 18-2 *Queen V* 3-3 Malta 185SFACB 17-4 SOC 7-7

AB501 2541 VC FF 24-1-42 CRD R-R 29-1 from VA WW M46 instal MM 28-7 R-R13-12 M61 instal con to LF IX. Used for dev of M61 & 66 eng. AFDU Witt 6-10 R-R 29-10 M66 instal CRD DeH 11-2-44 prop trls. HAL 25-2-44 FAF 17-7-47

AB502 2541 VBT FF 28-1-42 6MU 13-2 C&C 20-2 *Denmark* 11-3 Tak 9-5 ME 5-6 Aboukir filter fitt 224 wng s/dn by bf109 Tunisia 16-4-43 Air Com Gleed kld

AB504 2508 VCT FF 24-1-42 del flt to R-RH 28-1-42 RNDA GAL 12-3-42 trlinstal of fold wng mods. ROS VA 19-10 R-R 31-12 GAL 12-3-43 310S 405 e/fd i/sea nr Eddystone Lighthouse 30-6

AB505 2521 VC FF 25-1-42 CRD R-R 28-1 from VA WW M46 instal AFDU 26-4 R-R 7-5 con to HF IX M61 instal AFDU Horn for trls. 64S 4-6-42 Sqdn trls R-R 11-7 M77 with Rotol Mk XHCR six blade contra prop instal VA 17-7-43 mods to fin and rud lateral instability with normal F IX empennage prompted dev of increased area unit, retractable tailwheel. BDn 10-9 evaluation and comp trls with Spitfire F VIII. Stroboscopic effect of c/ps produced a white circle of approx 3° Pilots soon became accustomed to this AST 26-11 con to standard F IX 611S 13-7-44 VA 15-9 mods 312S 8-10 strk rear of MH357 at Bradwell Bay CE 8-12

AB507 2535 VC Spcl M46 FF 28-1-42 CRD R-RH 13-2 con to F IX 64S 4-6-42 for service trls RAF BH11 29-6 Tang 15-7 HAL 23-9 331S 30-4-43 CE ops 1-6-43

AB508 2536 VC FF 28-1-42 24MU 31-1 R-R 28-4 con to F IX M61 611S 28-11 AST 5-4-43 mods 316S 12-4-43 FTR ops 22-8-43 FH275.15

AB509 2542 VC FF 28-1-42 24MU 31-1 66S 15-3 AST 16-9 131S 31-12 412S 23-1-43 310S 3-3 144AF 3-3-44 SAL 20-3 402S 22-5 53 OTU 29-9 SOC 31-5-45

AB510 2543 VC FF 1-1-41 37MU 11-2 WAL 5-5 M46 instal 66S 21-9 to 3649M 11SoTT 2-4-43

AB511 2544 VC Spcl M64 FF-1-42 24MU 13-2 R-R 28-4 con to F IXC M61 340S 10-1-43 331S 10-1 AST 25-10 mods FA CB 5-11 AST 84GSU 3-4-44 611S o/s ldg str k MH333 CE 14-9

AB512 2545 VC Spcl M46 FF 31-1-42 5MU 13-2 66S 8-3-42 VSM 6-5-43 mods 315S 1-7-43 611S 6-7 hvy ldg cartwheeled CE 31-12 FH388.45

AB514 2572 EA VC Spcl M46 FF 7-2-42 8MU 12-2 66S 8-3-42 FTR ops 19-8

AB515 2564 VC M46 FF 6-2-42 8MU 13-2 66S 8-3 313S 3-12 CAC ops 66S 4-2 e/fd w/u ldg nr Wembury Devon CE 22-5 FH244.35

AB517 2574 EA VC Spcl M46 FF 7-2-42 33MU 12-2 66S 8-3 FTR ops 19-8 FH244.35

AB518 2575 EA VC M46 FF 8-2-42 33MU 20-2 501S 5-5 504S 27-10 310S 5-2-43 65S air coll with Blenhiem cd nr Porth CE dbf 16-4 FH244.50

AB519 2577 EA VC M46 FF 14-2-42 33MU 12-2 310S 24-11 FTR ops 29-1-43 FH289.00

AB520 2594 EA VC M46 FF 14-2-42 33MU 20-2 8MU 20-5 Malta 1-8 e/a CB 26-9 C3 ops 29-11 FH48.05

AB521 2587 EA VC M46 FF 12-2-42 37MU 15-2 66S 15-3-42 FAAC 21-3ROS 605S 20-6 AST 9-7 129S 19-2-43 e/fd f/ld CE 6-3

AB522 2593 EA VC M46 FF 14-2-42 37MU 15-2 R-R 28-4 con to F IX M63 332S 8-11 401S 9-12 4-2S 31-12 403S 25-1-43 AST 10-2 mods CB ops 12-3 GAL 405ARF 7-9 165S 29-9 131S 19-4-44 AST 31-3 310S 11-9 CB ops 12-3-45 recat C SOC 23-5

AB524 2597 EA VC M46 FF 16-2-42 37MU 20-2 66S 15-3 ASTH 16-10 19S 9-2-43 402S 5-5 FACE 3-1-44 ROS 53 OTU 2-9 288S 24-5-45 AST 29-11

AB525 2602 EA VC Spc l FF 20-2-42 37MU 24-2 R-R 30-4 con to F IX M61 WAL 306S 28-11 316S 14-3 AST mods 17-3 FTR ops 4-5

AB526 2604 EA VC Spcl M46 FF 21-2-42 39MU 24-2 *Emp Dar* 29-6 Malta 4-8 e/e CE 28-1-43 FH72.50

AB531 2607 EA VC Spcl M46 FF 21-2-42 9MU 24-2 47MU 7-6 *Emp Shack* 12-6-42 Malta 1-8 SOC 11-9

AB532 2613 EA VC FF 21-2-42 8MU 25-2 con to VCT 22-3 47MU 6-6 *Emp Shack* 12-6 Malta 1-9 C3 ops 19-10 NA USAAF 31-10-43 MAAF 31-1-44 EAF GR 2/33 2-5

AB535 2614 VC Spc l M46 FF 22-2-42 8MU 26-2 con to VCT 23-3 *Emp Cuba* 28-8 Gib 14-9 Malta 1-11 ME 1-9-43 FACE 6-2-44

AB536 2618 EA VC Harimau FF 25-2-42 8MU 26-2 con to VCT 11-5 47MU 21-6 *Emp Tern* 1-7 Malta 1-8 CE ops 8-11-43

AB779 9MU 29-7-41 92S 21-8 FTR ops 3-10

AB780 45MU 25-7-41 602S 6-8 FTR 21-9

AB781 8MU 31-7-41 452S 7-8 VA 19-11 602S 13-3-42 411S 25-3 dam ops 8-6 ROS 71S 7-6 VSM 31-8 fuel syst mods 222MU 25-10 *Harp* 30-10 USSR 24-3-43

AB782 LF VB M45M 37MU 9-8-41 111S 24-8 312S 31-12-42 602S 26-9-43 118S 10-10-43 132S 25-1-44 VSM 9-3 fuel syst mods Merlin 'Basta' mods 53 OTU 8-9 PAL 4-10-45 SOC 13-10

AB783 9MU 29-7-41 71S 27-8 CE ops 9-1-42 SOC 10-1

AB784 8MU 1-8-41 485S 7-8 CB ops 17-11 ASTE 452S 21-4-42 93S 4-6 VSM 17-3-43 fuel syst mods wng stiff 312S 4-6 AST 19-6 504S 30-6 313S 22-9 e/fd f/ld Hampton Middx

AB785 38MU 27-7-41 452S 4-8 FTR ops 19-8

AB786 38MU 27-7-41 611S 6-8 64S 14-11 GAL 21-3-42 401S 2-6 65S 16-7 303S 22-8 CB ops 13-11 AST 453S 4-4-43 129S 17-7 310S 14-8 VSM 20-12 fuel syst mods 13 OTU 26-4-45 FACE 87 Grp CF E/Fld a/c aban cd Chaules France 9-5-46

AB787 38MU 9-8-41 609S 18-8 AST 20-9 FACB 13-4-42 ROS recat E SOC 24-4

AB788 8MU 2-8-41 484S 9-8-41 CE ops 25-1-42 SOC

AB789 45MU 315S 31-8-41 HAL 24-10-41 Fitt TT hook FA CB 16-5-42 67Grp 22-11-43 AST 19-9-44 41 OTU o/s ldg std o/t Poulton CE 11-3-45 SOC 17-3

AB790 8MU 31-2-41 452S 5-8 308S 1-4-42 e/fd w/u ldg Everidge Kent CE 16-4 ASTH SOC 38MU 13-4-43 VSM 21-4 fuel syst mods wng stiff 504S 29-6 165S 1-7 308S 10-10 FACB 6-3-44 'Basta' mods 130S 22-6 530TU 15-8 FAAC 8-2-45 ROS recat E SOC 25-5-45

AB791 9MU 3-8-41 CBAF 20-8 412S 15-3-42 CB ops 28-3 AST 5USA 5-9 453S 13-9 CE ops 11-10

AB792 37MU 27-7-41 452S 5-8-41 412S 15-3-42 CB ops 28-3 AST 5USA 453S 13-9 CE ops 11-10

AB793 45MU 111S 22-8-41 121S 21-4-42 CE ops 25-4 SOC FH185.10

AB794 LF VB M45M 37MU 27-7-41 452S 5-8 GAL 20-8 602S 8-3-42 331S 7-4 FAAC 24-4 ROS 132S 35-5 P&P SM 12-2-43 308S 24-8 FAAC 1-10 ROS 610S 10-11 130S 30-1-44 222S 16-2 322S 17-3 CE ops 12-6

AB795 37MU 9-8-41 616S 18-8 FTR over e/tr 30-9

AB796 37MU 9-8-41 111S 26-8 ASTH 6-9-41 124S 15-12 FA 11-2-42 452S 12-5 93S 4-6 FAAC 11-6 ROS FA FTR 7-8

AB797 38MU 6-8-41 92S 10-8 AST 29-8 602S 14-10 417S 14-2-42 242S 21-4 strk fire tender on t/o Ouston CE 22-6 SOC 28-6

AB798 12MU 14-8-41 111S 18-8 e/fd on t/o f/ld strk house nr NWld 18-12 AST 13-1 recat E 20-5

AB799 8MU 1-8-41 485S 7-8 4-3S 5-4-42 FTR ops 2-6 FH106.20

AB800 12MU 14-8-41 91S 20-8 CAC ops 2-3-42 HAL 129S 29-4 FTR ops 19-8

AB801 222S 22-8-41 FTR ops 14-9

AB802 8MU 13-8-41 609S 21-8 dam ops 15-1-42 ROS 71S 26-3-42 412S 5-6 AST 23-7 416S 6-2-43 411S 23-3

AB803 8MU 13-8-41 222S 20-8 FAAC 29-12 ROS 401S 2-6-42 308S 5-8 167S 12-8 610S 14-10 131S 25-1-43 SAL 13-3 VSM 25-5 fuel syst mods 308S 21-7 322S 22-7 CE ops 16-8 SOC 31-8 FH392.20

AB804 45MU 15-8-41 71S 6-9 411S 24-12 CE ops 25-4-42

AB805 9MU 16-8-41 222S 24-8 PSO FTR ops 8-12

AB806 9MU 18-8 72S 22-8 401S 21-10 72S 23-3-42 s/dn by Spit FTR 1-7

AB807 9MU 16-8-41 222S 22-8 SOC 30-4-42

AB808 8MU 25-8-41 54S 29-8 FTR ops

AB809 37MU 24-8-41 306S 11-9 316S 13-12 HAL 30-5-42 41S 27-7 CA ops 22-8 AST con to Sea IB-NX963 28-5-43

AB810 12MU 17-8-41 71S 26-8 FTR ops 12-4-42

AB811 9MU 16-8-41 71S 26-8 403S 31-12 GAL 25-5-42 309S FTR ops 19-8

AB812 M46 6MU 20-8-41 71S 26-8 FAAC 27-3-42 fuel syst mods wng stiff 65S 16-4 132S 23-5 362S 28-6 CE 30-6 ROS 306S 3-10 FAAC 1-1-44 ROS HAL mr 18-3 1 AGS 5-2-45 SOC 3-9-46

AB813 9MU 15-8-41 403S 20-8 54S 25-8 FTR ops 17-9 FH25.0

AB814 M45M 6MU 17-8-41 403S 22-8 54S 25-8 124S 17-11 340S 20-8 453S 6-11 222S 31-3-43 167S 19-5 322S 1-1-44 VSM 9-3 fuel syst & 'Basta' mods SOC 22-9

AB815 6MU 20-8-41 71S 26-8 dam by bf109 cd New Romney 7-9 61 OTU 16-9 to 2697M SOC 22-9

AB816 37MU 24-8-41 234S 18-9 CE ops 26-2-42 SOC

AB817 24MU 24-7-41 72S 30-8 AST 7-12 121S 1-6-42 165S 20-2-43 FAAC 25-5 SAL 350S 9-10 322S 11-1-44-FTR ops 1-2 FH3-4.40

AB818 8MU 25-8-41 72S 29-8 452S 5-3-42 457S 22-3 64S 7-4 152S 26-4AST 16-5-43 con to Sea IB-NX948

AB819 8MU 25-8-41 54S 29-8 124S 17-9 FTR ops 25-4-42 FH203.30

AB820 12MU 27-8-41 315S 31-8 FACE dbf 8-9 SOC 13-9

AB821 24MU 24-8-41 616S 31-8 65S 6-10 FTR ops 13-10

AB822 24MU 24-8-41 72S 30-8-41 FTR ops 26-10

AB823 45MU 22-8-41 306S 3-9-41 303S 3-10 CE SOC 30-10

AB824 5MU 30-8-41 306S 14-9 303S 6-10 HAL 11-3-42 303S FTR ops 4-4-42

AB825 45MU 22-8-41 308S 9-9 316S 13-12 CE 13-2-42 SOC 25-2

AB826 33MU 29-8-41 41S 1-9 FTR ops 13-10

AB827 37MU 24-8-41 71S 10-9 FTR ops 20-10

AB828 LF LR VB M45M Assam VII 45MU 13-9-41 501S 26-9 R-R 6-12 mods 118S 17-5-42 154S 22-6 340S 20-7 VSM 19-9 fuel syst & rud mods wng stiff 316S 6-11-42 277S 2-9-44 FACB 25-1-45 recat E 13-2 SOC 23-3

AB841 45MU 25-7-41 452S 8-8 FTR ops 20-9

AB842 The Staffordian 38MU 6-7-41 452S 5-8-41 i/sea ops 8-11

AB843 6MU 22-7-41 72S 28-7 FTR ops 27-9

AB844 45MU 23-7-41 602S 3-8-41 FTR ops 12-8

AB845 9MU 27-7-41 403S 20-8 54S 25-8 124S 17-11 CAC ops 17-12 129S 19-8-42 602S 29-11 66S 19-2-43 234S 19-4-43 312S 29-6 RNDA 21-2-44 COAL 22-2 hook fitt Yeov 22-7

AB846 9MU 20-7 602S 31-7 118S 15-9 302S 15-10 CB ops 17-4-42 WAL SOC E 27-4 RTS

AB847 9MU 27-7-41 92S 21-8 ASTE 6-12 411S 20-8-42 air coll with R6897 cd Alby Lincs CAC 5-9-42 SOC E 28-1-43

AB848 M46 39MU 24-7-41 72S 28-12 CAC ops 5-5-42 ROS 332S 20-8 VSM 28-8 mods 411S 20-11 19S 5-5-43 34-S 15-12 41 OTU 21-9-44 SOC 6-6-45

AB849 LF LR VB M45M 33MU 27-7-41 602S 9-8 340S 4-5-42 41S 20-11 316S 15-3-43 306S 16-3 FACB 31-3 ROS 315S 2-7 AST 610S 6-9 316S 16-12 130S 27-4-44 FAAC 30-4 ROS 287S 27-8-45

AB850 Canterbury 37MU 27-7-41 485S 9-8 ASTH 28-9 134S 8-2-42 FACB 27-3 ASTH 131S 20-8 FTR ops 24-10

AB851 39MU 24-7-41 602S 30-7 485S 265S 26-1-42 452S 1-3 411S 10-4 WAL 18-5 91S 9-8 i/sea ops 19-8 FH226.25

AB852 8MU 30-7-41452S 5-8 FTR ops 13-10

AB853 8MU 2-8-41 485S 9-8 HAL 20-9 CE ops 27-11 SOC 29-11

AB854 9MU 20-7-41 72S 27-7 AST 23-8 234S 8-12 FTR ops 30-12

AB855 38MU 27-7-41 611S 6-8 72S 24-10 FTR ops 8-11

AB856 8MU 30-7-41 485S 9-8 FTR ops 21-9

AB857 37MU 27-7-41 452S 6-8 401S 1-3-42 CAC ops 13-3 ROS 501S 7-4 RNAS Stret 5-9 AST 13-10 hook fitt mods LoS 2-11

AB858 33MU 27-7-41 41S 1-9 FA tl wrk CE 19-11 SOC 21-11

AB859 8MU 2-8-41 610S 22-8 609S 17-1-42 ASTE 22-6 122S 29-8 FTR ops 16-9 FH235.10

AB860 37MU 27-7-41 485S 9-8 54S 8-4-42 167S 31-5 610S 14-10 131S 25-1-43 FAAC 22-3 AST M46 instal 412S 17-6 317S 28-6 453S 5-9 341S 3-11 329S 1-2-44 HAL 6-4 AST mr 13-5 recat E

AB861 9MU 27-7-41 602S 2-8 FTR ops 13-10 FH53.30

AB862 M45M 39MU 24-7-41 602S 30-7 316S 11-10 306S 12-12 FACB 1-5-42 GAL 4USA 15-1-43 WAL 340S 23-8-43 67Grp 22-11 DeH 17-6-44 84GCS 5-4-45 R&S refurb to Port 28-4-47

AB863 9MU 6-8-41 401S 27-9 FTR ops 21-10 FH14.05

AB864 9MU 308041 72S 30-9 AST 23-12 234S 26-4-42 FTR ops 23-7-44 FH189.05

AB865 9MU 26-8-41 403S 12-9 FAAC 4-5-42 WAL

AB866 M46 8MU 12-8-41 ROS 602 14-10 R-R 22-11 MM 20-1-42 315S 25-5-42 317S 5-9-42 124S 2-4-43 19S 4-7 FAAC 14-9 ROS VSM 20-12 fuel syst mods CGS 28-9-44 SOC 27-12-45

AB867 38MU 9-8-41 616S 12-8 65S 6-10 ASTH 16-10 222S 29-4-42 242S 11-8 COAL 26-6-43 con to train RNDA 19-1-43 SOC 15-5-45

AB868 12MU 14-8-41 111S 19-8 HAL 5-6-42 GAL 25-10 222S 27-10 *C o Lil* 8-12 for USSR dam in transit RTP SOC 5-3-43

AB869 8MU 13-8-41 222S 24-8 FTR ops 29-2-42

AB870 Hawkers Bay I 8MU 2-8-41 485S 7-8 HAL 3-10 72S 18-11 308S 24-8-42 VAM 25-6-43 fuel syst & elev mods Mk III IFF 349S 25-12 eng fire a/c aban cd Battle Sussex CE 30-1-44

AB871 111S 24-8-41 403S 20-1-42 CB 8-3 HAL cd on f/f 28-5 ROS 5 USA 8-9 504S 30-9 FAAC 29-10 ROS 501S 20-6-43 130S 29-6 349S 19-7 to 4353M 2 SoTT 6-12 extant RAF STA as AR514 (4354M)

AB872 12MU 14-8-41 41S 20-8 131S 9-1-42 609S 14-4 302S 10-9 FACB ROS CAC ops 3-3-43 132S 28-6 flew i/hill nr Shoreham Sussex 18-8

AB873 37MU 9-8-41 111S 24-8 AST 20-9 610S 8-12 Farn drag red trls can removed, whip aerial fitt spcl finish. RNAS Stret 1-9-42 CE 23-9 ASTH

AB874 37MU 9-8-41 452S 18-8 FACE dbf 7-9 SOC 23-9

AB875 LF LR VB 45MU 20-8-41 71S 27-8 hvy ldg MHth u/c clpse CE 28-3-42 ASTE recat B 308S 9-3-43 DeH 12-4 350S 9-10 322S 11-1-44 FACE 21-3 LMS CGS 30-9 SOC 27-12-45

AB892 45MU 22-8-41 315S 30-8 FAA 21-4-42 recat E SOC 30-4

AB893 12MU 14-8-41 72S 20-8 FA i/sea 8-11

AB894 The Hallow Spitfire 9MU 6-8-41 CBAF 21-8 452 20-9 CE ops 18-12 AST VSM 31-8-42 fuel syst mods Farn Jan'43 Ftr Com VHF aerial trls FTR ops 8-3 FHA166.30

AB895 45MU 15-8-41 315S 30-8 HAL 29-9 65S 10-9-42 167S 13-9 610S 14-10 131S 25-1-43 310S 30-6-43 313S 29-7 222MU 12-11 *Pandor* 25-11 port 8-12

AB896 45MU 10-8-41 71S 27-8 403S 31-12 131S 10-5-42 5USA 5-9 215MU 7-11 *Bar Inch* 18-12 USSR 24-3-43

AB897 6MU 20-8-41 71S 26-8 SOC 20-10 71S 31-12 FAAC 2-4-42 ROS 5USA 5-9 VSM 2-5-43 fuel syst mods wng stiff 317S 207 402S 12-10 air coll with AA880 21-3-44 CE ops 10-6

AB898 45MU 15-8-41 315S 30-8 GAL 26-5-42 HAL 11-12 411S 17-4-43 CAC ops 25-6-43 ROS 125AF 10-8 341S 17-10-43 USAAF 9-5-44 SOC 29-11-45

AB899 12MU 17-8-41 306 9-9 303S 6-10 FAAC 2-5-42 ROS 317S 29-5 HAL 9-8 334S 11-2-43 COAL 23-6 hook fitt (called Seafire) RNDA 16-1-44

AB900 6MU 20-8-41 71S 26-8 s/dn by Bf109 over France 9-9 SOC 30-11

AB901 38MU 9-8-41 609S 18-8 610S 10-12 FACB 12-2-42 WAL FAAC 28-6 ROS 76MU *C o Lil* 8-12 USSR 16-2-43

AB902 6MU 16-8-41 222S 22-8 1CRU 17-2-42 65S 24-7 93S 13-9 FAAC 27-9 ASTH 15-2-43 con to Sea IB-NX889

AB903 9MU 24-8-41 485S 2-9-41 FTR ops 18-9

AB904 LF VB 45MU 22-8-41 315S 30-8 WAL 17-1-42 322S 28-9-43 FAAC 25-11 53 OTU 27-6-44 FAAC 19-10 ROS to 5349M 5SoTT 14-7-45 SOC rtp

AB905 6MU 17-8-41 111S 24-8 FTR ops 21-7-422

AB906 38MU 24-8-41 306S 2-9 303S 3-10 HAL 10-11 AST 16-5-42 332S 30-6 FTR2-8

AB907 6MU 20-8-41 71S 26-8 FAAC 14-1-42 AST 2USA 22-8 CE 18-6-43

AB908 37MU 22-8-41 71S 10-9 ROS 21-11 FAAC 13-1-42 ROS 121S 25-3 VSM 29-7 fuel syst mods 131S 14-8 FAAC 18-8 WAL AST con to Seafire IB-NX892 21-2-43

AB909 6MU 16-8-41 71S 26-9 s/dn by Bf109 over France 7-9 SOC 30-11

AB910 92S Aug'42 ME 1-9 VSM 7-6-43 fuel syst mods wng stiff 416S 1-7-43 53 OTU took off Hibald with WAAF Margaret Horton on tail 4-4-45 sold Air Com Wheeler M45M instal G-AISU BoB Flight QJ-J Strk Hendy Heck at Wolverhampton 17-10-47 extant BofB Flight

AB911 CRU Reps 9-10-41 37MU 27-1-42 603S 7-4 332S 8-4 SAL CE 24-5 SOC FH36.30

AB912 38MU 27-8-41 306S 3-9 303S 6-10 ASTE 350S 19-6-42 e/fd i/sea 27-8

AB913 38MU 24-8-41 315S 29-8 HAL 26-1-42 RNAS Strt 5-9 SAL 30-9 hook fitt RNAS Don 13-4-44

AB914 45MU 22-8-41 315S 30-8 GAL 7-10 317S 5-9-42 FAAC 24-9 ROS e/fd f/ld Ormskirk Lancs CE 1-12

AB915 8MU 25-8-41 92S 29-8 i/sea ops 17-9

AB916 M45M 9MU 24-8-41 CBAF 5-9 313S 26-10 CAC ops 30-12 AST 152S 24-4-42 FACB 19-6 S&H 411S 19-8-43 341S 17-10 453S 27-10 602S 25-1-44 118S 13-3 58 OTU 17-5 1TEU 27-6 57 OTU 18-8 recat E SOC 15-2-45

AB917 The Inspirer 39MU 6-7-41 Star Fam dis 401S 4-1-42 CE ops 28-4 SOC 30-4 FH133.50

AB918 Wellington I 45MU 6-7-41 485S 10-8 GAL 14-2-42 312S 5-8 5USA 9-8 67th Obs Grp FACB 16-11 AST 131S 15-4-43 310S 30-6 313S 29-7

AB919 45MU 10-8-41 316S 30-10 ROS 28-11 610S 22-12 coll with AD247 ldg Hutton Cranswick CE 7-1-42 AST 8-4-43 con to Sea IB-NX918

AB920 37MU 24-8-41 308S 11-9 316S 13-12 306S 16-3-43 to 2656M 9-4 6th Army Ftr Wng USAAF

AB921 M45M 9MU 24-8-41 611S 7-9 64S 14-11VSM 3-9-42 fuel syst mods 165S 22-12 122S 15-7-43 FAAC 13-8 ROS 234S 3-9 FAAC 1809 ROS 303S 24-5-44 57 OTU 2-8 strk by BR391 when parked Boul CE 22-2-45 SOC 1-3

AB922 8MU 25-8-41 72S 29-8 ROS 29-9 401S 26-10 FTR ops 8-11

AB923 24MU 24-8-41 610S 31-8 315S 1-9 FTR ops 16-9

AB924 33MU 29-8-41 111S 3-9 FACE ttl wrk 28-9 AST 3-10 SOC 6-10

AB925 M46 5MU 30-8-41 308S 10-9 HAL 22-9 317S 17-3-42 HAL 19-5 132S 25-10 122S 21-5-43 310S 4-12 306S 4-3-44 277S 5-6 SOC 17-2-45

AB926 33MU 29-8-41 41S 1-9 65S 27-12 hit gunpit ldg Debden CE 26-1-42 SOC

AB927 39MU 28-8-41 315S 31-8 SOC 28-9

AB928 5MU 30-8-41 266S 13-9 WAL 24-4-42 130S 23-6 FAAC 10-7 ROS AST 27-11 COAL con to Sea IB-NX951 1-3-43

AB929 39MU 28-8-41 306S 3-9 3-3S 6-10 FAAC 29-1-42 ASTH 14-7 hook fitt 334S USA 1-10 VSM 30-6-43 fuel syst mods Mk III IFF RNDA 21-1-44

AB930 9MU 24-8-41 308S 10-9 HAL 22-9 FTR ops 8-11

AB931 LF LR VB M45M 38MU 24-8-41 315S 29-8 111S 26-7-42 VSM 26-1-43 fuel syst mods wng stiff 350S 11-1-44 e/fd i/sea 21-3 FH411.30

AB932 M45M 39MU 28-8-41 222S 2-9 ASTH 14-11 242S 11-8-42 CB ops 19-8 AST 131S 22-3-43 165S 9-8 308S 10-10 AST 10-1-44 504S 27-4 FAAC 16-6 ROS 57 OTU 2-8 SOC 3-1-46

AB933 5MU 30-8-41 266S 13-9 154S 11-2-42 FAAC 29-3 ROS 313S 8-6 VSM 10-10 fuel syst mods AST 13-2-42 con to Seafire IB-NX887

AB934 12MU 27-8-41 315S 31-12 CAC ops 16-9 HAL FTR ops 23-11

AB935 Gingerbread 12MU 27-8-41 92S 3-9 417S 7-2-43 242S 21-4 243S 6-6 232S 9-10 65S 28-10 130S 31-3-43 S&H 20-6 *Emp Ort* 6-10 PAL 19-10

AB936 5MU 30-8-41 306S 14-9 303S 3-10 AST 18-12 421S e/fd hit obst ldg Fairwood Common 30-5-42 41S 2-6 VSM 12-9-43 fuel syst & elev mods wng stiff S type pt Mk IFF bomb carr 269S 1-3-44 CE 4-3-46 SOC 24-3

AB937 12MU 27-8-41 315S 3-9 HAL 20-9 FTR ops 23-11

AB938 33MU 7-9-41 111S 16-9 FTR ops 1-6-42

AB939 LF VB 24MU 4-9-41 266S 13-9 312S 6-6-42 VSM 12-8 mods HAL 18-2-43 302S 21-6 19S 1-7 340S 28-9 485Sm 11-11 4ATU 7-1-44 FAF 19-1-45

AB940 6MU 7-9-41 403S 12-9 AST 4-9-42 hook fitt RNAS SOC 19-9

AB941 38MU 3-9-41 308S 9-9 ASTH 30-10 71S 15-3-42 334S 1-10 i/sea ops 27-1-43

AB960 6MU 31-8-41 111S 7-9 FAAC 5-5-42 AST 501S 6-11 flew into hill Slieve Greeba Mntn Co Down 18-2-43

AB961 LF LR VB M45M 38MU 2-9-41 ROS 4-9 616S 28-3 316S 22-5 FACB 12-10 ROS 306S 16-3-43 26S 3-4-44 FTR ops 23-6

AB962 39MU 29-8-41 111S 3-9 SOC 22-9

AB963 12MU 7-7-41 403S 12-9 GAL 7-10 402S 9-3-42 421S 8-5 FACE 30-5 SOC 7-6 FH32.0

AB964 M45M 8MU 7-9-41 266S 13-9 154S 12-3-42 FAAC 21-4 ROS 91S 17-5 AST 5-6 VSM 13-10 fuel syst mods wng stiff 167S 29-3-43 315S 26-6 CAC ops 14-7 ROS 611S 30-7 FACE 9-4-44 SOC 17-10-45

AB965 Palembang Oeloe III 45MU 13-9-41 501S 26-9 FACE 27-3-42 SOC 4-4

AB966 37MU 8-9-41 452S 19-9 PSO FTR over France 8-12

AB967 9MU 10-9-41 452S 20-9 R-RH 15-11 mods 457S 22-3-42 485S 26-3 118S 11-5 41S 20-6 350S 6-7 VSM 4-9 mods COAL 1-6-43 hook fitt alloc as Sea IB-NX964 cancel RNDA 19-1-44 LoS

AB968 24MU 4-941 308S 11-9 AST 12-12-42 19S 10-6 131S 6-9 P&P SM 21-10 131S 17-11 VSM fuel syst mods AST 8-4-43 con to Sea IBNX917

AB969 33MU 29-8-41 111S 3-9 FTR ops 21-9

AB970 M46 45MU 31-8-41 266S 13-9 FACB 20-1-42 AST 2USA 22-8 67Grp USAAF 4-4-43 345S 6-6-44 CE ops 8-6

AB971 LF VB 45MU 31-8-41 19S 30-10 316S 17-1-42 FAAC 25-8-42 350S 27-3-43 FACB 6-4-43 SAL 322S 20-7-43 DeH 27-11 26S 2-8-44 58 OTU 29-3-45 to 5719M 16-10

AB972 9MU 10-9-41 452S 20-9 R-RH 8-11 mods 452S 9-11 485S 26-3-42 118S 11-15 131S 14-6 FAAC 6-10 ROS 165S 31-12 122S 15-7-43 FH378.50

AB973 8MU 7-9-41 266S 13-9 R-RH 3-11 mods 616S 31-1-42 R-R 14-2-42 mods DeH 10-6 412S 26-9 421S 31-1-43 FTR ops 15-5 FH435.55

AB974 B B & C.I Railway 33MU 12-9-41 401S 26-9 FAAC 29-3-42 ROS 91S 18-4 121S 20-8 335S USA 1-10 302S 23-3-43 132S 28-6 FAAC 30-6 312S 13-11 443S 27-2-44 58 OTU 30-3 SOC mr 18-9-45

AB975 45MU 31-8-41 609S 7-7 121S 20-8-42 335S USA 1-10 VSM 6-7-43 fuel syst & elev mods wng stiff S type pt MkIII IFF M46 instut 411ARF 21-2-44 277S 26-5 CE 25-6

AB976 M46 6MU 30-8-41 306S 6-9 303S 6-10 ASTH 3-12 67Grp USAAF 16-10-42 31ATG 26-5 -44 SAL 7-7 2nd TAF Com S 7-2-45

AB977 37MU 6-9-41 118S 16-9 CE 16-12 SOC 26-12

AB978 12MU 7-9-41 403S 12-9 FTR ops 25-4-42 FH182.05

AB979 33MU 7-9-41 72S 4-4-42 FAAC 13-4 WAL react E

AB980 12MU 8-9-41 452S 24-9 ASTH 25-10 350S 31-7-42 e/td e/tr 16-8

AB981 6MU 7-9-41 403S 12-9 FAAC 10-2-43 SAL 165S 1-7 501S 19-7 504S 15-12 129S 26-1-44 278S 17-6 SOC 15-5-45

AB982 6MU 7-9-41 403S 12-9 ASTE 17-11 65S 13-8-42 309S 11-8 308S 15-8 VSM 1-10 fuel syst mods FTR ops 6-12

AB983 Singawang (NEI) 24MU 14-8-41 401S 27-9 FTR ops 27-10 FH50.55

AB984 West Borneo III (NEI) 5MU 13-9 611S 2-10 CE ops 5-11 Farn Jan'42 VHF trls

AB985 39MU 21-9-41 302S 11-10 FTR ops

AB986 M45M 9MU 10-10-41 CRD VA 31-12 for con to sea-Spitfire dam on f/f 165S 8-6-42 FAAC 25-8 ROS 93S 1-10 312S 31-12 132S 15-4-43 122S 21-5 234S 15-8 345S 3-4-44 53 OTU 11-8 Gosport Ftr Circus 30-9 SOC mr 28-5-45

AB987 45MU 7-10-41 234S 17-3-42 FTR ops 16-4 FH47.45

AB988 M45MA 45MU 7-10-41 310S 17-12 65S 22-3-42 FAAC 17-8 ROS 340S 9-9 SAL 25-10 336S USA 3-2-43 67Grp USAAF 22-11 Gosport Ftr Circus 23-10-44 R&S refurb to Port 15-10-47

AB989 M45M 38MU 26-8-41 306S 3-9 303S 6-10 HAL 8-11 452S 23-3-42 124S 1-6 501S 22-6-44 61 OTU 2-8 SOC 12-4-45

AB990 12MU 27-8-41 315S 31-8 FTR ops 21-9

AB991 Brierly Hill 5MU 13-9-41 401S 22-9 FTR ops 27-10 FH26.45

AB992 MXX 9MU 6-10-41 452S 14-10 FACE 22-1-43 SOC

AB993 6MU 30-8-41 306S 6-9 FTR ops 16-9 FH9.45

AB994 Gingerbread 45MU 31-8-41 401S 27-9 ROS 7-11 452S 18-11 457S 22-3-42 FTR ops 4-4 FH106-30

AD111 9MU 15-8-41 92S 28-8 GAL 3-10 71S 26-4-42 FACB 1-8 AST 306 31-8-43 302S 3-10-43 322S 25-11 222S 1-1-44 VSM 9-3 fuel syst 'Basta' MODS 276S 17-6 FRU 14-9 57 OTU 25-3-45 577S 4-6 SOC 25-10

AD112 6MU 20-8-41 71S 26-8 SOC 30-11

AD113 6MU 16-8 222S 22-8 64S 5-4-42 GAL 23-4 FACE 5-8 ROS 307S USA 19-8 350S 12-9 401S 7-12 402S 12-12 416S 23-3-43 421S 20-5 DeH 28-7 COAL 7-11 hook fitt RNDA 9-2-44

AD114 45MU 31-8-41 485S 7-9 FACA 12-3-42 463S 5-4 CB ops 2-6-42 MM mods RNAC Train Estb 30-6

AD115 6MU 30-8-41 306S 7-9 611S 8-3-42 243S 2-6 222S 11-8 FAAC 21-8 ROS FACE 12-12

AD116 Twickenham I 6MU 19-9-41 306S 24-9 303S 6-10 GAL 18-2-42 FACB 15-4 GAL 5S USA 8-9 504S 30-9 501S 19-10 f/ld Eire dbr 27-11 S&H react E 21-12 FH277.55

AD117 12MU 22-9-41 411S 3-10 FTR 16-12

AD118 24MU 4-9-41 266S 13-9 154S 11-2-42 FAAC 13-3 ROS 317S 27-5 GAL 340S 20-8 453S 6-11 FACB 20-12 AST 67 Reco Sq USA 17-10-43 AFDU 14-6-44 62 OTU 19-10 SOC 30-7-45

AD119 38MU 31-8-41 308S 5-9 316S 13-12 CB ops 29-4-42 CE ops 5-5 SOC

AD120 33MU 7-9-41 118S 17-9 ASTH 20-10 601S 14-3-42 133S 9-4 CAC ops 26-6 WAL VSM 4-2-43 fuel syst mods wng stiff COAL con to Seafire IB-NX966 31-5-43

AD121 12MU 7-9-41 403S 12-9 FACB 31-4-42 ROS 222S 26-5 FTR ops 31-5

AD122 38MU 31-8-41 610S 11-8 FTR ops 21-9

AD123 6MU 16-8-41 71S 26-8 cd Woodford Essex 15-10 SOC 27-10 Farn Jan'42

AD124 8MU 19-8-41 222S 20-8 602S 27-11 167S 6-4-42 CB ops 8-4 ROS 167S 8-8 222S 27-8 401S 7-12 91S 9-12 317S 1-5-43 hit sea off Levistone Suffolk ops CE 12-5

AD125 45MU 20-8-41 92S 21-8 417S 6-2-42 242S 21-4 243S 6-6 WAL 15-3-43 VSM 28-6 fuel syst & elev mods S type pt Mk III IFF wng stiff bomb carr. RNDA 16-1-44 269S 3-11 CE ber 21-1-46 SOC 24-1

AD126 24MU 34-8-41 41S 28-8 i/sea ops 18-9 FH22.25

AD127 M45M 37MU 6-9-41 118S 16-9 WAL 29-10 71S 27-4-42 CAC ops 19-8 ROS 334S 27-10 FACB 17-11 DeH VSM 22-6-43 fuel syst & elev mods wng stiff S type pt Mk III IFF COAL 3-1-44 mods hook fitt RNAS Hens 13-4

AD128 222S 22-8-41 GAL 26-9 504S 4-1-42 FACB 22-1 recat E 5-3

AD129 24MU 4-9-41 501S 15-9 FTR ops 17-11

AD130 38MU 31-8-41 308S 5-9 HAL 1-10 316S 13-12 CE ops 12-4-42 SOC FH188.40

AD131 6MU 18-9-41 222S 22-9

AD132 Bihar III 33MU 12-9-41 411S 2-10 WAL 18-5-42 402S 25-3-43 19S 5-5 64S 7-3-44 AST 8-12 FAF 1-2-45

AD133 M46 6MU 16-8-41 222S 22-8 FACA 30-11 64S 31-3-42 26S 27-7-44 41 OTU 25-1-45 58 OTU 22-3 631S 21-6 SOC 30-8

AD134 39MU 28-8-41 72S 30-8 CAC ops 17-3 ROS 401S 17-3-42 FTR 1-5 FH169.55

AD135 33MU 29-8-41 41S 1-9 AST 4-9 hook fitt 504S 26-9 287S flew i/grd Green Hailey Bucks 17-2-43

AD136 6MU 20-8-41 609S 29-8 CE ops 21-10 SOC 1-11 FH44.05

AD137 37MU 8-9-41 609S 30-9 HAL 18-5-42 VSM 5-2-43 fuel syst mods wng stiff 412S 2-5 317S 28-6 FTR ops 26-7 FH55.00

AD138 9MU 24-8-41 306S 7-9 303S 6-10 DeH 10-5-42 M46 instal 332S 4-2-43 340S 5-9-43 COAL 10-2-44

AD139 24MU 26-10-41 121S 31-1-42 411S 25-3 CAC ops 5-6 ROS VSM 26-9 fuel syst mods wng stiff 350S 15-3-42 610S 27-3 FTR 29-7 FH385.20

AD140 3065 317S F/hd Bolt Head Devon CE 15-3-42

AD176 6MU 19-9 71S 24-9 ASTH 7-12 411S 26-3-42 FACB 9-7 SAL 82MU 8-11 *Bar Inch* 18-12 USSR 24-3-43

AD177 37MU 5-12-41 308S 21-12 FTR ops 12-3-43

AD178 8MU 7-9-41 266S 18-9 R-R 24-10 mods flew i/high grd nr Sedgewick N'land 29-10 SOC 1-11 FH65.0

AD179 6MU 30-8-41 303S 6-10 FTR ops 25-3-42

AD180 37MU 14-9-41 234S 11-10 R-RH 7-12 mods 611S 11-2-43 316S 16-3 302S 3-10 402S 27-3-44 CE ops 22-6

AD181 38MU 14-9-41 485S 24-9 ASTH 4-10 67Th Obs Sq 24-3-43 FACE 6-12

AD182 LF VB 313S 21-10-41 64S 21-11 ASTH 29-3-42 152S 26-4 VSM 28-6-43 mods 610S 13-11 130S 30-1-44 222S 16-2 322S 17-3 350S 11-5 AST 19-5 R&S 15-1-47 SOC 10-2

AD183 9MU 20-9-41 72S 30-9 ROS 27-10 FACE 15-3-42 SOC 17-3

AD184 45MU 7-10-41 19S 30-10 616S 11-3-42 SAL 16-6 111S 26-7 VSM 13-5-43 mods con to Sea IB-PA118

AD185 LF VB M45M 45MU 8-10-41 19S 30-10 FAAC 10-2-42 ROS 93S 31-8 CGS 4-10 41S 6-11 WAL 15-3-43 602S 29-6 504S 10-10 129S 26-1-44 VSM 18-2-44 fuel syst mods 277S 12-5 DeH 19-7 1 AGS 5-12PAL 8-9-45 SOC 18-9

AD186 9MU 8-9-41 609S 20-9 HAL 2-11 402S 29-4-42 421S 8-5 AST 18-7 421S 13-11 402S 3-2-43 416S 23-3 421S 20-5 VSM 22-12 fuel syst mods FAF 9-10-47

AD187 13MU 10-9-41 118S 16-9 457S 22-3-42 485S 28-3 309S 16-7 FAAC 23-1-43 ROS AST 28-7 hook fitt RNDA 16-1-44

AD188 45MU 13-9-41 501S 2-10-41 FTR ops 8-11

AD189 9MU 6-10-41 602S 13-10 ROS 26-11 CE ops 12-3-42 SOC 31-3

AD190 45MU 15-10-41 19S 27-10 Stn Flt Colt 5-1-42 GAL 19-3 FA on f/f 11-7 ROS 215MU 12-11 *Nank* 28-11 USSR 6-2-43

AD191 37MU 12-10-42 19S 25-10 CAC ops 26-1 GAL 124S 28-4 602S 22-7 164S 11-9 341S 21-2-43 131S 21-4 310S 30-6 313Ss 26-7 HAL 17-6-44 R&S refurb to Port 18-4-47

AD192 LF LR VB 313S 21-10-41 ASTE 21-11 FACB 22-11 42 GAL VSM 26-3-43 mods 308S 15-7 349S 29-10 FAAC 1-3-44 ROS 63S 26-5 SOC 25-5-45

AD193 6MU 27-9-41 129S 1-10 ROS 7-3-42 CE ops 16-4 SOC

AD194 37MU 15-9-41 111S 1-10 403S 21-1-42 FAAC 3-4 118S 10-5 222S 21-6 CB ops 13-7 82MU 24-10 *Bar Inch* 18-12 USSR 24-3-43

AD195 45MU 25-9-41 411S 10-10 CE ops 13-2-42

AD196 38MU 31-8-41 71S 10-9 FTR ops 27-8-42

AD197 8MU 7-9-41 129S 14-10 313SD 25-2-42 CE ops 27-3

AD198 12MU 7-9-41 403S 12-9 WAL 8-1-42 303S 17-6 FACB 27-7 GAL 91S 3-1-43 19S 6-6 65S 30-6 130S 15-8 303S 15-2-44 coll with BL462 ldg Bally CE25-3

AD199 33MU 7-9-41 71S 19-9 145S 15-11 380S 11-2-42 403S 17-3 FAAC 2-4 ROS 121S 31-5 VSM 5-11-43 fuel syst mods 277S 4-3-44 MAL 17-8 Marshalls FS 24-10-45 SOC

AD200 37MU 7-9-41 501S 19-9 u/s ldg coll with BL752 & BL921 Ibsley 26-4-42 AST SOC 3-5

AD201 24MU 3-9-41 129S 11-9 FAAC 24-4-42 WAL CE

AD202 9MU 8-9-41 609S 20-9 111S 22-8 FTR ops 27-8

AD203 8MU 7-9-41 234S 14-9 FTR ops 20-10 SOC 31-10 FH 38.25

AD204 M45M The Andoverian 12MU 10-9-41 118S 16-9 ASTH 14-2-42 111S 29-8 340S 28-8-43 485S 11-11 SAL 4-3-44 303S 19-5 CAC ops 23-7 ROS 308S 27-8 26S 15-9 58 OTU 22-3-45 29MU 10-8

AD205 12MU 10-9-41 234S 14-9 ASTH 7-12 609S 28-1-42 FTR 25-4 FH96.0

AD206 12MU 7-9-41 403S 12-9 FTR 28-3-42 FH29.30

AD207 6MU 7-9-41 403S 12-9 SOC 30-9 FH16.15

AD208 6MU 7-9-41 403S 12-9 FTR ops 2-6-42 FH243.10

AD209 33MU 2-9-41 118S 17-9 FTR ops 25-4-42 FH163.10

AD210 Aruba (NEI) 33MU 12-9-41 118S 30-9 452S 1-10 FAAC 17-2-42 ROS FTR ops 30-4 FH118.20

AD225 5MU 12-9-41 111S 11-10 26MU 31-10 *C o Lil* 8-12 USSR 16-2-43

AD226 9MU 21-9-41 412S 6-10 WAL 20-4-42 152S 31-8 AST 23-7-43 con to Sea IB-NX 966 RNDA 16-1-44

AD227 M45M Ayre Spitfire 12MU 11-9-41 234S 19-9 FAAC 14-3-42 ROS VSM 23-7-43 mods 130S 15-1-44 222S 16-2 322S 17-3 345S 25-4 FACB 16-8 58 OTU 22-3-45 527S 27-9 RWE Watton 18-4-46 sold J Dale

AD228 Cheshire County II 12MU 22-9-41 401S 27-9 CB ops 8-1-42 WAL 350S 24-5 453S 16-12 FACE 18-1-43

AD229 12MU 21-9-41 SOC E 22-1-42

AD230 Palembang Oeloe IV no record

AD231 West Borneo II 5MU 13-9-41 19S 26-10 R-R 30-10 mods FACB 14-2-42 ASTH 307S USA 26-8 350S 12-9 401S 7-12 403S 25-1-43 FTR ops 15-2 FH114.0

AD232 Bihar I 33MU 12-9-41 401S 26-9 CE ops 29-3-42 SOC 31-3

AD233 West Borneo I 37MU 15-9-41 222S 1-10 FTR ops 25-5-42 Rodeo No.51 s/dn by Fw190 over France S/l Jankiewiez kld

AD234 Gerfalcon (Emmetts) 33MU 12-9-41 401S 26-9 AST 22-2-42 CE 13-3 SOC 31-3

AD235 12MU 11-9-41 118S 16-9 R-R 5-12 mods 222S 21-6-42 FA dbf 1-10 SOC

AD236 Bihar II 24MU 14-9-41 602S 23-9 81S 5-4-42 132S 7-5 FACB 12-7 SAL 222MU 1-11 *Nank* 28-11 USSR 6-2-43

AD237 M45M Dhanabad Jharia 45MU 12-9-41 501S 26-9 133S 2-8-42 401S 28-8 222S 26-9 FAAC 20-12 130S 31-3-43 19S 15-5 126AF 19-8 303S 3-12 strk by AD295 during scramble Bally CE 8-4-44

AD238 M45M Borough of Barnes 38MU 16-9-41 485S 26-9 54S 21-4 167S 31-5 FAAC 8-9 ROS 610S 29-10 131S 25-1-43 FAAC 9-4 ROS 130S 16-5 349S 19-7 345S 13-4-44 AST 3-7 FAF 19-1-45

AD239 Hoeloesoengai (NEI) 45MU 13-9-41 118S 18-9 CE 13-2-42

AD240 38MU 14-7-41 315S 10-9 GAL 18-2-42 hit telegraph pole nr North f/ld CB 8-3 recat E 13-3

AD241 Twickenham II 8MU 20-9-41 111S 1-10 602S flew i/high grd with AD256 Titsey Hill Surrey 23-11 GAL 129S 19-8-42 602S 29-11 66S 19-2-43 SAL 3-4 AST 27-5 con to Sea IB-NX982

AD242 Bihar IV 5MU 13-9-41 452S 15-10 i/sea ops 6-11

AD243 Tapanoeli (NEI) 37MU 14-9-41 302S 11-10 FACE 9-3-42 ASTE 20-5

AD244 6MU 26-9-41 616S 1-10 65S 6-10 FA 5-2-42 AST 65S 18-5 SAL 27-12 66S 23-3-43 CAC 14-4- LMS 341S 26-10 329S 23-2-44 63S 13-3 26S 27-4 57OTU 13-8 SOC 1-6-45

AD245 37MU 14-9-41 11S 1-10 ASTH 7-12 234S 26-4-42 CE ops 4-6 SOC 5-6 FH103-55

AD246 39MU 18-9-41 129S 24-9 CAC ops 12-4-42 recat E

AD247 Rajna Gar 24MU 14-9-41 129S 21-9 610S 30-11 coll with AB919 ldg Hutton Cranswick CE 17-1-42 SOC 23-1 AST 20-5-42 610S 16-8 670bs Grp USA 12-4-43 303S 25-3-44 CE ops 26-7

AD248 M45M Cheshire County I 24MU 14-9-41 485S 22-9 616S 25-3-42 ASTE 30-3 610S 27-2-43 350S 27-3 303S 6-1-44 130S 7-6 61 OTU 19-10 CGS 27-2-45 to 5591M FAF 11-3-46

AD249 45MU 22-9-41 401S 25-9-41 FAAC 23-12 ROS 222S 11-2-42 FTR ops 28-4 SOC

AD250 39MU 18-9-41 129S 24-9 sortie to shoot down dirfting balloon. I/sea off Littlehampton 28-10 SOC 30-10

AD251 Willenhall 39MU 18-9-41 602S 22-9 FAE ttl wrk 23-11 SOC 30-11

AD252 38MU 17-9-41 611S 25-9 64S 14-11 ASTH 21-3-42 2 SLG 26-4 111S 27-7 ASt con to Sea IB-PA128 15-6-43

AD253 6MU 19-8-41 401S 27-9 ASTH 7-5-42 FACB 19-1-43 ROS VSM 29-7 fuel syst mods wng stiff Mk III IFF S type pt bomb carr 24-9 Grp 22-3-44 269S 27-4 CE BER 20-3-46 SOC 28-3

AD254 39MU 18-9-41 401S 28-9 FAAC 29-14 ROS 154S 1-3-42 FTR ops 3-6

AD255 39MU 18-9-41 92S 19-10 401S 21-10 e/fd cd/ld Bluebell Hill Maidstone Kent CB 21-11 SOC 29-11

AD256 6MU 19-9-41 602S 24-9 flew i/high grd with AD241 Titsey Hill Surrey 23-11 ttl wrk SOC 30-11

AD257 Borough of Willesden 33MU 21-9-41 302S 11-10 610S 26-11 302S 31-12 ftr ops 5-6-42

AD258 8MU 20-9-41 403S 1-10 FAE SOC 17-1-42

AD259 LF VB M45M Ilford 12MU 26-9-41 411S 11-10 FACB 25-3-42 65S 24-7 165S 23-9 DeH 28-10 412S 30-9-43 AST 27-4-44 EFCS 10-10 SOC scr

AD260 Miss ABC 4 8MU 27-9-41 111S 1-10 AST 21-12 308S 24-8-42 DeH 4-11 VSM 9-6-43 fuel syst rud & elev mods wng stiff Mk III IFF 66S 12-10 coll with EP639 Perr CE 23-10 FH191.45

AD261 12MU 29-9-41 411S 10-10 AST 14-12 91S 18-4-42 VSM 26-8 mods FTR ops 9-2-43 FH325.35

AD262 38MU 14-9-41 315S 27-9 317S 5-1-42 FAAC 13-3 DeH 122S 3-7-43 234S 15-8 VSM 29-1-44 fuel syst mods 278S 18-4 e/fd f/ld Woodbridge Suffolk CE 11-5

AD263 Miss ABC II 12MU 29-9-41 411S 10-10 CAC ops 19-5-42 AST VSM 1-10 mods 52 OTU 9-6-43 FLS 2-2-44 SAL 7-4 AST 15-9 'Basta' mods CGS 22-2-45 SOC 29-11

AD264 Paisley 8MU 27-9-41 411S 2-10 PSO FTR ops 8-12

AD265 Cheshire County III 33MU 21-9-41 316S 26-10 306S 12-12 FACB 2-5-42 CBAF recat E SOC FH153.45

AD266 8MU 20-9-41 111S 11-10 FAAC 24-2-42 ROS 504S 10-7 501S 19-10 S&H mr 27-3-43 411S 10-7 126AF 10-8 341S 17-10 602S 25-1-44 287S 17-1-45

AD267 8MU 20-9-41 616S 24-9 65S 6-10 FTR ops 21-10

AD268 LF VB M45M 8MU 20-9-41 616S 24-9 65S 6-10 Farn 27-3-42 dvng trls 303S 22-8-42 306S 18-8-43 302S 3-10 322S 25-11 222S 1-1-44 26S 26-6 595 AACS 18-1-45

AD269 Trl Spit with 2×20mm can 4×.5in mgs 24MU 6-10-41 317S 13-10 AST 8-12 CAC ops 14-4-42 315S 4-9 303S 30-11 FACE 15-12

AD270 9MU 20-9 412S 6-10 FTR ops 8-11

AD271 9MU 21-9-41 611S 30-9 64S 14-11 ASTH 21-3-42 41S 27-7 FACB 29-8 WAL 312S 31-11 AST 30-3-43 con to Sea IB-NX956

AD272 6MU 29-9-41 302S 13-10 dbf on grd 25-12 SOc 27-12

AD273 12MU 21-9-41 403S 30-9 Ce ops 12-12 SOC 25-2-42

AD274 6MU 26-9-41 6-9s 11-10 72S 11-10 CB ops 5-4-42 ASTH 309S 31-7 FAAC 6-8 AST con to Sea IB-NX926 9-5-43

AD288 33MU 22-9-41 412S 8-10 71S 29-4-42 FACB 2-8 AST VSM 10-10 fuel syst mods 350S 19-7-43 ROS 26-8 DeH 16-6-44 to 5599M FAF 3-3-46

AD289 33MU 21-9-41 121S 15-11 FTR ops 28-4-42 FH151.25

AD290 33MU 31-9-41 602S 13-11 SOC 5-1-42 cancel AST 8-1 602S 29-6-43 CE ops 15-7 SOC FH64.10

AD291 45MU 27-9-41 412S 14-10 CE dbf 11-12 SOC 17-12

AD292 The Cannock Chase 6MU 27-9-41 411S 2-10 609S 19-11 ROS 18-3-42 FAAC 21-4 AST 332S 29-3-43 349S 19-8 hit trees cd Bridlington CE 12-10 FH409.35

AD293 39MU 29-9-41 92S 4-10 FA dbf 15-11 SOC 16-11

AD294 M46 Miss ABA III 6MU 26-9-41 118S 3-10 FAE 16-11 SOC 29-11 AST 8-1-42 350S 12-9 485S 22-12 122S 2-2-43 710S 18-2 RNDA 2-4-44 BC Ins 9-12 ASTH 17-7-46 M45M instal R&S refurb to Port 28-4-47

AD295 LF VB 45MU 1-10-41 317S 12-10 ROS 28-11 315S 4-9-42 VSM 13-10 fuel syst mods 130S 24-10 412S 31-1-43 e/fd w/u ldg Redhill CE 6-6-43 AST recat B 349S 3-1-44 303S strk AD327 in scramble Bally CAC 8-4 ROS 61 OTU 17-5-45 631S 31-6-45 SOC 19-9

AD296 24MU 13-10-41 71S 24-10 ASTH 27-11 flew i/mntn Lachanbreck Balmachie 15-3-42 R A Porter ATA kld

AD297 45MU 1-10-41 302S 14-10 hvy ldg o/t warm CE 15-4-42 ASTE SOC 23-4

AD298 45MU 15-10-41 134S 8-1 81S 4-4 243S 4-7 453S 10-9 CE ops 11-10

AD299 M45M 45MU 27-9-41 411S 11-10 292S 25-9-42 133S 29-9 336S 1-10 335S 15-2-43 303S 23-3 315S 6-6 e/fd w/u ldg Hutton Cranswick Ce 22-6 AST 12-4-44 58 OTU 22-3-45 to 5717M 16-10

AD300 6MU 28-9-41 91S 3-10 CAC ops 9-4-42 ROS FAAC 16-6 FTR ops 12-7 FH192.55

AD301 37MU 4-9-41 130S 31-12 AST 14-8-42 222MU 30-10 *C o Lil* 18-12 for USSR dam in transit rtp 5-3-43

AD302 M45M 39MU 29-9-41 92S 3-10 417S 7-2-42 e/fd cd Tain CE 9-3 SOC 31-3

AD303 National Federation of Hosiery Manufacturers Assoc 8MU 2-10-41 316S 11-10 FTR ops 9-11

AD304 37MU 4-9-41 316S 14-10 306S 12-12 FTR ops 26-4-42 FH147.10

AD305 12MU 30-9-41 412S 10-10 IPRU FAE 10-4-42

AD306 24MU 12-10-41 317S 19-10 CE ops 30-12 SOC

AD307 9MU 12-10-41 19S 23-10 FTR ops 25-3-42

AD308 45MU 1-10-41 317S 15-10 CB ops 16-3-42 ASTE recat E 20-5

AD309 Miss ABC IV 6MU 26-9-41 118S 3-10 GAL 7-4-42 65S 24-7 130S 31-3-43 CE 24-5

AD310 8MU 27-9-41 452S 1-10 CE ops 13-10 130S strk by BL515 on ldg Bally CE 24-5-43

AD311 45MU 1-10-41 316S 30-10 306S 12-12 FACB 28-4-42 CBAF SOC FH113.10

AD312 Cambridge 8MU 27-9-41 611S 1-10 64S 14-11 stld on ldg cd Horn SOC 30-11

AD313 45MU 1-10-41 317S 14-10 ROS 6-1-42316S 3-5 124S 28-7 FACE 28-8 SOC 5-9

AD314 37MU 4-9-41 308S 2-11 316S 13-12 hit disp pen on t/o CB 24-1-42 SOC 403S 7-6 416S 3-6-43 SAL 17-7 350S 9-10 CE ops 20-12 FH596.10

AD315 6MU 29-9-41 AFDU 9-10 FACB 18-1-42 AST 167S 28-2-43 316S 7-5-43 310S 17-8 504S 24-9 FACE 17-12

AD316 39MU 29-9-41 92S 3-10 FAAC 10-1-42 ROS 417S 14-2 242S 21-4 243S 6-6 SAL 6-11 VSM 8-9-43 fuel syst & elev mods wng stiff S type pt Mk III IFF bomb carr RNDA 16-1-44 as train

AD317 LF VB M45M 8MU 27-9-41 403S 1-10 FACB 27-3-42 AST 302S 4-7 CB ops 11-10 AST 19S 26-7-43 412S 30-9 303S 3-12 58 OTU 17-5-44 1TEU 27-6 FAAC 10-5-45 ROS recat E SOC 22-5

AD318 412S 7-10-44 R-R 15-11 mods 1st prod a/c fitt Neg G carb AFDU 8-1-42 R-R 12-5 AFDU 31-12 FAAC 12-5-43 ROS AFDU 23-5-43 FAAC 8-9-44 ROS 57 OTU 11-8-45 to 5683M 22-9 SOC 5-5-49

AD319 12MU 17-10-41 92S 30-10 417S 7-2-42 242S 18-4 243S 6-6 222MU 11-11 *Harp* 19-12 USSR 17-3-43

AD320 Palembang Oeloe 24MU 14-9-41 308S 20-9 130S 23-10 FAAC 1-6 AST VSM 11-10 fuel syst mods wing stiff 610S 19-4-43 AST 22-7

AD321 Firefly 24MU 6-10-41 317S 130-10 FACB 25-1-42 ROS CE ops 16-3 ASTE recat B 67 Obs Grp 4-6-43 130S 28-7-44 41 OTU 9-9-44 SOC 6-6-45

AD322 Everite 9MU 6-10-41 92S 13-10 ROS 15-12 350S 25-2-42 CE ops 5-8

AD323 37MU 13-10-41 R-R 24-10 mods 19S 25-10 coll with BL682 on t/o Ludham Ce 19-2-42 SOC

AD324 M45M 24MU 13-10-41 72S 24-10 FACE 12-2-42 GAL 121S 21-8 335S 1-10 501S 23-3 CB ops 27-6-44 ROS FAF 10-1-45

AD325 Westmorland II 12MU 29-11-41 310S 13-12 154S 23-5-42 312S 8-6 332S 3-8 FTR ops 19-8

AD326 9MU 14-10-41 234S 31-10 SOC 15-11 FTR ops

AD327 Solaire Ross 38MU 16-10-41 74S 23-11 232S 8-4-42 SAL 11-12 VSM 23-7-43 fuel syst rud & elev mods wng stiff S type pt Mk III IFF bomb carr 222S 1-1-44 234S 22-6 SOC 29-5-45

AD328 Saugre Charrua 45MU 15-10-41 310S 4-12 FACE 15-7-42 AST SOC 31-7 FH183.0

AD329 LF VB 12MU 30-9-41 412S 10-10 AST 19-12 M55M instal 403S 24-4-42 416S 3-6-43 610S 13-6 308S 3-7 130S 22-8 FACE 25-11 FH530.05

AD330 37MU 4-9-41 308S 4-11 316S 13-12 i/sea ops 28-2-42

AD331 45MU National Federation Hosiery Manufacturers (Nottingham & Mansfield). 45MU 7-10-41 310S 16-11 ROS 20-4-42 234S 29-7 GAL 11-9-42 FAAC 20-1-43 165S 27-1-43 AST VSM 22-6 fuel syst mods wng stiff 66S 24-8 CAC ops 8-10 ROS 441S 5-3-44 26S 30-3 FACB 14-4 LMS CGS 3-10 GAL 9-2-45

AD332 12MU 12-10-41 19S 24-10 CE ops 12-2-42 SOC 20-2

AD348 LF VB MXX Alas Del-Uruguay 9MU 6-10-41 609S 13-10 131S 31-3-42 CAC ops 19-8 AST 501S 6-11 S&H 21-1-43 VSM 28-3-43 fuel syst mods wng stiff M45M instal 610S 15-7-43 FAAC 5-10 ROS 130S 30-1-44 222S 16-2 322S 17-3 57 OTU 5-10 FACE 1-2-45 SOC 15-2

AD349 8MU 2-10-41 412S 7-10 u/S ldg cd Wellingore CE 9-12

AD350 24MU 6-10-41 317S 13-10 f/ld nr Prawle Devon strk AD351 on grd CE 16-3-42

AD351 Montevideo 45MU 8-10 317S 18-10 strk by AD350 CE 16-3-42

AD352 9MU 6-10-41 609S 13-10 FAAC 24-1-42 411S 10-6 402S 25-3-43 FAAC 6-4 ROS 315S 30-9 VSM 20-12 fuel syst mods 17SFTS 7-10-44 SOc 31-5-46

AD353 12MU 12-10-41 313S 22-10 FACB 10-1-42 AST 4USA 27-8 82GRP USAAF 18-11 SAL 12-4-43 CE ops 12-7-44

AD354 37MU 4-9-41 316S 14-10 ASTEx 19-11 306S 12-12 VSM 21-10-42 fuel syst mods wng stiff HAL 27-1-43 con to PRXIII M32 541S Ben 21-4 FACB 27-4-44 HAL SOC 28-3-45

AD355 9MU 10-10-41 485S 15-10 HAL 29-1-42 331S 7-4- VSM 23-9 CE ops 2-10

AD356 9MU 10-10-41 Black Eagle 411S 16-10 ROS 18-4-42 41S 9-5-42 FTR ops 22-5-42 FH132.0

AD357 Leicester Division 8MU 2-10-41 412S 7-10 GAL 19-5-42 309 USA 30-7 VSM 27-4-43 mods con to Sea IB-PA112

AD358 6MU 21-10-41 609S 28-10 FACB 29-1-42 WAL 93S 29-8 AST 15-3-43 conv to Seafire IB-NX902

AD359 8MU 19-10-41 611S 22-10 AST 31-12 403S 9-6-42 USAAF 11-7 ldg coll with AB270 CB 27-7 SAL 33MU 27-9-43 hook fitt RNDA 16-1-44 AST 28-3 RNAS Belfast 17-6

AD360 12MU 17-10-41 130S 21-10 CAC ops 19-8-42 ROs 130S 4-9 AST 20-11 COAL 21-6-43 hook fitt RNDA 16-1-44

AD361 38MU 15-10-41 313S 21-10 FACB 12-2-42 ROS 317 23-3 CE ops 2804

AD362 24MU 22-10-41 266S 6-12 312S 6-6-42 AST 19-10 421S 4-2-43 412S 5-3 602S 19-4 FAAC 14-9 AST 501S

3-7 61 OTU 2-8 FAAC 24-4-45 ROS 631S SOC 21-9

AD363 45MU 15-10-41 308S 29-10 316S 13-12

AD364 Turnall 24MU 6-10-41 ROS 26-11 Stn Flt Woodvale 16-5-42 FAAC 2905 ROS 317S 4-10 SAL 15-10 P&P SM 13-3-43 mods con to Sea IB-PA109

AD365 F.IB 45MU 8-10-41 310S 19-11 FAAC 12-4-42 AST con to Sea IB-NX919 8-4-43 ret RAF Dec '44

AD366 F.IB Wigtonsire 45MU 23-10-41 310S 16-11 234S 29-7-42 SAL 11-12 316S 14-3-43 340S 6-12 239S 16-2-44 63S 13-3 277S 26-5 SOC E 21-2-45

AD367 F.IB 24MU 6-10-41 317S 13-10 WAL mr 23-1-42 91S 3-4 CA ops 10-4

AD368 F.IB Prestwick 317S 20-4-41 cd nr Dartmouth Devon after sweeep Ce 15-3-42 ASTE Coal con to Sea IB-NX957 31-3-43

AD369 F.IB Kano II 12MU 17-10-41 130S 23-10 FAAC 5-3-42 ASTE recat E 20-5

AD370 Endeavour 37MU 13-10-41 130S 31-12 AST 17-11-42 303S 14-3-43 e/fd w/u ldg West Dean nr Friston 30-5

AD371 9MU 10-10-41 CRD VA 31-12 con to 2nd proto Sea Mk IIc Farn 25-2-42 catapult trls MFSU Speke 9-9 RNAS 11-8 778S Arb

AD372 Sandwich 317S 20-10-41 e/fd cd Exeter CE 1-12 SOC 10-12 cancel AST 8-1-42 313S 24-6-42 FTR ops 15-7

AD373 12MU 25-10-41 121S 4-12 ASTE 13-3 o/s ldg NWld std cd 2-10

AD374 45MU 30-10-41 310S 3-12 ASTE 12-8 602S 4-3-44 118S 13-3 61 OTU 19-10 SOC E 19-1-45

AD375 The Normanton 24MU 22-10-41 616S 8-11 FAAC 16-3-42 ROS 72S 23-3 CE ops 12-4 SOC 28-4 FH16-1-45

AD376 6MU 452S 22-11 SOC 24-11 52 OTU 23-11 42 to 2799M FAF

AD377 19S 23-10-41 e/fd cd/ldg Hickling Broad Norfolk CE 1-4-42 SOC FH168.0

AD378 45MU 28-10-41 310S 18-11 FAAC 23-11 GAL 5USA 6-9-42 504S 30-9 501S 19-10 FACB 6-11 S&H CE 21-12

AD379 37MU 17-10-41 91S 1-11 FACB 30-5-42 CA ops 21-1-42 165S 21-1-43 132S 22-7 350S 19-9 DeH 31-3-44 PAL 8-9-45 SOC 17-9

AD380 313S 24-10-41 152S 24-4-42 FTR ops 30-7

AD381 The Plessey Spitfire 12MU 27-11-41 412S 16-12 VSM 15-9-42 mods 64S 28-1-43 453S 2-4 129S 17-7 313S 15-8 FLS Mlfld 10-2-44 FAAC 7-6 AEAF Com Sq 20-9 FACB 23-6-45

AD382 45MU 29-10-41 310S 17-11 mr 3-2-42 232S 14-8 P&P SM 3-10 ASTH 10-7-43 hook fitt RNDA 18-1-44 53 OTU 3-7

AD383 M45M 303S 23-10-41 FAAC 24-7-42 ROS 453S 23-12 CAC ops 14-1-43 ROS 222S 31-3 167S 19-5 322S 29-10 SAL 7-11 26S 3-4-44 FAAC 29-8 AST 84GCS 4-2-45 R&S refurb to Port 15-4-47

AD384 Geo S Parker 12MU 12-10-41 313S 21-10 dam ops 12-4-42 ROS mr 313S 9-5

AD385 45MU 15-10-41 19S 30-10 WAL 317S 26-8-42 315S 4-9 336S 23-11 HAL 4-11-43 USAAF 23-11 RNDA 23-2-44 COAL 22-4 con to train RNAS Hens 1-8

AD386 9MU 14-10-41 315S 23-10 ASTH 7-11 72S 5-4-42 133S 15-6 453S 1-9 AST 17-12 RNDA 30-3-43 340S FFS 8-5-43 FACB 23-8 345S 3-4-44 53 OTU 11-8 u/s ldg o/l Hibald CE 13-2-45 SOC 26-2

AD387 North Star 45MU 15-10-41 316S 28-10 306S 12-12 VSM 28-7-42 mods GAL 12-9 AST con to Sea IB-NX899 14-3-43

AD388 12MU 17-10-41 130S 23-10 WAL 27-11 121S 5-5-42 VSM 22-8 eng change 335 USA 1-10 132S 23-3- air coll with P8548 cd nr Sittingbourne Kent dbf CE 14-4-43 SOC FH 272.05

AD389 24MU 13-10-41 71S 29-10 CAC ops 26-4-42 ROS 91S 20-5 FACB 19-7 AST VSM 20-10 fuel syst mods wing stiff HAL 3-5-43 con to PRXIII M32 4S 30-12 SOC 22-4-45

AD390 313S 24-10-41 CAC ops 29-3-42 ROS 152S 20-4 RNDA 28-5-43 AST 31-5 mods

AD391 24MU 13-10-41 130S 26-10 FACE 23-2-42 AST SOC 4-3

AD392 37MU 12-10-41 130S 2-11 ROS 5-11 145S 17-11 AST 12-1-42 411S 27-8 FAAC 28-9 ROS FACE 20-11 FH116.55

AD393 Goentoer (NEI) 37MU 25-1-42 132S 10-3 SAL 18-12 VSM 11-3-43 mods con to Sea IB-PA105

AD394 37MU 28-1-42 132S 16-3 FAAC 4-9 ROS SAL 25-11 VSM 11-3-43 mods con to Sea IB-PA107

AD395 6MU 28-11-41 16FPP strk high grd Thornhill Dumfries on f/f to 331S Skea Pilot A Scott ATA kld Ce 15-3-42

AD396 Ardjoeno (NEI) 8MU 17-1-42 609S 13-2 152S 24-4 FACE SOC 3-5 FH83.0

AD397 37MU 28-1-42 317S 17-3 CAC ops 1-6 ROS GAL 6-7 VSM 15-10 fuel syst mods wng stiff con to Sea IB-PA102

AD411 39MU 31-10-41 65S 15-11 AST 23-12 FACB 18-2-42 WAL 131S 16-5 FAAC 8-7 ROS 412S 3-8 VSM 12-10 FTR ops 29-11 FH145.35

AD412 45MU 26-10-41 310S 15-1 FTR ops 4-2

AD413 37MU 2-11-41 HAL 9-11 130S 1-7-42 HAL spcl invest 30-7 P&PSM 12-1-43 VSM 27-3 fuel syst mods wng stiff 416S 2-9 186S 17-2-44 FAAC 26-3 ROS 1687 Ftr Affil Flt 30-10 FACE cd f/l nr Howden Yorks dbf 11-1-46 pilot kld SOC 23-1

AD414 45MU 24-10-41 310S 17-11 FACE 14-2-42 SOC 27-2

AD415 37MU 4-11-41 312S 1-12 SAL 16-12 416S 1-3-42 CB ops 30-3 SAL 129S 30-6 FTR ops 18-8

AD416 38MU 15-10-41 19S 23-10 WAL 5-6-42 307S 31-7 93S 13-9 91S 17-3-43 132S 1-5 122S 21-5 FACE 4-7 SOC FH416.40

AD417 M45M YR Hen Bont 37MU 13-10-41 130S 8-12 FAAC 19-5-42 ROS VSM 13-10-43 fuel syst & elev mods wng stiff S type pt Mk III IFF bomb carr USAAF 9-5-44 AST 30-5 41 OTU 19-9 FAAC 6-9-45 recat E SOC 27-9

AD418 38MU 15-10-41 401S 22-10 AST 14-6-42 82MU 24-10 *Bar Inch* 19-12 USSR 24-3-43

AD419 Kano No.I CRD VA 17-10-41 CBAF for 3 months for trl instal ASTH 24-9-42 CRD DeH 31-12 VSM 28-6-43 fuel syst mods wng stiff 416S 30-8 131S 7-9 310S 24-9 315S 1-2-44 CE ops 16-6

AD420 Kano I 45MU 16-10-41 310S 17-11 FACE 12-4-42 SOC ASTH FH129.50

AD421 37MU 17-10-41 401S 1-11-41 FACB 30-3-42 ASTH 5-4 con to Sea IB-NX882 17-2-43

AD422 45MU 16-10-41 310S 15-11 2USA 22-8-42 247Grp 22-3-44 269S 27-4 CE ber 15-3-46 SOc 28-3

AD423 45MU 16-10-41 310S 21-7-42 SAL 6-5-44 'Basta' mods FLs Mlfld 24-5 12GRP Com Flt 9-11 SOC mr 12-11-45

AD424 8MU 19-10-41 CE ops 11-1-42 SOC 16-1

AD425 Ardua Spitfire 8MU 19-10-41 611S 22-10 ASTH 14-11 131S 14-4-42 VSM 8-6 mods M46 instal MHth 30-6 131S 31-12-43 312S 4-12 441S 27-2-44 56 OTU 30-3 1TEU 25-5 ROS 61 OTU 25-6 to 5544M 9-8-45

AD426 9MU 21-9-41 412S 6-10 FAAC 19-1-42 RNAS Stret 1-9 AST 24-9 hook fitt LoS 13-10 ROS 5-11 bboc RAF 13-4-45 1PTS 31-1-46

AD427 6MU 26-9-41 234S 3-10 PSO FTR ops 5-12

AD428 39MU 29-9-41 302S 10-10 FACE 24-4-42 AST VSM 31-8 fuel syst mods 403S 26-9 416S 3-6-43 SAL 350S 9-10 322S 11-1-44 FACE 16-1

AD429 412S 7-10-41 FACB 10-3-42 GAL 243S 29-7 SAL 18-11 VSM 15-5-43 fuel syst mods wng stiff 504S 24-8 313S 22-9 144AF 25-2-44 443S 27-2 FAAC 1-3 ROS 57 OTU 15-9 695S 21-11-45 SOC 27-12

AD430 9MU 10-10-41 452S 14-10 i/sea ops 6-11

AD449 37MU 2-11-41 603S 27-12 FAAC 16-3-42 ROS 332S 15-5 i/sea ops 29-6

AD450 38MU 10-12-41 65S 2-1-42 hvy ldg Debden CE 20-2 SOC

AD451 12MU 28-11-41 602S 5-1-42 FAAC 12-2 ROS reported miss 25-3 FAAC ROS 4-1S 12-7 317S 4-9 336S 23-11 DeH 16-6-44 10AGS 8-6-45 SOC 27-6-46

AD452 38MU 2-1-42 6711S 13-2 243S 2-6 222S 11-8 64S 31-3-43 baulked on app o/s tip on to nose CE 17-6 FH567.0

AD453 24MU 2-1-42 54S 1-3 167S 31-5 610S 14-10 131S 25-1-43 FACA 29-1 310S 30-6 to 4122M 10SoTT 3-9 CE 4-10-44

AD454 38MU 6-11-41 122S 18-11 234S 25-5-42 FTR ops 23-9

AD455 38MU 2-11-41 303S 9-12 FTR ops 4-4-42

AD456 12MU 1-11-41 616S 8-11 CE ops 12-4-42 SOC FH 181.20

AD457 37MU 31-10-41 610S 7-12 AST 17-7-42 421S 24-1-43 412S 3-2 FAAC 23-3 ROS 317S 8-5-43 412S 29-6 303S 3-12 FTR believed hit high grd in Eire 29-12

AD458 39MU 7-11-41 19S 22-11 FAAC 5-6-42 91S 22-10 FTR ops 31-10

AD459 37MU 31-10-41 616S 23-11 FACE 27-3-42 SOC

AD460 37MU 17-10-41 121S 4-11 FTR ops 4-5-42 FH159.50

AD461 19S 23-10-41 CAC ops 29-3-42 ROS 76MU 31-10 *C o Lil* 8-12 USSR 16-2-43

AD462 45MU 16-10-41 310S 16-11 ASTE mr 2-5-42 91S 9-8 CB ops 21-8 AST VSM 11-1-43 fuel syst mods wng stiff 402S CE ops 19-6

AD463 37MU 19-10-41 121S 4-11 CB ops 6-2-42 234S 18-4 FTR ops 24-4 FH58.10

AD464 45MU 16-10-41 310S 16-11 WAL 14-2-42 M55MA instal FAAC 28-6 ROS 308S 28-7 71S 12-8 334 USA 1-10 HAL 12-7-44 10AGS 8-6-45 R&S refurb to Port 4-7-47

AD465 M45M 9MU 14-3-41 313S 21-10 AST 9-7-42 91S 28-12 412S 1-5-43 308S 17-5 501S 27-8 HAL 12-11 61 OTU 2-8-44 SOC 29-11-45

AD466 24MU 26-10-41 610S 25-11 FTR over e/tr 12-12

AD467 12MU 24-10-41 72S 28-10 ASTH 28-11 154S 13-6-42 strk truck ldg Redhill CE 29-10 FH144.50 AST 10-12 COAL 7-7-43 hook fitt RNDA 16-1-44 RNAS Belfast 10-2

AD468 45MU 28-10-41 310S 17-11 spun off climb t/o cd ttl wrk 8-12 SOC 17-12

AD469 65S 30-10-41 ASTH 16-11 FAAC 6-6-42 ROS 222S 9-6 FACB 5-7 WAL 610S 22-2-43 350S 27-3 FACB 12-7 SAL 316S 18-12 118S 27-4-44 FACB 9-4-44 ASTH CGS 13-10 FAAC 20-3-45 recat E SOC 26-3

AD470 8MU 2-11-41 131S 7-11 MM 16-6-42 412S 22-8 CAC ops 17-11 ROS 402S 31-12 412S 2-1-43 132S 9-1 AST 7-7 234S 6-1-44 FAAC 12-4 ROS 57 OTU 12-10 e/fd f/ld nr Esh CE 13-3-45

AD471 8MU 2-11-41 121S 7-11 FAAC 13-2-42 CBAF CE FH110.10

AD472 145S 17-11-41 350S 7-2-42 hvy ldg Warm 19-4-42 WAL recat E SOC

AD473 5MU 9-11-41 74S 28-11 232S 8-4-42 FACB 9-6 222MU 27-12 *C o Lil* 8-12 USSR 16-2-43

AD474 45MU 30-10-41 64S 18-11 AST 22-2-42 331S 30-6 VSM 16-10 fuel syst mods M55 instal 453S 16-11 222S 31-3-43 167S 19-5 322S 20-7 349S 8-10 FACE 2-11 AST 61 OTU 11-8-44 AST 26-5-45 SOC 30-7

AD475 M45M 45M 29-10-41 145S 15-11 FAAC 3-1-42 ROS 350S 11-2 CAC ops 19-8 ROS 485S 9-1-43 453S 29-1 222S 31-3 VSM 5-4 mods 167S 19-5 322S 1-1-44 VSM 1-3 fuel syst & 'Basta' mods 275S 4-5 ASR SOC 22-2-45

AD476 39MU 8-11-41 19S 24-11 FACB 16-5-42 WAL CE 27-5

AD477 39MU 7-11-41 41S 24-12 CE ops 12-11 SOC AST H

AD478 39MU 7-11-41 19S 11-12 CAC ops 8-2-42 AST 129S 17-4 CAC ops 4-5 ROS 129S ran off runway tip onto nose Grimsetter CE 17-10 SOC 29-10 FH275.45

AD498 24MU 23-10-41 121S 30-11 FTR ops 17-4-42 FH129.55

AD499 M45M 24MU 22-10-41 616S 8-11 19S e/fd o/t w/u ldg nr Matlaske CB 15-11 AST 302S 24-3-42 CN ops 26-6 AST VSM 9-11 fuel syst mods wng stiff 350S 16-3-43 610S 27-3 WAL 24-1-44 13 OTU 28-9 R&S refurb to Port -6-5-47

AD500 19S 23-10-41 FACE 15-11 SOC 28-11

AD501 12MU 25-10-41 121S 4-11 s/dn CE 10-6-42 VSM 31-8 fuel syst mods wng stiff AST 9-4-43 con to PRXIII M32 RNDA 3-3-44

AD502 8MU 19-10-41 603S 22-10 332S 25-4-42 133S FTR ops 19-5

AD503 8MU 19-10-41 603S 22-10 e/fd hit bank in f/ ldg Drum Oak Aberdeen CE 12-1-42 SOC 23-1

AD504 Notts Miner 8MU 19-10-41 611S 22-10 R-R 5-11 mods 64S 14-11 41S 10-5-42 SOC 12-6

AD505 Condor 12MU 23-10-41 92S 30-10 417S 6-2-42 242S 6-5 243S 6-6-43 FAAC 10-7 ROS SAL 16-7 315MU 7-11 *Bar Inch* 18-12 USSR 24-3-43

AD506 Miss Herrin 6MU 28-1-41 412S 1-11 HAL 15-12 401S 3-5/42 taxy coll with BM372 Graves CE 1-6 WAL 67th Obs Grp USA 19-4-43 SAL 12-4-44 1TEU 57 OTU 17-8 95S 22-6-45 SOC 6-9

AD507 6MU 22-10-41 609S 22-10 FTR ops 15-11

AD508 38MU 6-11-41 74S 24-11 232S 8-4-42 VSM 24-9 fuel syst mods 308S 12-10 air coll with BM328 ld nr Cranswick CB 4-5-43 to 559M 3-10-45 FAF 11-3-46

AD509 6MU 28-10-41 412S 1-11 331S 17-3-42 dam ops 8-10 ROS 416S 4-11 411S 23-3 FAAC 14-7-43 ROS 412S 4-9 recat E 8-1-44

AD510 38MU 6-11-41 122S 15-11 412S 14-4-42 AST mr 25-6 152S 29-8 AST 16-5-43 con to Sea IB-NX947

AD511 9MU 8-11-41 122S 15-11 CB ops 14-3-42 AST 121S 6-6 VSM 25-9 fuel syst mods 1ADF Croydon 9-1- 335 USA 1-10 FAAC 21-5-43 222MU 26-9 *Emp Ort* 19-10

AD512 37MU 2-11-41 610S 7-12 FACE 18-5-42 SOC 24-5-42 FH158.45

AD513 6MU 28-10-41 121S 2-11 GAL 1-12 CAC ops 15-4-42 ROS 390S 31-7 131S 27-10 FAAC 10-11 ROS 165S 8-12 132S 26-7-43 118S 25-10 SAL 15-3-44 610 OTU 13-8 FAAC 9-12 SOC CE 14-6-45

AD514 M45M 19S 23-10-41 WAL 16-6-42 RNAS Stret 5-9 VSM 13-6-43 fuel syst mods wng stiff 402S 31-3-44 AST 30-4 FAF 19-1-45 GC 2/18

AD515 603S 6-11-41 ROS 29-1-42 GAL 421S 10-6 412S 3-2-43 ASTE mr 12-8 485S 3-1-44 234S 5-1 CAC ops 29-5 ROS 695S 21-6-45 SOC 1-10

AD516 Sir Robert 37MU 17-10-41 401S 1-11 FTR ops 22-11

AD517 39MU 31-10-41 452S 12-11 457S 22-3-42 308S 19-4 20S 17-6 CB ops 24-6 VSM 15-11 fuel syst mods AST 13-2-43 con to Sea IB-NX884

AD535 5MU 6-11-41 302S 15-11 74S 31-12 234S 8-4-42 VSM 24-9 fuel syst mods 302S 13-10 FACB 3-11 HAL COAL 26-6-43 hook fitt RNDA 16-1-44 RNAS Belfast 30-1

AD536 5MU 6-11-41 234S 26-11 ROS 17-12 602S 25-1-42 111S 25-3 41S 6-9 FACB 17-11 ROS 65S 2-2-43 130S 31-3 19-7 COAL 15-11 RNDA 22-3-44

AD537 33MU 22-11-41 457S 15-12 452S 23-3-42 CE ops 3-5 SOC FH124.50

AD538 38MU 6-11-41 501S 23-11 FACE 10-1-42 CE ops 24-4 WAL SOC 1-5

AD539 5MU 9-11-41 312S 7-12 air coll with BL293 cd nr New Mills CE 19-12 SOC 27-12

AD540 Blue Peter 24MU 22-10-41 122S 15-11 242S 23-4-42 broke up in dive nr Carsphairn Kirkcudbright 23-5

AD541 37MU 2-11-41 312S 6-12 FAAC 7-1-42 234S 18-4 FTR ops 23-7 FH171.35

AD542 6MU 28-10-41 308S 2-11 AST 14-12 310S 7-6-42 FAA 10-6 412S 29-7 FACB 26-8 AST VSM 8-3-43 fuel syst mods wng stiff 118S 10-9 64S 15-9 FAAC 7-5-44 AST WAL 31-10 SOC 22-5-45

AD543 12MU 1-11-41 616S 9-11 CE ops 13-4-42 SOC FH209.0

AD544 24MU 26-10-41 131S 10-12 FACB 4-1-42 65S 13-7 FACE 21-11 SOC

AD545 122S 15-11-41 cd Rosedale Yorks CE 25-1-42

AD546 24MU 26-10-41 616S 8-11 FACB 15-1-42 SOC 21-1

AD547 39MU 30-10-41 313S 6-11 FACE 22-1-42

AD548 Delhi III 12MU 25-10-41 121S 4-11 GAL 31-5-42 91S 1-8 i/sea ops 12-10

AD549 37MU 2-11-41 610S 7-12 AST 18-7-42 308S 11-1-43 CE ops 2-2

AD550 24MU 18-11-41 145S 17-12 350S 10-2-42 VA mr 6-5 ROS VSM 15-9 mods FTR ops 12-12 FH182.10

AD551 9MU 25-11-41 95S 17-12 FTR 25-3-43 SOC 28-3

AD552 9MU 20-11-41 74S 28-11 131S 9-5-42 FACB 7-9 SAL AST 16-5-43 con to Sea IB-NX949

AD553 37MU 4-11-41 312S 7-12 CE dbf ops 27-4-42 SOC FH113.40

AD554 24MU 19-11-41 131S 10-12 ROS 13-5-42 FAAC 4-6 FTR 15-8

AD555 5MU 6-11-41 302S 17-11 CE ops 18-12 SOC 21-12 recat B 9-1-42 AST 22-1 316S 15-6 VSM 24-1-43 mods FAAC 26-1 ROS AST 27-3 15FPP to VSM flap fail o/s ldg cd CE 8-9

AD556 24MU 26-10-41 ROS 28-11 19S 15-2-42 DeH 25-9 VSM 13-1-43 fuel syst mods wng stiff HAL 21-3 con to PRXIII M32 1PRU Ben 29-4 543S 16-5 400S 25-12 SOC 27-2-45

AD557 39MU 30-10-41 611S 7-11 603S 11-11 FAAC 8-1-42 ROS 332S 17-4 VSM fuel syst mods wng stiff 416S 29-1-43 411S 9-6 126AF 10-8 341S 17-10 SAL 1-3-44 504S 15-7 41 OTU 4-9 FAAC 30-1-45 ASTH 21-6-47

AD558 39MU 30-10-41 222S 7-11 FACB 27-2-42 SOC 6-3

AD559 9MU 1-11-41 616S 8-11 i/sea off Sheringham Norfolk 20-6-42 SOC 15-7

AD560 37MU AST 7-12-41 610S 26-5-42 FACB 23-6 AST 416S hit sea fly low 20 miles of Dung 28-2-43

AD561 37MU 23-11-41 122S 5-2-42 e/fd w/u ldg nr Darlington 11-2 SOC 18-2

AD562 M45M 12MU 21-11-41 124S 10-12 CAC mr 27-3-42 ROS 41S 22-7 316S 15-3-43 306S 16-3 302S 26-8 302S 3-10 316S 15-12 234S 18-12 VSM 25-1-44 fuel syst mods 278S 24-4 u/c clpse ldg Redhill CAC 13-4-45 recat E SOC 26-4

AD563 9MU 23-11-41 452S 5-12 307S coll on app with EN832 CE 10-7-42

AD564 9MU 1-12-41 124S 16-12 AST 23-12 71S 19-4-42 334 USA 1-10 cd nr Newport 26-5-43

AD565 9MU 1-12-41 74S 24-12 232S 8-4-42 coll with BL290 in pract ldg Llanb 2-6 AST VSM 24-9 fuel syst mods wng stiff AST 9-1-43 312S 17-5 AST 20-6 64S 26-10 CE ops 18-4-44

AD566 9MU 1-12-41 412S 15-12 FAAC 9-1-42 AST StA 20-6 308 USA 1-8 FAAC 11-8 HAS AST con to Sea IB-NX922

AD567 9MU 4-12-41 610S 5-1-42 FAAC 26-3 ROS 312S 31-12 AST 8-4-43 con to Sea IB-NX915 ret RAF Dec '44

AD568 9MU 74S 24-12-41 CE ops 8-2-42 SOC 28-2

AD569 9MU 8-12-41 74S 21-12 FACB 28-12 WAL 133S 13-6-42 401S 15-6 AST 6-7 121S 5-8 FTR ops 19-8

AD570 9MU 14-11-41 457S 24-11 452S 23-3-42 93S 4-6 dvd i/sea off Calf of Man 29-6 FH136.30

AD571 9MU 14-12-41 123S 28-12 167S 15-4-42 165S 3-6 FAAC 28-7 ROS 27-8 AST 402S 26-4-43 19S 5-5 65S 30-6 130S 15-8 VSM 18-2-44 fuel syst mods FACB 3-5-45 recat E SOC 14-5

AD572 37MU 31-10-41 312S 7-12 FACB 23-6-42 303S 3-2-43 19S 26-6 501S 22-7 485S 14-11 FACB 9-1-44 LMS 61 OTU hit high grd nr Loggerheads Staffs CE 16-1-45 SOC 20-3

AD573 45MU 29-10-41 145S 15-11 350S 11-2-42 AST 23-5 332S 20-8 335 USA 23-11 VSM 22-12-43 fuel syst mods DeH 6-6-44 SOC 12-10-50 to 5855M

AD574 45MU 20-10-41 310S 18-11 GAL 25-1-42 308S 24-8 41S 12-9 dvd i/sea off Newcastle Co Down CE 24-9 S&H 15-10 SOC 19-10

AD575 9MU 2-11-41 616S 9-11 FACB 28-1-42 GAL 111S 2-6 CA ops 21-7 610S 23-2-43 i/sea off Bognor 14-3 FH132.40

AD576 12MU 1-11-41 616S 8-11 FACB 13-1-42 19S 1-7 FAAC 10-11 ROS 131S 16-1 165S 21-1 302S 9-9 CAC ops 13-12 278S 7-10-44 SOC 25-5-45

AD577 LF VB 38MU 11-11-41 92S 23-11 417S 6-2-42 242S 6-6 AST 9-11 VSM 18-2-43 fuel syst mods wng stiff ROS 15-9 222S 16-2-44 CE 10-9-44

AD578 12MU 1-11-41 616S 8-11 FAAC 16-5-42 317S 26-8 HAL 23-9 315S 28-9 CB ops 16-11 HAL ASTH 10-7-43 hook fitt RNDA 18-1-44

AD579 6MU 13-11-41 504S 8-1-42 FAAC 16-2 S&H 315S 4-9 501S 19-10 SAL 22-1-43 AST con to Sea IB-NX904 12-3

AD580 37MU 23-11-41 131S 12-12 WAL 25-1-42 StA 28-3 308S 24-8 41S 12-9 FACB 29-10 AST 11-4-43 con to Sea IB-NX914

AD581 12MU 21-11-41 118S 11-12 FAAC 26-3-42 ROS 306S 16-6 e/fd cd in f/ldg 19-8 SOC 25-8

AD582 12MU 21-11-41 310S 4-12 AST 1-8 38MU 21-10 AST 18-2-43 con to Sea IB-NX890

AD583 37MU 23-11-41 130S 12-12 RNAS Stret 1-9-42 AST 18-9 RNAS LoS 3-10 ROS 5-11

AD584 37MU 23-11-41 130S 12-12 RNDA Stret 1-9-42 AST 24-9 hook fitt RNAS LoS 13-10 ROS 24-3-44

AR274 39MU 15-12 41 129S 2-1-42 CAC ops 26-3 ROS 501S 6-4 412S 19-5 SAL 6-8 222S 11-10 air coll with AB144 cd Dreghorn Ayr CE 8-1-43 SOC 13-1 FH351.05

AR275 M45M 9MU 16-12-41 cd on f/f 17-12 ROS 308S 18-9-42 222S 11-10 411S 22-4-43 401S 17-10 SAL 27-4-44 234S 27-7 57 OTU 13-8 FACB e/fld f/ld 27-3-45 recat E SOC

AR276 M46 9MU 5-1-42 C&C 21-2 *SS441* 20-3 ME 17-6 CE ops 17-6 SOC 19-6 FH6.05

AR277 9MU 5-1-42 C&C 21-2 *SS441* 20-3 Malta 1-7 SOC 29-7

AR278 M46 not counted on RAF contract, DTD contract CRD Farn 5-2-42 until June '43 gyro gunsight; elev trls 9MU 12-5-44 31ATG USAAF 31-5 1695 BD Flt SOC 5-12-45

AR279 6MU 5-1-42 317S 6-2 CE ops 16-3 WAL SOC 5-4

AR280 6MU 5-1-42 602S 26-1 302S 22-4 VSM 13-8 mods FTR ops 7-9

AR281 6MU 5-1-42 602S 26-1 222S 30-3 111S 30-3 CB ops 25-9 GAL VSM 24-10 fuel syst mods wng stiff 313S 16-3-43 66S 4-7 FTR 4-9

AR282 33MU 12-1-42 C&C Malta 1-7 SOC 23-7

AR283 33MU 12-1-42 61S 8-2 301S 14-7-43 307S 23-1 HAL 7-4 VSM 19-8 fuel syst & elev mods wng stiff Mk III IFF bomb carr 416S 3-12 186S 10-2-44 130S 18-4 303S CAC ops 26-7 ROS 61 OTU 14-4-45 SOC 22-5

AR284 VC 33MU 12-1-42 C&C 23-2 *SS437* 22-3 ME 206Grp 1-7 SOC 29-6

AR285 33MU 13-2-42 234S 19-4 FTR ops 23-7 FH123.20

AR286 38MU 25-1-42 82MU 26-2 *SS437* 12-3 ME 1-7 FACB 27-6 NAAF 218Grp 30-11-43 SOC 8-3-44

AR287 *SS440* Tak 15-3 ME 1-7 SOC 29-8-46

AR288 38MU 25-1-42 82MU 26-2 *SS440* Tak 15-3 ME 1-4 SOC 25-7

AR289 38MU 25-1-42 C&C 26-2 *SS441* 20-3 ME 1-7 SOC 1-2-44

AR290 38MU 25-1-42 82MU 26-2 *SS440* 21-3 Tak ME 1-7 145S CE ops 5-9 NAAF 218Grp 30-11-43 SOC 8-3-44

AR291 38MU 25-1-42 331S 15-3 FTR ops 21-4

AR292 38MU 26-1-42 91S 18-4 VSM 19-9 fuel syst mods wng stiff 308S 17-7-43 349S 29-10 64S 6-4-44 57 OTU swg on ldg o/t Boul CE 19-2 SOC 1-3

AR293 38MU 26-1-42 331S 15-3 VSM 12-8 mods SAL 25-10 VSM 27-3-43 fuel syst mods wng stiff 349S 8-10 602S 6-3-44 118S CE ops 28-3

AR294 38MU 30-1-42 331S 17-3 501S 27-4 130S 18-5 FTR ops 25-6 FH49.0

AR295 38MU 26-1-42 222S 28-2 e/a CB 2-7 VSM 10-10 fuel syst mods 501S 24-12 AST 25-10-43 M46 instal 31ATG 2-6-44 SAL 5-7 1688CU 30-9 SOC E 4-9-47

AR296 38MU 26-1-42 331S 27-3 VSM mods 453S 12-10 HAL 17-12 501S 23-3-43 ROS 7-6 411S 30-6 341S 25-1-44 118S 13-3 SAL 16-3 234S FACE 17-6

AR297 38MU 31-1-42 331S 10-4 CB ops RNAS LoS 4-9 884S AST 10-9 hook fitt ROS 15-2-44

AR298 38MU 2-2-42 331S 22-2 FTR ops 19-6

AR318 M45M 1st F Mk V built WAL 38MU 31-1-42 303S 16-4 FAAC 11-8 GAL 222S 13-1-43 64S 31-3 FAA 20-5 ROS 118S 25-9 SAL 19-10 3507RSU 27-1-44 COAL 1-2 hook fitt RNAS Hens 13-4

AR319 38MU 2-2-42 402S 18-4 4-5 FACB 19-5 AST VSM 24-8 fuel syst mods wng stiff HAL 29-12 con to PRXIII M32 Ben 6-4-43 541S 25-4 HAL 26-8 AST 2-3-45 SOC 6-3

AR320 M45M 8MU 12-2-42 122S 14-2 401S 16-4 111S 5-8 WAL 19-10 401S 12-3-43 FAAC 14-4 ROS 65S 30-6 130S 15-8 CRU 28-2-44 'Basta' mods AST 1-6 1AGS 26-11 FACE 26-1-45

AR321 8MU 7-2-42 82MU 24-2 *Katanga* 12-3 Tak 22-3 ME 1-7 FACB 5-7 SOC 1-2-44

AR322 8MU 7-2-42 C&C 20-2 *SS437* 22-3 ME 206Grp 1-7 SOC 29-6 FH10.05

AR323 M45M 8MU 12-2-42 611S 8-3 242S 2-6 222S 11-8 64S 31-3-43 FAAC 24-4 ROS 118S 25-9 67Grp USAAF 6-1-44 130S 24-5 FACB 12-6 AST 1AGS 30-11 u/c clpse ldg Barrow CE 9-4-46

AR324 M45M 7-2-42 C&C 20-2 *Katanga* 12-3 Tak ME 1-7 FA C3 29-4-43

AR325 38MU 7-2-42 331S 1-3 FACB 20-7 AST VSM 25-2-43 fuel syst mods wng stiff 118S 1-6 FTR ops 21-6

AR326 38MU 7-2-42 331S 1-3 CE ops 17-5 SOC 24-5

AR327 LF LR VB M45M 38MU 11-2-42 306S 16-4 VSM 11-9 mods 315S 24-9 316S 1-10 306S 16-3-43 CAC ops 9-9 ROS 322S 11-11 57 OTU 17-8 SOC 3-1-46

AR328 LF LR VB M45M 38MU 11-2-42 331S 15-3 SAL 25-10 VSM 24-3-43 fuel syst mods wng stiff 308S 17-7 349S FAAC 22-10 ROS 222S 2-3-44 322S 17-3 345S 25-4-44 DeH 19-7 FAF 9-10-47

AR329 38MU 11-2-42 317S 24-3 FTR ops 14-4

AR330 38MU 13-2-42 124S 20-4-43 FAAC 23-5 VSM 18-6 mods 401S 21-7 111S 26-7 312S 31-12 VSM 9-6-43 fuel syst mods wng stiff 66S 19-8 CAC ops 4-10 ROS 18-12 CE ops 27-5-44

AR331 M45M 38MU 14-2-42 41S 13-4 FACB 25-8 91S 31-12 317S 1-5-43 412S 29-6 FAAC 2-7 ROS 401S 18-8 M45M instal 132S 25-2-44 504S 15-3 CAC ops 13-6 310S 15-7 410TU 4-9 30-5-45

AR332 38MU 14-2-42 317S 20-3 FTR ops 29-4

AR333 38MU 16-2-42 350S 1-8 FTR ops 23-5

AR334 38MU 16-2-42 403S 19-4 FTR ops 19-8

AR335 38MU 16-2-42 303S 15-4 CB ops 5-6 AST 5USA 5-9 VSM 21-4-43 fuel syst mods wng stiff 131S 2-7 310/S 24-9 FTR ops 24-9 FH149

AR336 38MU 16-2-42 306S 17-4 133S 29-9 336S 1-10 CB ops 28-1-43 AST VSM 30-5 fuel syst mods wng stiff 611S 26-7 FTR ops 6-8

AR337 SR VB 38MU 18-2-42 501S 27-4 306S 18-5 VSM 9-10 fuel syst mods 315S 24-10 401S 4-3-43 416S 3-6 504S 11-6 FACB 12-7 MM mods M46 instal RNDA 3-3-44 con to train

AR338 38MU 24-2-42 310S 24-3 243S 12-8 SAl 6-11 402S 7-4-43 FAAC 18-4 ROS 124S 12-6 19S 4-7 315S hit high grd in form with BL469 W3427 Clady Corner Co Antrim CE 11-9

AR339 38MU 24-2-42 118S 1-4 129S 20-6 FTR ops 19-8

AR340 LF VB 38MU 24-2-42 317S 20-3 dam ops 19-8 VSM 23-9 fuel syst mods 315S 8-10 453S 23-11 222S 31-3-43 167S 19-5 FAAC 20-8 ROS 167S 17-9 322S 5-11 to 4430M 5SoTT 30-12-44 SOC 28-9-47

AR341 38MU 24-2-42 331S 28-3 CAC ops 29-7 ROS 133S 29-9 336S 1-10 CE ops 13-2-43

AR342 38MU 27-2-42 FA 15-4 52 OTU 2-2-43 FLS 2-2-44 SAL 7-11 'Basta' mods 1TEU 16-6 61 OTU 28-9 FAAC 28-1-45 ROS SOC 28-5

AR343 38MU 27-2-42 310S 7-6 VSM 1-8 fuel syst mods wng stiff 331S 28-8 416S 14-8-43 FACE 3-1-44 AST 234S 31-5 SOC 27-7

AR344 33MU 27-2-42 129S 9-5 602S 29-11 SAL 18-12 VSM 28-5-43 mods 313S 26-6 66S 4-7 340S 15-11 239S 16-2-44 63S 13-3 AST 21-6 1667CU 16-11 Bom Com 27-11-45 SOC E 8-12

AR345 33MU 27-2-422 403S 5-5 FACE 11-7 SOC 16-7 FH78

AR346 33MU 28-2-42 306S 26-4 FACB 11-8

AR347 33MU 9-3-43 72S 2-5 CB ops 8-6 WAL 167S 5-3-43 FACB 22-3 AST recat E 21-5

M45M 38MU 7-3-42 65S 28-4 453S 12-7-43 222S 31-3 VSM 7-4 mods 167S 19-5 FAAC 2-9 ROS 322S 3-10 222S 1-1-44 57 OTU 17-8 61 4-2-45 SOC 22-5 BBOC 5-6 SOC 22-6

AR363 38MU 7-3-42 340S 27-3 CAC ops 12-4 ROS FTR ops 30-7 FH67.50

AR364 38MU 7-3-42 19S 29-3 234S 7-9 FACB 5-10 132S 22-12 VSM 14-6-43 fuel syst mods wng stiff S type pt Mk III IFF bomb carr 611S 17-11 234S 6-8-44 63S 5-10 41 OTU 8-5-45 OTU 22-6 SOC 16-7

AR365 38MU 7-3-42 118S 19-4 FAA 23-4 FTR ops 9-5 FH15.30

AR366 LF LR VB M45M 38MU 7-3-42 306S 16-4 FAAC 6-6 ROS 303S 28-7 CB ops 19-8 ROS 412S 2-11 VSM 20-11 fuel syst mods 610S 18-3-43 350S 27-3 26S 7-4-44 FAAC 9-9 ROS 595S 18-1-45 R&S refurb to Port 15-4-47

AR367 M46 Scotia 38MU 7-3-42 91S 27-4 152S 3-5 FAAC 7-6 react E 222MU 22-10-43 *Pandor* 25-11 Port 18-12

AR368 38MU 7-3-42 403S 1-4 FTR ops 25-4 FH47.20

AR369 38MU 7-3-42 501S 27-4 222S 1-6 FTR ops 29-6

AR370 38MU 14-3-42 91S 2-4 FTR ops 15-6

AR371 38MU 14-3-42 303S 15-4 FAA 21-7 ROS GAL mr 14-1-43 VSM fuel syst mods wng stiff 131S 20-7 i/sea 19-8 SOC 31-8 FH149

AR372 38MU 14-3-42 501S 1-4 312S 25-6 VSM 17-8 mods 332S 28-8 133S 29-9 336S 29-9 AST 18-12-44 FCCS North 9-2-45 SOC 27-12

AR373 38MU 19-3-42 350S 17-6 CAC ops 19-8 ROS 453S 9-12 222S 31-3-43 167S 19-5 SAL 5-8 611S 9-11 61 OTU 23-7-44 S&H 4-12 FAF 16-3-46

AR374 38MU 14-3-42 234S FTR ops 17-4 FH26

AR375 38MU 14-3-42 501S 27-4 312S 25-6 CAC ops 11-8 AST 403S 22-8 408S 23-8 416S 3-6-43 222S 18-7 AST 21-7 mr M46 instal 312S 15-11 443S 272-44 58 OTU 30-3

AR376 38MU 17-3-42 303S 15-4 403S 26-2-43 411S 19-8 341S 17-10 602S 25-1-44 118S 13-3 SAL 12-5 'Basta' mods FAF 19-1-45

AR377 38MU 17-3-42 41S 13-4 CE ops 10-6 SOC 12-6 ASTH 16-6 302S 29-3 132S 28-6 118S 10-10 345S 26-6-44 std i/sea off Littlehampton 22-7

AR378 38MU 17-3-42 151S 17-6 131S 31-12 165S 3-2-43 122S 15-7 234S 15-8 303S 11-1-44 53 OTU 11-8 ROS 30-1-45 695S 21-6 SOC 25-10

AR379 38MU 17-3-42 322S 20-4 FTR ops 1-7

AR380 38MU 17-3-42 350S 20-7 FTR ops 19-8

AR381 38MU 17-3-42 306S 16-4 FAAC 1-5 FTR ops 22-8

AR382 416S air coll with EP108 cd Ashford CE 27-4-43 ASTEx 30-6

AR383 38MU 26-3-42 234S 26-4 AST 8-12 VSM 31-5-43 416S 7-7 FAAC 27-9 ROS 57 OTU 17-8-44 FACB 14-1-45 recat E SOC 27-1

AR384 38MU 26-3-42 65S 8-4 FACB 19-5 GAL RNAS Stret 5-9 ASTH hook fitt 1-10 LoS 19-10

AR385 38MU 26-3-42 302S 17-4 VSM 15-9 mods air coll with EN828 ld North Coates 24-4-43

AR386 38MU 26-3-42 91S 12-4 FACB 18-6 VSM 212-4-43 fuel sust mods wng stiff M46 instal 313S 30-6 66S 14-8 341S 3-11 CA ops 7-1-44 FLS 23-2 FAAC 28-5 AST CGS 14-10 FACE 5-7-45 SOC 16-7

AR387 38MU 25-3-42 91S 12-4 FA 18-4 HAL VASM 30-9 mods 118S 2-7-43 64S 25-9 AST mr 2-5-44 CGS 10-10 FACE 20-3-45 SOC 30-3

AR388 38MU 26-3-42 65S 8-4 FTR ops 21-7 SOC

AR389 38MU 27-3-42 403S 15-4 FTR ops FH32.25

AR390 M45M 27-3-42 452S 17-4 FACB 21-5 93S 4-6.

AR276: A flying career of just over six hours.

AST 21-1-43 317S 19-2-43 SAL 22-4 USAAF 8-5-44 MAL mr 21-7 1687 Flt 13-5-46 SOC 4-9-47

AR391 38MU 28-3-42 65S 28-4 CE ops 1-6 SOC 3-6

AR392 38MU 1-4-42 91S 18-4 41S 2-11 453S 23-12 AST 2-4-43 222S 7-4 421S 12-4 416S 23-5 401S 1-6 HAL 13-11 501S 28-6-44 61 OTU 2-8 SOC 18-5-45

AR393 SR VB 38MU 1-4-42 118S 19-4 154S 22-6 ROS 10-7 315S 29-7 41S 23-8 610S 12-3-43 350S 27-3 FAAC 27-7 ROS 67Grp USAAF 6-1-44 HAL 17-6 M46 instal 83GSU 3-10 SOC 12-4-45

AR394 38MU 1-4-42 41S 13-4 CAC ops 3-5 CE 11-5 WAL

AR395 M45M 38MU 1-4-42 81S 7-6 317S 15-6-43 412S 29-6 CAC ops 3-10 303S 3-12 SAL USAAF 10-5-44 1653CU 1-12 FACE 20-3-45 SOC 30-3

AR396 LF LR VB M46 38MU 4-4-42 602S 7-5 FAAC 11-5 ROS 402S 22-5 350S 14-8 CAC ops 19-8 ROS 412S 7-12 453S 31-1-43 167S 19-5 132S 13-2-44 504S 15-3 310S 23-7 53 OTU 6-11 flaps up during ldg o/s cd CE 20-2-45 M55M instal during service

AR397 38MU 6-4-42 313S 26-4 FTR ops 2-6

AR398 38MU 6-4-42 81S 3-6 AST 6-8 52 OTU 2-2-43 e/fd cd Nth Wroxhall wilts CE 6-9 SOC 11-9

AR399 38MU 6-4 154S 8-6 122S 23-6 AST mr 16-8 P&P SM 21-10 52OTU 5-2-43 FLS 2-2-44 SAL 7-4 'Basta' mods M46 instal 85 OTU 29-3-45 to 5720M 16-10

AR400 38MU 7-4 122S 6-5 FTR ops 17-5

AR401 38MU 8-4-42 402S 23-5 hit sea dam prop cd/ ldg nr Hailsham Sussex 30-7 SOC 11-9

AR402 38MU 7-4-42 122S 9-6 FTR ops 27-8

AR403 38MU 11-4-42 131S 16-5 165S 9-8 65S 23-9 dvd i/grd Westruther Berwicks dbf 16-1-43

AR404 M45M 38MU 11-4-42 124S 9-6 2USA 22-8 cd Thornton Abbey Lincs CE 24-10 AST 416S 22-4-43 FAAC 16-5 ROS 313S 9-9 USAAF 9-11 R&S refurb to Port 12-6-47

AR405 38MU 13-4-42 222S 2-6 CB ops 19-6 421S 1-10 412S 3-2-43 6-2S 30-6 345S 7-4-44 CB ops 17-7 1 FU 5-1-45 FAF 19-1 M50M instal GC 2/18

AR406 38MU 13-4-42 CRD Exeter 14-5 ROS 21-9-43 AST 22-2-44 41 OTU 21-2 58 OTU 22-3-45 SOC 17-7 to 5394M

AR422 38MU 13-4-42 19S 17-6 hit hill cd St Austell Cornwall CE 25-8 FH82.35

AR423 M46 38MU 13-4-42 485S 16-6 121S 17-6 FAAC 15-7 ROs 121S 28-7 CB ops 2-9 VSM 24-10 fuel syst mods wng stiff 118S 19-3-43

AR424 LF LR VB M45M 38MU 13-4-42 317S 1-6 315S 4-9 222S 1-12 64S 31-3-43 118S 25-9 SAL 16-10 132S 13-2-44 504S 15-3 310S 4-9 SOC 25-10-45

AR425 38MU 13-4-42 222S 1-6 242S 11-8 FTR ops 29-8

AR426 38MU 16-4-42 41S 13-6 cd during low aero Breighton Yorks Ce 20-6 SOC 25-6

AR427 38MU 17-4-42 611S 27-4-44 53 OTU 6-8 61 OTU 17-5-45 SOC mr 25-6

AR428 38MU 20-4-42 313S 17-6 AST 24-7 VSM 11-8 mods 306S 12-8 316S 1-10 602S 30-6-43 CE ops 15-7 SOC FH327

AR429 M46 20-4-42 129S 9-6 FAA 30-7 2USA 22-8 501S 19-3-43 R-R 6-7 AST 25-10 RNDA 28-3-44 350S 16-6 57 OTU 23-7 SOC 27-9-45

AR430 38MU 20-4-42 401S 4-6 65S 11-8 421S 13-9 CAC ops 27-10 ROS 602S air coll with Mustang AP181 cd nr Odiham Hants CE 19-4-43

AR431 38MU 20-4-42 154S 14-6 315S 21-7 317S 5-9 cd nr Finningley CE 31-3-43

AR432 38MU 20-4-42 313S 14-6 VSM 11-8 mods 331S 12-8 302S 20-11 132S 28-6-43 ASTH 31-7 349S 8-10 strk by EP354 while parked CE 12-2-44

AR433 38MU 20-4-42 317S 9-6 WAL 26-11 VSM 28-2-43 fuel syst mods wng stiff 118S 5-5 FTR ops 15-9 FH324

AR434 38MU 25-4-42 316S 15-6 315S 17-6-43 AST 26-6 'Black Boy' mods AST 3-7-43 hook fitt RNDA 16-1-44 Hens 11-2

AR435 5MU 25-4-42 65S 2-6-43 FAA 25-7 2USA 22-8 3257S 20-2 234S 5-9-43 DeH 23-11 41 OTU 3-3-45

AR436 5MU 25-4-42 403S 3-6 Mart Hth 16-6 FACB 17-6 AST VSM 7-3-43 fuel syst mods wng stiff 312S 27-5 234S 4-7 504S 30-6 313S 22-9 FACB 24-1-44 AST 41 OTU 24-5-45 to 5334M 14-7 SOC 16-6-50

AR437 LF LR VB M45M 5MU 27-4-42 403S 3-6 FAAC 19-6 ROS 416S 3-6-43 SAL 20-7 308S 26-9 349S 29-10 222S 2-3-44 322S 17-3 63S 3-5 118S 22-6 CAC ops 25-7 ROS 611S 3-10 61 OTU 12-4-45 SOC 22-6-45

AR438 5MU 27-4-42 403S 3-6 CAC ops 3-43 ROS 401S 27-3 FAA 12-4 ROS 416S 3-6 310S 7-6 52 OTU 24-6 VSM 9-7 M46 instal ARF 2-12 FAAC 15-4-44 ROS CGS 16-1-45 R&S refurb to Port 16-9-47

AR439 5MU 27-2-42 403S 3-6 FTR ops 19-8

AR440 5MU 27-2-42 403S 3-6 FA 22-9 SOC FH145.45

AR441 LF LR M45M 9MU 30-4-42 312S 21-6 130S 16-8 403S 14-6-43 313S 19-8 SAL 16-10 132S 13-2-44 504S 15-3 310S 15-7 CE ops 1-8

AR442 9MU 4-5-42 AST 20-5 VA 26-6 AST con to Sea IB-MB 439

AR443 9MU 4-5-42 AST 17-5 con to Sea IB-MB437

AR444 M46 9MU 4-5-42 AST 16-5 M45 instal con to Sea IB-MB344

AR445 9MU 4-5-42 AST 17-5 con to Sea IB-MB345

AR446 9MU 7-5-43 R-R Mer dev trls AST 20-5 con to Sea IB-MB 346

AR447 9MU 8-5-42 118S 4-6 air coll with EP191 ld nr Colt CE 29-7-43

AR448 LR VB 38MU 14-5-42 501S 5-6 CAC ops 11-8 ROS 118S 24-9 350S 4-12 610S 27-3-43 FACE 23-1-44 FH464.10

AR449 38MU 14-5-42 118S 3-6 FTR ops 20-6 FH15.25

AR450 38MU 16-5-42 118S 11-6 CB ops 4-9-43 129S 29-1-44 power dive i/grd just after t/o CE 8-8

AR451 38MU 16-5-42 66S 5-6 118S 23-9 350S 6-1-43 FACB 20-3 303S 20-5 315S 6-6 19S 26-6 67Grp USAAF 26-1-44 AST 6-6 CGS 28-9 to 5592M FAF 11-3-46

AR452 38MU 18-5-42 66S 5-6 118S 24-9 350S 4-12 610S 27-3-43 AST 2-4 132S 24-8 308S 11-10 2nd TAF Com Sq 8-6-44 420RSU 6-7 414S 27-7 1651CU 25-4-45 SOC 3-1-46

AR453 M45M 38MU 18-5-42 66S 5-6 118S 21-6 FAAC 12-6-43 CAC ops 18-9 ROS 277S 19-5-44 CAC ops 4-6 277S 16-7 276S 22-2-45 SOC 29-11

AR454 33MU 18-5-42 416S 30-6 602S 15-7 164S 11-9 burst tyre o/t Peterhead CE 19-10 SOC 25-10 FH62.40

AR455 LR VB 33MU 18-5-42 501S 14-6 118S 14-6 FTR ops 20-6 FH6.-5

AR456 33MU 18-5-42 501S 15-6 118S 16-6 FACE 22-9 FH115.

AR457 WAL contract 124305/40 AST 18-5-42 con to Sea IB-MB357

AR458 WAL contract 125305/40 ASTH 26-5-42 VA 4-7 AST 11-9 con to Sea IB-MB358

AR459 WAL contract 124305/40 ASTH 20-5-42 VA 23-6 AST con to Sea IB-MB348

AR460 WAL AST 15-6-42 con to Sea IB-MB 360

AR461 WAL AST 15-6-42 con to Sea IB-MB 361

AR462 M46 38MU 1-5-42 WAL 22-5 310S 19-7 AST 5-9 610S 20-4-43 FAAC 7-5 FTR into sea 11-6 FH280.45

AR463 LR VB 38MU 16-5-42 VSM 15-6 fuel syst mods M46 instal 602S 26-1-43 19S 1-6 315S 26-6 611S 6-7 FACB 23-11 402S 26-6-44 61 OTU 17-5-45 691S 21-6 SOC 5-10

AR464 VC M46 38MU 16-5-42 82MU 6-6 Malta 1-8 NWA 1-5-43

AR465 VC M47 38MU 18-5-42 47MU 28-6 *Hen Jasp* 9-8 Tak 3-9 ME 14-10 FACB 14-10

AR466 VC M47 38MU 18-5-42 R-RH Mer trls 52MU 1-7 *Emp Clan* 19-7 Malta 3-8 SOC 14-12 FH75.10

AR467 LR NV 38MU 26-5-42 R-RH Mer trls M46 instal 312S 9-8 CAC ops 17-5-43 234S 4-7 504S 5-7 FACB 2-8 DeH 611S 28-5-44 AST 15-6 M45M instal 53 OTU o/s ldg Hibald CE 1-1-45 SOC 15-1

AR468 VC 38MU 26-5-42 310S 19-7 AST 10-11 234S 3-12 602S 17-1 FTR i/sea 28-3 FH217.25

AR469 VC 38MU 28-5-42 215MU 2-7 *Belnov* 5-8 Tak 13-9 ME 14-10 NAASC 31-10-43 SOc 8-3-44

AR470 VC M46 39MU 1-6-42 52MU 10-7 *Emp Clive* 19-7 Malta 3-8 FTR ops 15-10-43

AR471 VC M46 39MU 1-6-42 52MU 9-7 *Emp Clive* 19-7 Malta 3-8 SOC 16-10

AR488 VC M46 39MU 1-6-42 52MU 9-7 *Emp Clive* 19-7 Malta 3-8 SOC 16-10

AR489 VC M46 39MU 1-6-42 76MU 29-7 Malta 1-8 CE ops 14-10

AR490 VC M46 39MU 1-6-42 308S 19-8 322S 22-7 CAC ops 16-8 249S 29-10

AR491 LF LR VC M45M 39MU 8-6-42 310S 19-7 FAAC 2-1-43 ROS FAAC 30-6 AST 402S 24-12 61 OTU 9-9-44 to 5268M 27-6-45 SOC 4-7-50

AR492 LF LR M46 39MU 12-6-42 313S 24-7 FACB 7-6 FACB 7-6 AST M45M instal 350S 9-10 FAAC 28-12 ROS 41 OTU 2-9-44 SOC 15-10-45

AR493 VC M46 38MU 12-6-42 313S 29-7 402S 19-6-43 to 4697M 10SoTT 27-3-44

AR494 VC M46 39MU 10-6-42 222MU 11-8 *Nakambo* 23-8 Tak 23-9 ME 29-10 FAC3 4-5-43

AR495 VCT M46 39MU 15-6-42 310S 21-7 CE ops 22-9 SOC FH78

AR496 VC M46 39MU 12-6-42 76MU 9-8 *Emp Cabot* 28-8 Tak Gib 14-9 Malta 18-12 FAC3 FH38.06

AR497 VCT M46 39MU 15-6-42 52MU 10-7 *Emp Clive* 19-7 Malta 3-8 NWA 21-6-45 ME 21-6 CE 13-7 SOC 13-9

AR498 LF LR VC 8MU 13-6-42 310S 23-7 WAL 18-2-43 M46 instal 350S 1610 FAAC ROS M45M instal 322S 11-1-44 air coll with AA853 i/sea CE 30-4

AR499 VC M46 8MU 17-6-42 310S 23-7 AST 5-11 FACB 29-1-43 AST 131S 13-8-43 315S 4-3-44 CGS 18-12 e/fd w/u ldg nr Burstwick Yorks 12-1-45 SOC 20-1

AR500 VC M46 8MU 17-6-42 313S 21-8 FACB 26-8 WAL M45M instal 131S 31-12 412S 23-1-43 427S 31-1 310S 3-3 2-7 186S 8-4-44 130S 18-4 CE ops 25-6

AR501 VC M46 8MU 22-6-42 310S 19-7 AST 1-12 GA strk by Mosquito Exeter WAL 23-3-43 504S 18-8 312S 16-10 422S 27-2-44 58OTU 30-3 FACB 9-9 AST CGS 24-4-45 Dept Aeronautical Eng Loughboro 21-3-46 Shuttleworth Trust as G-AWII BoB film extant codes NN-D 310S

AR502 VC M46 8MU 22-6-42 310S 21-7 CE ops 7-11 FH68

AR503 VC M46 8MU 22-6-42 310S 19-7-43 504S 3-4 165S 8-7 AST 9-8 308S 10-10 130S 22-6-44 345S 15-8 61 OTU 28-9 FACB 6-2-45 ROS 691S 21-6 SOC 30-8

AR504 VC M46 38MU 22-6-42 312S 9-8 CAC ops 17-10 AST FAAC 16-11 ROS 441S 27-2-44 56 OTU 30-3 FAAC 7-5-45 ROS recat E SOC 25-5-45

AR505 M46 38MU 22-6-42 19S 4-9 402S 26-4-43 FFAAC 24-8 ROS e/fd f/ld Barnerk Pk Surrey CE 11-11

AR506 VC M46 38MU 25-6-42 FSM 4-3-43 fuel syst mods HAL 29-4 not required for con 310S 7-6 131S 2-7 FTR 18-8 FH88-35

AR507 LR VC M46 38MU 25-6-42 610S 21-8 167S 14-10 132S 19-5-43 19S 25-5 315S 26-6 611S 6-7 FACB 23-4-44 AST 53 OT 27-9 FAAC 21-3-45 SOC 29-5

AR508 VC M46 38MU 29-6-42 610S 21-8 FACE 26-9 SOC 30-9 FH61.30

AR509 VC M46 38MU 29-6-42 610S 21-8 167S 14-10 310S 7-3-43 FAAC 3-4 ROS 132S 19-5 19S 25-5 315S 26-6 611S 6-7 FTR ops 9-11

AR510 VC M46 38MU 29-6-42 VSM 8-9 fuel syst mods 52MU 5-10 *Waroonga* 13-10 Aust 24-12

AR511 VC M46 38MU 29-6-42 312S 23-8 234S 4-7-43 504S 5-7 mr 23-8 416S 24-12 186S 1-2-44 130S 18-4 AST 16-5 M45M instal R&S 7-10-46

AR512 VC M46 38MU 29-6-42 313S 26-8 strk train during mock attack cd Blackford Somerset CE 4-6-43

AR513 LF LR M46 38MU 29-6-42 VSM 17-9 fuel syst mods 504S 24-11 CAC ops 16-9-43 ROS 19S 25-5 315S 26-6 611S 6-7 CB ops 16-9 AST M45M instal 129S 4-3-44 303S 24-4 FAAC 1-6 ROS 17SFTS 29-11 SOC 19-7-46

AR514 VC M46 9MU 3-7-42 P&P SM 17-9 310S 11-2-43 131S 2-7 310S 11-2-43 131S 2-7 310S 24-9 FAAC 14-11 ROS 64S 22-6-44 61 OTU 28-9 SOC 7-2-45

AR515 VC M46 9MU 6-7-42 VSM 17-9 fuel syst mods 350S 30-11 CB ops 12-12 412S 5-5-43 317S 28-6 64S 26-10 u/s ldg Ford strk obst CE 8-2-44 402S 3-7 CE 9-11

AR516 VC M46 9MU 3-7-42 VSM 15-9 fuel syst mods 19S 27-10 402S 5-5-43 416S 7-6 186S 16-3-44 FACB 9-4 61 OTU 7-9 FAAC 8-11 ROS SOC 27-6-45 M45M instal during service

AR517 VC M46 9MU 7-7-42 VSM 15-9 fuel syst mods 19S 13-10 FAAC 3-5-43 ROS 402S 18-6 FACB 30-6 611S 22-3-44 R&S 24-9-46

AR518 VC M46 33MU 6-7-42 313S 24-7 AST 5-4-43 66S 9-9 340S 15-11 52 OTU 25-1-44 567S 7-6-45 SOC 26-9

AR519 LR VC M46 33MU 7-7-42 312S 12-8 Farn 2-9 CAC ops 10-3-43 ROS 234S 4-7 504S 5-7 FAAC 25-8 AST R-R 6-11 165S 30-11 306S 24-4-44 501S 19-5 345S 15-8 577S 30-7-45 to 5523M

AR520 VC M46 33MU 7-7-42 313S 30-7

AR521 VC M46 33MU 7-7-42 310S 21-7 412S 24-4-43 FTR ops 7-6

AR522 VC M46 33MU 10-7-42 312S 31-7 FAAC 9-8 ROS 412S 23-4-43 s/dn by Mustang CE 17-6

AR523 VC M46 38MU 13-7-43 VSM 8-9 fuel syst mods 215MU 27-9 *Waro* 13-10 Aust 24-12 457S A58-2 NWA 28-2-43 shot down 30-6-43

AR524 VC M46 38MU 13-7-42 VSM 17-8 fuel syst mods 76MU 6-10 *SS626* 20-10 Gib 6-1 NWA 28-2-43 FAF 1-10 GC 1-7 PRO 14 FA C3 22-3-44

AR525 VCT M46 33MU 11-7-42 P&P SM 17-8 222MU 10-9 *SS620* 15-10 GIB 1-11 NWA 30-4-43

AR526 VC M46 38MU 11-7-42 VSM 9-9 fuel syst mods 215MU 27-9 *Waro* 13-10 Aust 24-12 457S (A58-3)

AR527 VC M46 38MU 13-7-42 VSM 4-9 fuel syst mods 66S 11-10 129S 19-2-43 CE ops 5-4

AR528 VC M46 38MU 13-7-42 610S 22-8 FACB 1-11 421S 11-4-43 446S 23-5 401S 1-6 FACE 14-8-44 LMS recat E 30-8

AR529 VC M46 38MU 13-7-42 313S 30-7 VSM 20-8 fuel syst mods 402S 14-5-43 dam ops ROS 501S 20-11 53 OTU 22-2-45 e/td on t/o o/t in w/u ldg CE 24-4-45 SOC 4-5

AR530 VC M46 38MU 13-7-42 VSM 20-8 fuel syst mods 222MU 16-9-43 *SS621* 16-10 GIB 1-11 C3 ops 4-12

AR531 VC M46 38MU 13-7-42 VSM 20-8 fuel syst mods 82MU 13-9 *SS622* 1-11 ME 30-11-44 SOC 31-5-45

AR532 VC M46 38MU 17-7-42 VSM fuel syst mods 215MU 27-9 *Waro* 13-10 Aust 24-12

AR546 VC M46 33MU 17-7-42 313S 26-7 CAC ops 15-10 ROS air coll with EP449 i/sea 15-1-43

AR547 VC M46 33MU 17-7-42 313S 30-7 FTR ops 8-3-43

AR548 VC M46 33MU 20-7-42 312S 23-8 hvy ldg Chu St disin 6-1-43 FH111

AR549 VC M46 33MU 17-7-42 313S 26-7 ROS 12-11 317S 18-8-43 64S Tang strk by BL472 while parked CE 18-10 FH357.55

AR550 VC M46 33MU 20-7-42 312S 31-7 FACB 6-9 AST 234S 29-11 602S 25-1-43 412S 19-4 317S 28-6 312S 4-10 442S 27-2-44 26S 25-3 130S 22-6 61 OTU 2-11 SOC 17-3-45

AR551 VCT M46 33MU 19-7-42 82MU 13-8 *Emp Fran* 30-8 Gib 14-9 Malta 1-11

AR552 VC M46 38MU 20-7-42 19S 4-9 167S 30-12 CAC ops 1-4-43 AST 504S 16-8 313S 22-9 442S 27-2-44 56 OTU 30-3 53 OTU 27-6 loss of power on t/o Redbourne Lincs w/u ldg strk tree CE 21-3-45 SOC 30-3

AR553 VCM46 38MU 20-7-42 VSM 2-8 fuel syst mods 82MU 26-9 *Par Sea* 30-10 Tak ME 16-12 SOC 1-2-44

AR554 VC M46 38MU 27-7-42 VSM 22-8 fuel syst mods 82MU 18-9 *Molaja* 1-10 lost at sea 3-10

AR555 VC M46 38MU 2-7-42 VSM fuel syst mods 82MU 22-9 *Lorca* 6-10 Tak 14-12 ME 28-2-43 Malta C3 ops 25-4 SOC

AR556 VCT M46 39MU 25-7-42 52MU 13-8 *Emp Cabot* 28-8 Gib 14-9 Malta 1-11 C3 ops 18-3 SOC 20-3

AR557 VCT M46 39MU 25-7-42 82MU 1-9 *SS621* 16-10 Gib 1-11 NWA 28-2-43

AR558 VCT M46 39MU 25-7-42 FAAC 16-8 ROS 215MU 15-9 *Porow* 9-10 Aust 457S A58-5 21-11

AR559 VCT M46 39MU 25-7-42 76MU 14-8 *Emp Cab* 28-8 Gib 14-9 Malta 1-11 249S C3 ops 27-2-43

AR560 VC M46 38MU 27-7-42 52MU 13-8 *Emp Cab* 28-8 Gib 14-9 Malta 1-11 C3 ops 29-6-43

AR561 VC M61 39MU 27-7-42 76MU 9-8 *Emp Cab* 28-8 Gib 14-8 CE ops 30-1-43 SOC 1-2 FH75.30

AR562 VC M46 27-7-42 82MU 1-9 *SS621* 16-10 Gib 1-11 NWA 28-2-43 ME 30-11-44 RHAF 25-4-46

AR563 VC M46 39MU 27-7-42 47MU 16-8 *Port Syd* 9-9 Aust 29-11

AR564 VC M46 39MU 4-8-42 FA f/f 16-8 ROS

47MU 17-12 *Suss* 9-3-43 Aust 16-4

AR565 VC M46 39MU 4-8-42 82MU 26-8 *Emp Fran* 30-8 Gib 14-9 Malta 1-11 ME 1435S C3 ops 18-12

AR566 VC M46 39MU 4-8-42 82MU 1-9 *SS620* 18-10 Gib 1-11 E Af FTR ops 14-1-43

AR567 VC M46 38MU 4-8-42 VSM 11-9 fuel syst mods 66S 11-10 129S 19-2-43 FAAC 29-5-43 ROS 453S 17-7 340S 13-12 329S 16-2-44 26S 22-3 57OTU 27-6 FACB 30-8 LMS 81 OTU 7-5-45 R&S 7-10-46

AR568 VC M46 38MU 4-8-42 666S 21-9 FACB 27-9 CE ops 13-10 SOC FH7.40

AR569 VC M46 38MU 4-8-42 VSM 20-8 fuel syst mods 82MU 13-9 *SS621* 16-10 Gib 1-11

AR570 VC M46 38MU 4-8-42 VSM 8-9 fuel syst mods 310S 8-10 61 OTU 26-4-45 to 5357M 10-7-45

AR592 VC M46 38MU 4-8-42 VSM 15-9 fuel syst mods 350S 2-12 FTR ops 23-1-43 FH31.50

AR593 VC M46 39MU 9-8-42 222MU 4-9 *SS620* 15-10 Gib 1-11 NWA 28-2-43 SOC 29--44

AR594 VC M46 39MU 10-8-42 82MU 13-9 *SS622* 17-10 Gib 1-11

AR595 VC M46 39MU 11-8-42 82MU 26-8 *Emp Fran* 30-8 Gib 14-9 Malta 1-11 ME 28-4-45 GACE 1564 Flt Strk tractor Istres France 8-6-46 SOC 27-6

AR596 VC M46 39MU 11-8-42 82MU 13-9 *SS622* 17-10 Gib 1-11 MAAF FTR ops 30-3-44

AR597 M46 39MU 13-8-42 con to VCT 82MU 18-9 *SS621* 16-10 Gib 1-11 NWA 28-2-43 SOC 31-7

AR598 VC M46 38MU 12-8-42 VSM 17-8 fuel syst mods 222MU 30-9 *Ocean Cour* 7-11 ME 7-12 con to VCT 4-10-45 SOC 29-8-46

AR599 VC M46 38MU 20-8-42 Stn Flt Port 17-9 i/sea ops 17-4-43 FH95.15

AR600 VC M46 39MU 17-8-42 VSM 11-9 fuel syst mods 52MU 25-2 *Ess Trad* 10-4-43 Casa 25-4 NWA 31-5 USAAF 31-8 FAF 10-9-47

AR601 VC M46 39MU 16-8-42 222MU 4-9 *SS622* 17-10 Gib 1-11

AR602 VC M46 39MU 20-8-42 76MU 19-4 *SS621* 16-10 Gib 1-11 NWA USAAF 31-7-43 FAF 1-10 SOC 26-4-45

AR603 VC M46 39MU 17-8-42 76MU 10-10 *Catrin* 20-11 Tak 27-12 ME 13-4-43 FAC3 13-12

AR604 VC M46 39MU 17-8-42 19S 13-10 402S 22-4-43 FAAC 25-8 ROS 63S 22-5-44 41 OTU 8-2-45 SOC to 5399M 17-7 5SoTT 29-11

AR605 VC M46 39MU 20-8-42 610S 9-10 167S 14-10 132S 19-5-43 19S 25-5 611S 3-8 10SoTT 21-10 to 4244M SOC 3-1-47

AR606 VC M46 38MU 20-8-42 501S 13-9 504S 19-10 313S 21-10 CE ops 18-11

AR607 VC M46 38MU 20-8-42 FACB 7-9 VSM 7-9 mods 129S 1-3-43 453S 17-7 341S 3-11 61 OTU 13-8-44 SOC 22-5-45

AR608 LR VC M46 38MU 24-8-42 19S 11-9 315S 26-6-43 611S 6-7 64S 10-7-44 53 OTU 17-7 FAAC 10-2-45 ROS SOC 29-5

AR609 VC M46 38MU 24-8-42 501S 19-9 504S 19-10 FAAC 19-3-43 ROS 165S 8-7 CE ops 25-7 FH284.55

AR610 VC M46 38MU 24-8-42 310S 15-9 CB ops 2-1-43 315S 1-7 611S 6-7 FTR ops 25-7 FH130

AR611 VC M46 39MU 24-8-42 76MU 22-9 *SS621* 16-10 GIB 1-11

AR612 VC M46 39MU 24-8-42 610S 11-9 167S 14-10 FTR ops 13-12 FH109.50

AR613 VC M46 39MU 24-8-42 76MU 16-10 *Emp Day* 22-10 Gib 9-11 242S C3 ops 1-1-43

AR614 LR VC M46 39MU 24-8-42 312S 11-9-42 ROS 7-11 CAC ops 14-5-43 AST 610S 20-11 130S 30-1-44 222S 16-2 FAAC 21-2-44 ROS 53 OTU 2-9 FAAC 16-9 ROS to 5378M 13-7-45 later 6371M & 7555M extant Ontario Canada

AR615 VC M46 39MU 28-8-42 76MU 19-9 *SS621* 16-10 Gib 1-11 NWA 28-2-43 SOC 8-2-45

AR616 VC M46 39MU 29-8-42 501S 13-9 504S FAAC 24-10 ROS DeH 11-4-43 131S 1-9 310S 24-9 441S 27-2-44 58 OTU 30-3 FAAC 2-7 ROS SOC 9-1-45

AR617 VC M46 39MU 2-9-42 82MU 25-9 *SS621* 16-10 Gib 1-11

AR618 VC M46 3-9-42 76MU 13-10 *Catrin* 20-11 Tak 27-12 Malta 1-7-43 NWA 31-8 ME 1-9 SOC 26-4-45

AR619 VC M46 39MU 3-9-42 215MU 5-10 *Suss* 19-10 Aust 28-11 54S s/dn over Darwin 15-3-43

AR620 VC M46 39MU 7-9-42 215MU 6-10 *Suss* 19-10 Aust 28-11 54S s/dn over Darwin 15-3-43

AR621 VC M46 39MU 7-9-42 215MU 5-10 *Suss* 19-10 Aust 28-11

BL serials all F.Mk.VB with Merlin M45 unless otherwise indicated

BL231 9MU 23-11-41 312S 7-12 ROS 11-12 CE ops 2-5-42 SOC FH63.46

BL232 M45M 24MU 30-11-41 64S 9-1-42 152S 26-4-42 FACB 3-4-42 FACB 30-4 S&H VSM 28-3-43 fuel syst elev & rud mods 611S 2409 FACE 1-11 MAL 63S 3-7-44 310S strk by MA228 ldg NWld CAC 23-10 ROS 41 OTU 8-2-45 e/fd on t/o fire pilot kld CE 12-3-45 SOC

BL233 37MU 23-11-41 131S 10-12 CAC ops 24-3-42 ROS 232S 21-7 VSM 24-9 fuel syst mods 453S 9-12 FAA 18-1-43 222S 31-3 167S 19-5-43 234S 5-1-44 FAAC 4-2 485S 12-3 CE ops 4-7

BL234 12MU 28-11-41 121S 321-12 CE ops 31-7-42 to 3337M Halton 8-8

BL235 33MU 7-2-42 302S 22-4 FAAC 13-3-43 AST VSM 9-8 mods 234S 5-1-44 63S 12-10 cd nr Kelvedon Essex CE 24-10

BL236 8MU 8-11-41 122S 15-11 WAL 12-12 401S 15-6-42 111S 26-7 222S 27-10 dvd from h/a cd nr Kilmaurs Ayr CE 15-1-43 FH141

BL237 9MU 9-4-41 122S 15-11 mr 14-4-42

BL238 Scott of Mafeteng 37MU 2-11-41 131S 10-12 FACB 20-2-42 154S 13-6-43 315S 21-7 317S 5-9 AST 23-7-43 con to Sea IB retained RAF serial 611S 5-8 RNDA 18-1-44 SAL 16-5

BL239 8MU 2-11-41 121S 7-11 ASTH 7-12 RAAA 7-2-42 e/fd cd nr Ramsgate 25-4 AST con to Sea IB NX981 27-5-43

BL240 9MU 1-11-41 501S 7-11 306S 18-5-42 FAAC 17-6 ROS 133S 29-9 336S 1-10 CAC ops 13-1-43 ROS CE ops 12-3

BL241 9MU 15-12-41 234S 5-1-42 f/ld nr Bodmin Cornwall after sortie with AA725, 726, BL668 CE 15-3

BL242 9MU 22-12-41 412S 28-1 CAC ops 9-3 AST CE 10-4

BL243 9MU 22-12-41 133S 5-1-42 74S 26-1 232S 8-4 222S 3-1-43 64S 31-3 USAAF 17-1-44 WAL 18-8 58 OTU 31-3-45 SOC 8-12

BL244 9MU 26-12-41 129S 6-1-42 CE ops dbf 19-6 SOC 25-6

BL245 9MU 4-1-42 411S 4-2

BL246 9MU 11-4-42 316S 5-6 FAAC 11-6 ROS coll with Beaufighter EL394 in circuit CE 22-11 SOC FH180.40

BL247 M45M 24MU 1-12-41 129S 14-2-42 CAC ops 19-8 ROS 303S 16-2-43 340S 28-9 485S 11-11 USAAF 9-5-44 SOC 19-11-45

BL248 9MU 26-11-41 41S 5-12 SOC 27-4-42 FH110.40

BL249 37MU 23-11-41 131S 10-12 FTR ops 28-3-42

BL250 12MU 1-12-41 131S 12-12 ROS mr 6-4-42 CE ops 5-6 SOC 7-6

BL251 38MU 6-11-41 122S 18-11 strk hill Mill Farm Upsall ttl wrk 5-12

BL252 37MU 2-11-41 312S 30-11 FACB 12-2-42 VSM 24-10 fuel syst mods AST 10-7-43 hook fitt RNDA 19-1-44

BL253 9MU 1-11-41 616S 8-11 ROS 28-8-42 AST 4-9 hook fitt & mods RNAS LoS 19-9

BL254 37MU 2-11-41 312S 7-12 ROS 28-5-42 152S 27-7 DeH 29-8 P&PSM 24-10 AST 9-5-43 con to Seafire IB-NX927

BL255 37MU 5-12-41 611S 16-2-42 FACB 7-4 SAL 133S 29-9 336S 1-10 FAAC 26-11 ROS WAL 14-3-43 610S 25-9 118S 22-5-44 611S 3-10 61 OTU 19-10 SOC 22-5-45

BL256 9MU 2-11-41 616S 8-11 129S 30-4-42 AST 21-7 412S 23-7 131S 19-11 610S 27-1-43 FTR ops 10-2

BL257 5MU 5-11-41 610S 26-11 FACB 15-6-42 WAL VSM 3-10 fuel syst mods 215 MU 8-11 *Bar Inch* 18-12 USSR 24-3-43

BL258 Canadian Pacific I 12MU 2-11-41 616S 11-11 FACB 19-2-42 AST M46 instal 401S 30-6 350S 5-8 485S 20-12 421S 12-2-43 FACB 7-3-43 VSM 25-6 mods 131S 24-8 310S 24-9 441S 5-3-44 58 OTU 30-3 61 OTU 25-6 FAAC 24-10 ROS 691S 21-6-45 SOC 13-9

BL259 M46 9MU 9-11-41 412S 23-11 FACB 15-5-42 ROS 131S 16-3-43 FAAC 28-4 SAL 131S 21-8 310S 24-9 315S 4-3-44 53 OTU 30-9

BL260 38MU 18-11-41 312S 10-12 AST 12-8-42 con to Sea IB-NX880 12-2-43

BL261 33MU 18-11-41 71S 30-11 CE ops 29-3-42 SOC

BL262 33MU 7-2-42 St Frm dis 610S 9-4 FAA 4-6 41S 16-7 CAC ops 21-7 ROS 340S 12-8 SOC 21-8 FH164.10

BL263 8MU 17-1-42 609S 13-2 FACB 30-3 AST VSM 12-10 fuel syst mods wng stiff 167S 26-3-43 132S 19-5 19S 25-5 315S 26-6 611S 1-7 FACB 30-7 ROS 234S 6-8-44 SOC 13-6-45

BL264 12MU 27-11-41 118S 11-12 FTR 19-5-42 FH142.20

BL265 8MU 4-1-42 310S 7-2 CE 3-7

BL266 8MU 4-1-42 129S 15-11 hit lorry ldg Westh CE 2-1-42 SOC 9-1

BL267 5MU 6-11-41 610S 26-11 FAAC 18-1-42 72S 29-7 222S 15-8 FAAC 10-12 ROS 65S 18-2-43 130S 31-3 349S 22-8 USAAF 6-1-44 1695CU 30-9 SOC 27-12-45

BL285 8MU 4-1-41 129S 15-11 spun into grd nr Thaxted 12-12 SOC 19-12

BL286 37MU 2-11-41 130S 12-12 i/sea off Falmouth 31-12

BL287 8MU 2-11-41 71S 6-11 CB ops 29-4-42

BL288 5MU 9-11-41 602S 15-12 222S 30-3-42 FTR 1-5

BL289 9MU 23-11-41 312S 7-12 SAL 23-7-42 215MU 17-11 *Bar Inch* 18-12 USSR 24-3-43

BL290 SR VB 5MU 9-11-41 74S 5-12 232S 8-4-42 FAAC 3-5 ROS air coll with AD565 ld Llanb CE 2-6 AST 129S 12-4-43 303S port wng fail cd Islington Cemetery London CE 14-6

BL291 LR VB 38MU 9-11-41 145S 18-11 350S 10-2-42 FAAC 20-3-42 ROS 308S 3-7 VSM 21-1-43 fuel syst mods wng stiff 312S 4-5 AST 16-5 234S 4-7 504S 30-6 26S 21-12-44 58 OTU 22-3-45 SOC 17-7 to 5389M

BL292 8MU 9-11-41 71S 15-11 65S 24-4-42 453S 11-7 222S 5-8 312S 31-12 602S 27-6-43 118S 10-10 132S 25-1-44 303S 24-5 41 OTU 19-4-45 SOC 6-6

BL293 9MU 23-11-41 312S 7-12 air coll with AD539 cd nr New Mills CE 19-12 SOC 27-12

BL294 LF VB M45M 24MU 30-11 457S 12-2-42 452S 23-3 93S 4-6 FAAC 10-9 WAL 332S 18-4-43 FACB 3-7 AST 118S 23-12 132S 22-12 275S 26-4-44 ROS 8-12 SOC 20-2-45

BL295 24MU 1-12-41 417S 14-2-42 416S 6-4 602S 15-7 164S 11-9 SAL 7-11 165S 16-12 hit trees nr Bridge of Don Aberdeen CE 6-6-43 FH328-35

BL296 12MU 10-2-42 611S 26-3 242S 2-6 SAL 27-10 VSM 18-5-43 mods con to Sea IB-PA120

BL297 8MU 17-1-42 118S 6-2 FTR ops 25-4 FH160.15

BL298 39MU 9-11-41 92S 19-11 FA FTR 10-1-42

BL299 24MU 21-11-41 131S 10-12 FAAC 16-4-42 41S 30-9 e/fd f/ld Chorlton Lodge Farm Cheshire CE 28-2-43

BL300 9MU 9-11-41 412S 23-11 e/fd hit shelter Wellingore aerodrome CE 15-4-42 AST SOC

BL301 37MU 18-11-41 130S 8-12 131S 10-12 HAL 21-12 234S 18-4-42 FAAC 22-5 AST con to Sea IB-NX895 10-3-43

BL302 LF VB 39MU 7-11-41 92S 18-11 610S 30-1-42 VSM 10-10 fuel syst mods 453S 3-1-43 222S 31-3 167S 19-5 FTR on ops 10-6 FH429.40

BL303 M45M 33MU 16-2-42 316S 14-4 dam ops 3-5 GAL VSM 26-1-43 fuel syst mods wng stiff 118S 14-4 CAC ops 24-5 ROS 64S 25-9 flaps fail w/u ldg somersaulted Colt CE 23-3-44 FH503.45

BL304 LF VB M45M 8MU 26-2-42 402S 23-3 610S 10-5 41S 16-7 CAC ops 19-8 ROS 412S 8-9 421S 31-1-43 BDn 12-7 comp level speed tests with and without spcl curved windscreen. Max speed increased by 2 mph. ASTE 12-12 602S 5-3-44 118S 13-3 FAF 19-1-45 GC 2/18

BL311 33MU 16-2-42 130S 26-3 FAAC 2-8 ROS 64S 24-12 453S 3-5-43 129S 17-7 DeH 28-7 501S 26-1-44 FTR ops 22-2 FH319.15

BL312 33MU 16-2-42 222S 14-4 FTR ops 30-7

BL313 33MU 16-2 234S 26-4 e/fd strk hut Perran CE 12-7 AST SOC FH9.30

BL314 LR VB 37MU 7-12-41 603S 27-12 FAAC 20-2-42 ROS 332S 17-4 FACB 12-7 AST VSM 5-2-43 fuel syst mods wng stiff 312S 19-4 234S 4-7 504S 30-6 313S 22-9 SOC 3-7-45

BL315 33MU 16-2-42 340S 17-3 CB ops 5-5 SOC 9-5 FH58.30

BL316 37MU 7-12 FAAC 4-3 ROS 19S 28-3 CB ops 26-4 recat E

BL317 37MU 23-11-41 131S 10-12 f/ld on beach Ton Fannau Merioneth CE 11-5 AST

BL318 24MU 24-11-41 72S 15-12 CAC ops 12-4-42 SOC E

BL319 24MU 18-11-41 504S 13-1-42 SAL 12-10 610S 16-2-43 FACB 11-3 P&PSM VSM 20-7 fuel syst mods wng stiff 504S 30-8 313S 22-9 443S 27-2-44 56 OTU 30-3 MAL 3-8 FACE 11-1-45 SOC 20-1

BL320 9MU 9-11-41 122S 15-11 FACB 30-1-42 WAL 91S 1-8 FA FTR 27-8 FH96.50

BL321 33MU 18-11-41 124S 28-11 71S 8-6-42 FAAC 1-7 AST con to Sea IB-NX955 4-3-43

BL322 39MU 9-11-41 92S 22-11 elect fault dbf 1-2-42 SOC 6-2

BL323 39MU 9-11-41 315S 26-11 i/sea ops 8-12

BL324 38MU 16-11-41 609S 22-11 CB ops 19-4-42 SOC E 24-4

BL325 8MU 15-11-41 74S 23-11 504S 22-4-42 hit tree w/u ldg Tanderagee Co Armagh CB 24-5 S&H SOC E 3-6 FH72.50

BL326 39MU 9-11-41 122S 15-11 130S 23-11 power fail on t/o hit Tomahawk CE 9-2-42 SOC 21-2

BL327 37MU 18-11-41 131S 13-12 82MU 21-10-42 *Bar Inch* 18-12 USSR

BL328 39MU 9-11-41 92S 22-11 417S 6-2-42 FACB 20-2 AST 242S 17-4 243S 6-6 222S 28-10 FAAC 7-2-43 SAL 611S 3-8 DeH 7-6-44 SOC 3-7-46

BL329 LF LR VB 33MU 7-2-42 340S 17-3 FACB 22-5 GAL M50 instal 308S 3-1-43 126S 19-8 412S 14-8 132S 1-3-44 504S 15-3 118S 3-7 611S 3-10 FAF 29-1-45 M45M instal

BL330 37MU 6-12-41 124S 16-12 CE ops 304042

BL331 8MU 12-12-41 72S 8-1-42 616S 8-1 ASTE 16-3 recat E 20-5

BL332 8MU 7-12-41 118S 12-12 FACE SOC 9-2-42

BL333 38MU 30-11-41 457S 21-12 452S 23-3-42 93S 4-6 ASTH 4-10 91S 3-1-43 i/sea ops 20-1-43 FH257

BL334 LF LR VB M45M 33MU 22-11-41 222S 5-12 72S 26-4-42 411S 18-5 242S 25-9 VSM 25-5-43 fuel syst mods wng stiff 308S 10-7 349S 29-10 602S 6-3-44 313S 3-10 61 OTU 19-10 SOC 13-2-45

BL335 LF VBA M45M 38MU 15-11-41 609S 22-11 165S 3-6-42 FAAC 23-6 222S 22-10 FAAC 7-1-43 SAL 165S 23-6 132S 26-7 118S 10-10 132S 25-1-44 57 OTU 13-8 FAAC 19-8 LMS recat E 23-9

BL336 33MU 15-11-41 124S 28-11 CE ops 28-1-42

BL337 8MU 15-11-41 403S 22-11 CE ops 12-2-42 SOC 25-2

BL338 8MU 15-11-41 72S 21-11 FACB 14-3-42 AST H 308 USA FTR 19-8

BL339 8MU 15-11-41 74S 23-11 232S 8-4-42 AST mr 9-6 332S 20-8 421S 21-11 412S 3-2-43 FAAC 3-4 ROS 416S 23-5 401S 1-6 dvd i/grd Underhill Frm Buckland CE 3-8

BL340 38MU 24-12-41 312S 1-2-42 FTR on ops 3-6 FH100

BL341 37MU 21-11-41 130S 12-12 air coll on convoy patrol i/sea off St Eval 3-6-42 FH170.40

BL342 M45M 6MU 23-12-41 133S 5-1-42 131S 11-1 FACB 18-3 VSM 12-10 fuel syst mods 132S 9-3-43 122S 21-5 234S 15-8 350S 3-7-44 57 OTU 23-7 FACE 9-4-45 SOC 26-4

BL343 12MU 23-11-41 312S 4-12 AST 24-6-42 RNDA 4-9 ASTH 28-9 hook fitt RNAS LoS 23-10

BL344 37MU 30-11-41 145S 17-12 FACB 26-1-42 GAL 121S 30-4 VSM 24-7-43 fuel syst & rud mods Mk III IFF wng stiff bomb carr 501S 22-10 i/sea ops 25-2-44 FH87

BL345 8MU 12-12-41 72S 8-1-42 616S 8-1 CE ops 15-3 SOC 31-3

BL346 24MU 13-12-41 485S 12-1-42 FAAC 15-4

BL347 8MU 26-2-42 411S 20-4-43 234S 11-1-44 CB ops 27-44 AST CGS 1-10 SOC 27-2-45

BL348 37MU 29-3-42 122S 18-4 FTR ops 17-5
BL349 9MU 20-11-41 65S 27-11 CAC ops 19-4 SOC E 23-4
BL350 SR VB 24MU 5-12-41 129S 14-2-42 602S 29-11 129S 22-1-43 66S 19-2 CB ops 7-3 ROS 234S 12-5 312S 29-6 317S 4-10 FAAC 7-1-44 ROS 'Basta' mods 28-2 CGS 13-10
BL351 9MU 24-11-41 457S 11-12 452S 23-3-42 air coll with AB244 CE 8-5 SOC FH145.30
BL352 37MU 23-11-41 131S 10-12 76MU 31-10-42 *C o Lil* 8-12 USSR 16-2-43
BL353 37MU 23-11-41 130S 12-12 DeH 14-7 222MU 25-10 *Harp* USSR 17 3 43
BL354 37MU 17-1-42 611S 16-2 FACE 28-2 SOC 8-3
BL355 37MU 23-11-41 130S 12-12 FACB 4-3-42 WAL 332S 20-8 222MU 27-11-43 *Dromare* 9-1-44 Port 28-1
BL356 37MU 23-11-41 130S 12-12 FTR ops 19-8-42 FH171.15
BL365 24MU 18-11-41 610S 13-2-42 403S 16-7 FAAC 25-5-43 RoS 421S 17-7 340S 21-9 67Grp USAAF 26-1-44 26S 18-12 58 OTU 22-3-45 to 5381M 13-7 SOC 5SoTT 29-11
BL366 29MU 23-11-41 FACB 14-4-42 ASTE hook fitt 4-9 RNAS LoS 19-9
BL367 24MU 1-12-41 611S 7-2-42 FACB 18-4 LMS 91S 23-2-43 616S 1-5 52 OTU 2-7 FLS 2-2-44 SAL 7-4 'Basta' mods 41 OTU 21-9 FAAC 8-2-45
BL368 12MU 21-11-41 416S 1-3-42 602S 15-7 164S 11-9 126S 10-8-43 186S 3-2-44 USAAF 9-5 R&S refurb to Port 15-12-47
BL369 9MU 20-11-41 74S 28-11 232S 8-4-42 FAA 16-8 VSM 24-9 fuel syst mods 132S 19-10 340S 28-9-43 485S 11-11 303S 28-2-44 VSM 28-3 mods 345S 30-8 61 OTU 28-9 SOC 17-5-45
BL370 37MU 23-11-41 130S 8-12 224S 28-4-42 130S 31-12 610S 20-2-43 350S 27-3 FACB 11-5 SAL 118S 3-8 64S 25-9 53 OTU 11-8-44 CE 30-9
BL371 37MU 31-11-41 131S 10-12 FAAC 3-5-42
BL372 5MU 12-12-41 65S 24-12 cd during aero Cutless Green Thaxted CE 2-5-42 AST SOC FH102.40 BBOC ASTH 8-10 332S 30-8-43 e/fd w/u ldg Little Waltham Essex
BL373 5MU 12-12-41 300S 2-1-42 123S 3-1 167S 15-4 165S 27-5 65S 23-9 SAL 26-12 AST con to Seafire IB-NX897 21-1-43
BL374 LF VB M45M 24MU 1-12-41 504S 8-1-42 FACB 8-3 S&H VSM 27-3-43 fuel syst mods wng stiff 118S 10-9 64S 25-9 1688Flt 12-10-44 R&S refurb to Port 24-6-47
BL375 37MU 22-12-43 303S 10-2-42 FTR ops 6-5
BL376 5MU 12-12-41 71S 31-12 CAC ops 27-2-42 ROS 334 USA 1-10 CAC ops 15-12 ROS 335S 28-1-43 315S 22-9 VSM 22-12 fuel syst mods 278S 18-4-44 376S 18-1-45
BL377 M45M 24MU 25-11-41 504S 5-1-42 501S 19-10 308S 4-1-43 322S 14-8 222S 1-1-44 VSM 9-2 fuels syst M 46 with 'Basta' mods 277S 6-5 coll with lorry Shoreham u/c des CE 16-8 290S 7-1-45 FAAC 6-11 SOC 16-11
BL378 24MU 23-11-41 54S 16-3-42 FAA 7-5 167S 31-5 610S 14-10 AST 27-11 VSM 26-1-43 mods HAL 30-3-43 con to PRXIII M32 Farn 24-1-44 anti-G trls. Speed trls with 'Spider Crab' (Vampire) over Farn-Basingstoke speed course. ETPS 15-5 MM Cowley Aug '44. Power boost trls Farn. CFE Tang 22-12-44 BDN 4-10-45 anti-G trls SOC 6-12
BL379 37MU 21-11-41 603S 27-12 FACB 10-3-42 SAL 17-3 308S 24-8 332S 21-12 52 OTU 4-4-43 FLS 2-2-44 FAAC 8-2 ROS VSM 10-4 fuel syst mods M46 with 'Basta' mods 276S 10-6 FAAC 16-4-45
BL380 9MU 25-11-41 19S 13-12 308S 17-10-42 FAA 17-11 COAL 27-7-43 to 4002M
BL381 9MU 23-11-41 312S 1-12 ASTE 24-3-42 FAAC 2-5 CE 15-5
BL382 29MU 23-11-41 64S 9-1-42 FAAC 13-2 ROS 152S 26-4 FACE 29-5 SOC 17-6
BL383 9MU 20-11-41 74S 28-11 232S 8-4-42 FAA 8-9 GAL 336 USA 13-2-43 RNDA 21-2-44 COAL 16-5 Hens 15-6 as train
BL384 12MU 27-11-41 457S 11-12 452S 23-3-42 i/sea off St Bees Hd Cumberland 10-4 FH80.30
BL385 LF LR VB M45M 24MU 28-11-41 485S 13-1-42 FACB 12-3 ROS 411S 30-6 VSM 17-4-43 fuel syst mods wng stiff 611S 19-7 308S 29-7 349S 29-10 303S 6-3-44 Met Com Sq 25-10 FAAC 16-3-45 SOC 24-11
BL386 VBT 27MU 22-11 603S 22-12 332S 22-4-42 FTR ops 31-7
BL387 39MU 16-12 6FPP cd del flt to 39MU CE SOC 20-12
BL388 6MU 13-12-41 504S 5-1-42 FACB 8-3-42 ROS 501S 19-10 59S e/fd w/u ldg Orford CE 25-5-43
BL389 12MU 14-12-41 123S 25-12 167S 11-4-42 165S 27-5 65S 23-9 130S 31-3-43 349S 19-7 pilot thrown out of a/c in dive ld safe cd Rutland CE SOC FH378.10
BL390 39MU 16-12-41 111S 27-3-42 WAL 19-10 122S 9-2-43 132S 6-2 AST 22-2 mods 122S 21-5 602S 15-8 504S 10-10 129S 26-1-44 VSM 18-2 fuel syst mods 17SFTS 5-9-45 SOC 4-7-46
BL391 37MU 22-12-41 610S 31-1-42 FACE 3-2 to AST con to Sea IB-NX888
BL403 29MU 23-11-41 41S 24-12 AST 16-2-42 331S 30-6 FAA 19-7 VSM 16-10 fuel syst mods 302S 6-11 FACE 5-12
BL404 29MU 23-11-41 41S 27-12 CE ops 4-5-42 WAL
BL405 24MU 24-11-41 41S 24-12 CE ops 14-5-42
BL406 37MU 23-11-41 131S 13-12 ROS 6-4-42 41S 30-8 FACB 19-4-43 AST 317S FTR ops 11-9
BL407 VBT 27MU 22-11-41 74S 15-12 cd nr Llanb believed struct fail dbf 24-12 SOC

Personalised codings on BL450.

BL408 12MU 22-12-41 222S 4-1-42 FACE 27-1
BL409 38MU 5-12-41 41S 24-12 FACB 24-1-42 308S 24-8 DeH 8-11-43 M46 instal 501S 13-4-44 345S 15-8 340S 9-11 DeH 1-12 CB recat E 2-1-45 SOC 8-1
BL410 24MU 24-11-41 e/a 6-1-42 WAL 317S 20-3 FAAC 20-5 ROS VSM 19-9 mods 315S 30-9 91S 26-1-43 CE ops 24-3
BL411 37MU 23-11-41 131S 10-12 FACE 23-3-42 SOC 3-4
BL412 cd f/f 22-11-41 ROS 12MU 10-1-42 122S 9-2 FAAC 4-5 ROS 308S 30-5 CE 2-2-43
BL413 6MU 23-12-41 306S 10-1-42 CAC ops 18-4 WAL recat E SOC FH68-15
BL414 6MU 13-12-41 504S 1-1-42 SAL 12-10 AST con to Sea IB-NX907 12-3-43
BL415 M45M 24MU 23-12-41 54S 7-3-42 FAA 7-5 167S 31-5 610S 14-10 AST 27-11 VSM 15-2-43 fuel syst mods wng stiff 412S 15-6 317S 28-6 312S 4-10 441S 27-2-44 234S 20-5 17SFTS 18-11 SOC 4-7-46
BL416 12MU 24-12-41 130S 11-1-42 AST mr 9-3 M46 instal 402S 10-4 421S 8-5 412S 3-2-43 602S 19-4 118S 28-4 611S 3-10-44 61 OTU 19-10 FACE 16-12 M45M instal during service
BL417 33MU 17-12 111S 5-1-42 FTR ops 27-4 FH185
BL418 M45M 37MU 9-4-42 485S 6-5 FAAC 14-5 ROS 457S 30-5 611S 30-7 72S 4-8 71S 2-8 FAAC 1-9 SAL 66S 23-3-43 411S 26-3 FAAC 18-10 ROS 341S 12-11 453S 11-12 602S 25-1-44 FACE 20-1 FH364.40
BL419 8MU 26-2-42 402S 17-3 FAAC 5-5 RNDA 1-9 AST 24-9 hook fitt RNAS LoS 1710 FTR ops 31-12-43
BL420 9MU 28-2-42 VSM 10-10 fuel syst mods AST con to Sea IB-NX910 21-3-43
BL421 9MU 28-2-42 RNAS Stret 1-9 as train ROS 17-10
BL422 37MU 29-3-42 457S 28-4 611S 30-5 71S 3-8 334USA 1-10 FAAC 25-10 52 OTU 29-1-43 411S 16-9 FTR ops 20-9
BL423 12MU 7-12-41 111S 17-12 91S 6-11-42 FTR ops 1-4-43
BL424 38MU 10-12-41 452S 23-12 CA ops 29-3-42 SOC 31-3
BL425 24MU 25-11-41 145S 17-12 FACB 15-1-42 AST 65S 9-6 FACB 23-7 S&H 91S 22-1-43 317S 6-4 412S 29-6 DeH 20-11 M46 instal 501S 15-8-44 OTU 28-9
BL426 38MU 24-12-41 234S 6-1-42 FAAC 9-8 SAL 132S 14-2-43 66S 15-8 340S 15-11 FAAC 1-12 ROS 341S 1-2-44 52 OTU 6-2 37 OTU 14-9 SOC 29-11-45
BL427 24MU 1-12-41 FACB 12-1-42 AST 234S 26-4 CE s/dn by HMS Kineserey pilot baled out nr Plymouth ops 28-7 FH137
BL428 24MU 6-12-41 41S 14-2-42 FAAC 11-6 ROS VSM con to Sea IB-PA116 20-11
BL429 37MU 1-12-41 111S 5-1-42 CE 14-3 SOC 31-3
BL430 38MU 24-12-41 134S 7-1-42 81S 8-4 132S 7-5 VSM 14-1-43 fuel syst mods wng stiff 310S 4-4 411S 7-6 416S 10-6 FTR over Holland 3-11 FH460.35
BL431 38MU 30-11-41 603S 13-12 FAAC 16-2-42 ROS 215MU 13-11 *Nank* 28-11 USSR 6-2-43
BL432 38MU 5-12-41 303S 16-12 FACE 19-2-42 SOC 24-2
BL433 24MU 1-12-41 131S 9-1-42 FACE 14-4 SOC
BL434 24MU 1-12-41 417S 14-2-42 RAF Tain 28-3 416S 6-4 CB ops 19-6 SAL 453S 29-6 AST 31-5-43 con to Sea IB-NX986
BL435 37MU 1-12-41 65S 28-1-42 411S 22-8 AST 25-9 VSM 8-2-43 fuel syst mods wng stiff 610S 1-4-43 FTR ops 4-4
BL436 37MU 8-12-41 308S 1-1-42 FAAC 25-10 HAL VSM 29-1-43 fuel syst mods wng stiff 313S 5-5 66S 4-7 FTR ops 30-7 FH378
BL437 5MU 10-12-41 222S 2-1-42 CB ops 25-3 ASTH 71S 21-8 334USA 1-10 403S 23-3-43 411S 16-9 341S 17-10 602S 25-1-44 R&S refurb to Port 1-8-47
BL438 24MU 23-12-41 154S 27-2-42 FACE 8-5 SOC 24-5
BL439 St Lucia ASTH 6-1-42 39MU 11-1 317S 27-1 154S 11-2 CB ops 16-3 ROS 610S 19-5 421S 3-2-43 602S 19-4 std ldg Selsey CE 11-6 FH394.30
BL440 24MU 4-1-42 54S 13-3 FACB 16-3 recat E reduced to scr 28-4
BL441 24MU 23-12-41 611S 18-2-42 242S 2-6 222S 11-8 222MU 7-11 *C o Lil* 8-12 dam in transit RTP 5-3-43
BL442 37MU 23-12-41 65S 28-1-42 FTR ops 27-4
BL443 9MU 15-3-42 RNDA 1-9 ASTH 3-10 mods hook fitt LoS 28-10 SAL 3-5-44 Hens 14-7

BL444 6MU 27-12-41 133S 5-1-42 74S 26-1 FACB 20-3
BL445 LF VB M45M 9MU 4-1-42 611S 12-2 FACB 20-10 SAL 308S 15-2-43 132S 19-8 118S 10-10 VSM 9-3-44 fuel syst 'Basta' mods 277S 6-5 ASTE 21-11 527S 16-4-45 sold scr 3-9-47
BL446 12MU 12-1-42 131S 28-7 FAAC 16-8 VSM 16-10 fuel syst mods wng stiff HAL 27-3-43 con to PRXIII M32 4S 30-12 SOC 28-3-45
BL447 8MU 26-2-42 121S 14-3 CB ops 12-4 CE 17-4 SOC
BL448 9MU 22-12-41 504S 9-1-42 FA FTR believed i/sea off St Johns Point Devon 29-6 FH109
BL449 24MU 5-12-42 71S 26-2 CAC ops 1-6 ROS 344USA 1-10 FACB 30-12 WAL 222MU 22-10-43 *Panador* 25-11 Port 8-12
BL450 12MU 1-12-41 122S 7-12 340S 24-5-42 421S 26-9 FAAC 9-10 ROS 10RS 13-1-43 FA del flt CAC ROS 41 OTU 8-2-45 SOC 17-7 to 5390M
BL461 37MU 6-12-41 145S 17-12 e/fd f/ld Catt CE 6-2-42
BL462 37MU 9-12-41 122S 1-3 reported miss 24-4 SOC BBOC 303S taxy coll with AD198 Bally CE 15-3-4
BL463 Berar I 37MU 27-12-41 FACE 16-3-42
BL464 LF LR VB M45M 24MU 24-12-41 118S 14-2-42 FAAC 17-3 ROS 411S 27-3 350S 26-7-43 303S 7-3-44 504S 15-3 CAC ops 12-5 ROS 303S 25-5 414S 3-8 53 OTU 28-9 695S 21-6-45 SOC 25-10
BL465 12MU 1-12-41 121S 13-12 403S 31-12 121S 22-1-42 CB ops 9-3 ASTE recat E SOC 20-5
BL466 12MU 7-12-41 412S 15-12 FACB 7-2-42 AST recat E 20-5
BL467 12MU 1-12-41 457S 12-12 452S 23-3-42 93S 4-6 82MU 23-11 *Bar Inch* 18-12 24-3-43
BL468 12MU 1-12-41 457S 12-12 452S 23-3-42 4-6 317S 29-4-43 DeH 18-6 M45M instal 412S 29-6 303S 3-13 SAL 11-1-44 M55M instal 501S 29-4 61 OTU 2-8 SOC 20-1-45
BL469 38MU 23-12-41 134S 7-1-42 81S 5-4 340S 4-5 FACB 12-2-43 AST VSM 16-2 fuel syst mods wng stiff 19S 29-5-43 DeH 18-6 315S hit hill in form with AR338&W3427 Clady Corner Co Antrim CE 11-9
BL470 24MU 6-12-41 312S 6-1-42 s/dn CE 2-5 SOC
BL471 9MU 22-12-41 411S 10-1-42 FTR ops 25-3
BL472 38MU 5-12-41 41S 23-12 FACB 24-2-42 AST 130S 23-7 ASTH 25-9 VSM 14-1-43 fuel syst mods wng stiff 167S 29-3 132S 19-5 19S 25-5 315S 26-6-43 611S 1-7 taxy coll with AR549 Tang CAC 18-10 ROS 53 OTU 23-11-44 SOC 8-1-45
BL473 37MU 7-12-41 308S 26-1-42 FAAC 7-7 ROS 91S 15-10 616S 1-5-43 52 OTU 16-7 FLS 2-2-44 DeH 26-2 'Basta' mods 53 OTU 14-12 61 OTU 28-6-45 SOC 15-10
BL474 M45M 12MU 9-12-41 123S 27-12 167S 16-4-42 165S 27-5 CAC ops 5-6 ROS FACB 22-1-44 &H 17SFTS 29-5-45 FAAC 14-1-46 recat E SOC 31-1-46
BL475 37MU 10-12-41 308S 10-1-42 e/fd on t/o cd CE 8-4 AST SOC
BL476 12MU 9-12-41 602S 24-12 350S 1-4-42 FTR ops 23-5
BL477 M45M 38MU 8-12-41 41S 24-12 121S 1-10-42 64S 23-3-43 453S 2-4 129S air coll with EN780 ldg Horn CAC 5-7 ROS 234S 22-8 350S 29-3-44 26S 15-9 41 OTU 25-1-45 FAAC 7-3-45 recat E SOC 30-3
BL478 8MU 26-2-42 601S 14-3 222S 29-3 FTR ops 17-4
BL479 316S Oct '42 308S Dec 504S 13-4-44 SAL 1-7 w/o 17-10-45
BL480 33MU 3-1-42 313S 15-1 FTR 10-4-42
BL481 37MU 15-3-42 616S 28-3 316S 22-5 FAAC 4-6 ROS 317S 4-7 315S 4-9 222S 1-12 64S 31-3-43 118S 25-9 USAAF 6-1-44 SOC E 27-11-46
BL482 38MU 28-12-41 308S 30-1-42 FACE 6-7 SOC 25-7 FH177.50
BL483 12MU 9-12-41 602S 21-12 FAAC 18-2-42 ASTH RNAS LoS 5-9 as train Yeov 3-7-43
BL484 12MU 9-12-41 610S 15-1-42 FACB 4-5 CE 5-5
BL485 24MU 23-12-41 54S 1-3-43 167S 31-5 FACB 10-7 SAL 215MU 29-10 *Nank* 28-11 USSR 6-2-43
BL486 LF LR VB M45M 12MU 9-12-41 609S 24-12 129S 29-4-42 FACB 3-6 CB ops 20-8 ROS 412S 3-9 VSM 21-10 fuel syst mods 421S 31-1-43 416S 23-5 401S 14-6 126S 10-8 132S 16-2-44 504S 15-3 FAAC 3-5 ROS 310S 15-7 SOC 6-6-45
BL487 12MU 9-12-41 RNDA 4-9-42 FACE 14-9
BL488 24MU 5-12-41 71S 8-2-42 334USA 11-10-43 VSM 16-11 fuel syst elev & rud mods S type pt Mk III IFF

bomb carr RNDA 26-2-44 COAL 23-3 RNAS Hens 23-6 as train

BL489 6MU 13-12-41 504S 1-1-42 501S 19-10 132S 31-12 122S 21-5-43 COAL 1-11 RNDA 9-2-44 LoS 8-3 as train

BL490 24MU 12-12-41 134S 16-1-42 81S 5-4 121S 6-5 i/River Blackwater Essex 23-6 SOC FH133

BL491 12MU 12-12-41 457S 7-1-42 i/sea off Ramsey IoM 8-3 SOC 31-3

BL492 37MU 7-12-41 74S 2-1-42 601S 4-4 133S 7-4 412S 18-5 CAC ops 4-9 ROS WAL 9-12 VSM 27-4-43 fuel syst mods wng stiff con to Sea IB-PA111

BL493 9MU 18-1-42 416S 2-4 ASTH mr 8-7 312S 31-12 AST con to Sea IB-NX906 17-3-43

BL494 33MU 3-1-42 74S 14-2 232S 8-4 FACB 27-6 AST 611S 5-2-43 308S 16-3 234S 22-8 to 4258M

BL495 33MU 3-1-42 310S 16-2 FAAC 15-3 ROS dam e/a 17-6 AST 332S 3-8 ASST 17-3-43 con to Sea IB-NX903

BL496 M45M 6MU 8-1-42 72S 26-1 65S 26-1 FACB 1-5 ROS 655S 23-5 412S 5-6 122S 29-8 453S 12-10 FAAC 17-11 ROS 610S 20-2-43 350S 27-2 345S 7-4-44 CAC ops ROS 57 OTU 17-8 132 OTU 3-2-45 R&S refurb to Port 20-5-47

BL497 38MU 26-12-41 310S 8-2-42 FACE 12-4 AST SOC FH61.40

BL498 6FPP cd del flt to 38MU strk trees Bisley Glos dbf 10-12-41 SOC

BL499 8MU 9-12-41 74S 15-12 416S i/sea off Selsey Bill thought coll with BL893 27-6-42

BL500 8MU 9-12-41 122S 11-12 FACE 18-12 CE ops 1-3-42 SOC 5-3

BL509 33MU 17-12-41 129S 5-1-42 i/sea Apl '42 SOC FH62.40

BL510 37MU 7-12-41 603S 27-12 FACE 26-3-43 SOC

BL511 24MU 12-12-41 122S 15-2-42 91S 8-6 FTR ops 11-9

BL512 12MU 14-12-41 312S 24-12 FAAC 23-6 ROS 67 Obs Grp 9-2-43 RNDA 5-3-44 COAL 23-3 Hens 15-6 as train

BL513 VBT 24MU 13-12-41 485S 12-1-42 CAC ops 12-4 ROS 129S 1-5 FACB 29-6 82MU 20-11 *Palma* 5-12 USSR 30-1-43

BL514 8MU 12-12-41 41S 24-1-42 RNAS Stret 5-9-42 ASTH 26-9 hook fitt LoS 24-10 SOC 29-5-45

BL515 38MU 10-12-41 123S 29-12 167S 16-4-42 165S 27-5 65S 23-9 130S 31-3-43 strk AD309 on ldg CE 24-5 349S 19-7 VSM 15-11 fuel syst mods SAL 9-6-44 CE 2-11 BBOC 1AGS w/u ldg Llangendeirne Carmathern CB 10-2-45 recat E SOC 24-2

BL516 LF VB M45M 12MU 14-12-41 312S 24-12 WAL 72S 13-5-42 5USA 6-9 453S 19-9 222S 31-3-43 167S 24-5 ROS 6-8 322S 13-8 FAA 27-10 ROS 402S 26-6-44 57 OTU 19-10 595S 14-6-45 FAAC 9-8 SOC E 20-8

BL517 39MU 16-22-41 314S 24-1-42 310S 25-1 AST mr 4-6 CE ops 23-6 SOC FH147

BL518 5MU 12-12-41 313S 28-12 154S 24-6-42 71S 18-7 flew i/hill with BM573 & R7296 Tarrennendre Merioneth 22-10

BL519 37MU 22-12-41 61S 29-1-42 242S 2-6 CE ops 18-9 SOC 19-10

BL520 M45M 39MU 16-12-41 134S 1-2-42 CA ops 11-2-42 ROS 232 8-4 VSM 16-9 fuel syst mods 308S 19-10 91S 15-4-43 501S 20-5 303S 8-1-44 VA 27-3 SAL 31-3 761S CE ops 19-6-44

BL521 24MU 12-1-42 91S 26-2 HAL 10-8 ASTH con to Sea IB-NX881 17-2-43

BL522 33MU 3-1-42 74S 14-2 232S 8-4 FAAC 29-6 VSM 24-9 fuel syst mods 132S 6-10 DeH 12-12 AST 5-5-43 con to Sea IB-NC941

BL523 24MU 4-1-42 91S 2-2 CAC ops 8-3 AST 133S 13-6 VSM 16-9 mods 336S 1-10 132S 23-3-43 234S 15-8 to 4368M 29-11-43 at 6RS Bolton

BL524 6MU 27-12-41 504S 5-1-42 FAB 6-7 S&H VSM 18-5-43 mods con to Sea IB-PA121

BL525 LR VB M45M Elcardo the Thistle 5MU 4-1-42 308S 28-1 FAAC 5-7 AST VSM 18-6 mods 308S 11-1-43 132S 9-9 602S 26-2-44 118S 13-3 313S 21-7 61 OTU 12-10 ROS 7-3-45 SOC 20-8

BL526 39MU 16-12-41 234S 2-1-42 VSM 14-1-43 fuel syst mods wng stiff HAL 25-3 con to PRXIII M32 RNDA 3-3-44

BL527 12MU 24-12-41 134S 8-1-42 81S 4-4 91S 24-5 P&PSM 18-6 FAAC 21-10 WAL VSM 3-3-43 mods con to Sea IB-PA100

BL528 38MU 17-12-41 65S 2-1-42 o/s ldg i/ditch Debden CE 27-1 SOC

BL529 12MU 14-12-41 312S 24-12 CB ops 24-1-42 GAL 610S 8-6 111S 17-7 AST 27-2-43 con to Sea IB-NC984

BL530 M45M 33MU 17-12-41 123S 2-1-42 167S 11-4 165S 27-5 FAAC 27-8 334USA 17-12 336S 15-2-43 WAL 350S 29-12 FAAC 6-1-44 AST USAAF 9-5 3507SU 28-1-45 288S 15-2 SOC 14-9

BL531 12MU 14-12-41 123S 28-12 167S 12-4-42 165S 27-5-43 lost wngs in dive cd Auchmillan Hill Frm Ayr 8-6 SOC 22-6 FH92.10

BL532 38MU 24-12-41 306S 5-2-42 CB ops 29-6 GAL VSM 18-2-43 fuel syst mods wng stiff 416S 28-8 FTR ops 4-9

BL533 24MU 12-12-41 611S 19-2-42 332S 12-4 FACB 8-5 recat E SOC 20-5 FH52.25

BL534 37MU 22-12-41 308S 1--0-1-42 FACE 17-5 SOC 21-5

BL535 38MU 17-12-41 123S 28-12 167S 10-4-42 CE 16-5 SOC 21-5

BL536 24MU 12-1-42 234S 14-2 129S FAAC 26-3 ROS VSM 15-9 mods 91S 1-10 FTR ops 6-12

BL537 Pekalangan 12MU 9-1-42 603S 19-1 FACB 28-2-43 LMS RNDA 4-9 AST 29-11 mods RNAS EA 27-2-43 VSM 5-11 fuel syst mods wng stiff Hens 6-9-44

BL538 Ambon (NEI) 8MU 17-1-42 401S 13-2 FACE 9-3 SOC 31-3

BL539 Landstorm (NEI) 33MU 4-1-42 504S 29-1 FAAC 16-5 S&H AST 15-5-43 con to Sea IB-NX944

BL540 37MU 17-1-42 148S 5-2-42 350S 11-2 VSM 17-8 mods M46 instal 164S 8-12 341S 21-2-43 340S 23-3 FAAC 17-4 ROS RNDA 20-2-44 57 OTU 595S 14-6-45 SOC 6-9

BL541 M45M 6MU 13-12-41 504S 5-1-42 501S 19-10 FACB 25-11 S&H 332S 9-3-43 310S 14-8 504S 24-9 611S 27-4-44 53 OTU 6-8 FAAC 9-12 695S 21-6-45

BL542 12MU 14-12-41 124S 6-1-42 FACB GAL 411S 7-6 FTR ops 19-8

BL543 37MU 23-12-41 317S 10-1-42 f/ld nr Prawle Devon CE 16-3

BL544 37MU 22-12-41 308S 10-1-42 315S 17-4 317S 5-9 232S 2-10 602S 16-4-43 FTR ops 15-5

BL545 37MU 22-12-41 308S 26-1-42 336S 27-10 USAAF 9-10-43 HAL 10-4-44 26S 17-6 41 OTU 8-2-45 287S 8-2 SOC 28-8

BL546 37MU 27-12-41 616S 7-2-42 VSM 24-9 fuel syst mods AST con to Sea IB-NX893 21-2-43

BL547 12MU 28-12-41 134S 8-1-42 81S 5-4 340S 4-5 CAC ops 11-5 ROS 302S 10-11 strk by R6888 ldg Heston CE 20-12 1AGS 20-1-45 PAL 4-9 SOC 10-9

BL548 6MU 6-1-42 602S 26-1 CAC ops 20-2 452S 9-3 457S 22-3 cd Kingston nr Worth Matravers Dorset CE 4-5 AST SOC

BL549 Ambarawa (NEI) 6MU 22-1-42 FTR ops 23-7

BL550 12MU 5-1-42 412S 5-1 FAAC 9-3 ASTH 71S 29-8 334USA 1-10 52 OTU 5-10-43 FLS 2-2-44 SAL 7-4 'Basta' mods 41 OTU 21-9 SOC 11-6-45

BL551 37MU 22-12-41 308S 16-1-42 132S 23-3 hit by Beaufighter X7937 while parked Sumburgh CE 2-5 129S 14-11 602S 29-11 66S 19-2-43 234S 12-5 312S 29-6 317S 4-9 53 OTU 5-10 FLS 2-2-44 SAL 12-4 M46 instal 'Basta' mods Morocco 10-4-45 MAAF 21-6 FAF 9-10-47 Dest.16-8-48

BL562 37MU 22-12-41 132S 10-3-42 FACE 2-5 SAL VSM 30-6-43 fuel syst mods S type pt Mk III IFF bomb carr RNDA 16-1-44 Hens 28-1 as train

BL563 6MU 23-12-41 317S 6-1-42 CE ops 16-3 VSM 13-8 mods 315S 4-9 131S 29-11 66S 27-1-43 350S 27-3 FAAC 22-6 ROS 234S 9-1-44 ASTH 26-9 FAF 19-1-45 GC 2/18

BL564 M45M 37MU 22-12-41 610S 5-2-42 AST 17-7 335USA 10-3-43 501S 23-3 504S 12-1-44 129S 26-1 VSM 19-2 fuel syst mods 17SFTS 16-10 FAAC 27-10 ROS SOC 31-7-46

BL565 9MU 21-2-42 5USA 5-9 504S 30-9 501S 19-10 349S 28-10-43 FTR ops 3-1-44

BL566 37MU 22-12-41 19S 14-2-42 340S 9-9 SAL 28-10 VA 9-6-43 ASTH 18-6 con to sea IB-PA129

BL567 SR VB 6MU 27-12-41 71S 17-1-42 FAAC 14-2 ASTH 303S 17-5 CAC ops 19-8 ROS 234S 4-7-43 504S 30-6 350S 17-7 e/td w/u ldg nr Dunstable Beds CAC 2-9 COAL 5-2-44 mods RNDA 3-4

BL568 9MU 21-12-41 501S 5-1-42 FACE 10-1-42 FACE 10-1-42 SOC 18-1

BL569 Berar II 12MU 24-12-41 130S 11-1-42 FACE 30-4

BL570 6MU 23-12-41 504S 5-1-42 FACB 12-7 S&H COAL 5-5-43 con to sea IB-NX958 Farn for trls

BL571 37MU 15-3-42 64S 13-4 AST 20-5 154S 12-7 AST 15-10 341S 30-3-43 313S 21-8 67Grp 22-11 SAL 12-4-44 FAAC 2-10 SOC 18-5-45

BL572 37MU 20-2-42 308S 2-4 316S 15-10 306S 16-3-43 FACB 4-6 DeH 13-6 222MU 24-9 Port 19-10

BL573 37MU 15-3-42 19S 13-4 CAC ops 19-8 ROS VSM 13-6-43 fuel syst elev & rud mods wng stiff 302S 27-9 306S 30-9 275S 7-7-44 SOC 20-2-45

BL574 8MU 25-4-42 303S 11-6 FTR ops 19-8

BL575 FF PJS 8-4-42 9MU 11-4 602S 21-5 416S 16-7 CAC ops 17-10 ROS 416S 24-10 i/sea ops 24-10

BL576 37MU 27-12-41 fitt hook deck suit trls *HMS Illust* Dec'41 308S 26-1-42 FAAC 12-4 WAL SOC E 27-4

BL577 38MU 28-12-41 308S 28-1-42 Farn 3-4-42 acc invest

BL578 9MU 24-12-41 FACB 29-1-42 WAL 130S 7-6 VSM 11-2-43 fuel syst mods wng stiff 610S 20-4-43 416S 10-6 FAAC 5-7 ROS 306S 30-9 315S FACB 22-3-44 1689 Bd Flt 15-1-45 PAL 4-10 SOC 9-10

BL579 M45M 38MU 23-12-41 504S 6-1-42 308S 30-1 310S 5-5 AST 13-7 VSM 1-8 fuel syst mods 332S 13-8 501S 29-1-43 CAC ops 5-7 ROS 504S 12-1-44 129S 26-1 26S 28-4 FACE 5-4-45 SOC 18-4

BL580 38MU 24-12-41 FAAC 6-1-42 ROS 118S 17-2 CB ops 9-5 recat E SOC FH102.10

BL581 Moesi-Ilir (NEI) 8MU 3-11-42 313S 17-1 ASTH 30-3 152S 26-4 VSM 27-3-43 fuel syst mods wng stiff 118S 25-8 CE ops 12-4-44

BL582 38MU 24-12-41 308S 28-1-42 FAAC 25-3-42 ASTH 71S 21-8 334USA 1-10 RNDA 24-3-44 COAL 12-5 mods RNAS Hens 20-6 as train SOC 21-3-45

BL583 6MU 28-12-41 71S 17-1 ASTH 31-8 VSM 17-4-43 fuel syst mods wng stiff 313S 24-6 66S 14-8 FAAC 27-8 340S i/sea on patrol off Lizard Point 17-11 FH385.30

BL584 33MU 3-1-42 St Frm dis 27-2 610S 1-4 111S 16-7 FTR ops 25-7 SOC 27-7

BL585 37MU 27-12-41 308S 26-1-42 FACE 13-2 SOC 27-2

BL586 38MU 10-1-42 65S 28-4 453S 12-7 AST 16-12 VSM 15-5-43 con to sea IB-PA115 ret RAF Dec'44

BL587 37MU 25-1-42 412S 28-3 CE ops 19-8

BL588 Grimsby I 12MU 9-1-42 134S 30-1 81S 4-4 331S 19-5 FTR 27-8

BL589 Legion of Imperial Frontiersmen 9MU 11-1-42 412S 26-4 421S 31-1-43 FAAC 24-2 ROS 416S 26-5 401S 16-4 126S 10-8 FACB 25-9 26S 26-4-44 41 OTU 25-1-45 58 OTU 22-3 to 5525M 30-7 M55M instal during service

BL590 6MU 9-1-42 403S 26-1 FTR ops 17-4 FH96.40

BL591 M45M ASTH 6-1-42 38MU 9-1 310S 17-2 234S 29-7 FAAC 12-9 340S 28-9-43 485S 11-11 VSM 9-3-44 'Basta' and fuel syst mods 277S 12-5 10AGS 5-6-45 FACE cd lnd Barrow 8-3-46 SOC 9-4

BL592 12MU 24-12-41 504S 9-2-42 501S 19-10 S&H 6-2-43 401S 10-8 HAL 19-6-44 42 OTU 9-12 FACB 2-3-45 recat E SOC 26-3-45

BL593 24MU 3-1-42 611S 18-2 FAAC 24-4 453S 11-7 222S 4-8 VSM 24-10 fuel syst mods AST 19-2-43 con to Sea IB-NX891

BL594 9MU 29-3-42 242S 21-4 FAAC 2-5 ROS 303S 15-7 FAAC 3-5-43 ROS 308S 25-6 AST 27-7 234S 5-1-44 CE ops 9-4

BL595 38MU 9-1-42 41S 10-2 81S 12-2 FTR ops 12-4 FH64.20

BL596 8MU 4-1-42 129S 7-2 FTR ops 28-7 FH220.50

BL597 Fort de Kock 38MU 26-1-42 121S 18-4 VSM 13-8 mods 121S dam f/ld CB 17-9 AST 20-3-43 con to Sea IB-NX912

BL598 Sanitor 8MU 17-1-42 401S 13-2 CAC ops 13-3 FTR ops 28-4 FH24.30

BL599 12MU 5-1-42 610S 15-1 AST 18-7 222S 25-10 i/sea ops 21-11

BL600 M45M 9MU 25-1-42 131S 15-2 FAAC 11-4 ROS VSM 10-10 mods 340S 25-1-43 341S 26-3 FAAC 11-4 ROS 401S 28-8 118S 24-5-44 313S FAAC 14-8 ROS 611S 3-10 FAF 1-2-45

BL613 I.M.C (NEI) 5MU 4-1-42 308S 28-1 VSM 28-8 fuel syst mods wng stiff 303S 30-11 FAAC 11-3-43 AST VSM 12-7 elev mods Mk III IFF S type pt bomb carr COAL 2-12 con RNDA 21-2-44 LoS as train

BL614 8MU 4-1-42 611S 7-2 CB ops 8-3 242S 2-6 222S 11-8 64S 31-3-43 ROS 30-8 118S 25-9 to 4354M 23-11 6SoTT 6-12 M46 instal Manchester Air & Space Museum 1983 extant

BL615 9MU 4-1-42 504S 6-2-42 501S 19-10 FACE 17-1-43 SOC FH214.15

BL616 M45M 12MU 28-12-41 134S 8-1-42 81S 5-4 91S 24-5 VSM 5-9 mods GAL 19-10 306S 29-8-43 316S 31-10 234S 15-12 VSM 25-1-44 fuel syst mods 276 ASR S 1-5 SOC 6-7-45

BL617 M45M 12MU 28-12-41 134S 13-1-42 81S 26-4 41S 4-5 CB ops 6-6 AST 6-7 Obs Grp 9-2-43 303S 9-4-44 CE ops 22-6

BL618 French Hope The First 38MU 6-1-42 10-2 242S 2-6 215MU 7-11 *Bar Inch* 18-12 USSR 24-3-43

BL619 38MU 9-1-42 222S 28-2 FTR ops 30-4

BL620 12MU 22-1-42 124S 17-3 FTR ops 25-4 FH56.50

BL621 Poerwokerto (NEI) 9MU 25-1-42 350S 19-2 CA ops 23-5 FACB 4-8 AST 222MU 27-10 *C o Lil* 8-12 dam in transit RTP 5-3-43

BL622 Serang (NEI) 9MU 25-1-42 350S 19-2 s/dn ops CE 25-4

BL623 24MU 4-1-42 234S 14-2 FTR ops 24-4 FH96.55

BL624 5MU 4-1-42 308S 28-1 FACE 6-7 SOC 9-7 FH35.55

BL625 5MU 4-1-42 412S 26-1 FACB 5-2 82MU 31-10 *Bar Inch* 13-12 USSR 24-3-43

BL626 39MU 3-1-42 312S 30-1 FTR ops 3-6 FH122.55

BL627 37MU 10-142 317S 17-2 CE ops 31-7

BL628 12MU 25-1-42 401S 1-4 308S 5-8 167S 12-8 610S 14-10 COAL 19-6-43 hook fitt RNDA 16-1-44 RNAS Belfast 30-1 to Aust extant, Victoria

BL629 Garontalo (NEI) 9MU 25-1-42 131S 14-4 FACE 11-6 AST VSM 12-10 fuel syst mods ADV Flt 15-10-43 57 OTU 5-9-44 eng trouble after dive w/u ldg nr Belford N'land CE 26-3-45

BL630 M45M Blythe Spirit 24MU 25-1-42 124S 14-3 453S 23-7 65S 16-12 130S 31-3-43 349S 19-7 303S 9-4-44 FAAC 13-5 ROS 414S 27-7 53 OTU 23-9 ASTE 17-11 recat E 2-1-45 SOC 8-1

BL631 6MU 27-1-42 316S 22-2 306S 16-3-43 DeH 18-7 66S 11-10 340S 15-11 239S 16-2-44 63S 13-3 26S 9-4 350S 10-6 57 OTU 23-7 FACB 25-9 LMS FAF Morocco 10-4-45

BL632 37MU 28-1-42 CAAF 25-2 mods 412S 20-4 FACB 18-1-42 421S 31-1 504S 29-4 350S 17-5 317S 1-6 412S 29-6 VSM 26-10 mr M55 instal 501S 27-3-44 FAAC 5-4 ROS 61 OTU 7-12 SOC 30-6-45

BL633 39MU 5-1-42 452S 29-1 457S 22-3 124S 28-4 e/a SOC 2-5 FH66.25

BL634 24MU 10-1-42 611S 19-2 603S 19-2 332S 10-4 FACB 28-6 ROS miss 31-7 AST 12-11 340S 28-9-43 485S 11-11 hit sea dam airframe a/c aban i/sea 21-12 FH313.50

BL635 Salatiga (NEI) 39MU 3-1-42 19S 13-2 3501SU 28-8 302S 17-10 HAL 28-10 ASTH 10-2-43 con to sea IB-NX879

BL636 Borough of Acton 12MU 10-3-43 457S 27-3 611S 30-5 72S 4-8 71S 13-8 FAAC 28-8 SAL 315S 12-2-43 FAAC 3-4 ROS 222MU 18-12 *Emp Corm* 3-1-44 Port 17-2

BL637 Stone 24MU 25-1-42 331S 12-4 CE ops 19-6 SOC

BL638 LF VB 9MU 4-1-42 411S 28-1 CB ops 24-3 ASTH M55M instal VSM 10-10 fuel syst mods M46 instal 453S 30-12 222S 31-3-43 167S 19-5 322S 22-6 26S 3-4-44 air coll with AA850 & W3314 cd Old Alresford Hants CE 22-7 SOC 16-8

BL639 37MU 9-1-42 616S 12-2 SAL 23-6 5USA 31-7 COAL 5-5-43 con to sea IB-NX959

BL640 39 MU 3-1-42 134S 8-2 81S 5-4 FTR ops 5-5 FH76.15

BL641 6MU 6-1-42 91S 10-2 HAL 11-3 4USA 5-8 67

Grp USA 22-11 602S 4-3-44 118S CB ops 21-5 ASTH CE ops 26-9

BL642 LF LR VB M45M Han Oman (NEI) 5MU 4-1-42 308S 28-1 FAAC 26-3 ROS 316S 23-12 FAAC 20-3-43 ROS 306S 30-4 349S 28-12 303S 6-3-44 FACE 15-3

BL643 37MU 25-1-42 412S 31-3 FTR ops 12-4

BL644 M45M 9MU 18-1-42 303S 18-12-43 DeH 29-2-44 mods VSM 24-3 fuel syst & 'Basta' mods 61 OTU 13-8 SOC 30-9-45 con to RIAP

BL645 8MU 17-1-42 111S 7-2 ASTH 27-1-43 CE ops 19-5 AST recat B 76MU 10-11 *Palma* 5-12 USSR 30-1-43

BL646 8MU 28-1-42 316S 3-3 VSM 26-7-43 fuel syst & elev mods wng stiff Mk III IFF bomb carr FAAC 30-11 ROS 234S 9-10-44 2GSU 16-6-45 MWW 16-2-46 R&S refurb to Port 13-4-47

BL647 8MU 4-1-42 65S 7-2 FTR ops 1-6 SOC

BL655 9MU 4-2-42 416S 24-3 FAAC 3-4 ROS 602S 15-7 164S 11-9 341S 3-2-43 SAL 4-3 VSM 30-3 fuel syst mods wng stiff 129S 30-5 416S 11-6 cd nr Dig CE 1-7

BL656 8MU 6-2-42 303S 16-2 CE ops 13-3

BL657 8MU 25-1-42 412S 13-2 CE ops 26-4

BL658 12MU 25-1-42 401S 15-3 FACE 24-3 111S 20-8 421S 13-3-43 CE ops 3-4

BL659 39MU 6-2-42 130S 26-2 610S 19-12 131S 25-1-43 e/fd i/sea off Wick CE 1-3 FH285

BL660 12MU 16-5-42 307S 1-10 ROS HQ 8th Ftr Com 21-10

BL661 Menado (NEI) 8MU 28-1-42 403S 8-2 FTR ops 8-3

BL662 6MU 6-1-42 91S 10-2 FTR ops 15-7 FH214.95

BL663 9MU 18-1-42 611S 19-2 242S 2-6 222S 11-8 FAAC 18-11 ROS 64S 31-3-43 118S 25-9 67Grp USA 6-1-44 SAL 15-6 57 OTU 17-7 61 OTU 12-4-45 SOC mr 29-5

BL664 Tegal (NEI) 12MU 22-1-42 123S 24-3 167S 17-4 165S 27-5 65S 23-9 SAL 4-3-43 VSM 2-6 fuel syst elev & rud mods wng stiff 222MU 26-9 Port 19-10

BL665 24MU 10-1-42 91S 26-2 CB ops 22-7 DeH 132S 8-2-43 CAC ops 15-5 ROS 52 OTU 2-7 VSM 20-1-44 fuel syst mods FLS 2-2 AST to 5595M FAF 3-3-46

BL666 37MU 10-1-42 132S 13-3 dam by Beaufighter X7937 Sumburgh CAC 2-5 129S 22-10 602S 29-11 66S 19-2-43 234S 19-4-43 312S 29-6 317S 4-10 VSM 5-11 fuel syst mods 277S 25-3-44 FAAC 31-3- AST CGS 3-10 e/fd w/u ldg nr Catf CE 1-10-45 SOC 4-10

BL667 12MU 10-1-42 416S 1-3 602S 15-7 132S 14-7 CE ops 22-8

BL668 39MU 26-1-42 234S 28-2 f/ld nr Bodmin Cornwall after sortie with AA725, 726 BL241 CE 15-3

BL669 38MU 26-1-42 402S 1-4 421S 8-5 FAAC 10-9 ROS 122S 15-7-43 234S 15-8 FAAC 2-10 303S 27-1-44 SAL 18-4 53 OTU 2-9 f/ld std cd Ashey nr Scunthorpe CE 1-1-45 SOC 15-1

BL670 Ever Ready 6MU 31-1-42 303S 16-2 FAA 7-7 315S 11-6-43 USAAF 17-1-44

BL671 M45M 37MU 28-1-42 132S 10-3 453S 23-12 222S 31-3-43 hvy ldg u/d clpse MHth CE 10-4 FH337.50SAL 4-5 504S 17-7 ROS 28-8 313S 25-10 FAAC 11-5-44 AST R&S refurb to Port 29-11-47

BL672 8MU 28-1-42 303S 16-2 CB ops 14-4 SOC E

BL673 M45M 9MU 25-1-42 132S 13-3 242S 23-6 222S 11-8 CB ops 19-8 GAL 336USA 23-1-43 AST 27-11 64S 3--4-44 345S 22-5- 57 OTU 17-8 275S SOC 20-2-45

BL674 6MU 31-1-42 41S 19-2 CB ops 18-9 AST 308S 23-2-43 132S 19-8 CAC ops 27-9 VSM 7-11 fuel syst mods 277S 8-4-44 CAC ops 10-5 ROS SOC 22-4-45

BL675 38MU 15-1-42 BDn Apl '42 radio, hand and fuel syst trls 322S 30-4 FAAC 3-6 VSM 31-8 fuel syst mods wng stiff AST 10-10 con to Sea IB-NX916

BL676 VBT Bondowoso AST 10-1-42 first Spit con to Sea IB-MB328 BDn hand and syst trls

BL677 38MU 26-1-42 402S 2-4 302S 6-5 FTR ops 31-5

BL678 AST con to Sea IB-MB330

BL679 AST con to Sea IB-MB339 31-1-42

BL680 LF VB 6MU 31-1-42 616S 18-2 USAAF 15-11-43

BL681 38MU 26-1-42 331S 15-3 VSM 5-10 mods CA ops 24-10 SAL 18-11 VSM 8-7-43 fuel syst elev & rud mods S type pt wng stiff Mk III IFF bomb carr 501S 5-11 e/fd on t/o Hawk cd i/trees CE 22-12 FH261.35

BL682 39MU 26-1-42 19S 13-2 coll with AD323 Ludham CE 19-2 SOC

BL683 5MU 31-1-42 91S 13-3 P&P SM 18-6 mods FTR ops 4-8 FH2-4.15

BL684 38MU 26-1-42 306S 1-4 VSM 28-7 fuel syst mods 316S 1-10 FAAC 29-10 HAL 17-11 mods 82MU 28-9-43 Port 9-11

BL685 Brastagi (NEI) 8MU 26-1-42 401S 14-2 CB ops 13-3 DeH 19-3 82MU 31-10 *Bar inch* 18-12 USSR 24-3-43

BL686 24MU 9-1-42 19S 25-2 611S 12-2-43 FAAC 27-4 ROS 4-3S 26-5 411S 4-9 341S 17-10 453S 27-10 FAAC 7-11 ROS 602S 25-1-44 FACE 7-3 57 OTU 7-12 FAAC 27-2-45 SOC E 12-3

BL687 AST con to Sea IB-MB329

BL688 M45M 9MU 25-1-42 132S 13-3 CAC ops 16-3 610S 14-10 335USA 11-3-43 501S 23-3 air coll with P8741 ldg Bally CA 12-4 CRD R-R 14-7 SAL 9-10 316S 31-2-44 63S 1-5 FAAC 4-11 ASTE 16-11 58 OTU 16-3-45 cd Walmersley nr Bury lancs CE 29-5-45

BL689 AST 10-1-42 con to Sea IB-MB340

BL690 M46 37MU 24-1-42 317S 17-3 VSM 11-9 fuel syst mods 315S 18-9 CA ops 16-11 HAL 308S 2-12 FACB 1-5-43 WAL 222MU 22-10 Port 18-12

BL691 6MU 22-1-42 610S 13-2 AST 17-7 VSM 10-10 611S 31-12 FACE 27-1-43 SOC

BL692 37MU 22-1-42 402S 8-3 FAAC 15-3 VA 232S 10-5 VSM 24-9 fuel syst mods 332S 6-10 334USA 22-11 AST 1-4-43 VSM 22-7 wng stiff MkIII IFF bomb carr 611S 23-12 234S 6-8-44 Tarrant Rushton 5-10 67MU Trans Com 7-3-46

BL693 24MU 25-1-42 234S 17-3 FACE 18-4 SOC 23-4

BL694 Sagle AST con to Sea IB-MB331

BL695 8MU 14-3-42 222S 1-6 e/a 29-6 P&P SM 24-9 fuel syst mods VA 18-4-43 con to Sea IB-PA110

BL696 9MU 11-4-42 AST 18-4 350S 1-7 P&PSM 26-8 416S 13-12 411S 23-3-43 341S 17-10 453S 27-10 602S 25-1-44 118S 13-3 57 OTU 25-8 577S 7-6-45

BL697 M45M 12MU 5-4-42 611S 21-4 242S 2-6 222S 11-8 WAL 26-9 91S 29-12 341S 1-7-43 306S 29-7 302S 3-10 234S 4-11 303S 28-4-44 57 OTU 2-8 air coll with P7884 cd CE 15-9

BL698 LF LR VB M45M 37MU 29-3-42 402S 2-5 122S 21-7 AST 20-10 312S 31-12 VSM 17-7-43 fuel syst & rud mods wng stiff Mk III IFF bomb carr 316S 29-11-43 65S 3-5-44 CE 30-6

BL699 9MU 12-2-42 485S 9-5 FTR ops 31-5 SOC FH16-45

BL707 6MU 31-1-42 403S 13-2 FTR ops 2-6 FH68.45

BL708 6MU 31-1-42 CB ops 25-4 recat E 5-5

BL709 St Ives Cornwall 33MU 7-2-42 340S 1-3 FAAC 14-5 SOC E 5-6-43 FH75-45

BL710 38MU 25-1-42 310S 25-2 234S 29-7 CE ops 29-10 SOC FH 169.10

BL711 9MU 7-2-42 132S 23-3 FTR ops 12-5

BL712 LF VB M45M 38MU 25-1-42 130S 23-2 ASTH 4-10 421S 16-1-43 412S 3-2 602S 19-4 BDn 25-7 rogue a/c sqdn reported it unstable flicked out of gentle turns eng vibration. Flown by ETPS who found no faults 504S FACB 25-10 ROS 41 OTU 1-2-45 58 OTU 22-3 to 5385M SOC 29-11

BL713 12MU 25-1-42 74S 15-2 VSM 24-9 fuel syst mods 132S 6-10 FTR ops 1-12

BL714 24MU 11-2-42 54S 16-3 167S 31-5 FAC 31-7 ROS 14-10 131S 25-1-43 SAL 5-2 M46 instal 23-3 FAAC 26-4 ROS 52 OTU 2-7 FAAC 12-1-45 recat E SOC 1-2-45

BL715 9MU 17-2-42 416S 25-3 FAAC 4-5 AST 322S 31-43 grd coll with AB904 CE 25-11 FH164.40

BL716 M45M 37MU 10-2-42 132S 1-4 ROS 17-3-43 616S 13-5 52OTU 2-7 340S 28-9 485S 11-11 VSM 17-3-44 fuel syst mods AST 9-5 17SFTS 25-9 SOC E 19-6-46

BL717 9MU 30-4-42 64S 4-6 154S 12-7 AST 10-8 132S 2-7-43 234S 15-8 129S 26-1-44 VSM 18-2 fuel syst mods 61 OTU 13-8 FAAC 16-9 ROS SOC 22-5-45

BL718 Rindsjani (NEI) 9MU 25-1-42 132S 10-3 FAAC 12-3 ROS 122S 21-5-43 234S 15-8 602S 4-3-44 118S 13-3 611S 3-10 FACB 12-12 AST SOC 15-1-45

BL719 M45M 9MU 25-1-42 132S 23-3 122S 21-5-43 234S 15-8 26S 3-4-44 41 OTU 25-1-45 58 OTU 22-3 to 5386M 18-7-45

BL720 Gedeh (NEI) 25-1-42 54S 15-3 167S 31-5 FAAC 13-6 ROS 1-4S 21-10 341S 21-2-43 340S 23-3 FAAC 30-8 ROS 234S 31-5-44

BL721 Garut (NEI) 6MU 27-1-42 72S 22-2 FTR ops 4-4 SOC FH35.50

BL722 38MU 22-1-42 222S 28-2 CB ops 4-6 WAL 306S 30-8 133S 29-9 336S 1-10 57 OTU 17-8-44 t/o coarse pitch hit obst CE 12-10

BL723 39MU 26-1-42 402S 5-3 CAC ops 19-4 SOC E

BL724 5MU 30-1-42 64S 2-4 FTR ops 8-4 FH8.50

BL725 M45M 8MU 6-2-42 64S 16-2 222S 2-5 CAC ops 25-5 ROS 242S 11-8 SAL 8-11 602S 21-7 504S 10-10-43 129S 26-1-44 VSM 19-2 fuel syst mods 277S 17-5 2nd TAF 1-3-45 FAAC 26-4

BL726 34MU 25-1-42 401S 14-3 CE ops 15-4 133S 15-6 FACB 5-7 ROS 65S 10-8 317S 2-9 315S 4-9 AST 13-2-43 con to Sea IB-NX885

BL727 9MU 6-2-42 132S 17-3 FAA 11-9 SAL 501S 8-6-43 411S 4-7 341S 17-10 453S 27-10 602S 25-1-44 SOC 27-10-45

BL728 9MU 12-2-42 72S 15-3 CAC ops 8-4 ROS 111S 16-5 FTR ops 1-6

BL729 M45M 9MU 5-2-42 222S 26-5 242S 11-8 93S 23-9 340S 28-9 485S 11-11 SAL 28-2-44 USAAF 9-5 1654CU 30-11 SOC 8-9-45

BL730 24MU 8-2-42 54S 13-3 167S 31-5 FACB 18-9 SAL AST 14-6-43 con to Sea IB-PA125

BL731 9MU 10-2-42 132S 15-3 CAC ops 10-11 610S 5-2-43 FTR ops 21-4 FH313.25

BL732 24MU 8-2-42 54S 16-3 167S 31-5 CE ops 10-9

BL733 39MU 10-2-42 72S 4-4 FAAC 25-4 ASTH 3-6S 20-5 FTR ops 31-7 FH145.45

BL734 12MU 11-2-42 416S 7-3 602S 15-7 FACB 20-7 SAL 91S 16-2-43 CAC ops 15-3 WAL 118S 10-9 64S 25-9 17SFTS 9-5-45 SOC 19-3-46

BL735 39MU 14-2-42 601S 14-3 411S 3-5 402S 25-3-43 19S 4-5 65S 20-6 130S 15-8 DeH 18-2-44 611S 28-6 64S 10-7 SOC 31-1-46

BL736 33MU 12-2-42 130S 25-3-42 AST 24-3-43 con to Sea IB-NX 954

BL748 12MU 28-1-42 603S 17-2 332S 16-4 FAAC 1-5 ROS 303S 28-7 night ldg dummy aerodrome Tofts Grange Q site Lincs CE 23-9 SOC FH122.55 AST 24-12 64S 3-5-43 65S 29-4 132S 23-5 302S 28-6 306S 3-10 SOC 31-7-46

BL749 12MU 25-1-42 504S 20-2 e/fd w/u ldg nr Comber Co Down CE 12-3

BL750 12MU 25-1-42 412S 4-4 411S 6-4 FAAC 14-8 308S 21-10 DeH 7-11 AST 10-3-43 con to Sea IB-NX896

BL751 5MU 20-1-42 cd in trans 315S CAC 13-3 ROS hit obst fly low Birkdale Sands Lancs CE 15-8 SOC 21-8

BL752 37MU 20-2-42 402S 15-3 strk by AD200 while parked Ibsley CE 26-4

BL753 LF LR VB M45M 9MU 30-1-42 401S 6-4 CAC ops 14-6 ROS 65S 11-8 132S 12-9 P&PSM 19-10 VSM 5-7-43 fuel syst elev & rud mods wng stiff S type pt Mk III IFF bomb carr 316S 28-11 63S 1-5-44 FTR ops 25-6

BL754 37MU 28-1-42 616S 28-3 e/fd i/sea of Dung 15-4

BL755 LFM45M 5MU 31-1-42 19S 24-4 CAC ops 23-6 ROS 130S 1-8 WAL 132S 19-8-43 118S 10-10 132S 25-1-44 VSM 9-3 fuel syst & 'Basta' mods 350S 10-6 FAAC 30-7 ROS 61 OTU 2-9 FAF 16-3-46

BL756 8MU 31-1-42 401S 2-5 FAAC 2-7 ROS RNAS LoS 6-9 ASTh 20-10 hook fitt

BL757 12MU 25-1-42 122S 17-2 118S 22-4 AST 25-6 65S 14-8 FAAC 19-8 ROS 340S 7-9 CAC ops 29-12 AST con to SEA IB-NX967

BL758 6MU 6-2-42 AST 6-3 124S 8-3 CE ops 13-3 SOC

BL759 12MU 11-2-42 416S 1-3 6-2S 15-7 164S 11-9 SAL 15-11 COAL 31-5-43 hook fitt RNDA 16-1-44 called Seafire by Admiralty

BL760 24MU 8-3-42 54S 13-3 167S 31-5 610S 14-10 131S 25-1-43 FAAC 25-3 ROS 310S 30-6 313S 29-7 FAAC 6-8 ROS 504S 12-1-44 129S 26-1 186S 13-4 130S 25-6 CAC ops 5-10 57 OTU 10-5-45 SOC 25-10

BL761 33MU 8-2-42 304S 1-3 FTR ops 10-4 SOC 14-4 FH26.30

BL762 12MU 14-2-42 504S 11-3 501S 19-10 VSM 26-6-43 mods 66S 809 FTR ops 3-10

BL763 M45M 33MU 8-2-42 72S 26-4 CB ops 26-4 340S 18-5 DeH VSM 3-9 fuel syst mods 421S 10-11 412S 3-2-43 602S 19-4 64S 27-4-44 61 OTU 28-9 FACE 21-2-45 SOC 28-2

BL764 9MU 25-1-42 VSM 29-8 fuel syst mods 222MU 24-10 *Halagus* 19-12 USSR 17-3-43

BL765 39MU 26-1-42 340S 2-3 FAAC 17-7 ROS 412S 12-10-43 FTR ops 13-12 FH247

BL766 8MU 6-2-42 129S 16-2 CE ops 28-3 SOC

BL767 24MU 8-2-42 54S 16-3 167S 31-5 61-S 14-10 131S 25-1-43 310S 30-6 313S 26-7 FACB 13-9 FLS 31-1-44 402S 17-6 527S 15-7 SOC 31-1-45

BL768 8MU 6-2-42 222S 16-2 FTR ops 29-6

BL769 8MU 31-1-42 312S 16-2 222S 18-6 242S 11-8 131S 22-9 610S 27-1-43 CE ops 6-2

BL770 33MU 7-2-42 Farn 10-4 acc invest with W3248 41S 2-6 2USA 22-8 CAC 3-11 VSM 18-4-43 con to Sea IB-PA113

BL771 24MU 8-2-42 54S 17-3 FAAC 12-4 SAL 222MU 13-11 *Halagus* 19-12 USSR 17-3

BL772 39MU 10-2-42 402S 5-3 421S 8-5 FACB 5-6 GAL VSM 11-10 fuel syst mods wng stiff 610S 4-4-43 26S 27-7-44 CE ops 21-11

BL773 6MU 4-2-42 72s 22-2 GAL mr 15-3 15-3 133S 15-6 CAC ops 19-8 VSM 19-9 mods 336S 1-10 AST 10-11 M45M instal CB ops 14-1-43 317S 11-6 412S 29-6 CRD MWW 23-9-45 con to dron A/c SOC 15-4-48 used as study a/c in acc prevention film

BL774 6MU 6-2-42 452S 14-2 FTR ops 29-3 SOC

BL775 31MU 10-2-42 132S 13-3 DeH 4-2-43 315S 6-4 303S 6-6 313S 19-8 to 4362M 25-11 5SoTT SOC 15-3-44

BL776 M45M39MU 14-2-42 145S 13-6 133S 30-9 336 1-10 DeH 18-8-43 COAL 28-2-44 con RNAS Hens 9-4 as train

BL777 38MU 13-2-42 41S 13-4 FTR ops 19-8

BL778 12MU 11-2-42 416S 1-3 FACB 6-5 SAL 4S 1-8 501S 2-12 USAAF 20-4-43 FACA 20-5 ROS 350S 20-7 RNDA 21-2-44

BL779 9MU 25-1-42 416S 1-3 FTR ops 4-4

BL781 9MU 10-2-42 132S 15-3 FTR ops 19-11

BL780 8MU 31-1-42 401S 14-2 FAAC 5-5 ROS 416S 27-2-43 411S 23-3 314S 17-10 602S 25-1-44 350S 3-4 CB ops 11-6 ROS 61 OTU 13-8 SOC 21-9-45

BL782 24MU 8-2-42 401S 14-3 FTR ops 13-7 FH167.30

BL783 8MU 31-1-42 118S 7-3 CAC ops 20-4-43 SOC E FH40.55

BL784 39MU 10-2-42 601S 8-3 412S 31-3-43 FTR ops 25-4

BL785 24MU 8-2-42 54S 1-3 124S 8-3 CE ops 10-3 SOC

BL786 33MU 8-2-42 340S 18-3 FTR ops 27-4

BL787 M45M 8MU 6-2-42 64S 16-2 222S 2-5 AST 27-5 RNAS Stret 6-9 VSM 26-5-43 fuel syst mods wng stiff 610S 30-6 602S 4-3-44 118S 13-3 FAF Morocco 18-12

BL788 33MU 7-2-42 340S 7-4 CAC ops 1-5 ROS 341S 26-3-43 610S 11-9 234S 11-5-44 53 OTU 17-7 FAAC 7-1-45 ROS 527S 24-5 sold scr 3-9-47

BL789 33MU 8-2-42 Star Fm dis 27-2 501S 25-3 FTR 5-4

BL801 24MU 10-2-42 317S 20-3 308S 1-4 FAAC 27-5 76MU 8-11 *Palma* 30-1-43

BL802 33MU 7-2-42 317S 23-3 hvy ldg o/t North CB 17-5 SOC 21.5

BL803 33MU 13-2-42 340S 17-3 CAC ops 15-7 ROS lost over e/tr 5-9 FH176.05

BL804 12MU 11-2-42 416S 7-3 FACB 3-4 ROS FACE 28-2-43

BL805 6MU 14-2-42 317S 7-3 f/ld Bolt Head CE 15-3

BL806 38MU 13-2-42 232S 13-4 VSM 24-9 fuel syst mods 222S 30-11 FAAC 26-1-43 SAL VA 9-6-43 con to Sea IB-PA126 ret RAF 3-10

BL807 39MU 14-2-42 601S 9-3 133S 14-4 FACA 24-5 FACE 28-7 SOC 13-8

BL808 12MU 14-2-42 416s 7-3 FACB 25-6 215MU 8-11 *Bar Inch* 10-12 USSR 24-3-43

BL809 45MU 2-4-42 81S 30-4 64S 3-5-43 118S 25-9 VSM 5-11 fuel syst mods M46 instal 17SFTS 7-10-44 FACB 2-5-45 recat E SOC 17-5

BL810 FF PJS 2-4-42 37MU 5-4-42 457S 19-5 611S

30-5 72S 4-8 303S 1-6-43 315S 6-6 19S 26-6 315S 1-7 234S 21-6-44 sold J Dale 8-7-48 M46 instal during service

BL811 45MU 2-4-42 81S 26-4 air coll with BM463 cd Hastings CE 2-6 SOC 7-6

BL812 Lichfield 9MU 25-3-42 402S 30-4 122S 1-9 416S 14-11 FACE 6-2-43

BL813 37MU 29-3-42 122S 18-4 FTR ops 24-4

BL814 37MU 29-3-42 122S 18-4 i/sea ops 7-6

BL815 45MU 2-4-42 485S 19-6 FTR ops 22-7

BL816 45MU 28-5-42 91S 2-7 FTR ops 22-7 FH28-45

BL817 FF PJS 2-4-42 45MU 7-4 81S 3-5 e/fd f/ld N'land 13-5 SOC 23-5

BL818 38MU 24-5-42 166S 23-9 ASTH 4-9 hook fittd dam trail ldg *HMS Rav* 165S 16-4-44

BL819 24MU 8-2-422 154S 27-2 313S 8-6 332S 3-8 FTR ops 19-8-43

BL820 9MU 21-2-42 402S 16-4 412S 6-5 FTR ops 26-11 FH64.50

BL821 38MU 6-2-42 331S 8-3 VSM 12-8 fuel syst mods FACA 16-5-43 313S 7-10 443S 27-2-44 58 OTU 30-3 1TEU 26-4 FACA 10-5 ROS 61, OTU 25-6 R-RH 27-7-45 new eng R&S refurb to Port 17-4-47

BL822 6MU 6-2-42 22-2 CAC ops 9-3 350S 1-4 FTR ops 1-6

BL823 12MU 11-2-42 416S 7-3 FACB 24-4 Lms 222MU 6-11 *C o Lil* 8-12 USSR 16-2-43

BL824 39MU 8-2-42 340S 15-3 CE 30-4 AST SOC 6-5 FH52.45

BL825 33MU 8-2-42 Star Fm dis 27-2 412S 18-6 FTR ops 19-7

BL826 LF LR VB 37MU 10-2-42 132S 10-3 FACB 2-5 SAL 421S 16-1-43 416S 23-5 401S 1-6 e/a CB 29-7 316S 7-12 63S 27-4-44 FAAC 14-5 ROS 41 OTU 8-5-45 SOC to 5398M 17-7 5SoTT 29-11

BL827 Elizabeth 33MU 8-2-42 304S 1-3 FTR ops 30-4 FH54.35

BL828 24MU 10-2-42 234S 20-3 FTR ops 24-4

BL829 6MU 24-2-42 401S 7-5 222S 26-9 FAAC 18-2-43 ROS 64S 31-3 118S 25-9 129S 3-2-44 276S 9-10 CA ops 14-3-45

BL830 Skagen Ind 6MU 14-2-42 129S 8-3 602S 29-11 66S 19-2-43 19S 1-5 FACE 20-5 65S 29-6 313S 21-10 442S 27-2-44 58 OTU 30-3 FACE 15-9

BL831 Skagen Ind 24MU 16-2-42 234S 5-4 FTR ops 24-4

BL832 Eleanor 12MU 22-2-42 401S 14-3 309S 12-8 HAL 26-10 132S 31-12 i/sea CE 23-2-43

BL833 33MU 13-2-42 331S 17-3 FTR ops 21-7

BL846 39MU 14-2-42 310S 23-3 FACB 10-6 VSM 18-10 fuel syst mods 412S CAC on ops 10-12 ASTH 20-3-43 con to Sea IB-NX913

BL847 37MU 12-2-42 417S 10-3-42 132S 1-9 FTR ops 28-1-43

BL848 24MU 8-2-42 54S 1-3 167S 31-5 FAAC 8-10 ROS VSM 21-3-43 fuel syst mods wng stiff 302S 7-7 31st ATG 9-6-44 1689Flt 6-10 fast ldg o/t cb 3-2-45 SOC 10-2

BL849 39MU 8-2-42 402S 5-3 401S 6-5 CE ops 5-6-43 SOC 6-6 FH113.45

BL850 LF LR VB M45M 6MU 14-2-42 402S 9-3 312S 4-5 41S 13-8 308S 30-5-43 610S 19-9 CAC ops 14-11 ROS 316S 25-12 118S 27-4-44 313S 21-7 611S 3-10 61 OTU 12-10 BAFO Com Sq 13-9-45 R&S refurb to Port 6-2-47

BL851 LF LR VB 12MU 14-2-42 416S 1-3 CAC ops 15-4 SAL M55M instal 242S 20-8 411S 23-9 FACB 27-10 ROS 402S 25-3-43 19S 21-5 317S 17-6 412S 29-6 126S 10-8 132S 7-3-44 504S 15-3 310S 15-7 strk by Martinet taxy Haw CE 6-9-44

BL852 6MU 14-2-42 402S 9-3 312S 3-5 403S 21-8 416S 3-6-43 19S 7-6 315 e/fd cd/ld Bally CE 8-7

BL853 9MU 1-3-42 VSM 29-8 fuel syst mods 91S 30-9 FTR ops 7-12 FH46

BL854 37MU 22-2-42 ROS 25-3 19S 28--3 CAC ops 19-5 ROS 340S 20-8 FTR over e/tr 5-9 FH147

BL855 Niels Ebbesen 24MU 16-2-42 234S 5-4 FAAC 25-4 WAL mr AST 22-4-43 con to Sea IB-NX920

BL856 M45M 6MU 16-2-42 RNDA 1-3 for con to Sea cancel ROS 501S 7-7-43 303S 20-2-44 57 OTU 17-8 FAAC 10-11 SOC 1-6-45

BL857 9MU 5-2-42 72S 15-4 CAC ops 12-4 SOC CE 20-4

BL858 39MU 6-2-42 340S 1-3 e/fd cd/ld Girvan Ayr CE 21-3 SAL RNDA 4-9 ASTH 1-10 hook fitt LoS 19-10

BL859 39MU 6-2-42 340S 1-3 CAC ops 15-7 ROS 412S 25-7 CE ops 5-8 SOC 11-8

BL860 37MU 17-2-42 317S 16-3 VSM 28-7 fuel syst mods 315S 4-9 332S 14-1-43 130S 13-9 FACE 23-1-44 FH550.40

BL861 33MU 8-2-42 316S 4-6 AST 24-1-43 VSM 18-5 con to Sea IB-PA123

BL862 M46 39MU 6-2-42 340S 1-3 334S 2-11 602S 25-1-43 331S 13-4 310S 14-8 504S 24-9 VSM 20-12 fuel syst mods 53 OTU 11-8-44 FAAC 5-10 ROS taxy i/obst Hibald CE 29-3-45

BL863 24MU 8-2-42 54S 15-3 167S 31-5 610S 14-10 VSM 24-7-43 fuel syst mods wng stiff S type pt Mk III IFF bomb carr 341S 26-12 FLS 23-3-44 57 OTU 14-9 FACB 18-11 recat E

BL864 9MU 12-2-42 72S 17-3 FACB 13-4 SOC E

BL887 37MU 10-2-42 417S 13-3 416S 6-4 602S 15-7 164S 11-9 341S 212-43 340S 23-3 504S 20-12 head on coll with P8785 cd nr Hatton Aberdeen CE 28-12 FH491.05

BL888 24MU 10-2-42 54S 17-3 167S 31-5 610S 14-10 131S 25-1-43 FAAC 27-4 ROS 310S 30-6 M46 instal 313S 29-7 315S 17-10 USAAF 17-1-44 AFDU 11-6 61 OTU 19-10 SOC 10-4-45

BL889 39MU 6-2-42 234S 28-2 FTR ops 17-4 FH67.45

BL890 33MU 12-2-42 130S 26-3 118S 23-11 316S 12-12 306S 16-3-43 82MU 27-9 *Bar For* 16-10 Port 9-11

BL891 6MU 6-2-42 331S 12-3 FAA 24-10 SAL VSM 12-7-43 fuel syst & elev mods wng stiff Mk III IFF bomb carr RNDA 21-1-44 as train

BL892 8MU 10-2-42 316S 3-3 FAAC 27-9 SAL 234S 31-3 312S 29-6 317S 4-10 52 OTU 5-10 FAAC 20-12 ROC DeH mods 'Basta' 26-2-44 FAAC 19-4 63S 15-9 58 OTU 22-3-45 to 5392M SOC 17-7

BL893 12MU 19-2-42 416S 28-3 i/sea off Selsey Bill beleived coll with BL449 27-6 FH127.30

BL894 12MU 14-2-42 603S 26-3 332S 15-8 CB ops 19-8 HAL AST 23-4-43 con to Sea IB-NX921

BL895 9MU 17-2-42 122S 15-3 242S 6-6 312S 31-12 COAL 12-7-43 hook fitt RNDA 16-1-44 RNAS Belfast 12-2-44

BL896 37MU 17-2-42 402S 15-3 421S 8-5 FTR ops 8-11

BL897 37MU 20-2-42 601S 31-3 412S 31-3 FACB 26-8 ROS 421S 9-2-43 CACops 13-2 ROS 416S 19-3 411S 23-3 401S 14-8 FACB 21-2-44 LMS BSDU 11-12 SOC 23-6-45

BL898 12MU 14-2-42 2USA 22-8 FAAC 11-3-43 ROS HAL 16-6-44 M45MA instal R&S refurb to Port 23-1-48

BL899 24MU 10-2-42 610S 15-3 65S 7-5 453S 11-7 VSM 24-10 fuel syst mods CE ops 10-12

BL900 The Canadian Policeman 5MU 17-2-42 403S 8-4 FACB 4-5 CE 11-5

BL901 9MU 10-2-42 316S 3-4 FACB 11-9 GAL COAL 5-5-43 con to Sea IB-NX960

BL902 9MU 14-2-42 303S 3-4 FAAC 14-4 CE 30-4 SOC

BL903 38MU 13-2-42 331S 8-3 FTR ops 19-8

BL904 12MU 11-2-42 416S 1-3 FAAC on f/f to 416S ROS 607S 13-8 184S 11-9 FAAC 11-9 SASL VSM 6-6-43 con to Sea IB-PA127

BL905 6MU 16-2-42 scheduled con to SEA IB cancel 14-2 154S 12-6 CA ops 21-6 340S 20-7 41S 20-11 VSM 19-6-43 fuel syst & rud mods 302S 21-8 306S 3-10 FACB 28-12 recat E 16-1-44

BL906 12MU 11-2-42 601S 10-3 412S 31-3 FACB 15-4 SOC E 15-4

BL907 LF LR VB M45M 33MU 7-2-42 Star Fm dis 27-2 222S 14-4 CB ops ROS ASTH 610S 29-1-43 350S 27-3 133S 17-2-44 132S 7-3 504S 15-3 ld on top of AD577 Haw CAC 10-9 AST 23-9 FACE 27-245 SOC 15-3

BL908 33MU 12-2-42 340S 17-3 CAC ops 14-4 FTR ops 23-8 FH160.45

BL909 33MU 13-2-42 340S 17-3 FTR ops 10-4 FH18.20

BL918 12MU 11-2-42 124S 14-3 CE ops 27-4 SOC recat B 13-10 288S 8-2-45 SOC 14-9

BL919 38MU 13-2-42 331S 15-3 FTR ops 21-7

BL920 12MU 11-2-42 416S 5-3 602S 15-7 164S 11-9 USAAF 11-6-43 FACE 9-9

BL921 6MU 14-2-42 402S 9-3 strk by AD200 while parked CE 26-4

BL922 12MU 11-2-42 611S 25-3 242 2-6 FACB 28-8 416S 29-1-43 411S 23-3 310S 3-5 cd nr Bally during base defence exercise CE 5-10

BL923 5MU 17-2-42 310S 7-3 FACB 15-6 AST 28-7 FAAC 30-8 ROS 453S 11-10 CE ops 31-10

BL924 Valdemar Atteday 24MU 16-2-42 234S 5-4 FTR ops 24-4 FH23.45

BL925 M45M 38MU 13-2-42 302S 24-3 Farn Apl'42 186S 23-3-44 FAAC 14-4130S 22-4 61 OTU 9-11 SOC 30-4-45

BL926 8MU 22-2-42 91S 3-3 FAAC 303S 4-4 CE ops 12-4 SOC 15-1-43

BL927 37MU 17-2-42 311S 17-3 CB ops 19-8 VSM 26-8 mods 315S 15-9 308S 2-12 FAAC 13-5-43 ROS 306S 3-10 316S 3-10 345S 31-3-44 57 OTU 17-8 SOC 27-12-45

BL928 8MU 28-8-42 485S 17-3 602S 25-3 CE ops 27-4 416S 16-7 strk by BM419 t/o 7-11 AST 52 OTU 27-5-43 strk by EP726 Charmy Down CE 27-6

BL929 5MU 17-2-42 402S 14-3 air coll with second a/c cd/ld Fairwood Common CE 27-5 ASTH SOC FH18. recat B 302S 21-3-43 302S 21-6 132S 28-6 SOC 25-7 FH231

BL930 37MU 17-2-42 132S 4-4 VSM 12-10 fuel syst mods 132S 6-11 ast 28-5-43 con to Sea IB-NX983

BL931 6MU 16-2-42 RNDA 1-3 RNAS LoS 1-12 train for instruction of maint personnel AST 13-2-43 con to Sea IB-NX888

BL932 12MU 22-2-42 417S 15-3 416S 6-4 602S 15-7 FTR ops 19-8 FH58.25

BL933 9MU 27-2-42 504S 10-4 FACB 12-5 ROS 315S 4-8-43 303S 6-12 VSM 20-12 fuel syst mods m46 instal 276S 25-4-44 FRU 14-9

BL934 5MU 16-2-42 129S 27-3 CE ops 19-8

BL935 8MU 23-2-42 72S 3-3 FTR ops 4-4 FH29.55

BL936 6MU 24-2-42 350S 24-5 FTR ops 1-6

BL937 24MU 16-2-42 416S 6-4 602S 15-7 CE ops 17-8 FH141.30

BL938 39MU 22-2-42 601S 9-3 133S 8-4 FTR ops 31-7

BL939 37MU 21-2-42 reported miss ops 29-3 234S 8-12 VSM 8-9-43 fuel syst mods wng stiff S type pt Mk III IFF bomb carr 269S 11-2-45 FAAC 23-11 recat E 24-1-46

BL940 LF VB M45M 9MU 14-2-42 305S 16-4 308S 25-6 130S 27-1-44 222S 16-2 FAAC 5-3 LMS 56 OTU 12-7 Farn 19-8 CRD Weston Zoyland 13-9 SOC 3-7-45

BL941 6MU 24-3-42 72S 13-4 411S 18-5 FAAC 29-6 ROS 453S 21-6 FACB 11-8 317S 4-2-43 412S 29-6 126S 10-8 FACB 8-10 MAL 313S 28-7 611S 3-10 GA CE 10-1-45

BL956 LF VB M45M 12MU 22-2-42 131S 13-3 FAB 19-6 AST 93S 31-8 VSM 31-8 fuel syst mods 122S 4-1-43 610S 18-2 R-R 18-4 mods 485S 1-5 R-R 20-5 for inspection 19-S 1-7 83GSU 8-6-44 R&S 25-10-46

BL957 8MU 22-2-42 402S 9-3 312S 4-5 FAAC 9-7 ROS 222S 19-7 242S 11-8 131S 22-9 WAL 5-2-43 91S 12-4 310S 1-5 315S 26-6 411S 10-7 341S 17-10 602S 25-1-44 118S 13-3 SAL 9-5 'Basta' mods 1665HCU 16-3SOC 12-12

BL958 5MU 17-2-42 129S 27-3 FAAC 10-6 ROS S&H 15-8 AST 14-3-43 con to Sea IB-NX898

BL959 37MU 20-2-42 315S 16-3 CE ops 23-8

BL960 12MU 19-2-42 603S 11-3 332S 18-4 FTR ops 31-7

BL961 12MU 19-2-42 601S 10-3 133S 30-4 FTR ops 31-5

BL962 M45M 39MU 22-2-42 601S 9-3 133S 16-4 306S 22-8 501S 29-1-43 USAAF 9-5 13 OTU 23-9 SOC 20-11-45

BL963 5MU 17-2-42 121S 13-3 CB ops 24-3 AST recat E 20-5 SOC 31-7

BL964 5MU 22-2-42 64S 28-3 FACB 3-4 30S FTR ops 26-7

BL965 LF LR VB M45M 24MU 16-2-42 234S 17-3 FAAC 26-8 26--8 ROS 421S 27-1-43 FACB 2-2 602S 605 501S 5-11 CAC ops 21-12 ROS 63S 1-5-44 57 OTU 19-10 eng fire in air o/t cd/ld nr Lowick N'land CE 3-3-45 SOC E 26-3

BL966 5MU 24-2-42 402S 14-3 133S 7-4 308S 7-5 41S 8-12 131S 14-3-43 FAAC 8-6 ROS 310S 23-8 504S 24-9 VSM 5-11 fuel syst mods 53 OTU 5-9-44 SOC E 23-1-45

BL967 12MU 19-2-42 601S 8-3 133S 10-4 FACE 7-5

BL968 6MU 27-2-42 411S 27-3 242S 25-9 DeH 12-10 VSM 8-2-43 fuel syst mods 129S 11-4-43 453S 17-7 strk by AB213 end of ldg run Bradwell Bay CB 14-7 recat E 3-8 129S 11-2-44 SOC 21-5-46

BL969 M45M 12MU 22-2-42 504S 11-3 501S 19-10 VSM 8-9-43 mods 129S 8-4-44 130S 10-5 403S 5-6 CE ops 22-6

BL970 5MU 24-2-42 504S 11-3 313S 30-1 152S 26-4 308S 30-1-43 315S 31-3 FAAC 6-5 ROS 19S 26-6 M46 instal 'Basta' mods 28-2-44 290S1-3-54 R&S 9-10-46 M45MA instal refurb to Port 6-8-47

BL971 33MU 26-2-42 152S 29-8 421S 20-11 412S 3-2-43 602S 19-4 CE ops 15-7 SOC FH243.25

BL972 M45M 37MU 24-2-42 412S 15-3 CAC ops 26-7 ROS 416S 23-5-43 401S 1-6 CAC ops 15-7 ROS 186S 22-3-44 130S 18-4 CB ops 27-4 ROS CGS 30-9 FACE 2-5-45 SOC 11-5

BL973 5MU 28-2-42 312S 30-3 FTR ops 17-5

BL974 5MU 28-2-42 501S 14-3 SAL 23-4-44 'Basta' mods FTR ops25-4

BL975 LF LR VB M45M 39MU 14-2-42 601S 9-3 133S 8-4 71S 19-5 334USA 1-10 132S 28-6-43 118S 25-1-44 504S 15-3 277S 8-7 SOC 17-2-45

BL976 M45M 9MU 27-2-42 VSM 29-8 fuel syst mods 122S 21-1-43 303S 21-2-43 CAC ops 28-5 ROS 308S 25-6 130S 22-8 DeH 18-2 290S 14-1-45 R&S refurb to Port 3-6-47

BL977 9MU 1-4-42 308S 1-6 VSM 8-8 mods 316S 4-8 CE ops 2-2-43

BL978 12MU 19-2-42 616S 15-3 65S 16-7 CAC ops 21-7 ROS 309S 11-8 340S1 12-9 341S 26-3-43 222MU 19-11 Port 28-1-44

BL979 5MU 24-2-42 401S 13-3 72S 4-4 CAC ops 5-6 AST 610S 18-2-43 350S 27-3 VSM 5-11 fuel syst mods 64S 10-6-44 to 5376M 13-7-45

BL980 8MU 22-2-42 411S 3-3 SOC 6-5

BL981 M45M 8MU 22-2-42 402S 9-3 WAL 29-3 222S 25-7 242S 11-8 411S 23-9 FACB 1-11 ROS 402S 25-3-43 FACB 8-4 WAL 610S 11-11 234S 7-6-44 R&S refurb to Port 23-7-47

BL982 39MU 22-2-42 601S 9-3 133S 12-4 FTR ops 31-7

BL983 AST con to Sea IB NX911

BL984 39MU 22-2-42 118S 14-3 FTR ops 6-6 FH86.40

BL985 26-2-42 616S 6-4 332S 28-5 FTR ops 19-8

BL986 8MU 28-2-42 121S 14-3 CA ops 21-7 ROS 335USA 1-10 GAL 7-12 AST 16-3-43 con to Sea IB-NX908 ret RAF Jan'45

BL987 LF VB M45M 6MU 27-2-42 CRD BDn 11-4 ASTH 3-5 331S 7-6 FACB 23-9 GAL VSM 27-5-43 mods 504S 24-8 222S 16-2-44 322S 17-3 63S 3-5 FTR ops 25-6

BL988 12MU 26-2-42 601S 10-3 133S 7-4 CE ops 19-5

BL989 37MU 25-2-42 402S 8-3 e/td i/sea nr Hollwick Light Bristol Channel 29-3 SOC 31-3

BL990 LF VB M45M 12MU 26-2-42 302S 15-3 FACB 3-7 SAL VSM 19-4-43 fuel syst mods wng stiff 610S 28-6 130S 30-1-44 222S 16-2 322S 17-3 FAAC 14-5-44 ROS A HQ BAFO 1-1-46

BL991 37MU 25-2-42 601S 15-3 133SD 9-4 ASTH 23-5 340S 12-9 234S 2-11 FACB 19-11 132S 22-12 485S 18-6-43 19S 1-7 340S 28-9 e/td i/sea nr Isle of May Firth of Forth 19-10 FH334

BL992 37MU 25-2-42 402S 8-3 FACB 17-3 GAL 242S 20-8 411S 23-9 FACB 5-4-43 AST VSM 2-9 fuel syst mods wng stiff S type pt Mk III IFF bomb carr 234S 24-1-44 SOC 30-7-45

BL993 12MU 22-2-42 504S 12-3 501S 19-10 FAAC 30-10 ROS 19S 25-5-43 315S 1-7 USAAF 31-5-44 LMS 23-7 M46 instal FAF 1-2-45

BL994 Nigeria 37MU 1-3-42 417S 13-3 601S 13-3 133S 10-4 CAC ops 20-7 ROS 91S 27-8 HAL 2-11 AST 31-5-43 con to Sea IB-NX989

BL995 12MU 26-2-42 601S 10-3 133S 13-4 dam by Do215 during night patrol a/c aban CE 28/29-4

BL996 39MU 22-2-42 601S 9-3 133S 7-4 308S 6-5 FTR ops 31-5

BL997 M45M 6MU 13-3-42 64S 25-4 SOC 306S 5-3-43 310S 17-8 504S 24-9 DeH 28-10 26S 2-4-44 CAC ops 11-6 recat E 23-5-45

BL998 33MU 26-2-42 41S 13-4 FTR ops 21-5 FH63.55

All F.Mk.VB with Merlin 45 unless otherwise indicated.

BM113 37MU 8-3-42 602S 26-3 FAAC 6-5 ROS 65S 4-6 453S 12-7 FACE 23-8 VSM 27-6-43 fuel syst mods wng stiff Mk.III IFF bomb carr 312S 20-12 441S 27-2-44 58 OTU 30-3 61 OTU 25-6 hit target drogue i/sea Dee Estuary 24-7-44

BM114 M46 5MU 1-3-42 602S 18-3 FTR ops 17-5

BM115 6MU 28-2-42 313S 14-4 FAAC 16-4 recat E SOC 16-4

BM116 M46 Red Rose I 39MU 9-3-42 485S 27-4 PO Falls aban a/c Cap Griz Nez France 1-5

BM117 5MU 28-2-4-42 313S 30-3 154S 8-6 611S 17-6 72S 4-8 AST 29-10 mr M50M instal 610S 23-3-43 485S 20-4 19S 1-7 340S 28-9 234S 21-6-44 SOC 29-5-45

BM118 6MU 27-2-42 234S 26-4 CE 22-5 SOC 3-6 AST recat A 341S 30-3-43 FAAC 12-6 ROS 340S 28-9 air coll with EP506 during exercise cd Dirleton E Lothian CE 27-10

BM119 12MU 26-6-42 485S 19-3 129S 27-3 CE ops 12-4 FH28.25

BM120 6MU 28-2-42 64S 25-4 154S 13-7 CB ops 27-8 AST 52 OTU 26-1-43 coll with N3121 taxy ADn CA 19-8 VSM 20-1-44 fuel syst mods CGS 5-10 SOC 29-11-45

BM121 cd del flt to 33MU AC 26-2-42 33MU 17-3 616S 11-4 412S 22-5 swg off flarepath NWld strk AB267 CAC 11-6 AST VSM 12-10 fuel syst mods wng stiff 310S 31-3-43 131S 1-7 310S 24-9 61 OTU 13-8-42 ran into BM327 Mount Br CAC 16-12 recat E 15-1-45

BM122 12MU 13-3-42 457S 1-4 611S 30-5 72S 4-8 FACB 14-8 SAL VSM 12-6-43 fuel syst elev & rud mods wng stiff Mk III IFF 277S 20-12 SOC 14-6-45

BM123 M46 8MU 28-2-42 403S 14-3 FTR ops 27-4 FH40.30

BM124 Queen Salote 37MU 14-3-42 602S 16-3 FAAC 13-7 ROS 81S 21-9 501S 19-7 303S 8-1-44 402S 26-6 345S 15-8 CAC ops 30-8 ROS 63S 5-10 SOC 25-4-46

BM125 33MU 27-2-42 72S 4-4 FTR ops 24-4 FH24.40

BM126 M46 37MU 8-3-42 602S 26-3 DeH 29-3 332S 21-4 FTR ops 7-6

BN127 5MU 28-2-42 313S 30-3 CAC ops 30-4 154S 8-6 122S 25-6 FACB 21-7 VSM 27-6-43 fuel syst elev & rud mods wng stiff MK III IFF 341S 24-10 239S 16-2-44 63S 13-3 BER 25-1-45

BM128 12MU 10-3-42 485S 18-3 602S 25-3 416S 16-7 CE ops 3-2-43

BM129 M46 45MU 2-4-42 64S 20-5 154S 15-7 VSM 29-7 fuel syst mods M45 instal 310S 28-2-43 132S 6-3 122S 21-5 234S 4-1-44 CAC ops 24-2 ROS 30-4 CB ops 10-6 ASTE SOC 3-1-46

BM130 12MU 1-4-42 122S 16-4 FTR ops 8-6

BM131 LF VB M50 6MU 19-4-42 317S 4-5 315S 4-9 FAAC 11-10 HAL 501S 5-12 FACA 29-1-43 AST M45M instal 610S 11-11 611S 7-6-44 234S 6-8 R&R refurb to Port 15-10-47

BM132 M45M 9MU 20-4-42 313S 18-5 154S 8-6 64S 15-6 154 19-7 CA ops 24-8 485S 7-12 CAC ops 12-3-43 ROS 611S 27-4 130S 5-9 118S 23-5-44 313S 21-7 FACE 31-7 BBOC 61 OTU 16-10 flew i/grd nr Rednal CE 2-2-45 SOC 9-2

BM133 45MU 27-4-42 416S 11-6 602S 15-7 164S 11-9 341S 21-2-43 340S 23-3 coll with W3569 Athelstone Ford E Lothian CE 6-4

BM134 37MU 13-3-42 402S 2-5 u/c clpse on t/o Redhill CE 22-6 SOC AST FH63.25 recat B 52 OTU 5-2 VSM 20-1-44 fuel syst mods 1688Flt 6-10 FAAC 19-1-46 recat E SOC 31-1

BM135 FF PJS 31-3-42 38MU 3-4 402S 24-5 122S 11-8 FTR ops 27-8

BM136 M46 37MU 8-3-42 485S 26-3 602S 26-3 416S 16-7 52 OTU 26-1-43 SAL 2-2 'Basta' mods 61 OTU 16-9-44 ASTE 29-12 recat E SOC 8-1-45

BM137 37MU 17-3-42 313S 18-4 154S 8-6 611S 17-6 81S 29-7 VSM 9-6-43 fuel syst mods wng stiff M46 instal 308S 3-8 CB ops 16-8 DeH 129S 4-2-44 FACE 13-2 FH160

BM138 33MU 17-3-42 122S 26-4 FTR ops 5-8

BM139 12MU 13-3 602S 27-3 485S 28-3 lost over France 26-4 FH48.10

BM140 6MU 27-2-42 315S 12-3 FACE 17-3

BM141 M46 37MU 8-3-42 602S 26-3 FAAC 13-7 ROS 81S 22-7 FTR ops 29-7

BM142 37MU 1-3-42 602S 19-3 416S 16-7 i/sea 25-7

BM143 6MU 27-2-42 452S 14-3 457S 22-3 611S 3-5 72S 4-8 HAL 3-11 i/sea ops 28-3-43 FH181.55

BM144 5MU 28-2-42 303S 30-3 315S 1-6 CA ops 12-6 e/fd w/u ldg nr Bangor Co Down CE 9-10-43

BM145 M46 39MU 18-6-42 312S 16-9 FAAC 15-10 ROS 234S 4-6-43 504S 30-6 FTR ops 26-7 FH288

BM146 M46 8MU 28-2-42 403S 14-3 FTR ops 14-4 FH40.50

BM147 M46 37MU 8-3-42 602S 28-3 485S 28-5 19S 1-7 VSM 5-11-43 fuel syst mods M45M instal 186S 26-5-44 118S 31-5 FACB 12-6 LMS sold scr bou 3-9-47

BM148 M46 8MU 23-2-42 485S 17-3 602S 25-3 FTR ops 28-3 SOC 31-3

BM149 6MU 28-2-42 111S 27-3 CAC ops 29-5 ROS 65S 6-6 t/o in coarse pitch Graves cd CE 25-7

BM150 M46 37MU 8-3-42 402S 2-5 FTR ops 17-5 FH22-45

BM151 M46 39MU 9-3-42 485S 28-3 lost over Channel 27-4 FH40.35

BM152 LF VB 12MU 26-2-42 611S 13-3 FAAC 15-4 453S 25-7 222S 31-3-43 167S 19-5 SAL 30-6 M50M instal 402S 30-8 CE ops 27-9

BM153 6MU 28-2-42 64S 25-4 FAAC 16-5 recat E SOC 21-5 FH28.05

BM154 37MU 8-3-42 64S 12-4-CAC ops 8-6 ROS 602S 20-6 82MU 27-10 *Bar Inch* 18-12 USSR 24-3-43

BM155 Joe and Roy 12MU 13-3-42 602S 27-3 485S 27-3 64S 5-5-43 315S 31-10 VSM 20-12 fuel syst mods M46 instal 442S 7-3-44 53 OTU 3-7 ROS 19-3-45 41 OTU 24-5-45 to 5347M 14-7 5SoTT SOC rtp 24-1-46

BM156 M46 37MU 8-3-42 602S 25-3 416S 22-9 Farn June'42 neg 'G' trls 411S 23-3-43 BDn Oct exhaust flame damping Farn Feb'43 341S 17-10 303S 25-3-44 61 OTU 3-9 290S 4-1-45 SOC 30-7 M50 instal during service

BM157 M46 37MU 8-3-42 602S 18-3 FAAC 23-5 416S 16-7 350S 30-11 485S 7-12 FACB 19-4-43 501S 20-5 e/fd w/u ldg nr Bexhill Kent CE 30-6 ASTH M45M instal 186S 22-3-44 130S 18-4 303S 23-11 FAAC 29-3-45 ROS 61 OTU 26-4 SOC 22-5

BM158 M46 39MU St Frm 9-3-42 81S 17-5 ROS 27-5 341S 10-11 350S 23-7-43 501S 11-1-44 FAAC 20-3 ROS 63S 17-5 58 OTU 22-3-45 to 5375M 18-7 5SoTT 29-11 SOC

BM159 12MU 13-3-42 457S 1-4 FTR ops 27-4 FH40.35

BM160 Assam IX 12MU 20-3-42 485S 18-3 602S 25-3 CA ops 2-6-43 recat E 28-7

BM161 Butafogo 12MU 10-3-42 485S 18-3 602S 25-3 CB ops 6-5 recat E 13-5

BM162 5MU 28-2-42 64S 2-4 CAC ops 12-4 403S 4-5 FTR ops 2-6 FH27.30

BM176 9MU 21-3-42 609S 28-4 350S 30-4 CB ops 30-7 316S 21-12 91S 24-4-43 65S 1-5 308S 17-5 350S 20-5 FAAC 7-7 LMS 222MU 13-12 *Emp Corm* 31-1-44 Port 17-2

BM177 9MU 4-3-42 RNAS 1-9 VSM 29-5-43 fuel syst elev & rud mods wng stiff 222MU 29-9 *Emp Cort* Port 19-10

BM178 9MU 20-3-42 152S 22-5 VSM 4-4-43 fuel syst mods wng stiff 416S 1-7 FACB 7-10 345S 3-4-44 CAC ops e/a 1-1-45 ROS SOC 19-2

BM179 9MU 18-3-42 501S 28-4 302S 1-6 VSM 29-7 fuel syst mods FACB 7-9 recat E 5-10

BM180 9MU 22-3-42 457S 30-4 FTR ops 9-5

BM181 M46 9MU 22-3-42 457S 30-4 611S 30-5 81S 30-7 67Grp USAAF 23-6-43 COAL 6-2-44 M45 instal

BM182 12MU 15-3-42 602S 26-3 FTR ops 13-7

BM183 37MU 13-3-42 485S 6-5 FTR ops 3-8 FH139

BM184 12MU 10-3-42 485S 27-3 FACB 31-5 GAL 82MU 6-11 *Bar Inch* 18-12 USSR 24-3-43

BM185 M46 39MU 9-3-42 403S 29-3 FAAC 21-4 111S 23-6 CAC ops 12-9 GAL 82MU 6-11 *Bar Inch* 18-12 USSR 24-3-43

BM186 M46 37MU 8-3-42 602S 24-3 FAAC 1-5 recat E 7-5

BM187 M46 39MU 9-3-42 602S 23-3 FTR ops 25-4 FH40.15

BM188 12MU 13-3-42 457S 1-4 FTR ops 1-5

BM189 12MU 13-3-42 457S 8-4 611S 30-5 72S 4-8-42 hit h/t cables in mock attack w/u ldg Dalmellington Ayr CA 6-8 SAL 215M 7-11 *Bar Inch* 18-12 USSR 24-3-43

BM190 M46 39MU 9-3-42 Star Fm dis 457S 10-5 611S 30-5 81S 30-7 65S 27-6-43 130S 15-8 M45M instal USAAF 9-5-44 CGS 30-9 SOC 4-9-45

BM191 6MU 28-2-42 64S 27-3 FTR ops 4-4 FH15.20

BM192 12MU 10-3-42 452S 27-3 457S 28-3 611S 30-5 72S 4-8 HAL 9-11 VSM 18-6-43 fuel syst & rud mods wng stiff 302S 28-8 to 5542M SOC E 6-5-49

BM193 12MU 10-3-42 457S 27-3 611S 30-5 71S 3-8 334USA 1-10 CE ops 20-10 FH219-10

BM194 6MU 13-3-42 25-4 FAAC 12-6 ROS 154S 15-7 FTR ops 30-7

BM195 M46 8MU 14-3-42 452S 25-3 611S 30-5 72S 29-7 610S 27-12 131S 25-1-43 ROS 9-4 310S 30-6 313S 29-7 129S 3-2-44 63S 11-6 41 OTU 1-8 58 OTU 22-3-45 SOC 6-7

BM196 Borough of Brentford & Chiswick 12MU 10-3-42 602S 27-3 485S 27-3 FTR ops 9-5 FH60.50

BM197 Lulu of Maketeng 12MU 10-3-42 485S 3-4 CE ops 26-4 FH30.45

BM198 39MU 14-3-42 485S 27-4 402S 8-7145S 12-8 52 OTU 5-2-43 VSM 18-4-44 fuel syst mods 345S 10-6 61 OTU 17-5-45

BM199 M46 37MU 8-3-42 485S 27-3 421S 27-2-43 416S 1-6 126S 10-8 CE ops 18-9

BM200 M45M 37MU 15-3-42 485S 28-4 FAAC 6-6 ROS 411S 16-7 341S 17-10 602S 25-1-44 234S 28-4 SOC 27-7

BM201 12MU 16-3-42 602S 3-4 416S 16-7 FAAC 21-7 ROS VSM 12-7-43 fuel syst elev & rud mods wng stiff Mk III bomb carr M46 instal 63S 11-6-44 58 OTU 22-3-45 FAAC 28-3 ROS to 5395M SOC 17-7 5 SoTT 29-11

BM202 Flying Scotsman (LNER) 6MU 13-3-42 222S 27-3 242S 27-3 AST 27-5 mods 611S 10-11

BM203 6MU 13-3-42 313S 18-4 154S 8-6 122S 14-6 FAAC 31-7 AST 485S 22-3-43 19S 1-7 611S 12-11 PAL 1-11-45 SOC 2-11

BM204 M46 6MU 13-3-42 602S 2-5 CAC ops 6-5 HAL 416S 16-7 e/td i/sea off Herne Bay Kent 25-1-43

BM205 LF LR VB M45M Nova Scotia 12MU 15-3-42 485S 27-3 e/a 27-4 HAL FAAC 19-5-43 ROS 401S 5-10 504S 10-11 129S 26-1-44 402S 30-3 53 OTU 20-7 SOC 29-5-45

BM206 5MU 23-3-42 71S 20-4 FTR ops

BM207 LF VB M45M Dominant Factor 9MU 13-3-42 313S 6-5 154S 8-6 VSM 29-6-43 fuel syst elev & rud mods wng stiff bomb carr 130S 25-1-44 222S 16-2 322S 17-3 303S 17-4 CGS 3-10 FACB 3-2-45 recat E SOC 9-2

BM208 M46 37MU 8-3-42 485S 27-3 FAAC 16-12 ROS FTR ops 4-4-43 FH361.15

BM209 9MU 13-3-42 313S 17-4 f/ld Bennington Kent CE 5-5

BM210 33MU 17-3-42 St Frm dis 122S 26-4 FTR ops 5-5

BM211 9MU 13-3-42 457S 8-4 611S 30-5 72S 4-8 416S 29-3-43 421S 30-5 FAAC 10-6 ROS 402S 5-10 CB ops 21-5-44 AST CGS 5-10 FACE 25-4-45 SOC 3-5

BM227 37MU 15-3-42 313S 18-4 154S 8-6

BM228 12MU 10-3-42 485S 18-3 602S 25-3 FTR ops 25-4 FH43.20

BM229 Silver Blue Bird 12MU 16-3-42 485S 27-3 CB ops 21-5 WAL 129S 19-8 CAC ops 8-10 SAL 234S 7-4-43 312S 29-6 317S 4-10 310S 19-10 USAAF 6-1-44 FAF 1-2-45 GC 2/18

BM230 Gerfalcon II 37MU 15-3-42 402S 2-5 350S 17-8 CE ops 21-9 FH162.45

BM231 12MU 15-3-42 485S 27-3 lost over e/tr 4-4

BM232 6MU 14-3-42 485S 3-5 FTR ops 30-11 FH209-10

BM233 LF LR VB M45M B B & C I Railway V 39MU 14-3-42 485S 29-4 19S 1-7-43 412S 24-9 402S 27-4-44 CAC ops 22-6 ROS 53 OTU 30-9 to 5337M SOC 14-10-50 Trans to FFS

BM234 Hope of Cheadle 12MU 15-3 485S 27-3 etd t/ld CE 27-4 FH41.55

BM235 33MU 17-3-42 602S 8-4 aban over Channel 26-5

BM236 Fellowship of the Bellows 8MU 14-3-42 602S 29-5 FTR ops 25-6 FH48.15

BM237 12MU 16-3-42 122S 10-4 CAC ops 17-4 CE rts 4-5

BM238 M45M 33MU 17-3-42 485S 6-4 CAC ops 4-4-43 ROS 19S 1-7 501S 8-11 CB ops 21-12 AST 234S 22-6-44 87Grp Com Flt Gat 28-12-44 e/td f/ld GAT at base 17-5-46 soc 22-6

BM239 39MU 14-3-42 485S 2-5 FAB 9-6 FTR ops 1-9-43 FH130

BM240 Clifton Cameras 8MU 14-3-42 452S 25-3 CAC ops 27-4 ROS 602S 9-6 CAC ops 26-6 ROS 416S 17-9 350S 20-7-43 CAC ops 27-8 ROS 65S 13-9 FTR ops 17-1-44 FH234.35

BM241 El Conquistador 12MU 16-3-42 122S 14-4 FTR ops 1-5

BM242 9MU 13-3-42 313S 24-4 54S 8-6 122S 20-6 FTR ops 30-7

BM243 37MU 13-3-42 457S 2-5 FAAC 7-5 ROS 122S 22-7 VSM 9-6-43 fuel syst & rud mods wng stiff 453S 19-8 341S 3-11 CAC ops 10-1-44 ROS 239S 16-2 Met Com Flt Hendon 17-11 FAAC 18-3-45 recat E SOC 28-3

BM244 Spen Valley Spitfire 37MU 15-3-42 122S 16-5 FTR ops

BM245 8MU 14-3-42 602S 27-3 416S 16-7 VSM 1-10 fuel syst mods. Lost over France 1-2-43 FH286.15

BM246 37MU 17-3-42 402S 2-5 FACB 23-6 AST P&PSM 1-10 mods 52 OTU 1-2-43 AST 18-9-44 'Basta' mods 58 OTU 22-3-45 to 5721M 16-10

BM247 Delphi IV 12MU 15-3-42 485S 2-4 FTR ops 2-8

BM248 6MU 14-3-42 313S 17-4 154S 8-6 CE 27-8

BM249 5MU 23-3-42 71S 29-4 FTR ops 2-6 FH45

BM250 Hornsey 39MU 14-3-42 485S 29-4 FAA 29-4 recat E

BM251 33MU 17-3-42 457S 8-4 FTR ops 1-5

BM252 M45M Bombay City 37MU 17-3-42 122S 6-5 FACB 16-9 ROS 222S 19-5 316S 22-11 130S 27-4-44 CRD Willmot Rowan 9-3-45 SOC 6-9

BM253 M46 37MU 15-3-42 501S 13-5 72S 16-5 65S 4-8 165S 23-9 e/td t/ld nr Coolham Sussex CE 17-12

BM254 6MU 14-3-42 64S 25-4 FTR ops 29-6 FH83.10

BM255 FF PJS 26-3-42 5MU 23-3 41S 26-5 453S 11-7 HAL 17-12 ASTH 10-7-43 hook fitt RNDA 18-1-44

BM256 M46 Dorothy Hans (Mary) 37MU 15-3-42 501S13-5 72S 16-5 65S 4-8 165S 29-9 FAAC 9-12 ROS 64S 4-9-43 118S 25-9 501S 3-3-44 26S 15-9 58 OTU 22-3-45 to 5384M 13-7 SOC 24-4-47 5SoTT

BM257 LF VB M45M 9MU 25-3-42 402S 30-4 165S 23-9 132S 19-7-43 118S 10-10 BDn 30-10 rogue a/c flew left wng low. Ails in bad state ret to sqdn fault free 132S 25-1-44 VSM 17-3 fuel syst mods FAF 19-1-45 GC 2/18

BM258 5MU 26-3-42 310S 14-4 312S 30-7 130S 16-8 52 OTU 5-2-43 DeH 9-4-44 'Basta' mods 501S 17-6 CE 6-11

BM259 12MU 26-3-42 485S 3-4 CE ops 4-5 FH55.05

BM260 Popeyes Pal 5MU 25-3-42 133S 12-4 FTR ops 17-5

BM261 6MU 14-3-42 313S 14-4 FTR ops 5-5

BM262 Lincolnshire Poacher 37MU 15-3-42 402S 30-4 CB ops 15-7 ROS 52 OTU 1-2-43 SAL 7-4 'Basta' mods FAF 19-1-44 GC 2/18

BM263 The Lord Mayor (York) 5MU 23-3-42 133S 12-4 CAC ops 18-8 ROS 165S 8-9 CE 19-9 FH135.05

BM264 Shetlander 5MU 23-3-42 133S 12-4 FTR ops 27-4

BM265 The Pride of Newport 5MU 25-3-42 331S 9-4 72S 12-5 CAC ops 26-7 ROS 243S 30-8 222S 28-10 strk Botha L6488 ldg Prestwick CE 2-12

BM266 33MU 17-3-42 Star Fm dis 122S 26-4 FTR ops 30-7

BM267 12MU 16-3-42 485S 3-4 lost over Channel 26-4 FH40.30

BM268 M46 45MU 1-4-42 310S 14-4 64S 21-5 FTR ops 8-6

BM269 12MU 26-3-42 122S 10-4 L/A 5-5

BM270 Pride of Puerto Rico 9MU 18-3-42 122S 6-5 FAAC 20-8 ROS 222MU 2-11 *Co Lil* 8-12 USSR 16-2-43

BM271 LF VB M45M Kenya Daisy 5MU 26-3-42 133S 12-4 72S 15-6 65S 29-3 130S 17-8-43 453S 31-1-44 118S 13-3 288S 15-2-45 SOC mr 2-1-46

BM272 LF VB M45M 9MU 25-3-42 402S 30-4 350S 19-8 165S 23-9 302S 4-4-43 118S 10-10 132S 25-1-44 VSM 9-3 fuel syst & 'Basta' mods FAF 19-1-45

BM273 5MU 23-3-42 154S 13-4 313S 8-6 165S 4-8 316S 19-9 312S 31-12 65S 30-6-43 130S 15-8 VSM 18-2-44 fuel syst mods 277S 26-5 276S 22-2-45

BM274 5MU 25-3-42 154S 14-14 FTR ops 4-5

BM289 12MU 26-3-42 64S 15-4 154S 19-7 VSM 20-7-43 fuel syst mods wng stiff Mk III IFF S type pt bomb carr RNDA 16-1-44 as train

BM290 FF PJS 25-3-42 12MU 26-3 485S 3-4 lost over Continent 26-4 FH39.40

BM291 5MU 25-3-42 340S 12-4 CAC ops 3-6 air cover Dieppe raid e/fd i/sea 19-8 FH134.05

BM292 45MU 29-3-42 113S 2-6 602S 15-6 416S 16-7 CE ops 4-12

BM293 5MU 25-3-42 71S 20-4 334USA 1-10 P&PSM 2-4-43 504S 26-8 313S 22-9 CE ops 7-9

BM294 12MU 29-3-42 64S 12-4 CE 22-4 FH65

BM295 5MU 26-3-42 154S 24-4 313S 8-6 331S 12-8 VSM 16-10 fuel syst mods 331S 8-12 64S 4-9 118S 25-9 443S 7-3-44 58 OTU 2-4 FAF Morocco 10-4-45

BM296 37MU 17-3-42 402S 25-5 CE ops 15-7 SOC 28-7 FH63.30

BM297 9MU 25-3-42 402S 30-4 350S 17-8 FTR ops 27-8

BM298 M45M 25-3-42 402S 30-4 CE ops 17-5 VSM 24-8 fuel syst mods 52 OTU 27-5-43 10AGS 8-6-45 R&S refurb to Port 8-10-46

BM299 45MU 27-3-42 81S 6-6 111S 7-12 485S FTR ops 14-4-43 FH517

BM300 5MU 27-3-42 133S 12-4 72S 15-6 CAC ops 16-6 ROS M46 instal 65S 4-8 165S 23-9 FAAC 13-12 ROS 222MU 8-11-43 *Pandor* 25-11 Port 3-12

BM301 Admiration 6MU 14-3-42 313S 14-4 154S 8-6 611S 17-6 CE ops 28-6

BM302 33MU 17-3-42 124S 19-8 602S 29-11 VSM 22-6-43 fuel syst mods wng stiff 504S 18-8 CE ops 27-8 SOC 31-8 FH232.15

BM303 37MU 17-3-42 457S 2-5 611S 305 FTR ops 8-6

BM304 12MU 26-3-42 485S 2-4 VSM 26-6-43 wng stiff MkIII IFF bomb carr 501S 22-10 345S CB ops 5-8-44 ASTE 61 OTU 17-5-45 695S 28-6 SOC 25-10

BM305 33MU 17-3-42 457S 8-4 611S 30-5 71S 3-8 FTR ops 31-8

BM306 FF PJS 24-3-42 12MU 28-3 313S 10-4 CB ops 5-5 recat E 17-5

BM307 5MU 27-3-42 FTR ops 29-4

BM308 F/Lt B E Finucane 37MU 28-3-42 122S 18-4 dam ops 2-6 AST FTR ops 15-7 FH97

BM309 12MU 28-3-42 122S 10-4 335S 29-1-43 315S 23-3 303S 6-4 313S 27-9 COAL 28-11 RNAS Hens 9-4-44 as train

BM310 5MU 28-3-42 129S 29-4 602S 29-11 FACE 30-12

BM311 M46 37MU 28-3-42 122S 6-5 e/a CB 17-5 AST 222MU 6-10-43 *Bar Forb* 16-10 Port 9-11

BM312 5MU 26-3-42 340S 12-4 CB ops 26-8 HAL 26-2-43 501S 6-5 FAAC 23-6 MAL 345S 12-4-44 CE ops 7-6

BM313 5MU 28-3-42 331S 9-5 72S 12-5 234S FAAC 4-6 LMS 222MU 27-11 *Dremore* 9-1-44 Port

BM314 5MU 27-3-42 616S 18-4 412S 22-5 COAL 26-3-43 con to Seafire IB-NX950

BM315 45MU 27-3-42 81S 1-5 ASTE 15-12 Flt Deff 9-10-43 CRD Deff 30-8-45 SOC 15-1-46

BM316 45MU 27-3-42 485S 2-6 611S 8-7 11S 2-8 421S 6-2-43 416S 23-5 401S 1-6 M46 instal HAL 12-11 M45M instal USAAF 10-5-44 17SFTS 12-10 FAAC 25-9-45 recat E SOC 4-10

BM317 12MU 28-3-42 313S 11-4 CB ops 1-4-43 AST VSM fuel syst mods wng stiff M46 instal 129S 12-4 453S 17-7 341S 3-11 coll with W3935 while taxy dbt CE 5-1-44 FH370

BM318 45MU 27-3-42 350S 17-4 313S 8-6 122S 9-7 310S 14-8-43 504S 24-9 USAAF 26-1-44 57 OTU 30-9 FACB 21-12 M46 & M45M instal during service

BM319 5MU 26-3-42 129S 17-4 FTR ops 4-5-42 FH36.25

BM320 12MU 1-4-42 164S 16-4 FTR ops 17-5 FH56.55

BM321 37MU 28-3-42 122S 18-4 FTR ops 5-5

BM322 45MU 27-3-42 313S 8-5 154S 8-6 64S 17-6 154S 12-7 19S air coll with BM539 cd Millbank Farm CE 9-7-43 VSM 3-8 fuel syst & rud mods wng stiff M46 instal 317S 21-8 312S 4-10 56 OTU 4-7-44 61 OTU 28-9 to 5601M 7-9-45 FAF 3-3-46

BM323 FF PJS 26-3-42 12MU 29-3 313S 11-4 154S 3-6 DeH 29-10 485S 11-4-43 CE ops 9-7 FH262.25

BM324 5MU 27-3-42 340S 12-4 SAL 25-10 52 OTU 1-5-43 SAL 23-4 M46 instal 'Basta' mods S&H CB 14-10 81 OTU 6-5-45 FAAC 16-5 recat E 2-7

BM325 The Canadian Policeman FF PJS 24-3-42 12MU 28-3 457S 27-4 602S 24-5 416S 16-7 CAC ops 23-1-43 ROS CE ops 3-2

BM326 M46 5MU 28-3-42 501S 11-5 75S 14-5 65S 4-8 Farn Sept'42 LOX eng boost trls 165S 23-9 e/fd cd nr Horsham Sfurey CE 24-12 FH160.15

BM327 M45M 45MU 29-3-42 72S 10-5 AST 16-7 92S 18-7 66S 17-4-43 SAL 7-3-44 64S 22-5 61S OTU 5-12 strk by BM121 on t/o Mount Br CE 16-12

BM328 12MU 28-3-42 313S 11-4 154S 8-6 122S 29-6 FACB 31-7 ROS 611S 11-12 308S 16-3-43 air coll with AD508 nr Hutton Granswick CE 4-5 FH248.35

BM329 12MU 28-3-42 123S 10-4 FTR ops 15-7

BM343 LF LR VB M45M FF PJS 26-3-42 5MU 28-3 340S 29-4 VSM 18-9 fuel syst elev & rud mods S type pt wng stiff Mk II IFF bomb carr M55M instal 322S 11-1-44 350S 13-3 CAC ops 7-6 ASTE 1687Flt Bomber Defence T.F 2-12 R&S refurb to Port 9-6-47

BM344 LF LR VB 5MU 28-3-42 403S 26-4 416S 3-6-43 SAL mr 20-7 350S 4-10 322S 11-1-44 287S 2-11 SOC 15-9-45

BM345 FF PJS 25-3-42 5MU 28-3 331S 9-5 72S 12-5 AST 16-5 312S FAAC 19-8 VSM 9-6-43 fuel syst mods wng stiff 611S 24-8 CAC ops 12-6 ROS 57 OTU recat E 15-2-45 SOC

BM346 5MU 28-3-42 403S 26-4 CAC ops 1-6 ROS 401S coll with W3839 Yorks CE 17-2-43 FH259.15

BM347 FF PJS 25-3-42 37MU 28-3 64S 13-4 154S 12-7 AST 11-10 52 OTU 30-11-43 DeH 29-2 'Basta' mods 57 OTU 27-6 FAAC 1-1-45 recat E 12-1

BM348 FF PJS 25-3-42 12MU 28-3 64S 12-4 154S 12-7 P&PSM 11-8 mods M46 instal 52 OTU 4-2-43 315S 22-9 303S 25-3-44 CAC ops 17-7 ROS 61 OTU 17-5-45 605S 28-6 SOC 25-10

BM349 12MU 29-3-42 122S 14-4 FTR ops 9-8

BM350 FF PJS 25-3-42 37MU 28-3 402S 30-4 CB ops 11-6 AST VSM 15-10 fuel syst mods wng stiff HAL 31-12 con to PRXIII M32 542S Ben 25-4-43 coll with AA971 Nettlebed Oxen CE 6-6

BM351 FF PJS 27-3-42 45MU 29-3 81S 1-5 52 OTU 29-12 SAL 12-4-43 M46 instal 'Basta' mods 57 OTU 19-10 53 OTU 13-2-45 FAAC 24-3 ROS PAL 2-10 SOC 5-10

BM352 12MU 29-3-42 122S 10-4 FTR ops 30-7

BM353 M45M 45MU 29-3-42 133S 10-5 485S 14-6 FACB 21-7 ROS 19S 1-7-43 350S 16-9 DeH 3-11 611S 28-6-44 61 OTU 23-7 SOC 14-5-45

BM354 FF PJS 26-3-42 45MU 29-3 CBAF 27-5 AST 29-5 485S 5-8 FACB 24-4-43 AST 322S 15-7 222S 1-1-44 VSM 9-3 'Basta' mods 53 OTU 30-9 to 5335M 14-7-45

BM355 M45M FF PJS 25-3-42 5MU 28-3 602S 13-5 416S 16-7 411S 23-3-43 CAC ops 3-4 ROS 322S 10-11 504S 18-11 129S FACB 23-1-44 SAL 186S 8-4 130S 18-4 FTR ops 21-5

BM356 Champion 12MU 29-3-42 64S 12-4 120S 3-6 154S 12-7 HAL 26-10 52 OTU 6-2-43 SAL 6-4-44 'Basta' 290S 17-1-45

BM357 12MU 29-3-42 313S 11-4 CE ops 24-4 AST

BM358 45MU 29-3-42 4FP&P cd nr Dyce on del flt CE 2-4 SOC 20-4 bboc 510S 21-6 P&PSM 11-11

BM359 Warminster 5MU 27-3-42 616S 14-4 316S 18-6 18-6 FACB 27-6 AST M46 instal 82MU 13-11 *Bar Inch* 18-12 USSR 24-3-43

BM360 12MU 29-3-42 313S 11-4 FTR ops 17-5

BM361 37MU 1-4-42 435S 11-7 41S 26-7 72S 28-7 71S 2-8 FTR ops 19-8 SOC 21-8

BM362 FF PJS 28-3-42 12MU 1-4 64S 12-4 154S 12-7 AST 6-10 421S 13-4-43 416S 23-5 401S 1-6 126S 10-8 FACE 15-10

BM363 45MU 29-3-42 81S 4-6 52 OTU 31-1-43 FACB 20-12 AST M46 instal 350S 19-5-44 CE ops 8-6

BM364 45MU 1-4-42 81S 30-4 VSM 6-7-43 fuel syst & rud mods 222MU 28-9 *Emp Ort* Port 19-10

BM365 37MU 1-4-42 65S 17-4 CB ops 21-7 VSM 3-10 fuel syst mods 222MU 6-11 *C o Lil* 8-12 USSR 16-2-43

BM366 45MU 1-4-42 457S 12-5 611S 30-5 HAL 6-6 mr M46 instal 72S 29-7 41S 2-8 FACB 28-10 VSM 5-7-43 fuel syst & elev mods wng stiff S type pt Mk III IFF bomb carr M45M install 345S 13-4-44 FAAC 12-9 AST recat E 2-1-45 SOC 9-1

BM367 FF PJS 28-3-42 AST con to Sea IB-NX961

BM368 M45M 5MU 28-3-42 403S 26-4 129S 26-4 FACB 5-6 ROS 412S 29-8 421S 31-1-43 401S 9-6 611S 14-4-44 53 OTU 6-8 SOC 25-5-45

BM369 45MU 28-3-42 81S 30-4 DeH 9-10 VSM 9-5-44 fuel syst & rud mods wng stiff S type pt Mk III IFF bomb carr M46 instal 53 OTU 11-8 e/fd f/ld nr Ottringham Yorks 15-5-45

BM370 37MU 1-4-42 124S 28-4 e/fd cd nr Fakenham Kent CE 14-7 AST SOC 28-7

BM371 FF PJS 28-3-42 45MU 1-4 309S 30-6 CB ops FAAC 4-7 ROS MMOx 31-1-44 mods RNDA 9-2 LoS 23-2 as train

BM372 12MU 12-4-42 401S 30-4 coll with AD506 taxy Graves CAC GAL 76MU 28-10 *C o Lil* 8-12 USSR 16-2-43

BM373 FF PJS 27-3-42 45MU 29-3 64S 13-4 122S 6-6 Farn Oct'42 AST 27-10 308S 21-1-43 91S 26-1 19S 29-5 65S 30-6 out of fuel i/sea off Brighton 27-7

BM374 FF PJS 27-3-42 12MU 29-3 313S 11-4 154S 8-6 64S 14-6 154S 12-7 FTR ops 30-7

BM375 12MU 1-4-42 129S 13-4 CE ops 2-5-43 FH45.50

BM376 37MU 5-5-42 402S 2-5 FAAC 8-7 ROS 81S 31-7 CAC ops 26-8 ROS 52 OTU 27-2-43 MMO 25-5 CRD Gunnery Res Unit Exeter 31-8 ROS 21-9 SAL mr 8-8-44 2nd TAF Com Sq 25-1-45

BM377 FF PJS 14-4-42 6MU 3-4 124S 29-4 312S 24-7 152A 24-8 AST 26-11 AST 11-3-43 con to Seafire 1B-NX901

BM378 12MU 5-4-42 81S 29-4 MMO 8-12 610S 23-3-43 485S 20-4 flew i/sea nr Worthing 30-5

BM379 45MU 10-4-42 132S 28-4 FACB 21-7 ROS FTR ops 10-6-43 FH119

BM380 37MU 5-4-42 131S 7-6 245S 22-8 ASTH 20-12-43 132S 15-2-44 FAAC 27-4-45 ROS SOC 5-11

BM381 LF LR VB FF PJS 31-3-42 37MU 1-4 350S 17-4 485S 20-12 FAAC 28-5 19S 1-7 132S 17-2-44 504S 15-3 310S 15-7 FAAC 25-8 ROS 61 OTU 6-11 SOC 14-5-45 M50 & M45M instal during service

BM382 FF PJS 2-4-42 38MU 5-4 81S 3-6 52 OTU 18-2-43 SAL 6-4 'Basta' mods 64S 17-6-44 57 OTU 24-5-45 SOC 25-10

BM383 38MU 3-4-42 485S 24-5 FTR ops 31-5 FH25

BM384 37MU 1-4-42 72S 17-4 FTR ops 9-5 FH153.25

BM385 12MU 5-4-42 602S 27-4 CAC ops 8-6 ROS 416S 16-7 CB ops 24-7 GAL VSM 27-6-43 fuel syst elev & rud mods wng stiff S type pt Mk III IFF bomb carr 501S 5-11 ops 23-5-44 ASTE 41 OTU 28-2-45 58 OTU 22-3 FAAC 8-6 recat E SOC 3-7

BM386 37MU 5-4-42 71S 29-4 FTR ops 1-6 FH37

BM399 M46 Upper Ward of Lanarkshire 33MU 17-3-42 Star Fm dis 122S 26-5 52 OTU 30-1-43 FACB 20-2 350S 29-4 coll with EN680 on ldg CE 11-7

BM400 39MU 18-4-42 310S 25-4 312S 30-7 340S 19-8 FTR ops 5-9 FH119.15

BM401 8MU 24-4-42 121S 5-5 FTR ops 19-8

BM402 9MU 20-4-42 72S 15-5 Farn June '42 neg 'G' and exhaust flame damping trls 602S 11-7 611S 21-7 VSM 20-10 fuel syst mods wng stiff M46 instal 310S 13-4-43 57 OTU 31-12 o/s ldg Esh o/t CE 1-2-45 SOC 15-2

BM403 45MU 29-3-42 313S 7-5 122S 8-5 e/fd f/ld Landwick Farm Essex CE 19-6 AST SOC 1-7

BM404 12MU 1-4-42 122S 14-4 FTR ops 5-5

BM405 FF PJS 1-4-42 33MU 3-4 121S 17-6 FTR ops 19-8

BM406 FF PJS 31-4-42 9MU 2-4 411S 7-6 FTR ops 19-8

BM407 M45M FF PJS 2-4-42 37MU 5-4 122S 18-4 ROS mr 10-7 416S 14-11 411S 23-3-43 ROS 3-8 340S 28-9 FAAC 31-10 485S 29-11 303S 30-4-44 CE ops 15-6

BM408 37MU 9-4-42 315S 7-5 FACB 12-7 LMS 335USA 3-2-43 331S 23-3 349S 1-8 VSM 5-11 fuel syst mods 57 OTU 8-9-44 ASTH 14-6-45

BM409 12MU 5-4-42 64S 15-4 FAA 16-5 154S 19-7 64S 1-8 122S 19-9 312S 31-12 VSM 3-6-43 fuel syst mods wng stiff 502S 4-7 306S 3-10 CGS 8-10 to 5539M

BM410 12MU 5-4-42 81S 29-4 strk by BM468 CE 2-6 SOC 6-6

BM411 45MU 5-4-42 132S 28-4 CAC ops 17-4-43 ROS 502S 26-5 FAAC 12-7 ASTE 66S 9-11 340S 15-11 FACB 19-12 USAAF 9-5-44 DeH 16-6 to 5600M FAF 3-4-45

BM412 45MU 5-4-42 133S 2-6 485S 3-6 FAAC 16-4-43 MMO 66S 14-8 340S 15-11 52 OTU 6-2-44 FAF 19-1-45 GC 2/18

BM413 45MU 5-4-42 611S 16-4 72S 4-8 CAC ops 29-8 ROS 232S 23-9 65S 19-10 SAL mr 3-4-43 VSM 27-6 fuel syst elev & rud mods bomb carr

BM414 39MU 26-4-42 421S 2-6 FAAC 28-3-43 ROS 418S 27-7 118S 7-8 64S 25-9 276S 9-10 FTR 5-4-45

BM415 38MU 5-4-42 64S 24-5 154S 12-7 FTR ops 28-8

BM416 FF PJS 3-4-42 12MU 5-4 64S 15-4 FACB 19-4 61 OTU strk by o/s BM461 when turning off runway Rednal CE 16-12-44 FH12.30

BM417 FF PJS 3-4-42 45MU 7-4 308S 24-8 FACE

BM418 45MU 5-4-42 37MU 9-4 133S 10-5 CAC ops 1-6 ROS 72S 15-6 65S 4-8 165S 23-9 u/s ldg Tang cd CE 16-12 AST recat B M46 instal VSM 19-7-43 fuel syst elev & rud mods wng stiff Mk III IFF M45M instal 306S 24-4-44 278S 26-5 SOC 27-6-46

BM419 5MU 10-4-42 154S 31-5 313S 8-6 416S 22-8 e/fd on t/o coll with BL 928 & EP279 CE 9-11 FH226.55

BM420 FF PJS 4-4-42 12MU 5-4 131S 25-4 CA ops 7-8 AST Wal 17-1-43 AST 22-4 con to Sea IB-NX923

BM421 12MU 5-4-42 129S 13-4 FTR ops 4-5 FH51.20

BM422 LF LF VB M45M 37MU 9-4-42 315S 7-5 319S 5-9 AST 27-2-43 411S 4-5 CB ops 4-7 recat E AST 322S 14-1-44 350S 13-3 FAAC 21-3 ROS CE ops 10-6

BM423 FF PJS 3-4-42 12 MU 5-4 81S 29-4 MMO 14-10 M46 instal 421S 25-2-43 416S 23-5 401S 1-6 26S 10-8 CAC ops 3-10 ASTH M45M instal 118S 30-3-44 611S 3-10 1AGS 12-12 MWW 11-2-46 dev of high speed targets CE for scr 3-3-47

BM424 FF PJS 8-4-42 5MU 10-4 154S 31-5 313S 8-6 VSM 11-8 306S 12-8 FTR ops 14-8

BM425 M45M 37MU 9-4-42 452S 12-5 93S 4-6 FAAC 3-10 ROS 64S 24-1-43 FACB 7-2 AST 19S 14-5 65S 30-6 130S 15-8 VSM 1-3-44 fuel syst & 'Basta' mods 1661CU 29-11-44 SOC

BM426 FF PJS 7-4-42 45MU 10-4 602S 13-5 FTR ops 17-5

BM427 45MU 10-4-42 54S 7-5 167S strk by jett hood of second Spit f/ld Castletown Caithness 24-3-43 610S 4-9 ROS 23-9 ASR duty strk water cd off Lizard Point 4-11 FH102.35

BM428 LF LR VB M45M FFPJS 8-4-42 5MU 10-4 403S 26-4 FAAC 4-6 ROS AST 17-7 131S 17-7 610S 27-1-43 350S 29-3 132S 18-2-44 504S 15-3 FAAC 19-4 ROS 310S 15-7 45 OTU 4-9 SOC 25-5-45

BM429 FF PJS 8-4-42 12MU 11-4 401S 30-4 CB ops 6-5 ROS FTR ops 26-7 FH59.10

BM430 FF PJS 4-4-42 45MU 5-4 242S 26-6 FACB 26-7 LMS 132S 18-4-43 122S 21-5 234S 6-7 USAAF 6-5-44 SAL 12-8 595S 18-12 SOC 6-9-45

BM447 FF PJS 4-4-42 5MU 10-4 134S 20-4 390S 31-7 FAAC 9-8 WAL VSM 10-10 fuel syst mods wng stiff HAL con to PRXIII M32 Ben 5-4-43 542S 12-7 ROS HAL SOC 27-2-45

BM448 234S VSM 25-1-44 fuel syst mods

BM449 45MU 11-4-42 416S 8-4 FTR ops 27-6 FH65.10

BM450 45MU 11-4-42 416S 8-4 FTR ops 27-6 FH65.10

BM451 45MU 11-4-42 416S 11-6 602S 15-7 FTR ops 19-8 FH58.25

BM452 5MU 10-4-42 154S 31-5 313S 8-6 e/fd cd i/ Channel 31-7

BM453 FF PJS 9-4-42 45MU 11-4 154S 15-6 form coll with P8757 on ldg CB 29-6 RNDA 1-9-43 RNAS Stret 4-9 ASTH 8-10 hook fitt LoS 31-10

BM454 FF PJS 11-4-42 37MU 12-4 308S o/s downwind ldg Atcham o/t CB 28-6 AST CE SOC 28-7

BM455 12MU 11-4-42 81S 29-4 CB ops 28-7 AST VSM 10-10 fuel syst mods 52 OTU 26-1-43 DeH 18-3 'Basta' mods 61 OTU 18-8 SOC 29-11-45

BM456 FF PJS 9-4-42 12MU 11-4 602S 27-4 FA FTR 1-5

BM457 12MU 11-4-42 416S 29-4 602S 15-7 164S 11-9 341S 3-2-43 FACB 19-2 SAL VSM 9-5 con to Sea IB PA124 23-5

BM458 37MU 12-4-42 402S 6-5 122S 31-7 312S 31-12 VSM 3-6-43 fuel syst & elev mods wng stiff 165S 5-9 308S 1-10 FAAC 4-3-44 277S 26-4 CAC ops 23-7 ROS SOC 17-2-45

BM459 M46 cd del flt to 45MU CAC 12-4-42 ROS 45MU 21-4 485S 2-6 FACB 15-9 ROS ASTH 1-10 M45M instal 19S 1-7-43 316S 5-10 303S 18-12 SAL mr 20-3-44 303S 28-6 CAC ops 2-7 ROS 53 OTU 10-8 695S 28-6-45 SOC 11-10

BM460 45MU 12-4-42 82MU 7-11 *Bar Inch* 18-12 USSR 24-3-43

BM461 45MU 12-4-42 81S 3-5 FACB 6-9 SAL 335S 29-1-43 SAL 7-7-44 CGS 13-10 to 5593M 23-10-45 FAF 3-3-46

BM462 FF PJS 10-4-42 cd del flt to 45MU CA 11-4-42 ASTE 38MU 24-8 222 MU 7-11 *C o Lil* 8-12 16-2-43

BM463 12MU 12-4-42 81S 30-4 air coll with BL811 cd Hastings CE 2-6 350S May '44 found nr wreckage of Marauder (believed collided) West Firle Scotland 8-6-44

BM464 LF LR VB M45M 37MU 12-4-42 485S 28-4 CAC ops 14-6 ROS coll with BM522 after ldg Wansford CB 30-7 AST 222S 15-1-43 64S 31-3-43 118S 25-9 132S 18-2-44 504S 15-3 61 OTU 13-8 FACB 19-9 recat E 13-10

BM465 M46 45MU 12-4-42 64S 19-5 154S 12-7 52 OTU 2-23-43 VSM 20-1-44 fuel syst mods 53 OTU 11-8 ROS 16-5-45 recat E SOC 25-5

BM466 FF PJS 11-4-43 37MU 12-4 402S 30-5 FTR ops 23-5 FH30

BM467 FF PJS 10-4-42 12MU 12-4 81S 29-4 CE 27-5 AST SOC 5-6

BM468 FF PJS 11-4-42 12MU 12-4 81S 30-4 o/s ldg Horn strk BM410 CB 2-6 GAL 52 OTU 9-2-43 350S 16-10 FTR 28-12 FH247-30

BM469 FF PJS 11-4-42 5MU 13-4 602S 13-5 FTR ops 8-6 FH50-15

BM470 FF PJS 10-4-42 45MU 12-4 133S 12-5 72S 15-6 52 OTU 5-2-43 FACB 3-4 DeH 315S CE ops 11-8-44

BM471 M45M 12MU 12-4-42 81S 30-4 FACB 27-8 AST VSM 21-10 fuel syst mods wng stiff 504S 30-4-43 416S 11-6 350S 24-9 FAAC 7-10 ROS 416S 2-2-44 186S 10-2 57 OTU 17-8 strk H/T cables after power loss cd nr Stockton on Tees CE 31-8

BM472 37MU 12-4-42 308S 21-6 FAAC 19-8 308USA FTR ops 24-10

BM473 5MU 13-4-42 81S P&PSM 14-3 NWA FTR 24-10

BM474 5MU 14-4-42 65S 2-6 164S 13-9 341S 3-2-42 SAL 23-2 350S 10-4 VSM 7-11 fuel syst mods 276S 26-4-44 MAL 10-8 BC Instr Sch Finningley 11-12 Bom Com Wire Sch 5-1-45 FAAC 3-5 recat E SOC 18-5

BM475 FF PJS 13-4-42 6MU 15-4 64S 25-4 FA FTR 17-4 FH29.20

BM476 6MU 14-4-42 64S 25-4 154S 14-7 165S 28-2-43 122S 4-8 234S 15-8 303S 16-1-44 SAL 20-3 26S 58 OTU 22-3 FACB 18-4 recat E SOC 29-5-43

BM477 6MU 15-4-42 402S 30-4 FAAC 22-6 AST VSM 25-9 fuel syst mods 167S 29-1-43 CE ops 5-5 FH192

BM478 6FPP fast ldg o/s cd on del flt to 37MU CE 16-4-42 SOC 28-4

BM479 5MU 13-4-42 71S 2-6 111S 9-7 2USA 21-10 65S 2-3-43 130S 1-4 222MU 22-10 *Pandor* 25-11 Port 8-12

BM480 LF VB M45M 45MU 16-4-42 154S 12-6 402S 18-6 122S 11-8 FAAC 11-9 ROS 165S 24-9 411S 4-9-43 341S 17-10 453S 20-11 234S 21-6-44 53 OTU 5-10 41 OTU strk lorry taxy at Chil CE 23-5-45 SOC 31-5

BM481 12MU 17-4-42 401S 30-4 317S 5-8 315S 4-9 AST 1-11 VSM 29-3-43 fuel syst mods wng stiff M50 instal 118S 31-5 64S 25-9 Met Com Sqn 15-11-44 57 OTU 24-4-45 577S 7-6 SOC 27-12

BM482 33MU 17-3-42 485S 1-7 FTR ops 13-2-43

BM483 FF PJS 29-3-42 9MU 1-4 313S 6-5 154S 8-6 122S 25-6 flap tail ldg strk obst MHth CE 29-6 AST SOC 7-7

BM484 9MU 1-4-42 72S 16-5 FAAC 4-7 ROS 13-7 FTR ops 26-7

BM485 9MU 1-4-42 72S 16-5 65S 14-8 FACE 15-9

BM486 9MU 13-4-42 64S 4-6 M46 instal 154S 13-7 FTR ops 15-7

BM487 M46 FF PJS 13-4-42 9MU 15-4 66S 30-5 129S 1-6 CAC ops 19-6 ROS 602S 29-11 129S 22-1-43 66S 19-2 VSM 24-6 fuel syst elev & rud mods wng stiff Mk III IFF bomb carr 315S 24-5-44 57 OTU 14-9 FAC3 15-2-45 recat E SOC 26-2

BM488 LF VB M46 9MU 16-4-42 81S 30-4 64S 4-6 154S 15-7 CAC ops 27-8 M45M instal 306S 7-8 302S 3-10-43 322S 6-12 SAL 10-5-44 'Basta' mods 57 OTU 18-7-44 SOC 14-6-45

BM489 M46 9MU 10-4-42 122S 21-5 FTR ops 8-6

BM490 LF M45M 45MU 2-4-42 132S 2-6 72S 15-6 322S 3-8 130S 15-8 222S 1-1-44 402S 24-5 FAAC 8-6 ROS 61 OTU 17-5-45 695S 28-6

BM491 M46 FF PJS 18-4-42 6MU 24-4 421S 10-5 411S 4-7-43 130S 15-8 FAAC 22-10 VSM 1-3-44 fuel syst M45M instal 'Basta' mods 278S 23-5 87 Grp Com Sqn 26-7-45 FAAC 27-8

BM492 9MU 26-4-42 132S 27-5 72S 15-6 FAAC 20-8 ROS VSM 18-8-43 fuel syst & elev mods wng stiff Mk III IFF S type pt bomb carr COAL 7-2-44

BM493 M46 FF PJS 17-4-42 37MU 16-4 122S 6-5 52 OTU 26-1-43 FAA 27-2 AST M45M instal 602S 1305 504S 10-10 CB ops 3-12 SAL 118S 28-4-44 CB ops 2-6 501S 15-8 61 OTU 12-1- FAAC 20-2-45 recat E SOC 30-3

BM508 12MU 5-4-42 129S 13-4 CE ops 5-6 FH97-05

BM509 M45M 37MU 9-4-42 402S 3-5 485S 31-7 19S 1-7-43 MMO 31-8 118S 30-3-44 616S 3-10 61 OTU 19-10 SOC E 1-3-45

BM510 9MU 12-4-42 313S 14-5 154S 8-6 611S 17-6 71S 3-8 334USA 1-10 VSM M46 instal 602S 15-7-43 CAC ops 17-8 118S 10-10 132S 25-1-44 VSM 17-3 fuel syst mods wng stiff M45M instal 277S 19-5 611S 3-10 2nd TAF Com S 1-3-45 SOC 28-4

BM511 FF PJS 16-4-42 9MU 18-4 FACE 16-7 SOC 25-7

BM512 5MU 13-4 315S 18-8-43 USAAF 17-1-44 AEAF Com Sqn 13-8

BM513 39MU 16-4-42 402S 2-5 350S 19-8 185S 18-9 FAAC 9-1-43 ROS 485S 23-1 FTR 12-2

BM514 M45M FF PJS 24-4-42 37MU 26-4 452S 12-5 93S 4-6 FAAC 16-8 ROS 610S 6-11 131S 25-1-43 VSM 13-5 fuel syst mods wng stiff 118S 2-7 64S 25-9 AEAF Heston 15-10-44 SHAEF Com Sqn 3-5-45 R&S refurb to Port 25-7-47

BM515 LF VB M45M 45MU 18-4-42 133S 16-5 72S 15-6 65S 4-8 165S 23-9 322S 3-8-43 222S 1-1-44 130S 24-5 CAC ops 20-6 ROS 61 OTU 19-8 GAAC 4-2-45 recat E

BM516 M46 16-4-42 72S 10-5-42 65S 14-8 165S 23-9 WAL 27-2-43 M50M instal 485S 27-4 19S 1-7 340S 28-9 12-3-44 AST 9-5 M45M instal 'Basta' mods CGS 5-10 SOC 27-12-45

BM517 FF PJS 15-4-42 39MU 16-4 313S 6-5 CAC ops 2-6 ROS 313S 13-6 91S 15-6 AST mr 3-9 CAC ops 10-12 AST swerved ldg Hawk o/t CE 5-4-43

BM518 FF PJS 14-4-42 45MU 16-4 133S 14-5 72S 15-6 65S 4-8 165S 23-8 CE ops 9-2 FH190.30

BM519 6MU 15-4-42 402S CB ops 6-7 CE 12-7

BM520 FF PJS 16-4-42 9MU 18-4 122S 19-5 FACB 13-7 ROS 82MU 10-11 *Bar Inch* 18-12 USSR 24-3-43

BM521 FF PJS 14-4-42 45MU 16-4 602S 10-6 spun i/grd Cuckford Sussex CE 17-6

BM522 M45M FF PJS 16-4-42 8MU 17-4 485S 2-5 form coll with BP858 ldg Kingscliffe CE 15-7 AST coll with BM464 after ldg 30-7 312S 31-12 19S 22-7-43 118S 25-10 132S 25-1-44 VSM 27-3 fuel syst and 'Basta' mods 277S 26-6 mr 23-11 recat E SOC 2-1-45

BM523 M55 37MU 16-4-42 133S 13-6 71S 29-6 4USA 28-8 FAAC 2-9 ROS 332S 8-11 122S 21-5-43 USAAF 6-9 443S 7-3-44 58 OTU 30-3 9 Grp Com Flt 18-7 ASTH 14-6-45

BM524 FF PJS 16-4-42 12MU 17-4 602S 7-5 FACE 22-5

BM525 FF PJS 15-4-42 12MU 17-4 401S 30-4 91S 28-7 AST 21-11 411S 22-3-43 402S 25-3 FAAC 2-4 to 3689M 4-5 CB 6-11-44 recat E 2-1-45

BM526 M46 FF PJS 17-4-42 39MU 19-4 19S 7-6 412S 9-9 421S 31-1-43 CRD Farn Feb/Mar '43 gyro gunsight trls FAAC 27-9 AST 31ATG 5-6-44 405RCU 13-7 ASTE 18-7 SOC 19-7-45

BM527 FF PJS 15-4-42 12MU 17-4 416S 29-4 FAAC 25-6 ROS 234S 27-7 416S 31-7 CE ops 29-10

BM528 M46 FF PJS 19-4-42 6MU 24-4 411S 7-5 FAAC 26-5 ROS VA M45M instal 453S 21-6 FACB 13-13 65S 26-5-43 130S 15-8 FAAC 8-9 ASTH M55M instal 186S 21-7-44 FAAC 18-6 57 OTU 3-10 SOC 1-6-45

BM529 M45M FF PJS 17-4-42 45MU 16-4 133S 14-5 72S 14-6 65S 4-8 165S 23-9 FAAC 9-1-43 ROS 602S 2107 504S 10-10 129S 26-1-44 SAL 8-2 FAAC f/f to 6MU ROS 303S 3-7 57 OTU 2-8 577S 2-6-45 SOC 3-7-46

BM530 LF VB M45M FF PJS 16-4-42 39MU 18-4 132S 7-6 FAAC 24-10 ROS 308S 21-5-43 215S FAAC 3-11 ROS 130S 26-1-44 222S 16-2 FAAC 8-3 ROS 53 OTU 27-6 587S 7-6-45 ASTH 10-10 SOC dbr 25-10

BM531 8MU 18-4-42 305S 7-5 303S 7-5 315S 6-6-43 19S 26-6 FACB 2-9 recat E 4-10

BM532 M45M 39MU 24-4-42 307S 21-6 FACE 12-7 AST 610S 20-2-43 10 Grp Com Flt 23-5 316S 29-6 65S 27-8 64S 27-8 118S 25-9 VSM 7-11 fuel syst mods 278S 24-4-44 287S 22-2-45 SOC 11-9

BM533 FF PJS 17-4-42 39MU 18-4 302S 3-4 FAAC 5-5 129S 9-6 FAAC 15-6 41S 14-7 lost on sortie land Wexford Eire out of fuel 21-8

BM534 FF PJS 16-4-42 8MU 18-4 421S 10-5 164S 23-11 SAL 23-1-43 CE 9-2

BM535 8MU 17-4-42 222S 10-5 242S 11-8 411S 23-9 FAAC 20-12 402S 25-3-43 19S 5-5 AST 18-6 402S 5-10 345S 13-4-44 CB ops 8-6 AST CGS 14-1-45 eng/fld aban cd nr Beverley Yorks obf CE 13-6

BM536 39MU 19-4-42 130S 3-6 FTR ops 25-6 FH49

BM537 M46 39MU 18-4-42 306S 30-4 HAL 23-8 133S 29-9 DeH 14-1-43 124S 29-3 19S 4-7 CRU 28-2-44 'Basta' mods SAL mr 14-4 53 OTU 11-8 recat B 16-4-45 recat E 22-5 SOC

BM538 M45M 9MU 18-4-42 308S 1-6 71S 14-7 401S 5-12 412S 12-12 421S 31-1-43 VSM 6-5 fuel syst mods wng stiff 610S 1-7 602S 4-3-44 118S 13-3 strk AR293 on t/o Sumburgh CE 28-3

BM539 LF VB 12MU 20-4-42 242S 16-6 FACB 27-9 ASTH 610S 9-4-43 R-R 18-4 mods 485S 6-5 R-R 20-5 inspection 19S 1-7 air coll with BM323 cd nr 125 SLG CE 9-7 FH136.45

BM540 8MU 18-4-42 305S 9-5 303S 7-5 164S 23-11 303S 31-12 e/td t/ld Pevensey Bay Sussex CB 11-2-43 USAAF 28-6 FACE 12-11

BM541 FF PJS 16-4-42 AST con to Sea IB-NX988

BM542 39MU 18-4-42 19S 7-6 FTR ops 19-8

BM543 M45M 12MU 14-4-42 139S 14-6 91S 15-6 CA ops 22-6 WAL 132S 26-4-43 122S 21-5 234S 15-8 FAAC 16-10 ROS MMO mr 16-1-44 350S 31-5 CGS 2-10 AST 23-10-45 SOC 20-10

BM556 M45M 12MU 24-4-42 152S 8-5 HAL mr 21-11 VSM 17-3-43 fuel syst mods wng stiff 402S 3-7 CE ops 4-9 recat B 11-9 245S 12-4-44 FAAC 27-5 ROS 57 OTU 17-8 FACE 3-5-45 SOC 15-5

BM557 FF PJS 17-4-42 12MU 24-4 152S 8-5 FACE 18-5

BM558 FF PJS 18-4-42 8MU 24-4 91S 5-5 FTR ops 20-8 FH180.45

BM559 6MU 19-4-42 BDn 30-4 hand & stab characteristics when recovering from dives. Steep turns to assess aeroelastically stresses. Comp trls with X4266 fitt DeH and Rotol props. Trls with and without 6¼lb int/wt in elev syst DeH prop superior to Rotol. 5USA 6-9 AST 15-5-43 con to Sea IB-NX945

BM560 FF PJS 17-4-42 39MU 19-4 111S 2-6 4USA 27-8 332S 8-11 P&PSM 10-3-43 VSM 12-7 fuel syst & rud mods wng stiff FTR ops 22-8 FH200.40

BM561 12MU 24-4-42 315S 30-4 317S 5-9 FAAC 2-2-43 340S 5-9 RNDA 20-2-44 COAL 9-5 mods Hens as train 2-6 RNDA 16-8

BM562 FACE on ferry flt SOC 10-7-42

BM563 37MU 1-5-42 307S 20-6 FACE 10-7 AST SOC FH20.20

BM564 6MU 19-4-42 350S 30-4 AST 27-12 501S 4-4-43 VSM 6-6 fuel syst elev & rud mods wng stiff 302S 22-9 306S 3-10 FACE 15-11 AST 22-11

BM565 M45M FF PJS 18-4-42 45MU 24-4 310S 25-6 421S 25-7 ROS 25-9 303S 2-4-43 315S 11-6 19S 26-6 501S 24-9 DeH 21-11 303S CE ops 21-5-44

BM566 6MU 19-4-42 41S 4-5 CAC ops 25-7 ROS 317S 3-8 FACE 29-8 SOC 9-9

BM567 FF PJS 18-4-42 39MU 19-4 111S 3-6 4USA 27-8 332S 8-11 314S 5-3-43 SAL 30-7 312S 20-10 443S 27-2-44 58 OTU 30-3 GAAC 27-2-45 recat E Soc 5-4

BM568 8MU 24-4-42 306S 3-5 FAAC 30-6 SAL 129S 22-10 602S 29-11 FAAC 9-12 ROS 340S 26-4-43 e/fd w/u ldg nr Backford Perths CB 15-7 SAL recat E 3-9

BM569 6MU 24-4-42 421S 10-5 FACE 21-7 SOC 27-7 FH81.32 AST recat B 16-11 VSM 19-3-43 fuel syst mods wng stiff 504S 10-5 FAAC 26-6 ROS P&P 19-8 57 OTU 12-9-44 577S 7-6-45 to 5520M 30-7 recat E SOC 21-2-49

BM570 FF PJS 21-4-42 8MU 24-4 421S 10-5 FAAC 26-9 VSM 1-3-43 con to Sea IB-PA101

BM571 45MU 24-4-42 416S 6-6 602S 15-7 e/fd o/t in f/ld CE 27-7 SOC 4-8

BM572 LF LR M45M FF PJS 21-4-42 45MU 24-4 453S 23-6 FACB 12-9 SAL 340S 24-4-43 611S 26-4-44 FAAC 18-5 ROS 41 OTU 24-5-45 to 5350M 14-7 SOC 5SoTT 29-11

BM573 37MU 2-5-42 610S 8-6 41S 17-7 flew i/hill with BL518 & R7296 Tarren Hendre Merioneth CE 23-10

BM574 FF PJS 22-4-42 12MU 26-4 501S 12-5 118S 23-9 FACB 29-11 recat E 28-12

BM575 8MU 24-4-42 421S 10-5 flew i/mountain nr St Johns Colloery Maesteg Glam CE 29-9 FH188.40

BM576 FF PJS 21-4-42 6MU 24-4 421S 10-5 COAL 28-6 fitt hook RNDA 19-1-44 RNAS Belfast 29-1

BM577 M46 FF PJS 22-4-42 45MU 24-4 232S 4-6 FACB 5-8 LMS VSM 16-7-43 fuel syst elev & rud mods wng stiff bomb carr 316S 22-11 63S 1-5-44 57 OTU 3-5 SOC 6-12-45

BM578 LF LR VB M45M FF PJS 18-4-42 6MU 19-4 121S 5-5 CB ops 19-5 ROS 64S 23-3 453S 2-4 222S 5-4 129S 17-7 118S 25-9 132S 19-2-44 504S 15-3 310S 15-7 41 OTU 4-9 FAAC 29-11 SOC 6-6-45

BM579 12MU 25-4-42 331S 4-6 FAAC 14-7 ROS CE ops 19-8

BM580 Dsfd 37MU 26-4-42 154S 12-6 412S 29-12 cd Anglesley 11-2-43 AST 23-4 con to Seafire IB-NX924

BM581 LR VB M50 FF PJS 24-4-42 37MU 26-4 121S 28-6 CA ops 21-7 335USA 1-10 P&P 2-4-43 con to Tech trng standard M46 instal 317S 22-9 312S 4-12 441S 27-2-44 56 OTU 30-3 595S 21-1-45 SOC 6-9

BM582 37MU 26-4-42 154S 12-6 CE 24-10

BM583 M45M 6MU 30-4-42 411S 7-5 402S 25-3-43 19S 22-4 65S 30-6 130S 15-8 453S 2-12 602S 25-1-44 SAL 2-3 350S 19-5-44 CB ops 7-8 AST 17SFTS 20-11 FACB 30-4-45 ROS SOC 4-7-46

BM584 33MU 24-4-42 340S 1-6 FTR ops 30-7 FH54.25

BM585 6MU 1-5-42 H Ercall 20-6 DeH 20-12-43 BDU Newm 10-1-44 FAAC 17-5 ROS SOC 15-11-45

BM586 FF PJS 30-4-42 6MU 1-5 309USA MMO 21-13-43 M46 instal COAL 11-3-44 mods RNDA 3-3 as train

BM587 LF LR VB M45M 6MU 7-5-42 304S 12-9 501S 2-11 S&H 27-3-43 VSM 4-7 fuel syst & elev mods wng stiff Mk III IFF bomb carr

BM588 LF LR VB M45M FF PJS 21-4-42 39MU 24-4 154S 13-6 4 USA 27-8 332S 8-11 SAL VSM 27-6-43 fuel syst & elev mods S type pt Mk III IFF bomb carr 316S 29-11 63S 1-5-44 FACB 14-7 58 OTU 30-7 to 5524M SOC 4-7-50

BM589 6MU 24-4-42 421S 10-5 BDn Aug'42 hand & stab recovery from steep dvs trls FACE 23-8 SOC 3-9

BM590 Olga 121S 335USA Sept'42

BM591 FF PJS 21-4-42 39MU 24-4 72S 7-6 133S 15-6 CAC ops 31-7 AST 421S 25-11 VSM 14-1-43 fuel syst mods wng stiff HAL 31-3 con to PRXIII M32 RNDA 3-5-44 718S Hens

BM592 8MU 25-4-42 121S 19-6 FTR 23-6

BM593 M45M 39MU 24-4-42 154S 13-6 FAAC 25-7 ROS 232S 15-10 164S 11-11 FAAC 5-12 341S 3-2-43 340S 23-3 FAAC 24-5 ROS 67Grp 20-12 501S 31-5-44 CB ops 13-8 ASTE 1653CU 28-11 SOC 16-8-45

BM594 M45M 39MU 24-4-42 403S 3-6 FACE 20-12 recat B SAL 308S 19-4-43 FAAC 21-6 DeH 611S 14-11

BM590 in the markings of 121 Squadron.

1696Flt 24-11 R&S refurb to Port 29-4-47

BM595 8MU 25-4-42 421S 12-5 AST 7-7 76MU 27-10 *C o Lil* 8-12 16-2-43

BM596 8MU 25-4-42 340S 8-5 CB ops 17-2 ASTH 13-2-43 con to Sea IB-NX886

BM597 37MU 26-4-42 315S 7-5 FACB 13-2-43 DeH VSM 26-6 fuel syst elev & rud mods wng stiff S type pt Mk III IFF bomb carr 222MU 41-44 58 OTU 2-4-45 to 5718M 16-10-45 11-3-67 Henlow for BoB film 1972 Chu Fen as BM597 Extant PR-0 of 609S

BM624 FF PJS 24-4-42 39MU 26-4 154S 15-6 421S 25-7 412S 3-2-43 602S 19-4 ASTH 2-9 82MU 24-9 *Ortolan* 6-10 Port 19-10

BM625 FF PJS 23-4-42 12MU 25-4 152S 8-5 AST con to Sea IB-NX900

BM626 12MU 25-4-42 152S 8-5 HAL 23-11 AST 26-11 VSM 12-3-43 con to Sea IB-PA104

BM627 FF PJS 24-4-42 33MU 26-4 421S 10-5 416S 27-2-43 401S 1-6 126S 10-8 FACE 26-9

BM628 LF LR VB M45M FF PJS 24-4-42 33MU 26-4 316S 4-6 FACB 28-2 VSM 3-6 fuel syst mods 118S 7-7 64S 25-9 FACB 2-10 MAL 132S 10-2-44 504S 15-3 FTR FA 14-4

BM629 5MU 29-4-42 111S 23-5 CAC ops 1-6 MMO RNAS Stret 3-9 ASTH 26-9 hook fitt LoS 24-10

BM630 FF PJS 24-4-42 33MU 26-4 124S 9-5 312S 23-7 121S 5-9 335USA 1-10 MAL 10-8-44 1AGS 3-11 SOC 13-9-46

BM631 39MU 26-1-42 41S 2-6 453S 11-7 AST con to Sea IB-NX928 9-5-43

BM632 FF PJS 24-4-42 45MU 27-4 137S 7-6 FACB 20-6 con to Sea IB-NX940 5-5-43

BM633 M45M 39MU 26-4-42 234S 7-6 FAAC 27-8 ROS 122S 21-5-43 HAL 20-8 416S 10-10 FAAC 1-11 ROS 186S 13-2-44 130S 30-4 310S 28-7 SOC 25-5-45

BM634 O Bandeirante 6MU 3-5-42 111S 13-6 FAAC 20-6 ROS 132S 27-4-43 122S 21-5 FTR ops 18-7 FH136

BM635 8MU 7-5-42 H Ercall 21-6 FACB 20-7 ROS 65S 2-12 DeH 1-11-43 61 OTU 23-9-44 SOC mr 13-2-45

BM636 LF LR VB M45M 12MU 9-5-42 HQ 8th Ftr Com 21-10 347S 14-12 FAAC 17-12-ROS 132S 21-2-44 504S 15-3 41 OTU 4-9 cd low fly pract dbf CE 16-3-45 SOC 23-3

BM637 9MU 10-5-42 41S 11-6 245S 22-8 WAL 23-3-43 con to TT standard MIII instal COAL 6-5 to 3688M airfield construction wng 7-8

BM638 12MU 9-5-42 152S 10-6 FTR ops 26-8

BM639 33MU 13-5-42 129S 1-6 CA ops 3-6 SOC E 5-6 FH212.35

BM640 FF PJS 15-4-42 12MU 17-4 81S 30-4 CAC ops 15-7 ROS 52 OTU 9-2-43 130S 13-9 DeH 18-2-44 53 OTU 11-8 SOC 5-6-45

BM641 LF LR VB M45M 9MU 9-5-42 504S 15-7 501S 19-10 FAAC 8-9-43 ROS 611S 26-4-44 DeH 20-6-61 OTU 23-7 53 OTU 6-8 coll with BL416 o/s Rednal CE 16-12 SOC 6-1-45

BM642 9MU 23-4-42 485S 30-5 WAL 14-3-43 602S 31-5 504S 10-10 FACE 6-12 57 OTU 17-8-44 SOC 29-8-45

BM643 9MU 26-4-42 122S 14-5 416S 14-11 411S 23-3-43 a/c aban believed defective cont cd Tonbridge Kent CE 5-7 FH350

BM644 M46 FF PJS 25-4-42 9MU 30-4 122S 8-6 52 OTU 9-2-43 FLS 2-2-44 61 OTU 28-9

BM645 9MU 9-5-42 64S 7-6 81S 7-6 122S 4-7-43 FAAC 13-7 ROS 602S 23-8 DeH 19-9 402S 27-3-44 53 OTU 20-7 FACE SOC 3-3-45

BM646 9MU 2-5-42 133S 13-6 FTR ops 31-7-43

BM647 FF PJS 25-4-42 45MU 27-4 453S 23-66 FACE 28-8 SOC 9-9

BM648 LF VB M45M 9MU 5-5-42 302S 5-6 308S 25-5 118S 10-10 132S 25-1-44 VSM 9-3 fuel syst 'Basta' mods AST 9-5 FAF 19-1-45 GC 2/18

BM649 SR VB 9MU 6-5-42 129S 31-7 602S 29-11 FAAC 6-1-43 ROS 66S 7-3 234S 12-5 312S 29-6 COAL 8-2-44 mods RNAS Hens 6-5 as train

BM650 9MU 15-542 133S 13-6 401S 15-6 FTR 13-7 FH47.05

BM651 9MU 11-5-42 121S 5-6 302S 5-6 132S 28-6 FAA 1-7 ROS 118S 25-10 132S 25-1-44 SAL 303S 3-7 SAL mr 26-9 CRD WW 20-3-45 Malcolms WWal dev of high speed targets 71MU CE scr 20-3-47

BM652 9MU 15-5-42 401S 17-6 411S 17-6 CB ops 19-8 AST 402S 25-3-43 19S 22-4 65S 30-6 FAAC 4-7 350S 9-10 FTR ops 13-11

BM653 9MU 16-5-42 401S 18-6 FAAC 22-6 ROS 72S 12-7 315S 4-9 501S 5-12 CAC ops 16-6-43 P&PSM 29-6 M46 instal 310S 26-10 315S 4-3-44 275S 3-6

All F. Mk VC Merlin 46 unless otherwise indicated

BP844 250 M45 FF 24-1-42 6MU 4-2 C&C 10-2 *Queen V* 2-3 Malta 126S 24-4 FTR ops 3-4 FH17.05

BP845 2527 M45 FF 25-1-42 6MU 4-2 C&C 10-2 *Queen V* 2-3 Malta 2-4 CB ops 9-5 SOC 24-11

BP846 2538 VBT Spcl FF 28-1-42 6MU 4-2 C&C 13-2 *Queen V* 2-3 Malta 2-4 CB ops 35-4 SOC 2-5

BP847 2565 VBT Spcl FF 10-2-42 6MU 11-2 39MU 11-2 C&C 27-2 *Denmark* 14-3 Tak ME 12-6 145S 16-9

BP848 2547 VBT Spcl FF 31-1-42 6MU 4-3 C&C 10-2 TAK 9-5 ME 5-6 145S FACB 32-9

BP849 2558 M45 FF4-2-42 8MU 6-2 C&C 19-2 *Queen V* 2-3 Malta 1-4 FACE 22-4 SOC 6-5

BP850 2559 VBT Spcl FF 4-2-42 8MU 6-2 C&C 18-2 *Queen V* 2-3 Malta 1-4 CB ops 25-4 SOC 5-5 FH8.40

BP851 2569 M45 for spcl committment FF 10-2-42 8MU 13-2 e/a 21-2 *Sobo* 20-4 Tak 1-5 ME 17-6 FTR ops 5-7

BP:852 2567 M45 FF 10-2-42 8MU 11-2 C&C 27-2 *Denmark* 14-3 Tak ME 16-5 CB ops 16-6 601S cd o/s ldg 19-8 to 4178M

BP853 2568 VBT Spcl FF 10-2-42 8MU 11-2 CRDS WDn 25-2 39MU 25-3 *Ripley* 30-4 TakME SOC 1-8

BP854 2595 CHA FF 14-2-42 8MU 17-2-3 SLG 2-4 con to VCT 11-5 1FPP lost in cloud strk trees a/c aban cd nr Cherrington Winchester CE dbf 15-8 SOC 5-8

BP855 2557 LR VCT Spcl FF 4-2-42 8MU 6-2 5091 FTR ops 5-8

BP856 2566 VCT Spcl FF 10-2-42 8MU 11-2 66S 17-4 CB ops 24-7 AST 312S 31-5-43 504S 5-7 313S 22-9 FTR 24-9

BP857 2570 VC Spcl FF 10-2-42 39MU 13-2 66S FACE 8-3

BP858 2583 CHA FF 12-2-42 39MU 16-2 485S 12-3 457S 31-5 611S 31-5 485S 8-7 form coll with BM522 ldg CE 15-7 SOC 21-7 FH98.30

BP859 2596 CHA FF 14-2-42 39MU 16-2 452S 12-3 457S 22-3 FTR ops 4-4 FH15.50

BP860 2598 VC Spcl FF 15-2-42 39MU 24-2 47MU 17-5 *Hopetown* Malta 1-7 NWA 1-5-43 USAAF 31-10 ME 15-3-45 SOC 29-8

BP861 2600 VC Spcl FF 17-2-42 CHA 39MU 24-2 82MU 18-5 *Hopetown* Malta CE ops 19-7 SIC 22-7 FH54.20

BP862 2601 VC Spcl FF 18-2-42 CHA 39MU 24-2 66S 16-4 tyre burst ldg o/t Ibsley CB 22-5 AST SOC E 1-6 FH14.20

BP863 2605 VCT Spcl FF 21-2-42 CHA 39MU 24-2 St Frm dis FACB 20-5 SAL 312S 30-10-43 411S 27-2-44 56 OTU 30-3 57 OTU 27-6 e/fd w/u ldg Monkseat N'land CE 18-4-45 SOC 29-4

BP864 2607 VC Spcl FF 21-2-42 CHA 39MU 24-2 66S 16-4 FACB 29-12 AST 504S 26-6-43 165S 8-7 308S 10-10 1660CU 7-12-44 R&S 24-9-46

BP865 2628 CHA FF 28-2-42 39MU 8-3 C&C 23-3 *Alderamin* 4-5 Tak ME 26-6-C3 ops 4-8-43 SOC 27-9

BP866 2621 VCT CHA FF 27-2-42 BDn 28-2 comp trop trls AB320 with 90-gal o/ld tank 29MU 15-3 Malta 1-5-43 185S Malta FAC218-3-44 SOC 28-4-45

BP867 2622 CHA FF 27-2-42 6MU 8-3 47MU 22-5 *Hopetown* 26-5 Malta 1-8 249S CE ops 15- SOC 16-9

BP868 2629 CHA FF 28-2-42 8-3-42 82MU 21-5 *Hopetown* 26-5 Malta 1-8 SOC 24-6-43

BP869 2630 CHA FF 28-2-42 6MU 8-3 82MU 20-5 *Hopetown* 26-5 Malta 1-8 SOC FH8.25

BP870 2640 CHA FF 7-3-42 8MU 9-3 47MU 23-3 *Emp Hth* 29-3 Tak 4-4 Malta 8-6 C3 ops 10-1-43 FH130.40

BP871 2641 CHA FF 7-3-42 8MU 26-3 *Emp Hth* 30-3 Tak 4-4 Malta 8-6 229S FTR ops 25-8 FH91

BP872 2642 CHA FF 7-3-42 8MU 17-3 82MU 26-3 *Emp Hth* 31-3 Tak 4-4 Malta 8-6 SOC 13-8

BP873 2643 CHA FF 7-3-42 8MU 17-3 82MU 26-3 *Emp Hth* 31-3 Tak 4-4 Malta 8-6 C3 ops 16-10

BP874 2644 CHA FF 7-3-42 8MU 24-3 RAF Abb 6-4 f/f Malta e/a CE 24-4 SOC 6-5

BP875 2654 CHA FF 8-3-42 6MU 15-3 82MU 23-3 *Emp Hth* 30-3 Tak 4-4 Malta 8-6 CE ops 10-6 SOC 12-6 FH26.25

BP876 2656 CHA FF 10-3-42 6MU 15-3 47MU 27-3 *Emp Hth* 29-3 Tak 4-4 Malta 8-6 185S CB ops 2-7 SOC 15-7 FH55.30

BP877 2665 CHA FF 13-3-42 6MU 15-3 82MU 26-3 *Emp Hth* 30-3 Tak 4-4 Malta CE ops 12-5 SOC 15-5

BP878 2668 CHA FF 13-3-42 6MU 15-3 47MU 27-3 *Emp Hth* 31-3 Tak 4-4 Malta CE ops 15-5 FH5.10

BP950 2676 CHA FF 14-3-42 8MU 15-3 47MU 24-3 *Emp Hth* 30-3 CE ops 1-6 SOC Malta 7-7 FH20 15

BP951 2677 CHA FF 14-3-42 8MU 15-3 47MU 24-3 *Emp Hth* 29-3 CE ops 17-5 SOC 18-5 FH12.10

BP952 2681 CHA FF 17-3-42 8MU 19-3 82MU 28-3 *Gib Guido* 7-4 Malta 8-6 C3 ops 17-11

BP953 2682 CHA FF 17-3-42 39MU 19-3 82MU 29-3 *Gib Guido* 7-4 Malta 8-6 SOC 26-5

BP954 2687 CHA FF 19-3-42 39MU 20-3 RAF Abb 11-4 f/f Malta SIC 5-5 FH6.45

BP955 2688 CHA FF 17-3-42 39MU 20-3 RAF Abb 10-4 f/f Malta FTR ops 17-10

BP956 2689 CHA FF 18-3-42 39MU 23-3 RAF Abb 11-4 f/f Malta e/a CE 20-4 SOC 6-5

BP957 2671 HEA FF 13-3-42 6MU 23-3 47MU 28-3 *Emp Hth* 31-3 Tak 4-4 Malta 8-6 CE ops 9-7 SOC 10-7 FH34.10

BP958 CHA FF 19-3-42 6MU 20-3-42 RAF Abb 10-4 f/f Malta 20-4 did not arrive Sgt Walcott missing

BP959 2697 CHA FF 20-3-42 6MU 23-3 47MU 28-3 *Sobo* Tak 1-5 ME 29-6 NAASC 31-1-43

BP960 2647 HEA FF 7-3-42 8MU 12-3 82MU 23-3 *Emp Hth* 31-3 Tak 404 FACE 10-5 SOC 12-5

BP961 2711 CHA FF 23-3-42 6MU 24-3 RAF Abb 9-4 f/f Malta 609S CB ops 24-4 SOC

BP962 2712 CHA FF 23-3-42 6MU 24-3 RAF Abb 8-4 f/f Malta 603S CA ops 1-5 SOC 5-5

BP963 2713 CHA FF 23-3-42 6MU 25-3 RAF Abb 10-4 f/f Malta e/a CE 22-4 SOC 6-5

BP964 2716 CHA FF 24-3-42 6MU 25-3 RAF Abb 10-4 f/f Malta CE ops 11-5 SOC 13-5 FH18.25

BP965 2718 CHA FF 25-3-42 6MU 26-3 RAF Abb 8-4 f/f Malta 29-4 CE ops 10-5 SOC 17-5

BP966 2725 CHA FF 26-3-42 8MU 28-3 RAF Abb 7-4 f/f Malta 1-5- ME 21-6 CE SOC 13-9

BP967 2726 CHA FF 26-3-42 8MU Malta SOC 6-5

BP968 2738 CHA FF 28-3-42 8MU 29-3 Malta SOC 5-5 FH5.50

BP969 2739 CHA FF 28-3-42 8MU 29-3 RAF Abb 8-4 f/f Malta CE ops 22-4 SOC 5-5

BP970 2740 CHA FF 28-3-42 8MU 29-3 RAF Abb 8-4 f/f Malta FTR ops 22-4 FH6.30

BP971 2748 CHA FF 29-3-42 8MU 1-4 3SLG 2-4

BP972 2749 CHA FF 29-3-42 8MU 1-4 3SLG 2-4

BP973 2755 CHA FF 1-4-42 8MU 2-4 RAF Abb 11-4 f/f Malta CE ops 25-4 SOC 10-6

BP974 2756 CHA FF 1-4-42 8MU 2-4 RAF Abb 11-4 f/f Malta e/a CE 21-4 SOC 6-5

BP975 2757 CHA FF 1-4-42 8MU 13-4 RAF Abb 11-4 f/f Malta CB ops 20-4 NWA USAAF 31-8-43 SOC 26-4-45

BP976 2758 CHA FF 1-4-42 8MU 2-4 Malta 601S 11-4 FTR ops 21-4 SOC 24-4 FH7.05

BP977 2759 CHA FF 1-4-42 39MU 2-4 RAF Abb 11-4 39MU 25-4 Malta 8-6 601S FACB 26-6 ME 1-7 NAAF 1-11-43

BP978 2760 CHA FF 1-4-42 39MU 2-4 47MU 17-4 Malta 7-5 SOC 16-5 ME 145S FAC2 17-12 Malta 1-8-43 CE ops 18-11

BP979 2779 CHA FF 7-4-42 39MU 4-4 RAF Abb 11-4 Malta 601S CB ops 30-4 SOC 7-7 FH43.20

BP980 2787 CHA FF 7-4-42 39MU 8-4 Ren 27-4 f/f Malta 8-6 SOC 13-8

BP981 2781 CHA FF 7-4-42 39MU 8-4 47MU 17-4 *SS485* 9-5 Ind ME 415S FTR ops 4-4-43

BP9982 2785 CHA FF 8-4-42 6MU 10-4 47MU 16-4 *SS485* 9-5 Ind ME 1-8 CB ops 22-8 Malta 602S 7-3-43 FAC2 1-11-43

BP983 2786 CHA FF 8-4-42 6MU 10-4 47MU 15-4 *Ripley* 26-4 Tak ME 20-6 FACB 17-7 to 4382

BP984 2797 CHA FF 10-4-42 6MU 12-4 82MU 18-4 *SS483* 9-5 ME SOC 23-9

BP985 2798 CHA FF 10-4-42 6MU 12-4 47MU 20-4 *SS485* 9-5 Ind ME 1-8 mods at 103MU Aboukir for H/A interception see page SOC 27-10-44

BP986 2799 CHA FF 10-4-42 6MU 1204 47MU 20-4 *SS485* 9-5 Ind ME C3 ops 22-10

BP987 2795 CHA FF 11-4-42 6MU 12-4 82MU 17-4 *SS483* 9-5 P Sudan 1-8-43 SOC 29-8-46

BP988 2803 CHA FF 11-4-42 6MU 12-4 32MU 17-4 *SS483* 9-5 ME 1-8-43 FAC3 26-8

BP989 2812 CHA FF 13-4-42 8MU 14-4 RAF Abb 26-4 f/f Malta 8-6 C3 ops 16-10

BP990 2821 CHA FF 15-4-42 16-4 RAF Abb 26-4 f/f Malta 249S 8-6 CE ops 7-7 SOC 8-7 FH55.10

BP991 2815 CHA FF 14-4-42 8MU 15-4 Malta 27-4 CE ops 11-5 SOC 13-5 FH13.20

BP992 2828 CHA FF 16-4-42 8MU 17-4 Malata 27-4 CA ops 14-7 CB ops 17-10

BP993 2822 CHA FF 15-4-42 8MU 16-4 RAF Abb 26-4 Malta 8-6 CE ops 18-6SOC

BR series all VCT M46 unless otherwise indicated

BR106 2636 HPA FF 7-3-42 8MU 8-3 47MU 23-3 *Emp Hth* 31-3 Tak 4-4 Malta 8-6 SOC 21-6 FH13.20

BR107 2635 HPA FF 3-3-42 8MU 8-3 47MU 23-3 *Emp Hth* 31-3 Tak 4-4 Malta 8-6 CB ops 18-9 SOC 5-2-43 FH122.25

BR108 2637 HPA FF 7-3-42 8MU 8-3 47MU 23-3 *Emp Hth* 31-3 Tak 4-4 Malta 8-6 603S s/dn by bf109 CE 8-7 F/lt Sanders safe SOC FH35.05 wreck found by divers Marsalform Bay 1968 main parts salvaged extant Valletta Museum Malta

BR109 2638 HPA FF 7-3-42 39MU 9-3 47MU 24-3 *Emp Hth* 31-3 Tak 4-4 Malta 8-6 C3 ops 21-3-43 SOC 21-3

BR110 2663 HPA FF 14-3-42 39MU 14-3 47MU 24-3 *Emp Hth* 31-3 Tak 4-4 Malta 8-6 CB ops 30-7 NWA 1-5-43 ME 15-3-45 SOC 29-8-46

BR111 2639 HPA FF 7-3-42 39MU 14-3 47MU 24-3

Emp Hth 29-3 Tak 4-4 Malta 8-6 FTR ops 11-7 SOC 12-7 FH56.15

BR112 2669 HPA FF 13-3-42 39MU 15-3 RAF Abb 10-4 f/f Malta 185S CB ops 6-5 CE ops 9-9 SOC 10-9

BR113 2678 HPA FF 14-3-42 39MU 16-3 82MU 28-3 *Sobo* 18-4 Tak 1-5 ME 601S 22-6 C2 ops 2-10-43 NAAF 1-11 sold Turk 29-3-45

BR114 2664 HPA Irene FF 12-3-42 39MU 14-3 C&C 23-3 mods *Alderamin* 4-5 Tak ME 26-6 CB ops 13-9 mods at 103 Aboukir for H/A interception MAAF 31-3-44 SOC 31-8 FAF CR 2/33 11-7-44 Dest by Hak 1-8-44

BR115 2667 HPA FF 13-3-42 39MU 16-3 47MU 28-3 Tak 4-4 Malta 126S 8-6 CB ops 7-7 SOC 1-8

BR116 2668 HPA FF 13-3-42 6MU 19-3 RAF Abb 8-4 f/f Malta CE ops 6-5 SOC 8-6

BR117 2700 HPA FF 20-3-42 6MU 23-3 RAF Abb 8-4 f/f Malta 185S CE ops 20-7 SOC 21-7 FH68.35

BR118 2684 HPA FF 17-3-42 6MU 23-3 47-MU 29-3 *Ripley* 29-4 ME 22-6 601S CE ops 2-9 SOC 23-9

BR119 2701 HPA FF 20-3-42 6MU 24-3 82MU 28-3 *Gib Guido* 7-4 Malta 185S 8-6 FACB 10-7 MAAF 21-6-45 SOC 23-8

BR120 2696 HPA FF 19-3-42 25-3 RAF Abb 10-4 f/f Malta SOC 6-8

BR121 2702 HPA FF 20-3-42 6MU 25-3 RAF Abb 8-10 f/f Malta SOC 29-6

BR122 2692 HPA FF 19-3-42 39MU 24-3 82MU 26-3 Tak 8-4 126S CE ops 9-8 10-8

BR123 2703 HPA FF 20-3-42 8MU 24-3 82MU 26-3 RAF Abb 7-4 f/f Malta SOC 21-5

BR124 2719 HPA FF 25-3-42 9MU 26-3 82MU 26-3 RAF Abb 6-4 f/f Malta 603S e/a SOC 28-4 F44.50

BR125 2730 HPA FF 25-3-42 28-3 RAF Abb 8-4 f/f Malta CE ops 26-4 SOC 5-5 FH15.50

BR126 2731 HPA FF 25-3-42 8MU 28-3 RAF Abb 12-4 f/f Malta 185S 8-6 CB ops 15-6 SOC 31-7 FH39.30

BR127 2732 HPA FF 27-3-42 8MU 28-3 Malta CE ops 12-5 SOC 7-7

BR128 2750 HPA FF 30-3-42 8MU 1-4 3SLG 2-4 Malta 29-4 CE ops 12-5 23-7 FH68.10

BR129 2733 HPA FF 8MU 28-3 RAF Abb 8-4 f/f Malta e/a CE 22-4 SOC 6-5

BR130 2743 HPA FF 28-3-42 8MU 29-3 Malta 1-5 C2 ops 14-10 NWA FACE 1-10-43 USAAF 31-10

BR131 2751 HPA FF 29-3-42 8MU 1-4 3SLG 2-4 Malta 27-4 CB ops 12-5 FTR ops 10-4-43 FH157.50

BR132 2764 HPA FF 1-4-42 8MU 2-4 47MU 16-4 *SS485* 9-5 Ind ME 601S cd P/o Llewellyn safe 31-10

BR133 2777 HPA FF 3-4-42 8MU 4-4 RAF Abb 26-4 Malta 8-6 FACE 10-5 SOC FH8.20 NAASC 31-10-43 SOC 8-3-44

BR134 2768 HPA FF 2-4-42 8MU 3-4 82MU 20-4 *SS483* 9-5 ME 1-8 NAAF 1-11-43 FAF CR 2/33 2-5-44 Des by bomb dropped from P-40 13-5-44

BR135 2778 HPA FF 3-4-42 82MU 18-4 *SS483* 9-5 ME SOC 10-12

BR136 2769 HPA FF 2-4-42 39MU 3-4 RAF Ren 28-4 f/f Malta 8-6 ME 1-7 FAC3 2-4-43

BR137 2780 HPA FF 3-4-42 39MU 4-4 RAF Ren 28-4 f/f Malta 8-6 SOC 15-5

BR138 2784 HPA FF 8-4-42 39MU 10-4 R-RH 7-5 con to MkIX M61 12MU 28-2-43 403S 16-3 FAAC 3-4 ROS 416S 28-4 AAST 7-5 mods 421S 15-5 CAC opsROS 405ARF HAL 18-8 165S 6-10 131S 19-3-44 Farn 3-7 grd resonance and vibrograph trls, comp with AB196, fitt mock-up eng.

BR139 2782 HPA FF 10-4-42 R-RH 12-4 con to MkIX M61 contract R-R M32D/aircraft/2140 9MU 9-6 611S 25-7 e/fd c/s ldg Martlesham o/t 29-8 SOC 17-9

BR140 2788 HPA FF 10-4-42 R-RH 12-4 con to MkIX M61 12MU 19-6 64S 24-6 AFDU Dux 3-8 AST 7-3-43 mods 453S 2-4 129S 17-7 AST 7-8 303S 22-9-44 CAC ops 28-12 ROS 441S 3-5-54 80 OTU 6-9 FAF 14-3-45

BR141 2800 HPA FF 10-4-42 R-RH 12-4 con to MkIX M61 12MU 19-6 64S 24-6 CAC ops 23-1-43 ROS 122S 10-5 222S 19-5 AST 17-6 M63 instal 19S 24-8 CB ops 9-10 recat E 18-10

BR142 2806 HPA FF 11-4-42 R-RH 12-4 con to MkIXC M61 12-6 64S 22-6 dam ops 31-8 AST FTR ops 13-2-43 FH196.40

BR143 2807 HPA FF 11-4-42 R-RH 12-4 con to MkIX M61 306S 13-11 ROS 30-11 316S 14-3-43 FTR ops 17-6

BR160 2625 EA M45M Bangalore I FF 17-2-43 9MU 28-2 501S 14-5 118S 2-8 504S 19-10 ROS 13-3-43 165S 8-7 AST 5-10 26S 13-3-44 53 OTU 4-10 ROS 3-1-45 PAL 14-9 Fire in air f/ld CAC SOC 21-9

BR161 2789 EA FF 10-4-42 39MU 12-4 RAF Ren 28-4 Malta 8-6 C3 ops 3-3-43

BR163 2631 EA FF 28-2-42 39MU 15-3 47MU 29-3 Tak 4-4 CE ops 16-6 SOC 18-6 FH19.40

BR165 2634 HPA Holmewood III FF 2-3-42 39MU 15-3 47MU 24-3 Tak 4-4 Malta 219S 4-6 CE ops 7-7 SOC 8-7 FH26.25

BR166 2652 EA FF 7-3-42 8MU 15-3 47MU 24-3 Tak 4-4 Malta 8-6 FAF 31-10-43 CE ops 19-9-44

BR168 2632 EA Hamadryad FF 28-2-42 9MU 8-3 501S 7-5 FTR ops i/sea 7-9 FH95.15

BR169 2650 EA FF 7-3-42 8MU 15-3 82MU 25-3 *Emp Hth* 29-3 Tak 4-4 Malta 8-6 603S CA ops 17-5 FACE 18-8 SOC FH68.25

BR170 2651 EA FF 7-3-42 8MU 15-3 82MU 17-3 *Guido* 7-4 Gib Malta 8-6 SOC 7-8 FH62.35

BR173 2660 EA FF 12-3-42 39MU 15-3 82MU 25-3 *Emp Hth* 31-3 Tak 4-4 Malta 8-6 C3 ops 14-10

BR175 2658 EA FF 12-3-42 39MU 15-3 82MU 25-3 *Emp Hth* 31-3 Tak 4-4 Malta 8-6 ME 1-7 C2 ops 1-9 CE 14-12-44 BBOC 21-6-45 SOC 29-8-46

BR176 2679 EA FF 16-3-42 6MU 17-3 RAF Abb 9-4 f/f Malta C3 ops 15-10 Farn Jly'44

BR177 2680 CHA FF 15-3-42 6MU 17-3 82MU 28-3 *Emp Hth* 31-3 Tak 4-4 Malta 4-6 SOC 19-4-43 FH159.10

BR179 2674 EA FF 13-3-42 39MU 15-3 47MU 24-3 *Emp Hth* 29-3 Tak 4-4 SOC 26-6

BR180 2686 EA FF 18-3-42 8MU 18-3 RAF Abb 10-4 f/f Malta FACE 22-4 SOC 6-5

BR182 2690 EA FF 19-3-42 39MU 23-3 RAF Abb 8-4 f/f Malta SOC 29-6

BR183 2691 EA FF 19-3-42 39MU 23-3 RAF Abb 8-4 f/f Malta SOC 29-6

BR184 2699 EA FF 21-3-42 8MU 24-3 RAF Abb 7-4 f/f Malta 249S 2-7 CE ops SOC 3-7 FH54.50

BR185 2695 EA FF 19-3-42 8MU 26-3 f/f Malta CA ops 3-5 SOC 12-5

BR187 2704 EA FF 21-3-42 8MU 24-3 RAF Abb 8-4 f/f Malta CE ops 4-5 SOC 6-5 FH17.05

BR188 2714 EA FF 24-3-42 8MU 25-3 82MU 26-3-42 Malta e/a CE 22-4 601S s/dn F/Sgt Schofield aban a/c inj 2-9

BR190 2705 EA FF 21-3-42 8MU 20-3 39MU 23-3 RAF Abb 10-4 f f Malta SOC 13-8 FH13.20

BR192 2717 EA FF 23-4-42 8MU 26-3 RAF Abb 8-4 f/f Malta 17-4 CA ops 29-4 ME 1-7 FACB 9-8 NAASC 31-10-43 SOC 26-4-45

BR194 2723 EA FF 26-3-42 8MU 28-3 RAF Abb 7-4 f/f Malta 249S cd Tak May '42 ME 1-7-43

BR195 2724 EA FF 26-3-42 8MU 27-3 RAF Abb 6-4 f/f Malta SAL 2-5 82MU 1-10 *Heribonaka* 30-10 Tak 1-12 ME 31-12 NA 30-11-43 MAAF 30-6-45

BR196 2728 EA FF 27-3-42 39MU 27-3 RAF Abb 11-4 f/f Malta 8-6 SOC 15-5

BR198 2729 EA FF 27-3-42 39MU 29-3 RAF Ren 26-4 *Emp Con* 10-6 Malta CE ops 8-7 SOC FH17.35

BR199 2736 EA FF 27-3-42 39MU 28-3 RAF Abb 11-4 f/f Malta CE ops 26-4 SOC 17-9

BR201 2742 EA FF 28-3-42 8MU 29-3 47MU 20-4 *SS485* 9-5 Ind ME 1-8 NAAF 218Grp 30-11-43 SOC 8-3-44

BR202 2752 EA LF VC FF 1-4-42 B&P 1-4 first Spit to be tested with 170-gal slipper o/ld fuel tank. Oil tank mods., BDn 10-6 fuel cons and range tests with 170-gal tank plus an additional 29-gal internal tank. Ttl fuel tankage 284-gals. B&P 6-7 M47 instal Farn 18-8 BDn 30-8 as rogue Spit 9MU 11-12 82MU 15-4-43 Casa 2-5 SOC 26-4-45

BR203 2747 EA FF 29-3-42 39MU 1-4 RAF Abb 11-4 f/f Malta 185S CE ops 20-7 SOC 23-7 FH29.30

BR204 2765 EA FF 1-4-42 39MU 3-4 RAF Abb 11-4 f/f Malta e/a CE 22-4 SOC 6-5

BR226 2710 HEA FF 23-3-42 39MU 29-3 RAF Abb 12-4 f/f Malta 8-6 CB ops 18-5 NA 1-6-43 Malta 1-11 CE ops 4-5-45 SOC 26-5 BBOC 21-6 SOC 30-8

BR227 2735 HEA FF 27-3-42 29-3 RAF Abb 11-4 f/f Malta 249S CB ops 8-7 SOC 9-7 FH7.45

BR228 2761 HEA FF 1-4-42 37MU 3-4 47MU 18-4 *SS485* 9-5 Ind ME 1-8 NA 218Grp 30-11-43 SOC 8-3-44

BR229 2811 HEA FF 12-4-42 39MU 14-4 RAF Ren 29-4 Malta 8-6 SOC 15-5

BR230 2793 HEA FF 10-4-42 39MU 18-4 RAF Ren 29-4 *Emp Con* 10-6 Malta CE ops 16-6 SOC 18-6 FH17.50

BR231 2870 HEA FF 27-4-42 39MU 29-4 VA tropicalised 3-5 47MU 6-5 *Emp Con* 10-5 Malta CE ops 8-6 SOC 9-6

BR232 2873 HEA FF 30-4-42 39MU 30-4 VA tropicalised 3-5 47MU 6-5 *Emp Con* 10-6 ME 1-7 601S FTR ops 6-7

BR233 2912 HEA FF 6-5-42 39MU 7-5 47MU 16-5 *Hopetarn* 26-5 Malta 249S CE ops 8-7 SOC 9-7 FH25.05

BR234 2979 HEA FF 27-5-42 39MU 28-5 82MU 10-6 *Nigers* 20-6 Tak 28-7 ME 1-8 SOC 13-9 M61 HA fitd plus other mods at 103MU Aboukir for H/Alt interception

BR235 3006 HEA FF 31-5-42 8MU 2-6 47MU 18-6 *Nigers* 20-6 Tak ME 22-7 74S C2 ops 6-9 NA 218Grp 30-11-43 SOC 29-6-44

BR236 3024 M45 HEA FF 5-6-42 8MU 8-6 55MU 8-7 *Emp Clive* 19-7 Malta 3-8 SOC 27-11 FH79.50

BR237 3038 HEA FF 13-6-42 8MU 22-6 215MU 19-7 Aust 23-10

BR238 3069 HEA FF 21-6-42 6MU 22-6 215MU 19-7 *Hoperidge* 4-8 Aust 23-10 457S A58-16

BR239 3080 HEA FF 24-6-42 6MU 26-6 47MU 16-7 Aust 18-10

BR240 3109 HEA FF 30-6-42 6MU 1-7 215MU 24-7 *Hoperidge* 4-8 Aust 23-10

BR241 3111 HEA FF 1-7-42 6MU 4-7 215MU 25-7 *Hoperidge* 4-8 Aust 23-10

BR242 2753 EA FF 1-4-42 39MU 2-4 RAF Abb 11-4 f/f Malta 8-6 126S SOC 17-7

BR244 2774 EA FF 3-4-42 8MU 4-4 RAF Abb 26-4 f/f Malta 8-6 126S SOC 11-7

BR245 2771 EA FF 2-4-42 8MU 3-4 82MU 18-4 *SS483* 9-5 ME 601S 1-8 CB ops 2-9 SOC 8-2-45

BR246 2766 EA FF 2-4-42 8MU 3-4 RAF Abb 12-4 47MU 3-5 *Emp Con* 10-6 Malta 249S CE ops 13-8 SOC 14-8 FH35.15

BR248 2773 EA FF 3-4-42 8MU 4-4 RAF Abb 26-4 f/f Malta 8-6 CE ops 9-5 SOC 10-5 FH12.15

BR249 2783 EA FF 7-4-42 CRD VA WD 12-4 CE 13-5 SOC 22-5 Farn 29-1-43 BDn 22-8 trop mods & gun heat trls. Spin trls wityh 30-gal jett tanks. Comp trls with BR288

BR251 2790 EA FF 10-4-42 39MU 12-4 RAF Ren 28-4 Malta 8-6 CB ops 9-5 CE ops 7-7 SOC 8-7 FH26.25

BR253 2791 EA FF 10-4-42 39MU 12-4 82MU 20-4 *SS483* 9-5 ME 1-7 SOC 9-8-45

BR254 2792 EA FF 10-4-42 39MU 12-4 47MU 4-5 *Emp Con* 10-6 Malta 1-7 C3 ops 15-10

BR256 2802 EA FF 11-4-42 39MU 12-4 SAL 6-5 45MU 1-10 4FPP e/fd w/u ldg on del flt Kinloss-H Ercall nr Ballater Angus 28-11-42

BR282 2805 EA FF 11-4-42 39MU 12-4 RAF Ren 27-4 Malta CE ops 10-5 SOC 12-5 BDn Jan '43 cool trls and comb rating in connection with trop mods

BR283 2814 EA FF 14-4-42 39MU 15-4 RAF Ren 28-4 f/f Malta 8-6 SOC 8-4 FH54

BR284 2809 EA FF 11-4-42 39MU 12-4 82MU 20-4 *SS483* 9-5 ME 6-10 SOC 26-3-43

BR285 2813 EA FF 14-4-42 39MU 15-4 RAF Ren 29-4 Malta 8-6 CE ops 2-6 SOC 3-6 FH65.05

BR288 2823 EA FF 15-4-42 CRD V WDn 16-4 BDn 22-7 trop mods; gun heat trls; spin trls with 30-gal jett tanks. 27-9 mods to ammunition heat syst; cool trls at comb rating comp trls with BR251. 222MU 7-12 *Hamble VI* 20-12 Gib 13-1-43 NWA 28-2 Malta 43S 1-7 FTR ops 4-7

BR290 2827 EQA FF 16-4-42 8MU 17-4 Malta 27-4 CB ops 15-5 NWA 1-5-43 Malta 1-7 Sicily 1-8 ME 30-9 SOC

BR291 2824 EA FF 15-4-42 8MU 16-4 RAF Abb 26-4 f/f Malta 8-6 CE ops 14-5 SOC 15-5 FH15.40

BR292 2834 EA FF 17-4-42 8MU 18-4 Malta 185 S 27-4 e/a CB 24-5 CE ops 14-8 FH61.45

BR293 2847 EA FF 20-4-42 6MU 26-4 RAF Ren 29-4 Malta 9-6 CB ops 12-5 SOC 14-10 bboc 14-10 C3 ops 30-11 FH25.40

BR294 2835 EA FF 17-4-42 8MU 17-4 Malta 185S 30-4 CE ops 2-7 SOC 3-7 FH55.10

BR295 2858 EA FF 25-4-42 6MU 26-4 47MU 4-5 *Emp Con* 10-6 Malta 185S 1-7 CE ops 18-7 SOC 8-12 FH55.55

BR296 2840 EA FF 18-4-42 8MU 19-4 SOC no trace 22-6-46

BR299 2862 EA FF 25-4-42 6MU 26-4 RAF Ren 28-4 SAL mr 5-5 215MU 22-11 *Bluff V* 3-12 Gib 31-1 NWA 28-2-43 Malta 1-6 NA 1-1-44 ME 21-6-45 SOC 30-4-47

BR300 2859 EA FF 25-4-42 6MU 26-4 RAF Ren 29-4 Malta 8-6 CE ops 10-6 SOC 11-6 FH16.30

BR301 2853 EA FF 24-4-42 6MU 25-4 RAF Ren 28-4 f/f Malta 249S 8-6 CE ops 29-7 SOC 31-7 FH54.20

BR303 2860 EA FF 25-4-42 6MU 26-4 RAF Ren 28-4 f/f Malta 8-6 CE ops 28-7 SOC 30-7

BR305 2879 EA FF 29-4-42 39MU 30-4 CHA 3-5 47MU 7-5 *Emp Con* 10-6 Malta 185S FACE 19-7 SOC 20-7 FH45.25

BR306 2863 EA FF 6MU 25-4-42 6MU 26-4 RAF Ren 29-4 f/f Malta 8-6 CE ops 15-6 SOC 16-6 FH47.45

BR308 2880 EA FF 29-4-42 39MU 30-4 CHA 3-5 allot Malta on *Emp Con* missing f/f from Porth 3-6

BR311 2901 EA FF 5-5-42 6MU 5-5 RAF Ren 6-5 47MU 7-5 *Emp Con* 10-6 Malta 1-7 C2 ops 4-10 C3 26-10

BR312 2884 EA FF 30-4-42 39MU 1-5 VA 3-5 8MU 6-5 47MU 7-5 *Emp Con* 10-6 Malta CE ops 8-6 SOC 7-7

BR313 2881 EA FF 30-4-42 39MU 1-5 allot Malta on *Emp Con* missing f/f from Porth 3-6

BR315 2893 EA FF 3-5-42 39MU 3-5 47MU 6-5 *Emp Con* 10-6 CE ops 27-6 SOC 29-6

BR316 2894 EA FF 3-5-42 39MU 3-5 47MU 6-5 *Emp Con* 10-6 Malta 249S CB ops 27-7 SOC FH39.25

BR317 2900 EA FF 5-5-42 6MU 5-5 RAF Ren 6-5 47MU *Emp Con* 10-6 Malta 185S FACB 3-7 CE ops 7-7 SOC 8-7 FH13.55

BR320 2902 EA FF 5-5-42 8MU 5-5 47MU 7-5 *Emp Con* 10-6 Malta CE ops 29-6 SOC 30-6 FH28.05

BR321 2903 EA FF 6-5-42 8MU 6-5 47MU 8-5 *Emp Con* 10-6 Malta 185S CE ops 2-8 SOC FH74.55

BR322 2904 EA FF 6-5-42 8MU 6-5 47MU 7-5 allot Malta on *Emp Con* miss f/f from Porth 3-6

BR323 2905 EA FF 6-5-42 8MU 6-5 82MU 17-5 *Hopetarn* 26-5 Malta 249S CE ops 12-7 SOC FH44.05

BR324 2906 EA FF 6-5-42 6MU 6-5 38MU 12-5 47MU 17-5 *Hopetarn* 26-5 Malta 249S CE ops 12-7 SOC FH27.40

BR325 2907 EA FF 7-5-42 6MU 7-5 82MU 16-5 *Hopetarn* ME 601S 1-7 FTR ops 10-7

BR327 2924 EA FF 9-5-42 6MU 9-5 47MU 17-5 *Hopetarn* 26-5 Malta SOC 7-7 FH13-30

BR328 2926 EA FF 10-5-42 6MU 11-5 47MU 17-5 *Hopetarn* 26-5 Malta 1-7 FACB 9-10 SOC 12-2-43

BR344 2829 CHA FF 11-5-42 6MU 18-4 RAF Ren 28-4 Malta 8-6 SOC 17-5

BR345 2837 CHA FF 17-4-42 6MU 19-4 RAF Ren 27-4 Malta 8-6 C3 ops 21-3-43 SOC 22-3

BR346 2838 CHA FF 18-4-42 6MU 19-4 RAF Ren 27-4 f/f Malta 8-6 SOC 15-5-43

BR347 2839 CHA FF 18-4-42 6MU 19-4 RAF Ren 27-4 Malta 8-6 SOC 15-5 FH59.40

BR348 2848 CHA FF 22-4-42 6MU 24-4 RAF Ren 28-4 Malta 8-6 SOC 10-6

BR349 2849 CHA FF 22-4-42 6MU 24-4 RAF Ren 28-4 Malta 8-6 CE ops 14-5 SOC 15-5 FH17.50

BR350 2850 CHA FF 22-4-42 6MU 24-4 RAF Ren 29-4 Malta 8-6

BR351 2854 CHA FF 24-4-42 BDn 26-8-42 cool and comb rating trls with trop mods in comp with BR288 39MU 6-11 222MU 5-12 *SS647* 19-12 Gib 6-2-43 NWA 25-2 Malta 1-7 Sic 1-9 NAASC 31-10 SOC 30-6-44

BR352 2855 CHA FF 22-4-42 6MU 25-4 RAF Ren 28-4 Malta 8-6 SOC 18-5

BR353 2856 CHA FF 25-4-42 6MU 25-4 RAF Ren 28-4 Malta 8-6 SOC 18-6

BR354 2857 CHA FF 25-4-42 6MU 25-4 RAF Ren 28-4 Malta 8-6 FTR 25-5 FH19.30

BR355 2868 CHA FF 26-4-42 39MU 27-4 47MU 4-5 *Emp Con* 10-6 Malta 126S FTR ops 9-7

BR356 2875 CHA FF 29-4-42 39MU 30-4 47MU 5-5 *Emp Con* 10-6 Malta 126S FTR ops 2-7 SOC 3-7 FH31.10

BR357 2888 CHA FF 1-5-42 8MU 2-5 47MU 5-5 *Emp Con* 10-6 Malta 126S 8-6 CE ops 4-8 SOC 6-8

BR358 2895 CHA FF 4-5-42 8MU 5-5 47MU 7-5 allot Malta on *Emp Con* miss on f/f from Porth 3-6

BR359 2876 CHA FF 29-4-42 39MU 30-4 CHA 3-5 tropicalised 47MU 7-5 *Emp Con* 10-6 Malta 1-7 SOC 26-8 FH57.15

BR360 2877 CHA FF 30-4-42 39MU 1-5 CHA 3-5 tropicalised 47MU 7-5 *Emp Con* 10-6 Malta 1-7 CE ops 15-6 SOC 18-6

BR361 2885 CHA FF 30-4-42 8MU 2-5 47MU 13-6 *Nigers* 20-6 ME 30-9 SOC 1-12-43

BR362 2889 CHA FF 1-5-42 8MU 2-5 47MU 5-5 *Emp Con* 15-6 Malta 185S CB ops 2-8 SOC 3-8 FH27-60

BR363 2890 CHA FF 2-5-42 39MU 5-5 47MU 7-5 *Emp Con* 10-6 Malta 1-7 601S FTR Sgt Lusty missing 31-8

BR364 2899 CHA FF 6-5-42 6MU 6-5 47MU 7-5 *Emp Con* 10-6 Malta 249S CE ops 9-7 SOC 11-7 FH25.25

BR365 2909 CHA FF 7-5-42 6MU 7-5 82MU 19-5 *Hopetarn* 26-5 Malta 1-7 CB ops 2-7 NA 1-6-43 ME 25-2-45 SOC 1-1-46

BR366 2910 CHA FF 7-5-42 6MU 7-5 47MU 17-5 *Hopetarn* 26-5 Malta 126S CE ops 10-8 SOC 17-8

BR367 2916 CHA FF 8-5-42 6MU 8-5 82MU 19-5 *Hopetarn* 26-5 Malta 249S CE ops 30-6 SOC 2-7 bboc 124S air cool with BR319 ldg Houghton Sussex CAC 15-10 FH14.50

BR368 2917 CHA FF 9-5-42 6MU 9-5 47MU 17-5 *Hopeturn* 26-5 Malta 185S 1-7 FACB 10-8 C3 ops 12-10

BR369 2816 HPA FF 14-4-42 R-RH 16-4 con to MkIX M61 340S 29-11 AST mods 22-2-43 341S 9-3 e/fd on app BHll w/u ldg CB 25-3 recat E

BR370 2817 HPA FF 14-4-42 R-RH 16-4 con to MkIX M61 12MU 26-6 64S 9-7 AST mods 18-2-43 453S fuel shortage cd/ld Southchurch Essex CE 29-3

BR371 2820 HPA 15-4-42 R-RH 16-4 M61 con to MkIX 6FPP e/fd on t/o Huck on del flt BHll w/u ldg CE 13-10 SOC 19-10

BR372 2830 HPA FF 16-4-42 CRD HAL 17-4 fitt double trailing edge braking flaps one section moved up other down. Farn 5-5-43 for trls in response to RAF request for some form of air brake to enable Spit to decelerate and prevent overshooting during comb. HAL 30-6 instal of upper surface dive brakes & drag reduction mods. Farn 22-10 for trls with same. Flaps took one second to actuate at 200mph, four secs at 400mph closing flaps took two and 8 secs respectively. Wt penalty 110lb Dive brakes always used in conjunction with flaps. Peak deceleration of 5G at 400mph but pilots reported target could be kept in gun sight during comb manoeuvres. BDn AFDU 9-3-44 service trls with 57 & 61 OTU Fus bomb rack fitt and dive bombing trls using brake and flaps continued until Feb '45 57 OTU 8-2-45 CE 8-6 SOC 3-8 The strengthened flaps were fitt to a number of F MkVIII airframes and proved operationally useful for steepening dvs onto grd targets

BR373 2833 HPA FF 17-4-42 8MU 17-4 47MU 7-6 *Emp Shack* 12-6 Malta 1-8 C2 ops 15-10 SOC 9-2-43 FH14-10

BR374 2844 HPA FF 18-4-42 9MU 20-4 82MU 6-6 *Guido* 12-6 Malta 1-8 185S CE ops 13-9 SOC 14-9

BR375 2845 HPA FF 22-4-42 9MU 23-4 501S 15-5 47MU 7-6 *Emp Shack* 12-6 Malta 1-8 NA 1-6-43 ME 1-8-44 SOC 9-8-45

BR376 2846 HPA FF 22-4-42 9MU 23-4 82MU 6-6 *Guido* 12-6 Malta 1-8 185S CB ops 14-9 FTR ops Dec '42 FH91.05

BR377 2846 HPA FF 26-4-42 9MU 27-4 VA tropicalised 47MU 7-5 *Emp Con* 10-6 Malta 1-7 CB ops 2-7 C3 12-10

BR378 2864 HPA FF 25-4-42 9MU 26-4 47MU 8-6 *Emp Dar* 29-6

BR379 2867 HPA FF 26-4-42 6MU 27-4 82MU 16-5 *Hopetarn* 26-5 Malta 249S 1-7 CB ops 14-7 CE ops 4-10 SOC 5-10

BR380 2896 HPA FF 4-5-42 6MU 4-5 RAF Ren 6-5 47MU 6-5 *Emp Con* 10-6 Malta 1-7 NEA 1-5-43 Italy 1-11 ME 15-3-45 SOC 27-6-46

BR381 2882 EA FF 30-4-42 6-5 47MU 8-5 *Emp Con* 10-6 CE ops 16-6 SOC 18-6

BR382 2883 HPA FF 30-4-42 6MU 6-5 82MU 17-5 *Hopetarn* 26-5 Malta CE ops 25-6

BR383 2897 HPA FF 4-5-42 6MU 4-5 RAF Ren 6-5 47MU 6-5 *Emp Con* 10-6 Malta 1-7 SOC 25-9

BR384 2898 HPA FF 5-5-42 9MU 5-5 47MU 7-5 *Emp Con* 10-6 Malta 1-7 ME 601S 21-6-45 CE 15-8 SOC 13-9

BR385 2911 HPA FF 7-5-42 9MU 7-5 82MU 16-5 *Hopetarn* 26-5 CE ops 23-6 SOC 24-6 FH19.10

BR386 2923 HPA FF 9-5-42 39MU 10-5 47MU 4-6 *Stir Cas* 19-6 Aust 25-8

BR387 2925 HPA FF 9-5-42 39MU 10-5 47MU 16-5 *Hopetarn* 26-5 Malta 1-7 FAC2 16-3-43 NA 1-7 FAF GR 2/33 2-5-44 SOC 12-7-45

BR388 2929 HPA FF 11-5-42 11-5 82MU 16-5 *Hopetarn* 26-5 Malta e/e 9-6 SOC 7-7

BR389 2934 HPA FF 14-5-42 37MU 15-5 82MU 13-6 *Nigers* 20-6 Tak 28-7 ME 1-8 FAC3 16-12-43

BR390 2935 HPA FF 12-5-42 37MU 15-5 82MU 10-6 *Nigers* 20-6 Tak Me 18-7 FAC2 29-9 SOC 30-9

BR391 2946 HPA FF 16-5-42 37MU 17-5 FACA 24-5 234S 29-11 602S 25-1-43 412S 19-4 317S 26-8 312S 26-8 FAAC 14-1-444 ROS 441S 27-2 56 OTU 30-3 57 OTU 27-6 strk rear of AB921 Boul CAC 22-2-45 ROS 567S 7-6 SOC 21-12

BR392 2958 HPA FF 20-5-42 37MU 22-5 82MU 14-6 *Nigers* 20-6 Tak ME 18-7 FTR ops 4-10

BR393 2959 HPA FF 20-5-42 37MU 24-5 47MU 12-6 *Nigers* 20-6 Tak 4-8 ME 17-8 FTR ops 13-1-43

BR459 2918 CHA FF 9-5-42 39MU 9-5 47MU 17-5 *Hopetarn* 26-5 ME 601S 1-7 CE ops 16-7 SOC 25-7

BR460 2919 CHA FF 9-5-42 39MU 10-5 47MU 16-5 *Hopetarn* 26-5 Malta 185S CE ops 20-7 SOC 21-7 FH32.50

BR461 2930 CHA FF 13-5-42 39MU 14-5 82MU 18-5 *Hopetarn* 26-5 Malta 1-7 C2 ops Sep '42 NA 1-6-43 SOC 26-4-45

BR462 2944 CHA FF 16-5-42 39MU 16-5 47MU 2-6 *Stir Cast* 19-6 Aust 25-8 457S A58-23

BR463 2942 CHA FF 15-5-42 39MU 16-5 47MU 20-5 *Hopetarn* 26-5 Malta 185S 1-7 CB ops 2-7 SOC Jan '43

BR464 2943 CHA FF 15-5-42 6MU 17-5 47MU 22-5 *Hopetarn* 26-5 Malta 1-7 C3 ops 12-10

BR465 2951 CHA FF 16-5-42 6MU 17-5 82MU 21-5 *Hopetarn* 26-5 Malta 126S CE ops 3-7 SOC 6-7

BR466 2952 CHA FF 19-5-42 6MU 19-5 82MU 1-6 *Nigers* 20-6 Tak ME 15-7 FA 26-8 SOC 11-9

BR467 2957 CHA FF 20-5-42 6MU 20-5 82MU 14-6 *Nigers* 20-6 Tak ME 92S 16-7 FAC2 27-8 SOC 30-9

BR468 2945 CHA FF 16-5-42 5MU 17-5 215MU 23-6 *Hoperange* 4-8 Aust 23-10 457S A58-24

BR469 2950 CHA FF 16-5-42 8MU 17-5 47MU 15-6 *Nigers* 20-6 Tak 28-7 ME 1-8 SOC 29-3-46

BR470 2964 CHA FF 21-5-42 8MU 22-5 82MU 4-6 *Nigers* 20-6 Tak ME 18-7 601S FTR ops 31-8 SOC 23-9 salvaged 1-12 SOC 29-8-46

BR471 2963 CHA FF 20-5-42 8MU 21-5 47MU 1-6 *Stir Cast* 14-6 Aust 25-8 Malta C3 ops 15-10

BR472 2965 CHA FF 21-5-42 6MU 22-5-42 47MU 15-6 *Nigers* 20-6 Tak 30-7 ME 7-10 FA FTR 23-2-43

BR473 2969 CHA FF 22-5-42 6MU 22-5 82MU 4-6 *Nigers* 20-6 Tak 18-7 ME 23-9 FAC2 13-9 SOC 31-10-43

BR474 2970 CHA FF 22-5-42 6MU 24-5 47MU 16-6 *Nigers* 20-6 Tak ME 22-7 90S FACE 1-9 SOC 23-9

BR475 2982 CHA FF 27-5-42 6MU 29-5 82MU 17-6 *Nigers* 20-6 Tak 28-7 ME 92S 1-8

BR476 2983 CHA FF 28-5-42 6MU 31-5 47MU 16-6 *Nigers* 20-6 Tak ME 24-7 FA 3-12 NA 30-11-43 FAC3 11-12

BR477 2984 CHA FF 28-5-42 6MU 31-5 47MU 15-6 *Nigers* 20-6 Tak ME 24-7 FTR ops 5-11

BR478 2985 CHA FF 28-5-42 6MU 30-5 47MU 14-6 *Nigers* 20-6 Tak ME 15-7 FTR 29-9

BR479 2989 EA FF 29-5-42 6MU 31-5 47MU 14-6 *Nigers* 20-6 Tak ME 22-7 FTR ops 12-10

BR480 2990 CHA FF 30-5-42 6MU 31-5 215MU 23-6 *Hoperange* 4-8 Aust 23-10

BR481 2992 CHA FF 30-5-42 6MU 31-5 47MU 18-6 *Nigers* 20-6 Tak ME 18-7 FTR 5-11

BR482 3003 CHA FF 31-5-42 6MU 1-6 38MU 6-7 215MU 8-7 *Emp Clive* 19-7 Malta 31-7 CE ops 17-8 SOC 19-8 FH7.45

BR483 3004 CHA FF 31-5-42 6MU 2-6 47MU 17-6 *Nigers* 20-6 Tak 25-8 ME 12-9 SOC 1-12-43

BR484 3007 CHA FF 2-6-42 6MU 4-6 47MU 17-7 *Eury* 30-7 Aust 18-10

BR485 3009 CHA FF 3-6-42 6MU 4-6 47MU 17-7 *Eury* 30-7 Aust 18-10

BR486 3010 CHA FF 4-6-42 6MU 7-6 215S 8-7 *Emp Clive* 19-7 Malta 3-8 229S CE ops 15-9 SOC 16-9

BR487 3023 CHA FF 4-6-42 6MU 8-6 47MU 17-6 *Nigers* 20-6 Tak 28-7 ME 1-8 NA 30-11-43 FA FTR 11-2-44

BR488 3025 CHA FF 6-6-42 8-6 215MU -8-7 *Emp Clive* 19-7 Malta 3-8 CE ops 29-8 SOC 31-8 FH10.15

BR489 3011 CHA FF 6-6-42 cd ff del to 39MU 6-6-42 AST SOC July

BR490 3026 CHA FF 7-6-42 6MU 8-6 47MU 17-6 *Eury* 30-7 Tak 28-7 ME 54S 1-8 Aust 457S A58-29 18-6-43 452S s/dn over Darwin FTR 30-6-43

BR491 3029 CHA FF 9-6-42 10-6 47MU 16-6 *Nigers* 20-6 Tak ME 16-7 C3 ops 13-10

BR492 3030 CHA FF 9-6-42 39MU 10-6 47MU 17-6 *Nigers* 20-6 Tak ME 92S FAC2 25-8 SOC 30-9

BR493 3031 CHA FF 11-6-42 39MU 13-6 47MU 30-6 *Eury* 26-7 Aust 18-11 457S A58-30

BR494 3035 CHA FF 12-6-42 39MU 13-6 47MU 18-6 *Nigers* 20-6 Tak ME 1-8 92S C3 ops 26-9 BAF 30-11-44 SOC 26-9-46

BR495 3036 CHA FF 13-6-42 39MU 14-6 47MU 1-7 *Eury* 30-7 Aust 18-10 NWA 28-2-43

BR496 3037 CHA FF 13-6-42 8MU 14-6 52MU 8-7 *Emp Clive* 19-7 Malta 3-8 229S FTR ops 26-8 FH12.12

BR497 3041 CHA FF 13-6-42 8MU 14-6 47MU 14-7 *Eury* 29-7 Aust 18-10

BR498 3050 CHA FF 15-6-42 8MU 14-6 52MU 8-7 *Emp Clive* 19-7 Malta 3-8 ME 31-1-45 CE SOC 13-9

BR499 3048 CHA FF 13-6-42 8MU 15-6 47MU 16-7 *Eury* 20-7 Aust 18-10 457S A58-33 FACA 11-7-43

BR515 2975 HPA FF 22-5-42 8MU 26-5 82MU 18-6 *Nigers* 20-6 Tak ME 24-7 92S FTR ops 2-9 SOC 23-9

BR516 2793 HPA FF 22-5-42 8MU 23-5 82MU 18-6 *Nigers* 20-6 Tak ME 22-7 FAC3 29-7-43

BR517 2794 HPA FF 22-5-42 8MU 23-5 47MU 16-6 *Nigers* 20-6 Tak 29-7 NAASC 31-10-43 SOC 29-2-44

BR518 2786 HPA FF 28-5-42 8MU 29-5 47MU 15-6 *Nigers* 20-6 Tak ME 24-7 92S CE ops 21-8 SOC 10-9

BR519 2993 HPA FF 30-5-42 8MU 1-6 82MU 13-6 *Nigers* 20-6 Tak ME 15-7 C2 22-10 NAAF 1-11-43 SOC 26-4-45

BR520 2994 HPA FF 30-5-42 39MU 1-6 47MU 16-6 *Nigers* 20-6 Tak ME 11-8 Malta FAC2 18-1-43 Sic 1-8 SOC 29-8

BR521 3000 HPA FF 31-5-42 39MU 1-6 47MU 17-6 *Nigers* 20-6 ME 27-9 SOC 26-9

BR522 3014 HPA FF 3-6-42 39MU 5-6 82MU 14-6 *Nigers* 20-6 Tak ME 13-7 C3 ops 19-10

BR523 3015 HPA FF 3-6-42 39MU 5-6 82MU 14-6 *Nigers* 20-6 Tak 22-7 SOC 29-8

BR524 3016 HPA FF 5-6-42 39MU 8-6 82MU 16-6 *Nigers*20-6 Tak ME 22-7 FACE 24-7

BR525 3042 HPA FF 13-6-42 6MU 14-6 215MU 8-7 Aust 23-10

BR526 3021 HPA FF 6-6-42 39MU 8-6 82MU 16-6 *Nigers* 20-6 Tak ME 24-7 SOC 29-8

BR527 3043 HPA FF 13-6-42 6MU 14-6 215MU 8-7 *Hoperidge* 4-8 Aust 23-10 457S A58-35

BR528 3044 HPA FF 13-6-42 6MU 14-6 215MU *Hoperidge* 4-8 Aust 23-10 54S s/dn over Darwin FTR 30-6-43

BR529 3053 HPA FF 15-6-42 6MU 16-6 215MU 8-7 *Emp Clive* 19-7 Malta 3-8 e/a SOC 19-8 FH44.40

BR530 3045 HPA FF 13-6-42 14-6 215MU 3-7 *Hoperidge* 4-8 Aust 23-10 54S s/dn over Darwin FTR 30-6-43

BR531 3062 HPA FF 20-6-42 6MU 21-6 215MU 21-7 *Hoperidge* 4-8 Aust 23-10 457S A58-38

BR532 3060 HPA FF 18-6-42 8MU 20-6 47MU 11-7 *Eury* 30-7 Aust 18-10

BR533 3063 HPA FF 20-6-42 8MU 21-6 47MU 11-7 *Eury* 30-7 Aust 18-10 457S A58-40

BR534 3064 HPA FF 20-6-42 39MU 21-6-42 52MU 9-7 *Emp Clive* 19-7 Malta 3-8126S FACE 4-9

BR535 3076 HPA FF 23-6-42 39MU 25-6 47MU 16-7 *Hoperidge* 4-8 Aust 28-10

BR536 3077 HPA FF 23-6-42 25-6 8MU 215MU 20-7 *Hoperidge* 4-8 Aust 23-10

BR537 3086 HPA FF 25-6-42 8MU 26-6 215MU 14-7 *Hoperidge* 4-8 Aust 23-10

BR538 3087 HPA FF 25-6-42 8MU 26-6 47MU 25-7 *Hoperidge* 4-8 Aust 23-10 457S A58-44

BR539 3088 HPA FF 27-6-42 8MU 30-6 215MU 24-7 *Hoperidge* 4-8 Aust 23-10

BR540 3105 HPA FF 29-6-42 8MU 2-7 47MU 25-7 *Hoperidge* 4-8 Aust 23-10 457S A58-46

BR541 3117 HPA FF 2-7-42 39MU 4-7 215MU 21-7 *Hoperidge* 4-8 Aust 23-10 457S A58-47 452S 1-43 457S 5-43

BR542 3125 HPA FF 5-7-42 39MU 7-7 215MU 21-7 *Hoperidge* 4-8 Aust 23-10 457S A58-48

BR543 3136 HPA FF 7-7-42 39MU 8-7 215MU 24-7 *Hoperidge* 4-8 Aust 23-10

BR544 3137 HPA FF 9-7-42 39MU 8-7 215MU 24-7 *Hoperidge* 4-8 Aust 23-10

BR545 3155 HPA FF 11-7-42 45MU 13-7 47MU 29-7 *Hoperidge* 4-8 Aust 23-10

BR546 3163 HPA FF 14-7-42 16-7 47MU 25-7 *Hoperidge* 4-8 23-10

BR547 3171 HPA FF 17-7-42 6MU 20-7 47MU 25-7 *Hoperidge* 4-8 Aust 23-10

BR548 3172 HPA FF 17-7-42 6MU 20-7 47MU 24-7 *Hoperidge* 4-8 23-10

BR549 3188 HPA FF 22-7-42 6MU 24-7 47MU 29-7 *Hoperidge* 4-8 Aust 23-10

BR562 2933 EA FF 14-5-42 39MU 15-5 82MU 18-5 *Hopetarn* 26-5 Malta 1-7 603S CB ops 31-7 C3 ops 18-1-43 FH130.25

BR564 2938 EA FF 15-5-42 39MU 16-5 47MU 19-5 *Hopetarn* 26-5 Malta 126S CE ops 3-7 SOC 6-7

BR565 2940 EA FF 16-5-42 39MU 16-5 47MU 19-5 *Hopetarn* 26-5 Malta 1-7 NWA USAAF 1-10-433 ME 15-3-45 SOC 29-8-46

BR566 2941 EA FF 16-5-42 39MU 16-5 82MU 20-5 *Hopetarn* 26-5 Malta 126S CE ops 7-7 SOC 8-7

BR568 2955 EA FF 18-5-42 39MU 21-5 47MU 2-6 *Stir Cast* 19-6 Aust 25-8

BR570 2953 EA FF 19-5-42 8MU 20-5 47MU 1-6 *Stir Cast* 19-6 Aust 25-8

BR572 2956 EA FF 19-5-42 8MU 20-5 47MU 1-6 *Stir Cast* 19-6 Aust FTR 25-8

BR573 2968 EA FF 21-5-42 6MU 23-5 82MU 1-6 *Nigers* 20-6 Tak 2-8ME 11-8 SOC 23-9

BR574 2961 EA FF 20-5-42 8MU 17-8 215S 31-8 *Tekoa* 17-9 Aust 2-12

BR576 2962 EA FF 20-5-42 6MU 22-5 82MU 1-6 *Nigers* 20-6 Tak ME 18-7 SOC 1-2-44

BR580 2981 EA FF 27-5-42 8MU 29-5 47MU 16-6 *Nigers* 20-6 Tak ME 24-7

BR582 2987 EA FF 28-5-42 8MU 29-5 47MU 15-6 *Nigers* 20-6 Tak 5-8 ME 11-8FAC3 29-8 59RSU

BR583 2988 EA FF 29-5-42 8MU 30-5 82MU 18-6 *Nigers* 20-6 Tak ME 145S 16-7 FTR ops 27-10

BR584 2995 EA FF 30-5-42 8MU 1-6 215MU 23-6 *Hoperidge* 4-8 Aust 23-10

BR586 3001 EA FF 31-5-42 39MU 1-6 47MU 12-6 *Nigers* 20-6 Tak ME 24-7 RHAF 25-4-46

BR589 3018 EA FF 5-6-42 8MU 6-6 215MU 2-7 *Hoperidge* 4-8 Aust 23-10

BR591 3017 EA FF 5-6-42 8MU 7-6 52MU 8-7 *Emp Clive* 19-7 Malta 3-8 C2 ops 26-10 NA 1-7-43 Italy 1-11 ME 30-11-44

BR621 3096 R-R con to MkIX M61 FF 27-6-42 9MU 27-6 611S 24-7 CAC ops 2-11 ROS 340S 25-1-43 FTR ops 11-2 FH88.10

BR622 3097 R-R con to MkIX M61 FF 27-6-42 9MU 28-6 611S 24-7 FTR ops 2-11

BR623 3098 R-R con to MkIX M61 FF 27-6-42 9MU 5-7 611S 24-7 72S 24-7 401S 27-7 403S 25-1-43 AST mods 22-4 421S 13-6-43 AST 25-8 312S 27-3-45 FAAC 11-6 to 6018M 26-7-46 2SoTT 14-10-50 FFS SonH

BR624 3122 R-R con to MkIX M61 FF 4-7-42 33MU 5-7 64S 19-7 AST mods 22-3-43 453S 2-4 FTR ops 28-5

BR625 3151 R-R con to MkIX M61 FF 4-7-42 33MU 5-7 403S FTRm ops 13-3-45

BR626 3152 R-R con to MkIX M61 FF 6-7-42 9MU 8-7 72S 24-7 401S 27-7 CB ops 15-8 GAL Farn 29-5-43 416S 6-4 CE ops 13-5

BR627 3153 R-R con to MkIX M61 FF 8-7-42 8MU 10-7 611S 25-7 AST mods 4-4-43 332S 13-4 struct fail port wng in spin cd nr Lyng Norfolk CE 12-5

BR628 3154 R-R con to MkIX M61 FF 10-7-42 39MU 72S 24-7 401S 27-7 FTR ops 28-8

BR629 3160 R-R con to MkIXX M61 FF 15-7-42 8MU 19-7 611S 25-7 CB ops 9-11 GAL 416S 6-4-43 3206 Sc Odiham 15-4 129S 28-7 mods 27-8 303S 31-8 308S 16-11 e/fd d/ld North CE 30-12

BR630 3159 R-R con to MkIX M61 FF 15-7-42 39MU 19-7 72S 24-7 401S 27-7 CAC ops 17-8 GAL 401S air coll with AB460 cd Swanage Bank Hospital Surrey CAC 19-9 ROS 403S 25-1-43 332S 29-6 FTR ops 15-8

BR631 3187 R-R con to MkIX M61 FF 21-7-42 611S 23-7 315S 9-4-43 303S 6-6 308S 16-8 CAC ops 25-4-44 recat E 15-9

BR632 3190 R-R con to MkIX M61 FF 23-7-42 6MU 16-7 FA 26-7 611S 3-8 AST mods 24-2-43 403S 6-4 CB ops 27-5 ROS 316S 29-9 312S 20-4-45 CFE Tang 30-8 to 6037M 2-8-46

BR634 3215 R-R con to MkIX M61 FF 29-7-42 402S 31-7 FTR ops 17-8

BR635 3199 R-R con to MkIX FF 24-7-42 M61 6MU 27-7 611S 30-7 402S 9-12 AST mods 24-12 402S 12-1-43 416S 23-3 CE ops 19-4 premature w/u t/o at Ken FH218.05

BR636 3214 R-R con to MkIX M61 FF 29-7-42 402S 31-7 HAL 23-8 for invest dam ops 30-8 122S 12-3-43 AST mods 21-4 222S 19-5 FTR ops 27-5

BR637 3237 R-R con to MkIX M61 FF 9-8-42 402S 12-8 416S 23-3-43 FACB 27-3 ROS AST 10-5 403S 2-6 FTR ops 20-6 FH201.50

BR638 3225 R-R con to MkIX M61 FF 5-8-42 133S 10-8 FTR ops 30-9

BR639 3224 R-R con to MkIX M61 FF 4-8-42 64S 6-8 AST 24-8 HA Flt North 16-9 FA 21-9 HAL SS Sqn North 31-12 e/fd on t/o strk BR181 CE 21-1-43 SOC 28-1 AST 15-2 405ARF 24-10 AST 31-5-44 VA mods 15-11-44 58 OTU 8-4-45 sold H Bath 10-11-49

BR640 3258 R-R con to MkIX M61 FF 14-8-42 133S 16-8 AST mr 7-9 133S FTR ops 30-9

BS Series All VCT M46 unless otherwise indicated

BS158 3054 CHA FF 16-6-42 39MU 18-6 47MU 30-6 *Eury* 30-7 Aust 18-10 FACA 11-2-43

BS160 3055 CHA FF 17-6-42 39MU 18-6 52MU 8-7 *Emp Clive* 19-7 Malta 3-8 1435S CE ops 29-8 SOC 31-8 FH19

BS161 3056 CHA FF 17-6-42 39MU 20-6 52MU 9-7 *Emp Clive* 19-7 Malta 3-8 NA USAAF 31-8-43

BS162 3072 CHA FF 21-6-42 6MU 22-6 47MU 16-7 *Eury* 30-7 Aust 18-10

BS163 3073 CHA FF 21-6-42 6MU 22-6 47MU 16-7 *Hoperidge* 4-8 Aust 23-10

BS164 3074 CHA FF 21-6-42 8MU 22-6 215MU 19-7 *Hoperidge* 4-8 Aust 23-10

BS165 3083 CHA FF 24-6-42 39MU 26-6 47MU 16-7 *Hoperidge* 4-8 Aust 23-10

BS166 3084 CHA FF 25-6-42 39MU 26-6 47MU 16-7 *Hoperidge* 4-8 Aust 23-10

BS168 3085 CHA FF 25-6-42 39MU 26-6 52MU 10-7 *Emp Clive* 19-7 Malta 3-8 NA 1-6-43 SOC 30-6-45

BS169 3094 CHA FF 27-6-42 39MU 28-6 47MU 26-7 *Hoperidge* 4-8 Aust 23-10

BS171 3110 CHA FF 30-6-42 39MU 3-7 215MU 19-7 *Hoperidge* 4-8 Aust 23-10

BS173 3114 CHA FF 2-7-42 15MU 3-7 47MU 24-7 *Hoperidge* 4-8 Aust 23-10

BS174 3115 CHA FF 2-7-42 15MU 3-7 47MU 31-7 *Hoperidge* 4-8 Aust 23-10 452S A58-68 20-6-43 s/dn

BS175 3124 CHA FF 5-7-42 15MU 6-7 47MU 28-7 *Hoperidge* 4-8 Aust 23-10

BS178 3132 CHA FF 8-7-42 6MU 11-7 47MU 25-7 *Hoperidge* 4-8 Aust 23-10

BS181 3134 CHA FF 11-7-42 8MU 13-7 47MU 25-7 *Hoperidge* 4-8 Aust 23-10

BS182 3135 CHA FF 11-7-42 8MU 13-7 47MU 25-7 *Hoperidge* 4-8 Aust 23-10

BS184 3141 CHA FF 11-7-42 39MU 13-7 47MU 25-7 *Hoperidge* 4-8 Aust 23-10

BS186 3166 CHA FF 15-7-42 6MU 17-7 47MU 25-7 *Hoperidge* 4-8 Aust 23-10

BS187 3167 CHA FF 15-7-42 6MU 17-7 47MU 25-7 *Hoperidge* 4-8 Aust 23-10

BS188 3174 CHA FF 17-7-42 6MU 19-7 47MU 29-7 *Hoperidge* 4-8 Aust 23-10

BS190 3179 CHA FF 19-7-42 6MU 20-7 47MU 25-7 *Hoperidge* 4-8 Aust 23-10

BS191 3180 CHA FF 19-7-42 6MU 20-7 47MU 29-7 *Hoperidge* 4-8 Aust 23-10

BS193 3191 CHA FF 23-7-42 8MU 27-7 215MU 14-8 *Teak* 17-8 Aust *14-11*

BS197 3205 CHA FF 24-7-42 39mU 28-7 47MU 31-7 *Hoperidge* 4-8 Aust 23-10

BS199 3207 CHA FF 26-7-42 39MU 29-7 215MU 5-8 *Teak* 17-8 Aust 14-11

BS201 3210 CHA FF 31-7-42 8MU 1-8 47MU 18-8 *Port Syd* 9-9 Aust 29-11

BS218 3147 HEA FF 11-7-42 8MU 12-7 47MU 25-7 *Hoperidge* 4-8 Aust 23-10

BS219 3176 HEA FF 18-7-42 8MU 19-7 47MU 20-7 *Hoperidge* 4-8 Aust 23-10

BS220 3246 HEA FF 12-8-42 6MU 13-8 47MU 20-8 *Port Syd* 9-9 Aust 29-11

BS221 3249 HEA FF 14-8-42 8MU 15-8 215MU 22-8 *Raranga* 29-8 Aust 10-11

BS222 3297 HEA FF 24-8-42 8MU 26-8 215MU 10-9 *Port Wynd* 9-10 Aust 21-11

BS223 3311 HEA FF 30-8-42 39MU 1-9 215MU 26-9 *Port Wynd* 9-10 Aust 21-11

BS224 3317 HEA FF 31-8-42 39MU 1-9 215MU 26-9 *Port Wynd* 9-10 Aust 21-11

BS225 3322 HEA FF 31-8-42 39MU 1-9 215MU 23-9 *Waro* 13-10 Aust 24-12

BS226 3333 HEA FF 5-9-42 6MU 7-9 215MU 13-9 *Port Wynd* 9-10 Aust 21-11

BS230 3202 HEA FF 25-7-42 6MU 26-7 47MU 30-7 *Hoperidge* 4-8 Aust 23-10

BS231 3211 HPA FF 26-7-42 6MU 28-7 215MU 12-8 *Teak* 17-8 Aust 11-11 452S A58-92 s/dn over Darwin C.O. S/Ldr Thorold-Smith kld 15-3-43

BS232 3232 HPA FF 9-8-42 6MU 11-8 47MU 17-8 *Port Syd* 9-9 Aust 29-11

BS233 3243 HPA FF 12-8-42 6MU 12-8 215MU 21-8 *Raranga* 29-8 Aust 11-11

BS234 3244 HPA FF 13-8-42 6MU 14-8 215MU 22-8 *Raranga* 29-8 Aust 10-11 1FW RAAF CRIC

BS235 3256 HPA FF 14-8-42 39MU 16-8 215MU 1-9 *Tekoa* 17-9 Aust 2-12

BS236 3261 HPA FF 16-8-42 39MU 17-8 215MU 1-9 *Tekoa* 17-9 Aust 2-12

BS237 3272 HPA FF 19-8-42 39MU 20-8 215MU 6-9 *Tekoa* 17-9 Aust 2-12

BS238 3312 HPA FF 30-8-42 39MU 31-8 215MU 13-9 *Port Wynd* 9-10 Aust 21-11

BS271 3273 R-RH con to MkIX M61 FF 20-8-42 64S 26-8-42 Spcl Flt North 6-9 as BF271 124S 25-1-43 331S 20-4-43 FACB 15-5 GAL SOC 25-7-46

BS272 3255 R-RH con to MkIX M61 FF 13-8-42 133S 15-8 331S 29-9 FACB 12-12 GAL 332S 31-12 122S 11-8-43 AST 28-9 M61 instal mods 84GSU 22-4-44 FAAC 12-12 ROS CE 27-5-48

BS273 3259 R-RH con to MkIX M61 FF 14-8-42 64S 16-8 AFDU Dux 16-8 Cranfield 27-8 Spcl Flt North 5-9 Wood prop, armour removed, arma red to 2 × 20mm can lightweight pt finish, operated under code 'Windgap' reached height of 45,000ft.

BS274 3247 incorrectly serialised BF274 Canadian Pacific retained until scr. Off CRD contract not to be included in count. R-RH con to MkIX M61 FF 12-8-42 BDn 13-8 climb and level speed perf and positional error. 6-10 range det with 170gal o/ld tank. Normal tankage range 589 miles 170gal tank only 762 Max range with max tankage @ 15000ft @ 170ASI 1372 miles. Endurance 1.95 hr @ 20000ft @ 250mph Guns removed for cool trls fuel cooler in port wing root 13-10 fuel cons trls. CRD Stav 11-1-43 AST 18-1-44 mr mods at Flight Refuelling for fighter towing trls July '44 58 OTU 16-5-45 sold Vickers 11-1-47 con to Type 509 Two-seat train RNeAF as H-98 22-3-48 See main text for details.

BS275 3238 R-RH con to MkIX M61 FF 9-8-42 133S 12-8 FTR ops 30-9

BS276 3227 R-RH con to MkIX M61 FF 7-8-42 133S 12-8 FTR ops 6-9

BS277 3270 R-RH con to MkIX M61 FF 18-8-42 402S 20-8 CE ops 4-12

BS278 3294 R-RH con to MkIX M61 FF 25-8-42 6MU 27-8 64S 4-9 FTR ops 27-1-43 FH108.05

BS279 3260 R-RH con to MkIX M61 FF 16-8-42 133S 17-8 FTR ops 30-9

BS280 3282 R-RH con to MkIX M61 FF 22-8-42 64S 23-8 AST 31-3-43 mods 453S 2-4 129S 17-7 405ARF 5-9 131S 27-9 VAO 20-12-44 mods to 6021M 26-7-46

BS281 3308 R-RH con to MkIX M61 FF 28-8-42 15MU 1-9 122S 25-9 222S 19-5-43 AST 25-5 33S 25-5-44 310S 8-7 303S 22-7 VA 26-10-44 mods

BS282 3283 R-RH con to MkIX M61 FF 22-8-42 64S 25-8 e/a CB 18-1-43 ROS 453S 2-4 AST 29-4 mods 129S 17-7 331S 28-8 165S 29-9 131S 19-3-44 611S 8-10 SOC 10-4-45

BS283 3313 R-RH con to MkIX M61 FF 30-8-42 15MU 1-9 122S 19-9 AST 10-11 AST 10-2-43 mods CE ops 17-4-43

BS284 3289 R-RH con to MkIX M61 FF 24-8-42 6MU 27-8 CB ops 12-12 GAL 405ARF 18-8-43 19S 22-8 CAC ops 18-10 274S 29-5-44 CB ops 28-7 recat E 3-11

BS285 3306 R-RH con to MkIX M61 FF 29-8-42 15MU 1-9 122S 25-9 FTR ops 15-10 FH16.15

BS286 3331 R-RH con to MkIX M61 FF 3-9-42 8MU 5-9 122S 19-9 AST 4-11 222S 19-5-43 AST 25-5 mods 65S 24-8 CB ops 7-11 AST 310S 8-7-44 504S 15-7 229S 13-2-45 310S 16-6 312S 27-8 to 6020M 26-7-46

BS287 3328 R-RH con to MkIX M61 FF 31-8-42 33MU 6-9 401S 12-12 403S 25-1-43 lost cont cd Marsham Kent 25-2 FH127.15

BS288 3329 R-RH con to MkIX M61 FF 1-9-42 33MU 3-9 306S 17-9 FACB 10-12 GAL 31-12 403S 8-6-43 AST 12-7 mods 405RSU eng fire a/c aban cd Forest Row E Grinstead CE 15-12

BS289 3394 EA R-RH con to MkIX M61 FF 15-9-42 12MU 17-9 47MU 28-11 GIB 7-12

BS290 3361 R-RH con to MkIX M61 FF 9-9-42 8MU 12-9 122S 25-9 FACB 20-10 GAL 403S 18-5-43 421S 20-5 AST 8-6 mods 421S 16-6 CE ops 9-8 FH118

BS291 3229 CHA FF 6-8-42 39MU 11-8 47MU 16-8 *Port Syd* 9-9 Aust 29-11

BS293 3235 CHA FF 9-8-42 39MU 11-8 47MU 16-8 *Port Syd* 9-9 Aust 29-11

BS295 3236 CHA FF 9-8-42 39MU 11-8 47MU 20-8 *Raranga* 29-8 Aust 10-11

BS298 3254 CHA FF 14-8-42 8MU 16-8 215MU 28-8 *Tekoa* 17-8 Aust 2-12

BS300 3265 CHA FF 17-8-42 6MU 18-8 215MU 23-8 *Raranga* 29-8 Aust 10-11

BS305 3286 CHA final MkV variant built by Super FF 23-8-42 6MU 26-8 215MU 6-9 *Tekoa* 17-9 Aust 2-12

BS335 3330 R-RH con to MkIX M61 FF 2-9-42 33MU 4-9 306S 1809 CAC ops 15-12 ROS AST 20-3-43 mods FTR ops 4-4

BS336 3350 R-RH con to MkIX FF 6-9-42 M61 8MU 9-9 122S 22-9 FACB 19-11 GAL 316S 24-7-43 AST 28-9 FAAC 17-10 CC.OR 31-12 recat E FH207-10

BS337 3358 R-RH con to MkIX M61 FF 8-9-42 12MU 10-9 47MU 28-11 *SS647* 19-12 GIB 6-2-43 NWA 31-3 SOC 31-8-44

BS338 3372 R-RH con to MkIX M61 FF 11-9-42 15MU 12-9 541S 1-10 VAWD 19-11 con to PR standard 47MU 25-1-43 *SS670* 24-3 Gib 12-4 ME FAC3 21-8 MAAF 27-4-44 SOC 15-3-45

BS339 3360 R-RH con to MkIX M61 FF 9-9-42 15MU 11-9 541S 2-10 28-1-43 *SS657* 19-2-43 Gib 9-3 Malta 1-8 ME 30-9 NA 31-8-44 REAF SOC 26-9-46

BS340 3432 R-RH con to MkIX M61 FF 20-9-42 8MU 24-9 401S 8-10 CAC ops 3-11 ROS 122S 2-12 GAL 10-3-43 315S 21-5 303S 6-6 AST 28-7 410ARF 15-12 501S 15-4-44 229S 29-5 SOC mr 26-2-45

BS341 3389 R-RH con to MkIX M61 FF 14-9-42 12MU 16-9 47MU 28-11 *SS646* 7-12 Gib 7-12

BS342 3414 R-RH con to MkIX M61 FF 18-9-42 12MU 21-9 47MU 21-10 *Algenib* 20-12 Alexandria 31-12 Suez 17-3-43 FAC3 13-11

BS343 3359 R-RH con to MkIX M61 FF 8-9-42 12MU 9-9 47MU 21-10 *Algenib* 31-12 Suez 17-3-43 ME 31-3 NA 31-8-44 SOC 23-10

BS344 3407 R-RH con to MkIX M61 FF 17-9-42 12MU 24-9 47MU 29-11 *SS647* 19-12 GIB 6-2-43 NWA 28-2 ret to UK 28-1-45 SAAF M63 instal 18-7-47

BS345 3433 R-RH con to MkIX M61 FF 23-9-42 122S 25-9 e/a CAC 8-11 ROS AST 7-5-43 mods 222S 19-5 403S 24-8 274S 16-6-44 to 5951M 12-6-46

BS346 3434 R-RH con to MkIX M61 FF 23-9-42 122S 25-9 FTR i/sea ops 6-12 FH49.50

BS347 3415 R-RH con to MkIX M61 FF 18-9-42 122S 21-9 Farn Nov'42 stab and neg 'G' trls 222S 19-5-43 65S 24-8 AST 13-10 mods to 6036M 12-4-49

BS348 3453 R-RH con to MkIX M61 FF 29-9-42 122S 1-10 222S 19-5-43 421S 24-8 405RSU 33S 28-5-44 310S 3-7 303S CAC ops 23-7 ROS VA 15-11 mods Scr train Flt Drem 25-1-45 WAL mr 22-8 SOC 7-7-49

BS349 3450 R-RH con to MkIX M61 FF 27-9-42 122S 30-9 FTR ops 8-11

BS350 3451 R-RH con to MkIX M61 FF 27-9-42 122S 30-9 FTR ops 2-12 FH52.30

BS351 3452 R-RH con to MkIX M61 FF 27-9-42 122S 1-10 402S 25-1-43 CE ops 13-3

BS352 3468 R-RH con to MkIX M61 FF 6-10-42 340S 8-10 FAAC 25-10 611S 23-11 AST 11-3-43 mods 341S 1-4 AST 4-4 mods 222S 29-7 403S 15-8 CAC ops 20-8 AST CRD BDn 4-12 pilot error measurements SAL 19-3-45 RHAF 13-5-48

BS353 3466 R-RH con to MkIX M61 FF 5-10-42 340S 9-10 402S 13-12 AST 12-3-43 mods 416S 21-3 402S 23-3 421S 20-5 CAC ops 17-6 ROS 307S 13-7 403S CAC ops 31-7 ROS 274S 21-6-44 CFE 11-1-45 80 OTU 5-7 CE 24-6-46

BS354 3554 R-RH con to MkIX M61 FF 19-10-42 19-10 BDn 28-10 trls with M61 with lower blower peak. 5-11 Mer RM-9SM (M70) instal Dec'42m trls wilth new eng and MkXII rud. It was proposed to instal this rud on FVIII,VII and IX prod. Spit. Oil cool and rad suit trls 5-12. Jan'43 comp perf trls with BS543 (M66 RM-10 SM) & BS551 (M70 RM-11 SM) high and low alt Merlin respectively. All eng had an improved supercharger with the first stage rotor increased to 12ft. A Bendix-Stromberg carb injected petrol into the eye of the supercharger these mods raising compression ratio. Level speeds at 30,000ft were BS 354 387mph 543 395 551 413. All a/c had the standard VC wing and BS354 although having an additional 50bhp was 7mph slower at S/L. This a/c was dam during trls GAL 28-1-43 for repairs. 47MU 5-4 *SS686* 24-4 Casa 17-5 ME 1-7 REAF 30-1-47

BS530 3460 R-RH con to MkIX M61 FF 2-10-42 331S 4-10 GAL 26-5-43 222MU 18-9 *Emp Mar* 7-10 Casa 19-10 NA 30-11 FTR ops 21-9-44

BS531 3454 R-RH con to MkIX M61 FF 30-9-42 331S 3-10 CAC ops 4-3-43 FTR ops 4-5

BS532 3467 R-RH con to MkIX M61 FF 5-10-42 340S 8-10 341S 7-4-43 222S 28-7 421S 24-8 reported miss 3-10 BDn Dec'44 pitot head measurements

BS533 3461 R-RH con to MkIX M61 FF 4-10-42 340S 8-10 CAC ops 22-1-43 ROS 403S 19-4 AST 29-4 mods FAAC 9-10 AST to 6205M 22-11-46

BS534 3515 R-RH con to MkIX M61 FF 14-10-42 401S 18-10 403S 25-1-43 AST 28-2 mods 33S 23-5-44 310S 8-7 504S 15-7 VA 21-9 mods 303S CE ops 13-10

BS535 3483 R-RH con to MkIX M61 FF 10-10-42 340S 11-10 FTR ops 31-10 FH11.50

BS536 3481 R-RH con to MkIX M61 FF 8-10-42 401S 12-10 CE ops 4-12

BS537 3484 R-RH con to MkIX M61 FF 10-10-42 332S 11-10 FACE 20-11 SOC 30-11

BS538 3482 R-RH con MkIX M61 FF 9-10-42 340S 11-10 AST mods 341S 26-3-43 CB ops 5-5 GAL 501S 6-12 313S 14-9-44 611S 5-10 SAAF 4-12-48

BS539 3596 R-RH con to MkIX M61 FF 6-11-42 64S 15-11 453S 2-4-43 AST 5-4 mods 129S coll with MA598 on t/o Horn CB 15-7 AST 411ARF 8-1-44 501S CB ops 29-2 VAOX 58 OTU 12-4-45 FAF 12-9-46

BS540 3517 R-RH con to MkIX M61 FF 17-10-42

332S 18-10 CAC ops 12-12 AST 9-2-43 mods FTR ops 2-5

BS541 3514 R-RH con to MkIX M61 FF 14-10-42 453S 18-5 e/fd on t/o f/ld Averley, Essex CE 1-6

BS542 3516 R-RH con to MkIX M61 FF 15-10-42 340S 17-10 FAAC 16-1-43 CAC op 28-2 ROS 341S 6-4 FAAC 17-1 ROS 303S 14-10 AST 19-10 mods 308S 22-10 FAF 14-3-46

BS543 3534 R-RH con to MkIX M61 FF 22-10-42 23-10 AFDU Dux 8-11 BDn 13-12 M66 (RM-10 SM) instal Comp trls with BS534 & BS551. See BS534 for details.CRD VA 22-2-43 403S 9-6 611S 10-6 AST 19-6 mods 485S 6-7 FTR on ops 22-8

BS544 3518 R-RH con to MkIX M61 FF 17-10-42 64S 21-10 FACB 12-4-43 GAL M63 instal 421S 24-2-44 310S 9-1-45 312S 2-9 FAF 17-10-46

BS545 3545 Brazil No I R-RH con to MkIX M61 FF 24-10-42 122S 27-10 CAC ops 1-5-43 ROS 403S 16-6 229S FAAC 22-6-44 274S FAAC 8-8 ROS VA 10-11 mods FAF 24-5-46

BS546 3546 O Guaran R-RH con to MkIX M61 FF 24-10-42 122S 27-10 AST 10-12 mods SOC 28-2-43 FH6.50

BS547 3607 R-RH con to MkIX M61 FF 8-11-42 611S 10-11 341S 21-4-43 AST 24-12 mods 229S 16-6-44 VA 15-9 mods sold Vickers 5-12-49

BS548 3576 R-RH con to MkIX M61 FF 31-10-42 340S 7-11 AST 10-12 mods 402S 31-1-43 CAC ops 12-3 ROS 341S 2-4 FTR ops 17-4

BS549 3577 R-RH con to MkIX M61 FF 31-10-42 315S 7-11 401S 9-12 FAAC 23-12 ROS AST 11-4-43 mods 403S 16-4 341S 20-7 FAAC 9-10 313S 29-8-44 611S 8-10 303S 22-3-45 441S 5-4 80 OTU 23-7 SOC 9-6-47

BS550 3624 R-RH con to MkIX M61 FF 16-11-42 12MU 20-11 *SS647* 19-12 GIB 6-2-43 NWA 28-2

BS551 3578 R-RH con to MkIX M61 FF 31-10-42 CRD R-RH 1-11 M70 (RM-9SM) instal comp trls with BS354 & 543 See BS354 for details. FACE 4-1-43 FH12.05

BS552 3547 R-RH con to MkIX M61 FF 24-10-42 27-10 AFDU Dux 21-11 WAL 27-6-45 recat E SOC 17-9

BS553 3623 R-RH con to MkIX M61 FF 10-11-42 9MU 17-11 47MU 29-11 *SS647* 19-12 GIB 6-2-43 NWA 28-2 Malta 1-7 Sic 1-8 NWA FAC3 18-10

BS554 3375 R-RH con to MkIX M61 FF 29-10-42 315S 6-11 AST 10-12 mods FTR ops 15-5-43

BS555 3597 R-RH con to MkIX M61 FF 7-11-42 9MU 17-11 47MU 28-11 *SS646* 7-12 GIB 17-12 SAL 13-4-43 VA 6-11-44 mods 303S 16-11 310S 3-5-45 FAF 27-7-46

BS556 3598 R-RH con to MkIX M61 FF 7-11-42 611S 10-11 AST 4-4-43 mods 315S 9-4 FTR ops 4-5 80S 29-5-44 FAAC 4-7 274S 17-7 FAAC 11-8 ROS sold H Bath 18-11-49

BS557 3630 R-RH con to MkIX M61 FF 18-11-42 9MU 20-11 47MU 29-11 *SS646* 7-12 GIB Malta 8-2-43 26-6

BS558 3635 R-RH con to MkIX M61 FF 21-11-42 9MU 23-11 47MU 29-11 *SS647* 19-12 GIB 16-2-43 NWA 28-2 FAF 1-10 reported missing 12-11-44 RHAF 29-5-49

BS559 3599 R-RH con to MkIX M61 FF 7-11-42 9MU 17-11 47MU 28-11 *SS647* 19-12 GIB 16-2-43 FAAC 6-3 SOC 20-9-45

EE series all F VC Merlin 46 unless otherwise indicated

EE600 33MU 4-9-42 R-RH Merlin trls 130S 6-11 65S 31-3-43 132S 23-5 302S 28-6-43 to 4187M

EE601 33MU 11-9-42 66S 21-10 129S 19-2-43 CAC ops 307 306S 7-10 61 OTU 20-9-44 SOC 19-3-45

EE602 LFVC Central Railways Uruguayan Staff 33MU 11-9-42 66s 21-10 129S 19-2-43 453S FACE 17-7 bboc 21-3-45 FACB 18-3

EE603 33MU 14-9-42 504S 10-11 165S CE ops 25-7-43 41S strk by MB844 on runway CE TAng 4-12 FH283.10

EE604 6MU 14-9-42 82MU 16-10 Gib 6-11 NWA 28-2-43 ret UK 91S air coll with MB859 cd E Grinstead CE 6-12

EE605 6MU 14-9-42 215MU 26-9 *Port Wynd* 9-10 Aus 21-11

EE606 6MU 14-9-42 215MU 23-9 *Port Wynd* 9-10 Aus 21-11

EE607 6MU 14-9-42 215MU 25-9 *Sussex* 19-10 Aus 28-11 452S RAAF A58-107 s/dn over Darwin 20-6-43

EE608 6MU 15-9-42 215MU 23-9 *Port Wynd* 9-10 Aus 21-11

EE609 6MU 15-9-42 215MU 27-9 *Port Wynd* 9-10 Aus 21-11

EE610 6MU 15-9-42 215MU 23-9 *Port Wynd* 9-10 Aus 21-11

EE611 33MU 19-9-42 66S 15-10 129S 19-2-43 FACB 14-8 HAL CRD BDn 16-4-44 SOC 18-5-45

EE612 33MU 19-9-42 130S 8-11 610S 5-4-43 FACB 21-5 recat E

EE613 LFLRVC 33MU 21-9-42 66S 15-10 19S 20-1-43 402S 26-4 FACB 23-8 AST M45M instal 322 11-2-44 350S 13-3-41 OTU 2-9 SOC 22-5-45

EE614 33MU 21-9-42 504S 24-11 FTR ops 4-4-43

EE615 9MU 21-9-42 130S 10-11 65S 31-3-43 610S 12-6 131S 31-7 e/fld w/u ldg Pitney CE 5-11

EE616 9MU 21-9-42 234S 13-11 602S 25-1-43 FTR ops 3-4

EE617 9MU 21-9-42 130S 10-11 65S 31-3-43 132S 23-5 302S 28-6 313S 4-12 443S 27-2-44 o/t t/o Dig CE 3-3

EE618 9MU 21-9-42 130S 10-11 65S 31-3-43 132S 23-5 302S 28-6 453S 8-10 341S 3-11 61 OTU 3-9-44 SOC 14-5-45

EE619 39MU 21-9-42 501S 10-10 504S 19-10 165S 8-7-43 CE ops 25-8

EE620 39MU 26-9-42 504S 19-10 165S 5-7-43 FAAC 27-7 AST 222MU 29-9 *Ortolan* 6-10 Port 19-10

EE621 39MU 25-9-42 504S 19-10 FTR i/sea on ops 24-6-43

EE622 39MU 26-9-42 602S 19-10 129S 29-11 234S 25-1-43 66S 19-4 313S 4-7 310S 26-7 611S 24-8-53 OTU 6-8-44 DeH recat E 2-1-45

EE623 39MU 28-9-42 66S 15-10 129S 19-2-43 453S 17-7 CB ops 4-8 LMS M45M instal 14-4-44 SOC 9-11-45

EE624 39MU 28-9-42 501S 10-10 165S 3-9-43 315S 28-11 CGS 13-10-44 SOC STR 15-11-49

EE625 39MU 28-9-42 501S 10-10 504S 16-3-43 303S 7-3-44 FACE 16-5-44

EE626 LFLRVC 39MU 28-9-42 310S FACB 3-2-43 AST M45M instal 316S 24-12 63S 1-5-44 587S 14-6-45 SOC 14-8

EE627 38MU 28-9-42 602S 19-10 29S 29-11 FAAC 23-1-43 52 OTU 6-2-44 57 OTU 31-12 61 OTU 3-5-45 SOC 5-6

EE628 38MU 28-9-42 130S 10-11 65S 31-3-43 FACE 11-4 FH118.50

EE629 38MU 130S 24-1065S 31-3-43 dvdi/sea off Lands End 1-5

EE630 38MU 28-9-42 66S 21-10 453S 17-7 FTR ops 15-8

EE631 33MU 3-10-42 602S 21-10 129S 29-11 234S 25-1-43 66S 19-4 313S 4-7 310S 26-7 131S 27-8 443S 27-2-44 CGS 27-2-44 CGS 28-9 SOC 25-10-45

EE632 33MU 2-1-42 130S 27-10 FTR ops 26-1-43 FH68.35

EE633 33MU 2-10-42 234S 17-11 air coll with EE682 ldg base CAC 23-1-43 502S 19-2 FTR ops 11-4

EE634 33MU 3-10-42 130S 21-11 610S 5-4-43 FTR ops 21-4 FH115.30

EE635 39MU 3-10-42 504S 19-10 310S 5-2-43 FTR ops 21-4 FH203

EE636 39MU 6-10-42 215MU 21-10 *Taranaki* 24-11 Aus 23-1-43

EE637 39MU 6-10-42 602S 21-10 129S 29-11 66S 19-4-43 313S 4-7 310S 26-7 416S 9-9 186S 8-3-44 FACA 17-3 AST 61 OTU 13-9 FACB 17-1-45 SOC 9-2

EE638 39MU 6-10-42 602S 7-11 129S 29-11 234S 25-1-43 66S 19-4 313S 4-7 310S 26-7 FAAC 29-7 453S 19-8 130S 17-6-44 58 OTU 22-3-45 SOC 27-12

EE639 39MU 6-10-42 215MU 21-10 *Taranaki* 24-11 Aus 23-1-43

EE640 38MU 6-10-42 66S 24-10 129S 19-2-43 453S 17-7 DeH 29-10 61 OTU 19-10-44 SOC 22-5-45

EE641 38MU 10-10-42 130S 24-10 65S 31-3-43 132S 23-5 e/fld a/c aban isea off Exmouth 30-5 FH206.50

EE642 38MU 12-10-42 130S 2-11 65S 31-3-43 132S 23-5 302S 28-6 52 OTU 1-2-44 OTU 28-9 691S 21-6-45 SOC 30-8

EE643 38MU 12-10-42 602S 9-11 129S 29-11 234S 25-1-43 66S 19-4 313S 4-7 310S 26-7 165S 21-8 308S 1-10 t/o in coarse pitch cd Coolham Woods CE 18-4-44

EE644 38MU 12-10-42 602S 31-10 129S 29-11 234S 25-1-43 66S 19-4 302S 22-9 306S 3-10 CAC ops 9-11 26S 13-4-44 CAC ops 6-7-44 41 OTU 8-2-45 to 5521M 30-7 SOC 4-7-50

EE657 39MU 12-10-42 504S 21-10 CE on ops 8-11 FH9.15

EE658 39MU 12-10-42 504S 19-10 FAAC 6-3-43 165S 8-7 130S 17-6-44 Sold J Dale 8-7-48

EE659 39MU 12-10-42 602S 19-10 129S 29-11 234S 25-1-43 66S 19-4 313S 4-7 310S 26-7 504S 25-8 363S 22-9 SOC 19-11-45

EE660 39MU 12-10-42 504S 19-10 CRD DeH 9-1-43 M45M instal AST 5-5 308S 20-7 322S 22-7 349S 29-10 CB ops 14-12 611S 27-5-44 53 OTU 6-8 SOC 28-8-45

EE661 LVFC 39MU 12-10-42 602S 21-10 129S 29-11 234S 25-1-43 66S 19-4 313S 4-7 310S 26-7 402S 9-9 53 OTU 27-9 FAE SOC 15-1-45

EE662 39MU 12-10 130S 6-11 65S 31-3-43 132S 23-5 302S 28-6 306S 3-10 303S 26-6-44 57 OTU 2-8 691S 21-6-45 SOC 4-8

EE663 33MU 19-10-42 222MU 28-12 *Atlan City* 2-1-43 Tak 11-3 ME 23-4 Malta 1-7 Sic 1-8 SOC 30-9

EE664 33MU 19-10-42 82MU 23-1-43 **SS682** 12-4 Casa 25-4 NWA 31-5 USAAF 31-7 325 ME 15-3-45 SOC 27-6-46

EE665 33MU 19-10-42 234S 17-11 602S 17-1-43 412S 19-4 317S 17-7 611S 25-9

EE666 33MU 19-10-42 234S 17-11 602S 25-1-43 412S 19-4 317S 28-6 52 OTU 24-1-44 AST 17SFTS 7-10 5AFU 14-7-45 SOCE 19-7-46

EE667 33MU 19-10-42 76MU 1-1-43 *Nairn* 10-2 Tak 11-3 ME 10-5 SOC 14-3-46

EE668 33MU 19-10-42 222MU 22-12 **SS652** 2-1-43 Gib 18-1 NWA 28-2 Malta 15-6 SOC FH110.45

EE669 6MU 20-10-42 215MU 2-11 *Aust Star* 27-1-43 Aus 11-3

EE670 6MU 20-10-42 215MU 6-11 *Taranaki* 24-11 Aus 23-1-43

EE671 6MU 27-10-42 215MU 17-11 *Port Durn* 19-12 Aus 28-2-43

EE672 6MU 20-10-42 215MU 8-11 *Taranaki* 24-11 Aus 23-1-43

EE673 6MU 27-10-42 82MU 14-11 *Port Durn* 19-12 Aus 28-2-43

EE674 6MU 27-10-42 215MU 6-11 *Taranaki* 24-11 Aus 23-1-43

EE675 39MU 27-10-42 215MU 21-11 *Port Durn* 19-12 Aus 28-2-43

EE676 39MU 27-10-42 215MU 16-11 *Sarp* 24-11 Aus 24-2-43

EE677 39MU 27-10-42 215MU 16-11 *Sarp* 24-11 Aus 24-2-43

EE678 39MU 27-10-42 215MU 8-11 *Sarp* 24-11 Aus 24-2-43

EE679 6MU 27-10-42 130S 6-11 65S 31-3-43 132S 23-5 302S 28-6 306S 3-11 130S 22-6-44 57 OTU 26-4-45 287S 7-6 MarCam 8-11 SOC 9-11

EE680 LFLRVC M46 39MU 27-10-42 130S 6-11 312S 1-2-43 234S 4-7 504S 5-7 402S 13-4-44 345S 15-8 CAC ops 26-8 ROS recat E 24-5-45 M45M instal during service

EE681 39MU 27-10-42 234S 17-11 602S 25-1-43 412S 19-4 317S 28-6 312S 4-10 442S 27-2-44 56 OTU 30-3 61 OTU 13-8 FACB 21-12 SOC 10-1-45

EE682 39MU 27-10-42 234S 20-11 602S 17-1-43 air coll with EE663 i/sea 23-1 FH53

EE683 39MU 2-11-42 130S 8-11 65S 31-3 43 132S 23-5 302S 28-6 CAC ops 28-6 ROS 306S FTR ops 27-9

EE684 39MU 31-10-42 130S 8-11 132S 23-5-43 412S 20-6 317S 28-6 FTR ops thought i/sea off Lizard Point 16-7 FH33.55

EE685 39MU 2-11-42 130S 8-11 65S 31-3-43 132S 23-5 416S 10-6 186S 22-2-44 130S 18-4 s/dn by Allied warships off Normandy 10-6 recat E 17-6

EE686 39MU 2-11-42 234S 17-11 602S 25-1-43 412S 19-4 e/fld f/ld nr Perr 20-4 FH144.30 402S 27-9 2nd TAF Com S 20-3-45 FAAC 17-4

EE687 39MU 7-11-42 234S 17-11 602S 25-1-43 e/fld isea off Lizard Point 26-2 FH114

EE688 39MU 2-11-42 234S 17-11 FTR ops 23-12

EE689 39MU 6-11-42 234S 17-11 CE on ops 23-12

EE690 39MU 2-11-42 130S 16-11 FTR ops 6-3-43 FH80.15

EE713 39MU 6-11-42 215MU 18-11 *Sarp* 24-11 Aus 22-2-43

EE714 6MU 9-11-42 234S 20-11 602S 25-1-43 412S 19-4 317S 28-6 DeH 17-9 61 OTU 16-9-44 691S 28-6-45 SOC mr 3-8

EE715 6MU 9-11-42 234S 23-11 412S 11-6-43 317S 28-6 312S 4-10 402S 28-5-44 57 OTU 2-8 strk by W3521 Esh CE 25-8

EE716 6MU 9-11-42 66S 3-12 129S 19-2-43 453S 17-7 52 OTU 31-1-44 57 OTU 16-9 FACE 14-10

EE717 6MU 9-11-42 234S 23-11 602S 25-1-43 412S 19-4 317S 28-6 FTR ops 3-8

EE718 39MU 17-11-42 215MU 14-12 *Emp Stren* 11-1-43 Aus 11-4

EE719 VAWD 9-11-42 wts & load of WAL prod a/c 39MU 17-11 215MU 14-12 *Emp Stren* 11-1-43 Aus 11-4

EE720 39MU 9-11-42 234S 17-11 602S 25-1-43 CAC on ops 12-4 412S 2-5 FTR ops 12-6

EE721 39MU 9-11-42 234S 30-11 602S 25-1-43 412S 19-4 312S 4-10 130S 19-6-44 CE ops 17-4

EE722 39MU 9-11-42 234S 20-11 602S 25-1-43 CB ops 11-3 130S 17-6-44 441S blown onto nose by wind ldg CB 8-1-45

EE723 LFLRVC 38MU 9-11-42 350S 13-12 610S 23-2-43 FACB 21-3 350S 9-10 322S 11-1-44 350S 13-3 CE ops 14-6

EE724 38MU 16-11-42 131S 15-1-43 610S 27-1 FTR ops 10-2

EE725 38MU 16-11-42 131S 15-1-43 610S 17-1 421S 31-1 310S 3-3 e/fld a/c aban i/sea off Beachy Head 28-3 FH11.30

EE726 38MU 9-11-42 350S 9-12 610S 27-3-43 CAC ops 4-4 FTR ops 22-6 FH 161.30

EE727 38MU 16-11-42 350S 13-12 453S 16-9-43 attempt o/s Perr std cd CE 13-9

EE728 39MU 17-11-42 215MU 20-12 *Emp Stren* 11-1-43 Aus 11-4

EE729 39MU 17-11-42 215MU 14-12 *Emp Stren* 11-1-43 Aus 11-4

EE730 39MU 23-11-42 602S 22-2-43 e/fld a/c aban isea off Lizard Point 23-2 FH3.00

EE731 39MU 17-11-42 215MU 14-12 *Emp Stren* 11-1-43 Aus 11-4

EE732 LFLRVC 39MU 17-11-42 66S 3-12 167S 5-5-43 132S 19-5 25-5 315S 26-6 611S 6-7 CAC ops 27-7 FTR ops 9-11

EE733 8MU 16-11-42 215MU 8-12 *Emp Stren* 11-1-43 Aus 11-4

EE734 8MU 16-11-42 215MU 22-12 *Aust Star* 27-1-43 Aus 11-3

EE735 8MU 20-11-42 215MU 8-12 *Emp Stren* 11-1-43 Aus 11-4

EE736 8MU 23-11-42 215MU 11-12 *Emp Stren* 11-1-43 Aus 11-4

EE737 8MU 23-11-42 215MU 10-12 *Emp Stren* 11-1-43 Aus 11-4

EE738 39MU 23-11-42 350S 9-12 610S 27-3 43 FTR ops 22-6 FH199.30

EE739 39MU 23-11-42 504S 8-12 350S 9-12 610S 23-3 43 i/sea ops 18-3

EE740 39MU 1-12-42 47MU 30-5-43 **LS514** 17-6 Tak 16-7 ME 15-9 MAAF 21-6-45 SOC 25-7-46

EE741 39MU 1-12-42 76MU 30-12 *Atlan City* 20-1-43 Tak 11-3 ME 20-4 Malta 1-7 Italy 1-11 NA 30-11 C3 on ops 24-4-44

EE742 LFLRVC 39MU 23-11-42 504S 8-12 350S 9-12 118S 15-4-43 167S 15-4 229S 23-11-44 61 OTU 26-4-45 691S 21-6 SOC 4-8

EE743 38MU 26-11-42 350S 9-12 610S 27-3 43 FTR ops 27-6 FH183.50

EE744 38MU 26-11-42 350S 13-12 610S 27-3-43 26S 6-4-44 CE ops 7-6 M45M instal

EE745 38MU 26-11-42 350S 9-12 610S 27-3-43 308S 19-8 349S 29-10 485S 8-6-44 2nd TAF Com Wg 5-7-45 E Sq BAFO Com Wg 13-9 sold J Dale 8-7-48

EE746 38MU 26-11-42 131S 21-12 412S 23-1-43 421S 31-1 310S 3-3 131S 2-7 FTR ops 4-9 FH 238.35

EE747 38MU 26-11-42 131S 12-12 350S 31-12 610S

27-1-43 606S 4-3 602S 7-3 412S 19-4 FTR ops 7-5 FH 140.30

EE748 39MU 2-12-42 215MU 22-12 *Aust Star* 27-1-43 Aus 11-3

EE749 39MU 1-12-42 222MU 22-12 **SS652** 2-1-43 Gib 15-1 NWA 28-2 412S FTR ops 7-6

EE750 39MU 1-12-42 222MU 29-12 *Atlan City* 20-1-43 Tak 11-3 ME 27-4 NAAF 1-11 SOC 14-12

EE751 39MU 1-12-42 215MU 29-12 *Emp Stren* 11-1-43 Aus 11-4

EE752 39MU 1-12-42 76MU 14-1-43 *Fort Senn* 13-2 Tak 11-3 ME 2-4 NA 30-11 Malta 118MU 31-1-44 ME 31-8 SOC 26-9-46

EE753 38MU 1-12-42 350S 14-12 610S 27-3-43 303S 22-4-44 166CU 20-11 SOC 27-12-45

EE766 38MU 1-12-42 350S 14-12 610S 22-3-43 FTR isea ops 28-3 FH99.30

EE767 38MU 1-12-42 131S 21-12 610S 27-1-43 FTR ops 10-2

EE768 38MU 1-12-43 131S 11-1-43 412S 23-1 421S 31-1 310S 3-3 131S FTR 27-8 FH197.55

EE769 38MU 1-12-42 131S 15-12 610S 27-1-43 606S 4-3 602S 7-3 412S 19-4

EE770 6MU 2-12-42 76MU 17-12 **SS652** 3-1-43 Gib 18-1 243S C3 ops 3-2

EE771 6MU 7-12-42 76MU 15-12 **SS652** 2-1-43 Gib 18-1 NWA 28-2 SOC

EE772 6MU 7-12-42 76MU 20-12 **SS652** 3-1-43 Gib 18-1 232S C3 ops 31-1

EE773 6MU 10-12-42 222MU 20-12 **SS652** 2-1-43 Gib 18-1

EE774 8MU 10-12-42 76MU 20-12 **SS652** 3-1-43 Gib 18-1 NWA 28-2 Malta 1-7 Sicily 1-9 NA 30-11 To Turk 29-3-45

EE775 8MU 10-12-42 76MU 18-12 **SS652** 3-1-43 Gib 18-1 NWA 28-2 C3 ops 18-4

EE776 8MU 7-12-42 76MU 15-12 **SS652** 3-1-43 Gib 18-1 NWA 28-2 C3 ops 17-4

EE777 8MU 7-12-42 76MU 15-12 **SS652** 3-1-43 Gib 18-1 NWA 28-2

EE778 8MU 7-12-42 82MU 12-12 **SS652** 2-1-43 Gib 18-1 e/a C3 2-2

EE779 33MU 7-12-42 222MU 22-12 *South* 30-12 Gib 13-1-43

EE780 33MU 7-12-42 76MU 9-1-43 *Nairn* 10-2 Tak 11-3 ME 23-4

EE781 33MU 14-12-42 82MU 1-2-43 *Fort Senn* 13-2 Tak 11-3 ME 22-4 Malta 1-7 Sicily 1-8 NAASC 31-10 Soc 26-4-45

EE782 33MU 14-12-42 222MU 30-12 *Atlan City* 20-1 Tak 11-3 ME 1-6 CE 13-9-45

EE783 33MU 14-12 43 82MU 10-1-43 *Atlan City* 20-1 Tak 11-3 ME 30-9 SOC 29-8-46

EE784 39MU 14-12 42 82MU 3-1-43 *Atlan City* 20-1 Tak 11-3 ME 18-4 NAAF 1-11 USAAF 31-1-44 ME 31-1-45

EE785 39MU 14-12-42 82MU 31-12 *Atlan City* 20-1-43 Tak 11-3 ME 23-4 Malta 1-7 IS SAAF CE ops 19-7

EE786 39MU 15-12-42 52MU 11-1-43 *Fort L M* 12-3 Tak 20-4 ME 25-5 FTR ops 28-9

EE787 39MU 4-1-43 222MU 26-1 *Alphard* 5-3 Tak 20-4 ME 10-3 118MU Malta 31-1-44

EE788 39MU 15-12-42 76MU 30-12 *Atlan City* 20-1-43 Tak 11-3 ME 18-4 NAAF 1-11 Malta 31-1-44

EE789 VC(T)M56 6MU 24-12-42 82MU 15-1-43 *Snd Fish* 5-2-43 Tak 12-3 ME 28-4 SOC 10-11-46

EE790 M56 6MU 24-12-42 222MU 9-1-43 *Nairn* 10-2-43 Tak 11-3 ME 29-3 Malta 1-7 NA 1-8 FAC3 7-12

EE791 M56 6MU 24-12-42 82MU 14-1-43 *Mer Prin* 18-1 Gib 6-2 NWA 25-2 Malta 1-7 Sic 1-8 NAASC 31-10 ME 15-3-43 FAF 14-2-46

EE792 M56 6MU 24012-42 82MU 14-1-43 *Sil Ash* 14-2 Tak 10-3 cd/ld C3 17-4

EE793 M56 33MU 24-12-42 82MU 15-1-43 *Sil Ash* 14-2 Tak 10-3 ME FACE 26-5

EE794 M56 33MU 24-12-42 222MU 26-3-43 *SS679* 1-4 Casa 25-4 NWA 31-5 USAAF 31-7

EE795 M56 33 MU 24-12-42 82 MU 15-1-43 *Sil Ash* 14-2 Tak 10-3 ME FAC3 31-3

EE796 M56 33 MU 30-12-42 76 MU 16-1-43 *Fort Senn* 13-2 Tak 11-3 ME 7-4 CE 18-1-45

EE797 M56 6MU 24-12-42 52MU 14-1-43 *Fort L M* 12-3 Tak 20-4 ME 25-7 SOC 1-4-44

EE798 M56 6MU 24-12-42 82MU 14-1-43 *Sil Ash* 14-2 Tak 10-3 ME 1-5 RHAF 25-4-46

EE799 M56 6MU 24-12-42 76MU 7-1-43 *Nairn* 10-2 Tak 11-3 ME 8-5 C3 ops 16-9 NA 30-11 SOC 29-2-44

EE800 M56 6MU 24-12-42 82MU 11-1-43 *Fort Senn* 13-2 Tak 11-3 ME FAC3 31-3

EE801 M56 6MU 24-12-42 222MU 9-1-43 *Nairn* 10-2 Tak 11-3 ME 30-4 SOC 31-8-44

EE802 M56 33MU 24-12-42 76MU 15-1-54 *Fort Senn* 13-2 Tak 11-3 ME 18-4 NAASC 31-10 ME 15-3-45 SOC 27-6-46

EE803 M56 33MU 30-12-42 82MU 27-1-43 *Fort Senn* 13-2 Tak 11-3 Malta 1-7 ME FA SOC 2-8

EE804 M56 33MU 30-12-42 82MU 5-12 *Fort Posk* 19-2 Gib 9-3 NA 31-3

EE805 M56 33MU 30-12-42 82MU 1-2-43 *Fort Senn* 13-2 Tak 11-3 ME 25-4 CE ops 26-11-44

EE806 33MU 8-1-43 82MU 1-2 *Fort Senn* 13-2 Tak 11-3 ME 1-5 NAASC 31-10 ME FAC3 3-1-44

EE807 39MU 2-1-43 215MU 24-12 *Suss* 9-3 Aus 16-4

EE808 39MU 2-1-43 222MU 4-2 *Alphard* 5-3 Tak 20-4 ME 9-8 NAF 11-1-44 C3 ops 23-4

EE809 39MU 2-1-43 76MU 24-1 *Fort Senn* 13-2 Tak 11-3 ME 30-3 FAC3 30-5-44

EE810 39MU 2-1-43 82MU 24-1 *SSLS230* 9-2 Tak 28-3 ME 20-4 Malta 1-8 NA 30-11 318S C3 ops 9-8-44

EE811 39MU 2-1-53 222MU 25-1 *Alphard* 5-3 Tak 20-4 ME 25-5 NAAF 11-1-44 SOC 26-4-45

EE834 6MU 4-1-43 215MU 15-1 *Tijuca* 4-2 Aust 13-4

EE835 6MU 4-1-43 215MU 14-1 *Tijuca* 4-2 Aust 13-4

EE836 6MU 4-1-43 215MU 15-1 *Tijuca* 4-2 Aust 13-4

EE837 6MU 8-1-43 222MU 26-1 FAAC 27-1 ROS *LS117* Aust 14-6

EE838 33MU 8-1-43 47MU 27-1 *Fort Senn* 13-2 Tak 11-3 ME 31-3 FAC3 21-4

EE839 33MU 8-1-43 76MU 31-1 *Fort Senn* 13-2 Tak 11-3 ME 30-3 SOC 1-1-44

EE840 33MU 8-1-43 82MU 1-2 *Fort Senn* 13-2 Tak 11-3 ME 31-3 FTR ops 2-7

EE841 39MU 23-1-43 215MU 9-2 *Alphard* 5-3 Yak 20-4 ME 27-5 SOC 20-6-45

EE842 39MU 23-1-43 222MU 6-2-43 *Sil Bch* 4-3 for Aust lost at sea 14-4

EE843 39MU 23-1-43 222MU 6-2 *Sil Bch* 4-3 as for 842

EE844 39MU 23-1-43 215MU 5-2 *Suss* 9-3 Aust 16-4

EE845 6MU 27-2-43 215MU 9-2 *Suss* 9-3 Aust 16-4

EE846 6MU 23-1-43 222MU 4-2 *Alphard* 5-3 Tak 20-4 ME 25-5

EE847 6MU 23-1-43 222MU 4-2 *Alphard* 5-3 Tak 20-4 ME 26-5 SOC 25-6-44

EE848 6MU 23-1-43 222MU 4-2 *Sil Beech* 4-3 for Aust lost at sea 14-4

EE849 8MU 23-1-43 215MU 5-3 *Suss* 9-3 Aust 16-4

EE850 8MU 23-1-43 215MU 4-2 *Suss* 9-3 Aust 16-4

EE851 8MU 23-1-43 215MU 5-3 *Suss* 9-3 Aust 16-4

EE852 8MU 27-1-43 215MU 4-2 *Suss* 9-3 Aust 16-4

EE853 8MU 23-1-43 215MU 8-2 *Suss* 9-3 Aust 16-4 **79S RAAF A58-146 SOC 19-3-44 Kilawina Island recovered 1974 rebuilt extant Adelaide**

EE854 33MU 23-1-43 82MU 6-2 *SS658* 22-2 Gib 7-3 NWA 31-3

EE855 33MU 23-1-43 76MU 14-2 *Fort L M* 12-3 Tak 20-4 ME 29-5 RHAF 25-4-46

EE856 M45 33MU 23-1-43 82MU 5-2 *SS657* 19-2 Gib 9-3 NWA 31-3 FAF 31-10

EE857 M45 23-1-43 82MU 5-2 *SS657* 19-2 Gib 9-3 NWA FTR ops 19-4

EE858 M45 33MU 23-1-43 82MU 5-2 *SS657* 19-2 Gib 9-3 NWA 31-3 NAASC 31-10 USAAF 29-3-44

EE859 VC(T)M45 39MU 26-1-43 82MU 5-2 *SS658* 22-2 Gib 7-3 NWA 31-3 SOC 26-4-45

EE860 M45 39MU 2-2-43 76MU 27-2 *Fort McCl* 21-3 Casa 6-4 NWA FTR ops 25-4

EE861 VC(T)M45 39MU 26-1-43 82MU 9-2 *SS658* 22-2 Gib 7-3 NWA 31-3

EE862 VC(T)M45 33MU 26-1-43 FAAC 2-3 ROS 47MU 9-3 *Gerrard Dow* 25-8 Casa 10-9 ME 21-6-45 CE 13-9

EE863 VC(T)M45 33MU 26-1-43 82MU 5-2 *SS657* 19-2 Gib 9-3 dam by sea water after e/a ret to UK CE 24-4

EE864 M45 33MU 6-2-43 ROS 12-3 *SS685* 2-5 Casa 17-5

EE865 M45 33MU 4-2-43 52MU 5-3 *SS680* 11-4 Casa 25-4 NA 1-10 USAAF 29-2-44 to Turkey 30-11

EE866 VC(T)M45 33MU 2-2-43 82MU 28-2 *SS682* 12-4 Casa 25-4 NA dam ops 11-6 Malta SOC 13-6 FH21

EE867 M45 39MU 2-2-43 82MU *Tyne* 2-3 Gib 24-3 NWA 30-4 ME 26-4-45 SOC 29-8-46

EF series All F Mk VC unless otherwise indicated Engines specified

EF526 M45 39MU 2-2-43 82MU 20-2 *Tyne* 2-3 Gib 24-3 NWA 30-4 ME 25-2-45 SOC 29-8-46

EF527 M45 39MU 2-2-43 82MU 20-2 *Tyne* 2-3 Gib 24-3 SOC 26-4-45

EF528 M45 39MU 5-2-43 76MU 27-2 *Harpol* 22-3 Casa 6-4 Malta 1-5 FTR ops 5-7

EF529 M45 39MU 5-2-43 76MU 27-2 *Harpol* 22-3 Casa 6-4 NWA 31-5 USAAF 31-8

EF530 M45 6MU 4-2-43 ROS 18-2 82MU 20-2 *SS686* 24-4 Casa 17-5 NWA 1-10 SOC 28-4-45

EF531 M45 6MU 4-2-43 222MU 12-2 *Fort McCl* 21-3 Casa 6-4 NWA 30-4 Malta 1-7 Sic 1-8 MAAF 21-6-45 SOC 19-7

EF532 M45 6MU 4-2-43 82MU 19-2 *Tyne* 2-3 Gib 24-3 NWA 31-4 Italy 1-11 SOC 26-4-45

EF533 SOC 26-4-45 no record

EF534 M45 6MU 8-2-43 52MU 22-2 *Harpol* 22-3 Casa 6-4 Malta SOC 10-7

EF535 M45 33MU 8-2-43 52MU 3-3 *SS680* 11-4 Casa 25-4 NWA 31-5 ME 1-7

EF536 M45 33MU 8-2-43 52MU 25-2 *Ess Trad* 10-4 Casa 25-4 ME 1-8 NAAF 1-11 C3 ops 9-6-44

EF537 M45 33MU 8-2-43 82MU 10-3 *SS682* 12-4 Casa 25-4 NWA 31-5 Malta 1-7 ME 1-9

EF538 M45 33MU 9-2-43 ROS 22-2 NWA USAAF 31-7 FAF 341S 31-10 ME 31-12 SOC 30-6-44 bboc 21-4-45 32S SOC 10-1-46

EF539 M45 33MU 8-2-43 52MU 3-3 *Harpol* 22-3 Casa 6-4 NWA 31-5 Malta C2 on ops 13-6 ME 1-7 to Turk 28-12-44

EF540 M45 39MU 8-2-43 82MU 27-2-45 *Emp Clive* 23-3 Casa 6-4 NWA 31-5 USAF 3-11 MAAF FAC3 26-1-44

EF541 M45 39MU 16-2-43 VA 1-3 AST 24-5 165S 21-8 314S 28-2-44 57 OTU 12-10 577S 14-6-45 to 5518M 28-7-45 SOC 7-7-48

EF542 VC(T)M45 39MU 13-2-43 82MU 9-3 *Emp Prin* 23-3 Casa 6-4 NWA 31-5 ME 31-1-45 to Turk 22-2

EF543 VC(T) 39MU 13-2-43 215MU 1-3-43 *Aspha* 5-3 Aust 17-5

EF544 M46 39MU 24-2-43 215MU 9-3 *LS117* 28-3 Aust 14-6

EF545 M46 6MU 15-2-43 215MU 24-2 *Aspha* 5-3 Aust 17-5

EF546 M46 6MU 15-2-43 215MU 24-2 *Aspha* 5-3 Aust 17-5

EF547 M46 6MU 15-2-43 215MU 18-2 *Ess Trad* 10-4 Casa 25-4 NWA 31-5

EF548 M46 6MU 15-2-43 52MU 26-2 *Ess Trad* 10-4 Casa 2504 NWA 1-10 MAAF 21-6-45

EF549 M46 6MU 15-2-43 76MU 27-2 *Fort McC* 21-3 Casa 6-4 NWA 30-5 Malta 1-7 Sic 1-8 FAC3 9-9

EE853 LF LR VB was shipped to Australia and lost on operations in early 1944. The remains were found at Kiriwana Islands, off New Guinea, 30 years later. They were shipped back to Australia and rebuilt as UP-O. Now with Langdon Badger, Adelaide.

EF550 M46 8MU 15-2-43 52MU 1-3 *Harpol* 22-3 Casa 6-4 ME 1-8 FAC3 23-9 NAAF 1-11 SOC 30-11

EF551 VC(T)M46 8MU 18-2-43 82MU 4-3 *Emp Prin* 23-3 Casa 6-4 NWA 31-5

EF552 VC(T)M46 8MU 18-2-43 82MU 4-3 *Emp Prin* 23-3 Casa 6-4 NWA 31-5 ME 30-11 SOC 13-9-45

EF553 VC(T)M46 8MU 16-2-43 52MU 1-3 *Harpol* 22-3 NWA 31-5 SOC 26-4-45

EF554 M46 8MU 24-2-43 222MU 17-3 *SS679* 10-4 Casa 25-4 FAC3 19-2-44

EF555 M46 39MU 24-2-43 82MU 10-3 *Emp Prin* 23-3 Casa 6-4 Malta 1-5 FAC3 1-10

EF556 M46 39MU 25-2-43 215MU 9-3 *LS117* 28-3 Aust 14-6

EF557 M46 39MU 24-2-43 215MU 9-3 CB ops 23-3 AUS 215MU 18-6 *LS627* 25-6 Aust 2-8

EF558 M46 39MU 24-2-43 215MU 9-3 *LS117* 28-3 Aust 15-6

EF559 M46 39MU 25-2-43 215MU 9-3 *Tekoa* 11-4 Aust 4-7

EF560 M46 6MU 24-2-43 215MU 9-3 *LS117* 28-3 Aust 14-6

EF561 M46 CRD B Dn 27-2-43 AST 10-8-44 57 OTU 4-1-45 SOC 5-6

EF562 M46 6MU 20-2-43 215MU 9-3 *Tekoa* 11-4 Aust 4-7

EF563 M46 6MU 28-2-43 215MU 9-3 *Tekoa* 11-4 Aust 4-7

EF564 M46 6MU 25-2-43 215MU 8-3 *Sussex* 9-3 Aust 16-4

EF565 M45 8MU 1-3-43 215MU 14-3 *Tekoa* 11-4 Aust 4-7 M46 instal

EF566 M45 8MU 1-3-43 82MU 19-3 *SS682* 12-4 Casa. 25-4 NWA 31-5 M46 instal. ME 30-11-44 RHAF 25-4-46 FACE 335S 2-10 dvd i/grd Langaja Greece Pilot HLD dbf 2-10

EF567 M45 39MU 1-3-43 215MU 22-3 *SS682* 12-4 Casa 25-4 Malta 1-7 Sicily 1-8 ME 30-9 NA 249S 1-11 FTR ops 11-6-44

EF568 M45 39MU 1-3-43 222MU 19-3 *SS679* 1-4 Casa 24-4 NWA 31-5 USAAF 31-12

EF569 M46 6MU 7-3-43 82MU 18-3 *SS682* 12-4 Casa 25-4 Malta 229S C3 ops 13-6 FH45.5

EF570 M45 6MU 1-3-43 82MU 12-3 *Fort McCl* 21-3 Casa 6-4 NA 31-5 Malta 1-6 ME 1-7 SOC 26-4-45

EF584 M45 6MU 1-3-43 82MU 12-3 *Emp Prin* 23-3 Casa 6-4 ME 31-8-44 FACE 22-2-45 M46 instal

EF585 M45 6MU 1-3-43 82MU 12-3 *Emp Prin* 23-3 Casa 6-4 NWA 31-5 Malta 1-8 NAAF 1-11 SOC 31-5-44

EF586 M45 6MU 1-3-43 47MU 14-3 *Orient C* 13-4 Casa 25-4 ME 15-3-45 SOC 27-9 M46 instal

EF587 M45 6MU 1-3-43 215MU 11-3 *Tekoa* 11-4 Aust 4-7 M46 instal

EF588 M46 39MU 8-3-43 215MU 22-3 *Tekoa* 11-4 Aust 4-7

EF589 M46 39MU 8-3-43 215MU 22-3 *Tekoa* 11-4 Aust 4-7

EF590 M46 39MU 8-3-43 215MU 29-3 *Nestor* 4-5 Aust 10-8

EF591 M46 39MU 8-3-43 222MU 26-3 *SS679* 1-4 Casa 25-4 NWA 31-5 ME 1-7 NAAF 1-11 Malta 118MU 31-1-44

EF592 M46 39MU 8-3-43 222MU 31-3 *Emp Bar* 2-5 Casa 17-5 NWA USAAF 31-7

EF593 M46 6MU 8-3-43 82MU 18-3 *SS682* 12-4 Casa 25-4 NWA 31-5 Malta 1-7 Sic 1-8 ME FTR ops 13-8

EF594 M46 6MU 8-3-43 82MU 18-3 *SS682* 12-4 Casa 25-4 NWA 31-5 Malta 1-7 Sic 1-8 NAAF 1-11 Malta SOC 1-3-44

EF595 M46 6MU 8-3-43 222MU 17-3 *SS679* 12-4 Casa 25-4 NWA 31-5 Malta FAC2 23-7 ME 1-9 SOC 2-10

EF596 M46 6MU 8-3-43 82MU 18-3 *SS682* 12-4 Casa 25-4 NWA 31-5 Malta 1-7 Sic 1-8 C3 ops 4-9

EF597 M46 6MU 8-3-43 82MU 18-3 *SS682* 12-4 Casa 25-4 ME 25-2-45 CE 31-5

EF598 M50 8MU 10-3-43 47MU 26-3 *Orient C* 13-4 Casa 25-4 ME C3 ops 26-5

EF599 M50A 8MU 11-3-43 215MU 30-3 *Emp Bar* 2-5 Casa 17-5 NWA 31-5 Malta 1-8 Sic NAAF 1-11

EF600 VC(T) M50 8MU 15-3-43 47MU 1-4 *SS686* 24-4 Casa 17-5 NWA 31-5

EF601 VC(T) M50A 8MU 15-3-43 215MU 30-3 *Emp Bar* 2-5 Casa 7-5 NWA 31-5 ME 21-6 SOC 13-9-45

EF602 M50 8MU 13-3-43 47MU 13-4 *Orient C* 13-4 Casa 25-4 NWA 31-5 FAF 30-11 USAAF

EF603 M50 33MU 15-3-43 222MU 5-4 *Emp Bar* 2-5 Casa 17-5 ME 1-8 SOC 13-9-45

EF604 M50 33MU 15-3-43 47MU 11-4 *Liberian* 5-5 Tak 27-4 ME 23-6 NAASC 31-10 SOC 31-5-45

EF605 M45 33MU 15-3-43 222MU 7-4 *Emp Bar* 2-5 Casa 17-5 ME 1-7 NAAF 1-11 SOC 29-8-46

EF606 NAAF 21-6-45 FAF 9-10-47

EF607 M45 33MU 15-3-43 222MU 7-4 *Emp Bar* 2-5 Casa 17-5 ME 1-7 NAAF 1-11 CE ops 6-4-44

EF608 M45 39MU 15-3-43 222MU 31-3 *Emp Bar* 2-5 Casa 17-5 ME 31-8-44 FACE 9-2-45

EF609 M45 39MU 20-3-43 52MU 6-4 *Fort Rup* 11-4 Casa 25-4 NWA 31-5

EF610 M45 39MU 20-3-43 222MU 8-4 *Emp Bar* 2-5 Casa 17-5 ME 1-9 NAAF 1-11 FACE 14-3-44

EF611 M45 39MU 22-3-43 52MU 6-4 *Emp Bar* 2-5 Casa 17-5 NWA 31-5 Malta 1-8 C3 ops 23-12

EF612 M45 39MU 22-3-43 222MU 6-4 *Emp Bar* 2-5 Casa 17-5 Malta 1-8 NAAF 1-11 ME 28-2-45 SOC 29-8-46

EF613 M45 6MU 22-3-43 215MU 2-4 *Emp Bar* 2-5 Casa 17-5 NWA 31-5 ME 1-9

EF614 M45 6MU 22-3-43 215MU 2-4 *Emp Bar* 2-5 Casa 17-5 NWA 31-5 USAAF 31-7 SOC 31-10

EF615 M50 6MU 29-3-43 82MU 10-4 *SS686* 24-4 Casa 17-5 NWA 31-5 Malta 1-8 FAC3 26-10

EF616 M45 8MU 23-3-43 222MU 4-4 *Emp Bar* 2-5 Casa 17-5 Malta 1-7 Sic 1-8 NAAF 1-11 SOC 29-2-44

EF629 VC(T) M45 8MU 26-3-43 82MU 8-4 *SS686* 24-4 Casa 17-5 Malta 1-8 NAASC 31-10 ME 30-11 SOC 29-6-44

EF630 VC(T) M46 8MU 26-3-43 47MU 4-4 *Emp Bar* 2-5 Casa 17-5 SOC 26-4-45

EF631 VC(T) M46 33MU 24-3-43 47MU 11-4 *Liber* 5-5 Tak 29-5 ME 16-7 C3 ops 12-4-44

EF632 VC(T) M46 33MU 29-3-43 222MU 10-4 *SS687* 29-4 Casa 17-5

EF633 VC(T) M46 39MU 29-3-43 47MU 26-4 *Liber* 5-5 Tak 29-4 ME 10-6 SOC 29-8-46

EF634 VC(T) M50 39MU 29-3-43 47MU 17-4 *Liber* 5-5 Tak 29-5 ME 10-6 SOC 29-8-46

EF635 M50 6MU 24-3-43 82MU 14-4 *SS686* 24-4 Casa 17-5 NAAS 31-10 32S MAAF 31-6-45

EF636 M50 6MU 24-3-43 82MU 10-4 *SS686* 24-4 Casa 17-5 NWA 31-5 Malta 118MU 31-1-44 SOC 26-11-45

EF637 VC(T) M46 8MU 24-3-43 82MU 8-4 *SS686* 24-4 Casa 17-5 ME 1-7 NAAF 1-11 SOC 31-10-45 M50 instal

EF638 VC(T) M50 8MU 2-4-43 82MU 12-4 *SS686* 24-4 Casa 17-5 Malta 1-11 NWA SOC 17-11

EF639 M50 33MU 5-4-43 82MU 22-4 *SS687* 29-4 Casa 17-5 ME 1-9 NAAF 1-11 SOC 29-2-44

EF640 M50 33MU 5-4-43 76MU 14-5 *SS702* 2-6 Casa 15-6 NWA 1-7 ME 1-9 NA 30-11 SOC 26-4-45

EF641 VC(T) M50 33MU 5-4-43 47MU 18-4 *Rook* 19-5 Tak 16-6 ME 24-7 SOC 31-5-45

EF642 M50 39MU 5-4-43 47MU 7-5 *Rook* 19-5 Tak 16-6 ME 16-7 SOC 29-8-46

EF643 VC(T) M50 39MU 5-4-43 47MU 4-5 *Rook* 19-5 Tak 16-6 ME 13-7 NWA SOC 1-10

EF644 M50 39MU 10-443 Farn 14-4 Monica I instal, trls in conjunction with Ju88 fitt Flensburg. Gun firing and A.I radar. Comp perf trls of improved surface pnt finish with EF731, EN946 and JL227(FIX). Drag red trls. 39MU 6-7 222MU 26-8 ROS *Card Gib* 3-9 Casa 20-9 NA 30-11 FAF 31-12 C3 ops 9-3-44

EF677 M50 39MU 14-5-43 47MU 9-6 *Glenb* Tak 30-7 ME 13-9

EF678 VC(T) M50 39MU 14-5-43 82MU 2-6 to 4203M 10SoTT 30-10 CE 29-10-44

EF679 M50 39MU 26-5-43 47MU 6-6 *SS707* Casa 29-6 NWA USAAF 1-10 12/52 lost in Italy 24-1-44

EF680 VC(T) M50 39MU 14-5-43 82MU *LS517* Tak 16-4 ME 22-8 SOC 13-9-45

EF681 M50 33MU 17-5-43 222MU *SS705* Casa 15-6 NWA 30-6 ME 1-8 NAAF 1-11 Malta 118MU 31-1-44 SOC 29-2

EF682 M50 33MU 17-5-43 222MU *SS705* Casa 15-6 NWA 1-10

EF683 M45 33MU 20-5-43 222MU *SS707* Casa 29-6 NAASC 31-10 ME 15-3-45 SOC 27-6-46

EF684 VC(T) M50 33MU 18-5-43 82MU 30-5 *SS703* Casa 15-6 ME 1-8 NAAF 1-11

EF685 M50 33MU 21-5-43 215MU 1-6 *SS708* Casa 29-6 Face 10-9 NAAF 1-11 SOC 8-3-44

EF686 VC(T) M46 6MU 25-5-43 222MU 1-6 *SS708* Casa 29-6 FAF 1-10 MAAF 21-6-45 FAF 10-9-47

EF687 M45 6MU 26-5-43 76MU 1-6 *SS708* Casa 29-6 NWA 1-10 SOC 28-4-45

EF688 M50 6MU 26-5-43 222MU 1-6 *SS708* Casa 29-6 NWA 1-10

EF689 M50 8MU 31-5-43 82MU 18-6 *SS710* Casa 14-7 ME 1-9 NWA 1-11 SOC 8-3-44

EF690 M50 Rotol Ltd. 2-6-43 8MU 18-6 82MU 24-6 *La Pampa* Casa 14-7 ME 1-9 NAAF 1-11 to Turk 30-11-44

EF691 VC(T) M50 8MU 7-6-43 222MU 18-6 *Fort Verc* Casa 14-7 USAAF 31-12 lost over Italy 19-12 SOC 29-2-44

EF692 VC(T) M50 33MU 9-6-43 47MU 23-6 *Fort Verc* Casa 14-7 NWA FAF 1-10 CE ops 29-10-44

EF693 VC(T) M50 33MU 9-6-43 47MU 23-6 *Fort Verc* Casa 14-7 NWA USAAF 1-10 lost in Italy 7-2-44

EF694 VC(T) M50 39MU 9-6-43 52MU 21-6 *La Pampa* Casa 14-7 ME 1-9 NAAF 30-11 9S FTR 25-10-44

EF695 VC(T) M50 39MU 10-6-43 82MU 23-6 *La Pampa* Casa 14-7

EF696 VC(T) M50 33MU 11-6-43 222MU 24-6 *La Pampa* Casa 14-7 ME 15-3-45 SOC 27-6-46

EF697 VC(T) M50 33MU 17-6-43 234S 13-7 222MU 20-8 *Ger Don* 25-8 Casa 10-9 NA 30-11 FAF GR 2/33 25-6-44 SOC 26-4-45

Tropicalised EF704 was transferred to the USAAF in 1944.

EF645 M50 6MU 10-4-43 76MU 23-4 *Fort Thom* 3-5 Casa 17-5 Malta 1-7 Sic 1-8 NAAF 1-11 SOC 29-8-46

EF646 M50 6MU 13-4-43 76MU 23-4 *Fort Thom* 3-5 Casa 17-5 Malta 1-10 SOC 26-6-45

EF647 M50 VAWD 12-4-43 wts & CG load of WAL prod a/c 6MU 14-4 82MU 26-4 *Fort Jer* 11-5 Casa 30-5 Malta 1-8 NA 30-10 USAAF 30-11 lost France 9-2-44 12/52

EF648 M50 8MU 13-4-43 82MU 23-4 *Fort Thom* 3-5 Casa 17-5 ME 1-9 FTR ops 2-12

EF649 M50 8MU 13-4-43 82MU 23-4 *Fort Jer* 11-5 Casa 30-5 NWA 1-7 MAAF 21-6-45 IAF 27-6-46 as MM4053

EF650 M50 8MU 13-4-43 82MU 23-4 *Emp Bar* 2-5 Casa 17-5

EF651 VC(T) M50 8MU 17-4-43 82MU 27-4 *Fort Jer* 11-5 Casa 30-5 NWA 1-7 ME 1-9 NAAF 1-11 ME 31-1-45 to Turk 22-2

EF652 M50 8MU 19-4-43 222MU 2-5 *Fort Stle* 16-5 Casa 30-5 NWA 1-7 MAAF 21-6-45

EF653 M50 39MU 10-4-43 47MU 7-5 *Pen Cast* 3-6 Tak 27-6 ME 20-9 SOC 16-7-46

EF654 M50 39MU 29-4-43 47MU 18-5 *Pen Cast* 3-6 Tak 27-6 ME 24-7

EF655 M50 39MU 19-4-43 47MU 9-5 *Pen Cast* 3-6 TAk 27-6 ME 6-9 C3 ops 24-4-44

EF656 VC(T) M50 39MU 27-4-43 47MU 13-5 *Rockley* 19-5 Tak 16-6 ME 17-7 NAAF 30-11 SOC 26-4-45

EF671 M50 6MU 27-4-43 222MU 5-5 *Fort Stle* 16-5 Casa 30-5 NWA 1-7 NAASC 31-10 ME 30-11 SOC 29-8-46

EF672 M50 6MU 27-4-43 222MU 5-5 *Fort Stle* 16-5 Casa 30-5 NWA 31-5 NAASC 1-10 ME 31-8-44 SOC 13-9-45

EF673 M50 6MU 27-4-43 222MU 5-5 *Fort Stle* 16-5 Casa 30-5 ME 1-9 NAAF 1-11

EF674 VC(T) M50 8MU 14-5-43 82MU 4-6 *SS707* Casa 29-6 s/dn by Allied fire 11-9 NAAF 1-11

EF675 VC(T) M50 8MU 14-5-43 222MU 1-6 *SS707* Casa 29-6 ME 1-8 NAAF 30-11 ME 31-8-44 SOC 28-9-46

EF676 VC(T) 8MU 14-5-43 82MU 4-6 *SS707* Casa 29-6 ME 1-9 FTR 9-12

EF698 VC(T) M55 33MU 22-6-43 234S 12-7 82MU 17-8 *Ger Don* 25-8 Casa NA 30-11 USAAF 31-1-44 SOC 31-8

EF699 VC(T) M55 33MU 22-6-43 234S 12-7 82MU 17-8 *Ger Don* 25-8 Casa 10-9 NA 30-11 USAAF 31-1-44

EF700 VC(T) M55 33MU 22-6-43 234S 12-7 222MU 23-8 *Card Gib* 3-9 Casa 20-9 NAAS 31-10 USAAF 31-1-44 lost in Italy 19-2

EF701 M55 39M& 22-6-43 234S 12-7 82MU 14-8 *Ger Don* 25-8 Casa 10-9 NA 30-11 USAAF 31-1-44 ME 15-3-45 SOC 29-8-46

EF702 VC(T) M45 234S 14-7-43 39MU 5-8 82MU 14-8 *Ger Don* 25-8 Casa 10-9 NA 30-11 MAAF 21-6-45 SOC 30-8

EF703 VC(T) M55 39MU 28-6-43 234S 14-7 82MU *Ger Don* 25-8 Casa 10-9 NAASC 31-10 USAAF 31-1-44 lost in Italy 19-3

EF704 VC(T) M55 39MU 28-6-43 234S 16-7 82MU 13-8 *Ger Don* 25-8 Casa 10-9 NAASC 31-10 USAAF 29-2-44 ME 25-2-45 SOC 29-8-46

EF705 M55 39MU 30-6-43 130S 20-7 82MU 14-8 *Ger Don* 25-8 Casa 10-9 NA 30-11 FACE 13-2-45

EF706 VC(T) M55 33MU 12-7-43 130S 24-7 82MU 27-8 *Ger Don* 25-8 Casa 10-9 NA 30-11 USAAF 31-1-44 ME 30-11 SOC 29-8-46

EF707 VC(T) M55 33MU 13-7-43 130S 24-7 82MU 18-8 *Ger Don* 25-8 Casa 10-9 NA 30-11 USAAF 31-1-44 lost in Italy 19-2

EF708 VC(T) M55 33MU 13-7-43 82MU 21-7 *SS732* Casa 18-8 NWA 1-10 USAAF 31-12 SOC 26-4-45

EF709 VC(T) M55 33MU 16-7-43 82MU 23-7 *SS732* Casa 18-8 NA 30-11 USAAF 31-1-44 SOC 28-4-45

EF710 VC(T) M55 33MU 17-7-43 82MU 27-7 *SS732* Casa 18-8 NA 30-11 USAAF 31-1-44 w/o in Italy 19-2

EF715 M55 39MU 28-7-43 222MU 11-8 *Ger Don* 25-8 Casa 10-9 NAASC 31-10

EF716 M55 39MU 29-7-43 326S 82MU 11-8 *Fort Thom* Casa 1-9 NAASC 31-10 USAAF 29-2-44 326S FTR 11-6

EF717 M55 39MU 4-8-43 82MU 21-8 *Ger Don* 25-8 Casa 10-9 NA 30-11 USAAF 31-1-44

EF718 M55 39MU 5-8-43 82MU 21-8 *Ger Don* 25-8 Casa 10-9 NAASC 31-10 ME 28-12-44 SOC 10-1-46

EF719 M55 39MU 7-8-43 222MU 19-8 *Ger Don* 25-8 Casa 10-9 NAASC 31-10

EF720 M55 39MU 11-8-43 82MU 21-5 *Card Gib* Casa 20-9 NAASC 31-10 SOC 30-3-45

EF721 VC(T) M55 33MU 12-8-43 82MU 18-8 *Ger Don* 25-8 Casa 10-9 NAASC 31-10 SOC 31-8-44

EF722 VC(T) M55 33MU 21-8-43 47MU 28-8 *Card Gib* Casa 20-9 NAASC 31-10 40S CE ops 5-8-44

EF723 VC(T) M55 39MU 16-8-43 215MU 27-8 *Card Gib* Casa 20-9 NAASC 31-10 MAAF 21-6-45

EF724 VC(T) M55 39MU 17-8-43 215MU 27-8 *Card Gib* Casa 20-9 NAASC 31-10

EF725 VC(T) M55 39MU 21-8-43 47MU 1-9 *Emp Grebe* Casa 29-9 NAASC 31-10 CE ops 8-1-44

EF726 VC(T) M55 33MU 21-8-43 47MU 26-8 *Card Gib* Casa 20-9 NAASC 31-10 SOC 26-4-45

EF727 VC(T) M55 33MU 24-8-43 82MU 30-8 *Emp Grebe* Casa 29-9 NAASC 31-10

EF728 M55 33MU 2-9-43 47MU 12-9 *Ocean Rid* Casa 10-10 NAASC 31-10 40S CE ops 6-3-44

EF729 M55 39MU 31-8-43 82MU 9-9 *Craw W L* 22-9 Casa 10-10 NAASC 31-10

EF730 M55 39MU 2-9-43 82MU 8-9 *Craw W L* 22-9 Casa 10-10 NAASC 31-10

EF731 LFVCM55M enlarged rad desert cam upper/ sky blue u/s Glos A/C Brockworth SS tank trls over Farn speed course. Farn Sep '43 with spcl finish for comp trls with EF644 and EN946. BDn 7-11 trls with normal and armoured leading edge Rotol Jablo prop. Edge of blade reinforced with wire insert. Farn June to July '44 for Gyro gunsight trls. R-RH 14-6-45 CAC 14-1-46 to 5803M 12SoTT 30-1 SOC 6-5-49

EF732 M55 33MU 2-9-43 82MU 9-9 *Craw W L* 22-9 Casa 1-10 NAASC 31-10 40S CE ops 28-7-44

EF733 M55 33MU 2-9-43 47MU 8-9 *Ocean Rid* Casa 10-10 NAASC 31-10 MAAF 21-6-45 Trg Del 4-10

EF734 M55 39MU 7-9-43 47MU 17-9 *Ionian* Casa 19-10 USAAF 29-2-44 MAAF 21-6-45 Trg Del 27-9-48

EF735 M55 39MU 8-9-43 222MU 15-9 *Craw W L* Casa 10-10 NAASC 31-10 SOC 26-4-45

EF736 M55 39MU 11-9-43 47MU 21-9 *Ionian* Casa 19-10 NA 30-11 FAF GR2/33 2-5-44

EF737 M55 33MU 17-9-43 222MU 22-9 *Emp Mar* Casa 19-10 NA 31-11 ME FACE 23-11

EF738 M55 33MU 17-9-43 82MU 20-9 *Emp Mar* Casa 19-10 NA 30-11 40S C3 ops 13-6-44

EF739 M55 39MU 28-9-43 47MU 9-10 *Char Hall* Casa 17-11 NA 30-11 USAAF 29-2-44

EF740 M55 39MU 1-10-43 82MU 19-10 *Mont City* 15-11 Casa 29-11 USAAF 29-2-44 253S FTR 11-5-44

EF741 M55 39MU 5-10-43 47MU 25-10 *Mont City* 15-11 Casa 29-11 USAAF 29-2-44 of 12/52 lost in Italy 15-2

EF742 M55 33MU 5-10-43 47MU 16-10 *Mont City* 15-11 Casa 29-11 USAAF 29-2-44 ME 28-12

EF743 M55 33MU 5-10-43 47MU 16-10 *Mont City* 15-11 Casa 29-11 MAAF 21-6-45 FAF 14-2-46

EF744 M55 33MU 7-10-43 47MU 15-10 *Char Hall* Casa 17-11 NA 30-11 USAAF 29-2-44 ME 31-1-45 SOC 28-9-46

EF745 M55 39MU 7-10-43 222MU 10-10 *Mont City* 15-11 Casa 29-11 USAAF 29-2-44 MAAF 21-6-45 FAF 10-9-47

EF746 M55 39MU 12-10-43 82MU 21-10 *Mont City* 15-11 Casa 29-11 USAAF 29-2-44 of 12/52 lost in Italy 19-2

EF747 M55 39MU 13-10-43 47MU 22-10 *Mont City* Casa 29-11 USAAF 29-2-44

EF748 M55 33MU 19-9-43 82MU 5-11 *Mont City* Casa 29-11 SOC 30-6-45

EF749 M55 33MU 19-9-43 47MU 13-11 *Fort Geo* Casa 22-12 USAAF 29-2-44 SOC 28-4-45

EF750 M55 33MU 22-9-43 82MU 10-11 *Fort Geo* Casa 22-12 ME 25-2-45 SOC 22-3

EF751 M55 39MU 26-10-43 222MU 9-11 *Fort Geo* Casa 22-12 USAAF 29-2-44 of 12/56 lost in Italy 17-3

EF752 M55 39MU 31-10-43 222MU 9-11 *Fort Geo* Casa 22-12 225S FTR 8-1-44 recat A ME 31-1-45 SOC 13-9

EF753 M55 39MU 5-11-43 76MU 22-11 *Fort Geo* Casa 22-12 USAAF 29-2-44

EN seris all F Mk VB Merlin 45 unless otherwise indicated. Rolls-Royce conversion contract 19713/39.

EN112 3608 R-R to FIX M61 FF 13-11-42 9MU 17-11 47MU 29-11 *SS646* 7-12 Gib 24-12

EN113 3649 R-R to FIX M61 FF 21-11-42 9MU 28-11 47MU 5-12 Malta 14-12 CE ops 6-2-43

EN114 3650 R-R to FIX M61 FF 21-22-42 CRD R-RH 28-11 flight trls with SU fuel injection pump cd Rearsby Leicester CE 29-12 FH13.55

EN115 3666 R-R to FIX M61 FF 27-11-42 12MU 1-12 47MU *Hamble VI* 20-12 Gib 13-1-43 NWA 28-2 ME 9-8-45 REAF 31-7-47 SOC 5-2-48

EN116 3634 R-R to FIX M61 FF 21-11-42 12MU 25-11 47MU 5-12 *SS647* 19-12 Gib 6-2-43 NWA 28-2 SOC 31-7

EN117 3665 R-R to FIX M61 FF 25-11-42 6MU 1-12 47MU 10-12 *Emp Tow* 23-12 Gib 13-1-43 FAC3 31-1

EN118 3667 R-R to FIX M61 FF 27-11-42 12MU 1-12 47MU 9-12 Gib 13-1-43 NWA 25-2

EN119 3699 R-R to FIX M61 FF 1-12-42 6MU 7-12 47MU 10-12 *Emp Tow* 23-12 Gib 13-1-43 NWA 28-2 FTR ops 25-4

EN120 3698 R-R to FIX M61 FF 30-11-42 12MU 7-12 47MU 19-12 *South* 30-12 Gib 3-1-43 NWA 28-2

EN121 3709 R-R to FIX M61 FF 4-12-42 6MU 7-12 47MU 11-12 *Emp Tow* 230-12 Gib 13-1-43 CE ops 21-1

EN239 3794 R-R to FIX M61 FF 24-12-42 12MU 4-1-43 47MU 240-1 *Emp Tide* 3-2 Gib 16-2 Malta 1-7 Sic 1-8 NAASC 31-10 MAAF 21-6-45 SOC 26-6-47

EN240 3711 R-R to FIX M61 FF 1-12-42 6MU 14-12 47MU 20-12 *South* 30-12 Gib 13-1-43 NWA 28-2 FACE 9-4-45

EN241 3697 MXX R-R to FIX M61 FF 30-11-42 6MU 7-12 47MU 12-12 *Emp Tow* 23-12 Gib 13-1-43 NWA 28-2 Malta 1-8 NAAF 11-11 SOC 8-3-44 bboc ME 21-6-45 SOC 5-2-48

EN242 3771 R-R to FIX M61 FF 20-12-42 12MU 24-12 47MU 9-1-43 *Mer Prin* 18-1 Gib 6-2 NWA 28-2 SOC 11-4-46

EN243 3757 R-R to FIX M61 FF 17-12-42 12MU 24-12 47MU 9-1-43 *Mer Prin* 18-1 Gib 6-2 NWA 28-2 C3 ops 5-4

EN244 3712 R-R to FIX M61 FF 4-12-42 6MU 14-12 47MU 22-12 *South* 30-12 Gib 13-1-43 NWA 28-2 72S 26-4 ME 21-2-45 FACE 9-4 SOC 14-6

EN245 3713 R-R to FIX M61 FF 4-12-42 9MU 14-12 47MU 3-1-43 *Mer Prin* 18-1 Gib 6-2 NWA 28-2 C3 ops 2-3

EN246 3739 R-R to FIX M61 FF 10-12-42 12MU 21-12 47MU 9-1-43 *Mer Prin* 18-1 Gib 6-2 72S C3 ops 25-2

EN247 3763 R-R to FIX M61 FF 20-12-42 12MU 24-12 47MU 9-1-43 *Mer Prin* 18-1 NWA 31-3 Malta 1-7 Sicily 1-8

EN248 3733 R-R toFIX M61 FF 7-12-42 9MU 14-12 12FPP SI nd u/c clpse running onto soft grd CE 11-1-43

EN249 3745 R-R to FIX M61 FF 13-12-42 9MU 21-12 47MU 11-1-43 *Emp Time* 3-2 Gib 16-2 NWA 31-3 SOC 10-1-44

EN250 3752 R-R to FIX M61 FF 16-12-42 9MU 21-12 47MU 3-1 *Mer Prin* 18-1 Gib 6-2 NWA 28-2 72S C3 ops 3-4

EN251 3773 R-R to FIX M61 FF 20-12-42 47MU 11-1-43 *Mer Prin* 19-1 Gib 6-2 NWA 28-2 SOC 18-8-44

EN252 3870 R-R to FIX M61 FF 11-1-43 6MU 25-1 *Well Crt* 18-2 Gib 7-3 Malta 1-7 Italy 1-11 CE 6-9-45

EN253 3795 R-R to FIX(T) M61 FF 29-12-42 Ben 4-1-43 47MU 5-1 *SS657* 19-2 Gib 9-3 ME 5-7-45 REAF 26-9-46

EN254 3803 R-R to FIX M61 FF 31-12-42 6MU 12-1-43 47MU 15-1 *Emp Hav* 19-1 Gib 6-2 Malta 1-7 ME RHAF 30-1-47

EN255 3836 R-R to FIX M61 FF 8-1-43 6MU 12-1 47MU 15-1 *Emp Tide* 3-2 Gib 16-2 NWA 31-3 USAF 12-31 lost in Italy 19-11

EN256 3793 R-R to FIX M61 FF 30-12-42 12MU 12-1-43 47MU 21-1 *Well Crt* 18-2 Gib 7-3 NWA 31-3

EN257 3871 R-R to FIX M61 FF 11-1-43 12MU 26-1 47MU 9-2 *Llan* 11-3 Gib 24-3 NWA 30-4 FA FTR 25-6

EN258 3844 R-R to FIX M61 FF 8-1-43 12MU 26-1 47MU 4-2 *SS657* 19-2 Gib 9-3 Malta 1-7 Sic 1-8 NAASC 31-10 C3 ops 18-12

EN351 3804 R-R to FIX M61 FF 31-12-42 6MU 4-1-43 47MU 11-1 *Emp Hav* 19-1 Gib 6-2 NWA 31-3 FAF 1-10 SOC 18-10-45

EN352 3843 R-R to FIX M61 FF 4-1-43 6MU 21-1 47MU 29-1 *SS657* 19-2 Gib 9-3 NWA 31-3 FAF 1-10 SOC 31-4-45

EN353 3845 R-R to FIX M61 FF 9-1-43 12MU 26-1 47MU 9-2 *SS657* 19-2 Gib 9-3 NWA 31-3

EN354 3872 R-R to FIX M61 FF 13-1-43 12MU 29-1 47MU 9-2 *Fort Hud* 20-2 Gib 7-3 NWA 31-3 SOC 15-3-45

EN355 3911 R-R to FIX M61 FF 15-1-43 12MU 26-1 47MU 14-2 *Llan* 11-3 Gib 24-3 NWA FAC3 6-4 SOC 8-4-44

EN356 3908 R-R to FIX M63 DFF 23-1-43 12MU 1-2 47MU 11-2 *Llan* 11-3 Gib 24-3 NWA 30-4 Malta 1-7 SOC 11-7

EN357 3912 R-R to FIX M61 FF 15-1-43 12MU 1-2 VAWD wts and CG load of R-R prod a/c 28-1 47MU 11-2 *Llan* 11-2 Gib 24-3 Malta 1-7 Sic 1-8 NAASC 31.10 ME 31-5-45 SOC 2-8

EN358 3380 R-R to FIX M63 FF 15-1-43 9MU 24-1 47MU 4-2 *SS657* 15-2 Gib 9-5 NWA 31-3 Malta 1-7 72S FTR ops 26-7

EN359 3882 R-R to FIX M63 FF 17-1-43 6MU 1-2 47MU 9-2 *Llan* 11-3 Gib 24-3 SOC 5-6-45

EN360 3899 R-R to FIX M61 FF 22-1-43 9MU 24-1 47MU 4-2 *SS657* Gib 9-3

EN361 3900 R-R to FIX M63 FF 23-1-43 12MU 26-1 47MU 6-2 *SS658* 22-2 Gib 7-3 NWA 31-3 Malta C3 ops 10-7 SOC 8-3-44

EN362 3901 R-R to FIX M61 FF 23-1-43 12MU 26-1 47MU 5-2 *SS657* 19-2 Gib 9-3 NWA 31-3

EN363 4044 R-R to LFIX M66 FF 27-2-43 341S 28-2 ROS 611S 17-5 CAC ops 11-6 ROS Flt Refuel Stav 31-1-44 APC South 21-2 FLS 5-6 to 6038M RAF Cosford SOC 14-10-50 FFS SoH

EN364 3926 R-R to FIX M63 FF 26-1-43 12MU 4-2 47MU 16-2 *Harmat* 10-3 Gib 26-4 NWA 31-5 ME 1-8 SOC 31-1-46

EN365 3903 R-R toFIX M61 FF 23-1-43 12MU 6-2 47MU 12-2 *Llan* 11-3 Gib 24-3 NWA 30-4 Malta 1-7 Sic 1-8 NAASC 1-11 232S FACE 1-5-45 SOC 30-8

EN366 3925 R-R to FIX M63 FF 26-1-43 12MU 3-2 47MU 14-2 *Llan* 11-3 Gib 24-3 NWA 30-4 SOC 22-11-45

EN367 R-R to FIX M63 FF 28-1-43 6MU 1-2 47MU 9-2 *Fort H H* 25-2 Gib 7-3 83MU ROS 165S 23-12 303S 3-9-44 FTR i/sea ops 25-2-45

EN368 3936 R-R to FIX M63 FF 28-1-43 6MU 2-2 47MU 9-2 *Llan* 11-3 Gib 24-3 NWA 30-4 SOC 31-7

EN369 3930 R-R to FIX M63 FF 29-1-43 39MU 1-2 47MU 9-2 *Fort H H* 20-2 Gib 7-3 NWA 31-3 USAAF 31-1-44 FACE 3-6-45

EN370 3937 R-R to FIX M63 FF 29-1-43 12MU 3-2 47MU 12-2 *Llan* 11-3 Gib 24-3 NWA 30-4 Malta 1-7 Sic 1-8 e/a C3 11-8

EN515 3957 R-R to FIX M63 FF 3-2-43 BDn comp trls with three types prop reduction gear combinations 12MU 9-2 47MU 19-2 *Harmat* 10-3 Gib 26-4 NWA 31-5

EN516 3938 R-R to FIX M63 FF 30-1-43 12MU 6-2 47MU 16-2 *Harmat* 10-3 Gib 26-4 NWA 31-5

EN517 3958 R-R to FIX M63 FF 4-2-43 12MU 10-2 47MU 24-2 *Wand* 12-3 Gib 24-3 NWA 30-4 ME 2-8-45 SOC 9-8

EN518 3962 R-R to FIX M63 FF 6-2-43 12MU 10-2 47MU 25-2 *Wand* 12-3 Gib 24-3 NWA 30-4 Malta 1-7 SOC 13-7 bboc 21-6-45 SOC 26-9-46

EN519 3947 R-R to FIX M63 FF 4-2-43 12MU 8-2 47MU 15-2 *Harmat* 10-3 Gib 26-4 NWA 31-5 Malta 1-6 FACE 20-8

EN520 3972 R-R to FIX M63 FF 11-2-43 9MU 13-2 47MU 25-2 *Wand* 12-3 Gib 24-3 Malta 1-7 Sic 1-8 CE ops 12-8 SOC 3-8-44

EN521 3965 R-R to FIX M63 FF 8-2-43 9MU 13-2 47MU 25-2 *Wand* 12-3 Gib 24-3 NWA 30-4 SOC 309-10 bboc for REAF 21-6-45

EN522 3986 R-R to FIX M63 FF 12-2-43 64S 16-2 453S 2-4 AST mods 7-5 331S 12-11 AST 8-1-44 611S 14-7 FACE 28-7

EN523 4096 R-R to FIX M63 FF 11-3-43 15MU 13-4 47MU 29-3 *SS680* 11-4 Casa 25-4 NWA 31-5 Malta 1-6 FAC2 19-10 SOC 1-11

EN524 4003 R-R to HFIX M70 FF 19-2-43 Bdn 21-2 oil cool & rad suit trls. VC Univ wing with mod upper can blisters. R-RH 24-7 M61 instal with exp exhaust manifold. Dev trls. FAAC 24-8-44 AST BDn 25-1-45 comp trls with three types prop reduction gear. Tailplaine incidence increased by 2° standard wint tips. ASTEx 33MU 8-7 Pers 5-9-47 S Africa 11-9 SAAF 25-9

EN525 3973 R-R to HFIX M70 Central Uruguayan Railways Uruguayan Staff FF 11-2-43 64S 13-2 BDn trls with three types of prop reduction gears; oil cool and rad suit ROS 12-7 129S 29-7 412S 26-8 AST 8-1-44 FAAC 7-4 ROS sold Vic 5-12-49

EN526 3990 R-R to FIX M63 FF 14-2-43 306S 18-2 Stn Flt North 23-2 AST 24-9 33S 8-7-44 504S 15-7 303S 4-2-45 CAC ops 8-2 to 5802M RAF Gat 3-1-46

EN527 3991 R-R to FIX M63 FF 14-2-43 306S 5-3 316S 14-3 302S 28-9 CB ops 3-11 33S 28-5-44 310S 8-7 504S 15-7 303S 13-8 CE ops

EN528 4002 R-R to FIX M63 FF 18-2-43 4MU 21-2 47MU 12-3 *SS670* 24-3 Gib 12-4 NWA 31-5 Malta 1-7 ME 1-9 NAASC 31-10 SAAF FTR 6-11-44

EN529 4032 R-R to LFIX M66 FF 24-2-43 OC Tang 28-3 611S ROS 20-5 485S 4-7 FTR ops 16-9-45

EN530 4035 R-R to FIX M63 FF 26-2-43 12MU 28-2 47MU 10-3 *SS670* 24-3 Gib 12-4 NWA 31-5 Malta 1-7 Sic 1-8 NAASC 31-10 MAAF 26-4-45 SOC 26-9-46

EN531 4053 R-R to FIX M63 FF 28-2-43 9MU 5-3 47MU 16-3 *SDS680* 11-4 Casa 25-4 NWA 31-5 Malta 1-6 CE ops 25-4-45

EN532 4054 R-R to FIX M63 FF 1-3-43 12MU 6-3 47MU 20-3 *SS680* 11-4 Casa 25-4 Malta 126S C3 ops 4-6 FH20.20

EN533 4033 R-R to FIX M63 FF 25-2-43 12MU 28-2 47MU 10-3 *SS670* 24-3 Gib 12-4 Malta 1-6

EN534 4034 R-R to FIX M63A FF 25-2-43 12MU 28-2 47MU 9-3 *SS670* 24-3 Gib 12-4 NA 31-5 Malta 1-8 Sic 31-10 SOC 30-6-44

EN551 4106 R-R to FIX M63 FF 16-3-43 9MU 18-3 Malta C3 ops 29-5

EN552 EN552 4107 R-R to FIX M63 16-3-43 9MU 18-3 47MU 4-4 *SS 686* 24-4 Casa 17-5 NWA 32S 31-5 FTR ops 2-4-44

EN553 4162 R-R to FIX M63 FF 30-3-43 12MU 47MU 10-4 *Emp Bar* 2-56 Casa 17-5 ME 1-8 NAAF 1-11 SOC 29-2-44

EN554 4205 R-R to LFIX M66 FF 12-4-43 611S 15-4 485S 4-7 CB AST 23-3-44 317S 24-9 308 FTR 18-9

EN555 4083 R-R to LFIX M66 F 7-3-43 611S 9-3 R-RH 31-5 ROS 341S 207 CAC ops 13-9 AST 441S 24-8-44 WAL SOC 16-6-45

EN556 4180 R-R to FIX M63 FF 1-4-43 6MU 6-4 47MU 12-4 *SS687* 29-4 Casa 17-5 ME 1-9 NAASC 31-10 SOC 14-3-44

EN557 4058 R-R to LFIX M66 7-3-43 611S 9-3 FTR ops 14-5

EN558 4082 R-R to LFIX M66 FF 7-3-43 611S 9-3 FTR ops 14-5

EN559 4084 R-R to LFIX M66 FF 10-3-43 611S 12-3 485S 4-7 ROS 3-8 FTR ops 20-10

EN560 4085 FF 10-3-43 no record. To RNAF as H-54 to H119 BAF 1952 as spares

EN561 4136 R-R to FIX M63 FF 23-3-43 6MU 47MU 5-4 *SS686* 24-4 Casa 17-5

EN562 4108 R-R to LFIX M66 FF 16-3-43 611S FTR ops 30-5

EN563 4109 R-R to LFIX M66 FF 18-3-43 611S 20-3 485S 4-7 66S FACB 15-4-44 FRU 6-8 SOC 15-8

EN564 4130 R-R to LFIX M66 FF 21-3-43 611S 49MU 26-3 485S 4-7 USAAF 8/67 FTR 14-7 France.

EN565 4131 R-R to LFIX M66 FF 22-3-43 611S 26-3 CAC ops 17-5 ROS 485S 4-7 FAAC 1-9 ROS 66S 2-12 FACB 24-4 1 CRU recat E 15-9

EN566 4135 R-R to LFIX M66 FF 23-3-43 611S 26-3 CAC ops 14-4 GAL 25-5 165S 1-8-44 VA mods 26-10-45 sold R. J. coley 6-2-50

EN567 4147 R-R to LFIX M66 FF 26-3-43 611S 1-4 FTR ops 4-5

EN568 4161 R-R to LFIX M66 FF 29-3-43 Stn HQ BH11 17-4 485S 23-9 66S FAAC 30-12 ROS SAL 30-3-45 13Com Flt Inverness 19-7-45 RAF 19-8-47 as SM-6

EN767, production VC with four Hispano cannon, after repair, June 1944. Returned to 57 OTU.

EN569 4169 R-R to LFIX M66 FF 2-4-43 485S 4-7 Stn Flt BH11 23-9 341S 10-10 411S 17-10 FAAC 16-3-44 AST 401S 23-11-44 CE ops 1-3-45

EN570 4181 R-R to LFIX M66 FF 3-4-43 15MU 8-4 76MU 21-4 611S 15-5 FTR ops 11-6

EN571 4206 R-R to LFIX M66 FF 13-4-43 611S 14-4 FTR 18-4

EN572 4236 R-R to LFIX M66 FF 19-4-43 611S 30-4 486S 4-7 FTR ops 6-9

EN573 4248 R-R to LFIX M66 FF 21-4-43 485S 1-7 FTR ops 15-7

EN574 4258 R-R to LFIX M66 FF 28-4-43 611S 30-4 FTR 17-5

EN575 4268 R-R to LFIX M66 FF 1-5-43 611S 6-5 485S 4-7 66S FTR ops 25-1-44 FH245.45

EN576 4273 R-R to LFIX M66 FF 2-5-43 611S 6-5 485S 4-7 CAC 30-7 341S 31-1-44 ROS MAL 21-10 3APU 4-5-45 MAAF 10-9 SOC 29-3-47

EN577 4286 R-R to LFIX M66 FF 7-5-43 33MU 13-5 82MU 11-6 *SS708* 14-6 Casa 29-6 NAAF 1-11 FACA 19-4-44

EN578 4285 R-R to LFIX M66 FF 7-5-43 39MU 13-5 82MU 11-6 *SS708* 14-6 Casa 29-6 NAAF 185S 1-11 CE ops 5-9-44

EN579 4299 R-R to LFIX M66 FF 11-5-43 39MU 15-5 341S 15-6 411S 17-10 308S 21-12-44 411 RSU 15-2-45 DeH 14-3 sold Turk 21-8-47

EN580 4330 R-R to LFIX M66 FF 16-5-43 6MU 22-5 611S 28-5 82MU 14-6 *SS708* 14-6 Casa 29-6 NAAF 1-11 SOC 20-9-45

EN581 4306 R-R to LFIX M66 FF 14-5-43 6MU 19-5 82MU 16-6 *La Pampa* 20-7 Casa 24-7 MAAF 21-6-44 SOC 14-3-46

EN582 4364 R-R to LFIX M66 FF 26-5-43 33MU 29-5 82MU 11-6 *SS708* 14-6 Casa 29-6 73S C3 ops 2-3-44

EN583 4331 R-R to LFIX M66 FF 19-5-43 8MU 22-5 222MU 9-6 *SS708* 14-6 Casa 29-6 IAF 30-5-46 as MM4038

EN628 4338 R-R to LFIX M66 FF 21-5-43 9MU 27-5 341S 26-6 411S 17-10 VEA 16-4-47 sold Int All 10-11-49

EN629 4363 R-R to LFIX M66 FF 26-5-43 33MU 29-5 341S 16-6 411S 17-10 FAAC 8-11 401S FTR ops 20-12 FH138.15

EN630 4371 R-R to LFIX M66 FF 26-5-43 33MU 31-5 341S 13-6 AST 28-9 83GPSU 24-3-44 FAAC 20-5 412RSU 8-6 DeH 18-8 VA 12-3-45 mods pers 21-4 MAAF 14-5 IAF 26-6-47 as MM4103

EN631 4389 R-R to LFIX M66 FF 30-5-43 45MU 6-6 611S 5-7 485S 6-7 FTR ops 22-8

EN632 4372 R-R to LFIX M66 FF 28-5-43 33MU 31-5 222MU 14-6 *SS708* 4-6 Casa 29-6 218Gp NA 30-11 IAF 30-5-46 as MM4051

EN633 4385 R-R to LFIX M66 FF 29-5-43 6MU 4-6 341S 16-6 FAAC 25-9 ROS 411S 23-10 VAOx mods 21-9-44 ASTE 21-2-45 sold Turk 30-7-47

EN634 4393 R-R to LFIX M66 FF 1-6-43 45MU 5-6 611S 2-7 485S FTR 22-8

EN635 4400 R-R to LFIX M66 FF 2-6-43 46MU 9-6 341S 23-6 DeH 18-8-44 VAO mods 22-2-45 MAAF 24-4 IAF 26-6-47 as MM4106

EN636 4394 R-R to LFIX M66 FF 1-6-43 46MU 6-6 341S 15-6 411S 17-10 VA mods 15-9-44 FAAC recat ASTH 19-3-45 sold Turk 15-10-47

EN637 4414 R-R to LFIX M66 FF 3-6-43 46MU 7-6 341S 18-6 CA 25-7

EN686-695 and 710-759 cancel in favour of 60 Seafire F.IIC as NM910-949 and 963-982.

EN763 VC 33MU 26-4-42 421S 10-5 ASTH to Seafire IB NX942 5-5

EN764 5MU 29-4-42 131S 24-5 WAL 7-9 P&PSM 6-3-43 to Seafire IB PA106

EN765 45MU 27-4-42 310S 25-6 421S 25-7 412S 3-2-43 602S 19-4 610S 25-9 602S 4-4-44 118S 13-3 287S 21-11 SOC 8-9-45

EN766 M46 5MU 28-4-42 41S 11-6 FACA 25-7 2USA 22-8 RNDA 28-3-44 ASTE 4-6 64S 10-6 53 OTU 17-7 577S 14-6-45 FA cd 12-7 SOC 21-7

EN767 VC M46 BDn 31-5-42 CBAF 8-6 6MU 4-10 VSM 12-10 fuel syst mods 167S 4-2-43 FAC 26-3 ROS 19S 25-5 416S 7-8 402S 2-9 CB ops 27-6-44 ROS 57 OTU 6-2-45 FACE 20-4 SOC 28-4

EN768 39 MU 26-4-42 19S 7-6 121S 16-9 335S 15-10 602S 29-6 ASTH 234S 24-1-44 e/fd a/c aban i/sea nr Eddystone Lighthouse 19-6

EN769 6MU 1-5-42 350S 31-7 hit o/hd cable f/ld nr Lewes CE 13-8 SOC 20-8

EN770 12MU 1-5-42 242S 27-5 243S 6-6 LMS 10-8 P&PSM 26-2-43 to Seafire IB PA103

EN771 FF PJS 24-4-42 33MU 26-4 91S 1-8 CE ops 26-8 ASTH VSM 15-5-43 fuel syst mods 313S 25-6 66S 4-7 FACB 22-8 41 OTU 24-2-45 58 OTU 22-3 SOC 10-1-47

EN772 FF PJS 25-4-42 12MU 26-4 111S 4-6 2USA 22-8 cd dbf Rowton Salop 17-1-43

EN773 M45M 5MU 29-4-42 131S 24-5 CAC ops 17-6 ROS 350S 15-10 VSM 16-2-43 fuel syst mods wng stiff 504S 29-3 165S 1-7 308S 11-10 1689 BD Flt 5-12-44 PAL 19-10-45 SOC 20-10

EN774 33MU 29-4-42 124S 26-5 453S 22-7 FACE 1-8 SOC 15-8

EN775 M55MA 33MU 29-4-42 124S 26-5 312S 23-7 453S 17-8 FACA 18-9 65S 15-10 130S 31-3-43 FACB 6-10 350S 22-6 R&S 15-1-47 refurb Port 3-12

EN776 FF PJS 27-4-42 45MU 28-4 307S 20-6 CB ops 19-8 AST VSM 31-8-43 fuel syst mods wng stiff S Type pt MkIII IFF bomb carr 234S 25-1-44 CGS 8-10 FAAC 19-4-45 ROS SOC 1-11

EN777 33MU 30-4-42 421S 10-5 FA i/sea 24-1-43

EN778 45MU 28-4-42 Ercall 21-6 309S FTR ops 19-8

EN779 33MU 30-4-42 421S 10-5 FTR ops 8-11

EN780 FF PJS 27-4-42 12MU 30-4 610S 21-5 41S 17-7 122S 14-3-43 222S 19-5 air coll with BL477 CE 5-7 FH367.00

EN781 M45M FF PJS 27-4-42 12MU 1-5 133S 13-6 124S 15-6 41S 25-7 131S 8-9 CAC ops 19-11 610S 27-1-43 350S 27-3 308S 19-8 349S 29-10 FAAC 14-5-44 recat E

EN782 45MU 2-5-42 91S 6-6 FTR i/sea ops 29-12 FM141.40

EN783 12MU 30-4-42 610S 21-5 308S 15-7 309S 24-8 71S 12-8 334USA 1-10 AST M46 instal 30-3-43 VSM 26-6 fuel syst mods 66S 3-11 340S 15-11 CAC ops 7-12 1TEU 16-6-44 57 OTU 12-9 e/fd t/o w/u ldg nr Felton N'land CE 2-5-45 SOC 30-5

EN784 12MU 7-5-42 308USA 21-6 FACA 9-7 317S 21-10 412S 29-6-43

EN785 37MU 1-5-42 315S 25-5 FAAC 11-6 76MU 8-11 *La Pampa* 5-12 3-2-43

EN786 12MU 30-4-42 331S 4-6 CE ops 1-11

EN787 FF PJS 28-4-42 6MU 30-4 154S 12-6 FTR ops 21-6

EN788 12MU 30-4-42 152S 4-5 315S 16-12 FAAC 2-6-43 ROS 19S 25-6 595S 18-12-44 SOC 6-9-45

EN789 M46 FF PJS 28-4-42 6MU 30-4 350S 24-5 222S 7-6 64S 31-8 118S 11-12 HAL to 4259M Western Airways SOC 3-12-46

EN790 12MU 1-5-42 93S 16-10 VSM 17-4-43 to Seafire IB PA114

EN791 45MU 2-5-42 137S 6-6 FTR ops 22-10

EN792 12MU 30-4-42 RAF Atcham 20-6 Ken 1-8 FTR ops 19-8

EN793 12MU 1-5-42 137S 15-6 121S 15-6 72S 28-7 306S 20-8 133S 29-9 336USA 1-10 CAC ops 22-1-43 SAL M46 instal 317S 9-9 312S 4-10 443S 27-2-44 1TEU 26-4 61 OTU 25-6 SOC 14-5-45

EN794 6MU 3-5-42 360S 5-6 316S 21-12 FACB 19-2-43 VSM 29-5 fuel syst mods wng stiff 66S 30-9 340S 15-11 52 OTU 25-1-44 FLS 2-2 FACE 24-6

EN795 45MU 2-5-42 232S 4-6 65S 2-10 SAL 4-3-43 VSM 31-5 fuel syst mods wng stiff 453S 19-8 341S 3-11 239S 16-2-44 329S 23-2 26S e/fd t/o w/u ldg Hutton Cranswick CE 15-3

EN796 M46 6MU 1-5-42 350S 2-6 CAC ops 19-8 ROS HAL 52 OTU 26-1-43 FLS 2-2-44 VSM 10-4 fuel syst 'Basta' mods AST 25-4 1689 BD Flt 28-9

EN797 FF PJS 29-4-42 45MU 2-5 403S 7-6 HAL 8-8 *Marmat* 19-12 USSR 17-3

EN798 M46 37MU 1-5-42 154S 12-6 111S 18-7 CAC ops 21-8 ROS 412S 11-10 421S 31-1-43 416S 23-5 610S 20-11 Stn Flt Exeter 4-3-44 SOC 23-1-45

EN799 45MU 2-5-42 HQ 8th Ftr T S USA 21-10 61 OTU cd nr Stafford 15-12 SOC 24-12

EN800 M45M FF PJS 29-4-42 12MU 1-5 133S 13-6 308S 15-6 234S 29-8 350S 4-7-44 57 OTU 23-7 R&S 24-10-46 refurb Port 3-7-47

EN821 45MU 16-5-42 243S 27-6 65S 28-10 FACB 15-12 SAL VSM 28-6-43 fuel syst mods wng stiff S Type Pt Mk III IFF bomb carr COAL 4-11 RNDA LoS 9-2-44 as train

EN822 33MU 14-5-42 211S 3-6 611S 11-1-43 cd Westerham Water Works CE 27-1 SOC

EN823 5MU 15-5-42 H Ercall 21-6 309S FACB 13-8 VSM 2-9-43 fuel syst mods wng stiff S Type pt MkIII IFF bomb carr 269S 31-1-44 247 Grp 22-3 SOC 12-7-45

EN824 45MU 17-5-42 463S 23-6 222S i/sea ops CE 10-12

EN825 5MU 21-5-42 222S 11-6 242S 11-8 FACB 6-11 AST 17-3-43 to Sea IB NX905

EN826 45MU 29-5-42 118S 1-7 306S 2-7 4S 52 Pst Grp USA 306S 26-7 FTR ops 23-8

EN827 38MU 23-5-42 41S 14-7 AST 13-3-43 VASM 28-6 fuel syst mods wng stiff Mk III IFF 312S 25-10 144AF HQ 9-4-44 288S 15-5-45 SOC 27-12

EN828 LFLRVB 45MU 3-5-42 41S 4-6 FAAC 6-8 302S 14-3-43 air coll with AR385 nr N Coates Ce 22-4 132S 28-6 316S 30-11 635S 1-5-44 63S 10-6 58 OTU 22-3-45 to 5391M 4SoTT 24-4-77

EN829 6MU 17-5-42 82MU 4-6 *Emp Shack* 12-6 Malta 1-8 SOC 26-8 FH52.50

EN830 FF PJS 30-4-42 37MU 1-5 131S 8-6 FAAC 25-8 f/ld France 18-11-43 to Daimler Benz Aktiengellschaft. DB605A inverted eng instal to test cool system. Arma removed for comp trls with bf109G, DB601A instal for further trls

EN831 6MU 1-5-42 350S 24-5 412S 10-6 FTR ops 19-8

EN832 12MU 4-5-42 308S 24-6 coll with AB563 on app CE 10-7 31st Sup Grp 28-7

EN833 12MU 8-5-42 RAF Atcham 20-6 FAAC 18-10 to 3414M 11SoTT 1-11 CE 28-6-48

EN834 6MU 4-5-42 133S 11-6 306S 22-8 HAL 25-8 USA 4-3 VASM 20-12 fuel syst mods wng stiff S Type pt Mk III IFF bomb carr 31ATG 9-6-44 SOC 25-10-45

EN835 6MU 5-5-42 350S 2-6 FTR ops 4-6

EN836 12MU 3-5-42 133S 13-6 124S 15-6 41S 22-7 FAAC 21-8 AST M46 instal VASM 16-10 fuel syst mods wng stiff 313S 22-3-43 66S 4-7 340S 15-11 303S 2503-44 ops 22-5

EN837 M45M LFLRVB 12MU 7-5-42 HQ 8th Ftr Com 21-10 P&PSM 2-7-43 fuel syst mods wng stiff 316S 22-11 63S 1-5-44 FTR ops 7-10

EN838 12MU 8-5-42 RAF Atcham 20-6 FAAC 24-6 308S 10-7 308USA 24-8 cd Arundel pilot kld wreck to Tang by VA CE 17-10

EN839 12MU 14-5-42 RAF StA 20-6 308S 24-8 12th Obs USA CB ops 2-12 AST to Seafire IB NX 925 23-4-43

EN840 12MU 3-5-42 315S 15-6 317S 5-9 421S 29-3-43 602S 19-4 CE ops 15-7 SOC FH365.00

EN841 M45M 6MU 6-5-42 312S 15-6 302S 2-9 FACE 18-2-43 WAL 602S 29-6 122S 6-7 504S 10-10 129S 26-1-44 VASM 18-2 fuel syst mods 276S 1-5 e/fd i/sea of Bolt Head 23-7

EN842 M45M 45MU 10-5-42 308S 24-8 340S 28-9 485S 11-11 57 OTU 31-12-44 FAAC 1-5-45 recat E SOC 14-5

EN843 VA to FIAX M63 9MU 16-6-43 82MU 23-6

La Pampa 2-7 Casa 14-7 ME 1-9 IAF 26-6-47 as M4138
EN844 6MU 4-5-42 91S 31-5 FTR 23-9
EN845 45MU 10-5-42 232S 4-6 FTR ops 10-6
EN846 37MU 9-5-42 65S 3-6 u/s ldg Great Sampford Essex CE 6-6 SOC 9-6
EN847 12MU 3-5-42 308th USA 9-6 std pn appr cd nr Atcham CE 29-6 AST 17-7 SOC FH5.15
EN848 8MU 7-5-42 124S 2-6 4S 52Pur Grp USA 12-7 struck R6623 ldg CE 28-7 SOC 4-8
EN849 M45M 37MU 10-5-42 65S 2-6 93S 13-9 65S 3-12 130S 31-3-43 402S 9-5 FAAC 4-8 277S 4-3-44 FAF 1-2-45 GC2/18 4-4
EN850 8MU 8-5-42 403S ftr ops 19-8
EN851 Lima Challenger 12MU 7-5-42 RAF St A 20-6 AST 16-11 COAL to Sea IB NX952 17-3-43
EN852 M45M 37MU 10-5-42 302S 2-6 306S FAAC 26-5-43 315S 2-10 VASM 22-12 fuel syst mods 276S 26-4-44 e/fd f/.ld nr aerodrome Bolthead CE 29-7-44
EN853 12MU 10-5-42 401S 4-6 121 (E)S 5-8 335S 8th SUA 1-10 CE ops 23-1-43 SOC
EN854 LFLRVB M46 12MU 7-5-42 HQ 8th Ftr Com 21-10 401S 9-3-43 AST 16-6 M45M instal 350S 5-10 322S 11-1-44 FACE 29-3 FH413.50
EN855 12MU 8-5-42 RAF Atcham 20-6 307S CE ops 19-8
EN856 M46 37MU 9-5-42 315S 25-5 FACE 24-77 317S 5-9 412S 29-6-43 308S 3-12 flew into hill nr. Snafell IoM 14-12
EN857 12MU 7-5-42 412S 6-6 421S 31-1-43 416S 23-5 401S 1-6 126S 10-8 17Sect RCAF FAAAC 13-6-44 403S 2-11 416S 7-12 SOC 25-4-45
EN858 M45M 8MU 8-5-42 403S 2-6 FAAC 2-8 416S 3-6-43 132S 13-6 302S 28-6 234S 6-1-44 53 53 OTU 5-10 FAAC 1-1-45 recat E SOC 8-1
EN859 45MU 10-5-42 71S 2-6 82MU 7-7 *C o Der* 1-11 USSR 10-1-43
EN860 5MU 9-5-42 111S 25-6 FAAC 24-7 S&H 350S 7-6-43 FACE 11-7
EN861 37MU 9-5-42 302S 3-6 FACE 8-9 GAL VASM 10-5-43 fuel syst mods 416S 26-6 CB ops 27-7 AST Ex 234S 22-12 dam by AA fire off Normandy 17-6-44 ROS 53 OTU 11-8 cd Nettleton Top nr Caister Lincs CE 31-12
EN862 M45M 8MU 8-5-42 65S 11-6 2USA 22-8 26S 10-4-44 FAAC 11-8-41 OTU 25-1-45 58 OTU 22-3 to 5397M 5SoTT 28-8-47
EN863 M45M 12MU 10-5-42 308S 24-8 VASM 22-10 fuel syst mods wng stiff S Type pt MkIII IFF 350S 3-4-44 CGS 1-10-45 SOC 20-10
EN864 5MU 9-5-42 670bs Grp USA FACE 23-11 COAL to Sea IB NX962 28-5-43
EN865 M45M 37MU 9-5-42 302S 2-6 132S 28-6-43 130S 14-3-44 222S 31-3 345S 25-4 FACE 29-4
EN866 37MU 9-5-42 129S 8-6 CAC ops 25-6 ROS 602S 29-11 129S 22-1-43 66S 19-2 234S 19-4 312S 29-6 CB 28-9 DeH RNDA 27-2-44 COAL 11-3 RNAS Hens as train 13-6
EN867 34S coll on runway with Beaufighter X7924 Colt CE 23-11-42
EN888 5MU 9-5-42 130S 23-6 CE ops 19-7 SOC 23-7
EN889 37MU 13-5-42 340S 5-6 131S 27-10 i/sea 11-11
EN890 12MU 14-5-42 RAF StA 20-6 33MU 31-10 307S AST 16-3-43 to Seafire IB NX909
EN891 33MU 13-5-42 124S 26-5 FTR ops 31-5 FH7.05
EN892 12MU 10-5-42 315S 16-6 FACB 14-7 313S 26-6-43 66S 4-7 FTR 12-9 FH113.05
EN893 37MU 10-5-42 131S 4-6 306S 29-1-43 316S 14-3 313S 10-1-44 AST 6-6 M45 instal Morocco 2-4-45 FAF 29-10-47
EN894 37MU 13-5-42 71S 3-6 4USA 27-8 313S 9-9-43 453S 17-10 239S 16-2-44 63S 13-3 53 OTU 11-8 VAC 26-2-45 61 OTU 17-5 695S 28-6
EN895 45MU 10-5-42 232S 5-6 65S 2-10 FACE 5-1-43 402S 26-6 303S 22-6-44 SOC 8-1-45
EN896 12MU 10-5-42 317S 6-6 315S 4-9 136S 26-11 610S 27-1-43 FTR 18-2
EN897 12MU 16-5-42 RAF Atcham 22-6 8th Ftr Grp USA 24-3 FACB 18-11 COAL con to train RNAS Hens 30-4-44
EN898 45MU 12-5-42 167S 24-6 61-S 14-10 131S 25-1-43 310S 30-6 504S 24-9 ASTE 22-11 RNDA 24-2-44
EN899 LFLRVB M45M 5MU 4-5-42 71S 2-6 501S 4-4-43 CB ops 11-9 132S 26-2-44 504S 15-3 310S 15-7 FAAC 16-8 61 OTU 28-9 SOC 10-5-45
EN900 M45M 37MU 10-5-42 154S 12-6 CAC ops 18-7 ROS 334S 7-12 SAL 1-8-44 1696Flt 24-11 sold J Dale 8-7-48
EN901 9MU 13-5-42 610S 7-6 332S 25-7 CAC ops 20-8 222MU 27-10 *C o Lil* 8-12 alloc USSR dam in transit rtp 5-3-43
EN902 12MU 14-5-42 307S 21-6 FACB 5-8 1CRU VASM 14-10 fuel syst mods wng stiff HAL 25-1-43 con to PRXIII M32 RNDA 3-3-44 SOC 27-2-45
EN903 M45M 37MU 10-5-42 RAF Atcham 20-6 308S 24-8 VASM 24-7-43 fuel syst mods wng stiff S Type pt MkIII bomb carr 234S 11-1-44 R&S 24-10-46 refurb Port 9-6-47
EN904 5MU 21-5-42 416S 30-6 602S 15-7 164S 11-9 341S 3-2-43 340S 5-4 USAAF Mount Farm 15-11 CE 26-3-45
EN905 LFVB M45M 37MU 24-5-42 66S 3-4 FACB 16-8 WAL 167S 14-1-43 91S 10-3 124S 28-4 322S 20-7 222S 1-1-44 CAC ops 8-1 57 OTU 13-8 SOC 28-3-45
EN906 5MU 14-5-42 1 CRU 21-6 SAL 8-8-44 1689Flt 5-12 PAL 27-9-45 SOC
EN907 33MU 14-5-42 91S 1-8 CAC ops 29-6 416S 10-2-43 411S 23-3 FTR ops 14-4 FH60.00
EN908 37MU 13-5-42 340S 5-6 411S 3-11 FACB 14-3-43 416S 12-6 lost over e/tr 25-11 FH261.50
EN909 5MU 14-5-42 H Ercall 21-6 FACE 1-10 SOC
EN910 37MU 13-5-42 332S 13-6 501S 2-12 S&H 27-3-43 332S VA to Sea IB PA122 30-5
EN911 M46 38MU 3-6-42 76MU 4-7 *C o Der* 1-11 USSR 10-1-43
EN912 33MU 13-5-42 303S 3-6 CAC ops 17-7 COAL 12-3-43 to Sea IB NX953
EN913 M45M 5MU 14-5-42 39MU 26-10 *La Pampa* 5-12 alloc USSR VASM 30-6-43 fuel syst mods wng stiff S Type pt MkIII IFF bomb carr 316S 7-12 63S 1-5-44 58 OTU 22-3-45 to 5380M 5SoTT 29-11
EN914 12MU 14-5-42 41S 4-6 CA ops 11-6 453S 11-7 CB ops 31-10 Hal COAL 7-7-43 fitt arrester hook RNDA 18-1-44
EN915 37MU 17-5-42 154S 12-6 71S 19-7 234USA 1-10 CAC 1-12 SAL 13-4-43 ADC Flt TFU Deff 1-10 lost cont a/c aban cd High Church Glos CE 1-2-45
EN916 33MU 15-6-42 303S 23-6 308S 22-10 CB HAL 7-12 VASM 21-8-43 fuel syst mods wng stiff 308S 21-8 FTR ops 22-9 FH159.25
EN917 LFVB M45M 33MU 15-5-42 316S 4-6 306S 19-3-43 CAC ops 24-9 ROS 222S 10-11 130S 24-5-44 CAC ops 21-7 61 OTU 3-9 SOC 19-7-45
EN918 33MU 15-5-42 121S 3-6 CA ops 18-6 P&P 121S 23-6 CB ops 14-9 335S 8th USA 1-10 CE ops 5-2-43
EN919 M45M 37MU 14-5-42 317S 5-6 FAAC 19-7 315S 26-12 303S 6-6-43 340S 20-9 485S 11-11 VASM 8-4-44 fuel syst mods 277S 17-6 58 OTU 29-3-45 SOC 29-11
EN920 12MU 15-5-42 RAF Atcham 21-6 31FG Merston attached 131S strk lorry on t/o CB 28-7 SOC 8-8
EN921 M45M 5MU 14-5-42 309S 21-6 FACB 24-7 412S 3-9 421S 31-1-43 416S 23-5 401S 1-6 126S 10-8 504S 10-11 129S 26-1-44 17SFTS 6-12 SOC 21-5-46
EN922 12MU 14-5-42 302S 4-6 CB ops 23-11 132S 28-6-43 129S 25-1-44 277S 30-8 57 OTU 1-3-45 595S 14-6 SOC 6-9
EN923 45MU 16-6-42 309S 30-6 FACB 8-7 WAL *Palma* 5-12 USSR 3-2-43
EN924 33MU 15-5-42 133S 13-6 CAC ops 22-8 VASM 20-11 fuel syst mods wng stiff CRD DeH 7-4-43 277S 12-10-44 57 OTU 1-3-45 SOC 29-11
EN925 6MU 17-5-42 cd on f/f to 47MU CE 26-5 AST 53MU 28-1-43 *SS657* 19-2 Gib 9-3 NWA 30-4 ME 20-11-44 REAF 29-3-45
EN926 37MU 17-5-42 118S 5-6 FTR ops 4-4
EN927 33MU 15-5-42 130S 7-6 AST 26-11 COAL 7-7-43 hook fitt RNDA 18-1-44
EN928 M45M 12MU 16-5-42 308S 24-8 CB 6-10 RNDA 20-2-44 DeH 13-7 R&S 24-10-46 refurb Port 24-6-47
EN929 45MU 16-5-42 RAF Atcham 20-6 307S FTR ops 20-8
EN930 45MU 16-5-42 453S 23-6 FACB 28-7 SAL 215MU 13-11 *Nank* 28-11 USSR 6-2-43
EN931 VB(T) 8MU 21-5-42 82MU 7-6 *Guido* 12-6 SAL 20-11 222MU 24-2-43 *Fort LM* 12-3 Tak 20-4 ME 20-5 FACE 18-11-44 SOC 28-12
EN932 33MU 18-5-42 602S 27-9 118S 11-11 CE ops 29-1-43 FH66.30
EN944 45MU 21-5-42 308S 24-8 131S 12-8 610S 27-1-43 421S 11-6 340S 7-8 FACE 11-10
EN945 45MU 21-5-42 RAF Atcham 22-6 67Obs Grp USA FACE 14-6-43
EN946 38MU 23-5-42 ROS 30-7 CRD Farn 30-7 ext renovation for drag reduction. Modified lead edge boundary layer trls comp trls with EF644, EN498 and JL227(FIX). Speed gain with cleaner airframe 4-5mph. Fitt Vickers curved, conical w/s; speed increase 5-12mph Smooth waxed finish. BDn 1943 for further drag reduction trls. FACB 17-5-43 AST 310S 9011 442S 30-3-44 277S 12-10 57 OTU 1-3-45 587S 14-6 M46 instal SOC 5-7
EN947 45MU 28-5-42 451S 7-7 222S 31-3-43 167S 19-5 CAC ops 7-6 504s 5-8 313S 22-9 17SFTS 28-9-44 FAAC 20-12 SAL CE
EN948 9MU 5-6-42 111S 16-7 308S 21-4-43 234S 22-8 303S 3-7-44 130S 13-8 278S 13-10 53 OTU 22-2-45 FAAC recat E SOC 25-5 Farn 1946 for static grd ejector seat trls
EN949 45MU 30-5-42 310S 25-6 312S 30-7 129S 22-8 602S 29-11 129S 22-1-43 66S 19-2 RNDA 30-5 as train
EN950 M45M 45MU 30-5-42 453S 23-6 FAAC 14-10 222S 31-3-43 167S 19-5 322S 20-7 416S 12-10 CB ops 13-11 1CRU M50M instal 350S 19-5-44 CE ops 6-6
EN951 LFVB M45M 33MU 17-5-42 133S 13-6 303S 20-4 315S 6-6-43 CAC ops 11-7 504S 10-10 129S 26-1-44 VASM 20-3-44 fuel syst mods CGS 27-9 to 5516M 28-7-45
EN952 12MU 16-5-42 RAF Atcham 23-6 HQ 8th Ftr Com 2-10 FACE 22-11
EN953 33MU 19-5-42 118S 18-6 FACB 27-2-43 504S 15-3 FTR ops 5-6
EN954 VB(T) 6MU 18-5-42 47MU 26-5 *Emp Shack* 12-6 Malta 1-8 C3 ops 11-10
EN955 6MU 17-5-42 47MU 26-5 *Emp Shack* 12-6 Malta 1-8 NA 1-6-43
EN956 37MU 17-5-42 501S 30-5 CE ops 27-8 SOC 1-9
EN957 M46 London Transport 45MU 22-5-42 308s 24-8 ASTE 14-3-44 350S 16-6 57 OTU 23-7 FAAC 9-8 recat E 23-10
EN958 33MU 17-5-42 501S 29-5 CE ops 27-8 SOC 1-9
EN959 M46 45MU 22-5-42 118S 16-6 504S 29-8-43 313S 22-9 443S 27-2-44 56 OTU 30-3 61 OTU 28-6-45 SOC 13-10
EN960 M46 37MU 24-5-42 66S 3-6 129S 19-2-43 133S 6-3 310S 22-3 FTR ops 3-5 FH322.00
EN961 M46 City of Wells 45MU 22-5-42 501S 9-6 CAC ops 20-6 66S 12-11 129S 12-2-43 CAC ops 4-3 312S 4-10 442S 27-2-44 1689Flt 3-10 SOC 13-7-45
EN962 37MU 24-5-42 222S 4-6 FAAC 15-7 91S 20-12 501S 27-8-43 485S 14-11 AST 9-5-44 M46 instal 57 OTU 4-1-45 SOC 5-7
EN963 37MU 17-5-42 601S 19-8 CE ops 27-8 SOC 19-9
EN964 LRVB 33MU 19-5-42 501S 14-6 118S 14-6 CB ops 25-8 313S 15-4-43 66S 4-7 COAL 8-11 RNDA 14-2-44 RAF 12-5-45 52MU 17-9 to 5585M FAF 27-2-46
EN965 37MU 17-5-42 118S 5-6 FACB 26-6 131S 29-12 610S 27-1-43 312S 19-4 234S 4-5 504S 30-6 10-10 RNDA 20-2-44 as train
EN966 Fiducia 45MU 22-5-42 501S 12-6 118S 16-6 CAC ops 15-11 AST FTR ops 19-7 FH374.50
EN967 45MU 30-5-42 76MU 8-7 *C o Der* 1-11 USSR 10-1-43
EN968 VB(T) 39MU 23-5-42 82MU 8-6 *Guido* 12-6 Malta 1-8 NA 1-6-43 435S SOC 26-4-45
EN969 5MU 20-5-42 66S 30-6 118S 23-9 cd nr Happisborough Norfolk CE 24-2-43 FH200.55
EN970 45MU 23-5-42 82MU 7-7 *C o Lil* 8-12-43 USSR 16-12
EN971 5MU 20-5-42 19S 28-6 234S 15-9 AST i/sea ops 3-5-43 FH260.00
EN972 8MU 23-5-42 82MU 6-6 *Guido* 12-6 Malta 1-8 FACB 22-9 C2 ops 16-10 C3 ops 1-12 FH37 10
EN973 VB(T) 8MU 23-5-42 82MU 6-6 *Lublin* 13-6 Malta 1-8 244S CE ops 9-8 SOC 6-10
EN974 45MU 30-5-42 501S 15-6 CB ops 27-10 310S 21-2-43 132S i/sea ops 17-4 FH12.00
EN975 5MU 19-5-42 118S 2-6 FTR ops 6-6 FH6.15
EN976 VB(T) 6MU 21-5-42 47MU 4-6 *Guido* 12-6 Malta 249S FTR ops 25-8 FH38.20
EN977 45MU 29-5-42 76MU 7-7 *C o Der* 1-11 USSR 10-1-43
EN978 VB(T) 8MU 23-5-42 47MU 6-6 *Emp Shack* 12-6 Malta 1-8 C3 ops 12-10
EN979 8MU 23-5-42 47MU 6-6 *Emp Shack* 12-6 Malta 1-8 C3 ops 14-10
EN980 VB(T) 39MU 24-5-42 82MU 6-6 *Guido* 12-6 Malta 1-8 FAC3 19-12-43 FH90.45
EN981 38MU 23-5-42 82MU 7-7 Gib 29-9 SOC 950Unit 31-1-43

EP series are all F Mk VB Merlin 46 unless otherwise indicated.
EP107 38MU 31-5-42 111S 26-7 350S 30-11 485S 7-12 FTR ops 13-2-43

EP120 was damaged during the ill-fated Dieppe operation. It was relegated to 5377M at St.Athan and took part in the Battle of Britain film. It is extant at Wattisham and seen here at RAF Wilmslow, Cheshire.

EP108 M45 38MU 1-6-42 222S 25-7 242S 11-8 411S 23-9 316S 6-4-43 air coll with AR382 cd Ashford CE 27-4 FH177.35

EP109 45MU 4-6-42 313S 20-6 403S 22-8 416S 3-6-43 602S 4-8 115S 10-10 501S 3-3-44 CAC ops 3-7 61 OTU 3-9 SOC 21-9-45

EP110 33MU 6-6-42 602S 24-6 416S 16-7 52 OTU 1-2-43 FAAC 18-6 313S 27-8 SAL 16-6-44 M45M instal 57 OTU 17-7 c/fld hit H/T cables w/u ldg nr Morpeth CE12-8

EP111 12MU 6-6-42 RAF Atcham 21-6 307S 20-8 FTR ops 20-8

EP112 M45 33MU 7-6-42 111S 25-6 2USA 22-8 332S 8-11 FACB 10-6 288S 10-2-45 burst tyre on t/o tip onto nose Chu Fen CE 22-2 SOC 28-2

EP113 12MU 11-6-42 602S 29-6 416S 16-7 FTR ops 29-7

EP114 45MU 1-7-42 416S 28-7 403S 2-3-43 FACB 18-5 AST M45M instal 416S 24-9 129S 2-2-44 402S 17-6 53 OTU 20-7 strk P7438 ldg KinL CE 15-10 61 OTU 12-4-45 SOC 13-10

EP115 37MU 16-6-42 402S 24-6 485S 13-8 CAC ops 28-11 ROS FTR ops 13-2-43

EP116 6MU 19-6-42 310S 24-7 316S 5-8 302S 3-10-43 234S 4-12 303S 11-1-44 AST 8-3 M45M instal 287S 2-12 MFS 25-10-45 SOC 23-10

EP117 M45 6MU 30-5-42 47MU 6-6 *Emp Shack* 12-6 Malta CE ops 15-7

EP118 LRVB 45MU 23-5-42 501S 12-6 CE ops dbt 16-9 SOC FH106.30

EP119 City of Wakefield 38MU 23-5-42 118S 21-6 66S 23-9 167S 9-11 FACB 17-2-43 234S 4-7 453S 17-10 341S 3-1-44 52 OTU 6-2 CGS 28-9 FAAC 12-12 SOC 15-2-45

EP120 45MU 23-5-42 501S 4-6 strk AB403 on runway Ibsley CAC 16-7 ROS CAC ops Dieppe 19-8 19S 9-9 402S 22-4-43 53 OTU 12-10-44 to 5377M St A 13-7 then 8070M BoB film 18-4-68 Wattisham, extant

EP121 LRVB 37MU 24-5-42 501S 30-5 FACB 24-7 VASM 10-10 fuel syst mods 131S 29-12 602S 7-3-43 412S 19-4 416S 10-6 o/s std cd Digby CE 29-6

EP122 VB(T) M45 39MU 24-5-42 47MU 8-6 *Guido* 12-6 Malta 1-8 SOC 4-4-43

EP123 M45 38MU 24-5-42 130S 1-7 118S 1-12 FTR ops 24-2-43 FH169.30

EP124 M50 45MU 23-5-42 118S 16-6 e/fld w/u ldg nr Colt 6-7-43

EP125 LFLR M45 38MU 23-5-42 FAAC 25-6 AST M46 instal VASM 12-10 fuel syst mods M45M instal 234S 6-2-43 312S 29-6 317S 4-10 340S 30-10 132S 7-3-44 504S 14-3 310S 15-7 41 OTU 4-9 58 OTU 19-4-45 SOC 6-7

EP126 LRVB 38MU 24-5-42 510S 23-6 CA ops 5-8 118S 17-10 FTR ops 16-8-43

EP127 38MU 24-5-42 82MU 8-7 VASM 25-9 fuel syst mods 310S 21-11 e/fld a/c aban cdr Beach Head 4-5-43 FH205.00

EP128 38MU 24-5-42 501S 21-6 FTR ops 11-8

EP129 45MU 28-5-42 66S 12-6 118S 21-6 501S 24-9 504S 19-10 167S 7-11 313S 25-3-43 CB ops 2-4 310S 24-9 444S 27-2-44 58 OTU 30-3 61 OTU 25-6 S&H 4-12 SOC 5-9-45

EP130 37MU 24-5-42 119S 4-6 501S 24-9 504S 19-10 19S 25-10 130S 10-11 132S 13-6-43 302S 28-6 CB 30-9 HAL RNDA 20-2-44 COAL 28-2-44

EP131 6MU 30-5-42 47MU 5-6 *Emp Shack* 12-6 Malta 1-8 NWA 1-5

EP132 VB(T) 39MU 24-5-42 82MU 7-6 *Guido* 13-6 Malta 1-8 NWA 1-6-43

EP133 39MU 24-5-42 118S 2-6 501S 24-9 CAC ops 4-10 ROS 504S 19-10 165S 1-7-43 308S 10-10 1TEU 20-5-44 2MPRU 25-9 CE

EP134 45MU 4-6-42 118S 16-6 FTR ops 20-6 FH6.25 cancel 21-6-45 SOC 28-9-46

EP135 6MU 30-5-42 42MU 4-6 *Lublin* 16-6 Malta 1-8 FAC2 15-10 SOC 2-12 FH84.10

EP136 VB(T) 6MU 29-5-42 82MU 4-6 *Emp Shack* 12-6 Malta 1-8 229S CB ops 25-9 NA 1-6-43

EP137 M45 6MU 28-5-42 47MU 6-6 *Emp Shack* 12-6 185S CE ops 3-7 SOC 1-8 FH13.45

EP138 6MU 30-5-42 82MU 4-6 *Emp Shack* 13-6 Malta 1-8 C3 ops 1-11

EP139 VB(T) 6MU 29-5-42 47MU 5-6 *Emp Shack* 12-6 Malta 1-8 C3 ops 12-10

EP140 VB(T) 39MU 24-5-42 82MU 7-6 *Guido* 12-6 Malta 1-8 249S FAC3 3-3-43 SOC 10-3

EP141 ASTH 30-5-42 VA 7-7 to Sea IB MB359

EP142 ASTH 30-5-42 VA 8-7 to Sea IB MB362

EP143 M45 37MU 14-6-42 RAF Atcham 20-6 FAAC 6-7 HQ 8th Ftr Com 21-10 FLS 31-1-44 FACB 14-3 SAL recat E 27-3

EP144 M45 ASTH 29-5-42 VA 7-7 to Sea IB MB363

EP145 8MU 18-6-42 76MU 7-7 *Ban Shah* 23-10 USSR 11-1-43

EP146 M45 ASTH 29-5-42 VA 4-7 to Sea IB MB364

EP147 M45 ASTH 30-5-42 VA 8-7 to Sea IB MB365

EP148 M45 ASTH 29-5-42 FA ff to VA 5-7 to Sea IB MB356 17-11

EP149 38MU 30-5-42 76MU 8-7 *C o Der* 1-11 USSR 10-1-43

EP150 37MU 14-6-42 76MU 6-7 *Canada* 3-12 USSR 1-3-43

EP151 38MU 30-5-42 76MU 4-7 *C o Der* 1-11 USSR 10-1-43

EP152 M45 9MU 31-5-42 215MU 6-7 *Emp Clive* 19-7 a/c aban after t/o *HMS Furious* in Med Sgt Sullivan safe 17-8

EP164 M45 9MU 17-5-42 152S 25-6 FTR ops 26-8-44

EP165 M45 9MU 21-5-42 65S 13-7 CB ops 15-9 SAL 222MU 7-11 *Hathagus* 19-12 USSR 17-3-43

EP166 M45 39MU 28-5-42 111S 16-7 VA 28-5-43 to Sea IB PA117

EP167 VA Csfd 9MU 22-5-42 133S 13-6 FACE 19-9 SOC 25-9

EP168 M45 9MU 27-5-42 133S 13-6 FTR ops 20-6

EP169 LFLR M45M 9MU 31-5-42 121S 7-7 FACB 29-7 S&H RNDA Stret 14-5-43 401S 28-8 CB ops 18-10 132S 23-2-44 504S 15-3 310S 15-7 41 OTU 4-9 58 OTU FAAC 24-4-45 to 5396M 5SoTT 17-7

EP170 M45 9MU 31-5-42 313S 21-6 FACB 11-7 RNDA 16-1-43 ASTH hook fitt RNAS Belfast 5-2-44

EP171 M45M 9MU 3-6-42 308S 8-7 340S 28-9-43 485S 11-11 VASM 17-3-44 Fuel syst and 'Basta' mods FRU 16-3-44 276S 2-11 SOC 29-11-45

EP172 M45 9MU 2-6-42 H Ercall 20-6 165S 9-1-43 e/fld f/ld on beach nr Newton Aberdeen Ce 18-4 SOC 29-4 FH171.00

EP173 M45M 9MU 4-6-42 308S 24-8 416S 27-1-43 411S 23-3 126AF 10-8 CB 30-8 129S 31-1-44 402S 17-6 CAC ops 7-7 83GSU 53 OTU 17-8 SOC 29-8-45

EP174 9MU 6-6-42 RAF ATcham 23-6 FAAC 19-8 308S 24-8 FLS 5-2-44 RNDA 23-3 for train

EP175 M45 9MU 7-6-42 RAF Atcham 24-6 308S 24-8 VASM 16-8-43 fuel syst mods wng stiff Type Spt MkIII IFF bomb carr RNDA 16-1-44 269S 27-4 CE 4-3-46 SOC 28-3

EP176 M45 9MU 10-6-42 H Ercall 21-6 8th Ftr Com 27-10 345S 30-11 FAAC 8-12 344S USA 15-1-43 109S 21-11 FAAC 18-5 LMS recat E 14-7-44

EP177 9MU 13-6-42 332S 26-6 CB ops 31-7 AST 421S 19-2-43 FTR ops 1-4

EP178 M45M 9MU 14-6-42 222S 15-7 242S 11-8 411S 23-9 402S 25-3-43 19S 22-4 65S 30-6 130S 15-8 VASM 11-3-44 fuel syst 'Basta' mods 2nd TAF 19-5-45

EP179 M45 9MU 14-6-42 71S 20-7 334S USA 1-10 CB AST 31-3-44 1 OADU 8-1-45 FAF 19-1

EP180 M45 9MU 16-6-42 133S 31-7 165S 29-8 65S 23-9 130S 31-3-43 349S 19-7 COAL 5-11 hook fitd RNDA 9-2-44

EP181 9MU 16-6-42 72S 10-9 602S 18-12 CAC 19-2-43 VASM 21-6 fuel syst mods Mk III IFF 129S 4-2-44 57 OTU 13-8 ASTH 14-6-45 SOC

EP182 9MU 30-6-42 81S 9-9 52 OTU 31-1-43 FACB 2-10 COAL for con 17-3-44

EP183 9MU 21-6-42 302S 10-8 72S 10-9 610S 25-3-43 485S 29-4 19S 1-7 322S 10-9 222S 1-1-44 USAAF 9-5

EP184 38MU 1-6-42 76MU 6-7 *Canada* 2-12 USSR 1-3-43

EP185 38MU 30-5-42 47MU 9-7 *C o Der* 1-11 USSR 10-1-43

EP186 9MU 1-6-42 215MU 6-7 *Emp Clive* 19-7 Malta 3-8 NA 1-6-43 FAF 9-4-47

EP187 38MU 1-6-42 52MU 26-6 *Emp Dar* 29-6 Malta 1-8 NA 1-7-43 SOC 28-4-45

EP188 9MU 31-5-42 215MU 6-7 *Emp Clive* 14-7 Malta 3-8 FTR ops 30-4-43 FH 125.30

EP189 VB(T) 38MU 1-6-42 82MU 19-6 *Emp Tern* 1-7 Malta CE ops 28-7 SOC 30-7

EP190 6MU 20-5-42 47MU 5-6 *Emp Shack* 12-6 Malta 1-8 FTR ops 26-8 FH50.15

EP191 M45 45MU 4-6-42 453S 23-6 FAAC 18-7 510S 14-9 501S 3-10 118S 31-12 air coll with AR447 cd nr Colt. CE 29-7-43

EP192 9MU 31-5-42 215MU 14-7 *Emp Cam* 10-5 Tak 15-9 ME 17-9 Sicily 1-8 C3 ops 1-10

EP193 9MU 2-6-42 76MU 6-8 *Emp Sun* 19-8 Tak 13-9 ME 7-10 SOC 8-3-44

EP194 6MU 7-6-42 52MU 25-6 *Emp Dar* 29-6 cd over Port side *HMS Furious* in Med Sgt Fleming kld 17-8

EP195 9MU 31-5-42 82MU 22-6 *Emp Kes* 2-7 Gib 31-12 ME 31-8-44 to Turk 23-9

EP196 6MU 31-5-42 82MU 5-6 *Emp Shack* 12-6 Malta 1-8 CB ops 29-8 SOC 21-10

EP197 38MU 31-5-42 82MU 22-6 *Emp Tern* 1-7 Malta 149S FACE 13-8 SOC15-8

EP198 12MU 17-6-42 610S 9-7 FTR ops 19-8

EP199 9MU 31-5-42 215MU 6-7 *Emp Clive* 14-7 Malta 3-8 FTR ops 16-11

EP200 6MU 30-5-42 82MU 5-6 *Emp Shack* 12-6 Malta 185S FTR ops 29-8 FH57.30

EP201 38MU 31-5-42 82MU 22-6 *Emp Kest* 2-7 Malta 18-4 NA 1-6-43 ME 30-11-44

EP202 33MU 1-6-42 118S 18-6 FAAC 13-9 ROS 421S 8-11 FACE 24-1-43

EP203 38MU 1-6-42 52MU 26-6 *Emp Dar* 29-6 Malta 1-8 1435S C3 ops 14-10

EP204 38MU 20-6-42 215MU 21-7 *Emp Puma* 17-8 Tak 23-9 ME 22-10 NAAF 31-10-43 FAF 9-10-47

EP205 VB(T) M45 9MU 31-5-42 82MU 19-6 *Emp Kes* 2-7 Malta 1-8 NA 1-6-43 C3 ops 12-7-44

EP206 LRVB M45 33MU 1-6-42 118S 18-6 416S 19-7-43 e/fld a/c aban i/sea 12-8

EP207 VB(T) 9MU31-5-42 82MU 19-6 *Emp Kes* 2-7 Malta 249S CE ops 14-8 SOC 16-8 FH23.30

EP208 38MU 7-6-42 222MU 31-8 Gib 27-9 ME 10-11

EP209 6MU 4-6-42 47MU 26-6 *Emp Gem* 1-7 Malta 1-8 CB 13-10

EP210 9MU 2-6-42 82MU 7-7 *Ban Shap* 23-10 USSR 11-1-43

EP211 9MU 1-6-42 76MU 6-8 *Emp Sun* 19-8 Tak 13-9 FACE 21-9

EP212 38MU 4-6-42 82MU 7-7 *C o Lil* 8-12 USSR 16-2-43

EP213 33MU 1-6-42 82MU 6-7 *C o Der* 1-11 USSR 10-1-43

EP226 33MU 1-6-42 118S 18-6 Farn Oct '42 for neg 'G' trls 129S 19-2-43 dvd i/sea from form flight 40 miles off Warm Dorset 4-4

EP227 M45 33MU 1-6-42 602S 11-9 118S 11-11 CAC ops 11-3-43 340S 26-12 57 OTU 27-6-44 CB LMS 21-9 recat E 2-10

EP228 38MU 6-6-42 310S 19-7 118S 8-11 s/dn by Harwich AA fire on return from sweep pilot kld 18-3-43 FH191.10

EP229 36MU 4-6-42 VASM 23-9 fuel syst mods HAL 16-11 VASM 12-2-43 wing stiff 542S 11-6 HAL 26-8-44 to PRXIII M32 39MU Star Fan dis 31-3-45

EP230 38MU 4-6-42 76MU 5-7 *C o Der* 1-11 USSR 16-1-43

EP231 12MU 5-6-42 82MU 8-7 *C o Der* 1-11 USSR 10-1-43

EP232 12MU 5-6-42 82MU 8-7 *Ban Shah* 23-10 USSR 11-1-43

EP233 45MU 4-7-42 82MU 8-7 VASM 23-9 fuel syst mods 310S 10-11 131S 1-7-43 310S 24-9 DeH 18-10-43 26S 10-6-44 FACE 6-10-44

EP234 45MU 4-6-42 118S 15-6 FTR ops 20-6 FH6.30

EP235 12MU 5-6-42 610S 9-7 FAAC 27-7 ROS 167S 14-11 FTR 1-1-43

EP236 12MU 28-8-42 222MU 20-9 *SS621* 16-10 Gib 1-11 NWA 28-2-43

EP237 12MU 5-6-42 82MU 8-7 3PATP 19-9

EP238 39MU 19-6-42 610S 9-7 FACA 21-7 313S 14-3-43 2TEU 17-6-44 57 OTU 27-6 595S 21-6-45 FAAC 20-8 recat E SOC 29-8

EP239 33MU 5-6-42 82MU 7-7 *Ban Shah* 23-10 USSR 11-1-43

EP240 45MU 5-6-42 510S 16-6 118S 16-6 CAC ops 9-9 312S 11-143 350S 5-10 FTR ops 13-11 FH288.15

EP241 33MU 7-6-42 82MU 7-7 *City o Der* 1-11 USSR 10-1-43

EP242 38MU 6-6-42 82MU *Ban Shah* 23-10 dam f/f AST 6-11 M45M instal 129S 12-3-43 453S 17-7 341S 3-11 350S 29-3-44 ECFS 21-9 R&S 3-1-47 refurb Port 17-12-47

EP243 38MU 6-6-42 76MU 6-7 *C o Der* 1-11 USSR 10-1-43

EP244 33MU 5-6-42 416S 30-6 602S 15-7 164S 11-9 341S 21-2-43 340S 23-3 FAAC 17-6 SAL M45 instal 501S 2-11 CAC ops 12-6-44 1696Flt 24-11 R&S 31-10-46 refurb Port 3-7-47

EP245 12MU 6-6-42 610S 9-7 167S 14-10 FAAC 21-3-43 AST 453S 16-9 341S 3-11 329S 6-4-44 SOC 21-9-45

EP246 33MU 6-6-42 76MU 6-7 *C o Der* 1-11 USSR 10-1-43

EP247 38MU 6-6-42 76MU 6-7 *C o Der* 1-11 USSR 10-1-43

EP248 38MU 6-6-42 76MU 6-7 *C o Der* 1-11 USSR 10-1-43

EP249 33MU 5-6-42 416S 15-6 602S 16-7 164S 11-9 341S 23-2-43 340S 23-3 USAAF 15-11 12FU 13-1-45 1 OADU 17-1 FAF 19-1

EP250 12MU 6-6-42 610S 9-7 167S 14-10 310S 22-3-43 131S 2-7 310S 24-9 WAL 19-1-44 17SFTS 7-10 5AFU 14-7-45 to 5939M 12SoTT 11-4-46 SOC 4-7

EP251 12MU 6-6-42 610S 11-7 167S 14-10 FTR ops 13-11

EP252 12MU 6-6-42 82MU 8-7 350S 29-11 FACB 7-3-43 1 CRU 453S 11-8 CE ops 8-10

EP257 served from Malta.

EP253 12MU 6-6-42 610S 9-7 167S 14-10 FAAC 9-3-43 19S 25-5 341S 15-11 350S 16-6-44 453S u/c cl psc ldg Swannington CE 15-1-45
EP254 38MU 14-6-42 215MU 1-7 *Emp Cam* 10-8 ME 17-9 FTR ops 7-11
EP255 VB(T) 6MU 11-6-42 52MU 21-6 *Emp Dar* 29-6 Malta 1-8 185S CE ops 31-7 SOC 1-8 FH10.00
EP256 9MU 9-6-42 76MU 7-7 *Ban Shah* 23-10 USSR 21-11
EP257 VB(T) 6MU 7-6-42 52MU 21-6 *Emp Dar* 29-6 Malta 1-8 NA 1-5-43 SOC 30-11-44
EP258 VB(T) 38MU 7-6-42 76MU 9-9 *SS620* 15-10 ME 5-11 Malta 1-12-43 to Turkey 29-3-45
EP259 38MU 7-6-42 52MU 26-6 *Emp Dar* 29-6 Malta 1-8 NA 30-11-43 SOC 24-4-45
EP260 38MU 7-6-42 52MU 26-6 *Emp Dar* 29-6 Malta 1-8 C3 ops 19-11
EP275 37MU 15-6-42 402S 25-6 FACB 22-7 AST C3 ops 19-11 recat E 16-8-43
EP276 37MU 15-6-42 611S 1-7 65S 16-9 FAAC 16-9 ROS 52 OTU 14-2-43 FAAC 27-7 VA ADn FLS 2-2-44 w/u ldg Glentrees Peebles CE 25-6
EP277 37MU 15-6-42 611S 1-7 350S 28-8 485S 18-9 FAAC 2-12 19S 1-7-43 501S 29-12 CAC ops 23-5-44 AST M50 instal 165HCU SOC 7-9-45
EP278 12MU 16-6-42 602S 29-6 416S 16-7 411S 23-3-43 FAAC 29-4 401S 13-6 FACA 25-7 VASM 18-4-44 fuel syst mods 53 OTU 27-9 61 OTU 17-5-45 605S 28-6 SOC 3-1-46
EP279 33MU 27-6-42 416S 21-7 strk by BM419 t/o Prestwick CE 9-11 SAL SOC 24-11 FH130.35
EP280 8MU 18-6-42 602S 8-7 416S 16-7 FAAC 22-1-43 3501SU 7-8 FACE 5-9
EP281 8MU 21-6-42 416S 31-8 411S 23-3-43 CAC ops 12-6 ROS 501S 15-8-44 61 OTU 28-9 PAL 10-9-45 SOC 29-9
EP282 38MU 25-6-42 82MU 14-11 *Bar Inch* 18-12 USSR 24-3-43
EP283 LFVB M45M 6MU 20-6-42 332S 26-6 412S 2-12 421S 31-1-43 416S 23-5 401S 1-6 322S 10-11 222S 1-1-44 287S 17-1-45 SOC 2-9
EP284 15MU 10-8-42 19S 20-8 402S 5-5-43 345S 14-4-44 61 OTU 28-9 M45M instal 3501SU 22-2-45 SOC 30-7
EP285 33MU 25-6-42 72S 28-7 52 OTU 27-1-43 315S 22-9 USAAF 6-1-44 FACB 12-2 VASM 18-4 fuel syst mods M45 Instal cd VASM during tests 4-5 FRU 16-8 276S 4-10 SOC 29-11-45
EP286 38MU 7-6-42 222MU 31-8 Gib 27-9 NWA 20-2-43 Malta 1-5 Italy 1-11 MAAF 21-6-45 FAF 16-2-46
EP287 12MU 16-6-42 310S 20-7 FAAC ops 27-2-43 FH225.00
EP288 Canadian Pacific II 37MU 14-6-42 402S 25-6 122S 12-8 350S 29-11 610S 27-3-43 hit trees in low level flight CE Axminster Devon 1-2-44 FH409.00
EP289 9MU 9-6-42 118S 18-6 CB ops 26-6 2SIG 21-9 501S 8-10 504S 19-10 167S 7-11 FA FTR 1-1-43
EP290 6MU 9-6-42 52MU 21-6 *Emp Dar* 29-6 Malta 1-8 NWA 1-6 FAF 31-10 ME 30-11-44 SOC 29-8-46
EP291 ASTH 14-6-42 VA 26-7 to Sea IB MB366
EP292 9MU 9-6-42 76MU 7-7 416S 16-7 *C o Der* 1-11 USSR 10-1-43
EP293 ASTH 14-6-42 VA 21-7 to Sea IB MB367
EP294 ASTH 10-6-42 VA 11-7 to Sea IB MB368
EP295 ASTH 14-6-42 VA 15-7 to Sea IB MB369
EP296 ASTH 11-6-42 VA 15-7 to Sea IB MB370
EP297 VB(T) 6MU 14-6-42 52MU 26-6 *Emp Dar* 29-6 Malta FTR ops 27-7
EP298 12MU 9-6-42 610S 9-7 167S 14-10 132S 19-5-43 19S 25-5 315S 26-6 611S 1-7 e/fld off coast during sweep a/c aban nr Yarmouth 22-9 SOC 30-9 FH583.35
EP299 ASTH 11-6-42 VA 18-7 to Sea IB MB371 25-7
EP300 37MU 12-6-42 118S 19-6 FAAC 31-7 501S 15-8 167S CA ops 8-11 322S 13-7-43 611S 8-10 57 OTU 19-10-44 61 OTU 3-5-45 695S 28-6 SOC 3-1-46
EP301 ASTH 16-6-42 VA 14-7 to Sea IB MB372
EP302 ASTH 11-6-42 VA 19-7 to Sea IB MB373 4-8
EP303 VB(T) 8MU 14-6-42 215MU 1-7 *Belmor* 5-8 Tak 13-9 ME 28-9 SOC 10-4-43
EP304 ASTH 10-6-42 VA 17-7 to Sea IB MB374
EP305 6MU 12-6-42 52MU 21-6 *Emp Dar* 29-6 Malta 1-8 NWA 1-6-43 SOC 30-9
EP306 VB(T) 6MU 14-6-42 52MU 25-6 *Emp Dar* 29-6 Malta 6-9 C2 23-9 NA 1-6-43 SOC 26-4-45
EP307 VB(T) 8MU 21-6-42 SLG3 23-6 FAAC 2-7 47MU 8-7 *C o Der* 1-11 USSR 1-1-43
EP308 ASTH 10-6-42 VA 14-7 to Sea IB MB375
EP309 VB(T) 8MU 14-6-42 21MU 2-7 *Belmor* 5-8 Tak 13-9 ME 14-10 FTR ops 20-3-43
EP310 VB(T) 8MU 23-6-42 76MU 28-7 RAF Abb 30-7 f/f Malta 6-9 C3 ops 15-11
EP311 33MU 20-6-42 82MU 6-7 *Canada* 3-12 USSR 1-3-43
EP312 9MU 16-6-42 222MU 11-8 *Moradian* 29-8 Tak 25-10 ME 10-8-43 SOC 10-1-46
EP313 VB(T) 38MU 16-6-42 52MU 26-6 *Emp Dar* 29-6 Malta 1-8 C2 26-10 SOC Jan'43 FH114.45
EP314 33MU 16-6-42 82MU 6-7 *Ban Shah* 23-10 USSR 11-1-43
EP315 VB(T) 8MU 14-6-42 215MU 2-7 *Belmor* 5-8 Tak 13-9 NAASC 31-10 USAAF 31-1-44
EP316 VB(T) 39MU 14-6-42 52MU 26-6 *Emp Dar* 29-6 Malta 1-8 CE ops 13-10
EP327 VB(T) 8MU 12-6-42 FAAC 2-7 215MU 2-7 *Emp Cam* 19-8 ME 17-9 FAC3 23-7-43
EP328 37MU 14-6-42 118S 22-6 66S 24-9 310S 31-10 234S 3-12 602S 25-1-43 412S 19-4 317S 28-6 FTR ops 26-7 FH55.10
EP329 VB(T) 6MU 14-6-42 215MU 6-7 *Emp Clive* 19-7 Malta 13-8 C2 ops 14-10 C3 ops 29-10
EP330 38MU 17-6-42 52MU 26-6 *Emp Dar* 29-6 Malta 1-8 SOC 19-4-43 bboc ME 21-6-45 SOC 29-8-46
EP331 VB(T) 39MU 14-6-42 52MU 26-6 *Emp Dar* 29-6 Malta 1-8 1435S CE ops 3-8 SOC 5-8
EP332 9MU 14-6-42 215MU 6-7 *Emp Clive* 19-7 Malta 3-8 NWA USAAF 31-8-43
EP333 VB(T) 8MU 18-6-42 76MU 7-7 *C o Der* 1-11 USSR 10-1-43
EP334 VB(T) 8MU 18-6-42 82MU 8-7 ME 17-10 NAAF 1-11-43 SOC 30-6-45
EP335 12MU 17-6-42 610S 14-7 FAAC 4-8 313S 27-10 52 OTU 6-2-43 VAWD 31-5 wts & CG load Port 19-10
EP336 VB(T) 39MU 14-6-42 52MU 26-6 *Emp Dar* 29-6 Malta 1-8 1435S CE ops 8-8 SOC 10-8
EP337 VB(T) 8MU 20-6-42 76MU 7-7 *C o Der* 1-11 USSR 10-1-43
EP338 9MU 14-6-42 52MU 27-6 *Emp Dar* 29-6 Malta 1-8 C3 ops 16-10
EP339 VB(T) 39MU 14-6-42 52MU 26-6 *Emp Dar* 29-6 Malta 1-8 229S CE ops 27-8 SOC 28-8 FH60.50
EP340 9MU 14-6-42 215MU 5-7 *Emp Clive* 19-7 Malta 3-8 C3 15-10
EP341 VB(T) 6MU 14-6-42 47MU 26-6 *Emp Gem* 1-7 Malta 1-8 SOC 18-10
EP342 VB 12MU 16-6-42 610S 11-7 FTR ops 19-8
EP343 VB(T) 39MU 14-6-42 52MU 26-6 *Emp Dar* 29-6 Malta 1-8 185S CB ops 31-9 ME 1-6-43 NAASC 31-10 32S FTR ops 31-8-44
EP344 38MU 17-6-42 52MU 26-6 *Emp Dar* 29-6 Malta 1-8 144S CE ops 30-7 SOC 1-8
EP345 9MU 14-6-42 215MU 5-7 *Emp Clive* 19-7 Malta 3-8 C3 ops 18-10
EP346 12MU 17-6-42 610S 11-7 130S 29-3-43 64S 5-4 132S 23-5 302S 28-6 306S 3-10 CGS 30-9-44 u/c clpse ldg Catf CE 29-8-45 SOC 4-9
EP347 37MU 14-6-42 310S 6-11 131S 2-7-43 ASTE 22-8 OTU 1-2-44 FLS 10-2 61 OTU 23-9 290S 4-1-45 SOC 30-7-45
EP348 33MU 17-6-42 76MU 6-7 *C o Lil* 8-12 USSR 16-2-43
EP349 12MU 17-6-42 610S 11-7 167S 14-10 FTR ops 13-11
EP350 VB(T) 8MU 18-6-42 167S 16-1-43 CB ops 18-2 195S 20-5 82MU 26-9 Port 19-10
EP351 33MU 17-6-42 82MU 6-7 *C o D* 1-11 USSR 10-1-43
EP352 39MU 19-6-42 312S 5-8 313S 1-6-43 FACA 16-5 66S 4-7 FACE 23-9 SOC 30-9 FH431.35
EP353 VB(T) 8MU 21-6-42 76MU 7-7 *Ban Shah* 23-10 USSR 11-1-43
EP354 33MU 20-6-42 167S 16-1-43 132S 19-5 19S 25-5 FACB 11-6 308S 26-9 349S 29-10 coll with AR430 on t/o Friston CE 12-2-44
EP355 6MU 20-6-42 610S 14-7 310S 24-7 e/fld w/u ldg on beach Brixham CE 31-7 SOC 10-8
EP356 33MU 20-6-42 76MU 6-7 *Canada* 3-11 USSR 1-3-43
EP357 6MU 20-6-42 82MU 8-7 *Ban Shah* 23-10 USSR 11-1-43
EP358 6MU 21-6-42 76MU 7-7 *City o Der* 1-11 USSR 10-1-43
EP359 VB(T) 8MU 21-6-42 76MU 7-7 *Ban Shah* 23-10 USSR 11-1
EP360 39MU 18-6-42 610S 11-7 167S 14-10 FACB 29-12 412S 18-6-43 317S FTR ops 24-6
EP361 39MU 19-6-42 610S 11-7 167S 14-10 CB ops 23-1-43 453S 17-7 341S 25-8 cd during exercise dbf CE Perr 23-10 FH416.10
EP362 33MU 20-6-42 82MU 8-7 65S 31-3-43 132S 23-5 302S 28-6 CAC 18-8 306S 3-10 PAL 28-3-46 to spares
EP363 6MU 20-6-42 76MU 7-7 *Canada* 3-12 USSR 1-3-43
EP364 LRVB 33MU 27-6-42 82MU 310S 1-8 129S 29-4-43 453S 17-7 f/ld i/sea by Bf110 F/Lt Ewins safe 8-10
EP365 9MU 20-8-42 VSM 17-9 fuel syst mods 82MU 18-2 *Fort L M* 12-3 Tak 20-4 ME 23-5 FAC3 29-4-44
EP366 6MU 21-6-42 76MU 7-7 *Ban Shah* 23-10 USSR 11-1-43
EP380 LFVB 8MU 21-6-42 416S 26-7 downwind t/o strk tree MHth CE 31-7 AST M45 instal 602S 13-5-43 118S 10-10 132S 25-1-44 USAAF 9-5-42 OTU 27-9-44 to 5931M 5SoTT 23-4-45 RTGA 28-8-47
EP381 39MU 26-6-42 111S 26-7 416S 28-7 CB ops 19-8 ROS 165S 20-9 CE ops 8-11
EP382 39MU 5-7-42 1 SLG 11-8 82MU 28-10 *Bar Inch* 18-12 USSR 24-3-43
EP383 33MU 27-6-42 416S 30-7 CB ops 22-7 VSM 14-9 fuel syst mods 222MU 6-11 *Nank* 28-11 USSR 6-2-43
EP384 33MU 27-6-42 416S 25-7 e/fld hit trees on app Earls Colne CE 25-8 AST 131S 15-1-43 602S 14-5 247S 25-5 FTR ops 6-6
EP385 33MU 23-6-42 122S 11-8 416S f/ld Earls Colne 22-8 52 OTU 20-10 315S 2-10-43 61 OTU 28-9-44 SOC 8-1-45
EP386 39MU 5-7-43 2SLG 14-9 82 MU *Bar Inch* 18-12 USSR 24-3-43
EP387 8MU 2-7-42 402S 25-7 350S 28-8 485S 18-9 FACB 12-6-43 AST M45M instal 322S 11-1-44 350S 13-3 CAC ops 7-6 57 OTU 23-7 FACB 29-12 recat E SOC 10-1-45
EP388 45MU 1-7-42 111S 26-7 416S 28-7 CAC ops 23-1-43 411S 23-3 610S 19-9 FAAC 13-2-44 501S 21-3 M45M instal e/fld & fire w/u ldg nr Bridgenorth Salop CE 2-11
EP389 33MU 20-6-42 82MU 7-7 *Ban Shah* 23-10 USSR 11-1-43
EP390 12MU 22-6-42 610S 11-7 FTR ops 2-9 FH84.5
EP391VB(T) 8MU 20-6-42 28SLG 23-6 215MU 7-11 *Bar Inch* 18-12 USSR 24-3-43
EP392 6MU 21-6-42 76MU 7-7 *C o Der* 1-11 USSR 10-1-43
EP393 12MU 22-6-42 610S 11-7 132S 19-5-43 19S 25-5 315S 26-6 611S 1-7 FTR ops 23-8 FH527.50
EP394 6MU 21-6-42 313S 30-7 FAAC 13-1-43 19S 26-4 CE ops 8-6
EP395 12MU 22-6-42 610S 11-7 167S 14-10 FACB 26-10 AST M45M instal 310S 31-1-43 131S 2-7 310S 24-9 510S 27-3-44 345S 12-8 CAC 21-9 SOC 27-6-45
EP396 8MU 22-6-42 47MU 8-7 *C o Der* 1-11 USSR 10-1-43
EP397 8MU 24-6-42 21MU 23-7 *Emp Puma* 17-8 Tak 23-9 ME 22-10 SOC 10-12
EP398 12MU 22-6-42 610S 14-7 167S 14-10 132S 19-5-43 19S 25-5 416S 10-6 FAAC 8-7501S 29-4-44 CE ops 14-7 M45M instal during service
EP399 39MU 25-6-43 76MU 2-8 *Emp Sun* 19-8 Tak 13-9 FTR ops 31-10
EP400 8MU 22-6-42 76MU 27-7 *City of Der* 1-11 USSR 10-1-43
EP401 VB(T) 38MU 22-6-42 215MU 19-7 *Emp Cam* 19-8 Tak 3-9 ME 28-9 NAAF 1-11-44 SOC 28-4-45
EP402 8MU 21-6-42 82MU 8-7 *C o Der* 1-11 USSR 10-1-43
EP403 6MU 21-6-42 76MU 7-7 *Ban Shah* 23-10 USSR 11-1-43
EP404 8MU 24-6-42 222MU 20-8 *Emp Fran* 30-8 Gib 14-9 Malta 1-12 143S NA 1-6-43 HWA USAAF 1-10 SOC 28-4-45
EP405 9MU 26-6-42 76MU 2-8 *Emp Sun* 19-8 Tak 13-9 ME 7-10 SOC 5-1-43
EP406 39MU 25-6-42 215MU 1-7 *Emp Puma* 19-8 Tak 23-9 ME 24-10 RHAF 25-4-46
EP407 39MU 24-6-42 76MU 4-8 *Emp Sun* 19-8 Tak 13-9 Mombassa 29-9
EP408 33MU 28-6-42 47MU 8-7 *C o Der* 1-11 USSR 10-1-43
EP409 33MU 27-6-42 82MU 8-7 453S 18-8-43 FAAC 8-10 341S 3-11 52 OTU 25-1-44 FLS 2-2 CGS 1-10 FACE 14-10
EP410 VB(T) 38MU 23-6-42 52MR 11-7 RAF Abb 29-7 f/f Malta 185S CE ops 15-8 SOC 16-8 FH17.35
EP411 33MU 26-6-42 310S 23-7 AST 26-2-43 M45M instal 317S 29-6 312 4-10 FAAC 14-1-44 411S 27-2 303S 22-5 42 OTU 5-11 R&S 14-1-47 refurb Port 23-12-47
EP412 VB(T) 8MU 23-6-42 52MU 12-7 *Emp Clive* 19-7 Malta 3-8 GIB 2-12 520S 23-3-44 GE ops 25-4
EP413 LRVB 12MU 22-6-42 310S 19-7 CB ops 10-8 118S 15-9 FTR ops 27-6-43
EP414 33MU 23-6-42 82MU 7-7 *Ban Shah* 23-10 USSR 11-1-43
EP415 38MU 25-6-42 82MU 7-7 *Co o Der* 1-11 USSR 10-1-43
EP416 38MU 25-6-42 82MU 6-7 *Co o Der* 1-11 USSR 10-1-43
EP417 38MU 25-6-42 47MU 7-7 *Co o Der* 1-11 USSR 10-1-43
EP431 33MU 24-6-42 76MU 3-7 *Canada* 31-12 USSR 1-3-43
EP432 LRVB 38MU 25-6-42 312S 6-8 313S 9-5-43 66S 4-7 FACB 9-8 129S 4-22-44 53 OTU 8-9 61 OTU 17-5-45 Mar Cam 6-12 SOC 5-12
EP433 39MU 25-6-42 52MU 14-8 *Emp Hth* 29-8 Gib 14-9 Malta 1-11 NA 1-6-43 FAF 9-10-47
EP434 33MU 24-6-42 47MU 9-7 *Co o Der* 1-11 USSR 10-1-43

EP455 with 601 Squadron, abandoned November 1942.

EP435 LRVB 39MU 26-6-42 213S 5-8 CAC ops 31-5-43 AST 302 19-8 306S 4-3-44 2775 5-5 83 GSU 1-3-45 FAAC 17-5

EP436 9MU 26-6-42 FAAC 30-6 ROS 82MU 26-8 *Emp Fran* 3--8 Gib 14-9 Malta 1-12 NA 1-6 43 SOC 26-4-45

EP437 38MU 28-6-42 215MU 21-7 *Emp Cam* 19-8 Tak 12-9 ME 19-9 FA FTR 13-10

EP438 39MU 24-6-42 76MU 5-8 *Nigerian* 29-8 Tak 28-10 SOC 5-1-43

EP439 9MU 28-6-42 76MU 5-8 *Co o Ath* 29-8 Tak 23-9 ME 29-10 FTR ops 31-8-44

EP440 9MU 28-6-42 76MU 5-8 *Emp Sun* 19-8 Tak 13-9 ME 23-9 FTR ops 10-7-43

EP441 9MU 25-6-42 76MU 4-8 *Emp Sun* 19-8 Tak 13-9 ME 28-9 SOC 13-12

EP442 9MU 25-6-42 76MU 6-8 *Co o Ath* 29-8 Tak 23-9 ME 22-10 FA FTR 22-3-43

EP443 39MU 25-6-42 610S 8-8 167S 14-10 FTR ops 12-12 FH181.45

EP444 VB(T) 38MU 27-6-42 52MU 14-8 *Emp Cab* 28-8 Gib 14-9 Malta 1-12 C3 ops 19-7-43

EP445 VB(T) 38MU 3-7-42 19S 16-8 402S 22-4-43 FACB 11-3-44 530TU 11-8 SOC 29-5-45

EP446 38MU 28-6-42 47MU 9-7 *Co o Der* 1-11 USSR 10-1-43

EP447 39MU 25-6-42 19S 10-8 402S 26-4-43 CB ops 4-6 504S 25-8 313S 22-9 53 OTU 30-11-44 FAAC 17-3-45 PAL 4-10 SOC 13-10

EP448 9MU 28-6-42 76MU 28-7 Malta 6-9 C3 ops 2-11 bboc SOC 1-12 FH67.50 NWA 1-5-43 FAC 24-1-44

EP449 39MU 26-6-42 313S 24-7 air coll with AR546 i/sea 15-1-43

EP450 38MU 28-6-42 82MU 5-7 *Canada* 3-12 USSR 1-3-43

EP451 9MU 28-6-42 76MU 3-8 *Emp Sun* 19-8 Tak 13-9 C3 ops 17-10 ME 27-10 FTR ops 13-11

EP452 33MU 26-6-42 82MU 8-7 310S 2-8 FACE 24-8 AST SOC 31-10 recat B 167S 24-12 19S 25-5-43 416S 7-6 186S 14-2-44 FAAC 9-3 63S 1-5 290S 7-1-45 R&S 31-10-46 refurb Port 6-5-47

EP453 45MU 1-7-42 310 14-7 FTR ops 11-9 FH75

EP454 33MU 27-6-42 FACB 7-7 SAL 45MU 11-9 *Nank* 28-11 USSR 6-2-43

EP455 9U 28-6-42 76MU 8-7 *Mokambu* 29-8 Tak 23-9 ME 13-10 601S F/O Allen-Rowlandson aban a/c 2-11

EP456 9MU 5-7-42 222MU 11-8 *Mokambu* 29-8 Tak 23-9 ME 2-10 FAC2 14-12 NAASC 31-10-43 SOC 27-6-46

EP457 VB(T) 27-6-42 76MU 26-7 RAF Abb 31-7 f/f Malta 185S CE ops 17-8 SOC 18-8 FH20.35

EP458 VB(T) 38MU 27-6-42 215MU 21-7 *Emp Puma* 19-8 Tak 23-9 ME FAC2 6-1-43 MAAF 31-3-44 SOC 16-7-46

EP459 VB(T) 38MU 3-7-42 RAF Abb 3-8 f/f Malta 6-9 ME 9-10 Italy 1-11-43 NAAF C3 ops 26-11 SOC 25-7-46

EP460 VB(T) 27-6-42 76MU 26-7 *Emp Hth* 29-8 Gib 14-9 Malta C3 ops 18-1-43 FH49.15

EP461 LFVB 8MU 2-7-42 RAF Exeter 4-8 SAL 27-10 303S 7-3-44 CE ops 21-5-44

EP462 33MU 27-6-42 82MU 7-9 *Canada* 3-12 USSR 1-3-43

EP463 9MU 26-6-42 76MU 27-7 *Emp Sun* 19-8 Tak 13-9 ME 31-6-45 SOC 10-1-46

EP464 45MU 1-7-42 38MU 9-7 310S 1-8 FTR ops 29-1-43 FH 213

EP465 VB(T) 38MU 3-7-42 19S 16-8 FACE 16-3-43 402S 5-5 u/c clpse hvy ldg Dig 18-6 SAL recat E 27-6

EP466 38MU 28-6-42 47MU 9-7 *C o Der* 1-11 USSR 10-1-43

EP467 38MU 28-6-42 76MU 26-7 RAF Abb f/f Malta 6-9 C3 24-10

EP468 38MU 28-6-42 76MU 6-7 *Canada* 3-12 USSR 1-3-43

EP469 38MU 28-6-42 76MU 6-7 *C o Der* 1-11 USSR 10-1-43

EP470 45MU 1-7-42 82MU 8-7 *Emp Cab* 28-8 Gib 14-8 NWA 28-2-43

EP471 VB(T) 38MU 28-6-42 76MU 26-7 RAF Abb 30-7 f/f Malta 6-9 185S C3 ops 3-3-43

EP472 VB(T) 38MU 28-6-42 76MU 26-7 RAF Abb 31-7 f/f Malta 108S dam ops 13-8 SOC 15-8

EP473 8MU 2-7-42 52MU 14-8 *Emp Cab* 28-8 Gib 14-9 Malta 1-11 SOC 9-2-43 FH103.45

EP485 45MU 1-7-42 485S 31-3-43 64S 19-8 118S 25-9 132S 13-2-44 504S 15-3 310S 15-7 41 OTU 15-7 strk by AB202 Haw CE 8-9

EP486 39MU 3-7-42 82MU 28-10 *Bar Inch* 18-12 USSR 24-2-43

EP487 38MU 19-7-42 310S 4-9 303S 30-11 HAL 8-4-43 VASM 4-8 fuel syst mods MkIII IFF S type pt bomb carr 411ARF 2-12 130S 16-8-44 FAAC 20-3-45 SOC 4-9-47

EP488 39MU 16-7-42 82MU 28-10 *Bar Inch* 18-12 USSR 24-3-43

EP489 33MU 26-7-42 416S 21-8 411S CAC ops 22-1-43 FTR ops 14-4 FH150.00

EP490 39MU 5-7-42 82MU 28-10 *Bar Inch* 18-12 USSR 24-3-43

EP491 6MU 19-7-42 312S 3-8 350S 6-8 165S 23-9 65S 15-7-43 130S 15-8 FAAC 3-2-44 VASM 1-3 fuel syst and 'Basta' mods M45M instal 1S 8-4 61 OTU 13-8 OTU 13-8 coll with EP757 CAC 4-12 recat E SOC 9-2-45

EP492 38MU 19-7-42 501S 2-9 5USA 13-9 164S 21-9 341S 3-2-43 340S 23-3 FAAC 25-6 SAL 82MU 27-9 Port 19-10

EP493 9MU 21-6-42 416S 29-8 ops 24-10 ROS CE ops 3-2-43

EP494 9MU 21-6-42 222MU 21-11 *Palma* 5-12 USSR 30-1-43

EP495 9MU 21-6-42 222MU 6-11 *C o Lil* 8-12 USSR 10-2-43

EP496 M45M 9MU 27-6-42 BDn 22-8 91S 10-3-43 340S 5-9 67 Recce Grp 2-11 28S 21-11-44 SOC 13-9-45

EP497 39MU 28-6-42 82MU 7-11 *Bar Inch* 18-11 USSR 24-3-43

EP498 9MU 2-7-42 VASM 27-9 fuel syst mods 82MU 25-10 *Bar Inch* 18-12 USSR 24-3-43

EP499 9MU 16-6-42 R-R to FIX M63 47MU 25-6-43 *Fort Ver* 14-7 Casa 24-7 ME 31-12 SOC 30-4-47

EP500 M45M 9MU 28-6-42 91S 20-8 317S 1-5-43 412S 29-6 126S 10-8 611S 22-6-44 42 OTU 24-5-45 587S 7-6 to 570M 5-10 CGS recat E SOC 24-9-49

EP501 9MU 1-7-42 222MU 9-11 *Haducus* 19-12 USSR 17-3-43

EP502 9MU 2-7-42 VASM 9-10 fuel syst mods 222MU 6-11 *Nank* 28-11 USSR 6-2-43

EP503 9MU 2-7-42 65S 10-9 165S 23-9 FACB 23-12 VASM 28-6-43 fuel syst mods wng stiff 165S 24-8 308S 1-10 345S 17-6-44 130S 15-8 61 OTU 19-8 SOC 9-2-45

EP504 LFVB 9MU 6-7-42 65S 10-9 prop hit grd on t/o somersaulted CE Graves 17-9 AST 303S 14-4-43 315S 6-6 19S 26-6 63S 3-7-44 61 OTU 9-11 SOC 22-5-45

EP505 9MU 8-7-42 222MU 6-11 *C o Lil* 8-12 USSR 16-2-43

EP506 9MU 20-7-42 VASM 10-8 fuel syst mods 65S 10-9 165S 23-9 19S 22-7-43 340S 28-9 air coll with BM118 cd Dirleton E Lothian CE 27-10

EP507 9MU 20-7-42 VASM 10-8 fuel syst mods 65S 10-9 165S 23-9 FACB 16-12 AST 65S 26-6-43 130S 15-8 222S 15-2-44 VASM 13-3 M45M instal 'Basta'mods 275S 4-4 SOC 20-2-45

EP508 9MU 20-7-42 91S 20-8 i/sea after mock comb Hawker Typhoon 17-12 FH124.5

EP509 LFLRVB 9MU 20-7-42 VSM 13-8 fuel syst mods M45M instal 65S 10-9 165S 23-9 509S 19-7-43 CAC ops 16-8 349S 3-1-44 303S 6-3 1688Flt 15-12 Sold Brooklands Av broken up 27-2-47

EP510 VB(T) 9MU 22-7-42 VSM 10-8 fuel syst mods 76MU 8-11 *Palma* 5-12 USSR 30-1-43

EP511 VB(T) 9MU 24-7-42 VSM 10-8 76MU 8-11 *Palma* 5-12 dam in transit SOC rts 17-2

EP512 VB(T) 9MU 1-8-42 VSM 10-8 fuel syst mods 76MU 11-11 *Palma* 5-12 USSR 30-1-43

EP513 VB(T) 9MU 29-7-42 VSM 10-8 fuel syst mods 76MU 8-11 *Palma* 5-12 USSR 30-1-43

EP514 VB(T) 9MU 1-8-42 VSM 13-8 fuel syst mods 76MU 10-11 *Palma* 5-12 USSR 30-1-43

EP515 M45M 9MU 8-8-42 VSM 27-9 fuel syst mods 118S 26-4-43 453S 3-1-44 602S 25-1 118S 13-3 CAC ops 20-5 3213S 21-7 611S 26-10 13Grp Com flt 11-11 FACE 21-9-45 SOC 5-10

EP516 9MU 1-8-42 19S 28-8 FACB 1-10 130S 28-3-43 65S 31-3 132S 23-5 302S 28-6 ops 30-6

EP517 9MU 1-7-42 76M 29-7 Malta Aug '42 249S FACE 15-8 SOC 16-8

EP518 39MU 6-7-42 312S 5-8 WAL 12-11 M45M instal CB ops 31-5-43 1CRU 416S 14-10 186S 13-2-44 130S 18-4 57 OTU 19-10 Face 1-12

EP519 9MU 1-7-42 76MU 29-8 Malta 6-9 C3 ops 11-3

EP520 VB(T) 38MU 28-6-42 76MU 16-8 *Emp Cab* 28-8 Gib 19-9 Malta 1-11 NA 1-6-43 USAAF 30-11

EP521 8MU 2-7-42 RAF Abb 31-7 f/f Malta 6-9 C3 ops 17-10

EP522 8MU 2-7-42 510S 8-9 509S 19-10 P&PSM 25-3-43 277S 14-1-44 CAC ops 8-6 ROS 61 OTU 16-3-45 691S 21-6 SOC 8-8

EP523 33MU 26-7-42 19S 10-8 FTR ops 19-8

EP536 8MU 2-7-42 222MU 20-8 *Emp Gran* 30-8 Gib 14-9 NWA 28-2-43 SOC 30-4

EP537 8MU 2-7-42 222MU 20-8 *Emp Cab* 28-8 Gib 14-9 NWA 28-2-43 SOC 31-3

EP538 8MU 3-7-42 501S 6-8 504S 19-10 CAC ops 24-3-43 165S 1-7 DeH 14-7 Port 19-10

EP539 45MU 1-7-42 82MU 8-7 312S 4-8 CE ops 14-5-43 FH259.10

EP540 45MU 1-7-42 82MU 8-7 *Canada* 3-12 USSR 1-3-43

EP541 39MU 2-7-42 76MU 28-7 185S FACB 1-9 Malta 6-9 FAC3 16-10

EP542 8MU 2-742 42MU 10-9 *SS621* 16-10 Gib 1-11 NWA 28-2-43 C3 ops 18-4

EP543 VB(T) 1-7-42 222MU 11-8 *Nigerian* 29-8 Tak 3-10 ME C2 28-12 NAAF 1-11-43 COC 8-3-44

EP544 45MU 1-7-42 222MU 5-12 *SS647* 19-12 Gib 6-2-43 NWA 28-2

EP545 VB(T) 38MU 1-7-42 82MU 4-9 *SS620* 15-10 Gib 1-11 E AF FTR ops 28-12

EP546 9MU 23-7-42 76MU 29-8 Malta 126S CE ops 17-8 SOC 19-8

EP547 9MU 3-7-42 76MU 26-7 312S 4-8 FACB 4-1-43 310S 29-3 131S 2-7 CE 27-8

EP548 LF LR VB 9MU 3-7-42 19S 10-8 402S 26-4-43 416S 19-8 FAAC 20-5-44 M45M instal LMS 53 OTU 29-11-44 SOC 5-6-45

EP549 LRVB 33MU 5-7-42 118S 3-9 64S 25-9-43 FTR ops 14-1-44 FH498

EP550 VB(T) 39MU 3-7-42 RAF Abb 21-7 f/f Malta 6-9 SOC 14-10

EP551 VB(T) 56MU 5-7-42 52MU 8-7 *Emp Clive* 19-7 Malta 3-8 C3 ops 15-1-43

EP552 VB(T) 38MU 3-7-42 19S 28-8 FACB 13-3-43 453S 17-8 312S 6-11 306S 4-2-44 84Grp Com S 24-4 1689 Flt 30-9

EP553 VB(T) 39MU 3-7-42 RAF Abb 31-7 f/f Malta 6-9 SOC 12-10

EP554 VB(T) 39MU 3-7-42 RAF Abb 30-7 f/f Malta 6-9 SOC 12-10 FH81.00

EP555 VB(T) 38MU 3-7-42 501S 12-9 504S 19-10 FACA 23-10 165S 1-7-43 CE ops 25-7 SOC FH310.25

EP556 VB(T) 8MU 2-7-42 82MU 26-8 *Emp Fran* 30-9 Gib 16-9 NWA 28-2-43

EP557 VB(T) 38MU 5-7-42 82MU 4-9 *SS622* 17-10 Gib 1-11 SOC 31-12 e/a 106 R&SU

EP558 8MU 5-7-42 312S 11-8 65S 1-5-43 132S 23-5 302S 28-6 CB ops 8-9 313S 4-2-44 1695Bd Flt 5-12 swg off runway o/t Dalton CE 3-2-45 SOC 9-2

EP559 LRVB(T) 38MU 3-7-42 312S 2-8 CAC ops 21-8 234S 4-7-43 FACB 17-7 AST M45M instal 501S 20-11 FTR ops 21-12 FH300.40

EP560 39MU 3-7-42 313S 29-7 FAAC 29-8 412S 4-5-43 317S 28-6 CAC ops 14-7 341S 3-11 239S 16-2-44 AST 13-3 M45M instal 1696Flt 21-11 R&S 12-11-46 refurb Port 31-7-47

EP561 VB(T) 39MU 3-7-42 RAF Abb 31-7 82MU 4-9 *SS622* 17-10 Gib 1-11 e/a SOC 31-12

EP562 VB(T) 8MU 5-7-42 47MU 24-8 *Emp Hth* 29-8 Gib 14-9 FACA 27-10 ROS 215MU 31-3-43 GIB 17-5 SOC 23-10-44 RHAF 25-10-46

EP563 VB(T) 8MU 5-7-42 47MU 24-8 *Emp Hth* 29-8 Gib 14-9 NWA 28-2-43

EP564 8MU 5-7-42 312S 11-8 AST 29-10 M45M instal 131S 7-1-43 610S 27-1 606S 4-3 602S 7-3 412S 19-4 416S 10-6 186S 10-2-44 CAC ops 21-5 SOC 7-9-45

EP565 33MU 5-7-42 47MU 9-7 *C o Der* 1-11 USSR 10-1-43

EP566 33MU 5-7-42 47MU 9-7 *C o Der* 1-11 USSR 10-1-43

EP567 9MU 5-7-42 52MU 16-8 *Emp Cab* 28-8 Gib 14-9 Malta 1-11 FTR 10-4-43 FH93.30

EP568 9MU 3-7-42 76MU 9-8 *Emp Cab* 28-8 Gib 14-9 NWA 28-2-43 SOC 1-7

EP569 VB(T) 38MU 5-7-42 76MU 20-8 *Emp Hth* 29-8 Gib 14-9 SOC 31-12

EP570 LRVB 9MU 3-7-42 312S 6-8 CAC ops 28-2-43 308S 3-11 CGS 1-10-44 to 5538M 4-8-45

EP571 VB(T) 38MU 5-7-42 52MU 14-8 *Emp Hth* 29-8 Gib 14-9 C3 ops 19-11

EP572 33MU 5-7-42 310S 21-7 FTR ops 27-2-43 FH203

EP573 VB(T) 6MU 5-7-42 52MU 9-7 *Emp Clive* 19-7 Malta 3-8 NA 1-1-44 CE 24-5-45

EP574 9MU 5-7-42 222MU 11-8 *Nigerian* 29-8 Tak ME 31-12 NAAF 1-11-43 SOC 8-3-44

EP575 LRVB 33MU 5-7-42 313S 24-7 CAC ops 20-8 312S 5-4-43 234S 4-7 504S 30-7-43 FAAC 27-8 402S 3-7-44 53 OTU 20-7 SOC 25-6-45

EP576 VB(T) 6MU 19-7-42 94S FAAC 7-8 47MU 21-8 Tak 12-10 ME 22-10 C3 ops 9-4-43 bboc 21-6-45 SOC 29-3-46

EP577 12MU 30-7-42 47MU 2-9 *SS625* 20-10 Gib 6-11 C3 26-11

EP578 VB(T) 38MU 5-7-42 47MU 26-8 *Atlan City* 8-9 Tak 29-10 ME 29-10 ME FAC2 1dg 29-10

EP579 VB(T) 38MU 5-7-42 47MU 26-8 *Atlan City* 8-9 ME 30-10 Malta 1-7-43 Sic 1-8 NAASC 31-10

EP594 6MU 19-7-42 312S 6-8 303S 12-8 FACB 23-9 52OTU 26-3-43 306S 16-9 302S 3-10-43 e/fld hit fence ldg Leasowe Cheshire 7-3-44 130S 8-8 SOC 22-5-45

EP595 12MU 20-7-42 485S 5-8-42 FTR ops 28-11 FH127.45

EP596 12MU 30-7-42 222MU 7-11 *Nank* 28-11 USSR 6-2-43

EP597 33MU 27-7-42 72S 30-8 VSM 21-6-43 fuel syst mods wng stiff M45M instal 66S 9-9 CAC ops 27-9 ROS 340S 15-11 239S 16-2-44 63S 13-3 10ADU 14-1-45 FAF GC2/18

EP598 8MU 23-7-42 222MU 6-11 *Nank* 28-11 USSR 6-2-43

EP599 8MU 24-7-42 FAAC 10-8 WAL 82MU 31-10 *Bar Inch* 18-12 USSR 24-3-43

EP600 LRVB 33MU 26-7-42 312S 5-8 FAAC 4-4-43 131S 2-7 416S 28-9 186S 13-2-44 130S 18-4 o/s ldg strk obst CE 28-4

EP601 39MU 26-7-42 19S 16-8 402S 22-4-43 FAAC 10-9 64S 27-4-44 276S 2-11 M45M instal SOC 29-11-45

EP602 12MU 29-7-42 276MU 31-10 *Palma* 5-12 USSR 30-1-43

EP603 39MU 29-7-42 19S 16-8 CE ops 19-1-43 FH138.35

EP604 12MU 31-7-42 VSM 24-9 fuel syst mods 19S 11-12 FACB 23-1-43 165S 26-8 308S 1-10 61 OTU 28-9-44 to 5053M SOC 10-8-45

EP605 45MU 1-8-42 19S 20-8 FACB 6-10 129S 7-3-43 453S 17-7 341S 3-11 2 Grp Com Flt 5-7-45 R&S 12-11-46 refurb Port 29-11-47

EP606 VB(T) 6MU 5-7-42 52MU 9-7 *Emp Clive* 19-7 o/e aban after t/o *HMS Furious* in Med Sgt McDougal safe 17-8

EP607 VB(T) 8MU 5-7-42 52MU 26-8-42 *Emp Fran* 20-8 Gib 14-9 FTR ops 11-2-43

EP608 12MU 19-7-42 313S 29-7 FACB 1-10 167S 28-2-43 FTR ops 4-4

EP609 8MU 2-8-42 82MU 14-8 *Emp Fran* 30-8 Gib 14-9 C3 ops 8-11-43 SOC 9-11

EP610 45MU 16-8-42 76MU 6-9 *SS622* 1-11 Gib

EP611 39MU 5-7-42 610S 1-8 FTR ops 19-8

EP612 VB(T) 6MU 5-7-42 38MU 9-7 *Emp Clive* 19-7 Malta 3-8 NWA 1-5-43 ME 1-8 NAAF 1-11 SOC 8-3-44 bboc 21-6-45 SOC 29-8-46

EP613 6MU 19-7-42 76MU 28-7 *Emp Sun* 19-8 Tak 13-9 ME 14-10 601S C3 ops 21-1-43 salvaged bboc 1-11 RHAF 25-4-46

EP614 39MU 5-7-42 313S 30-7 FAAC 3-1-43 310S 1-5

131S 2-7 CE ops 3-8 SOC 31-8 FH354.50

EP615* VA con to FIX M63 39MU 16-6-43 CAC 22-6 ROS 222MU 20-9 *Emp Mead* 2-10 Casa 19-10 NA 30-11 USAAF 31-1-44 of 12/31 lost in Italy 7-2 *original a/c crashed Willenhall 18-7-42 on test flt. A. Henshaw safe. Serial re-allocated.

EP616 VB(T) 8MU 24-7-42 cd/ldg nr Willenhall during f/f Csfd-CBAF Alex Henshaw safe 18-8 47MU 24-8 FTR ops 10-11

EP617 38MU 19-7-42 76MU 20-8 *Emp Hth* 29-8 Gib 14-9 NWA 28-2-43 MAAF 21-6-45 SOC 30-8

EP618 6MU 16-7-42 76MU 30-7 *Emp Sun* 19-8 Tak 13-9 NWA 28-2-43 ME 30-11-44 SOC 15-6-45

EP619 VB(T) 6MU 5-7-42 52MU 9-7 *Emp Clive* 19-7 Malta 25-7 ME 18-10 NWA FAC3 24-11-43

EP620 9MU 17-7-42 76MU 8-8 *Emp Cab* 28-8 Gib 14-9 C3 ops 154S 28-1-43

EP621 VB(T) 6MU 5-7-42 52MU 9-7 *Emp Clive* 19-7 Malta 3-8 NWA 28-2-43 ME 1-7 SOC 1-9

EP622 9MU 18-7-42 76MU 16-8 *Emp Cab* 28-8 Gib 24-9 Malta 1-11 NA 1-6-43 HOS SAAF SOC 28-4-45

EP623 39MU 26-7-42 82MU 27-10 *Bar Inch* 18-12 USSR 24-2-43

EP624 VB(T) 38MU 19-7-42 76MU 20-8 *Emp Hth* 29-8 Gib 14-9 NWA 28-2-43 SOC 30-4-43

EP636 6MU 18-7-42 8 OTU 30-7 313S 17-12 66S 4-7-43 CB ops 20-7 341S 11-1-44 FLS 22-2 FACE 2-5

EP637 39MU 16-7-42 310S 9-8 19S 8-12 402S 22-4-43 R-RH 24-7 M45M instal 402S FAAC 23-11 ROS CB ops 15-5-44

EP638 6MU 16-7-42 76MU 30-7 *Emp Sun* 19-8 Tak 13-9 ME 29-9 SOC 28-7-46

EP639 38MU 19-7-42 19S 20-8 402S 24-4-43 FACB 27-5 66S 6-9 coll with AD260 dbl CE Perr 23-10 FH313.00

EP640 6MU 18-7-42 FACB 17-8 350S 26-11 FTR i/sea 28-3-43 FH116.30

EP641 38MU 19-7-42 52MU 16-8 *Emp Cab* 28-8 Gib 14-9 SOC 17-2-43 FH77.20

EP642 9MU 17-7-42 76MU 6-8 *Emp Cab* 28-8 Gib 14-9 242S FAC3 4-1-43

EP643 9MU 17-7-42 76MU 4-8 *Emp Sun* 19-8 Tak 13-9 ME 2-10 CE ops 30-10

EP644 33MU 19-7-42 313S 31-7 CAC 3-12 453S 20-8-43 341S 3-11 239S 16-2-44 63S 13-3 17SFTS 12-10-44 FACE dbf 25-10

EP645 6MU 24-7-42 FACB 31-7 76MU 31-10 *Caterine* 20-11 Tak 27-12 ME 18-1-43 MAAF 28-12-44 CE SOC 6-9-45

EP646 M45 35MU 19-7-42 FAAC 7-9 AST M46 instal 118S 24-9 84Grp Com S 24-4-44 57 OTU FAAC 13-10 SOC 12-2-45

EP647 12MU 20-7-42 82MU 2-9 *SS630* 15-10 Gib 1-11

EP648 12MU 30-7-42 47MU 26-8 *Atlan City* 5-9 Tak ME 16-12 NAAF 1-11-43 SOC 28-4-45

EP649 VB(T) 12MU 20-7-42 47MU 26-8 *Atlan City* 8-9 ME 30-10 NAAF 1-11-43 SOC 8-3-44

EP650 6MU 26-7-42 76MU 8-8 *Emp Cab* 28-8 Gib 14-9 243S 28-2-43 SOC 28-2

EP651 38MU 19-7-42 501S 22-8 504S 19-10 FAAC 17-4-43 WAL M45M instal 602S 7-3-44 303S 30-4 1AGS 30-11 10AGS 5-6-45 FACB out of fuel cdf/ld Firrie W'moreland 4-1-46 recat E SOC 23-1

EP652 9MU 18-7-42 76MU 16-8 *Emp Cab* 28-8 Gib 14-9 Malta 1-11 NA 1-10-43 ME 25-2-45 REAF 29-3

EP653 took the route to Malta via Takoradi.

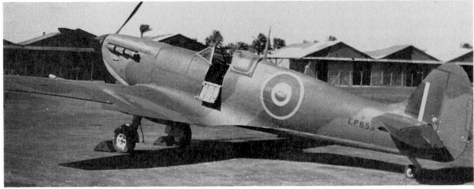

EP653 6MU 16-7-42 215MU 21-7 *Emp Puma* 19-8 Tak 23-9 Malta 1-8-43 Sic C3 ops 27-1-44 SOC 25-7-46

EP654 VC BDn 13-8-42 carb mon cockpit contam levels after firing guns, results negative 39MU 14-10 82MU 26-10 *SS634* 4-11 Gib 23-11 NWA 28-2-43 SOC

EP655 6MU 19-7-42 312S 3-8 *City of Ath* 29-8 Tak 23-9 ME 1-11 SOC 24-2-43 salvaged 30-9 SOC 8-3-44

EP656 6MU 19-7-42 47MU 5-5 Tak 14-10 NAASC 1-11-43 FAF GR.2/33 3-6-44 ME 26-4-45 SOC 29-8-46

EP657 VB(T) 38MU 19-7-42 47MU 26-8 *Atlan City* 8-9 ME 29-10 SOC 1-6-43

EP658 38MU 19-7-42 82MU 26-8 *Emp Frank* 30-8 Gib 14-9 Malta 1-12 NAASC.31-10-43 FAF 14-3-46

EP659 6MU 19-7-42 222MU 5-8 *Mokambu* 29-8 Tak 23-9 ME 18-10 C3 ops 14-12

EP660 LFLRVB 6MU 19-7-42 312S 3-8 FAAC 29-10 313S 4-2-43 FACB 16-5 AST M45 instal 611S 21-7 308S 31-7 349S 29-10 222S FAC2 7-3-44

EP661 12MU 19-7-42 313S 30-7 FAAC 24-12 AST 441S 27-2-44 FACB 25-3 DeH M45M instal BSDO 11-12 S7 OTU 10-3-45 SOC 29-11

EP662 6MU 14-7-42 222MU 19-8 *Emp Cab* 28-8 Gib 14-9 NWA 28-2-43

EP663 9MU 24-7-42 76MU 29-8 Malta 6-9 229S CE ops 17-9 SOC 18-9

EP664 LFLRVB 12MU 19-7-42 313S 30-7 AST 22-6-43 M45M instal 312S 15-9 350S 9-10 322S 11-1-44 277S 2-9 FACB 19-5-45 AST recat E SOC 21-6-45

EP665 6MU 22-7-42 47MU 22-8 ME 23-10 NAAF 1-11 CE 13-9-45 SOC 13-9

EP666 VB(T) 12MU 20-7-42 47MU 26-8 *Atlan City* 8-9 Malta 1-7-43 ME 1-9 NWA 1-10 MAAF 21-6-45

EP667 6MU 19-7-42 222MU 17-8 *Emp Cab* 28-8 Gib 14-9 SOC 31-12

EP668 12MU 1-8-42 47MU 1-9 *SS620* 15-10 Gib 1-11 NWA 28-2-43 FA dbf 16-5

EP669 9MU 27-7-42 Malta 6-9 SOC 27-4-43 bboc SOC 30-8-45

EP682 6MU 23-7-42 76MU 3-8-42 *Emp Sun* 19-8 Tak 13-9 ME 26-9 1S FAC3 11-2-43

EP683 33MU 21-7-42 76MU 10-9 *SS622* 1-11 NWA 28-2-43

EP684 6MU 22-7-42 47MU 26-8 *Atlan City* 8-9 Tak ME 22-10 FTR ops 3-1-43

EP685 9MU 24-8-42 Malta 6-9 C3 ops 23-10

EP686 12MU 25-7-42 66S 20-8 312S 31-10 FAAC 21-11 313S 9-3-43 66S 4-7 AST 17-10-43 RNDA 20-2-44 for train

EP687 8MU 24-7-42 66S 16-8 CE ops 2-10 SOC 9-10 recat B AST M45M instal 312S 14-3-43 509S coll Whitley EB292 ldg Hurn CB 10-7 350S 6-4-44 132 OTU 3-2-45 CE 18-6-46 SOC 21-6

EP688 LFLRVB Babs 38MU 27-7-42 47MU 26-8 *Atlan City* 8-9 40S SAAF 30-10 clip wng Aboukir filter F24 camera Malta 1-7-43 Sic 1-8 Italy 26-4-45

EP689 6MU 21-7-42 47MU 26-8 *Atlan City* 8-9 ME 30-10 Malta 1-7-43 Sic NAAF 30-11

EP690 9MU 22-7-42 47MU 26-8 *Atlan City* 8-9 ME 30-10 Malta 1-7-43 i/sea ops 18-7

EP691 9MU 23-7-42 47MU 29-7 Malta 6-9 C3 ops 23-1-43 FH186.25

EP692 6MU 23-7-42 76MU 3-8 *Emp Sun* 19-8 Tak 13-9 ME 23-9 SOC 3-3-44 bboc 21-6-45 SOC 26-9-46

EP693 12MU 27-7-42 47MU 7-9 *Corab* 15-9 ME 5-11 FAC3 18-8-43 SOC 8-3-44

EP694 6MU 24-7-42 47MU 22-8 Tak ME 21-6-45 RHAF 25-4-46

EP695 9MU 24-7-42 76MU 29-7 Malta 229S FTR ops 25-8 FH17.45

EP696 VB(T) 26-7-43 RAF Abb 30-7 f/f Malta 6-9 C3 ops 22-11

EP697 9MU 25-7-42 76MU 29-7 Malta 6-9 SOC 4-11

EP698 9MU 24-7-42 76MU 29-7 Malta 1-11 NWA USAAF 1-7-43 SOC 1-4-44

EP699 12MU 28-7-42 76MU 29-7 VSM 21-9 fuel syst mods 350S 30-11 CB ops ROS 610S 5-5-43 RACB 14-6 HAL 82MU 28-9 Port 19-10

EP700 38MU 25-7-42 RAF Abb 30-7 f/f Malta 6-9 C3 ops 12-10

EP701 38MU 25-7-42 RAF Abb 30-7 f/f Malta 6-9 FAC3 19-1-43 FH47.5

EP702 VB(T) 39MU 9-8-42 222MU 7-9 Gib 27-9

EP703 38MU 27-7-42 RAF Abb 3-8 SEU FACB 19-9 SAL 215MU 31-7-43 *SS732* 5-8 Casa 18-8 ME 31-1-45 SOC 16-1-46

EP704 12MU 27-7-42 76MU 23-9 *Cam Leith* 2-11 Tak 14-12 ME SOC 31-3-43

EP705 8MU 24-7-42 501S 23-8 i/sea ops 7-9 FH19.50

EP706 38MU 25-7-42 RAF Abb 3-8 f/f Malta 6-9 249S C2 ops 12-10 C3 ops 3-3-43

EP707 12MU 25-7-42 66S 20-8 312S 31-10 167S 9-11 132S 19-5-43 416S 4-7 SAL 13-2-44 M45M instal 501S 13-4 345S 15-8 61 OTU 28-9 CAC 22-11 AST SOC 30-7-45

EP708 9MU 25-7-42 47MU 29-8 Malta 6-9 NWA 1-5-43 ME 1-7 fire in air W/U HO CAT AR 15-2-45 RHAF 25-4-46

EP709 VB(T) 38MU 26-7-42 RAF Abb 3-8 dam on del flt SOC 30-8 FH22.20 bboc Malta 25-9 C2 ops 23-12 SOC 12-5-43 FH96.30

EP710 33MU 25-7-42 66S 3-8 129S 19-2-43 CE ops 23-5 FH249.30

EP711 38MU 26-7-42 76MU 28-7 Malta 6-9 ME 1-7 SOC 1-1-44

EP712 6MU 25-7-42 76MU 28-7 Malta 6-9 NA 1-7-43 USAAF 31-10

EP713 VB(T) 12MU 27-7-42 47MU 2-9 *SS620* 15-10 Gib 1-11-43

EP714 VB(T) 8MU 26-7-42 RAF Abb 30-7 f/f Malta 6-9 ME 15-3-45 SOC 25-7-46

EP715 33MU 25-7-42 19S 11-8 e/fld on t/o cd nr Sherborne, Dorset 17-3-43

EP716 6MU 25-7-42 76MU 28-7 Malta 6-9 C2 ops 24-10 FTR ops 13-4-43 FH84.5

EP717 8MU 26-7-42 RAF Abb 30-7 f/f Malta 6-9 SOC 4-3-43

EP718 6MU 29-7-42 RAF Abb 31-7 f/f Malta 6-9 C3 17-10

EP719 VB(T) M45 38MU 12-7-42 222MU 31-8 Gib 27-9

EP720 6MU 9-8-42 82MU 14-8 *Emp Fran* 30-8 Gib 14-9 Malta 1-11 FTR ops 8-2-43 cancel FAF GR.2/33 2-5-44 SOC 10-1-46

EP721 VB(T) 8MU 30-7-42 76MU 13-8 *Emp Cab* 28-8 Gib 14-9 Malta 1-11 SOC 19-4-43

EP722 VB(T) 8MU 30-7-42 RAF Abb 31-8 f/f Malta 6-9 NWA 1-5-43 ME 1-6 NAAF 1-11 FAC3 13-4-44

EP723 VB(T) 8MU 30-7-42 RAF Abb 31-7 strk house on t/o cd Ren CE 1-8 SOC

EP724 VB(T) 38MU 31-7-42 76MU 30-8 *Emp Hth* 29-8 Gib 14-9 CE ops 14-11

EP725 39MU 1-8-42 222MU 19-8 *Emp Fran* 30-8 Gib 14-9 NWA 28-2-43 FAC3 26-8

EP726 12MU 1-8-42 47MU 2-9 *SS625* 20-10 Gib 6-11 NWA 28-2-43 52 OTU jumped chocks hit BL928 CAC Charmy Down 27-7-43 (52 OTU info suspect)

EP727 6MU 29-7-42 RAF Abb 31-7 f/f Malta 6-9 FAC3 12-10-45

EP728 VB(T) 9MU 31-7-42 52MU 16-8 *Emp Cab* 28-8 Gib 14-9 Malta 1-11 NWA USAAF 31-8-43 SOC 28-4-45

EP729 VB(T) 38MU 31-7-42 82MU 26-8 *Emp Fran* 20-8 Gib 14-9 e/a SOC 31-12

EP747 39MU 1-8-42 501S 25-8 66S 23-9 129S 19-2-43 CE ops 13-6

EP748 45MU 12-8-42 6FPP miss on f/f last seen by Obs Corp Girvan 12-8

EP749 45MU 1-8-42 19S 20-8 flew i/hill Mary Tavy Devon 2-12

EP750 45MU 1-8-42 167S 20-2-43 132S 19-5 CAC ops 27-5 165S 7-8 308S 1-10 61 OTU 28-6-45 SOC 20-10 bboc 31-10 67MU 29-11 SOC

EP751 VB(T) 33MU 22-7-42 CRD Folland A/C 2-8 con to floatplane M45 6MU 14-8 Helensburg 27-8 *Perr Cast* 30-9 Alexandria ME SOC 28-12-44

EP752 6MU 14-8-42 47MU 24-8 *Emp Hth* 29-8 Gib 14-9 e/a SOC 30-12

EP753 VB(T) 6MU 24-7-42 82MU 30-8 *SS622* 17-10 Gib 1-11 242S SOC 31-12

EP754 33MU CRD Folland A/C 6-4-42 con to floatplane M45 *Perr Cast* 30-9 Alexandria ME

EP755 45MU 19-8-42 76MU 6-9 *SS622* 1-11 SOC 31-12

EP756 45MU 12-8-42 19S 20-8 CAC ops 18-1-43 402S 16-5 CE ops 31-8 129S 3-2-44 M50 instal 234S 10-6 CE ops 5-7

EP757 15MU 10-8-42 313S 31-10 66S 4-7-43 501S 8-11 CAC ops 9-11-43 345S 15-8-44 61 OTU 28-9-44 hit by EP491 awaiting t/o Rednal CE 4-12

EP758 VB(T) 8MU 14-8-42 47MU 7-9 *Corab* 15-9 Tak ME 9-11 MAAF 21-6-45 IAF 27-6-46

EP759 9MU 1-8-42 VASM 9-10 fuel syst mods 52 OTU 26-3-44 'Basta' mods 1TEU 16-6

EP760 9MU 1-8-42 222MU 7-11 *C o Lil* 8-11 USSR 16-2-43

EP761 9MU 1-8-42 222MU 9-11 *Harp* 19-12 USSR 17-3-43

EP762 9MU 16-8-42 ASTH 4-9 hook fitt RNAS LoS 28-10

EP763 9MU 17-8-42 VASM 9-10 fuel syst mods FACA 31-10 52 OTU 23-2-43 cd Little Somerford Drove Chippenham dbf 21-5

EP764 9MU 1-8-42 VASM 10-8 fuel syst mods 76MU 8-11 *Palma* 5-12 30-1-43

EP765 9MU 1-8-42 VASM 10-8 fuel syst mods 76MU 9-11 *Palma* 5-12 30-1-43

EP766 9MU 10-8-42 416S 29-8 FAAC 26-1-43 421S 9-4 401S 1-6 126S 10-8 234S 6-1-44 MAL 21-7 M45M instal 1668NCU 6-10-45 M55MA instal R&S 16-12-47 refurb Port 28-1-48

EP767 9MU 10-8-42 81S 30-8 485S 16-2-43 19S 1-7 411S 24-9 341S 17-10 602S 25-1-44 CB ops 7-3 LMS 73 BSDU 11-12 M45M instal R&S 31-10-46 refurb Port 3-6-47

EP768 9MU 9-8-42 154S 29-8 131S 22-4-43 313S 30-6 67Grp Mount Farm 20-12 AST 11-8-44 ECFB 21-9 FAAC 11-4-46 recat E SOC 8-7

EP769 9MU 17-8-42 P&PSM 27-9 52 OTU 20-3-43 331S 2-4 31-S 14-8 504S 24-9 67Grp USAAF 6-1-44 VASM 18-4-44 fuel syst mods M45M instal 277S 10-6 SOC 25-4-46

EP770 9MU 10-8-42 416S 29-8 CE opsAST FH108.25 cancel VA 16-7-43 341S 15-1-44 FLS 11-2 FAAC 11-5 ROS CFE Tang to 5400M 17-7-45

EP771 9MU 17-8-42 82MU 26-8 *Emp Fran* 30-8 Gib 14-9 NWA 28-2-43

EP772 VB(T) 9MU 16-8-42 47MU 24-8 *Emp Hth* 29-8 Gib 14-9 NWA 1-10 ME 21-6-45 RHAF 25-4-46

EP689 LF VB of the SAAF, Sicily, August 1943. It had the Special Merlin and Aboukir filter. No 601 Squadron badge appears on fin.

EP891, built as Mk V, crashed on delivery flight. Repaired and Merlin 63 installed. Converted to F Mk IX. Shot down 5 March 1945.

EP773 VB(T) 9MU 23-8-42 82MU 7-9 *SS621* 16-10 Gib 1-11 FAC2 12-12

EP774 9MU 21-8-42 82MU 4-9 *SS620* 15-10 Gib 1-11 NWA 28-2-43 USAAF 31-11 of 12 last 29-12 in med SOC 29-2-44

EP775 VB(T) 9MU 24-8-42 82MU 8-9 *SS620* 10-10 Gib 1-11 NWA 28-2-43 SOC

EP776 VB(T) 9MU 24-8-42 82MU 7-9 *SS620* 15-10 Gib 1-11 NWA 28-2-43

EP777 VB(T) 9MU 24-8-42 47MU 7-9 *Corab* 15-9 Tak ME 5-11 SOC 24-2-43

EP778 9MU 28-8-42 222MU 7-9 Gib 27-9 NWA 28-2-43

EP779 VB(T) 9MU 29-8-42 47MU 14-9 *Emp Lib* 19-9 ME CE ops 10-12 NAAF 30-11-43 SOC 8-3-44

EP780 VB(T) 9MU 29-8-42 82MU 21-9 *SS620* 15-10 Gib 1-11 111S C3 ops 6-1-43

EP781 VB(T) 9MU 29-8-42 222MU 17-9 *Molaja* 1-10 lost at sea 3-10

EP782 VB(T) 9MU 30-8-42 82MU 14-9 *Emp Lib* 19-9 Tak 14-10 Malta 1-8 NA 30-11 C3 ops 24-11

EP783 12MU 1-8-42 222MU 6-9 Gib 27-9

EP784 VB(T) 8MU 30-7-42 82MU 3-9 *SS620* 15-10 Gib 1-11

EP785 39MU 26-7-42 313S 2-8 312S 2-12 234S 4-7-43 504S 30-8 341S 18-1-44 FLS 11-2 FAAC 2-8 SAL M45M instal 132 OTU 3-2--45 R&S 2-12-46 refurb Port 16-9-47

EP786 6MU 29-7-42 RAF Abb 31-7 82MU 19-9 *Molaja* 1-10 lost at sea 3-10

EP787 6MU 10-8-42 52MU 14-8 *Emp Hth* 29-8 Gib 14-9 CE ops 11-10

EP788 VB(T) 38MU 31-7-42 47MU 7-9 *Corab* 15-9 Tak ME 6-11 USSR 31-3-43

EP789 8MU 1-8-42 222MU 3-9 Gib 27-9

EP790 6MU 10-8-42 76MU 14-8 *Emp Cab* 24-8 14-9 Malta 1-11 NAASC 31-10-43 ME 31-1-45 SOC 29-8-46

EP791 VB(T) 9MU 31-7-42 82MU 14-8 *Emp Fran* 30-8 Gib 14-9 Malta 1-11 NWA 31-2-43 USAAF 1-10 SOC 14-3-46

EP792 8MU 1-8-42 47MU 26-8 *Atlan City* 8-9 ME 30-10 C3 ops 19-4-43 SOC 13-9-45

EP793 8MU 1-8-42 47MU 26-8 *Atlan City* 8-9 ME 30-10 FTR ops 3-12

EP794 12MU 1-8-42 47MU 2-9 *SS625* 30-10 Gib 6-11 FA SOC 31-12

EP795 12MU 1-8-42 82MU 2-9 *SS621* 16-10 Gib 1-11 NWA USAAF 31-7-43 ME 31-1-45 CE 26-4 SOC

EP812 VB(T) 39MU 9-8-42 76MU 20-8 *Emp Hth* 29-8 Gib 14-9 NA 1-6-43 SOC 27-7-44 bboc ME 21-6-45 SOC 9-5-46

EP813 39MU 1-8-42 222MU 4-9 Gib 27-9 NWA USAAF 31-7-43

EP814 39MU 1-8-42 47MU 7-9 *Emp Lib* 19-9 Tak ME 5-11 NAASC FAC3 8-12-43

EP815 VB(T) 8MU 9-8-42 82MU 1608 *Emp Fran* 30-8 Gib 14-9 NWA 28-2-43 MAAF 21-4-45 SOC 30-6-46

EP816 39MU 1-8-42 2 SLG 12-8 FACA 2-9 82MU 13-9 *SS622* 1-11 for Gib

EP817 VB(T) 39MU 1-8-42 766MU 20-8 *Emp Cab* 28-8 Gib 14-9 NWA 28-2-43

EP818 9MU 2-8-42 82 6-8 *Emp Fran* 30-8 Gib 14-9 Malta 1-11 NWA 1-5-43 FACE 9-2-45 SOC 22-2

EP819 45MU 17-8-42 76MU 6-9 *SS622* 1-11 NWA SOC 31-7-43

EP820 8MU 1-8-42 82MU 29-8 *SS620* 4-10 Gib 15-10

EP821 8MU 2-8-42 82MU 31-8 *SS622* 17-10 Gib 1-11 NWA 28-2-43

EP822 8MU 2-8-42 47MU 26-8 *Atlan City* 8-9 ME 12-11 NAASC 31-10-43 SOC 26-4-45

EP823 6MU 9-8-42 52MU 14-8 *Emp Cab* 28-8 Gib 14-9 C3 ops 19-11

EP824 8MU 2-8-42 222MU 4-9 Gib 27-9 NWA USAAF 1-10-43 ME 28-4-45 SOC 29-8-46

EP825 VB(T) 12MU 6-8-42 47 1-9-42 *SS620* 15-10 Gib 1-11 SOC 26-4-45

EP826 12MU 12-8 47MU 6-9 *Corab* 15-9 Tak 14-10 ME 1-12 Malta 1-8-43 Sic NAAF 1-11-43 SOC 29-8-46

EP827 VB(T) 39MU 9-8-42 47MU 23-8 ME 1-10 NAASC 31-10-43

EP828 8MU 2-8-42 FACA 2-9 *Emp Fran* 30-8 Gib 14-9 249S MAAF 21-6-45 IAF 27-7-46

EP829 8MU 2-8-42 82MU 16-8-43 *Emp Fran* 30-8 Gib 14-9 249S MAAF 21-6-45 IAF 27-6-46 as MM4069

EP830 6MU 9-8-42 FAAC 28-8 ROS 82MU 1-12 Gib 31-12 NWA 28-2-43 Malta 1-7 ME 1-9

EP831 8MU 2-8-42 222MU 3-9 Gib 27-9

EP832 6MU 9-8-42 76MU 14-8 *Emp Cab* 28-8 Gib 14-9 C3 ops 23-11

EP833 VB(T) 6MU 9-8-42 76MU 20-8 *Emp Hth* 29-8 Gib 14-9 Malta 1-12 1435S C3 ops 11-5-43 FH172.50

EP834 8MU 2-8-42 52MU 14-8 *Emp Hth* 29-8 Gib 14-9 Malta 1-12 NA 1-6-43 SOC 26-4-45

EP835 6MU 10-8-42 52MU 14-8 *Emp Hth* 29-8 Gib 14-9 Malta 1-11 USAAF 31-10-43 ME 31-1-45 SOC 10-1-46

EP836 VB(T) 39MU 9-8-42 82MU 1-9 *SS621* 16-10 Gib 1-11 C3 ops

EP837 VB(T) 4-8-42 222MU 3-9 Gib 27-9

EP838 VB(T) 39MU 9-8-42 222MU 6-9 Gib 27-9 NWA 28-2-43 NAASC 31-10 FAC3 21-1-46

EP839 VB(T) 8MU 9-8-42 222MU 3-9 Gib 27-9 SOC 10-8 bboc 21-6-45 SOC 26-9-46

EP840 VB(T) 39-MU 2-9 *SS621* 16-10 Gib 4-11 FTR ops 4-12

EP841 VB(T) 39MU 9-8-42 222MU4-9 Gib 27-9

EP842 VB(T) 8MU 9-8-42 82MU 14-8 *Emp Fran* 20-8 Gib 14-9 Malta 1-11 C3 ops 21-5-43 FH168.15

EP843 6MU 9-8-42 52MU 14-8 *Emp Cab* 28-8 Gib 14-9 Malta 1-11 USAAF ME 1-9-43 SOC 31-5-45

EP844 6MU 9-8-42 82MU 29-8 *SS621* 16-10 Gib 1-11 Malta 1-12 ME 15-3-45 RHAF 25-4-46

EP845 VB(T) 6MU 13-8-42 222MU 19-8 *Emp Fran* 26-8 Gib 14-9 SOC 31-12

EP846 12MU 13-8-42 47MU 13-9 *Emp Lib* 19-9 Tak ME 5-11 SOC 1-11-43

EP847 12MU 21-8-42 76MU 16-9 ROS 9-10 *SS620* 15-10 Gib 1-11

EP869 VB(T) 38MU 16-8-42 47MU 7-9 *Emp Lib* 19-9 Tak ME 12-11 SOC 26-6-43

EP870 12MU 15-8-42 47MU 6-9 *Corab* 15-9 Tak ME 5-11 SOC 1-6-43

EP871 15MU 10-8-42 501S 1-9 FTR ops 17-9 FH25.15

EP872 12MU 21-8-42 82MU 2-9 *SS620* 15-10 Gib 1-11 NAASC 31-10-43 SOC 8-3-44

EP873 46MU 18-8-42 222MU 9-9 *SS622* 15-10 Gib 1-11 NWA 282-43

EP874 46MU 18-8-42 222MU 9-9 *SS620* 15-10 Gib 1-11

EP875 12MU 23-8-42 82MU 2-9 *SS621* 16010 Gib 1-11 NWA 28-2-43 SOC 8-3-44

EP876 45MU 28-8-42 76MU 12-9 *SS620* 15-10 Gib 1-11 NWA 28-2-43

EP877 12MU 21-8-42 52MU 2-9 *SS621* 16-10 Gib 1-11 NWA 28-2-43 SOC 28-2-43

EP878 LFLRVB(T) 9MU 24-9-42 40S SAAF ME 28-2-43 clip wng, smooth finish covered skin joints, Aboukir filter F24 camera C3 ops 22-3

EP879 12MU 21-8-42 47MU 14-9 *Emp Lib* 19-9 Tak NAAF 1-11-43 SOC 31-3-44

EP880 VB(T) 12MU 24-8-42 47MU 15-9 *Emp Lib* 19-9 Tak 11-11 Malta 1-7--43 Sic 1-8 SOC 8-3-44 bboc 21-6-45 SOC 29-8-46

EP881 46MU 27-8-42 222MU 14-11 FTR ops 17-2-43

EP882 45MU 28-8-42 222MU 19-9 *Molaja* 1-10 lost at sea 3-10

EP883 45MU 22-8-42 76MU 6-9 *SS622* 17-10 Gib 1-11

EP884 VB(T) 45MU 29-8-42 82MU 15-9 *SS622* 17-10 Gib 1-11 SOC 31-1-43

EP885 46MU 26-8-42 215MU 26-9 *Camarata* 2-11 Tak 14-12 FAC2 6-1-43 ME 18-2

EP886 VB(T) 38MU 11-8-42 82MU 15-9*Emp Lib* 19-9 Tak 9-11 Malta 1-7-43 MAAF 21-6-45 IAF 27-6-46 as MM4071

EP887 VB(T) 8MU 9-8-42 82MU 16-8 *Emp Fran* 30-8 Gib 14-9 FAC2 3-1-43 NWA 1-5 Malta 1-11 CE SOC 13-9-45

EP888 45MU 16-8-42 76MU 9-9 *SS622* 17-10 Gib 1-11

EP889 12MU 15-8-42 222MU 6-9 Gib 27-9 NWA 28-2-43

EP890 12MU 11-8 52MU 2-9 *SS620* 15-10 Gib 1-11 Malta 1-7-43 Sic 1-8 NAAF 1-11

EP891 R-R con to FIX M63 cd on test flt Aug'42 rebuilt CBAF 39MU 11-6-43 52MU 19-6 *La Pampa* 2-7 Casa 14-7 ME 1-9 NAAF 1-11 FTR ops 5-3-45

EP892 VB(T) 39MU 9-8-42 82MU 26-8 *Emp Fran* 30--8 Gib 14-9 NWA 28-2-43

EP893 12MU 10-8-42 47MU 14-9 *Emp Lib* 19-9 Tak 12-11 Malta 1-7-43 Sic 1-8 NAASC 1-11 SOC 30-6-45

EP894 12MU 10-8-42 47MU 13-9 *Emp Lib* 19-9 Tak Malta 1-7-43 SOC 30-7

EP895 12MU 10-8-42 47MU *Corab* 15-9 Tak ME 7-11 Malta 1-7-43 NAAASC 31-10

EP896 12MU 10-8-42 47MU 6-9 *Corab* 15-9 Tak ME 5-11 1S C2 ops 13-12 NAAF 1-11-43 SOC 8-3-44

EP897 VB(T) 14-8-42 47MU 7-9 *Corab* 15-9 Tak ME NAAF 1-11-43 SOC 8-3-44

EP898 VB(T) 39MU 9-8-42 82MU 1-9 *SS622* 6-10 Gib 1-11 FAC2 24-12 NWA 28-2-43 SOC 30-4-43

EP899 VB(T) 11-8-42 76MU 10-9 *SS622* 15-10 Gib 1-11

EP900 6MU 9-8-42 82 29-8 *SS620* 15-10 Gib 1-11 NWA 28-2-43

EP901 38MU 12-3-42 222MU 30-8 *SS612* 19-9 Gib 27-9

EP902 12MU 12-8-42 FACA 1-9 82MU 1-9 *SS621* 16-10 Gib 1-11 FAC3 11-12

EP903 12MU 10-8-42 47MU 26-8 *Atlan City* 8-9 ME 1-11 SOC 1-6-43bboc 21-6-45 FAF 14-2-46

EP904 38MU 12-8-42 82MU 26-8 *Emp Fran* 30-8 Gib 14-9 C2 5-1-43 NWA 28-2 SOC 26-4-45

EP905 46MU 16-8-42 82MU 12-9 *SS622* 17-10 Gib 1-

11 NWA 28-2-43 SOC 26-4-45

EP906 12MU 15-8-42 82MU 1-9 *SS622* 17-10 Gib 1-11 NWA 28-2-43

EP907 38MU 12-8-42 FACB 26-8 AST 222MU 21-12 *SS117* 4-1-43 Gib 18-1 USAAF 31-1 44 SOC 30-6

EP908 12MU 12-8-42 82MU 4-9 *SS622* 17-10 Gib 1-11 SOC 31-12

EP909 12MU 10-8-42 47MU 1-9 *SS620* 15-10 Gib 1-11 NWA 28-2-43 Malta 1-12 CE ops 13-9-45

EP910 12MU 13-8-42 82MU 1-9 *SS621* 16-10 Gib 1-11

EP911 12MU 15-8-42 47MU 2-9 *SS625* 20-10 Gib 1-11 SOC 31-12

EP912 12MU 13-8-42 82MU 3-9 *SS622* 17-10 Gib 1-11 USAAF NWA 1-10-43 SOC 29-2-44

EP913 12MU 11-8-42 82MU 3-9 *SS601* 16-10 Gib 1-11 NWA 28-2-43

EP914 12MU 15-8-42 76MU 16-9 *SS622* Gib 1-11 NWA 28-2-43 FAF SOC 29-2-44

EP915 VB(T) 6MU 13-8-42 222MU 22-8 *Emp Fran* 30-8 Gib 14-9 Malta 1-12 C3 ops 17-2-43 FH112.40

EP951 VB(T) 6MU 13-8-42 222MU 20-8 *Emp Fran* 30-8 Gib 14-9 NWA 28-2-43 NAASC 31-10 SOC 26-4-45

EP952 45MU 16-8-42 76MU 9-9 *SS621* 16-10 Gib 1-11 NWA 28-2-43 SOC 30-4

EP953 VB(T) 13-8-42 47MU 21-8 Tak 145S ME 24-10 C2 ops 5-1-43 RHAF 25-4-46

EP954 VB(T) 14-8-42 82MU 13-9 *SS622* 17-10 Gib 1-11 dam LMS 22-2-43 215MU 17-5 Casa 15-6 NWA 1-7 ME30-9

EP955 46MU 20-6-42 82MU 10-9 *SS621* 16-10 FTR ops 17-10 FH45.15

EP956 12MU 15-8-42 82MU 15-9 *Molaja* 1-10 lost at sea 3-10

EP957 VB(T) 34MU 14-8-42 47MU 7-9 *Corab* 15-9 Tak ME 7-11 NAAF 30-11-43 SOC 8-3-44

EP958 46MU 17-8-42 82MU 10-9 *SS620* 15-10 Gib 1-11 NWA 28-2-43 SOC 31-3

EP959 12MU 15-8-42 222MU 6-9 Gib 27-9 NWA 28-2-43 SOC 26-4-45

EP960 VB(T) 8MU 14-8-42 47MU 6-9 *Corab* 15-6 Tak 11-11 NAAF 30-11-43 SOC 31-3-44

EP961 VB(T) 38MU 14-8-42 82MU 1-9 *SS620* 15-10 Gib 1-11 FAC3 25-3-43

EP962 VB(T) 38MU 14-8-42 47MU 3-9 *SS625* 20-10 Gib 6-11 NWA 28-2-43

EP963 VB(T) 38MU 14-8-42 82MU 26-8 *Emp Fran* 30-8 Gib 14-9 NWA 28-2-43 ME 30-11-44

EP964 46MU 18-8-42 82MU 10-9 *SS621* 16-10 Gib 1-11 SOC 31-1-43

EP965 12MU 15-8-42 82MU 2-9 *SS621* 16-10 Gib 1-11 241S C3 ops 25-3-43

EP966 VB(T) 8MU 14-8-42 47MU 7-9 *Corab* 15-9 Tak 17-11 Malta 1-7-43 FACB 12-7

EP967 45MU 19-8-42 76MU 9-9 *SS620* 15-10 Gib 1-11 NWA 28-2-43

EP968 45MU 16-8-42 82MU 19-9 *Lorca* 6-10 Tak 14-12 ME 1-8-43 FTR ops -8-2-44

EP969 45MU 17-8-42 82MU 12-9 *SS622* 17-10 Gib 1-11 SOC 28-4-45

EP970 Argentevil 46MU 27-8-42 FAAC 6-9 ROS 215MU 13-2-43 *Harmat* 20-3 Gib 26-4 SOC 26-4-45

EP971 9MU 18-8-42 222MU 9-9 *SS621* 16-10 Gib 1-11 USAAF NWA 31-7-43 SOC 28-4-45

EP972 9MU 20-8-42 82MU 14-9 *Emp Lib* 19-9 Tak 30-11 Malta 1-7 Sicily 1-8 SOC 26-4-45

EP973 45MU 16-8-42 76MU 9-9 *SS622* 17-10 Gib 1-11 NWA 28-2-43 SOC 28-4-45

EP974 46MU 16-8-42 82MU 11-9 *SS622* 17-10 Gib 1-11

EP975 46MU 17-8-42 82MU 10-9 *SS621* 16-10 Gib 1-11 NWA 28-2-43 C3 ops 10-4-43

EP976 46MU 20-8-42 222MU 9-9 *SS620* 15-10 Gib 1-11 C2 ops NWA SOC 31-7-43

EP977 12MU 18-8-42 222MU 16-9 *SS622* 17-10 Gib 1-11

EP978 46MU 17-8-42 222MU 19-9 *SS620* 15-10 Gib 1-11 NWA 28-2-43 NAASC 31-10 USAAF 31-1-44 ME 21-6-45 SOC 29-8-46

EP979 12MU 21-8-42 222MU 16-9 *SS620* 15-10 Gib 1-11 SOC 26-4-45

EP980 45MU 19-8-42 FAAC 6-9 76MU 6-9 ROS *SS620* 15-10 Gib 1-11 NWA 28-2-43

EP981 12MU 18-8-42 222MU 31-8 *SS621* 16-10 Gib 1-11 NWA 28-2-43

EP982 46MU 24-8-42 222MU 18-10 *Ocean Cour* 7-11 Tak 21-12 SOC 31-5-45

EP983 12MU 22-8-42 3FPP cd on del flt Saighton nr Chester 17-9 FH2.50

EP984 45MU 21-8-42 222MU 19-9 *Molaja* 1-10 lost at sea 3-10

EP985 46MU 20-8-42 222MU 19-9 *SS621* 16-10 Gib 1-11

EP986 45MU 19-8-42 222MU 11-9 *SS620* 15-10 Gib 1-11

EP987 12MU 22-8-42 222MU 6-9 AST 21-9 82MU 1-12 *Bluff V* 3-12 C2 ops 6-1-43 SOC 28-4-45

EP988 12MU 22-8-42 47MU 2-9 *SS625* 20-10 Gib 6011 NWA 28-2-43

EP989 12MU 23-8-42 82MU 11-9 *SS622* 17-10 Gib 1-11 ME 15-3-43 SOC 29-8-46

EP990 46MU 20-8-42 222MU 20-9 *SS621* 16-10 Gib 1-11

ER series All F Mk VB Merlin M46 unless otherwise indicated

ER114 45MU 1-9-42 47MU 16-9 *Molaja* 1-10 lost at sea 3-10

ER115 45MU 1-9-42 47MU 16-9 *Molaja* 1-10 lost at sea 3-10

ER116 VB(T) 6MU 4-9-42 47MU 6-9 *Corab* 15-9 Tak 9-11 FTR ops 16-4-43

ER117 6MU 3-9-42 47MU 6-9 *Atlan City* 8-9 ME 30-10 SOC 3-1-43

ER118 VB(T) 6MU 4-9-42 82MU 8-9 *SS622* 17-10 Gib 1-11 FTR ops 4-1-43

ER119 VB(T) 33MU 7-9-42 82MU 9-10 *SS628* 25-10 Gib 9-11

ER120 VB(T) 6MU 4-9-42 76MU 9-9 *SS620* 15-10 Gib 1-11 5th Ftr S USAAF NWA SOC 31-7-43

ER121 VB(T) 7-9-42 82MU 9-10 *SS626* 28-10 Gib 1-11 SOC 31-12

ER122 46MU 9-9-42 222MU 19-9 *SS621* 16-10 Gib 1-11 SOC 31-12

ER123 VB(T) 9MU 16-9-42 222MU 27-10 *SS634* 4-11 Gib 23-11 NWA 28-2-43 CE ops 11-1-45

ER124 46MU 10-9-42 2223MU 19-9 *SS620* 15-10 Gib 1-11 NWA SOC 31-7-43

ER125 VB(T) 33MU 7-9-42 82MU 8-10 *SS628* 25-10 Gib 9-11 NWA 28-2-43 NAASC 31-10 SOC 26-4-45

ER126 VA to FIX M63 9MU 10-6-42 47MU 26-6 *Fort Ver* 1-7 Casa 14-7 NA 30-1-43 FTR ops 3-10

ER127 VB(T) 12-9-42 82MU 25-9 *SS622* 17-10 Gib 1-11

ER128 VB(T) 38MU 17-9-42 76MU 25-9 *Ocean Cour* 7-11 Tak 28-12 Malta 1-7-43 Sic 1-8 NAASC 31-10 RHAF 25-4-46

ER129 VB(T) 12MU 12-9-42 215MU 26-9 *Camarata* 2-11 Tak 16-12 ME 1-1-43 SOC 8-3-44

ER130 38MU 18-10-42 82MU 25-10 *SS634* 4-11 Gib 23-11 NWA 28-2-43 SOC 29-2-44

ER131 6MU 7-11-42 82MU 18-11 *Hamble V* 1-12 Gib 8-1-43 NWA 28-2-43 SOC 28-4-45

ER132 VB(T) 12MU 12-9-42 215MU 26-9 *Camarata* 2-11 Tak 14-12 ME 17-1-43 Malta 1-7 NAAF 1-11 SOC 31-8-44

ER133 12MU 16-9-42 215MU 26-9-42 *Camarata* 2-11

ER120, February 1943 52nd Fighter Group, USAAF. Badly damaged by flak but salvaged and returned to service.

Tak 14-12 ME 1-9-43 FAC3 27-4

ER134 46MU 23-8-42 222MU 1-10 *Ocean Cour* 7-11 Tak ME 28-12 Malta 1-7-43 Sic 1-8 C3 ops 14-9

ER135 45MU 21-8-42 22MU 5-9 Gib 27-9 SOC 31-12

ER136 45MU 21-8-42 76MU 6-9 *SS622* 17-10 Gib 1-11 NWA 28-2-43 ME 1-8 NAAF 29-9 USAAF 31-10 RHAF 25-4-46

ER137 46MU 20-8-42 222MU 19-9 *SS622* 17-10 Gib 1-11

ER138 46MU 21-8-42 CB 9-9 SAL 215MU 6-3-43 *SS672* 25-3 Gib 12-4 Malta 1-11 MAAF 21-6-45 SOC 19-7

ER139 45MU 21-8-42 FACB 15-9 AST 76MU 27-10 *Catrine* 20-11 Tak ME 3-1-43 FACE 15-9-44

ER140 45MU 21-8-42 76MU 6-9 *SS621* 16-10 Gib 1-11 FTR ops 4-1-43

ER141 VB(T) 12MU 24-8-42 47MU 14-9 *Emp Lit* 19-9 Tak ME 1-12 Malta 1-7-43 Sic 1-8 NAAF 1-11

ER142 12MU 21-8-42 76MU 19-9 *SS621* 16-10 Gib 1-11 FAC2 27-12 Malta 1-7-43 Sic 1-8 NAAF 1-11 SOC 30-6-45

ER143 46MU 24-8-42 82MU 23-10 *Catrine* 28-11 Tak 27-12 ME 17-4-43 SOC 26-4-45 bboc 21-6-45 SOC 10-1-46

ER144 12MU 22-8-42 222MU 9-9 *SS620* 15-10 Gib 1-11 C3 ops 28-1-43

ER145 12MU 22-8-42 222MU 21-9 *SS620* 15-10 Gib 1-11

ER146 12MU 24-8-42 76MU 19-9 *SS622* 17-10 Gib 1-11 C2 ops 13-11

ER159 12MU 21-8-42 82MU 15-9 *Molaja* 1-10 lost at sea 3-10

ER160 45MU 22-8-42 82MU 13-9 *SS621* 16-10 Gib 1-11

ER161 46MU 24-8-42 222MU 19-9 *SS620* 15-10 Gib 1-11 NWA USAAF 31-7-43 SOC 26-6-45

ER162 VB(T) 12MU 24-8-42 47MU 13-9 *Emp Lib* 19-9 Tak ME 12-11 SOC 24-2-43

ER163 36MU 27-8-43 82MU 6-9 *SS620* 15-10 Gib 1-11 NWA 28-2-43 Malta 1-7 Sic 1-8 ops 7-8 SOC 3-3-44

ER164 12MU 22-8-42 22MU 9-9

ER165 45MU 22-8-42 76MU 9-9 *SS621* 16-10 Gib 1-11

ER166 12MU 22-8-42 47MU 13-9 *Emp Lib* 19-9 Tak ME 1-12 SOC 24-2-43

ER167 45MU 23-8-42 47MU 12-9 *Emp Lib* 19-9 Tak NAASC 20-10-43 ME 30-11-44 SOC 31-10-46

ER168 12MU 26-8-42 47MU 14-9 *Emp Lib* 19-9 Tak FTR ops 17-12-43

ER169 38MU 27-8-42 82MU 17-9 *SS622* 17-10 Gib 1-11 SOC 31-12

ER170 46MU 24-8-42 215MU 26-9 *Ger-y-Bryn* 17-10

ER167 VB(T) went to North Africa in October 1943 and was SOC three years later. It is seen at Eastleigh, Nairobi at the time of SOC in natural metal finish and dark green Vokes filter.

ME 12-12 SOC 29-10

ER171 VB(T) 12MU 24-8-42 47MU 12-9 *Emp Lib* 19-9 ME 5-11-43 NAAF 30-11 SOC 26-4-45

ER172 45MU 22-8-42 76MU 9-9 *SS621* 16-10 Gib 1-11 FAC2 21-1-43 NWA FAC3 4-5

ER173 38MU 26-8-42 82MU 9-9 *SS621* 16-10 Gib 1-11 NWA 28-2-43 326S 19-5-45 81 R&SU 28-6 FAF 27-11

ER174 Forward I 38MU 27-8-42 82MU 6-9 *SS620* 15-10 Gib 1-11 NWA 28-2-43

ER175 38MU 28-8-42 47MU 13-9 *Emp Lib* 19-9 Tak 14-10

ER176 VB(T) Forward II 38MU 27-8-42 82MU 6-9 *SS620* 15-10 Gib 1-11 C3 13-12

ER177 VC 9MU 31-8-42 222MU 28-11 *Bluff V* 3-12 Gib 31-12 FTR ops 19-3-43

ER178 38MU 28-8-42 82MU 12-9 *Emp Lib* 19-9 Tak ME 1S SAAF C2 ops 14-12 Malta 1-7-43 Italy 1-11 SOC 30-6-45

ER179 45MU 22-8-42 82MU 19-9 *Molaja* 1-10 lost at sea 3-10

ER180 9MU 27-8-42 76MU 10-9 *SS621* 16-10 Gib 1-11 FAC2 26-11 NWA 28-2-43 Malta 1-7 NAASC 31-10 SOC 30-6-45

ER181 46MU 29-8-42 215MU 5-10 *Camarata* 2-11 Tak 14-12 ME 1-6-43 Malta 1-7 Sicily 1-8 SOC 8-3-44

ER182 12MU 24-8-42 47MU 14-9 *Emp Lib* 19-9 Tak 14-10 SOC 5-1-43

ER183 33MU 4-9-42 76MU 3-10 ME 1-11 FACB 21-12 NWA 31-8-43 SOC 26-4-45

ER184 VB(T) 38MU 29-8042 47MU 16-9 *Molaja* 1-10 lost at sea 3-10

ER185 46MU 29-8-42 222MU 19-9 *SS620* 15-10 Gib 1-11 NWA 28-2-43 SOC 31-3

ER186 9MU 26-8-42 82MU 8-9 *SS621* 16-10 Gib 1-11 NWA 28-2-43 FTR ops 13-4

ER187 9MU 27-8-42 82MU 19-9 *SS622* 17-10 Gib 1-11 NWA 28-2-43

ER188 VB(T) 15MU 10-9-42 222MU 17-9 *Ocean Cour* 7-11 Tak ME 28-12 SOC 30-9-43

ER189 9MU 31-8-42 222MU 16-9 *Molaja* 1-10 lost at sea 3-10

ER190 12MU 25-8-42 76MU 19-9 *SS621* 16-10 Gib 1-11 SOC 31-12

ER191 9MU 28-842 76MU 10-9 *SS620* 15-10 Gib 1-11

ER192 9MU 31-8-42 82MU 14-9 *Emp Lib* 19-9 Tak Malta 1-7-43 Sicily 1-8 ME 21-6-45 SOC 19-8-46

ER193 45MU 28-8-42 215MU 23-9 *Cam Leith* 2-11 Tak 14-12 ME 11-1-43 NAAF 28-8 SOC 31-3-44 bboc 25-10

ER194 VC 12MU 28-8-43 47MU 14-9 *Emp Lib* 19-9. Tak 14-10 ME FAC2 19-1-43 NAASC 31-10 CE ops SOC 9-4-45

ER195 46MU 26-8-42 215MU 30-9 *Cam Leith* 2-11 Tak 14-12 ME 6-1-43 SOC 3-3

ER196 Flt Lt B Moreland Denny 9MU 27-8-42 76MU 10-9 *SS621* 16-10 Gib 1-11 NWA 28-2-43

ER197 VB(T) Allcia 9MU 29-8-42 76MU 10-9 *SS620* 15-10 Gib 1-11

ER198 46MU 1-9-42 215MU 10-10 *SS628* 25-10 Gib 9-11 C2 ops 8-1-43 SOC 30-4

ER199 33MU 4-9-42 76MU 3-10 *Ocean Cour* 7-11 Tak ME 31-12 NWA FTR ops 31-3-43

ER200 12MU 28-8-42 76MU 16-9 *SS621* 16-10 Gib 1-11

ER206 Borough of Islington 46MU 29-8-42 215MU 10-10 *SS628* 25-10 Gib 9-11 FACE 31-12 SOC 28-2-43

ER207 9MU 31-8-42 47MU 14-9 *Emp Lib* 19-9 Tak 14-10 ME 31-1-43 REAF 29-3-45

ER208 VB(T) 39MU 9-9-42 82MU 14-9 *Emp Lib* 19-9 Tak 14-10 ME 1-12 SOC 23-10-44

ER209 12MU 28-8-42 222MU 16-9 *SS621* 16-10 Gib 1-11 SOC 31-1-43

ER210 9MU 27-8-42 82MU 11-9 *SS621* 16-10 Gib 1-11 NWA 28-2-43

ER211 VB(T) 45MU 30-8-42 222MU 11-9 ROS *SS621* 16-10 Gib 1-11

ER212 46MU 29-8-42 222MU 1-10 *Ocean Cour* 7-11 ME 1-1-43 SOC 26-3

ER213 Coulsden and Purley 12MU 28-8-42 76MU 9-9 *SS621* 16-10 Gib 1-11 NAASC 31-10-43 ME 31-8-44 SOC 29-3-45

ER214 6MU 2-9-42 47MU 6-9 *Corab* 15-9 Tak ME 5-11 FAC3 3-8-43

ER215 9MU 31-8-42 82MU 21-9 *SS621* 16-10 Gib 1-11

ER216 45MU 28-8-42 82MU 19-9 *Molaja* 1-10 lost at sea 3-10

ER217 9MU 31-8-42 222MU 19-9 *SS621* 16-10 Gib 1-11 NWA 28-2-43

ER218 VB(T) 39MU 6-9-42 82MU 13-9 *Emp Lib* 19-9 Tak ME 17-11 SOC 22-3-43 cancel NAASC 31-10 ME 28-4-45 SOC 29-8-46

ER219 9MU 31-8-42 222MU 21-9 *SS620* 15-10 Gib 1-11 NWA SOC 30-4-43

ER220 9MU 31-8-42 47MU 14-9 *Emp Lib* 19-9 Tak ME 7-11 FTR ops 17-4-43

ER221 46MU 29-8-42 FACA 3-9 *Cam Leith* 2-11 Tak 14-12 ME 1-9-43 FAC3 3-2-44

ER222 9MU 31-8-42 47MU 15-9 *Emp Lib* 19-9 Tak ME 10-11 Malta 1-7-43 BAF 1-10 SOC 23-8-45

ER223 45MU 1-9-42 215MU 23-9 *Cry-Y-Bryn* 13-10 Tak ME 8-12

ER224 9MU 31-8-42 42MU 14-9 *Emp Lib* 19-9 Tak ME 7-11 SOC 26-3-43

ER225 VB(T) 6MU 6-9-42 222MU 12-9 *SS620* 15-10 Gib 1-11 C2 ops 23-12 SOC 31-12-43

ER226 8MU 3-9-42 82MU 12-9 *SS621* 16-10 Gib 1-11 C2 ops 12-11 NAASC 31-10-43 ME 21-6-45 SOC 29-8-46

ER227 8MU 3-9-42 222MU 17-9 *Ocean Cour* 7-11 Tak ME 20-12 Malta 1-7-43 Sicily 1-8 SOC 8-3-44

ER228 VB(T) 39MU 6-9-42 47MU 13-9 Tak NAAF 1-11-43 ME 30-11-44 SOC 3-8-45

ER229 9MU 31-8-42 47MU 14-9 *Emp Lib* 19-9 Tak ME 11-11 601S C2 ops 16-12 NAAF 1-11-43 SOC 28-2-44

ER245 6MU 2-9-42 47MU 6-9 *Atlan City* Tak NAAF 1-11-43 SOC 8-3-44

ER246 9MU 31-8-42 82MU 19-9 *SS622* 17-10 Gib 1-11 NA 30-11 SOC 15-3-45

ER247 8MU 3-9-42 82MU 12-9 *SS621* 16-10 Gib 1-11 NWA 28-2-43 FA 31-3

ER248 VB(T) 6MU 4-9-42 222MU 8-9 Gib 27-10 PSOC 1-1-47 disposed of by Air Attache Madrid SOC 30-4-48

ER249 VB(T) 6MU 4-9-42 76MU 9-9 *SS621* 16-10 Gib 1-11 NWA 28-2-43 FAF 31-7 SOC 26-4-45

ER250 33MU 4-9-42 76MU 15-10 *Emp day* 23-10 Gib 9-11 C2 ops 24-11 NWA 28-2-43 Malta 1-7 MAAF 21-6-45 SOC 22-11-45

ER251 VB(T) 6MU 4-9-42 222MU 8-9 *SS622* 17-10 Gib 1-11

ER252 VB(T) 6MU 4-9-42 82MU 8-9 *SS621* 16-10 Gib 1-11 C2 ops 1-12 SOC 25-4-45

ER253 8MU 3-9-42 82MU 12-9 *SS621* 16-10 Gib 1-11 NWA 28-2-43

ER254 VB(T) 8MU 4-9-42 82MU 12-9 *SS622* 17-10 Gib 1-11 NWA 28-2-43

ER255 VB(T) 8MU 4-9-42 222MU 17-9 *Molaja* 1-10 lost at sea 3-10

ER256 6MU 6-9-42 222MU 10-9 *SS621* 16-10 Gib 1-11

ER257 33MU 4-9-42 82MU 8-10 *SS625* 20-10 Gib 1-11 SOC 31-1-43

ER258 33MU 6-9-42 82MU 19-9 *Molaja* 1-10 lost at sea 3-10

ER259 VB(T) 6MU 6-9-42 82MU 12-9 *SS623* 17-10 Gib 1-11

ER260 VB(T) 6MU 6-9-42 222MU 12-9 *SS620* 15-10 Gib 1-11

ER261 33MU 4-9-42 82MU 18-9 *Molaja* 1-10 lost at sea 3-10

ER262 VB(T) 6MU 6-9-42 76MU 9-9 *SS620* 15-10 Gib 1-11 NWA 28-2-43

ER263 VB(T) 6MU 4-9-42 82MU 13-9 *SS620* 15-10 Gib 1-11 FAC3 26-11

ER264 33MU 6-9-42 76MU 15-10 *SS625* 20-10 Gib 6-11 SOC 31-12

ER265 Csfd VC VA Ston 16-9-42 CBAF 26-9 45MU 21-10 *Hamble II* 19-11 C3 ops 18-1-43

ER266 VB(T) 6MU 4-9-42 FACA 9-9 ROS *SS620* 15-10 Gib 1-11

ER267 8MU 6-9-42 82MU 19-9 *Molaja* 1-10 lost at sea 3-10

ER268 8MU 6-9-42 222MU 17-9 *Molaja* 1-10 lost at sea 3-10

ER269 VB(T) 15MU 10-9-42 82MU 19-9 *Molaja* 1-10 lost at sea 3-10

ER270 8MU 6-9-42 76MU 30-9 *Lorca* 3-10 ME 1-1-43 NAAF 1-11

ER271 VB(T) 39MU 6-9-42 82MU 13-9 *Emp Lib* 19-9 Tak ME 7-11 FTR ops 12-1-43

ER272 VB(T) 39MU 6-9-42 47MU 13-9 *Emp Lib* 19-9 Tak ME 9-11 SOC 5-1-43

ER273 6MU 8-9-42 222MU 13-9 *SS621* 16-10 Gib 1-11

ER274 46MU 9-9-42 215MU 26-9 *Cam Leith* 2-11 Tak 14-12 ME 9-2-43 SOC 1-11

ER275 39MU 9-9-42 222MU 16-9 *Molaja* 1-10 lost at sea 3-10

ER276 8MU 6-9-42 222MU 17-9 *Molaja* 1-10 lost at sea 3-10

ER277 VB(T) 6MU 8-9-42 222MU 12-9 *SS621* 16-10 Gib 1-11 NAASC USAAF 31-1-44 ME 31-8 to Turk 28-9

ER278 VB(T) 39MU 9-9-42 47MU 14-9 *Emp Lib* 19-9 Tak ME 12-11 1S C3 ops 14-12 Malta 1-7-43 Sic NAAF 1-11 SOC 29-8-46

ER279 6MU 9-9-42 47MU 14-9 *Emp Lib* 19-9 Tak ME 12-11 FTR ops 11-1-43

ER280 VB(T) 15MU 10-9-42 47MU 14-9 *Emp Lib* 19-9 Tak ME 5-11 FTR ops 25-3-43

ER281 VC(T) 15MU 11-9-42 76MU 2-10 *Ocean Cour* 7-11 Tak ME 16-12 NAAF 1-11-43 SOC 31-11

ER282 VB(T) 6MU 6-9-42 82MU 11-9 *SS621* 16-10 Gib 1-11 NWA 28-2-43 SOC 31-7-43

ER283 VB(T) 39MU 6-9-42 82MU 13-9 *Emp Lib* 19-9 Tak ME 7-11 FAC3 12-7-43

ER299 Dsfd 38MU 18-9-42 76MU 23-9 *SS621* Gib 1-11 C5 15-1-43 CE 25-2-44

ER300 VB(T) 38MU 17-9-42 76MU 22-9 *SS621* 16-10 Gib 1-11

ER301 6MU 22-9-42 82MU 27-9 *Parib* 30-10 Tak ME 16-12 SOC 26-9-46

ER302 6MU 22-9-42 82MU 27-9 *Parib* 30-10 Tak ME 16-12 FAC3 26-5-44

ER303 VB(T) 8MU 23-9-42 82MU 4-10 *Catrina* 20-11 Tak 27-12 ME 31-1-43 Malta 1-8 Sic NAASC 31-10 C3 ops 19-3-44

ER304 VB(T) 8MU 23-9-42 82MU 2-10 *Parib* 30-1o Tak ME 16-12 Malta 1-7-43 Sicily NAASC 31-10 FAF FACE 21-4-45 SOC 26-4

ER305 12MU 24-9-42 215MU 5-10 *Cam Leith* 10-10 Tak 14-12 ME 31-1-43 SOC 8-3-44

ER306 VB(T) 39MU 25-9-42 76MU 6-10 *Ocean Cour* 7-11 Tak ME 22-12 NAASC 3-10-43 USAAF 31-1-44

ER307 45MU 24-9-42 215MU 16-10 *SS628* 25-10 Gib 9-11 FAC2 5-1-43 NWA 28-2 FTR ops 5-4

ER308 Dsfd 12MU 25-9-42 82MU 15-10 *SS628* 25-10 Gib 9-11 SOC 28-4-43

ER309 Dsfd 45MU 26-9-42 215MU 11-10 *SS628* 25-10 Gib 9-11

ER310 Dsfd 45MU 30-9-42 ROS 82MU *SS634* 4-11 Gib 23-11 NWA 28-2-43 875S Sic FA FTR 2-2-44

ER311 VB(T) 9MU 30-9-42 47MU 14-9 ROS *Molaja* 1-10 lost at sea 3-10

ER312 9MU 3-9-42 82MU 26-9 *Zorca* 6-10 ME 1-6-43

ER313 9MU 3-9-42 82MU 26-9 *Parib* 30-10 Tak ME 16-12 FTR ops 14-7-43

ER314 9MU 4-9-42 76MU 15-10 *SS625* 20-10 GIB 6-11 NWA USAAF 31-7-43 NAASC 31-10

ER315 9MU 4-9-42 76MU 6-10 *SS625* 20-10 Gib 6-11 NWA 28-2-43 Malta 1-7 Sic NAAF 1-11 ME 31-1-45 FAF 14-2-46

ER316 9MU 9-9-42 82MU 28-9 *Parib* 30-10 Tak ME 16-12 FAC3 3-7-43

ER317 9MU 9-9-42 82MU 28-9 *Parib* 30-10 Tak SOC 26-3-43

ER318 VB(T) 9MU 9-9-42 82MU 30-9 *Parib* 20-10 Tak ME 30-12 Malta 1-7-43 NA 21-6-45 SOC 26-9-46

ER319 VB(T) 9MU 10-9-42 82MU 26-9 *Lorca* 6-10 ME 23-12 NAAF 23-12 FAF 29-2-44 to Turk 28-8

ER320 VB(T) 9MU 13-9-42 82MU 6-10 *SS625* 20-10 Gib 6-11

ER321 VB(T) 9MU 13-9-42 76MU 6-10 *SS626* 20-10 Gib 6-11 NWA 28-2-43

ER322 9MU 12-9-42 47MU 14-10 *SS625* 20-10 Gib 6-11

ER323 Csfd VB(T) 9MU 17-9-42 82MU 21-10 *Catrine* 20-11 Tak 27-12 ME 10-2-43 Malta Sic 1-9 SOC 8-3-44 bboc 21-6-45 SOC 27-6-46

ER324 Csfd VB(T) 9MU 16-9-42 222MU 25-10 *SS634* 4-11 Gib 23-11 NWA 28-2-43

ER325 Csfd 9MU 18-9-42 82MU 9-10 *SS626* 20-10 Gib 6-11 USAAF NWA 1-10-43 ME 31-8-44 SOC 15-11-45

ER326 Dsfd 9MU 18-9-42 76MU 16-10 *SS626* 20-10 Gib 6-11 SOC 26-4-45

ER327 Dsfd 9MU 19-9-42 82MU 6-10 *SS625* 20-10 Gib 6-11 C3 ops 26-11

ER328 9MU 19-9-42 82MU 8-10 *SS626* 20-10 Gib 6-11 E Afr FTR ops 19-1-43

ER329 9MU 19-9-42 76MU 15-10 *SS625* 20-10 Gib 6-11 NWA 28-2-43 NAASC 31-10 SOC 26-4-45

ER330 VB(T) 9MU 24-9-42 82MU 9-10 *SS626* 20-10 Gib 6-11 C3 ops 5-12-43

ER331 9MU 26-9-42 76MU 16-10 *SS625* 20-10 Gib 6-11 C3 ops 26-11

ER332 9MU 26-9-42 47MU 15-10 *SS625* 20-10 Gib 6-11 ME 31-12 NWA 28-2-43

ER333 9MU 26-9-42 76MU 16-10 *SS625* 20-10 Gib 6-11 C3 ops 3-12

ER334 9MU 26-9-42 76MU 16-10 *SS625* 20-10 Gib 6-11 NWA 28-2-43

ER335 VB(T) 39MU 13-9-42 76MU 23-9 *Lorca* 3-10 ME 13-1-43 C3 ops 4-9

ER336 8MU 11-9-42 222MU 17-9 *Molaja* 1-10 lost at sea 3-10

ER337 15MU 10-9-42 222MU 17-9 *Molaja* 1-10 lost at sea 3-10

ER338 6MU 11-9-42 82MU 14-9 *Emp Lib* 19-9 Tak ME 6-11-43 NAAF SOC 29-8-46

ER339 VB(T) 15MU 10-9-42 222MU 17-9 *Molaja* 1-10 lost at sea 3-10

ER340 VB(T) 6MU 11-9-42 82MU 14-9 *Emp Lib* 19-8 Tak ME 9-11 SOC 8-3-44

ER341 46MU 10-9-42 215MU 25-9 *Cam Leith* 2-11 Tak 14-12 ME 31-1-43 NAAF 1-11 SOC 15-3-45

ER342 39MU 8-9-42 82MU 14-9 *Emp Lib* 19-9 Tak ME 5-11 Malta 1-7-43 i/sea ops 2-10 SOC 29-2-44

ER343 VB(T) 6MU 11-9-42 82MU 14-9 *Emp Lib* 19-9 Tak ME 31-12 FTR ops 19-4-43

ER344 VB(T) 39MU 9-9-42 47MU 14-9 *Emp Lib* 19-9 Tak ME 4-11 FTR ops 17-12

ER345 VB(T) 6MU 11-9-42 82MU 14-9 *Emp Lib* 19-9 Tak ME 4-11 FTR ops 19-4-43

ER461 VB(T) 6MU 11-9-42 82MU 14-9 *Emp Lib* 19-9 Tak ME 9-11 FTR ops 14-12

ER462 38MU 10-9-42 47MU 14-9 *Emp Lib* 19-9 Tak ME 12-11 SOC 1-12

ER463 9MU 13-9-42 82MU 11-10 *SS634* 4-11 Gib 23-11 NWA 28-2-43 NAASC 31-10 RHAF 25-4-46

ER464 VB(T) 8MU 11-9-42 82MU 30-9 *Parib* 20-10 Tak ME 19-12

ER465 VC(T) 15MU 10-9-42 47MU 14-9 *Emp Lib* 19-9 Tak ME 11-11 Malta Sic 1-8-43 NAAF 1-11 C3 ops 8-2-44

ER466 9MU 13-9-42 47MU 15-10 *SS625* 20-11 Gib 6-11 NWA 28-2-43 Malta 1-7 MAAF 21-6-45 FAF 28-2-46

ER467 VB(T) 8MU 11-9-42 76MU 20-9 *Lorca* 3-10 ME 6-10 Tak 14-12 NWA28-2-43 SOC 8-3-44

ER468 6MU 11-9-42 82MU 14-9 *Emp Lib* 19-9 Tak ME 17-11 SOC 29-8-46

ER469 38MU 12-9-42 47MU 16-9 *Molaja* 1-10 lost at sea 3-10

ER470 12MU 18-9-42 215MU 6-10 *Cam Leith* 2-11 Tak 14-12 C3 ops 1-1-43 ME 13-1 Malta Sic 1-8

ER471 VB(T) 45MU 13-9-42 215MU 27-9 *Cam Leith* 2-11 Tak 14-12 ME 31-1-43 SOC 26-9-46

ER472 VB(T) 8MU 11-9-42 222MU 17-9 *Molaja* 1-10 lost at sea 3-10

ER473 VB(T) 6MU 11-9-42 47MU 14-9 *Emp Lib* 19-9 Tak ME 9-11 SOC 13-9-45

ER474 12MU 18-9-42 215MU 28-9 *Cam Leith* 2-11 Tak 16-12 ME 6-1-43
ER475 6MU 25-9-42 76MU 2-10 *Ocean Cour* 7-11 Tak ME 31-12 NAAF 1-1-44 SOC 26-4-45
ER476 Canadian Lad VB(T) 45MU 16-9-42 215MU 27-9 *Cam Leith* 2-11 Tak 14-12 ME 31-12 to Turk 26-4-45
ER477 9MU 13-9-42 47MU 15-10 *SS625* 17-10 Gib 6-11 USAAF 31-7-43 NWA 1-10 SOC 27-6-46
ER478 VB(T) 38MU 12-9-42 82MU 15-9 *Emp Lib* 19-9 Tak ME 7-11 NAAF 1-11-43 SOC 26-4-45
ER479 38MU 12-9-42 47MU 16-9 *Molaja* 1-10 lost at sea 3-10
ER480 8MU 11-9-42 82MU 18-9 *Molaja* 1-10 lost at sea 3-10
ER481 6MU 11-9-42 47MU 14-9 *Emp Lib* 19-9 Tak ME 12-11 to Turk 22-2-45
ER482 VB(T) 12MU 12-9-42 215MU 26-9 *Ger-Y-Bryn* 13-10 Tak ME 6-12 Malta Sic 1-8-43 C3 ops 24-8
ER483 6MU 13-9-42 222MU 17-9 *Molaja* 1-10 lost at sea 3-10
ER484 VB(T) 38MU 12-9-42 82MU 19-9 *Molaja* 1-10 lost at sea 3-10
ER485 12MU 12-9-42 82MU 23-9 *SS622* 17-10 Gib 1-11
ER486 39MU 15-9-42 76MU 24-9 *Ocean Cour* 7-11 Tak ME 30-12 FTR ops 8-2-44
ER487 VB(T) 45MU 16-9-42 215MU 6-10 *Ger-Y-Bryn* 13-10 Tak ME 11-12 SOC 5-4-45
ER488 46MU 21-9-42 215MU 15-10 *SS628* 25-10 Algiers FTR ops 17-12-43
ER489 VB(T) 45MU 16-9-42 215MU 23-9 *Ger-Y-Bryn* 13-10 Tak ME 6-12 FAC2 8-12 CE 2-11-44
ER490 9MU 13-9-42 76MU 6-10 *SS625* 20-10 Gib 6-11 NWA 28-2-43 Malta 1-10 FTR 17-10-44
ER491 VB(T) 39MU 13-9-42 76MU 24-9 *Lorca* 6-10 Tak ME 28-12
ER492 39MU 13-9-42 76MU 24-9 *Lorca* 6-10 ME 31-12 Malta Sic 1-8-43 SOC 8-3-44
ER493 VB(T) 39MU 13-9-42 76MU 24-9 *Ocean Cour* 7-11 Tak ME 31-12 SOC 8-3-44
ER494 12MU 25-9-42 222MU 10-10 *SS626* 20-10 Gib 6-11 C2 ops 9-1-43 ME C3 ops 3-7-43
ER495 VB(T) 45MU 17-9-42 215MU 25-10 *SS634* 4-11 Gib C2 ops 26-12 C3 ops 17-4-43
ER496 VC 8MU 16-9-42 82MU 4-10 *Perib* 30-10 Tak ME 16-12 C3 ops 17-4-43
ER497 9MU 13-9-42 222MU 17-10 *SS626* 20-10 Gib 6-11 93S SOC 31-12-43
ER498 VB(T) 45MU 16-9-42 82MU 16-10 *SS628* 25-10 Gib 9-11 Malta 31-5-43 Sic 1-10 NA 1-1-44 SOC 26-4-45
ER499 33MU 19-9-42 82MU 15-10 *Emp Day* 22-10 Gib 9-11 FAC3 24-11
ER500 VB(T) 45MU 16-9-42 47MU 21-10 *Emp Day* 22-10 Gib 9-11 NWA 28-2-43 SOC 26-4-45
ER501 45MU 16-9-42 215MU 27-9 *Cam Leith* 2-11 Tak 14-12 ME 28-2-43 CE 17-4-44
ER502 VB(T) 45MU 17-9-42 215MU 30-9 *Cam Leith* 2-11 Tak 14-12 ME 1-1-43 FTR ops 16-4
ER503 38MU 18-9-42 76MU 22-9 *SS620* 15-10 Gib 1-11
ER504 VB(T) 8MU 17-9-42 82MU 2-10 *Perib* 30-10 Tak ME FAC2 17-12 NWA 28-2-43 SOC 26-4-45
ER505 33MU 19-9-42 76MU 15-10 *SS625* 20-10 Gib 6-11 SOC 31-12
ER506 45MU 23-9-42 47MU 20-10 *SS628* 25-10 NWA 28-2-43
ER507 VB(T) 45MU 16-9-42 215MU 6-10 *Cam Leith* 2-11 Tak 14-12 ME 31-12 SOC 26-3-43
ER508 VB(T) 38MU 17-9-42 76MU 23-9 *SS621* 16-10 Gib 1-11 81S C3 ops 1-1-43
ER509 Csfd 12MU 18-9-42 215MU 26-9 ROS *Belnor* 30-11 Tak 3-2-43 ME 5-3 NAASC 31-10 FA FTR 5-3-44
ER510 VB(T)38 MU 26-9 *SS620* 10-10 Gib 1-11 NWA USAAF 31-7-43
ER524 33MU 19-9-42 82MU 9-10 *SS626* 20-10 Gib NWA 28-2043 SOC 27-7-44
ER525 12MU 21-9-42 215MU 3-10 *Catrine* 20-11 Tak ME 21-1-43 NWA 28-2 SOC 29-8-46
ER526 46MU 19-9-42 215MU 13-10 *SS628* 17-10 Gib 9-11 C2 ops 27-12 recat 3 1-1-43
ER527 VB(T) 6MU 23-9-42 222MU 6-10 *Ocean Cour* 7-11 Tak 7-12 ME SOC 3-3-43
ER528 38MU 21-9-42 222MU 30-9 *Ocean Cour* 7-11 Tak ME 23-12 NAAF 1-11 C3 ops 27-1-44
ER529 VB(T) 33MU 18-9-42 76MU 15-10 *Emp Day* 22-10 Gib 9-11 SOC 31-12
ER530 46MU19-9-42 215MU 15-10 *SS628* 25-10 Gib 9-1 NWA 28-2-43 SOC
ER531 12MU 18-9-42 82MU 1-10 *Perib* 3-10 Tak ME 20-12 NAAF 1-11043 208S FTR ops 4-8-44
ER532 VB(T) 8MU 17-9-42 82MU 30-9 *Perib* 3-10 Tak ME 16-12 FAC3 24-8-43
ER533 6MU 25-9-42 82MU 30-9 *SS626* 20-10 Gib 6-11 NWA 28-2-43 SOC
ER534 8MU 23-9-42 82MU 4-10 *Catrine* 20-11 Tak 27-12 FTR ops 6-7-43
ER535 33MU 19-9-42 82MU 10-10 *SS626* 20-10 Gib 6-11 C2 17-1-43 SOC 31-12
ER536 8MU 18-9-42 82MU 25-9 *SS622* 17-10 Gib Algiers FTR ops 6-12
ER537 12MU 25-9-42 222MU 10-10 *SS626* 20-10 Gib 6-11 SOC 31-12
ER538 45MU 23-9-42 222MU 11-10 *SS626* 20-10 Gib 6-11
ER539 8MU 18-9-42 82MU 30-9 *Perib* 30-10 Tak ME 16-12 CE SOC 13-9-45
ER540 6MU 19-9-42 76MU 15-10 *SS625* 20-10 Gib 6-11 NWA 28-2-43
ER541 VB(T) 8MU 2-10 *Perib* 30-10 Tak ME FAC3 24-5-43
ER542 45MU 23-9-42 215MU 11-10 Gib 9-11 NWA 28-2-43 SOC
ER543 12MU 21-9-42 82MU 1-10 *Perib* 30-10 Tak ME 16-12 SOC 26-3-43
ER544 VB(T) 38MU 23-9-42 222MU 30-9 *Ocean Cour* 7-11 Tak CE ops 28-12
ER545 12MU 31-9-42 47MU 7-10 *SS625* 20-10 Gib 6-11 C3 ops 28-12
ER546 6MU 1-10-42 222MU 8-10 *Ocean Cour* 7-11 Tak ME 23-12 NAAF 30-11-43 SOC 31-8-44
ER547 VB(T) 6MU 23-9-42 82MU 1-10 *Perib* 30-10 Tak ME 20-12 Malta Sic 1-8-43 NAASC 31-10 SOC 26-4-45
ER548 8MU 22-9-42 222MU 6-10 *Ocean Cour* 7-11 Tak ME 28-12 SOC 1-11-43
EER549 12MU 21-9-42 82MU 1-10 *Perib* 30-10 Tak ME 16-12 Malta Sic 1-8-43 NA 30-11 SOC 26-4-45
ER550 6MU 30-9-42 76MU 10-10 *Ocean Cour* 7-11 Tak ME 20-12 NAASC 30-10-43 CE ops 4-7-44
ER551 46MU 21-9-42 76MU 13-10 *SS634* 4-11 Gib FAC2 28-12 recat 3 1-1-43
ER552 6MU 25-9-42 222MU 6-10 *Ocean Cour* 7-11 Tak C3 ops 5-12 SOC31-12
ER553 33MU 30-9-42 76MU 15-10 *Emp Day* 22-10 Gib 9-11
ER554 VB(T) 6MU 23-9-42 222MU 18-10 *Ocean Cour* 7-11 Tak ME 21-12 Malta Sic 1-8-43 NAASC 31-10 FACE SOC 24-4-45
ER555 45MU 23-9-42 222MU 11-10 *SS625* 20-10 Gib 6-11 SOC 31-1-43
ER556 VB(T)38MU 23-9-42 222MU 30-9 *Ocean Cour* 7-11 Tak 7-12 ME 31-12 Malta Sic 1-8-43 NAAF 1-11 SOC 25-7-46
ER557 38MU 6-10-42 47MU 14-10 *SS626* 20-10 Gib 6-11 NWA 28-2-43 USAAF 29-2-44 ME 25-2-45 SOC 26-9-46
ER558 38MU 21-9-42 222MU 30-9 *SS626* 20-10 Gib 6-11 Tak ME 23-12 NWA SOC 31-12-43
ER559 45MU 27-9-42 222MU 11-10 *SS626* 20-10 Gib 6-11 NWA SOC 31-7-43
ER560 33MU 26-9-42 82MU 10-10 *SS626 20-10* Gib 6-11 NWA 28-2-43
ER561 VB(T) 6MU 25-9-42 222MU 6-10 *Ocean Cour* 7-11 ME 7-1-43 NAAF 1-11
ER562 38MU 29-9-42 82MU 8-10 *SS625* 20-10 Gib 6-11 NWA 28-2-43
ER563 no record
ER564 33MU 26-9-42 76MU 15-10 *SS626* 20-10 Gib 6-11 NWA 28-2-43 C3 ops 11-4
ER565 VB(T) 39MU 27-9-42 76MU 6-10 *CO Der* 1-11 Basr 16-1-43 Malta 1-7 Sic NAAF 1-11 USAAF 31-1-44
ER566 12MU 25-9-42 215MU 13-10 *Catrine* 20-11 Tak 27-12 ME 28-1-43 NAAF 1-11 SOC 14-2-46
ER567 VB(T) 6MU 24-9-42 76MU 2-10 *Ocean Cour* 7-11 Tak 24-12 ME 28-12 FACE 20-2-45
ER568 6MU 24-9-42 76MU 2-10 *Ocean Cour* 7-11 ME 23-12 NWA 28-2-43 NAAF1-11
ER569 VB(T) 38MU 23-9-42 76MU 29-11 *Bluff V* 3-12 Gib 31-12 NWA 28-2-43
ER570 45MU 25-9-42 215MU 11-10 *SS628* 17-10 Gib 9-11 NWA USAAF 31-7-43 CE 14-6-45
ER571 45MU 26-9-42 215MU 11-10 *SS628* 25-10 Gib 9-11 C3 ops 13-1-43
ER583 39MU 30-9-42 76MU 13-10 *Catrine* 20-11 Tak ME 18-1-43 NAAF 1-11 FACE 18-7-44
ER584 9MU 8-10-42 82MU 24-10 *Catrine* 20-11 Tak 27-12 ME 29-1-43 Malta Sic 1-8 SOC 30-9
ER585 33MU 30-9-42 82MU 9-10 *SS626* 20-10 Gib 6-11 NA 31-5-43 Malta 1-6 FAC2 10-7-43
ER586 45MU 4-10-42 215MU 16-10 *SS628* 25-10 Gib 9-11 72S C2 ops 31-12 NWA 28-2-43
ER587 9MU 9-10-42 82MU 21-10 *Catrine* 20-11 ME 18-1-43 NAAF 1-11 MAAF 21-6-45 SOC 30-5-46
ER588 Dsfd 33MU 30-9-42 82MU 9-10 *SS626* 20-10 Gib 6-11 NWA 28-2-43 405S C3 ops 1-2-44
ER589 33MU 30-9-42 82MU 9-10 *SS625*20-10 Gib 6-11 SOC 31-1-43
ER590 39MU 18-10-42 76MU 27-10 *Catrine* 20-11 Tak ME 18-1-43 Malta 1-9 NA 1-11 to Turk 30-11-44
ER591 39MU 2-10-42 82MU 11-10 *SS634* 4-11 Gib SOC 31-1-43
ER592 38MU 2-10-42 82MU 11-10 *SS626* 20-10 Gib 6-11 E Afr FTR ops 3-1-43
ER593 45MU 8-10-42 47MU 21-10 *SS628* 25-10 Gib 9-11 NWA 28-2-43
ER594 38MU 2-10-42 222MU 11-10 Gib 6-11 C3 ops 5-12
ER595 45MU 28-11-42 215MU 11-12 *Hamble V* 20-12 Gib 13-1-43 FAC 9-2
ER596 45MU 8-10-42 215MU 21-10 *SS628* 25-10 Gib 9-11 NWA 28-2-43
ER597 45MU 29-10-42 222MU 12-11 *Bluff IV* 21-11 Gib 8-12 NWA 28-2-43 ME 1-9 NAASC 31-10
ER598 VB(T) 12MU 10-10-42 222MU 15-10 *SS626* 20-10 Gib 6-11 ME 23-12 NWA 28-2-43 250S C3 ops 20-3
ER599 VB(T) 12MU 10-10-42 47MU 16-10 *SS628* 25-10 Gib 9-11 C3 ops 28-12
ER600 45MU 30-9-42 222MU 11-10 *SS626* 20-10 Gib 6-11 NWA 28-2-43 SOC 30-4
ER601 WAL VB(T) 33MU 27-9-42 82MU 9-10 *SS626* 20-10 Gib 6-11 FTR ops 6-12
ER602 12MU 25-9-42 47MU 14-10 *Emp Day* 22-10 Gib 9-11 C2 ops 6-12 wrecked by Allied AA 22-12 SOC 31-12
ER603 38MU 10-10 *SS625* 20-10 Gib 6-11 SOC 31-12
ER604 8MU 1-10-42 76MU 10-10 *SS625* 20-10 Gib 6-11 ME 20-12 FAC2 3-1-43 Sic 1-8 SOC 8-3-44
ER605 38MU 27-9-42 222MU 6-10 *SS625* 20-10 Gib 6-11 CE ops 28-12
ER606 33MU 25-9-42 82MU 16-10 *SS626* 20-10 Gib 6-11 Malta 1-7-43 NWA 28-2 ME 1-9 NAASC 31-10
ER607 33MU 26-9-42 82MU 16-10 *Emp Clive* 11-12 Tak 23-1-43 ME 18-2 NWA SOC 28-2
ER608 38MU 27-9-42 76MU 6-10 *Ocean Cour* 7-11 Tak ME 21-12 NA 30-11-43 FAC 3-8-44
ER609 12MU 25-9-42 215MU 10-10 *Catrine* 20-11 Tak 27-12 ME 27-2-43 SOC 14-3-46
ER610 38MU 2-10-42 76MU 15-10 *SS625* 3-10 Gib 6-11 NWA 28-2-43 SOC 31-3
ER611 VB(T) 39MU 27-9-42 76MU 6-10 *Ocean Cour* 7-11 Tak ME 31-12 SOC 29-8-46
ER612 45MU 29-9-42 76MU 16-10 *SS626* 20-10 Gib 6-11 ME FTR ops 13-1-43
ER613 VB(T) 39MU 27-9-42 76MU 6-10 *Catrine* 20-11 Tak 27-12 ME 19-1-43 NAAF 1-11 SOC 26-4-45
ER614 VC(bomber) Wad Medoni/Blue Nile 6MU 22-1-43 222MU 24-1 *Well Crt* 18-2- Gib 7-3 NA 31-3 USAAF 31-10 SOC 29-2-44
ER615 WAL 9MU 21-9-42 82MU 16-10 *SS625* 20-10 Gib 6-11 FAC2 30-11 111S C3 ops 28-2-43
ER616 29-11-42 222MU 7-12 *SS647* 19-12 Gib 6-2-43 FAC3 21-2-44
ER617 WAL 9MU 21-9-42 82MU 16-10 *Emp Day* 22-10 Gib 9-11 111S C3 ops 3-2-43
ER618 30-9-42 82MU 9-10 *SS626* 20-10 Gib 6-11 NWA SOC 30-4-43
ER619 8MU 1-10 *Perib* 30-10 Tak 16-12 NAAF 1-11-43 SOC 29-2-44 bboc 14-6-45 trg del 13-9
ER620 VB(T) 33MU 2-10-42 222MU 16-10 *SS625* 20-10 Gib 6-11 C2 ops 17-12 SOC 31-1-43
ER621 12MU 3-10-42 47MU 16-10 *Emp Day* 22-10 Gib 9-11 NWA 31-5-43
ER622 6MU 30-9-42 222MU 13-10 *Ocean Cour* 7-11 Tank 20-12 NWA SOC 30-4-43 to Turk 22-2-45
ER623 33MU 1-10-42 82MU 17-10 *Emp Day* 22-10 Gib 9-11 FAC2 27-12 SOC 30-1-43
ER624 William 12MU 2-10-42 222MU 12-10 *SS625* 20-10 Gib 6-11 NWA 28-2-43 154S C3 ops 30-3
ER625 6MU 30-9-42 82MU 9-10 *SS626* 20-10 Gib 6-11 NWA 28-2-43 NAASC 31-10 ME 25-2-45 REAF 29-2-45
ER626 38MU 10-10-42 222MU 17-10 *SS625* 20-10 Gib 6-11
ER634 8MU 1-10-42 82MU 11-10 *Ocean Cour* 7-11 Tak ME 30-12 FTR ops 19-4-43
ER635 12MU 6-10-42 82MU 16-10 *Emp Day* 22-10 Gib 9-11 NWA 28-2-43 Malta 1-7 Sic 1-10 SOC 26-4-45
ER636 PG Spitfire 38MU 2-10-42 76MU 15-10 E Afr C3 ops 4-12
ER637 33MU 1-10-42 82MU 16-10 *SS625* 20-10 Gib 6-11 E Africa FAC3 1-12 SOC 18-11-44
ER638 8MU 10-10-42 47MU 15-10 *Emp Day* 22-10 Gib 7-11 NWA 28-2-43 SOC
ER639 12MU 10-10-42 222MU 13-10 *SS625* 20-10 Gib 6-11 FAC2 30-12 NWA 28-2-433 SOC 26-4-45
ER640 VB(T) 38MU 6-10-42 76MU 10-10 *Ocean Cour* 7-11 Tak ME 23-12 REAF 29-3-45
ER641 38MU 30-9-42 82MU 15-10 *Emp Day* 22-10 Gib 9-11 Ind 1-12 NWA 28-2-43 SOC
ER642 12MU 3-10-42 222MU 15-10 *SS626* 20-10 Gib 6-11 111S C2 ops SOC 28-2-43
ER643 VB(T) 38MU 6-10-42 76MU 15-10 *SS625* 20-10 Gib 6-11 NWA 28-2-43 Malta 1-9 NAASC 31-10 to Turk 26-4-45
ER644 VB(T) 38MU 6-10-42 76MU 16-10 *Emp Day* 22-10 9-11 NWA SOC 28-2-43
ER645 38MU 10-10-42 47MU 17-10 *SS628* 25-10 Gib 9-11 FAC3 20-12 recat 2 Malta 1-7-43 NWA FAC3 5-7 Sic ME FAC3 4-8-43
ER646 6MU 30-9-42 82MU 14-10 *Perib* 30-10 Tak FA FTR 6-3-43
ER647 33MU 1-10-42 82MU 16-10 *SS625* 20-10 Gib 6-11 Malta 1-12 USAAF 20-2-44 MAAF 21-6-45 trg del 27-9-45
ER648 46MU 7-10-42 FACA 10-10 215MU 13-11 *Belnor* 30-11 Tak 3-2-43 ME 9-3 Malta 1-7 Sic NAASC 31-10 SOC 26-6-45
ER649 12MU 3-10-42 215MU 15-10 *SS628* 25-10 Gib 9-11 81S FAC3 2-1-43
ER650 8MU 1-10-42 82MU 11-10 *Perib* 30-10 Tak ME 12-12 NWA 28-2-43 SOC 30-4
ER651 12MU 2-10-42 222MU 13-10 *SS626* 20-10 Gib 6-11 Algiers FTR ops 17-12
ER652 12MU 3-10-42 222MU 13-10 *SS625* 20-10 Gib 6-11 NWA 28-2-43 C3 ops 18-4
ER653 VB(T) 38MU 6-10-42 766MU 15-10 *SS626* 20-10 Gib 6-11 NWA 28-2-43 USAF 12-52 lost in Med 10-1-44
ER654 VC 12MU 9-10-42 222MU 17-10 *SS628* 25-10 Gib 9-11 NWA 28-2-43 SOC 30-4
ER655 VC 12MU 9-10-42 215MU 16-10 *SS628* 25-10 Gib 9-11 NWA USAAF 31-7-43 MAAF 21-6-45 IAF 27-6-46 as MM4055
ER656 VB(T) 6MU 30-9-42 222MU 17-10 *SS626* Gib 6-11 Algiers FTR ops 15-12
ER657 38MU 10-10-42 222MU 17-10 *SSS625* 20-10 Gib 6-11 SOC 31-12-43
ER658 VB(T) 38MU 6-10-42 47MU 14-10 *SS626* 20-10 Gib 6-11 NWA 28-2-43
ER659 38MU 8-10-42 222MU 17-10 *SS626* 20-10 Gib 6-11 Algiers FTR ops 16-12

ER660 46MU 8-10-42 215MU 15-10 *SS628* 25-10 Gib 9-11 NWA 28-2-43 SOC 28-4-45
ER661 12MU 6-10-42 222MU 10-11 *Emp King* 30-11 Tak 10-2-43 ME 7-3 Malta 1-7 Sic NAAF 1-11 to Turk 29-3-45
ER662 VB(T) 6MU 30-9-42 47MU 15-10 *Emp Day* 22-10 Gib 9-11 111S SOC 31-12 bboc 21-6-45 SOC 29-3-46
ER663 38MU 6-10-42 47MU 14-10 *SS625* 20-10 Gib 6-11 NWA 28-2-43 Malta 1-7ME 1-9 NAASC 31-10 CE 11-1-45
ER664 38MU 6-10-42 47MU 14-10 *SS625* 20-10 Gib 6-11 SOC 31-1-43
ER665 38MU 6-10-42 47MU 14-10 *SS626* 20-10 Gib 6-11 FTR ops 28-11
ER666 VC 39MU 17-11-42 82MU 1-12 *Emp Clive* 11-12 Tak 23-1-43 ME 8-3 NAASC 31-10 C3 ops 1-6-44 recat A to Turk 22-2-45
ER667 VB(T) 38MU 6-10-42 76MU 15-10 *SS625* 20-10 Gib 6-11 NWA 28-2-43 SOC
ER668 46MU 7-10-42 47MU 16-10 *SS628* 25-10 Gib 9-11 NWA 28-2-43 ME 31-1-45 CE SOC 13-9
ER669 46MU 7-10-42 82MU 16-10 *Emp Day* 22-10 Gib 9-11 SOC 31-1-43
ER670 VB(T) 6MU 10-10-42 82MU 14-10 *SS626* 20-10 Gib 6-11 NWA 28-2-43
ER671 46MU 8-10-42 215MU 15-10 *SS628* 25-10 Gib 9-11 FTR ops 15-12
ER672 45MU 9-10-42 47MU 21-10 *SS628* 25-10 Gib 9-11 AST 3-2-43 *SS703* 1-6 Casa 15-6 NWA 1-7 NAAF 1-11 SOC 26-4-45
ER673 12MU 9-10-42 82MU 16-10 *SS625*20-10 Gib 6-11 NWA 28-2-43 C3 ops 16-12
ER674 46MU 8-10-42 242S 22-10 47MU 27-10 Gib 9-11 NWA 28-2-43 FAF 31-7-43 601S FTR ops 11-12
ER675 8MU 10-10-42 47MU 15-10 *Emp Day* 22-10 Gib 9-11 NWA 28-2-43 NAASC 31-10 SOC 31-8-44
ER676 45MU 9-10-42 82MU 16-10 *SS628* 25-10 Gib 9-11 NWA 28-2-43 FTR ops 25-4
ER677 Csfd VB(T) 9MU 27-9-42 82MU 26-10 *SS634* 4-11 Gib 23-11 NWA 28-2-433 ME 15-2-45 SOC 25-7-46
ER678 Csfd 9MU 27-9-42 222MU 27-10 *SS634* 4-11 SOC 31-1-43
ER679 Csfd 9MU 1-10-42 82MU 16-10 *Emp Day* 22-10 Gib 9-11 E Afr FTR ops 8-1-43
ER695 Csfd 9MU 1-10-42 82MU 16-10 *Emp Day* 22-10 Gib 9-11 NWA 28-2-43 245S C3 ops 20-3
ER696 46MU 11-10-42 47MU 16-10 *Emp Day* 22-10 Gib 9-11
ER697 Csfd 9MU 8-10 42 222MU 27-10 *SS634* 4-11 Gib 23-11 NWA 28-2-43 SOC
ER689 Csfd 9MU 3-10-42 222MU 27-10 *SS634* 4-11 Gib 23-11 NWA 28-2-43 111S C3 ops 3-4
ER699 VB(T) 38MU 10-10-42 222MU 17-10 *SS628* 25-10 Gib 9-11 E Afr FAC3 23-11
ER700 9MU 9-10-42 47MU 26-10 *SSK-55* 3-11 Gib 23-11
ER701 VB(T) 38MU 10-10-42 76MU 15-10 *SS626* 20-10 Gib 6-11 FA SOC 31-12
ER702 39MU 18-10-42 82MU 26-10 *SS634* $-11 Gib 23-11 SAL 22-4-43 215MU 7-5-43 Casa 30-5 NWA 1-7 SOC 26-9-46
ER703 39MU 18-10-42 76MU 25-10 *Catrine* 20-11 Tak ME 17-1-43 SOC 26-4-45
ER704 46MU 11-10-42 82MU 16-10 *Emp Day* 22-10 Gib 9-11 SOC 26-3-43
ER705 39MU 18-10-42 76MU 28-10 *Catrine* 20-11 Tak ME 31-1-43 USAAF 31-1-44 FACE 15-2-45
ER706 39MU 18-10-42 76MU 28-10 *Catrine* 20-11 Tak 27-11 ME 29-1-43 Malta 1-7 CE ops 16-7
ER707 6MU 18-10-42 82MU 20-11 *SS634* 4-11 Gib E Afr 4-12 CE ops 30-1-43
ER708 6MU 19-10-42 *SS634* 26-10 Gib 4-11 E Afr C3 ops 34-12-43
ER709 12MU 20-10-42 82MU 27-10 *Hamble V* 19-11 Gib 8-12 NWA 28-2-43 2443S C3 ops 5-3
ER710 12MU 1-11-43 222MU 10-11 *Bluff IV* 21-11 Gib 8-12 152S E Afr C3 ops 8-2-43
ER711 46MU 25-10-42 222MU 16-11 *Bluff IV* 21-11 Gib 8-12 NWA 28-2-43 SOC
ER712 46MU 25-10-42 222MU 14-11-43 *Hamble V* 1-12 Gib 8-1-43 1676Flt NWA FAF 31-7 ME 21-6-45 SOC 10-1-45
ER713 39MU 16-6-43 VA con to FIX M63 222MU 25-6-43 Casa 14-7 E Afr 26-9-46
ER714 46MU 25-10-42 222MU 16-11 *Bluff IV* 21-11 C3 ops 28-12
ER715 46MU 7-11-42 215MU 30-11 *Bluff IV* 3-12 Gib 31-12 NWA 21-2-43 ret UK AST 9-11 RNDA 20-2-44 COAL 15-5 RNAS Hens 10-6
ER716 VB(T) 12MU 10-10-42 47MU 16-10 *SS628* 25-10 Gib 9-11 C3 ops 243S 26-2-43 Malta 1-7 FAC3 4-7
ER717 46MU 11-10-42 82MU 16-10 *Emp Day* 22-10 Gib 9-11 NWA 28-2-43 NAASC 31-10 ME 30-11 RHAF 25-4-46
ER718 VB(T) 12MU 10-10-42 82MU 16-10 *Emp Day* 23-10 Gib 9-11 NWA 28-2-43 ME 28-4-45 SOC 29-8-46
ER719 12MU 15-10-42 47MU 26-10 *Emp Day* 23-10 Gib 9-11
ER720 46MU 11-10-42 82MU 16-10 *SS628* 25-10 Gib 9-11 111S FAC3 3-2-43
ER721 38MU 19-10-42 82MU 25-10 *SS634* 4-11 Gib 23-11 E Afr FAC3 5-12
ER722 45MU 16-10-42 215MU 30-1- *Catrine* 20-11 Tak 27-12 ME 31-1-43 SOC 30-9
ER723 45MU 16-10 82MU 26-10 *SS634* 4-11 Gib 23-11 NWA 28-2 43 FTR ops 12-4
ER724 38MU 19-10-42 82MU 25-10 *SS634* 4-11 Gib 23-11 E Afr FTR ops 2-3-43
ER725 38MU 21-10-42 82MU 31-10 *Catrine* 20-11 Tak ME 13-1-43 SOC 31-12
ER726 33MU 27-10-42 82MU 8-11 *Bluff IV* E Afr FTR ops 2-1-43
ER727 33MU 27-10-42 82MU 8-11 *Bluff IV* 21-11 Gib 8-12 NWA 28-2-43 Malta 1-7 Sic NAASC 31-10 ME 21-6-45 SOC 27-6-46
ER728 12MU 31-10-42 222MU 10-11 *Emp King* 30-11 Tak 10-2-43 ME 9-3 Malta 1-7 Sic NAASC 31-10 336S CD f/lnd Voulu Greece 9-2-46 SOC 14-2
ER729 33MU 27-10-42 82MU 13-11 *Bluff IV* 21-11 Gib 8-12 NWA 28-2-43 ME 31-8-44 SOC 12-4-45
ER730 33MU 27-10-42 82MU 13-11 *Bluff IV* 21-11 Gib 8-12 NWA 28-2-43 USAAF 1-10 5 FRU FACE 17-10-44
ER731 6MU 7-11-42 7-11-42 82MU 22-11 *Bluff IV*3-12 Gib 31-12 NWA 28-2-43 Malta 1-7-43 Sic ME 1-11 NAASC 31-10 SOC 14-3-46
ER732 12MU 9-10-42 47MU 14-10 E Afr 72S SOC 31-12
ER733 VC38MU 76MU 24-10-42 *Catrine* 20-11 Tak 27-12 ME 27-1-43 NAASC 31-11 MAAF 31-3-44 SOC 28-4-45
ER734 8MU 12-10-42 82MU 16-10 *Emp Day* 22-10 Gib 9-11 NWA 28-2-43 SOC 30-4
ER735 VB(T) 8MU 13-10-42 215MU 11-12 *Emp Stren* 11-1-43 Aus 11-4
ER736 45MU 9-10-42 82MU 20-10 *SS628* 25-10 Gib 9-11 93S E Afr C3 ops 26-2-43
ER737 VB(T) 39MU 10-10-42 47MU 15-10 *Emp Day* 22-10 Gib 9-11 NWA 28-2-43
ER738 12MU 9-10-42 47MU 14-10 *Emp Day* 22-10 Gib 9-11 NWA 28-2-43
ER739 VC 12MU 9-10-42 215MU 17-11 *Guinean* 20-11 Tak 28-12 ME 21-1-43 NAAF 1-11 SOC 26-4-45
ER740 VC 46MU 11-10-42 47MU 16-10 *SS628* 25-10 Gib 9-11 NWA 28-2-43
ER741 45MU 9-10-42 47MU 21-10 *SSK-55*3-11 Gib 28-11 NWA 1-1-43 SOC 28-4-45
ER742 6MU 12-10-42 82MU 17-10 *Emp Day* 22-10 Gib 9-11 143S CE ops 15-7-44
ER743 46MU 11-1042 47MU 16-10 *Emp Day* 22-10 Gib 9-11 E Afr C3 ops 28-12
ER744 VB(T) 6MU 11-10-42 82MU 17-10 *Emp Day* 22-10 Gib 9-11 NWA 28-2-43 ME 21-6-45 SOC 14-3-46
ER758 9MU 8-11-42 47MU 20-11 *Emp Day* 22-10 Gib 9-11 ME 1-12 Tak 16-7-43 SOC 8-3-44
ER759 VB(T) 39MU 10-10-42 47MU 15-10 *Emp Day* 22-10 Gib 9-11 NWA 28-2-43
ER760 VC 8MU 12-10-42 215MU 24-10 *Taranki* 24-11 Aus 23-1-43
ER761 VB(T) 6MU 11-10-42 47MU 15-10 *Emp Day* 22-10 Gib 9-11 NWA 28-2-43
ER762 VC NW Railway II Punjab 45MU 18-10-42 82MU 1-11 *Hamble IV* 19-11 Gib 22-5-42 1676Flt
ER763 no record
ER764 6MU 12-10-42 82MU 17-10 *Emp Day* 22-10 Gib 9-11 Algiers FTR ops 11-12
ER765 VC 8MU 22-1-43 82 26-1 *Fort Senn* 13-2 Tak 11-3 ME 1-5 Iraq 1-6
ER766 VB(T) 8MU 13-10-42 82MU 16-10 *Emp Day* 22-10 E Afr FTR ops 6-12
ER767 6MU 4-10-42 VWD wts & CG. load 215MU 28-2-43 *Ess Trad* 10-4 Casa 25-4 NWA 31-5 ME 1-7 NA 30-11 SOC 30-6-45
ER768 46MU 11-10-42 47MU 16-10 *Emp Day* 20-10 Gib 6-11 NWA 28-2-43 SOC
ER769 46MU 7-11-42 215MU 20-11 *Bluff IV* 3-12 Gib 31-12 NWA 28-2-43 NA1-7 SOC 8-3-44 bboc 21-6-45 to VC 9-8 SOC 29-8-46
ER770 6MU 12-10-42 82MU 17-10 *Emp Day* 22-10 Gib 9-11 SOC 31-12
ER771 VC Albrina 45MU 16-10-42 215MU 7-11 *Hamble IV* 19-11 FAC2 17-1-43 SOC 30-4
ER772 12MU 24-10-42 215MU 4-11 *Hamble IV* 19-11 Gib 8-12 NWA 28-2-43 NAAF 1-11 ME 21-6-45 335S Cd L/d Sedes Greece 17-4-46 SOC 25-4
ER773 46MU 11-10-42 82MU 21-10 *Catrine* 20-11 Tak ME 21-1-43 NWA SOC 30-4 bboc 21-6-45 RHAF 25-4-46
ER774 46MU 11-10-42 e/a SOC 31-12
ER775 8MU 12-10-42 82MU 17-10 C2 ops 12-12 ME SOC 26-4-45
ER776 VC(T) 33MU 18-10-42 47MU 26-10 *Catrine* 20-11 Tak 30-12 ME 31-1-43 SOC 29-8-46
ER777 VC 45MU 31-10-42 82MU 16-11 *Bluff IV* 21-11 E Afr C3 ops 16-1-43
ER778 Spirit of Beverley 45MU 18-10-42 215MU 25-10 *SS634* 21-11 E Afr C3 ops 242S 2-1-43
ER779 VB(T) 39MU 10-10-42 47MU 14-10 *Emp Day* 22-10 Gib 9-11 NWA 28-2-43 Malta 1-7 ME 1-9 NAAF 1-11 SOC 28-4-45
ER780 46MU 11-11-42 FAAC 24-10 SAL 215MU 27-3-43 *SS679* 14-4 Casa 25-4 NWA 31-5 USAAF 31-7 SOC 28-4-45
ER781 VC 45MU 18-10-42 82MU 25-10 *SS634* 4-11 Gib 23-11 NWA 28-2-43
ER782 VC Assam X 38MU 15-10-42 82MU 6-11 *Hamble IV* 19-11 Gib 8-12 NWA 27-2-43 ME 28-4-45 FAF 13-3-46
ER783 Lima Challenger II 45MU 16-10-42 215MU 8-11 *Hamble IV* 19-11 Gib 8-12 NWA 28-2-43 MAAF 21-6 249S FAF 3-7-45
ER784 12MU 24-10-42 215MU 6-11 *Hamble IV* 19-11 E Afr FAC2 3-1-43 SOC 28-2-42
ER785 8MU 12-10-42 82MU 16-10 *Emp Day* 22-10 Gib 9-11 NWA 28-2-43 SOC 305
ER786 38MU 16-10-42 82MU 26-10 *SS634* 4-11 E Afr C3 ops 18-12
ER787 VC Hissar IV Punjab 45MU 18-10-42 215MU 8-11 *Hamble IV* 19-11 Gib 8-12 NWA 28-2-43 Malta SOC 12-6 FH75.45
ER788 8MU 12-10-42 47MU 15-10 Gib 9-11 NWA 28-2-43 SOC 26-4-45
ER789 6MU 12-10-42 82MU 17-10 *Emp Day* 22-10 Gib 9-11 NWA 28-2-43
ER790 33MU 18-10-42 47MU 20-10 *SSK-55* 3-11 Gib 23-11
ER791 12MU 24-10-42 215MU 4-11 *Hamble IV* 19-11 E Afr C3 ops 3-1-43

ER810 served from Malta and was transferred to Turkey in 1944.

ER804 VC(T) 39MU 15-10-42 76MU 27-10 *Catrine* 20-11 Tak 27-12 ME 16-2-43 CE SOC 13-9-45

ER805 VC(T) 33MU 18-10-42 76MU 26-10 *Catrine* 20-11 Tak 27-12 ME 31-1-43 SOC 26-4-45

ER806 VC 45MU 6-11-42 82MU 16-11 *Bluff IV* 21-11 E Afr FAC2 21-12 NWA 28-2-43 SOC

ER807 12MU 24-10-42 82MU 7-11 *Hamble* 19-11 Gib 8-10 NWA 28-2-43 243S FTR ops 3-5

ER808 9MU 15-10-42 222MU 25-10 *SS634* 4-11 ME 19-1-43 NWA 28-2-43

ER809 39MU 25-10-42 222MU 6-11 *Hamble IV* 19-11 Gib 8-12 NWA 28-2-43FAF 1-10 ME 15-3-45 SOC 29-8-46

ER810 3879 Inca 45MU 16-10-42 82MU 1-11 *Hamble IV* 19-11 Gib 8-12 NWA 28-2-43 Malta 1-7 NAAF 1-9 to Turk 28-12-44

ER811 BB & CI Railway 46MU 13-11 *Bluff IV* 21-11 111S E Afr C2 ops 1-2-43 C3 ops 5-2 FH10.15

ER812 12MU 18-10-42 82MU 20-10 *SS634* 4-11 Malta 1-12 E Afr C3 ops 17-1-43 NWA 28-2 ME 31-10 SOC 26-4-45

ER813 12MU 26-10-42 47MU 26-10 *SSK-553*-11 Gib 23-11

ER814 38MU 21-10-42 76MU 7-11 *Emp King* 30-11 Tak 10-2-43 ME 9-3

ER815 NW Railway III Punjab 45MU 18-10-42 82MU 25-10 *SS634* 20-11 Gib E Afr C2 ops 22-12 93S FAC3 25-2-43 NWA USAAF 31-7

ER816 Dhanbad Jharia II 38MU 24-10-42 76MU 2-11 *Hamble IV* 19-11 Gib 8-12 FACE 21-10-43

ER817 12MU 18-10-42 82MU 27-10 *SS634* 4-11 Gib E Afr C2 ops 3-12 SOC 31-12 bboc ME 22-2-45 FACE 28-4-46 SOC 27-6

ER818 33MU 21-10-42 76MU 31-10 *Catrine* 20-11 Tak ME 18-1-43 SOC 29-8-46

ER819 33MU 18-10-42 47MU 26-10 *SSK-55* 3-11 Gib 23-11 NWA 28-2-43 ME 21-6-45 SOC 13-9

ER820 33MU 21-10-42 47MU 27-10 *Hamble IV* 19-11 E Afr C3 ops 22-12

ER821 6MU 24-10-42 76MU 18-11 *Guinean* 20-11 Tak 28-12 ME 31-1-43 NAASC 1-11 MAAF 21-6-45 IAF 27-6-46 as MM4068

ER822 Ambala III Punjab 45MU 18-10-42 82MU 1-11 *Emp King* 30-11 Tak 10-2-43 ME 27-3

ER823 Gurdaspur II Punjab 45MU 18-10-42 215MU 24-10 *SS634* 4-11 Gib 23-11 NWA 28-2-43 NAAF FAC3 1-3-44

ER824 LFLRVB Nigeria Kabala Province 46MU 18-10-42 82MU 18-11 *Emp King* 30-11 dam in transit repair Canada 12-2-43 P&P 2-7 442S 23-2-44 12Grp Com Flt 23-4 Sold J Dale 8-7-48

ER825 Gurgaon III Punjab 46MU 18-10-42 FAAC 7-12 ROS 215MU 20-12 *Hamble VII* 30-12 Gib 18-1-43 NWA 28-2 SOC

ER826 33MU 21-10-42 47MU 26-10 *SSK-55* 3-11 Gib 23-11

ER827 33MU 21-10-42 47MU 26-10 *Hamble IV* 19-11 Gib 8-12 NWA 28-2-43 NA 1-7 SOC 8-3-44 bboc 21-6-45 SOC 29-8-46

ER828 6MU 24-10-42 82MU 6-11 *Emp King* 30-11 Tak 10-2-43 ME 8-3 SOC 8-3-44

ER829 9MU 20-11-42 222MU 7-12 *Hamble VI*20-12 Gib 13-1-43 NWA 28-2

ER830 33MU 18-10-42 47MU 26-10 *SSK-55* 3-11 Gib 23-11 SOC 28-4-45

ER831 38MU 21-10-42 76MU 6-11 *Guinean* 30-11 Tak 28-12 ME 28-2-43 FACE 1-5

ER832 33MU 27-10-42 82MU 9-11 *Bluff IV* 21-11 E Afr CE ops 4-1-43

ER833 Nigeria Benue Prudence 46MU 18-10-42 82MU 13-11 *Bluff IV* 21-11 Gib 8-12 NWA 28-2-43 FTR ops 2-4

ER834 12MU 21-10-42 47MU 26-10 *SSK-55* 3-11 Gib 23-11

ER846 33MU 21-10-42 47MU 26-10 *Hamble IV* 19-11 E Afr C3 ops 28-12

ER847 9MU 17-11-42 222MU 7-12 *SS647* 19-12 Gib 6-2-43 NWA 31-3 SOC 26-4-45 bboc 21-6 SOC 11-4-46

ER848 12MU 24-10-42 215MU 29-10 *Catrine* 21-11 Tak ME 18-1-43 Malta 1-8 NAASC 31-10 ME 31-8-44 SOC 7-6-45

ER849 38MU 21-10-42 82MU 6-11 *Hamble IV*21-11 Gib 8-12 NWA 28-2-43 CE ops 8-5

ER850 39MU 25-10-42 222MU 6-11 *Hamble IV* 19-11 Gib 8-12 NWA 28-2-43 152S C3 ops 1-3

ER851 12MU 24-10-42 215MU 6-11 *Hamble IV* 19-11 Gib 8-12 E Afr 241S C3 ops 3-2-43

ER852 Spirit of Uruguay II 38MU 21-10-42 82MU 6-11 *Hamble IV* 9-11 Gib 8-12 NWA 28-10-43 SOC 26-4-45

ER853 6MU 25-10-42 222MU 9-11 *Catrine* 20-11 Tak 27-12 ME 31-1-43 FAC3 6-3-44

ER854 VC 45MU 1-11-42 222MU 16-11 *Emp King* 30-11 Tak 10-2 ME 407 FTR ops 25-4

ER855 Bihar VIII 38MU 29-10-42 76MU 6-11 *Emp King* 30-11 Tak ME 19-1-43 Malta 1-7 Sic SOC 8-3-44

ER856 12MU 24-10-42 215MU 4-11 *Hamble IV* 19-11 Gib 8-12 NWA 28-2-43 Malta 1-7 NE FTR ops 10-7

ER857 12MU 24-10-42 215MU 6-11 *Hamble IV* 19-11 243S E Afr CE ops 7-6-43

ER858 6MU 25-10-42 222MU 6-11 *Emp King* 30-11 Tak 10-2-43 ME 9-3 FTR ops 16-4

ER859 Spirit of Uruguay II 38MU 24-10-42 76MU 18-11 *Bluff V* 3-12 Gib 31-12 NWA 30-4-43 NAASC 31-10 SOC 26-4-45

ER860 VC(T)MXX 38MU 31-10-42 82MU 13-11 *Bluff IV* 22-12 E Afr FAC3 22-12

ER861 6MU 25-10-42 222MU 6-11 *Emp King* 20-11 Tak 10-2-43 ME 11-3 NAASC 31-10 SOC 26-4-45

ER862 38MU 21-1042 222MU 7-11 *Hamble IV* 19-11 81S E Afr C2 4-1-43 NAASC 31-10 SOC 26-4-45

ER863 38MU 24-10-42 76MU 16-11 *Hamble IV* 1-12 Gib 8-1-43 NWA 30-4 SOC 30-6

ER864 6MU 7-11-42 82MU 17-11 *Hamble V* 1-12 Gib 8-1-43 NWA 28-2 Sic 1-8 ME 1-9 SOC 29-2-44

ER865 VC 46MU 26-10-42 82MU 14-11 *Hamble V* 1-12 Gib 8-1-42

ER866 VC 46MU 26-10-42 FAAC 26-10 VA 82MU 16-11 *Bluff IV* 21-11 Gib 8-12 NWA 28-2-43 Malta 1-7

ER867 39MU 26-10-42 82MU 6-11 *Emp King* 30-11 Tak 10-2-43 ME 13-3 CE 2-8-45 SOC 11-8

ER868 6MU 25-10-42 222MU 6-11 *Emp King* 30-11 Tak 10-2-43 ME 8-3 C3 ops

ER869 38MU 24-10-42 76MU 18-11 *Guinean* 30-11 Tak 28-12 ME 22-1-43 SOC 10-4

ER870 VB(T) 38MU 31-10-42 82MU 13-11 *Bluff IV* 21-11 Gib 8-12 NWA 28-2-43 SOC 8-2-45

ER871 39MU 25-10-42 222MU 6-11 *Emp King* 30-11 Tak 10-2-43 ME 11-3 Malta 1-7 Sic NAAF 1-11 SOC 31-5-45

ER872 VC 12MU 31-10-42 215MU 13-11 *Belnor* 30-11 Tak 3-2-43 ME 9-3 NAAF 1-1-44 C3 ops 26--3-44

ER873 6MU 25-10-42 82MU 6-11 *Emp King* 30-11 Tak E Afr C3 ops 27-1-43

ER874 6MU 25-10-42 82MU 6-11 *Emp King* 30-11 Tak E Afr C3 ops 27-1-43

ER875 6MU 7-11-42 82MU 20-11 *Hamble V* 1-12 Gib 8-1-43

ER876 6MU 25-10-42 222MU 31-10 *Catrine* 20-11 Tak 27-12 ME 9-2-43 NWA 28-2 FTR ops 30-3

ER877 VC 39MU 7-11 222MU 29-11 AST 47MU 30-1-43 *Fort Senn* 13-2 Tak 11-3 ME 24-3 SOC 26-4-45

ER878 39MU 25-10-42 82MU 21-10 *Catrine* 21-11 E Afr 31-1-43 SOC

ER879 VC 45MU 6-11-42 215MU 25-11 *Bluff V* 3-12 Gib 31-12 NWA SOC 28-2-43

ER880 VC 39MU 7-11-42 222MU 20-11 *Bluff V* 3-12 Gib 31-12 NWA 28-2-43 USAAF 31-1-44 SOC 30-6-45

ER881 12MU 27-10-42 82MU 11-11 *Emp King* 30-11 dam in trans rtp Ottawa Canada 12-2-43

ER882 6MU 25-10-42 222MU 6-11 *Emp King* 30-11 Tak 10-2-433 ME 9-3 FTR ops 22-5

ER883 12MU 26-10-42 82MU 7-11 *Hamble IV* 19-11 E Africa C2 ops NWA 28-2-43 C3 ops 2-3-44

ER884 VC 45MU 31-10-42 215MU 18-11 *Hamble V* 1-12 E Afr FTR ops 19-1-43

ER885 VC 39MU 7-11-42 76MU 22-11 *Bluff V* 3-12 NWA FACE 15-3-43

ER886 46MU 4-12-42 222MU 8-12 *Hamble VII* 30-12 Gib 18-1-43 NWA 28-2 USAAF 31-1-44 ME 30-9 SOC 14-3-46

ER887 VC 6MU 18-11 42 82MU 1-12 *Emp Clive* 11-12 Tak 23-1-43 ME 11-3 SOC 31-5-45

ER888 45MU 6-11-42 222MU 16-11 *Bluff IV* 21-11 Gib 8-12 NWA 28-2-43

ER889 VC 6MU 8-11-45 222MU 18-11 *Hamble V* 1-12 Gib 8-1-43 1676Flt 29-4 ME 31-1-45 SOC 29-3

ER890 6MU 6-11-42 222MU 15-11 *Bluff IV* 21-11 Gib 8-12 NWA 28-2-43 Malta 1-7 ME 15-3-45 RHAF 25-4-46

ER891 46MU 6-11-42 222MU 28-11 *Emp Clive* 18-12 Tak 23-1-43 ME 9-2 NAAF 1-11 SOC 31-8-44

ER892 VC(T) 38MU 31-10-42 82MU 13-11 *Bluff IV* 21-11 E Afr FAC3 12-1-43

ER893 45MU 7-11-42 215MU 20-11 *Bluff V* 3-12 Gib 31-12 NWA 28-2-43 Malta 1-8 ME 1-9 NAAF 1-11 IAL 27-6-46

ER894 VC(T) 38MU 31-10-42 76MU 16-11 *Hamble V* 1-12 Gib 18-1-43 NWA 28-2-43 Malta 1-7 SOC 27-4-44 bboc 10-7 SOC 28-9-46

ER913 VC 6MU 6-11-42 222MU 15-11 *Bluff IV* E Afr FTR ops 3-1-43

ER914 VC 39MU 6-11-42 76MU 17-11 *Hamble V* 1-12 Gib 8-1-43 NWA 28-2 Malta 1-7 NAAF 1-11 73S FTR ops 26-6-44

ER915 46MU 7-11-42 222MU 21-11 *Guinean* 30-11 Tak ME 17-1-43 SOC 29-8-46

ER916 39MU 7-11-42 222MU 20-11 *Guinean* 30-11 Tak ME 17-1-43 CE 12-7-45 SOC 5-8

ER917 VC 6MU 6-11-42 222MU 18-11 *Hamble V* 1-12 Gib 8-1-43 FAC3 3-7-44

ER918 VC 39MU 7-11-42 76MU 17-11 *Hamble V* 1-12 Gib 8-1-43 1676Flt 29-4 SOC 28-6-45

ER919 VC(T) 38MU 31-10-42 82MU 13-11 *Bluff IV* 21-11 Gib 8-12 NWA 28-2-43

ER920 VC 45MU 8-11-42 215MU 17-11 *Guinean* 30-11 Tak ME 17-1-43 SOC 28-1-44

ER921 VC 46MU 4-12-42 222MU 8-12 *Emp Tow* 25-12 Gib 225S CE ops 2-2-43

ER922 46MU 6-11-422 215MU 21-11 *Bluff V* 3-12 Gib 31-12 Malta 1-7 ME CE ops 17-7

ER923 46MU 7-11-42 215MU 17-11 *Hamble V* 1-12 Gib 8-2-43 NWA 28-2-43 SOC 28-4-45

ER924 VC 38MU 28-11-42 82MU 7-12 *Bluff VI* 16-12 Gib 13-1-43

ER925 46MU 6-11-42 215MU 17-11 *Bluff IV* 21-11 Gib 8-12 NWA 28-2-43 SOC 31-5-45

ER926 46MU 20-11-42 222MU 7-12 *Hamble VI* 20-12 Gib 13-1-43 NWA USAAF 31-7

ER927 VC 45MU 6-11-42 215MU 17-11 *Hamble V* 1-12 Gib 8-1-43 NWA 28-2 SOC 29-2-44

ER928 VC 39MU 6-11-42 76MU 17-11 *Bluff V* 3-12 Gib 31-12 NWA 28-2-43 Malta 1-7 FAC3 20-9 bboc 31-5-45 ME 21-6-45 SOC 22-11

ER929 45MU 31-10-42 222MU 11-11 *Bluff IV* 21-11 E Afr SOC 31-1-43

ER930 46MU 6-11-42 82MU 23-11 *Zarian* 5-12 lost at sea 18-1-43

ER931 VC 6MU 6-11-42 222MU 18-11 *Hamble V* 1-12 Gib 8-1-43 NWA USAAF 31-7 ME 30-11-44 327S 12-5-45 81RSU 17-5 328S 21-6 FAF 27-11

ER932 VC 39MU 6-11-42 76MU 17-11 *Hamble V* 1-12 Gib 8-1-43

ER933 VC 38MU 8-11-42 76MU 17-11 *Bluff V* 3-12 Gib 31-12 NWA 28-2-43 FTR ops 6-5

ER934 VC 6MU 8-11-42 76MU 17-11 *Guinean* 30-11 Tak 26-12 ME 31-1-43 C3 ops 20-9

ER935 VC 12MU 15-11-42 215MU 15-12 *SS652* 2-1-43 Gib 18-1 NWA 28-2

ER936 VC 12MU 15-11-42 215MU 23-11 *Emp Clive* 11-12 Tak 23-1-43 ME 31-3 FACE 16-9-44

ER937 VC 46MU 6-11-42 215MU 18-11 *Hamble V* 1-12 Gib 8-1-43 NWA 28-2 ME 25-2-45 SOC 13-9

ER938 8MU 17-11-42 215MU 23-11 *Emp Clive* 11-12 Tak 23-1-43 ME 25-2 Malta 1-7 Sic NAASC 31-10 Turk 22-2-45

ER939 VC 45MU 11-12-42 215MU 6-1-43 *Mer Prin* 18-1 Gib 6-2 NWA 28-2 FAC3 11-4

ER940 VC 6MU 6-11-42 82MU 1-12 *Bluff V* 3-12 Gib 31-12 NWA 28-2-43

ER941 38MU 8-11-42 76MU 26-11 *Emp Clive* 11-12 TAk 23-1-43 ME 25-2 NAAF 1-11 USAAF 31-1-44 SOC 26-4-45

ER942 45MU 7-11-42 222MU 16-11 *Bluff IV* 21-11 E Afr FAC3 11-1-43

ER943 45MU 13-11-42 82MU 23-11 *Zarian* 5-12 lost at sea 18-1-43

ER944 VC 6MU 8-11-42 76MU 16-11 *Guinean* 30-1 Tak 28-12 ME 21-1-43 NAAF 1-11 Soc 26-4-45

ER945 12MU 10-12-42 82MU 23-12 *SS652* 2-1-43 Gib 18-1 NWA 28-2

ER946 39MU 6-11-42 76MU 16-11 *Guinean* 30-11 ME 28-1-43 Malta 1-8 Sic SOC 1-12-43

ER947 VC 46MU 6-11-42 6FPP u/s ldg Sherburn-in-Elmet hit obst CE 7-11 SOC 19-11

ER948 VC 45MU 7-11-42 215MU 22-11 *Zarian* 5-12 lost at sea 18-1-43

ER960 45MU 8-11-42 215MU 20-11 *Bluff V* 3-12 Gib 31-12 NWA 28-2-43

ER961 45MU 8-11-42 82MU 26-11 *Zarian* 5-12 lost at sea 18-1-43

'Nigeria Benue Prudence', ER833, a presentation aircraft.

ER962 6MU 14-12-42 82MU 23-12 *Bluff VII* 2-1-43 E Afr 72S C3 ops 5-1

ER963 45MU 25-11-42 222MU 5-12 Gib 6-2-43 NWA 28-2 SOC 31-7

ER964 6MU 7-11-42 FAAC 17-11 ROS 82MU 16-4-43 *SS687* 29-4 Casa 17-5 Malta 1-7 Sic MAAF 21-6-45 SOC 25-7-46

ER965 46MU 8-11-42 82MU 22-11 *Zarian* 5-12 lost at sea 18-1-43

ER966 45MU 25-11-42 222MU 11-12 *Hamble VI* 20-12 Gib 13-1-43

ER967 12MU 20-11-42 215MU 7-12 *Hamble VI* 20-12 Gib 13-1-43 NWA 28-2 Malta 1-7 Sic NAAF 1-11 SOC 29-3-44

ER968 45MU 8-11-42 215MU 18-11 *Hamble V* 1-12 Gib 8-1-43 NWA 28-2 Malta 1-4 Sic NAAF 1-11-43 Trans Com ME 6-9 SOC 31-6-46

ER969 46MU 8-11-42 82MU 22-11 *Zarian* 5-12 lost at sea 18-1-43

ER970 39MUa 6-12-42 222MU 8-12 *Hamble VI* 20-12 Gib 13-1-43

ER971 45MU 8-11-42 82MU 23-11 *Zarian* 5-12 lost at sea 18-1-43

ER972 38MU 17-11-42 76MU 21-11 *Amstel* 29-11 Tak NWA 28-2-43 ME FTR ops 9-4

ER973 38MU 17-11-42 222MU 29-11 *Emp Clive* 11-12 Tak 23-1-43 ME 26-2 NAASC 31-10 SOC 8-3-44 bboc 29-3-45 REAF 29-3

ER974 9MU 13-12-42 222MU 30-12 *Bluff VII* 4-1-43 Gib 18-1 NWA 28-2

ER975 46MU 26-11-42 222MU 8-12 *Hamble VII* 30-12 Gib 18-1-43

ER976 VC 9MU 19-12-42 222MU 7-1-43 *SS653* 19-1 Gib 6-2 NWA 28-2 USAAF 31-10 FACE 22-10-44

ER977 46MU 8-11-42 222MU 23-11 *Zarian* 5-12 lost at sea 18-1-43

ER978 46MU 7-11-42 215MU 19-11 *Hamble V* 1-12 Gib 8-1-43 NWA 28-2-43 Malta 1-7 Sicily ME 30-9 NAAF 30-11 MAAF 21-6-45 SOC 11-4-46

ER979 46MU 7-11-42 215MU 17-11 *Hamble V* 1-12 Gib 8-1-43 NWA 28-2 CE ops 17-4 ME 30-11

ER980 9MU 8-11-42 222MU 22-11 Tak ME 19-1-43 NAAF 30-11 ME 15-3-45 SOC 29-8-46

ER981 9MU 8-11-42 222MU 28-22 *Emp Clive* 18-12 Tak 23-1-43 ME 25-2

ER982 9MU 8-11-42 222MU 23-11 *Emp Clive* 18-12 Tak 23-1-43 NA 30-11 ME 21-6-45 SOC 13-9

ER983 9MU 13-11-42 82MU 26-11 *Emp Clive* 18-12 Tak 23-1-43 ME 28-2 FTR ops 25-4

ER984 9MU 22-11-42 82MU 12-12 *SS652* 2-1-43 Gib 18-1

ER985 9MU 13-11-42 222MU 28-11 *Emp Clive* 18-12 Tak 23-1-43 ME 14-2 NAASC 31-1- to Turk 30-11-44

ER986 9MU 13-11-42 82MU 29-11 *Emp Clive* 11-12 Tak 23-1-43 ME 1-12 MAAF 21-6-45 Trg del 20-9

ER987 9MU 15-11-42 82MU 2-12 *Emp Clive* 18-12 Tak 23-1-43 ME 28-2 FAC3 15-4

ER988 9MU 20-11-42 222MU 7-12 *Hamble VII* 30-12 Gib 18-1-43

ER989 VC 9MU 22-11-42 222MU 7-12 *Hamble VII* 30-12 Gib 18-1-43 NWA SOC 31-7

ER990 VC 9MU 21-11-42 222MU 7-12 *Emp Tow* 23-12 Gib 13-1-43 NWA 28-2 SOC 28-4-45

ER991 9MU 20-11-42 222MU 5-12 *Bluff IV* 16-12 FAAC 3-3-43 SAL 215MU 21-4 *SS732* 5-8 Casa 18-8 NA 30-11 REAF 22-2-45

ER992 9MU 22-11-42 82MU 13-12 *SS652* 2-1-43 Gib 18-1

ER993 VC 9MU 22-11-42 222MU 7-12 *Hamble VII* 30-12 Gib 18-2-43 NWA SOC 31-7

ER994 9MU 22-11-42 82MU 12-12 *SS652* 2-1-43 Gib 18-1 ME 28-4-45 SOC 25-7-46

ER995 45MU 4-12-42 215MU 6-12 *Hamble VI* 20-12 Gib 13-1-43 NAASC 31-10 Malta SOC 1-2-44

ER996 45MU 4-12-42 ROS 222MU 8-12 *Hamble VI* 20-12 Gib 13-1-43 Malta 21-5-43 ME 1-7 SOC 26-43-45

ER997 45MU 4-12-42 ROS 18-12 222MU 8-12 *Hamble VI* 20-12 Gib 13-1-43 ME 31-8-44 SOC 10-1-46

ER998 VC 45MU 4-12-42 82MU 9-12 *SS652* 2-1-43 Gib 18-1 FAF 31-10

ES series all F Mk VC Merlin 46 unless otherwise indicated

ES105 VB 45MU 4-12-42 215MU 9-12 *Hamble VI* 20-12 Gib 13-1-43 NWA 28-2 FACE 9-7

ES106 VB 45MU 4-12-42 215MU 8-12 *Hamble VI* 20-12 Gib 13-1-43

ES107 R-R con to FIX M61 39MU 10-2-43 47MU 30-3 *Ess Trad* 10-4 Casa 25-4 NWA 31-5 Malta 1-6 Sic NA 30-11 SOC 13-9-45

ES108 6MU 8-11-42 82MU 20-11 *Hamble V* 1-12 Gib 8-1-43 NWA 28-2-43 ME CE ops 14-12-44

ES109 33MU 8-11-42 76MU 25-11 *Zarian* 5-12 lost at sea 18-1-43

ES110 45MU 6-11-42 215MU 20-11 *Bluff V* 3-12 Gib 31-12 NWA 28-2-43 MAAF 21-6-45 SOC 30-5-46

ES111 38MU 10-11-42 76MU 26-11 FAAC 26-11 ROS *Emp Tide* 3-2-43 Gib 16-2 NWA 3103 SOC 29-2-44

ES112 38MU 10-11-42 76MU 26-11 *Bluff V* 3-12 E Afr C2 ops 6-1-43 Sic 1-8 NAAF 1-11 SOC 8-3-44

ES113 33MU 8-11-42 76MU 22-11 *Zarian* 5-12 lost at sea 18-1-43

ES114 33MU 8-11-42 76MU 16-11 *Guinean* 30-11 TAk NWA FAC2 9-1-43 ME 31-3 SOC 1-12

ES115 9MU 10-11-42 82MU 26-11 *Emp Clive* 18-12 Tak 23-2-43 ME 9-2 SOC 10-1-44

ES116 45MU 8-11-42 215MU 18-11 *Guinean* 30-11 Tak 28-12 ME 28-1-43 Malta 1-7 Sic NAASC 1-11 ME 26-4-45 SOC 31-5

ES117 VB 46MU 18-11-42 76MU 21-11 *Emp King* 30-11 dam in trans rtp Ottawa Canada 12-2-43

ES118 38MU 8-11-42 76MU 29-11 *Hamble VI* 20-12 Gib 13-1-43 NWA 28-2 111S C3 ops 3-4

ES119 45MU 8-11-42 82MU 23-11 *Zarian* 5-12 lost at sea 18-1-43

ES120 33MU 8-11-42 76MU 22-11 *Emp Clive* 11-12 Tak 23-1-43 Gib 25-2 SOC 18-8

ES121 38MU 8-11-42 76MU 17-11 *Guinean* 30-11 Tak 28-12 ME 31-1-43 NAASC 31-10 MAAF 21-6-45 Trg del 4-10

ES122 VB 39MU 10-11-42 76MU 22-11 *Hamble V* 1-12 Gib FAC3 24-1-43 AST 20-4 *Ocean Rid* 23-9 Casa 10-10 NAASC 31-1- CE 7-6-45 SOC 2-7

ES123 VB 39MU 10-11-42 76MU 22-11 *Hamble V* 1-12 Gib 8-1-43 USAAF 31-10 SOC 26-4-45

ES124 12MU 13-11-42 222MU 21-11 *Guinean* 30-11 Tak 28-12 ME 17-1-43 NAASC 31-1- ME 30-11-44 SOC

ES125 VB 38MU 10-11-42 222MU 30-11 *Hamble V* 1-12 Gib 8-1-43 NWA 28-2 SOC 30-6-44

ES126 VB 39MU 6-11-42 222MU 23-11 *Bluff V* 3-12 Gib 31-12 NWA 28-2-43 111S C3 ops 3-4

ES127 39MU 10-11-42 82MU 27-11 *Emp Clive* 11-12 Tak 23-2-43 NA 30-11 261S second cockpit instal Catania Sicily 1944 SOC 9-20-47

ES128 VB 6MU 10-11-42 76MU 17-11 *Guinean* 30-11 Tak 28-12 ME 31-1-43 SOC 1-7

ES129 39MU 17-11-42 82MU 1-12 Gib 6-2-43 NWA 28-2 MAAF 21-6-45 FAF 12-2-46

ES130 VB 45MU 8-11-42 215MU 20-11 *Guinean* 30-11 Tak 28-12 ME 31-1-43 NAASC 31-10 SOC 26-4-45

ES131 6MU 17-11-42 82MU 1-12 *Emp Clive* 11-12 Tak 23-1-43 ME 25-2 SOC 1-9

ES132 38MU 10-11-42 76MU 23-11 *Zarian* 5-12 lost at sea 18-1-43

ES133 VB 46MU 13-11-42 222MU 26-11 *Emp Clive* 18-12 Tak 23-1-43 ME 20-2 CE ops 27-10-44

ES134 45MU 16-11-42 FACA 18-11 47MU 11-6-43 *Glenb* 3-7 Tak 30-7 ME 10-9

ES135 VB 39MU 10-11-42 222S 21-11 *Guinean* 30-11 Tak 28-12 ME 5-3-43 FTR ops 23-4

ES136 12MU 13-11-42 222S 20-11 *Guinean* 30-11 Tak 28-12 ME 31-1-43 Malta 1-7 Sic NAAF 1-11 MAAF 20-9-45 SOC 8-11

ES137 6MU 9-12-42 82MU 12-12 *SS652* 2-1-43 Gib 18-1 NWA 28-2 241S C3 ops 11-3

ES138 39MU 10-11-42 76MU 23-11 *Skelder* 10-1-43 Gib 6-2 NWA 28-2 FTR ops 24-4 USAAF 31-8

ES139 39MU 6-12-42 76MU 17-12 *SS362* 3-1-43 Gib 18-1 NWA 28-2 Malta 1-8 ME FTR ops 30-9

ES140 8MU 16-11-43 222MU 29-11 *Emp Clive* 11-12 Tak 23-1-43 ME 24-3 MAAF 31-3 SOC 26-4-45

ES141 9MU 15-11-42 82MU 2-12 *Emp Clive* 11-12 TAk 23-1-43 ME 31-3 NA 30-11 SOC 29-2-44

ES142 33MU 8-11-42 76MU 29-11 *Emp Tide* 3-2-43 Gib 16-2 NWA 31-3 ME 1-8 SOC 30-6-45

ES143 45MU 8-11-42 82MU 28-11 *Emp Clive* 18-12 NWA CB ops 17-2-43

ES144 VB 46MU 16-11-42 215MU 22-11 *Emp Clive* 11-12 Tak 23-1-43 ME 22-2 Malta 1-8 NAAF 1-11 RHAF 25-4-46

ES145 38MU 28-11-42 222MU 8-12 *Hamble VI* 20-12 Gib 13-1-43 NWA 28-2 SOC 29-2-44

ES146 6MU 17-11-42 82MU 5-12 *Hamble VI* 20-12 Gib 13-1-43 NWA 28-2

ES147 VB 45MU 16-11-42 222MU 11-12 *Hamble VI* 20-12 Gib 13-1-43 NWA 28-2 FTR ops 12-4

ES148 33MU 9-12-42 82MU 20-12 *Inch* 11-1-43 Tak 7-2 ME 8-3 Sic 1-8 NAAF 1-11 MAAF 21-6-45 SOC 30-8

ES149 38MU 6-12-42 82MU 12-12 *SS652* 2-1-43 Gib 18-1

ES150 45MU 20-11-42 222MU 2-12 *Emp Clive* 11-12 Tak 23-1-43 ME 21-2 Sic 1-8 FAC3 21-6-44 SOC 22-2-45

ES151 VB 46MU 13-11-42 222MU 23-11 *Zarian* 5-12 lost at sea 18-1-43

ES152 38MU 13-11-42 76MU 23-11 *Zarian* 5-12 lost at sea 18-1-43

ES153 45MU 13-11-42 82MU 23-11 *Zarian* 5-12 lost at sea 18-1-43

ES154 12MU 13-11-42 222MU 20-11 *Guinean* 30-11 Tak 28-12 ME 31-1-43 NAASC 30-10 SOC 31-8-44

ES168 45MU 13-11-42 82MU 23-11 *Zarian* 5-12 lost at sea 18-1-43

ES169 VB 38MU 17-11-42 76MU 23-11 *Zarian* 5-12 lost at sea 18-1-43

ES170 VB 12MU 13-11-42 222MU 10-11 *SS647* 19-12 Gib 6-2-43 NWA FTR ops 20-4

ES171 46MU 13-11-42 15MU 22-11 *Zarian* 5-12 lost at sea 18-1-43

ES172 VB 38MU 10-11-42 76MU 26-11 *Emp Clive* 11-12 Tak 23-1-43 ME 31-4 Malta 1-7 Sic NAASC 31-1- SOC 26-4-45

ES173 VB 38MU 17-11-42 222MU 29-11 *Emp Clive* 11-12 TAk 23-1-43 ME 18-7 SOC 13-9-45

ES174 46MU 13-11-42 215MU 22-11 *Zarian* 5-12 lost at sea 18-1-43

ES175 VB 45MU 13-11-42 82MU 28-11 *Emp Clive* 11-12 Tak 23-1-43 ME 14-2 NAAF 1-11 SOC 26-4-45

ES176 VB 39MU 6-12-42 222MU 9-12 *Hamble VII* 30-12 Gib 20-1-43 NWA 28-2 ME 1-9 NAASC 31-10 RHAF 25-4-46

ES177 VB 46MU 19-11-42 82MU 6-12 *Hamble VI* 29-12 Gib 13-1-43 NWA 28-2 USAAF 31-7 FAC3 26-10

ES178 9MU 10-1-42 FAAC 24-1 222MU 26-1-43 ROS *SS686* 24-4 Casa 17-5 SOC 28-4-45

ES179 VB 46MU 20-11-42 222MU 7-12 *Hamble VII* 20-12 Gib 18-1-43 NWA 28-2 241S C3 ops 2-3

ES180 VB 45MU 25-11-42 215MU 2-12 *Hamble VI* 20-12 Gib 13-1-43 NWA 28-2 FTR ops 22-4

ES181 VB 46MU 25-11-42 222MU 8-12 *Hamble VII* 30-12 Gib 18-1-43 NWA 28-2 FAC3 11-3

ES182 9MU 22-12-42 222MU 9-1-43 *Mer Prin* 18-1-43 Gib 6-2 USAAF 12-31 lost at Malta 30-6

ES183 9MU 31-12-42 82MU 11-1-43 43S E Afr FTR ops 2-2

ES184 VB 39MU 6-12-42 222MU 8-12 *Hamble VI* 20-12 Gib 13-1-43

ES185 VA to FIX M63 39MU 11-6-43 52MU 21-6 *La Pampa* 2-7 Casa 16-7 ME 1-9 NAAF 1-11

ES186 VB 46MU 4-12-43 82MU 13-12 *SS652* 2-1-43 CA ops 9-2 1676 Flt Gib 29-4 NA 29-9 USAAF 31-10 SOC 28-4-45

ES187 no record

ES188 VC(T) 12MU 21-1-43 47MU 30-1 *Fort Senn* 13-2 Tak 11-3 ME 8-5 NAAF 1-11 SOC 21-1-46

ES189 VB 46MU 4-12-42 222MU 9-12 *Hamble VII* 30-12 Gib 18-1-43

ES190 VB 46MU 20-12-42 82MU 14-1-43 *Mer Prin* 18-1 Gib 6-2 NWA 28-2 SOC 26-4-45

ES191 VB 46MU 4-12-42 82MU 12-12 *SS652* 2-1-43 Gib 18-1 NWA 28-2 ME 20-22-44

ES192 VB 39MU 6-12-42 222MU 8-12 *Hamble VI* 20-12 Gib 13-1-43 NWA 28-2 FAF 1-1- ME 26-4-45 SOC 28-2-46

ES193 VB 46MU 4-12-42 215MU 7-12 *SS652* 2-1-43 Gib 18-1 NWA 28-2 SOC 21-7

ES194 VB 45MU 9-12-42 215MU 3-1-43 *SS653* 19-1 Gib 6-2

ES195 12MU 20-12-42 215MU 31-12 *Skeld* 10-1-43 Gib 6-2 NWA 28-2 FAF 31-10 USAAF 31-5-44 ME 30-11

ES196 46MU 21-11-42 82MU 6-12 *Atlan City* 20-1-43 Tak 11-3 ME 31-3

ES197 6MU 17-11-42 FACB 23-11 WAL 47MU 6-6-43 Tak 16-7 ME 23-8 SOC 31-8-44

ES198 12MU 15-11-42 215MU 30-12 *Atlan City* 20-1-43 Tak 11-3 ME 22-4 Malta 1-7 Sic NAAF 1-11 FAC3 31-1-44

ES199 6MU 17-11-42 82MU 1-12 *Emp Clive* 11-12 Tak 23-1-43 ME 20-2 C3 ops 13-9

ES200 39MU 17-11-42 76MU 24-11 *Emp Clive* 11-12 Tak 23-1-43 ME 16-2 SOC 26-3-45

ES201 VB 6MU 17-11-42 82MU 21-11 *Amstal* 29-11 Tak ME 1-8-43 Sic NAASC 31-10 SOC 18-10-45

ES202 CRD VA 15-11-42 39MU 22-8-43 *Emp Grebe* 15-9 Casa 29-9 NAAF 1 SAAF FTR ops 13-12

ES203 VB 12MU 13-11-42 222MU 20-11 *Emp Clive* 18-12 Tak 23-1-43 ME 14-2 SOC 1-12

ES204 46MU 13-11-42 215MU 22-11 *Emp Clive* 11-12 Tak 23-1-43 ME 22-2 C3 ops 28-9

ES205 45MU 16-11-42 82MU 23-11 *Zarian* 5-12 lost at sea 18-1-43

ES206 12MU 15-11-42 215MU 23-11 *Emp Clive* 11-12 Tak 23-1-43 ME 20-2 Malta 1-8 SOC 8-2-44

ES207 45MU 16-11-42 222MU 29-11 *Emp Clive* 11-12 Tak ME 15-3-45 SOC 20-8-46

ES208 12MU 15-11-42 215MU 23-11 *Zarian* 5-12 lost at sea 18-1-43

ES209 45MU 20-11-42 222MU 28-11 *Emp Clive* 18-12 Tak ME 18-2-43 NAAF 1-11 SOC 26-9-46

ES210 45MU 13-11-42 82MU 23-11 *Zarian* 5-12 lost at sea 18-1-43

ES211 8MU 16-11-42 76MU 30-11 *Emp Clive* 11-12 Tak 23-1-43 ME 20-2 SOC 13-9-45

ES212 39MU 17-11-42 82MU 29-11 *Emp Clive* 11-12 Tak 23-1-43 ME 25-2 92S FTR ops 30-3

ES213 6MU 18-11-42 82MU 22-11 *Zarian* 5-12 lost at sea 18-1-43

ES214 45MU 21-11-42 222MU 29-11 *Emp Clive* 18-12 Tak 23-1-43 ME 9-2 SOC 10-4

ES227 VB 8MU 16-11-42 222MU 6-12 *SS647* 19-12 Gib 6-2-43 NWA 28-2 ME 21-6-45 SOC 13-9

ES228 VB 12MU 20-11-42 215MU 7-12 *Hamble VI* 20-12 Gib 13-1-43 NWA SOC 30-4

ES229 46MU 18-11-42 222MU 5-12 *SS647* 19-12 Gib 6-2-43 NWA 28-2 93S C3 ops 16-3 bboc 21-4-45 FAF 14-3-46

ES230 VB 33MU 9-12-42 222MU 21-12 *SS625* 2-1-43 Gib 18-1 SOC 26-4-45

ES231 12MU 20-11-42 22MU 3-12 *Emp Clive* 11-12 Tak 23-1-43 ME 9-3 NAASC 31-10 MAAF 21-6-45 Trg del 6-9

ES232 6MU 28-11-42 215MU 6-12 *Emp S Tren* 11-1-43 Aust 11-4

ES233 12MU 20-11-42 222MU 5-12 *Emp Clive* 11-12 Tak 23-1-43 ME 21-2 SOC 29-8-46

ES234 VB 6MU 18-11-42 82MU 22-11 *Zarian* 5-12 lost at sea 18-1-43

ES235 VB 39MU 17-11-42 222MU 29-11 *Emp Clive* 11-12 Tak 23-1-43 ME 14-2 FACB 9-12

ES236 46MU 21-11-42 82MU 6-12 *SS647* 19-12 Gib 6-2-43 NWA 28-2 SOC 28-4-45

ES237 8MU 16-11-42 82MU 1-12 *Emp Clive* 11-12 Tak 23-1-43 ME 20-2 SOC 10-4

ES238 6MU 29-11-42 215MU 7-12 *Port Dun* 19-12 Aust 28-2-43

ES239 VB 46MU 28-11-42 82MU 13-12 *SS652* 2-1-42 Gib 18-1 NWA 28-2 SOC 26-4-45

ES240 VB 12MU 25-11-42 222MU 30-12 *Atlan City* 20-1-43 Tak 11-3 ME 26-3 C3 ops 2-2-44

ES241 38MU 6-12-42 222MU 9-12 *Hamble VI* 18-12 Gib 13-1-43 NWA 28-2

ES242 46MU 28-11-42 76MU 26-12 *Atlan City* 20-1-43 Tak 11-3 ME 10-7 NAAF 1-11

ES243 45MU 6-12 FAAC 20-12 ROS ME 31-6-43 to Turk 29-3-45

ES244 VB 12MU 29-11-42 82MU 23-12 *SS652* 2-1-43 Gib 18-1 NWA USAAF31-7 103MU SOC 12-3-46

ES245 38MU 28-11-42 222MU 7-12 *SS647* 19-12 Gib 6-2-43 NWA 28-2 SOC 31-7

ES246 VB 6MU 28-11-42 82MU 11-12 *SS652* 2-1-43 Gib 18-1 NWA 28-2 Malta 1-7 Sic NAAF 1-11 ME 25-2-45 SOC 27-6-46

ES247 6MU 18-11-42 76MU 20-11 *Zarian* 5-12 lost at sea 18-1-43

ES248 VB 46MU 21-11-42 215MU 12-4-43 *SS686* 24-4 Cassa 17-5 NWA 1-7 ME 25-2-45 SOC 14-3-46

ES249 6MU 28-11-42 215MU 7-12 *Port Dun* 19-12 Aust 28-2-43

ES250 45MU 20-11-42 215MU 25-11 *Emp Clive* 11-12 Tak 23-1-43 ME 14-2 RHAF 25-4-46

ES251 6MU 18-11-42 82MU 23-11 *Emp Clive* 11-122 Tak 23-1-43 ME 15-2 Malta 1-7 Sic to Turk 22-2-45

ES252 VB 45MU 20-11-42 222MU 28-11 *Emp Clive* 14-12 Tak 23-1-43 ME 16-8 NAAF 1-11 SOC 26-4-45

ES253 46MU 21-11-42 222MU 9-12 *SS652* 2-1-43 Gib 18-1 E Afr C3 ops 5-2

ES254 12MU 28-11-42 222MU 7-12 *Hamble VI* 20-12 Gib 13-1-43 CE ops 11-9-46

ES255 VB38MU 28-11-42 82MU 6-12 *SS647* 19-12 Gib 6-2-43 NWA 28-2 152S C3 ops 19-3

ES256 VB 46MU 10-12-42 76MU 20-12 *Hamble VII* 30-12 Gib 18-1-43 NWA 28-2 AST E CE 11-4 Casa 27-9 NAASC 31-10 SOC 26-4-45

ES257 12MU 21-11-42 215MU 8-3-43 *SS672* 25-3 Gib 12-4 Malta 1-5 NAAF 21-6-45 IAF 27-6 as MM4013

ES258 45MU 4-12-42 82MU 12-12 *SS652* 2-1-43 Gib 18-1 NWA 28-2 SOC 28-4-45

ES259 6MU 28-11-42 215MU 5-12 *Port Dun* 19-12 Aust 28-2-43

ES260 45MU 4-12-42 7FPP downwind app banked steeply std cd CE Dyce 11-12

ES261 VB 38MU 28-11-42 82MU 6-12 *Bluff V* 16-12 Gib 13-1-43 NWA SOC 31-7

ES262 VB 12MU 28-11-42 222MU 5-12 *SS647* 19-12 Gib 6-2-43 Malta 1-10 FAC3 30-5-44

ES263 9MU 11-12-42 82MU 28-12 *SS653* 19-1 Gib 6-2-43

ES264 VB 38MU 6-12-42 76MU 9-12 *Hamble VI* 20-12 Gib 13-1-43 USAAF NWA 1-10 FAC3 20-7-44

ES276 VB 46MU 225-11-42 222MU 7-12 *Hamble VI* 20-12 Gib 13-1-43 USAAF 31-10 ME 31-1-45 SOC 9-5-46

ES277 46MU 9-12-42 222MU 15-12 *Emp Tow* 23-12 Gib 13-1-43 NWA SOC 30-4

ES278 46MU 9-12-42 ROS 215MU 21-1-43 *Well Crt* 18-2 Gib 7-3 NWA 31-3 SOC 28-4-45

ES279 38MU 9-12-42 76MU 18-12 *Hamble VII* 30-12 Gib 18-1-43 73 OTU Fayid Egypt 1944

ES280 38MU 6-12-42 222MU 9-12 *Hamble VI* 18-12 Gib 13-1-43 NWA 28-2 ME 1-8 SOC 26-4-45

ES281 38MU 9-12-42 76MU 18-12 *Hamble VI* 30-12 Gib 18-1-43 NWA 31-3 Sic 1-8 NAAF 1-11 FACE 24-8-44

ES282 38MU 6-12-42 82MU 12-12 *Hamble VII* 30-12 Gib 18-1-43 Malta 1-7 93S FTR ops 13-7

ES283 VB 12MU 28-11-42 82MU 12-12 *SS652* 2-1-43 Gib 18-1

ES284 12MU 28-11-42 222MU 7-12 *SS647* 19-12 Gib 6-2-43 NWA 28-2 USAAF ME 31-1-45 REAF 29-3-45

ES285 12MU 24-1-43 222MU 4-2 *SS657* 19-2 Gib 9-3 MAAF 21-6-45 FAF 28-2-46

ES286 VB 46MU 10-12-42 215MU 23-12 *Inch* 11-1-43 Tak 7-2 ME 1-6 FTR ops 2-3-44

ES287 46MU 28-11-42 82MU 113-12 FAAC 8-12 *SS652* 2-1-43 Gib 18-1 Malta 1-7 Sic NAAF 1-11

ES288 38MU 6-12-42 GAL 18-12 82MU 24-1-43 *SSLS230* 9-2 Tak 28-3 ME 28-4 Malta SOC 21-5

ES289 46MU 4-12-42 222MU 18-12 *Emp Tow* 23-12 Gib 13-1-43 NA 31-11 C3 ops 22-1-44

ES290 45MU 4-12-42 222MU 18-12 *SS652* 2-1-43 Gib 18-1 ME 31-1-45

ES291 R-R to FIX M63 332S 16-2-43 FTR ops 5-4

ES292 46MU 10-12-42 76MU 21-12 *SSJ52* 3-1-43 Gib 18-1 ME 1-10 C3 ops 23-1-44

ES293 33MU 9-12-42 82MU 20-12 *SS652* 2-1-43 Gib 18-1 NWA FACE 31-7 ME 15-3-45 SOC 29-8-46

ES294 6MU 29-11-42 222MU 5-12 *SS647* 19-12 Gib 6-2-43 NWA 28-2 Malta 1-7 Sic SOC 8-3-44 bboc 21-6-45 FAF 10-6-47

ES295 45MU 9-12-42 82MU 9-1-43 *Atlan City* 20-1 Tak 11-3 ME 28-4 Malta 1-7 Sic NAAF 1-11 to Turk 29-3-45

ES296 12MU 29-11-42 82MU 13-12 *Hamble VII* 30-12 Gib 18-1-43 USAAF 31-12 SOC 27-2-44

ES297 45MU 10-12-42 76MU 23-12 *SSJ52* 3-1-43 Gib 18-1 NWA 28-2 USAAF 31-10

ES298 38MU 15-12-42 222MU 21-12 *SS652* 2-1-43 Gib 18-1 NWA 225S C3 ops 3-4

ES299 6MU 9-12-42 82MU 12-12 *SS652* 2-1-43 Gib 18-1 NWA 28-2 FTR ops 23-6-44

ES300 33MU 9-12-42 222MU 20-12 *SS652* 2-1-43 Gib 18-1 Malta 1-8 ME 30-11-44 to Turk 28-12

ES301 VB 6MU 22-11-42 82MU 22-12 *Hamble VII* 30-12 Gib 18-1-43 SOC 26-4-45

ES302 38MU 6-12042 222MU 9-12 *Emp Tow* 23-12 Gib 13-1-43 152S FTR ops 24-3

ES303 12MU 29-11-42 76MU 29-12 *Atlan City* 20-1-43 Tak 11-3 ME 6-5 NAAF 30-11 SOC 8-3-44

ES295, Sicily August 1943, Pachino Airfield. Sold to Turkey, March 1945.

ES304 6MU 29-11-42 222MU 5-12 *SS647* 19-12 6-2-43 NWA 28-2 C3 ops 2-5

ES305 6MU 28-11-42 82MU 6-12 *SS647* 19-12 Gib 6-2-43 NWA 28-2 ME 30-11-44 to Turk 28-12

ES306 33MU 9-12-42 82MU 20-12 *SS652* 2-1-43 Malta 1-10 MAAF FTR ops 16-12-45

ES307 6MU 29-11-42 215MU 6-12 *Emp Stren* 11-1-43 Aust 11-4

ES308 33MU 20-12-42 222MU 31-12 *Mer Prin* 18-1-43 Gib 6-2 RGS a/c pool FAC3 10-3

ES309 9MU 11-12-42 82MU 28-12 *Skeld* 10-1-43 Gib 6-2 NWA 28-2

ES310 VC(T) 45MU 21-1-43 215MU 5-2 FAAC 3-2 *Liberian* 5-5 Tak 29-5 FAC3 22-6

ES311 46MU 9-12-42 FACB 9-12 CRU 47MU 8-4-43 *Emp Bar* 2-5 Casa 17-5 NWA 1-10 SOC 26-4-45

ES312 46MU 9-12-42 47MU 29-12 *SS653* 19-1-43 Gib 6-2

ES313 46MU 9-12-42 215MU 29-12 *Atlan City* 20-1-43 Tak 11-3 ME 11-4 Malta 3-6 SOC FH69.40

ES314 39MU 6-12-42 82MU 14-12 *SS652* 2-1-43 Gib 18-1 NWA 28-2 SOC 31-7

ES315 46MU 4-12-42 82MU 17-12 *Inch* 11-1-43 Tak 7-2 ME 9-3 Malta 1-8 Sic ME 15-2-45 SOC 27-6-46

ES316 12MU 29-11-42 222MU 12-12 *Hamble VI* 20-12 Gib 13-1-43

ES317 46MU 9-12-42 76MU 17-12 *SS117* 4-1-43 Gib 18-1

ES318 46MU 10-12-42 FACB 21-12 AST 76MU 21-2-43 *Fort l M* 12-3 Tak 20-4 ME 27-5

ES335 46MU 9-12-42 82MU 1-1-43 *Atlan City* 20-1 Tak 11-3 ME 21-4 SOC 30-6-45

ES336 ME 21-2-43 FAC3 28-2-44

ES337 38MU 9-12-42 76MU 18-12 *Hamble VII* 30-12 Gib 18-1-43 NWA SOC 31-7

ES338 45MU 9-12-42 222MU 18-12 *SS652* 2-1-43 Gib 18-1

ES339 38MU 6-12-42 82MU 12-12 *SS652* 2-1-43 Gib 18-1 NWA 28-2 FTR ops 6-4

ES340 45MU 6-12-42 222MU 18-12 222MU 18-12 *SS652* 2-1-43 Gib 18-1 USAAF 12-31 lost over Sicily 11-7

ES341 45MU 9-12-42 222MU 29-12 *Atlan City* 20-1-43 Tak 11-3 ME 27-4 SOC 29-8-46

ES342 45MU 9-12-42 215MU 6-1-43 *SS653* 19-1 Gib 6-2 NWA 1-10 73S FTR ops 27-6-44

ES343 38MU 9-12-42 82MU 14-12 *Hamble VII* 30-12 Gib 18-1-43 C3 ops 8-1-44

ES344 38MU 9-12-42 76MU 18-12 *Hamble VII* 30-12 Gib 18-1-43

ES345 45MU 9-12-42 76MU 24-12 *SS652* 3-1-43 Gib 18-1 FAC2 18-1 Malta 1-11 NA 1-1-44 SOC 28-4-45

ES346 12MU 29-11-42 222MU 21-12 *SS652* 2-1-43 Gib 18-1 E Afr FAC3 6-2

ES347 45MU 9-12-42 222MU 20-12 *SS652* 2-1-43 Gib 18-1 NWA 28-2 C3 ops 24-4

ES348 45MU 4-12-42 82MU 10-12 *Emp Tow* 23-12 Gib 13-1-43 1676Flt 29-4 ME 31-1-45 to Turk 22-2-45

ES349 45MU 9-12-42 222MU 31-12 *SS653* 19-1-43 Gib 6-2

ES350 12MU 10-12-42 82MU 23-12 *SS652* 2-1-43 Gib 18-1

ES351 45MU 6-12-42 82MU 17-12 *Bluff VII* 4-1-43 Gib 18-1 NWA 28-2 FAC/28-2

ES352 46MU 10-12-42 222MU 29-12 *Emp Hav* 19-1-43 Gib 6-2 Malta 1-7 Sic 43S NAAF 1-11 SOC 8-3-44

ES353 6MU 9-12-42 76MU 15-12 *Hamble VII* 30-12 Gib 18-1-43 NWA SOC 31-7

ES354 38MU 6-12-42 76MU 11-12 *Hamble VII* 30-12 Gib 18-1-43

ES355 6MU 9-12-42 82MU 12-12 *SS652* 2-1-43 Gib 18-1 NWA 28-2 FTR ops 18-6 FH95.45

ES356 45MU 6-12-42 76MU 18-12 *Bluff VII* 4-1-43 Gib 18-1 FTR ops 2-3

ES357 45MU 6-12-42 76MU 23-12 *Bluff VII* 4-1-43 Gib 18-1 Malta 1-6 SOC 28-4-45

ES358 33MU 20-12-42 82MU 10-10-43 *Atlan City* 30-1 Tak 11-3 ME 18-4 NAASC 31-10 CE 12-12-44

ES359 VB HCR GPO 6MU 20-12-42 222MU 8-1-43 *Atlan City* 30-1 Tak ME 20-3 to Turk 29-3-45

ES360 39MU 15-12-42 76MU 21-12 *Bluff VII* 4-1-43 Gib 18-12

ES361 9MU 11-12-42 82MU 28-12 *Skeld* 10-1-43 Gib 6-2 NWA 28-2 225S FAC3 21-3

ES362 45MU 11-12-42 222MU 31-12 *SS653* 19-1-43 Gib 6-2 USAAF NA 30-11 32S SOC 26-4-45

ES363 45MU 9-12-42 215MU 26-12 *SS652*2-1-43 Gib 18-1 NWA USAAF 31-7 ME 31-1-45 eng fire a/c aban CE 15-3

ES364 12MU 10-12-42 222MU 27-12 *Skeld* 10-1-43 Gib 6-2 NWA 28-2 SOC 28-4-45

ES365 6MU 15-12-42 82MU 13-1-43 *Nairn* 10-2 Tak 11-3 ME 21-4 Malta 1-7 Sic ME 417S C2 ops 10-8 SOC 8-3-44

ES366 46MU 10-12-42 82MU 23-12 *Bluff VII* 4-1-43 Gib 18-1

ES367 8MU 14-12-42 215MU 22-12 *Aust Clan* 27-1-43 Aust 11-3

ES368 38MU 20012-42 76MU 28-12 *SSK117 4-1-43* Gib 18-1 E Afr CE ops 5-2

ES369 46MU 10-12-42 76MU 18-12 ROS *SS682* 12-4-43 Casa 24-5 118MU Malta 31-1-44

JG series all F Mk Vc Merlin 46 unless outherwise indicated.

JG713 46MU 10-12-42 82MU 21-12 Gib 18-1-43 NWA 28-2 SOC 29-2-44

JG714 45MU 11-12-42 82MU 14-8 India 3-11-43 FTR ops 5-2-44

JG715 46MU 10-12-42 47MU 29-12 *SS653* 19-1-42 Gib 6-2 Malta 1-7 Sic SOC 29-2-44

JG716 6MU 9-12-42 76MU 15-12 Gib 9-3-43 NWA 31-3

JG717 38MU 24-12-42 82MU 25-1-43 *Bluff VIII* 18-2 Gib 7-3 NWA 31-3 SOC 31-10

ES352, struck off charge March 1944.

JG718 38MU 15-12-42 76MU 24-12 *AAJ52* 3-1-43 Gib 8-1 NWA SOC 31-7

JG719 38MU 15-12-42 76MU 21-12 *Bluff VIII* 4-1-43 Gib 18-1 NWA SOC 1-7

JG720 39MU 17-12-42 215MU 31-12 *Atlan City* 20-1-43 Tak 11-3 ME 17-4 Malta 1-7 Sic NAAF 1-11 SOC 28-4-45

JG721 46MU 15-12-42 82MU 10-1-43 *Atlan City* 20-1 Tak 11-3 ME 9-5 NAAF 1-11 SOC 26-4-45

JG722 VA to FIX M63 39MU 11-6-43 82MU 23-6 *La Pampa* 14-7 NWA C3 ops 25-12

JG723 12MU 10-12-42 82MU 28-12 *Inch* 11-1-43 Tak 7-2 ME 9-3 SOC 10-1-46

JG724 39MU 15-12-42 76MU 20-12 *Bluff VIII* 4-1-43 Gib 18-1 NWA 1-7 Sic 1-8 NAASC 31-10 SOC 31-8-44

JG725 46MU 11-12-42 215MU 20-12 *SS622* 2-1-43 Gib 18-1 NWA 28-2 FTR ops 25-4

JG726 9MU 11-12-42 222MU 24-12 *Inch* 11-1-43 Tak 7-2 ME 14-3

JG727 12MU 10-12-42 222MU 20-12 *SS652* Gib 18-1-43 NWA 28-2 43S C3 ops 13-5

JG728 46MU 15-12-42 215MU 24-2-43 *Asphalian* 5-3 Aust

JG729 39 MU 15-12-42 76MU 23-12 *SSJ52* 3-1-43 Gib 18-1 NWA 28-2 USAAF SOC 26-4-45

JG730 6MU 14-12-42 222MU 24-12 *South* 30-12 Gib 13-1-43

JG731 39MU 17-12-42 215MU 30-12 *Aust Star* 27-1-43 Aust 11-3 54S FTR ops 6-7

JG732 38MU 21-1-43 222MU 25-1 *Alphard* 5-3 Tak 20-4 ME 10-6 NAAF 1-11

JG733 38MU 15-12-42 76MU 29-12 *Atlan City* 20-1-43 Tak 11-3 ME 9-5 NA 30-11 32S to Turk 29-3-45

JG734 46MU 15-12-42 215MU 28-1-43 *Alph* 5-3 Tak 20-4 ME 1-6 SOC 29-8-46

JG735 6MU 14-12-42 222MU 24-12 *South* 30-12 Gib 13-1-43

JG736 39MU 15-12 76MU 23-12 *SSJ62* 3-1-43 Gib 18-1 NWA 25-2 ME 29-3-45 SOC 29-5-46

JG737 38MU 15-12-42 76MU 23-12 *SSJ62* 3-1-43 Gib 18-1 NWA 25-2

JG738 El Obeid Kurdofan 39MU 22-1-43 222MU 25-1-43 *Alph* 5-3 Tak 20-4 ME 7-5 NA 30-11 SOC 29-8-46

JG739 VA to FIX M63 6MU 13-6-43 76MU 23-6 *La Pampa* 2-7 Casa 14-7 ME 1-9 NAAF 1-11 SOC 18-10-45

JG740 8MU 14-12-42 215MU 29-12 *Aust Star* 27-1-43 Aust 11-3

JG741 39MU 17-12-42 82MU 22-12 *SSK117*4-1-43 Gib 18-1 NWA 25-2 C3 ops 11-5

JG742 38MU 15-12-42 76MU 21-12 *SSJ52* 3-1-43 Gib 18-1 NWA 28-2 SOC 29-2-44

JG743 38MU 15-12-42 76MU 28-12 *Atlan City* 20-1-43 Tak 11-3 ME 20-5

JG744 38MU 14-12-42 76MU 23-12 *SSK117* 4-1-43 Gib 18-1 to Turk 28-12-44

JG745 46MU 23-12-42 82MU 15-1-43 *Mer Prin* 18-1-43 Gib 6-2-43 NWA 28-2 SOC 26-4-45

JG746 39MU 15-12-42 76MU 21-12 *SSJ62* 3-1-43 Gib 18-1 NWA 28-2 Malta 1-7 Sic ME 30-9 NAASC 31-10

JG747 38MU 15-12-42 222MU 15-1-43 *Emp Tide* 3-2 Gib 16-2 FA FTR 22-3

JG748 38MU 14-12-42 76MU 21-12 *SSK117* 4-1-43 Gib 18-1

JG749 33MU 15-2-43 52MU 1-3 *Harpal* 22-3 Casa 6-4 NWA 30-4 SOC 26-4-45

JG750 JG7538MU 15-12-42 222MU 30-12 *Skeld* 10-1-43 Gib 4-2 NWA 28-2 SOC 28-4-45

JG751 38MU 14-12-42 76MU 21-12 *SSJ53* 3-1-43 Gib 18-1 NWA 28-2 Malta 1-7 SOC 13-7

JG752 8MU 14-12-42 52MU 1-1-43 *SS653* 19-1 Gib 6-2 NWA 28-2 C3 ops 243S 26-3

JG769 6MU 14-12-42 52MU 30-12 *Skeld* 10-1-43 Gib 6-2 NWA 28-2 Malta 1-7 Sic NAAF 1-11 FAC3 7-4-44

JG770 46MU 29-12-42 82MU 14-1-43 *Emp Hav* 19-1 Gib 6-2

JG771 46MU 23-12-42 222MU 13-1-43 *Emp Tide* 3-2 Gib 16-2 NWA 31-2 Malta 1-7 SOC 14-7

JG772 6MU 14-12-42 222MU 24-12 *South* 30-12 Gib 20-1-43

JG773 38MU 2-1-43 222MU 10-2 *Fort Hus* 20-2 Gib 7-3 NWA 31-3

JG774 45MU 9-12-42 215MU 3-1-43 *SS653* 19-1 Gib 6-2 NWA 28-2 ME 30-11-44 SOC 29-8-46

JG775 38MU 2-1-43 82MU 25-1 *Well Crt* 18-2 Gib 7-3

JG776 38MU 2-1-43 222MU 13-1 *Emp tide* 3-2 Gib 16-2 NWA 28-2 FTR ops 30-8-44

JG777 46MU 14-1-43 215MU 27-1 *Clear* 28-1 Gib 25-2 NWA CE ops 13-4

JG778 38MU 2-1-43 222MU 13-1 *Emp Tide* 3-2 Gib 16-2 NWA 28-2 FAF 31-7 SOC Oct '44

JG779 38MU 21-12-42 222MU 7-1-43 *SS653* 19-1 Gib 6-2 USAAF NWA 1-10 MAAF 21-6-45 Trg del 6-9-45

JG780 38MU 21-12-42 222MU 31-12 *SSK117* 4-1-43 Gib 18-1 NWA USAAF 31-7 FAF 14-2-46

JG781 12MU 6-1-43 82MU 15-1 *SSLS230* 9-2 Tak 28-3 ME 1-7 Malta Sic 1-8 SOC 29-8-46

JG782 38MU 2-1-43 222MU 13-1 *Emp Tide* 3-2 Gib 16-2 NWA 28-2 SOC 28-4-45

JG783 46MU 6-1-43 47MU 28-1 *Well Crt* 18-2 Gib 7-3 NWA 31-3 CE ops 3-3-44

JG784 46MU 26-1-43 215MU 1-6 *SS707* 10-6 Casa 29-6 ME 1-8 NAAF 1-11

JG785 12MU 21-1-43 215MU *Alph* 5-3-43 Tak 20-4 ME 10-6 SOC 1-11-44

JG786 12MU 21-1-43 47MU 30-1 *Fort Senn* 13-2 Tak 11-3 ME 9-5 MAAF 1-11 SOG 21-4-45

JG787 12MU 21-1-43 215MU 30-1 *Fort Senn* 13-2 Tak 11-3 ME 30-3 FAC3 27-12

JG788 45MU 29-1-43 215MU 3-2 *Alph* 5-3 Tak 20-4 ME 23-5 Turk 30-11-44

JG789 M50 46MU 15-3-43 215MU 29-3 *Emp Bar* 2-5 Casa 17-5 ME 1-7 NAAF 1-11 SOC 26-4-45

JG790 45MU 22-1-43 215MU 3-2 *Alph* 5-3 Tak 20-4 ME 20-5 Malta 1-9 Sic

JG791 46MU 29-1-43 222MU 4-2 *SS657* 19-2 Gib 9-3 dam by sea water due e/a CE ret to UK 17-7

JG792 46MU 26-1-43 215MU 28-2 *SS672* 25-3 Gib 12-4 NWA 30-4 Malta 1-7 Sic NAAF 1-11 SOC 26-4-45

JG793 45MU 29-1-43 215MU 18-2 *SS661* 10-3 Gib 26-4 Malta 1-7 ME 1-10 SOC 26-4-45

JG794 12MU 14-12-42 215MU 18-12 *SS653* 19-1-43 Gib 6-2 NWA SOC 31-7

JG795 8MU 14-12-42 215MU 27-12 *Aust Star* 27-1-43 Aust 11-3

JG796 8MU 14-12-42 215MU 27-12 *Aust Star* 27-1-43 Aust 11-3

JG797 39MU 17-12-42 47MU 29-12 *SS653* 19-1-43 Gib 6-2 NWA 28-2

JG798 12MU 17-12-42 215MU 7-1-43 *Atlan City* 20-1 Tak 11-3 ME 2-4 SOC 13-1-46

JG799 38MU 15-12-42 76MU 28-12 *SSK117* 4-1-43 Gib 18-1 ME 1-9 NAASC 31-10 SOC 8-3-44

JG800 39MU 22-1-43 76MU 27-1-43 *Clear* 25-2 Gib 31-3 USAAF 31-10 FTR ops 26-5-44

JG801 46MU 15-12-42 222MU 30-12 *SSK117* 4-1-43 Gib 18-1 NAAF 31-1-44 ME 25-2-45 SOC 31-5-45

JG802 45MU 24-1-43 215MU 9-2 *Alph* 5-3 Tak 20-4 ME 1-7 NAASC 31-10 CE 13-9-45 SOC 26-3-46

JG803 38MU 15-12-42 222MU 29-12 *Atlan City* 30-1-43 Tak 11-3 ME 23-4 SOC 26-3-46

JG804 39MU 21-12-42 82MU 2-1-43 *SS653* 19-1 Gib 6-2 NWA 28-2 NAAF 1-11 SOC 29-2-44

JG805 12MU 17-12-42 215MU 15-1-43 *Well Crt* 18-2 Gib 7-3 NWA CE ops 14-4

JG806 Port Sudan Kassala 15MU 22-1-43 76MU 28-1 *Clear* 5-2 Gib 25-2 NWA 31-4 Malta 1-7 Sic NAAF 1-11 SOC 31-8-44

JG807 39MU 17-12-42 215MU 3-1-43 *Tijuiga* 4-2 Aust 1-10-45

JG808 38MU 20-12-42 76MU 28-12 *Atlan City* 20-1-43 Tak 12-3 NWA CE ops 22-4-43

JG809 38MU 15-12-42 76MU 21-12 *SSJ52* 3-1-43 Gib 18-1 NWA 28-2 SOC

JG810 38MU 20-12-42 76MU 25-12 *SSK117* 4-1-43 Gib 18-1

JG835 6MU 31-12-42 82MU 14-1-43 *Mer Prin* 18-1 Gib 4-2 SOC 31-7

JG836 Lake St John 33MU 29-12-42 82MU 29-12 *Atlan City* 20-1-43 Tak 11-3 ME 8-5 352S FAC3 17-9 FTR ops 5-9-44

JG837 33MU 20-12-42 82MU 6-1-43 *Atlan City* 20-1-43 Tak 11-3 ME 1-5 NAAF 1-11 SOC 27-6-46

JG838 46MU 23-1-43 215MU 1-3 *SS672* 25-3 Gib 12-4 NA Malta 1-5 CB ops 5-7

JG839 38MU 21-1-43 82MU 26-1 *Fort Som* 13-2 Tak 11-3 ME 31-3

JG840 12MU 4-1-43 215MU 13-1-43 *Mer Prin* 18-1 Gib 6-2 NWA 28-2 SOC 21-4-45

JG841 6MU 31-12-42 82MU 9-1-43 *Emp Tide* 3-2 Gib 16-2 NWA 1-10 FAF 29-2-44 SOC 30-6

JG842 45MU 3-2-43 215MU 20-2 *Ess Trad* 10-4 Casa 25-4 FAF NWA 31-7 SOC 30-6-45

JG843 39MU 21-12-42 76MU 30-12 *SSK117* 4-1-43 Gib 18-1

JG844 45MU 21-1-43 215MU 28-1 *Alph* 5-3 Tak 20-4 ME 10-5 SOC 1-11

JG845 15MU 21-12-42 76MU 6-1-43 *Nairn* 10-2-43 Tak 11-3 ME 26-3 SOC 1-7

JG846 15MU 21-12-42 76MU 6-1-43 *Nairn* 10-2 Tak 11-3 ME 27-3 FA i/sea 23/6

JG847 12MU 22-12-42 215MU 7-1-43 *Mer prin* 18-1 Gib 6-2 NWA 28-2

JG848 12MU 17-12-42 222MU 30-12 *Skeld* 10-1-43 Gib 6-2 FAF 31-10 NAME 30-11 SOC 14-3-46

JG849 15MU 23-12-42 76MU 11-1-43 *Nairn* 10-2 Tak 11-3 ME 27-3 FTR ops 27-9

JG850 33MU 21-1-43 76MU 27-1 *Well Crt* 18-2 Gib 1-3 NWA 31-3

JG851 38MU 21-1-43 82MU 24-1 *Emp Tide* 3-2 Gib 16-2 NWA 30-4 Malta 1-7 Sic NAAF 1-11 ME 30-11 Turk 28-12-44

JG852 12MU 22-12-42 215MU 2-1-43 *SS653* 19-1 Gib 6-2 NWA 28-2

JG864 6MU 21-12-42 222MU 10-1-43 *Atlan City* 10-1 Tak 11-3 ME 20-4 Malta 1-7 Sic Gib def flt 23-10 dam on ops ldg Tangier Morocco interned 7-2-44

JG865 39MU 21-12-42 222MU 7-1-43 *SS653* 19-1 Gib 8-2 AST 6-4 *Chyel* 17-7 India 18-8 615S FTR ops 15-6-44

JG866 6MU 21-12-42 222MU 7-1-43 *Atlan City* 20-1 Tak 11-3 ME 11-4 Mala 1-7 Sic NAAF 1-11 CE 11-1-45

JG867 15MU 21-12-42 76MU 6-1-43 *Nairn* 10-2 Tak 11-3 ME 1-5 Malta 1-7 NAASC 31-10 C3 ops 20-1-44

JG868 46MU 31-12-42 82MU 15-1-43 *Mer Prin* 18-1 Gib 6-3 NWA SOC 31-7

JG869 12MU 22-12-42 215MU 2-1-43 *SS265* 18-1 Gib 6-2 NWA 28-2 Malta 1-5 Sic 1-8 SOC 23-10-44

JG870 12MU 22-12-42 215MU 2-1-43 *SS653* 19-1 Gib 6-2 NWA 31-3 FAF 1-10 SOC 26-4-46

JG871 38MU 24-12-42 82MU 14-1-43 *Emp Tide* 3-2 Gib 16-2 NWA 31-2 Malta 1-8 Sic NAAF 1-11

JG872 15MU 22-12-42 76MU 15-1-43 *Nairn* 10-2 Tak 11-3 ME 26-3 SOC 1-11

JG871 took the route to Malta via 'Gib'.

JG873 39MU 21-12-42 76MU 30-12 *SSK117* 4-1-43 Gib 18-1 NWA 28-2

JG874 46MU 21-1-43 47MU 28-1 *Fort Senn* 13-2 Tak 11-3 ME 1-5 Malta 1-7 SOC 8-3-44 bboc 21-6-45 SOC 29-8-46

JG875 Bem Te VI 15MU 21-12-42 76MU 31-12 *Atlan City* 20-1-43 Tak 11-3 ME 1-11 CE 13-9-45

JG876 15MU 23-12-42 76MU 10-1-43 *Nairn* 18-2 Tak 11-3 ME 22-4 Sic 1-8 RHAF 25-4-46

JG877 33MU 20-12-42 47MU 29-12 *SS653* 19-1-43 Gib 6-2 NWA 31-7

JG878 38MU 21-1-43 82MU 24-1 *Emp Tide* 3-2 Gib 16-2 NWA 31-3 ME 28-4-45 SOC 25-7-46

JG879 12MU 30-12-42 222MU 15-1-43 *Emp Hav* 19-1 Gib 6-2 NWA C3 ops 12-5

JG880 6MU 21-12-42 222MU 15-1-43 *Atlan City* 20-1 Tak 11-3 ME 8-5 NAASC 31-10 SOC 8-3-44 bboc 21-6-45 1563 flt e/fld on t/o cd nr Benina Libya 9-1-46 CE 31-1

JG881 9MU 29-12-42 82MU 21-1-43 *Fort Senn* 13-2 Tak 11-3 ME 8-5 C3 ops 18-9

JG882 12MU 16-2-43 82MU 26-2 *Fort McCl* 31-3 Casa 6-4 Malta 1-5 FACB 18-8 recat E 13-9

JG883 38MU 24-12-42 82MU 12-1-43 *Emp Tide* 3-2 Gib 16-2 NWA 31-3 USAAF 31-8 SOC 26-4-45

JG884 46MU 12-1-43 CAC 13-1 215MU 24-2 *Asphalian* 5-3 Aust 17-3

JG885 6MU 22-12-42 52MU 2-1-43 *Fort L M* 12-3 Tak 20-4 ME 19-5 NA 30-11 326S 19-5-45 FAF 27-11

JG886 46MU 31-12-42 222MU 10-1-43 *Alph* 5-3 Tak 20-4 ME 8-5 NA 30-11 C3 ops 14-2-44

JG887 9MU 24-12-42 82MU 15-1-43 *Silv Ash* 14-2 Tak 10-3 ME 22-3 FAC3 9-4

JG888 9MU 24-12-42 82MU 15-1-43 *Emp Hav* 19-1 Gib 6-2 SOC 29-2-44

JG889 15MU 23-12-42 76MU 9-1-43 *Nairn* 10-2 Tak 11-3 ME 27-4 Iraq 1-6

JG890 12MU 4-1-43 215MU 16-1 *Alph* 5-3 Tak 20-4 ME 13-7 NAASC 1-11 SOC 31-3-44 bboc 25-10 SOC 29-3-46

JG891 39MU 2-1-43 215MU 21-1 *Tijuga* 4-2 Aust 13-4

JG892 15MU 21-12-42 76MU 6-1-43 *Nairn* 10-2 Tak 11-3 ME 25-5 SOC 1-12

JG893 9MU 24-12-42 82MU 15-1-43 *Silv Ash* 14-2 Tak 10-3 ME 22-3 NA 30-11 73S C3 ops 11-5-44

JG894 12MU 30-12-42 222MU 15-1-43 *Snd Fish* 5-2 Tak 12-3 ME 22-3 C3 ops 9-9

JG897 39MU 2-1-43 215MU 13-1 *Suss* 9-3 Aust 16-4

JG898 12MU 20-12-42 222MU 13-1-43 *Alph* 5-3 Tak 20-4 ME 27-5 SOC 1-11

JG899 12MU 30-12-42 215MU 10-1-43 *Mer Prin* 18-1 Gib 6-2 NWA FAF 31-7

JG912 39MU 2-1-43 215MU 13-1 *Tijuga* 4-2 Aust 13-4

JG913 9MU 24-12-42 82MU 15-1-43 *Silv Ash* 14-2 Tak 10-3 ME 1-9 SOC 29-8-46

JG914 33MU 2-1-43 76MU 11-1 *Mer Prin* 6-2 USAAF NWA 1-10 SOC 26-4-45

JG915 46MU 31-12-42 222MU 10-1-43 *Alph* 5-3 Tak 20-4 ME 9-5 NAAF 1-11 ME 25-2-45 SOC 26-4

JG916 Omdurman/Khartoum 8MU 22-1-43 82MU 26-1 *Snd Fish* 5-2 Tak 12-3 ME 22-4 SOC 31-3

JG917 33MU 2-1-43 82MU 15-1 *Silv Ash* 14-2 Tak 10-3 ME 21-4 Malta 1-7 Sic NAAF 1-11 SOC 29-2-44

JG918 46MU 21-1-43 215MU 30-1 *Alph* 5-3 Tak 20-4 ME 20-5 Malta 1-1-44 NAAF SOC 8-8-46

JG919 33MU 21-1-43 76MU 29-1 *Fort Som* 13-2 Tak 11-3 ME 29-4 NA 30-11 CE 26-4-45

JG920 38MU 24-12-42 52MU 25-1-43 *Well Crt* 18-2 Gib 7-3 NA 1-5 Italy 1-11 SOC 27-7-44

JG921 45MU 4-12-42 9MU 6-12 *SS653* 19-1-43 Gib 10-2 NWA 28-2

JG922 46MU 6-12-42 82MU 12-12 *Hamble VII* 30-12 Gib 18-1-43

JG923 46MU 9-12-42 76MU 18-12 *Hamble VII* 30-12 Gib 18-1-43

JG924 46MU 9-12-42 76MU 18-12 3FPP hit telegraph pole fly zero feet 21-12

JG925 46MU 9-12-42 215MU 20-12 *Hamble VII* 30-12 Gib 18-1-43 FAF 29-2-44 REAF 22-2-45

JG926 9MU 11-12-42 82MU 23-12 *SSK117* 4-1-43 Gib 18-1 USAAF NWA 31-7 MAAF 21-6-45 SOC 19-7

JG927 9MU 11-12-42 82MU 23-12 *SSK117* 4-1-43 Gib 18-1 NWA 28-2 SOC 31-7

JG928 9MU 13-12-42 222MU 31-12 *SS653* 19-1 Gib 6-2 Malta ME 1-9 NAAF 1-11 185S CE ops 1-9-44

JG929 9MU 19-12-42 82MU 23-12 *SS653* 19-1 Gib 6-2

JG930 9MU 21-12-43 222MU 7-1-43 *SS653* 19-1 Gib 6-2 NWA 28-2

JG931 9MU 22-1-43 222MU 26-1 *Alph* 5-3 Tak 20-4 ME 9-5 NAAF 1-11 SOC 8-3-44 bboc 25-10 CE 13-9-45

JG932 9MU 22-1-43 222MU 26-1 *Clear* 5-2 Gib 25-2 NWA 31-3 ME 1-11 MAAF 21-6-45 SOC 25-7-46

JG933 9MU 22-1-43 222MU 3-2 *Alph* 5-3 Tak 20-4 ME 19-6 CE 13-9-45
JG934 9MU 22-12-42 82MU 14-1-43 *Emp Hav* 19-1 Gib 6-2
JG935 9MU 21-12-42 222MU 4-1-43 *SS653* 19-1 Gib 6-2 SOC 28-4-45
JG936 VA to FIX M63 6MU 7-6-43 222MU 14-6 *Fort Ver* 1-7 Casa ME 1-9 NAAF 1-11 FTR 7-2-44
JG937 9MU 7-2-43 82MU 20-2 *Tyne* 2-3 Gib 24-3 NWA 30-4 Malta 1-7 Sic SOC 26-4-45
JG938 9MU 1-1-43 82MU 21-1 *Silv Ash* 14-2 Tak 10-3 ME 30-3 NAAF 30-11-44 to Turk 29-3-45
JG939 9MU 21-12-42 222MU 8-1-43 *Atlan City* 20-1 Tak 11-3 Malta 1-7 Sic SOC 26-4-45
JG940 9MU 1-1-43 82MU 15-1 *Emp Hav* 19-1 Gib 6-2
JG941 9MU 1-1-43 82MU 14-12 *Emp Hav* 19-1 Gib 6-2 Malta 1-8 Sic NAAF 1-11 SOC 30-6-44
JG942 9MU 22-1-43 222MU 3-2 *Alph* 5-3 Tak 20-4 ME 10-6 NAAF 1-11 SOC 26-4-45
JG943 9MU 1-1-43 82MU 14-1 *Bluff VIII* 16-1 NA 19-1 Gib 6-2 SOC 26-4-45
JG944 9MU 24-12-42 82MU 14-1 *Emp Hav* 19-1 Gib 6-2 NWA 31-7 FAF 1-10 RAF NA 30-11 SOC 25-7-46
JG945 M45 15MU 21-1-43 76MU 4-2 *Fort Senn* 13-2 Tak 11-3 ME 22-3 Malta 1-7 FTR ops 10-7
JG946 46MU 31-12-42 82MU 15-1-43 *Sil Ash* 14-2 Tak 10-3 ME 22-4 Malta 1-7 NAASC 31-10 118MU Malta 31-1-44 SOC 8-3
JG947 12MU 30-12-42 222MU 13-1-43 *Alph* 5-3 Tak 20-4 ME 16-5 SOC 26-9-46
JG948 no record
JG949 6MU 2-1-43 82MU 15-1 *Mer Prin* 18-1 Gib USAAF 31-10
JG950 Kassala Town and Province 6MU 22-1-43 222MU 25-1 *Well Crt* 18-5 Gib 7-3 NWA 31-3 NAASC 31-10 FACE 28-4-45
JG951 6MU 31-12-42 82MU 14-1-43 *Mer Prin* 18-1 Gib 6-2 NWA 25-2
JG952 12MU 4-1-43 82MU 14-1 *Emp Tide* 3-2 Gib 16-2 NWA 31-3-44 SOC 28-4-45
JG953 12MU 10-1-43 215MU 12-1 *SS686* 24-1 Casa 17-4-45 ME 31-1 CE 2-8
JG954 6MU 2-1-43 215MU 13-1 *Sussex* 9-3 Aus 16-4
JG955 12MU 10-1-43 47MU 24-1 *Hamble VII* 3-2 Gib 16-2 NWA 31-3 Malta 1-10 ME 30-11-44 to Turk 28-12
JG956 38MU 23-1-43 ME 31-3 NAAF 1-11 SOC 8-3-44
JG957 39MU 2-1-43 215MU 13-1 *Tijuga* 4-2 Aus 13-4
JG958 12MU 10-1-43 76MU 25-1 *Fort Senn* 13-2 Tak 11-3 ME 28-4
JG959 12MU 10-1-43 76MU 29-1 *Fort Senn* 13-2 Tak 11-3 ME 24-3 NA 30-11 SOC 10-1-46
JG960 33MU 2-1-43 76MU *SS657* 19-2 NWA 31-3 SOC 28-4-45

JK series All F Mk VC Merlin 46 unless otherwise indicated

JK101 12MU 4-1-43 215MU 13-1 *Mer Prin* 18-1 Gib 6-2 NWA 43S 28-2 Malta 1-7 Sic NAAF 1-11 SOC 30-6-44 bboc 21-6-45 SOC 29-3-46
JK102 39MU 2-1-43 222MU 9-1 *Mer Prin* 18-1 Gib 6-2 USAAF NWA 1-10 RAF 30-11-45 ME RHAF 25-4-46
JK103 33MU 2-1-43 76MU 11-1 *Mer Prin* 18-1 Gib 6-2 NWA 28-2 Malta 1-7 ME 1-10
JK104 46MU 21-1-43 82MU 24-1 *Clear* 5-2 Gib 25-2 NWA 21-3 ME 1-11 SOC 26-4-45
JK105 46MU 21-1-43 82MU 24-1 *Clear* 5-2 Gib 25-2 SOC 26-4-45
JK106 46MU 21-1-43 47MU 28-1 *Fort Senn* 13-2 Tak 11-3 ME 30-3 FAC3 7-5-44 bboc 21-6-45 SOC 20-8-46
JK107 33MU 2-1-43 76MU 11-1 *Mer Prin* 18-1 Gib 4-2 NWA 28-2 NAAF FTR ops 24-4
JK108 12MU 10-1-43 215MU 25-1 *Alphard* 5-3 Tak 20-4 ME 29-5 C3 ops 18-3-44
JK109 39MU 22-1-43 76MU 27-1 *Clear* 5-2 Gib 25-2 NWA FTR ops 24-4
JK110 46MU 29-1-43 82MU 14-13 *Mer Prin* 18-1 Gib 6-2
JK111 46MU 31-12-42 82MU 14-1-43 *Emp Tide* 3-2 Gib 16-2 NWA 28-2 FAF NAASC 31-10 ME 21-6-45 SOC 3-1-46
JK112 45MU 21-1-43 82MU 27-1 *Clear* 5-2 Gib 25-2 NWA 30-4 225S ME 21-6-45 SOC 14-3-46
JK113 12MU 24-1-43 222MU 4-2 *SS657* 19-2 Gib 9-3 NWA 31-3 Sic 1-8 NAASC 31-10 ME 30-11-44 SOC 29-8-46
JK114 39MU 22-1-43 76MU 26-1 *Well Crt* 18-2 GIb 7-3 NWA 31-3 SOC 30-6-46
JK115 46MU 21-1-43 215MU 29-1 *Alph* 5-3 Tak 28-4 ME 27-5 CE 13-9-45
JK116 45MU 21-1-43 47MU 26-1 *Well Crt* 18-2 Gib 7-3 NWA 31-3
JK117 33MU 21-1-43 76MU 27-1 *Well Crt* 18-2 Gib 7-3 NWA 31-3 SOC 31-7
JK118 46MU 21-1-43 215MU 28-1 *Alph* 5-3 Tak 20-4 ME 29-5 CE ops 4-11-44
JK119 33MU 21-1-43 76MU 27-1 *Well Crt* 18-2 Gib 7-3 NWA 13-3
JK120 38MU 21-1-43 82MU 24-1 *Emp Tide* 3-2 Gib 16-2 NWA 31-3
JK121 45MU 21-1-43 215MU 28-1 *Alph* 5-3 Tak 20-4 ME 22-5 NAAF 1-11 SOC 2-3-44 bboc 21-6-45 SOC 4-5-46
JK122 15MU 22-1-43 76MU 27-1 *Clear* 5-2 Gib 25-2 Malta 1-5 FAC 24-10 229S FAC2 2-7-44
JK123 6MU 22-1-43 52MU 22-2 *Fort Park* 19-2 Gib 9-3 NWA 31-3 SOC 31-7
JK124 33MU 21-1-43 76MU 27-1 *Well Crt* 18-2 Gib 7-3 NWA 31-3 Malta 229S C3 5-7
JK125 15MU 29-1-43 76MU 13-2 *Fort L M* 12-3 Tak 20-4 ME 16-5 FTR ops 29-8
JK126 6MU 22-1-43 222MU 25-1 *Emp Tide* 3-2 Gib 16-2 NWA 31-3
JK127 8MU 22-1-43 82MU 26-1 *Fort Som* 13-2 Tak 11-3 ME 30-3 NAASC 31-10 RHAF 25-4-46
JK128 46MU 30-1-43 82MU 9-2 *SS658* 22-2 Gib 7-3 NWA 31-3 ME 30-11 SOC 31-12
JK129 15MU 20-1-43 76MU 4-2 *Fort Som* 13-2 Tak 11-3 ME 2-4 NAAF 30-11 SOC 8-3-44
JK130 33MU 20-1-43 47MU 27-1 *Fort Som* 13-2 Tak 11-3 ME 30-3 NAAF 21-6-45 IAF 27-6-46 as MM4001
JK131 15MU 20-1-43 76MU 30-1 *Fort Som* 13-2 Tak 11-3 ME 8-5
JK132 El Fisher/Darfur Province 6MU 22-1-43 52MU 27-1 *Well Crt* 18-2 Gib 7-3 NWA 31-3 Malta 1-7 Sic NAAF 1-11 154S SOC 29-6-44
JK133 15MU 22-1-43 76MU 27-1 *Clear* 5-2 Gib 25-2 NWA31-3
JK134 Juba Province 39MU 22-1-43 76MU 27-1 *SS702* 7-6 Casa 15-6 NWA 1-7 FAF 1-10 SOC 23-1-45
JK135 33MU 20-1-43 222MU 1-2 *Alph* 5-3 Tak 20-4 ME 22-5 NA 30-11 SOC 27-6-46
JK136 38MU 23-1-43 47MU 30-1 *Fort Senn* 13-2 Tak 11-3 ME 22-4 Iraq 1-6 NA 30-9
JK137 33MU 21-1-43 222MU 1-2 *Alph* 5-3 Tak 20-4 ME 7-5 SOC 1-12
JK138 45MU 29-1-43 215MU 3-2 *Alph* 5-3 Tak 20-4 ME 27-5 CB ops 8-11
JK139 15MU 20-1-43 76MY 30-1 *Fort Som* 13-2 Tak 11-3 ME 26-3 NWA Malta 1-7 Sic to Turk 29-3-45
JK140 33MU 22-143 222MU 1-2 *Alph* 5-3 Tak 20-4 ME 27-5 C3 ops 18-9
JK141 15MU 22-1-43 76MU 27-1 *Clear* 5-2 Gib 25-2 NWA 31-3
JK142 33MU 21-1-43 82MU 1-2 *Fort Som* 13-2 Tak 11-3 ME 30-3 SOC 27-6-46
JK143 15MU 22-1-43 76MU 30-1 *Fort Som* 13-2 Tak 11-3 ME 1-5 Malta 1-7 Sic FAF 28-2-46
JK144 M50A 9MU 15-2-43 222MU 6-2 *Fort L M* 12-3 Tak 20-4 ME 10-5 NWA C3 ops 13-4 NAAF 1-6 SOC 31-5-45
JK145 38MU 28-1-43 76MU 4-2 *Fort Som* 10-2 Tak 11-3 ME 27-3 SOC 26-9-46
JK159 39MU 15-2-43 82MU 1-3 *Emp Prin* 23-3 Casa 6-4 FAF 30-11 SOC 26-4-45
JK160 38MU 29-1-43 222MU 10-2 *Fort Hud* 20-2 Gib 7-3 NWA 31-3 USAAF 12/52 31-12 lost France 9-2-44
JK161 VWD wts & CG load 20-1-43 tare 5107; t/o 6851; with 30gal o/ld tank 7142; with 90gal o/ld tank 7641lb Trls with drag flaps 2-2 38MU 29-1 82MU 9-2 *SS658* 22-2 Gib 7-3 NWA 31-3 SOC 29-2-44
JK162 15MU 22-1-43 76MU 28-1 *Clear* 5-2 Gib 25-2 NWA 31-3 USAAF 31-8 CE ops 8-11-44
JK163 45MU 24-1-43 215MU 4-2 *Alph* 25-2 Tak 20-4 ME 7-5 to 4391M 28-2-44
JK164 VC(T) 38MU 28-1-43 76MY 4-2 *Fort L M* 12-3 Tak 20-4 ME 25-5 to Turk 28-12-44
JK165 46MU 27-1-43 47MU 4-3 *SS670* 24-3 Gib 12-4 NWA 30-4 NAAF 31-10 IAF 27-6-46 as MM4005
JK166 46MU 19-2-43 215MU 3-3 *SS672* 25-3 Gib 12-4 Malta 1-10 NAASC 31-10 CE 7-4-45
JK167 8MU 1-2-43 222MU 8-12 *Well Crt* 18-2 Gib 7-3 NWA 31-3 USAAF 1-10
JK168 38MU 29-1-43 222MU 9-12 *Well Crt* 18-2 Gib 7-3 NWA 31-3 SOC 31-8-44
JK169 8MU 22-1-43 82MU 26-1 *Fort Som* 13-2 Tak 11-3 ME 27-3 Malta 1-7 SOC 20-7
JK170 38MU 23-1-43 82MU 4-2 *Fort Som* 13-2 Tak 11-3 ME 26-3 NAAF 1-11 SOC 8-3-44 bboc 21-6-45 RHAF 25-4-46
JK171 12MU 24-1-43 222MU 4-2 *SS657* 19-2 Gib 9-3 NWA 31-3 USAAF 12/52 lost in Med 3-4
JK172 38MU 23-1-43 52MU 5-2 *Fort LM* 12-3 Tak 20-4 ME 27-5 SOC 1-12
JK173 45MU 29-1-43 222MU 4-2 *SS657* 19-2 Gib 9-3 NWA 31-3 Malta 1-7 Sic SOC 15-11-44
JK174 12MU 24-1-43 222MU 6-2 *Silv Bch* for AUS lost at sea 14-4
JK175 15MU 20-1-43 76MU 11-2 *Fort LM* 12-3 Tak 20-4 ME 18-5 SOC 1-11
JK176 12MU 24-1-43 222MU 6-2 *Silv Bch for* Aus lost at sea 14-4
JK177 45MU 24-1-43 215MU 3-2 *Alph* 5-3 Tak 20-4 ME 16-5 NAAF 1-11 FACE 8-3-45 SOC 26-4
JK178 8MU 7-2-43 222MU 8-2 *Well Crt* 18-2 Gib 7-3 NWA 31-3 FAR 1-10
JK179 46MU 1-2-43 82MU 6-2 *Fort Hud* 20-2 Gib 7-3 NWA 31-3 FAF 1-10 SOC 30-6-44
JK180 VC(T) 38MU 29-1-43 82MU 9-2 *Fort LM* 12-3 Tak 20-4 ME 12-5 NAAF 1-11 MAAF 21-6-45 SOC 18-10
JK181 VC(T) 38MU 28-1-43 222MU 9-2 *Silv Bch* for Aust lost at sea 14-4
JK182 VC(T) 15MU 30-1-43 76MU 8-2 *Fort LM* 12-3 Tak 20-4 ME 1-6 Malta 1-7 Sic NAAF 1-11 118MU Malta 31-1-44 SOC 26-4-45
JK183 45MU 24-1-43 222MU 3-2 *SS657* 19-2 Gib 9-3 NWA CE ops 25-4 USAAF 1-10
JK184 33MU 23-1-43 222MU 10-2 *Silv Bch* for Aus lost at sea 14-4
JK185 VC(T) 38MU 29-1-43 82MU 4-2 *Fort Park* 19-2 Gib 9-3 NWA 31-3 FAF 31-10 ME 31-12 SOC 5-12-44
JK186 38MU 6-2-43 82MU 1-3 *Fort Liv* 20-3 Gib 12-4 NWA 31-5 Malta 1-7 ME 1-9 NAASC 31-10 SOC 27--6-46
JK187 8MU 1-2-43 47MU 11-2 *SSLS290* 503 Tak 2-4 ME 8-7 FTR ops 8-8
JK188 Khartoum City and Province 46MU 1-2-43 47MU 12-2 *Copac* 5-3 Tak 2-4 ME 1-5 NA 30-11 USAAF 31-1-44 ME 30-11 32S SOC 14-3-46
JK189 CV(T) 38MU 28-1-43 222MU 9-2 *Fort Hud* 20-2 Gib 7-3 NWA 31-3 Malta 1-7 Sic CE ops 18-8
JK190 46MU 3-2-43 215MU 15-2 *Narratrio* 10-3 Gib 10-3 ME 31-8-44 to Turk 22-2-45
JK191 Malakal/upper Nile 15MU 6-2-43 76MU 21-2 *Fort LM* 12-3 Tak 20-4 ME 1-6 NAAF 1-11 SOC 29-8-46
JK192 46MU 1-2-43 82MU 6-2 Gib 7-3 NWA 31-3 SOC 31-7
JK193 46MU 1-2-43 82MU 9-2 Gib 7-3 73SA C3 ops 20-6-44
JK194 46MU 4-2-43 82MU 18-2 Gib 24-3 NWA 30-4 SOC 28-4-45
JK195 45MU 6-2-43 215MU 18-2 *Copac* 5-3 Tak 2-4 ME 1-11 NAAF Malta 118MU 31-1-44 REAF 22-2-45
JK214 CV(T) 45MU 25-1-43 215MU 109-2 *Well Crt* 18-2 Gib 7-3 249S C3 ops 11-8044
JK215 VC(T) 12MU 24-1-43 47MU 30-1 *Fort Som* 13-2 Tak 11-3 ME 8-5
JK216 VC(T) 45MU 28-1-43 215MU 4-2 *SSLS237* 5-3 Tak 20-4 ME 26-5 NAAF 30-11 SOC 29-8-46
JK217 45MU2-2-42 215MU 18-2 *Harmat* 15-3 Gib 26-3 NWA 31-5 Malta 1-8 Sic FTR ops 4-9
JK218 15MU 3-2-43 76MU 13-2 *Harpal* 22-3 Casa 6-4 NWA 30-4 USAAF
JK219 45MU 1-2-43 222MU 4-2 *SS657* Gib 9-3 dam by water e/a CE 24-3 SOC 10-4
JK220 45MU 2-2-43 215MU 9-2 *SS661* Gib 26-4 NA 31-5 Malta 1-11 SOC 19-7-45
JK221 45MU 2-2-43 82MU 19-2 *Tyne* 2-3 Gib 24-3 NWA 30-4 Malta 1-7 Sic ME 30-9 NAAF 1-11 CE ops 5-11 bboc 21-6-45 SOC 14-3-46
JK222 VC(T) 33MU 13-2-43 NWA 31-5 USAAF 1-10 RAF 29-2-44 SOC 26-4-45
JK223 2-2-43 215MU 31-2 *SS661* 10-3 Gib 26-4 ME 31-12
JK224 45MU 2-2-43 215MU 21-2 *Harmat* 10-3 Gib 26-4 1676Flt MAAF 21-6-45 SOC 11-4-46
JK225 15MU 3-2-43 33MU 14-2 *Asphadian* 5-3 Aus 17-5
JK226 15MU 3-2-43 76MU 21-2 *Harpal* 22-3 Casa 6-4 NWA 30-4 308S USAAF 32S RAF RHAF 25-11-46
JK227 15MU 3-2-43 76MU 20-2 *Fort L M* 12-3 Tak 20-4 ME 16-5 Malta 1-7 NAASC 1-11 FTR ops 29-2-44
JK228 33MU 9-2-43 76MU 25-2 *Harpal* 22-3 Casa 6-4 NWA 30-4 C3 ops 21-11
JK229 39MU 9-2-43 215MU 22-2 *Suss* 9-3 Aus 16-4
JK230 39MU 9-2-43 82MU 19-2 *Tyne* 2-3 Gib 24-3 Malta 1-5 NAASC 31-10 MAAF 21-6-45 SOC 19-7-45
JK231 39MU 9-2-43 215MU 19-2 *Suss* 9-3 Aus 16-4
JK232 VC(T) M50A 33MU 15-2-43 52MU 3-3 *SS680* 11-4 Casa 25-4 NWA 31-5 Malta 1-8 ME 30-9 NAASC 31-10
JK233 33MU 9-2-43 76MU 25-2 *Harpal* 22-3 Casa 6-4 NA 31-5 229S FTR ops 12-7
JK234 VC(T) M50 33MU 15-2-43 82MU 28-2 *Emp Prin* 23-3 Gib 6-4 NWA 31-5 ME 1-7 NAAF 1-11 RHAF 25-4-46
JK235 9MU 2-3-53 222MU 12-3 *SS679* Casa 25-4 NWA 31-5 USAAF 31-7
JK236 9MU 1-4-43 VA 11-4 M50 instal 222MU 31-8 *Card Gib* 3-9 Casa 20-9 NAASC 31-10 to Turk 26-4-45
JK249 15MU 29-1-43 76MU 13-2 *Fort L M* 12-3 Tak 20-4 ME 27-5 FACE 6-9-44
JK250 45MU 28-1-43 82MU 20-2 *Fort Liv* 20-3 Gib 12-4 NWA 30-4 ME 10-11-44 CE 4-10-45
JK251 46MU 6-2-43 82MU 16-2 *Fort Liv* 20-3 Gib 12-4 FAF ME 1943 SOC 26-4-45
JK252 15MU 6-2-43 76MU 8-3 *Harpal* 22-3 Casa 6-4 NWA 30-4 USAAF 31-7
JK253 46MU 6-2-43 47MU 18-2 *Copac* 5-3 Tak 2-4 CE 9-4
JK254 VC(T) 38MU 29-1-43 82MU 9-2 *Fort L M* 12-3 Tak 20-4 ME 11-6 CE ops 13-8

JK254 had a short life in the Middle East.

JK255 Barakat/Blue Nile 46MU 27-1-43 215MU 15-2 *Ess Trad* 10-4 Casa 25-4 NWA 31-5 USAAF 12/52 31-8 lost in Med 13-1-44
JK256 46MU 4-2-43 215MU 19-2 *Harmat* 10-3 Gib 26-4 ME 30-11-44 SOC RHAF 25-4-46
JK257 VC(T) 38MU 29-1-43 82MU 9-2 *Silv Bch* for Aus lost at sea 14-4
JK258 VC(T) M50A 38MU 29-1-43 47MU 18-2 *Silv Bch* for Aus lost at sea 14-4
JK259 46MU 3-2-43 215MU 13-2 *Copac* 5-3 Tak 2-4 NWA 16-1 FACB 1-7-44 SOC 27-6-46

JK260 Atbara 46MU 27-1-43 47MU 20-2 *Orient C* 13-4 Casa 24-4 NWA 31-5 Malta 1-7 Sic NAAF 1-11 CE 5-3-45

JK261 45MU 3-2-43 215MU 18-2 *Nomatris* 10-3 Gib 26-4 NWA USAAF 31-7 ME 28-4-45 SOC 29-8-46

JK262 45MU 6-2-43 215MU 3-3 *SS672* 25-3 Gib 12-4 NWA 30-4 SOC 31-7

JK263 15MU 6-2-43 76MU 4-3 *Harpal* 22-3 Casa 6-4 NWA 31-5 ME 1-9 SOC 29-6-44

JK264 46MU 1-2-43 47MU 18-2 *Copac* 5-3 Tak 2-4 ME 27-9 RHAF 25-4-46

JK265 46MU 2-2-43 47MU 18-2 *Copac* 18-2 Tak 2-4 ME 10-9

JK266 M15 46MU 4-2-43 215MU 18-2 *SS672* 25-3 Gib 12-4 NWA 30-4 FAF NAASC 31-10 249S FTR ops 10-6-44

JK267 45MU 3-2-43 82MU 20-2 *Fort Liv* 20-3 Gib 12-4 NWA 30-4 FAF 1-10 USAAF ME 31-8-44 SOC 14-3-46

JK268 46MU 3-2-43 47MU 20-2 *Orient C* 13-4 Casa 24-4

JK269 45MU 3-2-43 215MU 24-2 *Emp Trad* 10-4 Casa 25-4 NWA 31-5 SOC 30-9

JK270 VC(T) M50A 38MU 28-1-43 82MU 9-2 *Sansu* 8-3 Tak 2-4 ME 28-4 FAC3 16-2-44

JK271 46MU 3-2-43 215MU 11-2 *Copac* 5-3 Tak 2-4 ME 12-4 SOC 26-4-45

JK272 46MU 4-2-43 215MU 18-2 *Ess Trad* 10-4 Casa 25-4 ME 1-9 NAAF 30-11 SOC 26-4-45

JK273 VC(T)M45 38MU 29-1-43 222MU 9-2 *Silv Bch* for Aus lost at sea 14-4

JK274 15MU 6-2-43 76MU 25-2 *Harpal* 22-3 Casa 6-4 NWA 31-5 232S FTR ops 28-7

JK275 8MU 1-2-43 222MU 8-2 *Fort Hew* 20-2 Gib 7-3 NWA 31-3 Malta 1-7 Sicily NAAF 1-11 ME 15-3-45 RHAF 25-4-46

JK276 M50 8MU 1-2-43 47MU 1-2 *Isipan* 5-3 Tak 2-4 ME 1-3 CE 28-12-44

JK277 38MU 2-2-43 222MU 13-2 *Fort McL* 21-3 Casa 6-4 ME 21-6-45 SOC 27-6-46

JK278 46MU 3-2-43 47MU 3-3 *Orient C* 13-4 Casa 25-4 NWA USAAF 31-7 MAAF 21-6-45 Trg del 1-11-45

JK279 VC(T)M45 38MU 29-1-43 47MU 13-2 *Isipan* 5-3 Tak 2-4 NA 30-11 C3 ops 16-6-44

JK280 9MU 1-3-43 82MU 9-3 *Fort Liv* 20-3 Gib 12-4 1676Flt CAC ops 3-8 6MU 3-5-44 M45M instal 130S 28-5-44 CE ops 17-6

JK281 M50A 38MU 2-2-43 222MU 11-2 *Fort Hud* 20-2 Gib 7-3 NWA 31-3 SOC 26-4-45

JK282 46MU 3-2-43 215MU 17-2 *Copac* 5-3 Tak 2-4 ME 18-4 Malta 1-5 Sic NAASC 31-10 SOC 14-3-46

JK283 38MU 2-2-43 222MU 13-2 *Isipan* 5-3 Tak 2-4 ME 26-4 FAC3 28-4

JK284 45MU 2-2-43 215MU 9-2 Harmat 10-3 Gib 26-4 NWA 31-5 USAAF 31-7

JK285 45MU 4-2-43 82MU 19-2 *Tyne* 2-3 Gib 24-3 NWA 30-4 Malta 1-7 Sic ME 1-9 SOC 26-9-46

JK303 46MU 1-2-43 215MU 18-2 *Ess Trad* 10-4 Casa NAASC 31-10 SOC 11-4-46

JK304 45MU 3-2-43 215MU 6-3 *Ess Trad* 10-4 Casa 25-4 NWA 1-10 SOC 28-4-45

JK305 45MU 6-2-43 82MU 16-2 *Fort Liv* 20-3 Gib 12-4 NWA 31-5 ME 152S FTR ops 12-7

JK306 M50A 33MU 4-2-43 76MU 22-2 *Harpal* 22-3 Casa 6-4 NWA 30-4 Malta 1-7 Sic NAAF 1-11 RHAF 25-4-46

JK307 46MU 3-2-43 215MU 18-2 *Harmat* 10-3 Gib 26-4 Malta 1-7 NAASC 1-11 SOC 26-4-45

JK308 45MU 6-2-43 82MU 19-2 *Tyne* 2-3 Gib 24-3 Malta 1-5 C3 ops 13-6 FH47.30

JK309 38MU 2-2-43 222MU 13-2 *Fort Mcl* 21-3 Casa 6-4 NWA 30-4 Sic 1-8 USAAF NAAF 30-11 C3 ops 19-12

JK310 46MU 4-2-43 215MU 5-3 *SS672* 25-3 Gib 12-4 NWA 30-4 Malta 232S FTR ops 5-6

JK311 M50A 33MU 1-2-43 222MU 9-2 *Well Crt* 18-2 Gib 7-3 NWA 31-3 SOC 28-12-44

JK312 46MU 4-2-43 47MU *Orient C* 13-4 Casa 25-4 NWA 31-5

JK313 46MU 4-2-43 215MU 1-3 *SS679* 12-4 Casa 25-4 SOC 29-2-44

JK314 M50A 46MU 4-2-43 215MU 1-3 *SS670* 24-3 Gib 12-4 NWA 30-4 ME 29-3-45 SOC 29-8-46

JK315 ME 21-6-45 SOC 29-8-46

JK316 8MU 7-2-43 82MU 22-2 *Fort L M* 12-3 Tak 20-4 ME 27-5 SOC 25-7-46

JK317 12MU 6-2-43 47MU 21-2 *SS670* 24-3 Gib 12-4 NWA 30-4 SOC 28-4-45

JK318 8MU 2-2-43 82MU 18-2 *Clyde* 2-3 Gib 24-3 NWA FTR ops 12-4

JK319 45MU 4-2-43 215MU 18-2 *Copac* 5-3 Tak 2-4 ME 11-4 NAAF 1-11 SOC 30-6-45

JK320 46MU 2-2-43 215MU 11-2 *Copac* 5-3 Tak 2-4 ME 17-4 Malta FAC3 22-5 SOC 18-6

JK321 46MU 3-2-43 44MU 13-2 *Fort L M* 18-3 Tak 25-4 ME 7-5 FAC3 29-9 NAAF 1-11 SOC 29-2-44

JK322 6MU 6-2-43 82MU 19-2 *Tyne* 2-3 Gib 24-3 Malta 1-7 Sic 81S dam en bombs 1-8 NAAF 1-11 118MU Malta 31-1-44 USAAF

JK323 9MU 28-12-42 82MU 11-1-43 *Mer Pri* 18-1 Gib 6-2 NWA 28-2 SOC 20-4-46

JK324 9MU 28-12-42 82MU ME 30-9 NAASC 31-10 SOC 27-3-45 RHAF 25-4-46

JK325 9MU 21-1-43 222MU 26-1 *Well Crt* 18-2 Gib 7-3

JK326 9MU 4-1-43 82MU 15-1 *Emp Hav* 19-1 Gib 6-2

JK327 9MU 10-1-43 222MU 26-1 *Claar* 25-2 NWA 31-3 Malta 1-7 Sic ME 30-9 NAASC 31-10 RHAF 25-4-46

JK328 VC(T) 9MU 22-1 47MU 3-2 *Fort Som* 13-2 Tak 11-3 ME 27-3 SOC 25-7-46

JK329 VC(T) 45MU 27-1-43 215MU 4-2 *Alph* 5-3 Tak 20-4 ME 22-5 NAAF 1-11 FTR ops 20-12-44

JK330 VC(T) 45MU 27-1-43 215MU 4-2 *Alph* 5-3 Tak 20-4 ME 25-5 NAAF 1-11 SOC 26-9-46

JK331 VC(T) 9MU 22-1-43 222MU 5-2 *Silv Bch* for Aus lost at sea 14-4

JK332 9MU 10-1-43 222MU 26-1 *Emp Tide* 3-2 Gib 16-2 NWA 31-3 Malta 1-7 ME 1-9 NAAF 1-11 SOC 26-4-45

JK333 45MU 30-1-43 215MU 9-2 *Harmat* 10-3 Gib 26-4 NWA 31-5 Malta 1-6 NA 1-10

JK334 9MU 21-1-43 222MU 26-1 *Silv Pl* 5-2 Gib 25-2 NAAF FTR 31-3

JK335 9MU 16-2-43 222MU 3-3 *SS679* 12-4 Casa 25-4 NWA 31-5 ME 1-8 NAAF 30-9 FAC3 17-10

JK336 45MU 30-1-43 222MU 4-2 *SS657* 19-2 Gib 9-3 dam by sea water due en/ac CE 24-3

JK337 VC(T) 9MU 4-2-43 222MU 3-3 *Fort Mcl* 21-3 Casa 6-4 NWA 30-4 325 rd nr Athens 15-10-44 Sgt Gooch kld

JK338 VC(T) 45MU 28-1-43 215MU 3-2 *SS682* 12-4 Casa 25-4 NWA 31-5 73S FTR 3-5-44

JK339 VC(T) 45MU 29-1-43 82MU 4-2 *Fort Pask* 19-2 Gib 9-3 NWA SOC 31-7

JK340 45MU 1-2-43 215MU 9-2 *Harmat* 10-3 Gib 26-4 ME 1-7 NAASC 31-10 32S to Turk 26-4-45

JK341 9MU 2-2-43 82MU 12-2 *Fort H H* 20-2 Gib 7-3 NWA 31-3

JK342 9MU 2-2-43 82MU 12-2 *Fort H H* 20-2 Gib 7-3 NWA 31-3 SOC 26-4-45

JK343 VC(T)9MU 4-2-43 222MU 11-2 *Fort Mcl* 21-3 Casa 6-4 NWA 242S FTR ops 7-5

JK344 45MU 1-2-43 215MU 9-2 *Harmat* 10-3 Gib 26-4 MAAF 21-6-45 Trg del 27-9

JK345 9MU 2-2-43 82MU 12-2 *Fort H H* 20-2 Gib 7-3 NWA 31-3 Malta 1-7 Sic ME 30-9 SOC 8-3-44

JK346 46MU 27-1-42 47MU 3-3 *SS670* 24-3 Gib 12-4 NWA 30-4

JK359 VC(T)M50A 33MU 13-2-43 52MU 1-3 *SS680* 11-4 Casa 25-4 NWA 21-5 Malta 1-8 NAASC 31-10 ME 30-11 SOC 31-5-45

JK360 VC(T)M50 33MU 15-2-43 222MU 11-2 *Fort Mcl* 21-3 Casa 10-4 NWA 31-5 USAAF 31-7 MAAF CE ops 26-2-45

JK361 VC(T)M50 33MU 15-2-43 52MU 1-3 *Harpal* 22-3 Casa 6-4 NWA 31-5

JK362 6MU 28-2-43 82MU 9-3 *SS682* 12-4 Casa 25-4 NWA 31-5 Malta 1-8 Sic NAAF 1-1 118MU Malta 31-1-44 to Turk 30-11

JK363 VC(T) 12MU 18-2-43 82MU 28-2 *Emp Prin* 23-3 Casa 6-4 NWA 31-5 SOC 29-3-45

JK364 6MU 23-2-43 52MU 3-3 *Harpal* 22-3 Casa 6-4 NWA 30-4 Malta 1-7 Sic NAAF 1-11 SOC 26-4-45

JK365 6MU 28-2-43 52MU 3-3 *SS657* 22-3 Casa 6-4 NWA 30-4 Malta 1-7 Sic NAASC 1-11 SOC 8-3-44 cancel ME 21-6-45 SOC 29-8-46

JK366 6MU 23-2-43 52MU 3-3 *Harpal* 22-3 Casa 6-4 NA 31-5 Malta 1-6 Italy 7-11 ME 30-11-44

JK367 6MU 23-2-43 52MU 2-3 *SS680* 11-4 Casa 25-4 NWA 31-5 USAAF 31-7 SOC 26-4-45

JK368 38MU 2-2-43 76MU 12-3 *Harpal* 22-3 Casa 6-4 NA 31-5 Malta 1-6 NA 1-1-44 185S CE ops 29-4-44

JK369 M45 9MU 11-4-43 82MU 18-4 *SS687* 29-4 Casa 17-5 ME 1-7 USAAF June '44

JK370 15MU 26-2-43 76MU 10-3 *Harpal* 22-3 Casa 6-4 NWA 30-4 Malta 1-7 Sic 1-8 NAAF 1-11 SOC 31-12

JK371 46MU 27-2-43 47MU 16-3 *Orient C* 13-4 Casa 25-4 ME 25-2-45 REAF

JK372 M50A NAAF 25-4-43

JK373 46MU 27-2-43 47MU 18-3 *Orient C* 13-4 Casa 25-4 NWA 31-5 Malta 1-8 Sic C3 ops 28-8

JK374 12MU 28-2-43 82MU 5-3 *Fort Liv* 20-3 Gib 12-4 NWA 30-4 ME 30-11-44 SOC 29-3-45

JK375 VC(T)M50 6MU 2-3-43 82MU 11-3 *Emp Prin* 20-3 Casa 6-4 NWA 30-4

JK376 VC(T)M50 45MU 13-3-43 215MU 20-3 *Ess Trad* 10-4 Casa 25-4 NWA 31-5 Malta 10-8 Italy 1-11 ME 30-11 RHAF 25-4-46

JK377 VC(T)M50 6MU 2-3-43 82MU 11-3 *Emp Prin* 23-3 Casa 6-4 NWA 31-5

JK378 VC(T) 6MU 6-3-43 47Mu 15-3 *Orient C* 13-4 Casa 25-4 M50 instal NAASC 31-10 SOC 26-4-45

JK379 no record SOC 29-2-44

JK380 VC(T)M50 6MU 2-3-43 82MU 11-3 *Fort Liv* 20-3 Gib 12-4 NWA 30-4 USAAF 29-2-44 FAF 9-10-47

JK381 VC(T) 6MU 7-3-43 47MU 14-3 *Orient C* 13-4 Casa 25-4 SEAC 25-9-44 MAAF 27-10 to Turk 30-11

JK382 VC(T)M50 6MU 2-3-43 82MU 12-3 *Emp Prin* 23-3 Casa 4-4 NWA 31-5 ME 15-3-45 SOC 29-3-46

JK383 38MU 2-2-43 47MU 13-2 *Isipan* 5-3 Tak 2-4 ME 9-5 NAAF 30-11 FAF 25-4-46

JK384 46MU 3-2-43 215MU 15-2 *Fort L M* 18-3 Tak 20-4 ME 4-6 SOC 1-2-44

JK385 45MU 4-2-43 215MU 21-2 *Harmat* 10-3 Gib 21-4 NWA USAAF 31-8 SOC 19-7-45

JK386 no record SOC 29-2-44

JK387 8MU 7-2-43 82MU 13-2 *Fort L M* 12-3 Tak 20-4 ME 26-4 Malta 1-7 2SAAF S FTR ops 29-11

JK388 45MU 6-2-43 82MU 16-2 *Tyne* 2-3 Gib 24-3 2SAAF S FTR ops 9-1-44

JK389 38MU 4-2-43 76MU 12-2 *Harpal* 22-3 Casa 6-4 M50A instal NWA 30-4 Malta Sic 1-8 ME 30-9 SOC 26-4-45

JK390 15MU 3-2-43 76MU 13-2 *Harpal* 22-3 Casa 6-4 NWA 30-4 USAAF

JK391 12MU 6-2-43 47MU 14-3 *SS670* 24-3 Gib 12-4 NWA 30-4 Malta 1-6 FAC2 8-10 Italy 1-11 ME 31-1-45 SOC 31-5

JK392 12MU 67-2-43 215Mu 20-2 *Harmat* 10-3 Gib 24-4 NWA 31-5 IAF 27-6-46 as MM4067

JK393 8MU 7-2-43 82MU 13-2 *Sansu* 5-3 Tak 2-4 ME 23-4 Malta 1-7 Sic NAAF 1-11 to Turk 30-11-44

JK394 45MU 4-2-43 215MU 21-2 *Harmat* 10-3 Gib 26-4 Malta FTR ops 18-7

JK396 12MU 7-2-43 215MU 20-2 *Harmat* 10-3 Gib 26-4 NWA 31-5 31-5 USAAF 31-7

JK397 45MU 4-2-43 215MU 18-2 *Harmat* 10-3 Gib 26-4 NWA 31-5 ME 1-7 SOC 1-11

JK398 46MU 4-2-43 215MU 3-3 *670* 24-3 Gib 12-4 NWA 30-4 Malta 1-1-44 C3 ops 3-4

JK399 8MU 7-2-43 82MU 16-2 *Fort LM* 12-3 Tak 20-4 ME 23-5 NAAF 1-11 185S Malta FTR ops 21-9-44

JK400 Persian Gulf 33MU 10-2-43 52MU 21-2 *Fort LM* 12-3 Tak 20-4 ME 10-5 FAC3 11-1-44

JK401 38MU 2-2-43 222MU 13-2 *Fort McL* 21-3 Cassa 6-4 NWA 30-4 FTR ops 17-11

JK402 33MU 9-2-43 52MU 20-2 *Harpal* 22-3 Cassa 6-4 NWA 30-4 USAAF 31-7 ME 30-11-44 SOC 29-3-45

JK403 12MU 6-2-43 215MU 20-2 *Harmat* 1-3 Gib 26-4 NWA 31-5 Malta 1-8 USAAF

JK404 46MU 3-2-43 47MU 18-2 *Copac* 5-3 Tak 2-4 ME 17-4 Malta 23-4 C3 ops 12-8

JK405 38MU 6-3-43 82MU 11-2 *Tyne* 2-3 Gib 24-3 NWA 30-4 2S SAAF FTR ops 4-12

JK406 8MU 7-2-43 82MU 19-2 *Sansu* 5-3 Tak 2-4 ME 23-4 Iraq 1-6 Malta 1-7 CE ops 27-9-44

JK407 8MU 7-2-43 82MU 20-2 *Fort LM* 12-3 Tak 20-4 ME 23-5 NAAF 30-11

JK408 33MU 10-2-43 52MU 21-2 *Fort LM* 12-3 Tak 20-4 ME 26-5 RHAF 25-4-46

JK425 45MU 11-2-43 215MU 24-2 *Fort LM* 12-3 Tak 20- 4ME 27-5 NAAF 30-11 To Turk 31-5-45

JK426 6MU 6-2-43 82MU 18-2 *Tyne* 2-3 Gib 24-3 NWA 30-4 SOC 30-5-46

JK427 M50A 33MU 7-2-43 76MU 19-2 *Harpal* 22-3 Cassa 6-4 NWA 31-5 ME 1-8 NAAF 30-9 FAC3 19-10 185S Malta 1-1-44 253S FTR ops 6-7

JK428 M50A 33MU 7-2-43 76MU 19-2 *Harpal* 22-3 Cassa 6-4 Malta 7-5 NA 1-10

JK429 R-RH to FIX M63 12MU 1-3-43n 47MU 12-3 *SS670* Gib 12-4 NWA 31-5 Malta 1-7

JK430 6MU 6-2-43 82MU 18-2 *Tyne* 2-3 Gib 24-3 NWA 30-4 Malta 1-7 Sic ME 30-9 SOC 26-4-45

JK431 46MU 7-2-43 215MU 1-3 *SS672* 25-3 Gib 12-4 NWA 31-1-45 SOC 26-4

JK432 46MU 6-2-43 215MU 5-3 *SS672* 25-3 Gib 12-4 NA Malta 1-5 ME 1-9 NWA FAC3 9-11

JK433 15MU 6-2-43 76MU 2-3 *Harpal* 22-3 Cassa 6-4 NWA 30-4 MAAF 21-6-45 Trg del 13-9

JK434 no record SOC 26-4-45

JK435 VC(T)M50A 38MU 13-2-43 52MU 23-2 *Fort LM* 12-3 Tak 20-4 ME 13-12 SOC 13-9-45

JK436 VB 39MU 7-2-43 76MU 20-2 *Fort LM* 12-3 Tak 20-4 ME 20-9 SOC 13-9-45

JK437 12MU 11-2-43 215MU 25-2 *SS672* 25-3 Gib 12-4 NWA 30-4 USAAF 31-7 NAAF 21-6-45 Trg del 13-9-45

JK438 8MU 7-2-43 82MU 20-2 *Fort LM* 12-3 Tak 20-4 CE 18-5

JK439 8MU 7-2-43 82MU 19-2 *Fort LM* 12-3 Tak 20-4 ME 27-5 NA 30-11 SOC 14-3-46

JK440 12MU 7-2-43 215MU 20-2 *Harmat* 10-3 Gib 236-4 NWA 31-5 FAF SOC 31-8-44

JK441 VC(T)M50 38MU 13-2-43 52MU 23-2 *Fort LM* 12-3 Tak 20-4 ME 9-5 SOC 29-8-46

JK442 12MU 7-2-43 215MU 19-2 *Harmat* 10-2 Gib 26-4

JK443 38MU 6-2-43 82MU 16-2 *Tyne* 2-3 Gib 24-3 NWA 30-4 NAASC 31-10 SOC 29-2-44

JK444 46MU 7-2-43 47MU 3-3 *SS670* 24-3 Gib 24-3 NWA 31-5 SOC 26-4-45

JK445 M50A 33MU 7-2-43 76MU 19-2 *Harpal* 22-3 Casa 6-4 NWA 31-5 ME 28-4-45 SOC 25-7-46

JK446 M50A 33MU 7-2-43 76MU 19-2 *Harpal* 22-3 Casa 6-4 NWA 30-4

JK447 12MU 7-2-43 215MU 20-2 *Harmat* 10-3 Gib 26-4 NWA 31-5 FTR ops 16-10-44

JK448 46MU 7-2-43 215MU 1-3 *SS672* 25-3 Gib 12-4 NWA 30-4 Malta 1-7 ME 1-9 SOC 30-11-44 extant, Belgrade

JK449 8MU 7-2-43 82MU 19-2 *Sansu* 5-3 Tak 2-4 ME 21-4 Malta 1-7 Sic NWA 1-10 FAF 31-10 SOC 26-4-45

JK450 M50A 7-2-43 76MU 19-2 *Harpal* 22-3 Cassa 6-4 NWA 30-4 Malta 1-7 NAAF 1-11 SOC 236-4-45

JK451 VC(T)M50 15MU 16-2-43 76MU 6-3 *Harpal* 22-3 Cassa 6-4 NWA 30-4 ME 30-11-44 SOC 29-3-46

JK452 45MU 11-2-43 215MU 24-2 *Fort LM* 12-3 Tak 20-4 ME 8-5 NA 30-11

JK453 45MU 11-2-43 215MU 24-2 *Fort LM* 12-3 Tak 20-4 ME 6-5

JK454 VC(T))M50 38MU 17-6 234S 29-6 130S 20-7 222MU 19-8 *Ger Don* 25-8 Cassa 10-9 NA 30-11 SOC 30-6-44

JK455 VC(T)M50A 12MU 16-2-43 215MU 28-2 *Ess Trad* 10-4 Cassa 25-4 NWA 31-5 SOC 23-10-44

JK456 39MU 7-2-43 82MU 17-2 *Fort LM* 12-3 Tak 20-4 ME 26-5 NAAF 1-11 C3 ops 11-3-44

JK457 8MU 7-2-43 82MU 19-2 *Fort LM* 12-3 Tak 20-4 ME 10-5 NAAF 1-11

JK458 45MU 11-2-43 215MU 1-3 *Ess Trad* 10-4 Cassa 25-4 ME 30-11-44 to Turk 28-12

JK459 12MU 7-2-43 47MU 21-2 *SS670* 24-3 Gib 12-4 NWA 30-4 FAC3 18-6

JK460 VC(T)M50 38MU 13-2-43 222MU 27-2 *Ess*

Trad 10-4 Casa 25-4 NWA 31-5 ME 1-8 NAAF 30-9 SOC 29-8-46

JK461 VC(T)M50A 12MU 13-2-43 47MU 24-2 *Copac* 5-3 Tak 2-4 ME 12-4 Malta 1-7 154S FTR ops 25-7

JK462 VC(T)M50A 33MU 13-2-43 82MU 28-2 *Emp Prin* 23-3 Casa 6-4 ME 1-7 92S i/sea during aero nr Venice Italy pilot kld 30-5-46 SOC 29-8

JK463 R-RH to FIX M63 12MU 6-3-43 47MU *Fort Rup* 11-4 Casa 25-4 185S Malta FTR 25-5 FH11.15

JK464 45MU 11-2-43 215MU 3-3 *SS672* 25-3 Gib 12-4 NWA 30-4 USAAF SOC 11-4-46

JK465 M50 15MU 16-2-43 76MU 28-2 *Fort McL* 21-3 Casa 6-4 Malta 1-5 Italy 1-11 Trg del 13-945

JK466 VC(T)M50 38MU 13-2-43 52MU 23-2 *Fort LM* 12-3 Tak 20-4 ME 25-5

JK467 12MU 11-2-43 215MU 25-2 *SS672* 25-3 Gib 12-4 NAAF 93S FTR ops 7-5

JK468 45MU 19-2-43 215MU 3-3 *SS670* 24-3 Gib 12-4 NWA 30-4 Malta 1-7 Sic ME 30-9 NAAF 1-11 SOC 29-8-46

JK469 M50 33MU 14-2-43 52MU 1-3 *Harpal* 22-3 Casa 6-4 NWA 30-4

JK470 VC(T)M50 12MU 16-2-43 82MU 1-3 *Emp Prin* 23-3 Casa 6-4 NWA 31-5 SOC 26-4-45

JK471 VC(T)M50A 33MU 13-2-43 82MU 28-2 *Harpal* 22-3 Casa 6-4 NWA 31-5 601S FTR ops 3-12

JK472 12MU 11-2-43 47MU 24-2 *SS670* 24-3 Gib 12-4 NWA 31-5 ME 29-3-45 SOC 13-9

JK506 48MU 222MU 4-2-43 *SS657* 19-2 Gib 9-3 NWA 31-3 SOC 11-4-46

JK507 VC(T) 45MU 27-2-43 215MU 5-2 *SS682* 12-4 Casa 25-4 NWA 31-5 SOC 26-4-45

JK508 46MU 27-1-43 215MU 28-2 *SS670* 25-3 Gib 12-4 NWA 30-4 Malta 1-7 Sic NAAF 1-11 SOC 8-3-44

JK509 Wadi Halfa 6MU 6-2-43 82MU 18-2 *Tyne* 2-3 Gib 24-3 NWA 30-4 Malta 1-10 FAF MAAF CE ops 7-11-44

JK510 46MU 2-2-43 215MU 13-2 *Harmat* 10-3 Gib 26-4 NWA 31-5 Malta 1-8 Sic NAAF 1-11 118MU Malta 31-1-44 SOC 29-2

JK511 VC(T) 45MU 29-1-43 222MU 4-2 *SS657* 19-2 Gib 9-3 NWA 31-3 Malta 1-7 152S FTR ops 12-7

JK512 15MU 29-1-43 76MU 13-2 *Fort L M* 12-3 Tak 20-4 ME 19-6 NAASC 1-11 SOC 29-8-46

JK513 38MU 1-2-43 222MU 10-2 *Fort H H* 20-2 Gib 7-3 NWA 31-3

JK514 12MU 6-2-43 215MU 20-2 *Harmat* 10-3 Gib 20-4 FACE 26-5

JK515 45MU 1-2-43 215MU 9-2 *Harmat* 10-3 Gib 26-4 1676Flt CE ops 23-8

JK516 9MU 8-2-43 82MU 17-2 *Thom Holt* 25-3 Tak 209-43 ME 7-5 SOC 29-2-44

JK517 9MU 12-2-43 52MU 23-2 *Fort L M* 12-3 Tak 20-4 ME 26-5 SOC 1-11

JK518 9MU 8-2-43 82MU 20-2 *Fort Liv* 20-3 Gib 12-4 NWA 30-4 Malta 1-7 Sic ME 1-11 NAASC 31-10 SOC 29-8-46

JK519 VC(T) 38MU 13-2-43 52MU 27-2 *Ess Trad* 10-4 Casa 25-4 NWA FAF 1-1 SOC 18-8-44

JK520 M45 9MU 18-2-43 52MU 23-2 *Fort L M* 12-3 Tak 20-4 ME 23-6 NAAF 1-11 SOC 26-4-45

JK521 9MU 15-2-43 222MU 3-3 *SS679* 10-4 Casa 25-4 NWA 31-5 Malta 1-8 NAASC 31-10 SOC 28-4-45

JK522 M45 9MU 16-2-43 82MU 9-3 *SS682* 12-4 Casa 25-4 NA 31-5 Sic 1-10 NAAF CE ops 26-11

JK523 9MU 15-2-43 222MU 3-3 *SS679* 12-4 Casa 25-4 NWA 31-5 USAAF 31-7

JK524 9MU 23-3-43 52MU 6-3 *SS680* 11-4 Casa 25-4 NWA USAAF 31-7 FAF NAASC 31-10

JK525 9MU 15-2-43 222MU 3-3 *SS679* 12-4 Casa 25-4 Malta Sic 1-8 ME 30-9

JK526 9MU 19-2-43 3-3 *SS679* 12-4 Casa 25-4 NWA 31-5 USAAF 31-7 ME 30-11-44 to Turk 29-3-45

JK527 9MU 1-3-43 47MU 26-2 *Orient C* 13-4 Casa 25-4 NWA 31-5 ME 1-8 NAAF 30-9 CE SOC 19-7-45

JK528 9MU 29-2-43 82MU 9-3 *Fort Liv* 20-3 Gib 12-4 NWA 30-4 USAAF NAASC 31-10 ME 30-11-44 RHAF 25-4-46

JK529 9MU 19-2-43 82MU 6-3 *Emp Prin* 23-3 Casa 6-4 NWA 31-5 Malta 1-8 FAC2 26-10 NAF 1-11

JK530 VC(T) 6MU 7-3-43 47MU 15-3 *Orient C* 13-4 Casa 25-4 NWA 31-5 USAAF 31-7 RHAF 25-4-46 336S cd on t/o Sedes Greece 20-6

JK531 38MU 13-3-43 222Mu 28-3 *SS679* 12-4 Casa 25-4 145MU FTR ops 10-5 cancel NA 1-7 118MU Malta 31-1-44 ME 21-6-45 SOC 4-10

JK532 38MU 13-3-43 47MU 1-7 *Ess Trad* 10-4 Casa 25-4 NWA 31-5 C3 ops 30-3-44

JK533 VC(Y)M50 15MU 14-3-43 47MU 22-3 *SS682* 12-4 Casa 25-4 NWA 31-5 ME 31-1-45 SOC 29-8-46

JK534 VC(T)M45 15MU 22-3-43 76MU 12-4 *Fort Thom* 3-5 Casa 17-5 ME 1-8 NAASC 31-10 SOC 18-8-44

JK535 M45 R-RH to FIXC M66 23-4 VWD 26-11 M63A instal ACR and contraprops. Ext trls for perf and vibration. F21 tailplane fit R-RH 10-2-44 for gnrl dev 1CRU Cowley 18-6-456 recat E SOC 2-7

JK536 46MU 9-3-43 47MU 24-3 *Orient C* 13-4 Casa 25-4 NWA 31-5 Malta FAC2 4-8 SOC

JK537 M45 45MU 18-3-43 76MU 1-4 *SS 680* 11-4 Casa 25-4 NWA 31-5 USAAF 31-7

JK538 M50 9MU 18-4-43 38MU 21-4 *Fort Jer* 11-5 Casa 30-5 NWA 1-7 ME 1-9 NAAF 30-11 SOC 28-4-45

JK539 M45 15MU 18-3-43 76MU 1-4 *SS680* 11-4 Casa 25-4 NWA 31-5 Malta Sicily 1-8 ME 1-9 NAAF 1-11 SOC 13-9-45

JK540 46MU 29-4-43 45MU 2-5 *Fort Stle* 16-5 Casa 30-5 NWA 1-7 ME 14-7 C3 ops 15-9

JK541 VC(T) 15MU 14-3-43 76MU 26-3 *SS682* 12-4 Casa 25-4 NWA 31-5 ME 1-7 FAC3 11-8 NAAF 1-11 118MU Malta 31-1-44

JK542 VC(T)M50 39MU 20-3-43 222MU 29-3 *SS680* 11-4 Casa 25-4 31-5 USAAF NAASC 31-10. Served with Yugoslav Sq. Attach Tact Wng Balkan A/F SOC 31-12

JK543 VC(T)M50 39MU 20-3-43 82MU 29-3 *SS680* 11-4 Casa 25-4 NWA 31-5 USAAF NWA 31-7 Trg del 25-10-45

JK544 VC(T)M55 33MU 16-5-43 47MU 8-6 *Glenb* 3-7 Tak 20-7 ME 15-9 SOC 26-4-45

JK545 MJ50 38MU 6-5-43 76MU 21-5 *SS702* 2-6 Casa 15-6 NWA 1-7 SOC 28-4-45

JK546 VC(T) M50 15MU 22-3-43 76MU 4-4 *SS680* 11-4 Casa 25-4 NWA 31-5 SOC 30-6-45

JK547 VC(T)M50 45MU 14-5-43 82MU 22-5 *SS703* 1-6 Casa 15-6 NWA 1-7 ME 1-9 NAAF 1-11 to 4708MU 18-5-44

JK548 VC(T)M50 15MU 22-3-43 NWA 31-5 FTR ops 27-11

JK549 M45 15MU 22-3-43 82MU 7-4 *SS686* 24-4 Casa 17-5 Malta 1-8 Italy 1-11

JK550 M45 45MU 26-3-43 215MU 6-4 *SS687* 29-4 Casa 17-5 NWA USAAF 31-7 FAF 14-2-46

JK551 M45 12MU 27-3-43 82MU 6-4 *SS686* 24-4 Casa 17-5 NWA 31-5 USAAF 31-7

JK600 M50 33MU 14-2-43 52MU 3-3 *SS680* 11-4 Casa 25-4 NWA 31-5 SOC 26-4-45

JK601 VC(T)M50 38MU 15-2-43 52MU 23-2 *Fort LM* 12-3 Tak 20-4 ME 12-5 NAAF 1-11 SOC 8-3-44

JK602 M50 33MU 14-2-43 52MU 3-3 *SS680* 11-4 Casa 25-4 NWA 31-5 USAAF 12/52 31-8 lost in France 27-1-44

JK603 VC(T)M50 15MU 14-2-43 76MU 4-2 *Fort McL* 21-3 Casa 6-4 NWA 30-4 Malta 1-7 Sic NAAF 1-11 SOC 8-3-44

JK604 VC(T)M50 15MU 16-2-43 76MU 4-3 *Fort McL* 21-3 Casa 6-4 NWA 30-4 ME 1-8 USAAF 31-10 MAAF 21-6-45 SOC 18-10

JK605 15MU 24-2-43 76MU 6-3 *Harpal* 22-3 Casa 6-4 73S FTR ops 26-5-44

JK606 45MU 18-2-43 215MU 3-3 *SS672* 25-3 Gib 12-4 NWA 30-4 Malta 1-7 Sic ME 1-11 NAASC 31-10 SOC 9-3-44

JK607 VC(T) 15MU 18-2-43 76MU 2-3 *Fort McL* 21-3 Casa 6-4 NWA 30-4 USAAF 30-11 SOC 26-4-45

JK608 VC(T)M50 15MU 14-2-43 76MU 25-2 *Fort LM* 12-3 Tak 20-4 ME 7-5 SOC 26-4-45

JK609 VC(T) 39MU 18-2-43 82MU 1-3 *Emp Prin* 23-2 casa 6-4 NWA 31-5 USAAF 12/31 lost over Italy 5-11

JK610 VC(T)M50 12MU 16-2-43 82MU 1-3 *Emp Prin* 23-3 Casa 6-4 NWA 1-5 Malta 1-6 Sic NAAF 1-11 SOC 29-2-44

JK612 VC(T) 12MU 16-2-43 82MU 28-2 *SS682* 12-4 Casa 25-4 NWA 31-5 Malta 1-7 Sic NAAF 1-11 USAAF 31-1-44

JK613 VC(T)M50 38MU 15-2-43 222MU 27-2 *Ess Trad* 10-4 Casa 25-4 NWA 31-5 Malta 1-8 Sic NAAF 1-11 ME 30-11 SOC 25-7-46

JK614 VC(T) 15MU 16-2-43 76MU 3-3 *Fort McL* 21-3 Casa 6-4 NWA 31-3 Malta 1-7 Sic NAASC 31-10 MAAF 21-6-45 SOC 30-8

JK615 M50A 9MU 15-2-43 82MU 27-2 *Fort LM* 12-3 Tak 20-4 ME 26-5 NAAF 1-11 SOC 1-4-44

JK616 M50A 9MU 15-2-43 82MU 27-2 *Emp Prin* 23-3 Casa 6-4 NWA 31-5 Malta 1-8 Sic C2 ops NA 30-11 SOC 28-4-45

JK617 VC(T)M5υ 38MU 15-2-43 WAL 47MU 7-6 *Glenb* 3-7 Tak 30-7 ME 13-9 451S FAC3 16-2-44 SOC 22-2-45

JK618 38MU 21-2-43 82MU 8-3 *SS671* 20-3 Gib 12-4 NWA 30-4 SOC 26-4-45

JK619 45MU 18-2-43 215MU 7-3 *SS670* 24-3 Gib 10-4 NWA 30-4

JK620 R-RH to FIX M66 612S 12-3-43 e/fld w/u ldg Tunbridge Wells CB 26-3 AST 313S FAAC 29-5-44 3501SU 9-7 MAAF 5-3-45 cd France en route to ME CE 6-3-45

JK637 VC(T) 15MU 18-2-43 76MU 3-3 *Harpal* 22-3 Casa 6-4 NWA 30-4 Malta 1-7 Sic FTR ops 4-8

JK638 (MU 15-2-43 82MU 3-3 *Emp Prin* 23-3 Casa 6-4 NWA 31-5 ME 1-9 NAASC 1-11 SOC 26-4-45

JK639 38MU 21-2-43 82MU 6-3 *Fort Liv* 20-3 Casa 12-4 NWA 30-4

JK640 M50A Central Province of Behar VII 38MU 21-2-43 82MU 12-3 *Emp Prin* 23-3 Casa 6-4 NWA 31-5 Malta 1-10 ME 31-1-45 SOC 27-6-46

JK642 46MU 19-2-43 47MU 4-3 *SS670* 24-3 Gib 12-4 NWA 30-4 Malta 1-7 Sic ME FTR ops 18-8

JK643 45MU 18-2-43 215MU 7-3 *SS672* 25-3 Gib 12-4 NWA 30-4 Malta 1-7 ME 1-10 NAAF 125S FTR ops 16-12

JK644 38MU 21-2-43 52MU 3-3 *SS680* 11-4 Casa 25-4 Tak 20-4 ME 6-5 C3 ops 17-10 NA 3-11 SOC 29-2-44

JK645 VC(T)M50 38MU 15-2-43 52MU 23-2 *Fort LM* 12-3 Tak 20-4 ME 6-5 C3 ops 17-10 NA 30-11 SOC 29-2-44

JK646 45MU 26-2-43 47MU 15-3 *Orient C* 13-4 Casa 25-4 Malta 229S C3 ops 8-6

JK647 8MU 23-2-43 82MU 4-3 *Fort L M* 20-3 Gib 12-4 NWA 30-4 Malta 1-11 SOC 26-4-45

JK648 M50A 39MU 19-2-43 47MU 28-2 *Orient C* 13-4 Casa 25-4 NWA 31-5 USAAF 31-7 MAAF 31-1-44 REAF 23-2-45

JK649 VC(T)M45 15MU 16-2-43 76MU 4-3 *Fort McL* 21-3 Casa 6-4 NWA 30-4 Malta 1-7 Sic ME 30-9 NAAF 1-11 FAF 14-2-46

JK651 38MU 28-2-43 82MU 12-3 *Fort Liv* 20-3 Gib 12-4 NWA 31-5 Malta 1-8 Sic NAAF 1-11 ME 25-2-45 FTR 12-7

JK652 46MU 20-2-43 47MU 4-3 *SS670* 24-3 Gib 12-4 NWA 30-4 ME 30-6 32S RHAF 25-4-46

JK653 12MU 24-2-43 215MU 3-3 *SS672* 25-3 Gib 12-4 Malta 1-5 NA 1-7 Sicily ME 30-9 NWA USAAF 1-10 SOC 8-3-44

JK654 VC(T) 15MU 18-2-43 76MU 28-2 *Fort McL* 21-3 Casa 6-4 NWA 30-4 SOC 31-7

Short span wings Mk Vs with wheel well strengthening strakes on upper wing surfaces.

JK655 46MU 19-2-43 47MU 4-3 *SS670* 24-3 Gib 12-4 SOC 30-6-45

JK656 39MU 23-2-43 47MU 4-3 *Fort Liv* 20-3 Gib 12-4 NWA 30-4 Malta 1-7 Sic NAAF 1-11 118MU Malta 31-1-44 RHAF 25-4-46

JK657 46MU 19-2-43 47MU 4-3 *SS670* 24-3 Gib 12-4 1676Flt

JK658 VC(T) 39MU 18-2-43 82MU 1-3 *Emp Prin* 23-3 Casa 6-4 SOC 23-10-44

JK659 R-RH to FIX M63 15MU 13-3-43 47MU 26-3 *Orient C* 13-4 Casa 25-4 NWA 31-5 FTR ops 23-2-45

JK660 46MU 28-2-43 47MU 14-3 *Orient C* 13-4 25-4 CE ops 10-8-44

JK661 46MU 19-2-43 47MU 14-3 *SS670* 24-3 Gib 12-4 NWA 30-4 USAAF 31-7 RAF 31-5-44

JK662 6MU 27-2-43 82MU 9-3 *Fort Liv* 20-3 Gib 12-4 NWA 30-4 SOC 31-7

JK663 VC(T) 39MU 18-2-43 82MU 27-2 *Fort L M* 12-3 Tak 20-4 ME 7-5 SOC 1-11

JK664 6MU 21-2-43 82MU 1-3 *Emp Prin* 23-3 Casa 6-4 NWA 31-5 ME 15-3-45 to Turk 29-3

JK665 6MU 21-2-43 82MU 1-3 *Emp Prin* 23-3 Casa 6-4 NAASC 31-10 ME 30-11-44 to Turk 28-12

JK666 12MU 24-2-43 215MU 6-3 *SS672* 25-3 Gib 12-4 NWA 31-5 Malta 1-7 Sic

JK667 VC(T)M50 8MU 21-243 82MU 27-2 *Fort McL* 21-3 Casa 6-4 NWA 30-4 ME 1-8 CE ops 27-9

JK668 R-RH to FIX M63 12MU 4-4-43 47MU 9-4 *SS687* 29-4 Casa 17-5 NWA USAAF 31-7

JK669 M50A 38MU 21-2-43 82MU 12-3 *Emp Prin* 23-3 Casa 6-4 NWA 31-5 ME 29-6 FAC3 24-6

JK670 VC(T) M50 8MU 21-2-43 82MU 27-2 *Fort McL* 21-3 Casa 6-4 Malta 1-7 Sic SOC 18-8-44

JK671 VC(T) M50 8MU 21-2-43 82MU 27-2 *Fort L M* 12-3 Tak 20-4 ME 7-5 SOC 30-9

JK672 12MU 25-2-43 82MU 5-3 *Fort Liv* 20-3 Gib 2-4 Malta 1-5 Sic 1-10 SOC 30-8-45

JK673 12MU 24-2-43 215MU 3-3 *SS672* 25-3 Gib 12-4 NWA 31-5 USAAF SOC 26-4-45

JK674 15MU 25-2-43 76MU 2-3 *Harpal* 22-3 Casa 6-4 NWA 30-4 Malta 1-7 FTR ops 2-12

JK675 VC(T)M50 8MU 21-2-43 82MU 27-2 *Harpal* 22-3 Casa 6-4 NWA 30-4 CE 21-6-45

JK676 33MU 1-3-43 47MU 30-3 *Ess Trad* 10-4 Casa 25-4 NWA 31-5 C3 ops 7-3-44 bboc 23-10 to Turk 30-11

JK677 VC(T)M50 8MU 21-2-43 82MU 27-2 *Fort L M* 12-3 Tak 20-4 ME 7-5 SOC 1-11

JK678 6MU 23-2-43 52MU 28-2 *Harpal* 22-2 Casa 6-4 NWA 31-5 SOC 31-5-45

JK705 33MU 27-2-43 82MU 12-3 *Emp Prin* 23-3 Casa 6-4 USAAF 12/52 29-2-44 w/o France 27-1 (USAAF records)

JK706 M50 45MU 26-2-43 215MU 11-3 *SS670* 24-3 Gib 12-4 NWA 31-5

JK707 VC(T)M50 15MU 24-2-43 76MU 10-3 *Harpal* 22-3 Casa 6-4 NWA 30-4

JK708 6MU 26-2-43 82MU 7-3 *Fort Liv* 20-3 Gib 12-4 NWA 30-4 Malta 1-7 Sic NAAF 1-11 CE ops 28-10-44

JK709 33MU 23-2-43 47MU 11-3 *Orient C* 13-4 Casa 25-4 NWA 31-5 ME 1-7 C3 ops 20-3-44

JK710 8MU 23-2-43 82MU 4-3 *Fort Liv* 20-3 Gib 12-4 NWA 30-4 ME 1-9 to Turk 28-12-44

JK711 39MU 23-2-43 82MU 4-3 *Fort Liv* 20-3 Gib 12-4 NWA 31-5 USAAF ME 31-5-45 SOC 14-3-46

JK712 VC(T)M50 15MU 24-2-43 76MU 7-3 *Harpal* 22-3 Casa 6-4 NWA 30-4 FAF NAASC 31-10 SOC 26-4-45

JK713 12MU 25-2-43 82MU 5-3 *Fort Liv* 20-3 Gib 12-4 NWA 30-4 SOC 26-4-45

JK714 no record

JK715 15MU 24-2-43 76MU 7-3 *Harpal* 22-3 Casa 6-4 NWA 30-4 Malta 1-7 Sic NA 30-11 SOC 26-4-45

JK716 M50 46MU 26-2-43 215MU 8-3 *SS670* 24-3 Gib 12-4 NWA 31-5 USAAF NWA 31-7 ME 28-12-4 SOC 26-9-46

JK717 VC(T)M50 12MU 25-2-43 215MU 4-3 *SS672* 25-3 Gib 12-4 NWA 31-5 USAAF 31-8

JK718 45MU 28-2-43 47MU 17-3 *Orient C* 13-4 Casa 25-4

JK719 12MU 25-2-43 215MU 6-3 *SS672* 25-3 Gib 12-4 NWA 31-5 USAAF 31-7

JK720 45MU 26-2-43 215MU 11-3 *SS679* 13-4 Casa 25-4 Malta Sic 1-8 IAF 27-6-46 as MM4061

JK721 45MU 26-2-43 215MU 12-3 *SS672* Gib 12-4 NWA ME 1-7 FTR ops 13-11

JK722 45MU 26-2-43 215MU 12-3 *SS672* Gib 12-4 NA 1-5 ME 1-9 Malta Sic 1-10 NAAF 1-11 SOC 8-3-44 bboc 29-3-45 REAF

JK723 45MU 28-2-43 215MU 14-3 *SS672* Gib 25-3 Gib 12-4 NWA 30-4 Malta 1-7 Sic NA 30-11 SOC 8-3-44

JK724 45MU 26-2-43 215MU 11-3 *SS679* 13-4 Casa 25-4 NWA 31-5 USAAF 31-7 SOC 28-4-45

JK725 33MU 27-2-43 82MU 10-3 *Fort Liv* 20-3 Gib 12-4 NWA 31-5 Malta 1-8 SOC 26-4-45

JK726 45MU 26-2-43 47MU 17-3 *Orient C* 13-4 Casa 25-4 NWA 31-5 ME 1-8 NAAF 30-9 C3 ops 16-2-44

JK727 6MU 26-2-43 82MU 7-3 *Emp Prin* 23-3 Casa 16-4 NWA 31-5 ME 30-11 SOC 8-3-44 Trg del 27-9-45

JK728 45MU 26-2-43 215MU 11-3 *SS670* 24-3 Gib 12-4 Malta Sic 1-8 NA 30-11 253S FTR ops 28-10-44 cancel REAF 22-2-45

JK729 33MU 27-2-43 82MU 7-3 *Fort Liv* 20-3 Gib 12-4 NWA 30-4

JK730 M50 46MU 27-2-43 215MU 8-3 *SS670* 24-3 Gib 12-4 NWA 30-4

JK731 46MU 26-2-43 215MU 5-3 *SS670* 24-3 Gib 12-4 NWA 31-5 ME 30-1-44 CE 24-7-45

JK732 33MU 27-2-43 82MU 12-3 *Emp Prin* 23-3 Casa 6-4 USAAF NWA 1-10 253S C3 ops 7-8-44

JK733 46MU 28-2-43 47MU 16-3 *Orient C* 13-4 Casa 25-4 FAC3 14-9

JK734 VC(T) 45MU 6-3-43 215MU 14-3 *SS672* 25-3 Gib 12-4 USAAF NAASC 31-10 FAC 31-3-44

JK735 38MU 28-2-43 82MU 9-3 *Emp Prin* 23-3 Casa 6-4 NWA 31-5 USAAF 1-10 FTR ops 2-9-44

JK736 15MU 26-2-43 76MU 12-3 *Harpal* 22-3 Casa 6-4 NWA 31-5 USAAF 31-8

JK737 45MU 28-2-43 47MU 17-3 *Orient C* 13-4 Casa 25-4 NWA SOC 31-5

JK738 46MU 28-2-43 215MU 9-3 *SS679* 13-4 Casa 25-4 SOC 25-7-46

JK739 46MU 26-2-43 215MU 9-3 *SS679* 13-4 Casa 25-4 NWA 31-5 ME 25-2-45 REAF

JK740 6MU 27-2-43 82MU 9-3 *Fort Liv* 20-3 Gib 12-4 NAAF 1-11 SOC 22-2-45

JK741 46MU 28-2-43 215MU 9-3 *SS672* 25-3 Gib 12-4 NWA 30-4 FTR 21-10-44

JK742 M50 15MU 2-3-43 76MU 15-3 *Harpal* 22-3 Casa 6-4 NWA 30-4 Malta 1-7 Sic ME 1-11 SOC 25-10-44

JK756 6MU 27-2-43 82MU 9-3 *Fort Liv* 20-3 Gib 12-4 NWA 126S C3 ops 10-2-44

JK757 M50 33MU 27-2-43 82MU 10-3 *Emp Prin* 23-3 Casa 14-14 NWA 31-5

JK758 33MU 1-3-43 82MU 7-3 *Fort Liv* 20-3 Gib 12-4 NWA 30-4 Malta 1-7 Sic NAASC 31-10 40S FTR 1-9-44

JK759 15MU 1-3-43 47MU 13-3 *SS670* 24-3 Gib 12-4 CE ops 23-7-44

JK760 45MU 28-2-43 215MU 12-3 *SS679* 12-4 Casa 25-4 ME 31-8-44 SOC 28-12

JK761 33MU 1-3-43 222MU 15-3 *SS679* 12-4 Casa 25-4 NWA 31-5 SOC 29-2-44

JK762 R-RH to LFIX M66 RAF B Hll 26-3-43 611S 17-4 485S 4-7 FTR ops 20-10

JK763 38MU 28-2-43 *SS671* 20-3 Gib 12-4 NWA 30-4 USSAF NAASC 31-10 C3 ops 2-2-44

JK764 45MU 10-3-43 215MU 22-3 *Ess Trad* 10-4 Casa 25-4 ME 1-8 SOC 19-7-45

JK765 M45 33MU 1-3-43 47MU 11-3 *SS670* 24-3 Gib 12-4 NWA 31-5 USAAF 31-10 SOC 26-4-45

JK766 VC(T)M45 39MU 6-3-43 82MU 16-3 *Emp Prin* 23-3 Casa 6-4 ME 31-8-44 CE 11-1-45

JK767 VC(T)M50 38MU 6-3-43 222MU 16-3 *SS679* 12-4 Casa 25-4 NWA 31-5 NAAF 1-8

JK768 VC(T)M50 45MU 6-3-43 47MU 17-3 *Orient C* 13-4 Casa 25-4 NWA 31-5 USAAF 31-7 MAAF 31-1-44

JK769 R-RH to LFIX M66 RAF B Hll 27-3-43 611S 1-4 485S 4-7 FTR ops 3-10

JK771 33MU 1-3-43 82MU 12-3 *Emp Prin* 23-3 Casa Malta 31-5 NAASC 31-10 SOC 25-7-46

JK772 VC(T)M50A 39MU 6-3-43 82MU 16-3 *SS685* 12-4 Casa 25-4 NWA 31-5 USAAF 31-8

JK773 15MU 5-3-43 222MU 19-3 *SS679* 12-4 Casa 25-4 Malta 1-7 Sic SOC 20-9-46

JK774 45MU 28-2-43 47MU 15-3 *Orient C* 13-4 Casa 25-4 NWA 31-5 USAAF 31-7

JK775 38MU 28-2-43 222MU 14-3 *SS679* NWA USAAF 313-7 RAF 1-10

JK776 VC(T)M50 45MU 6-3-43 47MU 17-3 *Orient C* 13-4 Casa 25-4 NWA USAAF 31-7

JK777 VC(T) 38MU 6-3-43 222MU 17-3 *SS679* 12-4 Casa 25-4 NWA 31-5 USAAF 31-7 SOC 22-11-45

JK778 45MU 10-3-43 215MU 19-3 *SS679* 12-4 Casa 25-4 NWA 31-5 1-7 SOC 10-11-44

JK779 VC(T) 15MU 7-3-43 76MU 12-3 *SS679* 12-4 Casa 25-4 NWA 31-5 ME 15-3-45

JK780 VC(T)M50 38MU 6-3-43 222MU 16-3 *SS679* 12-4 Casa 25-4 NWA 31-5 USAAF 31-7 FAF NAASC 31-10 SOC 29-2-44

JK781 VC(T)M50 45MU 6-3-43 47MU 17-3 *Orient C* 13-4 Casa 25-4 NWA 31-5 ME 1-8 NAAF 30-9 SOC 30-11-44

JK782 VC(T) 38MU 6-3-43 222MU 16-3 *SS679* 12-4 Casa 25-4 Malta 1-7 Sic ME 1-11 RHAF 25-4-46

JK783 VC(T)M45 38MU 6-3-43 47MU 27-3 *Orient C* 132-4 Casa 25-4 FAF 1-10 NAASC 31-10 SOC 29-2-44

JK784 VC(T)M50 6-3-43 47MU 15-3 *Orient C* 13-4 Casa 25-4 NWA 1-10 IAF 27-6-46 as MM4065

JK785 15MU 4-3-43 76MU 18-3 *SS682* 12-4 Casa 25-4 NWA 31-5 Malta Sicily 1-8 NA 30-11 253S C3 ops 15-5-44

JK786 VC(T)M45 8MU 7-3-43 222MU 19-3 *SS679* 12-4 Casa 25-4 NWA 31-5 Malta Sic 1-8 NAASC 31-10 225S FTR ops 10-2-44

JK787 VC(T)M50 39MU 6-3-43 82MU 14-3 *Emp Prin* 23-3 Casa 6-4 NWA 31-5 ME 1-7 NA 30-11 SOC 14-12-44

JK788 VC(T) 39MU 6-3-43 222MU 14-3 *SS679* 12-4 Casa 25-4 NWA 31-5 USAAF 31-7 ME 31-8 SOC 14-3-46

JK789 12MU 7-3-43 47MU 16-3 *Orient C* 13-4 Casa 25-4 NWA 31-5 ME 1-7 NAASC 1-11 SOC 30-6-45

JK790 VC(T)M50 8MU 7-3-43 222MU 19-3 *SS679* 12-4 Casa 25-4 NWA 31-5 Malta 1-8 ME 1-10 NAAF 1-11 SOC 30-6-45

JK791 12MU 7-3-43 47MU 16-3 *Orient C* 13-4 Casa 25-4 NWA 31-5 USAAF

JK792 VC(T)M50 33MU 13-3-43 222MU 26-3 *SS679* 12-4 Casa 25-4 NWA 31-5 SOC 26-4-45

JK793 VC(T)M45 33MU 13-3-43 47MU *Glenb* 3-7 Tak 25-7 ME 14-9

JK794 VC(T) 39MU 6-3-43 222MU 19-3 *SS679* 12-4 Casa 25-4 NWA 31-5

JK795 R-RH to LFIX M66 RAF B Hll 27-3-43 611S 1-4 CAC ops 7-5 411S 17-10 AST 401S 24-8-44 FTR 21-9

JK803 9MU 12-2-43 82MU 4-3 *Emp Prin* 25-3 Casa 6-4 Malta 1-5 Italy 1-11 CE ops 4-11-44

JK804 9MU 26-2-43 222MU 12-3 *SS679* 12-4 Casa 25-4 NWA 31-5 Malta Sic 1-8 NWA USAAF 31-8 ME 31-1-45

JK805 9MU 27-2-43 82MU 9-3 *Fort Liv* 20-3 Gib 12-4 NWA 31-5 SOC 30-8-45

JK806 9MU 28-2-43 222MU 12-3 *SS679* 12-4 Casa 25-4 NWA 31-5 FAF 31-8 USAAF to Turk 30-11-44

JK807 9MU 1-3-43 222MU 12-3 *SS679* 12-4 Casa 25-4 NWA 31-5 Malta Sic 1-8 FAC3 2-10-43

JK808 15MU 4-3-43 76MU *SS682* 12-4 Casa 25-4 W Afr CE 22-4

JK809 33MU 23-2-43 47MU 11-3 *SS670* 24-3 Gib 12-4 NWA 30-4 USAAF 31-1-44 ME 30-11 RHAF 25-4-46

JK810 12MU 25-2-43 82MU 11-3 *Fort Liv* 20-3 Gib 12-4 NWA 31-5 Malta 1-7 Sic NA 30-11 USAAF 31-1-44

JK811 9MU 1-3-43 82MU 9-3 *SS671* 20-3 Gib 12-4 NWA 31-5 USAAF 31-8 SOC 15-3-45

JK812 9MU 1-3-43 222MU 12-3 *SS679* 12-4 Casa 25-4 NWA 31-5 C3 ops 24-7 Malta Sic 1-8

JK813 9MU 1-3-43 82MU 9-3 *Fort Liv* 20-3 Gib 12-4 NWA 30-4 USAAF 31-7

JK814 38MU 28-2 82MU 12-3 *Fort Liv* 20-3 Gib 12-4 SOC 26-4-45

JK815 12MU 8-3 215MU 17-3 *SS679* 12-4 Casa 25-4 NWA 31-5 Malta Sic 1-8 NA 30-11 SOC 26-4-45

JK816 12MU 8-3-43 82MU 22-3 *SS682* 12-4 Casa 25-4 Malta C3 ops 25-5 FH13.10

JK817 12MU 8-3-43 47MU 16-3 *Orient C* 13-4 Casa 25-4 NA 30-11-44

JK818 46MU 15-3-43 222MU 29-3 *SS680* 11-4 Casa 25-4 NWA 31-5 USAAF 31-7 RAF 29-2-44

JK819 46MU 15-3-43 222MU 29-3 *SS680* 11-4 Casa 25-4 NWA 31-5

JK820 38MU 13-3-43 222MU 23-3 *SS679* 11-4 Casa 25-4 NWA 31-5 Malta 1-8 FAC2 7-11 NA 1-1-44 SOC 28-4-45

JK821 M45 9MU 19-3-43 222MU 27-3 *SS679* 11-4 Casa 25-4 NWA 31-5 FAC3 18-2-44

JK822 M45 9MU 21-3-43 222MU 30-3 *SS680* 11-4 Casa 25-4 NAAF FTR ops 7-11

JK823 M45 9MU 21-3-43 82MU 3-4 *Fort Rup* 11-4 Casa 25-4 NWA FAF 1-10 NAASC 328S 12-5-45 81RSU 25-7-45 M50 instal FAF 27-11

JK824 M50 9MU 21-3-43 222MU 30-3 *SS680* 11-4 Casa 25-4 NWA 31-5

JK825 M50 9MU 1-4-43 222MU 30-4 *Fort Stle* 16-5 Casa 30-5 NWA 1-7 FAF GR2/33 1-10 CE 11-7-44 SOC 18-8

JK826 M50 9MU 21-3-43 82MU 3-4 *SS686* 24-4 Casa 17-5 Malta Sicily 1-8 FAC3 10-9

JK827 M45 45MU 28-3-43 82MU 5-4 *SS686* 24-4 Casa 17-5 USAAF 31-10 ME 15-3-45 SOC 27-6-46

JK828 M45 45MU 26-3-43 215MU 6-4 *SS687* 29-4 Casa 17-5 NWA 31-5 USAAF 31-7

JK829 M45 8MU 28-3-43 47MU 5-4 *SS686* 24-4 Casa 17-5 NWA 31-5 Malta Sic 1-8 NAASC 31-10 SOC 8-3-44 bboc 25-10 FTR 27-12

JK830 M45 8MU 28-3-43 47MU 5-4 *Emp Bar* 2-5 Casa 17-5 NAASC 31-10 C3 ops 30-12

JK831 M45 45MU 26-3-43 215MU 7-4 *SS687* 29-4 Casa 17-5 Malta Sic 1-8 NAASC 31-10

JK832 M50 8MU 28-3-43 82MU 4-4 *SS686* 24-4 Casa 17-5

JK833 M50 33MU 31-3-43 82MU 9-4 *SS686* 24-4 Casa 17-5

JK834 M50 38MU 2-4-43 222MU 16-4 *Fort Thom* 3-5 Casa 17-5 Malta Sic 1-8 NA 30-11 ME 25-2-45 REAF 29-3

JK835 M50 45MU 3-4-43 222MU 14-4 *SS687* 29-4 Casa 17-5 ME 15-3-45 SOC 30-4-47

JK836 M50 46MU 27-4-43 82MU 3-5 *Fort Jer* 10-5 Casa 30-5 NWA 1-7 ME 1-9 NAASC 1-11 SOC 30-6-44

JK837 VC(T)M50 38MU 2-4-43 47MU 17-4 *Emp Bar* 2-5 Casa 17-5 NAAF 1-11 185S CE ops 28-4-44

JK838 VC(T)M50 38MU 1-4-43 47MU 9-4 *SS686* 24-4 Casa 17-5 NWA 1-10 SOC 30-6-45

JK839 M50 46MU 3-4-43 215MU 10-4 *SS686* 24-4 Casa 17-5 NWA 31-5 USAAF 31-7 CE 19-10-44

JK840 VC(T)M50 R-RH to LFIX M66 23-5-43 39MU 19-3-44 84GSU 29-4 313S 8-6

JK841 VC(T)M50 33MU 21-5-43 222MU 31-5 *SS703* 1-6 Casa 15-6 NWA 30-6 ME 6-8 SOC 26-4-45

JK842 VC(T)M50 33MU 5-4-43 47MU 21-4 *Rook* 19-3 Tak 16-6 ME 18-7

JK860 VC(T)M50 33MU 222MU 1-3-43 RAF B Hll R-RH 1-4 to LFIX M66 485S 4-7 e/fld on t/o B Hll f/ld CB 31-8 recat E 14-9

JK861 15MU 7-3-43 222MU 19-3 *SS679* 11-4 Casa 25-4 NWA 31-5 USAAF 31-78 NAASC 31-10 118MU Malta 31-1-44 SOC 29-2-44

JK862 M50 6MU 6-3-43 47MU 14-3 *Orient C* 13-4 Casa 25-4 NWA 31-5

JK863 12MU 11-3-43 47MU 23-3 *Ess Trad* 10-4 Casa 25-4 NWA 31-5 Malta Sic 1-8 Soc Oct '44

JK864 VC(T)M50 8MU 7-3-43 222MU 17-3 *SS679* 11-4 Casa 25-4 NWA 1-10 USAAF 31-10

JK865 VC(T)M50 15MU 7-3-43 222MU 19-3 *SS679* 11-4 Casa 25-4 NWA 31-5 ME 1-8 SOC 1-9

JK866 M50 6-3 47MU 14-3 *Orient C* 13-4 Casa 25-4 NWA 31-5 ME 1-7 MAAF 1-11 NA 30-11 SOC 26-4-45

JK867 VC(T)M50 39MU 12-3-43 82MU 22-3 *SS682* 12-4 Casa 25-4 NWA 31-5 ME 6-8 SOC 26-4-45

JK868 VC(T)M45 15MU 7-3-43 222MU 19-3 *SS679* 11-4 Casa 25-4 Malta Sic 1-8 NA 30-11 SOC 26-4-45

JK869 VC(T)M45 8MU 7-3-43 222MU 17-3 *SS679* 11-4 Casa 25-4 NWA 30-4 ME 28-4-45 SOC 20-8-46

JK870 12MU 11-3-43 47MU 22-3 *Ess Trad* 10-4 Casa 25-4 NWA 31-5 NWA 31-5 USAAF 12/31 31-7 lost over Italy 2-12

JK871 46MU 10-3-43 47MU 21-3 *Ess Trad* 10-4 Casa 25-4 NWA 31-5 Malta Sic 1-8 SOC 28-4-45

JK872 VC(T)M50 39MU 12-3-43 82MU 22-3 *SS682*

12-4 Casa 25-4 NWA 31-5 ME 1-7 NAAF 1-11 C3 ops 24-2-44

JK873 M50 MAAF 25-4-44 32S FTR ops 23-10

JK874 M45 46MU 8-33-43 215MU 1-4 *Emp Bar* 2-5 Casa 17-5 NWA 31-5 ME 1-7 NAAF 1-11 118MU Malta 31-1-44 SOC 29-2

JK875 VC(T)M50 15MU 7-3-43 76MU 20-3 *SS682* 12-4 Casa 25-4 NWA 31-5 USAAF 1-10 RAF 31-5-44 FAC 9-3-45 SOC 30-8

JK876 45MU 10-3-43 215MU 19-3 *SS679* 11-4 Casa 25-4 NWA 31-5 SOC 31-8-44

JK877 VC(T)M50 8MU 7-3-43 222MU 17-3 *SS679* 11-4 Casa 25-4 NWA 31-5 ME 1-7 SOC 29-8-46

JK878 45MU 10-3-43 215MU 19-3 *Ess Trad* 10-4 Casa 25-4 ME 31-8 SOC 31-5-45

JK879 VC(T)39MU 12-3-43 47MU 24-3 *Orient C* 12-4 Casa 25-4 NA 31-5 Malta 1-6 Sic 1-10 ME 29-3-45 SOC 29-8-46

JK880 R-RH to FIX M63 9MU 47MU 15-4 *Fort Thom* 3-5 Casa 17-5 Malta Sic 1-8 FTR ops 10-9 SOC 8-3-44

JK885 VC(T)M45 39MU 12-3-43 222MU 29-3 *SS680* 11-4 Casa 25-4 NWA 31-5 Malta Sic 1-8 MAAF 1-11 ME 30-11 RHAF 25-4-46 cd F/Lndg Nr Tirnavos 27-9

JK886 12MU 11-3-43 47MU 22-3 *Orient C* 13-4 Casa 25-4 NWA 31-5 SOC 5-4-45

JK887 12MU 11-3-43 47MU 22-3 *Orient C* 13-4 Casa 25-4 NWA 31-5 ME 1-7 FAC2 27-10 Malta 1-11 NAASC 31-10 SOC 26-4-45

JK888 46MU 10-3-43 47MU 23-3 *Ess Trad* 10-4 Casa 25-4 NWA 31-5 ME 1-8 NAAF 30-9 FTR ops 26-11

JK889 46MU 14-3-43 215MU 21-3 *Ess Trad* 10-4 Casa 25-4 NA 31-5 Malta 1-6 FAC3 7-1-44

JK890 VC(T)M45 39MU 12-3-43 215MU 22-3 *Ess Trad* 10-4 Casa 25-4 NWA 31-5 ME 1-8 FACE 13-4-45 SOC 26-4

JK891 VC(T)M50 12MU 14-3-43 215MU 21-3 *SS679* 11-4 Casa 25-4 NWA 31-5 ME 1-7 NAASC 1-11 FACE 27-2-45

JK892 VC(T)M45 39MU 14-3-43 215MU 21-3 *SS679* 11-4 Casa 25-4 NWA 31-5 ME 1-8 NAAF 30-9 CE 13-9-45

JK922 VC(T)M50 38MU 12-3-43 82MU 21-3 *SS682* 12-4 Casa 25-4 NWA 31-5 4S CE ops 8-2-44

JK923 M45 45MU 26-3-43 215MU 7-4 39MU 18-5 M46 instal 76MU 1-7 Casa 29-7

JK924 VC(T)M50 38MU 12-3-43 222MU 27-3 *SS679* 11-4 Casa 25-4 Malta 1-7 Sic ME 30-9 NAASC 1-11 SOC 26-4-45

JK925 VC(T)M50 33MU 13-3-43 47MU 22-3 *Ess Trad* 10-4 Casa 25-4 NWA 31-5 ME 1-7

JK926 VC(T)M50A 33MU 13-3-43 47MU 21-3 *SS680* 11-4 Casa 25-4 NWA 31-5 Malta 1-8 Sic ME 25-2-45 CE 13-9

JK927 12MU 12-3-43 47MU 22-3 *Orient C* 13-4 Casa 25-4 NWA 31-5 ME 15-3-45 SOC 30-4-47

JK928 12MU 20-3-43 215MU 29-3-43 *Ess Trad* 10-4 Casa 25-4 NWA 31-5 Malta 1-7 SOC 5-7

JK929 VC(T)M45 15MU 14-3-43 76MU 26-3 *SS682* 12-4 Casa 25-4 Malta 1-6 ME FTR ops 4-7 SOC 18-8-44

JK930 M45 38MU 23-3-43 47MU 9-4 *Emp Bar* 2-5 Casa 17-5 Malta 1-8 Sic NAASC 31-10 118MU Malta 31-1-44 SOC 26-4-45

JK931 VC(T)M50 12MU 14-3-43 215MU 21-3 *SS679* 20-3 Casa 25-4 NWA 31-5 Malta Sic 1-8 NA 30-11 ME 31-1-44 to Turk 28-12

JK932 9MU 16-3-43 47MU 26-3 *Orient C* 13-4 Casa 25-4 NWA 31-5 SOC 26-4-45

JK933 46MU 14-3-43 47MU 24-3 *Orient C* 13-4 Casa 25-4 NWA 31-5 FAC3 21-1-44

JK934 VC(T)M50 14-3-43 76MU 29-3 *SS682* 12-4 Casa 25-4 NWA 31-5 Malta Sic 1-8 ME FAC3 11-8 NA 30-11 SOC 8-2-44

JK935 39MU 14-3-43 222MU 29-3 *SS680* 11-4 Casa 25-4 Malta 1-7 Sic NAASC 31-10 118MU Malta 31-1-44 ME 15-3-45 SOC 29-8-46

JK936 VC(T)M45 45MU 23-3-43 215MU 5-4 *SS687* 29-4 Casa 17-5 Malta 1-7 Sic NA 30-11 C3 ops 22-3-44

JK937 9MU 17-3-43 222MU 27-3 *SS679* 12-4 Casa 25-4 NWA 31-5

JK938 15MU 20-3-43 222MU 31-3 *SS680* 11-4 Casa 25-4 NWA 31-5 SOC 25-7-46

JK939 M45 45MU 15-3-43 215MU 6-4 *SS687* 29-4 Casa 17-5

JK940 M45 MWW 24-7-43 fitt tow hook CRD Farn 31-8 DeH 4-3-44 9MU 26-8 17SFTS 15-10-44 RAF BHill trls with 'Hasty-Hitch' towing Hotspur glider. Lost in fog out of fuel a/c aban cd Blackburn Lancs CE 23-12

JK941 VC(T)M50 12MU 14-3-43 215MU 21-3 *SS679* Casa 25-4 NWA 31-5 USAAF 1-10 C3 ops 21-5-44

JK942 M45 15MU 20-3-43 222MU 8-4 *Emp Bar* 2-5 Casa 17-5 NWA 31-5 FAC3 17-3-44

JK943 Shorts Effort 9MU 16-3-43 47MU 26-3 *Orient C* 13-4 Casa 25-4 NWA 31-5 ME 1-7 CE 13-9-45

JK944 9Mu 17-3-43 47MU 26-3 *Orient* 13-4 Casa 25-4 NWA 31-5 SOC 29-8-46

JK945 M50 15MU 20-3-43 76MU 1-4 *SS680* 11-4 Casa 25-4 ME 1-8 SOC 29-8-46

JK946 VC(T)M50 33MU 13-3-43 222MU 28-3 *SS680* 11-4 Casa 25-4 NWA 31-5 Malta Sic 1-8 NAASC 31-10 FAF 28-2-46

JK947 15MU 20-3- 43 222MU 31-3-43 *SS680* 11-4 Casa 25-4 253S FAC3 2-6-44

JK948 M50 45MU 15-3-43 215MU 7-4 *Emp Bar* 2-5 Casa 17-5 NWA 31-7 USAAF 12-52 lost over France 27-1-44

JK949 M45 R-RH to LFIX M66 27-3-43 33MU 25-6 82MU 1-7 *SS717* Casa 29-7 73S 29-1-48 137MU SOC 10-6

JK950 VC(T)M45 15MU 14-3-43 76MU 29-3 *SS682* 12-4 Casa 25-4 NA 31-5 Malta 1-6 Sic 1-10 NAAF i/sea ops 16-11

JK967 VC(T)M45 39MU 20-343 82MU 29-3 *SS680* 11-4 Casa 25-4 NWA 31-5 ME 1-8 NA 30-9 FTR ops 16-1-44

JK968 VC(T) 12MU 14-3-43 47MU 22-3 *Orient C* 13-4 Casa 25-4 NWA 31-5 REAF 22-2-45

JK969 15MU 18-3-43 76MU 222-3 *SS682* 12-4 Casa 25-4 NA 31-5 Malta 1-6 185S FAC2 4-7 ME 1-10 SOC 27-6-46

JK970 M45 15MU 18-3-43 76MU 1-4 *SS680* 11-4 Casa 25-4 NWA 31-5 ME 1-8 NAAF 30-9 SOC 26-4-45

JK971 VC(T)M45 39MU 20-3-43 82MU 29-3 *SS680* 11-4 25-4 NWA 31-5

JK972 15MU 20-3-43 222MU 31-3 *SS680* 11-4 Casa 25-4 NA 31-5 Malta 1-6 FACB 17-8 ME 1-10 Trg del 27-9-45

JK973 12MU 20-3-43 215MU 29-3 *Emp Trad* 10-4 Casa 25-4 ME 30-9NAAF 1-11 FTR ops 31-12

JK974 M45 15MU 20-3-43 76MU 1-4 *Fort Rup* 11-4 Casa 25-4 Malta 1-7 Sic NA 30-11 SOC 29-2-44

JK975 VC(T)M45 The Scottish James 38-MU 20-3-4 47MU 5-4 *SS686* 24-4 Casa 17-3 NWA 31-5 Malta Sic 1-8 118MU Malta 31-1-44

JK976 9MU 17-3-45 222MU 27-3 *SS679* 11-4 Casa 25-4 NWA 31-5 USAAF ME 15-3-45 SOC 28-9-46

JK977 12MU 20-3-43 215MU 29-3 *Ess Trad* 10-4 Casa 25-4 ME 1-9 NAAF 1-11 CE ops 19-10-44

JK978 M50 33MU 24-3-43 222MU 2-4 *Emp Bar* 2-5 Casa 17-5 ME 31-1-45 SOC 30-5-46

JK979 R-RH to LFIX M66 485S 31-7-43 232S 25-5-44 FRU AST 4-6 84GSU 30-10

JK981 Borough of Wood Green 12MU 20-3-43 215MU 29-3 *Ess Trad* 1-4 Casa 25-4 FAC3 2-4-44

JK982 15MU 20-3-43 76MU 1-6 *SS703* 1-6 Casa 15-6 NWA 1-7 ME 1-9 NAAF 1-11 SOC 26-4-45

JK983 M45 6MU 28-3-43 82MU 3-4 *SS686* 24-4 Casa 17-5 Malta Sic 1-8 NA 30-11 SOC 14-3-45

JK984 M45 45MU 2-4-43 222MU 14-4 *Fort Thom* 3-5 Casa 17-5 NWA 1-10 REAF 22-2-45

JK985 VC(T)M45 45MU 7-4-43 215MU *Fort Doug* 29-4 Casa 17-5 Malta 1-7 Sic ME 1-11 SOC 8-3-44

JK986 VC(T) 38MU 20-3-43 222MU 2-4 *Emp Bar* 2-5 Casa 17-5 Malta 1-7 Sic NAASC 31-10 SOC 29-2-44

JK987 38MU 20-3-43 47MU 31-3 *SS680* 11-4 Casa 25-4 NAASC 31-10 ME 25-2-45 CE 13-9

JK988 VC(T)M45 38MU 20-3-43 9-4 *Emp Bar* 205 Casa 17-5 SOC 18-8-44

JK989 M50 38MU 23-3-43 82MU 8-4 *SS686* 24-4 Casa 17-5 SOC 26-4-45

JK990 VC(T)M45 38MU 20-3-43 222MU 5-4 *Emp Bar* 2-5 Casa 17-5 Malta Sic 1-8 NWA FAC3 28-10

JK991 M45 38MU 23-3-43 47MU 9-4 *SS686* 24-4 Casa 17-5 NWA 31-5 FAC3 3-4-44

JK992 VC(T)M45 15MU 22-3-43 NWA 31-5 Malta 1-7 Sic NAASC 31-10 118MU Malta 31-1-44 SOC 29-2

JL series All F Mk VC(T) Engine as specified

JL104 M50 9-4-43 215MU 17-4 *Fort Doug* 29-4 Casa 17-5 NWA 31-5 ME 15-3-45 1415 Flt w/u Ld Habbaniya Iraq 6-1-46

JL105 M50 45MU 9-4-43 222MU 18-4 *Fort Thom* 3-5 Casa 17-5 NAASC 31-10

JL106 M45 R-RH to LFIX M66 10-4-43 (eng rated as RM 14 SM (Mer 100) gen dev CRD R-R 23-7 Mer 112 (RM 16 SM) instal. ASTH 7-7-45 29MU 16-1-46 to Turk 11-7-47

JL107 M45 R-RH to LFIX M66 10-4-43 FLS Mlfld 15-3-44 CFE Tang FAAC 10-4-45 ROS sold VA 28-11-49

JL108 M45 9MU 30-5-43 82MU 28-8 C3 ops 20-6-44

JL109 M50 R-RH to LFIX M66 10-4-43 341S 411S 17-10 132S FTR ops 30-4-44

JL110 M50 R-RH to LFIX M66 10-4-43 9MU 16-8 222MU 24-8 *Ger Don* 25-8 Casa 10-9 218Gp NA 30-11 SOC 3-5-45

JL111 M50 R-RH to LFIX M66 11-4-43 9MU 16-8 222MU 24-8 *Ger Don* 25-8

JL112 M50 33MU 18-4-43 47MU 26-4 *Liber* 5-5 Tak 29-5 ME 16-7 to 4390M 28-2-44

JL113 M50 45MU 21-4-43 215MU 28-4 *Fort Jer* 11-5 Casa 30-5 NWA 1-7 NAAF 30-11 SOC 26-4-45

JL114 M50 45MU 25-4-43 215MU 12-6 *Fort Ver* 1-7 Casa 14-7 NWA FAF 1-10

JL115 M50 38MU 27-4-43 76MU 28-5 *SS703* 1-6 Casa 15-6 NWA 1-7 FTR ops 31-9-44

JL116 M50 46MU 27-4-43 47MU 4-5 *Fort Jer* 1-5 Casa 30-5 NWA 1-7 ME 1-9 NAAF 1-11 SOC 30-6-45

JL117 M50 15MU 30-4-43 47MU 11-5 *Parn Cast* 5-6 Tak 27-6 ME 24-7 SOC 22-2-45

JL118 M50 46MU 2-5-43 47MU 11-5 *Fort Stle* 16-5 Casa 30-5 Malta 1-7 NWA 1-8 Italy 1-11

JL119 M50 46MU 4-5-43 47MU 11-5 *Fort Stle* 16-5 Casa 30-5 NWA 1-7 ME 1-8 NAAF 1-121 SOC 31-12

JL120 M50 46MU 4-5-43 215MU 13-5 *SS702* 2-6 Casa 15-6 NWA 1-7 ME 1-8 NAAF 1-11 SOC 3-3-44

JL121 M50 38MU 5-5-43 76MU 22-5 *SS702* 2-6 15-6 NWA 1-7 327S 12-5-45 FAF 27-11

JL122 M50 38MU 5-5-43 76MU 24-5 *SS702* 2-6-43 Casa 15-6 NWA 1-7 ME 1-8 NA 30-11 C3 ops 12-1-44

JL123 M50 12MU 5-5-43 47MU 12-5 *Fort Stle* 26-5 Casa 30-5 NWA 1-7 ME 1-10 MAAF 1-11 Trg del 1-11-45

JL124 M50 12MU 21-3-43 215MU 2903 *Ess Trad* 10-4 Casa 25-4 NA 31-5 Sic 1-10 SOC 29-2-44

JL125 M50 15MU 22-3-43 76MU 8-4 *Fort Thom* 3-5 Casa 17-5 Malta 1-7 FTR 17-7

JL126 M45 12MU 30-3-43 47MU 9-4 *Emp Bar* 2-5 Casa 17-5 ME 1-8 NA 30-11

JL127 M50 33MU 24-3-43 222MU 2-4 *Emp Bar* 2-5 Casa 17-5 Malta Sic 1-8 NAASC 31-10 CE ops 15-10-44

JL128 M45 15MU 22-3-43 82MU 4-4 *SS686* 24-4 Casa 17-5 NWA 1-10 FTR ops 28-11

JL129 M46 6MU 28-3-43 52MU 6-4 *Emp Bar* 2-5 Casa 17-5 NWA 31-5 USAAF 31-8

JL130 M46 9MU 5-4-43 82MU 13-4 *SS686* 24-4 Casa 17-5 NWA FAC3 8-6

JL131 M45 15MU 22-3-43 66MU 1-4 *SS680* 11-4 Casa 25-4 NWA 31-5 ME 1-9 USAAF 1-10 32S RAF SOC 15-12-44

JL132 M50 R-RH to LFIX M66 27-4-43 9MU 26-6 222MU 1-7 *Fort Nak* Casa 29-7 218Gp NA 30-11 225S FTR ops 29-8-44

JL133 M45 15MU 22-3-43 76MU 8-4 *Fort Thom* 3-5 Casa 17-5 NWA 31-5 Sic 1-8 NA 30-11 USAAF 31-1-44

JL139 M46 6MU 28-3-43 82MU 6-4 *SS680* 24-4 Casa 17-5 Malta Sicily 1-8 ME 1-11 SOC 8-3-44 bboc 21-6-45 RHAF 25-4-46

JL140 45MU 22-3-43 222MU 31-3 *SS680* 11-4 Casa 25-4 MAAF 31-1-44 SOC 26-4-45

JL159 M50 R-RH to LFIX M66 27-3-43 33MU 25-6 47MU 5-7 *Fort Chest* 11-7 Casa 29-7 NAASC 31-10 SOC 15-3-45

JL160 M45 33MU 31-3-43 222MU 7-4 *SS687* 29-4 Casa 17-5 FAF 9-10-47

JL161 M46 6MU 8-4-43 76MU 23-4 *Fort Thom* 3-5 Casa 17-5 MAAF 1-8 ME 21-2-45 SOC 29-8-46

JL162 M45 12MU 3-4-43 MAAF 31-1-44 Trg Del 6-9-45

JL163 M50 R-RH to LFLX M66 6MU 6-7-43 222MU 17-7 *Fort Rup* 25-7 Casa 16-8 218Gr NA 30-11 45S CE ops 28-8-44

JL164 M45 8MU 28-3-43 82MU *SS686* 24-4 Casa 17-5 ME 30-9 CE 24-7-45

JL165 M45 R-RH to LFIX M66 27-3-43. Spcl eng for dev of injector pump carb. BDN 12-11 trls of eng at +25lb boost ('Basta') and four blade Rotol prop. 150 Octane fuel. Cool trls Dec to Jan '44 AST 3-6-44 6MU 26-10 82MU 10-11 *Guinean* 22-12 Casa 15-1-45 ME 19-7 SOC 28-8-47

JL166 M45 38MU 2-4-43 82MU 11-4 *Emp Bar* 2-5 Casa 17-5 SOC 31-10

JL167 M45 45MU 23-3-43 215MU 7-4 *SS687* 29-4 Casa 17-5 Malta 1-8 NA 1-11 SOC 30-5-46

JL168 M45 33MU 31-3-43 222MU 11-4 *SS687* 29-4 Casa 17-5 ME 1-7 NAASC 1-11

JL169 M50 38MU 2-4-43 222MU 11-4 *SS687* 29-4 Casa 17-5 ME 1-8 NAAF 1-11 C3 ops 7-4-44

JL170 M46 12MU 30-3-43 215MU 7-4 *SS708* 14-6 Casa 29-6 ME 1-7 NWA FAC3 27-10

JL171 M45 DeH 28-3-43 AST 2-1-44 39MU 24-2-44 3501SU 23-6 53 OTU 2-9-44 SOC 18-5-45

JL172 M50 R-RH to LFIX M66 27-3-43 39MU 30-6 76MU 18-7 *Fort Rup* 25-7 Casa 16-8 73S CE ops 17-11-44

JL173 M45 12MU 3-4-43 NWA ME 1-7 NAASC 31-10 SOC 26-4-45

JL174 M46 8MU 28-3-43 82MU 6-4 *SS686* 24-4 Casa 17-5 NWA 31-5 ME 1-7 C3 ops 10-9

JL175 M46 46MU 27-3-43 215MU 5-5 *Emp Bar* 2-5 Casa 17-5 NWA 31-5 Malta Sic 1-8 NAASC 31-10 SOC 26-4-45

JL176 M46 6MU 28-3-43 82MU 5-4 *SS686* 24-4 Casa 17-5 NWA 1-10 ME 30-11-45 RHAF 25-4-46

JL181 M46 39MU 2-4-43 47MU 11-4 *SS686* 24-4 Casa 17-5 Malta Sic 1-8 NAASC 31-10 SOC 28-4-45

JL182 M45 33MU 30-3-43 222MU 7-4 *SS687* 29-4 Casa 17-5 NAAF 1-11 USAAF 31-1-44

JL183 M46 33MU 31-3-43 222MU 11-4 *SS687* 29-4 Casa 17-5 NWA USAAF 31-7

JL184 M45 39MU 2-4-43 47MU 27-4 *Liber* 5-5 Tak 29-5 ME 19-6 FAC3 18-9

JL185 M45 6MU 28-3-43 52MU 6-4 *Emp Bar* 2-5 Casa 17-5 NWA 31-5 FAF 31-10

JL186 M45 45MU 28-3-43 FACB 9-4 12MU 30-6 222MU 22-7 *Fort Rup* 25-7 Casa 16-8 NA 30-11 SOC 26-4-45

JL187 M50 46MU 3-4-43 215MU 15-4 *SS687* 29-4 Casa 17-5 MAAF 31-1-44 SOC 28-4-45

JL188 M50 46MU 3-4-43 215MU 12-4 *Emp Bar* 2-5 Casa 17-5 Malta 1-7 Sic NAASC 31-10 SOC 26-4-45

JL208 M45 39MU 2-4-43 47MU 12-4 *Liber* 5-5 Tak 29-5 ME 19-6 SOC 29-8-46

JL209 M45 39MU 2-4-43 222MU 12-4 *SS687* 29-4 Casa 17-5 ME 1-8 NAAF 1-11 ME 29-3-45 SOC 29-8-46

JL210 M50 45MU 2-4-43 222MU 14-4 *Fort Thom* 3-5 Casa 17-5 NWA FAF 1-10 ME 31-8-44 to Turk 28-9

JL211 M50 46MU 4-4-43 215MU 15-4 *SS687* 29-4 Casa 17-5 NAAF 1-11 SOC 26-4-45

JL212 M46 33MU 4-4-43 47MU 15-4 *Liber* 5-5 Tak 29-5 ME 23-6 SOC 1-12

JL213 M50 2-4-43 47MU 12-4 *Fort Thom* 3-5 Casa 17-5 ME 1-8 NAASC 1-11 SOC 18-8-44

JL214 M50 46MU 4-4-43 215MU 16-4 *Fort Doug* 29-4 Casa 17-5

JL215 M50 45MU 2-4-43 222MU 14-4 *SS687* 29-4 Casa 17-5 ME 1-9 NAASC 31-10 SOC 31-12

JL216 M46 39MU 10-4-43 47MU 21-4 *Liber* 5-5 Tak 29-5 ME 23-6 C3 ops 24-4-44

JL217 M50 R-RH to FIX M66 21-4-43 9MU 3-9 222MU 10-9 *Craw W L* 22-9 Casa 10-10 NAASC 31-10 FAC3 4-4-44

JL218 M50 46MU 4-4-43 82MU 16-4 *SS687* 29-4 Casa 17-5 NWA 1-10 SOC 26-4-45

JL219 M50 46MU 3-4-43 215MU 12-4 *Emp Bar* 2-5 Casa 17-5 Malta 1-7 Sic SOC 26-4-45

JL220 M50 46MU 4-4-43 215MU 16-4 *Fort Doug* 29-4 Casa 17-5 Malta 1-7 Sic NA 30-11 ME 15-3-45

JL221 M50 38MU 16-4-43 52MU 1-5 *Fort Stle* 16-5 Casa 30-5 NWA 30-9 NAASC 31-10 USAAF 31-1-44 ME 28-12 FAF 28-2-46

JL222 M46 33MU 5-4-43 222MU 15-4 *Fort Thom* 3-5 Casa 17-5 ME 28-4-45 SOC 26-9-46
JL223 M45 R-RH to LFIX M66 18-4-43 485S 24-7 FTR ops 22-8
JL224 46MU 4-4-43 FAAC 8-4 215MU 21-7 *SS732* 5-8 Casa 18-8 NWA 1-10 SOC 26-9-46
JL225 M50 46MU 4-4-43 82MU 15-4 *SS687* 29-4 Casa 17-5 FTR ops 6-2-44
JL231 M45 33MU 4-4-43 47MU 15-4 *Liber* 5-5 Tak 29-5 ME 19-6 NAASC 31-10 ME 15-3-45 SOC 23-8-46
JL232 12MU 16-4-43 215MU 2-5 *Fort Jer* 11-5 Casa 30-5 Malta Sic 1-8 ME FTR ops 249
JL233 M50 45MU 2-4-43 222MU 14-4 *Fort Thom* 3-5 Casa 17-5 ME 25-2-45 SOC 21-9-46
JL234 M50 R-RH to LFIX M66 11-4-43 33MU 21-8 47MU 30-8 *Emp Grebe* 15-9 Casa 29-9 328S 5-4-45 81RSU 25-4
JL235 M50 45MU 4-4-43 222MU 14-4 *Fort Thom* 3-5 Casa 17-5 Malta 1-7 Sic NAASC 32S 31-10 Trg del 25-10-45
JL236 M50 45MU 8-4-43 222MU 23-4 *Fort Thom* 3-5 Casa 17-5 NWA 1-7 ME 1-11 237S SOC 10-4-46
JL237 M45 33MU 4-4-43 222MU 14-4 *Fort Thom* 3-5 Casa 17-5
JL238 M45 12MU 19-4-43 215MU 4-5 *Fort Thom* 11-5 Casa 30-5 NWA ME 1-7 FA FTR 3-5-45
JL239 M45 R-RH to LFIX M66 39MU 22-8-43 222MU 2-9 *Emp Grebe* 15-9 Casa 29-9 SOC 21-9-45
JL240 M50 38MU 16-4-43 76MU 1-5 *Fort Stle* 16-5 Casa 30-5 NAASC 31-10 118MU Malta 31-1-44 ME 31-8 to Turk 22-2-45
JL241 M50 R-RH 11-4-43 15MU 14-4 76MU 5-5 *Fort Stle* 16-5 Casa 30-5 NWA 1-7 SOC 19-7-45
JL242 M50 33MU 16-4-43 47MU 3-5 *Rook* 19-5 Tak 16-6 ME 16-7 FAC3 28-2-44
JL243 M50 12MU 12-4-43 215MU 24-4 *Fort Thom* 3-5 Casa 17-5 Malta Sic 1-8 NA 30-11 C3 ops 24-3-44
JL244 M50 33MU 11-4-43 47MU 21-4 *Liber* 5-5 Tak 29-5 ME 2-7 NAASC 31-10 USAAF 31-1-44 ME 25-2-45 SOC 14-3-46
JL245 M50 12MU 14-4-43 215MU 23-4 *Fort Thom* 3-5 Casa 17-5 ME 25-7 Malta Sic 1-8 NA 30-11
JL246 M50 39MU 10-4-43 47MU 19-4 *Liber* 5-5 Tak 29-5 ME 19-6 123S SOC 27-7-44
JL247 8MU 19-4-43 47MU 25-4 *Kent* 10-5 Aus 3-7
JL248 46MU 19-4-43 47MU 23-4 *Fort Jer* 11-5 Casa 30-5 Malta 1-8 29S SOC 30-6-45
JL249 M45 39MU 9-4-43 47MU 26-4 *Rook* 19-5 Tak 16-6 ME 16-7 SOC 1-2-44
JL250 M45 15MU 11-4-43 76MU 26-4 *Fort Stle* 16-5 Casa 30-5 NWA 1-7 Malta 185S 1-1-44 ME 25-2-45 SOC 14-3-46
JL251 M50 38MU 16-4-43 52MU 1-5 *Fort Stle* 16-5 Casa 30-5 NWA 30-7 FAF 31-10 IAF 27-6-46 as MM4012
JL301 M50 45MU 20-5-43 215MU 30-5 *SS702* 2-6-43 Casa 15-6 NWA 1-7 ME 1-8 NAAF 1-11 Malta 118MU 31-1-44 USAAF
JL302 M50 33MU 6-6-43 47MU 14-6 *Glenb* 3-7 Tak 30-7 ME 10-9 FAC3 8-12
JL303 M45 9MU 27-6-43 222MU 12-7 *Martand* 26-7 Ind 27-8 ACSEA 21-8-45 SOC 13-9
JL304 M50 12MU 7-5-43 215MU 18-5 *SS703* 1-6 Casa 15-6 NWA 31-6 FAF 1-10 253S 29-2-44 FTR 24-10
JL305 M50 45MU 7-5 215MU 15-5 *SS703* 1-6 Casa 15-6 NWA 1-7 ME 1-9 NAAF 1-11 ME 31-8-44 SOC 26-9-46
JL306 M50 39MU 11-5-43 47MU 20-5 *Mearb* 3-6 Tak 8-7 ME 9-8 FACE 30-4-45
JL307 M50 39MU 11-5-43 47MU 20-5 *Emp Fran* 3-6 Tak 16-7 ME 28-8 M45 instal SOC 1-1-44
JL308 M50 39MU 11-5-43 76MU 21-5 *Mearb* 3-6 Tak 8-7 ME 28-8 FACE 15-9-44
JL309 M50 45MU 15-5-43 82MU 22-5 *SS702* 3-6 Casa 15-6 NWA 1-7 NAAF 1-10 ME 25-3-45 SOC 27-6-46
JL310 M50 45MU 14-5-43 76MU 22-5 *SS702* 3-6 Casa 15-6 NWA 1-7 ME 1-8 232S SOC 29-6-44
JL311 M50 12MU 7-5-43 215MU 17-5 *SS703* 1-6 Casa 15-6 NWA 30-6 ME 1-9 NAAF 1-11 ME 1-9 ME 31-8-44 SOC 30-6-45
JL312 M50 46MU 13-5-43 215MU 21-5 *SS702* 3-6 Casa 15-6 ME 1-9 74S SOC 10-4-45
JL313 M50 39MU 22-5-43 47MU 31-5 *Emp Fran* 3-6 Tak 6-7 ME 13-8 SOC 25-7-46
JL314 M50 6MU 31-5-43 215MU 8-6 *SSLS 627* 26-6 Aus 2-8
JL315 M50 no record SOC 26-9-46
JL316 M50 46MU 6-5-43 315MU 17-5 *SS703* 1-6 Casa 15-6 NWA Jy '43 FAF Corsica 31-10
JL317 M50 6MU 28-5-43 82MU 4-6 *SSLS98* 28-6 Ind 23-8 FACE SOC 2-5-45
JL318 M50 46MU 15-5-43 222MU 29-5 *SS703* 1-6 Casa 15-6 NWA 1-7 USAAF 31-12
JL319 M50 6MU 15-5-43 47MU 23-5 *SSLS98* 28-6 Ind 23-8 SOC 23-9-44
JL320 M50 6MU 15-5-43 47MU 23-5 *SSLS98* 28-6 Ind 23-8 615S FAC 3 16-5-44
JL321 M50 9MU 13-6 47MU 26-6 *Chyel* 17-7 Ind 18-8 73S 23-1-45
JL322 M50 6MU 17-5-43 76MU 30-5 *Fort Enter* 18-7 Ind 23-8 615S FTR ops 15-6-44
JL323 M50 39MU 17-6-43 234S 29-6 82MU 27-6 *SS732* Casa 18-8 NWA USAAF 1-10 MAAF SOC 30-6-45
JL324 M50 46MU 13-5-43 222MU 22-5 *SS702* 3-6 Casa 156 NWA 1-7 ME 1-8 SOC 28-4-45
JL325 M50 33MU 19-5-43 82MU 27-5 *SS702* 3-6 Casa 15-6 NWA 1-7 ME 1-8 NA 30-11 32S 352S FTR ops 19-10-44
JL326 M50 39MU 21-5-43 47MU 29-5 *Emp Fran* 3-6 Tak 16-7 ME 1-8 451S SOC 27-9-45
JL327 M50 39MU 21-5-43 47MU 29-5 *Emp Fran* 3-6 Tak 16-7 ME 13-8 FA SOC 3-4-45
JL328 M50 39MU 21-5-43 47MU 29-5 *Emp Fran* 3-6 Tak 16-7 ME 10-9 SOC 13-9-45
JL329 M50 39MU 21-5-43 47MU 29-5 *Emp Fran* 3-6 Tak 16-7 ME 13-8 FTR ops 21-11
JL330 M50 39MU 22-5-43 47MU 31-5 *SSLS514* 17-6 Tak 16-7 ME 31-8 NAAF FACE 20-9
JL331 M50 9MU 27-6-43 315MU 7-7 *Martand* 26-7 Ind 29-8 SOC 10-9-44
JL332 M50 39MU 22-5-43 47MU 29-5 *Emp Fran* 3-6 Tak 16-7 ME 10-8 SOC 10-1-46
JL333 M50 33MU 30-6-43 130S 18-7 82MU 18-8 *Ger Don* 25-8 Casa 10-9 NA 30-11 FAF 31-2 USAAF
JL334 M50 6MU 26-5-43 76MU 1-6 *Fort Enter* 18-7 Ind 23-8 ACSEA SOC 6-9-45
JL335 M45 R-RH 15-5-43 88MU 30-5 76MU 1-6 *SS703* 1-6 Casa 15-6 NWA 30-7 ME 1-8 NAAF 1-11 FTR ops 2-1-44
JL336 M50 33MU 30-6-43 130S 18-7 82MU 18-8 *Ger Don* 25-8 Casa 10-9 NA 30-11 SOC 29-2-44
JL337 M50 39MU 1-7 234S 17-7 39MU 5-8 82MU 14-8 *Ger Don* 25-8 Casa 10-9 NA 30-11 SOC 29-2-44 recat MAAF 25-3 REAF 29-3-45
JL338 M50 39MU 26-5-43 82MU 2-6 *SSLS5* 1-6 Tak 16-7 ME 23-9 C3 ops 14-2-44
JL346 M50 12MU 25-5-43 82MU 2-6 *Fort Jer* 12-5 Casa 30-5 Malta 1-8 Italy 1-11
JL347 M45 R-RH to LFIX M66 10-4-43 341S 27-7 FTR ops 3-10
JL348 9MU 19-4 47MU 23-4 *Nestor* 4-5 Aus 10-8
JL349 M45 R-RH to LFIX M66. Rotol Ltd 18-4-44 trls with contra props. Translational bearings failed after 48.45hr Farm 15-11 CE 29-7-45
JL350 M50 15MU 11-4-43 76MU 22-4 *Fort Thom* 3-5 Casa 17-5 FTR ops 17-4-44
JL351 M45 R-RH to LFIX M66 17-4-43 39MU 30-8 47MU 5-9 *Ocean Rid* 23-9 Casa 10-10 NAASC 31-10 SOC 14-3-46
JL352 M50 15MU 11-4-43 76MU 5-5 *Fort Stle* 16-5 Casa 30-5 Malta Sic 1-8 NAASC 31-1- SOC 31-8-44
JL353 M50 R-RH to LFIX M66 21-4-43 33MU 26-8 47MU 2-9 *Ocean Rid* 23-9 Casa 10-10 NAASC 31-1- 111S CE ops 9-11-44
JL354 M45 R-RH to LFIX M66 10-4-43 33MU 21-8 47MU 30-8 *Emp Grebe* 15-9 Casa 29-9 SOC 26-9-46
JL355 M50 45MU 9-4-43 222MU 18-4 VA 12-5 to LFIX M66 39MU 19-3-44 GAL 10-11 MAAF 3-2-45 ME 31-5 SOC 30-8
JL356 M50 R-RH to LFX M66 18-4-43 33MU 7-9 82MU 15-9 *Craw W L* 22-9 Casa 10-10 NAASC 31-10 94S FACE 31-7-44
JL357 M50 33MU 18-4-43 47MU 3-5 *Rook* 19-5 Tak 16-6 ME 16-7 SOC 29-8-46
JL358 M50 33MU 18-4-43 47MU 26-4 *Rook* 19-5 Tak 16-6 ME 13-7 FAC3 1-1- NAAF 1-11 SOC 26-4-45
JL359 M50 R-RH to LFIX M66 21-4-43 AFDU Witt 3-8 FAAC 7-9 ROS Farn Dec '43 comp trls with Fw190; Bf109; Mustang Mk III; Tempest and Spit MkXIV JL359 with univ wng and normal fuel load lacked endurance but proved the better all-round a/c COAL 1-5-45 mods CFE Tang 7-6 FAAC 13-6 ROS AFDS 4-10 FAAC 3-11 ASTH 19-11 to Turk 24-1-48
JL360 9MU 19-4-43 47MU 25-4-43 *Nestor* 4-5 Aus 10-8
JL361 M45 R-RH 18-4-43 to LFIX M66 Farn 6-8 SU carb trls. Sept weather trls. BDn March '4. Rotol Stav prop pitch indicator instal. Trls with SU carb until Apl '44. Achieved 418mph at 21000ft Farn Benito trls with JL 227. ASTH 20-11-45 29MU 27-3-46 NorAF 31-7-47
JL362 M50 15MU 11-4-43 76MU 26-4 *Fort Stle* 16-5 Casa 30-5 Malta Sic 1-8 111S FTR ops 12-12
JL363 M63 45MU 27-4-43 215MU 7-5 *Fort Stle* 16-5 Casa 30-5 NWA 1-7 SOC 30-6-45
JL364 M50 R-RH 18-4-43 to LFIX M66 33MU 2-9-43 47MU 6-9 *Ocean Rid* 23-9 Casa 10-10 NAASC 31-10 SOC 22-11-45
JL365 M45 39MU 10-4-43 47MU 19-4 *Liber* 5-5 Tak 29-5 ME 5-8 94S FTR ops 23-10-44
JL366 M50 R-RH 18-4-43 to LFIX M66 33MU 10-9-43 82MU 18-9 *Emp Mar* 7-10 Casa 19-10 NA 30-11 ME 9-8-45 REAF 31-10-46
JL367 M50 39MU 13-4-43 47MU 19-4 *Liber* 5-5 Tak 29-5 ME 19-6 NAAF 1-11 253S C3 ops 28-5-44
JL368 M50 112MU 27-4-43 215MU 14-5 *SS703* 1-6-44 Casa 15-6 NWA 30-6 ME 1-9 NA 30-11 ME 28-4-45 SOC 26-9-46
JL369 M50 15MU 11-4-43 R-RH to LFIX M66 9MU 16-8 52 MU 3-9 *Emp Grebe* 15-9 Casa 29-9 ME 31-5-45 SOC 9-8
JL370 M50 R-RH 11-4-43 to LFIX M66 82MU 31-8 *Emp Grebe* 15-9 Casa 29-9 SOC 31-8-44
JL371 M50 8MU 19-4-43 47MU 25-4 *Kent* 15-5 Aust 8-7
JL372 M50 R-RH to LFIX M66 11-4-43 39MU 24-8 222MU 4-9 *Craw W L* 22-9 Casa 10-10 NAASC 31-10 C3 ops 18-4-44
JL373 M50 R-RH to LFIX M66 15-4-43 341S 24-7 411S 20-10 FACB 9-12 to 4267M 1SoTT 19-4-44
JL374 46MU 215MU 30-4-43 *Fort Jer* 11-5 Casa 30-5 NWA 1-7 ME 1-8 FAF 31-10 USAAF to Turk 30-11-44
JL378 M50 8MU 19-4-43 47MU 25-4-43 *Kent* 10-5 Aust 3-7
JL379 33MU 16-4-43 47MU 29-4 *Rook* 19-5 Tak 16-6 ME 24-7 SOC 27-6-46
JL380 M50 9MU 20-4-43 47MU 28-4 *Nastra* 4-5 Aus 10-8
JL381 38MU 13-4-43 82 MU 26-4 *Fort Jer* 11-5 Casa 30-5 Malta USAAF 1-8 ME 25-2-45 SOC 27-6-46
JL382 M50 8MU 19-4-43 47 MU 25-4 *Kent* 10-5 Aus 3-7
JL385 M50 R-RH to LFIX M66 22-4-43 33MU 23-10 222MU 7-1-44 *City* 21-1-44 Casa 17-2 SOC 30-4-47
JL386 33MU 20-4-43 215MU 29-5 *SS627* 26-6 Aus
JL387 46MU 19-4-43 215MU 30-4 *Fort Jer* 11-5 Casa 30-5 NWA 1-7 FAF 1-10 NAASC 31-10 SOC 26-4-45
JL388 M50 38MU 13-4-43 222MU 23-4 *Fort Thom* 3-5 Casa 17-5 Malta Sic 1-8 92S ME C3 ops 25-9
JL389 M50 45MU 25-4-43 47MU 12-5 *Fort Stle* 16-5 Casa 30-5 Malta USAAF 1-8 SOC 26-4-45
JL390 M50 45MU 23-4-43 215MU 5-5 *Fort Jer* 11-5 Casa 30-5 NWA 1-7
JL391 M50 46MU 29-4-43 82MU 3-5 *Fort Jer* 11-5 Casa 30-5 NWA 1-7 USAAF 31-8
JL392 33MU 19-4-43 47MU 22-4 *Nestor* 4-5 Aus
JL393 46MU 19-4 215MU 30-4 *Fort Jer* 11-5 Casa 30-5 NWA 1-7 ME 1-9 NAAF 30-11 SOC 26-4-45
JL394 M50 9MU 20-4-43 47MU 28-4 *Kent* 10-5 Aus 3-7
JL395 M50 R-RH to LFIX M66 21-4-43 33MU 27-8 82MU 31-8 *Emp Grebe* 13-9 Casa 29-9 243S C3 ops 5-6-44

LZ series All F MkVC(T) Merlin M50 unless otherwise indicated

LZ807 VC 46MU 28-3-43 82MU 5-4 *SS686* 24-4 Casa 17-5 Malta 1-7 Sic NA 30-11 SOC 30-6-45
LZ808 VC 46MU 28-3-43 215MU 5-4 *SS687* 29-4 Casa 17-5 Malta 1-7 229S C3 ops 19-7
LZ809 VC M45 9MU 1-4-43 82MU 11-4 *SS686* 24-4 Casa 17-5 Malta 1-8 NA 1-10 USAAF 31-12
LZ810 VC M46 46MU 28-3-43 215MU 5-4 *Emp Bar* 2-5 Casa 17-5 Malta 1-7 ME 1-9 NAAF 1-11 SOC 26-4-46
LZ811 VC 9MU 1-4-43 82MU 11-4 *SS686* 24-4 Casa 17-5 Malta 1-8 SOC 20-1-44
LZ812 VC 9MU 28-3-43 82MU 11-4 *Emp Bar* 2-5 Casa 7-5 ME 1-7 ME 1-7 C3 ops 4-8 NAASC 31-10 118MU Malta 31-1-44 SOC 1-2
LZ813 VC 9MU 28-3-43 82MU 6-4 *SS686* 24-4 Casa 17-5 SOC 29-2-44
LZ814 VC 9MU 1-4-43 82MU 14-4 *SS686* 24-4 Casa 17-5 ME FAC3 7-6
LZ815 VC M45 9MU 1-4-43 82MU 14-4 *SS686* 24-4 Casa 17-5 32S ME 15-3-45 SOC 26-9
LZ817 VC M45 9MU 1-4-43 82MU 13-4 *SS686* 24-4 Casa 17-5 Malta 1-8 FTR ops 15-2-44
LZ818 VC M45 9MU 4-4-43 82MU 15-4 *SS686* 24-4 Casa 17-5
LZ819 VC 9MU 5-4-43 82MU 14-4 *SS687* 29-4 Casa 17-5 Malta 1-7 SOC 2-10
LZ820 VC 9MU 5-4-43 82MU 15-4 *Emp Bar* 2-5 Casa 7-5 USAAF 12/52 w/u ldg Borgataro Italy 19-12 SOC 29-2-44
LZ821 VC 9MU 7-4-43 82MU 18-4 *Emp Bar* 2-5 Casa 17-5 Malta 1-8 FACB 15-9
LZ822 33MU 11-4-43 47MU 21-4 *Liber* 5-5 Tak 29-5 ME 13-6 NAAF 1-11 SOC 18-8-44
LZ823 33MU 11-4-43 47MU 18-4 *Liber* 5-5 Tak 30-5 ME 2-7 NA 30-11 SOC 29-2-44
LZ824 33MU 11-4-43 47MU 18-4 *Liber* 5-5 Tak 29-5 ME 23-6 NA 30-11 FAC3 2-2-44
LZ825 33MU 11-4-43 47Mu 21-4 *Liber* 5-5 Tak 29-5 ME 19-6 NAAS 31-10 118MU Malta 31-1-44 SOC 29-2-44
LZ826 VC 9MU 14-4-43 82MU 11-5 *SS702* 2-6 Casa 15-6 NWA 1-7 ME 1-9 NAAF 1-11 118MU Malta 31-1-44 SOC 28-4-45
LZ827 VC 9MU 4-4-43 82MU 20-4 *Fort Thom* 3-5 Casa 27-5 ME 28-4-45 SOC 27-6-46
LZ828 M45 6MU 18-8-43 215MU 27-8 *Card Gib* 309 Casa 20-9 NAASC 31-10 ME 21-6-45 RHAF 25-4-46
LZ829 VC 9MU 16-4-43 222MU 29-4 *Fort Stle* 16-5 Casa 30-5 NA 1-7 ME 1-8 118MU Malta 31-1-44 to Turk 30-11
LZ830 VC 9MU 17-4-43 222MU 30-4 *Fort Stle* 16-5 Casa 30-5 NWA 1-7 SOC 1-1-47
LZ834 9MU 29-4-43 215MU 4-5 *Bris Star* 15-5 Aus 30-6
LZ835 15MU 25-4-43 215MU 19-5 *Tongaris* 16-6 Aus 18-8
LZ844 VC 38MU 20-4-43 47MU 26-4 *Kent* 15-5 Aus 2-7
LZ845 VC 8MU 19-4-43 47MU 25-4 *Kent* 15-5 Aus 3-7
LZ846 VC 33MU 23-4-43 105 OTU 2-5 215MU 8-5 Aus 30-6
LZ847 VC 45MU 23-4-43 215MU 5-5 *Fort Jer* 11-5 Casa 30-5 NWA 1-7 ME 1-8 C3 on ops 31-8 NAAF 31-10 SOC 29-2-44
LZ848 VC 9MU 25-4-43 215MU 4-5 *Bris Star* 18-5 Aus 30-6
LZ862 33MU 23-4-43 215MU 29-5 *SSLS267* 26-6 Aus 8-8
LZ863 VC 12MU 27-4-43 215MU 5-5 *Fort Jer* 11-5 Casa 30-5 NWA 1-7 USAAF 12/52 31-1-44 lost in Med 29-1 (USAAF records)
LZ864 VC M50A 38MU 23-4-43 82MU 4-5 *Fort Jer* 11-5 Casa 30-5 NWA 1-7 ME 1-8 NAAF 1-11 RHAF 25-4-46
LZ865 VC 33MU 18-4-43 47MU 24-4 *Nestor* 4-5 Aus 10-8
LZ866 VC 33MU 23-4-43 215MU 30-4 *Bris Star* 18-5 Aus 30-6
LZ867 VC 33MU 19-4-43 47MU 22-4 *Nestor* 4-5 Aus 10-8

LZ868 VC 33MU 23-4-43 105 OTU 2-5 215MU 8-5 *SSLS617* 18-5 Aus 30-6

LZ869 VC 45MU 27-4-43 215MU 7-5 *Fort Stle* 16-5 Casa 30-5 NWA 1-7 ME 1-8 NAAF 1-11 USAAF 31-1-44 SOC 31-8

LZ870 VC 9MU 24-4-43 215MU 6-5 *Bris Star* 18-5 Aus 30-6

LZ871 VC 46MU 27-4-43 47MU 5-5 *Fort Jer* 11-5 Casa 30-5 Malta SOC 8-7

LZ872 VC 12MU 25-4-43 82MU 7-5 *Fort Jer* 11-5 Casa 30-5 Malta 1-8 NA 30-11 SOC 26-4-45

LZ873 VC 33MU 20-4-43 47MU 24-4 *Bris Star* 18-5 Aus 30-6

LZ874 VC 9MU 1-5-43 215MU 8-5 *Bris Star* 18-5 Aus 30-6

LZ875 VC 38MU 23-4-43 47MU 23-5 *SS702* 2-6 Casa 15-6 NWA 1-7 249S FTR ops 4-7-44

LZ876 VC 12MU 25-4-43 82MU 7-5 *Fort Jer* 11-5 Casa 30-5 NWA 1-7 FAF 31-10

LZ877 VC 46MU 27-4-43 47MU 8-5 *Fort Stle* 16-5 Casa 30-5 ME 1-7 NAAF 1-11 FA SOC 20-3-45

LZ878 VC 45MU 27-4-43 215MU 17-5 *Fort Stle* 16-5 Malta 1-7 NWA 1-8 SOC 8-8-44

LZ879 45MU 3-5-43 47MU 10-5 *Fort Stle* 16-5 Casa 30-5 Malta 1-7 NWA 1-8 FAC3 24-7-44

LZ880 38MU 30-4-43 82MU 17-5 *SS702* 2-6 Casa 15-6 NWA 1-7 ME 1-9 NAAF 1-11 C3 ops 16-12

LZ881 VC 9MU 23-4-43 215MU 4-5 *Bris Star* 18-5 Aus 30-6

LZ882 VC 15MU 7-5-43 47MU 19-5 *Pen Cast* 3-6 Tak 27-6 ME 24-7 FAC3 13-4-44

LZ883 6MU 12-5-43 215MU 18-5 *Tongariro* 16-6 Aus 18-8

LZ884 6MU 2-5-43 215MU 9-5 *Bris Star* 18-5 Aus 30-6

LZ885 VC 45MU 27-4-43 215MU 7-5 *Fort Stle* 16-5 Casa 30-5 NWA 1-7 ME 1-8

LZ886 46MU 2-5-43 215MU 9-5 *Bris Star* 18-5 Aus 30-6

LZ887 45MU 2-5-43 215MU 9-5 *Fort Stle* 16-5 Casa 30-5 NWA 1-7 SOC 30-6-45

LZ926 15MU 1-5-43 215MU 19-5 *Tongariro* 16-6 Aus 18-8

LZ927 M63 12MU 1-5-43 47MU 10-5 *Fort Stle* 16-5 Casa 30-5 NWA 1-7 FAF 31-8 to Turk 30-11-44

LZ928 38MU 30-4-43 76MU 18-5 WAL 22-5 *Char Hall* 26-10 Casa 17-11 NA 30-11 ME 30-11-44 RHAF 25-4-46

LZ929 38MU 2-5-43 76MU 28-5 *SS702* 2-6 Casa 15-6 NWA 1-7 ME 1-8 NAAF 1-11 SOC 8-3-44

LZ930 38MU 2-5-43 215MU 26-5 *SS702* 2-6 Casa 15-6 NWA 1-7 SOC 29-2-44

LZ931 VC 46MU 3-5-43 47MU 11-5 *Fort Stle* 16-5 Casa 30-5 NWA 1-7 Malta 1-11 C3 ops MAAF 27-4-44

LZ932 VC 12MU 6-5-43 215MU 17-5 *SS703* 1-6 Casa 15-6 NWA 1-7 ME 1-8 RHAF 25-4-46

LZ933 VC 46MU 3-5-43 47MU 11-5 *Fort Stle* 16-5 Casa 30-5 Malta Sic 1-8 NA 30-11 SOC 8-3-44

LZ934 15MU 1-5-43 215MU 22-5 *SS627* 26-6 Aus 2-8

LZ935 45MU 2-5-43 47MU 10-5 *Fort Stle* 16-5 Casa 30-5 NWA 30-7 ME 1-8 CE ops 2-4-44

LZ936 VC 15MU 7-5-43 47MU 19-5 *Penr Cast* 3-6 Tak 27-6 ME 24-7 to 4212M

LZ937 45MU 14-5-43 47MU 20-5 *SS702* 2-6 Casa 15-6 NWA 1-7 ME 1-9 C3 ops 13-9 NAAF 31-10 SOC 31-12

LZ938 VC 12MU 7-5-43 215MU 18-5 703s 1-6 Casa 15-6 NWA 1-7 ME 1-8 NAASC 31-10 SOC 13-9-45

LZ939 6MU 15-5-43 47MU 23-5 *SSLS98* 28-6 Ind 23-8 SEAAC C3 ops 5-12

LZ940 33MU 16-5-43 47MU 23-5 *Meers* 3-6 Tak 8-7 ME 9-8 FAC3 13-8

LZ941 39MU 11-5-43 47MU 21-5 *Emp Fran* 3-6 Tak 16-7 ME 13-8 SOC 17-9-45

LZ942 39MU 11-5-43 47MU 21-5 *Emp Fran* 3-6 Tak 16-7 ME 13-8

LZ943 33MU 16-5-43 47MU 27-5 *Emp Fran* 3-6 Tak 16-7 ME 28-8 FACE 19-2-45 SOC 22-2

LZ944 12MU 14-5-43 76MU 22-5 *SS702* 2-6 Casa 15-6 NWA 1-7 ME 15-3-45 SOC 29-5-46

LZ945 12MU 14-5-43 82MU 24-5 *SS702* 2-6 Casa 15-6 NWA 1-7 ME 1-8 SOC 1-11

LZ946 45MU 2-5-43 215MU 12-5 *Fort Stle* 16-5 Casa 30-5 Malta Sic 1-8 ME 30-9 NAASC 31-10 SOC 26-4-45

LZ969 39MU 15-5-43 222MU 27-5 *Meers* 3-6 Tak 8-7 ME 10-8

LZ970 VC 15MU 7-5-43 76MU 25-5 *SS702* 2-6 Casa 15-6 NWA 1-7 ME 1-9 NAAF 1-11 SOC 31-5-45

LZ971 6MU 15-5-43 47MU 23-5 *Pegu* 15-6 Ind 20-8 FAC3 20-11

LZ972 6MU 15-5-43 76MU 27-5 *Fort Enter* 18-7 Ind 23-8 C3 ops 23-11

LZ973 VC 9MU 9-5-43 47MU 20-5 *Pegu* 15-6 Ind 20-8 61S FA FTR 13-11

LZ974 39MU 15-5-43 222MU 27-5 *Meers* 3-6 Tak 8-7 ME 10-8

LZ975 6MU 15-5-43 47MU 23-5 *Pegu* 15-6 Ind 25-8 SOC 31-5-45

LZ976 46MU 15-5-43 222MU 22-5 *SS702* 2-6 Casa 15-6 NWA 1-7 MAAF 21-6-45 SOC 19-7

LZ977 39MU 15-5-43 47MU 25-5 *Meers* 3-6 Tak 8-7 ME 30-7 SOC 29-8-45

LZ978 33MU 16-5-43 47MU 23-5 *Meers* 3-6 Tak 8-7 ME 10-8 SOC 29-8-46

LZ979 39MU 21-5-43 47MU 30-5 *Emp Fran* 3-6 Tak 16-7 ME 10-8 to Turk 26-4-45

LZ980 38MU 15-5-43 82MU 30-5 *SS703* 1-6 Casa 15-6 NWA 1-7 C3 ops 14-2-44

LZ981 46MU 14-5-43 215MU 22-5 *SS703* 1-6 Casa 15-6 NWA 1-7 ME 1-9 NAASC 31-10 SOC 29-8-46

LZ982 45MU 20-5-43 47MU 1-6 *SS703* 1-6 Casa 15-6 NWA 1-7 ME 1-8 NAAF 1-11 SOC 26-9-46

LZ983 38MU 15-5-43 52MU 29-5 *SS702* 2-6 Casa 15-6 NWA 1-7 SOC 31-5-45

LZ984 33MU 16-5-43 47MU 24-5 *Meers* 3-6 Tak 8-7 ME 10-8 C3 ops 27-9

LZ985 33MU 16-5-43 82MU 27-5 *Meers* 3-6 Tak 8-7 ME 10-8 FAF 14-2-46

LZ986 39MU 15-5-43 47MU 25-5 *Meers* 3-6 Tak 8-7 NWA CE 6-8

LZ987 38MU 21-5-43 FAAC 25-5 ROS 222MU 21-7 *Fort Rup* 25-7 Casa 16-8 NWA 1-10 FAF 31-10 MAAF 21-6-45 Trg del 4-10

LZ988 33MU 18-5-43 47MU 24-5 *Meers* 3-6 Tak 8-7 ME 9-8 FAC3 1-10

MA series All F Mk VC(T) Merlin otherwise indicated

MA261 38MU 15-5-43 82MU 30-5 *SS703* 1-6 Casa 15-6 NWA 1-7 ME 1-8 NAAF 1-11 SOC 31-8-44

MA262 38MU 15-5-43 82MU 30-5 *SS705* 1-6 Casa 15-6 NWA 1-7 ME 1-8 NAAF 1-11 Malta 31-1-44 SOC 29-1-44

MA263 33MU 16-5-43 222MU 23-6 *Chyel* 17-7 Ind 18-8 FAC3 25-2-44

MA264 no record

MA265 33MU 19-5-43 222MU 1-6 *SSLS98* 28-6 Ind 23-8 ACSEA SOC 19-8-45

MA266 33MU 19-5-43 47MU 31-5 *SSLS514* 17-6 Tak 16-7 ME 10-9 SOC 26-4-45

MA279 38MU 15-5-43 76MU 1-6 *SS703* 1-6 Casa 15-6 NWA 30-6 ME 1-7 NAASC 1-11 USAAF 31-12

MA280 33MU 19-5-43 47MU 31-5 *SSLS514* 17-6 Tak 16-7 ME 10-9 SOC 28-2-46

MA281 33MU 18-5-43 82MU 27-5 *SS702* 1-6 Casa 15-6 NWA 1-7 ME 1-8 NAAF 1-11 FACE 16-9-44

MA282 38MU 27-5-43 76MU 3-6 *SS703* 1-6 Casa 15-6 NWA 1-7 ME 1-8 NAAF 1-11 SOC 14-3-46

MA283 45MU 20-5-43 215MU 1-6 *SS707* 10-6 Casa 29-6 SOC 31-10

MA284 6MU 30-5-43 222MU 24-7 *Behar* 11-9 Ind 9-11 61S FTR ops 17-6-44

MA285 39MU 22-5-43 47MU 30-5 *Emp Fran* 3-6 Tak 16-7 ME 23-8 SOC 26-4-45

MA286 9MU 27-5-43 222MU 1-6 *SSLS78* 28-6 Ind 23-8 SOC 26-4-45

MA287 39MU 22-5-43 47MU 30-5 *SSLS514* 17-6 Tak 16-7 ME 31-9 to VB(T) 1-11-45 SOC 29-8-46

MA288 9MU 27-5-43 222MU 1-6 *SSLS98* 28-6 Ind 23-8 FAC3 15-11

MA289 45MU 20-5-43 215MU 30-5 *SS702* 2-6 Casa 15-6 NWA 1-7 ME 1-8 NAAF 1-11 SOC 20-1-46

MA290 9MU 10-6-43 82MU 22-6 *Chye* 17-7 Ind 18-8 ACSEA SOC 27-9-45

MA291 45MU 20-5-43 47MU 1-6 *SS703* 1-6 Casa 15-6 NWA 1-8 NAASC 31-10 32S FTR ops 25-8-44

MA292 9MU 27-5-43 222MU 1-6 *SSLS98* 28-6 Ind 23-8 SOC 10-7-44

MA293 39MU 25-5-43 47MU 31-5 *SSLS514* 17-6 Tak 16-7 ME 13-9 FA FTR 29-7-44

MA294 33MU 25-5-43 82MU 2-6 *SSLS517* 17-6 Tak 16-7 ME 23-8 SOC 1-2-44

MA295 9MU 29-5-43 47MU 4-6 *SS707* 10-6 Casa 29-6 ME 1-8 NAAF 1-11 SOC 31-8-44

MA296 9MU 27-5-43 222MU 1-6 *SSLS98* 28-6 Ind 23-8 FTR ops 20-1-44

MA297 6MU 28-5-43 47MU 4-6 *SSLS98* 25-6 Ind 23-8 SOC 7-2-45

MA298 R-RH 27-5-43 to LFIX M66 39MU 3-7 234S 14-7 RAF Mlfld 17-3-44 VSM 21-10-46 to 6462M 13-10-47 RDAF 28-7-48

MA328 9MU 18-4-43 38MU 21-4 *Fort Stle* 16-5 Casa 30-5 NWA 1-7 ME FTR ops 29-11

MA329 VC R-RH to LFIX M66 22-4-43 33MU 23-10 CRD VWD 25-10 CRD VWD 25-1-44 443S 27-7 410RSU 30-11 165S 2-9-46 sold R J Coley 3-2-50

MA330 VC 9MU 18-4-43 222MU 29-4 *Fort Stle* 16-5 Casa 30-5 NWA 1-7 ME 1-8 NAAF 1-11 C3 ops 29-11

MA331 12MU 19-4-43 215MU 29-4 *Fort Jer* 11-5 Casa 30-5 NWA 1-7 ME 1-8 SOC 31-5-45

MA332 VC 9MU 27-4-43 222MU 6-5 *Fort Stle* 16-5 Casa 30-5 Malta 1-7 ME 1-10 249S FTR ops 10-8-44

MA333 VC 9MU 27-4-43 76MU 6-5 *Fort Stle* 16-5 Casa 30-5 NWA 1-7 SOC 26-4-45

MA334 VC 9MU 29-4-43 222MU 4-5 *Fort Stle* 16-5 Casa 30-5 NWA 1-7 ME 30-11-44

MA335 VC 9MU 27-4-43 222MU 6-5 *Fort Stle* 16-5 Casa 30-5 NWA 30-6 USAAF 12/52 1-10 lost in Med 29-12 SOC 29-2-44

MA336 VC 9MU 27-4-43 76MU 6-5 *Fort Stle* 16-5 Casa 30-5 Malta 1-7 NAASC 31-10 USAAF 30-11 ME 31-1-45 SOC 10-1-46

MA337 38MU 1-5-43 82MU 17-5 *SS702* 2-6 Casa 15-6 NWA 1-7 ME 1-8 NAAF 1-11 FACE 21-9-44

MA338 12MU 1-5-43 82MU 17-5 *SS702* 2-6 Casa NWA 1-7 253S FTR ops 4-5-44

MA339 VC 12MU 6-5-43 215MU 23-5 *SS703* 1-6 Casa 15-6 NWA 30-6 ME 1-8 NAAF 1-11 SOC 26-4-45

MA340 VC 12MU 6-5-43 215MU 14-5 *SS702* 2-6 Casa 15-6 NWA 1-7 ME 1-9 NAAF 1-11 MAAF 21-6-45 SOC 11-4-46

MA341 VC 9MU 9-5-43 47MU 21-5 *Pegu* 15-6 Ind 20-8 SOC 25-4-46

MA342 VC 15MU 7-5-43 76MU 25-5 *SS702* 2-6 Casa 15-6 NWA 1-7 ME 1-8 SOC 1-12

MA343 VCM45 9MU 8-5-43 76 MU 19-5 *SS707* 10-6 Casa 29-6 ME 1-9 NAAF 31-10 SOC 28-8-46

MA344 VC 9MU 9-5-43 76MU 20-5 *SS702* 2-6 Casa 15-6 NWA 1-7 USAAF 31-8 ME 30-11-44 SOC 12-7-45

MA345 VC 9MU 8-5-43 76MU 19-5 *SS702* 2-6 Casa 15-6 NWA 1-7 ME 1-8 NAAF 1-11 SOC 18-8

MA346 38MU 13-5-43 76MU 28-5 *SS703* 1-6 Casa 15-6 NWA 1-7 ME 1-9 NAAF 1-11 118MU Malta 31-1-44 SOC 29-2-44

MA347 6MU 15-5-43 47MU 23-5 *SSLS98* 28-6 Ind 23-8 SOC 30-8-45

MA348 6MU 15-5-43 47MU 23-5 *SSLS98* 28-6 Ind 23-8 SOC 12-2-45

MA349 6MU 15-5-43 47MU 23-5 *SSLS98* 28-6 Ind 23-8 FTR ops 26-12

MA350 M45 33MU 16-5-43 47MU 24-5 *Meers* 306 Tak 8-7 ME 13-12 SOC 29-8-46

MA351 33MU 16-5-43 47MU 23-5 *Emp Fran* 3-6 Tak 16-7 ME 28-8 SOC 4-9-45

MA352 9MU 29-5-43 215MU 4-6 *SSLS627* 26-6 Aus 2-8

MA353 9MU 30-5-43 215MU 8-6 *SSLS627* 26-6 Aus 2-8

MA354 9MU 29-5-43 215MU 4-6 *SSLS627* 26-6 Aus 2-8

MA355 6MU 31-5-43 215MU 8-6 *SSLS627* 26-6 Aus 2-8

MA356 6MU 2-6-43 215MU 11-6 *SSLS627* 26-6 Aus 2-8

MA357 CRD R-RH 2-6-43 to LFIX M66. M65 Spcl instal 19-3-44 used by R-R for ext filtration tests of various Vokes air filters. One was standardised on Type 378 Spit FIX(T). 58MU 4-12-46 SOC 12-12

MA358 33MU 6-6-43 47MU 14-6 *Glenb* 3-7 Tak 30-7 ME 10-9 SOC 26-4-45

MA359 33MU 6-6-43 47MU 17-6 *Glenb* 3-7 Tak 30-7 ME 31-8 FTR ops 2-3-44

MA360 33MU 6-6-43 47MU 14-6 *Glenb* 3-7 Tak 30-7 ME 10-9 SOC 27-6-46

X MA361 6MU 3-7-43 47MU 8-7 *Marts* 26-7 Ind 29-8

MA362 39MU 1-7-43 234S 14-7 39MU 12-8 82MU 30-8 *Ger Don* 25-8 Casa 10-9 NA 30-11 SOC 26-4-45

MA363 33MU 6-6-43 47MU 14-6 *Glenb* 7-7 Tak 30-7 ME 11-9 SOC 29-8-46

MA364 M55 9MU 25-7-43 47MU 7-8 *Ocean Ves* 16-8 Ind 27-9 SOC 25-1-45

MA365 6MU 3-7-43 222MU 10-7 *Marts* 26-7 Ind 29-8 C3 ops 20-1-44 SOC 7-2-45

MA366 9MU 9-6-43 215MU 20-6 *SS627* 26-6 Aus 2-8

MA367 39MU 11-6-43 222MU 24-6 *Chyel* 17-7 Kar 18-8 607S FTR ops 9-2-44

MA368 39MU 11-6-43 222MU 24-6 *Chyel* 17-7 Ind 18-8 ACSEA 21-6-45 SOC 25-4-46

MA383 6MU 28-5-43 47MU 4-6 *SSLS98* 28-6 Ind 23-8 SOC 10-7-44

MA384 6MU 2-7-43 47MU 12-7 *Martand* 26-7 Ind 29-8 SOC 28-9

MA292 of No 615(NZ) Squadron, India August 1943. Note fern leaf motif under exhaust stubs.

MA385 9MU 6-6-43 215MU 16-6 *SSLS627* 21-6 Aus 2-8

MA386 6MU 1-6-43 47MU 10-6 *SSLS98* 26-6 Ind 23-8 C3 ops 26-12 SOC 14-6-45

MA387 6MU 1-6-43 215MU 8-6 *SSLS627* 26-6 Aus 2-8

MA388 6MU 1-6-43 47MU 10-4 *SSLS98* 28-6 Ind 2-8 SOC 12-2-45

MA389 6MU 2-6-43 215MU 11-6 *SSLS627* 26-6 Aus 2-8

MA390 9MU 30-5-43 47MU 4-6 *SSLS98* 28-6 Ind 23-8 SOC 11-6-45

MA391 6MU 6-6-43 222MU 16-6 *Chyel* 17-7 Ind 18-8 SOC 26-4-45

MA392 9MU 30-5-43 47MU 4-6 *SSLS98* 28-6 Ind 23-8 SOC 12-2-45

MA393 6MU 1-6-43 47MU 10-6 *SSLS98* 28-6 Ind 23-8 SOC 30-8-45

MA394 9MU 5-6-43 215MU 15-6 *SSLS627* 26-6 Aus 2-8

MA395 9MU 30-7-43 215MU 8-8 *Durham* 14-8 Aus 18-10

MA396 6MU 6-6-43 82MU 12-6 *Chyel* 17-7 Ind 18-8 SOC 13-9-45

MA397 39MU 20-6-43 234S 29-6 130S 25-7 82MU 18-8 *Ger Don* 25-8 Casa 18-9 NAASC 31-10 FAF 31-12 ME 30-11-44 SOC 29-3-45

MA643 38MU 21-5-43 82MU 30-5 *SS703* 1-6 Casa 15-6 NWA 1-7 ME 1-8 C3 ops 8-11

MA644 33MU 20-5-43 47MU 4-6 *Glenb* 3-7 Tak 30-7 ME 10-9 FTR ops 8-10-44

MA645 R-RH 23-5-43 to LFIX M66 RAF Mlfld 14-3-44 FAAC AST 83CSU 26-9m 302S 10-12 FACE 1-1-45

MA646 R-RH 23-5-43 to LFIX M66 RAF Mlfld 24-3-44 to 6070M 2-8-46 recat E 12-4-49

MA647 39MU 23-5-43 47MU 31-5 *SSLS514* 17-4 Tak 16-7 ME 10-9 SOC 28-9-46

MA648 R-RH 23-5-43 to LFIX M66 instal with SU MkII fuel injection pump. BD 21-10 trls with pump. Fuel was injected into eye of supercharger. Syst tested initially on W3322, but completely redesigned and fitt new air intake carb combining temperate and trop filters. Decrease in fuel cons of 11 to 17% in comp with normal M66. ROS 2-2-44 CRD R-R 22-9 SOC 2-7-45

MA649 39MU 23-5-43 82MU 206 *SSLS517* 17-6 Tak 16-7 ME 18-12 FAC3 19-1-44

MA650 9MU 27-5-43 222MU 1-6 *SSLS98* 28-6 Ind 23-8 FAC3 10-11

MA651 R-RH to LFIX M66 30-5-43 RAF Mlfld 14-3-44 e/fld w/u ldg nr East Fortune aerodrome CE 29-5-44

MA652 9MU 28-5-43 47MU 3-6 *SSLS98* 28-6 Ind SOC 7-2-45

MA653 39MU 1-6-43 234S 30-6 130S 20-7 82MU 21-8 *Ger Don* 25-8 Casa 10-9 NA 30-11 MAAF SOC 11-4-46

MA654 39MU 6-6-43 47MU 16-6 *Chyel* 17-7 Ind 18-8 SOC 26-4-45

MA655 R-RH 6-6-43 to LFIX M66 instal with SU MkII fuel injector pump. Subsequent history parallels MA648. CRD R-R 19-3-44 58MU 18-4-46 SOC 31-5-46

MA656 39MU 1-6-43 47MU 10-6 *Glenb* 307 Tak 30-7 ME 10-9 SOC 26-4-45

MA657 R-RH 1-6-43 to LFIX M66 final R-R MkV airframe. RAF Mlfld 14-3-44 VSM 17-10-46 sold to VA

MA670 9MU 10-6-43 82MU 23-6 *Marts* 28-7 Ind 29-8 C3 ops 14-4-44

MA671 39MU 17-6-43 234S 29-6 130S 20-7 82MU 19-8 *Ger Don* 25-8 Casa 10-9 NA 30-11 FAF 31-12 ME SOC 29-8-46

MA672 9MU 13-6-43 82MU 25-6 *Chyel* 17-7 Ind 18-8 FACE 14-11-44 SOC 27-11

MA673 6MU 19-6-43 47MU 27-6 *Chyel* 17-7 Ind 18-8 SOC 22-6-45

X MA674 9MU 13-6-43 82MU 25-6 *Chyel* 17-7 Ind 18-8 SOC 26-4-45

MA675 M50A 6MU 29-6-43 222MU 7-7 *Marts* 26-7 Ind 29-8 SOC 26-4-45

MA676 6MU 19-6-43 47MU 27-6 *Chyel* 17-7 Ind 18-8 SOC 7-2-45

MA677 M50A 6MU 29-6-43 222MU 7-7 *Chyel* 17-7 Ind 18-8 SOC 5-7-45

MA678 39MU 20-6-43 234S 29-6 130S 20-7 82MU 18-8 *Ger Don* 25-8 Casa 10-9 NA 30-11 FAF 31-12 MAAF FAC 3-3-44

MA679 39MU 21-6-43 234S 29-6 130S 20-7 222MU 23-8 *Ger Don* 25-8 Casa 16-9 NAASC 31-10 FAF 29-2-44

MA680 33MU 21-6-43 82MU 29-6 *SS717* 5-7 Casa 29-7 ME 31-1-45 SOC 13-9

MA681 33MU 12-6-43 222MU 25-6 *La Pampa* 2-7 Casa 16-7 ME 1-9 NAAF 1-11 SOC 13-2-45

MA682 33MU 22-6-43 82MU 29-6 *SS717* 5-7 Casa 29-7 ME 1-9 NAAF 1-11 ME 28-4-45 SOC 29-8-46

MA684 33MU 12-6-43 234S 14-7 82MU 18-8 *Ger Don* 25-8 Casa 10-9 NAASC 31-9

MA685 9MU 12-6-43 215MU 25-6 *Port Dun* 15-7 Aus 27-9

MA686 33MU 12-6-43 222MU 23-6 *Chyel* 17-7 Ind 18-8 SOC 12-2-45

MA688 6MU 20-6-43 222MU 1-7 *Chyel* 17-7 Ind 18-8 SOC 23-1-45

MA689 9MU 12-6-43 215MU 20-6 *SSLS627* 26-6 Aus 2-8

MA691 33MU 17-6-43 222MU 25-6 *La Pampa* 2-7 Casa 14-7 253S FTR ops 8-3-44

X MA692 6MU 20-6-43 82MU 2-7 *Chyel* 17-7 Ind 18-8 SOC 28-2-46

MA694 6MU 20-6-43 222MU 1-7 *Chyel* 17-7 Ind 18-8 615S FTR ops 15-6-44

MA695 39MU 23-6-43 234S 30-6 130S 23-7 82S 24-8 82MU 24-8 *Card Gib* 3-7 Casa 20-9 NAASC 31-10 FAF 29-2-44 USAAF ME 30-11 RHAF 25-4-46

MA696 M55 6MU 24-7-43 82MU 6-8 *Behar* 11-9 Ind 9-11 SOC 30-8-45

MA697 M55 6MU 6-8-43 215MU 13-8 *Corn* 20-8 Aus 16-11

MA698 9MU 8-8-43 82MU 3-9 *Emp Grebe* 15-9 Casa 29-9 NAASC 31-10 USAAF 21-12 52S 31-5-44 FTR ops 25-10

MA699 M55 6MU 7-8-43 215MU 14-8 *Horor* 14-9 Aus 21-10

MA700 33MU 25-6-43 234S 19-7 82MU 18-8 *Ger Don* 25-8 Casa 10-9 NA 30-11 ME 30-11-44 to Turk 28-12

MA701 33MU 25-6-43 130S 19-7 82MU Ger Don 25-8 Casa 10-9 NA 30-11 ME 31-8-44 SOC 10-1-46

MA702 M55M 39MU 4-7-43 234S 16-7 130S 23-7 82MU 13-8 *Ger Don* 25-8 Casa 10-9 NA 30-11 USAAF 31-1-44 SOC 26-9-46

MA703 39MU 27-6-43 234S 16-7 82MU 13-8 *Ger Don* 25-8 Casa 10-9 NA 30-11 FAF 31-12 to Turk 30-11-44

MA704 M55 33MU 1-7-43 234S 14-7 82MU 18-8 *Ger Don* 25-8 Casa 10-9 NA 30-11 FAF 29-2-44 ME 15-3-45 RHAF 25-4-46

MA850 M55M 9MU 1-7-43 130S 8-7 82MU 16-8 *Ger Don* 25-8 Casa 10-9 NA 30-11 USAAF 29-2-44 ME 31-1-45 SOC 29-8-46

MA851 M55 6MU 29-6-43 52MU 7-7 *Marts* 26-7 Ind 29-8 C3 ops 15-1-44 SOC 7-2-45

MA852 M55 6MU 29-6-43 222MU 7-7 *Chyel* 17-7 Ind 18-8 SOC 28-9-44

MA853 39MU 27-6-43 234S 14-7 82MU 13-8 *Ger Don* 25-8 Casa 10-9 NA 30-11 SOC 26-4-45

MA855 M55 39MU 29-6-43 234S 14-7 CRD BDn 16-8 VWD 26-2-44 BDn 28-2 FACE 20-3 ASTH 53 OTU 2-3-45 to 5379M 12-2-45

MA856 M55M 39MU 1-7-43 82MU 28-7 *SS732* 5-8 Casa 18-8 NWA 1-10 ME 28-4-45 SOC 27-6-46

MA857 M55 6MU 29-6-43 222MU 7-7 *Chyel* 17-7 Ind 18-8 SOC 12-2-45

MA858 M55 33MU 1-7-43 130S 16-7 234S 23-7 222MU 21-8 *Ger Don* 25-8 Casa 10-9 NAASC 31-10 SOC 26-4-45

MA859 M55 39MU 16-7-43 82MU 28-7 *SS732* 5-8 Casa 18-8 NWA 1-10 ME 28-4-45 SOC 29-8-46

MA861 M55 39MU 17-7-43 82MU 30-7 *SS732* 5-8 Casa 18-8 NWA 1-10 USAAF 31-12

MA862 M55M 9MU 1-7-43 130S 23-7 82MU 16-8 *Ger Don* 20-8 Casa 10-9 NA 30-11 USAAF 31-1-44 253S C3 ops 19-5-44

MA863 6MU 8-8-43 215MU 16-8 *Horor* 14-9 Aus 21-10 RAAF A58-246, extant Melbourne

MA877 M55 39MU 17-7-43 82MU 30-7 *SS732* 5-8 Casa 18-8 NWA 1-10 C3 ops 30-12

MA880 M55 39MU 17-7-43 82MU 30-7 *SS732* 5-8 Casa 18-8 NWA 1-10 ME 31-8-44 SOC 25-7-46

MA881 39MU 17-7-43 82MU 8-8 *Fort Thom* 14-8 Casa 1-9 ME FTR ops 26-9

MA882 M55 33MU 18-7-43 82MU 28-7 *SS732* 5-8 Casa 18-8 1676Flt Gib 22-9 FAF GR2/33 13-8-44

MA883 M55 9MU 8-8-43 222MU 29-8 *Card Gib* 3-9 Casa 20-9 NAASC 31-10 USAAF 12th AF 31-12 lost over France 9-2-44

MA885 M55 33MU 18-7-43 82MU 28-7 *SS732* 5-8 Casa 18-8 NA 30-11 237S FA FTR

MA886 M55 33MU 22-7-43 82MU 6-8 *Fort Thom* 14-8 Casa 1-9 NA 30-11 USAAF 29-2-44 SOC 26-4-45

MA887 M55 33MU 22-7-43 222MU 31-7 *Fort Thom* 14-8 Casa 1-9 NA 30-11 USAAF 29-2-44 SOC 26-4-45

MA888 M55 33MU 24-7-43 222MU 5-8 *Fort Thom* 14-8 Casa 1-9 NA 30-11 ME 21-6-45 SOC 29-8-46

MA889 M55 33MU 18-7-43 82MU 27-7 *SS732* 5-8 Casa 18-8 NA 30-11 USAAF 29-2-44 326S lost at sea 6-6

MA890 M55 39MU 26-7-43 222MU 19-8 *Ger Don* 25-8 Casa 10-9 NAASC 31-10 USAAF 31-1-44 w/o Italy 19-2

MA891 M55 33MU 22-7-43 222MU 31-7 *Fort Thom* 14-8 Casa 1-9 NA 30-11 SOC 26-4-45

MA892 M55 33MU 24-7-43 222MU 31-7 *Fort Thom* 16-8 Casa 1-9 NA 30-11 ME 21-6-45 SOC 13-9-45

MA893 M55 33MU 24-7-43 222MU 30-7 *SS732* 5-8 Casa 18-8 USAAF 29-2-44 MAAF 21-6-45 FAF 9-10-47

MA894 M55 33MU 24-7-43 222MU 31-7 *Fort Thom* 14-8 Casa 1-9 NA 30-11

MA895 M55 39MU 26-7-43 82MU 16-8 *Ger Don* 25-8 Casa 10-9 NA 31-11 MAAF 21-6-45 SOC 11-4-46

MA896 6MU 15-8-43 47MU 29-8 *Card Gib* 3-9 Casa 20-9 NA 30-11 SOC 26-4-45

MA897 M55 6MU 14-8-43 222MU 30-8 *Card Gib* 3-9 Casa 20-9 NAASC 31-10 SOC 26-4-45

MA898 39MU 23-6-43 234S 29-6 130S 23-7 82MU 20-8 *Ger Don* 25-8 Casa 18-9 NA 30-11 FAF 29-2-44 ME 30-11 SOC 11-10-45

MA899 9MU 27-6-43 82MU 8-7 *Marst* 26-7 Ind 29-8 C3 ops 31-12

MA900 33MU 26-6-43 130S 16-7 82MU 18-8 *Ger Don* 25-8 Casa 10-9 NA 30-11 SOC 23-10-44

MA901 33MU 26-6-43 130S 19-7 222MU 21-8 *Ger Don* 25-8 Casa 10-9 NA 30-11 FAF 29-2-44 ME 30-11 SOC 26-9-46

MA902 9MU 27-6-43 215MU 7-7 *Marst* 26-7 Ind 29-8 C3 ops 19-2-44

MA903 9MU 27-6-43 82MU 8-7 *Marst* 26-7 Ind 29-8 FTR 28-2-46

MA904 M50A 39MU 29-6-43 234S 14-7 82MU 13-8 *Ger Don* 25-8 Casa 19-9 NA 30-11 ME 21-6-45 RHAF 25-4-46

MA905 M55 33MU 30-6-43 130S 16-7 222MU 20-8 *Ger Don* 25-8 Casa 10-9 FTR ops 16-12

MA906 M55 39MU 1-7-43 234S 14-7 222MU 16-8 *Ger Don* 25-8 Casa 10-9 NA 30-11 SOC 26-4-45

MH series All VC(T) Merlin 55 unless otherwise indicated

MH298 39MU 1-7-43 234S 19-7 82MU 14-8 *Ger Don* 25-8 Casa 10-9 NA 30-11 SOC 30-11-44 bboc 21-6-45 RHAF 25-4-46 335S flew Mountain Greece Pilot kld 18-12

MH299 6MU 16-7-43 47MU 23-7 *SSLS808* 26-7 Ind 29-8 SOC 13-12-44

MH300 6MU 16-7-43 47MU 20-7 *SSLS808* 26-7 Ind 27-8 SOC 26-4-45

MH301 9MU 18-7-43 222MU 25-7 *Behar* 11-9 Ind 9-4 SOC 10-7-44

MH302 9MU 18-7-43 222MU 23-7 *Behar* 11-9 Ind 9-11 615S C3 ops 20-6-44

MH303 9MU 18-7-43 222MU 23-7 *Behar* 11-9 Ind 9-11 SOC 26-4-45

MH304 39MU 18-7-43 82MU 11-8 *Fort Thom* 14-8 Casa 1-9 NA 30-11 MAAF 21-6-45 FAF SOC 30-8-45

MH305 9MU 18-7-43 222MU 22-7 *Marst* 26-7 Ind 27-8 SOC 10-7-44

MH306 M50 9MU 31-7-43 215MU 13-8 *Corn* 20-8 Aus 16-11

MH307 39MU 18-7-43 82MU 13-8 *Ger Don* 25-8 Casa 10-9 NA 30-11 CE ops 1-4-44

MH308 9MU 18-7-43 222MU 22-7 *Marst* 26-7 Ind 29-8 SOC 2-10-44

MH309 39MU 19-7-43 47MU 1-8 *Fort Thom* 14-8 Casa 17-9 NA 30-11 FAF 29-2-44 RNAF 1948 as H-57 BAF 10-52 as SM-34

MH310 39MU 25-7-43 82MU 28-7 *Ger Don* 25-8 Casa 10-9 NA 30-11 FAF 31-12 SOC 26-4-45

MH311 6MU 24-7-43 222MU 30-7 *Behar* 11-9 Ind 9-11 SOC 7-2-45

MH564 M55M 39MU 29-7-43 82MU 11-8 *Fort Thom* 14-8 Casa 1-9 NA 30-11 USAAF 31-1-44

MH565 39MU 26-7-43 222MU 19-8 *Ger Don* 25-8 Casa 10-9 NA 30-11 USAAF 31-1-44

MH566 6MU 30-7-43 215MU 8-8 *Durham* 14-8 Aus 18-10

MH567 9MU 18-8-43 222MU 18-9 *Craw W L* 22-9 Casa 10-10 253S FTR ops 6-6-44

MH568 M55M 33MU 31-7-43 82MU 12-8 *Ger Don* 25-8 Casa 10-9 NA 30-11 ME SOC 22-12-44

MH581 M55M 39MU 28-7-43 222MU 11-8 *Fort Thom* 14-8 Casa 1-9 NA 30-11 USAAF 31-1-44 ME 25-2-45 SOC 29-8-46

MH582 M55M 33MU 30-7-43 222MU 10-8 *Fort Thom* 14-8 Casa 1-9 NA 30-11 REAF 29-3-45

MH583 M55M 33MU 30-7-43 82MU 7-8 *Fort Thom* 14-8 Casa 1-9 NA 30-11 SOC 26-4-45

MH584 M55M 33MU 30-7-43 82MU 12-8 *Ger Don* 25-8 Casa 10-9 NAASC 31-10 SOC 26-4-45

MH585 6MU 31-7-43 215MU 8-8 *Durham* 14-8 Aus 18-10

MH586 6MU 7-8-43 215MU 14-8 *Corn* 20-8 Aus 16-11

MH587 6MU 7-8-43 215MU 14-8 *Horor* 14-9 Aus 21-10

MH588 6MU 5-8-43 215MU 13-8 *Horor* 14-9 Aus 21-10

MH589 9MU 8-8-43 215MU 18-8 *Horor* 14-9 Aus 21-10

MH590 9MU 8-8-43 82MU 3-9 *Emp Grebe* 15-9 Casa 29-9 NAASC 1-11 ME 21-6-45 RHAF 25-4-46 335S Dam by AA fire co f/ld nr Dendelita Yugoslav 6-9

MH591 9MU 8-8-43 215MU 18-8 *Horor* 14-9 Aus 21-10

MH592 6MU 14-8-43 47MU 5-9 *Ocean Rid* 23-9 Casa 10-10 NAASC 31-10

MH593 6MU 14-8-43 222MU 30-8 *Card Gib* 3-9 Casa 20-9 USAAF 29-2-44 253S FTR ops 22-5

MH594 6MU 14-8-43 222MU 30-8 *Card Gib* 3-9 Casa 20-9 NA 30-11 USAAF 29-2-44 MAAF 21-6-45 FAF 9-10-47

MH595 VC 6MU 13-8-43 47MU 31-8 *Card Gib* 3-9 Casa 20-9 NA 30-11 SOC 26-4-45

MH596 6MU 15-8-43 47MU 30-8 *Card Gib* 3-9 Casa 20-9 NA 30-11 FAF GR2/33 15-6-44 SOC 31-8

MH600 VC 6MU 22-8-43 215MU 27-8 *Card Gib* 3-9 Casa 20-9 NAASC 31-10 SOC 26-4-45

MH605 VC M63 9MU 29-8-43 47MU 10-9 *Ocean Rid* 23-9 Casa 10-10 NAASC 31-10 USAAF 12/52 31-11 lost over Italy 19-12

MH637 9MU 25-7-43 47MU 7-8 *Ocean Ves* 16-8 Ind 27-9 SOC 26-7-45

MH638 9MU 25-7-43 47MU 7-8 *Ocean Ves* 16-8 Ind 27-9 FAC3 12-4-44

MH639 9MU 25-7-43 47MU 7-8 *Ocean Ves* 16-8 Ind 27-9 SOC 2-2-45

MH640 9MU 25-7-43 47MU 7-8 *Ocean Ves* 16-8 29-7 SOC 10-7-44

MH641 M55M 6MU 28-7-43 82MU 6-8 *Behar* 11-9 Ind 9-11 SOC 27-9-45

MH642 6MU 31-7-43 215MU 9-8 *Durham* 14-8 Aus 18-10

MH643 6MU 31-7-43 215MU 8-8 *Durham* 14-8 Aus 18-10

MH644 9MU 31-7-43 215MU 10-8 Durham 14-8 Aus 18-10

MH645 9MU 31-7-43 215MU 11-8 *Corn* 20-8 Aus 16-11

MH646 9MU 31-7-43 215MU 14-8 *Corn* 20-8 Aus 16-11 Last FV variant built at CBAF

MH750 to LFIX M66 33MU 19-9-43 405ARF 28-9 19S FAAC 7-10 317S 3-11 Air test FACB 27-11 WAL for repainting 24-2-44 302S 30-4 308S 83GSU 15-6 mods GAL mods 12-12 MAL 18-4-45 Czech AF 6-12-46

MH751 to LFIX M66 39MU 19-9-43 222MU 6-10 *Char Hall* 24-10 Casa 7-11 218Gp 30-11 237S FTR ops 25-9-44

MH752 to LFIX M66 39MU 18-9-43 47MU 3-10 *Char Hall* 24-10 Casa 17-11 218Gp 30-11 SOC 23-12-44

MH753 to LFIX M66 33MU 18-9-43 222MU 6-10 349S 8-6-44 340S 22-6 84GSU 29-6 402S 11-8 91S 12-4 1S 12-4-45 FAAC 22-10-45 VSM 17-10-46 sold VA

MH754 to LFIX M66 33MU 18-9-43 405ARF 28-9 411S CAC ops 22-5-44 412S 22-6 CB ops 29-6

MH755 to LFIX M66 39MU 18-9-43 52MU 30-9 *Char Hall* 24-10 Casa 17-11 218Gp 30-11 SOC 13-9-45

Spitfire Mk I converted to Mk V standard.

The following Mk Is were converted at Hucknall by Rolls-Royce between December 1940 and October 1941; K9788, N3053, R6761, 6770, 6776, 6809, 6833, 6882, 6889, 6890, 6897, 6904, 6908, 6917, 6919, 6923, 6960, 7142, 7143, 7158, 7161, 7195, X4062, 4106, 4257, 4272, 4279, 4342, 4476, R6889, 6917 and X4106 were converted to Mk Vs by No 1 CRU at the Morris Works, Cowley, Oxford with conversion sets supplied by Rolls-Royce. R6905 was converted by Heston Aircraft Ltd. Total 32.

The following Mk Is were converted by Air Service Training, Hamble, Westland Aircraft Ltd, Yeovil, General Aircraft Ltd, Feltham, Scottish Aviation Ltd, Prestwick and No 1 CRU Oxford; K9825, 9871, L1004, 1028, 1031, 1061, 1096, N3044, 3059, 3098, 3121, 3124, 3242, 3270, 3281, 3292, P9367, 9397, 9448, 9540, 9556, 9563, 9565, R6602, 6623, 6720, 6722, 6759, 6801, 6817, 6887, 6888, 6913, 6957, 6964, 6992, 7022, 7060, 7116, 7126, 7127, 7192, 7194, 7205, 7211, X4021, 4028, 4064, 4172, 4173, 4180, 4238, 4258, 4280, 4331, 4353,

4389, 4421, 4485, 4488, 4606, 4615, 4621, 4660, 4671, 4672, 4709, 4721, 4766, 4784, 4821, 4846, 4902, 4907, 4908, 4922, 4930, 4931, 4937, 4941, 4942, 4989, 4997, AR231. Total 84.

The same group of Companies also converted the following Spitfire Mk IIs to Mk V standard; P7287, 7297, 7299, 7308, 7316, 7324, 7447, 7498, 7505, 7532, 7619, 7629, 7672, 7686, 7692, 7789, 7846, 7849, 7906, 7909, 7920, 7964, 7965, 7986, 8036, 8038, 8086, 8095, 8099, 8167, 8195, 8236, 8237, 8239, 8246, 8259, 8262, 8324, 8339, 8436, 8438, 8445, 8517, 8545, 8549, 8563, 8589, 8595, 8645, 8706 and 8725. Total 51.

Rolls-Royce also converted a total of 18 PR Mk IIIs to Mk V standard, these Spitfire's having been, originally, Mk Is before the initial conversion: N3111, 3241, P9550, R6900, 6902, 6905, X4333-4335, 4383-4385, 4491-4494, 4497 and 4672.

One Mk IX LZ894, was also converted to Mk V standard. L1004 went on for conversion to the PR Mk XIII prototype. The majority of Rolls-Royce Mk Is were converted to Mk VB with cannon wings. One was loaned to the Admiralty as a hooked Spitfire in 1942. R4258 spent practically all its working life at Farnborough and Boscombe Down. P9563, R6720, 7022 and X4021 were recorded as being destroyed during the Battle of Britain.

Hooked Spitfire. P8537, 8707-8708, W3136, 3457, 3522, 3618, 3756, 3769, 3775, 3796, 3846, 3933, 3938, 3941, 3953, AA742, 866, 872, 904, 913, 964, 971, AB190, 213, 273, 845, 857, 899, 913, 929, 940, 967, AD113, 114, 127, 135, 187, 359, 360, 382, 426, 467, 535, 578, 584, AR297, 318, 384, 434, BL252, 253, 343, 366, 419, 443, 514, 576, 628, 756, 759, 818, 858, 895, BM255, 453, 576, 629, EN914, 927, EP170, 180 and 762.

To Royal Navy; R7207, 7231, 7301, 7305, 7335, W3113, 3229, 3328, 3370, 3437, 3602, 3646, 3681, 3939, AA730, 739, 758, 966, 974, AB201, 215, 867, AD125, 294, 316, 385, 386, 501, 514, 536, 583, AR337, 429, BL238, 383, 421, 483, 487-489, 512, 526, 537, 540, 562, 567, 582, 613, 776, 778, 787, 856, 891, BM289, 309, 371, 561, 586, 591, 649, EN766, 821, 866, 897, 898, 902, 949, 964-965, EP130, 174-175, 686 and 715.

For limited emergency service life only i.e. 5 minutes. The *Basta* modification was a Merlin engine boosted to +25lb/sq in. *Basta* Mk Vs were; P8700, 8748, W3432, 3518, 3760, AA918, 920, 931, AB208, 782, 790, 814, AD111, 263, 423, 475, AR320, 342, 399, BL350, 367, 377, 379, 445, 473, 550, 551, 591, 644, 755, 892, 957, 970, BM136, 246, 258, 262, 272, 324, 347, 351, 354, 356, 382, 425, 455, 488, 491, 516, 522, 537, 648, EN796, EP171, 178, 491, 507 and 759.

Danish Air Force; MA298.

French Air Force; P8718, 8748, 8782, R7220, 7336, W3229, 3322, 3328, 3426, 3619, 3632, 3718, 3899, 3931, 3939, 3957, AA718, 738, 751, 875, 881, 911, 965, 969, AB133, 139, 140, 199, 202, 339, 532, 939, AD132, 186, 227, 238, 248, 288, 324, 328, 366, 373, 376, 386, 451, 508, 514, AR328, 373, 376, 402, 405, 451, 524, 567, 600, 602, BL304, 329, 376, 426, 540, 551, 563, 567, 591, 600, 631, 634, 639, 665, 716, 720, 755, 787, 827, 887, 991, 993, BM117, 229, 257, 262-263, 272, 295, 322, 411-412, 461, 516-517, 561, 567-569, 571-572, 593, 648, BR114, 124, 140, 387, BS528, 539, 542, 544-545, 555, EE791, 856, EF538, 602, 606, 644, 697, 716, 736, 743, 745, EN637, 842, 849, 893, 919, 944, 964, EP179, 186, 204, 249, 286, 290, 433, 597, 644, 656, 658, 666, 720, 813, 903, 914, ER173, 249, 304, 315, 319, 466, 595, 606, 674, 712, 782-783, 809, 931, 998, ES129, 192, 229, 285, 294, JG778, 780, 841-842, 848, 870, 885, 896, 899, JK134, 143, 159, 178-179, 185, 251, 266-267, 326, 342, 380, 440, 449, 507, 509, 519, 524, 550, 649, 712, 783, 823, 825, 946, JL114, 121, 160, 185, 210, 221, 234-235, 244, 304, 316, 374, 387, LZ876, 927, 985, 987, MA397, 678, 679, 695, 703-704, 882, 889, 893, 898, 901, MH304, 309-310 and 594.

USAAF; R7256, 7271, 7297-7298, W3114, 3229, 3236, 3245, 3439, 3505, 3619, 3636, 3797, 3815, 3825, 3834, 3837, 3902, 3939, X4669, AA728, 752, 756, 764, 841, 877, 903, 964, 966, 969, 982, AB199, 257, 264, 789, 862, 898, 907, 918, 920, 929, 970, 974, AD116, 118, 247, 321, 353, 378, 385, 388, 417, 422, 511, AR278, 323, 335, 390, 393, 395, 404, 435, 451, 600, BL247, 267, 338, 365, 368, 376, 481, 488, 516, 530, 545, 564-565, 641, 663, 670, 673, 680, 688, 692, 729, 778, 888, 898, 920, 975, 993, BM181, 190, 193, 229, 293, 316, 318, 408, 411, 430, 510, 512, 523, 560, 567, 578, 581, 588, BP860, 975, BR130, 565, EE529, 664, 784, 794, 858, EF538, 540, 568, 592, 602, 614, 647, 693, 698-701, 703-704, 706-710, 716-717, 739-742, 744-747, 749, 751, 753, EN369, 772, 793, 799, 826, 838, 847, 853, 864, 900, 904, 945, EP110, 112, 167, 176, 183, 249, 285, 315, 332, 380, 401, 404, 520, 615, 698, 712, 728, 768-769, 774, 791, 795, 813, 824, 835, 843, 907, 912, 971, 978, ER120, 136, 161, 306, 314, 325, 477, 510, 557, 565, 569-570, 614, 647, 655, 705, 730, 780, 815, 880, 886, 926, 931, 941, 976, ES123, 138, 177, 186, 195, 244, 276, 284, 296-297, 362-363, JG729, 779-780, 800, 803, 914, 926, 949, JK102, 167, 183, 188, 218, 222, 226, 235, 252, 255, 261, 267, 278, 284, 309, 322, 360, 367, 369, 385, 390, 396, 402-403, 437, 464, 523-524, 526, 528, 530, 537, 542-543, 550-551, 602, 604, 607, 612, 648, 653, 661, 668, 673, 705, 716-717, 719, 724, 732, 734-736, 763, 765, 768, 772, 774-777, 780, 788, 791, 804, 806, 809-811, 813, 818, 827-828, 839, 861-862, 864, 870, 875, 941, 976, JL129, 131, 133, 182-183, 221, 244, 301, 318, 323, 333, 374, 381, 389, 391, LZ809, 863, 869, MA279, 335-336, 344, 695, 698, 702, 850, 861-862, 883, 886-887, 889-890, 893, MH564-565, 581, 593-594 and 605.

Norwegian Air Force; JL;361.

Transferred to Russia via Basrah P8755, 8783, W3818, AA908, AB781, 868, 896, 901, AD176, 190, 194, 225, 236, 301, 319, 418, 461, 473, 505, BL257, 289, 327, 352-353, 431, 441, 467, 485, 513, 618, 621, 625, 645, 685, 764, 771, 801, 808, 823, 974, BM154, 184-185, 189, 270, 359, 365, 371-372, 460, 462, 520, 595, EN785, 797, 859, 901, 911, 913, 923, 930, 967, 970, 977, EP145, 149-151, 165, 184-185, 210, 212-213, 230-232, 239, 241, 243, 246-248, 256, 282, 292, 307, 314, 333, 337, 351, 353, 356-359, 363, 366, 382-383, 386, 389, 391-392, 396, 400, 402-403, 408, 414-417, 431, 434, 446, 450, 454, 462, 466, 468-469, 486, 488, 490, 494-495, 497-498, 501-502, 505, 510, 512-514, 540, 565-566, 596, 598-599, 602, 623, 760-761, 764-765 and 788.

Portugal; P8791, W3128, 3180, 3248, 3430, 3431, 3518, 3519, 3641, 3648, 3803, 3902, 3951, AA728-729, 753, 756, 862, 881, 946, 967, 979, AB133, 191, 203, 487, 862, 873, 895, 988, AD191, 294, 383, 464, 499, 511, AR366-367, 404, 438, BL355, 368, 374, 437, 449, 496, 572, 636, 646, 664, 671, 684, 690, 821, 850, 890, 898, 970, 976, 978, 981, BM131, 176-177, 298, 300, 311, 313, 343, 364, 479, 514, 594, 624, EE620, EN775, 800, 903, 928, EP242, 244, 335, 350, 411, 452, 492, 538, 560, 605, 699, 766-767 and 785.

To Australia; AR510, 523, 526, 532, 558, 563-564, 619-621, 628, BR237-241, 468, 471, 480, 484-485, 490, 493-495, 499, 526-528, 530-533, 535-549, 568, 570, 572, 574, 584, 589, BS158, 162-166, 169, 171, 173-175, 178, 181-182, 184, 186-188, 190-191, 193, 197, 199, 201, 218-220, 222-226, 230-238, 291, 293, 295, 298, 300, 305, EE605-610, 636, 639, 669-678, 713, 718-719, 728-729, 731, 733-737, 748, 751, 807, 834-837, 844-845, 849-853, EF543-546, 556-560, 562-565, 587-591, ER735, 760, ES232, 238, 249, 259, 307, 367, JG728, 731, 740, 795-796, 807, 884, 891, 897, 912, 925, 954, 957, JK225, 229, 231, JL247, 314, 348, 360, 371, 378, 380, 382, 386, 392, 394, LZ834-835, 844-846, 848, 862, 865-868, 870, 873-874, 881, 883-884, 886, 926, 934, MA352-356, 366, 385, 387, 389, 394-395, 685, 689, 697, 699, 863, MH306, 566, 585-589, 591 and 642-646.

South African Air Force; BS344, 538, EE785, EN524, 528, EP688, ER178, ES202, JK387-388 and 405.

Netherlands Air Force; W3250 and BS274.

Royal Hellenic Air Force; AB321, 324, AR562, BS352, 558, EE798, 855, EF566, EN254, EP406, 562, 613, 694, 708, 772, 844, 953, ER128, 463, 717, 773, ES144, 176, 250, JG876, JK102, 127, 170, 226, 234, 256, 264, 275, 306, 324, 327, 376, 408, 528, 530, 550, 656, 782, 809, 885, JL139, 176, LZ828, 864, 928, 932, MA695, 704, 904, MH298 and 590.

Turkish Air Force; AB345, EE774, 865, EF539, 542, 651, 690, EN759, 633, 636, EP195, 258, ER277, 319, 476, 481, 590, 622, 643, 661, 666, 810, 938, 985, ES243, 251, 295, 300, 305, 348, 359, JG733, 744, 851, 938, 955, JK139, 164, 190, 236, 340, 362, 381, 393, 425, 526, 664-665, 676, 710-711, 806, 931, JL106, 210, 240, 359, 374, LZ829, 927, 979, MA700 and 703.

Indian Air Force; ER641, JG714, 865, JL303, 317, 319-322, 331, 334, LZ939, 971-973, 975, MA263, 284, 286, 288, 290, 292, 296-297, 341, 347-349, 361, 364-365, 367-368, 383-384, 386, 388, 390-393, 396, 650, 652, 654, 670, 672-677, 686, 688, 692, 694, 696, 851-852, 857, 899, 902-903, MH299-303, 305, 308, 311 and 637-641.

Czechoslovakian Air Force; MH750.

Royal Egyptian Air Force; BS339, 354, EN115, 253, 521, 925, EP652, ER207, 625, 640, 713, 973, 991, ES284, JK195, 371, 648, 722, 728, 739, 834, 968, 984, JL337, 366 and MH582.

Italian Air Force; EF649, EN583, 630, 632, 635, 843, EP758, 829, 886, ER655, 821, 893, ES257, JK130, 165, 392, 720, 784 and JL251.

Belgium Air Force; EN568.

Converted to PR IV Type D, R7029-7033, 7035-7036, 7038, 7040, 7042-7043 and 7055-7056.

Converted to PR V R7039 and 7034.

Converted to PR VII Type G R7308 and 7335.

Converted to F VII AB450 and 499.

Converted to F IX at Rolls-Royce Hucknall; AB196-197, 501, 505, 507-508, 511, 522, 525, BR138-143, 369-371, 621-640, BS271-290, 335-354, 530-559, EN112-121, 239-258, 351-370, 515-534, 551-559, 561-583, 628-637, EP499, JK429, 463, 620, 659, 668, 762, 795, 840, 860, 880, 949, 979, JL106-107, 109-111, 132, 159, 163, 165, 172, 223, 234, 239, 347, 349, 351, 353-356, 359, 361, 364, 366, 369-370, 372-373, 385, 395, MA298, 329, 357, 645-646, 648, 651, 655, 657, MH750 and 755.

Converted by Vickers to F IX; EN843, ES185 and JG936.

Converted to PR XIII P8784, W3112, 3135, 3831, AA739, AD354, 389, 501, 556, AR319, BL378, 446, 526, BM350, 447, 591, EN902 and EP229.

Converted to Seafire IIC; AD371.

Lost at sea on SS *Zarian* 18-1-43; ER930, 943, 948, 961, 965, 969, 971, 977, ES109, 113, 119, 132, 151-153, 168-169, 171, 174, 205, 208, 210, 213, 234 and 247.

Lost at sea on SS *Molaja* 3-10-42; AR554, EP781, 786, 882, 956, 984, ER114-115, 159, 179, 184, 189, 216, 255, 258, 261, 267-269, 275-276, 311, 336-337, 339, 469, 472, 479-480 and 483-484.

Lost at sea on SS *Silver Beech* 14-3-43; EE483, 848, JK174, 176, 181, 184, 257-258, 273 and 331.

Spitfire Mk V.

Maintenance and instructional airframes, either M—— or ——M.

P8700(5517), R7224(4406), W3122(3457), W3127(5537), W3228(5939), W3229(5572), W3250(5938), W3318(3405), W3322(5584), W3328(5571), W3423(5383), W3445(5393), W3530(4871), W3656(5842), W3707(5931), W3764(3386), W3795(3655), W3798(4263), AA751(5583), AA927(3779), AA839(5348), AA848(5387), AA929(5382), AA969(5596), AB139(5589), AB140(5590), AB192(4462), AB193(5443), AB202(5597), AB265(5541), AB278(4467), AB488(4237), AB499(4243), AB510(3649), AB815(2697), AB871(4353), AB904(5349), AB920(2656), AB971(5719), AD248(5591), AD288(5599), AD299(5717), AD376(2799), AD425(5544), AD453(4122), AD508(5594), AD573(5855), AR340(4430), AR373(5588), AR399(5720), AR406(5394), AR436(5334), AR451(5592), AR491(5268), AR493(4697), AR519(5523), AR570(5357), AR604(5399), AR605(4244), AR616(5378), AR614(5378).

BL234(3337), BL291(5389), BL365(5381), BL380(4002), BL450(5390), BL494(4258), BL523(4368), BL589(5525), BL614(4354), BL665(5595), BL712(5385), BL719(5386), BL755(5570), BL775(4362), BL892(5392), BL979(5376).

BM155(5347), BM158(5375), BM192(5542), BM201(5395), BM233(5337), BM246(5721), BM256(5384), BM322(5601), BM354(5335), BM409(5539), BM411(5600), BM461(5593), BM525(3689), BM567(5520), BM572(5350), BM588(5524), BM597(5718), BM637(3688).

BP852(4178), BP983(4382).

BR623(6018), BR632(6037).

BS280(6021), BS286(6020), BS345(5951), BS347(6036), BS533(6205).

EE600(4187), EE644(5521).

EF678(4203), EF731(5803).

EN363(6038), EN526(5802), EN828(5391), EN833(3414), EN862(5397), EN913(5380), EN951(5516), EN964(5585).

EP120(5377), EP169(5396), EP250(5939), EP380(5931), EP570(5538), EP604(5053), EP770(5400).

JK163(4391), JK547(4708).

JL112(4390), JL373(4267).

LZ936(4212).

MA298(6462), MA646(6070), MA855(5379).

27 June 1941 and a VB returns after a sweep over France.

AERIAL SPIES

Development of the photo-reconnaissance Spitfire began as a somewhat haphazard affair with the Air Ministry firm in its conviction that a two-seat aircraft was required because of (1) the bulky camera equipment and (2) a two-man crew was essential, one to pilot the aircraft, the second to operate the cameras and navigate. In the period leading up to World War Two, two men, Sidney Cotton (an Australian by birth) and Wing Commander F. W. Winterbottham, a professional airman and head of Air Intelligence Branch (A.I 1(C)), the air component of MI6, were largely responsible for the PR activities of the RAF, and in particular the use of the Spitfire for the role. Cotton had promoted the cause of high speed PR sorties and thought that the new Spitfire would be an ideal aeroplane, but the Air Ministry differed in many instances to Cotton's views and to Cotton appeared unbending in their attitude.

Cotton was almost a free agent and could not understand the Air Ministry's cautious approach to the problem. He completely ignored the fact that they had to operate within the restraints of service etiquette and a chain of command, whereas he was used to acting on his own initiative.

In September 1938 Winterbottham was in close contact with the French 2nd Bureau and talks were in progress on the possibility of photographing sensitive areas of Germany, in particular the defences along the Rhine. It was finally agreed that the French, and the RAF, would purchase two Lockheed twin engined Model 12As and convert them for this purpose through the good offices of British Airways, both aircraft being delivered the following November. It was not possible for the French and British air forces to operate the Lockheeds over Germany; what was needed was a 'free agent'. As a result of this requirement Winterbottham met Cotton in Paris during November and it was agreed that Cotton would fly the converted aircraft. By February 1939 the Lockheeds were converted and painted paint pale green overall, one stationed at Heston, and to maintain secrecy for the project a private company known as the Aeronautical Research and Sales Corporation was established.

The first official sortie was made on the morning of 10 March 1939 when Mannheim was photographed. Taking off from Heston at 11 o'clock Cotton and his co-pilot had timed the flight to coincide with the arrival over the town with that of the morning air service from Strasbourg. In the event of interception by German aircraft the camera and other installations were to be jettisoned through a hole cut into the Lockheed's cabin floor. Three cameras were fitted and the sorties were usually at a height of 20,000ft, and eventually the whole of the Ruhr, numerous German aerodromes and other military installations were photographed. Cotton also installed a Leica camera in each wing leading edge, hiding them with sliding panels. He planned to use them for low level photography.

As a result of his activities Cotton was invited by the Air Ministry to take over command of an experimental unit, based at Heston, Middlesex, and called the Heston Flight, for the development of high speed photographic-reconnaissance as the RAF's official unit was not in a position to deliver photographs of an acceptable quality. He was given the rank of Squadron Leader (acting Wing Commander) and on 22 March was joined at Heston by Squadron leader A. Earle (photographic officer); Flight Lieutenant R. H. Niven (a Canadian, well known to Cotton and then on a short service RAF commission) and Flying Officer M. V. Longbottom for flying duties; Flying Officer J. H. Blyth (liaison); Pilot Officer H. G. Belcher (equipment), plus 18 other ranks. The new unit occupied the hangar and offices belonging to Airwork Ltd., and had the Aero Club and part of a local hotel as Officer's Mess and quarters. The unit came under direct command of Fighter Command for administration. From 26 July to the end of August a number of trips were made to Berlin and on one notable occasion Cotton, Longbottom and Niven made a flight along the coast of Eire on 4 October, landing at West Freugh, only to be detained as spies by Group Captain Smith-Piggott. They were released after two hours after a telephone call to Heston.

On 2 September, the day before England declared war on Germany, the new unit's Lockheed flew a sortie over the river Elbe at 4.10 in the afternoon. The Admiralty wanted details of the German fleet and the prints were ready for examination by the Director of Naval intelligence the same evening. The Air Ministry had not been informed of the flight until after the event and was displeased with Cotton's actions. The following October Winterbottham proposed to Air Vice Marshall Peck that the new unit be authorised as a Photographic Unit for the RAF and be used mainly for strategic missions. For this he suggested that three Blenheims and three Spitfires be provided. Peck, surprisingly, suggested that perhaps prototype aircraft might be more suitable as they could be the most advanced aircraft available. However, in the event the Blenheims were delivered.

X4786, an ex- F Mk I, was converted to PR Mk VII Type G standards with the Merlin 45 engine. It was armed with Browning guns and carried two F 24 vertical cameras in the rear fuselage. Radio was omitted.

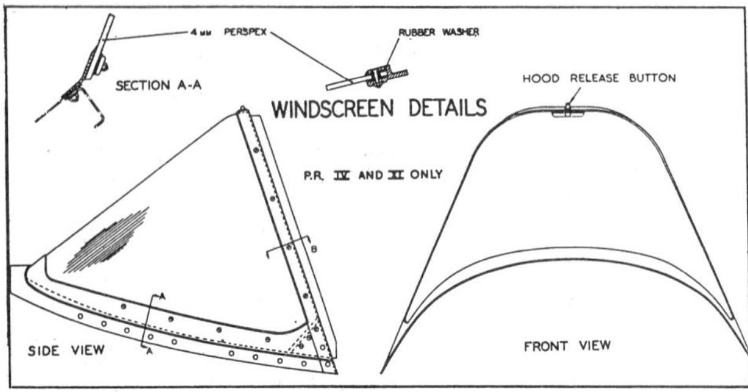

Windscreen details of the early PR aircraft. This windscreen was later to be specified for the PR Mk IV and XI only. The second drawing reveals details of the blister hoods for the IV and VII.

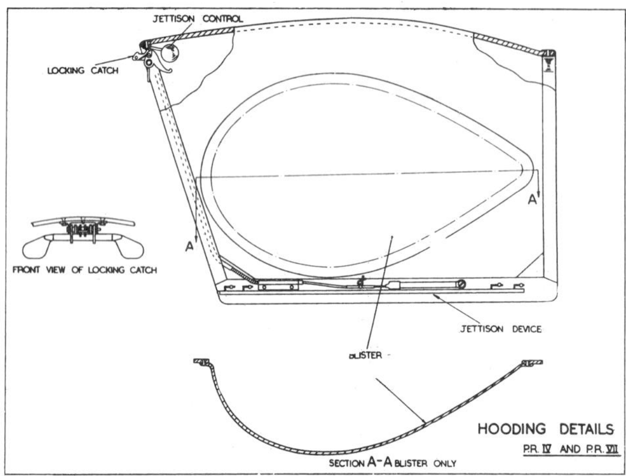

Cotton did not want Blenheims and said his thoughts were that a fighter with a clean airframe and superfluous weight removed would prove to be the ideal machine. The Air Ministry refused Cotton's request and the unit was instructed to modify the Blenheim by rubbing down the airframe and applying a smooth finish; fitting a spinner to the propellers which would help cool the engines without opening the cooling gills (the latter reduced maximum speed by as much as 30mph when extended); eliminating the front undercarriage fairing and fitting doors parallel with the underside of the engine nacelle. These modifications were to add 25mph to the overall speed.

After a lot of inter-departmental correspondence Cotton's request finally came to the attention of Air Marshal Dowding, and following upon a meeting between the two, at which Cotton again asked for Spitfires, N3069 and 3071 (Mk Is) were delivered to the Photographic Development Unit (PDU) at Heston early on the morning of 13 October. Cotton went to work immediately and they were stripped of guns, wireless and other equipment he thought superfluous. Gun ports were covered with metal plates and all plate and other joints filled in with plaster of paris. The normal RAF day fighter camouflage paint was removed and the Spitfires were repainted in the pale green finish cotton had named 'Camotint' and then polished to a hard gloss. This treatment increased the maximum speed to 390mph. Another camouflage scheme tested was a normal newsprint paper pasted on to the airframe. But it was too coarse and peeled off at the joints.

Both aircraft were then delivered to RAE, Farnborough, on 20 October for camera installation and Harold Stringer, acknowledged as an expert in his field, supervised the work. He had previously been experimenting with camera installations in damaged, ex-service Spitfire fuselages, including among many that of the prototype K5054. The Heston Spitfires were fitted with a single F24-5in camera in the position where the inner guns and ammunition boxes were originally fitted in each wing. The two cameras functioned simultaneously with slight overlap for stereoscopic effect, and trials commenced. Cotton had asked that a 30 gallon fuel tank be fitted under the pilot's seat, plus an oblique camera to be installed in the fuselage behind the cockpit, but it was thought it would upset the aircraft's CoG and the idea dropped. N3071 was delivered to No. 212(PR) Squadron and made the first Spitfire PR flight over Aachen, Germany, on 18 November 1939, piloted by Fly/Off. M. Longbottom. N3069 was damaged in a flying accident in August 1940 and struck off charge.

Although fuel capacity had not been increased Supermarine had been informed of the new requirement and on 16 October 1939 a copy of a report concerning modification for a revised Mk I Spitfire for PR duties landed on Cotton's desk. It read: (1) the aircraft is a Spitfire I fitted with Merlin III engine and Rotol airscrew. The leading edge is specially modified for use as a petrol tank and additional oil tankage is fitted. (2) All armament is omitted, but full armour protection (65lb) is provided. Wireless (55lb) has been retained—if omitted the weight is reduced by 30lb and tail ballast is required to compensate. (3) The total weight is made up as follows: Tare 4,819, service load 268, petrol (230 gal @ 7.5lb/gal) 1,722, oil (18½gal @ 9lb/gal) 166. Total 6,975lb. (4) The following are the estimated characteristics at the above loading. Take off run 320yds, time to 15,000ft 7mins, 25,000ft 16mins, service ceiling 29,000ft. Ranges, allowing for 20gal. for taxying, take off and residue after flight, and also allowing for amount used in climbing to the appropriate altitude; at 15,000ft 1,715 miles @ 250mph, 1,380 miles @ 300mph; at 20,000ft, 1,830 miles @ 250mph, 1,500 miles @ 300mph; at 25,000ft, 1,885 miles @ 250mph, 1,615 miles @ 300mph.

At a meeting at the Air Ministry shortly after Cotton had received his Spitfires the Air Staff noted: "That a special flight of high speed aircraft had been formed; it was equipped with cleaned up Spitfires, and it will expand to three flights based in France with a small operational flight in the UK. The Spitfire, cleaned up and with a special engine, is specially camouflaged white undersides with blue upper to operate at heights of 30,000ft plus. Range is being increased to 1,000 miles and external tanks will be fitted. The aircraft are operating from Rheims and are normally opposed by AA fire or enemy aircraft. On two occasions Bf109s have lain in wait at 30,000ft and tried to shoot the Spitfire down, but on both occasions the Spitfire shook the Bf off. The difference in speed seemed to be about 40mph".

The Heston flight was renamed No.2 Camouflage Unit* on 3 October and a detachment flight known as Special Survey moved to Seclin, near Lille, France, on 5 November and it was

R7143 was an ex-Mk I converted to PR Mk VII standards. As a Type G it carried the normal 'A' wing armament and is seen here with an F 24 oblique camera mounted behind the cockpit. It was photographed at Farnborough after the camera installation by Heston Aircraft, was painted pink overall and carried the legend Spitfire VII under the cockpit.

* *The Heston Flight operated in France as No. 212 Squadron as part of No. 11 Group, Fighter Command. It was controlled by the Directorate of Intelligence (Air Ministry).*

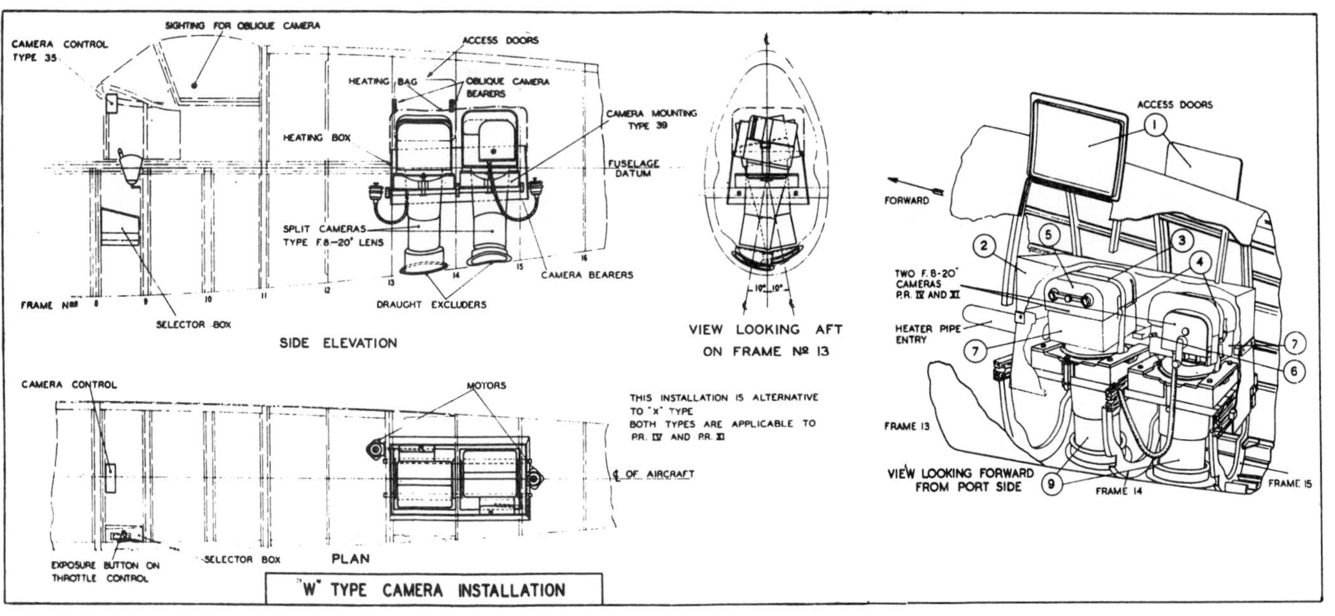

"W" TYPE CAMERA INSTALLATION

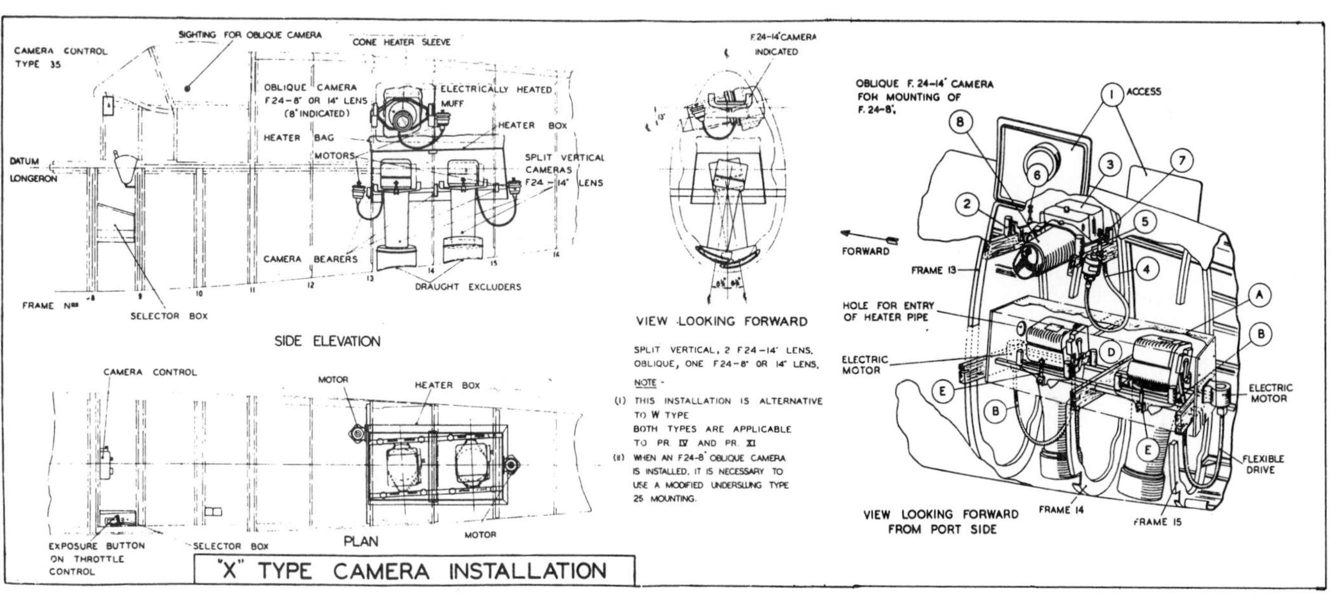

"X" TYPE CAMERA INSTALLATION

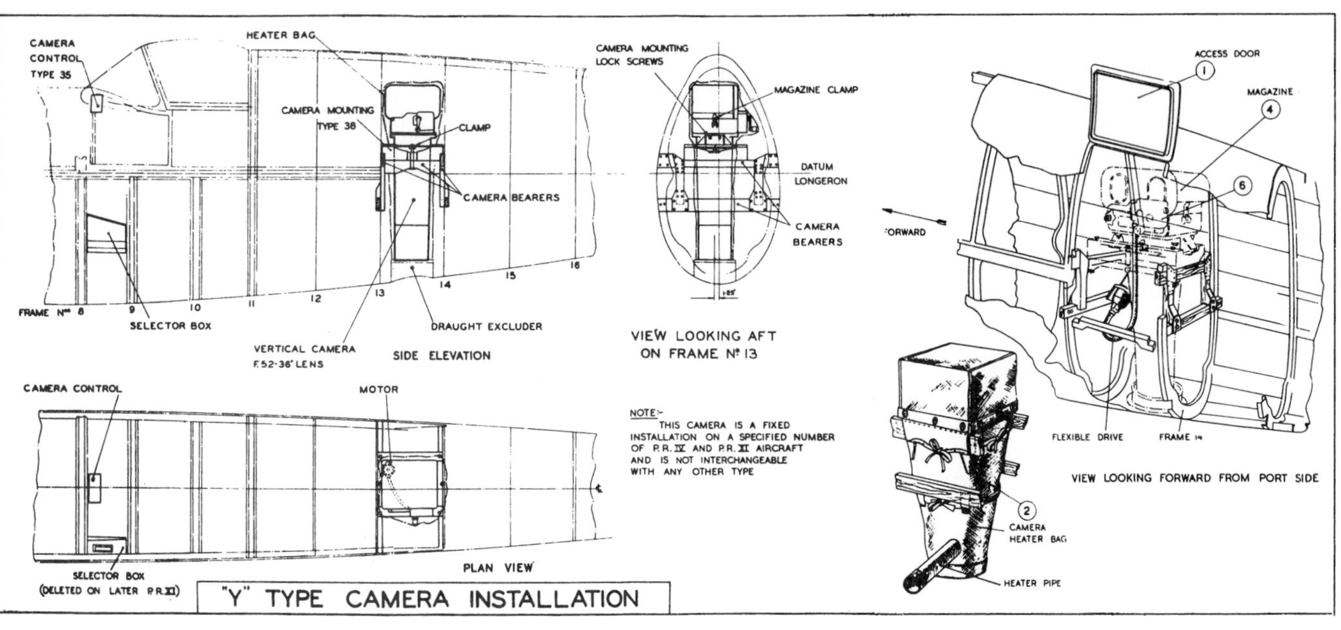

"Y" TYPE CAMERA INSTALLATION

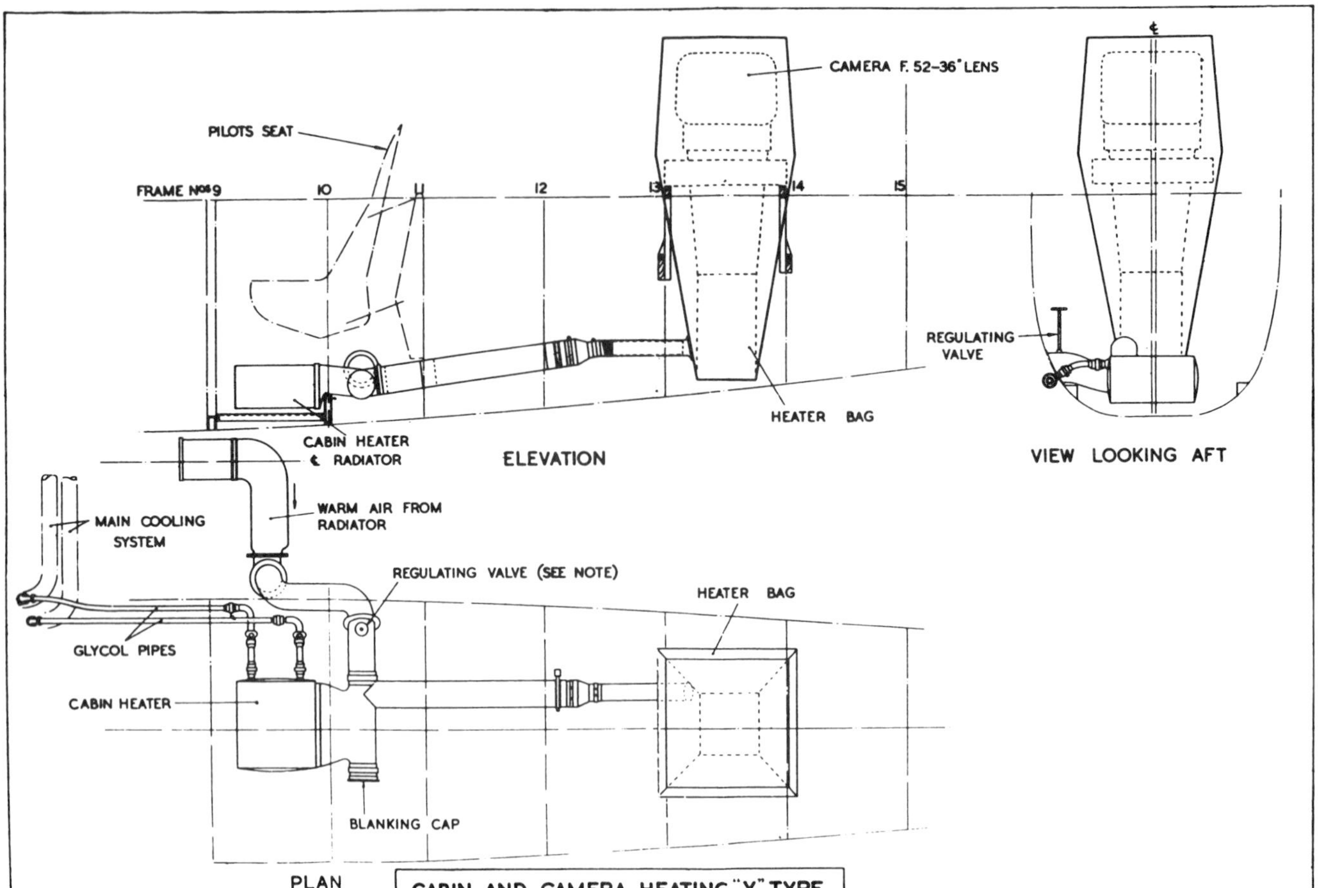

CABIN AND CAMERA HEATING, "Y" TYPE.

from there that the sorties mentioned above were launched. The Flight was transferred back to Heston on 1 January 1940. On 29 January RAE Farnborough was instructed by the Air Ministry to give six new Spitfires priority for conversion, the first two—N3116 and 3117—arriving at Heston on 4 February and the remaining four—P9307 to 9310—on the 11th. One, P9308, was sent direct to Supermarine for special modification at a cost of £1,700, while the remainder ended up at Farnborough for additional modifications to Type C. Modifications to P9308 were similar to those specified in the Supermarine report sent to Cotton on 16 October 1939 and the aircraft was designated the Type 353. Cameras were F24s with 8in lenses. This particular Spitfire went missing on operations on 19 May 1940 with P/O Coleman at the controls. A section of three PR Spitfires was transferred to Meaux, France, in April and during a short stay photographed every aerodrome in Belgium. It was the Heston Spitfires which sighted and photographed the German Panzer formations assembling in the Ardennes on May just before the break out into France.

It is interesting to note that Cotton approached the Belgian authorities the previous December to ask for permission to take the photographs, but his request was denied for the King refused on the grounds that it might provoke the Germans. Cotton also met his German agent in Brussels at the same time and obtained detailed information about the new German Acoustic and Magnetic mines, which he promptly turned over to British Intelligence on arrival back in England.

F24 vertical and oblique camera mountings in a PR Mk IV.

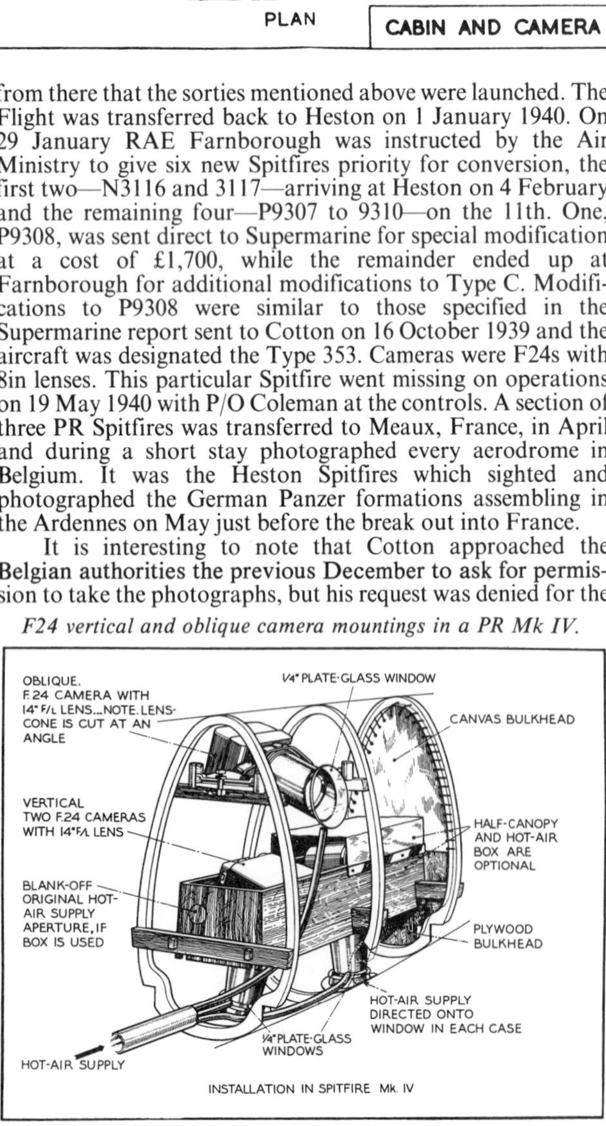

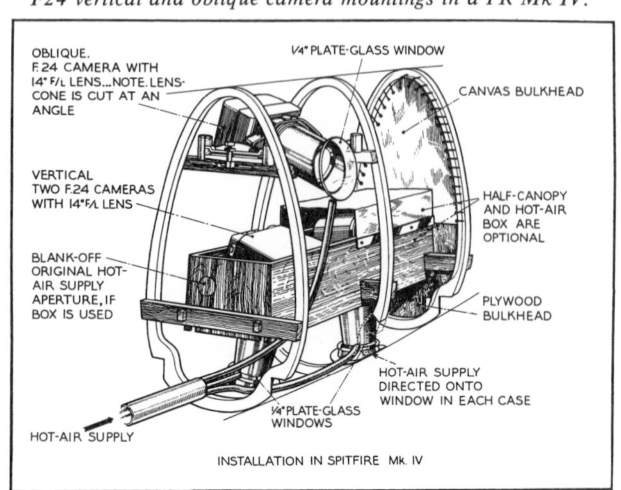

The question of delivery of the coverted Spitfires for PR clashed with the demands for fighter variants. Of the batch of 40 on order 15 had been delivered to Heston for camera installation during the critical period of the Battle of Britain. It was noted in a minute of a meeting held to discuss the situation that six converted aircraft had been destroyed in the German air raid on Woolston of September, and that three sets of PRU wings had been removed from their assembly jigs to make way for the F Mk IB cannon Spitfire wings, then urgently required. The minute stated that the PRU wings must be immediately returned to the assembly jigs and that delivery of three sets of wings must be completed every week. Supermarine were authorised to replace the destroyed Spitfires and an additional 12 were ordered, with the final aircraft having a Merlin XX engine installed for test purposes.

No. 2 Camouflage Unit had been expanded into the Photographic Development Unit in January 1940 with an establishment of 185 officers and men and was operating from either Heston or with No. 212 Squadron. The latter was formed in France as an offshoot of PDU and operated three Flights. By the spring of 1940 practically the whole of the Ruhr had been photographed and all the German Navy heavy ships and cruisers located for the Royal Navy. A total of 557 sorties was flown in the first three months and 12 aircraft (Spitfires) lost. Following the Dunkirk evacuation the unit was disbanded and aircraft and personnel re-absorbed by the PDU at Heston, and at the same time operational control was turned over to Coastal Command. The following month, July, it was renamed the Photographic Reconnaissance Unit (PRU).

In an exchange of letters between Air Marshal Saundby (Bomber Command) and Sholto-Douglas (Fighter Command) in July, the former wrote: "With reference to paras 2 and 3 of Minute 3 regarding increase in the establishment and organisation of the PDU to meet Bomber Command requirements, the work of converting the 30 additional Spitfires for the PDU is proceeding on high priority at RAE and the Heston Aircraft Company. The Ministry of Aircraft Production expects to have the first six aircraft ready within the next three

The PR Mk VI Type F, the early long-range reconnaissance Spitfire, carried some of its fuel in small underwing blisters. Seen here this aircraft is fitted with two F24 vertical and one F24 oblique cameras, the latter can be seen in the cockpit blister. Note the enlarged ventral oil tank.

weeks, and to complete them all in approximately six months.

"As regards fitting of Merlin XX engines, it was originally intended that the last ten of these 30 aircraft should be equipped with this engine, but the accelerated conversion programme has made this quite impracticable. The prototype Merlin XX installation has not been cleared technically and further, the conversion is an extensive one involving, amongst other things, a new engine mounting. It is estimated that Merlin XX Spitfires modified for PDU duties could be made available in 4 to 5 months, and unless, therefore, some of the 30 aircraft now being modified are held back to enable Merlin XX engines to be fitted, they will be delivered with Merlin III engines".

Sholto-Douglas made the briefest of replies: "Thank you. Do *not* hold up any of the 30 Spitfires for the Merlin XX. PS. I have just added another Flight of six Spitfires to the PRU. Will 30 be enough?". Saundby: "I imagine that the addition of a Flight of six Spitfires to the PRU will involve an increase of the number of aircraft required. We have, at the moment, asked for 30. Will you please advise me if we should ask for more to be modified and, if so, how many?". Sholto-Douglas: "In view of the increase of six Spitfires in the establishment of the PDU, I suggest that at least 10 more aircraft will be required and recommend that your order should be increased from 30 to 40. If the Merlin XX is released in time, I suggest that this mark should be fitted to the extra ten."

The next PRU to be formed was No. 3 at RAF Oakington on 16 November 1940 with an initial establishment of six Spitfires and two Wellingtons. The first Spitfire received was X4385 on 23rd of the same month and it was a Type C fitted with a 20in F8 camera in the fuselage and two, split 8in F24s in

the starboard wing. Additional fuel tanks of 30 gallons each were provided, one in the port wing and one immediately behind the pilot. A second Spitfire, X4386, was taken on charge the next day, and on the 29th Squadron Leader Ogilvie made the unit's first sortie by flying to Cologne. X4383 arrived on 17 December and was registered as a Type C with a split 8in F24 in the starboard wing and an F8 camera with 75cm Zeiss Likon telephoto lens in the fuselage. This camera was taken from a German reconnaissance aircraft shot down over England in August 1940. X4386 flew to Bremen on 4 January 1941 and both it, and the pilot, Flt/Lt. H. C. Marshall were posted missing. Marshall was later to be a POW.

No. 2 PRU was formed on 1 June 1941 at Heliopolis, Egypt, with two Hurricanes, a Lockheed Model 12A, and received its first three Spitfires (PR Mk IVs)—AB312, AB421 and BP904 a year later. They were designated the F Mk VD. The first operation was flown by Flt/Lt Pearce to Patras, Greece. The Spitfire (BP882) had many local modifications such as extended wing tips, engine changes, special finish and camouflage. After a long period of exposure in the sun a wing fuel tank burst due to expansion, resulting in the local development of vent pipes on the wing upper surface.

The question arose of putting the PRU organisation under

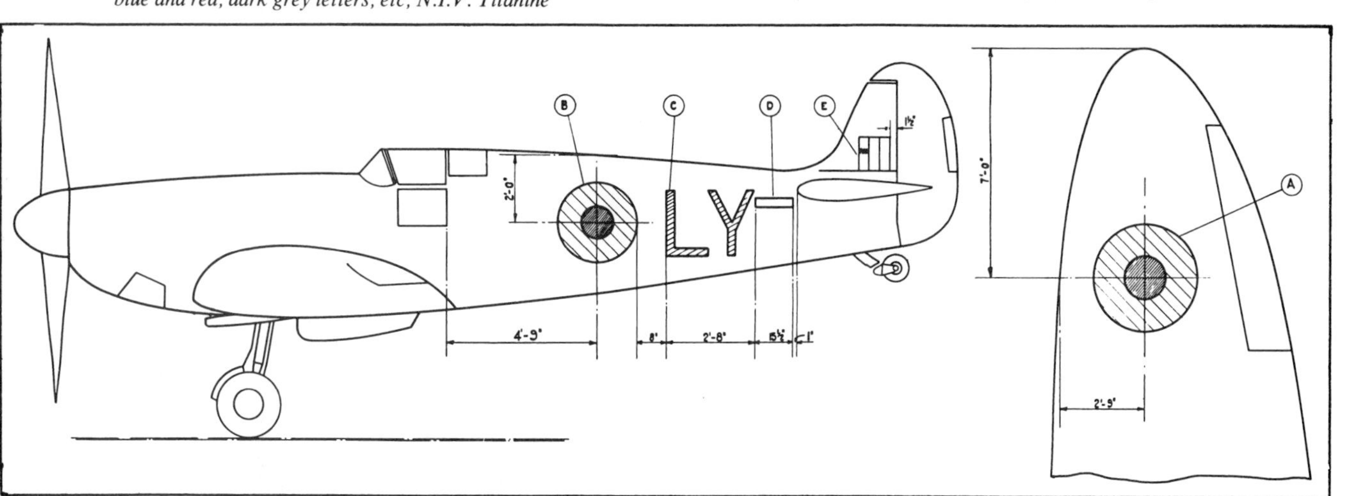

National markings as applied to PR Spitfires after standard colour of PR Blue was adopted. Legend- A, *outer blue 40in dia; inner red 16in.* B, *outer blue 30in; inner red 12.* C, *2ft high, 1ft 4in wide, stroke 3in wide, colour grey.* D, *serial No. 4in high, digits 2½in wide, stroke ½in wide.* E, *fin flash 1ft wide, strokes red, white, blue 4in wide. Port and starboard fuselage markings similar. Wing roundels upper surface only. Aircraft sprayed with Titanine special cellulose lacquer PRU blue. Roundels Night blue and red, dark grey letters, etc, N.I.V. Titanine*

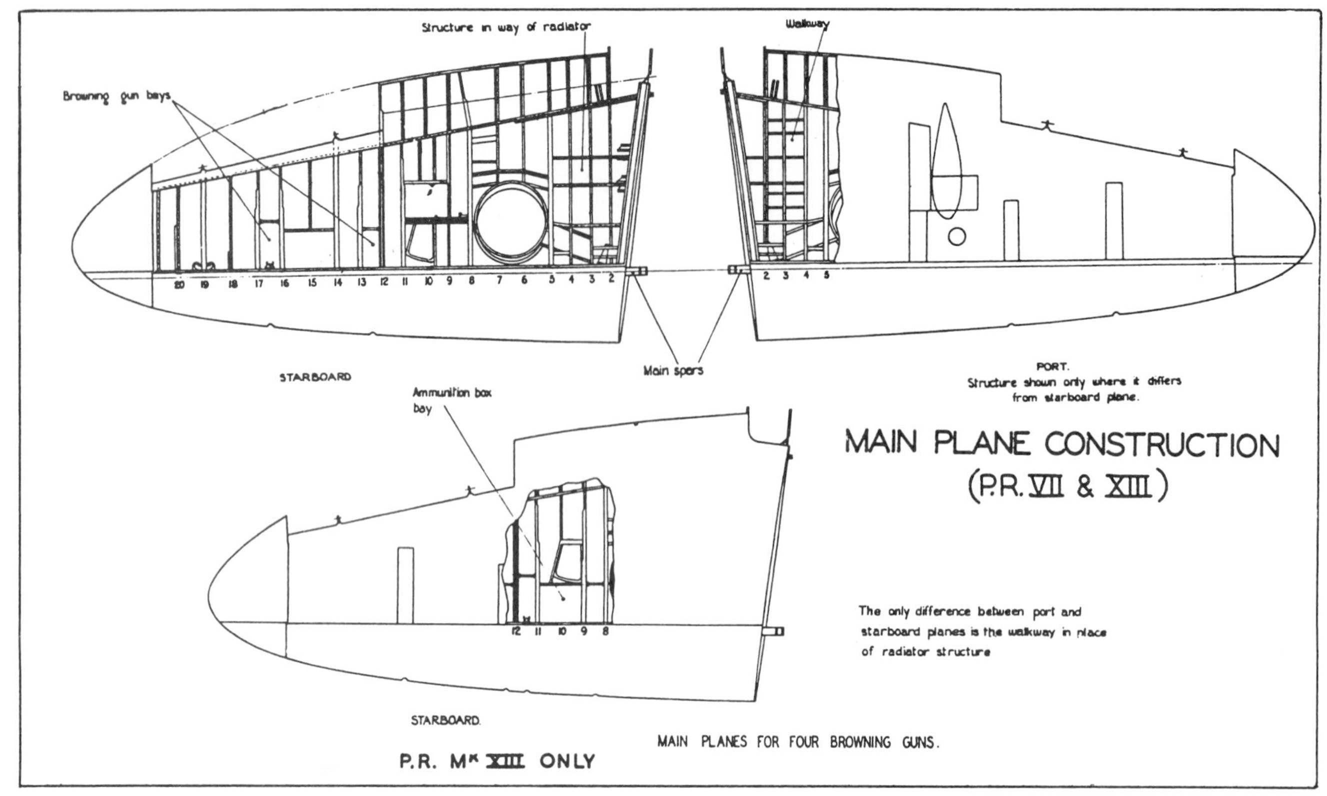

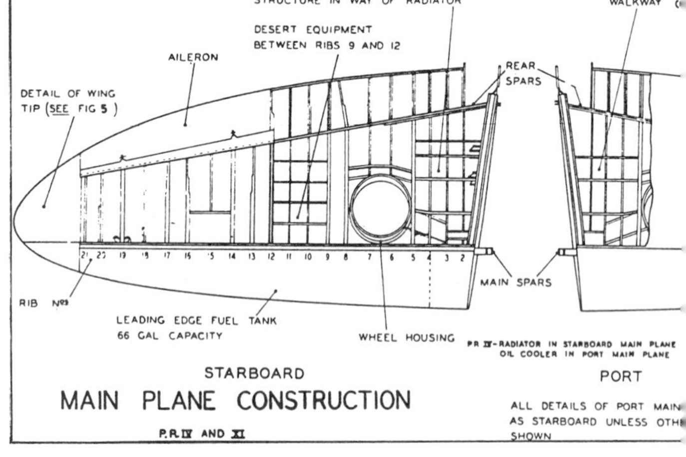

the direct control of Bomber Command, but Cotton wanted it to remain an independent unit until he was satisfied with its performance. Cotton's attitude was beginning to disturb the Air Staff for he had little patience with going through channels and said: "The Air Ministry is not geared to deliver goods over the counter". Although this might have been true the Air Ministry replied that a considerable amount of delay in supplying PDU's requirements were mainly due to Cotton's personality which aroused hostility. Air Marshal Portal, CinC, Bomber Command, suggested three separate PRUs for Bomber (No. 3), Coastal (No. 1) and General HQ Home Forces, but Admiral Dudley-Pound rejected this for he wanted control of his own PRU aircraft. Cotton did little to cool the situation for on several occasions Dudley-Pound approached him direct for special assignments, and even made provision for direct contact in the future for emergency situations. The last straw was when Cotton, rather than wait for Air Ministry approval, had entered into a personal commitment for photographic equipment costing £10,000.

It was time for a firm hand for the Air Ministry could not tolerate a serving officer to act on his own initiative, and the instructions of a sister service, without their acknowledgement of the fact. On 4 May 1941 the decision was taken to centralise all PRU activities. Cotton, although not demoted, had control of the unit taken out of his hands and a new CinC was appointed. Headquarters was located at Benson (a Bomber Command station) with detachments at Wick and St. Eval and an establishment of 32 Long Range Spitfires and eight Blenheims formed a nucleus around which the PRU was built. It was to provide a common service for the Army, Navy and Air Force, with operational control resting with the Air Ministry. Cotton could not beat the system, but without his flair and

R7020 was one of the first Mk Is converted to PR standards (PR Mk III Type C) and as such was unarmed. Note the Heston camera (F52) installation in the radio bay; the blister hood and the clear windscreen. It, too, was painted pink overall and is seen at Farnborough for use as a trials aircraft. No radio fitted.

foresight the successful development of the PRU would have taken much longer than it did.

A number of Spitfires did eventually have the Merlin XX installed, but those built on the production lines were normally fitted with the Merlin 45 or 46. There was a whole plethora of Type numbers allocated to the early converted and production aircraft, and confusion reigned until the Air Ministry issued role prefixes came into general use. Before this event seven of the early variants were known as the Types A to G, the letters generally defining camera installation, engine, armament and fuel arrangements, as specified in a letter from MAP to Supermarine dated 13 February 1942.

Spitfire Type A Merlin III. Retrospectively allocated to the first camera installations in the wings of N3071 and 3069 by RAE Farnborough. These were to become PR Mk IIIs. Normal Spitfire fuel load; one F24 camera in each wing; one 'spotting' camera behind pilot.

Type B (SR) (Short range) (PR IB) Merlin III. Allotted to the first two aircraft after addition of a 29 gallon petrol tank under the pilot's seat. Also to PR Mk III. Camera as Type A with 8in focal length lens and installed under wing blisters.

Type C (LR) (Long range) (PR IC). The original two Spitfires converted once again to accept a rear fuselage mounted camera/s (one Eagle or IX), plus the 2 × F24s 8in lens in starboard wing under blister. Extra fuel tanks were added: 30 gallons in a fixed blister under the port wing and 30 below the pilot's seat. These three designations applied to Spitfires converted to the modifications tested on the two original aircraft. The additional 40 Spitfires mentioned by Saundby and Sholto-Douglas in July 1940 carried the last designation mentioned. It is interesting to note that such was the urgency for delivery that two aircraft had Merlin II engines and one a Merlin XII. Eventually redesignated PR Mk III. The conversions to PR standards was carried out equally by Heston Aircraft and RAE Farnborough and many alternative colour schemes were tested, such as white, pink, blue and green. A blue grey, known as PR blue with 4 inch serial numbers was eventually adopted as standard. A large number were eventually converted to Type F standards.

Type D (Special L R) (or Super Long range). A number of important modifications were made to these aircraft including installation of two F8 20in and F24 14in focal length cameras. Early aircraft had the Eagle IV in the rear fuselage. Cameras were normally mounted in the rear fuselage and inclined so that two, overlapping photographs could be taken simultaneously. The 'D' wing with leading edge fuel tanks of $66\frac{1}{2}$ gallons in each was standard and total fuel load, including 30 gallons behind the pilot, amounted to 218 gallons. Hot air camera heaters were included and additional oil was carried in a blister tank under the port wing. Redesignated PR Mk III. Air Marshal Portal of Bomber Command wanted to return his Type D, one per week, to Rolls-Royce from 7 March 1941, for installation of the Merlin 45. He said: "I will have to risk the Germans getting hold of a Merlin 45 in order to obtain results". A bold statement when the Merlin 45 was a top priority engine for the forthcoming Mk V Spitfire. Type D production aircraft were eventually fitted with the Merlin 45 or 46 and three

F24 camera mounting in first conversion of PR Spitfire, October 1939.

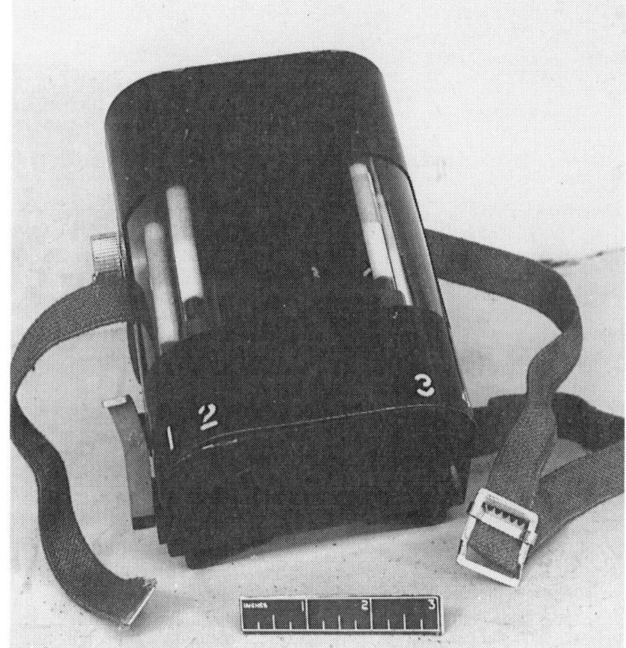

Silica gell pack as installed in early PR aircraft.

standard camera arrangements known as the W, X and Y were specified. Details of these are included in the Leading Particulars at the end of this chapter. Other equipment included a TR1133 R/T set, a K-Type dinghy and drinking water. A small batch of this type went to the Middle East and were fitted with the Aboukir filter. Redesignated PR Mk IV and V. A one off variant of this type was produced for low-altitude work for oblique closeups. It had an F24 camera installed under each wing in a bulged fairing with the lenses at right angles to the line of flight and pointing slightly below the horizontal.

Type F (LR). Conversions by Heston Aircraft Ltd, in

BR419, PR IV, lost in flying accident, January 1944.

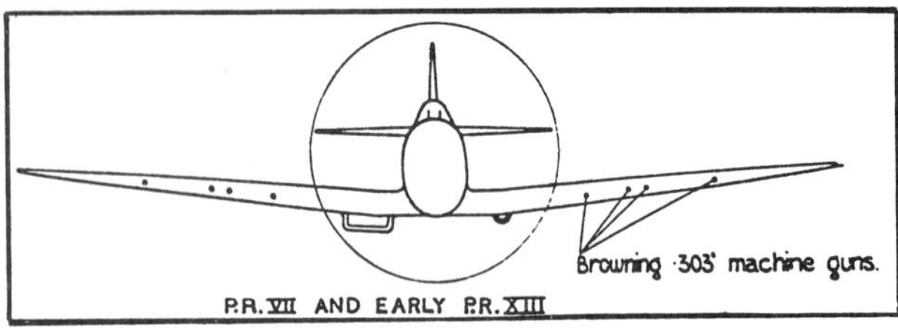

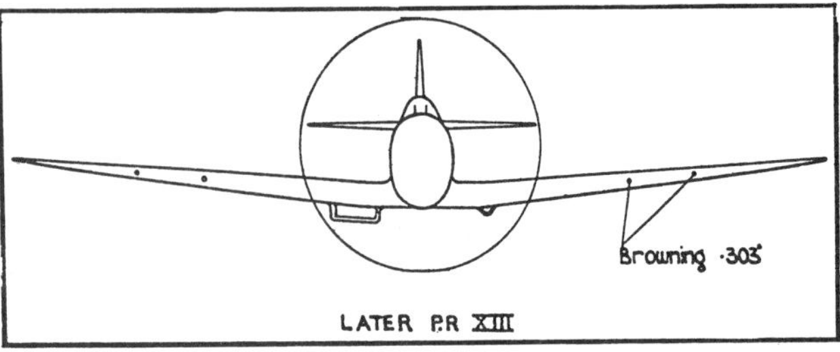

1941/42 with camera installation of one vertical F8 20in, or two F8 20in, or two F24 20in vertical and one F24 14in oblique. Oxygen economisers, the latter feeding only when the pilot took in oxygen; when he breathed out a valve closed cutting off supply. Tear drop blisters in cockpit hood sides*; a 20 gallon fuel tank under the pilot's seat and 30 gallon blister tanks under the wings; deeper nose cowling due to larger oil tank. Redesignated PR Mk VI.

Type G. The first armed PR Spitfire with standard 'A' wing (8 × .303in m/gs). All conversions by Heston Aircraft and fitted with two independently operated vertical (F24 5in forward; F24 14in rear) in rear fuselage, mounted port and starboard. If needed a third F24 could be mounted in the rear fuselage for downward views from the port hatch door. Bullet proof windscreen; cockpit hood teardrops; standard reflector sight; armour plate. Redesignated PR Mk VII. A number of these conversions (ie PR Mk XIII) were later fitted with the Merlin 32 engine. All subsequent PRs with this arrangement became the PR Mk XIIIs. Also, a small batch of Mk I Spitfires were due to be fitted with the Merlin 32 and be designated the PR Mk VIII, but this was abandoned when the Air Ministry issued its list of official designations and it would have clashed with the F Mk VIII fighter.

The weighing and CoG determination of a production PR Mk IV (Type D), BP927, took place at Worthy Down on 9 April 1942. It was armed with the 'A' wing and three loads were calculated – Load (2 x F24 14in cameras) 6,560lb; Load 2 (as per 1 but with 20lbs armour on rear fuel tank) 6,580; Load 3 (as Load 2 rear tank empty) 6,371. Certificate of Design for the PR Mk IV (Type 333) was issued by the Air Ministry on 24 February 1943 for production aircraft and it covered the basic F VB airframe with armament deleted.

'Pampa Flight' of No. 251 Squadron, part of Coastal Command (Met Recce) began operations over Germany in late 1942 to gather Met data for Bomber Command. The Squadron was based at Bircham Newton.

After the disaster of Convoy PQ17 in July 1942 when only eleven out of a total of 35 merchant ships arrived at Archangel, Russia, it was accepted that photo-reconnaissance intelligence was needed, and as a result three Spitfire PR Mk IVs of No. 1 PRU were despatched from Benson to North Russia where they could keep watch on the German surface raiders. Under the code name *'Orator'* the flight was commanded by Flt Lt. E. A. Fairhurst, and the ground party left the UK for Russia on 13 August with the aircrews and Spitfires flying out on 1 September, eventually to locate their base at Vaenga. The PRU Mk IVs carried the Red Star insignia and were painted in 'Camotint' green. The first PR Spitfire operation took place on 10 September over Alten fjord, in Norway and the first casualty was Fly Of. Walker on 27 September, when he failed to return from Alten. The flight returned to England in November. A second PRU detachment consisting of three PR IVs flew to

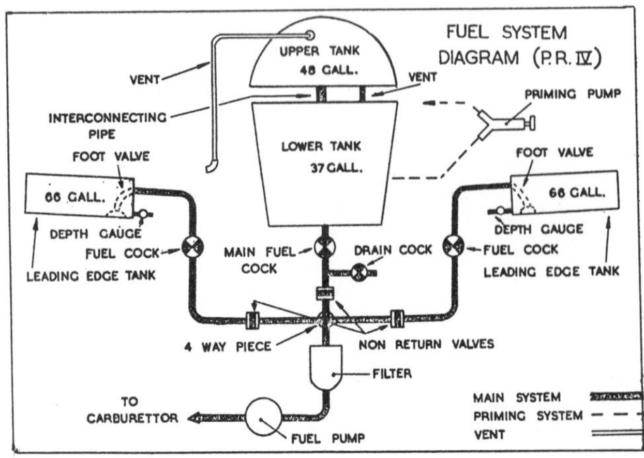

Williamson Manufacturing was one of a number of suppliers of cameras to the R.A.F. The Eagle was one of several types of camera employed by the P.R.U., hence the trade mark.

Engine control quadrant PR IV, VII and XII when mixture control was fitted

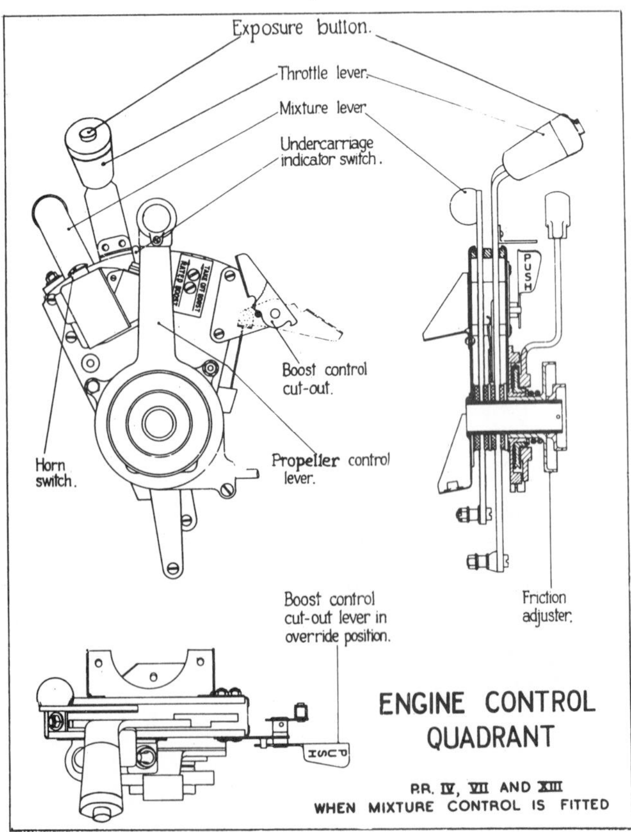

* *The blister was devised by Cotton in May 1939 and after taking out a patent he licensed production to Triplex. Cotton's royalty was 10/- (50 pence) per unit, but he generously waived payment.*

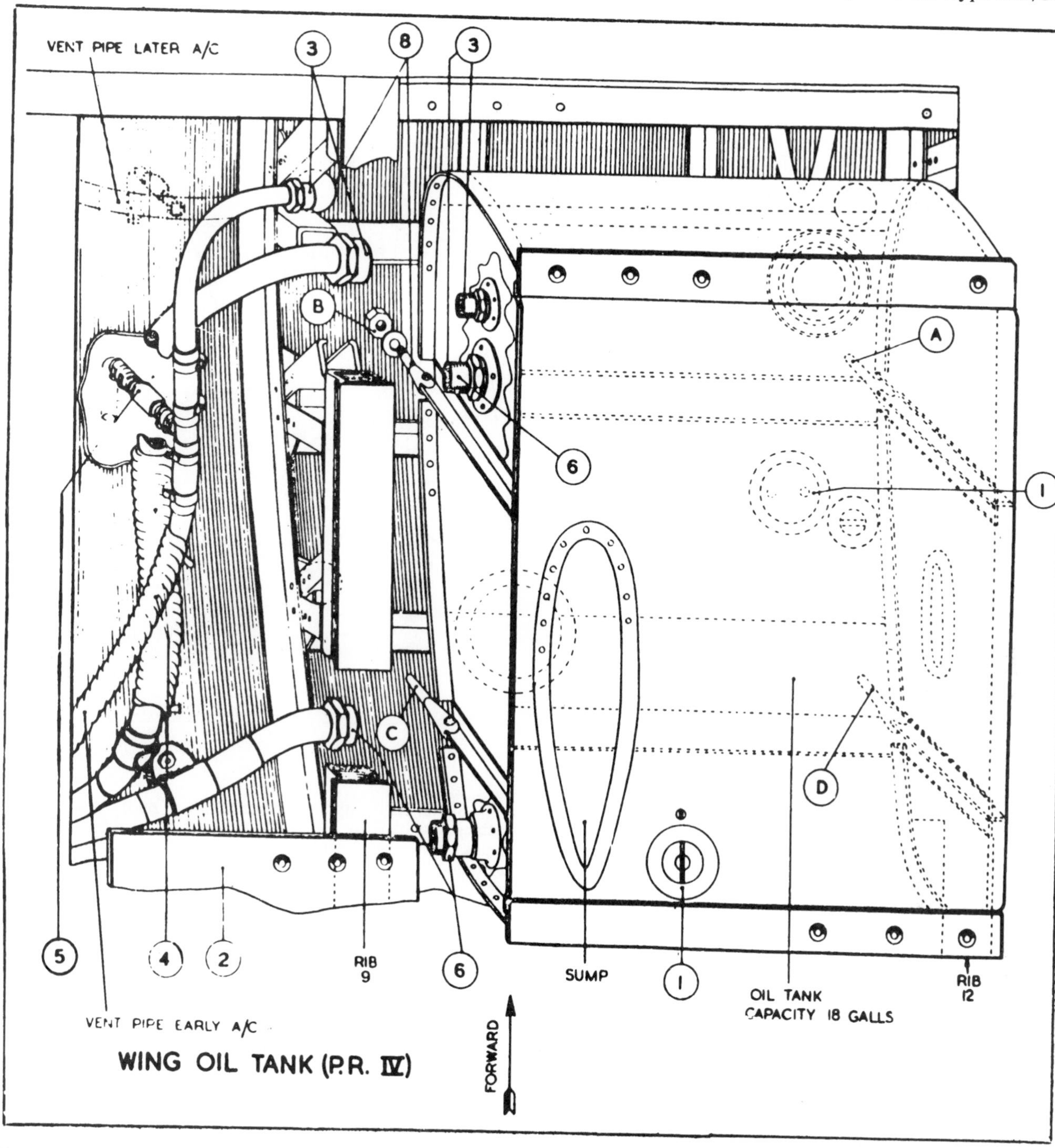

VENT PIPE LATER A/C

VENT PIPE EARLY A/C

RIB 9

SUMP

OIL TANK CAPACITY 18 GALLS

RIB 12

FORWARD

WING OIL TANK (P.R. IV)

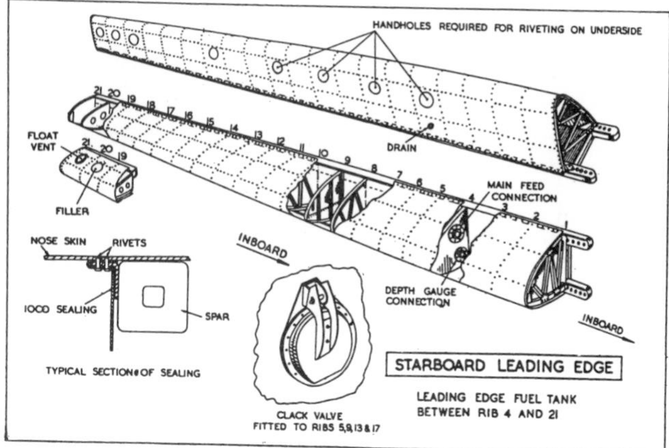

Vaenga in early April 1943 and was code named *'Source'*. The aircraft were from Squadron 543 and the PR flights led to the attack by midget submarines on the *Tirpitz* on 22 September, when the warship was badly damaged. The final PR operation was *Tungsten* in early 1944 and three Mark V Spitfires of 542 Squadron flew to Russia in February of that year. Operations began on 12 March but the unit was recalled in the following May, all ground equipment and aircraft being handed over to the Russians.

A number of converted Mk I Spitfires had to be returned to Heston Aircraft by Benson because of stress wrinkling of the mainplanes. K9787 (G), X4491 (F) and X4492 (C) were fitted with new wings. A number of PR Mk IV Type Ds had bad rivetting to top dorsal skin and Supermarine had to send a working party to Coastal Command to re-rivet them in October 1941. AA874, 963 and 968 were inadvertently delivered to squadrons with hollow wing root bolts and were grounded by an Air Ministry Signal on 20 November 1941. AA799 was used as a test bed for two propeller types. The weighing and CG determination of AR244 on 26 March 1942 revealed a tare of 5,066lb, auw (less cameras) 6,556, with cameras 6,654. Cameras were F24 14in oblique, 5in vertical, 14in vertical. These early production and converted aircraft were eventually replaced by the PR Mk X, Mk XI, Mk XII, Mk XIII and XIX.

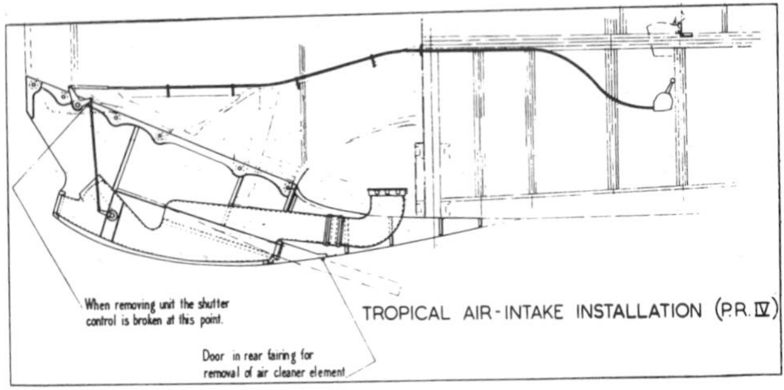

PR Mk IV

Wing. Planform elliptical; section NACA 2200 Series; incidence° root + 2, tip − ½; dihedral° 6; thickness % root 13.2, tip 6; aspect ratio 5.68; area nett 220, gross 242; chord (geo) 6.38, (ma) 7.01. Ailerons. Area 18.9; chord; movement° up 26, down 19; droop ⅜. Flaps area 15.6; movement° down 85. Wing loading 36.0; power loading.

Tailplane. Area 31.46; chord (ma) 4.0; incidence° root 0, tip ± ½; dihedral° 0. Elevators. Area 13.26; movement° up 28, down 23. Tab area 0.38; movement° up 20, down 7. Fin area 4.61. Rudder area 8.23; movement° each way 28. Tab area 0.35; movement° port 6, starbd 18.

Undercarriage. Wheels Dunlop AH2061; tyres Dunlop IJ 13 or 17. Oleo pressure 355; tyre pressure 55. Tailwheel, fixed castoring. Wheel Dunlop AH 2184/IX; tyre Dunlop TA 11, 12 or 14. Oleo pressure 214; tyre pressure 43.

Engine/s Merlin 45
Electric starting
Merlin 46
Other units installed.

Propeller/s. Rotol 3-blade RX5/10 pitch range 35°, fine pitch or, de Havilland Type 5/39B 3-blade (Merlin III) pitch range 20° fine pitch 30°. Diameter of both 10ft 9in.

Coolant. 70% distilled water, 30% Glycol. 14 gals in system.

Fuel. YY 100 octane. Capacity fuselage (upper) 48 gals, lower 37, wing leading edge 2 × 66.5. Total 218. Flow controlled by cocks on both sides of cockpit.

Oil. 18 gals in port wing between ribs 9 and 12.

Armour. Nil.

Armament. Nil. Plain windscreen.

Radio. TR1133 or TR1143.

Camera installation. Differed on early converted a/c but standardized later as follows – W installation 2 × F8 20in split vertical fanned, between fuselage frames 13 and 15 inclined 10° to the vertical and 20 to each other. Heating hot air. X installation. X F24 14in split vertical fanned and 1 × F24 8 or 14in oblique mounted as W with oblique over front F24. Inclined at 8½° to the vertical and 17 to each other. Heating electric. Y installation. 1 × F52 36in vertical used for bomb damage assessment. Mounted between frames 13 and 14. Heating hot air. This was a fixed installation for a specified number of PR Mk IVs and not interchangeable.

Weights. Tare 4,953lb, take off (W) 7,148 (X) 7,155 (Y) 7,119.5; max permissable 6,500. Tail ballast 17.5. PR Mk IV(T) tare 5,000. In the PR IV the CoG moved aft as fuel in wing tanks was consumed, after which it moved forward as fuselage fuel used.

Alternative to W installation. X. 2 x F24 14in split vertical fanned and 1 x F24 8 or 14in oblique mounted as W with oblique over front F24. Inclined at 8½° to the vertical and 17° to each other. Heating electric. Alternative to W. Y. 1 × F52 36in vertical used only for bomb damage assessment. Mounted between frames 13 and 14. Heating hot air. Fixed installation for a specified number of PR Mk IV. Not interchangeable.

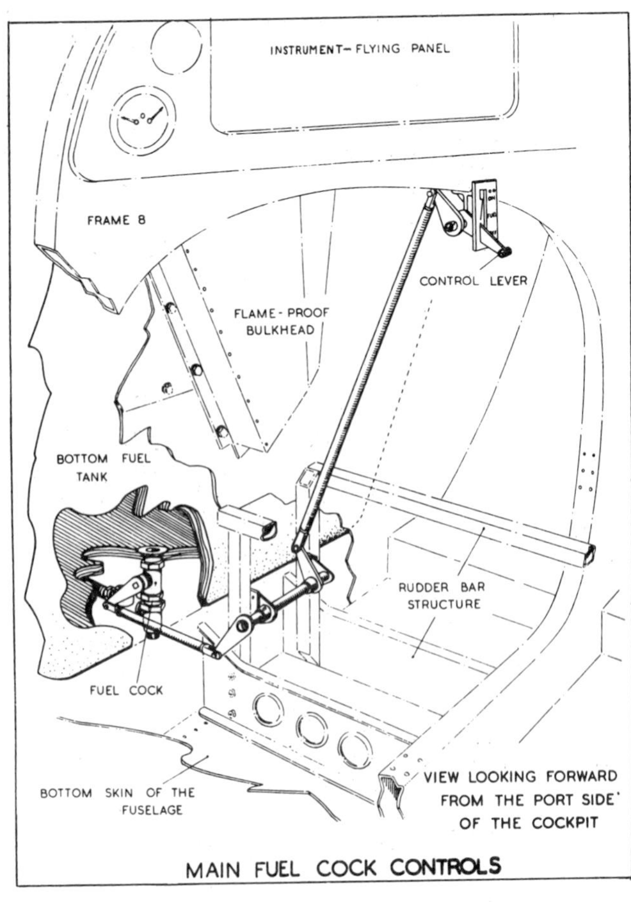

MAIN FUEL COCK CONTROLS

Signal pistol clipped starboard side of pilot's seat. Oblique cameras sighted by graticule engraved on cockpit hood and black markings at end of aileron. No indentification lights installed. CoG moves aft as wing fuel consumed, then forward was fuselage tanks emptied.

MODIFICATIONS TO PR AIRFRAME.

476 D wing. To fit immersed wing fuel pump 17-11-42; 552 Provide tropicalisation 10-2-42; 553 Fit door in starboard wing 10-3-42; 650 Strengthen mountings for Merlin 45, 46, 47 3-6-42; 735 Introduce balloon hood (retrofit only) 22-9-42; 743 Fit Westland convex elevator (not PR. IV (TROP) 20-10-42; 747 Provide external sump oil tank 6-10-42.

Spitfire PR Mk VII

Leading particulars as for PR IV except for the following variations.

Propellers. Rotol RX5/14, 3-blade CS VP, de Havilland Type 5/29 CS VP 3-blade or, Type 5/39 pitch range 20° or, Type 5/39A.

Fuel capacity. Upper fuselage 48 gals, lower 37, rear fuselage 29. Total 114.

Oil in tank under engine 5.8 gals.

Armour. Nil.

Armament. A wing (some a/c)

Radio. Nil.

Weights. Tare 4,985lb, take off 6,584, max permissible 6,590. CoG moved forward as fuel consumed.

Camera installation. G installation 1 × F24 5 or 8in vertical (front) and 1 × F24 8 or 14 in vertical (rear) between frames 13 and 14, and 1 × F24 8 or 14 in oblique mounted above front camera. heating electric.

One only upward indentification light fitted.

SERIAL NUMBERS

Supermarine Aviation (Vickers) Ltd.

Contract No. B19713/39

First order for 450 Spitfire Mk I, **R6595 to 7350, dated 9 August 1940. Built as Mks I/V/VA/PR IV. The following serials apply to PR IVs built to this** order; R7053-7044 and 7055-7056(12).

Fourth order for 500 Spitfire Mk I, **AA718 to AB536, dated 19 July 1940. Built as Mks VB/VC/VI/PR IV between** August 1941 and February 1942. The **following serials apply to PR IVs built to** this order; AA781-815, AB118-132, 300-319 and 421-430(80) and AB466.

Fifth order for 1,100 Spitfire Mk IA/IB, BP844 to BS559, dated October **1940. Built as; PR IV/F VB/VC/VI/VII/ PR XI between February and November** 1942. The following serials apply to **PR IVs built to this order; BP879-892,** 904-937, BR410-435, 641-670, BS355-367, 489-490, 492-497, 500 and 503-505(129).

Seventh order for 500 Spitfire Mk **VC, EN112 to 759, dated 23 August 1941. Built as PR IV/F VI/VII/F XII** between November 1942 and August 1943. **The following serials apply to PR IV built** to this order; EN155, 262, 264 and 386-389(8). Total built 229.

Westland Aircraft Ltd.

Contract No B124305/40

First order for 300 Spitfire Mk I dated August 1940. Built as Mks I/VB/ VC between July 1941 and September 1942. The following serials apply to PR Mk IV/V built to this order. AR257, AR258, AR260

Total Mk IV/V constructed 229.

All PR Mk IV Type D unless otherwise indicated. Engines specified. Fixed camera type installation in brackets.

Spitfire Mk V converted to PR standards R7035-7044, 7055-7056. Originally designated F Mk V (PR.C) they were redesignated PR IV Type D from R7035.

R7029 1688 HEA/HAL 22-5-41 1PRU 14-7 FACE 27-4-42
R7030 1694 HEA 1PRU Ben 24-5-41
R7031 1714 HEA 1PRU Ben 29-5-41
R7032 1715 HEA 1PRU Ben 30-5-41
R7033 1738 HEA 1PRU Ben 7-6-41 ttl wrk 5-10
R7034 1755 HEA 1PRU Ben 10-6-41
R7035 1838 HEA 1PRU Ben 3-7-41
R7036 1856 HEA 1PRU Ben 8-7-41
R7037 1901 HEA FF 16-7-41 1PRU Ben 31-7
R7038 1922 HEA FF 19-8-41 1PRU Ben 9-8
R7039 1943 FF 1-8-41 1PRU Ben 16-8 FTR 10-9
R7040 1944 HEA FF 2-8-41 1PRU Ben 12-8 FTR 2-12
R7041 1945 HEA FF GP 6-8-41 CHA 16-8 1PRU Ben 17-8 541S FTR 1-12-43
R7042 1946 HEA FF GP 8-8-41 CHA 16-8 dd 18-8
R7043 1971 HEA FF 9-8-41 1PRU 21-8 FTR 30-9
R7044 1972 HEA FF 13-8-41 dd 22-9
R7055 1996 HEA FF 24-8-41
R7056 1997 HEA FF 24-8-41

AA Series All PR IV Type D unless otherwise indicated. Engines specified. Fixed camera installation in brackets. Fuselage built Vincents Garage, Reading; wings and tailplane Great Western Motors; engines installed at Vincents and at Star Road Factory, Caversham, Reading. First flight and tests Henley Aerodrome nr Wargrave, Berks.

AA781 1998 HEA FF 21-8-41 1PRU 28-8 FAAC 6-1-42 ROS FTR ops 1-8

AA782 1999 M45 HEA FF 22-8-41 1PRU 30-8 FACB 12-11 SOC 29-11

AA783 2000 M45 HEA FF 24-8-41 1PRU 30-8 HAL 8-11 Ben 6-2-42 FTR ops 14-3

AA784 2005 M45 HEA FF 26-8-41 1PRU 30-8 HAL 26-1-42 M46 instal CB ops 11-6 1PRU 24-6 542S 30-9 80TU 5-5-43 FAAC 17-6 SOC 30-12-44

AA785 2018 M45(W) HEA FF 27-8-41 1PRU 30-9 HAL 13-10 3SLG 12-4-42 Ben 2-10 542S 8-12 1 OADU 15-9-43 Ind Nov '43 ME SOC 5-6-45

AA786 2031 M45 HEA FF 29-8-41 1PRU 6-9 HAL 2-1-42 mods 1PRU 11-1 FAAC 12-2 Ben 5-2-43 1 OADU 6-9 Ind 3PRU 7-10 FACE 5-4-45 SOC 31-5

AA787 2044 HEA FF 4-9-41 1PRU 6-9 FTR 23-2-42

AA788 2052 M45 HEA FF GP 4-9-41 Henley 8-9 1PRU 9-9 HAL 13-10 Ben 17-9-42 8OTU 27-9 FACB 6-6-43 HAL recat E 14-8-44

AA789 2053 M45 HEA FF 5-9-41 1PRU 9-9 12-12 mods PRU Leuch 26-1-42

AA790 2074 M45(X) HEA FF GP 12-9-41 Hen 1PRU 13-9 FACB 6-6-42 HAL 541S 30-9 540S 9-1-43 8OTU 21-6 VSM 8-9 external sump wng oil tank recat E SOC 1-1-45

AA791 2075 M45(X) HEA FF 12-9-41 1PRU 13-9 FAAC 22-4-42 CRD VWD 13-10 Ben 19-11 542S 14-12 air coll with BM350 cd Nettlebed Oxon CE 6-6-43

AA792 2077 M45 HEA FF 13-9-41 1PRU 13-9 FTR ops 7-12

AA793 2091 M45(X) HEA FF 15-9-41 1PRU 18-9 FAC 16-5-42 542S 30-9 FACB 18-12 1OADU 5-5-43 Ind 31-5 FTR ops Bombay 30-9

AA794 2094 (X)HEA FF 16-9-41 1PRU 18-9 HAL 7-11 mods 1PRU 18-11 8OTU 27-9-42 c/fld w/u ldg. Fraser CE 12-7-43 FH341.55

AA795 2113 HEA FF 1PRU 25-9 HAL 10-12 FTR ops 24-4-42 FH40

AA796 2115 HEA GP 20-9-41 CHA 1PRU 25-9 HAL 12-12 mods 1PRU 12-12 FTR ops 30-12

AA797 2148 HEA FF 30-9-41 1PRU 1-10 HAL 30-11 mods 1PRU 10-12 CE ops SOC 3-4-42

AA798 2143 M45 HEA FF 29-9-41 1PRU 1-10 GAL 2-2-42 PRU St Eval 6-2 FACE 12-4 FH44.30

AA799 2144 M45 HEA FF GP 29-9-41 Hen 1PRU 2-10 Heston 11-2-43 Ben 20-5 1OADU 9-6-43 Ind 16-6 SOC 5-10-44

AA800 2145 M45 HEA FF GP 29-9-41 Hen 1PRU 1-10 HAL mods 1PRU 8-12 SOC 31-7-42 FH155.10

AA801 2146 M45 HEA FF 29-9-41 HP 1PRU 7-10-41 struct fail cd nr Watchfield Berks 29-10 Farn Jan '42 for acc invest SOC 5-11

AA802 2147 M45 HEA FF 30-9-41 Hen 1PRU 5-10 FTR ops 7-9-42 SOC 8-9 FH25.55

AA803 2160 M45(W) HEA FF 2-10-41 1PRU 5-10 CB ops 15-1-42 534S 30-9 1OADU 11-3-43 f/f NA 14-3 C3 ops a/c aban 682S 5-5

AA804 2166 M45 HEA FF 6-10-41 1PRU 7-10 HAL 30-11 mods 1PRU 7-12 FTR ops 28-12

AA805 2167 M45 HEA FF 1PRU Ben 7-10 o/s ldg o/t CB 13-2-42 recat E SOC 22-2

AA806 2195 M45 HEA FF 14-10-41 1PRU 19-10 543S 30-9-42 FTR 28-10 FH238

AA807 2176 M45(W) HEA FF 9-10-41 1PRU 13-10 CE ops 19-2-42 541S 30-7 CB ops 16-4-43 543S 21-6 HAL 19-10 M46 instal 4S 19-3-44 SOC 12-3-45

AA808 2185 M45(W) HEA FF GP 11-10-41 1RU 13-

AA801, PR IV, Type D, after structural failure in the air. It crashed at Watchfield, Berkshire on 20 October 1941 and went to Farnborough for accident investigation.

PR IV and PR XI, nearest camera. (R C Cussons).

Spitfire PR Mk IV (Ashworth).

10 HAL 18-2-42 mods 541S 30-9 FAAC 15-2-43 CB ops 4-3 543S 7-7 AST 10-8

AA809 2207 M45 HEA FF 17-10-41 1PRU 19-10 543S 30-9-42 CE ops 13-2-45

AA810 2203 M45 HEA FF 17-10-41 1PRU 19-10 FTR ops 5-3-42

AA811 2208 M45(W) HEA FF 19-10-41 1PRU 20-10 534S 7-11-42 FTR ops 3-7-43

AA812 2213 M45 HEA FF 1PRU 24-10 FACE 24-10 HAL 10-4-42

AA813 2219 M45 FF GP 24-10-41 1PRU 28-10 hit snowbank ldg Topcliffe CE 24-1-42 SOC 27-1

AA814 2221 M45 HEA FF 25-10-41 1PRU 26-10 FTR ops 17-8-42

AA815 2234 PRIV(T) M45 HEA FF 28-10-41 1PRU 30-10 FAAC 11-4-42 HAL 1OADU 29-4-43 ME 1-5 SOC 31-5-45

AB series All PR IV Merlin 45

AB118 2244 HEA FF 30-10-41 1PRU 3-11 542S 30-9-42 FAAC 27-10 140S TAF 4-2-43 HAL 11-12 M46 instal SOC 22-4-45

AB119 2259 HEA FF 31-10-41 1PRU 6-11 CAC ops 11-1-42 ROS FTR ops 18-4 FH76.45

AB120 2270 HEA FF 5-11-41 1PRU 6-11 FTR ops 11-8-42

AB121 2271 HEA FF 7-11-41 5MU 11-11 dis at North 11-12 VA 3-1-42 1PRU 27-6 542S 30-9 CE ops 21-10 SOC FH49.55

AB122 2281 HEA FF 8-11-41 5MU 11-11 dis at North 11-12 VA Hen 9-3-42 142S 22-6 CA ops 19-7 HAL M46 instal 8OTU 7-11 FAAC 15-9-43 VSM 6-11 external pump wng oil tank SOC 16-3-45

AB123 2282 HEA FF 8-11-41 5MU 12-11 VA 3-1-42 1PRU 16-4 542S 30-9 Ben 21-1-44 8OTU 2-2 SOC 16-11

AB124 2297 HEA FF 16-11-41 5MU 18-11 VA 29-4-42 1PRU 24-7 542S 30-9 540S 9-1-43 8OTU 20-6-43 flew i/ clouds FTR 14-10 FH283.10

AB125 2304 HEA FF 15-11-41 5MU 26-11 dis at North 11-12 VA Hen 19-5-42 Ben 8-10 543S 22-1-43 FTR ops 10-2 FH23.35

AB126 2298 HEA FF 15-11-41 8MU 17-11 dis at North 11-12 VA 14-5-42 140S 4-7 FAAC 22-3-43 HAL FACE 5-8

AB127 2299 HEA FF 15-11-41 8MU 18-11 VA Hen 27-2-42 1PRU 20-4 FA FTR 10-5

AB128 2300 HEA FF 15-11-41 8MU 18-11 VA Hen 27-2-42 1PRU 8-3 543S 30-9 CE ops 28-2-43

AB129 2318 HEA FF 20-11-41 8MU 23-12 VA Hen 27-2-42 1PRU 8-3 CE ops 20-5 FH45.5

AB130 2325(Y) HEA FF 22-11-41 8MU 23-11 1PRU 26-1-42 140S instrument fail i/cloud a/c aban cd Sussex CE 26-8 SOC 31-8

AB131 2326 HEA FF 22-11-41 6MU 7-12 1401 Met Flt 16-2-42 222S FTR ops 12-4 FH9.55

AB132 2342 HEA FF 26-11-41 FACB 27-2 HAL 542S 30-9 Orater A/C 17-11 packed for ME

AB300 2341 HEA FF 26-11-41 5MU 30-11 Ben 17-1-42 packed for overseas ME 2PRU 1-3 Malta 1-4 69S CE ops 19-9 SOC 20-9

AB301 2357 HEA FF 30-11-41 5MU 5-12 FACB 17-12 HAL 1PRU 5-4-42 FTR ops 30-7

AB302 2358 HEA FF 30-11-41 5MU 4-12 1PRU 3-1-42 CAC ops 15-2 541S 30-9 8OTU 21-6-43 VSM 31-12-43 external sump wng oil tank SOC 26-3-45

AB303 2360 HEA FF 30-11-41 5MU 5-12 1PRU 31-1-42 542S 30-9 309FTU FAAC 4-11-43 Ben 23-12 8OTU 7-1-44 SOC 16-3-45

AB304 2374 HEA FF 5-12-41 5MU 7-12 Ben 28-1-42 packed for overseas ME 2PRU 19-3 Gib FACE 1-4

AB305 2375 (Y) HEA FF 5-12-41 6MU 7-12 1PRU 17-1-42 CB ops 13-3 HAL 3-9 M46 instal mods CA ops 16-9 541S 30-9 140S TAF 24-12 HAL 28-9-43 M45 instal 4S 5-3-44 41S 15-5 CE 8-12 SOC 15-5-45

AB306 2379 (WS) FF6-12-41 6MU 7-12 Ben 26-8 1PRU 14-9 543S 30-9 BDn 16-12 trls with mods c/s unit and DeH Hydromatic prop 521S 5-1-43 FACB 24-3 1OADU 14-8 Ind 7-10 SOC 26-4-45

AB307 2394 HEA FF 12-12-41 6MU 15-12 1PRU 17-1-42 CE ops 10-4 FH38

AB308 2395 HEA FF12-12-41 6MU 15-12 Ben 19-9-42 Farn Nov '42 photo trls 543S 21-2-43 FAAC 6-9 8OTU 7-1-44 SOC 16-3-45

AB309 2401 HEA FF 15-12-41 6MU 17-12 1PRU 9-3-42 541S 30-9 FTR ops 6-11

AB310 2402 HEA FF 16-12-41 9MU 23-12 Ben 13-1-43 1OADU 13-2 Malta 23-2 ME 1-7 FAC3 4-9

AB311 2405 HEA FF 18-12-41 dd 19-12 no record

AB312 2426 HEA FF 23-12-41 dd 27-12 no record 2PRU Egypt 17-3-42

AB313 2446 HEA FF 29-12-41 9MU 2-1-42 Farn 13-1 instrument and camera trls Ben hit hut in circuit cd dbf 30-3-43

AB314 2427 HEA FF 25-12-41 9MU 29-12 1PRU 3-5 CE ops 4-8

AB315 2428 HEA FF 25-12-41 12MU 29-12 1PRU 10-2-43 1OADU 18-3 ME 27-3 Ind 10-4 ME 1-5 SOC 31-8-44

AB316 2438 HEA FF28-12-41 12MU 29-12 Ben 20-3-43 Ind 5-6 FTR ops 15-12

AB317 2447 (Y) FF 29-12-41 12MU 3-1-42 1PRU 8-4 FTR ops 28-8

AB318 2458 FF 2-1-42 12MU 3-1 Ben 13-1-43 1OADU 27-2 Ind 1-4 CE ops 8-6

AB319 2450 HEA FF 31-12-41 12MU 3-1-42 Ben 13-1-43 1OADU 27-2 Ind 1-4 C3 ops 9-7

AB421 2454 FF 1-1-42 6MU 3-1 1PRU 27-1 ME 2PRU Heliopolis 17-3 C2 ops 13-10 CE ops 3-3-45 SOC 29-3

AB422 2469 (Y) FF 6-1-42 Hen 6MU 12-1 1PRU 17-2 FTR ops 28-8

AB423 2470 (W) FF 7-1-42 Hen 6MU 9-1 Ben 13-9 543S 7-11 SOC 5-12-43

AB424 2480 FF 9-1-42 Hen 6MU 12-1 1PRU 28-2 543S 30-9 HAL 3-9 mods FAAC 19-10 Ben overran runway u/c clpse CE 20-2-45

AB425 2481 FF 9-1-42Hen 6fMU 11-1 1PRU 28-2 FTR ops 23-4

AB426 2524 FF 25-1-42 8MU 28-1 1PRU27-2 FAAC 4-10 541S 19-12 10ADU 25-1-43 FAAC 26-1 NWA 28-2 ME 30-9 218Gp NA 30-11 SOC 30-11-44

AB427 2525 FF 25-1-42 8MU 28-1 1PRU 27-2 543S 30-9 Ben 22-10 SOC 5-12-43

AB428 2526 (W) FF 25-1-42 8MU 28-1 Ben 24-8 1PRU 3-9 FACB 24-9 541S 10-10 CB ops 5-3-43 10ADU 9-9 Ind 10-10 SOC 31-5-45

AB429 2528 FF 26-1-42 8MU 30-1 1PRU 28-2 FACE 26-3 SAL FH17

AB430 2529 FF 26-1-42 8MU 7-2 1PRU 27-2 542S 30-9 FTR ops 26-1-43

BP series All PR IV(T) Merlin 46 unless otherwise indicated

BP879 M45 (W) FF 28-1-42 9MU 30-1 Ben 29-8 541S 22-10 HAL 9-5-45 mods 542S 19-5 543S 7-7 309FTU e/fld on t/o w/u ldg CB 8-11 recat E

BP880 2551 FF 31-1-42 1PRU 6-2 cd en route to ME 16-3 HAL 20-6 Ben 13-1-43 India 23-9 FTR ops 5-3-44

BP881 2540 M45 (W) FF 28-1-42 9MU 30-1 Ben 28-8 1PRU 1-9 541S 30-9 FTR ops 8-2-43 FH74.70

BP882 2552 FF 31-1-42 1PRU 6-2 2PRU ME 15-3 Gib FACE 1-4

BP883 2553 FF 31-1-42 1PRU 6-2 2PRU ME 14-3 malta 6-9 SOC 19-10

BP884 2561 FF 7-2-42 8MU 15-2 1PRU 3-5 542S 30-9 HAL 18-6-43 M45 instal Ben 23-2-44

BP885 2562 FF 7-2-42 8MU 15-2 1PRU 14-3 1PRU ME 26-3 f/f Malta 1-4 69S ME 1-8 SOC 13-9-45

BP886 2550 HEA FF 31-1-42 8MU 14-2 1PRU 27-2 542S 30-9 8 OTU 3-6-43 VSM 8-9 external sump wng oil tank FAAC 25-4 SOC 23-4-45

BP887 2581 (W) HEA FF 11-2-42 8MU 13-2 CRD Farn 24-2 1PRU 18-4 FTR ops 17-8

BP888 2582 (W) HEA FF 11-2-42 8MU 14-2 Ben 22-8 FACB 28-8 HAL Ben 3-9 BDn May'43 8OTU 10-9 FAAC 27-10-44 recat E

BP889 2589 HPA FF 14-2-42 8MU 15-2 1PRU 7-5 543S 30-9 Orater A/C 17-11 Ben FTR ops 14-12

BP890 2608 HEA FF 21-2-42 1PRU 22-2 Ben f/f ME 22-2 cd en route FTR 18-3

BP891 2590 HPA FF 14-2-42 8MU 15-2 1PRU 7-5 541S 30-9 Orater A/C 17-11

BP892 2600 HEA FF 17-2-42 1PRU 22-2 f/f 1PRU ME 22-2 FACE in transit 1-4

BP904 2610 HEA FF 21-2-422 1PRU 22-2 Ben f/f 1PRU ME C2 ops 23-9 CE ops 23-1-45

BP905 2616 HEA FF 23-2-42 1PRU 25-2 Malta CB ops 1-4 f/f ME to UK 24-4 HAL Ben 27-11 Malta 7-12 Algiers 1-4-43 NA 1-6 ME 1-7 SOC 30-11

BP906 2623 HEA FF 27-2-42 1PRU 7-3 1PRU ME 29-3 FTR ops cd in neutral terr 2-4 FH9.20

BP907 2624 HEA FF 27-2-42 1PRU 7-3 Farn Apl'42 camera trls f/f 1PRU ME lost in transit 20-4 FH8-30

BP908 2633 HEA FF 28-2-42 1PRU 7-3 2PRU ME 14-4 69S SOC 8-3-46

BP909 2645 HEA FF 7-3-42 1PRU 8-3 f/f 2PRU ME 5-4 SOC 1-2-44

BP910 2646 HEA FF 7-3-42 6MU 12-3 Ben f/f 1PRU ME 1-5 Malta 8-2-43 SOC 13-3

BP911 2655 HEA FF 8-3-42 6MU 12-3 Ben f/f 2PRU ME 12-4 Malta 6-9 Ind 5-10 SOC 26-4-45

BP912 2672 (W) HEA FF 14-3-42 6MU 15-3 Ben 17-3 10ADU o/s ldg hit wall CE 17-4 Benson 18-5 47MU 31-8 *Molaja* 1-10 lost at sea 3-10

BP913 2670 (W) HEA FF 13-3-42 6MU 15-3 Ben f/f 2PRU ME 6-5 FA 18-12 SOc 1-6-43

BP914 2698 HEA FF 1PRU 25-3 Malta 3-5 CA ops 4-5 1PRU ME 69S FAC2 23-10 SOC 24-2-43

BP916 2707 HEA FF 20-3-42 1PRU 25-3 f/f 2PRU ME 5-6-43 FTR ops 17-6

BP917 2720 HEA FF 25-3-42 8MU 26-3 1PRU 30-4 CE 31-4 543S 30-9 HAL 30-6 mods Ben 23-2-44

BP918 2708 HEA FF 23-2-42 8MU 24-3 1PRU 3-8 542S 20-9 8 OTU 20-6-43 FAAC 17-9-44 recat E 11-10

BP919 2709 HEA FF 23-3-42 9MU 27-3 1401Flt 14-5 1PRU 14-6 541S 30-9 140S 24-12 FAAC 14-4-43 140S 26-6 Star Fmdis 39MU 31-3-45

BP920 2727 HEA FF 26-1-42 9MU 30-3 Ben 5-12 47MU 4-1-43 ME 1-8 SOC 31-5-45

BP921 2744 HEA FF 28-3-42 9MU 30-3 1PRU 3-5 FACE 18-7 SOC 31-7

BP922 2734 HEA FF 27-3-42 9MU 30-3 1PRU 5-5 541S 30-9 FAAC 29-10 HAL 415S 13-11 140S 24-11 ME 1-7-43 SOC 1-2-44

BP923 2741 HEA FF 28-3-42 9MU 30-3 1PRU 5-5 542S 30-9 Orater A/C 17-11

BP924 2762 (X) HEA FF 1-4-42 5MU 3-4 1PRU 16-4 FTR ops 28-8

BP925 2763 HEA FF 1-4-42 5MU 3-4 Farn 13-4 photo trls BDn Aug'42 33MU 19-9 Ben 27-10 81 OTU 9-12 FAAC 9-3-43 Hal Ben 19-8 544S Gib 3-9 FAAC 14-9 Ben 3-4-44 Stn Flt Gib 10-9 SOC 31-10-46

BP926 2770 HEA FF 2-4-42 5MU 3-4 1PRU 19-5 FACA 25-9 542S 31-10 8 OTU FACA 28-5-43 trs to HAL 22-6 106PRW 18-2-44

BP927 2775 (W) HEA FF 3-4-42 6MU 3-4 VA 17-5 M45 instal Ben 543S 31-10 8 OTU 22-10 FACB 31-8-44 recat E 23-9

BP928 2776 HEA FF 3-4-42 5MU 3-4 1401Flt 14-5 521S 31-12 Ben 5-4-43 ME 7-5 FA FTR 8-7

BP929 2794 M45 (W) HEA FF 10-4-42 38MU 13-4 1PRU 19-5 CB ops 10-9 543S 17-11 8 OTU 25-5 FAAC 26-8 HAL M46 instal 106PRW 16Gp 18-2-44

BP930 2808 M45 (W) HEA FF 11-5-42 38MU 13-4 Ben 28-11 Gib 25-12 NA 23-12

BP931 2796 M45 HEA FF 10-4-42 38MU 13-4 1401Flt 14-5 FAAC 28-8 521S 31-12 AL 16-9-43 M46 instal 8 OTU 27-1-45 SOC 21-8 to 4992M

BP932 2818 HEA FF 14-4-42 38MU 16-4 Ben 27-11 Malta 19-12 ME 1-9-43 SOC 31-5-45

BP933 2819 HEA FF 15-4-42 1PRU 18-4-42 ME 5-6 601S FACB 28-6 FTR ops 26-10

BP934 2831 HEA FF 16-4-42 1PRU 18-4 47MU 25-5 *Corab* 16-6 Tak 30-7 ME 11-8 FTR 13-10

Cologne, as photographed by F/Lt R C Cussons, No 541 Squadron, 16 December 1942, in BS499, PR XI.

N3187, converted to PR III, Type C, by Heston Aircraft, 4 February 1940. Trials at Farnborough in April. Merlin 45 installed, converted to PR V and joined PRU Benson 20 August 1941.

P9385 No. 2 PDU, originally converted to PR Mk III. Damaged by enemy bombs, Benson 27 February 1941. Merlin 45 installed by Heston Aircraft in May and brought up to Type F, PR Mk VI. (Ashworth).

X4784, ex Mk I and Mk V, converted finally to Type G, PR Mk VII, 17 January 1942. (Ashworth).

BP935 2832 HEA FF 17-4-42 1PRU 18-4 45MU 25-5 *Corab* 16-6 Tak 30-7 ME 11-8 Ind 5-10 FAC2 6-11 SOC 2-8-43

BP936 2841 HEA FF 18-4-42 1PRU 19-4 47MU 23-5 *Corab* 16-6 Tak 30-7 ME 3-11 Gib 30-9 SOC Apl'45

BP937 2872 (W) HEA FF 29-4-42 6MU 1-5 Ben 29-8 541S 30-9 Ben 16-8-43 Ind 9-10 SOC 26-3-45

BR series All PR IV(T) Merlin 46 unless otherwise indicated

BR410 2842 HEA FF 18-4-42 1PRU 19-4 FAAC 30-5 HAL ME 18-6 FAC3 15-12-43

BR411 2843 HEA FF 18-4-42 1PRU 19-4 Ben 19-4 ME 5-6 FA FTR 4-10

BR412 2874 (Y) HEA FF 30-4-42 6MU 2-5 39MU 13-5 543S 5-10 309Flt ADU 10-11-43 swg off runway ldg u/c clpse CE 13-3-45 SOC 26-3

BR413 2865 HEA FF 24-4-42 cd after swing on t/o to avoid Magister dbf test pilot kld. Liability accepted by Air Min after query received from MAP contracts

BR414 2869 HEA FF 25-4-42 1PRU 30-4 47MU 26-5 *Corab* 16-6 Tak 1-8 ME 11-8 C2 on ops 4-1-43 C3 ops 24-10

BR415 2891 (W) HEA FF 2-5-42 6MU 3-5 1PRU 8-6 CB ops 14-9 544S 16-11 541S 9-3-43 FACB 13-4 HAL Ben 25-4 Ind 3-9 FACB 29-1-44

BR416 2871 HEA FF 28-4-42 1PRU 2-5 47MU 13-7 *Amot E* 22-7 Tak 3-9 ME 19-10 SOC 13-9-45

BR417 2892 HEA FF 2-5-42 6MU 3-5 1PRU 15-6 CB ops 30-7 Ben 13-1-43 10ADU 18-2 flew i/high grd nr Cambourne Cornwall CE 17-2

BR418 2914 (W) HEA FF 8-5-42 9MU 10-5 Ben 17-9 47MU 3-10 *Catrine* 20-10 20-11 Tak 27-12 Ind 1-2-43 SOC 31-8-44

BR419 2920 HEA FF 9-5-42 9MU 10-5 1PRU 26-5 CB ops 2-8 543S 31-10 8 OTU 20-10-43 FA FTR 31-12 FH172.5

BR420 2921 HEA FF 9-5-42 9MU 10-5 1PRU 30-5 Tak 17-9 ME 19-9 SOC UK 12-3-45

BR421 2928 HEA FF 11-5-42 9MU 13-5 Ben 5-10 NWA 28-2-43 SOC 31-8-45

BR422 2947 M46M(Y) HEA FF 15-5-42 9MU 18-5 Ben 27-9 8 OTU 2-11 VSM external sump wng oil tank SOC 22-5-45

BR423 2936 (W) HEA FF 15-5-42 9MU 16-5 Ben 2-9 Gib 6-11 E Afr FTR ops 1-12

BR424 2984 (W) HEA FF 16-5-42 9MU 19-5 Ben 7-9 47MU 11-10 Porth 31-10 Malta 6-11 ME 6-11 CB ops 29-1-43 recat SOC 1-2 FH 209.50

BR425 2949 M45(Y) HEA FF 16-5-42 9MU 22-5 140S 13-7 FACB 19-7 HAL M46 instal 140S TAF 10-11 SOC 22-5-45

BR426 2971 (W) HEA FF 19-5-42 9MU 22-5 1PRU 6-9 47MU 12-10 Ben 31-10 Porth 6-11 f/f Malta 7-11 ME 11-11 69S FTR Sgt Howard dead in dinghy ops 18-12 FH111.10

BR427 2977 HEA FF 24-5-42 1PRU 28-5 47MU 27-6 *Amot E* 24-7 Tak 11-9 ME 14-9 Malta 1-6 SOC 31-5-45

BR428 2976 HEA FF 24-5-42 1PRU 28-5 47MU 6-7 *Amot E* 20-7 Tak 17-9 ME 31-1-43 SOC 30-11-44

BR429 2978 HEA FF 27-5-42 1PRU 28-5 47MU 27MU 27-6 *Sil Wil* 20-7 Tak 15-8 ME 29-9 SOC 31-8-44

BR430 2996 HEA FF 30-5-42 Ben 31-5 47MU 18-6 *Walloon* 21-7 Tak 15-8 ME 2-9 2PRU FAC2 21-9 682S FTR ops 14-2-44

BR431 3012 HEA FF 3-6-42 1PRU 8-6 9MU 28-6 ME 4-8 69S Malta 6-9 Ind 29-11 FAC2 13-12 SOC 31-5-45

BR432 3005 HEA FF 31-5-42 1PRU 2-6 47MU 27-6 *Amot E* 22-7 Tak 3-9 ME 1-10 CE 25-1-45

BR433 3020 HEA FF 6-6-42 1PRU 8-6 9MU 27-6 FACB 29-7 HAL Ben 6-8 ME 1-3-43 FTR over Greece 20-3-43

BR434 3033 (Y) HEA FF 10-6-42 1PRU 11-6 VA Ben 18-10 Porth 31-10 Gib 6-11 SOC 31-12

BR435 3034 HEA FDF 11-6-42 1PRU 14-6 47MU 6-7 *Wallsend* 21-7 Tak 15-8 MR 2-9 SOC 14-10

BR641 3051 HEA FF 14-6-42 1PRU 21-6 47MU 25-7 *Niger* 29-8 Tak 30-10 ME 2-11 Ind 1-12 SOC 13-12 FH55.45

BR642 3052 HEA FF 15-6-42 1PRU 18-6 47MU 14=7 *Niger* 24-8 Tak 27-10 ME 128S CE ops 29-11

BR643 3061 HEA FF 18-6-42 cd before delivery SOC 8-7

BR644 3068 HEA FF 20-6-42 1PRU 26-6 47MU 25-7 *Niger* 24-8 Tak 3-10 ME 1-12 FTR ops 26-9-43

BR645 3070 HEA FF 22-6-42 1PRU 24-6 47MU 15-7 *Niger* 24-8 ME 12-11 FACE dbf 26-9-43

BR646 3075 (W) HEA FF 22-6-42 45MU 23-6 Ben 3-9 47MU 12-10 Porth 6-11 f/f Malta 7-11 ME 13-11 SOC 16-11 FH28.15

BR647 3081 (X) HEA FF 24-6-42 45MU 26-6 Ben 7-9 Porth 6-11 ff Malta 7-11 ME 7-11 SOC 13-11 (crash f/f)

BR648 3082 HEA FF 24-6-42 45MU 26-6 140S TAF 3-7 e/tld a/c aban cd Varcombe Devon 16-8-43

BR649 3101 (W) HEA FF 27-6-42 45MU 29-6 Ben 2-9 Porth 31-10 Gib 6-11 C3 ops 20-11

BR650 3102 (W) HEA FF 28-6-42 45MU 1-7 Ben 26-8 542S 30-9 HAL 7-4-43 543S e/fld f/ld nr Polebrook Northants CE 11-5 SOC

BR651 3112 (Y) HEA FF 2-7-42 33MU 3-7 Ben 15-7 8 OTU 1-8 FAAC 27-8 FTR from H/A photo exercise 6-3-43

BR652 3123 (Y) HEA FF 4-7-42 33MU 8-7 VA 9-7 Ben 15-7 8 OTU 22-7 FACB 8-9 f/f ME 6-3-43 SOC 31-5-45

BR653 3138 (Y) HEA FF 8-7-42 Ben 16-7 ME 11-8 f/f Malta 12-8 Ind 1-2-43 SOC 2-8

BR654 3139 (Y) HEA FF 8-7-42 39MU 12-7 Ben 26-7 8 OTU 13-8 FAAC 24-8 HAL 3-9 Ben 27-3-43 ff ME 23-4 SOC 13-9-45

BR655 3140 (Y) HEA FF 10-7-42 12-7 Ben 28-7 8 OTU 16-8 FACE 11-9 SOC 17-9 FH75.40

BR656 3148 (W) HEA FF 11-7-42 33MU 12-7 Ben 22-12 f/f Malta 12-2-43 C3 ops dbf 13-4

BR657 3164 HEA FF 13-7-42 33MU 19-7 140S 25-7 Ben 545S 23-4 Porth 19-5 Ind 17-9 SOC 15-4-45

BR658 3165 HEA FF 15-7-42 21-7 1PRU 9-8 543S 30-9 FAAC 30-6-43 Ben 22-10 SOC 5-12

BR659 3175 HEA FF 17-7-42 19-7 140S 25-7 Ben 16-8-43 Ind 18-10 SOC 31-5-45

BR660 3178 (W) HEA FF 19-7-42 33MU 21-7 1PRU 5-8 541S 30-9

BR661 3184 (Y) HEA FF 21-7-42 33MU 22-7 1PRU Ben 5-8 541S 30-9 Ind 30-4-43 SOC 15-6-45

BR662 3189 HEA FF 23-7-42 1PRU 25-7 f/f ME 12-8

X4492 was one of four Spitfires operating in Canada during the war. It arrived at Rockcliffe in February 1943 and took part in high altitude trials before being fitted with a telescopic camera and flown by Flt Lt. T Percival to photograph the eclipse of the sun on 9 July 1945. It was converted to PR Mk VI standards.

FAC3 19-12

BR663 3195 HEA FF 24-7-42 1PRU 25-7 f/f ME 13-8 Malta 6-9 FTR ops 4-4-43

BR664 3197 HEA FF 25-7-42 1PRU 25-7 Ben 18-10 Porth 31-10 Gib 6-11 C3 ops 17-12 SOC 31-5-44

BR665 3196 HEA FF 25-7-42 1PRU 25-7 f/f ME 12-8 69S Malta 1-12-43 SOC 2-8-45

BR666 3221 (X) HEA FF 6-8-42 1PRU 9-8 Porth 26-9 f/f Gib 27-9 544S 30-10 CE ops 10-11 FTR

BR667 3228 (Y) HEA FF 8-8-42 1PRU 11-8 47MU 29-8 *Ripley* 8-9 Tak ME 27-10 f/f NWA SOC 1-11

BR668 3233 (W) HEA FF 9-8-42 6MU 10-8 Ben 20-9 544S 3-10 HAL 2-11-43 SOC 15-3-45

BR669 3245 HEA FF 12-8-42 39MU 13-8 Ben 20-9 544S 3-10 FTR ops 13-11

BR670 3250 (Y) HEA FF 14-8-42 39MU 15-8 Ben 7-9 541S 30-9 543S 3-2-43 e/fld w/u ldg CE 14-3

BR683 - 721, 745-772, 799-831, 849-877, 890-929, 954-976 cancel

BS series A11 PR IV(T) Merlin 46

BS355 3267 (W) HEA FF 17-8-42 6MU 18-8 Ben 31-8 Porth 31-10 Gib 6-11 NWA 28-2-43 SOC 1-3-47

BS356 3290 (W) HEA FF 6MU 24-8-42 6MU 25-8 Ben 30-8 Porth 3-10 Gib 6-11 C2 ops 20-11 recat 3

BS357 3291 (Y) HEA FF 24-8-42 6MU 26-8 Ben 17-9 8 OTU 9-10 FAAC 3-12 SOC 16-3-45

BS358 3292 (W) HEA FF 24-8-42 6MU 25-8 Ben 31-8 47MU 14-10 Porth 6-11 Malta 7-11 ME 14-11 NWA 1-5-43 SOC 8-3-44

BS359 3302 (X) HEA FF 28-8-42 6MU 29-8 Ben 8-9 47MU 11-10 Malta 6-11 69S FTR ops 15-11 P/o Jennett Msng

BS360 3332 (Y) HEA FF 28-8-42 1PRU 7-9 47MU 9-10 *Catrine* 20-11 Tak 27-11 SOC 1-3-44

BS361 3405 HEA FF 17-9-42 1PRU 19-9 Ben 10-11 Porth 29-11 NA 1-12 NWA 28-3-43 FAC3 10-2-44

BS362 3406 HEA FF 17-9-42 1PRU 19-9 340S 9-10 47MU 11-10 *Catrine* 20-11 Tak 27-12 NWA 30-4-43 NAASC 31-10 SOC

BS363 3408 HEA FF 19-9-42 1PRU 22-9 47MU 14-10 *Catrine* 20-11 Tak 27-12 SOC 6-12-45

BS364 3431 HEA FF 24-9-42 Ben 27-9 Porth 31-10 Malta 6-11 ME C3 ops 10-3-43

BS365 3449 HEA FF 30-9-42 1PRU 1-10 47MU 24-10 *Catrine* 20-11 Tak 27-12 FAC3 22-1-43

BS366 3478 HEA FF 10-10-42 1PRU 12-10 47MU 6-11 *Tynmouth* 30-11 Tak 22-2-43 ME 16-5 SOC 31-5-45

BS367 3492 HEA FF 16-10-42 1PRU 16-10 Malta 6-11 69S FTR ops 10-11 SOC Flt Lt. Coldbeck Pow SOC FH19.30

BS489 3502 HEA FF 16-10-42 1PRU 18-10 Porth 29-11 ME 1-12 NA 6-12 e/a 18-12

BS490 3520HEA FF 17-10-42 1PRU 21-10 Porth 29-11 ME 1-12 NA 6-12 FAAC 4PRU 31-12 SOC

BS491 3539 HEA FF 22-10-42 1PRU 27-10 542S 29-11 HAL 24-6-43 o/s ldg Sumburgh tip onto nose dbf 16-12-43

BS492 3560 HEA FF 27-10-42 1PRU 1-11 544S 6-12 HAL 11-8-43 SOC 22-5-45

BS493 3580 HEA FF 31-10-42 1PRU 2-11 47MU 17-12 *Inslanga* 11-1-43 Tak 7-2 SOC 13-9-45

BS494 3581 HEA FF 31-10-42 1PRU 2-11 Gib 25-12 NA 23-12 4PRU e/a C2 5-1-43

BS495 3594 HEA FF 6-11-42 1PRU 13-11 Porth 6-12 f/f Malta 2-12 4PRU e/a SOC 31-12

BS496 3648 HEA FF 21-11-42 1PRU Porth 3-12 f/f Malta 7-12 FAC3 3-3-43

BS500 3683 HEA FF 25-11-42 Benson 30-11 Porth 9-12 Malta C3 ops 12-1-43

BS503 3824 CHA FF 8-1-43 6MU 11-1 Ben 29-3 Porth 5-5 Ind 31-5 SOC 5-1-45

BS504 3828 CHA FF 8-1-43 6MU 11-1 1PRU 10-2 Porth 18-3 CE ops en route India 1-4

BS505 3862 M45 CHA FF 13-1-43 6MU 11-1 1PRU 10-2 Porth 18-3 Gib 27-3 C2 ops 7-7 HAL 8 OTU 7-3-44 CAC 12-11-44 recat E 16-11

EN series All PR IV engines specified

EN155 3770 M46 CHA FF 20-12-42 39MU 22-12 Ben 6-2-43 ME 14-3 SOC 31-5-45

EN262 3779 M46 CHA FF 22-12-42 39MU 24-12 Ben 6-2-43 FACB 5-3 HAL Ben 1-7 Ind 3-9 SOC 26-10-44

EN264 3796 M46 CHA FF 30-12-42 39MU 2-1-43 Ben 29-1 ME 27-3 FAC3 11-12

EN386 3918 M45 CHA FF 27-1-43 6MU 2-2 140S TAF 22-2 HAL 27-2-44 SOC 18-5-45

EN387 3948 M45 CHA FF 4-2-43 6MU 5-2 140S TAF 5-5 HAL 19-1-44 SOC 14-5-45

EN388 3953 M45 CHA FF 6-2-43 6MU 9-2 Ben 29-3 10ADU 29-4 SOC 31-5-45

EN389 3718 M46 BEN FF 6-12-42 1PRU Ben 7-12 Porth 31-12 Gib NWA 28-2 SOC 1-3-44

Although official Air Ministry records state that the above production PR IVs were built as such, manufacturer's records indicate that most consisted of the standard F MkV fuselage married to the Type D wing.

Conversions of standard Spitfires to Photo Reconnaissance.

Spitfire FMkI converted to Type C PR MkIII.
K9787, 9834, 9906, N3111, 3116, 3117, P9307, 9308, 9309, 9310, 9313, 9315, 9384, 9385, 9394, 9426, 9453, 9550, 9561, R6598, 6804, 6805, 6879, 6894, 6900, 6902, 6903, 6905, 6909, 6968, 7020, 7070, 7146, 7147, X4242, 4332, 4333, 4334, 4335, 4383, 4384, 4385, 4386, 4487, 4490, 4491, 4495, 4496, 4497, 4498, 4499, 4500, 4501, 4502, 4503, 4504, 4505, 4538, 4645, 4712, 4832, 4943, 4944, AR241, 259.

Spitfire MkI converted to Type C PR MkV all with Merlin 45 engines in place of the Merlin II or III. Later they were re-designated PR MkIV to bring them into line with true production PR MkIV.
N3111, 3117, 3241, P9550, R6900, 6902, 6905, 7198, X4333, 4334, 4335, 4383, 4384, 4385, 4411, 4491, 4493, 4494, 4497, 4498, 4499, 4500, 4501, 4502, 4503, 4504, 4505, 4538, 4555, 4596.

Spitfire F MkI converted to Type D PR V/IV.
R6910, 7142, X4492.

Spitfire MKI converted to Type F PR MKVI.
P9301, 9385, R6902, 6905, 6909, 7032, 7038, X4492, 4494, 4498,4499, 4501, 4502, 4505

Spitfire F MkV converted to Type PR MkVI.
R7032, 7038.

Spitfire F MkI converted to Type G PR MkVII.
N3113, 3241, P9328, 9505, 9518, 9565, R6910, 6964, 7028, 7059, 7116, 7130, 7139, 7143, 7197, 7211, X4021, 4162, 4333, 4384, 4411, 4555, 4596, 4599, 4600, 4645, 4660, 4672, 4766, 4784, 4786, 4839, 4907, AR234, 235, 239, 242, 244, 245, 257, 258, 260, 261.

Spitfire F MkV converted to Type G PR MkVII.
R7308, 7335.

Apart from a small production batch of PRMkIVs the early photo-reconnaissance Spitfires were conversions of the F MkIs and F MkVs listed. The conversions were spread between the Types A and G. A number of aircraft were converted many times by simple modifications, such as change of engine, armament or camera installation. This is why a number of Spitfires appear in more than one category.

Lost at sea on ss *'Molaja'*; BP912.

LOW LEVEL PHOTOGRAPHY

Early conversions of Spitfires to the PR role were concerned primarily with high altitude photo-reconnaissance and with their camera installations they were ideal for target identification before an attack and for damage assessment afterwards. But as the war progressed the need arose for tactical reconnaissance and that involved low altitude flying. The majority of the original PR Spitfires were unarmed as they relied upon speed to escape interception. At the lower altitudes they were more vulnerable and the term 'dicer' for this type of reconnaissance sortie was most appropriate. The 'dicer' Spitfires had to be able to defend themselves and there was the need for an armed version.

Prototype for the new PR Spitfire was the much modified Mk I L1004, originally converted to F Mk VA standards, and it was despatched to Heston Aircraft on 4 August 1942 for the installation of one F24 5 inch vertical and two F24 14 inch vertical and oblique cameras. It was transferred to Vickers on 10 December for armament and fuel system modifications and when weighed at Worthy Down on the 12th it had a Merlin 32 low altitude engine, a de Havilland propeller, the camera installation as mentioned and four .303 Browning machine guns. The tare weight was 5,085lb, auw 6,351 and with a 30 gallon overload fuel tank 6,642.

It arrived at Boscombe Down in March 1943 for weights and CoG loadings and the weights were tare 5,089lb, service 609, fuel 605, oil 52, auw 6,355. The centre of gravity range was from 7.8in and 8.0in aft; the latter limit was the aircraft in fully loaded condition. It was then put through a series of cooling tests with a temperate radiator similar to that fitted on the F Mk V, and as the tests proved acceptable it was next tested with a tropical radiator. These tests revealed that the tropical unit did not fully meet the dissipation requirements. To reduce temperatures to the stated limitations it was suggested that the aircraft be flown with the radiator flap opened one notch from the minimum drag position. For handling and spinning trials in April L1004 was fitted with an elevator incorporating an enlarged horn balance.

The Type Record 367/1 was issued on 30 September 1943, to be followed by the Certification of Design on 5 October. The Type Record specified the Merlin 32 engine and in the description stated that it covered the Spitfire F Mk VB production converted to PR Mk XIII production by the following modifications – deletion of two cannon guns, provision for cameras, adjustment of military load. The normal auw was quoted as 7,100lb and maximum level speed at 12,500 feet as 297mph. A list of conversions appears at the end of this chapter and it will be noticed that while the majority of conversions were to Mk V airframes P8784 was an ex Mk IIA and the last four R7308, X4021, 4660 and 4766 were all from PR VII, these originally converted from F Vs.

A total of 25 airframes were converted and the first – AD354 – entered service at Benson on 21 April 1943. They served with Nos 4, 400, 541 and 542 (PR) Squadrons, and twelve saw limited service with the Royal Navy from shore bases. All were withdrawn from service as obsolete in early 1945.

OFFICIAL REPORTS ON PR XIII

Boscombe Down, March 1943. L1004. Merlin 32. Prototype PR Mk XIII. Cooling tests with tropical radiator fitted. Oil cooling met requirements for tropical conditions under all flight conditions. Coolant temperatures on normal rating climb above limitations but can be brought within by climbing at an initial speed 20mph higher than the best climbing speed. On combat rating climb to 35,000ft the coolant temperatures failed to meet requirements. Coolant temperature failed to meet requirements for maximum cruising flight.

Seclin, nr Lille, France, 18 November 1939. Flt Lt. M Longbottom prepares for the first operational PR flight by a Spitfire, serial N3071. Target was Aachen, Germany.

Another PR variant (unknown) photographed in the Middle East with Aboukir filter.

Early conversion PR IV in pink 'Camotint'.

BP888 was a true production PR IV(T) which was originally seconded to Benson in February 1942 and is seen here at Boscombe Down in May 1943 for use as a trials aircraft. It was Cat E in November 1944.

BP932, a PR IV(T), is run up with a ground crew astride the tail unit. It was delivered to Malta in December 1942 and carries the dark, royal-blue PR finish applied to such aircraft in the area. Stripe under wing is a tape attached to the pitot head indicating that the head cover is in position.

An early PR Mk IV in the Middle East with the air filter modified by No 103 MU Aboukir. In addition to the 'Aboukir' filter the Spitfire had a filler applied to allow application of a smooth, gloss finish (despite the patchy colours shown here); extended wing tips and a specially tuned engine. It was used by 680 Squadron for sorties over Salonika.

Boscombe Down, March 1943. **L1004.** Climb and level speed performance and position error correction.

The performance results are summarised below:

	Normal rating	Combat rating
Max rate of climb (ft/min)	3780 at 7400 ft	4920 at 3000 ft
Rate of climb at 10,000ft (ft/min)	3350	3690
20,000	1900	2140
30,000	740	890
Time to 10,000ft (min)	2.7	2.25
20,000	6.6	5.8
30,000	14.8	12.9
Service ceiling (ft)	35,800	37,000
Estimated absolute ceiling (ft)	36,800	38,000
Max level speed (mph)	349 at 5400 ft	
Estimated (mph) speed	322	
Max speed 10,000ft (mph)	345	
20,000ft	335	

Spitfire PR Mk XIII

Leading particulars as for PR Mk IV with the following variations.

Engines. Merlin 32 1,645hp at 3,000rpm @ 2,500ft with + 18 lb boost. Coffman cartridge starting. Negative G carburetter.

Propeller/s. de Havilland Type 5/39 3-blade CS VP.

Fuel capacity. Upper fuselage 48 gals, lower 37. Total 85. Plus overload tanks of 30, 45 or 90 gals.

Armour. Bullet proof w/s with special gunsight consisting of a reflector sight graticule stencilled on the inner surface and a bead sight on top of the fireproof bulkhead.

Armament. A wing. Late production models with 350rpg. Production aircraft had four outer guns only.

Radio. TR.1133.

Performance.

Max speed @ 24,000ft 327mph, @ 20,000 335, @ 10,000 **345.5, @ 4,000 342, @ 2,000 332. Rpm at all speeds 3,000, boost ranged from + 1.4lb @ 24,000ft to + 18 @ 2,000.**

Rate of climb

height	mins	rate of climb ft/min	mph
2000	.55	3780	164
4000	1.05	3780	169
8000	2.1	3680	157
10,000	2.7	3350	154
20,000	6.65	1900	190.5
34,000	23.05	300	207.5

Estimated service ceiling 35,000; absolute 36,800. Rpm at **all heights and speeds 2,850; boost from + 12 @ 2,000 to – 5.5** @ 34,000. The above data is for the Merlin @ normal rating. At combat rating they started at

2000	.4	4920	164	3000rpm +18
to				
34,000	19.2	430	210.5	3000rpm –4.7

Camera installation. G as per PR Mk VII.

Weights. Tare lb 5085, take off 6353.5, max permissible 6500. Plus 30 gal o/ld tank 291, fibre tank 256; 45 gal 404, 90 gal 768. Tare weight with F 24 oblique 6385.5.

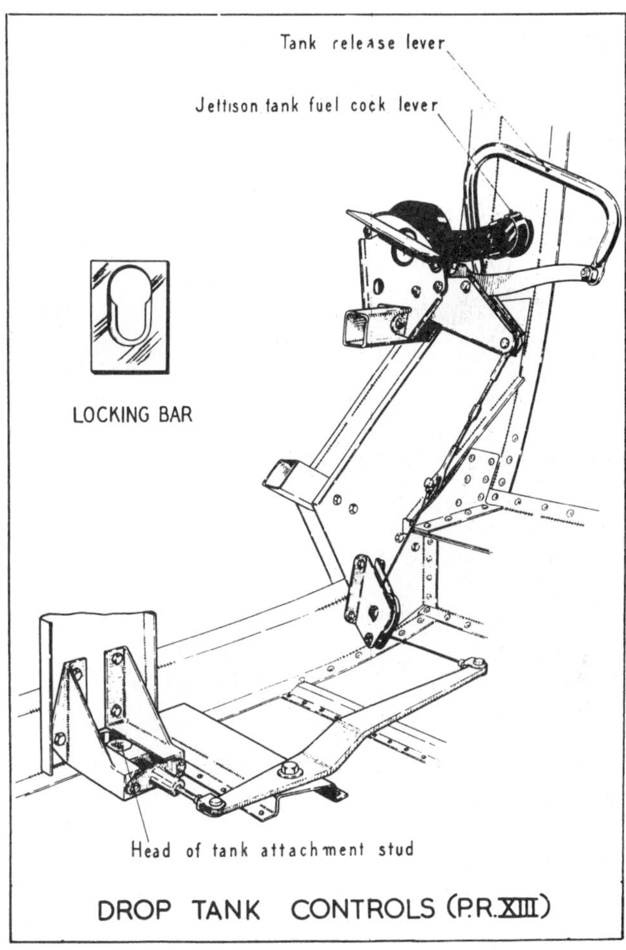

DROP TANK CONTROLS (P.R.XIII)

L1004, the ubiquitous ex Mk I, was converted to the prototype PR Mk XIII, below and page 252.

L1004 in its prototype PR Mk XIII guise.

"A NEW NAME IS JUSTIFIED"

It was in September 1941 that the problem of the numerous Spitfire versions forced both the Air Ministry and Supermarine to give urgent attention to the subject of designations to differentiate the various types. In fact, before the advent of the PR conversions it had been considered that Mark numbers were needed only for the most obvious design changes, such as the Mk I, built at Woolston, the Mk II built at Castle Bromwich, the Mk III Superiority Spitfire and the Mk IV Griffon. They were logical and orderly and the sub-designations, both prefix and suffix, were not considered.

But, the photo-reconnaissance conversions complicated matters as they were a mix of the Mks I, II and V, plus the true production aircraft. The Air Ministry wrote to Vickers saying – "It is necessary to decide if the conversion of 160 Spitfires for PRU duties be re-designated with new mark numbers, or they could be renamed, and it is considered in view of the differences (in camera, armament and fuel installations) a new name is justified. Up to the present, 19 September 1941, there is no separate contract for production of the PRU version, which will be obtained by conversion of the Mark V already on order. Up to the present they have been ordered on an ad hoc basis under direct supervision of the RAE.

"The firm (Vickers) feel it unnecessary to give the type a new name as it has, hitherto, been known by them as PRU Spitfire Type D. It is clear that some differentiation must be made and the following should be considered – (1) confirmation of the firm's unofficial designation PRU Type D; (2) a new mark number e.g. Spitfire Mk IX; (3) a new name. We can see no reason for the retention of the qualification Type D. Perhaps we could apply the designation Spitfire V (PRU)."

Vickers replied on 22 September and were of the opinion that Spitfire V (PRU) was the sensible solution for, as they argued – "It makes sense to have the role designation after the basic type Mk number". They also asked what mark number the General Purpose Spitfire with Merlin 61 (this was the prototype Mk III N3297, now with the new engine) would have, and confirmation that the new machine with Griffon engine (DP845, Mk IV) would not have a Spitfire mark number but be renamed. The Air Ministry replied to this – "It is agreed that the Griffon Spitfire should have a new name, but until decided we should continue to use the present designation Spitfire Mk IV. The General Purpose Spitfire, Merlin 61, without pressure cabin, will be called Mk VIII".

The date was now 7 October 1941 and the Air Ministry and Vickers' proposals, if adopted, would have resulted in the Mks I, II and III, a new name or Mk number for the PRU conversions and a new name for the Griffon Spitfire. But, a new name for the latter would have complicated matters still further for the Observer Corps had been advised about it and were informed it was to be called Spitfire. Two days later another Air Ministry letter stated – "PRUs will not be given a new Mark number but will be known by their normal Mark number with PRU after this, i.e. Spitfire V (PRU)". This would have resulted in Spitfire I (PRU), Spitfire II (PRU) and the Mk V as previously mentioned.

It appeared that the Vickers' viewpoint had prevailed but, not so, for on 12 December 1941 the Air Ministry wrote again to Vickers saying – "We should designate the existing PRU Spitfires as follows: Type C (PR Mk III), Type D (PR Mk IV), Type F (PR Mk VI), Type G (PR Mk VII) and Type H (PR Mk VIII). The next variations will be known as the Spitfire PR Mk IX". It seemed to be a most extraordinary mixture but must be borne in mind that camera, fuel and armament installations confused ordering of spares. On 24 January 1942 it was decided that in order to avoid confusion fighter Spitfires would be distinguished by the prefix F before the Mark number, i.e. Spitfire F Mk I, Spitfire F Mk II, etc, and this designation was to be retrospectively applied to all fighter Spitfires in service (and to other types, it is assumed). Vickers did query the reason for the prefix and were informed that the major reason for the prefix, instead of a suffix as suggested by Vickers, was that the former would act as an instantaneous recognition of the aircraft's role. This, it was claimed, would prevent a fighter being seconded to a bomber squadron. This ruling did make sense when applied to an aircraft such as the Mosquito, but apart from the PR variants seemed rather superfluous when applied to the Spitfire.

However, the designation muddle did not rest there for in early 1942 the decision was taken to develop a photographic reconnaissance version of the forthcoming F Mk VII, and in April the designation PR Mk X was allocated. At the same time the designation PR Mk XI was allocated to the PR version of the General Purposes Spitfire, the F Mk VIII. It was immediately pointed out that this would cause some confusion as the designation PR Mk VIII had been allocated to the Type H PR, one of the conversions of the F Mk V airframe. The result would have been two Mk VIII Spitfires, the F and PR. Also, through an oversight, the next conversion of the F Mk V to the PR role was to be called the PR IX.

There was a pause for thought and finally the Air Ministry decided that the PR Mk X variant of the F Mk VII would be acceptable, but the designations PR Mk VIII and PR Mk IX were abandoned. The PR Mk XI variant of the F Mk VII would also be abandoned in order that the Spitfire Mark numbers ran in some semblance from the F Mk I to the PR Mk VII; this is to be followed by the F Mk VII (no outcry about this Mk number), F Mk VIII and F Mk IX to the PR Mk X. Designating the Spitfires was not an easy task, as will be shown in later chapters. Finally, the few Spitfire Mk Is with two 20mm cannon and four .303 machine guns would not be allocated a retrospective mark number. It was not a serious matter for they would all be converted to F Mk VBs.

There it rested; through trial and error a workable system had evolved, but it was to be raised all over again, beginning with the Spitfire F Mk VI high altitude fighter. The Air Ministry issued the designation F Mk VIA for the variant with the 'A' wing; F Mk VIB with the 'B' wing and F Mk VIC with the universal wing on 11 July 1941. They then attempted to deal with the Spitfire F Mk VII in a similar manner, but as it had a new wing and different armament it was to be designated the F Mk VIIC. Vickers objected to this for they considered that a pressure cabin fighter should be designated to indicate its role, but the Air Ministry thought it was also a matter of ordering spares and the single designation would be sufficient for this.

Vickers then asked that the designation F Mk XIX be reserved for the developed Spitfire with the Mk VIII fuselage and Griffon engine. The Air Ministry would not agree for, as they pointed out, Vickers appeared to be in-filling between the F Mk XII and F Mk 20. Vickers was instructed to call the modified aeroplane F Mk 22, but it eventually became the F Mk XIV.

The Air Ministry now appeared to be inventing new suffixes for every Spitfire variant for, almost as an afterthought, they ordered that all fighters operating in the European war theatre were to carry the suffix 'Temp', for temperate fighter, and the tropicalised versions 'Trop'. This attempt to zonalise fighters failed for inevitably the suffix of both types was shortened to 'T' and confusion was widespread. Eventually 'Temp' and 'Trop' were abandoned and the 'T' suffix applied only to tropicalised fighters.

It was now 1943 and a whole range of sub designations was issued. Merlin engines with cropped supercharger impellers on the F Mk V was to result in the Spitfire LF Mk VA ('A' wing); LF Mk VB ('B' wing); LF Mk VC (universal wing). There was even a 'Special Duty', High Altitude, Mk V, a VD, VPC (pressure cabin?). In March 1944 the Spitfire F Mk IX with two cannons and .5in Brownings was to carry the designation LF Mk IX(G), this particular suggestion coming from the RAF maintenance units as a guide to ordering spare parts for this variant. The Air Ministry was very firm here and instructed all units that the suffix 'E' be applied for that version. It did appear that everyone concerned with the Spitfire waited until a new variant appeared before thinking seriously about a designation.

In an exchange of letters with Vickers beginning 27 January 1944 the Air Ministry suggested that – "In view of the imperative need of having a definite understanding as to the many new types of Spitfire and Seafire in design stage the following mark numbers will be applied from today. All rear view versions up to the Mk 21 to have the suffix RV. F Mk 23 (upturned leading edge version of the Mk 21); marks 24 to 39 to be reserved also for Mk 21 developments. Marks 41 to 49 reserved for naval versions of the F 21. Marks 51 to 59 reserved for PRU versions of Mk 21. Marks 61 to 99 reserved for any future developments of the Mk 21. Mark 101 Type 371 Production Merlin with five blade propeller. Mark 102 Type 371 Production Merlin with contra-props. Marks 103 to 109 reserved for future developments of the Type 371 with Merlin. Mark 112 Type 371 Production with Griffon and five blade propeller. Marks 114 to 119 reserved for further Griffon versions, and 121 to 129 reserved for Type 371 naval variants. Marks 131 to 139 reserved for variants of the Type 371 airframe converted to PRU duties, and the 'new name' for the Spitfire with laminar flow wing has been decided on. It will be called 'Valiant' (F 24)". It is assumed that the zero numbers, i.e., 40, 50, 60 etc, were reserved for prototype aircraft. "Three blocks of Mark numbers will be necessary for the Supermarine 'new name' and the following are recommended: (a) Marks 1-9 Merlin engined 'new name' and developments; (b) Marks 10-19 Griffon engined 'new name' and developments; (c) Marks 50 to 59 naval version of the 'new name', these applied to variants of the Valiant". The allocation of a block of mark numbers for PRU versions was not accepted and only the role letters were to be applied to modified airframes of a standard variant, i.e. PR XI for the F IX modified airframe.

Vickers replied to this letter and asked why their 'new' aeroplane could not still be called Spitfire, and as a result a meeting was arranged in order to discuss the situation in depth, this meeting taking place at Hursley Park on 11 February 1944. It was agreed that the naval version of the new aeroplane must have a new name, but none was suggested, and eventually the land based fighter was to be called Spiteful and the naval version Seafang because of the problems of identification. Vickers then asked that they be allocated blocks of ten mark numbers in advance of orders so that drawings and future designs could be identified in the offices and works. This was thought by the Air Ministry and MAP to be an extravagant use of mark numbers.

Joseph Smith was to receive a letter on 14 March informing him that Spitfires in the design and prototype stages were to be designated as follows: Griffon engined Types Mks 21 to 30; Merlin engined Types 31 to 40. The new laminar flow wing fighter, with Merlin Marks 1 to 9; with Griffon Marks 10 to 19; naval versions Marks 50 to 59.

In the event all the higher mark numbers after 24 were never used for the Spitfire and 'new name' variants as the jet age had begun and Mitchell's fighter, then eight years old, was to be replaced with more modern types. No mention was ever made of other Spitfire marks, such as the PR XIII, F Mk XIV, etc, but the designations must have been allocated on an automatic basis. The Seafire designations were a great problem for the first variants were known as the IB, IIC and III. A mark IV was proposed, but with the advent of the Griffon engine they jumped from III to XV, from XVII to the 47 with gaps in between in no apparent, logical order.

THE HIGH FLYERS

"At a meeting held at the Royal Aircraft Establishment, Farnborough, on 17 February 1941, the Air Ministry asked that a Spitfire should be provided with a pressure cabin capable of maintaining a differential pressure of 1lb per square inch at 40,000ft. The Marshall blower was to be used, and it was agreed that the sliding hood could be eliminated, provided that arrangements were made to allow the new hood to be jettisoned".

This was the opening statement of a report of this meeting and it determined the aspirations of the Air Staff of its need for a high altitude fighter, but it did not agree with the minutes of a similar meeting held at the Air Ministry on 31 August 1938. Then it was stated it was not practical to produce a pressure cabin fighter and pilots would have to use a suit. This thinking was in line with contemporary research, started in the 1920s when it was concluded: "If it (an aeroplane) were required to go much above 40,000ft it would be necessary to enclose the airman in an airtight dress, somewhat similar to an underwater diving dress but capable of resisting an internal pressure of, say, 130mm.Hg. This dress would be so arranged that even in a complete vacuum the contained oxygen would still have a pressure of 130mm.Hg. There would be no limit to the physiological height obtainable". The author John Scott Haldane, an American, had already successfully exposed a fellow American, balloonist Mark Ridge, in a modified diving suit to 84,000ft (17mm.Hg. abs).

By 1939 the Air Ministry had given the go ahead for the first development of a pressure cabin aircraft, for it was recognised that pressure suits were not very practical. The RAF's Medical Section was aware that exposure to low atmospheric pressure decreases the oxygen content of the blood and consequently dulled the senses, and the introduction of an oxygen mask into the new RAF fighters coming into service was the first essential for high flying. Initially the height at which it was considered safe to operate effectively without oxygen was 15,000ft. Breathing pure oxygen would begin at 42,000ft. Hence the 17 February meeting.

A report to the Aerodynamics Sub-Committee by Rolls-Royce on 29 July 1940 contained detailed flight trials with K9788, the second production F Mk I, and it was concerned with the raising of full throttle height of the Merlin II. Another Spitfire Mk I, N3171, Merlin III, was used at Boscombe Down for similar trials. The Spitfire could reach the desired altitude, but the pilot had to wear a close fitting oxygen mask.

To return to the report of February, it continued—"A Spitfire (R7120) completed and ready for flying was taken from the Mk V production line partially dismantled and two airtight bulkheads introduced into the fuselage. The forward bulkhead was fitted as close as possible to the rear of the petrol tanks with the rear immediately behind the rear perspex window at Frame 12. Seals and glands for controls were developed and tested using mainly Linatex rubber sheet. A specially designed, removable hood of $^{5}/_{16}$in Perspex clamped down onto a sponge rubber seal was fitted and the pilot's door blanked off, together with the rails carrying the normal sliding hood.

"A piping system for incoming air was introduced into the cockpit and it had small holes to project air on to the hood and windscreen. A control valve designed for a maximum pressure of 2lbs sq in was installed. All seams and joints, bolts, etc, were made airtight by painting them with a special rubber bituminous compound known as 'Trinasco'. Flight tests were carried out at 25,000ft to 40,000ft.

"Some difficulty was experienced in making the cabin completely airtight, particularly in the inaccessible corners, but the required degree of sealing was eventually attained. During flight trials pilots reported a great increase in mental and physical effort. The Marshall blower provided an air temperature of over 60° resulting in a cabin temperature of 8°C with an outside temperature of minus 55°C.

"The weather conditions during the flight tests were excellent, brilliant cloudless summer days, and the distribution of air from the blower over the transparent areas eliminated the misting and freezing usually encountered at this altitude".

The report concluded that pressurising of a Spitfire cockpit presented no insurmountable difficulties, the advantage greatly impressing the test pilots. Some slight alteration in design would be required of the glazing, together with modifications of hood attachment. Two altimeters were fitted to the aircraft, one connected to the outside and indicating true height and the other indicating the apparent height in the cabin. The pilot complained of distortion due to curvature of the hood sides and a new hood with straight sides and thicker Perspex was fitted. The engine, a Merlin 47, tended to surge at 38,000ft and new carburetter jets cured this.

X4942 was originally built as a Mk I and converted to the second prototype Spitfire HF Mk VI by Vickers Armstrong in July 1941. It is pictured here at Boscombe Down in the following September.

X4942 went to Vickers for various modifications needed to transform it into a high altitude fighter, including a revised cockpit area with perforated air discharge pipes. See also page 260.

Total estimated cost was £2,000 under Contract ACN/790/C23 (C) which called for a Mk V Spitfire modified to accept a differential pressure cabin and with a Merlin 61 installed R7120 was despatched to Farnborough for trials in June and it made its first flight on 24 August. Problems were experienced with the engine with the result that a new supercharger had to be fitted a few weeks into the trials programme. On 13 June a Supermarine Report, number 3116, outlined details of a production F Mk VI powered by a Merlin 60 driving a four blade Rotol Jablo propeller. The design incorporated an extended cowling to accept the longer engine; a Mk II radiator cowl under each wing; a larger oil tank; wing leading edge Mareng bags for additional fuel; the Universal wing with extended tips; a fuselage with strengthened centre section and an enlarged tail unit. The converted Mk III—N3297—appeared with corresponding modifications.

Three days later a meeting at Vickers, Oxford, was attended by executives from MAP, Rolls-Royce, Rotols and Supermarine in an attempt to formulate the entire Spitfire production programme, with particular emphasis on the pressure cabin model. It was decided to appoint an overall controller for the latter and R. C. Pilsbury was recruited. Supermarine proposed that all intermediate engines between the Merlin 45 and 60 be dropped from the programme, and also production of the Mk VI should commence in January 1942, with a gradual build-up to replace all previous Merlin engined Spitfires.

As the Air Ministry wanted to have two squadrons (60 aircraft) of the new type in service before that date Supermarine proposed that they could be produced by November or December; would have to be virtually hand-built prototypes; a Merlin 46 replacing the 60; a VB wing with extended tips, and no pressure cabin or cooling changes. Mr Hives, of Rolls-Royce, agreed in principle with the proposals and said the Merlin 48 would be dropped. He also pointed out that although Supermarine had planned to start production of the Mk VI in order to deliver the first models in January 1942, the Rolls programme for production Merlin 60 engines was not expected to begin until March that year. If the Air Ministry insisted with their demand for two squadrons of Mk VI aircraft, they would have to accept the Supermarine proposals for a Mk V conversion with the Merlin 46 or a short run of aircraft with Merlin 47s. A prototype of the Mk V conversion could be made ready for trials in a short period of time, and as a bonus a hybrid Merlin 45 with a Merlin XII crankcase would provide a cabin blower drive for pressurisation.

At a previous meeting of the same participants the Air Ministry had also stated that their aim was an introduction of the Mk VI powered by the Merlin 48, which was a Merlin 47 with intercoolers. This, too, had to be abandoned in order to concentrate on the forthcoming Merlin 60. Finally, it was also agreed that a bomber version of the Spitfire Mk VI with a Merlin 60 would be produced. Why the RAF would want to have a pressure cabin, high altitude fighter capable of carrying bombs is inexplicable. After the dust had settled it was agreed that Vickers would be responsible for the production of the first 350 examples of the Mk VI at Castle Bromwich, with Westland Aircraft taking over as the main contractor.

The two prototypes, R7120 and X4942, were converted by the RAE and Supermarine respectively. R7120 was converted from a Mk I and X4942 converted from a Mk VA (ex converted Mk I) with all its modifications completed by Supermarine on 26 June. The first to fly was X4942 on 4 July by J. K. Quill at Eastleigh with its hood off, followed on the same day by a second flight with the hood on to 25,000ft. The following day it was flown to Worthy Down reaching a height of 38,000ft.

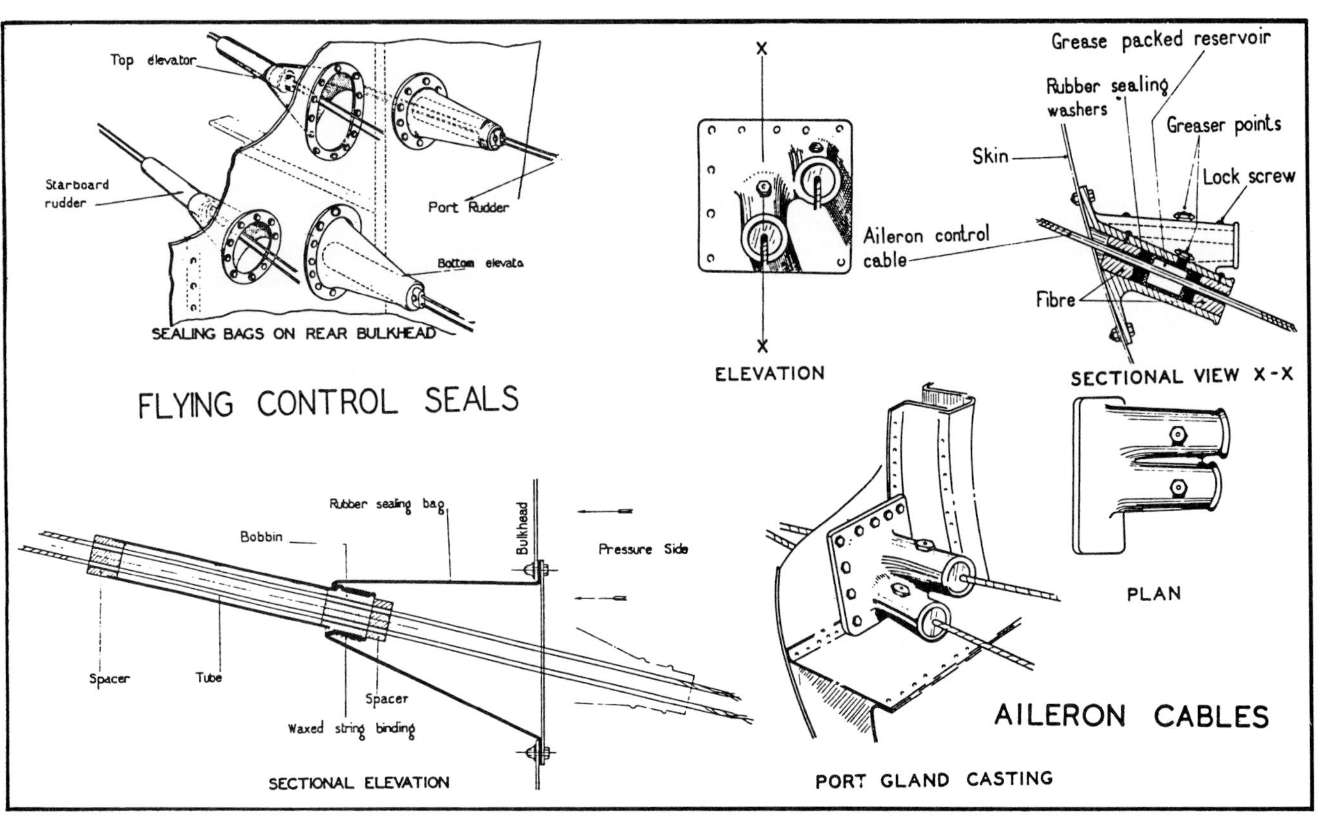

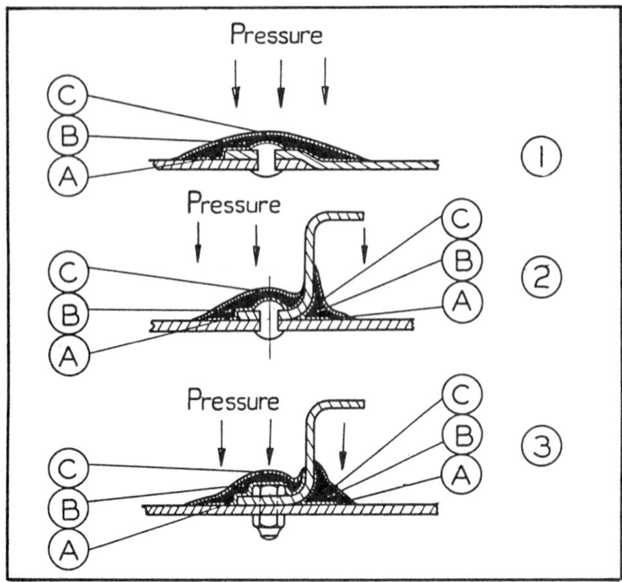

Typical Trinasco treatment to seal aircraft. A-Trinasco T.1 (medium); B-Trinasco T.2 (thick); C-Trinasco T.3 (thin).

Marshall blower installation (ribbed cylinder) and air cleaner (immediately to the rear). Second view is of the external air intake.

Balance tab and large horn on X4942's aileron. Trials at Boscombe Down April/May 1943.

R7120 first flew from the RAE on 25 August by S/Ldr H. J. Wilson AFC. The following day he reached a height of 35,000ft and on 7 September he achieved 39,500ft. X4942 was fitted with a Merlin 47 driving a four blade dural Rotol propeller. The wings had been 'borrowed' from N3297 and when weighed at Worthy Down on 13 August 1941 it had a tare of 5,211lb, and an auw of 6,610. To avoid confusion with other Spitfire types it was known as experimental aircraft No. 152 to the Royal Observer Corps.

Although the Air Ministry was committed to the pressure cabin research it was continuing with the individual pressure suit at the RAF Physiological Laboratory, but only as an interim measure for use at heights over 40,000ft until the pressure cabin Spitfire had completed Service trials and was in normal day-to-day use. Requirements of the suit were that it would provide freedom of movement, adequate vision, reasonable weight, suitable for inflation by a small air compressor, ease of putting on and taking off, not bulky when blown up. The first two prototypes were of a light material in one piece with a zip fastener down the front. Gloves were fingerless apart from the thumb and index finger, and the boots were an integral part. Weight was approximately 8 pounds, with the boots accounting for over half. Suit number three had a clear Perspex dome replacing the original fabric hood and was designed to be detachable.

R7120 was the subject of a Technical Note by the Structural & Mechanical Engineering Dept (SME) at Farnborough in November. The aircraft's fuel tanks for heights above 20,000ft, were pressurised, this being a standard feature on the later marks of Spitfire, and a Westland automatic cabin pressure regulating valve fitted. A specially shaped hood with an internal bullet-proof windscreen was fastened to the fuselage with four, quick release catches. No provision for heating cabin air was available. Flight trials revealed that the fixed hood deadened engine noise and the Merlin surged at high altitudes. On the third test flight it cut out at 35,000ft and the aircraft forced landed at Farnborough. A sliding hood was recommended to aid the pilot when landing.

The following month the aircraft was transferred to Boscombe Down for fuel consumption trials at all altitudes up to 37,300ft, and at high altitude with low rpm and weak mixture speed was 123mph @ 7.5mpg. The second prototype X4942 arrived and was now called a low pressure cabin aircraft. Performance trials consisting mainly of level speeds and climb to 30,000ft with a typical service load (6,550lb) produced a maximum rate of climb of 2,570ft/min up to 18,500ft and a service ceiling of 39,800ft. With weak mixture this was raised to 40,500ft at a maximum speed of 262mph. A duct was fitted between the radiator and under wing surface to improve air flow. With a full load little manoeuvring was possible at high altitude.

During December comparative tests with both prototypes were made with each aircraft being fitted in turn with a four blade Rotol and a three blade de Havilland propeller, with the former adding 1,200ft in ceiling over the latter. When fitted with the same propeller X4942 had an advantage of 600ft in height, but this was due to an increased wing span rather than propeller efficiency. R7120 was subjected to full performance and handling trials, and to speed deliveries of production Mk VIs MAP amended a contract for 500 Mk Is (of 19 July 1940) to cover construction of 100 examples of the pressure cabin variant, for which Rolls-Royce was to produce 100 Merlin 45 (Plus) Special engines. These aircraft were initially called Special Duty F Mk Vs and first delivery was requested for June 1942. Certification of Design was issued for the prototype X4952 (Contract 790/C, 23(c)), with a similar certificate for the production Type 350 with the designation Spitfire F Mk VI/P.I.

Weight was still the problem and Joseph Smith agreed that the engine mounting could be lightened and an investigation would be made into substituting magnesium for duralumin for the wing fillets, engine header tank, oil tank, ailerons, tailwheel doors and undercarriage fairings. A thinner engine cowling of 20 gauge material would be made up for trials and provision made for construction of a 12 gallon capacity elektron oil tank. The wing attachment bolts and spar flanges would be similar to those of the Griffon Spitfire so that the Griffon wings could be installed on the Mk VI fuselage. Gun tubes were to be reduced in thickness.

The weighing and CoG determination of the first production Mk VI (AB176) took place at Worthy Down on 21 December 1941 and with the Merlin 47 it had a tare of 5,181lb and an auw of 6,768. BR298, the first VI with a four blade Rotol dural propeller was weighed on 28 April 1942 and the tare had risen to 5,227lb; auw without overload tank 6,794, and with 30gal overload tank 7,085. Early production VIs with Merlin 47 could not have the universal wing as the strengthened wing spars were not ready in time, but aircraft with Merlin 61s did have it.

The first Mk VI accident occurred on 27 May 1942 when BR173 of No. 616 Squadron was leading a small formation. The formation had climbed to 16,000ft when one of the aircraft developed engine trouble and the pilot informed his leader that he proposed breaking formation and land. He received no acknowledgement of his message, the last communication from the leader having been received on the climb at 8,000ft. The remaining aircraft followed the leader into a diving turn to starboard, the speed of the dive increasing rapidly. There was a considerable cloud layer and the other Spitfire pilots decided to break formation, the leader diving out of sight into the cloud layer. It crashed near Welton, Lincolnshire, and ground witnesses said it had appeared below cloud cover at about 5,000ft with both wings missing. The pilot did not bale out and was killed, the fuselage caught fire on impact and burnt out. The tail unit had also broke off in the air and was found near the fuselage, but the wings were discovered some considerable distance away from the main wreckage. Upon inspection it was found that the primary failure occurred in the starboard wing which had failed under heavy load. The port wing broke off forwards at the root and the complete tail unit came away at the rear fuselage joint. Wheelwell strengthening had not been incorporated. Very little remained of the fuselage and it appears probable that the pilot had lost consciousness before the crash. The aft skin near the wheelwell was the first portion to fail.

Although the high altitude Spitfire was adequate for the role it was designed for its major failing was lack of a sliding hood. Before take off the hood had to be locked into position, having to be removed for pilot entry and exit. It could be jettisoned in flight, but in general pilots felt uneasy about the system and a sliding hood had to be perfected. Malcolm Aircraft had a factory at Slough, Buckinghamshire, producing sub-assemblies such as the Malcolm hood for the Spitfire, plus a small, experimental unit at White Waltham Aerodrome, near Maidenhead, Berkshire. Mr Marcelle Lobelle had been conducting trials with a version of the Malcolm hood for pressurised aircraft and the Air Ministry gave instructions for

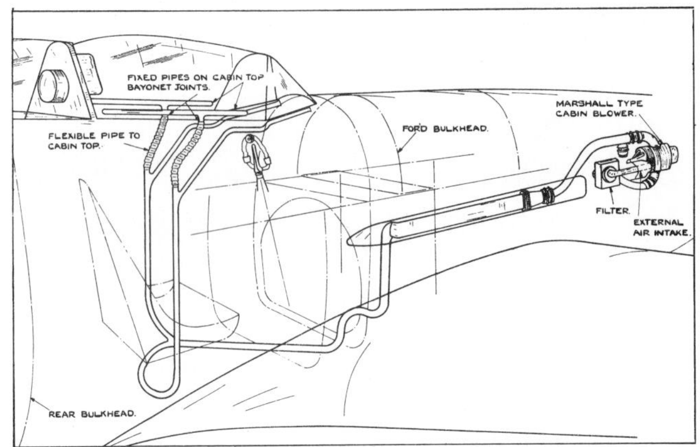

Schematic of the original pressure feed system to the cabin as installed on R7120.

On production HF VIs the pressure system was modified.

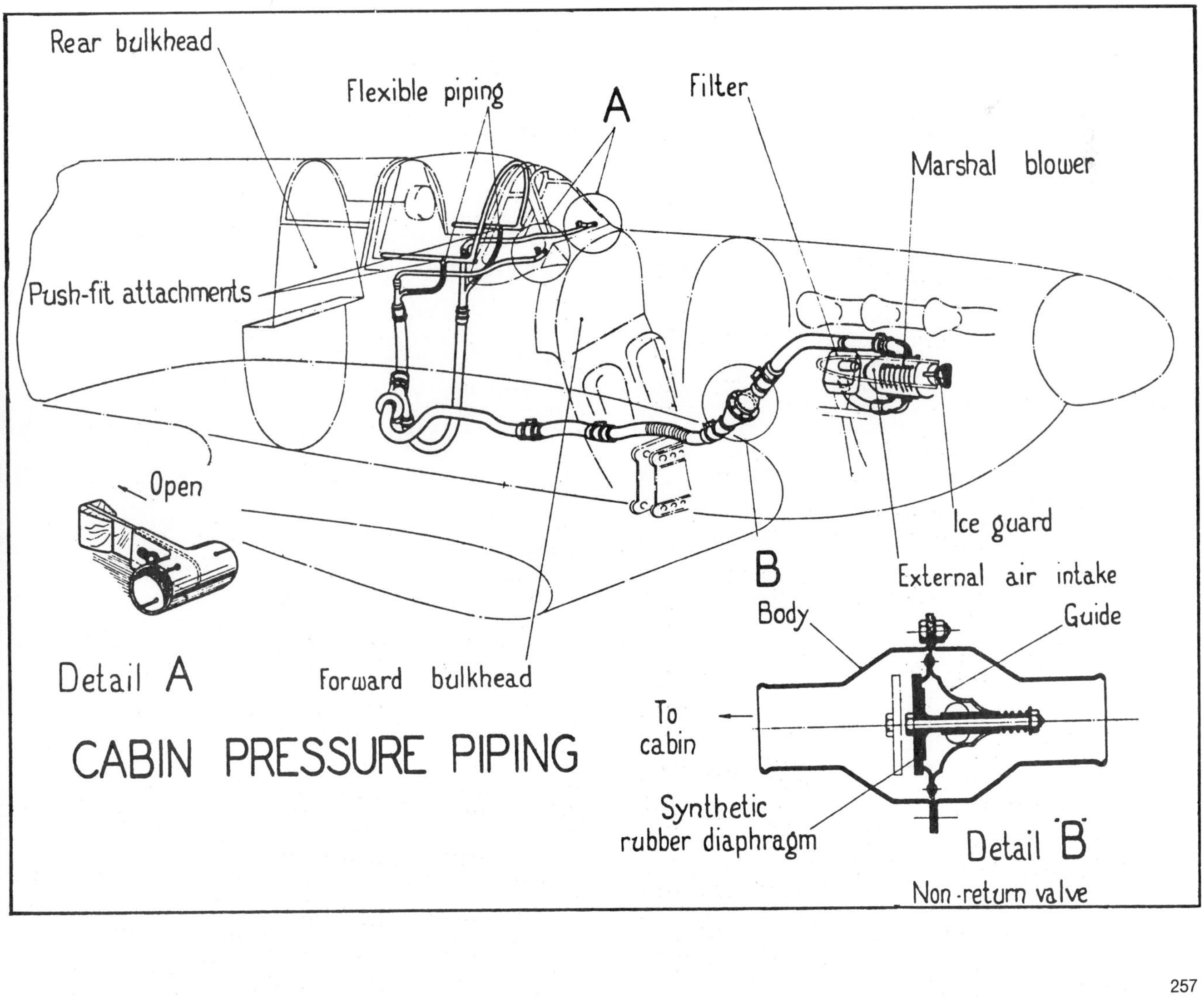

Standard production HF Mk VI of No. 124 Squadron. Cabin air intake is larger than that of prototype.

the work to be speeded up as the need was urgent. This hood eventually became known as the 'Lobelle'.

Mr Backhouse, designer at Malcolms, remembers when the fuselage of R7120, the original prototype Mk VI, arrived at White Waltham with all the rivet holes around the cockpit filled in. Job number 43 called for a pressurised, sliding hood based on the Malcolm and moulded from a single piece of Perspex. The first prototype was heat moulded to a wooden tool and then fitted into a rudder seal along the cockpit sides and at the rear. It was pressurised by a Marshall blower driven by the Merlin engine. One major problem was misting at height and the second development was a double layer hood with the inside bubble made of 5/16in material and the outer from 3/16. In the rear of the hood was a container of silica gel, across which cabin air was blown to remove moisture.

AB534 of No. 616 Squadron. It was transferred to Boscombe Down in May 1942 for cockpit contamination trials.

A second Mk VI, AB528, was modified at White Waltham in conjunction with RAE Farnborough and fitted with a third version of the hood with the direct vision panel on the port side deleted. The rear panel was also removed and replaced by a double layer, permanently sealed and containing dehydrated air. The sliding hood was the 'Lobelle' double layer with the inner layer resisting differential pressure and the interspace of atmospheric pressure. Initially, the interspace was vented to an expansion bag in the rear fuselage by means of rubber piping

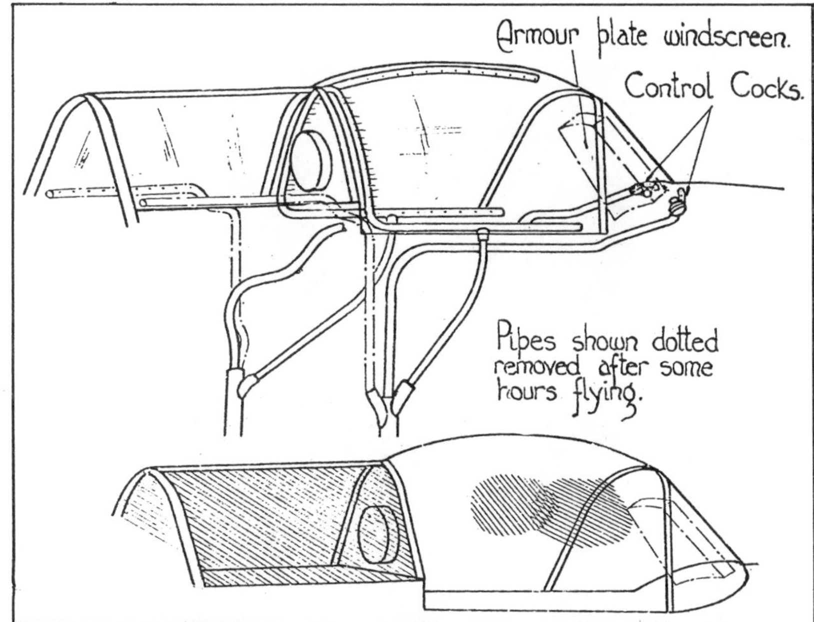

Trials to cure canopy misting were carried out at Boscombe Down and this drawing reveals the affected areas when air feed was changed. Photograph of hood demonstrates the full effect.

passing over pulleys, but this was discarded in favour of the silica gel drier forming the rear fairing of the hood. An inflatable rubber tube of special construction was used to seal the gap between the fuselage and hood, pressure for this tube being taken from a pitot tube inserted into the port air distribution tube inside the cockpit. From the tube a small pipe led to the seal via a tap which had two positions – pressure on and pressure off.

The hood jettisoning arrangement consisted of a powerful pre-loaded spring which when released forced the retaining rails outwards on their hinges, leaving the hood free. This spring was operated by pulling a knob on the instrument panel or pulling a flush fitting ring on the outside of the fuselage in the event of an emergency on the ground. It was additional to the normal release button on top of the mirror bracket. The small Vickers ventilator was removed and replaced by a larger unit, and the hand operated pressure control valve was replaced by a Westland automatic valve. A spill valve was thought unnecessary. Spraying of the supercharger air on to the hood and rear transparent panels was discontinued, the whole of the blower air being brought forward in the existing pipes and directed on to the windscreen and quarter panels. The taps at the forward ends of the pipes were retained.

Flight trials to check operation of the hood at various speeds and altitudes were started and as a result modifications had to be incorporated. Additional rollers were fitted and larger handles installed to the hood operating catch. To reduce back pressure on the supercharger, reduce seal pressure and also prevent air from the pipes bouncing from the windscreen into the pilot's eyes, the cabin piping was altered. A 'tee' piece was fitted into each vertical pipe and to enable the pilot to adjust seal pressure in flight four taps were made available. As a result of further flights these taps were fixed in the open position as this minimised back pressure and allowed the cabin seals to last longer. Hood jettisoning worked perfectly and during trials the unit would lift as soon as the pilot pulled the release knob, rising vertically to clear the radio mast and rudder, as shown in the photographs on page 264.

The F Mk VI was originally intended for high altitude interception of German aircraft over England, but five were shipped to the Middle East (BS106, 124, 134, 149 and one unidentified) in October 1942 to reinforce the modified high altitude Mk Vs of No. 252 Wing. The modified aeroplanes were more successful than the new Mk VIs, but only because the Ju86 was then able to fly at 50,000ft plus. The final production **Mk VI, EN189, left the production line in November 1942 and was sent to Worthy Down for weighing and CoG determination. It had a tare of 5,236lb and an auw of 6,803. Most Mk VIs spent their days after withdrawal from the RAF as trainers, with armament and pressurisation removed and the extended wing tips replaced by standard Mk I units.**

OFFICIAL REPORTS ON Mk VI

Farnborough November 1941. R7120. Pressurising of Spitfire cabin.

Boscombe Down 11 November 1941. R7120. F VI (converted Mk I) Merlin 47. Fuel consumption trials at all altitudes. Results indicated that the aircraft was operating at a higher specific fuel consumption than at the lower. Consumption was 32.5gal/hr.

Boscombe Down 1 December 1941. X4942. F VI (converted Mk I) Merlin 47. Performance tests with four blade Rotol Jablo **propeller. With an auw of 6,550lb and wide span wings (40ft 5in) the maximum speed was 350mph @ 30,000ft; climb 1,310ft/min** @ the same height. Service ceiling 40,500ft.

Boscombe Down 4 December 1941. X4942 and R7120. Comparative performance with three and four blade propellers.

	X4942		R7120	
	4B	3B	4B	3B
Max speed @ 30,00ft	350	350	342	—
@ 40,000	264	265	—	—
Rate of climb ft/min 10,000ft	2570	2590	2670	2620
38,000	320	190	325	100

Modifications to X4942 at Vickers for high altitude work.

Modified canopy with locking toggles.

Detail of canopy locking toggle.

Modified canopy in place. Note the hood vent.

Note lack of cockpit sliding rails.

Linatex sleeves in near bulkhead.

Rear bulkhead showing vacuum valve.

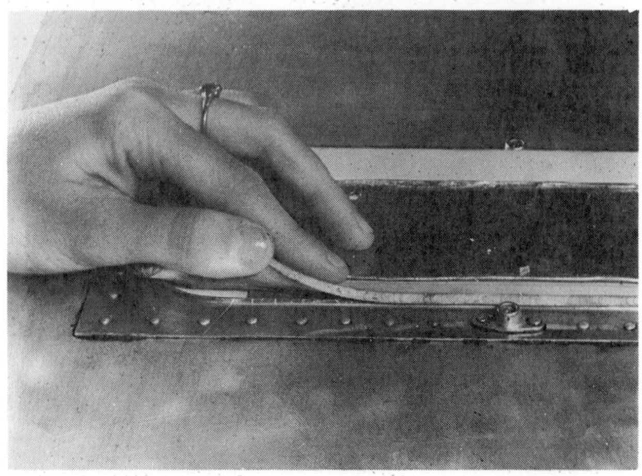

Application of rubber sealing strips.

Air discharge pipe in cockpit.

Views of X4942 at Farnborough, January 1943. Two photographs of the quick release fixture for the vacuum valve on the rear bulkhead. This was controlled by the pilot.

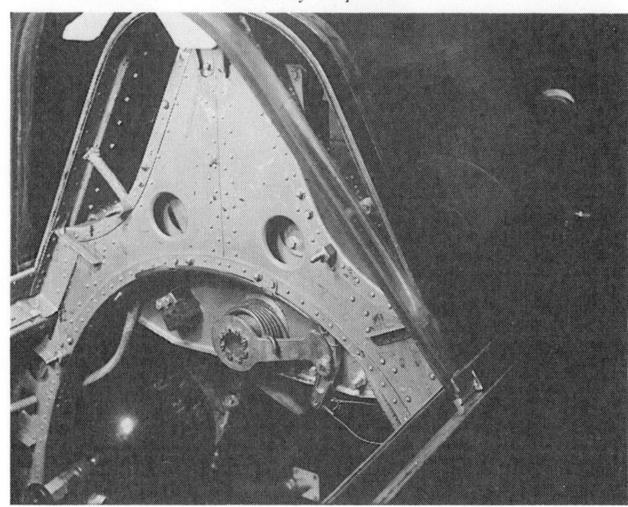

The four bladed prop gave an increase of about 1,200ft on ceiling over that obtained with the three blade. There was little difference in maximum speeds.

Boscombe Down December 1941. R7120. Performance and handling trials. Fitted with 3 and 4 blade propellers.

Boscombe Down March 1942. AB200. Second production F Mk VI. Carbon monoxide contamination tests. Aircraft free of carbon monoxide in flight.

Boscombe Down April 1942. AB200. Weights and CG loadings. Tare (lbs) 5,154, jettison tank 75, overload fuel 216, service load 927, internal fuel 605, oil 52. Take off weight 6,738. Max permissable 7,029.

Boscombe Down 25 June 1942. BR205 & BR287. Carbon

X4942, showing the 'Lobelle' hood and sliding rails.

Double skin construction of the 'Lobelle' hood shows clearly in these views. The Silica gel container is situated behind the pilot's head.

monoxide contamination tests. Tests required to determine extent of contamination after completion of specified flying hours. (55,130,150). Aircraft free at all times.

Boscombe Down 8 July 1942. AB200. Diving Trials. Preliminary tests of production Mk VIs produce violent recovery characteristics from dives and wings were being strained. Six dives made with AB200 and in one full forward trim had to be applied, followed by both hands pushing hard on control column. In spite of this the Spitfire pulled itself out of the dive violently causing pilot to black out. After five more dives examination of wings revealed stress rippling on upper surface near roots and a new pair of wings had to be fitted. It was then discovered that the tailplane shrouds did not conform to the tailplane contour but swept up at the trailing edge masking the flow of air to the trim tab.

Boscombe Down 9 July 1942. BR200, BR205, BR287. Intensive flying trials. BR200 completed 22.45hrs and crashed, to be replaced with BR287, which completed 150hrs. BR205 also completed 150hrs. All were new production Spitfire Mk VI with 'B' wing and negative G carburetter.

Boscombe Down 13 July 1942. AB200. Spinning trials. Spinning characteristics similar to normal Spitfire.

Boscombe Down 13 August 1942. AB200. Longitudinal stability and handling trials. Dynamic stability trials with a typical Service load under level flight and climb conditions at 10,000 and 36,000ft showed the aircraft stable at all conditions with no appreciable change with altitude.

Boscombe Down 16 July 1942. BR302. Handling tests of rogue aircraft. No. 616 Squadron reported that the aircraft was fit for straight and level flying only. Turns produced excessive shuddering and there was an increase of stall speed. It had completed 327 hours flying since manufacture. Buffetting due to poor fit of engine cowling.

Boscombe Down 30 September 1942. BR309. Fuel system tests with normal AVT.40 carburetter. Fuel system satisfactory for English conditions except summer.

Boscombe Down 13 October 1942. BR309. Fuel system tests with Rolls-Royce anti-negative G carburetter.

Farnborough January 1943. AB528. Flight trials of Malcolm pressure sliding hood.

Spitfire HF Mk VI

Boscombe Down 17 April 1943. Tests of ailerons with balance tab and horn balance. This Spitfire fitted with pair of special ailerons which incorporated a geared tab and an inset horn balance. At medium and high speeds the ailerons were moderately light. They overbalanced at low speeds.

Performance. Max speed 264mph @ 40,000; 364 @ 21,500; 300 @ 12,000; 292 @ 4,000. Cruise 132 @ 38,000; 180 @ 30,000 242 @ 20,000. Time to height. 5,000ft 2¼ mins; 10,000 4½; 20,000 8¾; 39,000 34¼. Rate of climb 1,310ft min @ 30,000; 320 @ 38,000; 2,750 @ 10,000. Speed on climb 170mph to 8,000ft; reduced by 2mph for every 100ft thereafter. Service ceiling 40,000ft. Stall flaps and u/c up 73mph, down 64. Landing 85, glide approach 95. Max speed u/c down 160mph, flaps ditto. Range 475 miles @ 150mph. Max dive 450mph.

Weights. Tare 5,227lb; take off 6,797; max permissible 6,850; landing 6,094 (minus 70lb with Jablo prop).

Pressure cabin differential maintained @ 2lb sq in @ 12,000ft. Manual valve operation on early a/c; automatic later models. At operating height air supply turned on in cabin. If red light appeared above 3,500ft oxygen was to be increased and aircraft descend.

Many types of exhaust stubs were experimented with in an effort to stop glare during night flying. The highly modified set was flown on a Mk VI in September 1942, as was the totally enclosed set.

Spitfire HF Mk VI.

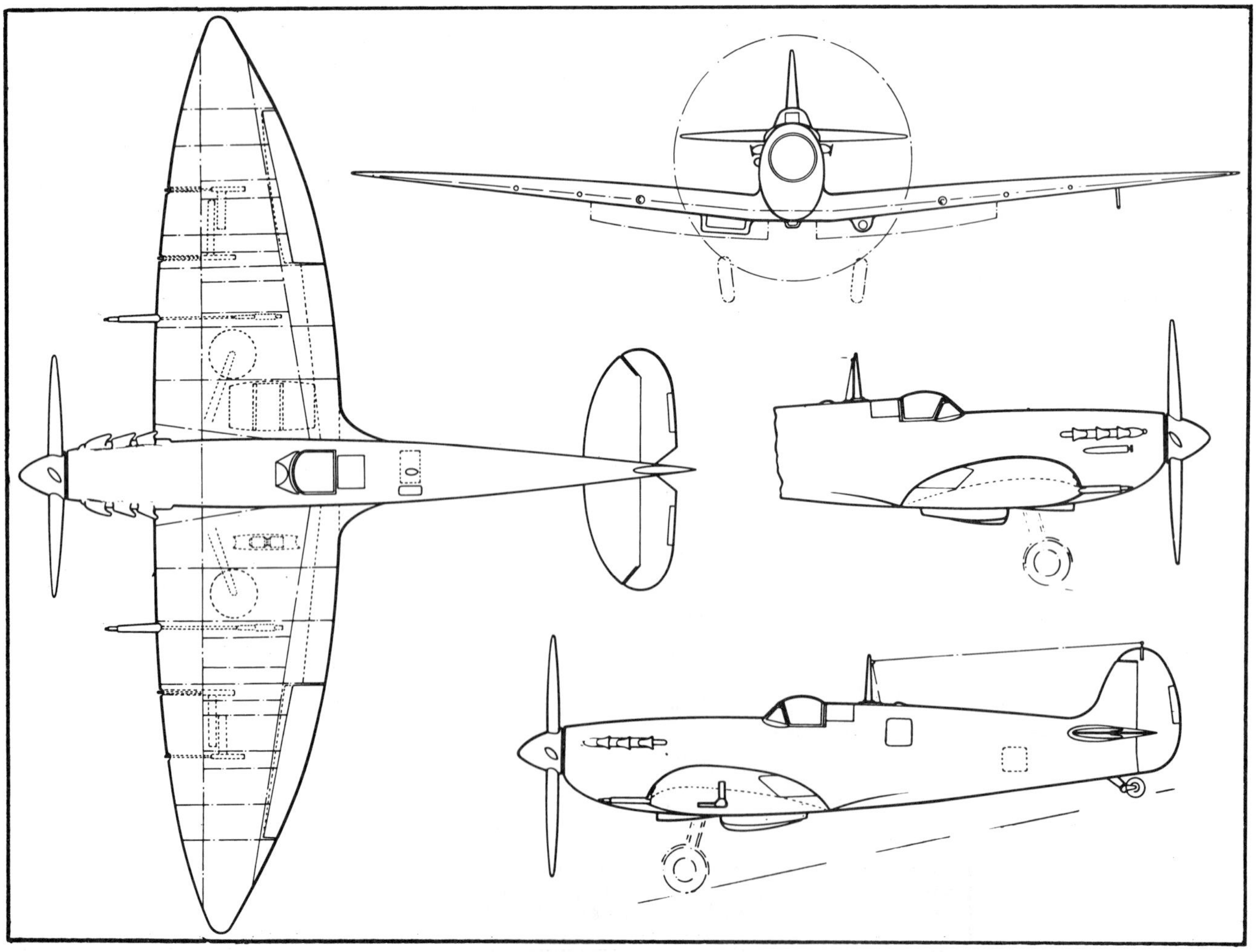

MAIN PLANE CONSTRUCTION
Structure in way of radiator
Walkway
Hispano gun bay
Non-slip Fitted Port & Starboard
Browning gun bays
Main Spars
Magazine bay
STARBOARD
PORT.
Landing lamp mounting
Structure shown only where different from starboard plane

Rear view mirror
Jettisonable hood
Bullet-proof windscreen
Dimming screen in up position
HOOD
Sealing rubber
Top locating spigot
ENLARGED SECTIONAL VIEW Q
Q

Waxed string
Linatex packing (if necessary)
Red-fibre washer
Linatex bag
Harness tube
TYPICAL BAG ASSEMBLY DETAIL B
Canvas bag
Red fibre washer
Fuselage datum
Red fibre washer (inside & outside)
Linatex bag with canvas bag outside
Detail B
Frame 8
9
10
SEE DETAIL A
SEALING MAIN HARNESS
Clip
Harness tube
Skin contour
Inboard
Bracket
DETAIL A

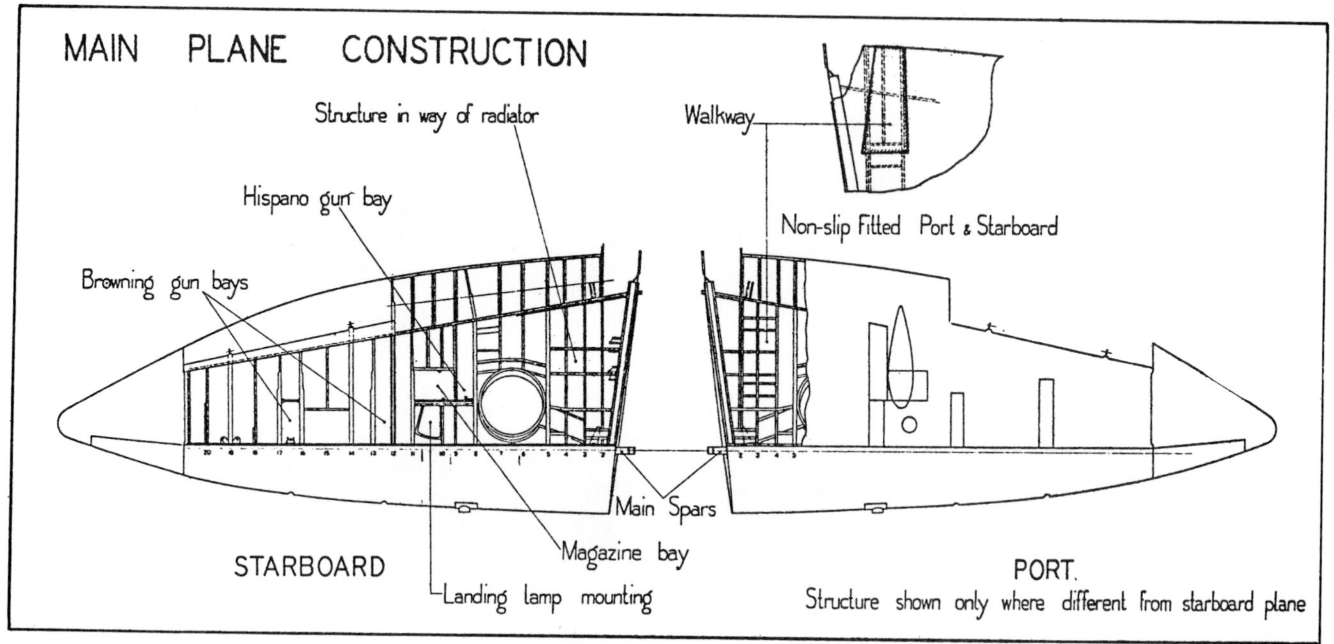

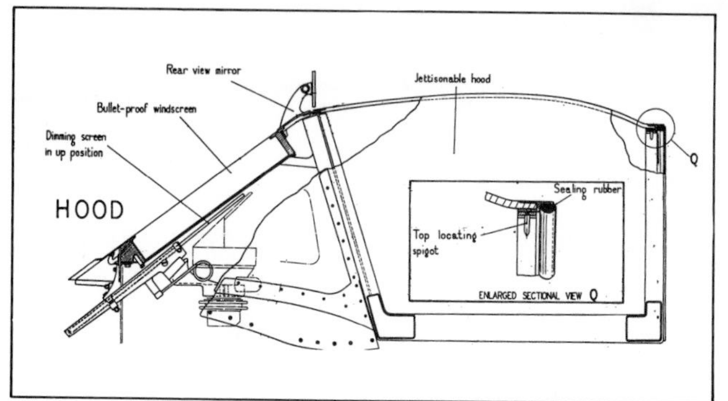

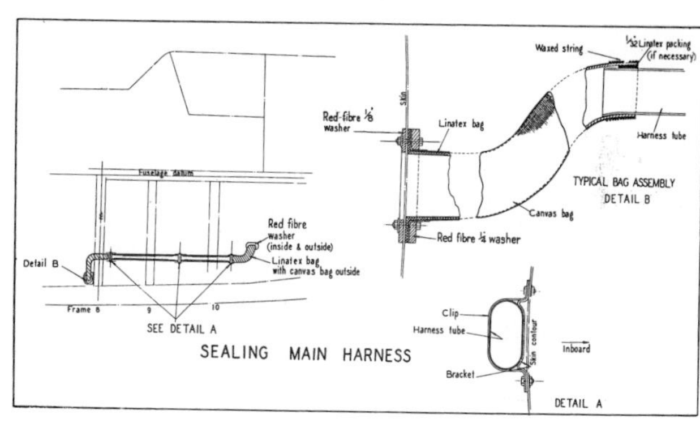

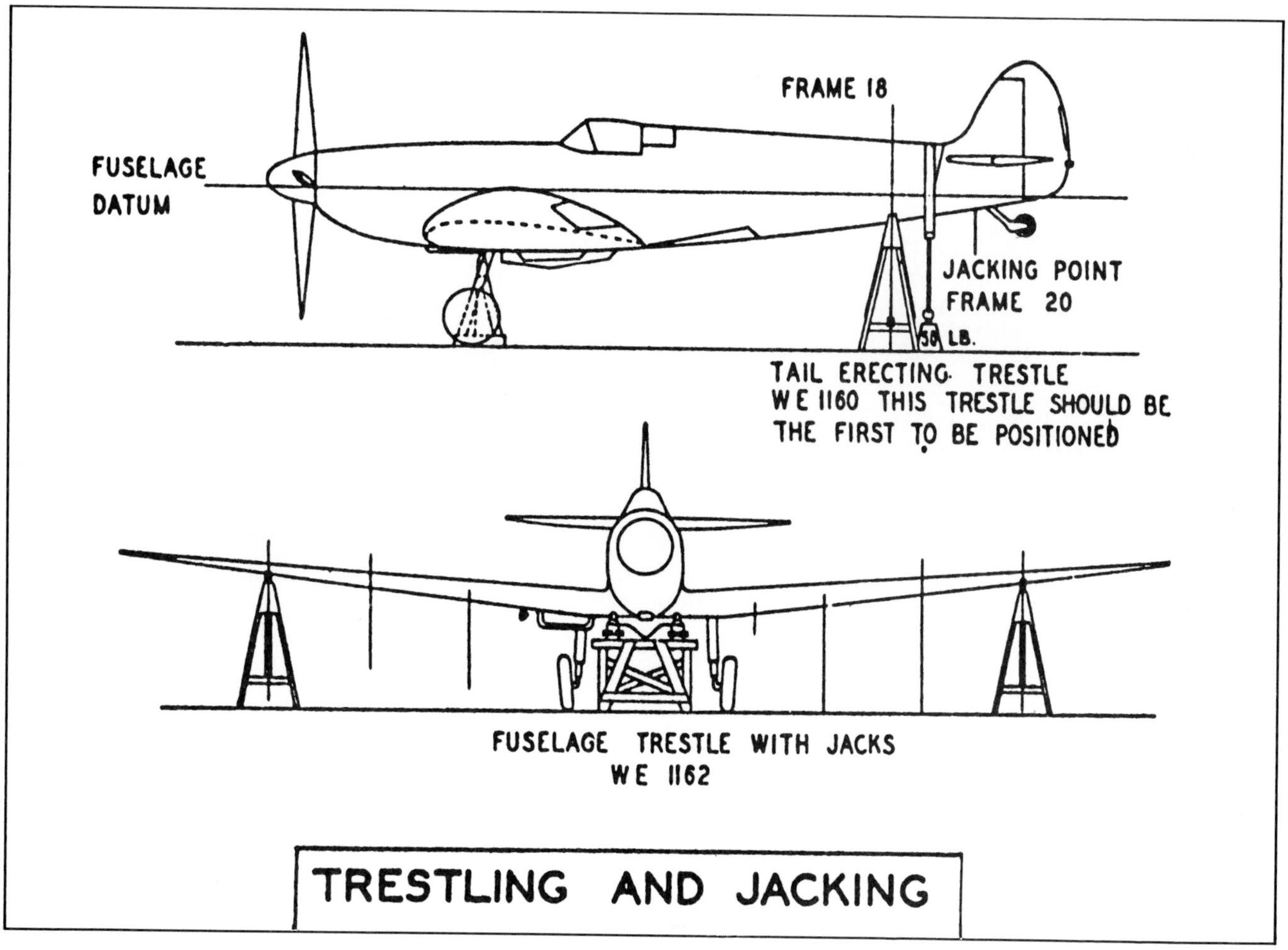

FRAME 18
FUSELAGE DATUM
JACKING POINT FRAME 20
56 LB.
TAIL ERECTING TRESTLE WE 1160 THIS TRESTLE SHOULD BE THE FIRST TO BE POSITIONED
FUSELAGE TRESTLE WITH JACKS WE 1162
TRESTLING AND JACKING

AB176, first pre-production Mk VI, at Eastleigh in late 1941. It was used as a trials aircraft by the makers before being seconded to No. 616 Squadron in January 1945.

Supermarine Aviation (Vickers) Ltd Contract No B19713/39 dated 9 August 1939.

Fourth order for 500 Spitfire Mk I dated 19 July 1940. Built as Mk VB/VC/VI/PR Mk IV between August 1941 and February 1942. The following serials apply to HF Mk VI built to this fourth order; AB176, 200, 211, 498, 503, 506, 513, 516, 523, 527-530 and 533-534.

Fifth order for 1,100 Spitfire Mk IA/B dated 24 October 1940. Built as: PR Mk IV/VB/VC/VI/VII/IX between February and November 1942. The following serials apply to Spitfire HF Mk VI built to this fifth order; BR159, 162, 164 167, 171, 172, 174, 178, 181, 186, 189, 191, 193, 197, 200, 205, 243, 247, 250, 252, 255, 286-287, 289, 297, 298, 302, 304, 307, 309-310, 314, 318-319, 326, 329-330, 563, 567, 569, 571, 575, 577-579, 585, 587-588, 590, 593, 595, 597-599, 979, 983-984, 987, BS106, 108, 111, 114-115, 117, 124, 133-134, 141, 146, 149, 228, 245, 436-437, 442, 448, 453, 460, 465, 472.

Seventh order for 500 Spitfire Mk VC dated 23 August 1941. Built as: Mks VC/PR Mk IV/VI/VII/IX/XII between November 1942 and August 1943. The following serials apply to HF Mk VIs built to this seventh order; EN176 and 189. Total built 97.

The following are listed VI in the Supermarine production list; BR110, 173, 175, 541, BS253, 359 and 427 but the RAF list them as quoted in the various chapters. On the other hand Supermarine lists BR159, 171-172 and 987 as VC.

Supermarine records state 100 Mk VI were delivered and RAF records 97.

All HF Mk VI (PC) Merlin 47 unless otherwise indicated

AB176 2386 39MU 501S 5-12-41 CRD VA 31-12 M47 instal Mal WW 15-2-43 Farn 31-8-44 hand trls; large tailplane instal Nov. Wts & CG load carb mono contam perf and cool trls. DTD for sqdn alloc. 616S 39MU 17-1-45

AB200 2531 M45 CRD BDn 29-1-42 M47 instal. Stab, hand, dives and recovery trls with normal span wng. Pilot blacked out and wings buckled during dive at 450 ASI. Wider span wngs (40ft 5in) fitt 455 ASI registered and pilot suffered no ill effects. Carb mono contam wts and CG load positional error and altimeter trls. VA 6-6-42 cabin sealing mods. 124S NWld 8-6-43 MMO 28-7 33MU 7-10

AB211 2515 9MU 5-2-42 124S 5-2 616S 4-3-43 124S 15-3 strk building low level pract Chigwell Essex CE 26-5-43

AB498 2546 M45 EA 6MU 5-2-42 421S 21-6 91S 22-6 124S 10-7 FTR ops 17-2-43

AB503 2554 24MU 6-1-42 616S 1-8 FACA 14-8 124S 25-1-43 lost cont in cloud overstressed in dive cd Sawbridgeworth Essex CE 3-6

AB506 2563 6MU 14-2-42 R-RH AFDU Dux 26-4 124S 7-9 FACA 20-4-43 616S 5-9 SOC 12-3-45

AB513 2584 EA 5MU 13-2-42 421S 15-7 124S 15-7 616S 15-9-43 MMO 30-12

AB516 2573 EA 5MU 13-2-42 421S 15-7 124S 15-7 FACB 8-3-43 616S 18-8 CRD BDn 15-9

AB523 2597 EA 37MU 15-2-42 616S 17-5 CAC ops 29-9 VSM 25-1-43 mods 1406Flt 8-4 519S 23-8-44

AB527 2588 EA 6MU 20-2-42 421S 13-6 91S 23-6 164S 5-9 602S 10-9 129S 29-11 FAAC 8-1-43 234S 24-2 66S 12-5 e/fld on t/o w/u ldg Skae CE 22-5 FH102.15

AB528 2611 EA 8MU 26-2-43 CRD Malcolms

The fixed hood was an undesirable feature on the early HA fighters and Malcolm's of White Waltham produced the 'Lobelle' sliding and quick release unit. It was flight tested on AB528, which is shown here during jettisoning trials.

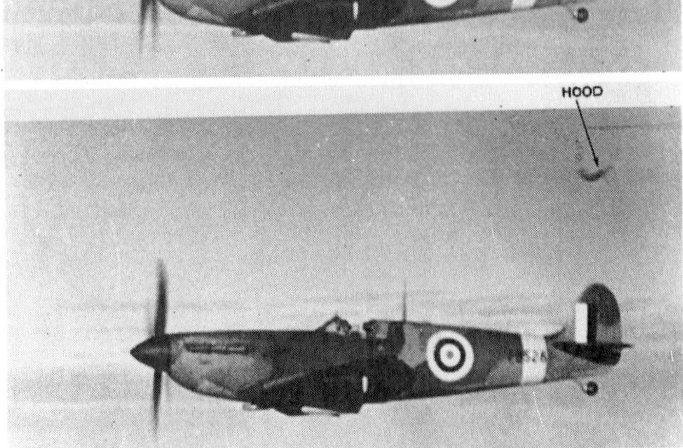

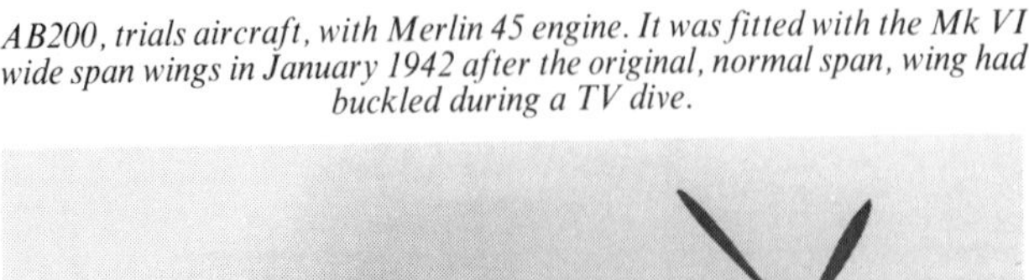

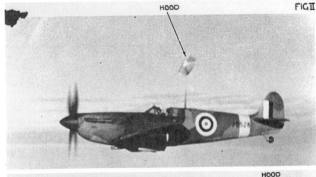

AB200, trials aircraft, with Merlin 45 engine. It was fitted with the Mk VI wide span wings in January 1942 after the original, normal span, wing had buckled during a TV dive.

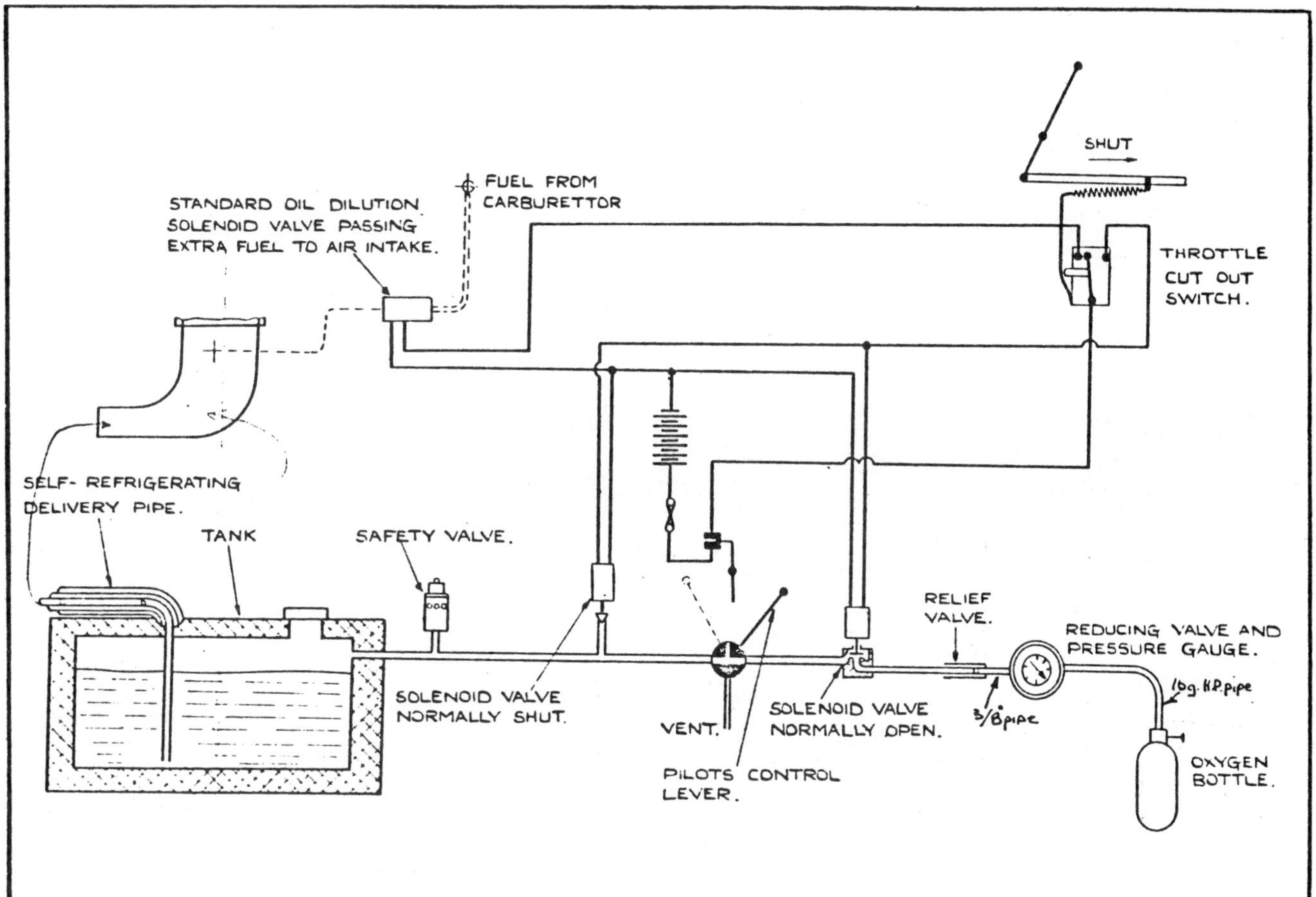

STANDARD OIL DILUTION SOLENOID VALVE PASSING EXTRA FUEL TO AIR INTAKE.

FUEL FROM CARBURETTOR

SHUT

THROTTLE CUT OUT SWITCH.

SELF- REFRIGERATING DELIVERY PIPE.

TANK

SAFETY VALVE.

SOLENOID VALVE NORMALLY SHUT.

VENT.

PILOTS CONTROL LEVER.

SOLENOID VALVE NORMALLY OPEN.

RELIEF VALVE.

3/8 pipe

REDUCING VALVE AND PRESSURE GAUGE.

1/8 g. H.P. pipe

OXYGEN BOTTLE.

LIQUID OXYGEN INJECTION SYSTEM
SPITFIRE VI

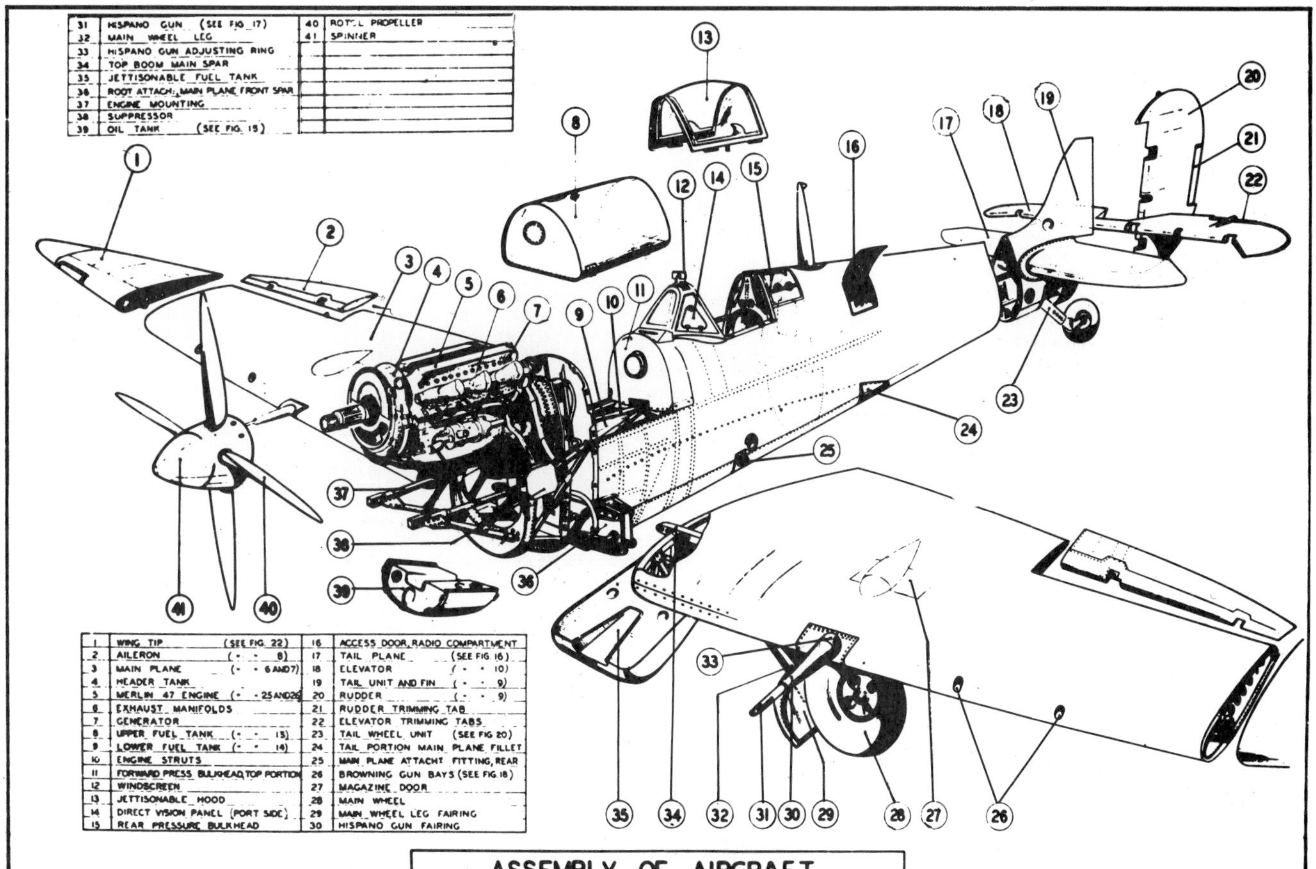

31	HISPANO GUN (SEE FIG 17)	40	ROTOL PROPELLER
32	MAIN WHEEL LEG	41	SPINNER
33	HISPANO GUN ADJUSTING RING		
34	TOP BOOM MAIN SPAR		
35	JETTISONABLE FUEL TANK		
36	ROOT ATTACH., MAIN PLANE FRONT SPAR		
37	ENGINE MOUNTING		
38	SUPPRESSOR		
39	OIL TANK (SEE FIG. 15)		

1	WING TIP (SEE FIG. 22)	16	ACCESS DOOR, RADIO COMPARTMENT
2	AILERON (" " 8)	17	TAIL PLANE (SEE FIG. 16)
3	MAIN PLANE (" " 6 AND 7)	18	ELEVATOR (" " 10)
4	HEADER TANK	19	TAIL UNIT AND FIN (" " 9)
5	MERLIN 47 ENGINE (" " 25 AND 26)	20	RUDDER (" " 9)
6	EXHAUST MANIFOLDS	21	RUDDER TRIMMING TAB
7	GENERATOR	22	ELEVATOR TRIMMING TABS
8	UPPER FUEL TANK (" " 13)	23	TAIL WHEEL UNIT (SEE FIG 20)
9	LOWER FUEL TANK (" " 14)	24	TAIL PORTION MAIN PLANE FILLET
10	ENGINE STRUTS	25	MAIN PLANE ATTACHT FITTING, REAR
11	FORWARD PRESS BULKHEAD, TOP PORTION	26	BROWNING GUN BAYS (SEE FIG. 18)
12	WINDSCREEN	27	MAGAZINE DOOR
13	JETTISONABLE HOOD	28	MAIN WHEEL
14	DIRECT VISION PANEL (PORT SIDE)	29	MAIN WHEEL LEG FAIRING
15	REAR PRESSURE BULKHEAD	30	HISPANO GUN FAIRING

ASSEMBLY OF AIRCRAFT

AB534 served briefly with 616 Squadron before going to Boscombe Down for carbon monoxide contamination trials.

Slough 11-6 'Lobelle' sliding hood instal (see page 257 for details). BDn CRD Farn 13-11 trls with hood. 124S 15-3-43 service trls. VA 30-3-43 new hood, mod instal. BDn comp trls with R7120 (proto press cabin a/c). Trls with three and four blade props. Farn Oct' 43 continuation of extns press cabin trls. MMO 11-11 SOC 3-5-65

AB529 2662 EA 8MU 2-4-42 421S 3-7 616S 29-7 FTR ops 19-8

AB530 2612 EA 8MU 29-3-42 124S 15-7 FTR ops 17-2-43

AB533 2649 EA 8MU 2-4-42 421S 1-7 91S 1-7 124S 10-7 FTR 17-2-43

AB534 2653 EA 8MU 26-3-42 616S 28-5 BDn Carb mono contam trls FACE 19-8 SOC 23-8

BR series All HF VI (PC) Merlin 47

BR159 2261 EA 8MU 26-3-42 616S 16-6 i/sea on ops 2-10 FH134.20

BR162 2685 EA 8MU 25-3-42 616S 26-5 VSM 25-1-43 124S 26-4 616S 15-9 39MU NEA 10-1-44 SOC 9-2-45

BR164 2675 EA 8MU 29-3-42 616S 24-5 CE ops 11-8 SOC 21-8 FH84.55

BR167 2648 EA 8MU 26-3-42 616S 19-6 FTR ops 30-7 FH42.25

BR171 2657 EA 8MU 29-3-42 421S 21-6 92S 22-6 124S 10-7 616S 1-9 124S 25-1-43 519S 14-4 mid-air fire a/c aban over Moray Firth CE 15-10

BR172 2659 EA 8MU 3-4-42 616S 16-5 cd Scampton CE 26-5 SOC FH17.20

BR174 2863 EA 6MU 29-3-42 616S 22-4 cd i/hill in bad visibility Nettle Combe IoW CE 1-11 FH153.30

BR178 2694 EA 6MU 24-3-42 616S 2-4 AST 27-5 FACB 29-6 124S 15-3-43 616S 31-8 519S 9-5-44 SOC 22-5-45

BR181 2706 EA 8MU 25-3-42 616S 9-5 AST 20-5 124S 25-1-43 e/fld on t/o NWld hit by BR639 CE 21-2 FH264.25

BR186 2715 EA 9MU 27-3-42 616S 4-5 FAAC 1-8 ROS CE ops 1-11 FH188

BR189 2721 HFVI(PC)SR EA 8MU 26-2-42 616S 16-5 FAAC 1-8 124S 25-1-43 310S 10-9 504S 24-9 39MU NEA 17-8-44 SOC 19-2-45

BR191 2722 EA 8MU 27-3-42 616S 16-5 FTR ops 3-6 FH25.15

BR193 2737 EA 8MU 29-3-42 616S 16-5 AST 20-5 124S 27-3-43 616S 31-8 SOC 18-5-45

BR197 2745 EA 8MU 1-4-42 616S 16-5 FACB 8-10 ROS 504S 3-11 ASTH 5-5-45

BR200 2746 EA BDn 1-4-42 comp perf trls with BR205 and BR287. Lost in cloud f/ld CB 13-4-42 MMO 616S 4-3-43 FAAC 15-4 ROS 39MU NEA 26-12 SOC 9-2-45

BR205 2754 EA BDn 2-4-42 Farn 29-5 press cabin trls. Trans to BDn June' 42 for ext dvng and perf trls with neg 'G' carb. Comp with BR287. Carb mono contam trls. Fitt DeH four blade Hydromatic prop for further trls with BR200 and BR287, Nov' 42 to Jan' 43. 39MU 7-5-43 1 CRU MMO 23-8-44 33MU 20-4-45 SOC 28-4

BR243 2767 EA 8MU 3-4-42 616S 9-5 CE ops 30-7 SOC 11-8 FH82.40

BR247 2836 EA BDn 18-4-42 9MU 26-5 616S 1-8 Farn Aug' 42 Marshall blower dev trls, later removed and replaced with Napier unit. FAAC 25-8-43 ROS SOC 20-4-45

BR250 2804 8MU 13-4-42 616S 8-5 FA 25-5 AST CRD Farn 31-7 Marshall blower dev trls. ETPS 29-1-43 SAC pumps instal. VHF radio trls. Airfield defence 3-2 Flown to 36,000ft to test Pesco press cabin pump. Zoomed to 45,000ft after TV dive by Flt Lt McClure. MMO 8-5-44 33MU 1-11-45 SOC 19-10

BR252 2801 HFVI(PC)SR EA 8MU 13-4-42 616S 29-5 602S 27-10 129S 29-11 234S 25-1-43 66S 12-5 313S 4-7 310S 29-7 504S 24-9

BR255 2810 EA 9MU 13-4-42 616S 6-5 CB ops 19-8 ROS SOC 9-2-45

BR286 2825 EA 9MU 17-4-42 616S 6-5 ASTH 6-10 FAAC 10-11 1402flt 17-3-43 33MU 23-11-44

BR287 2826 EA CRD BDn 17-4-42 trls with neg 'G' carb. Carb mono contam perf, hand and dives. Comp with BR200 and BR205. All three were testing cockpit warning lights which operated when cabin press dropped below 1lb sq in. De-mist apparatus in hood. WAL 24-6 521Met S 12-2-43 FAAC 9-1 1401Flt 5-9-44 33MU 7-11

BR289 2851 EA 8MU 24-4-42 AFDU Duxfd for tact trls. 23-5 BSM 10-9 fuel syst mods. Pilot requested fit of spcl fuel cock. 616S 1-10 SOC 14-3-45

BR297 2852 HFVI(PC)SR EA 5MU 24-4-42 164S 7-9 602S 10-9 129S 29-11 234S 25-1-43 66S 12-5 313S 4-7 310S 29-7 504S 24-9 SOC 2-5-45

BR298 2861 EA CRD VA 25-4-42 5MU 10-5 HAL 28-5 12MU 25-7 164S 30-8 602S 10-9 FACB 26-9 SOC 1-2-45

BR302 2886 EA 5MU 2-5-42 616S 8-6 ROS 13-2. Attacked with BS448 by Typhoons, air coll. Land at base, Ibsley. CAC 24-3-43. Sent to BDn as rogue a/c. Had completed 327.5hr fly time and 87.25hr since last major overall. Skin over star oleo leg broken; fus rear of star wng fillet badly dented; badly fitt engine cowling. Cowling sealed with fabric strips. 616S 12-8 39MU NEA 27-11 SOC 20-4-45

BR304 2878 HFVI(PC)SR 5MU 30-4-42 421S 1-7 91S 1-7 164S 5-9 612S 10-9 129S 29-11 234S 25-1-43 310S 17-8 504S 24-9 SOC 9-2-45

BR307 2887 EA 5MU 2-5-42 15MU 14-8 616S 16-9 FAAC 28-1-43 519S 23-10 SOC 22-5-45

BR309 2915 EA CRD BDn 8-5-42 fuel syst tests with normal AVT 40 carb. Super 8-7 neg 'G' carb and fuel de-aerator instal. BDn 15-9 fuel syst tests continued. CRD VA 12-8 1CRU 12-12 mods and mr 616S 6-5-43 519S 25-4-44 509S 30-5 SOC 9-2-45

BR310 2908 EA 5MU 8-5-42 616S 8-6 1CRU 11-12 mr and instal of new hood 616S 31-12 ROS FACE 18-2-43

BR314 2913 EA 8MU 8-5-42 124S 15-7 616S 25-1-43 CE dam by second a/c jett o/ld fuel tank a/c aban cd nr Waterlooville Hants 29-6-43

BR318 2920 EA 5MU 10-5-42 91S 30-6 421S 1-7 Spcl Flt North 16-9 616S 8-10 FAAC 18-1-43 39MU NEA 24-2-44 SOC 9-2-45

BR319 2927 EA 5MU 14-5-42 124S 9-7 CB ops 18-11 616S 18-5-43 124S air coll with BR567 a/c aban pilot miss 15-6 FH138.5

BR326 2931 EA 5MU 15-4-42 421S 28-6 91S 29-6 91S 28-6 Farn 4-9 LOX eng boost trls. Spcl Flt North 18-9 124S 25-1-43 616S 31-3 ROS 31-5

BR329 2932 EA 5MU 16-5-42 421S 11-7 124S 31-12 FACB 3-3-43 616S 5-7 CE ops 31-8 FH218.30

BR330 2939 EA 9MU 17-5-42 616S 20-8 ROS 13-2-43 FAAC 28-2-44 33MU 5-5

BR563 2937 EA 9MU 17-5-42 616S 6-8 FAAC 19-8 ROS 124S 6-12 MMO 25-8-43

BR567 2954 EA 21-5-42 421S 11-7 124S 9-7 CE dbf 15-9 SOC 2-10 FH73.25

BR569 2960 EA 5MU 21-5-42 124S 9-7 CAC ops 19-8 e/a i/sea 19-11 FH96.10

BR571 2966 EA 5MU 23-5-42 124S 9-7 CAC ops 21-8 FTR ops 17-2-43

BR575 2967 EA 5MU 23-5-42 421S 19-7 FTR ops 19-8

BR577 2991 HFVI(PC)SR EA 33MU 31-5-42 164S 29-8 602S 10-9 129S 29-11 234S 25-1-43 66S 12-5 313S 4-7 310-S 31-7 504S 24-9 SOC 24-4

BR578 2997 EA 33MU 1-6-42 421S 15-7 124S 15-7 CE 29-9 SOC FH46.5 cancel 616S 12-4-43 CB ops 23-5 39MU NEA 28-10-44

BR579 2980 HFVI(PC)SR EA 33MU 29-5-42 421S 19-7 124S 19-7 234S 13-2-43 66S 12-5 313S 4-7 310S 3-8 504S 24-9 Farn Sep'45

BR585 2998 EA 6MU 4-6-42 91S 28-6 CA ops 4-7 Spcl Flt North 16-9 124S 10-10 616S 25-1-43 f/ld CE 4-3 air coll with BS453 during Spartan exercise. e/fld on t/o 28-3

BR587 3013 EA 6MU 5-6-42 421S 19-7 124S 19-7 CE 28-9

BR588 3002 EA 6MU 2-6-42 124S 21-8 616S 26-6-43 FACB 8-9 39MU NEA 23-12

BR590 3019 EA 33MU 7-6-42 421S 19-7 124S 19-7 616S 25-1-43 e/fld i/sea off Swanage 18-4

BR593 3040 EA 33MU 14-6-42 421S 16-7 124S 16-7 CAC ops 30-7 39MU NEA 28-9-43 SOC 9-2-45

BR595 3046 EA 33MU 14-6-42 421S 16-7 124S 16-7 FAAC 26-8 616S 9-3-43 SOC 18-5-45

BR597 3091 EA EA AST mods 23-2-42 33MU 28-6 616S 21-7 FTR ops 30-7 FH8.35

BR598 3058 EA 9MU 20-6-42 616S 22-8 CAC ops 16-10 124S 31-10 616S 13-5-43 FACB 3-6 1401Flt 17-7-44 ASTH 13-5-45

BR599 3066 EA 9MU 23-6-42 616S 6-8 519S 23-2-44 CE ops 18-4

BR979 3090 EA 45MU 27-6-42 164S 1-9 602S 10-9 FAAC 22-9 234S 7-5-43 616S 15-5 SOC 24-4-45

BR983 3099 EA 33MU 5-7-42 616S 1-8 CB ops 19-8 WAL 24-8 521Met S 18-2-43 SOC 29-5-45

BR984 3108 EA 12MU 3-7-42 421S 17-7 124S 16-7 616S 25-1-43 39MU NEA 19-10

BR987 3116 EA 12MU 3-7-42 431S 17-7 124S 16-7 CAC ops 19-11 616S 27-3-43 FTR ops 16-8 FH295

BS series All HF VI (PC) Merlin 47

BS106 3119 EA 45mu 5-7-42 76MU 2-9 *Ripley* 8-9 Tak 3-10 ME 27-10 to reinforce BP985, H/A FV against Ju86P-2 sorties. 103MU mods to FR with F.8 oblique camera SOC 26-4-45

BS108 3120 EA 33MU 5-7-42 616S 22-7 FTR ops 30-7 FH7.25

BS111 3130 EA 33MU 11-7-42 616S 1-8 519S 8-2-44 CAC ops 15-2 ROS SOC 29-1-45

BS114 3131 EA 33MU 12-7-42 616S 1-8 FAAC 28-8 CE ops 16-4-43

BS115 3142 EA 8MU 12-7-42 616S 20-8 CAC ops 21-10 HAL e/fld i/sea off Christchurch Hants 22-8-43 FH182.15

BS117 3156 EA 8MU 14-7-42 616S 23-8 FACB 4-9 CE ops 31-8-43 FH218.30

BS124 3192 EA 15MU 26-7-42 76MU 2-9 *Ripley* 8-9 ME 28-10 FAC2 12-12 (see BS106)

BS133 3239 EA 6MU 13-8-42 76MU 1-9 *Ripley* 8-9 ME 28-10 SOC 26-4-45 (see BS106)

BS134 3263 EA 6MU 18-8-42 76MU 1-9 *Ripley* 8-9 ME 28-10 SOC 29-8-46 (see BS106)

BS141 3271 EA 33MU 21-8-42 602S 14-9 FAAC 12-11 ROS 234S 31-3-43 313S 4-7 310S 29-7 118S 24-12 AST 18-4-45

BS146 3281 HFVI(PC)SR EA 33MU 21-8-42 602S 25-9 129S 7-12 234S 22-1-43 224S 28-2 66S 12-5 313S 4-7 310S 29-7 504S 24-9 1401Met Flt 9-2-44 SOC 20-11-45

BS149 3280 EA 15MU 23-8-42 76MU 1-9 *Ripley* 8-9 ME 28-10 SOC 26-4-45 (see BS106)

BS228 3511 EA 38MU 27-10-42 521S 16-2-43 1401Flt 11-9

BS245 3499 EA 9MU 16-10-42 124S 12-12 616S 31-3-43 s/dn FTR 16-4

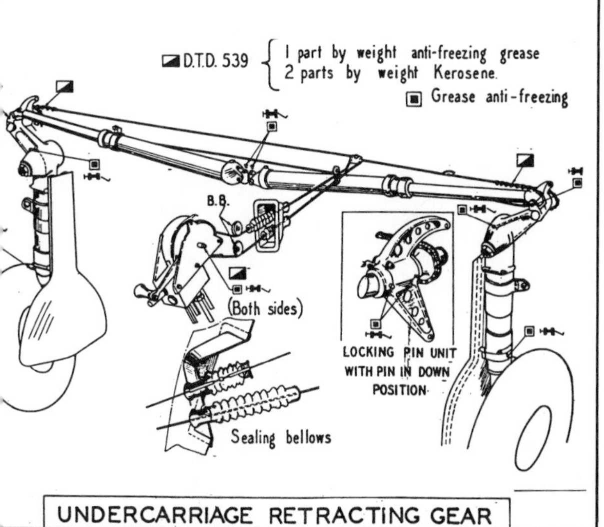
D.T.D. 539 { 1 part by weight anti-freezing grease
2 parts by weight Kerosene.
Grease anti-freezing
B.B.
(Both sides)
LOCKING PIN UNIT WITH PIN IN DOWN POSITION
Sealing bellows
UNDERCARRIAGE RETRACTING GEAR

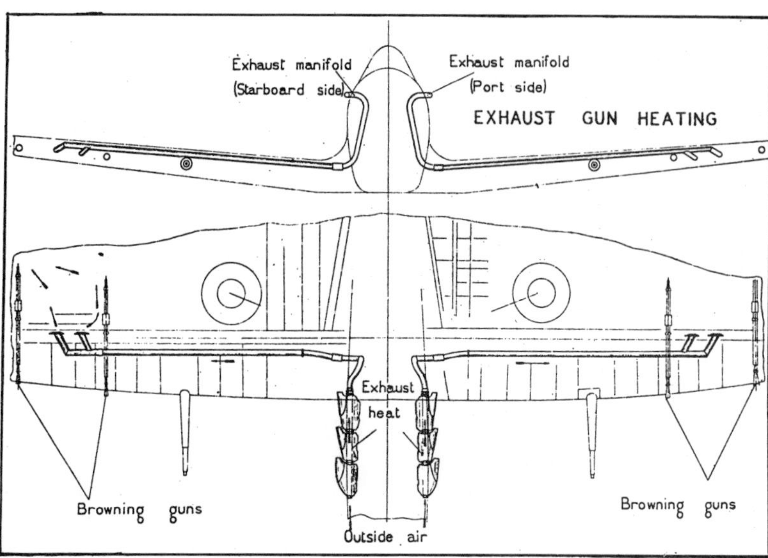
Exhaust manifold (Starboard side)
Exhaust manifold (Port side)
EXHAUST GUN HEATING
Exhaust heat
Browning guns
Browning guns
Outside air

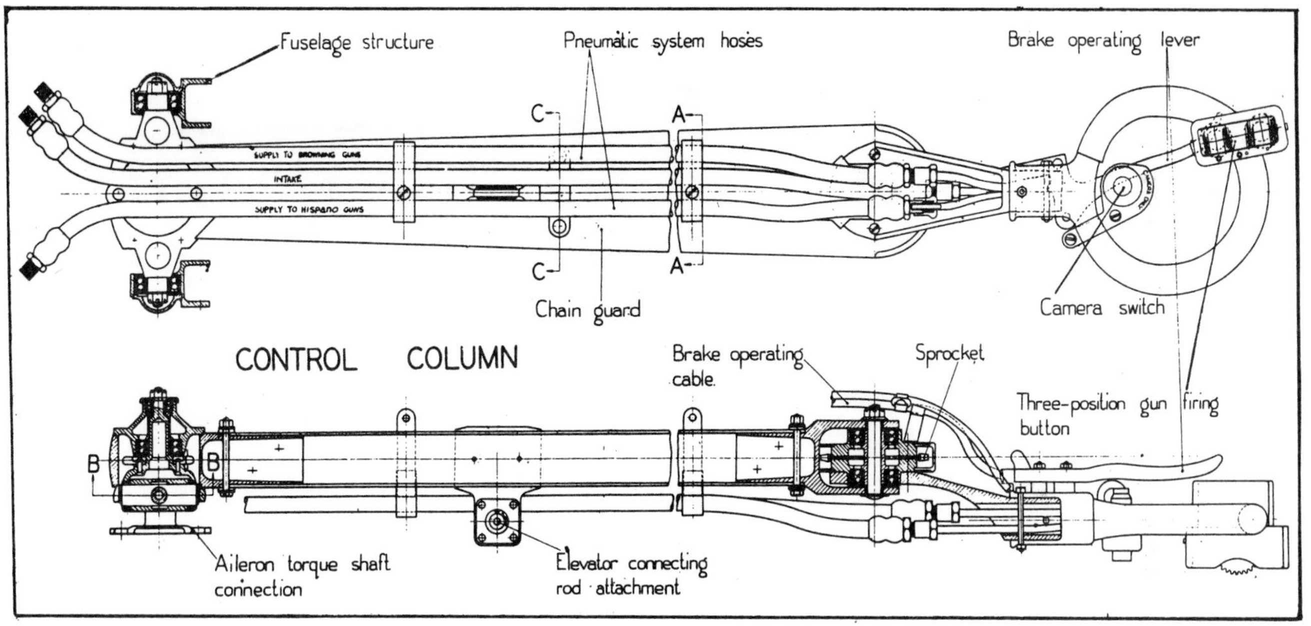
Fuselage structure
Pneumatic system hoses
Brake operating lever
SUPPLY TO BROWNING GUNS
INTAKE
SUPPLY TO HISPANO GUNS
Chain guard
Camera switch
CONTROL COLUMN
Brake operating cable
Sprocket
Three-position gun firing button
Aileron torque shaft connection
Elevator connecting rod attachment

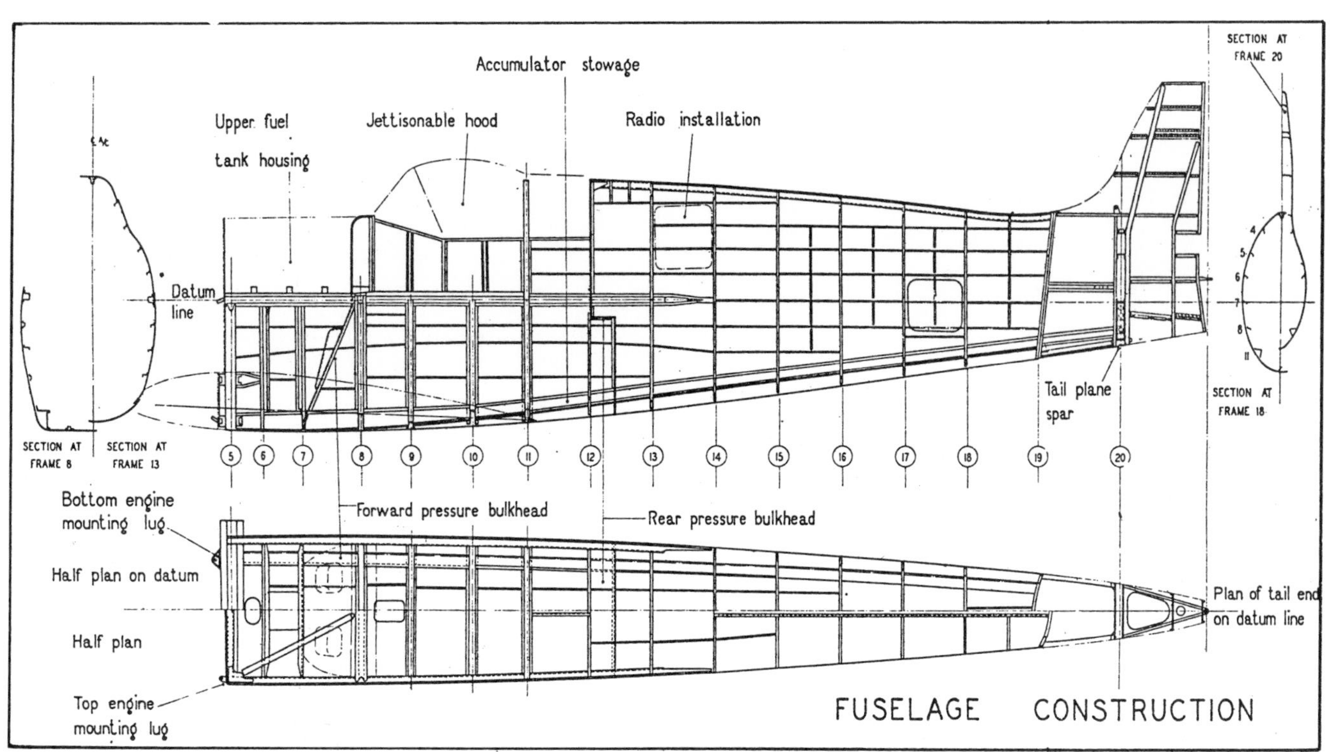
Accumulator stowage
Upper fuel tank housing
Jettisonable hood
Radio installation
SECTION AT FRAME 20
Datum line
SECTION AT FRAME 8
SECTION AT FRAME 13
Tail plane spar
SECTION AT FRAME 18
Bottom engine mounting lug
Forward pressure bulkhead
Rear pressure bulkhead
Half plan on datum
Half plan
Plan of tail end on datum line
Top engine mounting lug
FUSELAGE CONSTRUCTION

BS436 3349 EA 8MU 8-9-42 602S 24-9 swg off runway Skae o/s CE 21-10 SOC 29-10 SAL 31-12 39MU NEA 26-12 SOC 20-4-45

BS437 3347 HFVI(PC)SR EA 8MU 8-9-42 602S 26-9 FAAC 8-11 129S 8-12 234S 25-1-43 66S 12-5 313S 4-7 310S 29-7 504S 24-9 SOC 24-4-45

BS442 3375 HFVI(PC)SR EA 12MU 13-9-42 602S 24-9 129S 29-11 234S 25-1-43 66S 12-5-43 313S 4-7 310S 29-7 FACA 27-8 504S 24-9

BS448 3494 EA 39MU 14-10-42 CRD R-RH 27-10 616S 13-1-43 f/ld Ibsley CE 4-3 ROS attacked by Typhoons during Spartan exercise. Coll with BR302 a/c aban cd High Waterton Devon CE 24-3 FH83.05

BS453 3496 EA 8MU 14-10-42 616S 6-11 coll with BR858 during Spartan exercise cd nr Oxford CE 4-3-43 MMO 31-8 CRD Perfect Motors Elmdon 16-9 CRD VA 11-1-44 SOC 5-2-45

BS460 3498 EA 39MU 16-10-42 616S 10-11 ROS 20-3-43 CAC ops 11-2-44

BS465 3465 EA 39MU 14-10-42 R-RH 31-10 616S 13-1-43 f/ld during Spartan exercise CE 4-3-43 ROS CE ops 5-4

BS472 3472 HFVI(PC)SR EA 38MU 15-10-42 602S 17-11 129S 29-11 234S 22-1-43 66S 12-5 313S 4-7 310S 29-7 504S 24-9 39MU NEA 10-6-44 SOC 12-3-45

EN176 3615 M61 9MU 18-11-42 1402Flt 20-2-43 FAAC 10-2-45

EN189 3652 VWD 18-11-42 final prod FVI wts & CG load 39MU 29-11-42 124S 12-12 616S 31-3-43 39MU NEA 26-12-43

Spitfire Mk I converted to F VI X4942. F Mk V to F VI R7120

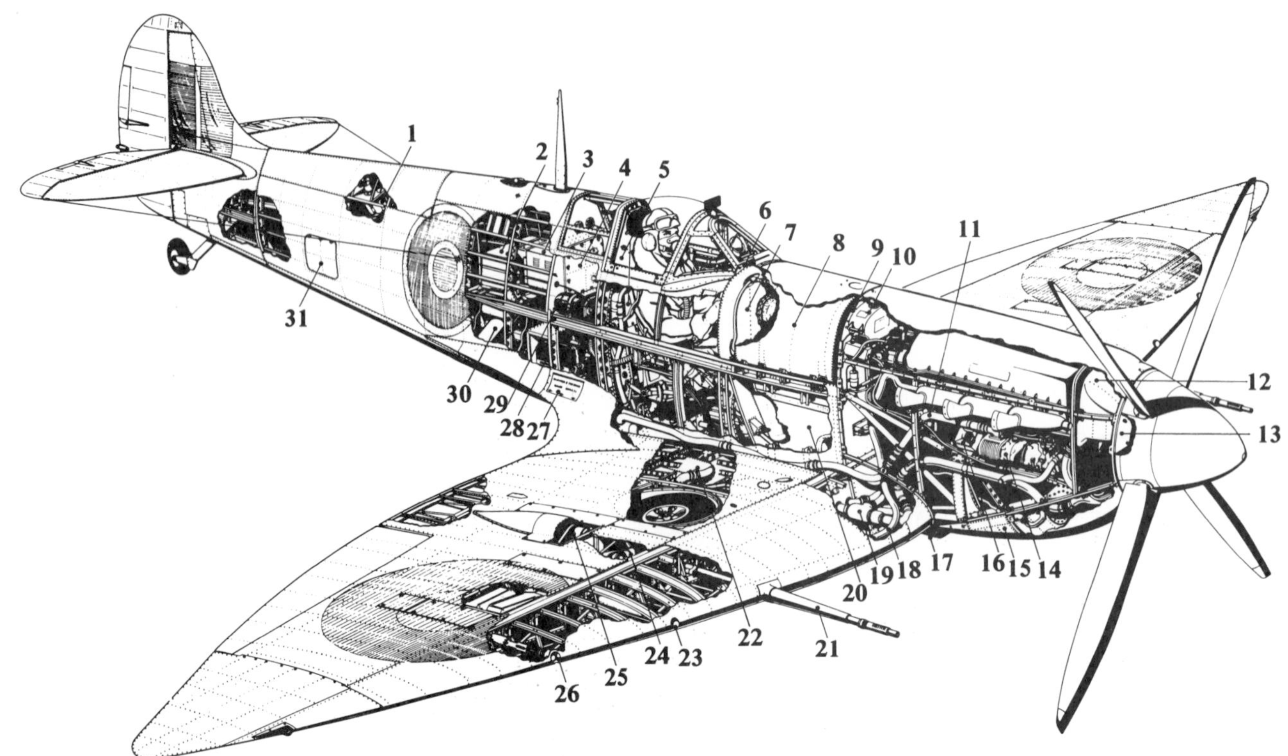

SPITFIRE VI AEROPLANE

Official cutaway drawing of the Spitfire F Mk VI. 1 Signal discharger, 2/3 radio sets, 4 panel in rear pressure bulkhead, 5/6/9/13 armour plate, 7 front pressure bulkhead, 8 upper fuel tank, 10 hydraulic system header tank, 11 air pipe to pressure cabin , 12 coolant header tank, 14 pressure cabin blower, 15 oil tank, 16 pressure cabin filter, 17 carburettor air intake, 18 gun heating pipe (exhaust), 19 coolant thermostat, 20 lower fuel tank, 21 Hispano cannon, 22 radiator, 23/26 Browning gun, 24 landing lamp, 25 Hispano gun magazine, 27 ground blower and pressure guage connections, 28 general services accumulator, 29 oxygen bottle, 30 flare chute, 31 access door.

"BLOW THE SPITFIRE"

With the advent of the two-stage, two-speed, inter-cooled Merlin 60 Series engines the original design of the Spitfire airframe was to undergo a fundamental change, and the resultant development and production types represented the peak of Spitfire/Merlin combination. The initial impetus given to the new breed of Spitfire came from Rolls-Royce who, during the research and development of superchargers, were made to recognise that any further increase in high altitude performance of the Merlin necessitated use of a two stage supercharger. It was a fairly easy operation to increase compression ratio (boost pressure at altitude), but to obtain more horse power the supercharger had to work more efficiently in order to, as it were, waste power driving the blower and to lower the excessive temperatures for compression ratio obtained.

Rolls-Royce had explored other alternatives such as exhaust turbos (as on the Republic P-47 Thunderbolt), and while attractive in lower fuel consumption under ideal cruising conditions they had little advantage in maximum power performance. Also, with the turbo system practically all the ejector exhaust effect would be lost. Weight was another drawback and the system would have been difficult to fit into current fighters like the Spitfire and other types on test. It also would mean careful, drag reducing design due to the numerous cooling ducts needed for the turbine. So, the mechanically driven, two-stage blower was chosen as the best method to develop.

It was erected on a static rig which accommodated two units simultaneously. The first stage was a modified Rolls-Royce Vulture blower, the second taken from a Merlin 46. On the rig the Vulture blower outlet was coupled up to the inlet of the Merlin. The gain in hp was excellent, 300 @ 30,000 ft as compared to the single stage Merlin 46. The next major problem was intercooling, for the charge temperature rise to the intake was 205°C at maximum rpm in FS gear, and this had to be reduced before passing to the second stage in order to get increased density of the charge to avoid premature detonation. Air cooled and liquid cooled intercoolers were investigated and flight tested, and it became evident that the water cooled type was most suited to the proposed design. And, in the Spitfire, it was an almost impossibility to use an air cooled intercooler in the space available. Theoretically, the more intercooling obtained (or lower temperature to the charge) means more engine power. But this also means installation of large radiators and the associated drag. It was discovered that there was a rapid increase in performance up to approximately 35% intercooling and after this it fell off. A 40% intercooling was chosen as it gave the best overall results.

The first Rolls-Royce engine produced to incorporate all the new features was the RM 6SM Merlin 60, specified for the high altitude Wellington bomber, another Vickers product. An example was installed in the Spitfire by Rolls-Royce because one of their engineers (Mr Hives) was curious enough to ask what would a Spitfire be like with the new engine. As a result a RM 8SM Merlin 61 was chosen which was similar to the 60 but had different supercharger drive gear ratios and two-piece cylinder blocks.

All this activity was taking place in 1941 and the Air Ministry wanted to see the results of a Spitfire with the new engine, the designation of which was to be the Spitfire F Mk VII. At a meeting at Hursley Park on 16 December 1941 the position regarding clearance for production of the new mark was discussed. Test beds were needed and three Spitfires were available, the first at Boscombe Down on CRD instructions, the second at Hucknall and the third held by Supermarine. The Mk VII was an important aeroplane as the whole of Supermarine production in the near future was going to be based upon the new design. It was decided that the aeroplane at Hucknall (R6700), called by now the General Purpose Spitfire, should be sent to Worthy Down and that Rolls-Royce should apply to Boscombe Down for the return of N3297, the much modified Mk III prototype. Owing to a shortage of Duralumin propeller blades it was also planned to take the opportunity to test, and then introduce, other materials. They were known by their trade names of Duramesh, Rotoload and Rayoid, all composite blades, some with metal sheaths.

The first true prototype F Mk VII was AB450, originally built as an F VB, and it was immediately transferred to CRD Rolls-Royce in July 1942. It had the normal pressure cabin and standard Mk V fuselage with small fin and rudder, the universal wing with extended tips, standard VC undercarriage and B armament. A retractable tailwheel, tail parachute fin guard and four blade dural Rotol propeller were non-standard. It had a Merlin 61 intercooled engine with twin radiators under the wings, plus an enlarged engine cowling which increased overall length to 31ft 3½in. Production aircraft were to have a Mareng fuel container in the leading edge of each wing, and to accommodate them nose ribs 6 and 7 had to be deleted and the top and bottom wing skin doubled. The fuel cells tended to collapse when all fuel was used due to suction, and the specification was modified to ensure that future production machines would have metal tanks. A vent was also fitted.

Certification of Design of the prototype Type 351 was

AB450 started life as a Mk VB and was converted to the prototype HF Mk VII. Seen here in original markings after first flight as Mk VII.

AB450, late 1942, with the High Altitude Flight, Northolt. Medium Sea Grey and PR blue camouflage, no cannons and extended wing tips.

EN470, seen here at Boscombe Down, was one of two F Mk VIIs used for LOX engine boost trials. The second Spitfire was EN465 and both had a LOX tank in the starboard wing in place of the normal fuel tank. With a Merlin 71 installed EN465 and 470 were seconded to RAE Farnborough, where a liquid oxygen boosted system was fitted in an attempt to increase high altitude and performance without the need for additional intercooling. The system was originally installed on a Mk II (see page 107).

EN470, LOX trials aircraft, in flight.

issued on 13 October 1942 and the general description was most interesting. It stated – This aeroplane is the prototype of the F Mk VII and F Mk VIII production Spitfires. Components of existing types with some modifications are used as indicated. Fuselage Spitfire Mk VI with forward bay reinforced for Merlin 61 engine. Spitfire F Mk 20 Tail unit. Spitfire F Mk 20 Tailplane, Spitfire F Mk V elevator and rudder. Mainplane, Spitfire F Mk VC with spar flanges reinforced and lead ballast added in outer portions of the wings. Main chassis, Spitfire F Mk VC leg and support structure. Spitfire F Mk VII production wheel and tyre equipment. Tail chassis, Spitfire F Mk VII production. Tare weight 5,201lb. Maximum all up 8,000.

AB450 arrived at Boscombe Down for trials ten days before certification on 4 October after short service trials with the RAF HA Special Flight at Northolt, where it had been painted a normal PR blue on the upper surfaces and deep Sky underneath. The first production contract was to Aircraft/ 1432/SAS/C. 23(c) as part of an original order for 1,100 Mk Is placed in October 1940. It called for five airframes serialled BS121, 142, 229, 253 and 427, the first two going to Northolt Special Flight, and BS229 to Boscombe Down for trials commencing 20 March 1943. A total of 140 examples was constructed, for by the time full scale production was reached it had been replaced in service by the Mk VIII and IX.

BS121 arrived at Worthy Down on 12 August 1942 for weighing and CoG determination. Tare was 5,919lb auw with 30 gal overload tank 7,909; auw with 90 gal tank 8,726. EN974 was fitted with a Merlin RM11SM 71 engine and .477 reduction gear driving a Rotol Hydulignum propeller at an auw of 7,870lb and was flight tested by Supermarine. Maximum level speed in FS gear 410mph at 25,300ft. Maximum rate of climb MS gear 4,460ft/min at 10,400ft. Maximum rate of climb FS gear 3,750ft/ min at 22,000ft. Operational ceiling (500ft/min) 40,900ft. Service ceiling (100ft/min) 42,800ft. Time to 40,000ft 14.9min.

Certification of the Type 351/1 F Mk VII/P I was on 9 June 1944 and production began. In an attempt to raise operating height of the Mk VII a number of experiments were carried out with MD176, which had started life equipped with a Merlin 61 engine. It arrived at Rolls-Royce, Hucknall, on 24 March 1944 to have the first of the RM16SM Series engines installed, this being the pseudo Merlin 112, a composite of a

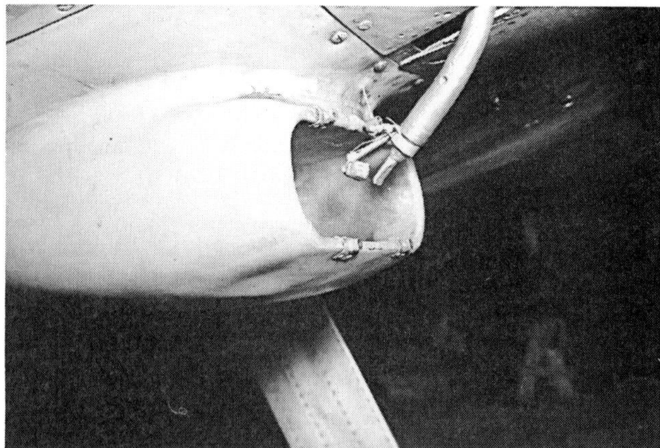

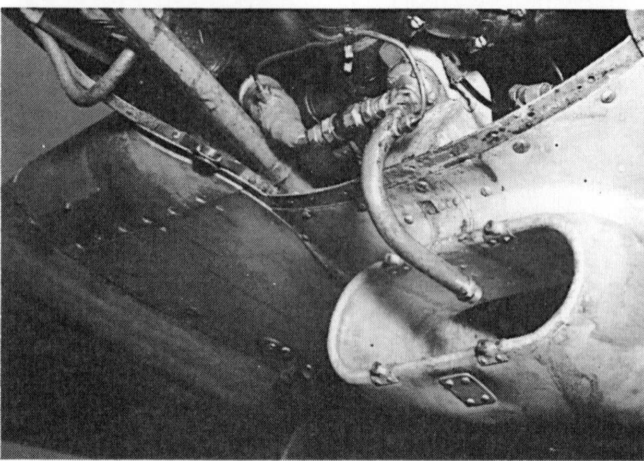

The LOX injection nozzle located in the carburetter air intake. Second view is of the nozzle and the mechanically operated flap valve controlled from the cockpit. Final view is of the flap valve.

Merlin 61 and RS 16SM. It was a project only and was similar to the Merlin 110 with provision for cabin blower. With the new engine this Spitfire was transferred to Boscombe Down in July for performance and cooling trials, during which time a Mk XII extended fin and rudder was installed. This aircraft was also used for trials of the RM11SM Merlin 71.

In order to boost engine power at high altitude two production Mk VII Spitfires—EN465 and 470—were seconded to RAE Farnborough to continue the development of a liquid oxygen (LOX) boosted system, which started with a Mk II—P8079—in April 1940 and a Mk V in October 1941. These early Spitfires did not have an intercooled Merlin so a modified system had to be used. The background to the early LOX experiments is worth recording. Trials were carried out by Rolls-Royce, Derby, in collaboration with Dr O. A. Saunders of Imperial College, London. The Merlin XX test engine was run at 3,000rpm in FS gear, and after injection of 3.9lbs of oxygen per minute the bhp was increased by 17.7% (from 600 to 706). A second test injecting 4.1lbs per minute increased the bhp from 750 to 855.

It was then decided to flight test the system and trials

BS229 at Boscombe Down for trials. Note the enlarged elevator horn.

revealed an increase of maximum speed of 30mph at 30,000ft, and the time of climb from 30,000 to 35,000ft reduced by two minutes. The limiting factor of the amount of oxygen injected was the capacity of the radiator to dissipate the increased heat. The LOX system weighed 110lb, including 60lb of LOX, and it was proposed to equip several squadrons of Spitfires for use as high altitude fighters. The British Oxygen Company was to provide and maintain the total installation, which consisted of a tank containing 21,000lb of LOX, a lorry fitted with a tank holding 1,600lb. Evaporation rate of LOX was estimated at 3½ to 4lbs per hour when in a Spitfire's tanks, and the lorry would be required to top up each aircraft every four hours.

By this time, January 1942, the pressure cabin Spitfires were under development and the LOX system was put on low priority, but in July 1942 interest was rekindled and the system installed in Spitfire Mk V, AB487, by Heston Aircraft Ltd.

BS142, second production Mk VII, September 1942. It went to RAF Northolt. On 15 May 1943 it shot down an Fw190.

Trials were carried out with, and without, LOX and consisted mainly of a number of climbs from 30,000 to 34,000ft. The table below details two typical trials.

Level flight at 32,000ft

Without oxygen		with oxygen		increase
ASI	true speed	ASI	true speed	mph
185	315	210	355	40
186	316	209	354	38

These figures should be compared with similar trials with the Mk II, during which the Merlin XII cut out at 38,000ft.

Level flight

Height (ft)	air Temp (°C)	true speed without oxygen	with	increase mph (true)
30,000	-32	296	306	10
32,000	-42	284	312	28
32,000	-44	284	314	30
32,000	-32	297	330	33
34,000	-42	271	295+	24+
34,000	-43	283	304+	21

Climb

30 to 35,000ft	without oxygen	7mins 40sec
	with oxygen	6mins 22secs
		5mins 34secs
		5mins 25secs
30 to 32,000ft		1min 50secs
30 to 34,000ft		4mins 5secs

Ceiling

Without oxygen	36,400ft
with	(i) 37,300ft
	(ii) 38,000ft

The developed systems fitted to the Mk VII Spitfire were installed by Heston Aircraft to RAE Farnborough instructions and flight trials began. The system now consisted of 80lbs LOX carried in the starboard wing fuel tank position. A self-refrigerating pipe delivered the LOX to a metering orifice fitted into the atmospheric end of the pipe where the oxygen was

EN474, HF Mk VII, Wright Field, USA, 24 February 1944.

discharged into the air intake. An emergency, manually-operated valve was installed for venting the LOX tank should the pressure rise above the norm of 6 to 9lb/sq in.

Injection of the LOX necessitated a proportionate increase in the supply of fuel to the engine in order to maintain the normal oxygen/fuel ratio necessary for satisfactory combustion. This additional fuel was supplied from a point near the carburetter entry to a solenoid valve through which the fuel passed. The power boosting was operated by the pilot by means of a control lever placed below the throttle lever. Weight of the complete power boosting installation was 130lb. In level flight at 40,000ft the speed increase was 27mph for a period of seven minutes, and an increase of 300hp.

Operation of the system was restricted to heights above 32,000ft in order that the normal maximum power output would not be exceeded. Both aircraft were then sent to AFDU, Wittering, for service trials, these consisting of full throttle at level speed at 40,000ft to test the effects of the system on rate of climb at heights above this, plus further attempts to increase ceiling. The trials were considered unsatisfactory and both Spitfires were returned to Heston Aircraft for further modifications. The trials, however, did prove that LOX injection provided a substantial increase in climb at high altitude for short periods, and it would provide the RAF with a fighter having rapid climb and acceleration for the interception of high flying enemy aircraft. But, handling problems with the liquid oxygen by service and maintenance engineers caused too many headaches. What was needed was a system which would provide a power boost of approximately 15 minutes and an overtaking speed of 50mph.

A number of Mk VIIs were adapted for meterological research and all surviving aircraft were withdrawn from service in 1947.

OFFICIAL REPORTS ON Mk VI

Boscombe Down October 1942. AB450. Merlin 60. Prototype F Mk VII (converted from Mk V). Carbon monoxide contamination tests. None found in cockpit during taxying and flight tests.

Boscombe Down October 1942. AB450. Performance and cooling tests with 0.42 propeller reduction gear. Rotol four blade dural prop, auw 8,000lb. Climb performance would have been better with 0.477 gear. Maximum speed @ 16,000ft in MS gear 390mph.

Boscombe Down 20 March 1943. AB229. Rate of roll measurement with reduced span ailerons. Ailerons reduced to 6ft 3in span in wide span wings. When compared with Spitfire with normal wings and ailerons the rate of roll was reduced at times by 40%.

Boscombe Down 21 March 1943. BS229. Carbon monoxide contamination tests. With ventilators closed contamination was nil. When open it was within excepted limits in level flight, nil in a dive but high during climb. Recommendations were to lock all ventilators.

Boscombe Down 14 May 1943. BS229. Rate of roll measurements with reduced span ailerons and normal Spitfire wing. Fitting of normal span wing tips increased rolling performance appreciably.

Boscombe Down March 1943. BS229. Stability tests. Both lateral and directional stability was poorer than previous Spitfire Marks, and longitudinal neutral and poorer than the the Mk V and VI. Increased horn balance on elevators.

Boscombe Down Feb-October 1943. BS229. Tests of landing flaps as air brakes. Four sets of flaps were used, the first failing after two dives (410 and 450mph). The port flap failed on the second set during a dive at 470mph. The third set had a number of ribs strengthened but three failed during dives at 470mph. The fourth, and final, set had all ribs strengthened and no damage occurred during dives at 470mph. Comparison dives were made with wing tips deleted.

Boscombe Down July-September 1944. MD176. HF Mk VII (RM.16SM, Merlin 112). Performance and cooling trials with pseudo Merlin 112 engine, a composite of a Merlin 61 and RM.16SM. Auw 7,990lbs. Maximum speed MS gear @

MD124, Boscombe Down, September 1944.

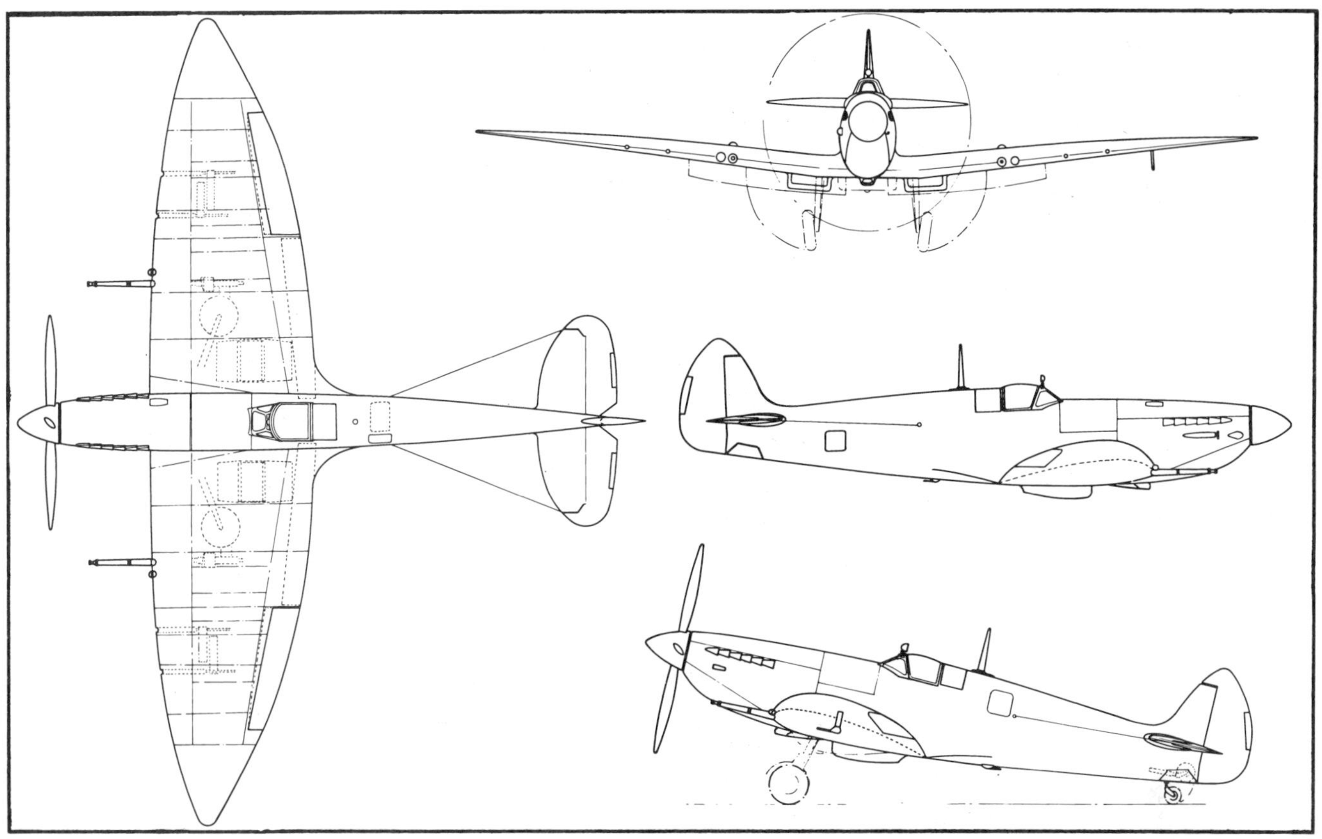

Spitfire HF Mk VII.

16,200ft, 400mph, FS gear @ 29,400 424, maximum rate of climb MS gear 4,060ft/min, FS gear 2,910, absolute ceiling 45,700ft. Service ceiling (100ft min) 45,100. engine with 18¼lb boost. The engine was a partially converted Merlin 71 driving a four blade Rotol R3/4F5/3 Jablo of 10ft 9in diameter. Coarse pitch 65°, fine 35°.

Farnborough May 1943. Application of the calculus of variations of propeller design to the Spitfire Mk VII Merlin 61. Purpose of investigation to discover whether any modifications could usefully be made to the normal planform and pitch distribution of a propeller. Design of blade shape indicated an improvement of efficiency at top speed of 2-3%. Four blade and six blade contra props utilised.

Farnborough November 1945. EN465 and EN470. Merlin 71. Liquid oxygen power boosting. A LOX boosting system, designed by RAE, was installed in both Spitfires by Heston Aircraft Ltd., in order to improve high altitude performance by increasing engine power output by 300bhp. In level flight at 40,000ft the system provided an additional 27mph for 7 minutes, and rate of climb above 41,000ft and ceiling were substantialy increased. Weight of the complete system, including LOX, was 130lb. Auw EN465 7,110lb, EN470 7,345.

F Mk VII and HF Mk VII

Wing. Planform elliptical; section NACA 2200 Series; Span 40ft 2in, incidence° root +2 to −½ 18ft 6in from CL a/c; dihedral° 6; thickness % root 13.2, tip 6; aspect ratio 6.49:1; area, gross 248.5; chord (geo) 6.38, (ma) 7.4. Ailerons. Area 18; chord (ma) movement° up 24, down 18; droop ⅜. Flaps. Area 15.6; movement° down 85. Wing loading 31.9lb sq ft; power loading 5.0716/hp.

Tailplane. Area 31.46; chord (ma) 4.0; incidence° root), tip ± ½; dihedral° 0. Elevators. Area 13.26; movement° up 28, down 23. Tab area 0.38; movement° up 20, down 7. Fin area 4.61. Rudder. Area 8.23; movement° each way 28. Tab area 0.35; movement° port 18, starbd 6.

Undercarriage. Wheels dunlop AH 10019; tyres Dunlop IK 13 or 17. Oleo pressure 415 or 510; tyre pressure 57. Tailwheel retractable castoring. Wheel Dunlop AH 2184/IX; tyre Dunlop Ecta TA12 or 14. Oleo pressure 265; tyre 57.

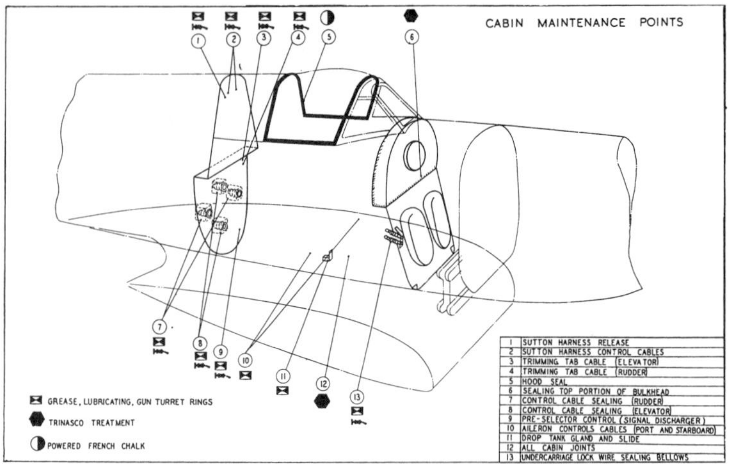

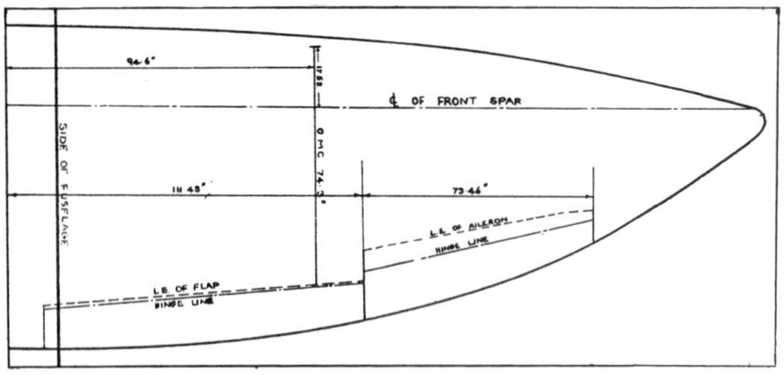

CABIN MAINTENANCE POINTS
GREASE, LUBRICATING, GUN TURRET RINGS
TRINASCO TREATMENT
POWERED FRENCH CHALK
1 SUTTON HARNESS RELEASE
2 SUTTON HARNESS CONTROL CABLES
3 TRIMMING TAB CABLE (ELEVATOR)
4 TRIMMING TAB CABLE (RUDDER)
5 HOOD SEAL
6 SEALING TOP PORTION OF BULKHEAD
7 CONTROL CABLE SEALING (RUDDER)
8 CONTROL CABLE SEALING (ELEVATOR)
9 PRE-SELECTOR CONTROL (SIGNAL DISCHARGER)
10 AILERON CONTROLS CABLES (PORT AND STARBOARD)
11 DROP TANK GLAND AND SLIDE
12 ALL CABIN JOINTS
13 UNDERCARRIAGE LOCK WIRE SEALING BELLOWS

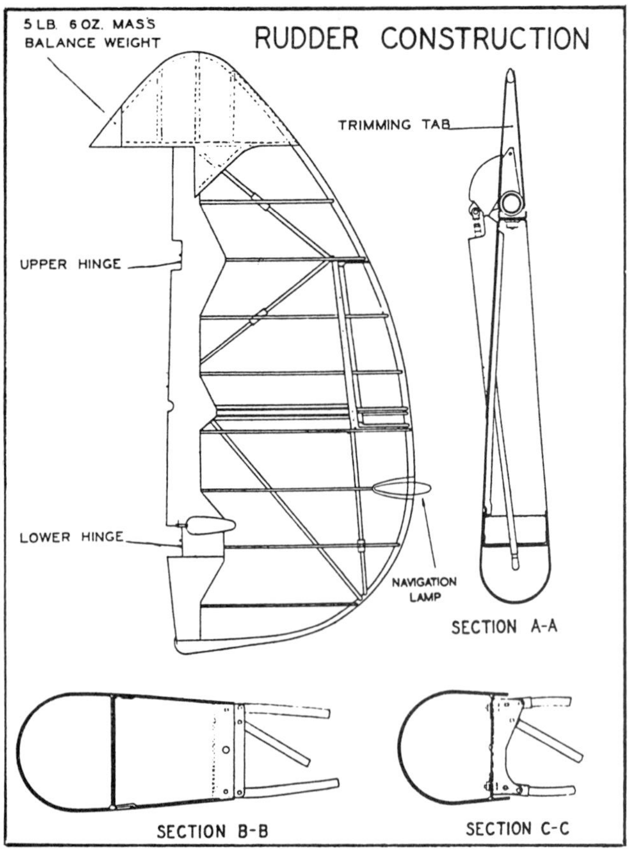

RUDDER CONSTRUCTION
5 LB. 6 OZ. MASS BALANCE WEIGHT
TRIMMING TAB
UPPER HINGE
LOWER HINGE
NAVIGATION LAMP
SECTION A-A
SECTION B-B
SECTION C-C

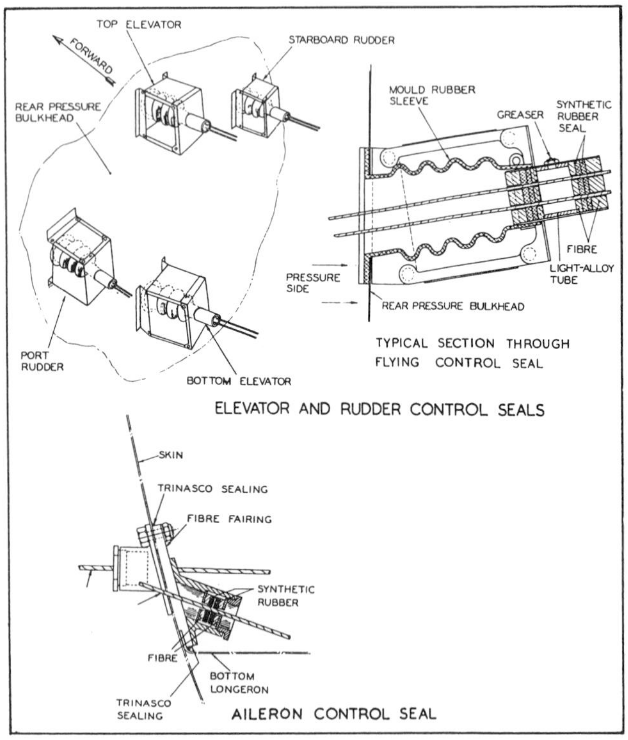

TOP ELEVATOR
FORWARD
STARBOARD RUDDER
REAR PRESSURE BULKHEAD
MOULD RUBBER SLEEVE
GREASER
SYNTHETIC RUBBER SEAL
FIBRE
LIGHT-ALLOY TUBE
PRESSURE SIDE
REAR PRESSURE BULKHEAD
TYPICAL SECTION THROUGH FLYING CONTROL SEAL
PORT RUDDER
BOTTOM ELEVATOR
ELEVATOR AND RUDDER CONTROL SEALS
SKIN
TRINASCO SEALING
FIBRE FAIRING
SYNTHETIC RUBBER
FIBRE
BOTTOM LONGERON
TRINASCO SEALING
AILERON CONTROL SEAL

94·6"
17·58
℄ OF FRONT SPAR
SIDE OF FUSELAGE
S.M.C. 74·3"
111·48"
73·46"
L.E. OF AILERON
HINGE LINE
L.E. OF FLAP
HINGE LINE

Wing of F Mk VII.

STRUCTURE IN WAY OF RADIATOR
WALKWAY
HISPANO GUN BAYS
NON-SLIP FITTED PORT AND STARBOARD
BROWNING GUN BAYS
MAIN SPARS
DOWNWARD IDENTIFICATION LAMP
AMMUNITION BOX BAYS
MAIN PLANE CONSTRUCTION
FUEL TANKS
STARBOARD
PORT
STRUCTURE SHOWN ONLY WHERE DIFFERENT FROM STARBOARD PLANE

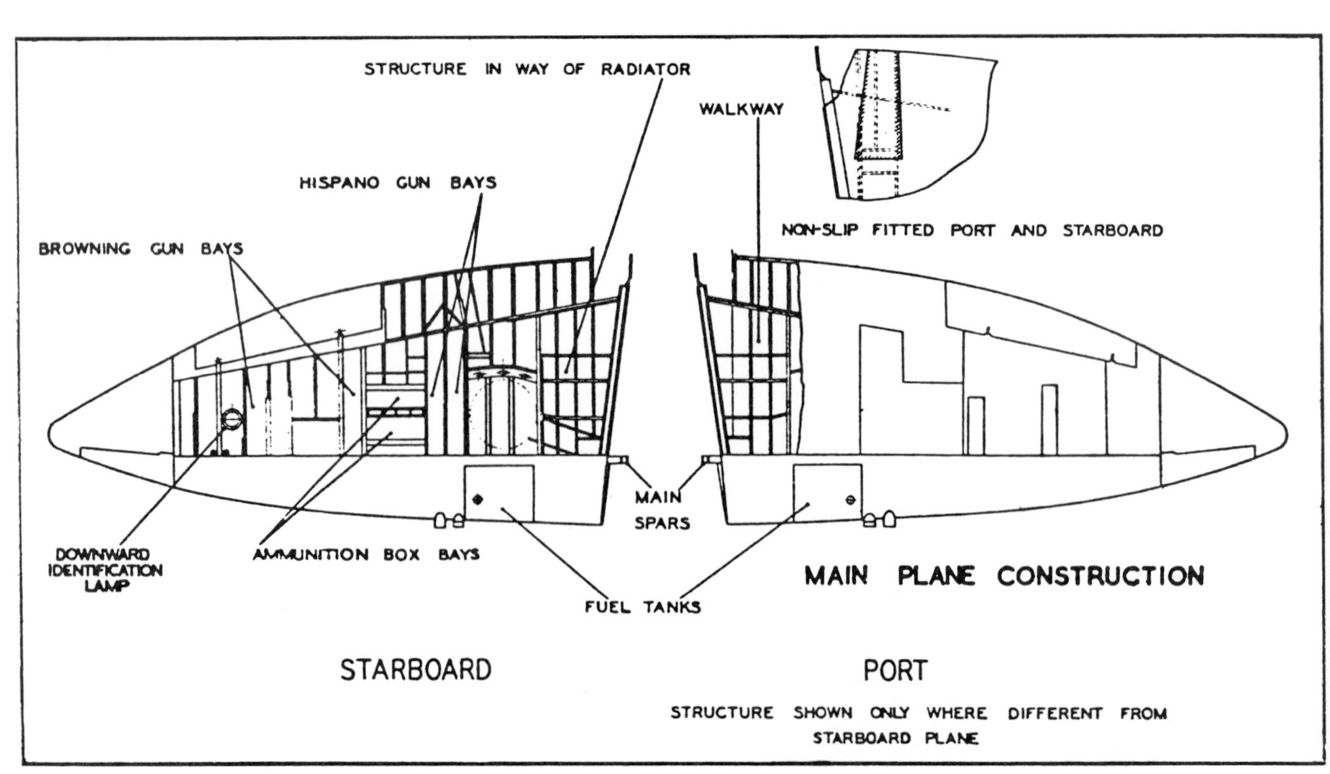

Engine/s. **Merlin/(F VII) 61 1,565hp @ 3,000rpm @ 1,225ft. Two stage, two speed. SU carb: Electric starting. Merlin 71 (HF VII) Normal climb 2,850rpm + 12; combat climb 3,000 + 18. Max speed (MS) + 18, FS + 8; Cruise (MS) 2,650 + 7. Merlin 64 1,710hp (F VII).**

Propellers. Merlin 61. Rotol 4-blade R3/4F5/2 Dural pitch range 35° fine pitch 31° 10' or; R3/4F5/3 Dural PR 35° FP 30° 10, or; R5/4F5/4 Jablo or Hydulignum PR 35° FP 20° 20'. Merlin 64. R12/4F5/4 Jablo or Hydulignum PR 35° FP 22° 20'. All 10ft 9in diameter.

Coolant. 70% distilled water, 30% Glycol. 12.5 gals in main system; 5.75 intercooler.

Fuel. Capacity Fuselage (upper) 47 gals, lower 49; wing leading edge 2 × $12\frac{3}{4}$, total $121\frac{1}{2}$ gals. Plus 30, 45, 90 and 170 o.ld tanks.

Oil. 7.5 gals in tank behind rear pressure bulkhead early a/c; 8.5 under engine later models.

Armour. 202lb.

Armament. B wing. Gunsight GM.2 reflector. Some a/c with Hispano Mk V cannon. Cine camera G.45 starbd wing.

Performance. F VII. Max speed 408mph @ 16,000ft; 374 @ 28,000; 424 @ 29,500. Stall @ normal take off wt 82 flaps up, down 74. Range 660 miles. Ceiling 43,000. HF VII. 400mph **@ 16,200ft 3,000rpm + $18\frac{1}{4}$ (MS); 424 @ 29,400, 3,000rpm + $18\frac{1}{4}$ (FS). Max climb 4,060ft min (MS); 2,910 (FS). Full throttle height (MS) 13,400ft; FS 26,800ft. Service ceiling 45,100, absolute 45,700. Change from MS to FS automatically @ 20,000ft. Time to 40,000ft 14.9min.**

Radio. TR1143, A1271, IFF ARI500 or 5025.

Weights. Tare (Lobelle hood) 5,947 (normal hood) 5,887, take off 7,928, max permissible 8,000. With CP tare 6,645, take off 8,614. With C wing take off 8,021.

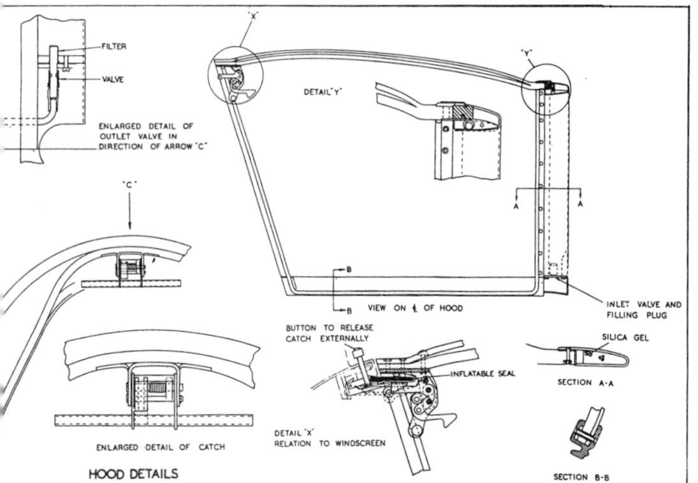

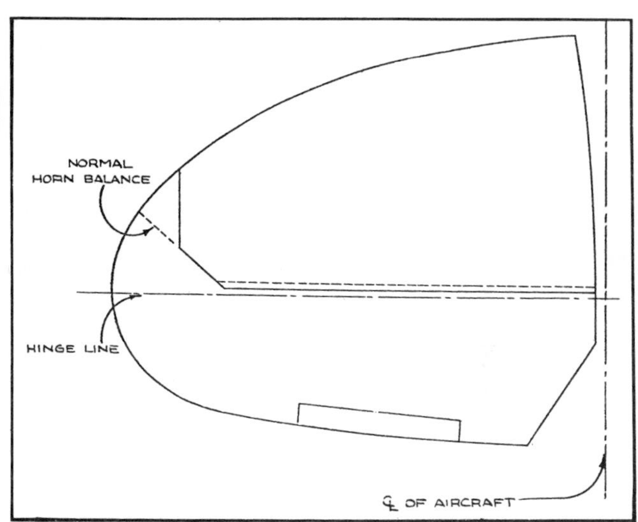

Elevator horn of BS229 was enlarged as indicated here.

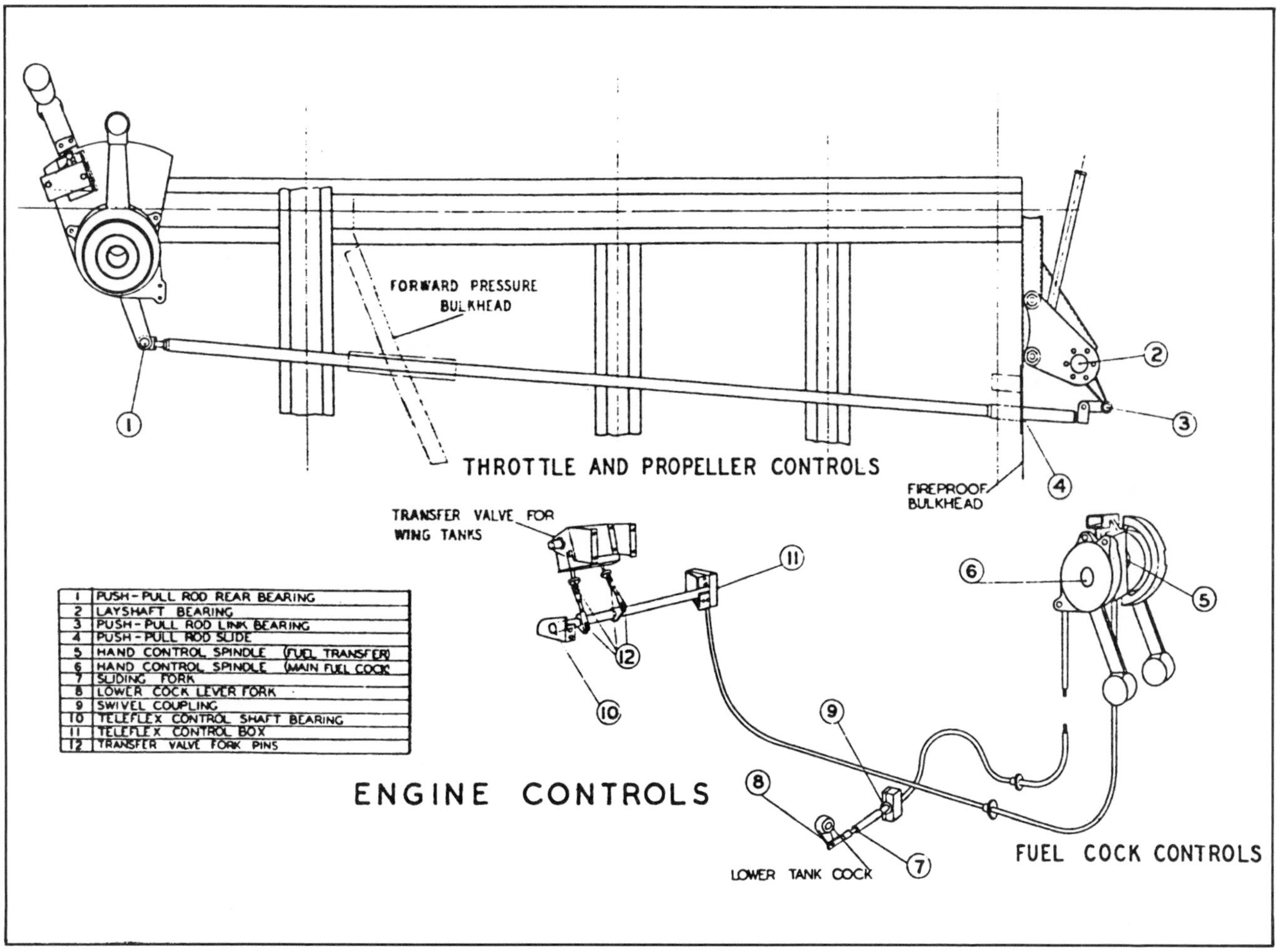

FORWARD PRESSURE BULKHEAD

THROTTLE AND PROPELLER CONTROLS

FIREPROOF BULKHEAD

TRANSFER VALVE FOR WING TANKS

1	PUSH-PULL ROD REAR BEARING
2	LAYSHAFT BEARING
3	PUSH-PULL ROD LINK BEARING
4	PUSH-PULL ROD SLIDE
5	HAND CONTROL SPINDLE (FUEL TRANSFER)
6	HAND CONTROL SPINDLE (MAIN FUEL COCK
7	SLIDING FORK
8	LOWER COCK LEVER FORK
9	SWIVEL COUPLING
10	TELEFLEX CONTROL SHAFT BEARING
11	TELEFLEX CONTROL BOX
12	TRANSFER VALVE FORK PINS

ENGINE CONTROLS

LOWER TANK COCK

FUEL COCK CONTROLS

SERIAL NUMBERS

Supermarine Aviation (Vickers) Ltd.

Contract No B19713/39.

Fifth order for 1,100 Spitfire Mk IA/IB dated 24 October 1940. Built as PR Mk IV/VB/VC/VI/VII/IX between February and November 1942. The following serial apply to F and HF Mk VIIs built to this fifth order; BS121, 142, 229, 253 and 427.

Seventh order for 500 Spitfire Mk VC dated 23 August 1941. Built as Mks PR IV/VI/VII/IX/X/XI/XII between November 1942 and August 1943. the following serials apply to F and HF Mk VIIs built to this seventh order; EN178, 192, 285, 297, 310, 457, 465, 470, 474,494-497, 499, 505-506, 509 and 511-512.

Tenth order for 426 Spitfire Mk VC dated 12 May 1942. Built as Mks VII/VIII/IX/X/XI/XII between July 1943 and March 1944. The following serials apply to F and HF Mk VIIs built to this tenth order; MB761-769,806, 808, 820-828, 883-887, 912-916, 929-935, MD100-146 and 159-190. Total built 141.

As in the case of the Mk VI there are differences between Supermarine and RAF records. Supermarine do not include; BS253, 427, EN178 and 496 but include BS150 and 604. RAF records are taken throughout in order that continuity is maintained

All HF VII. Engines specified.

BS121 3252 M61 EA CRD WD 5-9-42 H/A Flt North 23-9 123S 25-1-43 mr 22-5-44 recat E 15-6. First prod a/c to RAF

BS142 3385 M61 EA CRD WD 17-9-42 H/A Flt North 23-9 124S 25-1-43 FAAC 9-8 SOC 24-4-45 to 4419M fus only, CRD W Wal 4-12-43

BS229 3574 M61 EA CRD WD 2-11-42 BDn 20-3-43 rate of roll measurements with reduced span ails Down by 40% when comp with normal wng span Spit ails reversal estimated to be 470mph, a decrease of of approx 40mph. Carb mono contam tests. 14-5 rate of roll measurements with extended tips removed. Stab tests with increased horn balanced elev Oct'43 trls with ld flaps used as air brakes. Original flaps failed after two dives at 410 and 450mph. IAS. the second set failed after one dive at 410mph and two at 470mph. The third set had strengthened ribs and increased metal guage. They survived dives at 470mph. AFDU 2-2-44 Univ wng instal May'44 Stab trls with FV rud FAAC 5-9 ROS AFDU 1-2-45 AST 27-6

BS253 3524 M47 EA 33MU 24-10-42 616S 11-4-43 SOC 7-2-45

BS427 3299 M47 EA 6MU 29-8-42 76MU 1-9 *Ripley* 8-9 ME 28-10 SOC 25-5-44

EN series All HF VII. Merlin 61 unless otherwise indicated

EN178 3672 EA CRD R-RH 4-12-42 Hand Sq Hull 13-1-43 V VW 14-3 M71 instal gen dev H/A spit MMOF 19-12 124S 18-5-44 ASTH 26-5 SOC 29-11-45

EN192 3693 EA Hand Sq Hull 1-12-42 23MU 11-1-43 Mal WW 15-3 Aero-dynamic Flight Farn 5-7 C.O trls and Malcolm hood jett tests 124S 19-5-44 H/A trls SOC 9-12-48

EN285 3758 EA H/A Flt North 29-12-42 124S 25-1-43 1CRU 24-11-44 33MU 25-11 SOC 30-11 Shoe for trls with live AA ammunition to test explosive decompression of press cabin SOC 4-5-48

EN297 3765 EA CRD WW 231-12-42 Malcolm hood instal. Farn 14-4-43 CO trls BDn trls with conical and curved w/s, trls A.I radar 33MU 3-4-44 501SU 21-7 519S 16-7-45 sold Int All 1903047

EN310 3841 EA 33MU 11-1-43 124S 10-3 FACB 29-4 ROS 1CRU 30-10 124S 10-11 eng fire in flt f/ld Lashendon Kent CE 3-3-44

EN457 3906 EA 39MU 26-1-43 124S 9-3 e/fld at H/A glided to NWld o/s w/u ldg CE 21-5

EN465 3932 EA CRD HAL 7-2-43 mods for liquid oxygen eng inject Farn 28-8-43 M71 instal trls with same. 131S 28-8-44 ETPS trls with new eng and LOX; fuel pump trls. AFDU 30-8-44 39MU 4-12 AFDU 7-12 52MU 7-5-45 SOC 13-8

EN470 3961 EA CRD HAL 13-2-43 mods for liqid oxygen eng inject Farn 6-9 M71 instal trls with same. ETPS Oct'44 Lox eng boost trls 33MU 19-5-45

EN474 M64 EA 47MU 13-3-43 *Glenapp* 10-4 New York USA 2-5 issued to US Army HQ on trans 6-1-44 Freeman Field, Indiana 1946 as FE-400. Extant, displayed NASM Washington, DC.

EN477 3980 EA 33MU 15-2-43 MalWW 19-3 mods 39MU 24-9 616S 9-11 SOC 25-4-46

EN494 4090 M64 EA VWD 8-2-44 33MU 22-4 616S 26-6 HAA trls M71 instal SOC 9-12-48

EN495 4122 EA 39MU 22-3-43 124S 13-5 FACB 29-5 MMO 131S 2-8-44 HAA trls 9-12-48 SOC

EN496 4172 M64 EA 39MU 5-4-43 124S 15-4 dvd i/sea from H/A off Deal 14-5

EN497 4195 M64 EA 33MU 11-4-43 124S 18-4 FAAC 30-5 MMO 29MU 20-8-45 sold Int All 19-3-47

EN499 4224 M64 EA VWD 19-4-43 wts and CG load 33MU 28-4 124S 6-5 3501SU 6-7-44 131S 2-8 3GTS 11-10-45 39MU NEA 11-5-46

EN505 4267 M64 EA 33MU 4-5-43 124S 11-5 39MU 8-9-44 SOC H/A trls 9-12-48

EN506 4594 M64 EA 39MU 27-7-43 405ARF HAL 19-8 124S 17-8 MalWW 7-2-44 mods 33MU 13-5-45 519S FAAC 7-11 SOC 19-11

EN509 4279 M64 EA CRD 10-5-43 39MU 9-10 124S 9-11 SOC H/A trls 9-12-48

EN511 4290 M64 EA 9MU 15-5-43 R-RH 22-5 124S 7-8 CAC ops 26-4-44 SOC 9-2-45

EN512 4312 M64 EA 39MU 18-5-43 124S 10-5 e/fld w/u ldg Gillingham Kent 13-10 FH140.15

MB series All HF VII Merliln 64

MB761 4512 EA 33MU 4-7-43 124S 15-7 FAAC 23-12 1402Met Flt 28-10-44 SOC HAA trls 9-12-48

MB762 4547 EA 39MU 16-7-43 ROS 5-8 405ARF 1-9 616S 28-9 CAC ops 21-1-44

MB763 4568 EA 33MU 20-7-43 405ARF HAL 4-8 312S 11-8 118S 4-10 453S 27-10 Stn Flt Skae 8-11 FAAC 15-7-44 recat E 18-9

MB764 4593 EA 39MU 26-7-43 405ARF HAL 19-8 616S 14-10 CB ops 5-3-44 2AGS 3-3-45 sold Int All 19-3-47

MB765 4611 EA 33MU 10-8-43 405ARF 16-8 312S 18-8 118S 4-10 453S 27-10 Stn Flt Skae 8-11 CB ops SOC HAA trls 30-12-48

MB766 4635 EA 33MU 15-8-43 405ARF HAL 21-8 124S 28-8 3011 Service Echelon 4-2-44 CAC ops 124S 14-2-44

MB767 4641 EA 9MU 15-8-43 405ARF 22-8 616S 1-9 CAC ops ROS Ftr Com North 10-11-44 Shoe as target a/c SOC HAA trls 9-12-48

MB768 4647 EA 33MU 17-8-43 405ARF 27-8 616S 14-9 CE ops 12-6-44

MB769 4668EA 39MU 23-8-43 405ARF 8-9 616S 28-9 3GTS 11-10-45 39MU NEA SOC 11-5-46

MB806 4328 EA 9MU 14-5-43 R-RH 27-5 124S 23-8 Malcolms 7-2-44 mods 2AGS 22-3-45 sold scr 3-9-47

MB808 4359 EA 39MU 28-5-43 124S 6-6 CAC ops 14-2-44 616S 3-4 SOC HAA trls 30-12-48

MB820 4366 EA 39MU 28-5-43 124S 9-6 SOC HAA trls 30-12-48

MB821 4377 EA 39MU 30-5-43 124S 8-6 CB ops 26-6 Shoe as target a/c SOC 11-5-48

MB822 4392 EA 9MU 2-6-43 124S 28-6 CAC ops 11-1-44 ROS 616S 17-4 Shoe as target a/c SOC 26-5-48

MB823 4395 9MU 3-6-43 124S 10-7 FACB 29-8 11AGS 8-3-44 sold scr 3-9-47

MB824 4413 EA 39MU 6-6-43 124S 17-6 CAC 9-9 616S SOC HAA trls 30-12-48

MB825 4438 EA M61 33MU 16-6-43 124S 28-6 CA 22-10 11AGS 26-5-45 SOC 17-10-46

MB826 44426 EA 33MU 12-6-43 124S 21-6 3011 Service Echelon 30-11 124S 24-12 FAAC 7-4-44 SOC HAA trls 9-12-48

MB827 4448 EA 33MU 19-6-43 124S 4-7 VA 2-9 SOC 11-5-48

MB828 4482 EA 39MU 29-6-43 405ARF HAL 4-8 312S 11-8 118S 4-10 453S 27-10 Stn Flt Skae 8-11 SOC HAA trls 30-12-48

MB883 Stn 39MU 30-1-44 131S 24-2 FTR ops 7-6

MB884 STN 39MU 4-2-44 131S 22-6 11AGS 14-5-45 sold Int All 4-7-46

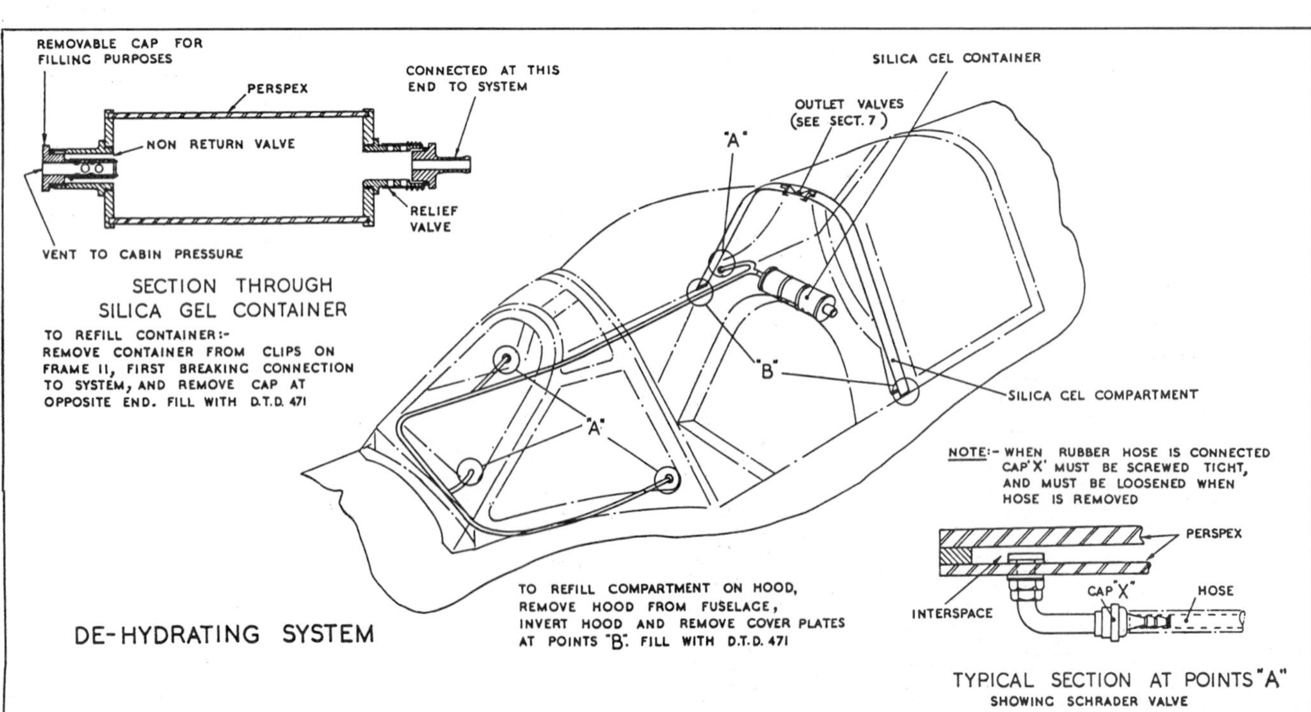

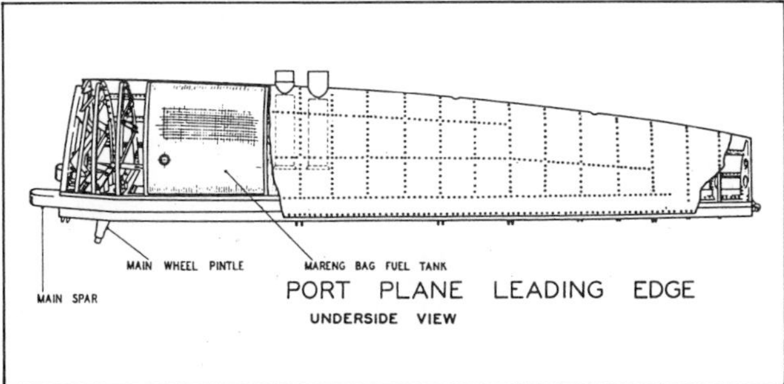
MAIN SPAR
MAIN WHEEL PINTLE
MARENG BAG FUEL TANK
PORT PLANE LEADING EDGE
UNDERSIDE VIEW

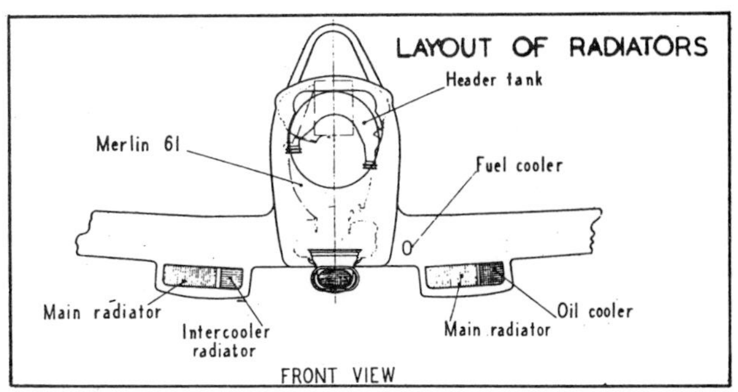
LAYOUT OF RADIATORS
Header tank
Merlin 61
Fuel cooler
Main radiator
Intercooler radiator
Oil cooler
Main radiator
FRONT VIEW

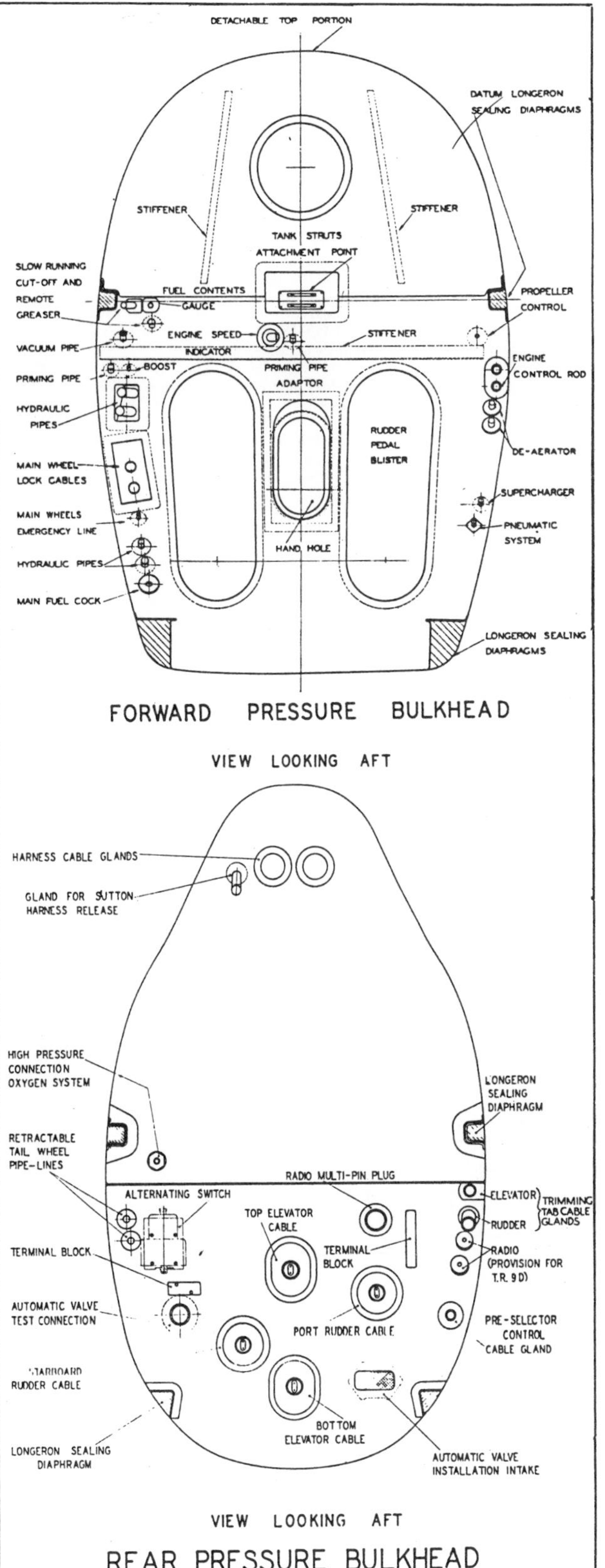
DETACHABLE TOP PORTION
DATUM LONGERON SEALING DIAPHRAGMS
STIFFENER
STIFFENER
TANK STRUTS ATTACHMENT POINT
SLOW RUNNING CUT-OFF AND REMOTE GREASER
FUEL CONTENTS GAUGE
PROPELLER CONTROL
VACUUM PIPE
ENGINE SPEED INDICATOR
STIFFENER
PRIMING PIPE
BOOST
PRIMING PIPE ADAPTOR
ENGINE CONTROL ROD
HYDRAULIC PIPES
RUDDER PEDAL BLISTER
DE-AERATOR
MAIN WHEEL LOCK CABLES
SUPERCHARGER
MAIN WHEELS EMERGENCY LINE
PNEUMATIC SYSTEM
HAND HOLE
HYDRAULIC PIPES
MAIN FUEL COCK
LONGERON SEALING DIAPHRAGMS
FORWARD PRESSURE BULKHEAD
VIEW LOOKING AFT
HARNESS CABLE GLANDS
GLAND FOR SUTTON HARNESS RELEASE
HIGH PRESSURE CONNECTION OXYGEN SYSTEM
LONGERON SEALING DIAPHRAGM
RETRACTABLE TAIL WHEEL PIPE-LINES
RADIO MULTI-PIN PLUG
ALTERNATING SWITCH
TOP ELEVATOR CABLE
ELEVATOR
RUDDER
TRIMMING TAB CABLE GLANDS
RADIO (PROVISION FOR T.R. 9D)
TERMINAL BLOCK
TERMINAL BLOCK
AUTOMATIC VALVE TEST CONNECTION
PORT RUDDER CABLE
PRE-SELECTOR CONTROL CABLE GLAND
RUDDER CABLE
BOTTOM ELEVATOR CABLE
LONGERON SEALING DIAPHRAGM
AUTOMATIC VALVE INSTALLATION INTAKE
VIEW LOOKING AFT
REAR PRESSURE BULKHEAD

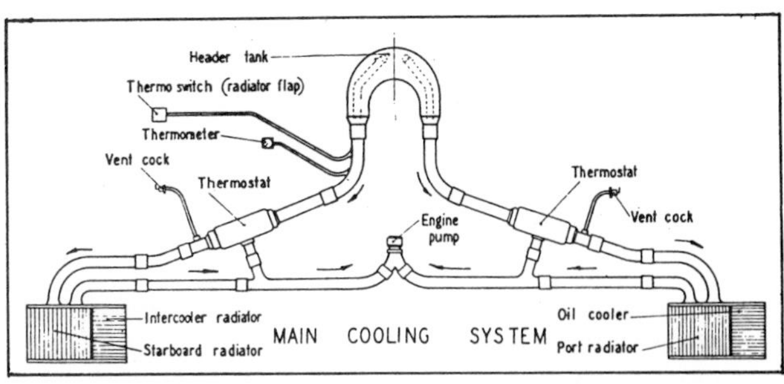
Header tank
Thermo switch (radiator flap)
Thermometer
Vent cock
Thermostat
Thermostat
Vent cock
Engine pump
Intercooler radiator
Starboard radiator
MAIN COOLING SYSTEM
Oil cooler
Port radiator

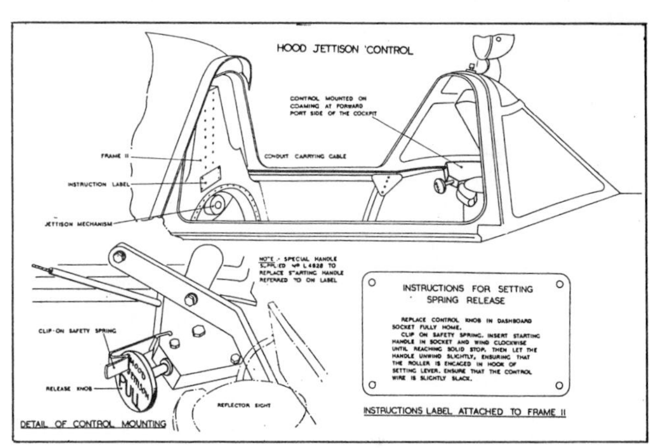
HOOD JETTISON CONTROL
INSTRUCTIONS FOR SETTING SPRING RELEASE
DETAIL OF CONTROL MOUNTING
INSTRUCTIONS LABEL ATTACHED TO FRAME 11

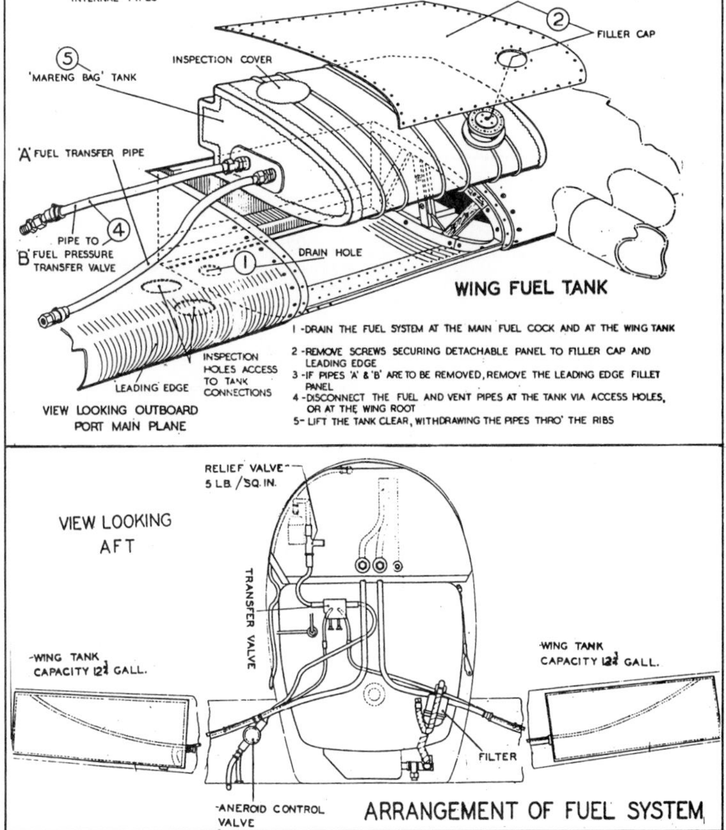
NOTE- THESE TANKS SHOULD BE HANDLED WITH CARE TO AVOID FRACTURING INTERNAL PIPES
SCREW FASTENED DETACHABLE PANEL
FILLER CAP
INSPECTION COVER
'MARENG BAG' TANK
'A' FUEL TRANSFER PIPE
PIPE TO
'B' FUEL PRESSURE TRANSFER VALVE
DRAIN HOLE
WING FUEL TANK
LEADING EDGE
INSPECTION HOLES ACCESS TO TANK CONNECTIONS
VIEW LOOKING OUTBOARD PORT MAIN PLANE
1 -DRAIN THE FUEL SYSTEM AT THE MAIN FUEL COCK AND AT THE WING TANK
2 -REMOVE SCREWS SECURING DETACHABLE PANEL TO FILLER CAP AND LEADING EDGE
3 -IF PIPES 'A' & 'B' ARE TO BE REMOVED, REMOVE THE LEADING EDGE FILLET PANEL
4 -DISCONNECT THE FUEL AND VENT PIPES AT THE TANK VIA ACCESS HOLES, OR AT THE WING ROOT
5- LIFT THE TANK CLEAR, WITHDRAWING THE PIPES THRO' THE RIBS
RELIEF VALVE 5 LB./SQ.IN.
VIEW LOOKING AFT
TRANSFER VALVE
WING TANK CAPACITY 12½ GALL.
WING TANK CAPACITY 12½ GALL.
FILTER
ANEROID CONTROL VALVE
ARRANGEMENT OF FUEL SYSTEM

MB885 STN 33MU 5-2-44 616S 15-5 2AGS 11-4-45 sold Int All 19-3-47

MB886 STN 33MU 5-2-44 124S 24-5 CB ops 14-6 11AGS 13-6-45 sold Int All 19-3-47

MB887 STN 39MU 7-2-44 131S 3-3 FTR ops 1-5

MB912 4739 EA 5-9-43 124S 17-9 CB 2-10 CRD BDn 25-5-44 1402Met Flt 12-9 FACE ff to 39MU 10-2-45 SOC 26-2

MB913 4807 EA 33MU 19-9-43 616S 4-10 CE ops 21-1-44 FH58.20

MB914 4779 EA 39MU 15-9-43 616S 30-10 Shoe as target a/c 21-5-48 SOC

MB915 4826 EAW 33MU 26-9-43 616S 7-11 SOC HAA trls 30-12-48

MB916 4838 EA 39MU 26-9-43 124S 9-11 CB 22-11-44 1CRU 2AGS 28-12-45 sold Int All 19-3-47

MB929 4873 EA 33MU 13-10-43 616S 21-10 e/fld i/sea off Portland Bill 5-11 FH7.30

MB930 4892 EA 33MU 13-10-43 616S 21-10 cd ldg bad visibility Exeter CE 3-12

MB931 4931 EA 39MU 20-10-43 3501SU 23-6-44 31S 9-7 19S 17-1-45 SOC HAA trls 9-12-48

MB932 STN 39MU 8-2-44 131S 20-3 FACB 19-4 recat E 23-9

MB933 STN 33MU 10-2-44 21 Base Def Wng 11-4 511FRU 13-7 18AGS 19-5-45 sold Int All 19-347

MB934 STN 33MU 12-2-44 3501SU 17-6 616S 9-7 2AGS 28-3-45 sold Int All 19-7-47

MB935 STN 39MU 15-2-44 131S 26-2 FTR ops 23-4

MD series All HF VII Merlin 64s

MD100 5034 EA 33MU 14-11-43 616S 25-11 CAC ops 18-4-44 2AGS 19-5-45 FAAC 6-6 ROS recat E SOC 22-6

MD101 5029 EA 33MU 14-11-43 616S 25-11 CAC ops 1-6-44 11AGS 9-5-45 sold Int All 10-3-47

MD102 5044 EA 39MU 16-11-43 616S 26-11 303S 17-1-44 CE 28-11

MD103 5061 EA 39MU 22-11-43 2AGS 25-3-45 sold Int All 19-3-47

MD104 5088 33MU 29-11-43 616S 14-12 CE ops 10-6-44

MD105 5071 EA 33MU 22-11-43 616S 2-12 RAF Exeter 13-3-44 SOC HAA trls 9-12-48

MD106 5096 EA 33MU 4-13-43 616S 24-12 FAAC 12-5-44 recat E 17-7

MD107 5112 EA 33MU 4-12-43 616S 23-12 33MU 22-7-44 MMO 16-11 SOC HAA trls 29-12-48

MD108 5126 EA 33MU 4-12-43 616S 25-12 FTR ops 22-5-44

MD109 5129 EA 9MU 23-12-43 3501SU 14-7-44 2AGS 5-4-45 FACE 20-4

MD110 5158 EA 9MU 22-12-43 131S 26-2-44 12AGS 11-3-45 sold scr 3-9-47

MD111 5159 EA 9MU 22-12-43 131S 7-2-44 CAC ops 18-6 154S 23-11 SOC HAA trls 7-12-48

MD112 5155 EA 39MU 20-12-43 124S 10-1-44 12AGS 16-3-45 FACE 29-11

MD113 5203 EA 39MU 24-12-43 124S 12-1-44 CRD 26-3-45 AFDU Tang 7-4 GRD SOC 31-12

MD114 5204 EA 39MU 24-12-43 Stn Flt Skae 9-2-44 FACE 20-2-44 CRD BDn 28-8 Shoe HAA trls 24-11-48 SOC

MD115 5183 EA 39MU 24-12-43 FACB 17-2-44 recat E 3-4

MD116 5206 EA 39MU 24-12-42 616S 31-1-44 131S 8-4 616S FACE 9-4

MD117 VA WD R-RH 21-1-44 VA 7-3 39MU 19-4 131S 22-5 CAC ops 4-7 11AGS 2-6-45 CE 7-10 SOC 9-8-46

MD118 5192 EA 33MU 27-12-43 Stn Flt Skae 2-1-44 sold Int All 19-3-47

MD119 5209 EA 33MU 24-12-43 131S 26-2-44 St Flt Culmhead 14-6 131S FTR ops 30-4-45

MD120 5210 EA 33MU 24-12-43 131S 26-2-44 FAAC 12-6 ROS 154S 23-11 ASTH 12-9 SOC 14-9

MD121 5231 EA 39MU 1-1-44 616S 31-1 FAAC 8-3 ROS CE ops 12-6

MD122 5231 EA 33MU 1-1-44 Stn Flt Skae 2-3 33MU 8-7-45 SOC 11-8

MD123 5239 EA 33MU 1-1-44 131S 29-2 FTR ops 12-6

MD124 39MU 6-1-44 131S 8-3 BDn 14-9 met recording trls One of the last FVIIs to retain MkII IFF retro-fit MkIV SOC 22-11-45

MD125 STN 39MU 7-1-44 131S 12-3 1AGS 23-4-45 sold Int All 19-3-47

MD126 STN 33MU 14-1-44 124S 26-3 2AGS 6-3-45 SOC 9-11

MD127 5202 EA 33MU 10-11-44 124S 30-4 SOC scr 29-7-46

MD128 STN 39MU 8-1-44 131S 22-5 CAC ops 12-6 recat E 18-9

MD129 STN 39MU 3-2-44 131S 26-2 154S 23-11 SOC 24-2-45

MD130 STN 33MU 20-1-44 124S 8-3 1402Met Flt 18-12 513S 14-9-45 Shoe SOC HAA trls 24-11-48

MD131 STN 39MU 20-1-44 131S 7-3 CAC ops 1-6 ROS recat E 17-7

MD132 STN 33MU 20-1-44 131S 13-3 154S 23-4 SOC 24-2-45

MD133 STN 39MU 23-1-44 616S 22-5 e/fld i/sea off Start Point 19-6

MD134 STN 39MU 23-1-44 131S 3-3 154S 23-11 strk by Dakota of 168S while parked B Hll dbf CE 25-1-45

MD135 STN 39MU 23-1-44 124S 12-3 SOC scr 29-7-46

MD136 STN 33MU 25-1-44 131S CB ops 14-6 FCCS 7-1-45 39MU NEA SOC HAA trls 9-12-48

MD137 STN 33MU 29-1-44 616S 22-6 CAC ops 13-7 131S 2-9 636S 7-12 recat E SOC 27-2-45

MD138 STN 39MU 29-1-44 Stn Flt Skae 7-3 sold Int All 19-3-47

MD139 STN 39MU 29-1-44 124S 24-2 2AGS 28-3 SOC 9-11-45

MD140 STN 33MU 30-1-44 616S 12-6 2AGS 16-3-45 Shoe HAA trls SOC 24-11-48

MD141 STN 33MU 6-2-44 3501SU 6-7 519S 31-8 CAC ops 6-1-45 ROS Shoe HAA trls SOC 24-11-48

MD142 STN 33MU 30-1-44 3501SU 6-7 8 OTU 14-12-45 to 6278M 4-3-47 6SoTT SOC 15-10-50 FFS SoH

MD143 STN 39MU 15-2-44 131S 3-3 154S 23-11 ASTH 12-9-45 SOC 14-9

MD144 STN 33MU 19-2-44 131S 5-3 CAC ops 8-7 154S 25-11 SOC 21-10-46

MD145 STN 33MU 20-2-44 124S 30-4 11AGS 5-3-45 SOC 11-4-46

MD146 STN 39MU 21-2-44 131S 8-3 154S 23-11 SOC 24-2-45

MD159 STN 39MU 22-2-44 131S 3-3 VA 28-3 616S FAAC 20-7 1420Met Flt 14-9-45 Shoe HAA trls SOC 24-11-48

MD160 STN 33MU 22-2-44 131S 2-3 CAC ops 12-6 RAF Leuch SOC 8-1-46

MD161 STN 39MU 3-3-44 124S 29-3 CA 12-4 11AGS 5-3-45 sold Int All 19-3-47

MD162 STN 33MU 2-3-44 124S 25-2 2AGS 26-5-45 sold Int All 19-3-47

MD163 STN 33MU 12-3-44 124S 19-5 HAA trls SOC 9-12-48

MD164 STN 33MU 2-3-44 124S 27-3 Shoe as target a/c SOC 23-4-48

MD165 39MU 3-3-44 3501SU 16-5 131S 17-6 154S 23-11 FACE 14-1-45 SOC 30-1

MD166 STN 39MU 4-1-44 131S FTR ops 17-5

MD167 STN 33MU 16-3-44 124S 30-4 12AGS 14-3 11AGS 9-6-45 sold Int All 19-3-47

MD168 STN 33MU 11-3-44 131S 27-3 154S 23-11 SOC 24-2-45

MD169 STN 33MU 16-3-44 131S 17-6 154S 23-11 11AGS 24-5-45 e/fld on t/o f/ld on beach Andreas CE 11-10 SOC 1-11

MD170 STN 33MU 16-3-44 3501SU 15-5 131S 17-6 154S 23-11 11AGS 1-2-45 to 6087M 4-9-46 allot 453S SOC 24-9-47

MD171 STN 33MU 14-3-44 3501SU 15-5 131S 17-6 FACE 25-8

MD172 STN 33MU 14-3-44 131S 7-4 CB ops 14-6 recat E 17-7

MD173 STN 39MU 15-3-44 131S 27-3 CAC ops 30-6 154S 23-7 HGU Tilstock 8-3-45 SOC scr 29-7-46

MD174 STN 39MU 19-3-44 616S 22-5 131S 22-9 154S 23-11 HAA trls SOC 9-12-48

MD175 33MU 11AGS 4-5-45 sold Int All 19-3-47

MD176 M61 STN CRD R-RH 28-3-44 Conv M71 instal which was a puesdo M112 composite of a M66 and RM 16 SM (110-114 series) with R-R SU injection pump. BDn July'44. Perf and cool trls Fitt FXII rud and Lobelle hood. 58Mu 19-9-45 CRD as pattern a/c SOC 20-9

MD177 M61 STN 33MU 4-4-44 616S 22-4 2AGS 26-3-45 sold Int All 19-3-47

MD178 M61 STN 33MU 9-4-44 616S 22-4 22-4 CAC ops 11-7 131S 2-8 3ADF e/fld in Cole circuit w/u ldg Ditteridge CE 1-3-45

MD179 M61 STN 33MU 13-4-44 124S 14-6 SOC 23-4

MD180 STN 39MU 16-4-44 519S FAAC 10-6-45 recat E SOC 26-6

MD181 STN 39MU 18-5-44 616S 14-6 1402Met Flt 6-12 518S 14-9-45 Shoe HAA trls SOC 24-11-45

MD182 M61 STN 39MU 9-4-44 616S 25-5 Shoe as target a/c SOC 1-6-48

MD183 M61 STN 39MU 13-4-44 131S 19-6 154S 23-11 HAA trls SOC 9-12-48

MD184 M61 STN 39MU 18-5-44 124S 7-6 2AGS 26-3-45

MD185 STN 39MU 19-5-44 3501SU 17-6 17-6 131S 12-7 154S 23-11 HAA trls SOC 9-12-48

MD186 STN 33MU 20-5-44 131S 11-6 154S 23-11 29MU 3-12-45 Shoe HAA trls SOC 24-11-48

MD187 STN 33MU 21-5-44 131S 7-6 CAC 7-7 154S 23-11 HAA trls SOC 9-12-48

MD188 STN 33MU 21-5-44 3501SU 14-6 131S 25-6 Stn Flt Culmhead 25-6 RAF Cole 9-10 HAA trls SOC 9-12-48

MD189 33MU 25-5-44 3501SU 8-6 616S 22-6 BDn 21-10-45 R&D 25-10 SOC 18-4-47 last prod FVII del to RAF 71MU 2-4-47 CE scr 7-7-47

MD190 STN 33MU 25-5-44 CRD BDn 27-5-44 SOC 30-1-47

Maintenance airframes BS142 (4419M) MD170 (6087M)

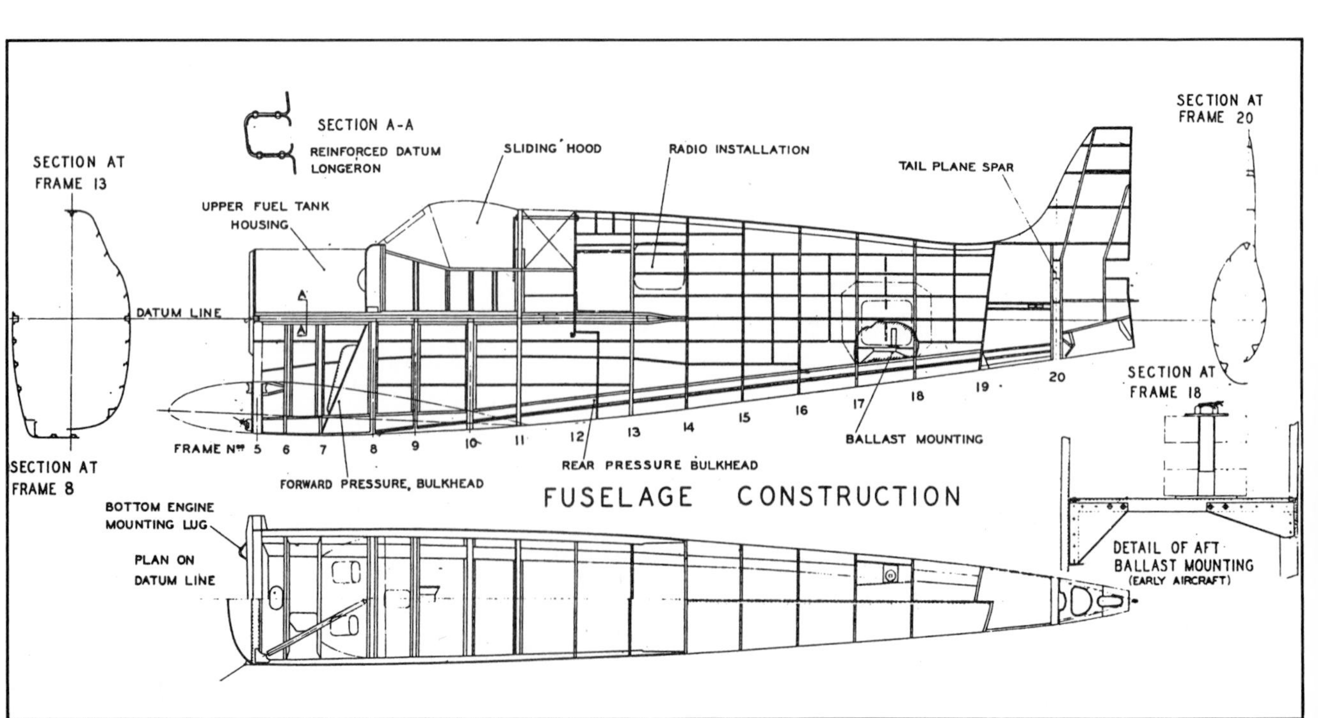

"A SIGNIFICANT AEROPLANE"

History does have a habit of repeating itself, albeit in an oblique manner on some occasions, and the month of September falls into this category so far as World War Two affected the Royal Air Force. It went to war on 3 September 1939; the peak of the Battle of Britain was reached during the same month one year later, and a third event occurred on 27 September 1941. Pilots returning from a sweep over Northern France reported the existence of a new, high performance, radial engined German fighter which was clearly superior to the Spitfire Mk V. RAF Intelligence was of the immediate opinion that it might have been the Curtiss Hawk fighter, a number of which had been supplied to France by America before the French Armistice.

As the file on the new fighter grew, and Spitfire losses mounted, it was obvious that the Luftwaffe possessed a superior weapon and an answer to it had to be found. Part of that answer came in the form of a 'present' from the Luftwaffe when an example of the new fighter, the superb Focke-Wulf Fw190 'Butcher Bird', inadvertently landed in England after the pilot had mistaken the coast of this country for France. Both RAE Farnborough and the Air Ministry had their theories about a radial engined, air cooled interceptor being inferior in performance to an in-line engine fighter violently overturned, for here was such an aeroplane superior to anything the RAF had in service.

This is not to say that the Air Ministry were lacking in foresight regarding up-dating the RAF's requirements for improved equipment, as plans were already well advanced for Spitfires powered by improved Merlin engines and, of course, the new generation Griffons. Also in the development stage were the new Hawker fighters – the Tornado and Typhoon to

JF299 was delivered to AFDU, Wittering, for handling trials and was then converted to have a reduced area rear fuselage and 'tear-drop' cockpit hood. It went to Boscombe Down for trials in September 1943; had a tropical air intake installed plus an enlarged rudder and extended wing tips. It was then shipped to North Africa for tropical trials, returned to Vickers and reverted to Mk VIII standards. A curved windscreen was fitted in front of the bullet proof panel.

be powered by the Napier Sabre engine.

The latest version of the Spitfire under development at that time was the F Mk VII, and the developed airframe and Merlin 60 Series engine would have enabled it to meet the Fw190 threat with some measure of success. But, it would be many months before sufficient production would provide enough for the RAF. What was needed was a new variant and a repetition of the Merlin 45 and eventual compromise Spitfire, the F Mk V. Fortunately for the RAF the sequence of events leading up to this 'new' Spitfire had begun when Rolls-Royce was experimenting with the intercooled Merlin 60 engine in modified F Mk I airframes, one of which was the Mk III prototype N3297.

It was used as a trials aircraft for the RM 8SM Merlin 61 engine with a much modified airframe and as such had flown for the first time on 20 September 1941. On Air Ministry instructions it had been despatched to Rolls-Royce, Hucknall, arriving there in April 1941 for installation of the RM2 SM Merlin 61. Performance trials at Boscombe Down took place in January to April 1942 and the speed range was (MS gear 330 mph at sea level, 368 at 10,000ft. FS gear, 400 mph at 23,700ft, 414 at 27,200 and 330 at 42,000. Maximum rate of climb was 3,200ft/min.

Supermarine realised there was not sufficient time to design a new Spitfire variant and the modifications dictated by trials with N3297 were incorporated into the F Mk VIII. The newest Spitfire variant was, in effect, an unpressurised version of the HF VII and intended for low altitude operations. JF274, which appeared 13 months after the Fw190 was recognised, was at Worthy Down on 9 November 1942 for weighing and CG determination. It had a Mk VII fuselage strengthened to cope with the various overload conditions, a retractable tail wheel and the universal wing. The figures (right) relate to the various loadings and configuration.

The Spitfire F Mk VIII was a significant aeroplane, for not only did it mark the transition point between the Merlin and Griffon powered aeroplane, it also introduced numerous design modifications which were incorporated as standard in the variants which followed it into production. There were three major versions of the Mk VIII – the F (fighter), HF (high altitude) and LF (low altitude fighter bomber), and the first production aircraft to reach the RAF were the latter. JF462 left

Condition of aeroplane	2 cannon & 4 Browning		4 cannon	
	Weight (lb)	CG (in)	Weight	CG (aft of datum)
Tare	5861	0.2	5861	0.2
Landing	6710	4.9	6885	5.0
Normal load	7831	5.9	8063	6.2
30 gal o/d tank	8131	6.4	8363	6.7
90 gal o/d tank	8648	7.0	8880	7.2
	With desert equipment			
Tare	5861	0.2	3861	0.2
Landing	6757	5.5	6932	5.5
Normal load	7878	6.4	8110	6.7
30 gal o/d tank	8178	6.85	8410	7.1
90 gal o/d tank	8695	7.4	8927	7.6

Merlin 61 engine with Rotol four blade Hydulignum propeller and rear fuselage oil tank. JF330 was weighed on 20 February 1943 and was lighter for it had a nose oil tank, a Merlin 63 and a wooden propeller and was without desert equipment. Tare 5772 lb, auw 'B' wing 7752, auw 'C' wing 7984.

the production line in April 1943 powered by a Merlin 66 (RM 10SM) with a .477 reduction gearing, and interconnected throttle/propeller controls. In an attempt to improve landing characteristics JF707 was fitted with an experimental undercarriage designed to eliminate toe-in and camber. It was forwarded to Castle Bromwich for trials on a hard surfaced runway to measure tyre wear. During the trials it was discovered that the modified axles had been assembled incorrectly to the oleos and only when changed (port to starboard) was toe-in eliminated. The aircraft then went to Boscombe Down who reported no adverse effects on take off, landing and taxying.

The Merlin 60 Series engines had resulted in a longer engine cowling and there was a tendency for pilots on landing to misjudge their attitude to the runway, and allowed the nose to tilt forward and then drop back to complete the landing run. Inevitably, the tilt forward resulted in the propeller striking the ground and damaged the tips. This was known as 'pecking' or 'bogging'. JG246 was sent to Rotol Airscrews for installation and trials of a cropped propeller to determine how short the blades could be without their characteristics being drastically altered. At 8ft 3in length there was a reduction in overall performance and at 7ft 11in this reduction became pronounced.

JF275, second production Mk VIII, was used for trials of the Supermarine tropical air intake. It served as a communucations aircraft at RAF Staff College and was finally sold in South America in 1947.

The results of the experiments were relayed to the service MUs and they did enable engineering personnel to ascertain if an aeroplane with a broken or damaged propeller could be air ferried for repair.

Short tactical trials of the Mk VIII took place at AFDU Wittering on 7 July 1943 when JF664 (Merlin 63) of No 332 Norwegian Squadron was made available. It was compared with the Spitfire Mk IX (the intended Mk VIII replacement) with the following results – up to 20,000ft the aircraft were comparable; to 30,000 the VIII was faster; to 36,000 it still had the edge over the IX. Climbing to 10,000ft the IX was superior.

In order to improve performance of the standard Mk VIII a Merlin 66 with 25 lb sq/in boost rating ('Basta'*) and 160 octane fuel was installed in JF275 (original engine Merlin 61) and flight tested by Supermarine. It had a Rotol Hydulignum propeller of 10ft 9in diameter, a standard wing with B armament, and it weighed 7,770lb at take off. Maximum speed in MS gear at 2,800ft was 374mph, and in FS gear at 14,000 it reached 409. Sea level speed was 362; rate of climb (MS) 5,580ft min at SL. In FS gear @ 11,00ft climb was 5,100ft/min; time to 25,000ft 5.8min. Level speeds and combat climb were made to compare 18 and 25lb sq in boost ratings and the tables below give comparative results –

	Level speed (mph)		
Height ft	+18 lb	+25	increase
0	338 MS	362 MS	24
2800	349	374*	25
9000	374*	387 FS*	13
12000	371 FS*	400*	29
14000	380*	409*	29
20200	405*	405	0

*FTH Full throttle height

	rate of climb ft/min		
0	4610 MS	5580* MS	970
3500	4610	5050	440
6400	4610*	5080 FS	470
11000	3960 FS	5100 FS*	1140
14000	3990	4600	610
17400	4010*	4010	0

Range was still a problem, even with an overload tank, because of drag. A 45 gallon torpedo shaped tank was developed and comparative trials with JF275 and BS118 (Mk IX), both with Merlin 61 engines, took place in September 1943. BS118 had the normal slipper tank and at maximum speed, MS gear, full throttle height was 10mph faster than JF275 with the streamlined tank.

Basta is Italian for 'more than enough', and also the German High Command's code name for Gibraltar

Test pilots had noticed that during the routine production flying test programme before delivery, the full throttle heights of current production engines varied considerably. In order that the tests could be related to a minimum FTH a number of Spitfires were tested again after the final acceptance flight. A total of 70 Spitfires from Supermarine production dispersal and 45 from Castle Bromwich were on test during May and June 1943. Results obtained were –

Aircraft	No of a/c tested	engine (Merlin)	air intake	level flight (ft) mean	max	min	climb (ft) mean	max	min
Mk VII	4	64	temp	12200	12600	11800	13500	–	–
Mk VIII	28	63	trop	11200	12000	10000	13000	13900	11800
Mk VIII	10	66	trop	8300	9000	6300	10200	10800	9600
Mk IX	45	63	temp	–	–	–	13500	14500	12300
PRXI	8	63	temp	13400	14000	12500	13250	13600	13100
Mk XII	9	Griffon III	temp	5500	6000	4600	4800	6300	3800

From previous tests it was known that about 800 to 1,000 feet was lost in FTH when the tropical air intake was fitted. Taking this fact into consideration it could be observed that 3,000 feet variation could exist on Merlin 63 Spitfires; 2,700 on Merlin 66 and 1,400 feet on Griffons.

Large numbers of the Mk VIII, all versions, were sent to the Middle East and Australia and they had to be tropicalised. The cumbersome Vokes desert filter as fitted to the F Mk V Spitfire had long since disappeared and the tropical F VIII was produced as the Type 360 with filter elements incorporated into the elegant, temperate intake. It was noted that there was a loss of FTH due to air leaking through the filters when the shutter was open. A blanking plate was fitted across the filter and the results showed an improvement in speed, thus –

aircraft	engine Merlin	s/c gear	with filter FTH ft	with filter V max mph	with blanking plate FTH ft	with blanking plate V max mph
JF275 VIII	61	FS	26800	397	27700	402
JL163 VIII	66	MS	8300	367	9500	372
JF707 VIII	66	MS	6900	363	8100	370
EN654 PR XI	63	MS	10200	381	11300	391.5
EN654 PR XI	63	FS	23000	410	24300	421

Major modifications were appearing on the Mk VIII as operational requirements flowed back to Supermarine via the services and MAP, and one of the most important was the pilot's rear view. This was never claimed to be exceptional as the cockpit and canopy faired into the rear fuselage decking. Peering into a mirror, identifying the enemy and reacting to the danger consumed vital seconds, and pilots needed to have a clearer view over their shoulders. As a result of this requirement JF299 was modified to have a clear view, tear drop canopy in place of the original Malcolm hood, and was sent to AFDU, Wittering, for service trials with personnel from all three services. All agreed the new canopy was an improvement over the old for pilots could see almost to the trailing edge of the elevator. Banking slightly during weaving the downward rear view was improved, while a new type of windscreen resulted in a better view forward. There were criticisms, one being that the curved windscreen picked up reflections, but this could be cured by a coat of matt, black paint on the engine cowling. The side panels of the screen were also considered to be too small and a pilot had to lean well forward to make full use of them, particularly when landing. The frames of the sliding hood were thought to be too wide, but they were deleted on subsequent models. Operation of the hood was considered to be unsatisfactory as it tended to jam at about five inches from the closed position. A winding device supplied the answer. The reflector sight was raised three inches and this improved the view for deflection shooting. Pilots were not happy about armour positioning and suggested it should be raised or, better still, replaced with bullet proof glass.

The same airframe was used for trials of the Pacitor fuel gauge, an electronic device which provided a more accurate reading of the fuel status. It remained steady in all flying attitudes and needle fluctuation during manoeuvres was two gallons either way. Trials of a 100 hour intensive flying session began on 5 August 1944 and four pilots took part. After 26 hours the original gauge stuck at around 60 gallons; the indicator needle was fouling the bezel, but when corrected it worked perfectly.

Reinforcement plans for the Middle East and Far East

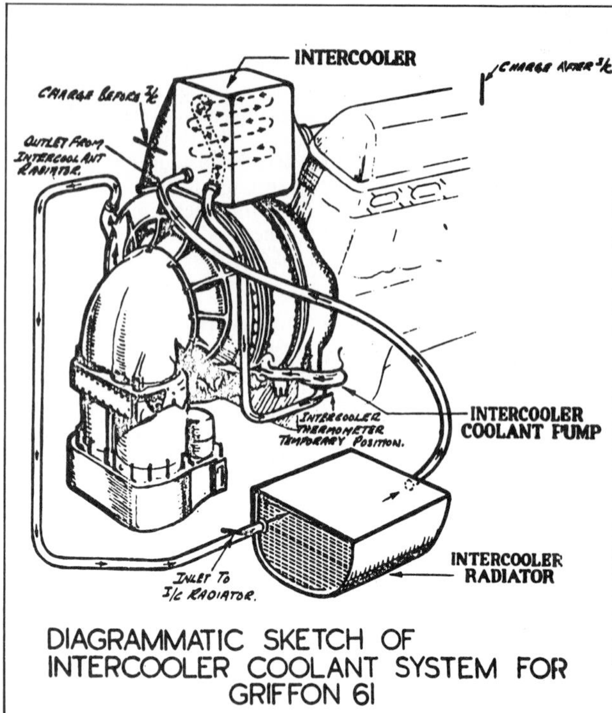

Drawing of the Mk VIII intercooling system as installed for trials. Trials aircraft was JF317, one of the prototype Mk XIVs.

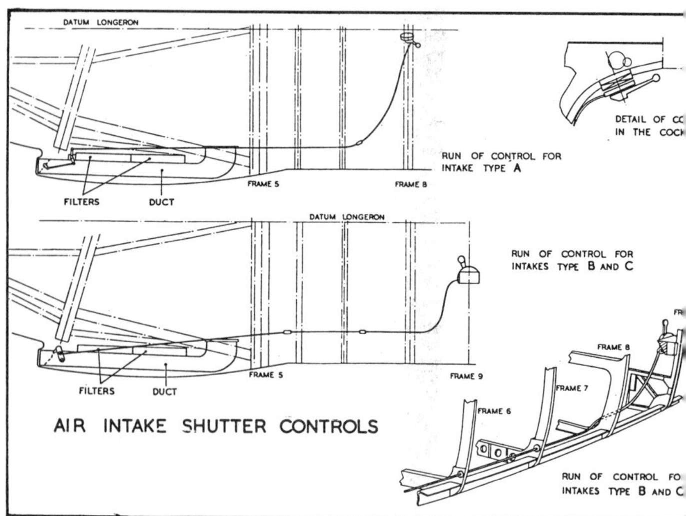

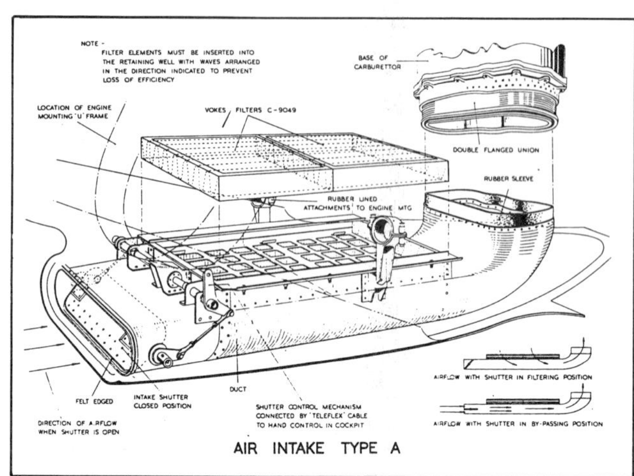

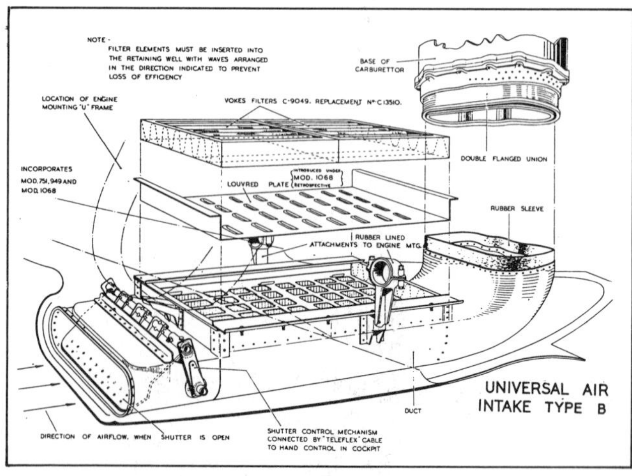

clashed with those for the build-up of equipment needed for the forthcoming invasion of Europe. Surface transport was at a premium and despite heavy shipment of Spitfires by sea alternatives had to be found. One method was ferrying the aircraft by air via Gibraltar, Malta and across North Africa via Takoradi. This did relieve the situation but air deliveries resulted in a lot of Spitfires arriving without guns and other equipment, as the weight penalties incurred with the installation of the overload drop tanks, such as the 170 gallon unit, did mean that armament, etc, had to go by surface. There was little point in developing bigger and bigger overload tanks and a new approach to the problem was required.

THE MALIANOWSKI WING

One was forthcoming. It was startling in concept and proposed by Messrs Cornwall and Clare of Heston Aircraft Ltd. They brought their proposals to Southampton on 13 December 1942. Termed the Malianowski Wing it was designed to be filled with fuel and towed along behind an aeroplane by means of twin booms attached to the wing trailing edge. This would provide a range of 2,100 miles at 250mph and ensure that the Spitfire could take-off at its maximum weight, fully armed with the overload fuel being lifted with practically no weight penalty. Towing forces were considered to be quite small with weight of the trailer containing 450 gallons of fuel at approximately 4,500lb this being carried by the trailer wing. Transfer of fuel was via an electric pump in the trailer and fed to the Spitfire's tank through the booms. Reinforcing of the Spitfire wing was minor and consisted of two universal joints installed on the upper surface at approximately mid wing and bolt plates carried the load to the rear of the front spar. Electrically fired explosive cartridges were to break the towing attachments simultaneously for jettison purposes. A modification to the fuel feed would take fuel directly to the forward tanks. The Heston Aircraft representatives left the meeting taking with them a complete set of drawings of the Mk VIII to study how best to adapt the wing for towing.

The towed wing was the brainchild of a Polish fighter pilot, Flight Lieutenant Malianowski, who was also an engineer, and he was introduced to Roxbee-Cox, of Farnborough, in 1941. He showed Roxbee-Cox plans of his invention and described its application to military aircraft. As originally conceived the trailer was to enable bomber range to be stretched, but RAE was able to produce figures proving to the inventor that his optimistic figures had not included drag; after all a combination of two monoplanes did add up to a form of biplane. But RAE did have a wing manufactured by a furniture company

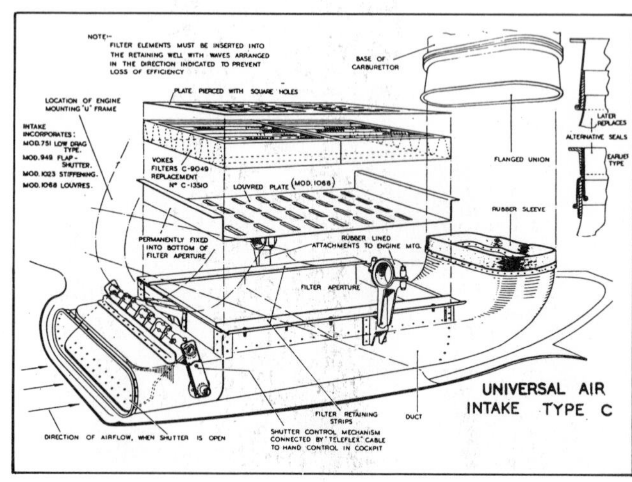

and Miles Aircraft flew it behind a Magister light trainer.

The first version was a rigid device with fixed fins and wheeled undercarriage. During initial trials both tug and trailer could not get airborne as the latter was constantly ground looping. One observer was almost killed by the device when it swung off the runway and headed straight for him. The booms had to be articulated directionally and they were, therefore, hinged and geared to a pair of rudders which replaced the fixed fins. It worked and was flown, following the Magister dociley. Performance analysis showed, however, that the most economic method to carry a fuel overload was in the accepted manner of hanging it in tanks under an aircraft's wings.

As fighter bombers the Mk VIIIs were able to carry a 500 lb GP bomb under the fuselage centre section, while another modification allowed carriage of one 250 lb bomb under each wing. They were then able to accommodate an overload tank on the centre section position. In the maximum permissible overload condition the Spitfire VIII could be equipped to carry 2 × 500 lb GP bombs under the centre section, each bomb being separated on release by one fifth of a second. In the full fighter bomber configuration the VIII had to sacrifice a quantity of fuel.

The additional power of the Merlin 60 Series engines was making take off more difficult for the powerful torque resulted in pilots having to apply full opposite rudder in order to keep the Spitfire in a straight line. It was decided to test an F VIII with a Merlin 66 driving Rotol six blade contra rotating propellers. JK535 eventually flew with a Merlin 63 with CR props and the modification was considered a success in spite of a weight penalty and mechanical complication. Another innovation was the installation of a laminar flow wing, but more on this later in the chapter.

A total of 438 LF Mk VIII Spitfires was scheduled to be produced with the contra-prop Merlin and laminar flow wing and on 6 December the DTD wrote to MAP – "I have seen the

Loading and C.G., VIII series.

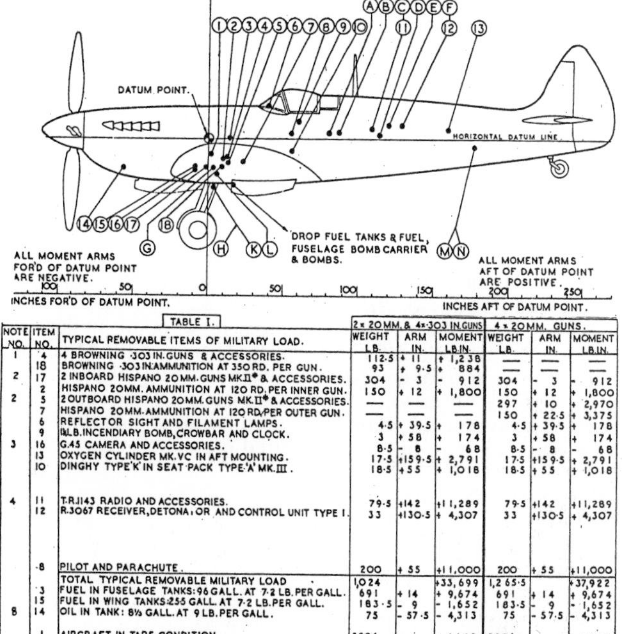

TABLE I.

NOTE NO.	ITEM NO.	TYPICAL REMOVABLE ITEMS OF MILITARY LOAD.	2 × 20MM. & 4×·303 IN.GUNS WEIGHT LB.	ARM IN.	MOMENT LB.IN.	4 × 20MM. GUNS. WEIGHT LB.	ARM IN.	MOMENT LB.IN.
1	4	4 BROWNING ·303 IN. GUNS & ACCESSORIES.	112·5	+ 11	+ 1,238	—	—	—
	18	BROWNING ·303 IN. AMMUNITION AT 350 RD. PER GUN.	93	+ 9·5	+ 884	—	—	—
2	17	2 INBOARD HISPANO 20 MM. GUNS MK.II* & ACCESSORIES.	304	- 3	- 912	304	- 3	- 912
	2	HISPANO 20MM. AMMUNITION AT 120 RD. PER INNER GUN.	150	+ 12	+ 1,800	150	+ 12	+ 1,800
2	5	2 OUTBOARD HISPANO 20 MM. GUNS MK.II* & ACCESSORIES.	—	—	—	297	+ 10	+ 2,970
	7	HISPANO 20MM. AMMUNITION AT 120 RD/PER OUTER GUN.	—	—	—	150	+ 22·5	+ 3,375
	6	REFLECTOR SIGHT AND FILAMENT LAMPS.	4·5	+ 39·5	+ 178	4·5	+ 39·5	+ 178
	9	1¼ LB. INCENDIARY BOMB, CROWBAR AND CLOCK.	3	+ 58	+ 174	3	+ 58	+ 174
3	16	G.45 CAMERA AND ACCESSORIES.	8·5	- 8	- 68	8·5	- 8	- 68
	13	OXYGEN CYLINDER MK.VC IN AFT MOUNTING.	17·5	+159·5	+ 2,791	17·5	+159·5	+ 2,791
	10	DINGHY TYPE 'K' IN SEAT PACK TYPE 'A' MK.III.	18·5	+ 55	+ 1,018	18·5	+ 55	+ 1,018
4	11	T.R.1143 RADIO AND ACCESSORIES.	79·5	+142	+11,289	79·5	+142	+11,289
	12	R.3067 RECEIVER, DETONATOR AND CONTROL UNIT TYPE I.	33	+130·5	+ 4,307	33	+130·5	+ 4,307
	8	PILOT AND PARACHUTE.	200	+ 55	+11,000	200	+ 55	+11,000
		TOTAL TYPICAL REMOVABLE MILITARY LOAD	1,024		+33,699	1,265·5		+37,922
	3	FUEL IN FUSELAGE TANKS: 96 GALL. AT 7·2 LB. PER GALL.	691	+ 14	+ 9,674	691	+ 14	+ 9,674
	15	FUEL IN WING TANKS: 25·5 GALL. AT 7·2 LB. PER GALL.	183·5	- 9	- 1,652	183·5	- 9	- 1,652
8	14	OIL IN TANK: 8⅓ GALL. AT 9 LB. PER GALL.	75	- 57·5	- 4,313	75	- 57·5	- 4,313
	1	AIRCRAFT IN TARE CONDITION.	5,806		+ 4,145	5,806		+ 4,145
		AIRCRAFT IN TYPICAL TAKE-OFF CONDITION.	7,779·5	+ 5·3	+41,553	8021	+ 5·7	+45,776

TABLE II

NOTE NO.	ITEM NO.	DROP TANKS AND FUEL, FUSELAGE BOMB CARRIER AND BOMBS.	WEIGHT LB.	ARM IN.	MOMENT LB.IN.
		30 GALL. BLISTER TYPE TANK.	57·5	+ 16	+ 920
		30 GALL. 100 OCTANE FUEL IN BLISTER TYPE TANK	216	+ 16	+ 3,456
		45 GALL. BLISTER TYPE TANK.	80	+ 13·5	+ 1,080
		45 GALL. 100 OCTANE FUEL IN BLISTER TYPE TANK	324	+ 13·5	+ 4,374
		50 GALL. TORPEDO TYPE TANK.	50	+ 13·5	+ 675
		50 GALL. 100 OCTANE FUEL IN TORPEDO TANK.	360	+ 13·5	+ 4,860
		FUSELAGE BOMB CARRIER AND ADAPTOR.	55	+ 19·5	+ 1,073
7		250 LB. BOMB ON FUSELAGE CARRIER.	250	+ 12	+ 3,000
7		500 LB. BOMB ON FUSELAGE CARRIER.	500	+ 12	+ 6,000
		90 GALL. BLISTER TYPE TANK.	120	+ 16	+ 1,920
		90 GALL. 100 OCTANE FUEL IN BLISTER TYPE TANK.	648	+ 13·5	+ 8,748

TABLE III.

NOTE NO.	ITEM NO.	ADDITIONAL AND ALTERNATIVE ITEMS OF REMOVABLE MILITARY LOAD.	WEIGHT LB.	ARM IN.	MOMENT LB.IN.
2	G	2 INBOARD HISPANO 20 MM GUNS MK.V & ACCESSORIES.	245·5	+ 2·5	+ 614
	L	WING BOMB CARRIERS.	22·5	+ 5	+ 113
7	H	250 LB. BOMBS ON WING CARRIERS.	500	+ 3·5	+ 1,750
7	K	SMOKE BOMBS ON WING CARRIERS.	240	+ 4	+ 960
	A	OXYGEN CYLINDER MK.VC IN FOR'D MOUNTING.	17·5	+ 81·5	+ 1,426
6	B	DESERT EQUIPMENT.	47·5	+ 87	+ 4,133
4	C	T.R.1133 RADIO AND ACCESSORIES.	72·5	+111·5	+ 8,084
	F	R.3002 RECEIVER, DETONATOR AND CONTROL UNIT.	32·5	+128	+ 4,160
5	E	A.1271 AMPLIFIER AND ACCESSORIES.	9	+119	+ 1,071
	D	RADIO BALLAST: 3 STANDARD WEIGHTS AT 17½ LB. EACH.	52·5	+114	+ 5,985
	M	TAIL BALLAST WEIGHTS, EACH.	17·5	+175·5	+ 3,071
	N	TAIL BALLAST MOUNTING.	5	+175·5	+ 878

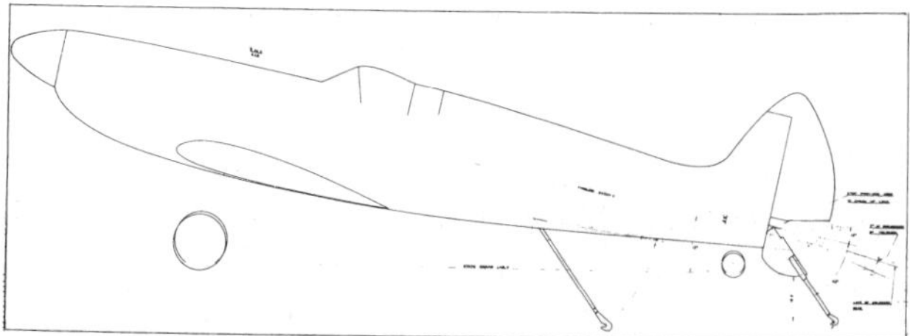

A small number of Mk VIIIs were converted for the Navy for deck landing trials at the Isle of Grain, the intention being to test the viability of the airframe and to eventually use the VIII for carrier operations. JG622 and 623 had this type of hook fitted and proofing trials took place at RNAS Arbroath from 27 April 1944. This much reduced Supermarine drawing gives an idea of the company's proposals for 'A' frame and sting hook.

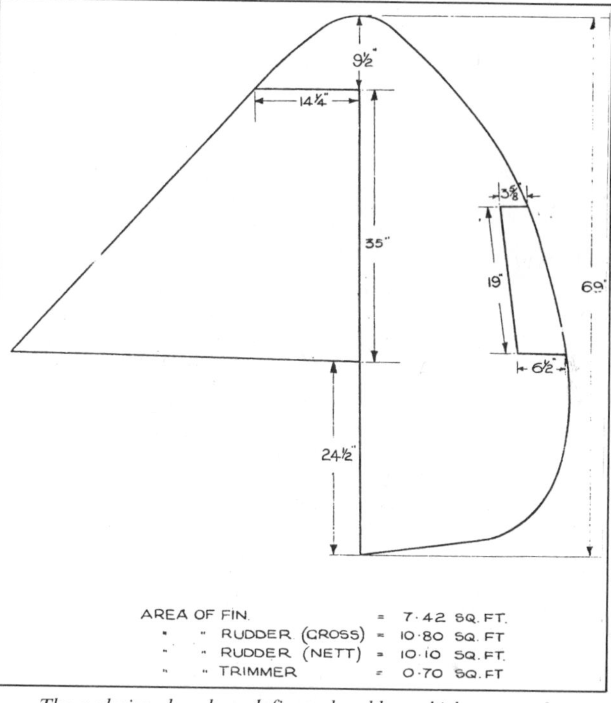

The redesigned, enlarged fin and rudder, which was to become standard on a large number of late production Spitfires, was originally tested on JF317. New fin/rudder area was 18.22 sq ft.

production programme which shows the LF Mk VIII Merlin 66 to come off the production line in November 1944 with laminar flow wings". At almost the same period Vickers wrote to Sorley (18 November 1943) saying that at a recent meeting with Rolls-Royce they were concerned to learn that *no* provision was being made for production of Merlins with contra-props. Joe Smith wrote to N. E. Rowe, of MAP, expressing the same sentiments. He also wrote – "You will recollect that Specifications F1/43 covers the supply of Spitfires with redesigned wings and CP Merlins or Griffons. We have to supply 438 Merlin CPs to F1/43 between November 1944 and August 1945 and there appears to be no corresponding programme covering supply of these engines". No explanation was ever forthcoming on the non-delivery of the CP engines and eventually MAP had to write to the DTD to the effect that *no* Spitfire Mk VIII, XIV or 21 would have the CP engine or the laminar flow wing. But, an entirely new aircraft with laminar flow wing and Merlin would go into production during November 1944 and with the Griffon engine in August 1944. This was the proposed Spitfire F23, or Victor.

At the time the first production F VIIIs were leaving the factories a lot of thought was being applied to the problem of improving wing efficiency, an improvement that was to lead to the proposed 'Super Spitfire', the Victor (F23). A basic VIII airframe was received by CRD, Vickers, in late September 1943 for fitment of a wing of modified section in which the centre of the leading edge was raised approximately one inch, and the nose contours adjusted accordingly. The object of the change was to improve performance by moving to the rear the air transition point. As the wings did not conform to the final, proposed new section, performance tests were not required, but

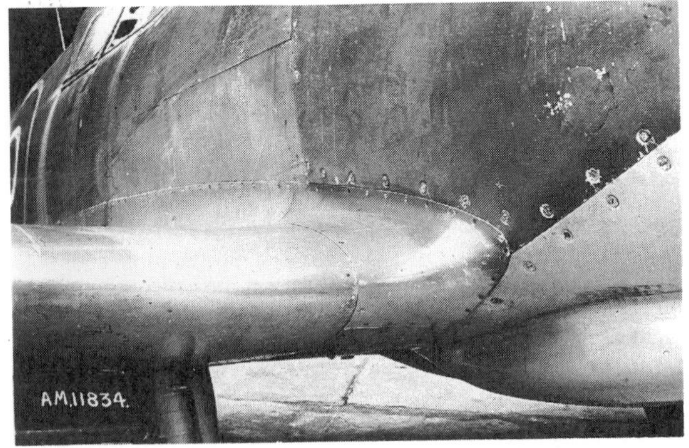

Top: Leading edge wing root of JG204 before and after modification to lift edge by two inches. Above: Flying view during trials.

handling checks were made to note if the change had made any appreciable improvement. In additional to the modified section a different type of fillet was added to the wing roots. New ailerons were attached by a 'piano' hinge, ie, a hinge that ran the complete length of the aileron. JG204 was flown at an auw of 7,945lb representing the normal service load. Longitudinal stability and control was appreciably worse than on the standard aircraft and it was more difficult to control in high speed level flight and dives. Stalling speed with flaps and undercarriage up was 78 mph, and the aircraft tended to drop its port wing. The usual warning buffet around the wing roots had disappeared and the main sign was onset of aileron snatch.

The most serious defects were lack of nose down elevator trim, particularly at altitude and excessive stick forces in and out of the dive. It was proposed to increase tailplane incidence and install a new wing with a second style of modified section, but trials were discontinued.

JF348, Merlin 63, delivered to North Africa in April 1943.

By late 1942 the Rolls-Royce Griffon was in full production and its first application to a major Spitfire variant was to the Mk XII, this version being based upon the experience gained from DP845, the prototype Mk IV. Other, more refined, Spitfires were being designed around the Griffon including the F Mk 21, and in order to gain experience with the engine prior to its introduction to the new aircraft it was decided to produce six test bed Spitfires with the Griffon RG 5SM G62, a modified RG 4SM Series, or Griffon III. The aircraft chosen were Mk VIIIs, JF316 to 321 to Contract 2904C of 25 March 1943. A seventh, NH636, was fitted with a Griffon 65 during the same year.

Supermarine produced a report on the modified airframes on 16 December 1942 and in addition to incorporating the raised leading edge of the wing it proposed relocation of the radiators from the original position to a point under the fuselage, just aft of the cockpit, similar to that of the Mustang. The carburetter intake was to be moved from under the engine cowling to just ahead of the wing leading edge. These, and other improvements would, claimed Supermarine, result in a speed increase of 30 mph but have required major redesign of both

JK535 was one of the small number of production Mk VIIIs fitted with a Merlin 63 Special engine and Rotol contra props. It is seen here at Rolls-Royce, Hucknall.

wings and fuselage. Another proposal was to submerge the radiators into the wing and have the intakes directly under the engine.

In the event only the lifted leading edge was adopted and by 17 January 1943 the first of the six experimental Spitfires, JF316, was weighed at Worthy Down. Fuselage and tail unit were standard Mk VIII and mainplane Mk VIII with Mk V tips. A Mk V tropical cowling replaced the temperate and the intercooler and main radiators deepened. There was 45 lb of ballast under the pilot's seat, plus another eight in the rear fuselage. Engine was a Griffon 61. Tare 6,274lb; take off (min) 7,462; landing (min) 6,895. When Supermarine reviewed the modified aeroplane they thought the combination to be – "A very useful interim type of aircraft and to be modified further by an improved air intake and propeller, radiators to provide tropical cooling, adjustment of equipment to delete ballast, use of Griffon 65 or 75 engine in lieu of the RG 5SM". All these modifications finally resulted in the appearance of the Spitfire F Mk XIV.

Maker's trials took place between January and 10 April when the engine was removed and a second installed with .51 gearing. Test pilot F. C. Furlong flew JF316, now with de Havilland CPs (tare 6,742lb, auw 7,462, landing 6,895) and he recorded these remarks – "There are certain things in this aeroplane which are far from standard, eg, small throttle box which includes automatic cut-off; certain engine gauges; fuel transfer system and dural tabs between wing and aileron which must have been put there by person or persons unknown for measuring upfloat at some time or another. The ailerons are not considered good; this is in keeping with ailerons on all contra rotating propellers which either have the misfortune to have been bad sets or else there is some peculiarity in this type of aeroplane which resists being banked in either direction with equal determination. The characteristic harshness and chatter associated with Rotol propellers was present here". The aeroplane was then delivered to Rolls-Royce, Hucknall, on 13 April.

JF321 was the final Mk VIII converted to F XIV prototype standard. It had a Griffon 61 and Rotol contra props and an extended fin and large chord rudder. The carburetter air intake was an early, original type. Little is known about this particular aircraft.

Brief performance tests of JF316 and 317 at an auw of 8,400lb were conducted by Supermarine for comparative purposes, both aircraft having the Griffon RG 5SM and a Rotol five bladed propeller. JF316 attained a maximum speed of 434 mph at 28,600 feet in FS gear; a climb rate of 4,260ft/min

MD249 failed to return from operations on 14 December 1944. It had been taken on charge the previous January.

at 5,000 feet in MS gear. JF317 returned figures of 423mph and 4,650ft/min. During cooling trials in June at Boscombe Down the test pilot reported that after application of about a quarter rudder alternately to port and starboard at 385 mph there was a change of trim, and on landing examination of the fuselage revealed appreciable buckling of the fuselage at frames 12, 13 and 14. The buckling was considered to be typical of that associated with the Spitfire, and in particular with tailwheel landing loads.

JF318 went to Boscombe Down on 26 May 1943 for 150 hours intensive flying and the Griffon failed after 104 hours had been logged, resulting in a forced landing. The experimental Rotol had to be replaced by a standard production unit after 88 hours. Engine change was long and difficult and took 140 man hours by skilled personnel, and as a result Rolls-Royce and Supermarine were asked to develop the whole unit – engine, mountings, etc – as a total power egg. With its new engine JF318 was returned to Boscombe on 25 August and after a further 54 flights of 47 hours 40 mins the aircraft crashed in Amesbury Cemetery. The pilot had climbed to 41,500 feet when the Griffon began running rough, and after experimenting with the throttle he put the aeroplane into a glide with smoke pouring from the port side. Oil spattered the windscreen and the top engine cowling began to vibrate with the result that the Spitfire was abandoned and caught fire on crashing. The remains were sent to Farnborough for accident investigation.

JF319 and 320 were fully converted to prototypes F Mk XIV, as was JF321. The latter was weighed at Worthy Down on 19 August with a Griffon 62 Rotol wooden, six bladed contra propeller; 180 lb fixed ballast between frames 18 and 19 and three additional ballast weights in the extreme rear fuselage. Tare was 6,645lb and auw 8,614.

The six converted F VIIIs were extensively flown by Furlong, Quill, Shea-Simmonds, R. E. Havercroft and P. Wigley of Supermarine as single or contra propeller aeroplanes, and some of their comments on the behaviour of the aircraft are worth recording.

JF319 (Furlong 12-7-44). Standard of vibration considered acceptable. Aeroplane not good enough to be sent to Boscombe Down without further check by Mr Quill. (Quill 13-7). Propeller aerodynamically balanced at Rotols and new constant speed units fitted. Bad vibration at low speeds. (Quill 14-7). Vibration particularly bad, especially around cockpit sides. (Furlong 17-7). Aeroplane still vibrating but decided to send it to Boscombe. It is considered they will complain about this.

JF321 (Shea-S 30-4-44). This Mk VIIIG (note suffix) fitted with a Rotol contra propeller was flown to Staverton for a check on what I consider to be undoubtedly propeller roughness and grinding noises. Bryan Greensted flew the aeroplane and his verdict was the engine as source of trouble. In spite of this I am still suspicious of the propeller. (Quill 30-4). Flown for vibration check. (Quill 7-5). New jets fitted to richen up weak mixture range. No marked improvement was observed.

Other F VIIIs flown by the same pilots are worthy of inclusion. JF299 (Shea-S 1-12-44). Handling flight to assess characteristics of Heston conversion type metal elevator. It is considered quite unacceptable and is overbalanced. JF299 (Havercroft 2-12). Heston metal elevator removed from Spitfire

A58-516, an HF Mk VIII. This aircraft shot down two Japanese fighters.

Mk XIV NH717 and fitted for comparison. In cruising flight the elevator hunts vigorously in an endeavour to stabilise but each time over corrects and sets up a series of sharp oscillations. JF299 (Quill 17-7-44). Revised type winding gear for rear vision hood. Perfectly OK for closing hood; unsatisfactory for opening. JF299 (Furlong 4-8). Pacitor petrol gauge fitted. Gauge takes about 45 secs to warm up and there are no criticisms. JF299 (Morgan 5-10). Flown to jettison rear vision winding hood. First attempt unsuccessful. Second attempt release pulled at 280 mph and hood flew off.

MT818 (Furlong 20-7-44). First Mk VIII with 75 gallon fuel tank behind pilot. Unstable but not viciously so. MT818 (Furlong 27-7). It is estimated that aeroplane becomes stable after 37 gallons have been used from rear tank. MT818 (Furlong 15-8). Long range Spitfire. Now has standard oil tank giving standard non-bulged bottom cowling. Flown with all tanks full. MT818 (Furlong). It is considered that the aeroplane might possibly be accepted by Boscombe Down. Deletion of the PRU oil tank and subsequent fitting of non-bulged cowling has improved stability.

A pair of Mk VIIIs of No.457 Sqdn, RAAF. Nearest aircraft was A58-614 and named Grey Moose.

Certificate of Design for the Mk VIII conversions was issued on 13 January 1945 as the Type 369; contract CTT/ACFT/C.23(c) and the following particulars noted. Engine Griffon 61, 65 or 85. General description. This aeroplane, basically Spitfire F Mk VIII Production, has been modified as indicated below. Engine mounting Spitfire F Mk 21 type equipment and frame 5. Special longerons and modified tail end. Mainplanes Spitfire F Mk VIII with modified cooling system fitted with standard tips. Tare 5,798, total 8,421lb.

JG204, which was the proposed F Mk 23 prototype, was constructed originally as an LF Mk VIII, and as such was weighed at Worthy Down on 30 September 1943 with a Merlin 66 engine and a Rotol four blade propeller. During Winter 1944/45 various modifications were incorporated and Quill flew it for a series of stall tests beginning 3 May 1943. The modified wing section had produced a different sequence of stall to the standard Spitfire wing, for on JG204 the stall commenced at the tip and spread inwards, the root being the last portion to stall. For the new series of tests the port wing was tufted and some root spoilers fitted, the object being to precipitate root stall and provide a more satisfactory stalling sequence of the entire wing. Straight stalls were carried out in two conditions – flaps and undercarriage up and down – and on both occasions the stall began a the root and spread outwards towards the cannons. As the stall reached this point tip stall began and spread towards the root to approximately one third of the aileron span.

JF318, third Mk VIII converted to F XIV prototype standards. It was used mainly for Griffon engine trials and finally burnt out after crashing in Amesbury Cemetery, Wilts.

JG204 was then compared with a standard Mk VIII, RB146, with both having tufts over the entire wing surface. Both aircraft were fitted with plain type, geared tab ailerons of identical design. Tests showed that the plain ailerons adversely affected stalling characteristics of the portion of the wing in front of the aileron, thus causing a loss in lateral stability at the stall. The raised leading edge of 204 reversed the sequence in which various portions of the wing stalled and caused the main stall to take place at the outer half of the wing before the inner half. The raised leading edge also caused the Spitfire wing to behave in a similar manner to that of the Spiteful.

During the last two years of the war USAAF aircraft were flying in their natural metal finish and the Air Ministry asked Supermarine to determine what weight penalty and performance there was concerning the Spitfire when painted. An LF Mk VIII, MT509, was weighed at Worthy Down, flown to Eastleigh and stripped of paint; reweighed at High Post, repainted at Eastleigh and again reweighed at High Post. Before stripping MT509 weighed 7,084lb, after 7,060. After repainting 7,075lb. Paint removed 24lb; fresh paint applied 15 lb. Performance figures were not available. MT818 was weighed at High Post to ascertain weight and CoG determination of a typical LF Mk VIII on 13 June 1944. Tare 5,085lb, auw 7,087. Merlin 66 engine, Rotol four blade wooden propeller. MT729 followed one month later and was weighed in the same condition – tare 5,806, auw 7,807lb.

Although the Admiralty was not interested in another Merlin powered Seafire they did want to know of the performance details of the Mk VIII, and Supermarine was instructed to modify an example for this purpose. JG663 was fitted with an 'A' frame arrester hook and 125 modifications incorporated. When weighed at High Post the tare was 5,979lb and auw 7,890. Final production F Mk VIII left the production line in February 1944 and although large numbers were produced they served, in the main, in overseas theatres and were never

MT881 Merlin 66 LF VIII, was despatched to Bombay, India, in October 1944. SOC, in India, July 1947.

employed against the threat they were built to counter, the Fw190. Another Spitfire took over this role, the Mk IX.

It is interesting to note that the Air Ministry, impressed by the Mk VIII, wanted a photo-reconnaissance version and MAP issued a contract on 21 April 1942 for the production of 70 PR Mk VIIIs with Merlin 61 engine. Serial numbers were to be LV643-681, LV726-756, but they were eventually produced as normal fighter variants with Merlin 66 engines.

OFFICIAL REPORTS ON Mk VIII

Boscombe Down May 1942. N3297 (Converted from Mk III). Prototype F Mk VIII. Merlin 61. Cooling trials. For tropical summer conditions the radiator suitability was within requirements for all conditions of flight Auw 7,225lb.

Boscombe Down May 1942. N3297. Measurement of plug voltages in flight. Tests were required for three types of magneto. Voltages recorded appeared reasonable and consistent.

Boscombe Down May 1942. N3297. Fuel consumption tests. Results showed that for weak mixture at cruising speed was normal, under maximum power conditions heavy.

Boscombe Down 26 May 1943. JF318. Griffon RG 5SM. Converted to F Mk XIV prototype. Intensive flying trials. 150 hours of intensive flying were required. Propeller was an experimental Rotol five blade. Flown between 26 May and 25 June for a total of 103hrs 50min (101 flights). The propeller failed at 87hrs 50mins, and the engine at 103hrs, resulting in a forced landing. Engine change took 140 man hours and as a result the demand was for development of the complete power egg. After 15 cowling removals the fasteners had to be replaced. Tyres were replaced after an average of 40 landings.

Boscombe Down 4 July 1943. JF318. Carbon monoxide contamination tests.

Boscombe Down 13 July 1943. JF317. Griffon RG 5SM. Converted to F Mk XIV prototype. Brief handling and tests of lateral and directional behaviour. Fitted with enlarged fin and rudder. Two propellers used – Rotol R.19/5F5/1, and second Rotol but with different pitch settings. Diameter 10ft 5in. Auw 8,375lb. Large changes in directional trim with speed and power.

Boscombe Down 25 August 1943. JF318. Further intensive flying trials. Following replacement of original Griffon a second series of trials was initiated. 100 hours required, during which the engine failed after trouble with ignition. Flown between 25 August and 25 September for a total of 54 hours 47 mins. The engine's main bearings failed after a climb to 41,500ft. Pilot experimented with throttle and put aircraft into glide. Smoke began issuing from port side oil sprayed windscreen and pilot had to bale out. The Spitfire crashed and burned out.

Boscombe Down 7 December 1943. JF319. Griffon RG 5SM. Converted to F Mk XIV prototype. Climb and level speed performance. Auw 8,400lb. Aircraft had high gloss paint finish, B wing and enlarged rudder. Maximum speed MS gear @ 5,500ft 391 mph, FS gear 3,600ft/min @ 21,800ft. Time to 10,000ft 2.3min, to 40,000ft 15.05 min. Ceiling 44,600ft.

Boscombe Down September 1943. JF319. Griffon RG 5SM. Converted to F Mk XIV prototype. Brief handling trials. Auw 8,400lb. Handling satisfactory.

Boscombe Down September 1943. JF229. F Mk VIII Merlin 61. Tests with modified hood. Top of the fuselage behind pilot was lower compared with standard Spitfire and the hood was a single, transparent panel. A curved windscreen panel forward of the bullet-proof glass was fitted.

A58-532, 4522 Sqdn, RAAF, Morotai, 1945.

Line up of Mk VIIIs of SEAC, on Cocos Islands, September 1945. Nearest the camera is MT657.

A58-303, RAAF, at Aircraft Research Development Unit, Laverton, Victoria, 1944.

A58-497, RG-V, "Grey Nurse", W/Cdr. R.H. Gibbes, 80th Fighter Wing.

This hood gave a great improvement in view and its operation could have been improved by the addition of a winding mechanism. This was fitted at a later date.

Boscombe Down 25 September 1943. JF319. Oil cooling and radiator suitability. Cooling was within requirements.

Boscombe Down 28**October 1943.** JF319. Determination of aftmost position of CoG. Aircraft satisfactory under all conditions of flight at CoG postions up to 7.4in aft of datum, **auw 8,450lb.**

Boscombe Down November **1943.** JF299. Directional behaviour tests with modified hood. Comparison with standard F VIII. No difference in behaviour could be detected.

Boscombe Down 12 June 1944. JF204. LF Mk VIII. Merlin 66. Handling tests with modified wing section. Centre of leading edge raised approximately one inch and nose contours adjusted. Object was to improve performance by moving back the transition point. New type of wing root fillet added, and piano hinge ailerons with balance tabs. Performance satisfactory. Tailplane incidence and different ailerons to be used on production aircraft with modifications*.

Boscombe Down 27 June 1944. JF707. Taxying, take off and landing trials with modified undercarriage. Experimental undercarriage with both camber and toe in removed to improve tyre wear. Auw **7,670lb.** Modification produced no adverse effects.

Vickers-Armstrong 29 March 1945. JG204. Comparison of stalling characteristics with RB145 (F Mk XIV). JG204 had the modified wing leading edge. Both aircraft had port wings tufted. Plain ailerons adversely affects stalling characteristics of wing area in front of ailerons, causing loss in lateral stability at the stall. On JG204 the sequence was reversed.

Vickers-Armstrong 3 May 1945. JG204. Stalling tests.

MODIFICATIONS TO F Mk VIII

600 Introduce the F Mk VIII 14-4,42; 723 Griffon 61 conversion (cancelled) T.I 16-12-42; 746 Delete downward red/green indentification lights 6-10-42; 751 Redesign tropical cowling and filter 20-10-42; 769 Introduce two cannon wing blisters 3-11-42; 841 Introduce Merlin 66 29-12-42; 856 Stiffen rear fuselage 9-3-43; 865 Introduce rear view fuselage 26-1-43; 875 Introduce Merlin 70 261-43; 877 Replace wobble with pulsometer pump 9-2-43; 885 Provide for tail towing 20-4-43; 897 Instal wobble pump until pulsometer available 9-2-43; 905 Introduce Merlin 63 23-2-43; 907 Introduce Merlin 63A 23-2-43; 914 Introduce Mk XII rudder as standard 23-2-43; 928 Delete dimming screen on gunsight 17-3-43; 934 Interim bomb carrying scheme 17-3-43; 948 Modify fuselage plating 4-5-43; 951 Provide fittings for under fuselage bomb; 971 Strengthen engine mounting 4-5-43; 989 Instal two additional downward indentification lights red/green 18-5-43; 1002 Standard in lieu of extended wing tips 1-6-43; 1005 Strengthen flaps, Class 2 urgency 15-6-43; 1008 T.I redesigned fuel transfer system 15-6-43; 1015 Fuselage bomb scheme 29-6-43; 1028 Interconncected throttle/airscrew control 29-6-43; 1058 Armour for frontal attack 24-8-43; 1081 Reinforce base of rudder; 1086 Instal arrester hook 21-9-43; 1110 Wing bomb installation 19-10-43; 1127 T.I Improved gun heating system 2-11-43; 1139 Iceguard on air intake 2-11-43; 1142 Increase gauge of tailplane skin 16-11-43; 1193 Split armour for rear protection 20-12-43; 1197 Contra-rotating propellers 11-1-44; 1201 **Winterisation** 11-1-44; 1248 T.I sting arrester hook 8-2-44; 1221 T.I 4×20mm Hispano 11-1-44; 1265 Mk V in lieu of Mk II guns in inboard position 22-2-44; 1293 T.I lightweight air system 21-3-44; 1436 Gyro gunsight Mk IID 22-8-44.

F Mk VIII, LF Mk VIII, HF Mk VIII

Wing. Planform elliptical; section NACA 2200 Series; span (F) 36′ 10″; incidence° root +2, tip $-\frac{1}{2}$; dihedral° 6; thickness % root 13.2, tip 6; aspect ratio 5.6:1 area nett 220; gross 242; chord (geo) 6ft 8in; (ma) 74.3. Ailerons. Area 18, movement° up 26, down 19; droop $\frac{3}{8}$. Flaps. Area 15.6; movement° down 85. Wing loading 32.1 lb/sq ft; power loading 4.97 lb/hp M61, 4.55 M63.

Tailplane. Area 31.46; chord (ma) 4.0; incidence° root 0, tip $\pm\frac{1}{2}$; dihedral° 0. Elevators. Area 13.26; movement° up 28, down 23. Tab area 0.76; movement° up 20, down 7. Fin area 4.61. Rudder area 8.23; movement° each way 28. Tab area 0.35; movement° port 18, starbd 6.

Undercarriage. Wheels Dunlop AH10019; tyres Dunlop IK13 or 17. Oleo pressure 400 or 415 (Trop) or, 490 or 510 (Trop). Tailwheel retractable castoring. Wheel Dunlop AH2184/IX; tyre Dunlop Ecta TA12 or 14. Oleo pressure 265; tyre pressure 55 or 57 (Trop).

Engine/s. Merlin 61 1,565hp. Merlin 63 1,710hp. Change to FS automatically @ 22,000ft. SU Neg G carb.

Propeller/s. M61. Rotol 4-blade R3/4F5/2 Dural 35° PR FP 31° 10′ or, Rotol R3/4F5/3 35° PR FP 30° 10′ or, Rotol R5/4F5/4

The proposed F23 Spitfire.

Supermarine Spitfire F/HF Mk VIII

Jablo or Hydulignum 35° PR FP 29° 20′. Merlin 63 & 63A Rotol 4-blade Jablo on Hydulignum 35° PR FP 22° 20′. All props 10ft 9in diameter.

Coolant. 70% distilled water, 30% Glycol.

Fuel. 100 octane.
Capacity Fuselage (upper) 47gals, lower 49, wing leading edge 2 × 14. Total 124gals. Plus 30, 45, 50 and 90 o/ld tanks. All tanks except l/edge self seal. Fuel system **pressurised.** At 20,000ft self sealing impaired.

Oil. 8.5gals.

Armour. 202lb.

Armament. B wing. Some a/c with Mk V Hispano cannon. Plus 2 × 250 or 1 500lb bombs.

Radio. TR1143, A1271, IFF ARI5000 or 5025 and/or smoke bombs.

Cine camera. G45 in starbd wing.

Performance. Max speed 408mph.

Ceiling 43,000ft. Range 660 miles.

Weights. Tare 5,806, take off 7,779, max permissable 8,000. With C wing take off 8,021.

LF Mk VIII as for F Mk VIII except for wing. Area 231sq ft.
Engine. Merlin 66 1,580hp. Change to FS @ 14,000ft; return @ 12,500ft (auto). Bendix Stromberg carb.
Propeller. Rotol 4-blade R12/4F5/4 pitch range 35°, fine pitch 22° 20′ Jablo on Hydulignum, diameter 10ft 9in.

Performance. Max speed 362 @ SL. Max rate of climb (MS) 5,580ft/min @ SL; (FS) 5,100ft/min @ 11,000ft. Time to 25,000ft 5.8mins.
With 25lb boost (Basta) and 160 octane fuel 374mph @ 2,800ft (MS); 409 @ 14,000 (FS).

Ceiling 41,500ft.

Weights. Tare 5,805lb, take off 7,807.

HF Mk VIII as for F Mk VIII except for: wing area 248.5 sq ft; chord 7ft 4.3in; incidence +2° root to $-\frac{1}{2}$ 18ft 5in from CL.

Engine. Merlin 70 1475hp.
Bendix Stromberg Carb: Fuel Injection.
Propeller Rotol 4-blade R12/4F5/4 pitch range 35°, fine pitch 22° 20′ Jablo or Hydulignum, diameter 10ft 9in.

Performance. Max speed 416mph.

Ceiling 44,000ft.

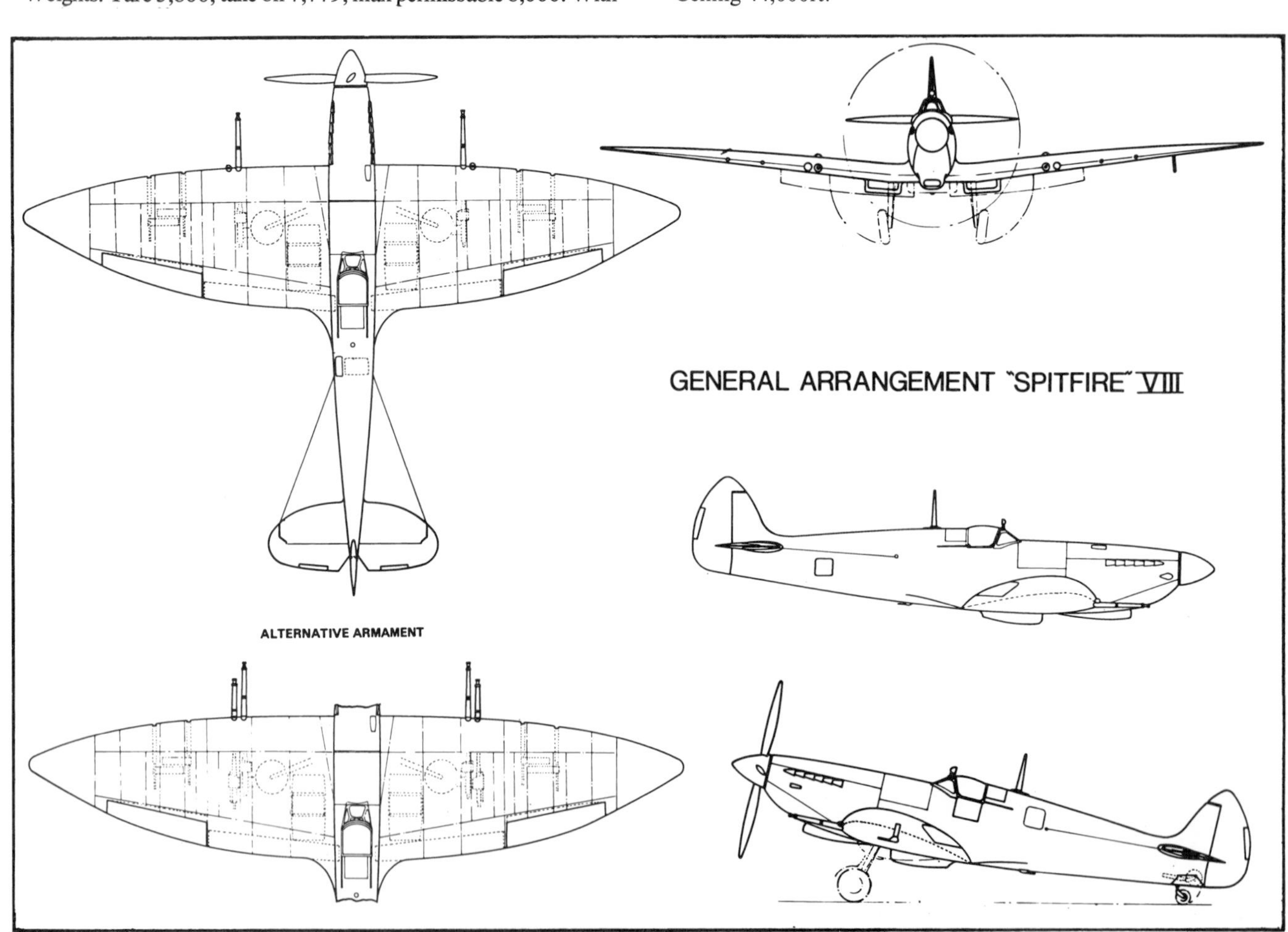

SERIAL NUMBERS

Supermarine Aviation (Vickers) Ltd. Contract No Aircraft/1877/C.23(C) First order for 800 Spitfire Mk VIII. Built as Mk VIIIs between November 1942 and April 1944; JF274-300, 316-364, 392-427, 443-485, 501-528, 557-592, 613-630, 658-676, 692-716, 740-789, 805-850, 869-902, 926-967, JG 104-124, 157-204, 239-275, 312-356, 371-387, 404-432, 465-500, 527-568, 603-624 and 646-695.

Contract No B19713/39.
Ninth order for 70 PR Spitfire with Merlin 61 dated 21 April 1942. Built as Mk VIII fighters between November 1943 and January 1944; LV 643-681 and 726-756.

Tenth order for 426 Spitfire Mk VC dated 12 May 1942. Built as Mk VII/VIII/IX/X/XI/XII between July 1943 and March 1944. The following serials apply to Mk VIIIs built to this tenth order; MB959-976, MD214-256, 269-303, 315-356 and 369-403 (173).

Contract Aircraft/1877/C.23(C).
Second order for 700 Spitfire Mk VIII dated 27 July 1942. Built as Mk VIIIs and XIVs between December 1943 and October 1944. The following serials apply to Mk VIIIs built to this second order; MT502-527, 539-581, 593-635, 648-689, 703-748, 761-802, 815-846, 872-915, 925-969, 981-999, MV112-156, 169-208, 231-245, 321-329, 342-346, 398-441, 456-487 and 499-514 (588).

Third order for 225 Spitfire Mk VIII dated 1 December 1942. Built as Mk VIII/XIV/XVIII between November 1944 and June 1945. The following serials apply to this third order; NH614-636 (23).

Total built; 1,654.

All F VIII up to and including JF662, engines specified. From JF663 to JF967 all LF VIII Merlin 66 unless otherwise indicated.

JF274 3660 M61 EA First prod FVIII FF 20-11-42 Hand S Hull 29-11 AST 21-6-43 VWD 9-11 wts & CG load 82MU 11-5-44 *Argyll* 1-6 Casa 13-6 MAAF 21-6-45 SOC 27-3-47

JF275 3632 M61 EA FF 21-11-42 CRD VWD 24-11 trls with Super trop air intake 6-2-43 1CRU 25-9 Com Flt Staff Coll 16-8-45 29MU 25-7 sold in Buenos Aires SA 13-6-47

JF276 3661 M61 EA FF 24-11-42 33MU 29-11 AST 222MU 20-8-43 *Ger Don* 25-8 Casa 10-9 NA 30-11 Ind 1-12 CE 14-6-45 SOC 30-8

JF277 3671 M61 FF 26-11-42 33MU 1-12 AST 222MU 10-8-43 *Fort Thom* 14-8 Casa 1-9 NAASC 31-10 ME 30-11 Ind 1-1-44 ACSEA 21-6-45 36sp cd f/ld nr Bankura Ind CE dbf SOC 5-2-46

JF278 3678 M61 EA FF 28-11-42 33MU 4-12 VA 15-7 39MU 6-9 NAASC 31-10 MAAF 21-6-45 CE SOC 20-7

JF279 3691 M61 EA FF 30-11-42 39MU 1-12 3206 Sc Stn Odiham 17-4-43 AST 222MU 24-8 Casa 20-9 NAASC 31-10 ME 30-11 Ind 1-12 FAC3 7-1-44

JF280 3724 M61 EA FF 8-12-42 15-12 AST 82MU 18-8 Casa 10-9 NAASC 31-10 FA FTR 5-1-44

JF281 3730 M61 EA FF 10-12-42 33MU 24-12 HAL 47MU 20-10-43 Casa 29-11 ME 21-6-45 SOC 31-12-46

JF282 3737 M61 EA FF 11-12-42 33MU 14-12 AST 47MU 27-8 Casa 20-9 NAASC 31-10 ME 31-10 Ind 1-12 SOC 10-7-44

JF283 3750 M61 EA FF 15-12-42 20-12 47MU 12-7 *Fort Nak* 14-7 Casa 29-7 NA 30-11 Ind 1-12 E/a CE 20-7-44

JF284 3759 M61 EA FF 19-12-42 38MU 24-12 WAL 222MU 8-8-43 Casa 1-9 NA 30-11 Ind 1-12 SOC 27-6-45

JF285 3785 M61 EA FF 23-12-42 38MU 29-12 WAL 47MU 16-7-43 Casa 16-8 NA 30-11 Ind 1-12 SOC 22-5-45

JF286 3797 M61 EA FF 30-12-42 38MU 2-1-43 MHth 4-5 FACB 17-6 recat E 24-6 1CRU 28-6 618S 26-8-44 SOC 9-11-48

JF287 3799 M61 EA FF 31-12-42 38MU 3-1-43 WAL 47MU 17-7 Casa 16-8 NA 30-11 Ind 1-12 FAC3 7-4-44 SOC 7-2-45

JF288 3816 M61 EA FF 1-1-43 38MU 8-1 WAL 82MU 16-8 Casa 18-8 NA 30-11

JF289 3817 M61 EA FF 8-1-43 13-1 WAL 215MU 31-7 Casa 18-8 NA 30-11 Ind 1-12 ACSEA 21-6-45 SOC 30-1-47

JF290 3840 M61 EA FF 8-1-43 38MU 13-1 AST 82MU 17-9 Casa 19-10 NAASC 31-10 925S C3 ops 15-6-44

JF291 3848 M61 EA FF 13-1-43 38MU 15-1 WAL 47MU 21-7 Casa 18-8 NA 30-11 Ind 3-12 C3 ops 15-2-44

JF292 3852 M61 EA FF 14-1-43 38MU 21-1 WAL 82MU 14-8 Casa 10-9 NAASC 31-10 Ind 1-1-44

JF293 3856 M61 EA FF 15-1-43 38MU 21-1 WAL 82MU 14-8 Casa 10-9 NA 30-11 SOC 30-6-44

JF294 3885 M66 EA FF 19-1-43 Casa Aug'43 Ind Oct'43 SAAF. Flew non-stop Cairo to Cape March 1944 extant Nat War Mus Johannesburg as 5501

JF295 3887 M61 EA FF 20-1-43 33MU 22-1 WAL 47MU 16-7 *Fort Rup* 25-7 Casa 16-8 NA 30-11 Ind 1-12 ACSEA 21-6-45 CE 19-7

JF296 3904 M61 EA FF 23-1-43 38MU 27-1 AST 17-9 mods 82MU 3-3-44 *Emp Day* 21-3 Casa 6-4 1CRU 14-9-45 to 5835M Csfd 27-2-46

JF297 3915 M61 EA FF 26-1-43 33MU 29-1 HAL 2-7 mods 82MU 18-8 *Ger Don* 25-5 Casa 10-9 NA 30-11

JF298 3933 M61 EA FF 30-1-43 33MU 3-2 WAL 82MU 26-7 *Card Gib* 3-9 Casa NA 30-11 92S C3 ops SOC 23-6-44

JF299 3934 M61 EA FF 30-1-43 AFDU Witt 8-8 hand trls BDn 16-9 reduced area rear fus and re-inforced tear drop hood with curved w/s. Jett trls. Trop intake replaced with temperate. Fitt FXII rud and extended wng tips. Casa Aug'43 for trop trls. Reverted to standard and ret VAWD for FVIII dev 9-12. VHP 5-10-44 comp trls with RM784 (FXIV) scr 1-6-45

JF300 3956 M61 EA FF 2-2-43 33MU 10-2 WAL 222MU 8-8 *Fort Thom* 14-8 Casa NA 30-11 Ind 1-12 FAC3 22-12 SOC 7-2-45

JF316 4386 Griffon III (RG 5 SM) CHA FF 20-1-43 JQ Con to 1st exp a/c Type 369, FXIV proto at VAHP Griffon 61 instal, Rotol 5-blade Jablo prop 17-1-43 CRD VAWD 13-4 wts and CG load Tare 6274, t/o 7402, land 6895lbs. R-RH 29-5 VA EA 20-4-44 G65 instal trls and gen dev with G65 and G67 AST 25-8-44 6MU 16-3-45 CRD DeH Prop 30-8 contra props instal trls RAF SoH 28-8-47 NEA fire fight demo SOC 29-4-48

JF317 4076 WDA FF 4-3-43 R-RH 6-3-43 Con to FXIV Griffon R G 5 SM. FVIII wng, Rotol five blade prop, extended cowling, larger air intake, fin and rud, balloon hood. BDn 7-9 climb, level speed, positional error, lateral and direct perf trls. R-RH 27-9 Griffon 65 instal VA EA 10-2-44 SOC 28-4-45 Rotol Stav 13-7 contra prop static trls Griffon with five blade prop considered 'unsatisfactory'. Scrap 13-8-45

JF318 4387 G61 CHA FF 29-5-43 ASTH 24-5-43 Con to FXIV. BDn 26-5 100 hrs ext fly trls plagued with continuous ignition problems. New eng instal, grnd clearance of prop on t/o 2.5in. Lateral and direct stab trls with mod tail unit. Carb mono contam tests. After 47hr second e/fld a/c f/ld. Extended wng tips fitt VAWD for a further 73 hrs fly. A/c aban when e/fld at H/A. Cd dbf Amesbury Cemetery 23-9-44 Remains to Farn Dec. SOC 1-6-45

JF319 4466 WDA R-RH con to FXIV 24-6-43 Griffon RG5-SM five blade Rotol prop; univ wng; mod fin and rud high quality finish; balloon hood; whip aerial. BDn 8-9 lateral and direct stab climb and level speed perf; positional error; deter of aftmost CG; carb mono contam oil cool and rad suit. Trls concluded 13-11. FACE SOC 2-5-45

JF320 4467 R-RH Con to FXIV G61 25-6-43 CRD WD for mkrs trls. Rotol Stav 2-11-44 ASTH 19-2-45 VA Stn 30-4-45 FACE 20-2-48 SOC 20-8

JF321 4663 WDA FF 20-8-43 R-RH 20-8 Con to FXIV G61 CRD WD 25-8

JF322 3959 M61 EA FF 8-2-43 33MU 9-2 WAL 222MU 12-7 *Fort Nak* 14-7 Casa 29-7 SOC 10-3-45

JF323 3950 M61 EA FF 4-2-43 33MU 7-2 WAL 215MU 10-7 *Fort Nak* 14-7 Casa 29-7 NA 30-11 Ind 1-1-44 SOC 21-4-45

JF324 3955 M61 EA FF 6-2-43 39MU 7-2 WAL 215MU 10-7 *Fort Nak* 14-7 Casa 29-7 NA 30-11 Ind 1-12 FAAC 21-6-45 SOC 19-7

JF325 3964 M61 EA FF 8-2-43 39MU 11-2 WAL 215MU 10-7 *Fort Nak* 14-7 Casa 29-7 NA 30-11 SOC 26-4-45

JF326 3999 M61 EA 27-2-43 82MU 5-3 *Fort Liv* 20-3 Gib 12-4 241S FTR ops 17-3-44

JF327 4017 M63 EA 6MU 25-2-43 82MU 5-3 *Fort Liv* 20-3 6Del Flt i/sea nr Conway Caerns 6-6

JF328 3981 M63 HFVIII EA 39MU 16-2-43 AST 47MU 4-9 *Ocean Rid* 29-9 Casa 10-10 NAASC 31-10 ME 30-11 Ind 1-1-44 SOC 2-5-45

JF329 3987 M63 EA 6MU 19-2-43 FAAC 21-4 ROS 2s TAF 31-5 HAL 3-7 mods 222MU 17-8 *Ger Don* 25-8 Casa 10-9 NAASC 31-10 ME 30-11 Ind 1-12 ACSEA 21-6-45 SOC 19-7

JF330 4000 M63 EA VAWD 20-2-43 wts and CG load with C wng t/o 7752lb. with D wng t/o 7984lb. 6MU 2-3 76MU 24-4 *Fort Stle* 16-5 Casa 30-5 NWA 1-7 ME 1-8 NAAF 1-11 SOC 26-4-45

JF331 4008 M61 EA 39MU 27-2-43 82MU 9-3 *Fort Liv* 20-3 Gib 12-4 NWA USAAF 31-7

JF332 4007 M63EA 39MU 2-3-43 82MU 29-4 *Fort Jer* 30-5 NWA 1-7 ME 1-8 NAAF 1-11 SOC 28-4-45

JF333 4014 M61 EA 25-2-43 82MU 9-3 *SS682* 12-4 Casa 25-4 NWA 31-5 USAAF 31-7 RAF 31-5-44 SOC 16-4-45

JF334 4015 M61 EA 6MU 26-2-43 76MU 29-4 *SS702* 2-6 Casa 15-6 NWA 1-7 ME 1-8 NAAF 1-11 SOC 30-6-45

JF335 4020 M61 EA 39MU 26-2-43 222MU 21-3 *Fort Thom* 3-5 Casa 17-5

JF336 4026 M63A EA 39MU 26-2-43 82MU 278-4 *Fort Jer* 1-5 Casa 30-5 NWA 1-7 ME 1-9 MAAF 1-11 417S C3 ops 8-12

JF337 4029 M63A EA 39MU 27-2-43 82MU 22-3 *Fort Thom* 3-5 Casa 17-5 NA 30-11 SOC 31-12

JF338 4036 M63 EA 6MU 28-2-43 82MU 29-4 *Fort Jer* 11-5 Casa 30-5 NWA 1-7 ME 5-7 SOC 31-12-46

JF339 4037 M63 EA 6MU 28-2-43 82MU 29-4 *Fort Thom* 3-5 Casa 17-5 SOC 31-8-44

JF340 4050 M63 EA 6MU 6-3-43 82MU 13-5 *Fort Stle* 16-5 Casa 30-5 USAAF 12/31 lost Italy 11-11

JF341 4055 M63A EA 39MU 6-3-43 47MU 29-4 *Fort Thom* 3-5 Casa 17-5 SOC 31-11

JF342 4056 M63A EA 39MU 6-3-43 47MU 12-4 *Fort Thom* 3-5 Casa 17-5 ME 1-8 NA 30-11 MAAF 21-6-45 183S SOC 29-9-45

JF343 4066 M63 EA 39MU 8-3-43 82MU 11-4 *SS686* 24-4 Casa 17-5 ME 1-8 NA 30-11 MAAF 21-6-45 92S SOC 27-3-47

JF344 4065 M63 EA 39MU 7-3-43 47MU 156-4 *Fort Thom* 3-5 Casa 17-5 NWA 1-10 FACE 15-2-44

JF345 4077 M63A EA 33MU 12-3-43 47MU 20-3 *Orient C* 13-4 Casa 24-4 NWA 31-5 USAAF 31-7

JF346 4073 M63A EA 33MU 7-3-43 222MU 15-3 *SS679* 12-4 Casa 25-4 ME 1-8 1S FTR ops 28-11

JF347 4074 M63 EA 33MU 7-3-43 82MU 17-3 *SS682* 12-4 Casa 25-4 NWA 31-5 USAAF 1-10 SOC 30-6-45

JF348 4079 M63 EA 33MU 12-3-43 47MU 20-3 *Orient C* 13-4 Casa 25-4 NWA 31-5 SOC 30-6-45

JF349 4097 M63 EA 38MU 14-3-43 222MU 19-4 *Fort Thom* 3-5 Casa 17-5

JF350 4091 M63 EA 45MU 18-3-43 215MU 2-7 *Fort Ver* 1-7 Casa 14-7 ME 1-9 NAASC 1-11 SOC 31-8-44

JF351 4092 M63A EA 45MU 14-3-43 215MU 31-3 *Emp Bar* 2-5 Casa 17-5 NWA 31-5 USAAF 31-7 SOC 31-8-44

JF352 4093 M63 EA 46MU 14-3-43 215MU 3-4 *Emp Bar* 2-5 Casa 17-5 Malta C3 ops 23-6 FH10.35

JF353 4094 M63A EA 46MU 14-3-43 215MU 7-4 *SS687* 29-4 Casa 17-5 ME 1-9 NAAF 1-11 MAAF 21-6-45 92S cd on t/o Zeltweg Austria FACE 25-11-46 SOC 28-11

JF354 4103 M63 EA 38MU 17-3-43 222MU 19-4 *Fort Thom* 3-5 Casa 17-5 ME 1-8 NAAF 1-11 MAAF 21-6-45 SOC 20-9

JF355 4123 M63 EA 38MU 22-3-43 25MU 29-3 *Emp Bar* 2-5 Casa 17-5 NA 30-11 Ind 1-1-44 SOC 26-4-45

JF356 4110 M63A 33MU 18-3-43 215MU 29-3 *Emp Bar* 2-5 Casa 17-5 ME 1-8 NAAF 1-11 SOC 4-4-45

JF357 4111 M63 EA 33MU 18-3-43 82MU 19-4 *La Pam* 2-7 Casa 14-7 ME 1-9 NAAF 1-11 SOC 18-8-44

JF358 4118 M63A EA 38MU 19-3-4 215MU 5-4 *SS687* 29-4 Casa 17-5 NA 30-11 Ind 1-1-44 C3 ops 13-3 SOC 7-2-45

JF359 4119 M63A EA 45MU 22-3-43 215MU 11-4 *SS687* 29-4 Casa 17-5 NWA USAAF 31-7

JF360 4120 M63 EA 45MU 22-3-43 215MU 4-7 *Fort Nak* 14-7 Casa 29-7 USAAF 31-10

JF361 4124 M63 EA 45MU 26-3-43 215MU 11-4 *SS687* 29-4 Casa 17-5 ME 1-8 NA 30-11 417S C3 ops 26-1-44

JF362 4125 M63A EA 45MU 26-3-43 82MU 14-4 *SS687* 29-4 Casa 17-5 ME 1-9 NA 30-11 C3 ops 22-1-44

JF363 4126 M63 EA 46MU 27-3-43 222MU 11-4 *SS687* 29-4 Casa 17-5 ME 1-8 MAAF 21-6-45 SOC 13-9

JF364 4139 M63A EA 46MU 27-3-43 215MU 11-4 *SS687* 29-4 Casa 17-5 NWA 31-7 32S SOC 30-6-45

JF392 4137 M63 EA 38MU 25-3-43 82MU 19-4 *SS687* 29-4 Casa 17-5 ME 1-9 NA 30-11 MAAF 21-6-45 SOC 28-2-46

JF393 4138 M63 EA 38MU 25-3-43 82MU 3-5 *Fort Jer* 11-5 Casa 30-5 NWA 1-7 ME 1-9 NA 30-11 FAC3 11-1-44

JF394 4140 M63A EA 33MU 27-3-43 222MU 14-4 *Fort Thom* 3-5 Casa 17-5 ME 1-8 MAAF 1-11 SOC 23-10-44

JF395 4144 M63 EA 33MU 27-3-43 82MU 6-4 *SS686* 26-4 Casa 17-5 MAAF 21-6-45 SOC 20-9-45

JF396 4145 M63 EA 46MU 27-3-43 222MU 11-4 *SS687* 29-4 Casa 17-5 ME 1-8 NAAF 1-11 SOC 23-10-44

JF397 4146 M63A EA 46MU 28-3-43 215MU 12-4 *Emp Bar* 2-5 Casa 17-5

JF398 4149 M63 EA 38MU 28-3-43 86MU 1-6 *SS707* 10-6 Casa 29-6 ME 1-8 NAAF 1-11 MAAF 21-6-45 SOC 31-12-46

JF399 4150 M63a EA 38MU 28-3-43 52MU 7-5 *Fort Stle* 16-5 Casa 30-5 NWA 1-7 Malta 1-8 SOC 31-8-44

JF400 4151 M63 EA 38MU 28-3-43 52MU 1-5 *Fort Stle* 16-5 Casa 30-5 NWA 1-7 ME 1-8 NAAF 1-11 USAAF 31-10 SOC 30-6-45

JF401 4152 M63 EA 45MU 20-3-43 215MU 12-4 *SS687* 29-4 Casa 17-5

JF402 4158 M63 EA 45MU 30-3-43 82MU 14-4 *SS686* 24-4 Casa 17-5 ME 1-8 NAAF 1-11 SOC 30-6-45

JF403 4159 M63 EA 30-3-43 82MU 19-4 *SS687* 29-4 Casa 17-5 NAAF 1-11 241S FTR ops 2-8-44

JF404 4163 M63 EA 38MU 2-4-43 82MU 23-5 *SS702* 2-6 Casa 15-6 NWA 1-7 SOC 29-8-46

JF405 4165 M63 EA 45MU 2-4-43 215MU 18-4 *Fort Thom* 3-5 Casa 17-5 CE ops SOC 2-9

JF406 4166 M63 EA 45MU 3-4-43 82MU 14-4 *SS687* 29-4 Casa 17-5 ME 30-9 NAAF 1-11 SOC 30-6-45

JF407 4167 M63A EA 46MU 3-4-43 82MU 15-4 *SS687* 29-4 Casa 17-5

JF408 4168 M63A EA 46MU 3-4-43 47MU 29-5 *SS703* 1-6 Casa 15-6 NWA 1-7

JF409 4171 M63 EA 33MU 3-4-43 222MU 12-4 *Fort Thom* 3-5 Casa 17-5 ME 1-8 NAAF 1-11 SOC 26-4-45

JF410 4173 M63 EA 33MU 3-4-43 82MU 14-4 *SS687* 29-4 Casa 17-5 C3 ops 2-2-44

JF411 4174 M63 EA 33MU 4-4-43 82MU 18-4 *SS687* 29-4 Casa 17-5

JF412 4260 M63 EA 33MU 3-5-43 47MU 12-5 *Fort Stle* 16-5 Casa 30-5 NWA 1-7 ME 1-8 FACE 19-11-44 SOC 14-6-45

JF413 4203 M63A EA 9MU 13-4-43 82MU 1-5 *Fort Jer* 11-5 Casa 30-5 NWA 1-7 ME 1-9 NAAF 1-11 92S FTR ops 13-9-44

JF414 4175 M63 EA 38MU 8-4-43 222MU 23-4 *Fort Stle* 16-5 Casa 30-5 NWA 1-7 ME 1-8 NAAF 1-11 SOC 31-8-44

JF415 4182 M63A EA 38MU 8-4-43 222MU 23-4*Fort Thom* 3-5 Casa 17-5

JF416 4183 M63 EA 38MU 8-4-43 82MU 4-5 *Fort Jer* 11-5 Casa 30-5 NWA 1-7 USAAF 30-11 185S CE ops 22-10-44

JF417 4189 M63 EA 45MU 11-4-43 215MU 28-4 *Fort Jer* 11-5 Casa 30-5 NWA 1-7 ME CE ops 5-9

JF418 4184 M63 EA 45MU 9-4-43 222MU 18-4 *Fort Thom* 3-5 Casa 17-5 ME CE ops 5-9

JF419 4185 M63 EA 45MU 9-4-43 215MU 21-4 SS687 2904 Casa 17-5 Malta 1-7 MAAF 21-6-45 SOC 29-8-46

JF420 4190 M63a EA 46MU 10-4-43 215MU 21-4 *Fort Thom* 3-5 Casa 17-5 ME 1-8 NAAF 1-11

JF421 4191 M63 EA 47MU 10-4-43 *Fort Thom* 3-5 Casa 17-5 Malta 1-8 ME 30-9 NAAF 1-11 SOC 23-10-44

JF422 4192 M63A EA 9MU 10-4-43 82MU 4-5 *Fort Jer* 11-5 Casa 30-5 NWA 1-7 ME 1-8 NAAF 1-11 SOC 30-6-44

JF423 4194 M63 EA 9MU 11-4 82MU 1-5 *Fort Jer* 11-5 Casa 30-5 NWA 1-7 ME 1-8 NAAF 31-10 MAAF 21-6-45 SOC 28-8

JF424 4193 M63 EA 12MU 10-4-43 215MU 23-4 *Fort Thom* 3-5 Casa 17-5 ME 1-11 NAAF 1-11 SOC 31-12-46

JF425 4196 M63 EA 12MU 13-4-43 215MU 23-4*Fort Thom* 3-5 Casa 17-5 ME 1-8 NAAF 1-11 SOC 30-6-44

JF426 4197 M63 EA 12MU 11-4-43 215MU 23-4 *Fort Thom* 3-5 Casa 17-5 ME 1-8 Malta 1-9 NAAF 1-11 SOC 26-4-45

JF427 4204 M63 EA 15MU 13-4-43 82MU 7-5 *Fort Jer* 11-5 Casa 30-5 NWA 1-7 ME 1-8 NAAF 1-11 SOC 31-8-44

JF443 4209 M63 EA 15-4-43 47MU 10-5 *Fort Jer* 11-5 Casa 30-5 NWA 1-7 ME 1-8 NAAF 1-11 SOC 31-12-46

JF444 4210 M63 EA 12MU 15-4-43 215MU 26-4*Fort Jer* 11-5 Casa 30-5 NWA 1-7 USAAF 30-11 241S CE ops 24-7-44

JF445 4211 M63 EA 12MU 17-4-43 315MU 26-4 *Fort Jer* 11-5 Casa 30-5 NWA 1-7 ME CE ops 3-9

JF446 4212 M63 EA 15MU 18-4-43 VA 15-5 76MU 11-6 *SS702* 18-6 Casa 27-6 ME 1-8 FTR ops 29-10

JF447 4213 M63 EA 17-4-43 76MU 18-6 *La Pam* 2-7 Casa 14-7 ME 1-8 NAAF 1-11 601S SOC 29-2-44

JF448 4222 M63 EA 15MU 18-4-43 47MU 10-5 *Fort Jer* 11-5 Casa 30-5 NWA 1-7 ME 1-8 C3 ops 7-12

JF449 4214 M63 EA 33MU 17-4-43 82MU 29-4 *Fort Jer* 11-5 Casa 30-5 NWA 1-7 ME 1-8 NAAF 1-11 SOC 30-6-45

JF450 4221 M63 EA 33MU 18-4-43 82MU 29-4 *Fort Jer* 11-5 Casa 30-5 NWA 1-7 ME 1-8 NAASC 31-10 MAAF 1-6-45 SOC 27-3-47

JF451 4223 M63 EA 38MU 18-4-43 82MU 24-5 *SS703* 1-6 Casa 15-6 NWA 1-7 ME 1-8 NAAF 1-11 SOC 13-8-44

JF452 4231 M63 EA 38MU 18-4-43 82MU 22-5 *SS702* 2-6 Casa 15-6 NWA 1-7 SOC 26-4-45

JF453 4233 M63 EA 46MU 21-4-43 82MU 3-5 *Fort Jer* 11-5 Casa 30-5 NWA 1-7 ME 2-8-45 SOC 10-8

JF454 4234 M63 EA 46MU 21-4-43 47MU 1-5 *Fort Stle* 16-5 Casa 30-5 NWA 1-7 SOC 30-6-45

JF455 4241 M63 EA 9MU 24-4-43 52MU 8-5 *Fort Stle* 16-5 Casa 30-5 NWA 1-7 USAAF 30-11 SOC 30-6-44

JF456 4235 M63 EA 9MU 21-4-43 47MU 4-5 *Fort Stle* 16-5 Casa 30-5 NWA 1-7 USAAF 30-11 SOC 30-6-44

JF457 4238 M63 EA 45MU 24-4-43 215MU 30-5 *SS702* 2-6 Casa 15-6 NWA 1-7 ME 1-8 NAAF 30-11 SOC 26-4-45

JF458 4239 M63A EA 45MU 23-4-43 47MU 2-5 *Fort Stle* 16-5 Casa 30-5 NWA 1-7 ME 1-8 241S CE ops 23-3-44

JF459 4240 M63 EA 45MU 24-4-43 47MU 4-5 *Fort Stle* 16-5 Casa 30-5 NWA 1-7 ME 1-8 MAAF 21-6-45 SOC 20-9

JF460 4244 M63 EA 45MU 25-4-43 47MU 5-5 *Fort Jer* 11-5 Casa 30-5 NWA 1-7 ME 1-8 NAAF 1-11 SOC 29-2-44

JF461 4254 M63 EA 9MU 24-4-43 47MU 11-5 *Fort Stle* 16-5 Casa 30-5 NWA 1-7

JF462 4266 LFVIII M66 EA 9MU 3-5-43 88MU 24-5 *SS702* 7-6 Casa 15-6 NWA 1-7 ME 1-9 NAAF 1-11 MAAF 21-6-45 i/sea 30-5-46

JF463 4255 M63 EA 15MU 30-4-43 47MU 15-5 *SS703* 1-6 Casa 15-6 NWA 1-7

JF463 was despatched to North Africa in May 1943.

JF464 4256 M63 EA 15MU 30-4-43 47MU 15-5 *SS703* 1-6 Casa 15-6 NWA 1-7 ME 1-8 NAAF 1-11 SOC 28-4-45

JF465 4259 M63 EA 12MU 1-5-43 47MU 11-5*Fort Stle* 16-5 Casa 30-5 NWA 1-10 ME 30-11 Ind 1-12 136S C3 ops 17-3-44

JF466 4261 M63 EA 12MU 30-4-43 82MU 9-5 Casa 30-5 NWA 1-7 ME 1-8 NAAF 1-11 185S FTR ops 12-1144

JF467 4262 M63 EA 33MU 30-4-43 47MU 12-5 *SS703* 1-6 Casa 15-6 NWA 1-7 ME 1-8 NAAF 1-11 MAAF 21-6-45 925 eng fail on t/o Treviso, Italy 4-3-46 SOC 25-4

JF468 4271 M63 EA 9MU 7-5-43 82MU 20-5 *SS702* 2-6 Casa 15-6 NWA 1-7 ME 1-9 NAAF 1-11 C3 ops 30-11

JF469 4272 M63 EA 9MU 3-5-43 76MU 17-5 *SS707* 2-7 Casa 29-7 ME 1-9 NAAF 1-11 C3 ops 8-12

JF470 4274 M63 EA 38MU 5-5-43 82MU 22-5 *SS702* 2-6 Casa 15-6 NWA 1-7 ME 1-8 NAASC 1-11 CE ops 1-10-44

JF471 4277 M63 EA 38MU 7-5-43 82MU 30-5 *SS703* 1-6 Casa 15-6 NWA 1-7 ME 2-9 NAAF 1-11 MAAF 21-6-45 SOC 13-9-45

JF472 4278 LFVIII M66 EA 15MU 7-5-43 76MU 11-6 *La Pam* 2-7 Casa 14-7 ME 1-9 NAAF 1-11 SOC 13-9-44

JF473 4280 M63 EA 15MU 7-5-43 76MU 29-5 *SS702* 2-6 Casa 15-6 NWA 1-7 ME 1-8 NAAF 1-11

JF474 4278 LFVIII M66 EA 15MU 11-5-43 76MU 1-6 *SS707* 15-6 Casa 29-6 NWA 1-8 NAAF 1-11 MAAF 21-6-45 SOC 27-3-47

JF475 4289 LFVIII M66 EA 15MU 13-5-43 76MU 29-5 *SS703* 1-6 Casa 15-6 NWA 1-7 ME 1-8 NAAF 1-11 USAAF 29-2-44

JF476 4298 M63A 4-R 6MU 13-5-43 82MU 21-5 *SS702* 2-6 Casa 15-6 NWA 1-7 ME 1-8 NAAF 1-11 92S C3 ops 14-2-44

JF477 4296 LFVIII M66 EA fire on test flight before del cd 31-5-43

JF478 4300 LFVIII M66 EA 6MU 14-5-43 82MU 23-5 *SS702* 2-6 Casa 15-6 NWA 1-7 NAAF 30-11 145S FACE 7-7-44

JF479 4315 M63A EA 8MU 15-5-43 222MU 31-5 *SS707* 15-6 Casa 29-6 ME 1-8 NAAF 1-11 417S SOC 1-1-47

JF480 4321 LFVIII M66 EA 8MU 14-5-43 76MU 29-5 *SS707* 15-6 CASA 29-6 ME 1-9 NAAF 1-11 VWd Dec '43 52MU Jan '44 RACF Test and Dev Centre Halifax Canada for Winterisation tests

JF481 4301 LFXIII M66 EA 8MU 14-5-43 82MU 25-5 *SS705* 2-6 Casa 15-6 NWA 1-7 ME 1-8 NAAF 1-11 FTR ops 2-1-44

JF482 4314 M63 EA 9MU 16-5-43 82MU 27-5 *SS707* 10-6 Casa 29-6 ME 145S FTR ops 15-8 SOC 8-3-44

JF483 4319 M63 EA 9MU 16-5-43 222MU 4-7 *Fort Nak* 12-7 Casa 29-7 NA 30-11 Ind 1-12 SOC 28-9-44

JF484 4317 M63 EA 9MU 16-5-43 222MU 7-7 *Fort Nak* 12-7 Casa 29-7 NA 30-11 Ind 1-12 SOC 27-6-45

JF485 4328 M63 EA 33MU 20-5-43 82MU 30-5 *SS703* 1-6 Casa 15-6 NWA 1-7 ME 1-8 MAAF 1-11

JF501 4329 M63 EA 33MU 20-5-43 82MU 28-6 *La Pam* 2-7 Casa 14-7 ME 1-9 MAAF 1-11 C3 ops 12-12

JF502 4333 M63 EA 33MU 22-5-43 82MU 30-5 *SS703* 1-6 Casa 15-6 NWA 1-7 ME 1-8 NAAF 1-11 92S SOC 26-4-45

JF503 4334 LFVIII M66 EA 33MU 22-5-43 222MU 31-5 *SS707* 10-6 Casa 29-6 ME 1-8 145S SOC 26-4-45

JF504 4332 LFVIII M66 EA 39MU 21-5-43 82MU 4-6 *SS707* 10-6 Casa 29-6 NAASC 3-10 C3 ops 24-1-44

JF505 4345 M63A EA 39MU 222-5-43 82MU 4-6 *SS707* 10-6 Casa 29-6 ME 1-8 NAAF 1-11 SOc 23-10-44

JF506 4344 ,73 EA 39MU 22-5-43 222MU 2-6 *SS707* 10-6 Casa 29-6 ME 1-8 NAAF 1-11 SOC 8-3-44

JF507 4316 M63A EA 39MU 25-5-43 222MU 2-6 *SS707* 10-6 Casa 29-6 ME 1-8 NAAF 1-11 SOC MAAF 21-6-45 SOC 13-9

JF508 4346 M63 EA 6MU 23-5-43 76MU 1-6 *SS707* 10-6 Casa 29-6 ME 1-8 NAAF 1-11 SOC 26-4-45

JF509 4347 M63 EA 6MU 23-5-43 82MU 8-6 *SS707* 10-6 Casa 29-6 ME 1-8 NAAF 1-11 C3 ops 26-1-44

JF510 4350 M63 EA 8MU 25-5-43 82MU 6-6 *SS707* 10-6 Casa 29-6 ME 1-8 NAAF 1-11 FTR ops 12-1-44

JF511 4351 M63 EA 8MU 25-5-43 82MU 6-6 *SS732* 5-8 Casa 18-8 NWA 1-10 USAAF 30-11

JF512 4357 M63 EA 6MU 26-5-43 47MU 1-6 *SS707* 10-6 Casa 29-6 ME 1-8 NAAF 1-11 SOC 30-6-45

JF513 4358 M63 EA 6MU 26-5-43 76MU 1-6 *SS707* 10-6 Casa 29-6 ME 1-8 NAAF 1-11 FTR ops 22-12-44 SOC

JF514 4362 LFVIII M66 EA 6MU 27-5-43 82MU 1-6 *SS707* 10-6 Casa 29-6 FAC3 14-9

JF515 4365 LFVIII M66 EA 8MU 28-5-43 215MU 25-6 *Fort Ver* 1-7 Casa 14-7 ME 1-9 NAAF 1-11 MAAF 21-6-45 SOC 20-9

JF516 4383 M63 EA ASTH 2-6-43 8MU 3-7 82MU 28-7 *SS732* 5-8 Casa 18-8 ME 30-11 Ind 1-12 SOC 26-4-45

JF517 4367 M63 EA 8MU 29-5-43 222MU 14-6 *SS708* 14-6 Casa 29-6 Me 1-8 NAAF 1-11 241S FTR ops 3-4-44

JF518 4363 M63 EA 9MU 30-5-43 215MU 28-6 *Fort Ver* 1-7 Casa 14-7 ME 1-9 NAAF 1-11 SOC 30-6-45

JF519 4373 M63 EA 9MU 30-5-43 222MU 28-6 *Fort Ver* 1-7 Casa 14-7 SOC 30-6-45

JF520 4378 M63 EA 39MU 31-5-43 222MU 9-6 *SS708* 14-6 Casa 29-6 ME 1-8 NAAF 1-11 SOC 8-3-44

JF521 4379 M63 EA 39MU 30-5-43 76MU 8-6 *SS708* 14-6 Casa 29-6 ME 1-8 NAAF 1-11 SOC 28-4-45

JF522 4380 M63 EA 39MU 30-5-43 76MU 8-6 *SS707* 10-6 Casa 29-6 NAASC 3-10 ME 30-11 Ind 1-12 615S SOC 22-5-45

JF523 4391 M63 EA 12MU 1-6-43 215MU 11-10 *Char Hall* 24-10 Casa 17-11 NA 30-11 SOC 28-4-45

JF524 4396 M63 EA 12MU 4-6-43 82MU 11-6 *SS708* 14-6 Casa 29-6 ME 1-8 NAAF FTR ops 29-10

JF525 4397 M63 EA 6MU 4-6-43 52MU 11-6 *La Pam* 2-7 Casa 14-7 ME 1-9 MAAF 1-11 SOC 20-9-45

JF526 4398 M63 EA 6MU 4-6-43 52MU 11-6 *SS708* 14-6 Casa 29-6 ME 1-8 NAAF 1-11 417S RCAF Italy 1944 SOC 14-6-45

JF527 4401 M63 EA 5-6-43 222MU 14-6 *Fort Ver* 1-7 Casa 14-7 ME 30-11 Ind 1-12 SOC 28-9-44

JF528 4402 M63 EA 9MU 6-6-43 215MU 28-6 *Fort Ver* 1-7 Casa 14-7 ME 1-9 MAAF 1-11 SOC 30-6-44

JF557 4403 M63 EA 9MU 5-6-43 215MU 28-6 *Fort Ver* 1-7 Casa 14-7 ME 1-9 NAAF 1-11 417S SOC 20-9-45

JF558 4411 M63 EA 9MU 6-6-43 215MU 28-6 *Fort Ver* 1-7 Casa 14-7 241S FAC3 i/sea 21-3-44

JF559 4412 M63 EA 6-6-43 82MU 14-6 *La Pam* 2-7 Casa 14-7 ME 1-9 NAAF 1-11 92S SOC 30-1-45

JF560 4418 M63 EA 33MU 9-6-43 222MU 18-6 *Fort Ver* 1-7 Casa 14-7 ME 1-9 NAAF 1-11 MAAF 21-6-45 73S SOC 18-10

JF561 4419 M63 EA 33MU 8-6-43 222MU 18-6 *Fort Ver* 1-7 Casa 14-7 ME 1-9 NAAF 1-11 SOC 30-6-44

JF562 4420 M63 EA 33MU 9-7-43 52MU 14-6 *La Pam* 2-7 Casa 14-7 ME 1-9 NAAF 1-11 FTR ops 23-2-44

JF563 4421 M63 EA 8MU 11-6-43 76MU 23-6 *La Pam* 2-7 Casa 14-7 ME 1-9 FTR ops 28-10

JF564 4422 LFVIII M66 EA 8MU 11-6-43 76MU 23-6 *La Pam* 2-7 Casa 14-7 ME 1-9 NAAF 1-11 MAAF 21-6-45 SOC 20-9

JF565 4423 LFVIII M66 EA 8MU 11-6-43 76MU 23-6 *La Pam* 2-7 Casa 14-7 ME 1-9 NAAF 1-11 145S SOC 30-6-44

JF566 4440 M63 38MU 12-6-43 52MU 21-6 *La Pam* 2-7 Casa 14-7 ME 1-9 NAAF 1-11 32S CE 3-11-44

JF567 4425 M63 EA 38MU 12-6-43 52MU 21-6 *La Pam* 2-7 Casa 14-7 NWA FTR ops 10-10

JF568 4431 LFVIII M66 EA 45MU 12-6-43 47MU 24-6 *Fort Ver* 1-7 Casa 14-7 ME 1-9 NAAF 1-11 145S FACE 8-7-44

JF569 4429 LFVIII M66 EA 45MU 12-6-43 215MU 21-6 *Fort Ver* 1-7 Casa 14-7 ME 1-9 NAAF 1-11 USAAF 31-1-44

JF570 4430 M63 EA 45MU 215MU 2-7 *Fort Ver* 1-7 Casa 14-7 ME 1-8 NAAF 1-11 C3 ops 25-1-44

JF571 4428 M63 EA 46MU 12-6-43 215MU 21-6 *Fort Ver* 1-7 Casa 14-7 ME 1-9 SOC 1-11

JF572 4444 M63 EA 20-6-43 47MU 30-6 *Fort Nak* 14-

7 Casa 29-7 NA 30-11 MAAF 21-6-45 SOC 20-9
JF573 4445 M63 EA 46MU 20-6-43 47MU 30-6 *Fort Nak* 14-7 Casa 29-7 NA 30-11 MAAF 1-12 152S FTR ops 13-3-44
JF574 4443 M63 EA 8MU 16-6-43 215MU *Fort Ver* 1-7 Casa 14-7 ME 1-9 NAAF 1-11 SOC 4-3-44
JF575 4455 M63 EA 12MU 23-6-43 222MU 4-7 *Fort Nak* 14-7 Casa 29-7
JF576 4456 M63 EA 12MU 22-6-43 45MU 26-6 215MU 5-7 *Fort Nak* 5-7 Casa 29-7 USAAF 31-10 185S MAAF 21-6-45 SOC 9-5-46
JF577 4462 M63 EA 12MU 25-6-43 215MU 6-7 *Fort Nak* 5-7 Casa 29-7 USAAF 30-11 FAC3 11-4-44
JF578 4382 M63 CHA 39MU 31-5-43 222MU 10-6 *SS703* 14-6 Casa 29-6 ME 1-8 NAAF 1-11 SOC 31-8-44
JF579 4390 M63 CHA 6MU 1-6-43 47MU 10-6 *SS708* 14-6 Casa 29-6 ME 1-8 NAAF 1-11 SOC 29-2-44
JF580 4399 M63 CHA 5-6-43 82MU 11-6 *SS708* 14-6 Casa 29-6 ME 1-8 NAAF 1-11
JF581 4415 M63 HPA 39MU 8-6-43 76MU 21-6 *La Pam* 2-7 Casa 14-7 ME 1-9 NAAF 1-11 FTR ops 27-2-44
JF582 4416 M63 CHA 39MU 8-6-43 76MU 23-6 *La Pam* 2-7 casa 14-7 ME 1-9 NAAF 1-11
JF583 4417 M63 CHA 39MU 8-6-43 76MU 21-6 *La Pam* 2-7 Casa 14-7 ME 1-9 NAAF 1-11 SOC 14-6-45
JF584 4424 M63 CHA FF 8-6-43 6MU 12-6 76MU 19-6 *La Pam* 2-7 Casa 14-7 MAAF 21-6-45 256S SOC 27-3-47
JF585 4432 M63 CHA FF 10-6-43 6MU 12-6 76MU 23-6 *La Pam* 2-7 Casa 14-7 ME 1-9 NA 30-11 FTR ops 24-1-44
JF586 4433 M63 CHA FF 10-6-43 6MU 13-6 76MU 23-6 *Fort Ver* 1-7 Casa 14-7 ME 1-9 NAAF 1-11 417S
JF587 4427 M63 CHA FF 9-10-43 12MU 13-6 215MU 23-6 *Fort Ver* 1-7 Casa 14-7 ME 1-9 NAAF 1-11 SOC 26-4-45
JF588 4434 M63 CHA FF 11-6-43 12MU 13-6 47MU 6-7 *Fort Ches* 11-7 Casa 29-7 ME 1-9 NAAF 1-11 SOC 26-4-45
JF589 4436 M63 CHA FF 12-6-43 12MU 13-6 47MU 20-6 *Fort Ver* 1-7 Casa 14-7 ME 1-8 NAAF 1-11 MAAF 21-6-45 SOC 29-8-46
JF590 4442 M63 HPA FF 12-6-43 38MU 16-6 47MU 25-6 *Fort Ver* 1-7 Casa 14-7 ME 1-9 NAAF 1-11 SOC 8-3-44
JF591 4450 M63 HPA FF 19-6-43 8MU 20-6 76MU 1-7 *SS717* 11-7 Casa 29-7 256S 18-3-44
JF592 4458 M63 HPA FF 22-6-43 38MU 23-6 76MU 2-7 *SS717* 11-7 Casa 29-7 ME 1-9 NAAF 1-11 C3 ops 24-1-44
JF613 4488 M63 HPA 12MU 28-6-43 47MU 9-7 *Fort Ches* 11-7 Casa 29-7 NWA C3 ops 5-12
JF614 4507 M63 HPA 39MU 3-7-43 76MU 18-7 *Fort Rup* 25-7 Casa 16-8 ME 30-11 SOC 31-12-46
JF615 4535 M63 HPA 39MU 12-7-43 82MU 23-7 *SS732* 5-8 Casa 18-8 ME 30-11 Ind 1-1-44 615S CE 30-11 SOC 14-4-45
JF616 4537 M63 HPA 33MU 16-7-43 82MU 24-7 *SS732* 5-8 Casa 18-8 92S SOC 30-11-44
JF617 4560 M63 HPA 33MU 16-7-43 215MU 6-8 *Malan* 16-9 Ind 9-11 CE 14-4-45 SOC 23-5
JF618 4591 M63 HPA 38MU 24-7-43 82MU 12-8 *Fort Thom* 14-8 Casa 1-9 ME 30-11 Ind 1-1-44 FTR ops 13-3
JF619 4588 LFVIII M66 HPA 12MU 27-7-43 215MU 9-8 *Fort Thom* 14-8 Casa 1-9 ME 30-11 Ind 1-1-44 136S FTR ops 29-4
JF620 4625 LFVIII M66 HPA 9MU 13-8-43 215MU 31-8 *Horor* 14-9 Aus 21-10
JF621 4628 LFVIII M66 HPA 9MU 14-8-43 215MU 31-8 *Horor* 14-9 Aus 21-10
JF622 4446 LFVIII M66 CHA 8MU 19-6-43 76MU 1-7 *SS717* 11-7 Casa 29-7 ME 30-11 Ind 1-12 FACE 15-7-44 SOC 7-2-45
JF623 4449 M63 CHA 8MU 20-6-43 76MU 1-7 *SS717* 11-7 Casa 29-7 ME 30-11 Ind 1-12 ACSEA 21-6-45 SOC 30-1-47
JF624 4459 M63 CHA 12MU 24-6-43 215MU 11-7 *Fort Nak* 18-7 Casa 29-7 MAAF 21-6-45 SOC 13-9
JF625 4480 M63 CHA 12MU 27-6-43 222MU 4-7 *Fort Nak* 18-7 Casa 29-7 ME 30-11 Ind 1-12 FACE 25-3-45 SOC 12-4
JF626 4493 M63 CHA 8MU 29-6-43 76MU 8-7 *Fort Ches* 11-7 Casa 29-7 ME 1-9 NAAF 1-11 SOC 29-2-44
JF627 4469 M63 CHA 8MU 27-6-43 76MU 7-7 *Fort Ches* 11-7 Casa 29-7 MAAF 21-6-45 SOC 14-3-46
JF628 4485 M63 CHA 8MU 29-6-43 Casa 29-7 USAAF 30-11 ME 21-6-44 SOC 31-12-46
JF629 4486 M63 CHA 12MU 29-6-43 47MU 7-7 Casa 29-7 ME 30-11 Ind 1-12 CE 23-4-45
JF630 4495 M63 CHA 12MU 1-7-43 215MU 11-7 Casa 29-7 ME 30-11 Ind 1-12 SOC 5-6-45
JF658 4497 M63 CHA 12MU 1-7-43 215MU 3-8 Casa 18-8 NWA 1-10 USAAF 30-11
JF659 4487 M63 CHA 12MU 29-6-43 47MU 11-7 Casa 29-7 SOC 3-6-46
JF660 4502 M63 CHA 38MU 2-7-43 47MU 12-7 Casa 29-7 USAAF 12/31 30-11 lost Italy 22-2-44
JF661 4503 M63 CHA 46MU 2-7-43 215MU 14-7 Casa 29-7 USAAF 31-10 SOC 31-8-44
JF662 4509 M63 CHA 45MU 4-7-43 215MU 5-8 Casa NWA 1-10 SOC 31-8-44
JF663 CHA 46MU 4-7-43 215MU 14-9 Ind 11-11 SOC 13-12-44
JF664 4518 M63 CHA AFDU 7-7-43 9MU 16-8 FAAC 82MU 26-12 Casa 21-1-44 CE ops 8-11
JF665 4519 CHA 39MU 7-7-43 222MU 19-7 Ind 29-8 FACE 18-8-44
JF666 4523 M63 CHA 39MU 12-7-43 222MU 25-7 Casa NA 30-11 Ind 1-12 152S FTR 14-44

JF672 is uncrated at Casablanca, North Africa, in November 1943.

JF667 4529 CHA 39MU 12-7 82MU 5-8 Casa 18-8 NA 30-11 Ind 1-1-44 SOC 31-5-45
JF668 4538 M63 CHA 39MU 16-7-43 82MU 5-8 Casa 18-8 NA 30-11 Ind 1-12 SOC 12-2-45
JF669 4539 M63 CHA 33MU 12-7-43 47MU 19-7 *Fort Rup* 25-7 Casa 16-8 NA 30-11
JF670 4534 M63 CHA 33U 12-7-43 82MU 5-8 *SS732* Casa 18-8 NWA 1-10
JF671 4541 CHA 33MU 16-7-43 82MU 5-8 *SS732* Casa 18-8 CE ops 2-9 Ind 1-1-44 SOC 13-5-45
JF672 4563 CHA 39MU 24-7-43 222MU 14-8 *Fort Thom* 1-9 NA 30-11 CE 4-1-45
JF673 4551 M63 CHA 39MU 17-7-43 82MU 5-8 *SS732* Casa 18-8 NA 30-11 Ind 1-12 CE 5-7-45
JF674 4553 CHA 12MU 18-7-43 82MU 5-8 *SS732* Casa 18-8 NWA 1-10
JF675 4562 CHA 12MU 23-7-43 82MU 12-8 *Fort Thom* 14-8 Casa 1-9 NA 30-11 SOC 23-2-45
JF676 4604 CHA 12MU 27-7-43 47MU 10-8 *Ger Don* 25-8 Casa 10-9 ME 30-11 Ind 1-12 CE 31-10-46
JF692 4578 CHA 38MU 25-7-43 52MU *SS722* 14-8 Casa 1-9 NA 30-11 MAAF 21-6-45 CE 20-9
JF693 4563 M63 38MU 23-7-43 82MU *Fort Geo* 4-13 Casa 22-12
JF694 4583 33MU 24-7-43 222MU *Bakar* 11-9 Ind 9-11 InAF 29-12-47
JF695 4584 M63 CHA 33MU 25-7-43 82MU *Fort Thom* 1-9 ME Ind 1-1-44 SOC 28-9
JF696 4610 CHA 33MU 5-8-43 82MU *Ger Don* 25-8 Casa 10-9 NA 30-11 MAAF 21-6-45 SOC 28-2-46
JF697 4600 CHA 38MU 30-7-43 82MU *Fort Thom* 14-8 Casa 1-9 NA 30-11 CE 4-1-45
JF698 4586 CHA 38MU 25-7-43 222MU *Fort Thom* 14-8 Casa 1-9 NA 30-11 Ind 1-1-44 SOC 31-5-45
JF699 4584 M63 CHA 38MU 27-7-43 82MU 15-11 *Fort Geo* 4-12 Casa 22-12 USAAF 31-1-44
JF700 4460 M63 EA 12MU 23-6-43 47MU *Fort Ches* 11-7 Casa 27-7 ME 1-9 NAAF 1-11 C3 ops 1-4-44
JF701 4454 M63 EA 45MU 21-6-43 215MU 2-7 *Fort Star* 6-7 Casa 14-7 ME 1-9 NAAF 1-11 SOC 18-8-45
JF702 4463 M63 EAQ 45MU 25-6-43 215MU 7-7 *Fort Nak* 14-7 Casa 29-7 ME 1-9 NAAF 1-11 C3 ops 15-3-44
JF703 4472 M63 EA 45MU 26-6-43 82MU 10-7 *Fort Nak* 14-7 Casa 29-7 ME 1-9 NAAF 1-11
JF704 4457 M63 EA 45MU 22-6-43 215MU 2-7 *Fort Ver* 1-7 Casa 14-7 ME 1-9 NAAF 1-11 SOC 28-10-44
JF705 4461 M63 EA 46MU 23-6-43 *Fort Nak* 14-7 Casa 29-7 NWA 1-10 SOC 26-4-45
JF706 4464 M63 EA 46MU 25-6-43 82MU 7-7 *Fort Nak* 14-7 Casa 29-7 USAAF 30-11
JF707 4473 EA CRD VA 27-6-43 exp u/c with wheel camber and toe-in removed to reduce tyre wear. BDn 27-6-44 for taxy t/o and ldg trls Less grd drag and no adverse effects on hand 33MU 9-8-44 215MU 2-5-45 *C of H K* 28-6 Ind 17-9 SOC 30-1-49
JF708 4470 M63 EA 38MU 25-6-43 52MU 4-7 *Fort Ches* 11-7 Casa 29-7 USAAF 31-10 SOC 30-6-44
JF709 4476 M63 EA 38MU 27-6-43 215MU 7-7 *Fort Nak* 14-7 Casa 29-7 MAAF 21-6-45 CE 26-9-45
JF710 4471 M63 EA 38MU 25-6-43 47MU 6-7 *Fort Ches* 11-7 Casa 29-7 ME 1-9 NAAF 1-11 C3 ops 16-12
JF711 4475 M63 EA 38MU 27-6-43 47MU 6-7 *Fort Ches* 11-7 Casa 29-7 NA 30-11 Ind 1-1-44 81S FTR ops 20-3-44
JF712 4474 EA 45MU 26-6-43 215MU 7-7 *Fort Nak* 14-7 Casa 29-7 NWA 1-10 CE ops 5-3-45
JF713 4477 EA 45MU 28-6-43 215MU 11-7 *Fort Nak* 14-7 Casa 29-7 NWA 1-10 SOC 26-4-45
JF714 4483 EA 45MU 28-6-43 82MU 10-7 *Fort Nak* 14-7 Casa 29-7 ME 145S C3 ops 26-1-44
JF715 4478 M63 12MU 27-6-43 82MU 9-7 *Fort Nak* 14-7 Casa 29-7 NA 30-11 Ind 1-2-44 SOC 26-1-44
JF716 4489 M63 EA 12MU 29-6-43 215MU 23-7 *SS732* 5-8 Casa 18-8 NWA 1-10 SOC 26-4-45
JF740 4484 EA 45MU 29-6-43 47MU 9-7 *Fort Ches* 9-7 Casa 29-7
JF741 4490 EA 12MU 29-6-43 215MU 19-7 *Marst* 26-7 Ind 29-8 SOC 31-5-45
JF742 4492 EA 46MU 30-6-43 47MU 21-7 *Marst* 26-7 Ind 29-8 e/fld cd/ld dbf CE 16-8-44 SOC 18-8
JF743 4498 M63 46MU 1-7-43 215MU 8-8 *Fort Thom* 14-8 Casa 1-9 Ind 1-12 SOC 29-3-45
JF744 4499 EA 8MU 1-7-43 76MU 9-7 *Fort Nak* 14-7 Casa 29-7 CE ops 4-11-44
JF745 4491 EA 8MU 1-7-43 76MU 9-7 *Fort Ches* 11-7 Casa 29-7 SOC 30-6-44
JF746 4500 EA 12MU 1-7-43 215MU 11-7 *Fort Nak* 14-7 Casa 29-7
JF747 4505 EA 12MU 3-7-43 215MU 11-7 *Fort Nak* 14-7 Casa 29-7 MAAF FTR ops 10-1-44
JF748 4504 EA 38MU 2-7-43 47MU 11-7 *Fort Rup* 25-7 Casa 16-8 NWA 1-10 417S C3 ops 16-6-44
JF749 4513 EA 38MU 3-7-43 82MU 11-7 *Fort Rup* 25-7 Casa 16-8 327S 12-5-45 339Wng 9-8 SNCAN 11-10
JF750 4511 EA 38MU 3-7-43 82MU 17-7 *Fort Rup* 25-7 Casa 16-8 NWA 1-10 MAAF 21-6-45 SOC 27-3-47
JF751 4514 EA 45MU 6-7-43 215MU 15-7 *Fort Rup* 25-7 Casa 16-8 NA 30-11 Ind 1-1-44 SOC 25-4-46
JF752 4515 EA 45MU 6-7-43 215MU 17-7 *Marst* 26-7 Ind 29-8 C3 ops 16-2-44
JF753 4516 EA 45MU 7-7-43 215MU 17-7 *Marst* 26-7 Ind 29-8
JF754 4522 EA 8MU 8-7 82MU 17-7 *Fort Rup* 25-7 Casa 16-8 NWA 1-10 C3 ops 24-1-44
JF755 4517 EA 12MU 7-7-43 47MU 18-7 *Marst* 26-7 Ind 29-8 SOC 14-2-45
JF756 4523 EA 12MU 8-7-43 215MU 20-7 *Fort Rup* 25-7 Casa 16-8 NWA 1-10 SOC 26-4-45
JF757 4524 EA 12MU 8-7-43 47MU 18-7 *Marst* 26-7 Ind 29-8 SOC 31-10-46
JF758 4525 EA 12MU 10-7-43 215MU 30-7 14-9 Ind 11-11 FAC3 3-1-44
JF759 4526 EA 33MU 10-7-43 47MU 18-7 *Marst* 26-7 Ind 29-8 SOC 11-4-46
JF760 4533 EA 33MU 10-7-43 47MU 18-8 *Marst* 26-7 Ind 28-8 SOC 30-1-47
JF761 4530 EA 33MU 10-7-43 47MU 18-7 *Marst* 26-7 Ind 28-8 C3 ops 17-3-44
JF762 4532 EA 33MU 12-7-43 47MU 18-7 *Marst* 26-7 Ind 28-8 SOC 12-2-45
JF763 4533 EA 38MU 12-7-43 76MU 22-7 *SS732* Casa 18-8 ME Ind 1-1-44 CE 2-8-45
JF764 4603 EA 38MU 26-7-43 82MU 6-8 *Fort Thom* 16-8 Casa 4-9 Ind 1-1-44 Fire in air 9-7 CE dbf 24-1-46
JF765 4542 EA 38MU 16-7-43 222MU 23-7 *SS732* 5-8 Casa 18-8 NWA 1-10 CE 13-9-45
JF766 4543 EA 38MU 16-7-43 82MU 26-7 *SS732* 8-8 Casa 18-8 Ind 1-1-44 SOC 20-4-45
JF767 4545 EA 39MU 18-7-43 47MU 29-7 *Ocean Ves* 16-8 Ind 27-9 SOC Jan '44
JF768 4544 EA 39MU 14-7-43 222MU 24-7 *SS732* 5-8 Casa Ind 1-1-44 SOC 22-5-45
JF769 4546 EA 33MU 16-7-43 82MU 26-7 *SS732* 5-8 Casa Ind 1-1-44 SOC 21-4-45
JF770 4548 EA 33MU 16-7-43 82MU 24-7 *SS732* 5-8 Casa 18-8 FTR ops 6-10
JF771 4556 EA 33MU 18-7-43 82MU 28-7 *Behar* 11-9 Ind 9-11 CE ops 8-8-44

JF772 4549 EA 33MU 16-7-43 82MU 24-7 *SS732* 5-8 Casa 18-8 NWA 1-10 C3 ops 15-2-44

JF773 4557 EA 33MU 18-7-43 222MU 30-7 *Behar* 11-9 Ind 9-11 SOC 19-1-45

JF774 4366 EA 39MU 20-7-43 82MU 7-8 *Behar* 11-9 Ind 9-11 SOC 28-4-46

JF775 4450 EA 39MU 16-7-43 222MU 2-8 *Behar* 11-9 Ind 9-11 SOC 30-1-47

JF776 4569 EA 39MU 22-7-43 222MU 31-7 *Behar* 11-9 Ind 9-11 SOC 10-7-45

JF777 4567 EA 39MU 20-7-43 47MU 1-8 *Ocean Ves* 16-8 Ind 27-9

JF778 4558 EA 39MU 18-7-43 222MU 24-3-44 *Kahroda* 8-4-44 Ind 3-6 CE 1-3-45

JF779 4570 EA 38MU 23-7-43 222MU 3-8 *Fort Thom* 14-8 Casa 1-9 NA 30-11 MAAF 21-6-45 CE 18-10

JF780 4511 EA 38MU 23-7-43 82MU 1-8 *Fort Thom* 15-8 Casa 1-9 NA 30-11 SOC 30-6-45

JF781 4580 EA 12MU 26-7-43 82MU 4-8 *Fort Thom* 15-8 Casa 1-9 NA 30-11 CE 27-12-44

JF782 4572 EA 12MU 26-7-43 222MU 17-8 *Ger Don* 25-8 Casa 10-9 Ind 1-1-44 25-8 RIAF u/c coll ld Miranshah FACE 23-4-46

JF783 4573 EA 12MU 23-7-43 82MU 4-8 *Fort Thom* 14-8 Casa 1-9 NA 30-11

JF784 4574 EA 12MU 23-7-43 82MU 4-8 *Fort Thom* 14-8 Casa 1-9 NA 30-11 MAAF 21-6-45 SOC 28-2-46

JF785 4575 EA 12MU 26-7-43 82MU 4-8 *Fort Thom* 14-8 Casa 1-9 Ind 1-1-44 SOC 25-4-46

JF786 4579 EA 12MU 26-7-43 215MU 9-8 *Fort Thom* 14-8 Casa 1-9 Ind 1-1-44 FAC3 18-2-44

JF787 4581 EA 33MU 26-7-43 222MU 31-7 *SS732* 5-8-43 Casa 18-8 NWA 1-10 C3 ops 31-12

JF788 4591 EA 33MU 25-7-43 215MU 6-8 Ind C3 ops 25-3-44

JF789 4592 EA 38MU 25-7-43 222MU 3-8 *Fort Thom* 14-8 Casa 1-9 Ind 1-1-44 FACE 151 OTU fire on app w/o ld Peshanar 22-8-46

JF805 4595 EA 38MU 27-7-43 82MU 6-8 *Fort Thom* 14-8 Casa 1-9 NAASC 31-10 C3 ops 23-1-44

JF806 4590 EA 38MU 25-7-43 47MU 9-8 *Ger Don* 25-8 Casa 10-9 NAASC 31-10 601S FTR ops 3-3-44

JF807 4596 EA 39MU 26-7-43 82MU 12-8 *Fort Thom* 14-8 Casa 1-9 NA 30-11 Ind 1-1-44

JF808 4597 EA 39MU 26-7-43 82MU 8-8 *Fort Thom* 14-8 Casa 1-9 NA 30-11 Ind 1-1-44 FA FTR 16-3-44

JF809 4598 EA 39MU 26-7-43 222MU 11-8 *Fort Thom* 14-8 Casa 1-9 India 1-1-44 SOC 30-5-45

JF810 4605 EA 33MU 26-7-43 82MU 10-9 *Craw Hon* 23-9 Casa 10-10 NAASC 31-10 SOC 23-10-44

JF811 4606 EA 33MU 7-8-43 222MU 14-8 *Ger Don* 25-8 Casa 10-9 India 1-1-44 FAC3 Sep'44

JF812 4607 EA 33MU 8-8-43 82MU *Ger Don* 25-8 CAsa 10-9 155S FTR 11-4-44

JF813 4619 EA 39MU 13-8-43 82MU 21-8-43 *Card Gib* 3-9 casa 20-9 NAASC 31-10 SOC 14-6-45

JF814 4616 EA 39MU 10-8-43 82MU 21-8 *Card Gib* 3-9 Casa 20-9 NAASC 31-10 SOC 31-7-47

JF815 4618 EA 39MU 12-8-43 82MU 21-8 *Card Gib* 3-9 Casa 20-9 NAASC 31-10 601S FTR ops 20-1-44

JF816 4621 EA CRD 16-8-43 AFDU Witt 22-10 9MU 26-11 47MU 25-12 *Fort Mich* 10-1-44 Ind 7-3 CE 1-11

JF817 4620 EA 6MU 12-8-43 47MU 20-8 *Behar* 11-9 Ind 9-11 SOC 30-1-47

JF818 4622 EA 6MU 13-8-43 222MU 20-8 *Ger Don* 25-8 Casa 10-9 Ind 1-1-44 C3 ops 17-3-44

JF819 4626 EA 6MU 13-8 222MU 21-8 *Ger Don* 25-8 Casa 10-9 Ind NA 30-11 FAC3 17-12

JF820 4633 EA 9MU 14-8-43 215MU 31-8 *Horor* 14-9 Aus 21-10

JF821 4634 EA 9MU 14-8-43 215MU 3-9 *Horor*14-9 Aus 21-10

JF822 4627 EA CHA 9MU 14-8-43 215MU 3-9 *Horor* 14-9 Aus 21-10

JF823 4642 EA 9MU 15-8-43 215MU 3-9 *Horor* 14-9 Aus 21-10

JF824 4644 EA 9MU 15-8-43 215MU 31-8 *Horor* 14-9 Aus 21-10

JF825 4643 EA 9MU 15-8-43 215MU 3-9 *Horor* 14-9 Aus 21-10

JF826 4649 EA 6MU 16-8-43 222MU 29-8 *Malan* 16-9 Ind 3-11 SOC 31-5-45

JF827 4648 EA 6MU 18-8-43 82MU 29-8 *Malan* 16-9 Ind 3-11 SOC 3-4-45

JF828 4651 EA 6MU 19-8-43 82MU 13-9 *Malan* 6-10 Ind 7-12 SOC Dec'44

JF829 4652 EA 6MU 19-8-43 82MU 24-8 *Malan* 16-9 Ind 3-11 SOC 31-5-45

JF830 4662 EA 6MU 21-8-43 47MU 27-8 *Malan* 16-9 Ind 3-11 CE 14-5-45

JF831 4655 EA 6MU 20-8-43 222MU 29-8 *Malan* 16-9 Ind 3-11 132 RSU e/fld on t/o Minealadon Burma 8-1-46 CE SOC 31-1-46

JF832 4656 EA 6MU 20-8-43 82MU 29-8 *Malan* 16-9 Ind 3-11 SOC 25-10-45

JF833 4658 EA PRVIII 6MU 20-8-43 47MU 29-8 *Malan* 16-9 Ind 3-11 FTR ops 14-3-44

JF834 4602 CHA 39MU 26-7-43 82MU 8-8 *Fort Thom* 14-8 Casa 1-9 NAASC 31-10 MAAF 21-6-45 SOC 27-3-47

JF835 4613 M63 CHA 39MU 9-8-43 222MU 27-8 *Card Gib* 3-9 Casa 20-9 NAASC 31-10 Ind 1-1-44

JF836 4585 CHA 39MU 25-7-43 47MU 1-8 *Fort Thom* 14-8 Casa 1-9 NA 30-11 MAAF 21-6-45 CE 18-10

JF837 4608 CHA 12MU 9-8-43 215MU 20-8 *Ger Don* 25-8 Casa 10-9 NAASC 31-10 MAAF 21-6-45 CE 13-9

JF838 4609 CHA 12MU 8-8-43 82MU 23-8 *Card Gib* 3-9 Casa 20-9 NAASC 31-10 SOC 25-4-45

JF839 4613 CHA 6MU 12-8-43 222MU 19-8 *Behar* 11-9 Ind 9-11 SOC 30-4-44

JF840 4617 CHA 6MU 12-8-43 47MU 20-8 *Behar* 11-9 Ind 9-11 FACE 1-5-44

JF841 4623 CHA 6MU 13-8-43 222MU 23-8 *Behar* 11-9 Ind 9-11 SOC 30-4-47

JF842 4624 CHA 6MU 13-8-43 222MU 25-8 *Malan* 16-9 Ind 3-11 SOC 30-4-47

JF843 46312 CHA 6MU 15-8-43 215MU 3-9 *Kohis* 14-9 Ind 11-11 SOC 1-6-47

JF844 4632 CHA 6MU 15-8-43 6FPP ff to 222MU cd bad weather Luckley Farm Stow on the Wold CE 20-8

JF845 4639 CHA 9MU 15-8-43 215MU 3-9 *Horor* 14-9 Aus 21-10

JF846 4654 CHA 9MU 21-8-43 215MU 3-9 *Horor* 14-9 Aus 21-10

JF847 4653 CHA 6MU 19-8-43 215MU 29-8 *Kohis* 14-9 Ind 11-11 SOC 31-4-47

JF848 4661 CHA 6MU 20-8-43 82MU 29-8 *Malan* 16-9 Ind 3-11 CE 13-9-44

JF849 4673 CHA 6MU 22-8-43 47MU 29-8 *Malan* 16-9 Ind 3-11 SOC 16-3-45

JF850 4673 CHA 6MU 22-8-43 47MU 29-8 *Malan* 16-9 Ind 3-11 SOC 16-3-45

JF869 4677 CHA 6Mu 23-8-43215MU 1-9 *Horor* 14-9 Aus 21-10

JF870 4674 CHA 6MU 26-8-43 215MU 30-8 *Horor* 14-9 Aus 21-10

JF871 4675 CHA 9MU 22-8-43 215MU 7-9 *Port Dar* 6-10 Aus 18-1-44

JF872 4676 CHA 9MU 22-8-43 215MU 8-9 *Port Dar* 6-10 Aus 18-1-44

JF873 4688 CHA 9MU 27-8-43 215MU 8-9 *Ocean Rid* 23-9 Casa 10-10 NAASC 31-10 USAAF 31-1-44 SOC 30-6

JF874 4701 CHA 33MU 27-8-43 82MU 2-9 *Craw W L* 22-9 Casa 10-10 NAASC 31-10 USAAF 31-1-44 417S 31-5 FTR ops 26-7

JF875 4691 CHA 33MU 27-8-43 82MU 2-9 *Craw W L* 22-9 Casa 10-10 NAASC 31-10 C3 ops 15-2-44

JF876 4645 HPA 17-8-43 215MU 3-9 *Horor* 14-9 Aus 21-10

JF877 4679 HPA 6MU 23-8-43 215MU 31-8 *Horor* 14-9 Aus 21-10

JF878 4698 HPA 33MU 30-8-43 47MU 4-9 *Ocean Rid* 23-9 Casa 10-10 NAASC 31-10 SOC 18-1-45

JF879 4717 HEA 39MU 30-8-43 82MU 9-9 *Craw W L* 22-9 Casa 10-10 NAASC 31-10 610S FA FTR 2-4-44

JF880 4728 HPA 39MU 3-9-43 47MU 11-9 *Ocean Rid* 23-9 Casa 10-10 NAASC 31-10 USAAF 31-1-44 MAAF 21-6-45 SOC 14-3-46

JF881 4729 HPA 33MU 3-9-43 47MU 8-9 *Ocean Rid* 23-9 Casa 10-10 NAASC 31-10

JF882 4756 HPA 6MU 11-9-43 222MU 16-9 *Emp Mast* 7-10 Casa 19-10 417S C3 ops 28-6-44

JF883 4787 HPA 9MU 17-9-43 215MU 30-9 *Leer* 13-12 Ind 26-1-44 SOC 3-12-46

JF884 4792 HPOA 6MU 18-9-43 215MU 26-9 *Papar* 13-11 Aus 30-12

JF885 4812 HPA 9MU 25-9-43 215MU 18-11 *Fort Phil* 11-12 Aus 16-1-44

JF886 4228 HPA 6MU 25-9-43 82MU 5-10 *Char Hall* 24-10 Casa 27-11 NA 30-11 MAAF 21-6-45 SOC 14-3-46

JF887 4846 HPA 6MU 1-10-43 222MU 8-10 *Mont City* 15-11 Casa 29-11 FACE 2-8-44

JF888 4991 EA 9MU 6-11-43 222MU 22-11 *Leer* 13-12 Ind 26-1-44 FACE 2-8

JF889 4985 CHA 9MU 9-11-43 222MU 18-11 *Leer* 13-12 Ind 26-1-44 SOC 13-12

JF890 5002 KEA 9MU 7-11-43 47MU 26-11 *Emp Reg* 29-12 Ind 18-2-44 SOC 19-7

JF891 4978 EA 9MU 3-11-43 47MU 17-11 *Leer* 13-12 Ind 26-1-44 SOC 25-4-46

JF892 4999 EA 9MU 3-11-43 82MU 17-11 *Leer* 13-12 Ind 26-1-44 SOC 31-12-46

JF893 5000 CHA 6MU 6-11-43 222MU 19-11 *Leer* 13-12 Ind 26-1-44

JF894 5010 M63 CHA 9MU 7-11-43 222MU 7-12 *Fan Hd* 24-12 Casa 8-1-44 MAAF 31-1 USAAF 29-2 CE ops 12-11

JF895 5009 M63 CHA 9MU 7-11-43 222MU 31-1-44 *Fort Lrd* 1-3-44 Casa 17-392S FTR ops 6-9

JF896 5017 M63 KEA 6MU 9-11-43 47MU 17-11 *Fort Geo* 4-12 Casa 22-12 FTR ops 20-8-44

JF897 5019 M63 6MU 11-11-43 222MU 24-11 *Fort Geo* 4-12 Casa 11-2 MAAF 21-6-45 CE 20-9-45

JF898 5018 M63 CHA 9MU 10-11-43 222MU 23-12 *Fan Hd* 24-12 Casa 8-1-44 MAAF 31-1 ME 21-6-45 SOC 31-12-46

JF899 5033 M63 KEA 6MU 13-11-43 215MU 2-12 *Fan Hd* 24-12 Casa 8-1-44 MAAF 31-1 USAAF 29-2 SOC 11-4-46

JF900 4665 M66 KEA 6MU 21-8-43 47MU 29-8 *Malan* 16-9 Ind 3-11 C3 ops 15-3-44

JF901 4464 M66 EA 9MU 22-8-43 47MU 7-9 *Kohis* 14-9 Ind 11-11 SOC Sept'44

JF902 4666 M66 EA 9MU 22-9-43 215MU 8-9 *Kohis* 14-9 Ind SOC 29-4-45

JF926 4667 M66 EA 9MU 22-8-43 47MU 7-9 *Kohis* 14-9 Ind 11-11 SOC 31-1-46

JF927 4671 EA 9MU 23-8-43 215MU 8-9 *Kohis* 14-9 Ind 11-11 SOC 27-12-45

JF928 4672 M66 EA 9MU 23-8-43 215MU 8-9 *Kohis* 14-9 Ind 11-11 SOC 31-5-45

JF929 4678 M66 EA 9MU 24-8-43 47MU 3-9 *Malan* 16-9 Ind 3-11 SOC 7-2-45

JF930 4681 M66 EA 9MU 24-8-43 82MU 8-9 *Craw W L* 22-9 Casa 10-10 NAASC 31-10 USAAF 31-1-44 ME 21-6-45 SOC 31-12-46

JF931 4682 M66 EA 9MU 24-8-43 47MU 7-9 *Ocean Rid* 23-9 Casa 10-10 NAASC 31-10 MAAF 21-6-45 SOC 29-3-47

JF932 4683 M66 EA 9MU 24-8-43 82MU 10-9 *Craw W L* 22-9 Casa 10-10 NAASC 31-10 USAAF 31-1-44 SOC 31-1-45

JF933 4684 M66 EA 6MU 25-8-43 215MU 3-9 *Oran* 11-10 Aus 28-11

JF934 4685 M66 EA 6MU 25-8-43 215MU 3-9 *Hasor* 14-9 Aus 21-10

JF935 4686 EA 6MU 25-8-43 215MU 3-9 *Hasor* 14-9 Aus 21-10

JF936 4689 EA 6MU 25-8-43 215MU 3-9 *Hasor* 14-9 Aus 21-10

JF937 4690 EA 6MU 27-8-43 215MU 7-9 *Hasor* 14-9 Aus 21-10

JF938 4694 EA 6MU 29-8 215MU 6-9 *Port Dar* 6-10 Aus 18-1-44

JF939 4707 EA 6MU 29-8-43 215MU 5-9 *Port Dar* 6-10 Aus 18-1-44

JF940 4700 EA 6MU 30-8-43 215MU 7-9 *Port Dar* 6-10 Aus 18-1-44

JF941 4695 EA 9MU 27-8-43 47MU 7-9 *Ocean Rid* 23-9 Casa 10-10 NAASC 31-10 C3 ops 29-3-44

JF942 4696 EA 9MU 30-8-43 215MU 14-9 *Orion* 11-10 Aus 28-11

JF943 4697 EA 9MU 30-8-43 222MU 10-9 *Malt* 6-10 Ind 18-12 CE 26-7-45

JF944 4711 EA 9MU 21-8-43 215MU 18-9 *Malt* 6-10 Ind 18-12 SOC 31-5-45

JF945 4708 EA 9MU 30-8-43 215MU 10-9 *Oran* 11-10 Aus 28-11

JF946 4708 EA 9MU 30-8-43 82MU 10-9 *Kohis* 14-9 Ind 11-11 SOC 28-4-44

JF947 4710 EA 9MU 30-8-43 82MU 10-9 *Kohis* 14-9 Ind 11-11 SOC 30-4-44

JF948 4712 EA 9MU 31-8-43 222MU 6-10 *Maihar* 29-10 Ind 10-1-44 SOC 12-9-46

JF949 4713 EA 38MU 31-8-43 47MU 7-9 *Ocean Rid* 23-9 Casa 10-10 NAASC 31-10 USAAF 31-1-44 SOC 31-8

JF950 4718 EA 38MU 31-8-43 47MU 6-9 *Char Hall* 24-10 Casa 17-11 NA 30-11 SOC 18-8-44

JF951 4720 EA 38MU 2-9-43 47MU 9-9 *Ocean Rid* 23-9 Casa 10-10 NAASC 31-10 USAAF 31-1-44 SOC Oct '44

JF952 4719 EA 33MU 31-8-43 47MU 8-9 *Ocean Rid* 23-9 Casa 10-10 NAASC 31-10 USAAF 31-1-44 FTR ops 11-12

JF953 4722 EA 39MU 2-9-43 82MU 9-9 *Craw W L* 9-9 Casa 10-10 NAASC 31-10 ME 30-11-44 MAAF 26-11-45 SOC 31-12-46

JF954 4721 EA 39MU 2-9-43 82MU 10-9 *Craw W L* 9-9 Casa 10-10 NAASC 31-10 USAAF 31-1-44 145S CE ops dbf 15-4-45

JF955 4723 EA 39MU 2-9-43 82MU 10-9 *Craw W L* 9-9 Casa 10-10 NAASC 31-10 341S FTR ops 17-8-44

JF956 4725 EA 39MU 2-9-43 82MU 10-9 *Craw W L* 9-9 Casa 10-10 NAASC 31-10 MAAF C3 ops 20-3-44

JF957 4726 EA 39MU 2-9-43 82MU 29-9 *Emp Har* 3-10 Casa 19-10 NAASC 31-10 ME FTR ops 24-4-44

JF958 4730 EA 39MU 4-9-43 82MU 15-9 *Craw W L* 9-9 Casa 10-10 NAASC 31-10 SOC 15-1-45

JF959 4731 EA 33MU 4-9-43 82MU 16-9 *Ocean Rid* 23-9 Casa 10-10 NAASC 31-10 CE ops 3-10-44

JF960 4742 EA 33MU 4-9-43 82MU 15-9 *Craw W L* 9-9 Casa 10-10 NAASC 31-10 417S FTR ops 9-5-44

JF961 4732 EA 39MU 4-9-43 47MU 14-9 *Ocean Rid* 23-9 Casa 10-10 NAASC 31-10 MAAF C3 ops 16-3-44

JF962 4741 EA 39MU 5-9-43 222MU 15-9 *Ocean Rid* 23-9 Casa 10-10 NAASC 31-10 SOC 30-6-44

JF963 4743 EA 39MU 5-9-43 47MU 14-9 *Ocean Rid* 23-9 Casa 10-10 NAASC 31-10 ME 5-7-45 SOC 31-12-46

JF964 4744 EA 39MU 5-9-43 222MU 15-9 *Ocean Rid* 23-9 Casa 10-10 NAASC 31-10 MAAF 21-6-45 92S strck building powerless app Treviso Italy pilot kld CE dbf 12-4-46

JF965 4749 EA 6MU 7-9-43 222MU 11-9 *Papan* 18-11 Aus 30-12

JF966 4750 EA 6MU 7-9-43 222MU 11-9 *Bris Star* 30-10 Aus 7-12

JF967 4752 EA 6MU 8-9-43 215MU 11-9 *Oran* 24-10 Aus 28-11

JG series All LF VIII Merlin 66 unless otherwise indicated

JG104 4751 EA 6MU 7-9-43 222MU 11-9 *Bris Star* 30-10 Aus 7-12

JG105 4755 CHA 6MU 9-9-43 215MU 14-9 *Oran* 24-10 28-11

JG106 4758 EA 6MU 10-9-43 215MU 11-10 *Tekoa* 30-10 Aus 4-2-44

JG107 4759 EA 6MU 10-9-43 215MU 16-9 *Oran* 24-10 Aus 28-11

JG108 4763 EA 6MU 11-9-43 222MU 16-9 *Emp Har* 3-10 Casa 19-10 NAASC 31-10 USAAF 31-1-44

JG109 4764 EA 6MU 11-9-43 222MU 16-9 *Emp Har* 7-10 Casa 19-10 C3 ops 10-4-44

JG110 4767 EA 9MU 13-9-43 222MU 20-9 *Emp Har* 7-10 Casa 19-10 NAASC 31-10 145S FTR ops 22-5-44

JG111 4766 EA 9MU 14-9-43 222MU 21-9 *Emp Har* 21-9-43 Casa 19-10 NAASC 31-10 MAAF 21-6-45 SOC 29-3-47

JG112 4768 EA 9MU 14-9-43 47MU 28-9 *Colleg* 26-10 Ind 16-12 FACE 21-6-44

JG113 4777 EA 9MU 14-9-43 222MU 20-9 *Maih* 29-10 Ind 16-1-44 SOC 30-1-47
JG114 4778 EA 9MU 14-9-43 82MU 25-9 *Nath* 6-10 Ind 7-12 SOC 30-1-47
JG115 4780 EA 9MU 15-9-43 222MU 25-9 *Emp Mar* 7-10 Casa 19-10
JG116 4782 EA 9MU 17-9-43 215MU 28-9 *C McBean* 22-11 Ind 7-1-44 CE Nov '44
JG117 4783 EA 9MU 17-9-43 82MU 7-10 *Colleg* 26-10 Ind 16-12
JG118 4790 EA 9MU 17-9-43 47MU 28-9 *Colleg* 26-10 Ind 16-12 SOC 3-12-44
JG119 4693 CHA 33MU 27-8-43 47MU 4-9 *Ocean Rid* 23-9 Casa 10-10 NAASC 31-10 SOC 31-8-44
JG120 4702 CHa 33MU 29-8-43 47MU 26-10 *Fort Geo* 4-12 Casa 22-12 USAAF 31-1-44
JG121 4703 CHA 33MU 31-8-43 47MU 8-9 *Ocean Rid* 23-9 Casa 10-10 NAASC 31-10 FACE 16-12-44
JG122 4704 CHA 39MU 31-8-43 82MU 8-9 *Nath* 6-10 Ind 7-12 SOC 30-1-47
JG123 4705 CHA 39MU 31-8-43 82MU 8-9 *Craw W L* 22-9 Casa 10-10 NAASC 31-10 USAAF 31-1-44 MAAF 25-4-45 FACE 26-4-45
JG124 4706 CHA 39MU 31-8-43 82MU 8-9 *Craw W L* 22-9 Casa 10-10
JG157 4724 CHA 33MU 2-9-43 47MU 8-9 *Ocean Rid* 23-9 Casa 10-10 NAASC 31-10 USAAF 31-1-44
JG158 4738 CHA 33MU 5-9-43 82MU 16-9 *Ocean Rid* 23-9 Casa 10-10 NAASC 31-10 MAAF FAC3 16-2-44
JG159 4733 CHA 39MU 4-9-43 47MU 18-9 *Ionian* 3-10 Casa 10-10 NAASC 31-10 CE ops 3-11-44
JG160 4734 CHA 39MU 4-9-43 222MU 15-9 *Craw W L* 15-9 Casa 10-10 NAASC 31-10 ME SOC 30-11
JG161 4740 CHA 33MU 6-9-43 47MU 11-9 *Ocean Rid* 23-9 Casa 10-10 NAASC 31-10 SOC Oct '44
JG162 4746 M63A CHA 33MU 5-9-43 222MU 13-9 *Ocean Rid* 23-9 Casa 10-10 NAASC 31-10 SOC 15-3-45
JG163 4745 CHA 39MU 4-9-43 47MU 14-9 *Ocean Rid* 23-9 Casa 10-10 NAASC 31-10 USAAF 31-1-44 MAAF FACE 12-10-44
JG164 4747 CHA 39MU 5-9-43 82MU 13-9 *Craw W L* 22-9 Casa 10-10 NAASC 31-10 SOC 23-10-44
JG165 4748 CHA 39MU 6-9-43 215MU 27-9 *Emp Mar* 7-10 Casa 19-10 NAASC 31-10 USAAF 29-2-44 SOC 31-8
JG166 4769 M63 CHA 6MU 11-9-43 222MU 16-9 *Emp Mar* 7-10 Casa 19-10 NAASC 31-10 ME 30-11 SOC 25-8-44
JG167 4765 CHA 6MU 11-9-43 222MU 16-9 *Emp Mar* 7-10 Casa 19-10 NAASC 31-10
JG168 4760 CHA 6MU 11-9-43 222MU 18-9 *Emp Mar* 7-10 Casa 19-10 NAASC 31-10 C3 ops 24-2-44
JG169 4770 CHA 9MU 14-9-43 215MU 28-9 *Leer* 19-12 Ind 26-1-44 FACE 26-5-45
JG170 4771 CHA 9MU 13-9-43 222MU 20-9 *Maih* 29-10 Ind 10-1-44 CE 2-6-45
JG171 4772 CHA 9MU 14-9-43 47MU 28-9 *Colleg* 26-10 Ind 16-12 CE 14-6-44 SOC 5-7-45
JG172 4776 CHA 9MU 14-9-43 47MU 28-9 *Colleg* 26-10 Ind 16-12 SOC 10-9-44
JG173 4781 CHA 6MU 14-9-43 82MU 20-9 *Emp Mar* 7-10 Casa 29-10 NAASC 30-10 SOC 26-4-45
JG174 4788 CHA 6MU 18-9-43 215MU 26-9 *Papan* 1-11 Aus 30-12
JG175 4793 CHA 6MU 18-9-43 215MU 26-9 *Papan* 1-11 Aus 30-12
JG176 4785 CHA 6MU 16-9-43 215MU 24-9 *Papan* 1-11 Aus 30-12
JG177 4794 CHA 6MU 18-9-43 215MU 27-9 *Papan* 1-11 Aus 30-12
JG178 4800 CHA 9MU 19-9-43 215MU 28-9 *C McBean* 22-11 Ind 7-1-44
JG179 4801 CHA 9MU 19-9-43 47MU 2-10 *Emp Mar* 7-10 Casa 19-10 NAASC 30-10 SOC 18-8-44
JG180 4802 CHA 9MU 20-9-43 *Maih* 29-10 Ind 10-1-44 SOC 24-5-45
JG181 4810 CHA 9MU 20-9-43 82MU 7-10 *Colleg* 26-10 Ind 16-12 155S FA FTR 5-9-44
JG182 4811 CHA 9MU 20-9-43 222MU 6-10 *Maih* 29-10 Ind 10-1-44 SOC 20-3-45
JG183 4814 CHA 9MU 22-9-43 222MU 4-10 *Maih* 29-10 Ind 10-1-44 SOC 31-5-45
JG184 4817 CHA 6MU 22-9-43 82MU 5-10 *Char Hall* 24-10 Casa 17-11 NA 30-11 SOC 30-6-44
JG185 4822 CHA 6MU 25-9-43 47MU 5-10 *Char Hall* 24-10 Casa 17-11 NA 30-11
JG186 4823 CHA 6MU 25-9-43 47MU 5-10 *Char hall* 24-10 Casa 17-11 NA 30-11 USAAF 31-1-44 SOC 30-6
JG187 4784 EA 6MU 16-9-43 215MU 21-9 *Papan* 13-11 Aus 30-12
JG188 4789 EA 6MU 17-9-43 215MU 24-9 *Papan* 13-11 Aus 30-12
JG189 4791 EA 6MU 17-9-43 215MU 24-9 *Papan* 13-11 Aus 30-12
JG190 4795 EA 6MU 20-9-43 82MU 27-9 *Emp Mar* 9-10 Casa 14-10 NAASC 30-10 SOC 29-2-44
JG191 4796 EA 6MU 18-9-43 215MU 26-9 *Papan* 13-11 Aus 30-12
JG192 4797 EA 6MU 17-9-43 215MU 24-9 *Papan* 13-11 Aus 30-12
JG193 4798 EA 9MU 19-9-43 222MU 6-10 *Maih* 29-10 Ind 10-1-44 CE 5-7-45
JG194 4805 EA 9MU 19-9-43 82MU 27-10 *Chyel* 3-12 Ind 12-1-44 CE ops 21-6-44
JG195 4806 EA 9MU 20-9-43 47MU 11-10 *Colleg* 26-10 Ind 16-12 FACE Mar '44
JG196 4808 EA 9MU 19-9-43 215MU 30-9 *Leer* 13-10 Ind 26-1-44 SOC 26-4-45
JG197 4809 EA 9MU 19-9-43 47MU 2-10 *Emp Mar* 7-10 Casa 19-10 NAASC 30-10 USAAF 30-1-44 MAAF 21-6-45 SOC 27-3-47
JG198 4815 EA 9MU 21-9-43 215MU 30-9 *Leer* 13-12 Ind 26-1-44 SOC 27-12-45
JG199 4816 EA 9MU 21-9-43 82MU 27-10 *Chyel* 3-12 Ind 12-1-44 SOC 30-1-47
JG200 4818 EA 9MU 23-9-43 82MU 11-10 *Chyel* 3-12 Ind 12-1-44 SOC 24-4-47
JG201 4819 EA 9MU 23-9-43 82MU 7-10 *Colleg* 26-10 Ind 16-12 607S FTR ops 18-5-44
JG202 4820 EA 9MU 24-9-43 47MU 11-10 *Char Hall* 24-10 Casa 17-11 NA 30-11
JG203 4821 EA 9MU 24-9-43 82MU 8-10 *Char Hall* 24-10 Casa 17-11 NA 30-11 145S FTR ops 7-10-44
JG204 4830 EA CRD VA 26-9-43 Farn full synthetic trop trls. BDn 12-6-44 trls with Spit F23 wng section. Lead edge raised one inch and nose contour adjusted; new root fillets; ails with trim tabs and piano hinges. Guns and can fairings on wng upper surface removed; curved w/s and balloon hood. The a/c was longitudinally unstable. Four can instal during trls Ext flown by Super test pilots. MPRD Cowley 4-10-46 SOC scr
JG239 4825 EA 6MU 24-9-43 215MU 6-10 *Papan* Aus 30-12
JG240 4834 EA 6MU 26-9-43 82MU 5-10 *Char Hall* 26-10 Casa 17-11 NA 30-11
JG241 4835 EA 6MU 26-9-43 82MU 14-11 *Fort Geo* 4-12 Casa 22-12 SOC 30-6-44
JG242 4836 EA 6MU 26-9-43 82MU 3-10 *Char Hall* 26-10 Casa 17-11 NA 30-11 USAAF 30-1-44 MAAF 21-6-45 SOC 26-7
JG243 4837 EA 6MU 26-9-43 82MU 5-10 *Char Hall* 26-10 Casa 17-11 NA 30-11 CE ops 11-12-44
JG244 4841 EA 6MU 26-9-43 82MU 5-10 *Char Hall* 26-10 Casa 17-11 NA 30-11 SOC 31-8-44
JG245 4842 EA 6MU 26-9-43 82MU 5-10 *Char Hall* 26-10 Casa 17-11 NA 30-11 USAAF 31-1-44
JG246 4848 EA 6MU 30-9-43 222MU 8-10 *Char Hall* 26-10 Casa 17-11 NA 30-11 SOC 18-3-44
JG247 4847 EA 6MU 29-9-43 215MU 6-10 *Char Hall* 26-10 Casa 17-11 NA 30-11 SOC 1-4-45
JG248 4849 EA 6MU 30-9-43 222MU 8-10 *Char Hall* 24-10 Casa 17-11 NA 30-11 USAAF 31-1-44 SOC 26-4-45
JG249 4850 EA 6MU 30-9-43 222MU 8-10 *Char Hall* 24-10 Casa 17-11 NA 30-11 CE ops 11-12-44
JG250 4851 EA 6MU 30-9-43 222MU 8-10 *Char Hall* 24-10 Casa 17-11 NA 30-11 MAAF 21-6-45 CE 26-2-45
JG251 4858 EA 9MU 1-10-43 222MU 13-10 *Maih* 29-10 Ind 10-1-44 SOC 31-10-46
JG252 4859 EA 9MU 1-10-43 222MU 15-10 *Chyel* 3-12 Ind 12-1-44 FACE 2-9-44
JG253 4863 EA 9MU 1-10-43 13-10 *Maih* 29-10 Ind 10-1-44 SOC 24-12-44
JG254 4864 EA 9MU 3-10-43 27-10 *Leer* 13-12 Ind 26-1-44 CE 14-8-44 recat B SOC 31-5-45
JG255 4865 EA 9MU 3-10-43 222MU 13-10 *Maih* 29-10 Ind 10-1-44 SOC 24-12-44
JG256 4860 EA 6MU 1-10-43 82MU 8-10 *Char Hall* 24-10 Casa 17-11 NA 30-11 SOC 30-6-45
JG257 4867 EA 6MU 3-10-43 82MU 11-10 *Char Hall* 24-10 Casa 17-11 NA 30-11 USAAF 31-1-44 6MU 2-6-45 215MU 15-7 *Co H K* 17-9 SOC 1-6-47
JG258 4868 EA 6MU 3-10-43 82MU 11-10 *Char Hall* 24-10 Casa 17-11 NA 30-11
JG259 4869 EA 9MU 3-10-43 82MU 20-10 *Chyel* 3-12 Ind 12-1-44 SOC 12-2-45
JG260 4889 EA 9MU 16-10-43 82MU 27-10 *Chyel* 3-12 Ind 12-1-44 SOC 19-7-45
JG261 4876 EA 9MU 7-10-43 82MU 27-10 *Chyel* 3-12 Ind 12-1-44 FACE 4-7-44
JG262 4877 EA 6MU 7-10-43 215MU 19-10 *Tekoa* 1-12 Aus 4-2-44
JG263 4878 EA 6MU 7-10-43 215MU 19-10 *Tekoa* 1-12 Aus 21-1-44
JG264 4882 EA 8-10-43 215MU 18-10 *Papan* 13-11 Aus 30-12
JG265 4886 EA 6MU 8-10-43 215MU 19-10 *Tekoa* 1-12 Aus 4-2-44
JG266 4883 EA 6MU 8-10-43 215MU 19-10 *Tekoa* 1-12 Aus 21-1-44
JG267 4888 EA 6MU 9-10-43 215MU 19-10 *Tekoa* 1-12 Aus 21-1-44
JG268 4890 EA 9MU 16-10-43 82MU 19-10 *Leerdan* 13-12 Ind 26-1-44 SOC 31-6-47
JG269 4874 KEA 6MU 3-10-43 215MU 21-10 *Tekoa* 1-12 Aus 21-1-44
JG270 4885 KEA 6MU 10-10-43 215MU 21-10 *Tekoa* 1-12 Aus 21-1-44
JG271 4891 KEA 6MU 10-10-43 215MU 22-10 *Papan* 13-11 Aus 30-12
JG272 4905 KEA 9MU 19-10-43 222MU 6-11 *Mon City* 15-11 Casa 29-11 417S C3 ops 4-9-44
JG273 4934 KEA 9MU 22-10-43 222MU 6-11 *Chyel* 3-12 Ind 12-1-44 SOC 25-4-46
JG274 4925 KEA 9MU 19-10-43 82MU 10-11 *Fort Geo* 4-12 Casa 22-12 SOC 23-10-44
JG275 4938 KEA 6MU 19-10-43 215MU 8-11 *Suff* 1-12 Aus 29-1-44
JG312 4960 KEA 6MU 28-10-43 82MU 9-11 *Fort Geo* 4-12 Casa 22-12 C3 ops 20-2-44
JG313 4970 KEA 9MU 6-11-43 222MU 25-11 *Emp Reg* 27-12 Ind 18-2-44 FAC3 3-5-44
JG314 4965 KEA 9MU 6-11-43 222MU 19-11 *Leer* 13-12 Ind 26-1-44 IOS RIAF D BR on LD SOC 1-6-47
JG315 4973 KEA BAIGACHI 3-4-46 9MU 6-11-43 FAAC 18-11 222MU 14-1-44 *Maih* 8-2 Ind 20-3 SOC 7-6-45
JG316 5030 CHA 6MU 13-11-43 215MU 26-11 *Fort Geo* 4-12 Casa 22-12 C3 ops 25-3-44
JG317 5037 KEA 6MU 16-11-43 47MU 2-12 *Fan Hd* 24-12 Casa 8-1-44 31-1 USAAF 29-2 SOC 31-12-46
JG318 5031 CHA 6MU 13-11-43 215MU 2-12 *Fort Geo* 4-12 Casa 22-12 241S FTR ops 9-6-44
JG319 5032 CHA 9MU 15-11-43 82MU 3-12 *Kaim* 22-12 Ind 18-2-44 SOC 25-4-46
JG320 5041 CHA 9MU 15-11-43 47MU 25-12 *Port Nip* 22-12 Ind 7-3-44 SOC 10-1-46
JG321 5051 KEA 9MU 16-11-43 82MU 4-12 *Kaim* 22-12 Ind 18-2-44 SOC 7-2-45
JG322 4995 KEA 9MU 6-11-43 222MU 25-11 *Emp Reg* 22-12 Ind 18-2-44 FTR 3-4-45
JG323 5047 CHA 9MU 15-11-43 222MU 13-12 *Kaim* 22-12 Ind 18-2-44 SOC 26-6-47
JG324 5074 KEA 9MU 2-12-43 47MU 19-12 *Kaim* 22-12 Ind 18-2-44 CE ops 16-6-44
JG325 5056 EA 9MU 25-11-43 222MU 13-12 *Kaim* 22-12 Ind 18-2-44 InAF 29-12-47
JG326 5075 KEA 9MU 28-11 43 222MU 13-12 *Kaim* 22-12 Ind 18-2-44 SOC 29-5-45
JG327 5062 EA 9MU 25-11-43 47MU 13-12 *Kaim* 22-12 Ind 18-2-44 SOC 10-7-44
JG328 5081 KEA 9MU 28-11-43 222MU 13-12 *Kaim* 22-12 Ind 18-2-44 SOC 2-2-45 (manufact break point)
JG329 4829 CHA 6MU 26-9-43 215MU 12-10 *Char Hall* 12-10 Casa 27-11 NA 30-11 CE ops 18-12-44
JG330 4843 CHA 9MU 29-9-43 47MU 20-10 *Leer* 13-12 Ind 26-1-44 SOC 26-5-45
JG331 4839 CHA 9MU 26-9-43 215MU 13-5-44 *C o Ag* 13-5 Ind 4-7 SOC 31-7-47
JG332 4844 CHA 9MU 1-10-43 215MU 21-10 *Tekoa* 1-12 Aus 21-1-44
JG333 4845 HPA 9MU 1-10-43 222MU 13-10 *Maih* 29-10 Ind 10-1-44 CE 21-6-45
JG334 4852 CHA 6MU 30-9-43 82MU 8-10 *Char Hall* 24-10 Casa 17-11 NA 30-11 SOC 31-12-46
JG335 4855 CHA 6MU 1-10-43 215MU 13-10 *Char Hall* 24-10 Casa 17-11 NA 30-11 MAAF C3 ops 9-2-44
JG336 4856 CHA 9MU 1-10-43 47MU 20-10 *Colleg* 26-10 Ind 16-12 SOC 10-9-44
JG337 4857 CHA 6MU 2-10-43 82MU 11-10 *Char Hall* 24-10 Casa 17-11 NA 30-11 MAAF 21-6-45 SOC 23-11
JG338 4869 CHA 6MU 3-10-43 215MU 12-10 *Char Hall* 24-10 Casa 17-11 NA 30-11 CE ops 2-9-44
JG339 4876 CHA 9MU 3-10-43 47MU 17-10 *Colleg* 26-10 Ind 16-12
JG340 4861 CHA 9MU 1-10-43 222MU 15-10 *Maih* 29-10 Ind 10-1-44 SOC 30-1-47
JG341 4871 CHA 9MU 3-10-43 47MU 17-10 *Colleg* 26-10 Ind 16-12 FACE 18-5-45
JG342 4879 CHA 9MU 7-10-43 215MU 27-10 *Perth* 14-12 Aus 3-2-44
JG343 4880 CHA 9MU 7-10-43 215MU 24-10 *Papan* 13-11 Aus 30-12
JG344 4887 CHA 9MU 9-10-43 82MU 27-10 *Chyel* 3-12 Ind 12-1-44 FAC3 24-3-44
JG345 4881 CHA 6MU 7-10-43 215MU 21-10 *Tabora* 7-12 Aus 21-1-44
JG346 4898 CHA 6MU 15-10-43 215MU 24-10 *Papan* 13-11 Aus 30-12
JG347 4897 CHA 6MU 15-10-43 215MU 25-10 *Tabora* Aus 21-1-44
JG348 4899 CHA 9MU 13-10-43 82MU 27-10 *Chyel* 3-12 Ind 12-1-44 81S C3 ops 19-4
JG349 4890 CHA 9MU 16-10-43 222MU 20-10 *Chyel* 3-12 Ind 12-1-44 CE 5-7-45
JG350 4891 CHA 9MU 17-10-43 215MU 29-10 *Perth* 14-12 Aus 3-2-44
JG351 4903 CHA 6MU 17-10-43 215MU 25-10 *Papan* 13-11 Aus 30-12
JG352 4913 CHA 6MU 17-10-43 215MU 25-10 *Papan* 13-11 Aus 30-12
JG353 4914 CHA 6MU 16-10-43 215MU 26-10 *Fort Phil* 11-12 Aus 16-1-44
JG354 4915 CHA 9MU 17-10-43 215MU 10-11 *Fort Phil* 11-12 Aus 16-1-44
JG355 4919 CHA 9MU 17-10-43 215MU 29-10 *Fort Phil* 11-12 Aus 16-1-44
JG356 4920 CHA 9MU 19-10-43 82MU 14-11 *Suff* 1-12 Aus 29-1-44
JG371 4922 CHA 17-10-43 215MU 24-10 *Papan* 13-11 Aus 30-12
JG372 4923 CHA 6MU 18-10-43 215MU 11-11 *Suff* 1-12 Aus 29-1-44
JG373 4924 CHA 6MU 17-10-43 215MU 25-10 *Perth* 14-12 Aus 3-2-44
JG374 4932 CHA 9MU 17-10-43 82MU 29-10 *Leer* 13-12 Ind 26-1-44 CE 5-7-45
JG375 4933 CHA 9MU 17-10-43 82MU 18-11 *Leer* 13-12 Ind 26-1-44 SOC 11-6-45
JG376 4948 CHA 6MU 24-10-43 215MU 15-11 *Fort Phil* 11-12 Aus 16-1-44
JG377 4943 CHA 6MU 24-10-43 215MU 8-11 *Perth* 14-12 Aus 3-2-44
JG378 4949 CHA 9MU 24-10-43 82MU 14-11 *Leer* 13-12 Ind 26-1-44 FACE 5-8-47
JG379 4957 CHA 9MU 27-10-43 222MU 13-12 *Kaim* 22-12 Ind 18-2-44 SOC 11-4-46
JG380 4958 CHA 9MU 27-10-43 222MU 11-11 *Leer* 13-12 Ind 26-1-44 FACE 16-8-44
JG381 4962 CHA 6MU 29-10-43 222MU 8-11 *Mont*

City 15-11 Casa 29-11 MAAF 21-6-45 CE 18-10
JG382 4964 CHA 6MU 27-10-43 215MU 9-11 *Suff* 1-12 Aus 29-1-44
JG383 4980 CHA 6MU 5-11-43 82MU 15-11 *Fort Geo* 4-12 Casa 22-12 SOC 30-6-44
JG384 4969 CHA 6MU 5-11-43 82MU 15-11 *Fort Geo* 4-12 Casa 22-12 USAAF 29-2-44 CE ops 4-7
JG385 4983 CHA 6MU 5-11-43 215MU 25-12 *Hind* 6-2-44 Aus 18-4
JG386 4984 CHA 9MU 5-11-43 215MU 17-11 *Fort Phil* 11-12 Aus 16-1-44
JG387 4994 CHA 9MU 7-11-43 215MU 19-11 *Suff* 1-12 Aus 29-1-44
JG404 5072 CHA 9MU 20-11-43 222MU 13-12 *Kaim* 22-12 Ind 18-2-44 SOC 30-1-47
JG405 5109 CHA 9MU 20-12-43 222MU 10-1-44 *Maih* 8-2 Ind 20-3 SOC 30-1-47
JG406 5078 CHA 9MU 25-11-43 222MU 5-3-44 *Berr* Ind 12-5 SOC 30-8-45
JG407 4893 EA 9MU 16-10-43 82MU 29-10 *Leer* 13-12 Ind 26-1-44 SOC 31-5-45
JG408 5230 AST 9MU 30-12-43 222MU 14-1-44 *Maih* Ind 20-3 SOC 31-12-46
JG409 4896 EA 9MU 16-10-43 222MU 2-11 *Chyel* 13-12 Ind 12-1-44 SOC 25-4-46
JG410 4894 EA 9MU 16-10-43 82MU 27-10 *Chyel* 13-12 Ind 12-1-44 SOC 12-12
JG411 4894 EA 9MU 16-10-43 82MU 29-10 *Leer* 13-12 Ind 26-1-44 SOC 24-1-47
JG412 4907 EA 9MU 18-10-43 215MU 6-11 *Leer* 13-12 Ind 26-1-44 SOC 19-7-45
JG413 4906 EA 9MU 13-12-43 215MU 6-11 *Leer* 13-12 Ind 26-1-44 SOC 30-1-47
JG414 4908 EA 6MU 15-10-43 215MU 26-10 *Papan* 13-11 Aus 30-12
JG415 4912 EA 6MU 17-10-43 215MU 5-10 *Tekoa* 1-12 Aus 21-1-44
JG416 4909 EA 6MU 15-10-43 215MU 23-10 *Papan* 13-11 Aus 30-12
JG417 4912 EA 6MU 15-10-43 215MU 22-11 *Papan* 13-11 Aus 30-12
JG418 4916 EA 9MU 18-10-43 47MU 30-11 *Kaim* 22-12 Ind 18-2-44 SOC 27-3-47
JG419 4917 EA 9MU 18-10-43 215MU 29-10 *Fort Phil* 11-12 Aus 16-1-44
JG420 4918 EA 29-1-43 215MU 6-11 *Perth* 14-12 Aus 3-2-44
JG421 4927 EA 6MU 17-10-43 215MU 24-10 *Papan* 13-11 Aus 30-12
JG422 4926 EA 6MU 17-10-43 215MU 24-10 *Papan* 13-11 Aus 30-12
JG423 4928 EA 6MU 18-10-43 215MU 24-10 *Perth* 14-12 Aus 3-2-44
JG424 4929 EA 6MU 17-10-43 215MU 28-10 *Fort Phil* 11-12 Aus 16-1-44
JG425 4930 EA 6MU 19-10-43 215MU 26-10 *Perth* 14-12 Aus 3-2-44
JG426 4939 EA CRD Rotol Airscrews Stav. cropped prop blade exp 20-10-43 29MU 15-5-46 scr 3-9-47
JG427 4940 EA 9MU 23-10-43 222MU 6-11 *Chyel* 3-12 Ind 12-1-44 SOC 30-1-47
JG428 4941 EA 9MU 22-10-43 222MU 11-11 *Leer* 3-12 Ind 26-1-44 FACE 14-5-45
JG429 4942 EA 9MU 24-10-43 215MU 11-11 *Fort Phil* 11-12 Aus 16-1-44
JG430 4946 EA 9MU 24-10-43 215MU 25-11 *Suff* Aus 29-1-44
JG431 4944 EA 9MU 24-10-43 215MU 13-11 *Fort Phil* 11-12 Aus 16-1-44
JG432 4945 EA 6MU 22-10-43 215MU 8-11 *Perth* 14-12 Aus 3-2-44
JG465 4950 EA 6MU 24-10-43 215MU 9-11 *Suff* 1-12 Aus 29-1-44
JG466 4952 EA 6MU 24-10-43 82MU 12-2-44 *Nanb* 22-2 Aus 19-5
JG467 4953 EA 6MU 24-10-43 215MU 11-11 Suss 5-1-44 Aus 29-2
JG468 4954 EA 6MU 24-10-43 215MU 9-11 *Fort Phil* 11-12 Aus 16-1-44
JG469 4955 EA 9MU 24-10-43 222MU 11-11 *Leer* 13-12 Ind 26-1-44 C3 ops 18-5
JG470 4959 EA 9MU 24-10-43 82MU 11-11 *Leer* 13-12 Ind 26-1-44 SOC 20-9-45
JG471 4990 EA 6MU 27-10-43 215MU 9-11 *Suff* 1-12 Aus 29-1-44
JG472 4966 EA 6MU 27-10-43 215MU 8-11 *Fort Phil* 11-12 Aus 16-1-44
JG473 4967 EA 6MU 27-10-43 215MU 8-11 *Fort Phil* 11-12 Aus 16-1-44
JG474 4968 EA 6MU 27-10-43 215MU 8-11 *Fort Phil* 11-12 Aus 16-1-44
JG475 4971 EA 6MU 30-10-43 222MU 13-11 *Fort Geo* 4-12 Casa 22-12 MAAF 21-6-45 SOC 28-2-46
JG476 4975 EA 6MU 30-10-43 222MU 9-11 *Fort Geo* 4-12 Casa 22-12 ME 30-6-45 SOC 31-12-46
JG477 4976 EA 9MU 3-11-43 82MU 17-11 *Leer* 13-12 Ind 26-1-44 SOC 1-6-47
JG478 5083 CHA 9MU 30-11-43 47MU 25-12 *Fort Mich* 10-1-44 Ind 7-3-44 FACE 27-5-45
JG479 5091 KEA 6MU 2-12-43 222MU 23-12 *C o Ad* 16-1-44 Ind 16-3-44 SOC 25-4-46
JG480 5054 EA CRD VAWD 12-12-43 52MU 28-1-44 RACF Test & Dev Unit, Halifax 26-2 Winterisation tests 3-3
JG481 5089 CHA 6MU 1-12-43 82MU 15-12 *Suss* 5-1-44 Aus 29-2
JG482 5059 EA 6MU 25-11-43 215MU 7-12 *Suss* 5-1-44 Aus 29-2
JG483 5101 KEA 6MU 2-12-43 82MU 15-12 *Kiam* 22-12 Ind 18-2-44 SOC 30-1-47
JG484 5093 CHA 6MU 1-12-43 215MU 15-12 *Suss* 5-1-44 Aus 29-2
JG485 5095 CHA 6MU 1-12-43 82MU *Ajax* 26-2-44 Aus 7-4
JG486 4997 EA 9MU 3-11-43 82MU 13-11 *Leer* 18-12 Ind 26-1-44 SOC 5-2-45
JG487 5001 CHA 6MU 6-11-43 47MU 16-11 *Fort Geo* 4-12 Casa 22-12
JG488 5015 EA 9MU 9-11-43 222MU 25-11 *Emp Reg* 27-12 Ind 18-2-44 SOC 31-5-45
JG489 5011 EA 9MU 7-11-43 222MU 25-11 *Emp Reg* 27-12 Ind 18-2-44 FACE 1S RIAF LD coll with MT987 Samuneli
JG490 4977 EA 9MU 5-11-43 82MU 18-11 *Fort Geo* 4-12 Casa 22-12 USAAF 31-1-44
JG491 4987 EA 6MU 3-11-43 222MU 14-11 *Fort Geo* 4-12 Casa 22-12 SOC 30-6-45
JG492 5035 M63 EA 6MU 13-11-43 222MU 24-11 *Fort Geo* 4-12 Casa 22-12 USAAF 29-2-44 241S FTR ops 20-4
JG493 5048 M63 EA 6MU 16-11-43 215MU 26-11 *Fort Geo* 4-12 Casa 22-12 ME 30-11-44 SOC 31-5-45
JG494 5049 M63 EA 6MU 17-11-43 215MU 2-12 *Fan Hd* 24-12 Casa 8-1-44 MAAF 31-1 SOC 31-8
JG495 5068 M63 EA 6MU 24-11-43 222MU 7-12 *Fan Hd* 24-12 Casa 8-1-44 MAAF 31-1 SOC 28-8-45
JG496 5076 EA 9MU 30-11-43 26-12 *Fort Mich* 10-1-44 Ind 7-3 SOC 11-4-46
JG497 5138 EA 9MU 20-12-43 222MU 14-1-44 *Maih* 8-2-44 Ind 20-3 SOC 30-1-47
JG498 5042 EA 9MU 14-11-43 82MU 3-12 *Kaim* 22-12 Ind 18-2-44 SOC 1-11-45
JG499 5043 EA 9MU 15-11-43 222MU 3-12 *Emp Reg* 27-12 Ind 18-2-44 SOC 30-1-47
JG500 5076 CHA 9MU 30-11-43 47MU 26-12 *Fort Mich* 10-1-44 Ind 7-3-44 SOC 31-7-47
JG527 5215 EA 6MU 4-1-44 222MU 13-1 *Maih* 8-2 Ind 20-3 3S RIAF fire on gd dbf Kolar FACE 11-4-46
JG528 5200 EA 9MU 22-12-43 82MU 7-1-44 *Samrain* 11-1 Ind 4-3 FACE 23-3-46
JG529 5201 EA 9MU 22-12-43 82MU 7-1-44 *Maihar* 8-2 Ind 20-3 SOC 12-2-45
JG530 5152 EA 9MU 20-12-43 82MU 7-1-44 *Samrain* 11-1 Ind 4-3 SOC 28-9
JG531 5069 EA 9MU 25-11-43 222MU 13-12 *Kaim* 22-12 Ind 18-2-44 SOC 12-12
JG532 5073 EA 9MU 30-11-43 47MU 24-12 *Fort Mich* 10-1-44 Ind 7-3 FACE 28-9
JG533 5136 EA 6MU 19-12-43 82MU 30-12 *Ajax* 26-2-44 Aus 7-4
JG534 5140 CHA 9MU 20-12-43 82MU 10-1-44 *Maih* 8-2 Ind 20-3 SOC 14-3-46
JG535 5146 EA 9MU 20-12-43 82MU 7-1-44 *Samrain* 11-1 Ind 4-3 FAC3 3-5
JG536 5151 EA 9MU 20-12-43 82MU 7-1-44 *Samrain* 11-1 Ind 4-3 SOC 31-5-45
JG537 5191 EA 9MU 22-12-43 82MU 7-1-44 *Samrain* 11-1 Ind 4-3 SOC 11-4-47
JG538 4988 EA 6MU 3-11-43 82MU 16-11 *Fort Geo* 4-12 Casa 22-12 USAAF 31-1-44 FACE 3-7 CE ops 30-4-45
JG539 4999 EA 9MU 5-11-43 47MU 22-11 *Fort Geo* 4-12 Casa 22-12
JG540 5003 EA 9-11-43 222MU 20-111 *Fort Geo* 4-12 Casa 22-12 241S FTR ops 30-3-44
JG541 5006 EA 6MU 7-11-43 47MU 17-11 *Fort Geo* 4-12 Casa 22-12 USAAF 2 9-2-44 MAAF 21-6-45 SOC 11-4-46
JG542 4979 EA 6MU 30-10-43 222MU 9-11 *Fort Geo* 4-12 Casa 22-12 USAAF 29-2-44 SOC 31-8
JG543 EA 6MU 22-2-43 82MU 4-3 *Lyca* 2-4 Aus 13-6
JG544 5242 EA 9MU 2-1-44 82MU 15-1 *Maih* 8-2 Ind 20-3 SOC 31-10-46
JG545 5022 EA 9MU 9-11-43 222MU 22-11 *Emp Reg* 27-12 Ind 18-2-44 SOC 15-1-45
JG546 5057 CHA 6MU 24-11-43 FACE del flt 1-12
JG547 5100 EA 9MU 30-11-43 47MU 18-12 *Kaim* 22-12 Ind 18-2-44 CE 24-5-45
JG548 5148 KEA 9MU 19-12-43 82MU 9-1-44 *Maih* 8-2 Ind 20-3 SOC 28-5-45
JG549 5211 EA 6MU 24-12-43 82MU 3-1-44 *Ajax* 26-2 Aus 7-4
JG550 9MU 21-1-44 222MU 6-2 *Fort Stik* 22-2 Ind 30-3 SOC 28-5-45
JG551 9MU 21-1-44 82MU 11-2 *Streaf* 26-3 Ind 11-5 CE ops 2-2-45
JG552 9MU 23-1-44 222MU 6-2 *Fort Stik* 22-2 Ind 30-3 SOC 25-4-46
JG553 9MU 9-2-44 222MU 5-3 *Berr* 29-3 Ind 12-5 SOC 11-1-45
JG554 9MU 9-2-44 82MU 26-3 *Streaf* 26-3 Ind 11-5 SOC 28-8-47
JG555 5082 EA 9MU 30-11-43 47MU 18-12 *Kaim* 22-12 Ind 18-2 FAC3 3-5
JG556 5164 CHA 6MU 12-2-44 82MU 23-2-44 *Clan Mac* 11-3 Aus 18-4
JG557 6MU 24-1-44 82MU 8-2 *Narb* 22-2 Aus 19-5
JG558 6MU 5-2-44 82MU 18-2 *Elamaf* 26-2 Aus 19-5
JG559 5012 EA 9MU 7-11-43 82MU 18-12 *Kaim* 22-12 Ind 18-2-44
JG560 5627 EA 9MU 14-11-43 222MU 3-12 *Emp Reg* 27-12 Ind 18-2 SOC 31-12-46
JG561 5050 CHA 9MU 15-11-43 82MU 3-12 *Kaim* 22-12 Ind 18-2-44 SOC 1-2-45
JG562 5046 CHA 9MU 15-11-43 82MU 3-12 *Kaim* 22-12 Ind 18-2-44 SOC 31-10-46
JG563 5025 CHA 9MU 15-11-43 222MU 13-12 *Kaim* 22-12 Ind 18-2 CE 20-9-45
JG564 5111 EA 9MU 22-12-43 82MU 7-1-44 *Maih* 8-2 Ind 20-3 SOC 17-8
JG565 5024 EA 9MU 16-11-43 222MU 14-12 *Kaim* 22-12 Ind 18-2-44 FAC3 30-5-44
JG566 CHA 6MU 19-12-43 47MU 30-12 *Miss Clu* 6-2-44 Aus 18-4
JG567 5053 CHA 6MU 16-11-43 82MU 3-12 *Kaim* 22-12 Ind 18-2-44 SOC 31-5-45
JG568 5128 CHA 6MU 13-12-43 222MU 30-12 *Fort Mich* 10-1-44 Ind 7-3 SOC 7-4-45
JG603 5058 EA 6MU 24-11-43 215MU 4-12 *Fort Phil* Aus 16-1-44
JG604 5084 EA 6MU 1-12-43 215MU 15-12 *Suss* 5-1-44 Aus 29-2
JG605 5116 EA 6MU 2-12-43 82MU 24-12 *Miss Clu* 6-2-44 Aus 18-4
JG606 5086 EA 9MU 30-11-43 47MU 24-12 *Fort Mich* 10-1-44 Ind 7-3 1S RIAF w/u ld Yelahanka dbf FACE burnt 24-4-46
JG607 5090 EA 6MU 1-12-43 215MU 15-12 *Suss* 5-1-44 Aus 29-2
JG608 5104 EA 6MU 4-12-43 222MU 23-12 *C o Ad* 16-1-44 Ind 16-3 CE 5-7-45
JG609 5097 CHA 6MU 2-12-43 82MU 25-12 *Hind* 6-2-44 Aus 18-4
JG610 5125 CHA 6MU 4-12-43 82MU 25-12 *C o Ad* 16-1-44 Ind 16-3 SOC 9-5-46
JG611 5117 EA 6MU 2-12-43 215MU *Suss* 5-1-44 Aus 29-2
JG612 5124 CHA 6MU 4-12-43 222MU 24-12 *C o Ad* 16-1-44 Ind 16-3 CE 4-1-45
JG613 5162 CHA 19-12-43 47MU 30-12 *Hind* 6-2-44 Aus 18-4
JG614 CHA 9MU 20-4-44 215MU 5-5 *C o Ad* 30-5 Ind 4-7 SOC 29-3-45
JG615 5007 M63 EA 6MU 7-11-43 47MU 15-11 *Fort Geo* 10-12 Casa 22-12 CE ops 1-8-44
JG616 5014 M63 EA 6MU 9-11-43 222MU 20-11 *Fort Geo* 10-12 Casa 22-12 MAAF 21-6-45 ME 16-8 SOC 31-12-46
JG617 5026 M63 EA 6MU 13-11-43 222MU 24-11 *Fort Geo* 10-12 Casa 22-12
JG618 5005 EA 9MU 7-11 222MU 30-11 *Emp Reg* 27-12 Ind 18-2-44 InAf 29-12-47
JG619 5028 M63 EA 6MU 13-11-43 215MU 26-11 *Fort Geo* 10-12 Casa 22-12 CE 13-11-44
JG620 5036 EA 9MU 14-11-43 47MU 30-11 *Emp Reg* 27-12 Ind 18-2-44 SOC 16-8-45
JG621 5079 CHA 9MU 30-11-43 47MU 28-12 *Fort Nip* 10-1-44 Ind 7-3 FAC3 30-5
JG622 5067 EA 6MU 24-11-43 215MU 4-12 *Clan Mac* 11-3-44 Aus 18-4
JG623 5099 KEA 9MU 20-12-43 222MU 11-1-44 *Maih* 8-2 Ind 20-3 SOC 25-9-47
JG624 STN 9MU 12-3-43 222MU 30-3 *C o Run* 8-4-44 Ind 18-5 SOC 27-3-47
JG646 KEA 9MU 23-3-44 215MU 3-4 *C o Run* 8-4 Ind 18-5 SOC 31-5-45
JG647 CHA 9MU 2-3-44 222MU 18-3 *Kal* 8-4 Ind 20-5 SOC 31-5
JG648 CHA 9MU 4-3-44 215MU 22-3 *Kal* 8-4 Ind 20-5 CE 23-12
JG649 CHA 9MU 4-3-44 215MU 22-3 *Kal* 8-4 Ind 20-5 CE ops 6-3-45
JG650 KEA 6MU 18-3-44 82MU 29-3 *Diamed* 19-4 Aus 27-6
JG651 CHA 9MU 6-3-44 82MU 22-3 *Kal* 3-4 Ind 20-5 CE 9-8-45
JG652 CHA 6MU 7-3-44 82MU 17-3 *Lyca* 2-4 Aus 13-6
JG653 KEA 6MU 3-3-44 82MU 15-3 *Lyca* 2-4 Aus 13-6
JG654 HPA 6MU 6-11-44 222MU 18-12 *Makhive* 22-1-45 Ind 19-2 SOC 28-2-46
JG655 CHA 6MU 11-3-44 82MU 20-3 *Lyca* 2-4 Aus 13-6
JG656 CHA 9MU 11-3-44 82MU 22-3 *Kalr* 8-4 Ind 20-5 InAF 29-12-47
JG657 KEA 9MU 20-3-44 82MU 13-9 *Mart* 30-10 Ind 8-12 SOC 9-5-46
JG658 CHA 9MU 12-3-44 215MU 26-3 *Kalr* 8-4 Ind 20-5 CE 9-8-45
JG659 CHA 12-3-44 82MU 20-3 *Lyca* 2-4 Aus 13-6
JG660 CHA 9MU 17-3-44 222MU 30-3 *C o Haid* 18-5 Ind 18-5 SOC 30-4-47
JG661 CHA sting hook (strengthened), retractable tailwheel instal. RNAS Crail 13-4-44. Deck land trls began 778S Arb with JG662 and 663 27-4. 9MU 11-8 to 5832M 26-2-46
JG662 CHA as per 661. 9MU 17-8 to 5833M 26-2-46
JG663 CHA as per 661. to 5834M 26-2-46
JG664 CHA 6MU 12-3-44 82MU 22-3 *Mit Park* 6-4 Aus 19-6
JG665 CHA 6MU 12-3-44 82MU 21-3 *Mit Park* 6-4 Aus 19-6
JG666 CHA 6MU 17-3-44 82MU 29-3 *Diamed* 19-4 Aus 27-6
JG667 CHA 9MU 14-3-44 222MU 28-3 *Kal* 8-4 Ind 20-5 SOC 2-2-45
JG668 CHA 6MU 18-3-44 82MU 27-3 *Mit Park* 6-4 Aus 19-6
JG669 CHA 9MU 20-3-44 215MU 10-4 *Fort Chur* 15-5 Ind 4-7 CE 4-10-45

JG670 CHA 9MU 20-3-44 222MU 31-3 *C o Shan* 9-4 Ind 18-5 SOC 25-4-46

JG671 CHA 9MU 21-3-44 215MU 31-3 *Fort Chur* 17-5 Ind 4-7 SOC 28-5-45

JG672 KEA 9MU 6-4-44 222MU 21-4 *Fort Chur* 17-5 Ind 4-7 SOC 14-2-46

JG673 CHA 9MU 23-3-44 82MU 3-4 *C o Shan* 9-4 Ind 18-5 SOC 30-9

JG674 CHA 9MU 23-3-44 82MU 7-4 *C o Shan* 9-4 Ind 18-5 CE 26-7-45

JG675 CHA 9MU 23-3-44 82MU 7-4 *C o Shan* 9-4 Ind 18-5 SOC 11-4-46

JG676 CHA 18-3-44 222MU 28-3 *C o Shan* 9-4 Ind 18-5 SOC 28-5-45

JG677 STN 9MU 20-3-44 82MU 14-4 *Fort Chur* 17-5 Ind 4-7 SOC 11-4

JG678 KEA 9MU 24-3-44 82MU 7-4 *C o Lin* 5-5 Ind 9-6 35 RIAF eng seized in flight 27-4-46 SOC 30-5

JG679 CHA 9MU 23-3-44 215MU 3-4 *C o Shan* 9-4 Ind 18-5 SOC 9-5-46

JG680 CHA 9MU 26-3-44 82MU 6-4 *C o Shan* 9-4 Ind 18-5 SOC 27-3-47

JG681 CHA 9MU 26-3-44 82MU 6-4 *C o Lin* 5-5 Ind 9-6 SOC 26-9-46

JG682 CHA 9MU 28-3-44 215MU 10-4 *Fort Chur* 17-5 Ind 4-7 SOC 27-6-46

JG683 CHA 9MU 28-3-44 215MU 10-4 *Fort Chur* 17-5 Ind 4-7 SOC 31-5-45

JG684 CHA 6MU 30-3-44 215MU 8-4 *Sap Park* Aus 10-7

JG685 CHA 6MU 28-3-44 82MU 13-4 *Sap Park* Aus 10-7

JG686 CHA 9MU 28-3-44 82MU 6-4 *C o Shan* 9-4 Ind 18-5 InAF 29-12-47

JG687 KEA 6MU 4-4-44 82MU 13-4 *Sap Park* 21-4 Aus 10-7

JG688 KEA 9MU 5-4-44 215MU 18-4 *Fort Chur* 17-5 Ind 4-7 SOC 26-8-47

JG689 KEA 6MU 4-4-44 82MU 14-4 *Diamed* 19-4 Aus 27-6

JG690 CHA 6MU 6-4-44 82MU 20-4 *Tee Park* 10-5 Aus 27-6

JG691 CHA 6MU 6-4-44 82MU 20-4 *Port M Q* 28-4 Aus 21-5

JG692 CHA 9MU 4-4-44 215MU 18-4 *Fort Chur* 17-5 Ind 4-7 CE 2-8-45

JG693 CHA 9MU 5-4-44 215MU 18-4 *Fort Chur* 17-5 Ind 4-7 SOC 19-7-45

JG694 CHA 9MU 5-4-44 215MU 18-4 *Fort Chur* 17-5 Ind 4-7 SOC 2-2-45

JG695 CHA 9MU 5-4-44 215MU 17-4 *Fort Chur* 17-5 Ind 4-7 SOC 26-4-45

LV series all F Mk VIII Merlin 66.

LV643 5123 STN 6MU 4-11-43 222MU *Karm* 22-12 Ind 18-2 SOC 31-12-46

LV644 5161 CHA 6MU 19-12-43 47MU *Hind* 6-2-44 Aus 29-4

LV645 5167 KEA 9MU 20-12-43 222MU 10-1-44 *Masir* 8-2 Ind 20-3 SOC 25-10-45

LV646 5166 KEA 9MU 20-12-43 82MU 7-1-44 *C o Ad* 16-1 Ind 16-3 SOC 11-1-45

LV647 5163 CHA 6MU 19-12-43 82MU 24-12 *Ajax* 26-2 Aus 7-4

LV648 5169 KEA 9MU 20-12-43 222MU 10-1-44 *Masir* 8-2 Ind 20-3 SOC 27-3-47

LV649 5171 CHA 6MU 9-12-43 82MU 1-1-44 *Ajax* 26-2 Aus 7-4

LV650 5137 STN 9MU 22-12-43 82MU 7-1-44 *Masir* 9-2 Ind 20-3 SOC 9-5-46

LV651 5173 CHA 6MU 19-12-43 222MU 30-12 *Fort Nip* 10-1-44 Ind 11-3 SOC 28-2-46

LV652 5156 STN 6MU 19-12-43 82MU 1-1-44 *Ajax* 26-2 Aus 15-4

LV653 5157 STN 6MU 13-12-43 52MU 24-12 *Fort Nip* 10-1-44 Ind 7-3 SOC 20-11-45

LV654 5197 CHA 9MU 27-1-43 222MU 11-1-44 *Masir* 8-2 Ind 20-3

LV655 5186 KEA 9MU 20-12-43 82MU 7-1-44 *Masir* 8-2 Ind 20-3 FACE 15-7 SOC 7-2-45

LV656 5178 STN 9MU 22-12-43 82MU 7-1-44 *Masir* 8-2 Ind 20-3 SOC 11-7-46

LV657 5172 CHA 6MU 19-12-43 47MU 31-12 *Hind* 6-2-44 Aus 29-4

LV658 5196 CHA 9MU 31-12-43 222MU 14-1-44 *Masir* 8-2 Ind 20-3 SOC 31-7-47

LV659 5221 CHA 6MU 30-12-43 82MU 24-1-44 *Fort Stik* 22-2 Ind 30-3 to USSR SOC 14-2-46

LV660 5206 STN 9MU 22-12-43 82MU 7-1-44 *Masir* 8-2 Ind 20-3 SOC 11-10

LV661 5234 CHA 9MU 1-1-44 82MU 15-1 *Masir* 8-2 Ind 20-3 FA SOC 7-1-45

LV662 KEA 9MU 21-4-44 215MU 5-5 *C o Ag* 30-5 Ind 4-7 SOC 9-8-45

LV663 STN 9MU 18-4-44 215MU 28-4 *C o Ag* 30-5 Ind 4-7 SOC 5-2-45

LV664 KEA 9MU 24-4-44 215MU 5-5 *C o Ag* 30-5 Ind 4-7 SOC 30-4-45

LV665 5180 CHA 9MU 20-12-43 222MU 11-1-44 *Masir* 8-2 Ind 25-3 155S FA FTR 3-9

LV666 5189 CHA 9MU 21-12-43 222MU 10-1-44 *Masir* 8-2 Ind 25-3 SOC 27-3-47

LV667 5187 CHA 9MU 22-12-43 222MU 10-1-44 *Masir* 8-2 Ind 25-3 SOC 25-7-46

LV668 5193 CHA 9MU 22-12-43 82MU 10-1-44 *Masir* 8-2 Ind 25-3 SOC 27-6-46

LV669 5198 CHA 9MU 31-12-43 52MU 24-1-44 *Fort Stik* 22-2 Ind 30-3 SOC 19-7-45

LV670 5207 CHA 9MU 22-12-43 222MU 15-1-44 *Masir* 8-2 Ind 30-3 SOC 31-12-47

LV671 5220 CHA 6MU 27-12-43 222MU 7-1-44 *Samlair* 11-1 Ind 4-3 CE ops 10-1-45 SOC 5-2

LV672 5227 CHA 6MU 26-12-43 82MU 12-6-44 *Lanark* 17-6 Aus 27-7

LV673 5213 CHA 6MU 24-12-43 FAAC 10-1-44 ROS 82MU 2-7 *Turkes* 28-7 India 5-9 CE 24-5-45

LV674 5175 EA FF 11-43 CRD WD 30-12 FAAC 19-4-44 BDn 5-5 intns fly trls fitt Pacitor Fuel gauge. FAAC 2-8-45 VAO 6MU 7-5-46 SOC scr 16-11-47

LV675 5181 STN 9MU 24-12-43 222MU 11-1-44 *Masir* 8-2 Ind 20-3 SOC 26-9-46

LV676 5222 CHA 6MU 20-12-43 222MU 7-1-44 *Samlair* 11-1 Ind 4-3 FACE 26-8 SOC 7-2-45

LV677 5229 KEA 6MU 6-1-44 82MU 24-1 *Fort Stik* 22-2 Ind 30-3 USSR SOC 29-8-46

LV678 5244 CHA 9MU 1-1-44 222MU 15-1 *Masir* 8-2 Ind 20-3 SOC 28-9

LV679 CHA 6MU 10-1-44 222MU 24-1 *Fort Stik* 22-2 Ind 30-3 FACE 11-8

LV680 CHA 6MU 8-1-44 222MU 24-1 *Fort Stik* 22-2 Ind 30-3 SOC 5-2-45

LV681 CHA 9MU 4-1-44 82MU 15-1 *Masir* 8-2 Ind 20-3 SOC 29-11-45

LV726 CHA 9MU 4-2-44 222MU 20-2 *Streef* 26-3 Ind 11-5 SOC 28-8-47

LV727 STN 6MU 21-1-44 82MU 31-1 *Hind* 6-2 Aus 18-4

LV728 KEA 9MU 24-4-44 82MU 11-5 *C o Ag* 30-5 Ind 4-7 SOC 31-5-45

LV729 LFVIII KEA 9MU 28-4-44 215MU 16-5 *Argyll* 1-6 Casa 13-6 FTR ops 8-4-45

LV730 KEA 9MU 28-4-44 215MU 16-5 *Argyll* 1-6 Casa 13-6 MAAF 21-6-45 SOC 14-3-46

LV731 KEA 9MU 1-5-44 82MU 24-5 *Argyll* 1-6 Casa 13-6 CE ops 3-10 bboc ME 5-7-45 SOC 13-9

LV732 5228 CHA 6MU 28-12-43 47MU 13-1-44 *Masir* 8-2 Ind 20-3 IS RIAF swung on t/o cd Samuneli 11-4-46 SOC 9-5

LV733 5217 KEA 6MU 30-12-43 222MU 7-1-44 *C o Ad* 16-1 Ind 16-2 SOC 6-3-45

LV734 KEA 6MU 4-1-44 222MU 13-1 *Masir* 8-2 Ind 20-3 FTR 5-7-45

LV735 5237 KEA 9MU 7-1-44 222MU 28-1 *Fort Stik* 22-2 Ind 30-3 SOC 30-3-47

LV736 CHA 9MU 22-2-44 82MU 12-3 *Berr* 29-3 Ind 12-5 SOC 11-4-46

LV737 5233 CHA 9MU 1-1-44 52MU 24-1 *Fort Stik* 22-2 Ind 30-3 e/fld cd dbf 11-4-46

LV738 5243 CHA 9MU 2-1-44 52MU 23-1 *Fort Stik* 22-2 Ind 30-3 85S FACE 17-10 SOC 15-11-45

LV739 KEA 9MU 7-1-44 222MU 20-1 *Masir* 8-2 Ind 20-3 CE ops 25-2-45 SOC 1-3

LV740 5213 STN 6MU 27-12-43 82MU 5-1-44 *Ajax* 26-2 Aus 7-4

LV741 5214 STN 6MU 27-12-43 47MU 13-1-44 *Masirah* 8-2 Ind 20-3 SOC 28-8

LV742 CHA 9MU 4-1-44 52MU 24-1 *Fort Stik* 22-2 Ind 30-3 SOC 23-9

LV743 KEA 9MU 7-1-44 82MU 24-1 *Fort Stik* 22-2 Ind 30-3 USSR SOC 30-5-46

LV744 CHA 6MU 10-1-44 82MU 25-1 *Fort Stik* 22-2 Ind 30-3 USSR SOC 27-3-47

LV745 CHA 9MU 30-1-44 222MU 17-2 *Streef* 26-3 Ind 11-5 SOC 5-7-45

LV746 CHA 6MU 14-1-44 222MU 30-1 *Fort Stik* 22-2 Ind 30-3 SOC 28-8-47

LV747 CHA 9MU 20-1-44 222MU 3-2 *Fort Stik* 22-2 Ind 30-3 SOC 28-9

LV748 STN 9MU 23-1-44 222MU 28-2 *Malika* 13-3 Ind 26-4 FTR ops 11-2-45

LV749 STN 6MU 29-1-44 215MU 11-2 *Streef* 26-3 Ind 11-5 SOC 26-1-45

LV750 STN 6MU 4-2-44 82MU 18-2 *Elen Af* 26-2 Aus 9-5

LV751 KEA 9MU 1-5-44 82MU 11-5 *Argyll* 1-6 Casa 13-6 327S 12-5-45

LV752 KEA 9MU 8-5-44 76MU 17-5 *Argyll* 1-6 Casa 13-6 CE ops 30-4-45 SOC 14-6

LV753 KEA 9MU 4-6-44 82MU 15-6 *Turkes* 28-7 Ind 5-9 SOC 18-10-45

LV754 KEA 9MU 10-5-44 52MU 26-5 *Argyll* 1-6 Casa 13-6 CE ops 417S 12-9

LV755 CHA 9MU 7-1-44 222MU 20-1 *Masir* 8-2 Ind 20-3 FACE 1-6

LV756 KEA 9MU 21-1-44 22MU 4-2 *Fort Stik* 22-2 Ind 30-3 SOC 31-5-45

MB & MD series all LF MkVIII Merlin 66

MB959 KEA 6MU 18-3-44 82MU 29-3 *Diomeds* 19-4 Aus 27-6

MB960 STN 6MU 28-1-44 82MU 11-2 *Elan Af* 26-2 Aus 9-5

MB961 KEA 9MU 20-3-44 52MU 3-4 *Hind* 9-4 Ind 18-5 SOC 27-3-47

MB962 KEA 9MU 23-3-44 82MU 6-4 *C o Shir* 9-4 Ind 18-5 disappeared over sea 31-10-46

MB963 KEA 9MU 20-3-44 82MU 6-4 *C o Lin* 5-5 Ind 9-6 SOC 26-12

MB964 KEA 9MU 21-3-44 52MU 3-4 *C o Shir* 9-4 Ind 12-5 SOC 15-10

MB965 KEA 9MU 21-3-44 52MU 3-4 *C o Shir* 9-4 Ind 18-5 SOC 16-1-47

MB966 KEA 9MU 24-3-44 82MU 6-4 *C o Shir* 9-4 Ind 18-5 SOC 27-3-47

MB967 KEA 9MU 5-4-44 215MU 18-4 *Fort Chur* 19-5 Ind 4-7 SOC 13-9-45

MB968 KEA 6MU 31-3-44 82MU 9-4 *Sap Park* 21-4 Aus 10-7

MB969 KEA 9MU 6-4-44 215MU 24-4 *Fort Chur* 17-5 Ind 4-7 SOC 11-7-46

MB970 KEA 6MU 6-4-44 82MU 20-4 *Fort MLar* 21-5 Aus 7-7

MB971 KEA 9MU 6-4-44 222MU 21-4 *Fort Chur* 17-5 Ind 4-7 FACE 25 RIAF c/ld Miranshah 13-6-46 casualty wastage return 27-6 SOC s11-7

MB972 KEA 6MU 9-4-44 82MU 22-4 *Fort MLar* 26-5 Aus 7-7

MB973 9MU 15-5-44 76MU 21-5 *Argyll* 1-6 Casa 13-6 MAAF 21-6-45 SOC 27-3-47

MB974 KEA 6MU 9-4-44 82MU 20-4 *Fort MLar* 21-5 Aus 7-7

MB975 KEA 9MU 21-4-44 222MU 3-5 *C o Ag* 30-5 Ind 4-7 SOC 31-5-45

MB976 KEA 9MU 21-4-44 22MU 3-5 *C o H K* 28-6 Ind 4-8 SOC 9-5-46

MD series, originally planned as F MkVII production

MD214 CHA 9MU 8-1-44 82MU 24-1 *Fort Stik* 22-2 Ind 30-3 SOC 9-8-45

MD215 KEA 9MU 2-1-44 82MU 24-1 *Fort Stik* 22-2 Ind 30-3 SOC 9-5-46

MD216 CHA 9MU 10-1-44 82MU 24-1 *Fort Stik* 22-2 Ind 30-3 SOC 25-7-46

MD217 5218 EA 6MU 27-12-43 82MU 3-1-44 *Ajax* 26-2 Aus 7-4

MD218 CHA 9MU 21-1-44 222MU 3-2 *Fort Stik* 22-2 Ind 30-3 SOC 31-10-46

MD219 STN 9MU 10-1-44 52MU 24-1 *Fort Stik* 22-2 Ind 30-3 25 RIAF cd f/ld Mirali FACE 17-5-46 CWR 23-5 SOC 13-6

MD220 CHA 6MU 20-1-44 222MU 3-2 *Fort Stik* 22-2n Ind 30-3 SOC 31-10-46

MD221 5060 EA 6MU 24-11-43 215MU 7-12 *Fort Phil* 11-12 Aus 16-1-44

MD222 5119 KEA 6MU 2-12-43 222MU 23-12 *C o Ad* 16-1-44 Ind 16-3 10S RIAF cd f/ld Panganj FACE 2-8-46 SOC 27-2-47

MD223 5065 EA 6MU 24-11-43 215MU 7-12 *Suss* 5-1-44 Aus 29-2

MD224 5122 CHA 6MU 4-12-43 222MU 23-12 *C o Ad* 16-1-44 Ind 16-3 SOC 30-7-45

MD225 5120 KEA 6MU 2-12-43 82MU 15-12 *Kiam* 22-12 Ind 18-2 SOC 26-6-47

MD226 5105 CHA 6MU 2-1-2-43 215MU 15-12 *Suss* 5-1-44 Aus 29-2

MD227 5107 EA 6MU 4-12-43 82MU 15-12 *Kiam* 22-10 Ind 18-2-44 FACE 9-2-45 SOC 13-3-45

MD228 5118 CHA 1-12-43 82MU 25-12 *Hind* 6-2-44 Aus 18-4

MD229 5132 KEA 6MU 5-12-43 222MU 23-12 *C o Ad* 16-1-44 Ind 16-3 SOC 9-10

MD230 5141 KEA 6MU 13-12-43 222MU 30-10 *Fort Nip* 1-1-44 Ind 7-3 SOC 26-4-45

MD231 5098 EA 6MU 2-12-43 215MU 15-12 *Hind* 6-2-44 Aus 18-4

MD232 5087 EA 6MU 2-12-43 215MU 15-12 *Suss* 5-1-44 Aus 29-2

MD233 5133 CHA 6MU 13-12-43 82MU 25-12 *C o Ad* 16-1-44 ind 16-3 SOC 16-2-45

MD234 5131 CHA 6MU 19-12-43 82MU 1-1-44 *Ajax* 25-2 Aus 7-4

MD235 5142 KEA 6MU 13-12-43 82MU 25-12 *C o Ad* 16-1 Ind 16-3 CE ops 2708 SOC 12-2-45

MD236 5148 KEA 6MU 13-12-43 82MU 25-12 *C o Ad* 16-1 Ind 16-3 SOC 30-1-47

MD237 5139 CHA 9MU 20-12-43 82MU 7-1-44 *Samlair* 11-1 Ind 4-3 FACE 25-6 SOC 7-2-45

MD238 5108 EA 6MU 1-12-43 215MU 15-12 *Suss* 5-1 Aus 29-2

MD239 5144 CHA 6MU 19-12-43 82MU 5-3-44 *Malika* 13-3 Ind 26-4 SOC 28-9 bboc 15-2-45 SOC 28-8-47

MD240 5145 CHA 13-12-43 222MU 30-12 *Fort Nip* 10-1-44 Ind 7-3 SOC 31-10-46

MD241 5115 EA 6MU 2-12-43 215MU 15-12 *Suss* 5-1-44 Aus 29-2

MD242 5147 EA 20-12-43 82MU 7-1-44 *Samlair* 11-1 Ind 4-3 CE ops 10-11 SOC 20-11

MD243 5154 CHA 6MU 13-12-43 222MU 30-12 *Fort Nip* 10-1-44 Ind 7-3 SOC 1-6-47

MD244 5143 CHA 6MU 13-12-43 222MU 30-12 *Fort Nip* 10-1-44 Ind 7-3 SOC 31-1-47

MD246 5241 EA 9MU 1-1-44 222MU 15-1 *Masir* 8-2 Ind 20-3 FTR 8-11

MD247 STN 9MU 2-1-44 82MU 15-1 *Masir* 8-2 India 20-3 CE ops 25-2-45 SOC 4-4

MD248 CHA 6MU 20-1-44 52MU 25-1 *Fort Stik* 22-2 Ind 30-3

MD249 STN 9MU 6-1-44 222MU 28-1 *Fort Stik* 22-2 Ind 30-3 FTR ops 14-12

MD250 STN 6MU 23-1-44 82MU 8-2 *Horor* 7-2 Aus 13-3

MD251 STN 6MU 28-1-44 82MU 7-2 *Narb* 22-1 Aus 19-5

MD252 STN 6MU 4-2-44 82MU 18-2 *Elenaf* 25-2-Aus 9-5

MD253 STN 6MU 23-1-44 82MU 3-2 *Hind* 6-2 Aus 18-4

MD254 STN 9MU 8-2-44 222MU 29-2 *Malika* 13-3 Ind 26-4 SOC 14-2-46

MD255 STN 6MU 29-1-44 82MU 7-2 *Fort Stik* 22-2 Ind 30-3 SOC 30-1-47
MD256 CHA 6MU 19-2-44 82MU 5-3 *Malika* 13-3 Ind 26-4 SOC 29-3-46
MD269 CHA 6MU 21-2-44 82MU 5-3 *Malika* 13-3 Ind 26-4 3S RIAF strk Bird f/ld nr Kohar FACE 17-9-46 SOC 31-10
MD270 KEA 6MU 19-2-44 215MU 9-3 *Bear* 29-3 Ind 12-5 SOC 9-8-45
MD271 CHA 6MU 19-2-44 82MU 1-3 *Malika* 13-3 Ind 26-4 SOC 28-3-46
MD272 STN 9MU 7-1-44 82MU 26-1 *Fort Stik* 22-2 Ind 30-3 Bas CE 14-7-45 SOC 26-7
MD273 CHA 6MU 20-1-44 222MU 31-1 *Fort Stik* 22-2 Ind 30-3 FACE 11-8
MD274 KEA 9MU 23-1-44 82MU 14-2 *Streef* 26-3 Ind 11-5 SOC 27-3-47
MD275 CHA 6MU 20-1-44 222MU 30-1 *Fort Stik* 22-2 Ind 30-3 SOC 10-1-46
MD276 KEA 9MU 21-1-44 222MU 6-2 *Fort Stik* 22-2 Ind 30-3 FACE 11-8 SOC 7-2-45
MD277 CHA 9MU 20-1-44 222MU 3-2 *Fort Stik* 22-2 Ind 30-3 SOC 27-3-47
MD278 CHA 9MU 28-1-44 82MU 12-2 *Streef* 26-3 Ind 11-5 SOC 25-7-46
MD279 CHA 9MU 28-1-44 222MU 15-2 *Streef* 26-3 Ind 11-5 SOC 9-5-46
MD280 KEA 9MU 23-1-44 82MU 9-2 *Fort Stik* 22-2 Ind 30-3 SOC 28-9
MD281 STN 6MU 21-1-44 82MU 3-2 *Horor* 7-2 Aus 13-3
MD282 KEA 9MU 8-2-44 82MU 2-3 *Bear* 29-3 Ind 12-5 SOC 11-4-46
MD283 STN 6MU 21-1-44 82MU 3-2 *Horor* 7-2 Aus 13-3
MD284 STN 9MU 21-1-44 222MU 3-2 *Fort Stik* 22-2 ind 30-3 SOC 9-5-46
MD285 STN 9MU 5-2-44 82MU 7-3 *Bear* 29-3 Ind 12-5 CE 24-2-45 bboc 21-6-46 SOC 25-7-46
MD286 CHA 6MU 5-2-44 82MU 21-2 *Clan MacL* 11-3 Aus 18-4
MD287 CHA 9MU 2-3-44 215MU 22-2 *Shahz* 8-4 Ind 20-5 SOC 27-3-47
MD288 STN 9MU 14-2-44 215MU 22-3 *Shahz* 8-4 Ind 20-5 SOC 30-5
MD289 STN 9MU 8-2-44 82MU 25-2 *Streef* 26-3 Ind 11-5 SOC 1-6-47
MD290 STN 6MU 10-2-44 52MU 23-2 *Malika* 13-3 Ind 26-4 SOC 12-2-45
MD291 KEA 6MU 20-2-44 82MU 1-3 *Streef* 26-3 Ind 11-5 11-5 SOC 31-1-46
MD292 CHA 6MU 20-2-44 82MU 1-3 *Malika* 13-3 Ind 26-4 FACE 12-8
MD293 KEA 6MU 20-2-44 82MU 3-3 *Bear* 29-3 Ind 12-5 FACE 11-8 bboc 7-11 SOC 6-9-45
MD294 CHA 9MU 21-2-44 222MU 3-3 *Bear* 29-3 Ind 14-5 SOC 29-3-45
MD295 STN 9MU 23-1-44 52MU 9-2 *Streef* 26-3 Ind 11-5 SOC 11-4-46
MD296 KEA 6MU 23-1-44 82MU 3-2 *Narb* 22-2 Aus 19-5
MD297 CHA 6MU 28-1-44 82MU 7-2 *Narb* 22-2 Aus 19-5
MD298 CHA 30-1-44 82MU 9-2 *Narb* 22-2 Aus 19-5
MD299 CHA 6MU 28-1-44 82MU 7-2 *Narb* 22-2 Aus 19-5
MD300 KEA 6MU 23-1-44 82MU 3-2 *Horor* 7-2 Aus 13-3
MD301 CHA 6MU 11-3-44 82MU 27-3 *Shahz* 8-4 Ind 3-6 SOC 26-7-45
MD302 CHA 9MU 28-1-44 82MU 14-2 *Streef* 26-3 Ind 11-5 CE ops 15-4-45
MD303 CHA 9MU 28-1-44 222MU 15-2 *Streef* 26-3 Ind 11-5 SOC 27-3-47
MD315 6MU 28-1-44 82MU 7-2 *Narb* 22-2 Aus 19-5
MD316 STN 6MU 29-1-44 82MU 8-2 *Streef* 26-3 Ind 11-5 FACE 6-9-46 SOC 31-10-46
MD317 STN 6MU 25-1-44 82MU 3-2 *Horor* 7-2 Aus 13-3
MD318 STN 6MU 29-1-44 82MU 7-2 *Streef* 26-3 Ind 11-5 SOC 31-10-46
MD319 STN 9MU 18-2-44 82MU 16-3 *Bear* 19-3 Ind 12-5 SOC 13-12
MD320 STN 6MU 9-2-44 52MU 24-2 *Malika* 13-3 Ins 26-4 FTR ops 4-10
MD321 STN 9MU 1-3-44 82MU 16-3 *Bear* 29-3 Ind 12-5 FACE 17-5-45 SOC 12-6
MD322 STN 6MU 11-3-44 47MU 17-3 *Bear* 29-3 Ind 12-5 SOC 28-5-45
MD323 STN 9MU 2-3-44 215MU 26-3 *Shahz* 8-4 Ind 20-5 SOC 31-12-46
MD324 STN 6MU 18-2-44 82MU 1-3 *Malika* 13-3 Ind 26-4 SOC 9-12
MD325 CHA 9MU 21-2-44 215MU 22-3 *Shahz* 8-4 Ind 20-5 SOC 13-6-46
MD326 6MU 20-2-44 CB 20-2 recat E VA Kee 3-3 215MU 19-8 *H Prince* 15-10 SOC 4-10-45
MD327 CHA 9MU 25-2-44 222MU 18-3 *Shahz* 8-4 Ind 20-5 SOC 2-4-45
MD328 STN 6MU 20-2-44 82MU 5-3 *Malika* 13-3 Ind 26-4 85 RIAF cd f/ld Ghanda 19-5-46 SOC 13-6
MD329 CHA 6-3-44 82MU 15-3 *Bear* 29-3 Ind 12-5 1S RIAF cd f/ld 10-7-46 SOC 31-10
MD330 CHA 9MU 11-3-44 VAOx 11-3 222MU 24-3 *C o Lin* 5-5 Ind 9-6 SOC 29-3-45
MD331 KEA 9MU 8-2-44 82MU 25-2 *Streef* 26-3 Ind 1-5 SOC 12-7-45
MD332 CHA 9MU 30-1-44 215MU 22-3 *Shahz* 8-4 Ind 20-5 SOC 12-2-45
MD333 CHA 9MU 5-2-44 82MU 7-3 *Bear* 29-3 Ind 12-5 10S RIAF u/c coll ld Hmawbi Burma 31-1-46 SOC 30-5
MD334 CHA 9MU 30-1-44 222MU 15-*Streef* 26-3 Ind 11-5 SOC 30-5-46
MD335 CHA 9MU 4-2-44 222MU 17-2 *Streef* 26-3 Ind 11-5 SOC 31-5-45
MD336 CHA 9MU 4-1-44 82MU 24-2 *Streef* 26-3 Ind 11-5 SOC 18-12
MD337 KEA 6MU 30-1-44 82MU 9-2 *Narb* 22-2 Aus 19-5
MD338 KEA 6MU 30-1-44 82MU 11-2 *Elenaf* 26-2 Aus 9-5
MD339 CHA 6MU 3-2-44 82MU 23-2 *Clan MacL* 11-3 Aus 18-4
MD340 CHA 9MU 8-2-44 82MU 1-7 *Turk* 28-7 Ind 5-9 FACE 155S w/u ld Medan Sumatra 17-8-46 SOC 20-8
MD341 KEA 6MU 5-2-44 FAAC 20-2 82MU 24-2 *Clan MacL* 11-3 Aus 18-4
MD342 9MU 8-2-44 ROS 14-2 82MU 24-2 *Bear* 29-3 Ind 12-5 SOC 12-9-46
MD343 STN 6MU 11-3-44 47MU 17-3 *Shahz* 8-4 Ind 20-5 SOC 29-1-45
MD344 STN 6MU 24-4-44 82MU 4-3 *Lyca* 2-4 Aus 13-6
MD345 STN 6MU 19-2-44 47MU 4-3 *Bear* 29-3 Ind 12-5 InAF 20-12-47
MD346 STN 9MU 12-3-44 82MU 22-3 *Shahz* 8-4 Ind 20-5 FACE 20-10 SOC 15-11
MD347 STN CRD BDn 2-3-44 VA 19-3 BDn 9-4 222MU 2-11 *Ingl* 1-1-45 Ind 4-2 SOC 27-6-46
MD348 CHA 9MU 14-3-44 215MU 3-4 Ind 18-5 FACE 15-7 SOC 7-2-45
MD349 KEA 9MU 8-5-44 47MU 21-5 *Argyll* 1-6 Casa 13-6 MAAF 21-6-45 SOC 31-12-46
MD350 KEA 9MU 11-5-44 82MU 31-5 *China P* 9-6 Ind 10-7 SOC 26-9-45
MD351 no record
MD352 KEA 9MU 14-5-44 215MU 26-5 *Argyll* 1-6 Casa 13-6 CE ops 7-11 bboc 30-8-45 deleted census agreement 23-3-46
MD353 KEA 9MU 14-5-44 215MU 31-5 *Fort Cham* 10-6 Ind 18-7 SOC 31-7-47
MD354 CHA 9MU 8-2-44 222MU 28-2 *Malika* 13-3 Ind 26-4 SOC 29-3-45
MD355 KEA 6MU 5-2-44 ROS 24-2 82MU 7-3 *Lyca* 2-4 Aus 13-6
MD356 CHA 9MU 8-2-44 222MU 29-2 *Malika* 13-3 Ind 26-4 SOC 14-1-45
MD369 CHA 9MU 5-2-44 82MU 24-2 *Streef* 26-4 Ind 11-5 SOC 31-10-46
MD370 STN 9MU 5-2-44 82MU 21-2 *Streef* 26-3 Ind 11-5 SOC 30-1-47
MD371 STN 9MU 5-2-44 222MU 21-2 *Streef* 26-3 Ind 11-5 SOC 28-8-47
MD372 KEA 6MU 8-2-44 82MU 18-2 *Elenaf* 26-2 Aus 9-5
MD373 CHA 9MU 8-2-44 47MU 26-2 *Malika* 13-3 Ind 26-4 CE ops 12-8
MD374 KEE 6MU 6-2-44 82MU 23-2 *Streef* 26-3 Ind 11-5 SOC 26-7-45
MD375 CHA 8-2-44 82MU 21-2 *Streef* 26-3 Ind 11-5 SOC 28-3-46
MD376 KEA 6-2-44 82MU 18-2 *Elenaf* 26-2 Aus 9-5
MD377 CHA 9MU 12-2-44 222MU 29-2 *Malika* 13-3 Ind 26-4 SOC 29-11-45
MD378 STN 9MU 8-2-44 82MU 23-2 *Streef* 26-3 Ind 11-5 FACE 11-3 SOC 7-2-45
MD379 CHA 9MU 11-3-44 82MU 22-3 *C o Shir* 9-4 Ind 18-5 SOC 27-3-47
MD380 STN 6MU 14-3-44 82MU 24-3 *Kit Park* 6-4 Aus 19-6
MD381 STN 6MU 14-3-44 82MU 21-3 *Kit Park* 6-4 Aus 19-6
MD382 STN 9MU 17-3-44 222MU 28-3 *C o Shir* 9-4 Ind 18-5 SOC 25-4-46
MD383 CHA 9MU 20-3-44 222MU 30-3 *C o Shir* 9-4 Ind 18-5 SOC 19-7-45
MD384 CHA 9MU 11-3-44 222MU 28-3 *Shahz* 8-4 Ind 20-5 FACE 10-1-47 SOC 30-1
MD385 KEA 6MU 5-3-44 82MU 15-3 *Lyca* 2-4 Aus 13-6
MD386 CHA 9MU 9-3-44 222MU 16-3 *Berr* 29-3 Ind 12-5 SOC 29-11-45
MD387 CHA 6MU 4-3-44 82MU 15-3 *Berr* 29-3 Ind 12-5 68 RIAF w/u ld Ranchi 18-9-46 SOC 24-4-47
MD388 KEA 6MU 18-3-44 82MU 27-3 *Kit Park* 6-4 Aus 19-6
MD389 STN 5-2-44 82MU 25-2 *Malika* 13-3 Ind 26-4 SOC 23-10
MD390 CHA 9MU 14-2-44 222MU 3-3 *Berr* 29-3 Ind 12-5 SOC 19-7-45
MD391 KEA 12-2-44 82MU 23-2 *Clan Mac* 11-3 Aus 18-4
MD392 STN 6MU 15-2-44 FAAC 22-2 82MU 20-7 *C o Lus* 16-8 Ind 28-8 SOC 19-7-45
MD393 CHA 9MU 16-2-44 215MU 12-3 *Berr* 29-3 Ind 12-5 CE ops 12-11 SOC 22-11
MD394 CHA 9MU 16-2-44 82MU 7-3 *Berr* 29-3 Ind 12-5 CE ops 19-6-45
MD395 CHA 9MU 16-2-44 82MU 16-3 *Berr* 29-3 Ind 12-5 SOC 7-2-45
MD396 STN 6MU 12-2-44 82MU 23-2 *Clan Mac* 11-3 Aus 18-4
MD397 STN 9MU 12-2-44 47MU 26-2 *Malika* 13-3 Ind 26-4 CE ops 18-8 SOC 7-2-45
MD398 STN 9MU 15-2-44 222MU 11-3 *Berr* 29-3 Ind 12-5 2S RIAF cd on t/o Miranshaw FACE 8-8-46 SOC 29-8
MD399 KEA 6MU 15-2-44 82MU 26-2 *Clan Mac* 11-3 Aus 18-4
MD400 KEA 6MU 18-2-44 47MU 5-3 *Berr* 29-3 Ind 12-5 1S RIAF cd/ld Samuneli 20-4-46 SOC 9-5
MD401 CHA 9MU 21-2-44 82MU 11-3 *Berr* 29-3 Ind 12-5 SOC 1-6-46
MD402 STN 9MU 12-3-44 215MU 26-3 *Shahz* 8-4 Ind 20-5 10S RIAF cd f/ld Burma 3-1-46 SOC 14-2
MD403 STN 9MU 12-3-44 82MU 22-3 *Shahz* 8-4 Ind 20-5 155S. Air coll with MU483 cd Arnhemia Sumatra DBF FACE b 26-2-46

MT series AII LF MkVIII Merlin 66

MT502 STN 6MU 30-3-44 82MU 8-4 *Sapp Park* 21-4 Aus 10-7
MT503 STN 6MU 4-4-44 82MU 13-4 *Sapp Park* 21-4 Aus 10-7
MT504 CHA 9MU 23-3-44 82MU 6-4 *C o Chy* 9-4 Ind 18-5
MT505 STN 9MU 20-3-44 222MU 31-3 *C o Chy* 9-4 Ind 18-5 SOC 30-1-47
MT506 STN 9MU 21-3-44 82MU 31-3 *C o Chy* 9-4 Ind 18-5 SOC 27-3-47
MT507 STN 9MU 24-4-44 215MU 5-5 *C o Ag* 305-5 Ind 9-7 SOC 27-2-47
MT508 CHA 6MU 30-3-44 82MU 6-4 *Sapp Park* 21-4 Aus 10-7
MT509 STN 6MU 6-4-44 82MU 14-4 *Diomed* 19-4 Aus 27-6
MT510 STN 6MU 9-4-44 82MU 20-4 *Port MacQ* 21-5 Aus 7-7
MT511 CHA 6MU 6-4-44 82MU 18-4 *Diomed* 19-4 Aus 27-6
MT512 CHA 6MU 31-3-44 82MU 13-4 *Sapp Park* 27-4 Aus 10-7
MT513 STN 6MU 30-3-44 82MU 13-4 *Sapp Park* 24-4 Aus 10-7
MT514 6MU 27-5-44 82MU 8-6 *Lanark* 17-6 Aus 27-7
MT515 STN 6MU 12-5-44 82MU 21-5 *Argyll* 1-6 Casa 13-6 CE ops 24-10

MD319, seen here at Boscombe Down, went to India in May 1944.

MT516 STN 9MU 18-4-44 222MU 22-2 *Fort Chu* 17-5 Ind 4-7 InAF SOC 27-11-47

MT517 STN 6MU 6-4-44 82MU 14-4 *Diomed* 19-4 Aus 27-6

MT518 CHA 6MU 6-4-44 82MU 14-4 *Diomed* 19-4 Aus 27-6

MT519 CHA 6MU 6-4-44 82MU 20-4 *Lea Park* 10-5 Aus 17-7

MT520 STN 9MU 21-4-44 215MU 5-5 *C o Ag* 30-5 Ind 4-7 6S FACE 15-4-47 SOC 26-6

MT521 STN 9MU 14-4-44 215MU 8-5 *C o Ag* 30-5 Ind 4-7 CE ops 24-5-45 bboc 12-7-45

MT522 CHA 9MU 20-4-44 215MU 30-4 *C o Ag* 30-5 Ind 4-7 SOC 16-1-47

MT523 STN 9MU 10-1-44 ROS 13-1 215MU 18-4 *Fort Chu* 17-5 Ind 4-7 SOC 28-2-46

MT524 STN 6MU 19-12-43 82MU 30-12 *Ajax* 26-2-44 Aus 7-4

MT525 STN 6MU 2-12-43 82MU 25-12 *Ajax* 26-2 Aus 7-4

MT526 KEA 6MU 15-2-44 82MU 1-3 *Malika* 13-3 Ind 26-4 SOC 31-12-46

MT527 STN 9MU 30-12-43 82MU 7-1-44 *Samlair* 11-1 Ind 4-3 FACE 14-7 SOC 7-2-45

MT539 KEA 6MU 21-2-44 82MU 9-3 *Lyca* 2-4 Aus 13-6

MT540 KEA 6MU 18-3-44 82MU 29-3 *Sapp Park* 21-4 Aus 10-7

MT541 KEA 29-2-44 82MU 10-3 *Lyca* 2-4 Aus 13-6

MT542 KEE 6MU 2-3-44 82MU 10-3 *Lyca* 2-4 Aus 13-6

MT543 KEE 6MU 29-2-44 82MU 9-3 *Lyca* 2-4 Aus 13-6

MT544 KEE 6MU 4-3-44 215MU 15-3 *Berr* 29-3 Ind 12-5 CE 24-5-45

MT545 STN 6MU 28-1-44 82MU 8-2 *Narb* 22-2 Aus 19-5

MT546 CBAF 6MU 19-5-44 215MU 28-5 *Argyll* 1-6 Casa 13-6 SOC 30-1-45

MT547 KEE 6MU 21-5-44 52MU 30-5 *Lanark* 17-6 Aus 27-7

MT548 KEE 6MU 25-5-44 82MU 2-6 *Tekoa* 9-6 Aus 9-8

MT549 KEE 6MU 22-5-44 82MU 31-5 *Lanark* 17-6 Aus 27-7

MT550 KEE 6MU 27-5-44 82MU 9-6 *Lanark* 17-6 Aus 27-7

MT551 KEE 6MU 27-5-44 82MU 21-6 *Samstu* 30-6 Casa 13-7 FTR ops 21-12

MT552 KEE 6MU 27-5-44 82MU 8-7 *Lanark* 17-6 Aus 27-7

MT553 KEE 6MU 27-5-44 82MU 21-6 *Samstu* 30-6 Casa 13-7 SOC 15-4-45

MT554 KEE 9MU 3-6-44 222MU 13-6 *C o H K* 28-6 Ind 4-8 SOC 46-6-47

MT555 KEE 9MU 4-6-44 222MU 13-6 *C 0 H K* 28-6 Ind 4-8 to Ins A/F SOC 27-11-47

MT556 KEE 9MU 3-6-44 82MU 15-6 *Clan Camp* 16-7 Ind 14-8 SOC 13-6-46

MT557 KEE 9MU 4-6-44 82MU 15-6 *Clan Camp* 16-7 Ind 14-8 SOC 23-8-45

MT558 KEE 9MU 7-6-44 82MU 15-6 *Clan Camp* 16-7 Ind 14-8 SOC 9-8-45

MT559 KEE 6MU 10-6-44 215MU 21-6 *Samstu* 30-6 Casa 13-7 SOC 23-8-45

MT560 KEE 9MU 15-6-44 222MU 25-6 *New Tex* 31-7 Casa 22-8 MAAF 21-6-45 ME 5-7 SOC 31-12-46

MT561 STN 6MU 15-6-44 52MU 27-6 *New Tex* 31-7 Casa 22-8 MAAF 21-6-45 SOC 27-3-47

MT562 KEE 6MU 17-6-44 52MU 27-6 *New Tex* 31-7 Casa 22-8 ME 30-6-45 SOC 9-8

MT563 KEE 9MU 17-6-44 82MU 2-7 *Taqh* 28-7 Ind 5-9 SOC 31-5-45

MT564 KEE 23-6-44 47MU 25-7 *Ocean War* 17-8 Ind 28-9 SOC 6-9-45

MT565 KEE 6MU 29-6-44 82MU 3-7 *New Tex* 31-7 Casa 22-8 SOC 29-2-45

MT566 KEE 10-7-44 82MU 22-7 *C o New* 16-8 Ind 29-9 SOC 26-7-45

MT567 KEE 9MU 4-7-44 82MU 17-7 *C o New* 16-8 Ind 28-9 SOC 30-5-46 used for RAF exhibitions

MT568 KEE 9MU 4-7-44 82MU 18-7 *C o New* 16-8 Ind 28-9 SOC 26-4-45

MT569 KEE 6MU 4-7-44 215MU 10-7 *New Tex* 31-7 Casa 22-8 SOC 16-4-45

MT570 KEE 6MU 6-7-44 47MU 14-7 *C o New* 16-8 Ind 28-9 SOC 13-6-45

MT571 KEE 6MU 6-7-44 47MU 14-7 *C o New* 16-8 Ind 28-9 SOC 29-11-45

MT572 KEE 6MU 8-7-44 82MU 18-7 *C o New* 16-8 Ind 28-9 SOC 16-1-47

MT573 KEE 9MU 14-7-44 76MU 29-7 *Ocean Wan* 17-8 Ind 28-9 SOC 28-9

MT574 KEE 9MU 16-7-44 76MU 29-7 *Ocean Wan 17-8* Ind 28-9 SOC 25-7-46

MT575 KEE 9MU 20-7-44 215MU 1-8 *C o Kim* 20-8 Ind 26-9 SOC 30-1-47

MT576 KEE 9MU 23-7-44 215MU 1-8 *C o Kim* 20-8 Ind 26-9 SOC 30-1-47

MT577 KEE 9MU 27-7-44 76MU 11-8 *Avris* 13-9 Ind 29-10 SOC 4-6-45

MT578 KEE 9MU 27-7-44 222MU 21-9 *LS2019* 3-10 Ind 4-11 SOC 26-9-45

MT579 KEE 9MU 27-7-44 76MU 11-8 *Avris* 13-9 Ind 29-10 SOC 31-5-45

MT580 KEE 6MU 27-7-44 76MU 10-8 *Avris* 13-9 Ind 29-10 SOC 13-6-46

MT581 9MU 14-8-44 82MU 29-8 *LS2019* 2-10 Ind 4-11 SOC 28-8-47

MT593 KEE 6MU 6-4-44 82MU 18-4 *Diomed* 17-4 Aus 27-6

MT594 CHA 6-4-44 82MU 25-4 *Rimu* 10-5 Aus 15-7

MT595 CHA 9MU 5-4-44 215MU 18-4 *Fort Chu* 17-5 Ind 4-7 SOC 31-12-47

MT596 CHA 6MU 6-4-44 82MU 20-4 *Fort MacQ* 21-5 Aus 7-7

MT597 CHA 9MU 11-4-44 215MU 27-4 *Fort Chu* 17-5 Ind 4-7 SOC 11-4-45

MT598 CHA 9MU 14-4-44 222MU 9-6 *C o H K* 28-6 Ind 4-8 SOC 18-5-45

MT599 CHA 9MU 18-4-44 215MU 2-5 *C o Ag* 30-5 Ind 4-7 SOC 11-4-46

MT600 CHA 9MU 11-4-44 215MU 23-4 *Fort Chu* 17-5 Ind 4-7 SOC 31-10-46

MT601 CHA sting hook (strengthened), retractable tailwheel. RNAS Crail 13-4-44 9MU 20-8 to 5829M 26-2-46 (see also JG661-663)

MT602 CHA as per MT601 11-8-44 to 5830M 26-2-46

MT603 CHA as per MT601 11-8-44 to 5831M 26-2-46

MT604 CHA 9MU 20-4-44 215MU 30-4 *C o Ag* 30-5 Ind 4-7 SOC 31-12-46

MT605 CHA 9MU 18-4-44 215MU 30-5 *C o Ag* 30-5 Ind 4-7 SOC 25-7-46

MT606 CHA 9MU 28-4-44 215MU 3-5 *C o Ag* 30-5 Ind 4-7 SOC 31-7-47

MT607 KEE 6MU 8-4-44 82MU 20-4 *Fort MacQ* 21-5 Aus 7-7

MT608 CHA 9MU 18-4-44 215MU 5-5 *C o Ag* 30-5 Ind 4-7 SOC 31-10-46

MT609 CHA 9MU 20-4-44 215MU 27-4 *C o Ag* 30-5 Ind 4-7 SOC 9-8-46

MT610 KEE 9MU 24-4-44 215MU 7-5 *C o Ag* 30-5 Ind 4-7 SOC 31-7-47

MT611 KEE 9MU 24-4-44 215MU 7-5 *C o Ag* 30-5 Ind 4-7 28 RIAF w/o ld Kohat CE ops 10-8-46 SOC 31-10

MT612 CHA 9MU 20-4-44 215MU 3-5 *C o Ag* 30-5 Ind 4-7 SOC 14-2-46

MT613 CHA 9MU 24-4-44 82MU 13-5 *Troil* 26-5 Ind 2-7 SOC 18-10-45

MT614 (P&S) CHA CRD Farn 21-4-44 drop tank trls 3PATP 24-11 *Emp Reg* 7-12 Ind 2-1-45 SOC 25-7-46

MT615 CHA 9MU 20-4-44 215MU 5-5 *C o Ag* 30-5 Ind 4-7 6S RIAF e/fld on t/o cd nr Ranchi FACE 9-3-46 SOC 25-4-46

MT616 KEE 9MU 24-4-44 222MU 5-5 *C o Ag* 17-5 Ind 4-7 SOC 11-4-46

MT617 CHA 9MU 22-4-44 215MU 5-5 *C o Ag* 30-5 Ind 4-7 SOC 14-6-45

MT618 CHA 6MU 23-4-44 82MU 1-5 *Rimu* 10-5 15-7

MT619 KEE 9MU 24-4-44 82MU 9-5 Troil 21-5 Ind 2-7 SOC 2-8-45

MT620 CHA 9MU 28-4-44 82MU 2-5 *Rimu* 10-5 Aust 15-7

MT621 CHA 6MU 29-4-44 82MU 9-5 *Tekoa* 9-6 Aus 9-8

MT622 CHA 6MU 28-4-44 82MU 9-5 *Tekoa* 9-6 Aus 9-8

MT623 CHA 8MU 26-4-44 215MU 5-5 *C o Ag* 30-5 Ind 4-7 SOC 27-3-47

MT624 CHA 6MU 28-4-44 82MU 5-5 *Fort MacQ* 24-5 Aus 4-7

MT625 222MU 12-5-44 *Argyll* 1-6 Casa 13-6 CE on ops 6-3-45

MT626 CHA 6MU 30-4-44 82MU 9-5 *Fort MacQ* 21-5 Aus 7-7

MT627 KEE 9MU 1-5-44 82MU 11-5 *Argyll* 1-6 Casa 13-6 328S 12-5-45 327S 4-10 FAF 27-11

MT628 KEE 6MU 30-4-44 82MU 10-5 *Troilus* 21-5 Ind 2-7 FACE 13-2-45 SOC 15-2

MT629 KEE 9MU 4-5-44 215MU 19-5 *C o Ag* 20-5 Ind 4-7 SOC 10-1-46

MT630 CHA 6MU 7-5-44 82MU 15-5 *Tekoa* 9-6 Aus 9-8

MT631 CHA 7-4-44 82MU 14-5 *Troil* 21-5 Ind 2-7 SOC 31-5-45 bboc 21-6 SOC 1-6-47

MT632 CHA 9MU 3-4-44 82MU 2-6 *Lanark* 17-6 Aus 27-7

MT633 CHA 6MU 7-4-44 76MU 14-5 *Argyll* 1-6 Casa 13-6

MT634 CHA 6MU 7-4-44 76MU 14-5 *Argyll* 1-6 Casa 13-6 FACE 18-5-45 SOC 30-8

MT635 CHA 6MU 7-5-44 82MU 15-5 *Tekoa* 9-6 Aus 9-8

MT648 CHA 9MU 20-4-44 82MU 52MU 27-5 *Samstu* 30-6 Casa 13-7 SOC 27-3-47

MT649 STN 6MU 26-4-44 82MU 3-5 *Fort MacQ* 21-5 Aus 7-7

MT650 CHA 6MU 28-4-44 215MU 1-5 *Tekoa* 9-6 Aus 9-8

MT651 CHA 9MU 22-4-44 222MU 5-5 *C o Ag* 30-5 Ind 4-7 SOC 30-1-47

MT652 STN 9MU 28-4-44 215MU 10-5 *C o Ag* 30-5 Ind 4-7 SOC 31-5-45

MT653 CHA 6MU 30-4-44 82MU 13-5 *Argyll* 1-6 Casa 13-6 FACE 30-6

MT654 STN 9MU 24-4-44 215MU 19-5 *C o Ag* 30-5 Ind 4-7 CE 24-5-45

MT655 CHA 6MU 23-4-44 82MU 1-5 *Rimu* 10-5 Aus 15-7

MT656 CHA 6MU 7-4-44 76MU 17-5 *Argyll* 1-6 Casa 13-6 417S CE ops 2-1-45

MT657 STN 9MU 17-4-44 215MU 29-4 *C o Ag* 20-5 Ind 4-7 SOC 30-1-47

MT658 CHA 6MU 29-4-44 82MU 82MU 9-5 *Tekoa* 9-6 Aus 9-8

MT659 STN 9MU 12-5-44 82MU 28-5 *Argyll* 1-6 Casa 13-6 SOC 20-1-45

MT660 STN 6MU 11-5-44 47MU 19-5 *Argyll* 1-6 Casa 13-6 CE ops 6-3-45

MT661 CHA 9MU 7-5-44 222MU 23-5 *Clan Macl* 1-6 Ind 6-7 SOC 29-8-46

MT662 CHA 9MU 7-5-44 215MU 15-56 *C o Ag* 30-5 Ind 4-7 FACE 1S 1-4-47 SOC 1-6

MT663 9MU 8-5-44 52MU 26-5 *Samstu* 30-6 Casa 13-7 SOC 29-2-45

MT664 STN 6MU 13-4-44 215MU 21-5 *Argyll* 13-6 ME 5-7-45 SOC 31-12-46

MT665 STN 6MU 14-5-44 215MU 24-5 *Argyll* 1-6 Casa 13-6 SOC 14-3-46

MT666 STN 9MU 8-5-44 222MU 21-5 *Argyll* 1-6 Casa 13-6 ME 30-6-45 SOC 30-12-46

MT667 ALD 6MU 26-5-44 82MU 21-6 *Samstu* 30-6 Casa 13-7 SOC 1-4-45

MT668 CHA 9MU 8-5-44 76MU 19-5 *Argyll* 1-6 Casa 13-6 SOC 26-9-45

MT669 STN 9MU 12-5-44 82MU 28-5 *Argyll* 1-6 Casa 13-6 FACE 26-6

MT670 STN 6MU 21-5-44 52MU 30-5 *Samstu* 30-6 Casa 13-7

MT671 STN 9MU 12-5-44 82MU 24-5 *Argyll* 1-6 Casa 13-6 CE ops 17-9

MT672 6MU 27-5-44 82MU 8-6 *Lanark* 17-6 Aus 27-7

MT673 STN 6MU 23-5-44 82MU 1-6 *Tekoa* 9-6 Aus 9-8

MT674 STN 9MU 3-6-44 82MU 14-6 *Truk* 28-7 Ind 5-9 SOC 4-10-45

MT675 HFVIII M7- STN 6MU 15-6-44 82MU 15-6 *Lanark* 17-6 Aus 27-7

MT676 STN 9MU 18-4-44 52MU 31-5 *Samstu* 30-6 Casa 13-7 CE ops 12-4-45 SOC 14-6

MT677 STN 6MU 18-5-44 215MU 25-5 *Samstu* 30-6 Casa 13-7 ME 2-8-45 SOC 10-8

MT678 no record

MT679 STN 9MU 7-6-44 82MU 15-6 *Turk* 28-7 Ind 5-9 SOC 13-6-46

MT680 STN 9MU 4-6-44 215MU 14-6 *Clan Camp* 16-7 Ind 14-8 SOC 13-9-45

MT681 STN 6MU 23-5-44 52MU 1-6 *Tekoa* 9-6 Aus 9-8

MT682 STN 6MU 26-5-44 82MU 8-9 *Lanark* 17-6 Aus 27-8

MT683 STN 9MU 3-6-44 215MU 11-6 *C o H K* 28-6 Ind 4-8 SOC 27-11

MT684 HFVIII M7- 6MU 27-6-44 82MU 8-7 *Claudia* 298 Aus 12-9

MT685 9MU 10-6-44 82MU 24-6 *Samstu* 30-6 Casa 13-7 SOC 13-4-45

MT686 6MU 10-6-44 82MU 28-6 *Samstu* 30-6 Casa 13-7 SOC 14-3-46

MT687 KEE 6MU 21-6-44 82MU 28-6 *Samstu* 30-6 Casa 13-7 SOC 29-2-45

MT688 9MU 10-6-44 82MU 21-6 *Samstu* 30-6 Casa 13-7 SOC 20-1-45

MT689 STN 6MU 11-6-44 215MU 21-6 *Samstu* 30-6 Casa 13-7 CE ops 20-3-45

MT703 6MU 27-5-44 82MU 12-6 *Lanark* 17-6 Aus 27-7

MT704 STN 9MU 2-6-44 82MU 15-6 *Turk* 28-7 Ind 5-9 i/sea SOC 5-7-45

MT705 STN 9MU 1-6-44 215MU 12-6 *Clan Camp* 16-7 Ind 14-8 SOC11-7-46

MT706 STN 9MU 3-6-44 82MU 15-6 *Turk* 28-7 Ind 5-9 SOC 27-6-46

MT707 STN 9MU 5-6-44 82MU 15-6 *Clan Camp* 16-7 Ind 14-8 SOC 27-3-47

MT708 STN 9MU 4-6-44 215MU 14-6 *Clan Camp* 16-7 Ind 14-8 SOC 24-5-45

MT709 STN 9MU 5-6-44 82MU 15-6 *Clan Camp* 16-7 Ind 14-8 SOC 31-7-47

MT710 STN 9MU 8-6-44 47MU 16-6 *Turk* 28-7 ind 5-9 SOC 23-8-45

MT711 (P&S) STN 6MU 21-6-44 52MU 26-6 *Samstu* 30-6 Casa 13-7 FTR 15-10 cancel ME 5-7-45 SOC 31-12-46

MT712 KEE 6MU 11-6-44 82MU 28-6 *Samstu* 30-6 Casa 13-7 FTR ops 15-10

MT713 STN 9MU 14-6-44 52MU 23-6 *Samstu* 30-6 Casa 13-7 ME 5-7-45 SOC 31-12-46

MT714 STN 9MU 15-6-44 52MU 24-7 *Samstu* 30-6 Casa 13-7 ME 30-11 MAAF 26-4-45 SOC 14-3-46

MT715 STN 9MU 15-6-44 52MU 24-6 *Samstu* 30-6 Casa 13-7 92S o/s u/c clpse ld Trevisio Italy 3-6-46 SOC 25-7

MT716 STN 9MU 16-6-44 215MU 29-6 *Clan Camp* 16-7 Ind 14-8 CE ops 25-2-45 SOC 1-3

MT717 STN 9MU 18-6-44 82MU 1-7 *Turk* 28-7 Ind 5-9 SOC 31-5-45

MT718 STN 9MU 20-6-44 82MU 8-7 *Turk* 28-7 Ind 5-9 SOC 31-5-45

MT719 STN 9MU 21-6-44 215MU 10-7 *Turk* 28-7 Ind 5-9 175 InAf 29-12-47 H-Banc 1977 Italy extant as I-SPIT

MT720 STN 9MU 22-6-44 82mU 8-7 *Turk* 28-7 Ind 5-9 SOC 31-5-45

MT721 STN 9MU 22-6-44 47MU 12-7 *C o New* 16-8 Ind 28-9 SOC

MT722 STN 9MU 23-6-44 82MU 8-7 *Turk* 28-7 Ind 5-9 SOC 22-5-45

MT723 STN 9MU 6-7-44 82MU 22-7 *C o New* 28-7 Ind 28-9 SOC 30-5-46

MT724 STN 9MU 7-7-44 82MU 22-7 *C o New* 16-8 Ind 28-9 SOC 29-8-46

MT725 CHA 9MU 9-12-44 215MU 9-1-45 *Angha* 22-1 Ind 19-2 SOC 27-3-47
MT726 STN 9MU 11-7-44 76MU 28-7 *Ocean Load* 17-8 Ind 28-9 SOC 9-5-46
MT727 STN 9MU 11-7-44 82MU 24-7 *C o New* 6-8 Ind 28-9 GACE 1-3-45 SOC 10-4
MT728 STN 9MU 14-7-44 222MU 23-8 *Ocean Load* 17-8 Ind 28-9 SOC 30-5-46
MT729 STN VAHP 13-7-44 9MU 28-7 76MU 11-8 Avris 13-9 Ind 20-10 SOC 9-5-46
MT730 STN 9MU 19-7-44 76MU 11-8 *Avris* 13-9 Ind 29-10 SOC 6-9-45
MT731 STN 9MU 22-7-44 76MU 11-8 *Avris* 13-9 Ind 29-10 SOC 19-7-45
MT732 STN 9MU 26-7-44 222MU 5-8 *SSLS2019* 2-10 Ind 4-11 SOC 29-11-45
MT733 STN 9MU 27-7-44 76MU 11-8 *Avris* 23-8 Ind 29-10 SOC 14-2-46
MT734 STN 9MU 15-8-44 222MU 21-9 *SSLS2019* 2-10 Ind 4-11 SOC 29-8-46
MT735 STN 9MU 15-8-44 *Ald Park* 26-9 ind 19-11 SOC 12-6-45
MT736 STN 9MU 18-8-44 82MU 2-9 *SSLS2019* 2-10 Ind 4-11 SOC 18-10-45
MT737 9MU 23-8-44 215MU 4-9 *H Prince* 4-9 Ind 15-10 SOC 25-7-46
MT738 6MU 28-4-44 82MU 2-9 *SSLS2448* 30-10 Ind 8-12 FACE 4-4-46 SOC 9-5
MT739 6MU 24-8-44 215MU 2-9 *Ald Park* 7-10 Ind 19-11 3S RIAF fire in air cd f/ld nr Kolar 2-3-46 SOc dbf 14-3
MT740 6MU 25-8-44 82MU 5-9 *Ingle* 1-1-45 Ind 4-2 SOC 12-7
MT741 9MU 29-8-44 215MU 8-9 *Ald Park* 7-10 Ind 19-11 SOC 26-9-46
MT742 6MU 1-9-44 222MU 12-9 *Ald Park* 26-9 Ind 19-11 to Ins A/F SOC 27-11-47
MT743 6MU 6-9-44 215MU 21-9 *Marta* 30-10 Ind 8-12 SOC 28-8-47
MT744 6MU 6-9-44 215MU 21-9 *Marta* 30-10 Ind 8-12 3S RIAF u/c coll ld Santa Cruz 12-5-46 SOC 30-5
MT745 STN 6MU 4-10-44 222MU 10-11 *Ing* 1-1-45 Ind 4-2 SOC 30-1-47
MT746 6MU 23-10-44 82MU 1-11 *Ing* 1-1-45 Ind 4-2 ME 14-3-46 InAF 31-12-47
MT747 6MU 9-10-44 222MU 16-10 *Marta* 30-10 Ind 8-12 SOC 30-1-47
MT748 HFVIII M70 6MU 10-9-44 82MU 27-9 *Port Fair* 15-10 Aus 24-11
MT761 STN 9MU 7-5-44 215MU 19-5 *C o Ag* 30-5 Ind 4-7 CE 29-12 SOC 12-2-45
MT762 KEE 9MU 14-7044 47MU 25-7 *Ocean Wan* 17-8 Ind 28-9 SOC 16-1-47
MT763 CHA 9MU 7-5-44 215MU 21-5 *Fort Cham* 10-6 Ind 18-7 SOC 23-2-45
MT764 CHA 9MU 8-5-44 215MU 16-5 *Argyll* 1-6 Casa 13-6 MAAF 21-6-45 SOC 14-3-46
MT765 KEE 9MU 8-5-44 76MU 19-5 *Argyll* 1-6 Casa 13-6 327S 12-5-45
MT766 215MU 29-9-44 *Marta* 30-9 Ind 8-12 SOC 31-10-46
MT767 STN 9MU 16-5-44 82MU 31-5 *Tekoa* 9-6 Aus 9-8
MT768 KEE 9MU 12-5-44 52MU 27-5 *Samstu* 30-6 Casa 13-7 CE ops 14-3-45
MT769 STN 6MU 11-5-44 47MU 19-5 *Argyll* 1-6 Casa 13-6 SOC 27-3-47
MT770 STN 9MU 12-5-44 82MU 28-5 *Argyll* 1-6 Casa 13-6 CE ops 16-3-45
MT771 CHA 9MU 18-5-44 82MU 9-6 *Lanark* 17-6 Aus 27-7
MT772 STN 6MU 11-5-44 222MU 28-6 *New Tex* 31-7 Casa 22-8 SOC 31-12-46
MT773 STN 9MU 14-5-44 215MU 26-5 *Argyll* 1-6 Casa 13-6 ME 30-6-45 SOC 31-12-46
MT774 STN 9MU 12-5-44 47MU 19-5 *Argyll* 1-6 Casa 13-6 CE 27-12 SOC 31-1-45 remains preserved at Santa Cruz
MT775 KEE 6MU 14-5-44 215MU 23-5 *Argyll* 1-6 Casa 13-6 ME 30-6-45 SOC 9-8
MT776 KEE 6MU 15-5-44 222MU 4-6 *Samstu* 30-6 Casa 13-7 SOC 14-3-46
MT777 STN 9MU 13-5-44 82MU 24-5 *Argyll* 1-6 Casa 13-6 CE ops 21-11
MT778 KEE 9MU 22-5-44 82MU 9-6 *Lanark* 17-6 Aus 27-7
MT779 CHA 9MU 22-5-44 82MU 31-5 *Tekoa* 9-6 Aus 9-8
MT780 KEE 9MU 24-5-44 215MU 31-5 *Fort Cham* 10-6 Ind 18-7 SOC 30-1-47
MT781 CHA 9MU 19-5-44 82MU 2-6 *Lanark* 17-6 Aus 27-7
MT782 CHA 9MU 22-5-44 82MU 8-6 *Lanark* 17-6 Aus 27-7
MT783 CHA 9MU 22-5-44 82MU 31-5 *China P* 9-6 Ind 10-7 155S cd F/ld nr Medan Sumatra 4-4-46 SOC 27-11-47
MT784 CHA 6MU 20-5-44 215MU 28-5 *Argyll* 1-6 Casa 13-6 SOC 11-5-45
MT785 STN 6MU 21-5-44 52MU 30-5 *Samstu* 30-6 Casa 13-7 SOC 20-4-45
MT786 CHA 6MU 27-5-44 82MU 20-6 *Samstu* 30-6 Casa 13-7 CE ops 2-10
MT787 CHA 6MU 25-5-44 82MU 1-6 *Tekoa* 9-6 Aus 9-8
MT788 CHA 6MU 25-5-44 82MU 2-6 *Lanark* 17-6 Aus 27-7
MT789 CHA 9MU 26-5-44 215MU 12-6 *Clan Camp* 16-7 Ind 14-8 SOC 31-5-45
MT790 CHA 9MU 1-6-44 215MU 12-6 *Clan Camp* 16-7 Ind 14-8 SOC 30-1-47
MT791 CHA 9MU 3-6-44 222MU 12-6 *C o H K* 28-6 Ind 4-8 FAF 25-4-46 SOC 30-5
MT792 CHA 9MU 3-6-44 82MU 15-6 *Turk* 28-7 Ind 5-8 SOC 16-1-47
MT793 STN 6MU 26-5-44 222MU 23-9 *Marta* 30-1 Ind 8-12 SOC 30-5-46
MT794 STN 6MU 26-5-44 82MU 80-6 *Lanark* 17-6 Aus 27-7
MT795 STN 9MU 8-6-44 222MU 12-6 *C o H K* 28-6 Ind 4-8 SOC 2-8-45
MT796 STN 9MU 2-6-44 222MU 12-6 *C o H K* 28-6 Ind 4-8 FACE 24-5-45 SOC 4-6
MT797 STN 9MU 7-6-44 215MU 16-6 *Clan Camp* 16-7 Ind 14-8 SOC 6-4-45
MT798 STN 9MU 7-6-44 52MU 24-6 *Marta* 30-10 Ind 8-12 SOC 30-1-47
MT799 STN 9MU 8-6-44 82MU 21-6 *Clan Camp* 16-7 Ind 14-8 SOC 13-9-45
MT800 STN 6MU 11-6-44 52MU *Samstu* 30-6 Casa 13-7 SOC 14-3-46
MT801 CHA 6MU 10-6-44 82MU 24-6 *Samstu* 30-6 Casa 13-7 CE 12-4-45 SOC 26-4
MT802 CHA 6MU 10-6-44 215MU 22-6 *Samstu* 30-6 Casa 13-7 SOC 20-9-45
MT815 STN 9MU 18-7-44 222MU 1-7 *Avris* 13-9 Ind 29-10 SOC 31-7-47
MT816 HFVIII M70 STN 6MU 15-6-44 82MU 24-6 *Chan* 1-8 Aus 12-9
MT817 HFVIII M70 STN 6MU 16-6-44 82MU 28-6 *Chan* 1-8 Aus 12-9
MT818 STN CRD VAHP 13-6-44 Farn oct'44 comp trls with PT452. Sold VA 21-6-47 Con to Type 502 Two-seat train B condition N32. Civil ref G-AIDN. Sold John Fairey Hamp Aero Club Sep '56 w/u ldg Coventry airport 6-2-78. Extan Oregon, USA. Further details see page 303.
MT819 HFVIII M70 CHA 6MU 30-6-44 82MU 8-7 *Chan* 1-8 Aus 12-9
MT820 HFVIII M70 STN 6MU 27-6-44 82MU 8-7 *Chan* 1-8 Aus 12-9
MT821 HFVIII M70 STN 6MU 20-6-44 82MU 28-6 *Chan* 1-8 Aus 12-9
MT822 HFVIII M70 STN 6MU 18-6-44 82MU 28-6 *Chan* 1-8 Aus 12-9
MT823 STN 9MU 27-6-44 215MU 10-7 *Turk* 28-7 Ind 8-9 FACE 20-5-45 SOC 19-7
MT824 STN 9MU 29-6-44 47MU 12-7 *C o New* 16-8 Ind 28-9 SOC 14-2-46
MT825 HFVIII M70 6MU 4-7-44 Farn Jly'44 82MU 18-7 *Chan* 1-8 Aus 12-9
MT826 STN 9MU 7-7-44 82MU 18-7 *C o New* 16-8 Ind 28-9 136S e/fld aban cd Kuala Lumpur Malaya FACE 15-4-46
MT827 STN 9MU 19-7-44 222MU 1-9 *Avris* 12-9 Ind 29-10 SOC 19-7-45
MT828 STN VA HP 20-7-44 9MU 5-8 215MU 27-8 *Ald Park* 7-10 Ind 19-11 SOC 27-2-47
MT829 HFVIII M70 6MU 7-7-44 82MU 16-7 *Chan* 1-8 Aus 12-9
MT830 HFVIII M70 6MU 6-7-44 82MU 18-7 *Chan* 1-8 Aus 12-9
MT831 HFVIII M70 6MU 14-7-44 82MU 20-7 *Chan* 1-8 Aus 12-9
MT832 STN 9MU 10-7-44 ROS 25-7 215MU 8-9 *Ald Park* 7-10 Ind 19-11 FACE Ambala 15-4-47 SOC 24-4
MT833 HFVIII M66 STN 6MU 7-7-44 82MU *Chan* 1-8 Aus 12-9
MT834 HFVIII M70 STN 6MU 8-7-44 82MU 18-7 *Chan* 1-8 Aus 12-9
MT835 HFVIII M70 STN Farn. VAHP 15-7-44 82MU 18-7 Farn Aug'44 *Bris Star* 30-1-45 Aus 5-3
MT836 9MU 31-12-44 215MU 14-1-45 *Clan For* Feb'45 Ind 28-3 SOC 1-6-47
MT837 6MU 24-12-44 215MU 7-1-45 *Malad* 22-1-45 Ind 19-2 SOC 25-10
MT838 9MU 3-1-45 215MU 22-1 *Emp Par* 13-2 Ind 3-4 SOC 26-9-46
MT839 (P&S) 9MU 3-1-45 215MU 27-1 *Clan For* Feb'45 Ind 28-3 SOC 29-11
MT840 FF 14-12-44 MJL 9MU 21-12-44 215MU 12-1-45 *Clan For* Feb'45 Ind 28-3 SOC 11-4
MT841 FF 21-12-44 MJL 9MU 31-1-45 215MU 2-2 *Emp Par* 13-2 Ind 12-4 FACE 29-1-47 SOC 27-2
MT842 CHA 6MU 21-1-45 222MU 26-4 *Emp Dyn* 16-5 Ind 7-6 SOC 13-6-46
MT843 6MU 21-12-44 215MU 9-1-45 *Malad* 22-1 Ind 19-2 SOC 31-7-47
MT844 CHA FF 22-1-45 MJL 9MU 30-1-45 3PATP 23-3 *Emp Dyn* 16-5 Ind 28-6 SOC 13-6-46
MT845 CHA 6MU 7-1-45 215MU 17-1 *Clan For* Feb'45 Ind 20-3 SOC 30-5-46
MT846 CHA 6MU 21-1-45 3PATP 21-4 *Emp Dyn* 16-5 Ind 7-6 SOC 13-6-46
MT872 9MU 17-8-44 215MU 7-9 *Ald Park* 7-10 Ind 19-11 FACE 2S RIAF f/ldon app Kohat 9-9-46 SOC 26-9
MT873 9MU 18-8-44 222MU 29-8 *SSLS2019* 2-10 Ind 4-11 1SFTS c/ldg Peshawar FACE 12-10-46 SOC 31-10
MT874 9MU 23-8-44 222MU 8-9 *SSLS2019* 2-10 Ind 4-11 SOC 9-5-46
MT875 9MU 23-8-44 82MU 2-9 *SSLS2019* 2-10 Ind 4-11 SOC 30-1-47
MT876 9MU 23-8-44 82MU 2-9 *SSLS2019* 2-10 Ind 4-11 SOC 30-8-45
MT877 9MU 25-8-44 215MU 9-9 *Ald Park* 25-9 Ind 19-11 SOC 30-8-45
MT878 9MU 25-8-44 222MU 8-9 *Ald Park* 25-9 Ind 19-11 SOC 10-1-46
MT879 6MU 25-8-44 82MU 3-9 *SSLS2019* 2-10 Ind 4-11 SOC 30-8-45
MT880 6MU 27-8-44 82MU 3-9 *SSLS2019* 2-10 Ind 4-11 SOC 12-6-45 sold InAF 31-12-47
MT881 6MU 27-8-44 82MU 3-9 *SSLS2019* 2-10 Ind 4-11 SOC 31-7-47
MT882 6MU 28-8-44 82MU 8-9 *SSLS2019* 2-10 Ind 4-11 SOC 14-2-46
MT883 9MU 5-9-44 215MU 13-9 *Ald Park* 7-10 Ind 19-11 SOC 11-10-45
MT884 9MU 6-9-44 82MU 20-9 *Marta* 30-10 Ind 8-12 SOC 13-6-46
MT885 9MU 5-9-44 82MU 12-9 *Marta* 30-10 Ind 8-12 SOC 1-6-47
MT886 6MU 6-9-44 82MU 12-10 *Marta* 30-10 Ind 8-12 SOC 30-1-47
MT887 9MU 10-9-44 FAAC 20-9 ROS 215MU 8-12 *Ing* 1-1-45 Ind 4-2 SOC 11-4-46
MT888 9MU 10-9-44 82MU 14-9 *Marta* 30-10 Ind 8-12 CE 21-6-45
MT889 KEE 6MU 17-4-44 222MU 4-10 *Marta* 30-10 Ind 8-12 SOC 30-1-47
MT890 HFVIII M70 6MU 9-9-44 82MU 21-9 *Sarp* 13-10 Aus 1-1-45
MT891 HFVIII M70 6MU 9-9-44 3PATP 23-3-45 *Fond* 18-4 Aus 14-6
MT892 HFVIII M70 6MU 10-6-44 82MU 3-9 *SSLS1965* 21-9 Aus 8-11
MT893 HFVIII M70 6MU 13-9-44 82MU 21-9 *Port Fair* 15-10 Aus 20-11
MT894 HFVIII M70 KEE 6MU 15-9-44 82MU 27-9 *Port Fair* 15-10 Aus 20-11
MT895 HFVIII M70 KEE 6MU 17-9-44 *Port Fair* 15-10 Aus 20-11
MT896 HFVIII M70 6MU 26-9-44 82MU 4-10 *Horor* 15-10 Aus 30-11
MT897 HFVIII M70 6MU 25-9-44 82MU 4-10 *Horor* 15-10 Aus 30-11
MT898 HFVIII M70 CHA 6MU 2-11-44 215MU 1-2-45 *N Z Star* 4-3 Aus 17-4
MT899 HFVIII M70 6MU 25-9-044 215MU 6-10 *Suss* 13-11 Aus 6-2-45
MT900 HFVIII M70 6MU 26-9-44 82MU 3-10 *Horor* 15-10 Aus 30-11
MT901 9MU 26-9-44 222MU 6-10 *Marta* 30-10 Ind 8-12 SOC 31-10-46
MT902 6MU 29-9-44 222MU 10-10 *Marta* 30-10 Ind 8-12 SOC 31-5-45
MT903 6MU 8-10-44 82MU 14-10 *Marta* 30-10 Ind 8-12 SOC 7-6-45
MT904 KEE 9MU 7-10-44 222Mu 18-10 *Marta* 30-10 Ind 8-12 SOC 13-6-46
MT905 KEE 9MU 7-10-44 222MU 23-10 *Marta* 30-10 Ind 8-12 SOC 9-5-46
MT906 6MU 16-10-44 222MU 23-10 *Marta* 30-10 Ind 8-12 SOC 13-6-46
MT907 6MU 29-10-44 3PATP 23-10 *Emp Reg* 7-12 Ind 2-1-45 SOC 27-3-47
MT908 9MU 30-10-44 82MU 18-11 *Ingl* 1-1-45 Ind 4-2 SOC 31-12-46
MT909 CHA 9MU 7-11-44 215MU 24-11 *Emp Reg* 7-12 Ind 2-1-45 SOC 8-6
MT910 HFVIII M70 6MU 23-10-44 215MU 5-1-45 *Bris Star* 30-1 Aus 5-3
MT911 KEE 9MU 9-11-44 222MU 24-11 *Ingl* 1-1-45 Ind 4-2 SOC 26-9-46
MT912 KEE 9MU 7-11-44 82MU 16-11 *Ingl* 1-1-45 Ind 4-2 SOC 28-8-47
MT913 KEE 9MU 9-11-44 215MU 24-11 *Emp Reg* 7-12 Ind 2-1-45 SOC 30-1-47
MT914 HFVIII M70 6MU 23-10-44 215MU 12-12 Aus 28-4-45
MT915 KEE 15-11-44 82MU 24-11 *Ingl* 1-1-45 Ind 4-2 SOC 31-7-47
MT925 no record
MT926 no record
MT927 no record
MT928 STN 6MU 11-6-44 52MU 22-6 *Samstu* 30-6 Casa 13-7 SOC 14-3-46
MT929 STN 6MU 13-6-44 82MU 24-6 *Samstu* 30-6 Casa 13-7 SOC 18-10-45
MT930 KEE 6MU 10-6-44 52MU 23-6 *Samstu* 30-6 Casa 13-7 SOC 26-4-45
MT931 KEE 9MU 11-6-44 82MU 1-7 *New Tex* 31-7 Casa 22-8 FTR ops 15-10
MT932 STN 6MU 18-6-44 52MU 28-6 *New Tex* 31-7 Casa 22-8 CE 16-12
MT933 STN 6MU 15-6-44 52MU 26-6 *Samstu* 30-6 Casa 13-7 328S
MT934 STN 9MU 18-6-44 82MU 1-7 *Turk* 28-7 Ind 5-9 SOC 30-1-47
MT935 STN 6MU 17-6-44 82MU 24-6 *Samstu* 30-6 Casa 13-7 SOC26-4-45
MT936 KEE 6MU 16-6-44 52MU 28-6 *New Tex* 31-7 casa 22-8 SOC 31-12-46
MT937 CHA 9MU 20-6-44 82MU 2-7 *Turk* 28-7 Ind 5-9 FACE 14-5-45 SOC 28-5
MT938 CHA 9MU 20-6-44 82MU 8-7 *Turk* 28-7 Ind 5-9 SOC 29-3-45
MT939 KEE 6MU 17-6-44 52MU 28-6 *New Tex* 31-7 Casa 22-8 SOC 31-1-46

MT947, despatched in July 1944, struck off charge in September 1946.

MT940 KEE 9MU 22-6-44 82MU 8-7 *Turk* 28-7 Ind 5-9 sold InAF 29-12-47
MT941 KEE 9MU 24-6-44 47MU 10-7 *Turk* 28-7 Ind 5-9 SOC 29-8-46
MT942 KEE 9MU 22-6-44 82MU 8-7 *Turk* 28-7 Ind 5-9 SOC 29-3-45
MT943 STN 9MU 25-6-44 82MU 8-7*Turk* 28-7 Ind 5-9 SOC 25-7-46
MT944 STN 9MU 24-6-44 82MU 8-7 *Turk* 28-7 Ind 5-9 SOC 31-5-45
MT945 STN 9MU 25-6-44 82MU 8-7 *Turk* 28-7 Ind 5-9 SOC 29-5-45
MT946 KEE 9MU 29-6-44 82MU 13-7 *Turk* 28-7 Ind 5-9 SOC 30-1-47
MT947 KEE 29-6-44 82MU 13-7 *Turk* 28-7 Ind 5-9 SOC 12-9-46
MT948 CHA 9MU 24-6-44 82MU 8-7 *Turk* 28-7 Ind 5-9 SOC 28S Malaya 2803046
MT949 KEE 9MU 10-7-44 82MU 22-7 *Co New* 16-8 Ind 28-9 SOC 31-5-45
MT950 KEE 9MU 16-7-44 215MU 5-8 *H Prince* 22-8 Ind 15-10 SOC 30-1-47
MT951 KEE 9MU 16-7-44 82MU 26-7 *Ocean Wand* 17-8 Ind 28-9 SOC 28-3-45
MT952 KEE 6MU 29-6-44 82MU 8-7 *New Tex* 31-7 Casa 22-8 SOC 31-8-45
MT953 STN 6MU 30-6-44 215MU 15-7 *New Tex* 31-7 Casa 22-8 SOC 11-4-46
MT954 STN 9MU 3-7-44 222MU 15-7 *Ocean Wand* 17-8 Ind 28-9 SOC 29-11-45
MT955 CHA 30-6-44 222MU 15-7 *Ocean Wand* 17-8 Ind 28-9 SOC 14-2-46
MT956 STN 9MU 29-6-44 47MU 9-7 *Turk* 28-7 Ind 5-9 SOC 9-12
MT957 STN 29-6-44 82MU 8-7 *New Tex* 31-7 Casa 22-8 ME 5-7-45 SOC 31-3-46
MT958 STN 9MU 3-7-44 82MU 24-7 *C o New* 16-8 Ind 28-9 SOC 14-3-46
MT959 STN 9MU 18-7-44 76MU 12-8 *Avristan* 13-9 Ind 29-10 SOC 11-4-46
MT960 KEE 9MU 20-7-44 47MU 30-7 *H Prince* 22-8 Ind 15-10 SOC 31-5-45
MT961 KEE 9MU 20-7-44 47MU 2-8 *H Prince* 22-8 Ind 15-10
MT962 STN 9MU 3-7-44 47MU 12-7 *Turk* 28-7 Ind 5-9 SOC 14-12-46
MT963 CHA 9MU 3-7-44 222MU 15-7 *Ocean Wan* 17-8 Ind 28-9 SOC 31-12-46
MT964 CHA 6MU 3-7-44 47MU 14-7 *C o New* 16-8 Ind 28-9 SOC 31-5-45
MT965 STN 9MU 10-7-44 82MU 24-7 *C o New* 16-8 Ind 28-9 SOC 9-1-45
MT966 CHA 6MU 7-7-44 47MU 14-7 *C o New* 16-8 Ind 28-9 FACE 28-5-45 SOC 13-6
MT967 STN 9MU 7-7-44 82MU 18-7 *C o New* 16-8 Ind 5-9 FACE 6-3-45 SOC 17-4
MT968 KEE 9MU 10-7-44 82MU 22-7 *C o New* 16-8 Ind 28-9 SOC 11-10-45
MT969 STN 6MU 7-7-44 82MU 17-7 *C o New* 16-8 Ind 28-9 SOC 30-1-47
MT981 STN 9MU 10-7-44 82MU 23-7 *C o New* 16-8 Ind 28-9 SOC 16-1-47
MT982 KEE 6MU 8-7-44 215MU 18-7 *Ocean Wan* 17-8 Ind 28-9 SOC 27-6-46
MT983 CHA 9MU 14-7-44 47MU 25-7 *Ocean Wan* 17-8 Ind 28-9 SOC 28-8-47 sold InAF 31-12
MT984 CHA 6MU 10-7-44 215MU 18-7 *Ocean Wan* 17-8 Ind 28-9 SOC 16-11-47
MT985 CHA 9MU 10-7-44 47MU 30-7 *H Prince* 22-8 Ind 15-10 SOC 27-6-46
MT986 CHA 6MU 10-7-44 225MU 18-7 *Ocean Wan* 17-8 Ind 28-9 SOC 26-5-45
MT987 CHA 9MU 10-7-44 82MU 22-7 *C o New* 16-8 Ind 22-9 CE 24-5-45 1s RIAF ld coll with JG489 *Samungli* 6-6-46
MT988 CHA 9MU 11-7-44 82MU 24-7 *C o New* 16-8 Ind 29-9 SOC 31-5-45
MT989 CHA 9MU 14-7-44 222MU 23-7 *Ocean Wan* 17-8 Ind 28-9 SOC 19-7-45
MT990 CHA 9MU 14-7-44 215MU 1-8 *H Princ* 19-8 Ind 15-10 SOC 1-2-45
MT991 6MU 31-7-44 76MU 8-8 *Avris* 24-8 Ind 29-10 SOC 2-8-45
MT992 CHA 9MU 17-7-44 76MU 29-7 *Avris* 13-9 Ind 29-10 SOC 20-3-45
MT993 KEE 9MU 16-7-44 47MU 2-8 *H Prince* 22-8 Ind 15-10 FACE 30-7-47 SOC 28-8
MT994 KEE 9MU 16-7-44 47MU 25-7 *Ocean Wan* 17-8 Ind 28-9 SOC 26-9-46
MT995 9MU 16-7-44 47MU 25-7 Ind 26-10 SOC 29-8-45
MT996 KEE 9MU 23-7-44 222MU 5-8 *SSLS2019* 2-10 Ind 4-11 SOC 28-3-46
MT997 9MU 22-7-44 222MU 8-8 *SSLS2019* 2-10 Ind 4-11 SOC 11-10-45
MT998 STN 9MU 26-7-44 222MU 3-8 *SSLS2019* 2-10 Ind 4-11 SOC 27-8-47
MT999 9MU 23-8-44 82MU 2-9 *SSLS2019* 2-10 Ind 4-11 SOC 30-8-45

MV series. All HF MkVIII Merlin M70 unless otherwise indicated

MV112 STN 6MU 12-7-44 *SSLS1968* 1-8-44 Aus 1 RAAF S 12-9 CAC 12-12-46
MV113 STN 6MU 13-7-44 82MU 29-7 *Sanauca* 30-7 Aus 7-9
MV114 STN 6MU 15-7-44 82MU 31-7 Aus 12-11
MV115 STN 6MU 22-7-44 82MU 28-7 *SSLS1961* 1-8 Aus 12-9
MV116 STN 6MU 23-7-44 82MU 12-9 *SSLS1965* 21-9 Aus 8-11
MV117 STN 6MU 13-8-44 82MU 21-8 Aus 12-11
MV118 LFVIII M66 STN 9MU 27-7-44 76MU 12-8 *Avris* 13-9 Ind 20-10 FACE 15-4-47 SOC 26-6
MV119 STN 6MU 15-7-44 82MU 23-7 *Sanauca* 30-7 Aus 7-9
MV120 STN 6MU 23-7-44 82MU 29-7 Aus 12-11
MV121 STN 6MU 29-7-44 82MU 7-8 Aus 12-11
MV122 LFVIII M66 STN 9MU 12-8-44 82MU 22-8 *SSLS2019* 2-10 Ind 4-11 SOC 27-2-47
MV123 STN 6MU 22-7-44 82MU 28-7 *SSLS1961* 1-8 Aus 12-9
MV124 STN 6MU 22-7-44 82MU 29-7 Aus 12-11
MV125 STN 6MU 28-7-44 82MU 6-8 Aus 12-11
MV126 LFVIII M66 CBAF 9MU 20-8-44 82MU 27-8 *SSLS2019* 2-10 Ind 16-11 SOC 31-5-45
MV127 LFVIII M66 STN 6MU 23-8-44 215MU 31-8 *SSLS2024* 7-10 Ind 19-11 SOC 29-8-46
MV128 STN 6MU 29-7-44 82MU 8-8 Aus 12-11
MV129 STN 6MU 29-7-44 82MU 7-8 Aus 12-11
MV130 LFVIII M66 STN 9MU 20-8-44 215MU 31-8 *SSLS2024* 7-10 Ind 19-11 SOC 30-5-46
MV131 LFVIII M66 23-8-44 47MU 27-8 *Ald Park* 29-9 Ind 19-11 SOC 21-6-45
MV132 STN 6MU 29-7-44 82MU 7-8 Aus 12-11 Tunisia
MV133 STN 6MU 20-8-44 82MU 26-8 *SSLS1964* 18-9 Aus 25-10
MV134 LFVIII M66 9MU 29-8-44 222MU 9-9 *Ald Park* 29-9 Ind 19-11 CE 19-4-45 SOC 4-10-45
MV135 STN 6MU 16-8-44 82MU 24-8 *SSLS1964* 18-9 Aus 25-10
MV136 STN 6MU 17-8-44 82MU 30-8 *SSLS1964* 18-9 Aus 25-10
MV137 6MU 5-9-44 82MU 14-9 *SSLS1965* 21-9 Aus 8-11
MV138 STN 6MU 18-8-44 82MU 24-8 *SSLS1964* 18-9 Aus 25-10
MV139 6MU 20-8-44 82MU 30-8 *SSLS1964* 18-9 Aus 25-10
MV140 6MU 31-8-44 82MU 10-9 *SSLS1965* 21-9 Aus 8-11
MV141 STN 6MU 20-8-44 82MU 30-8 *SSLS1964* 18-9 Aus 25-10
MV142 LFVIII M66 29-8-44 82MU 18-10 *Marta* 30-10 Ind 8-12 CE on ops 14-5-46 SOC 30-5
MV143 LFVIII M66 9MU 6-10-44 82MU 15-10 *Marta* 30-10 Ind 8-12 SOC 31-1-46
MV144 LFVIII M66 6MU 27-8-44 82MU *SSLS1964* 18-9 Aus 25-10
MV145 LFVIII M66 9MU 8-9-44 222MU 15-9 *Ald Park* 26-9 Ind 19-11 SOC 1-6-47
MV146 M66 6MU 7-9-44 82MU 15-9 *SSLS1965* 21-9 Aus 8-11
MV147 6MU 5-9-44 82MU 12-9 *SSLS1965* 21-9 Aus 8-11 155S w/u ld Medan Sumatra 14-5-46
MV148 6MU 31-8-44 82MU 10-9 *SSLS1965* 21-9 Aus 8-11
MV149 6MU 28-8-44 82MU 5-9 *SSLS1964* 18-9 Aus 25-10
MV150 ALD 6MU 3-10-44 215MU 12-10 *Ajax* 6-11 Aus 17-12
MV151 6MU 10-9-44 82MU 13-9 *SSLS1965* 21-9 Aus 8-11
MV152 6MU 31-8-44 82MU 10-9 *SSLS1965* 21-9 Aus 8-11
MV153 6MU 15-9-44 82MU 27-9 *Port Fair* 15-10 Aus 20-11
MV154 Australia A58-671 to UK as G-BKMI 23-12-82. Extant Bristol, under restoration.
MV155 6MU 10-9-44 82MU 13-9 *SSLS1966* 21-9 Aus 8-11 A53-61 extant Marshalls Airways Bankstown Sydney
MV156 6MU 15-9-44 82MU 29-9 *Port Fair* 15-10 Aus 24-11
MV169 CHA 6MU 20-9-44 82MU 28-9 *Horor* 15-10 Aus 30-11
MV170 6MU 24-9-44 82MU 4-10 *Horor* 15-10 Aus 30-11
MV171 6MU 10-9-44 82MU 21-9 *Sarpen* 13-10 Aus 13-1-45
MV172 ALD 6MU 20-9-44 82MU 29-9 *Horor* 15-10 Aus 30-11
MV173 6MU 25-9-44 82MU 4-10 *Horor* 15-10 Aus 30-11
MV174 6MU 24-9-44 82MU 4-10 *Horor* 15-10 Aus 30-11
MV175 6MU 25-9-44 215MU 5-10 *Horor* 15-10 Aus 25-11
MV176 6MU 12-10-44 215MU 23-10 *Ajax* 9-11 Aus 17-10
MV177 KEE 6MU 1-10-44 215MU 12-10 *Suss* 13-11 Aus 6-2-45
MV178 CHA 6MU 1-10-44 215MU 12-10 *Suss* 183-11 Aus 6-2-45
MV179 6MU 13-10-44 *SSLS1973* 18-11 Aus 23-12
MV180 6MU 24-10-44 82MU 17-12 *Marta* 6-1-45 Aus 28-3-45
MV181 6MU 1-11-44 215MU 7-2-45 *N Z Star* 4-3-45 Aus 17-4
MV182 6MU 25-9-44 82MU 4-10 *Horor* 15-10 Aus 30-11
MV183 CHA 6MU 1-10-44 215MU 12-10 *Suss* 18-11 Aus 6-2-45
MV184 M66 Super 6MU 1-11-44 215MU 24-11 *Parar* 31-12 Aus 6-4-45
MV185 6MU 9-11-44 215MU 7-2-45 *N Z Star* 4-3-45 Aus 12-4-45
MV186 6MU 27-10-44 215MU 21-1-45 *N Z Star* 4-3-45 Aus 17-4
MV187 6MU 24-10-44 215MU 12-12 *C o Cal* 18-1-45 Aus 27-2-45
MV188 CHA 6MU 14-11-44 215MU 7-2-45 *Clan Far* 10-3 Aus 4-5
MV189 6MU 9-10-44 215MU 14-10 *Ajax* 6-11 Aus 17-12
MV190 6MU 30-10-44 215MU 22-1-45 *N Z Star* 4-3 Aus 17-4
MV191 6MU 27-10-44 215MU 1-2-45 *N Z Star* 4-3-45 Aus 13-4
MV192 6MU 23-10-44 215MU 12-12 *C o Cal* 18-1-45 Aus 27-2
MV193 6MU 28-10-44 215MU 1-2-45 *N Z Star* 4-3 Aus 17-4
MV194 6MU 27-9-44 215MU 21-1-45 *N Z Star* 4-3 Aus 17-4
MV195 6MU 23-11-44 215MU 7-2-45 *Clan Far* 10-3 Aus 4-5
MV196 CHA 6MU 12-11-44 215MU 8-2-45 *N Z Star* 4-3 Aus 17-4
MV197 6MU 27-10-44 215MU 4-2-45 *N Z Star* 4-3 Aus 17-4
MV198 6MU 1-11-44 215MU 1-2-45 *N Z Star* 4-3 Aus 17-4
MV199 6MU 6-11-44 215MU 31-12 *C o Cal* 18-1-45 Aus 27-3
MV200 6MU 23-10-44 215MU 8-12 *Parar* 21-12 Aus 6-2-45
MV201 LFVIII M66 CHA 6MU 14-1-45 *Emp Dyn* 10-5 Ind 7-6 SOC 13-6-46
MV202 6MU 29-10-44 215MU 21-1-45 *N Z Star* 4-3 Aus 17-4
MV203 6MU 18-12-44 3PATP 3-3-45 *Clan Far* 10-3 Aus 6-5
MV204 CHA 6MU 14-10-44 215MU 13-2-45 *Clan Far* 10-3 Aus 6-5
MV205 LFVIII M66 CHA 6MU 2-12-44 82MU 17-12 *Mahad* 22-1-45 Ind 10-2 10S RIAF cd f/ld nr Jessore FACE 25-10-46 SOC 31-12
MV206 6MU 4-11-44 215MU 22-1-45 *N Z Star* 4-3 Aus 17-4
MV207 6MU 18-11-44 215MU 20-2-45 *Clan Far* 10-3 Aus 4-5

MV208 LFVIII M66 CHA 6MU 24-11-44 215MU 5-12 *Ing* 1-1-45 Ind 4-2 3S RIAF SOC 28-7 flew into gd Poridbidnur pilot kld 3-7-46

MV231 LFVIII M66 CHA 6MU 18-11-44 82MU 30-11 *Ing* 1-1-45 Ind 4-2 SOC 29-11

MV232 LFVIII M66 KEE 6MU 2-12-44 9MU 8-12 *Ing* 1-1-45 Ind 4-2 SOC 9-5-45

MV233 (P&S) CHA 6MU 18-11-44 215MU 27-2-45 *Clan Far* 2-3 Aus 4-5

MV234 LFVIII M66 9MU 21-11-44 215MU 21-2 *Ing* 1-1-45 Ind 4-2 SOC 29-8-46

MV235 6MU 6-11-44 215MU 2-1-45 *C o Cal* 4-1 Aus 27-2 Tunisia

MV236 LFVIII M66 CHA 6MU 18-11-44 82MU 30-11 *Ing* 1-1-45 Ind 4-2 9S e/fld on t/o Peshawar FACE 4-6-46 SOC 25-7

MV237 6MU 12-11-44 215MU 8-2-45 *N Z Star* 4-3 Aus 17-4

MV238 LFVIII M66 CHA 9MU 29-11-44 222MU 16-12 *Ing* 1-1-45 Ind 4-2 SOC 25-10

MV239 crash on test flt 6MU 20-3-45 23-4 *SSLS2820* 8-5 Aus 19-6 A58-758, Extant Scone, NSW, VH-HET.

MV240 6MU 16-10-44 215MU 23-10 *SSLS1973* 2-11 Aus 23-12

MV241 6MU 22-10-44 215MU 8-12 *Parar* 30-12 Aus 6-2-45

MV242 6MU 29-10-44 215MU 21-1-45 *N Z Star* 2-3-4 Aus 17-4

MV243 6MU 22-10-44 215MU 12-12 *SSLS2495* Aus 10-2-45

MV244 6MU 22-10-44 215MU 8-12 *Parar* 31-12 Aus 14-2-45

MV245 LFVIII M66 CHA 9MU 21-10-44 215MU 7-12 *Ing* 1-1-45 Ind 4-2-45 SOC 31-10-46

MV321 STN 6MU 15-9-44 82MU 26-9 *Horor* 15-10 Aus 30-11

MV322 6MU 8-10-44 215MU 14-10 *Ajax* 6-11 Aus 17-12

MV323 CHA 6MU 1-10-44 215MU 12-10 *Suss* 13-11 Aus 6-2-45

MV324 M66 6MU 13-10-44 215MU 23-10 *Suff* 18-11 Aus 23-12

MV325 KEE 6MU 1-10-44 215MU 7-10 *Suss* 13-11 Aus 14-2-45

MV326 LFVIII M66 KEE 9MU 1-10-44 82MU 15-10 *Marta* 30-10 Ind 8-12 SOC 5-4-46

MV327 LFVIII M66 CHA 9MU 5-10-44 82MU 15-10 *Marta* 30-10 Ind 8-12 CE SOC 21-6-45

MV328 LFVIII M66 KEE 9MU 9-11-44 82MU 18-11 *Ing* 1-1-45 Ind 4-2 SOC 30-1-47

MV329 LFVIII M66 KEE 9MU 7-11-44 82MU 18-11 *Ing* 1-1-45 Ind 4-2 SOC 25-4-46

MV342 6MU 27-10-44 215MU 2-1-45 *Bris Star* 4-1 Aus 5-3

MV343 LFVIII M66 9MU 6-11-44 215MU 4-12 *Ing* 1-1-45 SOC 27-3-47

MV344 6MU 29-10-44 215MU 1-2-45 *N Z Star* 4-3 Aus 17-4

MV345 LFVIII M66 KEE 6MU 2-11-44 222MU 11-11 *Ing* 1-1-45 Ind 4-2 155S ld f/ld Sumatra 13-2-46 SOC 30-1-47

MV346 CHA 6MU 10-11-44 215MU 13-2-45 *Clan Far* 10-3 Aus 4-5

MV398 LFVIII M66 CHA 9MU 22-7-44 222MU 30-7 *SSLS2019* 2-10 Ind 4-11 SOC 9-5-46

MV399 LFVIII M66 STN 9MU 27-7-44 76MU 12-8 *Avris* 13-9 Ind 29-10 SOC 24-4-47

MV400 LFVIII M66 KEE 6MU 29-7-44 76MU 11-8 *Avris* 13-9 Ind 29-10 SOC 31-5-45

MV401 LFVIII M66 STN 6MU 28-7-44 218MU 10-8 *H Prince* 1-9 Ind 15-10 SOC 18-10-45

MV402 LFVIII M66 CHA 9MU 25-7-44 215MU 2-10 *Ald Park* 27-10 Ind 19-11 SOC 5-7-45

MV403 LFVIII M66 6MU 1-8-44 76MU 8-8 *Avris* 13-9 Ind 29-10 is RIAF c/ld Indore 23-6-46 SOC 11-7

MV404 LFVIII M66 STN 9MU 29-7-44 76MU 11-8 *Marta* 30-10 Ind 8-12 SOC 1-6-47

MV405 LFVIII M66 KEE 6MU 29-7-44 76MU 11-8 *Avris* 13-9 Ind 29-10 SOC 11-10-45

MV406 LFVIII M66 STN 9MU 13-8-44 82MU 27-8 *SSLS2019* 2-10 Ind 4-11 FACE 20-6-47 SOC 31-7

MV407 LFVIII M66 6MU 30-7-44 76MU 6-8 *Avris* 13-9 Ind 29-10 SOC 18-10-45

MV408 LFVIII M66 KEE 6MU 29-7-44 76MU 11-8 *Avris* 13-9 Ind 29-10 SOC 14-2-46

MV409 LFVIII M66 CHA 28-7-44 76MU 12-8 *Avris* 13-9 Ind 29-10 SOC 30-1-47

MV410 LFVIII M66 KEE 6MU 12-8-44 215MU 21-8 *Ald Park* 7-10 Ind 19-11 SOC 27-9-45

MV411 LFVIII M66 STN 9MU 17-8-44 82MU 29-8 *SSLS2019* 2-10 Ind 4-11 FA FTR 5-4-45

MV412 LFVIII M66 9MU 18-8-44 215MU 27-8 *Ald Park* 7-10 Ind 19-11 SOC 11-4-46

MV413 LFVIII M66 STN 9MU 14-8-44 82MU 27-8 *SSLS2019* 2-10 Ind 4-11 SOC 30-1-47

MV414 LFVIII M66 9MU 2-8-44 82MU 29-8 *SSLS2019* 2-10 Ind 4-11 SOC 14-12-46

MV415 LFVIII M66 9MU 26-8-44 215MU 20-9 *Ald Park* 7-10 Ind 19-11 SOC 4-10-45

MV416 LFVIII M66 9MU 21-8-44 215MU 31-8 *Ald Park* 7-10 Ind 19-11 CE ops 31-5-45 SOC 6-6

MV417 LFVIII M66 6MU 26-8-44 82MU 2-9 *SSLS2019* 2-10 Ind 4-11 SOC 12-4-45

MV418 LFVIII M66 9MU 25-8-44 222MU 9-9 *Ald Park* 19-11 SOC 28-8-47

MV419 LFVIII M66 6MU 23-8-44 47MU 29-8 *Ald Park* 29-9 Ind 19-11 SOC 24-4-47

MV420 LFVIII M66 9MU 25-8-44 215MU 6-9 *Ald Park* 7-10 Ind 19-11 SOC 31-12-46

MV421 LFVIII M66 6MU 25-8-44 82MU 2-9 *SSLS2019* 2-10 Ind 4-11 SOC 30-1-47

MV422 LFVIII M66 6MU 25-8-44 82MU 8-9 *SSLS2019* 2-10 Ind 4-11 CE dbf SOC 10-1-46

MV423 LFVIII M66 9MU 24-8-44 215MU 3-9 *Ald Park* 7-10 Ind 19-11 SOC 31-12-46

MV424 LFVIII M66 9MU 24-8-44 82MU 2-9 *SSLS2019* 2-10 Ind 4-11 SOC 29-3-45

MV425 LFVIII M66 6MU 5-9-44 222MU 11-9 *Ald Park* 27-9 Ind 19-11 SOC 18-10-45

MV426 LFVIII M66 6MU 26-5-44 215MU 9-9 *Ald Park* 7-10 Ind 19-11 SOC 9-8-45

MV427 LFVIII M66 9MU 27-8-44 82MU 20-9 *Marta* 30-10 Ind 8-12 SOC 9-5-46

MV428 LFVIII M66 6MU 30-8-44 222MU 12-9 *Ald Park* 26-9 Ind 19-11 FACE 17-5-45 SOC 12-6

MV429 LFVIII M66 6MU 30-8-44 215MU 18-9 *Ald Park* 7-10 Ind 19-11 CE SOC 31-5-45

MV430 LFVIII M66 6MU 30-8-44 82MU 8-9 *Marta* 30-10 Ind 8-12 FACE 21-2-47 broken up SOC 26-6

MV431 LFVIII M66 6MU 8-8-44 222MU 12-9 *Ald Park* 27-9 Ind 19-11 SOC 7-6-45

MV432 LFVIII M66 6MU 5-9-44 215MU 9-9 *Ald Park* 7-10 Ind 19-11 SOC 1-6-47

MV433 LFVIII M66 9MU 31-8-44 222MU 9-9 *Ald Park* 26-9 Ind 19-11 SOC 26-7-45

MV434 LFVIII M66 6MU 30-8-44 82MU 8-9 *SSLS2019* 2-10 Ind 4-11 SOC for use as InsA/F 27-11-47

MV435 LFVIII M66 6MU 9-9-44 215MU 21-9 *Marta* 30-10 Ind 8-12 SOC 28-2-46

MV436 LFVIII M66 9MU 5-9-44 82MU 20-9 *Marta* 30-10 Ind 8-12 3S RIAF w/u ld Kolar 28-3-46 SOC 11-4

MV437 LFVIII M66 9MU 5-9-44 82MU 20-9 *Marta* 30-10 Ind 8-12 sold InAF 31-12-47

MV438 LFVIII M66 6MU 10-9-44 215MU 21-9 *Marta* 30-10 Ind 8-12 SOC 21-6-45

MV439 LFVIII M66 6MU 10-9-44 215MU *Marta* 30-10 Ind 8-12 SOC 25-7-46

MV440 LFVIII M66 9MU 8-9-44 82MU *Marta* 30-10 Ind 8-12 SOC 25-4-46

MV441 LFVIII M66 6MU 9-9-44 215MU 21-9 *Marta* 30-10 Ind 8-12 FACE 30-5-45 SOC 25-7

MV456 LFVIII M66 9MU 10-9-44 82MU 20-9 *Marta* 30-10 Ind 8-12 SOC 14-2-46

MV457 LFVIII M66 CHA 6MU 17-9-44 *Marta* 30-10 Ind 8-12 SOC 30-5-46

MV458 LFVIII M66 9MU 10-6-44 82MU 25-8 *Marta* 30-10 Ind 8-12 SOC 12-6-45

MV459 LFVIII M66 9MU 9-9-44 222MU 29-9 *Marta* 30-10 Ind 9-12 SOC 26-6-47

MV460 6MU 10-9-44 82MU 18-9 *SSLS1965* 21-9 Aus 8-11

MV461 6MU 11-9-44 82MU 18-9 *SSLS1965* 21-9 Aus 8-11

MV462 LFVIII M66 CHA 16-9-44 82MU 25-9 *Martaban* 30-10 Ind 8-12 SOC 31-7-47

MV463 6MU 16-8-44 82MU 13-9 *SSLS1965* 21-9 Aus 8-11

MV464 6MU 8-9-44 82MU 18-9 *SSLS1965* 21-9 Aus 8-11

MV465 6MU 10-9-44 82MU 21-9 *Sarpen* 26-9 Aus 1-1-45

MV466 M66 CHA 6MU 15-9-44 82MU 29-9 *Horor* 15-10 Aus 30-11

MV467 6MU 9-9-44 82MU 18-9 *SSLS1965* 21-9 Aus 8-11

MV468 6MU 10-9-44 82MU 21-9 *Port Fair* 15-10 Aus 24-11

MV469 6MU 15-9-44 82MU 27-9 *Port Fair* 15-10 Aus 24-11

MV470 CHA 6MU 15-9-44 82MU 27-9 *Port Fair* 15-10 Aus 24-11

MV471 CHA 6MU 16-9-44 82MU 27-9 *Port Fair* 15-10 Aus 24-11

MV472 CHA 6MU 18-9-44 82MU 27-9 *Horor* 15-10 Aus 30-11

MV473 KEE 6MU 17-9-44 82MU 27-9 *Horor* 15-10 Aus 30-11

MV474 CHA 6MU 17-9-44 82MU 27-9 *Horor* 15-10 Aus 30-11

MV475 KEE 17-9-44 82MU 26-9 *Port Fair* 15-10 Aus 24-11

MV476 CHA 6MU 18-9-44 82MU 28-9 *Horor* 15-10 Aus 30-11

MV477 6MU 23-9-44 82MU 29-9 *Horor* 15-10 Aus 30-11

MV478 6MU 25-9-44 82MU 4-10 *Horor* 15-10 Aus 30-11

MV479 6MU 25-9-44 82MU 3-10 *Horor* 15-10 Aus 30-11

MV480 LFVIII M66 9MU 23-9-44 215MU 6-10 *Marta* 30-10 Ind 8-12 SOC 27-3-47

MV481 6MU 29-9-44 215MU 6-10 *Suss* 13-11 Aus 6-2-45

MV482 6MU 21-10-44 82MU 17-12 *C o Cal* 18-1-45 Aus 27-2

MV483 LFVIII M66 6MU 27-9-44 222MU 3-10 *Marta* 30-10 Ind 8-12 155S air coll with MD403 cd Arnhemia Sumatra pilot kld FACE dbf 26-2-46 SOC 14-3

MV484 6MU 14-10-44 215MU 23-10 *Suff* 18-11 Aus 23-12

MV485 6MU 27-9-44 215MU 6-10 *Suss* 13-11 Aus 6-2-45

MV486 6MU 25-9-44 82MU 4-10 *Horor* 15-10 Aus 30-11

MV487 KEE 6MU 1-10-44 215MU 18-10 *SSLS1972* 6-11 Aus 17-2-45

MV499 CHA 6MU 1-10-44 215MU 12-10 *Suss* 8-11 Aus 6-2-45

MV500 CHA 1-10-44 215MU 12-10 *Suss* 13-11 Aus 6-2-45

MV501 CHA 6MU 1-10-44 215MU 12-10 *Suss* 13-11 Aus 6-2-45

MV502 6MU 13-10-44 215MU 23-10 *Suff* 18-11 Aus 23-12

MV503 CHA 6MU 2-10-44 215MU 14-10 *SSLS1972* 6-11 Aus 17-12

MV504 6MU 8-10-44 215MU 14-10 *Ajax* 6-11 Aus 17-12

MV505 6MU 13-10-44 215MU 23-10 *Ajax* 6-11 Aus 17-12

MV506 6MU 6-10-44 215MU *Suss* 13-11 Aus 6-2-45

MV507 6MU 15-10-44 215MU 23-10 *Suff* 18-11 Aus 23-12

MV508 no record

MV509 6MU 15-10-44 215MU 27-10 *Suff* 18-11 Aus 23-12

MV510 6MU 8-10-44 215MU 14-10 *Ajax* 6-11 Aus 17-12

MV511 6MU 15-10-44 215MU 27-10 *Suff* 18-11 Aus 23-12

MV512 6MU 15-10-44 215MU 23-10 *Suff* 18-11 Aus 23-12

MV513 6MU 15-10-44 215MU 27-10 *Suff* 18-11 Aus 23-12

MV514 6MU 15-10-44 215MU 9-12 *SSLS2495* 27-12 Aus 16-2

NH series all LF MkVIII Merlin M66

NH614 HFVIII M70 CHA 6MU 9-11-44 215MU 2-1-45 *C o Cal* 18-1 Aus 27-2

NH615 CHA 6MU 15-11-44 82MU 25-11 *Ing* 1-1-45 Ind 4-2 SOC 4-10

NH616 6MU 4-11-44 222MU 16-11 *Ing* 1-1-45 Ind 4-2 SOC 30-8

NH617 CHA 9MU 25-11-44 222MU 5-12 *Ing* 1-1-45 Ind 4-2 sold InA/F 29-12-47

NH618 CHA 6MU 18-11-44 82MU 24-11 *Ing* 1-1-45 Ind 4-2 SOC 26-6-47

NH619 CHA 9MU 18-11-44 215MU 29-11 *Ing* 1-1-45 Ind 4-2 2S RIAF en/fld on t/o Miranshaw pilot kld FACE dbf 12-9-46 SOC 30-1-47

NH620 KEE 6MU 14-11-44 215MU 27-11 *Ing* 1-1-45 Ind 4-2 SOC 11-4-46

NH621 KEE 9MU 20-11-44 222MU 30-11 *Ing* 1-1-45 Ind 4-2 SOC 11-4-46

NH622 M70 KEE 6MU 18-11-44 82MU 24-11 *Ing* 1-1-45 Ind 4-2 SOC 11-4-46

NH623 CHA 6MU 29-11-44 222MU 5-12 *Ing* 1-1-45 Ind 4-2 SOC 11-4-46

NH624 CHA 9MU 9-12-44 222MU 21-12 *Malad* 22-1-45 Ind 19-2 SOC 31-12-46

NH625 CHA 9MU 25-11-44 222MU 16-12 *Ing* 1-1-45 Ind 4-2 SOC 28-6

NH626 CHA 9MU 27-11-44 222MU 5-12 *Ing* 1-1-45 Ind 4-2 SOC 26-9-46

NH627 CHA 9MU 2-12-44 215MU *Malad* 22-1-45 Ind 19-2 SOC 31-10-46

NH628 CHA 6MU 29-11-44 215MU 9-12 *Ing* 1-1-45 Ind 4-2 SOC 31-10-46

NH629 CHA 6MU 24-11-44 215MU 6-12 *Ing* 1-1-45 Ind 4-2 SOC 30-1-47

NH630 KEE 9MU 2-12-44 215MU 25-12 *Malad* 22-1-45 Ind 19-2 SOC 31-12-46

NH631 LFVIII Griffon 65 KEE 6MU 16-12-44 222MU 5-1-45 *Malad* 22-1 Ind 19-2 sold InAF 31-12-47 extant InAF Mus Palam

NH632 CHA 9MU 8-12-44 222MU 21-12 *Ing* 1-1-45 Ind 4-2 SOC 28-6-45

NH633 6MU 17-12-44 222MU 31-12 *Malad* 22-1-45 Ind 19-2 SOC 31-7-47

NH634 9MU 3-1-45 *SSLS2545* 17-1 Ind 20-2 SOC 11-4-46

NH635 9MU 17-1-45 215MU 23-3 *Emp Dyn* 16-5-45 Ind 7-6 ACSEA 23-6 SOC 12-8-46

NH636 CHA 9MU 11-12-44 222MU 21-12 *Malad* 22-1-45 Ind 19-2 AFS strk by NH901 while parked Ambala 9-12-46 SOC 31-12

Sixth Order for 592 Spitfire Mk VIII dated 2 June 1943 Contract amended several times and finally reduced to PR XI and PR XIX. However, seven F MkVIII were also built to this order PA952 to 958 All LF M66

PA952 CHA 9MU 16-3-44 222MU 28-3 *C o Chy* 9-4 Ind 18-5 SOC 27-2-47

PA953 CHA 6MU 17-3-44 82MU 29-3 *Diomed* 19-4 Aus 27-6

PA954 CHA 6MU 17-3-44 82MU 27-3 *Kit Park* 6-4 Aus 19-6

PA955 STN 9MU 15-3-44 222MU 28-3 *C o Chy* 9-4 Ind 18-5 CE 24-5-45

PA956 CHA 9MU 6-3-44 82MU 12-3 *Berr* 29-3 Ind 12-5 SOC 12-2-45

PA957 KEE 6MU 18-3-44 82MU 27-3 *Kit Park* 6-4 Aus 19-6

PA958 CHA 6MU 12-3-44 82MU 21-3 *Kit Park* 6-4 Aus 19-6

Australia; JF820-825, 845-847, 869-872, 876-877, 884-885, 933-940, 942, 945, 966-967, JG104-107, 174-177, 191-192, 239, 262-267, 269-271, 275, 332, 342-343, 345-347, 350-356, 371-373, 376-377, 382, 385-387, 414-417, 419-425, 429-432, 465-468, 471-474, 481-482, 484-485, 543, 549, 556-557, 566, 603-605, 607, 609, 611, 613, 622, 650, 652-653, 655, 659, 664-666, 668, 684-685, 687, 689-691, LV644, 647, 649, 652, 657, 672, 727, 740, 750, MB959-960, 968, 970, 974, MD217, 221, 223, 226, 228, 231-232, 234, 238, 241, 251-253, 281, 283, 286, 296-300, 315, 317, 337-339, 344, 355, 372, 376, 380-381, 385, 388, 391, 396, MT502-503, 508-514, 517-519, 524-525, 539-543, 545, 547-550, 552, 593-594, 596, 607,618, 620-622, 624, 626, 630, 632, 635, 649-650, 655, 658, 672-673, 675, 681-682, 684, 703, 748, 767, 771, 778-779, 781-782, 787-788, 794, 816-817, 819-822, 829-831, 833-834, 890-900, 910, 914, MV112-117, 119-121, 123-125, 128-129, 132-133, 135-141, 144, 146-156, 169-200, 202-204, 206-207, 233, 235, 237, 239-244, 321-325, 342, 344, 346, 460-461, 463-479, 481-482, 484-487, 499-514, NH614, PA953-954 and 957-958.

French Air Force; JF296,591, JG257, MT627 and 791.

Indian Air Force; MT719, 746, 940, MV437, NH617 and 631.

Maintenance and Instructional Airframes; JF296(5835M), JG661(5832M), JG662(5833M), JG663(5834M), MT601(5829M), MT 602(5830M), MT603(5831M).

RNAS; JG661-663 and MT601-603.

Russia; LV677 and 743-744.

South African Air Force; JF294.

Two-seat trainer; MT818.

USAAF; JF345, 351, 354, 400, 416, 444, 456, 475, 511, 569, 576-577, 658, 660, 699, 706, 709, 873-874, 880, 894, 899, 930, 932, 949, 951-952, 954, JG108, 123, 157, 163, 165, 186, 242, 245, 248, 257, 317, 490, 492, 538 and 541.

JF661, Merlin 63, served with the USAAF in North Africa.

IN A SPITFIRE MEANT FOR TWO

When the Spitfire Mk I was delivered to the Royal Air Force in 1938 it was, at that time, an extremely sophisticated aeroplane. Training methods were based upon the biplane and new pilots were expected to make the transition with no experience of a fast monoplane with an enclosed cockpit, retractable undercarriage and a host of new innovations. That they were able to was a tribute to the training curriculum, but it was recognised that an interim type between the Spitfire fighter and the ab-initio trainer was a necessity for the pressure of war would result in a shorter period of training, and the subsequent switch to the monoplane fighter would raise many problems.

A two-seat training version of the Spitfire was originally conceived in 1941, some two years after the Hawker Hurricane was proposed in a similar form. There was a war-time, two-seat Spitfire, but this was a local, one-off modification converted by No 261 Squadron at Catania airfield, Sicily, in 1944. A second cockpit was installed in front of the original on a VC, and it was used mainly for communication duties. The Russians converted a Mk IX during the war by adding a second, closed cockpit behind the normal one. A photograph appears on page 324.

The idea of a two-seat trainer was revived in 1946 by Vickers and instead of a complete re-design it was decided to convert the basic Spitfire airframe for the role. First conversion was Mk VIII MT818 constructed in May 1944 and bought back from MAP. The conversion was completed at Chilbolton, Hampshire, and it first flew in August 1946 as N32.

MT818 was converted to the prototype T Mk VIII Trainer and carried the manufacturer's marks N32. It was later registered G-AIDN.

The Supermarine Specification 521 outlined details –

"The Supermarine two-seat trainer has been developed to fill a long-standing demand for a high-speed, single seat, fighter trainer. It is essentially a conversion of the Spitfire Mk VIII. The cockpits are of conventional layout with the front fully representative of an equivalent operational aircraft. It is normally occupied by the pupil and is placed 13½in further forward than on the standard Spitfire.

"The instructor's seat is mounted above that of the front and both cockpits having sliding and jettisonable hoods, the rear being more bulbous to allow a forward view along the side of the front cockpit. All essential instruments are duplicated. Fuel is carried forward of the front cockpit, with additional tanks in the wings."

On 22 August 1946 the new trainer had been registered as a civil aircraft with the marks G-AIDN, but was flown during the test flight period with B Condition marks N32. Mike Lithgow, Supermarine/Vickers test pilot, was of the opinion that the trainer differed from the fighter only in fore and aft stability control, and suggested that in order to prevent the aircraft tightening in turns with two pilots a 9½lb 'bob' weight be fitted in the elevator circuit. He said it was pleasant to fly with, or without, a passenger in the rear seat. One essential addition to the controls was an over-ride braking system in the instructor's cockpit. Access to the rear cockpit was difficult and it could not be opened in the air above 120mph. Empty weight was 6,020 lb with a maximum of 8,000.

In the Supermarine Specification provision was made for four .303 Browning machine guns. Lithgow pointed out there should be some provision for a gunsight in the rear cockpit. Lithgow put the prototype through a series of spinning trials and the aircraft behaved in a manner similar to that of the standard fighter. Following these trials G-AIDN was sent to Boscombe Down on 17 February for handling trials despite it being a civil type. It had a Merlin 66 engine, a Rotol four blade propeller and two machine guns in each wing. The tailplane was standard Mk VIII, but as a result of the early trials a length of angle metal 7¾in. long was fitted above and below the trailing edge of the elevator adjacent to the central cut-away. Maximum permissible speeds were Service 408 knots and Civil

348. Take off weight was 7,510lbs.

The Boscombe report stated – "The instructor's view was bad for take-off and landing and was unsuitable for gunnery instructions. A bad landing could be saved by instructions via the intercom, providing it was working. Both cockpits are cramped, particularly the rear, which was considered too narrow even for a pilot of average build. In the rear cockpit the undercarriage control lever, together with the trimmer wheel,

Semi cutaway drawing of Spitfire Mk VIII Trainer conversion as issued by Supermarine.

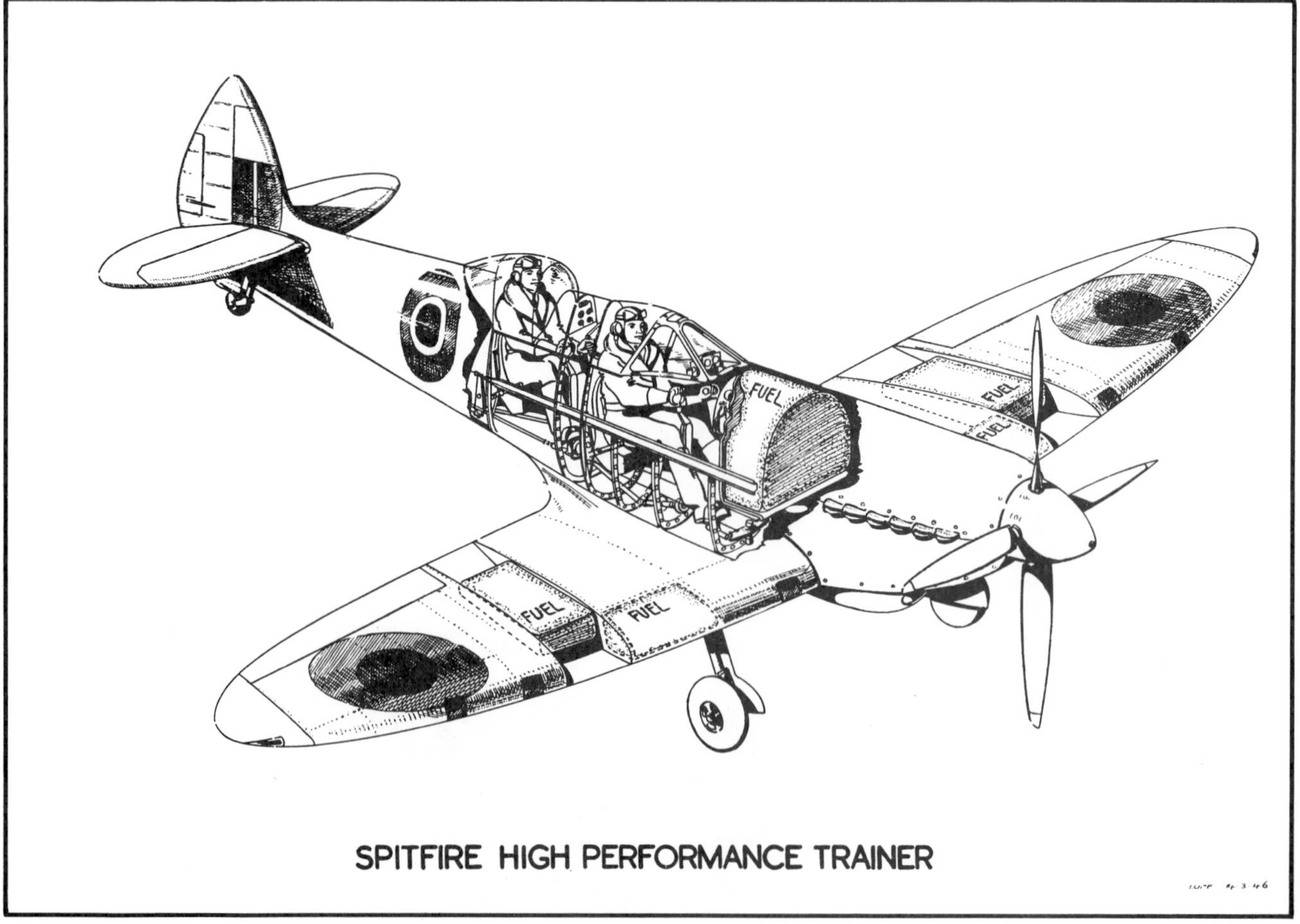

was almost out of reach. When the aircraft was flown from the rear cockpit there was a tendency for the tail to be raised too high on take-off. The rear windscreen gives a very distorted view and this was embarrassing when landing with the rear hood closed. The rear hood cannot be opened, or kept open, whilst the front hood is closed". The report concluded that the flying characteristics were satisfactory and similar to that of the Spitfire.

Flight Lieutenant L. R Colquhoun flew the new trainer to Belgium in June 1947 for demonstration and reported that the compass was approximately 15° out. The outward journey was made under contact conditions and a not very accurate compass course was steered. On the return, made above cloud and reliant upon the compass, it was a different story. When Colquhoun did break cloud he was still over sea and after a flight of 30 minutes was still over water. The compass deviation

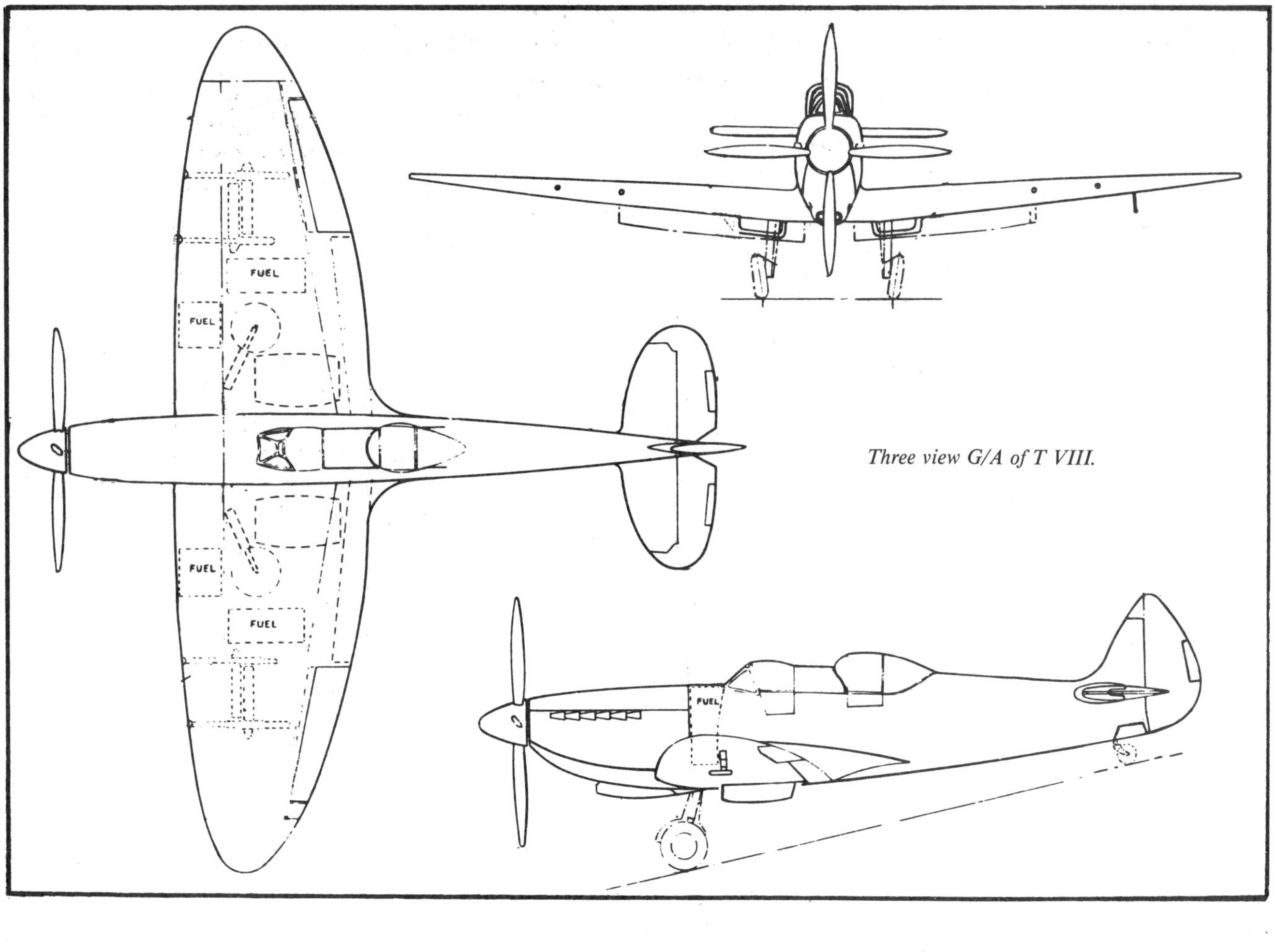

FUEL
FUEL
FUEL
FUEL
FUEL

Three view G/A of T VIII.

ranged between plus 2 and minus 9°. He reached England safely.

There was no demand for the Mk VIII Trainer and the only example built and flown was G-AIDN, but Quill visited Air Marshall Embry, Deputy Chief Training, on 2 February 1948, to discuss the possibility of supplying the RAF with a production version. Sir Basil made it clear that there was no question of the RAF requiring Spitfire Trainers. His reasons were (1) the Spitfire fighter was virtually extinct in RAF service, (2) as a basic advanced trainer the RAF was committed to certain types which had been designed to their specification. The Spitfire Trainer did not meet those requirements. (3) In reply to a suggestion that the Spitfire Trainer could be used by the Auxiliary Fighter Squadrons the answer was training methods of auxiliary pilots were about to be altered, and long term policy was to equip them with jet aircraft.

Sir Basil regretted that he could not present a case to the Air Ministry for asking for Spitfire Trainers and said that an order could be ruled out. As a matter of policy trainer versions of new operational fighters would be supplied concurrently with the single seat types. Quill tried again in December to get the RAF interested in the trainer for reserve units but policy was unchanged. However, at the end of March 1949 Fighter Command expressed an interest in the Spitfire Trainer as they thought there was a definite requirement for it in the Auxiliary Squadrons. Quill then visited Captain Charles Evans of the Royal Navy for a discussion on the Trainer as a possible replacement of the Harvard as an intermediate type. Quill did point out that RAF Reserve Command was re-considering its attitude towards the Supermarine aircraft and Captain Evans suggested a demonstration at the School of Naval Air Warfare.

G-AIDN was demonstrated to RAF Reserve Command at White Waltham aerodrome on 11 April and the outcome was a probable requirement for production models as a stepping stone between the Harvard and Spitfire 22 of the Auxiliary Squadrons. The requirement was for approximately 20 aircraft, and the only proviso was how best to present the case to the Air Ministry. Nothing did happen to produce an order for the Mk VIII trainer and it faded into history.

T Mk VIII

Wing. Planform elliptical; section NACA Series 2200; span 36′ 10″; incidence° root +2, tip $-\frac{1}{2}$; dihedral° 6; thickness% root 13.2, tip 6; aspect ratio 5.68; area sq ft nett 220, gross 242; chord (geometric) 6.38, mean aerodynamic 6ft 8in. Ailerons area sq ft 18.9; chord (ma); movement° up 26, down 19; droop $\frac{3}{8}$in. Flaps area sq ft 15.6; movement° down 85. Wing loading lb/sq ft 30·6; power loading lb hp 5·6.

Tailplane. Area sq ft 31.46; chord(ma) 4.1; incidence° root 0, tip $\pm\frac{1}{2}$; dihedral° 0. Elevators area sq ft 13.26; movement° up 28, down 23. Tab area sq ft 0.38; movement° up 20, down 7. Fin area sq ft 4.61. Rudder area sq ft 8.23;. Tab area sq ft 0.35; movement° port 12, starbd 12.

Undercarriage. Wheels Dunlop AH2061; tyres Dunlop 7-59-10; oleo pressure lb/sq in. Tailwheel fixed castoring. Dunlop AH2184; tyre Dunlop Ecta 3-00-4.

Engine/s. Merlin 66 1,315hp at take off.

Propeller/s. Rotol four blade. Diameter 10ft 9in.

Capacity. Fuselage tank 39 gals, wing leading edge 2 x 12¾, outer wing 2 x 14½. Total 93½ gals, plus 30 gal o/ld tank.

Oil. 7½ gals.

Armament. 4 x .303 Colt Browning machine guns.

Gunsight. Gyro.

Performance Max speed (FS), 393 mph @ 20,000ft; 362 (MS) @ 9,000; 326 (MS) @ SL. Rate of climb (FS) 3,890ft min @ 18,000; (MS) 4,570 @ 7,000; (MS) 4,540 @ SL. Service ceiling 40,600ft (100 ft min). Range cruise 240 miles (1.03 hr) @ 20,000ft. Average cruise speed 232 mph. Miles per gal 6.51. Take off 435 yards. Stall 80 mph. With 30 gal o/ld tank 418 miles.

Weights. Max permissible 7,400lb.

Several views of Spitfire Trainer N32 (ex MT818).

Bearing civil marks G-AIDN and race No.99, N32 became the property of the Hampshire Aeroplane Club.

G-AIDN in new paint scheme.

"OVER MY DEAD BODY"

"I understand that Rolls-Royce have suddenly produced the Merlin 61 out of the hat and claim for it a performance equivalent to the Merlin 45 at lower altitudes, and at higher altitudes to the Merlin 60. If the engine is proved in service to be capable of this performance it will be a most valuable advance, but we must have proper trials before we can swing over to it entirely. It is the ordinary Spitfire Mk V that I am worried about. This is the mainstay of the Spitfire first line strength for it is proving superior to the Me109 and we cannot run any risks with it. By the time the Merlin 61 is proved it seems to me we shall be into Spitfire F Mk IV production". Thus read an extract of the minutes of a meeting of the Air Staff on 24 June 1941, the speaker being the DTD Verney.

It was a most reasonable statement to make for the Spitfire V was, indeed, able to cope satisfactorily with enemy fighters when carrying the air war to the Continent, and there appeared no great urgency for a Spitfire with a re-worked Merlin engine. The new, Griffon-powered Mk IV was well into its test programme and production models had been promised by the end of the year. However, on 6 November that same year the DTD's message to the Air Staff was completely different in emphasis for he said – "I want to recommend to the Air Staff for adopting a new version of the Spitfire engined with the Merlin 61. The airframe is essentially the Spitfire Mk III (N3297). It is essential that the immediate aim would be to transfer all Spitfire production by Supermarine from the Spitfire Mk V to the new aircraft, and production deliveries could begin by mid-1942".

What event had occurred to make the normally cautious Verney issue such a statement which was diametrically opposed to that he had made almost five months previously? The event was, of course, the appearance of the Fw190, the 'Butcher Bird', which was to pose as big a threat to the Royal Air Force as did the 'Fokker Menace' that had swept all before it twenty-three years previously in the first World War. The Fw190 first appeared in September 1941 and it was painfully obvious that the Spitfire Mk V was no match for it. As related in the previous chapter the Spitfire Mk VIII was under development but owing to production difficulties would not be available for squadron service for a considerable time.

So serious was the Fw190 threat that the Air Staff was to issue a directive on 13 November 1941 halting all but essential RAF operations over Northern Europe, and a period of intensive pilot training embarked upon. Operations began once again in early 1942 and Fighter Command soon ran into problems with the new German fighter when two of the German Navy's capital ships sailed through the English Channel under an umbrella of Fw190s on 11 February 1942. After a breather, operations started once again the following month with RAF fighters concentrating on ground targets, and the battle continued for several months. At the end of the period Fighter Command had lost 335 aircraft, the majority of which were the Spitfire Mk V. This high rate of loss was unacceptable to Fighter Command, so much so that on 13 June Air Marshall Sholto-Douglas was instructed by the Air Staff to curtail all operations. The balance of air power had turned firmly against the RAF, and the decisive factor was the Fw190. What operations which did take place were limited to coastal targets, in much the same manner of operations being conducted by the Luftwaffe against South Coast English towns.

Although the situation seemed insoluble for the foreseeable future an event had taken place the previous April which was, eventually, to help overcome the Fw190 problem sooner than was expected. The F Mk III programme had been abandoned; the prototype N3297 returned to Rolls-Royce for use as a test bed. The engine currently under development was the Merlin 60, designed for use in an high altitude version of the Wellington bomber. Mr Hives had asked the question – "What would be the result if a Merlin 60 was installed in a Spitfire?" The answer was soon forthcoming and the Spitfire/Merlin 60 combination made its first flight on 27 September 1941, just seven days after the 'Butcher Bird' was reported in action.

The Air Ministry and Verney were informed of the event and their interest was immediate, and as a result the latter made his statement of 6 November, and to speed up the test flight programme a second Spitfire, R6700, a Mk I, arrived at Hucknall on 13 October for conversion and made its first flight with the new engine on 6 January 1942. Although at that time plans were still firm for large scale production of the F Mk VIII, an interim type (such as the Merlin 45 engined Mk Is while waiting for the production of F Mk III) was urgently needed, and official thinking was that a small conversion/production run of such a type with the Merlin 61 could serve the RAF successfully until the Mk VIII was available in quantity.

As a result of this thinking the Air Ministry decided to convert a number of their newest Spitfires, the Mk V, to the

N3297, prototype F Mk III, Merlin XX engine, was converted to the Mk IX prototype with the installation of a Merlin 61 and Rotol four blade propeller by Rolls-Royce in September 1941. It is seen here at Boscombe Down in October for initial trials.

AB197 was converted to the second prototype Mk IX by Rolls-Royce 24 May 1942. It had the Merlin 60 engine.

AB505, HF IX, with Merlin 77 and Rotol six blade contra-prop with a pitch range of 35°. Ballast was installed in the tail position to bring the CoG within acceptable limits. After trials at Boscombe Down the aircraft was returned to Supermarine, who removed the propeller unit and installed it on a second Mk IX.

AB499 with frontal, close fitting, anti-glare exhaust shrouds, Boscombe Down, March 1943.

BS139, Boscombe Down, December 1942, with multi-ejector, flame damping fishtails on exhaust system.

Merlin 61 configuration and to speed trials of the combination AB196 and 197 arrived at Hucknall on 7 and 12 December respectively, and both flew with their new engines on 26 February (AB186) and 27 March (AB197) 1942. In the intervening period R6700 had been transferred back to Supermarine on 7 January, the day after its first flight with a Merlin 61, and made two, short handling flights on the same day. It went into the works for minor modifications and was ready again for trials on 10 February. N3297 had been at Boscombe Down since 20 October 1941 and R6700 followed it on 4 March 1942. AB196 went to Vickers, Worthy Down, for trials, while AB197 followed the first two aeroplanes to Boscombe Down.

Official interest in the converted airframes had quickened and four more Mk Vs were chosen as development aircraft. AA873, the first production F Mk VC with the 4 × 20mm cannon wing, went to Rolls-Royce on 14 February; AB501 to Morris Motors, Oxford for conversion on 28 July; AB505 was converted by Rolls-Royce during May and AB507 arrived at Hucknall on 13 February. Thus was born the second most successful Spitfire variant, the F Mk IX.

It might appear that the Air Staff as a whole were satisfied with the new situation, but this was not so for one Air Marshall had serious reservations and went on record as saying that the Mk IX Spitfire would fly – "Over my dead body". It was a most unfortunate remark and, indeed, prophetic for he was to be killed in an accident soon after making his statement. Another senior staff member asked – "What loss of Spitfire production is likely during turnover from Merlin 46 to Merlin 61? It appears that the Spitfire with the Merlin 61 is not such a good a fighter as the Mk V with the Merlin 46 at 17-23,000 feet." But, Sholto-Douglas was convinced and ordered a further six Mk Vs converted to take the Merlin 61, and of these three were to go to Farnborough for – "engine thrashing" and three to Boscombe Down for high altitude trials.

The Air Ministry Certificate of Design for the Spitfire F Mk III, Merlin 61 conversion, N3297, and for R6700 'Spitfire Special', was issued on 1 April 1942. Both had Mark I wings without armament, an auw of 6,800lb and a maximum speed at 13,000 feet of 310mph. The weighing and CoG determination of AB196, the first Mk V conversion, took place at Worthy Down on 28 April and the results were – B wing, tare 5,730lb; auw 7,475; landing 6,750. A wing, tare 5,700lb; auw 7,241; landing 6,393 A total of 168 modifications had been made. R6700 returned to Worthy Down in August for propeller trials, the results of which were –

	Hydulignum	Dural	Jablo
Max speed @ 28,800ft	417	416	411
FS gear @ 35,000ft	404	402.5	397
MS gear @ 17,600ft	392	390.5	385
MS gear @ 23,000ft	387	384	378
Service ceiling (ft)	43,900	43,400	42,800
Operational	41,900	41,000	41,000
Rate of climb (ft/min)	2900 @ 27,600	2000	2800
FS gear	1400 @ 35,000	1020	1350
MS gear	3350 @ 14,500	3200	3400
	2700 @ 20,000	2740	2610
Time to height (mins) FS gear	16.1 (40,000ft)	20	16.9

The propellers were manufactured by Rotol and all had a diameter of 10ft 9in.

Cooling trials with N3297 were completed between January and April 1942, and fuel system tests with an immersed fuel pump by 1 May. Fuel was gravity fed into the bottom fuselage tank and then to the engine by pump, normal Spitfires having independent tanks and pumps. The fuel was heated before feeding into the tanks. It was clear that satisfactory operation of the Merlin 61 with a diaphragm or pressure carburetter would depend upon modification of the system. The self sealing tank and Mareng wing bags had made it more complicated. Fuel consumption trials followed and the results showed that for weak mixture cruising in level flight was normal, as applied to the Merlin 61, but at maximum power consumption was extremely heavy. Trials of weak mixture over 35,000ft were not possible because of engine surge. Final trials involved comparative tests with three types of propeller similar to those tested on R6700 and with .42 and .477 gears.

In order that the Royal Air Force could put a number of similar aircraft into service as quickly as possible Supermarine were ordered to instal Merlin 61 engines into 100 F Mk VC airframes on 18 April 1942, and all were to be delivered to Fighter Command by the end of June. In the event Supermarine converted 52 airframes and Rolls-Royce the remaining 48. Designation of the new Spitfire was F Mk IX and production proper began as off-sets from the Fifth Order of Contract B.19713/39, which was originally raised for Mk Is and later changed to Mk Vs and dated October 1940. The Spitfires were the BR and BS serial ranges and armament was either the 'B' and 'C' wing. First Squadrons to be equipped with the new mark were No. 64 at Hornchurch in June 1942, followed by No. 611 in July and Nos. 401 and 402 (Canadian) in August. The 'E' wing of two cannon and two .5in Brownings was introduced on to models at the end of the production run. Early production aircraft had the original Mk V fin and rudder, but later variants featured the broad-chord, pointed rudder. The reduced area fuselage and 'tear-drop' cockpit cover was another late innovation.

One of the first converted Mk Vs was delivered by Rolls-Royce to Worthy Down for weighing on 28 January 1943. The aircraft, EN357, had a Merlin 61 and Rotol four blade wooden propeller. Tare weight 5,605lb, auw 7,300; with 30 gal overload tank 7,591; landing 6,490. The weighing and CoG determination of the first production aircraft, BR581, took place at Worthy Down on 5 June 1943. With 'B' wing, tare 5,717lb, auw 7,407; with 30 gal overload tank 7,698; landing 6,624. 'A' wing, tare 5,687lb, auw 7,173; with 30 gal overload tank 7,447. The Certificate of Design for the Type 361 Production Spitfire F Mk IX was issued on 16 October and it stated – "This Type Record covers the modification of the Mark VC aeroplane by substitution of the Merlin 61 engine for the normal 45 or 46. To offset the increased weight of the powerplant the armament is limited to (a) 2 cannons and 4 Browning guns (b) 8 Browning guns. All up weight for (a) 7,400lb (b) 7,150. Maximum level speed at 9,750 feet 330mph." Addendum No. I covered the Spitfire Mk IX Production with the Merlin 61 boosted to 25lb sq in and HP raised from a maximum of 1,650 (18lb boost) at 9,750ft to 2,100hp at 10,500ft. Addendum No.3 was for the Mk IX with two .5in Brownings in lieu of the four .303s raising the auw to 7,500lb. The Addendum also covered the Spitfire F Mk IXE with standard fuselage and the Mk IXE with 'tear-drop' canopy and rear view fuselage, rear fuselage fuel tanks and clipped wings. Auw was 7,890lb (standard fus) and 7,950 (RV fus). Addendum No. 4 concerned the Mk IXE in the bomber and long range escort conditions. The table on page 310 lists various permissible loadings – F Mk IXE standard fuselage, rear fuel tank.

For the F Mk IXE with rear view fuselage, rear fuel tanks. As for standard fuselage except rear tank restricted to 66 gallons. In the nil overload condition with 66 gals in rear tank the bomb load was a 250 or 500lb bomb on a fuselage carrier. Later loadings could consist of 2 x 250lb wing, plus 1 x 500lb fuselage bomb, no overload fuel or rear tank, auw 9,059; or 2 x 250lb wing bombs plus 90 gal overload tank, no rear fuel, auw 9,250lb; or 1 x 170 gal overload tank only, auw 9,500lb.

The first production Mk IX from Castle Bromwich was JK395 and it was weighed at Worthy Down on 16 March 1943.

BS274 carried an incorrect serial number throughout its entire service life. There never was a BF serial range for the Spitfire and it is thought the mistake was a result of a misunderstood telephone conversation. It was used for many trials and is seen here at Boscombe Down after conversion from Mk V to Mk IX standard. It was eventually converted to the T Mk IX trainer configuration and sold to Holland.

Below: 'BS274 was used for trials with the 170 gallon overload tank. Right is the normal tank before modification to enable it to fit over the Mk IX's intake and left, after modifications.

O/ld fuel gals	rear tank	RPs inner	RPs outer	bombs wing	bombs fus
50	74	2 × 100lb (60lb head)	as inner	—	—
		or 1 × 180lb (60lb hd)	as inner	—	—
		or 1 × 300lb (100lb head)	—	—	—
90	—	as above	as above	—	—
90	74	2 × 100lb (60lb hd)	as inner . . .	or 1 × 120lb (smoke)	—
90	74	—	—	1 × 250lb (or on fus)	—
—	—	—	—	1 × 250lb or 1 × 120lb (smoke)	as wing

Merlin 63 and Rotol four blade wooden propeller and 226 modifications incorporated. It had a tare of 5,605 and an auw of 7,301lb. Castle Bromwich was now employing batteries of infra-red lamps for paint drying, which was reduced from hours to as many minutes. Also, the new system dried from the metal outwards expelling the paint solvents which were trapped by the normal method. This resulted in a longer lasting finish. EN498 in the same condition had the same tare but was eleven pounds over normal auw.

The new Mk II IFF was specified for the Mk IX and a contract placed with Ferranti Ltd., after approval of the unit by RAE Farnborough in January 1942. The first production set was ready by 3 March and in order that sufficient quantities would be ready for installation in the forthcoming production Mk IX airframes, examples of the set were sent to the British Purchasing Commission in August for quantity production in America. SME Mk I tensometers were to be issued to Spitfire Squadrons as standard equipment as from November 1942, and it was the Air Ministry's aim to re-equip all single engine fighter squadrons with the Mk IX from May 1943.

EXTENDING THE RANGE

Range of the Spitfire had always presented a problem and

Three views of BS428 during trials with a fuselage mounted 500 lb bomb, February 1943. Auw with Browning guns removed was 7,805lb.

EN314 was the trials aircraft for the MacLaren radiator protection scheme. It is seen here on test with a 200 gallon, torpedo, overload tank.

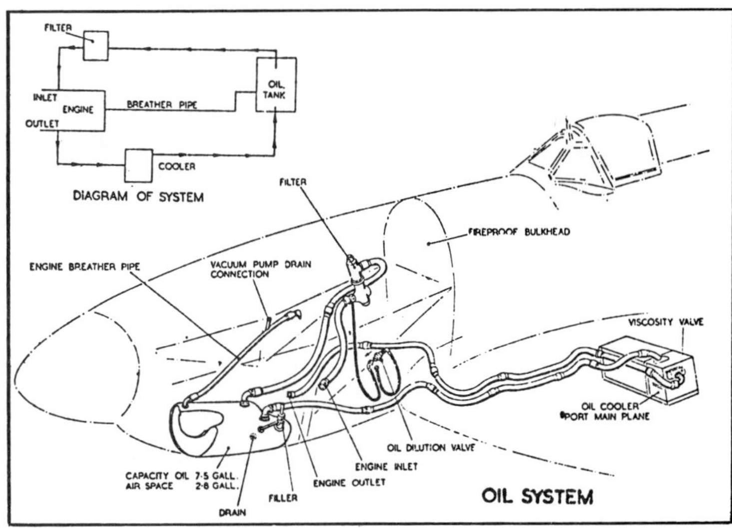

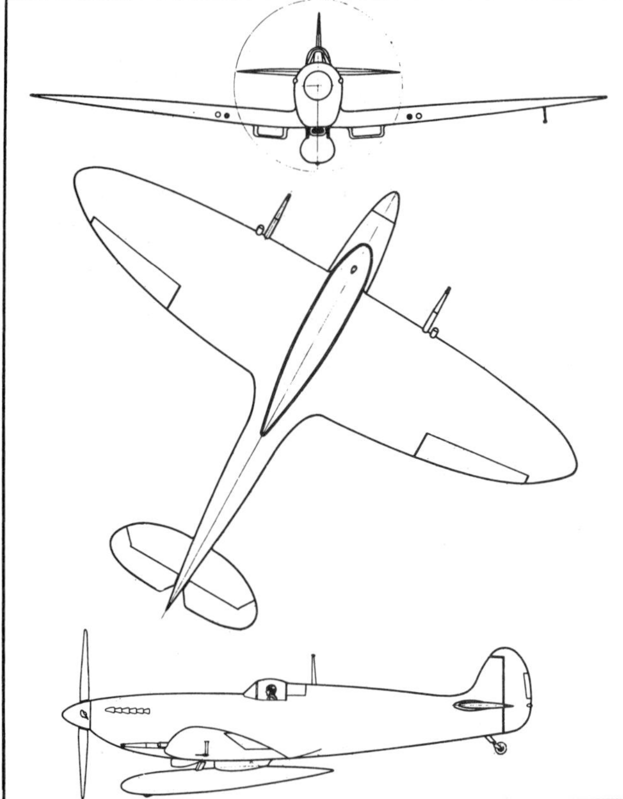

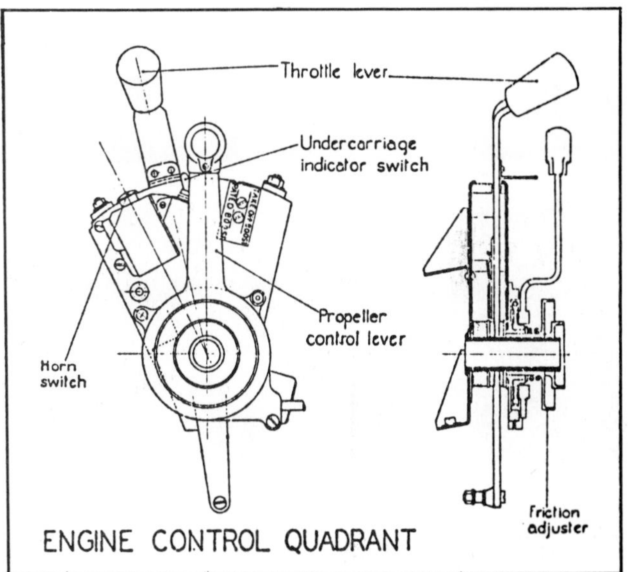

parallel with engine and airframe development went the jettisonable, flush fitting, overload 'slipper' tanks. One answer was development of the rear fuselage tank which could accommodate 72 gallons of fuel. A Technical report of Vickers describes the installation—The Vickers long-range fuel installation is partially represented by Spitfire IX ML186 which has the normal pressurised Spitfire IX 87 gallon main fuel tank, plus an additional 75 gallons (nominal) tank in the rear fuselage behind the pilot's seat. This feeds into the engine pump through an electrically driven immersed pump. In addition there is provision for carrying an under-fuselage 'slipper' drop tank of 90 gallons. Further increases of the fuel capacity are under consideration and these comprise fitting a Spitfire Mk VIII type leading edge tank of $13\frac{1}{2}$ gallons capacity in each wing, pressurised to feed into the main tanks, fitting a Mk VIII type main tank of 100 gallons capacity in lieu of the existing 87 gallon and increasing the oil tank size by three gallons. This equates to—Main fuel tank 87 gals, auxiliary rear fus tank 70gals, total internal capacity of ML186 157gals. Two L/E tanks of $13\frac{1}{2}$gals each 27gals. Additional fuel due to Mk VIII main tanks 13gals. Total proposed internal capacity 197gals. Auxiliary slipper drop tank 90gals. Total proposed capacity 287gals.

The problem with all this fuel, and associated increased weight, was stability for as fuel was burned off the CoG shifted, and before the Spitfire could begin to operate as a normal fighter the rear fuel tank had to be emptied. Flt Lt Havercroft was the first pilot to test ML186 on 17 January 1945 and fully loaded the Spitfire weighed 8,275lbs making it ride hard over rough ground. Take-off run was extended and the Spitfire reached 78mph before leaving the ground. Longitudinal instability started when a speed of 140mph was reached and as speed increased so pitching was more pronounced. When flaps and undercarriage were lowered pitching tended to disappear. During climb conditions the pilot had to fly the aircraft all the time for the control column could not be released or grip slackened without a divergence of course. At fast cruising , 245mph at 12,000ft, it was necessary to use the control stick continuously to damp out pitching and the aircraft could not be trimmed. In steep turns acceleration increased rapidly and a moderate push force was needed to prevent build up. If the push was overdone negative 'G' was experienced and pull had to be applied. After 35 gallons of fuel from the rear tank was used the aircraft stabilised.

A second scheme was a project by the Americans who modified two Spitfire Mk IXs, MK210 and MK317. In these the internal fuel capacity had been increased by fitting a 43 gallon tank in the fuselage behind the pilot's seat and two leading edge tanks, each of $16\frac{1}{2}$gals. Additional fuel was carried externally in two P-51 Mustang type drop tanks, each of 62gals capacity and suspended under the wings on P-51 bomb racks. With all this fuel the Spitfires weighed 10,150lb and the undercarriage was fully compressed. Also, oil tank capacity had been increased to 20gals. The still air range of the modified Spitfires was approximately 1,600 miles while the Vickers scheme was about 1,400, but the latter could be extended to 1,650 miles by an increase in internal fuel capacity. The American modified Spitfire handled better than the Vickers and was safer for reinforcing.

In addition to the large overload tanks a 30 and 45 gallon had been designed for the Mk IX and the loss of performance

The MacLaren scheme showing the front and side grids in position. These grids were made of bakelised linen sheets with electro-deposited copper moulded between the sheets. The grids were connected to the gunsight switch so that when a pilot was about to go into action, and there was the possibility of a radiator suffering damage, the protection scheme would operate. If the radiators were damaged a red light showed in the cockpit (see photo above) indicating the grid had been pierced. Soleniod relay switches then operated valves which cut off coolant flow through the damaged radiator and switched it to the undamaged unit. Photo, below, shows the coolant pump inlet equipped with special valves.

associated with the former's drag was between 5 and 12mph. The 30 gallon tank was tested on BS118, the 45 gallon on BS403 and a 90 gallon unit on EN498. BS403 was also flown with a 45 gallon Hurricane drop tank held in place by means of two straps and an adaptor bracket. This tank would not jettison from the Spitfire at speeds above 220mph.

Spitfire IX BS310 had a Merlin 66 engine installed for performance trials by the manufacturers and maximum speed in MS gear was a surprising 372mph at 8,200ft. In FS gear at 19,500ft it rose to 404. Rate of climb (MS) 4,850ft/min at 6,000ft and FS gear 4,500ft/min at 16,500ft. Auw 7,260lb. The Spitfire was then fitted with a Merlin 70 engine and performance improved to a maximum level speed (MS) 383mph at 13,400ft, FS gear 409 at 25,200ft. Maximum rate of climb (MS) 4,440ft/min at 11,000ft, FS gear 3,800ft/min at 21,000ft. Spitfire BS118 returned practically the same performance figures with a Merlin 61 engine (.42 reduction gear) and an 11ft 1in diameter Rotol hydulignum propeller for an auw of 7,280lb.

Large numbers of Spitfire Mk IXE were scheduled to serve in North Africa and the Far East and performance figures were required for a IX fitted with a tropical air filter. BS310 was fitted with a Spitfire Mk VIII intake and on trials maximum speed dropped from 381 to 375mph. An attempt to further increase top speed resulted in NH236 being modified with the installation of a specially calibrated Merlin 61 and a high speed, three blade de Havilland propeller. Thrust was measured by a pitot comb installation on the side of the engine cowling, plus four additional pitot heads on the wings. The propeller was effective up to heights of 15,000ft but after that the CS unit was unable to control the pitch. NH236 forced landed on one occasion at Wisley on 8 April 1948 and crashed on 14 September. Trials were discontinued.

Results obtained with BS310 with the two types of intakes were–

	Temperate	Tropical
(1) MS gear		
Max level speed (mph)	381	375
@ feet	15,700	14,900
Level speed @ SL (mph)	313	309
Level speed @ 20,000ft	376	369
(2) FS gear		
Max level speed (mph)	413	397
@ feet	28,000	25,600
Level speed @ 25,000ft	399	395
@ 30,000ft	411	392

Cooling drag of the aircraft with temperate intake was estimated at 8% of the total and at 12% for the tropical unit. The two stage supercharger complicated matters because of the need to cool the charge air after supercharging, for the size of intercoooling radiator block per HP dissipated was roughly twice the proportion needed in the main radiator. BS310 was next fitted with a Rolls-Royce RM 9SM engine with a .477 reduction gear, plus a Rotol, four blade, 10ft 9in diameter propeller with a fine pitch setting of 22° 20′ for performance tests on 23 February 1943. Results were—maximum speed (MS gear) 363mph @ 7,300ft; FS gear, 398 @ 21,000. Rate of climb (MS) 4,900ft/min @ 4,800ft, (FS) 4,050ft/min @ 18,000.

Supermarine and Rolls-Royce converted a total of 278 Mk Vs to the new standard and all had been delivered by March 1944, by which time the true production Mk IXs were also in service. No 64 Squadron, based at Hornchurch, was the first to be re-equipped after extensive trials with the converted aeroplanes. The first production aircraft reached the squadron on 6 July and operations with the type started on the 28th. Along with squadrons Nos 81, 122 and 154, No 64 took part in a sweep over France without contacting the enemy, but two days later the squadron met nine Fw190s and shot one down. Later the same day while escorting a bombing mission three more 190s were destroyed over the target and a fourth on the return flight. It augured well for the new Spitfire.

The Mk IX served in all theatres, including the Middle East, and after helping to chase the Afrika Korps out of North Africa was one of the first Allied fighters to land in Sicily. With the 8th Army the Mk IX crossed the Straits of Messina and pushed up the 'boot' of the Italian mainland. Meanwhile in anticipation of the Normandy landings, 'Operation Overlord', the new variant took part in the softening-up process which began building up from November 1943. The formation of the Allied Expeditionary Air Force was completed by 1 May 1944 with Air Chief Marshal Sir T. Leigh-Mallory as CinC. Concurrent with the softening-up period was 'Operation Pointblank' aimed at the reduction of fighters of the Luftwaffe, and by March 1944 2,950 had been destroyed. On 6 June 1944, D-Day,

MA235 leaving a Ferry Pilot's School for delivery. It went to No. 341 Squadron and was finally sold to the RHAF in March 1948.

nine Spitfire squadrons helped provide top cover for Allied troops and the first Mk IX to land in the bridgehead was MJ339 because of engine failure. On the same day 23 Spitfires of Nos 441, 442 and 443 Squadrons dropped 23,500lb bombs on the giant Wurzburg radar installations at Cap D'Antifer, scoring nine direct hits. Spitfires from Nos 26 and 63 Squadrons made 76 sorties on D-Day acting as spotters for naval gunfire. Forty-six squadrons were available for action on D-Day, plus nine for Home Defence. The first British Squadrons to land in France were Nos 130 and 303 at 1200hrs on D-Day plus four on a strip in the Gold Beach area.

By 10 June No 144 Wing comprising Nos 441, 442 and 444 Squadrons, RCAF, were operating from make-shift strips in the lodgement area, and as the ground forces continued their advance into France the long-awaited V-1 flying bomb assault against Southern England began on the 13th. 'Operation Crossbow' was launched to attack and destroy the launch sites for in the first nine days over 2,000 bombs were launched and their numbers increased every day. Among the many types of aircraft chasing them was the Tempest, Typhoon, Meteor and Spitfire Mk IX. The latter had to be pushed very hard to catch the 'Vengeance' weapon, but a number were stripped down to basic equipment; all surfaces cleaned of paint and polished, and 150 octane fuel used to boost performance. By the end of June the AEAF had 48 Squadrons of Spitfires in operation—two PR, two ASR and the remainder fighter/fighter bombers.

THE HIGH FLYING MK IX

As a result of the experience gained with the Spitfire Mk VIII, which had a limited production run, RAE Farnborough formulated the factors affecting the design of a high altitude fighter, these being weight, wing plan form, propeller efficiency and supercharged height at ceiling, the most promising stated as increasing supercharged height and wing span. Increasing solidity of the Spitfire propeller also increased overall efficiency by about 8% at heights above the supercharged heights. After allowances for increased weight, maximum rate of climb was increased by about 20% and absolute ceiling by 1,300ft. A larger diameter propeller provided a 25% increase in rate of climb at 30,000ft and a ceiling increase of 600ft. Weight was the major factor and the point made was that a twelve gun fighter is useless if it cannot operate at a ceiling at which four gun aircraft could. An increase in span produced a decrease in drag power over the whole range, but the weight factor had to be watched and propeller match to the aircraft became important.

Using the RAE Report as a basis the second variant of the F Mk IX was produced—the HF. The first HF IX was the now familiar conversion; the airframe chosen (AB505) fitted with a Merlin 61 at Hucknall in May 1942. Following upon the service trials at RAF Hornchurch it was returned to Hucknall in July and a Merlin 77 (similar to the Merlin 76 but with cabin blower)

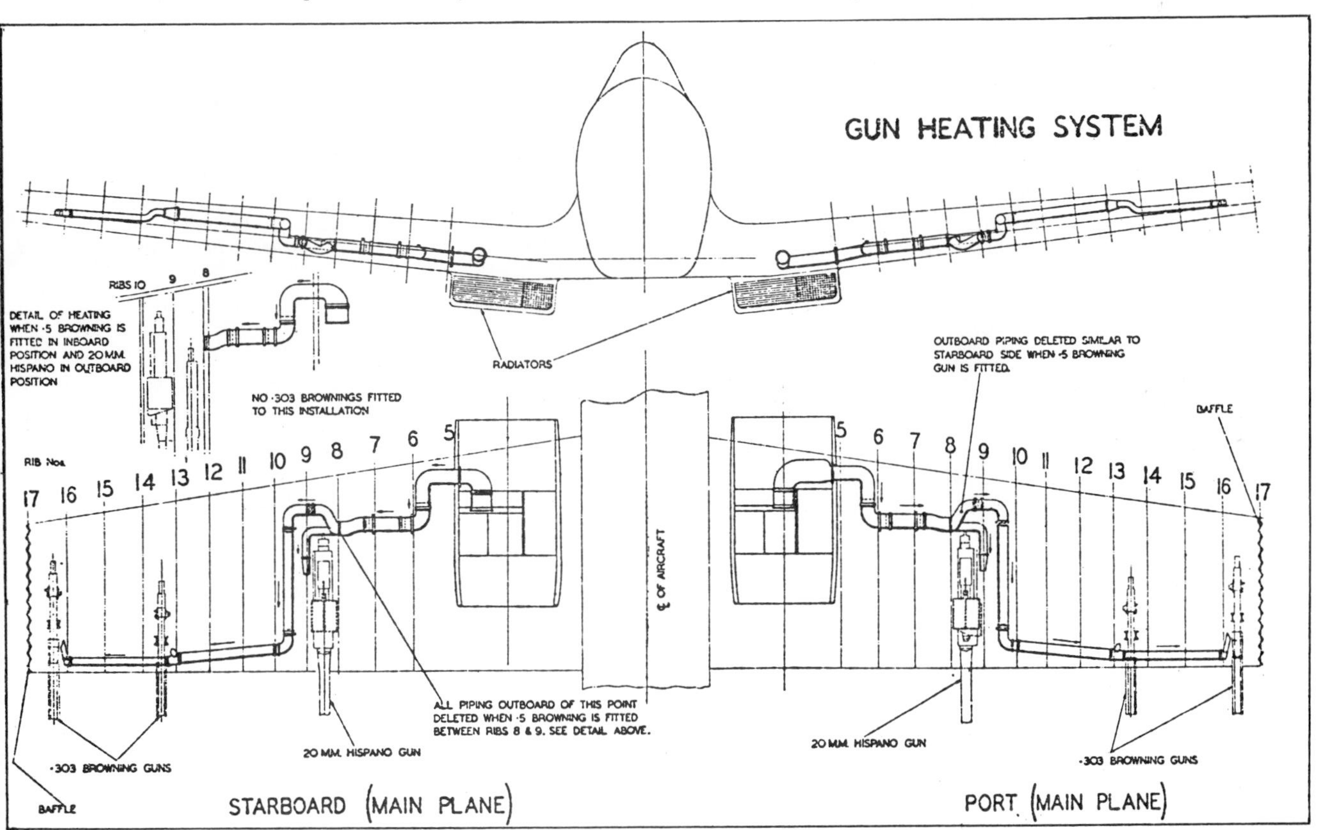

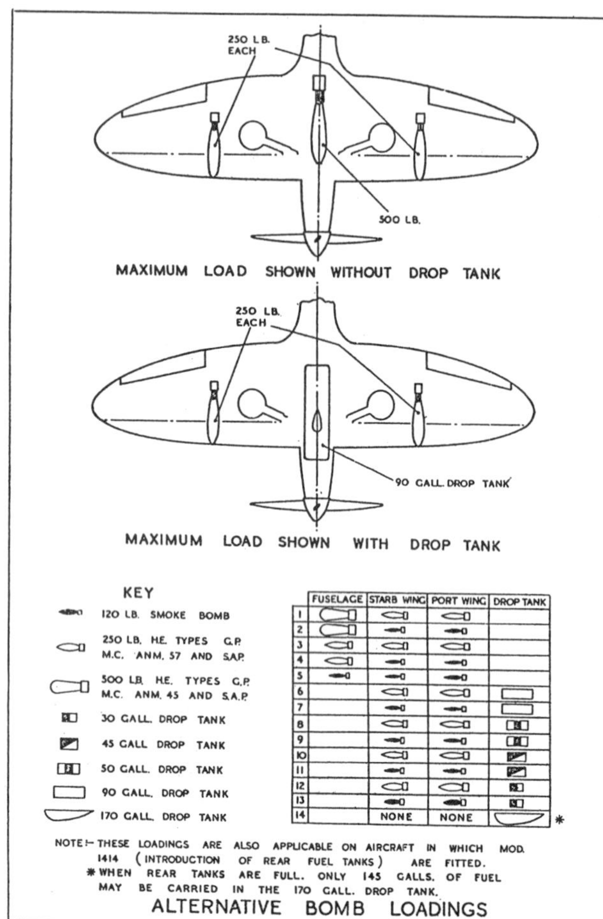

was fitted driving contra-props. After modification to the fin and rudder by Vickers it was sent to Boscombe Down for trials. It had two 20mm cannon only and was flown at a take-off weight of 7,440lb, and when taxying the control column had to be held to the rearmost position to avoid premature tail rise. The contra-props also eliminated all tendency for the aircraft to swing on take-off. After trials the Spitfire was returned to Vickers and the engine and propellers of MH874 fitted. The latter was originally equipped with the standard four blade propeller, which was to be replaced with a six blade Rotol contra rotating unit of 10ft 9in diameter.

Before the new high altitude Mk IX went into production a new German threat in the form of high altitude nuisance bombing had started with the appearance over England of the Ju86 bomber in August 1942. It could fly at heights above 40,000 feet and the RAF had nothing which could meet the challenge. After the initial raids a number of Mk IXs were stripped of all non-essentials and sent up after the Ju86s but were unable to affect the bombers in any way. On 28 August a

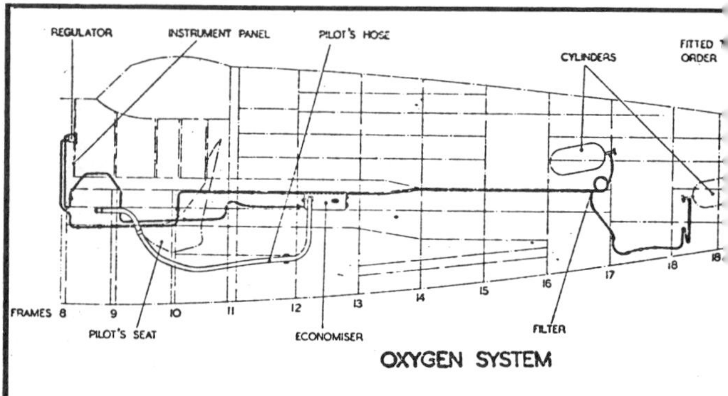

Ju86 bombed Bristol killing 48 people and injuring many more, and as a result of this incident Fighter Command formed the Special Service Flight at Northolt in order to produce an aeroplane and method to beat the German raiders. As a starter two F Mk IXs were converted to the HF specification: lightweight Jablo propellers, all armour protection and the four Browning guns removed, and painted PRU blue overall. The modified IXs were scrambled for the first time on 11 September with one of the fighters actually reaching 45,000ft, and the following day a Ju86 was attacked and damaged. Soon afterwards the high altitude raids ceased.

Following upon these trials with the two Spitfires an Air Ministry requirement of 1943 called for a Mk IX 'Type' Spitfire with contra-rotating propellers and rather than build a new aeroplane Supermarine decided to convert two standard Mk IXs. JK535 and JL349 were chosen, with the former going to Rolls-Royce on 23 April 1943 for installation of a Merlin 66. On 26 November it was again converted by Vickers at Worthy Down to take the Merlin 63A with Merlin 71 reduction gearing and Rotol six bladed contra-props. JL349 was not converted until 18 March 1944 by Rolls-Royce. MH874 can be regarded as the prototype Mk IX CP and the Type Record was issued on 22 February 1944. Certificate of Design for the type (covering JK535 and JL349) was issued on 12 September the same year. Take off weight of MH874 was 7,584lb.

EN524, a converted Mk VC, was the second HF Mk IX to be fitted with the Merlin 70 engine and it had smaller than standard upper cannon blisters. Initial trials at Boscombe were for oil cooling and radiator suitability, and both met the requirements for temperate and tropical conditions. It was tested with three types of propeller and associated reduction gear combinations, the differences in performance being minor. BS310 was once again converted to accept the installation of a Merlin 70 and performance trials were held in October 1943. The table opposite lists the performance of BS310 when fitted with the various engines.

MH434, LF Mk IX, M66, survived the war and was eventually sold to the RNAF for use as a target tug. Beyond this it served with COGEA in Belgium as 00-ARA. It returned to the UK as G-ASJV and had long span wings fitted. It is extant, based at Duxford.

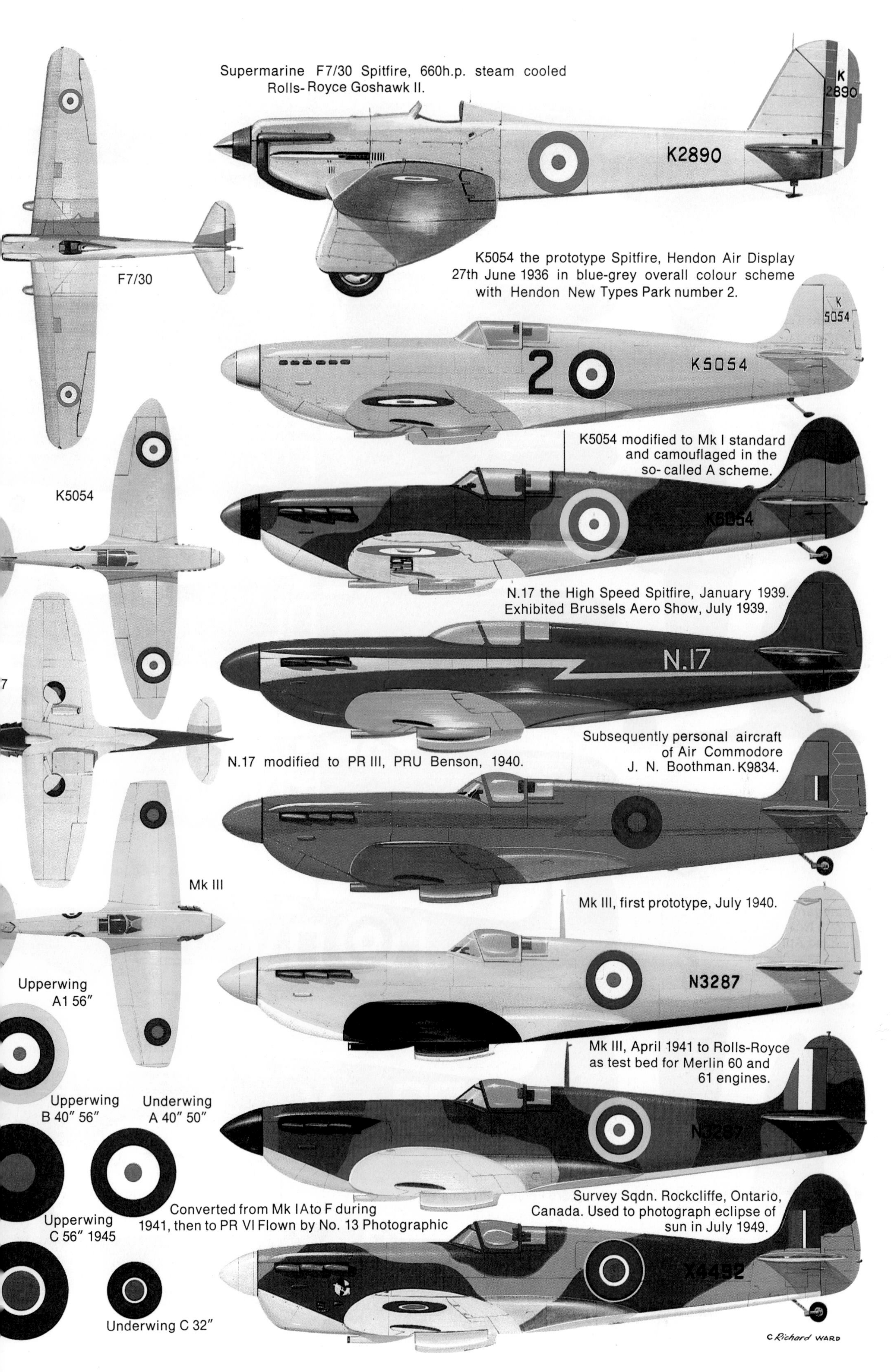
Supermarine F7/30 Spitfire, 660h.p. steam cooled Rolls-Royce Goshawk II.
K
2890
K2890
F7/30
K5054 the prototype Spitfire, Hendon Air Display 27th June 1936 in blue-grey overall colour scheme with Hendon New Types Park number 2.
K
5054
2
K5054
K5054 modified to Mk I standard and camouflaged in the so-called A scheme.
K5054
K5054
N.17 the High Speed Spitfire, January 1939. Exhibited Brussels Aero Show, July 1939.
N.17
7
Subsequently personal aircraft of Air Commodore J. N. Boothman. K9834.
N.17 modified to PR III, PRU Benson, 1940.
Mk III
Mk III, first prototype, July 1940.
N3287
Upperwing
A1 56″
Mk III, April 1941 to Rolls-Royce as test bed for Merlin 60 and 61 engines.
Upperwing
B 40″ 56″
Underwing
A 40″ 50″
N3287
Survey Sqdn. Rockcliffe, Ontario, Canada. Used to photograph eclipse of sun in July 1949.
Converted from Mk IA to F during 1941, then to PR VI Flown by No. 13 Photographic
Upperwing
C 56″ 1945
X4492
Underwing C 32″
C Richard WARD

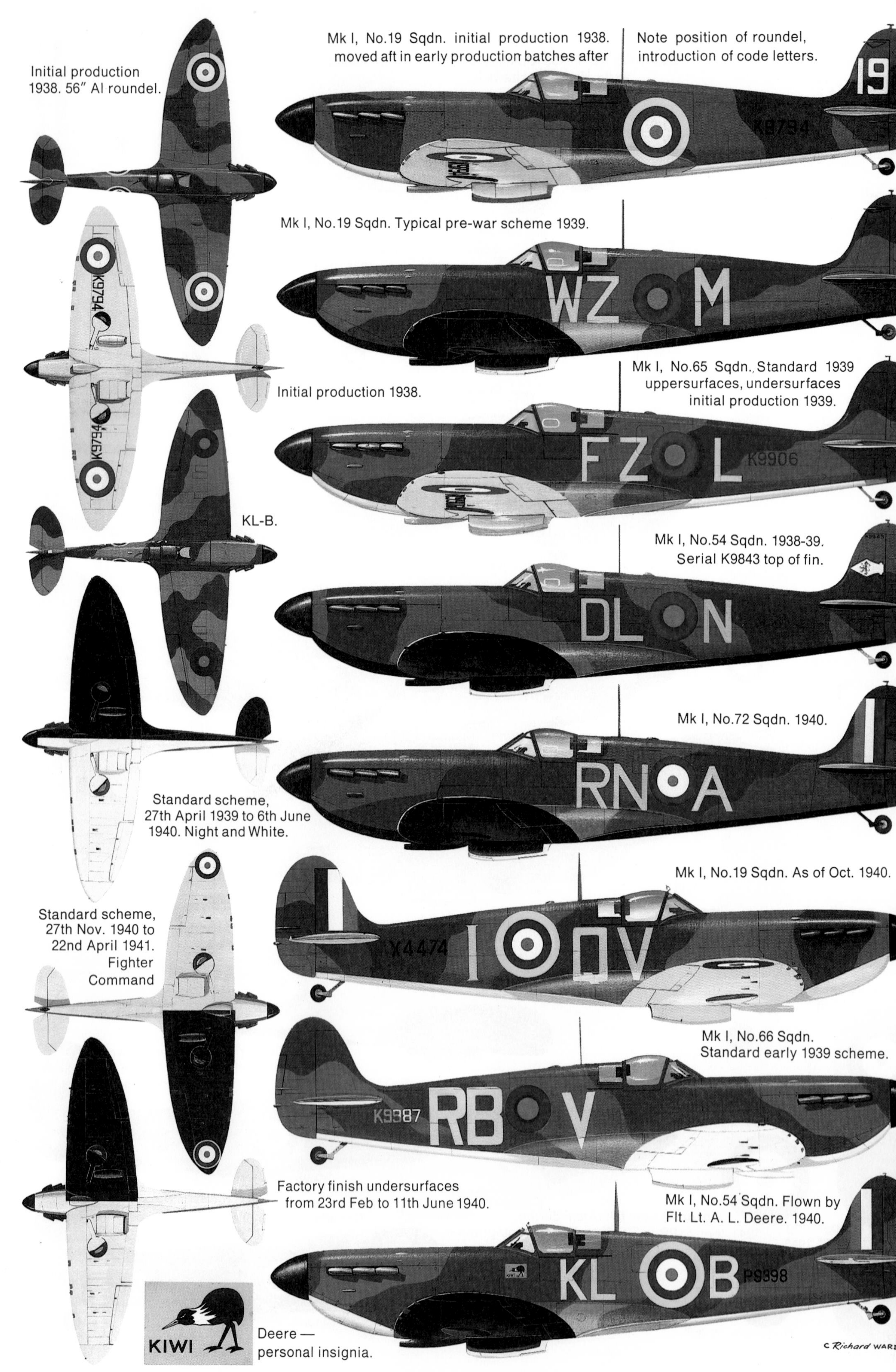

Initial production
1938. 56" Al roundel.
Mk I, No.19 Sqdn. initial production 1938.
moved aft in early production batches after
Note position of roundel,
introduction of code letters.
19
K9794
Mk I, No.19 Sqdn. Typical pre-war scheme 1939.
WZ M
K9794
K9794
Initial production 1938.
Mk I, No.65 Sqdn., Standard 1939
uppersurfaces, undersurfaces
initial production 1939.
FZ L
K9906
KL-B.
Mk I, No.54 Sqdn. 1938-39.
Serial K9843 top of fin.
DL N
Mk I, No.72 Sqdn. 1940.
RN A
Standard scheme,
27th April 1939 to 6th June
1940. Night and White.
Mk I, No.19 Sqdn. As of Oct. 1940.
X4474
I QV
Standard scheme,
27th Nov. 1940 to
22nd April 1941.
Fighter
Command
Mk I, No.66 Sqdn.
Standard early 1939 scheme.
K9987
RB V
Factory finish undersurfaces
from 23rd Feb to 11th June 1940.
Mk I, No.54 Sqdn. Flown by
Flt. Lt. A. L. Deere. 1940.
KL B
P9398
KIWI
Deere —
personal insignia.
c Richard WARD

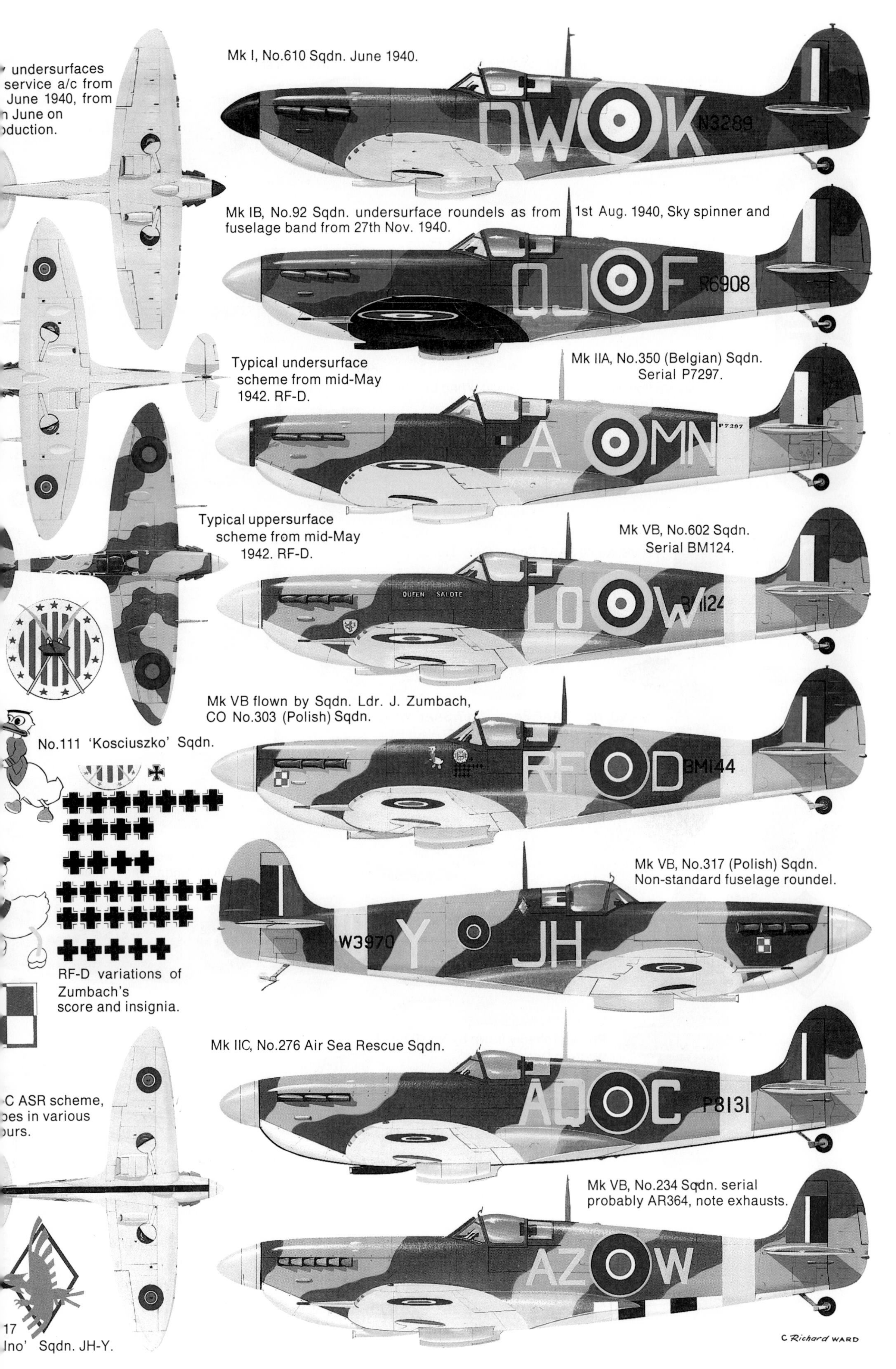

undersurfaces
service a/c from
June 1940, from
n June on
duction.
Mk I, No.610 Sqdn. June 1940.
DWOK
N3289
Mk IB, No.92 Sqdn. undersurface roundels as from 1st Aug. 1940, Sky spinner and fuselage band from 27th Nov. 1940.
QJOF
R6908
Typical undersurface scheme from mid-May 1942. RF-D.
Mk IIA, No.350 (Belgian) Sqdn. Serial P7297.
A OMN
P7297
Typical uppersurface scheme from mid-May 1942. RF-D.
Mk VB, No.602 Sqdn. Serial BM124.
QUEEN SALOTE
LOOW
BM124
Mk VB flown by Sqdn. Ldr. J. Zumbach, CO No.303 (Polish) Sqdn.
No.111 'Kosciuszko' Sqdn.
RF OD
BM144
Mk VB, No.317 (Polish) Sqdn. Non-standard fuselage roundel.
W3970
Y JH
RF-D variations of Zumbach's score and insignia.
Mk IIC, No.276 Air Sea Rescue Sqdn.
AQOC
P8131
C ASR scheme,
es in various
urs.
Mk VB, No.234 Sqdn. serial probably AR364, note exhausts.
AZOW
17
lno' Sqdn. JH-Y.
C Richard WARD

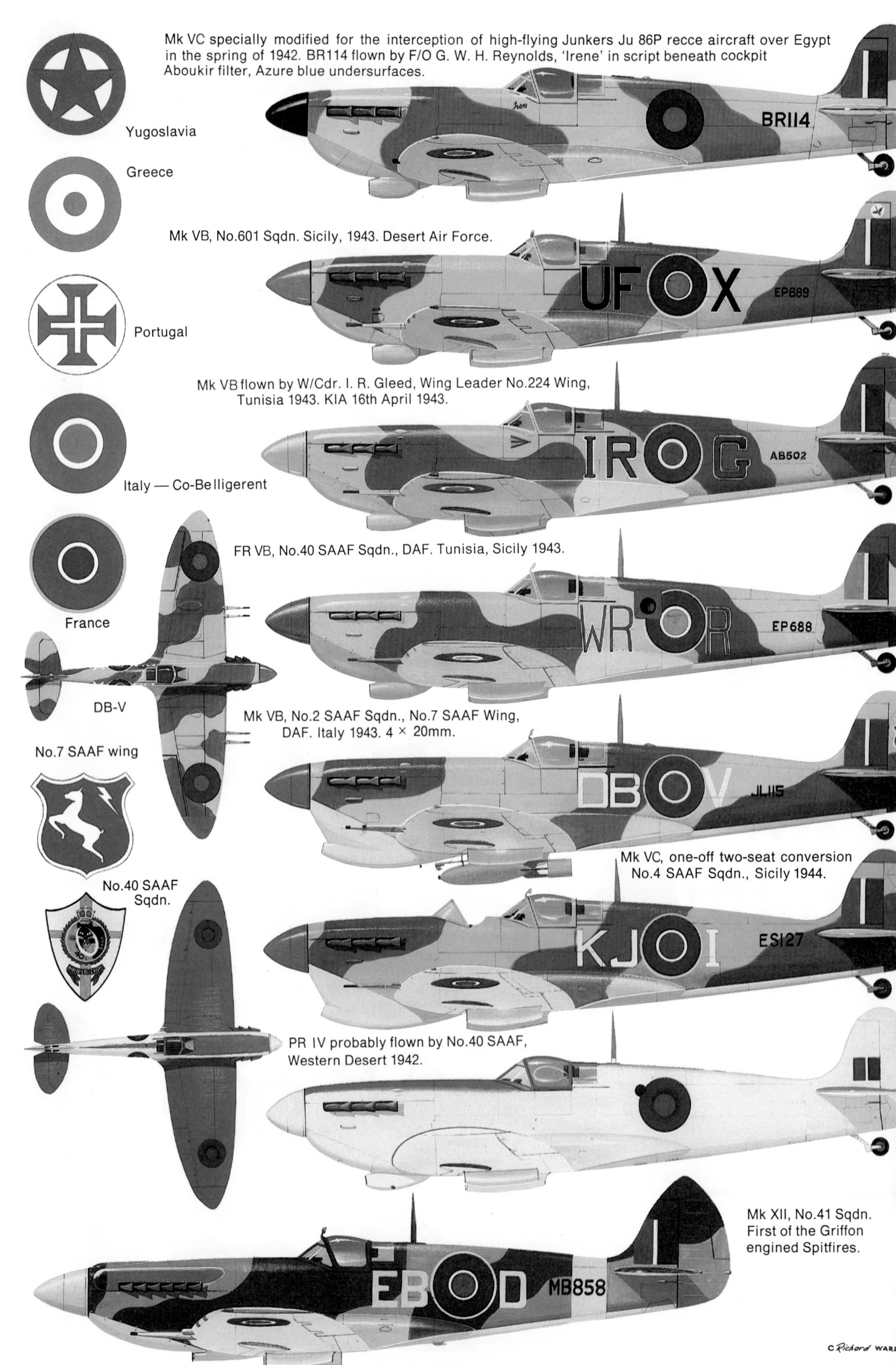

Mk VC specially modified for the interception of high-flying Junkers Ju 86P recce aircraft over Egypt in the spring of 1942. BR114 flown by F/O G. W. H. Reynolds, 'Irene' in script beneath cockpit AbouKir filter, Azure blue undersurfaces.
BR114
Yugoslavia
Greece
Mk VB, No.601 Sqdn. Sicily, 1943. Desert Air Force.
UF X
EP689
Portugal
Mk VB flown by W/Cdr. I. R. Gleed, Wing Leader No.224 Wing, Tunisia 1943. KIA 16th April 1943.
IR G
AB502
Italy — Co-Belligerent
FR VB, No.40 SAAF Sqdn., DAF. Tunisia, Sicily 1943.
WR R
EP688
France
DB-V
Mk VB, No.2 SAAF Sqdn., No.7 SAAF Wing, DAF. Italy 1943. 4 × 20mm.
No.7 SAAF wing
DB V
JL115
Mk VC, one-off two-seat conversion No.4 SAAF Sqdn., Sicily 1944.
No.40 SAAF Sqdn.
KJ I
ES127
PR IV probably flown by No.40 SAAF, Western Desert 1942.
Mk XII, No.41 Sqdn. First of the Griffon engined Spitfires.
EB D
MB858
c Richard Ward

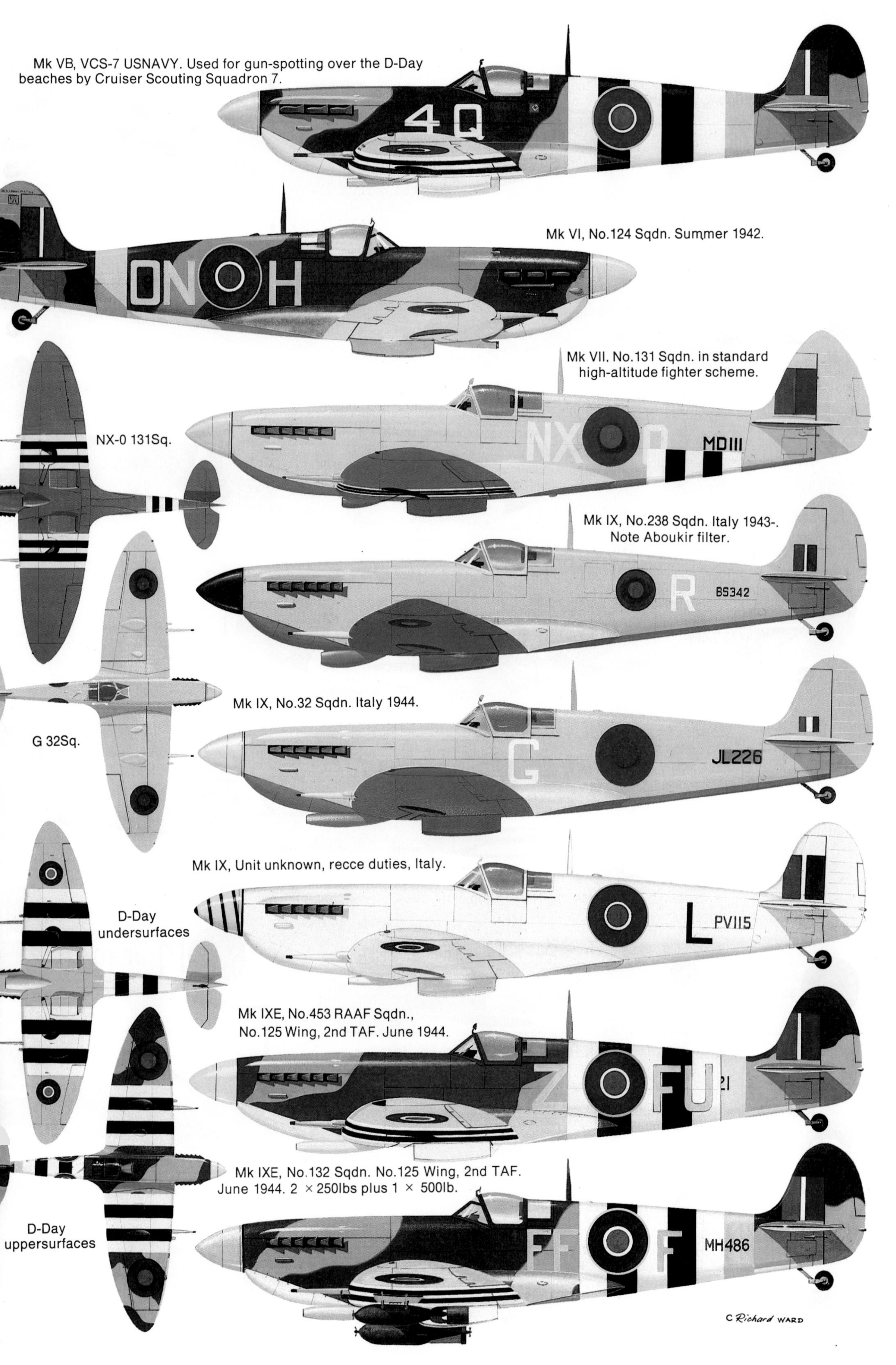

Mk VB, VCS-7 USNAVY. Used for gun-spotting over the D-Day beaches by Cruiser Scouting Squadron 7.
4Q
Mk VI, No.124 Sqdn. Summer 1942.
ON H
Mk VII. No.131 Sqdn. in standard high-altitude fighter scheme.
NX-0 131Sq.
NX
MD111
Mk IX, No.238 Sqdn. Italy 1943-. Note Aboukir filter.
R
BS342
Mk IX, No.32 Sqdn. Italy 1944.
G 32Sq.
G
JL226
Mk IX, Unit unknown, recce duties, Italy.
L
PV115
D-Day undersurfaces
Mk IXE, No.453 RAAF Sqdn., No.125 Wing, 2nd TAF. June 1944.
Z FU
21
Mk IXE, No.132 Sqdn. No.125 Wing, 2nd TAF. June 1944. 2 × 250lbs plus 1 × 500lb.
D-Day uppersurfaces
FF F
MH486
C Richard WARD

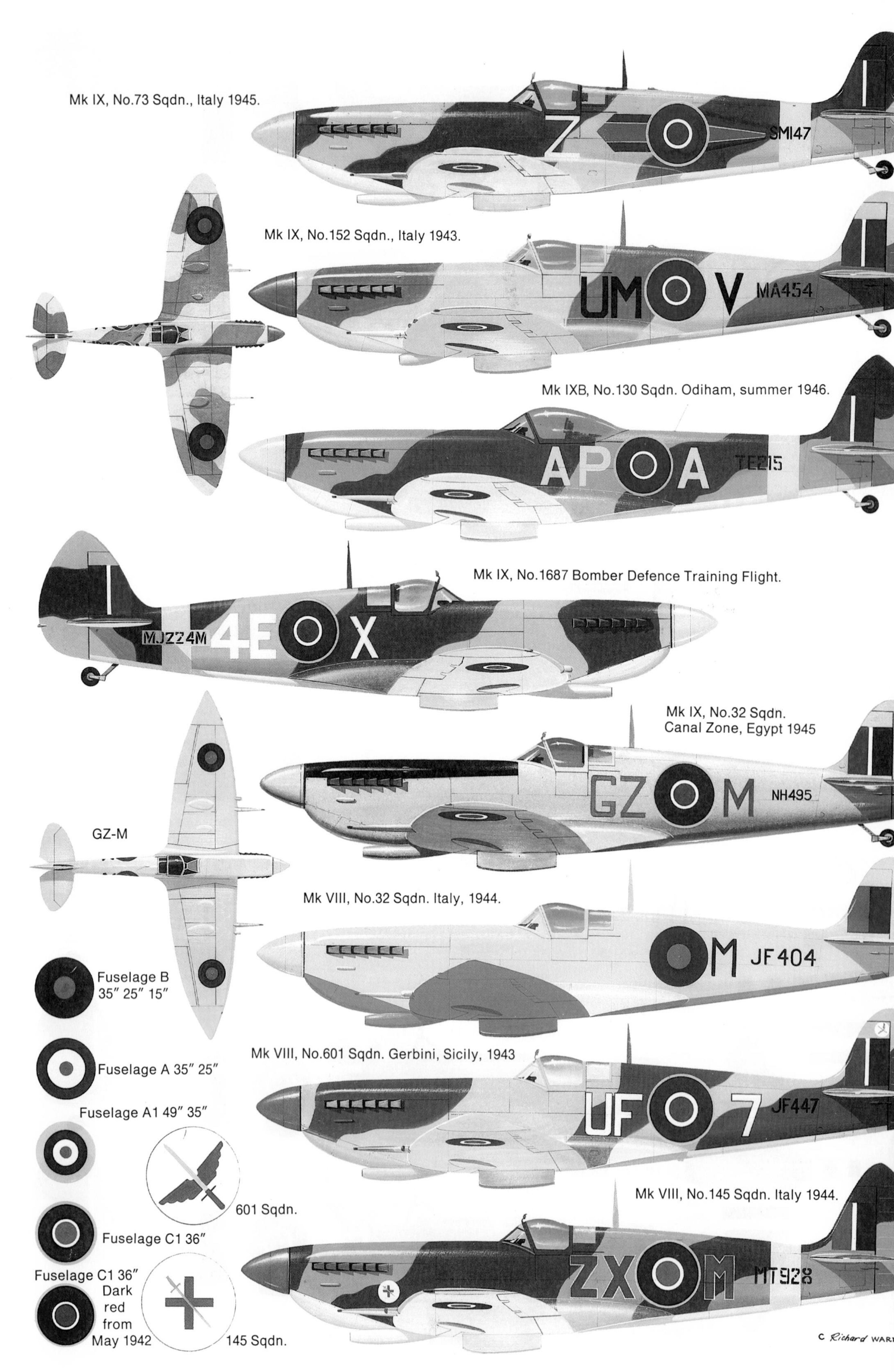
Mk IX, No.73 Sqdn., Italy 1945.
Mk IX, No.152 Sqdn., Italy 1943.
Mk IXB, No.130 Sqdn. Odiham, summer 1946.
Mk IX, No.1687 Bomber Defence Training Flight.
Mk IX, No.32 Sqdn.
Canal Zone, Egypt 1945
GZ-M
Mk VIII, No.32 Sqdn. Italy, 1944.
Fuselage B
35″ 25″ 15″
Mk VIII, No.601 Sqdn. Gerbini, Sicily, 1943
Fuselage A 35″ 25″
Fuselage A1 49″ 35″
601 Sqdn.
Mk VIII, No.145 Sqdn. Italy 1944.
Fuselage C1 36″
Fuselage C1 36″
Dark
red
from
May 1942
145 Sqdn.
C Richard WARD

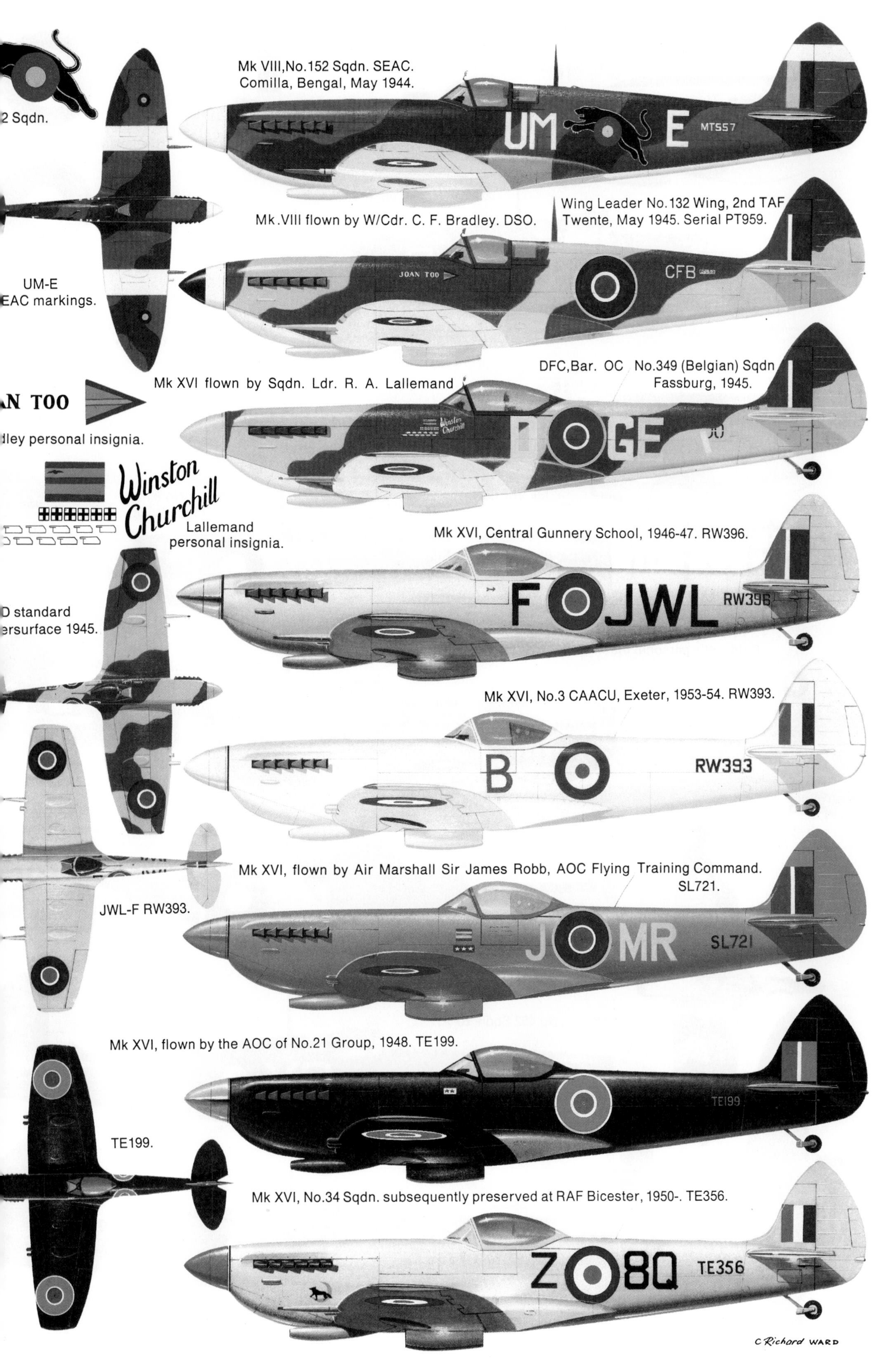
2 Sqdn.
Mk VIII,No.152 Sqdn. SEAC.
Comilla, Bengal, May 1944.
UM E
MT557
UM-E
EAC markings.
Mk.VIII flown by W/Cdr. C. F. Bradley. DSO.
Wing Leader No.132 Wing, 2nd TAF
Twente, May 1945. Serial PT959.
JOAN TOO
CFB
N TOO
lley personal insignia.
Mk XVI flown by Sqdn. Ldr. R. A. Lallemand
DFC,Bar. OC No.349 (Belgian) Sqdn
Fassburg, 1945.
D GE
Winston
Churchill
Lallemand
personal insignia.
Mk XVI, Central Gunnery School, 1946-47. RW396.
D standard
ersurface 1945.
F JWL
RW396
Mk XVI, No.3 CAACU, Exeter, 1953-54. RW393.
B
RW393
Mk XVI, flown by Air Marshall Sir James Robb, AOC Flying Training Command.
SL721.
JWL-F RW393.
J MR
SL721
Mk XVI, flown by the AOC of No.21 Group, 1948. TE199.
TE199
TE199.
Mk XVI, No.34 Sqdn. subsequently preserved at RAF Bicester, 1950-. TE356.
Z 8Q
TE356
C Richard WARD

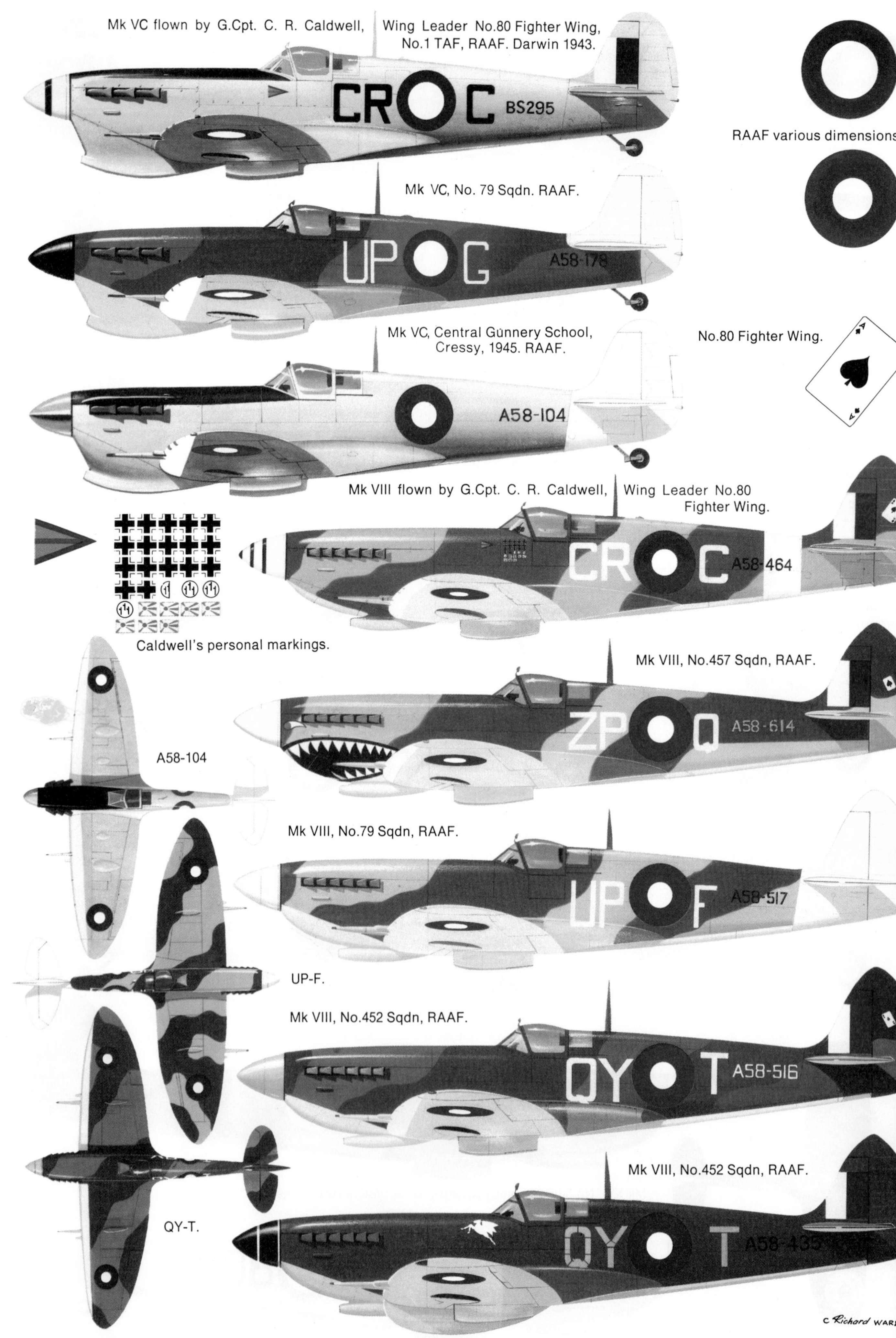

Mk VC flown by G.Cpt. C. R. Caldwell, Wing Leader No.80 Fighter Wing, No.1 TAF, RAAF. Darwin 1943.
CR C
BS295
RAAF various dimensions
Mk VC, No. 79 Sqdn. RAAF.
UP G
A58-178
Mk VC, Central Gunnery School, Cressy, 1945. RAAF.
A58-104
No.80 Fighter Wing.
Mk VIII flown by G.Cpt. C. R. Caldwell, Wing Leader No.80 Fighter Wing.
CR C
A58-464
Caldwell's personal markings.
Mk VIII, No.457 Sqdn, RAAF.
ZP Q
A58-614
A58-104
Mk VIII, No.79 Sqdn, RAAF.
UP F
A58-517
UP-F.
Mk VIII, No.452 Sqdn, RAAF.
QY T
A58-516
Mk VIII, No.452 Sqdn, RAAF.
QY T
A58-435
QY-T.
c Richard WAR

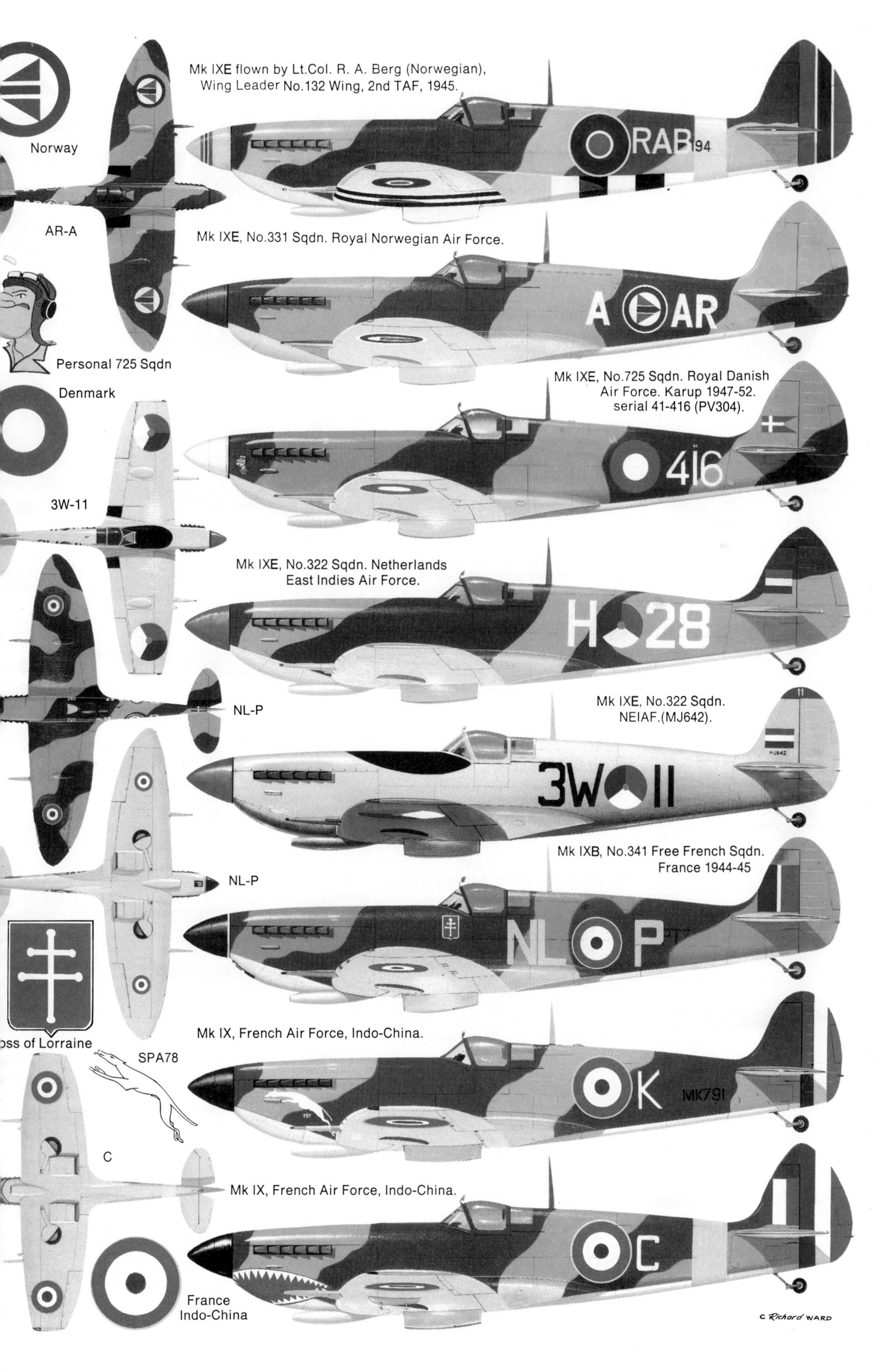
Mk IXE flown by Lt.Col. R. A. Berg (Norwegian),
Wing Leader No.132 Wing, 2nd TAF, 1945.
Norway
RAB
194
AR-A
Mk IXE, No.331 Sqdn. Royal Norwegian Air Force.
A AR
Personal 725 Sqdn
Denmark
Mk IXE, No.725 Sqdn. Royal Danish
Air Force. Karup 1947-52.
serial 41-416 (PV304).
416
3W-11
Mk IXE, No.322 Sqdn. Netherlands
East Indies Air Force.
H 28
NL-P
Mk IXE, No.322 Sqdn.
NEIAF.(MJ642).
3W 11
Mk IXB, No.341 Free French Sqdn.
France 1944-45
NL-P
NL P
oss of Lorraine
Mk IX, French Air Force, Indo-China.
SPA78
K
MK791
C
Mk IX, French Air Force, Indo-China.
C
France
Indo-China
c Richard WARD

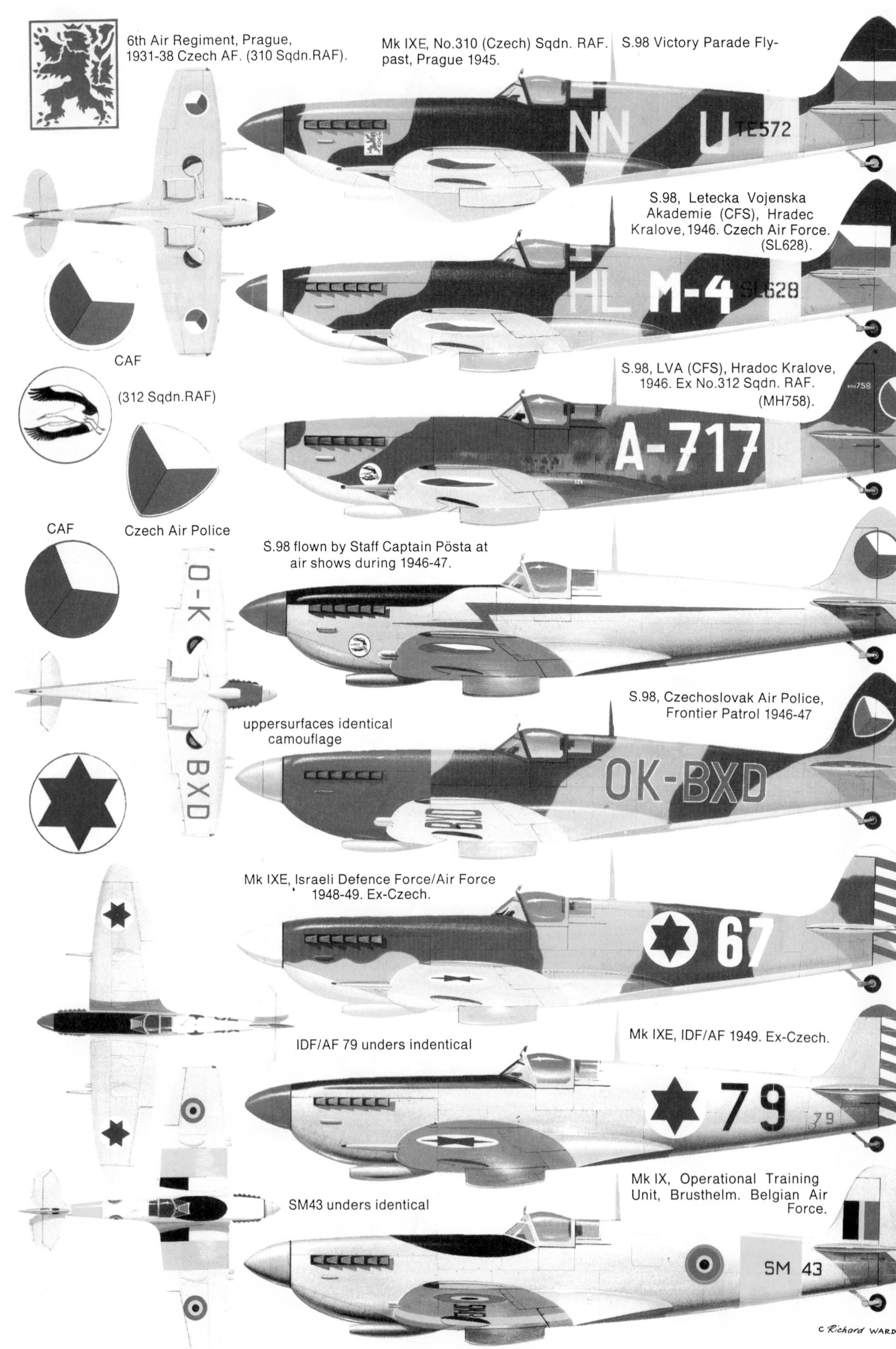
6th Air Regiment, Prague, 1931-38 Czech AF. (310 Sqdn.RAF).
Mk IXE, No.310 (Czech) Sqdn. RAF. S.98 Victory Parade Fly-past, Prague 1945.
NN U TE572
S.98, Letecka Vojenska Akademie (CFS), Hradec Kralove, 1946. Czech Air Force. (SL628).
HL M-4 SL628
CAF
(312 Sqdn.RAF)
S.98, LVA (CFS), Hradoc Kralove, 1946. Ex No.312 Sqdn. RAF. (MH758).
A-717
CAF
Czech Air Police
S.98 flown by Staff Captain Pösta at air shows during 1946-47.
O-K BXD
uppersurfaces identical camouflage
S.98, Czechoslovak Air Police, Frontier Patrol 1946-47
OK-BXD
Mk IXE, Israeli Defence Force/Air Force 1948-49. Ex-Czech.
67
IDF/AF 79 unders indentical
Mk IXE, IDF/AF 1949. Ex-Czech.
79
SM43 unders identical
Mk IX, Operational Training Unit, Brusthelm. Belgian Air Force.
SM 43
c Richard WARD

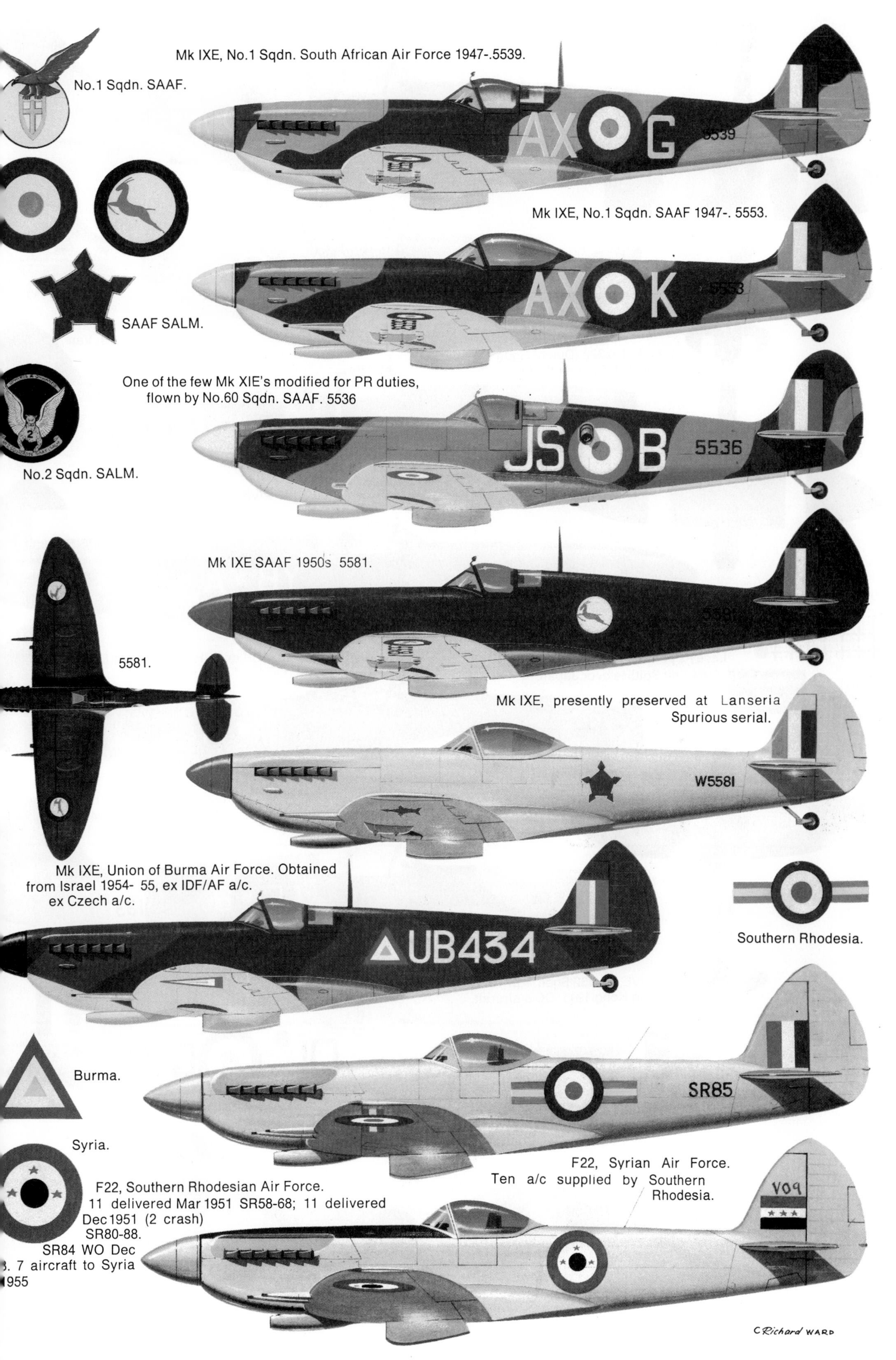

Mk IXE, No.1 Sqdn. South African Air Force 1947-.5539.

Mk IXE, No.1 Sqdn. SAAF 1947-. 5553.

One of the few Mk XIE's modified for PR duties, flown by No.60 Sqdn. SAAF. 5536

Mk IXE SAAF 1950s 5581.

Mk IXE, presently preserved at Lanseria Spurious serial.

Mk IXE, Union of Burma Air Force. Obtained from Israel 1954- 55, ex IDF/AF a/c. ex Czech a/c.

F22, Syrian Air Force. Ten a/c supplied by Southern Rhodesia.

F22, Southern Rhodesian Air Force. 11 delivered Mar 1951 SR58-68; 11 delivered Dec 1951 (2 crash) SR80-88. SR84 WO Dec . 7 aircraft to Syria 1955

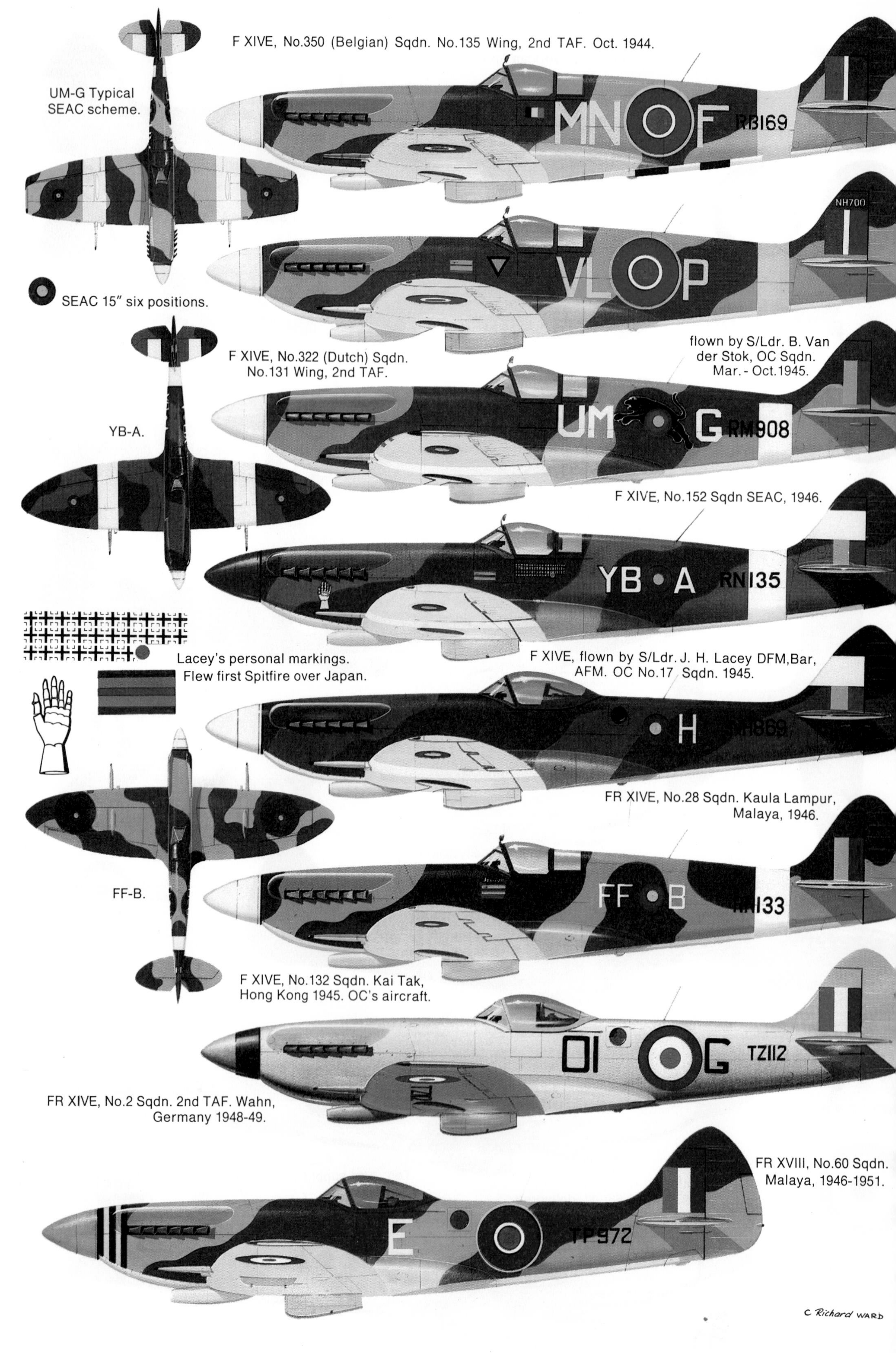
F XIVE, No.350 (Belgian) Sqdn. No.135 Wing, 2nd TAF. Oct. 1944.
UM-G Typical SEAC scheme.
MN F
RB169
NH700
VL P
SEAC 15" six positions.
F XIVE, No.322 (Dutch) Sqdn. No.131 Wing, 2nd TAF.
flown by S/Ldr. B. Van der Stok, OC Sqdn. Mar. - Oct.1945.
YB-A.
UM G
RM908
F XIVE, No.152 Sqdn SEAC, 1946.
YB A
RN135
Lacey's personal markings. Flew first Spitfire over Japan.
F XIVE, flown by S/Ldr. J. H. Lacey DFM,Bar, AFM. OC No.17 Sqdn. 1945.
H
FR XIVE, No.28 Sqdn. Kaula Lampur, Malaya, 1946.
FF-B.
FF B
RN133
F XIVE, No.132 Sqdn. Kai Tak, Hong Kong 1945. OC's aircraft.
OI G
TZ112
FR XIVE, No.2 Sqdn. 2nd TAF. Wahn, Germany 1948-49.
FR XVIII, No.60 Sqdn. Malaya, 1946-1951.
E
TP972
C Richard WARD

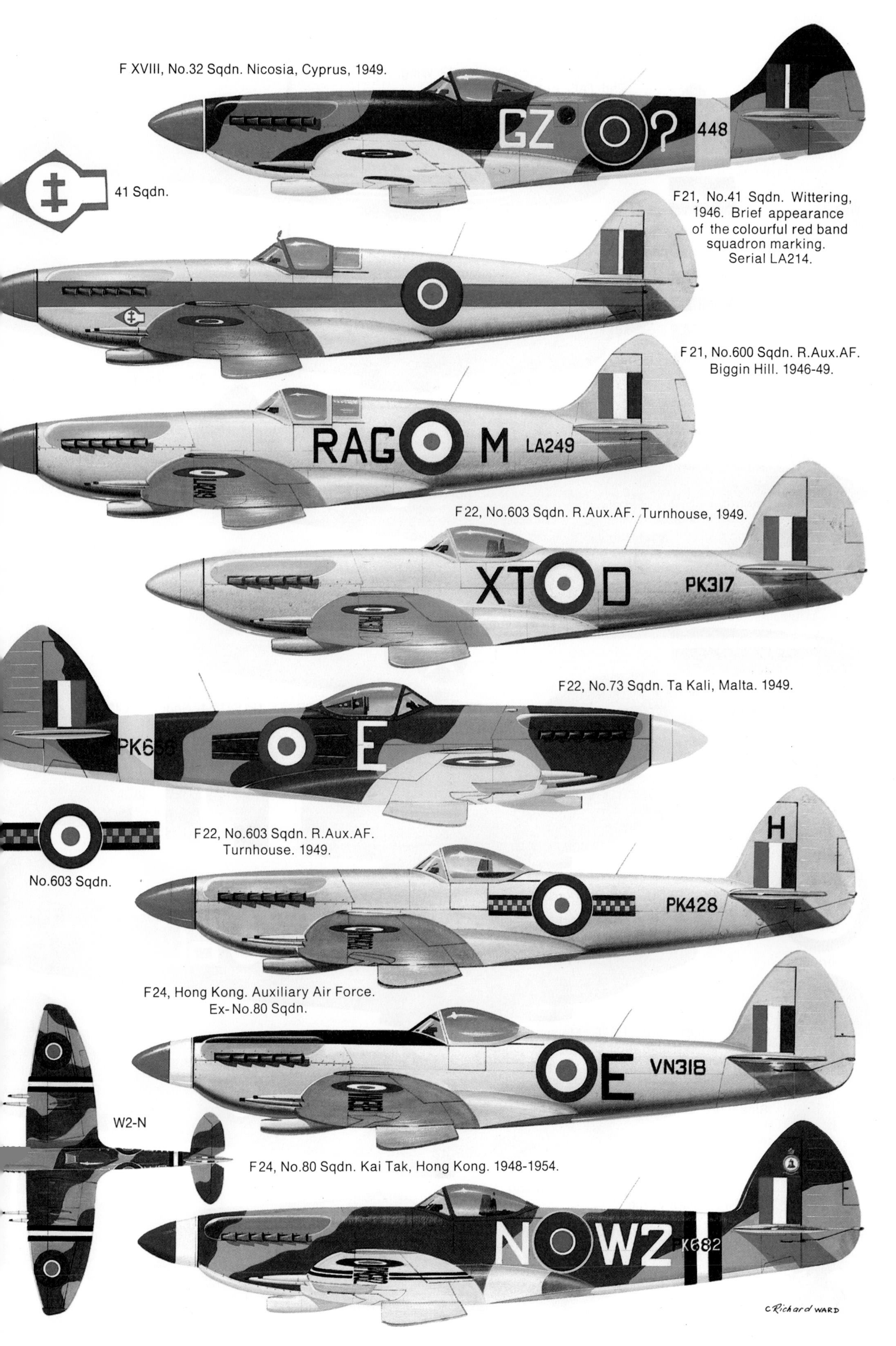
F XVIII, No.32 Sqdn. Nicosia, Cyprus, 1949.
GZ
448
41 Sqdn.
F21, No.41 Sqdn. Wittering, 1946. Brief appearance of the colourful red band squadron marking. Serial LA214.
F21, No.600 Sqdn. R.Aux.AF. Biggin Hill. 1946-49.
RAG M
LA249
F22, No.603 Sqdn. R.Aux.AF. Turnhouse, 1949.
XT D
PK317
F22, No.73 Sqdn. Ta Kali, Malta. 1949.
E
F22, No.603 Sqdn. R.Aux.AF. Turnhouse. 1949.
No.603 Sqdn.
H
PK428
F24, Hong Kong. Auxiliary Air Force. Ex-No.80 Sqdn.
E
VN318
W2-N
F24, No.80 Sqdn. Kai Tak, Hong Kong. 1948-1954.
N W2
K682
cRichard WARD

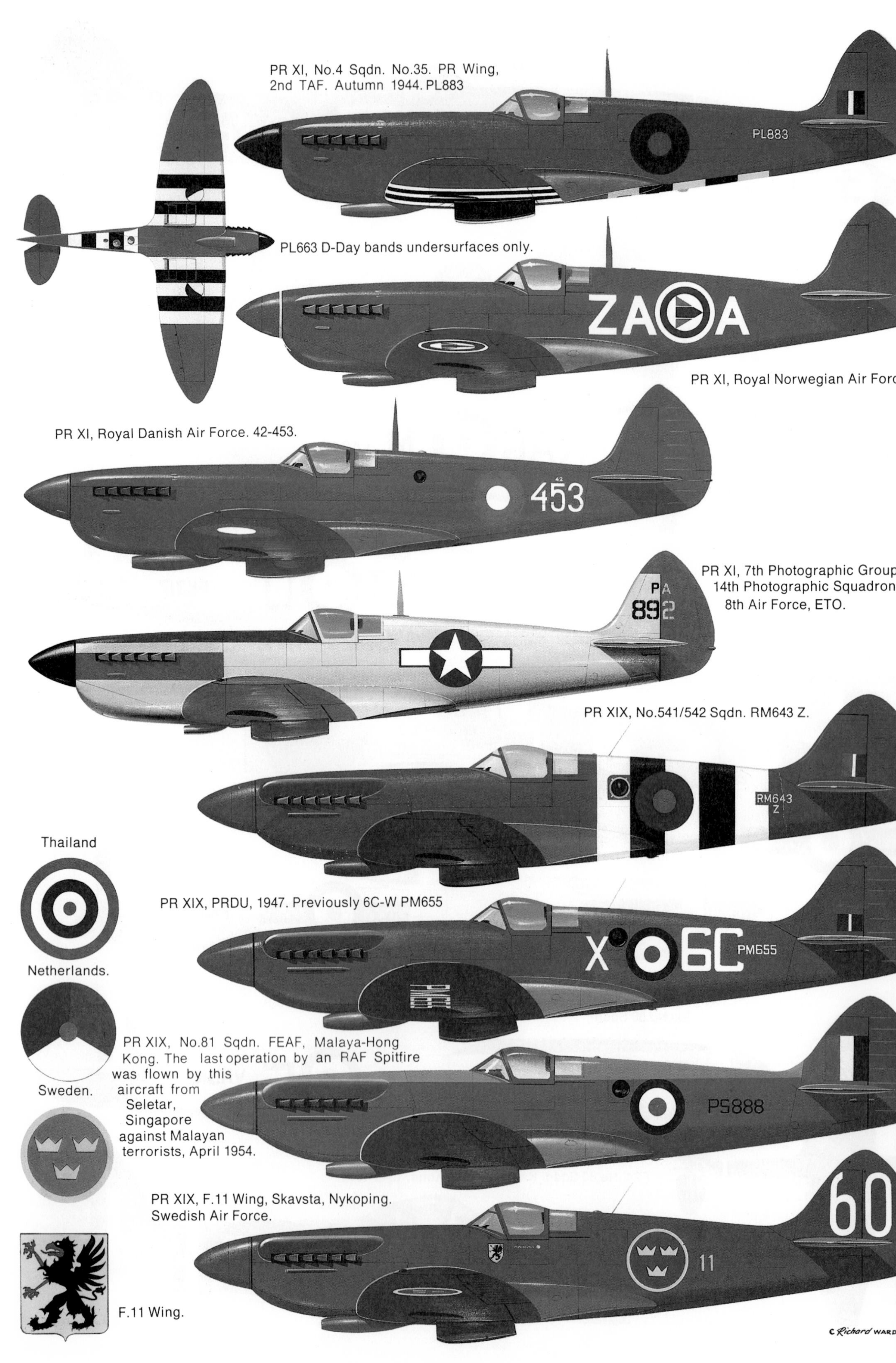

PR XI, No.4 Sqdn. No.35. PR Wing, 2nd TAF. Autumn 1944. PL883

PL663 D-Day bands undersurfaces only.

PR XI, Royal Norwegian Air Forc

PR XI, Royal Danish Air Force. 42-453.

PR XI, 7th Photographic Group, 14th Photographic Squadron, 8th Air Force, ETO.

PR XIX, No.541/542 Sqdn. RM643 Z.

Thailand

PR XIX, PRDU, 1947. Previously 6C-W PM655

Netherlands.

PR XIX, No.81 Sqdn. FEAF, Malaya-Hong Kong. The last operation by an RAF Spitfire was flown by this aircraft from Seletar, Singapore against Malayan terrorists, April 1954.

Sweden.

PR XIX, F.11 Wing, Skavsta, Nykoping. Swedish Air Force.

F.11 Wing.

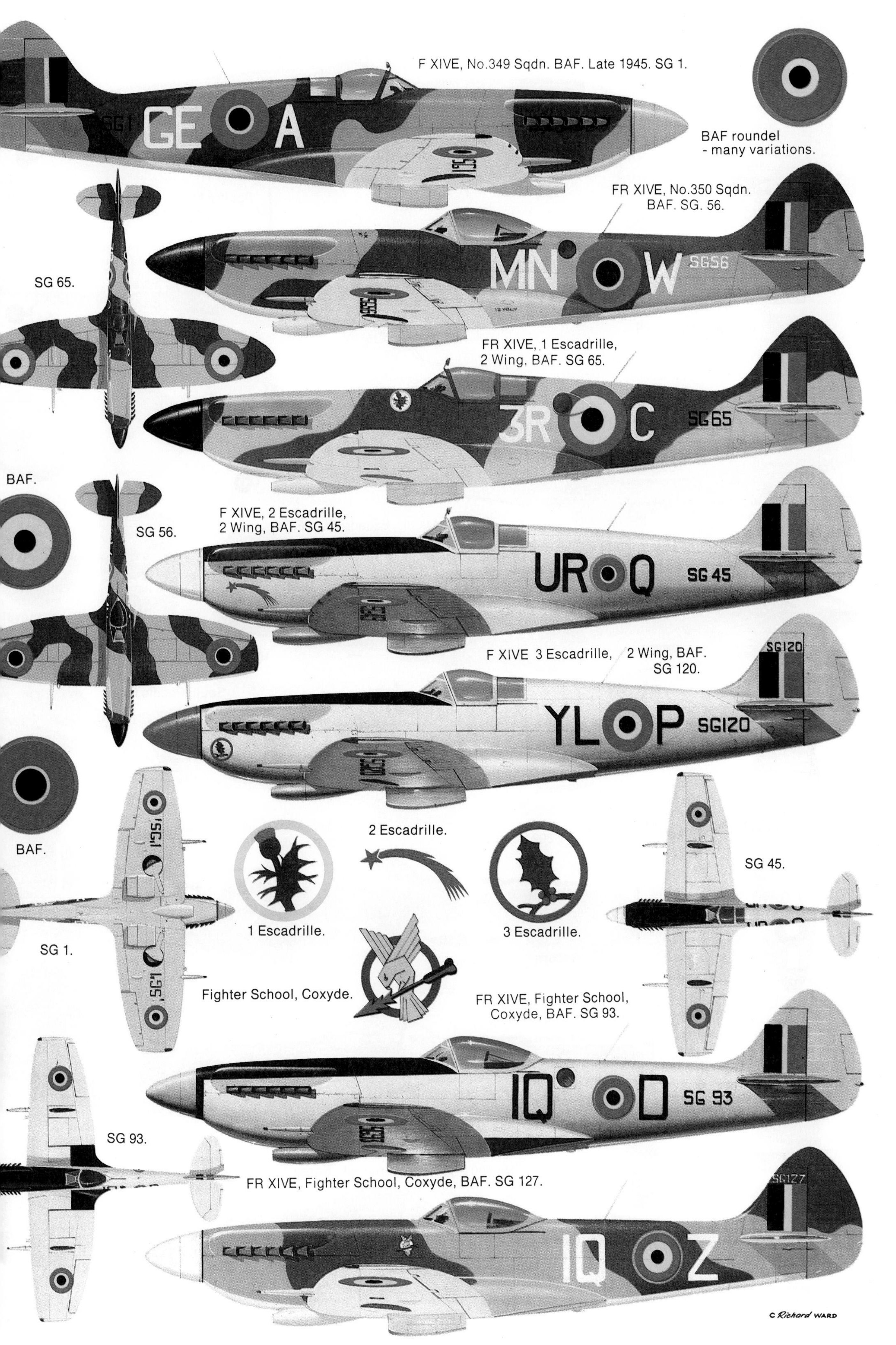

F XIVE, No.349 Sqdn. BAF. Late 1945. SG 1.
BAF roundel
- many variations.
FR XIVE, No.350 Sqdn.
BAF. SG. 56.
SG 65.
FR XIVE, 1 Escadrille,
2 Wing, BAF. SG 65.
BAF.
SG 56.
F XIVE, 2 Escadrille,
2 Wing, BAF. SG 45.
F XIVE 3 Escadrille, 2 Wing, BAF.
SG 120.
BAF.
2 Escadrille.
SG 45.
1 Escadrille.
3 Escadrille.
SG 1.
Fighter School, Coxyde.
FR XIVE, Fighter School,
Coxyde, BAF. SG 93.
SG 93.
FR XIVE, Fighter School, Coxyde, BAF. SG 127.
c Richard WARD

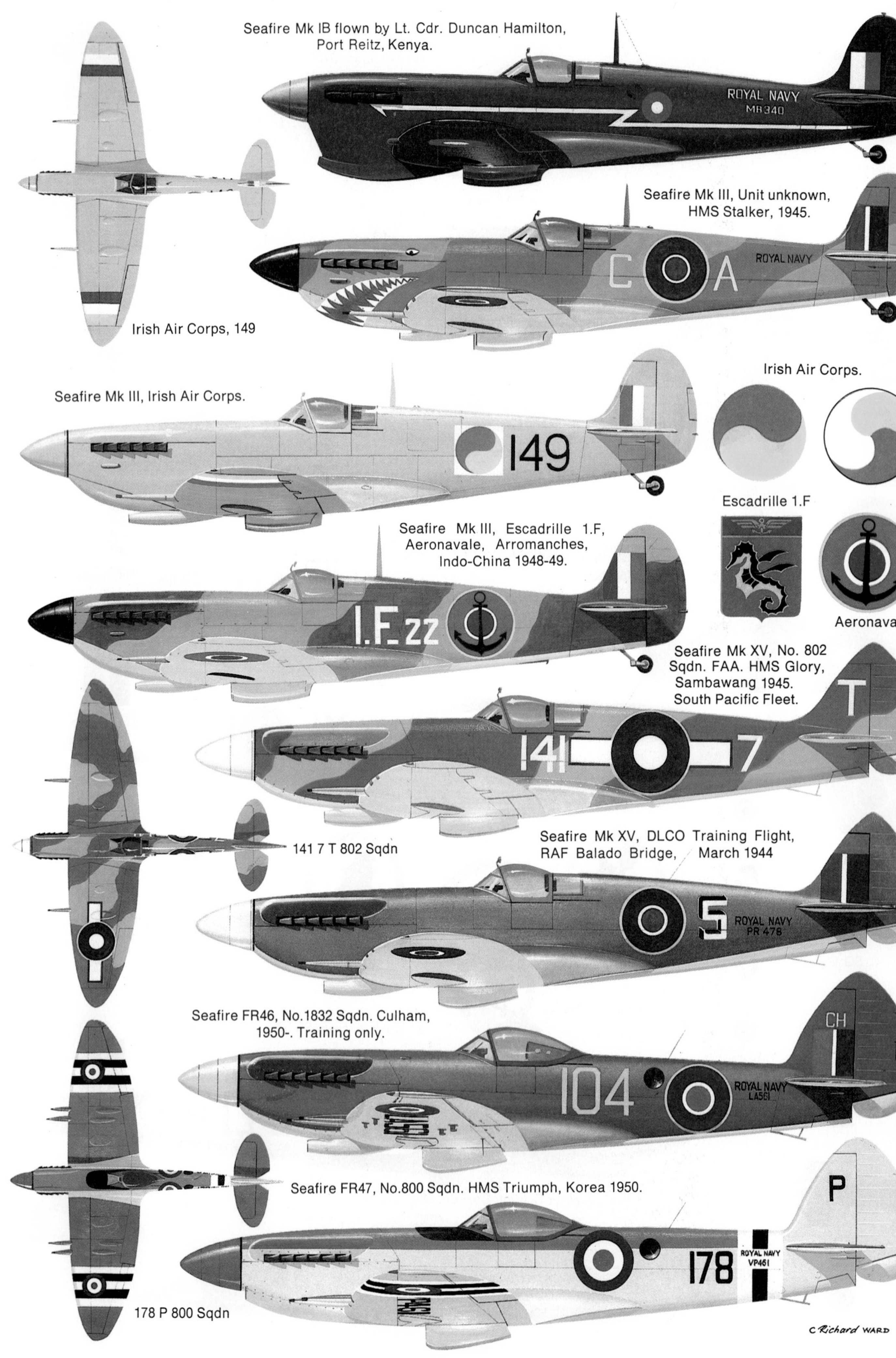
Seafire Mk IB flown by Lt. Cdr. Duncan Hamilton, Port Reitz, Kenya.
ROYAL NAVY
MB340
Seafire Mk III, Unit unknown, HMS Stalker, 1945.
C A
ROYAL NAVY
Irish Air Corps, 149
Seafire Mk III, Irish Air Corps.
149
Irish Air Corps.
Escadrille 1.F
Seafire Mk III, Escadrille 1.F, Aeronavale, Arromanches, Indo-China 1948-49.
1.F.22
Aeronaval
Seafire Mk XV, No. 802 Sqdn. FAA. HMS Glory, Sambawang 1945. South Pacific Fleet.
T
141 7
141 7 T 802 Sqdn
Seafire Mk XV, DLCO Training Flight, RAF Balado Bridge, March 1944
5
ROYAL NAVY
PR 476
Seafire FR46, No.1832 Sqdn. Culham, 1950-. Training only.
CH
104
ROYAL NAVY
LA561
Seafire FR47, No.800 Sqdn. HMS Triumph, Korea 1950.
P
178
ROYAL NAVY
VP461
178 P 800 Sqdn
C Richard WARD

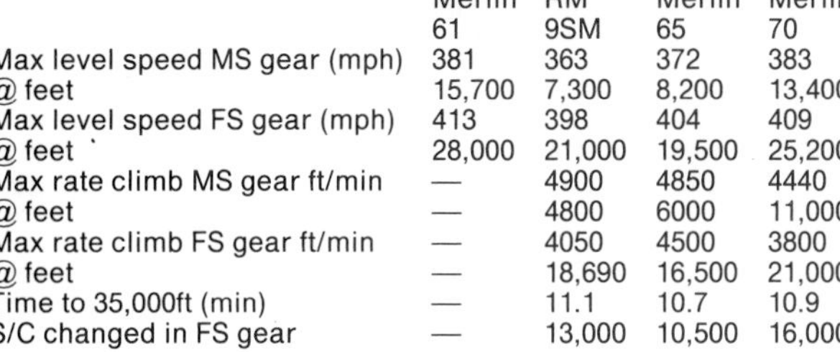

	Merlin 61	RM 9SM	Merlin 65	Merlin 70
Max level speed MS gear (mph)	381	363	372	383
@ feet	15,700	7,300	8,200	13,400
Max level speed FS gear (mph)	413	398	404	409
@ feet	28,000	21,000	19,500	25,200
Max rate climb MS gear ft/min	—	4900	4850	4440
@ feet	—	4800	6000	11,000
Max rate climb FS gear ft/min	—	4050	4500	3800
@ feet	—	18,690	16,500	21,000
Time to 35,000ft (min)	—	11.1	10.7	10.9
S/C changed in FS gear	—	13,000	10,500	16,000

The Mk IX with two large beer barrels 'Modification XXX' on the wing bomb carriers, was a typical propaganda effort of the period. The aircraft, MJ329 had little ground clearance at take off with full barrels. A second Mk IX carried the beer in a long range fuel tank.

When fitted with a tropical intake there was a speed reduction of between 6mph and 800ft in height in MS gear, and 16mph and 24000ft in height in FS gear.

THE LF MK IX

By far the most numerous of the Mk IXs were the low altitude versions, the LF with Merlin 66 engine as standard and with cabin blower deleted, .477 propeller reduction gear and throttle/propeller interconnected controls. The impetus given to large scale production came from Air Marshal Conningham,

LF IX MJ823. Handling trials at Boscombe Down with 2 x 250lb bombs under wing, March 1944.

CinC Air Forces in the Western desert. He originally asked for 'massive' supplies of LF VB/VC Spitfires as 80% of his operations were at low altitude. He also requested that all Mk Vs shipped to the Middle East from 10 April 1943 be delivered without the Vokes tropical filter. His MUs were going to install the smaller, and more efficient, Aboukir type in situ on arrival, and a production line had been set-up to produce the filter locally.

There was little point in building and shipping additional Mk Vs to the Middle East as future Spitfire production was devoted to the Mk IX, and the result was a low altitude variant to meet requirements. As related previously BS310 conducted trials with the Mk VIII tropical intake, but the prototype LF Mk IX can be considered as the converted Mk VC MA648, which arrived at Rolls-Royce, Hucknall, for conversion and installation of its new engine on 23 May 1943. This engine was also fitted with the SU Mk II single point, fuel injection pump, going to Boscombe Down for trials of the latter the following November. MA648 was fitted with a revised Mk VIII intake which combined temperate and tropical filtering systems controlled by a movable shutter.

The first production LF Mk IX (MJ823) arrived at Boscombe for handling trials with two 250lb GP bombs and two 120lb smoke bombs on wing racks. The bombs could be released at any speed up to the maximum diving, but there was a tendency towards a nose up change of trim, and any push force required to make the Spitfire dive had to be trimmed out before release to avoid excessive pull out stick forces. Trials were continued with a 500lb bomb or 2 × 90 gallon drop tanks beneath the fuselage. For these trials MJ823 had a most unusual modification for the .303 Brownings were removed, the gun ports sealed over and two .5in Browning machine guns installed in the empty Hispano cannon bays. Further trials with two 210lb GP and one 500lb MC bomb followed and the final ordnance trials were with two 210lb GP bombs and one 90 gallon overload fuel tank. Take off weight was 8,435 and 8,675lb respectively. There was a considerable change of longitudinal trim at speed but the aircraft was considered satisfactory for service use. MK810 was at Worthy Down on 6 March 1944 for weighing and a tare of 5,634 and an auw of 7,329lb was recorded. This aircraft was followed by PT452 on 25 July at High Post where the tare was lower at 5,565lb but the auw higher at 7,376. In the same condition, but with additional modifications, PV157 returned a tare of 5,614 and an auw of 7,426lb at High Post on 18 September. In the early months of 1944 one of the first Packard-built Merlin 266 engines became available

The modified conical, curved windscreen installed on EN498, Farnborough, September 1943. Fairings were of wood. The Spitfire was also used to tow the German Me162 rocket fighter to the old Wisley airfield and back.

for the Spitfire and it was installed in MK850. It was weighed at High Post on 13 June with a tare of 5,589 and an auw of 7,400lb.

Towards the end of the Mk IX production run, in particular the LF series, more range was demanded from the RAF's fighter bombers. Conditions in France made it difficult to store fuel on forward landing grounds and production of overload tanks had been stretched to the limit. Numerous studies had been made on the installation of additional, internal fuel for the Spitfire and a number of Mk IXs were modified to have a tank installed behind the pilot. Capacity ranged from 32 to 85 gallons and, as related earlier, the CoG moved to the rear and under certain conditions the aircraft was unsafe. Trials with ML186 established the aftmost limit of CoG at 9.9ins aft of the vertical datum, but before any further modifications were recommended for increasing fuel load the problem had resolved itself.

Also, as the Allied advance into France continued pilots flying the LF variant complained of skin wrinkling of the wings under certain conditions. No 125 Wing had many instances of buckled wings, all within a short period of time, usually due to the tactics used during the search and strike of targets. The operations involved a long, sustained dive in order to make it difficult for the enemy's anti aircraft fire to hit the Spitfire. Answers had to be found to the problem and field trials seemed the most logical, and as a result five Spitfires were fitted with V-g recorders. Trials started on 5 November 1944 and the maximum amount of 'G' recorded was four. The two main forms of attack suspected of causing skin wrinkling were armed reconnaissance and, as stated, dive bombing. For the latter the LF Mk IX could, and did, carry one 500lb bomb under the fuselage, and it could also carry two more 250lb bombs under the wings (as per the trials with MJ823 at Boscombe Down). On armed reconnaissance bombs were rarely carried and chief reliance placed upon cannon fire on soft skinned vehicles. The IXEs with .5in Brownings and cannon returned the best results, as demonstrated during the Falaise Gap period.

Method of attack was diving at an angle of between 45° to 60°, with 4lb engine boost, the lowest altitude being 1,000ft

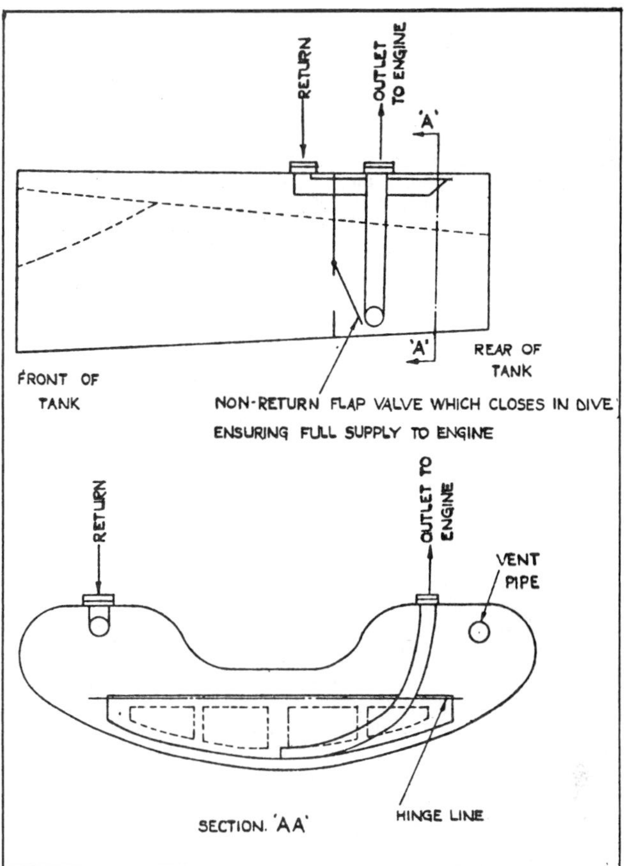

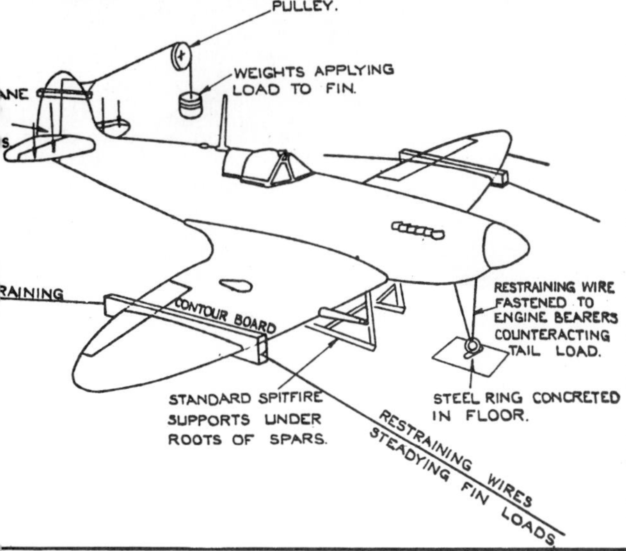

For measurements of tail loads at high speeds NH230 had an incidence vane fitted to the port pivot head. To record tail and fin deflections a number of holes were drilled in the tailplane upper surface. The small numbers, just visible, indicate the holes which were connected to instruments in the cockpit. Automatic observer cameras were installed behind the pilot, and a special tank (above right) ensured a full supply of fuel to the engine during dives. Second diagram shows the method of calibrating tailplane and fin loads in the static rig.

across roads. It was a rare event for a Spitfire to sweep along a road for such a manoeuvre enabled enemy AA fire to concentrate on the attacker. The Spitfire would, by then, be using rapid aileron rolls, weaving, tight turns and even inverted flight. Escape low down was not favoured. Pull out was far more severe than the dive with some pilots changing nose heavy trim during the manoeuvre, dropping both hands from the throttle to the trimming wheel. Others did not bother to alter trim until pull out was completed. Blacking out was a common occurrence but little attention was paid to it. When dive bombing the bomb weight increased speed and the Spitfire pilot tended to use the reflector sight as a bomb sight. The bombs were then released after a timed interval, judged by counting, from the start of the dive and while the target could be hidden by the Spitfire's engine cowling. Although this was fairly rough handling it did not produce excessive wrinkling and it was those pilots who held their height until the last possible moment and then dived almost vertically, pulling out late, who had most wrinkles. During this manoeuvre some pilots lost the stick and were liable to find themselves at around 1,600 feet before recovering full control. This, then, was the real reason for excessive wrinkling and pilots of the 'Bombfires' were advised to make a longer dive despite the chance of attracting more AA fire.

One Spitfire pilot actually bunted (outside looped) his aircraft and when it was examined at Air Service Training, Hamble, the aircraft, MA308, was found to have considerable buckling in the wing under surfaces in the region of the cannons. It was considered that the aircraft had been subjected to negative G. Engine mounting U frames were also buckling and 35 Spitfires from Biggin Hill were found to have this fault. EN554, Mk IXB, had to take violent evasive action with the result that the U frame was damaged as were the wings. EN560 was thought to have been subjected to over 10G with damage to engine mounts, buckled wings and port tailplane failure, the tip being displaced upward by six inches. MH692 was badly damaged in the rear fuselage, and two Mk IXs broke up in the air. MH349 was performing aerobatics at the end of a test flight when the centre section of one wing failed, and in the second aircraft the pilot had lost consciousness, probably due to lack of oxygen when flying at high altitude and had gone into a high speed dive, during which the port wing broke away.

The HF IX Spitfire was produced in small quantities when compared to total production, but the design did take into account most of the important factors in the RAE Report, and the largest numbers of true production HFs can be found in the PL serial groupings. Rate of production suggests they were ordered as and when needed.

What was the Mk IX like, performance wise, when compared with the Fw190? There was only one true method of finding out. A captured Fw190 was flown against a Spitfire up to heights of 35,000ft. Both pilots were carefully selected and the following figures emerged from the trials. At 2,000ft the Fw was 7-8mph faster than the Mk IX; at 5,000 both had virtually the same performance; at 8,000 the IX 8mph faster than the Fw; at 15,000 the IX faster by 5mph; at 18,000 the Fw 3mph faster; at 21,000 performance was similar and at 25,000 the Spitfire 5-7mph better. During climb to 23,000ft there was little difference between them, but above that height the 190 was falling off rapidly with the Spitfire increasing speed at a faster rate. The 190 dived faster and was more manoeuvrable than the Mk IX, except in the turning circle. The superior rate of roll of the Fw enabled it to avoid the Spitfire when attacked, and the IX's worst height for fighting was between 18 and 20,000ft and below 3,000. Both aircraft were 'bounced' and the Spitfire could not be caught if cruising at high speed. But the same circumstances applied to the 190.

BR592 was converted from a Mk V. It was lost on operations on 11 October 1942.

In order to improve the IX's performance it was recommended that 150 octane fuel be used, thus permitting increased boost. For this modification the engine mounting had to be strengthened; a 24-25lb boost gauge fitted; a throttle gate fitted to limit boost to 18lb if the aircraft was refuelled with 100 octane and a gate limiting boost to 14½lb fitted to prevent 25lb being used for take off. The exhaust manifolds burned out rapidly but the shorter life was accepted by the RAF.

PT465, HFIX, Merlin 70, after installation of its new engine and wing fillets. It was sent to North Africa, August 1944.

As with the Mk I and V a floatplane version of the IX was investigated and the chosen airframe, an LF Mk IXB MJ892, converted for trials during 1944. Full details of this conversion may be found in chapter 19. Flight towing by the Spitfire and of the aircraft were subjects of many experiments and these are dealt with on pages 162/3. Members of RAE Farnborough visited Supermarine in early December 1942 to discuss glider towing by the Mk IX. It was proposed to fit a shackle to the tailwheel, similar to that used in the 'Hasty Hitch' trials conducted with Mk I and V Spitfires. This was followed by a visit from Mr Lobelle and Mr Harper, of Malcolm Aircraft, to talk over the possibility of a Spitfire towing a 15,000 lb glider via the tailwheel.

SWEDEN'S DILEMMA SPITFIRES

An interesting incident concerning Spitfires, particularly the Mk IX, happened towards the end of the war in Europe. A number of the Allies were clamouring for fighter aircraft, most of all the Spitfire, and Turkey was promised a quantity in 1944. They were not delivered but 25 were definitely promised for Spring 1945. The Turkish Government was angry at not being able to get what they had asked for – a total of 1,198 aircraft of all types. They wanted most of all the Spitfire Mk IX but were offered Hurricanes and Spitfire Mk Vs. It was most difficult to get the Turkish Government to accept what was on offer, despite the British explaining that the latest Spitfires were needed for the forthcoming invasion of Europe, and that the Russians were pressing their claims for Spitfires, insisting they had priority.

But there was an underlying reason for delay in sending Spitfires to both countries at that time. At a meeting held in London on 25 April 1944 an offer was made to Sweden to equip a number of their fighter squadrons with Spitfires, conditional upon the cessation, or reduction, of ball bearing supplies to Germany. It seemed a straightforward offer. The Germans were being driven back in Russia and the Allied Invasion was imminent. But the Swedish Government was nervous because, mainly, of the German retreat in Russia. Large numbers were in Finland, on Sweden's border, and the Swedes thought that the German forces would not hesitate to cross that border if anything should happen to their vital supplies, such as bearings.

The British Spitfire offer was rejected on 30 April with the result that an approach was made by America and then by Russia, but still the Swedes refused, clinging desperately to their

PT470, HF IX, M70, after conversion to LF IX, Lydda, March 1945.

neutrality. Because of the refusal of America's offer Britain's own supply of Swedish ball bearings was jeopardised by an American refusal to supply Sweden with 100 octane aviation fuel.

A second meeting of Central Office of Supply (CoS) took place and the following resolution was passed – "If our negotiations are finally unsuccessful there must be no delay in reducing Swedish bearing output by other means. In these circumstances it is recommended that the sabotage proposals should be cleared by all departments concerned." What sabotage proposals were made is not known, but the Americans did hint that they, too, were prepared to end Swedish ball bearing production by bombing the factories.

The affair did not end there for the Swedes were aware that the German High Command had an inkling of what was happening. It was arranged with the British and American governments that in the event of German aggression through Finland into Sweden the RAF would fly fifteen Spitfire squadrons of Mk IXs to the Skane airbase. Additional Mk IXs were to be delivered as back up and would be flown by Swedish Air Force pilots to protect the central areas, leaving the RAF to deal with the initial onslaught. But, there had to be a quid pro quo. In exchange for the Spitfire commitment the Swedes had to allow long range radar to be installed in the British Consulate in Stockholm without delay. Nothing further was heard of this proposal, but the Swedes did ask for immediate delivery of 25 Spitfire IXs (the British promised 20) and they had to be in Sweden before 10 December 1944.

On VE day, 8 May 1945, the Mk IXs' combat career virtually came to an end, but numerous foreign air forces had a need for it and it eventually served with many. There were many exeriments and conversions with, and of, the Mk IX airframe, including the trial installation of a rocket propelled missile called Uncle Tom for air-to-ship attack. The prototype weapon had a head weighing 545lb and an auw of 980. Trials started on 15 August 1944 and by December the missile had been modified to take several different types of explosive head and was designated Uncle Tom Mk II.

Like the Mk V the IX was considered as a direct PR conversion and the configuration was discussed at Hursley Park on 23 September 1942, just a few weeks after N3297 had flown with the Merlin 60 engine. Oil capacity was set at the normal 8.5gal tank as supplies of the 14gal tank were not available. Fuel was specified as 84gals in the fuselage, plus 29 in the rear fuselage and 90 in an overload tank. The second arrangement was to be 84gals plus 90 in the drop tank. A 36in camera, no R/T, two cannon with 120rpg would all add up to an auw of approximately 8,000lb. The Mk IX conversion eventually became the PR Mk XI, but one aeroplane was converted to the above specifications – BS338. This was at Worthy Down on 19 November, and such was the urgency that it had been converted at No. 1 PRU Benson. The F 36in camera was installed in the radio compartment. Summary of weights and CoG loadings was –

Tare (lb)	5636 @ 0.15in forward of datum; 10.7 in below
Landing	6417 @ 4.2in aft of datum; 10.2in below
Normal load rear fuel tank dry	7352 @ 7.1in aft of datum; 9.1in below
30gal overload	7643 @ 7.4 aft of datum; 10.1 below
60gal overload	7926 @ 7.6in aft of datum; 11.1 below

MH477. Trials with the American M 10 tube, cluster rocket launchers. Arrows indicate angle pieces.

MK297, originally transferred to RNAF and then to COGEA as 00-ARB. Resold to UK and registered G-ASSD using parts of MH334 for restoration. It left the UK in April 1969 and was sold to Confederate Air Force as N1182. It is extant.

PHOTO-RECONNAISSANCE SPITFIRES FOR NORWAY AND EGYPT

During a visit by Jeffrey Quill to Oslo in October 1945, requirements for a photo-reconnaissance aircraft for the Royal Norwegian Air Force were discussed and formulated. Investigations into the best possible method of satisfying the requirements were carried out and the results were summarised in Supermarine Specification No. 517. This proposed that the existing Norwegian Mk IXs should be converted to low level Tac. R aircraft by removing the cannon armament and

Standard F IX outside RAF blister hangar.

installing fuel tanks in the cannon and ammunition bays. The incorporation of fixed fittings and wiring for a universal type camera installation similar to that in the Spitfire PR Mk XI. This required modification of the wings and the addition of three wing ribs, and installation in the wings of some of the equipment fitted into the fuselage. The Merlin 70 engine was specified in place of the 66, both engines being inter-changeable. An alternative was conversion to a high altitude Spitfire with pressure cabin and Merlin 71 engine.

The following data apply to (1) proposition one – **All up weight 7,600lb; with 90 gal o/ld tank 8,400. Fuel capacity,** fuselage 85gals, inner wing 26, outer wing 27, total internal capacity 138gals. Oil 7.5gals. Provision for carrying 4 × .303 Browning m/gs with 350rpg. Camera installations (i) 2 × F52 36in vertical (ii) 1 × F52 36in vertical (iii) 2 × F52 20in vertical (iv) 2 × F8 20in vertical and (v) 2 F24 14in vertical and one F24 14 or 8in port facing oblique. **Performance:**

	100 octane	160
FS Max speed	402mph	404
FTH	20,000ft	15,000
MS max speed	376	376
FTH	9000	3800
MS @ SL	337	358
Rate of climb FS	4090ft/min	5010
FTH	18,000ft	12,600
MS	4800ft/min	5730
FTH	7000ft	1900
MS @ SL	4790ft/min	5700

A-32, IAF, silver overall. Stato Maggiore Aerautica.

F IXE 5534 of the SAAF, based at AFS, Watokloƒ. Note rocket rail stubs and bomb carriers.

Service ceiling 42,100ft. Range Cruise 244mph normal fuel 800 miles. With 90 gal o/ld 250mph 1335 miles. Height 20,000ft. Engine Merlin 66.

Proposition (2)

	100 octane	160
MS Max speed	410mph	412
FTH	25,800ft	20,800
FS	388	388
FTH	14,100	8900
MS @ SL	330mph	351
rate of climb (MS)	3710ft/min	4630
FTH	24,700ft	19,300
FS	4630ft/min	5560

NH236, HF IX, M70, at Farnborough for propeller trials, August 1944. It went to de Havilland where an M61 was fitted but it crashed during tests.

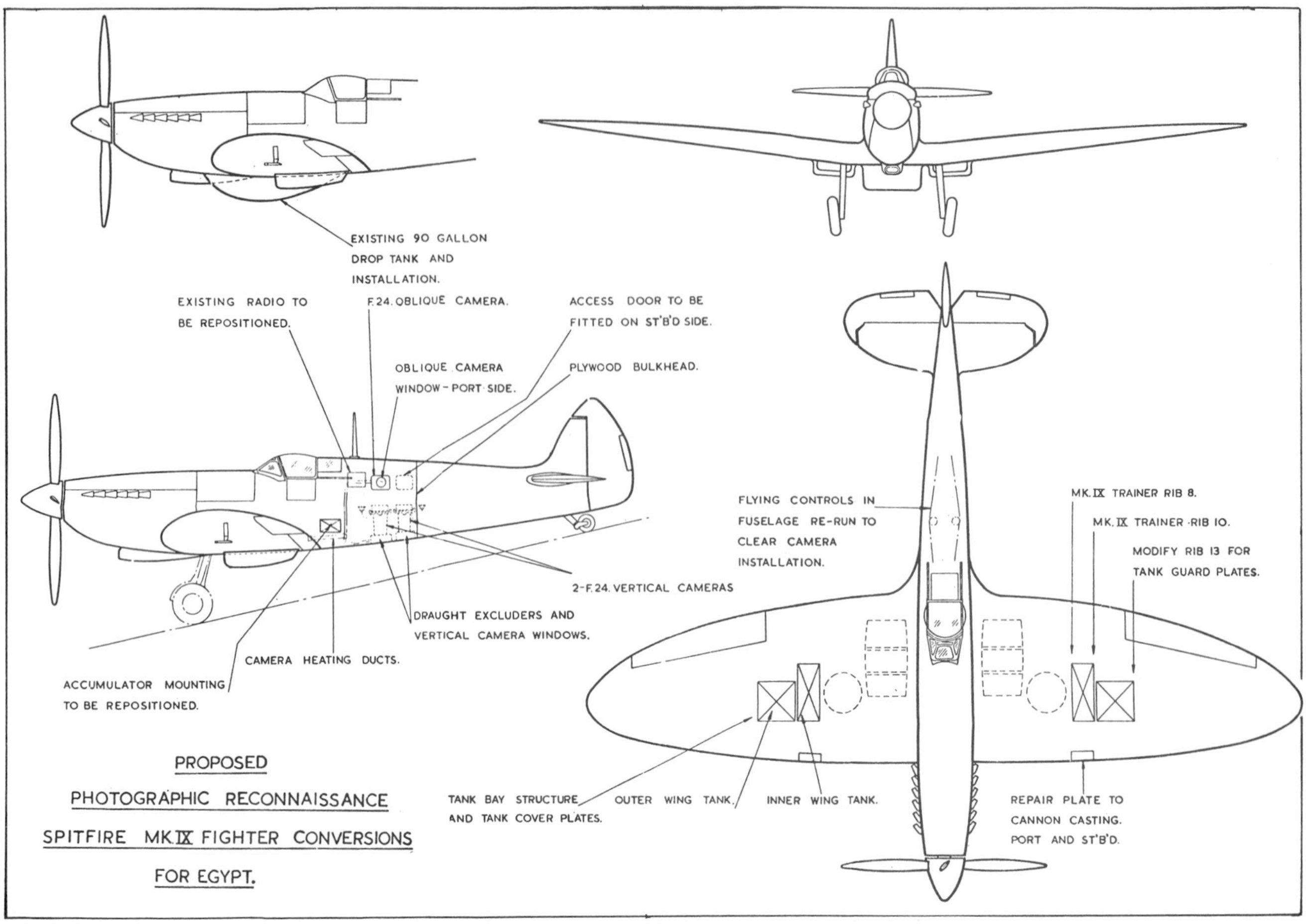

EXISTING 90 GALLON DROP TANK AND INSTALLATION.
EXISTING RADIO TO BE REPOSITIONED.
F.24. OBLIQUE CAMERA.
ACCESS DOOR TO BE FITTED ON ST'B'D SIDE.
OBLIQUE CAMERA WINDOW – PORT SIDE.
PLYWOOD BULKHEAD.
FLYING CONTROLS IN FUSELAGE RE-RUN TO CLEAR CAMERA INSTALLATION.
MK.IX TRAINER RIB 8.
MK.IX TRAINER RIB 10.
MODIFY RIB 13 FOR TANK GUARD PLATES.
2-F.24. VERTICAL CAMERAS
DRAUGHT EXCLUDERS AND VERTICAL CAMERA WINDOWS.
CAMERA HEATING DUCTS.
ACCUMULATOR MOUNTING TO BE REPOSITIONED.
TANK BAY STRUCTURE AND TANK COVER PLATES.
OUTER WING TANK.
INNER WING TANK.
REPAIR PLATE TO CANNON CASTING. PORT AND ST'B'D.

PROPOSED PHOTOGRAPHIC RECONNAISSANCE SPITFIRE MK.IX FIGHTER CONVERSIONS FOR EGYPT.

FTH	11,900	6800
MS @ SL	4560ft/min	5470
Service ceiling	42,200ft	

Range. Cruise 244mph normal fuel 800 miles; with 50gal overload tank 1,335 miles. Height 20,000ft.

An enquiry was also received from Egypt for the supply of 6 to 10 PR Mk IXs, but as they were not available an investigation was made into the possibility of converting the existing Egyptian Air Force F Mk IXs for the PR role. Supermarine Specification listed the full details and the data was as for the Norwegian conversions.

Several different types of Rolls-Royce engines were installed in service aircraft for trials under normal operating conditions. These included the Merlin 66 for the LF IXB; the Merlin 64; the Merlin 77 and one F IXE had a Merlin 46. Several odd designations also appeared including F IXC and the HF IXE. It is well known that six F Mk VIIIs were fitted with the Griffon 61 as development aircraft for the F Mk XIV, but what is not so well known is that a batch of seven LF Mk IXs were fitted with the G61 to help test the engine under normal service conditions.

SUPERMARINE'S TRIALS

Many flight trials were carried out by the Supermarine test pilot's team and a number are reproduced below.

Furlong 6-7-44. MH850. Merlin 266 (Packard Merlin) installed at Castle Bromwich. Rated climb and combat climb for boosts only.

Quill 12-8-44. PT452. Heavy ailerons and aircraft still fitted small rudder.

Quill 2-9-44. MJ636. Ailerons very heavy and aircraft left wing low. Engine surging which I would not refer to as surge. Something occurred very much on the lines of blower stalling. Not the type of surge we have on the Merlin 45 and 61 which takes place slowly and deliberately. I believe the engine is suffering from stalling of the rotor blades.

Furlong 6-9-44. MJ636. Merlin 66 interconnected throttle and propeller. It was found 18 months ago with Merlin 63s, 70s and 71s that a blower stall occurred if attempts were made to fly at high altitudes with too low revs and too high boosts.

Havercroft 30-11-44. ML186. Object of flight to determine limit of stability for combat with rear tank full. Take off and landing in this condition is without hazard but longitudinal instability in the climb is noticeable and in fast and slow level cruising. The aircraft must be flown deliberately and may not be left to itself even for a few seconds. In tight turns acceleration builds up and the aircraft is considered quite unacceptable in this state. The aircraft was further checked with 35 gallons in rear tank and it is acceptable for climb, fast and slow level cruising.

Quill 31-12-44. ML186. Main tanks and rear tanks full, with 90 gallon overload tank installed but empty. Object of flight to assess if aircraft is satisfactory for take off and formation flying. The aeroplane is just acceptable bearing in

NH314, IXE, M46 crashed during test flight. Rebuilt as HF IX, M70. It served with 34S Squadron, being declared Cat E in February 1945.

Line-up of Israeli LF IXs. Below '57', black IX in store. SOC 1955.

mind that the situation improves with each gallon of fuel used from the rear tank.

Quill 10-1-45. TB241. Aircraft is left wing low and propeller vibration considerable in dive.

Shea-Simmonds 1-6-45. RR232. Rear fuel Mk IX from the Handling Squadron at Hullavington. Ailerons excessively heavy throughout tests and could have done with 6in of trailing edge beading each side. With 25 gallons of fuel in rear tank it is just acceptable for combat.

Furlong 28-7-44. MK317. All tanks full. The engine is apparently running at about 65 gallons/hr. What have Rolls-Royce to say about this? Continuation of trials with one 62 gallon American drop tank on each wing (a) and with British 90 gallon slipper tank under fuselage (b). The British tank showed a superiority of speed of up to 12mph @ 10,000ft. It was also flown with American tanks empty and jettison tanks empty and rear tank full. Up to 10,000ft the aeroplane was perfectly stable.

OFFICIAL REPORTS ON Mk IX

Boscombe Down June 1942. AB197. Weights and loading data.

	'B' wing	'A' wing
Tare (includes 5 × 17.5lb ballast weights in tail	5749	5719
Service load	1008	798
Fuel	612	612
Oil	76	76
Take off	7445	7205

Boscombe Down 29 July 1942. N3297. Merlin 61 (converted from F I and F III). Comparative performance at normal and combat ratings with .42 and .447 reduction gears for three types of propeller. The change from normal to combat rating with .477 gears resulted in an average increase in rate of climb which varied from about 800ft/min at low altitude to about 200ft/min around 30,000ft. With .42 gears the increase was less marked but averaged about 300ft/min up to 30,000ft. Under all conditions the .477 gears gave better results than the .42, mainly because the rate of climb remained constant, or increased slightly with height up to full throttle height instead of decreasing all the way from ground level up. There was little

Post war export: 426 of the Royal Danish Air Force.

Mk IX modified in 1945 by No. 1 Aircraft Depot, Leningrad, for use as two-seat trainer.

JS-B, LF IX of SAAF (5536). Note oblique camera just aft of cockpit and fairing for vertical camera just behind rear of wing fillet. No armament.

difference in climb performance between the Hydulignum and Dural production propellers.

Boscombe Down 13 August 1942. N3297. Merlin 61. Fuel system tests. Auw 7,225lb. Tests to investigate behaviour of Spitfire with immersed fuel pump and pressure venting in fuel tanks. Tests proved that in all UK conditions either the pump or venting could maintain normal fuel pressure at the carburetter. Under tropical conditions both items were required to keep the engine running, but they could not maintain normal fuel pressure during climb.

Boscombe Down August 1942. AB197. Mk IXC. Interim maintenance report. This Spitfire was one of the first conversions of the F Mk VC airframe to Mk IX standards. Undercarriage. After nine landings (4hr 20min flying) the port tyre collapsed due to wall failure and both tyres were changed. After a further 16 landings (13hr 4min flying) the starboard tyre collapsed due to wall failure and both tyres changed. At 19hr flying time the port tyre burst. Total number of landings 60; flying hours 30. The tailwheel tyre burst at 64 landings; the port tyre after 37 hours flight and the starboard after 47. After 160 landings at the 60 hour inspection the starboard leg rake had moved forward ½in and deformed. After six more landings it was not possible to retract the u/c in flight. The port leg rake had moved forward 1¼in. Engine. Up to the 30hr inspection no faults. Airframe. No faults.

Boscombe Down 27 August 1942. BS139. Intensive flying trials. A period of 145 hours was carried out with this aircraft. The original engine failed after 117hrs. 258 landings were made and nine new tyres fitted.

Boscombe Down 27 September 1942. BS139. Fuel system tests. Tests showed the fuel system satisfactory for all conditions likely to be encountered in the UK.

Boscombe Down 1 October 1942. BF274. Determination of range with 170 gallon overload tank. Auw without o/ld tank 6,830lb, with tank 8,245. Distance flown using main tanks 589 miles, switching to overload tank a further 762 miles. Total still air range @ 15,000ft 1,372 miles.

Boscombe Down 10 October 1942. BF274. Fuel consumption trials. At auw 7,100lb in MS gear @ 174mph 6.76 air miles per gal; range 450 miles; endurance 1.95hrs at 20,000ft. FS gear @ 160mph 6.03 air miles per gal; range 375 miles; endurance 1.0hr @ 37,500ft. These results allow for climb to height.

Boscombe Down 18 October 1942. BS139. Carbon monoxide contamination trials.

Boscombe Down 22 October 1942. BF274. Climb and level speed performance and position error. Trials with and without 30 gallon overload tank. Without tank – Max rate of climb MS gear 3,200ft/min @ 13,500ft; FS gear 2,540ft/min @ 25,900ft. Service ceiling (100ft/min) 42,100ft. Time to 10,000ft 3.1 min; to 40,000ft 20.2 mins. Climb at combat rating MS gear 3,860ft/min @ 12,600ft; FS gear 3,020ft/min @ 25,200ft. Service ceiling 43,400ft. Time to 10,000ft 2.7 mins; to 40,000ft 16.6 mins. Max speed MS gear 380.5mph @ 15,400ft; FS gear 403mph @ 27,400ft. With tank – Max rate of climb MS gear 3,030ft/min @ 13,000ft; FS gear 2,360ft/min @ 25,900ft. Service ceiling (100ft/min) 42,400ft. Time to 10,000ft 3.3 mins; to 40,000ft 20.6 mins. Max speed MS gear 366mph @ 15,400ft; FS gear 389mph @ 27,400ft. Auw with tank 7,775lb, without 7,480.

Boscombe Down 4 November 1942. BF274. Engine cooling trials. On climb with best climbing speed and radiator flaps open cooling satisfactory. On climb in same condition but using combat power continuously cooling meets requirements for permitted five minute periods. In level flight @ 15,000ft MS gear and FS gear @ 27,000ft, radiator flaps shut, cooling meets requirements.

Boscombe Down 5 November 1942. BS139. Brief spinning trials. Auw 7,445lb. Spinning and recovery satisfactory, but a marked pitching and buffetting occurs.

Boscombe Down 9 November 1942. BS139. Tests of dive recovery characteristics. Considerably better than those of F Mk V.

Natal Squadron pilots, Mk IXs, of No. 222, June 1943.

F Mk IX, USAAF North Africa, September 1942.

TE308, HF IXC, M70, was sold to Vickers in July 1950 and converted to T.9 trainer, sold to Irish Air Corps as No.163, used in Battle of Britain film. Currently airworthy again in two-seat condition with Bill Greenwood, Aspen, Colorado.

RCAF pilot and ground crew, France, 1944.

RCAF pilot stands in the summer sun beside his Mk IX, France, 1944.

Mk IX and RCAF ground crew, France, August 1944.

RCAF Mk IX, wheels up landing, France August 1944. Soldier sweeps for mines.

Boscombe Down November 1942. BS354. Merlin RM 9SM, BS543 Merlin 66, BS551 Merlin 70. Performance of Mk IXs with high and low altitude versions of the intercooled Merlin. Two low altitude versions of the Merlin were designated RM 9SM and RM 10SM and a high altitude version was called the RM 11SM. The 10 and 11 were subsequently called the Merlin 66 and 70 respectively. All had Rotol propellers of 10ft 9in diameter and four blades. BS354 and 543 had the XH54D RM-S5; 551 the R5/4F5/4. Standard VC wings fitted. An improved type of supercharger was fitted to the Merlins with the diameter of the first stage rotor increased from 11ft 5in to 12ft. A Bendix-Stromberg carburetter injected fuel into the eye of the supercharger.

	BS354	BS543	BS551
Rate of climb @ S/L ft/min	4249	4620	4390
rate of climb full throttle height MS gear	4280	4700	4530
FS gear	3700 @ 18,200ft	3860 18,000	3480 24,700
Rate of climb @ 30,00ft ft/min	1925	2125	2600
Time to 10,000ft (min)	2.50	2.15	2.25
Time to 30,000ft (min)	9.15	8.4	8.05
Service ceiling (100ft/min)	40,500	40,900	41,000
Max speed @ S/L (mph)	329	336	329
Full throttle height MS gear	362	384	396
FS gear	398 @ 21,000ft	407 22,000	415.5 27,800
Level speed @ 30,000ft mph	387	395	413

The results showed that the RM 9SM in BS354 was inferior to the other two and the engine was dropped as a production unit.

Boscombe Down 9 December 1942. BS139. Flame damping trials with multi-ejector fish tail exhausts. Ground to air tests were conducted consisting of six runs at 300ft on a dark, cloudy night. Under all engine conditions the glow was so excessive that it was visible for over one mile as the Spitfire receded from the observers. The required distance was 100 yards.

Boscombe Down 23 December 1942. AB197. Gun heating tests with armament as installed in Spitfire VII and IX. The

SAAF Mk IX with 100 lb head RPs.

Line-up of Free French IXs, UK, 1944.

Spitfire of Free French Air Force, with the Mediterrean Allied Coastal Air Force.

BS183 at Centre de Perfectionment A' la Chasse (CPC), Morocco.

LF IXE with oblique camera port, FAF, post war.

French Mk IXs, Hanoi, Indo-China, 1947/48.

Mk IX carrying post war Aeronavale colours.

Free French HF IX, France, winter of 1944-45.

heating system collected hot air from the rear of each wing radiator and fed it to the gun bays. Although the heating did not fully meet with requirements it was considered good for the type of system utilised.

Boscombe Down December 1942. BS354. Merlin RM 9SM. Brief handling trials with F Mk XII rudder fitted. It was proposed to fit the Mk XII Spitfire rudder to Mk VII, VIII and IX production aircraft. Trials to determine the effect of the change of rudder on handling characteristics. The tendency of the Mk IX to swing to the left on take off was easier to control with the enlarged rudder.

Boscombe Down 5 December1942.BS354. Oil cooling and radiator suitability trials. Both met with requirements.

Vickers-Armstrongs December 1942. BS310. Comparative tests with Mk IX temperate and Mk VIII tropical air filter fitted. With the tropical filter speed was reduced by between 6 to 16mph.

Vickers-Armstrongs December 1942. BS310. Brief performance tests with Merlin 66 engine fitted. Max speed MS gear @ 8,200ft, 372mph; FS gear @ 19,500ft, 404. Rate of climb MS gear 4,850ft/min @ 6,000ft; FS gear 4,500ft/min @ 16,500ft.

Boscombe Down 14 January 1943. BS428. Brief handling trials with 250 and 500lb bomb fitted. The Universal No I Mk I bomb carrier was shortened. Auw with 250lb bomb 7,555lb; 500lb bomb 7,805. Bombs and carrier had little effect on flying characteristics.

Boscombe Down 29 January 1943. BS428. Level speed performance with and without 500lb bomb fitted. Max speed with bomb fitted 363mph @ 14,500ft. Without bomb 385 @ 14,750. Reduction in true air speed in MS gear was 22mph.

Boscombe Down 15 February 1943. BS428. Range determination with 500lb bomb fitted. The maximum still air range, dropping bomb at end of outward journey, was 450 miles, making no allowance for any combat periods.

Boscombe Down February 1943. BN524. HF Mk IX Merlin 70. Comparative performance trials with three types prop reduction gear combinations. (1) .477 gear 10ft 9in dia prop; (2) .42:1 gear, 10ft 9in prop, and .42.1 gear 11ft 1in prop.

	(1)	(2)	(3)
Rate of climb ft/min			
MS full throttle gear	4310	4030	4210
Time mins	2.3	2.5	2.4
FS gear (23,000ft°	3220	2930	3070
Time mins	5.6	6.75	6.45
Service ceiling	43,200ft	44,000	44,300
Max speed S/L	326	—	328
15,100ft MS gear	394	397	394
30,000ft FS gear	407	412	409

Boscombe Down 14 March 1943. AB499. Flame damping trials with frontal, close fitting anti-dazzle shrouds. At a range of 580 yards and 3,000ft altitude the exhaust glow was visible.

Boscombe Down 18 March 1943. BN524. Oil cooling and radiator suitability trials. Both met requirements.

Farnborough April 1943. P8441. Aileron tests in wind tunnel. Starboard wing of P8441 was tested and three methods of trimming used. (1) cord fixed to trailing edge (2) use of fixed tab (3) reflexing of trailing edge. Trial results needed for Mk IX Spitfires.

Boscombe Down May 1943. BN314. Handling tests with increased tailplane incidence. Incidence increased by 2° and elevator had enlarged horn balance. Change of incidence improved handling characteristics.

Boscombe Down 12 June 1943. AB197. Gun heating tests with armament as installed in Mk VIII. Four 20mm Hispano cannon. Did not meet requirements.

Farnborough June 1943. Wind tunnel tests on alternative Spitfire cabins. Tests to find the effect of drag of various modifications to Spitfire cabin. Cabins were mounted on a special body suspended from the upper balance and wind speeds of 80, 100, 120 and 140ft/sec recorded. Six windscreens and four hoods tested.

Farnborough 3 July 1943. Resonance tests of Spitfire F V and IX. A series of vibration-exciter tests were carried out on BR138 (Mk V) and AB196 (Mk IX) to examine the modes of vibration of single engine aircraft. The Mk V had a mock engine installed. It was noted that on some aircraft the wings flapped during ground run due to resonance, but it was not very noticeable on Spitfires. With a Mk IX running at high boost resonance did trouble some pilots. AB196 had its Merlin 61 installed during the trials and as a result it was recommended that rubber mounts be provided for engines.

Boscombe Down 17 August 1943. BS137. Rogue aircraft from No. 222 Squadron. Impossible to correct lateral trim and the aircraft crabbed sideways in flight. Heavy ailerons changed.

Farnborough September 1943. EN498. Effect of conical, curved windscreen on performance. Speed increase from 3mph @ Mach .43 to 12mph @ .79.

Boscombe Down September 1943. AB505. HF Mk IX

Mk IXs, India, 1944.

5621, LF IXE, of SAAF. Late production with rear view fuselage and large fin and rudder.

Merlin 77. Handling tests with contra-prop; fitted with enlarged fin and rudder (converted from Mk V). Rotol six blade CR 290F and 290R, 10ft 9in diameter. Auw 7,440lb. CPs eliminated swing on take off; aerobatics easier. All other manoeuvres normal.

Boscombe Down 23 October 1943. BS310. Comparative performance with 4 and 5 blade propellers.

	Diameter 10ft 9in	
	Rotol R 12/4F5/4 four blade	**Rotol Mk XH55 five blade**
Max rate of climb full throttle height MS gear ft/min	4470 @ 11,200ft	4500 @ 9,900
FS gear	3400 @ 22,700ft	3400 @ 21,700
Est Service ceiling	43,100ft	42,400
Max level speed @ full throttle height MS gear	388mph @ 14,600ft	ditto
FS gear	405mph @ 25,400ft	408 @ 24,600

Boscombe Down October 1943. BS310. Brief handling trials with CoG 5.8in aft of datum. Split armour moved CoG aft. Auw 7,320lb. Handling satisfactory.

Boscombe Down 12 November 1943. BS310. Determination of aftmost acceptable CoG. CoG approximately 9in from datum, when deterioration of longitudinal behaviour occurs.

Boscombe Down November 1943. MA648. LF Mk IX Merlin 66. Level speed trials with SU Mark II point fuel injection pump. Max speed @ 9,400ft full throttle height 379mph; FS gear @ 21,000ft 411.

Boscombe Down 20 February 1944. EN314. Merlin 61. Flight trials of Maclaren radiator protection scheme. Trials to examine maximum permissable power used in level flight with one main coolant radiator out of operation. Under temperate conditions radiator suitability remained above unity. Under tropical conditions flight almost impossible.

Boscombe Down 20 February 1944. EN314. F Mk IXC. Engineering and maintenance appraisal of Maclaren radiator scheme. Excellent results.

Airborne Forces Experimental Est. 31 March 1944. BS434. To assess suitability of Spitfire Mk IX as tug for fully loaded Hotspur glider. Auw 7,305lb. Take off speed 110mph. Performance as tug excellent.

Boscombe Down March 1944. BS310. Effect of Mach number on dive and recovery characteristics. Highest Mach number reached in dive was .83 and the aircraft developed a longitudinal pitching movement. Elevators became very heavy and there was considerable turbulence around the cockpit canopy.

Boscombe Down March 1944. MJ823. LF Mk IX Merlin 66. Handling trials with wing bombs. Bomb racks under wings held either (a) two × 250lb GP bombs or (b) two × 120lb Mk IIA smoke bombs. Auw 7,850 and 7,575lb respectively. Ordnance loads did not appreciably affect performance.

Farnborough April 1944. BS118, EN498, JL227. Flight tests on external misting of windscreen at high altitude. Complaints received from squadrons stated that in combat manoeuvres at high altitude external misting of the windscreen took place, caused, it was thought, by condensation of exhaust gas on cold screen. Deflectors of flat steel plates were installed on top of the exhaust stubs, the 'short' deflectors extending the length of the exhaust stubs while the 'long' extended further aft to about 21in of the wing chord. Misting never appeared in straight and level flight, but one or two degrees of sideslip could produce severe misting. The 'short' deflectors were superior to the 'long', and an added bonus was an increase in speed of approximately 6mph.

Farnborough 7 February 1944. BS403. Flight tests of 45gal Stanley Smith drop tank stability during aerobatics. Satisfactory.

Farnborough May 1944. Further jettison tests of Spitfire hoods in wind tunnel. Drawings show behaviour of hoods after leaving aircraft at various speeds.

Boscombe Down 3 June 1944. EN314. Coolant flow measurements with Maclaren radiator scheme. Measurements made with aircraft under normal conditions and with either radiator isolated by the protection scheme. During isolation flow of coolant was reduced by half, each cylinder block receiving an equal amount.

Boscombe Down 25 June 1944. MJ823. LF Mk IX. Handling trials with wing bombs and one 500lb bomb or a 90gal overload tank beneath fuselage. Auw with 2 × 250lb GP and 1 x 500lb MC bombs 8,435lb. With 2 x 210lb GP bombs and 1 x 90 gal overload tank 8,675. All trials satisfactory.

Boscombe Down 6 July 1944. AB197. Gun heating tests with a special manifold for heating armament as on Spitfire VIII.

Boscombe Down 6 July 1944. MK210. Effect of two underwing drop tanks on level speed performance and position-al error correction. Modifications installed at Wright Field, USA (1) 43gal tank behind pilot (2) two leading edge tanks of 16½gal (3) two Mustang type drop tanks of 62½gal. Auw with drop tanks empty 8,265lb; without tanks 8,155.

	mph without tanks	**with tanks**
Full throttle height MS gear	363 @ 9400ft	333 @ 8800
FS gear	392 @ 20,350ft	359 @ 19,600

Boscombe Down August 1944. MK210. Handling trials underwing drop tanks and tank dropping tests. Auw fuel tanks full 9165lb. Handling satisfactory. Starboard dropped @ 200mph. It swung clear of aircraft, bracing swept along wing undersurface but cleared tailplane. Port tank @ 250mph. Tank and bracing fell away clear. Starboard tank @ 300mph. Tail of tank forced up and dented undersurface of wing; bracing swept close to undersurface of tailplane.

Farnborough November 1944. V-g records for Spitfire Mk IX during operations in France and Belgium. A number of V-g recorders were installed in aircraft of a Spitfire Mk IX LF Wing on the North Western Front, in order to investigate skin wrinkling on mainplanes. Spitfires of No. 125 Wing had experienced a large number of buckled wings within the space of a few weeks. Aircraft involved in the tests were:– NL345,

Drawings of 'short' and 'long' engine exhaust deflectors on Mk IX Spitfire.

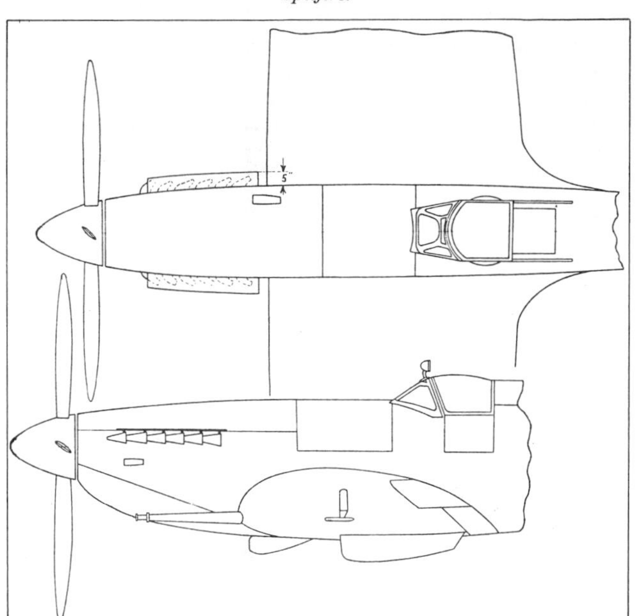

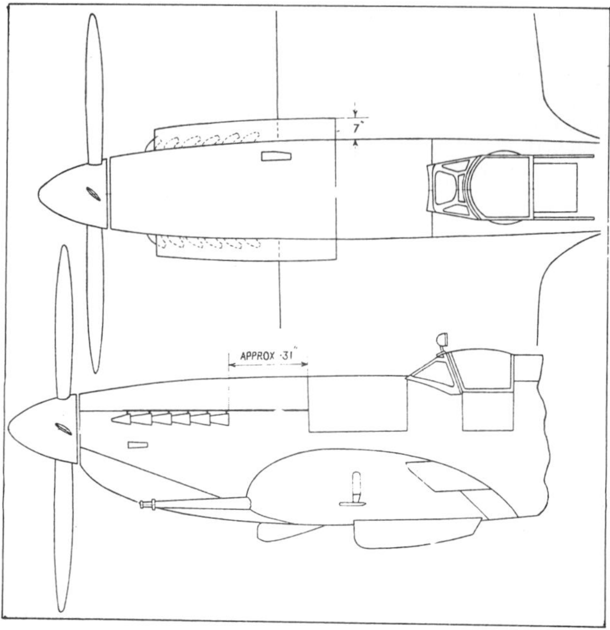

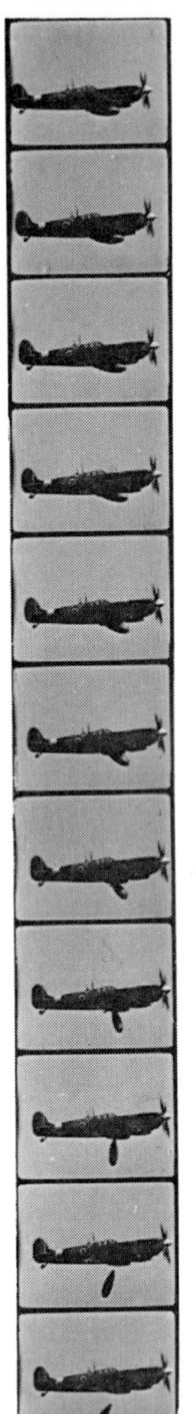

Jettison trials with MK210. At speeds in excess of 300mph the tanks fouled the aircraft, denting the under wing surfaces.

MK210 before and after receiving additional internal and external tanks. *Rear fuselage tank and Mustang underwing tanks (2 × 62½ gal) raised total fuel load to 200 gallons. On 20 September 1944 the Mk IXC flew the Atlantic non-stop from Newfoundland. Route was Bangor (Maine), Goose Bay (NFound), Reykjavik (Iceland). Pilots G. R. Avle and C. Lingquist USAAF. Second aircraft also modified was NK317, which made the journey in July 1944. It was modified at Wright Field, Ohio, USA. Close-up views show a tank with various venturi and wooden, steady plates. With a full fuel load MK210 weighed 9,165lb at take off.*

NH476, PT357. The two forms of attack suspected of causing wing damage were armed reconnaissance and dive bombing. For bombing one 500lb bomb was carried under the fuselage and two 250lb bombs under the wings. The pilots generally dived onto the target at an angle of 45 to 60°. Lowest altitude reached was about 1,000ft choosing one vehicle and diving across the road and not along it. Only in rare cases were roads swept with gun fire. After the attack the Spitfires were climbed immediately out of range of the heavy flak using rapid aileron rolls, weaving, tight turns and inverted flight. Escape low down was not favoured as the flak could concentrate easily at that height. The pull out was considered severe and and black out, a common occurrence, was ignored.

Boscombe Down 26 December 1944. BS352. Pitot error measurement.

Vickers-Armstrongs 17 January 1945. ML186. Effect of rear fuselage fuel tank (75 gallons) on handling qualities. Pilot R.L. Havercroft. Auw 8,275lb. CoG 12.2in aft of datum. Taxied without fear of nose over. Impossible to trim aircraft in climb and demanded pilot's complete attention. Aircraft acceptable for take off and landing and normal flying, but not for formation or combat.

Vickers-Armstrongs 29 January 1945. ML186. Stability for take off and formation flying. In the opinion of Quill, Morgan and Shea-Simmonds the aircraft with rear tank full was just about acceptable.

Boscombe Down January 1945. ML186. Handling with rear fuselage tank and metal elevators. The acceptable aftmost CoG position for combat manoeuvres was 9.9in aft of datum (34gals fuel used from rear tank). Metal elevators (hand made) improved performance. Inertia weight not recommended.

Boscombe Down 5 January 1945. MH477. Rocket firing trials with American M.10 tube cluster launchers. The firing of 4.5in rockets at speeds up to 450mph had no adverse effects on aircraft.

Boscombe Down 28 May 1945. TA822. F Mk IXE. Gun heating tests with NAFDU barrel cooling scheme. The cooling fitment was installed on the starboard .5in Browning gun.

Boscombe Down October 1945. EN314. Further tests of Maclaren radiator protection scheme.

Farnborough February 1946. NH230. Measurements of tail and fin loads by the deflection method in flight at high Mach numbers. Fully feathering propeller fitted with special counter balance weights at roots. Large rudder, incidence vane on starboard wing.

Farnborough April 1946. Wind tunnel tests on wooden Rotol propeller.

Flight Refuelling Ltd July 1944. BF274. Fighter Towing. (See page 162 for complete details).

Farnborough July 1949. NH236. Performance of a special de Havilland propeller in flight at high forward speeds. NACA

16 series blade section, three blades 11ft 0in diameter. Mach number of .82. Propeller efficiency over 80%. The Merlin 61 engine was specially calibrated, but the constant speed unit was unable to control propeller at altitudes above 15,000ft.

Farnborough July 1946. Flight tests of longitudinal stability and control characteristics of Mk IX with large tailplane fitted. Gross area of tailplane was 57% above that of the normal Mk IX. The large tailplane increased pitching moment due to sideslip. With a 20in long cord on the elevator the handling was better than that of the standard Mk IX.

Royal Air Force Squadrons operating the F Mk IX, including Fighter Command, are listed below.

The bad condition of the advanced air strips in Normandy were giving cause for concern and a Mr Marsh of Supermarine, Trowbridge designed a new type of undercarriage oleo leg in which the normal compression unit was helped by a bending movement. As the Supermarine Report stated – "To use Mr Marsh's analogy, you do not jump and land from a height with the legs straight, but with them bent a little". Problem was how to house the unit in the wing; as a result the idea was dropped.

Sqdn	Code	Period used
1	JX	Apl to Nov '44
6	JV	Dec '45 to Dec '46
19	QV	Aug '43 to Jan '44
28	BF	Aug to Sept '45
32	GZ	Aug '44 to May '47
33	5R	Dec '43 to Oct '44
43	FT	Jan '44 to May '47

Sqdn	Code	Period used
56	US	May to Jly '44
64	SH	Jly '42 to Jly '44
65	YT	Sept to Oct '42, Aug to Dec '43
66	LZ	May '43 to Apl '45, Sept '46 to Sept '47
72	RN	Feb '43 to Dec '46
73	TP	1944 to '47
74	ZP	1942 to '45

Winter, with snow and cold conditions (421 Squadron)...

... caused as many maintenance problems as did hot summer days and dust. France 1944.

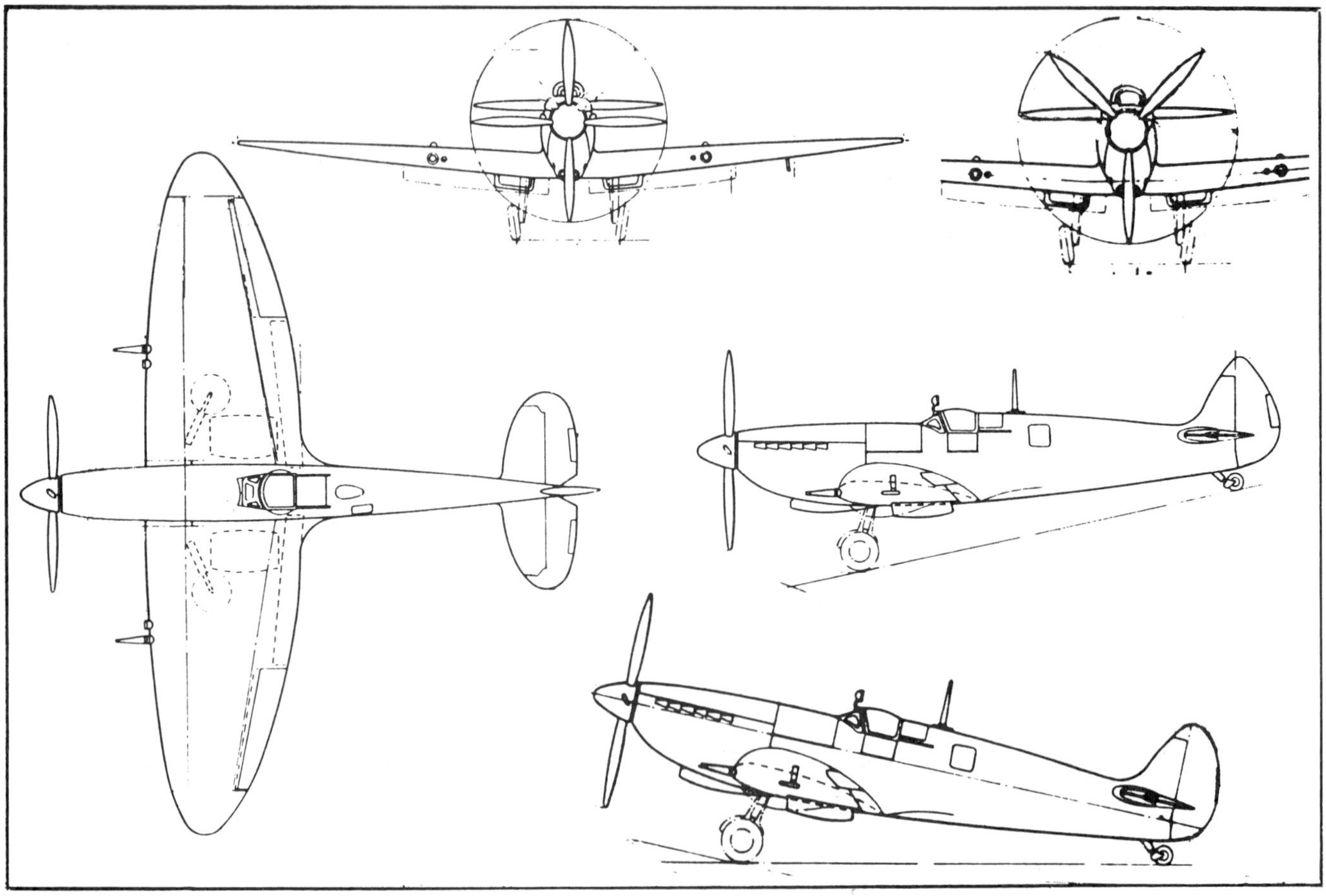

F Mk IX with four and three blade propeller; broad and normal chord rudder.

SPITFIRE F Mk IX, LF IX, LF IXE, HF IX, HF IXE

Wing span. (F) 36ft 10in; area 242sq ft. LF 32ft 2in; area 231sq ft.

Weights. F IX. Tare 5,800lb, take off 7,295.5, max permissible 7,500. Plus – 30 gal steel o/ld 281, fibre o/ld 256, wood o/ld 274, 90 gal o/ld 790. Bomb carrier 51 with 250 GP or SAP bomb, 500 GP, 500 MC, 500 SAP. Ballast 92.5.

Weights. F IXE. Tare 5,816lb, take off 7,181.5, max permissible 7,500, max o/ld 9,500. Plus ordnance as above, also 120 smoke bomb, or 45 gal o/ld 404, 50 gal o/ld 410, 170 gal ferry tank 1,414. Figures above are for a/c with Rotol 4-blade wood propeller. With Dural propeller tare weight 5,705, with split armour tare 5,648 (wooden prop), Dural prop tare 5,754.

Engines	Propeller
Merlin 61, 1,565hp.	Rotol 4-blade R.3/4F5/2 Dural 30° pitch.
Merlin 63, 1,650hp.	Rotol 4-blade R.5/4F5/3 Jablo or Hydulignum 30° or R.3/4F5/3 Dural 35. Diameter 10ft 9in.
Merlin 63A, 1,650hp.	Rotol R.12/4F5/4 Jablo or Hydulignum, or R.5/4F5/4 as above. Diameter 10ft 9in. 35°.

Merlin 61-63A with anti G carburettor and some with 18lb boost. Used on F IX.

Merlin 66, 1,580hp.	As Merlin 63A. Used for LF IX and LF IXE.
Merlin 70, 1,475hp.	As for Merlin 63A. Used for HF IX and HF IXE.

Fuel. 150 octane plus 25lb boost.

Fuel tankage. Fixed 48 gal upper and 37 lower fuselage in front of pilot. Total fixed 85 gals. Plus 30, 45, 50, 90 and 170 gal drop tanks. Late production models with 33 or 41 gal rear fuselage tank plus two 18 gal Mareng bags in wings. Fuel cooler in port wing root. Oil 7.5 gals normal, long range 14.4.

Armament. B wing F and LF IX. E wing LF IXE, C wing, two 20mm cannon and four .303 Brownings. Provision for 2 x 250lb or 1 x 500 bombs or mixture plus 120lb smoke bombs. Gun sight Gyroscopic Mk IID.

Radio. T.R. 1143, R3067, A1271. T.R. 1196A to special order only. ARI 15025 or ARI 5131 to special order only.

Armour. 200lb.

Cine camera. G.45 starboard wing.

Performance. Max speed F IX 408mph @ 25,000ft. HF 416 @ 27,000. LF 404 @ 21,000. Cruise (most marks) 324. Stall, flaps and U/C up 94, down 80. Rate of climb (most marks) 3,950ft min. Climb to 20,000ft 5.7 min. Ceiling (most marks) 43,000ft. Range between 434 to 980 with various fuel loads.

Tropicalisation Vokes 1943 Aero Vee.

Plan view of enlarged tailplane on Mk IX and comparison with standard tailplane.

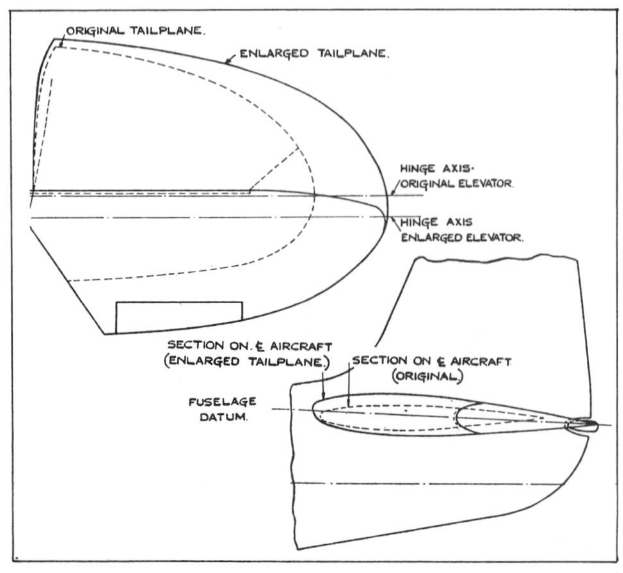

SERIAL NUMBERS

Supermarine Aviation (Vickers) Ltd
Contract No B.19713/39
Fifth order for 1,100 Spitfire Mk **IA/IB dated 24 October 1940. Built as** PR.IV/VB/VC/VI/VII/IX between February and November 1942. The following serials apply to Mk IXs built to this fifth order; BR581, 592, 594, 596, 600-605, 977-978, 980-982, 985-986, BS104-105, 107, 109-110, 112-113, 116, 118-120, 122-123, 125-132, 135-140, 143-145, 147-148, 150-152, 157, 159, 167, 170, 172, 176-177, 179-180, 183, 185, 189, 192, 194-196, 198, 200, 202, 227, 239-244, 246-252, 254-255, 292, 294, 296, 297, 299, 301-304, 306-319, 383-411, 428-435, 438-441, 443-447, 449-452, 454-459, 461-464, 466-471, 473-474 and 506-515.

Seventh order for 500 Spitfire Mk VC dated 23rd August 1941. Built as Mk VC/PR IV/VI/VII/IX/XI/XII between November 1942 and August 1943. The following serials apply to Mk IXs built to this seventh order; EN122-148, 152, 156, 171-175, 177, 179-188, 190, 191, 193-207, 259, 261, 265-270, 286-296, 298-309, 311-315, 329, 333-336, 339-340, 344-345, 349-350, 390, 392-394, 397-406, 444-456, 458-464, 466-469, 471-473, 475-476, 478-483, 490-493, 498, 500-502, 510, 513-514 and 617.

Vickers-Armstrongs (Castle Bromwich) Ltd
Contract No B981687/39
Sixth order for 989 Spitfire VB dated **23 January 1942. Built as Mks VC/** IX between December 1942 and April 1943. The following serials apply to Mk IXs built to this sixth order; JK395, 611, 641, 650, 770, 796, 881-884, 980, JL134-138, 177-180, 226-230, 252-256, 375-377 and 383-384.

Eighth order for 680 Spitfire Mk VC dated May 1942. Built as Mks VC/IX between March and June 1943. The following serials apply to this eighth order: LZ816, 831-833, 836-843, 861, 888-899, 915-925, 947-956, 989-998, MA221-260, 299-315, 369, 398-428, 443-487, 501-546, 559-601, 615-642, 683, 687, 690, 693, 705-713, 726-767, 790-819, 831-849, 854, 860, 878-879 and 884.

Supermarine Aviation (Vickers) Ltd
Contract No B19913/39
Tenth order for 426 Spitfire Mk VC **dated 12 May 1942. Built as Mks VII/** VIII/IX/X/XI/XII between July 1943 and March 1944. The following serial applies to a Mk IX built to this tenth order; MB807.

Ninth order for 2,190 Spitfire Mk VC dated 28th May 1942. Built as Mks VC/IX/XVI between July 1943 and May 1944. The following serials apply to Mk IXs built to this ninth order; MH312-336, 349-390, 413-456, 470-512, 526-563, 597-599, 601-604, 606-623, 635-636, 647-678, 691-738, 756-796, 813-856, 869-912, 924-958, 970-999, MJ114-156, 169-203, 215-258, 271-314, 328-369, 382-428, 441-485, 498-536, 549-555, 557-589, 602-646, 659-698, 712-756, 769-801, 814-858, 870-913, 926-967, 979-999, MK112-158, 171-213, 226-268, 280-326, 339-379, 392-428, 440-486, 499-534, 547-590, 602-646, 659-699, 713-756, 769-812, 826-868, 881-926, 939-969, 981-999, ML112-156, 169-216, 229-277, 291-323, 339-381 and 396-428.

Tenth order for 600 Spitfire Mk IX **dated 1 December 1942. Built as Mk** IXs between April and June 1944 as follows; NH148-158, 171-218, 230-276, 289-326, 339-381, 393-438, 450-496, 513-558 and 570-611.

Eleventh order for 800 Spitfire Mk **IXs dated 2 June 1943. Built as Mks** IX/F.22 between June 1944 and December 1945. The following serials apply to Mk IXs built to this eleventh order; PK991-998, PL123-169, 185-228, 313-356, 369-408, 423-466 and 488-499.

Twelfth order for 1,500 Spitfire Mk **21 dated 17 July 1943. Contract can**celled, then amended to 673 Mk IX. Built as Mk IX/XVI between June and October 1944. The following serials apply to Mk IXs built to this twelfth order; PT355-380, 395-436, 451-498, 523-567, 582-627, 639-683, 697-738, 752-795, 818-859, 873-915, 929-970, 986-999, PV115-160, 174-215, 229-270, 283-287, 289-294, 296-305, 308-326, 341-348 and 350-359.

Thirteenth order for 100 Spitfire Mk **IX dated 25 October 1943. Built as** Mks IX/XVI between August and October 1944. The following serials apply to Mk IXs built to this thirteenth order; RK798-819, 835-839, 841, 843-848, 850-858, 860-864, 867, 884-887, 889, 890, 894, 898-901, 906-909, 911, 912, 914-917, 919, 920 and 922-924.

Fourteenth order for 73 Spitfire Mk **IX dated 16 November 1943. Built as** Mk IXs between August and October 1944. The following serials apply to this fourteenth order; RR181-211, 228, 231-232, 235, 237-239, 241, 244, 246, 251-254, 258-260, 262 and 264.

Sixteenth order for 800 Spitfire Mk **21 dated 1 February 1944. Contract** cancelled in August 1944. Partially reinstated for 558 Spitfire Mk IX. Built as Mk IX/XVIs between September and November 1944. The following serials apply to Mk IXs built to this sixteenth order; SL594, 595, 625-635, 648-665, SM135-150, 170-177, 240, 425, 441-463, 486, 504-506, 508-510, 513-515, 517-537, 539-548, 563-597, 610-645, 647, 663, 666 and 668-669.

Seventeenth order for 1,884 Spitfire **Mk IX dated 19 April 1944. Built as** Mk IX/XVIs between December 1944 and June 1945. The following serials apply to Mk IXs built to this seventeenth order; TA738, 740, 742-758, 760-780, 793-808, 810-840, 844, 850-851, 854-888, 905-948, 960-999, TB115-129, 133-135, 142-150, 168-193, 195-197, 213-231, 233-236, 238-243, 249, 251, 253, 393, 413-450, 464-474, 477, 479, 482-491, 499, 500, 503, 516, 518, 523, 524, 527, 529-548, 563-571, 573, 575-577, 579, 584, 586, 587, 638, 640-659, 674, 676-701, 703, 708, 710-712, 717, 718, 736, 740, 771-808, 824-827, 830, 837-857, 909, 914, 918, 920, 924, 925, 938-959, 971-988, 992, 994, TD155, 175, 178-183, 192-213, 287, 290-292, 294-315, 352-368, 370, 371, 373, 374, 378, 379, 395, 399, 952-958, 970-999, TE115, 117, 118, 121-158, 197, 205, 211, 213, 215, 230-234, 236, 238, 289, 290, 292-299, 301, 303-309, 312, 313, 315, 329, 331, 333, 336, 337, 343, 493-535 and 549-578.

TOTAL 5,663. Supermarine 557 and Vickers-Armstrongs 5,117.

BR BS series all F IX Merlin 61 unless otherwise indicated.

BR581 3027 EA IXC FF 9-6-42 33MU 10-6 64S 22-6 CE ops 19-8

BR592 3028 EA FF 10-6-42 IXC 33MU 11-6 64S 8-7 FTR ops 11-10

BR594 3047 EA FF 11-6-42 33MU 28-6 64S 19-7 CAC ops 29-8 ROS 306S 16-9 64S 18-9 122S 12-12 331S 17-2 CE ops 2-5-43

BR596 3039 EA FF 13-6-42 33MU 16-6 64S 22-5 FTR ops 11-10

BR600 3079 IXC EA FF 24-6-42 45MU 26-6 64S 10-7 ROS 2-9 453S 14-11 FACB 27-5-43 AST BDn 11-2-44 SAL 4-10 80 OTU 24-5-45 sold H Bath 10-11-49

BR601 3057 EA FF 16-6-42 45MU 17-6 64S 10-7 FACB 21-10 GAL 453S 2-4-43 AST 16-4 mods 129S 17-7 316S 28-8 165S 28-9 AST 19-3-44 VA 1-3-45 mods MAL 25-4 *Clan McK* 27-1-49 SAAF 13-3-49. Auctioned in UK 10-86, extant.

BR602 3059 EA FF 18-6-42 45MU 21-6 64S 11-7 FTR ops 7-9 FH 74.35

BR603 3065 EA FF 20-6-42 12MU 23-6 64S 9-7 fuel shortage after sweep f/ld o/t Knighton Wembury Devon CE 27-9 SOC 9-10

BR604 3071 EA FF 21-6-42 12MU 23-6 64S 9-7 FTR ops 19-8

BR605 3078 IXC EA FF 25-6-42 12MU 26-6 64S 9-7 e/fd i/sea off Felixstowe Sgt Dickerson safe 1-8-42 SOC 4-8

BR977 3092 EA FF 27-6-42 45MU 28-6 64S 15-7 FTR ops 19-8

BR978 3093 EA FF 27-6-42 45MU 28-6 611S 25-7 FAAC 9-11 GAL 416S 11-4-43 AST 18-4 mods

BR980 3095 EA FF 27-6-42 45MU 28-6 AFDU 13-7 64S 4-8 Farn comp trls with Fw190 (MP499) FTR ops 5-9 FH 53.20

BR981 3103 EA FF 29-6-42 39MU 5-7 72S 24-7 401S 27-7 FTR 26-9

BR982 3104 EA FF 30-6-42 39MU 3-7 72S 24-7 401S 27-7 331S 5-12 AST 11-3-43 mods 611S 14-7-44 CE ops 5-9

BR985 3128 EA FF 6-7-42 39MU 7-7 72S 24-7 401S 27-7 CE ops 17-8 SOC 31-8

BR986 3118 EA FF 4-7-42 39MU 5-7 72S 24-7 401S 27-7 CB ops 28-8 ROS GAL 18-9 403S 22-3-43 AST 5-4 mods FTR ops 15-5 FH100.25

lBS104 3129 EA FF 8-7-42 12MU 16-7 72S 25-7 401S 27-7 403S 25-1-43 AST 11-3 mods FTR ops 13-5 FH256.5

BS105 3127 EA FF 6-7-42 39MU 7-7 64S 25-7 C3 ops 3-8 AST 122S 14-1-43 340S 28-2 AST 11-3 mods 341S 26-3 FTR ops 17-4

BS107 3145 EA FF 5-7-42 39MU 12-7 401S 27-7 FTR ops 19-8

BS109 3150 Ea FF 11-7-42 8MU 13-7 611S 24-7 FAAC 26-7 GAL 122S 19-9 AST 21-12 mods dvd i/grd from h/a nr Chelmsford Essex CE 24-10 FH103.10

BS110 3149 EA FF 8-7-42 8MU 12-7 611S 25-7 CB ops 23-10 GAL 340S 18-3-43 403S 19-3 FTR ops 4-4

BS112 3146 EA FF 9-7-42 8MU 12-7 611S 25-7 FTR ops 29-11

BS113 3158 EA FF 12-7-42 6MU 16-7 611S 24-7 FTR ops 2-11

BS116 3157 EA FF 12-7-42 6MU 16-7 611S 24-7 FAAC 16-1-43 ROS 403S 3-6 CB ops 14-3 GAL 274S 28-6-44 FLS 21-8-45 bou sold scr 3-9

BS118 3161 EA FF 25-7-42 VAWD 17-7 48hr trl BDn 19-11 VA HrPK comp test with normal and large elev tabs 2-10; exhaust flame deflectors instal directing hot gases to clear misted w/s at alt Serv trls adjudged failure. BDn 26-11-43 trls for drag effect of 30gal o/ld tank on level speeds. Assisted t/o trls (RATOG) and tail load at high mach numbers. Took over prog from EN498. Dvd to Mach .89 from 40,000ft. AST 20-6-44 33MU 14-10-44 VA 1-12 sold to R J Coley 3-2-50

BS119 3170 EA FF 16-7-42 33MU 21-7 72S 24-7 401S 27-7 CE ops 19-8

BS120 3177 EA FF 19-7-42 33MU 21-7 72S 24-7 401S 27-7 CB ops 19-8 GAL 403S FTR ops 4-4-43

BS122 3183 EA FF 20-7-42 33MU 23-7 402S 28-7 CE ops 21-8

BS123 3158 EA FF 12-7-42 33MU 23-7 402S 28-7 CAC ops 24-8 GAL 340S 20-2-43 AST 17-3-43 mods 341S 26-3 FAF FTR ops 17-5

BS125 3193 EA FF 23-7-42 6MU 24-7 611S 24-7 331S 4-4-43 AST 16-8 CB ops 3-10 ROS 313S 5-9-44 611S 3-10 312S 22-3-45 ASTE 3-4 SAAF 28-4-48

BS126 3200 EA FF 24-7-42 6MU 28-7 64S 14-9 CAC ops 10-11 GAL 416S 1-4-43 AST mods 4-4 421S 20-5 310S 19-9 CAC ops 26-9 ROS sold VA 30-4-47

BS127 3201 EA FF 25-7-42 6MU 26-7 402S 3-8 AST 7-3-43 mods M63 instal 416S 23-3 CB ops 13-5 GAL 165S 11-2-44 131S 19-3 313S 30-8 611S 8-10 310S 22-3-45 VA mods 312S 27-8 sold H Bath 27-10-49

BS128 3194 EA FF 23-7-42 611S 25-7 FAAC 20-12 ROS AST 26-1-43 mods M63 instal 340S 20-2 341S 26-3 AST 11-4 mods FACB 26-6 AST 274S 15-5-44 FAAC 7-8 ROS 86MU 3-9 FAF 10-4-46

BS129 3212 HFIX EA FF 27-7-42 8MU 27-7 133S 12-8 331S 29-9 CB ops 19-11 GAL 416S 3-5-43 421S 20-5 CAC

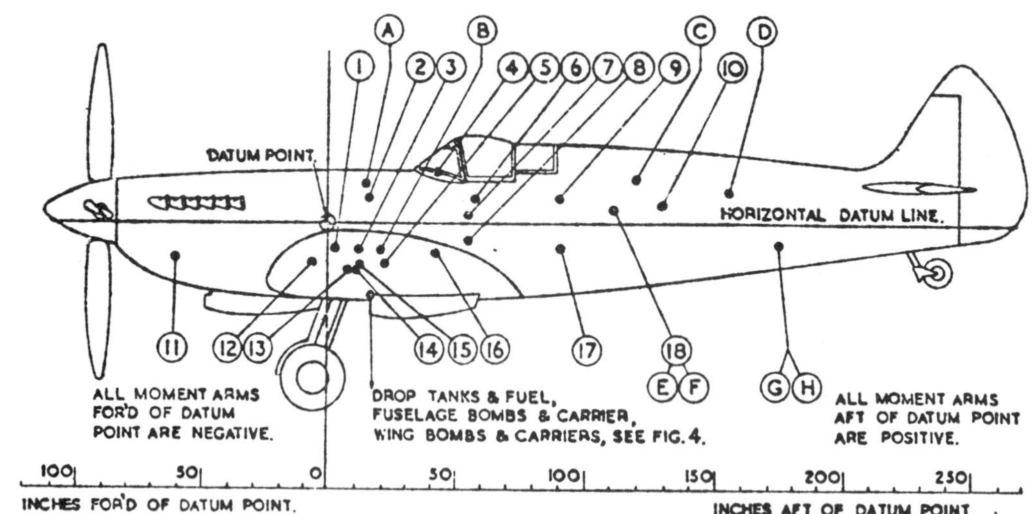

A B C D
1 2 3 4 5 6 7 8 9 10
DATUM POINT
HORIZONTAL DATUM LINE.
11 12 13 14 15 16 17 18
E F G H
DROP TANKS & FUEL,
FUSELAGE BOMBS & CARRIER,
WING BOMBS & CARRIERS, SEE FIG. 4.

TABLE I

NOTE NO.	ITEM NO.	TYPICAL REMOVABLE ITEMS OF MILITARY LOAD.	WEIGHT. LB.	ARM. IN.	MOMENT LB.IN.
1	14.	2 BROWNING ·50 IN. GUNS AND ACCESSORIES.	162·5	+ 10·5	+ 1,706
	15.	BROWNING ·50 IN. AMMUNITION AT 250 RD. PER GUN.	150	+ 12	+ 1,800
2	13.	2 HISPANO 20 MM. GUNS MK. II AND ACCESSORIES.	297·5	+ 7·6	+ 2,261
	5.	HISPANO 20 MM. AMMUNITION AT 120 RD. PER GUN.	150	+ 22·5	+ 3,375
	4.	GYROSCOPIC GUN SIGHT AND FILAMENT LAMPS.	8·5	+ 43	+ 366
	6.	1¼ LB. INCENDIARY BOMB, CLOCK AND CROWBAR.	3	+ 58	+ 174
	12.	G.45 CAMERA, ADAPTOR, FRONT FLANGE AND INDICATOR.	7	- 6	- 42
	16.	OXYGEN IN 3 CYLINDERS	7	+ 42	+ 294
	8.	DINGHY TYPE "K" IN SEAT PACK TYPE "A" MK. III.	18·5	+ 55	+ 1,018
3	18.	T.R.1143 RADIO AND ACCESSORIES.	80·5	+ 112	+ 9,016
	10.	R.3067 RADIO, DETONATOR AND CONTROL UNIT.	35	+ 130	+ 4,550
	7.	PILOT AND PARACHUTE.	200	+ 55	+ 11,000
		TOTAL TYPICAL REMOVABLE MILITARY LOAD.	1,119·5		+ 35,518
	2.	FUEL IN TOP FOR'D TANK: 48 GALL. 100 OCTANE AT 7·2 LB. PER GALL.	345·5	+ 15·1	+ 5,217
	3.	FUEL IN BOTTOM FOR'D TANK: 37 GALL. 100 OCTANE AT 7·2 LB PER GALL.	266·5	+ 10·8	+ 2,878
	9.	FUEL IN TOP REAR TANK: 41 GALL. 100 OCTANE AT 7·2 LB. PER GALL.	295	+ 89·5	+ 26,403
	17.	FUEL IN BOTTOM REAR TANK: 33 GALL. 100 OCTANE AT 7·2 LB. PER GALL.	237·5	+ 90·8	+ 21,565
5	11.	OIL IN TANK: 11·3 GALL. AT 9 LB. PER GALL.	101·5	- 60·2	- 6,110
	1.	AIRCRAFT IN TARE CONDITION.	5816		+ 14,962
		AIRCRAFT IN TYPICAL TAKE-OFF CONDITION.	8,181·5	+ 12·3	+ 100,433

TABLE II

NOTE NO.	ITEM NO.	ADDITIONAL AND ALTERNATIVE ITEMS OF REMOVABLE MILITARY LOAD.	WEIGHT LB.	ARM IN.	MOMENT LB.IN.
	D.	SIGNAL DISCHARGER, CONTROL & 6 CARTRIDGES.	13	+ 156	+ 2,028
	A.	EXHAUST GLARE SHIELDS & FITTINGS.	6·5	+ 15	+ 98
	B.	DESERT EQUIPMENT.	49	+ 22	+ 1,078
	E.	T.R. 1196 RADIO, MOUNTING TRAY & CONTROLLER.	39·5	+ 109	+ 4,306
4.	C.	A.1271 AMPLIFIER AND ACCESSORIES.	9	+ 120	+ 1,080
	F.	RADIO BALLAST: 3 STANDARD WEIGHTS.	52·5	+ 114	+ 5,985
	G.	STANDARD BALLAST WEIGHT AT AFT DOOR.	17·5	+ 175	+ 3,063
	H.	BALLAST MOUNTING AT AFT DOOR.	5	+ 175	+ 875

Loading and C.G., Mk IX E and Mk XVI.

ops 3-10 403S 24-10 33S 1-6-44 FAAC 16-6 ROS 611S 19-9 312S 8-10 VA0 26-10 mods 340S CAC ops 13-4-45 RHAF 20-4-48

BS130 3213 EA FF 30-7-42 8MU 402S 31-7 CAC ops 24-8 CE ops 17-1-43 ROS

BS131 3217 EA FF 1-8-42 402S 4-8 CB ops 6-9 GAL 341S 6-4-43 AST 21-4 mods 28-7 58 OTU 8-4-45 FAF 16-9-46 coll with ML422 19-6-47

BS132 3219 EA FF 4-8-42 402S 5-8 CE ops 4-12

BS135 3222 EA FF 7-8-42 RAF Ken 8-8 FTR ops 17-1-43

BS136 3223 EA FF 6-8-42 402S 9-8 FTR ops 24-8

BS137 3240 EA FF 11-8-42 133S 12-8 331S 29-9 FACB 5-1-43 GAL CAC on f/f to 6MU 2-5 ROS 222S 11-6 AST 16-6 mods BDn as rogue a/c from 22S rigged out of trim laterally with hvy ails 405ARF 24-8 131S 27-9 229S 25-6-44 FAAC 29-6 ROS 504S 3-8 611S 3-8 swg to port u/c clpse ldg CE Colt 13-9-44

BS138 3231 EA FF 8-8-42 133S 11-8 FTR 26-9

BS139 3248 EA FF 12-8-42 BDn 14-8 carb mono cockpit contam tests; 27-9 fuel syst trls; Oct '42 intns fly trls; 5-11 spin trls; 9-12 flame damping trls. The mult ejector fish tail manifolds produced excessive exhaust glow. After 117FH the M61 failed, and nine new tyres were fitt during a total of 258 ldg. Dive recovery behaviour tests. CRD R-RH for new eng. Trls with 30gal o/ld tank. FACE 23-12 FH159.10

BS140 3257 EA FF 14-8-42 133S 17-8 FTR ops 30-9

BS143 3262 EA FF 16-8-42 no record

BS144 3264 EA FF 16-8-42 133S 18-8 331S 29-9 CB ops 22-1-43 GAL 65S 10-8 AST mods 310S 12-9-44 u/s ldg std cd Bradwell Bay CE 19-2-45 SOC 22-2

BS145 3274 EA FF 20-8-42 401S 22-8 FAAC 11-1 ROS 403S 25-1-43 FTR ops 16-2 FH130

BS147 3275 EA FF 20-8-42 con to Type 509 two-seat train To Holland as H-99 23-3-48 to PH-NFN

BS148 3279 EA FF 22-8-42 402S 26-8 133S 6-9 FAAC 29-7 GAL 403S 29-3-43 AST mods 18-4 M63 instal 405 RSU 8-9 331S 17-10 FAAC 5-11 ROS 332S 5-12 CE ops 4-1-44

BS150 3825 EA FF 23-8-42 6MU 24-8 64S 30-8 FTR ops 5-9 FH6.25

BS151 3287 EA FF 24-8-42 402S 26-8 FACE 28-8 SOC 5-9

BS152 3293 EA FF 25-8-42 402S 26-8 AST 23-12 mods 416S 23-3-43 421S 20-5 ROS 12-7 to 5263M SOC 30-3-46

BS157 3100 CHA FF 27-6-42 45MU 28-6 72S 24-7 401S 27-7 FTR ops 19-8

BS159 3143 CHA FF 11-7-42 9MU 12-7 72S 24-7 401S 27-7 FTR ops 17-8

BS167 3113 CHA FF 2-7-42 9MU 3-7 402S 28-7 HAL 24-8 for invest 331S 20-4-43 AST mr M63 instal 28-9 229S 29-5-44 FTR ops 11-6

BS170 3121 CHA FF 4-7-42 8MU 6-7 611S 24-7 FTR ops 16-9

BS172 3133 CHA FF 9-7-42 39MU 11-7 72S 24-7 401S 27-7 AST 29-11 403S 25-1-43 FTR ops 27-2 FH167.30

BS176 3144 CHA FF 11-7-42 33MU 13-7 72S 24-7 401S 27-7 FAAC 5-12 ROS 332S 23-12 e/fd aban i/sea off Mans 10-2

BS177 3168 CHA FF 15-7-42 39MU 21-7 72S 24-7 401S 27-7 FTR ops 2-10 FH16.5

BS179 3169 CHA FF 15-7-42 19-7 611S 24-7 FTR ops 19-8

BS180 3173 CHA FF 17-7-42 33MU 19-7 72S 24-7 401S 27-7 CAC ops 16-3-43 GAL 341S 26-3 AST 18-4 mods 303S 31-7 FTR ops 23-9

BS183 3181 CHA FF 19-7-42 6MU 23-7 401S 18-8 403S 25-1-43 CAC ops 13-3 AST 131S 2-11 229S 25-9-44 AST mr 27-12 80 OTU 6-3-46 ME FAF 4-4

BS185 3182 CHA FF 20-7-42 6MU 23-7 611S 24-7 86MU 30-4 CE ops 30-8 SOC 11-9

BS189 3204 CHA FF 23-7-42 402S 28-7 HAL 611S 31-12 AST 10-2 mods 316S FTR ops 4-4

BS192 3203 CHA FF 24-7-42 611S 26-7 FACE 31-7 SOC GAL AST 14-1-43 mods 340S 1-3 341S 26-3 FACB 31-3 GAL 122S 14-8 FRU 6-7-44 FAF 3-6-47

BS194 3206 CHA FF 27-7-42 402S 29-7 416S 23-3-43 AST 27-3 mods FTR ops 3-4 FH220.25

BS195 3208 CHA FF 28-7-42 402S 29-7 CE ops 29-8

BS196 3209 CHA FF 31-7-42 402S 30-7 ROS 10-9 401S 27-10 403S 25-1-43 FTR ops 13-3

BS198 3218 CHA FF 1-8-42 402S 3-8 CE ops 24-8 SOC 31-8

BS200 3220 CHA FF 5-8-42 402S 9-8 306S 17-12 316S 14-3-43 FACB 26-3 GAL 129S 17-7 421S 26-8 AST 31-5-44 mr WAL 6-2-45 mods *Cal Mon* 6-1-48 SAAF 24-12

BS202 3230 CHA FF 7-8-42 402S 11-8 CAC ops ROS FTR ops 8-11

BS227 3462 IXC EA Magic Carpet FF 2-10-42 64S 9-10 AST 31-3-43 mods 453S 27-3 129S 17-7 332S 28-8 165S 29-9 274S 15-5-44 to 5322M 4-7-45 SOC rtp 24-1-46

BS239 3550 EA FF 24-10-42 340S 31-10 CAC ops 16-2-43 ROS 341S 26-3 CAC ops 15-7 HAL 405ARF 22-3-44 33S FAAC 22-6 CFE SOC 16-10-46

BS240 3475 EA FF 6-10-42 340S 8-10 Stn Flt BHll 29-11 CE ops 14-3-43

BS241 3458 EA FF 3-10-42 306S 5-10 Stn Flt BHll 4-12 FTR air coll with BS459 over Channel 26-1-43

BS242 3463 EA FF 3-10-42 340S 11-10 FACB 25-10 GAL 315S 22-4-43 AST 29-4 mods CAC ops 13-5 GAL 165S 14-2-44 19-3 313S 29-8 611S 22-3-45 441S 5-4 80 OTU air coll with BS403 13-12 SOC 29-12

BS243 3476 EA FF 9-10-42 340S 15-10 FTR ops 31-10 FH9.20

BS244 3473 EA FF 8-10-42 340S 11-10 ASTH 30-1-43 FTR ops 13-2 FH72.5

BS246 3474 EA FF 9-10-42 340S 11-10 FACB 24-10 ROS 611S 26-1-43 AST 5-4 mods 416S 11-4 403S 11-4 FTR ops 15-5 FH122.20

BS247 3477 EA FF 10-10-42 340S 11-10 CAC ops 13-2 ROS 332S 28-5 303S 3-3-45 441S 5-4 80 OTU 7-6 FAAC 2-12 FACE 13-12-46

BS248 3507 IXC EA FF 16-10-42 332S 17-10 AST 29-12 mods 313S 11-9-44 611S 8-10 310S 22-3-45 VAO 6-4 mods 60 6516M 20-2-48 RDAF 23-6

BS249 3512 EA FF 17-10-42 332S 18-10 ROS 16-2-43 317S 6-3-44 CB ops 10-2 AST 313S 30-8-44 611S 8-10 310S 22-3-45 VA 30-3 mods sold VA 5-6-47 to 6452M 15-10-47 SOC recat sc 8-8-49

BS250 3508 EA FF 16-10-42 332S 18-10 AST 27-2 mods 229S 1-8-44 VA 26-10 mods 229S 27-10 FAAC 8-11 ROS FAF 10-4-46

BS251 3509 EA FF 17-10-42 332S 18-10 struct fail in dive CE 30-1-43

BS252 3523 EA FF 18-10-42 332S 24-10 GAL 2-12 FTR ops 20-1-43

BS254 3519 EA FF 17-10-42 CRD Farn 8-11 stab & Neg G trls ETPS 18-3-43 weather tests & cool trls. Trans Wire & Elec Flt for exam of excessive generator heat GAL 8-5 332S 20-7 511FRU 3-8-44 Hatfield. Ret Farn contd generator cool trls VAO 19-10 mods 229S 20-10 FAF 21-8-46

BS255 3526 EA FF 20-10-42 332S 31-10 AST 27-1-42 mods FTR ops 2-5

BS292 3234 CHA FF 9-8-42 133S 11-8 FTR ops 6-9

BS294 3241 CHA FF 11-8-42 133S 13-8 FTR ops 30-9

BS296 3242 CHA FF 12-8-42 133S 14-8 331S 29-9 CE ops 29-11

BS297 3253 CHA FF 13-8-42 133S 16-8 CE ops 4-9 SOC 17-9

BS299 3266 CHA FF 17-8-42 133S 18-8 331S 29-9 according to VAWD records this a/c was con to FVII standards and tested for det of static longitudinal stab 4-2-43 FTR ops 13-4

BS301 3268 CHA FF 18-8-42 133S 19-8 FTR ops 30-8

BS302 3269 CHA FF 19-8-42 317S 21-8 306S 31-8 316S 16-3-43 AST mods CA ops 29-5 FTR ops 9-8 FH363

BS303 3277 CHA FF 401S 21-8-42 401S 23-8 o/s ldg strk disp pen CE Ken 24-10 FH61.5

BS304 3278 CHA FF 22-8-42 401S 23-8 u/s ldg strk trees Ken CE 18-11 SOC 25-11

BS306 3288 CHA FF 24-8-42 402S 26-8 FACA 20-9 AST 19-2-43 mods 416S 23-3 421S 20-5 air coll with EN180 nr Ken CAC 9-6 AST M63 install 411ARF 19-11 302S 27-12 FAAC 24-2-44 ROS 33S coll with MJ309 Mountfield Sussex CE 22-5

BS307 3296 CHA FF 26-8-42 401S 27-8 FACE dbf 5-10 SOC 15-10 FH8.40

BS308 3301 CHA FF 28-8-42 402S 30-8 CE ops 15-1-43 FH111.35

BS309 3310 CHA FF 30-8-42 402S 31-8 CB ops 4-12 GAL 82MU 21-4-43 *Fort Thom* 3-5 Casa 17-5 CE ops 14-12-44

BS310 3321 HFIX CHA FF 31-8-42 VAWD 11-11 comp trls of temperate & trop air intake and filter. Speed loss 4mph M66 install brief perf trls 1-3-43 CRD WD 22-5 RM.9SM torsional stiff tests of mod oleo leg links 31-8 BDn 31-10 det of aftmost CG position with four blade Rotol Jablo R12/4FS/4 and five blade Hydulignum Mk XH55 props with M70 (now instal). Also CG position for proposed instal of split armour. FXII rud and FVIII pilot head instal. 12-11 det of aftmost CG position; hand trls with same. March '44 trls to det effects of high Mach numbers in dive and recovery with eng/prop combinations. AST 4-4-44 mr 83GSU 19-8 FTR ops 27-9

BS311 3323 EA FF 31-8-42 401S 2-9 e/fd fuel short cd/ld Bolt Head Devon CE 28-9

BS312 3325 CHA FF 2-9-42 401S 4-9 FAAC 15-9 ROS 340S 28-10 FAAC 13-2-43 FTR ops 8-3

BS313 3344 CHA FF 5-9-42 401S 8-9 133S 8-9 FTR ops 30-9

BS314 3355 CHA FF 8-9-42 402S 10-9 AST 14-12 mods CE ops 17-1-43 FH84.25

BS315 3380 CHA FF 11-9-42 64S 13-9 CAC 10-10 453S 2-4-43 AST 22-4 mods 129S 17-7 131S 8-1-44 to 5941M 9-5-46 5SoTT SOC 20-3-50

BS316 3398 CHA FF 17-9-42 402S 17-9 FACE 29-11 FH58.5

BS317 3388 CHA FF 13-9-42 133S 16-9 401S 15-9 FTR ops 4-12

BS318 3399 CHA FF 17-9-42 611S 18-9 hit sea fly low on patrol south of Beachy Head FTR 11-2-43

BS319 3422 CHA FF 22-9-42 611S 25-9 AST 17-1-43 416S 2-4-43 412S 20-5 FTR ops 17-6

BS383 3423 CHA FF 22-9-42 401S 25-9 403S 25-1-43 AST 4-4 mods FTR ops 20-4 FH243.55

BS384 3403 CHA FF 18-9-42 306S 19-9 GAL 28-10 M63 instal 453S 12-5-43 AST 8-6 mods 129S 17-7 316S 28-8 302S 28-9 313S 5-9-44 611S 8-10 FAAC 16-1-45 ROS 312S 22-3 FAAC 23-7 sold H Bath 27-10-49

BS385 3435 CHA FF 24-9-42 RAF North 27-9 306S 30-9 402S 23-1-43 416S 23-3 AST 22-4 mods 421S struct fail in dive CE 19-5

BS386 3426 CHA FF 25-9-42 122S 27-9 ASST 8-1-43 mods 122S 12-1 R-RH 28-2 222S 19-5 313S 29-8-44 611S 8-10 303S 22-3-45 411S 5-4 84ARF 17-5 80 OTU 7-6 to 6157M 20-2-48 RDAF 10-6

BS387 3436 CHA FF 25-9-42 122S 1-10 CE ops 4-1-43 FH55.35 AST 24-2 delay due to lack of spares 611S 12-7-44 VA 3-10 mods 312S 8-10 FAF 20-7-46

BS388 3438 CHA FF 26-9-42 331S 27-9 AST 20-3-43 mods 331S 22-3 CAC ops 14-4 ROS FAAC 28-8-45

BS389 3444 CHA FF 28-9-42 331S 1-10 CE ops 12-12

BS390 3445 CHA FF 28-9-42 RAF Hand Sq Hull 1-10 FAAC 24-11 ROS FACB 4-8-43 AST CRD VA 5-3-44 hook instal RNAS Crail for deck land trls 19-4-44

BS391 3455 CHA FF 1-10-42 401S 3-10 FAAC 10-10 ROS FTR ops 8-11

BS392 3464 CHA FF 2-10-42 340S 8-10 AST 12-1-43 mods CAC ops 30-1 ROS 341S 26-3 129S 29-7 80S 16-6-44 310S unable to jett o/ld tank o/s ldg grd loop CE N Wld 9-9-44

BS393 3459 CHA FF 2-10-42 340S 8-10 AST 9-2 mods 341S 26-3 CAC ops 14-5 ROS 332S24-12 229S 29-5-44 VA 16-11 mods to 5354M 12-6-45 SOC 5-9-49

BS394 3465 CHA FF 3-10-42 340S 8-10 AST 8-11 341S 26-3-43 316S 22-8 302S 28-9 WAL for painting 23-1-44 312S 14-11 RHAF 29-4-48

BS395 3479 CHA FF 10-10-42 332S 13-10 AST 10-12 mods 83GSU 10-4-44 274S 29-5 GAL 23-11 57 OTU 3-5-45 sold H Bath 27-10-49

BS396 3485 CHA FF 10-10-42 332S 16-10 403S 30-1-43 FTR ops 24-6

BS397 3480 CHA FF 10-10-42 402S 11-10 FACB 8-11 recat E 18-11

BS398 3486 CHA FF 10-10-42 w/c Flying N Wld 13-10 332S AST 5-1-43 mods CB ops 27-3-43 GAL HAL 405ARF 6-8 421S 18-8 e/fd a/c aban over Kent 23-11 FH232.25

BS399 3490 CHA FF 11-10-42 332S 13-10 CE 24-11 SOC 30-11

BS400 3506 CHA FF 17-10-42 64S 18-10 453S 2-4 AST 18-4 mods CE ops 22-6

BS401 3529 CHA FF 21-10-42 332S 25-10 AST 21-12 mods FACB 21-5 GAL 303S 2-3-45 441S 5-4 80 OTU 7-6 FAF 14-3-46

BS402 3522 CHA FF 18-10-42 122S 22-10 bounced on ldg o/t Mans CE 22-11 GAL FH19-5

BS403 3530 CHA FF 21-10-42 306S 31-10 AST 2-2-43 CISU camera instal 316S 14-3-43 FACB 9-8 AST Farn Nov'43 gun firing and night fly trls with EN498 CRD BDn 23-12 endurance trls with O/ld tanks AST 27-4-44 mr 310S 26-9 CAC opos 102-45 80 OTU air coll with BS242 13-12 FAF 24-7-46

BS404 3531 CHA FF 21-10-42 306S 31-10 AST 23-1-43 mods struct fail in spin cd High St. Elstree CE 2-2 FH76

BS405 3543 CHA FF 21-10-42 122S 31-10 AST 29-4-43 mods 222S 19-5 FTR ops 13-6 FH198.5

BS406 3540 CHA FF 24-10-42 340S 31-10 FTR ops 9-1-43 FH49-30

BS407 3549 CHA FF 23-10-42 332S 31-10 FTR ops 8-4-43

BS408 3555 CHA FF 25-10-42 315S 31-10 ASTH 31-1-43 CB ops 15-4 GAL GRD Farn 4-12 gun firing trls AST 23-2-44 33S 1-6 310S 8-7 504S 15-7 303S coll with MH323 on t/o CAC 25-7 ROS CAL 10-11 mods M63 instal SAAF 23-6-48

BS409 3556 CHA FF 25-10-42 315S 31-10 ROS AST 12-1-43 mods 19S 21-8 e/a CAC 21-1-44 ROS 80S 29-5 310S 5-9 VAO 29-9 mods 312S 27-8-45 RHAF 6-5-48

BS410 3559 CHA FF 28-10-42 6-11 AST 15-3-43 mods FTR ops 13-5

BS411 3563 CHA FF 28-10-42 315S 6-11 AST 28-2-43 mods 303S 6-6 308S 16-11 FTR 19-11

BS428 3298 EA FF 26-8-42 402S 26-8 Farn Nov'42 neg G trls BDn 14-1-43 level speed perf with and without 500 lb bomb on mod carr 19-1 brief hand trls with 250 and 500lb bomb. Comp trls and range det Ice guard and guns removed; fuel cool instal in wing root. New carr of RAF design and manufacture instal 15-2 416S 23-3 AST 31-3 mods 421S 20-5 CAC ops 24-6 ROS 405ARF 14-9 611S 15-10-44 sold H Bath 24-11-49

BS429 3303 EA FF 27-8-42 317S 30-8 CE ops 6-9

BS430 3318 EA FF 31-8-42 402S 1-9 FAAC 25-1-43 ROS AST 10-2 mods 416S 23-3 CE ops 13-5

BS431 3309 EA FF 30-8-42 317S 30-8 306S FACB 30-11 GAL 82MU 27-8 *Card Grif* 3-9 Casa 20-9 ME 2-8-45 SOC 2-8

BS432 3319 EA FF 31-8-42 306S 1-9 FTR ops 8-11 FH49.20

BS433 3320 EA FF 31-8-42 402S 1-9 CAC ops 26-1-43 GAL 316S 10-7 AST 12-7 mods M63 instal 302S 28-9 611S 20-9-44 312S 8-10 SOC 22-2-45

BS434 3346 EA FF 6-9-42 402S 7-9 AST 27-2-43 mods 416S 23-3 FAAC 24-4 GAL CRD Mal WWal 25-12 tail wheel tow hook instal BDn 24-1-44 trls MAP Airborne Forces Exp Estb Sherburn in Elmet Feb '44 trls as tug for fully loaded Hotspur glider (Mer 63 eng). SAL 20-12-44 MWW 29-12-45 Farn 21-2-46 GAAC 3-4 SOC 31-10

BS435 3324 EA FF 31-8-42 611S 2-9 CE ops 5-2-43

BS438 3342 EA FF 5-9-42 306 S 10-9 CE ops 18-11 SOC 23-11 FH39.35

BS439 3343 EA FF 5-9-42 64S 8-9 GAL 13-10 316S 11-5-43 AST 15-5 mods M63 instal FACA 25-6 165S 28-9 AAST 4-12 CFE 16-9-44 FAAC 9-4-45 ROS to 5972M 2-7-46

BS440 3348 EA 6-9-42 402S 10-9 CE ops 16-2-43 FH160

BS441 3363 EA FF 9-9-42 64S 10-9 AST 17-3-43 mods 435S 2-4 129S 17-7 disin in high speed dive Jacobs Farm Maldon Essex 9-8 FH315.45

BS443 3364 EA FF 10-9-42 306S 12-9 CE ops 9-10 SOC 21-10 FH16.45

BS444 3365 EA FF 10-9-42 64S 12-9 FAAC 23-11 ROS 331S 23-12 VA/AST 23-1-43 mods 331S 26-1 CE ops 16-4

BS445 3373 EA FF 11-9-42 133S 13-9 331S 29-9 FACB 5-1-43 GAL M63 instal 332S 6-11 317S FAAC 20-2-44 ROS SOC 27-11-47

Mk IX ML417 was converted to Trainer status for the Indians, only to be deconverted by its present owner, Stephen Grey.

The front portion of a Mk IX was used to train pilots in operation of the gyro gunsight. Results were calculated by a computer linked to the sight.

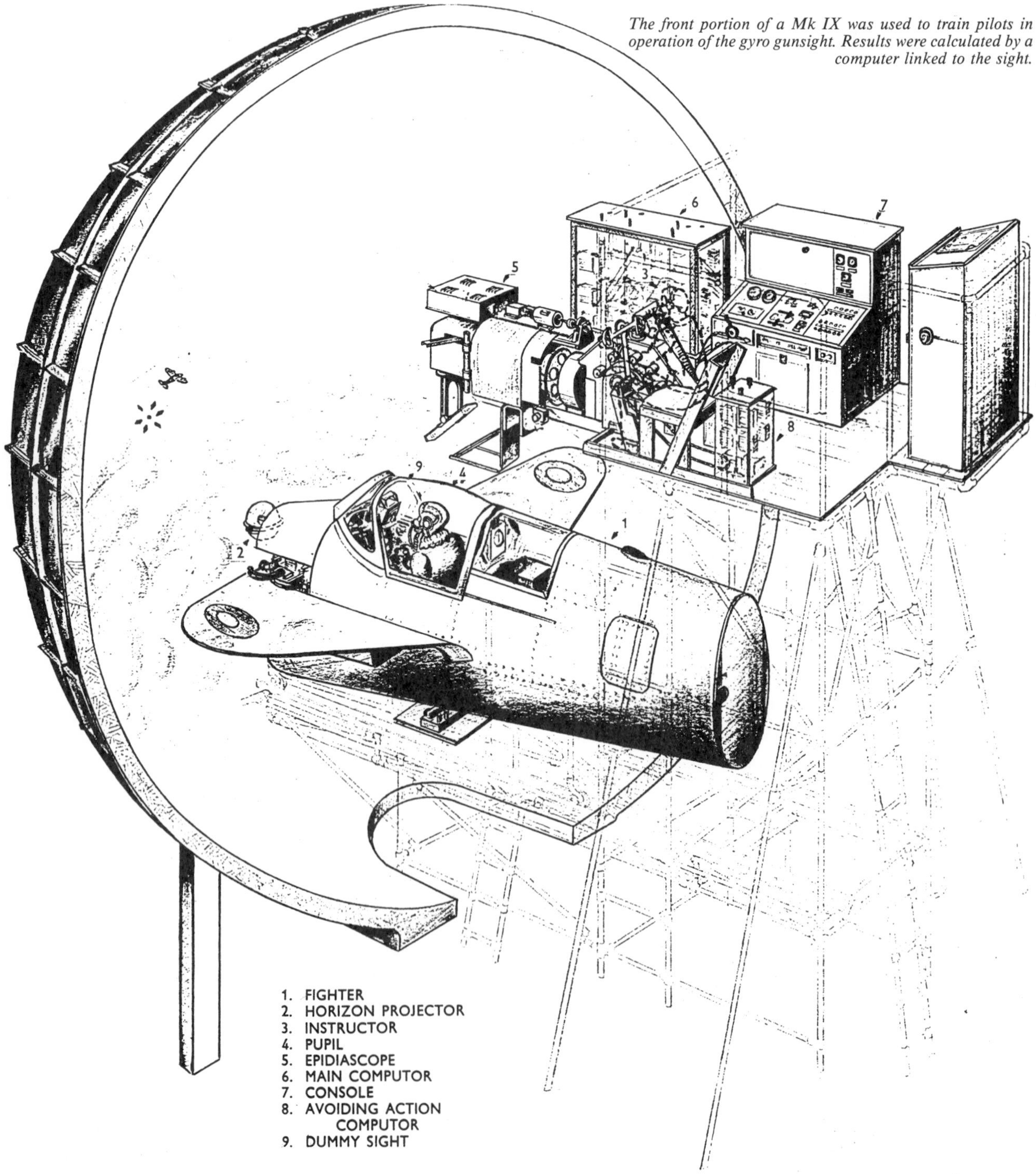

1. FIGHTER
2. HORIZON PROJECTOR
3. INSTRUCTOR
4. PUPIL
5. EPIDIASCOPE
6. MAIN COMPUTOR
7. CONSOLE
8. AVOIDING ACTION COMPUTOR
9. DUMMY SIGHT

BS452, ex Mk V, converted to Mk IX.

BS446 3374 EA FF 11-9-42 133S 13-9 FTR ops 30-9

BS447 3383 EA FF 11-9-42 133S 13-9 FTR ops 30-9

BS449 3384 EA FF 11-9-42 306S 15-9 e/fd on t/o tip onto nose CB 8-12 GAL 131S 27-9-43 FAAC 3-3-44 AST to 6035M 2-8-46

BS450 3386 EA FF 13-9-42 402S 15-9 CE ops 4-12

BS451 3393 EA FF 15-9-42 402S 16-9 FAAC 3-10 611S 29-11 AST 5-4-43 mods 315S 9-4 303S 6-6 308S 16-11 229S 26-1-44 VA 16-11 mods 229S 17-11 ASTE 12-2-45 SAAF 20-9-47

BS452 3395 EA FF 16-9-42 306S 17-9 FACB 21-10 GAL 65S 13-8-43 AST 30-9 mods FAAC 15-10 421S 23-2-44 53 OTU 8-6-45 sold VA 5-12-49

BS454 3396 IXC EA FF 16-9-42 cd on company test flt SOC 16-9

BS455 3400 EA FF 17-9-42 306S 18-9 FTR ops 31-12 FH89.30

BS456 3401 EA FF 18-9-42 306S 19-9 HAL 20-11 FTR ops 26-2-43 cancel AST 14-3 mods CAC ops 17-5 ROS 316S 12-7 FTR ops 22-8 FH314.45

BS457 3402 EA FF 18-9-42 VA WD 19-9 306S 24-9 Dtn Flt North 30-9 316S 14-3-43 AST 18-4 mods FTR ops 9-8 FH328.10

BS458 3410 EA FF 19-9-42 CRD R-RH 21-9 332S 15-10 AST 4-10-43 611S 17-7-44 CAC ops 23-8 ROS 312S 8-10 CRD VAO 25-11 mods FA 1-2-45 ASTE recat E SOC 18-4

BS459 3418 EA FF 24-9-42 306S 25-9 HAL FTR after coll with BS241 over Channel 26-1-43 FH102.35

BS461 3416 EA FF 23-9-42 122S 26-9 R-RH 19-3-43 222S 19-5 19S 24-8 AST 15-9 229S 1-7-44 FAAC 25-7 ROS CAC ops 14-9 303S 2-11 VAO 23-1-45 mods SCR train 25-1 GACB 26-6-45 recat E SOC 21-7

BS462 3408 EA FF 19-9-42 306S 25-9 316S 14-3-43 AST 31-3 mods 80S 29-5-44 CE ops 10-6

BS463 3419 EA FF 24-9-42 306S 26-9 316S 14-3-43 AST 7-4 mods CAC ops 11-6 ROS 331S 12-11 303S 25-9-44 CAC ops 25-2-45 ROS VAO 441S 5-4 80 OTU 7-6 FACE 13-12 SOC 10-1-46

BS464 3417 EA FF 23-9-42 122S 26-9 AST 12-1-43 mods 222S 19-5 312S 21-1-45 FAAC 8-4 FAF 21-8-46 extant Musee de l'Air Paris GW-S

BS466 3441 EA FF 26-9-42 331S 1-10 AST 17-2-43 mods 229S 24-5-44 o/s ldg strk obst nosed over Detling 28-5

BS467 3421 EA FF 25-9-42 331S 26-9 FACB 24-3-43 AST 47MU 14-9 *Ocean Rid* 23-9 Casa 10-10 NAASC 31-10 ME 5-4-45 SOC 5-2-48

BS468 3420 EA FF 25-9-42 331S 26-9 AST 9-2-43 mods FTR 13-4

BS469 3439 EA FF 26-9-42 331S 1-10 CE ops 12-12

BS470 3440 EA FF 26-9-42 331S 1-10 SAL 4-7-44 VAO 12-1-45 mods sold R J Coley 9-2-50

BS47173437 EA FF 26-9-42 331S 27-9 ASTH 31-1-43 FTR 205

BS473 3443 EA FF 29-9-42 543S 1-10 reported con to PRU standards by VA WD wts and CG load @ WD 27-10 47MU 21-2 *Llanb* 11-3 Gib 24-3 NWA 30-4 SOC 28-4-45

BS474 3457 HEA Canadian Pacific I FF 3-10-42 401S 8-10 403S 25-1-43 AST mods CAC ops 17-6 ROS 501S 8-3-44 274S 29-5 to 5955M 15-6-46

BS506 3636 EA FF 21-11-42 CRD Boulton Paul 29-11 VA 24-1-43 Boulton Paul 18-2 mods 9MU 18-3 315S 14-4 AST 7-5 mods 303S 6-6 308S 16-11 AST 8-1-44 mr 229S 17-6 CAC ops 23-6 ROS CFE 29-8 FAAC 13-2-46 recat E 24-6

BS507 3527 EA FF 21-10-42 332S 31-10 AST 23-1-43 mods e/fd w/u ldg o/t CE Rochester 4-6

BS508 3528 EA FF 21-10-42 332S 31-10 AST 8-1-43 mods 317S Llanb taxy into MA220 waiting t/o CE 29-2-44 AST 312S 23-2-45 332S 30-3-48 RHAF 1-4

BS509 3535 EA FF 22-10-42 402S 31-10 AST 17-2-43 mods 23-3 421S 20-5 403S 20-7 CE ops 27-7 FH291.45

BS510 3536 EA FF 22-10-42 611S 31-10 FTR ops 14-3-43

BS511 3542 EA FF 24-10-42 12MU 21-11 47MU 6-12 Malta 14-12 Gob 13-1-43 NWA 20-2 SOC 15-3-45

BS512 3551 EA FF 24-10-42 39MU 27-3-43 122S 11-5 AST 15-5 mods 222S 19-5 19S 24-8 80S 2-6-44 310S 5-9 VA 26-10 mods CAC ops 11-3-45 SAAF 15-5-47

BS513 3552 EA FF 24-10-42 315S 31-10 FAAC 22-1-43 AST 9-3 mods 303S 6-6 FAAC 7-10 308S 16-11 FAAC 2-3-44 33S 28-6 310S CAC ops 7-7 ROS to 6043M

BS514 3553 EA FF 25-10-42 315S 30-10 AST 8-1-43 mods FTR ops 4-4

BS515 3554 EA FF 27-10-42 315S 30-10 FTR ops 13-3-43

EN series engines specified

EN122 3564 M61 CHA FF 30-10-42 AST 17-2-43 mods M63S instal 341S 26-3 FAAC 5-7 332S 28-7 HAL 21 33S 28-6-44 310S 8-7 504S 15-7 303S FACB 15-8 DeH 80 OTU 8-6-45 FACB u/s lndg u/c coll Ouston 3-1-46 recat E SOC 16-1

EN123 3565 M61 CHA FF 30-10-42 315S 6-11 FAAC 12-2-43 ROS AST 24-2 mods 303S 6-6 308S 16-11 FAAC 11-12 AST 274S 26-5-44 CRD Farn 6-10 Army Coop trls a/c HAL 1-11 mods DTD Dux BAF 18-8-47 as SM-7 w/o 18-7-51

EN124 3582 M61 CHA FF 31-10-42 AST 315S 31-10 AST 3-2-43 mods FTR ops 4-4

EN125 3588 M61 CHA FF 336USA S 8-11 306S 22-11 FTR ops 31-12 FH36.10

EN126 3589 M61 CHA FF 336USA S 8-11 331S 23-11 AST 7-3-43 mods 165S 23-2-44 131S 19-3 FLS 29-8 FAAC 15-11 ROS CFE FAAC 3-12-45 ROS sold H Bath 27-10-49

EN127 3595 CHA FF 7-11-42 336USA S 8-11 401S 26-11 306S 28-11 HAL 7-12 AST 27-2-43 mods 316S 14-3 302S 11-1-44 80S 29-5 310S FTR ops 31-3-44

EN128 3610 M61 CHA FF 13-11-42 306S 17-11 316S 14-3-43 AST 22-3 mods FTR ops 26-6

EN129 3606 M61 CHA FF 10-11-42 401S 20-11 403S 25-1-43 ASTH 30-1 FACA 29-8 405 RSU 2-9 303S 25-1-45 441S 5-4 80 OTU 7-6 FAF 14-3-46

EN130 3622 M61 CHA FF 13-11-42 CAC ops 13-1-43 403S 25-1 AST 27-3 mods 331S 24-11 CE ops 7-1-44

EN131 3611 M61 CHA FF 13-11-42 315S 17-11 AST 27-1-43 mods

EN132 3613 M61 CHA FF 14-11-42 65S 17-11 e/td after t/o cd/ld CE Horn 24-3-43

EN133 3625 CHA FF 16-11-42 no record

EN134 3627 M61 FF 17-11-42 CHA 9MU 18-11 47MU 29-11 646S 7-12 GIB 17-12

EN135 3640 M61 CHA FF 21-11-42 9MU 22-11 47MU 5-12 647S 19-12 GIB 6-2-43 NW 28-2 Malta 1-7-43 Sic 1-8 ME 30-9 NAASC 1-11 MAAF 21-6-45 SOC 14-3-46

EN136 3541 M61 CHA FF 21-11-42 9MU 22-11 47MU 6-12 Gib 13-1-43 NWA 28-2 72S C3 ops 3-4

EN137 3642 M61 CHA FF 21-11-42 12MU 22-11 47MU 5-12 *SS647* 19-12 Gib 6-2-43 NWA 28-2 FAF 31-10

EN138 3643 M61 CHA FF 21-11-42 12MU 22-11 47MU 5-12 Malta 16-12 Gib 13-1-43 NWA 28-2 SOC 31-1-45

EN139 3676 M61 CHA FF 28-11-42 47MU 11-12 *Emp Tow* 23-12 Gib 13-1-43 NWA 28-2 SOC 29-2-44

EN140 3664 M61 CHA FF 25-11-42 9MU 28-11 47MU 22-2-43 *Harmajris* 10-3 Gib 26-4 Malta 1-7 Sic 1-8 CE ops 16-10-44

EN141 3687 M61 CHA FF 29-11-42 9MU 1-12 47MU 15-12 *Emp Tow* 23-12 Gib 13-1-43 81S FTR ops 24-3

EN142 3675 M61 CHA FF 29-11-42 9MU 1-12 47MU 8-12 *Emp Tow* 23-12 Gib 13-1-43 Malta 1-3 NWA 28-12 Malta C3 ops 22-5-44 FH52.35

EN143 3702 M61 CHA FF 4-12-42 9MU 5-12 47MU 28-12 *SS653* 19-1-43 Gib 6-2 Malta 1-7 Sic 1-8 ME 30-10 NAAF 1-11 RHAF 29-5-47

EN144 3703 MXX CHA FF 4-12-42 9MU 5-12 47MU 15-12 *Emp Tow* 23-12 Gib 13-1-43 NWA 28-2 Malta 1-7 Sic 1-8 NA 30-11 IAF 26-6-47 as 4115

EN145 3706 M61 CHA FF 5-12-42 39MU 6-12 47MU 14-12 *Emp Tow* 23-12 Gib 13-1-43 NWA 28-2 MAAF 26-4-45 IAF 26-6-47 as 4116

EN146 3721 M61 CHA FF 7-12-42 39MU 9-12 47MU 14-12 *Emp Tow* 23-12 Gib 13-1-43 Malta 1-3 NWA 28-2 ME 126S FAC3 dbt 13-4

EN147 3727 M61 CHA FF 9-12-42 39MU 11-12 47MU 2-1-43 *Shell* 10-1 Gib 6-2 Malta 1-7 Sic 1-8 NAAF FTR ops 14-12

EN148 3741 M61 CHA FF 11-12-43 9MU 20-12 47MU 9-1-43 *Mer Prin* 18-1 Gib 6-2 NWA 28-2 Malta 1-7 SOC 1-8

EN152 3748 M61 CHA FF 15-12-42 9MU 20-12 47MU 3-1-43 *Mer Prin* 18-1 Gib 6-2 NWA 31-3 Malta 1-7 Sic 1-8 ME 30-9 NAAF 1-11 SOC 14-3-46

EN156 3767 M61 CHA FF 20-12-42 22-12 47MU 2-1-43 *Mer Prin* 18-1-43 Gib 6-2 NAAF 1-11 SOC 8-3-44

EN171 3561 M61 EA FF 28-12-42 315S 31-10 306S 29-1-43 316S FTR ops 13-3 FH142.10

EN172 3562 M61 EA FF 30-10-42 315S 7-11 AST 21-1 mods 303S 6-6 308S 16-11 80S 29-5-44 DeH 5-7 mr VA 18-1-45 mods 584 TU Flt Cole 18-11-46 sold R J Coley 6-2-50

EN173 3570 M61 EA FF 30-10-42 315S 8-11 AST 21-12 mods 315S 29-12 303S 6-6-43 FTR 24-9

EN174 3573 EA FF 31-10-42 315S 7-11 306S 12-12 AST 27-1-43 mods cine camera instal 316S 14-3 FAAC 2-7 ROS 302S 28-9 229S 6-6-44 VA 9-11 mods FAF 10-4-46

EN175 3571 M61 EA FF 31-10-42 340S 7-11 AST 21-1-43 mods FTR ops 14-3

EN177 3572 M61 EA FF 31-10-42 332S 8-11 FAAC 2-10-43 FLS 20-8-44 M63 instal to 5969M 2-7-46 2SoTT recat E 12-4-49

EN179 3574 M61 EA FF 31-10-42 315S 7-11 AST 23-1-43 mods Stn Flt North 2-2 306S 23-2 316S 14-3 FTR ops 18-8 FH275.15

EN180 3590 M61 EA FF 6-11-42 336USA S 17-11 64S 22-11 CB ops 6-12 GAL 416S 13-5-43 421S 20-5 air coll with BS306 CE nr Ken 9-6

Laid down as a Mk V, BS464 joined the French Air Force in 1946. It is now displayed in the Musee de l'Air, Le Bourget, Paris.

EN181 3591 M61 EA FF 6-11-42 336USA S 17-11 332S 22-11 FACB 8-12 ROS 332S dvd i/grd from H/A Matching Green Essex 27-1-43

EN182 3601 M61 EA FF 9-11-42 336USA S 17-11 332S 22-11 AST 21-1-43 mods FAAC 15-5 GAL M63 instal 33S 9-6-44 310S 8-7 504S 15-7 303S CAC ops 18-9 ROS VA 26-10 mods 441S FACB 20-4-45 SAAF 27-8

EN183 3602 M61 EA FF 9-11-42 336USA S 17-11 401S 26-11 FTR ops 15-1-43 FH40.25

EN184 3603 M61 EA FF 10-11-42 336USA S 17-11 315S 23-11 AST 10-12 303S 6-6-43 FTR ops 24-3

EN185 3604 M61 EA FF 10-11-42 336USA S 17-11 315S 23-11 FTR ops 4-4-43

EN186 3614 M61 EA FF 13-11-42 12MU 24-11 47MU 5-12 *SS647* 19-12 Gib 6-2-43 Malta 1-7 Sic 1-8 NA 30-11 ME 2-8-45 SOC 9-8

EN187 3616 M61 EA FF 13-11-42 12MU 24-11 47MU 6-12 Malta 16-12 Gib 13-1-43 NWA 28-2 Sic 1-8 C3 ops 9-9

EN188 3617 M61 EA FF 14-11-42 12MU 24-11 47MU 6-12 Malta 16-12 Gib 13-1-43 NWA 28-2 Sic 1-8 4ADU FA FTR 14-10

EN190 3629 M61 EA FF 21-11-42 12MU 24-11 47MU 9-12 *Marsa* 20-12 Gib 13-1-43 NWA 28-2

EN191 3618 M61 EA FF 14-11-42 12MU 21-11 47MU 9-12 *Emp Tow* 23-12 Gib 13-1-43 NWA 28-2 CE ops 4-3-45

EN193 3637 M61 EA FF 21-11-42 9MU 24-11 47MU 6-12 Malta 16-12 Gib 13-1-43 NWA 28-2 CE ops 4-2-45 bboc MAAF 4-2 REAF 26-9-46

EN194 3638 M61 EA FF 21-11-42 9MU 26-11 47MU 5-12 *SS647* 19-12 Gib 6-2-43 NWA 28-2 SOC 14-3-46

EN195 3639 M61 EA FF 21-11-42 12MU 24-11 47MU 7-12 *Marsa* 20-12 Gib 13-1-43 NWA 28-2 Malta 1-7 Sic 1-8 SOC 29-2-44

EN196 3651 M61 EA FF 22-11-42 12MU 24-11 47MU 6-12 Malta 16-12 Gib 13-1-43 NWA 28-2 NA 30-11 CE ops 6-3-45 SOC 14-3-46

EN197 3662 M61 EA FF 24-11-42 9MU 29-11 47MU 5-12 Malta 16-12 Gib NWA 28-2-43 SOC

EN198 3663 M61 EA FF 25-11-42 29-11 47MU 5-12 *SS647* 19-12 Gib 6-2-43 NWA 28-2 SOC 31-7

EN199 3677 M61 EA FF 28-11-42 12MU 1-12 47MU 9-12 *Marsa* 20-12 Gib 13-1-43 NWA 28-2 C3 ops 24-4 Sic 1-8 NAASC 31-10 GACE blown away in gale 73S Luqa 23-12 SOC 30-1-47

EN200 3673 M61 EA FF 28-11-42 39MU 29-11 47MU 17-12 *Emp Tow* 23-12 Gib 13-1-43 Malta 1-3 126S C3 ops 25-3 SOC 26-3

EN201 3688 M61 EA FF 29-11-42 39MU 1-12 47MU 14-12 *Emp Tow* 23-12 Gib 13-1-43 NWA 28-2 USAAF 31-10 ME 19-7-45 SOC 13-9

EN202 3689 M61 EA FF 29-11-42 47MU 10-12 *Emp Tow* 23-12 Gib 13-1-43 NWA 28-2 SOC 14-3-46

EN203 3690 M61 EA FF 30-11-42 6MU 1-12 47MU 10-12 *Emp Tow* 23-12 Gib 13-1-43 NWA 28-2 Malta 1-7 Sic 1-8 ME 30-9 NAAF 1-11 SOC 15-3-45

EN204 3692 M61 EA FF 6MU 1-12 47MU 10-12 *Emp Tow* 23-12 Gib 13-1-43 NWA 28-2 Malta SOC 12-6 FH104.10

EN205 4016 HPA FF 24-2-43 15FPP e/fd cd/ld Battingsbourne Wilts del flt AST to 6MU CE 2-3-43

EN206 3700 M61 EA FF 1-12-42 6MU 6-12 47MU 11-12 *Emp Tow* 23-12 Gib 13-1-43 NWA 28-2 81S C3 ops 8-3

EN207 3701 M61 EA FF 2-12-42 6MU 6-12 47MU 10-12 *Emp Tow* 23-12 Gib 13-1-43 NWA 28-2 USAAF 31-8

EN259 3768 M61 CHA FF 20-12-42 6MU 22-12 47MU *Mer Prin* 18-1-43 Gib 6-2 NWA 28-2 Malta 1-7 SOC 5-7

EN260 3787 M61 CHA FF 24-12-42 30-12 1PRU Ben 21-1-43 541S 21-1 NA PRXI 27-3 Gib 1-6 NWA SOC 31-7

EN261 3788 M61 CHA FF 24-12-42 1PRU 29-12 39MU 14-1-43 *Glenpool* 5-2-43 Gib 25-2 NWA 31-3 Malta 1-7 Sic 1-8 NAASC 31-10 SOC 22-11-45

EN263 3810 M46 CHA FF 2-1-43 33MU 8-1 1PRU Ben M61 instal PRXI 2-3 ME 27-3 Malta 1-4

EN265 3801 M61 CHA FF 31-12-42 1PRU2-1-43 47MU 28-1 *Glenpool* 5-2 Gib 25-2 Malta 1-7 Sic 1-8 ME 30-9 CE ops 30-8-44

EN266 3860 HFIX M61 CHA FF 13-1-43 39MU 21-1 47MU *SS657* 19-2 Gib 9-3 83MU ROS 5-8 405ARF 21-11 AST 24-12 mods 611S 14-7-44 312S 26-10 VA 6-11 mods FAF 16-9-46

EN267 3864 M61 CHA FF 15-1-43 9MU 23-1 47MU 10-2 *Fort Hud* 20-2 Gib 7-3 NWA 31-3 Mlata 1-7 Sic 1-8 NAASC 31-10

EN268 3820 M61 CHA FF 8-1-43 9MU 13-1 47MU 26-1 *Clear* 5-2 Gib 25-2 Malta 1-7 NAASC Sic 30-10 MAAF SOC 14-3-46

EN269 3821 M61 CHA FF 8-1-43 9MU 13-1 47MU 26-1 *Clear* 5-2 Gib 25-2 Malta 1-7 NAASC Sic 31-10 FACE 9-2-44

EN270 3825 M46 CHA FF 8-1-43 9MU 15-1 47MU 11-2 *Llanb* 11-3 Gib 24-3 NWA 30-4

EN286 3715 M61 HEA FF 4-12-42 6MU 6-12 47MU 20-12 *Sheld* 10-1-43 Gib 6-2 NWA 31-3 Malta 1-7 Sic 1-8 NA 30-11 ME 2-8-45 RHAF 27-2-47

EN287 3705 M61 EA FF 4-12-42 6MU 6-12 47MU 10-12 *Emp Tow* 23-12 Gib 13-1-43 Malta 1-3 NWA 28-3 Malta FTR ops 12-7

EN288 3720 M61 EA FF 7-12-42 6MU 9-12 47MU 24-1-43 *SS657* 19-2 Gib 9-3

EN289 3735 M61 EA FF 11-12-42 39MU 14-12 47MU 20-12 *South* 30-12 Gib 9-3 FTR ops 4-3

EN290 3719 M61 EA FF 6-12-42 39MU 8-12 47MU 14-12 *Emp Tow* 23-12 Gib 13-1-43 Malta 1-3 NWA 28-2 Italy 1-11 SOC 31-5-45

EN291 3736 M61 EA FF 11-12-42 9MU 14-12 47MU 28-12 *Sheld* 10-1-43 Gib 6-2 NWA 28-2 Farn May'43 Malcolm hood instal. To Hull BDn Feb'44 MacLaren rad instal core trls with EN314. Trls included cool flow measurement. Italy, wrk after attack by USAAF Lightning 20-4-44

EN292 3742 M61 EA FF 12-12-42 39MU 20-12 47MU 31-12 *Sheld* 10-1-43 Gib 6-2 NWA 28-2 FTR ops 12-4

EN293 3751 EA FF15-12-42 39MU 20-12 47MU 31-12 *Sheld* 10-1-43 Gib 6-2 NWA 28-2

EN294 3753 M61 EA FF 17-12-42 39MU 20-12 47MU 29-12 *Sheld* 10-1-43 Gib 6-2 C3 ops 26-4

EN295 3754 M61 EA FF 17-12-42 39MU 20-12 47MU 29-12 *SS117* 4-1-43 Malta 1-3 NWA 28-2 C3 ops 10-7

EN296 3755 M61 EA FF 17-12-42 39MU 21-12 47MU 31 12 *Emp Tide* 3-2 Gib 16-2 NWA 31-3 Malta 1-7 ME 1-9 NA 30-11 CE ops exploded in sea 21-2-45

EN298 3760 M61 EA FF 19-12-42 12MU 23-12 47MU 10-1-43 *Emp Hav* 19-1 Gib 6-2 72S FTR ops 20-6 FH136

EN299 3761 M61 EA FF 19-12-42 12MU 23-12 47MU 14-1-43 *Emp Hav* 19-1 Gib 6-2 NWA FTR ops 28-4

EN300 3764 M61 EA FF 20-12-42 39MU 23-12 47Mu 2-1-43 *Sheld* 10-1 Gib 6-2 NWA 28-2 s/dn by RAF a/c CE 14-7

EN301 3766 M61 EA FF 20-12-42 39MU 21-12 47MU 2-1-43 *Mer Prin* 18-1 Gib 6-2 NWA 28-2 FTR ops 18-6 FH119

EN302 3778 M61 EA FF 22-12-42 9MU 23-12 47MU 26-1-43 *Well Crt* 18-2 Gib 7-3 NWA 31-3 USAAF ME 31-12 FACE 5-6-45

EN303 3783 M61 EA FF 23-12-42 9MU 24-12 47MU 15-1-43 *Emp Hav* 19-1 Gib 6-2 Malta 1-7 ME 1-9 FTR ops 22-9

EN304 3784 M61 EA FF 23-12-42 6MU 29-12 47MU 9-1-43 *Mer Prin* 18-1 Gib 6-2 NWA 31-3 Malta 1-7 NAASC Sic 31-10 ME 26-7-45 SOC 26-6-47

EN305 3790 M61 EA FF 23-12-42 543S 29-12 39MU 14-1-43 47MU 28-1 *Well Crt* 18-2 Gib 7-3 NWA 31-3

EN306 3851 M63 EA FF 13-1-43 39MU 21-1 47MU 3-2 *SS657* 19-2 NWA 31-3 Malta 1-7 Italy 1-11 NWA FAC3 18-11

EN307 3786 M61 EA FF 23-12-42 543S Ben 29-12 37MU 14-1-43 *Well Crt* 18-2 Gib 7-3 NWA 31-3 USAAF 31-12 lost over Italy 15-12

EN308 3798 M61 EA FF 30-12-42 39MU 2-1-43 47MU 9-1 *Emp Hav* 19-1 Gib 6-2 NWA 31-3 Malta 1-7 Sic 1-8 NAASC 31-10 SOC 18-10-45

EN309 3800 M61 EA FF 31-12-42 39MU 2-1-43 47MU 13-1 *Emp Hav* 19-1 Gib 6-2 Malta 1-7 FTR ops 16-7

EN311 3813 M61 EA FF 2-1-43 6MU 4-1 47MU 9-1 *Mer Prin* 18-1 Gib 6-2 NWA 28-2

EN312 3814 M61 EA FF 2-1-43 6MU 9-1 47MU 15-1 *Emp Hav* 19-1 Gib 6-2

EN313 3815 M61 EA FF 2-1-43 6MU 9-1 47MU 15-1 *Emp Tide* 3-2 Gib 16-2 NWA 31-3 Malta 1-7 Sic 1-9

EN314 M61 EA FF 8-1-43 VAWD 13-1 BDn May'43 hand trls with increased tailplane incidence (2°), enlarged elev horn balance. AST 20-7 mr 33MU 24-10 HAL 26-10 MacLaren rad instal. Stn Flt Heston 3-11 BDn 20-2-44 with EN291. Eng and maint trls of MacLaren rad. 20-2 flight trls of same. 3-6 cool flow measurements with MacLaren rad. Details to R-R.Trls end Oct'45. ASTH 18-12 MacLaren rad and mods removed M63 instal. Fuel syst trls with 200 gal torpedo-shape o/ld tank 33MU 8-7-46 SAAF 23-4-47

EN315 3819 M61 EA FF 8-1-43 6MU 11-1 47MU 25-1 *Clear* 5-2 Gib 25-2 Malta 1-7 SOC 16-7

EN329 3861 M61 EA FF 13-1-53 21-1 47MU 3-2 *SS658* 22-2 Gib 7-3 NWA 31-3 NA 30-11

EN333 3865 M61 CHA FF 15-1-43 39MU 21-1 47MU 6-2 *SS657* 19-2 Gib 9-3 NWA 31-3 Malta 1-7 Sic 1-8 NA 30-11 SOC 25-10-44

EN334 3876 M61 CHA FF 16-1-43 39MU 21-1 47MU 3-2 *SS657* 19-2 Gib 9-3 SOC 29-2-44

EN335 3883 M61 CHA FF 18-1-43 9MU 23-1 47MU 4-2 *SS657* 19-2 Gib 9-3

EN336 3888 M61 CHA FF 9MU 26-1-43 47MU 4-2 *SS657* 19-2 Gib 9-3

EN339 3890 M61 CHA FF 20-1-43 39MU 26-1 47MU 5-2 *Fort Hud* 20-2 Gib 7-3 NA 31-3 SOC 6-9-45

EN340 3893 M61 CHA FF 21-1-43 39MU 26-1 47MU 5-2 *Fort Hud* 20-2 Gib 7-3 NWA 31-3 ME 1-8

EN344 3917 M61 CHA FF 26-1-43 39MU 2-2 47MU 9-2 *Llanb* 11-3 Gib 24-3 NWA 30-4 Malta 1-8 185S C3 ops 23-1-44

EN345 3928 M61 CHA FF 29-1-43 39MU 2-2 47MU 9-2 *Llanb* 13-3 Gib 24-3 NWA 31-5 USAAF 31-7 ASTH 28-2-45 WAL 19-7 33MU 31-8 SAAF 14-5-49

EN349 3944 M63 CHA FF 3-2-43 6MU 10-2 47MU 20-2 *Harmat* 10-3 Gib 26-4 NWA 31-5 Malta 1-6 Sic 1-8 NA 30-11 fire on grnd CB 13-3-45 REAF 26-9-46

EN350 3945 M63 CHA FF 3-2-43 6MU 6-2 47MU 20-2 *Harmat* 10-3 Gib 26-4 NWA 31-5 Malta 1-6 Italy 1-11 SOC 5-6-45

EN390 3952 M63 CHA FF 5-2-43 6MU 7-2 47MU 18-2 *Harmat* 10-3 Gib 26-4 NWA 31-5 Malta 1-8 Sic 1-10 SOC 14-3-46

EN392 3954 M63 CHA FF 6-2-43 6MU 7-2 47MU 18-2 *Hapmat* 10-3 Gib 26-4 Malta 1-7 Italy 1-11 SOC 31-8-44 recat A 28-4-45 SOC 30-4-47

EN393 3970 M63 CHA FF 9-2-43 9MU 13-2 FACB 24-2 GAL M61 instal 39MU 26-1-44 84GSU 3-4 CAC ops 12-6 FRU 10-8 310S 12-10 FACB 23-12 SAL sold H Bath 24-11-49

EN394 3976 M63 CHA FF 11-2-43 9MU 15-2 47MU 28-2 *SS670* 24-3 Gib 12-4 Malta 1-7 SOC 2-10

EN397 3985 M63 CHA FF 13-2-43 332S 14-2 AST 9-3 mods 39MU 23-12 ROS 27-7-44 BDn 12-2-45 29MU 6-6-46 sold VA 5-12-49

EN398 3987 M63 CHA FF 13-2-43 402S 18-2 416S 23-3 Stn HQ Ken 4-4 AST mods 416S 16-4 421S 27-7 AST 26-8 CAC ops 24-9 AST 83GSU 23-3-44 SAL 22-8 9MU 9-1-45 80 OTU 24-5 29MU 21-3-46 sold H Bath 10-11-49 (W/C Johnson s/dn 16 of his final total of 34 e/a in EN398)

EN399 3997 M63 CHA FF 18-2-43 HAL 25-2 VA 18-3 6MU 22-3 *Emp Bar* 2-5 Casa 17-5 ME 1-7 SOC 26-8-45

EN400 4021 CHA FF 24-2-43 HAL 28-2 VA 18-3 6MU 22-3 47MU 29-3 *Orient C* 13-4 Casa 25-4 NWA 31-5

EN401 4040 M63 CHA FF 27-2-43 39MU 7-3 47MU 17-3 *Ess Trad* 10-4 Casa 25-4 NWA 21-5 Malta 1-6 ME 1-9

EN402 4060 M63 CHA FF 3-3-43 39MU 7-3 47MU 17-3 *SS680* 11-4 Casa 25-4 NWA 31-5 Malta 1-6 Sic 1-10 CE 24-10-44

EN403 4063 M63 CHA FF 4-3-43 6MU 9-3 47MU 17-3 *SS680* 11-4 Casa 25-4 NWA 1-6 C3 ops 7-8

EN404 4070 M63A CHA FF 6-3-43 6MU 9-3 47MU 17-3 *SS680* 11-4 Casa 25-4 NWA 31-5 Malta 1-6 FAC3 2-7

EN405 4095 M63A CHA FF 13-3-43 39MU 18-3 47MU 29-3 *Orient C* 13-4 Casa 25-4 ME 9-8-45 SOC 31-7-47

EN406 4128 M63 CHA FF 20-3-43 9MU 22-3 47MU 4-4 *SS686* 24-4 Casa 17-5 NWA 31-5

EN444 3837 M61 EA FF 8-1-43 9MU 15-1 47MU 3-2 *SS657* 19-2 Gib 9-3 ME CE ops 6-5

EN445 3839 M61 EA FF 8-1-43 12MU 13-1 47MU 28-1 *Well Crt* 18-2 Gib 7-3 Malta 1-7 Sic 1-8 NA 30-11 IAF 26-6-47 as MM4029

EN446 3838 M61 EA FF 8-1-43 9MU 15-1 47MU 26-1 *Clear* 5-2 Gib 25-2 Malta 1-7 Sic 1-8 NA 30-11 SOC 8-3-44

EN447 3842 M61 EA FF 9-1-43 12MU 13-1 47MU 28-1 *Well Crt* 18-2 Gib 7-3

EN448 3847 M61 EA FF 11-1-43 12MU 13-1 47MU 9-2 *Fort H H* 20-2 Gib 7-5 Malta 1-7 ME FTR ops 11-7

EN449 3849 M61 EA FF 13-1-43 39MU 21-1 47MU 3-2 *SS657* 19-2 Gib 9-3 NWA 31-3 Malta 1-7 FTR ops 4-8

EN450 3850 M61 EA FF 13-1-43 39MU 14-1 47MU 26-1 *Well Crt* 18-2 Gib 7-3 NWA 31-3 SOC 6-6-45

EN451 3854 M61 EA FF 14-1-43 39MU 21-3 47MU 4-2 *SS657* 19-2 Gib 9-3 SOC 8-3-44

EN452 3853 M61 EA FF 14-1-43 39MU 21-3 47MU 28-1 *Well Crt* 18-2 Gib 7-3 NWA 31-3

EN453 3855 M61 EA FF 15-1-43 39MU 21-1 47MU 28-1 *Well Crt* 18-2 Gib 7-3 NWA 30-4 USAAF 31-10

Now with the Confederate Air Force, based at Breckenridge, Texas, MK297 masqueraded for a whi 'Johnnie' Johnson's EN398.

Bombing-up and swinging into wind, France 1944.

The shark's mouth motif was popular with fighter pilots, particularly in the Far East war zone. A number of these Spitfires in the area were named "The Grey Goose".

EN454 3857 M61 EA FF 15-1-43 36MU 20-1 47MU 29-1 *Well Crt* 18-2 Gib 7-3

EN455 3858 M61 EA FF 16-1-43 6MU 20-1 47MU 5-2 *Fort H H* 20-2 Gib 7-3 Malta 1-7 Sic 1-8 NAASC 31-10 SOC 29-2-44

EN456 3884 M61 EA FF 18-1-43 6MU 21-1 47MU 28-1 *Well Crt* 18-2 Gib 7-3 NWA 31-3 Malta 1-7 Italy 1-11 REAF 26-9-46

EN458 3886 M61 EA FF 20-1-43 39MU 22-1 47MU 6-2 *SS658* 22-2 Gib 7-3 i/sea ops FTR 25-4

EN459 3894 M61 EA FF 21-1-43 39MU 22-1 47MU 5-2 *Fort H H* 22-2 Gib 7-3 NWA 31-3 Malta 1-7 Sic 1-8 NA 30-11

EN460 3905 M61 EA FF 23-1-43 9MU 3-2 47MU 11-2 *Llanb* 11-3 Gib 24-3 NWA 31-5 SOC 26-8-45

EN461 3907 M61 EA FF 23-1-43 9MU 29-1 47MU 10-2 *Llanb* 11-3 Gib 24-3 NWA 30-4 Malta 1-7 Sic 1-8 NA 30-11 CE ops 12-11-44 ME 30-11 SOC 6-9-45

EN462 3917 M61 EA FF 26-1-43 6MU 2-2 47MU 23-2 *Wand* 12-3 Gib 24-3 NWA 30-4 Malta 1-7 Sic 1-8 NAAF 1-11 SOC 28-3-46

EN463 3920 M61 EA FF 27-1-43 6MU 2-2 47MU 9-2 *Fort H H* 20-2 Gib 7-3 NWA 31-3 USAAF 1-10

EN464 3921 M63 EA FF 27-1-43 9MU 29-1 47MU 25-2 *SS670* 24-3 Gib 12-4 NWA 30-4 Malta 1-7 Sic 1-8 SOC 31-12

EN466 3931 M61 EA FF 29-1-43 9MU 7-2 47MU 16-2 *Harmat* 10-3 Gib 26-4 Malta 1-7 s/dn by Allied AA fire 10-7

EN467 3940 M63 EA FF 2-2-43 9MU 7-2 47MU 11-2 *Llanb* 11-3 Gib 24-3

EN468 3941 M61 EA FF 39MU 7-2 47MU 11-2 *Llanb* 11-3 Gib 24-3 NWA 31-5 Malta 1-6 FAC3 7-1-44

EN469 3946 EA FF 3-2-43 39MU 7-2 11-2 *Llanb* 11-3 Gib 24-3 NWA 31-5 Malta 1-8 Sic SOC 8-3-44

EN471 3951 M61 EA FF 5-2-43 39MU 7-2 47MU 15-2 *SS670* 24-3 Gib 12-4 NWA 30-4

EN472 3967 M61 EA FF 8-2-43 122S 13-2 FTR ops 26-2 FH6.50

EN473 3968 M61 EA FF 9-2-43 122S 13-2 222S 19-5 AST 15-8 M63 instal 405ARF 7-9 65S 1-11 33MU 2-2-44 3501SU 15-5 SAL 10-8 GAL 31-10

EN475 3982 M61 EA FF 13-2-43 340S 16-2 FTR ops 13-3

EN476 3988 M63 EA FF 13-2-43 9MU 16-2 47MU 28-2 *SS670* 24-4 Gib 12-4 USAAF 31-1-44 SOC 23-12

EN478 3995 M63 EA FF 17-2-43 39MU 18-2 47MU 1-3 *SS670* 24-3 Gib 12-4 Malta 1-7 Sic 1-8 SOC 1-2-44

EN479 4018 M63 EA FF 24-2-43 39MU 26-2 47MU 10-3 *SS670* 24-3 Gib 12-4 NWA 31-5 Malta 1-7 Sic 1-8 ME 2-8-45 SOC 9-8

EN480 4010 M63 EA FF 19-2-43 39MU 25-2 47MU 10-3 *SS670* 24-3 Gib 12-4 NWA 30-4

EN481 4009 M63 EA FF 20-2-43 CRD HAL 26-2 VA 23-3 47MU 1-4 *Ess Trad* 10-4 Casa 25-4 NWA 31-5 Malta 1-6 C3 ops 4-7

EN482 4027 M63 EA FF 20-2-43 CRD HAL 28-2 VA 23-3 47MU 1-4 *Emp Bar* 2-5 Casa 17-5 Malta 1-8 NAAF 1-11 REAF 31-10-46

EN483 4019 M63 EA FF 24-2-43 6MU 26-2 47MU 9-3 *SS670* 24-3 Gib 12-4 NWA 31-5 SOC 20-9-45

EN490 M63 EA FF 27-2-43 9MU 1-3 47MU 12-3 *SS670* 24-3 Gib 12-4 NWA 31-5 Malta 1-7 Sic 1-8 C3 ops 6-11

EN491 4028 M63A EA FF 26-2-43 9MU 1-3 47MU 29-3 *Orient C* 13-4 Casa 25-4 NWA 31-5 NWA 31-5 Malta 1-8 Sic SOC 19-1-45

EN492 4038 M63A EA FF 27-2-43 9MU 1-3 47MU 12-3 *SS670* 24-3 Gib 12-4 NWA 31-5 Sic 1-8 USAAF 31-1-44

EN493 4075 M63 EA FF 6-3-43 9MU 9-3 47MU 26-3 *Orient C* 13-4 Gib 25-4

EN498 4220 M61 WA FF 15-4-43 8MU 20-4 CRD Farn 24-3 trls of exhaust gas deflectors directing hot gas to clear misted-up w/s at H/A. Trls were fail VAWD 19-4 conical curved w/s instal as second step to clear misty w/s. Max speed gain of 5-12 mph. Hand and drag reduction trls. BDn June'45 cont of h/a misting trls with new w/s and mod exhaust gas deflectors. **M63 instal. Farn 28-8-44 Radar escort for Fw190;** escort (with X4258) to Ju88 fitt Leitchensen radar Oct; fitt Monica and used and used as radar target for Mosquito fitt with flexi fuel tanks. Night fly trls with BS403. Dec'44 Monica Mk1A instal for trls with Mosquito NA744 (also fitt Monica 1A). Monica trls with Beaufighter T4790 and Wellington HZ579. Medical research trls with Franks h/a pressure suit. Feb GGS trls. 8-3 flown by Major G DeHavilland as chase a/c for Spider Crab (proto Vampire MP838/G) 14-3 airfield defence a/c May fuel tank jett trls. P&P Sept instal of glider tug equip. Initial trls at BDn Ret Farn for use as glider tug for GAL GL56 tailless glider TS507. July'45 used as alternative tug with NH403 towing Me163 Komet rocket fighter to Wisley airfield and return. Towed Komet to BDn in Mar'46 Army coop trls in May. Rain repellant pt trls with NH403 and all-weather trls. Gust measurement trls with Vampire fitt with variable lift cont RAE census 31-7-47 29MU 19-7-48 sold H Bath 27-1-49

EN500 4232 M63 EA FF 17-4-43 8MU 20-4- 47MU 30-4 *Fort Stle* 16-5 Casa 30-5 Malta 1-8 Italy 1-11 NAAF SOC 26-9-46

EN501 4253 M63A EA FF 22-4-43 39MU 30-4 82-5 *SS702* 9-6 Casa 15-6 NWA 1-7 NAAF 1-11 SOC 31-3-44

EN502 4243 M63A EA FF 23-4-43 39MU 24-4 82MU 9-5 *Fort Stle* 16-5 Casa 30-5 Sicily 1-8 SOC 8-3-44

EN510 4281 M63A EA FF 6-5-43 39MU 12-5 82MU 20-5 *SS702* 9-6 Casa 15-6 NWA 1-7 NAAF 1-11 ItAF 30-5-46 as MM4036

EN513 4318 M63 EA FF 15-5-43 8MU 19-5 82MU 28-5 *SS702* 2-6 Casa 15-6 NWA 1-7 NAAF 1-11

Proof of the problems of following the official history cards: EN133 clearly in unit service, yet with no t of such in officialdom.

EN514 4326 M63 EA FF 18-5-43 9MU 21-5 82MU 27-5 *SS702* 2-6 Casa 15-6 NWA 1-7 NAAF 1-11 SOC 16-3-46

JK, JL and LZ series all Merlin 63 engine

JK395 1st prod CBAF a/c VAWD 16-3-43 wts & CG load 9MU 203 47MU 6-4-43 *SS686* Casa 17-5 NWA 31-5

JK611 9MU 23-3-43 47MU 31-3 *SS68-* 11-4 Casa 25-4 NWA 31-5 Malta 1-10 Sicly SOC 30-6-44

JK641 6MU 23-3-43 47MU 4-4 *SS686* 24-4 Casa 17-5 ME 1-7 NA 31-8-44 CE 20-9-45

JK650 9MU 16-3-43 47MU 29-3 *Ess Trad* 10-4 Casa25-4 FAC2 28-2-44 SOC 15-3-45

JK770 12MU 28-2-43 47MU 6-4 *Emp Bar* 2-5 Casa 17-5 Malta 1-7 Sic 1-8 NAASC 31-10 SOC 28-4-45

JK796 6MU 23-3-43 47MU 31-3 *Orient C* 13-4 Casa 25-4 Malta 1-7 Sic 1-8 NAASC 31-10 SOC 14-3-46

JK881 12MU 28-3-43 47MU 7-4 *SS686* 24-4 Casa 17-5 SOC 26-3-45

JK882 15MU 28-3-43 47MU 12-4 *SS687* 29-4 Casa 17-5 NWA 30-4-44 ME 1-8 NAAF 1-11 SOC 18-10-45

JK883 6MU 26-3-43 47MU 5-4 *SS686* 24-4 Casa 17-5 USAAF 31-7

JK884 12MU 27-3-43 47MU 6-4 *Emp Bar* 2-5 Casa 17-5 ME 1-7 NAASC 31-10 SOC 29-2-44

JK980 15MU 28-3-43 47MU 8-4 *Emp Bar* 2-5 Casa 17-5 ME 1-7 FAF 25-7-46

JL134 6MU 28-3-43 47Mu 6-4 *SS686* 24-4 Casa 17-5 NWA USAAF 31-7

JL135 15MU 28-3-43 47MU 12-4 *SS687* 29-4 Casa 17-5 NAASC 31-10 ASTH 23-3-45 29MU 27-7 sold VA 5-12-49

JL136 39MU 30-3-43 47MU 5-4 *Emp Bar* 2-5 Casa 17-5 ME 1-8 NAAF 1-11 CE ops 3-3-45

JL137 6MU 31-3-43 47MU 10-4 *Fort Thom* 3-5 Casa 17-5 ME 1-8 Malta NA 30-11 SOC 8-3-44

JL138 39MU 30-3-43 47MU 11-4 *SS687* 29-4 Casa 17-5 FACE 4-6-45

JL177 M66 15MU 2-4-43 47MU 12-4 *Fort Thom* 3-5 Casa 17-5 ME 1-8 REAF 29-8-46

JL178 39MU 5-4-43 47MU 12-4 *SS687* 29-4 Casa 17-5 ME 1-7 NAAF 1-11 ME FAC3 12-3-44

JL179 6MU 28-3-43 47MU 6-4 *Emp Bar* 2-5 Casa 17-5 ME 1-7 NAAF 1-11 SOC 28-4-45

JL180 39MU 31-3-43 47MU 11-4 *SS687* 29-4 Casa 17-5 Malta 1-7 Sic 1-9 NAASC 31-10

JL226 9MU 11-4-43 82MU 4-5 *Fort Jer* 11-5 Casa 30-5 NWA 1-7 ME 1-8 NAAF 1-11 CE ops 4-9-44

JL227 39MU 3-4-43 Farn Apl'43 comp drag reduction trls with EF731, EF644, EN946. 26-5 escort for Ju88 and Fw109 which were fitt with a radar device reacting to Monica tail warning radar instal in British bombers. The Wireless and Electrical Flt used JL227 for instns trls as they were under extreme pressure from the Air Min to find an answer to the problem and numerous a/c were pressed into service including **EN498 fitt AI radar; X4258, EF644, X4258 was also fitt with 'Relay' air-to-air homing equip Wellingtons HZ202 and HZ579 were fitt with Eureka/Babs. Mosquito DZ725 and DD619; Lanacster ED630; Fortress fitt with Oboe; Beaufighter T4790; Defiant AA539, and many other a/c types. 411AAF 19-11 302S 1-44 Farn Apl '44 for trls at h/a of exhaust gas w/s missing 80S 29-5-44 VA 23-10 mods 310S 23-10 312S 27-5-45 RHAF 20-4-48**

JL228 39MU 10-4-43 222MU 19-4 *Fort Thom* 3-5 Casa 17-5 ME 1-7 SOC 20-9-45

JL229 15MU 2-4-43 47MU 12-4 *Fort Thom* 3-5 Casa 17-5 NWA 1-10 USAAF 31-10 sold Turk 29-3-45

JL230 15MU 2-4-43 47MU 12-4 *SS687* 29-4 Casa 17-5 Malta 1-8 Sic ME 5-7-45 SOC 24-3-46

JL252 6MU 12-4-43 82MU 21-4 *Fort Thom* 3-5 Casa 17-5 Malta 1-8 NAAF 1-11 SOC 31-3-44

JL253 15MU 2-4-43 47MU 12-4 *SS687* 27-4 Casa 17-5 NAAF 1-11 USAAF 12/31 Lost in Italy 7-2-44

JL254 12MU 9-4-43 47MU 20-4 *Fort Thom* 3-5 Casa 17-5 SAAF FTR ops 13-11-44

JL255 9MU 10-4-43 82MU 30-4 *Fort Jer* 11-5 Casa 30-5 Malta 1-8 Sic NAASC 31-10 SOC 26-9-46

JK256 12MU 10-4-43 222MU 20-4 *Fort Thom* 3-5 Casa 17-5 Malta 1-8 NAAF 1-11 32S FTR ops 17-4-44

JL375 M60 6MU 11-4-43 47MU 19-4 *Fort Thom* 3-5 Casa 17-5 Malta 1-7 ME FTR ops 10-7

JL376 M60 6MU 11-4-43 47MU 19-4 47MU 19-4 *Fort Thom* 3-5 Casa 17-5 Malta 1-7 Sic 1-9 SOC 13-9-45

JL377 12MU 9-4-43 47MU 20-4 *Fort Thom* 3-5 Casa 17-5 ME 1-8 NAAF 1-11 FAF 31-11 FTR ops 26-4-45

JL383 39MU 13-4-43 222MU 21-4 *Fort Thom* 3-5 Casa 17-5 Malta 1-8 Sic NAASC 31-10 185S CE ops 13-2-45

JL384 9MU 11-4-43 82MU 4-5 *Fort Jer* 11-5 Casa 30-5 NWA 1-7 6MU 6-4-45 53 OTU 24-4 72S 29MU 5-8 sold H Bath 27-10-49

LZ816 LFIX M66 39MU 3-11-43 405ARF 12-11 AST 13-1-44 56S 10-6 402S out of cont i/sea off Selsey Sussex 19-7-44

LZ831 39MU 17-4-43 82MU 5-5 *Fort Jer* 11-5 Casa 5-6

LZ832 15MU 16-4-43 76MU 22-4 *Fort Stle* 16-5 Casa 30-5 30-5 Malta 1-8 NA 1-11 SOC 8-3-44 bboc ASTE 10-8-45 39MU 30-9 *Clan Chat* 28-4-48 SAAF 11-5

LZ833 M61 12MU 14-4-43 47MU 2-5 *Fort Thom* 3-5 Casa 17-5 ME 1-9 NAAF 1-11 SOC 28-4-45

LZ836 FIXT 8MU 24-4-43 82MU 18-5 *SS702* 2-6 Casa 15-6 NWA 1-7 ME 1-8 NAAF 1-11 ME 31-5-45 SOC 30-1-47

LZ837 39MU 14-4-43 222MU 2-5 *Fort Stle* 16-5 Casa 30-5 Malta 1-8 NAASC 31-10 FTR ops 28-12-44

LZ838 12MU 15-4-43 47MU 4-5 *Fort Stle* 16-5 Casa 30-5 Malta 1-8 Italy 1-11 MAAF C3 ops 23-3-44

LZ839 45MU 29-4-43 331S 7-5 FAAC 18-11 ROS 229S 25-9-44 310S 17-6-45 RHAF 31-3-48

LZ840 15MU 15-4-43 82MU 5-5 *Fort Jer* 11-5 Casa 30-5 FTR ops 11-7

LZ841 12MU 15-4-43 47MU 4-5 *Fort Stle* 16-5 Casa 30-5 NWA 1-7 ME 1-8 218Gr NA 30-11 MAAF 21-6-45 FACE u/c coll on ldg Innsbruck Austria 25-4-46 SOC 9-5

LZ842 232S SAAF 24-4-48 FA 27-4-50

LZ843 FAFF sold Turk 11-7-47

LZ861 6MU 17-4-43 82MU 26-4 *Fort Jer* 11-5 Casa 30-5 Malta 1-8 NAASC 31-10 C3 ops 3-7-44

LZ888 8MU 18-4-43 82MU 27-4 *Fort Jer* 11-5 Casa 30-5 NWA 1-7 NAASC 31-10 USAAF 29-2-44 MAAF 93S CE ops 4-4-45

LZ889 8MU 18-4-43 82MU 27-4 *Fort Jer* 11-5 Casa 30-5 Malta 1-8 Sic NAAF 1-11 ME SOC 26-9-46

LZ890 6MU 18-4-43 82MU 26-4 *Fort Jer* 11-5 Casa 30-5 NWA 1-7 ME 1-8 FAC3 5-7

LZ891 15MU 18-4-43 82MU 8-5 *Fort Jer* 11-5 Casa 30-5 NWA 1-7

LZ892 8MU 18-4-43 82MU 5-5 *Fort Jer* 11-5 Casa 30-5 Malta 1-8 NAAF 1-11

LZ893 6MU 18-4-43 82MU 26-4 *Fort Jer* 11-5 Casa 30-5 NWA 1-7 ME 1-8 NAAF 30-11 SOC 8-3-44

LZ894 6MU 17-4-43 82MU 30-4 *Fort Jer* 11-5 Casa 30-5 NWA 1-7 ME 1-8 NAASC 31-10 SOC 8-3-44 bboc 21-6-45 con to FVC 28-6 SOC 29-8-46

LZ895 39MU 17-4-43 82MU 5-5 *Fort Jer* 11-5 Casa 30-5 Malta 1-8 Sic NAASC 31-10 1435S FTR ops 26-4-44

LZ896 8MU 21-4-43 82MU 5-5 *Fort Jer* 11-5 Casa 30-5 Malta 1-8 Sic NAAF 1-11 C3 ops 4-4-44

LZ897 33MU 25-4-43 82MU 22-5 *Fort Jer* 11-5 Casa 30-5 NWA 1-7 ME 1-8 NAAF 1-11

LZ898 45MU 24-4-43 332S 9-5 FTR ops 11-9

LZ899 421S 30-5-43 403S 2-6 FTR 26-6 FH18.50

LZ915 33MU 25-4-43 82MU 22-5 *Fort Stle* 16-5 Casa 30-5 NWA 1-7 CE ops 17-3-45

LZ916 M61 46MU 28-4-43 331S 6-5 AST 27-6 M63 instal 3501SU 1-4-44 229S 26-6 VA 15-9 mods 310S 11-12 FACE 5-1-45

LZ917 46MU 28-4-43 331S CE 13-5

LZ918 33MU 25-4-43 82MU 22-5 *Fort Stle* 16-5 Casa 30-5 NWA 1-7 NAASC 31-10 FAF 30-11 RAF 29-2-44 SOC 23-10

LZ919 45MU 28-4-43 332S 14-5 CAC 27-7 273S 20-5-44 FLS 29-8 to 5952M 2SoTT 15-6-46

LZ920 38MU 28-4-43 331S 23-5 AST 23-2-44 611S 26-9 312S 8-10 Stn Flt Bradwell Bay 310S 22-3-45 e/fd f/ld hit tree nr Tang CE 2-5 SOC

LZ921 45MU 24-4-43 331S 14-5 3501SU 29-6-44 FLS 20-8 to 6012M 2-8-46 cancel M61 instal SOC 25-10-46

LZ922 38MU 27-4-43 332S dvd i/sea of Clacton 22-5

LZ923 FIXC 3MU 28-4-43 222MU 4-6 *SS707* 10-6 Casa 29-6 ME 1-8 NAAF 1-11 C3 ops 17-2-44 ME 16-8-45 107MU SOC 31-12-47 extant (N521R) California USA

LZ924 33MU 28-4-43 122S 6-5 222S 19-5 421S 24-8 FLS 16-9-44 CFE 5-3-45 FACE dbf 5-3 SOC 13-3

LZ925 FIXT 8MU 30-4-43 82MU 17-5 *SS702* 2-6 Casa 15-6 NWA 1-7 ME 1-8 NAAF 1-11 MAAF SOC 14-3-46

LZ947 46MU 28-4-43 332S 6-5 GAL 28-5 82MU 20-10 *Mont City* 15-11 Casa 29-11 MAAF 21-6-45 SOC 30-8

LZ948 46MU 29-4-43 332S CE 13-5

LZ949 FIXT 8MU 30-4-43 222MU 1-6 *SS707* 10-6 ME 1-8 NAAF 1-11 MAAF 21-6-45 IAF 30-5-46 as MM4074

LZ950 FIXT8MU 30-4-43 82MU 17-5 *SS702* 2-6 Casa 15-6 NVA 1-7 ME 1-8 NAAF 1-11 FTR ops 29-1-44

LZ951 39MU 30-4-43 341S 13-5 303S 31-7 308S 16-11 AST 2-2-44 mr 611S 13-7 312S 8-10 VA 29-11 mods FA FTR 9-2-45 SOC 22-2

LZ952 38MU 28-4-43 82MU 30-5 *SS703* 1-6 Casa 15-6 NWA 1-7 ME 1-8 NAAF 1-11 IAF 26-6-47 as MM4075

LZ953 39MU 1-5-43 82MU 22-5 *SS702* 2-6 Casa 15-6 NWA 1-7 ME 1-8 NAAF 1-11 SOC 8-3-44

LZ954 39MU 1-5-43 82MU 22-5 *SS702* 2-6 Casa 15-6 NWA 1-7 ME 1-8 NAAF 1-11 SOC 8-3-44

LZ955 39MU 29-4-43 403S 13-5 FTR ops 31-5

LZ956 FIXT 8MU 30-4-43 82MU 17-5 *SS702* 2-6 Casa 15-6 NWA 1-7 ME 1-8 NAAF 1-11 MAAF CE ber 6-9-45

LZ989 M61 316S 14-5-43 302S 28-9 FAAC 24-12 AST M63 instal 3501SU 29-6-44 274S 1-8 FAAC 11-8 ROS sold R J Coley 9-2-50

LZ990 315S 12-5-43 PSOC 1-1-47

LZ991 45MU 16-5-43 215MU 4-6 *SS707* 6-6 Casa 10-6 ME 1-8 NAAF 1-11 SOC 8-3-44 bboc MAAF 21-6-45 IAF 26-6-47 as MM 4142

LZ992 FIXT 8MU 30-4-43 82MU 18-5 *SS702* 2-6 Casa 15-6 NWA 1-7 NAASC 31-10 1435S FTR ops 8-3-44

LZ993 315S 12-5-43 303S 6-6 FTR ops 24-6

LZ994 45MU 15-5-43 215MU 4-6 *SS707* 10-6 Casa 29-6

LZ995 45MU 15-5 215MU 4-6 *SS707* 10-6 Casa ME 1-8 NAAF 1-11 C3 ops 14-12

LZ996 416S 12-5-43 421S 20-5 FTR ops 17-6

LZ997 39MU 29-4-43 403S 9-5 CE ops 17-8 FH123.50

LZ998 33MU 13-5-43 222MU 31-5 *SS707* 10-6 Casa 29-6 NWA 31-7

MA series Merlin 63 engine

MA221 6MU 12-5-43 82MU 19-5 *SS702* 2-6 Casa 15-6 NWA 1-7 ME 1-8 NAAF 1-11 317S strk BS508 taxy CAC Llanb 29-2-44

MA222 6MU 2-5-43 315S 10-5 305S 6-6 303S 10-6 CAC ops 3-11 308S 16-11 AAST 1-3-44 229S 6-10-44 229S 6-10 80 OTU 14-6-45 FAF 14-3-46

MA223 6MU 12-5 22MU 1-6 *SS707* 10-6 Casa 29-6 ME 1-9 NAAF SOC 8-3-44

MA224 341 11-5-43 222S 28-7 405ARF 131S 27-9 e/fd w/u ldg CE nr Tipton Cross Exeter 20-12 FH184.35

MA225 331S 11-5-43 33MU 10-4-44 M61 instal 3501SU 19-6 19-6 229S 1-7 FTR ops 15-9

MA226 12MU 15-5-43 421S 23-5 CA 26-6 ROS AST 23-2-44 3501SU 23-6 310S FTR ops 8-9

MA227 12MU 15-5-43 47MU 1-6 *SS703* 1-6 Casa 15-6 NWA 1-7 ME 1-8 MAAF 21-6 SOC 26-9-46

MA228 332S 11-5 CB 24-12 80S 6-6-44 310S 5-9 VA Ox 6-10 310S strk B1232 & W3820 ldg CE NWld 28-10 recat AC

MA229 453 11-5-43 129S 17-7 332S 28-8 3501SU 7-6-44 80S FAAC 24-6 310S 5-9 MAL 15-5-45 47MU 4-10-48 *Clan McK* 19-1-49 SAAF 23-1

MA230 45MU 27-5-43 453S 9-6 129S 17-7 421S 26-8 CB ops 18-10 AST 80S 31-5-44 310S 5-9 VA 15-9 mods FA FTR 23-2-45

MA231 12MU 15-5-43 215MU 1-6 *SS707* 10-6 Casa 29-6 ME 1-8 NAAF 1-11 MAAF 21-6-45 SOC 10-1-46

MA232 453S 11-5-43 129S 17-7 405ARF HAL 27-8 421S 20-2-44 611S 3-8 VAO 3-10 mods 312S 18-10 FAAC 7-11 ROS HAL 27-12 mr SAAF 4-7-47

MA233 33MU 27-6-43 47MU 4-7 *Fort Chest* 11-7 Casa 29-7 218Gp NA 30-11 C3 ops 23-3-45 SOC ME 2-8-48

MA234 45MU 15-5-43 215MU 4-6 *SS707* 6-6 Casa 29-6 ME 1-9 NAAF 1-11 FAC3 1-2-44

MA235 12MU 15-5-43 341S 24-5 316S 29-7 302S 28-9 AST 5-2-44 310S 7-12-44 312S 27-8-45 RHAF 31-3-48

MA236 9MU 7-6-43 82MU 16-6 *SS708* 14-6 Casa 29-6 ME 1-8 NAAF 1-11 MAAF 21-6-45 SOC 13-12

MA237 12MU 14-5-43 47MU 1-6 *SS703* 1-6 Casa 15-6 Malta 1-8 Sic NA 30-11

MA238 46MU 16-5-43 215MU 27-5 *SS702* 2-6 Casa 15-6 NWA 1-7 MAAF 21-6-45 SOC 9-9-46

MA239 33MU 13-5-43 222MU 27-5 *SS703* 1-6 Casa 15-6 NWA 1-7 ME 1-8 NAAF 1-11 FAC3 29-3-44

MA240 33MU 13-5-43 222MU 28-5 *SS703* 1-6 Casa 15-6 NWA 1-7 ME 1-8 NAAF 1-11 FA on F F 49MU to SAL 2-4-45 recat E SOC 17-5-45

MA241 122S 11-5-43 222S 21-5 403S 24-8 405RSU 29-9 403S hit trees ldg app CE Ken 20-12 FH182.25

MA242 6MU 12-5-43 82MU 19-5 *SS702* 2-6 Casa 15-6 NWA 1-7 USAAF 31-8

MA243 FIXT 33MU 13-5-43 82MU 27-5 *SS702* 2-6 Casa 15-6 NWA 1-7 ME 1-8 NAAF 1-11 SOC 18-10-45

MA244 FIXT 46MU 16-5-43 82MU 27-5 *SS703* 2-6 Casa 15-6 Malta 1-8 Sic NAASC 31-10 DeH 2-3-45 sold VA 5-12-49

MA245 46MU 16-5-43 215MU 27-5 *SS702* 2-6 Casa 15-6 NWA 1-7 ME 1-8 NAAF 1-11 SOC 20-9-45

MA246 39MU 16-5-43 222MU 29-5 *SS703* 1-6 Casa 15-6 NWA 1-7 ME 1-8 NAAF 1-11 SOC 29-2-44

MA247 39MU 16-5-43 215MU 25-5 *SS702* 2-6 Casa 15-6 NWA 1-7 ME 1-8 NAAF 1-11

MA248 39MU 16-5-43 222MU 28-5 *SS702* 2-6 Casa 15-6 NWA 1-7 USAAF 31-7 RAF ME 31-12 REAF 26-9-46

MA249 39MU 23-5-43 222MU 30-5 *SS707* 10-6 Casa 29-6 ME 1-8 NAAF 1-11 CE ops 185S 22-7-44

MA250 46MU 22-5-43 82MU 13-6 *SS708* 2-6 Casa 29-6 ME 1-8 NAAF FTR ops 14-12 SOC 14-3-46 cancel SOC wrongly reported 18-7-46

MA251 33MU 13-5-43 222MU 28-5 *SS703* 1-6 Casa 15-6 NWA 1-7 ME 1-8 NAAF 1-11 FAF 29-2-44 MAAF 31-5-45 REAF 26-9-46

MA252 45MU 17-5-43 215MU 6-6 *SS707* 10-6 Casa 29-6 ME 1-8 NAAF 1-11 C3 ops 3-12

MA253 39MU 23-5-43 222MU 31-5 *SS707* 10-6 Casa 29-6 ME C3 ops 9-9 NA 30-11 SOC 8-3-44

MA254 39MU 16-5-43 82MU 29-5 *SS703* 1-6 Casa 15-6 NWA 1-7 FAF 1-10 SOC 31-8-44

MA255 Uruguay X R-RH 18-6-43 HAL 3-6-44 GAL 29-10 mods 83GSU 4-11 412S CAC ops 27-12 ASTH 19-2-45 W Wal 18-12-46 to Turk

MA256 FIXT 33MU 21-5-43 22MU 1-6 *SS707* 10-6 Casa 29-6 ME 1-8 IAF 26-6-47

MA257 39MU 23-5-43 82MU 30-5 *SS703* 1-6 Casa 15-6 NWA 1-7 ME 1-8 NAASC 30-11 RHAF 30-1-47

MA258 46MU 22-5-43 215MU 1-6 *SS707* 10-6 Casa 29-6 NWA 1-10 ME 9-8-45 SOC 26-6-47

MA259 33MU 23-5-43 47MU 1-6 *SS707* 10-6 Casa 29-6 ME 1-8 NAAF 1-11 SOC 31-3-44

MA260 39MU 23-5-43 82MU 30-5 *SS703* 1-6 Casa 15-6 NWA 1-7 ME 1-8 NAAF 1-11 SOC 31-8-44

MA299 45MU 28-5-43 341S 7-6 303S 27-9 308S 16-11 AST 22-2-44 39MU 14-5 FLS 20-8 to 6038M 2-8-46

MA300 12MU 27-5-43 47MU 1-6 *SS703* 1-6 Casa 15-6 Malta 1-8 C2 3-8 SOC 10-9

MA301 332S 29-5-43 AST 16-1-44 80S 10-6 310S 5-9 VAO 21-9 mods ASTE 5-4-45 39MU 13-9 FAF 25-6-46

MA302 46MU 1-6-43 82MU 14-6 *La Pam* 2-7 Casa 14-7 ME 1-9 NAAF 30-9

MA303 332S 29-5-43 AST 8-2-44 3501SU 29-6 to 6034M 2-8-46 SOC 14-10-50 trans FFS SoH

MA304 315S 30-5-43 303S 6-6 308S 16-11 AST 13-2-44 229S 10-6 FTR ops

MA305 331S 29-5-43 FTR 27-9

MA306 12MU 27-5-43 47MU 1-6 *SS707* 10-6 Casa 29-6 ME 1-9 NAAF 1-11 SOC 8-3-44

MA307 45MU 28-5-43 222MU 14-6 *SS708* 14-6 Casa 29-6 ME 1-8 NAAF 1-11 FACE 12-5-45 SOC 23-8

MA308 331S 29-5-43 AST 25-10 39MU 27-1-44 RoS VA 21-8-45 Mods FAF 24-5-46

MA309 316S 30-5-43 302S 28-9 FAAC 19-10 ROS 332S 3-1-44 317S AST 23-3 mr 611S 27-9 312S 8-10 80 OTU 26-2-46 FAF 14-3

MA310 12MU 1-6-43 47MU 8-6 *SS708* 14-6 Casa 29-6 SOC MAAF 31-5-45

MA311 46MU 3-6-43 82MU 13-6 *SS708* 14-6 Casa 29-6 ME 1-8 NAAF 1-11 32S FACE 14-6-44

MA312 33MU 19-6 341S 5-7 411S 17-10 CE ops 23-11 i/Channel FH122.25

MA313 6MU 6-6-43 222MU 14-6 *SS708* 14-6 Casa 29-6 ME 1-8 CE ops 23-9

MA314 315S 30-5-43 303S 6-6 CAC ops 25-7 ROS FACB 7-10 AST 84GSU 3-4-44 229S 26-6 VA 1-11 312S 22-4-45 80 OTU 27-9-45 FAF 11-4-46

MA315 12MU 31-5-43 82MU 7-6 *SS707* 10-6 Casa 29-6 ME 1-8 NAAF 1-11 IAF 21-6-46

MA369 9MU 15-8-43 47MU 7-9 *Ocean Rid* 23-9 Casa 16-10 NAASC 31-10 IAF 30-5-46 as MM4023

MA398 39MU 27-3-43 222MU 30-5 *SS702* 1-6 Casa 15-6 NWA 1-7 ME 1-8 NAAF 1-11

MA399 FIXT 33MU 22-5-43 47MU 1-6 *SS707* 10-6 Casa 29-6 ME 1-8 FAC3 4-11

MA400 45MU 28-5-43 222MU 14-6 *SS708* 17-6 Casa 29-6 ME 1-8 NAAF 1-11 SOC 30-6-44

MA401 12MU 27-5-43 47MU 1-6*SS703* 1-6 Casa 15-6 NWA 1-7 ME 1-8 NAAF 1-11 151RU 9-3-45 328S 11-10 FAF 27-11

MA402 12MU 27-5-43 47MU 1-6 *SS703* 1-6 Casa 16-5 NWA 1-7 ME 1-8 NAAF 1-11 SOC 18-8-44

MA403 45MU 26-5-43 215MU 4-6 *SS707* 10-6 Casa 29-6 ME 1-9 NAAF 1-11 NA 31-8-44 CE ops 9-1-45

MA404 33MU 23-5-43 222MU 1-6 *SS707* 10-6 Casa 29-6 ME 1-8 NAAF 1-11 SOC 8-3-44

MA405 12MU 27-5-43 47MU 1-6 *SS703* 1-6 Casa 15-6 NWA 1-7 ME 1-8 SOC 28-4-45

MA406 33MU 25-5-43 222MU 1-6 *SS707* 10-6 Casa 29-6 ME 1-8 NAAF 1-11 SOC 28-8-47

MA407 45MU 26-5-43 222MU 14-6 *Fort Ver* 1-7 Casa 14-7 ME 1-9 FACE 14-3-45 SOC 29-8

MA408 33MU 26-5-43 222MU 7-6 *SS708* 10-6 Casa 29-6 NAAF 1-11 137MU 8-4-48 SOC 10-6

MA409 45MU 26-5-43 332S 6-6 FTR ops 15-7

MA410 33MU 25-5-43 222MU 20-6 *Fort Ver* 1-7 Casa 14-7 ME 1-8 NAAF 1-11 SOC 18-10-45

MA411 45MU 28-5-43 222MU 14-6 *SS708* 14-6 Casa 29-6 ME 1-8 NAAF 1-11 FACE 22-2-45 SOC 3-5

MA412 33MU 23-5-43 222MU 1-6 *SS707* 10-6 Casa 29-6 ME 1-8 NAAF 1-11 SOC 8-3-44

MA413 33MU 25-5-43 222MU 7-6 *SS707* 10-6 Casa 29-6 ME 1-9 NAAF 1-11 SOC 29-2-44

MA414 39MU 23-5-43 222MU 30-5 *SS703* 1-6 Casa 15-6 Malta 1-8 Sic NA 30-11 SOC Apl '45

MA415 33MU 25-5-43 222MU 7-6 *SS707* 10-6 Casa 29-6 ME 1-9 NAAF 1-11 ASR 18-5-45 VA 20-5 mods FAF 1-8-46

MA416 45MU 26-5-43 421S 6-6 CE 28-7 recat B AST 28-8 33S 30-6-44 310S 8-7 504S 15-7 VAO 6-10 mods 303S CAC ops 3-12 ROS SCR Trng FU 25-1-45 58 OTU 5-4 sold VA 8-12-49

MA417 45MU 26-5-43 222MU 14-6 *SS708* 14-6 Casa 29-6 ME 1-8 NAAF 1-11 SOC 14-3-46

MA418 12MU 27-5-43 47MU 1-6 *SS703* 1-6 Casa 15-6 NWA 1-7 ME 1-8 NA 30-11 SOC 28-4-45

MA419 M61 9MU 19-7-43 47MU 5-8 *Emp Prss* 5-8 Casa 18-8 218Gp NA 30-11 SOC 31-8-44

MA420 33MU 22-7-43 65S 5-8 122S EAAC 22-1-44 ROS 83GSU 27-3 303S 28-9 VAOx 6-10 mods 80 OTU 15-4-45 FAF 14-3-46

MA421 6MU 18-7-43 222MU 26-7 *SS732* 5-8 Casa 15-8 218Gp NA 30-11 USAAF 30-11

MA422 M61 6MU 18-7-43 AST 20-3-44 mr 511 FRU 6-4-44 33MU 13-8 303S 21-1-45 CAC ops 5-3-45 ROS 80 OTU 7-6-45 FAAC 19-10 ASTH RHAF 1-4-48

MA423 6MU 18-7-43 222MU 26-7 *SS732* 5-8 Casa 18-8 NWA 1-10 Malta 1-11 SOC 31-12-46

MA424 9MU 20-7-43 47MU 5-8 *Emp Prss* 5-8 Casa 18-8 NAASC 31-10 VA 21-8-45 mods REAF 26-9-46

MA425 39MU 21-7-43 82MU 7-8 *Fort Thom* 14-8 Casa 1-9 218Gp NA 30-11 241S CE ops 4-10-44

MA426 9MU 18-7043 47MU 27-7 *SS732* 5-8 Casa 28-8 218Gp NA 30-11 ME IAF 30-5-46 as MM4086

MA427 39MU 21-7-43 82MU 10-8 *Fort Thom* 14-8 Casa 1-9 218Gp 30-11 ME RHAF 27-3-47

MA428 9MU 19-7-43 47MU 5-8 *Emp Prss* 5-8 Casa 18-8 NWA 1-10 FAF RAF 29-2-44 SOC REAF 1946 fought in the Arab/Israeli conflict 1948

MA443 12MU 13-6-43 215MU 21-6 *Fort Ver* 1-7 Casa 14-7 ME 1-9 NAAF 1-11 CB ops 21-1-44

MA444 6MU 6-6-43 222MU 14-6 *Fort Ver* 1-7 Casa 14-7 ME 1-9 NAAF 1-11 C3 ops 72S 16-3-44 SOC 23-12

MA445 46MU 7-6-43 215MU 17-6 *Fort Ver* 1-7 Casa 14-7 ME 1-9 NAAF 27-4-44 SOC 28-4-45

MA446 ME MAAF 27-4-44 SOC 28-4-45

MA447 6MU 6-6-43 222MU 14-6 *Fort Ver* 1-7 Casa 14-7 ME 1-9 NAAF 1-11 IAF 305046 as MM 4030

MA448 6MU 6-6-43 222MU 14-6 *Fort Ver* 1-7-Casa 14-7 ME 1-9 NAAF 1-11 FAC3 15-9

MA449 45MU 6-6-43 82MU 17-6 *La Pam* 2-7 Casa 14-7 Mee 1-9 NAAF 1-11 SOC 14-3-46

MA450 9MU 7-6-43 82MU 22-6 *La Pam* 2-7 Casa 14-7 ME 1-9 NAASC 1-11 ME 30-11

MA451 46MU 3-6-43 82MU 13-6 *SS708* 14-6 Casa 29-6 ME 1-8 NAAF 1-11 SOC 6-9-45

MA452 6MU 6-6-43 222MU 14-6 *SS708* 14-6 Casa 29-6 ME 1-8 Malta NAAF 1-11 SOC 31-5-45

MA453 33MU 8-6-43 52MU 14-6 *La Pam* 2-7 Casa14-7 ME 1-9 NAAF 1-11 FTR ops 27-1-44 cancel bboc 21-6-45 IAF 3-5-45 as MM4031

MA454 33MU 8-6-43 47MU 15-6 *Fort Ver* 1-7 Casa 14-7 ME 1-9 NAAF 1-11 FTR ops 20-2-45

MA455 33MU 8-6-43 82MU 14-6 *La Pam* 2-7 Casa 14-7 ME 1-9 NA 31-8-44 SOC 5-10-45

MA456 39MU 10-6-43 52MU 21-6 *La Pam* 2-7 Casa 14-7 107MU SOC 31-12-47

MA457 9MU 8-6-43 215MU 28-6 *Fort Ver* 1-7 Casa 14-7 ME 1-8 NA 30-11 SOC 28-4-45

MA4548 33MU 8-6-43 47MU 15-6 *Fort Ver* 1-7 Casa 14-7 ME 1-9 NAAF 1-11 C3 ops 6-4-46

MA459 39MU 11-6-43 76MU 21-6 *La Pam* 2-7 Casa 14-7 253S FTR ops 11-3-44

MA460 39MU 9-6-43 52MU 19-6 *La Pam* 2-7 Casa 14-7 ME 1-9 NAAF 1-11

MA461 33MU 8-6-43 82MU 14-6 *La Pam* 2-7 Casa 14-7 NAAF FAC3 14-1-44

MA462 39MU 11-6-43 82MU 26-6 *La Pam* 2-7 Casa 14-7 ME 1-9 NAAF 1-11 ME 9-8-45 RHAF 27-2-47

MA463 6MU 6-6-43 222MU 14-6 *SS708* 14-6 Casa 29-6 ME 1-8 NAAF 1-11 SOC 8-3-44

MA464 39MU 10-6-43 76MU 6-7 *Fort Nak* 14-7 Casa 29-7 Malta 1-10 ME 28-12-44 SOC 13-12-45

MA465 FIXT 33MU 11-6-43 47MU 23-6 *Fort Ver* 1-7 Casa 14-7 ME 1-8 SOC 1-11

MA466 46MU 5-6-43 215MU 16-6 *Fort Ver* 1-7 Casa 14-7 ME 1-8 NAAF 1-11 SOC 13-8-44

MA467 403S 30-5-43 CAC ops 31-5 ROS 419RSU 21-3-44 312S 25-2-45 CAC ops 22-3 ROS RHAF 13-5-48

MA468 403S 31-5-43 FTR 3-10

MA469 45MU 4-6-43 222MU 14-6 *La Pam* 2-7 Casa 14-7 ME 1-9 NAAF 1-11 1435S C3 ops 17-1-44

MA470 12MU 1-6-43 47MU 8-6 *SS707* 10-6 Casa 29-6 ME 1-9 NWA C3 ops 19-11

MA471 45MU 3-6-43 82MU 17-6 *La Pam* 2-7 Casa 14-7 ME 1-9 NAAF 1-11 IAF 26-6-47

MA472 12MU 1-6-43 47MU 8-6 *SS708* 14-6 Casa 29-6 ME FAC3 21-8

MA473 12MU 1-6-43 82MU 7-6 *SS707* 10-6 Casa 29-6 ME 1-8 SOC 30-9 salvage bboc ME 1-11 NAASC 31-10 FTR ops 4-14-45

Polish units proudly displayed their national colours, either below the windscreen or as in this case, on the cowling.

MA474 46MU 7-6-43 215MU 16-6 *Fort Ver* 1-7 Casa 14-7 1435S FTR ops 8-3-44

MA475 12MU 1-6-43 47MU 8-6 *SS707* 10-6 Casa 29-6 ME 1-8 NAAF 1-11 CB ops 2-9-44

MA476 331S 26-6-43 AST 24-2-44 303S 1-3-45 441S 5-4 80 OTU 7-6 FAF 14-3-46

MA477 403S 31-5-43 421S 2-6 19S 16-11 410ARF 17-2-44 VA 16-11 mods 310S 25-1-45 CAC ops 13-3 SAAF 23-6-48

MA478 46MU 8-6-43 82MU 14-6 *La Pam* 2-7 Casa 14-7 ME 1-9 NAAF 1-11 ME 19-7-45 REAF 25-7-46

MA479 12MU 1-6-43 47MU 9-6 *SS708* 14-6 Casa 29-6 ME 1-8 SOC 12-3-45

MA480 46MU 1-6-43 82MU 14-6 *La Pam* 2-7 Casa 14-7 ME 1-9 FACB 10-10

MA481 12MU 31-5-43 82MU 7-6 *SS707* 10-6 Casa 29-6 ME 1-8 NAAF 1-11 FTR ops 5-4-45

MA482 6MU 6-6-43 222MU 14-6 *Fort Ver* 1-7 Casa 24-7 ME 1-9 NAAF 1-11

MA483 12MU 31-5-43 82MU 7-6 *SS707* 10-6 Casa 29-6 NWA 31-7 SOC 18-10-45

MA484 46MU 1-6-43 82MU 14-6 *La Pam* 2-7 Casa 14-7 ME 1-9 MAAF 23-12-44 SOC 26-9-46

MA485 6MU 6-6-43 222MU 14-6 *SS708* 14-6 Casa 29-6 NWA 31-7 MAAF 31-5-45 VA 21-8 mods SOC 30-4-47

MA486 46MU 7-6-43 215MU 17-6 *Fort Ver* 1-7 Casa 14-7 ME 1-9 NAAF FA FTR 15-10-44

MA487 45MU 5-6-43 82MU 17-6-43 *La Pam* 2-7 Casa 14-7 ME 1-9 NAAF 1-11 MAAF SOC 6-9-45

MA501 FIXT 33MU 11-6-43 222MU 20-6 *Fort Ver* 2-7 Casa 14-7 ME 1-8 NAAF 1-11 MAAF SOC 30-5-46

MA502 FIXT 33MU 11-6-43 76MU 20-6 *La Pam* 2-7 Casa 14-7 ME 1-9 NAAF 1-11

MA503 FIXT Uruguay VIII 6MU 12-6-43 76MU 19-6 *La Pam* 3-7 Casa 14-7 ME 1-9 NAAF 1-11 327S 5-4-45 81RSU 19-4

MA504 FIXT 33MU 13-6-43 222MU 22-6 *Fort Ver* 1-7 Casa 14-7 ME 1-9 SOC 28-2-46

MA505 12MU 13-6-43 215MU 20-6 *Fort Ver* 1-7 Casa 14-7 ME 1-9 NAAF 1-11

MA506 33MU 18-8-43 52MU 23-9 *Ionica* 3-10 Casa 19-10 218Gp NA 30-11-44 SOC 20-9-45

MA507 Uruguay XII 6MU 13-6-43 76MU 19-6 *La Pam* 2-7 Casa 14-7 ME 1-9 NAAF 30-11

MA508 FIXT 33MU 13-6-43 222MU 22-6 *Fort Ver* 1-7 Casa 14-7 ME 1-9 NA 20-11 SOC 11-12-45

MA509 12MU 13-6-43 215MU 20-6 *Fort Ver* 1-7 Casa 14-7 ME 1-8 NAAF 1-11 CB ops 7-2-44

MA510 FIXT 33MU 13-6-43 222MU 22-6 *Fort Ver* 1-7 Casa 14-7 218Gp NA 30-11 USAAF RAF 29-2-44 CE ops 3-9

MA511 Uruguay XI 6MU 13-6-43 76MU 23-6 *La Pam* 2-7 Casa 14-7 ME 1-9 NAAF 1-11 C3 ops 19-12

MA512 9MU 13-6-43 47MU 26-6 *Fort Ver* 1-7 Casa 14-7 ME 1-9 NAAF 1-11 SOC 30-11 151RU 29-3-45 327S 26-7 328S 4-10 FAF GC2/7 23-10-46

MA513 Uruguay VIII 6MU 13-6-43 76MU 19-6 *La Pam* 2-7 Casa 14-7 ME 1-9 NAAF 1-11 SOC 23-4-45

MA514 6MU 13-6-43 82MU 28-6 *La Pam* 2-7 Casa 14-7 alloc REAF but SOC 26-9-46

MA515 6MU 13-6-43 76MU 19-6 *La Pam* 2-7 Casa 14-7 ME 1-9 NAAF 1-11 IAF 26-6-47 as MM4081

MA516 12MU 14-6-43 215MU 21-6 *Fort Ver* 1-7 Casa 14-7 ME FTR i/sea 16-9

MA517 39MU 21-6-43 76MU 3-7 *SS717* 3-7 Casa 20-7 ME FACB 21-8

MA518 6MU 19-6-43 47MU 26-6 *Fort Ver* 1-7 Casa 14-7 ME 1-8 NAASC 30-11 ME FAC3 24-2-44

MA519 39MU 17-6-43 82MU 29-6 *La Pam* 2-7 Casa 14-7 ME 1-9 NAAF 1-11 SOC 8-3-44

MA520 39MU 17-6-43 82MU 29-6 *La Pam* 2-7 Casa 14-7 ME 1-9 FAC3 6-9

MA521 6MU 19-6-43 47MU 27-6 *Fort Ver* 1-7 Casa 14-7 ME 1-8 NAAF 1-11 FTR ops 17-3-44

MA522 39MU 27-6-43 82MU 29-6 *La Pam* 2-7 Casa 14-7 USAAF 31-1-44 RAF 31-5 ME 19-7-45 w/u ldg airstrip Al Faluja Palestine 25-3-47 SOC 30-4

MA523 39MU 17-6-43 222MU 25-6 *La Pam* 2-7 Casa 14-7

MA524 39MU 25-7-43 405ARF HAL 18-8 303S 1-9 308S 16-11 33S 20-5-44 FLS Mlfld 28-9 to 6214M 14SoTT 2-12-46

MA525 12MU 21-6-43 403S 26-6 e/fd over Ken f/ld in sandpit CE 13-7

MA526 9MU 12-6-43 47MU 1-7 *Fort Ver* 1-7 Casa 14-7 ME 1-8 NAAF 1-11 CE ops 16-10-44

MA527 9MU 13-6-43 82MU 28-6 *La Pam* 2-7 Casa 14-7 ME 1-9 NAAF 1-11 SOC 8-3-44

MA528 12MU 20-6-43 331S 4-7 VA 9-11-44 mods 303S 16-11 CAC ops 26-11 441S 5-4-45 80 OTU 7-6 FAF 14-3-46

MA529 39MU 19-6-43 47MU 6-7 *Fort Ches* 11-7 Casa 29-7 ME 1-9 NAAF 1-11 CE ops 17-8-44

MA530 39MU 19-6-43 52MU 3-7 *Fort Ches* 11-7 Casa 29-7 ME 1-9 NAAF 1-11 MAAF 31-10-46

MA531 33MU 17-6-43 47MU 28-6 *Fort Ver* 1-7 Casa 14-7

MA532 12MU 13-6-43 215MU 20-6 *Fort Ver* 1-7 Casa 14-7 NWA 31-7 MAAF 31-5 SOC 30-5-46

MA533 FIXT 33MU 17-6-43 47MU 28-6 *Fort Ver* 1-7 Casa 14-7 NWA 31-7 MAAF 31-5-45 SOC 30-5-46

MA534 6MU 19-6-43 47MU 23-6 *Fort Ver* 1-7 Casa 14-7 NAASC 31-10 FAF 30-11 CE ops 12-2-45

MA535 9MU 20-6-43 76MU 1-7 *SS717* 3-7 Casa 20-7 ME 1-9 NAAF 1-11 C3 ops 2-1-44

MA536 33MU 19-6-43 82MU 29-6 *SS717* 3-7 Casa 20-7 ME 1-9 NAAF 1-11 SOC 8-3-44

MA537 6MU 19-6-43 82MU 28-6 *La Pam* 2-7 Casa 14-7 ME 1-9 NAAF 1-11 SOC 20-9-45

MA538 6MU 20-6-43 47MU 30-6 *Fort Ver* 1-7 Casa 14-7 ME 1-9 NAAF 1-11 FTR ops 25-4-45

MA539 39MU 21-6-43 52MU 8-7 *Fort Ches* 11-7 Casa 29-7 NWA FAF 1-10 SOC 31-8-44

MA540 39MU 19-6-43 47MU 6-7 *Fort Ches* 11-7 Casa 29-7 ME 1-9 NAAF 1-11

MA541 6MU 20-6-43 82MU 28-6 *La Pam* 2-7 Casa 14-7 ME 1-9 NAAF 1-11 MAAF SOC 6-9-45

MA542 33MU 17-6-43 47MU 28-6 *Fort Ver* 1-7 Casa 14-7 ME 1-9 NAAF 1-11 SOC 13-9-45

MA543 12MU 21-6-43 421S 16-7 CE ops 19-8

MA544 39MU 19-6-43 76MU 3-7 *SS717* 5-7 Casa 29-7 MAAF SOC 6-9-45

MA545 33MU 20-6-43 47MU 28-6 *Fort Ver* 1-7 Casa 14-7 NWA 31-7 SOC 18-10-45

MA546 39MU 17-6-4o3 82MU 29-6 *La Pam* 2-7 Casa 14-7 ME 1-9 NAAF 1-11 ME 5-7-45 SOC 18-10

MA559 6MU 19-6-43 47MU 27-6 *Fort Ver* 1-7 Casa 14-7 NWA 31-7

MA560 6MU 20-6-43 76MU 1-7 *SS717* 5-7 Casa 29-7 ME 1-9 NAAF 1-11 72S i/sea ops 27-3-44

MA561 33MU 19-6-43 82MU 29-6 *SS717* 5-7-43 Casa 29-7 ME 1-9 NAAF 1-11 C3 ops 26-3-44

MA562 39MU 19-6-43 76MU 1-7 *SS717* 5-7 Casa 29-7 MAAF SOC 18-10-45

MA563 316S 25-6-43 302S 28-9 CB ops 21-1-44 FLS Mlfld 20-8 SAAF 28-9-48

MA564 12MU 20-6-43 403S CE ops 26-6

MA565 9MU 20-6-43 76MU 3-7 *SS717* 5-7 Casa 29-7 ME 1-9 NAAF 1-11 CE ops 5-3-45

MA566 316S 25-6-43 302S 28-9 302S e/fd cd/ld in field CE Fairwood Common 7-12

MA567 6MU 21-6-43 47MU 3-7 *SS717* 5-7 Casa 29-7 ME 1-9 NAAF 1-11 SOC 29-2-44

MA568 331S 25-6-43 AST 23-2-44 VA 4-9 229S 27-9 603S 1-3-45 CAC ops 23-3 FAF 25-6-46

MA569 9MU 21-6-43 222MU 7-7 *Fort Nak* 14-7 Casa 29-7 ME FAC3 21-8

MA570 39MU 21-6-43 52MU 8-7 *Fort Ches* 11-7 Casa 29-7 ME 1-9 NAAF 1-11 SOC 6-9-45

MA571 332S 25-6-43 ASTH 18-8 165S 4-1-44 FAAC 22-2 ROS 33S 16-5 FACB 26-5 AST 312S 25-5-45 FAF 18-10-46

MA572 33MU 20-6-43 222MU 25-6 *La Pam* 2-7 Casa 14-7 ME CE ops 31-8

MA573 403S 26-6-43 CE ops 13-11 FH172.45

MA574 33MZU 20-6-43 82MU 27-7 *SS732* 5-8 Casa 18-8 NWA 1-10 328S FAF 31-10

MA575 12MU 20-6-43 403S 5-7 421S w/u ldg after Ramrod sortie CE 27-8

MA576 39MU 21-6-43 52MU 3-7 *Fort Ches* 11-7 Casa 29-7 NWA 1-10

MA577 39MU 21-6-43 52MU 8-7 *Fort Ches* 11-7 Casa 29-7

MA578 6MU 19-6-43 VA 403S 27-6 AST 9-3-44 FLS Mlfld 2-9 CFE FAAC ROS sold H Bath 27-10-49

MA579 412S 26-6-43 FAAC 24-10 ROS 274S 15-5 DeH 11-7 584TU FAAC 30-4-45 ROS FACE CD F/ld nr Dunkerton Som SOC 28-2-46

MA580 6MU 21-6-43 52MU 7-7 *Fort Ches* 11-7 Casa 29-7 ME 1-9 NAAF 30-9 USAAF 31-10 MAAF SOC 28-4-45

MA581 9MU 20-6-43 222MU 1-7 *Fort Nak* 14-7 Casa 29-7 ME 1-9 NAAF 1-11 FTR ops 12-4-45

MA582 421S 25-6-43 ORAC 14-12 127AF 4-3-44 ROS 310S 5-4-45 312S 27-8 RHAF 29-4-48

MA583 9MU 24-6-43 47MU 4-7 *SS717* 5-7 Casa 29-7 ME 1-9 NAAF 1-11 FTR ops

MA584 303S 26-6-43 308S 16-11 FTR ops 30-11

MA585 403S 26-6-43 CB ops 21-10 AST 501S 22-4-44 274S 29-5 FLS Mlfld 21-8 FAAC 18-10 ROS cd in transit Mlfld-Witt CAC 6-1-45 RIS CFE 1-3 sold Int All 31-8-50

MA586 412S 25-6-43 CE 28-7 FH40.50

MA587 M77 CRD Rotol 24-6-43 trls with Rotol four and six blade c/props 230hr completed. 30hr oiling test of translational bearings. ROS 8-5-44 ASTE 17-5-45 33MU 8-10 SAAF 20-11-47

MA588 33MU 27-6-43 47MU 5-7 *Fort Ches* 11-7 Casa 29-7 ME SOC 30-7-47

MA589 33MU 24-6-43 82MU 29-6 *SS717* 5-7 Casa 29-7 ME 1-9 NAAF 1-11 FTR ops 22-1-44

MA590 33MU 27-6-43 47MU 4-7 *Fort Ches* 11-7 Casa 29-7 1-9 NAAF 1-11 MAAF SOC 31-8-45

MA591 421S 25-6-43 302S CAC ops 6-1-44 ROS FAF 25-6-46

MA592 412S 26-6-43 FAAC 31-8 CAC ops 3-10 313S 20-9-44 611S 8-10 MAL 6-6-45 SAAF 20-7-47

MA593 305S 26-6-43 CE 25-8 302S 31-8 AST recat E 20-9 AST 16-3-44 611S 13-7 VA 15-9 mods 312S 8-10 80 OTU 10-1-46 SAAF 30-9-48

MA594 453S 26-6-43 129S 17-7 331S 3-10 611S 14-7-44 312S 8-10 VA 31-10 mods AST sold R J Coley 3-9-50

MA595 9MU 30-6-43 215MU 7-7 Casa 29-7 NA USAAF 31-10

MA596 453S 25-6-43 CE 14-7 FH24

MA597 39MU 29-6-43 82MU 14-7 *Fort Rup* 25-7 Casa 16-8 218Gp NA 30-11 ME SOC Oct'44

MA598 222S 26-6-43 coll with BS539 on t/o CE Horn 15-7

MA599 39MU 27-6-43 82MU 14-7 *Fort Rup* 25-7 Casa 16-8 NWA 1-10 242S C3 ops 13-8-44

MA600 33MU 27-6-43 47MU 5-7 *Fort Ches*11-7 Casa 29-7 NWA 1-10 FAF 31-10 MAAF SOC 14-3-46

MA601 341S 26-6-43 129S 29-7 331S 28-8 FAAC 4-2-44 ROS 229S 8-9 57 OTU 26-4-45 53 OTU 3-5-45 80 OTU 17-5 FACB 14-7 recat E SOC 6-9

MA615 403S 26-6-43 CE 17-8 FH76.10 IAF as MM4043

MA616 39MU 27-6-43 82MU 15-7 *Fort Rup* 25-7 Casa 16-8 218Gp NA 30-11 USAAF 12-31 lost over Italy 15-12

MA617 M63A 29-6-43 76MU 7-7 *Fort Nak* 14-7 Casa 29-7 IAF 30-5-46 as MM4044

MA618 M63A 9MU 28-6-43 82MU 8-7 *Fort Nak* 14-7 Casa 29-7 IAF 30-5-46 as MM4045

MA619 33MU 27-6-43 47MU 4-7 *Fort Chest* 11-7 Casa 29-7 ME 1-9 NAAF 1-11 MAAF SOC 11-4-46

MA620 39MU 29-6-43 222MU 16-7 *Fort Rup* 25-7 Casa 16-8 NWA 1-10 ME 28-12-44 SOC 20-9-45

MA621 12MU 1-7-43 129S 11-7 332S 28-8 AST 4-3-44 1-7 std ldg app CE Swannington 13-7-45

MA622 M63A 9MU 28-6-43 215MU 7-7 *Fort Nak* 14-7 Casa 29-7 NWA 1-10 FAF 31-10

MA623 9MU 28-6-43 82MU 10-7 *Fort Nak* 14-7 Casa 29-7 218Gp NA 30-11 93S FTR ops 12-4-44

MA624 33MU 27-6-43 47MU 4-7 *Fort Chest* 11-7 Casa 29-7 ME 1-9 NAAF 1-11 SOC 23-10-44

MA625 9MU 28-6-43 82MU 8-7 *Fort Nak* 14-7 Casa 29-7 USAAF 12/31 lost over Italy 29-2-44

MA626 33MU 27-6-43 47MU 5-7 *Fort Ches* 11-7 Casa 29-7 ME 1-9 NAAF 1-11 242S C3 ops 22-6-44

MA627 33MU 27-6-43 52MU 7-7 *Fort Ches* 11-7 Casa 29-7 ME 1-9 NAAF 1-11 C3 ops 2-1-44

MA628 65S 6-8-43 CAC 3-11 ROS 405RSU 18-12 403S CAC ops 28-1-44 DeH 23-5-45 WAL 4-4-46 SAAF 15-9-48

MA629 33MU 1-7-43 82MU 8-7 *Fort Nak* 14-7 Casa 29-7 SOC 31-8-44

MA630 9MU 30-6-43 82MU 10-7 *Fort Nak* 14-7 Casa 29-7 ME 1-9 NAAF 1-11 IAF 26-6-47 as MM4049

MA631 6MU 29-6-43 222MU 7-7 *Fort Nak* 14-7 Casa 29-7 218Gp NA 30-11 SOC 31-8-44

MA632 6MU 29-6-43 222MU 7-7 *Fort Nak* 14-7 Casa 29-7 ME 1-9 NAAF 1-11 IAF 30-5-46 as MM4050

MA633 33MU 1-7-43 82MU 14-7 *Fort Rup* 25-7 Casa 16-8 NWA 1-10 MAAF SOC 23-11-45

MA634 9MU 27-6-43 82MU 8-7 *Fort Nak* 14-7 Casa 29-7 FACE 3-7-44

MA635 9MU 28-6-43 82MU 24-7 *SS732* 5-8 Casa 18-8 NWA 1-10 Malta 1-11

MA636 33MU 27-6-43 47MU 4-7 *Fort Ches* 11-7 Casa 29-7 ME 1-9 NAAF 1-11 C3 ops 27-1-44

MA637 39MU 27-6-43 76MU 11-7 *Fort Nak* 14-7 Casa 29-7 ME 1-9 NAAF 1-11 FTR ops 21-2-44

MA638 9MU 30-6-43 222MU 10-7 *Fort Nak* 14-7 Casa 29-7 218 Gp NA 30-11 FTR ops 20-10-44

MA639 12MU 1-7-43 316S 11-7 CE 28-7 AST 229S 6-6-44 80S 26-6 310S 5-9-44 FACB 11-12 ROS 32S ECFS 27-6-45 sold W F Lamont 8-9-49

MA640 33MU 30-6-43 47MU 16-7 *Fort Rup* 25-7 Casa 16-8 NWA 1-10 32S FTR ops 2-12-44

MA641 33MU 30-6-43 52MU 7-7 *Fort Ches* 11-7 Casa 29-7 NAASC 31-10 SOC 29-2-44

MA642 12MU 1-7-43 403S 11-7 CE ops 28-1-44 FH251.50

MA683 33MU 21-8-43 403S 31-8 308S 16-11 FACB 30-4-44 441S 5-4-45 WAL 29-8 HAL 20-10-47 sold Int All 29-8-50

MA687 33MU 23-8-43 47MU 2-9 *Emp Grebe* 15-9 Casa 29-9 93S CAC ops 27-3-44 ME 31-5-45 SOC 2-8

MA690 33MU 22-8-43 47MU 30-8 *Card Gib* 3-9 Casa 29-9 NAASC31-10 SOC MAAF 30-8-45

MA693 39MU 14-9-43 47MU 21-9 *Ionian* 3-10-45 Casa 19-10 NA 30-11 32S SOC ME 14-6

MA705 33MU 1-7-43 82MU 14-7 *Fort Rup* 25-7 Casa 16-8 NWA 1-10 USAAF 31-10 ME SOC 28-12-44

MA706 33MU 30-6-43 222MU 9-7 *Fort Nak* 14-7 Casa 29-7 SOC MAAF 30-8-45

MA707 6MU 28-6-43 222MU 7-7 *Fort Nak* 14-7 Casa 29-7 SOC 3-5-44

MA708 9MU 30-6-43 222MU 10-7 *Fort Nak* 14-7 Casa 29-7 NWA 1-10 MAAF 32S SOC 12-7-45

MA709 12MU 1-7-43 W/COM Fly Horn 15-7 129S 17-7 332S 28-8 coll with MH942 on t/o CB NWLD 25-10 AST ECFS 27-6-45 o/s ldg caught fire dvd i/grd pilot kld 1-4-48 SOC

MA710 33MU 1-7-43 82MU 14-7 *Fort Nak* 14-7 Casa 29-7 GACE 8-2-45

MA711 6MU 29-6-43 222MU 7-7 *Fort Nak* 14-7 Casa 29-7 NWA C3 ops 27-8 FAF 1-10

MA712 6MU 4-7-43 47MU 12-7 *Fort Nak* 14-7 Casa 29-7 ME 1-9 NAAF 1-11 32S SOC 30-6-44

MA713 12MU 1-7-43 421S 14-7 FAAC 5-1-44 AST 29-6 std cd avoid 2nd a/c Bradwell Bay CE 30-11

MA726 33MU 1-7-43 82MU 9-7 *Fort Nak* 14-7 Casa 29-7 FAC3 ME 16-9

MA727 39MU 3-7-43 76MU 18-7 *Fort Rup* 25-7 Casa 16-8 NWA 1-10 FAF 30-11 ME 31-12 FAC3 1-2-44

MA728 M63A 33MU 3-7-43 222MU 9-7 *Fort Nak* 14-7 29-7 FAF 30-11 ME 31-12 FTR ops a/c disin 28-1-45

MA729 39MU 1-7-43 82MU 14-7 *Fort Rup* 25-7 Casa 16-8 218Gp NA 30-11 ME 31-5-45 SOC 9-8

MA730 33MU 30-6-43 82MU 14-7 *Fort Rup* 25-7 Casa 16-8 218Gp NA 30-11 326S FAF FAC3 20-2-44

MA731 39MU 31-12-43 222MU 22-7 *SS732* 5-8 Casa 18-8 218Gp NA 30-11 FAF 31-12 MAAF Ce 12-3-45

MA732 M63A 39MU 3-7-43 82MU 7-8 *Fort Thom* 14-8 Casa 1-9 218Gp NA 30-11 ME SOC 30-11-44

MA733 33MU 3-7-43 82MU 14-7 *Fort Nak* 14-7 Casa 29-7 218Gp NA 30-11 SOC 31-8-44 bboc 5-6-45 SOC 30-5-46

MA734 39MU 4-7-43 82MU 28-7 *SS732* 5-8 5-8 Casa 18-8 NWA 1-10 USAAF 31-10 RAF NA 30-11 SOC Oct'44

MA735 M63A 222S 16-7-43 405ARF 24-8 131S 27-9 FACB 8-3-44 AST 39MU 31-5 FAF 16-4-46

MA736 33MU 3-7-43 82MU 14-7 *Fort Nak* 14-7 Casa 29-7 CE ops 13-2-45ME 31-5 SOC 2-8

MA737 39MU 18-7-43 47MU 29-7 *SS732* 5-8 Casa 18-8 NWA 1-10 ME SOC 1-3-44

MA738 33MU 3-7-43 82MU 14-7 *Fort Rup* 25-7 Casa 16-8 NWA 1-10

MA739 33MU 30-6-43 52MU 7-7 *Fort Ches* 11-7 Casa 29-7 ME 1-9 NAAF 1-11 SOC 28-4-45

MA740 303S 16-7-43 CAC 9-8 ROS 308S 16-11 AST 16-3-44 311S 30-8 313S 21-9 611S 8-10 FAAC 27-10 VAO 16-4-45 mods 312S 2-9-45 SOC 30-4-49

MA741 M61 39MU 3-7-43 82MU 23-7 *SS732* 5-8 Casa 18-8 218Gp NA 30-11 CE ops 25-3-45

MA742 316S 16-7-43 302S 28-9 ROS 11-11 274S 1-7-44 CB ops 9-7 ROS FLS Mlfd 29-8 to 5968 2SoTT 2-7-46

MA743 M61 39MU 4-7-43 82MU 14-7 *Fort Rup*25-7 Casa 16-8 218Gp NA 30-11 ME

MA756 421S 17-7-43 CB ops 13-9 AST CRD MWW 16-1-44 33MU 1-4 RAF Tang FAAC 2-7-45 ROS VA SAAF 18-6-47

MA757 222S 17-7-43 122S 24-8 FAAC 15-10 39MU 5-3-44 229MU 8-9 AST 27-12 mr ASTH 24-7-45 to scr 31-7-46

MA758 39MU 23-8-43 222MU 2-9 *Emp Grebe* 15-9 Casa 29-9 NAASC 31-10

MA759 33MU 18-7-42 82MU 29-7 *SS732* 5-8 Casa 18-8 218Gp NA 30-11 ME FA FTR 15-10-44

MA760 33MU 2-9-43 52MU 10-9 *Craw W L* 22-9 Casa 10-10 NAASC 31-10 SOC 13-6-44

MA761 6MU 18-7-43 222MU 26-7 *SS732* 5-8 Casa 18-8 218Gp NA 30-11 SOC 31-3-44

MA762 9MU 18-7-43 47MU 5-8 *Emp Prss* 5-8 Casa 18-8 218Gp NA 30-11 ME SOC 31-8-44

MA763 403S 23-7-43 CAC ops 17-7 AST 39MU 25-10 CRD BDn 6-12 ASTH 27-1-44 33S 22-6 310S 8-7 504S 15-7 303S FAAC 17-9 ROS 584ASTH 8-2-45 58 OTU WAL 1-8 sold VA 8-12-49

MA764 33MU 24-7-43 122S 10-8 FTR ops 25-11 FH102.30

MA765 33MU 18-7-43 82MU 26-7 *SS702* 5-8 Casa 18-8 NWA USAAF 1-10 MAAF SOC 6-9-45

MA766 39MU 18-7-43 52MU 31-7 *SS732* 5-8 Casa 18-8 NWA 1-10 ME 30-11 FACE 7-7-44

MA767 9MU 18-7-43 47MU 30-7 *SS732* 5-8 Casa 18-8 218Gp NA 30-11 241S FTR ops 21-3-44

MA790 9MU 18-7-43 47MU 30-7 *SS732* 5-8 Casa 18-8 218Gp NA 30-11 CE ops 21-3-45

MA791 33MU 21-7-43 405SU ARF HAL 4-8 316S 18-8 302S 28-9 ROS 20-1-44 FAAC 25-2 ROS SAL 14-7 RHAF 29-4-48

MA792 9MU 18-7-43 47MU 30-7 *SS732* 5-8 Casa 18-8 218Gp NA 30-11 ME SOC 31-10-46

MA793 IXE 6MU 19-7-43 47MU 27-7 *SS732* 5-8 Casa 18-8 NWA 1-10 USAAF 31-10 RAF 31-5-44 AST 23-5-45 47MU 9-2-48 *Clan Camp* SAAF as 5601 30-9-48 SOC 14-10-49 red to parts Nov'49 rebuilt as PT762 FE May'75 SAAF 6-5-76. Extant.

MA794 421S 17-7-43 9MU 20-4-44 AST 30-4 ECFS 22-6-45 FAAC 29-11 ROS sold J Dale 30-6-49

MA743 served with 218 Group in North Africa and later the Middle East.

MA744 316S 17-7-43 3501SU 28-7 Farn 27-11 wire & elect flt Nov'43 Monica I instal, flt trls with Halifax HZ228; Beaufighter X8218 and Halifax JD311 (last 3 a/c fitt Monica IIIA). Monica IIIA instal Jan'44, used for communications trls with R7034. weather trls wilth Spider Crab (proto Vampire) March eng ignition harness and gun firing trls 8-5-44 radar trls with Beaufighter KW392. June, cont of invest of ignition harness interference with Monica and VHF radio. Instal of 'Cheese Paired' battery 20-6. Accelerator trls, Fraser F(W.W.ACC). FACE 22-6-44 Trans BDn 3-7 Ret Farn 17-7 resonance tests on vibrgraph. To DTD Jan'45. Army Coop trls during which a/c cd Halton CE 5-2-45 SOC 12-2

MA745 39MU 3-7-43 76MU 18-7 *Fort Rup* 25-7 Casa 16-8 NWA 1-10 Malta 1-11 ME 31-5-45 SOC 9-3-46

MA746 M61 39MU 4-7-43 82MU 14-7 *Fort Rup* 25-7 Casa 26-8 218Gp NA 30-11 ME 2-8-45 SOC

MA747 M61 H E H Nizams State Railway No.11 129S 16-7-43 316S 28-8 302S 28-9 AST 8-1-44 274S 29-5 DeH 15-8 80 OTU 18-5-45 recat E 26-7-46

MA748 M61 331S 17-7-43 CE ops 9-9

MA749 M61 33MU 3-7-43 82MU 15-7 *Fort Rup* 25-7 Casa 16-8 NAASC 31-10 MAAF SOC 14-3-44

MA750 39MU 23-7-43 19S 21-8 AST 19-10 229S 28-6-44 u/c coll ldg CE Colt 3-9

MA751 M61 39MU 18-7-43 52MU 31-7 *SS732* 5-8 Casa 18-8 218Gp NA 30-11 ME IAF 26-6-47

MA752 LFIX M66 39MU 14-1-44 222MU 27-1 *Fort Lrd* 1-3 Casa 17-3 C3 ops 26-5

MA753 M61 39MU 4-7-43 222MU 25-7 *SS732* 5-8 Casa 18-8 218Gp NA 30-11 151RU 9-3-45

MA754 303S 17-3-43 e/fd cd/ld caught fire CE Rickmansworth Herts SOC 22-9

MA755 331S 17-7-43 AST 23-2-44 33MU 27-4 611S CE ops 14-8

MA795 322S 17-7-43 CAC 12-8 ROS 405ARF 3-10 19S 16-11 229S 29-5-44 FAAC 25-6 ROS 303S 3-8 CE ops 20-9

MA796 6MU 19-7-43 47MU 27-7 *SS732* 5-8 Casa 18-8 NWA 1-10 MAAF SOC 14-3-46

MA797 6MU 18-7-43 222MU 26-7 *Emp Prss* 5-8 Casa 18-8 218Gp NA 30-11

MA798 9MU 18-7-43 47MU 30-7 *SS732* 5-8 Casa 18-8 218Gp NA 30-11 ME 9-8-45 RHAF 27-2-47

MA799 129S 17-7-43 ROS 10-8 405ARF 7-9 131S 27-9 dvd i/gnd Eveley Farm nr Blandford CB recat E 1-12 FH80.5

MA800 9MU 20-7-43 47MU 10-8 *Ger Don* 25-8 Casa 10-9 NAASC 31-10 USAAF 31-1-44 RAF 241S FTR ops 21-3

MA801 33MU 20-7-43 222MU 30-7 *Fort Thom* 14-8 Casa 1-9 218Gp NA 30-11 ME FTR ops 22-3-45

MA802 6MU 19-7-43 47MU 27-7 *SS732* 5-8 Casa 18-8 218Gp NA 30-11 32S FTR ops 2-3-44

MA803 33MU 24-7-43 122S 13-8 39MU 9-3-44 VAOx 31-10 310S 4-1-45 to 6458M sold VA 13-5-47 RDAF 27-7-48

MA804 9MU 25-7-43 215MU 15-9 *Emp Mar* 2-10 Casa 19-10 218Gp NA 30-11 USAAF 31-12 RAF 31-5-44 SOC 23-12 bboc 21-6-45 SOC 14-8

MA805 33MU 21-7-43 82MU 29-7 *SS732* 5-8 Casa 18-8 218Gp NA 30-11 ME FTR ops27-7-44

MA806 39MU 23-7-43 19S 20-8 80S 29-5-44 e/fd on app f/ld hit tree CE WMall 10-7

MA807 33MU 25-7-43 405ARF 24-8 131S 27-9 165S 19-3-44 453S 11-4 33S 16-5 38S CE ops 19-6

MA808 9MU 20-7-43 82MU 5-8 *Fort Thom* 14-8 Casa 1-9 32S FTR ops 28-2-44

MA809 39MU 25-7-43 405ARF 26-8 131S 27-9 FAAC 3-3-44 SAL 22-2-45 16FU 5-6-46 Trans Com Csfd 13-6 CE 27-5-47

MA810 33MU 24-7-43 405ARF 16-8 332S 28-8 274S 29-5-44 SAL 23-6 VAO 20-12 FAF 24-5-46

MA811 33MU 20-7-43 82MU 29-7 *SS732* 5-8 Casa 18-8 Malta 1-10 Italy 1-11 241S C3 ops 25-6-44

MA812 33MU 22-7-43 65S 5-8 tyre burst ldg o/t dbf CE Graves 5-11 FH79.35

MA813 39MU 24-7-43 405ARF HAL 19-8 131S 27-9 165S 19-3-44 453S 11-4 33S 16-5 FAAC 24-5 AST 310S 16-5-45 FAF 17-8-46

MA814 9MU 25-7-43 122S 14-8 pilot overcome by fumes in circuit cd/ld CE Graves 1-4-44 AST 33S 28-5 310S 8-7 504S 303S FAAC 15-8 ROS VAO 6-10 mods 504S 13-10 FACE dbf 27-2-45

MA815 39MU 25-7-43 19S 20-8 122S 2-3-44 405RSU 20-4 ROS 19-8 611S 14-9 312S 8-10 ROS 26-10 CFE Tang 9-8-45 FAAC 31-8

MA816 33MU 22-7-43 66S 5-8 air coll over Kingsnorth aerodrome CE 22-9 FH78.40

MA817 39MU 26-7-43 405ARF HAL 18-8 403S 4-9 FAAC 16-10 AST 501S 15-4-44 229S 29-5 FTR ops 23-6

MA818 39MU 29-7-43 19S 20-8 410RSU 29-1-44 274S CB ops 7-6 RPS MAL 5-9 80 OTU 18-5-45 FAF 14-3-46

MA819 Barnley Chop 33MU 28-7-43 405ARF 14-8 19S 22-8 410RSU 18-12 65S 18-12 83GSU 4-1-44 FRU CB 23-8 310S 12-10 RHAF 20-4-48

MA831 33MU 21-7-43 405SU ARF HAL 4-8-43 412S 11-8 421S CAC ops 5-1-44 ROS AST 25-5 mr VA 1-2-45 mods FAF 25-4-46

MA832 9MU 25-7-43 405ARF HAL 18-8 403S 22-8 e/a 21-1-44 ROS 30S FAAC 20-5 ROS 80S 23-6 310S FACB 14-9 sold R J Coley 6-2-50

MA833 39MU 23-7-43 19S 21-8 out of fuel a/c aban i/sea off Bolt Head 3-9 FH30.20

MA834 6MU 25-7-43 405ARF HAL 6-8 129S 16-8 131S 27-9 dam in ldg trying to avoid wrk of MA860 CAC 4-2-44 312S 14-11 FAF 17-4-46

MA835 6MU 25-7-43 405ARF HAL 6-8 65S 15-8 FTR ops 3-1-44

MA836 33MU 26-7-43 122S 8-8 39MU 12-3-44 ROS 58 OTU 12-4-45 SOC 21-8

MA837 33MU 29-7-43 19S 20-8 122S 3-3-44 611S 3-8 AST 30-11 sold Int All 29-8-50

MA838 9MU 25-7-43 405ARF HAL 18-8 403S 22-8 CE ops 4-9

MA839 9MU 25-7-43 122S 14-8 FTR ops 9-9 FH45.25

MA840 39MU 28-7-43 405ARF HAl 17-8 403S 14-9 VA 7-4-44 317S FACE 17-4 AST 58 OTU 9-6-45 SOC 1-9-49 FFS 8-9

MA841 33MU 24-7-43 19S 19-8 410RSU 15-11 65S 18-12 19S 4-1-44 80S FACB 28-5 ASTH 312S 3-5-45 FAAC 13-7 ROS FAF 31-7-46

MA842 33MU 29-7-43 19S 20-8 80S 29-5-44 CE ops 10-6

MA843 39MU 25-7-43 405ARF 16-8 316S 27-8 302S 28-9 AST 23-3-44 mr 313S 29-8 611S 8-10

MA844 33MU 28-7-43 405ARF 16-8 403S 1-9 CAC ops 28-1-44 1S 26-6 310S 8-7 504S 15-7 303S 19-10 58 OTU 19-10 58 OTU 6-6-45 FAF 11-7-46

MA845 33MU 26-7-43 65S 5-8 CB ops 25-11 AST 80S 6-6-44 310S 5-9 VA 6-10 mods swg to port ldg strk FIDO burner o/t CE Mans 6-4-45 SOC 19-4

MA846 6MU 26-7-43 122S 11-8 ROS 10-9 FLS Mlfld 16-9-44 CFE tyre burst taxy tip onto nose CE W Raynham 8-10-45 recat B ECFS 3-5-46 49MU 1-4-49 sold scr 13-4

MA847 33MU 26-7-43 65S 8-8 FAAC 16-10 FTR ops 2-1-44

MA848 6MU 27-6-43 129S 4-8 4055 ARF HAL 27-8 131S 27-9 165S 19-3-44 453S 11-4 33S 16-5 Stn Flt North 23-5 310S 8-7 504S 15-7 58 OTU 5-4-45 sold VA 22-1-47 con to two-seat train (M66) G-15-2 @ SM 3-6-48 to InAF as HS534

MA849 39MU 28-7-43 405ARF HAL 17-8 421S 14-9 91S e/fd f/ld Gloucester Hill Amble 8-3-44 229S 20-9 ROS 13-6 FAAC 16-6 AST WAL 6-2-45 VA 21-8 mods SAAF 11-5-48

MA854 39MU 30-8-43 47MU 10-9 *Ocean Rid* 23-9 Casa 10-10 NAASC 31-10 SOC 31-8-44

MA860 33MU 21-8-43 405ARF 27-8 131S 27-9 cd/ld dbf pilot safe CE 4-2-44 FH110.15

MA878 33MU 22-8-43 47MU 30-8 *Emp Grebe* 15-9 Casa 29-9 NAASC 31-10 FTR ops 12-11-44 cancel bboc 20-1-45 recat A ME 1-5-45 MAAF 31-5 CE 6-9

MA879 39MU 26-9-43 405ARF 9-10 AST 19-10 33S FAAC 26-6-44 FLS Mlfld 21-8-46 sold VA 24-11-47

MA884 39MU 18-9-43 215MU 30-9 *Emp Mar* 5-10 Casa 19-10 218Gp NA 30-11 USAAF 31-1-44 MAAF SOC 30-8-45

MB807 4404 EA M63A 39MU 5-6-43 82MU 18-6 *La Pam* 2-7 Casa 14-7 ME 1-9 NAASC 31-10 SOC 31-3-44 recat A 31-1-45 MAAF SOC 26-7-45

MH series F IX Merlin 63 unless otherwise indicated

MH312 33MU 29-7-43 82MU 12-8 *Ger Don* 25-8 Casa 10-9 SOC 15-9-45

MH313 33MU 24-7-43 316S 14-8 302S 28-9 e/fd after t/o cd/ld Allan Fields Farm nr Hailsham Sussex CE 7-4-44 bboc recat B 28-6-45

MH314 39MU 28-7-43 405ARF HAL 18-8 Stn Flt North 29-9 302S 16-11 229S 29-5-44 VAO 13-10 mods 312S 16-12 RHAF 6-5

MH315 39MU 28-7-43 405ARF HAL 18-8 131S 27-9 165S 19-3-44 453S 4-5 33S 16-5 Stn Flt North 23-5 310S 8-7 504S 15-7 312S 16-11 VAOx 23-11 mods CAC ops 7-12 ROS to 5199M Sch Aeronaut Eng Hendon 5-4-45

MH316 33MU 28-7-43 19S 19-8 122S 3-3-44 ROS 28-8 127S CAC ops 2-10 420RSU 5-10 132Wg 19-10 FAF 5-7-64 des 25-6-47

MH317 no record

MH318 33MU 24-7-43 122S 15-8 421S 20-2-44 DeH 2-9 SCR584 TU Drem 27-3-45 FAAC 25-5 ROS to 6184M 8-11-64 cancel SOC 14-10-50 FFS

MH319 39MU 28-7-43 19S 21-8 80S 29-5-44 CB ops 22-6 recat E 14-7

MH320 33MU 31-7-43 405ARF 16-8 19S 7-9 410RSU 29-1-44 303S 30-8 CE ops 18-9

MH321 33MU 30-7-43 82MU 12-8 *Ger Don* 26-8 Casa 10-9 218Gp NA 30-11 ME 242S FTR ops 28-7-44

MH322 M61 39MU 31-7-43 405ARF HAL 19-8 131S 27-9 3132S 29-8-44 611S 8-10 151RU 1-3-45 VAO 16-4-45 mods RHAF 6-5-48

MH323 39MU 26-7-43 405ARF HAL 18-8 131S 27-9 ROS 19-2-44 310S 19-9 FACE 15-6-45 SOC 28-6

MH324 33MU 30-7-43 82MU 10-8 *Fort Thom* 14-8 Casa 1-9 218Gp NA 30-11 ME 93S CE ops 8-9-44

MH325 39MU 29-7-43 222MU 15-9 *Ocean Rid* 23-9 Casa 10-10 NAASC 31-10 MAAF 21-6-45 SOC 26-9-46

MH326 33MU 31-7-43 405ARF 17-8 131S 27-9 165S 19-3-44 453S 11-4 33S 16-5 CB ops 14-6 ROS 91S 2-9 GAL 3-11 mods VA 1-3-45 mods FAF 31-7-46

MH327 33MU 26-7-43 316S 14-8 302S 28-9 e/fd f/ld Reynoldston Glam CE 13-12

MH328 M61 5-8-43 6MU 18-2-44 313S 30-3 611S 8-10 303S 22-3-45 441S 5-4 WAL 27-6 M63 instal RAF Delegation Paros 24-12-46 sold Int All 29-8-50

MH329 33MU 29-7-43 82MU 7-8 *Fort Thom* 14-8 Casa 1-9 218Gp NA 30-11 FAC3 5-4-44

MH330 FIXE 9MU 13-8-43 19S 21-8 e/ac 21-4-44 ROS 83GSU 27-3 313S 21-9 310S 22-3-45 VA 30-3-45 mods FACE dbf 15-6 SOC 28-6

MH331 M61 65S 6-8-43 403S 25-10 274S 29-5-44 CAC ops 24-7 GAL VA 1-2-45 mods 80 OTU 28-2-46 FAF 14-3 des 25-3-49

MH332 M61 122S 9-8-43 611S 17-7-44 312S 3-10 FAAC 23-10 ROS VAO 9-2-45 mods WAL 14-8 SAAF 22-8-47

MH333 39MU 4-8-43 405ARF HAL 18-8 131S 27-9 129S f/ld out of fuel Tolleshunt D'Arcy Essex 25-10 AST Stn Flt Cole 27-2-44 501S 14-4 229S 29-5 strk by AB511 ldg while parked CB Colt 14-9 VA 18-1-45 mods 58 OTU 3-6 sold VA 8-12-49

MH334 39MU 29-7-43 421S 24-8 CE ops 3-9

MH335 39MU 30-7-43 403S 24-8 403RSU 25-10 310S 5-9-44 TU Drem 28-5-45 FAAC 25-6 ROS sold R J Coley 9-2-50

MH336 33MU 30-7-43 82MU 7-8 *Fort Thom* 16-8 Casa 1-9 218Gp NA 30-11 SOC 28-4-45

MH349 M63 33MU 31-7-43 316S 14-8 302S 28-9 274S 29-5-44 CAC ops 25-7 ROS 611S 29-8 312S 8-10 VAO 20-10 mods MAL 30-12 mr wng coll during aero eng fire dvd i/grd pilot kld CE 8-2-45 SOC

MH350 LFIXE M66 349S 331S RNorAF extant Oslo, coded FN-M

MH351 LFIX M66 33MU 405ARF 25-8-43 485S 6-9 FA into sea 3-10

MH352 M61 39MU 31-7-43 19S 24-8 611S 14-9-44 312S 8-10 VA 10-11 mods DeH 1-5-45 Trs to 1CRU 5-6 FAF 10-4-46 des 4-7-49

MH353 39MU 29-7-43 405ARF HAL 16-8 316S 27-8 302S 28-9 AST 24-4-44 mr 611S 3-8 ROS 312S 8-10 VAO 23-10 mods CAC ops 26-11 80 OTU 24-5-45 FAF 14-3-46

MH354 M61 39MU 31-7-43 19S 21-8 611S 14-7 312S 8-10 CE ops 31-12 SOC 15-1-45

MH355 33MU 31-7-43 19S 19-8 FACB 9-2-44 AST 22-2 M61 instal 485S 6-7 CAC ops ROS 310S 11-9 CAC ops 2-3-45 151RU 11-3 MAL 5-7 SAAF 17-3-49

MH356 M61 39MU 31-7-43 403S 21-8 FACB 12-10 AST 3501SU 24-6-44 VAOx 29-9 mods 229S 19-10 312S 22-4-45 FAF 11-8-46

MH357 M61 31-7-433 405ARF HAL 18-8 131S 27-9 FACB 9-11 AST 84GSU 3-4-44 302S CAC ops 25-4 611S 3-8 312S 8-10 CE ops 8-12

MH358 M61 65S 7-8-43 dam during t/o CB 30-11 511FRU 6-12 AST 14-5-44 M63 instal 229S 21-6 GAL 28-11 mods 58 OTU 10-6-45 SOC FFS 8-9-49

MH359 M61 39MU 31-7-43 222MU 15-9 *Ocean Rid* 23-9 Casa 10-10 NAASC 31-10 32S RHAF 29-5-47

MH360 LFIX M66 341S 6-8-43 CB ops 24-9 AST 84GSU 5-5-44 132S CAC ops 21-5 recat E 14-7 Farn Jan'45 neg G trls to Brussels 20-4-45

MH361 33MU 31-7-43 405ARF 16-8 403S 10-9 CE ops 18-11 FH74

MH362 M61 65S 7-8-43 AST 25-10 501S 16-4-44 274S 29-5 FTR ops 19-6

MH363 M61 39MU 4-8-43 405ARF HAL 18-8 131S 27-9 611S FTR ops 16-9-44

MH364 LFIX M66 485S 6-8-43 CE dbf ops 20-10

MH365 M61 39-MU 31-7-43 19S 20-8 CAC ops 6-1-44 recat E 1-9 sold R J Coley 3-2-50

MH366 LFIX M66 405ARF 8-8-43 341S 22-8 411S 17-10 WAL 10-10 Farn June to Sept'44 ails up-float trls 165S 8-6-45 88GSU 7-6 128W 18-7 129S 14-2-46 BAF 2-9-47 as SM-12 w/o 2-9

MH367 M61 65S 7-8-43 CAC ops 9-10 410RSU 18-12 229S 3-9-44 312S 16-12 ROS 5-7-45 ASTH 7-12 M63 instal EFS Hull 11-4-47 u/c clpse ldg CB 27-7-48 CE 17-8

MH368 122S 9-8-43 e/a CE 22-1-44 AST 313S 20-9-44 611S 8-10 FAAC 2-1-45 ROS 441S 15-2 FAF 17-7-47 GC 2/3 Des GC 1/6 5-7-50 FH347.05

MH369 122S 9-8-43 FACB 3-12 HAL 229S 4-6-44 CB ops 25-7 recat E 4-8

MH370 LXIX M66 405ARF HAL 10-8-42 485S 21-8 FACB 9-9 AST 443S 13-3-44 3501SU 1-7 322S 7-9

MH371 LFIX M66 222S 13-8-43 349S 8-6-44 421RSU 15-6 84GSU 15-6 SAL 11-8 MAAF 8-3-45 FTR ops 13-4

MH372 M66 65S 7-8-43 CAC ops 13-12 410RSU 18-12 ROS 229S 29-5-44 310S 5-10 CAC ops 2-3-45 151RU 11-3 sold VA 5-12-49

MH373 65S 5-8-43 air coll with MA816 over Kingsnorth aerodrome CAC 22-9 122S 3-3-44 33S 20-6 310S 8-7 504S 15-7 303S FAAC 9-8 ROS VA 18-1-45 mods 584TU 5-4 FACB 19-9 ASTH SAAF 18-6-47

MH374 LFIX M66 341S 6-8-43 CB ops 31-8 AST 30-4-44 308S 83GSU 15-6 mods 331S 15-6 126S 24-7 FCCS North 8-2-45 HAL 14-11 sold Turk 15-10-47

MH375 122S 9-8-43 ROS 21-10 122S 19-11 19S 7-12 313S FTR ops 24-1-44

MH376 65S 5-8-43 CB ops 7-11 AST 80S 16-6-44 310S 5-9 VAO 6-10 FAAC 10-11 ROS CE ops 22-2-45

MH377 LFIX M66 33MU 11-8-43 129S 14-8 504S e/a CE 22-2-44 FH169

MH378 65S 7-8-43 122S 20-1-44 80S 29-5 312S 20-6-45 FAF 26-6-46 GC1/6

MH379 122S 7-8-43 274S 10-6-44 FLS Mlfld 21-8 29MU 21-9-46 SOC 29-11-47

MH380 122S 9-8-43 FACB 28-1-44 AST 274S 1-8 FLS Mlfld 21-8 RAF Tang FACB 2-7-45 ASTH SAAF 20-9-47

MH381 LFIX M66 405S 8-8-43 341S 28-8 411S 17-10 CB ops 30-1-44 229S 11-5 MAL 27-12 mr 165S 24-5-45 66S 2-9-46 sold R J Coley 9-2-50

MH382 122S 9-8-43 421S 23-2-44 313S 5-9 611S 8-10

MH383 122S 7-8-43 tyre burst on t/o after striking Drem light, somersault CB Graves 29-11 410RSU recat E FH128.50

MH384 LFIX M66 405S 8-8-43 129S 18-8 504S e/a CE 22-2-44 FH384

MH385 LFIX M66 129S 14-8-43 e/fd cd/ld on coast South Foreland Kent CE 31-8

MH386 LFIX M66 405ARF 8-8-43 129S 22-8 504S e/a CE 22-2-44 FH152.35

MH387 LFIX M66 CRD 17-8-43 9MU 31-4-45 165S 1-6 66S 5-9-46 sold R J Coley 3-2-50

MH388 65S 7-8-43 3501SU 30-5-44 229S FAAC 29-6 ROS 303S 19-10 VAO 22-2-45 mods 80 OTU 3-5 FACE dbf 31-8 SOC 13-9

MH389 LFIX M66 39MU 18-8-43 405ARF 29-8 222S FTR ops 8-9 FH5.45

MH390 LFIX M66 405ARF 8-8-43 222S 21-8 FTR 27-9 FH51.35

MH413 LFIX M66 405ARF 8-8-43 222S 21-8 AST FRU CE 22-6-44

MH414 LFIX M66 129S 11-8-43 CE ops 5-9 AST 504S 22-2-44 511FRU 9-3 1S 26-6 CAC ops 6-7 VA 15-9 mods 64S GAL 16-12 GA by 2nd Spit CB 29-1-45 ASTH sold Tur 3-9-47

MH415 LFIXB M66 to RNAF 3/53 as H-65 later H-108 BAF as SM40 Target tug with COGEA as OO-ARD to G-AVDJ, N415MH Extant Big Springs, Texas (used in film "The Longest Day")

MH416 LFIX M66 33MU 11-8-43 222S 14-8 CAC ops 22-4-44 84GSU 22-6 SAL 11-8 VA 1-3-45 mods MAAF 19-5 RHAF 27-2-47

MH417 LFIX M66 405ARF HAL 8-8-43 341S 22-8 FTR ops 27-8

MH418 LFIX M66 33MU 11-8-43 129S 14-8 135AF 14-1-44 322S 20-8 328S 19-4-45 FAF GC1/1

MH419 LFIX M66 33MU 12-8-43 FTR ops 17-8

MH420 LFIX M66 9MU 15-8-43 47MU 7-9 *Ocean Rid* 23-9 Casa 10-10 NAASC 31-10

MH421 LFIX M66 341S 9-8-43 ROS 21-8 AST 12-9 341S 3-2-44 recat E 24-4

MH422 LFIX M66 122S 9-8-43 485S 9-8 129S FTR over e/tr 6-9 FH32.55 confirmation from 66S cd Southend 26-11 HAL 7-12 GAL 21-9-44 83GSU 6-10 412S 23-11 VASM 17-10-46 to 6454M 4SoTT

MH423 LFIX M66 222S 14-8-43 308S 83GSU 15-6-44 mods 332S 15-6 3501SU 14-7 MAAF 26-2-45 FTR 16-4

MH424 LFIX M66 33MU 11-8-43 222S 14-8 84GSU 15-6-44 DeH 22-8 RNAF 5-9-46 as H-53 to H-106 BAF as SM32 8-52

MH425 LFIX M66 129S 12-8-43 CE ops 22-12

MH426 LFIX M66 9MU 15-8-43 82MU 8-9 *Craw W L* 22-9 Casa 10-10 NAASC 31-10 FA FTR 8-3-45

MH427 LFIX M66 39MU 19-8-43 405ARF 29-8 132S 7-9 CAC ops 22-12 ROS 405 RSU 20-4-44 112S CE ops 11-5

MH428 LFIX M66 33MU 11-8-43 222S 14-8 350S FTR ops 30-1-44 FH131.20

MH429 LFIX M66 222S 11-8-43 FTR ops 31-8 FH16.05

MH430 LFIX M66 222S 15-8-43 84GSU 15-6-44 SAL 28-9 3501SU 23-2-45 VAOx 23-2 mods 3APU Llan 2-4 MAAF 3-5 137MU u/c coll lndg Hal Far Malta CE 7-5-46 SOC 30-5

MH431 LFIX M66 9MU 15-8-43 341S CAC ops 19-8 405ARF 10-9 132S 22-9 83GSU 15-6-44 CE ops 411S 31-7 DeH recat B 10-2-45 3APU 15-4 MAAF 6-5 Tak stor 29-1-48 SOC 10-6

MH432 LFIX M66 222S 13-8-43 84GSU 20-5 AST 442S 11-1-45 401S 22-3 130S 17-5 sold VA 17-10-46 VASM cov to two-seat train 13-5-48

MH433 LFIX M66 129S 12-8-43 CE 25-10 FH80.50

MH434 LFIX M66 FF AH 222S 13-8-43 shot dn FW190 Sept: 84GSU 15-6-44 ROS 7-7-44 76MU 27-7-46 RNAF 17-3-47 as H-68 332S as H-68 WUL later H-105 BAF as SM-41 3-53 sold COGEA as civil 00-ARA target tug sold T

Davies G-ASJV sold A Swire AC-S normal wing fitted used as photo a/c in BoB film extant G-ASJV reported M76 instal

MH435 LFIX M66 222S 12-8-43 strk by MH451 on t/o dbf CE Horn 1-9 1MPRD Cowley FH27.55

MH436 LFIX M66 39MU 11-8-43 129S 14-8 504S e/a CE 22-2-44 FH151.40

MH437 LFIX M66 222S 12-8-43 FACB 30-8 AST 84GSU 24-3-44 126S FTR ops 6-6 cancel 165S 14-9 ROS 14-11 CE ttl wrk ops 5-1-45

MH438 LFIX M66 39MU 11-8-43 129S 14-8 504S e/a 22-2-44 511FRU 9-3 274S 11-5 421S e/fd i/sea off Lyme Regis 6-6

MH439 LFIX M66 222S 13-8-43 84GSU 15-6 DeH 19-8 VAO 22-2-45 mods RNAF 26-7-46 as H-56 BAF as SM-33 8-52 w/o 13-1-54

MH440 LFIX M66 129S 14-8-43 CE ops 27-9 FTR ops FH10.40

MH441 LFIX M66 129S 14-8-43 CE ops 22-12

MH442 LFIX M66 129S 14-8 CE ops 6-9

MH443 LFIX M66 222S 15-8-43 ROS 27-9 129S 2-1-44 135AF 14-1 453S 15-6 64S 29-9 GAL 12-12 mods GAAC gale dam 16-3-47 sold 22-8

MH444 LFIX M66 9MU 15-8-43 47MU 14-9 *Ocean Rid* Casa 10-10 NAASC 31-10 USAAF 31-1-44 SAAF 3S FTR ops 20-2-45

MH445 LFIX M66 129S 14-8-43 504S 22-2-44 FH166.5

MH446 LFIX M66 129S 13-8-43 CE ops 4-9 e/a i/sea FH26.15

MH447 LFIX M66 129S 12-8-43 504S FACB 5-2-44 ROS 83GSU 20-5 441S FTR ops 12-6

MH448 LFIX M66 222S 15-8-43 Stn Flt Horn 4-10 132S CB ops 3-6-44 349S 15-6 350S 14-7 ROS 8-8 322S 7-9 VAOx 23-4-45 mods 595AACS 16-5-46 SOC 8-3-48

MH449 LFIX M66 129S 14-8-43 453S FAAC 15-3-44 ROS 83GSU 22-8 453S 30-10 FTR ops 2-11

MH450 LFIX M66 222S 15-8-43 FACB 30-8 AST 83GSU 16-5-44 412S FAAC 11-6 ROS 83GSU ComS 4-1-45 401S 8-3 CAC ops 16-3 39RecceWg 29-3 414S 5-4 126Wg 12-4 411S 10-5 sold VA 16-4-47 to 6461M 13-10 RDAF 28-7-48

MH451 LFIX M66 222S 15-8-43 strk MH435 while t/o CB Horn 1-9 AST 11-3-44 84GSU 1-11 308S 13-1-45 411RSU 15-2 3BRU FA SOC 1-3

MH452 LFIX M66 9MU 15-8-43 405ARF 15-9 132S 22-9 AST 20-2-44 401S 6-7 CB ops 16-8 410RSU 24-8 AST 5-9 WAL 13-2-45 mods MAAF 28-6 SOC 29-8-46 SOC in error for ER468 FV RHAF 27-2-47

MH453 LFIX M66 39MU 19-8-43 405ARF 14-9 132S 26-9 CAC ops 14-1-44 ROS 405RSU 9-2 132S e/fd w/u ldg nr Fairwood Common CE 15-3 FH92.20

MH454 LFIX M66 129S 14-8-43 CAC ops 3-10 135Af 14-1-44 3501SU 1-7 SAL 15-8 VAOx 20-12 mods MAAF 3-3-45 CE ops 12-4 SOC 14-6

MH455 LFIX M66 222S 14-8-43 CAC ops 5-9 ROS 485S 25-10 66S CE ops 30-5-44

MH456 LFIX M66 39MU 21-8-43 405ARF 29-9 602S 6-10 453S FACB 8-2-44 511FRU 5-5 GAL 19-6 442S 9-12 402 22-3-45 130S 17-5 recat E 20-5-46 SOC 23-7

MH470 LFIX M66 39MU 17-8-43 485S 26-8-43 FTR ops 24-9

MH471 LFIX M66 33MU 19-8-43 129S 26-8 FTR ops 5-9 FH13.40

MH472 6376 LFIX M66 129S 14-8-43 FTR over e/tr 24-9 FH61.25

The name 'Red Rose', was first applied to MH489 as 'Red Rose II'. MH819 became 'Red Rose III', seen here with Squadron Leader J G Saunders at Squires Gate, October 1943. MH972 of No. 132 Squadron was 'Red Rose IV'. It was lost on operations on 21 May 1944.

MH473 LFIX M66 33MU 20-8-43 485S 27-8 FAAC 15-10 ROS NFDW Ford 22-2-45 to 6142M RNAF 10-10-46 as Instructional airframe

MH474 LFIX B M66 39MU 19-8-43 405ARF 14-9 132S 22-9 FAAC 13-3-44 ROS 84GSU 18-4 312S 8-6 126S 3-7 VAOx 10-10 CE ops 28-11

MH475 LFIX M66 39MU 18-8-43 405ARF 4-9 132S 22-9 eng trouble w/u ldg Lodge Farm nr Newchurch Kent CE 21-12

MH477 LFIX M66 33MU 16-8-43 341S 20-8 411S 17-10 AST 30-5-44 USAAF 25-11 BDn Feb'45 rocket (4.5in.) firing trls with American M.10 tube cluster launchers. CGS 4-4-46 RNAF 31-7 as H-6

MH478 LFIX M66 39MU 19-8-43 405ARF 30-8 341S 7-9 HQ Flt B Hill 10-10 17APC 30-5-44 MAL 29-6-45 FCC S North 25-6-46 to 6383M 28-7-47 Scrap 26-6-52

MH476 LFIX M66 222S 15-8-43 350S CE dbr 30-1-44 FH107.5

MH479 LFIX M66 39MU 18-8-43 405ARF 1-9 602S 14-9 AST 83GSU FAAC 26-7-44 FRU 27-7 401S 24-8 CAC ops 29-9 411S 10-5-45 SOC 9-7

MH480 LFIX M66 39MU 17-8-43 405ARF 129S 12-9 CE ops 9-2-44 FH113

MH481 LFIX M66 39MU 21-8-43 405ARF 20-9 132S 6-10 CE ops 18-10

MH482 LFIX M66 39MU 19-8-43 405ARF 31-8 602S 14-8 FTR ops 21-12 cancel 84GSU 27-4-44 329S 8-6 145Wg 15-6 126S 3-7 FACB 20-8 ROS 132S 12-10 451S 15-12 326S 15-4-45 81RSU 14-6 SNCAN 21-6

MH483 LFIX M66 33MU 19-8-43 405ARF 24-8 341S 1-9 CAC 24-9 ROS USAAF 19-10 410S FAAC 9-3-44 40S CB ops 7-5 401S FTR ops 7-5

MH484 LFIX M66 33MU 18-8-43 405ARF 24-8 222S 6-9 hit obst ldg Horn 18-10 222S e/fd w/u ldg CE Rainham Essex 5-11 as H-51 later H-102 BAF as SM-30 6-52

MH485 LFIX M66 39MU 18-8-43 405ARF 27-8 129S 12-9 CB ops 20-10 AST 84GSU 27-4-44 66S FACE 21-5 MNO 22-11-45 RNAF 17-10-46

MH486 LFIX M66 39MU 21-8-43 405ARF 14-9 132S 26-9 83GSU 15-6-44 403S 30-8 MH487 LFIX M66 33MU 17-8-43 405ARF 24-8 129S 5-9 453S CE ops 13-6-44

MH487 LFIX M66 33MU 17-8-43 405ARF 24-8 129S 5-9 453S CE ops 13-6-44

MH488 LFIX M66 33MU 18-8-43 405ARF 24-8 602S 7-9 coll with MJ152 while taxy CB Detling 25-11 GAL 29-9-44 mods 124S eng cut after switch tanks just after t/o i/sea nr Ramsgate 12-10 bboc GAL 24-10 66S 2-11 84GSU 30-11 74S 24-12 411RSU 25-1-45 331S 15-3

MH489 LFIX M66 Red Rose II 33MU 28-9-43 485S 8-10 CE ops 222S 5-11 66S e/fd cd nr Tang 21-5-44

MH490 LFIX M66 33MU 20-8-43 405ARF 29-8 485S 7-9 FTR ops 3-10

MH491 LFIX M66 33MU 21-8-43 405ARF 25-7 222S 6-9 349S CE ops 10-5-44

MH492 LFIX M66 39MU 19-8-43 405ARF 1-9 602S 14-9 FTR ops 21-12

MH493 LFIX M66 39MU 31-8-43 47MU 14-9 *Ocean Rid* 23-9 Casa 10-10 NAASC 31-10 MAAF 21-6-45 SOC 30-8

MH494 LFIX M66 33MU 18-8-43 405ARF 26-8 222S 6-9 AST 5-10 332S 5-2-44 CE 26-3 FH92.25

MH495 LFIX M66 33MU 19-8-43 405ARF 26-8 129S 8-9 e/a CE 504S 22-2-44 FH117.20

MH496 LFIX M66 33MU 21-8-43 222S 26-8 CAC ROS 23-10 350S 30-1-44 313S 12-2 84GSU 22-6 FCCS 22-3-45 f/ld cd dbf CE Somerset 24-1-47

MH497 LFIX M66 39MU 21-8-43 405ARF 20-9 132S 6-10 FAAC 5-12 511FRU 12-12 VAO 21-9-44 mods 64S 22-9 GAL 12-12 MAL 8-4-45 sold R J Coley 3-9-50

MH498 LFIXB 33MU 20-8-43 405ARF 25-8 341S 7-9 FAAC 3-10 ROS 411S 23-10 64S 6-8-44 MAL 9-4-45 FAF 17-8-46

MH499 LFIX M66 33MU 19-8-43 405ARF 24-8 222S 6-9 312S 8-6-44 350S 9-1 322S 6-9 SAL 28-9 VAO 10-1-45 mods MAAF 26-2 SOC 26-9-46

MH500 33MU 3-9-43 47MU 11-9 *Ocean Rid* 23-9 Casa 10-10 NAASC 31-10 FAC3 17-2-44

MH501 LFIX M66 33MU 20-8-43 485S 24-8 SAL 3-10-44 VAO 15-3-45 mods FSU Dyce 29-6 130S 28-2-46 VA 30-4 mr recat E 24-6

MH502 LIXC M66 39MU 21-8-43 405ARF 14-9 132S 26-9 coll with MH856 ldg CE Detling 7-11 AST 84Gp Com S 29-6-44 317S 15-3-45 CAC ops 16-4 411RSU 19-4

MH503 LFIX M66 39MU 23-8-43 47MU 4-9 *Emp Grebe* 15-9 Casa 29-9 NAASC 31-10 SOC 28-4-45

MH504 LFIX M66 39MU 21-8-43 405ARF 18-9 602S 26-9 453S CB ops 21-2-44 442S 24-8 401S 31-8 511FRU 12-10 130S 17-5-45 595AAC S 16-5-46 FAAC 20-10-47 recat E SOC scr 27-11

MH505 LFIX M66 39MU 21-8-43 405ARF 18-9 132S 6-10 CB 18-2-44 AST 317S 29-6-44 CB ops 23-3-45 ASTE sold VA 28-11-49

MH506 33MU 21-8-43 405ARF 26-8 222S 12-9 e/fd w/u ldg CE Broadstairs Kent 24-10 FH50

MH507 LFIX M66 39MU 22-8-43 222MU 2-9 *Emp Grebe* 15-9 Casa 29-9 NAASC 31-10 MAAF 21-6-45 SOC 14-8

MH508 LFIX M66 33MU 21-8-43 405ARF 27-8 602S 14-9 CAC ops 15-12 118S FACB 1-2-44 64S 2-9 CB ops 27-9 SAL MAAF 2-7-45 RHAF 27-2-47

MH509 LFIX M66 33MU 23-8-43 82MU 31-8 *Emp Grebe* 15-9 Casa 29-9 NAASC 31-10 43S FTR ops 13-6-44

MH510 LFIX M66 33MU 24-8-43 222MU 30-8 *Card Gib* 3-9 Casa 20-9 NWA 31-7 SOC 21-9-45

MH511 LFIX M66 33MU 22-8-43 222MU 2-9 *Emp Grebe* 15-9 Casa 29-9 NAASC 31-10 SOC 5-6-45

MH512 LFIX M66 39MU 21-8-43 405ARF 22-9 602S 6-10 FTR ops 1-7-44

MH526 LFIX M66 39MU 21-8-43 405ARF 22-9 602S 6-10 SAL 3-10-44 MAAF 30-4-45 IAF 26-6-47 as MM4037

MH527 LFIX M66 33MU 23-8-43 222MU 31-8 *Emp Grebe* 15-9 Casa 29-9 NWA C3 ops 11-10

MH528 LFIX M66 39MU 16-9-43 317S 27-9 FACE 11-12

MH529 LFIX M66 39MU 22-8-43 47MU 1-9 *SS751* 15-9 Casa 29-9 NAASC 31-10 CE 26-2-45

MH530 LFIX M66 33MU 22-8-43 222MU 30-8 *Emp Grebe* 15-9 Casa 29-9 NAASC 31-10 ME 18-8-45 SOC 13-9

MH531 LFIX M66 33MU 22-8-43 47MU 30-8 *Card Gib* 3-7 Casa 20-9

MH532 LFIX M66 33MU 22-8-43 82MU 31-8 *Craw WL* 22-9 Casa 10-10 NAASC 31-10 CE ops 23-4-45

MH533 LFIX M66 33MU 24-8-43 82MU 31-8 *Emp Grebe* 15-9 Casa 29-9 NAASC 31-10 SOC 30-6-44

MH534 LFIX M66 33MU 24-8-43 222MU 30-8 *Emp Grebe* 15-9 Casa 29-9 NAASC 31-10 SOC 23-10

MH535 LFIX M66 39MU 23-8-43 222MU 2-9 *Emp Grebe* 15-9 Casa 29-9 NAASC 31-10 C3 ops 7-4-44

MH536 LFIX M66 39MU 23-8-43 222MU 2-9 *Emp Grebe* 15-9 Casa 29-9 NAASC 31-10 SOC 3-5-45

MH537 LFIX M66 39MU 22-8-43 222MU 1-9 *Emp Grebe* 15-9 Casa 29-9 NAASC 31-10 4S C3 ops 5-3-44

MH538 LFIX M66 39MU 22-8-43 47MU 1-9 *Emp Grebe* 15-9 Casa 29-9 NAASC 31-10 111S FTR ops 4-6-44

MH539 LFIX M66 33MU 23-8-43 222MU 30-8 *Emp Grebe* 15-9 Casa 29-9 NAASC 31-10 SOC 22-11-45

MH540 LFIX M66 33MU 26-8-43 47MU 6-9 *Emp Grebe* 15-9 Casa 29-9 NAASC 31-10 FTR ops 2-5-45

MH541 LFIX M66 39MU 23-8-43 82MU 8-9 *Craw WL* 22-9 Casa 10-10 NAASC 31-10 SOC 30-6-44

MH542 39MU 29-8-43 82MU 8-9 *Craw WL* 22-9 Casa 10-10 NAASC 31-10 NA 31-8-44 ME 31-5-45 SOC 2-8

MH543 LFIX M66 33MU 24-8-43 222MU 31-8 *Emp Grebe* 15-9 Casa 29-9 NAASC 31-10 FACE 4-3-45

MH544 39MU 27-8-43 222MU 4-9 *Craw WL* 22-9 Casa 10-10 NAASC 31-10 MAAF SOC 30-8-45

MH545 39MU 2-9-43 82MU 10-9 *Craw WL* 22-9 Casa 10-10 NAASC 31-10 FAF 28-8-46

MH546 LFIX M66 33MU 24-8-43 47MU 2-9 *Emp Grebe* 15-9 Casa 29-9 NAASC 31-10 SOC 28-4-45

MH547 LFIX M66 33MU 27-8-43 82MU 2-9 *Craw WL* 22-9 Casa 10-10 NAASC 31-10 ME 6-9-45 REAF 29-8-46

MH548 LFIX M66 33MU 27-8-43 22MU 31-8 *Emp Grebe* 15-9 Casa 29-9 NAASC 31-10 FTR ops 25-8-44

MH549 LFIX M66 39MU 47MU 10-9-43 *Ocean Rid* 23-9 Casa 10-10 NAASC 31-10 SOC 15-5-45

MH550 LFIX M66 39MU 27-8-43 47MU *Ocean Rid* 23-9 Casa 10-10 NAASC 31-10 SOC 6-9-45

MH551 33MU 27-8-43 47MU 2-9 *Emp Grebe* 15-9 Casa 29-9 NAASC 31-10 SOC 31-1-46

MH552 39MU 29-8-43 222MU 4-3-44 *Emp Raj* 21-3 Casa 6-4 MAAF 21-6-45 ME 26-6-47 137MU stor 12-2-48 SOC 10-6

MH553 LFIX M66 33MU 26-8-43 47MU 2-9 *Emp Grebe* 15-9 Casa 29-9 NAASC 31-10 SOC 13-3-44

MH554 LFIX M66 33MU 24-8-43 82MU 31-8 *Emp Grebe* 15-9 Casa 29-9 NAASC 31-10 FACE 5-6-45

MH555 39MU 29-8-43 47MU 5-9 *Ocean Rid* 23-9 Casa 10-10 NAASC 31-10 ME FAC3 5-12

MH556 39MU 29-8-43 82MU 8-9 *Craw W L* 22-9 Casa 10-10 FTR ops 20-3-45

MH557 LFIX M66 33MU 24-8-43 82MU 31-8 *Emp Grebe* 15-9 Casa 29-9 NAASC 31-10 CE ops 28-12-44

MH558 9MU 29-8-43 47MU 14-9 *Ocean Rid* 23-9 Casa 10-10 NAASC 31-10 SOC 31-8-44 bboc ME 21-6-45 RHAF 31-7-47

MH559 9MU 29-8-43 222MU 18-9 *Craw W L* 22-9 Casa 10-10 NAASC 31-10 MAAF 21-6-45 SOC 14-3-46

MH560 9MU 29-8-43 47MU 15-9 *Ionian* 3-10 Casa 19-10 NA 30-11

MH561 33MU 27-8-43 82MU 31-8 *Emp Grebe* 15-9 Casa 29-9 NAASC 31-10 FTR ops 14-6-44

MH562 39MU 29-8-43 222MU 4-9 *Craw W L* 22-9 Casa 10-10 NAASC 31-10 USAAF 31-1-44 73S CE ops 23-9

MH563 39MU 27-8-43 82MU 8-9 *Craw W L* 22-9 Casa 10-10 NAASC 31-10 CE ops 2-9-44

MH597 39MU 30-8-43 82MU 8-9 *Craw W L* 22-9 Casa 10-10 NAASC 31-10 USAAF 31-1-44 MAAF FAC3 29-2

MH598 39MU 30-8-43 82MU 8-9 *Craw W L* 22-9 Casa 10-10 NAASC 31-10 FACE 14-5-45

MH599 LFIX M66 33MU 23-8-43 47MU 30-8 *Emp Grebe* 15-9 Casa 29-9 NAASC 31-10 SOC 31-3-44 recat A 31-1-45 IAF 26-6-47 as MM4284

MH601 39MU 1-10-43 405ARF 12-10 165S 8-11 453S 11-4-44 33S 16-5 FTR ops 30-5

MH602 33MU 2-9-43 222MU 13-9 *Craw W L* 22-9 Casa 10-10 NAASC 31-10 IAF 30-5-46 as MM4041

MH603 39MU 15-10-43 405ARF Croydon 25-10 331S 3-1-44 274S 2-6 FLS Mlfld 21-8 CFE Tang FACB 1-6-45 ASTH SAAF 10-3-49

MH604 39MU 9-9-43 47MU 21-9 *Ionian* 3-10 Casa 19-10 NA 30-11 USAAF 31-1-44 MAAF IAF 30-5-46 as MM4042

MH606 33MU 7-10-43 131S 21-10 165S 19-3-44 453S 11-4 CAC 16-5 ROS 33S 26-5 ASTH 30-9-45 SAAF 26-9-48

MH607 33MU 3-9-43 82MU 15-9 *Emp Mar* 7-10 Casa 19-10 NA 30-11 ME 28-12-44 137MU stor 12-2-48 SOC 10-6

MH608 39MU 31-8-43 82MU 9-9 *Craw W L* 22-9 Casa 10-10 NAASC 31-10 241S FTR ops 12-4-44

MH609 33MU 3-9-43 82MU 15-9 *Craw W L* 22-9 Casa 10-10 NAASC 31-10 SOC 30-6-44

MH610 LFIX M66 33MU 23-1-44 349S 1-3 FTR ops 28-4

MH611 33MU 5-9-43 82MU 13-9 *Crawe W L* 22-9 Casa 10-10 NAASC 31-10 USAAF 31-1-44 MAAF 21-6-45 SOC 22-11

MH612 LFIX M66 39MU 22-8-43 82MU 3-9 *Emp Grebe* 15-9 Casa 29-9 NAASC 31-10 7S C3 ops 13-5-44

MH613 LFIX M66 39MU 22-8-43 47MU 1-9 *Emp Grebe* 15-9 Casa 29-9 NAASC 31-10 MAAF 21-6-45 SOC 30-8

MH614 LFIX M66 39MU 23-8-43 222MU 2-9 *Emp Grebe* 15-9 Casa 29-9 NAASC 31-10 FACE 19-11-44

MH615 LFIX M66 39MU 23-8-43 47MU 2-9 *Emp Grebe* 15-9 Casa 29-9 NAASC 31-10 USAAF 29-2-44 IAF 26-6-47

MH616 33MU 8-10-43 405ARF 19-10 274S 10-6-44 CAC ops 8-8 ROS 310S FTR ops5-9-44

MH617 LFIX M66 39MU 29-10-43 405ARF 8-11 412S 21-11 FTR ops 10-5-44

MH618 33MU 8-9-43 82MU 15-9 *Emp Mar* 7-10 Casa 19-10 NA 30-11 USAAF 31-1-44 RAF 31-5 SOC 5-6-45

MH619 39MU 14-9-43 215MU 30-9 *Emp Mar* 7-10 Casa 19-10 NA 30-11 MAAF 21-6-45 IAF 26-6-47 as MM4046

MH620 33MU 19-9-43 222MU 11-10 *Char Hall* 24-10 Casa 17-11 NA 30-11 SOC 23-12

MH621 LFIX M66 39MU 31-8-43 82MU 9-9 *Craw W L* 22-9 Casa 10-10 NAASC 31-10 IAF 30-5-46 as MM4047

MH622 LFIX M66 9MU 29-8-43 222MU 10-9 *Craw W L* 22-9 Casa 10-10 NAASC 31-10 SOC 18-8-44

MH623 39MU 14-9-43 47MU 29-9 *Ionian* 3-10 Casa 19-10 NA 30-11 93S FTR ops 16-4-44

MH635 33MU 11-9-43 82MU 18-9 *Emp Mar* 7-10 Casa 19-10 NA 30-11 MAAF 21-6-45 IAF 26-6-47 as MM4052

MH636 39MU 17-9-43 52MU 25-9 *Ionian* 3-10 Casa 19-10 NA 30-11 FTR ops 27-1-44

MH647 39MU 22-8-43 82MU 7-10 *Char Hall* 24-10 Casa 17-11 NA 30-11 CE ops 22-12-44

MH648 39MU 22-8-43 47MU 14-9 *Ocean Rid* 23-9 Casa 10-10 NAASC 31-10 MAAF 31-1-44 IAF 26-6-47 as MM4134

MH649 39MU 23-8-43 47MU 1-9 *Emp Grebe* 15-9 Casa 29-9 NAASC 31-10 SOC 14-6-45

MH650 39MU 23-8-43 47MU 1-9 *Emp Grebe* 15-9 Casa 29-9 NAASC 31-10 SOC 14-3-46

MH651 39MU 23-8-43 82MU 3-9 *Craw W L* 22-9 Casa 10-10 NAASC 31-10 MAAF 31-1-44 USAAF SOC 22-11-45

MH652 39MU 23-8-43 82MU 3-9 *Emp Grebe* 15-9 Casa 29-9 NAASC 31-10 C3 ops 16-2-44

MH653 39MU 23-8-43 47MU 1-9 *Emp Grebe* 15-9 Casa 29-9 NAASC 31-10 MAAF FAC3 bboc 11-2-44 REAF 29-8-46

MH654 33MU 25-8-43 47MU 2-9 *Emp Grebe* 15-9 Casa 29-9 NAASC 31-9 USAAF 31-1-44 MAAF CE ops 21-10

MH655 33MU 29-8-43 47MU 4-9 *Ocean Rid* 23-9 Casa 10-10 NAASC 31-10 USAAF 31-1-44 RAF 31-5 MAAF 21-6-45 SOC 6-9

MH656 33MU 29-8-43 222MU 7-9 *Craw W L* 22-9 Casa 10-10 NAASC 31-10 ASTH 29-5-46 'Gem' mods REAF 26-9

MH657 39MU 2-9-43 82MU 10-9 *Craw W L* 22-9 Casa 10-10 NAASC 31-10 C3 ops 27-1-44

MH658 39MU 2-9-43 82MU 10-9 *Craw W L* 22-9 Casa 10-10 NAASC 31-10 MAAF 21-6-45 SOC 30-8

MH659 39MU 3-9-43 47MU 13-9 *Ocean Rid* 29-9 Casa 10-10 NAASC 31-10 43S FTR ops 5-2-44

MH660 33MU 4-9-43 82MU 20-9 *Emp Mar* 7-10 Casa 19-10 NA 30-11 SOC 23-10-44

MH661 39MU 5-9-43 47MU 20-9 *Ocean Rid* 23-9 Casa 10-10 NAASC 31-10 242S FTR ops 20-5-44

MH662 33MU 4-9-43 47MU 11-9 *Ocean Rid* 23-9 Casa 10-10 NAASC 31-10 SOC 15-3-45

MH663 39MU 5-9-43 215MU 27-9 *Emp Mar* 7-10 Casa 19-10 NA 30-11 ASTE 1-6-45 SAAF 13-3-49

MH664 39MU 5-9-43 222MU 6-1-44 *Lds City* 21-1 Casa 17-2 M66 instal CE ops 6-4

MH665 33MU 10-9-43 405ARF CAC 19-9 403S 5-10 FTR ops 24-10

MH666 39MU 4-9-43 405ARF 15-9 165S 29-9 FAAC 1-12 ROS 453S 11-4-44 33S 16-5 310S 8-7 504S 15-7 VA 9-11 mods

MH667 33MU 4-9-43 52MU 10-9 *Craw WL* 22-9 Casa 10-10 NAASC 31-10 SOC 15-3-45

MH668 M63A 39MU 5-9-43 82MU 3-10 *Char Hall* 26-10 Casa 17-11 NA 30-11 232S FTR ops 29-4-44

MH669 33MU 5-9-43 47MU 14-9 *Ocean Rid* 23-9 Casa 10-10 NAASC 31-10

MH670 M63A 39MU 5-9-43 222MU 15-9 *Craw WL* 22-9 Casa 10-10 NAASC 31-10 FACE 18-12

MH671 33MU 11-9-43 303S 26-9 308S 16-11 80S 29-5-44 SAL 23-6 GAL 31-10 FAF 25-4-46

MH672 33MU 9-9-43 82MU 17-9 *Emp Mar* 7-10 Casa 30-11 FACE 11-2-45

MH673 33MU 9-9-43 47MU 14-9 *Ocean Rid* 23-9 Casa 10-10 NAASC 31-10

MH674 33MU 9-9-43 165S CAC 25-9 ROS 131S 21-12 453S 7-4-44 303S 23-11 FACB 29-11 ROS 414S 5-4-45 441S 11-5 FACB SAAF 18-6-47

MH675 33MU 11-9-43 82MU 19-9 *Emp Mar* 7-10 Casa 19-10 NA 30-11 USAAF 31-1-44

MH676 39MU 14-9-43 47MU 24-9 *Ionian* 3-10 Casa 19-10 NA 30-11 SOC 23-10

MH677 33MU 11-9-43 47MU 19-9 *Ionian* 3-10 Casa 19-10 NA 30-11 USAAF 31-1-44 CE 19-7-45 REAF 26-9-46

MH678 33MU 10-9-43 82MU 17-9 *Emp Mar* 7-10 Casa 19-10 NA 30-11 C3 ops 28-12

MH691 33MU 10-9-43 82MU 18-9 *Emp Mar* 7-10 Casa 19-10 NA 30-11 USAAF 31-1-44 IAF 26-6-47 (as MM4136)

MH692 33MU 10-9-43 165S 28-9 AST 2-12 453S 11-4-44 33S 16-5 310S 3-7 ROS 8-8 VA 15-11 mods 303S 25-2-45 CB ops DeH 24-9-45 SAAF 26-11-48

MH693 39MU 14-9-43 47MU 21-9 *Ionian* 3-10 Casa 19-10 NA 30-11 MAAF 21-6-45 SOC 14-3-46

MH694 M63A 33MU 10-9-43 165S 28-9 453S 11-4-44 33S 16-5 310S 8-7 504S 15-7 303S 17-11 CAC ops 9-2-45 441S 5-4 WAL 27-6 SAAF 16-11-48

MH695 33MU 11-9-43 215MU 6-10 *Mont City* 15-11 Casa 29-11 FTR ops 27-10-44

MH696 39MU 14-9-43 76MU 24-9 *Ionian* 3-10 Casa 19-10 NA 30-11 MAAF 21-6-45 SOC 26-9-46

MH697 39MU 14-9-43 47MU 3-10 *Char Hall* 24-10 Casa 17-11 NA 30-11 REAF 26-9-46

MH698 33MU 10-9-43 82MU 17-9 *Emp Mar* 7-10 Casa 19-10 NA 30-11 ME 21-6-45 RHAF 27-3-47

MH699 39MU 14-9-43 82MU 26-9 *Emp Mar* 7-10 Casa 19-10 NA 30-11 SOC 31-3-44 recat A 31-1-45 SOC 20-9

MH700 33MU 11-9-43 82MU 18-9 *Emp Mar* 7-10 Casa 19-10 NA 30-11 SOC 29-11-45

MH701 33MU 15-9-43 82MU 20-9 *Emp Mar* 7-10 Casa 19-10 NA 30-11 USAAF 31-1-44

MH702 33MU 14-9-43 82MU 20-9 *Emp Mar* 7-10 Casa 19-10 NA 30-11 ASTH 21-3-45 SOC 23-8

MH703 39MU 14-9-43 47MU 24-9 *Ionian* 3-10 Casa 19-10 NA 30-11 SOC 29-6-44

MH704 39MU 14-9-4 47MU 24-9 *Ionian* 3-10 Casa 19-10 NA 30-11 USAAF 31-1-44 MAAF CE ops 26-3-45

MH705 39MU 14-9-43 47MU 24-9 *Ionian* 3-10 Casa 19-10 NA 30-11 CE ops 4-12-44

MH706 39MU 14-9-43 52MU 26-9 *Ionian* 3-10 Casa 19-10 NA 30-11 FA FTR 21-4-44

MH707 33MU 11-9-43 82MU 18-9 *Emp Mar* 7-10 Casa 19-10 NA 30-11

MH708 LFIX M66 33MU 15-9-43 405ARF 22-9 602S 6-10 SAL 22-8-44 302S 18-1-45 317S 8-2 84Gp ARF 22-3 327S 31-5 FACE 13-9

MH709 LFIX M66 33MU 14-9-43 405ARF 19-9 602S 6-10 FTR ops 16-6-46

MH710 33MU 15-9-43 47MU 20-9 *Emp Mar* 7-10 Casa 19-10 NA 30-11 USAAF 31-1-44

MH711 39MU 14-9-43 76MU 24-9 *Ionian* 3-10 Casa 19-10 NAASC 31-10 USAAF 31-1-44 SOC 25-2-45

MH712 LFIX M66 39MU 14-9-43 317S 27-9 FACB 10-2-44 AST 84GSU 31-5 mods 302S CAC ops 18-6 411RSU 22-6 e/a 1-1-45 WAL recat E SOC 20-6

MH713 LFIX M66 39MU 15-9-43 405ARF 25-9 317S 15-10 332S CAC ops 11-6-44 420RSU 15-6 MAL 25-8 MAAF 15-2-45 SOC 20-2

MH714 LFIX M66 33MU 16-9-43 317S 25-9 coll with hut taxy North CB 1-10 AST 39MU 6-1-44 403S 31-1

MH715 LFIX M66 39MU 15-9-43 405ARF 30-9 485S 6-10 CA ROS 14-10 66S 8-6-44 MAL 18-7 83GSU FACB 14-9 ASTH MAAF 24-4-45 REAF 30-4-47 109MU stor 11-3-48 SOC 13-5

MH716 LFIX M66 39MU 14-9-43 405ARF 25-9 602S 15-6-44 CAC ops 15-7 AST MAAF NAAF 10-5-45 SOC 10-6-48

MH717 LFIX M66 33MU 16-9-43 317S 24-9 SAL 15-6-44 326S 5-4-45 FAF 27-11

MH718 LFIX M66 33MU 14-9-43 405SARF 19-9 132S 6-10 602S 15-6-44 442S 10-8 CB ops 15-8 410RSU 1ATC 24-45 DeH 29-3 recat E 20-9

MH719 LFIX M66 39MU 15-9-43 405ARF 25-9 443S CE ops 7-5-44

MH720 LFIX M66 33MU 16-9-43 405ARF 22-9 317S 7-10 332S FAAC 26-3-44 420RSU 15-6 FAAC 4-7 511FRU 26-7 DeH 1-8 3APU Lan 4-4-45 MAAF 24-4 IAF 26-6-47 as MM4062

MH721 LFIX M66 33MU 15-9-43 405ARF 19-9 602S 6-10 FTR ops 21-12

MH722 LXIX M66 33MU 15-9-43 405ARF 21-9 602S 6-10 out of fuel i/sea off Dung 7-1-44

MH723 LXIX M66 39MU 14-9-43 317S 27-9 e/a 10-1-44 66S 17-2 SAL 15-8 317S 18-1-45 CAC ROS mr eng change RNAF 30-9-46 as H-7

MH724 LFIX M66 33MU 16-9-43 405ARF 22-9 602S 6-10 CB ops 4-11 ROS 331S air coll with MH938 cd Berry Farm Ongar Essex CE 19-2-44 401S 29-5 MAL 4-10 76MU 20-1-45 MAAF 15-2 SOC 31-10-46

MH725 LFIX M66 39MU 1-10-43 317S 12-10 GAL 22-7-44 401S 24-8 CB ops 1-10 ROS RNAF 15-5-47 as H-63 later H-112 BAF as SM38

MH726 LFIX M66 33MU 19-9-43 317S 26-9 318S CB ops 5-1-44 AST 18-1 302S 15-6 301S FACB 26-7 420RSU 3-8 511FRU 10-8

MH727 LFIX M66 39MU 15-9-43 317S 27-9 AST 3-6-44 82MU 4-11 *Sil Lch* 13-11 Casa 23-11 RHAF 30-1-47

MH728 LFIX M66 33MU 17-9-43 317S 24-9 GAL 23-9-44 mods 442S 11-1-45 CAC ops 24-1 410RSU 1-2 401S CE ops 30-3-45

MH729 LFIX M66 39MU 14-9-43 317S 28-9 FACE 21-4-44 sold BAF as target tug SM-43 later 00-ARB

MH730 LFIX M66 33MU 16-9-43 405ARF 22-9 602S 6-10 CE ops 18-10

MH731 LFIX M66 39MU 15-9-43 405ARF 24-9 317S 7-10 332S 8-6-44 SAL 21-6 GAL 30-11 84GSU 20-1-45 345S 15-2 411RSU 1-3 ROS 19-3 345S 28-3 to 6026M 29-7-46 8SoTT

MH732 LFIX M66 39MU 17-9-43 52MU 29-9 *Char Hall* 24-10 Casa 17-11 NA 30-11 C3 ops 18-4-44 bboc 5-6 45 FAF 28-3-46

MH733 LFIX M66 39MU 18-9-43 47MU 3-10 *Fort Geo* 4-12 Casa 20-12 C3 ops 4-5-44

MH734 LFIX M66 33MU 16-9-43 405ARF 21-7 341S 2-10 411S 17-10 FAAC 24-12 412S e/fd f/ld nr Knock Kent CE 14-2-44 FH121.5

MH735 LFIX M66 39MU 17-9-43 52MU 29-9 *Char Hall* 24-10 Casa 17-11 217Gp NA 30-11 FACE 30-5-45

MH736 LFIX M66 33MU 16-9-43 405ARF 22-9 602S 15-6-44 410RSU 25-6 GAL 9-11 mods 215MU 6-1-45 *Tanele* 13-1 Casa 25-1 REAF 31-10-46

MH737 LFIX M66 33MU 18-9-43 405ARF 28-9 602S FAAC 6-7-44 405RSU 13-7 AST 18-7 82MU 21-11 *Guinean* 22-12 Casa 15-1-45 43S o/s lndg Tissano Italy FACE 23-9-46 SOC 31-10

MH738 LFIX M66 33MU 18-9-43 405ARF 28-9 132S FTR ops 21-12

MH756 LFIX M66 33MU 19-9-43 317S 26-9 FAAC 17-11 39MU 12-3-44 441S FTR ops 3-7

MH757 LFIX M66 33MU 24-9-43 82MU 6-10 *Char Hall* 24-10 Casa 17-11 218Gp NA 30-11 SOC 18-8-44

MH758 LFIXE M66 33MU 18-9-43 405ARF 28-9 132S 15-6-44 511FRU 13-7 403S 12-10 421S 7-12 327S 5-4-45 ME SOC 30-8 Letecka Vojenska Akademic (CFS) Czech AF 1946

MH759 LFIX M66 39MU 21-9-43 47MU 3-10 *Char Hall* 24-10 Casa 17-11 218Gp NA 30-11 232S C3 ops 12-6-44

MH760 LFIX M66 33MU 19-9-43 CAC 25-9 ROS 332S FTR ops 14-4-44

MH761 LFIX M66 33MU 19-9-43 317S 26-9 332S 27-4-44 AST 7-5 83GSU 28-9 401S 9-12 CE ops 14-1-45

MH762 LFIX M66 39MU 19-9-43 215MU 27-9 *Emp Mar* 7-10 Casa 19-10 218Gp NA 30-11 USAAF 31-1-44

MH763 LFIX M66 33MU 22-9-43 82MU 28-9 *Emp Mar* 7-10 Casa 19-10 218Gp NA 30-11 MAAF 21-6-45 SOC 19-7

MH764 LFIX M66 39MU 52MU 30-9-43 *Char Hall* 26-10 Casa 17-11 218Gp NA 30-11 FACE 15-6-45

MH765 LFIX M66 39MU 19-9-43 52MU 29-9 *Char Hall* 24-10 Casa 17-11 218Gp NA 30-11 MAAF 21-6-45 SOC 14-3-46

MH766 LFIX M66 39MU 23-9-43 82MU 23-9 *Char Hall* 26-10 Casa 17-11 218Gp NA 30-11 MAAF 21-6-45 SOC 13-9

MH767 LFIX M66 39MU 19-9-43 222MU 6-10 *Char Hall* 24-10 Casa 17-11 218Gp NA 30-11 C3 ops 9-8-44

MH768 LFIX M66 39MU 19-9-43 52MU 30-9 *Char Hall* 24-10 Casa 17-11 218Gp NA 30-11 CE ops 23-10-44

MH769 LFIX M66 33MU 21-9-43 222MU 3-10 *Char Hall* 24-10 Casa 17-11 218Gp NA 30-11 SOC 30-6-44

MH770 LFIX M66 39MU 19-9-43 52MU 30-9 *Char Hall* 24-10 Casa 218Gp NA 30-11 MAAF 21-6-45 SOC 26-9-46

MH771 LFIX M66 33MU 24-9-43 222MU 4-10 *Char Hall* 24-10 Casa 17-11 218Gp NA 30-11 SOC 20-9-45

MH772 LFIX M66 39MU 19-9-43 52MU 29-9 *Char Hall* 24-10 Casa 17-11 218Gp NA 30-11 ME 9-8-45 REAF 27-11-47 109MU stor 11-3-48 SOC 27-5

MH773 LFIX M66 39MU 19-9-43 47MU 21-10 *Mont City* 15-11 Casa 29-11 MAAF 21-6-45 SOC 14-3-46

MH774 LFIX M66 33MU 19-9-43 405ARF 5-11 FAAC Bg Hll 20-12 412S 6-7-44 1S 12-10 RHAF 19-5-45

MH775 LFIX 33MU 24-9-43 47MU 2-10 *Char Hall* 24-10 Casa 17-11 218Gp NA 30-11 SOC 14-3-46

MH776 M66 33MU 22-9-43 222MU 4-10 *Char Hall* 26-10 Casa 17-11 218Gp NA 30-11 41S FTR ops 23-3-44

MH777 LFIX M66 33MU 28-9-43 165S 6-10 AST 26-11 453S 11-4-44 33S 16-5 310S 8-7 504S 15-7 VA 16-11 mods 441S 5-4-45 MAL 10-9 WAL 21-9 SAAF 24-11-48

MH778 LFIX M66 39MU 21-9-43 52MU 29-9 *Char Hall* 24-10 Casa 17-11 218Gp NA 30-11 USAAF 31-1-44 RAF 31-5 601S CE ops 2-9

MH779 LFIX M66 39MU 1-10-43 129S 12-10 453S 15-6-44 403S CAC ops 14-7 127W 24-8 ASTE 5-10 MAAF 9-4-45 IAF 20-6-47 as MM4107

MH780 LFIX M66 39MU 23-9-43 47MU 5-10 *Char Hall* 24-10 Casa 17-11 218Gp NA 30-11 ME 16-8-45 SOC 23-8

MH781 LFIX M66 33MU 23-9-43 47MU 3-10 *Emp Mar* 7-10 Casa 19-10 218Gp NA 30-11 ME 31-5-45 SOC 2-8

MH782 LFIX M66 39MU 24-9-43 47MU 5-10 *Char Hall* 24-10 Casa 17-11 218Gp NA 30-11 FTR ops 28-12-44

MH783 LFIX M66 39MU 24-9-43 222S FTR ops 3-10 FH5.38

MH784 LFIX M66 39MU 24-9-43 47MU 5-10 *Char Hall* 24-10 Casa 17-11 218Gp NA 30-11 ME 26-6-47

MH785 LFIX M66 33MU 22-9-43 82MU 28-9 *Emp Mar* 7-10 Casa 19-10 218Gp NA 30-11 SOC 31-3-44 recat A 23-4-45 IAF 26-6-47 as MM4066

MH786 LFIX M66 33MU 21-9-43 82MU 28-9 *Empire Marlow* 7-10 Casa 19-10 218Gp NA 30-11 SOC 18-8-44

MH787 LFIX M66 39MU 24-9-43 47MU 5-10 *Char Hall* 24-10 Casa 17-11 218Gp NA 30-11 SOC 19-1-45

MH788 LFIX M66 33MU 24-9-43 47MU 2-10 *Char Hall* 24-10 Casa 17-11 218Gp NA 30-11

MH789 LFIX M66 39MU 24-9-43 82MU 5-10 *Char Hall* 24-10 Casa 17-11 218Gp NA 30-11 SOC 4-10-45 bboc 21-10 137MU stor 29-1-48 10-6

MH790 33MU 26-9-43 165S 8-10 453S 11-4-44 33S 16-5 FAAC 14-6 ROS 33S 15-7 FACE 20-8

MH791 LFIX M66 33MU 23-9-43 47MU 2-10 *Char Hall* 24-10 Casa 17-11 218Gp NA 30-11 FAC3 16-3-44

MH792 39MU 27-9-43 222MU 6-10 *Char Hall* 24-10 Casa 17-11 ME 1-12 FAC3 30-3-44

MH793 LFIX M66 33MU 24-9-43 222MU 9-10 *Char Hall* 24-10 Casa 17-11 218Gp NA 30-11 SOC 28-4-45

MH794 LFIX M66 33MU 23-9-43 47MU 2-10 *Char Hall* 24-10 Casa 17-11 218Gp NA 30-11 USAAF 31-1-44 MAAF 31-3 FTR ops 15-4-45

MH795 33MU 25-9-43 215MU 3-10 *Char Hall* 24-10 Casa 17-10 218Gp NA 30-11 USAAF 31-1-44 ME 23-12 REAF 26-9-46

MH796 33MU 26-9-43 165S 6-10 CE ops 20-1-44

MH813 33MU 25-9-43 215MU 6-10 *Char Hall* 24-10 Casa 17-11 218Gp NA 30-11 SOC 31-8-44

MH814 LFIX M66 33MU 25-9-43 222MU 3-10 *Char Hall* 24-10 Casa 17-11 218Gp NA 30-11 USAAF 31-1-44 RAF 31-5 SOC 13-9-45 cancel 611S a/c aban in cloud cd nr Kirby Stephen Yorks 3-7-48

MH815 39MU 25-9-43 165S 5-10 e/fd after t/o Chu Stan cd CE 24-10 FH19.40

MH816 39MU 27-9-43 47MU 9-10 *Char Hall* 24-10 Casa 17-11 218Gp NA 30-11 USAAF 29-2-44 RAF SOC 30-6

MH817 39MU 27-9-43 47MU 9-10 *Char Hall* 24-10 Casa 17-11 218Gp NA 30-11 SOC 15-3-45

MH818 33MU 25-9-43 47MU 2-10 *Char Hall* 24-10 Casa 17-11 218Gp NA 30-11 CE ops 21-2-45

MH819 LFIX M66 Red Rose III 33MU 26-9-43 485S 8-10 CAC 3-11 ROS 310S 12-6-44 420RSU 15-6 332S 22-6 CE 29-6 22-10-45

MH820 LFIX M66 33MU 25-9-43 47MU 2-10 *Char Hall* 24-10 Casa 17-11 218Gp NA 30-11 ME 26-7-45 SOC 10-9

MH821 M63S 33MU 26-9-43 215MU 3-10 *Char Hall* 24-10 Casa 17-11 218Gp NA 30-11 SOC 15-3-45

MH822 33MU 26-9-43 165S 6-10 CB ops 20-1-44 AST 16-5 mods 310S 8-2 504S 15-7 303S CE ops 31-8

MH823 39MU 26-9-43 165S 5-10 FAAC 4-2-44 ROS 453S 4-5 33S 16-5 310S 8-7 303S e/fd t/o Merston strk by BS408 CE 25-7 29-10-43

MH824 39MU 1-10-43 405ARF 12-10 65S 27-10 274S FAAC 19-5 ROS FLS Mlfld 21-8 CFE FAAC 11-6-45 SOC 30-1-47

MH825 39MU 24-9-43 131S 9-10 CAC 25-10 AST 229S 15-5-44 DeH 18-10 58OTU 7-6-45 sold H Bath 27-10-49

MH826 33MU 25-9-43 165S 6-10 453S 11-4 274S 29-5 hit balloon cable cd Fenpond Kent CE 9-7

MH827 LFIX M66 33MU 9-10-43 405ARF 18-10 401S 8-11 FTR ops 9-1-44 FH67.10

MH828 33MU 28-9-43 331S 5-10 80S 29-5-44 SAL 16-8 VA STN CSA 20-8-47 to VASM in error 27-8 bdn CSA 1-10 6MU 18-1-48 sold Int All 28-8-50

MH829 39MU 24-9-43 405ARF 9-10 403S 22-10 229S 29-5-44 CB ops 17-6 3501SU 14-11 FAF 9-7-46

MH830 33MU 28-9-43 332S 5-10 331S 3-1-44 FAAC 30-5-44 ROS 504S 10-8 312S 16-11 WAL 9-8-45 SAAF 22-10-48

MH831 33MU 1-10-43 405ARF 9-10 403S 22-10 308S CAC ops 25-4-44 ROS 411RSU 2-6 310S 11-7-45 RHAF 20-4-48

MH832 39MU 1-10-43 405ARF 9-10 421S 22-10 310S 8-9-44 CAC ops 6-10 ROS 312S 233-11 DeH 1-5-45 SAAF 22-8-47

MH833 33MU 26-9-43 215MU 3-10 *Char Hall* 24-10 Casa 17-11 218Gp NA 30-11 ME 2-8-45 SOC 9-8

MH834 39MU 24-9-43 9-10 *Char Hall* 24-10 Casa 17-11 218Gp NA 30-11

MH835 33MU 1-10-43 405ARF 9-10 403S 24-10 CAC ops 20-12 ROS 317S 5-3-44 229S 29-5 CAC ops 8-9 ROS MAL 6-1-45 sold H Bath 24-11-49

MH836 LFIX M66 ERD 39MU 22-10-43 52MU 8-11 *Mont City* 15-11 Casa 29-11 242S FTR ops 3-6-44

MH837 33MU 17-10-43 222MU 29-10 *Mont City* 15-11 Casa 29-11 ME FAC3 25-3-44

MH838 M63A 39MU 27-9-43 47MU 9-10 *Char Hall* 24-10 Casa 17-11 218Gp NA 30-11 con to LFIX M66 3-8-45 SOC 26-8-45

MH839 310S e/fd ldg app std cd Bradwell Bay 12-10-44

MH840 33MU 1-10-43 405ARF 9-10 403S 24-10 CAC ops 1-1-44 AST 317S 7-6 80S 1-7 310S 5-9 FACB 6-10 DeH 13-10 80OTU 6-3-46 FAF 4-4

MH841 LFIX M66 39MU 1-10-43 405ARF 12-10 401S 8-11 out of fuel return from sweep f/ld nr Worthing 2-5-44

MH842 39MU 1-10-43 405ARF 11-10 403S 22-10 302S std on finals cd Deanland Wood Sussex 7-4-44

MH843 39MU 1-10-43 405ARF 19-10 122S 18-12 AST 31-3-44 310S 8-9

MH844 39MU 1-10-43 405ARF 9-10 403S 22-10 317S CAC 1-5-44 FLS Mlfld 4-9 to 5970M 2-7-46 2SoTT recat E 12-4-49

MH845 LFIX M66 39MU 1-10-43 405ARF 19-10 401S 8-11 FTR ops 20-12 FH47.40

MH846 LFIX M66 33MU 1-10-43 317S 9-10 332S 8-6-44 511FRU 20-6 64S CB ops 30-9 recat E 15-10

MH847 LFIX M66 39MU 1-10-43 317S 12-10 332S 15-6-44 511FRU 20-7 174S 28-9 401S 4-1-45 CB ops 17-4

MH848 LFIX M66 39MU 16-10-43 405ARF 27-10 401S 8-11 e/fd f/ld hit trees Hawk CE 29-5-44

MH849 FIXA M63 33MU 28-9-43 165S 6-10 17APC South 1-3-44 FLS Mlfld 5-10 1S 5-10 CFE e/fd w/u ldg Raynham CE 7-5-46 SOC 29-5

MH850 LFIX M66 39MU 1-10-43 405ARF 12-10 411S 27-10 C Brom M266 instal 443S FTR ops 7-6-44

MH851 39MU 1-10-43 405ARF 11-10 65S 27-10 3501SU 20-3-44 611S 3-8 312S 8-10 FTR ops 16-11 cancel AST 19-1-45 bboc 47MU 10-3-48 SAAF 11-5

MH852 39MU 1-10-43 405ARF 18-10 131S 8-11 AST 23-8-44 453S 4-5 229S 29-5 FTR ops 17-6

MH853 33MU 1-10-43 405ARF 9-10 302S 8-11 274S 29-5 DeH 15-8 RHAF 20-5-48

MH854 LFIX M66 33MU 1-10-43 317S 11-10 332S e/fd after t/o f/ld Stanford River Essex CE 29-3-44

MH855 39MU 13-10-43 405ARF 20-10 501S 16-11 229S 29-5-44 312S 16-12 SAAF 1-10-48

MH856 LFIX M66 39MU 1-10-43 405ARF 12-10132S 27-10 strk by MH502 on ldg CE Detling 7-11

MH869 39MU 2-10-43 405ARF 19-10 302S 27-12 274S FACB 17-5-44 ROS FLS Mlfld 21-8 SAAF 21-5-49

MH870 39MU 1-10-43 405ARF 12-10 332S 8-10 317S FTR ops 14-2-44

MH871 33MU 1-10-43 405ARF 9-10 19S 27-10 CB ops 3-11 AST WAL for painting 9-2-44 229S 29-5 FAAC 23-6 ROS 229S hvy ldg u/c clpse CE 16-8 AST WAL 2-12 mods SAAF 11-5-48

MH872 LFIX M66 Red Rose IV 33MU 1-10-43 485S 8-10 FAAC 18-6-44 412S 401S 29-6 FTR ops cd/ld behind lines F/O Ashley safe 1-7

MH873 33MU 1-10-43 405ARF 9-10 65S 1-11 122S 20-1-44 FACA 29-5 CAC ops 8-8

MH874 CRD WD 8-10-43 M63A trls with Rotol c/props Feb'44. R-RH con the Mer 63A by adding Mer 71 reduction gear, transforming the original basic eng to c/prop DeH 15-6-45 to 6170M 1-11-46 SOC 12-11

MH875 39MU 2-10-43 405ARF 18-10 122S 27-10 611S 5-9-44 312S 8-10 CB ops 21-10 AST 58OTU 9-6-45 SAAF 21-6-48

MH876 39MU 2-10-43 405ARF 12-10 332S 3-1-44 274S 29-5 DeH 15-8 80OTU 18-5-45 FACB 16-6 AST 17-7 con to LFIX M66 SAAF 22-8-47

MH877 33MU 1-10-43 405ARF 11-10 165S 21-11 FTR ops e/tr 24-3-44

MH878 33MU 8-10-43 405ARF 18-10 308S 12-12 80S 29-5-44 FAAC 22-6 310S 4-9

MH879 LFIX M66 33MU 3-10-43 129S 11-10 504S e/a 22-2-44 FH110.5

MH880 39MU 8-10-43 405ARF 19-10 308S 27-12 80S FAAC 25-5-44 ROS 229S 10-6 AST 2-1-45 ECFS 7-6-48 hit H/T cables fly low cd nr Winterbourne Glos CE 7-2-47 SOC 21-3

MH881 39MU 2-10-43 405ARF 12-10 322S 8-11 274S 29-5-44 310S 5-9 SAL 28-9 FAAC 4-4-44 151RU 12-6

MH882 LFIX M66 39MU 3-10-43 405ARF 12-10 602S 28-10 FAAC 17-3-44 ASTH 27-3 83GSU 19-8 412S 12-10 39 Recce Wg 29-3-45 411S 12-4 126Wg 10-5 sold VA 5-12-49

MH883 LFIX M66 39MU 7-10-43 405ARF 26-10 ROS 16-2-44 412S 30-4 AST 302S 19-10 CB ops 2-1-45 DeH 14-2 sold Tur 16-1-47

MH884 LFIX M66 ERD 33MU 22-10-43 47MU 7-11 *Mont City* 15-11 Casa 29-11 MAAF 21-6-45 72S coll with NH453 cd aban Rutterfeld Austria FACE dbf 15-4-46

MH885 LFIX M66 39MU 3-10-43 405ARF 19-10 412S 21-11 401S CAC ops 4-12 FACE 29-6-44

MH886 LFIX M66 33MU 5-10-43 405ARF 18-10 401S 21-11 CE ops 26-11 SOC FH21.50

MH887 LFIX M66 33MU 17-10-43 82MU 18-11 *Fort Geo* 4-12 Casa 22-12 MAAF 21-6-45 SOC 29-8-46

MH888 33MU 5-9-43 82MU 17-9 *Emp Mar* 7-10 Casa 19-10 218Gp NA 30-11 C3 ops 27-3-44

MH889 LFIX M66 33MU 4-9-43 82MU 18-9 *Emp Mar* 7-10 Casa 19-10 218Gp NA 30-11 USAAF 31-1-44 MAAF FACE 14-2-45

MH890 33MU 8-9-43 82MU 18-9 *Ocean Rid* 23-9 Casa 10-10 NAASC 31-10 SOC 15-3-45

MH891 39MU 11-9-43 47MU 18-9 *Ionian* 3-10 Casa 19-10 218Gp NA 30-11 FTR ops 4-4-45

MH892 39MU 11-9-43 222MU 19-9 *Emp Mar* 3-10 Casa 19-10 218Gp NA 30-11 CE ops 12-4-45

MH893 39MU 11-9-43 47MU 21-9 *Ionian* 3-10 Casa 19-10 218Gp NA 30-11 SOC 14-6-45

MH894 39MU 18-9-43 82MU 5-10 *Char Hall* 24-10 Casa 17-11 326S 17-4-45

MH895 39MU 11-9-43 47MU 21-9 *Ionian* 3-10 Casa 19-10 218Gp NA 30-11 USAAF 31-1-44 MAAF FTR ops 8-2-45

MH896 33MU 14-9-43 76MU 22-9 *Ionian* 3-10 Casa 19-10 218Gp NA 30-11 USAAF 31-1-44 IAF 26-6-47 as MM4072

MH897 39MU 17-9-43 215MU 27-9 *Emp Mar* 7-10 Casa 19-10 218Gp NA 30-11 USAAF 31-1-44

MH898 39MU 18-9-43 82MU 5-10 *Char Hall* 24-10 Casa 17-11 218Gp NA 30-11 USAAF 31-1-44

MH899 39MU 19-9-43 229MU 29-9 *Emp Mar* 7-10 Casa 19-10 218Gp NA 30-11 MAAF 26-4-45 SOC 28-8-47

MH900 39MU 19-9-43 222MU 29-9 *Emp Mar* 7-10 Casa 19-10 218Gp NA 30-11 FTR ops 26-8-44

MH901 33MU 24-10-43 82MU 12-11 *Fort Geo* 4-12 Casa 20-12 SOC 4-1-45

MH902 33MU 22-9-43 47MU 26-7 *Ionian* 3-10 Casa 19-10 218Gp NA 30-11 USAAF 29-2-44 RAF 31-5 SOC 11-3-46

MH903 39MU 23-9-43 405ARF 5-10 421S 14-10 FTR 20-12 FH63.35

MH904 33MU 24-9-43 47MU 2-10 *Char Hall* 24-10 Casa 17-11 218Gp NA 30-11 FTR ops 13-4-45

MH905 33MU 28-9-43 165S 6-10 FTR over e/tr 26-11 FH62.15

MH906 33MU 1-10-43 405ARF 11-10 302S 27-10 FAAC 24-1-44 FLS Mlfld 20-3 sold scr 3-9-47

MH907 39MU 26-9-43 405ARF 9-10 421S 23-10 3501SU 17-6-44 229S 26-6 CE ops 29-8

MH908 39MU 26-9-43 405ARF 9-10 65S 1-11 310S 9-3-45 RHAF 29-4-48

MH909 33MU 29-9-43 165S 8-10 CAC ops 4-2-44 ROS 229S 29-5 310S 22-3-45 80OTU FACE e/fld on t/o Ouston 4-1-46 SOC 28-2

MH910 39MU 1-10-43 405ARF 12-10 332S 8-11 229S 29-5-44 ROS 27-7 3030S 3-8 FTR ops 1-11

MH911 LFIX M66 33MU 3-10-43 405ARF 9-10 401S 8-11 FTR ops i/sea 30-11 FH33.25

MH912 39MU 14-9-43 47MU 24-9 *Ionian* 3-10 Casa 19-10 218Gp NA 30-11 USAAF 31-12

MH924 39MU 14-9-43 76MU 22-9 *Ionian* 3-10 Casa 19-10 218Gp NA 30-11 ME 21-6-45 RHAF 30-11-47

MH925 33MU 17-9-43 52MU 10-9 *Ionian* 3-10 Casa 19-10 218Gp NA 30-11 CE 6-9-45

MH926 39MU 16-10-43 165S 3-11 453S 11-4-44 33S 16-5 FTR ops test flt 5-6

MH927 39MU 26-9-43 303S 9-10 308S 16-11 FTR ops 14-1-44

MH928 LFIX M66 33MU 28-12 416S 10-2-44 403S CE ops 29-6

MH929 LFIX M66 39MU 23-11-43 82MU 30-11 *Fort Geo* 4-12 Casa 22-12 43S FTR ops 4-3-44

MH930 33MU 19-9-43 47MU 26-9 *Ionian* 3-10 Casa 19-10218Gp NA 30-11 USAAF 31-1-44 40S SAAF CE ops 17-10

MH931 33MU 19-9-43 52MU 8-10 *Char Hall* 24-10 Casa 17-11 218Gp NA 30-11 ME 21-6-45 REAF 29-3-46

MH932 33MU 21-9-43 47MU 26-9 *Ionian* 3-10 Casa 19-10 218Gp NA 30-11 MAAF 21-6-45 REAF 26-9-46

MH933 39MU 23-9-43 405ARF 9-10 303S 8-11 16-11 274S FAAC 28-5-44 ROS 229S CE ops 2-10

MH934 39MU 24-9-43 47MU 2-10 *Char Hall* 24-10 Casa 17-11 218Gp NA 30-11 SOC 18-8-44

MH935 39MU 23-9-43 331S 3-10 332S 22-10 FAAC 7-11 ROS 274S 29-5-44

MH936 39MU26-9-43 331S 9-10 SAL 2-7-44 recat E 1-9 bboc Mar'46 FAF 26-7 GC1/4

MH937 33MU 25-9-43 47MU 2-10 *Char Hall* 24-10 Casa 17-11 218Gp NA 30-11 SOC 20-6-45

MH938 LFIX M66 39MU 28-10-43 310S 12-2-44 331S air coll with MH724 cd Berry Farm Ongar Essex CE 12-4 AST 84CSU 29-3 302S 19-10 e/a CE 1-1-45

MH939 33MU 3-10-43 405ARF 9-10 421S 26-10 501S 15-4-44 274S 29-5 FLS Mlfld 21-8 CFE FAAC 18-7-45 ASTH SAAF 11-10-47

MH940 39MU 26-9-43 331S 9-10 611S 17-7 312S 8-10 VAO 23-11 ROS 18-4-45 CFE 9-8 to 6146M 3-10-46 RNAF as instructional airframe

MH941 LFIX M66 33MU 14-1-44 405ARF 24-2-44 132S FAAC 13-3 AST 317S 17-8 411RSU 21-9 MAAF 25-2-45 SOC 10-5-46

MH942 39MU 26-9-43 332S 9-10 coll with MA709 on t/o CE Wld 25-10

MH943 9MU 30-8-43 222MU 18-9 *Craw W L* 22-9 Casa 10-10 NAASC 31-10 SOC 10-4-44

MH944 LFIX M66 9MU 31-8-43 222MU 10-9 *Craw W L* 22-9 Casa 10-10 NAASC 31-10 CE ops 13-4-45

MH945 39MU 29-8-43 47MU *Ocean Rid* 23-9 Casa 10-10 NAASC 31-10 IAF 26-6-47 as MM4285

MH946 33MU 28-9-43 82MU 2-9 *Emp Grebe* 15-9 Casa 29-9 NAASC 31-10 ME 21-6-45 con to LFIX M66 24-7-45 RHAF 30-1-47

MH947 33MU 26-8-43 47MU 2-9 *Emp Grebe* 15-9 Casa 29-9 NAASC 31-10 IAF 30-3-46 as MM4073

MH948 LFIX M66 9MU 30-8-43 47MU 14-9 *Ocean Rid* 23-9 Casa 10-10 NAASC 31-10

MH949 39MU 27-8-43 222MU 4-9 *Craw WL* 22-9 Casa 10-10 NAASC 31-10 SOC 14-2-46

MH950 LFIX M66 9MU 30-8-43 222MU 10-9 *Craw WL* 22-9 Casa 10-10 NAASC 31-10 FAC3 5-4-44

MH951 LFIX M66 9MU 29-8-43 222MU 10-9 *Craw WL* 22-9 Casa 10-10 NASSC 31-10 ME SOC 1-4-44

MH952 LFIX M66 33MU 30-8-43 47MU 6-9 *Ocean Rid* 23-9 Casa 10-10 NAASC 31-10 MAAF 21-6-45 SOC 11-4-46

MH953 LFIX M66 33MU 30-8-43 222MU 7-9 *Craw WL* 22-9 Casa 10-10 NAASC 31-10 SOC 30-4-47

MH954 LFIX M66 33MU 30-8-43 82MU 8-9 *Craw WL* 22-9 Casa 10-10 NAASC 31-10 MAAF 21-6-45 IAF 26-6-47 as MM4141

MH955 LFIX M66 9MU 29-8-43 82MU 10-9 *Craw WL* 22-9 Casa 10-10 NAASC 31-10 41S FTR ops 25-7-44

MH956 LFIX M66 33MU 2-9-43 82MU 13-9 *Craw WL* 22-9 Casa 10-10 NAASC 31-10 SOC 18-10-45

MH957 LFIX M66 33MU 30-8-43 82MU 10-9 *Craw WL* 22-9 Casa 10-10 NASSC 31-10 2S C3 ops 14-6-44

MH958 LFIX M66 33MU 30-8-43 47MU 6-9 *Ocean Rid* 23-9 Casa 10-10 NAASC 31-10

MH970 LFIX M66 33MU 30-8-43 222MU 7-9 *Craw WL* 22-9 Casa 10-10 ME 2-8-45 SOC 28-8-47

MH971 LFIX M66 39MU 2-9-43 47M 14-9 *Ocean Rid* 23-9 Casa 10-10 NAASC 31-10 7S C3 ops 3-7-44

MH972 LFIX M66 RED ROSE IV 39MU 4-9-43 405ARF 14-9 602S ROS 10-2-44 132 FTR ops 21-5-44

MH973 LFIX M66 39MU 31-8-43 82MU 9-9 *Craw WL* 22-9 Casa 10-10 NAASC 31-10 SOC 14-6-45

MH974 LFIX M66 39MU 31-8-43 82MU 9-9 *Craw WL* 22-9 Casa 10-10 NAASC 31-10 FTR ops 20-4-45

MH975 LFIX M66 33MU 2-9-43 82MU 10-9 *Craw WL* 22-9 Casa 10-10 NAASC 31-10 CE ops 3-8-44

MH976 LFIX M66 33MU 29-8-43 47MU 6-9 *Ocean Rid* 23-9 Casa 10-10 NAASC 31-10 USAAF 31-1-44 MAAF CE ops 13-11

MH977 LFIX M66 33MU 30-8-43 47MU 6-9 *Ocean Rid* 23-9 Casa 10-10 NAASC 31-10 SOC 14-3-46

MH978 LFIX M66 33MU 3-9-43 405ARF 13-9 132S 22-9 CAC ops 22-12 i/sea ops 14-1-44

MH 979LFIX M66 39MU 31-8-43 47MU 17-9 *Ionian* 3-10 Casa 19-10 218Gp NA 30-11 ME 20-6-47 73S u/c jam w/u ldg Takali Malta 5-9-47 SOC 30-10

MH980 33MU 3-9-43 47MU 9-9 *Ocean Rid* 23-9 Casa 10-10 NAASC 31-10 FTR ops 29-4-45

MH981 LFIX M66 38MU 31-8-43 82MU 9-9 *Craw W L* 22-9 Casa 10-10 NAASC 31-10 CE ops 3-5-45 SOC 30-8

MH982 LFIX M66 33MU 2-9-43 82MU 10-9 *Craw W L* 22-9 Casa 10-10 NAASC 31-10

MH983 33MU 3-9-43 52MU 10-9 *Craw W L* 22-9 Casa 10-10 NAASC FTR ops 13-12-44

MH984 LFIX M66 33MU 30-8-43 *Craw W L* 22-9 Casa 10-10 NAASC 31-10 SOC 30-8-45

MH985 39MU 5-9-43 222MU 15-9 *Craw W L* 22-9 Casa 10-10 NAASC 31-10 ME 5-7-45 con to LFIX M66 3-8 IAF 26-6-47

MH986 33MU 3-9-43 47MU 14-9 *Ocean Rid* 23-9 Casa 10-10 NAASC 31-10 SOC 31-3-44

MH987 LFIX M66 39MU 3-9-43 322S 13-9 222S i/Channel on escort duty 23-9 FH12.35

MH988 33MU 4-9-43 82MU 6-10 *Char Hall* 24-10 Casa 17-11 218Gp NA 30-11 USAAF 29-2-44 RAF 31-5 328S 26-7-45 FAF 27-11

MH989 39MU 4-9-43 47MU 14-9 *Ocean Rid* 23-9 Casa 10-10 NAASC 31-10

MH990 33MU 10-9-43 82MU 17-9 *Emp Mar* 7-10 Casa 19-10 218Gp NA 30-11 SOC 13-9-45

MH991 39MU 4-9-43 215MU 30-11 *Fort Geo* Casa 22-12 ME SOC 25-5-44

MH992 39MU 4-9-43 47MU 14-9 *Ocean Rid* 23-9 Casa 10-10 NAASC 31-10 SOC 15-3-45

MH993 33MU 4-9-43 52MU 10-9 *Craw W L* 22-9 Casa 10-10 NAASC 31-10 RHAF 27-3-47

MH994 39MU 5-9-43 222MU 15-9 *Craw W L* 19-9 Casa 10-10 NAASC 31-10 SOC 31-8-44

MH995 39MU 5-9-43 47MU 14-9 *Ocean Rid* 23-9 Casa 10-10 NAASC 31-10 CE ops 20-10-44

MH996 M61 39MU 15-9-43 47MU 24-9 *Ionian* 3-10 Casa 19-10 218Gp NA 30-11 ME 31-5-45 RHAF 27-2-47

MH997 39MU 4-9-43 47MU 14-9 *Ocean Rid* 23-9 Casa 10-10 NAASC 31-10 USAAF 31-1-44 IAF 30-5-46 as MM4092

MH998 39MU 5-9-43 222MU 15-9 *Ocean Rid* 23-9 Casa 10-10 NAASC 31-10 USAAF 31-10 SOC 10-4-44 bboc ME 21-6-45 SOC 27-7

MH999 M63A 39MU 5-9-43 222MU 29-9 *Emp Mar* 7-10 Casa 19-10 218Gp NA 30-11 USAAF 31-12 lost Italy 18-3-44

MJ series all LF IX Merlin 66 engine

MJ114 33MU 6-10-43 405ARF 15-10 401S 8-11 ROS 411S CAC ops 12-5-44 412S 317S 4-1-45 327S 31-5 FAF 27-11

MJ115 33MU 7-10-43 405ARF 18-10 401S 8-11 e/fd a/c aban i/sea off Bradwell Bay 30-11 FH20.25

MJ116 M63 33MU 18-10-43 47MU 26-10 *Mont City* 15-11 CE ops 18-9-45

MJ117 CP 39MU 13-10-43 405ARF 20-10 501S 16-11 FTR ops 24-11 FH11.25

MJ118 33MU 8-10-43 222S 18-10 313S 8-6-44 84GSU 29-6 64S 6-8 MAL 29-8 MAAF 10-2-45 ME SOC 31-10-46

MJ119 39MU 6-10-43 405ARF 18-10 412S 8-12 401S FACE 16-3-44 FH147

MJ120 33MU 16-10-43 331S 25-10 AST 26-11 33S 16-5-44 310S 8-7 303S e/fd f/ld nr Westh CE 10-8 SAL 25-9

MJ121 33MU 21-10-43 76MU 19-11 *Fort Geo* 4-12 Casa 22-12 4S FTR ops 24-1-44

MJ122 39MU 7-10-43 405ARF 401S 8-11 f/ld CE Knott Hill Farm nr Kingsdown Kent 1-12 FH16.15

MJ123 39MU 8-10-43 47MU 21-10 *Mont City* 15-11 Casa 29-11 7S C3 ops 16-5-44

MJ124 LFIX 39MU 7-10-43 405ARF 19-10 401S 8-11 CE 19-4-44

MJ125 39MU 17-10-43 411ARF 6-11 SAL 27-7-44 GAL 10-11 MAAF 12-3-45 SOC 14-3-46

MJ126 39MU 6-10-43 405ARF 19-10 412S 8-11 401S FTR ops 15-3-44 FH149.45

Mk IX from 340 'Ile de France' Squadron, Free French Air Force.

MJ127 39MU 16-10-43 405ARF 27-10 401S 8-11 421S 5-10-44

MJ128 39MU 8-10-43 47MU 21-10 *Mont City* 15-11 Casa 29-11 SOC 15-3-45

MJ129 M63 39MU 13-10-43 405ARF 20-10 501S 16-11 FAAC 19-3-44 ROS 274S 3-6 229S 28-7 303S 6-11 ASTE SAAF 14-11-47

MJ130 M63 39MU 18-10-43 222MU 9-11 *Fort Geo* 6-12 Casa 22-12 SOC 18-8-44

MJ131 39MU 17-10-43 401S 22-6-44 FTR ops 3-7

MJ132 39MU 17-10-43 411ARF 6-11 602S e/fd w/u ldg CB Etchingham Sussex 18-5-44 recat E 2-6

MJ133 39MU 17-10-43 405ARF 8-11 411S 21-11 133S FAAC 12-10-44 216S 127Wg 19-10 421S 7-12 SNCAN 21-6-45 SOC 21-6-47

MJ134 39MU 8-10-43 47MU 21-10 *Mont City* 15-11 Casa 29-11 SOC 6-12-45

MJ135 39MU 16-10-43 405ARF 25-10 412S 21-11 CE ops 11-5-44

MJ136 39MU 16-10-43 405ARF 25-10 412S 21-11 CE ops 11-5-44

MJ137 33MU 18-10-43 129S 4-11 504S e/a CE 22-2-44 FH78.10

MJ138 39MU 13-10-43 401S 8-11 302S 18-1-45 317S 8-2 CE ops 4-5-45

MJ139 33MU 17-10-43 129S 4-11 AST 13-11 FACB 24-12 AST VA for painting 17-3-44 443S 5-10 416S 30-11 AST 18-12 FAF 16-8-46

MJ140 39MU 17-10-43 405ARF 14-11 410S FAAC 22-2-44 411S CE ops 27-4

MJ141 39MU 10-10-43 405ARF 26-10 412S 21-11 401S FACB 11-1-44 AST 416S CE ops 12-7

MJ142 33MU 17-10-43 47MU 8-11 *Mont City* 15-11 Casa 29-11 GACE 22-12-44

MJ143 LFIXC 33MU 16-10-43 485S 25-10 66S CAC 19-5-44 AST 3-12 RNAF 17-7-46 as H-1 extant Soesterberg Museum

MJ144 39MU 17-10-43 405ARF Croydon 25-10 412S 21-11 401S 5-12 412S CB ops 30-5-44 322S 20-9 414S 4-1-45 CB ops 25-2-45

MJ145 39MU 13-10-43 401S 8-11 i/Channel ops 24-1-44 FH87.10

MJ146 33MU 16-10-43 405ARF 29-10 132S 15-6-44 421S 24-8 FTR ops 27-9

MJ147 33MU 16-10-43 405ARF 29-10 602S FAAC 421S 6-7-44 401S 24-3 411S 31-8 126Wg 10-9 132Wg 5-10 ASTE 10-2-45 WWal 18-12-46 sold Turk

MJ148 39MU 17-10-43 405ARF 25-10 412S 21-11 CB ops 18-6-44 recat E 15-9

MJ149 33MU 16-10-43 405ARF 25-10 412S 21-11 FTR ops 16-3-44 FH35.50

MJ150 33MU 19-10-43 222MU 28-10 350S FAAC 24-1-44 ROS 66S 8-6 CE ops 26-8

MJ151 33MU 20-10-43 222MU 21-10 *Mont City* 15-11 Casa 29-11 FTR ops 20-3-44

MJ152 33MU 16-10-43 405ARF 29-10 317S 12-12 CAC ops 5-1-44 ROS 401S FAAC 1-6 ROS 84GSU 16-8 RNAF 28-5-47 as H-31 w/o H-4-50

MJ153 33MU 16-10-43 405ARF 29-10 602S taxy coll with MH488 CB Detling 25-11 recat E 5-12

MJ154 33MU 16-10-43 485S 25-10 66S e/fd f/ld Great Chesterford Cambs 25-1-44 FH38.45

MJ155 33MU 18-10-43 47MU 8-11 *Mont City* 15-11 Casa 29-11 FTR ops 14-3-45

MJ156 33MU 21-10-43 47MU 14-11 *Fort Geo* 4-12 Casa 22-12 SOC 4-1-45

MJ169 39MU 16-10-43 405ARF 26-10 412S 21-11 FTRm ops over e/tr 29-11 FH16.50

MJ170 33MU 24-10-43 405ARF 11-11 132S FTR ops 29-4-44

MJ171 39MU 16-10-43 411ARF 6-11 AST 27-2-44 443S 22-6 416S 20-11 MAL 23-2-45 2APU 7-7-45 MAAF 7-8 REAF 27-11-46

MJ172 33MU 24-10-43 405ARF 11-11 401S FTR ops 29-2-44 FH20.25

MJ173 33MU 18-10-43 405ARF 29-10

MJ174 39MU 16-10-43 405ARF 27-10 317S 11-1-44 332S 8-6 FTR ops 4-7

MJ175 33MU 16-10-43 485S 4-11 349S 16-3-44 FACE 66S 2-4

MJ176 33MU 16-10-43 485S 25-10 66S FAAC 5-6-44 420RSU 8-6 3501SU 12-10

MJ177 39MU 16-10-43 340S 23-1-44 421S 8-6 34Wg Test Flt 28-9 sold VA 16-4-47 VASM to EA con to two-seat train 11-5-48

MJ178 33MU 17-10-43 47MU 8-11 *Mont City* 15-11 Casa 29-11 238S FTR ops 11-6-44

MJ179 33MU 18-10-43 222MU 29-10 *Mont City* 15-11 Casa 29-11 SOC 20-9-45

MJ180 33MU 16-10-43 485S 4-11 66S CB ops 9-2-44 83GSU 11-5 401S 22-6 410RSU 29-6 SAL 19-4-45 new eng sold

MJ181 39MU 24-10-43 412S 28-11 ROS 30-11 403S FACE 18-3-44 FH106.35

MJ182 33MU 16-10-43 485S 3-11 66S FTR ops 21-5-44

MJ183 39MU 18-10-43 82MU 6-11 *Mont City* 15-11 Casa 29-11 111S C3 ops 7-2-44

MJ184 33MU 17-10-43 222MU 7-11 *Fort Geo* 4-12 Casa 22-12 FAC3 16-3-44

MJ185 39MU 19-10-43 47MU 8-11 *Mont City* 15-11 Casa 29-11 C3 ops 20-3-44

MJ186 39MU 19-10-43 47MU 8-11 *Mont City* 15-11 Casa 29-11 237S FTR ops 20-5-44

MJ187 LFIXB 33MU 16-10-43 405ARF 412S 21-11 401S FACB 22-2 AST 403S CB ops 18-7 127Wg HQ 22-6 416S 20-7 403S 27-7 421S 7-12 443S 21-12 411S 8-2-45 FACE 22-2

MJ188 9MU 5-11-43 82MU 14-11 *Emp Arc* 23-12 Hap 9-1-45

MJ189 39MU 19-10-43 47MU 8-11 *Mont City* 15-11 Casa 29-11 111S FTR ops 4-6-44

MJ190 FF 12-10-43 by A Henshaw. e/fd aban a/c. another airframe substituted 39MU 12-12-43 82MU 24-12 *Co Lds* 26-1-44 Casa 17-2 72S FTR ops 30-5 cancel recat A 28-4-45 MAAF 21-6 SOC 19-7

MJ191 33MU 21-10-43 222MU 25-11 *Fort Geo* 4-12 Casa 22-12 ME 31-5-45 REAF 26-9-46

MJ192 39MU 20-10-43 47MU 8-11 *Mont City* 15-11 Casa 29-11 MAAF 21-6 SOC 20-9

MJ193 33MU 18-10-43 405ARF 28-11 421S 29-11 CAC ops 14-6-44

MJ194 39MU 30-10-43 76MU 12-11 *Fort Geo* 4-12 Casa 22-12 USAAF 31-1-44 SOC 31-8

MJ195 33MU 5-11-43 82MU 1-11 *Fort Geo* 4-12 Casa 22-12 SoC 29-4-45

MJ196 33MU 5-11-43 47MU 27-11 *Fam Head* 24-12 Casa 8-1-44 MAAF 31-1 FTR ops 19-3

MJ197 39MU 16-10-43 411ARF 6-11 317S 2-12 332S FAAC 3-5-44 331S 8-6 84GSU 25-7 ASTH 3-1-45 con to FXIX oblique cameras FAF 15-8-46

MJ198 39MU 17-10-43 405ARF 27-120 412S 21-11 312S CB ops 24-5-44 34Wg SU prep flt 27-7 327S 19-4-45 FAF 27-11 GC1/1

MJ199 39MU 24-10-43 47MU 9-11 *Fort Geo* 4-12 Casa 22-12 FAC3 8-8-44

MJ200 39MU 22-10-43 47MU 8-11 *Mont Bay* 15-11 Casa 29-11 SOC 10-4-45

MJ201 39MU 16-10-43 222S 6-11 310S 8-6-44 331S 15-6 91S 28-9 CAC ops 8-12 302S 18-1-45 GCAB 13-3-45 FAF 16-9-46

MJ202 9MU 5-11-43 83GSU 26-8-44 401S 14-9 CAC ops 19-11 to 5691M 2-10-45 SOC 24-1-51

MJ203 39MU 21-10-43 82MU 6-11 *Mont City* 15-11 Casa 29-11 CE ops 10-1-45

MJ215 M63 33MU 1-10-43 405ARF 9-10 19S 27-10 FTR ops 7-11 FH13.20

MJ216 M63 33MU 1-10-43 165S 8-10 453S 16-5-44 310S 8-7 504S 15-7 303S FAAC 18-8 ROS ASTE 6-10 ECFS 9-7-45 sold W F Lamont 8-9-49

MJ217 9MU 20-1-44 331S 9-2 420RSU CAC 19-7 331S 22-7 66S 3-8 WAL 19-10 165S 10-6-45 128Wg 19-7

MJ218 33MU 7-10-43 405ARF 18-10 401S 21-11 CAC ops 23-12 MEAF Commd 511FRU 9-1-44 332S CE ops 7-6

MJ219 M63 33MU 1-10-43 405ARF 7-10 302S 27-10 CAC ops 5-11 229S flew into hill in cloud IoW 11-6-44

MJ220 M63 33MU 1-10-43 322S 15-10 229S FAAC 11-5-44 ROS 611S 9-8 CAC ops 1-9 AST SAAF 28-4-48

MJ221 6MU 22-4-44 3501SU 26-5 165S 10-6 CAC ops 8-12 302S 18-1-45 317S 8-2 FACB 30-4 411RSU 3-5 SOC 3-4-47

MJ222 M63 33MU 1-10-43 405ARF 15-10 122S 27-10 229S 29-5-44 e/fld i/sea off Dung 30-7

MJ223 9MU 1-2-44 83GSU 12-3 132S 15-6 412S 20-7 453S CE ops 29-9

MJ224 M63 33MU 11-10-43 331S 9-11 611S 14-7-44 CAC ops 24-7 58 OTU 24-4-45 FACB 30-5 SAAF 24-4-48

MJ224 went to the SAAF in April 1948.

MJ225 33MU 11-10-43 331S 25-10 611S 3-8 CAC ops 10-9 SAL FAAC 26-2-45 312S 6-3 SAL 12-3 SAAF 2-1-49

MJ226 M63 33MU 18-10-43 82MU 4-11 *Mont City* 15-11 Casa 29-11 FACE 8-6-45 MAAF SOC 28-6

MJ227 M63 33MU 18-10-43 222MU 7-11 *Fort Geo* 4-12 Casa 22-12 ME 21-6-45 REAF 29-8-46

MJ228 33MU 18-10-43 405ARF 29-10 412S fast ldg coll with a/c on runway BHll 3-3-44 FH65.30

MJ229 33MU 18-10-43 405ARF 5-11 411S i/Channel ops 2-6-44

MJ230 33MU 18-10-43 405ARF 4-11 349S 8-6-44 84GSU 22-6 412S 22-6 421S 5-10

MJ231 9MU 12-2-44 83GSU 30-3 401S 22-6 410S CE ops 24-7-44 FTR ops 25-7

MJ232 33MU 18-10-43 222S 28-10 313S 8-6 84GSU 29-6 350S 24-7 322S 4-9

MJ233 39MU 21-10-43 82MU 6-11 *Mont City* 15-11 Casa 29-11 SOC 28-4-45

MJ234 39MU 21-10-43 82MU 6-11 *Mont City* 15-11 USAAF 31-1-44 SOC 14-3-46

MJ235 39MU 24-10-43 401ARF 9-11 317S 11-1-44 332S FTR ops 12-6

MJ236 39MU 24-10-43 401ARF 9-11 411S FTR ops 1-12 FH7.20

MJ237 39MU 16-10-43 405ARF 27-10 403S 29-6-44 CAC ops 18-7 441S 13-7 403S 27-7 AST 5-10 MAAF 27-2-45 ME SOC 26-9-46

MJ238 39MU 12-3-43 83GSU 27-4 GAL 23-11 MAAF 10-3-45 32S eng fail on t/o Ramat David Palestine CE 29-6-46 SOC 30-4-47

MJ239 39MU 27-10-43 411ARF 16-11 602S CB ops 16-6 441S 6-7 442S 20-7 401S 31-8 602S FACB 25-10 MAAF 20-6-45 SOC 18-10

MJ240 39MU 24-10-43 82MU 6-11 *Mont City* 15-11 Casa 29-11 SOC Oct'44

MJ241 39MU 28-7-44 82MU 10-8 *Melam* 20-8 Casa 3-9 ME 345S SOC 26-9-46

MJ242 9MU 5-11-43 52MU 21-11-44 *SS267* 1-12-44 Hap 9-1-45

MJ243 9MU 14-11-43 3501SU 13-6-44 350S 9-7 322S tyre burst hvy ldg u/c clpse CE Deanland 9-8

MJ244 9MU 5-11-43 91S 7-9 ROS 6-11 1S 12-4-45 HAL 29-8 BAF 2-9-47 as SM-11

MJ244 39MU 16-10-43 411ARF 6-11 317S 1-1-44 332S CAC ops 15-5 AST 83GSU 17-10 401S CE ops 8-12

MJ246 39MU 18-10-43 411ARF 6-11 401S 22-6-44 CE ops 28-6

MJ247 39MU 19-10-43 222MU 9-11 *Fort Geo* 4-12 Casa 22-12 MR 26-6-47 73S e/fd t/o cd Takali Malta 15-8-47 SOC 25-9

MJ248 ERD 38MU 23-10-43 82MU 26-11 *Fort Geo* 4-12 Casa 22-12 CE ops 11-12-44

MJ249 9MU 5-11-43 82MU 28-5-44 *Arabis* 29-6 Bas 12-8

MJ250 ERD 39MU 22-10-43 82MU 8-11 *Fort Geo* 4-12 Casa 22-12 SOC 5-6-45

MJ251 ERD 33MU 22-10-43 47MU 8-11 *Mont City* 15-11 Casa 29-11 USAAF 31-1-44 ME SOC 26-9-46

MJ252 33MU 20-10-43 47MU 8-11 *Mont City* 15-11 Casa 29-11 SOC 13-12-45

MJ253 39MU 18-10-43 222S 6-11 332S 15-6-44 CE ops 30-6

MJ254 ERD 33MU 22-10-43 47MU 7-11 *Fort Geo* 4-12 Casa 22-12 11-4-46

MJ255 33MU 24-10-43 405ARF 8-11 412S 21-11 CE ops 11-6-44

MJ256 33MU 20-10-43 47MU 7-11 *Mont City* 15-11 Casa 29-11 ME 9-8-45 65 FACE u/c clpse ldg Ramat David Palestine 6-6-46 SOC 25-7

MJ257 33MU 2-10-43 47MU 12-11 *Fort Geo* 4-12 Casa 22-12 USAAF 29-2-44 RAF 31-5 SOC 28-4-45

MJ258 39MU 20-10-43 82MU 6-11 *Mont City* 15-11 Casa 29-11 SOC 14-3-46

MJ271 LFIXC 33MU 2-10-43 411ARF 132S FACB 9-5-44 AST 401S 23-11 CAC ops 14-12 410RSU 21-12 ROS 23-2-45 RNAF 25-11-46 as H-8 extant Aviodome, Amsterdam

MJ272 39MU 20-10-43 47MU 8-1 *Mont City* 15-11 Casa 29-11 FTR ops 19-3-45

MJ273 39MU 18-10-43 82MU 6-11 *Fort Geo* 412 Casa 22-12 SOC 28-4-45

MJ274 39MU 29-10-43 82MU 16-11 *Mont City* 15-11 Casa 29-11 SOC 13-12-45

MJ275 33MU 20-10-43 44S 30-1-44 CAC ops 13-5 AST 83GSU 19-9 412S 23-11 CAC ops 16-2-45 FTR ops 30-3

MJ276 39MU 3-11-43 405ARF 12-11 602S FTR 15-6-44 SOC cancel bboc 405RSU 453S FAAC 18-8-44 441S 14-9 82Gp Com S 19-7-45 sold VA 16-4-47 con to two seat train 11-5-48

MJ277 33MU 20-10-43 47MU 8-11 *Mont City* 15-11 Casa 29-11 SOC 31-8-44

MJ278 39MU 20-10-43 222MU 8-11 *Mont City* 15-11 Casa 29-11 SOC 23-12-44

MJ279 33MU 5-11-43 82MU 11-11 *Fort Geo* 4-12 Casa 22-12

MJ280 ERD 39MU 23-10-43 82MU 8-11 *Fort Geo* 4-12 Casa 22-12 SOC 23-10-44

MJ281 33MU 17-10-43 129S 25-10 FACB 3-11 AST GAL 8-8-44 84GSU 23-8 302S 21-9 308S FTR ops 1-1-45

MJ282 33MU 20-10-43 222MU 8-11 *Mont City* 15-11 Casa 29-11 ME SOC 26-9-46

MJ283 33MU 24-10-43 405ARF 12-11 AST 25-5-44 83GSU 24-10 442S 28-12 401S 22-3-45 130S 17-5 ASTH 25-2-46 165S 12-9 FAF 1-5-47

MJ284 39MU 19-10-43 82MU 6-11 *Mont City* 15-11 Casa 29-11 SOC 31-12

MK959, painted as 'MJ289' in 167 Squadron colours, displayed at Eindhoven, Netherlands.

MJ285 9MU 3-11-43 322S 20-9-44 84GSU 9-11 327S 5-4-45 81RSU 19-4

MJ286 33MU 24-10-43 442S 13-3-44 17APC strk in rear by Martinet EM588 of 17APC CE South 23-5 602S 22-6 FTR ops 19-7

MJ287 39MU 24-10-43 411ARF 16-11 e/fd cd CE BH11 21-12 FH17.15

MJ288 39MU 24-10-43 405ARF 8-11 411S 21-11 FTR ops 1-12 FH20-.50

MJ289 33MU 24-10-43 405ARF 10-11 401S 21-11 83GSU 6-7-44 SAL 8-8 485S Apl'44 cd after sortie over Arnhem 30-9 GAL 3-11 mods *Taneli* 13-1-45 Casa 25-1 CE ops 13-4

MJ290 ERD 33MU 22-10-43 47MU 8-11 *Mont City* 15-11 Casa 29-11 25S C3 ops 3-3-44

MJ291 33MU 24-10-43 310S 24-1-44 84GSU 22-6 64S e/fd ldg app f/ld nr Harrow CE 11-7

MJ292 33MU 24-10-43 405ARF 10-11 39MU 7-4-44 83GSU 7-5 313S 8-6 412S 6-7 453S 28-9 MAAF 9-7-45 RHAF 30-1-47

MJ293 39MU 24-10-43 411ARF 16-11 317S 2-12 FACB 26-11 511FRU 13-12 313S 8-6-44 332S 15-6 420RSU 29-6 CB ops 8-8 DeH 16-8 MAAF 5-3-45 FTR ops 16-4

MJ294 33MU 23-1-44 349S 16-2 84GSU 15-6 mods 332S 15-6 602S 5-10 3APJ 15-4-45 MAAF 17-5 SOC 6-12

MJ295 33MU 24-10-43 405ARF 421S 6-7-44 127Wg HQ cd en route 10ADO CE 3-2

MJ296 39MU 24-10-43 411ARF 2-12 349S e/fd w/u ldg Boxing Farm West Dean Sussex CB 29-4-44 recat E

MJ297 39MU 27-10-43 47MU 11-11 *Fort Geo* 4-12 Casa 22-12 IAF 30-5-46 as MM4015

MJ298 39MU 24-10-43 76MU 14-11 *Fort Geo* 4-12 Casa 22-12 FAF 28-3-46

MJ299 39MU 24-10-43 411ARF 16-11 317S 2-12 332S FTR ops 8-3-44

MJ300 33MU 24-10-43 405ARF 21-11 FACB 3-3-44 AST 83GSU 30-6 412S 24-8 401S CE ops 2-10

MJ301 9MU 8-11-43 GAL 22-8-44 84GSU 10-9 441S FTR 1-11

MJ302 33MU 24-10-43 405ARF 8-11 412S 21-11 CE ops 28-1-44 FH72.5

MJ303 39MU 24-10-43 405ARF 8-11 412S 21-11 CAC ops 4-1-44 ROS 405RSU 9-2 602S FTR ops 10-5

MJ304 39MU 24-10-43 412S 23-11 FTR ops 2-8-44

MJ305 39MU 3-11-43 405ARF 21-11 118S FAAC 5-2-44 ROS 511FRU 8-6 602S 15-6 FTR ops 7-7

MJ306 33MU 24-10-43 405ARF 11-11 412S FTR ops 4-3-44 FH19

MJ307 33MU 24-10-43 405ARF 11-11 132S FTR ops 30-3-44

MJ308 39MU 24-10-43 52MU 8-11 *Mont City* 15-11 Casa 17-11 FTR ops 24-3-45

MJ309 39MU 1-10-43 405ARF 12-10 131S 8-11 165S 19-3-44 453S 11-4 33S coll with BS306 Mountfield Sussex CE 22-5

MJ310 33MU 7-10-43 405ARF 18-10 229S 29-5-44 ROS 6-6 WAL 8-6 recat E SOC 4-2-45

MJ311 M63 33MU 8-10-43 405ARF 18-10 501S 16-11 CAC ops 27-4-44 80S 29-5 FAAC 16-6 310S spun into grd from cloud St Michaels at Wade Braintree Essex 3-9 W/o Sv Kach kld

MJ312 39MU 15-10-43 405ARF 26-10 412S 21-11 CB ops 29-11 AST 83GSU 26-4-44 403S FACB 28-5 AST 412S 23-11 FTR ops 21-1-45

RDAF 407, ex PL375, entered service in February 1949.

MJ313 39MU 16-10-43 401S 21-11 411S 22-6-44 410RSU 12-7 126S 2-9 SAL 21-2-45 sold Turk 26-6-47

MJ314 39MU 16-10-43 405ARF 27-10 302S 21-11 CAC 21-4-44 274S FAAC 15-5 ROS FLS Mlfld 21-8 SOC 16-10-46

MJ328 M63 33MU 20-10-43 82MU 8-11 *Fort Geo* 4-12 Casa 22-12 SOC 29-8-46

MJ329 ERD 33MU 23-10-43 405ARF 8-11 412S 23-11 FAAC 20-3-44 MAL 18-7 410RSU 2-11 ASTE 9-2-45 to 6370M 10-7-47 RDAF 15-7-47 34MU Scrap 10-47

MJ330 ERD 24-10-43 222MU 9-11 *Fort Geo* 4-12 Casa 22-12 208S FTR ops 7-4-44

MJ331 33MU 24-10-43 405ARF 8-11 412S 21-11 FTR over e/tr 29-11 FH19.5

MJ332 33MU 24-10-43 GAL 8-8-44 84GSU 25-8 308S 19-10 CAC ops 5-12 409RSU 14-12 sold BAF 18-11-47 as SM-14

MJ333 33MU 24-10-43 129S 8-11 453S 15-6-44 421S 26-7 410RSU 28-9 MAL 5-10 MAAF 16-2-45 RHAF 31-7-47

MJ334 33MU 25-10-43 411ARF 17-11 412S 22-6-44 410RSU 12-7 443S 5-10 CAC ops 23-10-43 411S CE ops 20-4

MJ335 9MU 31-10-43 52MU 2-11 *SS268* 20-12 Hap 9-1-45

MJ336 9MU 31-10-43 82MU 14-11 *Emp Arch* 12-12 Hap 9-1-45

MJ337 9MU 2-11-43 82MU 13-11-44 *Emp Arch* 12-12 Hap 9-1-45

MJ338 9MU 31-10-43 3501SU 13-6-44 229S 28-6 359S CAC ops 7-7 ROS GF Gat 2-9 453S 26-10 2APU Filton 2-6-45 MAAF 25-6 SOC 26-9-46

MJ339 33MU 3-11-43 405ARF 13-11 FACB 13-5-44 602S FTR ops 7-6 (w/u ldg Normandy beach head) ASTH 30-7 1ATC 10-8 MAAF 7-4-45 SOC 30-8

MJ340 9MU 2-11-43 83GSU 28-8-44 443S 5-10 401S 1-2-45 130S 17-5 WAL 18-6 sold R J Coley 3-2-50

MJ341 AST 33MU 7-3-45 MMO 21-3 FAF 31-7-46

MJ342 9MU 16-11-43 GAL 25-3-44 84GSU 12-9 308S 19-10 CB ops 3-2-45

MJ343 9MU 29-11-43 3501SU 13-6-44 322S FTR ops 1-9

MJ344 9MU 29-11-43 313S FACE 26-4-44 441S 405RSU 403S 15-10 CB ops 19-11 AST sold Turk 17-1-47

MJ345 39MU 22-11-43 222MU 6-12 *Fan Head* 24-12 Casa 8-1-44 MAAF 31-1 81rsu 12-4-45 326S 10-5 FAF 27-11

MJ346 9MU 14-11-43 222MU 26-5-44 83GSU 23-8 AST 27-9 411S 28-9 132S 5-10 326S 5-4-45 FAF 4-12

MJ347 39MU 23-11-43 416S 31-1-44 CE ops 1-6

MJ348 33MU 17-11-43 83GSU 13-3-44 127Wg HQ 22-6 403S 27-7 CB ops 14-8 410RSU 17-8 421S 5-10 327S 5-4-45 81RSU 3-5 SNCAN 17-5 CG1/1 Cd 3-12-48

MJ349 39MU 23-11-43 222MU 15-12 *Fan Head* 24-12 Casa 8-1-44 MAAF 31-1 USAAF 29-2 RAF 31-5 73S SOC 30-4-47

MJ350 33MU 17-11-43 84GSU 25-5-44 401S 22-6 410RSU 29-6 412S 6-7 CE ops 14-8 recat B 17-8

MJ351 39MU 23-11-43 340S 13-2-44 84GSU 13-7 mr 28-12 414S FTR ops 19-3-45

MJ352 39MU 23-11-43 421S 5-2-44 403S FACE 12-4

MJ353 33MU 25-11-43 349S 16-2-44 CAC ops 11-6 GAL 15-12 mods 129S 17-5-45 sold BAF 17-8-47 as SM-2 w/o 17-5-50

MJ354 33MU 27-6-44 47MU 9-7 *Samm A A* 17-7 Hap 27-7

MJ355 LFIXB 33MU 25-11-43 405ARF 11-2-44 11-2-44 403S fail to pull out of dive bomb pract strk MJ820 CE 25-3 FH50.25

MJ356 LFIXB 39MU 23-11-43 421S 5-2-44 403S FTR ops 8-3 FH30 cancel recat AC 83GSU 3-3-45 FAF cd 1-2-49

MJ357 33MU 25-11-43 222MU 20-1-44 *Euryb* 2-3 Hap 23-4 Basr 6-5

MJ358 39MU 23-11-43 222MU 15-12 *Fan Head* 24-12 Casa 8-1-44 MAAF 31-1 CE ops 1-7 recat A 28-4-45 IAF 30-5-46 as MM4021

MJ359 45MU 8-5-44 AST 26-5 410RSU 6-8 FACE 15-8

MJ360 9MU 29-11-43 222MU 26-5-44 322S 20-9 327S 5-4-45 FAF 27-11 GC1/1

MJ361 33MU 20-11-43 313S 16-2-44 84GSU 29-6 322S 16-8 AST 5-12 COAL 15-5-45 mods 29MU 15-5-46 RNAF 25-11 as H-20

MJ362 33MU 30-11-43 222MU 20-1-44 *Euryb* 2-3 Hap 23-4 Basr 6-5

MJ363 33MU 30-11-43 84GSU 24-3-44 341S 8-6 421RSU 29-6 341S 6-7 CAC ops 3-3-45 414S 22-3 39Recce S 26-4 130S 17-5 SOC 30-11

MJ364 no record

MJ365 8MU 19-5-44 MAL 6-6 308S 22-6 1ATC 24-8 MAAF 26-2-45 SOC 2-8

MJ366 33MU 30-11-43 443S 11-3-44 CAC ops 27-6 410RSO 29-6 453S 23-11 *Farele* 5-1-45 Casa 25-1 SOC 16-2 bboc 16-8 SOC 5-2-48

MJ367 33MU 2-12-43 82MU 23-12 *Lds City* 21-1-44 Casa 17-2 CE ops 6-9

MJ368 39MU 2-12-43 47MU *Fan Head* 24-12 Casa 8-1-44 MAAF 31-1 SOC 18-8

MJ369 33MU 19-12-43 349S 16-2-44 ROS 16-4 416S 28-9 WAL 2-3-45 sold Turk 22-7-47

MJ382 9MU 6-11-43 GAL 31-8-44 83GSU 26-9 401S 18-11 CAC ops 19-11 HAL 139S 29-7-46 257S 3-10 FCCS 30-7-48 sold J Dale 30-6-49

MJ383 39MU 5-11-43 47MU 19-11 *Fort Geo* 4-12 Casa 22-12 FTR ops 27-9

MJ384 39MU 30-10-43 405ARF 11-11- 411S 21-11 421S FTR ops 17-6-44

MJ385 39MU 3-10-43 405ARF 12-11 401S CE ops 10-5-44

MJ386 9MU 5-11-43 83GSU 26-8-44 412S 14-9 FAAC 21-9 401S 28-9 CAC ops 29-1-45 ASTH sold Turk 3-11-47

MJ387 9MU 3-11-43 83GSU 26-8-44 416S 28-9 CAC ops 22-11 443S 14-12 WAL 8-10-45 sold Turk 7-8-47

MJ388 slave eng instal 9MU 3-11-43 229S FAAC 29-6-44 83GSU 29-8 403S 5-10 443S 14-12 411S 17-5-45 WAL 22-6 sold Turk 10-4-47

MJ389 39MU 27-10-43 47MU 11-11-*Fort Geo* 4-12 Casa 22-12 USAAF 29-2-44 RAF 31-5 SOC 30-6

MJ390 9MU 6-11-43 GAL 31-8-44 83GSU 26-9 401S 18-11 3BRU CE 17-9-45

MJ391 39MU 3-11-43 411ARF 1 2-11 317S 25-1-44 332S 8-6 GAL 29-11 mods MAAF 15-3-45 ME 16-8 RHAF 27-2-47

MJ392 39MU 3-11-43 405ARF 12-11 421 S 6-7-44 SAL 10-10 MAAF 15-4-45 NWA 18-4 ME SOC 31-10-46

MJ393 9MU 3-11-43 83GSU 26-8-44 401S 21-9 412S FAAC 3-10 ROS 453S 26-10 MAAF 25-5-45 ME 23-8 325 FACE f/fld of t.o Ramat David Palestine 5-7-46 SOC 29-8

MJ394 9MU 5-11-43 83GSU 26-8-44 421S 7-9

MJ395 9MU 3-11-43 83GSU 23-5-44 317S 11-1-45 411RSU 29-3 326S 28-6 SNCAN 16-8

MJ396 9MU 6-11-43 MAL 27-6-44 83GSU 1-8 308S 17-8 317S 22-3-45 ASTH 24-5 sold Turk 20-3-47

MJ397 9MU 3-11-43 GAL 17-9-44 83GSU 9-10 442S CE ops 29-10

MJ398 39MU 3-11-43 132S 20-11 602S 15-6-44 453S 6-7 602S 20-7 FTR f/ld France after attack by Mustangs 17-8

MJ399 9MU 3-11-43 MAL 27-6-44 83GSU 19-8 308S 14-9 411RSU 19-10 SOC 9-2-45

MJ400 9MU 5-11-43 82MU 13-11-44 *Emp Arch* 12-12 Hap 9-1-45

MJ401 33MU 3-11-43 82MU 11-11 *Fort Geo* 4-12 Casa 22-12 43S FTR ops 31-5-44

MJ402 9MU 3-11-43 CRD VA 18-4-44 9MU less mainplanes 23-4 ROS 14-6 MAAF 10-2-45 SOC 20-9

MJ403 39MU 27-10-43 405ARF 8-11 412S 21-11 e/fd f/ld Seddlescombe nr Hastings 22-3-44

MJ404 39MU 3-11-43 411ARF 2-12 Flt Refuel 3-11 mods RAF South 18-2 17APC SAL 25-7 39MU 5-1-45 MAAF 16-2 IAF 20-6-47 as MM4098

MJ405 slave eng instal 9MU 3-11-43 83GSU 29-8-44 FACE 22-2-45

MJ406 33MU 3-11-43 47MU 14-11 *Fort Geo* 4-12 Casa 22-12

MJ407 39MU 3-11-43 47MU 15-11 *Fan Head* 24-12 Casa 8-1-44 MAAF 31-1 SOC 18-8

MJ408 slave eng instal 9MU 3-11-43 83GSU 7-10-44 327S 5-11-45 81RSU 12-4 FAF 27-11 GC2/7

MJ409 9MU 6-11-43 441S 30-11-44 WAL 17-3-45 sold RNofAF 10-9-48

MJ410 33MU 5-11-43 47MU 14-11 *Fort Geo* 4-12 Casa 22-12 SOC 23-10-44

MJ411 9MU 5-11-43 GAL 18-8-44 84GSU 10-9 417S 23-9 1S FAAC 13-3-45 FACE 3-8 SOC 24-8

MJ412 9MU 5-11-43 83GSU 26-8-44 46S 14-9 410RSU 28-9 a/c reported FTR 25-9 wrk found Arnhem. pilot dead but was identified. To 402 Research & Eng Unit Oct'46

MJ413 9MU 5-11-43 FACE 7-8-44

MJ414 9MU 5-11-43 83GSU 26-8-44 416S 23-9 MAAF 10-3-45 SOC 20-9

MJ415 9MU 5-11-43 322S 5-9-44 328S 5-4-45 81 RSU 30-8 SNCAN 7-9 FAF GC1/3

MJ416 33MU 5-11-43 47MU 15-11 *Fan Head* 24-12 Casa 8-1-44 MAAF 31-1 ME 2-8-45 FAF 25-7-46

MJ417 39MU 5-11-43 411ARF 19-11 132S FTR ops 28-5-44

MJ418 9MU 3-11-43 GAL 8-8-44 84GSU 25-8 308S 19-10 FACB 19-1-45 ASTH SNCAN 5-7-45 sold RNorAF 16-6-47

MJ419 9MU 5-11-43 3501SU 21-6-44 441S FTR ops 6-8

MJ420 9MU 5-11-43 AST 31-5-44 441S 10-8 419RSU 20-8 511FRU 22-8 AST 29-8 MAAF 7-2-45 SOC 13-12

MJ421 9MU 2-11-43 AFDU COAL 7-4-45 mods CFE Tang 10-5 R-RH 20-6 HAL 22-10 sold BAF 26-8-47 as SM-9 w/o 4-8-50

MJ422 9MU 5-11-43 3501SU 17-6-44 1S 22-6 CE ops 30-7

MJ423 9MU 3-11-43 GAL 25-8-44 84GSU 14-9 317S 2-11 84Gp ARF 22-3-45 327S 19-4-45 339 French Wg 2-8 327S 9-8 328S 3-10 FAF 4-12

MJ424 9MU 3-11-43 405ARF 21-11 118S FACB 5-2-44 AST 350S CAC ops 14-7 ROS AST 31-8 MAAF 3-3-45 SOC 19-7

MJ425 9MU 5-11-43 GAL 9-9-44 83GSU 30-9 442S 12-10 411S 22-3-45 130S 17-5 WAL 31-5 sold VA 8-12-49

MJ426 33MU 5-11-43 82MU 11-11 *Fort Geo* 4-12 Casa 22-12 CE ops 4-1-45 bboc MAAF 21-6 SOC 14-346

MJ427 33MU 5-11-43 47MU 14-11 *Fort Geo* 4012 Casa 22012 MAAF 21-6-45 SOC 20-9

MJ428 9MU 5-11-43 401S FTR ops 29-6-44

MJ441 9MU 6-11-43 83GSU 29-8-44 442S 14-9 602S 28-9 1ADF Redhill FAAC 8-1-45

MJ442 33MU 25-11-43 222MU 14-12 *Fan Head* 24-12 Casa 8-1-44 MAAF 31-1 C3 ops 12-8

MJ443 9MU 12-11-43 83GSU 23-8-44 421S 12-10 6MU 21-12 FAF des 12-10-50

MJ444 9MU 5-11-43 83GSU 26-8-44 411S 21-9 410RSU 28-9 403 19-10 443S 14-12 FTR 18-1-45

MJ445 33MU 25-11-43 47MU *Fan Head* 24-12 Casa

MJ452, France, 1944, in the colours of 412 Squadron.

8-1-44 MAAF 31-1 FAC3 16-2 SOC 31-3-45

MJ446 9MU 5-11-43 GAL 25-8-44 83GSU 18-9 441S CAC ops 25-9 419RSU 28-9 1FU Persh 10-6-45 MAAF 25-6 RHAF 27-2-47

MJ447 39MU 5-11-43 47MU 16-11 *Fort Geo* 4-12 Casa 22-12 71MU ROS 27-2-44 USAAF RAF 31-5 SOC 18-8

MJ448 9MU 7-11-43 83GSU 29-8-44 401S 21-9 CB ops 1-3-45 ASTH sold Turk 2-5-47

MJ449 39MU 8-11-43 222MU 19-11 *Fort Geo* 4-12 Casa 22-12 MAAF 21-6-45 SOC 22-11

MJ450 39MU 7-11-43 411ARF 2-12 Flt Refuel Ltd 31-1-44 RAF Southend 18-2 17APC e/fd u/s South CE 19-4

MJ451 39MU8-11-43 411ARF 19-11 443S 13-3-44 431S 15-6 84GSU 21-7 34Wg Sprt Unit Prep flt 27-7 38S 4-1-45 CAAC 19-2 sold VA 30-10-46 con to two-seat train 26-5-48

MJ452 9MU 1-11-43 GAL 29-8-44 83GSU 9-9 412S 23-11 130S 17-5-45 ASTH to 6081M 15-8-46 5SoTT 26-6-47 SOC rtga

MJ453 9MU 29-11-43 222MU 26-5-44 GAL 25-8 83GSU 18-9 441S 28-9 CE 16-11

MJ454 39MU 7-11-43 411ARF 2-12 411S 22-6-44 410RSU 29-6-44 64S 6-8 FTR ops 8-6-45

MJ455 33MU 16-11-43 443S 13-3-44 FTR ops 8-6

MJ456 33MU 14-11-43 84GSU 5-5 412S 22-6 CAC ops AST 308S 4-1-45 317S 22-3 328S 31-5 327S 3-10 FAF 4-12

MJ457 9MU 83GSU 29-8-44 401S 14-9 442S 28-9 602S 28-9 328S 17-5-45 FAF 4-12

MJ458 9MU 13-11-43 MAL 27-6-44 83GSU 19-8 302S 21-9 308S 5-10 411RSU 8-2-45 CB ops 24-2 317S 12-4 81RSU 31-5 326S 28-6 FAF 4-12 GC2/1

MJ459 9MU 7-11-43 82MU 11-11-44 *Fort High* Hap 8-12

MJ460 9MU 10-11-43 322S 9-9-44 CE ops 16-9

MJ461 9MU 8-11-43 83GSU 23-8 412S 21-9-44 FAAC 29-9 ROS GAL 29-11 MAAF 12-5-45 SOC 14-3-46

MJ462 39MU 7-11-43 29MU 7-11 FAAC 15-11 Farn Mar'44 66S 8-6 453S 5-10 3501SU 9-10 2APU 7-6-45 MAAF 26-6 ME 26-7 REAF 26-9-46

MJ463 9MU 13-11-43 GAL 9-9-44 83GSU 6-10 442S24-10 410RSU 29-3-45 FTR 27-3

MJ464 9MU 13-11-43 AST 20-6-44 84GSU 6-7 441S 17-8 FAAC 21-9 409RSU 26-10 442S 25-1-45 CAC ops 22-3 FTR 24-2

MJ465 9MU 6-11-43 83GSU 7-10-44 326S 5-4-45 FAF 4-12 GC1/1

MJ466 9MU 10-11-43 GAL 30-8-44 442S 19-10 CE ops 28-10

MJ467 9MU 13-11-43 GAL 19-6-44 83GSU 19-8 308S 31-8 CE ops 1-1-45

MJ468 33MU 16-11-43 405ARF 24-2-44 411S FAAC 410RSU 29-6 411S 13-7 AST 22-9 MAAF 20-4-45 ME 2-8 RHAF 27-3-47

MJ469 9MU 8-11-43 GAL 25-8-44 469S CAC ops 26-11 RNAF 30-7-46 as H-9 322S w/o 22-2-52

MJ470 9MU 10-11-43 GAL 29-8-44 412S 23-11 CAC ops 29-12 412S 11-1-45 CB ops 8-2-45 sold H Baty 10-11-49

MJ471 33MU 14-11-43 442S 13-3-44 602S 28-9 WAL 14-10 331S 30-4-45

MJ472 33MU 22-11-43 82MU 3-12 *Lds City* 21-1-44 Casaa 17-2 SOC 31-5-45

MJ473 33MU 15-11-43 84GSU 23-3 441S CE ops 5-5

MJ474 9MU 30-11-43 83GSU 20-5-44 411S 22-6 CAC ops 18-8 411S 28-9 132S 5-10 SAL 4-1-45 MAAF 2-6 RHAF 30-1-47

MJ475 39MU 13-11-43 GAL 8-8-44 308S 19-10 317S 29-8-45 326S 31-5 FAF 4-12 GC2/7

MJ476 33MU 18-11-43 84GSU 23-3-44 331S 8-6 453S 1-10 3501SU 9-11 FCCS North 31-5-45 sold VA 5-12-48

MJ477 33MU 16-11-43 129S 29-12 504S 3-3-44 310S 8-6 441S 13-7 443S 24-8 83GSU Com S 1-3-45 MAL 6-3 sold R J Coley 9-2-50

MJ478 9MU 13-11-43 83GSU 28-8-44 127Wg HQ 31-8 421S 21-12 326S 5-4-45 FAF GC1/4

MJ479 9MU 29-11-43 52MU 26-5-44 GAL 25-8 401S 12-10 FACB 9-12 FACB f/f to 39MU 14-3-45 RNAF 12-7-46 as H-10 w/u 10-7-53

MJ480 33MU 14-11-43 405ARF 11-2-44 403S CE ops 19-5

MJ481 9MU 29-11-43 3501SU 17-6-44 1S 26-6 FTR ops 28-9

MJ482 9MU 13-11-43 MAL 27-6-44 83GSU 19-8 131Wg HQ 31-8 317S CB ops 14-10 4FSCU Duce 17-5-45 165S 66S 2-9-46 sold BAF 10-7-48 as SM-19

MJ483 39MU 15-11-43 47MU 24-11 *Fort Geo* 4-12 Casa 22-12 43S FTR ops 4-5-44

MJ484 33MU 22-11-43 84GSU 23-3-44 MAL 30-11 129S 16-5-45 FACE 8-11

MJ502, 'Prince Tongi Tonga No. II'.

MJ485 33MU 14-11-43 84GSU 23-3-44 412S 22-6 FTR 12-8

MJ498 39MU 24-11-43 341S 9-2-44 FTR ops 22-6 bboc 84GSU 9-7 402S 11-8

MJ499 33MU 25-11-43 84GSU 23-3 312S out of fuel cd attempt ldg CE Portsmouth 11-6 413RSU 15-6

MJ500 9MU 12-11-43 GAL 29-8-44 FAAC 21-9 ROS 10ADU 19-1-45 FACB 25-2 ASTH 23-5 FAF 13-8-46

MJ501 9MU 17-11-43 AST 6-6-44 317S 22-6 ROS 12-9 AST 22-9 MAAF 5-4-45 CE ops 20-4

MJ502 Prince Tongi Tonga No II 33MU 17-11-43 485S 20-1-44 349S 8-6 332S 22-6 SAL 6-12 MAAF 5-4-45 CE ops 14-4 SOC 14-6

MJ503 33MU 15-11-43 308S 3-5-44 84GSU 22-6 132S CAC ops 7-7 453S 20-7 FTR ops 27-7

MJ504 9MU 17-11-43 441S 29-6-44 421S 5-10 e/a 21-10 412S 15-2-45 CE ops 28-4

MJ505 39MU 23-11-43 82MU 3-12 *Fan Head* 24-12 Casa 8-1-44 MAAF 31-1 USAAF 29-2 FACE 3-6

MJ506 33MU 22-11-43 82MU 3-12 *Fan Head* 24-12 Casa 8-1-44 MAAF 31-1 USAAF 29-2 RAF 31-5 SOC Oct'44

MJ507 9MU 29-11-43 GAL 29-6-44 308S CAC ops 6-9 411RSU 21-12 MAAF 1-6-45 RHAF 27-2-47

MJ508 33MU 22-11-43 222MU 20-1-44 *Eury* 2-3 Hap 23-4 Bas 6-5

MJ509 39MU 18-11-43 310S CAC 15-5-44 ROS recat E 18-9

MJ510 39MU 28-11-43 222MU 27-1-44 *Eury* 2-3 Hap 23-4 Bas 6-5

MJ511 39MU 23-11-43 222MU *Lds City* 21-1-44 Casa 17-2 237S FTR ops 26-5

MJ512 33MU 22-11-43 222MU 3-12 *Fan Head* 24-12 Casa 8-1-44 MAAF 31-1 FACE 12-12-45 SOC 28-2-46

MJ513 33MU 22-11-43 222MU 30-11 *Fan Head* 24-12 Casa 8-1-44 MAAF 31-1 SOC Oct 44

MJ514 33MU 25-11-43 84GSU 25-5-44 443S CE 25-7

MJ515 33MU 22-11-43 442S 13-3-44 WAL 14-10 1APU 3-5-45 MAAF 26-5 SOC 6-12

MJ516 33MU 17-11-43 340S 20-1-44 e/fd after t/o i/ sea off Perr FTR 25-2 FH25.25

MJ517 9MU 29-11-43 215MU 5-9-44 Stn HQ Mans 5-10 151RU 2-8-45 3BRU CE 29-6-46

MJ518 33MU 22-11-43 340S 7-2-44 84GSU 13-7 414S 6-8 CAC ops 2-11 ASTH 3-2-45 sold VA 30-11-46 con to two-seat train 11-5-48

MJ519 33MU 22-11-43 410ARF 11-2-44 441S FTR ops 25-4 cancel 401S CB ops 1-7 410RSU 6-7 MAAF 2-8-45 RHAF 27-3-47

MJ520 9MU 17-11-43 132S 15-6-44 442S 15-6 421RSU 22-6 442S 27-7 CAC 18-8 ASTE 5-2-45 FAF 12-9-46 GC1/2 des Indo-China 1-6-47

MJ521 9MU 29-11-43 350S 350S 9-7-44 322S 4-9 MAAF 12-4 FTR ops 2-5-45

MJ522 39MU 2-12-43 341S 23-2-44 CAC ops 17-6 ROS 421RSU 13-8 602S 28-10 SAL 6-2-45 MAAF 21-6 RHAF 30-1-47

MJ523 33MU 22-11-43 222MU 14-12 *Fan Head* 24-12 Casa 8-1-44 MAAF 31-1-44 SOC 13-12-45

MJ524 39MU 29-11-43 329S 28-2-44 84GSU 6-7 CAC ops 23-9 recat E 20-11

MJ525 39MU 30-11-43 82MU 15-12 *Fan Head* 24-12 Casa 8-1-44 MAAF 31-1 USAAF 29-2 IAF 27-6-46 as MM4087

MJ526 33MU 22-11-43 222MU 3-12 *Fan Head* 24-12 Casa 8-1-44 MAAF 31-1 to 6079M 15-8-46

MJ527 39MU 24-11-43 82MU 23-12 *Lds City* 21-1-44 Casa 17-2 IAF 26-6-47 as MM4127

MJ528 33MU 22-11-43 442S 13-3-44 CAC ops 28-6 602S 28-9 326S 5-4-45

MJ529 9MU 30-11-43 GAL 29-6-44 403S CAC ops 18-8 340S FACE 25-8 AST recatE 18-9

MJ530 39MU 30-11-43 310S 8-3-44 313S 18-3 FACB 15-6 SAL GAL 31-10 458S 11-1-45 332S 1-3 74S 17-5 81 RSU 2-6 327S 31-5 228S 4-10 FAF 4-12

MJ531 39MU 19-12-43 82MU 18-1-44 *Eury* 2-3 Hap 23-4 Bas 6-5

MJ532 33MU 22-12-43 82MU 16-1-44 *Fort Lrd* 1-3 Casa 17-3 FTR ops 27-12

MJ533 39MU 23-11-43 82MU 30-12 *Fort Geo* 4-12 Casa 22-12 FTR ops 15-4-45

MJ534 39MU 24-11-43 331S 5-2-44 FTR ops 25-2

MJ535 39MU 2-12-43 82MU 15-12 *Fan Head* 24-12 Casa 8-1-44 MAAF 31-1- SOC 14-3-46

MJ536 39MU 24-12-43 411S 29-6-44 CB ops 2-9 410RSU 28-9 RNAF 19-5-47 as H-66 later H-106 w/o 10-48

MJ549 33MU 2-12-43 82MU 27-12 *Co Lds* 26-1-44 Casa 17-2 SOC 15-3-45

MJ550 39MU 18-3-44 52MU 16-4 *Afghan* 12-5 Hap 5-7

MJ551 39MU 2-12-43 331S 27-1-46 FAAC 23-4-44 AST 19-10

MJ552 39MU 2-12-43 47MU 15-12 *Fan Head* 24-12 Casa 8-1-44 MAAF 31-1 USAAF 29-2 RAF 31-5 CE ops 3-7

MJ553 33MU 12-12-43 312S 4-2-44 414S 10-8 CE ops 7-11

MJ554 33MU 12-12-43 412S 26-1-44 CE ops 7-6

MJ555 9MU 19-12-43 52MU 4-11-44 *Fort Mass* 11-11 Hap 8-12

MJ557 8MU 24-4-44 MAL 17-5 mods 308S 15-6 410RSU AST 26-8 WAL 28-12 MAAF 23-2-45 SOC 20-9

MJ558 33MU 12-12-43 313S 24-1-44 FTR ops 19-4

MJ559 8MU 24-4-44 84GSU 22-5 66S 8-6 416S CAC 18-7 1ATC 7-9 AST 20-9 BAF 1-9-48 as SM-22

MJ560 33MU 19-12-43 52MU 17-4-44 *Inver* 6-5 Hap 6-7

MJ561 33MU 22-12-43 416S 26-1-44 FAAC 28-4 410S FACB AST 341S 8-6 222MU *Guinean* 20-12 Casa 15-1-45 IAF 26-6-47 as MM4131 (lost over France 18-11-44 USAAF 9-1 records)

MJ562 33MU 19-12-43 82MU 30-1-44 *Fort Lrd* 1-3 Casa 17-3 SOC 20-9-45

MJ563 39MU 25-1-44 405ARF 11-2 403S CB ops 8-3 AST 411S 24-8 401S 31-8 501S CE ops 22-9

MJ564 33MU 12-12-43 341S 29-1-44 ROS 3-4 84GSU 24-7 FAF 12-11 GR2/33

MJ565 46MU 27-4-44 MAL 14-6 401S 10-8 AST 16-10 3APU 10-5-45 MAAF 16-7 SOC 28-8-47

MJ566 33MU 21-12-43 410ARF 11-2-44 410S FAAC 7-5 126S 6-8 FAAC ROS MAL 23-2-45 sold Turk 15-4-47

MJ567 33MU 22-12-43 331S 26-1-44 CAC ops 27-4 ROS 331S 20-5 CB ops 83Gp Com S 29-6 e/a CE 1-1-45 ASTH sold Turk 9-10-47

MJ568 39MU 1-5-44 52MU 13-5 *Arabis* 29-6 Bas 12-8

MJ569 33MU 19-12-43 349S 16-2-44 CAC ops 25-4 421S 29-6 CE ops 26-11

MJ570 39MU 24-12-43 403S 5-2-44 CE ops 14-7

MJ571 33MU 22-12-43 312S 31-1-44 FACB 17-3 317S 24-8 411RSU 19-10 MAAF 10-3-45 IAF 26-6-47 as MM4102

MJ572 33MU 22-12-43 84GSU 13-3 312S FAAC 30-4 SAL 312S 22-7-45 sold Czechslovakia 30-8-45

MJ573 39MU 24-12-43 222MU 7-1-44 *Lds City* 21-1 Casa 17-2 ME SOC 26-9-46

MJ574 39MU 24-12-43 82MU 8-1-44 *Lds City* 21-1 Casa 17-2 FACE 7-8-45 SOC 22-11

MJ575 39MU 24-11-43 403S 31-1-44 421S CAC ops 7-5 416S 27-7 CAC ops 26-9 AST 33MU 19-6-45 sold Turk 2-9-47

MJ576 33MU 30-11-43 222MU 20-1-44 *Eury* 2-3 Hap 23-4 Bas 6-5 MJ577 39MU 4-12-43 47MU 18-12 *Fan Head* 24-12 Casa 8-1-44 MAAF 31-1- USAAF 29-2 ME 5-7-45 RHAF 29-5-47

MJ578 39MU 24-11-43 47MU 18-12 *Fan Head* 24-12Casa 8-1-44 MAAF 31-1 SOC 11-4-46

MJ579 33MU 22-11-43 82MU 3-12 *Fan Head* 24-12 Casa 8-1-44 MAAF 31-1 USAAF 29-2 SOC 14-3-46

MJ580 9MU 29-11-43 165S 22-6-44 ASTH 12-2-45 RNAF 27-10-48

MJ581 39MU 23-11-43 66S 7-3-44 FAAC 14-6 421RSU 15-6 ROS 326S 5-4-45

MJ582 33MU 25-11-43 222MU 14-12 *Fan Head* 24-12 Casa 8-1-44 MAAF 31-1 USAAF 29-2

MJ583 39MU 29-11-43 331S 23-1-44 84GSU 25-7

MJ584 9MU 29-11-43 84GSU 26-5-44 132S 15-6 441S 10-8 ROS 14-12 SAL 13-3-45 VASM 30-10-46 sold

MJ585 39MU 29-11-43 82MU 23-12 *Lds City* 21-1-44 Casa 17-2 FTR ops 22-2-45

MJ586 9MU 30-11-43 84GSU 26-5-44 602S 15-6 127Wg HQ 17-8 FAAC 14-9 AST 29-12 4FSCU Dyce 17-5-45 165S 7-6 FACB e/fld f/ld disused airfield Northamstead 17-5-46 to 5948M 4SoTT 4-6-46

MJ587 33MU 25-11-43 47MU 15-12 *Fan Head* 24-12 Casa 8-1-44 MAAF 31-1 IAF 26-6-47 as MM4019

MJ588 33MU 25-11-43 47MU 15-12 *Fan Head* 24-12 Casa 8-1-44 MAAF 31-1 CE ops 18-3-45 recat A 28-4

MJ589 9MU 4-12-43 GAL 25-8-44 302S 19-10 317S 26-10 CB ops 18-3-45 sold Turk 16-10-47

MJ602 39MU 29-12-43 341S 31-1-44 CE ops 17-3 FH33.25

MJ603 33MU 10-1-44 82MU 31-1 *Fort Lrd* 1-3 Casa 17-3 MAAF 21-6-45 SOC 30-8

MJ604 39MU 24-11-43 410ARF 13-2-44 84Gp Com S FAAC 9-6 ROS GAL 2-9 83GSU 4-10 401S 18-11 FACE 20-11

MJ605 39MU 2-12-43 310S 27-1-44 602S 6-7 441S 10-8 411S 31-8 412S 7-9 453S 28-9 327S 5-4-45 FAF 27-11

MJ606 39MU 29-11-43 82MU 20-1-44 *Eury* 2-3-44 Hap 23-4 Bas 6-5

MJ607 33MU 13-12-43 82MU 23-1-44 *Eury* 2-3 Hap 23-4 Bas 6-5

MJ608 33MU 24-11-43 442S 13-3-44 CE ops 7-6

MJ609 39MU 30-11-43 82MU 15-12 *Fan Head* 24-12 Casa 8-1-44 MAAF 31-1 FTR ops 20-4-45

MJ610 9MU 30-11-43 82MU 28-5-44 *Arabis* 16-6 Hap 29-6 Bas 12-9

MJ611 9MU 30-11-43 416S CAC ops 10-7-44 410RSU 13-7 127WG 5-10 MAAF 25-5-45 SOC 28-8-47

MJ612 9MU 30-11-43 84GSU 26-5-44 313S 8-6 GAL 12-12 mods sold R J Coley 6-2-50

MJ613 33MU 26-11-43 47MU 21-12 *Lds City* 21-1-44 Casa 12-2 FACE 29-10 ME 31-5-45 MAAF 30-6 SOC 2-8

MJ614 9MU 30-11-43 322S 10-7-44 414S 15-3-45 429MU 29-7 RNAF 3-10-46 as H-2 w/o 27-8-50

MJ615 33MU 12-12-43 222MU 30-12 *Lds City* 21-1-44 Casa 17-2 SOC 28-4-45

MJ616 33MU 24-4-43 341S 29-1-44 touched down short of runway u/c torn off CE Perr 20-3 FH47.20

MJ617 39MU 29-11-43 341S 31-1-44 FAAC 10-6 421RSU 15-6 414S 10-8 DeH 8-2-45 BAF 1-9-48 as SM-23 w/o 25-6-52

MJ618 39MU 24-11-43 82MU 13-12 *Fan Head* 24-12 Casa 8-1-44 MAAF 31-1 SOC 31-4 recat A 31-1-45 SOC 20-9

MJ619 9MU 30-11-43 84GSU 26-5-44 414S CAC ops 11-12 409RSU 14-12 CB ops 28-3-45 FAF GC1/1

MJ620 39MU 30-11-43 82MU 15-12 *Fan Head* 24-12 Casa 8-1-44 MAAF 31-1 C3 ops 2-6

MJ621 33MU 4-12-43 222MU 13-12 *Fan Head* 24-12 Casa 8-1-44 SOC 14-3-46

MJ622 9MU 16-12-43 52MU 21-11-44 *Thom Scott* 18-12 Hap 9-1-45

MJ623 39MU 4-1-44 310S 27-1 ROS 17-3 33S 16-5 126S 17-6 91S 16-11 FTR ops 9-3-45

MJ624 39MU 24-11-43 47MU 18-12 *Fan Head* 24-12 Casa 8-1-44 MAAF 31-1 REAF 26-9-46

MJ625 39MU 13-12-43 82MU 26-12 *Lds City* 21-1-44 Casa 17-2 ME 31-5-45 MAAF 20-6 SOC 2-8

MJ626 33MU 2-12-43 47MU 20-12 *Lds City* 21-1-44 Casa 17-2 SOC 18-8

MJ627 9MU 4-12-43 GAL 18-8-44 441S 28-9 FACE 9-3-45 bboc recat B 11-9 AST sold VA as NEA 19-7-50 con to Type 509 two-seat train (T9). IAC 5-6-51 as 158 Apl'60 to G-ASOZ sold Film Aviation Services 13-11-63. Stor BH11 dismantled Feb'64. Wings to Belgium 1-4-64 for MJ772. Sep'64 sold T A Davies as spares for Spit G-ASJV. Mar'65 reg G-ASOZ cancel rts Elstree for G-ASJV. Wings sent to Belgium mated to fus of BAF 159 extant UK G-BMSB

MJ628 39MU 2-12-43 82MU 23-12 *Lds City* 26-1-44 Casa 17-2 CE ops 28-7

MJ629 39MU 29-11-43 82MU 13-12 *Fan Head* 24-12 Casa 8-1-44 MAAF 31-1- ME 28-12 SOC 30-4-47

MJ630 9MU 30-11-43 GAL 17-8-44 317S 19-10 411RSU 2-11 MAAF 12-5-45 IAF 26-6-47 as MM4133

MJ631 33MU 2-12-43 47MU 20-12 *Lds City* 23-1-44 Casa 17-2 SOC 14-3-46

MJ632 39MU 21-7-42 82MU 15-12 *Fan Head* 24-12 Casa 8-1-44 MAAF 31-1 CE ops 10-4-45

MJ633 39MU 29-11-43 331S 31-1-44 414S 26-10 e/a CB 1-1-45 409RSU 18-1 ASTE 25-4-45 sold RNAF 7-3-47

MJ634 33MU 2-12-43 47MU 20-12 *Lds City* 21-1-44 Casa 17-2 ME 13-9-45 SOC 26-9-46

MJ635 33MU 13-12-43 82MU 20-1-44 *Eury* 2-3 Hap 23-4 Bas 6-5

MJ636 33MU 2-3-44 84GSU 23-3 313S CAC ops 21-5 412S11-1-45 CB ops 31-3 FAF GC2/1

MJ637 39MU 312S 23-1-44 e/f std ld app Mendlesham CE 11-3-44

MJ638 39MU 19-12-43 222MU 31-1-44 *Eury* 2-3-44 Hap 23-4 Bas 6-5

MJ639 LFIXB 33MU 10-12-43 Flt Refuel Ltd 7-2-44 RAF South 17APC 29-2 132S FTR 6-6 cancel VA 6-5-46 recat E 24-6 RCO

MJ640 33MU 13-12-43 82MU 20-1-44 *Eury* 2-3 Hap 23-4 Bas 6-5

MJ641 39MU 2-12-43 82MU 24-12 *Lds City* 21-1-44 Casa 17-2 SOC 31-8

MJ642 9MU 4-12-43 GAL 31-8 83GSU 26-9 401S 18-11 RNAF 16-1-47 as H-11 3W-11

MJ643 39MU 30-11-43 82MU 15-12 *Fan Head* 24-12 Casa 8-1-44 FTR ops 17-4-45

MJ644 9MU 30-11-43 47MU 21-4-44 *Argyll* 1-6 Casa 13-6 FTR ops 9-3-45

MJ645 39MU 29-11-43 403S 5-2-44 CE ops 21-5

MJ646 39MU 30-11-43 82MU 15-12 *Fan Head* 24-12 Casa 8-1-44 USAAF 31-1 RAF MAAF FAC3 30-1-45

MJ659 39MU 2-12-43 222MU 3-1-44 *Lds City* 21-1 Casa 17-2 FTR ops 17-1-45

MJ660 9MU 4-12-43 GAL 25-8 83GSU 19-2 443S 413S 8-2-45 FAAC 19-3 FTR ops 26-3

MJ661 33MU 2-12-43 47MU 15-12 *Fan Head* 24-12 Casa 8-1-44 MAAF 31-1

MJ662 39MU 2-12-43 341S 9-2-44 FTR 10-6 cancel 401S 22-6 CAC ops 26-6 410RSU 22-6 CE ops 31-7

MJ712 in post war Dutch service, here in the colours of 322 Squadron.

MJ663 39MU 2-12-43 310S 23-1-4 FTR ops 21-5
MJ664 39MU 2-12-43 408S 5-2-44 CAC 13-8 410RSU 24-8 403S 23-11 AST 18-12 232MU M63 instal FAF 23-4-47
MJ665 39MU 2-12-43 82MU 15-12 *Fan Head* 24-12 Casa 8-1-44 MAAF 31-1 SOC 21-9-45
MJ666 33MU 12-12-43 82MU 23-12 *Lds City* 21-1-44 Casa 17-2 87S C3 ops 16-6
MJ667 33MU 13-12-43 82MU 20-1-44 *Eury* 2-3 Hap 23-4 Bas 6-5
MJ668 9MU 30-11-43 84GSU 26-5-44 313S 8-6MAL 18-7 441S 17-8 FTR ops 23-8 cancel AST 18-9 MAAF 7-4-45 IAF 26-6-47 as MM4058
MJ669 33MU 2-12-43 47MU 15-12 *Fan Head* 24-12 Casa 8-1 MAAF 31-1 FAF 28-3-46
MJ670 39MU 4-12-43 47MU 15-12 *Fan Head* 24-12 CAsa 8-1 MAAF 31-1 SOC 20-9-45
MJ671 39MU 2-12-43 341S 18-2-44 421RSU 13-7 421S 5-10 CAC ops 3-12 401S 28-12 CAC ops 24-1-45 MAL 26-3-45 FAF 12-9-46
MJ672 33MU 2-12-43 82MU 17-12 *Lds City* 26-1-44 Casa 17-2 SOC 14-2-46
MJ673 39MU 2-12-43 52MU 24-12 *Lds City* 21-1-44 Casa 17-2 IAF 30-5-46 as MM4059
MJ674 39MU 12-12-43 222MU 3-1-44 *Lds City* 21-1 Casa 17-2
MJ675 39MU 13-12-43 82MU 3-1-44 *Lds City* 21-1 Casa 17-2 SOC 18-8
MJ676 39MU 12-12-43 82MU 24-12 *Lds City* 21-1-44 Casa 17-2 SOC 5-6-45
MJ677 39MU 4-12-43 47MU 15-12 *Fan Head* 24-12 MAAF 31-1-44 SOC 30-6
MJ678 39MU 4-12-43 47MU 15-12 *Fan Head* 24-12 Casa 8-1-44 MAAF 31-1 AST 28-6-45 SOC 31-10-46
MJ679 9MU 2-12-43 3501SU 8-8-44 51 OTU 18-8 12Gp Com Flt 28-9 6MU 22-7-47 SOC 16-11
MJ680 39MU 11-12-43 82MU 23-12 *Lds City* 21-1-44 Casa 17-2 CE 5-11
MJ681 39MU 13-12-43 222MU 26-12 *Lds City* 21-1-44 Casa 17-2 SOC 15-3-45
MJ682 9MU 16-12-43 GAL 25-8-44 83GSU 21-9 302S 10-12 308S 4-1-45 CB ops 13-2-45 CFE Tang 22-7 130S 12-9-46 SOC 16-11-47
MJ683 33MU 13-12-43 222MU 20-1-44 *Eury* 2-3 Hap 23-4 Bas
MJ684 33MU 13-12-43 AST 30-12 VA for camouflage 15-3-44 ASTH 31-5 302S 22-6 CB ops 28-11 3BRU 25-1-45 84Gp ARF 8-3 317S 5-4 CE ops 19-4
MJ685 39MU 4-12-43 47MU 15-12 *Fan Head* 24-12 Casa 8-1-44 MAAF 31-1 USAAF 29-2 RAF 21-5 FACA 4-9
MJ686 33MU 12-12-43 222MU 23-12 *Lds City* 21-1-44 Casa 17-2 328S
MJ687 33MU 13-12-43 222MU 26-2-44 *Eury* 2-3 Hap 23-4 Bas 6-5
MJ688 33MU 2-12-43 47MU 20-12 *Lds City* 21-1-44 Casa 17-2 2S C3 ops 25-5
MJ689 39MU 11-12-43 52MU 24-12 *Lds City* 21-1-44 Casa 17-2 154S FTR ops 12-6
MJ690 39MU 19-12-43 82MU 25-1-44 *City of East* 10-2 Hap 5-4 Bas 7-4
MJ691 9MU 16-12-43 91S 3-9-44 CAC ops 2-3-45 151RU 15-3 FACE 7-5
MJ692 39MU 10-12-43 82MU 23-12 *Lds City* 21-1-44 Casa 17-2 4S C3 ops 17-5
MJ693 33MU 20-12-43 222MU 18-1-44 *Eury* 2-3 Hap 23-4 Bas 6-5
MJ694 33MU 24-12-43 82MU 24-1-44 *Fort Lrd* 1-3 Casa 17-3 SOC 30-8-45
MJ695 33MU 12-12-43 222MU 20-1-44 *Eury* 2-3 Hap 23-4 Bas 6-5
MJ696 39MU 12-12-43 82MU 24-12 *Lds City* 21-1-44 Casa 17-2 REAF 29-8-46
MJ697 33MU 13-12-43 82MU 29-1-44 *City of East* 10-2 Hap 5-4 Bas
MJ698 33MU 13-12-43 82MU 20-1-44 *Eury* 2-3 Hap 23-4 Bas 6-5
MJ712 33MU 20-12-43 331S 26-1-44 84GSY 10-8 151RU 3-5-45 326S 24-5 SNCAN 28-6. Dutch service not recorded.

MJ713 33MU 12-12-43 222MU 8-1-44 *Lds City* 21-1 Casa 17-2 CE ops 1-7 DeH 20-6-45
MJ714 33MU 20-12-43 310S 31-12 421S CE ops 19-5-44 310S 8-6 421S 27-7 RNAF 26-7-46 as H-67 later H-117 BAF as SM-35 1-53
MJ715 33MU 11-12-43 222MU 24-12 *Lds City* 21-1-44 Casa 17-2 ME 9-8-45 SOC 26-6-47
MJ716 33MU 12-12-43 52MU 22-5-44 *Emp Gla* 6-6 Hap 9-7
MJ717 33MU 13-12-43 222MU 20-1-44 *Eury* 2-3 Hap 23-4 Bas 6-5
MJ718 39MU 12-12-43 222MU 26-12 *Lds City* 21-1-44 Casa 17-2 ME 31-5-45 SOC 2-8
MJ719 39MU 12-12-43 82MU 30-12 *Lds City* 21-1-44 Casa 17-2 MAAF 31-5-45 SOC 14-3-46
MJ720 39MU 12-12-43 82MU 24-12 *Lds City* 21-1-44 Casa 17-2 SOC 18-10
MJ721 33MU 13-12-43 222MU 23-1-44 *Eury* 2-3 Hap 23-4 Bas 6-5
MJ722 33MU 20-12-43 310S 31-1-44 412S CAC ops 15-7 410RSU 20-7 411S 28-9 132S 5-10 MAAF 26-5-45 ME 16-8 SOC 24-3-46
MJ723 33MU 20-12-43 341S 29-1-44 84GSU 3-8 411S 4-1-45 FAAC 24-4 409RSU 26-11
MJ724 33MU 12-12-43 331S 10-2-44 FACE 19-2
MJ725 33MU 12-12-43 82MU 22-12 *Lds City* 21-1-44 Casa 17-2 RHAF 29-5-47
MJ726 39MU 21-12-43 312S 12-2-44 AST 31-3 6MU 442S 24-8 401S 31-8 CE ops 2-10
MJ727 39MU 11-12-43 82MU 23-12 *Lds City* 21-1-44 Casa 17-2 4S C3 ops 14-5-45
MJ728 33MU 24-12-43 331S 31-1-44 FTR ops 15-6
MJ729 9MU 16-12-43 83GSU 26-8-44 406S CAC ops 30-9 416S 28-9 411RSU 5-10 MAAF 11-2-45 RHAF 30-4-47
MJ730 33MU 12-12-43 222MU 24-12 *Lds City* 21-1-44 Casa 17-2 ME 30-11 MAAF 31-5-45 IAF 27-6-46 as MM4094 Ex-Israeli Air Force No.66. Registered G-BLAS 1982, extant, Sussex.
MJ731 9MU 16-12-43 FACB 24-8-44 DeH 30-8 6MU 11-3-45 MAAF 3-5 IAF 37-6-46 as MM4063
MJ732 39MU 29-12-43 331S 20-1-44 732Wg 22-6 33MU 19-8 414S 9-11 409RSU 16-11 CE ops dbf 6-1-45
MJ733 33MU 4-1-44 82MU 24-1 *Fort Lrd* 1-3 Casa 17-3 451S C3 ops 29-6 MMO 31-3-45
MJ734 6MU 28-3-44 332S 8-6 1S 5-10 3501SU 12-10 91S 23-11 FAAC 25-6-45 ROS 1S 26-7 3APS 13-9 FAAC 27-7-46 recat E SOC 30-1-47
MJ735 9MU 16-12-43 3501SU 26-8-44 Mans 12-10 FTR ops 2-2-45
MJ736 33MU 20-12-43 222MU 11-2-44 *Fort Lrd* 1-3 Casa 17-3 SOC 18-8
MJ737 39MU 16-12-43 82MU 30-12 *Lds City* 21-1-44 Casa 17-2 FAF GC2/1
MJ738 39MU 13-12-43 82MU 26-12 *Lds City* 21-1-44 Casa 17-2
MJ739 39MU 13-12-43 82MU 26-12 *Lds City* 21-1-44 Casa 17-2 SOC 23-12
MJ740 39MU 19-12-43 222MU 14-2-43 *Samana* 12-3 Hap 28-4
MJ741 33MU 20-12-43 443S 13-3-44 CB ops 30-7 410RSU 6-8 FACE 6-8
MJ742 9MU 16-12-43 83GSU 26-8-44 416S 23-9
MJ743 39MU 12-12-43 82MU 30-12 *Lds City* 21-1-44 Casa 17-2 232S C3 ops 7-5
MJ744 33MU 20-12-43 340S 7-2-44 84GSU 6-7 114S 30-11
MJ745 39MU 22-12-43 222MU 10-1-44 *Lds City* 26-1 Casa 17-2 SOC 20-9-45
MJ746 39MU 21-12-43 340S 9-2-44 FAAC 20-4 2nd TAF Com S 6-7 414S 10-8 CAC ops 24-12 409RSU 22-2-45 sold Int All 27-3-50
MJ747 33MU 13-12-43 82MU 20-1-44 *Eury* 2-3 Hap 23-4 Bas 6-5
MJ748 33MU 20-12-43 349S 16-2-44 CE ops 7-6
MJ749 39MU 19-12-43 82MU 25-1-44 *Samana* 12-3-Hap 28-4
MJ750 33MU 13-12-43 222MU 23-1-44 *Eury* 2-3 Hap 23-4 Bas 6-5
MJ751 33MU 19-12-43 312S 4-2-44 CAC ops 21-5 84GSU 22-6 91S 16-11 FACB 1-12 recat E 20-12
MJ752 33MU 20-12-43 241S 31-1-44 421S CAC ops 7-5 403S 27-7 127Wg 31-8 AST 14-12 313S 16-7-45 Czech AF 30-8
MJ753 39MU 20-12-43 222MU 27-1-44 *Eury* 2-3 Hap 23-4 Bas 6-5
MJ754 33MU 10-1-44 222MU 5-2 *Fort Lrd* 1-3 Casa 17-3 12S CE ops 27-7 recat A 31-8
MJ755 33MU 10-1-44 Casa Feb'44 RHAF 1947 restored and extant Tatoi Mus RHAF
MJ756 39MU 19-12-43 222MU 18-1-44 *Eury* 2-3 Hap 23-4 Bas 6-5
MJ769 39MU 13-12-43 222MU 26-12 *Lds City* 21-1-44 Casa 13-2 SOC 6-12-45
MJ770 33MU 20-12-43 416S 30-1-44 SAL 4-10 9MU 19-3-45 3APU Llan 21-4 MAAF 16-5 SOC 15-1-46
MJ771 39MU 20-12-43 82MU 23-1-44 *Samana* 12-3 Hap 28-4
MJ772 33MU 20-12-43 341S 20-1-44 CAC ops 18-6 340S 22-6 33MU 19-8 83GSU 27-9 FAAC 20-1-45 49MU 25-

MJ755, RHAF, extant and displayed at the Tatoi Museum, Greece.

1 HAL 19-7 sold VA as NEA 19-7-50 con to two-seat train 31-5-51 IAC 5-6 as 159 SOC IAC Jan'60 BHill 13-11 stor Cogea Belgium Mar'64 part payment for G-ASSD. Sold A Samuelson 3-1-66 Reg G-AVAV. Spec CofA issued 9-8-67 Shoreham 20-7-70 refurb extant Mesa USA as N8R

MJ773 33MU 16-12-43 82MU 20-1-44 *Eury* 2-3 Hap 23-4 Bas 6-5

MJ774 33MU 20-12-43 331S 10-2-44 443S 5-10 FRU 19-10 MAAF 23-2-45 SOC 30-4-47

MJ775 39MU 22-12-43 82MU 12-11-44 *Lds City* 21-1 Casa 17-2 2S C3 ops 13-6

MJ776 39MU 20-12-43 82MU 23-1-44 *Eury* 2-3 Hap 23-4 Bas 6-5

MJ777 39MU 19-12-43 82MU 25-1-44 *Co East* 10-2 Hap 5-4 USSR

MJ778 33MU 1-1-44 222MU 9-2 *Fort Lrd* 1-3 Casa 17-3 IAF 26-6-47 as MM4137

MJ779 33MU 19-12-43 443S 13-3-44 410RSU 25-7 127Wg 6-8 443S 23-9 CE

MJ780 33MU 20-12-43 341S 29-1-44 421RSU 15-6 84RSU 3-8 414S 28-9 CAC ops 11-10 409RSU 12-10 DeH 26-3-45 sold Turk 24-10-47

MJ781 33MU 13-12-43 82MU 20-1-44 *Eury* 2-3 Hap 23-4 Bas 6-5

MJ782 39MU 20-12-43 222MU 27-1-44 *Eury* 2-3 Hap 23-4 Bas 6-5

MJ783 LFIXC 39MU 21-12-43 83GSU 27-4-44 132S 15-6 403S 27-7 CE ops 5-8 BAF SM-15 2-48 extant Brussels Mus

MJ784 39MU 21-12-43 83GSU 27-7-44 132S 15-6 403S 27-7 CE ops 5-8

MJ785 39MU 20-12-43 165S 11-8-44 CAC ops 31-12 ROS MAL 21-2-45 165S FACE dbf 28-7

MJ786 33MU 20-12-43 341S 31-1-44 421S CE ops 21-5

MJ787 39MU 21-12-43 416S 31-1-44 CB ops 17-6 39MU 29-10 GAL 28-11 349S 25-1-45 435S 8-2 308S FTR ops 15-3

MJ788 39MU 22-12-43 222MU 7-1-44 *Lds City* 21-1 Casa 17-2 CE ops 5-10

MJ789 33MU 20-12-43 403S 31-1-44 453S FTR ops 11-6

MJ790 39MU 19-12-43 56S 17-6-44 350S 9-7 322S 4-9 414S 4-1-45 CAC ops 24-2 308S CB ops 11-3 411S 26-4

MJ791 39MU 19-12-43 82MU 18-1-44 *Co East* 10-2 Hap 7-4 USSR

MJ792 39MU 8-1-43 312S 22-1 416S CB ops 12-7 GAL 3-11 308S 15-2-45 sold RNo AF 9-5-47

MJ793 33MU 20-12-43 403S 31-1-44 421S 27-7 39CAF CAC ops 6-3-45 3BRU 22-3 recat E

MJ794 39MU 21-12-43 66S 7-3-44 CB ops 28-5 AST 302S 8-2-45 317S 22-3 CAC ops 11-4 sold VA 17-10-46

MJ795 39MU 21-12-43 340S 23-1-44 ROS FACB 5-6 GAL 23-9 222S 9-11 412S 25-1-45 CE ops 28-4

MJ796 39MU 29-12-43 1S 25-4-44 FTR ops 22-5

MJ797 9MU 20-12-43 GAL 18-8-44 317S 19-10 e/a CE 1-1-45

MJ798 39MU 7-1-44 310S 31-1 FTR ops 21-5

MJ799 39MU 28-12-43 312S 13-2-44 453S 13-7 421S 27-7 416S e/a CB 21-10 SAL 21-1-45 sold Turk 23-1-47

MJ800 39MU 19-12-43 82MU 18-1-44 *Eury* 2-3 Hap 24-4 Bas 6-5

MJ801 39MU 21-12-43 313S 25-1-44 CB ops 20-5 AST 302S 23-11 e/a 1-1-45 317S 8-2 CAC ops 8-4 ASTH sold Turk 14-10-47

MJ814 LFIXB 39MU 22-12-43 Flt Refuel 6-2 RAF South 18-2 17APC 2-3 FAAC 29-5 ROS FLS Mlfld 5-10 CFE 22-3-46 to 6183M 8-11 6SoTT

MJ815 39MU 21-12-43 485S 23-1-44 341S 8-6 511FRU 13-7

MJ816 33MU 24-12-43 82MU 7-1-44 *Fort Lrd* 1-3 Casa 17-3 SOC 30-4-47

MJ817 33MU 4-1-44 82MU 30-1 *Fort Lrd* 1-3 Casa 13-3

MJ818 39MU 24-12-43 82MU 8-1-44 *Lds City* 2-11 Casa 17-2

MJ819 33MU 20-12-43 82MU 25-1-44 *Co East* 10-2 Hap 5-4 Bas 7-4

MJ820 33MU 24-12-43 405ARF 24-2-44 421S dam by MJ355 in dive CAC 25-3 CE ops 18-8

MJ821 39MU 20-12-43 222MU 27-1-44 *Eury* 2-3 Hap 23-4 Bas 6-5

MJ822 39MU 20-12-43 340S 9-2 402S 17-7 91S 12-10 327S 15-4-45 339 French Wg 2-8 306S 11-10 FAF 4-12 GC2/1

MJ823 M61 CRD WD 21-2-44 BDn 19-3 trls with 2 × 250lb GP and 2 × 120lb MkIIA smoke bombs under wngs. Comp trls with 4 and 5 blade props. M66 instal, m/gns removed 25-6 further trls with 2 × 250lb GP and 1 × 500lb MC bomb; 2 × 210lb smoke bombs and 90gal o/ld tank. 33MU 2-12 12FU 12-1-45 MAAF 5-2 SOC 14-3-46

MJ824 33MU 20-1-44 405ARF 25-2 416S CE ops 13-6

MJ825 39MU 4-1-44 310S 22-1 340S 15-6 402S 17-7 326S 5-4-45 FAF GC1/6

MJ826 33MU 10-1-44 222MU 9-2 *Fort Lrd* 1-3 Casa 17-3 154S FTR ops 13-6

MJ827 33MU 22-12-43 331S 31-1-44 403S CE ops s/dn by AA fire off Normandy 9-6

MJ828 39MU 20-12-43 416S 31-1-44 CAC ops 25-9 416S 5-10 39MU 13-3-45 RNAF 19-5-47 as H-30 to PH-NFR

MJ829 38MU 24-12-43 310S 26-1-44 442S 20-7 410RSU 17-8 AST 5-9 MAAF 20-4-45 IAF 26-6-47 as MM4108

MJ830 39MU 22-12-43 222MU 6-1-44 *Lds City* 21-1 Casa 17-2 IAF 26-6-47 as MM4070

MJ831 LFIXB 33MU 29-12-43 416S 6-2-44 411S CE ops 15-5

MJ832 33MU 24-12-43 416S 30-1-44 CE ops 21-5

MJ833 LFIXB 33MU 22-12-43 421S 26-1-44 FACE 9-3 FH40.40

MJ834 33MU 24-12-43 331S 26-1-44 FTR ops 11-6

MJ835 33MU 22-11-43 222MU 30-11 *Fan Head* 24-12 Casa 8-1-44 MAAF 31-1 FTR ops 26-3-45

MJ836 33MU 22-11-43 82MU 3-12 *Fan Head* 24-12 Casa 9-1-44 MAAF 31-1 SAC 14-3-46

MJ837 39MU 24-11-43 222MU 30-11 *Fan Head* 24-12 Casa 8-1-44 MAAF 31-1 FACE 18-1-45 SOC 21-8

MJ838 39MU 24-11-43 *Fan Head* 24-12 Casa 8-1-44 MAAF 31-1 USAAF 29-2 RAF 31-5 SOC 20-9-45

MJ839 33MU 26-11-43 47MU 21-12 *Lds City* 21-1-44 Casa 17-2 ME 25-2-45 RHAF 27-3-47

MJ840 39MU 24-11-43 312S 18-2-44 flew i/hill in low cloud Barnes Farm nr Washington sussex CE 11-6 41RSU 15-6

MJ841 9MU 28-11-43 412S 22-6-44 AST 16-7 MAAF 6-5-45 IAF 26-6-47 as MM4109

MJ842 9MU 28-11-43 82MU 28-5-44 *Arabis* 16-6 Hap 29-6 Bas 12-8

MJ843 9MU 28-11-43 56S 17-6-44 442S 14-9 FCCS port wg and tailplane broke away in loop cd Bovington pilot kld CE 16-9-46 SOC 8-10

MJ844 9MU 29-11-43 AST 6-6-44 412S FTR 20-8

MJ845 9MU 29-11-43 82MU 28-5-44 9MU 21-6 33MU 9-1-47 SOC 7-8

MJ846 9MU 1-12-43 82MU 28-5-44 *Arabis* 16-6 Hap 29-6 Bas 12-8

MJ847 9MU 1-12-43 47MU 21-5-44 222MU 20-12 *Guinean* 22-11 Casa 15-1-45 ME 28-4 REAF 29-8-46

MJ848 9MU 4-12-43 602S 28-9-44 327S 5-4-45 FAF 27-11

MJ849 9MU 4-12-43 411S 7-9-44 CAC ops 26-9 401S 5-10 FACB 4-11 MAAF 5-4-45 IAF 26-6-47 as MM4139

MJ850 9MU 18-12-43 52MU 21-11-44 *Thom Scott* 15-12 Hap 9-1-45

MJ851 9MU 12-12-43 410S 28-9-44 FTR ops 22-2-45

MJ852 9MU 18-12-43 411S 14-9-44 CB ops 27-9 401S 5-10 410S FTR ops 25-12

MJ853 33MU 24-12-43 340S 9-2-44 FTR ops 29-2 FH19

MJ854 9MU 14-12-43 443S 12-10-44 CAC ops 14-1-45 401S 25-1 CAC ops 11-2 443S 1-3 CAC ops 17-4

MJ855 LFIXB 39MU 22-12-43 416S 10-2-44 ORAC 29-2 421S 27-7 WAL 19-10 165S 24-5-45 332S 15-11

MJ856 39MU 19-12-43 222MU 31-1-44 *Eury* 2-3 Hap 23-4 Bas 6-5

MJ857 33MU 28-12-43 FAAC 29-1-44 ROS 83GSU 30-5 411S FTR 27-6

MJ858 39MU 19-12-43 222MU 18-1-44 *Eury* 2-3 Hap 23-4 Bas 6-5

MJ870 39MU 4-1-44 403S 27-1 421S CE ops 25-6

MJ871 39MU 28-12-43 341S 9-2-44 CAC 1-7 414S 2-11 e/a 24-12 DeH 1-5-45 sold Turk 1-10-47

MJ872 39MU 24-12-43 416S 31-1-44 AST 2-2 SAL 17-8 WAL 26-1-45 sold Turk 25-9-47

MJ873 39MU 24-12-43 340S 11-2-44 ROS 27-2 FAAC 27-4 421RSU 15-6 602S 19-10 1S 8-2-45

MJ874 33MU 28-12-43 416S 26-1-44 FTR ops 29-9

MJ875 39MU 24-12-43 82MU 8-1-44 *Lds City* 21-1 Casa 17-2 FTR ops 1-4-45

MJ876 LFIXB 33MU 24-12-43 403S 26-1-44 405ARF 9-2 403S CE ops 8-3 FH24.45

MJ877 39MU 24-12-43 416S 1-2-44 CB ops 7-5 AST 83GSU 15-10 412S 14-12 FTR ops 8-1-45

MJ878 39MU 22-12-43 222MU 7-1-44 *Lds City* 21-1 Casa 17-2

MJ879 33MU 28-12-43 349S 16-2-44 332S 15-6 420RSU CAC 6-7 FAAC 20-7 83GSU 15-10 453S 9-11 SAL 23-11 MAAF 14-7-45 RHAF 30-1-47

MJ880 39MU 7-1-44 421S 23-1 CAC 12-7 421S 27-7 CE ops 23-8

MJ881 33MU 24-12-43 312S 7-4 322S 20-9 FAAC 29-9 414S 1-3-45 CAC 26-3 WAL 10-4 recat E 23-5

MJ882 39MU 24-12-43 416S 23-1-44 FAAC 28-6 416S 20-7 6130SE 5-10 132S FAAC 13-10 ROS 326S 5-4-45

MJ883 LFIXB 33MU 24-12-43 Flt Refuel 7-2-44 17APC South 29-2 317S 2-11 CB ops 1-1-45 AST W Wal 15-12-46 sold Turk

MJ884 39MU 28-12-43 312S 12-2-44 CAC 21-5 310S 8-6 602S 13-7 412S CE ops 27-9

MJ885 39MU 22-12-43 222MU 7-1-44 *Lds City* 21-1 Casa 17-2

MJ886 33MU 29-12-43 83GSU 18-5-44 403S CAC 9-6 83GSU 23-8 GAL 15-11 mods MAAF 3-3-45 ME 16-8 SOC 18-10

MJ887 33MU 8-1-44 410ARF 11-3 403S CAC ops 7-5 SAL 16-6 441S 4-11 329S 5-4-45 COAL 13-6-45 mods CGS 12-7 VASM 17-10-465 to 6455M 15-109-47 4SoTT SAOC 27-9-49

MJ888 39MU 28-12-43 310S 31-1-44 CAC 20-4 AST 308S 10-12 CB ops 1-1-45 ASTH sold Turk 23-7-47

MJ889 33MU 8-1-44 ROS 31-1 349S 16-2 FAAC 21-3 874G Com S 15-6 FTR ops 25-11

MJ890 39MU 28-12-43 341S 9-2-44 SAL 6-12 RAF Persh FACE 2-4-45 SOC 12-4

MJ891 33MU 24-12-43 403S 30-1-44 421S 27-7 AST 19-9 MAAF 16-5-45 73S flew l/grd ldg app CE Takali Malta 12-8-47

MJ892 LFIX M66 con to Type 385 floatplane MkIXB see page XXX. CRD Stav 29-12-43 9MU 15-9-44 ASTH recat E 25-9-45 SOC 22-11

MJ893 39MUI 8-1-44 312S 25-1 CB ops 23-3 AST GAL 5-8 302S 19-10 AST 28-11 RNAF 26-7-46 as H-69 later H-110 BAF as SM-42 w/o 6-5-54

MJ894 33MU 1-1-44 47MU 10-2 *Fort Lrd* 1-3 Casa 17-3 SOC 30-11-47

MJ895 33MU 4-1-44 222MU 9-2 *Fort Lrd* 1-3 Casc 17-3 FTR ops 31-12

MJ896 39MU 1-1-44 340S 9-2 414S 6-8 AST 9-11 sold Int All 29-8-50

MJ897 33MU 1-1-44 222MU 10-2 *Fort Lrd* 1-3 Casa 17-3 339Wg 31-5-45 FACE 4-12 FAF GR2/33 17-6-44

MJ898 33MU 4-1-44 222MU 6-2 *Fort Lrd* 1-3 Casa 17-3 MAAF SOC 30-6-45

MJ899 33MU 8-1-44 410ARF 11-2 411S 29-6 CE ops 18-8

MJ900 33MU 4-1-44 84GSU 24-3 312S 8-6 322S 6-9 SAL 6-12 MAAF 16-5-45 SOC 21-9

MJ901 33MU 4-1-44 47MU 29-1 *Fort Lrd* 1-3 Casa 17-3 CE ops 28-3-45

MJ902 39MU 4-1-44 82MU 31-1 *Co East* 10-2 Hap 5-4 USSR

MJ903 33MU 1-1-44 82MU 30-1 *Fort Lrd* 1-3 Casa 17-3 SOC 5-6-45

MJ904 39MU 29-12-43 222MU 10-1-44 *Lds City* 21-1 Casa 17-2 SOC 18-8

MJ905 33MU 8-1-44 410ARF 11-2 118S CAC ops 28-2 411S CE ops 2-6

MJ906 39MU 8-1-44 310S 23-1 420RSU 310S std on final app CE 136AF 7-6 511FRU 15-6

MJ907 39MU 7-1-44 312S 22-1 FTR ops 21-5

MJ908 39MU 4-1-44 331S 22-1 FAAC 11-3 ROS 151RU 29-3-45 WAL 10-4 Pers 2-6-47 FAF 3-6 GC2/1 FTR nr Zaaf (Algeria) 12-9-50

MJ909 33MU 4-1-44 82MU 31-1 *Fort Lrd* 1-3 Casa 17-3 CE ops 20-6-45

MJ910 39MU 4-1-44 341S 31-1 FTR 15-6 SOC cancel 414S 13-7 CAC ops 17-10 e/a CB 1-1-45 sold R J Coley 6-2-50

MJ911 39MU 10-1-44 ROS 13-1 39MU 3-3 341S 6-4 421RSU FACE 12-5

MJ912 39MU 4-1-44 431S 31-1 ROS 22-2 329S 8-6 414S 10-8 FTR 18-9

MJ913 33MU 1-1-44 222MU 9-2 *Fort Lrd* 1-3 Casa 17-3 4S FACB 26-5

MJ926 39MU 24-12-43 82MU 8-1-44 *Lds City* 21-1 Casa 17-2 FTR ops 24-10

MJ927 39MU 24-12-43 222MU 7-1-44 *Lds City* 21-1 Casa 17-2 SOC 28-4-45

MJ928 39MU 28-12-43 403S 2-3-44 421S ops 21-5-44

MJ929 39MU 23-1-44 405ARF 2-3 416S CE ops 8-6

MJ930 33MU 20-1-44 331S 4-3 FAAC 3-8 411S 26-4-45 sold J Dale 2-1-50

MJ931 33MU 4-1-44 312S 31-1 AST 25-5 302S 9-11 AST 8-12 331S 10-5-45

MJ932 39MU 30-12-43 82MU 12-1-44 *Fort Lrd* 1-3 Casa 17-3 SOC 15-3-45

MJ933 33MU 10-1-44 222MU 29-1 *Fort Lrd* 1-3 Casa 17-3 40S FTR ops 4-9

MJ934 6MU 22-4-44 317S 3-5 CAC ops 21-5 FTR ops 28-5

MJ935 46MU 27-4-44 MAL 16-5 302S 15-6 1ATC 24-8 DeH 29-8 3APU 3-5-45 MAAF 25-5 RHAF 27-3-47

MJ936 39MU 1-5-44 52MU 13-5 *Emp Gla* 21-5 Hap 9-7

MJ937 39MU 1-5-44 52MU 13-5 *Arabis* 14-6 Hap 29-6 Bas 12-8

MJ938 33MU 28-12-43 331S 10-2-44 FACE 19-2

MJ939 33MU 24-12-43 405ARF 11-2 403S FACE 29-5

MJ940 39MU 22-12-43 313S 15-2-44 FACB 19-2 ROS 313S 31-3 312S 20-4 FTR 10-6

MJ941 38MU 24-12-43 222MU 31-1 *Fort Lrd* 1-3 Casa 17-3 FTR ops 27-7

MJ942 33MU 23-12-43 405ARF 11-3-44 403S FACB 29-5 411S 8-6-45 511FRU SOC 21-2

MJ943 33MU 4-1-44 47MU 9-2 *Emp Ray* 21-3 Casa 6-4 237S FTR ops 9-6

MJ944 39MU 21-1-44 421S 5-2 403S CE ops 20-2

MJ945 46MU 28-4-44 AST 23-5 84GSU 31-5 302S 15-6

MJ946 33MU 29-4-44 52MU 12-5 *Arabis* 14-6 Hap 29-6 Bas 12-8

MJ947 39MU 14-1-44 312S 31-1 e/fd f/ld nr Chil CE 4-2 AST GAL 8-8 302S CE ops5-11

MJ948 33MU 14-1-44 82MU 31-1 *Fort Lrd* 1-3 Casa 17-3 4S C3 ops 17-5

MJ949 33MU 21-1-44 52MU 6-4 *Marsd* 22-4 Hap 29-5 Bas 10-6

MJ950 33MU 10-1-44 82MU 24-1 *Fort Lrd* 1-3 Casa 17-3 SOC 30-6

MJ951 39MU 24-12-43 421S 22-1-44 403S CB ops 9-6 401S 29-6 442S 31-8 602S 28-9 WAL 14-10 401S CAC ops 11-11 331S 17-5

MJ952 33MU 10-1-44 82MU 31-1 *Fort Lrd* 1-3 Casa 17-3 328S 5-4-45

MJ953 39MU 20-1-44 416S 18-2 CAC ops 18-7 403S 27-7 410RSU 19-10 RNAF 23-7-46 as H-12

MJ954 33MU 4-1-44 403S 24-1 421S CB ops 8MU 29-6 ROS 3-7 308S 19-10 328S 5-4-45

MJ955 33MU 20-1-44 349S 16-2 CAC ops 12-6 421RSU 15-6 403S 27-7 CAC 17-8 29MU 3-2-45 MAF 12-3 IAF 21-6 w/o 29-11-47

MJ956 39MU 20-1-44 222MU 13-2 *Fort Lrd* 1-3 Casa 17-3 FTR ops 23-1-45

MJ957 33MU 20-1-44 443S 27-7 410RSU 21-12 RNAF 20-5-47 as H-24

MJ958 39MU 20-1-44 47MU 1-2 *Fort Lrd* 1-3 Casa 17-3 SOC 13-10-45

MJ959 33MU 28-1-44 405ARF 24-2 412S 22-6 WAL 6-2-45 mods 328S 5-4 FAF GC1/1

MJ960 39MU 23-1-44 340S 9-2 332S 6-7 84GSU 5-10
MJ961 33MU 21-1-44 52MU 1-3 *St Cl* 3-4 Hap 16-5
MJ962 33MU 20-1-44 349S 16-2
MJ963 6MU 2-2-44 313S 16-2 CAC ops 29-5 64S 29-9 WAL 1-3-45 W Wal 18-12-46 sold Turk
MJ964 39MU 21-1-44 485S 7-2 349S 8-6 ROS 26-6 322S 8-9 AST 15-12 CRD COAL 2-5-45 mods CGS 27-4-46 SOC 30-1-47
MJ965 39MU 23-1-44 222MU 9-2 *Fort Lrd* 1-3 Casa 17-3 237S CE ops 25-7
MJ966 39MU 25-1-44 485S 9-2 340S 8-6 414S 10-8 CAC ops 12-9 SAL 11-4-45 ASTE FAF 27-7-46
MJ967 33MU 29-1-44 442S 13-3 swg on ldg strk MK149 & 181 CE Funtin 8-5
MJ979 39MU 7-1-44 313S 22-1 FAAC 6-4 26-4
MJ980 39MU 14-1-44 421S 31-1 403S CB ops 28-5 AST 401S 12-12 FTR ops 20-4-45
MJ981 39MU 10-1-44 403S 18-2 405ARF 28-2 602S 15-6 CAC ops 23-6 411RSU 29-6 66S 13-7 CE ops 22-9
MJ982 LFIXB 39MU 7-1-44 421S 23-1 CAC ops ROS 401S FTR ops 27-4
MJ983 39MU 14-1-44 47MU 1-2 *Fort Lrd* 1-3 Casa 17-5 FTR ops 13-4-45
MJ984 33MU 10-1-44 82MU 24-1 *Fort Lrd* 1-3 Casa 13-3 328S SOC 23-10
MJ985 39MU 10-1-44 421S 27-1 403S FAAC 4-5 411S 22-6 132S 5-10 451S SAL 4-1-45 MAAF 20-6 ME 16-8 SOC 27-11-47
MJ986 39MU 10-1-44 421S 27-1 403S CB ops 7-5 83GSU 7-10 328S
MJ987 39MU 7-1-44 403S 22-1 421S 29-6 CE ops 25-7
MJ988 39MU 25-1-44 403S 11-2 CE ops 28-6
MJ989 33MU 10-1-44 52MU 10-2 *Fort Lrd* 1-3 Casa 17-3 SOC 30-8-45
MJ990 33MU 4-1-44 52MU 10-2 *Fort Lrd* 1-3 Casa 17-3 FTR ops 25-2-45
MJ991 33MU 10-1-44 215MU 13-2 *Fort Lrd* 1-3 Casa 17-3 213S FTR ops 13-5
MJ992 33MU 10-1-33 222MU 5-2 *Fort Lrd* 1-3 Casa 17-3 FTR ops 5-1-45
MJ993 33MU 10-1-44 82MU 24-1 *Fort Lrd* 1-3 Casa 17-3 FTR 6-11
MJ994 39MU 14-1-44 421S 31-1 411S 29-6 511FRU 14-9 AST 19-9 MAAF 16-5-45
MJ995 33MU 8-1-44 52MU 10-2 *Fort Lrd* 1-3 Casa 17-3 FAF GR2/33 17-6-46
MJ996 33MU 10-1-44 222MU 9-2 *Fort Lrd* 1-3 Casa 17-3 IAF 27-6-46 as MM 4079
MJ997 33MU 10-1-44 82MU 31-1-44 *Fort Lrd* 1-3 Casa 17-3
MJ998 39MU 10-1-44 312S 25-1 AST 4-6 308S 21-12 CAC ops 23-1-45 317S CAC ops 1-4-45 recat E SOC 3-4-47
MJ999 39MU 14-1-44 47MU 9-2 *Fort Lrd* 1-3 Casa 17-3 C3 ops 1-6

MK series all LF IX Merlin 66 engine

MK112 39MU 8-1-44 340S 31-1 FAAC 22-4 ROS SAL 4-7 GAL 3-10 mods 222MU 20-12 *Tendi* 12-1-45 Casa 25-1 SOC 18-10
MK113 33MU 10-1-44 82MU 24-1 *Fort Lrd* 1-3 Casa 17-3 CE ops 13-3-45
MK114 6MU 30-1-44 482 11-2 R-RH 31-5 RAF Mlfld 23-7 FACB 3-5-45 VA 15-5 FAF 9-9-46
MK115 33MU 20-1-44 340S 2-3 56S 9-5 9-5 340S 8-6 MAL 18-7 421S CE ops 23-8
MK116 39MU 14-1-44 310S 31-1 FTR ops 21-5
MK117 39MU 7-1-44 415S 22-1 CE ops 10-7
MK118 33MU 10-1-44 222MU 11-2 *Fort Lrd* 1-3 Casa 17-3 SOC 31-9 cancel 73S cd/ld CE Takali Malta 27-1-48
MK119 39MU 14-1-44 222MU 11-2 *Fort Lrd* 1-3 Casa 17-3 ME 26-6-47 FACB 27-1-48 137MU stor 12-2-48 SOC 11-3
MK120 39MU 7-1-44 403S 23-1 421S u/s ldg u/c clpse Tang CE 10-6
MK121 6MU 30-1-44 411ARF 12-2 331S 8-6 421S 12-10 AST 2-1-45 COAL 15-5 mods CGS 22-7 29MU 15-5-46 RNAF 20-9 as H-18
MK122 39MU 10-1-44 313S 22-1 FTR ops 20-4
MK123 39MU 10-1-44 340S 31-1 350S eng fell out a/c disin in dive cd Normanhurst Sussex CE 8-7
MK124 33MU 20-1-44 222MU 22-2 *Emp Ray* 21-3 Casa 6-4 SOC 30-6
MK125 39MU 14-1-44 222MU 31-1 *Fort Lrd* 1-3 Casa 17-3 ME SOC 26-9-46
MK126 LFIXE 39MU 14-1-44 126S 30-5 56S FAAC 17-6 126S 4-1-45 MAL 165S 18-6 130S 14-6 FAAC 17-6-46 SIC 27-11
MK127 39MU 14-1-44 340S 9-2 CAC ops 7-6 421RSU 8-6 340S 15-6 414S 23-9 39(R)Wg 12-4-45 328S 20-9 FAF 4-12
MK128 DeH 14-1-44 9MU 30-9 453S 3-11 29MU 22-2-45 FCCS 15-7 GAAC 25-7 39MU 31-1-46 RNAF 25-11 as H-3 w/o 25-4-51
MK129 39MU 10-1-44 331S 31-1 FTR ops 9-2
MK130 33MU 23-1-44 349S 17-2 CE ops 28-5
MK131 39MU 2-2-44 313S 15-2 FACB 6-3
MK132 39MU 21-1-44 485S 9-2 329S 8-6 421RSU 22-6 329S 29-6 412S 10-8 414S 5-10 411S 19-4-45 326S 26-7 FAF 4-12 GC2/7
MK133 39MU 23-1-44 222MU 9-2 *Fort Lrd* 1-3 Casa 17-3 SOC 19-7-45 FAF GC1/4
MK134 39MU 14-1-44 222MU 31-1 *Fort Lrd* 1-3 Casa 17-3 SOC 23-12
MK135 33MU 8-1-44 349S 17-2 FACB 25-2 AST 39MU 3-5 441S 6-7 GAL 23-12 MAL 6-4-45 Czech AF 4-12-46
MK136 33MU 21-1-44 349S 17-2 e/fd u/s CE Westh 15-4
MK137 39MU 25-1-44 222MU 9-3 *Fort Lrd* 1-3 Casa 17-3 ME SOC 31-10-46
MK138 33MU 10-1-44 222MU 3-3 *Emp Ray* 21-3 Casa 6-4 SOC 30-6
MK139 39MU 20-1-44 416S 1-2 FAAC 5-8 127Wg HQ 10-8 416S 7-9 CE
MK140 39MU 8-1-44 340S 9-2 FTR ops
MK141 33MU 21-1-44 442S 13-3 CE ops 13-8
MK142 33MU 10-1-44 222MU 31-1 *Fort Lrd* 1-3 Casa 17-3 SOC 13-12-45
MK143 39MU 14-1-44 47MU 9-2 *Fort Lrd* 1-3 Casa 17-3 SOC 27-9-45
MK144 33MU 20-1-44 410ARF 11-2 132S 15-6 602S 20-7 442S 24-8 602S 28-9 sold R J Coley 3-2-50
MK145 33MU 29-1-44 222MU *Emp Ray* 21-3 Casa 6-4 CE ops 26-6-45 SOC 14-7
MK146 39 2-2-44 ROS 8-2 39MU 19-2 *Arabis* 10-3 Hap 15-5
MK147 LFIXB 39MU 14-1-44 416S 10-2 CAC ops 20-3 ROS 322S 28-9 WAL 24-5-45 29MU 26-9 sold Turk 1-10-47
MK148 33MU 21-1-44 349S 16-2 FAAC 25-4 349S 11-6 CE ops FRU 29-6 GAL 23-11 126S FTR ops 13-1 2 cancel recat A 6MU 21-12 MAAF 6-2-45 ME SOC 31-10-46
MK149 33MU 23-1-44 442S 13-1 strk by MJ967 ldg CE Fujntin 8-5
MK150 6MU 29-1-44 411ARF 12-2 310S FACE 26-4
MK151 39MU 25-1-44 222MU 12-2 *Fort Lrd* 1-3 Casa 17-3 FAF 28-3-46
MK152 39MU 23-1-44 222MU 12-2 *Fort Lrd* 1-3 Casa 17-3 SOC 18-10-45
MK153 33MU 29-1-44 349S 1-3 329S 15-6 414S 6-8 CAC ops 3-9 414S 14-9 GAL 20-12 9MU 6-1-45 MAL 6-2 BAF 20-11-48 as SM-28
MK154 33MU 20-1-44 222MU 22-2 *Fort Lrd* 1-3 Casa 17-3 IAF 27-6 as MM4083
MK155 39MU 4-1-44 82MU 15-2 *Fort Lrd* 1-3 Casa 17-3 IAF 26-6-47 as MM4117
MK156 LFIXB 8MU 12-2-44 441S 13-3 FACB 23-3 AST 308S 31-8 SAL 13-2-45 MAAF 23-3 IAF 30-5-46 as MM4004
MK157 33MU 20-1-44 442S 13-3 FAAC 12-5 442S 8-6 CE ops
MK158 39MU 30-1-44 *Fort Lrd* 1-3 Casa 17-3 ME 26-6-47 73S e/fd t/o CE Takali Malta 8-9-47 SOC 30-10
MK171 39MU 21-1-44 82MU *Fort Lrd* 1-3 Casa 17-3 CE 2-2-45 ME 31-5 SOC 2-8
MK172 6MU 20-1-44 485S 11-2 R-RH 27-5 CFE Tang 24-5 sold VA 21-10-46 to EA con to two-seat train 24-5-48
MK173 6MU 29-1-44 411ARF 12-2 313S e/fd f/ld CE 11-3
MK174 39MU 26-1-44 82MU 14-2 *Fort Lrd* 1-3 Casa 17-3 4S FTR ops 18-7
MK175 33MU 28-1-44 349S CE ops 12-6 421RSU 15-6 SOC June'44
MK176 LFIXB 6MU 29-1-44 Flt Refuel 11-2 RAF South 17APC 29-2 FAAC 3-7 ROS FLS Mlfld 5-10-46 sold VA 24-10 EA 28-2-47
MK177 8MU 441S 12-3-44 CE ops 15-6 recat B 22-6 302S 2-1-45 FTR ops 20-1-45
MK178 6MU 20-1-44 485S 11-2 349S 8-6 331S 15-3 420RSU 26-7 66S 3-8 132S 5-10 ASTE 10-2-45 sold Turk 9-10-47
MK179 38MU 21-1-44 405ARF 24-2 403S CE ops 3-5 into sea
MK180 9MU 28-1-44 485S 23-2 312S 8-6 322S 22-6 453S 26-10 SAL 28-11 MAAF 7-8-45 ME 26-6-47 SOC 28-8
MK181 33MU 23-1-44 442S 13-3 strk by MJ967 ldg CE Funtin 8-5
MK182 33MU 30-1-44 331S 4-3 FTR ops 7-5
MK183 39MU 23-1-44 430S 11-2 FTR ops 20-6 414S 12-10 DeH 1-5-45 sold 11-7-47
MK184 LFIXB 6MU 30-1-44 Flt refuel 8-2 17APC South 26-2 FLS Mlfld 5-10 to 5969 2SoTT recat E 12-4-46
MK185 39MU 25-1-44 215S 9-2 *Fort Lrd* 1-3 Casa 17-3 SOC 22-12
MK186 CRD W D 25-1-44 CRDVA CHA 28-2 AST 10-6
MK187 39MU 26-1-44 215MU 9-2 *Fort Lrd* 1-3 Casa 17-3 SOC 23-12
MK188 39MU 2-2-44 313S 15-2 GAL 12-12 mods RNAF 14-8-48 as H-23 w/o 25-3-53
MK189 9MU 28-1-44 485S 23-2 313S 8-6 322S CB ops 13-9 AST MAAF 31-3-45 SOC 20-9
MK190 33MU 28-1-44 331S 4-3 CB ops 29-4 AST 131Wg HQ 31-8 317S 21-9 CE ops 1-1-45
MK191 39MU 26-1-44 405ARF 11-2 602S FACE 16-3 FH29.10
MK192 39MU 26-1-44 411ARF 11-2 350S 17-2 349S CE ops 21-5
MK193 33MU 20-1-44 442S 13-3 CB ops 3-7 350S 1-9 322S 4-9 6MU 1-3-45 MAAF 5-4 IAF 30-5-46 as MM4008
MK194 33MU 23-1-44 83GSU 13-3 403S CAC ops 10-6 127Wg HQ 29-6 442S 13-7 AST 1-8 MAAF 29-2-45 IAF 30-5-46 as MM4010
MK195 33MU 23-1-44 405ARF 2-3 401S 22-2 412S CAC ops 16-9 132S 5-10 AST 12-12 sold Turk 17-1-47
MK196 39MU 28-1-44 340S 3-3 CAC ops 13-5 421RSU 22-6 401S 28-9 CAC ops 18-12 ASTH FAF 27-7-46 sold VA EA con to two-seat train 10-5-48
MK197 BDn 11-2-44 33MU 22-1-45 MWW 24-1 MAAF 12-5 SOC 31-7-47
MK198 6MU 30-1-44 485S 11-2 FAAC 23-4 310S 8-6 66S 15-6 i/sea ops 4-7
MK199 33MU 23-1-44 405ARF 2-3 412S CE ops 2-7
MK200 9MU 4-2-44 443S 11-3 CAC 26-4 ROS 317S 24-8 302S 31-8 CB ops 31-12
MK201 33MU 23-1-44 341S 12-2 CAC ops 22-6 GAL 441S 17-8 AST 12-2-45 sold Turk 13-8-47
MK202 9MU 28-1-44 485S 23-2 340S 8-6 414S 6-8 CAC ops 6-11 39MU 5-12 RNAF 12-4-47 as H-32
MK203 46MU 12-2-44 GAL 31-8 83GSU 30-9 CAC 3-11 401S 18-11 130S 17-5-45 WAL 20-6 33MU 27-9 sold R J Coley 3-2-50
MK204 6MU 30-1-44 485S 11-2 340S 8-6 FTR ops 20-6
MK205 39MU 28-1-44 313S 17-2 CAC ops 21-4 205S 29-6 332S 27-6 453S 5-10 AST 4-12 RNAF 29-9-46 as H-52 to H-101 BAF as SM31 w/o 11-10-52
MK206 33MU 30-1-44 442S 13-3 CAC ops 13-4 442S strk by Mosquito DD758 of 441S CE Ford 9-6
MK207 39MU 26-1-44 416S 13-2 CAC ops 26-7 AST 222MU 11-12 *Guinean* 22-12 Casa 15-1-45 IAF 26-6-47 as MM4120
MK208 9MU 28-1-44 313S 16-2 322S 4-9 CE ops 16-9
MK209 33MU 23-1-44 52MU 3-3 *Marsd* 22-4 Hap 29-5 Bas 10-8
MK210 LFIXC M61 R-RH eng trls Jan '44 39MU 30-1 47MU 14-2 mods for trls with increase fuel loads. Two underwing o/ld tanks of American design. *Carnarvon Castle* 25-2 Wright Field USA. Trls for range det Fuel syst drastically mod Ret UK by air non-stop. 200gals fuel carried, all military equip deleted. Flew from Newfoundland. BDn Aug '44. Trls to det effect of underwing tanks on level speed perf and position error correction. Hand trls. Mer 66 instal by R-RH 28-9 Trls with Bendix-Stromberg carb. 13SoTT Halton 22-1-45 to 4988M
MK211 6MU 30-1-44 313S 16-2 126S 27-7 DeH 16-1-45 CFE Tang 12-7 4S FAAC 5-12 recat E 22-1-46 SOC 31-1
MK212 9MU 28-1-44 443S 11-3 short of fuel after sweep w/u l/d nr Spettisbury Dorset CB 25-4 recat E 15-9
MK213 39MU 5-2-44 340S 3-3
MK226 39MU 22-12-43 47MU 31-1-44 *Fort Lrd* 1-3 Casa 17-3 SOC 31-8
MK227 33MU 24-12-43 82MU 24-1-44 *Fort Lrd* 1-3 Casa 17-3 IAF 27-6-46 MM4082
MK228 39MU 24-12-43 310S 5-2-44 CAC ops 22-5 66S 8-6 403S 5-10 WAL 16-2-45 33MU 1-6 sold Turk 18-7-47
MK229 33MU 24-12-43 82MU 11-1-44 *Fort Lrd* 1-3 Casa 17-3 MAAF 21-6-45 SOC 20-9
MK230 33MU 24-12-43 349S 1-3-44 401S 20-7 442S 31-8 602S 28-9 ASTE 16-1-45 9MU 18-6 RNAF 14-8-46 as H-58 later H-114 to spares
MK231 33MU 24-12-43 222MU 8-1-44 *Lds City* 21-1 Casa 17-2 2S C3 ops 26-6
MK232 LFIXB 9MU 20-1-44 416S 1-2-44 FACB 4-2 602S 15-6 401S 10-8 CAC ops 19-8 421S 22-8 CE ops 3-12-46

MK177 failed to return on 20 January 1945, while in service with 302 (Polish) Squadron.

MK233 33MU 29-12-43 349S 16-2-44 FAAC 13-4 416S 28-9 421S 1-12 FAAC 28-12 WAL 25-9-45 SOC 31-10

MK234 39MU 4-1-44 340S 31-1 ROS 13-2 332S 6-7 326S 5-4-45 FAF

MK235 9MU 1-2-44 504S 25-2-45 421S CE ops 13-6

MK236 39MU 2-1-44 331S 31-1 FAAC 2-4 AST sold J Dale 2-1-50

MK237 LFXIC 33MU 10-1-44 AST 18-2 412S 22-6 CAC ops 1-7 410RSU 28-9 CAC ops 27-9

MK238 39MU 4-1-44 341S 23-1 CE ops 10-6 AST 222MU 10-12 *Guinean* 22-12 Casa 10-1-45 CE ops 12-4 SOC 14-6

MK239 33MU 10-1-44 47MU 9-2 *Fort Lrd* 1-3 Casa 17-3 SOC 22-11-45

MK240 33MU 14-1-44 405ARF 24-2 83Gp Com S 29-6 e/a CE 1-1-45

MK241 33MU 14-1-44 442S 13-3 CAC ops 2-5 recat E 28-6

MK242 9MU 20-1-44 310S 8-2 91S 23-11 CAC ops 5-12 1S 12-4-45 3APS 13-9 SOC 24-9-46

MK243 33MU 10-1-44 222MU 11-2 *Fort Lrd* 1-3 Casa 17-3 SOC 30-8-45

MK244 9MU 20-1-44 312S 8-2 602S 6-7 CE ops 15-8

MK245 9MU 20-1-44 485S 6-2 FACB 27-7-45 recat E 6-9

MK246 9MU 20-1-44 485S 6-2 FAAC 25-3 ROS 126S 9-9 VAO 26-10 mods 126S 27-10 SAL 16-2-45 129S 15-11 FAAC 10-11 sold Turk 17-1-47

MK247 LFIXB 9MU 20-1-44 416S 10-2 AST 18-5 83GSU 18-10 308S 9-11 e/a dbf 1-1-45

MK248 9MU 20-1-44 312S 1-2 FTR ops 19-4

MK249 9MU 20-1-44 485S 6-2 349S 8-6 329S 22-6 414S 10-3 401S 26-4-45 FAAC 1-6 ROS RNAF 30-7-46

MK250 33MU 29-1-44 442S 13-3 AST 5-9 MAAF 12-3-45 SOC 14-3-46

MK251 33MU 28-1-44 331S 4-3 403S 5-10 AST 8-12 MAAF 12-4-45 FTR ops 24-4

MK252 39MU 25-1-44 485S 13-2 349S CE ops 8-6

MK253 33MU 29-1-44 405ARF 25-2 412S 22-6 CAC 18-7 442S 27-7 602S 19-10 2APU 9-5-45 MAAF 1-6 SOC 28-11-46

MK254 6MU 2-2-44 411ARF 16-2 313S CAC ops 29-5 312S 15-6 602S CAC ops 8-7 CB ops 9-8 511FRU 17-8 recat E 28-9

MK255 39MU 29-1-44 410ARF 18-2 602S 15-6 442S 24-8 MAAF 16-5-45 SOC 14-3-46

MK256 6MU 30-1-44 485S 11-2 ROS 16-4 317S 24-8 302S 31-8 308S CAC ops 5-12 e/a dbf 1-1-45

MK257 39MU 12-2-44 312S CAC 8-6 GAL 441S 24-8 91S 8-3-45 CAC ROS 12-12-46 Czech AF 10-6-47

MK258 6MU 2-2-44 504S 25-2 64S CE ops 24-7

MK259 9MU 4-2-44 83GSU 28-3 SAL 3-10 345S 1-3-45 327S 5-4

MK260 9MU 4-2-44 504S 25-2 453S 15-6 FTR ops 6-7

MK261 9MU 7-2-44 443S 11-3 MAAF 5-3-45 SOC 18-10

MK262 33MU 10-2-44 52MU 8-3 *Avris* 30-3 Hap 15-5

MK263 9MU 7-2-44 401S CB ops 22-6 AST 322S 25-1-45 485S 30-4 12Gr Com Flt 25-10 SOC scr 16-11-47

MK264 6MU 11-2-44 329S 28-2 FACB 5-3 AST 131Wg HQ 302S 31-8 e/a CE 1-1-45

MK265 6MU 5-2-44 329S 28-2 322S 20-8 414S 4-1-45 4CATC CE 9-3-45

MK266 39MU 12-2-44 312S FACB 12-4 AST 442S 24-8 401S 31-8 CAC ops 26-10 ROS 67MU 31-10 74S 8-2-45 CAC ops 9-2 317S 12-4 CAC ops 4-5 327S 31-5 FAF 27-11

MK267 33MU 15-2-44 no record

MK268 39MU 20-2-44 52MU 5-3 *St Cl* 3-4 Hap 15-5

MK280 39MU 25-1-44 485S 9-2 310S 8-6 629S 15-6 329S 22-6 340S 22-6 414S 7-8 recat E 2-10

MK281 9MU 28-1-44 504S 25-2 453S FACE 18-3 FH17.15

MK282 33MU 23-1-44 52MU 1-3 *Avris* 30-3 Hap 15-5

MK283 39MU 7-2-44 329S 28-2 411S 14-9 sold VA 5-12-49

MK284 6MU 2-2-44 504S 25-2 453S 15-6 401S 6-8 CAC ops 14-8 AST MAAF 12-3-45 ME 19-7 SOC 22-11

MK285 9MU 28-1-44 504S 25-2 453S 15-6 416S 27-7 443S 3-8 AST 18-12 FCCF North 6-7-45 to 6382M 25-7-45 Scrap 26-6-52

MK286 LFIXB 6MU 30-1-44 Flt Refuel 13-2 17APC South 5-3 442S 11-3 17APC FACE 23-5

MK287 9MU 28-1-44 504S 25-2 CAC ops 20-5 AST 308S 3-2-45 317S 29-3 326S 28-6 FAF 4-12

MK288 9MU 4-2-44 504S 25-2 453S FACB 9-6 GAL 23-9 mods 485S 16-11 435S 22-2-45 74S 1-3 345S FAAC 26-3 ROS 245S 2-7-46 sold Turk 1-5-47

MK289 39MU 7-2-44 84GSU 14-3 e/a CB 1-1-45 39MU 13-6 ROS 22-11 sold R J Coley 6-2-50

MK290 39MU 2-2-44 340S 3-3 CAC ops 6-6 414S 10-8 e/a CB 1-1-45 recat E 22-4 SOC 7-5

MK291 6MU 2-2-44 313S 16-2 64S CB ops 6-8 recat E 18-3-45

MK292 9MU 27-1-44 313S 14-2 420RSU 8-6 326S 5-4-45 339S 24-5 326S 28-6 FAF 4-12

MK293 6MU 29-1-44 485S 11-2 FAAC 31-3 329S 8-6 402S 17-7 FTR in trans 83RSU 2-1-45

MK294 6MU 30-1-44 340S 13-2 FAAC 4-5 421RSU 511FRU 22-6 602S 29-10 453S 30-10 DeH 28-2-45 WAL 24-9 sold Turk 24-10-47

MK295 33MU 23-1-44 442S 13-3 CAC 23-4 602S 28-9 327S 5-4-45 326S 11-10 FAF GC2/1

MK296 39MU 23-1-44 52MU 9-2 *Fort Lrd* 1-3 Casa 17-3 SOC 14-3-46

MK297 still wearing Belgian identity, prior to becoming G-ASSD. It flies today in Texas as N11RS.

MK297 6MU 30-1-44 411ARF 12-2 66S 17-2 ASTH 12-2-45 RNAF 27-9-46 as H-55 later H-116 BAF 9-53 SM43 to COGEA 00-ARB To G-ASSD with parts of MH434 civil reg cancel 18-4-69. To USA as N1882, later NX9BL. Extant Confederate A/F, Breckenridge, Texas, as N11RS.

MK298 39MU 4-2-44 329S 29-2 FAAC 7-6 341S 22-6 322S CAC ops 5-9 ROS 222MU 11-12 FLS CFE Tang 10-5-45 sold VASM 31-10-46 con to two-seat train 24-5-48

MK299 9MU 28-1-44 504S 25-2 453S 15-6 132S 20-7 403S 27-7 CE ops 17-8

MK300 39MU 30-1-44 405ARF 12-3 401S 22-6 FAAC 4-8 411S 31-3 401S 12-10 CE ops 29-12

MK301 6MU 29-1-44 485S 11-2 329S 8-6 13-7 350S e/fd f/ld o/t CE Westh 7-9 AST

MK302 39MU 28-1-44 485S 13-2 349S 8-6 332S 22-6 CB ops 13-9 33MU 13-1-45 MAAF 29-3 IAF 26-6-47 as MM4017

MK303 39MU 26-2-44 341S 13-2 FAAC 28-4 AST 442S 9-12 VASM 31-10-46 to 6456M 4SoTT 15-10-47 SOC 18-11-53

MK304 LFIXE 39MU 23-1-44 310S 7-2 442S 13-7 412S CE ops 2-8 WAL 14-10 19MU 20-4-45 331S FACE 21-9

MK305 39MU 2-2-44 329MU 7-3 FACB 29-5 recat E 6-7

MK306 39MU 28-1-44 405ARF 11-2 GAL 28-9 412S 14-12 FAAC 29-5-45 151RU 9-8 3BRU recat E 4-7-46

MK307 33MU 10-2-44 52MU 5-3 *St Cl* 3-4 Hap 15-5

MK308 6MU 4-2-44 340S 18-2 341S 13-7 34WSU HQ Flt 23-11 1401 Met Flt 25-2-45 ASTH 19-9 sold Turk 6-8-47

MK309 33MU 29-1-44 442S 13-3 453S 22-6 511FRU 26-6 126S 6-8 sold Turk 23-8-47

MK310 38MU 21-2-44 52MU 13-3 *St Cl* 2-4 Hap 15-5

MK311 39MU 7-2-44 ROS 3-5 411S 22-6 CAC ops 28-6 401S 6-7 FTR ops 26-7

MK312 LFIXB 9MU 26-1-44 Flt Refuel 8-2 17APC South 29-2 FLS CFE Mlfld 5-10 FAAC 13-2-45 58MU u/c coll ld Haw FACB 2-10-46 recat E 10-2-47

MK313 39MU 28-1-44 222MU 11-2 *Fort Lrd* 1-3 Casa 17-3 SOC 20-9-45

MK314 39MU 2-2-44 215MU 18-2 *Emp Ray* 21-3 Casa 8-4 FTR 1-8-45 cancel ME 26-6-47 SOC 31-7

MK315 9MU 6-2-44 443S 11-3 410RSU 23-9 CB ops 27-9 403S 23-11 AST 8-12 MAAF 10-5-45 dam in trans C3 28-5 rtp 20-7

MK316 9MU 28-1-44 329S 3-3 FACB 17-4 AST 308S 15-6 CB ops 1-10 AST 3APU Llan 9-5-45 MAAF 16-7 107MU strk vehicle taxy Kasfareet Egypt 2-11-46 ME 26-6-47 SOC 31-7

MK317 39MU 30-1-44 47MU 14-2 *Carnarvon Castle* 25-2 New York 10-3 Wright Field USA with MK210 1-7 Ret UK ASTH 24-9-45 Farn Sept '45 fuel cons trls. ETPS Farn Jan to Feb '45 trls with Bendix-Strom carb 29MU 6-4-46 con to standard FIX sold Turk 22-8-47

MK318 39MU 4-2-44 329S 3-3 341S 22-6 165S 20-9 CAC ops 9-11 151RU 9-3-45 sold VA 8-12-49

MK319 9MU 4-2-44 329S 3-3 421RSU 15-6 322S CAC ops 17-8 AST WAL 1-12 mods MAAF 4-3-45 FACE 13-7

MK320 9MU 28-1-44 313S 18-5 FAAC 322S CAC ops 20-8 326S 22-9

MK321 9MU 12-2-44 443S 11-3 out of fuel ret from sweep w/u ldg Puddleton Dorset CE 25-4

MK322 9MU 4-2-44 329S 3-3 CB ops 12-5 332S 13-7 16S 20-7 34WSU 19-10 ROS 9-12 AST 2-1-45 611S 4-2 CB ops 4-2 MAAF SOC 30-1-47

MK323 9MU 1-2-44 329S 3-3 AST 84GSU 30-10 FA cd Ryde IoW CE 11-11

MK324 6MU 2-2-44 504S 25-2 453S FTR ops carrying bomb for spcl target 14-4

MK325 6MU 2-2-44 504S 25-2 453S CB ops 23-4 recat E 15-9

MK326 38MU 5-2-44 442S 13-3 CE ops 13-5

MK339 39MU 2-2-44 222MU 23-2 *Fort Lrd* 1-3 Casa 17-3 ME 26-6-47 SOC 28-8

MK340 39MU 7-2-44 82MU 18-2 *Fort Lrd* 1-3 Casa 17-3 SOC 30-6

MK341 6MU 30-1-44 405ARF 11-2 403S CAC ops 19-5 332S e/fd a/c aban i/sea off Hastings 19-6

MK342 LFIXB 9MU 4-2-44 329S 3-3 strk Tiger Moth DE808 on t/o CE Perr 16-4

MK343 9MU 4-2-44 443S 11-3 CB ops 17-6 322S 9-11 414S 18-1-45 CE ops 27-2

MK344 9MU 4-2-44 313S 16-2 FACE 26-4

MK345 38MU 10-2-44 52MU 13-3 *St Cl* 3-4 Hap 15-5

MK346 6MU 4-2-44 329S 28-2 air coll in cloud with MK373 cd Wappington Farm Horsham Sussex CB 26-4 AST 332S 15-6 ASTH 14-10 308S 9-11 CB ops 2-1-45 recat E 12-3-45

MK347 6MU 30-1-44 485S 11-2 329S 8-6 ROS 414S 10-8 CB ops 28-9 302S 12-10 ASTE 11-5-45 sold Turk 1-10-47

MK348 39MU 9-4-44 82MU 18-2 *Fort Lrd* 1-3 Casa 17-3 4S CE ops 13-7

MK349 33MU 8-2-44 52MU 5-3 *St Cl* 3-4 Hap 15-5

MK350 6MU 4-2-44 441S 11-3 602S 22-6 402S FTR ops 17-7

MK351 33MU 5-2-44 52MU 5-3 *St Cl* 3-4 Hap 15-5 Bas 20-5

MK352 39MU 20-2-44 52MU 3-3 *Avris* 30-3 Hap 15-5

MK353 33MU 15-2-44 82MU 26-2 *Emp Ray* 21-3 Casa 6-4 72S C3 ops 26-6

MK354 6MU 4-2-44 349S 16-2 341S 22-6 66S 19-7

MK355 6MU 4-2-44 504S 25-2 453S 15-6 412S 10-8 401S 5-10 83GSU 15-3-45 FACE 29-3 SOC 12-4

MK356 9MU 4-2-44 443S 11-3 83GSU 6-8 to 5690M RAF Halton 2-10-45 BoB film extant RAF StA

MK357 39MU 4-2-44 FAAC 17-2 ROS 215MU 28-2 *Emp Ray* 21-3 Casa 6-4 ME 16-8-45 RHAF 30-147

MK358 46MU 12-4-44 MAL 17-4 mods 302S 15-6 84GSU 25-1-45 ROS ASTE 24-9 sold VA 5-10-49

MK359 39MU 4-2-44 329S 29-2 414S 10-8 CAC ops 6-11 151RU 25-1-45 ASTH 12-2 sold H Bath 27-11-49

MK360 6MU 9-2-44 329S 28-2 CE ops 26-4

MK361 6MU 7-2-44 126S 7-5 313S 8-6 ROS 20-7 222MU 20-12 *Taneli* 13-1-45 Casa 25-1 ME 16-8 RHAF 30-1-47

MK362 6MU 4-2-44 349S 16-2 66S 8-6 FAAC 26-8 CB ops 23-9 DeH 165S 20-5-45 FAAC 21-8-46 recat E SOC scr dump 8-11

MK363 6MU 4-2-44 349S 16-2 CE ops 6-6 74S 14-5-45

MK364 39MU 20-2-44 132S CE ops 12-6 411RSU 15-6

MK365 39MU 2-2-44 341S 18-2 349S 22-6 421S 6-7 CAC ops 2-10

MK366 39MU 15-2-44 132S 15-6 602S 20-7 AST 23-7 126Wg HQ 17-8 401S 412S 31-8 453S 5-10 328S 5-4-45

MK367 9MU 7-2-44 443S 11-3 132S 22-6 CB ops 4-7 AST 222MU 15-11 *Guinean* 22-12 Casa 15-1-45 SOC 31-12-46

MK368 33MU 8-2-44 52MU 14-3 *Avris* 30-3 Hap 15-5

MK369 33MU 23-6-44 329S 3-8 327S CAC ops 28-8 329S 31-8 CAC ops 21-2-45 345S 1-3 BAFO 14-3-47

MK370 33MU 4-2-44 302S 3-5 341S 15-6 CAC ops 18-7 ROS 302S ftr ops 7-12

MK371 33MU 9-2-44 52MU 26-3 *Marsd* 22-4 Hap 29-5

MK372 33MU 8-2-44 27-2 *Emp Ray* 21-3 Casa 6-4 CE ops 18-4 ME SOC 14-6

MK373 6MU 7-2-44 329S 28-2 air coll in cloud with MK346 f/ld Wappingdton Farm Horsham Sussex CE 26-4

MK374 39MU 7-2-44 329S 28-2 414S 10-8 CAC ops 18-11 e/a CB 1-1-45 recat E SOC 3-4-47

MK375 39MU 9-2-44 441S 11-3 222MU 22-12 *Guinean* 22-12 Casa 15-1-45 IAF 27-6-46 as MM4077

MK376 33MU 24-2-44 82MU 6-3 *Emp Ray* 21-3 Casa 6-4 601S FTR ops 18-7

MK377 33MU 21-2-44 52MU 8-3 *St Cl* 3-4 Hap 15-5

MK378 39MU 4-2-44 56S 20-5 CB ops 30-6 GAL MAAF 11-2 FAF 28-3-46

MK379 39MU 11-2-44 453S 15-6 421S 23-7 CAC ops 13-8 AST MAAF 16-5-45 ME SOC 26-9-46

MK392 8MU 12-2-44 441S 13-3 443S 27-7 403S 23-11 416S 11-1-45 401S CE ops 20-4

MK393 33MU 8-2-44 82MU 26-2 *Emp Ray* 21-3 Casa 6-4 ME 26-7-45 SOC 28-3-47

MK394 8MU 20-2-44 441S 13-3 CE ops 26-4

MK395 33MU 20-2-44 52MU 8-3 *St Cl* 3-4 Hap 15-5

MK396 33MU 10-2-44 215MU 10-3 *Emp Ray* 21-3 Casa 6-4 SOC 31-12

MK397 9MU 7-2-44 443S 11-3 FTR ops 16-6

MK398 39MU 11-2-44 FACB 19-2 AST 308S 11-1-45 CAC ops 14-2 FAF GC1/6

MK399 8MU 12-2-44 441S 13-3 FACE 15-6

MK400 33MU 15-2-44 47MU 1-3 *Emp Ray* 21-3 Casa 6-4 SOC 30-6

MK401 39MU 15-2-44 52MU 28-2 *Marsd* 22-2 Hap 29-5

MK402 33MU 15-2-44 222MU 26-2 *Emp Ray* 21-3 Casa 6-4 SOC 18-10-45

MK403 46MU 12-2-44 ASTH 25-5 302S 15-6 317S 11-1-45 GACB 15-3-45 MAL 26-3 RNAF 19-5-48 as H-29

MK404 33MU 9-2-44 222MU 26-2 *Emp Ray* 21-3 Casa 6-4 SOC 12-9-45

MK405 39MU 15-2-44 222MU 28-2 *Emp Ray* 21-3 Casa 6-4 FTR ops 3-3-45

MK406 33MU 12-2-44 47MU 1-3 *Emp Ray* 21-3 Casa 6-4 FTR ops 5-10

MK407 46MU 12-2-44 421S CAC ops 30-6 FA SOC 26-2-45

MK408 33MU 21-2-44 222MU 2-3 *Emp Ray* 21-3 Casa 6-4 7S C3 ops 21-7

MK409 39MU 15-2-44 52MU 28-2 *Avris* 30-3 Hap 15-5

MK410 33MU 15-2-44 82MU 27-2 *Emp Ray* 21-3 Casa 6-4 SOC 31-1-45

MK411 39MU 25-2-44 222MU 12-3 *Emp Ray* 21-3 Casa 6-4 FACE 8-6

MK412 39MU 11-2-44 222MU 22-2 *Emp Ray* 21-3 Casa 6-4 FAF 29-3-46

MK413 39MU 10-2-44 AST 14-3 9MU 23-5 AST 23-7 recat E 1-9 MAAF 10-4-45 IAF 26-6-47 as MM4124

MK414 39MU 20-2-44 222MU 2-3 *Emp Ray* 21-3 Casa 6-4 CE ops 6-3-45

MK415 39MU 24-2-44 441S 11-3 CAC ops 1-7 ROS MAAF 2-2-45 REAF 30-4-47 ME 27-11 SOC 26-2-48

MK416 6MU 15-2-44 no record

MK417 6MU 9-2-44 441S 12-3 416S 28-9 CB ops 8-12 410RSU 16-12

MK418 6MU 15-2-44 329S 28-2 453S 15-6 329S 22-6 3501SU 9-7 126S 27-7 e/a CE 8-12-45

MK419 33MU 21-2-44 82MU 5-5 *Emp Ray* 21-3 Casa 6-4 IAF 17-6-46 as MM4085

MK420 39MU 20-2-44 441S 11-3 CE ops 6-6 GAL recat B 17-10 442S e/a CE 1-1-45

MK421 8MU 20-2-44 83GSU 24-3 453S 15-6 421S 27-7 CB ops 6-8

MK422 39MU 15-2-44 222MU 28-2 *Emp Ray* 21-3 Casa 6-4 SOC 23-10

MK423 8MU 12-2-44 331S FAAC 6-6 511FRU 8-6 411S 29-6 1S 7-7 AST 29-9 VAO 22-12 mods 317S 25-1-45 AST 25-2 MAAF 5-4 SOC 2-8

MK424 39MU 24-2-44 222MU 4-3 *Emp Ray* 21-3 Casa 6-4 232S ops 11-6

MK425 46MU 12-2-43 501SU12-6 165S 22-6 CAC ops 11-9 ROS CE dbf ops 5-1-45

MK426 39MU 25-2-44 165S 30-3 91S 23-11 1S 12-4-45 VASM 31-10-46 new eng 6MU 1-9-47 to 6459M 13-10 RDAF 28-7-48

MK427 39MU 25-2-44 52MU 12-3 *Avris* 20-3 Hap 15-5

MK428 33MU 25-2-44 52MU 20-3 *Marsd* 22-4 Hap 29-5

MK440 39MU 25-2-44 222MU 12-3 *Emp Ray* 21-3 Casa 6-4 SOC 20-9-45

MK441 39MU 25-2-45 222MU 12-3 *Emp Ray* 21-3 Casa 6-4 SOC 13-9-45

MK442 33MU 24-2-44 52MU 12-4 *Afghan* 12-5 Hap 5-7

MK443 6MU 20-2-44 441S 11-3 AST 14-5 215MU 10-12 *Tarelle* 13-1-45 Casa 25-1 ME 26-4 SOC 28-8-47

MK444 33MU 15-2-44 222MU 22-2 *Emp Ray* 21-3 Casa 6-4 ME 28-12 MAAF 31-5-45

MK445 33MU 24-2-44 82MU 5-3 *Emp Ray* 21-3 Casa 6-4 ME 31-3-45 MAAF 30-6 SOC 2-8

MK446 39MU 28-2-44 52MU *St Cl* 3-4 Hap 15-5

MK447 39MU 22-2-44 222MU 3-3 *Emp Ray* 21-3 Casa 6-4 FTR ops 6-3-45

MK448 33MU 21-2-44 222MU 3-3 *Emp Ray* 21-3 Casa 6-4 ME 9-8-45 SOC 26-9-46

MK449 39MU 20-2-44 66S 7-3 CE ops 15-7

MK450 39MU 20-2-44 52MU 3-3 *St Cl* 3-4 Hap 15-5

MK451 33MU 21-2-44 52MU 8-3 *St Cl* 3-4 Hap 15-5

MK452 33MU 21-2-44 52MU 8-3 *St Cl 3-4* Hap 15-5

MK453 6MU 15-2-44 329S 28-2 3501SU 9-7 402S 11-8 91S FTR ops28-10

MK454 33MU 1-3-44 215MU 14-3 *Emp Ray* 21-3 Casa 6-4 FACE 6-2-45

MK455 39MU 1-3-44 52MU 7-3 *Marsd* 23-4 Hap 29-5 Bas 29-6

MK456 33MU 15-2-44 215MU 14-3 *Emp Ray* 21-3 Casa 6-4 AST 24-5-45 FAF 25-6-46 GC1/6

MK457 33MU 1-3-44 52MU 20-3 *Marsd* 22-2 Hap 29-5 Bas 10-6

MK458 33MU 21-2-44 215MU 20-3 *Emp Pea* 21-4 Casa 12-5 SOC 10-4-45

MK459 33MU 21-2-44 222MU 3-3 *Emp Ray* 21-3 Casa 6-4 SOC 30-4-47

MK360 8MU 20-1-44 441S 24-3 e/fd t/o f/ld Chessels Farm Handon Sussex CB 8-6 recat E 28-6

MK461 39MU 21-2-44 52MU 7-3 *St Cl* 3-4 Hap 15-5

MK462 39MU 2-3-44 83GSU 6-5 411S 29-6 CE ops 15-7

MK463 33MU 25-2-44 215MU 9-3 *Emp Ray* 21-3 Casas 6-4 SOC 20-9-45

MK464 39MU 5-3-44 442S 27-7 CAC ops 14-8 602S 28-9 WAL 12-10 FAAC 1-12 1S 3-2-45 SAL 22-4 FAF 16-9-46

MK465 8MU 2-2-44 441S 13-3 s/dn into Channel ops 6-6

MK466 8MU 20-2-33 441S 13-3 tyre burst on t/o o/t Ford CE 12-6 411RSU 15-6

MK467 39MU 29-2-44 47MU 18-3 *Emp Pea* 21-4 Casa 12-5 SNCAN 21-6-45

MK468 8MU 20-2-44 83GSU 24-3 421S 6-7 440S 13-7 443S 27-7 CE ops 23-8

MK469 39MU 1-3-44 222MU 14-3 *Emp Ray* 21-3 Casa 6-4 SOC 18-10-45

MK470 33MU 20-2-44 52MU 8-3 *St Cl* 3-4 Hap 15-5

MK471 39MU 2-3-44 165S 30-3 FTR ops 12-6

MK472 39MU 28-2-44 83GSU 24-3 421S CB ops 15-6 recat E 21-6

MK473 39MU 24-4-44 215MU 12-3 *Emp Pea* 21-4 Casa 12-5 FTR 27-2-45

MK474 39MU 21-2-44 66S 7-3 CAC ops 27-8 66S 7-9 453S 5-10 451S 15-12

MK475 39MU 2-3-44 56S 9-5 CAC ops 3-6 ROS 402S 24-8 64S 11-9 GAL 12-12 mods SAL 2-3-45 RNAF 15-4-48 as H-28 to PH-NFO

MK476 39MU 20-2-44 47MU 29-2 *Emp Ray* 21-3 Casa 6-4 CE ops 20-2-45 29MU 21-5-46 sold VA 28-11-49

MK477 33MU 21-2-44 52MU 13-3 *St Cl* 3-4 Hap 15-5

MK478 39MU 28-2-44 215MU 12-3 *Emp Ray* 21-3 Casa 6-4 MAAF 26-4-45 ME 26-6-47 SOC 28-8

MK479 33MU 21-2-44 222MU 2-3 *Emp Ray* 21-3 Casa 6-4 SOC 14-3-46

MK480 39MU 2-3-44 165S 11-4 403S CE ops 19-5 bboc MAL 7-2-45 19MU 20-4 331S 30-4 FACE 26-5 recat E 10-7 SOC 30-7

MK481 33MU 1-3-44 82MU 13-3 *Emp Raj* 21-3 Casa 6-4 SOC 18-8

MK482 39MU 1-3-44 222MU 13-3 *Emp Raj* 21-3 Casa 6- SOC 14-3-46

MK483 39MU 25-2-44 84GSU 14-3 312S 8-6 64S coll on runway with MK720 CAC Harrow 10-7 ROS MAL 20-11 39MU 4-3-45 MAAF 21-6 RHAF 29-5-47

MK484 39MU 28-2-44 341S 6-4 CAC ops 6-7 421S 5-10 328S 5-4-45 130S e/fd w/u ldg Marsh Farm Metheringham Lincs 26-5

MK485 33MU 25-2-44 82MU 7-3 *Emp Raj* 21-3 Casa 6-4 2S CE ops 1-3

MK486 38MU 24-2-44 82MU 8-3 *Emp Raj* 21-3 Casa 6-4 FACE 6-11

MK499 39MU 24-2-44 52MU 8-3 *Marsd* 22-4 Hap 29-5 Bas 10-6

MK500 39MU 24-2-44 215MU 9-3 *Emp Raj* 21-3 Casa 6-4 SOC 20-9-45

MK501 33MU 25-2-44 82MU 7-3 *Emp Raj* 21-3 Casa 6-4 ME 31-5-45 SOC 2-8

MK502 39MU 25-2-44 52MU 9-3 *Avris* 20-3 Hap 15-5

MK503 8MU 20-2-44 441S 13-3 FAAC 18-4 ROS 3501SU 21-8 Stn HQ Mans 5-10 411S 29-3-45 3BRU 9-8 CE

MK504 39MU 24-2-44 441S 11-3 FAAC 18-4 83GSU 17-8 416S e/a 21-10 SAL 16-2-45 165S 25-5 66S 2-9-46 SOC scr 16-11-47

MK505 33MU 21-2-44 52MU 13-2 *Marsd* 22-4 Hap 29-5 Bas 10-6

MK506 33MU 1-3-44 52MU 15-4 *Inver* 21-5 Hap 6-7

MK507 39MU 4-3-44 83GSU 6-5 403S CE ops 15-5

MK508 39MU 2-3-44 165S 29-3 e/fd w/u ldg nr Penzance CB 12-5 recat E 30-5

MK509 39MU 25-2-44 52MU 9-3 *St Cl* 3-4 Hap 15-5

MK510 39MU 28-244 453S 15-6 127Wg HQ 10-3 CAC ops 2-10 421S 12-10 SOC 17-1-45

MK511 39MU 1-3-44 222S 14-4 CAC ops 19-5 FTR ops 1-12

MK512 33MU 6-3-44 222MU 31-3 *Emp Pea* 21-4 Casa SOC 18-8-45

MK513 33MU 25-2-44 82MU 13-3 *Emp Raj* 21-3 Casa 6-4 SOC 20-9-45

MK514 39MU 3-3-44 165S 28-3 ASTH 12-2-45 SOC scr 16-10-47

MK515 39MU 24-2-44 441S 11-3 FAAC 15-6 91S 8-3-45 1S Mans 12-4 6MU NEA 15-1-47 SOC scrap 16-11-47

MK516 33MU 4-3-44 420RSU 14-9 332S 21-9 403S 9-11 1CRU Cowley 2-3-45 FSU Dyce 27-6-45 130S 16-9 595S 30-5-46 SOC OA 24-8-48

MK517 39MU 2-3-44 56S 9-5 402S 17-7 ROS 8-8 Stn Flt Hawk 5-10 SAL 19-3-45 sold Turk 23-10-47

MK518 33MU 25-2-44 222MU 13-3 *Marsd* 22-2 Ban 10-6

MK519 8MU 28-2-44 441S 13-3

MK520 33MU 19-3-44 302S 1-5 341S 15-6 145S 29-6 3501SU 9-7 322S 4-9

MK521 33MU 1-3-44 222MU 21-3 *Emp Pea* 21-4 Casa 12-5 SOC 30-6

MK522 39MU 24-2-44 52MU 9-3 *Avris* 30-3 Hap 15-5

MK523 33MU 8-3-44 52MU 6-4 *Marsd* 22-4 Hap 29-5 Bas 10-6

MK524 39MU 2-3-44 CAC 26-3 83GSU 24-5-44 441S CB ops 29-6 511FRU 13-7 126S 6-8 130S 8-6-45 595S 2-5-46 to 6583M 24-8-48 RAF Henlow 24-8-48

MK525 39MU 22-2-44 52MU 8-3 *Marsd* 22-4 Hap 29-5 Bas 10-6

MK526 39MU 24-2-44 52MU 8-3 *Marsd* 22-4 Hap 29-5 Bas 10-6

MK527 33MU 2-3-44 52MU 13-4 *Afghan* 12-5 5-7

MK528 33MU 25-2-44 222MU 3-3 *Emp Raj* 21-3 Casa 6-4 SOC 30-4-47

MK529 9MU 5-4-44 308S 3-5 16S 22-6 CB ops 7-8 485S 11-1-45 FTR ops 9-2-45 cd in Holland

MK530 38MU 24-2-44 82MU 7-3 *Emp Raj* 21-3 Casa 6-4 FTR ops 8-2-45

MK531 39MU 1-3-44 83GSU 26-5 411S CE ops 25-6

MK532 33MU 5-3-44 313S CAC ops 21-5 SAL 20-11 MAAF 16-5-45 RHAF 27-2-47

MK533 39MU 28-2-44 52MU 14-3 *St Cl* 3-4 Hap 15-5

MK534 33MU 12-3-44 84GSU 26-3 FAAC 30-11 ROS WAL 14-6-45 sold Turk 25-9-47

MK547 LFIXB 6MU 16-2-44 504S 25-2 453S CAC 15-4 ROS GAL 12-8 308S CAC ops 14-10 MAAF 21-4-45

MK548 39MU 20-2-44 52MU 29-2 *Avris* 30-3 Hap 15-5

MK549 33MU 16-2-44 222MU 20-3 *Emp Pea* 21-4 Casa 12-5 FTR ops 20-3-45

MK550 39MU 20-2-44 52MU 5-3 *St Cl* 3-4 Hap 20-5

MK551 39MU 20-2-44 47MU 29-2 *Emp Raj* 21-3 Casa 6-4 SOC 28-4-45

MK552 39MU 21-2-44 82MU 5-3 *Emp Raj* 21-3 Casa 6-4 ME 31-5

MK553 39MU 21-2-44 47MU 29-2 *Emp Raj* 21-3 Casa 6-4 SOC 18-10-45

MK554 39MU 1-3-44 52MU 14-3 *Inver* 21-5 Hap 6-7

MK555 33MU 24-2-44 222MU 3-3 *Emp Raj* 21-3 Casa 6-4 IAF 26-6-47 as MM4114

MK556 39MU 21-2-44 52MU 8-3 *Marsd* 23-4 Hap 29-5 Bas 10-6

MK557 39MU 1-3-44 222MU 13-3 *Emp Raj* 21-3 Casa 6-4 IAF 27-6-46 as MM4101

MK558 39MU 2-3-44 222MU 13-3 *Emp Raj* 21-3 Casa 6-4 SOC 20-9-45

MK559 39MU 1-3-44 341S FAAC 19-6 416S 27-7 e/a CB 21-10 sold Turk 17-1-47

MK560 33MU 4-3-44 401S 22-6 CAC ops 24-7 442S 31-8 416S 19-10 FAAC 18-11 ASTH 3-2-45 FAF 27-7-46 GC1/4

MK561 39MU 3-3-44 341S 6-4 FAAC 10-6 33MU 23-8

MK562 39MU 1-3-44 82MU 18-3 *Emp Pea* 21-4 Casa 12-5 SOC 18-8-45

MK563 39MU 12-3-44 83GSU 15-6 mods 329S 15-6 3501SU 9-7 350S 11-8 322S 4-9 414S 4-1-45 CE ops 25-3

MK564 39MU 5-3-44 165S 29-3-44 341S 25-5 403S CE ops 15-6 453S 13-7 403S 14-8 443S 1-3-45 401S 29-3 sold Turk 14-10-47

MK565 39MU 1-3-44 no record

MK566 39MU 1-3-44 452S FTR ops 21-5

MK567 39MU 5-3-44 165S 28-3 FTR ops 12-6

MK568 39MU 12-3-44 302S 3-5 412S 20-7 AST 1-9 WAL 15-12 mods MAAF 5-2-45 SOC 30-4-47

MK569 39MU 12-3-44 66S 8-6 453S 5-10 1CRU Cowley 4-1-45 3APU 13-4 MAAF 16-5 IAF 26-6-47 as MM4122

MK570 33MU 18-3-44 84GSU 5-5 403S FTR ops 18-6

MK571 33MU 4-3-44 215MU 15-3 *Emp Raj* 21-3 Casa 6-4 RHAF 30-4-47

MK572 39MU 12-3-44 56S 9-5 402S 17-7 91S CAC ops 20-8 ROS 1S 13-1-45 FACB 14-1 Com Flt Bovington 6-9-46 to 6379M 2-1-48 SOC 12-10-49

MK573 39MU 12-3-44 421S CAC ops 30-6 FAAC 3-11 CAC ops 29-11 411S 8-2-45 Sch of AS Old Sarum 41Gp HQ 26-4-45 to 5236M SOC 23-5-50

MK574 6MU 4-4-44 86MU 3-9

MK575 39MU 12-3-44 453S 15-6 443S 26-7 MAL 4-1-45 MAAF 16-5 ME 26-6-47 137MU 26-2-45 RHAF 27-5-48

MK576 33MU 19-3-44 412S 22-6 CAC ops 29-6 CE ops 13-8

MK577 6MU 4-4-44 329S 8-6 MAL 18-7 411S 24-3 401S 31-8 SAL 4-3-45 BAF 11-8-48 as SM-21

MK578 33MU 18-3-44 302S 30-4 308S 15-6 FTR SOC 16-6 cancel AST 20-10 222MU 12-12 *Guinean* 22-12 Casa 15-1-45 REAF 31-10-46

MK579 6MU 4-4-44 132S 15-6 441S 132S CB ops 23-6 401S 6-7 WAL 10-12 mods FCC Flt North 22-6-45 sold VA 5-12-49

MK580 33MU 18-3-44 84GSU 27-4 recat E 16-7

MK581 8MU 26-3-44 331S 8-9 49MU CAC 8-7

MK582 33MU 18-3 329S 27-4 CE ops 2-5

MK583 33MU 19-3-44 1S 11-4 ROS 11-6 AST 11-9 WAL mods sold Turk 23-1-47

MK584 33MU 21-3-44 52MU 6-4 *Marsd* 22-4 Hap 29-5 Bas 10-6

MK585 8MU 26-3-44 56S 4-5 MAL 18-7 441S 28-9 FTR ops 23-1-45

MK586 8MU 24-3-44 66S 8-6 CAC ops 20-6 66S 27-7 453S 5-10 MAAF 9-7-45 IAF 26-6-47

MK587 6MU 4-4-44 329S 8-6 3501SU 9-7 402S 25-7 91S FTR 7-12

MK588 8MU 26-3-44 332S 5-5 420RSU CAC 6-7 332S 27-7 CE ops 17-9

MK589 8MU 26-3-44 165S 30-5 FTR ops 6-6

MK590 8MU 27-3-44 401S 22-6 412S 31-8 453S 28-9 ASREx 10-2-45 16FU tyre burst on t/o tip onto nose St Maw CE 12-9-46 SOC 29-1-47

MK602 9MU 2-1-44 ROS 28-1 443S 11-3 CAC ops 25-5 AST 441S FTR 6-11

MK603 39MU 23-1-44 222MU 12-2 *Fort Lrd* 1-3 Casa 17-3 326S 26-4-45 FAF 27-11-45 GC1/1 des 11-7-51

MK604 39MU 23-1-44 no record

MK605 9MU 1-2-44 443S 11-3 CAC 10-5 CE ops 8-6

MK606 9MU 29-1-44 313S 17-2 FACB 4-8 recat AC 322S 709 AST 5-12 RNAF 15-5-47 as H-50 later H-111 to spares

MK607 9MU 29-1-44 443S 14-3 FTR ops 16-6

MK608 9MU 1-2-44 411ARF 12-2 312S CE ops 15-5

MK609 9MU 1-2-44 313S 21-2 o/s ldg trk wall CE South 15-3

MK610 9MU 1-2-44 132S FAAC 11-4 ROS GAL 17-8 317S 2-11 e/a CE 1-1-45

MK611 9MU 1-2-44 603S FAAC 22-5 CB ops 16-6 511FRU 22-6 MAL 18-7 443S CE ops 30-11

MK612 9MU 1-2-44 602S 15-6 412S 24-8 CB ops 5-10 PCE 16-10

MK613 33MU 8-2-44 52MU 8-3 *Avrist* 30-3 Hap 15-5

MK614 9MU 6-2-44 83GSU 12-3 602S 15-6 FTR ops 1-8

MK615 33MU 8-2-44 52MU 1-3 *Avrist* 20-3 Hap 15-5

MK616 39MU 10-2-44 CE 10-2

MK617 cd on del flt CE 10-2-44 rtp not to be counted. Serial alloc to new a/c now in USSR 27-8 new a/c 39MU 24-5 52MU 14-6 *Avris* 29-6 Hap Bas 22-8

MK618 9MU 12-2-44 435S 12-3 CE ops 24-7

MK619 39MU 20-2-44 66S 7-3 AST 25-3 FAAC 7-7 AST 3501SU 16-10 328S 5-4-45 FAF GC1/1 des 16-10-48

MK620 33MU 24-2-44 215MU 14-3 *Emp Raj* 21-3 Casa 6-4 SOC 30-6

MK621 39MU 26-2-44 215MU 21-3 *Emp Pea* 21-4 Casa 12-5 FACE 3-7

MK622 9MU 20-2-44 412S 22-6 FTR ops 7-7

MK623 9MU 20-2-44 e/a 3-3 ROS AST 31-5 308S 15-6 CB ops 15-3-45 bou SOC 16-10-47

MK624 9MU 20-2-44 602S 12-3 SAL 10-7 mods recat E 11-6-45

MK625 33MU 24-2-44 82MU 9-3 *Emp Raj* 21-3 Casa 6-4 ME 27-9-45 SOC 28-8-47

MK626 39MU 26-2-44 52MU 12-3 *Avris* 20-3 Hap 15-5

MK627 39MU 26-2-44 215MU 9-3 *Emp Raj* 21-3 Casa 6-4 CE ops 12-11

MK628 9MU 20-2-44 132S 15-6 403S CAC 23-7 AST 8-12 sold Turk 15-4-47

MK629 39MU 26-2-44 215MU 9-3 *Emp Raj* 21-3 Casa 6-4

MK630 39MU 26-2-44 411S 24-8 442S 31-8 412S 7-9 602S AST 4-12 453S 3-12 RNAF 18-7-46 as H-19

MK6312 LFIXB 9MU 1-3-44 132S CE ops 14-6 411RSU 15-6 83GSU strk by taxy PL130 CE Thorney Island 2-10 AST 222MU 31-12 49MU CE 14-3-47

MK632 9MU 1-3-44 401S 29-6 412S 31-8 421S 19-10 AST 2-1-45 39MU 29-5 RNAF 17-7-46 as H-13

MK633 39MU 29-2-44 331S 8-6 443S 11-1 45 411S 1-3 FACE 17-4

MK634 39MU 29-2-44 222MU 14-3 *Emp Raj* 21-3 Casa 6-4 4S FTR 18-7

MK635 9MU 9-3-44 56S 17-6 402S 17-7 91S CE ops 1-9

MK636 9MU 9-3-44 443S 27-7 CAC ops 17-8 ASTH 30-8 12FU 12-1-45 MAAF 10-2 IAF 30-5-46 as MM4080

MK637 39MU 5-3-44 165S 28-3 9MU 23-3-45 MAAF 30-4 87S h/t trees l/f Treviso Italy 22-1 SOC 14-3-46

MK638 39MU 5-3-44 165S 30-3 CE ops 26-7

MK639 9MU 9-3-44 FLS CFE VA EA 2-5-46

MK640 39MU 12-3-44 66S i/sea ops 21-5

MK641 39MU 11-3-44 52MU 11-4 *Emp Gla* 10-6 Hap 9-7

MK642 39MU 11-3-44 52MU 13-4 *Marsd* 22-4 Hap 22-4 Bas 10-6

MK643 39MU 11-3-44 52MU 11-4 *Afgan* 12-5 Hap 5-7

MK644 33MU 17-3-44 1S 11-4 CB ops 22-5 ROS FACE 2-3-45

MK645 39MU 17-3-44 52MU 16-4 *Inver* 21-5 Hap 6-7

MK646 39MU 18-3-44 52MU 16-4 *Afgan* 12-5 Hap 5-7

MK649 33MU 17-3-44 1S 14-4 CAC ops 3-12 RSO GA jumped chocks strk two Spits CB 29-1-45 ASTH FAF 15-8-46 GC2/4

MK660 39MU 12-4-44 52MU 1-5 *Inver* 21-5 Hap 6-7

MK661 9MU 5-4-44 317S 3-5 CAC 28-5 421S 13-7 CE ops 26-8

MK662 39MU 28-2-44 222MU 14-2 *Emp Raj* 21-3 Casa 6-4 CE ops 14-9

MK663 33MU 7-3-44 222S 27-3 347S 7-9 FAAC 30-10 29MU 9-7-45 sold Turk 5-9-47

MK664 39MU 28-2-44 222MU 12-3 *Emp Raj* 21-3 Casa 6-4

MK665 33MU 25-2-44 52MU 20-3 *Avris* 30-3 Hap 15-5

MK666 39MU 2-3-44 56S 27-5 402S 17-7 ROS 29-7 126S 4-9 MAL 14-2-45 29MU 15-5 130S 21-3-46 strk gr while in cloud Hussey Farm nr Froyle Hants CE Pilot kld 20-8 SOC 29-8

MK667 39MU 11-3-44 331S 8-6 414S 21-12 CAC ops 24-3-45

MK668 39MU 25-2-44 215MU 21-3 *Emp Pea* 21-4 Casa 12-5 SOC 30-6

MK669 39MU 1-3-44 222S 2-4 332S 31-8 AST 8-12 1APU 6-5-45 MAAF 27-5 ME 9-8 SOC 28-2-46

MK670 HFIX M70 6MU 31-3-44 74S 16-5 312S 8-7 CAC ops 25-8 ROS 33MU 1-8-45 sold R J Coley 3-2-50

MK671 6MU 28-3-44 AST 6-6 317S 22-6 CAC ops 1-9 AST 20-9 329S 8-1-45 CAC ops 16-2

MK672 HFIX M70 6MU 28-3-44 74S 16-5

MK673 9MU 24-3-44 126S 10-5 FAAC 21-10 ROS WAL 14-2-45 165S 12-6 66S 2-9-46 sold R J Coley 3-2-50

MK674 HFIX M70 6MU 28-3-44 74S FACE 12-5

MK675 HFIX M70 6MU 30-3-44 1 27S 16-5 313S 8-7 118S 15-7 441S 15-2-45 SAL 20-3-45 47MU 14-1-48 SAAF 5-8

MK676 46MU 27-3-44 MAL 16-6 411S 6-8 401S 31-8 CAC ops 20-10 PCE 30-10

MK677 33MU 22-4-44 485S 3-5 CAC 20-8 ROS 341S 13-12 308S 11-1-45 349S 8-2 FAF 12-9-46

MK678 9MU 5-4-44 317S 10-5 402S 17-7 FAAC 4-8 ROS 1005SW Tang 12-10 WAL 3-3-45 9MU 28-6 sold Turk 1-10-47

MK679 9MU 14-4-44 308S 64S 30-11 39MU 24-2-45 MAAF 29-3 IAF 26-6-47 as MM4135

MK680 HFIX M70 46MU 30-3-44 127S 16-5 313S 8-7 118S 15-7 DeH 21-2-45 33MU 14-9 FAF 3-12

MK681 HFIX M70 6MU 28-3-44 74S 16-5 312S 312S 8-7 313S 5-10 CB ops 24-12 ASTH 6-1-45 RDAF 27-10-48 as 404 coll with 412 at Arreso 24-7-50

MK682 HFIX M70 6MU 28-3-44 74S 16-5 312S 8-7 CE ops 18-9

MK683 HFIX M70 9MU 5-4-44 118S CAC ops 1-11

91 Squadron Mk IX. Serial is MK73- or MK75-.

recat E 16-11 bboc 9-3-45 8 OTU 14-8 FACE SOC 26-9-46 to 6162M Ben 26-10

MK684 8MU 26-3-44 317S 1-5 322S FTR ops 30-8

MK685 33MU 4-4-44 52MU 26-4 *Inver* 21-5 Hap 6-7

MK686 6MU 31-3-44 66S CB ops 16-6 511FRU 22-6 GAL 6-11 411S 21-12 39 Recce Wg 29-3-45 414S 5-4 411S 12-4 MAL 27-6 FAF 31-7-46

MK687 6MU 31-3-44 411S 29-6 421S 25-6 411S 27-7 1ATC 10-8 ROS 21-8 10ADU 19-1-45 MAAF 2-2 CE ops 13-4

MK688 39MU 15-4-44 302S 3-5 83GSU 17-6 mods 64S CAC ops 31-7 ROS 64S 26-8 sold Turk 22-7-47

MK689 8MU 26-3-44 331S 8-6 33MU 2-9 414S 30-11 CB ops 24-3-45 FAF GC1/1

MK690 6MU 22-4-44 317S 3-5 411S 20-7 401S 24-7 411S 31-8 132S 5-10 ASTE 30-5-45 FAF 17-8-46 GC2/7 des 27-10-48

MK691 HFIX M70 6MU 30-3-44 74S 9-4 CAC ops 27-5 ROS 312S 9-6 eng cut after jswitch fuel tanks cd/ld 28-8

MK692 46MU 30-3-44 AST 21-6 401S CA ops 12-8 311S 31-8 132S 5-10 fire in air f/ld CE 15-2-45

MK693 6MU 31-3-44 403S 27-7 CAC ops 12-8 DeH 39MU 10-3-45 MAAF 2-8 RHAF 30-1-47

MK694 HFIX M70 6MU 30-3-44 74S 16-5 312S 8-7 313S 5-10 303S 11-12 VA Henley 30-8-45 ROS 29MU 15-3-46 RDAF 12-1-49 as 405

MK695 8MU 27-3-44 132S 15-6 403S 27-7 CAC ops 8-8 443S CE ops 3-12

MK696 HFIX M70 6MU 31-1-44 127S FAAC 8-5 ROS CE ops 27-5

MK697 HFIX M70 39MU 15-5-44 222MU 25-5 *Argyll* 1-6 Casa 13-6 SOC 6-9-45

MK698 9MU 5-4-44 317S 3-5 MAL 18-7 401S 31-8 412S FTR ops 5-12

MK699 33MU 15-4-44 52MU 29-4 *Inver* 21-5 Hap 6-7

MK713 33MU 24-2-44 82MU 7-3 *Emp Raj* 21-3 Casa 6-4 FAF GR2/33 30-9 DeH 18-5-45 9MU 21-6 FCCS 16-7 FAAC 21-5-46 SOC scr dump 29-7

MK714 33MU 1-3-44 215MU 16-3 *Emp Raj* 21-3 Casa 6-4 SOC 18-10-45

MK715 8MU 25-2-44 56S 9-5 402S 17-7 1S 12-4-45 6MU NEA 7-10-46 sold VA for spares 2-1-47 to Holland as H-97 Mar'48 con to two-seat train T9 23-3-48

MK716 FRIX 39MU 2-3-44 302S 3-5 83GSU 15-6 mods 312S FACB 24-6 ROS 34WSU Prep Flt 27-7 414S CB ops 2-3-45 FAF GC2/1

MK717 33MU 11-3-44 222S 2-4 CAC ops 1-5 ROS 485S 11-1-45 349S 8-2 308S 22-2 84Gr ARF 10-5 4S 12-7 326S 23-8 34Grp Com S 6-9 FACE 6-12

MK718 33MU 24-2-44 52MU 12-4 *Afghan* 12-5 Hap 5-7

MK719 39MU 2-3-44 302S 5-5 83GSU 15-6 mods 308S 15-6 332S CAC ops 7-7 ROS MAAF 21-6-45 RHAF 30-1-47

MK720 33MU 15-3-44 308S 3-5 420RSU 15-6 64S runway coll with MK483 CE Harrow 10-7 GAL 28-11 mods 332S 25-1-45 FTR ops 1-3

MK721 6MU 31-3-44 con to type 509 two-seat train 19-6-51 IAC as 160 29-6 cd 15-2-57

MK722 39MU 1-3-44 485S 21-4 CAC 8-6 e/a b 1-1-45

MK723 33MU 11-3-44 302S 3-5 83GSU 15-6 mods 16S 22-6-45 CE ops 22-6

MK724 33MU 1-3-44 215MU 10-3 *Emp Raj* 21-3 Casa 6-4 CE ops 19-9

MK725 33MU 15-3-44 1S 13-4 FAAC 20-4

MK726 39MU 15-3-44 1S 27-4 CAC ops 23-7 ROS ASTE 16-4-45 29MU 1-10 sold Turk 11-7-47

MK727 33MU 6-3-44 215MU 20-3 *Emp Pea* 21-4 Casa 12-5 SOC 18-10-45

MK728 33MU 8-3-44 215MU 20-3 *Emp Pea* 21-4 Casa 12-5 ME 16-8-45 SOC 27-11-47

MK729 33MU 5-3-44 84GSU 27-3 442S 27-7 602S 28-9 e/fd in circuit cd/ld CE Colt 14-10

MK730 39MU 2-3-44 403S CAC ops 16-7 e/a CB 2-10 443S 14-12 e/a CE 1-1-45 ASTE recat B 6-4 recat E SOC 28-4-45

MK731 33MU 11-3-44 331S 8-6 511FRU 15-6 33MU 19-8 414S FTR ops 28-11

MK732 RNAF as H-25 1948 4SoTT StA 1971 71MU Nov '71 RNAF RAF Coning 1974 spares for BoB Flt as 8633M. Extant RNAF Museum, Gilze-Rijen.

MK733 39MU 11-3-44 1S 14-4 FACE 20-4 ROS SAL 18-4-45 sold Turk 2-5-47

MK734 39MU 15-3-44 56S taxy coll with NH152CB Newchurch 21-5 ROS 402S 17-7 91S FAAC 15-3-45 326S 28-6 FAF 27-11

MK735 39MU 15-3-44 52MU 7-4 *Marsd* 22-4 Hap 29-5 Bas 10-6-45

MK736 33MU 11-3-44 132S 15-6 602S 6-7 CE 4-7 82MU 19-12 *Tanelle* 13-1-45 25-1 SOC 30-4-47

MK737 39MU 12-3-44 83GSU 8-5 132S 15-6 441S CE ops 30-6

MK738 33MU 15-3-44 ROS 16-6 1S 17-6 165S 4-7 412S CAC ops 14-8 ROS 165S 20-9 MAAF 16-5-45 SOC 26-6-47

MK739 33MU 1-3-44 215S 20-3 *Emp Pea* 21-4 Casa 12-5 FACE 14-5-45

MK740 33MU 7-3-44 52MU 12-4 *Afghan* 12-5 Hap 5-7

MK741 39MU 28-2-44 52MU 14-3 *St Cl* 3-4 Hap 15-5

MK742 33MU 2-3-44 84GSU 23-3 403S CE dbf ops 2-6

MK743 33MU 8-3-44 222MU 20-3 *Emp Pea* 21-4 Casa 12-5 FAF GC2/3

MK744 39MU 11-3-44 1S 14-4 FTR ops 17-8

MK745 39MU 28-2-44 312S 15-6 64S 3-9 ROS CE 3-11

MK746 39MU 28-2-44 Porth 3-4 165S 1-8 SAL 6-2-45 3APU 19-4 MAAF 21-6 RHAF 29-5-47

MK747 33MU 2-3-44 ASTH 31-5 308S 15-6 CB ops 26-9 sold Turk 10-10-47

MK748 39MU 28-2-44 52MU 14-3 *Avris* 30-3 Hap 15-5

MK749 39MU 5-3-44 165S 28-3 CE 23-6

MK750 39MU 1-3-44 47MU 18-3 *Emp Pea* 21-4 Casa 12-5 CE ops 1-7

MK751 39MU 2-3-44 165S 30-3 FTR ops 6-6

MK752 39MU 5-3-44 165S 30-3 e/fd w/u ldg Farthinghoe Kent CE 13-7

MK753 no record

MK754 .5in guns 33MU 5-3-44 485S 8-6 332S CAC ops 11-10 ASTH 15-2-45 sold Turk 30-4-47

MK755 39MU 28-2-44 215MU 9-3 *Emp Raj* 21-3 Casa 6-4 FACE 2-10

MK756 33MU 4-3-44 312S FAAC 27-4 AST 308S 9-11 CAC ops 1-1-45 326S 5-4 327S 4-10 FAF 4-12 GC2/1

MK769 39MU 1-3-44 222MU 13-3 *Emp Raj* 21-3 Casa 6-4 SOC 28-4-45

MK770 39MU 2-3-44 222MU 13-3 *Emp Raj* 31-3 Casa 6-4 IAF 26-6-47 as MM4604

MK771 33MU 8-3-44 215MU 20-3 *Emp Pea* 21-4 Casa 12-5 SOC 30-6

MK772 39MU 2-2-44 83GSU 30-5 442S CE ops 13-7

MK773 39MU 1-3-44 82MU 18-3 *Emp Pea* 21-4 Casa 12-5 SOC 30-6

MK774 39MU 3-3-44 222S 20-4 CE ops 29-9

MK775 33MU 4-3-44 84GSU 23-3 312S 8-6 3501SU 22-6 602S 13-7 64S 2-9 FTR 1-9

MK776 33MU 12-3-44 411S 22-6 CE ops 27-6

MK777 LFIXE 39MU 2-3-44 442S CAC ops 7-7 1ATC 24-8 AST 1-9 129S 17-5-45 257S 14-10-46 BAF 24-8-48 as SM-24

MK778 39MU 4-3-44 165S 30-3 CE ops 6-4

MK779 33MU 15-3-44 52MU 6-4 *Afghan* 12-5 Hap 5-7

MK780 39MU 4-3-44 401S CAC ops 23-6 403S 29-6

MK781 39MU 1-3-44 52MU 18-3 *Marsd* 22-4 Hap 29-5 Bas 10-6

MK782 39MU 2-3-44 Stn Flt Cole 3-4 ROS 12-9 64S 5-10 FAAC 5-11 SAL 29-3-45 COAL 25-6 mods & new eng CGS 25-7 SOC 27-11-47

MK783 33MU 7-3-44 222MU 20-3 *Emp Pea* 21-4 Casa 12-5 SOC 30-3-45

MK784 39MU 8-3-44 222S 16-4 349S 7-9 83GSU FACB 18-10 3APU 19-4-45 MAAF 14-5 137MU stor 29-4-48 SOC 24-6

MK785 33MU 4-3-44 52MU 12-4 *Afghan* 12-5 Hap 5-7

MK786 33MU 11-3-44 302S 3-5 312S 15-6 441S CAC ops 7-7 FAAC 11-12 ROS ASTE 12-2-45 sold Turk 16-11-47

MK787 33MU 11-3-44 222S 12-4 421RSU 22-7 349S 30-11 sold Turk 15-10-47

MK788 39MU 5-3-44 165S 29-3 CAC ops 22-5 GAL 3-10 mods 411S 16-11 to 5685M 28-9-45 SoH 26-4-50 SOC AFD 24-1-51

MK789 33MU 8-3-44 52MU 6-4 *Marsd* 22-4 Hap 29-5 Bas 10-6

MK790 33MU 2-3-44 56S 9-5 416S CE ops 29-6

MK791 39MU 2-3-44 ROS 6-4 401S 28-9 CAC ops 30-3-45 411S 24-5 FAAC 25-5 VAOx WAL 14-8 FAF 16-9-46

MK792 33MU 8-3-44 52MU 6-4 *Marsd* 22-4 Hap 29-5 Bas 10-6

MK793 39MU 4-3-44 332S CAC ops 15-6 420RSU 22-6 602S 29-10 1FU MAAF 23-4-45 CAC 29-4 ME 14-6 SOC 26-9-46

MK794 39MU 2-3-44 56S 27-5 402S 17-9 412S 24-5-45 recat E 11-6 SOC 5-9

MK795 33MU 5-3-44 310S CB ops 21-5 AST 401S FTR ops 19-9 cancel ASTH 29-9 411S 28-12 CAC ops 23-1-45 401S 1-2 FACB 24-2 sold VA 5-12-49

MK796 33MU 6-3-44 302S 30-4 1S FTR ops 22-5 421S 13-7 CE ops 25-7

MK797 33MU 5-3-44 222S 30-3 FTR ops 29-6
MK798 39MU 11-3-44 1S 14-4 FTR ops 1-6
MK799 39MU 19-8-44 222S 21-4 CAC 5-10 485S 11-1-45 349S 8-2 322S 22-2 RNorAF 14-12-47
MK800 33MU 11-3-44 433S 27-7 442S CAC 12-8 CE 14-9
MK801 39MU 11-3-44 165S 28-3 CAC ops 19-5 ROS AST 1-9 WAL 13-2-45 sold R J Coley 3-2-50
MK802 33MU 6-3-44 52MU 28-3 *Marsd* 22-4 Hap 29-5 Bas 10-6
MK803 33MU 7-3-44 215MU 20-3 *Emp Pea* 21-4 Casa 12-5 SOC 13-9-45
MK804 33MU 11-3-44 222S 2-4 349S 25-1-45 485S 22-2 326S 22-6 FAF 27-11 GC2/7
MK805 33MU 11-3-44 312S 8-6 64S 29-9 ROS DeH 16-10 3APU 13-4-45 MAAF 16-5 145S IAF 27-6-46 as MM4084 extant Italian AF Museum
MK806 33MU 11-3-44 17APC 1-4 FLS Mlfld 5-10 29MU 30-5-46 SOC 17-6
MK807 33MU 15-3-44 17APC 1-4 FLS Mlfld 5-10 CFE 27-8-45 mr 29-4-46 recat E 8-7
MK808 33MU 12-3-44 403S FAAC 22-6 421S CAC ops 11-7 AST 222MU 20-12 *Taele* 13-1-45 Casa 25-1
MK809 8MU 22-3-44 421S CAC ops 2-7 CE 13-7
MK810 VA WD 6-3-44 39MU 19-3 132S CAC ops 21-5 403S 27-7 CE ops 5-8
MK811 39MU 5-3-44 165S 29-3 CB ops 1-7 GAL 10-11 MAAF 25-2-45 SOC 5-10
MK812 39MU 11-3-44 332S 29-4 453S 5-10 3501SU 31-10 326S 5-4-45 CE 11-10
MK826 8MU 7-3-44 442S 27-7 CE ops 1-8
MK827 33MU 8-3-44 312S 8-6 GAL 18-7 416S CB ops 25-9 412S 26-4-45 FTR ops 3-5
MK828 39MU 17-3-44 52MU 16-4 *Inver* 21-5 Hap 6-7
MK829 33MU 11-3-44 222S 14-4 421RSU 15-6 recat E 15-9
MK830 39MU 17-3-44 222S 21-4 CAC ops 21-5 AST 331S 30-11 CAC ops 14-2-45 331S 22-2 349S FTR ops 27-4
MK831 39MU 11-3-44 165S 29-3 CAC ops 19-5 FTR ops 5-9
MK832 33MU 11-3-44 411S 22-6 132S 5-10 326S 5-4-45 FAF 4-12 GC2/3
MK833 33MU 11-3-44 222S 2-4 cAC ops 21-5 ROS AST 8-1-45 MAAF 28-6 ME SOC 28-8-47
MK834 39MU 12-3-44 411S CE ops 19-5
MK835 33MU 4-3-44 84GSU 5-5 416S 13-7 416S 12-10 to 5693M 2-10-45 SOC 24-1-51
MK836 33MU 8-3-44 82MU 27-3 *Emp Pea* 21-4 Casa 12-5
MK837 33MU 15-3-44 416S 27-7 e/a 12-10 416S FTR ops 22-11
MK838 8MU 30-3-44 165S 30-5 CAC ops 26-7 ROS 91S 18-12 SAL 23-4-45 39MU 21-7 sold Turk 3-11-47
MK839 33MU 11-3-44 302S 3-5 310S 15-6 329S 22-6 165S 20-9 MAL 7-2-45 331S 30-4
MK840 39MU 12-3-44 401S e/fd i/sea 50 miles off Selsey Bill 3-6
MK841 39MU 12-3-44 302S 5-5 84GSU 22-6 mods 602S 13-7 CAC ops 30-7 126Wg HQ 17-8 401S 411S 31-8 CB ops 27-9 AST MAAF 14-6-45 ME 2-8 REAF 26-9-46
MK842 FIXC M66 cd Mar'44 rebuilt as HFIX M70 8MU 15-5-44 3501SU 5-6 313S 7-1-45 cd 1-2 SOC 8-2 bboc DeH 2-3 WAL 4-9 Persh 17-6-47 SAAF 14-7-47
MK843 33MU 11-3-44 411S 22-6 64S FAAC 412S 20-7 401S 17-8 403S FTR ops 31-8
MK844 33MU 12-3-44 431S 8-6 443S 28-9 442S 8-2-45 412S 22-3 CE ops a/c aban 10-4
MK845 33MU 11-3-44 401S 22-6 FRU 6-7 12TU 12-1-45 MAAF 5-2 SOC 14-6
MK846 39MU 12-3-44 1S 14-4 ROS 3501SU 12-10 MAAF 16-5-45 SOC 22-11
MK847 39MU 21-3-44 52MU 23-4 *Afghan* 12-5 Hap 5-7
MK848 39MU 12-3-44 52MU 7-4 *Afghan* 12-5 Hap 5-7
MK849 39MU 19-3-44 485S 21-4 50MU 2607 ROS 31-7 11FU 6-1-45 MAAF 7-2 REAF 26-9-46
MK850 VAHP 3-7-44 39MU 3-8 R-RH 13-2-45 Bdn May'45 Merlin 266 (Packard Merlin 69 mods to M66 standards). Con to FXVI. Rad suit oil cool and com rating trls ASTH 9-10 FAF 16-9-46
MK851 33MU 15-3-44 52MU 13-4 *Afghan* 12-5 Hap 5-7
MK852 39MU 19-3-44 441S 13-7 405RSU CAC 3-8 49MU 29-11 SAL 21-2-45 sold Turk 9-10-47
MK853 39MU 11-3-44 412S FTR ops 10-5
MK854 39MU 11-3-44 165S 29-3 CAC ops 13-9 ROS 33MU 25-2-45 MAAF 21-6 ME 23-8 SOC 5-2-48
MK855 39MU 11-3-44 165S 11-4 FTR ops 7-6
MK856 39MU 12-3-44 52MU 8-4 *Afghan* 12-5 Hap 5-7 to 5690M StA
MK857 39MU 17-3-44 52MU 13-4 *Afghan* 12-5 Hap 5-7
MK858 33MU 15-3-44 52MU 4-5 *Inver* 21-5 Hap 6-7
MK859 8MU 22-3-44 FTR ops 14-6 cancel recat B 1ATC 10-8 AST 22-8 222MU 28-11 *Guinean* 20-12
MK860 39MU 20-3-44 52MU 29-4 *Inver* 21-5 Hap 6-7
MK861 39MU 12-3-44 52MU 8-4 *Afghan* 12-5 Hap 5-7
MK862 39MU 26-3-44 485S 25-4 421RSU 8-6 349S 22-6 33S 26-7 hit by AA fire out of fuel w/u l/d Coombe Head Sussex CE 3-8
MK863 .5in. guns 39MU 18-4-44 222S 8-6 CB ops 19-10 322S 9-11 DeH 9-3-45 WAL 24-9 sold Turk 20-10-47
MK864 9MU 5-4-44 GAL 16-5 412S 17-8 401S CAC ops 9-9 126AF 21-9 401S CAC ops 25-9 ROS 33MU 14-3-45 MAAF 27-5 RHAF 30-1-47
MK865 39MU 17-8-44 52MU 16-4 *Afghan* 12-5 Hap 5-7
MK866 39MU 9-5-44 222S 15-6 FAAC 13-11 485S 11-1-45 411S 3-5 FAAC 21-5 29MU 24-5 RNoAF 8-4-48
MK867 39MU 12-3-44 1S 14-4 FTR ops 28-9
MK868 33MU 15-3-44 17APC 4-4 FLS Mlfld 5-10 FSDS Tang FACA 22-4-45 CFE FACB 12-1-46 ASTH 7-2
MK881 39MU 17-3-44 403S CE ops 14-7
MK882 8MU 26-3-44 401S CAC ops 30-6 39MU 7-12 MAAF 17-2-45 SOC 6-9
MK883 33MU 5-3-44 222S 12-4 FTR i/sea 7-8
MK884 39MU 15-3-44 52MU 8-4 *Afghan* 12-5 Hap 5-7
MK885 33MU 15-3 411S 22-6 CB ops 7-9 4ATC 21-9 PCE
MK886 39MU 24-3-44 485S 21-4 ROS 20-6 DeH 24-11 331S 10-5-45
MK887 39MU 15-3-44 52MU 11-4 *Afghan* 12-5 Hap 5-7
MK888 39MU 17-3-44 312S CB ops 15-5 AST 24-5 401S 18-11 CAC ops 1-3-45 FTR ops 13-3
MK889 33MU 15-3-44 222S 4-4 349S 8-6 DeH 13-3-45 WAL 12-10 sold Turk 15-10-47
MK890 33MU 18-3-44 1S 14-4 FTR ops 22-5
MK891 33MU 30-4-44 52MU 20-5 *Arabis* 14-6 Hap 29-6 Bas 12-8
MK892 33MU 15-3-44 222S 4-4 CE ops 10-6
MK893 9MU 24-3-44 12S 10-5 DeH 8-1-45 sold Turk 22-7-47
MK894 39MU 17-3-44 52MU 16-4 *Afghan* 12-5 Hap 5-7
MK895 39MU 17-3-44 312S 8-6 64S CE ops 3-8
MK896 39MU 17-3-44 222S 14-4 308S 1-3-45 331S FAAC 22-3 AST 39MU 7-9 sold Turk 4-11-47
MK897 39MU 19-3-44 485S 25-4 CAC ops 28-9 6MU 31-3-45 332S 1-5
MK898 8MU 24-3-44 317S 1-5 CAC ops 29-5 ROS GAL 31-8 442S 9-12 CAC ops 8-2-45 442S 15-2 CE ops 18-4
MK899 8MU 4-4-44 AST 14-5 302S 15-6 CAC ops 17-8 1ATC 24-8 317S 19-10 SAL 14-4-45 29MU 9-11 sold Turk 3-11-47
MK900 39MU 18-3-44 52MU 16-4 *Afghan* 12-5 Hap 5-7
MK901 33MU 5-3-44 1S 13-4 CAC ops 19-7 ROS 165S 5-10 1S 19-10 AST 6-4-45 RNAF 5-7-46 as H-14 w/o 9-4-48
MK902 33MU 19-3-44 401S CE ops 7-6
MK903 39MU 17-3-44 52MU 8-4 *Afghan* 12-5 Hap 5-7
MK904 39MU 19-3-44 485S 1-5 222S 22-6 331S 4-1-45 34S 26-4 84ARF 30-4 WAL 22-6 29MU 8-11 RNoAF 28-8-47
MK905 39MU 20-3-44 302S 3-5 CAC ops 7-6 302S 22-6 84GSU mods 322S FTR ops 1-9
MK906 39MU 17-3-44 222S 26-4 33MU 14-11 MAAF 27-6-45 IAF 26-6-47 as MM4110
MK907 33MU 19-3-44 441S CAC ops 16-7 SAL 28-2-45 9MU 28-5 sold Turk 26-6-47
MK908 39MU 17-3-44 52MU 8-4 *Afghan* 12-5 Hap 5-7
MK909 8MU 24-3-44 56S 4-5 402S 17-7 91S FTR ops 15-8
MK910 39MU 19-3-44 84Gr Com S 16-5 485S 1-2-45 CAC 22-2 317S 15-3 SNCAN 28-6 FAF GC1/3 des Dung Khyet (Indo-china) 24-10-48
MK911 39MU 18-3-44 52MU 13-4 *Afghan* 12-5 Hap 5-7
MK912 8MU 24-3-44 312S 8-6 AST 30-11 RNAF 26-7-46 as H-59 later H-119 BAF 6-52 extant as SM-29 Saffraenberg Belgium
MK913 46MU 22-3-44 MAL 15-6 441S 21-9 SAL 13-3-45 RNAF 25-5-47 as H-34
MK914 33MU 13-4-44 485S 23-4 442S 27-7 411S CB ops 16-9 4ATC 21-9 PCE
MK915 FRIX 33MU 19-4-44 302S 3-5 83 GSU 15-6 mods 16S 22-6 2nd TAF Com S 30-11 e/a 1-1-45 AST 14-3 sold Turk 7-7-47
MK916 8MU 23-3-44 412S CAC ops 20-7 410RSU 27-7 AST 3-8 222MU 20-12 *Tardi* 13-1-45 Casa 25-1 IAF 30-5-46 w/o 23-9-47
MK917 8MU 24-3-44 329S FAAC 21-5 ROS 416S 23-9 39MU 5-5-45 sold R J Coley 6-2 50
MK918 33MU 19-3-44 302S 30-4 308S 15-6 421S 29-6 403S 27-7 e/a CB 21-10 SAL 28-3-45 recat E 11-6
MK919 33MU 19-3-44 1S 10-4 CB ops 22-5 ROS 1S 7-7 tailwheel torn off ldg swg u/c clpse CE Detling 12-9
MK920 33MU 18-3-44 421S 27-7 FRU CB 12-11 39MU 23-3-45 165S 17-5 66S 5-9-46 59S 8-1-48 43Gp DA CAC 19-2 recat E SOC 24-12
MK921 8MU 23-3-44 84Gp 30-4 CAC ops 5-10 e/a CE dbf 1-1-45
MK922 8MU 24-3-44 AST 14-5 317S 15-6 CB ops 21-10 CFE 21-7-45 to 5971M 2SoTT 2-7-46 recat E 12-4-49
MK923 9MU 24-3-44 126S 10-5 39MU 11-5-45 RNAF 19-5-47 as H-61 later H-104 BAF as target tug SM-37 2-53 COGEA OO-ARF extant Windsor, Ontario. NX521R
MK924 39MU 20-2-44 302S 3-5 84GSU 15-6 mods 331S 15-6 414S 5-10 CE ops 26-3-45
MK925 39MU 17-3-44 52MU 14-4 *Afghan* 12-5 Hap 5-7
MK926 9MU 24-3-44 1S 16-4 ROS 27-4 441S 7-12 WAL 20-4-45 sold Turk 23-10-47
MK939 6MU 4-4-44 AST 13-6 317S 17-8 CB ops 28-9 DeH 165S 20-5-45 66S 2-4-46 sold Int All 29-8-59
MK940 8MU 27-3-44 MAL 17-5 312S FTR ops 10-6
MK941 6MU 31-3-44 421S CB ops 26-6 441S 6-7 CE ops 7-8
MK942 6MU 31-3-44 453S 15-6 CB ops 25-6 AST 82MU 20-12 *Emp Arch* 22-12 Hap 9-1-45 FAF 7-7-46

MK842, M66, crashed during delivery flight. Rebuilt as HF IX, M70. To the South African Air Force in July 1947.

MK850 converted to Mk XVI standards with the installation of a Packhard Merlin 266.

MK943 8MU 12-4-44 AST 9-6 317S 17-8 FTR ops 12-9

MK944 9MU 31-3-44 GAL 16-5 317S 24-8 CB ops 21-10 recat E 26-3-45

MK945 39MU 12-4-44 52MU *Inver* 21-5 Hap 6-7

MK946 8MU 12-4-44 84GSU 29-5 CE 9-6 SOC

MK947 9MU 6-4-44 56S 22-6 403S 12-10 302S CB ops 5-11 ASTE 12-2-45 sold Turk 25-3-47

MK948 46MU 22-3-44 FACE 26-3 AST 12-4 317S 24-8 e/a CB 1-1-45 sold Turk 28-8-47

MK949 39MU 12-4-44 52MU 27-4

MK950 33MU 20-4-44 485S 30-4 412S 28-12 411S 28-12 CE ops 3-3-45

MK951 8MU 14-4-44 FACB 14-5 AST CRD R-RH 31-8 ASTH 14-9 CRD R-RH 19-9 453S 19-10 11SU 9-1-45 MAAF 17-2

MK952 39MU 19-3-44 52MU 16-4 *Afghan* 12-5 Hap 5-7

MK953 46MU 5-4-44 83Gp Com S 29-6 e/a CE 1-1-45

MK954 39MU 15-4-44 52MU 29-4 *Inver* 21-5 Hap 6-7

MK955 39MU 15-4-44 56S 9-5 CAC ops 22-5 ROS 402S 17-7 91S CE ops 26-3-45

MK956 39MU 15-4-44 52MU 20-5 *Arabis* 14-6 Hap Bas 12-8

MK957 39MU 18-4-44 52MU 1-5 *Inver* 21-5 Hap 6-7

MK958 39MU 18-4-44 302S 3-5 310S 15-6 16S 22-6 CAC ops 15-7 DeH 11-9 Pershore 24-3-45 MAAF 12-7 FACE 1-11 SOC 6-12

MK959 39MU 15-4-44 302S 3-5 329S 15-6 165S 30-8 SAL 6-2-45 29MU 13-4 RNAF 25-9-46 SOC 4-6-54 extant Eindhoven Holland H-15

MK960 39MU 18-4-44 52MU 29-4 *Inver* 21-5-45 Hap 6-7

MK961 39MU 18-4-44 52MU 6-5 *Emp Gla* 1-6 Hap 9-7

MK962 no record

MK963 8MU 21-4-44 AST 14-5 317S 15-6 DeH 29-8 317S CAC ops 9-11

MK964 8MU 21-4-44 310S 17-5 349S 14-6 403S 29-6 CB ops 18-8 DeH 29-8 MAAF 15-6-45 SOC 30-4-47

MK965 HFIX M70 39MU 13-4-44 127S 6-5 FAAC 31-5 ROS 313S 8-7 441S 15-2-45 WAL 9-8 29MU 4-2-46 RDAF 10-2-49 as 406

MK966 6MU 22-4-44 331S CE ops s/dn AA fire off Normandy 10-6 SOC 12-12

MK967 46MU 30-3-44 MAL 16-6 441S 17-8 329S 19-4-45 COAL 22-8-45 mods VA 6-5-46 SOC 17-6-48

MK968 39MU 13-5-44 AST 30-5 mods 317S 15-6 CAC ops 20-9 FACE 8-12

MK969 6MU 27-3-44 421S CE ops 27-6

MK981 9MU 14-4-44 308S 3-5 ROS 453S 20-10 33MU 21-12 MAAF 23-2-45 ME 9-8 RHAF 30-4-47

MK982 39MU 20-3-44 302S burst tyre t/o i/soft grnd CE Chailey Sussex 8-5

MK983 39MU 20-3-44 302S 3-5 84GSU 22-6 mods FRU CB 14-9 MAL 18-1-45 332S 10-5

MK984 33MU 1-5-44 AST 14-5 308S 15-6 e/a CE 1-1-45

MK985 39MU 20-3-44 52MU 25-4 *Inver* 21-5 Hap 6-7

MK986 9MU 25-3-44 1S 18-4 ROS 9-8 317S 2-11 FAAC 30-11 1S 11-1-45 ASTE 16-4 sold Turk 24-1-47

MK987 9MU 25-3-44 1S 16-4 421S CAC 15-6 DeH 29-1-45 3APU 5-4 MAAF 29-6 ME SOC 28-8-47

MK988 9MU 25-3-44 1S 16-4 ROS 15-7 ASTE 16-4-45 sold Turk 12-3-47

MK989 9MU 27-3-44 126S 10-5 CAC ops 19-6 453S 30-10 MAAF 25-2-45 FAF 25-7-46

MK990 8MU 27-3-44 421S 7-9 CAC ops 25-9

MK991 9MU 27-3-44 56S 23-4 Cb ops 6-5 VAOx 602S 30-10 MAAF 3-3-45 RHAF 27-2-47

MK992 8MU 27-3-44 441S CAC ops 30-6 403S 12-8 441S 17-8 411S 8-2-45 130S 17-5 VA 11-3-46 recat E 24-6

MK993 9MU 30-3-44 126S 10-5 AST 2-1-45 RNAF 15-5-47 as H-62 later H-115 w/o 7-1-49

MK994 9MU 6-4-44 126S 10-5 FACB 11-7 WAL 23-2-45 FCCS u/c coll ld Graveley 26-5-46 SOC 19-8

MK995 9MU 30-3-44 126S 10-5 CAC ops 2-9 ROS ASTE 12-2-45 sold Turk 20-3-47

MK996 9MU 6-4-44 222S 22-6 CB ops 19-10 ASTE 5-3-45 FAF 11-9-46 16FU St Mw w/u ld FACB 14-9 recat E 18-9

MK997 9MU 8-4-44 1S 16-4 CAC ops 5-7 ROS AST RNoAF 14-4-48 IAF as MM4092

MK998 9MU 6-4-44 56S 10-6 402S 17-7 91S 4-11 CAC 25-1-45 ASTE RNAF 5-7-46 as H-16

MK999 39MU 12-4-44 302S 3-5 83GSU 15-6 mods 332S 15-6 CAC ops 3-7 602S 5-10 FACE 18-12

ML series All LF IX Merlin 66 unless otherwise indicated

ML112 9MU 3-4-44 GAL 16-5 308S 27-6 CAC ops 25-12 e/a CE 1-1-45

ML113 39MU 13-4-44 308S 3-5 412S 13-7 CAC ops 16-8 411S 28-9 132S 5-10 FAAC 10-11 ROS FCCS 8-7-45 sold VA 16-4-47 con to two-seat train

ML114 39MU 12-4-44 52MU 1-5 *Inver* 21-5 Hap 6-7

ML115 39MU 12-4-44 56S 6-5 402S 17-7 91S CAC ops 5-12 ASTE 6-2-45 sold Turk 29-4-47

ML116 9MU 14-4-44 308S 3-5 CB ops 21-5 AST 82MU 23-11 REAF 26-9-46

ML117 8MU 24-3-44 1S 28-5 FAAC 2-6-44 ROSA 86MU 6-2-45 1S 22-4 to 5495M 25-7 321S ATC

ML118 8MU 24-3-44 AST 9-6 401S 6-8 CE ops 22-9

ML119 9MU 24-3-44 1S 4-4 Czech AF 6-12-46

ML120 8MU 26-3-44 132S 15-6 FTR 28-6

ML121 39MU 19-3-44 52MU 8-4 *Afghan* 12-5 Hap 5-7

ML122 8MU 26-3-44 1S 28-5 FAAC 6-7 ROS 165S 1-9 brake fail taxy strk bowser CE Mans 12-9

ML123 8MU 23-3-44 66S 8-6 CE ops 6-7

ML124 46MU 27-3-44 AST 25-5 302S 15-6 6MU 24-3-45 MAAF 21-6 107MU rep 26-2-48 storage RHAF 10-6

ML125 33MU 19-3-44 17APC 1-4 39MU 9-8-45 sold Turk 3-11-47

ML126 8MU 23-3-44 FAAC 8-4 ROS Hand Sq Hullav 15-3 416S 12-10 DeH 19-1-45 sold Turk 25-9-47

ML127 39MU 19-3-44 52MU 16-4 *Afghan* 12-5 Hap 5-7

ML128 46MU 22-3-44 MAL 17-5 mods 317S 22-6 CAC ops 16-3 CE ops 16-9

ML129 33MU 18-3-44 84GSU 5-5 VAO 13-6 401S 22-6 CAC ops 24-8 403S 7-9 FACB 24-9 MAAF 22-4-45 IAF 30-5-46 as MM4000

ML130 8MU 27-3-44 317S 1-5 FTR ops 12-6

ML131 8MU 24-2-44 442S CAC ops 28-7 AST 222MU 20-12 *Faele* 13-1-45 Casa 25-1 ME 16-8 SOC 26-6-47

ML132 8MU 28-3-44 AST 6-6 317S 6-7 332S 30-4-45

ML133 46MU 22-3-44 MAL 16-6 83GSU Com S 20-7 e/a CE 1-1-45

ML134 39MU 20-3-44 453S 15-6 CAC 25-6 AST 215MU 8-12 *Tanela* 13-1-45 Casa 25-1 IAF 30-5-46 as MM4002

ML135 33MU 19-3-44 401S 22-6 CE ops 1-7

ML136 46MU 30-3-44 AST 25-5 302S 15-6 e/a CE 1-1-45

ML137 46MU 22-3-44 350S 9-7 322S 4-9 ROS ASTH 18-1-45 FAF 8-8-46 GC1/2

ML138 8MU 24-3-44 453S 15-6 CAC 27-6 416S 27-7 CE 12-10

ML139 8MU 27-3-44 165S 20-6 FACB 30-8 AST MAAF 2-4-45 IAF 26-6-47 as MM4003

ML140 46MU 30-3-44 3051SU 21-6 421S 6-7 327S 5-4-45 FAF GC1/6

ML141 8MU 26-3-44 AST 9-6 414S 24-8 401S 21-12 CE ops 25-4-45

ML142 46MU27-3-44 3051SU 21-6 401S 27-7 1ATC 24-8 CAC recat B ASTH 30-8 WAL 2-12 mods MAAF 3-2-45 SOC 18-10

ML143 46MU 27-3-44 350S CAC ops 29-7 ROS MAL 10-5-45 sold Turk 1-10-47

ML144 6MU 27-6-44 332S 3-8 CAC ops 29-8 FTR ops 4-11

ML145 HFIX M70 8MU 27-3-44 123S 17-4 127S CB ops 23-5 ROS 313S 8-7 113S 15-7 CAC ops 26-11 313S 11-1-45 WAL 9-8 12-1-46 SAAF 28-4-48

ML146 6MU 28-3-44 453S 15-6 CE ops 13-7 MAAF 3-3-45 CE ops 26-4

ML147 6MU 31-3-44 453S 15-7 441S 10-8 WAL 4-4-45 sold Turk 1-4-47

ML148 HFIX M70 8MU 26-3-44 3501SU 16-5 74S 10-6 312S CAC ops 7-7 ROS DeH 1-5-45 47MU 24-2 SAAF 20-7-48

ML149 6MU 28-3-44 331S 8-6 FTR ops 30-6

ML150 HFIX M709 8MU 30-3-44 3501S 5-6 sold E Smelt 25-5-50

ML151 8MU 24-3-44 MAL 17-5 412S 22-6 39MU 11-12 10ADU 22-1-45 MAAF 7-2 ME 23-8 6S out of fuel cd nr Syrian Okhori Cyprus 5-12-46

ML152 6MU 28-3-44 132S 15-4 412S 20-7 442S 2-8 CAC ops 9-8 CE ops 19-8

ML153 6MU 28-3-44 443S 22-6 CAC ops 5-12 126Wg 28-12 e/a CE 1-1-45

ML154 HFIX M70 39MU 15-4-44 74S 25-5 312S 8-7 e/fd in circuit std cd CE NWld 28-8

ML155 33MU 5-4-44 52MU 17-4 *Inver* 21-5 Hap 6-7

ML156 9MU 6-4-44 GAL 16-5 mods 403S 17-8 FAAC 12-10 ASTH 5-4-45 sold Turk 14-10-47

ML169 9MU 5-4-44 17APC 25-4 56S CB ops 22-5 213MU 4-7-47 to 6365M 27-6 to 6389M 30-7 SOC scrap 30-5-50

ML170 6MU 30-3-44 AST 13-6 308S 17-8 CE ops 6-12

ML171 HFIX M70 6MU 28-3-44 74S 16-5 312S 8-7 313S 5-10 FAAC 7-1-45 ASTH 22-1 595S 26-7 to 6236M 24-1-47SoH 26-4-50 SOC 24-1-57

ML172 HFIX M70 8MU 5-4-44 132S 20-4 127S 16-5

ML173 6MU 4-4-44 AST 13-6 441S ASTE 15-5-45 WW 18-12-46 sold Turk

ML174 HFIX M70 9MU 6-4-44 127S 21-4 FAAC 20-6 ROS 313S 5-10 FACB 24-10 BDn 22-2-45 CRD ETPS 6MU NEA 16-4-47

ML175 9MU 5-4-44 165S 5-6 ops 5-8 ROS 1S 28-12 GA strk by Spit CAC 29-1-45 ROS WAL 26-7 sold Turk 3-11-47

ML176 39MU 21-4-44 485S 6-5 CB ops 3-9 AST MAAF 14-6-45 ME SOC 26-9-46

ML177 9MU 5-4-44 308S 3-5 602S 13-7 127Wg HQ 403S 17-8 FAAC 9-12 ROS GAL 14-2-45 403S 16-2 SAL 4-4 recat E 11-6

ML178 8MU 14-4-44 317S 1-5 MAL 18-7 403S FAAC 28-8 2ATC 31-8 AST 3-10 332S 12-5-45

ML179 HFIX M70 46MU 30-3-44 74S 312S 5-10 recat E 8-1-46 SOC 25-3

ML180 46MU 5-4-44 403S CB ops 16-7 AST WAL 1-12 11FU 9-1-45 MAAF 27-2 IAF 30-5-46 as MM4090

ML181 33MU 20-4-44 485S 30-4 AST 6-6 341S 9-11 274S 13-12 CB ops 9-2-45 sold Turk 5-9-47

ML182 HFIX M70 46MU 18-4-44 127S 15-5 313S 8-7 118S 15-7 CAC ops 18-9 recat E 19-9

ML183 39MU 13-4-44 308S 3-5 132S 29-6 403S 27-7 FTR 18-8

ML184 39MU 13-4-44 443S CAC ops 17-6 416S 30-11 SAL 29-3-45 sold Turk 4-11-47

ML185 HFIX M70 46MU 5-4-44 127S 16-5 313S 8-7 118S 15-7 SAL 21-2-45 595S 10-7 RAF Henlow 24-8-48 to 6585M

ML186 Flown by J Quill High Post-Scotland and ret non-stop 14-4-44 BDn 24-6 1st LFIX to have rear fus 72 gal fuel tank. Trls with metal elev Mer 61 instal. During hand with rear fus tank pilots were instructed to avoid violent manouvres before 34 gals used. Wt in rear fus made a/c unstable. Series of trls instigated to det aftmost CofG. HPA 25-8 VA 17-1-45 ext trls by test pilots to det suitable hand as a/c was considered unsafe for comb until sufficient fuel had been used. 29MU 11-7 sold Turk 15-10-47

ML187 HFIX M70 6MU 4-4-44 127S CB ops 22-5 DeH 8-8 313S 17-2-45 sold VA 5-12-49

ML188 33MU 4-44-44 52MU 23-4 *Inver* 21-5 Hap 6-7

ML189 8MU 5-4-44 56S 7-5 AST 6-6 222MU 1-12 *Guinean* 22-2 Casa 15-1-45 SOC 20-9

ML190 33MU 15-4-44 52MU 23-4 *Inver* 21-5 Hap 6-5

ML191 9MU 14-4-44 317S 3-5 GAL 22-7 441S 28-9 WAL 14-5-45 sold Turk 13-10-47

ML192 8MU 30-3-44 AST 2-6 317S 22-6 FTR 11-8

ML193 .5in guns 39MU 18-4-44 485S 8-6 FTR 22-6 cancel AST recat B 3-10 1APU 31-4-45 MAAF 14-5 IAF 26-6-47 as MM4009

ML194 6MU 31-3-44 GAL 29-11 mods 29MU 23-145 MAAF 6-4 ME 72S spun in on powerless app Zeltweg Austria 12-9-46 SOC 31-10

ML195 HFIX M70 46MU 18-4-44 74S 19-5 312S CAC ops 10-7 ROS 74S 28-7 313S 5-10 sold VA 28-11-49

ML196 HFIX M70 8MU 26-4-44 127S 22-5 313S 8-7 118S 15-7 FAAC 14-9 441S 15-2-45 313S 5-4 WAL 2-8 47MU 6-2-48 cd/ld del flt not TOC CAC SAAF 10-8

ML197 HFIX M70 39MU 18-4-44 312S 5-9 313S 5-10 WAL 2-8-45 29MU 22-12 SAAF 13-2-49

ML198 8MU 18-4-44 317S 1-5 FTR ops 20-6 cancel 132S 13-7 ASTH 30-7 WAL 15-12 mods SAL 29-3-45 recat E 11-6

ML199 9MU 6-4-44 3501SU 16-5 165S 20-6 recat E 15-9

ML200 HFIX M70 33MU 18-4-44 74S 4-5 CE ops 10-6

ML201 6MU 6-4-44 no record

ML202 6MU 31-3-44 332S 8-6 453S 5-10 DeH 28-2-45 sold Turk 24-10-47

ML203 33MU 4-4-44 52MU 17-4 *Inver* 21-5 Hap 6-7

ML204 46MU 5-4-44 165S 20-6 e/fd w/u ldg CE Hermitage Farm Aylesford Kent 17-8

ML205 33MU 6-4-44 441S CAC ops 13-7 411S 6-8 442S 10-8 602S 28-9 FACB 25-10 sold Turk 21-10-47

ML206 33MU 1-5-44 AST 14-5 mods 317S 15-6 CAC 20-6 411RSU 22-6 16S 13-7 CE ops 11-12

ML207 HFIX M70 33MU 13-4-44 74S 4-5 ROS 20-6312S 28-9 313S 5-10 FTR ops 25-10

ML208 6MU 6-4-44 ASTH 30-5 302S 15-6 CA ops 26-8 602S 26-10 WAL 4-6-45 29MU 7-9 sold Turk 16-4-47

ML209 HFIX M70 6MU 6-4-44 127S 1-6 313S 8-7 118S 15-7 CB ops 8-10 recat E 30-10

ML210 HFIX M70 39MU 15-4-44 127S 6-5 313S 8-7 118S 15-7 CAC ops 15-11 sold R J Coley 3-2-50

ML211 HFIX M70 6MU 6-4-44 127S 2-6 313S 8-7 118S 15-7 441S 15-2-45 329S 5-4 58OTU 19-4 SOC FFS 8-9-49

ML212 HFIX M70 33MU 15-4-44 74S 4-5 312S 8-7 MAL 9-9 39MU 17-2-45 sold R J Coley 6-2-50

ML213 8MU 27-4-44 MAL 15-5 441S CE ops 2-7

ML214 6MU 25-4-44 126S 7-5 FACB 10-10 ROS ASTE 5-2-45 FAF 14-8-46 GC1/3

ML215 33MU 6-4-44 302S 30-4 308S 10-5 FTR ops 21-5

ML216 HFIX M70 39MU 13-4-44 127S 6-5 FAAC 27-5 AST 313S 8-7 118S 15-7 441S 15-2-45 FA FTR 10-3

ML229 HFIX M70 39MU *Inver* 21-5 Hap 6-7

ML230 HFIX M70 33MU 6-4-44 74S 4-5 312S 8-7 313S 5-10 to 5200M 7-4-45 Sch of Aero Eng SOC 31-8-45

ML231 39MU 14-4-44 308S 5-5 416S 13-7 CAC ops 18-8 1ATC 24-8 ROS 416S 13-10 SAL 6-2-45 132Wg 19-7 FACE 7-9

ML232 HFIX M70 6MU 6-4-44 74S 26-5 312S 8-7 118S 2-8 FACE 10-4-45 SOC 26-4

ML233 HFIX M70 33MU 13-4-44 74S 20-5 312S 8-7 313S 7-10 29MU 19-8-45 sold H Bath 27-10-49

ML234 HFIX M70 6MU 18-4-44 127S 5-5

ML235 HFIX M70 39MU 13-4-44 127S 6-5 118S CAC ops 18-7 ROS DeH 21-2-45 329S 13-11 FAF 24-11

ML236 HFIX M70 33MU 6-4-44 74S 312S 8-7 313S 5-10 FAAC 29-1-45 sold R J Coley 3-2-50

ML237 33MU 13-4-44 52MU 29-4 *Inver* 21-5 Hap 6-7

ML238 HFIX M70 39MU 13-4-44 127S 6-5 313S 8-7 118S 15-7 SAL 17-2 SOC 16-11-47

ML239 6MU 28-4-44 ASTH 30-5 302S 15-6 CAC ops 6-10 AST MAAF 26-2-45 FACE 25-4-45 SOC 19-7-45

ML240 HFIX M70 33MU 23-4-44 74S 20-5 312S 8-7 CE ops 11-8

ML241 HFIX M70 33MU 20-4-44 74S 4-5 442S FACE 9-6 ROS 313S 5-10 SAL 5-4-45 recat E 11-6 SOC 5-9

ML242 8MU 31-4-44 165S 30-5 Persh 21-4-45 MAAF 21-6 318S o/s ldg Treviso Italy 26-3-46 SOC 28-3-46

ML243 HFIX M70 39MU 15-4-44 127S 6-5 FTR ops 30-5 313S 8-7 118S 15-7 DeH 21-2-45 SAAF 5-6-47

ML244 33MU 1-5-44 332S 8-6 602S 9-11 MAL 14-12 129S 19-5-45 ROS 7-1-46 recat E 24-6

ML245 HFIX M70 33MU 25-4-44 74S 4-5 312S 8-6 CE ops 25-8
ML246 HFIX M70 9MU 18-5-44 441S 5-3-45 313S 5-4 WAL 9-8 SAAF 17-11-48
ML247 HFIX M70 39MU 13-4-44 127S 6-5 313S 8-7 118S 15-7 SAL 21-2-45 595S 19-7 FAAC 12-2-48 recat E 24-12 trs to 3MU authority 18-8-49
ML248 46MU 18-4-44 403S FTR ops 28-6
ML249 HFIX M70 9MU 14-4-44 3501SU 16-5 441S 5-3-45 329S 5-4 58OTU 19-4 sold H Bath 27-10-49
ML250 8MU 21-4-44 317S 1-5 416S 13-7 FACE 2-12
ML251 HFIX M70 39MU 21-4-44 127S 5-6 313S 8-7 118S 15-7 441S 15-2-45 329S 5-4 58OTU 19-4 ASTH 30-4 sold H Bath 10-11-49
ML252 8MU 23-4-44 602S 15-6 FTR ops 4-7
ML253 HFIX M70 8MU 13-4-44 312S 2-8 118S 9-12 441S 15-2-45 329S 5-4 58OTU 19-4 sold VA 28-11-49
ML254 39MU 13-4-44 308S 5-5 FTR ops 21-5
ML255 HFIX M70 6MU 19-4-44 127S 5-5 ROS 8-6 313S 8-7 118S 15-7 FAAC 14-9 ROS 441S 3-2-45 313S 5-4 WAL 2-8 SAAF 16-11-48
ML256 33MU 26-4-44 52MU 7-5 *Inver* 21-5 Hap 6-5
ML257 9MU 21-4-44 GAL 16-5 302S 15-6 FTR ops 22-6
ML258 9MU 29-4-44 1S dam ops 8-6 ROS FTR ops 29-12
ML259 HFIX M70 33MU 13-4-44 74S 20-5 312S 8-7 FACB 7-8 313S 5-10 CAC ops 24-12 ROS MAL 5-7-45 SAAF 19-12-48
ML260 8MU 27-4-44 AST 14-5 mods 312S 15-6 442S 17-8 401S 31-8 CAC ops 26-11
ML261 HFIX M70 33MU 20-4-44 74S 4-5 312S 8-7 ROS 24-8 313S 12-10 sold VA 5-12-48
ML262 6MU 18-4-44 3501SU 21-6 602S 6-7 132S 27-7 e/a CB 21-10 416S 18-12 RNAF 25-11-46 as H-17
ML263 CRD VA CBAF 24-4 CE 22-1-46
ML264 8MU 27-4-44 MAL 17-5 mods 401S 22-6 442S 25-8 602S 28-9 WAL 1-3-45 sold Turkey 6-4-48
ML265 8MU 28-4-44 MAL 12-6 132S 10-8 CB ops 18-8 602S 14-9 442S CAC ops 6-10 412S 2-11 sold Turk 25-9-47
ML266 8MU 14-4-44 56S 9-5 CAC ops 13-6 ROS 322S CAC ops 17-9 ASTH WAL 2-9-45 sold Turk 30-7-47
ML267 6MU 25-4-44 26S 8-5 e/td t/o f/ld CE Culmhead 3-6
ML268 9MU 21-4-44 317S 3-5 414S 10-8 CAC ops 22-8 AST 411S 3-5-45 sold Turk 30-7-47
ML269 8MU 19-4-44 MAL 17-5 mods 441S FAAC 10-7 ROS AST 30-9 3APU 7-5-45 MAAF 21-6 RHAF 27-4-47
ML270 9MU 26-4-44 1S 16-5 662S 19-10 FTR ops 21-11 cancel 328S 25-4-45 327S 11-10 FAF 4-12 BE708 des nr Meknes 20-1-49
ML271 39MU 10-5-44 56S 7-6 MAL 18-7 441S 17-8 CAC ops 23-8 131Wg 8-3-45 CAC ops 18-4 SNCAN 28-6 GC 1/3 des Bao Ha 8-6-49
ML272 8MU 21-4-44 56S FACE 5-5
ML273 46MU 27-4-44 AST 26-5 302S 15-6 CAC ops 22-6 511FRU 29-6 411S 9-12 CB ops 23-1-45 sold Turk 15-9-47
ML274 46MU 18-4-44 AST 23-5 308S 15-6 CAC ops 26-8 AST 1APU 7-5-45 MAAF 23-6 ME SOC 26-9-46
ML275 6MU 18-4-44 317S 3-5 i/sea ops 18-5
ML276 46MU 18-4-44 56S 9-5 ROS 20-6
ML277 8MU 21-4-44 56S 9-5 e/td ldg app w/u ldg nr Newchurch CAC 11-6 GAL 28-9 mods 412S 23-11 FTR ops 20-1-45
ML291 30MU 15-4-44 52MU 1-5 *Inver* 21-5 Hap 6-7
ML292 33MU 6-4-44 416S CB ops 14-6 GAL 29-11 MAAF 2-2-45 ME 26-6 REAF 31-7-47
ML293 9MU 22-4-44 56S 10-5 GAL 10-11 mods 317S 16-1-45 CB ops 8-4 ROS VA 27-4 sold Turk 16-4-47
ML294 46MU 5-4-44 350S 9-7 322S FAAC 9-8 ROS 333S FACE 8-11
ML295 39MU 13-4-44 411S 22-6 CE ops 30-7
ML296 HFIX M70 33MU 18-4-44 74S 4-5 312S 8-7 CE ops 7-9
ML297 33MU 21-4-44 52MU 3-5 *Inver* 21-5 Hap 6-7
ML298 33MU 20-4-44 52MU 3-5 *Inver* 21-5 Hap 6-7
ML299 33MU 26-4-44 52MU 7-5 *Emp Gla* 1-6 Hap 9-7
ML300 8MU 24-4-44 411S 14-9 326S 5-4-45 FAF 4-12
ML301 39MU 1-5-44 52MU 16-5 *Argyll* 1-6 Casa 13-6
ML302 33MU 29-4-44 52MU 10-5 *Emp Gla* 1-6 Hap 9-7
ML303 33MU 4-5-44 83GSU 16-5 443S 27-7 CE ops 12-8
ML304 8MU 23-5-44 AST 9-6 317S 22-6 1ATC 10-8 411RSU 19-4-45
ML305 33MU 5-5-44 401S 22-6 421S 24-8 HAL 6-1-45 39MU 29-7 sold R J Coley 3-2-53
ML306 8MU 29-5-44 132S 15-6 GAL 10-11 mods MAAF 2-2-45 ME 380 MU u/c c/ld Pisa, Italy 25-1-46
ML307 33MU 6-5-44 602S 15-6 CAC ops 5-8 1ATC 24-8 ASTH 33MU 14-1-45 FAAC 3-3-45 MAAF 13-9 SOC 31-7-47
ML308 8MU 23-5-44 3501SU 21-6 421S 6-7 CE ops 27-8
ML309 46MU 8-5-44 AST 23-5 302S 15-6 CB ops 26-8 AST WAL 13-2-45 sold R J Coley 3-2-50
ML310 33MU 6-5-44 317S FTR ops 7-6
ML311 39MU 15-5-44 83GSU 22-2-45 to 5689M 2-10 recat scr SOC 13-10-49
ML312 45MU 8-5-44 AST 26-5 302S 15-6 CB ops 25-7 317S 24-8 308S 5-10 CAC ops 21-10 MAAF 2-8-45 SOC 28-8-47

ML307 with 'E' wing.

ML313 VA Dsfd 8MU 11-5-44 1S 26-5 CAC ops 18-6 ROS 165S 1-9 91S 28-12 FACB 14-1-45 ASTH 5-2 sold Turk 15-9-47
ML314 45MU 8-5-44 AST 26-5 84GP Com S 15-6 349S 8-2-45 485S 22-2 317S 1-3 FTR ops 10-4
ML315 39MU 13-5-44 MAL 27-6 mods 308S 31-8 CAC ops 1ATC 7-9 recat E 18-9-45
ML316 39MU 13-5-44 AST 26-5 308S CAC ops 3-9 1ATC 7-9 recat E 20-9
ML317 33MU 13-5-44 ASTH 31-5 441S 17-8 CE 2-12
ML318 39MU 15-5-44 403S 6-7 410RSU 27-7 127Wg 6-8 CAC ops 416S CE ops 26-9
ML319 39MU 18-5-44 83Gp Com S 29-6 FACB 26-8 ROS GAL 28-11 mods 332S 25-1-45 CAC ops 13-2 485S 26-4 74S 17-5 326S 28-6 FAF 4-12
ML320 8MU 19-5-44 ASTH 31-5 317S 22-6 CB ops 28-2-45 ASTH 29MU 29-5-46 sold Turk 21-8-47
ML321 39MU 15-5-44 66S FAAC 17-6 132Wg 22-6 66S 27-7 GACB 23-3-45 MAL sold Turk 15-10-47
ML322 33MU 18-5-44 ASTH 31-5 317S 17-8 CE ops 24-12
ML323 8MU 19-5-44 ASTH 31-5 308S 15-6 CB ops 1-10 AST MAAF 5-5-45 SOC 21-9
ML339 HFIX M70 8MU 19-4-44 312S 11-7 453S 26-10 303S 22-3-45 441S 5-4 58 OTU 12-4 sold VA 5-12-49
ML340 33MU 18-4-44 52MU 26-4 *Inver* 21-5 Hap 6-7
ML341 9MU 26-4-44 56S 10-5 402S 17-7 91S FACE 28-2-45
ML342 6MU18-4-44 2nd TAF com S 6-7 126Wg 442S 15-3-45 CE ops 17-4
ML343 HFIX M70 6MU 26-4-44 127S 5-5 313S 8-7 118S 15-7 DeH 21-2-45 FAF 3-12 GC2/7
ML344 33MU 20-4-44 52MU 3-5 *Inver* 21-5 Hap 6-7
ML345 8MU 28-4-44 MAL 12-6 441S 17-8 CAC ops 25-10 129S 16-5-45 to 6460M 17-5-46 sold VA 16-4-47 RDAF 30-7-48
ML346 39MU 25-4-44 485S 8-6 CB ops 17-7 recat E 511FRU 27-7
ML347 9MU 21-4-44 GAL 16-5 84GSU 26-6 FACB 17-7 322S 28-9 CB ops 30-9 AST MAAF 5-4-45 ME SOC 26-9-46
ML348 HFIX M70 8MU 21-4-44 127S 22-5 313S 8-7 118S 15-7 CB ops 5-8 recat E 17-8
ML349 8MU 19-4-44 AST 23-5 317S 31-12
ML350 6MU 25-4-44 317S 3-5 CAC ops 30-6 39MU 7-12 SAL 27-3-45
ML351 8MU 19-4-44 56S 9-5 CAC ops 18-5 ROS MAL 18-7 412S FTR ops 1-10
ML352 33MU 20-4-44 52MU 29-4 *Inver* 21-5 Hap 6-7
ML353 HFIX M70 8MU 19-4-44 313S 5-10 CB ops 29-11 FAF GC2/4
ML354 33MU 21-4-44 485S 15-6 CAC ops 24-8 ROS 82MU *Lafian* 12-11 Casa 23-11 SOC 14-3-46
ML355 33MU 20-4-44 485S 30-4 82MU 20-10 *Sil Lar* 18-11 Casa 23-11 SOC 14-8-45
ML356 HFIX M70 8MU 21-4-44 313S 1-3-45 CAC ROS 20-6 HAL SAAF 10-8-48
ML357 39MU 29-4-44 349S 24-5 485S 15-6 302S FTR ops 19-6 cancel 82MU 21-10 *Lafian* 13-11 Casa 23-11 SOC 11-4-46
ML358 8MU 27-4-44 ASTH 13-5 mods 302S 15-6
ML359 33MU 29-4-44 52MU 22-5 *Arabis* 14-6 Hap 29-6 Bas 2-8
ML360 9MU 21-4-44 GAL 16-5 mods 441S 17-8 CE ops 25-9
ML361 39MU 18-4-44 485S 1-5 421RU 22-7 e/a dbf CE 1-1-45
ML362 9MU 21-4-44 308S 3-5 16S 22-6 CAC ops 22-7 83GRU 26-10 414S 15-3-45 412S 26-4 WAL 22-6 sold Turk 25-9-47
ML363 46MU 25-4-44 AST 13-6 45MU 15-7 66S 31-8 CB ops 7-10 DeH 26-10 332S 12-5-45
ML364 HFIX M70 33MU 23-4-44 74S 4-5 312S 8-7 313S 5-10 CAC ops 5-1-45 SAL 5-4 SOC 5-9
ML365 39MU 26-4-44 341S 15-6 349S 21-7 33S 27-7 349S 11-1-45 485S 22-2 331S 1-3 66S 29-3 302S 19-4 74S 17-5 326S 28-6
ML366 6MU 28-4-44 126S 7-5 FTR ops 8-7
ML367 HFIX M70 9MU 22-4-44 127S CAC ops 20-5 AST 312S 23-1-45 sold Int All 29-2-50
ML368 .5in guns 39MU 18-4-44 485S 8-6 e/a CB 1-1-45 ASTH sold Turk 10-4-47
ML369 33MU 26-4-44 222MU 19-5 *Arabis* 14-6 Hap 29-6 Bas 12-8
ML370 9MU 22-4-44 GAL 16-5 441S 10-8 602S 19-10 401S 24-10 CAC ops 25-3-45 to 6414M 21-8-47 sold J Dale 12-1-50
ML371 8MU 25-5-44 AST 14-5 302S 15-6 CAC ops 10-8 131Wg 17-8 303S 9-11 CAC ops 5-12 MAAF 18-5-45 IAF 30-5-46 as MM4024
ML372 6MU 22-4-44 317S 3-5 64S eng trouble i/sea off Bolt Head 7-7
ML373 8MU 23-4-44 310S 8-6 16S 22-6 CAC ops 24-7 412RSU 24-7 GAL 23-11 mods FACB 10-2-45 ROS MAAF 21-6 SOC 28-8-47
ML374 6MU 18-4-44 317S 3-5 16S 27-7 602S 19-10 39MU 30-4-45 MAAF 29-6 SOC 26-6-47
ML375 6MU 6-5-44 82MU 28-5 *Arabis* 16-6 Hap 29-6 Bas 12-8
ML376 8MU 23-4-44 MAL 17-5 mods 308S 15-6 131Wg FAAC 23-12 84GSU 25-1-45 FAAC 23-2 MAL 28-4 sold Turk 25-9-47
ML377 33MU 23-4-44 485S 30-4 486S 16-11 GAL 23-11 mods SAL 29-3-45 recat E 11-6
ML378 8MU 23-4-44 17APC 1-6 FLS Mlfld 3-10 VA 22-3-46 SOC 17-6-48
ML379 HFIX M70 9MU 22-4-44 3501SU 16-5 CRD Deff 29-5-45 SOC 15-1-46
ML380 6MU 28-4-44 83Gp SU 7-5 CB ops 3-6 GAL 28-9 mods 345S 2-11 74S 13-12 CB ops 13-2-45 recat E SOC 21-3-45
ML381 39MU 12-5-44 329S 15-6 332S 13-7 602S 5-10 326S 5-4-45 FAF GC1/1
ML396 8MU 23-4-44 412S CAC ops 3-6 GAL 17-10 mods 84GSU 4-11 411S 12-12 SOC 27-4-46
ML397 6MU 25-4-44 FAAC 5-5 ROS 126S 30-5 FACB 8-8 ROS 132S 12-10 451S 15-2-45 328S 15-4 327S 15-4 327S 11-10 FAF 4-12
ML398 6MU 22-4-44 126S 8-5 FAAC 7-8 ROS 11-9 GAL 12-12 mods SAL 4-4-45 recat E 11-6
ML399 HFIX M70 46MU 27-4-44 118S 6-12 CAC ops 23-12 ROS 441S 15-2-45 329S 5-4 58OTU 19-4 recat E 18-1-46
ML400 33MU 22-4-44 485S 30-4 CAC ops 22-5 ROS 1-6 FAAC 17-9 ROS 9MU 5-1-45 MAAF 26-2 FA FTR 5-4
ML401 9MU 22-4-44 GAL 16-5 412S 24-7 401S 31-8 Persh 30-5-45 MAAF 16-6 SOC 26-6-47
ML402 33MU 29-4-44 52MU 10-5 *Emp Gla* 1-6 Hap 9-7
ML403 39MU 26-4-44 AST 13-6 132S 13-7 FTR 15-8
ML404 39MU 25-4-44 349S 15-6 CAC ops 4-8 132Wg 10-8 331S CAC ops 25-8 MAAF 23-2-45 SOC 31-5
ML405 HFIX M70 39MU 1-5-44 82MU 22-5 *Argyll* 1-6 Casa 12-6 318S c/ld Teviso Italy FACE 31-7-46 SOC 28-11
ML406 HFIX M70 8MU 21-4-44 127S FAAC 27-5 ROS 118S 1-8 FA FTR 23-8
ML407 33MU 23-4-44 485S 30-4 CAC ops 12-10 341S 4-1-45 308S 11-1 349S 8-2 345S 22-3 332S 19-4 sold VA NEA 19-7-50 con to Type 509 two-seat train 1951 IAC as 162 SOC July '60 Extant, Middle Wallop, G-LFIX.
ML408 33MU 26-4-44 52MU 4-5 *Emp Gla* 1-6 Hap 9-7
ML409 46MU 25-4-44 MAL 15-4 mods 317S 22-6 CB ops 18-7 MAAF 26-2-45 FAF 28-3-46
ML410 46MU 25-4-44 AST 26-5 308S 15-6 CAC ops 31-8 AST WAL 13-2-45 mods 3APU 26-4 MAAF 12-5 IAF 26-6-47 as MM4123
ML411 8MU 26-4-44 403S 27-7 CAC ops 24-8 127Wg

31-8 e/a CB 21-10 421S 7-12 302S 18-1-45 317S 8-2 sold Turk 14-10-47

ML412 33MU 22-4-44 485S 3-5 CAC ops 10-9 340S 19-10 345S 16-11 84Gr ARF 15-3-45 332S 29-3 CAC ops 1-4 485S 30-4 74S 17-5 MAL 25-5 sold H Bath 27-10-49

ML413 HFIX M70 8MU 27-4-44 127S 30-5 FRU 6-7 441S 25-3-45 595S 18-7 FAAC 22-8 ROS bou SOC 5-2-47

ML414 .5in guns 39MU 25-4-44 225S CB ops 13-6 421S CAC ops 1-7 401S 13-7 442S 25-8 602S 28-9 1S 8-2-45 WAL 19-4 sold Turk 10-4-47

ML415 46MU 27-4-44 403S FAAC 16-7 127Wg 6-8 416S e/a CB 12-10 recat E SOC 4-4-45

ML416 33MU 1-5-44 442S 13-7 SAL 10-8 412S 17-8 FAAC 2-9-45 1ATC 7-9 MAAF 15-4-45 NWA 18-4 IAF 26-6-47 as MM4125

ML417 6MU 28-4-44 443S 22-6 CAC ops 7-8 127Wg HQ 10-8 443S CAC ops 29-9 401S 12-10 411S 5-4-45 412S 12-4 sold VASM 31-10-46 to EA con to two-seat train 25-5-48 as G.15-11 to Indian AF as HS543 1-49 G-BJSG 7-8-80 extant again as single seater.

ML418 6MU 27-4-44 3501SU 23-5 165S 10-6 MAAF 29-5-45 ME 2-8 SOC 28-8-47

ML419 46MU 25-4-44 AST 24-5 317S 15-6 FTR 20-6 SOC cancel 13-7 127Wg HQ 17-8 401S 24-8 SAL 6-2-45 MAAF 21-6 ME 2-8-45 ME SOC 9-10-47

ML420 46MU 30-4-44 403S CB ops 17-7 recat E 1-8

ML421 9MU 26-4-44 56S 10-5 AST 6-6 329S 15-2-45 345S 1-3 317S 8-3 FTR ops 12-4

ML422 9MU 5-5-44 442S 27-7 CAC ops 3-8 126Wg 10-8 442S 132S 5-10

ML423 6MU 27-4-44 1S CAC ops 9-6 ROS WAL 14-8-45 29MU 22-12 BAF 9-7-48 as SM-18

ML424 8MU 23-4-44 AST 6-5 mods 443S 27-7 127Wg HQ 31-8 CAC ops 443S 19-10 412S 8-2-45 SAL 26-3 sold Turk 22-7-47

ML425 HFIX M70 39MU 29-4-44 82MU 21-5 *Argyll* 1-6 Casa 13-6 FTR ops 18-9

ML426 33MU 26-4-44 52MU 7-5 *Emp Gla* 1-6 Hap 9-7

ML427 9MU 29-4-44 3501SU 16-5 FLS 31-5 R-RH 7-6 new eng 29MU 27-8-45 VASM 31-10-46 to 6457M 4SoTT 15-10-47 extant Birmingham Mus

ML428 46MU 27-4-44 MAL 17-5 mods 302S 15-6 GACB 21-3-45 MAL 16FU 2-7 blown onto wng ldg nosed over CAC St Mw 16-9-46 recat E 18-9 SOC 16-1-47

NH series all LF IX Merlin 66 unless otherwise indicated

NH148 HFIX M70 33MU 28-4-44 312S 30-5 CAC ops 18-9 ROS 313S 5-10 FACE 1-2-45 SOC 8-2

NH149 33MU 30-4-44 52MU 13-5 *Emp Gla* 1-6 Hap 9-7

NH150 9MU 29-4-44 66S 8-6 602S 5-10 CE ops 2-12

NH151 8MU 30-4-44 329S 8-6 MAL 18-7 441S 17-8 CE ops 25-9

NH152 6MU 28-4-44 56S 17-5 taxy coll with MK734 CE Newchurch 21-5 AST 9MU 7-9 401S 9-12 CAC ops 24-2-45 410RSU 1-3 130S 17-5 recat E SOC 20-5-46

NH153 HFIX M70 46MU 28-4-44 ROS 4-5 118S 29-10 441S 8-2-45 329S 5-4 58 OTU 19-4 29MU 5-8 sold VA 8-12-49

NH154 LFIXE 9MU 26-4-44 GAL 11-5 308S 15-6 ASTE 7-2-45 COAL 14-6 mods CGS 16-7 RHAF 31-3-48

NH155 6MU 28-4-44 56S 17-5 402S 17-7 91S CAC ops 17-8 ROS 402S 2-9 ASTE 1-5-45 VA CBAF 19-7 ROS sold Turk 25-9-47

NH156 33MU 29-4-44 52MU 10-5 *Emp Gla* 1-6 Hap 9-7

NH157 6MU 27-4-44 443S 22-6 FTR ops 5-1-45

NH158 46MU 30-4-44 AST 24-5 2nd TAF Com S 8-6 Stn Flt North 26-7 AST 2-8 317S 11-1-45 CB ops 21-2 ASTE sold Turk 22-7-47

NH171 8MU 30-4-44 332S CAC ops 20-6 125Wg 9-7 602S CAC ops 13-7 412S 17-8 453S 23-9 GAL 30-11 mods 165S 20-5-45 332S 15-11

NH172 8MU 30-4-44 332S FTR ops 8-6

NH173 6MU 27-4-44 66S CAC ops 16-6 132Wg 22-6 453S 5-10 FAAC 19-10 ROS MAAF 3-7-45 208S coll with RK837 f/ld dbr Beirut Lebanon 10-5-46 SOC 25-7-46

NH174 8MU 28-4-44 310S 8-6 411S 3-7 132S 5-10 ASTE 10-2-45 Czech AF 6-12-46

NH175 8MU 28-4-44 MAL 12-6 441S FTR ops 13-8 recat AC 16-11 401S 26-4-45 412S 10-5 to 5692M 2-10 SOH 26-4-50 AFD SOC 24-1-51

NH176 46MU 30-4-44 MAL 20-6 441S CAC ops 11-8 FAAC 26-9 419RSU 5-10

NH177 39MU 1-5-44 52MU 13-5 *Arabis* 14-6 Hap 29-6 Bas 12-8

NH178 46MU 30-4-44 MAL 14-6 441S 10-8 FTR 13-8

NH179 8MU 30-4-44 310S 8-6 416S CAC ops 14-7 71MU 2-2-45 AST 1-3 33MU 23-6 sold Turk

NH180 33MU 31-4-44 52MU 15-5 *Emp Gla* 21-5 Hap 9-7

NH181 HFIX M70 6MU 6-5-44 74S 28-5 74S tyre burst t/o strk air raid shelter CE Lympne 30-6

NH182 9MU 29-4-44 412S 22-6 CAC ops 13-8 AST 39MU 18-1-45 MAAF 17-2 IAF 26-6-47 as MM4104

NH183 33MU 1-5-44 421S left form off St Catherines Point FTR 7-6

NH184 8MU 6-5-44 47MU 19-5 *Argyll* 1-6 Casa 13-6 IAF 24-6-47 as MM4118

NH185 33MU 1-5-44 52MU 11-5 *Arabis* 14-6 Hap 29-6 Bas 12-8

NH186 6MU 1-5-44 AST 18-5 308S 15-6 FTR ops 11-9

NH187 39MU 2-5-44 52MU 18-5 *Emp Gla* 1-6 Hap 9-7

ML427 was recategorised to 6457M. Now in Birmingham Museum.

NH188 6MU 1-5-44 AST 18-5 308S 15-6 CE ops 8-10 416S 30-11 47MU 17-9 RNAF 17-5-47 as H-64 later H-109 BAF 3-53 as SM-39 to COGEA as OO-ARC then Canada as CF1-NUS. Extant NAM, Rockliffe, Ontario.

NH189 33MU 1-5-44 132S 15-6 CAC 3-7 453S 27-7 412S 17-8 FTR ops 27-9

NH190 HFIX M70 33MU 8-5-44 127S 10-6 313S 8-7 118S 15-7 CB ops 30-10 ROS 441S 15-2-45 341S 22-2 329S 22-3 SAAF 10-8-48

NH191 9MU 5-5-44 AST 31-5 317S 29-6 FTR ops 8-8

NH192 39MU 2-5-44 52MU 16-5 *Emp Gla* 1-6 Hap 9-7

NH193 6MU 1-5-44 AST 18-5 308S 15-6 CAC ops 28-9 411RSU 19-10 FACB 13-4-45 ASTE RNoAF 14-12-47

NH194 no record

NH195 33MU 2-5-44 411S CE ops 11-6

NH196 33MU 5-5-44 411S 29-6 127Wg 28-9 132S 5-10

NH197 6MU 8-5-44 215MU 25-5 GAL 16-8 302S 2-11 308S 4-1-45 FAAC 20-3 RSO 47MU 9-1-47 RNAF 20-5 as H-33 w/o 18-11-49

NH198 6MU 1-5-44 AST 18-5 317S 15-6 CB ops 6-11 29MU 18-3-45 MAAF 16-5 73S lost part of prop blade f/ld Takali Malta 1-9-47 SOC 30-10

NH199 8MU 23-5-44 349S 15-6 CE ops 30-8

NH200 39MU 10-5-44 82MU 22-5 1S 3-8 FAAC 14-4-45 VAO WAL 26-7 29MU 8-11 sold Turk 6-12-47

NH201 9MU 9-5-44 313S 8-6 3501SU 9-7 1S 27-7 FTR ops 17-8

NH202 6MU 8-5-44 82MU 21-5 *Arabis* 16-6 Hap 29-6 Bas 12-8

NH203 33MU 8-5-44 602S FTR ops 10-6

NH204 9MU 5-5-44 421S FTR ops 23-6

NH205 45MU 8-5-44 AST 26-5 411S 6-8 CAC ops 24-8 126Wg 411S 31-8 132S 5-10 327S 5-4-45 FAF

NH206 45MU 25-5-44 MAL 7-6 302S 3-8 FAAC 10-2-45 FACB 15-4 ASTE 29MU 23-10 sold Turk 17-1-47

NH207 9MU 5-5-44 401S CE ops 21-6

NH208 33MU 8-5-44 453S 15-6 CAC ops 8-7 443S 25-7 WAL 20-5-45 RNoAF 9-5-47

NH209 6MU 6-5-44 82MU 19-5 GAL 17-5 1S 29-3-45 29MU 10-10 sold VA 28-11-49

NH210 39MU 9-5-44 222MU 25-5 *Argyll* 1-6 Casa 13-6 SOC 28-4-45

NH211 VA HPA 8-5-44 39MU 18-5 222MU 4-6 MAL 27-6 FAAC 5-7 ROS 302S 31-8 COAL 17-5-45 mods CGS 10-6 bou sold scr 3-9-47

NH212 33MU 5-5-44 132S 18-5 412S 20-7 453S 28-9 WAL 28-2-45 RNAF 22-4-48 Gs h-22

NH213 9MU 5-5-44 AST 6-6 453S 3-8 CAC ops 15-8 29MU 15-7-45 RNoAF 9-5-47

NH214 6MU 6-5-44 82MU 19-5 GAL 12-8 302S 19-10 ASTH 1-3-45 39MU 5-7 sold Turk 16-10-47

NH215 33MU 10-5-44 222S 15-6 CAC 21-9 ASTE sold VA 5-12-49

NH216 39MU 6-5-44 52MU 30-5 *Arabis* 14-6 Hap 29-6 Bas 12-8

NH217 9MU 9-5-44 83GSU 23-5

NH218 45MU 24-5-44 340S 29-6 345S 16-11 FTR ops 14-2-45

NH230 CRD Farn Apl' 44 measurements of tail and fin loads at high Mach numbers. Weather trls Aug '45. Feb to July '46 cont of fin and rud trls, with larger rud instal and full feathering prop. See page 317 for details. SOC Farn 25-3-48

NH231 8MU 15-5-44 403S CAC 20-6 FRU 6-7 s/d by Allied AA fire 19/7 GAL mods 39MU 12-2-45 MAAF 12-3

NH232 33MU 19-5-44 83GSU 30-5 403S FAAC 25-6 CAC ops 19-7 CE ops 17-8

NH233 45MU 8-5-44 AST 26-5 441S FTR ops 15-8

NH234 6MU 8-5-44 222MU 24-5 *Arabis* 18-6 Hap 29-6 Bas 12-8

NH235 33MU 5-5-44 403S FACB 17-6 33MU 4-1-45 MAAF 10-2 SOC 20-9

NH236 HFIX M70 33MU 8-5-44 3501SU 30-5 33MU 29-8 Farn 3-12 exhaustive prop trls cont through 1946/47. DeH Hatfield M61 instal 11-7-47 Farn 10-10. FA cd CE 14-9 49MU 27-10

Above: NH188 in 421 Squadron colours, when owned and flown by John Paterson as CF-NUS. Below: Same aircraft while in service with COGEA at Coxyde, Belgium.

NH237 39MU 6-5-44 52MU 18-5 *Arabis* 14-6 Hap 29-6 Bas 12-8

NH238 HFIXC M70 RNAF H-60 1948 later H-103 BAF as SM-36 1-53 COGEA as OO-ARE. USA as N238V 1972 Extant Bitteswell as G-MKIX.

NH239 39MU 10-5-44 82MU 22-5 165S 1-9 6MU 17-2-45 MAAF 21-6-45 208S Flew i/high gd pilot kld nr Haifa 30-1-47 SOC

NH240 8MU 20-5-44 411S 22-6 CAC 28-9 401S 12-10 CAC ops 24-2-45 SAL 26-3 9MU 23-6 FAF 12-9-46 EAA601

NH241 .5in. guns. 33MU 6-5-44 349S CAC ops 17-6 CE ops 19-11

NH242 33MU 18-5-44 52MU 30-5 165S 8-8 CAC ops 5-9 ROS 91S 21-12 9MU 31-3-45 MAAF 16-5 IAF 27-6-46 as MM4095:

NH243 33MU 5-5-44 411S 22-6 FRU 29-6 MAAF 28-2-45 73S Takali 29-1-48 SOC 10-6

NH244 33MU 10-5-44 453S 15-6 443S 26-7 FAAC 1-12 DeH sold Turk

NH245 9MU 9-5-44 AST 6-6 127Wg HQ 17-8 443S CE ops 27-9

NH246 33MU 17-5-44 1S 28-5 FACB 22-3-45 DeH 29MU 1-11-45 sold Turk 10-10-47

NH247 9MU 9-5-44 453S 15-6 401S 6-7 CAC ops 30-7 AST 39MU 23-11 MAAF 8-3-45 IAF 12-6-47 as MM4096

NH248 33MU 11-5-44 82MU 23-5 3501SU 17-8 411S 14-9 132S 5-10 327S 12-4-45 326S 4-10 FACE 27-11 FAF BE708

NH249 8MU 11-5-44 340S 8-6 414S 14-9 CAC ops 19-9

NH250 HFIX M70 39MU 13-5-44 312S 8-9 313S 5-10 FAAC 20-6-45 29MU 28-9 sold Turk 15-10-47

NH251 33MU 10-5-44 MAL 7-6 349S 31-8 AFDU Witt GACA 26-11 411S 12-4-45 130S 17-5 58OTU 12-7 66S 2-9-46 sold R J Coley 3-2-50

NH252 6MU 8-5-44 47MU 19-5 *Argyll* 1-6 Casa 13-6 111S e/fd cd/ld 31-8 SOC 23-10

NH253 LFIXE 33MU 8-5-44 1S 28-5 CAC ops 3-9 ROS HAL 21-7-45 29MU 11-2-46 RNoAF 19-12-47

NH254 8MU 11-5-44 66S 8-6 453S FAAC 4-10 DeH 12-10 recat E 28-11

NH255 33MU 18-5-44 1S 28-5 ROS 30-8 FAAC 9-10 WAL 17-4-45 sold Turk 15-10-47

NH256 HFIX M70 33MU 13-5-44 215MU 24-5 *Sam Stur* 30-6 Casa 13-7 ME 5-7-45 SOC 25-4-46

NH257 8MU 220-5-44 349S 15-6 CAC ops 11-10 ASTH 9MU 20-7-45 sold Turk 15-4-47

NH258 33MU 10-5-44 412S 22-6 FACB AST 33MU 11-3-45 sold R J Coley 3-2-50

NH259 39MU 12-5-44 132S 15-6 CE ops 14-7 s/dn by Mustangs 410RSU 7-9

NH260 33MU 10-5-44 401S 22-6 CE ops 18-8

NH261 39MU 9-5-44 349S 8-6 FAAC 31-3 485S 25-1-45 74S 1-3 332S 8-3 29MU 18-7 RNoAF 5-9-47

NH262 HFIX M70 33MU 10-5-44 215MU 28-5 *Argyll* 1-6 Casa 13-6 SOC 30-8-45

NH263 39MU 10-5-44 82MU 21-5 403S 24-8 443S 14-12 411S CE ops 3-5-45

NH264 39MU 11-5-44 222MU 4-6 *Arabis* 19-6 Hap 29-6 Bas 12-8

NH265 39MU 12-5-44 403S CE ops 16-7

NH266 39MU 12-5-44 403S FTR ops 18-8

NH267 HFIX M70 39MU 17-5-44 52MU 30-5 *Samstur* 30-6 Casa 13-7 CE ops 6-4-45 SOC 14-6

NH268 8MU 11-5-44 416S 27-7 CAC ops 13-8 ASTE 14-2-45 29MU 21-8 sold Turk 3-11-47

NH269 33MU 11-5-44 222MU 19-5 *Argyll* 26-5 Casa 13-6 SOC 14-8-46

NH270 33MU 11-5-44 341S 8-6 84GSU 3-8 414S 11-12 FAF GR 2/33 CAC ops 24-3-45

NH271 HFIX M70 33MU 16-5-44 215MU 28-5 *Argyll* 1-6 Casa 13-6 FACE 7-2-45

NH272 LFIXE 45MU 23-5-44 MAL 8-6 132S 13-7 CE ops 1-8

NH273 8MU 19-5-44 310S 15-6 421RSU 3-8 33S CB ops 17-9 CE 16-11

NH274 33MU 10-5-44 453S 15-6 CE ops 12-7

NH275 HFIX M70 9MU 10-5-44 313S 16-2-45 WAL 31-8 29MU 27-2-46 SAAF 5-8-48

NH276 39MU 13-5-44 1S 14-9 AST 12-10 33MU 21-12 MAAF (alloc) 15-2-45 12FU flew i/cliff with PT360 Kimmeridge Dorset CE 17-2 SOC bboc 24-3-45

NH289 39MU 13-5-44 83GSU 27-5 39MU 14-10 2AADA 2-11 328S

NH290 39MU 15-5-44 222MU 4-6 441S 24-8 1S 29-3-45 CE ops 19-4 SOC 8-5

NH291 39MU 16-5-44 215MU 1-6 *Arabis* 16-6 Hap 29-6 Bas 12-8

NH292 33MU 16-5-44 215MU 26-5 *Arabis* 16-6 Hap 29-6 Bas 12-8

NH293 HFIX M70 39MU 12-5-44 222MU 23-5 *Argyll* 1-6 Casa 13-6 CE ops i/sea 2-3-45

NH294 6MU 20-5-44 313S 22-6 127S 27-7 CB ops 28-9 SAL 10-10 9MU 26-2-45 MAAF 25-5 ME 14-8 SOC 30-10-47

NH295 33MU 16-5-44 3APU 15-4-45 MAAF 16-5 SOC 28-8-47

NH296 33MU 11-5-44 222MU 21-5 *Argyll* 1-6 Casa FTR ops 21-9

NH297 HFIX M70 33MU 15-5-44 222MU 25-5 *Argyll* 1-6 Casa 13-6 IAF 30-5-46 as MM4016

NH298 45MU 16-5-44 443S 22-6 CB 20-7 ROS 9MU 27-10 MAAF 10-2-45 FTR ops 30-6

NH299 33MU 17-5-44 83GSU 30-5 403S 22-6 1ATC 6-8 FRU CE 10-8

NH300 8MU 20-5-44 443S FTR ops 16-6

NH301 33MU 11-5-44 222MU 21-5 *Emp Gla* 1-6 Hap 9-7

NH302 33MU 16-5-44 GAL 8-8 317S 21-9 CB ops 6-10 AST 33MU 4-3-45 sold R J Coley 3-2-50

NH303 39MU 18-5-44 52MU 21-6 *Arabis* 17-6 Hap 29-6 Bas 12-8

NH304 8MU 15-5-44 332S 8-6 FTR ops 4-7

NH305 8MU 23-5-44 MAL 7-6 132S 13-7 CB ops 6-8 SAL 29MU 4-2-45 MAAF 5-4 SOC 18-10

NH306 39MU 15-5-44 441S 22-7 511FRU CB 17-8 ROS 2AAD 1-11 328S 12-4-45 327S 4-10 SNCAN 18-10

NH307 39MU 12-5-44 411S 22-6 222MU 20-12 *Tanela* 13-1-45 Casa 25-1 IAF 30-5-46 as MM4018

NH308 39MU 18-5-44 52MU 21-6 *Arabis* 17-6 Hap 29-6 Bas 12-8

NH309 RNAF as H-57 later H-113 BAF 10-52 as SM-34

NH310 HFIX M70 33MU 13-5-44 215MU 24-5 *Samstur* 30-6 Casa 13-7 ME 26-7-45 SOC 9-8

NH311 33MU 23-5-44 349S 15-6 131Wg 308S 22-2-45 331S 5-4 349S FACE 26-4

NH312 8MU 15-5-44 332S FTR ops 17-9 33MU 10-3-45 MAAF 20-6 SOC 28-8-47

NH313 HFIX M70 6MU 17-5-44 127S 2-6 313S 15-7 441S 8-2-45 329S 5-4 58 OTU 19-4 FAAC 14-6 ROS recat E 25-6 sold Turk 15-10-47

NH314 8472 FIXE M46 cd on test flt May '44 rebuilt at CBAF as HFIX M70 8MU 1-7-44 74S CAC ops 29-10 345S 13-12 FACE 6-2-45

NH315 39MU 12-5-44 222MU 23-5 GAL 12-8 317S 19-10 327S 12-7-45 FAF 27-11 GC2/1

NH316 39MU 19-5-44 313S 29-6 127S 27-7 DB ASTH 3-1-45 332S 1-5

NH317 39MU 13-5-44 411S 22-6 CAC ops 31-7 WAL 13-2-45 mods 129S 16-5 hit wall o/t taxy CE Hutton Cranswick 21-3-46 SOC 28-3

NH318 45MU 23-5-44 310S 15-6 33S 27-7 CE ops 17-9

NH319 8MU 20-5-44 310S 15-6 33S 27-7 AST 18-9 6MU 14-1-45 MAAF 31-3 NWA 15-4 IAF 27-6-46 as MM4019

NH320 45MU 16-5-44 441S 22-6 443S 28-9 CAC VA ROS 1-1-45 sold International Alloys 29-8-50

NH321 33MU 16-5-44 485S 8-6 e/a CE dbf 1-1-45

NH322 45MU 18-5-44 412S 22-6 FTR ops 25-8

NH323 33MU 16-5 349S 15-6 485S CAC ops 22-2-45 WAL 33MU 20-7 sold R J Coley 3-2-50

NH324 39MU 17-5-44 215MU 1-6 *Arabis* 16-6 Hap 29-6 Bas 12-8

NH325 8MU 15-5-44 442S 15-6 FTR ops 11-7

NH326 33MU 23-5-44 52MU 30-5 91S 19-8 Farn Dec '44 prop research & tail loads at high Mach numbers CAC 25-3-45 328S 26-4 FAF 27-11 BE-708

NH339 9MU 26-4-44 GAL 16-5 mods 308S 22-6 CAC ops 17-8 410RSU CE ops 6-11

NH340 6MU 25-4-44 126S 8-5 o/s strk NH402 in touch and go ldg Harrow CE 20-7

NH341 8MU 28-4-44 MAL 17-5 mods 411S 22-6 FTR ops 2-7

NH342 6MU 1-5-44 AST 18-5 317S 15-6 302S 9-11 317S 11-1-45 CB ops 28-2 MAL 9MU 15-6 156S 20-6-46 165S 27-6 66S 2-9 sold R J Coley 3-2-50

NH343 45MU 22-5-44 MAL 8-6 30S CB 17-12 AST HQ TTC Com Flt 28-11 to 6384M RAF Cranwell 5-8-47 SOC 14-9-51

NH344 33MU 1-5-44 421S CB ops 17-6 411S 29-6 CE FTR ops 27-7

NH345 45MU 19-5-44 602S 15-6 AST 16-7 66S strk H/T cables f/ld Hammond Farm nr Horsham 18-7 215MU 14-11 *Tanela* 13-1-45 Casa 13-8 6S e/fld on app Nicosia Cyprus 19-10-46

NH346 IXE D-wing (2 × 20mm can × 4 × .5in m/gs) original FV fin and rud 45MU 22-5-44 412S 22-6 1ATC 24-8 AST 1-9 485S CE ops 15-11 bboc 28-2-45 MAAF 3-3 87S SOC 30-4-47

NH347 8MU 23-5-44 443S 22-6 CAC ops 6-8 127Wg 17-8 FTR ops 29-9

NH348 6MU 26-5-44 310S 15-6 33S CAC ops 27-7 331S 4-1-45 CAC ops 28-2

NH349 45MU 25-5-44 AST 9-6 317S 22-6 FCCS North 11-7-45 33MU 4-6-48 sold Turk 26-7

NH350 45MU 30-5-44 MAL 15-6 132S CAC ops 20-6 132S 13-7 FTR ops 1-8-45 AST 25-11

NH351 8MU 20-5-44 56S 21-6 17-7 FAAC 20-1-45 recat FAF GC1/4

NH352 39MU 31-5-44 FACB 29-6 312S 19-10 ROS 30-10 215MU 11-12 *SSLS2495* 13-1-45 Casa 25-1 FTR ops 22-4

NH353 45MU 23-5-44 AST 10-6 412S 6-8 411S 10-8 129S 16-5-45

NH354 39MU 10-5-44 349S 15-6 511FRU 10-8

NH355 6MU 26-5-44 485S 15-6 331S CB ops 9-8 SAL 6MU 8-1-45 MAAF 16-2 FA flew i/sea CE SOC 30-8-45

NH356 6MU 8-5-44 215MU 21-5 91S 30-8 1S CE ops 19-4-45 SOC

NH357 45MU 30-5-44 MAL 15-6 453S 27-7 412S 28-9 CAC 19-10 411S 9-12 CAC ops 9-2-45 WAL RNoAF 31-7-47

NH358 45MU 30-5-44 312S 22-6 74S CAC 7-9 ROS 222MU 12-10 *Guinean* 22-12 Casa 15-1-46

NH359 39MU 5-6-44 453S 20-7 CAC ops 22-8 602S 31-8 442S CB ops 4-10 recat E SOC 14-2-45

NH360 HFIX M70 39MU 18-5-44 Farn 9-1-45 tail load and anti-G trls. FACB 17-7 ASTH 30-7 29MU 16-2-46 sold VA 5-12-49

NH361 39MU 31-5-44 AST 20-6 132S 13-7 CAC ops AST 29MU 18-5-45 sold Turk 24-3-47

NH362 HFIX M70 39MU 12-5-44 222MU 23-5 *Argyll* 1-6 Casa 13-6 FTR ops 5-3-45

NH363 39MU 13-5-44 66S 15-6 FAAC 25-8 AST 33MU 7-12 MAAF 16-2-45 FACE 20-6

NH364 45MU 5-6-44 485S 22-6 hit water performing aero off Port Talbot CE 15-11

NH365 39MU 18-5-44 AST 6-6 317S 22-6 FTR ops 27-8

NH366 39MU 5-6-44 MAL 28-6 602S 10-8 340S CE ops 3-9

NH367 6MU 20-5-44 312S 22-6 74S CE ops 11-8

NH368 8MU 23-5-44 222S 15-6 CAC 17-8 ROS 331S 19-10 30-4-45 317S 3-5 328S 31-5 327S 3-10 SNCAN 18-10 SOC 21-6-47

NH369 39MU 5-6-44 453S CAC 14-8 412S 5-10 CAC ops 28-10 442S 7-1 recat E SOC 1-4-45

NH370 33MU 30-5-44 MAL 7-6 123S 13-7 412S 5-10 CAC ops 18-1 MAL 29MU 23-1-45 MAAF 5-3 ME SOC 31-10-46

NH371 45MU 2-6-44 453S 27-7 412S 28-9 CAC ops 13-10 9MU 26-3-45 MAAF 16-5 SOC 30-5-46

NH372 39MU 15-6-44 341S 21-7 CB ops 7-10 SAL 332S 5-4-45 FAAC 23-8

NH373 6MU 26-5-44 312S 22-6 66S 11-12 FACE SOC 10-2-45

NH374 45MU 10-6-44 312S 29-6 CE ops 74S 16-8

NH375 45MU 12-6-44 310S 22-6 33S 27-7 FTR ops 24-8

NH376 45MU 12-6-44 340S 6-7 CE 7-9-45

NH377 45MU 12-6-44 33S 27-7 CAC ops 6-8 511FRU 24-8 326S 5-4-45

NH378 45MU 14-6 340S 6-7 CB ops 31-8 1ATC 7-9 33MU 26-12 12FU cd el flt MAAF 340S CE 7-3-45

NH379 33MU 23-6-44 127S 22-7 331S 31-8 FA i/sea CE 4-10

NH380 39MU 23-6-44 MAL 6-7 602S 17-8 CB ops 27-8 411S 5-10 CE ops 20-1-45

NH381 6MU 26-5-44 310S 22-6 333S 27-7 CB ops 11-9 345S 15-2-45 331S 12-4 84ARF 30-4 412S 3-5 130S 17-5 FA FTR 6-7

NH393 39MU 20-4-44 52MU 1-5 *Inver* 21-5 Hap 6-7

NH394 39MU 21-4-44 52MU 3-5 *Inver* 21-5 Hap 6-7

NH395 33MU 20-4-44 52MU 12-5 *Inver* 21-5 Hap 6-7

NH396 33MU 21-4-44 52MU 4-5 *Inver* 21-5 Hap 6-7

NH397 9MU 25-4-44 126S 10-5 CE ops 1-8

NH398 6MU 24-4-44 443S CB ops 17-7 AST 215MU 8-1-45 Casa 25-1 *Tanela* 13-1 ME w/u ld Marcianse Italy 27-2-46 SOC 31-10

NH399 39MU 20-4-44 52MU 3-5 *Inver* 21-5 Hap 6-7

NH400 6MU 24-4-44 317S 3-5 165S 30-11 ASTH 12-2-45 FAF 18-10-46

NH401 45MU 22-6-44 165S 6-7 FAAC 13-8 ROS 602S 27-10 91S 15-2-45 CAC ops 21-3 ROS 1S 5-4 HAL 29-8 RNoAF 15-11-47

NH402 9MU 25-4-44 126S 10-5 strk by NH340 when parked CE Harrow 20-7

NH403 9MU 24-4-44 126S 10-5 AST 28-12 Farn 26-7-45 prop research. Sept con to target tug, used for stab and cont trls while towing GAL tailless glider TS507 with EN498. ASTH mods for towing Me163 Komet rocket fighter. HPA 1946. Windscreen misting and assoc hand trls June'47. July, participant in gust prog Chase a/c for Vampire TG426 during latter's deck land trls. Jan'48 rain repellant prog with EN498 and all-weather trls. Gloster A/C Brockworth March. 31-8-48 Farn. Film making with Lancaster FM201 (Air Min Film Unit). SOC PEE Shoe 26-9-50

NH404 9MU 26-4-44 GAL 16-5 442S 6-8 401S 31-8 FTR ops 29-9

NH405 9MU 24-4-44 GAL 16-5 441S 17-8 FTR ops 14-9

NH406 9MU 26-4-44 126S 10-5 CE ops 14-9

NH407 9MU 26-4-44 GAL 16-5 441S CB ops 22-8 4APU 6-1-45 MAAF 18-2 SOC 30-8

NH408 NH409 6MU 27-4-44 416S CAC 28-6 127AF 6-7 CAC ops 9-10

NH409 9MU 26-4-44 132S 15-6 CAC 27-6 126S 6-8 FA FTR 8-12

NH410 9MU 28-4-44 GAL 16-5 302S 3-8 e/a CE 1-1-45

NH411 9MU 29-4-44 416S 6-7 CAC ops 27-9 443S 14-12 ROS 6MU 28-2-45 COAL 22-6 mods CGS 20-7 FACE e/fld t/o Lecon c/d Molecroft 28-1-46 SOC 5-2

NH412 33MU 2-5-44 421S CAC ops 8-7 440S 13-7 442S 20-7 CAC ops 18-8 CE 14-9

NH413 9MU 1-5-44 401S FACE 14-6

NH414 9MU 1-5-44 132S 15-6 441S 20-7 64S 2-9 GAL 12-12 mods SAL 12-3-45 sold Turk 23-1-47

NH415 9MU 1-5-44 421S CE ops 13-6

NH416 33MU 1-5-44 52MU 10-5 *Emp Gla* 1-6 Hap 9-7

NH417 FIXC 329S RDAF as 401 12-1-49.Extant Egeskov museum, Denmark as 41-401.

NH418 HFIX M70 9MU 18-5-44 441S 13-3-45 329S 5-4-45 58OTU 19-4 FAAC 24-5 ROS 29MU 11-8 sold VA 5-12-49

NH419 39MU 23-5-44 349S 15-6 CAC ops 2-8 33S 10-8 329S 4-1-45 435S 4-1-45 332S 8-3 GAAC 15-3 485S 26-4 sold Turk 13-10-47

NH420 HFIX M70 33MU 20-5-44 52MU 27-5 *Samstu* 30-6 Casa 13-7 SOC 5-6-45

NH421 45MU 24-5-44 FAAC 18-6 ROS 127S 27-7-45 485S 21-12 e/a CE dbf 1-1-45

NH422 HFIX M70 8MU 24-5-44 312S 29-9 313S 5-10 29MU 19-8-45 sold H Bath 10-11-49

NH423 33MU 23-5-44 310S 22-6 33S 27-7 331S 4-1-45

349S 26-4 412S 3-5 FACB 13-6 ASTH 16-1-46 RNoAF 28-8-47
NH424 6MU 26-5-44 441S 16-11 485S sold VA 2-5-47
NH425 39MU 23-5-44 310S 15-6 33S 27-7 CAC ops 29-11 349S 25-1-45 485S 22-2 332S 8-3 FTR ops 16-4
NH426 8MU 19-5-44 349S 15-6 CAC ops 11-9 DeH 3APU 13-4-45 MAAF 12-5 IAF 26-6-47 as MM4105
NH427 6MU 8-6-44 313S 22-6 127S CB ops 25-7 AST 74S 15-2-45 CAC ops 24-2 AST sold Turk 25-3-47
NH428 6MU 20-5-44 310S 15-6 CAC ops 24-6 33S 6-7 CAC ops 26-7 ROS 332S CB ops 13-10 recat E SOC 19-2-45
NH429 33MU 23-5-44 MAL 6-6 132S 13-7
NH430 33MU 24-5-44 313S 22-6 127S 27-7 341S e/a CE 30-12 DeH recat E SOC 26-2-45 1401 Met Flt SOC 20-9
NH431 8MU 23-5-44 72S 21-9 CAC ops 13-10 AST 9MU 31-3-45 MAAF 28-4 CAC 1-5 IAF 26-6-47 as MM4027
NH432 33MU 24-5-44 485S 22-6 e/a CE dbf 1-1-45
NH433 HFIX M70 8MU 26-5-44 504S 25-1-45 SAL 24-4 1401 Met Flt Eindhoven 2-9 33MU 24-9 sold R J Coley 3-2-50
NH434 33MU 24-5-44 349S 15-6 CAC 1-9 ROS SAL 19-3-45 W Wal 18-12-46 sold Turkey
NH435 45MU 23-5-44 AST 9-6 132S 13-7 FTR ops 9-8
NH436 33MU 23-5-44 313S 22-6 127S CB ops 28-9 29MU 7-3-45 MAAF 7-4 SOC 14-2-46
NH437 HFIX M70 6MU 23-5-44 441S 26-2-45 329S 5-4 58OTU hit lorry in dive attack nr Malpas Cheshire CE 30-5-45
NH438 6MU 26-5-44 310S 22-6 33S 27-7 349S 3-8 FAAC 25-8 ROS GAL 20-10 mods 411S 8-11 CE ops 24-3-45
NH450 HFIX M70 39MU 28-5-44 312S 5-9 313S 5-10 CE ops 28-1-45 SOC 8-2
NH451 6MU 26-5-44 GAL 12-6 132S 20-7 e/a 28-9 411S FAAC 13-10 ROS 132S 3-11 222MU *Talela* 13-1-45 Casa 25-1 ME 16-8 REAF 29-8-46 fought in Arab-Israeli war of 1948
NH452 45MU 23-5-44 AST 9-6 132S 13-7 CE ops 18-8
NH453 6MU 20-5-44 349S 15-6 CB ops 30-7 AST 33MU 7-12 MAAF 21-3-45 111S FACE coll with MA884 aban c/d Rutterfeld Austria complete wreck 15-4-46 SOC 25-4
NH454 33MU 20-5-44 349S 15-6 485S 10-8 FAAC 20-8 ROS GAL 20-10 mods 74S 6-11 CAC ops 10-12 DeH 165S 31-5-45 66S 2-9-46 abs SOC 5-2-47
NH455 8MU 20-5-44 310S 22-6 33S 27-7 CAC ops 12-10 1APU 6-5-45 MAAF 28-5 RHAF 27-3-47
NH456 39MU 23-5-44 349S 15-6 CAC ops 21-10 ASTH 39MU 11-7-45 sold Turk 14-10-47
NH457 39MU 23-5-44 340S 29-6 345S 16-11 CAC 11-2-45 ASTE 39MU 7-9 sold Turk 23-10-47
NH458 HFIX M70 33MU 24-5-44 213S 6-2-45 ROS 4-9 CFE 25-10 SOC 16-10-46
NH459 HFIX M70 9MU 27-5-44 312S 27-9 313S 5-10 sold H Bath 10-11-49
NH460 8MU 23-5-44 310S 15-6 33S 27-7 CAC ops 13-9 420RSU 21-9 39S 26-10 332S 10-5-45
NH461 6MU 26-5-44 312S 22-6 74S FTR ops 26-8
NH462 45MU 23-5-44 453S 15-6 412S 10-8 CAC ops 27-9 416S 19-10 MAL 8-4-45 sold Turk 18-11-47
NH463 45MU 23-5-44 MAL 8-6 317S 22-6 302S 9-11 e/a CE 1-1-45
NH464 6MU 23-5-44 349S 15-6 FAAC 27-8 ROS 441S 16-11 FACE 24-12
NH465 45MU 25-5-44 AST 9-6 132S 6-7 FACE 31-7
NH466 45MU 24-5-44 229S 22-6 1S 14-7 e/fd on Diver (VI) patrol w/u ldg Thane Kent CE 4-8
NH467 6MU 26-5-44 349S FAAC 16-6 511FRU 22-6 82MU 23-11 *Guinean* 22-12 Casa 15-1-45 ME 16-8 SOC 26-2-48
NH468 6MU 26-5-44 312S 22-6 74S CAC ops 25-8 AST WAL 10-12 mods 33MU 12-12 MAAF 20-4-45 IAF 30-5-45 as MM4004
NH469 45MU 24-5-44 FACB 20-6 GAL 17-10 mods 329S 30-11 74S 13-12 CB ops 1-3-45
NH470 33MU 23-5-44 602S 6-7 FTR ops 8-8
NH471 45MU 25-5-44 AST 10-6 132S 13-7 CAC ops 13-8 41S 17-8 411S 28-9 CAC ops 27-12 412S 4-1-45 sold VA 5-10-49
NH472 33MU 20-5-44 349S 15-6 ROS 28-8 329S 4-1-45 CAC ops 16-1 DeH sold Turk 23-10-47
NH473 45MU 23-5-44 AST 9-6 132S 13-7 CB ops 10-8 33S 24-8 411S 5-10 NFOW Ford 1-3-45 FACB 20-4
NH474 33MU 28-5-44 349S 15-6 CAC ops 4-8 132Wg 14-9 FACE 9-11
NH475 33MU 23-5-44 310S 15-6 33S 27-7 CAC ops 5-8 WAL 19-10 332S 31-4-45
NH476 39MU 27-5-44 GAL 12-6 132S 20-7 FTR 27-9
NH477 39MU 28-5-44 312S 22-6 CE ops 74S 11-10
NH478 HFIX M70 6MU 23-5-44 BDn 23-2-45 FACB 20-4 DeH 26-4 29MU 21-12 RDAF 12-1-49 as 402
NH479 6MU 26-5-44 313S 22-6 127S 27-7 126S 12-10 FTR ops 30-10
NH480 6MU 24-5-44 310S 22-6 33S CAC ops 26-7 FTR 12-10
NH481 8MU 24-5-44 MAL 7-6 132S 13-7 CB ops 3-8 341S 30-11 74S 13-12
NH482 HFIX M70 33MU 26-5-44 124S 14-7 9MU 23-2-45 sold H Bath 18-11-49
NH483 39MU 27-5-44 310S 15-6 33S 27-7 GAL 23-11 mods FACE 12FU f/f to 10ADU 10-2-45 SOC 24-2
NH484 39MU 27-5-44 349S CAC ops 15-6 dvd i/grd from H/A during comb nr Burgess Hill Sussex CE 12-7
NH485 6MU 26-5-44 349S 27-7 CB ops AST WAL 11-1-45 mods FSU 17-6 128Wg 19-7 FACE 11-8

NH491, No 485 Squadron, following a wheels up landing on test flight after repairs at AST. Recategorised E, SOC, February 1945.

NH486 HFIX M70 39MU 27-5-44 124S 14-7 9MU 15-3-45 MAAF 9-7 ret UK SOC 26-6-47
NH487 39MU 27-5-44 310S 15-6 33S 27-7 11FU 3-1-45 ROS 9-4 sold Turk 26-6-47
NH488 HFIX M70 33MU 30-5-44 124S 14-7 3S CE ops 6-10
NH489 39MU 27-5-44 GAL 12-6 132S 3-8 411S 28-9 442S 8-11 FTR ops 24-2-45
NH490 45MU 2-6-44 329S 29-6 FAAC 13-9 ASTH 33MU 28-7-45 sold Turk 9-6-47
NH491 39MU IXE 27-5-44 312S 15-6 485S 20-7 w/u ldg nr Hamble on test flt after rep AST CB 13-9 recat E SOC 6-2-45
NH492 6MU 31-5-44 215MU 8-6 6MU 12-6 GAL 17-8 317S 19-10 FACE i/sea 8-12
NH493 45MU 31-5-44 MAL 15-6 132S 20-7 FTR ops 15-8
NH494 39MU 27-5-44 AST 13-6 453S CE ops 25-7
NH495 6MU 26-5-44 313S 22-6 127S 27-7 CB 31-8 AST 33MU 11-2-45 MAAF 10-3 ME 16-8 REAF 27-11-47 109MU stor 11-3-49 SOC 27-5
NH496 45MU 26-5-44 313S 29-6 127S 27-7 FTR ops 25-8
NH513 HFIX M70 39MU 28-5-44 124S 14-7 595S 30-8-45 29MU 22-2-46 SAAF 26-847
NH514 39MU 31-5-44 340S 29-9 345S 16-11 485S CE dbf ops 6-1-45
NH515 6MU 31-5-44 312S 22-6 74S 25-8
NH516 39MU 27-5-44 310S 15-6 33S 27-7 332S 4-1-45 CB ops 17-4 ASTH FAF 16-9-46 GC1/2
NH517 39MU 30-5-44 MAL 6-7 CAC ops 11-8 132S 3-9 411S 28-9 FACB 26-11 19MU 26-4-45 4 FSCU 17-5 130S 31-5 FACE 4-7
NH518 HFIX M70 39MU 20-5-44 215MU 11-8 *Melam* 20-8 Casa 3-9 CE ops 9-2-45
NH519 33MU 31-5-44 329S 29-6 ROS 30-9 308S 22-2-45 332S 15-3 CAC ops 30-3 485S 30-4 74S 2-6 327S 21-6 SNCAN 28-6
NH520 45MU 26-5-44 313S 22-6 329S 3-8 CAC ops 1-9 71MU 11-1-45 ASTH 15-1 29MU 27-8 RNoAF 13-5-48
NH521 33MU 30-5-44 326S 6-7 CE ops 22-8
NH522 45MU 26-5-44 341S 29-6 FTR ops 26-8
NH523 33MU 31-5-44 MAL 7-6 132S CE ops 12-7 WAL 21-12 5FPP lost cont in cloud on f/f a/c aban cd CE Staton Wyreville Leics 21-12
NH524 6MU 26-5-44 312S 22-6 345S 30-11 CB ops 22-2-45 33MU 27-5 sold Turk 12-11-47
NH525 39MU 27-5-44 127S 31-8 CAC 28-9 CE ops 30-10
NH526 33MU 6-6-44 313S 29-6 127S 27-7 FTR ops 15-10 IAF as MM4037
NH527 33MU 31-5-44 312S 22-6 74S 14-9 CAC ops 341S 10-12 ROS 74S 16-2-45 33MU 23-4 sold R J Coley 8-2-50
NH528 HFIX M70 33MU 29-6-44 *New Tex* 31-7 Casa 22-8 SOC 30-8-45
NH529 33MU 30-5-44 132S 20-7 AST 12-8 222MU 20-12 Casa 15-1-45 ME SOC 26-9-46
NH530 39MU 27-5-44 485S 27-7 e/a dbf 1-1-45
NH531 33MU 31-5-44 341S 29-6 ROS 17-8 GAL 9-10 mods 329S 9-12 74S 13-12 332S 5-4-45 CE ops 6-4
NH532 39MU 2-6-44 82MU 30-11 *Guinean* 22-12 Casa 15-1-45 FTR ops 19-4
NH533 39MU 30-5-44 313S 22-6 127S 27-7 FACB 26-8 AST 6MU 10-3-45 MAAF 15-4 NWA 18-4 SOC 29-8-46
NH534 HFIX M70 31-5-44 124S 14-7 504S 20-1-45 MAL 14-4 6MU 28-7 SAAF 2-6-47
NH535 39MU 28-5-44 312S 22-6 FACB 74S 5-8 DeH 14-8 9MU 6-2-45 MAAF 15-3 SOC 29-8-46 IAF as MM4128
NH536 HFIX M70 6MU 3-6-44 504S 24-7 CAC ops 30-8 ROS 504S eng fire when grd running Mans dbf CE 15-9
NH537 39MU 6-6-44 MAL 25-7 602S 17-8 442S CAC ops 9-11 SOC 25-2-45
NH538 6MU 8-6-44 313S 22-6 127S 27-7 74S e/a 20-12 317S 11-1-45 349S CAC ops 9-2-46 485S 20-2-45 332S 1-3 327S 5-7 FAF 27-11 BE708 des 4-1-52
NH539 HFIX M70 33MU 5-6-44 124S 14-7 47MU 17-2-48 SAAF 5-8
NH540 45MU 30-5-44 329S 29-6 CAC ops 1-10 345S 1-3-45 331S 8-3 29MU 10-7 RnoAF 1-5-48
NH541 45MU 3-6-44 329S 29-6 CAC ops 17-9 e/a CB 1-1-45 recat E SOC 24-2
NH542 HFIX M70 8MU 5-6-44 124S 17-7 FAAC 1-9 ROS abs SOC 5-7-47
NH543 39MU 28-5-44 313S 22-6 127S 27-7 CE ops 1-9
NH544 45MU 31-5-44 332S 31-8 CE ops 4-1-45
NH545 HFIX 9MU 3-6-44 124S 14-7 595S 12-7-45 sold Sanger & Co 22-8-47
NH546 6MU 31-5-44 312S 22-6 74S FAAC 30-7 ROS 312S 11-8 341S 13-12 302S 18-1-45 DeH 8-2 sold R J Coley 3-2-50
NH547 HFIX M70 9MU 3-6-44 12S 14-7 124S FAAC 9-8 ROS 287S 16-3-45 9MU 26-8-46 SOC 16-10-47 bou 2MPRD
NH548 33MU 6-6-44 329S 6-7 FTR ops 26-8
NH549 39MU 8-6-44 MAL 6-7 602S 17-8 CB ops 9-9
NH550 45MU 31-5-44 312S 22-6 74S CAC ops 16-8 ROS GAL 6-10 mods 442S CAC ops 26-11 332S 10-5-45 414S FAAC 23-6
NH551 33MU 5-6-44 340S 6-7 345S 16-11 485S 4-1-45 308S 22-2 CAC ops 13-4
NH552 6MU 31-5-44 GAL 12-6 132S 3-8 411S 28-9
NH553 45MU 2-6-44 312S CAC ops 24-6 74S 6-7 FTR 27-8
NH554 45MU 31-5-44 313S 29-6 127S 27-7 485S 4-1-45 CAC ops 3-2 WAL 5-3 33MU 27-6 sold Turk 22-7-47
NH555 39MU 5-6-44 453S 3-8 ASTH 24-9 CE
NH556 39MU 5-6-44 602S 10-8 442S 28-9 FTR ops 7-11
NH557 39MU 5-6-44 AST 27-6 453S 20-7 CE ops 27-9
NH558 39MU 8-6-44 52MU 12-7 *Samedway* 11-8 Hap 27-8
NH570 33MU 30-5-44 310S 22-6 FTR ops 29-6
NH571 33MU 6-6 329S 29-6 CE ops 18-12
NH572 HFIX M70 8MU 5-6-44 124S 17-7 AST 29-8 595S 13-7-45 130S FAAC 20-5-46 abs SOC 5-2-47 FAF GC1/4
NH573 6MU 8-6-44 340S 6-7 FTR ops 14-8 ASTH 30-8 66S 19-10 6MU 29-12 MAAF 7-2-45 CE ops 20-3 SOC 18-10
NH574 6MU 6-6-44 331S 25-7 CAC ops 14-8 ROS GAL 28-11 mods 9MU 23-1-45 MAAF 18-3 ME SOC Jly '45
NH575 33MU 5-6-44 AST27-6 132S 20-7 CE ops 20-8
NH576 33MU 10-6-44 GAL 29-6 74S 26-3 341S 13-12 329S CB ops 16-2-45 ASTE 29MU 7-9 RNoAF 5-9-47
NH577 HFIX M70 6MU 6-6-44 504S 24-7 ROS 5-9 CE ops 21-11
NH578 HFIX M70 8MU 5-6-44 124S 17-7 287S 22-7-45 FACE 9-11 SOC 15-11
NH579 6MU 8-6-44 312S 22-6 74S CAC ops 26-8 AST 9MU 18-7-45 WAL 14-9 FAF 27-2-46 GC1/2
NH580 39MU 5-6-44 MAL 6-7 453S CB ops 28-8 511FRU 7-9 recat E 20-9
NH581 33MU 5-6-44 310S 29-6 MAAF 8-2-45 FTR ops 22-4
NH582 HFIX M70 6MU 6-6-44 504S 27-7 CAC ops 12-8 RNAS Arbr 29-5-45 33MU 5-7 RDAF 8-7-48 as 403
NH583 33MU6-6-44 313S 22-6 127S 27-7 FAAC SOC 15-1-45
NH584 45MU 6-6-44 312S 22-6 74S 16-11 345S CAC ops 7-12 332S 29-4-45
NH585 6MU 18-6-44 AST 23-6 132S 13-7 442S 23-11 326S 19-7-45 FAF 27-11
NH586 39MU 10-6-44 331S 24-7 FTR ops 14-8
NH587 HFIX M70 33MU 10-6-44 504S 14-7 CE ops fire in air cd 29-11
NH588 39MU 7-6-44 GAL 11-7 602S 31-8 442S CAC ops s/dn by Spit 6-10 411S 2-11 442S 11-11 CAC ops 21-1-45 ROS MAAF 28-6-45 SOC 28-8-47
NH589 33MU 17-6-44 33S 27-7 349S 10-8 CAC ops 21-1-45 ROS MAAF 28-6 SOC 28-8-47
NH590 33MU 6-6-44 329S 29-6 145Wg HQ en/ac 20-12 329S 4-1-45 345S 25-1 ROS mr 23-4 84GDC 30-8 sold J Dale 2-1-50
NH591 45MU 13-6-44 GAL 7-7 602S 17-8 442S 28-9 CAC 28-11 recat E SOC 3-4-47
NH592 45MU 9-6-44 329S 29-6 CB ops 10-7 GAL 11-11 mods 39MU 6-12 MAAF 2-4-45 SOC 30-8
NH593 33MU 12-6-44 340S 6-7 coll with PK991 t/o CAC Tang 16-8 ROS AST 11-10 33MU 25-2-45 MAAF 21-6 SOC 28-8-47
NH594 45MU 10-6-44 340S 6-7 CAC ops 21-10 345S 30-11 FTR ops 14-2-45
NH595 33MU 5-6-44 329S 6-7 CB ops 26-11

NH596 6MU 10-6-44 313S 29-6 127S 27-7 CE ops 1-9

NH597 39MU 10-6-44 331S 3-8 341S 4-1-45 322S FTR ops 8-4

NH598 45MU 10-6-44 329S 6-7 CE ops 8-8 DeH 29MU 6-2-45 MAAF 4-4 SOC 10-5-46

NH599 39MU 10-6-44 33S 3-8 FAAC 7-9 ROS 82MU 4-11 *Sil Lar* 12-11 Casa 28-11 IAF 30-5-46 as MM4040 (MM4130)

NH600 33MU 10-6-44 313S 29-6 127S 27-7 FTR ops 14-8

NH601 no record

NH602 6MU 10-6-44 340S 6-7 CAC ops 21-10 345S 16-11 e/a 20-12 3BRU 14-2-45

NH603 8MU 14-6-44 329S 22-7 FACB 1-11 ROS 9MU 22-3-45 MAAF 5-4 SOC 18-10

NH604 39MU 7-6-44 329S 29-6 FACB 17-7 485S 16-11 FAAC 26-12 6MU 19-7-45 new eng sold 11-7-47

NH605 6MU 8-6-44 341S 29-6 USAAF CAC ops N Italy, Borgotaru 5-8 VAO 29MU 6-2-45 MAAF 23-3

NH606 9MU 12-6-44 82MU 28-7 *New Tex* 31-7 Casa 22-8 ME 2-8-45 SOC 31-7-47

NH607 45MU 10-6-44 329S 29-6 340S 30-8 CAC ops 7-10 AST 39MU 18-4-45 sold Turk 14-10-47

NH608 33MU 10-6-44 MAL 27-6 302S 17-8 FTR ops 14-9

NH609 6MU 8-6-44 312S 22-6 74S CAC ops 2-11 341S 13-12 e/a 20-12 ASTH 6MU 5-7-45 sold 11-7-47

NH610 8MU 12-6-44 329S 6-7 ROS 26-8 DeH 2-9 29MU 28-2-45 MAAF 12-4 SOC 30-4-47

NH611 HFIX M70 9MU 14-6-44 504S 17-7 ROS 5-9 329S FAAC 11-4-45 ASTH 29MU 18-2-46 SAAF 18-3-48

PK,PL,PT,PV series all LF IX Merlin 66

PK991 6MU 10-8-44 340S FAAC 28-6 421RSU 29-6 340S strk by NH593 t/o CE Tang 16-8

PK992 39MU 10-6-44 MAL 6-7 132S 17-8 411S 28-9 FTR ops fire in air (a/c aban) 26-2-45

PK993 33MU 12-6-44 340S 6-7 CE ops 26-8

PK994 33MU 10-6-44 329S 29-6 FACB 14-1-45 ASTH 9MU 13-7 sold Turk 17-1-47

PK995 8MU 14-6-44 331S 26-7 FACB 13-8 33S 12-10 341S 4-1-45 308S 11-1 329S 1-2 74S 1-3 332S 29-3 327S 14-6 FAF 27-11 GC1/3 s/dn 11-9-49

PK996 9MU 19-6-44 341S FTR ops 15-8

PK997 8MU 15-6-44 331S 25-7 FTR ops 23-8

PK998 39MU 17-6-44 MAL 25-7 132S 17-8 511FRU 22-8 412S 5-10 CAC ops 12-12 WAL 11-6-45 sold VA 5-12-49

PL123 33MU 31-5-44 AST 23-6 329S 31-8 CAC ops 30-10 74S 13-12 CB ops 14-2-45 recat E 18-6

PL124 45MU 30-5-44 312S 22-6 74S 16-11 345S 13-12 CAC ops 22-12 ASTH 165S 10-6-45 FAAC 3-12 ROS sold Turk 22-7-47

PL125 33MU 16-6-44 453S 3-8 FACB 16-8 511FRU 17-8 331S 4-1-45 411S 3-5 29MU 29-6 sold Turk 15-10-47

PL126 33MU 16-6-44 453S 20-7 412S CAC ops 28-9 3APU 4-5-45 MAAF 28-5 ME SOC 26-9-46

PL127 45MU 19-6-44 82MU 22-7 *New Tex* 31-7 Casa 22-8 IAF 26-6-47 as MM4099

PL128 39MU 29-6-44 349S 10-8 CAC ops 26-8 ROS 82MU 27-10 *Sil Lar* 13-11 Casa 23-11 CE ops 6-8-45

PL129 33MU 17-6-44 329S 6-7 CB ops 23-1-45 33MU 16-6 sold Turk

PL130 45MU 19-6-44 GAL 21-7 132S 17-8 83GSU 30-10 412S coll with MK631 while taxy CE Thorney Island 19-11

PL131 8MU 22-6-44 331S 25-7 341S 4-1-45 302S 13-1 349S 4-2 FACE 3-3 recat E SOC 13-3

PL132 33MU 19-6-44 332S 3-8 317S CA ops 18-10 331S 1-2-45 e/d after dive f/ld hit ditch CE 21-3-45 SOC 26-3

PL133 33MU 24-6-44 GAL 25-7 485S 31-8 CAC ops 14-2-45 ROS 29MU 17-6 VA recat E 24-6-46

PL134 6MU 14-6-44 82MU 24-6 *New Tex* 31-7 Casa 22-8 SOC 31-5-45

PL135 8MU 17-6-44 453S CB ops 24-7 AST 39MU 10-11 11FU 3-1-45 MAAF 7-2 ME 16-8 RHAF 27-2-47

PL136 6MU 10-6-44 313S 22-6 127S 27-7 FACB 2-8 SAL GAL 18-11 mods 9MU 9-1-45 FAAC 1-2 ASTE sold Turk 25-9-47

PL137 33MU 19-6-44 341S FTR ops 9-7

PL138 8MU 22-6-44 329S 3-8 CAC ops 22-9 411RSU GAAC 11-2-45 74S 1-3 332S CAC 21-3 485S 30-4 74S 17-5 328S 31-5 FAF 4-12 GC1/7

PL139 45MU 10-6-44 341S 29-6 FTR ops 14-8 cancel 322S 21-9 341S 19-10 317S 11-1-45 331S 25-1 29MU 21-6-48 sold H Bath 27-10-49

PL140 45MU 12-6-44 33S 6-7 485S 11-1-45 317S CAC ops 28-2

PL141 39MU 8-6-44 341S 3-7 en/ac 29-11 3APU 1-5-45 MAAF 29-5 ME SOC 26-9-46

PL142 33MU 17-6-44 340S 6-7 FTR ops 20-8

PL143 8MU 20-6-44 MAL 6-7 222S 31-8 CAC ops 19-10 329S 25-1-45 CAC ops 14-2 ASTH sold Turk 14-10-47

PL144 33MU 27-6-44 52MU 12-7 *San Suva* 21-7 Hap 27-8

PL145 8MU 14-6-44 453S 3-8 411S 12-10 485S CAC ops 17-1-45 ASTE 33MU 21-4-45 129S 16-6 SOC 31-7-46

PL146 45MU 22-6-44 39MU eng trouble after t/o w/u ldg Cole o/ld tank fire CE 19-7

PL147 33MU 27-6-44 52MU 10-7 *San Suva* 21-7 Hap 27-8

PL148 33MU 27-6-44 47MU 9-7 *Sam Const* 17-7 Hap 27-9

PL149 33MU 23-6-44 453S 3-8 412S 28-9 ROS 8-11 SAL 6-2-45 129S 15-5 257S 24-10-46 BAF 26-8-47 as SM-8 w/o 16-10-48

PL150 33MU 27-6-44 52MU 10-7 *Samtred* 11-8 Hap 27-8

PL151 6MU 30-6-44 47MU 19-7 *New Tex* 31-7 Casa 22-8 FAF GR2/33 26-8 SOC 15-3-45

PL152 39MU 29-6-44 329S 10-8 CAC ops 11-2-45 74S 8-3 331S 12-4 349S 26-4 317S 3-5 328S 31-5 FAF 27-11 GC2/1

PL153 39MU 29-6-44 66S 31-8 341S 4-1-45 340S 15-2-45 345S 15-2 CE ops 10-4

PL154 6MU 30-6-44 47MU 19-7 *New Tex* 31-7 Casa 22-8 FAF GC2/3 20-2-50

PL155 45MU 30-6-44 GAL 22-7 602S FA FTR 29-8

PL156 6MU 30-6-44 47MU 19-7 *New Tex* 31-7 Casa 22-8 SOC 23-12

PL157 6MU 30-6-44 47MU 19-7 *New Tex* 31-7 Casa 22-8 FACE 1-12

PL158 6MU 30-6-44 82MU 24-7 *New Tex* 31-7 Casa 22-8 SOC 15-3-45 RHAF 31-7-47

PL159 45MU 30-6-44 MAL 2-8 453S 24-8 412S 28-9 CE ops 19-11

PL160 45MU 30-6-44 GAL 21-7 602S 17-8 DeH 10-5-45 29MU 22-10 sold Int All 27-3-50

PL161 45MU 17-7-44 349S 10-8 ROS 11-9 332S 19-10 CB ops 17-4-45 29MU 4-9 sold Turk 28-8-47

PL162 45MU 17-7-44 317S 22-2-45 331SD 13-3 FTR ops 13-3 a/c disin

PL163 45MU 17-7-44 33S 10-8 331S 4-1-45 CAC ops 19-4 485S 30-4 FAB 10-5 sold Turk 25-9-47

PL164 45MU 17-7-44 74S 15-8 FAAC 33MU 5-1-45 MAAF 23-2 ME 30-8 IAF 26-6-47

PL165 45MU 17-7-44 FAAC 17-8 222S 17-8 485S CAC ops 3-1-45 345S 25-1 CB ops 1-3 FAAC 3-4 ROS sold Turk 11-7-47

PL166 33MU 21-7-44 222MU 3-8 *Melam* 20-8 Casa 3-9 MAAF SOC 23-8-45

PL167 45MU 9-7-44 349S 17-8 332S 28-9 FTR ops 3-11

PL168 6MU 19-7-44 47MU 24-7 *Sil Sand* 9-8 Casa 23-8 ME 9-8-45 REAF 29-8-46

PL169 33MU 21-7-44 no record

PL185 8MU 12-6-44 329S 6-7 CAC ops 17-7 345S 15-2-45 332S 22-3 486S 30-4 74S 17-5 MAL 25-5 29MU 24-9 RNoAF 26-6-47

PL186 33MU 15-6-44 453S 27-7 CAC 10-9 412S 5-10 FTR ops 20-1-45

PL187 9MU 13-6-44 332S 3-8 CB ops 6-9 FACB 31-12 DeH 9-1-45 331S Norway

PL188 8MU 15-6-44 340S 6-7 FTR 14-9 cancel recat B 4-11 WAL 28-3-45 mods 129S 16-5 FACE 20-6

PL189 HFIX M70 8MU 12-6-44 124S 17-7 441S 29-3-45 329S 5-4 129S 17-5 FAF 24-11 GC1/1

PL190 8MU 12-6-44 329S 29-6 CAC ops 30-10 129S Lubeck 11-6-46 BAF 17-8-47 as SM-4

PL191 8MU 14-6-44 GAL 11-7 602S CAC ops 15-8 127Wg 7-9 FTR ops 9-11

PL192 HFIX M70 39MU 16-6-44 124S 14-7 441S 22-4-45 329S 26-4 ASTH 4-1-46 33MU 24-6-46 Persh 10-4-47 SAAF 23-4

PL193 33MU 12-6-44 341S 13-7 FTR ops 30-9

PL194 HFIX M70 8MU 12-6-44 124S CAC ops 5-1-45 287S 19-7 sold Argentine AF 1-9-47 codes LV-NMZ. VA serviced 170gal. o/ld tank instal plus 2 × 20gal in wngs. Total fuel 428gal 29-4-47 Flown by Capt J Storey Hurn-Gib 5-5; Dakar-Natal; Natal-Buenos Airies

PL195 39MU 16-6-44 52MU 12-7 *Sam Const* 17-7 Hap 27-8

PL196 33MU 1206044 AST 27-6 453S 20-7 AST 15-8 132S 24-8 74S 25-1-45 CAC 10-2 151RU 6-3 328S 9-8 FAF 27-11

PL197 9MU 13-6-44 52MU 12-7 *Sam Const* 17-7 Hap 27-9

PL198 8MU 17-6-44 MAL 6-7 411S 28-9 CE ops 23-11

PL199 39MU 16-6-44 52MU 12-7 *Sam Const* 17-7 Hap 27-8

PL200 39MU 14-6-44 82MU 14-7 *Sansuva* 21-7 Hap 24-8

PL201 33MU 12-6-44 GAL 29-6 453S 27-7 412S 5-10 CB ops 18-10 MAAF 30-4-45 ME 2-8 SOC 26-9-46

PL202 8MU 14-6-44 341S 21-7 FACB 4-8 511FRU 10-8 412S CB ops 29-9 222S 19-10 345S FTR ops 8-2-45

PL203 HFIX M70 9MU 14-6-44 504S 17-3 ASTE 5-4-45 SAAF 19-6-49

PL204 33MU 16-6-44 453S 27-7 412S 23-8 FTR ops 19-11

PL205 9MU 13-6-44 52MU 15-7 *Sam Const* 17-7 Hap 27-8

PL206 45MU 12-6-44 AST 23-6 453S CE ops 24-7 s/dn by Thunderbolts over France

PL207 8MU 16-6-44 MAL 6-7 602S 10-8 442S 28-9 CE ops 28-10

PL208 9MU 13-6-44 52MU 12-7 *Sam Const* 17-7 Hap 27-8

P209 LHFIX M70 9MU 15-6-44 345S 5-9 340S 23-11 341S 15-2-45 329S 22-3 Persh 24-11-47 SAAF 11-12

PL210 33MU 17-6-44 340S 6-7 345S 18-1-45 331S 5-4 349S 26-4 317S 3-5 326S 31-5 327S 2-8 FAF GC1/3

PL211 45MU 14-6-44 GAL 27-6 453S 27-7 CAC ops 2-8 412S 30-9 CB ops DeH Persh 1-6-45 MAAF 14-6 RHAF 30-2-47

PL212 33MU 12-6-44 341S 13-7 en/ac 20-12 ASTH FAF 9-9-46

PL213 8MU 15-6-44 MAL 6-7 602S 10-8 CB ops 20-8 511FRU 24-8 412S 29-3-45 29MU 16-9 sold Turk 30-7-47

PL214 8MU 16-6-44 341S CAC ops 21-7 ROS 332S 25-1-45 FTR ops 28-2

PL215 HFIX M70 33MU 16-6-44 504S 14-7 58 OTU 19-4-45 WAL 14-8 SAAF 21-6

PL216 8MU 15-6-44 329S 20-7 CE ops 30-7

PL217 39MU 15-6-44 331S 3-8 CE ops 29-12

PL218 HFIX M70 33MU 17-6-44 124S 18-7 CE ops 28-12

PL219 33MU 17-6-44 331S 3-8 CAC ops 18-10 FACE 5-1-45

PL220 33MU 16-6-44 453S 20-7 FTR ops 26-7

PL221 33MU 17-6-44 340S 6-7 FTR ops 26-7 cancel recat A 27-7 DeH 18-8 331S 10-5-45

PL222 HFIX M70 9MU 15-6-44 504S 17-7 FACE 31-8

PL223 8MU 15-6-44 341S 21-7 CAC ops 2-12-45 DeH WAL 3-1-46 sold Turk 16-10-47

PL224 8MU 15-6-44 453S 27-7 341S FTR ops 14-8 cancel 412S 28-9 ASTE 8-1-45 165S 10-6 66S 2-9-46 BAF 10-7-48 as SM-20 w/o 1-9-52

PL225 33MU 17-6-44 329S 6-7 411RSU CE 8-8 ASTE

PL226 33MU 17-6-44 MAL 6-7 132S CB ops 19-8 DeH 322S 12-5-45

PL227 33MU 17-6-44 453S FTR ops 25-7

PL228 33MU 23-6-44 331S 25-7 strk in rear by PL258 on ldg CE Funtin 8-89

PL246 45MU 17-6-44 GAL 1-7 341S 19-10

PL247 39MU 19-6-44 341S 24-7 CE ops 1-9

PL248 HFIX M70 39MU 17-6-44 504S 15-7 FAAC 28-1-45 ROS 151RU 23-3-45 sold Int All 2-11-49

PL249 HFIX M70 39MU 17-6-44 504S 15-7 DeH 18-8 124S 25-3-45 12Gp Com Flt 20-9 SOC scrap 16-10-47

PL250 8MU 16-6-44 341S 13-7 CAC ops 16-9 e/a 29-11 ASTH 313S 22-7-45

PL251 39MU 19-6-44 485S 31-e/a CE dbf 1-1-45

PL252 39MU 17-6-44 MAL 25-7-44 453S 24-8 412S 7-9 CE ops eng fire d fail in air a/c aban pilot kld CE 22-2-45

PL253 HFIX M70 8MU 29-6-44 124S 24-7 47MU 10-3-48 SAAF 11-5

PL254 16-6-44 453S 27-7 CB ops 16-8 AST MAAF 10-3-45 318S cd f/ld nr Treviso Italy 26-1-46 SOC 31-1

PL255 33MU 17-6-44 341S 13-7 ROS 30-8 33S 12-10 CB ops 3-11 AST 29MU 21-12-45 RNoAF 1-5-48

PL256 HFIX M70 39MU 20-6-44 504S 17-7 CAC ops 1-12 340S 11-1-45 341S 8-3 329S 22-3 to 6371M 10-7-47 RDAF 15-7 34MU scrap 10-47

PL257 45MU 19-6-44 GAL 1-7 132S 17-8 CE ops 27-9

PL258 39MU 17-6-44 331S 25-7 strk rear of PL228 ldg Funtin CAC 8-8 420RSU FTR ops 29-12

PL259 39MU 19-6-44 341S CAC 10-10 411FRU FACB 8-11 recat E SOC 20-2-45

PL260 45MU 19-6-44 602S 31-8 442S 28-9 33MU 3-1-45 ASTE 14-2 sold Turk 2-5-47

PL261 HFIX M70 33MU 22-6-44 124S 18-7 CAC ops 6-1-45 151RU 2-3 39MU 10-9-48 SAAF 13-2-49

PL262 8MU 24-6-44 331S 3-8 ROS 27-9 AST 17-10 WAL 13-2-45 mods 4FSCU Dyce 17-5 165S FACE 2-8-48

PL263 HFIX M70 33MU 19-6-44 504S 15-7 441S 5-4-45 329S 5-4 ASTH mr 22-2-46 SOC scr 16-10-47

PL264 39MU 19-6-44 MAL 25-7 602S 26-8 CE ops

PL265 39MU 6-5-44 215MU 18-5 GAL 12-8 317S 19-10 CAC ops 13-2-45 411RSU 84Gp ARF 22-3 327S 5-4 FACB 4-9 3BRU 13-9 P recat E 420RSU 10-8 FTR ops 29-12

PL266 9MU 6-5-44 56S 5-6 39MU 2-8-45 FAF 5-12-46

PL267 9MU 6-5-44 AST 6-6 302S 22-6 e/a CE 1-1-45

PL268 9MU 6-5-44 ASTH 13-5 mods 308S 15-6 CAC ops 13-10 411RSU 19-10 AST 31-10 Persh 7-4-45 MAAF 20-4 SOC 28-8-47

PL269 9MU 8-5-44 215MU 18-5 308S 15-6 FTR ops 26-8 bboc 11-1-45 WAL 15-3 sold R J Coley 6-2-50

PL270 39MU 18-5-44 52MU 21-6 *Arabis* 29-6 Hap 12-8

PL271 33MU 12-5-44 52MU 30-5 91S 26-8 CB ops 14-12 328S 10-5-45 FAF 27-11

PL272 9MU 8-5-44 AST 9-6 441S 17-8 ASTE 12-4-45 33MU 10-9 FAF 4-9-46 GC1/4

PL273 9MU 9-5-44 341S 8-6 66S 27-7 84GSU 15-10 MAAF 20-4-45 ME 9-8 FAF 25-7-46

PL274 FAF 26-9-46 132SMU swg on ldg hit Dakota KJ862 Ciampino Italy 13-9-46

PL275 39MU 15-5-44 412S CE ops 25-6

PL276 39MU 17-5-44 AST 6-6 403S 24-8 29MU 13-7-45 sold VA 5-12-49

PL277 33MU 18-5-44 17APC 28-5 FLS Mlfld 3-10 to 6041M 2-8-46

PL278 45MU 17-5-44 132S 15-6 453S 20-7 416S 24-8 CAC ops 27-9 401S 15-3-45 3BRU CE 17-9

PL279 8MU 20-5-44 MAL 6-6 308S 22-6 FTR 26-8

PL280 8MU 19-5-44 442S CAC ops 18-7 410RSU 401S 25-7 CAC ops 10-8 FTR ops 18-8

PL281 8MU 20-5-44 126S 7-6 FACB 21-8 DeH 411S 21-1-45 CAC ops 25-1 DeH Persh 28-5 MAAF 10-6 SOC 30-4-47

PL282 45MU 22-5-44 MAL 7-6 317S 22-6 511FRU 31-8 FACE 19-10

PL283 8MU 20-5-44 83Gp Com S 29-6 FAAC 18-7 ROS GAL 17-10 mods 411S 11-1-45 FTR ops 21-4

PL284 45MU 22-5-44 MAL 7-6 317S 29-6 e/a CE 1-1-45

PL285 39MU 24-5-44 52MU 11-6 *Arabis* 17-6 Hap 29-6 Bas 12-8

PL286 45MU 25-5-44 302S 17-8 317S 11-1-45 326S 28-6 SNCAN 4-10 FAF GC1/1

PL287 39MU 2-6-44 340S 6-7 CE ops 21-10

PL288 45MU 25-5-44 3501SU 22-6 350S 9-7 322S FTR ops 1-9

PL313 45MU 2-6-44 MAL 16-6 453S FTR ops 25-7

PL314 45MU 2-6-44 3501SU 22-6 350S 9-7 165S FAAC 14-8 ROS 91S 28-12 CB ops 23-1-45 French RSU 25-7 326S 20-9 FAF 27-11 GC2/7

PL315 6MU 2-6-44 GAL 12-6 453S 9-7 FTR ops 27-7

PL316 33MU 6-6-44 AST 23-6 132S 27-7 CE ops 25-9

PL317 39MU 7-6 340S 6-7 CB ops 16-9 33MU 11-3-45 165S 17-5 FACE 12-9

PL318 45MU 14-6-44 GAL 4-7 411S 5-10 CB ops 6-11 3BRU 8-3-45 ASTH 4-4 sold R J Coley 9-2-50

PL319 9MU 12-6-44 215MU 24-7 *New Tex* 31-7 Casa 22-8 FACE 28-5-45 SOC 30-8 FAF 24-11

PL320 39MU 7-6-44 ASTH 27-6 132S 20-7 411S 28-9 412S 5-4-45 ROS VA 10-5 sold Turk 26-6-47

PL321 9MU 12-6-44 82MU 24-7 *New Tex* 31-7 Casa 22-8

PL322 9MU 12-6-44 215MU *New Tex* 31-7 Casa 22-8 SOC 31-1-45

PL323 9MU 12-6-44 GAL 27-6 82MU 23-7 *New Tex* 31-7 Casa 22-8 FTR ops 20-10

PL324 6MU 13-6-44 602S 10-8 442S 28-9 FACE on del flt 28-1-45 412S GAAC 16-4

PL325 39MU 16-6-44 66S 3-8

PL326 8MU 17-6-44 127S 3-8 FTR ops 11-9

PL327 8MU 19-6-44 84GSU 5-7 FAAC 26-7 ROS 33S 12-10 485S 5-1-45 CB ops 6-1 29MU 26-5 RNoAF 28-8-47

PL328 45MU 21-6-44 IAF as MM4121

PL329 45MU 21-6-44 *Saman* 5-8 Hap 27-8

PL330 8MU 19-6-44 MAL 25-7 602S 24-8 442S 28-9 29MU 18-3-45 MAAF 12-5 IAF 26-6-47 as MM4020

PL331 33MU 27-6-44 52MU 12-7 *Samsuva 21-7 Hap 27-8*

PL332 8MU 22-6-44 341S CAC ops 1-9 e/a CB 29-11 411RSU 30-11 sold Turk 3-3-47

PL333 8MU 22-6-44 341S 24-7 CAC ops 26-8 ROS AST 9-10 3APU 4-4-45 MAAF 25-5 ME 9-8 SOC 26-2-48

PL334 8MU 24-6-44 222MU 28-7 *New Twx* 31-7 Casa 22-8 130S 17-5-45 ME 31-5

PL335 8MU 24-6-44 52MU 3-8 *Samcalia* 11-8 Hap 27-8

PL336 8MU 30-644 52MU 16-7 *S Tredi* 11-8 Hap 27-8

PL337 33MU 21-7-44 82MU 27-7 *Sil Sand* 9-8 Casa 23-8 SOC 6-12-45

PL338 33MU 22-6-44 222MU 5-8 *Sil Sand* 9-8 Casa 23-8 ME SOC 26-9-46

PL339 39MU 24-7-44 82MU 5-8 *Ad S Ot* 8-9 Hap 23-9

PL340 33MU 22-4-44 47MU 30-7 ROS 12-8 *Q Park* 13-9 Casa 23-9 225S e/fld on app Campoformido Italy 25-9-46 SOC 28-11

PL341 33MU 15-7-44 *Samyara* 1-8 Hap 27-8

PL342 9MU 15-7-44 82MU 23-7 *New Tex* 31-7 Casa 22-8 SOC 14-3-46

PL343 39MU 24-7-44 *Samyara* 1-8 Hap 27-8

PL344 8MU 1-7-44 GAL 19-7 602S CAC ops 12-8 442S 28-9 FACB 26-12 401S 19-4-45 88Gp HQ 16-9 129S FAAC 6-5-46 151RU 5-9 recat E 10-12. Extant, Hampshire, 1986

PL345 9MU 17-7-44 82MU 28-7 *Sil Sand* 9-8 Casa 23-8 FTR ops 7-10

PL346 39MU 24-7-44 *Samyara* 3-8 27-8

PL347 6MU 26-7-44 *Sil Sand* 9-8 Casa 23-8-45 ME 31-5

PL348 6MU 17-7-44 215MU 27-7 *New Tex* 31-7 Casa 22-8 SOC 13-12-45

PL349 33MU 21-8-44 74S 7-9 341S 13-12 e/a CB 21-12 AST BAF 11-8-47

PL350 30MU 24-7-44 52MU 3-8 *Samyara* 5-8 Hap 27-8

PL351 39MU 27-7-44 82MU 10-8 *Melam* 20-8 Casa 3-9 FTR ops 19-3-45

PL352 39MU 27-7-44 82MU 10-8 *Mealm* 20-8- Casa 3-9 CE ops 29-12

PL353 39MU 28-7-44 82MU 10-8 *Melam* 20-8 Casa 3-9 225S tyre burst on t/o Campoformido Italy ME SOC 31-10-46

PL354 39MU 29-7-44 52MU 10-8 *Samarit* 8-9 Hap 23-9

PL355 39MU 3-8-44 82MU 12-8 *Sil Gu* 22-8 Casa 11-9 FTR ops 10-3-45

PL356 39MU 29-7-44 341S 14-9 CAC ops 10-10 9MU 18-1-45 MAAF 12-3 ME 9-8 RHAF 30-1-47

PL369 33MU 22-6-44 331S 3-8 ROS 12-9 AST 22-9 Persh 2-4-45 MAAF 21-6 ME SOC 26-9-46

PL390 39MU 17-6-44 MAL 25-7 6-2 7-9 442S CAC ops 4-10 CE 14-1-45

PL371 HFIX M70 39MU 20-6-44 405S 17-7 441S 5-4-45 329S 5-4 to 5751M CDT&RE 4-12 SOC 1-11-47

PL372 HFIX M70 33MU 27-6-44 82MU 24-7 *New Tex* 31-7 Casa 22-8 601S FTR ops 13-11 ME SOC 26-9-46

PL373 45MU 20-6-44 GAL 4-7 411S 28-9 FAAC 13-10 ROS 67MU 31-10 MAAF 26-5-45 ME SOC 26-9-46

PL374 HFIX M70 33MU 21-6-44 124S 18-7 595S 3-9-45 33MU NEA 28-5-47 SOC 21-10

PL375 HFIX M70 33MU 21-6-44 504S 15-7 ROS 9-8 CAC ops 24-2-45 151RU RDAF as 407 9-2-49

PL376 HFIX M70 39MU 20-6-44 *New Tex* 31-7-Casa 22-8 ME 31-5-45 SOC 2-8

PL377 HFIX M70 33MU 21-6-44 222MU 24-7 *New Tex* 31-7 Casa 22-8 SOC 30-8-45

PL378 HFIX M70 8MU 20-6-44 504S 16-7 441S 29-3-45 29-3-45 329S 5-4 CAC ops 4-5 ROS 595S 16-8 FACB 25-6-46 recat E SOC 17-10-46

PL379 HFIX M70 9MU 23-6-44 504S 17-7 MAL 24-8 24-8 33MU 19-10 441S 26-3-45 FAF 24-11

PL380 HFIX M70 33MU 21-6-44 504S 15-4 swg strk PT627 ldg CE Mans 10-11

PL381 45MU 21-6-44 *Samannon* 5-8 Hap 27-8

PL382 39MU 25-6-44 52MU 12-7 *Sam Const* 17-7 Hap 27-8

PL383 8MU 24-6-44 52MU 3-8 *S Tredi* 11-8 Hap 27-8

PL384 HFIX M70 33MU 22-6-44 82MU 20-7 *New Tex* 31-7 Casa 22-8 SOC 31-5-45

PL385 HFIX M70 8MU 20-6-44 504S 16-7 FTR ops 7-8

PL386 HFIX M70 33MU 22-6-44 *New Tex* 31-7 Casa 22-8 SOC 31-1-45

PL387 HFIX M70 39MU 20-6-44 82MU 20-7 *New Tex* 31-7 Casa 22-8 43S FACE 8-10-46 a/c disin after dive nr Mortegliano pilot kld SOC 31-10

PL388 HFIX M70 39MU 21-6-44 82MU 28-7 *New Tex* 31-7 Casa 22-8 IAF 26-6-47 as MM4122

PL389 39MU 25-6-44 52MU 12-7 *Sam Su* 21-7 Hap 27-8

PL390 HFIX M70 39MU 21-6-44 441S 28-3-45 329S 5-4 FAF 24-11 BE708 des 23-11-51

PL391 8MU 23-6-44 39MU 17-7 *Samyara* 1-8 Hap 27-8

PL392 HFIX M70 33MU 24-6-44 124S 18-7 CAC 15-12 ROS 9MU 9-3-45 RDAF 7-4 as 408 cd Ringsted 22-9-51

PL393 33MU 23-6-44 331S 3-8 CAC ops 12-10 FTR ops 3-11 cancel bboc 25-1-45 331S 25-2 CE 12-4

PL394 33MU 23-6-44 84GSU 9-7 485S 14-12 CE ops 6-1-45

PL395 33MU 23-6-44 341S 10-8 FTR ops 26-8

PL396 HFIX M70 9MU 24-6-44 504S 17-7 CB ops 9-12 AST 595S 28-7-45 130S 30-5-46 bou SOC 27-1-47

PL397 33MU 25-6-44 52MU 10-7 *S Tredi* 11-8 Hap 27-9

PL398 33MU 22-6-44 GAL 25-7 132S 31-8 411S 28-9 CB ops 26-2-45 410RSU 1-3 33MU 12-10 sold Turk 24-1-47

PL399 45MU 27-6-44 *Panama* 30-7 Hap 27-8

PL400 HFIX M70 33MU 24-6-44 82MU 23-7 *New Tex* 31-7 Casa 22-8 FTR ops 6-4-45

PL401 33MU 22-6-44 82MU 24-7 331S strk by Marauder PN-N of 322B Gp while parked CE Ford 16-8 Casa 22-8

PL402 45MU 27-6-44 MAL 21-7 453S 3-8 412S 28-9 CB ops 28-12 401S 19-4-45 421S 10-5 326S 26-7 FACE 27-11 FAF 4-12

PL403 45MU 21-6-44 341S 21-7 421RSU 3-8 e/a CB 29-11 DeH 6MU 26-4-45 SOC 13-10 FAF

PL404 8MU 24-6-44 33MU 16-7 *Samcalia* 11-8 Hap 27-8

PL405 8MU 24-6-44 341S 22-7 CAC 19-9 ROS 82MU 20-12 Casa 25-1 FTR ops

PL406 39MU 25-6-44 52MU 10-7 *S Tredi* 11-8 Hap 27-8

PL407 8MU 24-6-44 33MU 16-7 *Saman* 30-7 Hap 27-8

PL408 33MU 23-6-44 331S 9-7 CB ops 11-11 AST 332S 5-5-45

PL423 33MU 24-6-44 GAL 25-7 341S CAC ops 12-9 442S 28-9 411S 29-3-45 ASTH 11-7 29MU 18-12 sold Turk 17-1-47

PL424 33MU 24-6-44 341S 21-7 FTR 14-8

PL425 33MU 25-6-44 82MU 14-7 *Sam Su* 21-7 Hap 27-8

PL426 39MU 29-6-44 331S 3-8 FTR ops 28-8

PL427 6MU 27-6-44 340S 31-8 345S CE 19-11

PL428 8MU 23-6-44 52MU 3-8 *S Tredi* 11-8 Hap 27-8

PL429 33MU 25-6-44 82MU 14-7 *Sam Su* 21-7 Hap 27-8

PL430 8MU 25-6-44 GAL 19-7 411S 28-9 CE ops 8-2-45

PL431 6MU 27-6-44 82MU 24-7 *New tex* 21-7 Casa 22-8 SOC 23-10

PL432 HFIX M70 8MU 24-6-44 504S FTR ops 19-10

PL433 33MU 24-6-44 GAL 25-7 132S 31-8 411S 5-10 CE ops 23-1-45

PL434 8MU 24-6-44 GAL 19-7 132S 17-8 411S 28-9 CAC ops 28-11 VAO recat E SOC 10-2-45

PL435 39MU 25-6-44 52MU 10-7 *Sam Su* 21-7 Hap 27-8

PL436 8MU 25-6-44 GAL 19-7 132S 10-8 602S 10-8 442S 28-9 CB ops 2-11 recat E SOC 29-1-45

PL437 39MU 25-6-44 341S 10-8 511FRU 8-9 CB ops 20-9 SAL CE ops

PL438 45MU 27-6-44 GAL 20-7 453S 24-8 412S CB ops 29-9 411S 4-1-45

PL439 6MU 24-7-44 *Sil Sand* 9-8 Casa 23-8 ME SOC 26-9-46

PL440 6MU 27-6-44 82MU 24-7 *New Tex* 31-7 Casa 22-8

PL441 45MU 27-6-44 MAL 22-7 453S FTR ops 7-8

PL442 8MU 30-6-44 52MU 3-8 *S Tredi* 11-8 Hap 27-8

PL443 8MU 27-6-44 222MU 23-7 *New Tex* 31-7 Casa 22-8 REAF 29-8-46

PL444 6MU 24-6-44 82MU 27-6 *New Tex* 31-7 Casa 22-8 SOC 11-4-46

PL445 33MU 27-6-44 52MU 12-7 *Sam Su* 21-7 Hap 27-8

PL446 39MU 25-6-44 52MU 10-7 *Sam Su* 21-7 Hap 27-8

PL447 33MU 27-6-44 52MU 12-7 *Sam Con* 17-7 Hap 27-8

PL448 39MU 29-6-44 MAAL 25-7 132S 17-8 411S 28-9 CAC ops 3-12 412S 5-4-45 130S 17-5

PL449 33MU 27-6-44 52MU 12-7 *Sam Su* 21-7 Hap 27-8

PL450 HFIX M70 9-8-44 345S 1-9 340S 23-11 CE ops 5-12

PL451 39MU 29-6-44 349S 10-8 332S 28-9 CB ops 8-4-45

PL452 HFIX M70 39MU 30-7-44 504S CE ops 16-9 4ATC 21-9 FAF GC1/1 des 27-2-50

PL453 33MU 1-7-44 33S 10-8 CAC ops 30-8 ROS 222MU 26-11 *Guinean* 22-12 Casa 15-1-45 SOC 31-5

PL454 33MU 29-6-44 GAL 25-7 132S CB ops 25-8 222S 12-10 CAC ops 28-10 74S 4-1-45 345S 15-3 331S 19-4 485S 30-4 c on f/f 81RSU CAC 26-5 FAF

PL455 9MU 1-7-44 82MU 23-7 *New Tex* 31-7 Casa 22-8 ME SOC 27-6-46

PL456 8MU 29-6-44 33MU 16-7 *Saman* 5-87 Hap 27-8

PL457 45MU 20-6-44 MAL 22-7 132S 24-8 CE ops 25-9

PL458 HFIX M70 39MU 20-6-44 *New Tex* 31-7 Casa 22-8 IAF 26-6-47 as MM4032

PL459 33MU 29-6-44 GAL 25-7 329S 25-8 CE

PL460 33MU 29-6-44 *Saman* 5-8 Hap 27-8

PL461 33MU 1-7-44 GAL 25-7 22S 24-8 CAC ops 6-10 29MU 12-2-45 3APU 4-4 MAAF 21-4 RHAF 27-2-47

PL462 45MU 30-6-44 ROS 25-7 GAL 12-9 341S 19-10 CB ops 4-11 AST sold Turk 15-10-47

PL463 8MU 29-6-44 66S 24-8 CAC ops 1-11 331S 5-4-45 349S CAC ops 24-4 RNoAF 28-8-47

PL464 39MU 29-6-44 341S 10-8 241S CE ops 26-9 FAF

PL465 8MU 29-6-44 33MU 16-7 *New Tex* 31-7 Casa 22-8 CE ops 11-12

PL466 33MU 29-6-44 GAL 25-7 132S 24-8 411S 28-9 412S FACB 4-11 1FU Persh 27-3-45 MAAF 12-4 ME 5-7 SOC 31-12-47

PL488 33MU 29-6-44 341S 10-8 CAC ops 7-10 e/a CE 20-12 SOC 1-4-45

PL489 HFIX M70 39MU 30-6-44 82MU 22-7 *New Tex* 31-7 Casa 22-8 CE ops 13-4-45

PL490 8MU 1-7-44 GAL 20-7 602S 10-8 442S FTR ops 28-9

PL491 6MU 1-7-44 47MU 19-7 *New Tex* 31-7 Casa 22-8 CE ops 23-4-45 SOC 31-5

PL492 8MU 30-6-44 349S 10-8 CAC ops 4-9 332S 28-9 CE ops 13-10

PL493 45MU 1-7-44 MAL 25-7 602S 17-8 402S CAC 6-10 410RSU 12-10 411S 23-11 39Rec Wg 29-3-45 414S 5-4 412S 12-4 WAL 22-6 sold Turk 20-1-47

PL494 39MU 30-6-44 52MU 3-8 *Sancalia* 11-8 Hap 27-8

PL495 8MU 30-6-44 GAL 2-8 602S 14-9 442S 28-9 CAC ops 4-11 411S 16-11 CB ops 25-2-45 FAF 9-9-46 GC2/4

PL496 39MU 30-6-44 *Saman* 5-8 Hap 27-8

PL497 8MU 30-6-44 MAL 25-7 74S 17-8 CAC ops 1-1-45 151RU 345S 15-3 332S 12-4 sold VA 8-12-49

PL498 45MU 1-7-44 GAL 8-8 411S 28-9 FAAC 22-10 ROS 12FU 1-1-45 MAAF 6-4 SOC 30-4-47

PL499 39MU 30-6-44 52MU 3-8 *Samcalia* 11-8 Hap 24-8

PT355 39MU 29-6-44 82MU 14-7 *San Su* 21-7 Hap 27-8

PT356 39MU 29-6-44 82MU 14-7 *San Su* 21-7 Hap 27-8

PT357 45MU 28-6-44 MAL 21-7 453S 10-8 412S 28-9 CAC ops 3-12 410RSU 412S FTR ops 30-3-45

PT358 39MU 29-6-44 82MU 14-7 *San Su* 21-7 Hap 27-8

PT359 8MU 30-6-44 33MU 16-7 222MU 23-7 *New Tex* 31-7 Casa 22-8 328S 5-4-45 FAF

PT360 8MU 30-6-44 349S 10-8 AST 15-9 39MU 6-1-45 12FU flew i/cliff top with NH276 CE Kimmeridge Dorset 17-2-45 SOC in error bboc 24-3 MAAF 15-6

PT361 9MU 1-7-44 215MU 24-7 *New Tex* 31-7 Casa 22-8 SOC 14-3-46

PT362 9MU 1-7-44 82MU 23-7 *New Tex* 31-7 Casa 22-8 SOC 14-3-46

PT363 8MU 30-6-44 33MU 16-7 *Samyara* 1-8 Hap 27-8

PT364 39MU 1-7-44 *New Tex* 31-7 Casa 22-8 SOC 30-8-45

PT365 9MU 1-7-44 82MU 24-7 *New Tex* 31-7 Casa 22-8 FAF GR2/33 30-9

PT366 9MU 17-7-44 82MU 1-8 *Sil Sand* 9-8 Casa 23-8 FTR ops 22-9

PT367 9MU 17-7-44 82MU 26-7 *Sil Sand* 9-8 Casa 23-8 328S 5-4-45 327S 3-10 SNCAN 11-11

PT368 9MU 17-7-44 82MU 31-7 *Sil Sand* 9-8 Casa 22-8 FACE 1-12 SOC 9-8-45

PT369 9MU 20-7-44 82MU 31-7 *Sil Sand* 9-8 Casa 23-8 ME 9-8 RHAF 2-3-47

PT370 9MU 20-7-44 82MU 4-8 *Sil Sand* 9-8 Casa 23-8 SOC 20-9-45

PT371 39MU 21-7-44 222MU 30-7 *Sil Sand* 9-8 Casa 23-8 FTR ops 22-3-45

PT372 39MU 21-7-44 222MU 30-7 *Sil Sand* 9-8 Casa 23-8 ME 31-5-45 SOC 9-8

PT373 33MU 22-6-44 *Samyara* 1-8 Hap 27-8

PT374 33MU 22-6-44 82MU 7-8 *Ad S Ot* 8-9 Hap 23-9

PT375 6MU 24-7-44 82MU 29-7 *Sil Sand* 9-8 Casa 23-8 CE ops 27-10

PT376 9MU 28-7-44 76MU 7-8 *Melam* 20-8 Casa 3-9 FAF 28-3-46

PT377 6MU 24-7-44 47MU 31-7 *Sil Sand* 9-8 Casa 23-8

PT465,HF IX, M70, at roll-out.

PT378 9MU 25-7-44 *Sil Sand* 9-8 Casa 23-8 SOC 23-10

PT379 8MU 29-6-44 222MU 23-7 *New Tex* 31-7 Casa 22-8 FACE 21-5-45 SOC 23-8

PT380 33MU 29-6-44 47MU 9-7 *Samconst* 17-7 Hap 27-7

PT395 8MU 30-6-44 349S 10-8 CE ops 6-10

PT396 45MU 1-7-44 MAL 28-7 602S 17-8 ROS 9MU 4-1-45 MAAF 12-4 IAF 26-6-47 as MM4025

PT397 8MU 30-6-44 *Sil Sand* 9-8 Casa 23-8 FTR ops 14-9

PT398 HFIX M70 8MU 1-7-44 MAL 7-9 595S 26-7-45 to 6584M Henlow 24-8

PT399 33MU 1-7-44 GAL 25-7 329S 31-8 74S 21-12 345S CAC ops 13-3-45 DeH RNoAF 9-6-47

PT400 8MU 8-7-44 *Sansara* 9-8 Hap 27-9

PT401 6MU 1-7-44 328S 5-4-45 327S 3-10 FAF 27-11

PT402 8MU 1-7-44 MAL 25-7 602S 24-8 442S 28-9 CB ops 27-12 410RSU DeH 16-2-45 sold Turk 30-4-47

PT403 39MU 30-6-44 215MU 27-7 *New Tex* 31-7 Casa 22-8 SOC 26-2-48

PT404 33MU 1-7-44 52MU 20-7 *S Tredi* 11-8 Hap 27-8

PT405 45MU 1-7-44 MAL 21-7 453S 3-8 412S 23-9 CAC ops 18-10 53MU 19-3-45 sold Turk 15-9-47

PT406 33MU 15-7-44 52MU 3-8 *Sancalia* 11-8 Hap 27-8

PT407 39MU 21-7-44 82MU 11-8 *Sil Gu* 22-8 Casa 11-9 FTR ops 4-3-45

PT408 33MU 15-7-44 *Saman* 30-7 Hap 27-8

PT409 6MU 17-7-44 47MU 24-7 *Sil Sand* 9-8 Casa 23-8 FTR ops 22-4-45

PT410 9MU 15-7-44 82MU 24-4 *New Tex* 31-7 Casa 22-8 CE ops 15-3-45

PT411 6MU 1-7-44 222MU *New Tex* 31-7 Casa 22-8 SOC 23-12

PT412 39MU 15-7-44 215MU 25-7 *New Tex* 31-7 Casa 22-8 SOC 5-6-45

PT413 B Down 16-7-44 33MU 11-5-45 W Wal 18-12-46 sold Turk

PT414 9MU 18-7-44 82MU 20-7 *Sil Sand* 9-8 Casa 25-8 IAF 27-6-46 as MM4026

PT415 6MU 1-7-44 ROS 4-8 33MU 1-3-45 sold Turk 23-8-48

PT416 9MU 14-7-44 82MU 23-7 *New Tex* 31-7 Casa 22-8 SOC 5-6-45

PT417 33MU 1-7-44 GAL 25-7 84GSU 15-8 127S 24-8 CE ops 27-9

PT418 39MU 17-7-44 52MU 3-8 *Samcalia* 11-8 Hap 17-8

PT419 6MU 17-7-44 *New Tex* 31-7 Casa 22-8 CE ops 4-11

PT420 6MU 17-7-44 47MU *New Tex* 31-7 Casa 22-8 SOC 30-4-47

PT421 6MU 1-7-44 82MU 23-7 *New Tex* 31-7 Casa 22-8 FTR ops 23-2-45

PT422 6MU 17-7-44 47MU 24-7 *Sil Sand* 9-8 Casa 23-8 FAF GR2/33 9-11

PT423 9MU 15-7-44 82MU 24-7 *New Tex* 31-7 Casa 22-8 ME 5-7-45 SOC 26-6-47

PT424 9MU 15-7-44 82MU 23-7 *New Tex* 31-7 Casa 22-8 SOC 13-9-45

PT425 33MU 15-7-44 *Samyara* 1-8 Hap 27-8

PT426 6MU 17-7-44 222MU 28-7 *Sil Sand* 9-8 Casa 23-8 CE ops 20-2-45

PT427 39MU 17-7-44 222MU 25-7 *New Tex* 31-7 Casa 22-8 ME 5-7-45 RHAF 27-3-47

PT428 33MU 15-7-44 52MU 3-8 *Samcalia* 11-8 Hap 27-8

PT429 39MU 17-7-44 *Saman* 5-8 Hap 27-8

PT430 39MU 15-7-44 *Saman* 5-8 Hap 27-8

PT431 39MU 17-7-44 *Saman* 5-8 Hap 27-8

PT432 HFIX M70 39MU 19-7-44 82MU 29-7 *Sil Sand* 9-8 Casa 23-8 FTR ops 26-9

PT433 6MU 17-7-44 215MU 27-7 *New Tex* 31-7 Casa 22-8 SOC 18-10-45

PT434 HFIX M70 8MU 1-7-44 ROS 9-8 504S 5-9 33MU 16-5-45 SAAF 23-2-49

PT435 39MU 17-7-44 *Samyara* 1-8 Hap 27-8

PT436 9MU 19-7-44 82MU 29-7 *Sil Sand* 9-8 Casa 23-8 328S 5-4-45

PT451 39MU 17-7-44 222MU 25-7 *New Tex* 31-7 Casa 22-8 SOC 22-11-45

PT452 VA HPA 24-7-44 Farn ETPS Nov'44 comp trls with MT818 9MU 28-5-45 MAAF 28-5-45 ME SOC 26-9-46

PT453 9MU 19-7-44 82MU 4-8 *Sil Sand* 9-8 Casa 23-8 SOC 29-12

PT454 9MU 18-7-44 82MU 21-7 *Sil Sand* 9-8 Casa 23-8 FAF

PT455 HFIX M70 39MU 27-7 *Sil Sand* 9-8 Casa 329S FTR ops 29-3-45

PT456 9MU 15-7-44 82MU 22-7 *New Tex* 31-7 Casa 22-8 SOC 15-5-45

PT457 9MU 19-7-44 47MU 30-7 *Sil Sand* 9-8 Casa 23-8 CE 15-12 SOC 22-11-45

PT458 33MU 18-4-44 222MU 11-8 *Sil Gu* 22-8 Casa 11-9 FAF 28-3-46

PT459 39MU 17-7-44 52MU 31-7 *Samyara* 1-8 Hap 27-8

PT460 HFIX M70 39MU 11-10-44 222MU 10-11 *Guinean* 22-12 Casa 25-2-45 IAF 30-5-46 as MM4033

PT461 9MU 19-7-44 82MU 28-7 *Sil Sand* 9-8 Casa 23-8

PT462 HFIX M70 39MU 21-7-44 215MU 31-7 *Sil Sand* 9-8 Casa 23-8 IAF 26-6-47 as MM4100 Israel 0607. Under restn. Sussex as Trainer G-CTIX.

PT463 HFIX M70 8MU 20-7-44 124S 7-8 ROS 14-8 504S 8-2-45 17APC Warm 12-4-45 HAL 22-10 29MU 11-2-46 RDAF 23-3-48 as 409

PT464 33MU 27-7-44 504S 31-8 412RSU 28-12 441S 5-4-45 329S 5-7 FAAC 14-9 ROS VAO recat E 20-5-46 SOC 19-7

PT465 HFIX M70 33MU 20-7-44 215MU 31-7 *Sil Sand* 9-8 Casa 23-8 FTR ops 24-4-45

PT466 HFIX M70 33MU 20-7-44 215MU 31-7 *Melam* 20-8 Casa 3-9 SOC 13-12-45

PT467 IXC 6MU 20-7-44 222MU 31-7 *Sil Sand* 9-8 Casa 23-8 328S 5-4-45 81RSU 12-4-45 FAF GC2/3

PT468 6MU 17-7-44 215MU 27-7-44 *New Tex* 31-7 Casa 22-8 SOC 11-4-46

PT469 33MU 14-8-44 52MU 25-8 *Samarit* 8-9 Hap 23-9

PT470 HFIX M70 39MU 19-7-44 82MU 27-7 *Sil Sand* 9-8 Casa 23-8 ME 19-2-45Com Flt Lydda w/u ldg CE Abu Sueir 14-5-47 SOC 3-7

PT471 39MU 17-7-44 52MU 2-8 *Sanyara* 5-8 Hap 27-8

PT472 39MU 26-8-44 345S 340S 23-11 39MU 19-4-45 SAAF 16-11-48

PT473 HFIX M70 39MU 20-7-44 215MU 31-7 *Sil Sand* 9-8 Casa 23-8 SOC 31-7-47

PT474 HFIX M70 33MU 20-7-44 222MU 29-7 *Sil Sand* 9-8 Casa 23-8 CE ops 25-4-45 SOC 19-7

PT475 39MU 2-7-44 222MU 30-7 *Sil Sand* 9-8 Casa 23-8 FTR ops 4-1-45

PT476 39MU 21-7-44 222MU 30-7 *Sil Sand* 9-8 Casa 23-8 SOC 23-10

PT477 33MU 31-7-44 215MU. 11-8 *Q Park* 13-9 Casa 23-9 CE ops 12-3-45 73S w/u ldg Takali Malta 19-8-47 SOC 25-9

PT478 39MU 24-7-44 47MU 408 *Melamp* 20-8 Casa 3-9 FTR ops 26-2-45

PT479 33MU 22-7-44 82MU 29-7 *Sil Sand* 9-8 Casa 23-8 SOC 14-3-46

PT480 HFIX M70 39MU 21-7-44 124S 3-8 CBAF 17-11 DeH 329S 23-9-45 FAAC 24-9 VA 1-10 mods SOC mr 8-2-46

PT481 HFIX M70 39MU 17-7-44 82MU 24-7 *New Tex* 31-7 Casa 22-8 IAF 26-6-47 as MM4126

PT482 9MU 19-7-44 82MU 31-7 *Sil Sand* 9-8 Casa 23-8 ME 23-8-45 SOC 26-9-46

PT483 6MU 19-7-44 222MU 31-7 *Sil Sand* 9-8 Casa 23-8 FACE 6-6-45 SOC 6-12-45

PT484 9MU 18-7-44 *Sil Sand* 9-8 Casa 23-8 FTR ops 22-12

PT485 9MU 19-7-44 82MU 1-8 *Sil Sand* 9-8 Casa 23-8 FTR ops 3-3-45

PT486 HFIX M70 33MU 20-7-44 82MU 29-7 *Sil Sand* 9-8 Casa 23-8

PT487 6MU 19-7-44 82MU 28-7 *Sil Sand* 9-8 Casa 23-8 FACE 12-6-45 SOC 8-10

PT488 HFIX M70 33MU 21-7-44 222MU 29-7 *Sil Sand* 9-8 Casa 23-8 ME SOC 10-6-48

PT489 39MU 21-7-44 47Mu 31-7 *Sil Sand* 9-8 Casa 23-8 SOC 20-9-45

PT490 6MU 24-7-44 47MU 31-7 *Sil Sand* 9-8 Casa 23-8 FTR ops 17-9

PT491 33MU 22-7-44 47MU 30-7 *Sil Sand* 9-8 Casa 23-8 FTR ops 21-11

PT492 33MU 22-7-44 222MU 5-8 *Sil Sand* 9-8 Casa 23-8 RHAF 30-4-47

PT493 HFIX M70 33MU 20-7-44 215MU *Sil Sand* 9-8 Casa 23-8 SOC 13-9-45

PT494 39MU 21-7-44 47MU 31-7 *Sil Sand* 9-8 Casa 23-8 ME 23-8-45 FAF 25-7-46 SOC 10-9-47

PT495 6MU 20-7-44 82MU 26-7 *Sil Sand* 9-8 Casa 23-8 CE ops 25-2-45

PT496 39MU 20-7-44 82MU 26-7 *Sil Sand* 9-8 Casa 23-8 328S 5-4-45 326S FAF 27-11

PT497 39MU 21-7-44 82MU 8-8 *Melamp* 20-8 Casa 3-9 CE ops 4-3-45

PT498 33MU 22-7-44 222MU 3-8 *Melamp* 20-8 Casa 3-9 FTR ops 16-4-45

PT523 39MU 3-8-44 82MU 11-8 *Sil Gu* 22-8 Casa 11-9 SOC 30-8-45

PT524 39MU 3-8-44 82MU 11-8 *Sil Gu* 22-8 Casa 11-9 ME SOC 26-9-46

PT525 33MU 8-8-44 485S 24-8 151RU 28-1-45 3BRU 8-3 29MU 10-7 sold Turk 25-9-47

PT526 39MU 3-8-44 82MU 12-8 *Q Park* 13-9 Casa 23-9 SOC 31-5-45

PT527 39MU 3-8-44 82MU 122-8 *Melamp* 20-8 Casa 3-9 SOC 18-12-45

PT528 39MU 3-8-44 52MU 16-8 *Samarit* 8-9 Hap 23-9

PT529 8MU 11-8-44 84GSU 23-8 66S 31-8 AST 20-11 332S 10-5-45

PT530 39MU 3-8-44 82MU 11-8 *Sil Gu* 22-8 Casa 11-9 CE ops 9-1-45 ME 31-5 SOC 9-8

PT531 39MU 4-8-44 82MU 12-8 *Q Park* 13-9 Casa 23-8 SOC 14-3-46

PT532 8MU 8-8-44 485S 31-8 1APU 7-4-45 MAAF 26-5 32S FACE c/ld Ramat David Palestine 7-9-46 SOC 26-9

PT533 33MU 12-8-44 52MU 26-8 *Emp Cel* 2-9 Hap 23-9

PT534 39MU 8-8-44 82MU 12-8 *Melamp* 20-8 Casa 3-9 FTR ops 30-1-45

PT535 45MU 14-8-44 VAOx 15-9 GAL 24-10 mods 83GSU 21-11 412S 28-1-45 39FSU CE 15-2

PT536 45MU 14MU 14-8-44 341S 31-8 FAAC 30-9 411RSU 331S 10-5-45

PT537 45MU 14-8-44 84GSU 30-8 132Wg 28-9 CAC ops 27-9 ASTH sold Turk 23-10-47

PT538 9MU 15-8-44 66S CAC ops 20-10 420RSU 341S 13-12 e/a 20-12 317S 11-1-45 331S 25-1 sold Turk 29-4-48

PT539 33MU 15-8-44 82MU 26-8 *Q Park* 13-9 Casa 23-9 SOC 14-3-46

PT540 45MU 18-8-44 84GSU 25-8 CE ops 19-11

PT541 61MU 17-8-44 82MU 31-8 *Q Park* 13-9 Casa 23-9 FTR ops 23-1-45

PT542 6MU 17-8-44 82MU 30-8-44 *Q Park* 13-9 Casa 23-9 CE ops 4-12

PT543 6MU 23-8-44 82MU 1-9 *Q Park* 13-9 Casa 23-9 FTR ops 27-2-45

PT544 33MU 18-8-44 52MU 1-9 *Emp Cel* 4-9 Hap 23-9

PT545 6MU 23-8-44 82MU 31-8 *Q Park* 13-9 Casa 23-9 CE ops 26-12

PT546 6MU 23-8-44 82MU 31-8 *Q Park* 13-9 Casa 23-9 SOC 22-12

PT547 6MU 23-8-44 82MU 31-8 *Q Park* 13-9 Casa 23-9 SOC 13-9-45

PT548 6MU 23-8-44 8GSU 1-9 74S 7-9 345S 13-12 e/a 10-12 4-11 RSU CAC 14-2-45 129S Lubeck 19-6-46 CE me SOC 22-10-46

PT549 45MU 24-8-44 127S 12-10 349S 14-12 CE ops 3-2-45

PT550 6MU 29-8-44 82MU 5-9 *Q Park* 23-9 SOC 31-5-45

PT551 39MU 25-8-44 33S 7-9 CAC ops 1-10 420RSU MAAF 8-3-45 137MU storage 29-1-48 SOC 10-6

PT552 6MU 29-8-44 52MU 13-9 *SSLS1225* 24-9 Casa 2-10 SOC 14-3-46

PT553 6MU 29-8-44 GAL 29-11 mods 81RSU 14-6-45 327S 23-7

PT554 6MU 29-8-44 332S 5-10 CB ops 4-11!SAL 16-11 33MU 27-3-45 sold R J Coley 3-2-50
PT555 39MU 29-8-44 84GSU 11-8 349S 21-9 CE ops 19-10
PT556 39MU 29-8-44 ROSVA 2-9 222MU 22-9 *Sil Lar* 13-11 Casa 23-11 FTR ops 25-2-45
PT557 39MU 29-8-44 82MU 9-8 *Q Park* 13-9 Casa 23-9 FTR ops 26-11
PT558 39MU 29-8-44 52MU 11-9 *SS257* 25-9 Hap 13-10 Murm 30-10
PT559 39MU 8-9-44 340S 5-10 345S 16-11 331S 12-4-45 412S 3-5 29MU 29-7 sold H Bath 27-10-47
PT560 33MU 31-8-44 33S CB ops 15-10 420RSU 3APU 15-4-45 MAAF 14-5 ME 9-8 SOC 27-3-47
PT561 39MU 5-9-44 Drfrd 18-9 19-11 *Thom Scott* 18-12 Hap 17-1-45
PT562 39MU 5-9-44 33MU 21-9 FTR 12-10
PT563 33MU 31-8-44 52MU 10-9 *SS257* 28-9 Hap 13-10 Murm 1-11
PT564 33MU 18-9-44 52MU 27-9 *SS256* 3-10 Hap 12-10 Murm 1-11
PT565 39MU 5-9-44 332S 28-9 CB ops 25-11 ASTH mods sold Turk 5-4-48
PT566 6MU 29-8-44 *Q Park* 13-9 Casa 23-9 CE ops burnt 30-3-45
PT567 33MU 29-8-44 52MU 8-9 *SS256* 30-9 Hap 13-10 Murm 1-11
PT582 6MU 20-7-44 222MU 31-7 *Sil Sand* 9-8 Casa 23-8 FAF GR2/33 130S 17-8-45 recat E 20-5-46
PT583 33MU 22-7-44 222MU 3-8 *Melamp* 20-8 Casa 3-9 FA FTR 5-11
PT584 6MU 24-7-44 47MU 31-7 *Sil Sand* 9-8 Casa 23-8 CE ops 30-4-45
PT585 33MU 21-7-44 215MU 25-7 *Sil Sand* 9-8 Casa 23-8 s/d by Mustangs nr Venice FTR 11-11
PT586 33MU 24-7-44 82MU 4-8 *Ad S Ot* 8-9 Hap 23-9
PT587 33MU 22-7-44 215MU 11-8 *Melamp* 20-8 Casa 3-9 241S 1-1-45 SOC 5-1
PT588 6MU 22-7-44 82MU 28-7 *Sil Sand* 9-8 Casa 23-8 CE ops 24-10
PT589 39MU 25-7-44 52MU 8-8 *Samarait* 8-9 Hap 22-9
PT590 33MU 22-7-44 82MU 29-7 *Sil Sand* 9-8 Casa 23-8 IAF 30-5-46 w/o 7-3-47
PT591 33MU 22-7-44 *Sil Sand* 9-8 Casa 23-8 SOC 19-7-45
PT592 33MU 22-7-44 ROS 31-7 ASTE 5-3-45 33MU 7-9 sold Turk 22-7-47
PT593 33MU 21-7-44 82MU 28-7-44 *Sil Sand* 9-8 Casa 23-8 SOC 20-9-45
PT594 39MU 25-7-44 *Sil Sand* 9-8 Casa 23-8 ME 9-8-45 SOC 31-10-46
PT595 39MU 21-7-44 47MU 31-7 *Sil Sand* 9-8 Casa 23-8 FTR ops 13-2-45
PT596 33MU 22-7-44 82MU 29-7 *Sil Sand* 9-8 Casa 23-8 FACE 1-8-45 SOC 30-8
PT597 33MU 22-7-44 222MU 5-8 *Sil Sand* 9-8 Casa 23-8 ME 2-8-45 SOC 9-8
PT598 6MU 24-7-44 *Sil Sand* 9-8 Casa 23-8 FA FTR 25-9
PT599 33MU 30-7-44 52MU 7-8 *Samarit* 8-9 Hap 23-9
PT600 33MU 22-7-44 82MU 28-7 *Sil Sand* 9-8 Casa 23-8 FTR ops 17-4-45
PT601 HFIX M70 33MU 22-7-44 504S 7-8 DeH 18-8 30MU 23-4-45 183S 23-6 234S 9-8 SAAF 5-8-48 5573
PT602 33MU 22-7-44 82MU 4-8 *Ad S Ot* 8-9 Hap 23-9
PT603 33MU 22-7-44 *Sil Sand* 9-8 Casa 23-8 CE ops 10-12-46
PT604 33MU 28-7-44 222MU 10-8 *Melamp* 20-8 Casa 3-9 ME 2-8-45 SOC RHAF 27-5-48
PT605 HFIX M70 33MU 24-7-44 504S 7-8 CAC ops 25-10 ROS 124S 4-1-45 441S 5-4 329S 5-4 FACE 25-7 SOC 1-8
PT606 6MU 24-7-44 222MU 30-7 *Sil Sand* 9-8 Casa 23-8 FTR 21-11
PT607 39MU 27-7-44 52MU 8-8 *Samarit* 8-9 Hap 23-9
PT608 HFIX M70 39MU 26-7-44 124S 14-8 CE ops 31-8 DeH recat E 18-9
PT609 8MU 25-7-44 74S CAC ops 26-8 329S 13-12 CAC ops 23-12 331S 2-4-45 sold H Bath 27-10-48
PT610 33MU 26-7-44 215MU 6-8 *Melamp* 20-8 Casa 3-9 ME 2-8-45 SOC 9-8
PT611 33MU 3-8-44 52MU 14-8 *Ad S Ot* 8-9 23-9
PT612 HFIX M70 39MU 24-7-44 504S 25-1-45 SAL 16-4 ASTE FAF Friedershaven 7-12
PT613 9MU 26-7-44 215MU 5-8 *Melamp* 20-8 Casa 3-9 SOC 31-1-45
PT614 HFIX M70 39MU 24-7-44 345S 8-9 340S 23-11 329S 22-3-45 WAL 23-5 SAAF 28-4-48
PT615 33MU 28-7-44 82MU 10-8 *Melamp* 20-8 Casa 3-9 SOC 28-2-46
PT616 33MU 24-7-44 82MU 4-8 *Ad S Pt* 9-9 Hap 23-9
PT617 39MU 28-7-44 47MU 4-8 *Melamp* 20-8 Casa 3-9 ME 28-12 RHAF 30-1-47
PT618 33MU 26-7-44 82MU 15-8 *Melamp* 20-8 Casa 3-9 ME 28-12 SOC 28-8-47
PT619 HFIX M70 33MU 22-7-44 504S 5-9 FACB 24-3-45 ROS 124S 19-4 WAL 29-8 SAAF 13-2-49
PT620 8MU 25-7-44 74S CAC ops 10-9 66S 21-9 CB ops 2-10 SAL 25-10 MAAF 29-5-45 SOC 28-8-47
PT621 8MU 26-7-44 340S 17-8 CAC ops 26-8 BASU 25-10 DeH 9-1-45 313S 19-7 Czech AF 30-8
PT622 6MU 24-7-44 76MU 10-8 *Melamp* 20-8 Casa 3-9 SOC 10-6-48
PT623 8MU 25-7-44 340S 17-8 345S 16-11 CB ops 8-2-45 126Wg 22-2
PT624 8MU 27-7-44 331S CB ops 15-10 420RSU 6MU 1-3-45 MAAF 29-3 CE ops 25-4
PT625 9MU 26-7-44 215S 5-8 *Melamp* 20-8 Casa 2-9 FTR ops 25-4-45 cancel IAF 30-5-46 as MM4048
PT626 39MU 25-7-44 82MU 3-8 *Samyara* 5-8 Hap 27-8
PT627 HFIX M70 39MU 25-7-44 504S 16-8 parked strk by PL380 ldg CE Mans 10-11
PT639 39MU 4-8-44 82MU 11-8 *Melamp* 20-8 Casa 3-9 ME 19-7-45 FAF 28-11-46
PT640 HFIX M70 39MU 27-7-44 504S 15-8 329S 19-7-45 to 5746M 17-11 RTGA 5SoTT 28-8-47
PT641 6MU 24-7-44 47MU 31-7 *Sil Sand* 9-8 Casa 23-8 CE ops 20-3-45
PT642 9MU 26-7-44 215S 5-8 *Melamp* 20-8 Casa 3-9 SOC 30-8-45
PT643 9MU 27-7-44 29MU 29-3-45 129S 17-5 257S 18-10-46 BAF 22-10-47
PT644 8MU 25-7-44 127S FAAC 16-8 ROS GAL 21-9 mods 442S 12-10 33MU 6-7-45 BAF 4-7-48
PT645 33MU 26-7-44 82MU 4-8 *Ad S Ot* 8-9 Hap 23-9
PT646 39MU 25-7-44 *Sil Sand* 9-8 Casa 23-8 SOC 5-6-45
PT647 no record RHAF 27-2-47
PT648 6MU 28-7-44 76MU 11-8 *Melamp* 26-8 Casa 3-9 FTR ops 10-11
PT649 8MU 28-7-44 127S CAC ops 28-8 420RSU 31-8 127S CE ops 8-11
PT650 HFIX M70 39MU 26-7-44 345S 5-9 340S 23-11 341S 15-2-45 329S 22-3 595S 5-10 eng out on t/o CE Pembrey 31-5-48
PT651 33MU 26-7-44 82MU 4-8 *Ad S Ot* 8-9 Hap 23-9 ret UK Mar'45
PT652 33MU 10-8-44 504S 31-8 33S CE ops 6-10 441S 5-4-45 329S 5-4 FACE 23-7 SOC 1-8
PT653 9MU 27-7-44 82MU 10-8 *Melamp* 20-8 Casa 3-9 IAF 27-6-46 as MM4093
PT654 6MU 28-7-44 82MU 9-8 *Melamp* 20-8 Casa 8-9 IAF 26-6-47 as MM4054
PT655 39MU 29-7-44 222MU 10-8 *Sil Gu* 22-8 Casa 11-9 SOC 10-6-48
PT656 39MU 27-7-44 82MU *Melamp* 20-8 Casa 3-9 IAF 26-6-47 as MM4129
PT657 HFIX M70 8MU 30-7-44 345S 1-9 340S 23-11 341S 15-2-45 329S 22-3 sold R J Coley 8-2-50
PT658 8MU 27-7-44 135Wg FAAC 24-8 39S 31-8 335S CE ops 29-10 33S 16-11 332S 10-5-45
PT659 39MU 3-8-44 82MU 11-8 *Sil Gu* 22-8 Casa 11-9 ME 31-5-45 SOC 2-8
PT660 33MU 28-7-44 22MU 10-8 *Melamp* 20-8 Casa 3-9 RHAF 27-2-47
PT661 8MU 28-7-44 84GSU 23-8 FTR 30-8
PT662 6MU 28-7-44 76GSU 11-8 *Melamp* 20-8 Casa 3-9 FTR ops 29-1-45
PT663 33MU 30-7-44 52MU 7-8 *Samarit* 8-9 Hap 23-9
PT664 33MU 28-7-44 215S 6-8 *SSLS210* 20-8 Casa 3-9 ME 31-5-45
PT665 39MU 28-7-44 82MU 8-8 *Melamp* 20-8 Casa 3-9 SOC 14-3-46
PT666 33MU 30-7-44 222MU 10-8 *Sil Gu* 22-8 Casa 11-9 IAF 26-6-47 as MM4056
PT667 39MU 29-7-44 82MU 8-8 *Melamp* 20-8 Casa 3-9 IAF 30-5-46 as MM4057
PT668 33MU 28-7-44 215MU 6-8 *Melamp* 20-8 Casa 3-9 CE ops 13-3-45
PT669 no record Persh 17-7-46 RNAF as H-5 w/o 9-6-49
PT670 39MU 5-8-44 82MU 17-8 *Ad S Ot* 8-9 Hap 23-9
PT671 6MU 28-7-44 76MU 11-8 *Melamp* 20-8 Casa 3-9 ME 25-2-45 FAF 28-3-46
PT672 33MU 28-7-44 215MU 11-8 *Melamp* 20-8 Casa 3-9 40S Italy SOC 30-4-47 SAAF rebuilt as WR-R from MA739 & 5601
PT673 8MU 28-7-44 84GSU 14-8 329S FTR ops 30-10
PT674 33MU 30-7-44 52MU 7-8 *Samarit* 8-9 Hap 23-9
PT675 39MU 30-7-44 52MU 10-8 *Samarit* 8-9 Hap 23-9
PT676 39MU 30-7-44 82MU 12-8 *Sil Gu* 22-8 Casa 11-9 ME SOC 10-6-48
PT677 39MU 29-7-44 82MU 8-8 *Melamp* 20-8 Casa 3-9 IAF 26-6-47 as MM4060
PT678 39MU 30-7-44 52MU 14-8 *Samarit* 8-9 Hap 23-9
PT679 33MU 30-7-44 215MU 12-8 *Q Park* 13-9 Casa 23-9 SOC 13-9-45
PT680 6MU 15-8-44 331S 31-8 C3 ops 9-2-45 33MU 11-6 sold Turk 6-5-47
PT681 6MU 28-7-44 76MU 11-8 *Melamp* 20-8 Casa 2-9 ME 28-12 MAAF 31-5-45 SOC 20-9
PT682 33MU 30-7-44 52MU 10-8 *Samarit* 8-9 Hap 23-9
PT683 33MU 3-8-44 52MU 14-8 *Ad S Ot* 8-9 Hap 23-9
PT697 33MU 3-8-44 52MU 13-8 *Samarit* 8-9 Hap 23-9
PT698 39MU 30-7-44 222MU *Sil Qu* 22-8-0 Casa 11-9 SOC 26-6-47
PT699 39MU 30-7-44 82MU 8-8 *Sil Gu* 22-8 Casa 11-9 SOC 31-12
PT700 33MU 3-8-44 222MU 11-8 *Sil Gu* 22-8 Casa 11-9 SOC 19-7-45
PT701 39MU 30-7-44 82MU 11-8 *Sil Gu* 22-8 Casa 11-9 FTR ops 20-11
PT702 33MU 3-8-44 222MU 11-8 *Sil Gu* 22-8 Casa 11-9 87S f/ld Treviso Italy 9-7-46 SOC 28-11
PT703 39MU 23-8-44 52MU 2-9 *Emp Cel* 9-9 Hap 23-9
PT704 33MU 4-8-44 331S 31-8 420RSU 2-11 FTR ops 29-12
PT705 33MU 1-8-44 222MU 11-8 *Sil Gu* 22-8 Casa 11-9 ME 5-7-45 REAF 29-8-46
PT706 6MU 5-8-44 215MU 16-8 *Q Park* 13-9 Casa 23-9 137MU stor 12-2-48 SOC 10-4
PT707 33MU 1-8-44 222MU 11-8 *Melamp* 20-8 Casa 3-9 e/fd cd dbf CE 17-11
PT708 33MU 1-8-44 222MU 11-8 *Melamp* 20-8 Casa 3-9 CE ops 25-4-45
PT709 33MU 1-8-44 222MU 11-8 *Sil Gu* 22-8 Casa 11-9 FTR ops 17-2-45
PT710 33MU 30-7-44 52MU 10-8 *Samarit* 8-9 Hap 23-9
PT711 39MU 1-8-44 52MU 15-8 *Ad S Ot* 9-9 Hap 23-9
PT712 39MU 3-8-44 82MU 12-8 *Sil Gu* 22-8 Casa 11-9 CE ops dbf 8-2-45
PT713 39MU 11-8-44 82MU 24-8 *Ad S Ot* 8-9 Hap 23-9
PT714 HFIX M70 8MU 9-8-44 345S 1-9 340S 23-11 341S 15-2-45 329S 22-3 33MU 19-4 RDAF 22-9-48 as 410
PT715 33MU 3-8-44 82MU 13-8 *Sil Gu* 22-8 Casa 11-9 FTR ops 19-12
PT716 33MU 3-8-44 82MU 13-8 *Q Park* 13-9 Casa 23-9 FTR ops 31-1-45
PT717 6MU 5-8-44 222MU 11-8 *Sil Gu* 22-8 Casa 11-9 ME 20-9-45 SOC 26-6-47
PT718 33MU 9-8-44 349S 31-8 CAC 21-9 420RSU 33S 28-9 222S FTR ops 13-10
PT719 39MU 3-8-44 52MU 15-8 *Ad S Ot* 8-9 Hap 22-9
PT720 6MU 4-8-44 FACB 10-8 222MU 10-8 *SSLS1225* 24-9 Casa 2-10 SOC 30-8-45
X PT721 39MU 5-8-44 332S 21-9 132Wg 12-10 FACB 21-1-45 ASTH 13-2 sold R J Coley 3-2-50
PT722 33MU 3-8-44 52MU 14-8-44 *Ad S Ot* 8-9 23-9
PT723 8MU 10-8-44 249S 31-8 CAC ops 9-11 332S 22-2-45 FTR ops 2-4
PT724 6MU4-8-44 76MU 11-8 *Melamp* 20-8 Casa 3-9 ME SOC 26-9-46
PT725 39MU 5-8-44 GAL 20-10 mods 84GSU 15-11 442S 11-1-45 CE ops 2-2
PT726 33MU 9-8-44 331S 31-8 420RSU 19-10
PT727 33MU 9-8-44 74S 31-8 FAAC 10-9 AST WAL 13-2-45 mods 331S 10-5
PT728 6MU 4-8-44 222MU 13-8 *Sil Gu* 22-8 Casa 11-9 CE ops 18-11
PT729 8MU 5-8-44 340S 31-8 345S 16-11 CAC ops 22-2-45
PT730 33MU 9-8-44 349S 31-8 CE ops 5-10
PT731 33MU 3-8-44 52MU 14-8 *Ad S Ot* 8-9 Hap 23-9
PT732 6MU 5-8-44 222S 24-8 CAC ops 15-10 84GSU 14-12 329S 25-1-45 345S CB ops 25-2 485S 26-4 74S 17-5 328S 11-10 FAF GC2/1
PT733 HFIX M70 8MU 9-8-44 340S 23-11 e/fd after t/o attempt circuit cd CE Drem 19-12
PT734 33MU 9-8-44 349S 28-9 ASTH 16-1-45 6MU 28-4 sold Turk 16-4-47
PT735 6MU 5-8-44 127S 31-8 74S 21-12 329S 21-12 CAC ops 3-2-45 ROS SOC FFS 1-9-49
PT736 6MU 5-8-44 331S 24-8 AST 8-12 9MU 19-3-45 MAAF 20-4 ME 16-8 SOC 31-10-46
PT737 8MU 9-8-44 340S 31-8 345S 16-11 CE ops 13-2-45 ASTH 9-3 FAF 4-12-46 GC2/4 des 20-3-48
PT738 6MU 5-8-44 340S 31-8 CE ops 11-10 411RSU
PT752 6MU 5-8-44 74S CAC ops 14-10 recat B AST 130S 5-6-45 595AAC S 16-5-46 mr SOC 14-10
PT753 HFIX M70 8MU 9-8-44 345S 1-9 240S FTR ops 18-11 cancel 595S 26-7-45 130S 15-8-46 con to target tug to 6140M 16-9
PT755 8MU 11-8-44 341S 31-8 FTR ops 10-10
PT756 HFIX M70 39MU 29-8-44 504S 11-12 441S 5-4-45 329S 5-4 SOC 21-9
PT757 9MU 12-8-44 82MU 25-8 *Q Park* 13-9 Casa 23-9 SOC 4-1-45
PT758 39MU 5-8-44 485S 24-8 FAAC 21-1-45 135Wg CAC ops 8-2 326S 14-6 FAF 27-11
PT759 39MU 14-8-44 52MU 25-8 *Ad S Ot* 8-9 Hap 23-9
PT760 HFIX M70 33MU 11-8-44 82MU 22-8 *Q Park* 13-9 Casa 23-9 SOC 30-3-45
PT761 HFIX M70 33MU 11-8-44 222MU 24-8 *Q Park* 13-9 Casa 23-9 FTR ops 23-4-45
PT762 8MU 10-8-44 66S 31-8 CAC 6-10 331S CAC ops 16-10 FTR ops 27-10
PT763 39MU 14-8-44 349S 7-9 CAC ops 21-10 420RSU 26-10 ASTH 12-1-45 sold Turk 16-1-47
PT764 HFIX M70 39MU 12-8-44 82MU 23-8 *Q Park* 13-9 Casa 23-9 CE ops 24-6-45
PT765 HFIX M70 33MU 11-8-44 82MU 30-8 *Q Park* 13-9 Casa 23-9 SOC 6-9-45

PT766 HFIX M70 33MU 11-8-44 345S 1-9 CAC 30-9 ROS ASTE 24-1-45 595S 15-7 dvd i/grd from cloud Bishoptom Glam pilot kld 21-3-46 dug up in Mar '75

PT767 33MU 18-8-44 52MU 5-9 *Q Park* 13-9 Casa 23-9 SOC 14-3-46

PT768 HFIX M70 39MU 17-8-44 82MU 26-8 *Q Park* 13-9 Casa 23-9 SOC 6-9-45

PT769 33MU 14-8-44 82MU 26-8 *Q Park* 13-9 Casa 22-8 FACE 4-10

PT770 8MU 11-8-44 84GSU 23-8 74S 31-8 CE ops 29-9

PT771 33MU 12-8-44 52MU 25-8 *Samarit* 8-9 Hap 23-9

PT772 8MU 11-8-44 84GSU 30-8 127S FTR ops 2-10

PT773 9MU 12-8-44 82MU 31-8 *Q Park* 13-9 Casa 23-9 SOC 5-6-45

PT774 9MU 12-8-44 222MU 24-8 *Q Park* 13-9 Casa 23-9 FTR ops 6-3-45

PT775 8MU 16-8-44 74S 31-8 CB ops 6-10 411RSU 12-10 AST 25-10 332S 12-5-45 88Gp Oslo 2-7

PT776 45MU 19-8-44 33S 7-9 CAC ops 22-9 SAL 29-9 45MU 29-12 ASTH 10-5-45 sold R J Coley 3-2-50

PT777 45MU 30-8-44 332S 28-9 429RSU 8-2-45

PT778 9MU 12-8-44 52MU 13-9 *SSLS1225* 24-9 Casa 2-10 SOC 23-8-45

PT779 39MU 4-8-44 84GSU 25-8 341S CAC ops 12-9 FTR ops 29-11

PT780 39MU 14-8-44 52MU 26-9 *Ad S Ot* 2-9 Hap 23-9

PT781 HFIX M70 33MU 15-8-44 345S 2-9 340S 23-11 341S 15-2-45 329S 22-3 SAAF 4-12-48

PT782 39MU 18-10-44 52MU 26-10 *Emp Stal* 14-11 Hap 8-12

PT783 8MU 8-9-44 66S 28-9 132Wg CAC 5-10 66S ops 4-11 331S 16-11 412S 3-5-45 326S 5-7 FAF 27-11

PT784 33MU 24-8-44 33S 14-9 84GSU 14-12 329S 15-2-45 3BRU 19-4

PT785 39MU 14-8-44 52MU *Samarit* 8-9 Hap 23-9

PT786 33MU 14-8 52MU 25-8 *Samarit* 8-9 Hap 23-9

PT787 HFIX M70 33MU 15-8-44 345S 1-9 CAC ops 30-9 ROS ASTE 18-1-45 Stn Flt Exeter 16-9 SAAF 13-2-49

PT788 39MU 14-8-44 127S 31-8 CB ops 12-10 511FRU 12-10 MAL 21-10 6MU 13-1-45 MAAF 17-2 SOC 14-3-46

PT789 39MU 14-8-44 82MU 27-8 *Q Park* 13-9 Casa 23-9 SOC 19-7-45

PT790 9MU 31-8-44 82MU 9-9 *SSLS1225* 24-9 Casa 2-10 92S flew i/hill in cloud nr St Gertraud Austria pilot kld 9-10-46 SOC 28-10

PT791 33MU 14-8-44 222MU 19-8 *Q Park* 13-9 Casa 23-9 CE ops 10-1-45

PT792 39MU 14-8-44 82MU 27-8 *Q Park* 13-9 Casa 23-9 SOC 20-9-45

PT793 9MU 12-8-44 82MU 25-8 *Q Park* 13-9 Casa 23-9 FTR ops 13-4-45

PT794 39MU 14-8-44 52MU 30-8 *Emp Cel* 2-9 Hap 23-9

PT795 39MU 17-8-44 52MU 28-8 *Emp Cel* 2-9 Hap 23-9

PT818 HFIX M70 33MU 15-8-44 345S 2-9 340S 23-11 341S 15-2-45 R-RH 1-4-47 SOC 7-6-49

PT819 8MU 16-8-44 127S 31-8 341S e/a 20-12 ASTH 19-1-45 FAF 27-7-46 GC1/2 des 15-9-47

PT820 6MU 16-8-44 82MU 27-8 *Q Park* 13-9 Casa 23-9 FTR ops 22-12

PT821 8MU 16-8-44 331S 31-8 ROS 5-10 82MU 28-11 *Guinean* 22-12 Casa 15-1-45 ME 16-8-45 SOC 27-3-47

PT822 33MU 17-8-44 215MU 29-8 *Q Park* 13-9 Casa 23-9

PT823 8MU 16-8-44 331S 31-8 431S 13-12 e/a 20-12 411RSU 84Gp ARF 12-4-45 332S 12-4 485S 30-4 74S 17-5 326S 29-5 SNCAN 28-6

PT824 39MU 24-8-44 52MU 2-9 *Emp Cel* 9-9 Hap 23-9

PT825 39MU 30-8-44 52MU 16-9 *SS257* 25-9 Hap 13-10 Murm 1-11

PT826 6MU 17-8-44 331S 31-8 ROS 27-9 AST 18-10 39MU 3-3-45 sold Turk 15-10-47

PT827 6MU 23-8-44 340S 14-9 341S 21-9 e/a CB 29-11 411RSU 332S 29-4-45 FACE 14-6

PT828 39MU 17-8-44 222MU 26-8 *Q Park* 13-9 Casa 23-9 FTR ops 3-1-45

PT829 33MU 17-8-44 52MU 5-9 *SS256* 24-9 Hap 13-10 Murm 30-10

PT830 6MU 17-8-44 349S 7-9 420RSU 11-12 e/a dbf 1-1-45

PT831 33MU 14-8-44 222MU 19-8 *Q Park* 13-9 Casa 23-9 FTR ops 17-11

PT832 39MU 17-8-44 52MU 26-8 *Ad S Ot* 8-9 Hap 28-9

PT833 6MU 15-8-44 341S 31-8 84GSU 21-9-46 331S 9-5-45

PT834 33MU 29-8-44 332S 21-9 FTR ops 3-4-45

PT835 HFIX M70 39MU 17-8-44 82MU 27-8 *Q Park* 13-9 Casa 23-9 ME REAF 18-5-46 RHAF 30-1-47

PT836 33MU 18-8-44 215S 29-8 *Q Park* 13-9 Casa 23-9 CE ops 28-4-45

PT837 33MU 24-8-44 52MU 1-9 *Emp Cel* 9-9 Hap 23-9

PT838 HFIX M70 33MU 8-9-44 441S 7-4-45 329S 12-4 FACE 29-8 SOC 30-8

PT839 33MU 17-8-44 222MU 29-8 *Q Park* 13-9 Casa 23-9 SOC 23-12

PT840 8MU 26-8-44 74S 14-9 341S e/a CE 20-12

PT841 8MU 23-8-44 349S 7-9 CE ops 19-10

PT842 6MU 17-8-44 340S 7-9 345S CB ops 4-11 AST sold Turk 17-4-47

PT843 6MU 17-8-44 331S CB ops 6-9 AST 39MU 22-2-45 SAL 17-3 sold Turk 25-3-47

PT844 HFIX M70 39MU 24-8-44 345S 12-9 340S 30-11 341S 15-2-45 329S 14-6 FAF 24-11

PT845 39MU 24-8-44 82MU 6-9 *Q Park* 13-9 Casa 23-9 SOC 14-6-45

PT846 39MU 23-8-44 82MU 5-9 *Q Park* 13-9 Casa 23-9 FAF 28-3-46

PT847 HFIX M70 33MU 24-8-44 345S 5-9 340S FTR ops 8-11

PT848 6MU 23-8-44 332S 21-9 CAC ops 11-10 AST 332S FTR ops 11-2-45

PT849 33MU 24-8-44 66S 14-9 CB ops 1-10 420RSU AST 15-4-45 MAAF 16-5 SOC 10-6-48

PT850 33MU 24-8-44 82MU 31-8 *Q Park* 13-9 Casa 23-9 SOC 20-9-45

PT851 33MU 24-8-44 349S 11-1-45 420RSU 25-1 sold Turk 1-4-47

PT852 6MU 23-8-44 33S 14-9 341S 4-1-45 308S 11-1 485S CAC ops 9-2 332S 22-2 CB ops 7-3 sold Turk 6-10-47

PT853 6MU 23-8-44 222S 7-9 CB ops 12-10 420RSU 165S 29-3-45 66S 2-9-46 BAF 25-5-47 as SM-16

PT854 45MU 26-8-44 33S CE ops 16-10

PT855 33MU 24-8-44 340S 7-9 345S 16-11

PT856 33MU 24-8-44 33S 21-9 CAC ops 5-10 420RSU 485S 11-1-45 CE ops 13-2

PT857 8MU 23-8-44 485S 7-9 e/a CE b 1-1-45

PT858 33MU 24-8-44 74S 7-9 329S 13-12 74S CAC ops 9-3-45 411RSU AST 10-4 RNoAF 8-5-47

PT859 39MU 24-8-44 52MU 8-9 *SS256* 24-9 13-10 Murm 1-11

PT873 6MU 23-8-44 222MU 14-9 485S 11-1-45 CAC ops 8-2 420RSU ASTH 5-3 RNAF 26-6-48 as H-26 w/o 14-7-50

PT874 33MU 17-8-44 52MU 25-8 *Samarit* 8-9 Hap 23-9

PT875 33MU 24-8-44 52MU 2-9 *Emp Cel* 4-9 Hap 23-9

PT876 HFIX M70 45MU 26-8-44 504S 18-11 CE ops 30-12

PT877 33MU 24-8-44 341S 19-10 e/a 29-11 411RSU 86MU 3-1-45 1APU 10-5 MAAF 21-6 107MU 18-12-47 RHAF 27-5-48 SOC 10-6

PT878 33MU 24-8-44 52MU 2-9 *Emp Cel* 9-9 Hap 22-9

PT879 39MU 24-8-44 52MU 8-9 *SS256* 13-10 Hap 30-10

PT880 33MU 24-8-44 *SS257* 30-9 hap 13-10 Murm 30-10

PT881 39MU 24-8-44 485S 14-9 420RSU 14-12

PT882 8MU 23-8-44 329S CB ops 12-9 421RSU AST 12-10 331S 10-5-45

PT883 33MU 24-8-44 127S 23-11 442S 14-12 CB ops 15-3-45 1CRU sold Turk 22-8-47

PT884 39MU 24-8-44 331S 14-9 CAC ops 22-2-45 420RSU 332S 24-3-45 FTR ops 24-3 cancel 29MU 9-7 RNoAF 7-5-47

PT885 33MU 24-8-44 84GSU 5-9 485S 7-9 FRU 18-1-45 FA SOC 6-3

PT886 39MU 25-8-44 82MU 5-9 *Q Park* 13-9 Casa 23-9 SOC 14-3-46

PT887 6MU 23-8-44 349S 14-9 CB ops 29-1 420RSU ASTH 5-3-45 129S 17-6-46 BAF 17-8-47 as SM-3 wo 11-7-50

PT888 HFIX M70 45MU 25-8-44 504S 13-12 CA ops 23-1-45 151RU 2-3 RDAF as 411 10-2-49

PT889 HFIX M70 45MU 23-8-44 74S 14-9 341S 23-9 CE ops 11-10 AST recat E 11-11

PT890 33MU 25-8-44 485S 14-9 e/a CE dbf 1-1-45

PT891 39MU 24-8-44 349S 7-9 420RSU 16-11

PT892 39MU 24-8-44 340S 7-9 FTR ops 20-9

PT893 33MU 29-8-44 52MU 8-9 *SS256* 24-9 Hap 13-10 Murm 1-11

PT894 39MU 24-8-45 340S 7-9 345S 16-11 CAC ops 16-2-45 FAF GC1/1

PT895 39MU 25-8-44 52MU 5-9 *SS256* 24-9 13-10 Murm30-10

PT896 33MU 24-8-44 485S 14-9 CB ops 14-9 420RSU SAL 21-10 MAAF 14-5-45 SOC 9-8

PT897 39MU 24-8-44 222MU 17-9 *SSLS1225* 24-9 Casa 2-10 CE ops 10-3-45

PT898 45MU 27-8-44 ROS 7-9 GAL 26-9 mods 345S CB ops 19-11 Persh 15-4-45 MAAF 1-5 ME 16-8 RHAF 27-2-47

PT899 39MU 27-8-44 52MU 11-9 *SS256* 25-9 Hap 13-10 Murm 30-10

PT900 6MU 30-8-44 52MU 13-9 *SSLS1225* 24-9 Casa 2-10 ME 31-5-45 SOC 2-8

PT901 39MU 24-8-44 52MU 2-9 *Emp Cel* 9-9 Hap 23-9

PT902 8MU 26-8-44 329S 14-9 CAC ops 30-10 411RSU 329S FTR ops 21-11

PT903 HFIX M70 45MU 25-8-44 345S 6-9 340S 23-11 341S 15-2-45 329S 22-3 595S 5-9 FACB 2-5-46 bou sold scr 3-9-47

PT904 HFIX M70 33MU 30-8-44 124S 8-9 332S FACE 28-2-45 595S 12-7 e/fd u/s f/ld CE nr St Fld CE nr St Florence Pembroke 16-8-46

PT905 HFIX M70 8MU 26-8-44 345S 7-9 340S 23-11 341S 15-2-45 329S 22-3 SAAF 16-4-49

PT906 33MU 25-8-44 33S 14-9 341S 4-1-45 317S 11-1 302S 18-1 332S 25-1 485S 30-4

PT907 HFIX M70 8MU 26-8-44 345S 7-9 340S CB ops 21-11 AST FAF 1-1-46 Persh 23-10-47 RDAF as 412 23-10 coll with 404 at Arreso 24-7-50

PT908 33MU 27-8-44 66S 14-9 CAC ops 1-10 420RSU 5-10 74S 21-12 341S 4-1-45 340S 15-2-45 329S 15-2 345S 1-3 332S 12-4 CAC ops 27-4 420RSU 30-4 327S 14-6 326S 4-10 FAF 27-11

PT909 45MU 26-8-44 331S 28-9 FTR ops 29-12

PT910 HFIX M70 39MU 29-8-44 504S 7-12 441S 5-4-45 329S 5-4 FAAC 29-9 ROS ASTH 22-7-46 Persh 11-4-47 SAAF 23-4

PT911 45MU 27-8-44 33S 21-9 CE ops 1-10

PT912 6MU 29-8-44 127S 19-10 74S 21-12 341S 4-1-45 340S 15-2 345S 15-2 331S 12-4 29MU 7-7 RNoAF 14-12-47

PT913 HFIX M70 45MU 26-8-44 345S 6-9 FTR ops 18-9

PT914 39MU 25-8-44 82MU 5-9 *Q Park* 13-9 Casa 23-9 SOC 14-3-46

PT915 HFIX M70 45MU 26-8-44 506S 11-9 441S 5-4-45 329S 5-4 FAF 24-11

PT929 HFIX M70 33MU 8-9-44 FAAF 27-2-45 FTR ops 12-4

PT930 6MU 27-8-44 66S 5-10 FTR ops 4-11

PT931 HFIX M70 8MU 26-8-44 345S 7-9 340S 23-11 341S 15-2-45 329S 22-3 RDAF as 413 8-7-48 cd Oresund 28-9-49

PT932 HFIX M70 8MU 29-8-44 345S 12-9 340S 23-11 341S 15-2-45 FACE 8-3 SOC 15-3

PT933 33MU 31-8-44 52MU 12-9 *SS256* 25-9 Hap 13-10 Murm 30-10

PT934 IXC 45MU 30-8-44 127S 5-10 FRU 19-10 AST 27-10 313S 31-4-45 FACE 15-7

PT935 9MU 31-8-44 222MU 19-9 *SSLS1225* 24-9 Casa 2-10 FTR ops 21-2-45

PT936 39MU 29-8-44 332S 21-9 CAC ops 11-10 420RSU 332S FTR ops 24-2-45

PT937 6MU 30-8-44 GAL 20-10 mods 341S 30-11 74S 13-12 345S CAC ops 15-3-45 ROS 29MU 8-7

PT938 8MU 26-8-44 485S 21-9 CAC ops 5-1-45 420RSU ASTH 8-3 sold Turk 7-7-47

PT939 33MU 27-8-44 341S 14-9 340S 21-9 AST 27-10 3APU 13-5-45 MAAF 21-6 RHAF 27-2-47

PT940 8MU 5-9-44 66S 28-9 CAC ops 11-10 420RSU 331S 30-4-45

PT941 HFIX M70 39MU 29-8-44 340S 11-12 341S 15-2-45 329S 22-3 1401Met Flt 30-8 SAAF 13-2-49

PT942 9MU 5-9-44 66S 5-10 3-11 345S 21-12 CAC ops 28-2-45 ASTE 21-3 RNoAF 18-11-47

PT943 8MU 26-8-44 222S 7-9 CB ops 6-10 AST MAAF 10-5-45 ME 9-8 RHAF 30-4-47

PT944 39MU 66S 5-10-44 341S 13-12 39MU 18-5-45 SOC 28-10-47

PT945 45MU 31-8-44 66S 19-10 331S 30-11 FTR ops 14-1-45

PT946 8MU 26-8-44 349S 7-9 CB ops fire in air 6-2-45 ASTE recat E SOC 12-3

PT947 33MU 27-8-44 329S 14-9 340S 21-9 345S 16-11 CAC ops 6-2-45 411RSU ASTE 4-5 sold Turk 20-1-47

PT948 6MU 29-8-44 GAL 26-9 mods 345S 2-11 74S CB ops 10-12 411RSU 165S 22-5 FAAC 8-6 ROS sold VA 5-12-49

PT949 45MU 30-8-44 GAL 26-9 mods 66S 2-11 FAAC 7-5-45 151RU RNoAF 15-11-47

PT950 33MU 29-8-44 52MU 5-9 *Q Park* 13-9 Casa 23-9 CE 26-1-45

PT951 39MU 29-8-44 332S 21-9 FAAC 26-1-45 420RSU

PT952 33MU 29-8-44 52MU 8-9 *SS256* 13-10 Hap Murm 30-10

PT953 45MU 27-8-44 329S 7-9 FACB 1-1-45 MAL FSU Dyce 19-6 165S 14-2-46 66S to 6263M 6SoTT 1-2-47

PT954 33MU 29-8-44 222MU 15-9 *SSLS 1225* 23-9 Casa 2-10 FTR ops 20-2-45

PT955 45MU 30-8-44 127S 12-10 CB ops 29-10 3APU 10-4-45 MAAF 12-5 SOC 28-8-47

PT956 6MU 29-8-44 331S 28-9 151RU 8-3-45 332S 15-3 FTR ops 3-4

PT957 39MU 30-8-44 82MU 10-9 *SSLS 1225* 24-9 Casa 2-10 IAF 30-5-46 as MM4076

PT958 39MU 29-8-44 52MU 12-9 *SS256* Hap 13-10 Murm 30-10

PT959 45MU 30-8-44 33S 19-10 329S 4-1-45 341S 22-3 66S 19-4 84ARF 30-4 411S 3-5 FAF 27-11

PT960 6MU 30-8-44 215MU 13-9 *SSLS1225* 24-9 Casa 2-10 blown to pieces in air 29-3-45

PT961 45MU 29-8-44 127S 19-10 CE ops 30-10 bboc 1CRU 15-1-45 129S 16-5 SOC 31-7-46

PT962 6MU 30-8-44 82MU 9-9 *SSLS1225* 24-9 Casa 2-10 FTR ops 17-4-45

PT963 45MU 29-8-44 349S 28-9 CE ops 3-11

PT964 6MU 5-9-44 GAL 25-9 mods 21-10 CE ops 31-12

PT965 45MU 31-8-44 341S 23-10 CE ops 26-11

PT966 39MU 29-8-44 127S 5-10 341S 13-12 e/a CB 20-12 411RSU AST 8-1-45 165S 31-5 66S 2-9-46 SOC scr 16-10-47

PT967 33MU 30-8-44 52MU 15-9 *SS257* 25-9 Hap 13-10 Murm 30-10

PT968 45MU 30-8-44 66S 28-9 349S 11-12 CAC ops 5-1-45 ASTH sold Turk 23-1-47

PT969 33MU 30-8-44 52MU 10-9 *SS257* 25-9 Hap 13-10 Murm 1-11

PT970 39MU 30-8-44 52MU 18-9 *SS257* 25-9 Hap 13-10 Murm 1-11

PT986 313S RNAF 1-10-48 to PH-NFP as target tug

PT987 33MU 30-8-44 523MU 12-9 *SS256* 25-9 Hap 13-10 Murm 30-10

PT988 6MU 30-8-44 215MU 12-9 *SSLS1225* 24-9 Casa 2-10 CE ops 18-4-45 MAAF SOC 31-5-45
PT989 33MU 31-8-44 52MU 8-9 *SS256* 24-9 Hap 13-10 Murm 1-11
PT990 33MU 5-9-44 52MU 10-9 *SS257* 25-9 Hap 13-10 Murm 30-10
PT991 6MU 5-9-44 74S 19-10 329S 13-12 345S 1-3-45 CB ops 7-4 FAF GC2/1
PT992 6MU 5-9-44 GAL 22-9 mods 16-10 CAC ops 22-12 410RSU 39MU 31-5-45 sold R J Coley 8-2-50
PT993 6MU 318-8-44 GAL 25-9 mods 127S 2-11 332S 18-1-45 74S 17-5 326S 28-6
PT994 33MU 30-8-44 82MU 10-9 *SSLS1225* 24-9 Casa 8-10 IAF 26-6-47 as MM4143
PT995 33MU 31-8-44 332S 19-10 CAC ops 6-1-45 420RSU 14-1-45 485S 30-4 74S 17-5 328S 31-5 327S 3-10 FAF 27-11 GC2/1
PT996 43MU 31-8-44 341S 5-10 FTR ops 20-10
PT997 33MU 30-8-44 82MU 8-9 *Q Park* 13-9 Casa 23-9 FACE fire in flt CE 31-10
PT998 39MU 5-9-44 341S 21-9 e/a CB 29-11 recat E SOC 3-1-45
PT999 6MU 16-9-44 74S 19-10 fire in air cd/ld dbf pilot safe CE 9-3-45

PV115 33MU 2-8-44 222MU 11-8 *Sil Hu* 22-8 Casa 11-9 Udim Camp Fordo Italy. White overall for PR duties. IAF 26-6-47 as MM4097
PV116 9MU 27-7-44 215MU 11-8 *Melamp* 20-8 Casa 3-9 SOC 5-1-45
PV117 IXE 9MU 24-7-44 215MU 11-8 *Melamp* 20-8 Casa 3-9 ME 26-7-45 208S SOC 25-4-46
PV118 9MU 28-7-44 82MU 11-8 *Sil Gu* 22-8 Casa 11-9 ME 19-7-45 RHAF 29-5-47
PV119 33MU 1-8-44 15-8 *Melamp* 20-8 Casa REAF 30-4-47 109MU stor 15-1-48 RHAF 27-5
PV120 9MU 29-7-44 215MU 11-8 *Melamp* 20-8 Casa 3-9 FTR ops 16-4-45
PV121 9MU 29-7-44 74S 17-8 CAC ops 13-10 411RSU Persh 17-3-45 MAAF 2-4 SOC 14-3-46
PV122 39MU 2-8-44 82MU 12-8 *Q Park* 13-9 Casa 22-9 IAF 27-6-46 as MM4088
PV123 33MU 2-8-44 222MU 11-8 *Sil Gu* 22-8 Casa 11-9 CE ops 31-1-45
PV124 33MU 2-8-44 222MU 11-8 *Sil Gu* 22-8 Casa 11-9 253S cd/ld CE Treviso Italy 14-2-47 SOC 27-3
PV125 33MU 2-8-44 52MU 10-8 *Samarit* 8-9 Hap 23-9
PV126 9MU 3-8-44 329S 18-1-45 CB ops 9-2-45 DeH sold Turk 9-5-47
PV127 33MU 2-8-44 222MU 11-8 *Sil Gu* 22-8 Casa 11-9 ME SOC 26-9-46
PV128 33MU 14-8-44 82MU 26-8 *Q Park* 13-9 Casa 23-9 FAF 28-3-46
PV129 33MU 14-8-44 52MU 25-8 *Emp Cel* 2-9 Hap 23-9
PV130 39MU 30-8-44 52MU 11-9 *SS257* 30-9 Hap 13-10 Murm 1-11
PV131 33MU 14-8-44 52MU 26-8 *Emp Cel* 2-9 Hap 23-9
PV132 39MU 30-8-44 52MU 10-9 *SS257* 30-9 Hap 13-10 Murm 30-10
PV133 33MU 5-8-44 52MU 26-8 *Emp Cel* 2-9 Hap 22-9
PV134 45MU 14-8-44 349S 31-9 CE ops 3-11
PV135 33MU 3-10-44 52MU 12-10 *Emp Stal* 4-11 Hap 8-12
PV136 9MU 31-8-44 *Q Park* 13-9 Casa 23-9 ME 16-8-45 6S c/ld Ramat Palestine 19-2 SOC 28-2-46
PV137 6MU 16-8-44 222MU 24-8 *Q Park* 13-9 Casa 48S CE ops 1-1-45
PV138 39MU 21-8-44 74S 7-9 CE ops 4-11 recat E SOC 1-4-45
PV139 33MU 9-9-44 127S CB ops 14-10 420RSU 6MU 23-3-45 MAAF 21-6 SOC 26-6-47
PV140 8MU 5-9-44 332S 28-9 CAC ops 11-10 420RSU FAAC 14-12 AST 3-1-45 29MU 31-4 sold Turk 15-10-47
PV141 8MU 5-9-44 332S 28-9 CE ops 17-3-45 SOC 2-4
PV142 6MU 31-8-44 332S 5-10 12FU 20-1-45 MAAF 8-2 cd en route to ME dbf 10-2
PV143 8MU 5-9-44 66S 21-9 345S 21-12 FTR ops 8-2-45
PV144 8MU 5-9-44 74S 19-10 411RSU 15-2-45 332S 15-3 485S CAC ops 23-4 81RSU 327S 5-7
PV145 39MU 5-9-44 222MU 23-9 *SSLS1353* 24-10 Casa 3-11 ME SOC 26-9-46
PV146 6MU 31-8-44 66S 5-10 329S 13-12 CB ops 14-2-45 sold Turk 17-1-47
PV147 33MU 5-9-44 127S 12-10 341S 14-12 340S 15-2-45 74S 1-3-45 345S 15-3 317S 10-5 328S 31-5 FAF 27-11
PV148 6MU 31-8-44 GAL 20-10 mods 84GSU 2-11 442S 12-2-45 411S122-3 FAAC 1-4-45 410RSU SOC 27-11-47
PV149 33MU 5-8-44 66S 18-9 331S 16-11 CB ops 4-2-45 ASTE sold Turk 29-6-47
PV150 39MU 5-9-44 52MU 18-9 *SS257* 30-9 Hap 13-10 Murm 1-11
PV151 HFIX M70 33MU 23-11-44 124S 1-2-45 6MU 17-10-47 sold E Smelt 25-5-50
PV152 6MU 30-8-44 222MU 11-9 *SSLS1225* 24-9 Casa 2-10 SOC 13-9-45
PV153 8MU 15-9-44 331S 19-10
PV154 6MU 30-8-44 GAL 25-9 mods 222S 19-10 442S 18-1-45 CE ops 24-1
PV155 6MU 5-9-44 GAL 26-9 mods 349S 28-10 CAC ops 5-1-45 420RSU 18-1 485S 8-2 345S 1-3 326S 9-8 FAF 27-11
PV156 33MU 5-9-44 485S 21-9 CAC ops 22-12 420RSU 485S 28-12 e/a CE dbf 1-1-45
PV157 VA HPA 16-9-44 6MU 30-9 215MU 6-10 *SSLS1353* 24-10 Casa 3-11 FACE 4-4-45
PV158 33MU 13-9-44 *SS255* 25-9 Hap 12-10 Murm 30-10
PV159 33MU 5-9-44 84GDC 30-8-45 39MU 12-9 sold Turk 4-11-47
PV160 6MU 5-9-44 33S 28-9 CE ops 6-10
PV174 39MU 16-9-44 52MU 3-10 *SS256* 7-10 Hap 12-10 Murm 30-10
PV175 39MU 5-9-44 331S 28-9 349S 30-4-45 317S 3-5 328S 31-5 FAF 27-11
PV176 8MU 8-9-44 341 e/a Cb 29-11 411RSU 33MU 28-3-45 sold Turk 18-9-47
PV177 33MU 5-9-44 341S 11-10 CE ops 411RSU 12-10
PV178 33MU 13-9-44 52MU 23-9 *SS257* 28-9 Hap 13-10 Murm 1-10
PV179 39MU 5-9-44 52MU 16-9 *SS257* 25-9 Hap 13-10 Murm 30-10
PV180 9MU 15-9-44 222S 14-12 74S 4-1-45 332S 15-3-45 328S 13-9 FAF 27-11 BE708
PV181 33MU 5-9-44 66S 5-10
PV182 39MU 35-9-44 52MU 4-10 *SS257* 7-10 Hap 16-10 Murm 30-10
PV183 39MU 16-9-44 *SS255* 25-9 Hap 12-10 Murm 1-11
PV184 39MU 15-9-44 *SS255* 30-9 Hap 12-10 Murm 30-10
PV185 39MU 5-9-44 2322S 14-12 341S 4-1-45 340S 15-2-45 345S 15-2 FRT ops 24-4
PV186 33MU 5-9-44 66S 23-S 23-9 FTR ops 26-9
PV187 8MU 16-9-44 341S 19-10 CAC ops 5-12 411RSU 74S 14-12 CB ops 14-2-45 FAF GC1/6
PV188 33MU 8-9-44 52MU 23-9 *SS256* 30-9 Hap 12-10 Murm 1-11
PV189 33MU 5-9-44 340S 21-9 CB ops 13-10 411RSU 129S 17-5-45 9MU 13-10 46 BAF 25-11-48 as SM-26 wo 25-6-52
PV190 8MU 15-9-44 442S 18-10 CAC ops 410RSU 331S 14-5-45
PV191 6MU 16-9-44 IAF as MM4119 26-6-47
PV192 8MU 15-9-44 no record
PV193 45MU 3-8-44 no record
PV194 33MU 13-9-44 *SS256* 30-9 Hap 13-10 Murm 30-10
PV195 39MU 21-9-44 82MU 28-9 *SS255* 7-10 Hap 20-10 Murm 1-11
PV196 39MU 16-9-44 52MU 29-9 *SS255* 2-10 Hap 12-10 Murm 30-10
PV197 39Mu 15-9-44 82MU 28-9 *SSLS1353* 24-10 Casa 3-11 e/td fire in flt CE 30-11 SOC 23-12
PV198 39MU 15-9-44 52MU 27-9 *SS255* 1-10 Hap 12-10 Murm 30-10
PV199 39MU 16-9-44 412S 12-10 CAC ops 5-12 AST 29MU 17-6-45 sold Turk 5-9-47
PV200 39MU 8-9-44 52MU 18-9 *SS257* 28-9 Hap 13-10 Murm 30-10
PV201 33MU 16-9-44 52MU 27-9 *SS256* 1-10 Hap 12-10 Murm 1-11
PV202 no early record sold VA 19-7-50 con to Type 509 two seat train IAC as 161 29-6-51 SOC Dec '60. To G-BHGH, later G-TRIX. Extant, Sussex
PV203 no record
PV204 39MU 15-9-44 *SS255* 25-9 Hap 12-10 Murm 30-10
PV205 8MU 16-9-44 332S 19-10 DeH 24-2-45 Persh 5-12-46 Czech AF 12-12
PV206 39MU 21-11-44 52Mu 30-11 *Hen Vil* 18-12 Hap 11-1-45
PV207 39MU 30-9-44 52Mu 15-10 *Emp Stal* 7-11 Hap 8-12
PV208 45MU 18-9-44 66S 9-11 332S 30-11 FTR ops 14-1-45
PV209 6MU 16-9-44 411S CAC ops 1-11 FTR ops 16-11
PV210 39MU 25-9-44 331S 19-10 FTR ops 26-11
PV211 HFIX M70 33MU 16-9-44 82MU 28-9 *SSLS1353* 24-10 Casa 5-11 CE ops 6-5-45 SOC 30-8
PV212 HFIX M70 9MU 18-9-44 124S FACE 15-2-45 SOC 22-2
PV213 33MU 21-9-44 332S 19-10 FTR ops 16-2-45
PV214 39MU 15-9-44 52MU 27-9 *SS255* 28-5 Hap 12-10 Murm 30-10
PV215 33MU 18-9-44 222S 19-10 CB ops 22-12 410RSU 485S 14-12 FSU Dyce 19-6-45
PV229 HFIX M70 8MU 16-9-44 345S 10-10 340S 23-11 341S 15-2-45 329S 22-3 FAF 24-11
PV230 33MU 18-9-44 66S CB ops 511FRU 222S 9-11 411S 11-1-45 sold H Bath 27-10-49
PV231 33MU 21-9-44 66S 19-10 CB ops 1-11 151 RU 29MU 7-7-45 sold Turk 2-9-47
PV232 HFIX M70 33MU 16-9-44 FAAC 23-9 ROS 222MU 7-12 FAAC 4-3-45 ROS 329S 12-10 FAF 24-11
PV233 39MU 21-9-44 412S 19-10 ROS 28-10 222MU 20-12 *Tanela* 13-1-45 Casa 25-1 FACE 9-6
PV234 33MU 21-9-44 412S 21-10 81RSU 14-6-45 326S 28-6 SNCAN 2-8
PV235 no record
PV236 39MU 23-9-44 82MU 4-10 *SS257* 9-10 Hap Murm 30-10
PV237 39MU 16-9-44 82MU 28-9 *SSLS1353* 24-10 Casa 3-11 ME SOC 26-9-46
PV238 HFIX M70 33MU 16-9-44 222MU 23-9 *SSLS1353* 24-10 Casa 3-11 ME SOC 26-9-46
PV239 no record
PV240 39MU 21-9-44 83GSU 5-10-44 411S CE ops 29-10
PV241 39MU 25-9-44 215MU 6-10 *SSLS1353* 24-10 Casa 3-11 SOC 14-3-46
PV242 33MU 25-9-44 82MU 29-9 *SS257* 2-10 Hap Murm 30-10
PV243 6MU 18-9-44 84GSU 10-10 FACE SOC 17-3-45
PV244 33MU 16-9-44 52MU 27-9 *SS255* 28-9 Hap Murm 30-11
PV245 33MU 23-9-44 83GSU 6-10 412S CE ops 19-11
PV246 6MU 16-9-44 82MU 26-9 *SSLS1353* Casa 3-11 ME 2-8-45 SOC 28-2-46
PV247 39MU 23-9-44 52MU 3-10 *SS255* 5-10 Hap Murm 30-10
PV248 39MU 23-9-44 82MU 28-9 *SS255* 1-10 Hap Murm 30-10
PV249 33MU 23-9-44 52MU 2-10 *SS255* 5-10 Hap Murm 30-10
PV250 39MU 21-9-44 52MU 29-9 *SS255* 3-10 Hap Murm 30-10
PV251 39MU 21-9-44 82MU 30-9 *SS255* 4-10 Hap Murm 30-10
PV252 39MU 23-9-44 82MU 28-9 *SS255* 3-10 Hap Murm 30-10
PV253 33MU 18-9-44 222S 19-10 33Gp Com S 25-1-45 412SD CB ops 22-3 410RSU recat E 16-4
PV254 39MU 23-9-44 82MU 28-9 *SS257* 2-10 Hap Murm 30-10
PV255 33MU 21-9-44 51MU 27-9 *SS255* 4-10 Hap Murm 30-10
PV256 39MU 23-9-44 52MU 30-9 *SS257* 5-10 Hap Murm 30-10
PV257 39MU 21-9-44 52MU 29-9 *SS255* 2-10 Hap Murm 30-10
PV258 39MU 23-9-44 82MU 30-9-44 *SS255* 4-10 Hap Murm 30-10
PV259 HFIX M70 33MU 23-9-44 215MU 3-10 *SSLS1353* 24-10 Casa 3-11 ME 26-7-45 con to LFIX M66 13-12-45 REAF 29-8-46
PV260 39MU 23-9-44 82MU 3-11 *Lafian* 13-11 Casa 23-11 FTR ops 25-4-45
PV261 HFIX M70 39MU 23-9-44 52MU 9-10 *SSLS1353* 24-10 Casa 3-11 SOC 20-9-45
PV262 39MU 25-9-44 82MU 6-10 *SS258* 9-10 Hap Murm 30-10
PV263 39MU 25-9-44 331S 19-10 CB ops 14-1-45 sold Turk 4-3-47
PV264 HFIX M70 6MU 26-9-44 124S 27-10 CE ops wrck 14-2-45 SOC 22-2
PV265 33MU 23-9-44 82MU 28-9 *SS257* 2-10 Hap Murm 30-10
PV266 39MU 23-9-44 52MU 29-9 *SS257* 2-10 Hap Murm 30-10
PV267 39MU 23-9-44 52MU 29-9 *SS257* 2-10 Hap Murm 30-10
PV268 33MU 23-9-44 82MU 28-9 *SS255* 1-10 Hap Murm 30-10
PV269 HFIX M70 8MU 25-9-44 183S 24-6-45 234S 26-7-45 SAAF 13-2-49
PV270 IXC 9MU 28-9-44 82MU 18-10 *SSLS2135* 21-10 Casa 3-11 253S coll with TA808 ldg Treviso Italy 16-1-47 IAF 26-6 as MM4014 sold VA 5-12-49
PV283 HFIX M70 45MU 2-11-44 504S 9-12 124S 25-1-45 29MU 4-9 sold VA 5-12-49
PV284 HFIX M70 9MU 25-9-44 17AC 21-11 329S 18-10-45 FAF 24-11 GC1/6
PV285 33MU 25-9-44 82MU 30-9 *SS255* 3-10 Hap Murm 30-10
PV286 HFIX M70 9MU 25-9-44 345S 12-10 340S 23-11 341S 15-2-45 329S 22-3 FAF 24-11 GC2/7
PV287 39MU 23-9-44 82MU 28-9 *SS257* 2-10 Hap Murm 30-10
PV289 33MU 26-9-44 329S 9-11 CE ops 22-1-45
PV290 HFIX M70 Farn 27-9-44 large tail plane instal for exhaustive trls of stick force per 'G' at forward CoG position. Con completed at CBAF. WD Feb'45 DTD Aug 6MU 6-9-45 bou SOC 12-2-47
PV291 39MU 23-9-44 84GSU 6-10 74S 19-10 CE ops 2-2-45
PV292 39MU 23-9-44 74S 19-10 CAC ops 31-13 329S 25-1-45 345S 8-3 317S 10-5-45 326S 31-5 FAF 4-12 GC1/6 EXTANT

PT986 after service with the RNAF, became PH-NFP.

PV293 39MU 25-9-44 340S 19-10 345S 16-11 74S 13-12 151RU 14-12 308S 15-2-45 317S 29-3 4S 12-7 451S 9-10 29MU 10-1-46 sold VA 5-12-49

PV294 33MU 26-9-44 84GSU 329S 9-11 74S 13-12 FTR 26-2-45

PV296 HFIX M70 25-9-45 124S 7-2-46 29MU 25-9 RDAF 25-10-48 as 414

PV297 39MU 27-9-44 82MU 4-10 *SS257* 13-10 Hap Murm 30-11

PV298 39MU 28-9-44 82MU 5-10 *SS257* 13-10 Hap Murm 30-11

PV299 HFIX M70 8MU 27-9-44 124S 5-2-45 GAAC 7-6 ROS 29MU 5-9 Farn 7-1-49 loaned as fus only for test SOC 11-8

PV300 HFIX M70 39MU 23-9-44 222MU 5-10 *SSLS1353* 24-10 Casa 3-11 CE ops 23-4-45

PV301 45MU 26-9-44 84GSU 21-10 Persh 15-4-45 MAAF 28-6 RHAF 31-7-47

PV302 45MU 27-9-44 66S CAC ops 4-11 332S 30-11 FTR ops 14-1-45

PV303 HFIXE M70 BHM 24 45MU 3-10-44 504S 22-12 124S 25-1-45 29MU 5-9 RDAF 20-11-48 as 415

PV304 HFIXE M70 6MU 30-9-44 11APC 4-11 29MU 29-7-45 RDAF 12-1-49 as 416

PV305 33MU 26-9-44 222S 19-10 CAC ops 3-11 485S 30-11 CAC ops 25-12 332S CAC ops 6-1-45 sold Turk 5-9-47

PV306 39MU 28-9-44 222MU 10-10 *SSLS1353* 14-10 Casa 3-11 FTR ops 21-3-45

PV308 HFIX M70 39MU 28-9-44 82MU 17-10 *SSLS1356* 13-11 Casa 23-11 1APC 19-7-45 SOC 14-3-46

PV309 39MU 25-9-44 82MU 6-10 *SS257* 13-10 Hap Murm 30-11

PV310 33MU 26-9-44 349S 9-11 CB ops 17-1-45 39MU 16-6 sold J Dale 2-1-50

PV311 BHM 24 8MU 3-10-44 74S 9-11 FTR ops 25-2-45

PV312 HFIX M70 45MU 26-9-44 124S 26-10 ROS Hutton Cranswick 23-8-45 VA EA 25-4-46 recat E

PV313 HFIX M70 9MU 27-9-44 17APC 4-11 FAAC 26-3-45 ROS 595S 6-9 to 6257M 6SoTT 26-3-47

PV314 8MU 28-9-44 127S CB ops 8-11 6MU 6-2-45 MAAF 23-2 FACE 8-6 SOC 28-6

PV315 BNHM 24 39MU 2-10-44 215MU 12-10 *SSLS1353* 24-10 Casa 3-11 SOC 23-8-45 bboc MAAF 30-8 ME 225S w/u ld Campoformido Italy 6-7-46 SOC 31-10

PV316 39MU 25-9-44 442S 9-12 CE 21-12

PV317 45MU 27-9-44 52MU 10-11 *Thom Scott* 18-12 Hap 9-1-45

PV318 HFIX M70 8MU 27-9-44 124S 5-2-45 ROS VAOx 16-3 124S dvd i/grd from cloud CE Full Sutton Yorks 29-5 SOC 31-5

PV319 BHM 24 39MU 2-10-44 82MU 9-10 *SS258* 9-10 Hap Murm 30-10

PV320 39MU 28-9-44 82MU 10-10 *SSLS1353* 24-10 Casa 3-11 SOC 23-9-45

PV321 BHM 24 HFIX M70 33MU 3-10-44 222MU 10-10 *SSLS1353* 24-10 Casa 3-11 ME SOC 10-6-48

PV322 BHM 24 39MU 30-9-44 82MU 7-10 *SS258* 15-10 Hap Murm 30-10

PV323 9MU 27-9-44 82MU 31-10 *Lafian* 13-11 Casa 23-11 ME 9-8-45 SOC 28-8-47

PV324 HFIX M70 39MU 28-9-44 82MU 10-10 *SSLS2135* 21-10 Casa 3-11 RHAFD 27-3-47

PV325 BHM 24 39MU 30-9-44 82MU 10-10 *SSLS2135* 21-10 Casa 3-11 RHAF 27-3-47

PV326 39MU 28-9-44 82MU 6-10 *SS258* 9-10 Hap Murm 30-10

PV341 39MU 28-9-44 82MU 5-10 *SS258* 15-10 Hap Murm 30-10

PV342 BHM 24 45MU 30-9-44 411S 5-11 410RSU 21-12 sold Turk 24-3-47

PV343 HFIX M70 8MU 27-9-44 504S 3-12 124S 25-1-45 329S 20-9 FAAC 15-11 FAF 24-11

PV344 BHM HFIX M70 9MU 2-10-44 124S 7-2-45 29MU 20-9 RDAF as 417 28-10-48

PV345 BHM 24 33MU 30-9-44 82MU 8-10 *Fort B* 1-11 Hap 8-12

PV346 HFIX M70 45Mu 30-9-44 222MU 12-10 *SSLS1353* 24-10 Casa 3-11 FTR ops 16-4-45

PV347 BHM 24 45MU 30-9-44 411S 28-10 CAC ops 16-4-45 410RSU 411S FAAC 23-5 ROS VAOx sold H Bath 27-10-49

PV348 39MU 28-9-44 82MU 6-10 *SS258* 7-10 Hap Murm 30-10

PV350 39MU 28-9-44 82MU 4-10 *SS257* 13-10 Hap Murm 30-10

PV351 BHM 24 39MU 30-9-44 82MU 7-10 *SS258* 9-10 Hap Murm 30-10

PV352 33MU 26-9-44 412S 2-11 SOC 21-6-47

PV353 BHM 24 8MU 30-9-44 66S 2-11 FA SOC 15-1-45

PV354 HFIX M70 45MU 29-9-44 124S 5-2-45 ROS 23-3 595S 6-9 RDAF as 418 28-10-48

PV355 45MU 27-9-44 82MU 21-11 *Emp Orch* 23-12 Hap 9-1-45

PV356 BHM 24 39MU 30-9-44 222MU 15-10 *SSLS1353* 24-10 Casa 3-11 ME 2-8-45 REAF 30-4-47 109MU storage 15-1-48 RHAF 27-5

PV357 BHM 24 39MU 3-10-44 52MU 12-10 *Emp Stal* 4-11 Hap 8-12

PV358 39MU 2-10-44 82MU 9-10 *SS258* 9-10 Hap Murm 30-10

PV359 39MU 12-10-44 222MU 19-10 *Sil Lar* 13-11 Casa 23-11 IAF 26-6-47 as MM4022

PV340-385, PV399-733 cancel

RK889, Edmonton II, served with No.313 Squadron as an HF IX.

RK,RR series all LFIX Merlin 66

RK798 33MU 18-9-44 52MU 27-9 *SS255* 1-10 Hap Murm 30-10

RK799 39MU 30-8-44 52MU 13-9 *SS257* 25-9 Hap Murm 30-10

RK800 9MU 27-9-44 215MU 7-10 *SSLS1353* 24-10 Casa 3-11 ME SOC 10-6-48

RK801 33MU 18-9-44 52MU 27-9 *SS255* 1-10 Hap Murm 30-10

RK802 39MU 5-9-44 33S 28-9 CAC ops 11-10 420RSU 349S 26-10 CB ops 4-11 420RSU

RK803 45MU 21-9-44 331S 19-10 CAC 13-2-45 349S 26-4 84ARF 30-4 401S 3-5 sold Turk 12-7-48

RK804 8MU 16-9-44 341S 19-10 FACE 20-12

RK805 33MU 18-9-44 52MU 27-9 *SS255* 1-10 Hap Murm 30-10

RK806 39MU 9-9-44 341S 12-10 e/a CB 29-11 411RSU DeH 9-1-45 129S 16-5 FAAC 8-11

RK807 39MU 15-9-44 52MU 27-9 *SS255* 28-9 Hap Murm 30-10

RK808 33MU 13-9-44 52MU 23-9 *SS256* 28-9 Hap Murm 30-10

RK809 45MU 21-9-44 349S 28-lo 485S 8-2-45 331S e/fd t/o hit bank o/t CE Oak Farm Tang 16-3 SOC 9-4

RK810 8MU 16-9-44 411S 12-10 CE ops 4-1-45

RK811 HFIX M70 6MU 16-9-44 345S 15-10 340S 23-11 341S 15-2-45 329S 22-3 595S 16-8 287S 22-11 RDAF 22-9-48 as 419 cd nr Skrystrup 27-2-50

RK812 8MU 16-9-44 FA SOC 7-3-45

RK813 33MU 18-9-44 82MU 28-9 *SS257* 2-10 Hap Murm 30-10

RK814 33MU 18-9-44 52MU 27-9 *SS255* 1-10 Hap Murm 30-10

RK815 39MU 23-9-44 52MU 30-9 *SS255* 4-10 Hap Murm 30-10

RK816 33MU 18-9-44 52MU 27-9 *SS257* 2-10 hap Murm 30-10

RK817 45MU 18-9-44 66S 2-11 331S 30-11 349S 26-4-45 412S 10-5 326S 5-7 FAF 27-11

RK818 39MU 23-9-44 52MU 30-9 *SS255* 5-10 Hap Murm 30-10

RK819 9MU 23-9-44 52MU 30-9 *SS255* 4-10 Hap Murm 30-10

RK835 BHM 24 8MU 2-10-44 341S 26-10 70S CE ops 10-12

RK836 BHM 24 33MU 30-9-44 82MU 5-10 *SS256* 7-10 Hap Murm 30-10

RK837 BHM 24 39MU 2-10-44 215MU 12-10 *SSLS1353* 24-10 Casa 3-11 ME 2-8-45 208S coll with NH173 f/ld DRR Beirut Lebanon 10-5-46 SOC 26-7

RK838 45MU 27-9-44 349S CE ops 30-11

RK839 BHM 24 33MU 30-9-44 82MU 5-10 *SS256* 13-10 Hap Murm 30-10

RK841 BHM 24 8MU 30-9-44 82MU 10-12 *Emp Cel* 23-12 Hap 9-1-45

RK843 BHM 24 33MU 2-10-44 52MU 11-10 *Emp Stal* 4-11 Hap 8-12

RK844 33MU 3-10-44 52MU 11-10 *Emp Stal* 4-11 Hap 8-12

RK845 33MU 3-10-44 52MU 11-10 *Fort Is* 11-11 Hap 8-12

RK846 BHM 24 39MU 2-10-44 82MU 10-10 *SSLS1353* 24-10 Casa 3-11 CE ops 23-2-45

RK847 BHM 24 39MU 30-9-44 52MU 9-10 *Fort B* 4-11 Hap 8-12

RK848 BHM 24 8MU 30-9-44 340S 19-10 345S CB ops 5-11 AST sold Turk 6-8-47

RK850 9MU 9-10-44 82MU 18-10 *SSLS2135* 21-10 Casa 3-11

RK851 BHM 24 45MU 30-9-44 349S 9-11 CAC ops 420RSU ASTE 21-2-45 VA 8-11 BAF 20-11-48 as SM-27 wo 22-11-51

RK852 BHM 24 39MU 1-10-44 52MU 12-10 *Fort B* 4-11 Hap 8-12

RK853 BHM 24 45MU 30-9-44 349S 9-11 FAAC 2-12 ROS 329S 25-1-45 341S 22-3 331S 19-4 349S 26-4 317S 3-5 FAF 27-11

RK854 BHM 24 45MU 3-10-44 52MU 19-11 *Thom Scott* 18-12 Hap 9-1-45

RK855 IXC 9MU 7-10-44 222MU 17-10 *Sil Lar* 3-11 Casa 23-11 Reltweg Austria 1946 SOC 30-4-47

RK856 BHM 24 39MU 2-10-44 222MU 12-10 *SSLS1353* 24-10 Casa 3-11 RHAF 30-1-47

RK857 BHM 24 9MU 2-10-44 82MU 10-10 *SSLS1353* 24-10 Casa 3-11 ME 26-7-45 SOC 28-7-46

RK858 BHM 24 33MU 2-10-44 52MU 11-10 *Emp Stal* 4-11 Hap 8-12

RK860 HFIX M70 8MU 12-10-44 124S 30-1-45 CE ops 25-3 SOC 8-5

RK861 BHM 24 8MU 3-10-44 84GSU 15-10 127S FTR ops 3-11

RK862 39MU 3-10-44 215MU 12-10 *SSLA2135* 21-10 Casa 3-11 SOC 28-2-46

RK863 39MU 3-10-44 82MU 18-10 *Fort B* 4-11 Hap 8-12

RK864 BHM 24 33MU 30-9-44 82MU 5-10 *SS256* 13-10 Hap Murm 30-10

RK867 33MU 3-10-44 52MU 11-10 *Emp Stal* 4-11 Hap 8-12

RK884 485S 25-1-45 332S 22-3

RK885 33MU 27-10-44 82MU 7-11 *Fort High* 11-11 Hap 8-12

RK886 BHM 24 39MU 2-10-44 *SSLS2135* 21-10 Casa 3-11 SOC 20-9-45

RK887 45MU 5-10-44 52MU 27-11 *SS268* 4-11 Hap 9-1-45

RK889 HFIX M70 Edmonton II 45MU 6-10-44 313S 10-5-45 ROS VA Henley RDAF as 420 26-10-48

RK890 39MU 12-10-44 82MU 25-10 *Lafian* 13-11 Casa 23-11 SOC 20-9-45

RK894 8MU 6-10-44 52MU 26-10 *Emp Stal* 4-11 Hap 8-12

RK898 39MU 10-10-44 52MU 17-10 *Fort B* 4-11 Hap 8-12

RK899 39MU 12-10-44 52MU 17-10 *Emp Stal* 4-11 Hap 8-12

RK900 45MU 5-10-44 412S 23-11 CAC ops 20-4-45 410RSU 327S 26-7 FAF 27-11

RK901 HFIX M70 6MU 17-10-44 1APC 19-7-45 6MU 15-10-47 sold E Smelt 25-5-50

RK906 8MU 6-10-44 345S 9-11 74S 13-12 CAC ops 31-12 411RSU 74S 24-2-45 345S 15-3 332S 12-4 74S 17-5 327S 14-6 328S 4-10 FAF GC1/7

RK907 6MU 9-10-44 82MU 18-10 *Lafian* 13-11 Casa 23-11 CE ops 25-4-45

RK908 HFIX M70 33MU 18-10-44 124S 24-1-45 ROS VA 12-3 sold H Bath 27-4-49

RK909 39MU 12-10-44 52MU 22-10 *Fort Is* 4-11 Hap 8-12

RK911 HFIX M70 8MU 12-10-44 124S 3-2-45 29MU 4-9 RDAF as 419 23-3-48 cd nr Ikast 12-1-49

RK912 HFIX M70 39MU 23-10-44 222MU 10-12 *Guinean* 22-12 Casa 15-1-45 FACE 7-6

RK914 33MU 19-10-44 82MU 4-11 *Fort High* 11-11 Hap 8-12

RK915 39MU 10-10-44 52MU 17-10 *Fort High* 4-11 Hap 8-12

RK916 HFIX M70 39MU 14-10-44 82MU 25-10 *Sil Lar* 14-11 Casa 23-11 CE ops 10-3-45

RK917 HFIX M70 45MU 10-10-44 3501SU 12-2-45 CFE 10-5 Ftr Com Sector Unit NWld 16-3 Essex Sector 584TU 27-6-46 SAAF 3-2-49

RK919 39MU 12-10-44 52MU 17-10-45 *Fort Is* 18-11 Hap 8-12

RK920 6MU 7-10-44 82MU 19-10 *SSLS2135* 21-10 Casa 3-11 SOC 31-1-46 bboc 14-2 SOC 30-4-47

RK922 39MU 12-10-44 82MU 17-10 *SSLS2135* 21-10 Casa 3-11 ME 26-7-45 SOC 25-7-46

RK923 39MU 12-10-44 52MU 22-10 *Fort B* 4-11 Hap 16-12

RK924 HFIX M70 8MU 12-10-44 30MU 4-1-45 6MU 26-4 234S 2-8 SAAF 10-9-48

RR181 CBAF 33MU 17-8-44 52MU 26-8 *Emp Cel* 2-9 Hap 23-9

RR182 39MU 25-8-44 332S 21-9 FACB 11-2-45 ASTE sold Turk 13-9-47

RR183 39MU 23-8-44 341S 7-9 c/a CB 29-11 411RSU AST 10-1-45 sold R J Coley 3-2-50

RR184 39MU 30-8-44 82MU 8-9 *Q Park* 13-9 Casa 23-9 CE ops 4-1-45

RR185 45MU 31-8-44 66S 28-9 CB ops 13-10 511FRU 19-10- 129S 16-5-45 SOC 31-7-46

RR186 9MU 31-8-44 222MU 15-9 *SSLS1225* 24-9 Casa 2-10 SOC 20-9-45

RR187 39MU 30-8-44 66S 21-9-44 341S 13-12 340S 15-2-45 74S 1-3 345S 8-3 CAC ops 13-4 411RSU 485S 26-4 327S 31-5 339 French Wg 2-8 FAF 27-11 GC 2/3

RR188 9MU 31-8-44 82MU 10-9 *SSLS1225* 16-9 Casa 2-10 SOC 114-46

RR189 9MU 5-9-44 215MU 10-9 *SSLS1225* 23-9 Casa 2-10 SOC FTR ops 3-1-45

RR190 9MU 5-9-44 215MU 13-9 *SSLS1225* 24-9 Casa 2-10 FACE 15-6

RR191 9MU 5-9-44 222MU 17-9 *SSLS1225* 24-9 Casa 2-10 IAF 26-6-47

RR192 9MU 5-9-44 82MU 14-9 *SSLS1225* Casa 2-10 ME 5-7-45 RHAF 30-4-47

RR193 9MU 11-10-44 82MU 18-10 *SSLS2135* 21-10 Casa 3-11 ME 26-6-47 RHAF 31-7-47

RR194 9MU 15-9-44 442S 19-10 FTR 4-11

RR195 CBAF 9MU 21-9-44 82MU 20-10 *Lafian* 18-11 Casa 23-11 REAF 31-10-46

RR196 CBAF 9MU 15-9-44 442S 19-10 412S 29-3-45 CAC ops 19-4 410RSU SOC 27-11-47

RR197 CBAF 9MU 16-9-44 222MU 28-9 *SSLS1353* 24-10 Casa 3-11 ME 5-7-45 RHAF 27-3-47

RR198 CBAF 9MU 16-9-44 82MU 26-9 *SSLS1353* 24-10 Casa 3-11

RR199 CBAF 9MU 16-9-44 222MU 28-9 *SSLS1353* 24-10 Casa 3-11 SOC 4-4-46

RR200 CBAF 15-9-44 33S 19-10 74S 4-1-45 345S 15-3 332S 22-3 CAC ops 5-4 81RSU 328S 3-10 FAF 27-11 GC1/7

RR201 CBAF 18-9-44 66S 9-11 411S 28-12 CB ops 30-4-45

RR202 CBAF 9MU 18-9-44 52MU 4-11 *Fort High* 11-11 Hap 8-12

RR203 9MU 27-9-44 82MU 20-10 *Sil Lar* 13-11 Casa 23-11 RHAF 27-7-47

RR204 9MU 18-9-44 222MU 28-9 *SSLS1353* 24-10 Casa 3-11 IAF 26-6-47 as MM4011

RR205 No record

RR206 HFIX M70 8MU 12-10-44 3501SU 16-2-45 CFE 10-5 SOC 27-11-47

RR207 9MU 12-10-44 222MU 18-10 *Sil Lar* 13-11 Casa 23-11 ME 5-7-45 RHAF 27-2-47

RR208 39MU 19-10-44 52MU 28-10 *Fort B* 4-11 Hap 8-12

RR209 HFIX M70 45MU 14-10-44 124S 5-2-45 FACB 7-6 ASTH RDAF as 421 28-10-48

RR210 9MU 12-10-44 82MU 12-10 *SSLS2135* Casa 3-11 FAAF CE 12-7-45

RR211 6MU 9-10-44 82MU 20-10 *Lafian* 13-11 Casa 23-11 SOC 6-9-45

RR228 HFIX M70 9MU 13-10 AFDU 15-2-45 fitt 75gal fuel tank rear fus 164S bou SOC 27-1-47

RR231 HFIX M70 14-10-44 82MU 25-10 *Sil Lar* 13-11 Casa 23-11 ME 5-7-45 SOC 25-7-46

RR232 HFIX M70 45MU 14-10-44 FAAC 26-10 ROS ECFS 17-3-45 VAO SAAF 5632 21-4-48 Extant, Nowra, Australia

RR233 Coll with SM212 at CBAF before delivery 19-10-44

RR235 HFIX M70 39MU 14-10-44 222MU 10-11 *Guinean* 22-12 Casa 15-1-45 IAF 26-6-47 as MM4112

RR237 33MU 19-12-44 *W R Gra* 21-2-45 Hap 26-3

RR238 HFIX M70 BDn 28-10-44 FAAC 24-5-45 ROS VAOx 1-6 BDn 30-8 VACBAF mr 20-3-46 recat E 24-6

RR239 HFIX M70 33MU 18-10-44 222MU 23-11 *Guinean* 22-12 Casa 5-1-45 IAF 30-5-46 as MM4091

RR241 HFIX M70 39MU 14-10-44 82MU 25-10 *Lafian* 13-11 Casa 23-11 87S FACE e/fld u/s ldg Treviso Italy 26-6-46 SOC 29-8

RR244 HFIX M70 33MU 18-10-44 82MU 26-10 *Lafian* 13-11 Casa 23-11 FTR ops 4-4-45

RR246 HFIX M70 39MU 6-11-44 215MU *Guinean* 22-12 Casa 16-1-45 43S FTR ops 14-4-45

RR251 HFIX M70 39MU 14-10-44 222MU 5-11 *Sil Lar* 13-11 Casa 23-11 IAF 26-6-47

RR252 HFIX E as MM4113 M70 39MU 19-10-44 124S 8-2-45 29MU 13-9 RDAF as 422 12-3-48 scrapped 1-9-53

RR253 39MU 18-10-44 52MU 26-10 *Emp Stal* 4-11 Hap 8-12

RR254 HFIX M70 33MU 18-10-44 222MU 29-10 *Sil Lar* 13-11 Casa 23-11 SOC 14-3-46

RR258 HFIX M70 33MU 18-10-44 *Melt Mob* 25-1-45 MAAF 17-2 SOC 30-8

RR259 HFIX M70 39MU 19-10-44215MU 28-11 *Guinean* 22-12 Casa 15-1-45 CE ops 10-4 SOC 14-6

RR260 HFIX M70 33MU 23-10-44 222MU 12-12 *Guinean* 22-12 Casa 10-1-45 ME SOC 26-9-46

RR262 HFIX M70 33MU 18-10-44 82MU 26-10 *Lafian* 13-11 Casa 23-11 SOC 30-8-45

RR264 HFIX M70 33MU 18-10-44 222MU 13-11 *Guinean* 22-12 Casa 10-1-45 SOC 6-9

SL and SM series all LIFX M66

SL5945 CBAF 33MU 19-7-45 310S 7-8 Czech AF 30-8

X SL595 CBAF 33MU 2-7-45 88GSU 21-9 CAC VAOx 27-9 RNAF 11-12-47 5MU 19-12 sold R J Coley 3-2-50

SL625 CBAF 33MU 16-6-45 312S 3-8 Czech AF 30-8

SL626 CSFD 39MU 19-6-45 312S 1-8 Czech AF 30-8

SL627 CBAF 39MU 18-6-45 312S 3-8 Czech AF 30-8

SL628 CSFD IXE 39MU 19-6-45 312S 3-8 Czech AF 30-8

SL629 CBAF 39MU 22-6-45 313S 19-7 Czech AF 30-8

SL630 CBAF 39MU 22-6-45 313S 19-7 Czech AF 30-8

SL631 CBAF 39MU 25-6-45 312S 1-8 Czech AF 30-8

SL632 CBAF 39MU 25-6-45 312S 4-8 Czech AF 30-8

SL633 CBAF 39MU 25-6-45 312S 2-8 Czech AF 30-8

SL634 CBAF 33MU 29-6-45 312S 17-9 Czech AF 30-8

SL635 CSFD 39MU 29-6-45 313S 9-8 Czech AF 30-8

SL648 CSFD 39MU 29-6-45 312S 4-8 Czech AF 30-8

SL649 CSFD 33MU 29-6-45 312S 16-8 Czech AF 30-8

SL650 CBAF 33MU 30-6-45 312S 23-8 Czech AF 30-8

SL651 CBAF 33MU 17-7-45 310S 7-8 Czech AF 30-8

SL652 CBAF 33MU 23-7-45 mans 7-8 313S 8-8 Czech AF 30-8

SL653 CBAF 33MU 19-7-45 312S 23-8 Czech AF 30-8

SL654 CBAF 33MU 19-7-45 312S 23-8 Czech AF 30-8

SL655 CSFD 39MU 24-7-45 310S 7-8 Czech AF 30-8

SL656 CSFD 39MU 24-7-45 312S 4-8 Czech AF 30-8

SL657 CSFD 39MU 24-7-45 313S 7-8 Czech AF 30-8

SL658 CBAF 33MU 2-8-45 313S 7-8 76MU 10-10 *Diomed* 29-11 FAF Sai I.C 19-1-46

SL659 CBAF 33MU 2-8-45 76MU 13-10 *Diomed* 29-11 FAF Sai IC 19-1-46 GC1/4 des 12-6-48

SL660 CBAF 33MU 25-7-45 310S 17-9 Czech AF 30-8

SL661 CSFD 39MU 14-8-45 sold Turk 28-8-47

SL662 CBAF 33MU 25-7-45 RAF Mans 7-8 Czech AF 30-8

SL663 CBAF 33MU 31-7-45 BDn 23-10 ETPS Farn FACB u/c jam w/u ld Granfield 8-4-46 VA 6-5 recat E 24-6

SL664 CBAF 33MU 23-7-45 Mans 7-8 313S 9-8 Czech AF 30-8

SL665 CBAF 33MU 31-7-45 88GSU 29-11 29MU 27-12 sold Turk 30-7-47

SM135 BAF 9MU 18-9-44 222MU 28-9 *SSLS1353* Casa 3-11 ME 5-7-45 RHAF 30-4-47

SM136 CBAF 9MU 18-9-44 215MU 28-9 *SSLS1335* 24-10 Casa 3-11 SOC 23-8-45

SM137 9MU 20-9-44 215MU 25-9 SSLS 24-10 Casa 3-11 ME 2-8-45 FACE 3-3-47 SOC 27-3

SM138 CBAF 9MU 21-9-44 222MU 29-9 *SSLS1353* 24-10 Casa 3-11 SOC 18-12-45

SM139 CBAF 9MU 22-9-44 127S 2-11 331S 30-11 78MU 29-3-45 sold Turk 16-10-47

SM140 39MU 23-9-44 52MU 30-9 *SS256* 7-10 Hap Murm 30-10

SM141 9MU 28-9-44 82MU 15-4 *SSLS2135* 21-10 Casa 3-11 SOC 30-4-47

SM142 33MU 23-9-44 82MU 28-9 *SS255* 12-10 Hap Murm 30-10

SM143 33MU 25-9-44 82MU 28-9 MAAF 17-2-45 SOC 14-3-46

SM144 33MU 25-9-44 82MU 28-9 *SS255* 4-10 Hap Murm 30-10

SM145 9MU 28-9-44 82MU 11-11 *Fort High* 18-11 Hap 8-12

SM146 BHM 24 9MU 30-9-44 52MU 4-11 *Fort High* 18-11 Hap 8-12

SM147 IXE BHM 24 9MU 30-9-44 82MU 31-10 *Lafian* 13-11 Casa 23-11 SOC 14-3-46

SM148 BHM 24 9MU 2-10-44 222MU 18-10 *Sil Lar* 13-11 Casa 23-11 CE ops 28-3

SM149 BHM 24 9MU 2-10-44 222MU 18-10 *Sil Lar* 13-11 Casa 23-11 CE ops 28-3

SM150 BHM 24 9MU 2-10-44 52MU 12-10 *SSLS1353* 24-10 Casa 3-11 FACE 31-3-45 SOC 14-6

SM170 BHM 24 9MU 2- 10-44 52MU 10-10 *SSLS1353* 24-10 Casa 3-11 CE ops

SM171 BHM 24 9MU 2-10-44 52MU 10-10 *SSLS1353* 24-10 Casa 3-11 IAF 30-5-46 as MM4006

SM172 BHM 24 9MU 2-10-44 *SSLS2135* 21-10 Casa 3-11 ME 27-9-45 RHAF 25-9-47

SM173 CBAF 5-10-44 52MU 10-10 *SSLS1353* 24-10 Casa 8-11 IAF 26-6-47 as MM4007

SM174 BHM 24 9MU 2-10-44 52MU 10-10 *SSLS1353* 24-10 Casa 9-11 IAF 27-6-47 as MM4089

SM175 9MU 9-10-44 82MU 18-10 *SSLS2155* 21-10 Casa 3-11 ME 20-9-45 RHAF 29-5-47

SM176 9MU 12-10-44 222MU 17-10 *Silver Lar* 13-11 Casa 23-11 CE ops 11-4-45 SOC 30-8

SM177 9MU 16-10-44 82MU 31-10 *Lafian* 13-11 Casa 23-11 SOC 22-11-45

SM240 CBAF 33MU 24-11-44 82MU 7-12 *J D Yea* 20-12 Hap 9-1-45

SM425 CBAF 39MU 25-11-44 82MU 20-12 *J D Yea* 20-12 Hap 9-1-45

SM441 9MU 12-10-44 82MU 18-10 *SSLS2155* 20-12 Casa 3-11 IAF 26-6-47 w/o 9-47

SM442 33MU 17-10-44 52MU 26-10 *Emp Stal* 4-11 Hap 8-12

SM443 9MU 16-10-44 82MU 31-10 *Lafian* 18-11 Casa 23-11 ME 26-7-45 SOC 27-11-47

SM444 9MU 16-10-44 82MU 31-10 *Lafian* 13-11 Casa 23-11 SOC 13-12-45

SM445 9MU 17-10-44 82MU 31-10 *Sil Lar* 18-11 Casa 23-11 IAF 30-8-46 as MM4028

SM446 9MU 17-10-44 82MU 31-10 *Sil Lar* 18-11 Casa 23-11 FACE 30-9-46 SOC 31-10

SM447 M77 39MU 23-10-44 52MU 3-11 *Fort B* 4-11 Hap 8-12

SM448 33MU 20-10-44 52MU 3-11 *Fort B* 4-11 Hap 8-12

SM449 39MU 23-10-44 52MU 3-11 *Fort Is* 4-11 Hap 8-12

SM450 39MU 2-11-44 82MU 9-11 *Fort High* 11-11 Hap 8-12

SM451 CBAF 33MU 27-10-44 82MU 6-11 *Fort High* 11-11 Hap 8-12

SM452 39MU 2-11-44 82MU 9-11 *Fort Mas* 11-11 Hap 16-12

SM453 CBAF 33MU 27-10-44 82MU 7-11 *Fort High* 11-11 Hap 8-12

SM454 33MU 4-11-44 52MU 10-11 *Fort High* 132-11 Hap 8-12

SM455 CBAF 33MU 27-10-44 82MU *Fort Is* 11-11 Hap 8-12

SM456 39MU 30-10-44 82MU 7-11 *Fort Is* 11-11-Hap 8-12

SM457 39MU 2-11-44 82MU 9-11 *Fort High* 18-11 Hap 8-12

SM458 39MU 4-11-44 52MU 9-11 *Fort High* 18-11 Hap 8-12

SM459 39MU 2-11-44 82MU 9-11 *Fort Mas* 18-11 Hap 8-12

SM460 33MU 1-11-44 82MU 9-11 *Fort Mas* 11-11-Hap 8-12

SM461 33MU 1-11-44 82MU 23-11 *Emp Cel* 26-12 Hap 9-1-45

SM462 3MU 1-11-44 82MU 9-11 *Fort High* 10-10 Hap 8-12

SM463 33MU 8-11-44 52MU 15-11 *Thom Scott* 18-12 Hap 9-1-45

SM486 CBAF HIFX M70 39MU 2-12-44 234S 8-8-45 FAAC 17-9 ROS 130S 14-2-46 bou SOC 12-2-47

SM504 CBAF HFIX M70 39MU 28-11-44 234S 2-8-45 130S 14-2-46 SOC 6-6

SM505 HFIX M70 33MU 23-11-44 183S 24-6-45 FAAC 12-11 ROS VA SAAF 13-2-49

SM506 HFIX M70 33MU 23-11-44 47MU 24-2-48 *Clan For* 10-3 SAAF 12-4

SM508 CBAF 39MU 24-11 82MU 18-1-45 *SS276* 20-1-45 Hap 13-2

SM509 33MU 23-11-44 52MU 1-12 *Hen Vill* 9-12 Hap 9-1-45

SM510 CBAF 39MU 25-11-44 52MU 5-12 *Hen Vill* 9-12

SM513 HFIX M70 33MU 23-11-49 183S 24-6-45 122S 9-8 sold H Bath 27-10-49

SM514 33MU 23-11-44 82MU 7-12-44 *Hen Vill* 15-12 Hap 9-1-45

SM515 HFIXE M70 33MU 23-11-44 124S 23-1-45 ROS VAO sold E Smelt 8-6-50

SM517 39MU 21-11-44 82MU 1-12 *Samarit* 25-12 Hap 17-1-45

SM518 HFIX M70 39MU 23-11-44 164S 24-4-45 on loan for BoB 29-8-46 bou sold scr 3-9-47

SM519 33MU 23-11-44 82MU 7-12 *Samarit* 23-12 Hap 9-1-45

SM520 HFIX M70 33MU 23-11-44 SAAF 21-6-48

SM521 CBAF 39MU 24-11-44 82MU 7-12 *J D Yea* 23-12 Hap 9-1-45

SM522 CBAF 33MU 24-10-44 82MU 7-12 *J D Yea* 23-12 Hap 9-1-45

SM523 CBAF M70 39MU 6-12-44 183S 24-6-45 ROS VAO 21-8 234S 27-9 FAAC 19-12 ASTH Persh 29-4-47 SAAF 17-5

SM524 LFIX G61 33MU 20-11-44 82MU 7-12 *Hen Vill* 15-12 Hap 9-1-45

SM525 LFIX G61 33MU 20-11-44 82MU 7-12 *Samarit* 10-12 Hap 9-1-45

SM526 CBAF 33MU 28-11-44 82MU 8-12 *J D Yea* 9-12 Hap 9-1-45

SM527 CBAF 39MU 24-11-44 82MU 7-12 *Emp Cel* 23-12 Hap 9-1-45

SM528 39MU 21-11-44 82MU 30-11 *Emp Cel* 23-12 Hap 9-1-45

SM529 LFIX G61 33MU 20-11-44 82MU 30-11 *Emp Cel* 26-12 Hap 9-1-45

SM530 33MU 23-11-44 82MU 7-12 *Samarit* 12-12 Hap 9-1-45

SM531 CBAF 39MU 24-11-44 82MU 7-12 *J D Yea* 23-12 Hap 9-1-45

SM532 CBAF 33MU 24-11-44 52MU 6-12 *Hen Vill* 9-12 Hap 9-1-45

SM533 CBAF 33MU 24-11-44 82MU 7-12 *J D Yea* 23-12 Hap 9-1-45

SM534 CBAF 33MU 24-11-44 82MU 7-12 *J D Yea* 20-12 Hap 9-1-45

SM535 LFIX G61 33MU 20-11-44 82MU 30-11 *Samarit* 23-12 Hap 9-1-45

SM536 33MU 4-12-44 82MU 1-1-45 *SS275* 19-1 Hap 13-2

SM537 CBAF 33MU 24-11-44 52MU 8-12 *Ed Fann* 23-12-Hap 9-1-45

SM539 39MU 21-11-44 52MU 30-11 *Hen Vill* 15-12 Hap 9-1-45

SM540 39MU 21-11-44 82MU 1-12 *Samarit* 23-12 Hap 9-1-45

SM541 CBAF 39MU 24-11-44 82MU 7-12 *J D Yea* 23-12 Hap 9-1-45

SM542 CBAF 39MU 29-11-44 82MU 20-12 *Emp Arch* 26-12 Hap 9-1-45

SM543 CBAF 39MU 25-11-44 52MU 5-12 *Emp Fann* 23-12 Hap 9-1-45
SM544 CBAF 39MU 25-11-44 82MU 7-12 *J D Yea* 23-12 Hap 9-1-45
SM545 CBAF 33MU 24-11-44 52MU 6-12 *Hen Vill* 18-12 Hap 9-1-45
SM546 CBAF 39MU 24-11-44 82MU 7-12 *J D Yea* 20-12 Hap 9-1-45
SM547 39MU 23-11-44 52MU 6-12 *Hen Vill* 15-12 Hap 9-1-45
SM548 CBAF 39MU 25-11-44 82MU 12-12 *Samarit* 23-12 Hap 9-1-45
SM563 CBAF 33MU 24-11-44 82MU 7-12 *J D Yea* 20-12 Hap 9-1-45
SM564 CBAF 33MU 24-11-44 82MU 10-12 *Emp Cel* 26-12 Hap 9-1-45
SM565 BHM 24 39MU 5-12-44 52MU 13-12 *Ed Fann* 23-12 Hap 9-1-45
SM566 CBAF 39MU 24-11-44 52MU 9-12 *Hen Vill* 15-12 Hap 9-1-45
SM567 CBAF 39MU 25-11-44 52MU 6-12 *Ed Fann* 23-12 Hap 9-1-45
SM568 CBAF 33MU 29-12-44 82MU 10-12 *Ed Fann* 23-12 Hap 9-1-45
SM569 CBAF 39MU 25-11-44 52MU 9-12 *Hen Vill* 18-12 Hap 9-1-45
SM570 CBAF 3MU 28-11-44 52MU 13-12 *Ed Fann* 20-12 Hap 9-1-45
SM571 39MU 25-11-44 52MU 5-12 *Ed Fann* 23-12 Hap 9-1-45
SM572 CBAF 33MU 29-11-44 82MU 10-12 *Emp Arch* 19-12 Hap 9-1-45
SM573 CBAF 39MU 25-11-44 52MU 5-12 *Hen Vill* 18-12 Hap 9-1-45
SM574 CBAF 33MU 7-12-44 *SS276* 25-1-45 Hap 13-2-45
SM575 LFIX G61 33MU 20-11-44 82MU 30-11 *Emp Cel* 26-12 Hap 9-1-45
SM576 CBAF 39MU 24-11-44 52MU 9-12 *Hen Vill* 18-12 Hap 9-1-45
SM577 CBAF 39MU 24-11-44 82MU 7-12 *J D Yea* 23-12 Hap 9-1-45
SM578 CBAF 33MU 24-11-44 82MU 7-12 *J D Yea* 20-12 Hap 9-1-45
SM579 CBAF 39MU 25-11-44 52MU 6-12 *Ed Fann* 23-12 Hap 9-1-45
SM580 CBAF 33MU 24-11-44 82MU 7-12 *J D Yea* 20-12 Hap 9-1-45
SM581 CBAF 33MU 24-11-44 82MU 12-12 *Emp Cel* 26-12 Hap 9-1-45
SM582 CBAF 33MU 24-11-44 82MU 7-12 *J D Yea* 20-12 Hap 9-1-45
SM583 CBAF 39MU 25-11-44 52MU 9-12 *Hen Vill* 15-12 Hap 9-1-45
SM584 CBAF 39MU 6-12-44 82MU 3-1-45 ROS 11-1 *SS276* 25-1-45 Hap 13-2
SM585 CBAF 33MU 28-11-44 82MU 10-12 *Emp Cel* 23-12 Hap 9-1-45
SM586 CBAF 39MU 24-11-44 52MU 9-12 *Hen Vill* 17-12 Hap 9-1-45
SM587 CBAF 39MU 25-11-44 52MU 5-12 *Ed Fann* 23-12 Hap 9-1-45
SM588 CBAF 33MU 29-11-44 82MU 19-12 *Emp Arch* 23-12 Hap 9-1-45
SM589 CBAF 39MU 28-11-44 52MU 6-12 *Ed Fann* 23-12 Hap 9-1-45
SM590 CBAF 33MU 29-11-44 52MU 8-12 *Ed Fann* 23-12 Hap 9-1-45
SM591 CBAF 33MU 24-11-44 82MU 7-12 *J D Yea* 20-12 Hap 9-1-45
SM592 CBAF 33MU 29-11-44 82MU *Emp Cel* 26-12 Hap 9-1-45
SM593 CBAF 24-11-44 82MU 7-12 *Emp Cel* 26-12 Hap 9-1-45
SM594 CBAF 28-11-44 52MU 5-12 *Hen Vill* 19-12 Hap 9-1-45
SM595 CBAF 33MU 29-11-44 82MU 19-12 *Emp Arch* 23-12 Hap 9-1-45
SM596 CBAF 33MU 29-11-44 82MU 10-12 *Hen Vill* 15-12 Hap 9-1-45
SM597 CBAF 33MU 28-11-44 82MU 12-12 *J D Yea* 23-12 Hap 9-1-45
SM610 CBAF 33MU 2-12-44 82MU 21-12 *SS273* 26-1-45 Hap 13-2
SM611 CBAF 39MU 23-11-44 52MU 5-12 *Ed Fann* 23-12 Hap 9-1-45
SM612 CBAF 33MU 29-11-44 52MU 8-12 *Ed Fann* 23-12 Hap 9-1-45
SM613 CBAF 33MU 28-11-44 82MU 12-12 *Emp Cel* 26-12 Hap 9-1-45
SM614 CBAF 39MU 28-11-44 52MU 5-12 *Ed Fann* 23-12 Hap 9-1-45
SM615 CBAF 39MU 29-11-44 82MU 11-12 *J D Yea* 20-12 Hap 9-1-45
SM616 CBAF 39MU 28-11-44 52MU 8-12 *Ed Fann* 23-12 Hap 9-1-45
SM617 CBAF 33MU 29-11-44 82MU 19-12 *Emp Arch* 23-12 Hap 9-1-45
SM618 CBAF 39MU 28-11-44 82MU 20-12 *SS275* 13-1-45 Hap 13-2
SM619 CBAF 33MU 29-11-44 19-12 *Emp Arch* 26-12 Hap 9-1-45
SM620 CBAF 33MU 9-2-44 82MU 10-12 *Hen Vill* 15-12 Hap 9-1-45
SM621 CBAF 33MU 28-11-44 52MU 6-12 *Ed Fann* 23-12 Hap 9-1-45
SM622 CBAF 33MU 29-11-44 82MU 10-12 *J D Yea* 20-12 Hap 9-1-45
SM623 CBAF 39MU 6-12-44 82MU 3-1-45 *SS276* 25-1-45 Hap 13-2
SM624 CBAF 39MU 2-12-44 52MU 3-1-45 *SS275* 19-1-45 Hap 13-2
SM625 CBAF 39MU 30-12-44 52MU 16-12 *Ed Fann* 23-12 Hap 9-1-45
SM626 CBAF 39MU 28-11-44 52MU 16-12 *Ed Fann* 23-12 Hap 9-1-45
SM627 CBAF 39MU 29-11-44 52MU 6-12 *Ed Fann* 23-12 Hap 9-1-45
SM628 CBAF 39MU 6-12-44 82MU 12-2-45 *Emp Stal* 13-2 Hap 20-3
SM629 CBAF 33MU 6-12-44 *SS275* 18-1-45 Hap 23-2
SM630 CBAF 39MU 28-11-44 82MU 20-12 *Emp Arch* 26-12 Hap 9-1-45
SM631 CBAF 39MU 2-12-44 82MU 12-2-45 *Fort Yuk* 27-2 Hap 20-3
SM632 CBAF 39MU 28-11-44 52MU 6-12 *Ed Fann* 23-12 Hap 9-1-45
SM633 CBAF 33MU 6-12-44 52MU 12-1-45 *SS274* 10-1 Hap 13-2
SM634 CBAF 39MU 2-12-44 82MU 3-1-45 *SS273* 26-1 Hap 13-2
SM635 CBAF 39MU 29-11-44 52MU 6-12 *Ed Fann* 23-12 Hap 9-1-45
SM636 CBAF 33MU 6-12-44 *SS275* 12-1-45 Hap 13-2
SM637 CBAF 33MU 6-12-44 82MU 18-12 *Emp Arch* 23-12 Hap 9-1-45
SM638 CBAF 33MU 7-12-44 *SS275* 12-1-45 Hap 13-2
SM639 CBAF 33MU 2-12-44 82MU 10-1-45 *SS276* 28-1 Hap 13-2
SM640 CBAF 33MU 6-12-44 82MU 13-2-45 *Emp Stal* 13-2 Hap 20-3
SM641 CBAF 39MU 30-11-44 52MU 13-12 *Ed Fann* 23-12 Hap 9-1-45
SM642 CBAF 33MU 6-12-44 52MU 13-1-45 *SS275* 19-1 Hap 13-2
SM643 CBAF 33MU 29-11-44 52MU 8-12 *Ed Fann* 23-12 Hap 9-1-45
SM644 CBAF 33MU 29-11-44 82MU 10-12 *Emp Cel* 26-12 Hap 9-1-45
SM645 CBAF 33MU 2-12-44 52MU 31-12 *SS274* 19-1-45 Hap 13-2
SM647 CBAF 33MU 29-11-44 82MU 10-12 *Hen Vill 15-12 Hap 9-1-45*
SM663 *CBAF 33MU 6-12-44 82MU Emp Arch* 23-12 Hap 9-1-45
SM666 CBAF 39MU 6-12-44 *Samarit* 30-3-45 Hap Murm 25-4
SM668 CBAF 39MU 5-12-44 331S 12-5-45
SM669 CBAF 33MU 8-12-44 *SS276* 25-1-45 Hap 13-2

TA, TB, TD, and TE series all LF IX Merlin 66 CBAF unless otherwise indicated

TA738 39MU 2-12-44 82MU 3-1-45 *SS273* 19-1 Hap 15-2
TA740 39MU 2-12-44 52MU 3-1-45 *SS274* 19-1-45 Hap 13-2
TA742 39MU 2-12-44 *W R Gra* 26-2-45 Hap 20-3
TA743 39MU 4-12-44 52MU 9-12 *Ed Fann* 23-12 Hap 9-1-45
TA744 39MU 2-12-44 82MU 3-1-45 *SS275* 11-1 Hap 13-2
TA746 39MU 5-12-44 Hvy ldg u/c clpse drop tank fire Cole 3-2-45 SOC 9-2
TA747 33MU 5-12-44 *SS275* 19-1-45 Hap 13-2
TA748 33MU 5-12-44 *SS275* 19-1-45 Hap 13-2
TA749 39MU 5-12-44 52MU 19-12 *Ed Fann* 23-12 Hap 9-1-45
TA750 33MU 4-12-44 82MU 8-12 *Emp Arch* 23-12 Hap 9-1-45
TA751 33MU 8-12-44 *SS276* 25-1-45 Hap 13-2
TA752 39MU 2-12-44 82MU 1-1-45 *SS273* 26-1-45 Hap 13-2
TA753 33MU 4-12-44 82MU 1-1-45 *SS273* 19-1 Hap 15-2
TA754 39MU 6-12-44 82MU 3-2-45 *W R Gra* 26-2 Hap 20-3
TA755 33MU 6-12-44 82MU 10-1-45 *SS275* 19-1 Hap 13-2
TA756 BHM 24 39MU 5-12-44 52MU 18-12 *SS275* 10-1-45 Hap 13-2
TA757 33MU 5-12-44 *SS276* 28-1-45 Hap 13-2
TA758 33MU 2-12-44 82MU 18-12 *Emp Arch* 23-12 Hap 9-1-45
TA760 33MU 12-1-45 *W R Gra* 20-2 Hap 20-3
TA761 39MU 7-12-44 82MU 3-1-45 *SS273 28-1 Hap 15-2*
TA762 39MU 21-1-45 82MU 26-2 *Fort Bag* 28-2 Hap 20-3
TA763 33MU 8-12-44 *SS275* 19-1-45 Hap 13-2
TA764 BHM 24 39MU 5-12-44 52MU 19-12 *Ed Fann* 23-12 Hap 9-1-45
TA765 BHM 24 39MU 5-12-44 52MU 19-12 *SS275* 19-1 Hap 13-2
TA766 33MU 8-12-44 *SS276* 25-1-45 Hap 13-2
TA767 39MU 5-12-44 5v2MU 19-12 *Ed Fann* 23-12 Hap 9-1-45
TA768 33MU 6-12-44 82MU 13-1-45 *SS276* 25-1 Hap 13-2
TA769 33MU 5-12-44 *W R Gra* 18-2 Hap 20-3-45
TA770 33MU 6-12-44 82MU 10-1-45 *SS276* 28-1 Hap 13-2
TA771 39MU 11-12-44 82MU 1-1-45 *SS273* 26-1 Hap 13-2
TA772 HFIX M70 33MU 9-12-44 MAAF 11-2-45 ME SOC 14-6
TA773 BHM 24 39MU 5-12-44 82MU 19-12 *Ed Fann* 23-12 Hap 9-1-45
TA774 33MU 9-12-44 82MU 22-1-45 *SS276* 25-1 Hap 13-2
TA775 39MU 9-2-45 *Samarit* 30-3 Hap Murm 25-4
TA776 33MU 9-12-44 *SS276* 25-1-45 Hap 13-2
TA777 39MU 7-12-44 *W R Gra* 26-2-45 Hap 20-3
TA778 33MU 9-12-44 *Fort B* 21-2-45 Hap 29-3
TA779 33MU 9-12-44*SS275* 19-1-45 Hap 13-2
TA780 HFIX M70 FACB 2-12-44 33MU 14-12-44 ROS VAO FAF 1-1-46
TA793 39MU 7-12-44 82MU 31-12 *SS275* 19-1-45 Hap 13-2
TA794 HFIX M70 39MU 18-12-44 MAAF 27-2-45 cd on f/f repaired Belgium 22-6 16FU 29-11 sold VA 5-12-49
TA795 HFIX M70 39MU 11-12-44 124S 23-1-45 CAC ops 9-3 DeH recat E 30-7 SOC 18-8
TA796 HFIX 39MU 12-12-44 124S 24-3-45 595S 6-9 130S 15-8-46 to 6139M 16-9
TA797 39MU 7-12-44 82MU 30-12 CAC ops 10-1-45 *SS276* 25-1-45 Hap 13-2
TA798 HFIX M70 39MU 13-12-44 *Mel Mob* 5-3-45 MAAF 19-3 SOC 14-3-46
TA799 39MU 18-12-44 82MU 31-1-45 *Fort Yuk* 27-2 Hap 20-3
TA800 HFIX M70 33MU 12-12-44 124S 16-3 329S 30-8 FAF 24-11 GC2/7
TA801 33MU 17-12-44 82MU 22-1-45 *SS273* 26-1 Hap 13-2
TA802 HFIX M70 33MU 9-12-44 183S 28-6-45 122S 16-8 FAAC 15-11 ASTH Persh 10-4-47 SAAF 16-5
TA803 33MU 8-12-44 82MU 25-1-45 *SS273* 26-1 Hap 13-2
TA804 HFIX M70 33MU 9-12-44 124S 25-3-45 FAAC 30-5 595S 2-9 130S 16-5-46 abs SOC 5-2-47
TA805 HFIX M70 39MU 3-1-45 183S 24-6 234S 2-8 SAAF 26-4-49
TA806 HFIX M70 33MU 12-12-44 *Mel Mob* 28-2-45 MAAF 11-4 SOC 20-9
TA807 HFIX M70 33MU 12-12-44 MAAF 10-3-45 ME 19-7 SOC 31-1-46
TA808 HFIX M70 39MU 18-12-44 *Mel Mob* 4-2-45 MAAF 12-2 con to LFXVI 253S coll with PV270 ldg Treviso Italy 16-1-47 SOC 30-1
TA810 HFIX M70 33MU 9-12-44 *W R Gra* 26-2-45 Hap 20-3
TA811 HFIX M70 39MU 11-12-44 124S 23-1-45 sold VA 28-11-49
TA812 HFIX M70 39MU 11-12-44 183S 25-6-45 122S 16-8 sold RDAF as 423 28-10-48 cd Holstebro 15-11-49
TA813 HFIX M70 39MU 11-12-44 124S 23-1-45 FAAC 5-2 ROS sold RDAF as 424 20-11-48
TA814 33MU 17-12-44 82MU 6-2-45 *W R Gra* 26-2 Hap 20-3
TA815 39MU 17-12-44 52MU 13-1-45 *SS275* 19-1 Hap 13-2
TA816 HFIX M70 39MU 11-12-44 *Mel Mob* 26-2-45 MAAF 8-3 ME 23-8 RHAF 30-4-47
TA817 HFIX M70 39MU 11-12-44 *Mel Mob* 4-2-45 MAAF 17-2 CE ops 26-4
TA818 33MU 17-12-44 82MU 22-1-45 *Emp Stal* 10-2 Hap 20-3
TA819 33MU 17-12-44 *W R Gra* 26-2-45 Hap 20-3
TA820 33MU 17-12-44 82MU 22-1-45 *SS273* 26-1 Hap 13-2
TA821 33MU 23-9-44 82MU 28-9 *SS255* 12-10 Hap Murm 30-10
TA822 LFIXE 45MU 21-9-44 AFDU 19-10 BDn 11-1-45 gun heat trls with NAFDU barrel cool scheme. ASTH 6-2-45 mods BDn 21-2 29MU 27-12 sold VA 5-12-49
TA823 9MU 23-9-44 222MU 11-10 *SSLS2353* 24-10 Casa 3-11 73S Takali Malta 137MU 29-1-48 RHAF 27-5
TA824 33MU 23-9-44 82MU 28-7 *SS255* 3-10 Hap Murm 30-10
TA825 HFIX M70 8MU 25-9-44 345S 10-10 340S 18-1-45 341S 15-2 329S 22-3 1401 Met Flt 15-9 84GDC 13-12 sold Int All 2-11-49
TA826 33MU 25-9-44 82MU 30-9 *SS255* 12-10 Hap Murm 30-10
TA827 45MU 20-9-44 52MU 11-11 *Fort High* 18-11 Hap 8-12
TA828 33MU 25-9-44 82MU 30-9 *SS255* 4-10 Hap Murm 30-10
TA829 39MU 28-9-44 82MU 10-10 *SSLS2135* 21-10 Casa 3-11 SOC 20-9-45
TA830 33MU 25-9-44 52MU 3-10 *SS255* 5-10 Hap Murm 30-10
TA831 33MU 25-9-44 82MU 30-9 MAAF 17-2-45 ME SOC 31-10-46
TA832 33MU 25-9-44 82MU 5-10 *SS257* 13-10 Hap Murm 30-10
TA833 BHM 24 45MU 2-10-44 33MU 10-11 *Thom Scott* 18-12 Hap 9-1-45
TA834 39MU 28-9-44 82MU 5-10 *SS257* 13-10 Hap Murm 30-10
TA835 39MU 28-9-44 82MU 5-10 *SS258* 7-10 Hap Murm 30-10
TA836 BHM 24 8MU 30-9-44 127S 2-11 74S e/a CB 12-10 411RSU AST 29-12 129S 17-5-45 BAF 25-11-48 as SM-25

TA837 BHM 24 8MU 2-10-44 349S 9-11 CE ops 5-2-45

TA838 BHM 24 45MU 30-9-44 127S 2-11 332S 30-11 FTR ops 4-1-45

TA839 BHM 24 45MU 2-10-44 411S 9-12 FTR ops 1-5-45

TA840 BHM 24 45MU 2-10-44 82MU 11-11 *Fort High* 18-11 Hap 8-12

TA844 39MU 27-10-44 no record

TA850 no record

TA851 39MU 27-10-44 no record

TA854 BHM 24 6MU 3-10-44 82MU 10-10 *SSLS1353* 26-10 Casa 3-11 ME 5-7-45 RHAF 27-2-47

TA855 BHM 24 45MU 2-10-44 FACB en route 84GSU 23-10 129S 16-5-45 ROS 27-5-46 BAF 26-8-47 as SM-10 wo 14-12-51

TA856 BHM 24 45MU 2-10-44 52MU 10-11 *Thom Scott* 10-12 Hap 9-1-45

TA857 BHM 24 6MU 3-10-44 82MU 11-10 *SSLS1353* 24-10 Casa 3-11 ME 26-7-45 SOC 28-2-46

TA858 BHM 24 45MU 2-10-44 411S 2-11 CB ops 24-12 410RSU sold Turk 3-11-47

TA859 BHM 24 6MU 3-10-44 82MU 12-10 *SSLS1353* 24-10 Casa 3-11 RHAF 29-5-47

TA860 BHM 24 45MU 2-10-44 82MU 10-11 *Fort High* 11-11 Hap 8-12

TA861 6MU 7-10-44 82MU 12-10 *SSLS2135* 21-10 Casa 3-11 SOC 19-7-45

TA862 6MU 7-10-44 82MU 18-10 *Sil Lar* 13-11 Casa 23-11 SOC 10-9-45

TA863 39MU 7-10-44 82MU 18-10 *Lafian* 10-11 Casa 23-11 ME 20-9-45 RHAF 29-5-47

TA864 39MU 7-10-44 82MU 18-10 *SSLS2135* 21-10 Casa 3-11 318S cd in flames 9-9-45 SOC 9-10

TA865 39MU 7-10-44 82MU 18-10 *Fort B* 4-11 Hap 8-12

TA866 39MU 12-10-44 82mU 17-10 *Sil Lar* 13-11 Casa 23-11 SOC 14-3-46

TA867 39MU 12-10-44 52MU 22-10 *Fort B* 4-11 Hap 8-12

TA868 33MU 16-10-44 52MU 26-10 *Emp Stal* 4-11 Hap 8-12

TA869 33MU 16-10-44 52MU 26-10 *Emp Stal* 4-11 Hap 8-12

TA870 33MU 17-10-44 52MU 29-10 *Fort Is* 4-11 Hap 8-12

TA871 39MU 27-10-44 82MU 4-11 *Fort Is* 11-11 Hap 8-12

TA872 39MU 19-10-44 52MU 3-11 *Fort Is* 4-11 Hap 8-12

TA873 33MU 23-10-44 *Fort Is* 11-11 Hap 8-12

TA874 39MU 19-10-44 52MU 28-10 *Fort B* 4-11 Hap 8-12

TA875 33MU 23-10-44 82MU 7-11 *Fort High* 11-11 Hap 8-12

TA876 33MU 23-10-44 82MU 7-11 *Fort High* 11-11 Hap 8-12

TA877 33MU 23-10-44 *Fort Is* 11-11 Hap 8-12

TA878 33MU 24-10-44 52MU 4-11 *Fort Mas* 11-11 Hap 8-12

TA879 33MU 24-10-44 52MU 4-11 *Fort Is* 11-11 Hap 8-12

TA880 39MU 30-10-44 82MU 4-11 *Fort Is* 11-11 Hap 8-12

TA881 39MU 27-10-44 82MU 4-11 *Fort Is* 11-11 Hap 8-12

TA882 39MU 2-11-44 82MU 9-11 *Fort Mas* 18-11 Hap 8-12

TA883 DSFD 39MU 28-10-44 82MU *Fort Is* 11-11 Hap 8-12 SAAF as TA999

TA884 39MU 27-10-44 82MU 4-11 *Fort Is* 11-11 Hap 8-12

TA885 39MU 27-10-44 82MU 4-11 *Fort Is* 11-11 Hap 8-12

TA886 33MU 30-10-44 82MU 7-11 *Fort Mas* 11-11 Hap 8-12

TA887 33MU 30-10-44 52MU 4-11 *Fort High* 11-11 Hap 8-12

TA888 39MU 2-11-44 82MU 9-11 *Fort Mas* 11-11 Hap 8-12

TA905 33MU 28-10-44 82MU 4-11 *Fort Is* 11-11 Hap 8-12

TA906 33MU 30-10-44 52MU 4-11 *Fort High* 11-11 Hap 8-12

TA907 33MU 30-10-44 *Fort High* 11-11 Hap 8-12

TA908 39MU 30-10-44 82MU 9-11 *Fort Mas* 11-11 Hap 8-12

TA909 39MU 30-10-44 82MU 6-11 *Fort High* 11-11 Hap 8-12

TA910 33MU 4-11-44 52MU 10-11 *Fort High*13-11 Hap 8-12

TA911 33MU 9-11-44 52MU 27-11 *J D Yea* 9-12 Hap 9-1-45

TA912 33MU 4-11-44 82MU 19-11 *Emp Arch* 23-12-Hap 9-1-45

TA913 39MU 1-11-44 82 9-11 *Fort Mas* 11-11 Hap 8-12

TA914 39MU 1-11-44 82MU 9-11 *Fort High* 11-11-Hap 8-12

TA915 33MU 4-11-44 52MU 10-11 *Fort High* 13-11 8-12

TA916 39MU 1-11-44 82MU 9-11 *Fort Mas* 8-11 Hap 8-12

TA917 33MU 7-11-44 82MU 7-12 *Hen Vill* 15-12 Hap 9-1-45

TA918 39MU 4-11-44 52MU 9-11 *Fort High* 13-11-Hap 8-12

TA919 39MU 4-11-44 52MU 10-11 *Fort High* 13-11 Hap 8-12

TA920 BHM 24 33MU 19-11-44 82MU *Emp Cel* 26-12 Hap 9-1-45

TA921 39MU 15-11-44 52MU 27-11 *J D Yea* 20-12 Hap 9-1-45

TA922 39MU 21-11-44 82MU 1-12 *Emp Arch* 23-12 Hap 9-1-45

TA923 39MU 21-11-44 52MU 30-11 *Hen Vill* 15-12 Hap 9-1-45

TA924 39MU 21-11-44 82MU 30-11 *Samarit* 23-12 Hap 9-1-45

TA925 39MU 21-11-44 52MU 2-12 *Hen Vill* 18-12 Hap 9-1-45

TA926 39MU 21-11-44 52MU 6-12 *Hen Vil* 16-12 Hap 9-1-45

TA927 39MU 21-11-44 82MU 7-12 *J D Yea* 23-12 Hap 9-1-45

TA928 39MU 21-11-44 82MU 1-12 *Emp Arch* 23-12 Hap 9-1-45

TA929 39MU 21-11-44 52MU 30-11 *Hen Vill* 10-12 Hap 9-1-45

TA930 33MU 28-11-44 82MU 10-12 *Emp Cel* 26-12 Hap 9-145

TA931 33MU 28-11-44 82MU 8-12 *Emp Cel* 26-12 hap 9-1-45

TA932 39MU 21-11-44 82MU 7-12 *J D Yea* 20-12 Hap 9-1-45

TA933 39MU 21-11-44 82MU 1-12 *Emp Arch* 23-12 Hap 9-1-45

TA934 39MU 23-11-44 52MU 6-11 *Hen Vill* 15-12 hap 9-1-45

TA935 33MU 28-11-44 82MU 13-12 *J D Yea* 20-12 Hap 9-1-45

TA936 39MU 2-12-44 52MU 3-1-45 *SS274* 10-1 Hap 13-2-45

TA937 33MU 30-11-44 82MU 13-12 *J D Yea* 20-12 Hap 9-1-45

TA938 39MU 2-12-44 52MU 12-1-44 *SS274* 10-1 Hap 13-2

TA939 33MU 4-12-44 82MU 31-12 *SS275* 13-1 Hap 13-2

TA940 33MU 30-11-44 562MU 8-12 *Ed Fann* 16-12 Hap 9-1-45

TA941 33MU 30-11-44 82MU 15-12 *Emp Arch* 26-12 Hap 9-1-45

TA942 33MU 30-11-44 82MU 10-12 *Tandi* 13-1-45 Casa 25-1

TA943 33MU 4-12-44 82MU 2-1-45 *SS275* 19-1 Hap 13-2

TA944 39MU 2-12-44 *W R Gra* 26-2 Hap 20-3

TA945 39MU 2-12-44 *SS273* 12-1-45 Hap 13-2

TA946 39MU 6-12-44 82MU 6-1-45 *SS273* 26-1 Hap 13-2

TA947 33MU 4-12-44 52MU 12-1-45 *SS274* 19-1 HAp 13-2

TA948 39MU 11-12-44 *SS273* 26-1-45 Hap 15-2

TA960 33MU 7-12-44 82MU 22-1-45 *SS276* 25-1 Hap 13-2

TA961 DSFD 39MU 18-12-44 82MU 17-1-45 *SS275* 19-1 Hap 13-2

TA962 DSFD 39MU 18-12-44 82MU 23-1-45 *SS273* 26-1 Hap 13-2

TA963 33MU 9-12-44 82MU 25-1-45 *SS273* 26-1-45 Hap 13-2

TA964 39MU 11-12-44 82MU 2-1-45 *SS275* 24-1 Hap 13-2

TA965 DSFD 39MU 18-12-44 82MU 13-1-45 *SS276* 25-1 Hap 13-2

TA966 39MU 7-2-45 *Park Ben* 30-3-45 Hap Murm 25-4

TA967 39MU 11-12-44 52MU 2-1-45 *SS275* 28-1 Hap 13-2

TA968 39MU 7-12-44 82MU 26-2-45 *Fort B* 28-2-Hap 20-3

TA969 39MU 31-12-44 82MU 7-2-45 *Fort B* 28-2 Hap 20-3

TA970 39MU 11-12-44 52MU 12-1-45 *SS274* 19-1 Hap 13-2

TA971 39MU 2-11-44 82MU 9-11 *Fort High* 11-11 Hap 8-12

TA972 33MU 6-11-44 52MU 15-11 *Thom Scott* 18-12 Hap 9-1-45

TA973 33MU 6-11-44 82MU 23-11 *Emp Arch* 23-12 Hap 9-1-45

TA974 33MU 16-11-44 82MU 27-11 *J D Yea* 20-12 Hap 9-1-45

TA975 33MU 9-12-44 *Samarit* 30-3-45 Hap Murm 25-4

TA976 33MU 16-11-44 52MU 27-11 *J D Yea* 20-12 Hap 9-1-45

TA977 33MU 25-11-44 82MU 12-12 *Samarit* 23-12 Hap 9-1-45

TA978 39MU 23-11-44 52MU 9-12 *Hen Vill* 18-12 Hap 9-1-45

TA979 33MU 24-11-44 82MU 7-12 *J D Yea* 20-12 Hap 9-1-45

TA980 G61 39MU 20-11-44 52MU 28-11 *Hen Vill* 18-12 Hap 9-1-45

TA981 39MU 23-11-44 52MU 9-12 *Hen Vill* 15-12 Hap 9-1-45

TA982 33MU 23-11-44 52MU 9-12 *Hen Vill* 15-12 Hap 9-1-45

TA983 39MU 23-11-44 52MU 9-12 *Hen Vill* 15-12 Hap 9-1-45

TA984 39MU 23-11-44 52MU 5-12 *Ed Fann* 20-12 Hap 9-1-45

TA985 33MU 1-12-44 *SS275* 12-1-45 Hap 13-2

TA986 33MU 24-11-44 82MU 7-12 *J D Yea* 20-12 Hap 9-1-45

TA987 39MU 29-11-45 52MU 6-12 *Ed Fann* 23-12 Hap 9-1-45

TA988 33MU 1-12-44 82MU 15-12 *J D Yea* 20-12 Hap 9-1-45

TA989 39MU 2-12-44 82MU 4-2-45 *Fort B* 28-2 Hap 20-3

TA990 39MU 29-11-44 82MU 11-12 *J D Yea* 20-12 Hap 9-1-45

TA991 39MU 29-11-44 82MU 11-12 *Emp Arch 23-12 Hap 9-1-45*

TA992 39MU 2-12-44 *W R Gra* 26-2-45 Hap 20-3

TA993 33MU 1-12-44 52MU 14-12 *Emp FAnn* 23-12 HAp 9-1-45

TA994 39MU 2-12-44 *Samarit* 30-3-45 Hap Murm 25-4

TA995 DSFD 39MU 18-12-44 82MU 13-1-45 *SS276* 25-1 Hap 13-2

TA996 39MU 3-1-45 *W R Gra* 26-2 Hap 20-3

TA997 33MU 4-1-45 82MU 13-2 *Fort Yuk* 24-2 Hap 20-3

TA998 DSFD 39MU 18-12-44 *SS276* 25-1-45 Hap 13-2

TA999 39MU 3-1-45 82MU 12-2 *Emp Stal* 13-2 Hap 20-3

TB115 33MU 4-1-45 82MU 13-2 *Fort Yuk* 27-2 Hap 20-3

TB116 39MU 31-12 82MU 17-1-45 *Joy KLil* 19-1-45 Hap 13-2

TB117 39MU 3-1-45 *SS276* 25-1 Hap 13-2

TB118 39MU 31-12 *SS276* 26-1-45 Hap 13-2

TB119 33MU 19-12-44 *Fort Mass* 16-2 Hap 20-3

TB120 *Emp Stal* 10-2-45 Hap 20-3

TB121 52MU 12-1-45 *SS274* 19-1 Hap 13-2

TB122 33MU 4-1-45 82MU 16-2 *Fort Mas* 15-2 Hap 20-3

TB123 33MU 4-1-45 82MU 12-2 *Fort Yuk* 27-2 Hap 20-3

TB124 39MU 31-12-44 82MU 23-1-45 *SS276* 25-1 Hap 13-2

TB125 33MU 12-1-45 *W R Gra* 20-2 Hap 20-3

TB126 39MU 5-1-45 82MU 31-1 *Fort Yuk* 27-2 Hap 20-3

TB127 DSFD 39MU 6-1-45 82MU 7-2 *W R Gra* 26-2 Hap 20-3

TB128 DSFD 39-MU 6-1-45 82MU 7-2 *Fort B* 28-2-Hap 20-3

TB129 33MU 4-1-45 82MU 10-2 *Emp Stal* 13-2 Hap 20-3

TB133 39MU 22-1-45 82MU 26-2 *Samarit* 30-3 Hap Murm 25-4

TB134 39MU 17-1-45 82MU 7-2 *W R Gra* 26-2 Hap 20-3

TB135 39MU 17-1-45 82MU 19-2 *Emp Stal* 13-2 Hap 20-3

TB142 39MU 17-1-45 82MU 12-2 *Fort Yuk* 27-2 Hap 20-3

TB143 39MU 17-1-45 *Emp Stal* 10-2 Hap 20-3

TB144 39MU 22-1-45 *W R Gra* 20-2 Hap 20-3

TB145 33MU 7-2-45 *Samarit* 30-3 Hap Murm 25-4

TB146 39MU 7-2-45 *Ben H H* 17-3 Hap Murm 25-4

TB147 39MU 10-2-45 *Ben H H* 17-3 Hap Murm 25-4

TB148 39MU 7-2-45 *Parkn Ben* 30-3 Hap Murm 25-4

TB149 39MU 22-1-45 *W R Gra* 26-2 Hap 26-3

TB150 39MU 7-2-45 *Emp Prow* 29-4 Hap Murm 22-5

TB168 33MU 17-12 44 *Emp Stal* 10-2-45 Hap 20-3

TB169 33MU 17-12-44 82MU *Fort B* 28-2-45

TB170 39MU 17-12-44 82MU 12-2-45 *Fort Yuk* 27-2 Hap 20-5

TB171 33MU 17-12-44 82MU 22-1-45 *SS276* 24-1 Hap 13-2

TB172 33MU 17-12-44 82MU 3-2-45 *W R Gra* 26-2 Hap 20-3

TB173 33MU 17-12-44 82MU 3-2-45 *Fort Yuk* 27-2 Hap 20-3

TB174 39MU 17-12-44 82MU 7-1-45 *SS276* 25-1-45 Hap 13-2

TB175 33MU 4-1-45 82MU 12-2 *Emp Stal* 13-2 Hap 20-3

TB176 33MU 17-12-44 82MU 31-1-45 *Fort Yuk* 27-2 Hap 20-3

TB177 33MU 17-12-44 *Fort Mas* 15-2 15-2 Hap 20-3

TB178 33MU 17-12-44 82MU 16-2-45 *W R Gra* 26-2 Hap 20-3

TB179 39MU 18-12-44 *SS275* 19-1-45 Hap 20-2

TB180 33MU 31-12-44 82MU 3-2-45 *Fort Yuk* 27-2 Hap 20-3

TB181 33MU 17-12-44 *W R Gra* 26-2 Hap 20-3

TB182 33MU 17-12-44 82MU 3-2-45 *W R Gra* 26-2 Hap 20-3

TB183 33MU 17-12-44 *Fort Yuk* 27-2-45 Hap 20-3

TB184 39MU 13-12-44 82MU 3-1-45 *SS273* 26-1 Hap 15-2

TB185 39MU 3-1-45 *W R Gra* 26-2 Hap 20-3

TB186 39MU 18-12-44 *SS275* 19-1-45 Hap 13-2

TB187 33MU 31-12-44 82MU 25-1-45 *SS276* 19-1 Hap 13-2

TB188 33MU 31-12-44 MAAF 25-5-45 111S dam during dive bomb pract cd nr Tissano FACE 4-11-46 SOC 28-11

TB189 39MU 3-1-45 82MU 12-2 *Emp Stal* 13-2 Hap 20-3

TB190 39MU 4-1-45 *W R Gra* 26-2 Hap 20-3

TB191 39MU 21-1-45 82MU 26-2 *Ben H H* 7-3 Hap Murm 25-4

TB192 39MU 3-1-45 *Fort Mas* 16-2 Hap 20-3

TB193 39MU 17-12-44 *SS275* 19-1-45 Hap 13-2

TB195 33MU 31-12-44 82MU 25-1-45 *SS274* 24-1 Hap 13-2

TB196 33MU 31-12-44 *Emp Stal* 16-2-45 Hap 20-3

TB197 HFIX M70 39MU 21-1-45 *Mel Mob* 24-2 MAAF 5-3 SOC 13-12

TB213 33MU 4-1-45 82MU 16-2 *Fort Mas* 15-2 Hap 20-3

TB214 39MU 18-12-44 82MU 23-1-45 *SS273* 26-1 Hap 13-2

TB215 39MU 3-1-45 *Emp Stal* 10-2 Hap 20-3

TB216 39MU 17-12-44 82MU 7-1-45 *SS275* 19-1 Hap 13-2

TB217 39MU 3-1-45 *W R Gra* 26-2 Hap 20-3

TB218 39MU 18-12-44 82MU 24-1-45 *SS274* 19-1 Hap 13-2

TB219 39MU 18-12-44 *SS275* 19-1 Hap 13-2

TB220 33MU 17-12-44 82MU 22-1-45 *SS276* 25-1-45 Hap 13-2

TB221 39MU 18-12-44 *SS276* 25-1-45 Hap 13-2

TB222 33MU 31-12-44 *Emp Stal* 10-2-45 Hap 26-3

TB223 39MU 28-12-44 82MU 24-12 *SS274* 19-1-45 Hap 13-2

TB224 39MU 3-1-45 *Fort Yuk* 27-2 Hap 20-3

TB225 39MU 18-12-44 82MU 12-2-45 *Emp Stal* 13-2 Hap 20-3

TB226 39MU 3-1-45 *W R Gra* 26-2 Hap 20-3

TB227 39MU 8-1-45 82MU 3-2 *W R Gra* 26-2 Hap 20-3

TB228 39MU 3-1-45 *Fort Yuk* 27-2 Hap 20-3

TB229 39MU 3-1-45 82MU 10-2 *Fort B* 28-2 Hap 20-3

TB230 33MU 31-12 *Emp Stal* 16-2 Hap 20-3

TB231 33MU 4-1-45 82MU 6-2 *W R Gra* 26-2 Hap 20-3

TB233 33MU 4-1-45 82MU 18-2 Hap 27-2

TB234 39MU 3-1-45 *W R Gra* 26-2 Hap 20-3

TB235 33MU 31-12-44 82MU 12-2 *Emp Stal* 12-2 Hap 20-3

TB236 39MU 8-1-45 82MU 24-1 *SS274* 19-1 Hap 13-2

TB238 33MU 4-1-45 82MU 12-2 *Fort Yuk* 27-2 Hap 20-3

TB239 33MU 31-12-44 82MU 12-2-45 *Emp Stal* 13-2 Hap 20-3

TB240 39MU 17-1-45 82MU 10-2 *W R Gra* 26-2 Hap 20-3

TB241(HPA 8-1-45 CBAF 22-2 FAAC 2-4-46 recat E SOC 22-7

TB242 33MU 31-12-44 *W R Gra* 26-2-45 Hap 20-3

TB243 39MU 18-12-44 *SS276* 25-1-45 Hap 13-2

TB249 33MU 31-12-44 82MU 25-1-45 *SS273* 26-1 Hap 13-2

TB251 39MU 3-1-45 *W R Gra* 26-2 Hap 20-3

TB253 39MU 4-1-45 *Fort Mas* 16-2 Hap 20-3

TB393 33MU 28-1-45 *Park Ben* 10-3 Hap Murm 25-4

TB413 CSFD 39MU 2-12-44 82MU 30-12 *SS275* 19-1-45 Hap 21-2

TB414 33MU 5-12-44 82MU 17-1-45 *SS275* 19-1 Hap 13-2

TB415 33MU 1-12-44 *SS276* 20-1-45 Hap 13-2

TB416 39MU 2-12-44 82MU 1-1-45 *SS273* 26-1 Hap 15-2

TB417 39MU 6-12-44 *W R Gra* 26-2-45 Hap 20-3

TB418 33MU 8-12-44 *SS276* 28-1-45 Hap 13-2

TB419 33MU 8-12-44 *SS276* 25-1-45 Hap 13-2

TB420 39MU 4-1-45 82MU 12-2 *Fort Yuk* 27-2 Hap 20-3

TB421 39MU 11-12-44 52MU 12-1-45 *SS274* 19-1 Hap 13-2

TB422 33MU 9-12-44 82MU 20-1-45 *SS276* 25-1-45 Hap 13-2

TB423 33MU 8-1-45 *W R Gra* 26-2 Hap 20-3

TB424 39MU 11-12-44 52MU 3-1-45 *SS275* 19-1 Hap 13-2

TB425 CSFD 39MU 12-12-44 82MU 9-1-45 *SS275* 19-1 Hap 13-2

TB426 CSFD 39MU 18-12-44 52MU 12-1-45 *SS275* 19-1 Hap 13-2

TB427 39MU 31-12-44 82MU 3-2-45 *Fort B* 28-2 Hap 20-3

TB428 CSFD 39MU 30-12-44 82MU 31-1-45 *Fort Yuk* 27-2 Hap 20-3

TB429 39MU 30-12-44 82MU 31-1-45 *Fort Yuk* 27-2 Hap 20-3

TB430 CSFD 39MU 30-12-44 82MU 24-1-45 *SS274* 19-1 Hap 13-2

TB431 33MU 30-12-44 *Emp Stal* 15-2-45 Hap 20-3

TB432 39MU 4-1-45 82MU 3-2 *Fort B* 28-2 Hap 20-3

TB433 39MU 31-12-44 *W R Gra* 26-2-45 Hap 20-3

TB434 33MU 1-1-45 82MU 31-1 *Fort Yuk* 27-2 Hap 20-3

TB435 39MU 4-1-45 82MU 12-2 *Fort Yuk* 27-2 Hap 20-3

TB436 39MU 4-1-45 82MU 3-2 *W R Gra* 26-2 Hap 20-3

TB437 33MU 5-1-45 *Fort Mas* 15-2 Hap 20-3

TB438 33MU 21-1-45 *Emp Stal* 10-2 Hap 20-3

TB439 CSFD 39MU 2-1-45 312S 4-8 Czech AF 30-8

TB440 33MU 20-1-45 *W R Gra* 26-2 Hap 20-3

TB441 33MU 20-1-45 *W R Gra* 26-2 Hap 20-3

TB442 33MU 5-1-45 *W R Gra* 26-2 Hap 20-3

TB443 33MU 7-2-45 *Park Ben* 11-3 Hap Murm 25-4

TB444 33MU 7-2-45 *Park Ben* 30-3 Hap Murm 25-4

TB445 33MU 10-2-45 52MU 1-4 *Fort High* 6-4 Hap Murm 22-5

TB446 33MU 9-2-45 *Park Ben* 30-3 Hap Murm 25-4

TB447 33MU 7-2-45 *Samarit* 6-3 Hap Murm 25-4

TB448 DSFD 39MU 19-2-45 52MU 4-4 *Ad SOc* 30-4 Hap Murm 23-5

TB449 33MU 9-2-45 *Ben H H* 10-3 Hap Murm 25-4

TB450 33MU 9-2-45 *Park Ben* 30-3 Hap Murm 25-4

TB464 33MU 7-2-45 *Samarit* 30-3 Hap Murm 26-4

TB465 33MU 20-2-45 *Samarit* 30-3 Hap Murm 25-4

TB466 DSFD 39MU 19-2-45 *Ad SOc* 30-4 Hap Murm 23-5

TB467 33MU 20-2-45 *Park Ben* 30-3 Hap Murm 25-4

TB468 33MU 9-2-45 *Park Ben* 30-3 Hap Murm 25-4

TB469 33MU 9-2-45 *Ben H H* 23-3 Hap Murm 25-4

TB470 DSFD 39MU 9-2-45 *Ben H H* 17-3 Hap Murm 25-4

TB471 33MU 10-2-45 *Ad SOc* 30-4 Hap Murm 23-5

TB472 33MU 10-2-45 *Emp Prog* 29-4 Hap Murm 22-5

TB473 33MU 20-2-45 82MU 18-3 *Park Ben* 30-3 Hap Murm 25-4

TB474 33MU 20-2-45 82MU 18-3 *Park Ben* 30-3 Hap Murm 25-4

TB477 DSFD 39MU 19-2-45 *Ben H H* 10-3 Hap Murm 25-4

TB479 DSFD 39MU 19-2-45 *Park Ben* 30-3 Hap Murm 25-4

TB482 33MU 20-2-45 *Samarit* 30-3 Hap Murm 25-4

TB483 33MU 20-2-45 *Ben H H* 24-3 Hap Murm 25-4

TB484 39MU 9-2-45 *Park Ben* 30-3 Hap Murm 25-4

TB485 DSFD 39MU 19-2-45 *Samarit* 30-3 Hap Murm 25-4

TB486 33MU 13-2-45 *Ad SOc* 30-4 Hap Murm 23-5

TB487 39MU 20-2-45 82MU 28-3 *Ad SOc* 30-4 Hap Murm 23-5

TB488 DSFD 39MU 21-2-45 *Emp Prow* 29-4 Hap Murm 22-5

TB489 33MU 13-2-45 *Emp Prow* 29-4 Hap Murm 22-5

TB490 DSFD 39MU 25-2-45 *Ben H H* 24-3 Hap Murm 25-4

TB491 39MU 21-1-45 82MU 2-4 *Ad SOc* 20-4 Hap Murm 23-5

TB499 39MU 28-1-45 *Fort Yuk* 27-2 Hap 20-3

TB500 39MU 4-2-45 *Park Ben* 30-3 Hap Murm 25-4

TB503 39MU 21-1-45 82MU 26-2 *Fort B* 28-2 Hap 20-3

TB516 39MU 22-1-45 *Emp Stal* 20-2 Hap 20-3

TB518 33MU 7-3-45 52MU 14-5 *Sannyth* 1-6 Hap Murm 12-6

TB523 33MU 28-1-45 *Ben H H* 17-3 Hap Murm 5-5

TB524 39MU 4-2-45 *Emp Stal* 20-2 Hap 20-3

TB527 33MU 28-1-45 *W R Gra* 26-2 Hap 20-3

TB529 30MU 28-1-45 *Fort B* 27-2 Hap 20-3

TB530 39MU 4-2-45 *Ben H H* 17-3 Hap Murm 25-4

TB531 39MU 13-2-45 ROS 17-3 82MU 19-3 *Samarit* 30-3 Hap Murm 25-4

TB532 HFIX M70 6MU 4-2-45 3501SU 16-3 BH11 3-5 HQ SE Sector Bromley Common SOC 18-4-47

TB533 39MU 10-2-45 *Ben H H* 24-3 Hap Murm 25-4

TB534 33MU 28-1-45 *Samarit* 20-3 Hap Murm 25-4

TB535 39MU 4-2-45 82MU 1-3 *Samarit* 30-3 Hap Murm 25-4

TB536 39MU 28-1-45 *W R Gra* 26-2 Hap 20-3

TB537 HFIX M70 30MU 5-2-45 183S 24-6 234S 23-8 130S 7-2-46 SOC 16-11-47

TB538 39MU 21-1-45 *Fort Yuk* 27-2 Hap 20-3

TB539 HFIX M70 39MU 1-2-45 *Mel Mob* 23-2 MAAF 5-3 137MU conv to LFIX M66 29-1-48 RHAF 27-5

TB540 HFIX M70 30MU 5-2-45 164S 26-6 to 6063M 4SoTT 12-8-46 SOC 27-6-47

TB541 39MU 28-1-45 82MU 2-3 *Ben H H* 24-3 Hap Murm 25-4

TB542 HFIX M70 30MU 5-2-45 alloc USSR Mar '45 164S 21-3-46 to 6061M 4SoTT 12-8

TB543 39MU 9-2-45 *Park Ben* 24-3 Hap Murm 25-4

TB544 HFIX M70 30MU 5-2-45 164S 24-6 to 6062M 4SoTT 12-8-46

TB545 HFIX M70 39MU 14-2-45 MAAF 18-4 93S 137MU con to LFIX M66 29-1-48 RHAF 27-5-48

TB546 HFIXE M70 39MU 11-2-45 MAAF 18-4 SOC 10-6-48

TB547 39MU 28-1-45 *Samarit* 30-3 Ham Murm 25-4

TB548 HFIX M70 30MU 5-2-45 164S 24-6 GACB onto nose when eng started Mid Wallop 29-8-46 recat E SOC 13-11

TB563 33MU 22-1-45 82MU 28-2 *Samarit* 30-3 Hap Murm 25-4

TB564 HFIX M70 6MU 4-2-45 CRD Leavesden 22-6 RDAF as 425 28-10-48

TB565 HFIX M70 30MU 5-2-45 164S 26-6 bou SOC 27-1-47

TB566 33MU 22-1-45 *Emp Stal* 3-3 Hap 20-3

TB567 HFIX M70 30MU 5-2-45 164S 24-6 abs SOC 5-2-47

TB568 HFIX M70 30MU 5-2-45 183S 24-6 234S 9-8 FAAC 12-12 Persh 13-5-47 SAAF 2-6

TB569 HFIX M70 30MU 5-2-45 183S 24-6 234S 26-7 FAAC 4-10 ASTH SAAF 11-12-48

TB570 HFIX M70 6MU 4-2-45 124S 3-3 RDAF as 426 26-10-48

TB571 39MU 10-2-45 *Park Ben* 30-3 Hap Murm 25-4

TB573 33MU 13-2-45 82MU 26-3 *Emp Prow* 29-4 Hap Murm 22-5

TB575 39MU 10-2-45 *Samarit* 30-3 Hap Murm 25-4

TB576 HFIX M70 39MU 14-2-45 164S 26-6 FACB 28-11 recat E SOC 30-11 bboc ASTH 28-12 Persh 10-4-47 SAAF 16-4-47

TB577 HFIX M70 39MU 18-2-45 Persh 5-4 MAAF 18-4 137MU con to LFIX M66 29-1-48 RHAF 27-5

TB579 39MU 28-1-45 *Emp Prow* 29-4 Hap Murm 22-5

TB584 HFIX M70 33MU 10-2-45 183S 24-6 122S 16-8 RDAF as 427 4-11-48 cd Bjerringbro 5-1-49

TB586 HFIX M70 30MU 5-2-45 164S 26-6 abs SOC 15-2-47

TB587 HFIX M70 39MU 14-2-45 164S 26-6 SOC 30-1-47

TB638 39MU 10-2-45 *Ben H H* 17-3 Hap Murm 25-4

TB640 33MU 10-2-45 *Ad S Oc* 30-4 Hap Murm 22-5

TB641 39MU 9-2-45 *Park Ben* 30-3 Hap Murm 25-4

TB642 39MU 10-2-45 *Park Ben* 30-3 Hap Murm 25-4

TB643 33MU 10-2-45 52MU 1-4 *Fort High* 5-5 Hap Murm 22-5

TB644 33MU 9-2-45 82MU 27-3 *Emp Prow* 29-4 Hap Murm 22-5

TB645 33MU 10-2-45 PATP 14-4 *Fort High* 5-5 Hap Murm 22-5

TB646 39MU 10-2-45 *Ben H H* 5-5 Hap Murm 25-4

TB647 33MU 14-2-45 52MU 1-4 *Fort High* 5-5 Hap Murm 22-5

TB648 33MU 9-2-45 *Ben H H* 17-3 Hap Murm 25-4

TB649 33MU 9-2-45 *Samarit* 26-3 Hap Murm 25-4

TB650 39MU 9-2-45 *Park Ben* 30-3 Hap Murm 25-4

TB651 33MU 10-2-45 *Samarit* 30-3 Hap Murm 25-4

TB652 39MU 10-2-45 *Samarit* 30-3 Hap Murm 25-4

TB653 33MU 10-2-45 *Park Ben* 30-3 Hap Murm 25-4

TB654 39MU 16-2-45 *Samarit* 30-3 Hap Murm 25-4

TB655 d39MU 10-2-45 *Samarit* 30-3 Hap Murm 25-4

TB656 33MU 9-2-45 *Ad S Oc* 30-4 Hap Murm 22-5

TB657 33MU 9-2-45 *Park Benjamin* 30-3 Hap Murm 25-4

TB658 39MU 25-2-45 PATP 9-4 *Fort High* 5-5 Hap Murm 22-5

TB659 33MU 10-2-45 *Samarit* 30-3 Hap Murm 25-4

TB674 39MU 13-2-45 *Ben H H* 5-5 Hap Murm 25-4

TB676 33MU 9-2-45 *Samarit* 30-3 Hap Murm 25-4

TB677 39MU 13-2-45 *Park Ben* 30-3 Hap Murm 25-4

TB678 33MU 10-2-45 *Emp Prow* 29-4 Hap Murm 22-5

TB679 82MU 10-2-45 *Ad S Oc* 30-4 Hap Murm 22-5

TB680 39MU 13-2-45 *Park Ben* 30-3 Hap Murm 25-4

TB681 39MU 21-2-45 *Ben H H* 24-3 Hap Murm 25-4

TB682 33MU 10-2-45 82MU 27-3 *Emp Prow* 29-4 Hap Murm 22-5

TB683 33MU 14-2-45 82MU 18-3 *Samarit* 30-3 Hap Murm 25-4

TB684 39MU 27-2-45 82MU 28-3 *Emp Prow* 29-4 Hap Murm 22-5

TB685 39MU 28-2-45 52MU 23-3 *Fort High* 5-5 Hap Murm 22-5

TB686 39MU 27-2-45 52MU 4-4 *Ad S Oc* 30-4 Hap Murm 22-5

TB687 39MU 13-2-45 *Ben H H* 24-3 Hap Murm 25-4

TB688 39MU 21-2-45 52MU 28-3 *Fort High* 5-5 Hap Murm 22-5

TB689 33MU 14-2-45 *Park Ben* 30-3 Hap Murm 25-4

TB690 33MU 13-2-45 52MU 2-4 *Fort High* 14-4 Hap Murm 22-5

TB691 39MU 25-2-45 *Ad S Oc* 30-4 Hap Murm 22-5

TB692 39MU 14-2-45 52MU 7-3 *Samarit* 30-3 Hap Murm 25-4

TB693 33MU 25-3-45 52MU 1-4 *Fort High* 5-5 Hap Murm 22-5

TB694 39MU 20-2-45 *Park Ben* 30-3 Hap Murm 25-4

TB695 39MU 20-2-45 *Samarit* 30-3 Hap Murm 25-4

TB696 39MU 21-2-45 52MU 28-3 *Fort High* 3-5 Hap Murm 22-5

TB697 52MU 3-4-45 *Fort High* 5-5 Hap Murm 22-5

TB698 33MU 11-3-45 52MU 5-5 *Sannyth* 5-5 Hap Murm 12-6

TB699 39MU 21-2-45 82MU 27-3 *Emp Prow* 29-4 Hap Murm 22-5

TB700 33MU 14-2-45 82MU 26-3 *Emp Prow* 29-4 Hap Murm 22-5

TB701 39MU 27-2-45 52MU 23-3 *Fort High* 5-5 Hap Murm 22-5

TB703 39MU 25-2-45 *Ad S OC* 30-4 Hap Murm 22-5

TB704 33MU 27-2-45 *Emp Prow* 29-4 Hap Murm 22-5

TB705 33MU 14-2-45 *Ben H H* 27-3 Hap Murm 25-4

TB706 39MU 27-2-45 52MU 23-3 *Fort High* 7-4 Hap Murm 22-5

TB707 33MU 25-2-45 82MU 7-4 *Emp Prow* 24-4 Hap Murm 22-5

TB708 39MU 27-2-45 52MU 4-4 *Ad S Oc* 20-4 Hap Murm 22-5

TB710 39MU 20-12-44 82MU 21-4 *Ad S Oc* 30-4 Hap Murm 22-5

TB711 33MU 27-2-45 *Ad S Oc* 30-4 Hap Murm 22-5

TB712 39MU 25-2-45 *Emp Prow* 29-4 Hap Murm 22-5

TB717 33MU 27-2-45 *Emp Prow* 29-4 Hap Murm 22-5

TB718 39MU 25-2-45 82MU 27-3 *Emp Prow* 29-4 Hap Murm 22-5

TB736 33MU 27-2-45 *Ad S Oc* 30-4 Hap Murm 22-5

TB740 39MU 21-3-45 *Park Ben* 30-3 Hap Murm 25-4
TB771 33MU 1-2-45 *Ben H H* 27-3 Hap Murm 25-4
TB772 33MU 8-1-45 *W R Gra* 26-2 Hap 20-3
TB773 33MU 17-1-45 *Ben H H* 27-3 Hap Murm 25-4
TB774 33MU 17-1-45 *W R Gra* 26-2 Hap 20-3
TB775 33MU 17-1-45 *Fort Yuk* 27-2 Hap 20-3
TB776 39MU 19-1-45 82MU 31-1 *Fort Yuk* 27-2 Hap 20-3
TB777 33MU 17-1-45 *Samarit* 30-3 Hap Murm 25-4
TB778 39MU 9-1-45 82MU 24-1 *SS274* 27-1 Hap 21-2
TB779 33MU 17-1-45 *Samarit* 30-3 Hap Murm 25-4
TB780 39MU 10-2-45 *Samarit* 22-3 Hap Murm 25-4
TB781 33MU 20-1-45 *Ben H H* 27-3 Hap Murm 25-4
TB782 33MU 19-1-45 *Ben H H* 27-3 Hap Murm 25-4
TB783 33MU 28-2-45 52MU 26-4 *Sannyth* 2-5 Hap Murm 12-6
TB784 33MU 19-1-45 *Samarit* 30-3 Hap Murm 25-4
TB785 33MU 19-1-45 *Park Ben* 23-3 Hap Murm 25-4
TB786 CSFD 39MU 1-2-45 82MU 1-3 *Ben H H* 27-2 Hap Murm 25-4
TB787 33MU 20-1-45 *Ben H H* 27-2 Hap Murm 25-4
TB788 33MU 3-2-45 82MU 28-2 *Fort B* 28-2 Hap 20-3
TB789 33MU 3-2-45 *W R Gra* 26-2 Hap 20-3
TB790 39MU 7-2-45 *Ben H H* 27-2 Hap Murm 25-4
TB791 33MU 1-2-45 *Samarit* 30-3 Hap Murm 25-4
TB792 33MU 5-2-45 *Samarit* 30-13 Hap Murm 25-4
TB793 33MU 9-2-45 *Park Ben* 30-3 Hap Murm 25-4
TB794 33MU 7-2-45 *Ben H H* 27-2 Hap Murm 25-4
TB795 CSFD 39MU 24-2-45 82MU 27-3 *Emp Prow* 29-4 Hap Murm 22-5
TB796 33MU 7-2-45 *Ben H H* 27-2 Hap Murm 25-4
TB797 33MU 13-2-45 *Emp Prow* 29-4 Hap Murm 22-5
TB798 33MU 9-2-45 ROS 19-3 82MU *Ben H H* 20-3 Hap Murm 25-4
TB799 33MU 7-2-45 *Ben H H* 27-3 Hap Murm 25-4
TB800 33MU 18-2-45 52MU 23-3 *Ben H H* 24-3 Hap Murm 25-4
TB801 33MU 10-2-45 82MU 27-3 *Emp Prow* 29-4 Hap Murm 22-5
TB802 33MU 13-2-45 *Park Ben* 24-3 Hap Murm 25-4
TB803 DSFD 39MU 21-2-45 82MU 27-3 *Emp Prow* 29-4 Hap Murm 22-5
TB804 39MU 21-2-45 82MU 23-4 *Ad S Oc* 30-4 Hap Murm 22-5
TB805 DSFD 39MU 25-2-45 52MU 4-4 *Ad S Oc* 21-4 Hap Murm 22-5
TB806 39MU 28-2-45 *Ad S Oc* 30-4 Hap Murm 22-5
TB807 39MU 21-2-45 ROS 2-3 82MU 21-4 *Ad S Oc* 30-4 Hap Murm 22-5
TB808 39MU 21-2-45 82MU 2-5 *Sannyth* 5-5 Hap Murm 12-6
TB824 DSFD 39MU 25-2-45 PATP 14-4 *Fort High* 5-5 Hap Murm 22-5
TB825 DSFD 39MU 25-2-45 PATP 14-4 *Fort High* 5-5 Hap Murm 22-5
TB826 DSFD 39MU 25-2-45 PATP 8-4 *Fort High* 5-5 Hap Murm 22-5
TB827 39MU 28-2-45 *Park Ben* 26-3 Hap Murm 25-4
TB830 39MU 28-2-45 82MU 31-4 *Fort Gra* 21-5 Hap Murm 11-6
TB837 39MU 28-2-45 52MU 25-4 *Sannyth* 2-5 Hap Murm 12-6
TB838 39MU 28-2-45 *Ad S OC* 30-4 Hap Murm 12-6
TB839 39MU 1-3-45 82MU 28-3 *Emp Prow* 29-4 Hap Murm 22-5
TB840 33MU 1-3-45 52MU 28-4 *Sannyth* 5-5 Hap Murm 12-6
TB841 33MU 6-3-45 *Emp Prow* 29-4 Hap Murm 22-5
TB842 39MU 1-3-45 *Emp Prow* 29-4 Hap Murm 22-5
TB843 33MU 5-3-45 *Emp Prow* 29-4 Hap Murm 22-5
TB844 HFIX M70 9MU 27-3-45 441S 28-3 329S 5-4 FAF 24-11
TB845 HFIX M70 9MU 27-3-45 441S 27-3 329S 5-4 FACE 31-7 ROS RDAF 29-9-48 as 427
TB846 HFIX M70 6MU 28-2-45 183S 24-6 FAAC 4-8 ROS 122S 20-9 port u/c clpse on t/o CE Hawk 10-10 SOC
TB847 HFIX M70 9MU 28-2-45 1401Met Flt 2-4 sold VA 28-11-49
TB848 33MU 7-3-45 82MU 22-4 *Fort High* 23-4 Hap Murm 22-5
TB849 33MU 7-3-45 82MU 28-4 *Samhasty* 19-5 Hap Bak 11-6
TB850 33MU 5-3-45 *Ben HH* 20-3 Hap Murm 25-4
TB851 33MU 8-3-45 52MU 23-4 *Sannyth* 5-5 Hap Mol 12-6
TB852 39MU 12-3-45 82MU 22-4 *Fort High* 28-4 Hap Murm 22-5
TB853 33MU 13-3-45 *Emp Prow* 29-4 Hap Murm 22-5
TB854 DSFD 39MU 13-3-45 82MU 21-4 *Ad S Oc* 23-4 Hap Murm 22-5
TB855 39MU 17-3-45 82MU 21-4 *Ad S Oc* 30-4 Hap Murm 22-5
TB856 33MU 16-3-45 82MU 22-4 *Fort High* 28-4 Hap Murm 22-5
TB857 33MU 16-3-45 82MU 7-5 *Fort Gra* 12-5 Hap Murm 11-6
TB909 HFIX M70 33MU 3-3-45 Persh 10-4 MAAF 14-5 IAF 26-6-47 as MM4111 (MM4140)
TB914 HFIX M70 9MU 25-2-45 441S 26-3 329S CE ops 6-4 SOC 19-4
TB918 HFIX M70 6MU 28-2-45 124S CE ops 30-3 RNAF 1946
TB920 HFIX M70 6MU 28-2-45 164S 26-6 to 6144M 3-10-46 RNAF as Instructional A/F
TB924 HFIX M70 6MU 1-3-45 164S 26-6 SOC 30-1-47
TB925 HFIX M70 9MU 28-2-45 164S 28-6 FAAC 14-6-46 recat E 27-6
TB938 CFSD 39MU 2-3-45 82MU 28-3 *Emp Prow* 29-4 Hap Murm 22-5
TB939 CFSD 39MU 24-2-45 82MU 27-3 *Emp Prow* 29-4 Hap Murm 22-5
TB940 33MU 24-2-45 82MU 26-4 *Emp Prow* 29-4 Hap Murm 22-5
TB941 33MU 13-2-45 *Samarit* 28-3 Hap Murm 25-4
TB942 CFSD 39MU 24-2-45 3 *Emp Prow* 29-4 Hap Murm 22-5
TB943 33MU 20-3-45 82MU 28-4 *Samtru* 19-5 Hap Bak 11-6
TB944 33MU 27-2-45 *Emp Prow* 29-4 Hap Murm 22-5
TB945 33MU 24-2-45 52MU 11-4 *Fort High* 6-4 Hap Murm 22-5
TB946 33MU 28-2-45 82MU 27-4 *Fort Gra* 5-5 Hap Murm 11-6
TB947 33MU 24-2-45 52MU 1-4 *Fort High* 7-4 Hap Murm 22-5
TB948 33MU 28-2-45 *Ad S Oc* 30-4 Hap Murm 22-5
TB949 39MU 2-3-45 *Samarit* 26-3 Hap Murm 25-4
TB950 33MU 28-2-45 82MU 26-4 *Fort Gra* 5-5 Hap Murm 11-6
TB951 39MU 2-3-45 52MU 29-4 *Sannyth* 5-5 Hap Molot 12-6
TB952 CSFD 39MU 2-3-45 *Samarit* 26-3 Hap Murm 25-4
TB953 39MU 1-3-45 82MU 28-3 *Emp Prow* 29-4 5-5 Hap Murm 22-5
TB954 CSFD 39MU 5-3-45 PATP 11-4 *Fort High* 5-5 Hap Murm 22-5
TB955 CSFD 39MU 2-3-45 *Samarit* 30-3 Hap Murm 25-4
TB956 33MU 15-3-45 52MU 12-5 *Sannyth* 12-5 Hap Molot 12-6
TB957 CSFD 39MU 5-3-45 *Ad S Oc* 30-4 Hap Murm 22-5
TB958 33MU 10-3-45 82MU 27-3 *Emp Prow* 29-4 Hap Murm 22-5
TB959 CSFD 39MU 5-3-45 52MU 23-4 *Sannyth* 5-5 Hap Mol 12-6
TB971 CSFD 39MU 5-3-45 82MU 27-3 *Emp Prow* 29-4 Hap Murm 22-5
TB972 33MU 8-3-45 52MU 23-4 *Sannyth* 5-5 Hap Mol 12-6
TB973 CSFD 39MU 5-3-45 *Emp Prow* 29-4 Hap Murm 22-5
TB974 39MU 16-4-45 82MU 30-4 *Sannyth* 19-5 Hap Mol 12-6
TB975 33MU 29-3-45 82MU 4-5 *Samtru* 12-5 Hap Bak 11-6
TB976 CSFD 39MU 12-3-45 *Emp Prow* 29-4 Hap Murm 22-5
TB977 33MU 22-3-45 52MU 16-5 *Samtru* 19-5 Hap Bak 11-6
TB978 33MU 15-3-45 82MU 30-4 *Samtru* 14-5 Hap Bak 11-6
TB979 33MU 22-3-45 52MU 15-5 *Samtru* 19-5 Hap Bak 11-6
TB980 33MU 20-3-45 52MU 28-4 *Sannyth* 5-5 Hap Mol 12-6
TB981 HFIX M70 9MU 25-2-45 441S 26-3 329S 5-4 FAF 24-11
TB982 HFIX M70 9MU 27-2-45 441S 27-3 329S 5-4 FAF 24-11
TB983 HFIX M70 33MU 3-3-45 MAAF 30-4 IAF 26-6-47 as MM4078
TB984 HFIX M70 9MU 27-2-45 308S CB ops 20-3 sold H Bath 18-11-49
TB985 HFIX M70 6MU 28-2-45 183S 28-6 122S 16-8 FAAC 27-8 ASTH SAAF 21-7-47
TB986 HFIX M70 6MU 28-2-45 164S 28-6 Persh 6-5-47 SAAF 28-5
TB987 HFIX M70 6MU 28-2-45 164S 26-6 Persh 14-5-47 SAAF 4-8
TB988 HFIX M70 6MU 1-3-45 1401Met Flt 31-3 ASTH 7-2-46 Persh 6-5-47 SAAF 22-5
TB992 HFIX M70 33MU 3-3-45 Persh 12-4 MAAF 28-5 SOC 22-1-46
TB994 HFIX M70 6MU 2-3-45 1401Met Flt 20-9 sold VA 5-12-49

TD155 39MU 7-5-45 82MU 12-5 *Sannyth* 26-5 Hap Mol 12-6
TD175 39MU 17-3-45 82MU 21-4 *Ad S Oc* 30-4 Hap Murm 22-5
TD178 39MU 16-3-45 *Ad S Oc* 30-4 Hap Murm 22-5
TD179 33MU 21-3-45 82MU 30-4 *Samtru* 19-5 Hap Bak 11-6
TD180 33MU 20-3-45 52MU 5-5 *Sannyth* 26-5 Hap Mol 12-6
TD181 33MU 20-3-45 82MU 30-4 *Samtru* 19-5 Hap Bak 11-6
TD182 33MU 20-3-45 82MU 28-4 *Fort Gra* 12-5 Hap Murm 22-5
TD183 33MU 22-3-45 82MU 2-5 *Samtru* 19-5 Hap Bak 11-6
TD192 39MU 24-3-45 82MU 21-4 *Ad S Oc* 28-4 Hap Murm 22-5
TD193 39MU 23-3-45 82MU 21-4 *Ad S Oc* 30-4 Hap Murm 22-5
TD194 33MU 26-3-45 82MU 2-5 *Sannyth* 19-5 Hap Mol 12-6
TD195 33MU 24-3-45 82MU 31-4 *Fort Gr* 19-5 Hap Murm 22-5
TD196 39MU 24-3-45 *Ad S Oc* 30-4 Hap Murm 22-5
TD197 39MU 29-3-45 82MU 22-4 *Fort High* 28-4 Hap Murm 22-5
TD198 33MU 26-3-45 52MU 12-5 *Sannyth* 12-5 Hap Mol 12-6
TD199 33MU 29-3-45 82MU 2-5 *Samtru* 19-5 Hap Bak 11-6
TD200 33MU 29-3-45 52MU 14-5 *Sannyth* 19-5 Hap Mol 12-6
TD201 39MU 30-3-45 82MU 26-4 *Fort Gra* 12-5 Hap Murm 22-5
TD202 39MU 30-3-45 82MU 28-5 *J JMcGr* 27-11 FAF Sai 27-11
TD203 39MU 31-3-45 82MU 26-4 *Fort Graham* 5-5 Hap Murm 11-6
TD204 39MU 30-3-45 82MU 22-5 *Sannyth* 26-5 Hap Mol 12-6
TD205 HFIX M70 33MU 29-3-45 14-1Met Flt 2-8 412RSU 13-12 sold H Bath 27-10-49
TD206 HFIX M70 33MU 29-3-45 14-1Met Flt 3-8 FAAC 28-10 412RSU
TD207 33MU 4-4-45 82MU 4-5 *Fort Gra* 19-5 Hap Murm 11-6
TD208 33MU 4-4-45 52MU 2-5 *Sannyth* 5-5 Hap Mol 12-6
TD209 33MU 4-4-45 52MU 11-5 *Sannyth* 12-5 Hap Mol 12-6
TD210 33MU 4-4-45 52MU 11-5 *Sannyth* 12-5 Hap Mol 12-6
TD211 33MU 4-4-45 52MU 23-5 *Samtra* 19-5 Hap Bak 11-6
TD212 39MU 11-4-45 82MU 26-4 *Fort Gra* 19-5 Hap Murm 11-6
TD213 39MU 11-4-45 82MU 24-4 *Ad S Oc* 19-5 Hap Murm 22-5 SAAF W5581 extant Johannesburg 1971
TD287 33MU 22-3-45 82MU 30-4 *Samtru* 19-5 Hap Bak 11-6
TD290 33MU 23-3-45 82MU 31-4 *Fort Gra* 19-5 Hap Murm 11-6
TD291 39MU 24-3-45 82MU 31-4 *Fort Gra* 19-5 Hap Murm 11-6
TD292 39MU 21-3-45 52MU 28-4 *Sannyth* 5-5 Hap Mol 12-6
TD294 39MU 23-3-45 52MU 29-4 *Sannyth* 5-5 Hap Mol 12-6
TD295 39MU 21-3-45 52MU 29-4 *Sannyth* 5-5 Hap Mol 12-6
TD296 39MU 26-3-45 82MU 22-4 *Fort High* 28-4 Hap Murm 22-5
TD297 39MU 26-3-45 82MU 22-4 *Fort High* 28-4 Hap Murm 22-5
TD298 33MU 20-3-45 82MU 31-4 *Samtru* 19-5 Hap Bak 11-6
TD299 39MU 23-3-45 82MU 21-4 *Ad S Oc* 22-4 Hap Murm 22-5
TD300 39MU 23-3-45 82MU 22-4 *Fort High* 25-4 Hap Murm 22-5
TD301 33MU 23-3-45 82MU 31-4 *Fort Gra* 19-5 Hap Murm 11-6
TD302 39MU 23-3-45 82MU 31-4 *Fort Gra* 19-5 Hap Murm 11-6
TD303 33MU 22-3-45 82MU 18-5 *Fort Gra* 19-5 Hap Murm 11-6
TD304 33MU 22-3-45 82MU 18-5 *Fort Gra* 19-5 Hap Murm 11-6
TD305 HFIX M70 39MU 31-3-45 234S 27-8 130S 7-2-46 to 6158M 12SoTT 18-10-46
TD306 39MU 26-3-45 82MU 22-4 *Fort High* 26-4 Hap Murm 23-5
TD307 39MU 24-3-45 82MU 23-4 *Fort Gra* 5-5 Hap Murm 11-6
TD308 39MU 26-3-45 82MU 23-4 *Fort Gra* 5-5 Hap Murm 11-6
TD309 39MU 24-3-45 82MU 22-4 *Fort High* 25-4 Hap Murm 22-5
TD310 HFIX M70 6MU 27-3-45 183S 24-6 234S 8-8 SAAF 23-2-49
TD311 39MU 27-3-45 82MU 21-4 *Ad S Oc* 28-4 Hap Murm 23-5
TD312 33MU 29-3-45 52MU 15-5 *Samtru* 19-5 Hap Bak 4-6
TD313 HFIX M70 33MU 30-3-45 695S 2-8 631S hit hedge on t/o cd nr Aberporth CE 14-9 SOC 27-9
TD314 HFIX M70 33MU 30-3-45 183S 24-6 234S 26-7 SAAF 12-5-48. Extant Ontario, Canada.
TD315 HFIX M70 39MU 29-3-45 183S 24-6 234S 26-7 SAAF 11-8-48
TD352 HFIX M70 39MU 29-3-45 234S 8-8 SAAF 10-3-49
TD353 HFIX M70 39MU 29-3-45 234S 8-8 ROS VA 13-S 28-3-46 Persh 13-5-47 SAAF 5-6
TD354 39MU 9-4-45 82MU 26-4 *Fort Gra* 5-5 Hap Murm 11-6
TD355 HFIX M70 39MU 29-3-45 Persh 23-10-47 RDAF as 428 23-10
TD356 HFIX M70 39MU 30-3-45 Persh 23-10-47 RDAF as 429 23-10
TD357 39MU 13-4-45 52MU 28-4 *Sannyth* 5-5 Hap Mol 12-6

TD358 HFIX M70 39MU 29-3-45 164S 26-6 to 6145M RNAF Langham 3-10-46 as instructional A/F

TD359 HFIX M70 39MU 31-3-45 183S 24-6 234S 9-8 FAAC 13-9 ROS 122S 25-10 attempt f/ld u/s hit obst Wick CE 1-11 SOC

TD360 39MU 30-3-45 82MU 30-4 *Samtru* 19-5 Hap Bak 11-6

TD361 HFIX M70 39MU 31-3-45 234S 20-8 130S 7-2-46 bou SOC 12-2-47

TD362 HFIX M70 6MU 5-4-45 287S 6-7 RDAF as 430 22-9-48

TD363 HFIX M70 33MU 5-4-45 164S 24-6 dvdi/grd from H/A nr Newm Suffolk CE pilot kld 10-7-46 SOC 25-7

TD364 33MU 16-4-45 82MU 25-5 *J J McG* 9-6 FAF Sai 3-1-46 GC 1/7

TD365 33MU 10-4-45 82MU 22-5 *Sannyth* 16-5 Hap Mol 12-6

TD366 HFIX M70 33MU 30-3-45 CRD Farn 25-7 anti-G trls 10-1-46 flew round trip in connection with anti-G trls to Buckeburg-Hamburg-Schlesweig-Lubeck-Celle-Fassburg-Celle-Buckeburg. Returned Farn 19-1 FAAC 28-7-46 recat E Oct '46 instrument representation. March '48 R-RH RAF Buckeburg 9-9

TD367 HFIX M70 39MU 31-3-45 RDAF as 431 29-9-48

TD368 39MU 9-4-45 82MU 22-4 *Fort Gr* 5-5 Hap Murm 11-6

TD370 HFIX M70 6MU 5-4-45 595S 11-7 13-S 16-5-46 abs SOC 5-2-47

TD371 33MU 10-4-45 82MU 24-5 *Sannyth 26-5* Hap Mol 12-6

TD373 33MU 14-4-45 82MU 22-5 Hap Mol 12-6

TD374 33MU 11-4-45 52MU 22-5 *Samtru* 26-5 Hap Bak 11-6

TD378 39MU 23-4-45 52MU 24-5 *Sannyth* 27-10 FAF Sai 3-1-46

TD379 39MU 21-4-45 82MU 24-5 *Sannyth* 26-5 Hap Mol 12-6

TD395 33MU 24-4-45 82MU 25-5 *Sannyth* 26-5 Hap Mol 12-6

TD396 39MU 1-5-45 82MU 29-5 *J J McG* 27-11 FAF Sai 3-1-46 GC 3/2 des 31-10-47

TD397 33MU 2-5-45 82MU 25-5 *J J McG* 27-11 FAF Sai 3-1-46 GC 3/2

TD398 39MU 27-4-45 52MU 1-6 *SAmsylv* 28-11 FAF Sai 3-1-46

TD399 33MU 25-5-45 82MU 2-6 *J J McG* 27-11 FAF Sai 3-1-46

TD952 33MU 22-3-45 52MU 11-5 *Sannyth* 12-5 Hap Mol 12-6

TD953 33MU 20-3-45 52MU 14-5 *Sannyth* 19-5 Hap Mol 12-6

TD954 39MU 31-3-45 82MU 26-5 *J J McG* 27-11 FAF Sai 3-1-46 GC2/7

TD955 33MU 20-3-45 82MU 26-4 *Fort Gra* 5-5 Hap Murm 11-6

TD956 39MU 21-3-45 52MU 4-4 *Fort High* 14-4 Hap Murm 22-5

TD957 39MU 23-3-45 82MU 21-4 *Ad S Oc* 28-4 Hap Murm 22-5

TD958 33MU 26-3-45 82MU 4-5 *Samtru* 19-5 Hap Bak 11-6

TD970 39MU 4-4-45 82MU 24-5 *Samtru* 21-5 Hap Bak 11-6

TD971 39MU 4-4-45 82MU 30-4 *Samtru* 19-5 Hap Bak 11-6

TD972 33MU 26-3-45 52MU 5-5 *Sannyth* 5-5 Hap Mol 12-6

TD973 33MU 26-3-45 52MU 11-5 *Sannyth* 12-5 Hap Mol 12-6

TD974 33MU 29-3-45 52MU 2-5 *Sannyth* 5-5 Hap Mol 12-6

TD975 39MU 4-4-45 82MU 19-5 *Fort Gr* 19-5 Hap Murm 11-6

TD976 33MU 4-4-45 82MU 18-5 *Fort Gr* 19-5 Hap Murm 11-6

TD977 39MU 4-4-45 82MU 31-4 *Sannyth* 17-5 Hap Murm 11-6

TD978 39MU 4-4-45 82MU 31-4 *Fort Gra* 18-5 Hap Murm 11-6

TD979 39MU 4-4-45 52MU 2-5 *Sannyth* 5-5 Hap Mol 12-6

TD980 33MU 21-4-45 82MU 23-5 *Sannyth* 26-5 Hap Mol 12-6

TD981 39MU 4-4-45 82MU 25-5 *J J McG* 9-6 FAF Sai 3-1-46 GC1/2 des 18-3-47

TD982 39MU 16-4-45 52MU 29-4 *Sannyth* 5-5 Hap Mol 12-6

TD983 39MU 4-4-45 52MU 11-5 *Sannyth* 12-5 Hap Mol 12-6

TD984 CSFD 39MU 2-5-45 82MU 15-6 *Diomed* 8-12 FAF Sai 19-1-46 GC1/2

TD985 33MU 5-4-45 82MU 15-6 *Samsylv* 28-11 FAF Sai 31-1-46 GC3/2

TD986 33MU 12-4-45 82MU 25-5 *J J McG* 27-11 FAF Sai 3-1-46 GC1/2

TD987 33MU 12-4-45 82MU 22-5 *Sannyth* 26-5 Hap Murm 12-6

TD988 39MU 13-4-45 82MU 27-4 *Fort Gra* 12-5 Hap Murm 11-6

TD989 39MU 16-4-45 52MU 2-5 *Sannyth* 5-5 Hap Mol 12-6

TD990 39MU 19-4-45 82MU 23-5 *Samtru* 26-5 Hap Bak 11-6

TD991 CSFD 39MU 30-4-45 82MU 28-5 *J J McG* 27-11 FAF Sai 3-1-46 GC1/7

TD992 CSFD 39MU 7-4-45 52MU 22-5 *Samtru* 26-5 Hap Bak 11-6

TD993 39MU 1-5-45 82MU 23-5 *Sannyth* 26-5 Hap Mol 12-6

TD994 33MU 24-4-45 82MU 2-6 *Diomed* 8-12 FAF Sai 19-1-46

TD995 33MU 23-4-45 82MU 24-5 *Samtru* 26-5 Hap Bak 11-6

TD996 33MU 23-4-45 82MU 2-6 *J J McG* 27-11 FAF Sai 3-1-46 GC1/2 des 12-2-47

TD997 33MU 27-4-45 52MU 1-6-45 *Samsylv* 28-11 FAF Sai 3-1-46

TD998 33MU 27-4-45 82MU 2-6 *J J McG* 27-11 FAF Sai 3-1-46 GC2/7 des 26-10-47

TD999 33MU 25-4-45 52MU 23-5 *Samtru* 26-5 Hap Bak 11-6

TE115 39MU 9-4-45 82MU 22-4 *Fort High* 28-4 Hap Murm 22-5

TE117 HFIX M7- 33MU 5-4-45 234S 2-8 130S 7-2-46 abs SOC 5-2-47

TE118 33MU 12-4-45 82MU 25-5 *Samtru* 26-5 Hap Bak 11-6

TE121 33MU 11a-4-45 82MU 2-6 *J J McG* 27-11 FAF Sai 3-1-46 GC1/4 des 10-11-47

TE122 33MU 14-4-45 82MU 24-5 *Samtru* 26-5 Hap Bak 11-6

TE123 33MU 16-4-45 82MU 29-5 *Samsylv* 28-11 FAF Sai 8-1-46 GC2/7

TE124 33MU 16-4-45 82MU 2-6 *Diomed* 8-12 FAF Sai 19-1-46 GC1/2 des Hanoi 12-2-47

TE125 39MU 17-4-45 82MU 22-5 *Samtru* 26-5 Hap Bak 11-6

TE126 39MU 19-4-45 52MU 22-5 *Samtru* 26-5 Hap Bak 11-6

TE127 39MU 19-4-45 52MU 22-5 *Samtru* 26-5 Hap Bak 11-6

TE128 39MU 21-4-45 52MU 22-5 *Samtru* 26-5 Hap Bak 11-6

TE129 DSFD 33MU 29-4-45 82MU 22-5 *Sannyth* Hap Mol 12-6

TE130 39MU 28-4-45 82MU 24-5-45 *Samtru* 26-5 Hap Bak 11-6

TE131 39MU 28-4-45 52MU 22-5 *Samtru* 26-5 Hap Bak 11-6

TE132 39MU 23-4-45 52MU 22-5 *Samtru* 22-5 Hap Bak 11-6

TE133 39MU 21-4-45 82MU 24-5 *Sannyth* 26-5 Hap Mol 12-6

TE134 33MU 23-4-45 82MU 23-4 *Sannyth* 26-5 Hap Mol 12-6

TE135 39MU 21-4-45 52MU 22-5 *Samtru* 26-5 Hap Bak 11-6

TE136 33MU 23-4-45 82MU 25-5 *Samtru* 26-5 Hap Bak 11-6

TE137 DSFD 39MU 27-4-45 82MU 24-5 *Fort Gra* Hap Murm 11-6

TE138 33MU 24-4-45 52MU 24-5 *Samsylv* 28-11 FAF Saigon 3-1-46

TE139 33MU 24-5-45 82MU 24-5 *Sannyth* 26-5 Hap Mol 12-6

TE140 DSFD 39MU 27-4-45 52MU 24-5 *Samsylv* 28-11 FAF Sai 3-1-46

TE141 DSFD 39MU 27-4-45 52MU 24-5 *Samsylv* 28-11 FAF Sai 3-1-46

TE142 DSFD 39MU 30-4-45 82MU 22-5 *Sannyth* 26-5 Hap Mol 12-6

TE143 DSFD 39MU 30-4-45 82MU 25-5 *J J McG* 27-11 FAF Sai 3-1-46

TE144 DSFD 39MU 30-4-45 82MU 25-5 *J J McG* 27-11 FAF Sai 3-1-46

TE145 39MU 1-5-45 82MU 6-6 *Sansylv* 28-11 FAF Sai 3-1-46 GC1/2

TE146 39MU 1-5-45 82MU 25-5 *Samtru* 26-5 Hap Bak 11-6

TE147 DSFD 39MU 30-4-45 82MU 28-5 *J J McG* 27-11 FAF Sai 3-1-46 GC3/2 des 6-1-47

TE148 DSFD 39MU 30-4-45 82MU 28-5 *J J McG* 27-11 FAF Sai 3-1-46 GC1/2 des 3-1-47

TE149 39MU 1-5-45 82MU 28-5 *Sansylv* 28-11 FAF Sai 3-1-46 GC2/7

TE150 39MU 1-5-45 82MU 24-5 *Samtru* 26-5 Hap Bak 11-6

TE151 39MU 7-5-45 52MU 23-5 *Samtru* 26-5 Hap Bak 11-6

TE152 33MU 7-5-45 52MU 23-5 *Samtru* 26-5 Hap Bak 11-6

TE153 39MU 28-5-45 88GSU 20-9 sold Turk 24-3-47

TE154 39MU 1-5-45 82MU 25-5 *Sannyth* 26-5-45 Hap Mol 12-6

TE155 33MU 23-5-45 82MU 9-6 *Sansylv* 28-11 FAF Sai 3-1-46 GC1/4

TE156 33MU 3-5-45 82MU 29-5 *Sansylv* 28-11 FAF Sai 3-1-46 GC1/2

TE157 33MU 7-5-45 82MU 24-5 *Sannyth* 26-5 Hap Mol 12-6

TE158 33MU 23-5-45 82MU 6-6 *J J McG* 27-11 FAF Sai 3-1-46 GC3/2 des 16-3-47

TE197 HFIX M70 39MU 16-5-45 122S 29-8 RDAF as 432 31-5-48

TE205 HFIX M70 33MU 15-5-45 Persh 29-7-47 SAAF 26-8-47

TE211 HFIX M70 33MU 23-5-45 122S 16-0-45 SAAF 16-5-47

TE212 HFIX M70 33MU 23-5-45 Persh 1-7-47 SAAF 4-7

TE213 HFIX M70 33MU 23-5-45 Persh 1-7-47 SAA 4-7 extant as 5518, SAAF Museum, Lanseria.

TE216 HFIXE M70 tear drop canopy 39MU 18-5-4 234S 12-10 130S 7-2-46 6MU 17-10 SAAF 22-8-47

TE230 HFIX M70 39MU 18-5-45 234S 12-10 130S 7 2-46 Persh 6-5-47 SAAF 27-8

TE231 HFIX M70 39MU 17-5-45 122S 30-8 RDA as 433 31-5-48

TE232 HFIX M70 39MU 16-5-45 122S 30-8 SAA 12-8-47

TE233 HFIX M70 39MU 16-5-45 122S 11-8 FAAC 6 9 ROS RDAF as 434 28-5-48

TE234 HFIX M70 39MU 17-5-45 122S 29-8 41S 11-4 46 SAAF 22-5-47

TE236 HFIX M70 39MU 17-5-45 122S 11-8 RDA as 435 31-3-48

TE238 HFIX M70 39MU 18-5-45 122S 9-3-46 SAA 25-9-47

TE289 HFIX M70 33MU 29-5-45 Persh 28-7-4 SAAF 21-8-47

TE290 HFIX M70 39MU 8-6-45 122S 10-9 SAAF 22 8-47

TE292 HFIX M70 39MU 1-6-45 122S 3-10 SAAF 23 8-49

TE293 HFIX M70 39MU 4-6-45 Persh 28-7-47 SAAF 21-8

TE294 HFIX M70 39MU 7-6-45 122S 10-4 FAAC 24 9 ROS SAAF 7-8-47

TE295 HFIX M70 33MU 31-5-45 234S 30-9 130S 7-2 46 sold Int All 29-8-50

TE296 HFIX M70 33MU 31-5-45 122S 16-9 RDAF as 436 31-5-48

TE297 HFIX M70 39MU 1-6-45 SAAF 20-4-49

TE298 HFIX M70 33MU 28-5-45 Persh 2-7-47 SAAF 7-8-47

TE299 HFIX M70 39MU 12-6-45 122S 4-10 13Go Com S 31-1-46 bou SOC 29-1-47

TE301 HFIX M70 33MU 4-6-45 Persh 28-7-47 SAAF 9-10

TE303 HFIX M70 39MU 1-6-45 SAAF 25-5-49

TE304 HFIX M70 33MU 1-6-45 GAAC 16-3-47 recat E SOC 31-7

TE305 HFIX M70 33MU 31-5-45 122S 17-9 SAAF 31-7-47

TE306 HFIX M70 39MU 12-6-45 122S 30-8 13Gp Com S 31-1-46 SAAF 17-7-47

TE307 HFIX M70 33MU 31-5-45 SAAF 23-6-48

TE308 HFIXC M70 no early record sold VA 19-7-50 con to Type 509 two seat train G-AWGB 1AC as 163 30-7-51 WOC 1961 BoB film with rear cockpit removed 1974 To CF-RAF, N92477. Extant Aspen, Colorado as N308WK.

TE309 HFIX M70 39MU 1-6-45 47MU 28-3-49 SAAF 12-10-49

TE312 HFIX M70 33MU 1-6-45 47MU 30-6-48 SAAF 27-10

TE313 HFIX M70 33MU 1-6-45 47MU 28-6-48 SAAF 24-11

TE315 HFIX M70 33MU 2-6-45 Persh 10-11-47 SAAF 11-12

TE329 HFIX M70 33MU 4-6-45 47MU 5-4-48 SAAF 23-6

TE331 HFIX M70 33MU 7-6-45 47MU 5-4-48 SAAF 3-11

TE333 HFIX M70 33MU 4-6-45 47MU 14-4-48 SAAF 23-6

TE336 HFIX M70 33MU 1-6-45 Persh 1-7-47 SAAF 4-7

TE337 HFIX M70 33MU 2-6-45 Persh 11-7-47 SAAF 31-7

TE343 HFIX M70 39MU 1-6-45 47MU 5-4-49 SAAF 8-9

TE493 33MU 27-4-45 82MU 22-5 *Samtru* 26-5 Hap Bak 11-6

TE494 39MU 10-5-45 52MU 1-6 *Sansyl* 28-11 FAF Sai 3-1-46

TE495 CSFD 39MU 30-4-45 82MU 24-5 *Samtru* 26-5 Hap Bak 11-6

TE496 LFIX G61 33MU 2-5-45 82MU 22-5 *Sannyth* 26-5 Hap Mol 12-6

TE497 33MU 4-5-45 82MU 22-5 *Sannyth* 26-5 Hap Bak 11-6

TE498 33MU 4-5-45 52MU 23-5 *Samtru* 26-5 Hap Bak 11-6

TE499 33MU 4-5-45 52MU 23-5 *Samtru* 26-5 Hap Bak 11-6

TE500 39MU 30-4-45 82MU 28-5 *J JMcG* 27-11 FAF Sai 3-1-46 GC3/2

TE501 39MU 30-4-45 82MU 28-5 *J J McG* 27-11 FAF Sai 3-1-46 GC3/2

TE502 39MU 30-4-45 82MU 28-5 *J J McG* 27-11 FAF Sai 3-1-46

TE503 no early record sold Turk 1-10-47

TE504 39MU 30-4-45 82MU 28-5 *J J McG* 27-11 FAF Sai 3-1-46 GC2/7

TE505 39MU 30-4-45 82MU 28-5 *J J McG* 27-11 FAF Sai 3-1-46 GC2/7

TE506 39MU 30-4-45 82MU 28-5 *J J McG* 27-11 FAF Sai 3-1-46 GC1/2

TE507 39MU 30-4-45 82MU 28-5 *J J McG* 27-11 FAF Sai 3-1-46

TE508 39MU 30-5-45 88GSU 20-9 Turk 24-3-47

TE509 39MU 25-5-45 82MU 3-6 *J J McG* 27-11 FAF Sai 8-1-46 GC3/2 des 22-3-48

TE510 39MU 30-5-45 310S 1-8 Czech AF 30-8-46

TE511 CSFD 39MU 31-5-45 88GFSU 16-9 Turk 10-4-47

TE512 39MU 1-6-45 310S 2-8 Czech AF 3--8-46
TE513 39MU 1-6-45 310S 2-8 Czech AF 9-8
TE514 33MU 12-6-45 76MU 10-10 *Diomed* 8-12 FAF Sai 19-1-46 GC1/3
TE515 33MU 16-6-45 312S 3-8 Czech AF 30-8
TE516 39MU 1-6-45 310S 2-8 Czech AF 9-8 extant
TE517 33MU 2-6-45 313S 25-7 Czech AF 30-8 Israel 2046, to UK G-BIXP later G-CCIX, extant.
TE518 CSFD 8-6-45 312S 3-8 Czech AF 30-8
TE519 33MU 9-6-45 310S 30-7 Czech AF 30-8
TE520 33MU 12-6-45 129S 19-6 BAF 18-8-47 as SM-5 wo 14-2-52
TE521 39MU 15-6-45 310S 2-8 Czech AF 9-8
TE522 33MU 14-6-45 312S 3-8 Czech AF 30-8
TE523 33MU 14-6-45 312S 2-8 Czech AF 30-8
TE524 33MU 16-6-45 312S 2-8 Czech AF 30-8
TE525 33MU 23-5-45 82MU 6-6 *J J Mc G* 27-11 FAF Sai 3-1-46
TE526 33MU 23-5-45 82MU 6-6 *J J Mc G* 27-11 FAF Sai 3-1-46 GC1/2 des 1-3-47
TE527 39MU 8-6-45 310S 1-8 Czech AF 30-8
TE528 DSFD 39MU 17-5-45 52MU 1-6 *Sansyl* 28-11 FAF Sai 3-1-46 GC3/2 des 22-1-47
TE529 DSFD 39MU 17-5-45 52MU 4-6 *Sansyl* 28-11 FAF Sai 3-1-46 GC2/7
TE530 33MU 15-5-45 82MU 6-6 *Samsyl* 28-11 FAF Sai 3-1-46
TE531 39MU 28-5-45 313S 20-7 Czech AF 30-8
TE532 33MU 1-6-45 313S 30-7 Czech AF 30-8
TE533 33MU 15-5-45 82MU 7-6 *Sansyl* 28-11 FAF Sai 3-1-46 GC1/2 FTR 22-3-47
TE534 DSFD 39MU 18-5-45 82MU 2-6 *Sansyl* 28-11 FAF Sai 3-1-46 GC1/3
TE535 DSFD 39MU 17-5-45 82MU 28-5 *J J McG* 27-11 FAF Sai 3-1-46 GC2/7
TE549 DSFD 18-5-45 52MU 4-6 *Sansyl* 28-11 FAF Sai 3-1-46 GC1/7
TE550 33MU 23-5-45 82MU 2-6 *Sansyl* 28-11 FAF Sai 3-1-46 GC1/7
TE551 39MU 7-6-45 310S 1-8 Czech AF 30-8
TE552 33MU 23-5-45 82MU 2-6 *Sansyl* 28-11 FAF Sai 3-1-46 GC3/2
TE553 DSFD 39MU 18-5-45 82MU 3-6 *Sansyl* 28-11 FAF Sai 3-1-46 GC2/7
TE554 33MU 26-5-45 310S 1-8 Czech AF 30-8 Israel AF as 57 7-52 171351 4X-FOG extant Israel airworthy
TE555 33MU 26-6-45 61 OTU 3-9 Czech AF 30-8
TE556 33MU 31-5-45 313S 19-7 Czech AF 30-8
TE557 33MU 31-5-45 313S 19-7 Czech AF 30-8
TE558 33MU 1-6-45 313S 19-7 Czech AF 30-8
TE559 33MU 1-6-45 310S 1-8 Czech AF 30-8
TE560 33MU 31-5-45 310S 30-7 Czech AF 30-8
TE561 33MU 1-6-45 313S 25-7 Czech AF 30-8
TE562 39MU 12-6-45 310S 1-8 Czech AF 30-8
TE563 DSFD 39MU 8-6-45 310S 1-8 Czech AF 30-8
TE564 33MU 7-6-45 313S 26-7 Czech AF 30-8
TE565 LFIXC 33MU 7-6-45 310S 30-7 extant Prague Military Mus Bulgaria
TE566 33MU 15-6-45 312S 3-8 Czech AF 30-8 **IDFAF 2032. To UK and extant as G-BLCK.**

TE567 33MU 25-6-45 310S 1-8 Czech AF 30-8
TE568 39MU 12-6-45 88GSFU 16-9 sold Turk 10-9-47
TE569 39MU 18-6-45 313S 20-7 Czech AF 30-8
TE570 39MU 12-6-45 313S 25-7 Czech AF 30-8
TE571 39MU 12-6-45 310S 2-8 Czech AF 9-8
TE572 39MU 15-6-45 310S 2-8 Czech AF 9-8
TE573 39MU 12-6-45 310S 25-7 Czech AF 30-8
TE574 39MU 22-6-45 313S 19-7 Czech AF 30-8
TE575 DSFD 39MU 20-6-45 312S 1-8 Czech AF 30-8
TE576 33MU 25-6-45 312S 3-8 Czech AF 30-8
TE577 33MU 25-6-45 312S 3-8 Czech 30-8
TE578 33MU 25-6-45 312S 2-8 Czech AF 30-8

OTHER AIR FORCES AND CONVERSIONS. MARK IX.

Belgium Air Force; EN123, MH366, 415, 434, 729, MJ244, 332, 353, 421, 482, 559, 617, 783, MK153, 577, 777, 923, ML423, PL149, 190, 224, 349, PT643, 644, 853, 887, PV189, RK851, TA836, 855 and TE520.

Built as F. Mk. V by Supermarine and converted to Mk. IX standards; AD366, BR581, 589, 592, 594 and 596.

Conversions by Vickers-Armstrongs; EN843, EP499, 615, ER713, ES185, JG722, 739, 936, JK882, LZ816, 893, MA687, 690 and 860.

Czechoslavakian Air Force; MH758, MJ572, 752, MK135, 257, ML119, NH174, PT621, PV205, SL594, 625-635, 648-657, 660, 665, TB439, TE510, 512-513, 515-519, 521-524, 527, 531-532, 551, 554-567, 569-578. Also believed PL250.

French Air Force; BS123, 128-129, 131, 183, 192, 250, 254, 386, 401, 403, EN129, 137, 174, 266, LZ843, 918, MA222, 251, 301, 308-309, 314, 401, 415, 420, 428, 476, 503, 505, 512, 528, 534, 539, 568, 571, 591, 600, 622, 711, 728, 730, 735, 810, 813, 818, 831, 834, 841, 844, 849, MH316, 326, 331, 352-353, 356, 363, 368, 371, 378, 380, 418, 482, 497-498, 545, 666, 671, 717, 732, 829, 840, 894, 936, 988, MJ114, 133, 139, 177, 197-198, 201, 230, 234-235, 241, 283, 285, 298, 341, 345-346, 348, 356, 360, 395, 408, 415-416, 423, 442-443, 456-458, 465, 475, 478, 500, 518, 520, 530, 564, 567, 605, 612, 614, 619, 636, 664, 669, 671, 686, 712, 723, 737, 746, 793, 822, 825, 848, 873, 897, 908, 952, 954, 959-960, 966, 984, 986, 995, MK114-115, 127, 132-133, 140, 151, 183, 196, 204, 234, 259, 266, 287, 292, 294-295, 297, 300, 320, 278, 398, 401, 412, 456, 467, 560, 603, 619, 659, 677, 680, 686, 689-690, 713, 716, 734, 743, 756, 791, 804, 832, 850, 910, 942, 989, ML137, 140, 214, 235, 270-271, 300, 304, 319, 343, 353, 362, 365, 381, 397, 422, NH203, 205, 208, 210, 218, 240, 248-249, 266, 270, 289, 306, 315, 326, 351, 368, 381, 400, 457, 514, 516, 519, 538-539, 551, 572, 579, 585, 593, 602, 607, PK991, 995, PL138, 151-152, 154, 189, 192, 196, 210, 212, 256, 266, 271-274, 286, 314, 319, 379, 390, 402-403, 450, 452, 454, 464, 495, PT359, 365, 367, 376, 401, 422, 454-455, 458, 467, 494, 496, 559, 582, 612, 623, 639, 650, 657, 671, 714, 732, 737-738, 758, 766, 783, 819, 823, 842, 844, 846, 894-895, 899, 905, 907-908, 912, 915, 959, 991, 995, PV127-128, 147, 155, 175, 180, 187, 229, 232, 234, 284, 286, 292, 343, RK853, 906, RR187, 200, SL658-659, TA780, 800, 825, TB844, 981-982, TD202-203, 364, 378, 395-399, 952, 954, 981, 984-986, 991, 994, 996-998, TE121, 123-124, 138, 140-141, 143-145, 147-149, 152, 155-156, 158, 494, 500-502, 504-506, 509-510, 514, 525-526, 528-530, 534-535, 549-550 and 552-553.

Irish Air Corps; MJ627, 772, MK721, ML407, PV202, and TE308.

Italian Air Force; EN144-145, 445, 510, LZ949, 952, 991, MA256, 315, 369, 426, 447, 453, 471, 515, 617-618, 630, 632, 751, MH526, 599, 602, 604, 615, 619, 621, 635, 648, 691, 720, 779, 785, 896, 945, 947, 954, 985, 997, MJ297, 358, 404, 525, 527, 561, 571, 578, 630, 668, 673, 730-731, 778, 829-830, 841, 849, 955, 996, MK154-156, 193-194, 207, 227, 302, 375, 413, 419, 555, 557, 569, 586, 636, 679, 770, 805, 906, 916, ML129, 134, 139, 180, 193, 371, 410, 416, NH182, 184, 242, 247, 297, 307, 319, 426, 431, 468, 590, PL127, 164, 328, 330, 388, 458, PT396, 414, 460, 462, 481, 590, 625, 653, 654, 656, 666-667, 677, 957, 994, PV115, 122, 191, 270, 359, RR191, 204, 235, 239, 251, SM171, 173-174, 441, 445, TB909 and 983.

Maintainance Airframes; BS227(5322M), BS386(6517M), BS449(6035M), BS474(5955M), BS499(5933M), BS513(6043M), LZ919(5952M), LZ921(6012M cancelled), MA299(6039M), MA303(6034M), MA524(6214M), MA742(5968M), MH422(6454M), MH450(6461M), MH478(6383M), MH731(6026M), MJ202(5691M), MJ329(6370M), MJ452(6081M), MJ526(6070M), MJ586(5948M), MJ814(6183M), MJ887(6455M), MK184(5969M), MK210(4988M), MK285(6382M), MK303(6456M), MK356(5690M), MK426(6459M), MK524(6583M), MK572(6379M), MK573(5236M), MK683(6162M), MK788(5685M), MK835(5693M), ML117(5495M), ML171(6236M), ML185(6585M), ML230(5200M), ML311(5689M), ML427(6457M), NH175(5692M), NH343(6384M), PL256(6391M), PL277(6041M), PL371(5751M), PT398(6584M), PT640(5746M), PT753(6140M), PT953(6263M), PV313(6257M), TB540(6060M), TB542(6061M), TB544(6062M), TB920(6144M), TD305(6158M), TD358(6145M), TA796(6945M).

Royal Danish Air Force; BS248, 386, MA803, MH450, MK426, 475, 681, 694, 965, ML345, NH417, 423, 478, 582, 392, PT463, 714, 888, 931, PV296, 303-304, 344, 354, RK889, 911, RR209, 252, TB564, 570, 584, 845, TD355-356, 362, 367, TE197, 231, 233, 236, and 296.

Royal Egyptian Air Force; EN193, 349, 456, 482, MA248, 251, 424, 428, 478, 653, 677, 697, 715, 736, 772, 795, 931, 932, MJ171, 191, 227, 462, 624, 696, 847, MK415, 578, 841, 849, ML116, 292, NH451, PL168, 443, PT705, PV259, and RR195

Royal Hellenic Air Force; BS129, 349, 508, EN143, 286, JL227, LZ839, MA235, 257, 422, 427, 462, 467, 532, 582, 791, 798, 819, MH314, 322, 359, 416, 452, 508, 558, 698, 727, 774, 831, 853, 855, 908, 924, 946, 993, 996, MJ292, 333, 391, 446, 468, 474, 507, 519, 522, 577, 725, 729, 755, 839, 879, 935, MK357, 361, 483, 571, 575, 691, 693, 719, 746, 864, 981, 993, ML124, NH154, 455, PL135, 138, 158, 211, 356, 461, PT369, 427, 492, 604, 617, 647, 660, 835, 877, 898, 939, 943, PV118-119, 301, 324, 356, RK856, RR192, 197, 203, 207, SM125, 172, 175, TA816, 823, 854, 859, 863, TB539, 545 and 577.

Royal Netherlands Air Force; BS147, 409, MH424, 434, 439, 473, 485, 723, 725, MJ143, 152, 271, 361, 469, 479, 536, 580, 614, 642, 714, 828, 893, 953, 957, MK121, 128, 188, 202, 205, 230, 249, 297, 403, 475, 532, 606, 630, 632, 715, 901, 912-913, 923, 959, 961, 998, ML262, 269, NH188, 197, 212, PT873, 986, SL595, TA812, and TB920.

Royal Norwegian Air Force; MH350, MJ409, 418, 633, 792, MK799, 866, 904, 997, NH193, 208, 213, 253, 261, 357, 401, 520, 540, 575, PL185, 255, 327, 463, PT399, 858, 884, 912, 937, 942 and 949.

Russia; MJ188, 242, 249, 335-337, 354, 357, 362, 400, 459, 508, 510, 531, 550, 555, 568, 576, 606-607, 610, 622, 635, 638, 640, 667, 683, 687, 690, 693, 695, 697-698, 716-717, 721, 740, 747, 749-750, 753, 756, 771, 773, 776-777, 781-782, 791, 800, 819, 821, 842, 846, 850, 856, 858, 902, 936-937, 946, 949, 961, MK146, 209, 262, 268, 282, 307, 310, 345, 349, 351-352, 368, 371, 377, 395, 409, 427-428, 442, 446, 450-452, 455, 457, 461, 470, 477, 499, 502, 505-506, 509, 518, 522-523, 525- 527, 533, 548, 550, 554, 556, 584, 613, 615, 617, 626, 641-643, 645-646, 660, 665, 685, 699, 718, 740-741, 748, 779, 781, 785, 789, 792, 802, 828, 847-848, 851, 856-858, 860-861, 865, 884, 887, 891, 894, 900, 903, 908, 911, 925, 942, 945, 952, 954, 956-957, 985, ML114, 121, 127, 155, 188, 190, 203, 229, 237, 256, 291, 297-299, 302, 340, 344, 352, 359, 369, 375, 402, 408, 426, NH149, 156, 177, 185, 187, 192, 192, 202, 216, 234, 237, 264, 291-292, 301, 303, 308, 324, 393-396, 399, 416, 558, PL144, 147-148, 150, 195, 197, 199-200, 205, 208, 270, 285, 329, 331, 335-336, 339, 341, 343, 346, 350, 354, 381-383, 389, 391, 397, 399, 404, 406-407, 425, 428-429, 435, 442, 445-447, 449, 456, 459, 494, 496, 499, PT355-356, 358, 363, 373-374, 380, 400, 404, 406, 408, 418, 425, 428-431, 435, 469, 471, 528, 533, 544, 558, 561, 563-564, 567, 586, 589, 599, 602, 607, 611, 616, 626, 645, 651, 663, 670, 674-675, 678, 682-683, 697, 703, 710-711, 713, 719, 722, 731, 759, 771, 780, 782, 785-786, 794-795, 824-825, 829, 832, 837, 859, 874-875, 878-880, 893, 901, 933, 952, 958, 967, 969-970, 987, 989-990, PV125, 129-133, 135, 150, 158, 174, 178-179, 182-184, 188, 194-196, 198, 200-201, 204, 206-207, 214, 236, 242, 244, 247-252, 254-258, 262, 265-268, 285, 287, 297-298, 309, 317, 319, 322, 326, 341, 345, 348, 350-351, 355, 357-358, RK798-799, 801, 805, 807-808, 813-818, 836, 839-840, 843-845, 847, 852, 854, 858, 863-864, 867, 885, 887, 894, 898-899, 909, 914-915, 919, 923, RR181, 202, 235, 253, SM140, 142, 144-146, 148, 240, 425, 442, 447-463, 508-510, 514, 517, 519, 521-537, 539-548, 563-597, 610-645, 647, 663, 666, 668-669, TA738, 740, 742-745, 747-758, 760-771, 774-778, 793, 797, 799, 801, 804, 810, 814-815, 818-821, 824, 826-828, 830, 832-835, 840, 856, 865, 867-888, 905-910, 912-941, 943-948, 960-999, TB115-129, 133-135, 142-150, 168, 170-187, 189-193, 195-196, 213-231, 233-236, 239-240, 242-243, 249, 251, 253, 393,413-438, 440-450, 464-474, 477, 479, 482-491, 499-500, 503, 516, 518, 523-524, 527, 529-531, 533-536, 538, 541, 543, 547, 563, 566, 571, 573, 575, 579, 638, 640-659, 674, 676-701, 703-708, 710-712, 717-718, 736, 740, 771-808, 825-827, 830, 837-843, 848-857, 938-959, 971-980, TD155, 175, 178-183, 192-201, 203-204, 207-213, 287, 290-292, 294-304, 306-309, 311-312, 354, 357, 360, 365, 368, 371, 373-374, 379, 395, 952-953, 955-957, 970-980, 982-983, 987-990, 992-993, 995, 999, TE115, 118, 122, 125-137, 139, 142, 146, 150-151, 154, 157, 493 and 495-498.

South African Air Force; BR601, BS125, 200, 408, 451, EN182, 314, LZ833, MA229, 477, 563, 587, 592-593, 628, 756, 849, MH332, 355, 373, 380, 444, 603, 606, 663, 674, 692, 694, 777, 830, 832, 851, 869, 871, 875-876, 939, MJ129, 220 224-225, MK675, 843, ML145, 148, 196-197, 243, 246, 255, 259, 356, NH190, 275, 534, 539, 611, PL192, 203, 209, 215, 253, 261, PT434, 472, 601, 614, 619, 672, 781, 787, 905, 910, 941, PV269, RK917, 924, RR232, SM505-506, 520, TA802, 805, 810, 883, TB569, 576, 985-988, TD310, 314-315, 352-353, TE205, 211-213, 215, 230, 232, 234, 238-239, 290, 292-294, 297-298, 301, 303, 305-307, 309, 312-313, 315, 329, 331, 333, 336-337 and 343.

Slave engine: MJ405

Turkish Air Force; JL229, MA255, MH375, 414, MJ147, 313, 344, 369, 386-388, 396, 448, 566-567, 575, 589, 780, 799, 801, 871-872, 883, 888, 894, 963, MK147, 178, 195, 201, 228, 246, 288, 294, 308-309, 317, 347, 517, 534, 559, 564, 583, 628, 663, 678, 688, 726, 733, 747, 754, 786-787, 838, 852, 863, 889, 893, 896, 899, 907, 915, 926, 947-948, 986, 988, 995, ML15, 125-126, 143, 147, 156, 173, 175, 181, 184, 186, 191, 202, 205, 208, 264-266, 268, 273, 293, 313, 320-321, 362, 368, 376, 411, 414, 424, NH155, 158, 179-180, 200, 214, 244, 246, 250, 255, 257, 268, 313, 349, 361, 414, 419, 427, 456-457, 462, 472, 487, 490, 524, 554, 589, 607, PK994, PL124-125, 129, 136, 143, 161, 163, 165, 213, 223, 260, 320, 332, 398, 423, 493, PT402, 405, 413, 415, 525, 537-538, 565, 592, 680, 734, 763, 826, 842-843, 851-852, 883, 938, 947, PV126, 140, 146, 149, 159, 176, 199, 231, 263, 305, 342, RK803, 848, RR182, SL661-662, 664, SM139, TA858, TE153, 503, 508 and 568.

Two-seat Trainers: BS147, MA848, MH415, 432, 434, MJ177, 276, 451, 518, 627, 772, MK172, 196, 298, 715, 721, ML113, 345, 407, 417, PV202 and TE308.

USAAF: EN180, 183-185, 201, 207, 302, 345, 453, 463, 476, 492, JK883, LZ888, MA242, 421, 453, 510, 522, 580, 595, 616, 705, 734, 765, 793, 800, 804, 884, MH477, 483, 562, 611, 615, 618, 651, 655, 675, 701, 04, 710-711, 762, 778, 794-795, 814, 816, 889, 897-898, 902, 912, 930, 988, 997, MJ194, 234, 251, 257, 349, 389, 447, 505, 506, 525, 552, 560, 577, 579, 582, 646, 685, 838, NH182, 184, 317, 319 and 605.

TWO INTO ONE – SECOND ATTEMPT

The reasons behind adaptation of the Mk IX airframe to the two-seat trainer role are many, but with the ending of hostilities a large number of superfluous Spitfires were sitting at MUs awaiting the breaker's yards. The same yardstick could be applied to the Merlin 266 Mk XVI, and with the experience gained with the Mk VIII trainer conversion Vickers arranged to buy back from MAP a number of redundant Spitfires with the aim of refurbishing and converting them to the training configuration.

The Mk VIII G-AIDN was used as a demonstrator and the first customer for the trainer conversions was Holland who ordered three Mk IXs. These were delivered as H-97, H-98 and H-99, ex MK715, BF274 and BS147 respectively, on 23 March 1948. The MkVIII conversion was allotted the Type number 502 and the Mk IX Type 509. The front cockpit was moved forward 13½ inches and the second cockpit was added behind it, slightly raised in order to give the pilot a reasonable view.

Vickers were a little uncertain about the position regarding flying unregistered civil Spitfires and the Registration Board supplied details. (a) Unregistered aircraft could be flown within a radius of ten miles of the parent aerodrome. If flown outside this radius they had to carry the nationality marking followed by a hyphen and digits. (b) The ten mile radius was to be increased. (c) It was advisable to identify all aircraft regardless of the radius limit. (d) For the purpose of carrying out demonstration or other flights with the Mk IX trainer the contractor to apply for Certificate of Registration, airworthiness and a licence to operate the wireless station. A petrol permit to be issued with the C. of A. (e) It was in order to use Vicker's own registration markings when test flying aircraft being prepared for sale to foreign governments, with flights confined to their own aerodromes. (f) Delivery flights of aircraft for foreign governments carrying foreign services markings arranged by the Air Attache of government represented.

Jeffery Quill was again discussing supply of the new mark of trainer with RAF Reserve Command and on 13 April 1949 he wrote to Group Capt. Newbiggin at White Waltham enclosing details of Mk IXs and XVIs at various MUs. No. 33 Lyneham, 33 Mk IX about to be reduced to spare parts. 39 MU Colerne, 16 Mk IX about to be reduced to spares, plus five Mk XVI fully maintained for issue to user units. 6MU Brize Norton, 9 Mk IX fully maintained. 29MU High Ercall, 19 Mk XVI fully maintained.

"All the above aeroplanes are without Mod 963 (the cutaway fuselage and teardrop hood). This is just as well as the Trainer conversion of an aircraft which has this modification would be more difficult and expensive. There are probably some more Mk IXs around somewhere, but as these are supposed to be obsolete 41 Group have no records of them. No doubt you will be able to delay the destruction of these aircraft whilst the question of the Spitfire trainers is under consideration. The fully maintained Mk XVIs are, so I understand, kept as reserve for user units."

Quill demonstrated the Mk VIII Spitfire Trainer to HQ Training Command at Bovingdon aerodrome, where it was also flown by a Wing Cdr McGuire and Sqdn Ldr Hughes, using both cockpits. McGuire told Quill that he had been visited by Captain Newbiggin, who had been emphatic about the necessity for the trainers in Auxiliary squadrons.

The next customer for the T9, as it was now called, was India, who purchased ten bearing the Indian Air Force numbers HS534 to 543. During a visit to IAF Maintenance Depot at Kanpur in July 1949 Quill was told that the IAF understood that 42 Spitfire Mk XVIII had been purchased and that the last four of these were to be converted into trainers by Supermarine at South Marston. This report cannot be confirmed.

It is, however, confirmed that Supermarine did some drawings for the Spitfire XVIII trainer under Type 518.

Quill and P. G. Roberts flew G-ALJM to Denmark and Norway, starting on 12 October 1949, to demonstrate the new trainer. Carrying a 50 gallon drop tank it left Eastleigh on the morning of the 12th and landed at Copenhagen at 13.40, having refuelled at Amsterdam. They flew on to Gotenburg, Sweden, after an attempt to reach Oslo, Norway, on the 16th failed due

Below: All three Dutch two-seaters. Bottom: H-99 carried its former identity, BS147, on the fin.

TE308, HF IXC, M70, was sold to Vickers in July 1950 and converted to T9 trainer standards. Sold to Irish Air Corps as 163 it was used during the 'Battle of Britain' film. Sold to Don Plumb of Windsor, Ontario, Canada, who had the rear cockpit faired over by Field Aviation in 1974. It is now with Bill Greenwood of Aspen, Colorado, as a two-seater.

to bad weather. They reached Oslo on 18 October, arriving back at Eastleigh on the 21st.

Quill wrote a report of his trip and said that as regards Service Aviation in Denmark the situation was very confused — "There are still separate Naval and Army Air Arms, each having its own Headquarters and administration." When Quill was in Denmark in 1946 he reported that all the Service Chiefs admitted the situation to be inefficient and uneconomic. However, the Single Air Service and Command was due to come into being on All Fools Day 1950. Influencing the Command's training policy was not easy. Chipmunks had been ordered for ab-initio training and it was proposed to use Harvards for intermediate, followed by a short period on Spitfire fighters. The next step was a short course on Meteor trainers with completion of training on the Meteor fighter.

It was a complicated training sequence and Quill thought he could persuade the Danish High Command to introduce the two-seat Spitfire immediately after ab-initio for he considered the training of jet fighter pilots lay not in bringing them up to the stage of proficiency to enable them to take off and land safely, but giving them experience of pilot navigation at high altitude and speed, instrument let-down and R/T homing procedure.

He considered it was an ideal situation for introduction of the Spitfire Trainer.

Quill was more optimistic regarding sales of the Spitfire Trainer to Norway. He delivered G-ALJM to the Commanding Officer of Gardemoen Air Base saying — "The standard of Norwegian Service Aviation is such that one can leave an aeroplane with them, invite them to fly it as much as they like, and go away and let them get on without anxiety". Although the visit produced no sales of the aircraft Quill mentioned that whilst talking with a Major Jorgstad of the RNoAF he was asked how many Spitfire Mk IXs Vickers would accept in direct exchange for one Spitfire Trainer.

Quill was asked to produce figures for converting Norwegian Mk IXs to the T9 configuration and he quoted £5,700 (approximately) each. For a large number of conversions the cost per aircraft could be held at £5,200. The Norwegian officials asked if it were possible for Supermarine to grant a licence for the conversions to be carried out in Norway and Quill said he would raise the point on his return to England. He was also asked about the possibility of utilising the Trainer as a target tug. He replied that such an interim conversion would be expensive for all flying controls would have to be removed from the rear cockpit and special storage arrangements made for the tow winch and sleeve targets. Quill promised that although no detailed study had been made of such a conversion Supermarine would be prepared to make a study and forward it without delay.

G-ALJM was then sold to Egypt as 684 arriving at Cairo 17 April 1950 for the Egyptian Air Force.

A final order for six conversions was obtained from Ireland in 1950 and delivered as 158 to 163 of the Irish Air Corps between 31 May and 30 July 1951.

This thus made a total of 20 Mk IX conversions though it could have totalled 36 if orders from Argentina for 10 conversions and Iraq for 6 had not been cancelled. Russia had also shown an interest, even though they had converted some.

"NOBODY'S CHILD"

With its long experience of designing and building float planes it would have come as no surprise if Supermarine had prepared a specification for a Spitfire capable of operating from water, but no such design was proposed by the company and when the idea was promoted in early 1940 both Supermarine and Hawker were asked for suggestions for putting Fighter Command's latest fighters on floats. On 22 April it was realised by all parties that it would not be possible to design and build a set of floats in the short time available and the decision was taken to fit floats originally intended for the Blackburn Roc float plane. Blackburn also elected to design a special pair of floats for the proposed Spitfire which would have a maximum speed of 300mph at 17,500ft, a rate of climb at sea level of 1,100ft/min up to 15,000ft, and 400ft/min at 20,000. Time to 15,000ft was estimated at eleven minutes, service ceiling 23,000ft and auw 6,960lb.

The Air Ministry asked Captain Slattery of the Admiralty if he would sanction release of 50 sets of Roc floats in order that there be no delay in Spitfire conversions should the experiment prove successful. Slattery replied in a positive manner by forwarding them to No 12 MU Kirkbride the following day. In the meantime Hawkers wrote to the Air Ministry on 27 April suggesting that the Osprey float would be a better proposition than the Roc because it was lighter and more suitable for the Spitfire. By now the 'Phoney War' on the Continent had hotted up and the signs were that Germany would not hesitate to protect its supply and sources of iron ore by invading Norway.

N. E. Rowe of MAP wrote to Joseph Smith on 28 April stating that a set of Roc floats was due to arrive at Woolston on the following day. The Air Ministry contacted Gloster Aircraft and requested that the company convert a Gladiator to operate on floats. Glosters were willing to go ahead with the conversion but did point out that the estimated speed would be approximately 228mph at 16,000ft.

Supermarine passed a Mk I Spitfire, R6722, over to Folland Aircraft, together with the Roc floats, and asked them to proceed with the conversion. De Havilland were ordered to supply a two pitch propeller converted for constant speed by 7 May. There was a tremendous flurry of activity with Supermarine, seemingly, to stand aloof. The Air Ministry ordered production of 16 Hurricanes, plus nine reserve aircraft, plus an additional 20 sets of Osprey floats on 20 May, and at the same time informed Supermarine that they were to discontinue work on the Spitfire conversion. Unfortunately, the project had gathered its own momentum for R6722 had been converted by Follands and it arrived at No 12 MU for flotation trials on 3 June. Supermarine received a cancellation of the project on 10 June and at the same time received instructions to complete the aeroplane. The horse had already left the stable and it was a very unstable mount, for when water trials were conducted by No 12 MU they showed that the Spitfire/Roc float combination was totally unsuitable for the job it was to do. R6722 was painted in the normal day fighter camouflage, including the under surface scheme of black and white. The aircraft was never flight tested and after the floats had been removed it was sent back to No 39 MU on 10 May 1941 for conversion to F Mk VA status.

There was an interesting sequel to this saga for RAE Farnborough had been instructed to conduct water tank tests of the Hurricane and Spitfire on Roc floats in June 1940, in particular porpoising and sea-worthiness. The Spitfire performed better than the Hurricane, which suffered from water splashing on flaps and radiator, and the under fuselage received heavy spray.

Despite the apparent fiasco of the Spitfire I (and Hurricane) float variant, known to all and sundry as the 'Narvik Nightmare', the Air Ministry was not deterred in its efforts to obtain a floatplane fighter, for just one year later, on 16 May 1941, Supermarine was awarded a contract for a floatplane development of the F Mk III Spitfire. The project was awarded the highest priority and to speed development Farnborough was again asked to conduct trials in their water tank on models of the Mk III. Initial trials took place in June in the wind tunnel to determine if the large, float carrying strut interfered with air flow to the radiator. These were followed by water tank tests in October that year, but by then the project had been cancelled.

The floats were considered to be not good enough for clean running, but were as good as the average float. They were kept as small as possible to reduce drag and had good porpoising characteristics. It was recommended that the fabric elevators be

General arrangement of the F Mk 1 floatplane conversion with Blackburn floats. It was never flown.

replaced by metal units to prevent damage by spray action. Two designs of floats were tested and our photographs show the model in the Farnborough tank. Four float settings were tested and the conclusions were that sea-worthiness of the final form of floats was inferior to that of the floats tested on the Spitfire Mk I, Hurricane and Barracuda.

It was all disappointing and the Air Ministry, MAP and the Royal Navy decided against further development, calling it "nobody's child'. The Supermarine contract included a proviso whereby – "If the Mk III project failed all design and development costings and effort could be diverted to conversion to the F Mk V airframe". Leading particulars of the Mk III floatplane were – all up weight 7650lb; wing area 243 sq ft; wing incidence to thrust and fuselage datum 2° at root; wing incidence to float datum 5° original, 4° modified. Float – length 24.60ft; forebody length 13.37ft; afterbody 11.23ft. Maximum beam of chines 3ft 4in. Track of floats 10ft 0in.

Supermarine continued to progress with a Spitfire floatplane and in agreement with the Mk III contract proviso submitted a proposal to the Air Ministry on 14 May 1941 for a production version of the F Mk V fighter on floats. Mr P. M. Shervall, of Supermarine, went along to Farnborough on 20 June to witness tank tests of the Type 344 float as designed and built by his company, and at the same time to talk about the Type 355 (Mk V) float. He reported his findings to Joseph Smith.

To test the validity of a production floatplane based upon the Mk V, a Mk VB, W3760, built at Southampton in July 1941, was sent via the DTD to Vickers and from there to Folland Aircraft, at Hamble, for installation of the Supermarine floats. To accomplish this the land undercarriage and retracting mechanism was removed and the float struts attached to a much strengthened wing spar. Additional area was added under the fin to conteract the de-stabilising effect of the floats and also to improve lateral stability, and a larger, redesigned rudder was incorporated.

The Air Ministry was not at all enamoured with the idea of a Mk V floatplane variant and was looking elsewhere. As a result they sent a cypher telegram to the RAF Delegation in Washington on 17 September 1941 – "Admiralty require floatplane fighter for support of opposed landings outside range of shore based fighters until latter can be established at captured aerodrome. Also to assist in defence of fleet anchorage where there is no suitable site for aerodrome. We do not

Studies of the Spitfire Mk III model floatplane under test in the Farnborough water tank reveal the effects of spray on the airframe during various stages of the speed runs.

GA of the proposed F Mk III conversion.

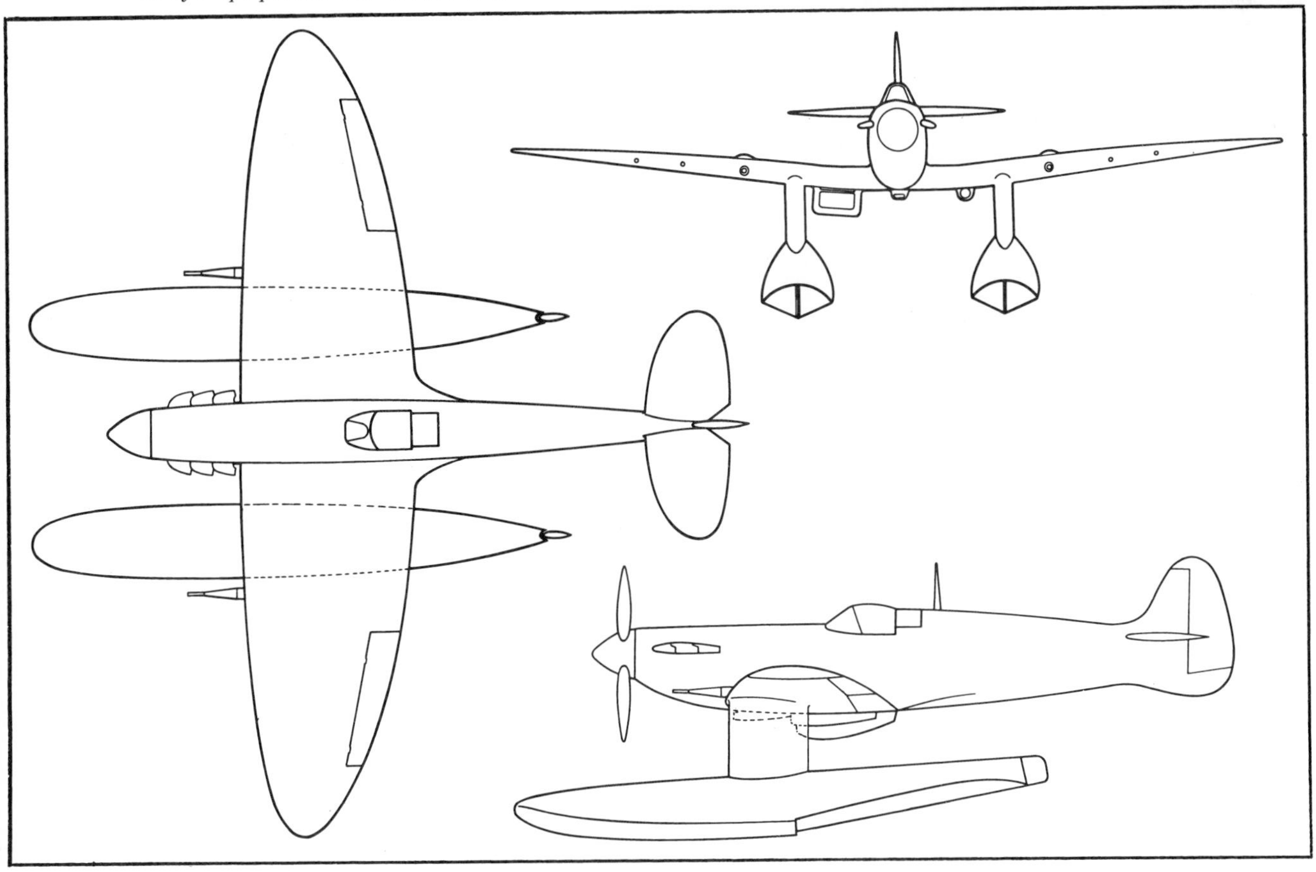

First prototype Mk VB conversion, EP751, at Folland Aircraft, Hamble, Hants, after modification. It had the original fin and rudder but lacked wing fillets. Strengthening strakes and sling points were fitted. A four blade propeller was installed.

deny that such an aircraft might not be of value in special circumstances such as operations against Atlantic Island. Spitfire is the only type which might be developed here. This should be undertaken without serious interference with other development work on this type which it is agreed has the higher priority. We are, therefore, anxious to know if any floatplane is in prospect in America".

The matter was again raised at a meeting held two months later on 7 November, during which it was suggested that the Curtiss Kittyhawk might be a more suitable type for conversion than the Spitfire. The Curtiss Company said they were able to supply a floatplane variant of the Kittyhawk – "If the need for this type justified the cost and delay in production of other types". But, basically, the Americans lacked enthusiasm and were reluctant to convert the Kittyhawk for the same reason the Air Ministry had for converting the Spitfire. Also, there was a heavy demand for the Kittyhawk in the Middle East and Russia, and Curtiss did not want to divert effort.

Supermarine Report 3373 of 1 May 1942 reviewed conversion of W3760 in the following manner – "It is understood that the prototype aeroplane will be a conversion from a standard Mark VB type. The alterations and additions to be carried forward are as follows: (1) addition of floats complete with trunk and mountings (2a) reinforcing of spar to suit (3) addition of front and rear attachment brackets to outer mainplane (3b-f) replacement and addition of ribs 5 to 8 (4c) auxiliary spar replaced by redesigned spar (4d) plating from rib 1 to 8 aft of spar back to auxiliary spar replaced by 14 guage skin (5a) rear spar frame in fuselage replaced by redesigned frame (5c) bottom longeron reinforced (6a) rear fuselage complete with tailwheel to be removed (6b) rear fuselage with added fin surface and no tail wheel (8) Rotol four blade 11ft 3in diameter propeller added (9) tropical air intake fitted (13) compressed air bottles removed to floats (15) tail ballast deleted (16) slinging gear and points added (17) aeroplane to be camouflaged to temperate sea scheme (21) addition of tail anti spin parachute (prototype only)". Two flap positions, 40 and 30°, were recommended.

GA of the Spitfire Mk VB conversions.

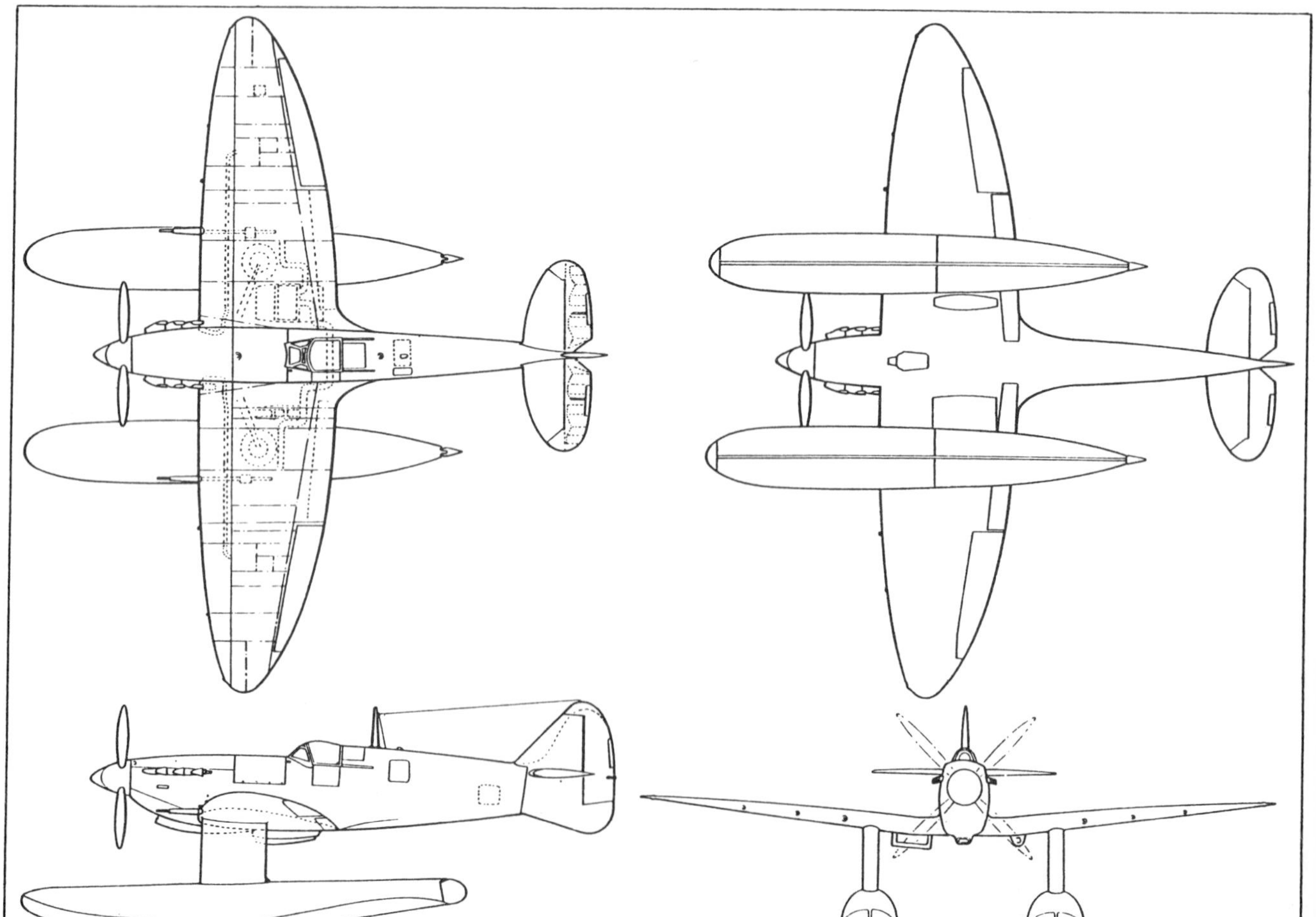

Second conversion of Mk VB was W3760 photographed taxying and at speed. The smooth line of the engine cowling is marred by the tropical filter, added for operations in the Middle East. Large amounts of spray swept the rear fuselage and during trials salt water corrosion was so bad that a new rear fuselage and tail unit had to be fitted.

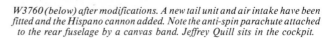

W3760 (below) after modifications. A new tail unit and air intake have been fitted and the Hispano cannon added. Note the anti-spin parachute attached to the rear fuselage by a canvas band. Jeffrey Quill sits in the cockpit.

All up weight for stressing was to be 8125lb. Performance (estimated) – max diving speed 420mph, level speed @ 18,250ft 240mph, stalling flaps up 97mph, down 86. W3760 was ready for trials in September 1942 and was weighed at Hursley Park on 1 October. It had a Merlin 45 engine with fish tail, non-heating exhaust manifolds, a Rotol four blade XH54W RRM H HE propeller of 10ft 9in diameter, a 6½lb inertia weight in the elevator control circuit, standard 'B' wing armament. Tare 5581lb, take-off 7418, landing 6717. An examination of the airframe revealed many faults: the float buffers were badly fitted as were the hand hole covers, the latter being considered to be totally unsuitable for high speed. The plating was highly criticised and in general the airframe was thought to be in poor condition.

Initial flight tests returned a maximum speed of 317mph @ 18,000ft, 253 @ sea level, maximum rate of climb (constant to 14,000ft) 2100ft/min, service ceiling 32,500ft, operational ceiling (500ft/min) 28,700ft. A Rotol XH54D RM SS propeller with cropped blades and a 10ft 9in diameter was installed resulting in an increase in the dorsal and ventral fin area, and the wing radiator had a redesigned entry to lesson water spray ingestion at take-off. The carburetter air intake under the nose was also extended. The Spitfire was delivered to the Marine Aircraft Experimental Establishment at Helensburgh in February 1943 for a series of tests beginning with maintenance, as a result of which the floats were fitted with air operated water rudders connected to the normal landplane braking system. A retractable mooring bollard was also installed.

Considerable trouble was experienced with leaking floats due to the caulking cracking and deflection of the floats during landing and taxying. Their condition was so bad that they were returned to Folland for modifications and repair. The aircraft was returned to Helensburgh for performance and cooling trials in June. Spinning tests in August showed the Spitfire to have similar characteristics to the landplane version at an auw of 7610lb.

Encouraged by those results the Air Ministry ordered two further Mk VB conversions – EP951 and 754, the former having been in store at 33 MU from 22 July. It was delivered to Follands on 4 August and after conversion was weighed at Hamble 16 days later revealing a tare of 5931lb and an auw of 7524.

It then went to No 6 MU on 14 August 1943 for the service equipment to be installed, after which it arrived at MAEE Helensburgh on 27th for trials. Brief performance tests revealed a maximum level speed of 331mph at 14,000ft with the Merlin 46 engine and a Rotol 10ft 9in diameter propeller, four blades, dural. At sea level speed was 281 and it had a maximum rate of climb of 3,050ft/min. EP754 was at 33 MU on 22 July 1942 and transferred to Follands for conversion on 4 August.

All three conversions arrived at No 52 MU on 27 September 1943 for packing and despatch to the Middle East on board *SS Penrith Castle*. The ship left the U.K. on 6 October and arrived at Alexandria, Egypt 24 days later. They were taken on charge at No 107 MU at Kasjareet in November, this unit being formed from 'C' Squadron of the famous No 103 MU based at Aboukir, and erected for service trials. Training was in the hands of Group Captain Wilson MacDonald, commander of the Gunnery School at Ballah at that time.

The float Spitfires were intended to operate against the Junkers Ju 52 tri-motor transports flying from Greece to Crete on refuelling missions. The Spitfires were to also operate in the same area and be supplied by Royal Navy submarines. The total flight would have consisted of a Walrus amphibian, two high speed launches, five pilots and fifteen ground staff. Test pilots included Flt. Lt. R F Martin and Fly. Off. Pugson and training started on the Great Bitter Lake in Egypt and difficulties were immediately encountered. Engine torque was so fierce that the aircraft usually buried one float under the

Third VB conversion was EP754.

water on the take off run, the water rudders being virtually useless. During landing the tail section was submerged towards the end of the run. Corrosion was rife and W3760 had to have a new tail unit sent out from England.

None of the Mk VBs saw operational service for the logistics of supplying the operational team put a strain on the submarine service. By November the aircraft had been returned to Alexandria and to the U.K. by the Summer of 1944, to be struck off charge on 28 December that year. The float Spitfire story did not end with the demise of the VBs for on 21 October 1943 Supermarine were asked by the R.T.O. for their views on the possible adaptation of the existing Type 355 floats to an F Mk VIII Spitfire. The following conclusions from report No. 3966 were in Air Ministry hands by 11 November –
1. Weight. The weight of a Mark VIII Seaplane conversion with existing floats would be approximately 8,600lb with two cannon, four Brownings, 124 gallons fuel and a dural propeller. The reserve buoyancy of the floats at this weight would be 66%. This was low when compared to the VB's 85%. 2. CG position. This would be satisfactory assuming a little re-disposition of equipment. (3) Propeller. It is considered that a propeller 11ft 3in diameter would be required and the tip water clearance would then be approximately 3in less than that of the existing Mk VB conversion with a propeller of the same diameter. (4) Fuel. The fuel carried in the leading edge of the Mk VIII landplane would require to be housed elsewhere. (5) Tail end. It is anticipated that the existing Type 335 unit would be satisfactory from the stability standpoint without alterations, but if necessary the new large rudder could be fitted. The strength is satisfactory. (6) Strength of floats and trunks; no major design modification required but detail stiffening necessary in places. (7) Design work involved. The layout of the Mark VIII wing is different from that of the VB and a certain amount of re-drawing would be required in this connection. With reference to Item 1, since we now have no aeroplane which could be overloaded and tested to this weight, it can only be a matter of conjecture as to whether the degree of sea worthiness and stability obtainable with existing floats at a weight of 8,600lb would meet requirements. In our opinion it is just possible that the existing floats could be over loaded successfully to this extent but we would not care to recommend their use without trial. In other words, *caveat emptor*. All up weight for stressing was estimated at 8125lb; max level speed @ 18,250ft 240mph and stalling speed 97mph, flaps down.

Nothing came of the proposed Mk VIII floatplane possibly because of the interest in the Mk IX conversion. Only one prototype IX was required and an LF IXB, MJ892, was delivered to Rotols, Staverton, on 29 December 1943 and was fully converted by May 1944. This conversion sprang from the Supermarine Specification No 506 for the Type 385. Engine was a Merlin 66, two speed, two stage unit driving a Rotol, dural, four bladed propeller of 11ft 3in diameter. Normal armament was two cannon (120rpg) and four Brownings (350rpg) and a fuel capacity of 84 gals; oil 7½ gals. If the cannon were deleted the fixed fuel capacity could be raised to 139 gals. Cameras for photo-reconnaissance could be accommodated. Wing span was 36ft 10in, area 242sq ft, loading 33.9lb sq ft. Length 35ft 6in. Max height over rudder (tail down on land) 10ft. Max width across floats 14ft 2in. Tare 6,500lb, normal auw 8,200, with 50 gal overload tank 8,610 Max permissible diving speed

The three modified VBs were despatched to the Great Bitter Lakes, Egypt, for service trials.

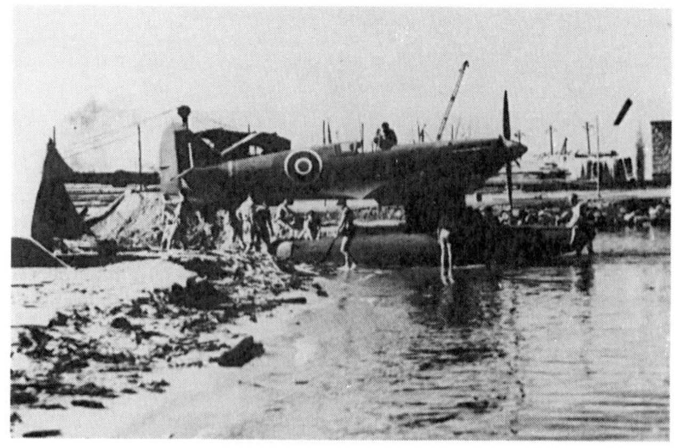

420mph. It was painted normal day fighter camouflage on all upper surfaces and yellow under surfaces on 22 May 1944.

MJ892 was at Beaumaris on 14 June 1944 for weighing and had a tare of 6,488lb and an auw of 8,179. CoG range at normal range was 2.5 to 3.2in. aft of vertical datum. The conversion had been undertaken by Folland Aircraft and it made its first flight from Beaumaris on 6 July with F. C. Furlong at the controls. At full load it was flown to 20,000ft and during level speed runs the oil pressure gauge fell to zero. Furlong returned to base to discover the gauge was faulty and reported that the aircraft was directionally unstable. The following day he did a series of take-offs and landings and reported that after the aircraft had been running on the step preparing to take-off – "A sort of lateral patter starts making the aeroplane waddle from side to side on each float". It was impossible to correct and the aircraft had to be brutally pulled off the water. He ended by saying that if the aeroplane was ever going to be taken seriously something had to be done about the waddle.

During a series of take off runs on 11 July Furlong could not get airborne for on every attempt the engine cut. He then closed the tropical intake shutter and cured the fault as water was getting into the engine. Trials were completed and the

F C Furlong in the prototype F Mk IX floatplane Spitfire, MJ892.

GA of F Mk IX floatplane.

Spitfire handed over to the RAF. It was returned to Folland for repair on 3 August 1945, but these were cancelled , the airframe **recategorised as E2 and struck off charge on 22 November.**

Trials with the Mk IX prototype seem to have rekindled interests in a floatplane Spitfire for a scheme was considered for the production of 12 Mk V conversions for use with a squadron to investigate the development and production of special equipment for the war against Japan. The report was dated 15 February 1944 and Supermarine were asked to submit a proposal. Supermarine wrote that at that time the three modified Mk Vs, together with two reserve sets of floats were still in the Middle East (ostensibly for the defence of the island of Kos) and eight sets of floats were still in the UK. What did the Air Ministry want to do about this situation?

The Air Ministry thought that all work on the proposed twelve floatplanes should be undertaken by Folland Aircraft, who were to convert a further eight Spitfire Mk V fuselages to accept the suplus floats. They would contact the Admiralty.

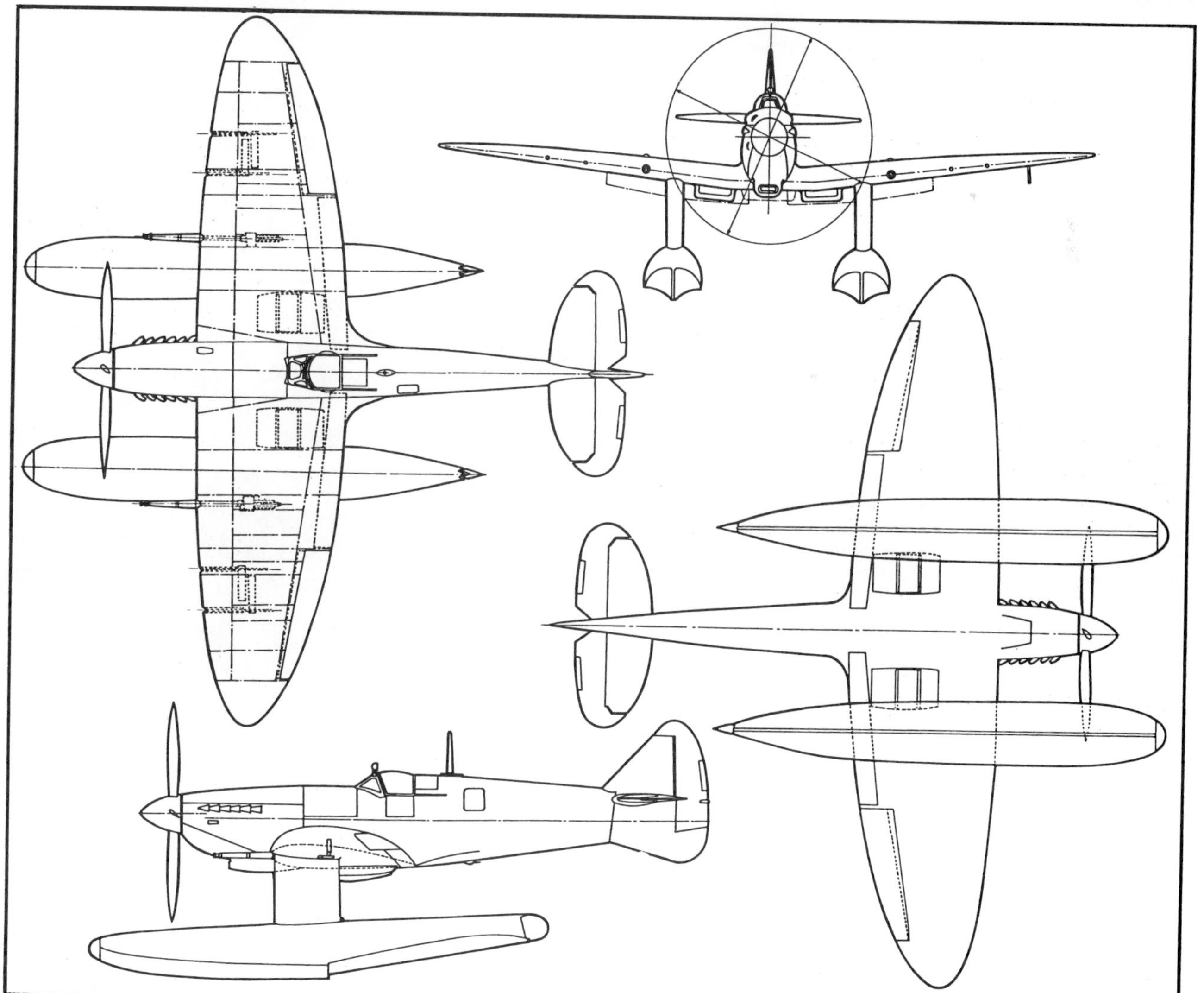

Flying views of MJ892.

MJ892 at Beaumaris.

The following month the Air Ministry reached a decision on the project – "The value of a seaplane fighter must always be limited on account of its inferior performance to the landplane, and it appears doubtful if Spitfire floatplanes would be of great value if operating within range of enemy shore-based fighters. Fitting of floats to a Spitfire involves a major modification involving the use of special jigs. We are, therefore, faced with the alternatives of going ahead with the construction of 12 seaplanes and storing them until required, or abandoning the project altogether. It is recommended that as these seaplanes will never be required, we cut our losses now and drop the project".

When the F 21 Super Spitfire was being issued to the RAF the Air Ministry asked Supermarine to submit a proposal for a float variant, but interest never progressed beyond the specification stage. The following details were applicable to the float F 21 –

Tare weight 7000lb, take off 9950, max permissible 11,415. Four 20mm cannon with 120rpg. Span 35ft 0in, area 210sq ft. Length 35ft 3½in. Height over fin on water 11ft 6in. Service ceiling 34,700ft. Max speed 353mph @ 12,000ft, 382 @ 25,000. Cruise @ 20,000ft 244mph, loiter 203mph. Time to 20,000ft 11min. Stall 85mph. Griffon 61 of 2080hp @ 8000ft, 1820 @ 21,000. Fuel 120 gals. Range 360 miles, with 180 gallon overload tank 912, loiter 1.5 hour, with overload tank 3hr 95min.

Despite the success of the Japanese float planes the Spitfire version was always a proposal, and with the F21 ended all attempts to produce a Spitfire on floats. Apart from design and specifications Supermarine had little to do with it, all the major conversion work being undertaken by Follands.

THE INTER-COOLED TEN

While development history of the Spitfire PR Mk X was uncomplicated the situation regarding its designation was more complex. The Royal Air Force had been operating converted Mk V aircraft and production built PR IVs for a considerable period, and when the Merlin 60 Series engines became available for the Spitfire it was decided to order a high flying PR machine with the inter-cooled Merlin 64. The basic design consisted of the F Mk VII fuselage fitted with PR Mk XI wings with the following modifications incorporated. (1) Armament and some armour plate deleted; (2) Spitfire PR XI production oil tank fitted; (3) PR Type military load; (4) Fuselage frame 5 and fuselage aft of frame 12 as Spitfire Mk XI production; (5) Fuselage frame 12 to special design, this being a pressure bulkhead. Auw 8150lb, maximum level speed at 12,500ft 325mph.

The Air Ministry allocated the designation PR Mk X to the new aeroplane, and at the same time allocated the designation PR Mk XI as the photo-recco version of the F VIII. It was pointed out that the designation PR Mk VIII had been allocated to the Type H PR, a proposed conversion of the Mk VB airframe, and that the next variant of the VB conversion to the PR role was to be called PR IX. There was a change of mind and the PR Mk X variant of the F Mk VII was confirmed and the PR Mk VIII and PR IX were abandoned. Also, the PR XI variant of the F VIII would be abandoned so that the PR Spitfire aircraft were from PR Mk III to VII, PR X. A slight confusion had also arisen about the timing of the PR X for it appeared after the PR XI went into service. This was because the latter was a conversion of the F Mk IX Spitfire, which was available before F VII airframes were ready for conversion to the former. Also, the Fw 190 problem was filling the production and conversion lines with Mk IX variants and a low priority was given to the development of a new PR aeroplane. It was not until May 1944 that the type was introduced into service.

The first PR Mk X (MD192) reached RAF Benson on 4 April 1944, to be followed by the remaining fifteen conversions, all reaching the RAF six weeks after the initial delivery. MD196 went to No 106 Wastage Group before return to Vickers for various trials. The Certificate of Design was issued on 8 May 1944 for the Type 387.

During a test flight with MD196 Quill reported that the aircraft with cabin de-pressurised and metal elevator fitted was pleasant to fly. This was 3 July 1944, and when he took it up again four days later, this time with the cabin pressurised, he noticed that the bulkhead seals caused minor elevator control problems due to friction. Summing up performance he said that the aircraft with metal elevator and no cabin seals was best, metal elevator and cabin seals better than the same situation but with fabric elevators.* The aeroplane was not a great success and after limited service with Nos 541 and 542 (PR) Squadrons, was withdrawn from service in September 1945.

ELEVEN BEFORE TEN

As related the PR Mk XI was originally intended as the photo-recce version of the F VIII, but because of a possible confusion of designations the PR XI finally emerged as a variant of the F Mk IX. No I PRU Benson, home of the photo-reconnaissance aeroplane, wanted a new Spitfire to replace their war-weary Mk V conversions and PR IV production PRs. The PR X was progressing slowly because of non-availability of the F VII airframe and the replacement programme had to be speeded up.

The Supermarine Type Record for the PR XI Type 365 defined the aircraft as: Engine. Merlin 61. Description. The Spitfire PR Mk XI is the Spitfire F Mk IX production with the following modifications: (1) Armament and some armour plating deleted; (2) Spitfire PR Mk IV L.E. fuel tanks fitted; (3) Oil tank of increased capacity fitted; (4) PR Type military load.

EN149 made its first flight on 15 December 1942 as a Mk IX and was immediately transferred to No 1 PRU Benson for conversion to PR XI standards. South Marston fitted the Universal camera installation and it was delivered to No 541 Squadron in October 1943.

No Specification was available and the Strength Requirements were based on the fighter version. Auw 7,800lb, maximum level speed at 9,750ft 330mph.

No I PRU produced fifteen conversions of the F Mk IX, beginning with BS487 in October 1942, the basic conversion being removal of all armament and ancilliaries and installation of cameras in the fuselage. It was not possible for the wing tanks to be installed at Benson as sealing was a major, skilled operation, so plans were made for the converted aircraft to be flown to Heston Aircraft. Thirty examples were ready for despatch to Heston when Supermarine agreed to convert them and future airframes allocated for PR duties on the F Mk IX assembly lines.

The RAF and other commands wanted the new PR Spitfire in a hurry and in order to build up supplies deliveries came from two sources – pre-production XIs from Mk IX airframes (Type 374) and normal production XIs (Type 365). The former were Mk IX airframes with Merlin 61, 63 and 63A engines, a fixed tailwheel and original rudder, armament and some armour removed. Later models had a retractable

**The first production PR Mk X was MD191 and this was weighed at High Post on 6 April 1944. It had a Merlin 64 engine and Rotol four blade wooden propeller. Tare weight was 5,812 and auw 8,159lb.*

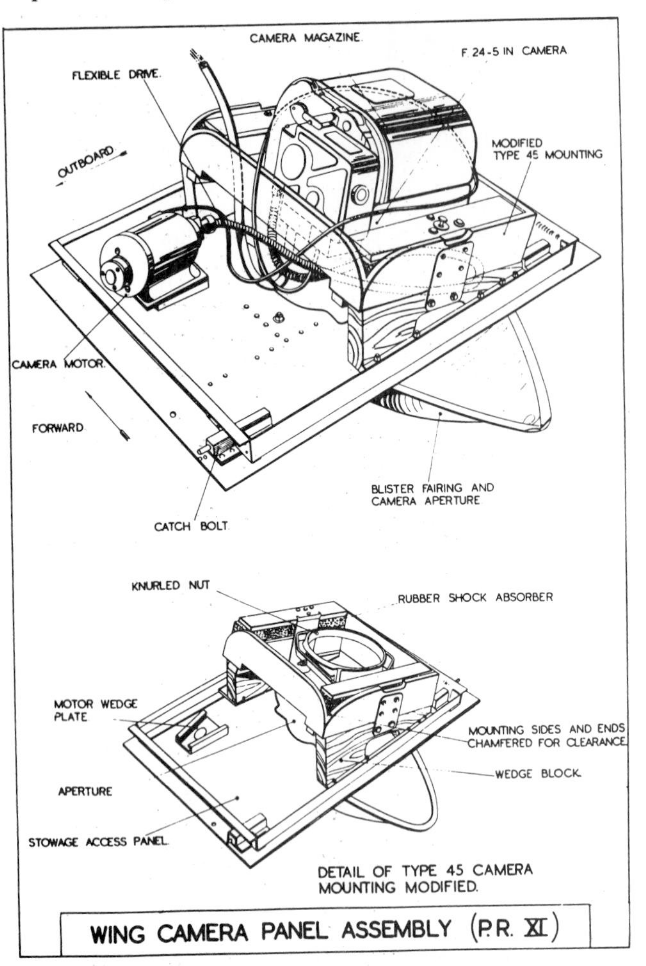

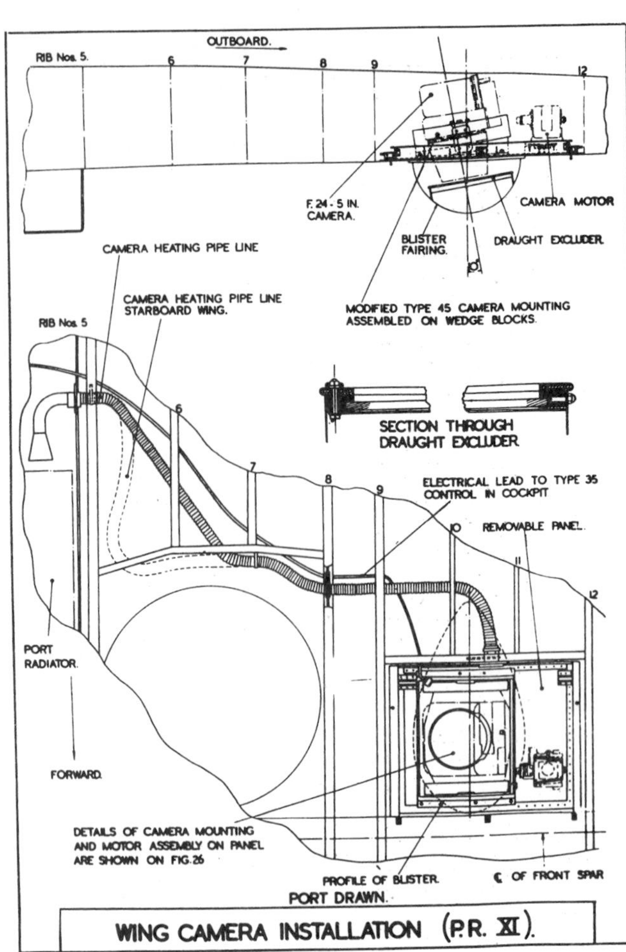

Wing camera installation.

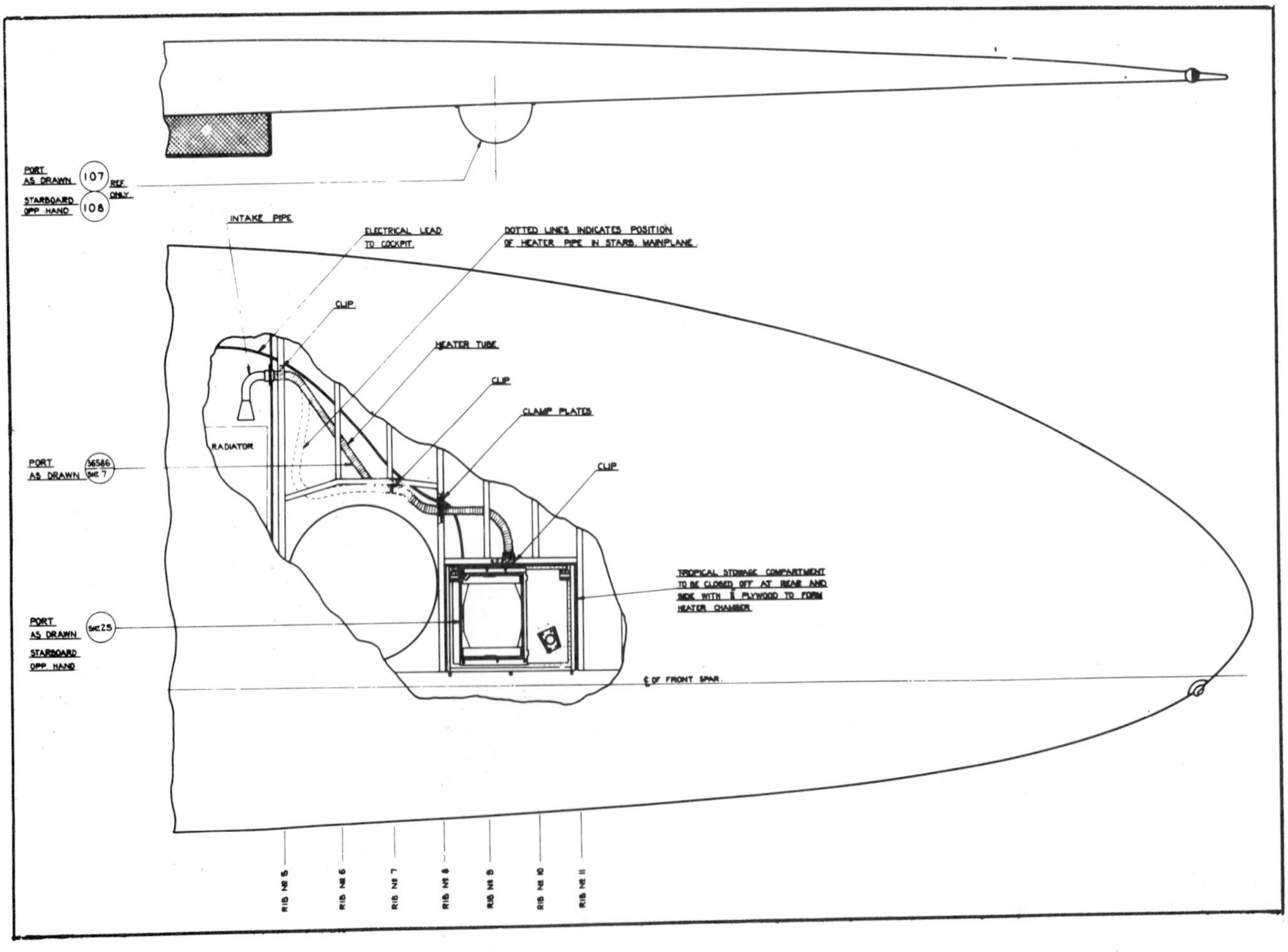

PORT AS DRAWN (107) REF. ONLY.
STARBOARD OPP. HAND (108)

INTAKE PIPE
ELECTRICAL LEAD TO COCKPIT
DOTTED LINES INDICATES POSITION OF HEATER PIPE IN STARB. MAINPLANE.
CLIP
HEATER TUBE
CLIP
CLAMP PLATES
CLIP
RADIATOR
PORT AS DRAWN (36586 SHT. 7)
TROPICAL STOWAGE COMPARTMENT TO BE CLOSED OFF AT REAR AND SIDE WITH ⅛ PLYWOOD TO FORM HEATER CHAMBER
PORT AS DRAWN (SK.25)
STARBOARD OPP. HAND
℄ OF FRONT SPAR

RIB No 5
RIB No 6
RIB No 7
RIB No 8
RIB No 9
RIB No 10
RIB No 11

EN409, the PR XI in which Squadron Leader Martindale reached a speed of almost Mach I in a dive, losing the entire propeller and gear unit. Top view shows the Spitfire at Farnborough before the flight; note high altitude Wellington in background. Second picture shows EN409 back at Farnborough with propeller and gear missing after the dive. A model on a plinth at Farnborough records the event. Joseph Smith stands almost below the model's tailplane.

tailwheel and a broad chord rudder. The first three aircraft had Merlin 61s, EN362 to PL762, 765 and 767 Merlin 63s. Installation of the Merlin 70 began with PL763, jumped to 768 and from thereonin to the final production the 70 was standard.

Camera installation was the Universal 2 × F 52-36in in the rear fuselage vertically fanned 5°-20′ to port and starboard of the aircraft's centre line, and staggered to each other on the centre line. The Mk XI could also carry two F 24 5in cameras, one in each wing, mounted in small blister fairings outboard.

The first converted PR IX, BS497, was weighed at Worthy Down on 17 November 1942. It had a Merlin 61 engine and Rotol four blade wooden propeller and 'Y' camera installation (1 × F 52 36 inch). Its tare was 5,553lb and auw 7,770. This was followed by EN343 on 30 January 1943 with a tare of 5,555, landing 6,220, with wing fuel tanks empty 6,787 and auw 7,790lb. 'Y' camera. EN419 had a Merlin 63 engine and the 'W' type camera installation of two F 8 20 inch units. Its tare was 5,623, landing 6,339, with wing tanks empty 6,906 and auw 7,909lb. PA859 had the universal camera installation and when weighed at Worthy Down on 3 January 1944 (Merlin 63) its tare weight was 5,602 and auw 7,913. The cameras installed were 2 x F 52 36 inch. PL907, tare 5,636, take off 7,898. Merlin 70, Rotol propeller.

MB798 with a Merlin 63 was seconded to Boscombe Down for level speed performance tests and positional error in August 1943, featuring a non-standard windscreen and two, rear view mirrors, one each side, internally, in the cockpit. At a take off weight of 8,040lb, the maximum speed in FS gear at 24,500ft was 417mph, maximum cruising FS gear at 31,000ft 397mph. At 38,000ft maximum speed was 387mph and cruising 378.

In January 1944 diving tests were conducted at Farnborough to compare performance of the PR XI with that of the North American P-51 Mustang, which had a laminar flow wing. Both aircraft had the pitot head removed from under the wing and replaced by one at one wing tip. A pitot comb 14 inches wide was mounted behind the trailing edge, recording pressures on a bank of airspeed indicators in the fuselage. All instruments were grouped and photographed at 1 to 1½ seconds during any dive. In the Mustang the pilot had to operate the camera by pressing the gun firing button; in the Spitfire it was automatic.

The dives were made from high altitude to obtain the highest possible Mach numbers, while keeping down indicated speeds and resultant loads. The Mustang's Allison engine was supercharged to only 10,000ft, and the dives were made from 28,000ft with guns and radio removed. The Spitfire dived from 40,000ft. The dive started by accelerating to maximum level speed at these heights, putting the nose down and setting engine controls to provide maximum permissible continuous boost. The dive angle was normally 45° and pull out at a gentle 2-3G. Both pilots were warned of large trim changes in the nose down dive and of possible ineffective elevator trim tab. They had to trim into the dive and when nose-down change appeared near the maximum Mach number hold the aircraft by stick force alone, ignoring the trimmer. The Spitfire reached .89 at 29,000 from 40,000ft, and the Mustang .80 at 17,000 from 28,000.

The Republic P-47 Thunderbolt took part later in the tests but the pilot said that he went out of control longitudinally and recovered only by putting his dive recovery flap down. The small spoiler flap under the Mustang's fuselage, intended to block radiator entry during glides to prevent over-cooling, permitted a higher Mach number to be reached in level flight, and a number of dives were made with it extended. The Thunderbolt's flap had to be used with great care.

The trials continued with Spitfire PL827 to measure pressure distribution over the wing at Mach numbers up to .85. A second pitot head was installed to the other wing tip and it had an incidence vane near the point. Small, 1/16in diameter holes were drilled into the outer wing sections, with ten on the upper and ten on the lower surfaces located at 98 inches from the aircraft's centre line. A further eight (four above and four below) were drilled into the inner wing sections, near the trailing edge, but there was no indication of flow separation at any Mach number up to .85. Profile drag measurements were next, with the Spitfire having a comb installed behind the wing trailing edge adjacent to the port aileron (page 390). This was the same comb as used during the Spitfire/Mustang trials, and it was to be replaced by a modified unit later in the trials (page 390).

The aircraft used in the profile drag trials was EN409, a pre-production Mk XI conversion, and it was a remarkable aircraft if only for the major accident it was involved in. The first incident took place in February 1944 when Sqdn. Ldr. A. F. Martindale dived it from 40,000ft over Farnborough and was able to keep it under control only by holding the control column with two hands. After landing the pilot found that a large number of wing rivets had popped. On 27 April Martindale again took off from Farnborough and climbed to 40,000ft, diving to 27,000ft, only to have the Rotol Jablo propeller and Merlin 61 reduction gear torn away. He managed to glide the Spitfire back to Farnborough. These extracts from Martindale's flight log report the situation –
"Yesterday, Thursday 27th April, I flew EN409 to make a

Camera heating bag for PR Mk XI.

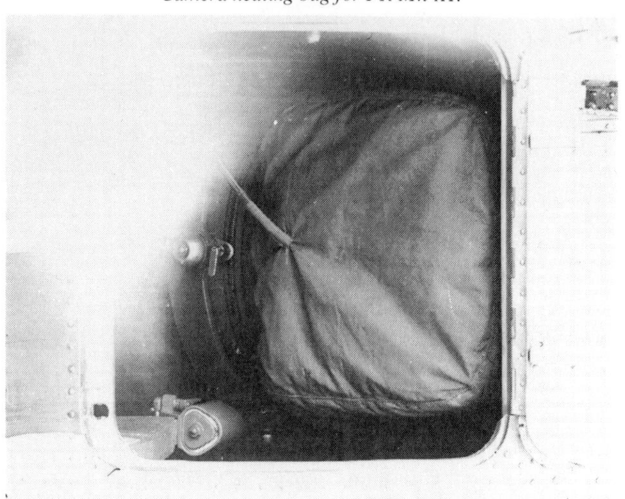

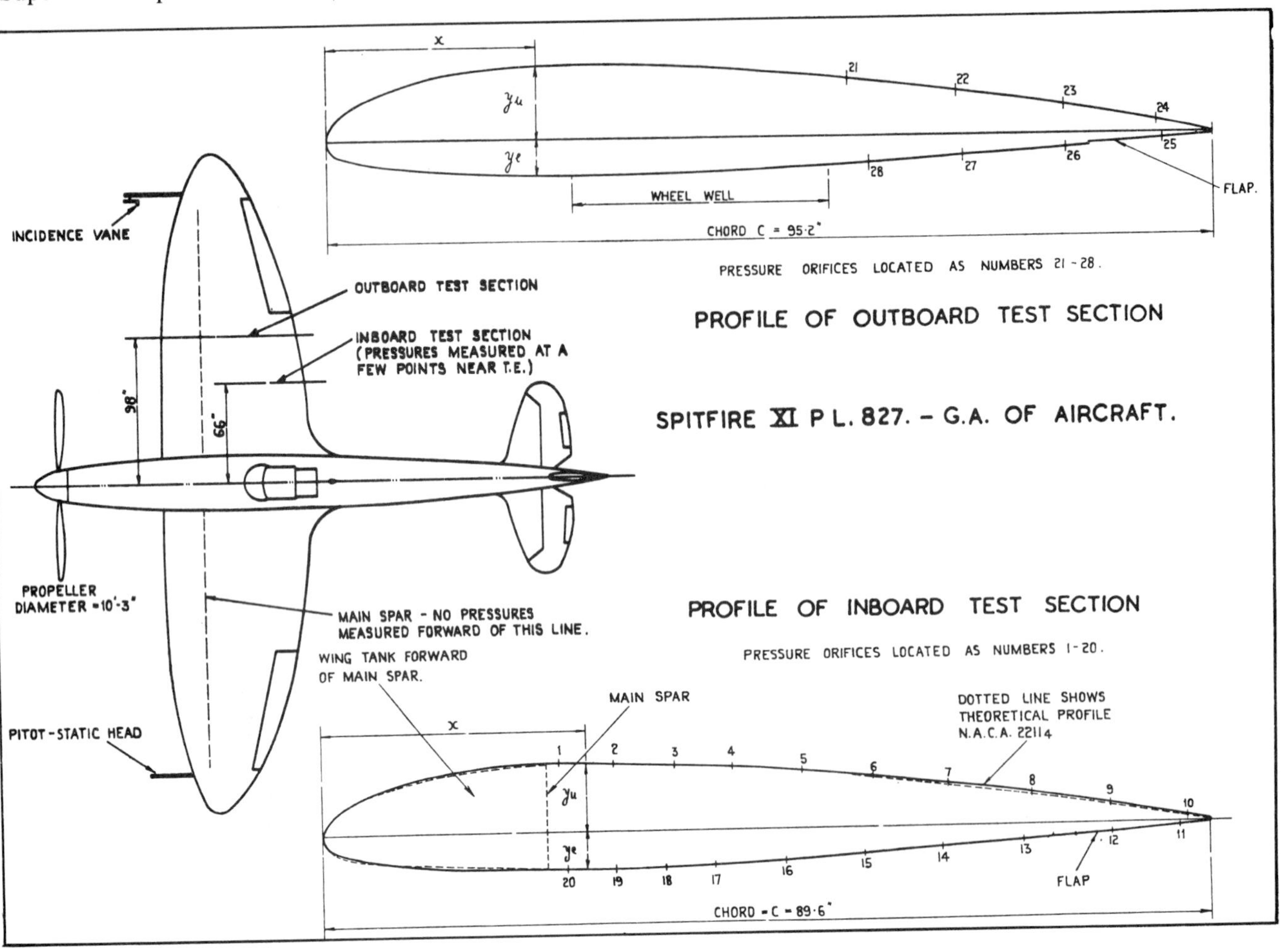

x

y_u

y_l

21 22 23 24 25 26 27 28

WHEEL WELL

FLAP.

CHORD C = 95·2"

INCIDENCE VANE

PRESSURE ORIFICES LOCATED AS NUMBERS 21 – 28.

OUTBOARD TEST SECTION

PROFILE OF OUTBOARD TEST SECTION

INBOARD TEST SECTION (PRESSURES MEASURED AT A FEW POINTS NEAR T.E.)

98"

66"

SPITFIRE XI P L. 827. – G.A. OF AIRCRAFT.

PROPELLER DIAMETER = 10'-3"

MAIN SPAR – NO PRESSURES MEASURED FORWARD OF THIS LINE.

PROFILE OF INBOARD TEST SECTION

WING TANK FORWARD OF MAIN SPAR.

PRESSURE ORIFICES LOCATED AS NUMBERS 1 – 20.

MAIN SPAR

DOTTED LINE SHOWS THEORETICAL PROFILE N.A.C.A. 22114

PITOT - STATIC HEAD

x

1 2 3 4 5 6 7 8 9 10 11 12 13 14 15 16 17 18 19 20

y_u

y_l

FLAP

CHORD = C = 89·6"

PL827 was used for trials to measure pressure distribution on a Spitfire wing in high speed flight. Drawing shows positions of pressure holes in wing surface at sections indicated. During dives at Mach 0.85 the supersonic region on the upper wing surface covered more than half the chord. Trials took place in August/September 1944.

EN409 took part in a series of trials to measure wing profile drag, and for these trials was fitted with two designs of a trailing edge comb which carried a series of small pitot heads to record pressure. The original comb proved unreliable as the supports created too much turbulence. The second type of comb (below) was a better proposition and was mounted in the position illustrated. The trials were adjudged a failure as the pitot heads needed to be installed close to the wing leading edge to be able to record true results.

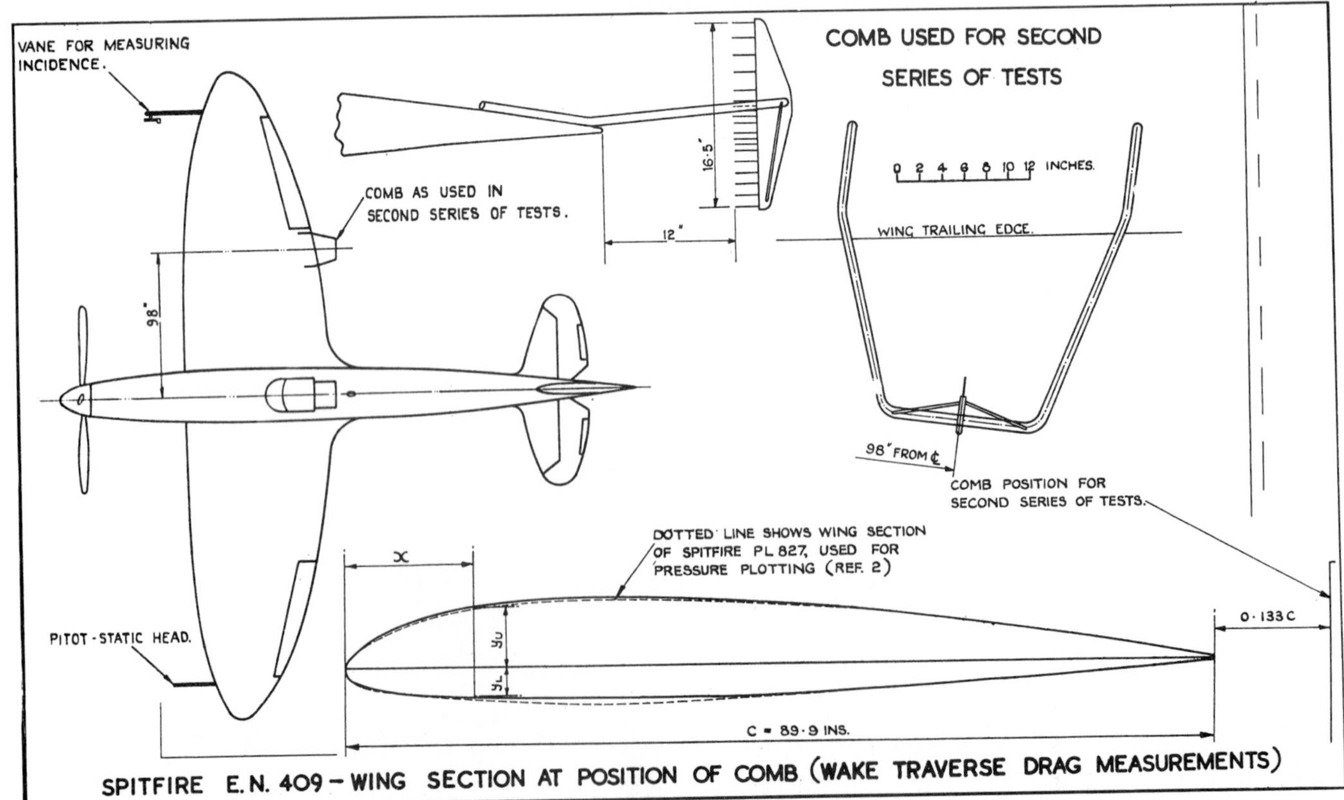

N74138, ex PL983, was converted for courier duties with the American Embassy, London, 1947. It is seen here being piloted by Lettice Curtiss, who used '138 to break the 100km closed-circuit record at 313.208mph.

N74138 was presented by Vickers to the Shuttleworth Trust in 1950 and was feried to Old Warden by John Jordan as G-15-109.

comparison between leading edge pitot-static, underwing pitot-static and static vent in a dive at the highest possible Mach number. I took off and climbed to 40,000 feet with altimeter at 1,013. At ceiling I began to feel slightly inoxic due to the low oxygen flow and flew level for a time at 2850rpm full throttle and worked the ASI round to 170mph. I then most carefully set the rudder and elevator trims, selecting an intermediate position on the latter between the extremes I have tried. I switched on camera and dived the aeroplane.

"I bunted steadily keeping the 'G' low so as to reduce drag and closed the throttle slightly. When I was down to 32,000 feet the altimeter was spinning merrily and the dive was very steep and I was pulling back on the stick in the usual way due to the change of trim at the shock stall.

"I glanced at the altimeter and saw it drop from 28,000 to 27,000 and knew I was past the high speed. I began to think of easing out of the dive when there was a fearful explosion and the aircraft became enveloped in white smoke. I incorrectly assumed that a structural failure had occurred as I knew this to be the danger. The aircraft shook from end to end and I knew I could not bail out at such speed so I sat still. The aircraft was doing nothing startling but the screen and hood were now quite black and I could see nothing. Automatically I eased the stick back and discovered by looking backwards through the oil film that I was climbing. The airspeed was falling as the noises were dying down. I realised I could now bail out and opened the hood, but the aircraft was under partial control at least and so I switched off the camera and began to think I might be able to get the aircraft down and save the film and other apparatus. I still did not know what had happened as I could not see through the windscreen.

"I pointed the aircraft towards base and called up on the radio. As I tried to look round the screen my goggles were whipped away, but the engine clearly was not going and I could see no propeller. Bits of engine were sticking out and it seemed to have moved sideways. I reported this to base. I consulted the Chief Test Pilot as to the advisability of lowering the wheels, supposing they would go down. The hydraulics were u/s and I had pressure for flaps. The CTP advised a wheels down landing and I glided 20 miles or so and saw I would reach base. This I reached at 6000 feet, the aircraft gliding very nicely without its propeller. On landing I saw that the propeller and engine reduction gear had gone and a main engine bearer had buckled".

Martindale then transferred back to PL827, which had arrived at Farnborough on 6 May 1944. It had a Merlin 70 and

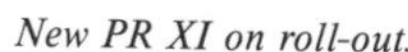

New PR XI on roll-out.

EN654, M63A, was used at a later stage in its life for use as a mail carrier.

a Rotol Dural propeller. On 15 August Martindale climbed to 36,000 feet before starting his dive. The engine oversped, probably because the CS unit failed, when he was at 24,000 feet and this time the supercharger burst with the result that the aircraft caught fire. At that time it was over the outskirts of London, at Ealing and Brentford, but he turned west towards Farnborough. The fire eventually died away but clouds of smoke billowed from the engine cowling. Nearing Farnborough Martindale discovered that the field was obscured by low cloud and he decided that a forced landing was safer. He aimed to put down in a field near Woking, in Surrey, but his windscreen was, by now, covered in engine oil and he failed to see high tension electricity wires directly across his approach until, virtually, the last moment. While attempting to avoid them he crash landed in a copse on Whitmore Common, and in getting clear found he had damaged his spine. Despite this he still managed to retrieve the recording cameras from the now burning wreck.

By March 1944 only four Mk XIs with Merlin 60 series engines were awaiting delivery and the first of the Merlin 70 series was about to be delivered. PL907 was weighed at High Post and tare weight was 5,636 and auw 7,898lb. The Mk XI was being forced to operate at heights above 40,000ft for lengthy periods and a pressure cabin was needed and the Merlin 16 SM was specified as the engine. But, production was unreliable and it was considered that the engine was unsuitable. Supermarine arranged to build and deliver 16 pressure cabin Mk XIs with the Mk VII fuselage and Merlin engine, the aircraft operating at a slightly lower altitude, and follow these with 22 Griffon powered XIs, the latter eventually becoming the PR Mk XIX.

In December 1945 the need arose to fly a standard PR Mk XI with the Merlin 70 for a distance of 2,240 miles for a long range escort mission. Duration of the flight was estimated at 5¼ hours and, as it was to be carried out at 27,000ft, a following tail wind of 110mph was assumed. Fuel was, therefore, required for a five hour flight and a range of 1,690 miles. A Mk IX with the Merlin 61 was used as the trials aircraft at Boscombe Down as the specific consumption of the Merlin 70 was about 5% lower than that of the 61, but the XI airframe was cleaner and lack of armament would improve the XI/70 combination by the same 5%.

Weight of the Mk XI with a 90 gallon overload tank was 8,440 lb and with 170 gallon ferry tank 9,080 lb. A total range of 2,301 miles was estimated with the 170 gallon tank, and as the range required was 2,240 there was a safety margin of 61 miles or 12 minutes flying.

Three PR Mk XIs served with the Royal Danish Air Force. They were PL974 numbered 451, PL833 (452) and PM134 (453). All served with 2 Luftlotille (No 2 Air Flotilla) of the Naval Air Service, Kastrup, before transfer to 4 Eskadrille (No 4 Squadron) of the Army Air Force. All were struck off charge on 1 June 1955 and scrapped.

There was a one-off PR XI worthy of mention, a civil version purchased by Captain James Storey. The description in the Supermarine Type Record states that the civil version was similar to the service aircraft with the addition of a standard 170 gallon overload fuselage tank and two PR Mk XIX type 19¼ gallon wing fuel tanks. The service version fuel consisted of 84 gallons in fuselage tanks and 133 gallons in wing leading edge tanks. With full fuel, including overload tank, the Spitfire weighed 9,700lbs. Maximum speed with o/ld tank was 312mph. Storey had served in the RAF during the war and returned to Argentina on demob to run an aerial photography company there. He decided the best aeroplane for the job was the Spitfire XI, with the Merlin 70, and he purchased one from the Ministry of Supply with only 20 hours flying time on the log book. Vickers converted it and installed three Williamson cameras—two vertical and one oblique.

He decided to fly it to Buenos Aires from Hurn, via Gibraltar, Dakar, Natal, Rio de Janeiro, Montevideo and Buenos Aires with a fuel load of 428 gallons and an endurance of approximately 11 hours. The longest leg across the Atlantic took 8½ hours in the company of a British South American Airways York 'Stag Glitter'. One incident was on the Gibraltar-Dakar leg, when Storey got lost and had to land on a beach.

Endurance of LV-NMZ was based upon the estimate of December 1945 and as the three longest legs of the journey were Lisbon/Dakar 1,730 miles, Dakar/Natal 1,860 and Natal/Rio 1,280 miles there was sufficient margin of safety. Take off and

LV-NMZ was purchased by Captain James Storey, refurbished by Vickers, who bought it from the MoS, and flown across the South Atlantic, non-stop, by Storey who used it for his aerial photography company. His flying distance and time was 1,800 miles and 8 hours 40 min. respectively at an average speed of 208mph. The fuel load was 428 gallons consisting of normal PR tanks, two additional 20 gallon tanks in the wings plus an 170 gallon slipper tank. Storey was accompanied on his long flight by a BSAA York.

climb on main tanks consumed 10 gallons, plus eleven from the 170 gallon ferry tank. Cruise on drop tank for a further 760 miles, release tank and switch to internal fuel for 1,250 miles. Totals 2,030 miles with a 9% margin. Ballasting was critical and was as follows. Without cameras and radio six standard weights of $17\frac{1}{2}$ lb to be carried; when cameras and/or radio carried ballast to be reduced as follows—for each F52 16 inch camera remove four standard weights; for each F52 20in or F8 remove three standard weights; for each F 24 camera remove one weight; for the TR 1143.

The PR XI became the work horse of Coastal Command during 1943/44 and was declared surplus to RAF requirements in February 1948.

OFFICIAL REPORTS ON THE Mk XI

Boscombe Down, August 1943. MB789. Merlin 63. Level speed performance and position error. Windscreen was non-standard. The position error correction varied from plus 5.5mph @ 140mph to minus 5.3mph @ 340. Maximum speed FS gear @ 24,500ft was 417mph, cruising (FS) 397 @ 31,000ft. Maximum speed @ 38,000ft was 387mph.

Boscombe Down, 28 February 1944. PL758. Cooling trails with reduced radiator exit duct areas. The PR XI operated from the UK with reduced radiator exit ducts as the Merlin 63 tended to be overcooled when cruising. Trials were needed to test the modification under tropical conditions, and they revealed that if the PR XI was to be used in hot climates the radiator modifications would have to be deleted.

Farnborough, June 1945. EN409. Profile drag measurements on Spitfire wing at high speeds. This is the report of the trials flown by Sqdn. Ldr. Martindale.

Farnborough, August 1945. PL827. Measurements of pressure distribution of Spitfire wing in flight at high speeds. Continuation of trials with pilot Martindale.

PR Mk X

Wing. Planform elliptical; section NACA Series 2200; span 36′ 10″;incidence° root +2, tip $-\frac{1}{2}$; dihedral° 6; thickness % root 13.2, tip 6; aspect ratio 5.68; area nett 220, gross 242; chord

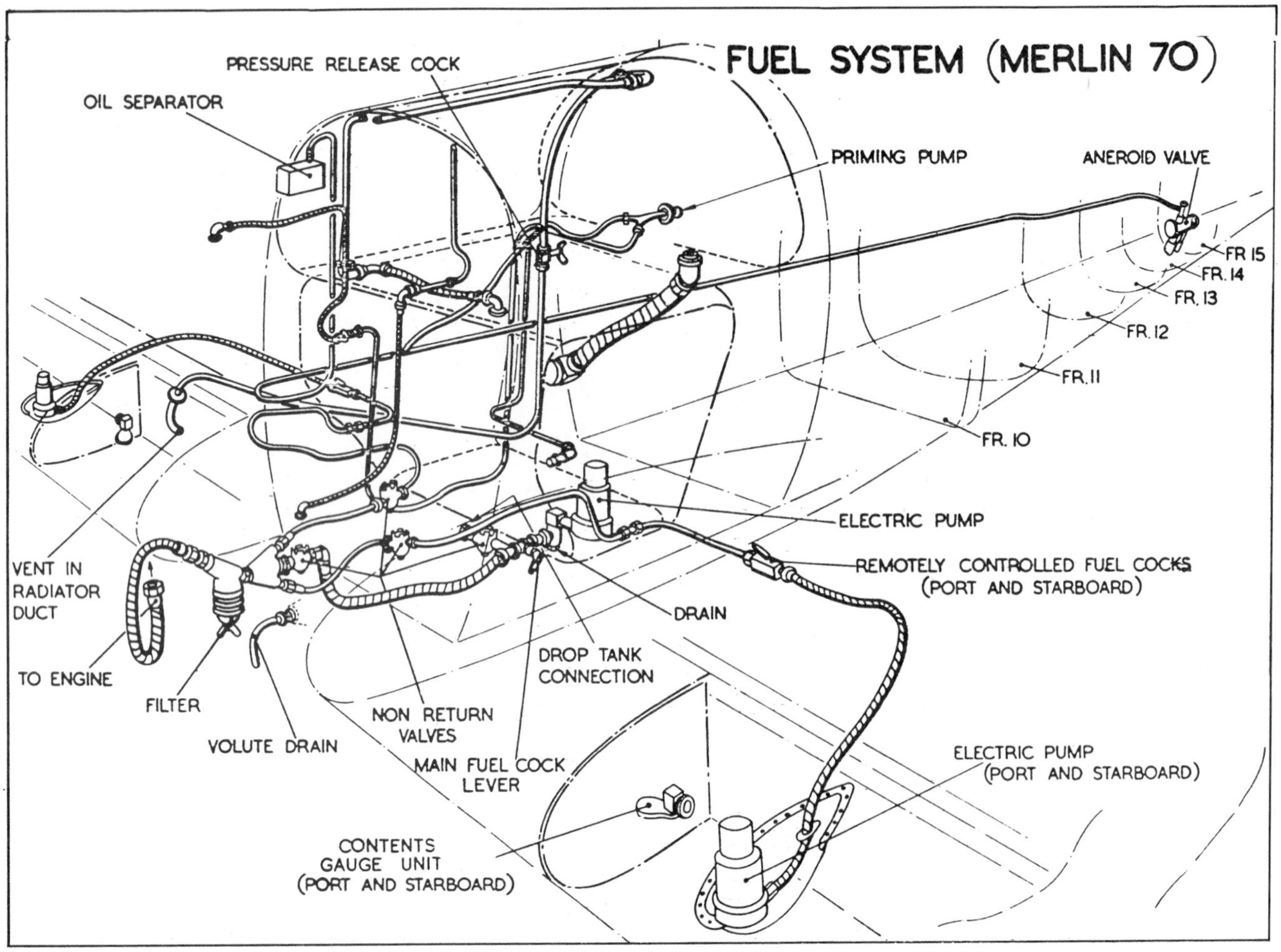

FUEL SYSTEM (MERLIN 70)

PRESSURE RELEASE COCK
OIL SEPARATOR
PRIMING PUMP
ANEROID VALVE
FR 15
FR. 14
FR. 13
FR. 12
FR. 11
FR. 10
ELECTRIC PUMP
REMOTELY CONTROLLED FUEL COCKS (PORT AND STARBOARD)
DRAIN
VENT IN RADIATOR DUCT
TO ENGINE
FILTER
VOLUTE DRAIN
NON RETURN VALVES
DROP TANK CONNECTION
MAIN FUEL COCK LEVER
ELECTRIC PUMP (PORT AND STARBOARD)
CONTENTS GAUGE UNIT (PORT AND STARBOARD)

Above: Fuel system diagram of the PR XI.

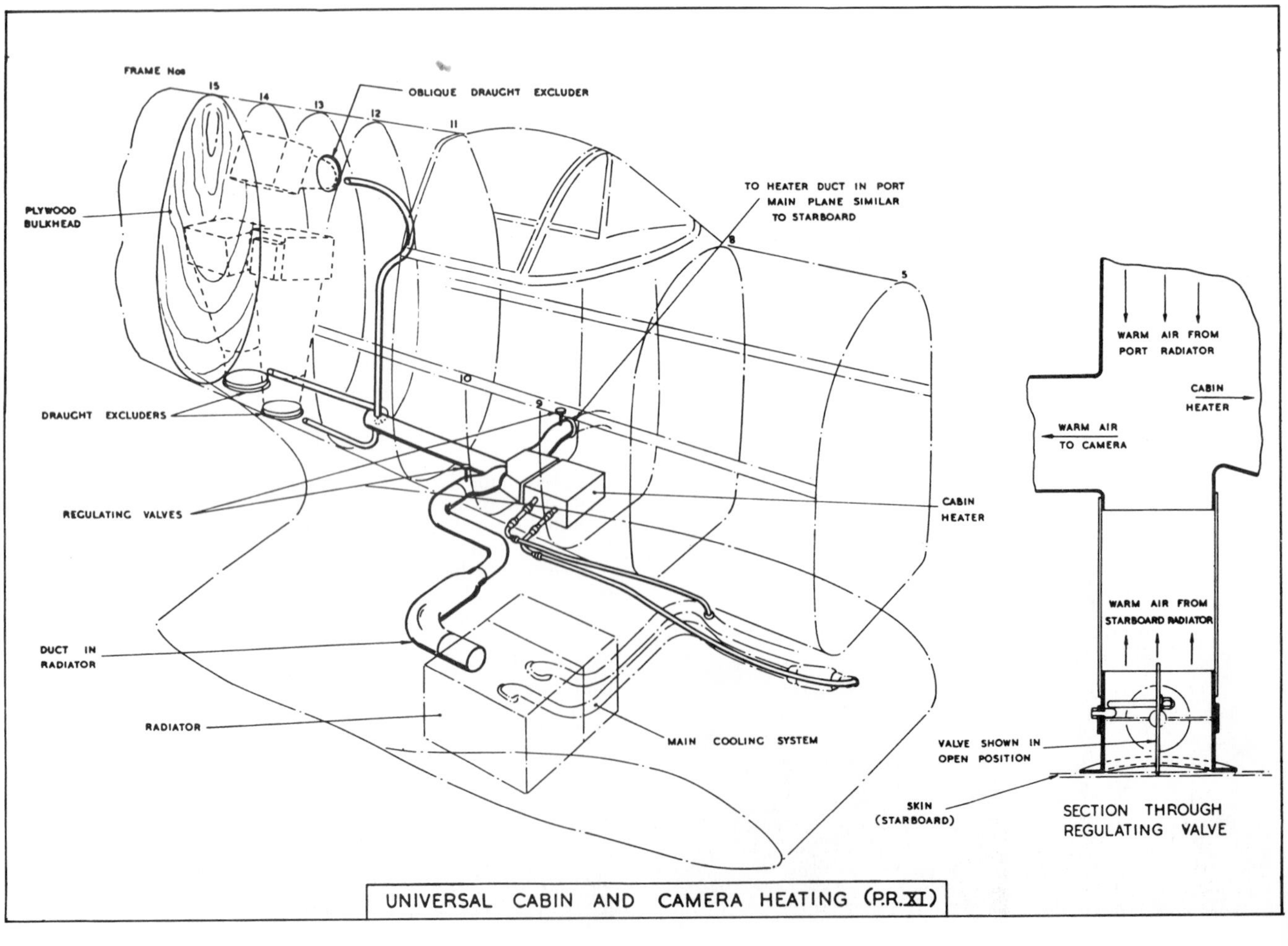

FRAME Nos
15
14
13
12
11
OBLIQUE DRAUGHT EXCLUDER
PLYWOOD BULKHEAD
TO HEATER DUCT IN PORT MAIN PLANE SIMILAR TO STARBOARD
8
5
10
9
DRAUGHT EXCLUDERS
REGULATING VALVES
CABIN HEATER
DUCT IN RADIATOR
RADIATOR
MAIN COOLING SYSTEM
WARM AIR FROM PORT RADIATOR
CABIN HEATER
WARM AIR TO CAMERA
WARM AIR FROM STARBOARD RADIATOR
VALVE SHOWN IN OPEN POSITION
SKIN (STARBOARD)
SECTION THROUGH REGULATING VALVE

UNIVERSAL CABIN AND CAMERA HEATING (P.R.XI)

PA961 served with 400 Squadron and was demobbed as late as August 1947.

(geo) 6.38, (ma) 7.01. Ailerons. Area 18.9; chord (ma) movement° up 26, down 19; droop ⅜. Flaps. Area 15.6; movement° down 85. Wing loading 33.7lb/sq ft; power loading 4.77lb/hp.

Tailplane. Area 31.46; chord (ma) 4.0; incidence° root 0, tip ± ½; dihedral° 0. Elevators. Area 13.26; movement° up 28, down 23; tab area 0.38; movement° up 20, down 7. Fin area 4.61. Rudder area 8.23; movement° 28 each way. Tab area 0.35; movement° port 6, starbd 18.

Undercarriage. Wheels Dunlop AH10019; tyres Dunlop IK13 or 17. Oleo pressure 430 or 530; tyre pressure 60. Tailwheel retractable castoring. Wheel Dunlop AH2184/IX; tyre TA 12 or 14. Oleo pressure 280; tyre pressure 60.

Engine/s. Merlin 64 1,710hp @ 3,000rpm @ 8,500ft MS, 1,510 @ 21,000ft FS.

Propeller/s. Rotol R12/4F5/4 4-blade Hydulignum pitch range 35° fine pitch 22° 20′.

Coolant. 70% distilled water, 30% Glycol. 13.5gals in main system. 3.2 intercooler.

Fuel. 100 octane. Capacity. Fuselage (upper) 47gals, lower 48.5. Wing leading edge 2 × 66. Total 228. Plus 90gal o/ld tank.

Oil. 14.4gals in tank under engine.

Armament. Nil.

Radio. TR1143 A2171.

Performance. Max speed FS. 417 @ 24,200ft (boost +18); 412 @ 28,000 (+13); 387 @ 38,000 (−9.5).

Weights. Tare 5,812, take off 8,159, max permissible.

Camera installation. 2 × F52 36in vertical mounted between frames 13 and 15. 10° 40′ between each camera and each 5° 20′

PR XI PL965 was delivered to the Dutch Technical School at Deelen in July 1947. It was later given Dutch markings and displayed at the National War and Resistance Museum, Overloon.

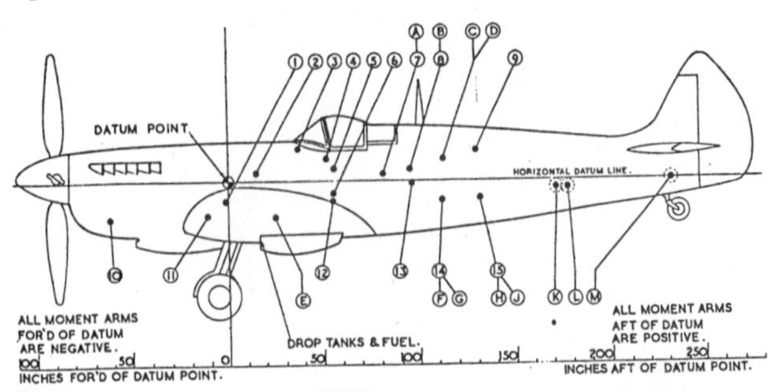

TABLE I

NOTE NO.	ITEM NO.	TYPICAL REMOVABLE ITEMS OF MILITARY LOAD.	WEIGHT LB.	ARM IN.	MOMENT LB.IN.
	12	1½ IN.SIGNAL PISTOL AND CARTRIDGES.	5.5	+ 54.5	+ 300
	4	1¼ LB.INCENDIARY BOMB, NAVIGATIONAL COMPUTOR, CLOCK, CROWBAR & RATIONS.	7.5	+ 51.5	+ 386
	3	CAMERA CONTROL UNIT TYPE 35.	4.5	+ 36.5	+ 164
1	14	FOR'D VERTICAL F.52 36 IN.CAMERA AND ACCESSORIES.	100.5	+112.5	+11,306
1	15	AFT VERTICAL F.52 36 IN.CAMERA AND ACCESSORIES.	100.5	+128.5	+12,914
	7	3 OXYGEN CYLINDERS MK.Vc.	58	+ 81	+ 4,698
	6	DINGHY TYPE 'K' IN SEAT PACK TYPE 'A' MK II.	15	+ 55	+ 825
	9	FIRST-AID OUTFIT.	2.5	+128.5	+ 322
5	8	T.R.1143 RADIO AND ACCESSORIES.	79	+ 94.5	+ 7,466
	13	A.1271 AMPLIFIER.	4.5	+ 95.5	+ 430
	5	PILOT AND PARACHUTE.	200	+ 55	+11,000
		TOTAL TYPICAL REMOVABLE MILITARY LOAD.	577.5		+49,811
8	10	OIL IN TANK: 14.4 GAL. AT 9 LB.PER GAL.	129.5	- 61	- 7,900
	2	FUEL IN FUSELAGE TANKS: 84 GAL. AT 7.2 LB.PER GAL.	605	+ 13.5	+ 8,168
	11	FUEL IN WING TANKS: 133 GAL. AT 7.2 LB.PER GAL.	958	- 11	-10,538
9	1	AIRCRAFT IN TARE CONDITION.	5,602		- 4,787
		AIRCRAFT IN TYPICAL TAKE-OFF CONDITION.	7,872	+ 4.4	+34,754

TABLE II.

DROP FUEL TANKS AND FUEL.	WEIGHT LB.	ARM IN.	MOMENT LB.IN.
30 GAL. FUEL IN DROP TANK.	216	+ 16	+ 3,456
30 GAL. DROP TANK.	60	+ 16	+ 960
45 GAL. FUEL IN BLISTER TYPE DROP TANK.	324	+ 13.5	+ 4,374
45 GAL. BLISTER TYPE DROP TANK.	80	+ 13.5	+ 1,080
90 GAL. FUEL IN BLISTER TYPE DROP TANK.	648	+ 13.5	+ 8,748
90 GAL. BLISTER TYPE DROP TANK.	120	+ 16	+ 1,920

TABLE III.

NOTE NO.	ITEM NO.	ADDITIONAL AND ALTERNATIVE ITEMS OF REMOVABLE MILITARY LOAD.	WEIGHT LB.	ARM IN.	MOMENT LB.IN.
	A	3 OXYGEN CYLINDERS MK V*.	44	+ 81	+ 3,564
6	E	DESERT EQUIPMENT.	40	+ 24	+ 960
5	B	T.R.1133 RADIO AND ACCESSORIES.	70.5	+ 95	+ 6,698
2	G	FOR'D VERTICAL F.8 20 IN. CAMERA AND ACCESSORIES.	79.5	+112.5	+ 8,944
2	H	AFT VERTICAL F.8 20 IN. CAMERA AND ACCESSORIES.	79.5	+129.5	+10,295
3	C	OBLIQUE F.24 8 IN. CAMERA AND ACCESSORIES.	32	+111.5	+ 3,568
4	D	OBLIQUE F.24 14 IN. CAMERA AND ACCESSORIES.	35.5	+111.5	+ 3,958
4	F	FOR'D VERTICAL F.24 14 IN. CAMERA AND ACCESSORIES.	35.5	+111	+ 3,941
4	J	AFT VERTICAL F.24 14 IN. CAMERA AND ACCESSORIES.	35.5	+130.5	+ 4,633
	K	BALLAST WEIGHT ON FOR'D PEG AT AFT ACCESS DOOR.	17.5	+171	+ 2,993
	L	BALLAST WEIGHT ON AFT PEG AT AFT ACCESS DOOR.	17.5	+177.5	+ 3,106
7	M	TAIL BALLAST WEIGHT ON MOUNTING ABOVE TAIL WHEEL.	17.5	+230	+ 4,025

Loading and CoG diagram Mk XI.

from the vertical, or 2 × F8 20in or F52 20in verticals, or 2 × F24 14in and 1 × F24 14 or 8in oblique. Installation of latter as in W. This type of installation was the U (universal). Heating hot air from radiator.

Wing. Planform elliptical; section NACA series 2200; span 36′ 10″; incidence° root 0, tip $-\frac{1}{2}$; dihedral° 0; thickness % root 13.2, tip 6; aspect ratio 5.68; area nett 220, gross 242; chord (geo) 6.38, (ma) 7.01. Ailerons. Area 18.9; chord (ma) movement° up 26, down 19; droop $\frac{3}{8}$. Flaps. Area 15.6; movement° down 85. Wing loading 31.9lb/sq ft; power loading 4.96lb/hp.

Tailplane. Area 31.46; chord (ma) 4.0; incidence° root 0, tip $\pm\frac{1}{2}$; dihedral° 0. Elevators. Area 13.26; movement° up 28, down 23. Tab area 0.38; movement° up 20, down 7. Fin area 4.61. Rudder area 8.23. Tab area 0.36; movement° port 6, starbrd 18.

Undercarriage. Wheels Dunlop AH2061; tyres Dunlop IJ13 or 17. Oleo pressure 380 or 465; tyre pressure 57. Tailwheel, 1st 45 a/c fixed; later models from MB794 retractable castoring. Wheel Dunlop AH2184/IX; tyre Dunlop TA 12 or 14. Oleo pressure 230; tyre pressure 45.

Engine/s. Merlin 61 1,565hp. Change to FS @ 15,250ft, back to MS @ 13,750; Merlin 63 1,650hp change to FS @ 21,000ft, back to MS @ 19,500; Merlin 63A 1,710hp FS/MS as above; Merlin 70 1,475hp. Change to FS @ 19,500ft, back to MS @ 18,000; All electric starting.

Propeller/s. Merlin 61. Rotol R3/4F5/2 4-blade, pitch range fine pitch or, R3/4F5/3 or R5/4F5/4. Merlin 63, 63A and 70. Rotol R12/4F5/4 4-blade Hydulignum pitch range fine pitch 22° 20′.

Coolant. 70% distilled water, 30% Glycol.

Fuel. YY 100 octane. Capacity. Fuselage (Upper) 48gals, lower 37, wing leading edge 2 × 66. Total 217. Plus 30, 45 or 90 gal o/ld tank. Consumption MS gear @ 20,000ft 160mph 5.76 gal/hr.

General arrangement of PR Mk XI.

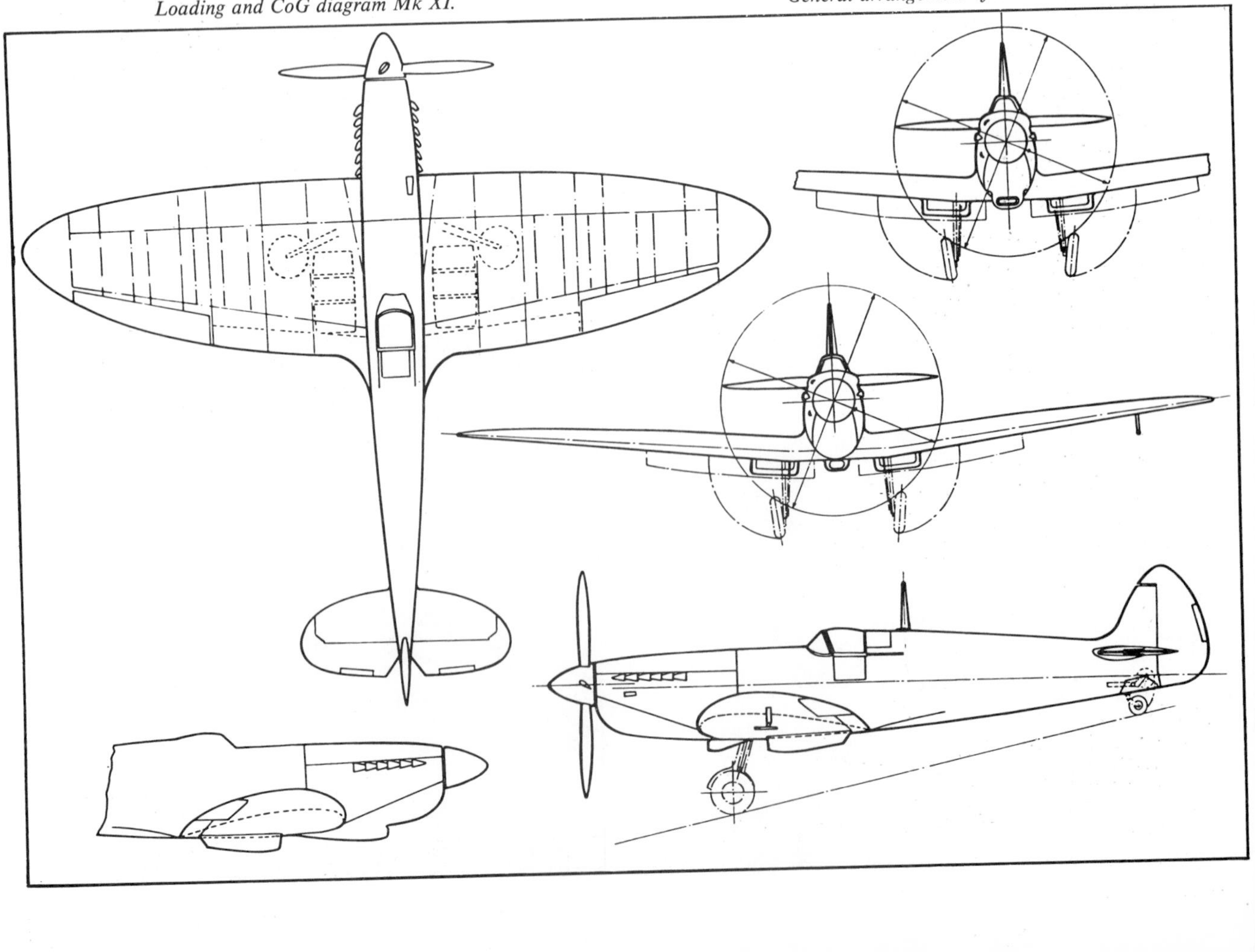

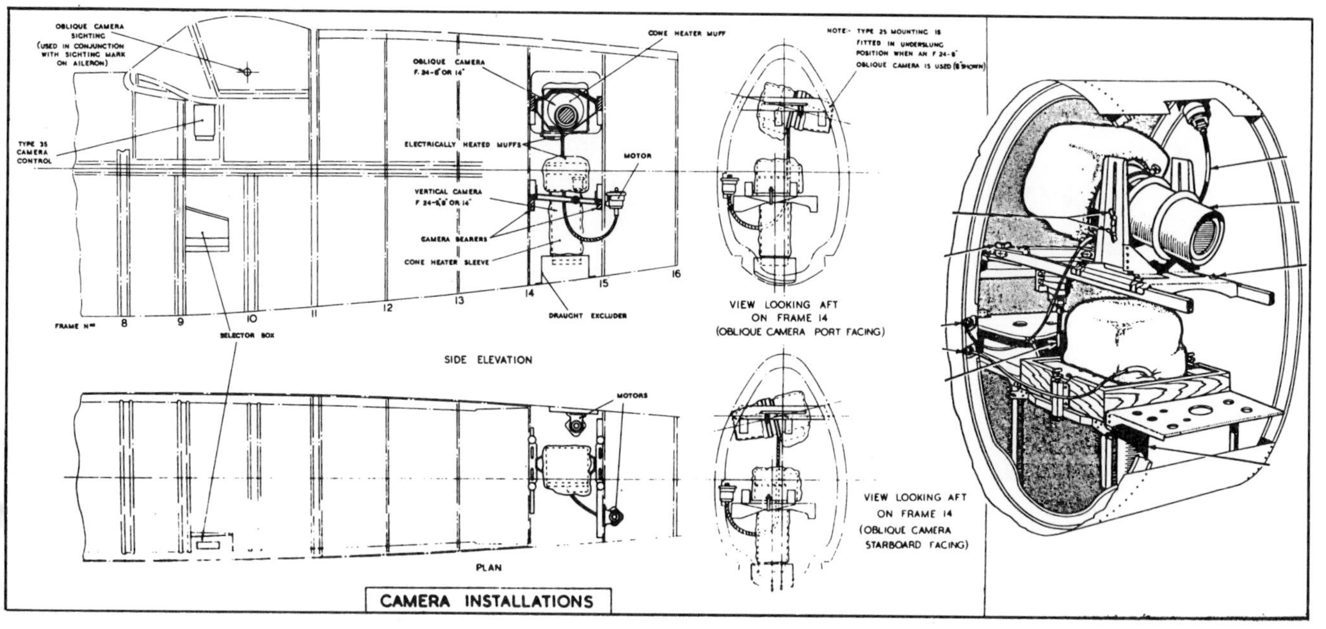

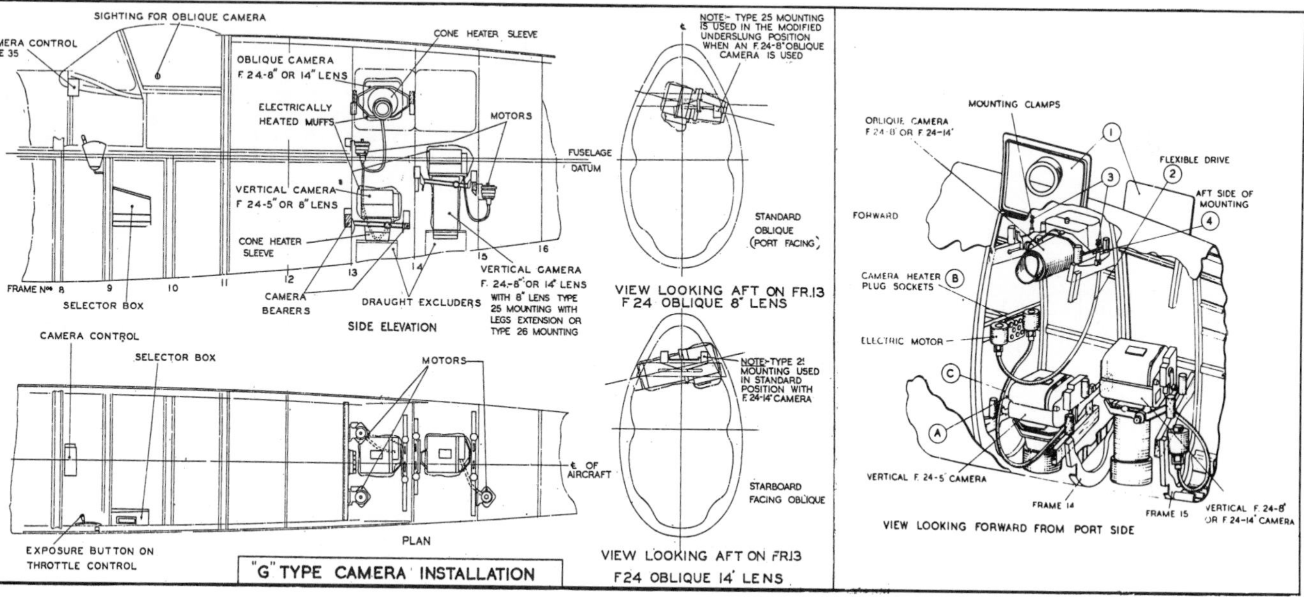

Camera port mud flap and control.

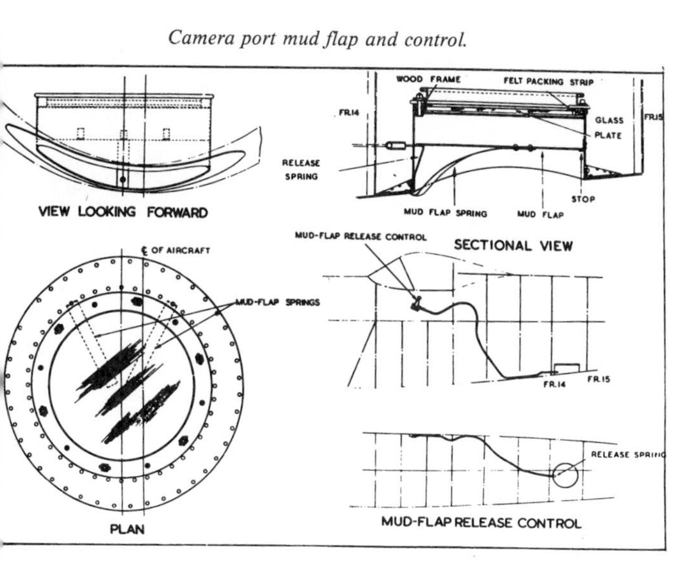

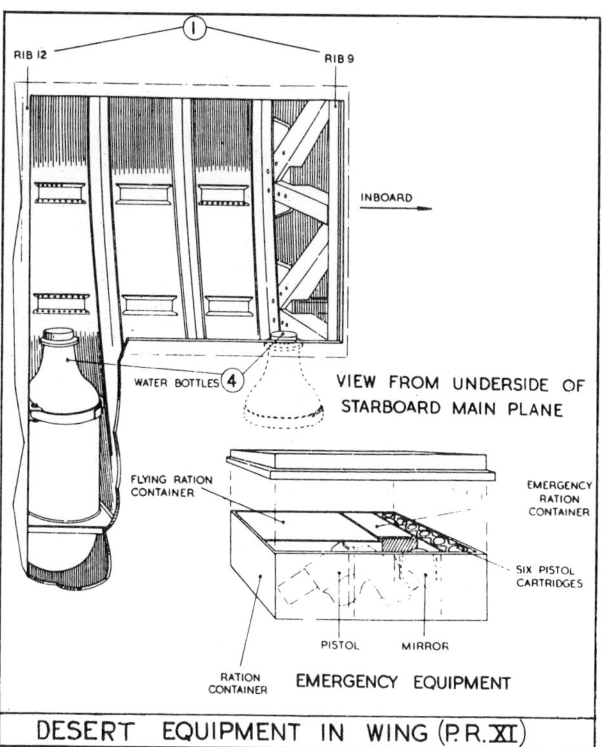

SIGHTING FOR OBLIQUE CAMERA
ACCESS DOORS
PLYWOOD BULKHEAD
CAMERA CONTROL TYPE 35
CAMERA MOUNTING TYPE 38
FUSELAGE DATUM
SPLIT CAMERAS TYPE F 52 36 LENS
DRAUGHT EXCLUDERS
FRAME Nos 8 9 10 11 12 13 14 15 16
SELECTOR BOX
SIDE ELEVATION
ANGLE OF CAMERAS
VIEW LOOKING AFT ON FRAME 13
CAMERA CONTROL TYPE 35
MOTORS
CAMERA RAILS
℄ OF AIRCRAFT
EXPOSURE BUTTON ON TROTTLE CONTROL
SELECTOR BOX
CAMERA BEARERS
PLAN
ACCESS DOORS
MAGAZINE
FORWARD
GEARBOX
CLAMPS ON TYPE 38 MOUNTING
PLYWOOD BULKHEAD
FRAME 13
FRAME 14
FRAME 15
FLEXIBLE DRIVE FROM MOTOR (NOT SHOWN) TO CAMERA
TWO F 52 36" CAMERAS
VIEW LOOKING FORWARD FROM PORT SIDE
UNIVERSAL TWO F. 52 CAMERA INSTALLATION (P.R.XI)

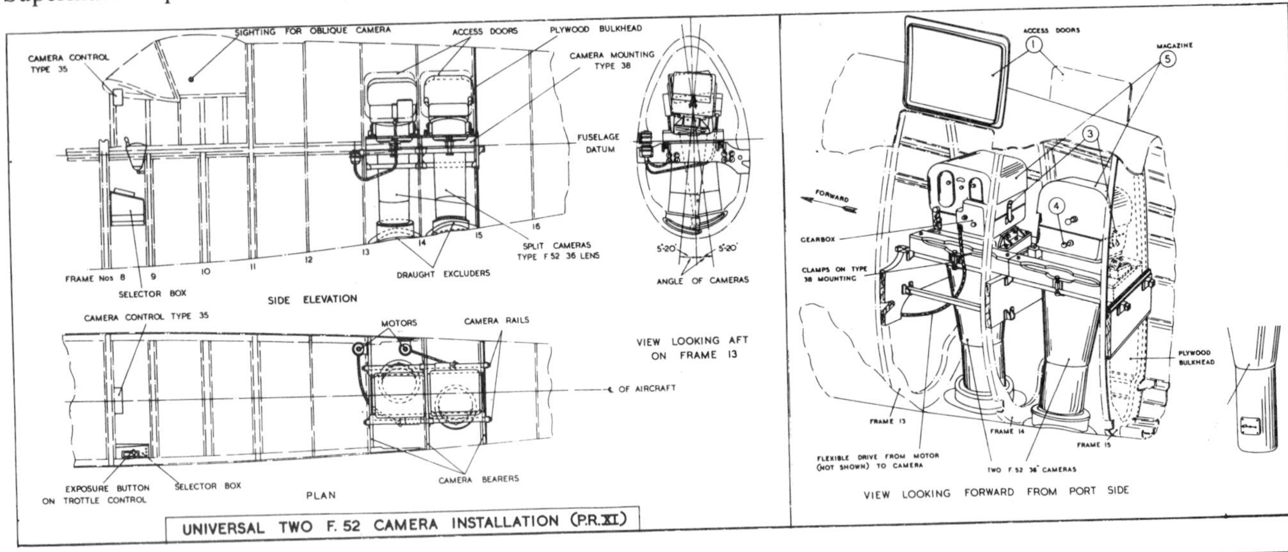

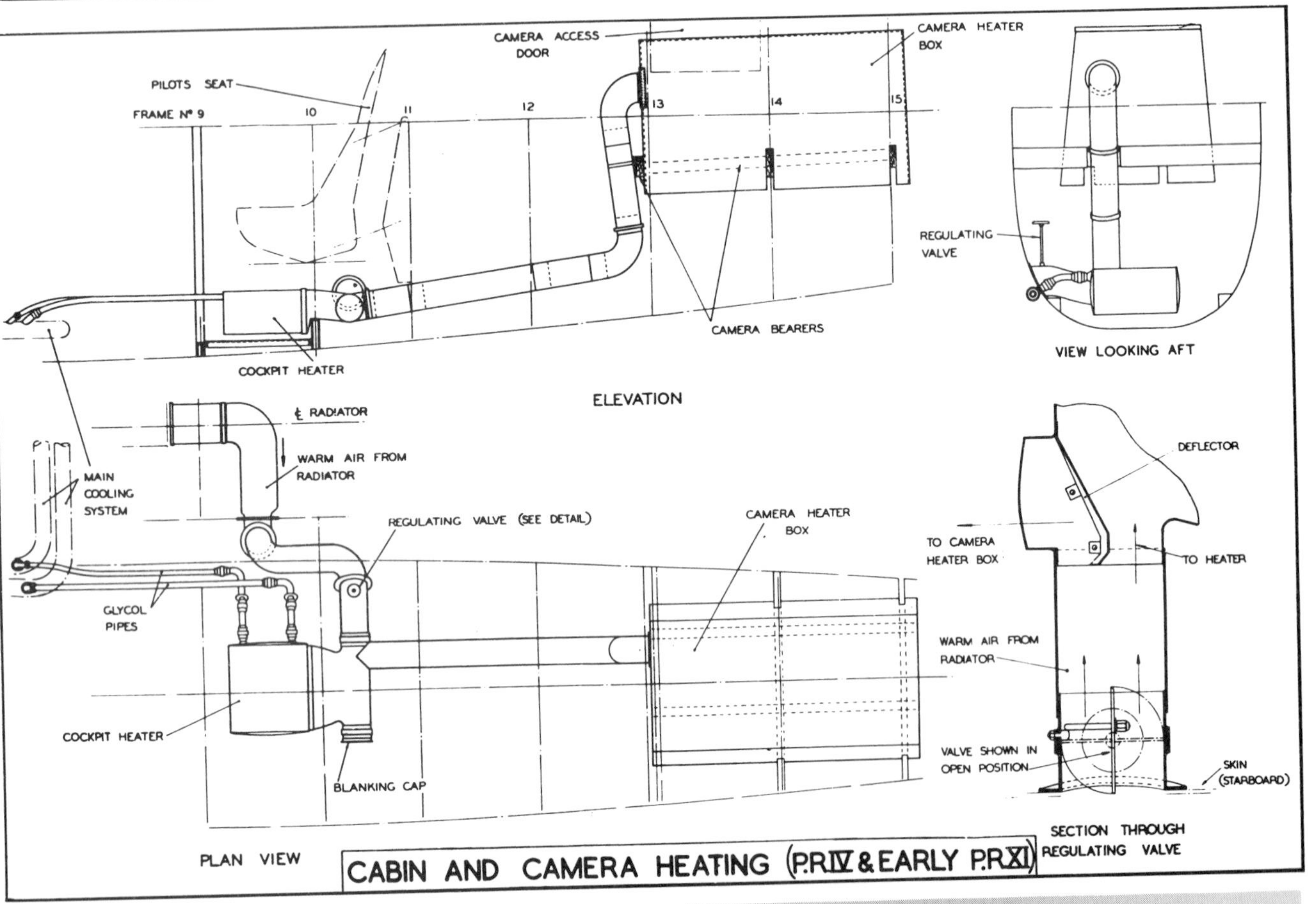

CAMERA ACCESS DOOR
CAMERA HEATER BOX
PILOTS SEAT
FRAME Nº 9
10
11
12
13
14
15
REGULATING VALVE
CAMERA BEARERS
COCKPIT HEATER
VIEW LOOKING AFT
ELEVATION
℄ RADIATOR
WARM AIR FROM RADIATOR
MAIN COOLING SYSTEM
REGULATING VALVE (SEE DETAIL)
CAMERA HEATER BOX
DEFLECTOR
TO CAMERA HEATER BOX
TO HEATER
GLYCOL PIPES
WARM AIR FROM RADIATOR
COCKPIT HEATER
VALVE SHOWN IN OPEN POSITION
SKIN (STARBOARD)
BLANKING CAP
PLAN VIEW
CABIN AND CAMERA HEATING (P.R.IV & EARLY P.R.XI)
SECTION THROUGH REGULATING VALVE

Oil. 14.4 gals under engine.

Armament. Nil. Plain windscreen.

Radio. TR1133, TR1143.

Performance. Max speed FS 417mph @ 24,200ft; max cruise 397 @ 31,000. Range (170 ferry) 2,301 miles, endurance 5.4hr. Rate of climb 4,350ft/min. Time to 20,000 5 min. Ceiling 44,000ft.

Weights. Tare 5,575lb, (T) 5,602; take off 7,731, (T) 7,872; max permissible 7,930.

Camera installation. U (universal mounting). 2 × F52 36in verticals or, 2 × F8 20in and 1 × F52 20in or, 2 × F24 8in and 1 × F24 8 or 14in. Heating hot air. Later production a/c had 1 × F24 5in camera located (one per wing) between ribs 9 and 12 aft of main spar. Covered by blister fairing incorporating a glass window covered by metal mud flap on take off.

LT

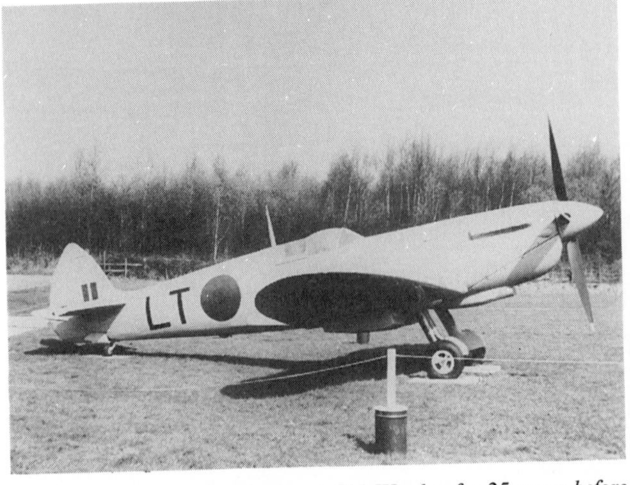

PL983 was displayed statically at Old Warden for 25 years before moving to Duxford in August 1975.

SERIAL NUMBERS

SUPERMARINE AVIATION (VICKERS) LTD.

Contract No. B19713/39

Tenth order for 426 Spitfire Mk VC dated 12 May 1942. Built as MkVII/VIII/IX/X/XI/XII between July 1943 and March 1944. The following serials apply to PR Mk X built to this order. MD191 to 199, MD213. Originally scheduled as F Mk VIIs.

Thirteenth order for six Spitfires MkVII dated 18 February 1944. Built as PR Mk X in May 1944. SR395 to 400. Total built 16. All Merlin 64 engines.

MD191 STN Ben 16-5-44 541S 23-5 HAL 12-2-45 mods Mar Cam 11-10 SOC 13-10

MD192 STN Ben 4-4-44 542S CB ops 29-5 HAL 6-6 Mar Cam 11-10 SOC 13-10

MD193 STN Ben 540S 8-5-44 106GPWP1 11-8 541S 23-9 HAL 22-2-45 mods cancel recat E 25-5

MD194 STN Ben 22-4-44 542S 25-5 HAL 15-7 Mar Cam 26-4-45 SOC 27-9

MD195 STN Ben 22-4-44 541S 23-5 HAL 5-12 Mar Cam 11-10-45 SOC 13-10

MD196 STN Ben 24-4-44 542S 30-5 106GPWP1 18-6 542S 23-9 Mar Cam 17-9-45 SOC 27-9

MD197 STN Ben 25-4-44 541S 25-5 HAL 15-7 CE ops 9-1-45 SOC 12-1

MD198 STN Ben 28-4-44 542S 30-5 HAL 15-7 believed M71C instal 542S 30-11 e/a dbf CE 1-1-45 SOC 12-1

MD199 STN Ben 30-4-44 541S 23-5 CB ops 13-1-45 HAL mods cancel recat E SOC 26-5

MD213 STN Ben 30-4-44 542S 21-6 CAC ops 5-8 HAL 21-8 Ben 9-3-45 SOC 5-6

SR395 HPA Ben 16-5-44 106Gp WP1 18-6 541S 11-8 HAL 30-11 mods Mar Cam 11-10-45 SOC 13-10

SR396 Ben 7-5-44 542S 10-6 hvy ldg u/c clpse CE 24-2-45

SR397 STN Ben 11-5-44 542S 11-6 HAL 22-3-45 mods cancel recat E 25-5 SOC 22-6

SR398 Ben 14-6-44 542S 16-6 HAL 5-4-45 mods Mar Cam 11-10

SR399 STN Ben 14-5-44 106Gp WP1 18-6 542S 16-8 8 OTU 4-5-45 50MU 3-8 SOC 8-8

SR400 STN Ben 14-5-44 106Gp WP1 18-6 542S 11-8 8 OTU 4-5-45 SOC 25-6

SUPERMARINE AVIATION (VICKERS) LTD.

Contract No. B197813/39.

Fifth order for 1,100 Spitfire IA/IB, BP844 to BS559, dated October 1940. Built as PR IV/FVB/VC/VI/VII/IX/XI between February and November 1942. The following serials apply to PRXIs built to this order; BS497-499 and 501-502.

Seventh order for 500 Spitfire Mk. VC dated 23 August 1941. Built as PR IV/VC/VII/IX/XI/XII between November 1942 and August 1943. The following serials apply to PR XI built to this seventh order as Type 365; EN149-151, 153-154, 260, 263, 330-332, 337-338, 341-343, 346-348, 385, 391, 395-396, 407-430, 503-504, 507-508 and 652-685.

Tenth order for 426 Spitfire Mk VC dated 12 May 1942. Built as Mks VII/VIII/IX/X/XI/XII between July 1943 and March 1944. The following serials apply to PR Mk XI built to this tenth order as Type 365; MB770-793, 888-911 and 936-958. MB952-958 completed to contract No. A/C 1877 C.23(c).

Fifth order for 100 Spitfire Mk VIII dated 9 April 1943 and under contract No. A/C 1877/C.23(c). Built as PR Mk XI and LF Mk VIII between November 1943 and March 1944 as; PA838-871, 884-913, 926-951 and 959-961.

Sixth order for 592 Spitfire Mk VIII dated 2 June 1943 and under contract No. A/C 1877/C.23(c). Contract amended several times and finally reduced to PR Mk XI and PR Mk XIX; the following serials apply to PR XIs built to this sixth order; PL758-799, 823-866, 881-925, 949-998 and PM123-160. Total 476.

BS497 3647 HEA 1PRU Ben. wts & CG ldgs of 1st con at WD 17-11-42 FF 21-11 Y camera instal 1PRU 23-11 542S 3-12 543S 26-7-43 HAL 23-10 8OTU 2-7-45 dived into grd nr Newmarket CE 25-7-46 SOC 28-7

BS498 3682 HEA FF 25-11-42 1PRU Ben 7-12 541S 26-3-43 CE ops 13-6

BS499 3684 HEA FF 29-11-42 1PRU Ben 7-12 541S 13-12 VASM 27-9-43 universal camera instal Ben 18-6-44 HAL 27-9 to 5933M 28-2-47

BS501 3716 BEN FF 1-12-42 1PRU Ben 7-12 542S 14-12 VASM 27-9-43 universal camera instal 541S 16-10-43

BS502 3717 HEA FF 6-12-42 1PRU Ben 7-12 542S 14-12 VASM 27-9-43 universal camera instal FTR ops 25-2-44

EN149 3747 M61 CHA FF 15-12-42 33MU 20-12 1PRU Ben 11-1-43 VASM 29-9 universal camera instal 541S 11-10 CB ops 9-2-44 ROS FRU to 84GSU 11-5 412RSU 15-6 4S 28-9 HAL 27-12 mr sold MoS 18-1-49

EN150 3762 M61 CHA FF 17-12-42 33MU 22-12 1PRU Ben 14-1-43 541S 9-2 16S 20-10 FAAC 5-4-44 HAL 1PP 13-4-45 8 OTU 30-4 CE 2-9-46 SOC 14-2-47

EN151 3769 M61 CHA FF 2--12-42 33MU 22-12 1PRU Ben 11-1-43 542S 1-2 FTR ops 26-2

EN153 3756 M61 CHA FF 19-12-42 39MU 20-12 1PRU Ben 13-1-43 Malta 12-2 C3 ops 18-7 Quoted as PRIV but M61 means PRXI

EN154 3774 M61 CHA FF 21-12-42 33MU 22-12 1PRU Ben 15-1-43 541S 21-2 FAAC 19-2 HAL 8 OTU 1-7-44 e/fd on t/o f/ld Woodbine Farm Haverford West CE 11-5-45 SOC 25-5

EN260 3787 M61 CHA FF 24-12-42 39MU 30-12 1PRU 30-12 1PRU Ben 21-1-43 541S 21-2 NA 27-3 Gib 1-6 NWA SOC 31-7

EN263 3810 M46 CHA FF 2-1-43 33MU 8-1 1PRU Ben M61 instal 2-3 ME 278-3 Malta 1-4

EN330 3830 M61 CHA FF 9-1-4 33MU 11-1 1PRU Ben 5-2 NWA 21-5 542S 9-7 FTR ops 10-4-44

EN331 3859 M61 CHA FF 13-1-43 33MU 21-1 1PRU Ben 5-2 1 OADU ff NA 10-3 Malta 1-4 SOC 18-10-45

EN332 3863 M61 CHA FF 14-1-43 45MU 23-1 1PRU Ben 24-2 542S 3-3 HAL 8-3 Ben 17-3 400S 19-1-44 CAC ROS 3-12-45 bou SOC 29-4-47

EN337 3877 M61 CHA FF 16-1-43 1PRU Ben 23-1 1OADU ff NA 2-3 Gib 1-6 ME Feb '45 SOC 26-9-46

PR XI Pre-Production Mk IX conversion sets to Type 374. All Merlin 61 unless otherwise indicated.

EN338 3889 CHA FF 20-1-43 33MU 27-1-43 Ben 9-3 10ADU 26-3 Malta 26-3 218Gp NA 30-11 682S FTR ops 24-8-44

EN346 3923 CHa 39MU 2-2-43 541S 15-3 FACB 17-6 HAL Ben 2-7 541S 20-9 VASM 2-10 univ camera instal 106Gp WPl 18-6-44 34WSU 29-5 sold MoS 18-1-49

EN347 3927 CHA 39MU 2-2-43 Ben 15-9 10ADU 10-3 NA 10-3 FTR ops 30-3

EN348 3939 CHA 33MU 2-2-43 Ben 18-2 542S 2-3 CAC ops 23-3 HAL 1-4 1PRU Ben 16S 15-10 400S 6-5-44 34WSU 29-8 1PP Ben 2-5-45 sold MoS 18-1-49

EN385 3708 HEA 1PRU Ben 7-12-42 541S 9-12 FTR 13-2-43

EN391 3949 CHA 46MU 7-2-43 Ben 5-3 1-ADU 22-3 Malta 2-4 NWA 1-10 ME 30-9 FACE 26-12-44

EN395 3977 CHA 45MU 14-2-43 Ben 17-3 542S 22-3 VASM 8-10 univ camera instal 542S 7-11 FAAC 15-3-44 ROS 1-6GP WPl 18-6 8 OTU FAAC 2-5-45 Sold Mos 18-2-49

EN396 3978 CHa 14-2-43 Stn Flt Ben 10-5 542S 23-5 VASM 10-9 univ camera instal 1-6Gp WPl 18-6-44 No.1 Cam Unit Stapleford 1-7 8OTU 28-3-45 to 5934M RAF Halton 15-4-46 SOC rtp 28-4-47

EN407 4207 CHA Ben 16-4-43 10ADU 5-5 NWA 31-5 C3 ops 25-5

EN408 4228 CHA Ben 21-4-43 10ADU 16-5 Malta 1-11 NWA 1-12 ME 30-9-45 SOC 26-6-47

EN409 4229 CRD Farn 21-4-43 eng calibration and efficiency trls. BDn May '43 wng drag and w/s misting trls. Farn Apl '44 compressibility trls and measurement of air-frame drag up to Mach .89 in dvs. A comb of 19 pitot heads instal behind wng on fus and connected to ASI behind pilot. They were photographed at 1½sec. intervals. During one dive on 27-4-44 Sq Ldr A. F. Martindale (ETPS) reached a speed of 600 ASA, severely dam his a/c. Details on page 389. EN409 was replaced by PL827. Hal 6MU 4-1-45 8OTU 27-2-45 FA FTR 7-4-45

EN410 4249 CHA 6MU 29-4-43 Stn Flt Ben 10-5 541S 23-5 1-6Gp WPl 18-6-44 34WSU 28-8 4S 2-11 HAL 19-12 SFU 7-3-46 sold MoS 18-1-49

EN411 3979 CHA 45MU 14-2-43 Ben 12-3 541S FTR ops 28-5

EN412 4005 CHA 45MU 25-2-43 Ben 12-3 Malta 1-5 ME 30-9 680S w/u Ldng Shaibah Iraq 23-4-46 SOC 28-2

EN413 4011 CHA 46MU 28-2-43 Ben 8-3 542S 14-4 106Gp WPl 18-6-44 8 OTU 1-7

EN414 4046 CHA 46MU 4-3-43 Ben 14-3 10ADU 5-4 NWA 8-4 CE ops 26-5-45 SOC 31-5

EN415 4024 CHA 46MU 28-2-43 Ben 8-3 542S 14-4 FAAC 13-2 ROS 106WPl 18-6 34WSU 10-8 sold MoS 18-1-49

EN416 4031 CHA 1PRU Ben 28-2-43 541S 18-3 FACA 29-8 VASM 29-8 univ camera instal 542S 17-4-44 8 OTU 1-7 FACB 1-1-45 HAL SFU Hen 22-2-46 sold MoS 22-8-47

EN417 4045 M63 CHA 1PRU Ben 3-3-43 542S 22-2 1-6Gp WPl 18-6-44 8 OTU 28-7 flew into trees after t/o Countesswells Farm Aberdeens CE 15-12-44

EN418 4064 M63A CHA 45MU 8-3-43 Ben 26-3 541S 8-4 VASM 29-9 univ camera instal HAL 13-3-44 Ben 16-2-45 FACE 10-4 SOC 18-4

EN419 4067 M63 CHA VAWD wts and CG load of pre-prod con a/c tare 5623, t/o 7909, land 6339lbs. W camera instal 45MU 24-3-43 VBen 17-4 land Furadouro, Portugal on f/f a/c and pilot safe. Assumed interned 5-5 10ADU 7-5 CE 7-5

EN420 4102 M63A CHA 6MU 26-3-43 Ben 4-4 1-ADU 24-4 Malta 1-5 ME 30-9 SOC 31-1-46

EN421 4104 M63 CHA Ben 23-3-43 10ADU 16-5 NA 19-5 SOC 29-2-44

EN422 4105 M63A CHA Ben 20-3-43 10ADU 14-4 NWA 30-4 SOC 28-2-46

EN423 4105 M63A CHA Ben 23-3-43 10ADU 5-5 NWA 31-5 SOC 28-2-46

EN424 4100 M63A CHA 6MU 15-3-43 1PRU Ben 25-3 543S 12-4 542S FTR ops 14-4-44

EN425 4114 M63 CHA 6MU 20-3-43 1PRU Ben 27-3 10ADU 29-4 Gib 1-6 ME 30-9 FTR 24-5-45

EN426 4115 M63A CHA Ben 2--3-43 543S 31-3 1-6Gp WPl 18-6-44 SOC 3-8-45

EN427 4129 M63A CHA Ben 23-3-43 1-ADU 2--4 f/f eng trouble ret Ben 25-4 MAL 1-7 FTR 29-8

EN428 4155 CHA Ben 30-3-43 10ADU 28-6 NA 22-7 SOC 31-7

EN429 4156 M63A Ben 2-4-43 10ADU 13-5 Gib 1-6 NWA 1-12 SOC 28-4-45

EN430 4187 CHA Ben 13-4-43 10ADU 13-5 MAL 21-6-44 SOC 27-3-47

EN503 4288 M63 EA 6MU 15-5-43 Ben 23-5 541S 1-6 VASM 1-9 univ camera instal FTR ops 21-1-44

EN504 4297 M63 EA 6MU 15-5-43 Ben 11-8 10ADU 27-8 NWA 1-10 FTR ops 21-1-44

EN507 4316 M63 EA 6MU 17-5-43 Ben 3-7 10ADU 2-8 MAL 5-8 Malta C3 ops 2-9

EN508 4323 M63 EA 6MU 20-5-43 Ben 11-8 10ADU 30-8 i/sea en route Gib 31-8 FH14

EN series all PR Mk XI Merlin 63

EN341 3892 M61 CHA 33MU 27-1-43 CRD VAWD 28-2 541S 17-4 542S 16-5 15FPP o/s ldg VASM strk fence u/c clpse on arrival for instal of univ camera 10-9

EN342 3897 M61 CHA 33MU 27-1-43 Ben 26-2 541S 18-3 541S 18-3 NWA 31-5 FAAC 2-9 HAL 6MU 8-1-44 SOC 3-8-45

EN343 3917 M61 CHA VAWD 30-1-43 wts and CG load of prod a/c with Y camera instal 39MU 5-2 Ben 15-2 NWA 31-5 VASM 29-8 univ camera instal 542S 25-9 8 OTU 1-7-44 CE 11-5-45 SOC 28-3-46

EN652 4370 CHA 6MU 25-6-43 ROS 22-7 Ben 23-7 542S 20-8 8 OTU 30-8 FA FTR 12-3-45

EN653 4381 CHA 6MU 31-5-43 Ben 15-6 541S 2-7 FTR ops 15-7

EN654 4408 M63A WD (T) VAWD wts and CG load of prod a/c with X camera instal 7-6-43 16S 21-10 ROS 412RSU 29-6-44 16S FACB 11-9 HAL Ben 5-6-45 as specially mod mail carrier North 10-11 SOld MoS 22-8-47

EN655 4409 (T) CHA 6MU 8-6-43 Ben 11-8 1OADU 31-8 MAAF No.7 Flt 4-9 ME 1-11 SOC 26-9-46

EN656 4410 (T) CHA 6MU 8-6-43 Ben 2-7 1OADU 7-8 MAL 12-8 RHAF 29-5-47

EN657 4437 (T) CHA Ben 16-6-43 1OADU 8-7 Malta 17-7 SOC 31-8-44

EN658 4435 (T) CHA Ben 16-6-43 1OADU 11-7 MAL 12-7 NWA 31-7 SOC 28-2-46

EN659 4441 (T) CHA Ben 16-6-43 1OADU 3-7 MAL 5-7 NWA C3 8-7

EN660 4447 (T) CHA Ben 22-6-43 1OADU 22-7 MAL 24-7 FTR ops 30-8

EN661 4451 (T) CHA Ben 23-6-43 1OADU 2-8 MAL 5-8 ME 30-9 Levant SC u/c coll taxy Lydda Palestine 21-8-46 SOC 27-3-47

EN662 4452 CHA 33MU 23-6-43 Ben 24-6 541S 10-7 106Gp Wpl 18-6-44 8 OTU 1-7 FACE i/sea 18-12

EN663 4465 CHA Ben 28-6-43 543S 22-7 CA ops 3-10 16S 29-10 FACB 9-8-44 CHA Ben 27-2-45 34WSU 23-3 4S 29-3 recat E SOC 18-7-45

EN664 4453 CHA Ben 24-6-43 541S 26-7 VASM 24-9 univ camera instal 106Gp Wpl 18-6-44 542S 23-9 HAL 5-4-45 recat E SOC 17-9

EN665 4479 CHA Ben 29-6-43 542S 26-7 FACB 2-12 HAL 34WSU 22-2-45 8 OTU 1-3 cd CE 8-5-46 sold H Bath 30-5

EN666 4481 CHA Ben 29-6-43 541S 22-7 8 OTU 11-9 FACE 24-4-45 SOC 26-4

EN667 4496 CHA Ben 3-7-43 542S 26-7 FAAC 25-2-44 HAL 34WSU 8-3-45 4S 22-3 recat E SOC 23-11

EN668 4506 CHA Ben 6-7-43 541S 4-8 FAAC 2-10 HAL Ben 1-2-45 34WSU 14-2

EN669 4520 CHA 6MU 11-7-43 Ben 23-7 541S 26-8 10ADU 4-10 FTR on cross country flt 18-12

EN670 4521 (T) CHA Ben 11-7-43 10ADU 7-8 MAL 12-8 Malta 1-98 C3 ops 2-10

EN671 4528 (T) CHA Ben 15-7-43 10ADU 11-8 MAL 14-8 FTR ops 25-12-44

EN672 4540 (T) CHA Ben 16-7-43 10ADU 9-8 MAL 14-8 SOC Apl'45
EN673 4552 (T) CHA Ben 25-7-43 10ADU 13-8 MAL 17-8 SOC 27-2-47
EN674 4554 (T) CHA Ben 20-7-43 10ADU 14-8 MAL 17-8 Malta 1-9 FAC3 13-9
EN675 4555 (T) CHA Ben 18-7-43 10ADU 20-8 MAL 28-8 SOC 18-10-45
EN676 4564 (T) CHA Ben 22-7-43 10ADU 22-8 MAL 24-8 Malta 1-9 ME 31-5-45 SOC 9-8
EN677 4599 (T) CHA 6MU 28-7-43 Ben 16-8 10ADU 9-9 MAL 7FC 17-9 NWA 1-10 SOC 28-4-45
EN678 4601 (T) CHA 6MU 29-7-43 Ben 9-8 10ADU 21-8 MAL 24-8 Malta 1-9 NWA 1-12
EN679 4587 (T) CHA 6MU 28-7-43 Ben 11-8 10ADU 17-9 Ind 30-9-44 SOC 27-12-45
EN680 4614 CHA 6MU 11-8-43 140S 7-9 coll with BM399 when ldg CAC 2-1-44 84GSU 5-4 4S 2-11 recat E SOC 26-11-45
EN681 4630 CHA 6MU 17-8-43 140S 7-9 400S 6-5-44 Ben 2-5-45 Western AC 5-6-45 HAL 7-6 recat E SOC 13-9-45
EN682 4629 CHA 6MU 17-8-43 Ben 2-9 ROS 7-9 542S e/fld w/u ldg nr Billingshurst Stn Sussex CE 2-8-44.
EN683 4636 CHA 6MU 15-8-43 Ben 2-9 541S 22-9 CAC ops 10-2-44 ROS 106Grp Wpl 18-6 400S 10-8 34WSU 23-4-45 GAAC 17-7 4S 26-7-2S 20-9-45 SOC 12-12
EN684 4637 CHA 6MU 15-8-43 542S 20-9 CB ops 23-11 Ben 3-2-45 8 OTU 13-4 recat E SOC 28-12
EN685 4638 CHA 6MU 15-8-43 Ben 2-9 543S 16-9 FTR ops 13-5-44

MB series all PR Mk XI(T) Merlin 63 unless otherwise indicated

MB770 4250 CHA Ben 28-4-43 10ADU 9-6 Malta 24-6 682S FTR ops 4-3-44
MB771 4257 CHA 6MU 29-4-43 Ben 10-5 542S 23-5 8 OTU 1-9-44 ROS 9-4-45 sold MoS 18-1-49
MB772 4264 CHA Ben 2-5-43 10ADU 7-7 Malta 1-8 CB ops 3-9 NWA 1-12
MB773 4265 CHA Ben 2-5-43 10ADU 31-5 Malta 1-6 218Gp NA 30-11 SOC 28-4-45
MB774 4275 CHA Ben 2-5-43 10ADU 25-5 Malta 1-6 ME 30-9 SOC 26-9-46
MB775 4282 CHA Ben 12-5-43 10ADU 31-5 NWA FACB 13-8
MB776 4291 M61 CHA Ben 12-5-43 10ADU 4-6 NWA 1-7 Malta 1-8 C2 ops 12-9 MAAF 21-6-45 SOC 18-10
MB777 4292 CHA Ben 12-5-43 10ADU 15-6 MAL 16-6 NWA 1-7 Malta 1-11 MAAF SOC 28-2-46
MB778 4293 CHA Ben 12-5-43 10ADU 15-6 NWA 1-7 Malta 1-8 FAC3 13-9
MB779 4295 M63A CHA Ben 12-5-43 10ADU 15-6 HAL 22-6 MAL 17-7 NWA 31-7 MAAF SOC 18-10-45
MB780 4302 M63A CHA Ben 15-5-43 10ADU 9-6 Malta 1-7 541S Ben 14-7 FAAC 25-11 MAAF 21-6-45 SOC 18-10
MB781 4304 CHA Ben 16-5-43 10ADU 21-6 NA 1-7 MAAF SOC 31-5-45
MB782 4310 CHA Ben 16-5-43 FTR in transit Porth to Gib 18-5
MB783 4311 CHA M63A Ben 18-5 10ADU 7-7 MAL 8-7 Malta 1-8 Italy 1-12 MAAF SOC 13-10-45
MB784 4312 M63A CHA Ben 18-5-43 10ADU 30-5 MAL 30-6
MB785 4333 M63A CHA Ben 18-5-43 10ADU 28-6 Malta 1-7 ME 30-9 CE SOC 12-7-45
MB786 4348 CHA Ben 25-5-43 10ADU 15-6 Malta 1-7 MAAF 21-6-45 SOC 28-2-46
MB787 4337 CHA 6MU 22-5-43 Ben 23-5 541S 3-6 VASM 26-8 univ camera instal 8 OTU 30-8-44 to 5935M 15-4-46 rpt 28-4-47
MB788 4343 M63 CHA Ben 23-5-43 542S 15-6 8 PTU 4-10-44 fire in air FAAC 6-11 HAL sold MoS 18-1-49
MB789 4352 CHA enlarged oil tank; spcl w/s, rounded and lacking metal formers. BDn 16-8-43 level speed perf and positional error at H/A Ben 25-5-43 542S 15-6 VASM 24-9 univ camera instal 542S 9-10 flew i/hill Stubbs Field, Turville, Oxon CE Homing bearing at wrong height 1-12
MB790 4353CHA Benson 26-5-43 CB ops 19-6 HAL VASM 15-9 univ camera instal 541S 30-9 photo sorties f/ld nr Buddock, Cornwall CE 18-12 AST SOC 5-1-44
MB791 4361 CHA Ben 28-5-43 543S 3-7 106Gp Wpl 18-6-44 34WSU 22-2-45 8 OTU 29-6 to 5936M 18-4-46 rtp 28-4-47
MB792 4360 M63A CHA Ben 27-5-43 541S 19-6 FTR 24-6
MB793 4369 CHA Ben 28-5-43 542S 21-6 CE ops 7-5-44
MB888 4650 CHA Ben 20-5-43 10ADU 1309 NWA 1-10 MAAF SOC 28-2-46
MB889 4657 CHA Ben 20-8-43 10ADU 15-9 Ind 30-9 SOC 12-6-45
MB890 4659 CHA Ben 20-8-43 10ADU 11-9 NWA 1-10 MAAF 21-6-45 SOC 14-3-46
MB891 4670 CHA Ben 22-8-43 10ADU 15-9 Ind 30-9 681S FTR ops 30-8-44 SOC 11-9
MB892 4669 CHA Ben 22-8-43 10ADU 7-10 MAL 12-10 NAASC 31-10 SOC 28-6-45
MB893 4687 CHA Ben 26-8-43 10ADU 15-9 Ind 21-10 SOC 31-8-44
MB894 4699 CHA Ben 27-8-43 10ADU 26-9 Ind 1-11 SOC 12-3-45
MB895 4692 CHA Ben 27-8-43 10ADU 25-9 Ind 11-10 CE SOC 26-7-45
MB896 4714 CHA Ben 31-8-43 10ADU 26-9 Ind 7-10 SOC 12-6-45
MB897 4715 CHA Ben 31-9-43 10ADU 26-9 MAL 12-10 41S lost w/u ldg Harty Marshes Sheppey Kent 12-2-44 MAAF 21-6-45 SOC 18-10
MB898 4716 CHA Ben 31-8-43 10ADU 26-9 Ind 17-10 SOC 31-8-44
MB899 4727 CHA Ben 3-9-43 10ADU 23-9 Ind 11-10 SOC 11-4-46
MB900 4736 CHA Ben 5-9-43 10ADU 2-10 Ind 21-10 SOC 30-5-46
MB901 4737 CHA Ben 5-9-43 10ADU 9-10 MAL 11-10 i/sea off Spanish Coast on ops 11-10 FH9.10
MB902 4753 CHA Ben 8-9-43 541S 10-10 16S dvd i/grd nr Devizes CE 29-3-44
MB903 4754 CHA Ben 9-9 541S 10-10 106Gp Wpl 18-6-44 34WSU 16-8 16S 2-3-45 sold MoS 18-1-49
MB904 4761 CHA Ben 11-9-43 Gib 25-10 ME 27-10 Ind 1-11 FTR ops 10-1-44
MB905 4762 CHA Ben 11-9-43 10ADU 12-9 ME 6-11 GA Ind 1-1-44
MB906 4773 CHA Ben 12-9-43 541S 13-10 106Gp Wpl 18-6-44 8 OTU 26-9 to5937M 15-4-46 rtp 28-4-47
MB907 CHA Ben 12-9-43 541S 13-10 106Gp Wpl 12-7-44 34WSU 16-8 4S FAAC 6-9 421RSU CE ops 19-11
MB908 4786 CHA Ben 16-9-43 541S 10-10 Ce op 4-11
MB909 4799 CHA Ben 19-9-43 10ADU 20-10 Gib 25-10 Ind 19-11 SOC 27-2-47
X MB910 4803 CHA Ben 19-9-43 10ADU 24-10 Gib 26-10 Ind 2-11 SOC 28-8-47
MB911 4804 CHA Ben 10-9-43 10ADU 24-10 Gib 26-10 Ind 10-11 SOC 29-6-45
MB936 4824 CHA Ben 25-9-43 10ADU 20-10 MAL 29-10 SOC MAAF 30-4-45
MB937 4831 CHA Ben 26-9-43 10ADU 23-10 MAL 25-10 682S C3 ops 23-11-44
MB938 4827 CHA Ben 26-9-43 10ADU 24-10 MAL 25-10 SOC MAAF 29-5-47
MB939 4832 CHA Ben 26-9-43 10ADU 9-11 MAL 12-11 FTR ops 3-10-44
MB940 4833 CHA Ben 26-9-43 10ADU 9-11 FAAC 10-11 218Gp NA 30-11 SOC 14-6-45
MB941 4853 CHA 140S 30-9-43 Ben 6-10 16S 21-4-44 34WSU 23-8 400S 14-9 FAAC 29-12 409RSU HAL 20-2-45 SOC 16-11-47
MB942 4854 M61 CHA 140S 30-9-43 Ben 6-10 400S 5-5-44 e/a CB 1-1-45 recat E 27-4
MB943 4862 CHA 140S 2-10-43 FAAC 2-11 HAL M61 instal 11-11 1PP Ben 1-5-44 sold MoS 18-1-49
MB944 4872 CHA 140S 3-10-43 16S 20-3-44 CAC ops 8-5 412RSU 16S 2-11-44 34WSU 14-12 HAL 3-2-45 sold Int All 31-3-49
MB945 4875 CHA Ben 7-10-43 USAAF 30-10 lost in Channel 1-3-44
MB946 4884 CHA Ben 9-10-43 USAAF 12-11 HAL 30-3-45 recat E SOC 5-7
MB947 4902 CHA 140S 15-10-43 400S 5-5-44 83GSU 19-4-45 34Gp OC(UK) 6-9 SOC 27-9
MB948 4904 CHA no record
MB949 4910 CHA Ben 16-10-43 USAAF 12-11 HAL 23-11 34WSU 30-8-44 4S 18-1-45 GAAC 3-8 84Gp OC(UK) 6-9 scr 16-11-47
MB950 4921 CHA Ben 18-10-43 USAAF 13-11 HAL recat E 5-7-45 SOC 13-9
MB951 4951 CHA Ben 24-10-43 16S 28-11 412RSU 22-7-44 34WSU 3-8 FAAC 11-4-45 sold MoS 18-1-49
MB952 4972 CHA Ben 5-11-43 7th Recc Gp 14th PRS 8thAF USAAF 23-11 lost over Holland 8-9-44
MB953 4937 CHA Ben 22-10-43 16S 22-11 AAC 6-9-44 412RSU HAL 4-11 sold MoS 18-1-49
MB954 4936 CHA Ben 20-10-43 16S 22-11 CAC ops 28-4-44 CE ops 18-9
MB955 4947 CHA Ben 5-11-43 USAAF 8-7 5-12 lost over Holland 19-9-44
MB956 4956 CHA Ben 5-11-43 USAAF 13-12 HAL 30-3-45 recat E 5-7 SOC 13-9
MB957 4963 CHA 16S 5-11-43 FAAC 27-9-44 412RSU 34WSU 12-10
MB958 4974 CHA 16S 5-11-43 CAC ops 13-8-44 ROS 34WSU 8-9 1PP Ben 10-3-45 HAL recat E 5-7 SOC 13-9

PA series all PR Mk XI(T) Merlin 63.

PA838 498 1 CHA 16S 3-11-43 151RU 14-6-45 49MU 28-6 mr SOC 14-9
PA839 4982 CHA 16S 5-11-43 FAAC 29-5-44 HAL 400S 10-8 1PP Ben 10-2-45 4S 20-3 412S 16S 9-8 26S 18-10 SOC 27-11-47
PA840 4992 CHA 16S 5-11-43 FACE 22-2-44
PA841 4993 Ben 6-11-43 USAAF 5-12 HAL 5-4-45 recat E SOC 13-9
PA842 4989 CHA Ben 5-11-43 USAAF 23-11 HAL 8-12-45 sold MoS 22-8-47
PA843 5004 M66 CHA no record
PA844 5008 CHA Ben 7-11-43 10ADU 1-1-44 MAL 31-1 MAAF SOC 18-10-45
PA845 5016 CHA Ben 15-11-43 10ADU 28-12 GIB 31-12 ME 1-2-44 SOC 26-9-46
PA846 5020 CHA Ben 9-11-43 10ADU 28-12 India 15-1-44 SOC 12-6-45
PA847 5021 CHA Ben 9-11-43 10ADU FTR on f/f Porth to Gib 14-12 FH6.10
PA848 5038 CHA Ben 15-11-43 10ADU 28-12 Ind 31-12 ACSEA 9-2-44 618S FTR ops 2-7-44
PA849 5039 CHA Ben 15-11-43 16S 9-12 CB ops 28-5-44 HAL 1PP Ben 10-2-45 4S 5-4 sold MoS 22-8-47
PA850 5080 CHA Ben 30-11-43 10ADU 31-12 Gib 5-1-44 ME 1-2 MAAF 31-5-45 SOC 29-8-46
PA851 4986 CHA Ben 5-11-43 USSAF 8-7 28-11 lost in North Sea 23-12
PA852 5199 CHA 6MU 19-12-43 4S 2-2-44 FAAC 7-8 412RSU ROS 26-4-45 sold MoS 22-8-47
PA853 5224 CHA Ben 27-12-43 10ADU 10-2-44 ACSEA 21-2 C3 ops 23-3
PA854 5223 CHA Ben 27-12-43 Gib 29-1-44 MAAF 31-1 s/dn by Spit FIX C3 7-4
PA855 5185 CHA Ben 21-12-43 542S 7-1-44 out of fuel f/ld nr Mans CE 25-2
PA856 5194 CHA Ben 21-12-43 541S 29-12 10ADU 29-1-44 MAL 30-1 Ind 8-2 SOC 12-6-45
PA857 5236 CHA Ben 1-1-44 4S 7-2 151RU 17-5-45 CAC 4-6 recat E SOC 16-11
PA858 5235CHA Ben 1-1-44 10ADU 5-2 MAL 6-2 MAAF 31-3 SOC 19-10-45
PA859 STN M70 Ben 1-3-44 541S 26-3 e/a CB 1-1-45 HAL 1401Met Flt 19-2-46 FACB cd f/lnd nr Crewe 2-4 SOC
PA860 5066 CHA Ben 24-11-43 10ADU 28-12 Ind 30-1-44 SOC 26-7-45
PA861 5040 CHA Ben 15-12-43 16S 25-12 CB ops 6-7-44 HAL 1PP Ben 21-3-45 SOC 23-8
PA862 5085 CHA Ben 4-12-43 FAAC 31-12 10ADU 12-6-44 ME 19-6 ACSEA 27-10-45 SOC 25-7-46
PA863 5045 CHA Ben 15-11-43 16S 24-12 FTR ops 8-3-44
PA864 5094 CHA Ben 2-12-43 541S 29-12 8 OTU 7-11-44 29MU 7-7-45 SOC 30-5
PA865 5064 CHA Ben 24-11-43 10ADU 2-1-44 Indiam 17-1 ACSEA SOC 13-6-46
PA866 5121CHA Ben 13-12-43 10ADU 20-1-44 MAAF 21-2 683S FTR ops 19-5
PA867 5063 CHA 24-11-43 ROS 8-2-44 MAL 7-3 SOC 18-10-45

MB789, Boscombe Down, August 1943, for performance trials. With a Merlin 63 and auw 8,040 lb it reached 417mph (FS gear) @ 24,200ft, and had a maximum cruising speed (FS) of 397 @ 31,000.

PA868 5106 CHA Ben 541S CB ops 5-7-44 HAL recat E 14-8
PA869 5127 CHA Ben 4-12-43 16S 3-1-44 HAL 6-10 1PP Ben 16-3-45 34WSUI e/fld w/u ldg Sandley nr Gillingham CE 128-6 SOC 21-7
PA870 5102 CHAM Ben 4-12-43 16S 3-1-44 CE ops 7-6
PA871 5134 CHA Ben 13-12-43 400S 19-1-44 FRU 14-12 34WSU 19-4-45 HAL 27-6 recat E SOC 15-9
PA884 5160 CHA 6MU 19-12-43 4S 18-1-44 412RSU 1-2 84GOC UK 6-9 to 5679M 21-9
PA885 5153 CHA Ben 21-12-43 542S 9-1-44 FTR ops 28-5
PA886 5150 CHA Ben 13-12-43 400S 19-1-44 HAL 23-2-45 6MU 28-8-47 sold Int All 31-3-49
PA887 5165 CHA 6MU 19-12-43 4S 1-2-44 34WSU 3-8 400S 14-9 e/a CB 1-1-45 HAL recat E 5-7 SOC 14-9
PA888 5170 CHA Ben 13-12-43 400S 25-4-44 CB ops

12-5 HAL 1PP Ben 1-2-45 29MU 24-6 SOC 30-5-46

PA889 5170 CHA 9MU 19-12-43 400S 24-1-44 CB ops 10-8 ROS 1PP Ben 4-2-45 4S 5-4 49MU 20-9 SOC 20-12

PA890 5182 CHA Ben 21-2-43 10ADU 6-2-44 Ind 26-2 ACSEA CE 12-3-45

PA891 5190 CHA Ben 20-12-43 4S 2-2-44 511FRU 15-6 ROS sold MoS 18-1-49

PA892 4996 Ben 6-11-43 USAAF 17-1-44 1PP Ben 3-4-45 HAL 17-4 recat E SOC 14-9-45

PA893 5219 CHA HAL 29-1-44 6MU 19-7 Ben 20-8 CE ops 20-9

PA894 CHA Ben 7-1-44 400S 7-2 e/a CE 1-1-45

PA895 5195 CHA Ben 24-12-43 10ADU 5-1-44 MAL Gib 6-2 MAAF 31-3 SOC 31-1-46

PA896 CHA Ben 4-1-44 10ADU 10-2 ACSEA 21-2 SOC 25-7-46

PA897 CHA Ben 29-1-44 4S 11-2 ROS 13-2-45 sold MoS 22-8-47

PA898 CHA Ben 14-1-44 10ADU 10-2 ACSEA 21-2 SOC 28-8-47

PA899 CHA Ben 29-1-44 4S 11-2 CAC ops 9-5 16S 20-7 CE ops 9-9

PA900 CHA Ben 400S 11-2-44 ROS HAL 16-4-45 recat E SOC 14-9

PA901 CHA Ben 29-1-44 4S 5-3 CE ops 10-4

PA902 CHA Ben 29-1-44 16S 12-3 511FRU e/fd in circuit f/ld Hartford Bridge 28-3 SOC 29-3 FH28.5

PA903 CHA Ben 29-1-44 400S 11-2 CB ROS 23-10 34WSU 2-2-45 VAEA 24-10-46 scr 28-11

PA904 CHA Ben 29-1-44 10ADU 5-3 5-3 MAL 8-3 SOC 18-10-45

PA905 CHA Ben 30-1-44 10ADU 1-3 MAL 2-3 FTR 29-12-45

PA906 CHA Ben 29-1-44 10ADU 28-2 ACSEA 10-3 SOC 1-12-46

PA907 CHA Ben 29-1-44 MAL 1-3 ME Feb'45 SOC 31-10-46

PA908 CHA Ben 10ADU 4-3-44 ACSEA 17-3 SOC 9-5-46 Indian AF inst M342. In store USAF Museum, Dayton. Extant.

PA909 CHA Ben 30-1-44 10ADU 29-2 MAL 1-3 SOC 18-10-45

PA910 CHA Ben 2-2-44 10ADU 29-2 MAL 1-3 SOC 27-2-47

PA911 5225 CHA Ben 29-1-44 10ADU 30-1 CAC ops 13-3 ROS MAAF 14-4 ME SOC 26-9-46

PA912 CHA Ben 29-1-44 PRDU 9-2 106GTp Wpl 18-6 542S 21-6 400S 21-9 sold MoS 22-8-47

PA913 Ben 19-2-44 10ADU 15-3 ACSEA 23-3 SOC 26-4-45

PA926 CHA Ben 29-1-44 10ADU 19-2 ACSEA 29-2 SOC 12-6-45

PA927 CHA Ben 9-2-44 84GSU 19-3 400S 15-6 sold MoS 22-8-47

PA928 CHA Ben 2-2-44 10ADU 1-3 ACSEA 11-3 SOC 12-6-45

PA929 CHA Ben 29-1-44 16S 12-3-44 cd Sandhill Farm Bletchingley CE 8-6 412RSU 15-6

PA930 CHA Ben 2-2-44 10ADU 19-2 Gib 20-2 MAAF 31-2 FTR 23-2-45

PA931 CHA Ben 2-2-44 4S 11-3 HAL 13-6 4S 31-8 ROS 5-3-45 SOC ABS 5-2-47

PA932 CHA Ben 20-2-44 10ADU 20-3 MAAF 25-3 ME 2-8-45 SOC 9-8

PA933 ALD Ben 12-2-44 16S 14-3 CE ops 31-5

PA934 CHA Ben 30-1-44 10ADU 1-3 ACSEA 23-3 SOC 27-2-47

PA935 Ben 19-2-44 10ADU 17-3 ACSEA 26-3 cd f/lnd Malaya 22-2-46 SOC 31-12

PA936 ALD Ben 24-2-44 10ADU 15-3 MAAF 31-2 SOC 18-10-45

PA937 CHA Ben 5-2-44 541S FAAC 9-10 ROS 8 OTU 24-11 SOC 30-5-46

PA938 Ben 20-2-33 10ADU 19-2 MAAF 25-3 CE ops 11-12

PA939 CHA Ben 400S 5-3-44 FAAC 20-3 HAL 16-5 1PP Ben 3-2-45 16S 5-4 83GOC 8-11 BAFO Com Wg 30-12 sold bou 3-9-47

PA940 ALD Ben 22-2-44 10ADU 24-3-44 ACSEA 3-4 SOC 1-1-45

PA941 CHA Ben 14-2-44 542S 19-3 CB ops 5-10 HAL 1PP Ben 12-5-45 sold MoS 22-8-47

PA942 CHA Ben 15-2-44 541S 14-3 400S 15-6 34WSU Trng Flt 14-9 out of fuel f/ld Eckington Worcs CE 31-10

PA943 CHA Ben 15-2-44 541S 14-3 8 OTU 7-11 e/fld H/A ditched Loch Connell Argyll CE 5-7-45 SOC 13-9

PA944 CHA Ben 14-2-44 USAAF 20-4 HAL 5-4-45 recat E SOC 13-9

PA945 CHA Ben 12-2-44 542S 14-3 FTR ops 5-10

PA946 CHA Ben 24-12-44 10ADU 10-4 ACSEA 17-4

PA947 CHA Ben 12-2-44 16S 14-3 400S 25-7 412RSU 22-7 16S 3-8 FTR ops 30-9

PA948 M70 ALD Ben 6-3-44 542S 23-3 6MU 23-8-45 sold MoS 22-8-47 FACB 3-8

PA950 ALD Ben 6-3-44 10ADU 12-4 MAAF 15-4 SOC 18-10-45

PA951 CHA Ben 20-2-44 10ADU 4-4 ACSEA 17-11 SOC 13-6-46

PA959 ALD Ben 29-2-44 10ADU 8-5 ACSEA 18-5 SOC 1-11-45

PA960 CHA Ben 14-2-44 10ADU 6-4 MAAF 15-4 ME 23-12 13S Fayid 8-1-48 109MU 5-2 SOC 6-8-50

PA961 ALD Ben 24-2-44 84GSU 19-3 400S 15-6 83GSU 17-5-45 sold MoS 22-8-47

PL series 758 to 762, 764 to 766, 770 Merlin 63 rest M70

PL775, 'A', of 541 Squadron, Benson, June 1944.

PL758 CHA BDn 28-2-44 cool trls wilth reduced area rad exit duct. Trop air intake by-passed when eng overcooled in temperate conditions. Fitt FXII rud Ben 20-8 4S 31-8 HAL 6-2-45 recat E SOC 3-9 bboc SFU Honiley 7-3-46 e/fld w/u ldg nr Warwick 19-7 FA SOC 25-7

PL759 ALD Ben 28-2-44 6MU 18-4 4S 15-6 412RSU 29-6 130AF CAC 6-7 ROS Ben 13-2-45 83GOC 6-9 SOC 19-9

PL760 CHA Ben 18-2-44 10ADU 19-3 MAAF 25-3 SOC 3-1-45

PL761 CHA Ben 28-2-44 4S 15-6 CAC ops 22-6 412RSU 29-6 1PP Ben 6-3-45 BAFO Com Wg 23-10 FACB strk Auster NJ934 lndg Valkenrure Holland 5-1-46 151RU 5-1 recat E SOC 31-1

PL762 ALD Ben 3-3-44 6MU 18-4 4S 15-6 CAC ROS 6-4-45 sold MoS 22-8-47

PL763 ALD Ben 12-3-44 10ADU 28-2 MAAF 11-4 SOC Oct'44

PL764 CHA Ben 28-2-44 84GSU 26-3 4S 15-6 FAAC 4-11 HAL sold MoS 22-8-47

PL765 CHA Ben 2-3-44 84RSU 19-3 4S 15-6 e/a CE 1-1-45

PL766 CHA Ben 12-3-44 542S 30-4 8 OTU 8-11 sold MoS 22-8-47

PL767 ALD Ben 23-3-44 7th Recc Gp 14th PR S 8th AF USAAF 20-4

PL768 ALD Ben 12-3-44 10ADU 6-4 ACSEA 21-4 SOC 29-2-47

PL769 ALD Ben 12-3-44 10ADU 21-3 ACSEA 20-4 SOC 9-5-46

PL770 CHA Ben 28-2-44 6MU 18-4 16S 6-5 FAAC 11-8 sold MoS 22-8-47

PL771 ALD Ben 18-3-44 10ADU 4-7 MAAF 19-4 SOC 18-10-45

PL772 ALD Ben 20-3-44 ACSEA 8-5 SOC 29-6-45

PL773 ALD Ben 20-3-44 10ADU 4-4 ACSEA 20-4 20-4 SOC 13-6-46

PL774 ALD Ben 27-3-44 10ADU 6-5 ACSEA 18-5 SOC 6-9-45

PL775 ALD Ben 22-4-44 541S 14-5 71MU 14-3-46 SOC 1-4

PL776 ALD Ben 23-2-44 1OADU 4-4 ACSEA 17-4 SOC 26-4-45

PL777 ALD Ben 27-3-44 MAAF 18-4 s/dn en route to Gib 18-4 disposed of by Air Attache Madrid 30-4-45

PL778 ALD Ben 16-4-44 10ADU ACSEA 20-5 SOC 31-1-46

PL779 ALD Ben 2-4-44 10ADU 26-4 ACSEA 8-5 SOC 1-11-45

PL780 ALD Ben 2-4-44 10ADU 26-4 ACSEA 8-5 SOC 27-2-47

PL781 CHA 6MU 6-4-44 Ben 9-9 ROS 10ADU 24-10 NWA 26-10 ACSEA 30-10 SOC 17-10-49

PL782 ALD Ben 2-4-44 USAAF 8-7 20-4 lost over Germany 5-9

PL783 ALD Ben 11-4-44 10ADU 28-4 ACSEA 20-5 SOC 11-1-45

PL784 ALD Ben 2-4-44 10ADU 26-4 ACSEA 11-5 SOC 27-2-47

PL785 ALD Ben 6-4-44 542S 30-4 sold MoS 22-8-47

PL786 ALD 6MU 24-4-44 Ben 14-5 4S 23-5 Ser Flt Odiham 14-8 CAC ROS 4S 25-9 400S 12-10 e/a CE 1-1-45 HAL 23-4 recat E 5-7

PL787 ALD 6MU 22-4-44 Ben 14-5 4S 25-5 eng fire a/c aban over Eng Channel 17-7

PL788 CHA 6MU 6-4-44 Ben 4-10 10ADU 14-10 MAAF SOC 18-10-45

PL789 ALD 6MU 25-4-44 Ben 5-9 54S 10-9 SOC 27-11-47

PL790 ALD Ben 6-4-44 USAAF 8/7 20-4 lost over England 15-6

PL791 ALD Ben 22-4-44 10ADU 31-5 ACSEA 12-6 SOC 26-4-45

PL792 CHA 6MU 30-4-44 Ben 12-5 4S 15-6 412RSU CAC 22-6 61S FAAC 30-9 ROS 400S CAC ops 24-2-45 4S 10-5 2S 6-9 SOC 27-11-47

PL793 ALD 6MU 30-4-44 Ben 20-5 4S 15-6 2S 6-9-45 SOC 26-3-46

PL794 ALD 6MU 18-4-44 Ben 14-5 4S 30-5 412RSU 29-8 Persh 18-8-47 RDanAF 23-8 as 451

PL795 ALD 6MU 23-4-44 Ben 20-5 84GSU 30-5 16S 8-6 FAAC 20-9 ROS 400S 4-1-45 HAL 10-5 recat E SOC 5-7

PL796 ALD 6MU 25-4-44 Ben 20-5 4S 15-6 CE ops 24-12

PL797 ALD 6MU 22-4-44 Ben 14-5 400S 23-5 CE ops 17-7

PL798 ALD Ben 11-4-44 10ADU 27-4 ACSEA 11-5 SOC 13-9-45

PL799 ALD 6MU 30-4-44 Ben 14-5 400S 25-5 CAC ops 22-3-45 SOC 29-8

PL823 ALD 6MU 10-5-44 Ben 20-5 84GSU 2-6 16S 8-6 FACB 17-7 412RSU 20-7 FACB 15-7-45

PL824 ALD 6MU 30-4-44 Ben 14-5 400S 30-5 SOC 6-9-45

PL825 ALD 6MU 20-5-44 Ben 16-8 542S 3-9 sold MoS 22-8-47

PL826 ALD 6MU 9-5-44 Ben 20-5 84GSU 2-6 400S 15-6 ROS 10-11 16S 29-3-45 FAAC 27-7 8 OTU 10-9 SOC 12-6-48

PL827 CHA Farn 6-5-44 replacement trls a/c for EN409. Rate of roll and contin of compressibility trls initiated with EN409. F/ld Whitmoor Common CB 15-8 HAL recat E 24-9

PL828 ALD 6MU 30-4-44 Ben 13-6 400S 6-8 FAAC 21-3-45 HAL recat E SOC 14-9-45

PL829 ALD M70 6MU 2-5-44 Ben 14-5 400S 25-5 eng fire in circuit Odiham hit tree cd dbf CE 28-7 pilot kld

PL830 ALD 6MU 25-5-44 Ben 13-6 16S 23-7 CAC ops 19-11 4S 26-7-45 BAFO CE 2-9-47

PL831 ALD M50 6MU 7-5-44 Ben 14-5 4S 30-5 eng fire in air CE 9-8

PL832 ALD 6MU 14-5-44 Ben 20-5 4S 15-6 CAC ops 19-10 412RSU 28-2 71MU 30-3-46 SOC 1-4

PL833 ALD 6MU 8-5-44 Ben 20-5 400S 8-6 HAL 15-8 No 2 Gp Guttersloh 3-1-46 Persh 6-1-47 RDanAF 1-9 as 452 scr 1-6-55

PL834 ALD 6MU 14-5-44 Ben 20-5 16S 8-6 CE ops 20-9

PL835 ALD 6MU 20-5-44 Ben 25-8 MAAF 19-9 SOC 6-9-45

PL836 ALD 6MU 14-5-44 Ben 20-5 16S 15-6 400S 10-8 CB ops 5-9 409RSU HAL 30-9 2Gp BAFO Com S 15-1-46 CE 28-9

PL837 ALD 6MU 22-5-44 Ben 13-6 400S 6-8 ROS 27-10 to 5453M 12-6-46

PL838 ALD 6MU 3-6-44 Ben 4-10 10ADU 15-9 NWA 19-10 ACSEA 23-10 SOC 24-12

PL839 ALD 6MU 22-5-44 Ben 13-6 34WSU 20-10 16S 4-1-45 26S 20-9 151RU 10-10 SOC 26-3-46

PL840 ALD 6MU 28-5-44 Ben 27-10 34WSU 16-11 4S 23-11 CAC ops 29-12 3BRU CE 29-6-46

PL841 ALD 6MU 29-5-44 Ben 9-9 10ADU 20-9 NWA 25-9 ACSEA 12-10 FTR ops 7-6-45

PL842 ALD 6MU 3-6-44 10ADU 30-11 NWA 2-12 MAAF SOC 13-10-45

PL843 ALD 6MU 5-6-44 Ben 13-6 4S 29-6 FAAC 15-12 400S 29-3-45 BAFO Com Wng 18-10 sold scr bou 3-9-47

PL844 ALD 6MU 1-6-44 Ben 27-10 10ADU 9-11 NWA 17-11 MAAF SOC 18-10-45

PL845 ALD 6MU 1-6-44 Ben 15-9 16S 5-10 FTR ops 18-11

PL846 ALD 6MU 8-6-44 Ben 9-9 MAAF 25-9 SOC 18-10-45

PL847 ALD 6MU 5-6-44 Ben 13-6 4S 29-6 HAL 28-8 541S 26-3-45 FAAC 14-6 8OTU 2-9-46 SOC 31-10

PL848 ALD 6MU 11-6-44 Ben 15-9 16S 28-9 CAC ops 25-10 HAL 23-2-45 recat E SOC 14-9

PL849 ALD 6MU 19-6-44 Ben 3-7 10ADU 22-7 MAAF 25-7 ACSEA 1-8 FTR ops 19-6-45

PL850 ALD 6MU 11-6-44 Ben 23-8 16S 16-11 FACB 13-12 HAL CFE 10-11-45 6MU NEA 13-1-47 sold MoS 22-8

PL851 ALD 6MU 11-6-44 Ben 15-9 16S 5-10

PL852 ALD 6MU 23-6-44 Ben 3-7 10ADU 22-7 MAAF 25-7 ACSEA 29-7 SOC 31-11-45

PL853 ALD 6MU 12-6-44 Ben 15-9 16S 5-10 FTR ops 14-1-45

PL854 ALD 6MU 17-6-44 Ben 25-8 16S 14-9 CAC ops 24-3-45 HAL 27-4 recat E SOC 14-9

PL855 ALD 6MU 21-6-44 Ben 3-7 10ADU 17-7 MAAF 20-7 ACSEA 27-9 SOC 25-10-45

PL856 ALD 6MU 12-6-44 Ben 16-8 541S 5-9 FTR ops 20-3-45

PL857 ALD 6MU 17-6-44 Ben 3-7 10ADU 25-7 MAAF 31-7 SOC 18-10-45

PL883 saw service with 400 Squadron.

PL858 ALD 6MU 19-6-44 Ben 3-7 10ADU 17-7 MAAF 20-7 ACSEA 8-8 SOC 6-9-45

PL859 ALD 6MU 24-6-44 Ben 3-7 10ADU 22-7 MAAF 25-7 SOC 19-1-45

PL860 ALD Ben 30-6-44 10ADU 24-7 NWA 27-8 ACSEA 6-9 fire in air i/sea on f/f SOC 30-12

PL861 trans to Royal Navy

PL862 ALD Ben 25-6-44 10ADU 12-7 MAAF 14-7 ACSEA 29-7 SOC 6-9-45

PL863 ALD Ben 25-6-44 10ADU 8-7 MAAF 12-7 ACSEA 29-7 SOC 31-10-46

PL864 ALD 6MU 7-7-44 Ben 9-9 NWA 21-9 CE 6-1-45

PL865 ALD 6MU 16-7-44 Ben 5-9 10ADU 26-9 NWA 27-9 ME Feb '45 SOC 31-10-46

PL866 ALD 6MU 8-7-44 295S 10-7 USAAF 8/7 lost 14-2-45

PL881 ALD 6MU 10-7-44 Ben 4-10 400S 26-10 BAFO Com Wg 27-9-45 FACE 19-10

PL882 ALD Ben 1-7-44 541S 22-7 FTR 5-12

PL883 ALD 6MU 3-7-44 400S CAC on ops 26-7 Ben 14-10 e/a CE 1-1-45

PL884 ALD Ben 30-6-44 10ADU 28-7 MAAF 29-7 ACSEA 8-8 SOC 12-7-45

PL885 ALD 6MU 2-7-44 Ben 25-8 MAAF 19-9 SOC 18-10-45

PL886 ALD 6MU 8-7-44 Ben 5-9 542HCU 9-9 SOC 23-8-45

PL887 ALD 6MU 11-7-44 Ben 27-10 541S 2-11 FTR ops 30-11

PL888 ALD 6MU 16-7-44 1PP Ben 14-10 ME 5-11 ACSEA 12-11 SOC 9-5-46

PL889 ALD 6MU 11-7-44 Ben 27-10 10ADU 10-11 NWA 16-11 ACSEA 22-11 SOC 27-2-47

PL890 ALD 6MU 10-7-44 Ben 27-10 34NSU 16-11 66S 23-11 16S 18-1-45 GAAC 25-2-45 26S 20-9 3BRU CE 29-6-46

PL891 ALD 6MU 10-7-44 Ben 4-11 34WSU 16-11 4S 24-12 ROS 23-2-5 BAFO Com Wg 1-1-46 RAF Berlin 6-2 SOC 27-11-47

PL892 ALD 6MU 16-7-44 1PP Ben 14-10 16S 9-11 26S 25-10-45 3BRU CE 29-6-46

PL893 ALD 6MU 16-7-44 Ben 16-11 10ADU 20-11 MAAF 28-11 ME 5-7-45 SOC 26-9-46

PL894 ALD 6MU 20-7-44 Ben 4-10 4S FAAC 6-11 1401 Met Flt 26-11-45 FACE cd on t/o pilot kld Celle 27-4-46 SOC 31-8

PL895 ALD 6MU 16-7-44 Ben 5-9 36MU 3-1-45 ROS 400S 26-7 BAFO Com Wg 20-9 151RU 18-10 scr bou sold 3-9-47

PL896 ALD 6MU 20-7-44 1PP Ben 14-10 542S 1-11 71MU 13-3-46 SOC 1-4

PL897 ALD 6MU 16-7-44 Ben 4-11 10ADU 25-11 ME 1-12 ACSEA 10-12 SOC 11-7-46

PL898 ALD 6MU 23-7-44 Ben 23-8 10ADU 8-9 ME 18-9 ACSEA 21-9 SOC 27-2-47

PL899 ALD 6MU 22-7-44 1PP Ben 14-10 541S 1-11 FTR ops 1-1-45

PL900 541S e/fd cd Surrey 6-1-45

PL901 ALD 6MU 28-7-44 Ben 16-8 542S 28-8 FACE 6-1-45 SOC 12-1

PL902 ALD 6MU 23-7-44 1PP Ben 14-10 4S 16-11 ROS 17-3-45 HPA 8-7 Met Com S 30-7 sold E Smelt 21-6-49

PL903 ALD Ben 28-7-44 34WSU 16-8 ROS 25-10 39WG 11-12 SOC 23-8-45

PL904 ALD 6MU 28-7-44 Ben 16-8 541S FTR ops 28-9

PL905 ALD 6MU 28-7-44 Ben 23-8 Northolt 8-9 16S 14-9 e/a CE 1-1-45

PL906 ALD 6MU 29-7-44 Ben 16-8 542S FTR ops 27-11

PL907 6MU 27-8-44 Ben 9-9 10ADU 16-9 NWA 18-9 ACSEA 24-9 SOC 1-6-47

PL908 ALD 6MU 29-7-44 Ben 16-8 542S 28-8 FA cd 24-7-45 ROS recat E SOC 23-11

PL909 6MU 14-8-44 Ben 25-8 10ADU 8-9 ME 17-9 ACSEA 21-9 SOC 30-5-46

PL910 6MU 21-8-44 Ben 28-9 542S 3-10 sold MoS 22-8-47

PL911 6MU 21-8-44 Ben 15-9 400S 28-9

PL912 6MU 21-8-44 Ben 15-9 16S 28-9 e/a 1-1-45 412RSU 25-1 82GOC 8-11 Neth SoTT 8-7-47 as Instructional A/F

PL913 6MU 23-8-44 Ben 5-9 16S 14-9 FACB 17-11 HAL 1401 Met Flt 16-1-45 FA f/lnd eng/fld Salzwedel 19-1-46

PL914 6MU 2-9-44 Ben 28-9 USAAF 2-10 1PP Ben 3-4-45 71MU 18-3-46 SOC 1-4

PL915 6MU 27-8-44 1PP Ben 8-10 10ADU 24-10 MAAF 27-10 c/lnd Hellopolis, Egypt 16-9 SOC 28-11-46

PL916 6MU 27-8-44 Ben 9-9 10ADU 16-9 NWA 18-9 FTR ops 8-10

PL917 6MU 29-8-44 1PP Ben 8-10 10ADU 24-10 NWA 2-11 ME 30-11 SOC 29-8-46

PL918 6MU 13-9-44 1PP Ben 27-9 10ADU 9-10 MAAF 11-10 SOC 20-9-45

PL919 6MU 29-8-44 Ben 28-9 541S 28-11 FTR ops 24-12

PL920 6MU 29-8-44 1PP Ben 8-10 10ADU 24-10 NWA 28-10 ACSEA 20-11 SOC 13-6-46

PL921 6MU 29-8-44 1PP Ben 8-10 542S 15-10 sold MoS 22-8-47

PL922 6MU 10-9-44 Ben 21-9 16S 12-10 CAC ops 17-12 412RSU HAL recat E SOC 13-9-45

PL923 6MU 2-9-44 1PP Ben 18-9 NWA 27-9 ME Feb '45 SOC 15-6

PL924 6MU 10-9-44 1PP Ben 15-9 10ADU 24-10 NWA 28-10 ME 29-10 ACSEA 6-11 SOC 28-2-46

PL925 6MU 9-9-44 Ben 21-9 400S 19-10 FTR ops 28-10

PL949 6MU 2-9-44 Ben 28-9 10ADU 7-10 NWA 10-10 SOC 28-2-46

PL950 9MU 18-9-44 CRD Farn 28-9 Ben 27-10 400S 9-11 e/a CB 1-1-45 HAL recat E SOC 13-9

PL951 ALD Ben 16-9-44 10ADU NWA 30-9 ACSEA 3-10 28-8-47

PL952 ALD 9MU 2-10-44 Ben 9-10 541S 19-10 6MU 13-9-45 SOC 1-4-46

PL953 6MU 2-9-44 Ben 21-9 4S 19-10 FTR ops 29-10

PL954 ALD 9MU 22-9-44 Ben 30-9 10ADU 9-10 NWA 12-10 ACSEA 18-10 MAAF 27-10 FTR ops 2-1-45

PL955 6MU 3-9-44 1PP Ben 15-9 10ADU 26-9 NWA 28-9 ME 20-9-45 SOC 28-2-46

PL956 ALD 9MU 1-10-44 1PP Ben 17-1-45 4S 22-2 SOC 16-11-47

PL957 6MU 2-9-44 Ben 21-9 4S 19-10 CE ops 19-11 412RSU 18-1-45 CAC ops 9-3 BAFO Com S 12-2-46 SOC 27-11-47

PL958 9MU 26-9-44 Ben 7-10 FAAC 14-10 HAL VAHP 5-6-45 71MU 14-3-46 SOC 1-4

PL959 ALD 9MU 15-9-44 1PP Ben 22-9 USAAF 27-9 sold E Smelt 21-6-49

PL960 6MU 9-9-44 Ben 21-9 10ADU 30-9 NWA 2-10 ME 8-10 ACSEA 8-10 SOC 27-2-47

PL961 ALD 9MU 1-10-44 1PP Ben 3-2-45 542S 26-3 SOC 16-11-47

PL962 9MU 24-9-44 USAAF 8/7 3-10 lost over France 15-1-45

PL963 9MU 26-9-44 Ben 7-10 544S 10-12 542S CAC ops 23-12 ROS 83Gp Com S 27-3-46 sold Int All 28-3-49

PL964 ALD 9MU 2-10-44 1PP Ben 17-1-45 16S 8-2 FAAC 5-8

PL965 9MU 9-10-44 Neth SoTT Extant Overloon National War & Resistance Museum.

PL966 9MU 9-10-44 1PP Ben 14-1-45 541S 21-1 26S 29-1-46 sold scr bou 3-9-47

PL967 ALD 9MU 3-10-44 1PP Ben 16-4-45 BAFO Com Wg 10-1-46 SOC 27-11-47

PL968 ALD 9MU 1-10-44 1PP Ben 14-1-45 541S 21-1 3BRU 20-3-46

PL969 9MU 9-10-44 Ben 4-11 10ADU 21-11 ME 1-12 ACSEA 10-12 SOC 6-9-45

PL970 ALD 9MU 2-10-44 1PP Ben 5-1-45 16S 18-1 FAAC 20-8 BAFO Com Wg 13-12 sold scr bou 3-9-47

PL971 no record

PL972 9MU 9-10-44 1PP Ben 7-2-45 106Gp 2-12 USAAF 9-3-46 sold VA 21-3-47

PL973 9MU 29-10-44 1PP Ben 6-11 10ADU 21-11 dam in France en route to ACSEA 27-11 ret UK by ship 25-6-45 HAL 1401 Met Flt 30-11 FAAC 14-3-46 SOC 5-2-47

PL974 Ben 12-10-44 4S 2-11 84Gp Com S 6-9-45 recat E 23-10 SOC 10-1-49 RDanAF as 451 23-8 SOC scr 1-6-55

PL975 9MU 16-10-44 1PP Ben 6-11 HAL 3-1-45 400S 25-1 BAFO Com Wg 25-10 CE 12-5-47

PL976 Ben 12-10-44 16S 23-11 e/a CE 1-1-45

PL977 6MU 21-10-44 Ben 10-11 10ADU ME 15-11 ACSEA 22-11 SOC 2-8-45

PL978 9MU 11-10-44 1PP Ben 6-11 16S 21-12 e/a 1-1-45 16S 18-1 CAC ops 22-3 26S 21-9 1401 Met Flt 15-4-46 Celle 84Gp Com Wg 28-10-46 Celle 84Gp Com Wg 28-10-46CE 6-8-47

PL979 5S Sept '45 trans to Royal Navy sold VA Jly '47. Extant R NorAF Gardermoen, as B-AZ

PL980 6MU 28-10-44 Ben 4-11 10ADU 21-11 NWA 29-11 SOC 28-2-46

PL981 6MU 2-11-44 Ben 4-11 400S 4-1-45 83Gp Com Wg 18-12 SOC 27-11-47

PL982 6MU 20-10-44 Ben 10ADU 4-12 ME 15-12 ACSEA 10-1-45 SOC 11-7-46

PL983 2S 6-9-45 6MU 12-1-46 22 OTU VA con high speed courier for American Embassy 27-1-48 as NC74138 to G.15-109 Shuttleworth 1950. Extant G-PRXI.

PL984 6MU 31-10-44 400S FACE 25-12

PL985 6MU 2-11-44 Ben 4-11 34WSU 16-11 16S 30-11 26S 20-9-45 sold scr bou 3-9-47

PL986 6MU 24-10-44 FTU 10ADU 10-11 NWA 12-11 SOC 28-2-46

PL987 6MU 2-11-44 400S 11-1-45 BAFO Com Wg 20-9 FACE 19-11

PL988 6MU 7-11-44 Persh 10ADU 29-11 ME 3-12 ACSEA 11-12 SOC 27-2-47

PL989 Ben 14-11-44 34WSU 23-11 e/a CE 1-1-45 409RSU 15-1 SOC 28-4

PL990 6MU 18-11-44 1PP Ben 24-11 10ADU 5-12 NWA 16-12 SOC 28-2-46

PL991 Ben 15-11-44 10ADU 7-12 NWA 14-12 FTR ops 29-1-45

PL992 ALD 1PP Ben 18-11-44 10ADU 2-12 ME 6-12 CAC 10-12 141RSU 22-7-45 SOC 23-7

PL993 Ben 14-11-44 4S 22-2-45 2S FAAC 4-9 412RSU 6-9 sold Int All 28-3-49

PL994 Ben 14-11-44 16S 13-12 e/a 19-3-45 Persh 15-7-47 RNorAF 31-7

PL995 ALD Ben 29-11-44 400S 11-1-45 BAFO Com Wg FAAC 13-9-45 3BRU 13-4-46 SOC 27-6

PL996 ALD 1PP Ben 18-11-44 MAAF 10-12 fire en route CE

PL997 Ben 25-11-44 10ADU 7-12 ME 17-12 ACSEA 10-1-45 7S FACE dbf 14-2-47 SOC 27-3

PL998 ALD 1PP Ben 18-11-44 400S 11-1-45 BAFO Com Wg 4-10 3BRU 2-4-46 Neth SoTT 8-7-47 as Instructional A/F

PM series all Merlin 70 except PM126, 127, 132 & 140 Griffon 65

PM123 ALD 1PP Ben 18-11-44 16S 11-1-45 e/a 19-3 AFDS CFE 15-11 SOC 8-4-48

PM124 ALD Ben 29-11-44 400S 4-1-45 ADLS FACB 14-9 SOC scr 16-11-47

PM125 ALD Ben 27-11-44 16S 20-9 FACB cd f/lnd Petersfield pilot kld 2-1-46 dbf on grd recat E SOC 31-1

PM126 ALD Ben 11-2-44 MAAF 27-12 SOC 18-10-45

PM127 ALD Ben 3-12-44 106Gp SR 2-2-45 542S 18-3 71MU 14-3-46 SOC 1-4

PM128 ALD Ben 27-11-44 400S e/a CB 1-1-45 409RSU 18-1 HAL 17-4 recat E SOC 3-9

PM129 Ben 25-11-44 10ADU 7-12 ACSEA 10-1-45 SOC 17-10-46

PM130 ALD Ben 5-12-44 1FU 10ADU 5-1-45 MAAF 14-1 SOC 26-9-46

PM131 ALD Ben 11-12-44 400S 11-1-45 FACB 18-7

PM132 ALD Ben 1-12-44 4S 11-1-45 CAC ops 21-1 412RSU 1401 Met Flt 6-2-46 25u/c coll lndg Ostend Belgium FACB 17-7 passed to Army Salvage SOC 10-8

PM133 ALD Ben 6-12-44 400S 4-1-45 BAFO Com Wg 18-10 NSoTT 8-7-47 as Instructional A/F

PM134 ALD Ben 26-12-44 4S 28-1-45 84Gp OC 6-9 268S 20-9 2S 27-9 Persh 18-89-47 RDanAF 12-9 as 453 722 FR.S 1954 sold scr 1-6-55

PM135 ALD M70 Ben 11-12-44 eng fire gnd running CE 31-12

PM136 ALD Ben 5-12-44 400S 4-1-45 BAFO Com Wg 27-9 CE 31-10-46 passed to Army Salvage 27-5-47

PM137 ALD Ben 17-12-44 400S 11-1-45 BAFO Com Wg 27-9

PM138 ALD Ben 20-12-44 400S 11-1-45 HAL 5-6 recat E 5-7

PM139 CHA Ben 13-1-45 541S 17-1 FAAC 15-3-46 SOC 30-5

PM140 ALD Ben 1-12-44 10ADU 2-1-45 MAAF 8-1 SOC 26-9-46

PM141 ALD Ben 11-12-44 10ADU 2-1-45 MAAF 8-1 13S Com Flt Fayid 11-12-47 Ismalia 27-5-48 109MU 10-6 SOC 11-12-50

PM142 ALD Ben 17-12-44 400S 18-1-45 CE ops 9-5

PM143 ALD Ben 8-1-45 541S 15-1 FAAC 8-6 SOC recat E 25-10

PM144 1PP Ben 7-1-45 541S 17-1 8 OTU 7-9-46 to 6249M 28-1-57 RAF Cranwell SOC 16-1-51

PM145 1PP Ben 14-1-45 541S 19-1 8 OTU 27-8-46 SOC sold BKL Alloys 27-4-48

PM146 1PP Ben 3-1-45 ROS 12-3 34WSU 26-3 400S 26-4 FAAC 1-3-46 recat E SOC 21-3

PM147 1PP Ben 20-1-45 16S 8-3 26S 20-9 SOC 27-11-47

PM148 1PP Ben 17-1-45 541S 23-1 FTR ops 8-3

PM149 1PP Ben 17-1-45 542S 29-1 1401 Met Flt 16-1-46 scr SOC 16-11-47

PM150 1PP Ben 20-1-45 106Gp 6-2 542S 71MU 13-3-46 SOC 1-4

PM151 1PP Ben 17-1-45 400S 15-2 BAFO Com Wg 20-9 FAAC 2-12

PM152 1PP Ben 22-1-45 4S 22-2 CE dbf on grd 22-3

PM153 ALD 1PP Ben 22-1-45 USAAF 4-2 BAFO Com Wg 17-1-46 FAAC 10-7 recat E 19-8

PM154 ALD 1PP Ben 3-2-45 106Gp 19-2 541S 18-3 8 OTU 3-7-46 to 6205M 28-1-47 RAF Cranwell SOC 16-1-51

PM155 1PP Ben 2-2-45 SOC 24-3

PM156 1PP Ben 20-1-45 400S 8-2 CAC ops 18-4 BAFO Com Wg FAAC 11-9 3BRU 16-4-46 CE 23-5-47

PM157 ALD MJL 1-2-45 1PP Ben 3-2 USAAF 22-2 BAFO Com Wg 16-1-46 cd/ld Buckenburg Germany CB 4-10-47 recat E 8-10

PM158 ALD Ben 1-1-45 106Hp SR 2-2 541S 16-3 SOC 27-11-47

PM159 CHA FF MJL 2-2-45 Ben 4-2 541S 24-3 8 OTU 31-7-46 CB 10-10-46 recat E 10-4-47

PM160 ALD dam in hvy ldg pre del trls 20-2 Ben 1-3-45 268S 9-1-46 SOC 27-11-47

LATER ALLOCATIONS.

Maintenance airframes; PA884(5679M), PL837(5453M), MB791(5936M), MB906(5937M), EN396(5934M), PM144(6249M), PM154(6250M).

Royal Danish AF; PL794.

Royal Navy; PL861 and 979.

Royal Norwegian Air Force; PL994.

USAAF; MB945, 949-950, 952, PA841-842, 851, 892, 944, PL767, 914, 959, 962, 972, PM153 and 157.

THE FIRST GRIFFON SPITFIRE

At the beginning of 1942 the Spitfire F Mk V was the main component part of the defensive and offensive arms of Fighter Command, but it was completely outclassed by the Luftwaffe's front line fighter, the Fw190. The Mk IX Spitfire was many months away from full production status and this was the situation confronting the Air Staff when it met in February 1942 to discuss the design and development of future fighter requirements. Sholto-Douglas said he was crystal gazing and that—"We must settle our minds on the type of day fighter which should be designed in 1943. The scheme should follow on the lines of the existing Spitfire, in particular the pressure cabin versions and the Griffon engined Mk IV. However, features which require improving are (1) landing speed (2) air brakes (3) manoeuvring flaps (4) endurance. Statistics show that many Spitfires crashed on landing due to high speeds of 80-90mph; also air brakes were vital. Failure to understand the fuel system resulted in 30% of crashes."

All present agreed that two classes of fighters were needed, a medium altitude—0-35,000 feet and a high altitude—30-50,000 feet, and firepower had to be increased. The 40mm cannon should be considered and instructions should be issued for a Spitfire to be tested with (1) 6 × 20mm cannon (this was produced eventually as a mock up on DP845, prototype Mk IV), (2) six cannon in wings and 2 × 40mm cannon in underwing containers, (3) 3 × 40mm cannon in wings with 50rpg or (4) 2 × 20mm and 2 × 40mm cannon as the best possible compromise, plus a provision for underwing bombs. It was recognised that the 40mm cannon had a slow rate of fire of 100 rounds per minute. If (1) was selected the aim was to achieve 200rpg. Item (4) was an adaptation of Dowding's 'short and crossbow' fighter of 1938.

Sholto-Douglas ended the meeting by saying—"At present I have to rely on the Spitfire Mk VB as my principle high performance day fighter. It is slightly inferior to the Bf109F in ceiling and rate of climb at altitude, partly due to the fact that it carries a superior armament. My main concern is that the present condition can be maintained until the Spring; by then the Germans might have produced a new fighter".

The Spitfire F Mk VIII had been developed in a race to meet the threat presented by the introduction of the Fw190 in September 1941, and the compromise F Mk IX eventually emerged to fulfill this role. But the VIII was indirectly to help provide the RAF with its first re-engined Spitfire, the F Mk XII. This had to combat not a new German fighter as forecast by Sholto-Douglas but an old foe in new guise.

It will be recalled that the Air Ministry had decided upon trials with the Rolls-Royce Griffon engine and had also chosen to convert six Mk VIII airframes to continue tests initiated by DP845 and DP851. The trials of the VIIIs were successful and it was decided that the converted VIIIs would serve as a useful interim type until a finalised production design powered by the Griffon appeared. However, before the modified VIIIs had even started trials with their new engines a low-level version of the Fw190 was making 'hit and run' raids against the South Coast of England from bases in Normandy. A test bed for the Griffon was urgently needed and one was at hand – DP845, the original prototype Mk IV now redesignated Mk XX. It was

DP485, prototype F Mk IV, was converted to the prototype F Mk XII. With a Griffon IIB engine it started trials at Boscombe Down in September 1942.

despatched to Boscombe Down on 3 September 1942.

When it arrived it still had the original style Mk I fin and rudder and handling trials, with a new type of wheel brake, were started to assess take off swing due to the torque of the Griffon and full left trim had to be used. The Boscombe report called DP845 Spitfire Mk XII, Griffon IIB, and it was flown extensively for many weeks. A full outline of this aircraft's Boscombe trials begins opposite. The Supermarine Type Record of 14 January 1943 for the Type 366/1 Production Spitfire F Mk XII contained the following reference – "Engine. Rolls-Griffon III. General description. This Type Record covers the modification of the F Mk VC aeroplane by substitution of the Griffon III engine for the normal Merlin 45 or 46". It would have been difficult to convert the standard VC airframe to take the Griffon engine as it required a beam mounting, was wider and the cowling higher. However, the Type Record stated that the auw was 7,400lb and maximum level speed at 1,500 feet was 350mph. Type 349 wings were specified. A Certificate of Design was issued at the end of the month.

Before DP845 was seconded to Boscombe, Supermarine had it under test at Hucknall. For operating under temperate summer conditions it was fitted with a tropical type Mk V QCY radiator and duct. The oil cooler was also a tropical V. Both radiators satisfied the specified conditions and the trials continued with a pair of Mk IA wings fitted with wooden, slotted flaps mounted on external hinge brackets, and a mock up windscreen having a curved front panel. This was later removed and the normal flat, bullet proof panel and flat side panels fitted. The Mk IA wings were then removed and Mk VC with four Brownings and two Hispano cannon installed, the latter having small blisters replacing the larger type covering the magazines. Streamlined fairings were also fitted over the inboard cannon leading edge mountings. Auw had now increased to 7,300lb.

The tail empennage with a retractable wheel was replaced by a Mk V unit with a fixed wheel, and a large chord rudder installed. The Rotol propeller was cropped to 10ft 5in diameter.

Numerous trials were carried out with DP845, the first series being comparative performance as a Mk XII with a Griffon III engine and .45 reduction gearing, and a Griffon IV with .51 gearing. Chase plane was the prototype F Mk IX, N3297, and the results showed that in .51 gear maximum level speed in FS was reduced by 8mph; the maximum rate of climb FS gear increased by 500ft/min and 700ft/min in MS gear. Time to 30,000 feet was reduced by 1.6 min. Cooling and perfor-

DP845 the prototype F Mk IV was converted to the prototype F Mk XII. It is seen here at Boscombe Down in September 1942 during trials.

Flying views of DP845 with original clipped wing and normal span.

mance trials with the Griffon RG 14 SM returned figures of maximum level speed FS gear 397mph at 14,200 feet; in MS gear 384 at 6,100 feet. Maximum rate of climb MS gear 5,320ft/min at 2,600 feet; in FS gear 4,500ft/min at 11,000 feet. The aeroplane was tested with the same engine and four and five bladed Rotol, Jablo propellers. With the five blade unit maximum level speed in MS gear actually decreased by 7mph to 377 at 6,000 feet. No gain in rate of climb in MS gear but a gain of 250 ft/min in FS gear. The full results of the Boscombe Down trials are summarised in tabular form on page 406.

The Supermarine test pilots thought the large chord rudder should have a large elevator horn balance as the standard type tended to de-stabilise the aircraft. It was flown with a yaw indicator installed in one of the Browning gun ports and with a new type of artificial horizon. Hydraulic brakes were fitted in place of the normal pneumatic and found to be useless; elektron covered ailerons were tested and laminar flow wing trials conducted.

Production started in the Summer of 1942 and the first aircraft off the line was EN221 and was weighed at Worthy Down on 13 October before despatch to Boscombe Down on 5 November for trials. The new Mk XII was one of the first Spitfires to have a flush riveted fuselage and EN221 was closely examined in order to assess external finish. The paint work was declared to be much smoother than previous Spitfires and the yellow leading edge strip the best example to date. Inspection hole cover could have been improved but the removable wing panels were found to be better than those on the average Spitfire although not as good as on contemporary American aircraft. The engine cowling was considered good and it was requested that the aerial mast be replaced by the whip type. Tare weight was 5,706lb, auw 7,389; with 30gal overload tank 7,680; in landing condition 6,579lb.

EN222 followed and EN223 went to Boscombe initially before delivery to AFDU, Duxford, after a request from the unit for a Mk XII for tactical trials. It reached Duxford on 21 December 1942. EN224 was used as a test aircraft to improve swing on take off; Quill was the pilot and the tests were carried out at Eastleigh on grass. By reducing engine boost from 12 to 7 lb/sq in the swing was reduced and take off run increased by only 10 yards. EN226 was an experimental Mk XII which had a temporary rear oil tank, standard wing tips and a Seafire Mk III A frame arrester gear fitted. It was intended for Admiralty trials and when weighed at Worthy Down on 12 February 1943 1943 it had a tare of 5,737lb; normal auw 7,419; with 30 gal overload tank 7,710; landing weight 6,609lb. EN228 was the first Mk XII to reach a fighter squadron when it was received at No 41 on 24 February. EN229 was weighed for comparative purposes at the same time and its weights were – tare 5,580lb; auw 7,278; with 30 gal overload tank 7,569; landing 6,468lb. MB800 was weighed on 7 May (tare 5,575lb; auw 7,277).

Only 100 examples of the F Mk XII were constructed, for continuous development of the Mk VIIIs with Griffon engine had produced its successor, the F Mk XIV. The XIIs went mainly to Nos 41 and 91 Squadrons (the first example to No 91 on 15 June 1943) and were restricted to home defence. EN226 was later to be used as the trials aircraft for the Seafire Mk XV and it was called a 'hooked Spitfire'. The XII was declared surplus to requirements and obsolete in February 1946.

OFFICIAL REPORTS ON THE Mk XII

Boscombe Down, 19 September 1942. DP845 F Mk XII prototype Griffon II. Oil cooling and radiator suitability. Auw 7,415 lb. On the climb at normal rating using best climb speed and radiator shutter fully open oil temperatures were within requirements for temperate summer conditions but not for tropical above 30,000ft. The radiator suitability was also satisfactory for summer temperate conditions but failed tropical requirements at all heights up to 34,000ft. The requirements were also satisfactory for level speed flight for temperate conditions but not for tropical.

Boscombe Down, 6 November. DP845. Brief handling trials. Special finish with all external surfaces flush riveted, joints filled and surface polished. New type brakes smooth and progressive in action. Swing on take-off to the right and needed correcting. Rudder not large enough to compensate.

Boscombe Down, 8 October 1942. DP845. Fuel consumption trials. Because engine surging occurred at low engine speeds and boost pressures, the main carburetter jets were replaced by larger diameter units. Auw 7,415lb with 95 gallons fuel.

EN621, first production Mk XII used for maker's trials before delivery to No. 41 Squadron.

Boscombe Down, 3 September 1942. DP845. Climb and level speed performances and position error correction. Results: –

Fuel consumption.

Height (ft)	weight (lb)	distance covered on climb (miles)	distance covered on cruise (miles)	max still air range (miles)
5000 (MS)	7040	5	420	425
20,000 (MS)	7000	35	430	465
20,000 (FS)	7000	35	405	440
30,000 (FS)	6960	85	355	440

Fuel consumption at 20,000 feet MS gear. Weight 7050 lb.

True air speed	rpm	boost lb sq in	fuel flow gals/hr	miles per gal.	mixture
354	2760	+1.2	74.9	4.73	rich
328	2400	-1.0	61.6	5.32	rich
299	2195	-2.3	44.7	6.70	weak
273.5	1990	-3.3	39.1	6.99	weak
F.C at 30,000 feet FS gear					
381	2760	+2.1	84.4	4.52	rich
354	2400	-0.8	60.6	5.85	weak
290	1990	-4.1	42.3	6.87	weak

Fuel consumption on climb, normal climb power (+9lb boost, 2750rpm). Weight 7415lb

Height (ft)	time (min)	ASI (mph)	fuel flow (gals/hr (gals used)	distance covered air miles
4000 (MS)	1.3	190	103 (2.5)	4.5
8000 (MS)	2.8	190	87 (4.5)	9.5
12,000 (FS)	4.5	190	105 (7)	16
20,000 (FS)	8.2	177	92 (13.5)	30
30,000 (FS)	15.5	141	71 (23)	59

Climb and level speed performance Griffon IIB. Take off weight 7415lb.

Performance on climb (combat rating). Supercharger gear changed at 11,200 feet.

Height(ft)	time from start (mins)	rate of climb ft/min	TAS(mph)	boost lb sq in	rpm	mixture
2000	.55	3760	196.5	12.0	2740	rich
4000	1.05	3600	202	10.8	2740	rich
8000	2.25	3130	215	7.8	2740	rich
14,000	4.35	2760	236	12.0	2740	rich
20,000	6.7	2230	242.5	7.8	2700	rich
30,000	12.95	1110	235	0.3	2700	rich
37,000	23.8	320	227.5	-4.2	2700	rich

Service ceiling 39,000 feet; estimated absolute ceiling 40,000

Level speed performance. Weight 7415lb

Height(ft)	TAS (mph)	boost (lb sq in)	rpm	mixture	super-charger gear
2000	355	12.0	2750	rich	MS
4000	364.5	12.0	2750	rich	MS
10,000	370.5	8.6	2750	rich	MS
16,000	388.5	12.0	2750	rich	FS
20,000	397	10.0	2750	rich	FS
24,000	392	6.6	2750	rich	FS

With Griffon VI. Rotol R13/4F5/6 four blade Jablo propeller

Performance on climb, radiator flap open. Take off weight 7320 lb.

Height(ft)	time(min)	rate of climb ft min	ASI(min)	boost lb sq in	rpm	S/C gear
1900	0.4	4960	180	+14.8	2750	MS
4000	0.8	4630	180	+13.0	2750	MS
10,200	2.25	4300	180	+14.8	2750	FS
20,000	5.05	2780	155	+ 6.1	2750	FS
30,000	10.3	1240	130	- 1.0	2750	FS
36,000	19.1	320	115	—	2750	FS

Service ceiling 37,350 feet. Estimated absolute ceiling 38,000.

Level speed performance. Radiator flap closed. Corrected to weight of 6960 lb.

Height(ft)	TAS(mph)	boost lb sq in	rpm	S/C gear
2000	362	+14.8	2750	MS
4650	375	+14.8	2750	MS
8000	373	+11.8	2750	MS
10,000	374	+14.8	2750	FS
20,000	383	+ 8.1	2750	FS
32,000	359	+ 0.6	2750	FS

Boscombe Down, 29 March 1943. DP845. Handling during take-off with reduced boost and modified propeller fine pitch setting. Owing to the violent swing to port on take-off the Mk XII prototype was returned to Supermarine to have the propeller fine pitch stop changed from 40° to 31°15′ to enable a higher rpm to be obtained with reduced boost. The original Griffon II was replaced by a IV in which the reduction gear was .51:1 instead of .45:1. As well as take-offs dives were made to ensure that over speeding did not occur. The swing on take-off was reduced and the report concluded that a further decrease was desirable for safe carrier operation where full throttle was more likely to be opened rapidly. The report did not qualify this last comment.

Boscombe Down, 7 April 1943. DP845. Griffon IV. Further cooling trials. The radiator flap installation was representative of a production Mk XII and cooling requirements for temperate conditions were met.

Boscombe Down, 16 April 1943. DP845. Brief spinning trials. Auw 7,420lb. Tests were made at 15,000ft and characteristics were similar to other Spitfire marks.

Boscombe Down, June 1943. DP845. Griffon VI. Climb and level speed performance with Griffon VI engine. Auw 7,320 lb. Engine was changed during trials. Maximum rate of climb

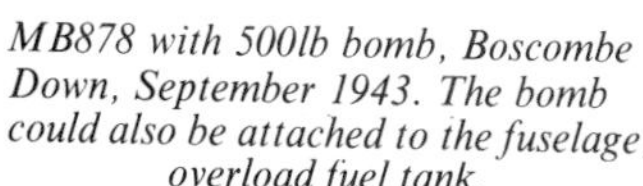

MB878 with 500lb bomb, Boscombe Down, September 1943. The bomb could also be attached to the fuselage, overload fuel tank.

MS gear 4,960ft/min @ 1,900ft, FS gear 4,300ft/min @ 10,200ft. Time to 10,000ft 2.2min, to 30,000ft 10.1min. Service ceiling **37,350ft. Maximum speed MS gear 375mph @ 4,600ft, FS gear 389 @ 12,800.**

Boscombe Down, 6 November 1942. EN221 and EN222. Intensive flying trials. A period of 150 hours intensive flying was required on production Mk XIIs with Griffon III engines. EN221 had normal universal wings, while 222 had a clipped wing. During the trials the wing tips of 221 were fitted to 222. 222 had a cropped hydulignum propeller and experimental stainless steel exhaust stubs. The aircraft had to force land during trials due to fuel shortage.

Boscombe Down, 30 November 1942. EN221. Oil cooling and radiator suitability trials. Auw 7,400lb. Satisfactory for both temperate and tropical conditions.

Boscombe Down, 4 February 1943. EN222. Oil cooling and radiator suitability with correct design radiator exit areas.

Boscombe Down, 13 February 1943. EN222. Carbon monoxide contamination tests. No contamination discovered in cockpit under any flying condition.

Boscombe Down, August 1943. EN624. Tests of alleged rogue aircraft. Aircraft belonged to No 91 Squadron who reported heavy aileron control with excessive up-float. Aileron shrouds were straightened, cables correctly tensioned, all reflexing removed. Faults were distortion of shrouds and too much reflexing.

Boscombe Down, September 1943. MB878. Effect of 500lb bomb and Universal Mk III bomb rack on level speed performance. Tests with and without bomb and bomb rack.

Condition	FS All out level				MS Cruising (Weak)			
	Max TAS mph	RPM	Boost lb/in²	FTH ft	Max TAS mph	RPM	Boost lb/in²	FTH ft
(a) Without bomb rack or bomb	394	2750	+12	18100	341	2400	5.8	8680
(b) With bomb rack	382	"		18000	333	"	"	8600
(c) With rack & bomb	371	"		17900	322	"	"	8520

Boscombe Down, February 1944. MB878. Oil system operations during manoeuvres involving application of negative and positive G manoeuvres which produced negative G resulted in drop in oil pressure. Positive G had no effect.

F Mk XII

Wing. Planform elliptical; section NACA Series 2200; span 32′ 7″; incidence° root +2, tip $-\frac{1}{2}$; dihedral° 6; thickness% root 13.2, tip 6; aspect ratio 5.68; area nett gross 231; chord (geo) 6.38, (ma) 7.01. Ailerons. Area 18.9; chord(ma) movement° up 26, down 19; droop $\frac{3}{8}$. Flaps. Area 15.6; movement° down 85. Wing loading 31.5 lb/sq ft

Tailplane. Area 31.46; chord(ma) 4.0; incidence° root 0, tip $\pm\frac{1}{2}$; dihedral° 0. Elevators. Area 13.26; movement° up 28, down 23. Tab area 0.38; movement° up to 20, down 7. Fin area 4.61. Rudder Area 8.23. Tab area 0.91; movement° port 12, starbd. 12.

Undercarriage. Wheels Dunlop AH2061; tyres Dunlop IJ 13 or 17. Oleo pressure 420 star 380 port, or 505 star 465 port; tyre pressure 57. Tailwheel retractable castoring. Wheel Dunlop AH2184/IX; tyre Dunlop TA 12 or 14. Oleo pressure 242; tyre pressure 47.

Engine/s. Griffon III

Griffon IV (24 engines only). 1,720hp @ SL (MS); 1,735 @ 1,000; 1,495 @ 14,500 (FS). A number of early a/c had the Griffon II

Starter Coffman cartridge, starbd side.

Propeller/s. Rotol R13/4F5/5 Dural 4-blade. Pitch range 35° fine pitch 31° 15′ first six a/c only or, R13/4F5/6 Jablo pitch range 35° fine pitch 26° 14′. Diameter of both 10ft 5in.

Coolant. 70% distilled water, 30% Glycol.

Fuel. Capacity (early a/c EN serials). Fuselage (upper) 48 gals, lower 37. Total 85. Later a/c (MB serials). 36 upper, 49 lower. Plus 30 gal o/ld tank. Consumption MS 5.96 gal/hr @ **5,000ft 215mph; 6.99 FS @ 20,000 200mph; 7.23 @ 30,000** 180mph.

Oil. 6 gal early a/c in fuselage behind pilot; later models 7 gal in fuselage forward of pilot.

Armament. Universal B wing Plus 1 × 250 lb GP or SAP or 1 × 500 ditto bombs.

Radio. TR9D, TR1133, R3002, A2171 BA

Cine camera. G42B or G45 in port wing.

Performance. Griffon IIB. Rotol XH/54D-RM-55. Max **speed @ 2,000ft (MS) 355mph; @ SL 346; 372 @ 8,000; 370 @ 12,000 392 @ 24,000. Rate of climb. 3,040ft/min (196.5mph) @ 2,000ft; 2,800 (208) @ 6,000; 2,340 (221.5) @ 10,000; 1,920 (242.5) @ 20,000; 420 (230) @ 35,000. Time to height.**

F Mk XIIs MB882, 858, 794, 840, 862 of No 41 Squadron, April 1944.

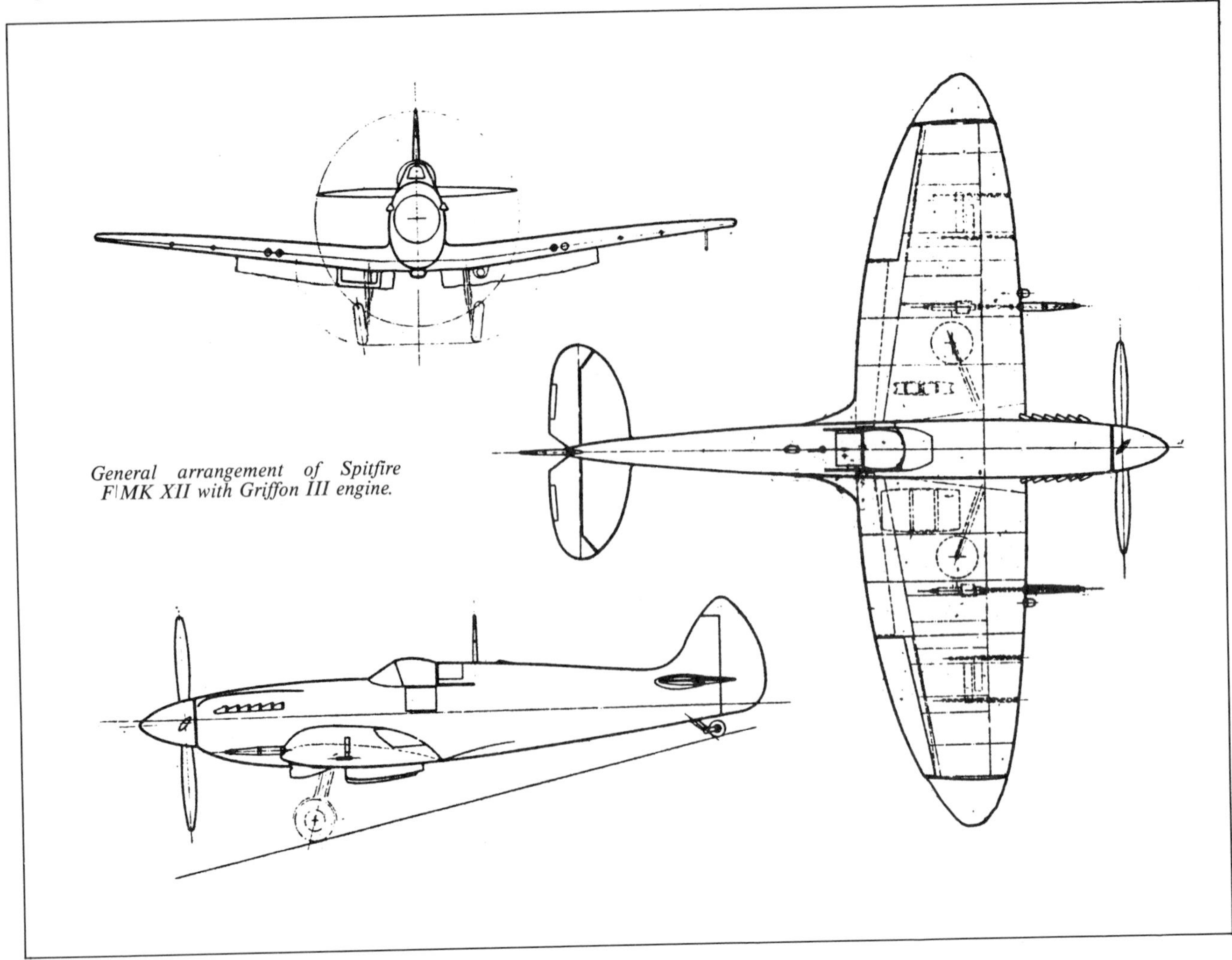

General arrangement of Spitfire F/MK XII with Griffon III engine.

0.65 mins 2,000; 2min 6,000; 3.55 10,000; 8.15 20,000; 23.35 35,000. Combat rating was faster.

Griffon VI Rotol R13/4F5/6. 352mph @ SL (MS); 362 @ 2,000; 373 @ 8,000; 370 @ 12,000. FS, 364 @ 8,000; 389 @ 12,500 383 @ 20,000; 359 @ 32,000. Rate of climb 4,960ft/min @ 1,900ft (180mph); 4,295 @ 8,000; 4,300 @ 10,200 (175); 2,780 @ 20,000 (155); 1,240 @ 30,000 (130); 320 @ 36,000 (115). Time to height, 0.8 mins 4,000ft; 1.75 8,000; 2.7 12,000; 5.05 20,000; 19.1 36,000. Service ceiling 37,350, absolute 38,000. Take off run 450yds, landing 690. Range 493 miles @ 263mph @ 20,000ft with 30gal o/ld tank. Normal fuel 329.

Weights. Tare 5,580lb, take off 7,280, max permissible 7,400. With Dural prop; tare 5,652; with Jablo 5,575.

SERIAL NUMBERS

SUPERMARINE AVIATION (VICKERS) LTD
Contract No B19713/39
Seventh order for 500 Spitfire Mk VC dated 23 August 1941. Built as Mk VC/PR IV/VI/VII/IX/XI/XII between november 1942 and August 1943. The following serials apply to LF XIIs built to this seventh order; EN221-238 and 601-637.

Tenth order for 426 Spitfire Mk VC dated 12 May 1942. Built as Mks VII/VIII/IX/X/XI/XII between July 1943 and March 1944. The following serials apply to LF XIIs built to this tenth order; MB794-805, 829-863 and 875-882. Total Mk XIIs built 100.

EN series All F XII Griffon III unless otherwise indicated

EN221 3495 HPA CRD VAWD 13-10-42 first prod a/c wts and CG load tare 5706; t/o 7389; with 30gal o/l tank 7680; land 6759lb. BDn 5-11 spcl finish for intns flying trls. Wng tips removed (instal on EN222); int/wt in elev syst. oil cool and rad suit trls in comp with EN222 and DP845. VACHA 11-3-43 8MU 31-5 41S 30-5-44 FAAC 27-6 ROS 39MU NEA SOC 14-5-46

EN222 3679 HPA CRD BDn 5-12-42 comp trls with EN221 and DP845. Standard clip wng fitt with EN222's tips. the metal Rotol prop was cropped after 'boggin' in land acc R-RH 13-2-43 stainless steel engine exhaust manifolds instal. BDn carb mono cockpit contam tests. 1CRU 3-3 rep VACHA 11-3 AFDU Witt 24-5 91S 4-3-44 33MU 25-3 SOC 22-12-45

EN223 3704 HPA CRD BDn 14-12-43 AFDU DUX 21-12 AST 26-6-43 mods AFDU 10-11 91S 20-11 CE ops 6-1-44 FH103.15

EN224 3740 HPA CRD Farn 15-12-42 hand trls ASTH 13-2-43 rep 41S 15-5-44 FAAC 27-6 AST WAL 15-12 mods 595S 14-5-45 College Aeronautics Cranfield 4-7-46

EN225 3812 GIV HPA 5MU 11-1-43 CRD VACHA 29-1 according to Super records this a/c (called 'hooked Spitfire') was fitt with arrester hook and used for trls. Wts and CG load 12-2 778S 28-2 (Royal Navy trials) Griffon III instal 91S 29-12 ASTH 28-1-44 rep 41S 16-6 FLS 20-9 AFDU 9-10 CFE SOC 23-11-45

EN227 3832 GIV HPA 45MU 21-1-43 VACHA 1-2 778S 28-2 (Royal Navy trials) VA 14-3 Griffon III instal 91S 29-12 strk by EN606 on runway Tang CB 20-1-44 ASTH 41S 8-6 FLS 20-9 AFDU 9-10 CFE SOC 23-11-45

EN228 3875 HPA 45MU 21-1-43 41S 24-2 FACB 14-5 ROS FLS 20-9-44 SOC 22-12-45

EN229 3983 HPA CRD CAWD 12-2-43 wt and CG load of prod A/C Tare 5680; t/o 7278; wilth 30gal o/l tank 7569; land 6468lb. 46MU 27-2 41S 13-3 CAC ops 17-5 ASTH 21-5 GIV instal 91S 4-3-44 41S 28-6 FLS 28-9 39MU NEA SOC 14-5-46

EN230 GIV AFDU 13-2-43 91S 24-5 CE ops 1-9 w/e

EN231 3998 HPA 46MU 25-2-43 41S 9-3 CAC ops 18-7 ETPS Farn 14-2-44 trls of ignition harness supressors to prevent interference with VHF radio. FTR 18-6-,44 of 41S into English Channel

EN232 4006 HPA CRD VA 24-2-43 15MU 23-4 41S 9-5 FACE f/lnd Friston 28-5

EN233 4043 HPA 41S 28-2-43 FTR ops 18-7 FH110.55

EN234 4051 HPA 41S 4-3-43 FAAC 8-10 ROS 91S 20-11 ASTH 9-3-44 33MU 11-3-45 lost height in slow roll cd Old Sarum CE 17-8 SOC 28-9

EN235 4052 HPA 41S 2-3-43 FTR ops 18-7 s/dn over France FH127.10

EN236 4053 HPA 41S 7-3-43 FTR ops 27-3 ROS 26-8 41S 3-9 PSOC 21-6-47

EN237 4081 HPA 41S 11-3-43 FTR ops 13-3-44 FH281.15

EN238 4087 HPA 41S 14-3-43 FACB 23-7 ASTH 3501SU 13-5-44 FLS 30-10 FAAC 30-10 to SoTT as 5670M 19-9-45 SOC 28-4-47 Scrap

EN601 4086 HPA 41S 14-3-43 FTR ops F/Lt Poynton missing Dieppe 23-4 FH19.40

EN602 4088 HPA 41S 14-3-43 FAAC 16-8 ROS 91S 20-12 41S 14-6-44 ASDT 22-9 39MU NEA 4-5-45 SOC 14-5-46

EN603 4113 CHA 41S 20-3-43 FACB 11-6 ROS AST 9-12 recat E 20-12

was the trials aircraft for the short span Mk XII.

EN604 4121 HPA 41S 22-3-43 CB ops 17-4 ASTH 405ARF HAL 14-8 91S 7-9 FACE 6-12

EN605 4117 CHA 41S 22-3-43 ROS 22-4 CAC 10-5-44 ROS AST 23-9 595S 19-5-45 SOC 30-5-46

EN606 4127 HPA 41S 22-3-43 ASTH 16-6 405ARF HAL 5-9 91S 29-9 coll with EN227 ldg Tangmere CE 20-1-44 FH139.45

EN607 4141 HPA 33MU 27-3-43 41S 20-4 CB ops 27-4 ASTH 4-5 CRD Malcolms WW 14-2-44 AST 13-6 595S 29-12 SOC 30-5-46

EN608 4142 HPA 33MU 27-3-43 41S 22-4 i/sea off Ford ops pilot safe 22-9

EN609 4116 CHA 41S 22-3-43 CB ops 26-9 ASTH FLS Mlfld 23-9-44 39MU NEA 26-10 SOC 16-5-46

EN610 4132 CHA 41S 24-3-43 e/fld cd nr Hawk on finals CE 24-4

EN611 4154 CHA 41S 30-3-43 i/sea ops 27-8 FH125.30

EN612 4157 CHA 41S 30-3-43 i/sea ops Deippe 3-5 s/dn by FW190 FH23.30

EN613 4143 HPA 33MU 27-3-43 91S 21-4 CAC ops 22-4 ROS AST 16-10 into sea ops 31-1-44

EN614 4160 HPA 15MU 2-4-43 91S 1-5 FTR ops s/dn il/sea off Dunkirk 19-9

EN615 4164 CHA 15MU 2-4-43 91S 1-5 AST 28-1-44 41S 2-9 FLS Mlfld 20-9 EAAS Manby 15-12 SOC 30-5-46

EN616 4208 CHA 15MU 3-4-43 CRD R-RH 6-5 develop a/c for GIII and GIV ASTH 29-3-45 recat E 28-5 SOC 18-7

EN617 4242 CHA 15MU 24-4-43 91S 29-5 i/sea 12m W Le Hay ops 16-9

EN618 4170 CHA 15MU 4-4-43 91S 7-5 i/sea ops 31-1-44

EN619 4179 HPA 15MU 5-4-43 91S 1-5 ROS 26-8 ASTH 24-10 41S 7-6-44 FAAC 21-6 ROS FLS Mlfld 28-9 SOC 14-12-45

EN620 4227 CHA 39MU 24-4-43 91S 13-5 ROS 26-8 41S 14-3-44 AST 4-6 39MU NEA 23-3-45 SOC 13-5-46

EN621 4197 HPA 8MU 11-4-43 91S 13-5 CAC ops 8-10 ROS 3-11 e/fld f/ld Reigate Hill CE 5-2-44 FH172.5

EN622 4200 CIV HPA 8MU 11-4-43 91S 13-5 CB ops 6-6 ASTH 3501SU 26-4-44 41S 27-7 FTR ops over Holland 3-9

EN623 4201 HPA 39MU 11-4-43 91S 9-5 ROS 26-8 AST 9-3-44 595S 15-6-45 e/fld i/sea Newquay Bay Cardigan CE 26-6 SOC 28-6

EN624 4218 HPA 39MU 18-4-43 91S 13-5 BDn Aug'43 Rogue Spitfire from 91S hvy ail control flew left wing low FACE crash 23-1-44

EN625 4219 HPA 8MU 18-4-43 91S 13-5 ASTH 9-3-44 3501SU 16-8 451S 15-9 FLS Mlfld 20-9 AFDU 19-10 e/fld f/ld lost star wing Norfolk CE 11-12

EN626 4225 CHA 8MU 19-4-43 405ARF HAL 26-8 91S 17-9 cd E Horsham ops 6-11

EN627 4226 CHA 39MU 19-4-43 91S 13-5 S/dn SE Dover 16-6 FH52.40

All these a/c EN221 to 627 had fixed tailwheel

MB series Griffon III MB794 to 856. Griffon IV thereon

MB794 4237 HPA 8MU 24-4-43 405ARF HAL 26-8 41S 29-9 FTR ops Normandy Beach Head 9-6-44

MB795 4245 HPA 8MU 27-4-43 405ARF HAL 27-8 41S 29-9 CAC ops 20-10 ROS to 4875M 15-9-44 SOC 1-1-48

MB796 4226HPA 39MU 27-4-43 41S 21-5 FTR ops a/c aban on fire 6-9

MB797 4247 HPA 39MU 27-4-43 405ARF HAL 1-8 41S 22-8 FACE cd/ld Harty Marshes 12-2-44 FH131.15

MB798 4263 HPA 8MU 1-5-43 405ARF HAL 22-8 41S 14-9 AST 39MU 22-9-44 595S 2-5-45 29MU 2-9-45 5919M 2-9 93S ATC 12-3-46 SOC 30-11-49

MB799 4269 HPA 8MU 6-5-43 405ARF HAL 22-8 41S 14-9 91S 16-9 a/c aban i/sea off Ramsgate 19-9

MB800 4270 HPA VAWD 7-5-43 wts & CG ld ngs prod a/c Tare 5575; t/o 7277lb. 39MU 11-5 41S 19-5 FTR s/dn by Fw190 F/Sgt May missing 19-9

MB801 4276 HPA 39MU 11-5-43 41S 11-5 ROS 26-8 FACE cd/lnd 20-11

MB802 4284 HPA 41S 11-5-43 FTR ops s/dn by AFW190 F/O Parry missing 24-9

MB803 4283 HPA 91S 13-5-43 HAL 23-10 61 OTU 41S 15-5-44 AST 21-6 39MU NEA 14-5-46

MB804 4322 HPA 39MU 18-5-43 405ARF HAL 1-8 41S 22-8 CB ops 16-7-44 ASAT Aberforth 2-5-45 595S 3-5 to 5920M 12-3-46 115S ATC

MB805 4320 CHA 91S 16-5-43 FTR ops 24-7

MB829 4294 HPA 41S 11-5-43 FAAC 3-5-44 AST WAL 1-12 39MU NEA SOC 16-5-46

MB830 4307 HPA 91S 17-5-43 CAC ops 2-9 ROS 41S 2-10 e/fd f/ld nr Frilston Bridge CE 23-6-44

MB831 4308 CHA 91S 17-5-43 CB ops 20-10 AST 3501SU 24-7-44 41S 13-8 FTR shot down ops over Holland 1-9

MB832 4309 HPA 91S 16-5-43 AST 6-6 91S 3-1-44 FTR ops 23-1 FH28.30

MB833 4303 CHA 9MU 15-5-43 91S 8-6 CAC 18-8 ROS 41S CE ops 12-6-44 w/o

MB834 4305 HPA 6MU 15-5-43 41S 1-6 FTR ops cd i/sea 3-10 FH152.40

MB835 4325CHA 9MU 18-5-43 91S FTR s/dn in Channel 16-6 FH12.20

MB836 4324 HPA 6MU 18-5-43 405ARF HAL 4-8 91S 22-8 ROS 19-11 33MU 20-3-44 3501SU 8-6 41S 26-6 FLS Mlfld 28-9 39MU NEA SOC 16-5-46

MB837 4336 CHA 6MU 22-5-43 405ARF HAL 4-8 41S 1-9 CB ops dam by exploding V.I. 8-7-44 AST 33MU 13-2-45 mods 595S 14-5 FAAC ff H Ercall 17-8 ROS 595S 1-11 29MU SOC 30-5-46

MB838 4339 HPA 8MU 27-5-43 ROS VA 31-5 41S 19-8 FACA 15-11 AST EAAS Manby 2-12-44 to 5921M 12-8-45 538S ATC SOC 28-347

MB839 4342 CHA 9MU 23-5-43 91S 11-6 AST 9-3-44 CE 24-9

MB840 4340 HPA 8MU 23-5-43 405ARF WAL 25-8 41S 19-10 FAAC 21-7-44 FLS Mlfld 20-9 33MU 26-10 FACB 1-2-45 recat E SOC 9-2

MB841 4341 HPA 8MU 23-5-43 405ARF HAL 25-8 91S 9-10 41S 15-5-44 CB ops 13-7 AST 2-8 39MU NEA SOC 16-5-46

MB842 4355 HPA 6MU 28-5-43 91S 19-6 CB ops 24-10 ROS 41S 7-3-44 FTR into Channel CE 12-6

MB843 4356 HPA 6MU 27-5-43 405ARF HAL 4-8 41S 1-9 FTR ops i/sea off Herm Island CI 2-6-44

MB844 4354 CHA 9MU 28-5-43 405ARF HAL 4-8 41S 18-8 fast ldg np flaps coll with EN603 Tangmere CB 4-12 AST EAAS Mamby 28-11-44 to 5922M 77S ATC 12-3-46 SOC 6-11-47

MB845 4374 HPA 33MU 30-5-43 41S 20-7 AST 4-6-44 595S 28-4-45 29MU 7-12 SOC 30-5-46

MB846 4375 HPA 33MU 30-5-43 41S 20-7 CE ops 1-12

MB847 4384 HPA 33MU 5-6-43 41S 20-7 AST 21-6-44 39MU NEA SOC 14-5-46

MB848 4376 HPA 33MU 30-5-43 91S 15-6 FAAC 18-3-44 595S 29-12 39MU 17-1-45 SOC 30-5-46

MB849 4388 HPA 33MU 3-6-43 Tangmere 22-6 91S 2-9 ROS 5-12 FACE cd Gloucester Hill Amble Northumb 8-4-44

MB850 4405 HPA 8MU 5-6-43 FA 15-8 405ARF HAL 2-9 41S 29-9 CB ops 20-10 AST 41S 24-7-44 FLS Mlfld 20-9 33MU 16-11 PSOC 20-6-47

MB851 4406 HPA 6MU 5-6-43 91S 19-6 33MU 20-3-44 3501SU 20-8 Ftr Com Com Flt Old Sarum 27-8-45 sold scrap 3-9-47

MB852 4407 HPA 9MU 7-6-43 405ARF HAL 18-8 91S FTR ops 8-9

MB853 4439 HPA 39MU 12-6-43 3501SU 1-7-44 41S 17-7 FLS Mlfld 20-9 AFDU 19-10 FLS 2-8-45 SOC 30-5-46

MB854 4468 HPA 38MU 25-6-43 3501SU 27-7-44 41S CB ops 17-8 ROS 33MU 3-1-45

MB855 4494 HPA GIV 39MU 4-7-43 CRD Malcolms WW 31-12 AST mr 12-3-44 GIII instal EAAS Manby 14-12 to 5923M 12-3-46 417S ATC SOC 14-6

MB856 4501 HPA 39MU 2-7-43 41S 23-6-44 CB ops 14-7 ROS FTR ops 9-9 cancel 410RSU 21-9 AST 30-4-45 recat E 23-5 SOC 18-7

MB857 4508 39MU 4-7-43 91S 30-2-44 3501SU 15-5 ROS 13-7

MB858 4536 HPA 38MU 16-7-43 405RSU ARF HAL 4-8 41S 7-9 FAAC 22-5-44 ROS 33MU 15-12

MB859 4559 HPA 33MU 18-7-43 91S 9-11 air coll with EN604 cd Forest Row E. Grinstead CE 6-12

MB860 4576 HPA 39MU 22-7-43 91S 22-1-44 41S CAC ops 28-7 ROS 39MU NEA SOC 16-5-46

MB861 4577 HPA 39MU 24-7-43 91S 1-2-44 41S CAC ops 21-7 ROS

MB862 4589 HPA 33MU 27-7-43 41S 7-8 CAC ops 30-8 ROS 595S FAAC 28-5-45 recat E 22-11 SOC 19-2-46

MB863 4615 HPA 33MU 10-8-43 41S 26-11 no flaps o/s grd loop Friston CE 20-3-44

MB875 4646 HPA 39MU 17-8-43 41S 23-6-44 eng trouble on t/o pilot braked a/c o/t CE Lympne 25-8

MB876 4660 HPA 3MU 21-8-43 405ARF 3-9 91S 29-9 AST 8-1-44 41S 15-5 FTR ops 18-6

MB877 4680 HPA 33MU 24-8-43 405ARF HAL 3-9 91S 29-9 41S 28-5-44 coll with Tioger Moth DE575 41S just after t/o Lympne CE 17-7

MB878 4735 HPA CRD BDn 4-9-43 trls with 500lb bomb on univ Mk FII fus rack. Speeds with bomb 363; without 383mph. trls oil syst under neg and pos G 33MU 20-3-44 3501SU 23-6 41S 14-7 CAC ops 26-8 ROS FLS Mlfld 28-9

MB879 4757 HPA 33MU 10-9-43 ADGB Tang 16-12 39MU 9-11-44 SOC 13-5-46

MB880 4775 HPA 33MU 12-9-43 41S 14-12 CAC ops 2-5-44 ROS s/dn by AA fire Sover i/sea 17-8

MB881 4813 HPA 33MU 21-9-43 41S 21-12 CE ops 7-1-44

MB882 4846 CHA 33MU 24-11-43 41S 21-12 ROS 15-5-44 FLS Mlfld 20-9

MAINTENANCE AIRFRAMES

EN238(5670M), MB804(5920M), MB838(5928M) and MB844(5922M).

MB882, April 1944, with slipper fuel tank.

"A USEFUL INTERIM TYPE"

The first series production Griffon engined Spitfire was the F Mk XIV, a combination of the F VIII airframe and new engine, and the design was extensively proved by converting six Mk VIIIs to the configuration. They were JF316 (GIII), JF317 (G61, first to fly), JF318 (G61), JF319 (G65), JF320 (G61) and JF321 (G61). The last went to Rotol at Staverton for trials with contra-rotating propellers. Although both Supermarine and the Air Ministry referred to all F VIII conversions as 'interim' types and regarded early production aircraft as 'stop gaps' until the Super Spitfire, the F Mk 21 was developed, large numbers of the Mk XIV were produced.

Before production of the Mk XIV began the RAF wanted to know what the new type could do and JF317 was sent to AFDU Wittering on 29 July 1943. A full report of the trials read as follows—

SHORT TACTICAL TRIALS OF EXPERIMENTAL SPITFIRE XIV

On instructions from Headquarters, Fighter Command, an experimental Spitfire XIV, JF317 (Griffon 61) was made available by A&AEE for three days for short tactical trials. The trials took the form of a direct comparison with a Spitfire VIII (Merlin 63) JF664, and flying took place from 27 to 29 July 1943. The aircraft used is a conversion of the Spitfire VIII. The larger engine involves a much longer engine cowling and the extra weight forward has been balanced by ballast in the tail. The fin has been increased in area to help directional stability and a large rudder is fitted. This aircraft had the normal wings of a Mk VIII with small span ailerons, but the extended wing tips had been replaced by the standard tips as on Mk IX. The engine is not representative of production as the FS gear is higher and the MS lower. A five blade propeller is fitted. The engine has a Bendix injection carburetter and boost for combat is limited to plus 15lbs. The Mk VIII weighed 7,760lb, the XIV 8,376.

Performance. Speeds near the ground are identical, at 10,000 and 15,000ft the VIII is faster, at 20/25,000ft similar, at 30,000 and over the XIV accelerated faster and was the superior aircraft. Climbs; Zero to 30,000ft the VIII is the better aircraft, at 30,000ft and over the XIV is by far the better.

The elevator control of the XIV was found to be much heavier than that of the VIII, unpleasantly so, and the other controls felt to be slightly heavier than on previous Spitfire Mks. In spite of heavy controls the XIV is more manoeuvrable than the VIII in turns at all heights. Spins were carried out in the XIV at 25,000ft. The aircraft did not spin voluntarily but had to be put into and held in the spin. On releasing the controls the aircraft automatically came out of the spin. Instead of spinning in the normal nose down attitude, the nose of the aircraft oscillated from an almost vertical position downwards to a position with the nose well above the horizon, so that the aircraft was tail down. It spent most of its time in this flat position from which, after four turns, recovery was fast by the normal method or slower if the controls were released. It never

Six F Mk VIIIs were converted to accept the Griffon engine and were used as prototypes for the F Mk XIV, itself an interim type until appearance of the F21. JF316 had the Griffon 61 and JF318 was the first conversion. Note the air intake shape.

JF321 was fitted with de Havilland contra-props and an enlarged fin and rudder. It was built by Supermarine as an F Mk VIII converted.

appears to become uncontrollable. Pilot's view is superior on the XIV due to the lower engine cowling. Both aircraft carry the same amount of fuel (96 gallons in the main tank and 27 gallons in two wing tanks). Refuelling checks made to compare consumption showed than when the two aircraft stayed together throughout the trials, the Griffon engine was using approximately 10-15 gallons more fuel per hour than the Merlin.

Conclusions. Of the two aircraft the Mk VIII is preferable at all heights up to about 25,000ft except for its turning capabilities. It is much lighter on the elevators and easier for the average pilot to fly. Its performance and fuel consumption are better. The Mk XIV is superior above 25,000ft and with its better turning characteristics it is more than a match for the VIII. The difficulties of trimming will probably be reduced as pilots gain familiarity.

The Certificate of Design for Type 369 was issued under Contract CTT/Acft/C.23(c) as the Spitfire F Mk VIII Conversion, and the General Description read—Griffon 61, 65 or 85. This aeroplane, basically Spitfire F Mk VIII production, has been modified as indicated. Engine mounting Spitfire F Mk 21 production type. Fuselage Spitfire F VIII production adapted to the F 21 type equipment at frame 5. Special longerons and modified tail end. Main planes Spitfire F VIII with modified cooling system and fitted with standard wing tips. Auw 8,600lb.

The Supermarine Specification No 472 for the Type 379 (Production) of 18 May 1943 was more specific. Spitfire F Mk XIV is basically an F Mk VIII fitted with a Griffon two stage engine—Griffon 65 high altitude or 75 low altitude. Airscrew Rotol five blade 10ft 5in diameter. A few aircraft may be fitted with counter rotating airscrews. Engine installation as test bed aircraft, Type 369, but a number of special test instruments will be omitted. Fuel tanks, fuselage tanks as Mk 21, wing tanks as Mk VIII. Total 115 gallons. Oil tank as Mk 21. Cooling systems similar to test beds (Type 369) but new cooling units and fairings are required. Main planes as Mk VIII but minor strengthening. Standard Mk VC wing tips, pintle bolts modified. Oleo legs as Mk VIII. Tail unit as Mk VIII with special ballast arrangements. Flight trials in hand may necessitate increased fin area and altered incidence. Main and tail wheels and tyres (inclined bulkhead) and equipment layout as Mk 21. The rear view cabin top will be introduced on this type as a modification. Armament two cannon and four Browning only. Provision for Mk V (short) cannon if available. Electrical, 12 volt earth return system as fitted to fifth test bed aircraft. Airscrew ground clearance 2.45in.

JF321, the last of the six test bed Mk VIIIs, was weighed at Worthy Down on 19 August 1943 in the following condition: Griffon 61 driving a Rotol six blade counter rotating propeller unit, 85 gallons fuel in fuselage tanks and 27 in wings. Nine gallons oil and three ballast weights totalling 150lb mounted between frames 18 and 19. It had a tare of 6,645lb and auw of 8,614. This is compared with the first production XIV, RB140 on 30 September. It had a Griffon 65 and Rotol five blade propeller, plus ballast of 90lb. Tare 6,580lb auw 8,489. NH706 in the same condition was weighed on 8 March 1944 with a tare of 6,591 and auw 8,489lb. RM766 had the E armament of two .5in Brownings replacing the .303s, plus the two Hispanos and it had a tare of 6,511lb and auw of 8,524. NH657 was fitted with de Havilland six blade contra props and 73½lb ballast in fin, plus 70lb between frames 18 and 19. When weighed at High Post on 23 August 1944 the tare was 6,866lb and auw 8,868.

Supermarine Specification No 478 introduced the FR XIV and long range versions on 29 November. The main modifications to the airframe were—rear fuselage fuel tanks, oblique and vertical camera and one rear tank, new wheels and tyres, strengthened wing spars and fuselage, new oleo legs, oblique camera and one rear tank. The applications of these modifications to the production programme was—stage 1, the standard Mk XIV; stage 2, rear view version; stage 3, rear view with oblique camera and 31 gallon rear tank. If certain minor modifications were omitted clipped wings were specified. Stage 4, rear view with oblique and vertical cameras and rear tank; stage 5, rear view with rear tanks.

The Certification of Design for all variants was issued on 29 November 1944 to Contract No CTT/Acft/1877/C.23 for the Spitfire Mk XIV/P.1, 2×20mm cannon and 2×.5in Browning. Addendum number 1 was for RB146 with plain ailerons and aileron circuit modified for same (24 January 1945). Addendum 2 for the Type 379 bomber (22 January) covered the XIV with rear view fuselage, carriage of bombs and standard drop tanks. Weight fully loaded but without bombs or drop tanks 8,600lb; as fighter bomber (2 x 250lb or 1 x 500) 9,685lb. With wing bombs (2 x 250lb) and 90 gallon drop tank 9,900lb, approved for target tug duties, J-Type winch, in tropics. Addendum 3 for FR XIV (31 January) covered the addition of oblique cameras, internal rear fuel (32 gals), carriage of bombs and drop tanks and Mk XII clipped wings. Fully loaded without rear fuel, bombs or drop tank 8,750lb; as fighter with rear fuel 8,980; with wing and fuselage bombs (2 x 250 plus 1×500lb) 10,065; wing bombs and 90 gals fuel tank 10,280lb. Bombs and drop tanks had to be jettisoned before landing. Flying above 15,000 feet with a full rear tank was prohibited. The RAF put forward a proposal for fitting RATOG and an arrester hook for operations from unimproved airfields.

A production F Mk XIVE, RM807, was weighed at High Post on 19 September and it had a tare weight of 6,599lb, auw 8,602. The increased loads affected a number of Mk XIVs to the extent of local skin buckling on wings and fuselage at load attachment points, and some pilots were nervously reporting the slightest wrinkle. Supermarine were of the opinion that these skin wrinkles had the advantage of showing that reasonably high loads had been applied and corrective measures could be taken. It did not, said Supermarine, imply that the aircraft was on the point of failure or that it had been seriously weakened. The RAF, however, decided that these possibilities had to be avoided and issued instructions that all Mk XIVs were to be retrospectively fitted with clipped wings. RM784, Mk XIVE rear view, clipped wings, was weighed at High Post on 2 October and had a tare weight of 6,577lb, auw 8,590. The first production XIVE with the improved rear view fuselage, NH741, was also weighed at High Post on 4 December. Tare 6,621, auw 8,628.

The next Supermarine Specification was covered in Report 4344 (29 December 1944) and related to JF317, JF320, JF321 and RB144 fitted with contra rotating propellers. This led to the Type Record 'Type 373' on 16 January 1945 with certification under Contract CTT/Acft/2601/C.23c, Griffon 85, auw 8,800lb. First production models reached the RAF in February 1945 and they had the conventional cockpit hood, full elliptical wings and 'C' armament. Late production models had the 'E' wing, reduced area rear fuselage, clear view canopy and some provision for camera mounting. A small number had the interconnected throttle and propeller, a device that was supposed to relieve the pilot of throttle setting.

NH717 was fitted with an Elektron engine cowling on 10 October 1944 to test its durability, but after ten hours' flying a crack appeared in the bottom panel near the wing fillets. After 35 hours the crack had enlarged and had to be repaired. After 50 hours the cowling was removed and returned to the manufacturer. The Elektron cowling was 30lbs lighter than the standard item, but its tendency to crack resulted in it being abandoned as a standard fitting. Jeffrey Quill tested RM784 for spin recovery and reported satisfactory results on 19 February 1945, and Shea-Simmonds flew the same aircraft a few days later to assess the handling characteristics of a production, rear view, Mk XIV. He reported that the rear view modification had a detrimental effect on directional stability and control, particularly in the climb. Shea-Simmonds thought the aircraft would meet with strong Service criticism in view of the poor directional stability and with (B) he thought it acceptable.

NH717 was returned to Vickers fitted with a tropical air intake shutter interconnected with the undercarriage lever, this being considered an operational necessity as there were occasions when the lowered undercarriage did prevent cooling air reaching the radiator in sufficient quantity and the engine overheated, particularly in the tropics. During test flights the original installation would not work and pilot F. C. Furlong had to use both hands to move the operating lever. A more powerful operating jack was fitted and it worked successfully. The same aircraft was then flown to check feed and fuel consumption with a 170 gallon overload tank. The system could not be faulted and jettison trials followed with drops up to 250mph being made in safety. RB146 had plain, tab-balanced ailerons in place of the standard Frise, and lateral control was considered to be far too light at low speeds, with a tendency to overbalance at high speeds. It was also flown with the Griffon at 25lbs boost.

Skin wrinkling had not been fully cured and a team from Supermarine visited RAF Wherwell on 15 March 1945. A

JF319, second Mk VIII conversion, had the true air intake configuration and the new, enlarged fin and rudder as proposed for the F 23 Valiant.

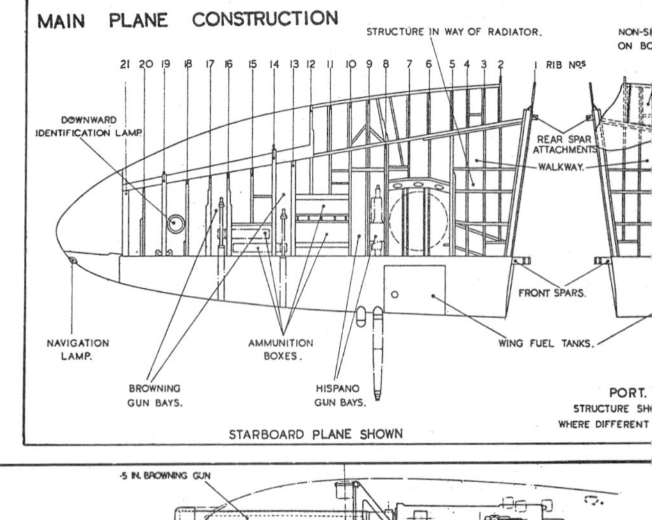

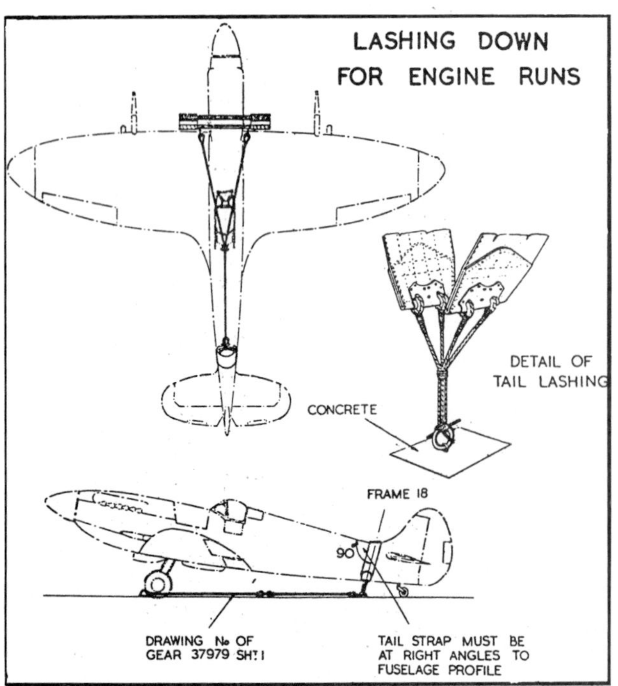

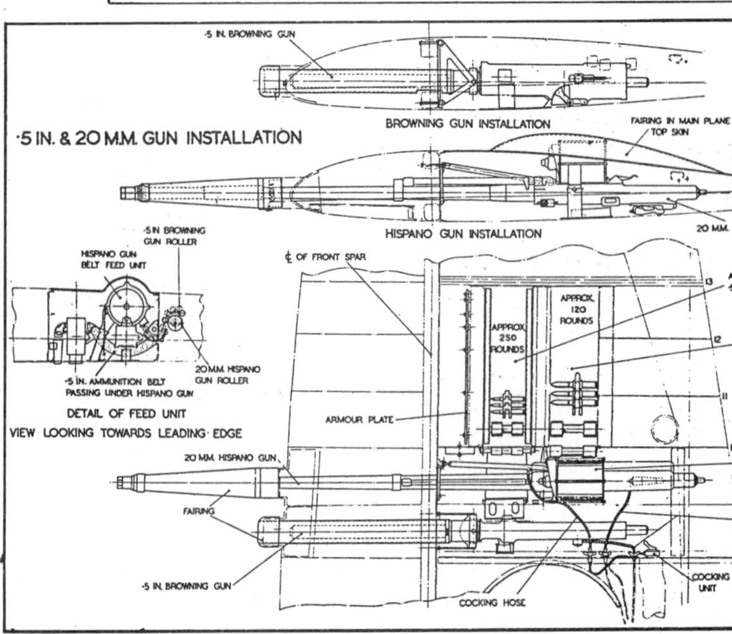

number of XIVEs were examined and found to have the defect in the top wing plating in the vicinity of the gun bays. The cause was thought to be the discontinuous spanwise stringers, the effect pulled rivets and wrinkling. A modification consisting of brackets at the end of the stringers was introduced and the RAF agreed to allow minimal wrinkling. The fault had come to light during a prolonged series of bombing practice with small bombs.

Clear view hood jettison trials were requested by the RAF as several instances had been reported of the released hood striking the airframe under certain conditions. Lieutenant Hill, RNVR, flew MV262 over Salisbury Plain and after release the hood shot off violently, striking and badly damaging the fin, rudder and tailplane. In addition it had ripped the top fuselage just aft of the cockpit for a distance of 12 inches and had badly scarred the starboard fuselage side. Hill reported—"Subsequent to an agreed signal (to the chase aeroplane) there was no hood jettison due to the pilot being unable to operate the gear. Both aircraft dived through cloud to 1,500ft, when the hood flew off. The sequence was so rapid as to be impossible to follow what happened in detail, but the hood appeared to rear as though attached to its back and I saw two distinct pieces fly back from the aeroplane, apparently passing just above the tailplane and certainly below the top of the fin. The perspex canopy seemed to be detached from the metal frame. I would suggest that the canopy broke in half when it reared up, with one half going each side of the fin and part, if not all, of the metal frame passing on one side". Subsequent examination revealed the damage as related above. See photograph and sequence drawings of hood jettison tests on page 160.

RM732 was returned to Supermarine from No 41 Group with trim reversal problems. The ailerons were extremely light up to 350mph when reversal from left to right became apparent and the aircraft flew left wing low. It was fitted with standard Frise units. Starboard wing incidence was decreased by 15mins of angle but no change of trim was effected. While it was at the company airfield in March 1945 it was decided to carry out a comparison of tuft behaviour at the stall with the Mk XIV and a Spiteful, NN664. Quill was the pilot and both aircraft had tufted wings, these revealing that the Spiteful wing was becoming stalled, particularly that in front of the ailerons, considerably in advance of the ultimate stall of the wing, or final collapse of lift. RM732, tufted in a similar manner, revealed that there was no sign of any collapse until a speed very much closer to the stall was obtained. The outstanding fact was that the Spiteful wing in front of the aileron stalled first, while on the Spitfire it stalled last, thought to be due to the gap in front of the Frise aileron. It was decided to continue the experiments with a second Mk XIV, RB146, which had plain ailerons and no gap. A sketch of the Spitfire and Spiteful wings appears on page 498.

Another 41 Group XIV with the same problem as RM732 was RM709. The fault seemed incurable and Quill, Shea-Simmonds, Morgan and Errington thought it was caused by a combination of wing and aileron deflection and slipstream effect. Adjustable ailerons such as those fitted to the Firefly and Mosquito were suggested as possible alternatives. A considerable number of F XIVs were delivered to de Havillands at

TZ138, FR XIVe, arrived at Fort Nelson, BC, Canada, in November 1946 for winterisation trials. While taxying the wheels of the aircraft broke through the snow surface and it nosed over, damaging the propeller. There was 18 inches of snow and the Spitfire could not operate at normal efficiency. A set of Tiger Moth skis were fitted and as a result additional engine power was required to maintain forward ground speed. For take off the aircraft was held on the ground until 120/150mph was attained. As the aircraft left the ground the skis dropped away. As a result of these trials it was recommended that single engine fighters should not operate with skis, but they were useful for emergencies. TZ138 is still in existence, in the USA.

RB144 was one of the few Mk XIVs with the de Havilland contra-props.

Hatfield for what was code named 'GEM' modifications. No details of these modifications have ever been released, but it is thought to have concerned engine output.

The personal flight log notes of the various Vickers/ Supermarine test pilots are worth recording—RM709 (Shea-S 27-2-45) Original ailerons recovered with thicker gauge skin. Slightly to considerably left wing low at speeds ranging from 170 to 470mph. Starboard aileron floating up to 470mph. No beneficial effect has resulted from alteration of starboard wing incidence.

RM732 (Shea-S 7-3-45) Flown following removal of the fitting from the port wing root and consequent restoration of port wing to its normal angle of incidence. The starboard wing still has the decrease of angle in incidence of 15mins. RM732 (Quill 10-3-45) This has the modified rear spar fitting on the starboard wing giving it 15mins decrease in incidence. Although left wing low there were no traces of aileron reversal. RM732 (Shea-S 20-3-45) Flight to photograph wool tufts now applied all over upper surface of port wing. The inboard wing section stalls first followed rapidly by tip. This leaves a much greater area of the wing and aileron outboard of cannons unstalled until a final breakdown of flow all over. It would appear that the Frise type aileron, presumably by virtue of the slot in front, does keep a considerable portion of the wing unstalled. RM732 (17-5-45) With the fitting to give an increase of 25′ to port wing incidence. No reversal of lateral trim but ailerons far too heavy.

RM766 (Quill 18-8-44) On first flight aircraft was right wing low but port gun panel had a lot of buttons undone and was lifting and some buttons were undone on the port side cowling.

NH657 (Furlong 24-8-44) A Mk XIV fitted with de Havilland contra-rotating propeller. Considered to be the best contra-propeller hitherto flown.

NH717 (Shea-S 14-10-44) Aircraft flown for purpose of jettisoning the 170 gallon long range tank. The tank was dropped in level flight at 250mph with satisfactory results. It is considered that the directional stability is adversely affected when flying with the tank. (24-10-44) Intensive flying elektron cowling. Max speed of 300mph @ 2400rpm @ 10,000ft (25-10-44) Level cooling and charge temperature in FS gear @ 25,000ft. (27-10-44) 35 mins extensive flying with elektron cowling. Maximum speed 400mph.

RH784 (Shea-S 5-10-44) Flight made in order to observe test of hood jettisoning by JF299. (29-11-44) Metal covered rudder. Directional control unacceptable. Hood jettison test failed. (30-11-44) Another unsuccessful test made to jettison hood at 300mph. (4-12-44) Fabric rudder and balance tab. Directional stability substantially better.

RB146 (Shea-S 7-12-44) Plain ailerons and plus 25lb boost engine. Flaps causing instability.

NH717 (Quill 7-11-44) Metal covered elevator, a vast improvement on that fitted to standard F XIV. The best metal elevator tested to date. (9-11-44) Aircraft dived to 470mph. considerable propeller vibration apparent throughout airframe, particularly at trailing edge port wing. Upfloat on starboard aileron. (29-11-44) Elevator light but ineffective up to 180 ASI, As speed increased it improved and at 450 it is very effective. (Morgan 8-1-45) Observations of first flight of Spiteful. Air-to-Air R/T successful.

RM732 (Morgan 18-12-44) One of the aircraft returned from 41 Group with reversal of trim. Ailerons extremely light up to 350mph when reversal from right to left becomes apparent and the aircraft left wing low at 470. (Shea-S 4-2-45) Port wing incidence increased by 15 mins. Altering incidence had no effect.

MV253 (24-12-44) Hood winding gear tests at Eastleigh by Quill. Satisfactory providing speed is low, maximum permissible is 200mph.

MV247 (Shea-S 17-1-45) Flown with 21 gallons in rear tank, main and wing tanks full. (19-1-45) Handling with rear tank full and auw 9030lb. Satisfactory for take off and normal flying and considered acceptable for combat in an emergency after half fuel in rear tank used. (20-1-45) Handling with 90 gallon drop tank and rear tank full. Directional stability poor, the rudder shows a marked tendency to over balance. Aircraft could be cleared for non-combat flying.

RM784 (Quill 8-1-45) Comparison of fabric and metal covered rudders. Auw 8580lb. With fabric rudder directional stability good, with metal unit quite unacceptable. With balance tab disconnected the situation improved.

RM784, Griffon 65, at Boscombe Down, March 1945, for spinning trials, after fitment of tear drop canopy and reduced area rear fuselage.

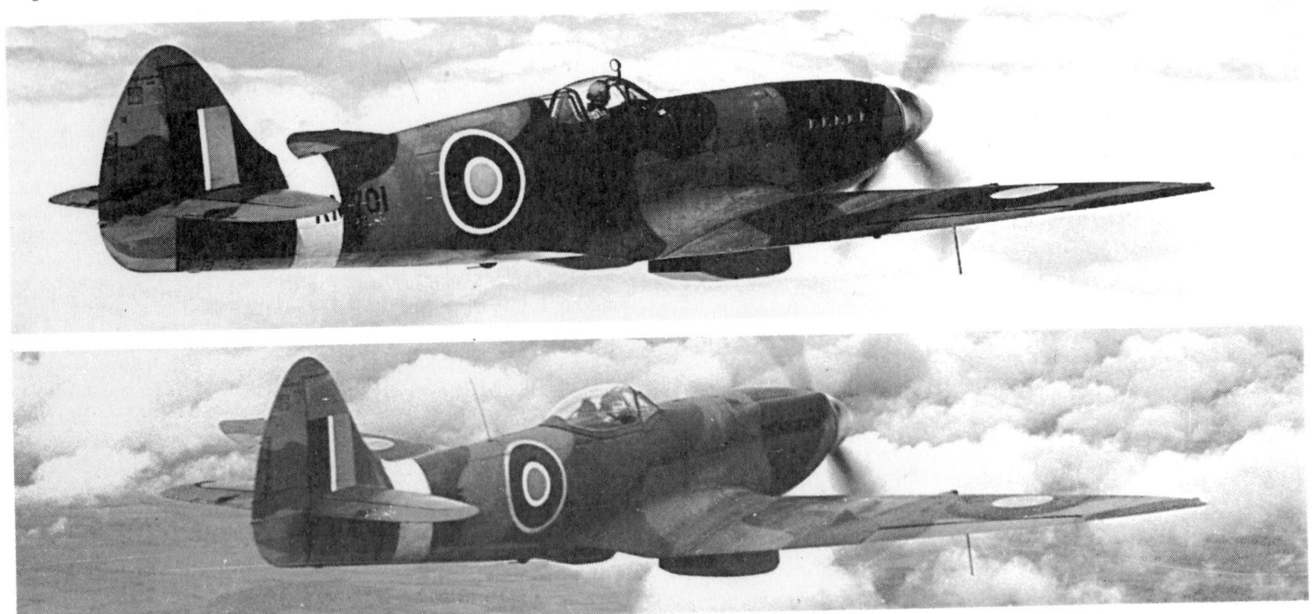

Compare the normal canopy of RM701 with the rear view of RM785.

RB146 (Morgan 10-1-45) Flown to photograph jettisoning rear vision hood. (Shea-S 3-2-45) Fitted Rolls-Royce circular type exhaust stubs. (27-3-45) Wool tufts fitted over whole of port wing upper surface. First indication of stall is elevator buffeting, the tufts between cannon and wing root going. As control column pulled back wing tip tufts affected. Has little effect on condition of aeroplane and lateral control can still be retained. There is a patch of wing forward of the inboard end of the aileron and extending to the wing leading edge outboard of the cannon which remains unstalled. If control column pulled further back this central part of wing stalls and tufts show a complete breakdown of flow. On landing the inboard tufts are beginning to show signs of stalling but the Spitfire wing is not really stalled when the aircraft lands.

RM732 (Shea-S 9-2-45) Flight to examine lateral trim and control with wing tips removed. It was observed that the port flap door in the wing upper surface was opening at speeds in excess of 400mph but it is thought this was due to a defect in the door spring.

NH717 (19-2-45 Wigley) Final report on elektron cowling. Total flying time now 90hr 35min. After 50hr 30mins the bottom panel was badly cracked and had to be repaired. After total of 64hr 10mins slight cracks developed at screw fastener holes, thought due to removal of cowling. After 90hr 35min top cowling and starboard side developed bad cracks and further flying was suspended. In the top cowling a crack 9 inches long had developed. From a pilot's viewpoint this was most serious for if the crack increased a dive to limiting speed could have ripped off the cowling with unpleasant results.

RM709 (Shea-S 27-2-45) Original ailerons covered with thicker gauge skin. Lateral trim reversal characteristics are less pronounced. (23-3-45) Normal ailerons refitted and 6in reflex on starboard unit in order to put aircraft in trim laterally on the climb. (Quill 10-3-45) Modified rear spar fitting on starboard wing giving it 15mins decrease in incidence. (Shea-S 29-3-45) Wool tufts on port wing upper surface. Aircraft with Frise type ailerons kept wing unstalled for longer periods than that measured on RB146. (Shea-S 6-5-45) Aircraft now has port wing fitting giving an increase of 25mins to the incidence. The 15mins decrease still to starboard wing. (18-5-45) Wing tips removed resulting in improved lateral control up to 350mph.

CR397 (Wigley 14-6-45) Intensive flying of Rotol contra rotating propeller. This propeller has completed a total of 127 hours and 30 minutes flying since the transfer bearing was stripped and rebuilt by Rotol Ltd on 13 March. In order to avoid loss of flying time due to aircraft inspections, the propeller was removed from JF321 after 79 hours, 20 minutes flying, and fitted to Spitfire F 21 LA218 on 16 May and to F 21 LA219 on 26 May. When the propeller was fitted to JF321 there was a very marked grinding vibration at low engine speeds as well as a certain amount of pure propeller vibration at all speeds. These faults were improved by enriching the mixture. I consider that this propeller vibration does not make flying particularly pleasant, especially over long distances. If it persists in similar contra props, it will draw unfavourable comment from the Service.

TP240 (Shea-S 2-10-45) Handling trials with six RPs on zero length rails. As a result of trials the FR Mk XIV is considered satisfactory in all flying conditions.

Mk XIV of the Royal Thai Air Force.

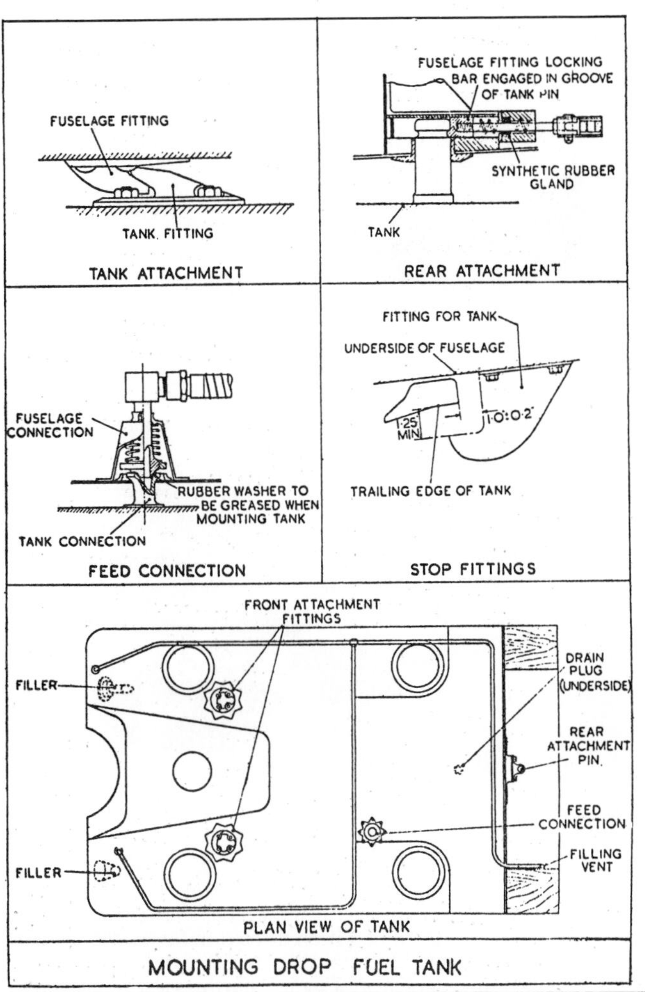

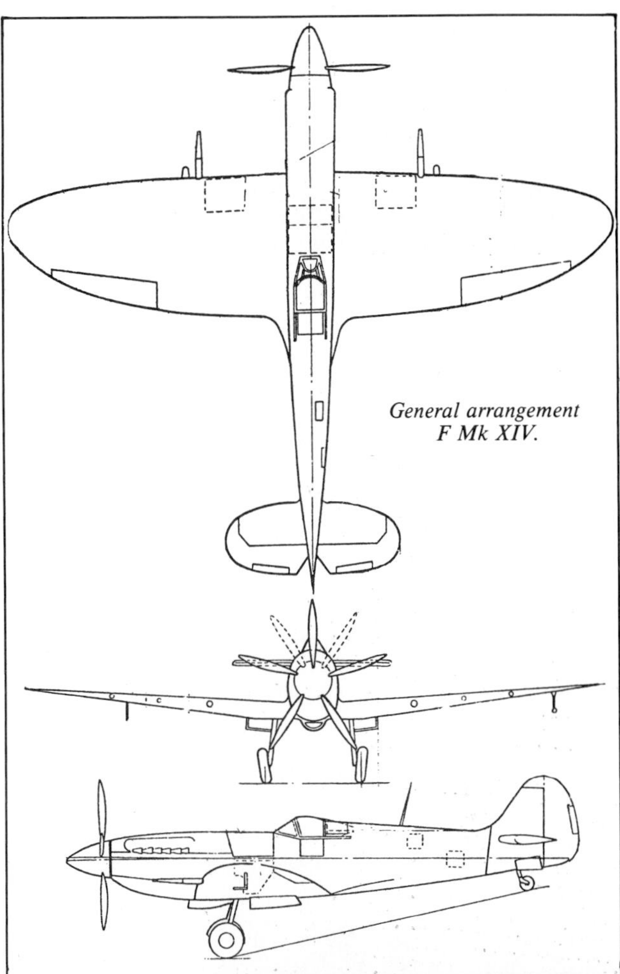
General arrangement F Mk XIV.

ITEM NO.	NOTE NO.	TYPICAL REMOVABLE ITEMS OF MILITARY LOAD.	4 x ·303 IN.+ 2 x 20MM. WEIGHT LB.	ARM IN.	MOMENT LB.IN.	2 x ·50 IN.+ 2 x 20MM. WEIGHT LB.	ARM IN.	MOMENT LB.IN.
6	1	4 BROWNING ·303 IN. GUNS & ACCESSORIES.	112·5	+ 11	+ 1,238	—	—	—
3		BROWNING ·303 IN. AMMUNITION AT 350 RD. PER GUN.	93	+ 9·5	+ 884	—	—	—
17	2	2 BROWNING ·50 IN. GUNS & ACCESSORIES.	—	—	—	165·5	+ 10	+ 1,655
8		BROWNING ·50 IN. AMMUNITION AT 250 RD. PER GUN.	—	—	—	150	+ 12	+ 1,800
15	3	2 INNER HISPANO 20MM. GUNS & ACCESSORIES.	304	- 3	- 912	—	—	—
7		HISPANO 20MM. AMMUNITION AT 120 RD. PER INNER GUN.	150	+ 12	+ 1,800	—	—	—
16	3	2 OUTER HISPANO 20MM. GUNS & ACCESSORIES.	—	—	—	297·5	+ 10·5	+ 3,124
18		HISPANO 20MM. AMMUNITION AT 120 RD. PER OUTER GUN.	—	—	—	150	+ 22·5	+ 3,375
5		REFLECTOR SIGHT MK.IIS AND 4 FILAMENT LAMPS TYPE 'B'.	4·5	+ 40	+ 180	4·5	+ 40	+ 180
9		1¼ LB. INCENDIARY BOMB MK.I, CLOCK MK.II AND CROWBAR.	3	+ 58	+ 174	3	+ 58	+ 174
14	6	G.45 CAMERA MK.I AND ACCESSORIES	8·5	- 8	- 68	8·5	- 8	- 68
12		OXYGEN CYLINDER MK.VC.	17·5	+ 187	+ 3,273	17·5	+ 187	+ 3,273
11		DINGHY TYPE 'K' IN SEAT PACK TYPE 'A' MK.II.	15	+ 55	+ 825	15	+ 55	+ 825
19	4	T.R.1143 RADIO AND ACCESSORIES.	79·5	+ 142	+ 11,289	79·5	+ 142	+ 11,289
20		R.3067 RECEIVER, DETONATOR NO. D64 MK.I AND CONTROL UNIT TYPE I.	35	+ 151.5	+ 5,302	35	+ 151·5	+ 5,302
10		PILOT AND PARACHUTE.	200	+ 55	+ 11,000	200	+ 55	+ 11,000
		TOTAL TYPICAL REMOVABLE MILITARY LOAD.	1,022·5		+ 34,985	1,126		+ 41,929
4		FUEL IN FUSELAGE TANKS: 85 GAL. 100 OCTANE AT 7·2 LB. PER GAL.	612	+ 15·5	+ 9,486	612	+ 15·5	+ 9,486
13		FUEL IN WING TANKS: 25¼ GAL. 100 OCTANE AT 7·2 LB. PER GAL.	183·5	- 9	- 1,652	183·5	- 9	- 1,652
1	5	OIL IN TANK: 9 GAL. AT 9 LB. PER GAL.	81	+ 1·0	+ 81	81	+ 1·0	+ 81
2	9	AIRCRAFT IN TARE CONDITION.	6,576		-12,201	6,511		-12,909
		AIRCRAFT IN TYPICAL TAKE OFF CONDITION.	8,475	+ 3·6	+ 30,699	8,513·5	+ 4·3	+ 36,935

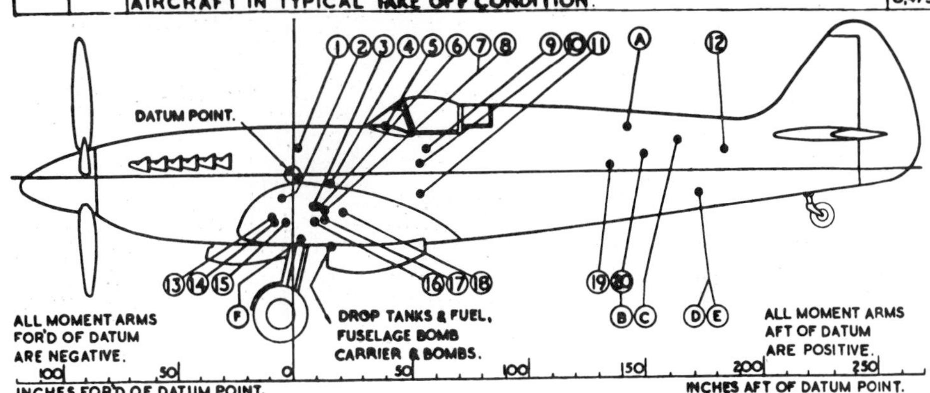

Extract from loading and centre of gravity diagram for Spitfire F Mk XIV and XIV(e).

OFFICIAL REPORTS ON Mk XIV

Boscombe Down, 19 September 1944. **RM766** F Mk XIVE. Gun heating test. Recommendations as for RB146.

Boscombe Down, 27 March 1945. MV247 FR XIV. F24 oblique camera installation. Camera located just aft of rear fuselage fuel tank. Able to photograph through glass portholes to either port or starboard. Some form of shock absorbent incorporated into mounting required to cure vibration.

Boscombe Down, 28 March 1945. MV247. Fuel functioning tests of rear 31 gallon fuselage tank. This tank gave an adequate supply of fuel to engine up to a height of 25,000ft, and it completely drained in 15 minutes. The tank was independent of the main fuel system with fuel supplied direct to engine, being controlled by a separate cock situated by the pilot's seat.

Boscombe Down, March 1945. MV247. Handling tests with full tanks and 90 gallon drop tank. Directional behaviour poor, especially with drop tank. Longitudinal behaviour unsatisfactory above 15,000ft. However, if rear fuel tank used immediately after take-off the aircraft was satisfactory with drop tank.

Boscombe Down, March 1945. **RM784. Spinning trials.** Reduced area rear fuselage. Slight increase in number of turns to recover from spin when compared with standard fuselage Spitfire.

Boscombe Down, March 1945. **RB146. Brief handling** trials with piano-hinge type ailerons. Ailerons gave a substantial improvement in manoeuvrability and lateral control over standard F XIV.

Piano hinges were fitted to the ailerons of RB146 for a series of handling trials. The ailerons had geared, balance tabs.

Central Fighter Establishment, Tangmere, 13 April 1945. **RB179**. Trials with American Mk V zero length R/P launchers. Normal handling unaltered but slight loss of speed in level flight. Directional stability in dive was poor and aircraft difficult to hold on to target. Considered acceptable for service use.

Boscombe Down, June 1945. RM784. Determination of aftmost acceptable CoG. Should be limited to 5.6in aft of datum.

Boscombe Down, 14 November 1943. RB141. Griffon RG 5SM. Brief handling trials of a production aircraft. Comparison with prototype JF319. Auw 8490 lb. There was little difference in handling but a number of criticisms were made; the visual indicators on the wing which showed when the undercarriage was down had been deleted in favour of cockpit electrical units. Reintroduction was recommended as they were vital during an emergency. Engine starting was considered complicated as both hands were required and the pilot had to hold the control column steady with his knees.

RB141 went to Boscombe in 1943 for trials when fitted with the F21 fin and rudder.

MB878 with 500lb bomb for trials at Boscombe Down.

Boscombe Down, November 1943. RB141. Weights and loading data. In basic configuration: – Tare 6578 lb, service load 1023, fuel 806, oil 81, totals 8488. Ordance and overload tanks produced many variations: – see data.

Boscombe Down, 25 November 1943. RB144. Griffon 56. Intensive flying trials. 150 hours required on a production XIV with Griffon 65. Aircraft flown by operational pilots, assisted by maintenance fitters. Auw 8445 lb, with 45 gallon overload tank 8845. Engine cowling deemed unsatisfactory as they took two skilled fitters 1hr 40min to change. Experimental stainless steel exhaust stubs had to be replaced by the normal mild steel units. At the start of trials the tail wheel retracted during taxying causing minor damage to bottom rudder. Two inspection panels in wing fairings were lifting in flight and were finally riveted down. Later, modified fairings with an improved type of panel were installed. Despite minor faults the aircraft was found to be 'most satisfactory'.

XIVe, RB140, with GEM engine mods.

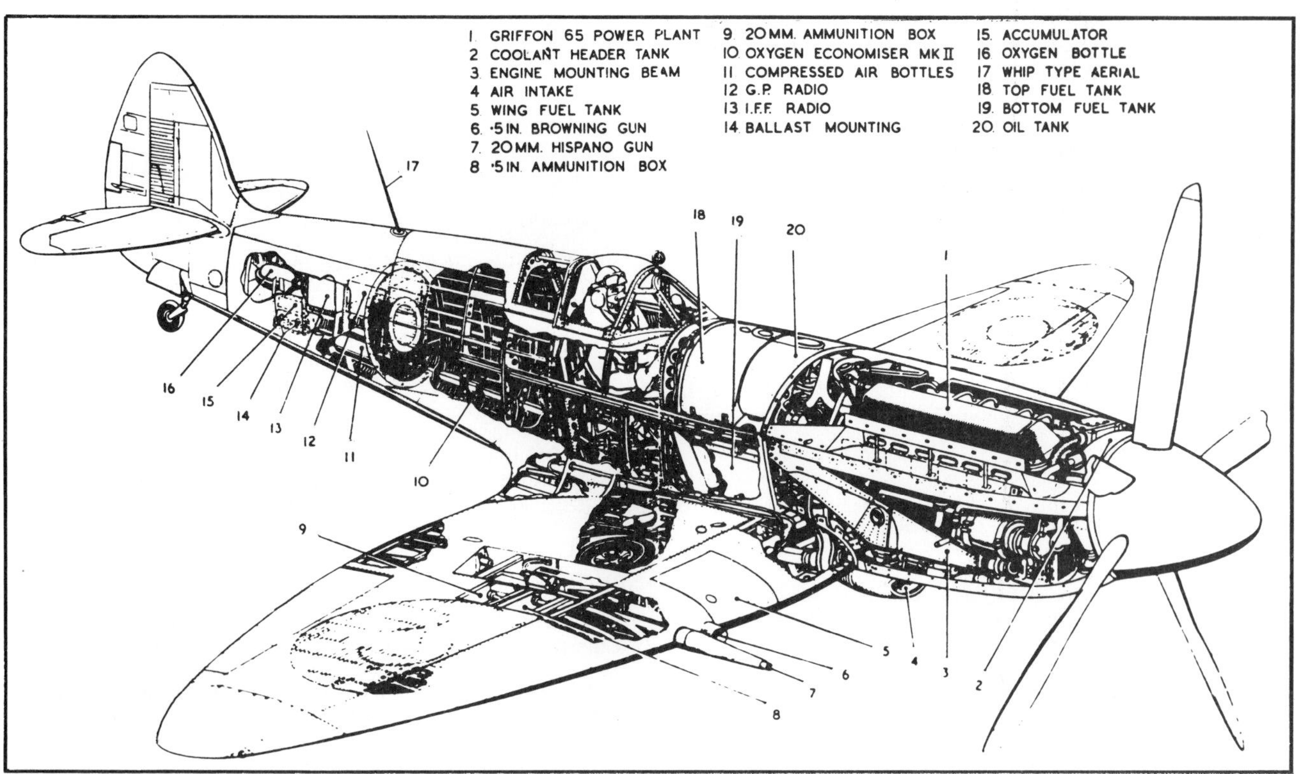

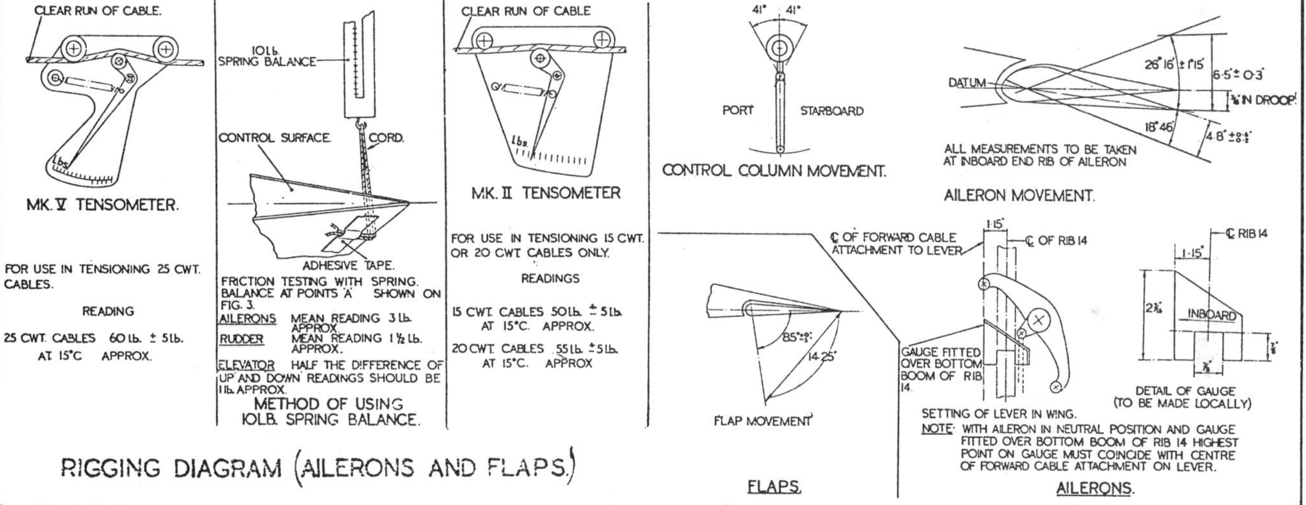

Three of the RB serial range XIVs were used for maker's and experimental trials. RB142 eventually went to No.616 Squadron. Note the transparent fairing next to cannon.

Supermarine Spitfire F Mk XIV

Boscombe Down, 21 April 1944. RB146. Gun heating tests. All gun temperatures were below requirements. Recommended that gun bays should be partitioned off from rest of wing and lagged, and plastic ducting be replaced by light alloy.

Boscombe Down, 7 May 1944. RB146. Fuel consumption trials. Auw 8,465 lb. Fuel 112 gallons.

Air miles per gallon

Height ft	Optimum specific air range AMPG	RPM	Boost lb/sq in	ASI mph	S/C gear
5000	5.28	1800	−2	200	MS
20000	5.32	1800	−2	195	FS
35000	4.99	2050	−1¾	195	FS

Climb @ 2600 rpm +9 lb boost

Conditions	At 5000ft Fuel used galls	At 5000ft Distance miles	20000ft Fuel used galls	20000ft Distance miles	35000ft Fuel used galls	35000ft Distance miles
Normal climbing power 2600 rpm +9 lb/in² boost Rad flaps open	3	5	13½	26	27	59
Max cruising power 2400 rpm +7 lb/in² boost Rad flaps closed	3	5	12	26	24½	61

Range

Height ft	S/C gear	Mean weight lb	Corrd specific air range AMPG	Dist covered on climb (miles)	Dist covered cruise (miles)	Max still air range (to nearest 5 miles)
5000	MS	8010	5.30	5	520	525
20000	FS	7980	5.35	26	476	500
35000	FS	7935	5.04	61	385	445

Endurance

Height ft	Fuel flow galls/hr	Endurance (hours)	S/C gear
5000	37.8	2.6	MS
20000	46.2	1.9	MS
20000	46.8	1.9	FS
35000	64.4	1.2	FS

F Mk XIV, XIVE, FR Mk XIV, FR Mk XIVE

Wing. Planform elliptical; section NACA Series 2200; span 36′ 10″; incidence° root +2, tip −½; dihedral° 6; thickness% root 13.2, tip 6; aspect ratio 5.68; area nett 220, gross 242; chord(geo) 6.38, (ma) 7.01. Ailerons. Area 18.9; movement° up 24, down 19; droop ⅜. Flaps. Area 15.4; movement° down 85. Wing loading 35 lb/sq ft; power loading 4.16 lb/hp. Propeller clearance at take off 8½in.

Tailplane. Area 33.84; chord(ma) 4.0; incidence° root 0, tip ±½; dihedral° 0. Elevators. Area 13.74; movement° up 28, down 23. Tab area 0.688; movement° up 20, down 7. Fin area 6.65. Rudder. Area 10.08; movement° 28½ each way. Tab area 0.7; movement° port 2½, starbd 27, setting 1.5in starbd.

Belgian SG-22, IQ-0 of OTU Coxyde. Ex RM791.

SG-56, also of the Coxyde OTU.

Undercarriage. Wheels Dunlop AH10019; tyres Dunlop IK 13 or 17. Oleo pressure 480P/520S lb/sq in. Tyre pressure 80 lb/sq in. Tailwheel retractable castoring. Wheel Dunlop AH2184/IX; tyre Dunlop TA12 or 14. Oleo pressure 265 lb/sq in; tyre pressure 80 lb/sq in.

Engine/s. Griffon 65, two speed, two stage super; 2,035hp @ 7,000ft, 1,540 @ take off (MS), 1,820 @ 21,000 (FS).

Griffon 85 2,055hp @ 2,750rpm @ 8,250ft.
Griffon 61 1,785hp @ take off (2,750rpm).
Coffman cartridge Mk V starter.

Propeller/s. G65. Rotol R19/5F5/1 5-blade Jablo pitch range 35° fine pitch 27° 15′. Diameter 10ft 5in. G85 Rotol 6-blade contra rotating Jablo or Hydulignum pitch range 35° fine pitch 31° 45′ and 30° 15′. Diameters 10ft 5in and 10 4in.

Coolant. 70% mains water, 30% Glycol. 15½ gals in main system. 3½ intercooler.

Fuel. 100 octane + 18 boost, 150 + 21 boost.
Capacity. Fuselage (upper) 36 gals, lower 48, wing leading edge 2 × 12¾, total 109½. Plus 30, 45, 50, 90 and 170 gal o/ld tanks.
Consumption (G65) 37.8 gal hr @ 5,000ft, 46.2 @ 20,000 (MS); 64.4 @ 35,000 (FS).

Oil. 9 gals in fuselage.

Armour. 180lb.

Armament. B wing.
Plus Mk IX rockets, 250, 500, 120 (smoke) bombs.

Radio. TRf1143, ARI 500 or 5025, A1271.

Cine camera G45 in starboard wing.

Gunsight. Mk II reflector or Gyro.

Performance. Max speed 439 @ 24,500ft (FS), 404 @ 11,000 (MS), 274 @ 30,000 (FS), 220 @ 35,000 (FS), 357 @ SL (MS). Normal cruise 362 @ 20,000. Max dive 470. Rate of **climb 4,580ft/min @ SL (MS), 3,700 @ 22,500 (FS), 4,700 @ 8,000 (MS). Time to 20,000 7 min. Service ceiling 43,000. Stall** flaps up 87mph, down 75. Landing 75. Range 460 miles normal, 850 max. Endurance 1.9hr. Stall flaps and u/ up 87, down 75.

Weights. Tare 6,576lb, take off 8,475, max permissable 8,500, max overload 10,280. With 30 gal o/ld tank (take off) 8,779; 250lb bomb 8,779; 90 gal tank 9,278; 500lb bomb 8,959.

F Mk XIVE. As for F Mk XIV except for – armament E wing. Rear fuselage fuel tank of 33 gals, total 142½ gals. Range 610 miles, duration 2.4hr.

FR Mk XIV. As for F Mk XIV except for – cameras.

FR Mk XIVE. As for FR Mk XIV except for – .5″ machine guns.

Weights. Take off 8,750, with rear fuel 8,980, max permissable (full ordnance) 10,065, max overload (ordnance and o/ld fuel 90 gal) 10,280.

Range. Normal fuel 610 miles, duration 2.4hr. Max miles 960.

With G85 CP. Weights. Tare 8,600lb, take off 8,800.

SERIAL NUMBERS

SUPERMARINE AVIATION (VICKERS) LTD.

Contract B980385/39.

Second order for 700 Spitfire Mk VIII dated 27 July 1942. Built as Mks VIII and XIV between December 1943 and October 1944. The following serials apply to Mk XIVs built to this second order; MT847-858, MV246-273, 286-320 and 347-386.

Third order for 225 Mk VIII dated 1 December 1942. Built as Mk VIII/XIV/XVIII between November 1944 and June 1945. The following serials apply to Mk XIVs built to this third order; NH637-661, 685-720, 741-759, 775-813, 831-846, 857-871, 873-875 and 892-929.

Fourth order for 144 Mk VIII dated 29 December 1942. Original order cancelled and serials NM776-810 re-allocated to Airspeed Oxford. Re-order for 10 Mk XIVs, built in March and April 1945; NM814-823 only 834-835 and 879-906 cancelled.

Eighth order for Mk XIV dated 14 August 1943. Built as Mk XIVs between October 1943 and March 1944; RB140-189.

Tenth order for 406 Mk XIV dated 23 October 1943. Built as Mks XIV and XIX between April 1944 and May 1945. The following serials apply to Mk XIVs built to this tenth order; RM615-625, 648-656, 670-713, 726-770, 783-825, 839-887, 901-943, 957-999, RN113-160 and 173-221.

Eleventh order for 150 Mk XI dated 12 February 1944. Built as Mks XIV and XVIII between February 1945 and January 1946. The following serials apply to Mk XIVs built to this eleventh order; SM812-842, 876-899 and 913-938.

Order for 473 Mk F21 (Victor), TP195-811, in August 1944. The following Mk XIVs were built to this order; TP236-240 and 256(6).

Order for 157 Mk F21 dated 23 February 1945 from Supermarine, TX974 to TZ240. Built as: TX974-998, TZ102-149, 152-176 and 178-199 FR XIV(120). The rest bult as FR XVIII.

MT/MV series All FRXIV Griffon 65 unless otherwise indicated

MT847 FR (Intm) KEE P/proto for intro of thicker skin at tailplane root 4-4-44 6MU 24-2-45 BDn 15-12-45 29MU 18-2-46 226 OCU 14-11-50 33MU 2-8-51 to 6960M 28-5-52 extant Cosford

MT848 STN P/proto to intro Vokes wet type Aeroply filter 22-8-44 9MU 7-3-45 215MU 17-5 *Samstu* 2-7 Ind 28-7 6S RIAF cd f/lnd nr Ranchi CE

MT849 KEE 33MU 13-2-45 222MU 29-4 *Emp Dyn* 16-5 Ind 7-6 28S cd lnd Ku Lu 17-12-46 SOC 30-1-47

MT850 KEE 33MU 21-2-45 84GSU 30-7 453S 6-9 CC 29-1-46 SOC 12-6

MT851 KEE 33MU 21-2-45 215MU 18-5 *Samstu* 2-7 Ind 28-7 SOC 29-11

MT852 KEE 33MU 29-3-45 84GSU 12-4 268S 19-4 16S 1-11 Dvd i/trees, Ceue pilot kld 15-2-46 SOC 35WSU 28-2

MT853 used by Super as P/proto 31-10-44 to RNAF as instructional airframe

MT854 KEE 33MU 24-2-45 76MU 4-10 *Clan MacB* 28-11 ret to 76MU for re-erection 28-11 34MU 26-5-47 sold rtp 1979

MT855 EA 6MU 1-3-45 613S 3-5-47 FAAC 30-7 recat sold scr E Smelt 30-12-48

MT856 KEE 33MU 5-3-45 215MU 18-5 *Samstu* 2-7 Ind 28-7 SOC 25-7-46

MT857 CHA 39MU 27-2-45 76MU 8-10 *Clan MacB* 29-11 ret to 76MU for re-erection 29-11 NEA 28-3-51 sold Cindalalum 30-8

MT858 (Intm) Kee Norton 25-2-45 used by Super as p/proto 8-1-46 Hull 28-1-47 to Pendine rocket firing trls. Farn 6-5-47 5MU 5-11 CFE 5-7-49 29MU scr 5-10 NEA 31-3-53 SOC 22-9

MV series

MV246 FRXIVE ALD MJL 23-11-44 9MU 29-11-44 BAF(SG-55) 24-8-48 cd II-10. Extant, Brussels Museum.

MV247 FRXIVE ALD CRD HPA 15-1-45 BDn 27-3 fuel funct tests of rear 31gal. fus tank. It supplied fuel to eng independent of main syst to 25,000ft (empty after 15 mins climb). Hand trls with full fuel and 90gal o/ld tank. Gun heat trls F24 oblique camera instal at VA BDN 27-3 trls proved instal unsuitable 29MU 24-5 84GSU 16-9 CC 25-10 ASTH 613S 4-11-46 FAAC 22-8-48 recat E

MV248 FRXIVE ALD 39MU 30-11-44 83GSU 5-3-45 430S 17-5 FAAC 15-10 BAF (SG-4) 25-4-47

MV249 STN 33MU 3-12-44 83GSU 5-3-45 41S 22-3 CB ops 24-4 recat E SOC 19-5

MV250 STN 39MU 13-3-45 83GSU 13-8 *D Bank* 6-9 Ind 14-10 Jap SOC 25-3-48

MV251 STN 33MU 3-12-44 130S 22-3 45 401S 10-5 411S 23-6 3BRU CE 29-6-46

MV252 STN 39MU 30-11-44 402S 26-4-45 412S 28-6 3BRU 6-4-46 2S 24-6-48 w/u ldg Wahn, Bzg CE 25-11

MV253 EA 39MU 10-1-45 AFDU Witt 31-1 CAC 22-1-46 ROS Super p/proto to intro winding mech for RV slide hood 2-4 cleared for prod 6-5 ETPS Farn 30-5 trls 602S 12-6-47 BCSU 22-4-48 CB surplus recat E 12-1-49

MV254 STN 33MU 16-12-44 41S 22-3-45 GACB 22-4 ASTH 612S 18-2-47 29MU 24-10-49 NEA 31-3-53 SOC 30-9

MV255 STN 33MU 18-12-44 41S 7-3-45 FACE 26-3 SOC 4-5

MV256 STN 39MU 26-12-44 402S 19-4-45 412S 28-6 BAF (SG-39) 22-3-48 arrived in bad condition replaced

MV257 STN 33MU 22-12-44 41S 9-3-45 416S 20-9 FACB 22-1-46 3BRU 21-3 recat E

MV258 STN 33MU 18-12-44 403S 9-3-45 FTR ops 25-3

MV259 STN 39MU 3-2-45 414S 10-5 430S 17-5 416S 15-11 2S BAFO 5-2-49 CAC 26-4 FAC3 4-10 SOC recat C 11-10

MV260 STN 39MU 22-12-44 41S 22-3-45 CAC ops 20-4-45 416S 20-9 FAAC 21-2-46 151RU 22-8 BAFO CE 12-6-47

MV261 FXIV(RV) STN used by Super as p/proto 5-9-44 39MU 18-12 416S 10-3-46 33MU 19-3 sold Belgium via VA 11-1-51

MV262 STN 9MU 8-3-45 *SSLS2861* 13-4-45 Ind 21-5 sold InAF 31-12-47 Ret UK 1978. Extant, Charles Church, Hampshire.

MV263 FRXIV(RV) Super p/proto for gun mounting mount mods 5-9-44 443S BAF (SG-77) 10-12-48 cd 18-7-50

MV264 STN 39MU 3-1-45 83GSU 12-3 41S 22-3 FACE 28-7

MV265 STN 39MU 3-1-45 402S 17-4 CAC ops 29-4 410RSU 412S 28-6 33MU NEA 9-11-49 sold Belgium via VA 15-1-51

MV266 EA FXIV 33MU 3-1-45 41S 22-3 CAC ops 11-4 409RSU 416S 20-9 33MU 19-3-46 sold British Lion Production Assetts 23-4-47

MV267 FXIV STN 33MU 41-45 41S 29-3 350S 14-6 29MU 20-2-46 NEA 31-7-50 sold Belgium via VA 25-8-50

MV268 FXIV STN 33MU 4-1-45 130S 29-3 401S 10-5 411S 28-6 cd f/lnd Celle 4-3-46

MV269 EA 39MU 14-1-45 83GSU 17-4 414S 26-4 FACE 6-7

MV270 STN 39MU 17-11-45 430S 10-5 29MU 12-9 151RU reserve 21-12 2S 7-9-46 BAFO D/A 29-10-48 NEA SOC 22-9-53

MV271 Super p/proto for metal ails mods 14-11-44 39MU 17-1-45 215MU 3-4 *Emp Dyn* 16-5 Ind 7-6 SOC 28-8-47

MV272 STN 39MU 22-1-45 350S 130S 10-5 401S 10-5 411S 28-6 FACE dbf 13-7

MV273 STN 39MU 5-2-45 268S 19-4 FAAC 14-6 151RU 9-8 3BRU recat E 4-7-46

MV286 (Intm) ST Super p/proto 7-10-44 39MU 3-2-45 222MU 12-5 *C o Chest* 7-6 Ind 25-6 SOC 25-9-47

MV287 STN 39MU 3-2-45 215MU 17-5 *Samstu* 2-7 Ind 28-7 SOC 27-121-47

MV288 STN 39MU 1-2-45 BAF (SG-30) 28-1-48 cd 10-8-51

MV289 KEE 39MU 10-2-45 215MU 8-7 *Emp Gam* 5-8 Ind 30-8 SOC 28-8-47

MV290 FRXIV(RV Intm) STN p/proto for cockpit wiring mods 25-7-44 to standardise top rear fus tank 14-11 to intro FRXIV intm variant 14-11 ASTH 15-4-45 6MU 6-5 76MU 14-9 *Fort Mich* 28-9 Ind 18-10 Jap SOC 25-3-48

MV291 KEE 39MU 7-2-45 FAAC 7-5 ROS 83GSU 15-6 61 OTU 21-3-46 SOC 12-3-48

MV292 KEE 39MU 10-2-45 215MU 1-7 ROS 9-7 *C o H K* 26-8 Ind 17-9 SOC 11-4-46

MV293 KEE p/proto for ails mods 25-7-44 33MU 1-3-45 215MU 20-8 *D Bank* 6-9 Ind 14-10 sold InAF 31-12-47 ret to UK as G-BGHB. Later G-SPIT, extant, Duxford with BJS Grey.

MV294 FRXIVE KEE 33MU 15-2-45 222MU 12-5 *C o Chest* 7-6 Ind 25-6 Jap 26-9-46 SOC 24-3-48

MV295 STN 39MU 15-3-45 82MU 27-8 *D Bank* 6-9 Ind 14-10 SOC 28-8-47

MV296 KEE 39MU 10-2 45 sold InT All 9-6

MV297 FRXIV(Intm) KEE p/proto to intro intm variant 14-11-44 Farn 28-2-45 222MU 30-4 *Emp Dyn* 16-5 Ind 29-6 SOC 28-8-47

MV298 CHA 39MU 15-2-45 47MU 20-9 *Ocean Ver* 7-11 Ind 2-12 ACSEA 28-4-46 Jap 24-4-47 SOC 24-3-48

MV299 STN 33MU 18-3-45 414S 12-4 2S 9-8 412RSU 16-8 FAAC 12-6-46 310S 10-7-47 39MU NEA 9-2-52 sold VA 15-8-48

MV300 KEE 33MU 23-2-45 215MU 15-5 *C o Chest* 7-6 Ind 25-6 ACSEA 5-7 Japan 24-3-48

MV301 KEE 33MU 24-2-45 215MU 27-6 *Emp Gam* 5-8 Ind 30-8 ACSEA 13-9 7S RIAF eng fail t/o Miranshah cd D&F 8-9-46

MV302 CHA 33MU 26-2-45 402S 26-4 412S 28-6 39MU 20-3-46 BAF(SG-36) 22-3-48

MV303 KEE Norton 25-2-45 611S 20-3-47 43Gp D/A CAC surplus 3-4-49 recat E 7-8-49 scr 9-9

MV304 STN 39MU 16-3-45 82MU 11-9 *Fort Pt* 11-9 Ind 16-10 ACSEA 26-10 SOC 28-5-47

MV305 FRXIV(Intm) STN Super p/proto 24-5-44 33MU 18-3 222MU 2-6 *Emp Gam* 6-8 Ind 30-8 SOC 1-6-47

MV306 CHA 33MU 26-2-45 47MU 24-9 *Sancouan* 8-12 Ind 3-1-46 ACSEA 31-1 Jap 24-4-47 SOC 24-3-48

MV307 FRXIV STN 33MU 18-3-45 2S 12-4 FACB 12-5 412RSU ASTH 14-12 615S 15-10-46 600S 19-10 613S 31-7-47 FAAC 13-3-48 recat E 6-12

MV308 KEE 9MU 3-3-45 215MU 8-6 *Samstu* 2-7 Ind 28-7 ACSEA 9-8 SOC 28-8-47

MV309 RV(intm) KEE p/proto to mod & strengthen blister good. Retrofit for most Mks 20-2-45 9MU 1-3-45 26S 15-7 611S 9-7-47 50RTC 12-9-49 NEA 22-9-50 sold VA 11-12

MV310 STN 9MU 8-3-45 402S 3-5 412S 28-6 33MU NEA 4-12-46 SOC 25-3-47

MV311 WIN 29MU 21-3-45 214S 26-4 FACE 29-4

MV312 EA 9MU 31-3-45 453S 6-11 29MU 24-4-46 BAF(SG-99) 22-6-49

MV313 (intm) STN p/proto Coffman starter mods 24-5-44. For eng cowling mods 5-9 29MU 22-3-45 268S 19-4 CE ops 3-5

MV314 6MU 25-3-45 414S 19-4 FA FTR 6-7

MV315 ALD 29MU 26-3-45 268S 12-4 16S 1-11 sold H Bath 10-11-49

MV316 STN 26-3-45 268S 19-4 16S 1-11 1 ARU flew i/grd Veldkapel pilot kld 5-4-46

MV317 EA 6Mu 31-3-45 76MU 4-10 *Tarata* 29-11 Ind 23-12 ACSEA 28-4-46 Jap 24-4-47 SOC 24-3-48

MV318 KEE 29MU 2-4-45 47MU 22-9 *Sancounan* 3-12 Ind 8-1-46 ACSEA 28-4 Japan 24-4-47 SOC 24-3-48

MV319 STN 39MU 31-3-45 *SSLS2561* 15-4 Ind 21-5 11S w/u ldg 18-7 SOC 18-10

MV320 STN Super p/proto 17-10-44 39MU 31-3-45

MV259 saw much squadron usage until withdrawal in 1949.

215MU 20-7 *C o H K* 26-8 Ind 17-9 ACSEA 27-9 28S eng fail f/lnd Kuala Lumpur 28-11-46 SOC 27-3-47

MV347 STN 33MU 2-4-45 222MU 17-4 *Emp Dyn* 16-5 Ind 7-6 ACSEA 22-6-46 SOC 28-8-47

MV348 (intm) STN Super p/proto 4-4-44 39MU 4-4-45 414S 26-4 2S 9-8 FAAC 10-11 123Wg HQ 23-1-46 2S BAFO 22-2-47 ROS 13-5-49

MV349 STN Super p/proto for mod oleo legs 18-4-44 33MU 4-4-45 222MU 17-4 *Emp Dyn* 16-5 Ind 7-6 ACSEA SOC 25-9-47

MV350 CHA 29MU 4-4-45 610S 30-9 sold VA 10-5-50

MV3512 CHA 29MU 4-4-45 268S 17-5 16S 1-11 2S BAFO 7-5-49 FAC3 19-3-50 SOC 26-10

MV352 STN 39MU 10-4-45 430S 10-5 SNCAN 3-1-46 350S 5-1 443S 14-1 613S 15-5-47 sold VA 12-5-48

MV353 STN 12-4-45 451S 4-10 FAAC 28-1-46 recat E SOC 19-7

MV354 EA 6MU 14-4-45 414S 10-5 430S 17-5 FAAC 27-7 ROS 33MU 5-9 cd f/lndg nr Lyneham 18-11-46 SOC 7-1-47

MV355 STN 33MU 19-4-45 82MU 1-7 *C o H K* 26-8 Ind 17-9 ACSEA 27-9 28S tyre burst t/o w/u lnd Kuala Lumpur 8-11-46 SOC 8-5-47

MV356 EA 29MU 20-4-45 222MU 15-5 *C o Chest* 7-6 Ind 25-6 ACSEA 12-7 SOC 8-11

MV357 (intm) STN p/proto for GM2 GGS 27-6-44 9MU 29-4-45 222MU 12-5 *C o Chest* 25-6 ACSEAS 5-7 Jap SOC 24-3-48

MV358 ALD 39MU 19-1-45 76MU 7-5 *Emp Sev* 27-5 New York USA 15-6 ret UK 47MU 22-1-47 sold J Dale 6-1-50

MV359 ALD 39MU 5-2-45 76MU 23-9 *Clan MacB* 29-9 ret 76MU 29-11 NEA 1-8-50 sold VA 15-11-50 to BAF

MV360 ALD 39MU 19-1-45 453S 29-6 FAAC 19-7 ROS sold BAF 9-3-49 cd on f/f to Belgium 25-3

MV361 ALD 39MU 19-1-45 76MU 16-5 *Emp Sev* 27-6 New York USA 15-6 ret UK 47MU 22-1-47 for sale for future recovery Cat scr 19-7-49

MV362 ALD 39MU 19-1-45 453S 29-6 FACE dbf 20-7

MV363 ALD FF MJL 2-2-45 39MU 5-2-45 222MU 24-4 *Emp Dyn* 16-5 Ind 7-6 ACSEA 28-6 Jap SOC 24-3-48

MV364 (intm) STN Super used as p/proto 11-7-44 39MU 22-1-45 215MU 17-5 *Samstu* 2-7 Ind 28-7 ACSEA 9-8 ROS 13-5-49

MV365 EA 39MU 17-1-45 215MU 17-5 *Samstu* 2-7 Ind 28-7 ACSEA 9-8 SOC 28-8-47

MV366 STN 39MU 22-1-45 215MU 8-7 *Emp Gam* 5-8 Ind 30-8 ACSEA 13-9 SOC 27-6-46

MV367 ALD 39MU 5-2-45 FCCS 2-2-46 SOC 25-3-48

MV368 LAD FF MJL 3-2-45 39MU 16-2-45 16S 1-11 SOC 2MPRD bou 8-8-46

MV369 ALD 39MU 5-2-45 268S 26-4 16S 5-4-46 BAF(SG-90) 8-2-49

MV370 KEE 39MU 10-2-45 82MU 30-8 *Ocean Gal* 4-9 Ind 14-10 ACSEA 29-11 sold InAF 31-12-47, G-FXIV 1980. Extant North Weald.

MV371 KEE 39MU 5-2-45 82MU 19-6 *Emp Gam* 5-8 Ind 30-8 FACE 13-2-47 SOC 27-3

MV372 ALD FF MJL 5-2-45 39MU 16-2-45 222MU 10-4 *Emp Dyn* 16-5 Ind 7-6 ACSEA 5-7 SOC 28-8-47

MV373 KEE 33MU 15-2-45 Rotol Ltd 24-4 215MU 9-5 *Samstu* 2-7 Ind 28-7 ACSEA 9-8 SOC 28-8-47

MV374 ALD FF MJL 4-2-45 39MU 16-2-45 82MU 27-8 *D Bank* 6-9 Ind 14-10 ACSEA 11-10 to 3490 8S RIAF swing on t/o u/c cllpse Kular 25-10-46 SOC 24-4-47

MV375 KEE 39MU 5-2-45 130S 3-5 401S 10-5 411S 28-6 3BRU CE 11-12-46

MV376 KEE 33MU 15-2-45 215MU 27-4 *Emp Dyn* 16-5 Ind 7-6 ACSEA 28-6 SOC 18-10

MV377 ALD 39MU 16-2-45 82MU 27-8 *D Bank* 6-9 ind 14-10 ACSEA 11-10 SOC 28-8-47

MV378 FRXIVE STN 39MU 23-1-45 412S 28-6 BAF(SG-50) 10-7-48

MV379 KEE 39MU 10-2-45 76MU 20-9 *Ocean Vic* 24-9 Ind 30-10 ACSEA 29-11 Jap SOC 24-3-48

MV380 ALD FF MJL 3-2-45 39MU 22-2-45 215MU 18-6 *C o Chest* 7-6 Ind 25-6 ACSEA 5-7 Jap SOC 24-3-48

MV381 ALD 39MU 23-2-45 84GAC 6-9 451S 4-10 BAF(SG-34) 10-3-48

MV382 STN 39MU 5-2-45 414S 26-4 2S 9-8 350S 18-10 125Wg HQ 6-6-46 BAF(SG-80) 17-12-48 wo 20-7-52

MV383 ALD 33MU 20-2-45 414S 10-5 430S 17-5 BAF(SG-95) 11-5-49 cd 20-7-54

MV384 ALD FF MJL 9-2-45 33MU 22-2-45 222MU 7-6 *Emp Gam* 5-8 Ind 30-8 ACSEA 12-9 sold InAF 29-12-47

MV385 CHA 33MU 22-2-45 414S 17-5 2S BAFO 11-10-47 FAC3 11-11-49 SOC 16-11

MV386 CHA 39MU 22-2-45 215MU 5-8 *C o H K* 26-8 Ind 17-9 ACSEA 27-9 SOC 27-11-47

NH series All FR XIV Griffon 65 FXIV NH653 to 745

NH637 EA 6MU 28-2-45 Airspeed Ltd 21-1-47 on loan for exhib RTOS 14-2 613S 22-12 NEA 31-3-53 SOC 22-9

NH638 STN 9MU 4-3-45 414S 12-4 2S 9-8 151RU 11-10 3BRU CE 29-6-46

NH639 CHA 6-3-45 268S 19-4-45 FACB 3-11 ASTH 615S 18-10-46 607S 29-7-47 CAC surplus 3-3-49 sold VA 10-5-50

NH640 STN 6MU 7-3-45 414S 19-4 2S 9-8 451S 4-10 443S 17-1-46 sold J Dale 1-6-49

NH641 (intm) STN Super p/proto 30-10-44 9MU 4-3-45 268S 5-4 151RU 4-9 3BRU CE 29-6-46

NH642 (INTM) EA Super p/proto 509-44 6MU 16-3-45 268S 26-4 151RU 4-9 3BRU CE 29-6-46

NH643 STN 9MU 12-3-45 268S 5-4 FACB 18-7 ASTH BAF(SG-26) 14-1-48 cd 23-7-51

NH644 STN 39MU 11-3-45 sold Int All 26-5-49

NH645 STN 39MU 18-3-45 215MU 22-6 *Emp Gam* 5-8 Ind 30-8 ACSEA 13-9 sold InAF 29-12-47

NH646 (intm) STN Super p/proto for wheel wells mods 13-6-44 29Mu 23-3-45 2S 12-4 FAAC 17-7 ROS 610S 14-9-48 sold VA 11-5-50

NH647 (intm) STN Super p/proto 25-7-44 6MU 26-3-45 268S 19-4 412RSU 26-4 151RU 11-10 3BRU CE 29-6-46

NH648 CGA 6MU 20-3-45 414S 19-4 CAC on ops 29-4 67MU 5-7 ROS 7-7 33MU NEA 26-2-52 sold VA 15-8-52

NH649 STN 9MU 24-3-45 2S 19-4 FAAC 16-5 2S 14-6 268S 9-8 3BRU CE 29-6-46

NH650 CHA 33MU 20-3-44 414S 12-4-45 151RU 28-6 3BRU CE 299-6-46

NH651 KEE 33MU 28-2-45 82MU 15-6 *Emp Gam* 5-8 Ind 20-8 ACSEA 7S RIAF tyre burst t/o cd Miranshah 14-2-46 SOC 24-4-47

NH652 CHA 29MU 25-3-45 268S 19-4 FACB 13-5 151RU 21-6 3BRU CE 29-6-46

NH653 STN 39MU 5-3-44 322S 29-3 DeH 'Gem' mods 9-5 610S 28-11 FACB 14-1-45 ASTH 29MU 11-2-46 NEA 14-9-53 sold MoS 13-5-54

NH654 STN 39MU 11-3-44 91S 27-3 AST 'Gem' mods 18-5 CAC ops 13-7 ROS 350S 22-2 CAC ops 23-2 ASTH BAF(SG-8) 25-4-47

NH655 STN 333MU 11-3-44 322S 26-3 1GRU 9-5 'Gem' mods 9MU 2-4 BAF(SG-1) 17-4-47 cd 7-11-49

NH656 STN 39MU 23-3-44 322S 1-5 AST 6-6 47MU 23-3-45 *Fern* 7-5 SOC 27-3-47

NH657 Flt trls VAHPA 24-8-44 CRD DeH 26-8 DH contra prop instal FACE 25-9 AST 9MU 26-3-45 411S 28-6 sold VA 10-5-50

NH658 STN 33MU 26-2-44 322S 6-4 350S 25-1-45 CAC ops 2-5 AST 607S 28-4-46 CAC surplus 28-1-49 NEA 31-7-50 sold VA 25-8 to Belgium

NH659 STN 33MU 26-3-44 222S 7-4 FAAC 2-5 ROS 322S 9-9 350S 18-1-45 CAC ops 2-2 recat E 16-8

NH660 STN DeH 'Gem' mods 6-4-44 33MU 30-4 MMO 1-6 610S 26-6 CAC ops 23-1-45 350S 12-4 CAC ops 19-4 412RSU 20-12 CE 14-1-46

NH661 STN DeH 'Gem' mods 6-4-44 33MU 30-3 322S 16-5 CB ops 19-6 ROS 610S 21-12 350S 8-3-45 3BRU CE 29-6-46

NH685 STN 33MU 18-4-44 610S 10-6 DeH 'Gem' mods 8-9 350S 15-2-45

NH686 STN 33MU 26-3-44 322S 7-4 FAAC 7-5 AST 'Gem' mods 9-5 350S 9-8 130S 5-10 350S 8-3-45 FTR ops 20-4

NH687 STN 39MU 26-3-44 24 Base Def Wg HQ 13-4 iGRU 'Gem' mods 23-4 322S FACE 31-5

NH688 STN 39MU 26-3-44 610S 12-4 DeH 18-7 CAC ops 18-8 ROS 130S 19-4-45 BAF(SG-16) 25-7-47 cd/ld W/O 3-7-50

NH689 STN 33MU 18-4-44 350S 18-1-45 443S 15-1-46 NEA 26-2-51 to 6836M 2-3

NH690 CBAF DeH 'Gem' mods 5-4-44 33MU 27-4 322S 10-6 CAC ops 30-6 ROS 350S 9-11 AST 14-3-45 NEA 7-10-49 sold VA 25-8-50 to Belgium

NH691 STN 39MU 21-4-44 322S 12-6 130S 9-4-45 CE ops 27-4

NH692 STN 33MU 29-4-44 MMO 1-6 322S 12-7 350S 9-8 41S 12-7-45 416S 20-9 3BRU CE 21-3-46

NH693 CBAF DeH 'Gem' mods 5-4-44 39MU 24-4 3501SU 24-5 3S 9-7 322S CB ops 3-8 350S 8-3-45 411S 16-8 151RU 6-2-46 3BRU CE 30-5

NH694 STN 39MU 21-4-44 DeH 10-6 322S 20-6 CAC ops 30-7 ROS ASTH CFE 30-5-46 swung cd on t/o 17-4-47 to 6340 BAF 24-7

NH695 STN 39MU 1-5-44 610S 26-5 DeH 4-7 350S 19-7 CAC ops 11-2-45 ASTH 1FPP hit tree fly low Button Oak Upper Arley Salop pilot kld 19-3-46 SOC 29-5

NH696 STN 33MU 9-4-44 322S 10-6 DeH 29-6 350S 9-8 130S 5-10 443S 14-1-46 sold MoS 16-2-53

NH697 STN 39MU 21-2-44 91S 8-3 DeH 16-6 130S 29-8 CAC ops 23-9 350S 8-3-45 3BRU CE 23-11-46

NH698 STN 39MU 21-2-44 91S 7-3 DeH 10-6 350S 1-3-45 CAC ops 9-4 ASTH sold VA 10-5-50 RThaiAF U14-10/93

NH699 STN 33MU 11-3-44 332S 13-3 ASTH 'Gem' mods 27-4 322S 3-5 CAC ops 4-8 ROS 130S 19-4-45 401S 10-5 3BRU CE 4-7-46

NH700 STN 39MU 4-3-44 322S 14-3 FACE 11-4

NH701 STN 33MU 28-2-44 91S 14-3 ASTH 'Gem' mods 10-5 130S e/fld ldg High Halden o/s CE 17-8

NH702 STN 39MU 28-2-44 322S 12-3 610S 5-9 350S 18-1-45 CB ops 8-2 ASTH CFE 29-5-46 600S 3-5-48 611S 3-10 CAC surplus 23-9-49 NEA 31-7-50 sold VA 25-8 to Belgium

NH703 CRD BDn 1-3-44 39MU 16-5 610S 10-6 DeH 4-7 91S 16-7 402S 9-11 3BRU CE 18-7-46

NH704 STN 33MU 28-2-44 322S FAAC 19-3 Swinderby 17-6-46 SOC 28-3-47

NH705 STN 33MU 2-3-44 91S 21-3 ASTH 'Gem' mods 14-5 DeH 16-5 2nd TAF rear HQ 18-1-45 CB ops 24-2 ASTH CFE 24-4-46 SOC 3-7-48

NH706 STN VAWD 6-3-44 mods R-RH 6-4 gen dev of G65 inter-connected controls 6MU 2-5-46 R-RH 30-11 58MU 8-7-47 SOC 9-7-49

NH707 STN 33MU 11-3-44 91S 20-3 SAL 2-7 130S 18-8 AST CS(A) BDn 3-7-46 trls with MkIX rocket projectiles FCHS 11-11 607S 9-2-48 615S 26-4 611S 8-1-49 recat E 14-7 sold J Dale 30-12

NH708 STN 33MU 11-3-44 322S 23-3 AST 'Gem' mods 9-5 Farn Feb'45 bombing trls NEA 28-2-51 to 6840M 19-6

NH709 STN 12-3-44 322S 20-3 ASTH 'Gem' mods 27-4 322S 3-5 CAC ops 7-7 ROS 610S std on ldg wng hit grd Lympne CE 18-9

NH710 STN 33MU 12-3-44 91S 2-3 DeH 16-6 130S 29-8 350S 4-10 FAAC 6-11 e/a CB 1-1-45 AST NEA 31-7-50 sold VA 25-8 to Belgium

NH711 STN DeH 'Gem' mods 6-4-44 33MU 9-5 322S 22-6-44 350S 9-8 FTR ops 23-1-45

NH712 STN DeH 'Gem' mods 6-4-44 39MU 1-5 2nd TAF Rear HQ Flt 18-1-45 41S 8-2 ROS VA BAF(SG-20) 22-9-47 w/o 16-1-48

NH713 STN 39MU 17-3-44 322S 3-4 DeH 'Gem' mods 23-5 130S CE ops 18-8 AST NEA 24-3-53 SOC 2-10

NH714 STN 39MU 18-3-44 322S 7-4 610S 11-1-45 350S CAC ops 19-4 ASTH sold VA 10-5-50 RThaiAF U14-9/93

NH715 STN 39MU 19-3-44 3501SU 24-5 DeH 20-6 322S 30-6 CAC ops 4-7 AST 41S 12-7-45 416S 20-9 MPRD CE Jly'46 Sea branch folder Apl'49

NH716 STN 33MU 26-3-44 322S 7-5 DeH 20-6 130S 29-8 350S 4-10-46 FTR 9-11

NH717 G61 VAHPA 25-7-44 to 8-1-45 jett trls with 170gal o/ld tank. 27-6-45 trls of Elektron eng cowling. No advantage over normal alloy. Max speed with new cowl 470mph in drive. Used as chase plane for FF Spiteful 8-1-45 ASTH 26-6 33MU 16-2-46 FAF GC2/7 NEA 26-5-52 sold VA 18-8

NH718 STN 33MU 23-4-44 DeH 12-6 322S 20-6 350S 9-8 CAC ops 7-2-45 ASTH BAF(SG-71) 25-11-48

NH719 STN 39MU 25-4-44 610S 26-5 DeH 25-8 RAF Friston 8-9 FTR ops 10-12

NH720 STN 33MU 23-4-44 91S 10-6 DeH 'Gem' mods 23-6 130S 29-8 hit by Allied AA fire CAC 18-12 BAF as SG-73 10-12-48 cd 14-6-51

NH741 ALD CRD VAHPA 3-12-44 wts & CG load prod a/c tare 6621; t/o 8628 73.5lb fixed ballast. First prod a/c with RV fus. 33MU 8-2-45 NEA 31-7-50 sold VA 10-1-51 to Belgium

NH742 EA to ALD MJL 23-11-44 ALD 6MU 29-11-44 NEA 15-8-50 sold VA 13-11 to Belgium

NH743 ALD 6MU 29-11-44 NEA 15-8-50 sold VA 10-11 to Belgium

NH744 Super p/proto to intro Mk3G IFF 25-1-44 33MU 3-100 402S 29-3-45

NH745 EA to ALD MJL 23-11-44 ALD 39MU 1-12-44 41S 23-3-45 CB ops 16-4 409RSU

NH746 KEE Norton 25-2-45 76MU 16-9 *Fort Mich* 23-9 Ind 18-10 ACSEA 30-5-46 Jap SOC 24-3-48

NH747 CHA 33MU 24-2-45 26S 14-6 3BRU 8-5-46 2S 20-10-47 SR CAC 12-10-48 recat E 16-10

NH748 ALD FF MJL 10-2-45 33MU 21-2-45 222MU 12-5 *C o Chest* 7-6 Ind 25-6 ACSEA 12-7 coll with MV354 Seletar 18-10 SOC 8-11

NH749 ALD 33MU 23-2-45 215MU 20-5 *Samstu* 2-7 Ind 28-7 ACSEA 9-8 sold InAF 29-12-47 to UK 1978 and G-MXIV. Extant as NX749DP Chino, California.

NH750 KEE 33MU 28-2-45 76MU 26-7 *Clan MacB* 29-11 ret 76MU for re-erection 6MU 21-6-48 Wunstorf 15-7-70 Res. Buskebury 31-7 2S 31-7 29MU 31-1-51 NEA 31-3-53 SOC 22-9

NH751 ALD 33MU 5-3-45 222MU 7-6 *Emp Gam* 5-8 Ind 20-8 ACSEA 13-9 SOC 28-11-46

NH752 ALD 33MU 28-2-45 Rotol Ltd. 24-4 402S 3-5 412S 28-6 CAC mr 11-3-46 3BRU CE 24-6-46

NH753 ALD 33MU 28-2-45 82MU 24-8 *Ocean Gal* 17-9 Ind 14-10 107MU e/fld a/c aban cd off Rhodes i/sea 8-7-47

NH754 ALD 33MU 3-3-45 451S 3-9 BAF(SG-56) 24-8-48 cd 5-6-50

NH755 ALD 33MU 28-2-45 222MU 2-6-45 *Emp Kum* 19-7 Ind 14-8 ACSEA 13-9 SOC 28-8-47

NH756 ALD 33MU 28-2-45 FAAC FF 26-2 ASTH 61 OTU 16-9 SOC 16-11-47

NH757 ALD 29MU 26-3-45 414S 26-4 2S 9-8 w/u lnd syst a/c 2-9-46 recat E 12-9

NH758 ALD 33MU 28-2-45 222MU 2-6 *Emp Kum* 19-7 Ind 14-8 ACSEA 23-8 SOC 28-8-47

NH759 ALD 6MU 3-3-45 76MU 14-9 *Ocean Vict* 24-9 Ind 20-10 FACE 30-7-47 SOC 28-8

NH775 KEE 33MU 28-2-45 453S 6-9 BAF as SG-91 8-2-49

NH776 KEE 33MU 26-2-45 222MU 7-6 *Emp Gam* 5-8 Ind 30-8 ACSEA 13-9 SOC 25-4-46

NH777 ALD 6MU 2-3-45 76MU 16-9 *Ocean Vict* 7-11 Ind 2-12 ACSEA 27-12 SOC 25-9-47

NH778 ALD 9MU 3-3-45 47MU 26-9 *Sancouan* 3-12 Ind 3-1-46 ACSEA 31-8 Jap 10-3-47 SOC 25-3-48

NH779 ALD 9MU 3-3-45 411S 25-10 610S 20-2-47 sold VA 15-8-50

NH780 KEE 33MU 28-2-45 451S 30-3 BAF(SG-74) 9-12-48

NH781 EA 6MU 3-3-45 76MU 14-9 *Fort Mich* 22-9 Ind 12-10 ACSEA 8-11 SOC 28-8-47

NH782 ALD 9MU 5-3-45 215S 17-5 *Samstu* 2-7 Ind 28-7 ACSEA 9-8 SOC 14-2-46

NH783 KEE 33MU 7-3-45 453S 6-9 2S 29-2-49 NEA 31-3-53 SOC 22-9

NH784 ALD 9MU 3-3-45 611S 1-1-47 surplus 4-8-49 to 6689M 12-8

NH785 ALD 9MU 3-3-45 615S 20-3-47 613S 25-9 sold E Smelt 25-8-49

NH786 KEE 6MU 1-3-45 47MU 15-9 *Ocean Vict* 24-9 Ind 30-10 1S fts cd f/lnd 2-8-46 SOC 26-9

NH787 ALD 9MU 3-3-45 215MU 9-6 *Samstu* 2-7 Ind 28-7 ACSEA 9-8 SOC 8-5-47

NH788 ALD 33MU 9-3-45 82MU 15-7 *C o H K* 26-8 ACSEA 27-9 CE SOC 28-8-47

NH789 CHA 6MU 2-3-45 76MU 2-10 *Clan MacB* 22-11 ret 76MU for re-erection NEA 1-8-50 sold VA 10-11 BAF(SG-108)

NH790 CHA 39MU 1-3-45 *Samp* 15-4 Ind 21-5 SOC 8-11 UK 1968 extant

NH791 ALD 33MU 8-3-45 451S 3-9 CE Army Salvage 23-10 SOC 25-10

NH792 EA 6MU 3-3-45 451S 6-12 615S 12-11-46 FAAC 13-4-47 ROS 607S 10-10 recat E 17-8-49 scr

NH793 ALD 33MU 12-3-45 82MU 27-7 *D Bank* 6-9 Ind 14-10 ACSEA 11-11 8S RIAF cd f/lnd Rojaveit Pilot kld 19-3-46 SOC 11-4

NH794 ALD 6MU 11-3-45 607S 4-11-46 RSCU 21-3-48 607S 1-7 CAC surplus 3-3-49 sold VA 10-5-50 RThiaAF U14-12/93

NH795 KEE 9MU 15-3-45 215MU 8-6 *Samstu* 2-7 Ind 28-7 ACSEA 9-8 4S RIAF u/s lnd hit obs Cochin 3-4-46 SOC 9-5

NH796 ALD 39MU 14-3-45 61 OTU 10-9 SOC 12-3-48

NH797 STN 6MU 9-3-45 414S 26-4 2S 8-8 GAAC 10-9 453S 4-10 451S 6-12 BAF(SG-75) 9-12 48

NH798 STN 9MU 10-3-45 83GOC 15-9 3BRU 29-4-46 Army Salvage BAFO 24-10 recat E 31-10

NH799 ALD 9MU 16-3-45 215MU 22-5 *Samstu* 2-7 Ind 28-7 ACSEA 9-8 49S FACE 27-2-47 sold InAF 29-12 Extant Duxford.

NH800 KEE 9MU 13-3-45 26S 14-6 FAAC 20-8 416S 1-11 612S 24-1-48 sold VA 10-5-50 RThaiAF U14-25/93

NH801 ALD 39MU 12-3-45 *Ocean Ch* 18-4 Ind 23-5 ACSEA 21-6 11S u/c clpse on t/o w/u ldg 24-7 SOC 1-11

NH802 ALD 9MU 13-3-45 222MU 11-5 *C o Chest* 7-6 Ind 25-6 ACSEA 12-7 sold InAF 31-12-47

NH803 CHA 6MU 13-3-45 76MU 17-9 *Ocean Vict* 24-9 Ind 30-10 ACSEA 29-11 SOC 26-6-47

NH804 KEE 33MU 16-3-45 82MU 9-7 *C o H K* 26-8 Ind 17-9 ACSEA 27-9 Jap 25-3-48

NH805 ALD 9MU 19-3-45 82MU 11-9 *Fort Per* 18-9 Ind 16-10 ACSEA 25-10 InAF 31-12-47

NH806 CHA 39MU 12-3-45 82MU 13-7 *C o H K* 26-8 Ind 17-9 ACSEA 27-9 7S RIAF bird strike cd Kohat pilot kld 3-7-46 SOC 29-8

NH807 ALD 9MU 19-3-45 268S 19-4 16S 1-11 FACE 5-6-46 bboc 6-4 BAF(SG-87) 13-1-49

NH808 KEE 33MU 21-3-45 414S 12-4 412S 27-9 FAAC 20-12 3BRU 24-1-46 recat E 30-5 rtp

NH809 ALD 39MU 19-3-45 76MU 20-9 *Ocean Vict* 24-9 Ind 20-10 ACSEA 29-11 Jap SOC 24-3-48

NH810 ALD 39MU 19-3-45 76MU 20-9 *Samcon* 9-12 Ind 3-1-46 ACSEA 21-1 Jap 13-2-47 SOC 24-3-48

NH811 ALD 39MU 19-3-45 61 OTU 15-9 29MU 19-946 SOC 12-3-48

NH812 KEE 29MU 24-3-45 414S 12-4 39 Rec Wg 10-5 414S hit fence in o/s o/t CE Warm 27-6 SOC 11-7

NH813 WIN 29MU 21-3-45 414S 5-4 FTR ops 24-4

NH831 CHA 29MU 26-3-45 268S 19-4 16S 1-11 BAF(SG-98) 11-5-49

NH832 KEE 33MU 2-4-45 41S 12-7 416S 20-9 FACE 28-11

NH833 CHA 29MU 27-3-45 451S 25-10 sold VA 10-5-50

NH834 WIN 29MU 2-4-45 268S 26-4 16S 1-11 29MU 5-4-46 sold VA 11-5-50

NH835 KEE 33MU 8-4-45 402S 3-4 FTR ops 3-5

NH836 KEE 33MU 2-4-45 268S 12-4 FACE 15-5

NH837 CHA 29MU 4-4-45 47MU 22-9 *Ocean Vict* 17-11 Ind 2-12 ACSEA 27-12 SOC 26-6-47

NH838 STN 33MU 4-4-45 268S 26-4 ROS sold VA 25-8-50 to Belgium

NH839 STN 33MU 3-4-45 268S 10-5 16S 1-11 FACE 18-12

NH840 (intm) STN Super p/proto top fuel tank mods 11-7-44; eng mount mods 29-11 39MU 10-4-45 83GSU 6-5

NH841 STN 33MU 12-4-45 215MU 15-5 *C o Chest* 7-6 Ind 25-6 ACSEA 5-7 Jap SOC 25-3-48

NH842 STN 39MU 15-4-45 33MU 21-11-49 NEA 29-2-52 sold VA 15-8

NH843 STN 33MU 20-6-45 82MU 24-8 *Ocean Gal* 7-9 Ind 14-10 ACSEA 8-11 SOC 25-8-47

NH844 STN 39MU 16-4-45 215MU 7-5 *Emp Dyn* 16-5 Ind 2-6 ACSEA 28-6 Jap SOC 24-3-48

NH845 EA 29MU 26-4-45 222MU 12-5 *C o Chest* 7-6 Ind 25-6 ACSEA 5-7 SOC 25-9-47

NH846 STN 9MU 23-4-45 215MU 17-5 *Samstu* 2-7 Ind 28-7 ACSEA 9-8 9S RIAF w/u lnd dbf Gurgoan 19-3-46 SOC 28-3

NH857 KEE 33MU 11-4-45 430S 10-5 29MU 28-9 BAF(SG-84) 15-1-49

NH858 CHA 33MU 14-4-45 76MU *Fort Mich* 28-9 Ind 18-10 ACSEA 29-11 SOC 28-8-47

NH859 CHA 33MU 14-4-45 215MU 15-5 *C o Chest* 7-6 Ind 25-6 ACSEA 5-7 Jap SOC 25-3-45

NH860 KEE 33MU 10-4-45 82MU 15-7 *C o H K* 26-8 Ind 17-9 ACSEA 27-9 SOC 31-1-46

NH861 STN 33MU 10-4-45 215MU 26-7 *C o H K* 26-8 Ind 17-9 ACSEA 27-9 SOC for Ins/af 27-11-47

NH862 KEE 33MU 21-4-45 411S 11-10 611S 6-8-48 CAC surplus 4-8-49 60MU 8-8 611S 23-8 NEA 31-3-53 SOC 22-9

NH863 CHA 33MU 10-4-45 84GOC 30-8 ROS 25-9 BAF(SG-93) 10-3-49

NH864 KEE 33MU 11-4-45 268S 17-5 16S 1-11 BAF(SG-67) 29-10-48 cd 28-3-51

NM821, named 'Fochinell', in the colours of 2 Squadron.

NH865 KEE 33MU 18-4-45 215MU 2-5 *Emp Dyn* 16-5 Ind 7-6 ACSEA 28-6 9S RIAF cd f/lnd nr Hungu 28-5-46 SOC 25-7

NH866 (intm) EA Super p/proto strenthen fus for FR & LR variants 14-1-44 33MU 14-4-45 215MU 15-5 *Samstu* 3-7 Ind 28-7 ACSEA 9-8 Jap SOC 24-3-48

NH867 KEE 33MU 18-4-45 215MU 15-5 *Samstu* 2-7 Ind 28-7 ACSEA 9-8 Jap SOC 24-3-48

NH868 KEE 6MU 18-4-45 222MU 10-5 *Emp Dyn* 16-5 Ind 7-6 ACSEA 5-4 SOC 31-1-46

NH869 KEE 6MU 18-4-45 215MU 27-4 *Emp Dyn* 4-5 Ind 7-6 ACSEA 28-6 SOC 25-9-47

NH870 KEE 9MU 21-4-45 215MU 7-5 *Emp Dyn* 4-5 Ind 7-6 SOC 28-8-47

NH871 KEE 29MU 26-4-45 222MU 12-5 *C o Chest* 7-6 Ind 25-6 ACSEA 5-7 Jap SOC 24-3-49

NH873 KEE 29MU 26-4-45 222MU 4-5 *Emp Dyn* 16-5 Ind 7-6 ACSEA 28-6 FACE 16-1-47 SOC 30-1

NH874 KEE 39MU 27-4-45 Hand S Hull 30-5 29MU 20-9 NEA 31-3-53 SOC 22-9

NH875 KEE 6MU 30-4-45 222MU 10-5 *Emp Dyn* 16-5 Ind 7-6 ACSEA 28-6 Jap SOC 24-3-48

NH892 CHA 39MU 21-3-45 453S 6-9 BAF(SG-65) 5-10-48 cd 14-12-53

NH893 ALD 33MU 18-4-45 215MU 17-5 *Samstu* 2-7 Ind 28-7 ACSEA 9-8 SOC 28-8-47

NH894 ALD 29MU 2-4-45 BAF(SG-94) 10-3-49

NH895 FRXIVE CHA 6MU 18-3-45 84GOC 30-8-45 451S 4-10 39MU 19-1-46 sold Int All 9-6-49

NH896 WIN 29MU 21-3-45 414S 12-4 2S 9-8 air coll with TZ196 over Celle, Germany cd kld pilot CE 31-1-47 SOC

NH897 WIN 29MU 22-3-45 2S 19-4 3BRU 5-9-46 2S e/fld cd in f/ldg pilot kld 10-12-48

NH898 ALD 29MU 24-3-45 2S 21-6 FACB 22-6 268S 2-8 610S 2-5-47 39MU surplus 1-6-49 CE scrap 16-7

NH899 KEE 29MU 24-3-45 414S 26-4 411S 27-9 FACE 1-12

NH900 CHA 33MU 18-3-45 414S CE ops 7-4

NH901 KEE 6MU 4-4-45 222MU 29-5 *Emp Kum* 19-7 Ind 14-8 ACSEA 23-8 sold InAF 29-12-47

NH902 ALD 29MU 24-3-45 414S 19-4 9MU 27-7-57 NEA 31-3-53 sold MoS 30-12

NH903 ALD 6MU 26-3-45 414S 5-4 2S 9-8 Celle 18-7-46 1BRSD 28-6-48 SOC 31-5-50

NH904 FRXIVE ALD 6MU 26-3-45 414S 15-4 CB ops ASTH 2-12 610S 4-11-46 ROS 26-7-48 6MU 2-5-49 NEA 1-2-50 sold VA 14-11 BAF(SG-108) extant UK Strathallen Collection S Flack 30-1-79 reflown as G-FIRE 14-3-81 extant

NH905 ALD 9MU 26-3-45 402S 26-4 412S 28-6 FACE 19-12

NH906 ALD 39MU 2-4-45 *Ocean Ves* 18-4 Ind 23-5 ACSEA Jap SOC 25-7-48

NH907 WIN 29MU 2-4-45 268S 26-4 FAAC 12-5 16S 1-11 29MU 5-4-46 35Wg hit sea off Cap Gris Nez 5-4-46 SOC pilot kld

NH908 CHA 29MU 25-3-45 47MU 22-9 *Ocean Ver* 7-11 Ind 2-12 ACSEA 27-12 SOC 25-9-47

NH909 (intm) STN Super p/proto 27-6-44 33MU 4-4-45 215MU 18-7 *Emp Gam* 5-8 Ind 20-8 ACSEA 24-8 SOC 25-8-47

NH910 CHA 33MU 30-3-45 2S 12-4 cd on t/o Celle CB 20-7-46 3BRU 1-8 recat E 28-9

NH911 ALD 39MU 2-4-45 47MU 25-9 *Sauconan* 3-12 Ind 8-1-46 ACSEA 31-1 Jap 13-2-47 SOC 25-3-48

NH912 STN 33MU 4-4-45 430S 10-5 29MU 10-9 2S 21-11-46 f/ld cd nr Celle Germany CE 2-4-47 SOC 30-4

NH913 ALD 39MU 6-4-45 *Ocean Ves* 18-4 Ind 23-5 ACSEA 21-6 Jap SOC 24-3-48

NH914 WIN 29MU 2-4-45 47MU 13-9 *Fort Mich* 22-9 India 18-10 ACSEA 29-11 Jap SOC 24-3-48

NH915 KEE 33MU 2-4-45 41S 12-7 416S 20-9 SOC 25-7-46

NH916 KEE 33MU 10-4-45 76MU 14-9 *Fort Mich* 22-9 Ind 18-10 ACSEA 29-11 SOC 28-8-47

NH917 KEE 33MU 28-4-45 82MU 31-8 *Ocean Gal* 17-9 Ind 14-10 ACSEA 29-11 sold InAF 29-12-47

NH918 KEE 29MU 2-5-45 26S 2-6 613S 20-10-47 NEA 1-8-50 sold VA 13-11 to Belgium

NH919 KEE 33MU 9-5-45 451S 4-10 226 OCU 9-2-50 NEA 26-9-51 sold scr MoS 13-5-54

NH920 KEE 29MU 4-5-45 222MU 1-6 *Emp Gam* 5-8 Ind 20-8 ACSEA 13-9 SOC 25-9-47

NH921 KEE 29MU 4-5-45 222MU 10-6 *Emp Gam* 5-8 Ind 20-8 ACSEA 13-9 SOC 27-3-47

NH922 KEE 33MU 3-5-45 451S 4-10 443S 17-1-46 BAF(SG-101) 21-7-49

NH923 KEE 33MU 3-5-45 451S 4-10 FAAC 10-10 412RSU 1-11 NEA 31-3-53 SOC 22-9

NH924 KEE 29MU 5-5-45 222MU 6-6 *Emp Gam* 5-8 Ind 30-8 ACSEA 13-9 SOC 28-2-46

NH925 (intm) EA Super p/proto for mod oleo legs 13-6-44 29MU 4-5-45 26S 26-4 FACE 29-11

NH926 KEE 6MU 24-5-45 215MU 22-6 *Emp Gam* 5-8 Ind 30-8 ACSEA 13-9 SOC 25-9-47

NH927 KEE 33MU 14-5-45 82MU 24-8 *D Bank* 6-9 Ind 14-10 ACSEA 18-10 SOC 28-8-47

NH928 KEE 33MU 16-5-45 82MU 27-8 *D Bank* 6-9 Ind 14-10 ACSEA 11-10 SOC 28-8-47

NH929 KEE 6MU 19-5-45 222MU 2-6 *Emp Kum* 17-7 Ind 14-8 ACSEA 30-8 SOC 28-8-47

NM series all FR XIV Griffon 65

NM814 ALD 29MU31-3-45 611S 20-6-47 CE 4-7-48

NM815 ALD 33MU 13-4-45 84GSU 23-4 FAAC 22-6 ROS 610S 18-6-47 sold VA 15-8-52

NM816 ALD 33MU 13-4-45 611S 6-11-46 CAC surplus 31-3-49 ROS sold R J Coley 3-2-50

NM817 ALD 33MU 16-4-45 215MU 10-5 *Emp Dyn* 14-5 Ind 7-6 ACSEA 28-6 Jap 11S u/s lnd 12-12-46 SOC 31-7-47

NM818 ALD 33MU 13-4-45 84GSU 23-4 FAAC 16-5 2S 1-6 tyre burst on t/o Wunstorf Germany 2-6-47 412RSU recat E SOC 26-6

NM819 ALD 33MU 18-4-45 222MU 12-5 *C o Ches* 7-6 Ind 25-6 ACSEA 12-7 11S Malaya o/s lndg Kuala Lumpur 26-1-46 SOC 27-2-47

NM820 ALD 33MU 18-4-45 222MU 12-5 *C o Ches* 7-6 Ind 25-6 ACSEA 5-7 SOC 27-2-47

NM821 EA 6MU 14-4-45 414S 26-4 2S 9-8 FAAC 5-9-47 BAFO D/A 6-9 2S w/u lndg Utersen CB 20-8-49 recat E 25-8

NM822 ALD 33MU 18-4-45 215MU 15-5 *C o Ches* 7-6 Ind 25-6 ACSEA 5-7 Jap SOC 24-3-48

NM823 ALD 33MU 26-4-45 222MU 12-5 *C o Ches* 7-6 Ind 25-6 ACSEA 5-7 28S u/c clpse lnd Malaya 14-6-46 SOC 31-12

G-FIRE, ex NH904, extant.

Mark XIV Serials

RB series all F XIV Merlin 65

RB140 5176 FXIVE STN F-21 fin and rud instal. First prod XIVE 39MU 20-12-43 616S 1-2-44 DeH 'Gem' mods 6-4 610S CE ops 30-10

RB141 5023 STN CRD DBn 14-11-43 F-21 fin and rud. Hand trls of prod a/c. Wts and CG load carb mono cockpit contam tests. R-R RG5-SM. VA 26-12-43 G65 instal. Red BDn for 150hrs comp fly trls with RB144, 2nd prod a/c. Trls with 90gal. o/ld tank. AFDU 31-1-44 322S 18-3 FTR ops 3-5

RB142 4935 STN 39MU 28-10-43 616S 1-1-44 610S 2-1 CAC ops 21-5 ROS 610S cd CE ops 12-7

RB143 4961 STN 39MU 28-10-43 Hand S Hull 14-11 39MU 11-5-44 41S 26-4-45 FAAC 7-5 409RSU 10-5 416S 20-9 VA 13-5-46 recat E 24-6

RB144 5013 STN CRD VAWD 7-11-43 BDn 25-11 Intns comp fly trls with RB141 VAHPA 27-3-44 mods ASTH 30-6-45 G85 instal. DeH Airscrews Hatfield 29-11 trls with various props including DeH six-blade contra prop. 45gal o/ld tank instal; burst during taxy when tailwheel retracted. SOC scrap 16-11-47

RB145 5052 STN 39MU 16-11-43 610S 3-1-44 CAC ops 4-7 ROS 350S FACE 8-12

RB146 5055 STN CRD VAWD 17-11-43 Five-blade prop instal. BDn 28-2-44 wts & CG load spin trls with tail parachute. 7-5 fuel cons trls and range det 21-4-44 gun heat tests and plastic ducting; latter replaced by light alloy pipes. March '45 'piano' type hinge instal on ails to examine prospects of fitt to prod a/c. Comp trls with RM766. VA HPA 7-12 Griffon with +25lb. boost (Basta) instal. Hood jett trls. New type, circular exhausts instal on Griffon; wool tufts on upper port wng surface. Comp tests with JG204. ASTH 12-6-45 for removalk of non-standard items and incorporation of outstanding FXIV mods FACB 19-6 on test flt. BDn 30-8 VA recat E 24-6-46

RB147 5110 STN 33MU 2-12-43 FAAC on f/f ROS 222S 22-3-44 AST 11-6 *Samsae* 15-4-45 Ind 21-5 Jap 26-9-46 SOC 31-7-47

RB148 5077 STN 33MU 2-12-43 610S 1-1-44 DeH 7-6 610S CE ops 27-12

RB149 5092 STN 39MU 29-11-43 616S 1-1-44 610S 2-1 DeH 30-5 610S CE 15-12

RB150 5113 STN 33MU 2-12-43 610S 1-1-44 FAAC 16-2 DeH 'Gem' mods 6-4 610S FTR ops 30-8

RB151 5114 FXIVE G55M STN 33MU 4-12-43 610S 16-1-44 1CRU 'Gem' mods 19-5 610S CAC ops 19-9 ROS 39MU 21-3-46 NEA 26-2-51 to 4841 2-7

RB152 5205 STN 39MU 27-12-43 610S 14-2-44 AST 8-5 'Gem' mods 610S CAC ops 24-6 ROS 350S 22-2-45 CAC ops 28-2 130S 5-4 3BRU CE 23-11-46

RB153 5168 STN 39MU 20-12-43 610S 6-1-44 AST 19-4 610S CE ops 9-7

RB154 5177 STN 39MU 20-12-43 610S 6-1-43 610S 6-1-44 DeH 'Gem' mods 12-5 610S eng fire in air 25-12 409RSU 350S 15-2-45 ASTH 28-9 BAF (SG-13) 24-7-47

RB155 5199 STN 39MU 24-12-43 DeH 23-8 350S 19-4-45 FAAC 21-9 412RSU RNeth SoTT 31-7-47

RB156 5212 STN 33MU 27-12-43 610S 9-2-44 eng trouble f/ld Harrow Somerset 12-2 DeH 'Gem' mods 13-5 610S CB ops 12-7 ROS ASTH 4-6-45 BAF (SG-68) 29-10-48 cd 14-5-52

RB157 5216 STN 33MU 28-12-43 610S CAC ops 9-7 ROS NEA 26-2-51 to 6842M 3-5

RB158 5240 STN 33MU 1-1-44 322S 20-3-44 ETPS Farn 30-4 AST 3-5 eng mods Farn Aug '44. During Aug '44 a priority order was passed to ETPS by Air Min for a method to boost eng to allow Spit to catch and destroy the VI pilotless bomb. A mixture of 150 octane fuel and methanol tested in RB158 proved useless. 130S 29-8 350S 4-10 3BRU CE 29-6-46 612 16-3-48 CE surplus 23-3-49

RB159 5232 STN 33MU 1-1-44 610S 17-2 DeH 'Gem' mods 4-6 610S cd out of fuel Moldeghem Belgium CAC 20-1-45 350S 15-2 CB ops 23-2 151RU 41S 26-4 416S 20-9 ASTH 21-11 sold H Bath 27-10-49

RB160 STN 33MU 7-1-44 322S 14-3 DeH 'Gem' mods 5-4 322S FAAC 31-5 ROS 3501SU 20-8 GAAC strk obst while being towed 23-2-45 ASTH CFE 29-5-46 FAAC 5-5-49 sold R J Coley 3-2-50

RB161 STN 33MU 8-1-44 91S 29-2 DeH 'Gem' mods 13-4 130S 29-8 350S 4-10 hit by enemy AA 24-12 CB 409RSU ASTH 2-5-45 BAF(SG-27) 14-1-48 cd 31-7-52

RB162 STN 39MU 20-1-44 610S 19-2 DeH 25-4 610S hit by enemy AA during sweep i/sea Flt Lt Percy aban a/c but was k/d 22-5

RB163 STN 39MU 20-1-44 610S 23-2 DeH 23-6 610S ops 19-9 ROS BAF (SG-5) 29-4-47

RB164 STN 39MU 30-1-44 610S 20-2 DeH 23-6 CAC ops 23-1-45 409RSU ASTH 23-4 sold VA 10-5-50

RB165 STN 33MU 3-2-44 91S 8-3 ASTH 'Gem' mods 14-5 130S 29-8 CB ops 6-9 AST CFE 20-6-46 611S 7-10-48 FAAC 29-3-49 ROS NEA 1-8-50 sold VA 9-11 to Belgium 15-11

RB166 STN 39MU 20-1-44 610S 23-2 DeH 'Gem' mods 25-4 610S CAC ops 14-5 ROS AST 5-9 BAF(SG-2) 22-5-47

RB167 STN 20-5-44 3501SU 1-7 310S 2-8 610S 14-12 FTR ops 26-1-45

RB168 STN 39MU 15-3-44 322S 3-4 ASTH 'Gem' mods 3-5 322S CAC ops 20-6 ROS 130S 8-9 350S 4-10 CE ops 11-11-45

RB169 STN 33MU 21-1-44 91S 29-2 DeH 'Gem' mods 26-4 130S 29-8 350S CAC ops 6-10 hit by Allied AA fire 23-12.f/ld nr base 25-12 AST CFE 136-46 612S 24-8-47 GACA 22-7-48 recat E 26-8

RB170 STN 39MU 17-3-44 610S 11-4 AST 14-4 NEA 26-2-51 to 6843M 29-5

RB171 STN VA WD 27-1-44 33MU 20-3 322S 27-3 AST 'Gem' mods 19-4 322S CAC ops 16-6 410RSU 84GDC 15-10-45 NEA 26-2-51 to 6837M 2-3

RB172 STN 33MU 23-1-44 91S 27-2CE ops 12-3

RB173 STN 33MU 30-1-44 DeH 'Gem' mods 29-5 91S 10-6 130S 29-8 350S 4-10 CAC 7-2-45 409RSU GA Eng Fire 28-2 ASTH 27-4 recat E SOC 17-5

RB174 STN 33MU 3-2-44 91S 27-2 AST for con 7-5 ASTH 26-6-45 sold VA 10-5-50

RB175 STN 39MU 4-2-44 610S FAAC 5-3 ROS hit by AA fire during sweep des in cd/ldg France 28-5

RB176 STN 33MU 5-2-44 610S 22-2 Farn 7-5 spin trls with tail para. June, perf and eng vibration tests. Aug, power boost trls. Nov, endur trls and Griffon dev with ETPS (7,9 and 19lbs eng boost with target of plus 25lb. Dev declared priority in Jan '45. Piston fail Feb. G65 replaced by G67 in June after five hours fly, 350S 29-3 ASTH 14-5. Farn 25-5 port wheel axle fail on ldg. tip onto nose broke back CE 28-7 SOC 25-8

RB177 STN 33MU 6-2-44 91S 27-2 AST 'Gem' mods 22-4 91S CAC ops ROS 443S 14-1-4-6 sold J Dale 16-9-49

RB178 STN 39MU 7-2-44 610S 23-2 cd/ld at base Flt Lt West kld CE 23-5

RB179 STN 33MU 12-2-44 AFDU Witt 27-2 trls with American R/Ps FAAC 29-8 NEA 26-2-51 to 6838M 2-3-51

RB180 STN 39MU 22-3-44 91S 7-3 AST 'Gem' mods 26-4 91S CAC ops 17-6 ROS 12-4-45 FAAC 25-6 419RSU recat E SOC 19-7

RB181 STN 33MU 14-2-44 91S 25-2 DeH 'Gem' mods 30-5 130S 4-10 443S 15-1-46 sold VA 10-5-50

RB182 STN 39MU 15-2-44 91S 26-2 ASTH 'Gem'mods 12-4 91S CAC ops 11-7 ROS ASTH 6-2-45 BAF (SG-69) 29-10-48

RB183 STN 39MU 18-2-44 91S 4-3 ASTH 19-4 130S 4-10 CAC ops 28-10 411RSU

RB184 STN 33MU 21-3-44 322S 6-4 DeH 'Gem'mods 23-4 322S FACB 11-5 AST 451S 29-6-45 sold VA 10-5-50 R Thai AF U14-3/93

RB185 STN 39MU 25-2-44 91S 12-3 AST 'Gem' mods 12-4 3501SU 24-7 350S 22-2-45 FTR ops P/O Cresswell-Turner 5-4

RB186 STN 33MU 25-2-44 322S 25-3 DeH 30-5 350S 18-1-45 CAC ops 11-2 ASTH BAF(SG40) 23-4-48

RB187 STN 33MU 20-2-44 91S 14-3 FTR patrol thought i/sea F/O Collis 29-4

RB188 STN 33MU 91S 29-2-44 AST 'Gem' mods 5-5 130S 29-8 350S 4-10 cd in bad weather nr Turn F/Sgt Ritchie kld 11-2-45 ASTH sold VA 10-5-50 R Thai AF U14-18/93

RB189 STN 39MU 4-3-44 222MU 18-3 AST 'Gem' mods 14-4 322S 28-4 out of fuel cd Moldeghem Belgium CAC 11-7 ROS 350S FAAC (originally reported missing over Channel) 29-12 409RSU CB ops 25-4-45 ASTH sold VA 10-5-50

RM series all FX IV G65 unless otherwise indicated

RM615 STN DeH 'Gem' mods 6-4-44 39MU 1-5 3501SU 24-5 91S 1-7 130S 29-8 350S 4-10 hvy ldg Lympne tip onto nose CE 25-10

RM616 33MU 9-4-44 322S FACB 10-7 AST *Samsacola* 15-4-45 Ind 31-5 SOC 25-9-47

RM617 STN 39MU9-4-44 91S 1-5 CE ops 28-6

RM618 STN 47MU 18-4-44 33MU 2-12 350S 15-2-45 FTR ops 24-4

RM619 STN 33MU 9-4-44 91S 12-7 130S 4-10 s/dn nr Aachen Germany pilot aban a/c to POW CE 16-1-45

RM620 STN 39MU 26-4-44 91S 28-6 130S 29-8 350S 4-10 FTR ops 25-10 recat AC 2-11 412RSU 350S CAC ops 10-12 e/a CB 1-145 ASTH 25-4 NEA 26-252 sold VA 15-8

RM621 STN 39MU 7-5-44 3501SU 7-6 91S 29-8 350S 4-10 e/a CB 1-145 AST sold VA 10-5-50

RM622 STN 33MU 7-5-44 3501SU 30-5 322S 28-6 350S 28-11 CAC ops 3-12 509RSU e/a CE 1-1-45

RM623 CHA 33MU 27-5-44 350S 16-8 130S 3-10 350S CAC ops 5-4-45 409RSU Res pl 28-2-46 NEA 26-5-51 to 6839M 15-3

RM624 CHA 39MU 10-6-44 91S 14-7 402S 9-11 CAC ops 11-2-45 410RSU 402S 22-2 CAC ops 18-4 410RSU 412S 28-6 3BRU CE 29-6-46

RM625 CHA 33MU 10-6-44 91S 7-8 402S 9-11 CAC ops 25-12 409RSU 23-12 ASTH 24-4-45 BAF (SG-46) 15-6-48 roll SG-37 14-1-49

RM648 STN 33MU 7-6-44 322S 17-7 350S 18-1-45 412RSU 27-9 3BRU CE 29-6-46

Cockpit of RM689.

RM649 CHA 33MU 10-6-44 91S 14-7 83GSU 5-10 FACE 28-10

RM650 STN 39MU 11-6-44 curved and conical w/s instal. Service trls AFDU Dux 8-8 comp trls with RM689. No marked advantage over normal w/s and maint more difficult EA eng fire CB 16-11 AST 27-11 recat E 18-12

RM651 STN 39MU 11-6-44 91S 14-7 402S 7-9 412S 28-6-45 151RU 16-8 3BRU CE 29-6-46

RM652 STN 39MU 13-6-44 402S 9-11 CAC ops 5-4-45 410RSU ASTH 24-4 CFE 16-5-46 SOC 6-7-48

RM653 STN 33MU 11-6-44 91S 14-7 CE ops 26-7

RM654 CHA 33MU 25-6-44 91S air coll with Tempest F/O Schade kld CE 31-7

RM655 STN 39MU 16-6-44 322S 5-8 350S 9-8 130S 5-10 409RSU 28-12 130S CAC ops 16-1-45 SOC recat E 4-5

RM656 CHA 33MU 19-6-44 91S 14-7 CE ops 3-8

RM670 STN 33MU 7-5-44 610S 26-6 FAAC 27-8 ROS ASTH 19-1-45 CFE 16-5-46 CE 20-8-48

RM671 CHA 39MU 20-5-44 322S 7-6 CAC ops 14-7 ROS 402S 25-9 130S 25-9 350S 4-10 CE ops 14-11

RM672 CHA 33MU 28-5-44 322S 7-6 CAC 3-7 ROS 350S 4-10 FTR ops 25-10 cancel AST 16-1-45 BAF(SG-11) 25-6-47 cd 5-8-53

RM673 CHA 39MU 23-5-44 MMO 2-6 3501SU 24-6 130S 20-8 350S 4-10 FTR ops 25-12

RM674 STN GRU Witt 30-7-44 BDn 9-5-45 33MU 10-11-49 NEA 31-7-50 sold VA 2-1-51 to Belgium 15-1

RM675 STN 39MU 13-6-44 350S 18-8 130S 5-10 CAC ops 22-12 409RSU 610S 8-2-45 130S CAC ops 25-4

RM676 CHA 33MU 28-5-44 322S 17-7 350S 11-1-45 CAC ops 11-2 BDn May'45 ASTH BAF(SG-21) 22-9-47 cd 19-2-48

RM677 CHA 39MU 29-5-44 610S CAC ops 18-7 ROS 610S FTR ops 14-2-45 wrk found deeply buried

RM678 CHA 33MU 2-6-44 3501SU 22-6 322S CB ops 12-7

RM679 STN 39MU 7-6-44 610S 14-7 CAC ops 19-9 ASTH BAF(SG-23) 20-10-47

RM680 CHA 39MU 10-6-44 41S 12-10 ROS 20-3-45 33MU 13-7 ASTH 21-8 BAF(SG-58) 209-48

RM681 STN 33MU 12-6-44 3501SU 10-7 610S 19-7 CAC ops 6-11 ROS NEA 26-1-51 to 6844M

RM682 STN 39MU 14-6-44 91S 14-7 402S CB ops 25-10 409RSU 2-11 ASTH 26-4-45 sold VA 10-5-50

RM683 STN 33MU 18-6-44 402S 26-8 151RU 15-3-45 ROS ASTH 9-7 BAF(SG-70) 11-11-45

RM684 CHA 39MU 30-6-44 402S CB ops 5-10 419RSU recat E SOC 28-4-45

RM685 CHA 39MU 27-6-44 402S FAAC 23-8 ROS ASTH 25-9-45 BAF(SG-15) 25-7-47

RM686 CHA 33MU 25-6-44 91S 18-7 402S hvy ldg u/c clpse o/ld tank fire CE Hawk 6-9 AST 19-10

RM687 STN 39MU 18-6-44 91S 14-7 402S CE ops 25-10 SOC 5-4-45

RM688 CHA 33MU 27-6-44 91S 18-7 AST 17-10

Based at East Midlands Airport, the Rolls-Royce Mk XIV, RM689, wore the serial RM619 at one time. Codes are of 130 Squadron.

401S 17-5-45 411S 28-6 29MU 2-4-46 sold MoS 16-2-53

RM689 CHA 39MU 3-7-44 curved and conical w/s instal. Trls AFDU Dux 5-8 with RM650 ROS 13-9 83GSU 24-2-45 350S 1-3 443S 14-1-46 sold MoS 9-2-49 R-RH FMar'49 to G-ALGT for BoB film 1968. extant as RM619 AP-D

RM690 CHA 33MU 12-7-44 3501SU 7-8 130S 14-9 350S 4-10 hit by en AA a/c aban FTR 24-12

RM691 CHA 39MU 7-7-44 3501SU 6-8 350S 4-10 CAC ops 18-12 409RSU AST 2-3-45 recat E SOC 11-3

RM692 CHA 33MU 4-9-44 83GSU 13-10 ASTH 1-10-45 sold VA 10-5-50 RThaiAF U14-24/93

RM693 130S 25-1-45 41S 19-4 416S 20-9 403RSU 25-1-46 SOC 19-7-46

RM694 CHA CFE hit by RM925 after ldg West Raynham 4-11-48 to 6640M Horn 25-2-49 extant Illinois USA fuselage only

RM695 CHA 33MU 22-7-44 350S 16-8 CB ops 1-9 recat E 9-9

RM696 CHA 15-7-44 322S 5-8 350S 9-8 41S 13-10 CE ops 24-4-45

RM697 CHA 33MU 20-9-44 FAAC 14-1-45 ROS 350S 22-11 443S 15-1-46 BAF(SG-42) 25-5-48 w/o 4-5-50

RM698 33MU 16-8-44 41S 15-9 CAC 3-2-45 130S 15-3 ASTH 25-4 recat E SOC 3-5

RM699 CHA 39MU 21-8-44 41S 15-9 hit by AA a/c aban cd dbf 18-12

RM700 CHA 39MU 16-7-44 322S 5-8 350S 9-8 130S 5-10 ROS 14-2-45 33MU NEA 31-7-50 sold VA 8-1-51 to Belgium 15-1

RM701 CHA 41S 350S BAF(SG-6) 3-5-47

RM702 39MU 21-3-46 sold Int All 26-5-49

RM703 STN 33MU 16-9-44 2S 23-11 414S 7-8-45 BAF(SG-78) 17-12-48 w/o 27-10-50

RM704 STN 39MU 21-8-44 350S ADGB 5-9 41S 13-10 CAC ops 4-12 409GSU 41S CACops 3-3-45 ASTH CFE 24-4-46 CE 28-7-48

RM705 39MU 26-8-44 41S 15-9 CAC ops 5-10 ROS ASTH 11-7-45 BAF(SG-66) 5-10-48 cd Mar'53

RM706 STN 39MU 21-9-44 2S 16-11 CE 26-1-45

RM707 39MU 21-8-44 41S 15-9 CAC ops 2-2-45 409RSU NEA 27-2 sold VA 15-1-51 to Belgium 31-1

RM708 39MU 30-5-44 2S 23-11 GAAC 2-2-45 2S CE ops 27-2

RM709 STN 39MU 23-9-44 BDn from 41Grp as rogue Spit Had ails reversal-right to left. Replaced by thicker guage metal types & stbd wg incidence decreased by 15min of angle. No apparent change. Port wg incidence increased by 15min of angle. Wng tips removed. VA HPA for tests 8-12 6MU 29-8-45 CFE 30-5-46 610S 22-8-47 sold MoS 16-2-53

RM710 33MU 27-8-44 41S 15-9 350S 5-10 CAC ops 31-12 409RSU ASTH 4-4-45 BAF(SG-59) 20-9-48 cd 6-4-51

RM711 FXIVE 39MU 3-9-44 130S 12-10

RM712 39MU 3-9-44 2S 23-11 FACB 27-5-45 412RSU recat E 27-12 BAF(SG-70) 16-1-48

RM713 FXIVE STN 33MU 1-10-44 130S 19-10 FAAC 31-12 409RSU 4-1-45 CE ops 30-3

RM726 FXIVE STN 39MU 18-6-44 91S 14-7 402S 7-9 CAC ops 11-10 419RSU 402S GACB 17-4-45 ASTH BAF(SG-14) 25-7-47 cd 8-9-52

RM727 CHA 33MU 25-6-44 91S 31-7 402S 9-11 CAC ops 10-3-45 405S 12-4 402S 26-4 3BRU CE 18-7-46

RM728 CHA 33MU 19-6-44 3501SU 6-7 130S CAC ops 25-8 ROS 350S 4-10 e/a CB 1-1-45 ASTH sold VA 10-5-50

RM729 CHA 33MU 25-6-44 130S 16-8 350S 4-10 CAC ops 11-4-45 409RSU ASTH SOC rts 30-11-46

RM730 CHA 33MU 25-6-44 83GSU 4-3-45 FA i/sea 21-4-45

RM731 CHA 33MU 27-6-44 91S 20-7 402S CAC 17-8 ROS 91S 9-1 402S CAC ops 26-12 409RSU 350S 11-1-45 61S 18-1 FTR ops 23-1

RM732 CHA 39MU 27-6-44 350S 9-8 BDn from 42Grp rogue Spit similar to RM709 wg incident increased at VAHPS by 15min. No effect on trim wng tips removed VA CHA sold R J Coley 1-6-49

RM733 CHA 39MU 3-7-44 130S 20-8 350S 4-10 610S 1-2-45 sold J Dale 1-6-49

RM734 CHA 39MU 27-6-44 91S 24-7 402S 9-11 ROS 67MU 2-12-45 NEA 26-2-52 sold VA 15-8

RM735 CHA 39MU 27-6-44 91S 14-7 402S CAC ops 17-10 409RSU recat E SOC 14-2-45

RM736 CHA 33MU 10-7-44 610S 19-8 FTR ops 18-12

RM737 CHA 39MU 8-7-44 91S 24-7 402S 9-11 FAAC 3-12 409RSU ASTH 21-2-45 CFE 30-5-46 FAAC 25-7-49 ROS to 6694M 2SoTT 24-8 SOC 15-5-54

RM738 CHA 33MU 4-9-44 322S 5-8 350S 3-10 130S 5-10 401S 10-5-45 411S 28-6 612S 14-2-48 Res pl 21-3-50 SOC C5 8-10

RM739 CHA 39MU 30-6-44 610S 24-7 FTR ops 25-10 cancel 24-1-45 610S CAC ops 24-1 350S CE ops 26-2

RM740 CHA 39MU 6-7-44 322S 1-8 350S 9-8 610S CB ops 27-12 409RSU ASTH 5-4-45 607S 16-3-48 FAAC 17-7 cd on test flt at Lubeck sold R J Coley 3-2-50

RM741 CHA 39MU 7-7-44 322S 4-8 350S 9-8 130S 5-10 CAC ops 22-3-45 41S 26-4 416S 20-9 VA 27-3-46 BAF(SG-18) 22-9-47

RM742 CHA 33MU 6-7-44 39MU 29-7 350S CB ops 24-8 AST *Ocean Ves* 18-4-45 Ind 23-5 ACSEA 21-6 InAF 29-12-47

RM743 CHA 33MU 11-7-44 91S air coll with VI fly bomb cd 26-7 402S 9-11 130S 19-4-45 401S 10-5

RM744 CHA 39MU 25-7-44 350S 21-8 130S 5-10 CAC ops 25-3-45 350S FTR ops 20-4

RM745 2S 28-12-44 CB ops 14-2-45 ASTH CFE 20-6-46 607S 4-9-47 CAC surplus 3-3-49 NEA 31-5-53 22-9

RM746 CHA 39MU 23-7-44 610S 26-9

RM747 CHA 33MU 17-7-44 322S 5-8 350S e/a CB 1-9 AST 451S 29-6-45 sold VA 10-5-50

RM748 CHA 33MU 13-7-44 322S 5-8 3350S 9-8 130S FACB 30-9 ROS AST 12-12 412S 28--6-45 sold Int All 26-5-49

RM749 CHA 39MU 27-7-44 350S ADGB 5-9 130S 5-10 s/dn Belgium 8-12

RM750 CHA 33MU 15-7-44 322S 5-8 350S 9-8 130S 5-10 FTR ops 2-3-45

RM751 CHA 39MU 16-7-44 322S 5-8 350S GA fire on starting eng CB 27-8 AST recat E 30-9

RM752 CHA 39MU 25-7-44 350S 23-8 130S CAC ops 7-10 409RSU 402S 12-4-45 FACB 3-9 recat E BAFO to Ins/af 29-8-46

RM753 CHA 33MU 18-7-44 322S 5-8 350S 9-8 130S 15-10 CAC ops 19-3-45 409RSU 350S 17-5 FAAC 10-10 ASTH 602S 4-3-47 recat SOC 11-8-47

RM754 CHA 33MU 16-7-44 350S 16-8 e/a CB 1-9 AST CFE 18-6-46 CE 28-7-48

RM755 CHA 33MU 25-7-44 322S 5-8 350S 12-8 130S 5-10

RM756 CHA 33MU 21-7-44 322S 5-8 350S 9-8 130S 5-10 hit by enemy AA over Ardennes 'Battle of the Bulge' CE 23-1-45

RM757 130S GAAC 1-4-45 409RSU ASTH 29-5 sold VA 10-5-50

RM758 no record

RM759 41S CE ops 5-4-45 ASTH BAF(SG-32) 11-2-48

RM760 CHA 33MU 28-7-44 350S 16-8 130S 5-10 FTR ops 31-12

RM761 CHA 33MU 28-7-44 350S 16-8 130S CE ops 30-9

RM762 33MU 11-8-44 350S 26-8 130S 5-10 FTR ops 16-1-45

RM763 39MU 18-8-44 350S 5-9 130S CE ops 5-10

RM764 33MU 14-8-44 350S 26-8 83GDC 15-9-45 ASTH 19-12 BAF(SG-38) 22-3-48 cd 24-2-52

RM765 39MU 25-8-44 41S 20-9 s/dn by Fw190 nr Munster pilot FTR 23-1-45

RM766 FXIVE CRD BDn 19-9-44 gun heat trls 130S 12-4-45 FTR ops 19-4

RM767 33MU 20-8-44 41S 15-9 CE 16-1-45 409RSU

RM768 CRD HP 11-9-44 33MU 13-9 130S 4-1-45 401S 10-5 411S 28-6 CAC ASTH 14-12 ROS BAF(SG-10) 21-6-47 cd 14-4-48

RM769 33MU FXIVE 33MU 18-9-44 41S 26-9 CB ops 18-12 409RSU ASTH 16-2-45 accepted by BAF pilot cd at 33MU 19-6-47 SOC 25-9

RM770 39MU 26-8-44 41S 15-9 CB ops 13-1-45 409RSU ASTH 18-1 BAF(SG-35) 10-3-48 cd 5-6-51

RM783 39MU 28-8-44 84GSU 20-10 2S 23-11 CAC ops 25-12 130S 1-3 ASTH 12-12 600S 25-3-47 613S 21-7 NEA 13-4-51 sold VA 10-10

RM784 FXIVE 33MU 27-9-44 HP 29-11 trls with metal rud direct stab bad. Hood jet trials. Hood broke into two striking rear fus and tailplane. Acted as chase plane to Spitfire NN664 20-2-45 BDn Mar'45 spin trls. Recovery longer than with normal fus Spitfire. Spin para and tail guard instal. June det of aftmost CG position. ASTH 9-7 29MU 6-4-46 BAF(SG-100) 22-6-49

RM785 (Maris) 30MU 22-10-44 401S 19-4-45 FACE 22-5 S/Ldr Klersy kld in crash

RM786 FRXIV STN 39MU 5-2-45 82MU 1-7 *C oH K* 26-8 Ind 17-9 ACSEA 27-9 1S FTS f/lnd out of fuel Khaital 13-5-46 i/sea off Miho Jap 24-7-47

RM787 39MU 26-8-44 41S 20-9 Stn Flt Lympne 16-11 130S 25-1-45 CB ops 30-3 409RSU ASTH 30-4 BASF(SG-28) 15-1-48 dbf 17-3

RM788 M66 6MU 27-8-44 41S 20-9 CAC ops 5-10 ROS ASTH 11-6-45 CFE 3-5-46 sold Int All 2-2-50

RM789 39MU 27-8-44 41S 15-9 CAC ops 5-1-45 409RSU 18-1 41S FTR ops 22-2

RM790 39MU 25-8-44 41S 15-9 ROS ASTH 30-4-45 CRD BDn 15-4-46 trls with MkIX RP instal 607S 9-3-48 CAC surplus 28-1-49 CFE 18-3 NEA 31-7-50 sold VA 25-8 to Belguim 31-8

RM791 38MU 26-8-44 41S 15-9 CAC ops 23-1-45 409RSU BAF(SG-22) 20-10-47

RM792 FXIVE 39MU 31-8-44 402S 12-10 FAAC 25-12 409RSU 610S 1-2-45 350S 17-9 443S 14-1-46 607S 3-6-47 CAC surplus 28-1-49 ROS NEA 31-7-50 sold VA 25-8 to Belgium 31-8

RM793 33MU 27-8-44 41S 18-9 prop strk grnd on t/o u/c retract o/ld tank fire Lympne CE 5-10

RM794 33MU 27-8-44 FRU 15-9 430S 15-3-45 611S 28-2-47 29MU 21-10-49 NEA 31-3-53 SOC 22-9

RM795 39MU 31-8-44 2S 23-11 130S rep FTR ops cancel 414S 7-8-45 1 BR&SD BAFO 3-1-49 Res pl 20-4 NEA 1-8-50 sold VA 10-11 to Belgium 15-11

RM796 FXIVE 33MU 7-9-44 41S 15-9 409RSU 25-1-45

RM797 ex16 RThaiAF extant as VH-XIV, Sydney, Aust.

RM798 FXIVE 33MU 9-9-44 2S 30-11 ASTH 26-9-45 NEA 31-3-53 SOC 22-9

RM799 FXIVE 33MU 9-9-44 41S 18-9 CAC 13-1-45 409RSU ASTH 28-5 CFE 3-5-46 CE 28-7-48

RM800 33MU 10-9-44 2S 9-11 NEA 31-3-53 SOC 22-9

RM801 FXIVE STN 39MU 5-10-44 VA EA 24-2-45 29MU 27-8 sold H Bath 27-10-49

RM802 FRXIV long span wg 33MU 13-9-44 2S 16-11 350S 17-9-45 412S 13-4-46 BAF(SG-44) 10-6-48 cd 23-12-53

RM803 FXIVE STN 33MU 22-9-44 2S 9-11

RM804 STN 33MU 6-10-44 402S 4-1-45 401S 24-5-45 411S 28-6 FACB 31-1-46 NEA 14-9-53 sold MoS 14-5-54

RM805 STN 33MU 16-9-44 2S 16-11 412RSU 28-12 CE ops 2S 8-2-45

RM806 FXIVE STN 33MU 22-9-44 83GSU 2-10-45 FACE 1-9

RM807 FXIVE STN 33MU 22-9-44 2S 21-12 CAC ops 3-3-45 409RSU 430S 15-3 CAC ops 2-5 409RSU NEA 31-3-53 SOC 22-9

RM808 FXIVE STN 39MU 23-9-44 150S 12-12 130S CAC ops 22-1-45 FTR ops 8-4

RM809 39MU 29-9-44 130S 2-11 402S 16-11 FAAC 23-11 610S 8-2-45 402S 22-3 GAAC 20-4 410RSU 412S 7-6 443S 5-7 411S 11-10 1BRSU 3-6-47 recat E 7-6

RM810 FXIVE 33MU 30-9-44 430S 30-11 607S 26-6-47 CAC surplus 3-3-49 ROS NEA 31-3-53 SOC 2-10

RM811 STN 39MU 21-9-44 2S 9-11 FTR ops 22-12

RM812 STN 39MU 23-9-44 2S 22-2-45 FTR ops 18-3

RM813 FXIVE STN 39MU 23-9-44 30MU 12-10 mods 2S 16-11 CB ops 14-1-45 ASTH CFE 10-5-46 FAAC 18-10 ROS SOC 12-3-48

RM814 33MU 28-9-44 402S 2-11 CAC ops 18-4-45 410RSU

RM815 39MU 8-10-44 130S 21-12 409RSU CE ops 16-1-45

RM816 WIN 29MU 20-2-45 222MU 13-3 *H Prince* Ind 15-5 SOC 31-7-47

RM817 FXIVE STN 39MU 1-10-44 430S 4-1-45 414S 19-7 607S 19-10-48 CAC surplus 28-1-49 ROS NEA 31-7-50 sold VA 25-8 to Belgium 31-8

RM818 FXIVE STN 39MU 1-10-44 430S 23-11 e/fld a/c aban pilot kld dbf 31-12

RM819 FXIVE 33MU 30-9-44 402s 12-12 FAAC 26-12 412S 25-1-45 FTR ops 13-2

RM820 30MU 22-10-44 430S 30-11 409RSU mr 28-4-45 BAF (SG-83) 18-1-49

RM821 30MU 22-10-44 430S 30-11 dvdigrd from cloud CE 26-4-45

RM822 33MU 29-10-44 430S 14-12 2S 1-3-45 ROS 2-7 BAF(SG-61) 30-9-48

RM823 30MU 27-10-44 540S e/fld cd 8-2-45

RM824 FXIVE 39MU 5-10-44 430S 4-1-45 hit by AA cd 14-2 151RU 2-3 611S 30-9-48 CAC surplus 29-3-49 NEA 16-2-51 sold VA 28-2

RM825 STN 39MU 3-10-44 84GSU 28-10 FACB 7-11 ROS 2S 22-2-45 CAC ops 10-4 412RSU 414S 7-8 613S 17-2-47 NEA 31-3-53 SOC 22-9

RM839 FXIVE STN 39MU 5-10-44 402S 9-11 409RSU 23-11 402S FTR ops 21-2-45

RM840 FXIVE STN 39MU 5-10-44 222MU 17-2-45 *Defend* 8-3 Ind 6-4 ACSEA 9-7-46 SOC 28-11

RM841 30MU 27-10-44 83GSU FAAC 16-11 BAF (SG-72) 26-11-48 cd 30-6-49

RM842 33MU 3-10-44 41S 18-1-45 FTR ops 10-2

RM843 FXIVE 39MU 8-10-44 402S 23-11 FAAC 29-12 410RSU 402S CAC ops 24-2-45 FTR ops 16-4

RM844 FXIVE 33MU 12-10-44 130S CE ops 1-12 409RSU 401S 10-5-45 411S 23-6 3BRU CE 29-6-46

RM845 33MU 12-10-44 402S 4-1-45 412S 28-6 403RSU 11-2-46 3BRU recat E 24-6-46

RM846 33MU 14-10-44 402S 4-1-45 CAC ops 16-2 410RSU

RM847 FXIVE 33MU 15-10-44 430S 4-1-45 401S 24-5 411S 23-6 403RSU 19-3-46 3BRU 8-5 recat E 5-6

RM848 30MU 22-10-44 mods 49MU 14-12 e/a CE 1-1-45

RM849 33MU 10-10-44 402S 9-11 CAC ops 17-11 409RSU 402S CE ops 18-12

RM850 33MU 14-10-44 430S 23-11 Ben 1-3-45 430S FTR ops 1-5

RM851 FXIVE 30MU 15-10-44 430S 30-11 613S 12-8-48 cd on ldg Ringway CE 12-12-48 SOC 2-3-49

RM852 FXIVE 30MU 15-10-44 430S 14-12 NEA 31-3-53 SOC 30-9

RM853 FXIVE 30MU 15-10-44 430S 11-1-45 NEA 31-3-53 SOC 30-9

RM854 30MU 23-10-44 mods 39MU 9-11 NEA 26-2-51

RM855 30MU 23-10-44 mods 84GSU 28-11 Fire on grnd 15-12 recat SOC 9-1-45 to 6845M 29-5-51

RM856 30MU 22-10-44 mods 430S 14-12 e/a CB 1-1-45 409RSU ASTH 19-2 NEA 26-2-51 to 6846M

RM857 30MU 23-10-44 mods 430S 30-11 e/a CB 1-1-45 ASTH BAF(SG-53) 22-7-48 W/O 30-6-49

RM858 33MU 31-10-44 451S 29-12 610S 18-1-45 402S 26-4 412S 28-6 3BRU 21-3-46 151RU 7-5 BAFO CE 23-11

RM859 30MU 22-10-44 VA EA 7-2-45 CFE 16-5-46 to 6523M 2-3-48

RM860 130S BAF(SG-37) 23-4-48 coll with SG-46 W/O 14-1-49.

RM861 33MU 28-10-44 610S 13-1-45 CAC ops 3-2 ASTH FLS CFE 26-9-46 613S 4-9-47 cd on ldg Ringway CE 26-6-48

RM862 33MU 27-10-44 402S 4-1-45 CB ops 29-3 ASTH FLS CFE 14-11-46 to 6350M 5-6-57 BAF 24-8-47

RM863 33MU 29-10-44 41S 28-11 CAC ops 21-2-45 ASTH BAF(SG-86) 19-1-49

RM864 39MU 2-12-44 401S 17-5-45 411S 28-6 SOC bou 12-2-47

RM865 39MU 10-9-44 130S 12-10 409RSU 1-3-45

RM866 FXIVE STN 39MU 23-9-44 430S 11-1-45 2S 1-3-45 ASTH 10-5 BAF(SG-41) 22-3-48 cd 30-4

RM867 STN 33MU 16-9-44 30MU 1-10 FACB 18-10 AST recat E 4-11

RM868 STN 33MU 16-9-44 84GSU 22-10 ROS 20-12 2S 15-2-45 FAAC 4-4 412RSU 414S 7-8 sold H Bath 27-10-49

RM869 FXIVE STN 39MU 1-10-44 610S 15-2-45 130S 15-3 409RSU 12-4 350S 26-4 GACB 9-6 recat E

RM870 FXIVE STN 39MU 5-10-44 VA EA 7-2-45 BAF(SG-12) 3-7-47 cd 5-1-50

RM871 FXIVE 33MU 30-9-44 30MU 11-10 mods 2S 23-11 CAC ops 13-2-45 412RSU 2S FTR ops 1-4

RM872 39MU 16-10-44 2S 4-1-45 CB ops 12-4 412RSU ASTH CFE 16-5-46 u/c clpse ldg West Raynham CAC 10-3-49 recat E 1-4

RM873 FXIVE 39MU 8-10-44 402S 25-10 CB ops 8-11 AST 130S 1-3-45 CAC ops 1-3 409RSU 401S 10-5 411S 26-7 sold VA 10-5-50 Thai U14-6/93, extant.

RM874 FXIVE 39MU 8-10-44 430S 14-12 409S 27-4-45 29MU 20-5 Brazilian Air Attache 19-12-52

RM875 FXIVE 33MU 15-10-44 402S 23-11 410RSU 15-2-45 402S FTR ops 20-4

RM876 FXIVE 39MU 8-10-44 430S 30-11 AST mr 3-5-45 BAF(SG-24) 14-11-47 cd 27-12-50

RM877 KEE 50MU FACE 17-10-44 ASTH 29-10

RM878 30MU 17-10-44 mods VA EA 24-2-45 NEA 31-5-53 SOC 30-9

RM879 FXIVE 33MU 15-10-44 41S 4-1-45 CAC ops 3-2 GAAC 13-3 ROS NEA 31-7-50 sold VA 15-1-51 BAF 31-3

RM880 39MU 1-11-44 610S 18-1-45 ROS 20-3 GAAC 23-7-46 ROS sold MoS 16-2-53

RM881 30MU 22-10-44 430S 18-1-45 NEA 31-3-45 NEA 31-3-53 SOH fire ftng ins/af 30-9 SOC

RM882 30MU 27-10-44 PRDU 26-11 2S 29-3-45 414S 7-8 BAF(SG-52) 27-7-48 dam ldg 7-1-49 w/u ldg W/O 16-3-51

RM883 30MU 22-10-44 83GSU 23-11 e/a CE 1-1-45

RM884 30MU 28-10-44 84GSU 4-2-45 NEA 26-2-51 to 6847M 19-6-51

RM885 33MU 7-11-44 41S 8-2-45 GAAC 13-3 ROS CFE 10-7-46 CE 9-7-48

RM886 33MU 31-10-44 82MU 20-12 *Maledin* 22-1-45 Ind 9-2 SOC 11-6

RM887 30MU 28-10-44 2S 4-1-45 CB ops 14-2 ASTH CFE 25-5-46 610S 4-9-47 FAAC 26-2-49 recat E

RM901 30MU 27-10-44 2S 18-1-45 414S 7-8 AST mr 11-12 612S 25-4-47 FAAC 12-5 eng dam ROS 29MU surplus 30-9-49 NEA 31-5-53 SOC 22-9

RM902 33MU 28-10-44 402S 4-1-45 412S 28-6 sold Int All 26-5-49

RM903 39MU 6-11-44 130S CAC ops 12-4-45 409RSU 350S 26-4 443S 14-1-46 NEA 14-9-53 sold MoS 14-5-54

RM904 33MU 30-10-44 FAAC 22-12 ASTH 5-1-45 402S 15-3 FTR ops 11-4

RM905 33MU 6-11-44 82MU 17-12 *Ing* 1-1-45 Ind 4-2 Japan 26-9-46 SOC 31-7-47

RM906 33MU 29-10-44 402S 4-1-45 FTR 25-2-45 cancel BAF(SG-19) 22-9-47 cd 16-1-48

RM907 33MU 31-10-44 2S 2-11 610S 13-1-45 CB ops 23-1 ASTH CFE 25-5-46 SOC 6-7-48

RM908 29MU 4-3-45 *H Prince* 29-3 Ind 15-5 ACSEA 26-6-46 SOC 27-2-47

RM909 30MU 4-11-44 2S 18-1-45 414S 7-8 IR&SD 1-1-49 2S BAFO 5-1 49MU for BoB 12-9 NEA 26-2-51 to 6848M 11-4

RM910 30MU 9-11-44 430S 11-1-45 FAAC 11-8 419RSU 416S 19-3-46 VA EA 23-5-46 NEA recat E 6-9

RM911 39MU 6-11-44 VA EA 12-2-45 NEA 31-3-53 SOC 2-10

RM912 CHA 39MU 20-11-44 82MU 17-12 *Ing* 1-1-45 Ind 4-2 SOC 24-4-47

RM913 39MU 9-11-44 610S 15-2-45 ROS 20-3 BAF(SG-62) 4-10-48

RM914 33MU 10-11-44 83GSU 9-2-45 CE ops 4-3

RM915 39MU 10-11-44 610S 8-2-45 41S 22-3 416S 20-9 3BRU 21-3-46 SOC 27-6

RM916 STN 39MU 29-11-44 41S 15-2-45 GAAC 13-3 ROS VA BAF(SG-3) 17-4-47 extant

RM917 33MU 14-11-44 610S 8-2-45 ROS VA 14-3 BAF(SG76) 10-12-48 cd 25-2-53

RM918 33MU 14-11-44 41S 1-2-45 GAAC 13-3 ROS NEA 31-7-50 to Belgium 8-1-51

RM919 33MU 15-11-44 130S 1-3-45 CAC ops 409RSU ASTH 7-5-45 CFE 24-4-46 607S 23-8-47 CAC surplus 28-1-49 NEA 31-3-53 sold MoS 30-12

RM920 30MU 15-11-44 2S 8-2-45 FACB 17-4 412RSU ASTH 4-5 BAF(SG-43) 29-5-48 cd 20-2-51

RM921 FRXIV BAF(SG-57) 24-8-48 extant Florennes as RL-D

RM922 30MU 21-11-44 2nd TAF rear HQ 18-1-45 83GSU 1-2 lost, f/ld Highfield House Farm Glos CE 26-2

RM923 30MU 24-11-44 430S 18-1-45 CAC ops 25-3 ASTH NEA 31-3 SOC 22-9

RM924 KEE 7-12-44 430S 15-3-45 2S 22-3 CAC ops 7-4 412RSU 610S 30-1-48 611S u/c clpse ldg Hooton Pk 19-3-49 recat E 19-7

RM925 STN 39MU 25-11-44 130S 1-3-45 CB ops 2-4 409RSU ASTH 27-4 CFE 3-5-46 strk RM 694 after ldg West Rayham 4-11-48 ROS recat E 28-2-49

RM926 39MU 20-11-44 82MU 17-12 *Ing* 1-1-45 Ind 4-2 SOC 31-7-47

RM927 29MU BAF(SG-25) 14-11-47 extant Illinois USA

RM928 39MU 24-11-44 41S 22-3-45 453S 22-11 411S 12-3-46 NEA 31-3-53 SOC 2-10

RM929 30MU 21-11-44 430S 11-1-45 ROS 25-4 NEA 26-2-51 trls of fire damping materials by RAF Res Board 15-4 to 6849M

RM930 39MU 20-11-44 222MU 16-2-45 *Defend* 8-3 Ind 6-4 SOC 14-1-46

RM931 KEE 39Mu 26-11-44 610S 15-2-45 41S 22-3 CAC ops 21-4 409RSU 41S FACE dbf 1-7

RM932 ALD 39MU 29-11-44 76MU 23-2-45 *Fern* 31-1 Ind 7-5 SOC 27-3-47

RM933 39MU 29-11-44 402S 26-2-45 CAC ops 26-3 410RSU ASTH 1-6 BAF(SG-60) 20-9-48

RM934 KEE 6MU 29-11-44 82MU 22-12 *Ing* 1-1-45 Ind 4-2 SOC 24-4-47

RM935 KEE 39MU 26-11-44 130S 12-2-45 401S 10-5 411S 28-6 FAAC 6-9 409RSU ASTH 7-12 BAF(SG-17) 22-9-47

RM936 STN 6MU 5-12-44 82MU 19-12 *Mahad* 22-1-45 Ind 29-2 SOC 31-7-47

RM937 30MU 25-11-44 2S 15-3-45 414S 7-8 BAF(SG-82) 18-1-49

RM938 FXIVE from EA KJL 23-11-44 ALD 30MU 6-12-44 2S 15-2-45 CAC ops 6-4 412SRSU Res pl 30-2-46 BAF(SG-92) 17-2-49

RM939 KEE 39MU 26-11-44 610S FAAC 26-2-45 ROS NEA 9-2-52 sold VA 31-8

RM940 CHA 9MU 8-12-44 222MU 7-1-45 *Mahad* 22-1 Ind 19-2 SOC 25-9-47

RM941 KEE 9MU 30-11-44 82MU 16-12 *Ing* 1-1-45 Ind 4-2 SOC 31-10-46

RM942 KEE 9MU 3-12-44 82MU 16-12 *Ing* 1-1-45 Ind 4-2 SOC 25-4-46

RM943 CHA 9MU 8-12-44 82MU 20-1-45 *Emp Pag* 12-2 Ind 12-4 SOC 24-4-47

RM957 STN 6MU 7-12-44 222MU 4-1-45 *Mahad* 22-1 Ind 19-2 ACSEA SOC 11-7-46

RM958 KEE 9MU 13-12-44 222MU 9-1-45 *Mahad* 22-1 Ind 19-2 SOC 25-9-47

RM959 STN 6MU 7-12-44 ret HPA for rectification 6-2-45 CFE 10-7-46 swng on ldg u/l cllpse W Raynham CB 30-6-49 recat E 1-9-49

RM960 KEE 9MU 7-11-44 222MU 7-1-45 *Mahad* 22-1 Ind 19-2 SOC 1-11

RM961 CHA 9MU 12-12-44 82MU 13-1-45 *Mahad* 22-1 Ind 19-2 SOC 25-9-47

RM962 KEE 9MU 5-12-44 222MU 9-1-45 *Mahad* 22-1 Ind 19-2 SOC 28-8-47

RM963 KEE 6MU 8-12-44 222MU 31-12 *Mahad* 22-1-45 Ind 19-2 Jap 26-9-46 SOC 31-7-47

RM964 CHA 9MU 5-1-45 222MU 23-1 *Emp Pag* 12-2 Ind 12-4 SOC 25-9-47

RM965 STN 6MU 7-12-44 222MU 5-1-45 *Mahad* 22-1 Ind 19-2 SOC 28-9-47

RM966 CHA 9MU 12-12-44 82MU 18-1-45 *Clan For* 20-1 Ind 20-3 Jap 26-9-46 SOC 24-3-48

RM967 KEE 6MU 9-12-44 82MU 15-1-45 *Emp Par* 12-2 Ind 12-4 17S eng fail a/c aban i/sea of Japan pilot kld 27-6-46 SOC 29-8

RM968 KEE 10-12-44 82MU 30-12 *Mahad* 22-1-45 Ind 19-2 SOC 14-11-46

RM969 STN Super p/proto for fus bomb instal 4-4-44; to intro wng bomb racks 27-6 9MU 7-12 222MU 14-2-45 *Defend* 8-3 Ind 6-4 24-4-47

RM970 STN Super p/proto improved tailplane and fin lead edge 16-5-44 9MU 7-12 222MU 20-1-45 *Emp Par* 12-2 Ind 12-4 SOC 7-3-47

RM971 STN 9MU 7-12-44 82MU 16-1-45 *Clan For* 26-1 Ind 20-3 SOC 27-2-47

RM972 EA Super p/proto can fairing mods 12-12-44 6MU 2-1-45 82MU 15-1 *Clan For* 26-1 Ind 20-3 Jap 26-9-46 CE 17S 18-12-47 SOC 20-1-48

RM973 KEE 6Mu 10-12-44 222MU 5-1-45 *Mahad* 22-1 Ind 9-2 SOC 28-8-47

RM974 KEE 6MU 12-12-44 82MU 19-1-45 *Emp Par* 12-2 Ind 12-4 365P cd en route to Ind from ACSEA FTR 20-6-46

RM975 KEE 6MU 12-12-44 222MU 5-1-45 *Mahad* 22-1 Ind 12-2 SOC 1-11

RM976 STN 9MU 13-12-44 82MU 16-1-45 *SSLS2545* 25-1 Ind 12-4 SOC 11-7-46

RM977 KEE 6MU 26-12-44 82MU 19-1-45 *Emp Par* 12-2 Ind 12-4 SOC 31-12-46

RM978 KEE 6MU 12-12-44 222MU 5-1-45 *Mahad* 13-1 Ind 19-2 SOC 27-3-47

RM979 CHA 6MU 19-12-44 222MU 5-1-45 *Mahad* 22-1 Ind 19-2 SOC 31-7-47

RM980 STN 6MU 18-12-44 222MU 9-1-45 *Mahad* 22-1 Ind 19-2 SOC 25-9-47

RM981 9MU 20-12-44 82MU 13-1-45 *Mahad* 22-1 Ind 19-2 Jap 26-9-46 17S w/u ldg Miho Jap CE 21-1-47 SOC 31-7

RM982 CHA 6MU 5-1-45 82MU 10-1 *Emp Par* 12-2 Ind 12-4 4CMU spun i/grd from low alt pilot kld Dum Dum CE 13-3-46 SOC 11-4

RM983 9MU 20-2-44 82MU 13-1-45 *Clan For* 20-1 Ind 20-3 SOC 31-7-47

RM984 KEE 6MU 26-12-44 82MU 16-1-45 *Clan For* 25-1 Ind 20-3 SOC 31-7-47

RM985 KEE 9MU 5-2-45 215MU 25-2 *Fort Cam* 17-3 Ind 11-5 JAp 26-9-46 n17S 24-7-47 f/ld in seawater lake CE SOC

RM986 CHA 9MU 5-1-45 82MU 20-1 *Emp Par* 12-2 Ind 12-4 Jap 26-9-46 SOC 24-3-48

RM987 STN 9MU 4-1-45 222MU 5-2 *Emp Par* 12-2 Ind 12-4 SOC 31-10-46

RM988 EA Super p/proto cool syst 2-5-44 6MU 31-12 82MU 15-1-45 *Clan For* 20-1 Ind 20-3 Ind 20-3 SOC 25-9-47

RM989 CHA 6MU 2-1-45 82MU 15-1 *Clan For* 30-1 Ind 20-3 SOC 9-8

RM990 KEE 9MU 6-1-45 222MU 22-1 *Emp Par* 12-2 Ind 12-4

RM921, in 414 Squadron colours, on the gate at Florennes, Belgium.

RM991 CHA 6MU 2-1-45 82MU 15-1 *Clan For* 20-1 Ind 20-3 Jap 26-9-46 SOC 24-3-48

RM992 KEE 6MU 2-1-45 82MU 19-1 *Emp Par* 12-2 Ind 12-4 SOC 31-2-47

RM993 CHA 9MU 8-1-45 222MU 5-2 *Emp Par* 12-2 Ind 12-4 SOC 27-9

RM994 KEE FF MJL 19-12-44 6MU 12-1-45 222MU 6-2 *Emp Par* 12-2 Ind 12-4 FTR 28S f/f en route Ind pres China Sea 17-6-46

RM995 KEE 6MU 5-1-45 82MU 19-1 *Emp Par* 12-2 Ind 12-4 SOC 31-7-47

RM996 KEE FF MJL 23-12-44 9MU 23-1-45 222MU 17-2 *Defend* 8-3 Ind 6-4 SOC 31-7-47

RM997 CHA 9MU 3-1-45 222MU 13-2 *Defend* 8-3 Ind 6-4 SOC 28-11-46

RM998 KEE 9MU 5-1-45 222MU 12-2 *Defend* 8-3 Ind 6-4 SOC 18-10

RM999 KEE 6MU 4-1-45 222MU 23-1 *Emp Par* 17-2 Ind 12-4 CE dbf 6-9

RN series All FX IV Griffon 65

RN113 30MU 4-11-44 2S 18-1-45 CAC ops 7-2 412RSU ASTH 30-4 BAF(SG-29) 15-1-48

RN114 30MU 4-11-44 2S FAAC 5-1-45 430S 25-1 414S 19-7 ASTH 26-9 610S 17-4-47 NEA 28-3-51 sold VA 15-10

RN115 30MU 6-11-44 2nd TAF rear HQ 18-1-45 430S 22-2 414S 14-6 BAF(SG-63) 4-10-48 w/o 31-7-51

RN116 30MU 21-11-44 83GSU FAAC 4-1-45 430S 1-2 CB ops 26-4 ASTH 24-5 BAF(SG-102) 21-7-49

RN117 33MU 9-11-44 130S 15-3-45 CB ops 25-3 ROS VA BAF(SG-47) 22-6-48 w/o 9-8-51

RN118 33MU 9-11-44 130S 15-3-45 CB ops 25-3 ROS VA BAF(SG-47) 1-7-48 cd 9-8-51

RN119 33MU 8-11-44 402S 8-2-45 CAC ops 21-3 412S 28-6 BAF(SG-45) 10-6-48

RN120 33MU 9-11-44 610S 8-2-45 FTR ops 11-2

RN121 39MU 10-11-44 610S 15-2-45 130S 15-3 CB ops 12-4 409RSU ASTH 1-6 Pers 30-4-47 BAF(SG-7) 1-5 cd 15-3-51

RN122 39MU 14-11-44 130S 15-3-45 CAC ops 30-3 3BRU 26-3-46 CE 4-6-47

RN123 39MU 14-11-44 83GSU 15-2-45 41S FTR ops 2-3

RN124 STN 25-11-44 41S 1-3-45 BAF(SG-96) 11-5-49

RN125 30MU 22-11-44 2S 8-2-45 CAC ops FTR 26-3

RN126 30MU 21-11-44 402S 15-3-45 CB ops 18-4 410RSU recat E SOC 12-12

RN127 FXIVE ALD 6MU 30-11-44 222MU 4-1-45 *Mahad* 22-1-45 Ind 19-2 SOC 24-4-47

RN128 CHA 9MU 5-1-45 222MU 19-2 *Defend* 8-3 Ind 6-4 Jap 26-9-46 17S eng fire a/c aban cd pilot kld nr Hiroshima 19-9-47

RN129 CHA 9MU 5-1-45 222MU 3-2 *Emp Par* 12-2 Ind 12-4 17S cd/ld CE Iwakuni Jap 17-9-47 SOC 31-12

RN130 CHA 9MU 8-1-45 222MU 1-2 *Emp Par* 12-2 Ind 12-4 36SP flew i/grd 2-5-46 nr Agra pilot kld ACSEA SOC 25-7

RN131 CHA 9MU 5-1-45 222MU 8-2 *Emp Par* 12-2 Ind 12-4 17S o/s ldg CE Kisarazu Jap 3-8-47 SOC 30-10

RN132 KEE 6MU 12-1-45 222MU 6-2 *Emp Par* 12-2 Ind 12-4 SOC 25-10

RN133 CHA 9MU 5-1-45 222MU 6-2 *Emp Par* 12-2 Ind 12-4 Jap 26-9-46 SOC 24-3-48

RN134 KEE 6MU 12-1-45 222MU 6-2 *Emp Par* 12-2 Ind 1 2-4 SOC 28-8-47

RN135 KEE 6MU 8-1-45 222MU 5-2 *Emp Par* 12-2 Ind 12-4 Jap 28-9-46 SOC 24-3-48

RN136 KEE 6MU 7-1-45 222MU 14-2 *Defend* 6-3 Ind 6-4 SOC 8-11

RN137 KEE 9MU 7-1-45 222MU 3-2 *Emp Par* 12-2-Ind 12-4 *HMS Vindex* Sept'46 SOC 24-4-47

RN138 CHA 9MU 8-1-45 222MU 11-2 *Defend* 8-3 Ind 6-4 SOC 18-11-46

RN139 CHA 9MU 9-1-45 222MU 16-2 *Defend* 8-3 Ind 6-4 SOC 31-7-47

RN140 STN 6MU 3-12-44 82MU 17-12 *Ing* 1-1-45 Ind 4-2 SOC 12-12-46

RN141 KEE 6MU 10-1-45 222MU 26-2 *Emp Par* 12-2 Ind 4-2 SOC 12-12-46

RN142 CHA 6MU 14-1-45 222MU 3-2-45 *Emp Par* 12-2 Ind 12-4 Jap 26-9-46 SOC 24-3-48

RN143 CHA 9MU 17-1-45 222MU 8-2 *Defend* 8-3 Ind 6-4 Jap 26-9-46 tropical exposure CE SOC 30-10-47

RN144 KEE 6MU 20-1-45 222MU 11-2 *Defend* 19-2 Ind 6-4 SOC Ins A/F 27-11-47

RN145 CHA 9MU 17-1-45 222MU 8-2 *Emp Par* 12-2 Ind 12-4 SOC 1-11

RN146 KEE 6MU 17-1-45 222MU 6-2 *Defend* 8-3 Ind 6-4 Jap 26-9-46 SOC 24-3-48

RN147 WIN 29MU 21-1-45 222MU 20-2 *Defend* 8-3 Ind 6-4 26-9-46 SOC 24-3-48

RN148 EA Super p/proto for Coffman Starter safety device 27-6-44 6MU 7-1-45 222MU 5-2 *Emp Par* 12-2-Ind 12-4 Jap 26-9-46 SOC 24-3-48

RN150 WIN FF MJL 13-1-45 29MU 21-1 222MU 23-2 *SSLS2850* 20-3 Ind 15-5 ACSEA 7S MAF o/s Ind Mahardjpur 12-4-46 SOC 25-7

RN150 WIN FF MJL 13-1-45 29-1-45 *Defend* 8-3 Ind 6-4 Jap 26-9-46 SOC 24-3-48

RN151 KEE FF MJL 13-1-45 29MU 3-2 222MU 1-3 *H Prince* 29-3 Ind 15-5 SOC 27-2-47

RN152 KEE 9MU 2-11-45 215MU 25-2 *Fort Carn* 17-3 Ind 11-5 17S Jap cd/ld CE Miho 23-7-47 SOC 30-10

RN153 KEE FF MJL 17-1-45 9MU 21-1 222MU 17-2 *Defend* 12-3 Ind 6-4 SOC 27-3-47

RN154 CHA 9MU 20-1-45 222MU 14-2 *Defend* 8-3 Ind 6-4 sold InAF 27-3-47 SOC 31-7

RN155 KEE 29MU 3-2-45 222MU 26-2 *H Prince* 29-3 Ind 15-5 SOC 28-8-47

RN156 CHA FF MJL 19-1-45 9MU 1-2 215MU 10-3 *Fort Carn* 20-3 Ind 11-5 Jap 26-9-46

RN157 KEE 3-2-45 222MU 23-2 *H Prince* 27-3 Ind 15-5 8S FACE 14-5-47 SOC 1-6

RN158 CHA FF MJL 19-1-45 6MU 21-1-45 222MU 6-2 *Emp Par* 8-3 Ind 11-5 Jap 26-9-46 SOC 24-3-48

RN159 KEE 29MU 3-2-45 222MU 4-3 *H Prince* 27-3 Ind 15-5 InAF 29-12-47

RN160 CHA 21-1-45 222MU 11-2 *Defend* 8-3 Ind 6-4 SOC 18-10

RN173' KEE 9MU 3-2-45 222MU 17-2 *Defend* 8-3 Ind 6-4 SOC 18-10

RN174 KEE 29MU 3-2-45 222MU 26-2 *H Prince* 31-3 Ind 15-5 ACSEA 28-11-46 SOC 25-9-47

RN175 KEE 9MU 3-2-45 76MU 28-2 *Fern* 31-3 Ind 7-5 Jap 26-9-46 SOC 24-3-48

RN176 FXIVE KEE 6MU 4-2-45 222MU 20-2 *Defend* 8-3 Ind 6-4 SOC 28-11-46

RN177 CHA 6MU 5-2-45 222MU 20-2 *H Prince* 31-3 Ind 15-5 Jap 26-9-46 SOC 24-3-48

RN178 CHA 6MU 4-2-45 222MU 16-3 *Defend* 8-3 Ind 6-4 6S FACE 26-4-47 SOC 28-8-47

RN179 KEE 6MU 5-2-45 222MU 20-2 *Defend* 8-3 Ind 6-4 SOC 28-8-47

RN180 CHA 9MU 20-2-45 402S 26-4 412S 28-6 3BRU 21-3-46 SOC 27-6-46

RN181 KEE 9MU 5-2-45 222MU 20-2 *Defend* 8-3 Ind 6-4 17S f/ld cd CE Aragawa Jap 5-5-47 SOC 31-7

RN182 CHA 6MU 4-2-45 222MU 20-2 *H Prince* 29-3 Ind 15-5 SOC 12-12-46

RN183 KEE 6MU 3-2-45 222MU 16-2 *Defend* 8-3 Ind 6-4 SOC 28-5-47

RN184 KEE FF MJL 31-1-45 6MU 3-2 222MU 20-2 *H Prince* 24-3 Ind 15-5 SOC 12-12-46

RN185 FXIVE KEE 6MU 5-2-45 222MU 16-2 *Defend* 8-3 Ind 6-4 Jap 26-9-46 SOC 24-3-48

RN186 CHA 9MU 20-2-45 222MU 7-3 *H Prince* 31-3 Ind 15-5 SOC 28-11-46

RN187 KEE 29MU 4-2-45 *Sam Sacola* 15-4 Ind 21-5 Jap 26-9-46 SOC 24-3-48

RN188 CHA 9MU 7-2-45 215MU 25-2 *Fort Carn* 17-3 Ind 11-5 Jap 26-9-46 SOC 31-7-47

RN189 KEE 6MU 4-2-45 222MU 20-2 *Defend* 8-3 Ind 6-4 FACE 19-7 SOC 6-9

RN190 KEE 6MU 5-2-45 222MU 20-2 *H Prince* 31-3 Ind 15-5 SOC 31-7-47

RN191 WIN 29MU 10-2-45 222MU 5-3 *H Prince* 29-3 Ind 15-5 SOC 28-8-47

RN192 CHA 29MU 7-2-45 222MU *H Prince* 27-3 Ind 15-5 FACE 27-4-47 SOC 26-6

RN193 WIN 29MU 10-2-45 222MU 16-3 *H Prince* 31-3 Ind 15-5 disposed of through DGD 25-9-47

RN194 KEE 9MU 20-2-45 215MU 13-3 *Fort Carn* 18-3 Ind 11-5 SOC 28-8-47

RN195 KEE 9MU 10-2-45 76MU 1-3 *Fern* 31-3 Ind 7-5 SOC 27-12

RN196 CHA 6MU 15-2-45 130S 29-3 409RSU 13-4

RN197 KEE 9MU 10-2-45 76MU 1-3 *Fern* 31-3 Ind 7-5 Jap 26-9-46 SOC 24-3-48

RN198 CHA 6MU 14-2-45 41S CAC ops 24-3 350S 19-7 443S 15-1-46 sold VA 10-5-50

RN199 KEE 9MU 20-2-45 215MU 14-3 *Sam Sacola* 18-4 Ind 21-5 7S FACE 21-2-47

RN200 KEE 9MU 20-2-45 215MU 12-3 *Emp Dyn* 16-4 Ind 7-6 ACSEA 28-6 390MU u/c jam w/u ldg Sele Sing 22-1-47 SOC 27-2

RN201 FXIVE KEE 350S BAF(SG-31) 11-2-48 hvy ldg cd 5-2-50 SOC extant Beauvechain. (CE-A)

RN202 KEE. 6MU 13-2-45 430S 5-4-412S 27-8 sold Int All 26-5-49

RN203 KEE 6MU 14-2-45 FAAC 28-2 ROS 130S FTR ops 19-4

RN204 FRXIV CHA 9MU 3-3-45 402S FTR ops 19-4

RN205 FXIVE WIN 29MU 20-2-45 222MU 16-3 *Sam Sacola* 15-4 Ind 21-5 17S Sele SOC 24-3-48

RN206 CHA 9MU 25-2-45 FAAC 28-2 ROS 451S 22-11 BAF(H-96) 22-9-47

RN207 WIN 29MU 21-2-45 222MU 16-3 *H Prince* 31-3 Ind 15-5 SOC 27-3-47

RN208 CHA 9MU 20-2-45 41S CE ops 16-4 SOC 3-5

RN209 WIN 29MU 20-2-45 222MU 18-3 *H Prince* 31-3 Ind 15-5 SOC 28-8-47

RN210 KEE 39MU 20-2-45 41S 22-3 CAC ops 25-4 ASTH FLS CFE 26-9-46 611S 23-8-47 dvd i/grd Freckleton Marsh Warton Lancs CE 8-5-48

RN211 KEE 39MU 21-2-45 402S 29-3 ASTH 4-6 NEA 9-2-52 sold VA 15-8

RN212 Csfd 39MU 24-2-45 130S CE dbf 11-4

RN213 KEE 9MU 21-2-45 350S 11-10 FAAC 26-4-46 3BRU SOC 16-10-47

RN214 9MU 24-2-45 412S 27-9 ROS 7-8--46 sold Int All 26-5-49

RN215 KEE 9MU 5-3-45 130S 12-4 11C ATC 17-5 ASTH BAF(SG-54) 19-8-48

RN216 STN 9MU 27-4-45 214MU 20-5 *Samstu* 2-7 Ind 28-7 ACSEA 9-8 SOC 25-9-47

RN217 (Intm) STN 33MU 30-4-45 61 OTU 6-9 to 6251M 10SoTT 27-1-47

RN218 FRXIV ALD 39MU 1-5-45 82MU 19-6 *Emp Gam* 5-8 Ind 30-8 ACSEA 6-9 SOC 27-3-47

RN219 FRXIVE ALD 39MU 1-5-45 82MU 19-6 *Emp Gam* 5-8 Ind 30-8 ACSEA 13-9 11S Yonago Jap strk grd during mock attack disin over sea pilot kld 30-5-47

RN220 FRXIV G66 STN 9MU 16-5-45 222MU 1-6 *Emp Kum* 19-7 Ind 14-8 ACSEA 30-8 SOC 26-6-47

RN221 FRIXV STN 33MU 2-5-45 215MU 20-8 *D Bank* 6-9 Ind 14-10 ACSEA 18-10 SOC 28-8-47

SM series All FR XIV Griffon 65 except SM812 to 842 F XIV

SM812 CHA 29MU 25-2-45 222MU 21-3 *H Prince* 24-3 Ind 15-5 SOC 24-4-47

SM813 KEE RAF Norton 24-2-45 47MU 8-3 *Fern* 23-3 Ind 7-5 SOC

SM814 CHA 29MU 4-3-45 350S FTR ops 19-4

SM815 WIN 29MU 18-3-45 *H Prince* 29-3 Ind 15-5 SOC 31-7-47

SM816 KEE 6MU 27-2-44 215MU 14-3 *Fort Carn* Ind 11-5 SOC 27-3-47

SM817 KEE 6MU 28-2-45 41S 5-4 416S 20-9 VA 18-4-46 recat E 8-7

SM818 EA6MU 1-3-45 130S FTR ops 5-4

SM819 KEE 29MU 9-3-45 *H Prince* 31-3 Ind 15-5 InAF 29-12-47

SM820 CHA 9MU 2-3-45 41S 5-4 416S 20-9 SOC 25-7-46

SM821 CHA 9MU 2-3-45 ROS 17-3 BAF(SG-51) 27-7-48 cd 5-5-49

SM822 KEE 29MU 9-3-45 222MU 18-3 *H Prince* 31-3 Ind 15-5 SOC 31-7-47

SM823 KEE 33MU 9-3-45 41S 12-4 416S 20-9 FACE 9-11

SM824 KEE 29MU 9-3-45 222MU 21-3 *H Prince* 31-3 Ind 15-5 ACSEA 30-5 SOC 25-9-47

SM825 KEE 6MU 10-3-45 350S CAC ops 2-5 409RSU 3BRU CE 29-6-46

SM826 CHA 4-3-45 41S 5-4 453S 22-11 CFE 10-7-46 600S 1-5-48 to 6626M 16-12 SOC 30-5-50

SM827 CHA 33MU 10-3-45 130S CE ops 19-4

SM828 KEE 6MU 9-3-45 130S 5-4 CAC ops 25-4 409RSU 401S 10-5 411S 28-6 SOC 28-5-46

SM829 CHA 33MU 8-3-45 41S CB ops 31-3 ASTH 615S 20-3-47 610S 12-1-48 NEA 1-8-50 sold VA 10-11 to Belgium

SM830 KEE 33MU 13-3-45 350S CE ops 15-4

SM831 KEE 33MU 18-3-45 411S 28-6 FAAC 18-9 403RSU 416S 1-11 NEA 26-2-52 sold VA 15-3-52

SM832 FXIVE CHA InAF sold D. Arnold Blackbushe July '78 G-WWII Extant Duxford.

SM833 KEE 33MU 13-3-45 130S 19-4 CB ops 2-5 409RSU 4-5 recat E SOC 13-6

SM834 KEE 9MU 18-3-45 222MU 16-4 *Emp Dyn* 16-5 Ind 7-6 ACSEA 5-7 SOC 27-2-47

SM835 KEE 9MU 13-3-45 3PATP 21-4 *Emp Dyn* 16-5 Ind 7-6 ACSEA 28-6 SOC 31-7-47

SM836 KEE 6MU 18-3-45 215MU 2-4 *Sam Sacola* 15-4 Ind 21-5 SOC 31-7-47

SM837 CHA 9MU 12-3-45 215MU 26-4 *Emp Dyn* 16-5 Ind 7-6 ACSEA 5-7 SOC 28-8-47

SM838 CHA 15-3-45 *Sam Sacola* 15-4 Ind 21-5 SOC 31-7-47

SM839 KEE 6MU 18-3-45 1PATP 13-4 *Ocean Ch* 18-4 Ind 23-5 ACSEA 30-5-46 SOC 25-9-47

SM840 KEE 6MU 22-3-45 *Sam Sacola* 15-4 Ind 21-5 355MU FACE 22-3-47 SOC 24-4-47

SM841 KEE 6MU 22-3-45 *Sam Sacola* 15-4 Ind 21-5 SOC to Ins AF 27347

SM842 CHA 6MU 22-3-45 3PATP 18-4 *Emp Dyn* 16-5 Ind 7-6 ACSEA 28-6 SOC 28-8-47

SM876 CBAF 29MU 23-4-45 26S 610S 12-4 TAAC 26-7-48 ROS sold MoS 16-22-53

SM877 ALD no record

SM878 ALD 39MU 18-4-45 222MU 10-5 *Emp Dyn* 16-5 Ind 7-6 ACSEA 5-7 SOC 24-4-47

SM879 CBAF 29MU 23-4-45 26S 13-6 3BRU 8-5-46 2S 3-7-47 CE 5-10-48

SM880 ALD 29MU 23-4-45 222MU 2-5 *Emp Dyn* 16-5 Ind 7-6 ACSEA 28-6 SOC 25-9-47

SM881 KEE 39MU 16-4-45 222MU 7-5 *Emp Dyn* 16-5 Ind 7-6 ACSEA 28-6 Japan SOC 25-3-48

SM882 KEE 33MU 22-4-45 61 OTU 2-9 SOC 12-3-48

SM883 KEE 29MU 25-4-45 222MU 24-5 *C o Ches* 7-6 Ind 25-6 ACSEA 5-7 SOC 25-9-47

SM884 WIN 29MU 27-4-45 412S 28-6 cd f/lndg Hetlingen 7-2-46 403RSU SOC 28-2 bboc VA 6-5 recat E 24-6

SM885 CBAF 29MU 23-4-45 222MU 4-5 *Emp Dyn* 16-5 Ind 7-6 ACSEA 28-6 SOC 27-2-47

SM886 WIN 29MU 27-4-45 26S 12-6 FAAC 27-11 403RSU 611S 26-6-47 CAC surplus 2-4-49 NEA 9-2-52 solkd VA 15-8

SM887 KEE 29MU 26-4-45 222MU 18-5 *C o Ches* 7-6 Ind 25-6 ACSEA 5-7 11S cd f/ld in Jungle Malacca 7-2-46

SM888 KEE 29MU 24-4-45 222MU 13-5 *C o Ches* 7-6 Ind 25-6 ACSEA 12-7 28S cd/ld CE Sele Sing 6-5-47 SOC 5-6

SM889 STN 39MU 1-5-45 82MU 15-6 *Emp Gam* 5-8 Ind 30-8 ACSEA 13-9 SOC 27-12

SM890 STN 239MU 1-5-445 82MU 18-7 *C o H K* 26-8 Ind 17-9 ACSEA 20-9 SOC 30-1-47

SM891 (Intm) STN Super p/proto 6-3-45 47MU 6-5 82MU 5-9 *Ocean Gal* 8-9 Ind 14-10 ACSEA 29-11 Jap SOC 24-3-48

SM892 STN 39MU 7-5-45 82MU 22-6 *Emp Gam* 5-8 Ind 30-8 ACSEA 13-9 SOC 14-2-46

SM893 STN 9MU 14-5-45 82MU 15-6 *Emp Gam* 5-8 Ind 30-8 ACSEA 13-9- 8 RIAF S a/c aban lost cd FTR 4-12-46

SM894 EA 9MU 17-5-45 215MU 13-6 *Emp Gam* 5-8 Ind 30-8 ACSEA 6-9 SOC 26-6-47

SM895 STN Super p/proto mainplane stiff 6-3-45 6MU 18-5 222MU 2-6 *Emp Kum* 19-7 Ind 14-8 ACSEA 23-8 SOC 25-9-47

SM896 ALD 39MU 7-5-45 451S FAAC 10-8 ROS 226 OCU 16-12-49 FAC3R 24-5-51 scrap 28-5

SM897 KEE 6MU 15-5-45 222MU 1-6 *Emp Kum* 19-7 Ind 14-8 ACSEA 23-8 8S RIAF swng on t/o stry obs Burma 21-1-46

SM898 ALD 9MU 16-5-45 82MU 16-6 *Emp Gam* 5-8 Ind 20-8 ACSEA 12-9 SOC 28-3-47

SM899 ALD 29MU 23-5-45 453S 6-9 226 OCU 30-12-49 FAC2 20-9-50 recat 4R to 6902M 30-9-52

SM913 KEE 29MU 26-5-45 61 OTU 3-8 FAAC 5-11 ROS to 6166M 12SoTT 30-10-46

SM914 FRXIVE KEE 29MU 29-5-45 61 OTU 3-8 612S 23-6-47 6MU surplus 24-10-49 sold VA 12-5-50 Thai U14-1/93, extant Bangkok.

SM915 KEE 29MU 2-6-45 222MU 12-7 *C oH K* 26-8 Ind 17-9 ACSEA 27-9 RIAF 27-2-47 SOC 28-8

SM916 KEE 9MU 23-5-45 82MU 24-8 *D Bank* 20-10 ACSEA Jap SOC 24-3-48

SM917 ALD 9MU 23-5-45 82MU 7-7 *C o H K* 26-8 Ind 17-9 ACSEA 27-9 105S FACE 12-12-46 SOC 28-12

SM918 KEE 6MU 5-6-45 215MU 29-6 *Emp Gam* 5-8 Ind 30-8 ACSEA 6-9 SOC 25-9-47

SM919 KEE 9MU 9-6-45 451S FACE 20-7

SM920 KEE 6MU 22-6-45 82MU 17-8 *C o H K* 26-8 Ind 17-9 ACSEA 27-9 Jap SOC 24-3-48

SM921 KEE 9MU 12-6-45 47MU 1-10 *Saucouan* 31-12 Ind 2-1-46 ACSEA 31-1 Jap 18-3-47 SOC 25-3-48

SM922 KEE 9MU 12-6-45 61 OTU 20-9 FACB 15-4-46 SOC 12-3-48

SM923 KEE 6MU 22-6-45 82MU 16-8 *Ocean Gal* 17-9 Ind 14-10 Jap SOC 24-3-48

SM924 KEE 9MU 25-6-45 47MU 26-9 *Saucouan* 3-12 Ind 3-1-46 ACSEA 31-11 Jap 24-4-47 SOC 24-3-48

SM925 KEE 9MU 29-6-45 47MU 21-9 *Ocean Vic* 24-9 Ind 30-10 Jap 4S FACE 11-6-47 SOC 31-7

SM926 (Intm) STM p/proto u/c mods 17-4-45 6MU 25-6 61 OTU 9-8 SOC 12-3-48

SM927 STN 9MU 2-7-45 76MU 17-9 1BR&SD Res pl 28-2-49 2S 5-3 NEA 31-5-53 SOC 22-9

SM928 KEE 6MU 30-6-45 61 OPTU 7-8 GAAC 10-10 SOC 12-3-48

SM929 KEE 9MU 9-7-45 607S 17-4-47 cd/ld Ouston CB 4-1-48 recat E 29-1 sold J Dale 5-8

SM930 KEE CRD HAL 7-7-45 MacClarens 30-8 HAL 14-6-46 NEA 1-8-50 sold VA 16-11 to Belgium

SM931 KEE 39MU 13-8-45 76MU 20-9 *Ocean Vac* 7-11 Ind 2-12 ACSEA 27-12 Jap SOC 24-3-48

SM932 KEE 6MU 17-7-45 82MU 13-8 *C o H K* 26-8 Ind 17-9 ACSEA 20-9 SOC 27-6-46

SM933 KEE 6MU 17-7-45 82MU 27-8 *D Bank* 6-9 Ind 4-10 ACSEA 11-10 RIAF 29-12-47

SM934 KEE 39MU 28-7-45 82MU 13-8 *Ocean Gal* 17-9 Ind 14-10 ACSEA 29-11 Jap SOC 24-3-48

SM935 (Intm) STN Super p/proto 13-6-44 9MU 17-7-45 451S 4-9 33MU 15-11-49 NEA 29-2-53 sold VA 15-8

SM936 KEE 39MU 27-7-45 82MU 30-8 *D Bank* 6-9 Ind 14-10 ACSEA 11-10 SOC 25-9-47

SM937 KEE 39MU 13-8-45 82MU 11-9 *Fort Per* 11-9 Ind 16-10 ACSEA 25-10 RIAF 29-12-47

SM938 KEE 39MU 9-8-45 84GOC 6-9 451S 4-10 BASF(SG-9) 3-6-47 cd 12-5-50

TP, TX TZ series All FR XIV Griffon 65

TP236 VA HPA 1-11-45 602S 24-10-46 607S 15-11-47 CAC surplus 3-3-49 sold VA 10-5-50

TP237 KEE 6MU 22-5-45 215MU 5-6 *Samstu* 2-7 Ind 28-7 ACSEA 9-8 SOC 28-8-47

TP238 KEE 9MU17-5-45 215MU 13-6 *Emp Gam* 5-8 Ind 30-8 ACSEA 6-9 SOC 27-3-47

TP239 KEE 6MU 22-5-45 215MU 3-6 *Samstu* 2-7 Ind 9-8 CE SOC 27-6-46

TP240 KEE 9MU 23-5-45 CFE Tang 6-9 FAAC 2-1-46 AST H BDn Oct'46 trls of MK IX RP instal 612S 9-1-47 FAAC 11-5 eng dam. Flew i/hill nr Durham pilot kld CE 3-9-48 SOC 17-9

TP256 KEE 6MU 22-3-45 82MU 19-6 *Emp Gam* 5-8 Ind 30-8 ACSEA 13-9 SOC 27-3-47

TX974 STN 29MU 23-8-45 47MU 22-9 *Ocean Ver* 7-11 Ind 2-12 ACSEA 27-12 9S RIAF explosion on start eng Peshawar CEdbf 16-8-46

TX975 KEE 39MU 13-8-45 76MU 20-9 *Ocean Vic* 24-9 Ind 30-10 ACSEA 29-11 Jap SOC 24-3-48

TX976 (intm) STN Super p/proto 5-9-44 33MU 11-8-45 82MU 5-9 *Ocean Gal* 17-9 Ind 14-10 ACSEA 9-11 1 SFTS sta on ldg Ambala CE 4-5-46 SOC 31-10

TX977 KEE 6MU 30-8-45 47MU 18-9 *Ocean Vic* 24-9 Ind 30-10 ACSEA 29-11 Jap SOC 24-3-48

TX978 KEE 33MU 5-8-45 76MU 16-9 *Fort Mich* 22-9 Ind 18-10 ACSEA 29-11 7S RIAF emercy Kohat 24-7-46

TX979 KEE 33MU 5-9-45 76MU 17-9 *Fort Mich* 22-9 Ind 18-10 ACSEA 8-11 Jap FACE 11-6-47 SOC 31-7

TX980 KEE CRD R—RH 6-9-45 G65 removed after perf trls G105 instal with 3-speed superhcarger for comp trls 52MU 20-10-48 CE 25-10

TX981 KEE 33MU 11-9-45 76MU 26-9 *Clan MacB* 29-11 ret 76MU for re-erection 615S 5-7-48 612S cd/ld CE Dyce 19-12

TX982 KEE 33MU 12-9-45 76MU 3-10 *Clan MacB* 22-11 ret 76MU for re-erection 6MU w/u ldg CB 30-12-48 sold E Smelt

TX983 KEE 33MU 5-10-45 513S 2-12-46 RCSU 14-4-48 sold VA 15-8-52

TX984 KEE 29MU 9-10-45 226 OCU 20-1-50 FAC3R 13-2 ROS NEA 31-3-53 sold MoS 14-12

TX985 STN 6MU 26-11-45 602S 26-11-46 RCCU 14-4-48 607S 21-11 CAC surplus 3-3-49 sold R J Coley 3-2-50

TX986 FRXIVE KEE 6MU 27-4-45 222MU 1-6 *Co Ches* 7-6 Ind 25-6 ACSEA 12-7 Jap SOC 24-3-48

TX987 ALD 29MU 3-5-45 222MU 8-6 *Emp Gam* 5-8 Ind 30-7 ACSEA 13-9 SOC 25-9-47

TX988 ALD 29MU 30-4-45 222MU 1-6 *Emp Kum* 19-7 ACSEA 23-8 9S FTR 19-2-47

TX989 KEE 29MU 2-5-45 451S 3-9 BAF(SG-88) 8-2-49

TX990 ALD 29MU 30-4-45 222MU 13-6 *OoHK* 26-8 India 17-9 ACSEA 27-9 RIAF 29-12-47

TX991 (intm) STN Super p/proto 5-9-44; for hood wind gear 6-3-45 1PP Ben 28-4 82MU 7-9 *Fort Mich* 23-9 Ind 18-10 ACSEA 29-11 8S FACE 15-3-47 SOC 24-4

TX992 ALD 29MU 30-4-45 26S 14-6 613S 14-4-48 NEA 1-8-50 sold VA 14-11 to Belgium 15-11

TX993 KEE 29MU 2-5-45 26S 12-6 411S 2-3-46 sold VA 10-5-50

TX994 ALD 29MU 3-5-45 222MU 10-6 *Emp Gam* 6-8 Ind 30-8 ACSEA 13-9 SOC 28-8-47

TX995 ALD 29MU 12-5-45 453S 6-9 BAF(SG-49) 10-7-48

TX996 STN 39MU 29-4-45 47MU 25-9 *Sancouan* 3-12 Ind 3-1-46 ACSEA 31-1 390MU SOC 13-1-48

TX997 ALD 6MU 3-5-45 222MUJ 30-5 *Emp Kum* 19-7 Ind 14-8 ACSEA 13-9 SOC 24-4-47

TX998 ALD 9MU 2-5-45 26S 14-6 602 29-7-47 29MU surplus 10-3-49 NEA 31-3-53 SOC 22-9

TZ102 ALD 6MU 3-5-45 215MU 17-5 *Samstu* 2-7 Ind 28-7 ACSEA 9-8 Jap SOC 24-3-48

TZ103 ALD 6MU 23-5-45 26S 14-6 613S 3-7-47 49MU BoB 12-9-49 NEA 22-9-50 sold VA 11-12

TZ104 KEE 29MU 6-5-45 FAAC 4-6 82MU 30-8 *Ocean Gal* 17-9 Ind 14-10 ACSEA 29-11 FACE dbf 18-3-47 SOC 26-6

TZ105 ALD 9MU 7-5-45 215MU 8-6 *Samstu* 2-7 Ind 28-7 ACSEA 9-8 SOC 28-9-47

TZ106 ALD 6MU 7-5-45 453S 28-6 DVD SOC 22-7 i/grnd nr Wichling Kent. Pilot kld 6-1-46

TZ107 ALD 6MU 11-5-45 222MU 2-6 *Emp Kum* 19-7 Ind 14-8 ACSEA 23-8 8S RIAF dbf on grnd Burma 15-1-46 SOC 31-1

TZ108 ALD 39MU 12-5-45 82MU 16-6 *Emp Gam* 5-8 Ind 30-8 ACSEA 6-9 7S RIAF swng lnd u/c cllpse Nahnajpur 29-3-46 SOC 25-4

TZ109 KEE 33MU 12-5-45 215MU 20-8 *D Bank* 6-9 Ind 14-10 ACSEA 18-10 SOC 28-8-47

TZ110 ALD 9MU 16-5-45 82MU 15-6 *Emp Gam* 5-8 Ind 20-8 ACSEA 13-9 6S RIAF u/s lnd Ranchi CE 3-8-46 SOC 25-9-47

TZ111 ALD 29MU 23-5-45 453S 6-9 BAF(SG-89) 8-2-49

TZ112 ALD 6MU 23-5-45 26S 13-6 FAAC 17-7 ROS 416S 25-10 33MU 19-3-46 1BR&SD Res pl 20-5-49 2S BAFO 1-6-50 6MU 31-1-51 NEA 31-3-53 sold MoS 30-12

TZ113 ALD 29MU 23-5-45 222MU 19-7 *CoHK* 26-8-45 Ind 17-9 ACSEA 27-9 RIAF 29-12-47

TZ114 ALD 29MU 23-5-45 222MU 12-7 *CoHK* 26-8 Ind 17-9 ACSEA 27-9 RIAF 29-12-47

TZ115 ALD 6MU 25-5-45 82MU 19-6 *Emp Gam* 5-8 Ind 30-8 ACSEA 13-9 11S Jap GACE 15-1-47 SOC 31-7

TZ116 KEE 29MU 28-5-45 453S 6-9 FAAC 18-10 151RU 607S 3-12-46 CAC surplus 3-3-49 NEA 14-7-50 sold J Dale 13-11

TZ117 ALD 9MU 27-5-45 82MU 5-7 *CoHK*26-8 Ind 17-9 ACSEA 27-9 SOC 13-3-47

TZ118 ALD 29MU 23-5-45 222MU 20-7 *CoHK* 26-8 Ind 17-9 ACSEA AFS cd lnd Ambala CE 25-9-46 SOC 31-10

TZ119 ALD 9MU 28-5-45 82MU 15-7 *CoHK* 26-8 Ind 17-9 ACSEA 27-9 SOC 25-8-47

TZ120 ALD 9MU 28-5-45 82MU 15-7 *CoHK* 26-8 Ind 17-9 ACSEA 27-9 InAF 28-11-46 SOC 30-11-47

TZ121 ALD 6MU 29-5-45 215MU 22-6 *Emp Gam* 6-8 Ind 30-8 ACSEA 13-9 SOC 28-8-47

TZ122 KEE 29MU 29-5-45 451S 3-9 FAAC 20-9 411RSU NEA 26-5-52 sold VA 15-8

TZ123 ALD 6MU 29-5-45 82MU 19-6 *Emp Gam* 5-8 Ind 30-8 ACSEA 13-9 SOC 28-8-47

TZ124 ALD 6MU 29-5-45 82MU 19-6 *Emp Gam* 5-8 Ind 30-8 ACSEA 6-9 SOC 31-2-46

TZ125 ALD 6MU 31-5-45 453 1-7 443S 17-1-46 613S 18-4-47 e/fld cd/ld nr Ringway CE 9-11 SOC 25-11

TZ126 ALD 6MU 1-6-45 2S 26-7 BAFO CE 5-10-48

TZ127 ALD 9MU 31-5-45 453S 6-9 BNAF(SG-81) 18-1-49

TZ128 ALD 6MU 1-6-45 26S 16-7 411S 25-10 CE 4-6-47

TZ129 ALD 6MU 2-6-45 2S 26-7 CD f/lnd Elbstorf 24-4-46 recat E 412 RSU

TZ130 ALD 9MU 2-6-45 453S FAAC 25-7 ROS recat E SOC 23-11

TZ131 ALD 9MU 2-6-45 453S 6-9 443S 16-1-46 FACB 4-2 VA recat E 24-6

TZ132 ALD 9MU 6-6-45 453S 6-9 443S 16-1-46 BAF(SG-48) 10-7-48

TZ133 ALD 29MU 14-6-45 47MU 22-9 *Ocean Ver* 30-10 Ind 2-12 ACSEA 27-12 SOC 25-9-47

TZ134 ALD 9MU 18-6-45 453S 6-9 613S 25-3-47 CE f/f 28-5-49 scrap 16-7

TZ135 KEE 6MU 30-6-45 61 OTU 23-8 to 6165M 30-10-46 12SoTT

TZ136 ALD 6MU 18-6-45 26S 3-7 3BRU 8-5 SOC 21-10-47

TZ137 ALD 9MU 3-7-45 453S 6-9 FAAC 4-10 ROS VA BAF(SG-33) 11-2-48 cd 5-6-51

TZ138 FRXIVE ALD R-RH prep for cold tests. 47MU Nov'45 RACF Edmonton Canada for cold tests. Eng replaced summer '46. Second trls began 26-11-46 end 28-2-47 Total fly time 41.55hrs a/c nosed over while taxy in snow and dam prop. Tiger Moth skis instal for t/o only, skis dropped Gun heat inadequate SOC 31-3-49 sold con to CF-GMZ. To Minneapolis USA 1960 extant as N138TZ Mass. Took part in Nat. Air Races Cleveland Ohio

TZ139 ALD 9MU 3-7-45 451S 3-9 FAAC 7-9 ROS 611S 2-9-47 CAC surplus 2-4-49 NEA 26-2-52 sold VA 15-8

TZ140 FRXIVE ALD 6MU 22-6-45 ASTH 20-7 VA EA 4-1-46 AMPR 3C 29-7 615S 5-7-48 612S 20-9 CAC surplus 30-9-49 NEA 31-3-53 SOC 11-8

TZ141 ALD 9MU 5-7-45 453S 6-9 443S 16-1-46 451S 17-1 600S 13-1-47 611S 18-10 FAAC 11-12-48 ROS scr 21-12-49

TZ142 ALD 6MU 9-7-45 451S 3-9 NEA 31-7-50 sold VA 25-8 to Belguim

TZ143 ALD 6MU 9-7-45 82MU 18-8 *C o H K* 26-8 Ind 17-9 ACSEA 20-9 SOC 26-9-46

TZ144 ALD 9MU 17-7-45 FAAC 23-8 ROS 610S 6-6-47 scr 30-1-50

TZ145 ALD 9MU 12-7-45 76MU 19-9 *Ocean Ver* 7-11 Ind 2-12 ACSEA 27-12 Jap 13-3-47 SOC 24-3-48

TZ146 KEE 33MU 13-7-45 215MU 20-8 *D Bank* 6-9 Ind 14-10 ACSEA 18-10 SOC 11-4-46

TZ147 ALD 9MU 11-7-45 47MU 19-9 *Ocean Ver* 7-11 Ind 21-2 ACSEA 27-12 Jap 24-4-47 SOC 24-3-48

TZ148 ALD 39MU 17-7-45 451S 4-10 FAAC 27-11 to 6562M 28-5-48 SOC 20-9-50

TZ149 ALD 33MU 17-7-45 76MU 22-9 *Ocean Ver* 7-11 Ind 7-12 ACSEA 27-12 SOC 25-9-47

TZ152 ALD 33MU 19-7-45 82MU 24-8 *Ocean Gal* 17-9 Ind 24-10 ACSEA 29-11 6S RIAF lost cont during Ftr affil. CD nr Namkum pilot kld 9-4-46 SOC 25-4

TZ153 ALD 39MU 20-7-45 82MU 13-8 *C o H K* 26-8 Ind 17-9 ACSEA 27-9 SOC 27-12

TZ154 ALD 33MU 17-7-45 76MU 4-10 *Clan MacB* 22-11 ret to 76MU for re erection BAF(SG-97) 11-5-49

TZ155 ALD 39MU 21-7-45 76MU 20-9 *Ocean Ver* 24-9 Ind 30-10 ACSEA 29-11 SOC 1-6-47

TZ156 ALD 39MU 25-7-45 82MU 13-8 *C o H K* 26-8 Ind 17-9 ACSEA 20-9 6S RIAF cd f/lnd Ranchi 8-1-46 SOC 14-2

TZ157 ALD 39MU 21-7-45 82MU 13-8 *C o H K* 26-8 Ind 17-9 ACSEA 30-5-46 SOC 24-4-47

TZ158 ALD 6MU 27-7-45 61 OTU 13-8 FAAC 10-10 SOC 12-3-48

TZ159 ALD 33MU 28-7-45 215MU 20-8 *D Bank* 6-9 Ind 14-10 SOC 30-5-46

TZ160 ALD 6MU 28-7-45 82MU 18-8 *C o H K* 26-8 Ind 27-9 ACSEA 20-9-46 SOC 30-1-47

TZ161 ALD 6MU 21-8-45 47MU 13-9 *Fort Mich* 22-9 Ind 19-10 SOC 31-7-47

TZ162 ALD 6MU 28-7-45 82MU 18-8 *Ocean Gal* 17-9 Ind 14-10 ACSEA 29-11 6S RIAF cd f/lng Guldar 5-3-46 SOC 25-4

TZ163 KEE 39MU 13-8-45 47MU 20-9 *Ocean Vic* 24-9 Ind 30-10 ACSEA 29-11 6S RIAF cd on t/o Ranchi CE 8-11-46 SOC 24-4-47

TZ164 ALD 6MU 21-8-45 76MU 28-9 *Clan MacB* 25-11 ret to 76MU for re erection 1BR&SD BAFO 18-12-49 2S 4-1-49 NEA 31-3-53 sold MoS 30-12

TZ165 ALD 33MU 27-8-45 76MU 14-9 *Fort Mich* 22-9 Ind 18-10 ACSEA 29-11 Jap SOC 25-3-48

TZ166 ALD 33MU 27-8-45 76MU 14-9 ASTH 26-10 BAF(SG-79) 17-12-48 cd 20-9-50

TZ167 ALD 6MU 27-8-45 47MU 18-9 *Ocean Vic* 26-9 Ind 30-10 ACSEA 29-11 1 SFTS cd f/lng Thanesar 11-4-46 SOC 5-5

TZ168 ALD 6MU 27-8-45 76MU 17-9 *Ocean Vic* 24-9 Ind 30-10 ACSEA 29-11 SOC 28-8-47

TZ169 ALD 6MU 29-8-45 47MU 5-9 *Fort Mich* 23-9 Ind 18-10 ACSEA 29-11 SOC 31-10-46

TZ170 ALD 6MU 31-8-45 76MU 17-9 *Ocean Vic* 24-9 Ind 30-10 ACSEA 29-11 SOC 28-8-47

TZ171 ALD 6MU 31-8-45 47MU 13-9 *Fort Mich* 22-9 Ind 18-10 ACSEA 29-11 IAF 31-12-47

TZ172 ALD 33MU 5-9-45 76MU 20-9 *Ocean Vic* 7-11 Ind 2-12 ACSEA 27-12 SOC 25-9-47

TZ173 ALD 33MU 7-9-45 76MU 16-9 *Fort Mich* 22-9 Ind 18-10 ACSEA 29-11 SOC 28-8-47

TZ174 ALD 6MU 12-9-45 76MU 28-9 *Clan MacB* 29-11 ret to 76MU NEA 1-8-50 sold VA 9-11 to Belguim

TZ175 STN 33MU 29-10-45 600S 7-11-46 612S 3-11-47 63MU SOC rtp 16-7-49

TZ176 STN 29MU 22-10-45 612S 7-7-47 o/s ldg lost cont CE Dyce 24-11-47 SOC 13-1-48

TZ178 KEE 29MU 27-12-45 607S 4-6-47 TAAC 21-9 ROS CE 14-10-48

TZ179 KEE 6MU 6-3-46 Long Kesh Ireland 12-9-46 SOC mr 22-10

TZ180 KEE 6MU 17-10-45 43Grp HQ 3-7-46 613S 6-1-48 2S 30-8-50 NEA 31-3-53 sold MoS 30-11

TZ181 G67 KEE 29MU 17-12-45 612S 2-5-47 FAAC 5-12-48 ROS NEA 31-3-53 SoH f ftng trls SOC 14-9

TZ182 G67 KEE 29MU 27-12-45 612S 5-9-47 GAAC 19-12-48 ROS NEA 31-3-53 SoH f ftng trls 14-9

TZ183 KEE 6MU 17-10-45 612S 4-11-46 sold VA 10-5-50

X TZ184 KEE 6MU 22-5-45 215MU 1-6 *Samstu* 2-7 ACSEA 9-8 SOC 25-9-47

TZ185 G66 STN 9MU 23-5-45 215MU 7-7 *Emp Gam* 5-8 Ind 30-8 ACSEA 6-9 AFS eng fail on app. w/u lnd Ambala CE 17-12-46 SOC 30-1-47

TZ186 KEE 6MU 22-5-45 215MU 3-6 *Samstu* 2-7 Ind 28-7 ACSEA 9-8 8S RIAF eng fail in crct Trichinopoly cd 9-6-46 SOC 31-10

TZ187 KEE 9MU 29-5-45 82MU 5-7 *Emp Gam* 30-8 ACSEA 13-9 SOC 25-9-47

TZ188 KEE 9MU 29-5-45 215MU 7-7 *Emp Gam* 5-8 Ind 30-8 ACSEA 6-9 dbf SOC 14-3-46

TZ189 KEE 29MU 31-5-45 76MU 20-9 *Ocean Ver* 7-11 ACSEA 27-12 Jap SOC 2-4-48

TZ190 KEE 29MU 8-6-45 82MU *Ocean Gal* 17-9 Ind 14-10 ACSEA 29-11 SOC 28-8-47

TZ191 KEE 29MU 2-6-45 222MU 5-7 *C o H K* 26-8 Ind 17-9 ACSEA 20S hit Thunderbolts in o/s Burma pilot kld 27-9 CE dbf 14-3-46

TZ192 FRXIVE KEE 29MU 1-6-45 453S 6-9 BAF(SG-64) 5-10-48 cd 23-10-52

TZ193 ALD 9MU 14-6-45 26S 16-9 411S 25-10 BAF(SG-85) 19-1-49

TZ194 KEE 6MU 7-6-45 26S 16-7 FAAC 14-1-46 403RSU sold scr bou 3-9-47

TZ195 KEE 29MU 2-6-45 222MU 12-7 *C o H K* 26-8 Ind 17-9 ACSEA 27-9 7S RIAF cd during dive bomb practice pilot kld FTR 21-8-46

TZ196 KEE 9MU 15-6-45 2S 26-7 air coll with NH896 over Celle Germany cd pilot kld CE SOC 31-1-47

FR XIVe TZ112 served with 2 Squadron post war.

TZ197 KEE 6MU 29-6-45 61 OTU 23-8 SoTT Langham 5-12-46 SOC 17-12-47

TZ198 ALD 9MU 18-6-45 451S 3-9 443S 17-1-46 Lubeck Germany 11-12 1BR&SD 26-11-48 2S BAFO 4-1-49 NEA 3-4-51 sold VA 12-10

TZ199 KEE 6MU 22-10-45 61 OTU 28-5-46 SOC 12-3-48

Interim; MT847, 858, MV290, 297, 305, 309, 313, 348, 364, NH641-642, 646-647, 840, 866, 909, 925, RN217, SM891, 926, 935, TX976 and 991.

'Gem' Mods programme De Hav and AST; NH653-655, 660-661, 685-688, 690, 693-699, 701, RB148, 150-152, 154-156, 159-166, 168-171, 173-174, 177, 180-186, 188-189, and RM615.

Prod proto.; MT847-848. MV253, 263, 271, 286, 290, 293, 297, 305, 309, 313, 320, 348-349, 364, NH641-642, 646-647, 744, 840, 866, 909, 925, RM970, 972, 988, RN148, SM891, 895, 926, TX976 and 991.

Maintenance airframes; MT847(6960), NH784(6689), RM623(6839), RM694(6629/6004), RM737(6140), RM884(6847), RM929(6849), RN217(6241), TZ135(6165) and TZ148(6562).

Belguim A.F.; MV256, 261, 265, 267, 288, 302, 312, 360, 369, 378, 381-383, NH643, 654, 658, 688, 742-743, 754, 780, 789, 797, 857, 863-864, 892, 894, 918, 922, RB154, 161, 163, 165-166, 182, RM625, 672, 674, 676, 679-680, 683, 685, 697, 700, 703, 707, 710, 712, 726, 741, 759, 764, 768-770, 784, 787, 790-792, 795, 802, 817, 820, 822, 857, 860, 862-863, 866, 870, 876, 879, 882, 906, 913, 916-918, 920-921, 927, 933, 935, 937-938, RN118-119, 121, 124, 201, 206, SM829, 930, TX992, 995, TZ111, 127, 132, 137, 142, 154, 174 and 192-193.

Indian A.F.; MV293, 384, NH645, 749, 799, 802, 805, 807, 831, 838, 917, RM742 and SM937.

RThaiAF; NH698, 714, 794, 800, RB184, 188, RM692 and 23 others as U14/1/93 to U14/30/93.

Right: Rolls-Royce's G-ALGT, the former RM689.
Below: Belgian Air Force SG-127. Former RAF serial is untraced.
Bottom: CF-GNZ, the former TZ138, for the 1949 Ohio Air Races.

A ROSE BY ANOTHER NAME

As production of the F Mk IX Spitfire quickened and Fighter Command squadrons were able to assess the qualities of the new mark, it became evident from combat reports that most interceptions were taking place at a lower level than previously encountered. The Commanding Officer of the Middle East fighter units requested that supplies of Spitfires be limited to the lower altitude examples and the production lines were hard put to meet demand. The final answer to this demand was the F Mk XVI, virtually a Mk IX airframe with the Rolls-Royce Packard Merlin engine.

The designation had not been applied just to differentiate between the UK-built engine and the American. The latter unit did have minor fitments to the former and the F XVI designation was an aid to the ordering of spares. Apart from this both aircraft were virtually identical.

The Merlin 266 Packard unit sprang from an original order placed with the American company in July 1940. The Packard company was second choice as originally it had been proposed that Ford of Detroit build the engine under licence. Before the outbreak of war arrangements were made for the Merlin to be produced in France by the French Ford offshoot. The Ford Detroit factory had access to a complete set of Merlin III drawings and on behalf of their French subsidiary had placed large orders in America for machine tools. But, with the outbreak of war and the defeat of France in early 1940 Henry Ford, founder of the company, was not at all certain it was a good idea to produce the Merlin engine. Like a lot of Americans at that time he thought that Germany would very soon defeat Britain, and although he did not object to building the Merlin for America he considered it politically unwise to do the same for Britain. There was another viewpoint, this time from Washington. Officials considered that the Ford company would be unable to match the fine limits of engineering required for the Merlin with their mass production methods.

In the event Ford withdrew in June 1940 and the negotiations then taking place with Packard were concluded. Capital and current production cost were to be shared by both American and British governments on a one third-two thirds basis respectively. An order was placed with Packard for 1,500 engines on a fixed price basis of cost, plus a fixed fee, after which any future orders would be negotiable. There was also an option to purchase a further 10,000 engines in two orders of 5,000 within six months of completion of the initial order. The British government had committed itself to the sum of £30 million and the first Packard engine would not be ready until the summer of the following year. It could be considered that both governments had faith in the British people being able to weather the storm, fighting a static war until supplies of material enabled them to beat the German war machine.

MK XVI RW396 carrying the four-letter Flying Training Command codes for the Central Gunnery School, with whom it served throughout its flying career.

Packard overcame all the difficulties associated with production of the Merlin engine and by the time the final delivery was made it had delivered 55,000 units at an average cost each of approximately $12,000. 25,000 engines reached England. The F IX and XVI were built, initially, on the same production line at Castle Bromwich and separate lines were established as production expanded.

Trials of the new variant were not as extensive as its twin and they are recorded below.

SM394 (Quill 5-12-44) General handling of aircraft showed it to be definitely unstable. (13-12-44) Flown at aft limit for type after wing tips fitted. No appreciable effect on longitudinal stability. (Shea-S 16-12-44) New elevator fitted after original found to be badly distorted. Wing tips removed; directional control still below standard.

SM205 (Quill 20-1-45) Flown to check effect on handling with Cluster Bomb No 6. Dived three times from 15,000ft at 450mph. Bomb thought to produce a deterioration in directional stability. (27-2-45 Shea-S) Flight checks with Bomb No 7. Satisfactory up to limiting diving speed.

TA759 (Shea-S 28-2-45) Rear view XVI. Flight to investigate effect of rear view modification upon handling. Longitudinal charactistics B......awful, but considered that modification not the cause and elevator might be the culprit. (2-3-45) Behaviour of aircraft puzzling and investigation into elevator system recommended. (21-3-45 Morgan) Two different CBAF elevators tested. Aircraft in similar condition as per original tests. (22-3-45 Shea-S) Flown at full load and with No 1 South Marston elevator. Stability showed great improvement and handling considered satisfactory. (22-3-45) Flown at full load with No 2 SM elevator. Satisfactory. (29-3-45 Shea-S) Flight to check operation of hood winding gear. Satisfactory up to speeds of 240mph.

SM410 (Shea-S 7-4-45) First CBAF rear view XVI, with rear tank full (67gals). Metal elevator. With CoG 11.8in aft of datum aircraft was unstable at this loading. Metal elevator is good. (18-4-45) Flight to determine most acceptable CoG for combat purposes @ 25,000ft. Take off with all tanks full, having started engine and taxied out on rear tank and continued on same to climb to 25,000ft. Continue to run on rear tank until such time CoG became acceptable for combat flying. (Quill 23-4-45) Elevator from ML186 fitted as it was thought original elevator might be responsible for loss of stability. Most obvious external reason for poor stability would seem to be the front engine cowling, which has a most exaggerated balloon shape. From tests carried out on Mk IXs it is known that this results in the reduction of fore and aft stability. (12-5-45) Flown with complete tail unit of ML186. Aircraft considered more satisfactory with the new stern. (18-4-45 Shea-S) Aircraft fitted with Maclaren radiators and delivered to that company at Heston.

TE910 (Shea-S 16-5-45) Flown with last of six CBAF

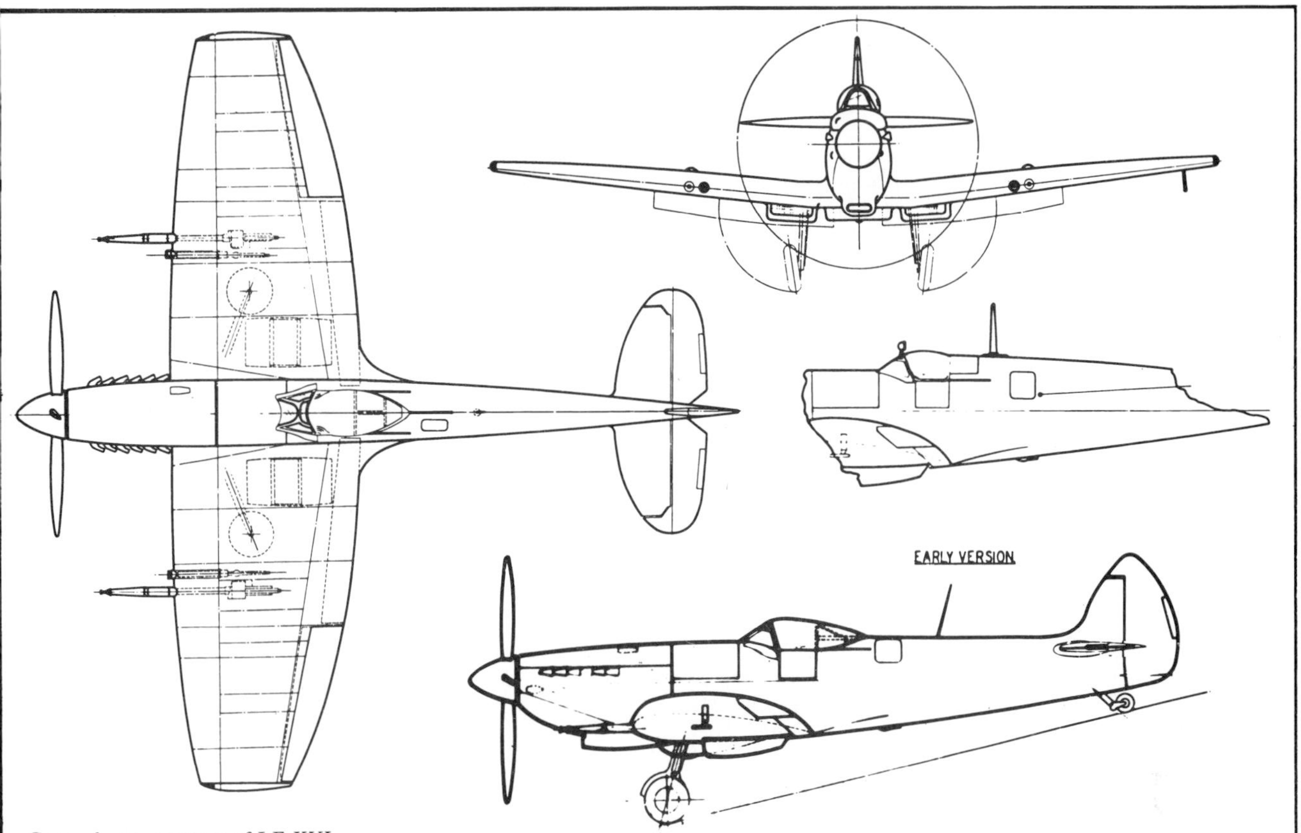
EARLY VERSION
LATER VERSION

General arrangement of LF XVI.

SL452 today guards the gate at RAF Coltishall. It is seen here in three different guises. Right: At Duxford in the colours of 64 Squadron. Below: Also thought at Duxford, this time in 65 Squadron markings. Bottom: In overall gloss scheme at an unknown location.

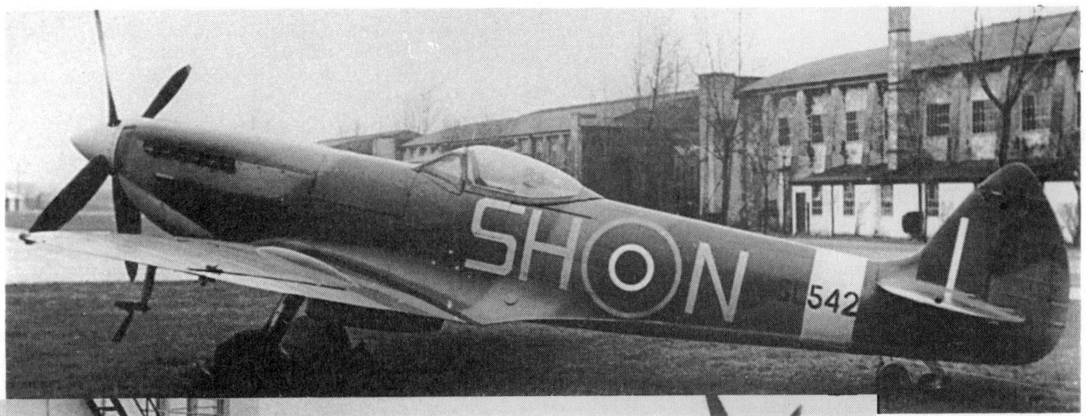
SHON
SL542

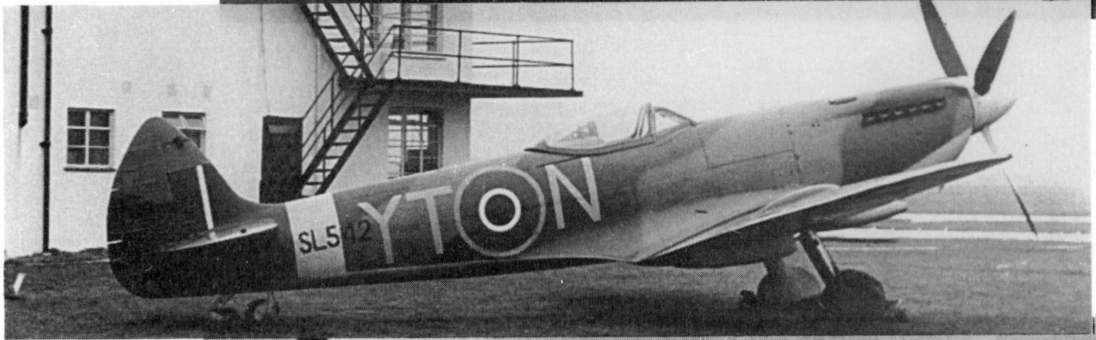
SL542
YTON

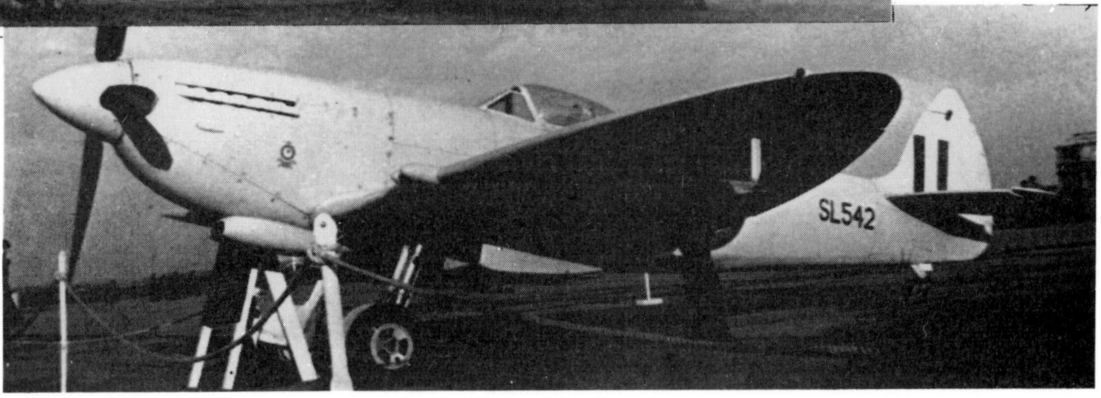
SL542

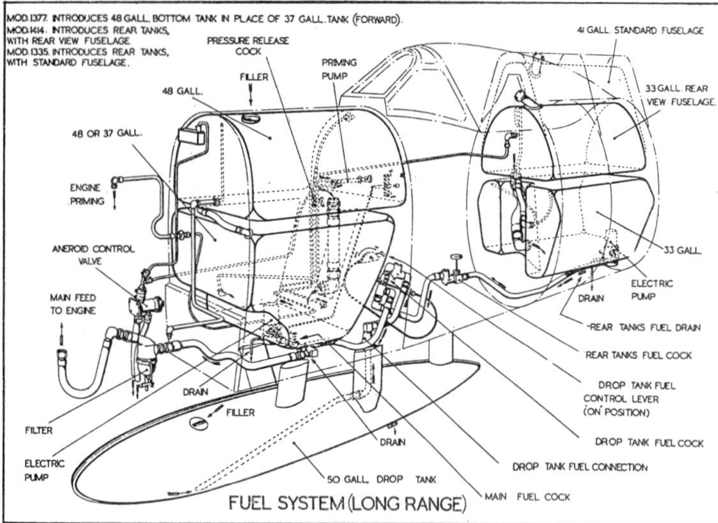

elevators. Bordered on over balanced and needed to have 6 inches of TE beading each side.

SM394 was at High Post on 7 November 1944 for weighing and CG determination and it had a tare weight of 5,607lb and auw of 7,419. SM420 was used to flight test the Maclaren radiator scheme and when weighed at High Post on 19 March 1945 the tare was 5,657lb and auw 7,549. The long range Mk XVI SM410 reached High Post on 28 March and was fitted with the improved rear view hood. Its tare was 5,894lb and auw 8,302, including all internal tanks full. TE190 was similar to SM410 but when weighed at High Post on 26 April its tare was 5,757lb and auw 7,558, and the full fuel load was not carried.

SL604 was fitted with a metal elevator and flown for trials in October 1945. The elevator was specially selected by A.I.D. inspectors and the handling qualities were described as excellent.

OFFICIAL REPORTS ON Mk XVI

Boscombe Down, November 1944. MK850. Merlin 266. Oil cooling and radiator suitability on climbs at combat rating. 100 and 150 octane fuel. Satisfactory.

Vickers-Armstrongs, 1 March 1945. SM205. Flight trials with various types of bombs. Handling trials with (a) 1 × 500lb cluster bomb slung under fuselage (No 6); (b) 1 × 500lb cluster bomb (No 7) slung under fuselage; (c) 3 × 200lb smoke floats carried under each wing and one under fuselage and (d) 4 × 10lb practice bombs carried on light series carriers, one under each wing making a total of eight bombs in all. A flight was made at each of the above conditions plus a dive to 470mph. No unusual effects were observed.

Vickers-Armstrongs, 27 April 1945. TB757. Handling trials with RPs on zero length rails, two 60lb RPs under each wing. Handling characteristics considered satisfactory.

Boscombe Down, June 1945. SM410. Brief spinning trials. Rear view fuselage and rear fuel tanks. Satisfactory.

Boscombe Down, June 1945. TB232. Handling with a 90 gallon drop tank and 2 × 250lb GP bombs under wings. With rear tank full the tests were made to simulate operational conditions. Owing to the sustained, short period, longitudinal pitching oscillation and bad directional characteristics, it was recommended that the aircraft would only be suitable for flying by experienced Spitfire pilots in good visibility. It was considered that aiming of bombs for accurate gunnery would be difficult under the conditions tested.

Boscombe Down, June 1945. TL757. Attitude measurements with Mk VIII RP installation. 8 × 60lb head RPs in tier on four zero length launchers. Auw 8,225lb.

Vickers-Armstrongs, 3 July 1945. SM410. Spinning trials. Auw 8,100lb. Spins at 20,000 and 30,000ft. Pre-stall wing root buffeting occurred during initial trials, this having an adverse effect on recovery. Trials postponed until modifications to engine cowling and fillets made. Satisfactory.

Boscombe Down, 11 June 1948. TE241. Mk4 Hispano cannon. Trials of Gyro Gunsight Mk4B installation. In the view of A&AEE the installation was unacceptable for service use.

Vickers-Armstrongs, 8 October 1945. Six Mk XVI Spitfires from CBAF fitted with the factory's elevators were tested at High Post for any inconsistency in handling which might have been attributable to variations in the elevators. Auws 7,450lb 6.2ins CoG. Only one elevator acceptable without trailing edge beading being fitted. Therefore, all Mk XVIs should have TE beading and the modification introduced ASAP.

F Mk XVI and LF Mk XVI

Wing. Planform elliptical; section NACA Series 2200; incidence° root +2, tip $-\frac{1}{2}$; dihedral° 6; thickness% root 13.2, tip 6; aspect ratio 5.68; area 220 nett, gross 242; chord (geo) 6.38, (ma) 7.01. Ailerons. Area 18.9; movement° up 26, down 19; droop ⅜. Flaps. Area 15.4; movement° down 85.

Below: SL669 served with No 501 Squadron.

Above: SL666, No 65 Squadron, RAF Wattisham, 1947.

Top: SL721 seen at Blackbushe in August 1973 when it was G-BAUP. Above: Seen while serving as the personal aircraft of ACM Sir James M. Robb, based at Northolt.

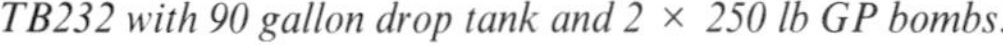
TB232 with 90 gallon drop tank and 2 × 250 lb GP bombs.

TE288 at Canterbury War Museum, New Zealand. It has since been replaced by a GRP replica and moved to Woodbourne.

Tailplane. Area. 31.46 (late a/c 33.84); chord (ma) 4.0; incidence° root 0, tip ± $\frac{1}{2}$; dihedral° 0. Elevators. Area 13.26 (late a/c 13.74); movement° up 28, down 23. Tab area 0.76 (later a/c 0.69); movement° up 20, down 7. Fin area 4.51. Rudder. Area 8.23 (later a/c 10.0); movement° 28 each way. Tab area 0.35 (later a/c 0.89); movement° port 18, starbd 6.

Undercarriage. Wheels Dunlop AH2061 or AH10019; tyres Dunlop IJ 13 or 17 or IK 13 or 17; Oleo pressure 465 (later a/c 380); tyre pressure 57 or 54. Tailwheel fixed castoring. Wheel Dunlop AH2184/IX, tyre TA 12 or 14. Oleo pressure 242; tyre pressure 47.

Engine/s. Packard Merlin 266. 1,372hp. Take off 1,372 (MS) @ 3,000rpm + 12lb boost; combat rating (max 5mins) 1,702 @ 3,000 @ 5,500 (MS) + 18; 1,630 @ 3,000 @ 16,500ft (FS) + 18; 1,410hp @ 2,850 @ 9,000ft + 12 (MS): 1,315 @ 2,850 @ 19,000 + 12 (FS). Electric starting.

Propeller/s. Rotol R12/4F5/4 4-blade Jablo or Hydulignum pitch range 35° fine pitch 22° 20′. Diameter 10ft 9in.

Coolant. 70% distilled water, 30% Glycol. Main system 14$\frac{1}{2}$ gals, intercooler 4$\frac{1}{2}$.

Fuel. 100 octane; 150 for +25lb boost.
Capacity fuselage (upper) 48 gals, lower 37. Total 85. Plus 45, 50, 90 and 170 gal o/ld tanks.

Oil. 7.5 or 14.4 for ferrying.

Weights. Tare 5,894, take off 8,288.5, max overload 9,500 LF Mk XVI.

SERIAL NUMBERS

VICKERS-ARMSTRONG (CASTLE BROMWICH) LTD.
Contract No. B1981687/39
Ninth order for 2,190 Spitfire Mk VC dated 28 May 1942. Built as Mks VC/IX/XVI between July 1943 and May 1944. A single **Mk XVI** built to this ninth order; MJ556.

Twelfth order for 1,500 Spitfire Mk 21 dated 17 July 1943. Contract cancelled, then amended to 673 Mk IX. Built as Mks IX/XVI between June and October 1944. The following serials apply to Mk XVIs built to this order; PV288, 295, 307, 327 and 349.

Thirteenth order for 100 Spitfire Mk IX dated 25 October 1943. Built as MKs IX/XVI between August and October 1944. The following serials apply to XVIs built to this order; RK840, 842, 849, 859, 865-866, 868, 883, 888, 891-893, 895-897, 902-905, 910, 913, 918, 921 and 925-926.

Fourteenth order for 73 Spitfire Mk IX dated 16 November 1943. Built as Mks IX/XVI between August and October 1944. The following serials apply to Mk XVIs built to this order; RR205, 212-213, 226-227, 229-230, 234, 236, 240, 242-243, 245, 247-250, 255-257, 261, 263 and 265.

Fifteenth order for 700 Spitfire Mk 21 dated 20 January 1944. Contract cancelled in August 1944. Partially re-instated for 40 Spitfire Mk IX. Built as Mk XVI between June and July 1945; RW344-359 and 373-396.

Sixteenth order for 800 Spitfire Mk 21 dated 1 February 1944. Contract cancelled in August 1944. Partially re-instated for 558 Spitfire Mk IX. Built as Mk IX/XVI between September and November 1944. The following serials apply to F Mk XVIs built to this order; SL541-565, 567-571, 573-579, 596-602, 604-605, 607-611, 613-618, 620-624, 666, 668-676, 678-681, 685, 687-690, 713, 715, 717-721, 724-725, 727-728, 733, 745, SM178-213, 226-239, 241-258, 273-316, 329-369, 383-424, 426-427, 464-485, 487-488, 503, 507, 511-512, 516, 538, 646, 648, 664-665, 667 and 670-671. Cancelled were; SL667, 682-684, 686, 722-723, 726, 729-732, 734-744, 746-747, 759-798, 812-857, 873-915, 928-959, 971-999, and SM112-134 (257)

Seventeenth order for 1,884 Spitfire Mk IX dated 19 April 1944. Built as Mks IX/XVI between December 1944 and June 1945. The following serials apply to Mk XVIs built to this order; TA739, 741, 759, 809, TB130-132, 136-141, 232, 237, 244-248, 250, 252, 254-256, 269-308, 326-349, 352-392, 394-396, 475-476, 478, 480-481, 492-498, 501-502, 515,; 517, 519-522, 525-526, 528, 549, 572, 574, 578, 580-583, 585, 588-598, 613-637, 639, 675, 702, 709, 713-716, 733-735, 737-739, 741-759, 828-829, 831-836, 858-868, 883-908, 910-913, 915-917, 919, 921-923, 989-991, 993, 995-999, TD113-154, 156-158, 176-177, 184-191, 229-267, 280-286, 288-289, 293, 316-325, 338-351, 369, 372, 375-377, 400-408, TE116, 119-120, 174-196, 198-204, 206-210, 214, 228-229, 235, 237, 239-259, 273-288, 291, 300, 302, 310-311, 314, 328, 330, 332, 334-335, 338-342, 344-359, 375-385, 387-408 and 434-471, 473-480(632). TE386 and 472 cancelled. Also TD409-428, 443-490, 515-546, 560-605, 618-649, 660-706, 720-766, 783-815, 829-866, 884-925 and 937-951. Total built 1,053.

All F XVI Spitfires were, basically, the F IX powered by the Packard/Merlin M266. They were primarily intended for the low to medium altitude role and carried the designation LF XVI. A small number were built for specialist operations and some had alternate engines. These are specified.

MJ556 First Spitfire to have M266 instal, Dec '43 19MU 7-5-45 19S 25-4-46 FAAC 15-8 RHAF 1-4-49

PV288 XVIE 8MU 13-10-44 322S 9-11 CB ops 24-3-45 WAL rect E SOC 23-5
PV295 XVIE 45MU 3-10-44 CFE 30-10 comp trls with FIX, perf identical AFDU 2-11 COAL mods 1-5-45 29MU 21-9-46 bou sold scrap 3-9-47
PV307 45MU 3-10-44 66S 30-11 FTR ops 15-12
PV327 XVIE BHAM 24 45MU 2-10-44 322S 9-11 420RSU 8-3-45 DeH 12-4 recat E SOC 23-5
PV349 BHAM 24 45MU 3-10-44 1277S 9-11 CAC ops 15-12 420RSU ASTH 20-2-45 567S 4-10 RHAF 4-5-49

RK840 BHAM 24 45MU 3-10-44 322S 9-11 FTR ops 28-1-45
RK842 BHAM 24 45MU 3-10-44 66S 30-11 CAC ops 1-4-45
RK849 BHAM 24 45MU 3-10-44 127S 1-11 17SFTS 4-4-46 air coll with TM862 nr Digby CA 30-4
RK859 BHAM 24-45MU 3-10-44 127S 9-11 CE ops 202-45 SOC 23-2
RK866 9MU 12-10-44 322S 9-11 FACE 3-2-45
RK868 33MU 9-10-44 66S 30-11 CE ops 10-12
RK883 45MU 7-10-44 66S 30-11 CAC ops 18-3-45 CE ops 24-4 411RSU 23-5
RK888 9MU 12-10-44 322S 9-11 FTR ops 1-4-45
RK891 45MU 7-10-44 66S 31-10 FACB 29-11 AST 308S 15-3-45 CAC ops 12-4 411RSU 317S 3-5 349S 4-4-46
RK892 33MU 9-10-44 322S 9-11 FTR ops 13-2-45
RK893 9MU 14-10-44 66S 11-12 420RSU 21-12 403S 21-6-45 EAAS(FTC) 17-11-48 CGS 19-11 FRS 19-12-49 scrap 26-4-50
RK895 39MU 7-10-44 322S 9-11 FTR ops 14-2-45
RK896 39MU 7-10-44 66S 9-11 127S 9-11 FTR ops 17-1-45
RK897 33MU 9-10-44 322S 9-11 FTR ops 1-4-45
RK902 8MU 14-10-44 322S 9-11 420RSU 29-3-45 recat E SOC 24-7
RK903 39MU 7-10-44 ROS 13-12 329S 1-3-45 341S 15-3 FACB 21-9
RK904 39MU 7-10-44 322S 9-11 420RSU 11-1-45 CAC ops 322S 24-3 FACE 24-7
RK905 33MU 9-10-44 66S 30-11 CB ops 23-3-45 420RSU 345S 10-5 435S 16-8 61 OTU 21-2-46 to 6419M 25-8-47
RK910 33MU 9-10-44 421S 28-12 CE ops 11-3-45
RK913 9MU 14-10-44 66S 30-11 RSU 22-3-45
RK918 9MU 12-10-44 66S 4-1-45 CE ops dbf 23-3-45
RK921 8MU 19-10-44 322S 9-11 FTR ops 13-2-45
RK925 8MU 13-10-44 322S 25-1-45 420RSU 26-4 FAAC 30-6 453S 25-10 3BRU 26-3-46 CE 7-5
RK926 6MU 19-10-44 127S 11-12 CB ops 23-1-45 ASTH recat E SOC 18-7

RR205 8MU 14-10-44 322S 9-11 312S 1-3-45 FACE 19-3
RR212 8MU 18-10-44 127S 23-11 CAC ops 31-12 420RSU 125S CE ops 6-4-45
RR213 8MU 13-10-44 322S 9-11 e/fd f/ld dbf 26-3-45
RR226 8MU 14-10-44 127S CB ops 18-11 ASTH 5(P)AFU 15-11 7SFTS 15-4-46 to 6180M 6-11 SOC 16-10-48
RR227 8MU 14-10-44 66S 9-11 127S 19-11 FA FTR 29-11
RR229 8MU 14-10-44 127S 9-11 FA FTR 29-11
RR230 8MU 14-10-44 322S 9-11 CAC ops 13-2-45 ASTE recat E SOC 1-6
RR234 9MU 14-10-44 127S 9-11 SOC 9-2-45
RR236 8MU 14-10-44 127S 9-11 FTR ops 23-1-45
RR240 8MU 13-10-44 322S 9-11 CE ops 5-3-45
RR242 39MU 23-10-44 127S 16-11 ASTH 24-4-45 recat E 23-5 SOC 17-7
RR243 8MU 14-10-44 322S 9-11 FAAC 24-9-45 412RSU 349S 1-11 FAAC 21-3-46 411RSU 22-2-46 SOC 28-3-46
RR245 6MU 18-10-44 66S 23-11 84ARF 30-4-45 411S 7-6 401S 28-6 5(P)AFU 13-11 17SFTS 4-4-46
RR247 8MU 19-10-44 66S 11-1-45 84ARF 30-4 340S 24-5 FACE 8-7
RR248 6MU 17-10-44 66S 9-11 127S 9-11 CB ops 26-3-45 1CRU 1-5 recat E 23-5 SOC 21-7
RR249 8MU 13-10-44 322S 9-11 FTR ops 1-4-45
RR250 9MU 14-10-44 127S 4-1-45 349S 26-4 317S 24-5 FACE 11-8
RR255 6MU 17-10-44 66S 9-11 127S 9-11 CE ops 29-12
RR256 39MU 27-10-44 403S 14-12 CAC ops 2-4-45 416S 12-4 FTR ops 19-4
RR257 6MU 17-10-44 127S 25-1-45 78MU 8-3 ROS 61 OTU 25-3-46 302AFS FAAC 3-9-47 NEA 14-11-48 sold Int All 28-3-49
RR261 8MU 14-10-44 66S 28-12 84ARF 30-4-45 485S 21-6 322S 27-9
RR263 66S broad chord rud instal RAF Ken 20-9-45 to 7216M extant France with serial TB597
RR265 6MU 17-10-44 84GSU 31-10 66S 9-11 127S 9-11 CAC ops 15-12 420RSU ASTH 27-2 recat E 28-5 SOC 17-7 Cat 4R — relaxed 61 OTU renamed 203AFS Dec'45 later to 226 OCU 8 OTU renamed 257 OCU Dec'46

RW344 XVIE 33MU 29-6-45 308S 30-8-46 CAC ops 3-9 350S 26-9 BAF BAFO on loan pend del FXIV 26-10
RW345 XVIE CBAF 39MU 26-6-45 33MU 13-10-49 3CAACU 4-6-51 CR Sch Mid Wallop 17-10 NES 13-12-54 RAF Ken for use in film 16-8-55 sold Cox & Darks 30-4-56
RW346 XVIE 39MU 28-6-45 102RFS 13-4-51 29MU 15-10 NES 14-12-54 sold H Bath 16-5-56
RW347 XVIE CBAF 33MU 29-6-45 RHAF 25-4-49
RW348 XVIE COAL mods 10-7-45 EAAS Manby 28-7 501S 15-4-47 f/ld cd CB Glos 6-7-47 recat E SOC 25-7
RW349 CBAF 39MU 30-6-45 103 FRS 17-5-51 BUC C4R 20-8 recat 5 to 6889M 7-9-52
RW350 XVIE CBAF 29MU 2-7-45 MacClarens HAL 1-3-46 65S 26-3-46 SOC area BS 5-2-47
RW351 XVIE CBAF VAHP 12-7-45 6MU 27-7 631S 28-11-47 C4R(S)25-4-51
RW352 XVIE 6MU 30-7-45 7605S 5-5-48 FAAC 20-6 ROS 63Grp Com Flt 10-5-49 AGT Gat refurb 19-1-51 1 OFU Abingdon 30-10-52 MAEF 28-11 187S 25-8-53 3CAACU 14-10 NES 16-8-56 sold En/RM 5-4-57
RW353 XVIE CBAF 39MU 30-6-45 RHAF 14-5-49
RW354 XVIE CBAF 49MU 25-7-45 HAL 21-3-46 65S 10-5 RHAF 13-1-49
RW355 XVIE CBAF 6MU 14-8-45 614S 6-2-47 air coll with TE314 cd Long Sutton Somer pilot kld dbf CE 7-12 SOC 8-1-48
RW356 CBAF 29MU 12-7-45 667S 2-8 61 OTU 27-12 FAAC 20-7-48 ROS recat E 16-11

RW382 became M7245. It now stands outside RAF Uxbridge.

TE330 was presented to the Museum of Air Power, Colorado Springs, USA, at a special ceremony at Odiham. It is now at the USAF Museum, Dayton, Ohio.

TL757 at Boscombe Down, June 1945, for trials of RP launchers. Close up shows 60lb heads.

RW393 gained its all-white colours with No 31 Squadron. It later became 7293M and now guards the gate at RAF Turnhouse (left).

RW357 CBAF 29MU 2-7-45 65S 15-3-46 WAL mods 2-3-49 scrap 20-2-50

RW358 CBAF 2-7-45 604S 8-2 FAAC 12-12-49 ROS CGS 17-12-50 3CAACU 16-11-53 NES 13-12-54 sold L Met 15-5-56

RW359 CBAF 6MU 2-8-45 604S 6-2-47 609S 27-10-49 FA3R 13-7-50 ROS to 6835M 19-2-51

RW373 CBAF 29MU 2-7-45 FATU 22-9 6 OTU 15-3-46 FAAC 1-7 ROS 61 OTU 2-6 20S 25-2-49 NES 19-5-53 C5(C) 29-7

RW374 CBAF 9MU 29-6-45 604S 15-4-47 TAAC 1-6-48 ROS recat E 2-7

RW375 6MU 20-7-45 RNAS LoS 31-1-46

RW376 CBAF 30-6-45 601S 15-4-47 NES 21-10-53 sold R J Coley 3-3-54

RW377 CBAF 9MU 18-7-45 631S 9-8 FAAC 29-9-47 ROS to 6555M 10-5-48 611S Woodvale 30-12-49 scrap 19-1-50

RW378 CBAF 6MU 20-7-45 614S 8-2-47 609S 8-10-48 StA SG1 to 6821M 29-1-51

RW379 CBAF 39MU 30-6-45 RHAF 8-4-49

RW380 29MU 21-3-46 RHAF 29-6-49

RW381 CBAF 6MU 20-7-45 151RU Res pl 3-10-46 GAAC 16-1-47 616S 31-5-48 609S 30-8-48 AGT Gat refurb 10-2-51 5CAACU 23-11-53 NES 13-12-54 sold L Met 15-5-56

RW382 XVIE 6MU 20-7-45 604S 1-4-47 3CAACU 12-6-51 to 7245M @ 609S 28-11-55 repainted as RW729 BoB film extant 8075M RAF Uxbridge

RW383 CBAF 6MU 21-7-45 601S 22-3-48 air coll with SL725 over Woking. F/lndg Shackleford CE 15-6-49 scrap 11-7

RW384 CBAF 29MU 3-8-45 126S 7-3-46 19S 21-3-46 41S 5-12 691S 24-7-47 TAAC 17-2-49 ROS 17S 13-7 3CAACU 15-3-51 FAC5(C) 5-6

RW385 CBAF 9MU 13-7-45 631S 11-8 air coll with SL614 lnd safe CE 16-2-49

RW386 XVIE 6MU 2-8-45 604S 25-3-47 mods 10-4-49 604S to 6944M RAF Tech Coll 24-8-49. To 6944M 14-1-52 (RAK-A). To G-BXVI, extant Bitteswell.

RW387 CBAF 6MU 31-7-45 203AFS 3-11-47 CAC 403GDA 11-8-48 ROS 5S 18-9-50 612S 1-4-51 102FRS 26-4-51 NES 3-4-53 sold J G Will 23-10

RW388 XVIE CBAF 6MU 18-7-45 667S 2-8 FA 30-11 612S 30-4-51 FA3R 3-1-52 offer to Mus New Zealand to 6946M 30-9 con to FMkV AB917 'The Inspirer' for BoB film 10-4-68 con back to RW388 6-10-69 Extant Stoke-on-Trent

RW389 CBAF 29MU 20-8-45 20S 18-7-50 5CAACU 25-9-51 NES 14-12-54 sold E Smelt 13-6-56

RW390 DSFD 29MU 28-8-45 61 OTU 14-1-45 FAAC 15-12-48 ROS recat E 23-3-49

RW391 6MU 30-7-45 501S 18-12-46 FAAC 7-3-48 ROS to 6552M 10-5 E&S Wg Digby

RW392 CBAF COAL mods 19-7-45 6MU 23-8 CGS 21-2-46 eng fail on t/o Lecon C3 3-12-49 ROS recat scr 13-1-50

RW393 602S 1956 personal a/c Air Marshall Sir Williams Elliot to 7293M 3CAACU painted white extant RAF Turnhouse

RW394 CBAF 6MU 25-7-45 601S 9-1-47 3CAACU 19-6 CR Sch M Wallop 17-10-52 FA3R 19-4 ROS FCCRS 25-6 NES 13-12-54 to 7280M @ 614S 10-10-55

RW395 9MU 18-7-45 8 OTU 17-12-46 cd/ldg CE Leuch 13-9-48 SOC

RW396 XVIE CBAF 29MU 24-7-45 CGS 2-4-46 eng fail cd f/lndg West Skipsea Ranges 6-1-49

SL541 CBAF 6MU 11-8-45 501S 1-2-47 FACA 9-11 scrap sold J Dale 9-1-50

SL542 XVIE DSFD 9MU 18-7-45 595S 30-8 695S 28-7-48 1 CAAC 7-12-50 29MU 11-6-51 2CAACU 1-3-54 Stn Flt Dux 1-4-55 58MU 31-1-57 to 8390M extant Coltishall

SL543 DSFD 29MU 25-8-45 Driffield 8-10 ROS 7-12 614S 16-1-47 FAAC 17-7-48 recat E 19-11

SL544 DSFD 29MU 25-8-45 61 OTU 7-3-46 FAAC 7-7-47 recat E 20-1 SOC 11-11

SL545 CBAF 29MU 24-7-45 66 OTU 12-2-46 61 OTU cd lndg Keevil CB 25-3 recat E SOC 19-8

SL546 CBAF 29MU 30-7-45 61 OTU 11-2-46 FAAC 6-4 SOC 29-5-47

SL547 CBAF COAL mods 19-7-45 6MU 29-8 CGS 2-12-46 flapless ldg u/c clpse CE Catf 6-5-47 SOC 29-5

SL548 CBAF 6MU 31-7-45 604S 1-4-47 FA3R 13-11-49 Ken Com Flt 24-11-50 NES 14-12-54 sold H Bath 1-5-56

SL549 6MU 30-7-45 12Grp Com Flt 3-10-47 595S 22-4-48 691S 21-10 17(AAC)S 11-2-49 RFS 21-3-51 45MU 16-11 sold J G Will 28-10-53

SL550 COAL 19-7-45 6MU 23-8 CRD North 21-3-46 Farn July'46 exhaustive gust measure prog with PS914 and PM501 33MU 14-8 FAAC 23-1-47 SOC 21-10

SL551 CBAF 6MU 1-8-45 61 OTU 12-5-47 NEA 14-12-54 sold H Bath 23-5-56

SL552 CBAF 29MU 24-7-45 CAC 26-4-48 sold Inter All 10-2-50

SL553 CBAF 6MU 8-8-45 501S 10-4-47 FTR in snowstorm pres i/sea in Solent off IoW 21-2-48

SL554 CBAF 33MU 5-9-45 203AFS 11-6-49 sold J Dale 13-11

SL555 CBAF 29MU 27-7-45 RHAF 27-6-49

SL556 CBAF 6MU 19-7-45 61 OTU 25-3-46 out of fuel f/ld nr South Molton Devon CE 5-1-48

SL557 CBAF 6MU 17-7-45 667S 2-8 61 OTU 27-12 FAAC 16-4-47 ROS 226 OCU 23-10 sold J Dale 13-11-50

SL558 CBAF 29MU 27-7-45 sold J Dale 1-6-49

SL559 CBAF 29MU 3-8-45 61 OTU 5-2-46 cd lndg pilot kld Keevil CE 14-3 SOC 28-3

SL560 CBAF 29MU 24-7-45 61 OTU 31-1-46 lost fly speed ldg u/s cd Keevil CE 16-4 SOC 25-4

SL561 CBAF 6MU 25-7-45 603S 4-3-47 609S 27-6-48 to 6823M 30-11-50 StA

SL562 DSFD 29MU 25-8-45 61 OTU 19-2-46 FAAC 30-7-47 NEA 15-9 SOC 19-3-48

SL563 CBAF 33MU 23-8-45 CBE 7-3-46 Cent Bomb Est Marham u/c jam w/u ldg CE 18-6 sold E Smelt 10-3-48

SL564 CBAF 6MU 21-7-45 603S 30-1-47 612S 27-1-49 AGT Gat refurb 17-7-51 NEA 14-12-54 sold E Smelt 31-6-56

SL565 CBAF 29MU 8-8-45 St Flt Cole 10-9 218MU 2-5-46 to 6333M 14-5-47

SL567 CBAF 29MU 27-9-45 631S 17-4-46 hvy ldg burst tyre o/t CE Llanb 17-6

SL568 CBAF 6MU 20-7-45 501S 1-2-47 FAAC 21-8 612S 20-5-49 eng fail cd f/lndg nr Dyce CE 27-9-49 scrap 6-10

SL569 CBAF COAL mods 3-8-45 6MU 2-9 CGS 30-9 45MU 21-10-52 NES 3-6-53 sold J G Will 28-10

SL570 COAL mods 19-7-45 6MU 18-2-46 CGS cd/ld Leconfield CB 16-9-48 recat E 30-9

SL571 CBAF 29MU 27-7-45 BCIS Finningley 3-7-46 501S 28-4-47 cd/ld CB 5-10 recat E 23-10 SOC 5-12

SL573 CBAF VA HPS 15-10-45 39MU 19-10 RHAF 31-1-49

SL574 XVIE 6MU 14-8-45 FAAC 28-10-48 CGS 19-7-49 Civilian AA Coop Unit w/u ldg Sth London Sept'49 to 8391M Extant, for San Diego Museum.

SL575 CBAF 6MU 20-7-45 61 OTU 25-3-46 203 AFS swung off peri track hit building Chivenor 23-10-47 39MU 30-11 sold J Dale 8-7-48

SL576 CBAF King Tupou I Tonga No.3 29MU 27-7-45 21 OTU 7-3-46 FAAC 1-7 202 CTU 8-5-47 501S 16-5 FAAC 2-12 ROS recat E 15-9-48

SL577 CBAF 29MU 28-7-45 61 OTU 19-2-46 FAAC 9-2-48 FACE 30-11

SL578 CBAF 6MU 31-7-45 603S 24-10-46 CE scrap 5-6-47

SL579 CBAF 29MU 27-7-45 61 OTU 11-2-48 FAAC 17-10 ROS 203AFS air coll with SL670 i/sea off Hartland Point Devon pilot kld CE 29-10-48

SL596 CBAF 6MU 27-8-45 151RU 1-10-46 349S 12-10 BAF on loan pend del FXIV 26-10 out of fuel f/ld SM 8-8-47 6MU 12-8 CE sold E Smelt 10-3-48

SL597 CBAF COAL mods 3-8-45 6MU 8-9 CGS 30-9 CLEA T2 14-3-50 sold J Dale 13-11

SL598 CBAF COAL mods 23-8-45 6MU 12-10 CRD North 22-11 ROS 14-2-46 33MU 3-12 SOC 7-8-47

SL599 CBAF 6MU 2-8-45 601S 18-10-46 604S 31-10 cd on t/o N Wld CE 23-7-49 scr 13-10

SL600 CBAF 29MU 8-8-45 595S 1-11 FA scrap 28-8-50

SL601 CBAF 33MU 23-8-45 126S 27-2-46 19S 21-3-46 cd ldng Lubeck CB 6-5 3BRU 9-5 recat E 12-6

SL602 CBAF 6MU 1-8-45 1689Flt ADn 28-4-47 NEA 12-4-48 sold Int All 29-3-49

SL604 CBAF VA HPA 31-8-45 29MU 23-10 61 OTU 6-2-46 strk cable cd Oxbridge Devon 9-12 SOC 16-12

SL605 CBAF COAL mods 27-8-45 6MU 11-10 CGS 11-2-46 BUC C3R 17-10-50 recat 5(S) 20-4-51

SL607 no record

SL608 CBAF 39MU 31-8-45 RHAF 30-4-49

SL609 CBAF 6MU 31-7-45 603S 6-6-47 609S 10-4-48 29MU 29-12-50 NES 14-12-54 sold H Bath 1-5-56

SL610 CBAF 33MU 23-8-45 126S 6-3-46 19S 21-3-46 FAAC 7-5 recat B 1-7 351RU 29-8 recat E 31-7

SL611 CBAF 33MU 20-8-45 111 OTU 27-9 29MU 3-1-46 603S 19-2-47 hit mountain f/f Haw-Turn 20-11 wreck found Scawfell Cumber 1-5-48

SL613 CBAF 6MU 10-8-45 FAAC 9-9-46 ROS 49MU 18-9 614S 6-12 604S 29-10-48 6MU 13-4-50 2CAACU 5-9-52 C5(C) 14-12-53

SL614 CBAF 6MU 14-8-45 577S 5-9 631S 27-6-46 20S air coll with RW385 i/sea of Harlech pilot kld 16-2-49 SOC 24-2

RW394 became 7280M in October 1955.

SL576, King Tupou I, Tonga No.3.

SL615 CBAF VA HPA 31-8-45 29MU 18-10 6-4 18-3-47 FACB 14-9-48 hit ldg light BHll 15-9 ROS 34MU 28-9 recat E 25-3-49

SL616 CBAF 6MU 10-8-45 17 OTU 9-9-46 1PRFU 18-8-47 FAC3R 5-4-51 to 6885M 31-8-51 14SoTT SOC 17-7-59

SL617 CBAF VA HPS 31-8-45 29MU 11-10 61 OTU 5-2-46 203AFS w/u ldg CAC Chivenor 8-1-48 NEA 9-2 sold Int All 28-3-49

SL618 CBAF 29MU 30-8-45 61 OTU 19-2-46 203AFS e/fd f/ld cd nr Buckfastleigh Devon CE 23-7-48

SL620 CBAF 1-8-45 501S 24-10-46 cd/ld CB 7-6-47 39MU 30-7 SOC 15-3-48

SL621 CBAF COAL mods 31-8-45 CGS 27-2-46 C3S/R 14-3-50 NES 3-6-53 sold J G Will 28-10

SL622 CBAF 6MU 2-8-45 151RU 8-10-46 CGS 18-8-47 EAAS 9-7-48 FAAC 22-10 ROS recat E 6-12

SL623 CBAF 29MU 8-8-45 RHAF 18-3-49 FA f/f 8-4 ROS Greece 21-6

SL624 CBAF 29MU 2-8-45 111 OTU 7-11 33MU 21-6-46 WAL mods 27-2-49 RHAF 4-7

SL666 CBAF 6MU 16-8-45 695S 5-9 NES 14-12-54 sold E Smelt 13-6-56

SL668 CBAF 33MU 23-8-45 126S 6-3-46 19S 21-3 226 OCU FA3(R) 28-10-49 recat scrap 9-5-50

SL669 CBAF 6MU 8-8-45 501S 24-3-47 FAAC 17-5 GACB 18-10-48 recat E 4-1-49

SL670 29MU 28-7-45 61 OTU 5-2-46 203AFS air coll with SL579 cd nr Bradworth Devon CE 29-10-48

SL671 CBAF 6MU 31-7-45 601S 18-10-46 FAAC 26-7-47 ROS 601S flew i/high grd in cloud Marley Commom Sussex pilot kld CE 12-2-48 SOC 25-2

SL672 CBAF 6MU 23-7-45 614S 22-1-47 FAAC 30-10 ROS 20S 19-4-51 5CAACU 1-10 C5(C) 27-4-54

SL673 CBAF 6MU 1-8-45 501S 29-5-47 CE on insp 4-10-48 AFD 4-1-49

SL674 XVIE 29MU 26-7-45 17 OTU 1-4-46 501S 7-8-47 FAAC 4-9-48 612S 29-4-49 to 8392M extant Biggin Hill

SL675 CBAF 6MU 1-8-45 17 OTU 2-4-46 614S 10-4-47 FAAC 25-11-47 recat E 614S dived i/sea from cloud nr Nells Point Glam pilot kld 17-4-48

SL676 CBAF COAL mods 3-8-45 6MU 29-8 CGS 30-9 air coll with Wellington BJ884 pilot kld co Yorks CE 26-7-46 SOC 8-8

SL678 CBAF 20-8-45 61 OTU 16-1-46 CGS FACE 26-7 SOC 17-8 bboc 6MU 14-10 695S 4-9-47 2CAACU 17-51 C5 9-9-51

SL679 CBAF 39MU 1-10-45 RHAF 9-2-49

SL680 CBAF 6MU 31-7-45 38MU 16-6-47 614S 22-7 612S 21-11-48 FCCS 4-7-51 NES 4-6-56 sold scr 22-10

SL681 CBAF COAL mods 3-8-45 6MU CGS 30-9 604S 6-11-46 FAAC 24-8-47 recat E 10-3-48 sold E Smelt

SL685 CBAF 29MU 27-7-45 61 OTU 5-2-46 43Grp D/A 23-3-49 to 6666M 24-5 Cancelled to 6675M 11-7

SL687 CBAF 33MU 20-8-45 126S 6-3-46 19S 21-3 6MU 1-11 SOC abs 5-2-47

SL688 CBAF 29MU 30-7-45 61 OTU 31-1-46 6MU 12-1-50 NES 28-3-51 sold Cimdal Aluminium 30-8

SL689 CBAF 29MU 20-8-45 61 OTU 11-2-46 63S 10-7-47 203 AFS 22-5-48 TAAF 6-7 ROS 43Grp D/A 25-3-49 recat E 13-4

SL690 DSFD 29MU 25-8-45 19S 13-5-46 9MU 13-11-46 SOC bou 16-10

SL713 CBAF 29MU 20-8-45 102RFS 11-4-51 45MU 30-10 2CAACU 29-4-52 C5 comps 21-12-53

SL715 CBAF VA HPA 6-9-45 29MU 15-10 61 OTU 19-3-46 SOC 22-2-49 sold Int All 1-2-50

SL717 CBAF 29MU 8-8-45 595S 13-9 WAL mods 28-1-49 RHAF 21-8

SL718 CBAF 6MU 27-8-45 26 QJU Wng 7-3-46 33MU 2-7 612S 19-5-49 NES 11-10-54 RAF Dux BoB C5(C) 9-11-54

SL719 CSFD 29MU 31-8-45 603S 10-2-47 609S 25-6-48 FAAC 2-1-49 ROS to 6676M 14-7 scrap 6-10

SL720 CBAF VA HPA 31-8-45 29MU 11-10-61 OTU 2-4-46 611S 27-2-50 236 OCU 4-1-51 FA3R 20-3 45MU dismantled 5-2-54 C5(S) 11-9

SL721 CBAF 6MU 27-8-45 FCCS North 10-10-46 VASM 29-10 Met Com S 5-2-48 FACA 17-7 VASM spcl finish; gun bays removed, con to luggage compartment. Del by M Lithgow to RAF Bovington for use of AOC Ftr Com 17-12 VASM Feb'49 repainted & mods 31S 11-4 CGS 4-8-51 NES 13-12-54 sold F Wilensk 11-2-55 USA 1966 as N8R Sold D Arnold as G-BAUP. Extant San Diego as N8WK

SL724 CBAF 6MU 27-8-45 FATU 28-11 4 OTU 21-3-46 61 OTU 22-5-47 203 AFS hit grd after recover from dive pilot kld Bideford Devon 19-1-48 SOC 22-1

SL725 CBAF COAL 27-8-45 6MU 29-9 CRD North Mar'46 33MU 4-7 601S 6-11 FAAC 12-8-48 ROS 601S air coll with RW383 over Woking cd Byfleet pilot kld 15-6-49 scrap 8-7

SL727 CBAF 29MU 11-8-45 614S 18-3-47 601S 8-10-48 6MU 28-3-50 1689Flt 14-2-51 car 3R 10-7 recat 4R sold MoS 9-11-53

SL728 CBAF 33MU 23-8-45 126S 6-3-46 19S 21-3 33MU 18-10 RHAF Arr 6-8-49

SL733 CBAF 6MU 27-8-45 FATU 28-11 EANS 9-1-47 EAAS 10-12-48 CGS 15-12 to 6701M 5-10-49

SL745 CBAF XVIE VA HPA 31-8-45 BDn 5-10 deter of aftmost CoG; comp trls with ML186 29MU 3-1-46 601S 1-2-47 502S 3-3-50 NES 13-12-54 RAF Ken 16-8-55 used for films sold scrap 30-4-56

SM178 8MU 19-10-44 127S 9-11

SM179 9MU 18-10-44 127S 9-11 CB ops 11-4-45 420RSU ASTH 24-4 recat E SOC 17-7

SM180 8MU 19-10-44 127S 30-11 CB ops 14-2-45 1CRU recat E 28-8 SOC 21-9

SM181 9MU 23-10-44 127S 11-12 CAC ops 1-4-45 349S 26-4 322S 18-10 84GDC 15-11 102FRS 20-4-51 FA3R 6-7 NES 19-5-53 C5 15-7

SM182 45MU 19-10-44 127S 4-1-45 420RSU 26-4 345S 17-5 FAAC 7-8

SM183 45MU 19-10-44 66S 23-11 FACB 13-12 420RSU recat E SOC

SM184 9MU 27-10-44 453S 9-11-hvy ldg u/c clpse CE Hawk 18-5-45 SOC 29-5

SM185 33MU 1-11-44 453S 23-11 183S 21-6-45 567S 5-7 587S SOC 26-7

SM186 6MU 17-10-44 127S 9-11 349S 26-4-45 317S 24-5 341S 18-10 350S 18-1-46 FACB 25-3 recat E 2-5

SM187 9MU 28-10-44 453S 9-11 CE ops 24-12

SM188 39MU 27-10-44 453S 23-11 CE ops 20-3-45 SOC 29-3

SM189 8MU 30-10-44 2nd TAF rear HQ 13-1-45 443S 1-2 GACB 19-4 410RSU

SM190 8MU 30-10-44 403S 14-12 AM(PR8) 14-6-45 GACB 6-9 403RSU

SM191 8MU 1-11-44 421S 28-12 CAC ops 3-2-45 410RSU 416S 5-7 83GOC 20-9 SOC 5-10

SM192 45MU 19-10-44 66S 23-11 151RU 22-3-45 SAL 4-4 recat E SOC 28-5

SM193 9MU 23-10-44 453S 9-11 183S 9-2-45 567S 5-7 to 5979M 3-7-46

SM194 CBAF 33MU 28-10-44 453S 10-11 CAC ops 4-12 AST 595S RHAF 5-3-49

SM195 39MU 24-10-44 ROS 10-11 302S 25-1-45 CB ops 16-2 recat E SOC 28-5

SM196 9MU 23-10-44 127S 21-11 420RSU 30-11 ASTH 12-2-45 recat E 28-5

SM197 8MU 19-10-44 84GDC 15-10-45 29MU 15-11 17SFTS 27-2-46 eng fail on app Barkston Heath CB 5-6 recat E SOC 20-6

SM198 9MU 6-11-44 229S 30-11 692S 16-8-45 691S 16-8 5S 3-4-50 3FRS 29-8-51 2CAACU 31-12-52 NEA 13-5-53 C5 29-7

SM199 BHAM 24 45MU 18-11-44 451S 8-2-45 577 S 23-6 bou sold scrap 3-9-47

SM200 8MU 30-10-44 416S 11-1-45 403S 15-2 416S 22-2 83GDC 4-10 SOC 23-10

SM201 8MU 30-10-44 421S CAC ops 27-12 410RSU 421S FTR ops 22-1-45

SM202 6MU 19-10-44 66S 23-11 CAC ops 8-2-45 410RSU recat E 23-5 SOC 21-7

SM203 8MU 30-10-44 403S 14-12 CAC ops 23-1-45 410RSU 403S 15-2 412S 24-5 402S 28-6 sold E Smelt 21-6-49

SM204 8MU 1-11-44 421S 28-12 443S 22-22-45 CE 403RSU 16-9 3BRU 4-10

SM205 CRD VA HPS 27-10-44 fly trls (J Quill) with No.6 Cluster Bomb (500lb under fus) with dive to 450ASI 20-1-45 repeat trls with No.7 Cluster bomb (500lb fus mount) 27-2 3 × 200lb. smoke floats, one under each wng, one fus; plus seperate trls with 4 × 10lb practice bombs on light carr Total of 8 bombs (Shea-Simmonds) 1-3 9MU 12-3 302S 5-4 SOC bou 24-10-47

SM206 33MU 30-10-44 403S 14-12 410RSU 4-1-45

SM207 39MU 23-10-44 453S 23-11 CAC ops 14-3-45 ROS 567S 5-7 to 5908M

SM208 8MU 30-10-44 403S 14-12 410RSU 25-1-45 403S FTR ops 19-3

SM209 9MU 23-10-44 66S 14-1-45 FACE 23-2-45

SM210 45MU 19-10-44 66S 14-12 cd Hoogerand Holland CB 6-2-45

SM211 39MU 23-10-44 66S 30-11 FTR ops 25-12

SM212 CBAF coll with RR223 at CB before del 19-10-44 33MU 10-2-45 340S 8-3 CE ops 9-3

SM213 6MU 23-10-44 66S 4-1-45 CB ops 23-3 151RU 341S 12-4 GACB 6-6 411RSU CE 14-6

SM226 6MU 27-10-44 127S 11-12 SOC E 19-2-45

SM227 45MU 1-11-44 416S 11-1 45 FTR ops 25-2

SM228 22MU 29-11-44 416S FTR ops 24-12

SM229 6MU 1-11-44 416S 21-1 403S 15-2-45 416S FTR ops 9-3

SM230 6MU 27-10-44 453S 9-11 183S 21-6-45 strk hanger on app CE Hawk 29-6 1-7

SM231 CBAF 33MU 27-10-44 66S CB ops 26-12 420RSU recat E SOC 5-3-45

SM232 8MU 30-10-44 416S 21-12 CAC ops 12-2-45 410RSU 416S DOD s/dn in flames by Mustangs FTR 31-3

SM233 39MU 27-10-44 453S 23-11 FTR ops 18-3-45

SM234 6MU 1-11-44 602S 20-11 FAAC 11-12 ROS CE ops 11-4-45 SOC 19-4

SM235 6MU 4-11-44 602S 20-11 17SFTS 1-12-45 SOC 10-2-47

SM236 9MU 23-10-44 66S 11-12 CB ops 6-2-45 recat E SOC 12-3

SM237 6MU 23-10-44 127S 11-12 409RSU 29-3-45 ASTH 4-5 recat E 23-5 SOC 17-7

SM238 8MU 30-10-44 421S CB ops 5-1-45 421S FTR ops 24-2

SM239 6MU 30-10-44 421S 28-12 CE ops 25-3-45 SOC 10-4

SM241 8MU 27-10-44 83GSU 26-11 FACE 18-12

SM242 9MU 30-10-44 421S 28-12 FTR ops 19-4-45

SM243 CBAF 33MU 28-10-44 453S 23-11 183S 21-6-45 567S 5-7 to 5964M Empire Rad Schl Debden

SM244 8MU 27-10-44 453S 9-11 FTR ops 21-2-45 SOC 1-3

SM245 8MU 27-10-44 3501SU 10-11 610TU 12-1-46 203AFS 1-7-47 226 OCU 14-6-49 scr 24-1-50

SM246 6MU 27-10-44 127S 4-1-45 FTR ops 1-4

SM247 39MU 23-10-44 66S 9-11 ROS COAL mods 11-7-45 CGS 2-9 to 6323 RNAF Langham 22-4-47

SM248 8MU 27-10-44 403S 14-12 416S 23-12 CE ops 24-3-45 SOC 28-4

SM249 45MU 30-10-44 453S 11-11 FAAC 1-3-45 recat E 28-5 SOC 21-7

SM250 45MU 30-10-44 453S 11-11 183S 21-6-45 567S 5-7 FAAC 14-9 recat E SOC 27-9

SM251 8MU 30-10-44 403S 14-12 CB ops 11-2-45 410RSU DeH 20-3 recat E SOC 21-6

SM252 9MU 30-10-44 421S 28-12 6MU 6-1-49 sold E Smelt 21-6

SM253 6MU 30-10-44 127S 16-11 340S 10-5-45 FAAC 7-8 420RSU 16-8 recat E 13-9

SM254 6MU 1-11-44 602S 23-11 FAAC 9-12 ROS 659S 19-10-45 619S 23-1-47 SOC 27-4-48 sold BRL Alloys 29-4

SM255 6MU 30-10-44 453S 20-11 FTR ops 21-2-45

SM256 29MU 30-10-44 453S 21-11 FAAC 11-5-45 recat E SOC 25-5

SM257 33MU 4-11-44 602S 27-11 CAC ops 1-12 FTR ops 10-2-45

SM258 CBAF 33MU 28-10-44 403S 14-12 410RSU 11-1-45 recat E 23-5 SOC 21-7

SM273 29MU 30-10-44 127S 11-12 CE ops 1-4-45 Farn Nov'48 weather trls Tang July'49 photo fly sessions wilth Lancaster FM201 Farn spin trls

SM274 8MU 4-11-44 416S 21-12 410RSU 11-1-45 DeH 28-3 recat E 22-4

SM275 6MU 4-11-44 421S 28-12 410RSU 25-2-45 ASTE 26-3 recat E SOC 1-6

SM276 CBAF 33MU 28-10-44 602S 23-11 5(P)AFU 15-11 17SFTS 14-1-46 to 6176M 6-11 6SoTT 16-10-48

SM277 8MU 27-10-44 416S FTR ops 27-12

SM278 CBAF 33MU 28-10-44 453S 10-11 183S 21-6-45 567S 5-7 hit high grd in bad weather Arden Great Moor Yorks 16-9 SOC 27-9

SM279 no record

SM280 CBAF no record

SM281 CBAF no record

SM282 CBAF 33MU 28-10-44 453S 10-11 183S 21-6-45 567S 5-7 ETPS Farn 15-4-47 hand trls; June'48 instrument displays High Ercall 4-11-49 radar app and land; spin trls 29MU 10-11 sold H Bath 9-11-50

SM283 CBAF 39MU 28-10-44 66S 11-12 CAC ops 23-1-45 420RSU CAC ops 13-2

SM284 CBAF 8MU 28-10-44 421S 28-12 412S 24-5-45 402S 23-6 to 6637M @ 612S 10-2-49

SM285 39MU 7-11-44 403S 14-12 CAC ops 31-3-45 410RSU 691S 30-8 bou sold scrap 3-9-47

SM286 6MU 28-10-44 83GSU std ldg u/c torn off drop tank fire CE Tang 11-12

SM287 9MU 30-10-44 602S 27-11 61 OTU 7-2-46 208AFS i/sea off Ilfracombe pilot kld 31-5-49 SOC 9-9

SM288 9MU 2-11-44 602S 27-11 17SFTS 1-12-45 e/fd after t/o a/c turned back to base w/u ldg short of runway CE Harlaxton 14-6-46 SOC 29-7

SM290 CBAF 33MU 28-10-44 403S 4-12 410RSU 4-2-45 NEA 1-7 sold H Bath 27-10-49

SM291 8MU 1-11-44 403S 14-12 CAC ops 2-3-45 412S 28-6 sold E Smelt 21-6-49

SM292 9MU 27-10-44 74S CAC ops 21-3-45 411RSU 127S 10-5 340S 17-5 84GDC 15-11 sold H Bath 27-10-49

SM293 8MU 30-10-44 421S 28-12 FACE 4-5-45

SM294 CBAF 33MU 28-10-44 403S 14-12 CAC ops 31-3-45 443S 12-4 CAC ops 24-4 410RSU

SM295 45MU 1-11-44 403S 14-12 CE ops 17-4-45

SM296 9MU 30-10-44 602S 23-11 66S 23-11 CE ops 4-1-45 420RSU AST 2-3 SOC 5-3

SM297 CBAF 39MU 28-10-44 66S 11-12 420RSU 14-12

SM298 39MU 28-10-44 66S 11-12 420RSU 14-12

SM299 CBAF 33MU 29-10-44 66S 11-12 CAC ops 22-1-45 151RU 30-8 3BRU

SM300 CBAF 9MU 29-11-44 403S 26-2-45 CB ops 24-3 DeH recat E SOC 21-6

SM301 9MU 2-11-44 602S 23-11 FAAC 28-12 ROS 61OTU 12-1-46 w/u ldg Chivenor 8-1-48 to 6553M 10-5-48

SM302 45MU 1-11-44 403S 14-12 410RSU 29-3-45

SM303 8MU 1-11-44 416S CE ops 26-12

SM304 CBAF 8MU 28-10-44 416S 21-12 CE ops 3-1-45

SM305 6MU 30-10-44 School of AS Old Sarum 11-1-45 302S 25-1 CB ops 3-3 recat E 23-4 SOC 15-5

SM306 9MU 6-11-44 229S 30-11 FTR ops 11-1-45

SM307 9MU 6-11-44 602S 25-11 CAC ops 19-1-45 ROS 17EFTS 3-12 to 6175M 6-11-46

SM308 8MU 4-11-44 416S CAC 24-12 410RSU 403S 15-2-45 203AFS 18-3-49 2CAACU 4-9-51 C5 16-12-53

SM309 45MU 6-11-44 421S 28-12 CAC ops 15-3-45 410RSU 17SFTS 11-22-46 eng fail w/u lndg Harlaxton CB 28-3 recat E SOC 23-5

SM310 45MU 1-11-44 416S 21-12 e/a dbf 1-1-45

SM311 9MU 2-11-44 421S 28-12

SM312 6MU 30-10-44 403S 14-12 410RSU 29-3-45

SM313 9MU 2-11-44 403S 14-12 FTR ops 15-3-45

SM314 33MU 4-11-44 421S 28-12 443S CAC ops 8-2-45 410RSU 443S FTR ops 31-3

SM315 6MU 1-11-44 403S 14-12 FACE 14-4-45

SM316 9MU 7-1-45 329S 1-3 341S 15-3 403S 19-4 609S 25-4-49 eng fail f/lndg ne Yeadon DBF CE 2-5 scrap 16-5

SM329 8MU 1-11-44 443S 18-1-45 FACB 4-10 151RU recat E SOC 14-2-46

SM330 6MU 6-11-44 83GSU CB ops 9-12 AST COAL mods 13-7-45 CGS 17-12-46 CFS 2-2-48 scrap 26-5-49

SM331 6MU 4-11-44 416S CB ops 24-12 410RSU AST 14-3-45 recat E SOC 17-7

SM332 8MU 28-10-44 3501SU 10-11 eng fire in air CB 21-1-45 ASTH 61 OTU 17-1-46 FACA 10-4 ROS recat SOC 29-8

SM333 39MU 30-11-44 451S 21-12 CE ops 14-1-45 SOC 31-1

SM334 9MU 6-11-44 229S 6-12 410RSU 28-12 recat E SOC 21-7-45

SM335 33MU 6-11-44 416S FTR ops 23-12 cancel recat B ASTH SOC 28-5-45

SM336 6MU 11-1-44 403S CB ops 18-12 410RSU 21-12 e/a CE 1-1-45

SM337 33MU 6-11-44 229S 1-12 603S CAC ops 15-3-45 ROS 17STFS 29-1-46 bou sold scrap 3-9-47

SM338 8MU 4-11-44 403S 14-12

SM339 6MU 6-11-44 229S 1-12 FAAC 30-12 ROS 303S 15-2-45 595S 8-11 WAL 4-3-49 mods; mods cancel scrap 20-2-50

SM340 9MU 6-11-44 229S 11-12 603S FAAC 14-2-45 ROS 287S 30-8 CFS 17-4-47 FAAC 13-11 ROS HQ MC Com S 23-3-48 sold E Smelt 21-6-49

SM341 39MU 7-11-44 602S 23-11 FAAC 3-2-45 ROS sold E Smelt 21-6-49

SM342 45MU 9-11-44 602S 22-12 VA 15-3-49 mods and con RHAF 22-7

SM343 9MU 2-11-44 602S 23-11 229S 30-11 AM(PR8) 2-9-45 SOC 11-3-46

SM344 33MU 4-11-44 229S 1-12 287S 30-8-45 SOC 10-10-46

SM345 6MU 4-11-44 416S 11-1-45 CAC ops 22-1-45 410RSU 443S 1-2-45 412S 24-5 402S 28-6 NEA 5-8 sold H Bath 27-10-49

SM346 45MU 6-11-44 451S 21-12 fire in flt f/ld cd CE 14-3-45

SM347 6MU 6-11-44 416S 11-1-45 CB ops 14-2 recat E SOC 28-5

SM348 9MU 6-11-44 229S 30-11 416S 28-12 603S 18-1-45 ROS 453S 22-3 183S 21-6 587S 5-7 691S 20-6-46 595S eng fail cd f/lndg nr Carmarthen CE SOC 31-1-49

SM349 9MU 2-11-44 416S 21-12 410RSU 4-1-45 DeH 3-4 recat E 23-5

SM350 33MU 4-11-44 602S 23-11 5(P)AFU 14-1-46 bou sold scr 3-9-47

SM351 6MU 6-11-44 602S 23-11 SOC 17-12-45

SM352 6MU 6-11-44 602S 23-11 coll with SM358 ldg CAC Swann 15-1-45 ROS 61 OTU 7-2-46 607S 27-2-50 sold J Dale 18-12

SM353 6MU 4-11-44 602S 23-11 air coll with 538 nr Swann CAC 15-3-45 ROS SOC 19-11

SM354 45MU 6-11-44 416S 21-12 CAC ops 27-2-45 410RSU AST 10-4 recat E SOC 23-5

SM355 45MU 2-11-44 84GSU 8-1-45 FAAC 16-1 420RSU 66S 1-2 FACE 5-3

SM356 BHAM 24 9MU 19-11-44 CFE 22-2-45 AFDS FAAC 15-10 ROS 61 OTU 21-22-46 17S 9-2-49 5S 6-4-50 C4R recat scr 5-5

SM357 9MU 6-11-44 229S 30-11 603S FAAC 18-1-45 ROS 595S 3-11-46 FAAC 11-2 ROS recat E SOC 6-8-48

SM358 45MU 15-11-44 602S 22-12 strk in rear by SM352 ldg CE Swann 15-1-45 ASTH RHAF 21-6-49

SM359 45MU 6-11-44 421S 28-12 612S 26-4-49 VA 27-9-50 recat 5(S) 29-1-53

SM360 229S 1-12-44 631S 23-8-45 FAAC 23-7-48 to 6597M 20-9

SM361 33MU 9-11-44 602S 23-11 ROS 13-12 CE ops 24-3-45 SOC 31-3

SM362 33MU 6-11-44 451S 29-12 164S 14-6-45 577S 28-6 SOC 6-9

SM363 39MU 7-11-44 403S CAC ops 18-12 410RSU recat E SOC 7-7-45

SM364 8MU 4-11-44 421S 23-11 CAC ops 13-1-45 410RSU FTR ops 26-4

SM365 9MU 6-11-44 416S 21-12 CB ops 21-2-45 410RSU DeH 12-4 recat E SOC 23-5

SM366 33MU 9-11-44 421S 28-12 412S 24-5-45 402S 28-6 sold J Dale 1-6-49

SM367 9MU 6-11-44 229S 30-11 631S 30-8-45 695S 3-10-46 TAAC 7-6-48 ROS 34S C4R 31-1-50 recat scr

SM368 9MU 9-11-44 83GSU 20-12 en/ac CE 1-1-45 410RSU SOC 28-3

SM369 9MU 6-11-44 416S 21-12 e/a CE 1-1-45

SM383 6MU 9-11-44 416S 11-1-45 443S 15-2 FTR ops 21-4

SM384 39MU 9-11-44 451S 21-12 CE ops 14-1-45 SOC 31-1

SM385 9MU 9-11-44 229S 6-12 603S CAC ops 10-3-45 ROS 287S 30-8 to 6008M RAF Selection Brd Framewood Manor SOC 28-5-51

SM386 33MU 30-11-44 416S 11-1-45 403S 15-2 s/dn in flames by Mustangs DOD FTR 31-3

SM387 39MU 9-11-44 416S CAC ops 25-12 410RSU e/a CE 1-1-45 DeH recat E SOC 23-5

SM388 39MU 10-11-44 602S 23-11 CB ops 17-3-45 recat E SOC 12-7

SM389 9MU 9-11-44 416S 11-1-45 403S 15-2 CB ops 2-3 ASTH recat E SOC 18-7

SM390 9MU 6-11-44 229S 6-12 FACB 23-12 AST WAL mods 15-5-45 5(P)AFU 2-11 7SFTS 15-4-46 to 6201M 15-11 6SoTT SOC 9-7-51

SM391 39MU 21-11-44 451S 21-12 164S 14-6-45 577S 30-6 to 6000M 2SoTT

SM392 9MU 9-11-44 421S 28-12 83GSU 26-7-45 SOC 12-9

SM393 9MU 9-11-44 421S 11-1-45 FTR ops 23-1

SM394 VA HPS 6-11-44 fly trls with Lithgow, Quill & Shea-Simmonds. Bad ails with longitud istab; wng tips fitt resulting in poor rate of roll. Mk V wng tips instal, a/c more unstable. New elev instal 16-12-44, wng tips removed 33MU 15-1-45 451S 13-2 164S 14-6 577S 28-6 to 6004M 2SoTT

SM395 BHAM 24 45MU 18-11-44 302S 25-1-45 CAC ops 26-4 411RSU 317S 18-5 FACB 20-5 recat E SOC 7-7

SM396 6MU 9-11-44 229S 1-12 603S air coll with TB396 nr Palling Norfolk CE 24-3-45 SOC 31-3

SM397 33MU 9-11-44 416S 11-1 403S 15-2-45 416S CAC ops 7-4 410RSU 67MU 9-8 ROS

SM398 33MU 9-11-44 302S 8-2-45 CB ops 3-3 DeH 5-5 recat E SOC 21-6

SM399 BHAM 24 9MU 9-11-44 410RSU 11-1-45 416S 1-2 403S 15-2 416S 22-2 CE ops 18-3

SM400 39MU 30-11-44 602S 20-12 11AGS 3-5-46 43Grp D/A surplus 23-10 NEA 22-11 SOC abs 5-2-47

SM401 9MU 9-11-44 229S 6-12 631S 30-8-45 611S caught fire during maintenance CE Sealand 21-11-47 SOC 11-12

SM402 6MU 9-11-44 453S 13-12 183S 12-6-45 452S 5-7 to 5973M 2-7-46 SOC 8-9-51

SM403 9MU 9-11-44 416S 21-12 a/c CE 1-1-45

SM404 9MU 9-11-44 416S 21-12 CAC ops 24-2 416S DOD CE wrecked by AA fire 17-3

SM405 6MU 9-11-44 229S 1-2-45 603S CAC 9-3 ASTE recat E 30-5

SM406 BHAM 24 6MU 19-11-44 341S 13-9-45 84GDC 15-11 17S 12-2-49 C4R scrap 25-9-50

SM407 45MU 9-11-44 302S 25-1-45 151RU 13-5-46 VA 13-6 recat E 9-6-47

SM408 BHAM 24 9MU 19-11-44 83GSU 5-1-45 FAAC 28-1 ROS 443S 1-3 CAG 25-4 410RSU bou

SM409 BHAM 24 6MU 19-11-44 302S 18-1-45 FACE 31-7

SM410 1st CBAF XVI with rear view fus and rear fuel tank CRD HPS 30-3-45 Trls a/c pilots Quill, Shea-Simmonds. Metal elev instal 7-4 trls with same, good results. Rear fuel tank full, a/c unstable @ 10,000ft. ML186's elev instal to cure fore and aft stab No change. Trls end 15-5 BDn 14-6 spin trls. High stall speed due to bad fitt eng cowl (Quill complained about this and said it had an exaggerated balloon shape). Complete empannage of ML186 instal. Tail para. Eng cowl covered fabric and doped. 33MU 20-8 102RFS 10-4-51 2CAACU 11-1-54 NES 4-6-56 sold British Aluminium 22-10

SM411 XVIE 421S 83GSU 103FRS 3CAACU BoB film later 7242M. Extant, Poland.

SM412 33MU 15-11-44 302S 18-1-45 FTR ops 13-2

SM413 6MU 9-11-44 229S 1-12 692S 16-8-45 691S 14-8 sold scr bou 3-9-47

SM414 45MU 9-11-44 416S 18-1-45 403S 15-2 412S 24-5 FACE 9-6 9-6 SOC 21-6

SM415 BHAM 24 45MU 18-11-44 10FPP ff to 83GSU strk by RN116 on ldg CE Westh 4-1-45

SM416 39MU 10-11-44 229S 1-12 603S FAAC 14-6-45 ROS 1362Flt 16-8 Stn Flt Turn 11-7-46 CE 19-8-48

SM418 39MU 30-11-44 451S 21-12 FAAC 9-2-45 ROS 164S 14-6 577S 5-7 695S 12-7 61 OTU 17-4-47 to 6417M 23-8-47

SM419 33MU 18-12-44 302S CAC ops 10-2-45 151RU 18-6-46 bou sold scr 3-9-47

SM420 HAL 24-11-44 VA HPA 15-3-45 MacLaren rad instal HAL 18-4 29MU 14-6-46 bou sold scr 3-9-47

SM421 33MU 19-11-44 421S 18-1-45 CAC ops 3-2 410RSU 403S CAC ops 28-3 410RSU VA mods 15-3-49 RHAF 6-8

SM422 BHAM 24 39MU 19-11-44 CAC ops 1-3-45 341S FTR ops 1-4

SM423 33MU 15-11-44 416S 11-1-45 410RSU SOC 21-2

SM424 39MU 10-11-44 602S 23-11 11AGS 2-5-46 203AFS 10-9-48 C4S 31-10-51 to 6931M 14SoTT 20-11

SM426 9MU 29-11-44 403S 25-2-45 412S 24-5 402S 28-6 to 6570M 25-6-48 SOC 6-4-49

SM427 BHAM 24 6MU 19-11-44 451S 21-12 66S 5-2-45 FAAC 4-3 164S 14-6 577S 5-7 bou sold scrap 3-9-47

SM464 BHAM 24 9MU 19-11-44 229S 6-12 FAAC 10-3-45 DeH recat E 23-5 SOC 21-6

SM465 BHAM 24 39MU 19-11-44 451S 21-12 CE ops 9-3-45 SOC 15-3

SM466 BHAM 24 9MU 18-11-44 416S 11-1-45 403S 15-2-45 412S 24-5 5(P)AFU 2-11 17STFS 4-4-46 bou sold scr 3-9-47

SM467 9MU 1-12-44 443S 1-2-45 CAC ops 26-3 410RSU bou 7-3-46

SM468 BHAM 24-6MU 19-11-44 83GSU 4-1-45 strk by RN116 on ldg CE westh 5-1 SOC 29-1

SM469 6MU 23-11-44 443S 13-1-45 FACB 13-3 410RSU ASTE 4-4 recat e 30-5

SM470 BHAM 24 6MU 19-11-44 416S 11-1-45 CAC ops 21-2 410RSU 83GDC 20-9 SOC 5-10

SM471 39MU 30-11-44 451S 3-1-45 164S 14-6 577S 5-7 FAAC 1-4-46 ROS to 6005M 2SoTT

SM472 BHAM 24 45MU 18-11-44 302S CAC ops 28-1-45 ASTH 631S 24-8 cd f/lndg CE Caennavon SOC 14-3-46

SM473 9MU 29-11-44 229S 6-1-45 603S cd in Holland ops 17-3 SOC 31-3

SM474 9MU 5-12-44 421S 18-1-45 CB ops 19-3 410RSU recat E SOC 10-4

SM475 BHAM 24 6MU 19-11-44 451S 21-12 FAAC 19-2-45 ROS 164S 14-6 577S 28-6 631S 27-6-46 SOC 3-6-48

SM476 9MU 29-11-44 421S 18-1-45 ASTH 12-5 recat E SOC 18-7

SM477 BHAM 24 6MU 19-11-44 451S 21-12 FAAC 20-2-45 recat E SOC 18-7

SM478 39MU 30-5-44 443S 1-2-45 FTR ops 24-2

SM479 BHAM 24 6MU 19-11-44 451S 21-12 164S 14-6-45 577S 28-6 to 6002M 2SoTT

SM480 39MU 30-11-44 451S 21-12 164S 14-6-45 577S 5-7 to 6003M 2SoTT

SM481 33MU 21-11-44 416S 11-1-45 1CRU 20-2 (P)AFU 15-11 17SFTS 26-6-46 to 6202M 6SoTT 15-11

SM482 BHAM 24 45MU 18-11-44 322S 8-3-45 349S 31-5 322S 18-10 102FRS 3-5-51 HQ HC Com S 7-7-52 NES 13-12-54 sold L Met 15-5-56

SM483 BHAM 24 45MU 18-11-44 403S 4-2-45 CE ops 3-3

SM484 BHAM 24 6MU 19-11-44 453S 8-1-45 183S 21-6 567S 29-6 to 5981M 3-7-46

SM485 BHAM 24 45MU 18-11-44 443S 18-1-45 412S 24-5 402S 28-6 612S 7-2-49 FAAC exercise foil VA rapid turn round 25-6-49 NEA 29-11-50 proof & exp section Shoe 15-5-51

SM487 BHAM 24 45MU 18-11-44 302S 18-1-45 CAC ops 28-1-45 ASTH recat E SOC 21-3

SM488 33MU 21-11-44 302S 11-1-45 CB ops 14-2 410RSU recat E SOC 1-4

SM503 39MU 30-11-44 416S 11-1-45 403S 15-2 29MU 27-9 RHAF 6-8-49

SM507 33MU 21-11-44 451S 29-12 164S 14-6-45 577S 5-7 to 5999M 6SoTT SOC 3-2-50

SM511 BHAM 24 39MU 18-11-44 451S 3-1-45 FAAC 17-1 ROS 577S 28-6 bou sold scr 3-9-47

SM512 39MU 30-11-44 443S 18-1-45 412S 24-5 402S 28-6 102FRS 26-4-51 FA C5(C) 8-9

SM516 33MU 7-12-44 451S 29-12 FAAC 7-5-45 ROS 567S 12-7 SOC 10-10-46

SM538 33MU 7-12-44 602S 4-1-45 air coll with SM353 cd nr Swann CE SOC 14-2

SM646 39MU 4-12-44 443S FAAC 22-1-45 410RSU 412S 7-6 402S 28-6

SM648 33MU 18-12-44 302S 14-2-45 CB ops 16-2 ASTH recat E SOC 18-7

SM664 39MU 7-12-44 443S 1-2-45 FTR ops 21-4

SM665 39MU 5-12-44 451S 12-2-45 164S 14-6 577S 28-6 to 6001M 2SoTT

SM667 9MU 1-12-44 302S 11-1-45 CB ops 24-2 AST recat E SOC 1-6

SM670 39MU 4-12-44 443S 1-2-45 FTR ops 6-4

SM671 9MU 1-12-44 403S 25-1-45 FA SOC 25-5

TA739 XVIE 9MU 1-12-44 416S FAAC 15-1-45 410RSU 403S 15-2 416S 22-2 CAC ops 21-4 443S FTR ops 25-4

TA741 XVIE 39MU 4-12-44 433S 18-1-45 CAC ops 28-2 410RSU 4-5-46

TA759 VA HPS 9-2-45 Trls a/c-pilots Shea-Simmonds, Morgan. Hand trls 28-2. Invest into elev syst and control surfaces. New elev instal 5-3. VASM elev instal 22-3 19MU 5-5 CGS 3-7 RHAF 11-5-49

TA809 CSFD 39MU 24-2-45 340S 4-4 FTR ops 9-4

TB130 XVIE 30MU 30-12-44 earmarked for Greece 1-9-46 FACB 24-4-49 RHAF 27-4

TB131 9MU 8-1-45 340S FTR ops 3-3

TB132 XVIE 6MU 3-1-45 302S 8-2 ASTH 4-4 recat E SOC 17-7

TB136 XVIE 6MU 4-1-45 302S 8-2 CE ops 22-3-46 SOC 10-4

TB137 XVIE 9MU 6-1-45 329S 1-3 341S 15-3 CAC ops 5-4 350S 15-1-46 SOC 29-1-48

TB138 XVIE 6MU 5-1-45 340S CE ops 25-2

TB139 XVIE 9MU 6-1-45 603S 13-2 ROS 26-3 631S 30-8 TAAC 5-7-59 recat scr 15-11

TB140 XVIE 9MU 7-1-45 302S 22-2 151RU 22-3 ASTE 1-5 recat E SOC 30-5

TB141 XVIE 39MU 4-1-45 302S 8-2 151RU 1-3 ASTE 4-4 recat E SOC 30-5

TB232 XVIE 30MU 30-12-44 BDn June '45 hand trls with 90gal drop tank and two 250lb bombs on underwing carr; two can blanked off. Recommended that with rear fuel tank full only experienced Spit pilots should fly a/c and in good visibility. RHAF 20-3-49

TB237 XVIE 6MU 4-1-45 83Grp Com S 22-2 FAAC 12-7 416S 19-7 83GDC 26-9 RHAF 9-2-49

TB244 XVIE 6MU 4-1-45 603S 9-2 ROS 7-6 631S 23-8 out of fuel f/ld on beach Tal-Y-Bont merioneth CE 3-4-46 SOC 14-4

TB245 XVIE 39MU 5-1-45 102FRS 13-4-51 1 OFU Abingdon 29-10-52 MEAF 28-11 3CAACU 11-11-53 NES 13-12-54 sold L Met 15-5-56

TB246 XVIE 6MU 3-1-45 302S 8-2 CB ops 24-2 ASTH 17-4 recat E SOC 1-6

Two views of TB252. Above shows it on the gate at RAF Acklington in fictitious markings. Below: Possibly at Boulmer.

TB247 XVIE 6MU 4-1-45 340S 15-2 84GDC 15-11 203AFC 11-6-49 NEA 28-3-51 sold Cindal Aluminium 30-8

TB248 XVIE 30MU 30-12-44 61 OTU 22-2-46 FACB 13-12 recat E SOC

TB250 XVIE 9MU 6-1-45 302S FTR ops 14-3

TB252 XVIE 9MU 6-1-45 329S 1-3 411RSU 8-3 341S 15-3 350S 15-1-46 151RU 15-10 61 OTU 29-5-47 Old Sarum 18-1-49 33MU 27-2-53 as 7257M Odiham 13-8-55 to 7281M 2-9 but cancelled Acklington 21-8-59 Boulmer 1-8-69 as 8073M 15-12 extant Bentley Priory.

TB254 XVIE 30MU 30-12-44 RHAF 3-8-49

TB255 XVIE 30MU 30-12-44 RHAF 30-4-48

TB256 XVIE 30MU 30-12-44 to 6369M 10-7-47 RDAF cancelled 6412M 16-8 SOC 11-11-47

TB269 XVIE 33MU 30-12-44 to 6369M 10-7-47 RDAF cancelled 6412M 16-8 Soc 11-11-47

TB270 XVIE 33MU 8-4-45 443S 15-2 bou 7-3-46

TB271 XVIE 6MU 5-1-45 421S 1-3 83GSU 26-7 sold J Dale 9-6-49

TB272 XVIE 6MU 5-1-45 340S 22-3 CB ops 411RSU 317S 24-5 GACB bou sold scr 3-9-47

TB273 XVIE 6MU 5-1-45 416S 1-3 412S 24-5 FAAC 16-6 ROS RHAF 29-3-49

TB274 XVIE 6MU 4-1-45 416S 1-3 CAC ops 12-4 410RSU recat E SOC 7-7

TB275 XVIE 30MU 5-1-45 RHAF 20-4-49

TB276 XVIE 6MU 4-1-45 403S 17-5-45 83Grp Com S 19-7 443S 27-9 Res pl 2-7-46 302S 12-7 bou SOC 24-10-47

TB277 XVIE 6MU 3-1-45 340S CB ops 22-2 DeH 7-4 recat E SOC 23-5

TB278 6MU 3-1-45 302S 25-1 307S 19-3-46 VA 15-4 recat 9-6-47

TB279 9MU 28-1-45 74S FAAC 21-3 411RSU 485S 17-5 84GDC 23-8 308S 6-9 SOC 7-8-47

TB280 9MU 6-1-45 340S 15-2 CAC ops 8-9 411RSU recat E SOC 21-7

TB281 6MU 5-1-45 421S 15-2 NEA 27-9 sold H Bath 27-10-49

TB282 30MU 30-12-44 103FRS 25-5-51 5CAACU 16-7-52 C4R 4-11-53

TB283 33MU 4-1-45 302S 8-9 FTR ops 3-3

TB284 6MU 3-1-45 340S 15-2 CB ops 28-2 ASTH recat E SOC 28-8

TB285 6MU 5-1-45 340S CB ops 16-2 AST recat E SOC 1-6

TB286 6MU 12-1-45 340S CAC ops 13-3 74S CAC ops 23-4 411RSU 317S 31-5 recat E 5-12-46

TB287 9MU 8-1-45 340S 15-2 127S 10-5 341S 17-5 612S 12-7-50 AGT Gat refurt 23-10-51 NES 25-11-54 to 7559M NWld to MHth as 5658M

TB288 30MU 5-1-45 601S 28-4-47 502S 8-3-50 278MU C5 25-2-52 recat (S)

TB289 6MU 4-1-45 340S 1-3 CE ops 21-3

TB290 6MU 7-1-45 340S FTR ops 27-2

TB291 30MU 5-1-45 SOC 12-3-48

TB292 6MU 3-1-45 302S 8-2

TB293 30MU 5-1-45 600S 11-9-51 33MU 26-9 NES 13-12-54 RAF Kenley for film 16-8-55 sold scr 30-4-56

TB294 30MU 3-1-45 609S 14-7-49 C5(S) 16-3-51

TB295 6MU 4-1-45 603S 9-2 287S 30-8 EAAS Manby 29-8-47 sold J Dale 5-8-48

TB296 30MU 5-1-45 AM Unit Exhibition 5-4-48 sold J Dale 9-1-50

TB297 6MU 8-1-45 340S 15-2 FTR ops 13-3

TB298 FACB on test flt 31-12-44 9MU 12-3-45 322S 29-3 FAAC 16-5 411RSU 17SFTS 29-1-46 bou sold scr 3-9-47

TB299 39MU 7-1-45 345S 12-4 302S 22-11 strck TB742 on gd Ahlhorn CB 18-6-46 RSU 308S 21-11-46 NEA 16-12 bou SOC 24-10-47

TB300 6MU 4-1-45 421S 15-2 403S 5-7 FAAC 24-7 ROS 34MU on loan for BoB film 31-2-49 3CAACU 6-6-51 NEA 16-2-53 sold H Bath 23-6

TB301 30MU 5-1-45 School Sea/Land/Air Warfare 10-5-46 FAAC 31-12-48 recat E 23-3-49

TB302 30MU 7-1-45 102FRS 2-5-51 3CAACU 29-9-53 NES 13-12-54 sold L Met 15-5-56

TB303 30MU 5-1-45 11AQS low flying over sea cd, coast Maughold Head IoM 30-3-47 Manston S HQ 13-9-49 NEA 22-3-51 sold Cindal Aluminium 30-8

TB304 9MU 7-1-45 453S 13-2-45 183S 21-6 587S 5-7 sold scr bou 8-9-47

TB305 9MU 7-1-45 340S 21-2 8GDC 15-11

TB306 6MU 6-1-45 341S FACE 14-3 411RSU

TB307 30MU 7-1-45 101FRS 17-5-51 29MU 11-10 NES 14-12-54 sold H Bath 16-5-56

TB308 30MU 5-1-45 CGS 15-6-50 3CAACU 28-10-53 NES 13-12-54 602S 12-8-55 to 7255M 6-3-58

TB326 9MU 6-1-45 302S 15-2-45 FACB 16-4 151RU recat E SOC 21-7

TB327 33MU 7-1-45 416S 22-3 410RSU FTR ops 12-4

TB328 9MU 7-1-45 322S 1-3 66S 15-3 17SFTS e/fd cd/ld CE on Hixon aerodrome 13-11 SOC 16-1-46

TB329 9MU 7-1-45 FACE 13-2

TB330 30MU 5-1-45 11AGS 14-5-46 flew i/high grd pilot kld CE Maughold IoM 20-3-47 SOC 18-4

TB331 39MU 10-1-45 322S 22-2 CB ops 25-2 DeH recat E SOC 21-6

TB332 9MU 7-1-45 451S 13-2 FAAC 3-3 recat E SOC 21-7

TB333 9MU 7-1-45 84GSU FAAC 18-2 ROS 345S 18-4 308S FACE 18-12

TB334 39MU 7-1-45 322S 1-3 CB ops 18-3 511FRU recat E SOC 1-6

TB335 9MU 6-1-45 340S 1-3 CE ops 1-4

TB336 9MU 7-1-45 84GSU FACE 20-2

TB337 6MU 17-1-45 322S 22-2 FACB 19-3 420RSU AST recat E SOC 17-7

TB338 9MU 6-1-45 340S 15-2 CAC ops 31-3 411RSU recat E 31-8

TB339 6MU 4-1-45 322S CAC ops 24-2 AST recat E SOC 17-7

TB340 39MU 7-1-45 403S 1-3 421S 5-7 RHAF 6-7-49

TB341 9MU 12-1-45 302S 22-2 FTR ops 24-2

TB342 9MU 6-1-45 340S 1-3 CAC ops 2-4 411RSU

TB343 6MU 17-1-45 329S 1-3 341S 15-3 FTR ops 1-4

TB344 9MU 7-1-45 84GSU FAAC 12-3 ROS 10 OTU 10-1-46 201 CTU 8-5-47 to 6331M 14-6

TB345 9MU 7-1-45 302S 22-2 VA 15-4-46 recat E 9-6-47

TB346 9MU 7-1-45 322S 22-2 420RSU 12-4 recat E SOC 21-7

TB347 6MU 7-1-45 340S CAC ops 25-2 MAL 5(P)AFU 2-11 7SFTS 15-4-46 u/c clpse t/o Hibald 22-5 SOC 30-7

TB348 6MU 12-1-45 74S 15-3 485S 17-5 345S 23-8 350S 17-1-46 BAF on loan pend del of FXIV 26-10 sold J. Dale 6-1-48

TB349 6MU 12-1-45 421S 15-2 CAC ops 20-4 410RSU 443S 5-7 bou 7-3-46

TB352 33MU 8-1-45 443S 15-2 308S 22-3 443S CAC ops 2-5 410RSU bou 7-3-46

TB353 9MU 18-1-45 74S CB ops 20-3 411RSU SAL recat E 28-5

TB354 9MU 12-1-45 CGS 11-7 17SFTS 28-5-46 FTC 31-7-37 SOC sold B K Alloys 29-4-48

TB355 9MU 12-1-45 74S CAC ops 20-3 411RSU 485S 17-5 349S 6-9 FACB 15-9 recat E 21-9

TB356 6MU 17-1-45 329S 1-3 341S 15-3 350S 18-1-46 FAAC 26-6 411RSU
TB357 6MU 12-1-45 603S 9-2 FAAC 24-2 ROS FAAC on f/f 31-5 recat E SOC 20-6
TB358 9MU 7-1-45 329S 1-3 341S 15-3 CB ops 25-4 151RU recat E SOC 19-6
TB359 6MU 12-1-45 340S 15-2 FTR ops 7-4
TB360 39MU 12-1-45 340S CB ops 21-2 151RU recat E SOC 6-6
TB361 9MU 24-1-45 302S 8-3 151RU 26-6-46 3BRU CE 11-7
TB362 9MU 4-2-45 322S 8-3 302S 27-8 NEA 16-12-46 SOC 29-1-48
TB363 6MU 17-1-45 340S CAC ops 1-3 151RU 13-3 recat E SOC 4-7
TB364 6MU 3-2-45 308S 22-3 SOC 30-10-47
TB365 30MU 28-1-45 DeH 8-3 10 OTU 7-1-46 17 OTU 25-9-46 201CTU to 6362M 13-5-47
TB366 9MU 12-1-45 3501SU 13-2 FACB 5-4 ASTE recat E SOC 1-6
TB367 30MU 23-1-45 FAAC f/f in transit from VA 28-1 ROS SOC 21-12
TB368 30MU 28-1-45 17SFTS 15-11 FAAC 27-12 recat E SOC 23-1-46
TB369 6MU 17-1-45 302S 22-2 FAAC 13-10 411RSU 21-6-47
TB370 9MU 12-1-45 302S 15-2 CB ops 18-3 WAL recat E SOC 23-6
TB371 9MU 12-1-45 329S 1-3 341S 15-3 FTR ops 20-4
TB372 9MU 12-1-45 329S 1-3 341S 15-3 FTR ops 25-4
TB373 6MU 12-1-45 329S 1-3 CAC ops 21-3 350S 21-2-46 BAF pend del FXIV 26-10
TB374 29MU 3-2-45 302S 2903 151RU 30-7-46 CE 23-5-47
TB375 9MU 21-1-45 329S CB ops 28-23 DeH recat E 23-5 SOC
TB376 9MU 12-1-45 603S 13-2 1353Flt 25-10 CFS 30-4-48 sold Int All 21-8-50
TB377 6MU 3-2-45 516S 22-3 FAAC 8-8 recat E SOC 24-8
TB378 9MU 21-1-45 84S 3-3 302S 8-3 FTR ops 9-4
TB379 6MU 4-2-45 421S 22-3 631S 3-2-49 NES 14-13-54 sold H Bath 1-5-56
TB380 6MU 13-2-45 631S 7-1-48 GAAC 25-1-49 ROS 20S 27-4-49 FA3R 14-8-51 ROS NES 14-12 sold E Smelt 13-6-56
TB381 9MU 28-1-45 341S CAC ops 24-3 Ce ops 10-4
TB382 no record BoB film to 7244M RAF Henlow extant RAF Abingdon

TB382 seen at Middleton St George, circa 1960.

TB383 9MU 4-2-45 322S 22-3 FACE 8-5
TB384 30MU 28-1-45 Doncaster 30-9 SOC 12-3-46
TB385 6MU 17-1-45 329S CE ops 28-2 SOC 26-3
TB386 6MU 17-1-45 329S 1-3 341S 15-3 350S 17-1-46 BAF pend del FXIV 26-10 sold J Dale 8-7-48
TB387 9MU 28-1-45 341S 29-3 CAC ops 9-4 411RSU ASTH recat E SOC 17-7
TB388 9MU 21-1-45 329S 1-3 FTR ops 21-3
TB389 6MU 17-1-45 FAAC 2-3 ROS 11AGS 2-5-46 EAAS 11-11-48 CGSD 19-7-49 3CAACU 2-7-51 G Radio Sch Mid Wallop 16-10 NES 14-12-54 sold H Bath 23-5-56
TB390 9MU 21-1-45 84GSU FACB 12-3 ASTH recat E SOC 18-7
TB391 9MU 4-2-45 451S 3-3 164S 14-6 577S 5-7 283S 3-7 SOC 30-1-47
TB392 no record
TB394 9MU 28-1-45 340S 8-3 411RSU 340S CE ops SOC 16-4
TB395 9MU 21-1-45 302S CB ops 13-3 151RU WAL recat E SOC 2-7
TB396 9MU 4-2-45 603S 13-3 air coll with SM396 i/sea off Palling Norfolk Ce 24-3
TB475 6MU 4-2-45 341S CB ops 3-4 151RU 345S 26-4
TB476 6MU 14-2-45 443S 15-3 bou 7-3-46
TB478 6MU 3-2-45 322S 8-3 SOC 18-4
TB480 9MU 4-2-45 308S 29-3 349S 20-8-46 SOC 29-1-48
TB481 39MU 10-2-45 443S CE ops 24-3
TB492 6MU 8-2-45 127S 8-3 349S 30-4 bou sold scrap 3-9-47
TB493 9MU 28-1-45 302S 1-3 CAC ops 31-3 FACE 12-4 411RSU recat E SOC 7-7
TB494 6MU 29-1-45 322S CB ops 25-2 ASTH recat E SOC 18-7
TB495 9MU 28-1-45 84S 3-3 74S 15-3 485S 17-5 SOC 10-9
TB496 6MU 17-1-45 340S CAC ops 9-3 FTR ops 1-4
TB497 6MU 29-1-45 329S 1-3 341S CAC ops 23-3 FTR ops 1-4

TB308 last served with No 602 Squadron, before becoming 7255M for display use.

TB498 6MU 29-1-45 322S 15-3 83GDC 3-11 RAF Andover 2-6-49 3CAACU 8-10-53 NES 14-12-54 sold Eng RM 28-6-56
TB501 29MU 3-2-45 66S 12-4 84ARF 30-4 443S 21-7 GACB 15-9 403RSU
TB502 9MU 21-1-45 CA ops 13-3 340S 22-3 NEA 17-12 sold H Bath 27-10-49
TB515 6MU 9-2-45 127S 5-3 349S 30-4 322S 18-10 sold E Smelt 21-6-49
TB517 6MU 9-2-45 61 OTU 7-3-46 FAAC 8-8-47 ROS 203AFS 6-11 to 6649M RAF Henlow 28-3-49 RAF Full Sutton 24-7-51 SOC 11-9
TB519 9MU 4-2-45 329S 8-3 341S 15-3 sold J Dale 1-6-49
TB520 9MU 21-1-45 453S 2-3 183S 14-6 587S 5-7 691S 20-6-46 FAAC 24-3-47 recat E SOC 29-4
TB521 29MU 3-2-45 66S 29-3 FTR ops 11-4
TB522 6MU 29-1-45 443S 5-4 RCIS Finningley 30-5-46 to 6262M 12-2-47 12SoTT
TB525 29MU 3-2-45 302S CB ops 18-3 ROS 17SFTS 27-12 FAAC 15-1-46 recat E SOC 30-1
TB526 6MU 9-2-45 61 OTU 22-2-46 203AFS e/fd f/ld Floreychurch Devon dbf 8-1-48
TB528 9MU 28-1-45 340S 1-3 CB ops 29-3 ASTH 30-4 recat E SOC 18-7
TB549 29MU 3-2-45 74S 15-3 FAAC 16-4 486S 17-5 601S 21-6-49 236OCU 11-6-50 dismantled 5-2-54 C5(S) 11-9
TB572 6MU 20-2-45 63S 22-3-48 695S 28-4 eng cut on app w/u ldg CE Detling 16-12 AFT SOC 17-1-49
TB574 29MU 3-2-45 66S 29-3 84ARF 30-4 74S 10-5 485S 17-5 61 OTU 16-1-46 NEAS 28-8-50 sold En/RM 11-1-51
TB578 30MU 28-1-45 17SFTS 31-1-46 recat E 9-10 to 6177M 6-11
TB580 33MU 21-2-45 340S 15-3 127S 17-5 349S 24-5 CE 29-11
TB581 6MU 4-2-45 66S CAC ops 18-3 349S FAAC 7-5 317S 24-5
TB582 29MU 3-2-45 340S 5-4 127S 17-5 317S 24-5 sold scr bou 3-9-47
TB583 29MU 3-2-45 308S CAC ops 26-3 ASTH recat E SOC 18-7
TB585 29MU 3-2-45 345S 12-4 127S 10-5 308S 29-11 CE SOC 25-7-46
TB588 9MU 4-2-45 84ADC 15-10 sold E Smelt 21-6-49
TB589 29MU 3-2-45 302S 8-3 317S 24-5 302S 8-10 Cd f/lndg nr Ahlhorn 13-2-46 SOC 28-2
TB590 29MU 25-2-45 66S 5-4 6127SE 30-4 74S 10-5 485S 17-5 341S 16-8 350S 6-2-46 6-1S 6-2-47 101FRS 29-8-51 NES 4-6-56 sold British Aluminium 22-10
TB591 6MU 3-2-45 340S 1-3 FCCS 24-1-49 609S 30-6-50 AGT Gat refurb 19-2-51 23CAACU 7-6-54 NES 4-6-56 sold British Aluminium 22-10
TB592 6MU 3-2-45 451S 7-3 164S 14-6 577S 5-7 288S 5-7 to 6080M
TB593 29MU 3-2-45 74S 15-3 FTR F/ld e/tr pilot believed in friendly hands 5-4
TB594 6MU 4-2-45 FACE 1-3 SOC 23-3
TB595 29MU 3-2-45 602S 26-3 17SFTS 6-12 sold J Dale 8-7-48
TB596 6MU 6-2-45 340S 15-3 127S 17-5 317S 24-5 sold scr bou 3-9-47
TB597 6MU 3-2-45 340S 8-3 CAC ops 26-3 FTR ops 1-4
TB598 6MU 6-2-45 74S CAC ops 24-3 DeH recat E SOC 21-6
TB613 29MU 3-2-45 127S 8-3 349S FAAC 20-5 3-8S 12-7 SOC 7-8-47
TB614 29MU 3-2-45 322S 15-3 FAAC 30-6 411RSU 5-7
TB615 6MU 3-2-45 341S 15-3 FAAC 30-6 411RSU
TB616 9MU 28-1-45 416S 10-5 83GDC 20-9 VA mods 15-3-49 RHAF 27-7
TB617 6MU 3-2-45 66S 19-4 84ARF 30-4
TB618 6MU 3-2-45 340S 8-3 CE ops 21-3 ASTH recat E SOC 18-7
TB619 6MU 19-2-45 453S 7-3 183S 21-6 587S 5-7 567S 4-10 RHAF 11-5-49
TB620 9MU 4-2-45 451S 1-3 164S 14-6 577S 5-7 288S 5-7 SOC ABS 5-2-47
TB621 29MU 3-2-45 443S CB ops 8-3 recat E SO 28-3
TB622 29MU 3-2-45 74S 16-3 485S 17-5 345S 23-349S 15-4-46 BAF pend del FXIV 14-11 sold J Dale 8-7-48
TB623 33MU 2-12-45 127S 8-3 FTR ops 27-4
TB624 6MU 3-2-45 83GSU FACE b 4-3
TB625 6MU 4-2-45 74S 15-3 CAC ops 31-3 485S 17-BAFO Com Wng 27-9 164S 19-7-46 603S 19-12 609S 13-5-4 coll with Anson NK715 taxy CB 13-8 recat E
TB626 9MU 4-2-45 322S 8-3 CAC ops 19-4 RHA 22-7-49
TB627 9MU 19-2-45 322S 22-3 FTR ops 23-4
TB628 19MU 7-3-45 345S 12-4 FACB 16-5
TB629 9MU 4-2-45 603S 13-3 287S 30-8 scr SOC 10-10-46
TB630 29MU 3-2-45 403S 5-4 691S 30-8 TAAC 24-11-47 ROS 691S 3-4-50 AGT Gatwick refurb 26-1-5 5CAACU 15-5-52 sold R J Coley 17-2-56
TB631 9MU 4-2-45 74S 15-3 485S 17-5 BAFO Com Wng 27-9
TB632 29MU 3-2-45 308S 22-3 SOC 7-8-47
TB633 29MU 25-2-45 ROS 7-5 667S 12-11 61 OTU 27-12 sold Int All 10-2-50
TB634 6MU 3-2-45 403S CAC ops 421S 15-3 sold H Bath 27-10-49
TB635 9MU 4-2-45 127S 8-3 349S 26-4 317S 24-SOC 7-8-47
TB636 6MU 9-2-45 308S 15-3 FACE 13-7
TB637 6MU 6-2-45 308S 22-3 bou sold scr 3-9-47
TB639 9MU 4-2-45 74S 15-3 203AFS 5-8-49 HQ RC Com S 5-5-50 FA5(C) 30-7-51
TB702 33MU 25-2-45 340S 26-4 103FRS 16-5-5 3CAACU FA3R 11-5-54 SOC 13-5
TB709 33MU 24-2-45 74S 29-3 127S 10-5 340S 24-FAAC 18-10 350S 17-4-46 BAF on loan pend FXIV 26-10
TB713 19MU 26-3-45 412S 7-6 402S 28-6 31S 16-3-49 1689 Flt ADn 23-7-51 Trans Com 3-6-52 FTU Ben 9-4-53
TB714 9MU 19-2-45 66S 29-3 FTR ops 1-4
TB715 6MU 19-2-45 308S 15-3 411RSU salvage dump 26-7
TB716 19MU 7-3-45 74S 4-4 GACE 28-4
TB733 9MU 19-2-45 308S CE ops 24-3
TB734 29MU 19-2-45 308S FTR ops 20-3
TB735 39MU 20-2-45 84GSU 12-3 66S 22-3 349S 30-4 412RSU 29-11
TB737 33MU 21-2-45 83GSU 4-3 403S 15-3 FTR ops 31-3
TB738 XVIE 9MU 19-2-45 84GSU 6-3 74S 15-3 341S 10-5 485S 16-8 61 OTU 18-2-46 bou SOC 24-10-47
TB739 XVIE 33MU 20-2-45 74S 15-3 CE on ops dbf 19-4
TB741 29MU 22-2-45 84GSU 8-3 74S 15-3 411RSU 19-4 485S 19-5 FACE 19-6
TB742 39MU 20-2-45 84GSU 12-3 302S 29-3 Strck by TB299 on grd Ahlhorn CE 18-6-46 SOC 27-6
TB743 33MU 24-2-45 453S 9-3 FAAC 13-6 49MU 18-6 recat E SOC 8-8
TB744 65FD 39MU 24-2-45 451S 16-3 164S 14-6 577S 5-7 288S 5-7 to 6048M 6-8-46 11AGS SOC 24-10-47
TB745 33MU 24-2-45 84GSU 12-3 202S CAC ops 1-4 411RSU bou 29MU 3-9-47 SOC
TB746 33MU 21-2-45 66S 12-4 84ARF 30-4 83GSU 443S 21-6 SOC 29-7-46
TB747 33MU 24-2-45 74S 29-3 485S 17-5 127S 17-5 322S 24-5 34MU BoB loan 31-8-49 2CAACU 12-5-52 FAC5(S) 23-7-53
TB748 XVIE 9MU 19-2-45 302S CAC ops 1-4 411RSU BAF on loan pend del FXIV 30-10-46 recat E 5-12
TB749 33MU 24-2-45 84GSU 9-3 308S 15-3 CE ops 9-4
TB750 19MU 25-2-45 124S 1-3 341S FTR ops 30-3
TB751 39MU 24-2-45 84GSU 12-3 302S eng fire taxy CB 24-3 recat E SOC 13-4
TB752 33MU 21-2-45 66S 25-3 409RSU 29-3 403S 19-4 CAC ops 26-4 410RSU 102FRS 19-4-51 to 7256M extant RAF Mans to 7279M then 8080M refurb at Rochester airport Jan '79 gate guardian Manston
TB753 19MU 27-2-45 340S 5-4 162S 25-7-46 164S 20-8 to 6904M 29-9-51
TB754 33MU 3-3-45 83GSU 17-3 4-3S 5-4 FTR 23-4
TB755 XVIE 29MU 19-2-45 127S 8-3 349S 30-4 FAAC 22-11 bou SOC 19-2-47

TB756 19MU 25-2-45 416S 5-7 11AGS 4-11-47 SOC -3-49

TB757 COAL mods 26-2-45 CRD HPA 4-3-45 BDn -3 attitude measure trls with MkVIII Type 3 RP instal × 60lb heads) on four zero length rails. Two 20mm can ther two sealed off). VA 27-4 hand trls with RP instal and ur RPs. Rud forces assymetric VA EA 21-8-46 29MU bou 9-47 sold scrap

TB758 39MU 27-2-45 84GSU 28-3 340S 5-4 411RSU)-5 11AGS 16-5-46 595S 4-10-48 691S 21-10 102FRS 24-4-51 old J G Will 28-1-53

TB759 XVIE 29MU 22-2-45 66S 29-3 84ARF 30-4 1S 21-6 401S 28-6 691S 30-8 Strck TB 993 taxy Chivenor B 1-2-49 recat E SOC 9-2

TB828 39MU 25-2-45 308S 29-3 3BRU 14-10-46 SOC -10

TB829 33MU 24-2-45 308S 15-3 FAAC 2-8

TB831 6MU 27-2-45 403S FTR ops 31-3

TB832 33MU 24-2-45 308S 15-3 FAAC 2-10 411RSU cat E 6-3-46

TB833 6MU 25-2-45 308S 22-3 CB ops 16-4 411RSU OC 3-4-47

TB834 6MU 25-2-45 302S 22-3 CE BAFO 22-5-47

TB835 29MU 25-2-45 421S CAC ops 1-5 410RSU EA 24-9 sold H Bath 27-10-49

TB836 33MU 25-2-45 66S 22-3 FTR ops 20-4

TB858 6MU 25-2-45 66S 29-3 340S 21-6 20S 19-4-51 CAACU 25-9 NES 14-12-54 sold E Smelt 13-6-56

TB859 33MU 24-2-45 74S 15-3 485S 17-5 RHAF 7-2-9

TB860 33MU 28-2-45 308S 22-3 3BRU CE 11-7-46

TB861 29MU 22-2-45 340S 22-3 102FRS 11-4-51 A3R 28-8 ROS 2CAACU 13-4-53 C5(C) 14-12

TB862 33MU 20-2-45 421S 5-4 17SFTS 11-2-46 air oll with RK849 nr Digby CE 30-4 SOC 14-5

TB863 453S 183S 657S 691S 17S Extant Duxford as G-CDAN.

TB864 29MU 22-2-45 341S CAC ops 1-4 411RSU ecat E SOC 23-5

TB865 no record but with 74S

TB866 CSFD 39MU 24-2-45 308S 29-3 349S 5-4-46 BAF on loan pend del FXIV 26-10 sold J Dale 8-7-48

TB867 9MU 10-3-45 345S 12-4 350S 24-11-46 BAF on loan pend del FXIV 26-10 SOC scr 16-11-47

TB868 XVIE 33MU 15-3-45 341S 12-4 350s 18-10-46 BAF on loan pend del FXIV 26-10 SOC 12-3-48

TB883 33MU 24-2-45 403S 29-3 CAC ops 14-4 10RSU

TB884 CSFD 39MU 24-2-45 66S 29-3 FTR ops 1-4

TB885 322S 2-45 UK 10-45 RAF Kenley extant Shoreham, APS

TB886 33MU 15-3-45 421S 19-4 RHAF 27-7-49

TB887 19MU 12-3-45 341S 26-4 SOC 30-5-46

TB888 29MU 25-2-45 41S 7-6 FAAC 4-7 443S 19-7 203AFS 12-2 for film work recat scr 28-4-50

TB889 XVIE 19MU 29-3-45 74S 19-4 CAC ops 19-4 411RSU 340S 3-5 317S 24-5 bou sold scrap 3-9-47

TB890 6MU 25-2-45 308S 29-3 412RSU AM PR8 25-10 to Warsaw for exhibition 302S 6-3-46 recat E 12-12

TB891 29MU 25-2-45 416S 22-3 FAAC 6-9 151RU 3-2S 11-7-46 NEA 16-12 bou SOC 19-2-47

TB892 19MU 25-2-45 341S 12-4 350S 17-1-46 BAF 26-10 on loan pend del FXIV SOC sold BKL Alloys 27-4-48

TB893 29MU 25-2-45 322S 5-4 317S 24-5 w/u lndg Ahlhorn AC 1-5-46 recat E 2-5

TB894 6MU 25-2-45 308S 15-3 recat E 28-8 SOC

TB895 19MU 25-2-45 322S CAC ops 5-4 420RSU RHAF 6-7-49

TB896 39MU 27-2-45 345S CAC ops 20-4 411RSU recat E 11-2-47

TB897 XVIE 6MU 16-3-45 345S 12-4 FAAC 10-5 recat E SOC 11-7

TB898 19MU 12-3-45 66S 12-4 317S 12-7 FACE 10-1

TB899 XVIE 19MU 16-3-45 20S 25-2-49 C4R 23-3-50 ROS NEA 14-12-54 sold H Bath 16-5-56

TB900 XVIE Winston Churchill 9MU 17-3-45 127S 12-4 349S 26-4 349(BAF)S RAF Fassburg Germany '46 SOC 30-5-46

TB901 XVIE 9MU 17-3-45 411S 21-6 FAAC 4-7 151RU Res pl 5-10 RHAF 22-2-49

TB902 19MU 12-3-45 341S 12-4 6-4S 29-7-49 NES 13-12-54 sold L Met 15-5-56

TB903 19MU 27-2-45 66S 5-4 6127SE 30-4 74S 17-5 17SFTS 29-1-46 recat E 9-10 to 6178M 6-11

TB904 19MU 27-2-45 603S 24-3 1353Flt 16-8 CE 24-8-46

TB905 33MU 25-2-45 416S 22-3 ASTH 11-10

TB906 19MU 25-2-45 127S 5-4 349S 30-4 SOC 29-1-48

TB907 29MU 25-2-45 322S 29-3 FTR ops 1-4

TB908 33MU 28-2-45 308S 29-3 FAAC 22-5 ROS RHAF 4-4-49

TB910 39MU 27-2-45 127S 5-4 349S 30-4 FAAC 18-12 412RSU 349S CE gd f/lndg nr Hannover 19-6-46

TB911 6MU 27-2-45 603S 15-3 609S 1-3-49 NES 14-12-54 sold H Bath 3-5-56

TB912 19MU 27-2-45 340S 2-4 CAC ops 6-4 411RSU recat E SOC 21-7

TB913 39MU 27-2-45 451S 24-3 166S 14-6 577S 5-7 288S 5-7 SOC 31-5-46

TB915 19MU 27-2-45 84GSU 21-3 66S FAAC 7-4 84ARF 30-4 421S 19-9 416S 26-7 443S 15-11 jumped by Thunderbolts. a/c aban cd Belmhusom CE 18-1-46

TB916 6MU 27-2-45 84GSU 13-3 322S 29-3 11AGS 26-4-46 236 OCU 18-4-51 to 6945M 28-1-52

TB917 6MU 27-2-45 84GSU 13-3 340S 29-3 CE ops 23-4

TB919 39MU 27-2-45 84GSU 28-3 345S 12-4 411RSU 19-4 340S 3-5 CE ops 1-4-46

TB921 19MU 27-2-45 302S 29-3 84GSU 21-3 CAC ops 411RSU 16-12-46 SOC 29-1-48

TB922 19MU 27-2-45 83GSU 25-3 403S 5-4 FAAC 26-5 FCCS 11-2-49 NEA 28-8-51 sold Cinda Aluminium 30-8

TB923 33MU 3-3-45 83GSU 16-3 443S 5-4 FTR ops 26-4

TB989 19MU 27-2-45 603S 16-3 287S 16-8 SOC scrap 10-10-46

TB990 6MU 3-3-45 322S 5-4 302S 31-5 NEA 16-12-46 SOC 29-1-48

TB991 6MU 27-2-45 ROS 9-4 345S 26-4 137S 17-5 349S 24-5 BAF pend del FXIV 26-10-46

TB993 6MU 5-3-45 603S 28-3 692S 16-8 691S strk TB759 taxy Chivenor 1-2-49 AFS EX 15-3-51 NEA 19-5-533 C5(R) 20-7

TB995 33MU 28-2-45 308S 29-3 SOC 7-8-47

TB996 33MU 8-3-45 345S CAC ops 20-4 411RSU SOC 3-4-47

TB997 6MU 7-3-45 322S 12-4

TB998 19MU 2-3-45 603S 27-3 1362Flt 16-8 FAAC 18-4-46 595S 7-7-48 5S dvd i/grd after inverting nr Ferryside pilot kld CE 17-6-49 scrap 15-11

TB999 6MU 1-3-45 308S 5-4 412RSU 3-10-46 recat E 12-12-46

TD113 6MU 1-3-45 66S 5-4 322S 30-4 SOC 12-11

TD114 6MU 1-3-45 403S 5-4 VA mods 15-3-49 RHAF 27-7

TD115 6MU 1-3-45 322S 5-4 CB ops 16-4 DeH recat E SOC 23-5

TD116 33MU 2-3-45 127S 5-4 349S 30-4 FAAC 20-9 412RSU NEA

TD117 19MU 2-3-45 322S 5-4 CAC ops 23-4 420RSU recat E SOC 7-7

TD118 6MU 1-3-45 308S 5-4 317S 26-4 302S 17-5 SOC 7-8-47

TD119 XVIE 19MU 26-3-45 345S 19-4 61 OTU 18-2-46 203AFS i/sea after recovering from dive Morte Bay ranges N Devon pilot kld 9-9-48

TD120 6MU 1-3-45 341S 5-4 FAAC 16-9 recat E

TD121 19MU 7-3-45 127S 12-4 349S 39-4 FAAC 13-2-46 recat E SOC 28-2-46

TD122 33MU 3-3-45 308S 5-4 SOC 7-8-47

TD123 6MU 5-3-45 602S 28-3 FAAC 5-4 ROS 61 OTU 7-2-46 GAAC 12-8 recat E SOC 4-2-47

TD124 6MU 7-3-45 345S 12-4 350S 18-1-46 cd l/lndg Darup CE 5-10

TD125 6MU 6-3-45 127S CAC 24-4 420RSU recat E SOC 21-6

TD126 9MU 10-3-45 421S 5-4 RHAF 26-1-49

TD127 19MU 5-3-45 602S 27-3 416S 5-7 17SFTS 29-11 SOC 10-2-47

TD128 19MU 7-3-45 345S 12-4 NEA 16-12-46 bou SOC 24-10-47

TD129 XVIE 33MU 22-3-45 416S 26-4 11AGS 16-5-46 NEA 22-11 SOC 29-1-48

TD130 33MU 2-3-45 403S 5-4 EAAS 17-11-48 CGS 29-9-49 NEA 28-3-51 sold Cindal Aluminium 30-8

TD131 6MU 2-3-45 322S 5-4 FACB 8-5 recat E SOC 7-7

TD132 19MU 7-3-45 603S 29-3 287S 30-8 63S 7-7-47 1(P)RFU Fly Trng Com 22-8-47 eng fire on app Finningley CE 21-2-49 AFD 28-3

TD133 XVIE 33MU 20-3-45 341S 26-4 FAAC 5-9 420RSU RHAF 19-3-49

TD134 XVIE 9MU 23-3-45 84GSU FAAC 31-5 ROS MacLarens HAL 23-3-46 65S 22-5 164S 26-9 63S 26-9 91S FACE 691S hit grd during practice attack a/c aban cd nr Cleave Cornwall 19-8-48 SOC

TD135 XVIE 604S to 6798M Irvington extant New York

TD136 XVIE 33MU 20-3-45 74S 19-4 485S 17-5 345S 16-8 61 OTU 7-2-46 203AFS 1-7-47 611S 27-2-50 609S 5-6 C3R 19-6 recat 5(C)

TD137 XVIE 39MU 15-3-45 322S 5-4

TD138 XVIE 33MU 22-3-45 345S CAC ops 13-4 340S 26-4 127S 17-5 317S 29-5 AM PR8 25-10 NEA 16-12-46 bou SOC 24-10-47

TD139 6MU 8-3-45 603S 29-3 341S FTR ops 17-4

TD140 9MU 10-3-45 127S 5-4 349S 26-4 BAF on loan pend del of FXIV 26-10-46 NEA 22-9-47 sold J Dale 9-1-50

TD141 29MU 9-3-45 403S 4-5 RHAF 15-3-49

TD142 29MU 8-3-45 127S 5-4 349S CAC ops 3-5 411RSU 317S 24-5 bou sold scrap 3-9-47

TD143 9MU 9-3-45 74S 5-4 485S 17-5 FAAC 19-6 411RSU 61 OTU 4-4-46 to 6418M 23-8-47

TD144 XVIE 33MU 15-3-45 127S 5-4 CB ops 11-4 420RSU recat E SOC 21-7

TD145 33MU 8-3-45 84GDC 15-10

TD146 XVIE 39MU 15-3-45 341S 5-4 345S 12-4 FACB 1-6 411RSU recat E SOC 11-7

TD147 9MU 10-3-45 443S 5-4 RHAF 8-6-49

TD148 XVIE 345S 26-7-45 317S 29-11 bou sold scrap 3-9-47

TD149 9MU 9-3-45 322S 5-4 317S 24-5 bou sold scrap 3-9-47

TD150 19MU 12-3-45 74S 12-4 485S 17-5 317S 6-9 NEA 16-12-46 bou SOC

TD151 29MU 9-3-45 603S 26-3 692S 16-8 691S 16-8 5S 3-4-50 APS Acklington 1-9-51 NES 14-12-54 sold E Smelt 13-6-56

TD152 29MU 9-3-45 453S 26-3 183S 21-6 567S 5-7 WAL mods 27-1-49 scrap 23-2-50

TD153 29MU 10-3-45 345S 12-4 308S hit truck taxy Ahlhorn AC 1-4-46 recat E 5-4

TD154 29MU 10-3-45 443S CB ops 22-4 410RSU recat E SOC 13-6

TD156 29MU 10-3-45 66S 6-4 CB ops 11-4 420RSU recat E SOC 21-7

TD157 29MU 10-3-45 322S 5-4 CE ops 24-4

TD158 6MU 10-3-45 340S 12-4 FACE 2-6

TD176 9MU 10-3-45 341S 5-4 RHAF 25-2-49

TD177 29MU 8-3-45 341S 5-4 FACE 3-5

TD184 XVIE 9MU 19-3-45 127S 26-4 349S 30-4 BAF on loan pend del FXIV 26-10-46 sold J Dale 1-6-49

TD185 XVIE 9MU 17-3-45 CFE 5-4 667S 22-11 61 OTU 10-1-46 recat E 16-12-48

TD186 XVIE 9MU 17-3-45 345S 12-4 443S 29-11 SOC ABS 5-2-47

TD187 XVIE 9MU 17-3-45 416S 19-4 164S 19-7-46 21 OTU 14-8 1687 BDT Flt 7-9 to 6224M 13-12 RNAF SoTT

TD188 XVIE 33MU 22-3-45 345S FAAC 16-4 350SD 17-1-46 BAF on loan pend del FXIV 26-10 SOC 12-3-48

TD189 XVIE 29MU 30-3-45 CFE 5-4 345S 26-4 127S 317S 24-5 sold scr 3-9-47

TD190 XVIE 6MU 24-3-45 84GDC 30-8 RHAF 29-6-49

TD191 XVIE 6MU 23-3-45 443S 26-4 RHAF 30-12-48

TD229 XVIE 9MU 26-3-45 403S 17-5 RHAF 26-1-49

TD230 XVIE 33MU 20-3-45 411S 7-6 FACB 23-6 410RSU

TD231 XVIE 19MU 24-3-45 341S 6-9 350S 15-1-46 BAF on loan pend del FXIV Fassburg Germany 26-10 to 6538M 4SoTT 31-3-48

TD232 XVIE 19MU 29-3-45 322S 26-4 127S 24-5 349S 18-10 FACE 17-12

TD233 XVIE 29MU 30-3-45 340S FTR ops 23-4

TD234 XVIE 39MU 11-4-45 84GSU 22-4 recat E 24-10 bou sold scr 3-9-47

TD235 XVIE 39MU 26-3-45 84GDC 15-10 226 OCU 31-10-46 RHAF 8-4-49

TD236 XVIE 39MU 20-4-45 CGS 10-7 to 6273M 27-3-47 6SoTT SOC 16-8-48

TD237 XVIE 9MU 22-3-45 322S 26-4 349S 18-10 BAF on loan pend del FXIV 26-10-46 sold J Dale 8-7-48

TD238 XVIE 19MU 26-3-45 302S 6-9 FAAC 5-12 151RU NEA 16-12-46 SOC 29-1-48

TD239 XVIE 9MU 27-3-45 443S 5-7 RHAF 13-1-49

TD240 XVIE 29MU 31-3-45 302S FACE 10-10

TD241 XVIE 33MU 30-3-45 340S 26-4 VA T.I & trls of GGS Mk IVB 18-11-47 Stored 18-8-48 RHAF 13-1-49

TD242 XVIE 29MU 31-3-45 308S 26-4 SOC 7-8-47

TD243 XVIE 6MU 21-4-45 412S 21-6 402S 28-6 RHAF 22-2-49

TD244 XVIE 29MU 30-3-45 84GSU 15-4 FAAC 23-5 MacLarens HAL 26-3-46 65S 18-6 164S 11-7 203AFS 8-4-48 sold Inter All 10-2-50

TD245 XVIE 9MU 29-3-45 416S 21-6 FACE 8-9

TD246 XVIE 19MU 4-4-45 443S 5-7 416S 29-7 RHAF 25-3-49

TD247 XVIE 19MU 4-4-45 322S 17-5 FAAC 7-7 151RU 12-7 recat E 4-7-46

TD248 XVIE M266 CBAF Con. No. 1X/4262 off contract and toc 11-5-45 6MU BNn for storage 695 Army Coop Sq 5-7 codes 8Q-T service on site by 54MU working party from Cambridge 31-12-47 ret to 695S new codes 4M-E 13-5 No.2 Civilian AA Coop Unit Little Snoring 31-8-51 9MU Csfd storage 27-5-54 NES 14-12 610 County of Chester RAAF Hooton Park as display a/c codes DW-A 4-1-55 R.AU.AF disbanded a/c awaiting disposal 1366 Chester ATC Sq at Sealand as 7246M 8-4-59 to 30MU Sealand for display 31-1-67 Colour scheme of u/s Ocean Grey & Dark Green, black prop 4in. yellow tips Sky spinner and fuse band 18in wide 4in forward of tailplane. Wing lead edge yellow 4in wide band from tip u/s roundel 32in dia overall. Dull red centre 'in wide white' in wide blue bands Fus roundel Type Cl 36in dia 2in white 8in blue bands fin flash 24in wide 8in wide stripes. Extant RAF Sealand DW-A 7246M

TD249 19MU 16-3-45 BCIS Finningley 5-7-46 614S 8-6-47 612S 21-11-48 swng on lndg u/c cllpse Dyce 12-5-49 recat E 29-6

TD250 29MU 10-3-45 341S 5-4

TD251 XVIE 9MU 17-3-45 416S 302S 18-6-46 NEA 6-12 SOC 29-1-48

TD252 XVIE 6MU 15-3-45 345S 12-4 302S 22-11 bou SOC 24-10-47

TD253 XVIE 19MU 16-3-45 345S 12-4 350S 18-1-46 alloc BAF dam CE in trans 24-10

TD254 19MU 12-3-45 74S 341S 10-5 127S 17-5 322S 24-5 631S 8-12-48 AGT Gatwick refurb 24-6-51 NES 14-12 sold E Smelt 13-6-56

TD255 XVIE 33MU 15-3-45 416S 5-4 612S 12-7-50 4CAACU 25-1-52 NES 14-12-54 sold E Smelt 13-6-56

TD256 XVIE 33MU 15-3-45 341S 5-4 GAAC 17-2 420RSU recat E 13-9

TD257 XVIE 39MU 15-3-45 403S 5-4 102FRS 19-4-51 2CAACU 1-3-54 NES 4-6-56 sold Br Al 22-10

TD258 XVIE 19MU 24-3-45 74S 12-4 485S 17-5 340S 2-8 SOC 14-12

TD259 XVIE 19MU 16-3-45 345S 12-4 127S 10-5 340S 17-5 FAAC 16-7 420RSU recat E 23-8

TD260 6MU 12-3-45 411S 7-6 401S 28-6 17SFTS 29-11 sold scrap bou 3-9-47

TD261 XVIE 39MU 15-3-45 340S 12-4 103FRS 16-5-51 5CAACU 7-5-53 NES 13-12-54 sold L Met 16-5-56

TD262 XVIE 39MU 15-3-45 74S 5-4 340S 24-5 FACB 11-6 411RSU CE 10CATC 21-6

TD263 XVIE 9MU 17-3-45 84GSU 12-4 ASTE 24-4 recat E SOC 30-5

TD264 XVIE 9MU 19-3-45 421S 26-4 FAAC 24-7 410RSU 416S 2-8 164S 19-7-46 63S 3-9 RNAF SoTT 8-7-47

TD265 XVIE 9MU 17-3-45 412S 7-6 402S 28-6 17SFTS 6-12 FAAC 18-6-46 recat E SOC 26-8-46

TD266 XVIE 19MU 16-3-45 421S 10-5 ECFS 9-7 20S 25-2-49 FA3R 30-6-50 recat scrap 27-7

TD267 XVIE 6MU 15-3-45 308S 13-9 NEA 16-12-46 bou SOC 24-10-47

TD280 XVIE 33MU 21-3-45 340S 12-4 17S 11-2-49 5S 3-4-50 recat 5(C) 6-3-52

TD281 XVIE 9MU 23-3-45 341S 25-10 350S 18-1-46 BAF on loan pend del FXIV 26-10 to 6540M 4SoTT 31-3-48

TD282 XVIE 6MU 20-3-45 443S 19-4 SOC 27-1-47

TD283 XVIE 9MU 17-3-45 322S 26-4 302S 1-11 cd f/lndg nr Cloppenburg

TD284 XVIE 9MU 21-3-45 CGS 11-7 17SFTS 28-5-46 CFSL 3-4-47 FAAC 20-1-48 ROS SOC 23-2

TD285 XVIE 9MU 23-3-45 340S 16-9 RHAF 11-4-49

TD286 XVIE 9MU 17-3-45 403S 5-4 317S 28-6 11AGS 15-5-46 SOC 19-3-48

TD288 XVIE 9MU 21-3-45 66S 26-4 349S 30-4 CE 23-5-47

TD289 XVIE 33MU 20-3-45 403S 19-4 11AGS 8-5-46 NEA 26-11-46 SOC 29-1-48

TD293 39MU 9-4-45 443S 3-5 FTR ops 4-5

TD316 9MU 5-4-45 317S 20-6-46 NEA 16-12 bou SOC 24-10-47

TD317 6MU 5-4-45 308S 20-4 SOC 7-8-47

TD318 19MU 29-3-45 340S 19-4 SOC scrap 22-7-46

TD319 9MU 27-4-45 CGS 11-7 w/u lndе Lecon C3 12-10-49 ROS to 6862M 15-5-51 B Hll 22-10-57

TD320 19MU 20-4-45 411S 7-6 401S 28-6 RHAF 13-1-49

TD321 19MU 30-4-45 61 OTU 29-1-46 FAAC 14-6-49 ROS recat scr 15-10

TD322 29MU 5-4-45 322S 26-4 349S 18-10 FAAC 21-3 411RSU SOC 25-2-46

TD323 29MU 20-4-45 601S 22-6-49 20S 14-10-50 5CAACU 25-9-51 C5 26-5-52

TD324 19MU 4-4-45 74S 26-4 341S 17-5 345S FACE dbf 15-10

TD325 19MU 4-4-45 341S 26-4 350S 17-1-46 BAF on loan pend del FXIV 26-10-46

TD338 39MU 9-4-45 345S 26-4 FACE 10-10

TD339 19MU 4-4-45 127S 26-4 349S 30-4 595S 4-10-48 5S 17-3-50 NES 6-6-56 sold Br Al 22-10

TD340 29MU 24-4-45 CGS 19-7 strck by Martinet EM617 on grnd Lecon 3R 8-11-49 recat scr 23-12

TD341 19MU 12-4-45 443S 3-5 SOC scr 29-7-46

TD342 6MU 21-4-45 84GDC 30-8 RHAF 19-3-49

TD343 6MU 16-4-45 403S 21-6 103FRS 16-5-51 FCCRS Sch Mid Wallop 18-6-52 NES 14-12-54 sold H Bath 17-5-56

TD344 6MU 1-5-45 695S 6-7 FACB 19-5-46 ROS 1CAACU 7-12-50 NES 4-6-56 sold Br Al 22-10-56

TD345 6MU 14-4-45 302S 16-5-46 SOC 29-11-48

TD346 29MU NEA 20-4-45 sold H Bath 27-10-49

TD347 6MU 14-4-45 340S 16-9 612S 20-10-49 FACR 14-5-50 recat scr 23-5

TD348 19MU 30-4-45 350S 24-1-46 349S 12-10 BAF on loan pend del FXIV 26-10

TD349 29MU 20-4-45 412S 7-6 402S 28-6 RHAF 11-4-49

TD350 39MU 17-4-45 RHAF 7-6-49

TD351 6MU 19-4-45 411S 7-6 401S 28-6 VA mods 15-3-49 RHAF 28-7

TD369 29MU 5-4-45 322S 26-4 302S 22-6-46 NEA 16-12 SOC 29-1-48

TD372 19MU 12-4-45 349S 17-5 BAF on loan pend del FXIV 26-10-46

TD375 19MU 12-4-45 BAFO Com Wng 2-8 FAAC 30-8 Res pl 302S 11-7-46 Farn Jly '46 anti-G trls NEA 16-12 SOC 29-1-48

TD376 85GSU 19-7-45 VA mods 15-3-49 RHAF 23-7

TD377 39MU 11-4-45 411S 7-6 401S 28-6 17SFTS to 6179M 9-10 recat E

TD400 6MU 18-5-45 61 OTU 5-2-46 sold int All 10-2-50

TD401 6MU 7-5-45 695S 5-7 691S 11-2-49 CE scrap 22-11

TD402 6MU 18-5-45 RNAF SoTT 8-7-47 at Deelen

TD403 19MU 15-5-45 CGS 6-7 614S 24-10-46 612S 25-11-49 FAC5 4-2-50 recat scr 9-3

TD404 9MU 16-5-45 CGS 11-7 RHAF 9-5-49

TD405 9MU 15-5-45 667S 20-7 1353Flt 28-9 FAAC 13-11 ROS NEA 23-1-47 sold scr 25-5-50

TD406 19MU 15-5-45 CGS 10-7 7SFTS 6-6-46 FAAC 15-7-47 ROS SOC sold BKL Alloys 27-4-48

TD407 9MU 16-5-45 667S 20-7 61 OTU 27-12 FAAC 22-6-48 to 6423M 30-8 sold scr SOC 24-12

TD408 9MU 23-5-45 667S 20-8 2 OTU 3-1-46 61 OTU 10-1 bou SOC 27-1-47

TE116 19MU 4-4-45 74S 21-4 CB ops 24-4 420RSU ASTEx recat E 28-5

TE119 19MU 13-4-45 308S 6-9 349S 16-1-46 AM PR8 21-3 350S 9-5 BAF on loan pend del FXIV 26-10 CE scr sold E Smelt 10-3-48

TE120 19MU 12-4-45 443S 3-5 FAAC 6-9 614S 15-1-48 GAAC 12-7-47 103FRS 16-5-51 NEA 19-5-53 C5 15-7

TE174 6MU 18-5-45 51 OTU 14-1-46 FAAC 17-2-48 recat E SOC 21-4

TE175 9MU 16-5-45 587S 3-8 691S 20-6-46 RFS Exeter 20-3-51 NEA 13-5-53 C5 25-7

TE176 6MU 16-5-45 61 OTU 5-2-46 FAAC 26-2-47 ROS recat E SOC 29-5-47

TE177 6MU 18-5-45 61 OTU 14-1-46 FAAC 22-8 ROS

TE178 6MU 24-5-45 2APS 16-2-46 1 OFU 29-10-52 MEAF 28-11 HQ Home Com S 7-9-53 NES 13-12-54 sold L Met 15-5-50

TE179 9MU 18-5-45 587S 20-8 691S 20-6-46 TACB 17-10 recat E SOC scr dump 22-5-47

TE180 9MU 23-5-45 695S 30-8 w/u ldg CAC H StFth 21-6-48 recat E 23-7

TE181 9MU 15-5-45 631S 9-8 FACB 8-7-46 recat E 11-7 SOC 1-10

TE182 6MU 17-5-45 61 OTU 14-1-46 FAAC 16-3-49 ROS C5R scr 24-1-50

TE183 6MU 23-5-45 61 OTU 17-1-46 std cd attempt ldg Keevil pilot kld CE 22-3 SOC

TE184 203AFS 1-7-47 226 OCU 14-6-49 607S to 6850M 1855S ATC. To Belfast. Extant

TE185 9MU 23-5-45 695S 20-8 t/ld cd nr H StFth CB 25-8-47 recat E SOC scrap 11-9

TE186 9MU 24-4-45 CGS 11-7 scrap 9-2-50

TE187 19MU 23-4-45 411S 7-6 401S 28-6 1PAFU 18-8-47 1FRS 12-11-49 C3R ROS NEA 13-5-53 C5 scrap 20-7

TE188 19MU 12-4-45 317S 13-5-46 bou sold scr 3-9-47

TE189 29MU 20-4-45 604S 16-6-47 TAAC 16-4-49 ROS Fly Wing Debden 15-11-50 NEA 22-10-53 sold R J Coley 3-3-54

TE190 VA HPS 21-4-45 trls a/c Metal elev with 6in beading each side 16-5 33MU 19-6 61 OTU 16-1-46 203 AFS i/sea nr Chivenor pilot kld CE 25-3-49

TE191 6MU 18-4-45 416S 10-5 83GDC 20-9 349S 1-1-46 AM PR8 12-2 FAAC 18-10 412RSU RHAF 22-2-49

TE192 29MU 24-4-45 CGS 19-7 SOC DBR 27-6-46

TE193 29MU 13-1-45 TAF 2nd Com S 5-7 CFS 29-4-49 eng fail o/s f/lndg South Cerney CE 1-7 cat scr 25-10

TE194 29MU 24-4-45 CGS 19-7 scrap 3-2-50

TE195 19MU 23-4-45 412S 7-6 402S 28-6 61 OTU 6-2-46 sold scr bou 3-9-47

TE196 29MU 24-4-45 CGS 20-7 11AGS 30-4-47 203AFS 25-8-48 scr 24-1-50

TE198 6MU 27-4-45 411S 7-6 FAAC 4-7 410RSU

TE199 XVIE 19MU 23-4-45 412S 7-6 402S 28-6 Staff Coll W Wal 25-7-46 FAAC 12-9 ROS 21Gp Com Flt FTC AOC's personal trans (glossy black, gold trim overall) to 6603M 30-12-48 SoH FFS gate guardian June '55

TE200 19MU 23-4-45 411S 7-6 401S 28-6 CFS 21-8-47 sold J Dale 8-6-50

TE201 19MU 20-4-45 411S 7-6 401S 28-6 SOC 30-5-46

TE202 19MU 20-4-45 412S 7-6 402S 28-6 MacLarens HAL 27-3-46 65S 17-7 164S 18-7 63S 3-9 631S 16-6-48 sold J Dale 30-12-49

TE203 19MU 28-4-45 411S 7-6 401S 28-6 1PRFU 14-7-47 101FRS 17-2-50 C5 14-9-54

TE204 19MU 23-4-48 411S FAAC 31-5 ROS 601S 9-6-47 FAAC 23-4-49 ROS 103FSR 16-5-51 NES 13-12-54 sold L Met 3-9-47

TE206 19MU 25-4-45 421S 5-7 302S 6-9 317S 11-10 bou sold scr 3-9-47

TE207 29MU 24-4-45 CGS 19-7 to 6272M 19-2-47 cancel 6SoTT 25-3 SOC 17-7-52

TE208 29MU 20-4-45 411S 7-6 401S 28-6 308S GAAC 23-10 614S 2-6-47 604S 30-9-48 RCMSDU mods 10-4-49 RAF College Lindholme 2-2-50 NES 4-6-54 sold BrAl 22-10

TE209 29MU 25-4-45 CGS 19-7 strk by Martinet on gd Lecon CB 14-1-46 recat E SOC 23-1

TE210 19MU 27-4-45 VA 10-5 631S 11-8 flew i/high grd Minera Mt nr Wrexham CE 31-8 SOC 13-9

TE214 XVIE extant Canada War Mus (once carried false serial TE353)

TE228 6MU 25-4-45 411S 7-6 401S 28-6 61 OTU 8-3-46 SOC 4-2-47

TE229 9MU 27-4-45 GCS 11-7 air coll with Wellington BK214 of CGS cd E Yorks pilot kld CE 27-6-46 SOC

TE235 19MU 30-4-45 RHAF 7-6-49

TE237 19MU 30-4-45 SOC 28-8-46

TE239 19MU 4-5-45 61 OTU 6-1-46 eng cut t/o w/u ldg Keevil CE 30-4 SOC 10-7

TE240 19MU 10-5-45 CGS 8-7 17STFS 28-5-46 e/fld u/s ldg strk garage CAC Hibld 26-7-47 recat E SOC 15-8

TE241 9MU 1-5-45 FAAC CGS 10-7 VA STN 4-6-48 BDn 11-6 trls of GCS FMk.4B sight instal. Unacceptable for service use owing to limited view over nose

TE242 29MU 1-5-45 CGS 12-7 EAAS 13-7-48 FAAC 22-12-48 ROS CGS 25-2-49 FAAC 12-5 6998M 8-9-52 recat 5(S) 13-11

TE243 6MU 31-5-45 164S 19-7-46 63S 3-9 FAAC 24-6-47 recat E SOC 18-7

TE244 19MU 30-4-45 61 OTU 29-1-46 GAAC 7-7-47 ROS 502S 28-4-49 to 6655M

TE245 19MU 30-4-45 RHAF 7-6-49

TE246 29MU 4-5-45 FATU 30-9 6 OTU 15-3-46 FAAC 15-5-48 ROS 236 OCU 11-9-48 CE on insp 8-7-49 scr 13-12

TE247 19MU 30-4-45 411S 7-6 401S 23-6 PRFU 28-8-47 FACS 1-5-50 AFD scr 12-5

TE248 6MU 1-5-45 695S 5-7 61 OTU 17-4-47 603S 27-2-50 34S 29-5 C5 SOC

TE249 6MU 1-5-45 EAAS Manby 24-6 RHAF 4-5-49

TE250 19MU 15-5-45 CGS 8-7 603S 19-10-46 609S 2-5-48 C4R 13-4-50 recat scrap 10-5-50

TE251 19MU 30-4-45 61 OTU 16-1-46 FACB 28-6 60 OTU 24-8 sold scr bou 3-9-47

TE252 39MU 1-6-45 RHAF 22-6-49

TE253 9MU 16-5-45 587S 25-7 691S 20-6-46 hit grd cloud CE Dartmoor pilot kld 3-1-47 SOC

TE254 6MU 7-5-45 AAS Manby 24-6 SOC 21-10-4

TE255 6MU 7-5-45 AAS Manby 24-6 to 6433M 10 47 SOC AFD 5-4-50

TE256 29MU 1-5-45 FATU 26-9 VA EA 10-4-46 b SOC 26-7

TE257 29MU 4-5-45 FATU 22-9 103FRS 16-5- NES 4-6-56 sold scr 24-10

TE258 6MU 15-5-45 61 OTU 16-1-46 FAAC 17 ROS 203AFS cd/ldg CAC Keevil 6-8-47 NEA 15-9 SOC 19-48

TE259 19MU 10-5-45 CGS 8-7 FATU 20-9 5(P)AF 21-3-46 surplus 8-3-50 NEA 28-3-51 sold Cindal Aluminiu 30-8

TE273 no record

TE274 6MU 18-5-45 151RU Res pl 27-9-46 349S 1 10 BAF on loan pend del FXIV 26-10 NEA 9-1-48 sold Smelt 25-5-56

TE275 9MU 18-5-45 287S 24-8 604S 5-11-47 cd f/ln nr Chigwell C4R 27-11-49 ROS recat E bou scr 29-12

TE276 9MU 16-5-45 667S 31-7 ROS 61 OTU 10-1- RHAF 26-11-48

TE277 6MU 23-5-45 164S 19-7-46 63S 3-9 595S 30-48 695S 23-7 2CAACU 17-8-51 C5 11-12-54

TE278 9MU 25-5-45 587S 26-8 691S 20-6-46 FAA 18-1-47 recat E SOC 30-1

TE279 9MU 15-5-45 667S 25-7 FAAC 10-9 recat 30-1-46

TE280 6MU 16-5-45 61 OTU 14-1-46 FAAC 29-4- SOC 29-5

TE281 9MU 18-5-45 667S 2-8 61 OTU 27-12 FAA 9-12-46 ROS 226 OCU 7-8-47 scrap 24-1-50

TE282 9MU 23-5-45 695S 9-8 air coll with TE376 Bawburgh Norfolk CE 2-10 SOC 11-10

TE283 29MU 24-5-45 667S 23-8 61 OTU 27-12 bc sold scr 3-9-47

TE284 29MU 2-6-45 349S Fassburg 23-8-46 BAF o loan del FXIV 26-10 RHAF 25-2-49

TE285 30-5-45 595S 13-9 FACB 10-11 recat E SO 17-9-46

TE286 6MU 24-5-45 MacClarens HAL 15-3-46 65 18-4 164S 11-7 691S 14-11 RFS Exeter 20-3-51 NEA 16-2-5 sold H Bath 23-6

TE287 9MU 27-5-45 691S 5-9 `e/fd f/ld on beac Morte Point nr Ilfracombe dbf 4-11-46

TE288 XVIE 61 OTU 501S 102SFTS to 7287M. Extant RNZAF Museum.

TE291 6MU 31-5-45 HAL 19-3-46 65S 2-5 SOC 30- 47

TE300 DSFD 9MU 9-7-45 595S 13-10 4CAACU 29 8-51 SOC 28-6-54

TE302 6MU 8-6-45 609S 18-8-48 AGT Gat refurb 10 2-51 1689Flt ADn 23-7 NES 14-12-54 sold scr 19-6-56

TE310 29MU 9-6-45 61 OTU 19-2-46 FAAC 13-3 t 7741M Tang recat E SOC scr dump 16-8

TE311 BoB film extant RAF Abingdon to 7241M (7741M) 6 OTU rename 236 OCU 631S rename 20S Dec'47

TE314 6MU 8-6-45 614S 23-6-47 air coll with RW a/ aban cd Long Sutton Somer 7-12 SOC 8-1-48

TE328 9MU 7-6-45 631S 7-9-48 SOC 2-11

TE330 601S to 7449M presented to USAAF 3-7-5 extant Wright Patterson Field Dayton Ohio

TE332 6MU 15-6-45 126S 27-2-46 19S 21-3 WAL mods 3-3-49 scr 23-2-50

TE334 39MU 12-6-45 61 OTU 19-2-46 CB during maintenance 25-3-49 recat E 16-7

TE335 9MU 14-6-45 605S 18-5-48 RC Com Sq 5-1 sold Trial & Exp Estb Shoe 21-5-51 SOC 13-9

TE338 9MU 12-6-45 609S 9-8-48 hit obs on app Yeadon CB 30-1-49 to 6642M 9-3 SOC AFD 4-4-51

TE339 29MU 9-6-45 236 OCU 1-8-46 cd/ld CB Kinloss 22-6-48 recat E 23-7

TE340 6MU 8-6-45 203AFS 3-3 hit trees pulling ou of dive Tibenham pilot kld C5 18-8-49 recat E scr 9-9

TE341 RAF Kenley 16-8-55 sold Pinewood Studios

TE342 9MU 2-6-45 APS Acklington 11-9-47 CR School Mid Wales 17-10-51 NES 16-12-54 sold H Bath 3-5-56

TE344 9MU 13-6-45 604S 15-4-47 20S 3-4-50 FAC3 2-6 ROS scrap 19-7-51

TE345 9MU 13-6-45 631S 15-12-47 NES 13-12-54 sold L Met 15-5-56

TE346 19MU 20-4-45 RHAF 26-11-48

TE347 9MU 20-6-45 21 OTU 7-3-46 202OTU 603S 28-7-47 609S 10-4-48 recat E 27-10

TE348 9MU 13-6-45 203AFS dvd i/grd nr Wirkleigh Devon pilot kld 28-5-48

TE349 39MU 4-6-45 101FRS 12-3-51 29MU 11-10 NES 4-6-56 sold BrAl 22-10-56

TE350 6MU 12-6-45 RHAF 30-12-48

TE351 9MU 12-6-45 61 OTU 12-1-46 TAAC 19-2-48 ROS 203AFS f/ld cd CE Westleight N Devon pilot kld 16-9-48 SOC

TE352 39MU 25-6-45 102FRS 23-4-51 TA3R 18-6 ROS to 6890M 7-9 SOC 13-6-52

TE353 9MU 13-6-45 203AFS 23-9-48 TAAC 1-6-49 recat E 9-8 to Canada (found to be TE214)

TE354 6MU 15-6-45 HAL 20-3-46 65S 2-5 164S 15-8 691S 30-4-48 RFS Exeter 15-3-51 NEA 12-6-53 sold J G Will 23-10

TE355 DSFD 9MU 10-7-45 203AFS 2-3-48 FAAC 10-3-49 ROS recat scr 6-10

TE356 695S 34S 2CAACU 71MU 11-3-67 to 6700M extant RAF Little Rissington to 7001M 15-9-52. Extant Bitteswell.

TE357 no record

TE358 9MU 13-6-45 Pers 16-4-47 29MU 29-5-48 103FRS 16-5-51 NEA 3-12-56 sold R J Coley 17-4-57

TE359 6MU 16-6-45 203AFS 22-3-48 603S 27-2-50 612S 25-5-50 20S 17-7-51 NEA 13-6-53 sold J G Will 28-10

TE375 9MU 13-6-45 EAAS(FTC) 11-11-48 CGS 29-9-49 FA scr 23-10-50

TE376 DSFD 6MU 9-7-45 695S 3-8 FAAC 23-8 ROS air coll with TE282 nr Bawburgh Norfolk CE SOC 2-10

TE377 6MU 31-7-45 203AFS 27-10-47 610S 27-2-50 NEA 12-10 sold Proof Exp Estb Shoe 24-1-51

TE378 9MU 14-6-45 203AFS 3-3-48 226 OCU w/u lndg Strad C3 20-10-49 recat scr 8-11

TE379 9MU 9-6-45 162S 25-7-46 164S 1-8 1PRFU 14-4-47 FA3R 21-2-51 recat 5(S) to Proof Exp Estb Shoe 2-7

TE380 DSFD 6MU 14-7-45 587S 3-8 691S 20-6-46 RFS Exeter 19-3-51 scr AFD 25-2-53

TE381 6MU 15-6-45 RHAF 5-12-48

TE382 6MU 16-6-45 10 OTU 27-2-46 17 OTU 28-2 FAAC 9-8 ROS WAL mods 1-3-49 RHAF 24-8

TE383 6MU 16-6-46 RHAF 30-12-48

TE384 XVIE 9MU CE 8-7-52 603S BoB film to 7207M To VH-XVI, extant, Queensland

TE385 9MU 13-6-45 614S 10-3-48 612S 21-11-48 4CAACU 4-2-52 NES 16-12-54 sold H Bath 17-2-56

TE387 6MU 20-7-45 19S 23-5-46 203AFS 27-10-47 w/u lndg Strad CB 28-7-49 recat E 18-8

X TE388 6MU 31-7-45 HQ MC Com Sq 3-5-48 FACB 23-4-49 sold R J Coley 3-2-50

TE389 9MU 15-6-45 1APS 4-2-46 19S 25-4 203AFS 8-7-49 610S 27-2-50 1CAACU FA3R 22-1-52 to 6990M 21-6 2258S ATC

TE390 6MU 14-6-45 595S 27-8-48 4CAACU 29-8-51 NES 14-12-54 sold E Smelt 18-6-56

TE391 29MU 8-8-45 126S 27-2-46 19S 21-3-46 WAL mods 9-2-49 RHAF 15-8

TE392 65S to 7000M Waterbeach 15-9-52 extant Bitteswell

TE393 6MU 16-6-45 126S 27-2-46 19S 21-3 WAL mods 25-1-49 scrap 20-2-50

TE394 29MU 20-6-45 65S 15-3-46 cd f/lndg nr Cambridge CB 15-7 recat E SOC 3-10

TE395 9MU 13-6-45 601S 15-4-47 HQ HC Com Sq 10-8-51 FA4R 13-8-53 C5(C)AFD 18-8

TE396 6MU 19-6-45 26 OTU 7-3-46 19S 21-3 103FRS 16-5-51 NEA 16-2-53 sold H Bath 23-6

TE397 29MU 9-6-45 65S 18-2-46 126S 27-2 19S 21-3 103FRS 16-5-51 5CAACU 4-7-52 C4R 4-11-53

TE398 29MU 20-6-45 65S 15-3-46 164S 29-8 63S 3-9 e/fd on app Mid Wallop hvy ldg u/c coll port wng torn away CE 6-12 SOC 18-4-47

TE399 29MU 22-6-45 631S 5-9 FAAC 2-12-47 sold J Dale 8-7-48

TE400 9MU 16-6-45 501S 7-5-48 612S 20-5-49 Radio Sch Mid Wal 12-2-52 NES 14-12-54 to 7240M 28-9-55

TE401 9MU 19-7-45 587S 26-8 691S 20-6-46 scrap 1-2-50

TE402 6MU 16-6-45 MacLarens HAL 7-3-46 65S 20-3 164S 11-7 63S 3-9 FAAC 24-6-47 ROS 395S 16-6-48 695S 28-7 1CAACU 7-12-50 FA3R 25-1-56

TE403 9MU 25-6-45 501S 5-2-47 FAAC 9-10-48 ROS CR Sch Mid Wal 17-10-51 C3R 16-10-52 ROS NES 14-12-54 sold H Bath 1-5-56

TE404 DSFD6MU 14-7-45 667S 30-7 FAAC 28-8 ROS recat E SOC 22-12

TE405 DSFD 29MU 17-7-45 CGS 2-4-46 NES 14-12-54 sold E Smelt 13-6-56

TE406 DSFD 9MU 9-7-45 61 OTU 7-3-46 203AFS flew i/high grd in bad weather Brent Moor Buckfastleigh Devon CE 23-10-47 SOC 5-12

TE407 6MU 15-6-45 MacLarens HAL 7-3-46 65S 8-4 164S 11-7 63S 3-9 203AFS 6-5-48 FA3R 31-10-56 sold L Met 29-1-57

TE408 9MU 16-6-45 126S 7-3-46 19S 21-3 WAL mods 8-2-49 scr 23-2-50

TE434 29MU 22-6-45 667S 23-8 61 OTU 27-12 bou sold scr 3-9-47

TE435 DSFD 29MU 25-7-45 631S 16-3-46 f/ld cd on beach Merioneth CE 24-11-48 SOC 3-8-49

TE436 6MU 2-8-45 614S 10-4-47 604S 30-9-48 1-3FRS 16-7-51 NEA 12-6-53 sold J G Will 23-10

TE347 9MU 16-6-45 603S 9-4-47 609S 22-3-48 FA3R 20-4-50 recat scrap 16-5

TE438 6MU 22-6-45 MacLarens HAL 7-3-46 65S 11-4 SOC ABS 5-2-47

TE439 9MU 19-6-45 604S 9-6-47 TAAC 1-6-48 ROS recat E 20-7

TE440 29MU 23-6-45 695S 22-7 61 OTU 17-4-47 203 AFS dvd i/grd nr Woolfardisbury pilot kld CE 18-1-49 SOC 1-2

TE441 6MU 1-8-45 203AFS 7-9-48 APS Acklington 6-12-49 F&T charge 20-MU 27-12-50 1689Flt 15-2-51 FA scr 17-4

TE442 6MU 31-7-45 501S 27-1-47 601S 28-1 cd/ld Villacoublay France CB 26-7-48 recat E 25-10

TE443 9MU 23-6-45 2APS 5-2-46 FAAC 5-9-47 ROS 63S 22-3-48 595S 4-5 f/ld cd Pembroke CE 29-5-48 SOC 31-5

TE444 DSFD 29MU 25-7-45 349S 27-8-46 63S 5-9 RAF on loan pend del FXIV 26-10

TE445 6MU 31-7-45 6MU ADn 28-4-47 NEA 14-10-48 sold Int All 28-3-49

TE446 6MU 22-6-45 MacLarens HAL 7-3-46 65s 4-4 164S 29-8 63S 3-9 cd f/lndg nr Neustadt CE SOC 10-10

TE447 6MU 22-6-45 126S 21-2-46 19S 21-3 WAL mods 26-1-49 RHAF 3-8

TE448 29MU 22-6-45 HAL 11-2-46 126S 7-3 65S 21-3 20S 5-8-49 C5 scr 21-4-53

TE449 29MU 23-6-45 695S 11-7 FAAC 1-4-47 C5(C) 13-11-52

TE450 29MU 23-6-45 695S 22-7 NEA 16-9-53 sold H Bath 23-9

TE451 29MU 23-6-45 65S 18-2-46 126S 17-2 19S 21-3 sold bou scr 3-9-47

TE452 9MU 25-6-45 595S 5-10-48 FA scr 2-8-50

TE453 29MU 22-6-45 MacLarens HAL 18-2-46 65S 20-3 164S 15-8 63S 3-9 cd f/lndg Ottenbuttel CE 10-9 SOC 26-9

TE454 29MU 22-6 65S 15-3-46 CE scrap 10-3-48 sold E Smelt 11-3

TE455 9MU 19-6-45 1PRFU 18-8-47 scr 11-8-50

TE456 XVIE 47MU 16-7-56 3CAACU Dishforth extant Auckland War Mus New Zealand

TE457 29MU 20-6-45 HAL 11-2-46 SF Horsham eng fire on starting dbf HSt Fth CE 9-9

TE458 6MU 22-6-45 126S 21-2-46 19S 21-3 scrap SOC 16-11-47

TE459 33MU 27-6-45 RAF College Bracknell 26-4-46 FAAC 15-6 Res Com CF W Wal u/c coll ldg 3-6-47 ROS recat E scr 11-3-48

TE460 9MU 18-6-45 CFS 11-4-47 FAAC 21-6 ROS recat E 14-9-48

TE461 9MU 29-6-45 601S 28-5-47 29MU 11-10-51 NES 14-12-54 sold H Bath 23-5-56

TE462 607S 101FRS to 7243M Ouston East Fortune extant Royal Scottish Museum of Flight

TE463 29MU 2-7-45 FATU 26-9 603S 9-7-47 609S 14-5-48 to 6822M 29-1-51

TE464 39MU 26-6-45 103FRS 16-5-51 NES 11-10-54 RAF Dux C5 9-11

TE465 39MU 12-7-45 SOC mr 27-11

TE466 33MU 30-6-45 131WG u/c cllpse lndg Eindhoven CB 2-9-46 recat E 11-2-47

TE467 33MU 27-6-45 604S 7-5-49 FACE 26-5 ROS 17S 16-10-50 RFS Exeter 19-3-51 NEA 13-5-53 C5 AFD 25-7-53

TE468 39MU 26-6-45 RHAF 9-2-49

TE469 9MU 25-6-45 bou SOC 29-4-47

TE470 29MU 20-6-45 19S 28-5-46 612S 17-2-50 FCCRS 4-7-51 FA scr 25-10

TE471 no record

TE472 to 6258M

TE473 9MU 29-6-45 601S 15-4-47 FAAC 15-5-48 ROS NEA 21-10-53 sold R J Coley

TE475 6MU 9-7-45 COAL mods 12-7 EAAS Manby 28-8 FAAC 16-7-48 ROS recat E 20-11

TE476 to 7451M Neatishead RAF Henlow 8071M BoB film extant RAF Northolt 1983

TE477 29MU 2-7-45 FATU 24-9 602S 28-3-47 609S 6-5-48 FA3R 18-2-50 ROS to 6820M 29-12

TE478 6MU 10-8-45 616S 7-6 609S 17-7 scr 18-6-51

TE479 COAL mods 19-7-45 CGS 21-2-446 61 OTU 14-5-47 to 6641M 2-3-49

TE480 CRD COAL mods 11-7-45 6MU 28-7 CGS 21-2-46 w/u ldg CB Lecon 6-4-48 sold H Bath 27-10-49

ON LOAN TO BELGIUM AIR FORCE PENDING DELIVERY OF F XVI RW344, SL596, TB348, 373, 386, 709, 748, 866-868, 892, 991, TD140, 184, 188, 231, 237, 253, 281, 325, 348, 372, TE119, 274 and 444.

MacLAREN MODS. RW350, SM421, TD134, 244, TE202, 407, 438, 446 and 453.

MAINTENANCE AIRFRAMES. RR229(6180M), RR263(7216M), RW382(7245M), RW393(7293M), RW386(6944M), RW388(6946M), SL542(8390M), SL565(6333M), SL674(8392M), SM193(5979M), SM276(6176M), SM385(6008M), SM402(6248M), SM411(7242M), SM484(5981M), SM899(6902M), TB252(7257M), TB308(7255M), TB382(7244M), TB522(6262M), TB578(6177M), TB752(7256M), TB753(6904M), TB903(6178M), TB916(6945M), TD135(6798M), TD236(6273M), TD248(7264M), TD280(6540M), TD319(6862M), TE184(6850M), TE199(6603M), TE207(6272M), TE311(7241M), TE330(7449M), TE338(6642M), TE352(6890M), TE356(7001M), TE384(7207M), TE392(7000M & 8074M), TE397(6700M), TE462(7243M), TE476(7451M & 8071M), TE477(6820M) and TE479(6641M).

ROYAL HELLENIC AIR FORCE. PV349, RW347, 379, SL623-624, 679, 717, TA759, TB130, 237, 254-255, 272, 274, 617, 859, 886, 895, 901, 908, TD114, 126, 133, 142, 145, 147, 176, 190-191, 229, 235, 239, 241, 243, 246, 285, 320, 342, 349-350, 376, 404, TE191, 235, 245, 252, 276, 284, 346, 350, 381-383, 391 and 447.

Above: TE357 clearly existed, although no official history card has been traced for it.

Below: TE356, wearing No 695 Squadron markings, on the parade ground at Bicester.

T Mk XVI

Wing. Planform elliptical; section NACA Series 2200; incidence° root +2, tip $-\frac{1}{2}$; dihedral° 6; thickness% root 13.2, tip 6; aspect ratio 5.68; area sq ft nett 220, gross 242; chord (geometric) 6.38, mean aerodynamic 6ft 6.8 Ailerons area sq ft 18.9; movement° up 26, down 19; droop in $\frac{3}{8}$. Flaps area sq ft 15.6; movement° down 85. Wing loading lb/sq ft 30.17; power loading lb/hp 4.17. Propeller clearance at take off 9.50in. (Wing span decreased by $3\frac{1}{2}$in when Air Ministry decided that tips should be detachable. New tips were less pointed.

Tailplane. Area sq ft 31.46; chord (ma) 4.1 incidence° root 0, tip $\pm\frac{1}{2}$; dihedral° 0. Elevators area sq ft 13.26; movement° up 28; down 23; tab area sq ft 0.38; movement° up 20; down 7. Fin area sq ft 4.61. Rudder area sq ft 8.23; tab area sq ft 0.35; movement° port 12; starbd 12.

Undercarriage. Wheels Dunlop AH2061; tyres Dunlop 7-59-10; pressure lb/sq in oleo pressure lb/sq in. Tailwheel, fixed castoring. Dunlop AH2184; tyre Dunlop Ecta 3-00-4.

Engine/s. Packard Merlin 266. Take off 1,325hp @ 3,000rpm (MS) 1,750 @ 3,000 @ 5,500ft; 1,372 @ 2,850 @ 9,000.

Propeller/s. Rotol 4-blade.

Diameter 10ft 9in.

Fuel 100 octane 130 octane. Fuselage 39 gals, inner wing $2 \times 14\frac{1}{2}$. Outer wing 2×13. Total 94 gals.

Performance. Max speed 386mph @ 20,000ft (FS), 360 @ 9,000 (MS), 322 @ SL (MS). Rate of climb, 3,970ft min @ 18,000ft (FS), 4,650 @ 7,000 (MS), 4,640 @ SL (MS).

Service ceiling 41,500 ft. Range @ 228mph @ 20,000ft 234 miles. Fuel consumption 6.40 mpg. Endurance 1.03 hr. Take off run 430 yds.

Weight. Take off 7,300lb.

General arrangement of T Mk XVI.

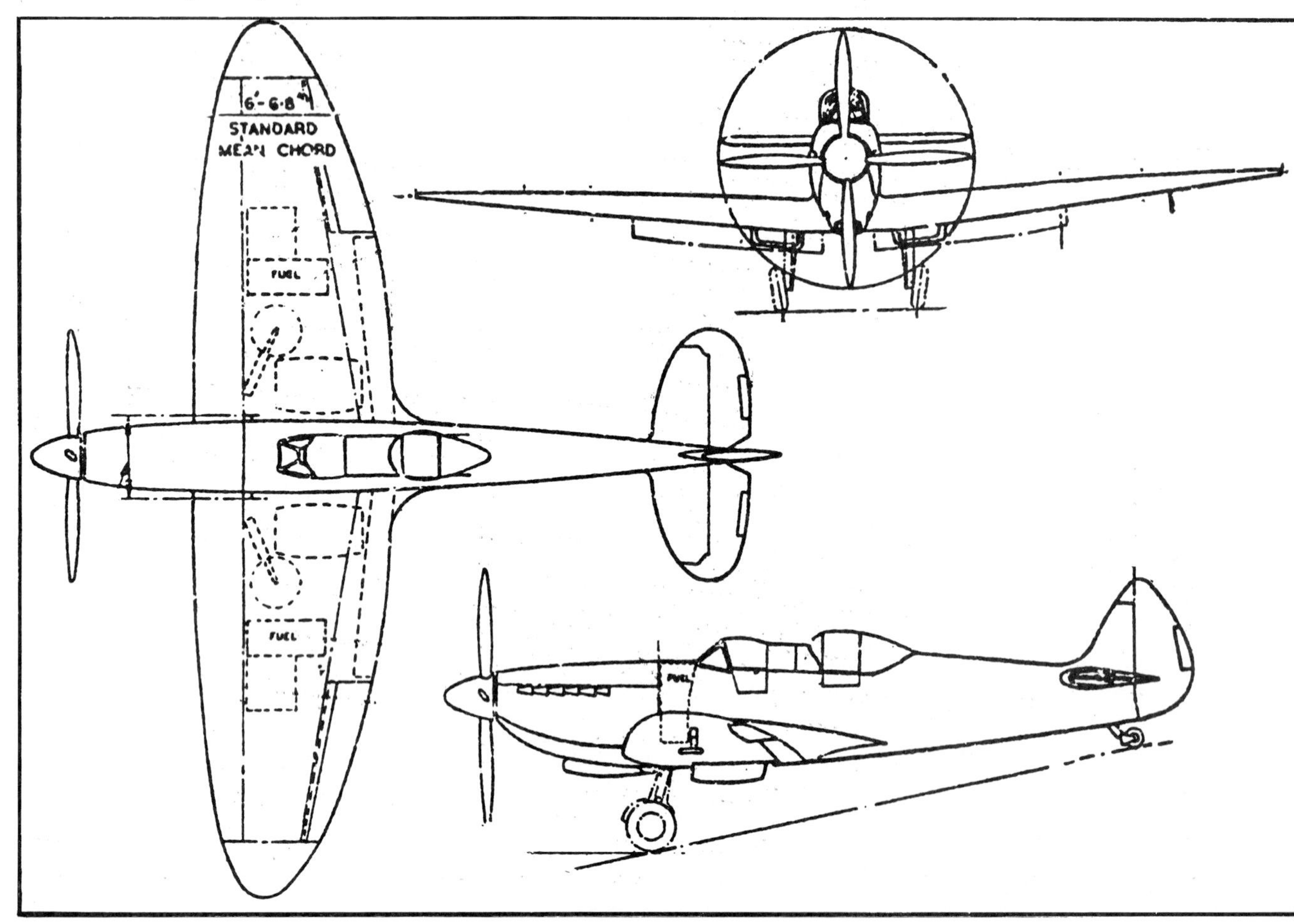

'SUPER SPITFIRE'

Towards the end of 1943 development of the so-called 'Super Spitfire' was started. Supermarine were aware that the time had arrived when new discoveries in aerodynamics meant that in order to keep the Spitfire as a front line fighter a decision had to be taken to (1) design a new aeroplane incorporating the laminar flow wing with an increased power Merlin or Griffon engine (2) produce yet another variant of the basic Spitfire design utilising the Griffon and modifying the fuselage and wing. Flight and static tests had proved that the F Mk VIII fuselage was capable of modification to accept more powerful engines, even though this would mean a much modified empennage to counteract torque. The modified fuselage could then be married to a redesigned wing.

The result of all considerations eventually resulted in the **Spitfire F Mk XVIII, and as already mentioned in chapter 23,** the interim aircraft for this variant, the F Mk XIV, was produced in greater numbers than the type which was to replace it.

Designation of the new variant posed a few problems for the Air Staff as the next logical mark number was XVIII, for the mark XVII had been allocated to a new Seafire and PR XIX for the latest photo-reconnaissance Spitfire. When the Mk XIV had been in service for some months the Air Staff informed Fighter Command that the designation FR Mk XVIII had been reserved for the forthcoming fighter-reconnaissance version of the fighter, but Fighter Command wrote back to say that two squadrons of the Second TAF were already equipped with retrofitted F XIVs with cameras and they were known as FR Mk XIVs. This was during November 1944 and the Air Staff did not like the unofficial designation that Fighter Command had chosen, and as a result decided that the retrofitted F XIVs should be known as 'Interim F Mk XIV, Oblique Cameras' It was clumsy and was ruled out for the 'Interim F Mk XIV' designation had already been allocated to the F Mk VIII airframes fitted with the Griffon engine. So, the obvious choice, the F Mk XVIII was finally agreed upon.

There was no specially-built prototype and the first production model, SM843, was used for maker's trials and it arrived at High Post aerodrome on 8 June 1945 to begin tests. It had been built to FR standards with two F24 cameras of varying focal length installed in the rear fuselage. The Type Record for the F and FR (Type 394/1) was issued on 17 May and the General Description read – This Type Record covers the Spitfire F & FR Mk XVIII which is structurally similar to the Mk XIV except that strengthening of the wings and main undercarriage has been introduced to cater for weight increases due to rear fuel and cameras. The Type Record also covers an increase in engine power to that corresponding to 25 lb/sq in boost and an increase in terminal velocity to 475 mph at 10,000 feet. No Specification has been issued and flight reserve factors are quoted on the Spitfire fighter basis. In the fighter bomber condition, reserve factors of 0.85 are regarded as acceptable. For the condition with drop tanks no flight reserve factors are quoted as the tank is regarded as dropped or its contents used before appreciable manoeuvring loads are imposed on the aeroplane. The requirements of AP 970 Chap 703, para 31 are at least satisfied.

Loading conditions	Weight lb	CoG aft of datum(in)	Stressing conditions
Fighter (A) Combat load, all internal tanks full except upper rear tank	8960	6.5	Landing
(B) (A) plus upper rear tank full	9190	8.6	Combat
(C) (B) plus 1 × 500 lb bomb & 2 × 250 lb wing bombs	10275	8.5	Bombing
(D) (B) plus 90 gal drop tank & 2 × 250 lb wing bombs	10940	8.7	Takeoff
Fighter Recco. (E) Combat load, all internal tanks full except rear tank	8770	4.7	Covered by fighter loading conditions
(F) (E) plus rear tank full	9000	6.9	Bombing
(G) (F) plus 1 × 500 lb fuselage bomb & 2 × 250 lb wing bombs	10085	7.0	
(H) (F) plus 90 gal drop tank & 2 × 250 lb wing bombs	10300	7.2	Covered by fighter loading conditions

Maximum level speed 385 mph

On 6 July Shea-Simmonds flew SM843 complete with a standard F Mk XIV rudder and he reported directional stability above 400 mph as poor and propeller vibration completely unacceptable. Investigation of the propeller revealed it had been damaged during the aircraft's delivery flight and not reported. The following day, flying with the propeller from TP279, plus its large chord rudder with split trimmer tab, SM843 was assymetric to port in climb and suffered from a reversal of directional trim at around 400 mph. It returned to base to have a four inch long strip fitted to the elevator trailing edge upper surface and this resulted in some improvement.

TP279 was the next Mk XVIII to arrive at High Post and Shea-Simmonds was rather scathing about its performance. He said – "It is my opinion that this aircraft should not have been passed during production tests for two reasons. (1) the ailerons are excessively heavy and there is some reversal of lateral trim from left to right. Note the degree of reversal is not serious but the aileron control weight renders the aircraft useless as a fighting proposition. (2) the slow running and tick over characteristics are not satisfactory, although typical. If the throttle is closed gently the tick over speed of the engine is too high, but if the throttle is opened slightly and them snapped closed sharply the tick over speed is then too low and the engine stops. There is also quite noticeable reversal of directional trim as speed is increased above 400 mph".

The first Mk XVIII to be delivered to the Royal Air Force was SM844 on 28 May 1945, reaching No 28 Squadron in Hong Kong. A total of 201 FR variants were completed for this role, and 99 aircraft were completed for the fighter/bomber role with provision for wing mounted bombs and rockets. No cameras were carried in this version, the first of which was NH782. A number of F XVIIIs were fitted with RATOG and an arrester hook as an aid to improve handling from unimproved airfields, but it was an experiment which did not progress beyond handling trials. In an attempt to extend the life of the variant Supermarine proposed a two-seat trainer version based on a modified airframe and retrofitting surplus XVIIIs to accept the second seat. Supermarine Type 518 detailed the necessary changes for the trainer version, which was to have been designated the T Mk XVIII.

The operational life of the Mk XVIII was limited owing to the cessation of hostilities shortly after it had entered service. Production was severely cut back and those built went mainly to India and the Far East, most of them directly into storage. The last Spitfire sortie was flown by No 60 Squadron as a strike against terrorists in the Kota Tinggi area of Johore on 1 January 1951.

OFFICIAL REPORTS ON Mk XVIII

Boscombe Down, 14 November 1945. TP279. Camera and gun heating trials. The aircraft fitted with canvas bulkheads fore and aft of the camera bay. Heating was adequate as were the gun temperatures.

Boscombe Down, 30 November 1945. TP279. F24 camera installation. Two split verticals ($8\frac{1}{2}°$ semi included angle) and one oblique. The verticals were mounted in tandem aft of the rear fuel tank on wooden bearer rails. Water penetrated the fuselage and contaminated the camera gear box. The oblique camera was mounted above the forward vertical. There was some vibration and the camera assembly was liable to strike against the glass viewing portholes on occasion. The report recommended improvement to mountings.

Boscombe Down, 12 May 1948. TP423. Trials of Gyro Gunsight Mk 4B installation. Satisfactory.

Boscombe Down, August 1945. NH872. Brief handling trials with 99 gallon drop tank and determination of aftmost position of GoG.

High Post, 15 July 1947. TP423. Handling with 170 gallon drop tank. All tanks full, except rear fuselage. Auw 10,390 lb, GoG 7.1in aft of datum. $6\frac{1}{2}$ lb inertia weight in elevator system.

SM970 was converted for use as a target tug. The winch and cable was stored in the fuselage tank. Tailwheel was protected from fouling of the cable by a strut. Cockpit view reveals cable status gauge (RH), padded and specially adapted joystick and gauge for speed control. Final view is of the winch.

SM843, FR XVIII trials aircraft, never saw squadron service and was sold as scrap in December 1949.

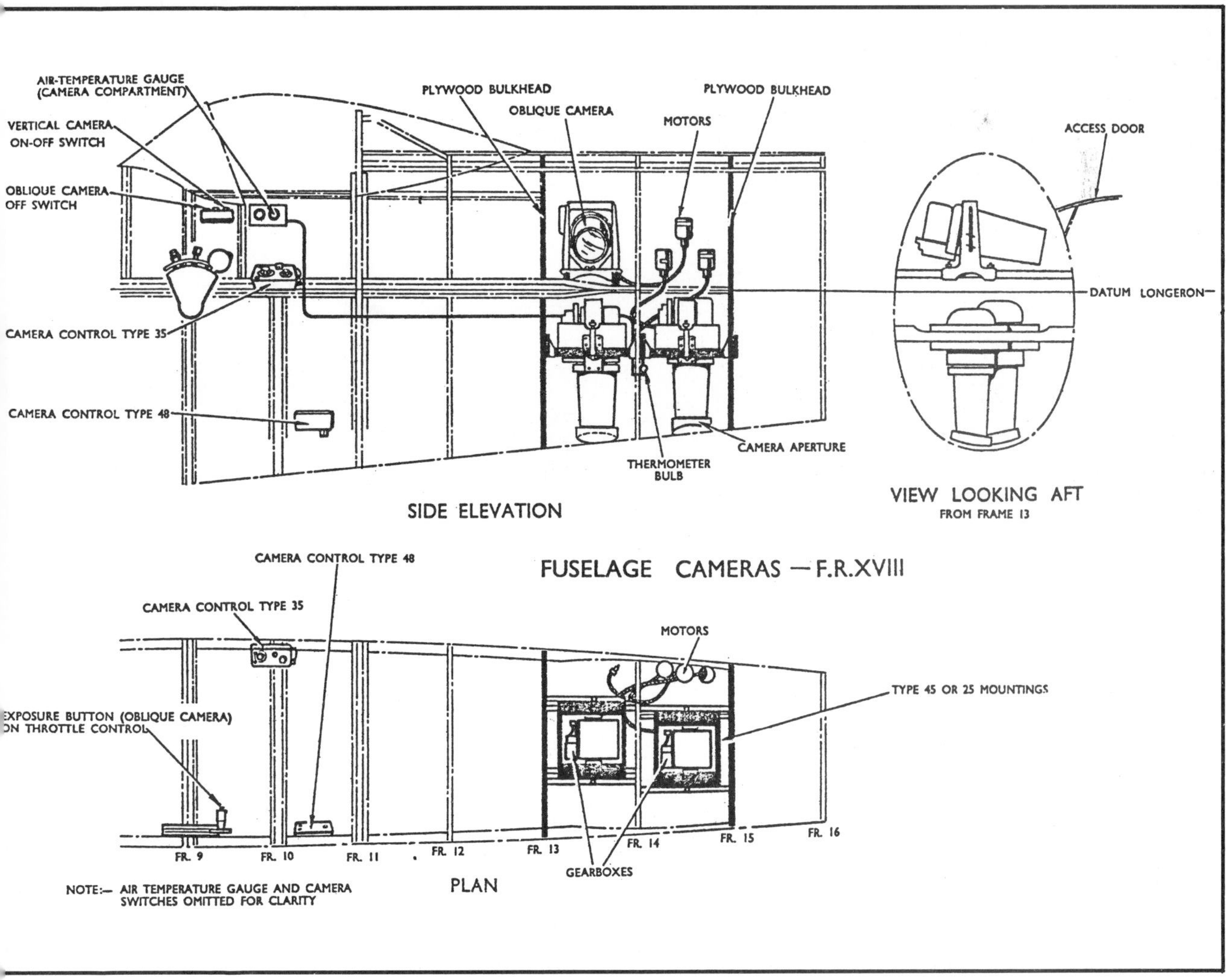

Aircraft dived to limiting speed with drop tank – 400 mph where it was unpleasant to fly. Suggested that limit of 320 mph be imposed.

F Mk XVIII and FR Mk XVIII

Wing. Planform elliptical; section NACA Series 2200; span 36′ 10″ incidence° root +2, tip $-\frac{1}{2}$; dihedral° 6; thickness % root 13.2, tip 6; aspect ratio 5.68; area sq ft nett 220, gross 242; chord (geometric) 6.38, mean aerodynamic 6ft 6.8in. Ailerons area sq ft 18.9; movement° up 24, down 19; droop $\frac{3}{8}$in. Flaps area sq ft 15.4; movement° down 85. Wing loading lb/sq ft 36.6; power **loading lb hp 4.35. Propeller clearance at take off 8½in** (Wing span decreased by $3\frac{1}{2}$in when Air Ministry decided that tips should be detachable. New tips were less pointed.

Tailplane. Area sq ft 33.84, chord (ma) 4.1, incidence° root 0, tip ± ½, dihedral° 0. Elevators area sq ft 13.74, movement° up 28, down 23, tab area sq ft 0.688, movement° up 20, down 23. Fin area sq ft 6.65. Rudder area sq ft 10.08, movement° port 28½, starbd 28½, tab area sq ft 0.7, movement° port 9, starbd 13½, setting 1.75m to starbd.

Undercarriage. Wheels Dunlop AH2061; tyres Dunlop. Tailwheel, fixed castoring. Dunlop AH2184; tyre Dunlop.

Engine/s. Griffon 65 2,035hp @ 2,750rpm @ 8,250ft. Griffon 67 2,375hp @ 2,750rpm @ 1,250ft.

Coffman cartridge starter.

Propeller/s. Rotol R19/5F5/1 5-blade Jablo pitch range 35°, fine pitch 27° 15″.

Coolant. 70% distilled water, 30% Glycol. Main system $15\frac{1}{2}$gals, in engine $4\frac{1}{2}$, intercoolers 4gal $5\frac{1}{2}$pts.

Fuel. 100 octane 18lb boost. 150 octane 25lb boost. Capacity upper fuselage 36gals, lower 48, $25\frac{1}{2}$ in wings (2 × $12\frac{3}{4}$), 66gal rear fuselage (2 × 33), total $175\frac{1}{2}$, plus 30, 45, 50, 90 o/ld tank 170.

Oil. 9gals in fuselage.

Armour. 180lb.

Armament. E wing. Plus 3 × 500lb GP bombs or Mk VIII and Mk IX RPs. Plus 60 (25lb head), 100 (60), 180 (60) lb rockets also 300 (180). 180 and 300 had triple motors.

Radio. TR1143, ARI 1262, ARI 5025, ARI 5151 special order only.

Cine camera. G45.

Gunsight. Gyro Mk IID.

Performance. Max speed 357mph @ SL (MS), 402 @ 11,000 (MS), 399 @ 15,900 (MS), 437 @ 24,500 (FS), 416 @ 34,000 (FS).

Rate of climb. SL (MS) 4,120ft/min; 8,000ft 4,200; 13,400 3,480; 17,500 (FS) 3,480; 22,500 3,285; 30,000 480.

Weights. Tare 6,845.5lb, take off 8,861.5, max permissible 9,100. max overload 11,000.

FR Mk XVIII

Total fuel $142\frac{1}{2}$

Cameras. 1 × F24 14 in and 2 x F24 20 in verticals. or 1 x F52 vertical.

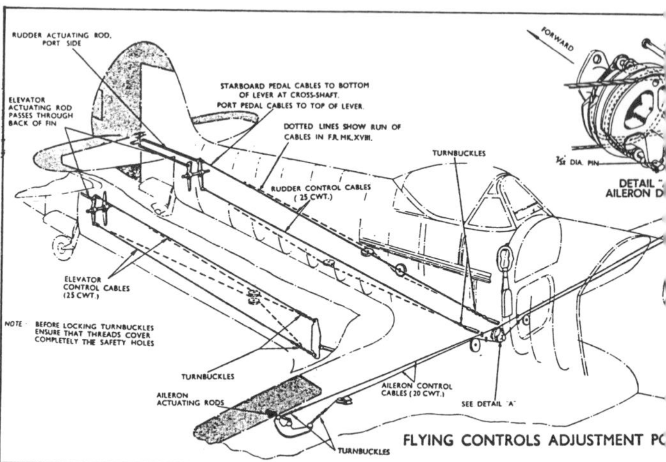

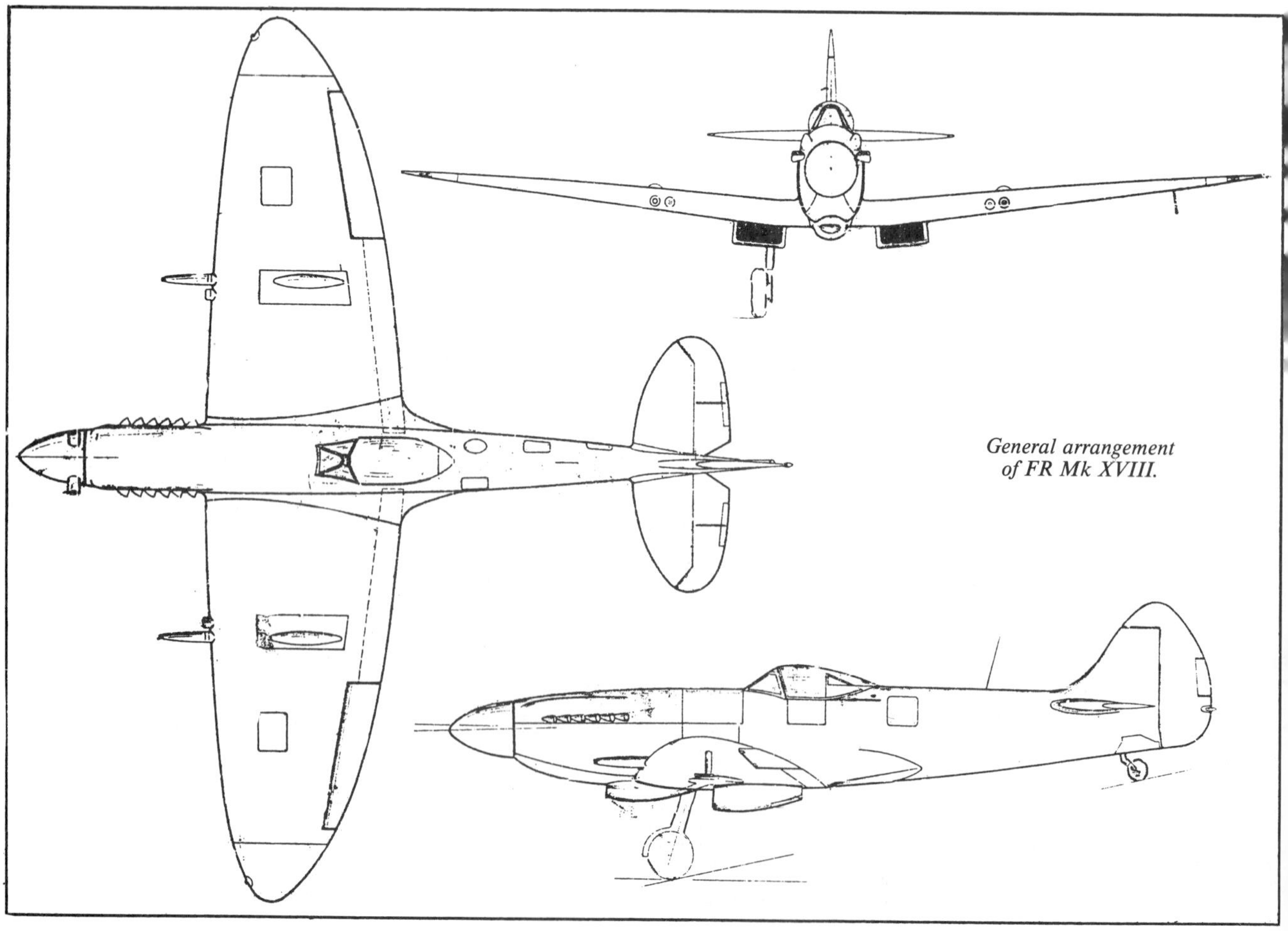

General arrangement of FR Mk XVIII.

Contract No. Air/1877/c.23(c).

Third order for 225 Spitfire Mk VIII, NH614 to NH929, dated 1 December 1942. Built as Mk VIII/XVI/XVIII between November 1944 and June 1945. The following serials apply to Mk XVIIIs built to this third order; NH847-856 and 872.

Eleventh order for 150 Spitfire Mk XI, SM812 to SM997, dated 12 February 1944. Built as Mk XIV/XVIII between february 1945 and January 1946. The following serials apply to Mk XVIIIs built to this eleventh order; SM843-845, 939-956 and 968-997.

Twelfth order for 300 Spitfire Mk XIV, TP195 to TP456, dated August 1944. Built as Mk XIV/XVIIIs between December 1945 and February 1946. the following serials apply to Mk XVIIIs built to this twelfth order; TP195-235, 257-298, 313-350, 363-408 and 423-456.

Thirteenth order for 157 Spitfire Mk XIV, TX974 to TZ240, dated 23 February 1945. Built as Mk XIV/XVIIIs between August 1945 and January 1946. the following serials apply to Mk XVIIIs built to this thirteenth order; TZ200-205 and 210-240. Total 300.

Production prototypes; NH849-850, SM844, 942, 945, 951, 955, 977, 979, 986, TP196, 295, 314, 342, 377, 398 and 400.

Burma A. F. NH853, SM943 and TP198(3).

India A. F. NH848, 855, SM845, 940-942, 944-946, 951, 969, 971, 974, 976, 979-986, 988-992, TP203, 257-260, 262-267, 269, 274, 276, 280, 287-290, 293-294, 296-298, 319, 325-326, 333, 338-339, 342, 344, 346, 363, 365, 367, 370, 379-380, 388, 392-393, 395-397, 401, 403-405, 425-426, 435-437, 439, 441-442, 444, TZ205, 217-219, 222, 224, 227, 231 and 235.

NH SM series all FX VIII Griffon 65

NH847 39MU 19-6-45 33MU 9-3-50 NEA 6-5-53 sold scr 18-1-54

NH848 STN 6MU 24-6-45 76MU 28-1-46 *Pent* 18-2 Ind 17-3 ACSEA 28-3 InAF 31-12-47

NH849 STN Super p/proto camera mount mods 29-9-44 33MU 30-6-45 76MU 16-1-46 *Megua* 29-1 Ind 25-2 ACSEA 4-3 MBFE stor 27-10-49 602S 16-2-50 C5(S) SOC 8-3-51

NH850 STN Super prod p/proto signal discharger mods 6-3-45 33MU 1-7 76MU 30-1-46 *Pent* 18-2 Ind 17-3 ACSEA 28-3 60S Sele 11-4-49 SHQ Semb 14-6 MBFE stor 11-1-51 C(S) SOC 8-3

NH851 STN 33MU 30-6-45 76MU 16-1-46 *Megua* 29-1 Ind 25-2 ACSEA 14-3 MBFE stor 21-3-50 FEAF 60S 29-8 SOC scr 8-3-51

NH852 STN 33MU 1-7-45 76MU 14-2-46 *Taran* 8-3 Ind 30-3 ACSEA 11-4 MBFE 9-12-49 60S 18-3-50 C(S) SOC 7-8

NH853 STN 39MU 8-7-45 76MU 18-2-46 *Taran* 8-3 Ind 30-3 ACSEA 11-4 Burma 22-4-48

NH854 STN 33MU 4-7-45 ROS NEA 6-5-53 sold MoS 12-1-54

NH855 STN 33MU 4-4-45 76MU 16-1-46 *Megua* 29-1 Ind 25-2-46 ACSEA 14-3 ret UK 31-7-47 sold R J Parkes 22-6-49 InAF 23-6-54

NH856 STN 39MU 8-7-45 76MU 13-2-46 *Taran* 8-3 Ind 30-3 ACSEA 11-4 Sele 25-8-49 FEAF SOC to 6680M but cancelled

NH872 STN Super prod proto for wng strength (particularly of FR and and long range a/c); for strength oleo legs; for strength fus for FR and L/R a/c 14-11-44 VA HPA 9-6-45 BDn 16-8 trls with 90 & 99gal O/L slipper tanks; det of aftmost CG with the additional 66gal rear fus fuel tank. Mod

NH872 was used exclusively as a trials aircraft.

rud as instal on F21 and contra props. Ret HPA 8-9 ECFS 10-10 Kee 16-1-46 33MU 13-2-50 NES 5-5-53 sold MoS 20-1-54

SM843 FR XVIII STN VA HPA 8-6-45 large chord rud and prop from TP279 July'45 33MU 4-1-46 WAL mods 11-2-49 NEA 31-3-53 sold scr MoS 30-12

SM844 FRXVIII(RV) G66 STN first XVIII to RAF 28-5-45 Super prod proto for strength wngs, fus and oleo legs 14-11-44 39MU 28-5-4547MU 10-5-50 *Cycl* 28-6 FEAF 19-7 S HQ Kai Tak stor 30-7 28S 18-10 reinforcement plan 31-3-51 C5 SOC 14-11-52

SM845 FRXVIII STN G66 39MU 28-5-45 76MU 13-12 *Sampenn* 19-1-46 Ind 11-2 ACSEA 28-2 ret UK 31-7-47 sold InAF 31-12

SM939 STN 33MU 10-7-45 76MU 12-1-46 *Megua* 29-1-46 Ind 25-2 ACSEA 14-3 MBFE 13-10-49 60S 15-3-50 C5(S) SOC 8-3-51

SM940 STN 33MU 11-7-45 76MU 29-12 *Sampenn* 19-1-46 Ind 11-2 ACSEA 28-2 ret UK 26-6-47 sold R J Parkes 13-7-49 InAF

SM941 STN ECFS Hull 25-7-45 39MU 9-8 76MU 12-1-46 *Megua* 29-1 India 25-2 ACSEA 14-3 ret UK 31-7-47 R J Parkes 14-6-49 InAF

SM942 STN Super prod proto 13-6-44 33MU 18-7-45 76MU 16-1-46 *Megua* 29-1 Ind 25-2 ACSEA 14-3 ret UK 31-7-47 R J Parkes 9-6-49 InAF

SM943 STN 33MU 23-7-45 76MU 31-1-46 *Taran* 8-3-46 Ind 30-3 ACSEA 11-4 60S w/u ldg Teng Sing 24-12-47 Burma 22-4-48

SM944 STN 39MU 23-7-45 76MU 16-1-46 *Megua* 29-1 Ind 25-2 ACSEA 14-3 ret UK 31-7-47 sold InAF 14-6-49

SM945 STN Super prod proto for stronger wheels, tyres and brakes 31-10-44 39MU 31-7-45 76MU 4-2-46 *Taran* 8-3-46 Ind 30-3 ACSEA 11-4 ret UK 31-7-47 InAF 31-12

SM946 STN 33MU 24-7-45 76MU 10-1-46 *Sampenn* 19-1 India 11-2 ACSEA 28-2 ret UK 26-6-47 R J Parkes 12-7-49 InAF

SM947 STN 39MU 31-7-45 76MU 28-1-46 *Pent* 18-2 Ind 17-3 ACSEA 28-3 Sele repairs 18-3-49 60S 24-10 FAC3 recat 5(C) SOC 21-12-50

SM948 STN 39MU 31-7-45 32MU for radio instal 3-1-50 FEAF 4-4 MBFE stor 18-5 60S 5-8 C5 14-11

SM949 STN 39MU 31-7-45 33MU 9-3-50 NEA 6-5-53 sold scr MoS 18-1-54

SM950 STN 33MU 18-8-45 76MU 16-1-46 *Megua* 29-1 Ind 25-2 ACSEA 14-3 MBFE storage 21-3-50 Cat comp BER 12-9

SM951 STN Super prod proto u/c mods 10-7-45 6MU 30-8 76MU 10-1-46 *Sampenn* 19-1 Ind 11-2 ACSEA 28-2 ret UK 26-6-47 R J Parkes 13-7-49 InAF

SM952 STN 33MU 22-8-45 76MU 14-2-46 *Taran* 2-3 Ind 30-3 ACSEA 11-4 InAF 31-12-47

SM953 STN 6MU 23-8-45 76MU 4-2-46 *Taran* 8-3 Ind 30-3 ACSEA 11-4 Sele 25-8-49 SOC

SM954 STN 6MU 23-8-45 76MU 31-1-46 *Taran* 8-3 Ind 30-3 ACSEA 11-4 Sele SOC 25-8-49

SM955 STN Super prod proto 17-4-45 33MU 6-9 76MU 6-2-46 *Taran* 8-3 Ind 31-3 ACSEA 17-10 MBFE stor 29-8-49 60S 16-11 SOC 8-3-51

SM956 STN 33MU 6-9-45 76MU 31-1-46 *Taran* 8-3 Ind 30-3 ACSEA 17-10 Sele SOC 25-8-49

SM968 KEE 6MU 28-8-45 76MU 30-1-46 *Pent* 18-2 Ind 17-3 ACSEA 17-10 390MU 13-4-48 Sele SOC 17-6-49

SM969 KEE 6MU 30-8-45 76MU 10-1-46 *Sampenn* 19-1 Ind 11-2 ACSEA 28-2 6S RIAF cd during aero Ranchi pilot kld 20-12-46 ret UK 26-6-47 R J Parkes 16-7-49 InAF ret UK July '78 sold D Arnold as G-BRAF, extant

SM970 KEE CRD Wilmot Mansion & Beaulieu 15-9-45 Farn May'47 target tow with PK513; Nov'48 winch trls Lasham. Type J BDn 31-7-47 SOC 31-3-49

SM971 KEE 6MU 17-9-45 76MU 4-1-46 *Sampenn* 19-1 Ind 11-2 ACSEA 28-2 ret UK 26-6-47 R J Parkes 27-6-49 InAF

SM972 KEE 33MU 11-9-45 76MU 6-2-46 *Taran* 8-3 Ind 30-3 ACSEA 11-4 Sele 15-1-49 60S 2-8 Sing AAF 10-5-51 SOC 27-2-53

SM973 KEE 33MU 11-9-45 76MU 16-1-46 *Megua* 29-1 Ind 25-2 ACSEA 17-10 MBFE 21-11-49 60S 2-3-50 SOC 8-3-51

SM974 KEE 6MU 17-9-45 76MU 4-1-46 *Sampenn* 19-1 Ind 11-2 ACSEA 28-2 ret UK 26-6-47 R J Parkes 1-7-49 inAF

SM975 KEE 33MU 5-10-45 76MU 30-1-46 *Pent* 18-2 Ind 17-3 ACSEA 17-10 Sele 25-8-49 60S 24-10 Fire Dog FAC4R 5-5-50

SM976 ALD 33MU 11-10-45 76MU 11-12 *Fort Sal* 18-1-46 Ind 12-2 ACSEA 28-2 ret UK 31-7-47 InAF 31-12

SM977 STN Super prod proto rud trim mods; rear spar mods port wing 20-2-45 33MU 11-1-46 76MU 14-2-46 *Taran* 2-3 Ind 11-4 ACSEA 17-10 Sele 24-2-49 SOC 13-8-59 to 6689 1M but cancelled

SM978 ALD 33MU 11-10-45 76MU 11-12 *Fort Sal* 18-1 India 12-2 ACSEA 28-2 MBFE 29-8-49 FAA scrap 10-1-50

SM979 STN Super prod proto 17-4-45 33MU 27-11 76MU 10-1-46 *Sampenn* 19-1 Ind 14-2 ACSEA 28-2 ret UK 26-6-47 R J Parkes 13-7-49 InAF

SM980 KEE 6MU 17-10-45 76MU 7-1-46 *Sampenn* 19-1 Ind 14-2 ACSEA 28-2 ret UK 31-7-47 InAF 14-6-49

SM981 STN 6MU 16-11-45 76MU 10-1-46 *Sampenn* 19-1 Ind 11-2 ACSEA 28-2 ret UK 31-7-47 R J Parkes 22-7-49 InAF

SM982 KEE 33MU 18-10-45 76MU 28-11 *Clan MacB* 14-12 Ind 31-1-46 ACSEA 14-2 ret UK 31-7-47 R J Parkes 22-7-49

SM983 KEE 33MU 18-10-45 76MU 19-11 *Samcon* 9-12 Ind 3-1-46 ACSEA 31-1 InAF 31-12-47

SM984 KEE 33MU 11-10-45 76MU 7-12 *Clan MacB* 16-12 Ind 31-1-46 ACSEA 14-2 ret UK 26-6-47 R J Parkes 16-7-49 InAF

SM985 G67 STN 33MU 11-10-45 76MU 7-12 *Clan MacB* 16-12 Ind 31-1-46 ACSEA 14-2 ret UK 26-6-47 R J Parkes 22-7-49 InAF

SM986 STRN Super prod proto 2-5-44 extant as HS986 InAF Museum

SM987 KEE 6MU 22-10-45 VA mods and recon 1-4-49 NEA 31-5-53 sold scr MoS 14-12

SM988 STN 6MU 27-10-45 76MU 16-1-46 *Megua* 29-1 Ind 26-2 ACSEA 14-3 InAF 31-12-47

SM989 KEE 6MU 22-10-45 76MU 10-1-46 *Sampenn* 19-1 Ind 11-2 ret Uk 26-6-47 R J Parkes 16-7-49 InAF

SM990 KEE 6MU 1-11-45 76MU 16-1-46 *Megua* 29-1 Ind 25-2 ACSEA 14-3 ret UK 31-7-47 InAF 31-12

SM991 KEE 6MU 1-11-45 76MU 3-1-46 *Sampenn* 19-1 Ind 11-2 ACSEA 14-3 InAF 31-12-47

SM992 STN 6MU 16-11-45 76MU 3-1-46 *Sampenn* 19-1 Ind 11-2 ret UK 31-7-47 R J Parkes 22-6-49 InAF

SM993 KEE 39MU 18-1-46 33MU 5-5-50 NEA 6-5-53 sold scr MoS 12-1-54

SM994 KEE 39MU 30-1-46 47MU 23-2-50 *Pyrrhus* 19-4 FEAF 10-5 MBFE stor 11-5 60S 21-10 SOC 14-11-52

SM995 KEE 39MU 30-1-46 33MU 14-3-50 NEA 6-5-53 sold scr 15-2-54

SM996 KEE 39MU 18-1-46 33MU 9-12-49 *Memson* 29-3-50 FEAF MBFE stor SOC 14-11-52

SM997 KEE 39MU 22-2-46 FEAF 30-3-50 MBFE stor S HQ Sele 30-6-51 C5 SOC 25-9-52

TP series FX VIII Griffon 65 up to and including TP234 FR XVIII thereon

TP195 KEE 39MU 17-12-45 76MU 302-46 *Taran* 8-3-46 Ind 30-3 ACSEA 11-4 Sele 1-2-49 60S 30-8 flew i/grd nr Kuala Lumpur pilot kld scrap SOC 17-12

TP196 STN Super prod proto to intro large chord rud 14-8-45 33MU 27-11-45 76MU 11-12 *Fort Sal* 8-1-46 Ind 12-2 ACSEA 28-2 ret UK 26-11-47 R J Parkes 9-6-49 InAF

TP197 KEE 39MU 28-1-46 RNAS Ren 20-6-49 Sele 12-8 Last RAF SQ to use Spit as strike a/c SOC 16-11-52

TP198 KEE 39MU 17-12-45 76MU 28-1-46 *Pent* 12-2 Ind 17-3 ACSEA 28-3 Burma 22-4-48

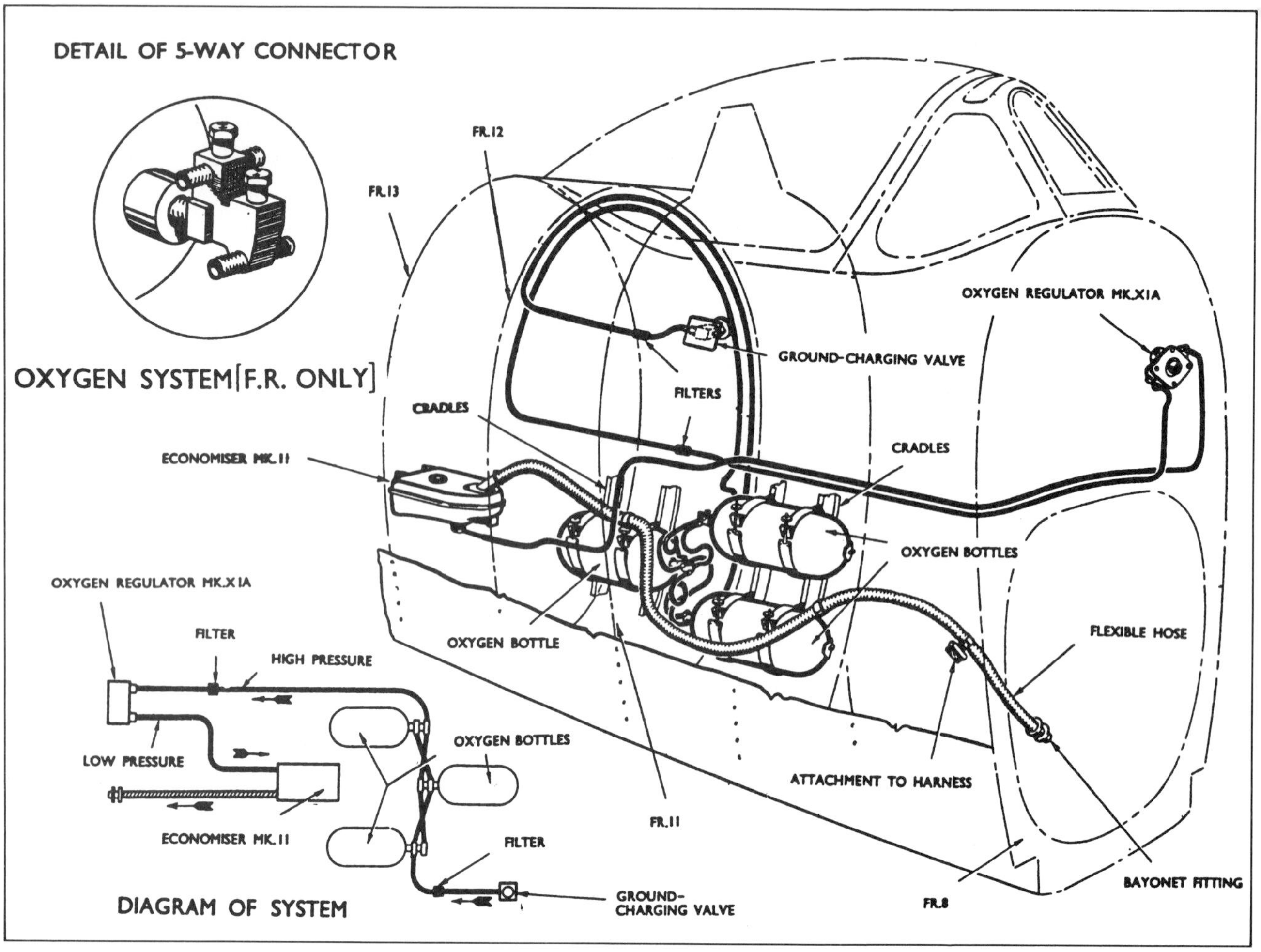

DETAIL OF 5-WAY CONNECTOR
OXYGEN SYSTEM[F.R. ONLY]
FR.13
FR.12
FR.11
FR.8
GROUND-CHARGING VALVE
OXYGEN REGULATOR MK.XIA
FILTERS
CRADLES
ECONOMISER MK.II
CRADLES
OXYGEN BOTTLES
OXYGEN BOTTLE
FLEXIBLE HOSE
ATTACHMENT TO HARNESS
BAYONET FITTING
OXYGEN REGULATOR MK.XIA
FILTER
HIGH PRESSURE
LOW PRESSURE
OXYGEN BOTTLES
ECONOMISER MK.II
FILTER
GROUND-
CHARGING VALVE
DIAGRAM OF SYSTEM

TRIMMING CONTROLS ADJUSTMENT POINTS
ALL CABLES ARE 5 CWT
TOP CABLES OUTBOARD
TURNBUCKLES
ADJUSTABLE FORK END
DETAIL OF ELEVATOR TAB JACK
TO RUDDER TAB
ADJUSTABLE FORK-END
RUDDER TRIMMING CONTROL
DETAIL OF RUDDER TAB JACK

RIB 5
·5 BROWNING GUN
20 M.M. HISPANO GUN
STARBOARD AS DRAWN
PORT OPPOSITE HAND
GUN-HEATING SYSTEM
RADIATOR
GUN-HEATING PIPE
RIB 8
RIB 10

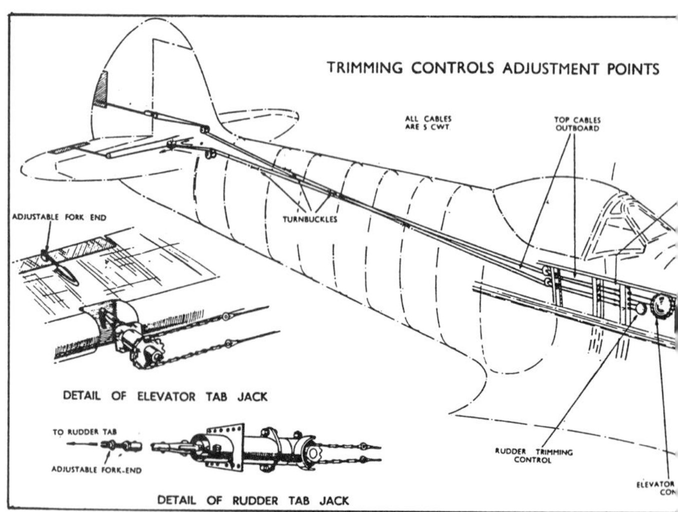

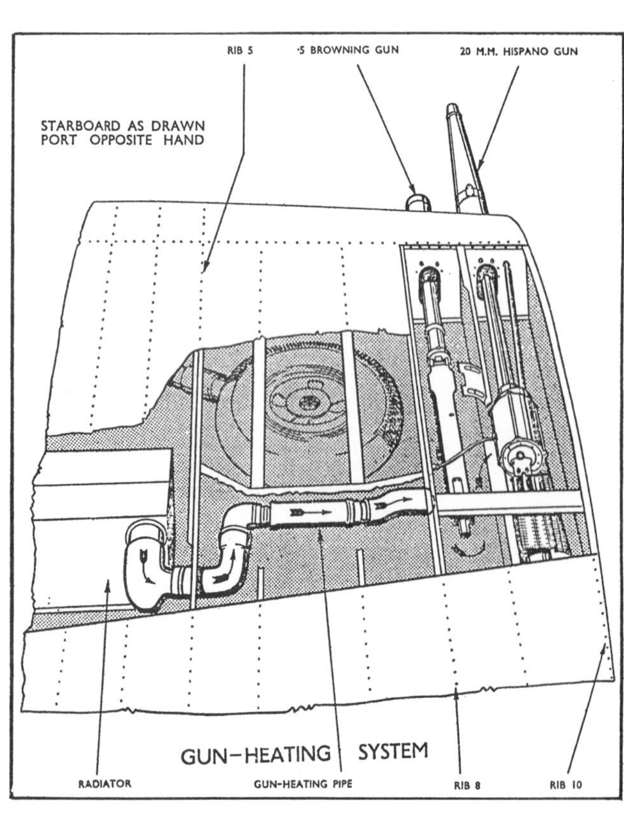

Camera port on TP279.

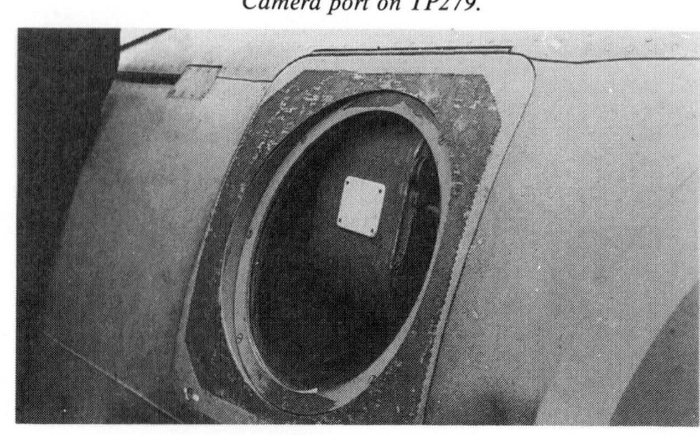

TP199 KEE 39MU 17-12-45 47MU 16-2-46 *Taran* 8-3 Ind 30-3 ACSEA 17-10 Sele 22-6-48 SOC 17-6-49

TP200 KEE 47MU 20-12-45 ROS 19-6-46 RNAS Ren 4-7-48 sele 12-8-49 60S 30-8 MBFE stor 11-1-51 C5 14-11-52

TP201 KEE 39MU 21-12-45 47MU 27-2-46 *Taran* 8-3 Ind 30-3 ACSEA 11-4 Sele 8-6-48 SOC 17-6-49 to 6681M 18-7 cancelled

TP202 KEE 39MU 5-1-45 76MU 21-2-46 *Taran* 8-3 Ind 30-2 ACSEA 11-4 60S cd/ld Teng sing CE 12-8-47 SOC 28-8

TP203 KEE 39MU 17-12-45 76MU 17-1-46 *Megua* 25-2 ACSEA 14-3 ret UK 1-1-48 R J Parkes 10-6-49 InAF

TP204 KEE 39MU 17-12-45 47MU 16-2-46 *Taran* 8-3 Ind 30-3 ACSEA 11-4 60S Teng Sing 8-6-48 SOC 17-6-49

TP205 KEE 6MU 5-1-46 47MU 25-8-47 *Maron* 24-9 Sing 18-10 ACSEA 27-11 390MU 29-1-48 60S 13-4-48 fire starting up Butterworth 1-12-49 MBFE 19-12 2nd Malayan Ftr S Penang 26-6-50

TP206 KEE 6MU 5-1-46 47MU 1-9-47 *Eury* 8-11 Sing 18-12 ACFE 28-12 60S 14-6-48 SOC 8-3-51

TP207 KEE 39MU 14-1-46 47MU 27-2 *Taran* 8-3 Ind 30-3 ACSEA 11-4 Sele 25-11-48 60S 26-8-49 FA 7-2-50 recat rogue a/c SOC

TP208 KEE 6MU 13-2-46 47MU 4-9-47 *Stent* 19-9 60S Teng Sing 3-11 ACFE 27-1-48 FAC3 21-10-49 MBFE SOC 8-3-51

TP209 KEE 39MU 14-1-46 76MU 14-2 *Taran* 30-3 ACSEA 11-4 60S Teng air coll with TP210 cd pilot kld 10-5

TP210 KEE 6MU 22-2-46 47MU 28-8-47 *Maron* 24-9 Sing 18-10 ACFE 27-11 60S Teng 9-4-48 air coll with TP209 a/c aban cd Johore 10-5

TP211 KEE 39MU 13-2-46 FEAF 5-6-50 NES 6-5-53 sold scr MoS 11-2-54

TP212 ALD 33MU 4-2-46 76MU 14-2 *Taran* 8-3 Ind 30-3 ACSEA 11-4 Sele 26-8-48 60S 31-1-49 FAAC 29-6-49 SOC 8-3-51

TP213 KEE 39MU 28-1-46 33MU 28-3-50 NEA 6-5-53 sold scr MoS 11-2-54

TP214 KEE 39MU 28-11-46 76MU 20-2 *Taran* 8-3 Ind 30-3 ACSEA 11-4-46 60S cd/ld Sele Sing 17-2-47 SOC 24-4

TP215 KEE 39MU 6-3-46 33MU 5-1-50 NEA 6-5-53 sold scr MoS 14-1-54

TP216 ALD 39MU 30-1-46 FEAF 27-3-50 MBFE stor 18-5 60S 10-6 SOC 14-11

TP217 ALD 33MU 4-2-46 76MU 14-2 *Taran* 8-3 Ind 30-3 ACSEA 11-4 Seletar 26-8-48 60S 31-12 FAAC 11-6-49 SOC 3-8-50

TP218 KEE 6MU 16-3-46 VA mods & con 29-3-49 Hand Sq 21-10 FEAF 3-5-50 MBFE stor 11-5 FA scr 24-4-51

TP219 KEE 6MU 7-3-46 FEAF 15-6-49 Sele 12-8 60S 20-8 FA scr 22-1-50

TP220 ALD 39MU 30-1-46 FEAF 3-5-50 MBFE stor 4-5 C5 14-11-52

TP221 KEE 6MU 22-2-46 47MU 1-9-47 *Eury* 8-11 Sing 18-12 ACFE 29-4-48 60S 14-5 FACB 21-3-49 C(5) SOC 8-3-51

TP222 ALD 39MU 4-2-46 NEA 9-8-50 sold J Dale 10-11

TP223 KEE 6MU 22-2-46 47MU 2-9-47 *stent* 25-9 Sing 3-11 ACFE 27-11 60S 14-5-48 TAAC 20-9 spun i/gnd nr Sembawang plt kld CE SOC 27-7-49

TP224 ALD 39MU 4-2-46 33MU 5-4-50 NEA 6-5-53 sold scr MoS 11-2-54

TP225 KEE 6MU 13-2-46 47MU 1-9-47 *Stent* 25-9 Sing 3-11 ACFE 27-11 60S 19-4-48 std recovering from dive cd nr Raub Malaya pilot kld 8-10

TP226 ALD 39MU 4-2-46 33MU 19-6-50 NEA 4-5-53 sold scr MoS 12-1-54

TP227 ALD 6MU 2-12-46 47MU 4-9-47 2FPP std ldg o/t CE Sealand 4-9 SOC 18-10

TP228 KEE 6MU 7-3-46 VA mods & con 29-3-49 226 OCU 29-11 NEA 6-5-53 sold scr MoS 18-1-54

TP229 ALD 6MU 7-3-46 VA mods & con 29-3-49 FEAF 30-3-50 60S 15-8 C(5) 14-11-52

TP230 KEE 6MU 6-3-46 *Titan* 18-8-48 ACFE 30-9-48 Sele 60S 5-11 FA3R 12-6-50

TP231 ALD 6MU 21-2-46 47MU 1-9-47 *Eury* 8-11 Sing 18-122 60S 14-5-48 hit trees recovering from bomb dive cd nr Serendah pilot kld 12-11-SOC 13-11

TP232 ALD 6MU 14-3-46 VA mods & con 1-4-49 NEA 31-3-53 sold scr MoS 30-12-55

TP233 ALD 6MU 19-3-46 VA mods & con 29-3-49 *Mennon* 29-3-50 FEAF 26-4 SOC 14-11-52

TP234 ALD 6MU 21-3-46 226 OCU 24-10 RNAS Ren 28-6-49 Sele 12-8 60S 6-10 FA scr 2-2-50

TP235 FRXVIIIE ALD 6MU 24-3-46 226 OCU 24-10 FCCRS 4-12-47 FEAF 60S Sele 29-9-49 C5(C) SOC 31-10-50

TP257 STN 39MU 29-5-45 47MU 117-1-46 *Megua* 29-1 Ind 25-2 ACSEA 14-3 ret UK 25-8-47 R J Parkes 27-6-49 InAF

TP258 STN 39MU 30-5-45 47MU 13-12 *Fort Sal* 18-1-46 Ind 12-2 ACSEA 28-3 InAF 31-11-47

TP259 STN 39MU 1-6-45 76MU 5-12 *Clan McW* 7-10 Ind 31-1-46 ACSEA 14-2 InAF 31-12-47

TP260 STN 39MU 1-6-45 76MU 5-12 *Clan McW* 16-12 Ind 31-1-46 ACSEA 14-2 InAF 31-12-47

TP261 STN 33MU 1-6-45 47MU 13-12 *Fort Sal* 18-1-46 INd 12-2 ACSEA 28-3 28S dvd i/grnd nr Semb Sing pilot kld 5-7-48 SOC 21-7

TP262 STN Super prod proto 17-10-44 33MU 2-6-45 47MU 28-11 *Clan MacB* 7-12 Ind 31-1-46 ACSEA 14-2 ret UK 1-1-48 R J Parkes 8-6-49 InAF

TP263 STN 33MU 3-6-45 47MU 2-12 *Clan MacB* 8-12 Ind 31-1-46 ACSEA 14-2 InAF 31-12-47

TP264 STN 33MU 3-6-45 47MU 13-12 *Fort Sal* 18-1-46 Ind 12-2 ACSEA 28-2 ret UK 23-10-47 R J Parkes 1-7-49 InAF

TP265 EA 33MU 11-6-45 76MU 16-1-46 *Megua* 29-1 Ind 25-2 ACSEA 14-3 ret UK 31-7-47 R J Parkes 16-6-49 InAF

TP266 STN 33MU 9-6-45ECFS 11-7 76MU 29-11 *Clan MacB* 29-11 Ind 31-1-46 ACSEA 14-2 InAF 31-12-47

TP267 STN 33MU 9-6-45 47MU 12-11-46 *Megua* 29-1 Ind 25-2 ACSEA 14-3 InAF 31-12-47

TP268 STN 39MU 5-6-45 76MU 2-2-46 *Taran* 8-2 Ind 30-2 ACSEA 11-4 SOC 30-1-48

TP269 ALD 39MU 13-6-45 47MU 29-1-46 *Pent* 19-2 Ind 17-3 ACSEA 28-3 ret UK 26-6-47 R J Parkes 12-7-49 InAF

TP270 ALD 39MU 13-6-45 o/s Ind RNAS Ren cd Silloth 5-7-49 CE scr 5-8

TP271 ALD 39MU 18-6-45 RNAS Ren 5-7-49 Sele 15-8 MBFE stor 31-8 28S 12-4-50 FA3R 24-4 SHQ Kia Tak 3-10 SOC 14-11-52

TP272 ALD 39MU 20-6-45 RNAS Ren 8-7-49 Sele 15-8 MBFE stor 29-8 28S 5-9 surplus 11-1-51 sold to be used as decoy 9-3

TP273 STN 33MU 14-6-45 MED(ME) 28-5-48 MEAF 6-1-50 FACB 20-1 ROS NEA 7-5-53 sold J G Will 28-10

TP274 ALD 39MU 18-6-45 47MU 1-12 *Clan MacB* 16-12 Ind 31-1-46 ACSEA 14-2 InAF 31-12-47

TP275 ALD 33MU 19-6-45 76MU 13-11 *Clan MacB* 29-11 31-1-46

TP276 ALD 33MU 20-6-45 47MU 13-12 *Fort Sal* 18-1-46 Ind 12-2 ACSEA 28-2 ret UK 31-7-47 bboc Mauripur 27-11 InAF 31-12 HS653. Extant Illinois.

TP277 STN 39MU 18-6-45 33MU 10-10-49 FEAF 8-3-50 28(FR)S 21-4 SHQ Kai Tak 14-6 reinforcement plan 31-3-51

TP278 ALD 33MU 19-6-45 MED(ME) 31-5-48 107MU 30-9 208S 24-2-49 MEAF 19-12-50 SOC 6-2-52

TP279 FR XVIIIE ALD VA HPA 30-6-45 trls a/c 5-7 large chord rud with split trim tab instal. Shea-Simmonds said in his report "in my opinion this a/c should not have been passed during production tests for two reasons 1) ailerons are excessively hvy and there is some reversal of lateral trim from right to left 2) slow running and tick over are not satisfactory." He also noted reversal of directional trim as speed increased above 400 mph IAS. BDn 19-9 camera and gun heat trls results satisfactory 30-11 camera trls minor mods recommendded. 38MU 1-5-46 WAL mods 14-2-49 cd on test flt 13-7-50

TP280 STN Super prod proto 20-3-45 39MU 19-6 76MU 1-1-46 *Taran* 8-3 Ind 30-3 ACSEA 11-4 bboc Mauripur 27-11-47 InAF 31-12 HS654. Extant Illinois

TP281 STN 39MU 19-6-45 76MU FACB 3-12 recat E 5-6-47

TP282 ALD 33MU 5-7-45 76MU 29-12 *Sampenn* 19-1-46 Ind 11-2 ACSEA 28-2 InAF 31-12-47

TP283 ALD 39MU 6-7-45 47MU 17-1-46 *Megua* 29-1 Ind 25-2 ACSEA 14-3 Sele stor 15-7-49 C5(S) SOC 8-3-51

TP284 ALD 39MU 6-7-45 47MU 17-1-46 *Megua* 29-1 Ind 25-2 ACSEA 14-3 Sele 16-12-48 28S Kai Tak 17-5-46 FAC4 3-7-50 rogue a/c excessive vibration in flt to BDn SOC to Ins GS

TP285 ALD 39MU 2-7-45 76MU 11-12 *Fort Sal* 18-1-46 Ind 12-2 ACSEA 28-2 bboc Mauripur 27-11-47 InAF

TP286 ALD 39MU 12-7-45 47MU 18-1-46 *Megua* 29-1 Ind 25-2 ACSEA 14-3 Sele 81S 6-10-49 60S 20-3-50 C5(S) SOC 8-3-51

TP287 ALD 33MU 3-7-45 76MU 7-11 *Clan MacB* 16-12 Ind 31-1-46 ACSEA 14-2 InAF 31-12-47

TP288 ALD 39MU 25-6-45 76MU 2-2-46 *Taran* 8-3 Ind 30-3 ACSEA 11-4 ret UK 26-6-47 R J Parkes 27-6-49 InAF 30-6

TP289 ALD 33MU 2-7-45 47MU 20-11 *Samer* 3-12 Ind 8-1-46 ACSEA 21-1 InAF 31-12-47

TP290 KEE 39MU 12-7-45 47MU 17-1-46 *Megua* 29-1 Ind 25-2 ACSEA 14-3 InAF 31-12-47

TP291 ALD 33MU 2-7-45 St Mw Rad Flt 26-6-46 NEA 19-2-48 sold E Smelt 25-5-50

TP292 ALD 6MU 16-7-45 MED(ME) 24-8-46 109MU 6-5-48 208S 9-12 air coll TP450 cd Gt Bitter Lake, Egypt. Pilot kld CE 14-7-49 SOC 28-7

TP293 ALD 33MU 14-7-45 47MU 13-12 *Fort Sal* 18-1-46 Ind 12-2 ACSEA 28-2 bboc Mauripur 27-11-47 InAF 31-12

Camera port clearly visible, TP265 had a similar career to TP297 above.

TP297 served from India, before joining the Indian Air Force.

TP294 ALD 33MU 25-7-45 76MU 19-11 *Clan McW* 16-12 Ind 31-1-46 ACSEA 14-2 InAF 31-12-47

TP295 ALD Super prod proto reintroduction of visual u/c indicator on wing 12-12-44 6MU 16-7-45 VA mods 1-4-49 MEAF 22-2-52 SOC 6-2-52

TP296 STN 9MU 23-7-45 76MU 5-12 *Clan MacB* 16-12 Ind 31-1-46 ACSEA 14-2 InAF 31-12-47

TP297 KEE VA HPA 18-7-45 76MU 7-11 *Clan MacB* 16-12 Ind 31-1-46 ACSEA 14-2 ret UK 26-6-47 R J Parkes 16-7-49 InAF

TP298 STN 9MU 17-7-45 47MU 13-12 *Fort Sal* 18-1 Ind 12-2 ACSEA 28-2 bboc Mauripur 27-11-47 InAF 31-2-47 Extant Wyoming

TP313 STN 6MU 24-7-45 St Mw 16-5-46 MED(ME) 17-7 208S SOC 31-12-47

TP314 ALD Super prod proto u/c mods 10-7-45 6MU 24-7 47MU 29-1-46 *Pent* 18-12 Ind 17-3 ACSEA 28-3 Sele 25-8-49 SOC

TP315 ALD 6MU 16-7-45 VA mods & con 1-4-49 226 OCU 29-9 NEA 6-5-53 sold scr MoS 15-2-54

TP316 ALD 6MU 27-7-45 LRS Mid Wal 3-3-47 NEA 19-2-48 sold E Smelt 25-5-50

TP317 ALD 6MU 25-7-45 St Mw 29-5-46 MED(ME) 1-8 109MU 25-11-48 208S 24-2-49 SOC 10-1251

TP318 ALD 6MU 27-7-45 VA mods & con 1-4-49 MEAF 19-2-50 208S 20-2-50 SOC 6-2-52

TP319 ALD 33MU 27-8-45 47MU 10-11 *Samcon* 2-12 Ind 3-1-46 ACSEA 31-1 InAF 31-12-47

TP320 ALD 6MU 28-7-45 St Mw 29-5-45 MED(ME) 26-9 208S 14-5-49 SOC 14-7

TP321 KEE 6MU 13-8-48 226 OCU 6-9 WAL mods 10-2-49 NEA 31-3-53 sold scrap MoS 30-12

TP322 ALD 6MU 28-7-45 47MU 4-2-46 *Taran* 8-3 Ind 30-3 ACSEA 11-4 Sele 25-8-49 SOC 13-9 unsuitable

TP323 ALD 6MU 28-7-45 RNAS Renf 28-6-49 28S FEAF 15-8-49 SQH reinforcement 26-2-51 SOC 16-11-52

TP324 ALD 6MU 28-7-45 76MU 9-2-46 *Taran* 8-3 Ind 30-3 ACSEA 11-4 28S strk by TZ230 ldg CE Kai Tak 20-1-48 SOC 22-1

TP325 KEE 33MU 21-8-45 76MU 10-11 *Clan MacB* 16-12 Ind 31-1-46 ACSEA 14-2-46 InAF 31-12-47

TP326 KEE 33MU 23-8-45 47MU 10-11 *Sancon* 3-12 Ind 3-1-46 ACSEA 31-1 InAF 31-12-47

TP327 ALD 6MU 31-8-45 47MU 1-1-46 4FP o/s Indg Sealand CAL 4-2 CBAF repair cancel recat E 9-6-47

TP328 ALD 6MU 5-9-45 RNAS Ren 23-6-49 28S FEAF 15-8 scr SOC 6-1-50

TP329 KEE 33MU 30-8-45 76MU 27-12 *Sampenn* 19-1-46 Ind 11-2 ACSEA 28-2 Sele 1-9-48 28S 8-4-49 o/t Indg Kuching Borneo CE en route Hong Kong 11-5 SOC

TP330 ALD 6MU 12-9-45 St Mw 3-6-46 MED(ME) 17-7 107MU 25-8-49 FA3R 2-3-50 208S 1-5 SOC 6-2-52

TP331 ALD 6MU 12-9-45 28S FEAF 30-6-49 SHQ stor 16-2-51 reinforcement plan SOC 20-4

TP332 ALD 6MU 5-9-45 St Mw 29-10-46 MED(ME) 30-1-47 208S 19-1-50 SOC 6-2-52

TP333 ALD 33MU 11-10-45 76MU 19-11 *Samcon* 9-12 Ind 3-1-46 ACSEA 31-1 InAF 31-12-47

TP334 ALD 208S w/u ldg Camat David Palestine 12-5-48

TP335 ALD 6MU 18-9-45 FEAF Sele 10-6-49 28S FTR into Sth China Sea 5-9

TP336 ALD 33MU 12-9-45 St Mw 11-5-46 MED(ME) 26-9 des on grd by REAF Ramat David Palestine 22-5-48 SOC 17-1-50

TP337 ALD 6MU 19-9-45 CRS Mid Wal 9-10-46 NEA 11-3-48 sold Int All 2-11-49

TP338 ALD 33MU 11-10-45 76MU 10-11 *Clan MacB* 29-11 Ind 31-1-46 ACSEA 14-2 ret UK 26-11-47 R J Parkes 10-6-49 InAF

TP339 ALD 33MU 11-10-45 76MU 19-11 *Clan MacB* 16-12 Ind 31-1-46 ACSEA 14-2 bboc Mauripur 27-11-47 InAF 31-12

TP340 G67 ALD 6MU 12-10-45 St Mw 28-6-46 MED(ME) 30-1-47 208S Nicosia 22-7-48 FACE 7-1-49 FTR after hostile action by Israeli ftrs 13-1

TP341 ALD 33MU 11-10-45 76MU 19-11 *Clan MacB* 29-11 Ind 31-1-46 ACSEA 14-2 Sele 25-8-49 SOC 13-9

TP342 FRXIV (intm) proto G67 STN 1st a/c with G67 eng 17-4-45 Super prod proto for relocation pilot harness in cockpit 23-1-45; ammunition anti-jam mods 1-5 6MU 27-11 47MU 29-1-46 *Pent* 18-12 Ind 17-3 ACSEA 28-3 ret UK 24-8-47 R J Parkes 1-7-49 InAF

TP343 G67 STN 6MU 19-10-45 St Mw 16-5-46 FAAC 4-7 SOC 12-8-47

TP344 KEE 33MU 18-10-45 47MU 20-11 *Samcon* 3-12 Ind 3-1-46 ACSEA 31-1 InAF 31-12-47

TP345 G67 ALD 6MU 12-10-45 St Mw 4-7-46 MED(ME) 26-9 107MU 24-2-49 208S 17-11 GA3R 17-5-50 SOC 6-2-52

TP346 G67 KEE 33MU 27-12-45 47MU 12-1-46 *Megua* 29-1 Ind 25-2 ACSEA 14-3 InAF 31-12-47

TP347 G67 ALD 6MU 13-10-45 47MU 4-9-47 *Stent* 25-9 Sing 3-11 28S 20-2-48 Kai Tak C5 SOC 2-10-50

TP348 G67 ALD 6MU 17-10-45 St Mw 31-7-46 MED(ME) 12-12 WAL mods 29-1-49 NEA 31-3-53 sold scr MoS 14-12

TP349 G67 ALD 6MU 12-10-45 Cole 4-10-46 CC&RS Rudloe Manor hvy ldg wing hit grd broke off CE 25-3-47 SOC 24-4

TP350 G67 KEE 33MU 17-12-45 76MU 4-2-46 *Taran* 8-3 Ind 30-3 ACSEA 11-4 FAC(S) 15-2-50 SOC 13-8

TP363 G67 KEE 33MU 18-10-45 76MU 28-11 *Clan MacB* 16-12 Ind 31-1-46 ACSEA 14-2 InAF 31-12-47

TP364 G67 ALD 6MU 17-10-45 St Mawgan 25-6-46 MED(ME) 32S des on grd by REAF Ramat David aircraft 22-5-48 SOC 10-12-51

TP365 G67 ALD 6MU 22-10-45 St Mw 1-8-46 MED(ME) 32S w/u ldg Dawson Field Transjordan CE 23-10-47 SOC 27-11

TP366 G67 ALD 33MU 22-10-45 47MU 2-12 *Clan MacB* 16-12 Ind 31-1-46 ACSEA 14-2 ETPS Fırn 27-6 weather tests InAF 31-12-47

TP367 G67 ALD 33MU 22-10-45 76MU 1-12 *Clan MacB* 29-11 Ind 31-1-46 ACSEA 14-2 InAF 31-12-47

TP368 G67 ALD 33MU 21-12-45 St Mw 11-5-46 MED(ME) 10-7 32S dvd i/grd nr Amman Jordan pilot kld CE 20-6-47

TP369 G67 ALD 39MU 6-12-45 St Mw 10-9-46 MED(ME) 31-10 208S 11-12-47 cd on t/o Nicosia 16-5-48 SOC 24-6

TP370 G67 ALD 33MU 6-11-45 76MU 28-12 *Sampenn* 19-1-46 Ind 11-12 ACSEA 28-2 ret UK 27-1-47 R J Parkes 10-6-49 InAF

TP371 G67 ALD 6MU 13-12-45 CRS Cole 2-10-46 GAAC 6-11 FCC&RS Flt Mid Wal FAAC 15-7-47 ROS VA mods & cons 1-4-49 MEAF 5-1-50 FACB recat scr 18-1

TP372 ALD 6MU 13-12-45 Sing 13-10-47 28S 19-4-48 FAAC 19-7-49 SOC 7-7-50

TP373 G67 ALD 39MU 6-12-45 St Mw 20-8-46 MED(ME) GAAC 30-9 SOC 24-6-48

TP374 G67 ALD 6MU 11-1-45 226 OCU 9-9-46 WAL mods 15-2-49 NEA 31-5-53 sold scr MoS 14-12

TP375 G67 ALD 39MU 8-12-45 FEAF 8-3-50 SHQ Kai Tak 3-10 SOC 14-11

TP376 G67 KEE 6MU 6-1-46 47MU 4-9-47 *Tant* 5-12 Sing 15-1-48 28S 4-8 cd on app pilot kld CE Semb Sing

TP377 FRXVIIIE EA Super prod proto strength fus & ails attachment 12-6-45 6MU 16-11 47MU 1-8-47 *Maton* 24-9 Sing 18-10 28S Hong Kong 1.1-3-48 surplus 11-1-51 SOC to be used as decoy 9-3

TP378 ALD 6MU 14-12-45 47MU 1-8-47 *Maton* 24-9 Sing 18-10 28S 2-3-48 C(5) SOC 2-10-50

TP379 G67 ALD 33MU 29-12-45 76MU 16-1-46 *Megua* 29-1 Ind 25-2 ACSEA 14-3 InAF 31-12-47

TP380 G67 STN 33MU 27-10-45 47MU 10-1-46 *Samp* 19-1-46 Ind 11-2 ACSEA 28-2 InAF 31-12-47

TP381 G67 ALD 39MU 8-12-45 St Mw 20-8-46 MED(ME) 9-10 109MU 11-11-48 SOC 3-3-49

TP382 G67 ALD 39MU 8-12-45 33MU 14-11-49 FEAF 22-3-50 28S 21-4 SHQ Kai Tak 14-6 reinforcement plan 16-11-52

TP383 G67 ALD 39MU 14-12-45 47MU 17-1-46 *Megua* 29-1 Ind 25-2 ACSEA 14-3 Sele 10-6-49 FA SOC 14-8-50

TP384 G67 ALD 39MU 14-12-45 33MU 23-6-50 NEA 6-5-53 sold scr MoS 20-1-54

TP385 KEE 33MU 18-1-46 St Mw 15-6 MED(ME) 1-8 FAAC 5-7-48 208S 24-5-50 SOC 6-2-52

TP386 G67 KEE 33MU 14-1-46 St Mw 11-5 MED(ME) 3-7 107MU 24-2-49 32S air coll with TZ229 cd Nicosia 11-10-51 SOC 6-2-52

TP387 G67 ALD 6MU 27-12-45 St Mw 4-7-46 MED(ME) 21-8 FACE 7-1-49 FTR hostile action by Israeli a/c 13-1

TP388 G67 ALD 39MU 6-12-45 76MU 12-1-46 *Megua* 29-1 Ind 25-2 ACSEA 14-3 ret UK 26-11-47 R J Parkes 8-6-49 InAF

TP389 G67 ALD 33MU 15-12-45 76MU 16-1-46 *Megua* 29-1 Ind 25-2 ACSEA 14-3 SOC 30-1-48

TP390 KEE 33MU 22-6-45 47MU 29-12 *Samp* 19-1-46 Ind 11-2 ACSEA 28-2 Sele 10-6-49 28S 12-4-50 FA SOC 12-4

FR XVIII at Kallang Airport, Singapore, 1949.

TP391 KEE 33MU 18-6-45 St Mw 31-7-46 MED(ME) 14-11 107MU 24-2-49 208S 27-3-50 SOC 10-12-51

TP392 KEE 33MU 18-6-45 76MU 7-11 *Clan MacB* 16-12 Ind 31-1-46 ACSEA 14-2 InAF 31-12-47

TP393 KEE 33MU 23-6-45 76MU 19-11 *Clan MacB* 16-12 Ind 31-1-46 ACSEA 14-2 InAF 31-12-47

TP394 KEE 39MU 21-6-45 FEAF 28-3-50 SHQ kai Tak 24-5 28S 14-6 GAC5 25-11

TP395 KEE 33MU 22-6-45 76MU 27-12 *Samp* 19-1-46 Ind 11-12 ACSEA 28-2 ret UK 27-11-47 R J Parkes 3-6-49 InAF

TP396 KEE 33MU 29-6-45 76MU 13-11 *Clan MacB* 16-12 Ind 31-1-46 ACSEA 14-2 ret UK 27-11-47 R J Parkes 8-6-49 InAF

TP397 STN 39MU 23-6-45 76MU 5-12 *Clan MacB* 16-12 Ind 31-1-46 ACSEA 14-2 InAF 31-12-47

TP398 STN Super prod proto chassis mods 17-4-45 39MU 25-6 76MU 7-12 *Clan MacB* 16-12 Ind 31-1-46 ACSEA 14-2 ret UK 25-8-47 R J Parkes 1-7-49 InAF

TP399 KEE 33MU 27-7-45 47MU 29-12 *Samp* 19-1-46 Ind 11-2 ACSEA 28-2 Seletar 25-8-49 SOC 13-8

TP400 STN Super prod proto 5-9-44 39MU 29-6-45 47MU 17-1-46 *Megua* 29-1 Ind 25-2 ACSEA 14-3 Sele s15-7-49 SOC 12-9-50

TP401 KEE 33MU 6-7-45 76MU 1-1-46 *Samp* 19-1 Ind 11-2 ACSEA 28-2 ret UK 27-1-47 R J Parkes 8-6-49 InAF

TP402 ALD 39MU 2-7-45 76MU 1-1-46 *Samp* 19-1 Ind 11-2 ACSEA 28-2 Sele 23-8-48 SOC 17-6-49

TP403 KEE 39MU 2-7-45 76MU 7-12 *Clan MacB* 16-12 Ind 31-1-46 ACSEA 14-2 InAF 31-12-47

TP404 KEE 39MU 2-7-45 76MU 10-10 *Clan MacB* 16-12 Ind 31-1-46 ACSEA 14-2 InAF 31-12-47

TP405 KEE 39MU 24-7-45 47MU 17-1-46 *Megua* 29-1 Ind 25-2 ACSEA 14-3 ret UK 26-6-47 R J Parkes 1-7-49 InAF

TP406 KEE 39MU 10-7-45 76MU 28-1-46 *Pent* 18-2 Ind 17-3 ACSEA 28-3 Seletar 3-6-48 28S 21-10 FACB 12-8-49 Kai Tak 16-8 surplus SOC 9-3-51 used as decoy

TP407 KEE 39MU 11-7-45 47MU 1-12 *Sampenn* 19-1-46 Ind 11-2 ACSEA 28-2 81S 20-7-48 60S 23-3-50 SOC 8-3-51

TP408 KEE 6MU 11-7-45 CRS Cole 2-10-46 to 6441M RAF Pembroke 25-9-47

TP423 KEE 6MU 11-7-45 VA HPA 11-4-47 trls 170gal o/ld tank BDn 3-5-48 trls of GGS Mk.4B instal. Acceptable for rocket and can ops VA mods & con 29-3-49 FEAF 27-3-50 28S 31-5 SHQ reinforcement plan 16-2-51 SOC 14-11-52

TP424 KEE 6MU 13-7-45 FEAF 13-6-49 28S 15-8 FA FTR 14-2-50

TP425 ALD 33MU 17-7-45 76MU 5-1 *Sampenn* 19-1-46 Ind 11-2 ACSEA 28-2 ret UK 27-11-47 R J Parkes 3-6-49 InAF

TP426 KEE 9MU 17-7-45 76MU 5-12 *Clan MacB* 16-12 Ind 31-1-46 ACSEA 14-2 InAF 31-12-47

TP427 KEE 6MU 23-7-45 47MU 11-9-47 *Eury* 8-11 Sing 18-12 ACFEU 18-12 Sele 3-6-48 28S 10-7 FAAC 26-9-49 Kai Tak FA4R 2-2-50 surplus used as decoy 9-3-51

TP428 KEE 6MU 28-7-45 47MU 4-9-47 *Eury* 8-11 Sing 8-12 Sele 3-6-48 28S 15-7 BDn Jly '48 trls with GGS Mk.4B FACE 13-8-49

TP429 KEE 6MU 23-7-45 St Mw 3-6-46 MED(ME) 1-8 325S Nicosia 9-7-48 325 Dvd i/grnd nr Lapithos – Cyprus pilot kld CE SOC 21-1-49

TP430 KEE 6MU 23-7-45 CRS Cole 9-10-46 FAAC 22-4-47 NEA 6-6 SOC 16-11

TP431 KEE 6MU 23-8-45 RNAS Ren 28-6-49 28S FEAF 15-8 Kai Tak SHQ reinforcement plan 26-2-51 SOC 14-11-52

TP432 KEE 6MU 28-7-45 VA mods & con 29-3-49 226OCU 27-8 NEA 6-5-53 sold scrap MoS 12-1-54

TP433 KEE 6MU 9-8-45 47MU 23-9-47 *Eury* 8-11-47 Sing 18-12 Sele 3-6-48 28S 28-10 SOC 9-3-51

TP434 KEE 6MU 21-8-45 226 OCU 6-9-46 CFE 21-8-47 FEAF 27-3-50 SHQ Kai Tak 14-8 28S 11-9-50 reinforcement plan SOC 16-11-52

TP435 KEE 33MU 28-8-45 47MU 10-1-46 *Sampenn* 19-1 Ind 11-2 ACSEA 28-3 InAF 31-12-47

TP436 KEE 33MU 6-9-45 76MU 7-11 *Clan MacB* 16-12 Ind 31-1-46 ACSEA 14-2 ret UK 26-6-47 R J Parker 28-6-49 InAF

TP437 KEE 33MU 11-9-45 47MU 1-12 *Clan MacB* 16-12 Ind 31-1-46 ACSEA 14-2 InAF 31-12-47

TP438 KEE 6MU 21-9-45 St Mw 31-7 MED(ME) 30-1-47 208S 22-7-48 Nicosia SOC 30-4-51

TP439 KEE 33MU 18-10-45 47MU 10-11 *Sancon* 31-12 Ind 3-1-46 ACSEA 31-1 InAF 31-12-47

TP440 ALD 6MU 19-9-45 St Mw 4-7-46 MED(ME) 26-9-46 109MU 10-6-48 32S 30-9 208S 1-9-49 SOC 17-11

TP441 ALD 33MU 11-10-45 47MU 20-11 *Sancon* 3-12 Ind 3-1-46 ACSEA 31-1 InAF 31-12-47

TP442 G67 KEE 33MU 18-10-45 76MU 13-11 *Clan MacB* 16-12 Ind 31-1-46 ACSEA 14-2 bboc 27-11-47 InAF 31-12

TP443 G67 ALD 6MU 19-10-45 St Mw 7-10-46 MED(ME) 31-10 32S des on grd by REAF Ramat David airfield 22-5-48

TP444 G67 ALD 33MU 27-10-45 76MU 15-12 *Sampenn* 19-1-46 Ind 11-2 ACSEA 28-2 ret UK 31-7-47 InAF 14-6-49

TP445 G67 ALD 6MU 12-1-46 47MU 6-8-47 *Maron* 24-9 Sing 18-10 28S 23-3-48 SOC 28-12-50

TP446 G67 ALD 6MU 12-1-46 St Mw 31-7 MED(ME) 31-10 32S des on grd by REAF Ramat David airfield 22-5-48 SOC 5-8

TP447 G67 33MU 16-1-46 St Mw 16-5 MED(ME) 26-9 208S 10-6 SOC 6-2-52

TP448 G67 ALD 33MU 16-1-46 St Mw 15-6 MED(ME) Arr Fayid 1-8 109MU 25-3-48 SOC 26-8

TP449 M67 ALD 33 MU 4-2-46 St Mw 15-6 MED(ME) 26-9 208S a/c aban after loss cont during aero cd dbf CE Megiddo Palestine 11-10-47

TP450 G67 ALD FF LRC 6-2-46 33MU 11-2 St Mw 11-5 MED(ME) 30-10-47 208S 11-12 dam on grd by REAF Ramat David airfield 22-5-48 Air Coll TF292 cd nr Abu Sultan Egypt pilot kld CE 14-7-49

TP451 G67 ALD FF LRC 6-2-46 33MU 12-2 e/fd f/ld cd CE 13-5-48 SOC 25-5

TP452 G67 ALD 33MU 22-2-46 MED(ME) 9-6-48 28S FEAF 27-3-50 SHQ reinforcement plan 26-2-51 SOC 14-11-52

TP453 G67 ALD 33MU 22-2-46 MED(ME) 30-9-48 109MU 13-1-49 208S 24-2 FAAC 18-3 SOC 30-4-51

TP454 G67 ALD CRD VA HPA 9-3-46 Hand Sq Hull 17-12 Ftr Com Com S 25-4-47 FCCRS i/sea off Bournemouth during low aero pilot kld CE 17-9-47

TP455 G67 ALD 33MU 8-3-46 RNAS Ren 28-6-49 28S 15-8 FACB Kai Tak 30-8-49 SOC used for decoy 9-3-51

TP456 G67 ALD 6MU 7-3-46 St Mw 28-6 MED(ME) 26-9 FACE 7-1-49 FTR after Israeli AF hostile action Egypt 13-1-49

TZ series all Griffon 67 FR XVIII

TZ200 ALD 33MU 8-12-45 47MU 27-12 *Sampenn* 19-1-46 Ind 11-2 ACSEA 28-2 28S cd emergency ldg Kluang Malaya CE 8-6-47 SOC 19-6

TZ201 ALD 33MU 19-12-45 76MU 1-2-46 *Taran* 8-3 Ind 30-3 ACSEA 11-4 28S e/fd a/c aban Seremban Malaya 9-1-48

TZ202 KEE 39MU 10-11-45 RNAS Ren 30-6-48 28S FEAF 15-8-49 onto nose running up Kai Tak CAC 2-11-49

TZ203 ALD 6MU 19-12-45 St Mw 28-6-46 MED(ME) 31-8 109MU 31-12-47 32S Nicosia 8-7-48 FAAC 20-8 208S 10-11-49 SOC 12-12-51

TZ204 KEE 33MU 10-11-45 St Mw 16-5-46 MED(ME) 1-8 109MU 10-6-48 208S 10-2-49 cd f/lnd nr Fayid Egypt CB 4-10 SOC 8-2-50

TZ205 ALD 33MU 14-12-45 76MU 29-12 *Sampenn* 19-1-46 Ind 16-2 ACSEA 28-2 InAF 31-12-47

TZ210 ALD 6MU 19-12-45 St Mw 21-6-46 MED(ME) 1-8 28S a/c aban 9-1-48 109MU C4R 31-1-50 SOC recat(S) 14-9

TZ211 ALD 6MU 19-12-45 St Mw 17-6-46 MED(ME) 6-8 32S 26-6-47 109MU 25-8-49 208S 25-3-50 FA3R 31-8-50 FA scrap 5-2-51

TZ212 ALD 33MU 5-1-46 St Mw 11-5 MED(ME) 21-8 109MU 25-11-48 208S 13-1-49 FA3R 29-10-49 SOC 10-12-51

TZ213 KEE 33MU 18-1-46 MED(ME) 8-6-48 FEAF 20-8-50 MBFE stor 23-8 SOC 14-11-52

TZ214 ALD 6MU 13-12-45 St Mw 21-6-46 MED(ME) 31-10 32S Palestine 26-6-47 109MU 11-8-49 208S 15-2-50 SOC 6-2-52

TZ215 KEE 33MU 30-1-46 16FU St Mw 5-6-46 MED(ME) 17-7 208S cd on t/o Ein Shemer Palestine CE 14-2-47

TZ216 KEE 33MU 30-1-46 St Mw 31-7 MED(ME) 18-9 208S FA scrap 24-10-50

TZ217 ALD 39MU 6-12-45 47MU 12-1-46 *Megua* 29-1 Ind 25-2 ACSEA 14-3 InAF 31-12-47

TZ218 ALD 33MU 12-12-45 47MU 29-12 *Sampenn* 19-1-46 Ind 11-2 ACSEA 28-2 InAF 31-12-47

TZ219 33MU 8-12-45 47MU 27-12 *Sampenn* 19-1-46 Ind 11-2 ACSEA 28-2 InAF 31-12-47

TZ220 ALD 6MU 27-1-46 St Mw 4-7 MED(ME) 6-8 SOC 24-6-48

TZ221 ALD 39MU 28-12-45 St Mw 20-8-46 MED(ME) 26-9 FAAC 109MU 31-10 SOC 28-8-47

TZ222 ALD 33MU 5-12-45 76MU 27-12 *Sampenn* 19-1-46 Ind 11-2 ACSEA 28-2 ret UK 31-7-47 R J Parkes 1-7-49 InAF

TZ223 ALD 33MU 5-12-45 76MU 15-12 *Sampenn* 19-1-46 Ind 11-2 ACSEA 28-2 28S f/ld cd CE Johore Bahru Malaya 21-7-47

TZ224 KEE 33MU 5-12-45 47MU 12-1-46 *Megua* 29-1-46 Ind 25-2 ACSEA 14-3 InAF 31-12-47

TZ225 ALD 33MU 8-12-45 47MU 27-12 *Sampenn* 19-1-46 Ind 1-2 ACSEA 28-2 28S cd/ld Kuching Sarawak CE 3-2-48

TZ226 KEE 33MU 17-12-45 76MU 16-1-46 *Megua* 29-1 Ind 25-2 ACSEA 14-3 Sele 2-7-48 SOC 17-6-49 to 6680M 18-7 cancelled

TZ227 KEE 33MU 17-12-45 76MU 4-1-46 *Sampenn* 19-1 Ind 11-2 ACSEA 28-2 InAF 31-12-47

TZ228 ALD 6MU 13-12-45 St Mw 4-7-46 MED(ME) 26-9 FTR after Israeli A/F action 7-1-49

TZ229 KEE 6MU 10-1-46 St Mw 12-7 MED(ME) 21-8 FACE 11-10-48 32S air coll with TP386 cd CE Nicosia 11-10 SOC 28-10

TZ230 KEE 33MU 17-12-45 47MU 10-1-46 *Sampenn* 19-1 Ind 11-2 ACSEA 28-2 28S strk TP324 ldg CB Kai Tak 20-1-48 SOC 22-1

TZ231 KEE 33MU 17-12-45 47MU 12-1-46 *Megua* 29-1 Ind 25-2 ACSEA 14-3 ret UK 21-8-47 R J Parkes 28-6-49 InAF

TZ232 KEE 33MU 16-1-46 St Mw 16-5 MED(ME) 26-9 32S e/fd t/o cd Ramat David Haifa Palestine 21-5-48 SOC 24-6

TZ233 ALD 33MU 4-2-46 MED(ME) 6-7-48 109MU 31-12-48 208S 10-2-49 SOC 10-12-51

TZ234 ALD 33MU 30-1-46 St Mw 15-6 MED(ME) 26-9 SOC 27-11-47

TZ235 ALD 33MU 27-12-45 76MU 16-1-46 *Megua* 29-1 Ind 25-2 ACSEA 14-2 InAF 31-12-47

TZ236 ALD 6MU 3-1-46 St Mw 12-7 MED(ME) 26-9 109MU 8-1-48 32S Ein Slemer 12-2-48 32S eng fail u/s f/lnd Nicosia Cyprus CE FA SOC 19-1-49

TZ237 ALD 33MU 12-1-46 St Mw 11-5 MED(ME) 26-9 208S e/fd on t/o CE Kisumu Kenya 10-9-47 SOC 30-10

TZ238 ALD 6MU 3-1-46 St Mw 28-6 MED(ME) 24-7 cd on f/f El Mas CAC 3-8 SOC 13-11

TZ239 ALD 6MU 1-1-46 St Mw 28-6 CAC 5-5-47 ROS to 6472M Morton in the Marsh 5-11 recat E SOC 25-6-49

TZ240 ALD 33MU 12-1-46 St Mw 16-5 MED(ME) 208S Gebel Hauz 12-7 cd in emergency ldg CE Kabriz Egypt 21-12-48 SOC 13-1-49

Stores container tested on a Mk XVIII at Farnborough, January 1943.

TZ203 in service with No 208 Squadron at Nicosia.

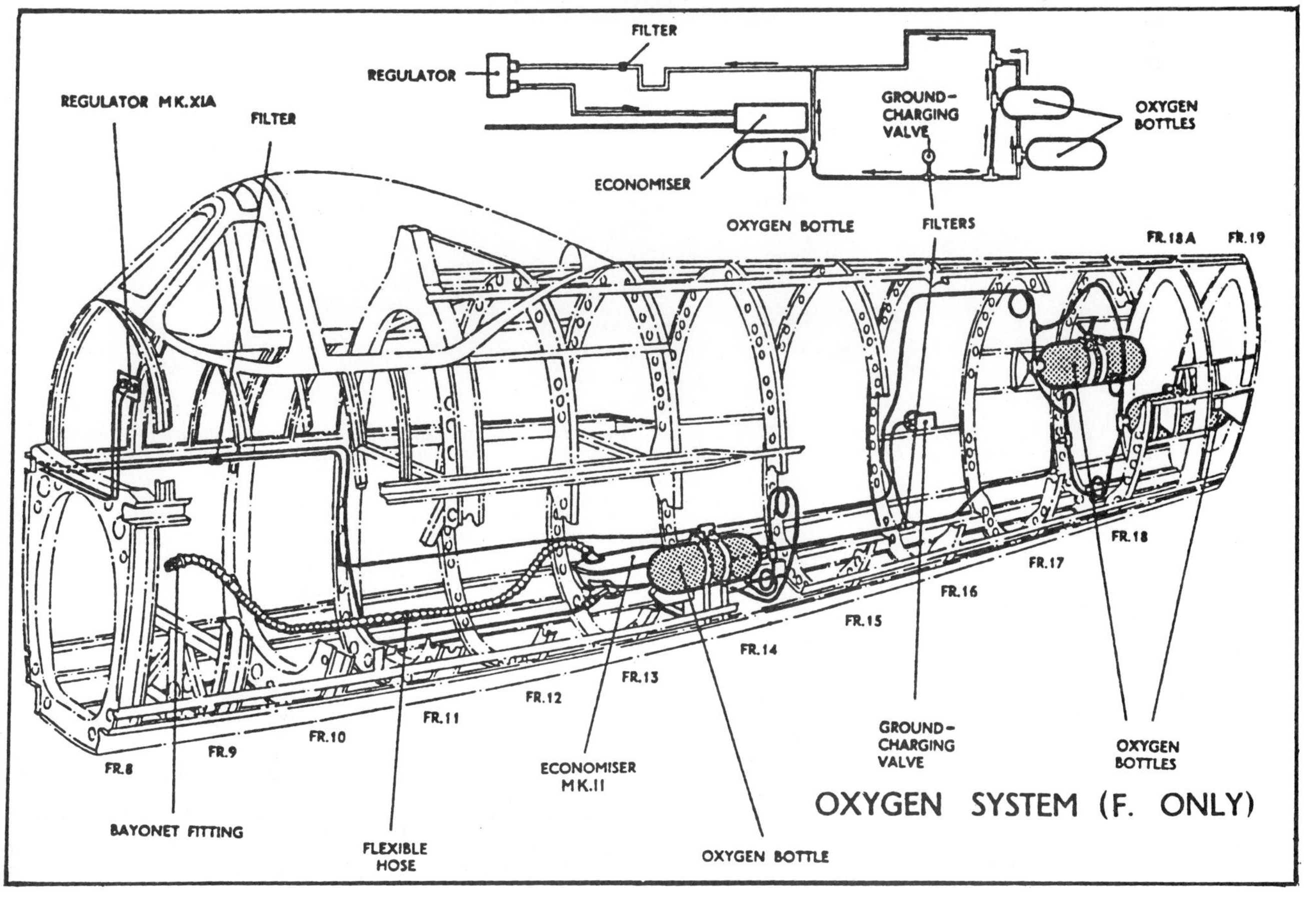

REGULATOR MK.XIA
FILTER
REGULATOR
FILTER
GROUND-CHARGING VALVE
OXYGEN BOTTLES
ECONOMISER
OXYGEN BOTTLE
FILTERS
FR.18A
FR.19
FR.18
FR.17
FR.16
FR.15
FR.14
FR.13
FR.12
FR.11
FR.10
FR.9
FR.8
GROUND-CHARGING VALVE
OXYGEN BOTTLES
ECONOMISER MK.II
BAYONET FITTING
FLEXIBLE HOSE
OXYGEN BOTTLE

OXYGEN SYSTEM (F. ONLY)

THE LATE 'TEEN PR SPITFIRE

Towards the end of the production run of the PR XI, squadrons operating the type were being forced to fly at higher altitudes in order to escape the attentions of enemy interceptors, and the Merlin 61/63 engines could not provide the power necessary for the Spitfire to reach these heights. A small number of airframes had been fitted with the Merlin 70, but it was realised that this was only a temporary measure until a better engine/airframe combination could be produced. Operating heights had risen to 40,000 feet plus and only the Griffon engine could provide the required power.

The Air Staff had been asking for a PR development of the Griffon powered Spitfire with a pressure cabin, and a prototype was eventually ordered. Supermarine thought that the designation for the new variant would be in the Mk 20 range, but the Air Ministry had informed the company that it was to carry the designation PR XIX, which Supermarine assumed would have been allocated to a fighter variant. The confusion over Mark numbers had arisen from the time when the Air Ministry had re-organised them at the period when the Mark V fighter had appeared.

The Supermarine Specification No 475 itemised details of major components of the new variant–
Main planes, PR Mk XI with DTD 273 booms (no alternative); Mk XIV u/c pintle. Provision for Mk XIV cooling and oil systems. Provision for additional 20 gallons petrol in each wing (not on first 22 a/c).
Chassis, Mk VIII. Tail end Mk XIV with adjustable ballast.
Fuselage, Mk XIV with pressure cabin and Lobelle sliding hood (first 22 a/c will have standard Mk XIV fuselage and cabin top with PR XI screen).
Universal camera installation. PR wireless equipment in Mk XIV positions.
Curved windscreen. Spar flange attachments to suit PR XI wings.
Fuel tanks (1) fuselage as Mk XIV (2) wings leading edge as PR XI. An additional 20 gallons to be provided in each wing with remote to transfer to fuselage tanks. (these tanks will not be fitted to first 22 a/c).
Immersed pumps for direct supply from leading edge tanks (3) drop tanks standard provision.

PM631, one of three PR Mk XIXs with the Battle of Britain Memorial Flight.

Fuel system, combination of PR Mk XI and Mk XIV. Oil tank and systems as Mk XIV.
Engine, Griffon 66 (first 22 a/c will have Griffon 65 without cabin blower). Airscrew, Rotol 5 blade R 19/5F5/1 as for Mk XIV. Engine installation as Mk XIV. Cooling system as Mk XIV. Cockpit heating on first 22 a/c.
Thermostats deleted after first 22 a/c. Wireless as for PR XI in Mk XIV position. Electrical as for Mk XIV with PR additions. Accumulator aft.
Armour protection, 10g over top fuel tank, rear armour only as Mk XIV.

In order to get a supply of aircraft to the RAF Supermarine arranged to supply sixteen pressure cabin PR XIs powered by the Merlin 63 in March 1944, and to follow these with 22 Griffon engined, non-pressurised Mk XIs as outlined in Specification 425. At one time consideration was given to powering the PR XIX with the Merlin 16 SM engine, but it could not meet production or performance requirements.

The first non-pressurised Mk XIX was RM626 with the

PS853 seen (below) back in PRU colours at Blackbushe in 1973. It is seen above in the colours it adopted after leaving the Woodvale-based 'Thum' Flight. It is today on charge with the Battle of Britain Memorial Flight at Coningsby.

PS858 was the trials Spitfire for the long range 170 gallon ferry fuel tank.

Griffon 65 engine driving a Rotol five blade wooden propeller, and when weighed at High Post on 27 April 1944 it had a tare weight of 6,363lb and an auw of 8,575. Initial deliveries of this type were made in May 1944. SW777, ordered on 18 March 1944, was selected as the pressurised version prototype and this had a Griffon 66 with the same type of Rotol propeller. It, too, was at High Post on 26 October for weighing and CoG determination and had a tare of 6,522lb and an auw of 9,001. PM661, when weighed at High Post on 18 June 1946 had a higher tare of 6,597 and auw of 9,031.

The contract for the pressurised XIX was placed on 27 March and specified use of (1) a basic FVIII fuselage with FVII pressure cabin (2) wings as for PR XI plus additional 40 gallons of fuel (2 × 20) in the wings (3) flying controls and universal camera installation as for PR XI. Price was to be a maximum of £7,500 each exclusive of stoppages of work due to air raids. This sum was raised to £8,980 in October and the specification then called for a prototype PR version of the F Mk XIV with pressure cabin.

SW777 was flown on 31 October 1944 by Shea-Simmonds for full service fuel and 90 gallon overload tank trials. With an auw of 9,000lb the pilot reported that the Spitfire had poor directional stability. Quill then flew it on 9 November without the overload tank at 40,000ft and it was still directionally unstable. He flew it the following day with the 90 gallon tank in position and thought that more work was required to make it an acceptable aeroplane.

Both pilots agreed that with wing tanks empty and with and without the overload tank fitted the aircraft was at its worst condition. It was then flown to Benson for fitment of a 170 gallon ferry tank preparatory for trials. Take off weight rose to 10,450lb and apart from a few minor criticisms the aircraft was thought to be acceptable for PR work. An attempt was made during the flight on 13 January 1945 to jettison the big tank but it would not leave the aircraft. The second test at Benson was after a new, short chord and deep blister hood had been installed. It was noisy and let in a draught. A second hood with

Above: PS890, production prototype Mk XIX, eventually served with the Thai Air Force.

PS934 of No 541 Squadron, 2nd TAF's post-war Spitfire PR unit.

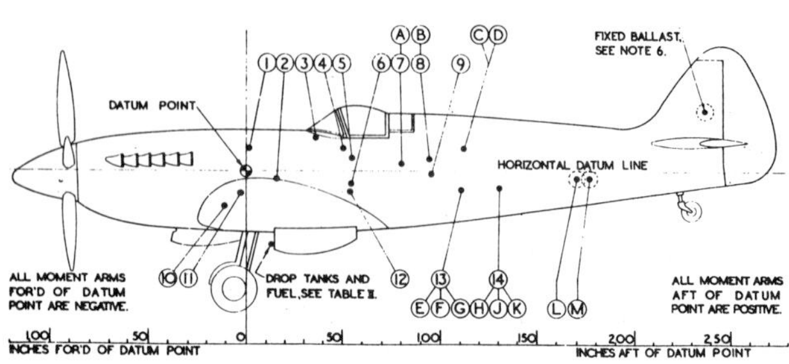

A B
C D
FIXED BALLAST. SEE NOTE 6.
1 2 3 4 5 6 7 8 9
DATUM POINT
HORIZONTAL DATUM LINE
ALL MOMENT ARMS FOR'D OF DATUM POINT ARE NEGATIVE.
10 11
DROP TANKS AND FUEL, SEE TABLE II.
12 13 14
E F G H J K L M
ALL MOMENT ARMS AFT OF DATUM POINT ARE POSITIVE.
100 50 0 50 100 150 200 250
INCHES FOR'D OF DATUM POINT
INCHES AFT OF DATUM POINT

TABLE I.

NOTE NO.	ITEM NO.	TYPICAL REMOVABLE ITEMS OF MILITARY LOAD.	WEIGHT LB.	ARM IN.	MOMENT LB.IN.
	12	1½ IN. SIGNAL PISTOL AND 8 CARTRIDGES.	5.5	+ 54.5	+ 300
	4	1¼ LB. INCENDIARY BOMB, NAVIGATIONAL COMPUTOR, CLOCK, CROWBAR AND RATIONS.	7.5	+ 51.5	+ 386
	3	CAMERA CONTROL UNIT TYPE 35.	4.5	+ 36.5	+ 164
1	13	FOR'D VERTICAL 36 IN. F.52 CAMERA AND ACCESSORIES.	100	+112.5	+11,250
1	14	AFT VERTICAL 36 IN. F.52 ..MERA AND ACCESSORIES.	100	+128.5	+12,850
	7	3 OXYGEN CYLINDERS MK. V C.	52	+ 81	+ 4,212
	6	DINGHY TYPE 'K' IN SEAT PACK TYPE 'A' MK.III.	18.5	+ 55	+ 1,018
4	3	T.R.1143 RADIO AND ACCESSORIES.	79	+ 94.5	+ 7,466
	9	A.1271 AMPLIFIER.	4.5	+ 95.5	+ 430
	5	PILOT AND PARACHUTE.	200	+ 55	+11,000
		TOTAL TYPICAL REMOVABLE MILITARY LOAD.	571.5		+49,076
5	1	OIL: 9 GALL. AT 9 LB. PER GALL.	81	+ 1	+ 81
	2	FUEL IN FUSELAGE TANKS: 85 GALL. 100 OCTANE AT 7.2 LB. PER GALL.	612	+ 15.5	+ 9,486
	10	FUEL IN WING TANKS: 133 GALL. 100 OCTANE AT 7.2 LB. PER GALL.	957.5	− 11	−10,533
6	11	AIRCRAFT IN TARE CONDITION.	6,353		−15,679
		AIRCRAFT IN TYPICAL TAKE-OFF CONDITION.	8,575	+ 3.8	+32,431

TABLE II.

DROP FUEL TANKS AND FUEL.	WEIGHT LB.	ARM IN.	MOMENT LB.IN.
45 GALL. BLISTER TYPE DROP TANK.	80	+ 13.5	+ 1,080
45 GALL. 100 OCTANE FUEL IN DROP TANK.	324	+ 13.5	+ 4,374
90 GALL. BLISTER TYPE DROP TANK.	120	+ 16	+ 1,920
90 GALL. 100 OCTANE FUEL IN DROP TANK	648	+ 13.5	+ 8,748

TABLE III.

NOTE NO.	ITEM NO.	ADDITIONAL AND ALTERNATIVE ITEMS OF REMOVABLE MILITARY LOAD.	WEIGHT LB.	ARM IN.	MOMENT LB.IN.
	A	3 OXYGEN CYLINDERS MK. V.	44	+ 81	+ 3,564
4	B	T.R.1133 RADIO AND ACCESSORIES.	70.5	+ 95	+ 6,698
1	E	FOR'D VERTICAL 20 IN. F.52 CAMERA AND ACCESSORIES.	90	+112.5	+ 10,125
1	H	AFT VERTICAL 20 IN. F.52 CAMERA AND ACCESSORIES.	90	+128	+ 11,520
2	F	FOR'D VERTICAL 20 IN. F.8 CAMERA AND ACCESSORIES.	79	+113	+ 8,927
2	J	AFT VERTICAL 20 IN. F.8 CAMERA AND ACCESSORIES.	79	+129.5	+ 10,231
3	G	FOR'D VERTICAL 14 IN. F.24 CAMERA AND ACCESSORIES.	34.5	+111.5	+ 3,847
3	K	AFT VERTICAL 14 IN. F.24 CAMERA AND ACCESSORIES.	34.5	+132	+ 4,554
3	C	OBLIQUE 14 IN. F.24 CAMERA AND ACCESSORIES.	34.5	+111.5	+ 3,847
3	D	OBLIQUE 8 IN. F.24 CAMERA AND ACCESSORIES.	30.5	+111.5	+ 3,401
	L	BALLAST WEIGHT ON FOR'D PEG AT AFT ACCESS DOOR (MAXIMUM: 4).	17.5	+171	+ 2,993
	M	BALLAST WEIGHT ON AFT PEG AT AFT ACCESS DOOR (MAXIMUM: 4).	17.5	+177.5	+ 3,106

Loading and C.G., PR Mk XIX (non-pressurised).

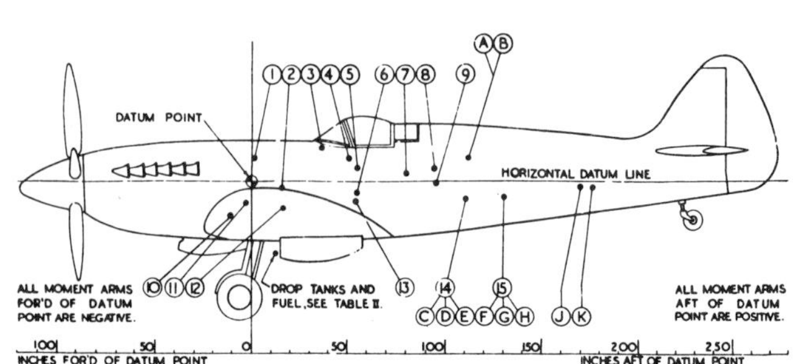

A B
1 2 3 4 5 6 7 8 9
DATUM POINT
HORIZONTAL DATUM LINE
ALL MOMENT ARMS FOR'D OF DATUM POINT ARE NEGATIVE.
10 11 12
DROP TANKS AND FUEL, SEE TABLE II.
13 14 15
C D E F G H J K
ALL MOMENT ARMS AFT OF DATUM POINT ARE POSITIVE.
100 50 0 50 100 150 200 250
INCHES FOR'D OF DATUM POINT
INCHES AFT OF DATUM POINT

TABLE I.

NOTE NO.	ITEM NO.	TYPICAL REMOVABLE ITEMS OF MILITARY LOAD.	WEIGHT LB.	ARM IN.	MOMENT LB.IN.
	13	1½ IN. SIGNAL PISTOL AND 8 CARTRIDGES.	5·5	+ 54	+ 297
	4	1¼ LB. INCENDIARY BOMB, TORCH, CLOCK AND CROWBAR.	4	+ 59	+ 236
	3	CAMERA CONTROL UNIT TYPE 35.	4·5	+ 37	+ 167
1	14	FOR'D VERTICAL 36 IN. F.52 CAMERA AND ACCESSORIES.	100	+112·5	+ 11,250
1	15	AFT VERTICAL 36 IN. F.52 CAMERA AND ACCESSORIES.	100	+128·5	+ 12,850
	7	3 OXYGEN CYLINDERS MK V C.	52	+ 81	+ 4,212
	6	DINGHY TYPE 'K' IN SEAT PACK TYPE 'A' MK III	18·5	+ 55	+ 1,018
4	8	T.F. 1143 RADIO AND ACCESSORIES.	80	+ 94	+ 7,520
	9	A.1271 AMPLIFIER.	4·5	+ 95	+ 428
	5	PILOT AND PARACHUTE.	200	+ 55	+11,000
		TOTAL TYPICAL REMOVABLE MILITARY LOAD	569		+48,978
5	1	OIL: 9 GALL. AT 9 LB. PER GALL.	81	+ 1·0	+ 81
	2	FUEL IN FUSELAGE TANKS: 82½ GALL. 100 OCTANE AT 7·2 LB. PER GALL.	594	+ 15·0	+ 8,910
	10	FUEL IN WING LEADING EDGE TANKS: 133 GALL. 100 OCTANE AT 7·2 LB. PER GALL.	957·5	− 10·9	−10,437
	12	FUEL IN INTER-SPAR TANKS: 38½ GALL. 100 OCTANE AT 7·2 LB. PER GALL	277	+ 17·4	+ 4,820
	11	AIRCRAFT IN TARE CONDITION.	6,522		−18,404
		AIRCRAFT IN TYPICAL TAKE-OFF CONDITION.	9,000·5	+ 3·8	+33,948

TABLE II

DROP FUEL TANKS AND FUEL.	WEIGHT LB.	ARM IN.	MOMENT LB.IN.
45 GALL. BLISTER TYPE DROP TANK.	80	+ 13·5	+ 1,080
45 GALL. 100 OCTANE FUEL IN DROP TANK.	324	+ 13·5	+ 4,374
90 GALL. BLISTER TYPE DROP TANK.	120	+ 16	+ 1,920
90 GALL. 100 OCTANE FUEL IN DROP TANK.	648	+ 13·5	+ 8,748
170 GALL. BLISTER TYPE DROP TANK.	190	+ 12	+ 2,280
170 GALL. 100 OCTANE FUEL IN DROP TANK.	1,224	+ 11·5	+ 14,076

TABLE III

NOTE NO.	ITEM NO.	ADDITIONAL AND ALTERNATIVE ITEMS OF REMOVABLE MILITARY LOAD.	WEIGHT LB.	ARM IN.	MOMENT LB.IN.
1	C	FOR'D VERTICAL 20 IN. F.52 CAMERA AND ACCESSORIES.	90	+ 112	+ 10,080
1	F	AFT VERTICAL 20 IN. F.52 CAMERA AND ACCESSORIES.	90	+ 128	+ 11,520
2	D	FOR'D VERTICAL 20 IN. F.8 CAMERA AND ACCESSORIES.	79	+ 113	+ 8,927
2	G	AFT VERTICAL 20 IN. F.8 CAMERA AND ACCESSORIES.	79	+ 129	+ 10,191
3	E	FOR'D VERTICAL 14 IN. F.24 CAMERA AND ACCESSORIES.	34·5	+ 111	+ 3,830
3	H	AFT VERTICAL 14 IN. F.24 CAMERA AND ACCESSORIES.	34·5	+ 132	+ 4,554
3	A	OBLIQUE 14 IN. F.24 CAMERA AND ACCESSORIES.	34·5	+ 112	+ 3,864
3	B	OBLIQUE 8 IN. F.24 CAMERA AND ACCESSORIES.	30·5	+ 111	+ 3,386
	J	BALLAST WEIGHT ON FOR'D PEG AT AFT ACCESS DOOR (MAXIMUM: 4)	17·5	+ 171	+ 2,993
	K	BALLAST WEIGHT ON AFT PEG AT AFT ACCESS DOOR (MAXIMUM: 4)	17·5	+ 178	+ 3,115

Loading and C.G., PR Mk XIX (pressurised).

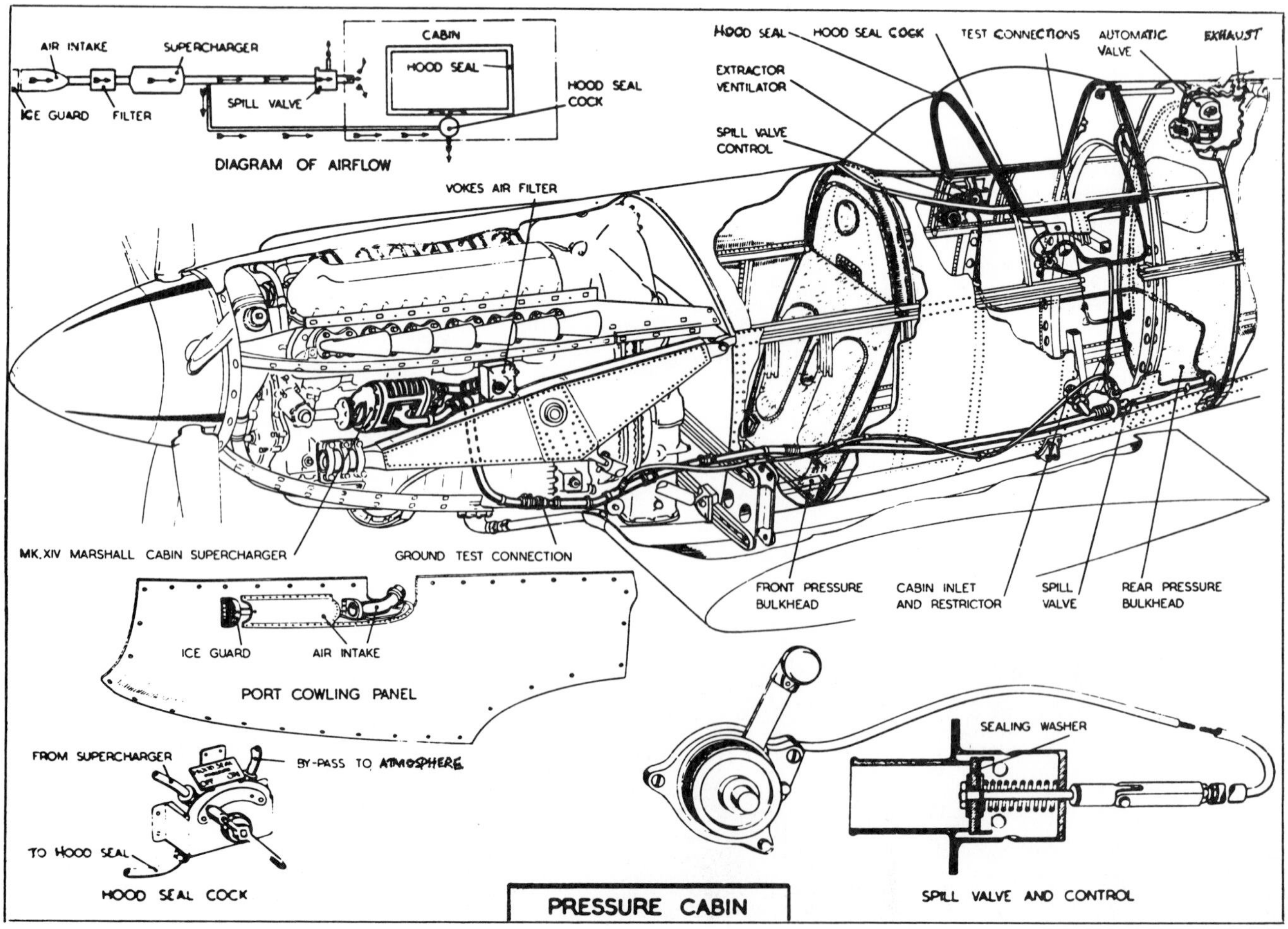

AIR INTAKE
SUPERCHARGER
CABIN
HOOD SEAL
HOOD SEAL COCK
SPILL VALVE
ICE GUARD
FILTER
DIAGRAM OF AIRFLOW
HOOD SEAL
HOOD SEAL COCK
TEST CONNECTIONS
AUTOMATIC VALVE
EXHAUST
EXTRACTOR VENTILATOR
SPILL VALVE CONTROL
VOKES AIR FILTER
MK.XIV MARSHALL CABIN SUPERCHARGER
GROUND TEST CONNECTION
FRONT PRESSURE BULKHEAD
CABIN INLET AND RESTRICTOR
SPILL VALVE
REAR PRESSURE BULKHEAD
ICE GUARD
AIR INTAKE
PORT COWLING PANEL
FROM SUPERCHARGER
BY-PASS TO ATMOSPHERE
TO HOOD SEAL
HOOD SEAL COCK
SEALING WASHER
PRESSURE CABIN
SPILL VALVE AND CONTROL

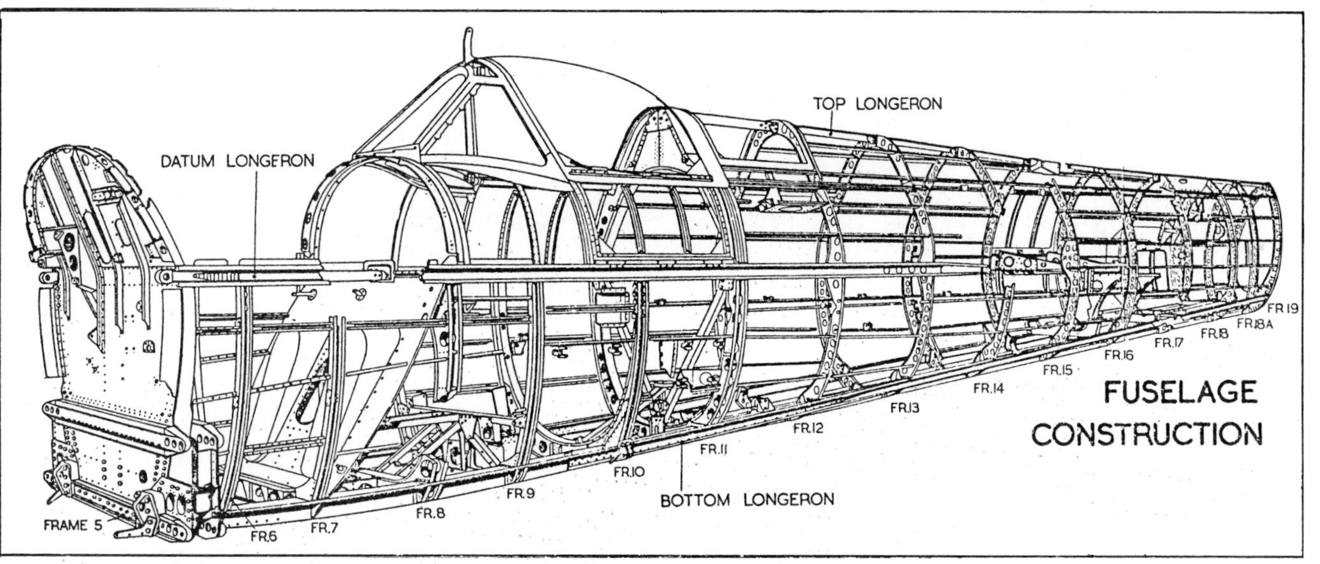

long chord and a shallow blister was fitted and tested; it was much quieter but the draught persisted.

The Certificate of Design for the Type 389 PR Mk XIX was issued on 5 June 1944 and the Type Record reflected details as in Supermarine Specn. 475. Type Record for the Type 390 (Pressure Cabin) was issued on 22 January 1945 and the main difference between both types was the F Mk VII pressure cabin with Lobelle hood for the 390. Certificate of Design was issued on the same day.

A production XIX, PS858, arrived at Boscombe Down on 19 March for fuel functioning tests with 90 and 170 gallon drop tanks and the A&AEE report's conclusions was that both tanks could be used satisfactorily at all heights. Handling trials with the same types of tanks were then commenced and in climbs altitude there was a noticeable deterioration in handling characteristics. Pilots thought the aircraft was unpleasant to fly, but very good without tanks. PM655 was at Eastleigh in April 1946 for a trial installation of vertical cameras in the wings.

Two hundred and twenty five examples of the PR Mk XIX were constructed and saw service in the European Theatre during the war with Bomber Command and a number saw service in the Far and Middle East. After the war 70 (later reduced to 50) were sold to Sweden and four to Turkey, and the last flight by an RAF Mk XIX was when PS853 took off from Woodvale, Lancashire, on a meteorological sortie. The pilot, Flt Lt J. Formby landed at 11.18am. This same aeroplane was to be used for tactical trials with the Lightning jet fighter in 1963. PM184-228, 245-288, 302-347 and 367-404 were cancelled, and it was intended to switch already allocated PR XIX serials PM419-466 and 478-495 to the Spiteful programme.

OFFICIAL REPORTS ON THE PR XIX

Vickers-Armstrongs, 13 January 1945. SW777. Take off and handling with 170 gallon overload tank. Flown to Benson for trials. Auw 10,450lb. Slightly longer take off run, climb to 35,000ft. Directional stability poor. At 22,000ft an attempt was made to jettison tank. The jettison lever could be moved but the tank remained attached to the aircraft.

Vickers Armstrongs, 2 March 1945. SW777. Handling with aircraft fitted special low altitude blister hood. Short chord and deep blister type hood. It was noisy and draughty. The long chord shallow blister hood was fitted and aircraft tested with it. Much quieter but still draughty. Dived at 470mph satisfactory. The long chord hood considered the better.

Boscombe Down, February 1945. PS858. Griffon 66. Handling trials with and without 90 and 170 gallon drop tanks. Pleasant to fly without tanks up to Mach .825. Directional behaviour was bad with either overload tank, particularly at high altitude with larger tank. Recommended that fuel from drop tank be used immediately after take off to enable tank to be dropped ASAP.

Boscombe Down, 19 March 1945. PS858. Fuel functioning tests with 90 and 170 gallon drop tanks. Both types could be used satisfactorily at all heights up to 40,000ft with complete drainage of tanks.

Vickers-Armstrongs, 18 June 1945. PM519. Handling of production aircraft. Tested and found satisfactory.

Boscombe Down, April 1943. L1004. Handling and spinning tests. Aircraft fitted with enlarged elevator horn balance. Auw 6,355lb.

RM632, one of the last Spitfires lost to enemy action in World War Two while in service with No 542 Squadron, 6 January 1945.

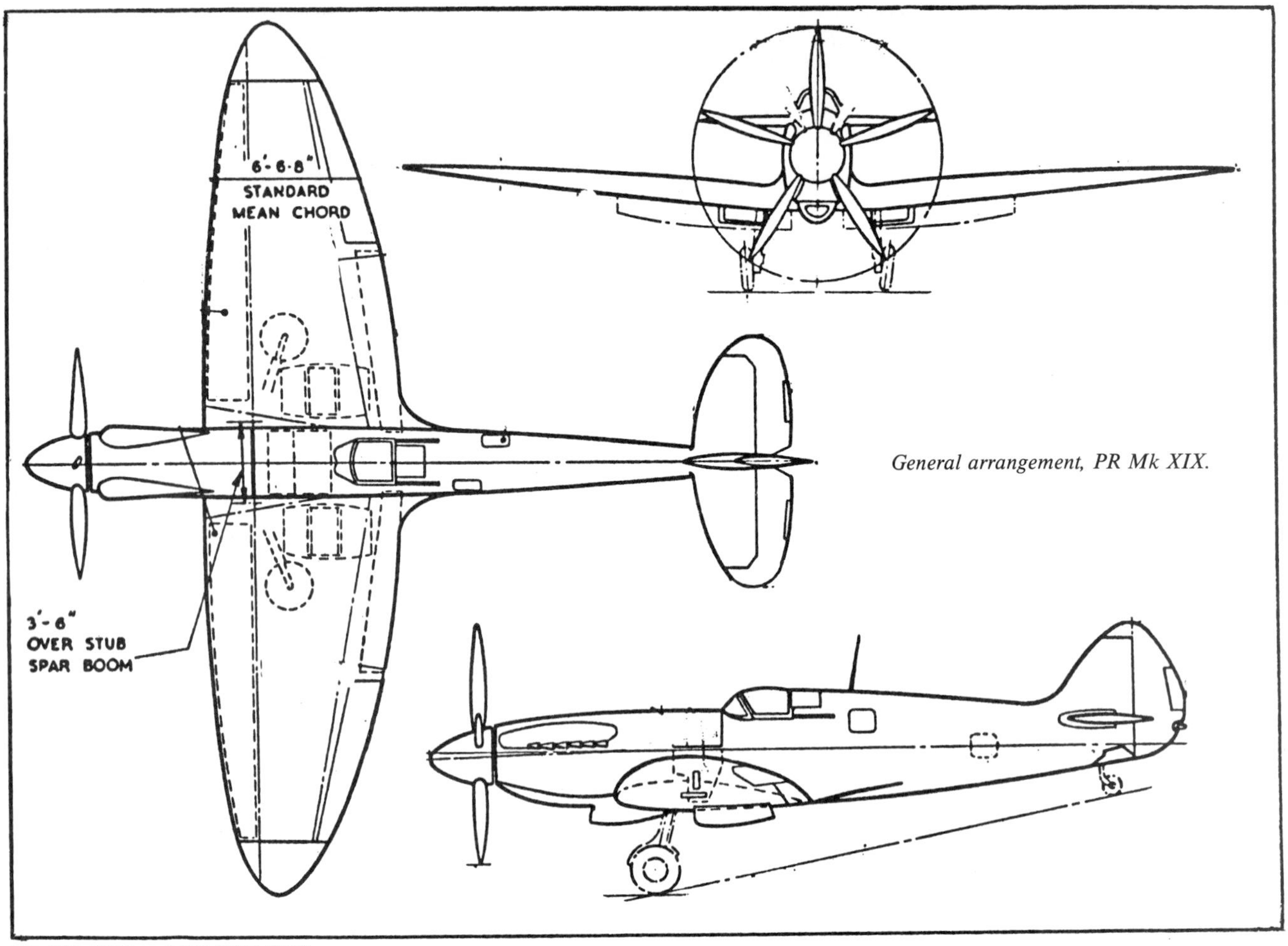

General arrangement, PR Mk XIX.

PR Mk XIX and PR XIX (PC)

Wing. Planform elliptical; section NACA Series 2200; span 36′ 10″;incidence° root +2, tip $-\frac{1}{2}$; dihedral° 6; thickness% root 13.2, tip 6; aspect ratio 5.68; area nett 220, gross 242; chord (geo) 6.38, (ma) 6ft 6.8″. Ailerons. Area 18.9; movement° up 26, down 19; droop $\frac{3}{8}$. Flaps. Area 15.4; movement° down 85. Wing loading 37.2; power loading 4.43. Propeller clearance @ take off $8\frac{1}{2}$in.

Tailplane. Area 33.84; chord (ma) 4.1; incidence° root 0, tip $\pm\frac{1}{2}$; dihedral° 0; Elevators. Area 13.74; movement° up 28, down 23. Tab. Area 0.688; movement° up 20, down 7. Fin area 6.65. Rudder. Area 10.08; movement° $28\frac{1}{2}$ each way. Tab area 0.7; movement° port 11, starbd $14\frac{1}{2}$. Set starbd 0.2in.

Undercarriage. Wheels Dunlop AH10019; tyres Dunlop IK13 or 17. Oleo pressure 570 stbd, 530 port; tyre pressure 80. Tailwheel retractable castoring. Wheel dunlop AH2184/IX; tyre Dunlop TA 12 or 14. Oleo pressure 255; tyre pressure 80.

Engine/s. Griffon 66 RG4 SM 2,035hp @ 2,750rpm @ 7,000ft (MS), 1,820 @ 21,000 (FS). Take off 1,520 @ 2,750rpm + 12lb boost to 7,000ft. Combat rating (5 mins) 2,035hp @ 2,750rpm + 18lb boost @ 7,000ft (MS), 1,820 @ 2,750 + 18 @ 21,000 (FS). 18 boost used with 130 octane fuel. Griffon 65 2,035hp first 26 a/c only. Coffman cartridge starter.

Propeller/s. Rotol R19/5F5/1 5-blade Jablo or Hydulignum 35° pitch range fine pitch 27° 15′. Diameter 10ft 5in.

Coolant. 70% mains water, 30% Glycol. Main system $14\frac{1}{2}$ gals, intercooler $4\frac{1}{2}$.

Fuel. 100 octane. Capacity. Fuselage (upper) $34\frac{1}{2}$. Lower 48, wing leading edge 2 × $66\frac{1}{2}$, inter spar tanks 2 × $19\frac{1}{4}$. Total 254. Plus 30, 45, 90, 170 o/ld tanks.

Oil. 9 gals in upper fuselage.

Armament. Nil.

Radio. TR1143 A1271.

Performance. Max speed 445mph @m 26,000ft (FS), 410 @ 12,000(MS), 355 @ SL(MS). Rate of climb 3,400ft min @ 22,000ft (FS), 43,3000ft min @ 9,000ft (MS), 4,400ft min @ SL (MS). Service ceiling 42,600ft (100ft min). Range Average cruise @ 325-360mph @ 35,000ft 1,010 miles, normal tankage. mpg 4.9, duration 2.7 to 3hr. With 90 gal o/ld tank @ 310-360mph 1,400 miles @ 35,000ft. mpg 4.1, duration 3.8 to 4.3hr. Take off run 600yds, landing 700. Cruise @ 250mph 1,120 miles; @ 375mph 680 miles. Time to 35,000ft 15.5 min. Cruise 250mph @ 35,000ft (FS).

Weights. Tare (non press) 6,550lb, 6,522 (PC), take off (NP) 8,575, (PC) 9,000. 5, max permissible 10,450.

Camera installation/s. Alternatives of – (1) 2 × F52 36in fanned vertical (2) 1 × F52 vertical (3) 2 × F52 20in fanned vertical (4) 2 × F8 20in fanned vertical (5) 2 × F24 14in vertical and 1 × F24 14 or 8in port facing oblique.

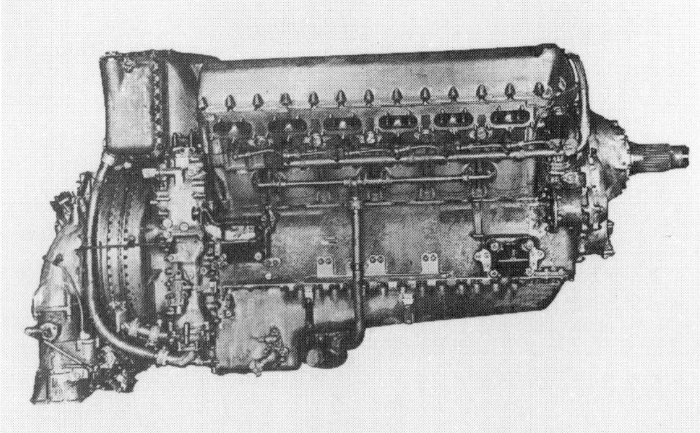

Griffon G65.

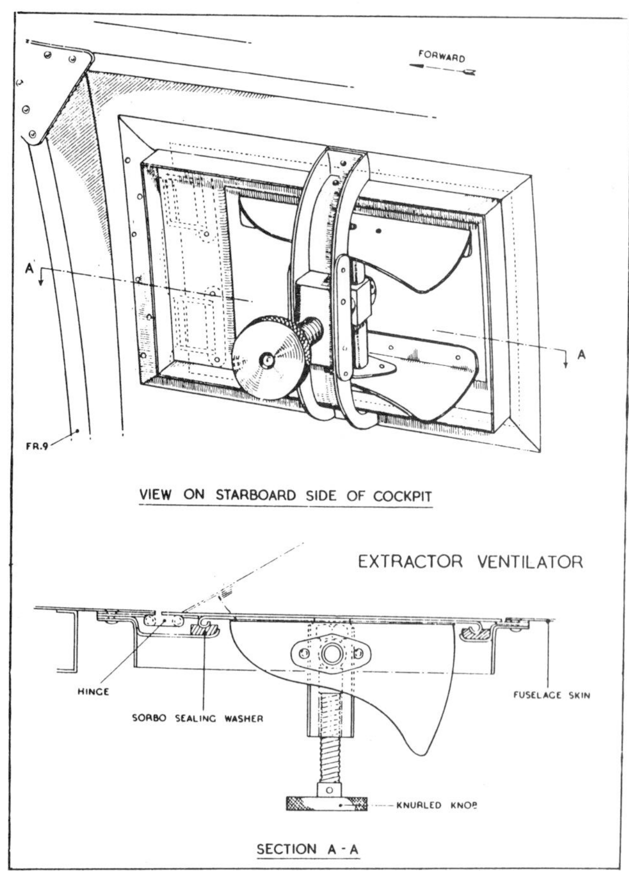

SW777, the trials aircraft for Mk XIX, went to Boscombe Down and R-R Hucknall for fuel consumption trials during 1946. Cat E September 1947.

JACKING ONE WHEEL ONLY
INNER NUT SLACKED OFF
BURST TYRE
VERTICAL ℄ OF JACK PARALLEL TO ℄ OF AIRCRAFT
FOUR LEGGED HYDRAULIC JACK REF. SUB-HEAD B8/5890
TAIL WHEEL
℄ AIRCRAFT
FIXED LEGS OF JACK PARALLEL TO LINE JOINING SOUND WHEEL TO TAIL WHEEL
BURST TYRE
SOUND WHEEL
PLAN SHOWING POSITION OF JACK LEGS

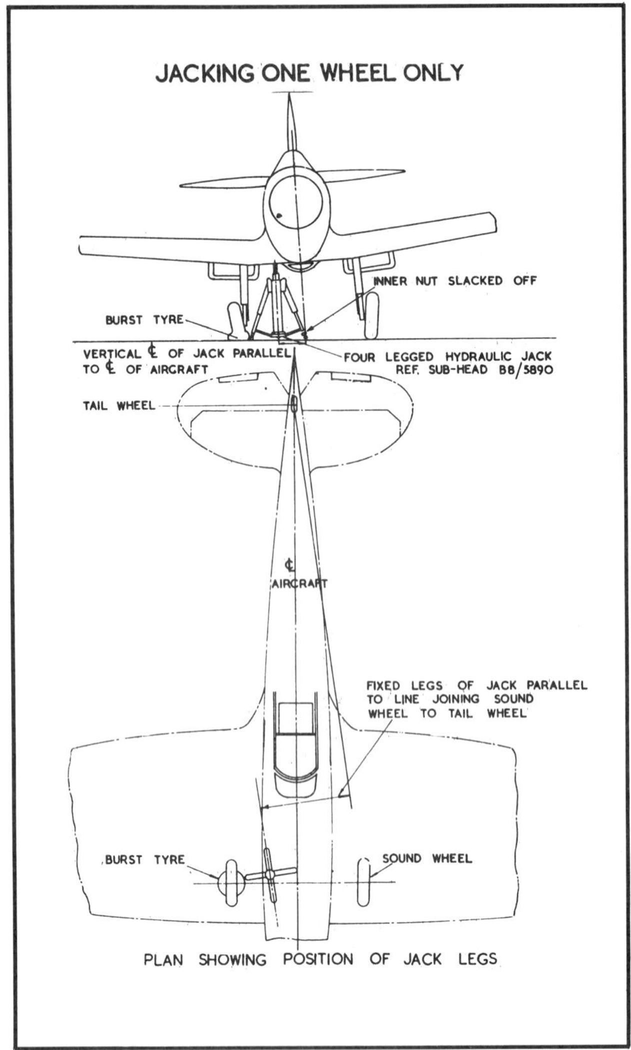

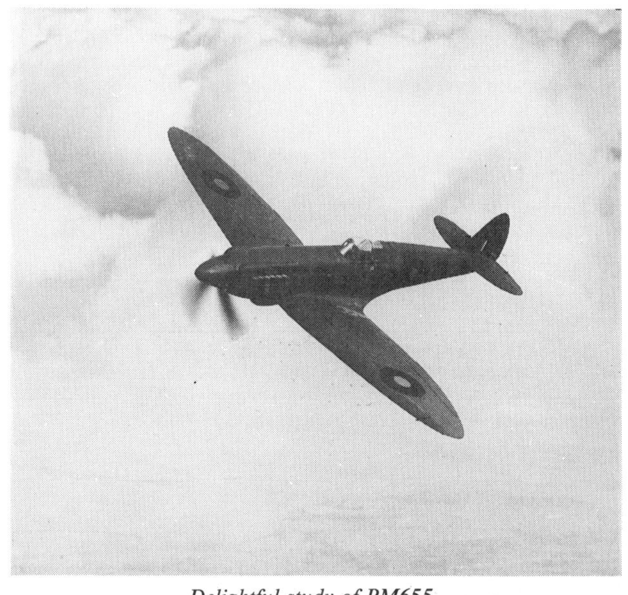

Delightful study of PM655.

DETAIL AT 'A'
DETAIL AT 'B' SHOWING ATTACHMENT TO LONGERON
TO LOCK CONTROLS
1. RAISE SEAT TO HIGHEST POSITION.
2. CLAMP LONG STRUT AT 'A' ON SPADE GRIP AND INSERT OTHER END 'C' INSIDE OF SEAT.
3. INSERT PIN OF SHORT ARM IN LUG.
4. INSERT LONG PIN OF LOWER BAR IN HOLE IN STARBOARD STARWHEEL BEARING.
5. INSERT SHORT PIN OF BAR IN EYEBOLT AT 'B'.
'A'
CROSS STAY
'B'
STBD. LONGERON
'C'
DETAIL 'C'
FLYING CONTROLS LOCKING GEAR
DETAIL PLAN OF COCKPIT
PILOT'S SEAT
CONTROL COLUMN
FR.8
FR.9
FR.10
FR.11
FRAME 8
FORWARD
FRAME 9
FRAME 10

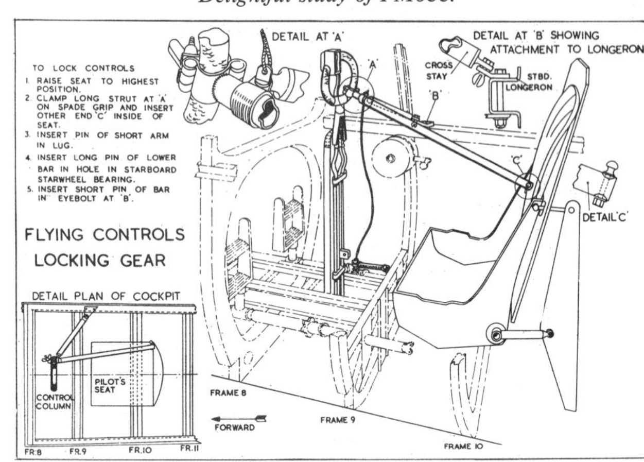

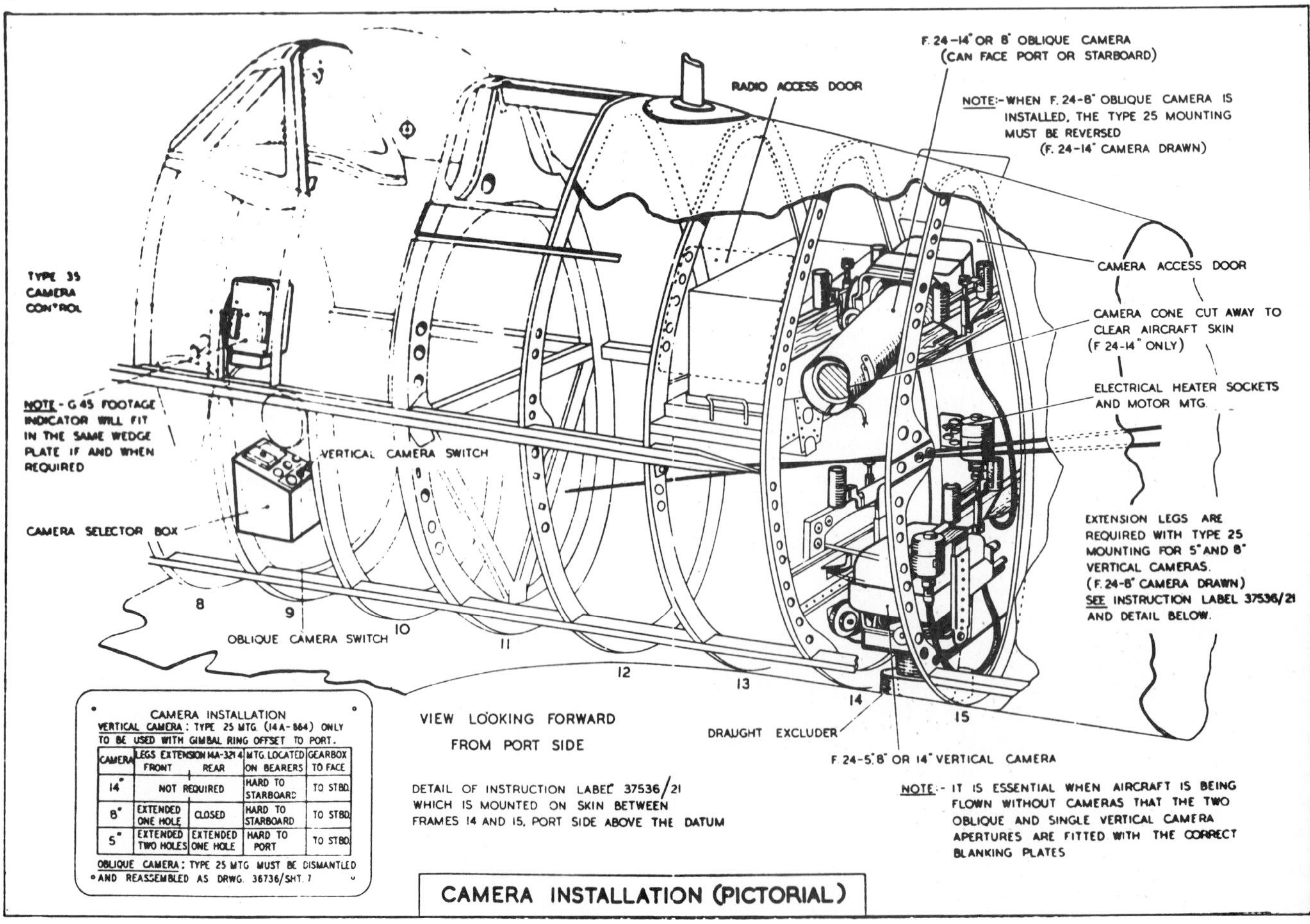

F. 24-14" OR 8" OBLIQUE CAMERA (CAN FACE PORT OR STARBOARD)
RADIO ACCESS DOOR
NOTE:- WHEN F. 24-8" OBLIQUE CAMERA IS INSTALLED, THE TYPE 25 MOUNTING MUST BE REVERSED (F. 24-14" CAMERA DRAWN)
TYPE 35 CAMERA CONTROL
CAMERA ACCESS DOOR
CAMERA CONE CUT AWAY TO CLEAR AIRCRAFT SKIN (F 24-14" ONLY)
ELECTRICAL HEATER SOCKETS AND MOTOR MTG.
NOTE - G.45 FOOTAGE INDICATOR WILL FIT IN THE SAME WEDGE PLATE IF AND WHEN REQUIRED
VERTICAL CAMERA SWITCH
CAMERA SELECTOR BOX
EXTENSION LEGS ARE REQUIRED WITH TYPE 25 MOUNTING FOR 5" AND 8" VERTICAL CAMERAS. (F. 24-8" CAMERA DRAWN) SEE INSTRUCTION LABEL 37536/21 AND DETAIL BELOW.
8
9
10
11
12
13
14
15
OBLIQUE CAMERA SWITCH
DRAUGHT EXCLUDER
F 24-5". 8" OR 14" VERTICAL CAMERA
CAMERA INSTALLATION
VERTICAL CAMERA: TYPE 25 MTG. (14A-864) ONLY TO BE USED WITH GIMBAL RING OFFSET TO PORT.
CAMERA | LEGS EXTENSION 14A-3214 FRONT | REAR | MTG. LOCATED ON BEARERS | GEARBOX TO FACE
14" | NOT REQUIRED | HARD TO STARBOARD | TO STBD.
8" | EXTENDED ONE HOLE | CLOSED | HARD TO STARBOARD | TO STBD.
5" | EXTENDED TWO HOLES | EXTENDED ONE HOLE | HARD TO PORT | TO STBD.
OBLIQUE CAMERA: TYPE 25 MTG MUST BE DISMANTLED AND REASSEMBLED AS DRWG. 36736/SHT. 7
VIEW LOOKING FORWARD FROM PORT SIDE
DETAIL OF INSTRUCTION LABEL 37536/21 WHICH IS MOUNTED ON SKIN BETWEEN FRAMES 14 AND 15, PORT SIDE ABOVE THE DATUM
NOTE:- IT IS ESSENTIAL WHEN AIRCRAFT IS BEING FLOWN WITHOUT CAMERAS THAT THE TWO OBLIQUE AND SINGLE VERTICAL CAMERA APERTURES ARE FITTED WITH THE CORRECT BLANKING PLATES
CAMERA INSTALLATION (PICTORIAL)

Supermarine Aviation (Vickers) Ltd

Sixth order for 592 Spitfire Mk VIII, PL758 to PM676, dated 2 June 1943, **reduced to 227 PR XI and 124 PR XIX.** Built between February 1944 and May 1946. The following serials apply to 536-581, 596-637 built to this order; PM496-519, 536-637 and 651-661.

Seventh order for 200 Spitfire Mk VIII, PS684 to PS935, dated 17 July 1943. Order amended to 121 Spiteful and **79 Spitfire PR XIXs. Built between November 1944 and May 1945. The following serials apply to PR XIXs built to this** seventh order; PS831-836, 849-893 and 908-935.

Tenth order for 406 Spitfire Mk XIV, RM615 to RN221, dated 23 October 1943. Built as Mk XIV and XIX between April 1944 and May 1945. The **following serials apply to PR XIXs built** to this tenth order; RM626-646. (22).

PR XIX prod. PM498, 506, 543, 548, 564, 569, 571, 599, 621, 623-624, 631, 653, 655-656, PS852-853, 866, 869-870, 880-881, 884, 890, 914, 916, 917 and 925.

To Bomber Command; PM580, 609-615, 618, 621, 628, 630, 658, PS858, 885, 908, 930 and 934.

To Indian AF. PM562-563, 565-566, 569-570 and 602-607.

To Maintenance Airframes; PM651(7758M), PS915(7548M).

To Royal Swedish AF. PM497-499, 502-503, 554, 556, 559-561, PS850, 859-865, 867-884, 886, 891, 893, 909, 923-924, 926-929, 931, 933 and 935.

To Royal Thai AF. PM630, PS836 and 888.

To USAAF. PM536 and 541.

PM and PS series all with Griffon 66

PM496 STN 6MU 23-5-45 FAAC 2-9-46 a/c PSD held 6MU 29-11-47 SOC 31-3-48 sold E Smelt 8-9

PM497 To Swed with Mks G-15-36 via Mars by Sgt Elmergard 19-1-49 became 31025

PM498 PR XIX (PC) Super p/proto desert equip 20-2-45 to Swed with Mks G-15-15 7-10-48 became 31004

PM499 To Swed with Mks G-15-41 via Mars by Lt Fyrlund 13-2-49 became 31040

PM500 STN 6MU 27-5-45 Ben 6-9-46 541S 7-9 CAC 17-11-48 ROS FAC3 21-2-50 recat 4R NEA 7-10 sold En R M 12-7-54

PM501 EA 6MU 28-5-46 Farn 11-9 ETPS 6-6-47 for Met Flt Farn Nov '49 hand & spin trls with 170 gal ventral o/ld fuel tank, MkXIV tail unit. Direct stab bad, particularly with tank at H/A. Pilots instructed to use o/ld tank immediately after t/o. Feb '50 gust prog with PS914 and SL550. BDn for trls, ret Farn April '51 for use as chase plane for DeH 108 TG183 which cd during trls on 1 May. Chil Aug IFF trls with Harvard FT375. Chase plane for Meteor EE476 fitt automatic dive brakes. H Ercal 6-2-52 NEA 7-10 sold En R M 7-7-54

PM502 To Swed with Mks G-15-35 via Mars by Lt Strom 12-2-49 became 31026

PM503 To Swed with Mks G-15-35 via Mars 7-10-48 became 31003

PM504 STN 1PP Ben 31-5-45 MAAF 28-6 ACSEA 4-7 cd SOC 27-6-46

PM505 STN 1PP Ben 1-6-45 MAAF 28-6 ACSEA CAC en route rts 15-8

PM506 PRXIX(PC) STN Super p/proto combined Coffman starter and breech on G66 20-2-45 1PP Ben 2-6 MAAF 30-7 ACSEA 7-8 SOC 11-4-46

PM507 STN 1PP Ben 2-6-45 MAAF 10-7 ACSEA 14-7 cd SOC 27-6-46

PM508 STN Ben 5-6-45 10ADU 26-6 MAAF 2-7 ACSEA 26-7 SOC 17-10-46

PM509 STN Ben 5-6-45 10ADU 26-6 MAAF 2-7 ACSEA 12-7 SOC 30-5-46

PM510 STN 1PP Ben 8-6-45 10ADU 29-6 MAAF 2-7 ACSEA 20-7 Ind 31-10-46 SOC 4-12

PM511 STN 1PP Ben 8-6-45 10ADU 28-7 MAAF 31-7 ACSEA 26-8 SOC 28-8-47

PM512 G65 1PP Ben 11-6-45 10ADU 26-7 MAAF 31-7 ACSEA 10-8 Ind 25-7-46 SOC to Ins A/F 27-3-47

PM513 G65 1PP Ben 11-6-45 MAAF 17-8 ACSEA 26-8 SOC 30-5-46

PM514 G65 1PP Ben 11-6-45 10ADU 28-7 MAAF 31-7 ACSEA 7-8 Ind 27-6-46 disposed of to Army Salvage 28-8-47

PM515 G65 1PP Ben 11-6-45 10ADU 26-7 MAAF 31-7 ACSEA 9-8 SOC 30-5-46

PM516 STN 1PP Ben 12-6-45 MAAF 25-7 ACSEA 3-9 SOC 28-8-47

PM517 STN Ben 18-6-45 10ADU 23-7 MAAF 8-8 ACSEA 18-8 Ind 31-10-46 SOC 4-12

PM518 STN Ben 18-6-45 10ADU 18-7 MAAF 25-7 ACSEA 9-8 SOC 11-7-46

PM519 STN VA HPA 18-6-45 tests of prod a/c 6MU 29-6 Ben 16-7 10ADU 17-9 MAAF 18-9 ACSEA 24-9 Ind 31-10-46 SOC 4-12

PM536 STN Ben 18-6-45 10ADU 1-9 MAAF 9-9 USAF Cairo 17-9 ACSEA 11-10 SOC 28-8-47

PM537 STN Ben 18-6-45 MAAF 17-8 ACSEA 10-9 SOC 27-3-47

PM538 STN Ben 18-6-45 10ADU 8-8 MAAF 17-8 ACSEA 9-9 Ind 15-8-46 SOC 29-8-46

PM539 STN Ben 18-6-45 10ADU 29-9 MAAF 8-10 ACSEA 21-10 SOC 23-8-47

PM540 STN 1PP Ben 22-6-45 10ADU 6-9 MAAF 10-9 ACSEA 5-10 Ind 29-6-46 SOC 28-8-47

PM541 STN 1PP Ben 22-6-45 10ADU 1-9 MAAF 9-9 USAF Cairo 17-9 ACSEA 5-10 SOC 28-11-46

PM542 STN Ben 23-6-45 10ADU 6-9 MAAF 12-9 ACSEA 17-9 disposed of to Army Salvage 28-8-47

PM543 (PC) STN Super p/proto u/c mods 17-4-45 6MU 25-6-45 Ben 16-7 10ADU 15-1-46 ACSEA 13-2 SOC 28-8-47

PM544 STN 6MU 30-6-45 Ben 29-8 10ADU 15-1-46 MAAF 5-2 ACSEA 13-2 Ind 31-10 SOC 4-12

PM545 STN 6MU 30-6-45 Ben 28-8 10ADU 15-1-46 MAAF 5-2 ACSEA 28-2 SOC 28-8-47

PM546 STN 6MU 30-6-45 Ben 16-7 10ADU 12-10 MAAF 18-10 ACSEA 24-10 Ind 29-8-46 disposed of to Army Salvage 28-8-47

PM547 STN 6MU 30-6-45 Ben 16-7 MAAF 28-10 ACSEA 5-11 Ind 27-6-46 disposed of to Army Salvage 28-8-47

PM548 (PC) STN Super p/proto fuel filter mods 24-5-45 6MU 30-6 Ben 16-7 151MU 17-1-46 Res pl 26S 17-3 sold VAEA 12-11

PM549 STN 6MU 30-6-45 Ben 24-8 2S BAFO 22-11 1BR&SD 23-8-48 Short Bros 10-4-51 19RFS FAC5(S) 4-5-52

PM550 STN 6MU 3-7-45 1PP Ben 21-8 10ADU 24-1-46 2S BAFO 11-7 FAC3(R) 21-12-50 work stopped contract 4917 raised rts 30-9-52

PM551 STN 6MU 3-7-45 Ben 29-8 10ADU 23-10 ME 1-11 SOC 29-8-46

PM552 STN 6MU 3-7-45 Ben 29-8 10ADU 2-10 MAAF 20-10 ACSEA 26-10 Ind 27-6-46 34S FACE complete wrk 12-10 SOC 31-12

PM553 STN 6MU 3-7-45 1PP Ben 21-8 10ADU 30-10 ME 15-11 SOC 29-8-46

PM554 6MU 7-7-45 1PRU Ben 24-8 151RU 14-11 25S 29-11 to Swed with Mks G-15-38 via Mars by Lt Mughow 11-2-49 became 31027

PM555 STN 6MU 6-7-45 Ben 24-8 2S 29-11 FAAC 5-6-47 eng repair FAC3 20-1-50 NEA 5-4 sold EnRM 15-7-54

PM556 To Swed with Mks G-15-42 via Mars by Lt Muchow 24-2-49 became 31031

PM557 STN 6MU 9-7-45 1PP Ben 21-8 10ADU 24-1-46 ME 30-1-47 SOC 28-8

PM558 STN 6MU 11-7-45 1PP Ben 21-8 FACE dbf 12-9 SOC 17-10

PM559 To Swed with Mks G-15-43 via Mars by Lt Hallander 24-2-49 became 31032

PM560 To Swed with Mks G-15-44 via Mars by Lt Carlsson 24-2-49 became 31033

PM561 To Swed with Mks G-15-45 via Mars by Lt Lundstrom 16-3-49 became 31034

PM562 STN to 6MU BNn as PM402 in error 13-7-45 earmarked for Ind Mar '46 sold VA 24-8-48

PM563 STN 6MU 14-7-45 earmarked for Ind Mar '46 sold VA 24-8-48

PM564 (PC) Super p/proto for QS pilot's harness in lieu of QK; to delete locking device and make quick release operative 23-1-45 6MU 18-7 Ben 24-8 2S 22-11 c/fd after t/o Mars cd/ld 29-10-46 SOC 31-10

PM565 STN 6MU 19-7-45 earmarked for Ind Mar '46 sold VA 24-8-48

PM566 STN 6MU 21-7-45 earmarked for Ind Mar '46 sold VA 24-8-48

PM567 STN 6MU 19-7-45 Ben 24-8 MAAF 29-10 ME 1-11

PM568 STN 6MU 18-7-45 1PP Ben 24-8 10ADU 7-1-46 ACSEA 24-2 SOC 31-12

PM569 STN Super p/proto 31-10-44 6MU 19-7-45 earmarked for Ind Mar '46 sold VA 24-8-48

PM570 STN 6MU 19-7-45 earmarked for Ind Mar '46 sold VA 24-8-48

PM571 STN Super p/proto for u/c mods 10-7-45 6MU 23-7 Ben 24-8 10ADU 24-9 MAAF Ed Adam 17-2-46 132MU 15-4 ME 25-4 SOC 29-8

PM572 STN 6MU 23-7-45 1PP Ben 24-8 MAAF 23-9 CAC eng change 108RSU 1-11 ret UK 12-5-46 sold J Dale 1-6-49

PM573 STN 6MU 24-7-45 1PP Ben 21-8 10ADU 16-11 ME 23-11 SOC 29-8-46

PM574 STN 1PP Ben 24-7-45 MAAF 27-9 ACSEA 23-10 81S SHQ Tengah 20-10-49 for short term service FEAF cat comp fwt SOC 25-1-50

PM575 STN 1PP Ben 24-7-45 10ADU 17-9 MAAF 21-9 SOC 29-8-46

PM576 STN CFE Tang 27-7-45 6MU 14-9 FEAF 23-12-50 MBFE storage 81S 6-9-52 FAC(S) c/fd ditched SOC 10-9

PM577 STN Ben 31-7-45 16S 29-8 268S 20-9 29MU 18-4-46 Short Bros mods for Met duties. Thum ascent 10-4-51 NEA 24-7-56 sold H Bath 5-11

PM578 STN Ben 28-7-45 MAAF 24-8 ME 30-8 SOC 29-8-46

PM579 STN Ben 28-7-45 16S 17-8 268S 20-9 61OTU 27-5-47 disbanded WEF 1-7-47 226OCU FA3(R) 24-10-49 ROS 9MU 25-8-50 NEA 7-10-53 sold scrap 14-6-54

PM580 STN Ben 31-7-45 16S 29-8 268S 20-9 16S 1-11 FAAC 6-5-46 ROS 541S 23-2-50 trans Bomb Com WEF 1-3 AGT Gat refurb 11-1-51 sold VA 6-2-53

PM581 STN 6MU 31-7-45 Ben 29-8 10ADU 14-12 MAAF 21-12 ACSEA 30-12 SOC 28-8-47

PM596 STN 6MU 31-7-45 Ben 29-8 MAAF 7-11 ACSEA 12-11 SOC 28-8-47

PM597 STN Ben 18-8-45 10ADU 23-10 ME Ismalia 4-12 SOC 29-8-46

PM598 STN Ben 22-8-45 10ADU 14-12 ME 132MU 19-12 SOC 29-8-46

PM599 STN Super p/proto 17-4-45 Ben 22-8 10ADU 30-10 ME 132MU 23-11 SOC 29-8-46

PM600 STN Ben 30-8-45 10ADU 16-11 ME 137MU 23-11 SOC 29-8-46

PM601 STN Ben 30-8-45 10ADU 15-12 ME 137MU 19-11 SOC 29-8-46

PM602 STN 6MU 30-8-45 earmarked for Ind Mar '46 sold VA 24-8-48

PM603 STN Super p/proto 6-3-45 6MU 12-9 earmarked for Ind Mar '46 sold VA 24-8-48

PM604 STN 6MU 31-8-45 earmarked for Ind Mar '46 sold VA 24-8-48

PM605 STN 6MU 31-8-45 earmarked for Ind Mar '46 sold VA 24-8-48

PM606 STN 6MU 6-9-45 earmarked for Ind Mar '46 sold VA 24-8-48

PM607 STN 6MU 6-9-45 earmarked for Ind Mar '46 sold VA 24-8-48

PM608 STN 6MU 12-9-45 1BRSD 10-11-48 2S BAFO 7-5-49 AGT Gat refurb 9-3-51 sold 6-2-53

PM609 STN 6MU 12-9-45 Leuch 31-3-49 541S 20-4 trans Bomb Com 1-3-50 AGT Gat refurb 1-5-51 sold 6-2-53

PM610 STN 6MU 15-9-45 Leuch 26-4-49 541S 13-5 trans Bomb Com 12-3-51 AGT Gat refurb 12-5 work stopped for recovery of spares. To 6995M Henley 25-8-52

Benson Wing PM555 during August 1945. Its carcass was sold to Enfield Rolling Mills in July 1954 for melting down.

PM611 STN 6MU 18-9-45 Leuch 20-12-48 237OCU 11-1-49 trans Bomb Com 18-9-50 63MU SR 10-2-51 C3R 16-2 ROS AGT Gat refurb 18-5 work stopped for recovery of spares 14-8-52 to 6996M Henley 25-8-52 SOC 31-1-53

PM612 STN 6MU 27-11-45 82S Ben 14-4-47 541S 3-12 FAAC 12-7-49 ROS trans Bomb Com 15-12 FA3R 12-5-50 ROS 541S 12-9 AFT Gat refurb 1-5-51 NEA 9-10-53 sold J G Will 24-4-54

PM613 STN 6MU 12-9-45 237(PR)OCU 25-9-48 trans Bomb Com 3-10-50 29MU 3-7-51 NEA 7-10-53 sold EnRM 15-7-54

PM614 STN 6MU 31-10-45 VA STN 27-1-48 T 1 of Mod 1677 FCCS 4-6 Leuch 2-9-49 237OCU 25-7-50 trans Bom Com 18-9 FA scr 8-2-51

PM615 STN 6MU 31-10-45 Leuch 26-1-49 237OCU 15-2 trans Bomb Com 18-9-50 NEA 7-10-53 sold EnRM 19-7-54

PM616 STN 6MU 15-10-45 BAFO Com Wng 7-8-47 2S 13-8 FA scr 6-7-50

PM617 STN Ben 26-11-45 2S BAFO 3-2-46 C4(RE) 24-10-50 NEA 9-5-51 sold H Bath 14-9

PM618 STN 6MU 19-10-45 Leuch 2-5-49 541S 26-5 trans Bom Com 1-3-50 FA scr 13-6-50

PM619 STN 29MU 3-12-45 61OTU 4-7-46 NEA 203AFS 17-9-47 sold VA 11-11-48

PM620 29MU 3-12-45 61OTU 5-7-46 203AFS 6MU 17-9-47 1BRSD 22-9-48 2S BAFO 9-10 9MU 15-5-51 NEA 7-10-53 sold scr 9-9-54

PM621 STN Super p/proto relocation pilot's harness 23-1-45 6MU 15-10 Leuch 13-7-49 237OCU 25-8 541S 7-9 trans Bomb Com 1-3-50 AGT Gat refurb 16-1-51 NEA 7-10-53 sold EnRM 9-7-54

PM622 STN 6MU 1-11-45 8OUTU Ben 17-12-46 237S Leuch lost wng during aero display pilot kld SOC 18-9-48

PM623 STN Super p/proto reintroduction visual u/c indicator wng u/s 12-12-44 6MU 31-10-45 82S Ben 25-6-47 541S 3-12-47 FAAC 6-4-48 recat E 6-4

PM624 STN 6MU 15-10-45 8OTU Ben 17-12-46 541S 17-6-48 FAAC 16-7 ROS trans Bomb Com 1-3-50 AGT Gat refurb 13-3-51 NEA 7-10-53 sold scr 19-9-54

PM625 STN 6MU 11-10-45 2S BAFO 4-2-50 NEA 7-10-53 sold scr 9-9-54

PM626 STN 6MU 19-10-45 Leuch 9-5-49 541S 31-5 air coll PM629 a/c aban cd nr Streatley Berks 23-8 SOC 6-9

PM627 6MU 20-9-45 15-6-52 BR&SD Res pl 26-5-49 2S BAFO 10-11 AGT Gat refurb 9-3-51 9MU sold AST 15-2-53 IAF HS964. To Canada and extant Linkoping, Sweden

PM628 STN 6MU 1-11-45 Leuch 11-5-49 54S 26-5 trans Bomb Com 1-3-50 AGT Gat refurb 1-5-51 Thum Flt Woodvale 16-7-52 FAC5 des 5-3-54

PM629 STN 6MU 1-11-45 61OTU 17-7-46 Leuch 26-2-49 541S 16-3 air coll PM626 c/lnd nr Pangbourne Berks CE SOC 23-8

PM630 STN BDn 26-11-45 speed & height tracking by radar dam CB 1-10-46 6MU 1-4-47 541S 4-2-49 trans Bomb Com 1-5-50 237OCU 15-2-51 FA3R 17-7 AGT Gat refurb cancel ROS FEAF 15-2-52 SOC 7-8-54 Thai AF 31-8 extant

PM631 (PC) STN Super p/proto 16-5-44 Coffman starter mods 15-5-45; pilot's harness mods 10-7 Hooton Pk Met Sectn BBMF Colt BoB film extant BBMF RAF Coningsby

PM632 STN 6MU 6-11-45 2S Celle 15-12-46 w/u ldg Buckeburg BZG CE 2-7-48

PM633 STN 6MU 6-11-45 FCCS 29-11 GAAC 9-9-46 RNAF SoTT to 6453M 6-11 RNAFS Langham SOC 17-12-47

PM634 G65 6MU 18-10-45 1PP Ben 27-11 2S 3-2-46 eng fail in crct cd nr Celle CB12-6 412RSU recat E 30-8 prov to 6160M cancel 17-10

PM635 STN Ben 26-11-45 10ADU 23-2-46 ACSEA 10-3 SOC 16-1-47

PM636 STN 29MU 3-10-45 61OTU 28-6-46 FACE 7-1-47 SOC 20-6

PM637 STN Super p/proto 5-9-44 29MU 3-12-45 61OTU 15-7-46 disbanded WEF 17-47 FAAC 8-4-49 ROS 17S 24-10 226OCU 22-2-50 NEA 7-10-53 sold scr 14-6-54

PM651 CRD W Wal 27-11-45 ML Aviation 31-7-47 6MU 30-9 AGT Gat refurb 15-1-51 Thum Flt Woodvale 15-3-54 FA3R 14-4 SOC 16-7 Ben 28-6-69 7758M BoB film RAF Benson extant WF

PM652 STN Ben 26-11-45 PROV 22-7-46 541S 29-7 237 OCU 30-4-48 APHDU 18-1-49 FAAC 17-5 ROS 49MU for spcl fitment 17-7-54 C5 21-1-45

PM653 (PC) STN Super p/proto filter in generator air duct 4-4-44 VA HPA 5-12-45 Ben 7-12 2S BAFO 27-7-46 Res pl Wunstorf 28-2-50 C4R 23-2-51

PM654 STN Farn 26-11-45 SME Flt press cabin trls 29MU 1-5-46 VAEA 12-11

PM655 (PC) STN Super p/proto 13-6-44 camera heating mods 20-3-45; intro split 5in vertical wing cameras 1-5; CRD VA EA 5-1-46 trl instal oxygen economiser 27-11; intro cabin heat. Ben 26-8-48 APHDU 30-6-50 9MU 31-1-51 NES 16-10-53 sold scr 16-9-54

PM656 EA Super p/proto new tail wheel 1-5-45; elev & rud mods 10-7. 29MU 21-3-46 VA EA 12-11

PM657 STN Mal WW 27-11-45 VA 27-4-46 EA 12-11

PM658 STN 29MU 2-4-46 82S Ben 16-1-47 541S 3-12 Farn 16-2-50 trans Bomb Com 1-3 29MU 12-1-51 NEA 7-10-53 sold En/RM 12-7-54

PM659 STNVAEA 20-7-46 on temp loan inspect purposes 6MU 20-12 VASM eng mods spcl paint finish Air Chief Marshall Robbs personal a/c 31S 18-9-48 Leuchars 27-4-49 APHDU 8-8 trans Bomb Com 1-3-50 AGT Gat refurb 1-5-51 sold scr

Above: PM651 guards the gate at RAF Benson, home of the PRU. Below: PM627 served the RAF and IAF, moved to Canada and is now in Sweden.

PM660 STN 6MU 9-5-46 Ben 22-1-47 Celle 5-5 2S BAFO 9-10-49 Res pl Wunstorf 29-12 recat 4R 31-1-51

PM661 HrPK 61 OTU 24-6-46 226 OTU C3R 7-2-50 recat 4R ROS 30-3-53

PS831 ALD PRU Ben 29-11-44 541S 22-1-46 106Grp 18-3 FACE 1-4-45 SOC 16-4

PS832 STN PRU Ben 2-12-44 542S 2-1-45 106Grp 18-3 151RU 17-1-46 2S Wunstorf 3-2-46 w/u ldg CE Celle 1-12-47

PS833 STN PRU Ben 31-12-44 34Wng 13-3-45 16S 22-3 268S 20-9 412RSU 4-10 3BRU CE 29-6-46 EA 8-3-50

PS834 STN PRU Ben 16-12-44 34Wng 13-3-45 16S 22-3 151RU 20-9

PS835 STN 1PP Ben 31-12-44 WSU 12-3-45 151RU 3-5 268S 20-9 29MU 9-4-46 sold MoS 8-7-49

PS836 STN 1PP Ben 31-12-44 542S 29-5-45 6MU 12-10 MBFE storage 1-1-51 FEAF 7-1 81S 16-1 SOC 12-3-54 ThaiAF 28-6 U14-27/97 extant Chieng Mei

PS849 STN 1PP Ben 3-1-45 16S 15-3 268S 20-9 2S 6-11-46 SOC 7-8-47

PS850 STN 1PRU Ben 3-1-45 541S 27-8 sold VA to Sweden with Mks G-15-61 via Mans by Fanrik Aulin 11-5-49 became 31050

PS851 STN Ben 7-1-45 PRDU 8-4 SOC 2-3-48 NEA 12-7 sold H Bath

PS852 (PC) STN Super p/proto metal ails mods 31-10-44 PRU Ben 9-1-45 541S 8-5 542S 27-8 81S 3-1-51 HKAAF 25-3-54 wu 21-4-55

PS853 VASM p/proto 5-9-44 AFDU CRU Ben 16S 268S final flt 9-7-57 CFE Binbrook to BoB Flt BHll Used in tactical trls with EE Lightning 1963 extant RAF BBMF

PS854 1PP Ben 14-1-45 542S 7-5 6MU 12-10 FEAF 23-12-50 MBFE storage 1-1-51 81S 31-1 HKAAF 6-8-54 SOC 16-9-55

PS855 STN 1PP Ben 20-1-45 MAAF 16-4 SOC 28-2-46

PS856 STN 1PP Ben 22-1-45 FACB 16-2 HAL BAFO Com S 1-1-46 FCCS GAAC 17-4-48 recat E 3-5

PS857 STN 1PP Ben 3-2-45 10ADU cd on f/f to Port CAC 13-6 108RSU ME 20-10 SOC 29-3-46

PS858 (PC) G65 STN BDn 5-2-45 trls with and without 90 and 170gal o/ld fuel tanks. G66 instal. Hand trls with both types fuel tank 6MU 22-4 541S Ben 12-9-46 82S 541S 11-12-47 trans Bomb Com WEF 1-3-50 29MU 31-1-51 NES 7-10-53 sold En/RM 9-7-54

PS859 EA 6MU 6-2-45 sold VA to Swed with Mks G-15-60 via Mars by Fanjunkore Molander 11-5-49 became 31049

PS860 KEE 6MU 10-3-45 sold VA 5-8-48 to Swed with Mks G-15-20 via Mars by Flt Ringborg 4-12-48 became 31009

PS861KEE 6MU 10-2-45 sold VA 16-8-48 to Swed with Mks G-15-24 via Mars by Flt Ringborg 19-1-49 became 31013

PS862 KEE 6MU 13-2-45 sold VA 20-8-48 to Swed with Mks G-15-26 via Mars by Sgt Auliss 19-1-49 became 31015

PS863 KEE 6MU 14-2-45 sold VA 9-8-48 to Swed with Mks G-15-29 via Mars by Lt Vangstrom 11-2-49 became 31018

PS864 KEE 6MU 14-2-45 sold VA 20-2-48 to Swed with G-15-28 via Mars by Lt Persson 11-2-49 became 31017

PS865 KEE 6MU 25-2-45 sold VA to Swed with Mks G-15-56 via Mars by Bwerstelojt Nant 11-5-49 became 31045

PS866 KEE Super p/proto Vokes wet type Aeroply fliter 22-8-44 6MU 22-2-45 sold VA 26-7-48 to Swed with Mks G-15-19 via Manston became 31006

PS867 EA 6MU 1-3-45 sold VA 22-10-48 to Swed with Mks G-15-57 via Mars by Lapten Ehrning 11-5-49 became 31046

PS868 KEE 6MU 26-2-45 sold VA 13-9-48 to Swed with Mks G-15-21 by Sgt Sundell 4-12-48 became 31012

PS869 EA Super p/proto 16-5-44 sold VA 12-8-48 to Swed with Mks G-15-32 via Mars by F/Lt Forsberg 4-12 became 31021

PS870 (PC) EA Super p/proto wing mods 31-10-44 6MU 1-3-45 sold VA 13-8-48 to Swed with G-15-34 by F/Lt Goliath 19-1-49 became 31023

PS871 KEE 6MU 27-3-45 sold VA 20-8-48 to Swed with Mks G-15-27 via Mars by Sgt Sundell 19-1-49 became 31016

PS872 EA 6MU 1-3-45 sold VA 29-10-48 to Swed with Mks G-15-40 via Mars by Lt Jawoel 12-2-49 became 31029

PS873 STN 6MU 3-3-45 sold VA 27-10-48 to Swed with Mks G-15-39 via Mars by Lt Norin 12-2-49 became 31028

PS874 STN 6MU 7-3-45 sold VA 29-7-48 to Swed with Mks G-15-17 via Mars by F/Lt Tyrling 5-11 became 31008

PS875 STN 6MU 9-3-45 sold VA 4-11-48 to Swed with Mks G-15-51 via Mars by Lt Ljoequist 13-4-49 became 31040

PS876 STN 6MU 9-3-45 sold VA 4-11-48 to Swed with Mks G-15-54 via Mars by Mr Morgan (VA test pilot) 20-4-49 became 31043

PS877 STN 6MU 11-11-48 to Swed with Mks G-15-55 via Mars by Mr Robarts (VA) 20-4-49 became 31044

PS878 EA 6MU 13-3-45 sold VA 6-8-48 to Swed with Mks G-15-16 via Mars by F/Lt Carlesson became 31007

PS879 EA 6MU 14-3-45 sold VA to Swed with Mks G-15-35 via Mars by P/O Tyrling 19-1-49 became 31024

PS880 (PC) STN Super p/proto Coffman starter mods

31040, Swedish Air Force. Ex PS875.

PS915 was taken off gate guardian duties in June 1984 for a restoration to flying condition by British Aerospace at Preston.

PS925, used as production prototype for fuel gauges by the Photographic Reconnaisance Development Unit, whose codes it wears.

5-9-44 6MU 15-3-45 sold VA 2-11-48 to Swed with Mks G-15-52 via Mars by Lt Ringborg 13-4-49 became 31041

PS881 (PC) EA Super p/proto coolant header tank mods 24-5-44; camera heat mods 5-10 6MU 18-3-45 sold VA 12-8-48 to Swed with Mks G-15-31 via Mars by Sgt Aulin 15-12-48 became 31020

PS882 EA 6MU 21-3-45 sold VA 17-11-48 to Swed with Mks G-15-59 via Mars by Lejtnat Hagg 11-5-49 became 31048

PS883 STN 6MU 22-3-45 sold VA 6-8-48 to Swed with Mks G-15-22 via Mars by P/O Tyrling 4-12-48 became 31011

PS884 (PC) STN Super p/proto eng cowl mods 31-10-44 6MU 24-3-45 sold VA 17-11-48 to Swed with Mks G-15-58 via Mars by Lt Hjelm 11-5-49 became 31047

PS885 STN 6MU 24-3-45 237(PR) OTU Ben 17-9-47 541S 16-4-48 TAA 30-9-49 trans Bomb Com 1-3-50 AGT Gat refurb 16-1-51 NEA 7-10-53 sold scr 9-9-54

PS886 EA 6MU 23-6-45 sold VA 25-11-48 to Swed with Mks G-15-46 via Mars by F/O Carlesson 16-3-49 became 31035

PS887 EA 6MU 2-4-45 PRU Ben 24-4 541S 19-7 FACB 27-9-46 3BRU 3-11 Ben 8-4-47 AGT Gat refurb 12-3-51 NEA 7-10-52 sold VA 9-9-54

PS888 EA 6MU 30-3-45 1PP Ben 24-4 542S 17-6 FEAF 23-12-50 FAC3 3-6-53 flew last RAF operat Spitfire sortie 81S 1-4-54 sold ThaiAF 3-6

PS889 STN 8-4-45 1PP Ben 9-6 EA 26-6 VASM 18-3-49 2PRS Buckeburg 22-11-50 NEA 7-10-53 sold scrap 14-6-54

PS890 (PC) STN Super p/proto eng mount mods 29-11-44 6MU 9-4-45 PRU Ben 30-4 542S 13-6 81S 22-1-51 ThaiAF 3-6-54 U14-26/97. To USA. extant Chino

PS891 STN 6MU 9-4-45 sold VA 17-8-48 to Swed with Mks G-15-33 via Mars by Lt Forsberg 15-12-48 became 31022

PS892 STN 6MU 19-4-45 1PP Ben 20-4 10ADU 8-6 MAAF 13-6 ACSEA 21-6 SOC 29-8-46

PS893 EA 6MU 24-4-45 sold VA 11-8-48 to Swed with Mks G-15-30 via Mars by F/Lt Goliath 5-11 became 31019

PS908 1PP Bens 24-4-45 542S 17-6 8 OTU 18-11-46 trans Bomb Com 18-9-50 AGT VA 13-7-51 NEA 7-10-53 sold Lawton Metals 1-10-54

PS909 STN 1PP Ben 28-4-45 541S 9-6 sold VA 7-12-48 to Swed with Mks G-15-47 via Mars by Lt Sunberg 17-3-49 became 31036

PS910 STN 1PP Ben 24-4-45 10ADU 4-6 MAAF 8-6 SOC 28-2-46

PS911 STN Ben 3-5-45 10ADU 14-8 MAAF 24-8 ACSEA 11-9 SOC 30-5-46

PS912 STN Ben 30-4-45 10ADU 4-6-45 MAAF 8-6 SOC 28-2-46

PS913 STN Ben 30-4-45 10ADU 6-6 MAAF 12-6 ME 14-6 SOC 30-8

PS914 (PC) STN Super p/proto rad mods 6-3-45 CRD VA 16-4 Farn ETPS cabin blower trls 17-4 at h/alt F/ld during trls November. Target a/c for Firebrand DK399 fitt A.C.R. trls navigation equip. Jan'46 autos. Feb, high speed target for Spit FVIII LV674. Jly gust prog with SL550 and PM501. Trls contd to Jan'48 then used as drone for high speed dives. 6MU 25-1-49 CAC 4-3 ROS sold scr MoS 21-7

PS915 STN 6MU 16-4-45 Ben 26-4 541S 21-6 PRDU 22-7-46 2S BAFO 7-7-48 Thum Flt Woodvale 4-6-54 B Hll 14-6-57 to 7548M & 7711M 10-12-57 extant BBMF

PS916 STN Super p/proto oleo leg mods 27-6-44; mainplane stiff 6-3-45 6MU 19-4 1PP Ben 20-4 MAAF 16-6 ACSEA 28-6 SOC 31-7-47

PS917 (PC) STN Super p/proto wheel well mods 17-10-44 1PP Ben 21-4-45 10ADU 4-6 MAAF 10-6 ACSEA 28-6 34S 30-1-46 o/s hit building Palam India pilot kld 26-11 complete wrk 26-11 SOC 30-1-47

PS918 STN 1PP Ben 21-4-45 MAAF 2-6-45 ACSEA 26-7 Ind 31-10-46 SOC 4-12

PS919 1PP Ben 24-4-45 MAAF 1-6 ACSEA 28-6 SOC 23-7-48

PS920 1PP Ben 24-4-45 541S 24-7 PRDU 27-7-46 82S 31-12 8 OTU 31-12 541S 30-4-48 236 OCU 12-7-48 NEA 7-10-53 sold E Smelt 26-8-54

PS921 1PP Ben 1-5-45 MAAF 9-8 ME 9-3-46 SOC 29-8

PS922 1PP Ben 1-5-45 10ADU 17-6 MAAF 19-6 SOC 28-2-46

PS923 STN 6MU 7-5-45 sold VA 27-7-48 to Swed with Mks G-15-18 via Mars by Sgt Elmegard 5-11 became 31005

PS924 (PC) STN 6MU 12-5-45 sold VA 7-12-48 to Swed with Mks G-15-48 via Mars by F/O Nilsson 16-3-49 became 31037

PS925 (PC) STN Super p/proto fuel guage instal 5-10-44 6MU 10-5-45 Farn Jly'45 APL.DU 25-3-48 237 OCU 27-1-49 spun in on app Leuchars pilot kld CE 1-7 SOC 19-7

PS926 STN 6MU 10-6-45 sold VA 13-12-48 to Swed with Mks G-15-49 via Mars by F/O Frosell 17-3-49 became 31038

PS927 STN 6MU 12-6-45 sold VA 16-12-48 to Swed with Mks G-15-53 via Mars by Lt Carlsson 13-4-49 became 31042

PS928 EA 6MU 14-6-45 sold VA 10-8-48 to Swed with Mks G-15-25 via Mars by P/O Palmquist 19-1-49 became 31014

PS929 STN 6MU 5-6-45 sold VA to Swed with Mks G-15-50 via Marston by Lt Hansson 17-3-49 became 31039

PS930 STN 6MU 15-5-45 541S Ben 24-10-46 82S 25-10 CAC 9-11-48 ROS trans Bomb Com WEF 1-3-50 AGT Gat refurb 12-3-51 NEA 7-10-53 sold scrap 9-9-54

PS931 STN 6MU 16-5-45 sold VA 27-7-48 to Swed with Mks G-15-13 became 31002

PS932 STN 6MU 17-5-45 BAFO Com Wng Buckeburg 9-7-47 sold Int All 2-2-50

PS933 STN 6MU 18-5-45 sold VA 10-8-48 to Swed with Mks G-15-23 via Mars by P/O Palmquist 4-12-48 became 31012

PS934 STN 6MU 27-5-45 Leuch (CC) 3-10-49 541S 21-11 trans Bomb Com WEF 1-3-50 29MU 31-1-51 NEA 16-10-53 sold En/RM 15-7-54

PS935 STN 6MU 22-5-45 earmarked for Ind Mar'46 sold VA 26-7-48 to Swed with Mks G-15-12 7-10-48 became 31001

RM series all Griffon 65

RM626 HPA Ben 16-5-44 1st PRXIX to RAF 106Grp wastage pl 26-6-44 Spec OUT 6-9 MAAF e/a CECE 27-11

RM627 STN Ben 30-4-44 541S 4-6 FTR ops 4-3-45

RM628 STN Ben 30-4-44 542S 2-6 first PRXIX sorties S/Ldr Bell Le Harve France 24-5-44 541S 27-8-45 82S CAC 17-4-47 recat E scr SOC 9-7

RM629 STN Ben 1-5-44 541S 2-6 FACB 15-7 HAL sold MoS 21-7-49

RM630 STN Ben 2-5-44 PRDU 21-6 106Gro wastage pl 30-6 MAAF 19-1-45 SOC 28-2-46

RM631 STN Ben 11-5-44 541S 2-6 FTR ops 9-3-45

RM632 STN Ben 6-5-44 542S 4-6 FTR ops 6-1-45

RM633 STN PRU Ben 6-5-44 541S 4-6 e/fd a/c aban i/sea off Mans 15-6

RM634 STN Ben 11-5-44 542S 11-6 ROS 14-11 to 6160M 17-10-46 SOH FFS SOC 13-10-49

RM635 STN Ben 13-5-44 541S 11-6 FACE 21-3-45 SOC 4-4

RM636 STN Ben 16-5-44 542S 11-6 541S 27-8-45 82S Eindhoven 5-11-46 3BRU 30-12 CAC recat E 22-3-48

RM637 STN Ben 21-5-44 106Gpwp 18-6 541S CAC ops 7-10 sold J Dale 1-6-49

RM638 STN Ben 21-5-44 542S 11-6 fire in flt CE 21-3-45 HAL to 5730M 24-10 8 OTU SOC 12-6-46

RM639 STN Ben 21-5-44 106Gpwp 6-7 spec dest 12-9 682S MAAF FTR ops 8-10

RM640 CHA Ben 23-5-44 106Gpwp 18-6 spec dest 6-9 FTR ops 9-2-45

RM641 CHA Ben 1-6-44 106Gpwp 6-7 MAAF Sep'44 CE ops 21-3-45 SOC 3-5

RM642 STN Ben 5-6-44 106Gpwp 12-7 NWA 14-12 SOC 6-9-45

RM643 CHA Ben 28-5-44 106Gpwp 21-6 541S 22-7 EA 26-1-49 AGT Gat refurb and mods 12-1-51 29MU 5-6 NEA 4-5-53 C5 9-9

RM644 CHA Ben 22-5-44 106Gpwp 18-6 541S 27-12 FAAC 20-6-46 82S 12-12 eng fail on t/o Ben SOC 26-12

RM645 STN Ben 5-6-44 106Gpwp 12-7 10ADU 25-10 NA 23-12 FTR ops 31-1-45

RM646 CHA Ben 2-6-44 106Gpwp 6-7 542S 2-1-45 541S 27-8 VA 26-1-49 29MU 16-1-50 NEA 4-5-53 C5 9-9

RM647 CHA Ben 2-6-44 106Gpwp 12-7 541S 12-3-45 1PP 30-12 84GCS BAFO 27-5-47 CE 15-8

A MAJOR REDESIGN

As related in previous chapters Supermarine and the Air Staff were aware that the basic Spitfire design as conceived by Mitchell needed updating if it was to continue to be employed for the role it was originally specified for—an interceptor capable of undertaking strike attacks against ground targets when required. The Royal Air Force had accepted a number of various marks which were, nominally, conversions and re-engined Mk I airframes and had been deprived of the first major redesign, the Mk III, because of the urgent need for the Mk V. The second major redesign was the Mk VIII and this, too, did not enter full scale production in time to meet the requirement it had been ordered for, combating the Fw190. But the lessons learned from this Spitfire variant were to be applied to practically every mark of Spitfire that followed, including the F21 and F24.

The Griffon engined F Mk XIV had a limiting speed of approximately 470mph IAS as the aileron problem, including upfloat of about ¾in, made it practically unmanageable at certain attitudes and speeds. The Supermarine test pilots' reports, as quoted in chapter 22, contained the numerous attempts made to cure these faults but the problem was never fully resolved. A new wing was necessary and design work on a completely revised unit started in February 1942, and the results of experiments carried out with JG204, a Mk VIII with the wing leading edge lifted by two inches, were utilised by Joseph Smith and his team. The original wing as designed by Mitchell had been built up around the torsion box leading edge formed by the built-up spar. Smith opted to retain this basic form but behind the spar was to incorporate a number of torque boxes with load bearing joints at openings such as wheel wells and inspection panels. The wing was still the familiar ellipse but the tips had evolved into a blunter profile.

Flight tests with JG204 had revealed that larger area ailerons were necessary, which in turn would mean an increased wing area, and Smith had to have a second look at the wing. Close liaison with Farnborough had resulted in the adoption of a laminar flow aerofoil (which led eventually to the Spiteful wing) and a modified version of the wing was installed on DP851, the second prototype F Mk IV. Supermarine report 3542 went into details of the cooling arrangements for DP851, which was to be the test bed for the F21.

"(1) The Griffon 61 engine for the prototype F21 aeroplane DP851 will have an engine intercooler suitable for approximately 40% intercooling. (2) The intercooler radiator provided by Supermarine will not provide the 55% i/c hoped for. (3) Supermarine produced results on the trials at Worthy Down of 1.2 sq ft intercooling on the Merlin 61. These were disappointing, but the safe limitations as in the case of the Griffon is imposed by the Merlin engine intercooler—that only about 40% i/c is possible without alternation to the intercooler. (4) The Griffon 61 engines for production F21 Spitfires were discussed and Rolls-Royce stated that for the next 18 months these would be Griffon 61 issue 2, dated January 1942, with lower M. S. supercharger gear. The counter rotating Griffon 61 engine will have the C envelope powers plus 55% i/c and 10,000 and 20,000ft blowers."

It has been suggested that a ventral fuselage radiator with 30% more area would meet requirements, for not only would it have improved cooling (and less drag), it would also be less vulnerable to combat damage. A study was made but the scheme involved a complete redesign of the fuselage.

Modified to the Type 356 configuration as an interim prototype, DP851 commenced trials on 4 October 1942. Powered by a Griffon 61 with 18lb boost it had an auw of 9,020lb, a maximum speed in FS gear of 441mph at 30,000ft and 387mph in MS gear at 8,000ft. The Griffon 61 (RG 5SM), number 3556, drove a five blade Rotol Jablo propeller of 11ft diameter, was beam mounted, lower and was several inches longer than the Merlin 61 installation.

A discussion took place at Supermarine on 9 November with officials of MAP and Mr Clifton present to examine DP851's performance with a change of engine/propeller gears. Captain Liptrot of MAP produced estimates which showed that by changing from a .45 gear to a .51, the higher the actual speed of the F21 the greater would be the speed loss. It was decided to wait for performance figures of the prototype before firming adoption of gearing.

On 1 May 1943 the Type Record for the prototype 356/1 Spitfire F Mk 21 was issued by Supermarine and the following details were relevant—Length 32.75ft, span 40.42ft, wheel track 5.75ft. Wing aerofoil section NACA 22 series of elliptical planform of Spitfire Mk I extended 1.67ft on each side. Incidence +2° to fuselage datum at root, tip -.62°. Dihedral 0° inboard of 31in from aircraft C_L +6°. Wing area 248.5sq ft, root chord 8.33ft, geometric mean chord 6.15ft, aspect ratio 6.57. Control surfaces movements and settings, aileron 26° 16′ up, 19° 34′ down, elevator 28° up, 23° down. Rudder ± 28°. Elevator tab 21° up, 8° down. Rudder tab –13°. Flap movement 75° down.

Fuel capacity, upper fuselage 36 gals, lower 49, wing tanks 112. Consumption (combat condition MS gear) 183 gal/hr. Oil 9 gals. Consumption 35 pints/hr maximum all out level flight. Cooling system, pressure water 14.8gals. Intercooler 3.56gals. Weights, normal auw 9,680lb, with 3 × 500lb bombs 11,290, with 4 × 300lb RPs and 90gal drop tank 11,930.

DP851 was weighed at Worthy Down on 29 November the previous year and returned a tare of 6,733lb with a four blade dural propeller and 6,737 with a five blade hydulignum. The wings had provision for 6 × 20mm Hispano cannon and the aircraft had a tail parachute fitted. DP851 was written off on 13 May 1943 when it crashed after its undercarriage failed during a

Below and opposite: DP851, ex prototype F Mk IV, was used as the prototype F21.

PP139, the production prototype F21 Victor.

Areas and Chords

Surface	Span ft	Mean chord ft	Balance area sq ft	Surface area sq ft
Aileron/side	5.76	1.29	2.17	7.45
Fixed tailplane	9.00	1.97	—	17.70
Elevator & tabs	10.50	1.31	1.56	13.76
Total tailplane and elevator	10.50	3.00	—	31.46
Elevator tab/ side	1.74	.22	—	.38
Fin	2.55	1.81	—	4.61
Rudder & tab	5.74	1.74	.49	10.00
Total Fin and Rudder	—	—	—	14.61
Rudder Tab	1.58	.43	—	.68
Brake flap/ side	9.40	1.13	—	10.62

70mph landing, but by this date the true prototype F21 Victor, as it was to be called, PP139, was in the advance stages of construction at South Marston works. By the following August PP139 was at Boscombe Down for trials. Before shipment to A&AEE it had been weighed at Worthy Down (23 July) and had a tare of 6,849 lb and an auw of 9,121. The CoG range with normal loads was quoted as 1.5 to 3.4in aft of the vertical datum.

No official Air Ministry Specification for the F21 was issued and Supermarine were advised to follow the defunct F Mk 20 (Mk IV) details. On 28 May 1943 Supermarine wrote to MAP confirming that they had been instructed to build 2,962 F 21s at Castle Bromwich and South Marston. MAP replied on 6 June and in their letter stated – "1,500 Spitfire F21 (Victor) aircraft for manufacture at the Castle Bromwich and South Marston factories additional to the 350 aircraft of this type at present under Instructions Nos B.981687/39/C.23(c) and Acft/1951/C.23(c). The serial numbers allotted to the additional aircraft are as follows—PS938-987, PT100-145, PT160-203, PT220-267, PT281-325, PT338-380, PT395-436, PT451-498, PT523-567, PT582-627, PT639-683, PT697-738, PT752-795, PT818-859, PT873-915, PT929-970, PT986-999, PV115-160, PV174-215, PV229-270, PV283-327, PV341-385, PV399-445, PV458-499, PV520-567, PV581-625, PV639-680, PV697-739, PV752-779, PV820-865, PV879-919, PV935-984, PW112-158, PW173-196, PW221-250."

The MAP letter made no reference to the original quantity as specified by Supermarine in their 28 May letter for the 350 aircraft on order as mentioned by MAP were referred to as 'Existing Contract Cover'. There could be no mistake on the part of Supermarine regarding the quantity of 2,962 for they had requested receipt of formal amendents "as soon as possible". The situation regarding contracts and orders for the F21 appeared to get more confusing with the passage of time as practically every instruction from MAP to Supermarine appeared to be contradictory to previous instructions. The name Victor was to be officially dropped when MAP then wrote to Vickers on 1 November 1943—"The F21 Victor aircraft on order are to be redesignated F21 Laminar flow wing".

In order to simplify production and reduce weight it was decided to ask Messrs Booths, a company producing main spar booms for the Spitfire, to experiment with the production of single extruded taper tube to replace the normal nest of tubes used for the wing. Main difficulty was to extrude the tube with tapered thickness walls in addition to the normal root to tip taper of the complete unit. The first scheme, intended for the F21, was examined on 29 June 1943 and Booths said they could start series production in six months. It was also decided to produce a similar boom for the Seafire with the boom in two parts, but in the event the scheme was abandoned except for experiments.

New radiators manufactured in light alloy instead of copper were to be provided by Messrs Gallay and the first deliveries were to be ready for the third prototype in early 1944. The radiators were supplied in small quantities and used on experimental aircraft only.

The Mk 21 prototype included many new innovations such as an armament of four 20mm Hispano Mk II cannon with 150

In 1944 Martin Baker Aircraft were working on the design of a pilot ejection device for the latest propeller and jet driven aeroplanes as ever increasing speeds made it difficult for a pilot to clear his machine in the event of an emergency. There were no precedents for the company to base their research on and the many problems were dealt with as and when they arose. Rumours soon began circulating about the work and stories of experiments with humans, alive and dead, were given credence. One of the major problems of ejecting a pilot from the aircraft currently in service, including the Spitfire, was that the cockpit was so small that the pilot could not be lifted from it in the sitting position and he had to assume an upright stance. The initial Martin Baker scheme was based on a swinging arm mounted on top of the fuselage with the rear end on a pivot just forward of the fin; the forward end was fitted with a 'U' shaped piece engaging rings on the pilot's parachute harness. When the mechanism was actuated a powerful spring swung the arm upwards, lifting the pilot from the seated to standing position and swinging him clear of the aircraft with the aid of aerodynamic forces acting on the arm. Our illustration shows the sequence of events.

A model of the scheme was demonstrated to Sir Stafford Cripps, MAP, and Sir Wilfred Freeman on 11 October 1944, and as a result a Defiant fighter, suitablity modified, made the first dummy ejection in flight at RAF Wittering on 11 May 1945 wilth Rotol's chief test pilot, Bryan Greensted, at the controls. Six more dummy ejections were made at speeds of up to 300mph on 17 May at Beaulieu. By now, however, it had become clear that the arm scheme incurred too great a weight penalty and the best method of escape from an aircraft was by forced ejection of the seat complete with pilot. James Martin developed the idea of fitting the pilot's seat with a controlled explosive charge and the device was ground tested on 24 January 1945. In the intervening period the same Defiant was fitted with the modified seat and airborne tests completed with a dummy seat and pilot later that year. The first Spitfire to be fitted with the seat was the F21 but no installation was ever made.

Loading and C.G., Mk 21.

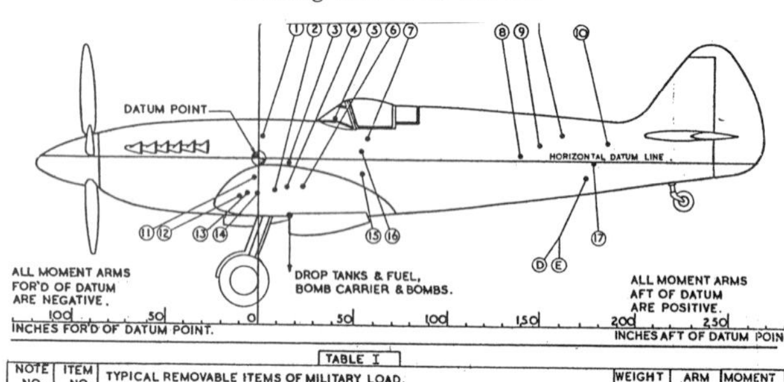

TABLE I

NOTE NO.	ITEM NO.	TYPICAL REMOVABLE ITEMS OF MILITARY LOAD.	WEIGHT LB.	ARM IN.	MOMENT LB.IN.
1	14	2 INBOARD HISPANO 20MM.GUNS AND ACCESSORIES.	290.5	- 0.5	- 145
1	2	2 OUTBOARD HISPANO 20MM.GUNS AND ACCESSORIES.	290	+ 8.5	+ 2,465
	4	AMMUNITION FOR INBOARD HISPANO 20MM.GUNS AT 150 RD. PER GUN.	187.5	+ 14	+ 2,625
	6	AMMUNITION FOR OUTBOARD HISPANO 20MM.GUNS AT 150 RD.PER GUN.	187.5	+ 23	+ 4,313
	5	REFLECTOR SIGHT MKIIS AND 4 FILAMENT LAMPS TYPE 'B'.	4.5	+ 40	+ 180
	7	1¼LB.INCENDIARY BOMB MKI, CLOCK MKII AND CROWBAR.	3	+ 58	+ 174
	13	G.45 CAMERA MKI, ADAPTOR TYPE 32, FRONT FLANGE AND INDICATOR TYPE 45.	7	- 5.5	- 39
	10	OXYGEN CYLINDER MK.Vc.	19.5	+187	+ 3,647
	15	DINGHY TYPE 'K' IN SEAT PACK TYPE 'A' MKII.	15	+ 55	+ 825
	17	FIRST-AID OUTFIT.	2.5	+175.5	+ 439
2	8	T.R.1143 RADIO AND ACCESSORIES.	79.5	+142	+11,289
	9	R.3067 RECEIVER, DETONATOR NO. D64 MK.I AND CONTROL UNIT ASSEMBLY TYPE 1.	35	+151.5	+ 5,302
	16	PILOT AND PARACHUTE.	200	+ 55	+11,000
		TOTAL TYPICAL REMOVABLE MILITARY LOAD.	1,321.5		+42,075
	3	FUEL IN FUSELAGE TANKS: 85 GAL.100 OCTANE FUEL AT 7.2 LB. PER GAL.	612	+ 15.5	+ 9,486
	12	FUEL IN WING TANKS: 34 GAL.100 OCTANE AT 7.2 LB. PER GAL.	245	- 9.5	- 2,328
3	1	OIL IN TANK: 9 GAL. AT 9 LB. PER GAL.	81	+ 1	+ 81
4	11	AIRCRAFT IN TARE CONDITION.	6,923		-14,607
		AIRCRAFT IN TYPICAL TAKE-OFF CONDITION.	9,182.5	+ 3.8	+34,707

TABLE II

DROP TANKS AND FUEL, BOMB CARRIER AND BOMBS.	WEIGHT LB.	ARM IN.	MOMENT LB.IN.
30 GAL. DROP TANK.	60	+ 16	+ 960
30 GAL. FUEL IN DROP TANK.	216	+ 16	+ 3,456
45 GAL. BLISTER TYPE DROP TANK.	80	+ 13.5	+ 1,080
45 GAL. FUEL IN BLISTER TYPE DROP TANK.	324	+ 13.5	+ 4,374
90 GAL. BLISTER TYPE DROP TANK.	120	+ 16	+ 1,920
90 GAL. FUEL IN BLISTER TYPE DROP TANK.	648	+ 13.5	+ 8,748
BOMB CARRIER AND ADAPTOR.	55	+ 18	+ 990
250 LB. BOMB.	250	+ 12	+ 3,000
500 LB. BOMB.	500	+ 12	+ 6,000

TABLE III.

NOTE NO.	ITEM NO.	ADDITIONAL AND ALTERNATIVE ITEMS OF REMOVABLE MILITARY LOAD.	WEIGHT LB.	ARM IN.	MOMENT LB.IN.
	B	R.3002 RECEIVER, DETONATOR NO. D39 AND CONTROL UNIT.	32.5	+151	+ 4,908
	A	A.1271 AMPLIFIER.	4.5	+131.5	+ 592
	C	1½IN. SIGNAL DISCHARGER, CONTROL AND 6 CARTRIDGES.	13	+164	+ 2,132
	D	1 STANDARD BALLAST WEIGHT ON MOUNTING AT AFT DOOR.	17.5	+175.5	+ 3,071
	E	DETACHABLE BALLAST MOUNTING AT AFT DOOR.	5	+175.5	+ 878

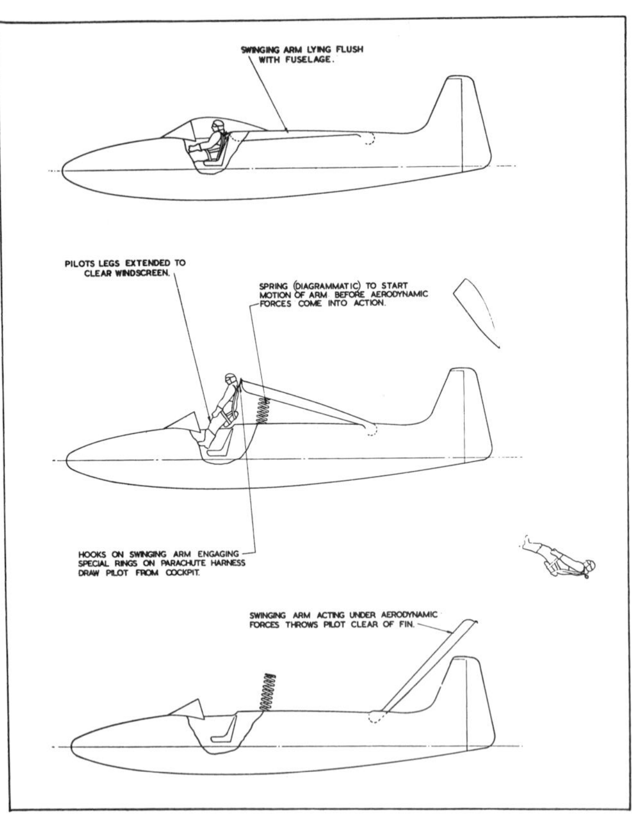

Martin Baker proposal for ejection seat in Spitfire.

Loading and C.G., Mk 21 contra-props.

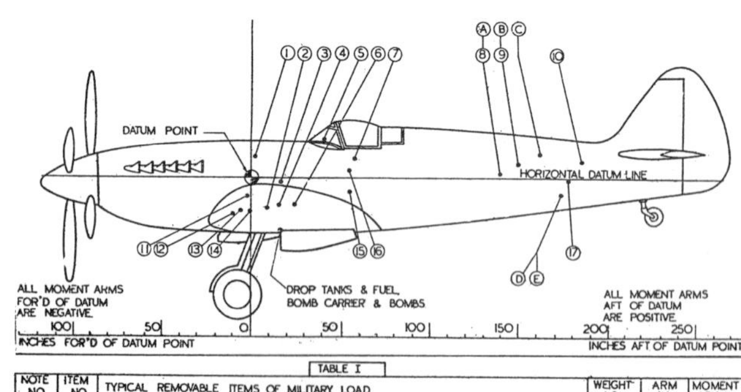

TABLE I

NOTE NO.	ITEM NO.	TYPICAL REMOVABLE ITEMS OF MILITARY LOAD.	WEIGHT LB.	ARM IN.	MOMENT LB.IN.
1	14	2 INBOARD HISPANO 20MM. GUNS AND ACCESSORIES.	290·5	- 0·5	- 145
1	2	2 OUTBOARD HISPANO 20MM. GUNS AND ACCESSORIES.	290	+ 8·5	+ 2,465
	4	AMMUNITION FOR INBOARD HISPANO 20MM. GUNS AT 150 RD. PER GUN.	187·5	+ 14	+ 2,625
	6	AMMUNITION FOR OUTBOARD HISPANO 20MM. GUNS AT 150 RD. PER GUN.	187·5	+ 23	+ 4,313
	5	REFLECTOR SIGHT MK IIS AND 4 FILAMENT LAMPS TYPE 'B'.	4·5	+ 40	+ 180
	7	1¼ LB. INCENDIARY BOMB MK I. CLOCK MK.II AND CROWBAR.	8	+ 58	+ 174
	13	G.45 CAMERA MK I, ADAPTOR TYPE 32, FRONT FLANGE AND INDICATOR TYPE 45.	7	- 5·5	- 39
	10	OXYGEN CYLINDER MK.Vc.	19·5	+187	+ 3,647
	15	DINGHY TYPE 'K' IN SEAT PACK TYPE 'A' MK II.	15	+ 55	+ 825
	17	FIRST-AID OUTFIT.	2·5	+175·5	+ 439
2	8	T.R.1143 RADIO AND ACCESSORIES.	79.5	+142	+11,289
	9	R.3067 RECEIVER, DETONATOR NO. D64 MK I AND CONTROL UNIT ASSEMBLY TYPE 1.	35	+151: 5	+ 5,302
	16	PILOT AND PARACHUTE.	200	+ 55	+11,000
		TOTAL TYPICAL REMOVABLE MILITARY LOAD.	1,321·5		+42,075
	3	FUEL IN FUSELAGE TANKS: 85 GAL. 100 OCTANE FUEL AT 7·2 LB. PER GAL.	612	+ 15·5	+ 9,486
	12	FUEL IN WING TANKS: 34 GAL. 100 OCTANE AT 7·2 LB. PER GAL.	245	- 9·5	- 2,328
3	1	OIL IN TANK: 9 GAL. AT 9 LB. PER GAL	81	+ 1	+ 81
4	11	AIRCRAFT IN TARE CONDITION.	7,136·5		- 18,065
		AIRCRAFT IN TYPICAL TAKE-OFF CONDITION.	9,396	+ 3·3	+31,249

TABLE II

DROP TANKS AND FUEL, BOMB CARRIER AND BOMBS.	WEIGHT LB.	ARM IN.	MOMENT LB.IN.
30 GAL. DROP TANK.	60	+ 16	+ 960
30 GAL. FUEL IN DROP TANK	216	+ 16	+ 3,456
45 GAL. BLISTER TYPE DROP TANK.	80	+ 13·5	+ 1,080
45 GAL. FUEL IN BLISTER TYPE DROP TANK	324	+ 13·5	+ 4,374
90 GAL. BLISTER TYPE DROP TANK.	120	+ 16	+ 1,920
90 GAL. FUEL IN BLISTER TYPE DROP TANK.	648	+ 13·5	+ 8,748
BOMB CARRIER AND ADAPTOR.	55	+ 18	+ 990
250 LB. BOMB.	250	+ 12	+ 3,000
500 LB. BOMB.	500	+ 12	+ 6,000

TABLE III

NOTE NO.	ITEM NO.	ADDITIONAL AND ALTERNATIVE ITEMS OF REMOVABLE MILITARY LOAD	WEIGHT LB.	ARM IN.	MOMENT LB. IN.
	B	R3002 RECEIVER, DETONATOR NO. D39 AND CONTROL UNIT	32·5	+151	+ 4,908
	A	A.1271 AMPLIFIER.	4·5	+131·5	+ 592
	C	1½ IN. SIGNAL DISCHARGER, CONTROL AND 6 CARTRIDGES.	13	+164	+ 2,132
	D	1 STANDARD BALLAST WEIGHT ON MOUNTING AT AFT DOOR.	17·5	+175·5	+ 3,071
	E	DETACHABLE BALLAST MOUNTING AT AFT DOOR.	5	+175·5	+ 878

LA188 was a trials aircraft (June 1945). View of cockpit reveals modified control column and Mach meter, plus accelerometer.

rounds each for the outer and 175 rounds for the inner, as tested on JF319, one of the six Mk VIIIs with Griffon engines.

Armour now totalled 190lb and all this additional weight resulted in a strengthened fuselage with the four, main longerons manufactured from stainless steel. The undercarriage oleos were lengthened, and strengthened, to cope with the large diameter propellers and the wheel track widened to 6ft 8in, but it still retracted outwards. Weights and CoG loadings revealed a tare of 6,853lb and normal take off of 9,124. Fuel capacity was 119 gallons with 85 in the fuselage in front of the pilot and 34 in wing tanks. Tests in the 24 foot RAE wind tunnel had indicated that the critical Mach number of a flat panelled windscreen was .4855 compared with .71 of a curved, and as a result Supermarine had added curved overlay panels to the front and sides of PP139's screen. But theory and practice do not always produce the same conclusions and although the new, shaped screen did add about six mph to the maximum speed, optical problems were greater than the speed advantage and the flat style was utilised on production models. During trials the Griffon 61 failed and had to be replaced by a G65. PP139 was then returned to Vickers for further modification. Brief level speed trials with the prototype at 2750rpm + 18lb boost revealed a maximum speed of 460mph at 25,600 feet (FS gear) and 432 at 12,200 (MS).

Even before production F21s had flown the RAF had announced plans for equipping two squadrons with the new Spitfire variant, and what was most unusual about the announcement was that the aircraft were to have contra-prop Griffons. The first five aircraft off the production lines, LA187 to 191, were utilised for extensive flying trials by the makers, Boscombe Down and Farnborough, and the following notes are extracts from all these sources, beginning with the prototype PP139.

Spitfire F Mk 21 (Victor) PP139 Boscombe Down September to November 1943. Level speed performance and position error correction. Griffon 61 with .45/1 propeller reduction gear. Curved windscreen and modified sliding hood, no rear view mirror. Modified wing with extended tips of thinner section. Metal covered ailerons with inset balance tabs. 4x20mm guns with muzzles sealed, ejection chutes open, individual bulges in top surface of wing above each gun. Bulge above each undercarriage wheel well, doors under wing completely enclosing wheels when retracted. Whip aerial aft of cockpit, no I.F.F aerials between fuselage and tailplane. Fin and rudder changed in shape compared with earlier Spitfire marks. 5 blade Rotol R19/5F5/1 propeller. Enlarged horn balance to elevator. All tests made at a take-off weight of 9,125lb. Position error correction, corrected to 95% of take-off weight was from plus 9mph at 130mph to minus 9.8mph at 380mph. True maximum airspeed in MS (medium supercharged) gear 434mph at 12,000ft, at 4000ft MS gear 390mph, at 20,000ft MS and FS (fully supercharged) 431mph, at 25,800ft FS gear 457mph, at 38,000ft MS gear 434mph. It has now been returned to Vickers for the production type of windscreen, sliding hood and rear view mirror. In addition a rudder, with a balance tab, will be fitted.

PP139 at Vickers 17-8-44 (Furlong). Flown with holes in underside of wing just in front of aileron hinges. Forward and upper end of ailerons had wooden block fitted in an attempt to smooth airflow through the holes, the idea being to simulate a slotted aileron. Straight stall, flaps and wheels up 90mph. This is 10mph better than LA187 with standard plain ailerons. It is considered that aileron control at slow speeds has improved with the new fitment, but it was impossible to fly the aeroplane at high speeds as it is seriously one wing low.

17-8-44. 400lb ballast added. Aileron gearing will have to be reduced as they are too light at high speeds. Cause might be holes under wing, removal of wing tips, incorrect aileron gearing.

18-8-44 (Quill). Flown twice – once with new slots in leading edge of ailerons and then with slots covered with fabric. Slots improve aileron control near the stall. It is thought that if this machine had the raised leading edge the improvement to be gained by these aileron slots would be more apparent because the aeroplane could be flown more slowly.

18-8-44 (Quill). Flown with one layer fabric over holes. No change in stall and gliding turns. Flown with three layers fabric over holes, plus clear dope and red paint. Results disappointing as there was no deterioration in aileron characteristics caused by 'bunging up' the slots.

26-9-44 (Shea-Simmonds). Tests discontinued owing to rpm and boost surge.

30-9-44. Subsequently discovered that the supercharger intercooler was leaking.

6-1-45 (Shea-Simmonds). Fitted once more with curved windscreen fairing for investigation of directional stability characteristics.

7-1-45 (Quill). Fitted with the old rounded windscreen but unlike the prototype did not have the flat sided hood, this being fitted to Spiteful NN660 at the time of crash. Balloon hood installed. Probable slight improvement with screen and hood but this line of development is not likely to be much use in curing the present trouble with the Spitfire F21.

17-1-45. Flown with standard F21 rudder, the balance tab gearing halved. It is felt that halving the tab gearing is a step in the right direction, but I do not consider the rudder acceptable in its present form.

15-3-48 (Shea-Simmonds). Brief check flight to test skid vane installation.
13-7-44 (Furlong) LA187 (first production). Taxi trials. High speed taxying, brakes somewhat ineffective.
31-7-44 (Furlong). Flown with new aileron tab gearing. Aileron buffetting as stall approaches very much improved by locking the tabs.
12-8-44 (Quill). Large chord metal rudder fitted. It vastly improves directional stability. Criticism:- insufficient rudder trim to left, still right wing low, rev. counter sticks and has to be tapped to produce accurate reading.
16-8-44 (Quill). Whilst diving to maximum speed hood and port door blew away.
9-10-44 (Quill). Spinning from 20,000ft with recovery at 15-17,000. Six spins, three to right, three to left. More difficult to recover from three spin turn than from two.
19-10-44 (Shea-Simmonds). Flown for final check prior delivery to Boscombe Down. Lateral trim incorrect, the aircraft being right wing low. Undercarriage 'up' lights u/s and cockpit sliding hood too stiff.
9-1-45 (Quill). Flown as received from Boscombe Down. Strong smell of petrol in cockpit. Directional stability bad. Starboard flap, and to a lesser extent, port flap, was coming open in high speed dives.
17-1-45 (Banner). Dived aircraft through 30,000ft at speeds between 250 and 350 indicated with flap lever in neutral and up position. Flaps remained closed. During a turn to port at 18,000ft port flap seen to open to 1½in, lever in neutral position. Flap came up again on selecting up.

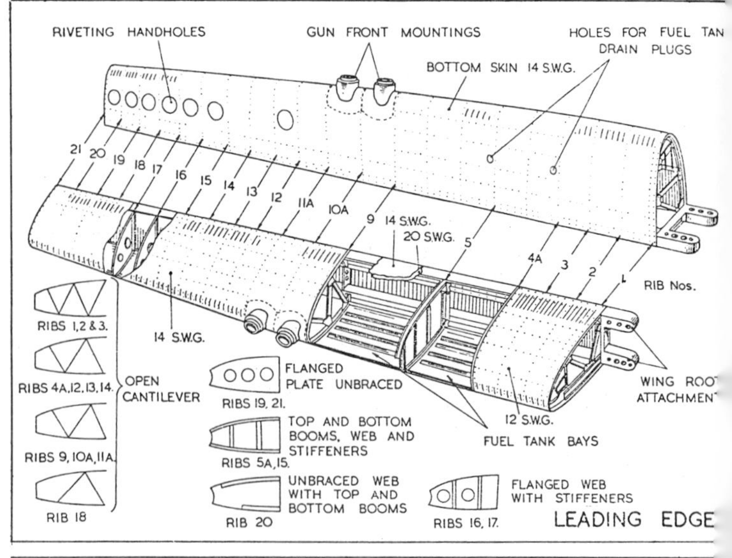

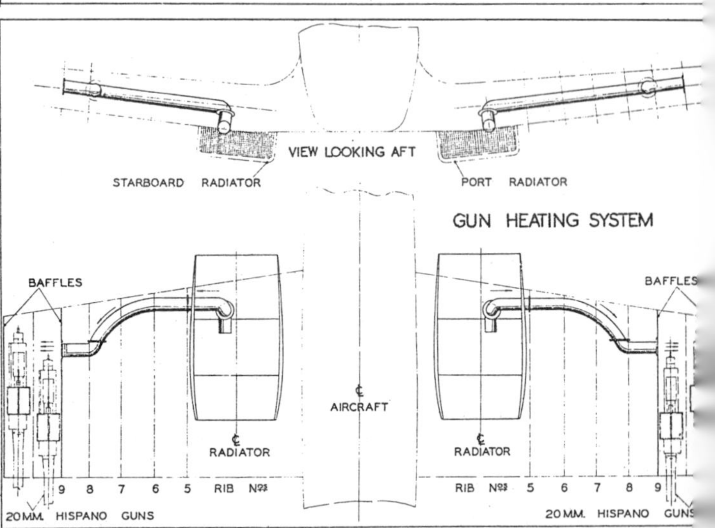

Spitfire F Mk 21 LA187 Boscombe Down, March to July 1945. Weights and loading data.

Load	A	B	C	D	E	F
Tare weight	6985	6985	6985	6985	6985	6985
Take-off	9302	9583	9713	10084	9607	9857

Load- A Typical service; B plus 30 gallon drop tank; C plus 45 gallon drop tank; D plus 90 gallon drop tank; E plus 1x250lb bomb; F plus 1x500lb bomb.
Fuel. Main fuselage 85 gallons. Wing (2) 39.5. Normal total 124.5 gallons.
Centre of gravity of the loads measured relative to the datum point and parallel to the datum line are A 3.6" aft., B 4ft aft., C 4.1" aft., D 4.4" aft., E 3.9" aft and F 4.1" aft.
Position error trials 3rd to 6th March. Corrected to 95% of take-off weight and to take-off weight less 95% of the disposable load. Correction varied from plus 7mph to minus 11½mph.

RIVETING HANDHOLES
GUN FRONT MOUNTINGS
HOLES FOR FUEL TAN
DRAIN PLUGS
BOTTOM SKIN 14 S.W.G.
14 S.W.G.
20 S.W.G.
RIB Nos.
WING ROO
ATTACHMEN
RIBS 1,2 & 3.
RIBS 4A,12,13,14.
OPEN CANTILEVER
RIBS 9,10A,11A.
RIB 18
FLANGED PLATE UNBRACED
RIBS 19, 21.
TOP AND BOTTOM BOOMS, WEB AND STIFFENERS
RIBS 5A,15.
UNBRACED WEB WITH TOP AND BOTTOM BOOMS
RIB 20
FLANGED WEB WITH STIFFENERS
RIBS 16, 17.
12 S.W.G.
FUEL TANK BAYS
LEADING EDGE

VIEW LOOKING AFT
STARBOARD RADIATOR
PORT RADIATOR
BAFFLES
BAFFLES
AIRCRAFT
RADIATOR
RADIATOR
RIB Nos
RIB Nos
20 MM. HISPANO GUNS
20 MM. HISPANO GUNS

GUN HEATING SYSTEM

RADIATOR
FLAP JACK
AMMUNITION BOXES
TRAILING RIB Nos
REAR SPAR ATTACHMENT
AILERON AND TAB
BOTTOM SKIN PLATING
RADIATOR FLAP CONTROL
STANDARD TIP
EXTENDED TIP (SPECIAL TO H.F. AIRCRAFT ONLY)
NON-SLIP WALKWAY (PORT ONLY)
AILERON CONTROL CABLES
RADIATOR RECESS STRUCTURE
UNDERCARRIAGE PINTLE
MAIN SPAR FORWARD ATTACHMENT
WING TIPS
LEADING EDGE
NAVIGATION LAMP
TOP SKIN
PICKETING TUNNELS
STARBOARD MAIN PLANE
CENTRE RIB Nos
LEADING EDGE FUEL TANKS
20 MM HISPANO GUNS
GAUGES OF PLATES ARE INDICATED IN CIRCLES THUS (22) = 22 S.W.G.
TOP DUCT PLATE 16 SWG.
RADIATOR FAIRING 20 SWG.
TOP SKIN PANELS
BOTTOM SKIN PANELS

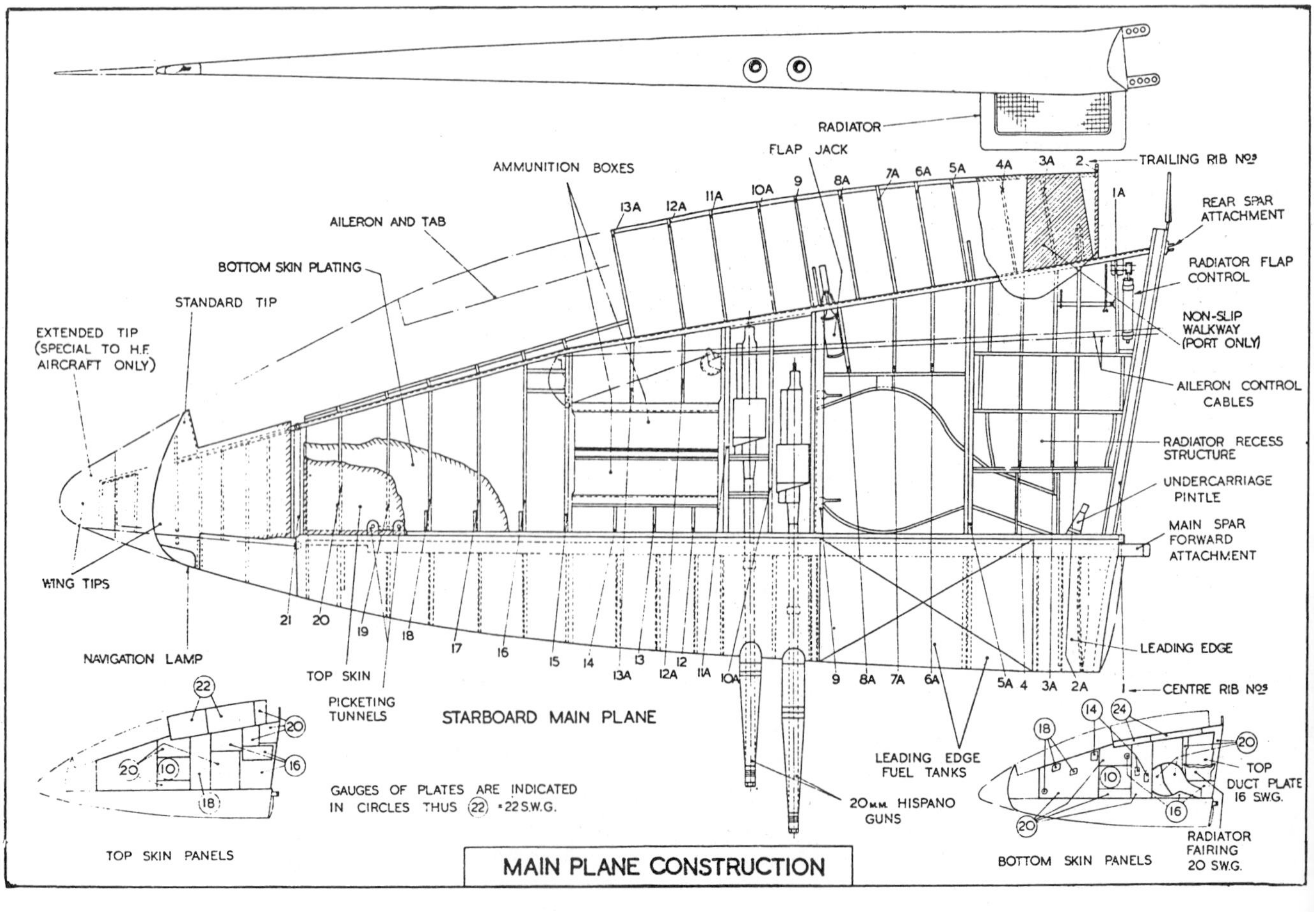

MAIN PLANE CONSTRUCTION

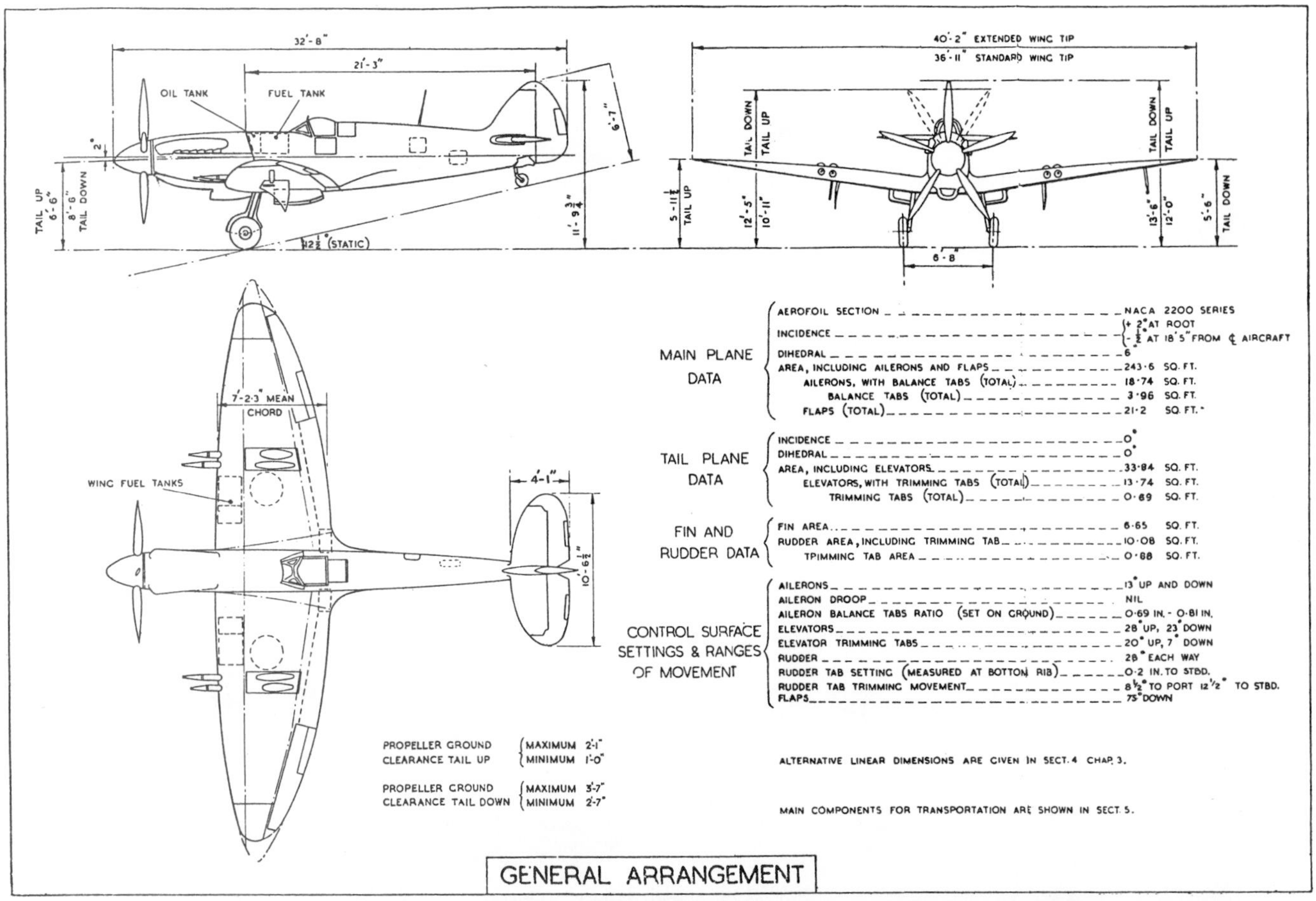

32'-8"
21'-3"
OIL TANK
FUEL TANK
2°
6'-7"
TAIL UP 6'-6"
8'-6" TAIL DOWN
11'-9¾"
12½° (STATIC)

40'-2" EXTENDED WING TIP
36'-11" STANDARD WING TIP
TAIL DOWN
TAIL UP
5-11½ TAIL UP
12'-5"
10'-11"
13'-6"
12'-0"
5'-6" TAIL DOWN
6-8"

7'-2·3" MEAN CHORD
WING FUEL TANKS
4'-1"
10'-6½"

MAIN PLANE DATA	AEROFOIL SECTION	NACA 2200 SERIES
	INCIDENCE	+ 2° AT ROOT - ½° AT 18'5" FROM ℄ AIRCRAFT
	DIHEDRAL	6°
	AREA, INCLUDING AILERONS AND FLAPS	243·6 SQ. FT.
	AILERONS, WITH BALANCE TABS (TOTAL)	18·74 SQ. FT.
	BALANCE TABS (TOTAL)	3·96 SQ. FT.
	FLAPS (TOTAL)	21·2 SQ. FT.
TAIL PLANE DATA	INCIDENCE	0°
	DIHEDRAL	0°
	AREA, INCLUDING ELEVATORS	33·84 SQ. FT.
	ELEVATORS, WITH TRIMMING TABS (TOTAL)	13·74 SQ. FT.
	TRIMMING TABS (TOTAL)	0·69 SQ. FT.
FIN AND RUDDER DATA	FIN AREA	6·65 SQ. FT.
	RUDDER AREA, INCLUDING TRIMMING TAB	10·08 SQ. FT.
	TRIMMING TAB AREA	0·88 SQ. FT.
CONTROL SURFACE SETTINGS & RANGES OF MOVEMENT	AILERONS	13° UP AND DOWN
	AILERON DROOP	NIL
	AILERON BALANCE TABS RATIO (SET ON GROUND)	0·69 IN. - 0·81 IN.
	ELEVATORS	28° UP, 23° DOWN
	ELEVATOR TRIMMING TABS	20° UP, 7° DOWN
	RUDDER	28° EACH WAY
	RUDDER TAB SETTING (MEASURED AT BOTTOM RIB)	0·2 IN. TO STBD.
	RUDDER TAB TRIMMING MOVEMENT	8½° TO PORT 12½° TO STBD.
	FLAPS	75° DOWN

PROPELLER GROUND CLEARANCE TAIL UP	MAXIMUM	2'-1"
	MINIMUM	1'-0"
PROPELLER GROUND CLEARANCE TAIL DOWN	MAXIMUM	3'-7"
	MINIMUM	2'-7"

ALTERNATIVE LINEAR DIMENSIONS ARE GIVEN IN SECT. 4 CHAP. 3.

MAIN COMPONENTS FOR TRANSPORTATION ARE SHOWN IN SECT. 5.

GENERAL ARRANGEMENT

Trials aircraft LA215 with and without Rotol contra-props.

Above and below: LA219 was also fitted with the Griffon 85 and contra-props. Boscombe Down, September 1945.

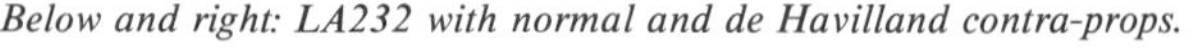

Below and right: LA232 with normal and de Havilland contra-props.

Climb and level speed performance. Results:- rate of climb at full throttle height MS gear plus 21lb boost 4440ft/min at 4900ft. Ditto with plus 9lb boost at 14,200ft 2740ft/min. Ditto FS gear 21lb boost 3615ft/min at 19,200ft. Ditto plus 9lb boost 2125ft/min at 29,000ft. Estimated service ceiling 42,400ft. Combat level speed (plus 21lb boost, 2750rpm) 406mph. MS gear full throttle height (7000ft). 442mph FS gear f.t.h. (21,800ft). 446mph FS gear f.t.h. (22,600ft). Level speed figures with new engine.
Cooling trials. Radiator suitability and oil inlet temperatures satisfactory for operation under tropical summer conditions.

LA188 at Vickers 2-9-44 en route Boscombe Down. (Quill). Aileron control too light, almost overbalanced. Tab gear ratio ridiculously light and should not have been passed out from the factory.
21-9-44 (Morgan). Ailerons now heavier are considered correct.
6-10-44 (Morgan). Photography of production Spitfire F21 from MAP Hudson.
3-11-44 (Shea-Simmonds). Delivery flight to Farnborough.
26-3-45 (Quill). Equipped with fabric covered small horn balance type of elevator and the rudder has had balance part of the operating of the tab deleted. The machine is going to Farnborough for high Mach number dives. However, it is badly left wing low and is being corrected before delivery to RAE. RAE requests that flap indicators be fitted to trailing edge of wing in order that behaviour of flaps in dives can be checked. Mechanical indicators to be fitted to show behaviour of wheel doors.

LA189 at Vickers. 16-9-44 (Morgan). Aircraft dived to 525 ASI after incorporation of modification to stern.

LA190 at Vickers. 22-8-44 (Quill). Comparison of standard F21 aileron with the modified unit on PP139.
24-8-44 (Furlong). Level speed at 30,000ft beside Spiteful for position error. Stalls:- flaps and wheels up buffetting starts 84mph. Flaps, etc, down 72mph.
31-8-44 (Quill). For checking before delivery to Boscombe. Ailerons too light. Port ammunition bay panel lifting at leading edge due to Oddie Fasteners coming undone.

LA189 and LA190. Boscombe Down 19 September 1944

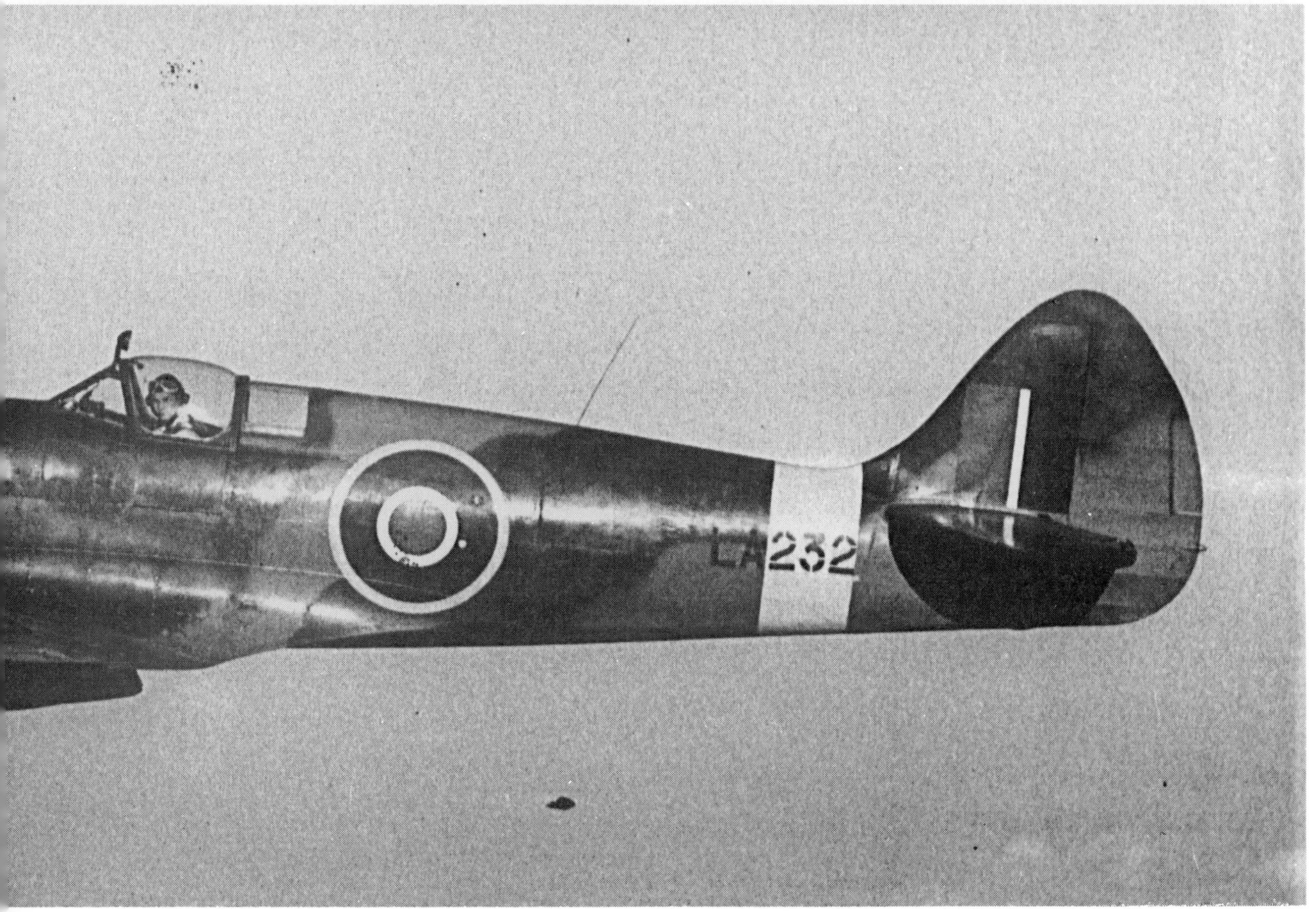

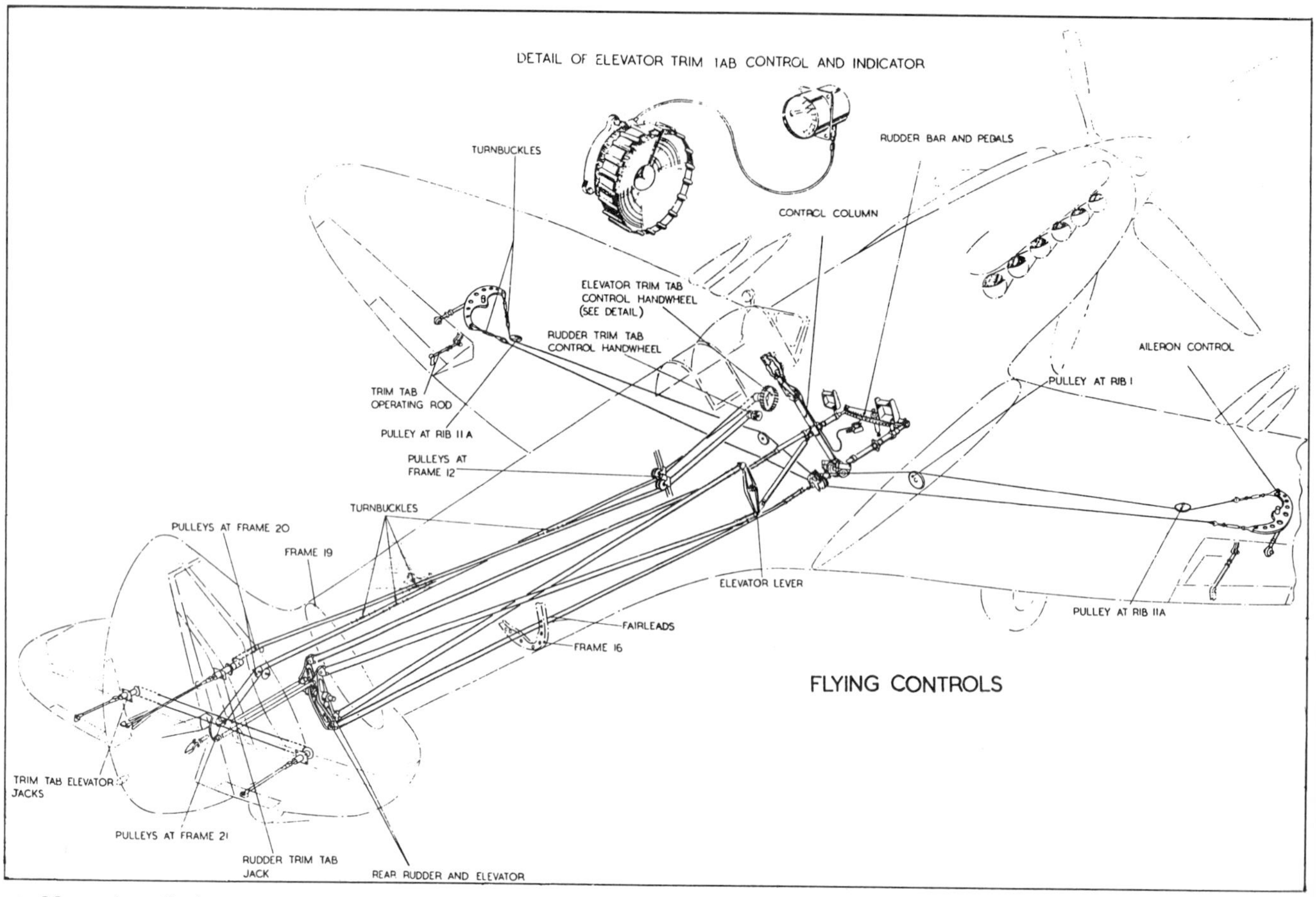

DETAIL OF ELEVATOR TRIM TAB CONTROL AND INDICATOR
TURNBUCKLES
RUDDER BAR AND PEDALS
CONTROL COLUMN
ELEVATOR TRIM TAB CONTROL HANDWHEEL (SEE DETAIL)
RUDDER TRIM TAB CONTROL HANDWHEEL
AILERON CONTROL
PULLEY AT RIB I
TRIM TAB OPERATING ROD
PULLEY AT RIB II A
PULLEYS AT FRAME 12
TURNBUCKLES
PULLEYS AT FRAME 20
FRAME 19
ELEVATOR LEVER
PULLEY AT RIB IIA
FAIRLEADS
FRAME 16
FLYING CONTROLS
TRIM TAB ELEVATOR JACKS
PULLEYS AT FRAME 21
RUDDER TRIM TAB JACK
REAR RUDDER AND ELEVATOR

to November. Carbon monoxide contamination tests. Results within acceptance limits.

LA190 at Vickers 20-3-45. Report on Gallay radiators fitted to F21. Flown for 2 hours 20mins when starboard radiator found to be leaking badly. Lower part of radiator lifted from matrix.

LA191 at Vickers 6-7-44 (Furlong). Level speeds at 14,000ft. Ignition or carburration wrongly adjusted. Propeller vibrates at 2000rpm.
8-7-44 (Quill). Delivered from South Marston prior to delivery to Boscombe.
12-7-44 (Furlong). Adjustments made to engine timing. Aileron tab adjustment jack incorrectly set. Alters flying controls.
17-7-44 Morgan). The available trimming adjustment is too coarse. Port wheel fairing door damaged in flight.
19-9-44 (Morgan). Check flight before delivery Boscombe.

LA192 at Vickers 19-9-44. (Morgan). Check flight before delivery to Boscombe after incorporation of modification to stern.
9-3-45 (Shea-Simmonds). Delivered from Handling Squadron Hullavington after complaints. Aircraft was damaged by Handling Squadron as a result of heavy landing. Port flap and wing tip bent. Aircraft then allegedly repaired by South Marston and faults became noticeable after same. Tendency for undercarriage selector lever to jam in midway position when selecting wheels down.
13-3-45 (Shea-Simmonds). Chassis operations carried out with port wheel being photographed by cine camera carried in 50 gallon drop tank.
20-3-45 (Shea-Simmonds). Chassis operation now satisfactory.

LA199 at Vickers 6-12-44. (Shea-Simmonds). Check flight before intensive trials.
20-1-45 (Quill). Fitted with enlarged or 'lash-up' fin with standard rudder and horn balance modified to give a shrouded instead of open balance. Better than standard F21. Excessive yaw at high speed. Decided to try disconnection of balance tab.
20-1-45 (Shea-Simmonds). New type enlarged fin. Above 380mph directional stability and control becomes rapidly worse.
2-2-45 (Quill). Balance tab inoperable for test flight. Much

LA228 serving with the Biggin Hill-based No 600 (City of London) Squadron, Royal Auxiliary Air Force.

F21s of No 600 Squadron in camouflage.

improvement and large fin improves directional stability at low and medium speeds.
14-2-45 (Quill). Improved directional stability up to nearly 400mph. Unfortunately no speed over 400 was reached for when applying yaw at 380-400 there was a considerable jerk and the starboard wheel door carried away damaging the aircraft. It would appear that in order to get this aircraft satisfactory we shall have too much horn which will destroy the pleasant feel of the control as it was when it had a smaller horn. Conclusion is the shielded type horn is not adequate for the work and something to the standard horn be tried with the enlarged fin.
27-8-45 (Quill). Level speeds to determine effect of fitting a modified type of nose intake.

LA211 at Vickers 18-12-44 (Errington). Handling check in connection with investigation regarding reversal with increased speed. At start of dive with speed approximating 350-400mph the aircraft was badly right wing low but, at the same time, the right hand aileron was seen to be upfloating to about $\frac{7}{8}$". Aircraft flying in an unusual crabwise manner, the side slip needle was well over to one side and the pilot was pressed against the cockpit side. It was then noted that the 'up' lights for the undercarriage had gone out and it can be presumed that one of the wheel doors had partially, or completely, opened. One door completely opened would produce yawed flight. The interesting feature is the ailerons which, with stick free, floated up approximately 100% more than when the wheel door was shut. There may be grounds to suggest that the slip-stream effects of the Griffon engine result in slightly yawed flight, this flight producing aileron upfloat on the leading edge side, with structural distortion. A change of flow at higher speeds may reverse the trim.
10-1-45 (Shea-Simmonds). Rudder balance tab gearing halved. Some doubt during flight as to position of main undercarriage and wheel doors at speeds above 250mph. Probable that either one, or both, wheel doors sucking open at high speed.
17-1-45 (Quill). Enlarged horn consisting of one extra lamination. Wheel doors are opening to a certain extent, as shown by indicators, during high speed dives.
22-1-45 (Quill). Balance tab out of operation, two extra laminations on horn balance. With this rudder the main handling objection were the powerful fore and aft changes of trim with speed. Decided to test aircraft on next flight with metal covered elevator.
28-1-45 (Quill). Metal elevator. Reduced fore and aft change of trim, but elevator overbalanced and quite unacceptable.
5-2-45 (Quill). During this flight confirmation that buffetting results from a small amount of G. at high speeds. I think it comes from the wheel doors and recommend that the aircraft be tested with wheel doors removed.
26-2-45 (Shea-Simmonds). Micro switches for undercarriage indicator lights repositioned so as to eliminate possibility of their going out through upper surface skin deflection.
26-2-45 (Shea-Simmonds). Delivered to Boscombe.

Spitfire LA211 F Mk 21 Boscombe Down, 18th May 1945. Weights and loading data.

Load	A	B	C	D	E	F
Tare	7102	7102	7102	7102	7102	7102
Service load	1322	1382	1402	1442	1627	1877
Fuel	915	1136	1246	1577	915	915
Oil	81	81	81	81	81	81
Take-off Wt.	9420	9701	9831	10202	9725	9975

Load A Typical service. B plus 30 gals. in fuselage drop tank., C plus 45 gal. blister tank., D plus 90 gal. blister tank., E plus 1 × 250lb. bomb., F plus 1 × 500lb bomb. Normal fuel load 124.5 gals. Oil 9 gals. Centre of gravity measured relative to datum point and parallel to datum line:- A 3.6" aft., B 3.9" aft., C 4ft. aft., D 4.3" aft., E 3.9" aft., F 4.1" aft.
LA211 Navigation. Equipped with P.8 compass. Conclusions. Compass position cannot be regarded as entirely satisfactory.

LA213 Rotol contra. at Vickers 5-4-45 (Quill). While cruising at zero rpm. and in auto, on moving the airscrew lever gently forward and changing auto into manual the propeller ran away and overspeeded up to 3100rpm. Throttle was closed and after short glide engine opened up gradually and normal constant speed action resumed. Flight lasted 15 minutes and in later stages propeller began to get extremely rough and aircraft landed.
12-4-45 (Quill). Propeller changed. At high speed end directional stability is not acceptable.
13--4-45 (Shea-Simonds). $1\frac{1}{2}$" added to rudder horn, no balance tab in operation, no trailing edge strips or beading fitted.
14-4-45 (Shea-Simonds). Flown in same condition as on previous flight except for addition of two 4" span metal strips fitted both above and below tab on trailing edge of rudder, one each side. Aeroplane is acceptable in present condition from a directional stability point of view up to an ASI of between 450 and 470mph.
16-4-45 (Quill). Flown with large chord metal covered rudder and $8\frac{1}{2}$" of horn depth and split trailing edge tabs internally reinforced by wood. At take-off noticeable high frequency vibration introduced by metal rudder which reflected propeller vibration and appeared to alter completely the resonance characteristics of the aeroplane. On reaching 400mph ASI a

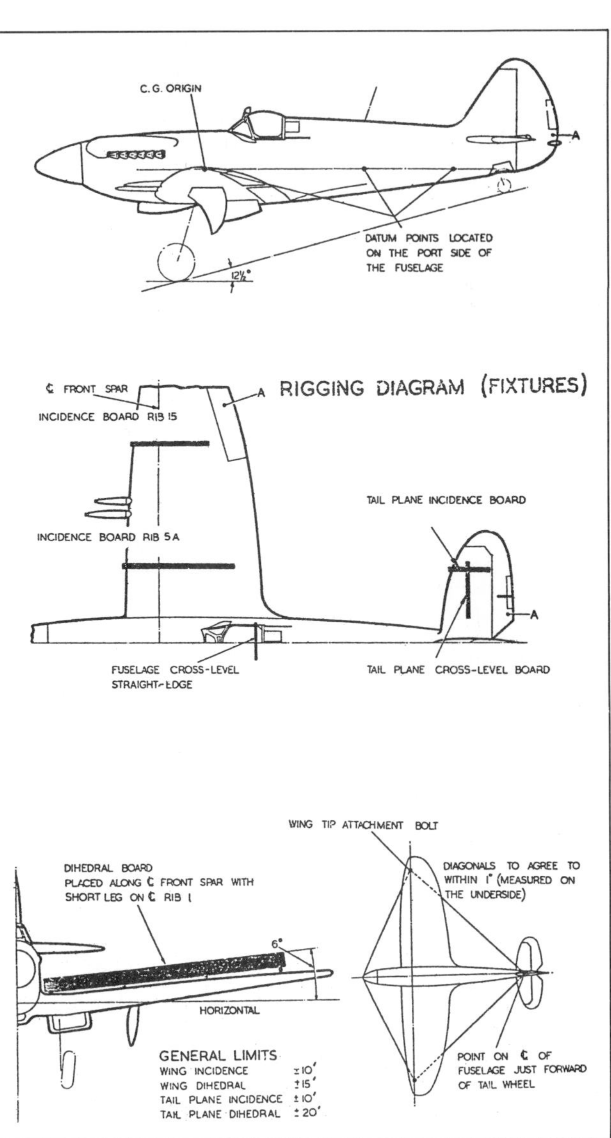

LA328 served operationally only with No 600 Squadron.

sudden commencement of what was thought tail flutter and at this stage impossible to stop aircraft from acceleration without putting on a fair amount of G, which was not considered advisable. The flutter was noticeable at both stick and rudder pedals and was causing movement throughout the cockpit giving the impression of sitting within jelly. I looked in the mirror and was able to see that the fin was moving considerably from side to side. From the general feel of the aircraft I formed that this flutter was in the form of a torsional movement of the whole empennage. The period during which the tail was fluttering was fairly long because it was considered safer to sit tight and let it flutter while the aircraft decelerated gradually rather than risk aggravating the flutter by increasing the G in an attempt to decelerate quickly.

4-5-45 (Shea-Simonds). Flown on following condition. Contra prop., rudder horn 12.3" depth., 26" of 5/16" diameter beading fitted each side of the rudder trailing edge above the trim tab. South Marston interim scheme 21 metal rounded horn elevator ex-PK312 fitted. Condition generally acceptable.

13-6-45 (Quill). Flown with de Havilland contra prop. Directional characteristics bad but aircraft not fitted with correct rudder.

LA214 at Vickers (allocated to Rotols) 20-2-45 (Quill). Propeller specially balanced. Asked to fly aeroplane and to state whether I thought there was any propeller vibration present. Conclusions:- the special balanced prop has not proved to be the solution to the problem of prop vibration on F21.

LA215 at Vickers 2-3-45 (Shea-Simonds). Fitted with modified metal elevator from LA211. I can see no reason why it should not go to Boscombe in its present condition.

9-3-45 (Shea-Simonds). Flown to check wheel door locking up following repairs after aircraft returned from CFE, who had lost a door in flight. Considered satisfactory.

LA216 at Vickers 23-4-45 (Quill). Contra F21 flown for directional stability check.

25-4-45 (Quill). Flown with 12.3" of horn depth and 20.5" of beading on both sides of rudder trailing edge instead of the split trailing edge strips of 20.5". Aircraft approved to go to Rotols with diving limitation of 450mph.

LA218 at Vickers 30-4-45 (Shea-Simonds). Fitted Rotol contra prop and rudder trailing edge beading.

2-5-45 (Quill). Trailing edge beading extended upwards by 6" making total 26½". Result was to cause a reduction in speed at which directional stability broke down in dive.

LA220 at Vickers 31-5-45 (Shea-Simonds). Flight to check directional stability of contra prop before delivery to Boscombe.

Spitfire LA219 F Mk 21 CR propeller. Boscombe Down September-October 1945. Griffon 85. Effect on level speed performance of a propeller spinner modified to prevent oil slinging. During early testing of contra-rotating propellers of Spitfire 21 aircraft by Messrs. Rotol Ltd., leakage of oil from behind the front spinner shell caused oil misting of the windscreen. In order to overcome this an anti-oil sling ring was fitted at the forward end of the rear shell. The loss in speed performance incurred by the modification amounted to 4mph EAS.

Intensive flying trials 19 June to 3 October 1945. An intensive flying programme of 100 hours was carried out on **each of two Spitfire 21 aircraft fitted with Rotol contra props** to test the propeller installation in particular. No defects were found on the propellers apart from one cracked spinner. Two aircraft LA219 and LA220 were **standard F21s.**

Spitfire LA220 F Mk 21 Boscombe Down. Weights and loading data.

Load	A	B	C	D	E	F
Tare weight	7158	7158	7158	7158	7158	7158
Service load	1107	1167	1187	1227	1162	1162
Bombs					250	500
Pilot, parachute and dinghy	215	215	215	215	215	215
Fuel	857	1073	1181	1505	857	857
Oil	81	81	81	81	81	81
Flying Wt.	9418	9694	9822	10186	9723	9973

Loads are:- A Typical service load., B plus 30 gal drop tank., plus 45 gal. blister tank., D plus 90 gal. blister tank., E plus 1 × 250lb. bomb., F plus 1 × 500lb. bomb. Weight limitations. Max. permissible take off 11,250.lbs. Max. landing 9250lb. Fuel total 119 gals. Oil 9 gals. Centre of gravity measured relative to datum point and parallel to datum line:- A 2.9" aft of datum point., B 3.3" aft., C 3.3" aft., D 3.7" aft., D 3.2" aft., F 3.4" aft.

LA219 and LA220. Carbon monoxide contamination tests. except during the condition of taxying with hood open both Spitfires complied with requirements.

LA232 (CP) at Vickers 20-8-45 (Quill). Handling check prior delivery to Service indicated a complete breakdown of directional stability at about 400mph. At 450 they were such as to render the aeroplane dangerous unless handled with great care. Partial opening of wheel doors in flight causes a total breakdown in directional stability. It would seem that the only immediate solution is to delete them.

LA329 at Vickers. 8-1-47 (Lithgow). Handling with 1 × 100lb. R.P. on each wing. It was considered possible that the limiting speed in a dive with one R.P. per wing at 425mph. could be raised. As a result of tests that it might be permissible to raise the diving speed to 440mph. Over this high lateral accelerations and low rudder forces make the aircraft unpleasant to fly and dangerous for low level rocket attacks.

Production of the F21 started, after considerable delays, in late 1944 and the Air Ministry said— "On the present programme it will continue until the end of 1944, although half the production stops at the end of 1944. It must be regarded as one of our main fighter types for the next two years or so." First deliveries reached the RAF in December, but by then the air war for fighters had shifted in emphasis with high altitude interception becoming rare and most of the activity taking place at under 20,000 feet and the majority of sorties were ground attack and support. LA187 was modified to a reduced span of 36ft 11in, and there was little interest in the contra-prop

Unknown F21 with personalised colour scheme. Possibly LA232.

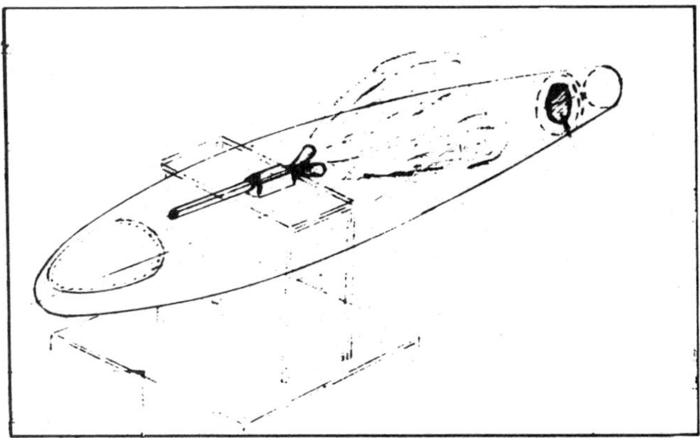

Sketch of the Vickers 34mm gun fitted to a Mosquito fuselage. PK378 had the gun fitted under a wing and was used for trials in June 1952 following high altitude trials. It was damaged, Cat 6 and declared surplus 3 December. A second Mk 22, PK481 was also fitted with the 34mm gun and the aircraft was damaged in the hangar on 16 December 1952, Cat 4. It was repaired and continued the trials at R.A.E. until it had engine failure and was damaged on landing.

version in spite of LA312 to 317 being retrofitted with CPs at South Marston. Only 120 examples were constructed and after service with Nos 1,41,91 and 122 squadrons the type was relegated to the auxiliary units as the improved F22s and 24s became available. The F21 was finally declared obsolete in May 1953.

The first South Marston production F21, LA187, was weighed at the works on 24 January 1944 and it had a Griffon 65 engine with five blade Rotol, Jablo propeller. Tare was 6,923lb and auw 9,183. LA188 was examined at High Post on 13 May after the test pilot had complained that the aileron control was most unsatisfactory (in fact most of the Supermarine test pilots had complained about this). The following points were noted (1) the balance tabs were twisted (2) the trailing edge of the tab projected about $\frac{1}{2}$ inch beyond the wing trailing edge (3) the trailing edge of the aileron was reflexed downwards (4) the under surface of the aileron was hollow (5) the aileron shroud was bent upwards in several places (6) the wing tip sections were bad and there was a bad bump on the top surface of both tips. It was realised that at high speed the wing tip was operating at a very small incidence and slight differences had the effect of doubling, or destroying, local lift.

During recovery from a dive at 500mph the cockpit hood and door on LA187 broke away and the aircraft was taken to High Post on 17 August for examination. The door had broken off at the hinges and before leaving the aircraft had swung, damaging the fuselage plating. The hood had also bent the whip aerial before striking the fin leading edge. It was considered that the door catches failed first.

Rotol were to supply a number of experimental propellers for the F21 production aircraft in an attempt to select the best possible unit for various Griffon engines. One new design was a six blade, wooden, counter rotating unit with NACA 16 section, plus a second unit with dural blades, both for the Griffon RG 4SM. Another Rotol unit was for an eight blade in dural for the RG 19ML (Griffon 1945) engine. A five blade paddle unit was also under design. At the same time, October 1944, de Havilland were to supply a number of Hamilton Super Hydromatic propellers they were building under licence. The first F21 with contra-props, LA213, was weighed at High Post on 23 March 1945 complete with Griffon 85 engine, a six blade CP and 32lb of ballast added between frames 18 and 19. Tare was 7,137lb and auw 9,411.

Two experiments with F21 airframes are worthy of mention. In March 1945 a drone conversion was used for TV dives. The system, designed in America, was originally tested on a drone F Mk V and was eventually intended for installation in naval aircraft. A second F21 had the Vickers Type 34mm recoilless gun fitted under its wings in April 1952. The installation and gun were code named 'Lockie' after Sqdn. Ldr. Lockie. Nothing came of this interesting experiment for the Spitfire, while being pushed out of the hangar, fell into a drain hole from which the cover had been removed and the gun was knocked off its mounting and badly damaged.

Original tests of the gun were made on a Mosquito fuselage with the gun positioned approximately six feet aft of the cockpit (see diagram). When the first round was fired, using nine instead of the specified $10\frac{1}{2}$lb propellant, a row of $\frac{1}{8}$in. alloy rivets at 1in. spacing and positioned two feet ahead of the gun's muzzle pulled out.

For the third round the gun was mounted $7\frac{1}{2}$in. above the fuselage with the muzzle four feet aft of the nose.

A Beaufighter fuselage was then used for a second series of experiments to test the gun's effects on a metal structure. With the gun $13\frac{1}{2}$in. above the fuselage and about 12 feet aft of the tail (facing aft), the first round resulted in skin damage and pulled rivets. During the second and third rounds fuselage frames and stringers were badly buckled. As a result it was decided that the blast tube should be of at least 8 inches diameter to permit reduction of gas pressure. The tests were conducted at Woolwich in November 1946 and by April 1952 the gun had been installed under the F21 Spitfire wing, and was then flown to calculate drag on a number of occasions. After the gun had been damaged it was decided not to continue with this most interesting series of trials.

SERIAL NUMBERS

Vickers-Armstrong (Castle Bromwich) Ltd
Contract No. B981687/39
Seventh order for 300 Spitfire Mk VC dated March 1942. Order cancelled in 1943. Re-established later that year to 120 Spitfire Mk 21. Built between July 1944 and December 1945. The following serials apply to Mk 21s built to this seventh order. LA187 to 236; 249 to 284, 299 to 332. Total 120

LA Series all F21 Griffon 61

LA187 G-65 HPA 27-1-44 maker's fly trls 1-4 A Henshaw G61 instal ret S Marston by Henshaw for instal of second G61. Initially fitt FVC wings. Test flights by Quill, Furlong, Shea-Simmonds and Banner July'44 until Jan'45. Taxi trls 13-7-44 det of CG 22-7 large chord metal rud instal 12-8 fore and aft stab not acceptable, and right wing low, cockpit hood and port door blew away during TV dive 16-8 spin trls 9-10 B Down 7-1-45 weights and CG loads. Ret VA after complaints of directional stab. Discovered that flaps were extending at high speed. Ret B Down 3-3-45 positional error, climb and level speed and cool trls. CB 17-12 ASTH for mods 2FPP Atcham for trans to 9MU 18-12-46 pilot lost f/ld crash disused airfield o/s strk obst. Crash in trans CE complete wreck 9-1-47 SOC. Colour scheme PR blue upper deep sky under

LA188 CRD VASM 26-4-44 maker's tests B Down 29-4 mods for high speed trls HPA 11-5 trls. Ret B Dn 1-9 by Capt Stedall ATA Farn 3-11 compressibility trls VA HPA Jan'45. Farn 30-8 VA 20-3-46 guns removed G65 instal dvd to Mach.89 CB 33MU 24-11-47 ETPS Farn Aug'48 compressibility trls WAL 28-2-49 mods 9MU 11-9-50 NES 16-6-53 SOC as wreck sold MoS 16-6-54

LA187, first production F21 prior to completion to full F21 standards.

LA189 4334 CRD B Dn 23-7-44 carb mon cockpit contam tests; fly trls Fin and Rud mods 16-9 dvd to 525 ASI 39MU 15-10-45 33MU 9-3-50 sold scr MoS 25-8-56

LA190 4335 G65 CRD Farn 18-8-44 B Down 19-9 G61 instal; hand trls 1s 22-9 VASM 26-9-46 33MU 7-11-47 3CAACU 8-10-51 sold scr 18-3-53

LA191 4336 CRD VA maker's tests 6-7-44 to 19-9 Furlong, Quill, Morgan. Eng and prop vibration R-R for checks. Port wheel door dam in flt 16-7 B Dn 19-9 high speed trls Farn Nov'44 vibration trls and stress analysis (vibrograph) 29MU 8-2-46 615S 16-4-47 SOC 5-12

LA192 4337 1st F21 to Handling S Hull. Del by Sq Ldr Stamson from VASM 30-8-44 B Dn 19-9 after fin and rud mods ret SM for paint 13-2-45 ret to Hull 21-2. Hvy land dam wing and flaps. Repair at VASM B Dn 30-8 AST Hamble 13-11 6MU 16-10-46 615S 1-4-47 600S 30-12-47 33MU 1-6-50 SOC 30-6

LA193 4452 VA HurPk 31-8-44 VASM 19-12-45 del by Flt/Lt Dwight to 29MU 5-1-46 602S 10-4-47 throttle jam open w/u land Woodvale CE 16-3-48 SOC 3-6 to 6564M 19-6 101 Reserve Centre, Bishopbriggs

LA194 4339 Test Flt/Lt Johnson 8-9-44 25mins 49MU Sealand 53 Wng 12-9 del by FO Lane ATA to 47MU for packing trls 16-9 33MU 5-3-45 122S 1-2-46 to 6373M for Medical Trng Dept Research Marsworth 17-7-47

LA195 4340 VASM del by FO Brown to 33MU 15-1-46 615S 25-4-47 FACB 19-8-48 6MU 27-10-49 33MU 15-10-51 NES 16-6-53 RAF Old Sarum used as target firing trls West Down 31-5-54

LA196 4341 test flown Flt/Lt Johnson VASM 25mins. 16-9-44 del 39MU by 1st Off Curtis ATA 25-9-44 91S 7-1-45 1S 15-2-45 122S 14-2-46 41S 13-4 RAF Llan 6-11-52 sold scr 17-3-54

LA197 4342 test flown Flt/Lt Johnson VASM 8mins 28-9-44 del 33MU by Capt Hughes ATA 2-10 91S 7-3-45 122S 17-1-46 9MU crash land Csfrd 23-9-47

LA198 4338 test flown Flt/Lt Johnson VASM 25mins 21-9-44 del 33MU by Capt Hughes ATA 2-10 1S 3-5-45 602S to 7118M Worcester 187S ATC BoB film 1968, 9 extant RAF Lauchars

LA199 4345 test flown Flt/Lt Johnson VASM 25mins 25-9-44 del 39MU Capt Hughes ATA 2-10 enlarged fin & rud instal ('lash-up' J Quill) 20-1-45 1S May'45 VA T1 2-stage Amber & Blue equip 7-12-49 33MU 8-9-50

LA200 4344 test flown Flt/Lt Johnson VASM 30mins 12-10-44 del 39MU by S/O Seear ATA 8-12 FA crash RAF Ludham 91S SOC 12-5-45

LA201 4346 test flown Flt/Lt Johnson VASM 10mins 14-10-44 del 39MU FO Hill ATA 7-11 CFE 21-11 AFDU 23-11 1S 1-2-45 91S 7-3-46 9MU 25-10 sold R J Coley 25-8-54

LA202 4329 test flown Flt/Lt Johnson 30mins VASM 23-10-44 del 33MU by FO Dutton ATA 7-11 1S 10-6-45 FACB 10-7 WAL 25-2-49 mods sold R J Coley 25-8-54

LA203 4348 TEST FLOWN Flt/Lt Johnson VASM 70mins 28-10-44 del 33MU by FO Harle ATA 7-11 91S 7-1-45 RAF Ludham CE 14-5 SOC 19-5

LA204 4351 test flown Sq Ldr Ellis VASM 10mins 4-1-44 Wng Com Gibson 10mins 15-11 del 39MU 1st Off Jordon 27-11 SM 28-6-45 mods 91S 10-10-46 sold R J Coley 25-8-54

LA205 4347 test flown Sq Ld Ellis VASM 15mins del 30MU by Mr Erewood 21-11 91S 18-1-45 SM 16-3 mods CBAF 27-7 615S 23-6-47 FACB 27-3-48 EA 12-4-50 sold En R/M 5-7-54

LA206 4359 test flown Flt/Lt Johnson VASM 10mins 15-1-44 del 33MU by Mr Sween 26-11 91S 9-12 FAAC 19-4-45 VA 122S 17-1-46 41S 5-9 CE SOC 22-8-47

LS207 4350 test flown Flt/Lt Johnson VASM 20mins VASM 9-11 del 39MU by Mr Stainer 21-11 91S 7-1-45 1S SOC 16-11-47

LA208 4353 test flown Flt/Lt Johnson VASM 20mins 10-11-44 del 39MU by Mr McDonald 26-11 91S 22-2-45 615S 2-6-47 FAC 25-1-48 RCMSU (RC) 8-7-49 C4(R) 11-11 VA recat 4RE RAF Llan 6-11-52 NES 16-6-53 sold L Met

LA209 4352 test flown Flt/Lt Johnson VASM 30mins 16-11-44 del 33MU by 1st Off Joss ATA 29-11 CFE Tang 18-2-45 91S 7-3-46 FAAC 27-6 41S 4-6-47 sold E Smelt 21-6-49

LA210 4354 test flown Flt/Lt Johnson VASM 15mins 21-11-44 del 33MU by Mr Kappeles ATA 30-11 91S 4-1-45 1S 25-7 CBAF 27-9 122S 17-1-46 41S 5-9 to 6413 Wattisham 19-8-47 SOC 1-11-49

LA211 4355 test flown Flt/Lt Johnson VASM 25mins 29-11-44 del HPA by 1st Off Curtis ATA 5-12 metal elev instal HPA. Jan '45. BDn 26-2-45 weights and CG loads; intns fly trls. FACB 27-2 March mods to interim stage with tail unit and instal of fin and rud from PP139 F21 proto. May, navigations trls with special compas replacing normal P8 39MU 23-5 1S 26-7 122S 14-2-46 612S 9-6-47 FA i/sea off Lancs pilot kld 21-7-47 SOC 22-8

LA212 4357 test flown Flt/Lt Johnson VASM 15mins 29-11-44 del 33MU by Mr Seear ATA 6-12 91S 4-1-45 SM 2-8 1S 18-10 122S 17-1-46 FAAC 29-6-46 3BRU 91S 11-7 CBAF 13-10 3CAACU 15-11-51 9MU 16-12 NES 2-12-53 sold scr MoS 17-3-54

LA192, first production F21 to the RAF.

LA213 4358 test flown Flt/Lt Johnson VASM 20mins 8-12-44 del HPA by P Hill 2-1-45 G68 instal with two, three blade Rotol c/props. Eng trouble 5-4-45 Stav rud mods 14-4 fitt DeH c/props 13-6-45 29-3-51 as Type 373 (FXIV Comp trls with LA220, latter fit fabric elev (later metal). Trls during same period with DeH c/props, instal at HPS 13-6-45 G85 instal 33MU 6-1-50 29MU 28-3-51 sold En RM 7-7-54

LA214 4356 test flown Flt/Lt Johnson VASM 15mins 8-12-44 HPA 15-12 alloc CRD Rotol Stav CRD VA EA 4-1-45 G68 instal and Rotol c/props VASM for trls with exp u/c 1-2 Flown by Henshaw as Type 373 (FXIV) ret Stav for eng/prop trls 13-2 33MU 7-10-46 615S 14-11-47 614S 15-8-49 9MU 25-5-50 sold E Smelt 25-8-54

LA215 4360 test flown Flt/Lt Johnson VASM 25mins 15-12-44 del CRD VA EA by Capt Stedal ATA 6-1-45 mod tail unit (Spiteful) instal and also mod metal elev from LA211. B Down 21-3 trls with new mods. Also fitt interim stage navigational equip. G68. Rotol c/props instal (Type 373 FXIV). CFE Tang 19-3 91S CRD VA 30-8 CFE FLS 25-4-46 615S 9-1-47 CB 3-6-48 6MU rts 14-7 sold Int All 2-11-49

LA216 4360 test flown Flt/Lt Johnson VASM 20mins 21-12-44 Del HPA 2-1-45 G68, Rotol c/props instal (Type 373 FXIV). Trls at Stav 25-4-45 EA & HPA July. CFE Tanmg 615S Jan '47 Farn 29-10 'Enemy a/c display sold scr Nov '49

LA217 4362 test flown Flt/Lt Johnson VASM 20mins 21-12-44 del CRD VA HPA by P Wgley ARA 2-1-45 NAFDS 29-6 CFE FLS 25-4-46 CE DeH 24-9 41S 18-6-47 615S B Hll 7-8-47 6MU 29-7-48 sold Int All 2-11-49

LA218 4363 test flown Flt/Lt Johnson VASM 20mins 30-12-44 del CRD VA EA Mr McDonald ATA 31-12 G85, Rotol c/props instal (Type 373 FXIV) Stav trls 1945/6 FACE 18-2-46 recat 14-8-47 SOC 22-8

LA219 4364 test flown Flt/Lt Johnson VASM 20mins 30-12-44 del CRD VA EA by Mr Twitabias ATA 4-1-45 G85, Rotol c/props instal (Type 373 FXIV) Rotol Stav 31-5 VA HPA 5-6 Rotol 15-6 mod spinner instal with oil ring on lead edge of rear shell to prevent oil slinging BDn Jly'45 hand trls Aug, carb mon cockpit contam tests 100 hours test fly 1S 25-10 o/s lnd Hutton Cranswick CB 1-4-46 recat E SOC 20-4

LA220 4365 test flown Flt/Lt Johnson VASM 30mins 5-1-45 Henshaw 9-1 del CRD VA EA by FO Fairley ATA 28-2 G85, Rotol c/props instal. BDn June to Oct '45. Fabric elev, comp trls with LA213; as per LA219. Main and flt trls with Ftr Com pilots and naval ground crews. Wts and CG loads. 100 perf tests. 1S 25-10 9MU 4-10-46 38MU 6-11-52 NES 24-2-53 sold scr 8-9-54

LA221 4366 test flown Flt/Lt Johnson VASM 20mins 10-1-45 allot CRD B Down 13-1 re-allot del 33MU by FO Pieper ATA 10-2 91S 24-2 VASM 15-6 mods test flown Henshaw 20mins 27-6 91S FAAC 29-6-46 recat E 27-2-47

LA222 4367 test Flt/Lt Johnson VASM 20mins 12-1-45 del 39MU by FO Garrod ATA 20-1 91S 5-3 CBAF 16-9 602S 18-7-47 f/ld crash CA Glenboig Lanarks 31-10-48 recat E 23-11

LA223 4368 test flown Flt/Lt Johnson VASM 20mins 18-1-45 del 39MU by Flt/Lt Fellows ATA 21-2 91S 13-3 CBAFs 27-9 600S 19-5-47 RCMSU(RC) C4 VA mr 15-5-50 NES 16-6-53 sold scr MoS 15-8-54

LA195 (RAV-E) of No.615 Squadron, R.Aux.AF.

LA224 4369 test flown Flt/Lt Lowern VASM 40mins 22-1-45 allot CRD VA HPA re-allot 33MU 3-2-45 del by FO Elliot ATA 27-2 91S 9-3 CBAF 27-9 Servicing Wng Dxfd 22-1-47 SOC 22-8

LA225 4370 test flown Flt/Lt Lowern VASM 10mins 22-1-45 del 39MU by FO Guest ATA 10-2 91S 7-3 VASM 16-7 mods 1S 18-10 122S 17-1-46 FAAC 25-2 ROS 41S 18-4 602S 6-6-47 FA scr 16-11-51 3CAACU Cat E 30-7-52

LA226 4371 FF 9-1-45 test flown Flt/Lt Johnson VASM 5mins 31-1-45 del 33MU by Flt/Lt Fellows ATA 21-2-45 91S 7-3 1st ops flt 13-4 VASM 15-6 mods 122S 17-1-46 9MU NES 15-12-47 3CAACU Exeter 18-9-51 to 5119M 18-1-54 2224S ATC CFS Little Rissington 9-2-58. Displayed at South Marston, extant Biggin Hill.

LA227 4372 test flown Flt/Lt Johnson VASM 25 mins 1-2-45 del 33MU by Flt/Lt Ellis ATA 21-2 1S 15-6 602S 25-2-49 FAAC 13-5 ROS sold Scr MoS 20-7-54

LA228 4373 test flown Flt/Lt Johnson VASM 15 mins 29-1-45 del 39MU by Flt/Lt Jopp ATA 20-2 91S 18-5 CBAF 27-0 91S 15-12 600S 11-6-47 33MU 30-6-50 3 CAACU 30-9-51 NES 11-11

LA229 4374 test flown Flt/Lt Johnson VASM 20 mins 2-2-45 del 39MU by Flt/Lt Jopp ATA 20-2 s/dn over Fresian Isles 11-3

LA230 4375 test flown Flt/Lt Johnson VASM 35 mins 4-2-45 del 39MU by FO Davidson ATA 28-2 91S 19-6 VASM 28-6 mods SOC 22-8-47

LA231 4376 test flown Flt/Lt Johnson VASM 15 mins 9-2-45 del 39MU by Flt/Lt Ellis ATA 2-12 1S 2-8 600S 28-4-47 FACB 31-1-48 VA Burmese Con Sq 26-1-53 NES 16-6 sold En RM 6-7-54

LA232 4377 test flown Flt/Lt Johnson VASm 13-2-45 allot 33MU del VASM 6-3 for prop trls; new eng instal. del CBAF by Sq Ld Ellis (CB test pilot) 4-5 contin of trlls. G85 Rotol c/props. Becme personal a/c TT AVM TC Traill HCCS lnd one u/c leg up WWal ce 30-10-49

LA200 (DL-E), 91 Squadron, 1945.

LA226 seen here at its birthplace, South Marston.

LA233 4378 test flown Flt/Lt Loweth VASM 25 mins 20-4-45 del 39MU by FO Drzewiect 30-4 NES 16-3-53 sold En RM 12-7-54

LA234 4379 test flown Flt/Lt Johnson VASM 25 mins 14-2-45 del 33MU by FO Elliot ATA 22-2 91S 9-3 s/dn over Fresian Isles 11-3 SOC 17-5

LA235 4380 test flown Sq Ld Ellis 15 mins 19-2-45 del 33MU by FO Andrew 24-2 91S 23-3 VASM 15-6 mods NES 23-11-52 sold scr MoS 17-3-54

LA236 4381 test flown Flt/Lt Johnson VASM 25 mins 21-2-45 del 33MU by Capt Stedall ATA 2-3 91S 23-3 122S 10-1-46 RAF Lland 30-10-49 FACB 17-1-53 ROS recat 5(S) 15-4

LA249 4382 test flown Flt/Lt Johnson VASM 25 mins 12-3-45 del 39MU by FO Llewellyn ATA 22-3 91S 27-9 CBAF 30-10 600S 2-7-47 AGT Gat refurb 3-3-51 NES 30-6-53 sold En RM 8-7-54

LA250 4383 test flown Flt/Lt Johnson VASM 15 mins 26-2-45 del 33MU by FO Dundamy 5-3 91S 30-5 VASM 28-6 mods FAAC 91S 29-6-46 602S 10-4-47 to 6833M RAF St Athan 24-1-51 8-1-52

LA251 4384 test flown Flt/Lt Johnson VASM 25 mins 13-3-45 del 39MU by FO Gasold ATA 22-3 1S 14-6 122S 14-2-46 eng fail i/sea off Lossie pilot kld 8-3 SOC 28-3

LA252 4385 test flown Flt/Lt Johnson VASM 25 mins 15-3-45 del 39MU by FO Simm ATA 22-3 91S 19-4 122S 17-1-46 41S FAAC 12-8 recat E SOC 22-8-47

LA253 4386 test flown Flt/Lt Loweth VASM 30 mins 22-3-45 del 39MU by FO Jordan ATA 10-4-45 34MU CAC 27-6 ROS VA STN 17-10 600S 3-6-48 RAF Lland 29-10-52 CFS FA5(C) 4-12 Prop hit grd on t/o o/t

LA254 4387 test flown Flt/Lt Loweth VASM 10 mins 27-3-45 del 33MU by FO Ball ATA 13-4 91S 30-6 CBAF 6-9 1S 18-12 91S 7-11-46 SOC 22-8-47

LA255 4388 test flown Flt/Lt Loweth FASM 30 mins 26-3-45 del 39MU by FO Fairley ATA 10-4 1S 29-6 91S VASM 19-7 mods CE 13-11-47 to 6490M 4-12 extant RAF Witt as JX-U 1S

LA256 4389 test flown Flt/Lt Loweth VASM 5 mins 29-3-45 del 39MU by FO Davidson 13-4 3CAACU 8-5-53 NES 23-11 sold E Smelt 14-6-54

LA257 H390 test flown Flt/Lt Loweth VASM 20 mins 5-4-45 del 39MU by FO Goodwin ATA 23-4 NES 19-1-54 sold E Smelt 14-6-54

LA258 H391 tet flown Sq Ld Ellis VASM 15 mins 12-4-45 del 39MU by Capt Cuthbert ATA 25-4 3CAACU 18-9-51 NES 31-3-54 sold E Smelt 25-8

LA259 4392 test flown Flt/Lt Loweth VASM 25 mins 8-4-45 del 39MU by FO Passold ATA 18-4 NES 16-6-53 RAF Old Sarum firing trls 25-5-54

LA260 4393 test flown Sq Ld Ellis VASM 20 mins 17-4-45 del 33MU by FO Ayres ATA 27-4 1S 30-4 FAAC 17-10 ASTH 41S 30-8-46b FAAC 15-5-47 ROS crash in transit 41S 24-2-48 VA RAF Lland 11-12-52

LA261 4394 test flown Sq Ld Ellis VASM 10 mins 14-4-45 del 39MU by FO Tamsay ATA 23-4 sold scr MoS 29-7-54

LA262 4395 test flown Sq Ld Ellis VASM 20 mins 19-4-45 del 33MU by Capt Turk ATA 28-4 1S 3-8 SOC 16-10-47

LA263 4396 test flown Flt/Lt Loweth VASM 25 mins 21-4-45 del 39MU by FO Nest ATA 28-4 3CAACU 18-9-51 NES 16-11-53 to 7131M 15-2-54 143S ATC

LA264 4397 test flown Flt/Lt Loweth VASM 25 mins 23-4-45 del 33MU by FO Drzewiecki ATA 2-5-45 VASM 6-7 mods NES 16-6-53 sold R J Coley 25-8-54

LA265 4398 test flown Flt/Lt Loweth VASM 20 mins 23-4-45 del 33MU by FO Fryer ATA 2-5 VASM 12-7 mods 91S 6-9 266 OCU 3-10-46 602S 14-9-48 FAAC 14-1-49 to 6834M 29-1-51

LA266 4399 test flown Flt/Lt Loweth VASM 25 mins 26-4-45 del 33MU by FO Dutton ATA 4-5 91S 30-6 CBAF 9-11 FACB 4-1-46 cd lndg Charterhall 25-1 recat E SOC 31-1

LA267 400 test flown Flt/Lt Loweth VASM 20mins 28-4-45 del 33MU by S/O Cowdry ATA 7-6 1S 30-9 602S 18-12-49 spun i/grnd Bishopton Renfrews pilot kld 3-4 NES 30-6-53 sold En/RM 12-7-54

LA268 4401test flown Flt/Lt Loweth VASM 20mins 27-4-45 del 33MU by FO Rogers ATA 4-5 1S FACB 4-9 ASTH refurb 602S 15-4-47 SOC 22-4-48

LA269 4402 test flown Flt/Lt Loweth VASM 20mins 3-5-45 del CRD Bdn by FO Hay ATA 15-5 33MU 22-9 602S 22-6-49 FA3R 13-11 ASTH refurb NES 16-6-53 sold J G Will 20-4-54

LA270 4403 test flown Flt/Lt Loweth VASM 20mins 4-5-45 del 39MU by FO Ayres ATA 16-5 NES 16-6-53 sold R J Coley 25-8-54

LA271 4404 test flown Flt/Lt Loweth VASM 25mins 11-5-45 del 39MU by FO Hosking ATA 24-5 sold MoS 20-7-54

LA272 4405 test flown Flt/Lt Loweth VASM 20mins 15-5-45 del 33MU by FO Symondson ATA 7-7 41S 5-12 19S 12-2-47 CB 13-10-48 VA NES 16-6-53 sold scr 21-6-54

LA273 4406 test flown Flt/Lt Loweth VASM 5mins 16-5-45 del 33MU by FO West ATA 30-5 1S 16-9 615S 13-5-47 ROS 14-5-48 NES 16-6-53 sold En/RM 8-7-54

LA274 4407 test flown Flt/Lt Loweth VASM 15mins 25-5-45 3 changes eng del 39MU by FO Symondson ATA 29-6 NES 16-6-53 sold R J Coley 25-8-54

LA275 4408 test flown Flt/Lt Loweth VASM 10mins 23-5-45 del 33MU by FO Jones ATA 7-6 1S 22-8 602S 2-4-48 FACE 18-6-49 scrap 9-8

LA276 4409 test flown Flt/Lt Loweth VASM 20mins 27-5-45 del 33MU by Capt Cuthbert ATA 7-6 1S 17-9 SOC 16-11-47

LA277 4410 test flown Flt/Lt Loweth VASM 20mins 30-5-45 del 39MU by FO Jones ATA 12-6 1S 19-9 FAAC 26-5-46 SOC 16-11-47

LA278 4411 test flown Flt/Lt Loweth VASM 20mins 1-6-45 del 33MU by FO Fryes ATA 19-6 FAAC 10-10 ROS 41S 13-4-46 600S 7-8-47 615S 2-9 NES 3-6-53 sold L Met 1-10-54

LA279 4412 test flown Flt/Lt Loweth VASM 25mins 5-6-45 del 33MU by FO Robins ATA 18-6 91S 26-9 1S 10-10-46 o/s land Abbots crash 28-8-48 VA recatE 3-3-49

LA280 4413 test flown Flt/Lt Loweth VASM 20mins 8-6-45 del 39MU by FO Couttendon ATA 18-6 VASM 11-7 mods NES 20-10-53 SOC 9-9-54

LA281 4414 test flown Flt/Lt Loweth VASM 20mins 12-6-45 alloc 39MU re-allot VA HPA 23-6 NES 16-6-53 RAF Old Sarum firing trls 31-5-54

LA282 4415 test flown Flt/Lt Loweth VASM 20mins 15-6-45 del 33MU by FO Drzewieck ATA 26-6 122S 9-2-46 41S std lnd u/c collpse CB Witt 23-4 SOC 31-5

LA283 4416 test flown Flt/Lt Loweth VASM 20mins 15-6-45 del 33MU by FO Njrordson ATA 3-7 122S 1-2-46 41S 602S 17-2-49 FAAC 12-3 VASM 5-7-51 mods NES 22-10-52 sold J G Will 29-5-54

LA284 4417 test flown Flt/Lt Loweth VASM 20mins 20-6-45 del 39MU by FO Ayres ATA 3-7 91S 9-11-46 CBAF 122S 28-2 41S swng on t/o tip onto nose CE Ackl 22-11 SOC 12-12

LA299 4418 test flown Flt/Lt Loweth VASM 30mins 22-6-45 del CBAF 25-6 McLarens HAL 30-8 VA HPA 10-1-46 1S 28-3 41S 30-5 615S 21-8-47 600S 2-9-47 to 6489M 4-12 SOC 14-9-50

LA300 4419 test flown Flt/Lt Loweth VASM 10mins 22-6-45 allot 33MU re-allot CRD McLarens HAL del by FO Netterton ATA 6-7 trls with new rad 33MU 21-3-46 WAL 18-2-49 mods NES 16-6-53 sold scr 9-9-54

LA301 4420 test flown Flt/Lt Loweth VASM 20mins 25-6-45 del 39MU by FO Ayres 3-7 1S 12-9 FAAC 12-9-46 recat E 14-8-47

LA302 4421 test flown Flt/Lt Loweth VASM 15mins 28-6-45 del 33MU by FO Younghusband ATA 6-7 1S 1-2-46 41S std on lnd drop star wng Ack 15-11-46 recat E SOC 13-12

LA303 4422 test flown Flt/Lt Loweth VASM 10mins 4-7-45 del 39MU by FO Ayres ATA 12-7 1S 12-9 FACE dbf 27-9 SOC 25-10

LA304 4423 test flown Flt/Lt Loweth VASM 20mins 6-7-45 del 39MU by SO Cowdry ATA 13-7 122S 4-2-46 41S 1-11 sold MoS 2-4-54

LA305 4424 test flown Flt/Lt Loweth VASM 25mins 7-7-45 del 39MU by Cmdr Leaver ATA 31-7 6368M 10-4-47 RDAF 15-7 cancel 11-8 to 6411M 18-8

LA306 4425 test flown Flt/Lt Loweth VASM 25mins 11-7-45 del 33MU 21-7 41S 23-4-46 615S 27-8 FACA 3-7-48 VA NES 16-6-53 sold MoS 17-3-54

LA307 4426 test flown Flt/Lt Loweth VASM 20mins 12-7-45 del 39MU by SO Symondson ATA 3-8 RAF Lland 11-12-52 NES 5-7-46 recat E SOC 22-8

LA308 4427 test flown Flt/Lt Loweth VASM 5mins 13-7-45 del 33MU by FO Jones ATA 3-8 1S 15-5-46 mr 5-7 recat E SOC 22-8

LA309 4429 test flown Flt/Lt Loweth VASM 25mins 31-7-45 del 33MU by FO Everleigh ATA 18-8 WAL 23-2-49 mods NES 16-6-53 sold scr 8-9-54

LA310 4429 test flown Flt/Lt Loweth VASM 20mins 1-8-45 del 33MU by FO Shuse ATA 10-8 WAL 17-2-49 mods NES 6-6-53 sold scr 8-9-54

LA311 4430 test flown Flt/Lt Loweth VASM 20mins 3-8-45 del 33MU 18-8 1S 25-5-46 recat E SOC 22-8-47

LA312 4431 test flown Flt/Lt Loweth VASM 20mins 2-8-45 del 33MU 11-8 WAL 22-2-49 mods NES 30-6-53 sold L Met 1-10-54

LA313 4432 test flown Flt/Lt Loweth VASM 25mins 8-8-45 33MU 17-8 615S 25-3-47 FACB 10-8-48 VA NES 16-6-53 sold En/RM 6-7-54

LA314 4433 test flown Flt/Lt Loweth VASM 20mins 9-8-45 del 39MU by FO French ATA 27-8 3CAACU 18-9-51 sold MoS 2-4-54

LA315 4434 test flown Flt/Lt Loweth VASM 20mins 27-8-45 del 33MU by FO Robins ATA 12-9 Stn Flt Witt 26-6-46 41S 28-11 602S 31-8-47 FAAC 11-1-48 GAC2 20-12 AGT Gat 6-4-51 sold D G Griffiths 3-3-54

LA316 4435 test flown Flt/Lt Loweth VASM 20mins 14-8-45 del 39MU by FO French ATA 27-8 FAAC 13-4-49 ROS NES 16-6-53 sold MoS 5-3-54

LA317 4436 test flown Flt/Lt Loweth VASM 20mins 20-8-45 VA Chil TI & flt trls GGS Mk 48 del 39MU by FO Ayres ATA 30-8 VA 16-9 NES 16-6-53 sold R J Coley 25-3-54

LA318 4437 test flown Flt/Lt Loweth VASM 20mins 21-8-45 del 33MU by FO Harrison ATA 11-9 WAL 16-7-49 mods NES 16-6-53 sold MoS 2-4-54

LA319 4438 test flown Flt/Lt Loweth VASM 20mins 31-8-45 del 33MU by FO Anderton RAF 17-9 602S 28-7-49 NES 16-6-53 sold R J Coley 25-8-54

LA320 4439 test flown Flt/Lt Loweth VASM 10mins 31-8-45 del 33MU by Flt/Lt Lever ATA 29-9 WAL 30-1-49 mods 3CAACU 8-10-51 NES 29-10-53 sold E Smelt 14-6-54

LA321 4440 test flown Flt/Lt Loweth VASM 5mins 7-9-45 del 39MU by Flt/Lt Lever RAF 3-10 3CAAVU 19-9-51 NES 1-12-53 sold MoS 2-4-54

LA322 4441 test flown A Henshaw VASM 20mins 12-9-45 del 39MU by Flt/Lt Major RAF 3-10 3CAACU 6-11-51 NES 1-12-53 sold MoS 17-3-54

LA323 4442 test flown Flt/Lt Loweth VASM 5mins 28-9-45 del 33MU by Flt/Lt Major RAF 11-10 600S 1-4-47 Std on app cd Thorney Island CE 18-6 CE scr 19-7-49

LA324 4443 test flown Flt/Lt Loweth VASM 15mins 27-9-45 del 33MU by Flt/Lt Rogers RAF 11-10 WAL 24-2-49 mods NES 16-6-54 sold MoS 14-6-54

LA325 4444 test flown G Huntley VASM 20mins 4-10-45 del 33MU by Flt/Lt Major RAF 1-11 WAL 31-1-49 mods RAF Lland 6-11-52 FA3R 20-11 ROS sold En/RM 9-7-54

LA326 4445 test flown Flt/Lt Brown VASM 20mins 16-10-45 del 33MU by Flt/Lt Watts RAF 14-11 CSA Defford replace Tempest as target a/c 12-3-48 B Dn trls Rotol 5-blade prop 4-10-49 Dam C.3 Soc (MoS) 7-11-51

LA327 4446 test flown Flt/Lt Brown VASM 5mins 16-10-45 del 39MU Flt/Lt Rogers RAF 8-11 sold MoS 30-7-54

LA328 4447 test flown Flt/Lt Loweth VASM 20mins 6-11-45 del 33MU by Flt/Lt Watts RAF 26-11 600S 9-4-47 sold MoS 9-9-56

LA329 4448 test flown Flt/Lt Loweth VASM 20mins 29-10-45 del 33MU by Flt/Lt Watts RAF 26-11 VA HPA 30-8-46 trls with 1x100lb RP under wings 602S 10-4-47 FAAC 5-5-50

LA330 4449 test flown Flt/Lt Loweth VASM 15mins 13-11-45 del 29MU by Flt/Lt Major RAF 28-12 41S 19-9-46 600S 23-1-47 o/s land BHill CE 8-5-49 scr 23-9

LA331 4450 test flown Flt/Lt Loweth VASM 20mins 6-12-45 del 29MU by Flt/Lt Fitz RAF 600S 15-5-47 Lland 23-10-52 C3 21-11-52 ROS NEA rts 15-4-54 sold D Bond 27-8

LA332 4451 test flown Flt/Lt Loweth VASM 20mins 7-12-45 del 29MU by Flt/Lt O'brien RAF 2-1-46 sold J Dale 8-7-48

PP139 G65 F21 proto (2nd) HPA Contract No CRD 2601. CRD BDn Nov'43 G61 instal (A&AEE Aero Note was entitled 'Victor'.) Speed trls and positional error; weights and CG loads. Thin section wing (see page 497) with extended tips. Metal ails; u/c wheel doors for wells; flush rivetted throughout. ASTH 29-6-45 FACB 21-3-46 CE 13-4 (Note: not to be included in RAF strength) Serial was same as on Sunderland PP139

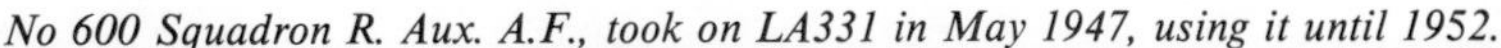

No 600 Squadron R. Aux. A.F., took on LA331 in May 1947, using it until 1952.

THE SAME BUT DIFFERENT

The Spitfire F Mk 22 was developed almost on a parallel to the F21 and differences in airframe design and engine were minor, the most obvious being the reduced area rear fuselage and installation of a clear view canopy. Supermarine had discussed the F22 with the Air Ministry and had wanted to use the designation F Mk XIX, but the Air Ministry had insisted on the Mark number of 22. As the aircraft (F21 and 22) were so similar to each other they bore the same Type number, 356, and all production F22s were offsets from the much amended F21 contracts*. There were two prototypes, SX549 and TM383, the latter being modified from F21 standards, then modified again to become the prototype Seafire Mk 46. SX549 was originally ordered as an F21 but built as an F22, the modification being carried out by Cunliffe Owen in November 1944.

The first production F22, PK312, was delivered to High Post aerodrome for trials in March 1945; reproduced below are the initial test pilot's notes. All were made by Shea-Simmonds (S-S).

30-4-45 (S-S). Fitted new production type interim scheme rounded horn elevator. Elevator far too light and I would suggest that 12in of beading on each side of the elevator at the trailing edge be tried to start with. The hood is not a good fit and the rear winding gear does not engage the final notch. Consequently it rolls back one notch and there is a tendency for the hood to lift at high speed. Brakes are feeble to the point of being virtually useless.

10-5-45 (S-S). Slightly left wing low and a noticeable reversal of directional trim at speeds in excess of 400mph with, I think, some lateral trim reversal from left to right. Has the rear view modification to the fuselage reduced the torsional stiffness of the tailplane?

11-5-45 (S-S). At 30,000ft the aircraft was unstable, although it would be acceptable for combat at this altitude. The rear view modification has a detrimental effect on directional stability, and although I do not consider it by any means unacceptable I anticipate trouble when carrying any form of drop tank or bomb.

18-6-45 (S-S). Recommend reintroduction of a rear view mirror fitted internally.

Spitfire PK312 F Mk 22 Boscombe Down 18 December 1945. Weights and CG loadings data. Griffon 61. Aircraft was prototype for the Mark fitted with a rear view hood, larger tail unit and representative of the first 250 production aircraft without rear fuselage tanks.

Load	A	B	C	D	E	F
Tare weight (lb)	7006	7006	7006	7006	7006	7006
Service load	1338	1338	1338	1338	1338	1338
30gal drop tank	—	60	—	—	—	—
30 gal fuel	—	219	—	—	—	—
45gal drop tank and fuel	—	—	408	—	—	—
90gal tank and fuel	—	—	—	777	—	—
1 × 250lb bomb & carrier	—	—	—	—	305	—
1 × 500lb bomb & carrier	—	—	—	—	—	555
Main fuel 85gals	621	621	621	621	621	621
Wing fuel 36gals	263	263	263	263	263	263
Oil 9gals	81	81	81	81	81	81
Flying weight (lb)	9309	9588	9717	10086	9614	9864

Maximum permissible take off weight 11,350lbs.

Centres of gravity relative to datum point and parallel to datum line: A 5.4" aft of datum point, B 5.7" aft, C 5.8" aft, D 6.2" aft, E 5.7" aft, F 5.8" aft.

The company's summing up of the trials were very frank—"The Spitfire XXII (sic) differs from the XXI (sic) in two respects which are likely to affect its handling characteristics. It has the cutaway type fuselage incorporating the rear vision hood and the large (Spiteful type) empennage. This represents an increase in tailplane and elevator of 27% and in fin and rudder of 28% over and above the XXI. PK312, which is not fitted with rear fuel tanks, is representative of the first 230-250 XXIIs, for which no rear fuel tanks are scheduled.

"Certain of the tests laid down in AP970** have not been repeated on this aeroplane since the full requirements were carried out on the XXI. Only such tests as were considered likely to have been affected by the changes in the XXII have been repeated. Ground handling is satisfactory but rudder loads are higher during taxying and as the elevator is mass balanced the stick tends to fall back under its own weight in the static condition—this tends to hinder access to the cockpit and the changed sign of the 'stick force' is noticeable during taxying.

"As the first 230 to 250 aircraft are being delivered without rear fuel tanks no attempt has been made to provide this machine with the reserve stability which would be required to cater for the rear fuel case. The full load CG without rear fuel comes out at 5.6in aft of the datum and the elevator has been so arranged to provide the requisite amount of stability at a loading of 5.9 in aft. The machine has been checked in general flights up to 35,000ft and the stick free stability, both static and dynamic, is considered satisfactory.

"A feature of the aircraft is, however, that it is statically unstable stick free (engine on) at low speeds. This is noticeable during climb, but as the dynamic stability remains positive it does not constitute a nuisance to the pilot. Engine off static stability is positive down to the stall and this results in higher stick force for tail down loading than is the case for the XXI. Directional stability is good and aileron characteristics remain the same as for XXI. The aircraft goes slightly left wing low at maximum.

"General. The tendency due to mass balancing the elevator for the control column to fall to the aft position when the aircraft is on the ground causes a certain amount of trouble when the pilot enters the cockpit. This could be rectified by incorporation of a bob weight. Wheel doors have caused trouble during dives and if not correctly closed in flight trim in all axes is affected. One of the causes is lowering the undercarriage at too high a speed."

On 9 October 1945 the order for F22s was reduced to a total of 627 and MAP requested that deliveries be made as follows: October 61, November 60, December 50, January 1946 30, February 25, March 25, April 25, May 25, June 25, July 19. August onwards 25 aircraft per month. In a further letter of 20 October the serials of the cancelled aircraft were listed—

PK664 with Griffon 85 and contra-props after being sold to Vickers in February 1954. It still survives, on the gate at Binbrook.

**In a letter to Supermarine on 25 January 1945 MAP reduced the F21 contract to 1,577 F22.*
***Air Publication No AP970.*

NG891-913, NG926-968, NG979-999, NH112-115, NG116-147, PV360-385, PV399-445, PV458-499, PV520-567, PV581-583, PW123-133. More was to follow for on November the order was again reduced from 627 to 287 aircraft. Supermarine were requested to supply MAP with a list of cancelled serial numbers: PK436-468, PK727-754, PK769-811, PK828-868, PK8832-926, PK949-990, NG757-798, NG813-856, NG868-890.

Trials with the prototypes continued and pilots complained of an abnormal increase in stick force required to hold an out of trim dive as the limiting diving speed was approached. Adding beading to the elevator tab upper surfaces had little effect, but beading on the elevator trailing edge considerably reduced stick force. It was concluded that the stick forces were due to elevator distortion and that the horn be strengthened.

PK684 fitted with a Griffon 87 engine and a six blade de Havilland contra prop was weighed at High Post on 21 February 1946, returning a tare of 7,526lb and an auw of 10,280. PK320 was at Vickers on 8 January 1947 for trials while fitted with an asymmetric RP load. Lithgow was the pilot. The 100lb RPs were fitted to the port wing and Lithgow reported that the load had no effect on lateral trim or control of the Spitfire from climbing to maximum diving speed. Stalling and baulked landing characteristics were not noticeably affected. PK428 and PK525 went to Vickers on 2 January 1948 and Colquhoun reported that the recent production tests showing unusual elevator characteristics were probably due to elevator

Southern Rhodesian Air Force F22s, one (below) armed with rockets.

Below: SX549 before delivery, as the prototype F22. It was originally ordered as the prototype F21.

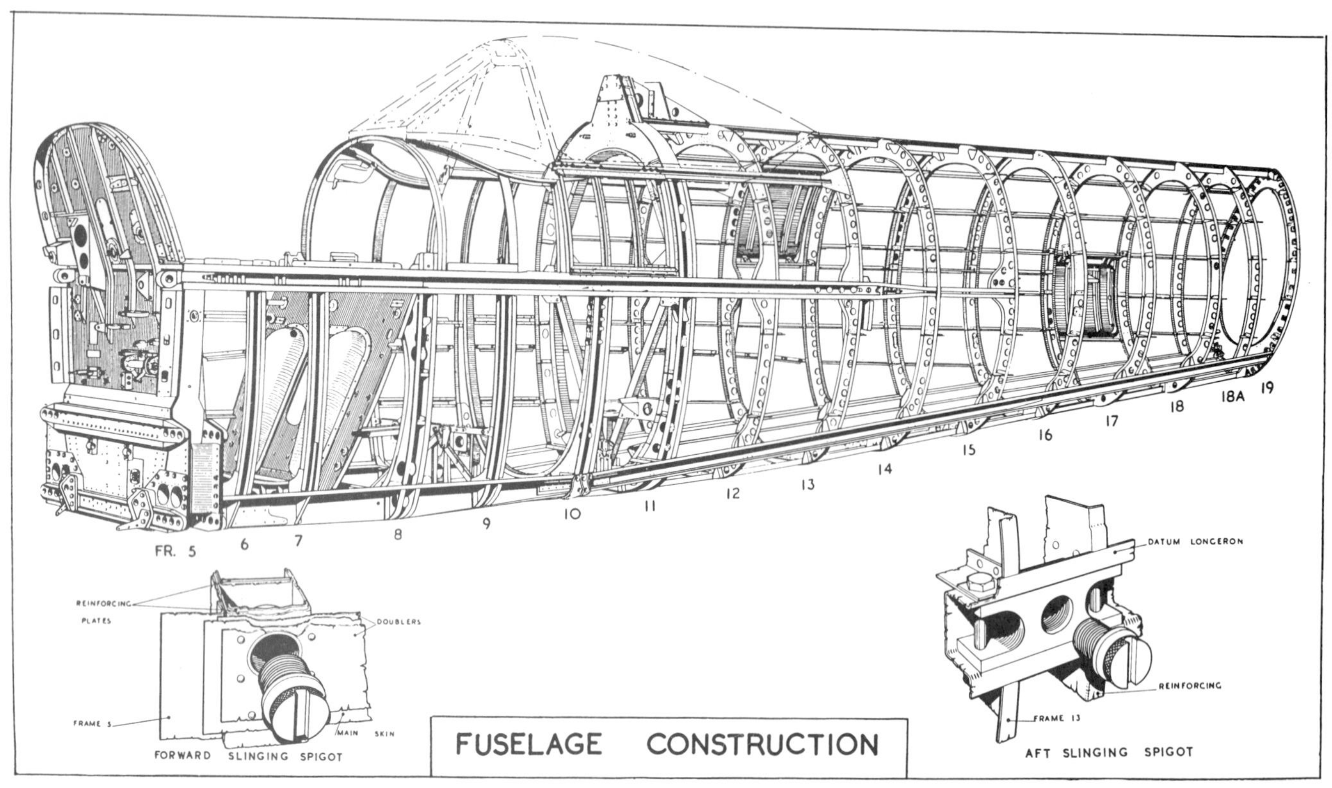

PK431 at South Marston following mods and conversions. It was sold as scrap in May 1954.

PK406 served with No 603 Squadron RAuxAF, from Ringway.

F22 (681) of Royal Egyptian Air Force.

distortion. As part of an experiment to allow the F22 to operate from unimproved airfields one example was fitted with an arrester hook and rear fuselage of a Seafire Mk 46.

Although the Mk 22 was issued to RAF squadrons as a front line service type, No 73 Squadron at Ta Kali, Malta, is an example, the majority were used by the Auxiliary Air Force and Flying Refresher Schools. The type was practically out of service by 1952; 80 went into storage and 63 sold abroad, and it was finally declared obsolete to all RAF requirements in May 1955.

On 1 May 1950 Vickers signed an agreement with the Egyptian Government for the supply of 20 F22s (ex British Government stocks which had been in service in the Royal Air Force) overhauled and supplied in accordance with Specification No 480. The total contract price was £239,000 to be paid in three instalments.

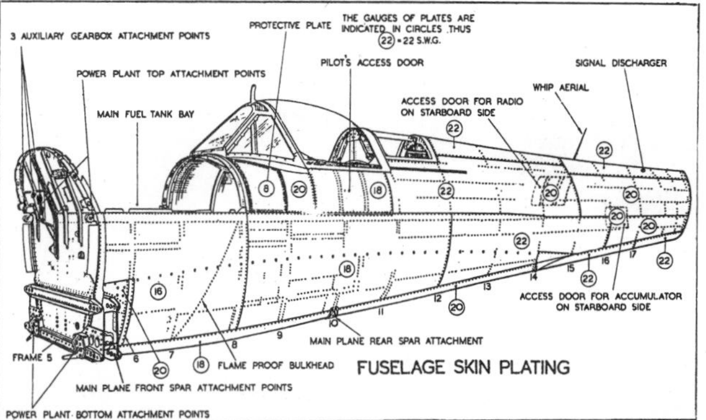

Armour. 315 lb.

Armament 4 × 20mm cannon Mk 2* 175rpg inner, 150 outer. Plus 3 × 500lb bombs three sets of rockets 60, 100, 2 × 60, 180, 2 × 100.

Radio. TR1143 R3067.
Cine camera. G45.
Gunsight Gyro.

Performance. 449mph @ 25,000 (FS) + 18, 450 @ 19,500 (FS) + 25, 413 @ 11,000 (MS) + 18, 412 @ 5,000 (MS) + 25, 366 @ SL + 18, 390 @ SL + 25. Rate of climb 3,600ft min @ 21,500ft (FS) + 18, 4,300 @ 17,000 (FS) + 25, 4,300 @ 8,000 (MS) + 18, 5,100 @ 2,000 (MS) + 25, 4,250 @ SL + 18, 5,100 @ SL + 25. Service ceiling (100ft min) 45,500ft. Range (normal tanks) 380 miles @ 20,000 @ 230-245 cruise, 4.92mpg, duration 1.54-1.63hr; with 90 gal o/ld tank 734 miles @ 20,000ft @ 225-245mph, 4.65mpg, duration 3-3.27hr. Take off run 670yds. Max dive 500mph. Landing 520. Economical cruise 245mph.

Weights. Tare 7,160, take off 9,000, max permissible 11,290. Landing 9,750.

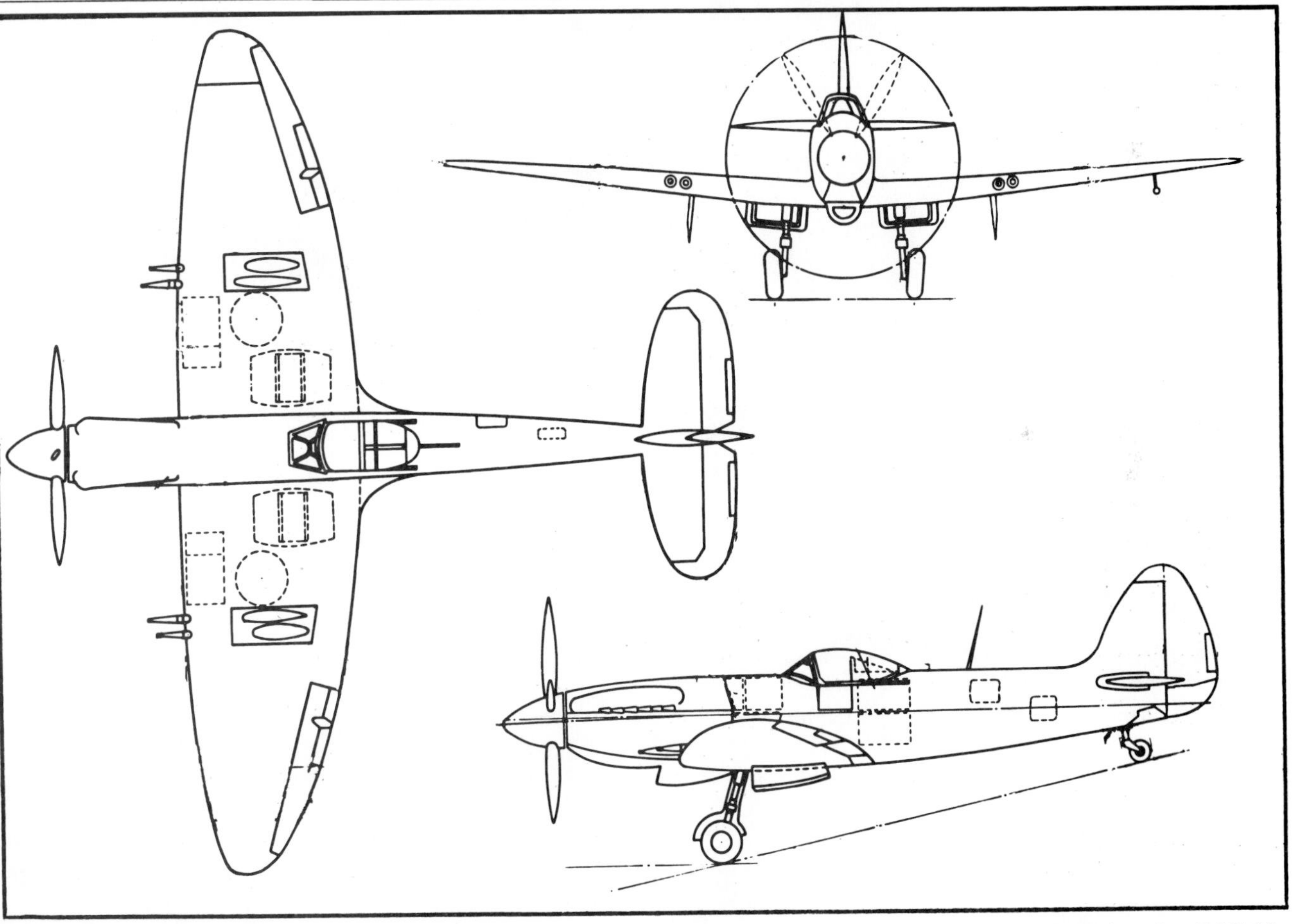

General arrangement, F Mk 22.

Rear view of an F Mk 22.

PK312 during maker's trials. It was fitted with Griffon 85 and contra props in September 1946 and the Spiteful type tail unit.

PK726 was ordered as an F22. It was the final Spitfire on the South Marston production line.

Hispano cannon loading bay.

PK542, carrying race number 100, taking part in the Daily Express Trophy Race with Quill as pilot.

Vickers-Armstrongs (Castle Bromwich) Ltd.

Contract No. B981687/39.

Eleventh order for 800 Spitfire Mk IX dated 2 June 1943. Built as Mks IX/22 between June 1944 and December 1945. Production transferred from Castle Bromwich, which closed down in December 1945, to Supermarine at South Marston. The following serials apply to Mk 22s built to this eleventh order. PK312-356, 369-412, 426-435, 481-525, 539-582, 594-635, 648-677, 680, 684 and 715. PK436-468 (33) cancelled. PK678-689 and 712-726 (27) completed as F24s.

Maintenance airframe; PK318 (6255M).

PK series all Griffon G61

PK312 CRD HPA 21-3-45 test flown Flt/Lt Loweth 10 mins VASM 18-4 mods VA HPA 27-4 del by Lt Underwood RN MoD BDn 30-11 metal elev instal 17.5 wghts and CG load; bomb instal tests. VA 5-9-46 G85, Rotol c/props instal, also Spiteful tail unit. VA HPA makers trls 6-2-47 (see page 488) CE SOC 18-4

PK313 CBAF test flown F/lt Johnson VASm 45 mins 10-3-45 CRD 17-3 del 33MU by F/O Ford ATA 13-9-46 VASM 18-9 con to proto F24 66gal, rear fus tank instal. FF as F.24 27-2-46 WAL 7-2-49 mods 9MU 4-11 29MU 11-1-50 NES 20-4-45 sold H Bath 30-10-56

PK314 CBAF test flown S/Ldr Morgan VASM 10 min 26-2-45 1st to RAF del 33MU by F/O Ford ATA 20-4-45 VASM 26-2-47 mods WAL 11-1-49 mods sold VA 9-2-50

PK315 CBAF 33MU 7-5-47 BDn 30-8 VASM del by S/Ldr Derry 14-10-46 mods 6MU 4-5-47 607S 13-1-49 FA FTR 4-12-49

PK316 CBAF 39MU 25-4-45 VASM 14-10-46 mods 6MU 16-1-47 502S 4-7-49 FAC3 4-6-50 ROS 226 OCU 5-3-51 102FRS 26-4 NES 16-6-53 sold scr MoS 19-2-54

PK317 CBAF 39MU 18-5-44 VASM 21-9-46 mods 6MU 4-11 603S 12-5-48 CAC 22-2-49 ROS FAAC 9-8 FAC3 21-5-51 VA refurb 25-7 NES 30-6-53 sold VA 4-2-54

PK318 CBAF CRD VA HPS 26-5-45 to 6255M RNeAF 31-1-47 SOC 11-11

PK319 CBAF 33MU 5-5-45 FAAC 12-6 ROS VA EA 3-10-46 mods 39MU 25-10 VA KEE 25-11-47 39MU 4-12 sold VA 22-12-49

PK320 CRD HPA G74 instal 19-5-45 BDn Oct'46 trls with MkIX Series 2 RP instal and other armament VA APA. Hand trls with asymetric RP load VASM 30-5-47 mods G61 instal 6MU 14-7-47 614S 27-7-48 AGT Gat refurb 11-1-51 9MU 17-7-52 NES 30-6-53 sold VA 4-2-54

PK321 CBAF 33MU 12-5-45 VA KEE 3-6-46 mods 33MU 11-11 mods 13-4-49 9MU 8-12 602S 25-5-50 FAC2 9-12 recat 3 ROS NES 16-6-53 sold Scottish Clover Industries 3-3-54

PK322 CBAF 33MU 20-5-45 VA KEE 29-5-46 mods 611S 8-2-49 FA scr 11-6-50 SOC 28-6

PK323 CBAF HAL 10-6-45 29MU 11-2-46 VA EA 15-7 33MU 4-10 WAL 14-1-49 mods 9MU 12-10 sold VA 9-2-50

PK324 CBAF 39MU 19-6-45 VA KEE 10-9-46 mods & con 33MU 26-11 610S 10-3-49 29MU 31-8-51 NES 30-6-53 sold scr 21-5-54

PK325 CBAF 33MU 5-7-45 VA KEE mods 13-8-46 6MU 16-1-47 608S 21-3-49 RCMSU 31-3 602S 30-9-50 AGT Gat refurb 29MU 5-6-51 NES 30-6-53 sold scr MoS 9-4-54

PK326 CBAF 33MU VASM 31-5-46 VA EA 4-6 33MU 14-8 Pers 26-11-47 ME 137MU storage 11-12 73S Takali 29-1-48 ret UK 14-10 CAC ROS 11-11 SRAF 19-12-51

PK327 CBAF 39MU 5-7-45 VASM 16-9-46 mods VA KEE 27-11-47 39MU 3-12 sold VA 29-12-49

PK328 CBAF 39MU 14-7-45 VA KEE 28-10-47 mods test flown S/Ldr Derry 504S 10-6-48 603S 25-1-50 222S 18-7 102FRS 14-9-51 NES 30-6-53 sold scrap MoS 27-8-54

PK329 39MU 13-7-45 VA KEE 29-4-47 mods 600S 30-9-48 615S 27-4-50 AGT Gatwick refurb 3-2-51 29MU NES 30-6-53 sold scr MoS 9-4-54

PK330 CBAF 33MU 5-7-45 VASM 18-6-46 mods 33MU 26-9-46 Pers 26-11-47 ME 137MU storage 29-1-48 ret UK 21-12 SRAF 25-3-51

PK331 CBAF 39MU 26-6-45 VA KEE 31-10-46 mods & con 613S 21-3-49 102FRS 30-4-51 FAC4 20-7 ROS NES 16-6-53 sold J G Will

PK332 33MU 5-7-45 VA KEE 29-5-46 33MU 10-9 WAL 17-3-49 mods NES 16-6-53 sold VA 4-2-54

PK333 M266 CBAF 30-8-45 VASM 21-3-47 mods & con 608S 8-7-48 RCMSU 25-8 C4R 15-12-49 VA recat 5(C) 17-3-53

PK334 33MU 21-7-45 VA KEE 1-7-46 mods 607S 13-1-49 RCMSU 102FRS 20-6-51 C3R ROS 27-10 NES 16-6-53 sold scr 8-9-54

PK335 33MU 5-7-45 VASM 23-5-46 VA EA 14-6 607S 13-1-49 AGT Gat refurb 10-7 NES 16-6-53 sold J G Will 20-4-54

PK336 33MU 28-7-45 VASM 20-5-46 VA EA 18-6 WAL 17-1-40 mods NES 16-6-53 sold E Smelt 14-6-54

PK337 39MU 5-7-45 VA KEE 21-4-47 mods 608S 21-6-48 613S 30-6-50 AGT Gat refurb 4-3-51 45MU 28-11 FA3R 6-12 4FPP cd on f/f to 45MU at 25MU 18-12 sold VA 5-5-53

PK338 33MU 22-7-45 VA EA 18-6-46 WAL 17-3-49 mods 9MU 6-4-50 Farn 16-1-51 trls with Beaufighter NT913 towing target sleeve AGT Gat refurb 17-9 NES 16-6-53 sold VA 4-2-54

PK339 33MU 24-7-45 VA KEE 3-7-46 mods 613S 30-12-48 AGT Gat refurb 5-3-51 45MU 28-11 NES 16-6-53 sold scr MoS 19-2-54

PK340 39MU 22-8-45 VA STN 14-4-47 mods 608S 3-7-48 613S 22-8-50 102FRS 2-5-51 NES 16-6-53 sold scrap MoS 21-4-54

PK341 33MU 6-9-45 VA KEE 16-4-47 mods 603S 15-4-48 C5A 7-9-49 ROS NES 16-6-53 sold J G Will 24-5-54

PK342 39MU 3-8-45 VA KEE 6-5-47 mods 603S 15-4-48 AGT Gat refurb 26-7-51 NES 16-6-53 sold scr J G Will 20-4-54

PK343 33MU 26-7-45 VA EA 11-7-46 33MU 1-10 GACB 9-11 SOC kdn 2-5-47

PK344 33MU 3-8-45 VA KEE 31-12-46 mods 6MU 16-1-47 SRAF 4-12-51 FA scr 7-12

PK345 33MU 3-8-45 VA EA 18-6-46 33MU 10-9 WAL 14-4-49 mods 9MU 6-6-50 NES 16-6-53 sold VA 4-2-54

PK346 39MU 11-8-45 VASM 29-10-46 mods & con 613S 30-12-48 FA scr 21-7-50

PK347 33MU 14-8-46 VA EA 16-8-46 mods 102FRS 31-7-51 NES 16-6-53 sold J G Will 24-5-54

PK348 33MU 1-8-45 VA EA 29-6-46 Pers 14-1-47 ME 137MU 10-6-48 ret UK 30-12 sold VA 27-4-53

PK349 33MU 21-7-45 VA EA 20-6-46 602S 14-10-48 ops to trng 28-4-49 C3R 19-10 602S 18-7-50 NES 16-6-53 sold scr 8-9-54

PK350 33MU 3-8-45 VA EA 18-6-46 Pers 15-7-47 ME 31-7 ret UK 28-10-48 SRAF 25-3-51 SR64. Crashed 26-3-82, parts survive.

PK351 33MU 3-8-45 VA KEE 12-7-46 mods & con 504S 16-3-49 408S 15-12 AGT Gat refurb 21-2-51 NEA 16-6-53 sold scr MoS 13-4-54

PK352 33MU 14-8-45 VA KEE 16-9-46 WAL 13-1-49 mods 29MU 12-9-49 NEA 16-6-53 sold scr MoS 9-4-54

PK353 33MU 28-7-45 VA KEE 8-7-46 mods & con 8-7-46 613S 6-1-49 RCMSU 25-8 NEA 16-6-53 sold scr MoS 13-4-54

PK354 39MU 27-8-45 VA KEE 17-4-47 mods 603S 13-5-48 FAAC 30-8 ROS C3R 26-4-50 ROS AGT VA 31-7-51 NES 16-6-53 sold VA 4-2-54

PK355 39MU 3-8-45 VASM 10-10-46 mods test flown Lithgow SOD SRAF 25-3-51 SR65 extant Harare.

PK356 39MU 3-8-45 VASM 9-10-46 mods WAL 13-1-49 mods sold VA 23-2-50

PK369 33MU 3-9-45 VASM 16-1-47 mods 602S 14-10-48 ops to trng 28-4-49 FACA 16-6 ROS AGT Gat refurb 28-2-51 NES 16-6-53 rts 6-10-54

PK370 39MU 10-8-45 VA KEE 5-12-46 VA KEE 5-12-46 mods SRAF 19-12-51

PK371 39MU 30-8-45 VASM 9-12-46 mods WAL 11-4-49 mods 102FRS 31-5-51 NES 16-6-53 sold J G Will 24-5-54

PK372 39MU 3-8-45 VA KEE 22-4-47 mods 615S 9-9-48 FACE 27-3-49 scr 5-5

PK373 CBAF 39MU 3-8-45 VA KEE 5-12-46 moids 502S 28-10-48 102FRS 31-7-51 NES 16-6-53 sold scrap MoS 9-8-54

PK374 CBAF 33MU 3-9-45 VA KEE 16-9-46 mods sold VA 8-12-49

PK375 CBAF 33MU 13-8-45 VA EA 13-9-46 mods & con 102FRS 19-4-51 FA3R 15-8 ROS NEA 16-6-53 sold J G Will 24-5-54

PK376 CBAF 3-9-45 VA EA 12-9-46 mods & con 614S 12-8-48 FAAC 28-4-49 ROS RCMSU 8-8 FAAC 18-8 ROS FA3R recat 4R 614S 18-1-50 FA3R 15-8 recat 5(C) 2-7-51

PK377 CBAF 39MU 27-8-45 VA SM 29-10-46 mods & con WAL 16-6-48 mods 102FRS 19-4-51 NES 16-6-53 sold J. G. Will 24-5-54

PK378 39MU 11-8-45 VA EA 5-7-46 WAL 21-3-49 mods VA 9-4-52 C3R 22-7 ROS NES 16-6-53 sold VA 6-3-54

PK379 CBAF 33MU 23-8-45 VA KEE 19-12-46 mods WAL 16-3-49 mods NES 16-6-53 sold VA 4-2-54

PK380 CBAF 27-8-45 VA EA 11-6-46 Pers 24-11-47 ME 137MU storage 8-1-48 73S Takali Malta 11-3 FAAC 20-9 ret UK 31-3-49 VA repair 25-8 NES 16-6-53 sold R. J. Coley 9-11-54

PK381 39MU 30-8-45 VA KEE 6-9-46 mods 611S 8-2-49 FAAC 3-5-49 ROS AGT VA refurb 8-5-52 NES 16-6-53 sold VA 4-2-54

PK382 33MU 27-8-45 VA KEE 8-8-46 mods 610S 17-3-49 ops to trng 25-4 FACE 26-6

PK383 39MU 30-8-45 VA KEE 5-12-46 mods plus new prop to cure vibration WAL 23-3-49 mods NES 25-10-51 sold D Squire 24-2-53

PK384 39MU 2-1-46 VA KEE 1-12-47 mods 607S 21-1-49 FAAC 27-3 ROS NES 16-6-53 sold scr MoS 3-5-54

PK385 33MU 6-9-45 VA KEE 8-8-46 mods & con 610S 17-3-49 FAC3 scrap 21-5-50

PK386 39MU 2-9-45 VASM 29-10-46 mods & con 613S 15-12-48 FACB 5-2-49 VA 10-8 33MU 8-10-51 sold VA 27-4-53

PK387 39MU 27-8-45 VA KEE 9-8-46 mods WAL 28-4-49 mods NES 16-6-53 sold VA 4-2-54

PK388 39MU 31-8-45 VA KEE Oct 46 mods 502S 13-10-48 226 OCU 12-3-51 NES 16-6-53 RAF Old Sarum fire trls 24-5-54

PK389 33MU 8-9-45 VASM 26-2-47 mods 600S 17-9-48 615S 21-4-50 AGT Gat refurb 12-3-51 45MU 10-1-52 FA3R cd Haw del flt ROS 21-5-52 sold VA 5-5-53

PK390 39MU 6-9-45 VA EA 27-9-46 RAF Debden BoB 13-9-49 sold VA 21-12

PK391 39MU 8-9-45 VA KEE 15-5-46 Pers 13-11-47 ME 317MU storage 11-12 ret UK CBAF 29-6-49 NES 26-9-50 sold VA 4-2-54

PK392 39MU 8-9-45 VA KEE 7-10-47 mods 600S 22-9-48 615S 21-4-50 AGT refurb 26-1-51 NES 16-6-53 sold VA 4-2-54

PK393 39MU 26-6-45 VASM 10-12-46 mods new eng 607S 8-2-49 TAAC 24-4 ROS FA scr 20-8-52

PK394 33MU 7-6-45 VASM 16-1-47 mods 607S 25-1-49 FA FTR 24-6-50

PK395 39MU 26-6-45 VA KEE 18-4-47 mods 504S 1-6-48 602S 17-1-50 AGT Gatwick refurb 23-2-51 NES 16-6-53 sold J. G. Will 24-5-54

PK396 33MU 26-6-45 VA KEE 8-7-46 mods & con 603S 12-5-48 FA3R 14-7-50 603S 23-9 AST NES 16-6-53 sold scrap MoS 26-5-54

PK397 33MU 19-7-45 VA EA 21-6-46 Pers 13-10-47 ME 137MU 11-12 73S Ta Kali Malta 29-1-48 ret UK 12-10 NES 16-6-53 sold Scottish Aero Industries 3-3-54

PK398 39MU 27-8-45 VA KEE 20-1-47 mods WAL 25-3-49 mods NES 16-6-53 sold VA 4-2-54

PK399 39MU 24-7-45 VA EA 28-3-47 mods 504S 1-6-48 TR-A C.3S/R 8-2-50 ROS recat 4R VA 102FRS 18-7-51 NES 16-6-53 sold scrap MoS 11-8-54

PK400 33MU 3-9-45 VA EA 8-8-46 mods 613S 14-12-48 FA3R 12-3-50 ROS Mar Cam refurb 25-2-51 NES 16-6-53 sold VA 4-2-54

PK401 33MU 5-8-45 VA EA 3-10-46 mods & con SRAF 19-12-51

PK402 39MU 3-8-45 VASM 18-12-46 mods 502S 11-10-48 226 OCU 9-3-51 AGT VA refurb 9-7 NES 16-6-53 sold J G Will 24-5-54

PK403 33MU 27-8-45 VA EA 15-8-46 mods & con 614S 28-7-48 FAAC 18-9-49 recat E scr 28-9-49

PK404 39MU 6-9-45 VASM 13-3-47 mods 608S 22-7-48 33MU 22-1-51 NES 16-6-53 RAF Old Sarum fire trls 31-5-54

PK405 39MU 23-8-45 VA EA 8-8-46 mods 600S 22-9-48 FACA 25-10 610S 1-6-50 NES 16-6-53 sold scr MoS 3-5-54

PK406 39MU 30-8-45 VA EA 8-8-46 mods 613S 5-11-48 102FRS 15-4-51 NES 16-6-53 sold scr J G Will 24-5-54

PK407 39MU 22-8-45 VA STN 11-4-47 mods 608S 22-7-48 Op Sq 1-6-50 602S 8-9 AGT Gatwick refurb 20-2-51 NES 16-6-53 sold scr 8-9-54

PK408 33MU 3-9-45 VA EA 3-10-46 mods & con BDn 5-2-47 trls with three 500lb bombs under fus & wngs VA 8-9-48 trls fuel syst 6MU 11-1-49 SRAF 25-3-51

PK409 39MU 30-8-45 VASM 9-1-47 mods & con 615S 8-12-48 AGT Gat refurb 9-2-51 NES 16-6-53 sold VA 4-2-54

PK410 39MU 31-8-45 VA KEE 17-1-47 mods & con 614S 1-9-48 AGT Gat refurb 6-2-51 NES 16-6-53 sold scr MoS 21-4-54

PK411 33MU 6-9-45 VA KEE 15-4-47 603S 15-4-48 C3R 12-8-48 ROS AGT VA refurb 18-7-51 NES 16-6-53 sold VA 4-2-54

PK412 39MU 6-9-45 VA KEE 16-8-46 mods 33MU 17-12-46 WAL 24-3-49 mods NES 16-6-53 sold VA 4-2-54

PK426 39MU 6-9-45 VA KEE 27-5-46 33MU 4-10 WAL 26-3-49 mods 102FRS 24-4-51 FA3R 2-7 ROS NES 16-6-53 sold J G Will 24-5-54

PK427 39MU 25-9-45 VA KEE 7-10-47 mods 613S 5-11-48 C3(R) 17-7-50 AGT VA refurb 20-3-51 NES 16-5-53 sold scr MoS 19-2-54

PK428 33MU 6-9-45 VA KEE 16-4-47 mods VA Chil 2-1-48 trls to cure elev instability 603S 5-5-48 ROS 22-2-49 FA3R 22-2-51 NES 16-6-53 sold scr MoS 26-5-54

PK429 33MU 27-9-45 VA EA 7-10-46 mods & con 4RS 15-9-49 102FRS 16-4-51 NES 16-6-53 sold scrap 6-9-54

PK430 33MU 18-10-45 VA EA 8-8-46 mods & con to F24 610S 17-3-49 102FRS 30-4-51 FA5(S) 6-7-51

PK431 33MU 18-10-45 VASM 19-3-47 mods & con 33MU 23-6-47 WAL 29-4-49 mods 102FRS 1-5-51 NES 16-6-53 sold J G Will 24-5-54

PK432 33MU 25-9-45 VA EA 12-9-46 mods & con SRAF 19-12-51

PK433 39MU 27-9-45 VA EA 30-4-47 mods & con 603S 18-5-48 AGT VA refurb 18-7-51 NES 16-6-53 sold J G Will 24-5-54

PK434 39MU 1-10-45 VA KEE 13-9-46 mods & con WAL 10-1-49 mods 614S 27-10 FA3R 24-7-50 ROS NES 16-6-53 sold L Met 1-10-54

PK435 39MU 3-10-45 VA KEE 18-6-46 mods 504S 11-5-48 cd/ld Bentwaters CE 4-9 sold VA 7-12-49

PK481 33MU 3-9-45 VA EA 10-12-47 mods 611S 11-2-49 AGT Gatwick refurb 16-6-51 CS(A) 19-8-52 free loan for 6 months trls with VA 34mm gun R.A.E. firing trls 16-12-52 dam eng fail 5-5-53 5MU 22-7-53 C3R VA 29-5-53 last official flt of Spit at Farn Mr Morgan (VA) took off at 14.40hrs for Chil NEA 19-8-53 sold RAFA Brighton 15-9-55 extant Bull Creek, Perth, Australia

PK482 33MU 31-8-45 VA KEE 5-11-46 mods & con SRAF 7-12-51 FAC(5) 16-12 cd by SRAF pilot

PK483 39MU 31-8-45 VA KEE 16-1-47 mods & con 502S 30-8-48 FA scrap 23-4-50

PK484 39MU 12-9-45 VA KEE 5-5-47 mods sold VA 7-12-49

PK485 33MU 5-9-45 VA EA 17-10-46 mods & con 611S 28-2-49 AGT Gat refurb 16-6-51 NES 16-6-53 sold scr MoS 19-2-54

PK486 33MU 5-9-45 VA KEE 8-8-46 mods 504S 4-6-48 VA C4R 30-3-51 recat 5C 18-3-53

PK487 33MU 31-8-45 VASM 9-10-46 mods & con 15-3-49 NES 16-6-53 sold VA 4-2-54

PK488 33MU 25-9-45 VA KEE 16-4-47 mods 502S 8-10-48 FACB 25-6-49 recat E 16-7

PK489 flown 6MU Brize Norton to East Lithgow 4-1-50

PK490 39MU 31-8-45 VA EA 31-7-46 WAL 18-3-49 mods NES 16-6-53 sold VA 4-2-54

PK491 39MU 15-9-45 VA KEE 6-5-47 mods 614S 9-8-48 607S 4-9-50 102FRS 14-6-51 NES 16-6-53 sold J G Will 24-5-54

PK492 33MU 5-9-45 VA EA 7-10 mods & con WAL 27-4-49 mods NES 16-6-53 sold VA 4-2-54

PK493 33MU 6-9-45 VA KEE 16-6-46 502S 13-10-48 AGT VA refurb 27-2-51 NES 16-6-52 sold J G Will 24-5-54

PK494 39MU 6-9-45 VA KEE 9-9-46 mods SRAF 19-12-51

PK495 39MU 12-9-45 VA KEE 22-4-47 mods 504S 5-5-48 R-RH FAAC 9-4-49 Farn from Ben 12-9-50 replacement for PK513 (cd Jly'50) on anti-G trls BDn 8-2-51 instruments presentation. Apl'51 I.F.F. trls FA3R 10--51 ROS Sch of Aviation Farn 31-5-52 NES 16-6-53 sold scrap 8-9-54

PK496 33MU 17-9-45 VA EA 5-12-46 mods & con 610S 8-4-49 ops to trng 25-4 NES 16-6-53 sold scr MoS 21-4-54

PK497 33MU 25-9-45 VA EA 5-11-46 mods & con 504S Hucknall 21-5-48 FAAC 29-8 ROS NES 16-6-53 RAF Old Sarum firing trls 24-5-54

PK498 33MU 11-9-45 VASM 16-10-46 mods & con 607S 28-1-49 FA scr 3-9-50

PK499 33MU 25-9-45 VA KEE 29-5-46 mods 502S 27-8-48 103FRS 27-4-51 NES 16-6-53 sold scr MoS 3-5-54

PK500 39MU 12-9-45 VA KEE 5-5-47 mods 614S 13-8-48 AGT Gat 18-1-50 NES 16-6-53 sold VA 4-2-54

PK501 33MU 17-9-45 VA KEE 15-4-47 mods 614S 9-8-48 607S 22-9-50 NES 16-6-53 sold scr MoS 21-5-54

PK502 39MU 19-9-45 VA KEE 22-4-47 mods 39MU 7-6-48 sold VA 16-12-49

PK503 39MU 19-9-45 VA EA 11-4-47 mods 20MU 23-10-51 NES 16-6-53 sold scrap MoS 3-5-54

PK504 33MU 7-9-45 VA KEE 15-4-47 mods e/fd test flt Flt Lt Colq f/ld East new eng 9-12 603S 5-5-48 FAAC 2-6 ROS NEA 16-2-53 sold VA 20-4-53

PK505 39MU 18-9-45 VASM 20-1-47 mods test flown S/Ldr Derry 30-3-47 615S 10-12-48 AGT Gat refurb 13-2-51 NES 16-6-53 sold R J Coley 25-8-54

PK506 39MU 12-9-45 VA KEE 15-4-47 mods 504S 16-6-48 SRAF 25-3-51

PK507 33MU 17-9-45 VA KEE 16-4-47 mods & con 20MU 24-10-51 NES 16-6-53 sold scr MoS 9-4-54

PK508 33MU 17-9-45 VASM 4-3-47 mods & con 610S 8-4-49 NES 16-6-53 sold R J Coley 25-8-54

PK509 39MU 21-9-45 VA KEE 8-10-47 mods sold VA 21-12-49

PK510 33MU 17-9-45 VA EA 4-10-46 mods & con 610S 17-3-49 NES 16-6-53 sold En/RM 19-6-56

PK511 39MU 1-10-45 VA KEE 27-5-46 33MU 4-10 WAL 22-3-49 mods 610S 12-6-50 NES 16-6-53 sold scr MoS 26-8-54

PK512 33MU 25-9-45 VA EA 8-8 mods & con sold VA 7-12-49

PK513 33MU 25-9-45 VA KEE 16-1-47 mods & con 33MU 18-7-47 Farn Sep'48 target towing duties with SM970 RAF Andover 21-9 Farn Aug'49 instrument presentation and anti-G trls Several flts aborted due to faulty equip MHth Oct'50 for anti-G and crash proof fuel tank trls cd/ld Abingdon Berks during anti-G trl C3R 24-7-50 replaced by PK495 recat scr 7-9

PK514 33MU 17-9-45 VA KEE 9-9-46 mods SRAF 25-3-51

Nine F22s of No 613 Squadron with PK533 in foreground.

PK524 39MU 21-9-45 VA KEE 2-10-47 mods sold VA 22-12

PK525 33MU 27-9-45 VA KEE 1-5-47 VA Chil 2-1-48 trls to cure elev instability 603S 31-3-48 AGT Gat refurb 1-9-51 NES 16-6-53 sold J G Will 24-5-54

PK539 39MU 27-9-45 VA KEE 27-5-46 603S 8-4-49 NES 20-7-51 sold scr MoS 27-4-54

PK540 33MU 10-10-45 VA 5-11-46 mods & con 611S 16-2-49 FA3R 3-4-50 ROS NES 16-6-53 sold VA 4-2-54

PK541 33MU 30-9-45 VA 8-7-46 mods & con sold VA 22-10-49

PK542 39MU 1-10-45 VA STN 11-4-47 mods 614S 29-7-48 AGT Gat refurb 19-1-51 fuel cons trls with old tanks 17-5 flown in Daily Express Trophy race by Quill 22-5 sold VA 30-4-53

PK543 39MU 27-9-45 VA KEE 24-4-47 mods 608S 21-6-48 FAAC 27-6-49 AGT Gat refurb 4-3-51 NES 16-6-53 sold J G Will 20-4-54

PK544 39MU 27-9-45 Pers 13-11-47 ME 28-11 73S Takali 31-12 ret UK 14-10-48 CB non-fly 22-3-49 NES 16-6-53 sold En/RM 7-7-54

PK545 33MU 27-9-45 VASM 26-11-46 mods & con WAL 25-4-48 mods cancel scr 16-2-50

PK546 39MU 1-10-45 VA KEE 20-1-47 mods & con AM PK3 Squires Gate 17-6-47 615S 26-11-48 AGT Gat refurb 12-3-51 NES 16-6-53 sold scr MoS 19-2-54

PK547 VA HPA 11-12-45 BDn 14-12 full gunnery acceptance trls Suspended due to misaligned ammo belts. Comp trls with VN329 VA 1-10-46 mods & con 608S 22-7-48 602S 3-6-50 NES 16-6-53 sold VA 4-2-54

PK548 33MU 27-98-45 VASM 20-5-46 VA EA 25-6 Pers 24-11-47 ME 11-12 137MU storage ret UK 31-3-49 SRAF 19-12-51

PK549 39MU 28-9-45 VA 11-9-46 mods WAL 20-4-49 mods 102FRS 23-4-51 NEA 16-2-53 sold VA 20-4

PK550 33MU 8-10-45 VA 19-9-46 mods & con 615S 7-5-49 AGT Gat refurb 10-3-51 NES 16-6-53 sold VA 4-2-54

PK551 33MU 8-10-45 VASM 20-1-47 mods & con WAL 8-4-49 mods NES 16-6-53 sold VA 4-2-54

PK552 39MU 1-10-45 VCA EA 17-6-46 611S 11-2-49 TACA 1-5 VA 102FRS 11-6-51 NES 16-6-53 sold J G Will 24-5-54

PK553 39MU 28-9-45 VA KEE 23-4-47 mods 607S 13-1-49 AGT Gat refurb 5-6-51 NES 16-6-53 sold J G Will 24-5-54

PK554 33MU 8-10-45 VA 19-9-46 mods 610S 14-7-49 FAAC 25-7 ROS FA4R 23-4-50 VA recat 5(C) 17-3-55

PK555 33MU 10-10-45 VASM 27-5-46 mods & con Pers 14-11-47 ME 27-11 73S Ta Kali 29-1-48 bomb carr detatched ld badly dam 27-8 recat E SOC 28-10

PK556 39MU 1-10-45 VA EA 11-6-46 Pers 13-11-47 ME 30-11 73S Ta Kali 29-1-48 607S 19-7-50 NES 16-6-53 sold scr MoS 21-4-54

PK557 33MU 8-10-45 VA EA 5-12-46 mods 607S 11-2-49 NES 16-6-53 sold scr MoS 13-4-54

PK558 39MU 1-10-45 VA KEE 27-5-46 NEA 12-2-53 sold D Squire 24-2

PK559 33MU 8-10-45 VA EA 6-12-46 mods & con WAL 26-4-49 mods NES 16-6-53 sold VA 4-2-54

PK560 39MU 10-10-45 VA KEE 16-5-46 602S 7-10-48 ops to trng 28-4-49 C3R 22-2-51 ROS NES 16-6-53 sold J G Will 25-5-54

PK561 33MU 8-10-45 VA EA 10-4-47 mods 502S 13-10-48 226 OCU 5-3-51 102FRS 24-4 NES 16-6-53 sold J G Will 24-5-54

PK562 39MU 1-10-45 VASM 9-1-47 mods & con 615S 6-9-48 FACB 14-11 sold VA 20-12-49

PK563 33MU 8-10-45 VA 18-9-46 mods 500S 29-5-48 FACB 2-11 ROS 613S 9-5-49 AGT Gat refurb 4-3-51 NES 16-6-53 sold scr MoS 27-8-54

PK564 39MU 19-10-45 VA KEE 13-5-46 613S 23-5-50 AGT Gat refurb 6-3-51 NES 16-6-53 sold scr MoS 19-2-54

PK565 33MU 8-10-45 VASM 16-10-46 mods & con 102FRS 20-4-51 NES 16-6-53 sold J G Will 25-5-54

PK566 33MU 8-10-45 VA EA 31-7-46 502S 22-10-48 FA3R 15-6-50 ROS AGT Gat refurb 17-2-51 NES 16-6-53 sold Scottish Aero Industries 3-3-54

PK567 33MU 13-10-45 VA EA 6-12-46 mods 502S 18-10-48 226 OCU 5-3-51 102FRS 24-4-51 NES 16-6-53 sold J G Will 24-5-54

PK568 33MU 10-10-45 VA 5-11-46 mods & con 610S 17-3-49 FA3R 29-5-50 Helliwells Ltd 7-3-52 C4R recat 5(C) 4-3-53

PK513 (above) had a varied trials life, including target towing duties at RAE Farnborough. PK523 (right) served at Thornaby with No 603 Squadron, RAuxAF.

PK515 VASM 29-11-46 con to F24 completed 29-1-47 33MU 3-3-47 WAL 10-3-49 mods NEA 14-12-54 sold scr E Smelt 13-6-56

PK516 33MU 27-9-45 VASM 4-3-47 mods & con WAL 14-3-49 mods sold VA 9-2-50

PK517 39MU 27-9-45 VA KEE 9-10-47 mods 39MU 16-7-48 sold VA 16-12-49

PK518 33MU 25-9-45 VASM 27-5-46 VA EA 12-6 Pers 24-11-47 ME 30-11 137MU 73S Takali 31-12 ret UK 21-2-49 NES 16-6-53 RAF Old Sarum firing trls 1-6-54

PK519 39MU 21-9-45 VA KEE 2-10-47 mods 615S 12-8-49 AGT Gat refurb 16-2-51 NES 16-6-53 RAF Old Sarum firing trls 1-6-54

PK520 39MU 19-9-45 VA KEE 16-1-47 mods & con 9MU 23-7-47 FAAC 16-9-48 ROS 611S 11-8-49 NES 16-6-53 sold En/RM 8-7-54

PK521 33MU 25-9-45 VA KEE 2-10-46 mods & con 611S 28-2-49 FACE 3-7 scr

PK522 33MU 27-9-45 VASM 20-5-46 NES 16-6-53 sold R J Coley 8-11-54

PK523 33MU 25-9-45 VA 5-11-46 mods & con 608S 28-5-49 AGT Gat refurb 4-6-51 NES 16-6-53 sold VA 16-2-54

PK569 33MU 10-10-45 VA KEE 13-8-46 mods & con 516S 31-8-48 AGT Gat refurb 5-3-51 NES 16-6-53 sold J G Will 25-5-54

PK570 33MU 10-10-45 VA EA 24-10-46 mods & con 603S 31-[illegible] 48 FAAC 2-5 ROS AGT VA refurb 19-7-51 NES 16-6-53 sold J G Will 25-5-54

PK571 33MU 8-10-45 VA KEE 8-3-46 mods & con 603S 12-5-48 C3R 21-4-50 ROS FA3R 18-9-50 AGT VA refurb 19-7-51 NES 16-6-53 sold VA 4-2-54

PK572 33MU 10-10-45 VA EA 2-7-46 Pers 6-12-47 ME 9-2-48 73S Ta Kali 25-3 ret UK 14-10-48 SRAF 19-12-51

PK573 33MU 18-10-45 VA STN 17-12-47 mods 613S 26-10-48 FAC2 11-6-50 recat 3R AGT Gat refurb 6-2-51 NES 16-6-53 sold En/RM 28-6-56

PK574 33MU 10-10-45 VA EA 245-7-46 613S 21-12-48 102FRS 14-4-51 NES 16-6-53 sold J G Will 24-5-54

PK575 33MU 10-10-45 VASM 9-12-46 mods & con SRAF 25-3-51

PK576 33MU 18-10-45 VA EA 10-4-47 Pers 18-11-47 ME 137MU storage 11-12 ret UK 21-12-48 SRAF 25-3-51

PK577 39MU 15-10-45 VASM 14-10-46 mods & con 610S 17-3-49 NES 16-6-53 sold scr 8-9-54

PK578 39MU 15-10-45 VA KEWE 6-10-47 mods 602S 30-9-48 FAAC 19-12-48 ROS AGT VA refurb 21-9-51 sold VA 5-5-53

PK579 33MU 18-10-45 VASM 27-5-46 VA EA 7-6 610S 4-3-49 NES 16-6-53 sold scr MoS 14-6-54

PK580 29MU 4-1-46 VA KEE 17-7-465 mods 102FRS 16-4-51 FA3R 16-8 ROS NES 16-6-53 sold scr 8-9-54

PK581 33MU 22-10-45 VASM 20-1-47 mods & con 102FRS 1-5-51 NES 16-6-53 sold J G Will 24-5-54

PK582 33MU 8-11-45 VA 19-9-46 mods & con 607S 8-2-49 sold E Smelt 26-8-54

PK594 39MU 15-10-45 VASM 22-5-46 VA EA 13-6 Pers 13-11-47 ME 27-11 73S Ta Kali 8-1-48 ret UK 12-1-48 SRAF 19-12-51

PK595 33MU 8-11-45 VASM 20-1-47 mods & con 504S 18-6-48 607S 7-7-50 flew i/high gnd nr Lowther Castle Penrith 20-8-50 scr

PK596 33MU 8-11-45 VA EA 10-4-47 mods 613S 10-11-48 103FRS 16-6-51 NES 16-6-53 sold J G Will 25-5-54

PK597 33MU 18-10-45 VA 30-9-46 mods CAC 10-11-48 ROS HQ MC Com Sq 18-8-49 NES 16-6-53 scr 6-10-54

PK598 33MU 22-10-45 VASM 16-1-47 mods & con Pers 26-11 FACB 7-12 sold VA7-12-49

PK599 33MU 8-11-45 VASM 30-10-46 mods & con 613S 1 0-11-48 FAC 20-11

PK600 29MU 6-12-45 VASM 14-6-46 sold VA 20-12-49

PK601 33MU 18-10-45 VA EA 14-8-46 502S 12-10-48 C3R 28-10-50 ROS NES 16-6-53 sold J G Will 24-5-54

PK602 39MU 27-10-45 VA KEE 2-12-47 mods 607S 27-1-49 FA3R 31-3-50 recat 4R VA FA during air test 19-8 recat 5(C) 5-3-53

PK603 39MU 27-10-45 VA KEE 25-4-47 mods & con 607S 11-2-49 NES 16-6-53 sold scr MoS 3-5-54

PK604 39MU 13-12-45 VA KEE 24-4-47 mods Chil on short term loan 10-2-48 614S 18-8-48 AGT Gat refurb 17-4-51 sold VA 5-5-53

PK605 33MU 18-10-45 VA EA 5-12-46 mods & con 502S 17-4-47 AGT Gatwick refurb 6-6-51 NES 16-6-53 sold J G Will 24-5-54

PK606 33MU 8-11-45 VASM 4-3-47 mods & con 504S 1-6-48 FAAC 25-9 ROS RCMSU 21-5-49 611S 7-1-50 608S 22-4 NES 16-6-53 sold E Smelt 14-6-54

PK607 33MU 29-11-45 VASM 31-5-46 Pers 24-11-47 ME 30-11 73S Ta Kali 29-1-48 ret UK 28-10 NES 16-6-53 sold R J Coley 25-8-54

PK608 39MU 27-10-45 NES 16-6-53 sold R J Coley 17-2-56

PK609 33MU 22-10-45 VA KEE 28-11-46 mods 610S 23-3-49 102FRS 27-4-51 NES 16-6-53 sold J G Will 24-5-54

PK610 39MU 27-10-45 VA KEE 23-1-47 mods & con NEA 12-2-53 sold D Squire 26-53

PK611 39MU 27-10-45 VA KEE 16-1-47 mods & con Pers 27-11 ME 11-12 73S Ta Kali 29-1-48 ret UK 14-10 FACA 17-7-49 NES 16-6-53 sold R J Coley 25-8-54

PK612 39MU 27-10-45 VA KEE 22-1-47 mods & con Pers 18-11 ME 11-3-48 73S 29-4 ret UK 28-10 NES 16-6-53 sold scr 21-6-54

PK613 39MU 27-10-45 VA KEE 3-6-46 mods 607S 3-1-49 RCMSU 24-5 AGT Gat refurb 14-9-51 NES 16-6-53 sold scrap MoS 19-2-54

PK614 33MU 1-1-46 VASM 4-3-47 mods & con CFE 13-11 603S 12-4-48 FACE 6-3-49 scrap 19-5

PK615 33MU 29-11-45 VA KEE 16-9-46 mods 102FRS 3-5-51 NES 16-6-53 sold J G Will 28-5-54

PK616 33MU 17-12-45 VASM 26-11-46 mods & con NES 16-6-53 sold D Squire 24-2-54

PK617 39MU 27-10-45 VASM 20-1-47 mods & con 608S 9-7-48 FACE 13-2-49

PK618 33MU 3-1-46 VASM 16-1-47 mods & con; new prop instal to cure vibration 615S 8-12-48 FAAC 25-1-49 ROS AGT VA refurb 26-1-51 NES 16-6-53 sold scr 19-2-54

PK619 39MU 5-12-45 VA EA 1-4-47 mods 614S 18-8-48 AGT Gat refurb 24-4-51 sold VA 5-5-53

PK620 33MU 29-11-45 VA EA 29-7-46 VASM 17-4-47 new prop instal to cure vibration 502S 12-10-48 102FRS 27-4-51 NES 16-6-53 sold scr MoS 27-4-54

PK621 39MU 27-10-45 VA KEE 21-1-47 mods & con 509S Hucknall 12-5-48 602S 15-1-50 AGT Gat refurb 21-2-51 sold VA 4-5-53

PK622 33MU 19-12-45 VASM 16-1-47 mods & con 102FRS 30-4-51 NES 16-6-53 sold scr MoS 22-9-54

PK623 no record

PK542, this time with a different race number – see page 483.

PK656 of No 73 Squadron, Ta Kali 1948. Returned to UK in 1949 and sold as scrap 1954.

PK624 33MU 21-12-45 VA EA 5-12-46 mods & con 614S 25-8-48 AGT Gat refurb 17-1-51 NES 16-6-53 sold VA 4-2-54 extant RAF Abingdon RAU-T (8072M)

PK625 33MU 19-12-45 VA EA 22-12-47 mods SRAF 25-3-51

PK626 39MU 27-10-45 VA EA 17-6-46 NES 16-6-53 sold R J Coley 25-8-54

PK627 33MU 11-2-46 VASM 15-5 mods & con to F24 by RAF @ 32MU 28-1-47 WAL 30-3-49 mods NES 14-12-54 sold En/RM 28-6-56

PK628 33MU 19-12-45 VA EA 3-10-46 mods & con 610S 8-4-49 FAC2 25-4 recat 3R ROS NES 16-6-53 sold scr 21-6-56

PK629 33MU 29-11-45 VASM 23-5-46 615S 6-9-48 AGT VA refurb 26-1-51 NES 16-6-53 sold En/RM 19-6-56

PK630 39MU 18-12-45 VA STN 9-4-47 mods 608S 20-7-48 602S 12-9-50 NES 16-6-53 sold scrap 28-6-56

PK631 39MU 13-13-45 VA EA 26-3-47 mods & con 611S 9-5-49 RCMSU 3-6 AGT Gat refurb 16-6-53 sold J G Will 24-5-54

PK632 33MU 19-12-45 VA STN 12-9-46 mods & con 611S 11-2-49 NES 16-6-53 sold J G Will 24-5-54

PK633 33MU 19-12-45 VA KEE 16-9-46 mods & con f/ld Ramsbury 4-1-47 600S 11-5-49 2ANS Thorney Isle 10-10-51 NES 16-6-53 sold scr MoS 29-7-54

PK634 39MU 31-10-45 VASM 22-1-47 mods & con 6MU 4-5-47 hit trees fly low bad visibility cd pilot kld nr BNn CE 3-12-48 SOC

PK635 33MU 17-12-45 VASM 9-12-46 mods HQ MC Com Flt 10-8-49 NES 16-6-53 slod scrap MoS 26-8-54

PK648 39MU 4-1-46 VASM 3-3-47 mods & con 614S 22-7-48 C3R 2-1-50 ROS recat 4R VA 30-3-51 react 5(C) 5-12-52

PK649 33MU 20-12-45 VASM 16-1-47 mods & con SRAF 19-12-51

PK650 33MU 3-1-46 VASM 7-10-46 mods & con 611S 16-2-49 AGT Gat refurb 18-7-51 sold VA 5-5-53

PK651 33MU 30-12-45 VASM 26-2-47 mods & con 608S 11-6-48 FAAC 17-10 ROS 602S 23-6-49 102FRS 1-5-51 NES 16-6-53 sold R J Coley 25-8-54

PK652 33MU 20-12-45 VA KEE 16-9-46 mods & con 611S 8-2-49 AGT Gat refurb 16-6-51 sold VA 24-4-53

PK653 33MU 20-12-45 VA EA 11-4-47 mods 608S 29-6-48 FA scr 25-3-50

PK654 39MU 13-12-45 VA EA 22-7-46 500S 27-5-48 FAAC 18-6 ROS 613S 6-11 FAC5 17-7-50

PK655 39MU 13-12-45 VASM 3-4-47 mods NEA 16-2-53 sold D Squire 24-2

PK656 29MU 6-12-45 VA EA 20-6-46 Pers 1-10-47 ME 5-1-48 73S Ta Kali 25-12 ret UK 14-10-49 NES 16-6-53 sold scr 21-6-54

PK657 39MU 13-12-45 VA KEE 24-1-47 mods & con 504S 15-6-48 607S 15-12 102FRS 15-6-51 FA3R ROS 15-8-51 NES 16-6-53 sold J G Will 22-4-54

PK658 39MU 3-12-45 VASM 3-3-47 mods & con C.BE Marsham 28-8 NEA 12-2-53 sold D Squire 26-2-58

PK659 29MU 6-12-45 VA WIN 6-6-46 611S 25-2-49 NES 16-6-53 sold scr 8-9-54

PK660 33MU 20-12-45 VA EA 17-12-46 mods & con 615S 26-11-48 FAAC 26-3-49 ROS AGT Gat refurb 1-3-51 sold VA 24-4-53

PK661 33MU 1-1-46 VA KEE 28-11 610S 8-6-48 NES 16-6-53 sold scr MoS 13-4-54

PK662 29MU 6-12-45 VA WIN 6-6-46 Pers 7-7-47 ME 31-7 TAAC Ajaccio Corsica en route f/f UK 18-10-48 ROS NES 16-6-53 sold R J Coley 25-8-54

PK663 33MU 1-1-46 VASM 4-1-47 mods & con 4-1-47 SRAF 25-3-51

PK664 39MU 5-12-45 VASM 21-3-47 mods & con 615S 11-5-49 RCMSU 16-5 TAAC 29-8 AGT Gat refurb 2-2-51 NES 16-6-53 sold VA 4-2-54 (reported G85 & c/props) extant RAF Binbrook V6-B (as 7759M)

PK665 33MU 3-1-46 VA KEE 28-11 608S 15-7-48 610S 22-6-50 RAF Kenley scrap fire ftng demos 27-5-54

PK666 29MU 6-12-45 VASM 3-6-46 Comm 296 Malta 11-7-47 FAAC ff (1FU Pers) 18-7-47 recat E SOC scr 22-8

PK667 39MU 5-12-45 VA KEE 28-4-47 mods & con 614S 18-8-48 607S 4-9-50 NES 16-6-53 sold scrap MoS 3-5-54

PK668 29MU 6-12-45 VA KEE 12-7-46 102FRS 27-4-51 sold VA 5-5-43

PK669 33MU 20-12-45 VA KEE 26-11-46 611S 28-2-49 AGT Gat refurb 16-6-51 NES 16-6-53 sold Scottish Aero Industries 3-3-54

PK670 33MU 1-1-46 VASM 4-1-47 mods & con VA HPS new prop instal to cure vibration 17-4 600S 23-9-48 508S 28-4-50 502S 24-6-50 NES 16-6-53 sold scr 8-9-54

PK671 39MU 3-12-45 VASM 24-3-47 mods & con 504S 1-6-48 TRA 608S 17-2-50 618S 22-7 AGT Gat refurb 4-5-51 sold VA 24-4-53

PK672 29MU 27-12-45 VA KEE 11-7-47 mods & con VA KEE 9-1-47 SRAF 25-3-51

PK673 33MU 1-1-46 VASM 9-12 NES 16-6-53 sold R J Coley 8-11-54

PK674 29MU 6-12-45 VA WIN 6-6-46 Pers 14-11-47 ME 20-11 73S Ta Kali 29-1-48 ret UK 28-10 NES 16-6-53 sold J G Will 24-5-54

PK675 Prod test J Derry 19-5-47

PK676 33MU 3-1-46 VA KEE 18-7 mods 102FRS 24-8-51 NES 16-6-53 sold J G Will 24-5-54

PK677 29MU 11-2-46 VA KEE 10-5-46 con to F24 by RAF @ 32MU 28-1-47 WAL 1-2-49 mods NEA 4-12-54 sold H Bath 2-11-56

PK680 33MU 11-2-46 VA 31-10 mods & con to F24 by RAF @ 33MU 28-1-47 WAL 7-3-49 mods NEA 14-12-54 sold scr 17-5-56

PK684 VA HPA 11-2-46 VASM 27-5 G87 instal, mods & con to F24 by RAF @ 33MU 28-1-47 WAL 9-3-49 mods NEA 14-12-54 sold H Bath 17-5-56

PK715 29MU 11-2 46 VASM 16-5 mods & con to F24 by RAF @ 33MU 28-1-47 WAL 29-3-49 mods NEA 14-12-54 sold H Bath

SX549 proto F24 G65 (not to be counted in summary). Originally ordered as F21 proto Apl '44 with rear view red area fus and 24 volt electric system. Cancelled COAL 8-11-44 (DTD) sold MoS 8-10-45

THE STILLBORN VALIANT

"It became obvious from flight tests on two Spitfire IX aeroplanes that there is a large increase in drag at Mach numbers at which future Spitfire types taking advantage of engine development should operate. These tests, although carried out in a somewhat rough method, gave results which showed general agreement with calculations which had been made at an earlier date." Thus ran the opening paragraph of Supermarine Report Number 3612 of 8 December 1942 and as a result of these, and other tests, the Super Spitfire and Spiteful were to finally evolve. The report continued:–

"It was also realised that a considerable reduction in wing profile drag is possible by delaying the point of transition from laminar to turbulent flow as far aft as practicable on both surfaces. There is little doubt that the present production wing has transition at the leading edge, and even if the finish is improved it is only possible, by virtue of the particular velocity distribution, to get transition at about 25% on the top surface whilst on the lower surface the point of transition remains practically at the leading edge. This latter phenomenon is due to the NACA 2200 Series section being over-cambered for CLs at which the Spitfire operates under conditions of maximum speed. This produces a peak in the velocity distribution very near the leading edge on the lower surface, which is in turn associated with the point of transition. The problem of designing a wing of improved aerodynamic form which would give an increase in performance both at sea level and at altitudes was therefore investigated.

"The available information in connection with the design of laminar flow, or low-drag and high speed wings is still very largely in the research stage. To enable advantage to be taken of the latest data available the Aerodynamics Department of the National Physics Laboratory had agreed that the design of aerofoil sections should be carried out by S. R. Hughes of Supermarine at the NPL under the supervision of Dr S. Goldstein. The planform for production considerations should have two straight tapers and calculations made by the Supermarine Aerodynamics Department show a wing area of 210 sq ft and 35ft span should give the best all round performance. From our estimates of performance, based on two envelopes of engine power (stages A and C of the Griffon 61/Dev) the maximum speeds, etc, are as follows:–

	Stage A	Stage C
Auw (lb)	8,500	8,700
V max sea level (mph)	361	368
Aeroplane CL at SL	0.12	0.12
V max at 35,000ft (mph)	466	516
Aeroplane CL at 35,000ft	0.235	0.20

"We were required to design for the highest possible Mach number without sacrificing performance at lower altitudes. The thickness/chord ratio (13%) at the root end was determined by accommodation and structural requirements. To obtain the amount of space between the leading edge and 40% chord which was required to house the wheel, it was impossible to design a section which would have a slope on the velocity distribution if we were to keep the critical Mach number as high as possible. The aerofoil thus developed is in fact a high speed section and not correctly a laminar flow type".

The Supermarine drawing of the proposed wing revealed it to be similar to that eventually adopted for the Spiteful, except that the latter was a true laminar flow type and called the Type 371 wing. The Type 372, Spitfire F23, was to make use of an interim wing which was the normal production type raised by 2in at the leading edge for two purposes (1) to improve the pilot's view and (2) to increase speed without increasing overall drag or pitching movement appreciably. Tests of the new incidence setting were made on a scale model Spitfire in the Farnborough 11½ft × 8½ft closed jet wind tunnel at a wind speed of 180fps. The new wing was set at 1.5°, 3.5 and 4.5 to the fuselage datum, the wing being rotated about a point .338c behind the leading edge of the centre line chord. The finalised setting provided a maximum critical Mach number of .722, representing 496mph at 31,000ft.

The F23 lifted LE wing was discussed at RAE on 23 June 1944 and it was agreed that the reduction in drag due to movement of the transition point was small on the top surface, while on the lower the movement of transition was 12%, equivalent to a speed increase of 4mph @ 25,000ft. It was also agreed that the onset of shock waves on the under wing surface would be delayed and there would be some gains, but the magnitude could not be estimated. JG204, a Mk VIII, was flown with the modified wing installed and the results found to be disappointing. This may have been due to the wing profile for as a note (3934) of 18 October 1943 reveals:– "Progress on the new Spitfire wing. New leading edge ribs had been made at Supermarine and the wings forwarded to the Pressed Steel Company at Oxford for the fitting of skin plating. The expected gain in performance could not be obtained from JG204 with the modified wing, as it was not made close enough to the correct profile. But, it was worthwhile flight testing for measurement of transition points".

Deletion of the underwing radiators and substitution of the fuselage unit was actively considered and the scheme was tested at Farnborough on a ¼in scale model of the forthcoming

PP139, prototype for the Valiant. On the rear of this photograph is the caption:-'Modifications include pointed wings of 40ft 6in span; special fin and rudder. Plans were prepared for a 6x20mm wing. The F23 was for high altitude interception'. it reverted to F21 standards and ended its days on the scrap heap at Eastleigh.

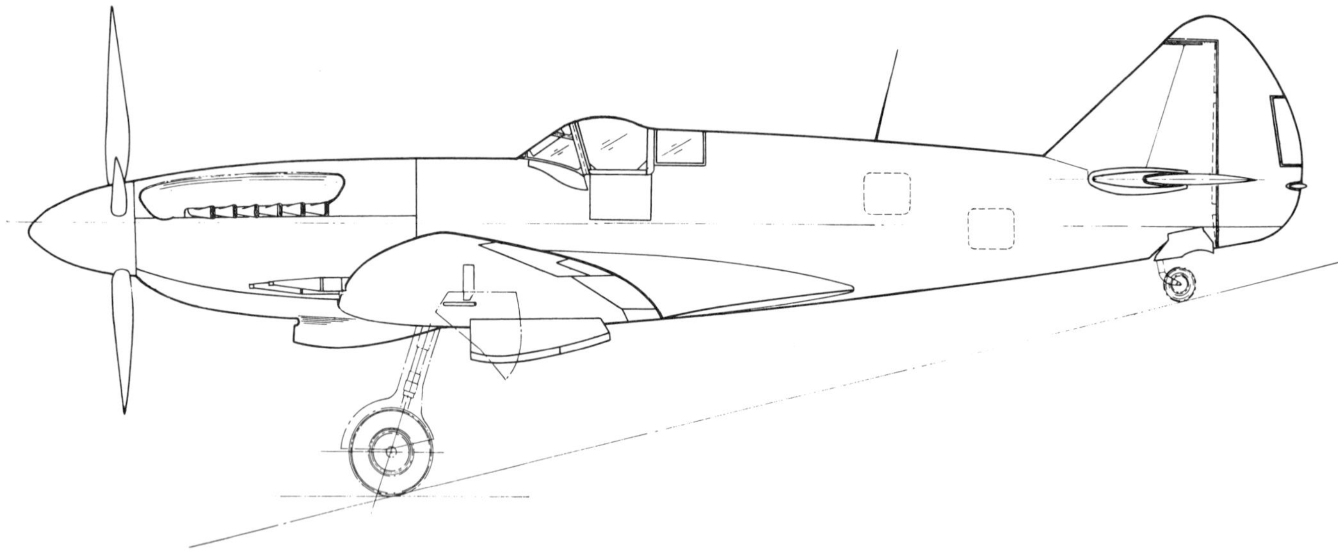

Only known drawing of the Valiant.

Supermarine F 1/43 (Spiteful). The conclusions reached were that the fixed entry duct would result in loss of performance and maximum rate of climb and level speed would suffer.

Further discussions at Supermarine and the RAE led to the decision to build a prototype F23 incorporating the revised, high speed wing but eventually the prototype F21 Victor, PP139 was used. The photographs depict PP139 in what is claimed to be the F23 configuration and it is interesting to note that the flying view shows the original, broad chord fin and rudder, while the ground view illustrates the same unit with increased area fin leading edge. If production had resulted from the prototype trials the F23 would have been known as the Supermarine Valiant. A decision was taken on this point at the Air Ministry on 2 February 1944, but by the time PP139 had made its initial flights in its new guise the Supermarine conversion F 1/43 prototype (NN664) had flown and the proposed F23 Valiant (Super Spitfire) faded into oblivion. A contract dated 23 October 1943 for 438 "laminar flow wing" LF VIII (F23) was subsequently cancelled.

The flight test reports on JG204 with the lifted LE wing make interesting reading, and they are reproduced below.

1-7-44 (Furlong). Handling at CG 7" aft. Aeroplane considered perfectly stable at the medium and lower altitudes. Further handling at 30,000ft and above necessary. Suggest aeroplane now goes to Boscombe Down.

6-7-44 (Furlong). Aeroplane has raised leading edge and 2° tailplane incidence. Handling carried out above 30,000ft. Dive recovery at these altitudes was satisfactory. Further trimming was carried out on the port aileron and the aeroplane is now perceptibly left wing low. It was delivered to Boscombe Down in this condition.

29-11-44 (Havercroft). Camera investigation of buffet and aileron snatch. Buffet started at 85 ASI; the aircraft is wallowing and slightly left wing low and it is possible that a little left aileron was applied. At 74 ASI the control column snatches smartly over to the right, the right wing dropping with the nose. Third run. Snatch occurred and control column held back. Right wing dropped smartly to an angle of 60-70° together with the nose until the aircraft was in a vertical attitude. Buffeting continued until the speed exceeded 87 ASI.

9-12-44 (Shea-Simmonds). Flown for the purpose of checking characteristics and behaviour at stall. With flaps and chassis raised there was no normal Spitfire buffetting as stall was approached, but at 81 ASI considerable aileron snatch developed which persisted as the control column was brought back. Tail buffett began just before the stall at 75-77 ASI, either wing and nose dropping sharply. With flaps and undercarriage down the stall was similar, less aileron snatch, with stall at 68-70 ASI. When gliding with flaps down there is a pronounced elevator hunt from 130-160 ASI. The elevator hunt and longitudinal instability at low speeds with flaps down is pronounced.

30-4-45 (Quill). Flown with two root spoilers and port wing tufted to check whether stall characteristics were altered. Tests with flaps and chassis up and down, and in both conditions the stall started at root, spreading out as far as the cannons. As the root stall reached the cannons the tip stalled and spread inwards until one third of the span of the aileron from the outboard end. The portion of wing in between remained unstalled until after landing speed was reached. This meant that the portion of wing in front of two thirds of the aileron span was virtually unstalled throughout. There was a marked increase of buffetting which preceded the stall.

Ground view of PP139 reveals increased area fin and rudder.

THE FINAL SPITFIRE

There was always more than a little confusion about the last Spitfire variant, the F Mk 24, for apart from minor modifications such as the short barrelled Hispano Mk V* cannon it was virtually identical to the F22 in much the same manner as were the first Spitfires, the Mks I and II. The new Mark was the final 24 uncompleted F22 airframes brought up to F24 standard by Supermarine, plus a small number of 22s converted by the RAF. Supermarine referred to them initially as F22s, but the RAF applied the correct designation.

The Supermarine Type Record issued on 12 March 1947 specified the F21, 22 and 24 as a common airframe with minor modifications to differentiate each variant. VN302 with a Griffon 61 engine and Rotol five blade wooden propeller was weighed at High Post on 25 May 1946 with a tare of 7,334 lb and an auw of 10,088. VN490 went to Chilbolton on 14 November 1947 and in a similar condition had a tare of 7,185 lb and an auw of 10,152. On 20 January 1948 VN492 weighed 7,419 tare and 10,147 auw.

VN329 arrived at Boscombe Down on 28 October 1946 to continue the full gunnery acceptance trials of the Mk V* cannon which had begun the previous January with PK547, a Mk 22. Twenty one air firing trips were made and although there were considerable problems with misaligned ammunition belts causing stoppages the Mk 22 and 24 were cleared for combat. During the trials the pilots of both aircraft complained of excessive vibration. As a result VN324 had a vibrograph installed to record the vibrations and the effect they might have on both guns and gyro gunsight. Routine production tests of VN324 and 481 revealed unusual elevator characteristics and the tests confirmed that the elevator finish was below standard, but removal of the inertia weight improved performance.

A complete series of trials with various loads were carried out on VN302, the pilots being Lithgow and Colquhoun, in the following conditions –

Load	auw (lb)	CG (ins aft datum) u/c down
(a) 3 × 500 lb MC bombs with long tails	11,710	9.8
(b) 3 × 200 lb smoke floats No 2 Mk II with No 27 nose and No 26 tail fairing	10,810	10.5
(c) 3 × 500 lb smoke bombs Mk II with No 25 nose fairing and No 81 tails	11,710	9.8
(d) 4 × 100 lb RPs plus 50 gal torpedo tank	10,870	10.5
(e) 4 × 300 lb RPs	11,450	8.7
(f) 4 × 300 lb RPs plus 50 gal torpedo tank	11,860	8.9
(g) 4 × 300 lb RPs plus 90 gal slipper tank empty	11,470	8.8
(h) as (g) slipper tank full	12,120	9.1

The rear fuel tank of the aircraft was full throughout the complete trials. The 50 gallon tank self jettisoned during one flight and as a result a modification was made to the attachment points. At each loading the Spitfire was dived to the approximate maximum permissible indicated air speed. No unsatisfactory features came to light during the trials and handling was considered to be acceptable. On loading (h), however, it was recommended that take off should be restricted to concrete runways; on grass it was most unpleasant as the run was increased and the aircraft was liable to become prematurely airborne, resulting in excessive strain on the undercarriage.

VN324 (Derry 16-6-47). Gyro gunsight vibration test. A recorder camera was carried and the worst vibration occurred at 18 lb boost and 2750 rpm. Several dummy rockets were carried. The sight was considered unacceptable.

VN481 (Morgan/Derry) 15-8-47). Investigation into unusual longitudinal behaviour. Fitted new spring tab elevator. During a test the aircraft felt excessively light, but at 475 violent fore and aft pitching started, resulting in both high negative and positive g. Derry thought that above 430 mph it was impossible to make small movements of the elevator without causing an initial jerk. The elevator was removed and sent to Hursley Park for check of mass balance. It was suggested that this elevator be fitted to another Spitfire – VN485 – have a new elevator fitted and the two aircraft test flown for comparison.

VN481 (Morgan/Derry 29-8-47). Aircraft fitted new stern and elevator. Found to be normal on first flight. Then fitted with original elevator and behaved as in previous tests. A rigging check revealed that the original elevator and tailplane were well outside the prescribed limits and there was considerable tail twist. VN324 was then fitted with the suspect tail unit and dived to 500 and 525 mph without a trace of trouble. During one flight a length of angle metal was fitted to the elevator trailing edge. The elevator was then fitted to VN490 and once again the original pitching began. When fitted with a new elevator the Spitfire behaved in a normal fashion. Fifteen F 24s had, by now, been fitted with the same type of elevator and flown without fault. A Mk 24 was also test flown with a Durestos plastic rudder in August 1951.

Production of the true F24 was confined to the Keevil works and the first two aircraft arrived at No 33MU on 30 April 1946, while the last, VN496, left South Marston after modifications of 24 February 1948 and was delivered on 4 April 1949. Early Mk 24s had the long barrelled Hispano cannon, but they were soon replaced by the short barrel Mk V* cannon. The new Spitfire saw limited service with home based squadrons, but sixteen examples were shipped to Hong Kong in 1950, serving with No 80 Squadron. Most went into long term storage in 1952 and were finally scrapped in 1956.

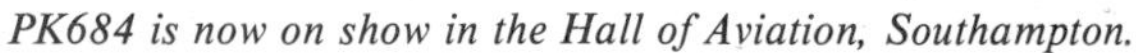

PK684 is now on show in the Hall of Aviation, Southampton.

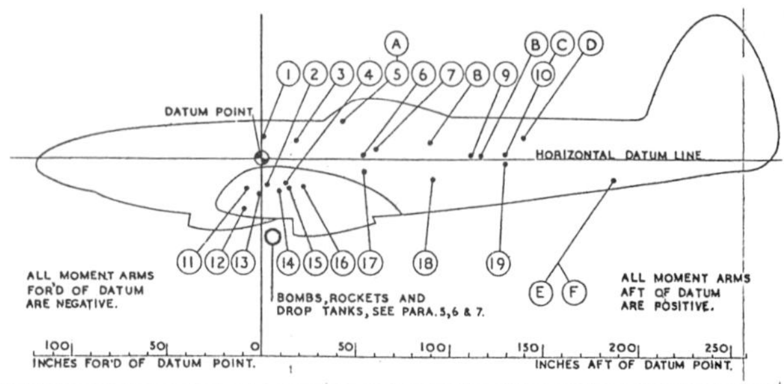

NOTE	ITEM	TYPICAL REMOVABLE ITEMS OF MILITARY LOAD.	WEIGHT LB.	ARM IN.	MOMENT LB.IN.
1	13	2 INBOARD HISPANO 20MM. GUNS MK. II AND ACCESSORIES.	290.5	− 0.3	− 87
1	14	2 OUTBOARD HISPANO 20MM. GUNS MK. II AND ACCESSORIES.	290	+ 8.6	+ 2,494
	15	AMMUNITION FOR INBOARD HISPANO 20MM. GUNS AT 150 ROUNDS PER GUN.	187.5	+ 14.2	+ 2,663
	16	AMMUNITION FOR OUTBOARD HISPANO 20MM. GUNS AT 150 ROUNDS PER GUN.	187.5	+ 23.2	+ 4,350
	5	GYROSCOPIC GUNSIGHT MK. II D.	8.5	+ 43	+ 366
	7	1¼ LB. INCENDIARY BOMB, CLOCK AND CROWBAR.	3	+ 61	+ 183
2	11	G.45 CAMERA AND ACCESSORIES	9	− 7	− 63
	19	OXYGEN IN 3 BOTTLES.	7	+129	+ 903
	17	DINGHY TYPE 'K' IN SEAT PACK TYPE 'A' AND WATER CUSHION.	23.5	+ 55	+ 1,293
3	9	T.R. 1143 RADIO AND ACCESSORIES.	81.5	+111	+ 9,047
4	10	S.C.R. 695 RADIO AND ACCESSORIES.	36	+129	+ 4,644
	6	PILOT AND PARACHUTE.	200	+ 55	+ 11,000
		TOTAL TYPICAL REMOVABLE MILITARY LOAD.	1,324.0		+ 36,793
	3	FUEL IN TOP FOR'D TANK: 36GALL. 100 OCTANE AT 7.2 LB. PER GALL.	259	+ 18.7	+ 4,843
	4	FUEL IN BOTTOM FOR'D TANK: 49GALL. 100 OCTANE AT 7.2 LB. PER GALL.	353	+ 12.9	+ 4,554
	8	FUEL IN TOP REAR TANK: 33GALL. 100 OCTANE AT 7.2 LB. PER GALL.	237.5	+ 89.5	+ 21,256
	18	FUEL IN BOTTOM REAR TANK: 33GALL. 100 OCTANE AT 7.2 LB. PER GALL.	237.5	+ 90.8	+ 21,565
	12	FUEL IN WING TANKS: 36GALL. 100 OCTANE AT 7.2 LB. PER GALL.	259	− 9.3	− 2,409
5	1	OIL IN TANK: 9 GALL. AT 9 LB. PER GALL.	81	+ 1	+ 81
	2	AIRCRAFT IN TARE CONDITION.	7,351		+ 22,791
		AIRCRAFT IN TYPICAL TAKE-OFF CONDITION.	10,102	+ 10.8	+109,474

NOTE	ITEM	ADDITIONAL AND ALTERNATIVE ITEMS OF REMOVABLE MILITARY LOAD.	WEIGHT LB.	ARM IN.	MOMENT LB.IN.
	A	REFLECTOR GUNSIGHT, ADAPTOR AND FILAMENT LAMP.	5	+ 44	+ 220
6	D	DESERT EQUIPMENT.	42	+139	+ 5,838
7	B	A.1271 RADIO AND ACCESSORIES.	12	+115	+ 1,380
8	C	R.3090 RADIO AND ACCESSORIES.	36	+129	+ 4,644
	E	TAIL BALLAST MOUNTING.	5	+187	+ 935
	F	STANDARD WEIGHT ON TAIL BALLAST MOUNTING (MAX.3).	17.5	+187	+ 3,273

Loading and C.G., Mk 24.

Wing. Planform elliptical; section NACA Series 2200; span 36' 11" incidence ° root + 2 to -½ 18ft 5in from CL a/c; dihedral° 6; thickness % root 13.2, tip 6; aspect ratio area nett 222, gross 243.6; chord (geo) 8.33, (ma) 7.23. Ailerons. Area 18.74; chord (ma) 0.25; movement° up 13, down 13; droop 0. Tabs area 3.96; setting 0.69-0.81. Flaps. Area 21.2; movement° down 75. Wing loading 40.5; power loading 3.94. Propeller clearance ° t/o 1ft.

Tailplane. Area 42.56; chord (ma) 4.09; incidence° root 0, tip ± ½; dihedral° 0. Elevators. Area 17.39; movement° up 28, down 23. Tab area 0.69; movement° up 20, down 7. Fin area 9.95; under rudder 2.31. Rudder. Area 10.55; movement° 28°15′ each way. Tab area 0.68; movement° 1.68in, starbd 1.44, setting 1.72 starbd.

Undercarriage. Track 6ft 8in wheels Dunlop; tyres Dunlop; tyre pressure 75 lb/in².

Tailwheel retractable castoring. Wheel Dunlop; tyre 105 Pressure 95.

Engine/s. Griffon 61 RG 4SM 2,050hp @ 8,250ft (MS), 1,780 @ 22,000 (FS). Max power 30 mins 1,480 @ 13,500 (MS) @ 2,600rpm + 9 boost, 1,320 @ 27,000 + 9 @ 2,600rpm (FS). Take off 1,520hp @ 2,750rpm + 12, 2,373 @ 2,057rpm @ 1,250ft + 25 (150 octane) 5mins, 2,035 @ 2,750 @ 7,000 + 18.

Griffon 64

Coffman cartridge starter.

Griffon 85 2,340hp @ 750ft (MS) 2,120 @ 12,250 (FS), 24 volt electrical system.

Propeller/s. Rotol R14/5F5/2 5-blade Jablo pitch range 35° fine pitch 28° 30'. Diameter 11ft 10in.

Coolant. 70% distilled water, 30% Glycol. 4½ engine, 3½ intercooling, total 15¾gals.

Fuel capacity. Fuselage (upper) 36gals, lower 48, inboard wing 2 × 5½, outboard 2 × 12½ total 120. Plus upper rear fuselage 33, lower 33. Gross total 275, plus 45,50,90 gal o/ld tanks.

Oil. 9gals.

Armour. 190lb.

Armament. 4 x 20mm Hispano Mk II cannon, 175rpg inboard, 150 outboard, plus 3 × 500lb bombs. or rockets or Mk V* guns.

Radio. R3090, A1271.

Cine camera. G45 stabd wing.

Performance. Max speed 454mph @ 26,000ft (FS), 420 @ 12,000 (FS), 412 @ 5,000 (MS). Rate of climb 4,900ft min @ 2,000 (MS) 4,100ft min @ 17,000 (FS), service ceiling (100ft min) 43,000ft. Range (normal fuel), 390mph @ SL, cruise 245. Max dive 500.

Take off run 700yds, landing 560.

Weights. Tare 7,351lb, take off 10,102, max permissible 10,150, max overload 12,150 to include:
with full rear fuel (take off) 9,900; plus 4 x 300lb RPs 10,920; with 3 × 500lb bombs 11,290; with 4 × 300lb RPs and 90gal o/ld tank 11,930; with 3 × 500lb bombs and 90gal tank 11,740; with 170gal ferry tank 11,330.

24 volt system.

General arrangement of F Mk 24 in the markings of No 80 Squadron.

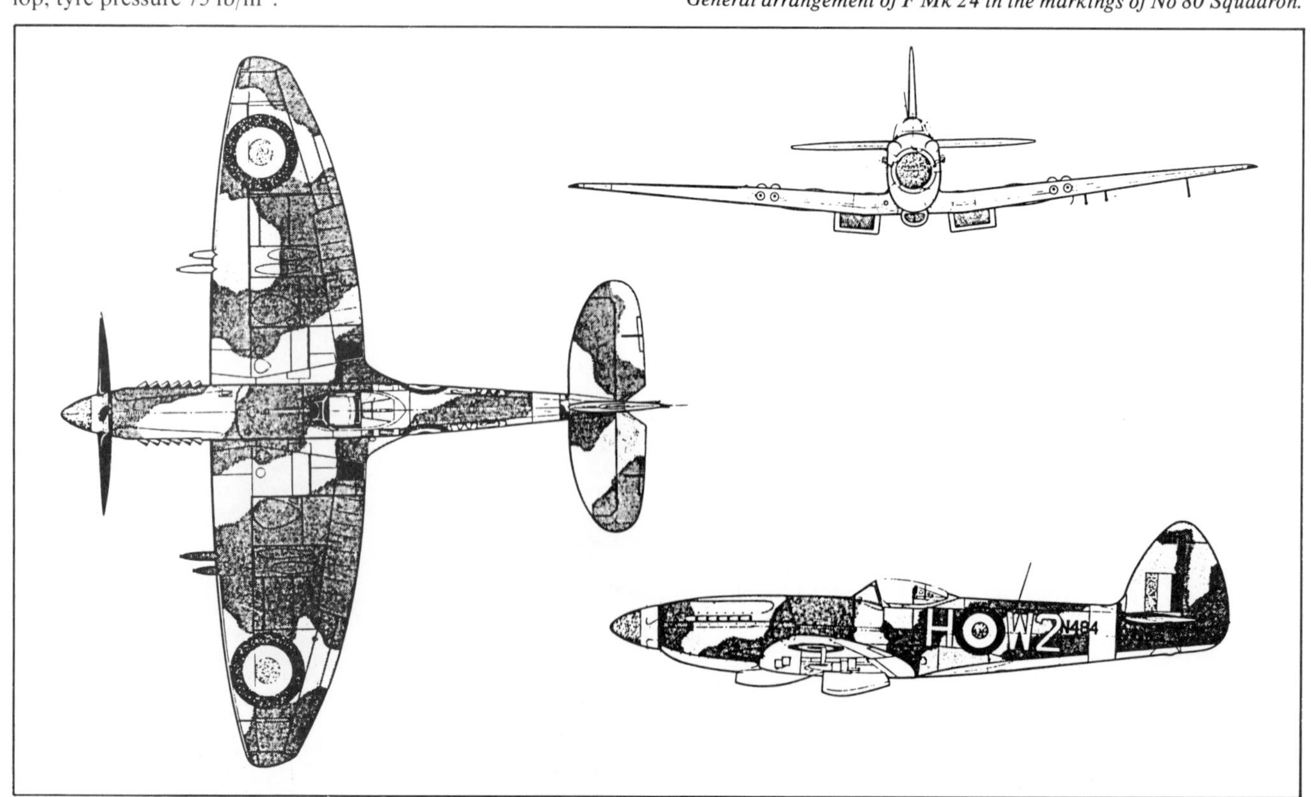

SERIAL NUMBERS

Vickers-Armstrong (Castle Bromwich) Ltd.

Contract No. B981687/39.

Eleventh order for 800 Spitfire Mk IX dated 2 June 1943. Built as Mks IX/22 between June 1944 and December 1945. Production of Mk 22 transferred to Supermarine at South Marston. The following serials apply to Mk 22s completed as Mk 24; PK678-679, 681-683, 685-689, 712-714 and 716-726.

Contract No. A/C 5795/C.23(c).

Order for 150 Spitfire Mk 22 dated 15 November 1945, transferred to Supermarine at South Marston. 54 aircraft built as Mk 24 between April 1946 and February 1948 as; VN301-334 and 477-496. The following were cancelled; VN335-348, 364-397, 413-439 and 456-476. A fixed price contract, the final for the Spitfire, was delivered to Supermarine, Winchester, on 13 August 1947. It called for the supply of 54 aircraft at a fixed price of £7,442 each, plus £14.10s per flight per aircraft. The PK series were supplied on a cost plus profit basis.

Converted from Mk 22s to Mk 24 standards; PK515, 627, 677, 680, 684 and 715.

Maintenance airframes: PK724(7288M) and PK653 (7150M).

PK and VN series all with Griffon G61 engine

PK678 SM t/fln F/O Brown 20min 27-2-46 6MU 29-11 80S 6-2-48 NES 16-6-53 sold J G Will 24-5-54

PK679 SM t/fln W J G Morgan 15min 8-3-46 33MU 25-10 WAL 28-3-49 mods NEA 14-12-54 sold E Smelt 13-6-56

PK681 SM t/fln F/Lt Wigey 25min 8-3-46 33MU 28-11 RNAS Renfrew 29-6-49 Sele Sing 12-8 MBFE 11-9-50 Sing AAF 20-7-51 390MU(S) 7-3-52 SOC 15-4-54

PK682 SM t/fln L R Colq 20min 19-2-46 33MU 13-8 1BR&SD 22-9-48 80S 29-9 FEAF 2-7 FA3R 3-7-50 SOC 28-8-51

PK683 SM t/fln L R Colq 15min 19-2-46 33MU 13-8 *Pyrrhus* 12-8-50 FEAF 7-9 MBFE storage 12-9 FA3R 24-7-51 Sing AAF 24-7 390MU(S) 10-2-53 SOC 15-4-54 ATC Malaya as 7150M extant Hall of Aviation, Southampton

PK685 SM t/fln W J G Morgan 20min 27-2-46 33MU 13-9 WAL 3-2-49 mods NEA 14-12-54 sold E Smelt 13-6-56

PK686 SM t/fln W J G Morgan 15min 27-2-46 33MU 30-10 WAL 18-1-49 mods NEA 14-12-54 sold En/RM 28-6-56

PK687 SM t/fln F/Lt Wigley 15min 6-3-46 33MU 18-10 FEAF 28-3-50 MBFE storage 18-5 SHQ Kai Tak 3-10 80S 5-9-51 HKAAF 15-5-52 SOC 11-12-53

PK688 SM t/fln W Brown 20min 19-2-46 33MU 30-10 WAL 12-4-49 mods NEA 14-12-54 sold H Bath 17-2-56

PK689 SM t/fln F/Lt Wigley 20min 27-2-46 33MU 27-9 emergency during del flt u/c door and star oleo would not retract WAL 7-1-49 mods HQ BAFO Com S 8-8-51 NEA 14-12-54 sold En/RM 28-6-56

PK712 SM t/fln F/O Brown 15min 6-3-46 33MU 26-11 RNAS Ren 4-7-48 80S FEAF 15-8 390MU(S) 1-3-52 SOC 1-7-53

PK713 SM t/fln W J G Morgan 20min 19-2-46 33MU 11-9 emergency during del flt port oleo would not retract WAL 4-2-49 mods NEA 14-12-54 sold H Bath 2-11-56

PK714 SM t/fln L R Colq 15min 8-3-46 33MU 11-11 WAL 24-1-49 mods NEA 14-12-54 sold H Bath 2-11-56

PK716 SM t/fln F/Lt Wigley 20min 33MU 30-9-46 RNAS Renfrew 4-7-49 Sele 2-8 80S 5-9 FA scrap 27-2-50 SOC

PK717 SM t/fln L R Colq 20min 33MU 11-10-46 WAL 5-4-49 mods NEA 14-12-54 sold En/RM 28-6-56

PK718 SM t/fln F/O Brown 15min 33MU 9-10-46 WAL 27-3-49 mods HQ 2Grp Com Flt 9-12-52 NEA 14-12-54 sold H Bath 2-11-56

PK719 SM t/fln L R Colq 15min 6-3-46 33MU 9-10 FEAF 28-3-50 MBFE storage 18-5 80S Kai Tak 20-9 HKAAF 15-5-52 FAC5 SOC 12-6-54

PK720 SM t/fln L R Colq 15min 6-3-46 33MU 10-10 FEAF 28-3-50 SHQ Kai Tak 24-5 80S 20-7 HKAAF 15-5-52 FAC5 SOC 16-8-53

PK721 SM t/fln F/Lt Wigley 20min 19-2-46 33MU 5-11 WAL 5-4-49 NEA 14-12-54 sold E Smelt 13-6-56

PK722 SM t/fln W J G Morgan 20min 19-2-46 33MU 27-9 WAL 8-3-49 mods NEA 14-12-54 sold En/RM 28-6-50

PK723 SM t/fln F Brown 20min 27-2-46 33MU 26-11 RNAS Renfrew 4-7-49 80S FEAF 15-8 stld on app cd Kai Tak pilot kld CE 23-8 SOC

PK724 SM t/fln F/Lt Wigley 20min 27-2-46 33MU 30-10 WAL 1-4-49 mods NEA 14-12-54 RAF Brize Norton as 7288M 4-11-55 extant RAF Mus Hendon

PK725 SM t/fln F/Lt Wigley 20min 27-2-46 33MU 13-9 WAL 2-2-49 mods NEA 14-12-54 sold En/RM 28-6-56

PK726 SM t/fln F/Lt Wigley 15min 6-3-46 33MU 5-11 WAL 31-3-49 mods at CBAF Originally F22 fus but finish as F24

PK713 saw no service use, having an eventful ferry flight to No 33 MU at Lyneham on 11 September 1946, subsequent mods, storage and sold for scrap in November 1956.

VN301 F22 KEE t/fln L R Colq 14-3-46 33MU 3-4 VA HrPK 6-5 con to F24 80S 15-1-48 NEA 13-2-54 sold L Met 15-5-56

VN302 KEE t/fln L R Colq SM 14-3-46 Mid Wallop 19-9 CRD VA 30-11 VA HPA 22-1-47 hand with external stores:- 3x500lb bombs; 3x200lb No. 2 MkII smoke floats; 3x500lb MkII smoke bombs; 4x100lb RPs & 50gal torpedo o/ld tank; 4x300lb RPs & 50gal tor o/ld tank; 4x300lb RPs & 90gal slipper o/ld tank (empty); 4x300lb RPs & 90gal slip o/ld tank (full). Rear fus tank full during trls. The 50gal tank self jett during trls; fitting mods. At each load a/c dived to max per speed. B Dn 3-1-47 CFE 20-4-48

VN 303KEE 33MU 10-7-46 80S BAFO 23-2-48 FAAC 20-7 VA NES 13-12-54 sold R J Coley 17-2-56

VN304 KEE t/fln L R Colq 20-3-46 33MU 30-4 VA HrPK 6-5 80S BAFO 18-2-48 VA 15-10 FEAF 2-7-49 Kai Tak 20-9-50 SOC 4-10

VN305 KEE 33MU 12-7-46 80S Wunstorf 29-9-48 FEAF 2-7-49 80S eng fail aban i/sea off Hong Kong pilot kld C3 13-10-49 FA FTR 28-12

VN306 KEE VA HPA 17-4-46 VA KEE 28-9 mods & cons 80S 16-8-48 flew i/grd nr Gutersloh pilot kld CE 7-3-49

VN307 KEE 33MU 26-4-46 VA HrPK 6-5 80S BAFO 23-2-48 FEAF 2-7-49 FA3R 24-1-51 SOC scr 5-7

VN308 KEE 33MU 30-4-46 VA HrPK 6-5 80S 15-1-48 FEAF FEAF 2-7-49 Kai Tak 13-12 HKAAF 15-5-52 FA3R 15-6 SOC 11-12

VN309 KEE 33MU 30-4-46 VA HrPK 6-5 1BR&SD BAFO 20-1-49 80S 17-1 FEAF 2-7 SOC 22-8-51

VN310 KEE 33MU 26-7-46 80S 15-1-48 FEAF 15-8-49 FA FTR 12-1-51

VN311 KEE 33MU 26-7-46 80S 15-1-48 NEA 13-12-54 sold L Met 15-5-56

VN312 KEE 33MU 26-7-46 80S BAFO 9-2-48 FEAF 15-8-49 FA3R 9-6-50 SOC 7-7

VN313 KEE t/fln L R Colq 28-2-46 33MU 14-8 res pl BAFO 2-5-49 80S 10-6 FEAF 2-7 FAC4 13-12 Kai Tak 13-12 HKAAF 15-3-52 SOC 3-10-53

VN314 F22 KEE t/fln L R Colq 20-3-46 Ald 33MU 30-4 VA HrPK 6-5 con to F24 80S BAFO 28-3-49 FEAF 15-8 SOC 12-2-51

VN315 F22 KEE bdn 9-7-46 Hand Sq Hull 11-6-47 80S 6-2-48 VASM 12-10 con to F24 80S 6-2-49 NEA 14-12-54 G BEE fitment 10-11-55 Thum Flt Woodvale 24-1-56 NEA 25-5 sold H Bath 30-10

VN 316F22 KEE t/fln L R Colq Ald 2-4-46 con to F24 27-4 ECFS 3-5 FAAC 7-6 VA WAL 21-1-49 mods HQ 2Grp Com Flt 20-8-51 FA3R 11-7-52 NEA 13-12-54 sold L Met 15-5-55

VN317 KEE ECFS 18-7-46 1BR&SD 1-1-49 80S 12-1 w/u lnd Renfrew CF 2-7 scr 22-7

VN318 KEE Farn Jly'46 CRD VA HPA 30-11 80S 23-2-48 HKAAF 1-4-52 w/u 21-4-55

VN319 KEE 33MU 4-7-46 80S 18-2-48 air coll with VN323 cd Hombrink Lezze B2G Germany pilot kld CE 28-10

VN320 KEE 33MU 29-7-46 80S BAFO 1-3-48 NEA 14-2-54 sold E Smelt 13-6-56

VN321 KEE t/fln L R Colq 22-7-46 33MU 29-7 instal 22-12-49 NEA 13-12-54 sold R J Coley 17-2-56

VN322 KEE t/fln L R Colq 23-7-46 33MU 29-7 80S BAFO 18-2-48 scr 8-9-49 NEA 16-6-53 sold MoS 19-2-54

VN323 KEE t/fln L R Colq 23-7-46 33MU 29-7 80S 9-2-48 air coll with VN319 cd/ld Hombrink Lezze Germany CE 28-10

VN324 STN t/fln L R Colq 13-7-46 VA CRD 30-11 VA HPA 16-6-47 GGS vibration tests pilot Derry bdn 31-12 full gunnery acceptance trls (MkV can) VA stored until 1950 Farn 12-10-50 on loan VA for Lympe air races NEA 14-12-54 sold En/RM 25-6-56

VN325 KEE t/fln L R Colq 26-7-46 33MU 29-7 WAL 12-3-49 mods NEA 14-12-54 sold H Bath 31-10-56

VN326 KEE 33MU 11-11-46 WAL 20-1-49 mods FEAF 2-9-50 MBFE storage 8-12 390MU 29-2-53 SOC 18-2-54

VN327 KEE t/fln L R Colq 6-9-46 33MU 21-9 WAL 19-1-49 NEA 11-5-56 sold H Bath 31-10

X VN328 KEE t/fln L R Colq 9-9-46 33MU 21-9 WAL 11-3-49 NE/Stock 14-12-54 sold H Bath 31-10-56

VN329 KEE t/fln L R Colq 30-9-46 VA HPA 11-10 Bdn 28-10-46 full gunnery acceptance trls with MkV*can Problems with misaligned ammo belts. Comp trls with PK547, the latter acting as chase plane at time. VA STN 1-10-47 WAL 6-4-49 mods NEA 14-12-54 sold H Bath 17-2-56

VN330 VA HrPK t/fln S/Ldr Derry SM 10min 9-10-46 33MU 4-11 WAL 6-1-49 mods FEAF 15-11-50 390MU 28-2-53 SOC 18-2-54

VN331 HrPK VA t/fln S/Ldr Derry 10min SM 19-3-47 VA HPA 19-3 9MU 11-6 RNAS Ren 29-6 Sele 12-8-49 SHW Kai Tak 3-10-50 80S 1-8-51 SOC 1-7-53

VN332 VA HrPK t/fln W R Morgan 15min SM 25-3-47 47MU 28-5 Task 322 London *Beaverlake* to Canada RCAF Winter Estb Edmonton Alberta 24-8 cocooning and winterisation trls re-cocooned Aug'48, dismantled Sept'49 sold in Canada 21-3-51 registered as N7929A

VN333 KEE 6MU 16-1-47 VASM mods 6MU 9-3-40 for completion of mods 33MU 10-10-51 NEA 13-12-54 sold L Met 15-5-56

VN334 KEE 6MU 16-1-47 VASM mods to 6MU 9-3-49 for completion of mods 45MU 19-10-51 FEAF 29-10-51 NEA 14-12-54 sold H Bath 31-10-56

VN477 t/fln S/Ldr Derry 15min SM 12-5-47 6MU 7-8 VASM 10-3-49 mods 45MU 19-10-51 FEAF 3-11-52 NEA 14-12-54 fitment 12-7-55 sold Aluminium Refineries 19-6-56

VN478 VA HrPK t/fln S/Ldr Derry 30min SM 23-6-47 6MU 7-8 VASM 9-3-49 mods 45MU17-10-51 FEAF 26-11-52 NEA 11-5-56 sold scrap 31-10

VN479 VASM 6-4-48 6MU 30-5 FEAF 8-8 MBFE storage 16-8 SOC 18-2-54

VN480 VA HrPK 9MU 28-8-47 RNAS Ren 29-6-49 Sele 12-8 80S 27-12 SOC 10-12-51

VN481 VA HrPK VAHPA 15-8-48 invest of longitud behaviour (see page 489) 9MU 3-9 RNAS Ren 29-6-48 Sele 12-8-49 SHQ Kai Tak 14-8-50 80S 5-9 SOC 1-9-52

VN482 VA HrPK 9MU 3-10-47 RNAS Ren 29-6-49 Sele 29-6 SOC 15-1-51

VN483 VA HrPK t/fln L R Colq 15min SM 23-7-47 6MU 7-8 VASM 3-3-40 mods FEAF 27-3-50 SHQ Kai Tak 24-5 80S 26-7 390MU(S) 1-3-52 SOC 1-7-53

VN484 VA HrPK t/fln L R Colq 20min SM 19-6-47 6MU 7-8 VASM 28-2-49 mods FEAF 27-3-50 MBFE Kai Tak 14-8 80S 27-10 390MU(S) 1-3-52 SOC 1-7-53

VN485 VA HrPK t/fln S/Ldr Derry 25min SM 27-8-47 9MU 4-9 RNAS Ren Sept'49 Sele SHQ Kai Tak 3-10-50 80S 5-9-51 Hong Kong AAF 13-5-52 last flt 15-1-55 FH241.40 to 7326M extant Kai Tak 10-4-56

VN486 VA HrPK t/fln L R Colq 10min SM 15-7-47 6MU 7-8 VASM 3-3-49 mods FEAF 27-3-50 80S Kai Tak 24-5 390MU 1-3-52 SOC 10-2-53

VN487 SM t/fln L R Colq 10min 2-9-47 9MU 11-9 RNAS Renfrew 11-9 Seletar 12-8 MBFE stld on app cd Seletar C2 7-12 SOC scr 7-12

VN488 VA HrPK t/fln S/Ldr Derry 10min SM 19-9-47 6MU 10-10 VASM 28-6-49 mods 80S 15-8 FAAC 29-3 Kai Tak 29-8 SOC 28-8-51

VN489 VA HrPK t/fln L R Colq 10min SM 2-10-47 6MU 27-10 VASM 9-3-49 RNAS Ren 28-6 Sele 12-8 80S FEAF 27-12 SOC 10-12-51

VN490 VA HrPK t/fln W R Morgan 15min SM 14-11-47 6MU 15-12 VASM 17-3-49 mods RNAS Ren 28-6 Sele 12-8 SOC 27-11-50

VN491 VA HrPK t/fln L R Colq SM 20min 16-10-47 6MU 27-10 VASM 10-3-49 mods RNAS Ren 28-6 Sele 12-8 80S FEAF 27-12 FA scrap 26-7-50

VN492 VA HrPK t/fln W R Morgan 40min SM 15-12-47 9MU 23-12 Chil on short term loan CSA charge 15-1-48 RNAS Ren 29-6-49 Sele 12-8 SHQ Kai Tak 3-10-50 80S 1-2-51 HKAAF 15-5-52 FEAF 3-10-53 SOC 19-7-54

VN493 VA HrPK t/fln L R Colq 10min SM 24-11-47 6MU 11-12 RNAS Ren 30-6-48 VASM 4-4-49 mods 80S FEAF 15-8 SOC 28-8-51

VN494 VA HrPK t/fln W R Morgan 10min SM 19-12-47 9MU 14-1-48 FEAF 22-10-50 MBFE storage 26-10 Sing AF 23-7-51 SOC 18-2-54

VN495 VA HrPK 9MU 21-1-48 RNAS Ren 29-6-49 Sele 12-8 80S 5-9 FAC4 13-12 Kai Tak SOC 28-8-51

VN496 VA HrPK final Spit variant to leave SM prod line 24-2-48 del to 6MU BNn by W R Morgan 4-4-49 RNAS Ren 30-6 80S FEAF 15-8 C5 SOC 15-12-50

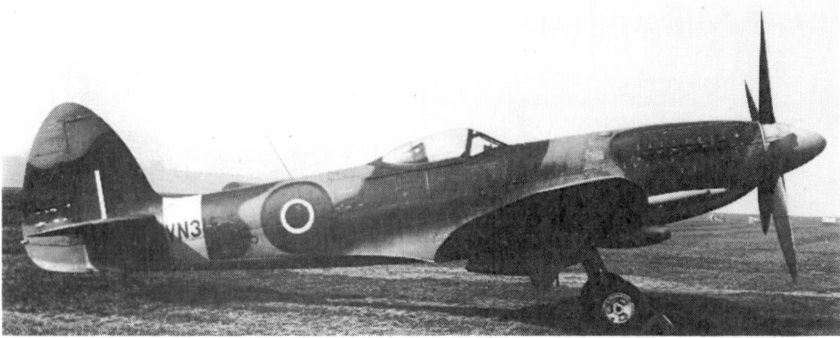

Above and right: VN315 served with No 80 Squadron and in early 1956 was examined for use with the Woodvalve-based 'Thum' Flight.

VN479 was issued to the Far East in August 1948, but was to remain in storage at Seletar.

VN318 heads a line-up of F24s of the HKAAF at Kai Tak in 1955.

PHOENIX TO ASHES

Towards the end of 1942 Supermarine were investigating the means by which the aerodynamics of the Spitfire wing (perfectly adequate for the speeds at which aircraft were flying mid-way through the war) could be improved. It had faults, the worst being the inherent aeroelasticity due to the light structure behind an immensely strong torsion box leading edge. This secondary structure had to be light because of power/weight considerations for the first Merlin engines produced approximately 950bhp., and every pound saved was that much less for the engine to pull through the air.

Inevitably engine power increased and the Spitfire wing was able to cope with the additional stresses by constant modification and strengthening. But, the time was fast approaching when a radical change had to be made if the Spitfire was to fly faster and higher and to utilise its power more efficiently

Even before Supermarine had initiated experiments a paper had been published by the RAE, Farnborough, in February 1942. Written by A.D. Young it was a survey of compressibility effects in aeronautics, and for his references Young had read material dating back to 1927. His paper's conclusions were that at speeds below that at which shock waves appear the effects of compressibility on pressure distribution, lift and pitching moments on thin aerofoils at small incidences were predictable. Compressibility causes a slight increase in the drag coefficient.

As speed increased beyond that at which shock waves appeared flow breakaway generally occurred and a rapid rise in drag, fall in lift and change in pitching moment followed. It was possible to reduce some of these adverse effects by boundary layer control. It was also important to delay the onset of shock waves on a high speed aeroplane to as high a speed as was possible.

To achieve this happy state wing sections would have the maximum thickness and camber positions considerably nearer the mid-chord point than was the case with the, then, current aerofoils. Camber lines had to be so designed to give the most desirable loading while the thickness had to be as small as possible and the nose section approach that of an ellipse.

The Supermarine design staff under Joseph Smith were aware of all these facts and by November 1942 was working on designs of a new wing for the Spitfire. It was acknowledged that experience of the new sections was limited and that any new wing would have to be produced to fine tolerances. Rather than embrace the new technology immediately Supermarine decided to first, produce a new high speed wing by modifying the original design and lift the leading edge by two inches. Depending on the results obtained from tests, a completely new, laminar flow wing would then be designed. The former was fitted to an F Mk VIII (JG204) with the intention of adopting it for the so-called 'Super Spitfire', the F Mk 23, while the latter was more successful and eventually led to the Type 371 Spiteful.

Supermarine Specification No 469 (September 1942) outlined what was the first step towards the Type 371 design. It read - "An investigation of the Air Staff outline requirements for a high performance, single seat day fighter has been made and the conclusions reached that the Spitfire Mk 21 airframe with a suitably rated Griffon engine meets these requirements. Estimates of speed and performance are – maximum level speed at 17,500 feet, 420mph, rate of climb (ft/min) 4,500 at 10,000ft, 1,980 at 34,000ft. Proposals for a new wing of lower drag, and a windscreen with better rearward view, have been tentaively discussed with MAP. These improvements could be applied to the F21 airframe at a suitable stage in production."

After additional information was available on the new wing Specification No.470 was issued on 30 November – "A new wing has been designed for the Spitfire with the following objects (1) To raise as much as possible the critical speed at which drag increases, due to compressibility, become serious. (2) To obtain a rate of roll faster than any existing fighter. (3) To reduce wing profile drag and thereby improve performance.

"The wing area has been reduced to 210 sq ft (Spiteful) and a thickness chord ratio of 13% has been used over the inner portion of the wing where the equipment is stored. Outboard the wing tapers to 8% thickness/chord at the tip. The aerofoil section has been calculated under the supervision of Dr. Goldstein at the National Physics Laboratory. It is anticipated that the speed corresponding to the critical Mach number will be 55mph higher than with the present Spitfire wing. In addition laminar flow is anticipated back to 6° on the outer part of the wing where there is no slipstream or cannon barrel to cause forward transition. Attention is being concentrated on making the wing simple to build, with straight tapers, so that a smooth and accurate contour may be achieved in production. For this reason the wing covering is comparitively thick which has the further advantage of providing high torsional rigidity necessary for good aileron control at high speed. An aileron reversal speed of 850mph is aimed at.

"The wing has been designed for fitting to the F21 Spitfire. It is not possible to make it inter-changeable with the existing wing as some adjustment of the front and rear spar attachments has been necessary for reasons of balance. The chassis has a wide track and retracts inwards". Main particulars were – wing span 35ft 0in, area 210sq ft; auw(lb) 8,670; wing loading (lb sq ft) 41.3; critical Mach number at wing root .72. Propeller, counter rotating of 11ft 0in diameter with six blades. Apart from the fuselage it was an embryo Spiteful.

The limiting speed (terminal velocity) was quoted as 525mph; level speed 360; flaps down 180; stall 118. From production considerations it was thought advisable to keep the chord lines straight in elevation. The original layout by the project office had indicated an increase in dihedral at the 'kink' in plan form and it was thought necessary to increase the whole dihedral angle on production aircraft. The prototype was to be built with 3° of angle.

There was an extensive flow breakaway from the roof of the entry duct in the high condition of the original design of Spiteful radiators and wind tunnel tests were conducted at the RAE Farnborough to improve the design. The entry duct was lengthened; duct roof shape modified; by-passing the wing boundary layer over the radiator matrix; a guide vane used to obtain better flow distribution. A, is the original duct, the full lines showing entry and exit; broken lines flap positions for maximum entry and exit areas. B, lengthened entry duct with alternative shapes of diffuser. C, original entry duct with modified diffuser. D, complete by-pass ducts with exits on upper surface of wing.

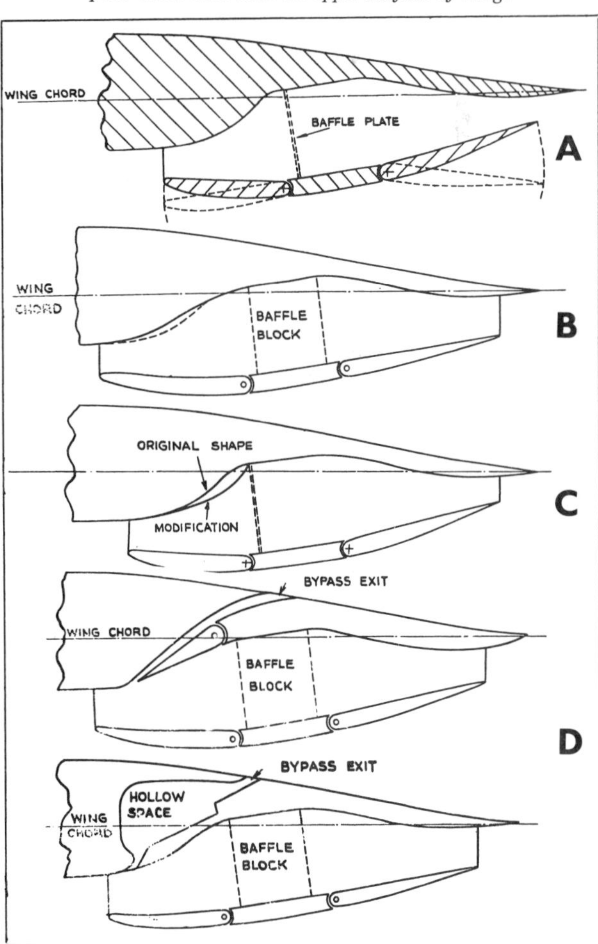

The Air Ministry was impressed by the specification and in February 1943 issued their own, F 1/43, which called for a single seat fighter with the laminar flow wing. It specified that the fuselage was to be based upon that of the F Mk VIII Spitfire, and in keeping with its association with the Royal Navy the Air Ministry asked that the aeroplane should be designed – "So that a wing folding scheme to meet possible FAA use without extensive modification should be provided". Contra rotating propellers, an armament of 4×20mm cannon, good view forward and rear, and a Rolls-Royce Griffon engine were also demanded. The F1/43 prototype was regarded by the Air Ministry as an experimental type for the purpose of trying out the laminar wing and contra-props as quickly as possible. Originally these items were to be installed in the F Mk VIII airframes using either the Merlin or Griffon and, in fact, some modification was made to four Mk VIIIs. The Type 371 F 1/43 'Valiant' production aircraft was to incorporate all the new modifications as standard, and if the Griffon engine was not available Merlin RM16 SM units were to be used as an interim measure.

In a letter of 29 December to Supermarine the Air Ministry spelled out its proposed programme for F 1/43 development – First prototype to Spec. F 1/43 to have F Mk VIII fuselage (amended in a subsequent letter to a Mk XIV fuselage) with counter rotating Griffon, plus laminar flow wing to be designated F Mk XIV with laminar flow wings; second prototype to be representative of the F 1/43 production aircraft Supermarine Type 371, with new, standard fuselage and counter rotating Griffon; third prototype to be similar to second prototype but with the Merlin single rotation engine. This is a single rotation type prototype as there is no production programme for the Merlin CR; a fourth F 1/43 for arrester gear trials. This will be the Type 371 with Griffon CR engine and hook. Supermarine are to begin producing the Type 371 with Griffon CR in August 1944 when the F Mk XIV begins to taper. At the end of 1944 they start producing the Type 371 with single rotation engine and F Mk VIII production begins to taper. Both Castle Bromwich and South Marston will begin production of the Type 371 CR in late 1945.

A contract for 'Three Spitfire F Mk VIII aircraft with redesigned, high performance wings' was issued, serial numbers NN660, 664 and 667, at a cost of £45,000. This covered components purchased; actual wages; overhead charges and a profit calculated at the approved rate. A fourth prototype – RT464 – was also ordered for use as the navalised Spiteful. In the event it was not completed as the fuselage was appropriated by the DTD for structural tests in May 1946. Final invoice for the four prorotypes was a staggering £339,450.

From past experience with the Spitfire Supermarine knew that wind tunnel tests were a vital part of the research needed for the Type 371, and one of the first tests was made during December 1942 on the effect of using a radiator flap to increase area for landing. In accordance with the specification's demand for a contra prop installation tunnel tests were carried out at Farnborough in October 1943 to determine the stability of the design with the six blade unit. Both longitudinal and directional instability were encountered due to the large, de-stabilising effects of the propellers. A larger fin and rudder was needed.

The tunnel tests continued with a five blade single unit and two wing settings. Increasing wing setting by 1° had no effect on the longitudinal stability and the five blade propeller was only marginally better than the worst effects of the contra-prop. A Supermarine Report of 30 December 1943, Number 3984, concerned performance comparison of both wing and fuselage radiator schemes. The fuselage scheme was estimated to provide 7% more intercooling than the wing installation, but laminar flow over the whole of the cowling was turbulent. It was decided to test the fuselage radiator (and adapt it for use on the Spitfire) on a $\frac{1}{4}$ scale model of the F 1/43 in the Farnborough wind tunnel, and the results showed limiting speeds to be low. In addition the scheme was not suitable for tropical conditions, and the wing installation was superior under all conditions.

Half wing models of the wing were also tested in the wind tunnel over a range of incidence and aileron angles with two control surface curvatures – normal and flat. As tabs would have had to be used with either type there appeared to be no definite advantage. Supermarine tested ailerons made of alclad and elektron, purely as a weight saving exercise, and it was proposed using elektron as trailing edge strip. The weight saved was 5.92lb but it was considered that the problems of assembling the components with all contact surfaces treated with a varnish and assembled wet were too great.

A mock-up of F 1/43 was inspected by the Air Ministry on 1 March 1944 and on the 4th Vickers had written to them asking that the name Spiteful be considered for the new aeroplane. The Air Ministry wanted to call it the Valiant, but eventually agreed to the Vickers' suggestion. A few weeks later it was agreed by both parties that the Merlin 14SM engine would not be used for one of the prototype aircraft and all efforts were to be concentrated on the Griffon. First flight of the pseudo Type 371 Spiteful had been planned for 15 March, but the new wing was not ready and delivery dates began to slip. Reasons for the delay were many – the pilot's view over the nose was considered unsatisfactory and one of the remedies suggested was an increase of 2° wing incidence. There was disagreement about the merits of a flat or curved windscreen.

Although it had been agreed that the Merlin engine be dropped as a possible power plant for the Spiteful investigations were still being made for use of the Merlin 15.SM at +18lb boost driving either a single five or six blade propeller or similar bladed contra-props with a diameter of 11ft 8in. The same investigation also considered five or six blade 11ft diameter propellers for the Griffon engine. Dropping the Merlin engine from the design was not a major problem because the fuselage had been designed to accept both engines

The first Type 371 wing was fitted to NN660, a Spitfire Mk XIV fuselage as flown by Jeffrey Quill on 30 June 1944. It crashed the following September.

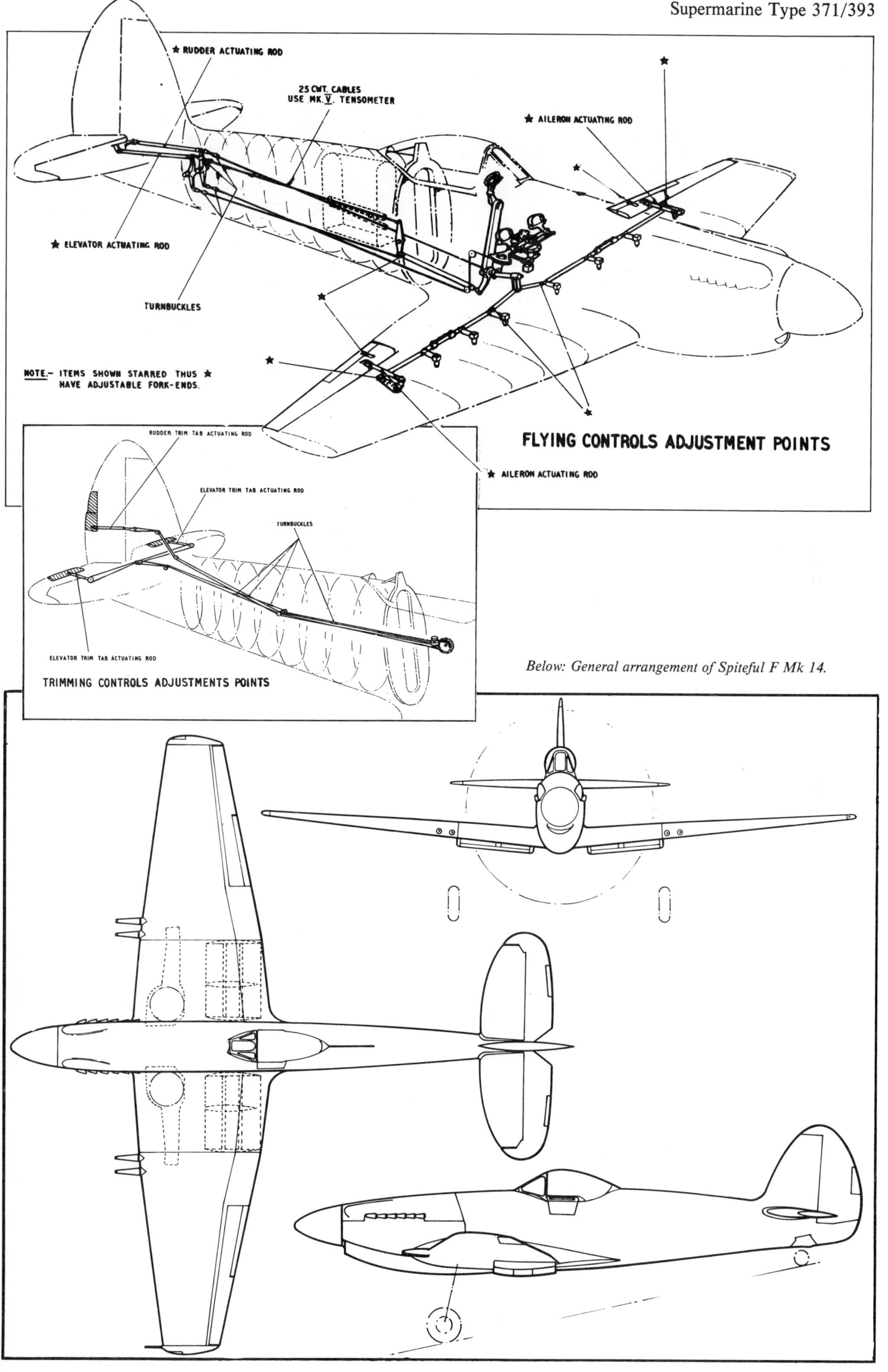

Below: General arrangement of Spiteful F Mk 14.

Prototype Spiteful, NN664, flew for the first time on 8 January 1945 with the normal Spitfire large chord fin and rudder. The larger unit was installed in April/May. Note Royal Navy legend on fuselage.

as outlined by Joseph Smith in Technical Note 3859 of 12 August 1943.

Weight saving was a major factor and the following points were mentioned as being capable of modification – extra machining of wing main spar flanges. Twenty-three pounds could be saved if the wing skin was reduced in thickness by .005in. Building the oleo legs of duralumin would save 33.5lb with a further fifty five pounds saved by deletion of the starting mechanism and relying on external starting. The alloy MG9, once considered for the Supermarine F 7/30 prototype, would save pounds when used in place of duralumin in oil and water tanks. Light alloy gills and radiator tubes saved 105lb, and the use of electricity or hydraulics for the pneumatic system would have saved 25lb. The total amount of weight saved by these methods was 442.8lb.

By April 1944 the first of the new laminar wings was ready for installation on to a Spitfire F Mk XIV fuselage, NN660. It had a Griffon 61 engine and five blade Rotol propeller, and on 30 June Jeffrey Quill took off from High Post for the first flight. Tare weight was 6,746lb and for flight trials it was to be loaded to the Spiteful estimated auw – 9,000lb. NN660 had a very short life for it crashed at High Post on 13 September killing the test pilot Frank Furlong. The accident report tells the story –

"During accident investigations in respect of NN660 it has been found that in the aileron circuit as arranged in the prototype, the possibility is present of the aileron control jamming or becoming disconnected in flight. Under positive 'G' the push-pull rods will move down in relation to the wing ribs and protuberances on the rods may catch up on the rib cut-out. Movement of the control by the pilot may then (a) pull back the sleeve (protuberance) and possibly disconnect the circuit (b) cause jam at or near the neutral position (c) cause jam with aileron 84% up preventing a return to neutral. Under negative 'G' the rods will move up in relation to the ribs, and in aileron operation the pin may then catch up on the inboard end of the tophat section attached to the gun door. This would cause jam with aileron 14% up preventing a return to neutral. Evidence on two previous flights showed the pilot felt some temporary obstruction in operating the ailerons. The aileron circuit for the second aircraft is being redesigned".

On the day following the accident an ejector seat for the Spiteful was discussed and the plan was for the pilot and seat to be ejected through the fuselage door. This was later amended to ejection in the accepted fashion via the jettisoned canopy, and it was planned to introduce this major modification to the airframe when series production started.

Supermarine Report 4540 provided details of a wing profile modification to improve handling characteristics. It read – "Preliminary handling tests may show that a prototype aeroplane has unexpected and undesirable handling characteristics due to some fault in the aerodynamic shape of the wing or empennage. In such cases, where improvement necessitates change in aerofoil section, reliable evidence in the form of flight tests is desirable before becoming finally committed to the

RB515 made a second forced landing, this time at Farnborough, sustaining substantial damage.

First production Spiteful was RB515 which also had the F21 Spiteful fin and rudder. Four days after its first flight it had to make a wheels up landing at Boscombe Down. Following repairs it was fitted with the larger fin.

First production Spiteful, RB515, which made its maiden flight on 2 April, 1945.

serious changes in design involved. It is also desirable that a rapid reversion to the original shape should be possible if occasion demands. A case in point occurred with the F 1/43 Spiteful; the prototype showed unsatisfactory lateral stability just above stalling speed.

"Wind tunnel tests suggested this might be due to the effect on the ailerons of the reflex curvature over the trailing half of the section and it was proposed to modify the profile in way of the ailerons, eliminating the reflex. It was decided to fit wooden fairings over the regions involved, these fairings being narrow, chordwise strips. Initial tests were made using yellow pine in 1½ and 3in wide strips. These tended to break away in flight and balsa wood was substituted". Our drawings show the modified wing profile and area involved.

By this time the first true prototype Spiteful, NN664, was nearing completion and to test the revised aileron circuit a series of stiffness and loading tests were carried out and concluded satisfactorily. Modification of the circuit delayed the first flight and Rowe, of MAP, wrote to Joseph Smith on 16 December – "I expect news of the first flight before Christmas as a Christmas present". But, Supermarine would not be hurried and the aircraft was flown by Jeffrey Quill on 8 January 1945, still in an unpainted state.

NN664 had many faults – aileron snatch at speeds preceeding the stall with wing dropping at the same time, and many experiments were carried out to eradicate them in the form of reduced span ailerons, modified wing section near the ailerons, wing spoilers and, as tested in the Farnborough wind tunnel, an enlarged fin and rudder and enlarged tailplane and elevator. With the new empennage it was first flown on 24 June 1945.

A Supermarine Report of 22 May detailed these, and other modifications. The wing was modified by sticking strips of balsa wood to the upper surface, but this did not improve matters. Tufts were fitted from wing tip to the inboard edge of the bulge and they indicated that the whole of the outer portion of the wing became stalled about 10 to 20mph above the main stall. The entire upper surface of the port wing was then tufted

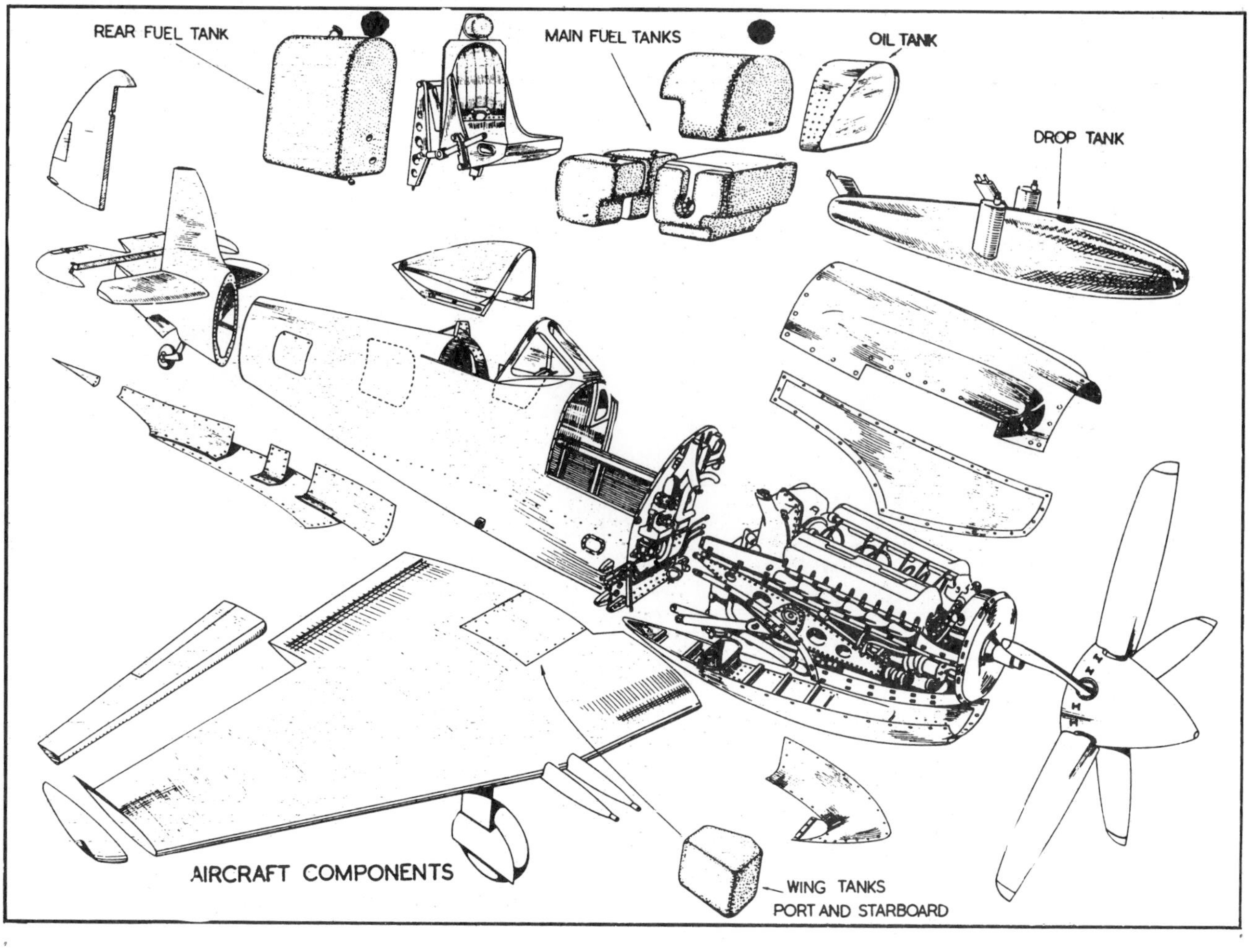

REAR FUEL TANK
MAIN FUEL TANKS
OIL TANK
DROP TANK
AIRCRAFT COMPONENTS
WING TANKS
PORT AND STARBOARD

and in flight it revealed that the whole of the portion of the wing in front of the ailerons stalled before main lift had broken down. To speed trials similar tests were made on Spitfire wings and included plain and Frise ailerons, raised leading edge section, root spoilers.

Slotted ailerons were then fitted and they had small area, geared balance tabs. Quill and his fellow pilots thought that an increase in wing dihedral angle would contribute towards better lateral control throughout the speed, and in particular at low speed.

The first production Spiteful RB515 made its maiden flight of fifteen minutes on 2 April 1945 with Jeffrey Quill at the controls. It was fitted with the small, F 21 type fin and rudder. On 6 April Quill flew it for 40 minutes on aileron trials. Three days later while making level speed runs he experienced some vibration and he had to make a wheels up landing at Boscombe

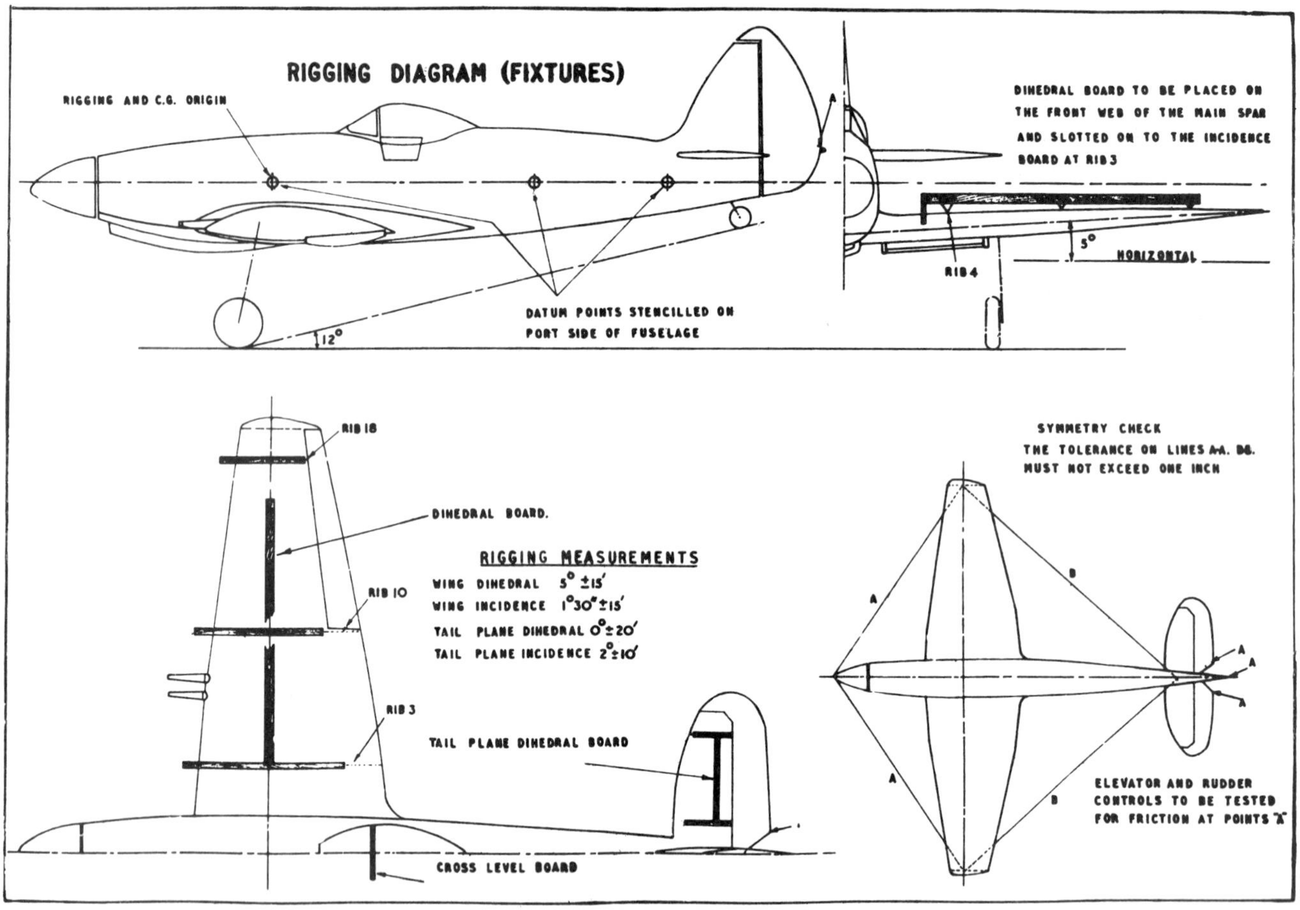

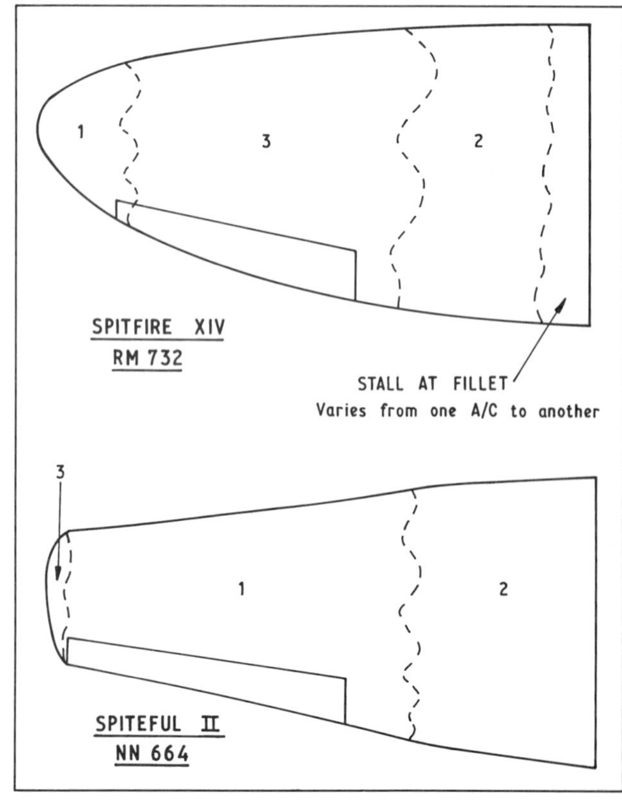

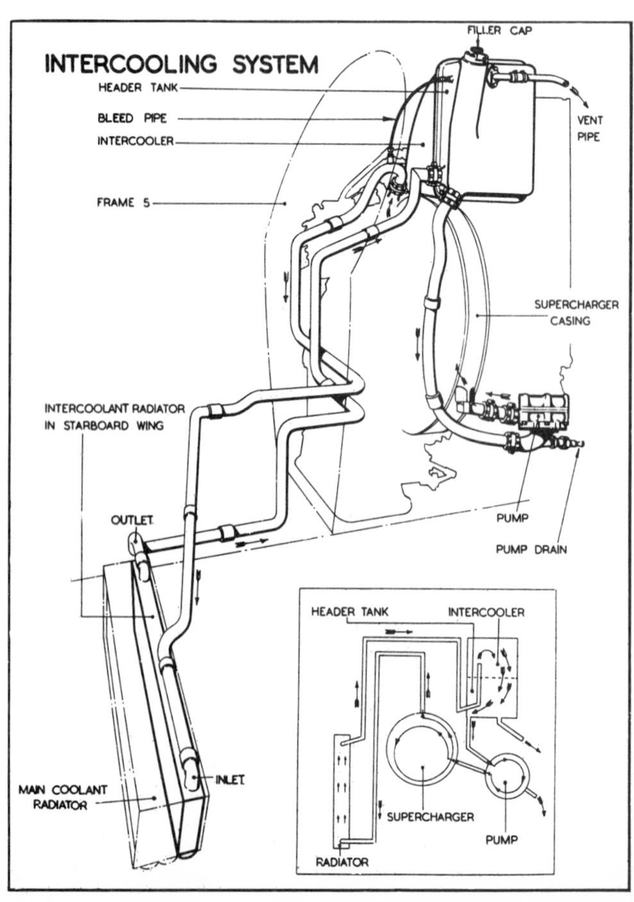

Down. The aircraft was sent back to the workshops for repair and while there the larger tail unit was installed. Fitted with wing root spoilers it flew again on 21 May. These were removed upon landing and it was transferred to Farnborough two days later.

In the meantime Supermarine had received a letter from MAP on 12 April informing them that the order for F Mk XIV Spiteful had been reduced by 150, leaving a total of 650. Supermarine replied asking that MAP should reconsider as the company was expecting an order for a quantity of Seafang aircraft, and it would be wasteful to cancel 150 sets of castings, etc.

Flight trials with RB515 continued and on 27 September the supercharger impellers burst when it was at high altitude. The engine began vibrating until the propellers stopped rotating and the pilot, Shea-Simmonds, stalled the aircraft with the result that the fuselage split under the cockpit door. A wheels up landing was made at Farnborough resulting in further damage to the bottom longerons and plating, and as a result of this an external stiffening strip 1½ inches wide was fitted under the cockpit. Weight increase was also causing concern for when RB515 was first weighed on 31 March the auw was 8,650lb, and this had risen to 9,222 by the time of its second accident. Production aircraft were to have provision for a strengthened tail wheel and an enlarged empennage; a rear fuel tank and system (64½ gals); provision for drop tanks; racks for 2 × 100lb bombs; provision for 4 × 300lb rocket packs.

An FR and PR variant was also proposed but as of 1 November 1945 no trial installation or prototype had been authorised. The MAP was of the opinion that introduction of these variants would overload Supermarine and jeopardise introduction of the fighter version. Supermarine urged that an FR and PR Spiteful be authorised without delay in order to maintain the, then, target force of twelve FR Squadrons. The FR variant was to have the rear fuel capacity reduced to 43 gallons; two vertical F24 20 inch and one F24 14 inch cameras, plus the ancilliaries, plus provision for carrying an offensive load. If required a 1,780 gallon overload fuel tank could be carried, but the take off limitation would have risen to 12,400 lb.

The third prototype, NN667, differed from its immediate predecessor in having an extended carburetter air intake just behind the propeller, and after its first flight it went to Boscombe Down on 27 March 1946. The report of the engineering and maintenance appraisal concluded "In poor condition and badly constructed". This Spiteful was put through a series of trials by Derry and Lithgow with a set of Spitfire F21 and Spiteful wing fillets fitted. Dives were made to Mach .83 and there was little difference in performance with either type of fillet. Pilot's reports on the Spiteful pointed to two unpleasant aspects of longitudinal trim (1) a large change of trim occurred with operation of the radiator flaps for cooling, and of radiator flaps and landing flaps for landing and (2) an unusually large force was required to get the tail down when landing. Use of the trim tab partially cured condition (1) but (2) was more complicated. Due to fuel consumption the CoG moved forwards and a spring mechanism had to be introduced into the elevator system to raise the elevator in conjunction with fuel consumption.

Griffon engine and mounting showing the cartridge engine starter and breech.

The original order for the Spiteful was 650 examples and the first cancellation removed 260 aircraft in the serial ranges NM824-852, 879-906, PM161-168, 184-228, 245-284, RB841-843,857-898,912-954,965-987. A second cancellation reduced the 390 on order to 80- serials PM671-676,PS684-725,739-781,795-830,RB598-615,628-667,691-725,739-783,796-827,828-840. The final cancellation reduced from 80 on order to 22 machines; serials deleted were RB526,532,534,537-557,571-578 582-597,668,669,683-690.

By mid-March 1946 the Air Ministry was beginning to lose interest in the Spiteful and the DTD wrote to Joseph Smith saying that they were only interested in the Spiteful as a low altitude attack aircraft, and unless it was cleared for this production would be abandoned. It was a bitter blow to Smith and his colleagues, but the Air Ministry's decision was inevitable as jet powered fighters were beginning to reveal their superiority over the propeller driven types.

The second production Spiteful, RB516, was weighed at high Post on 5 February 1946 and with a Griffon 69 engine and Rotol five blade wooden propeller its tare was 7,556lb and auw

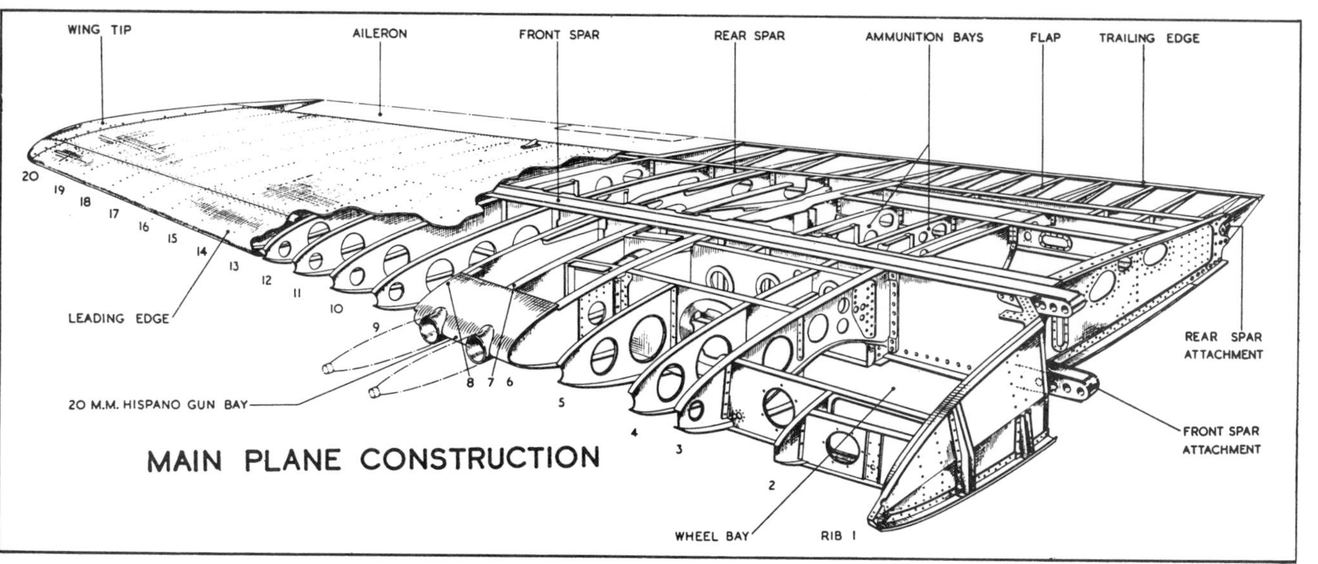

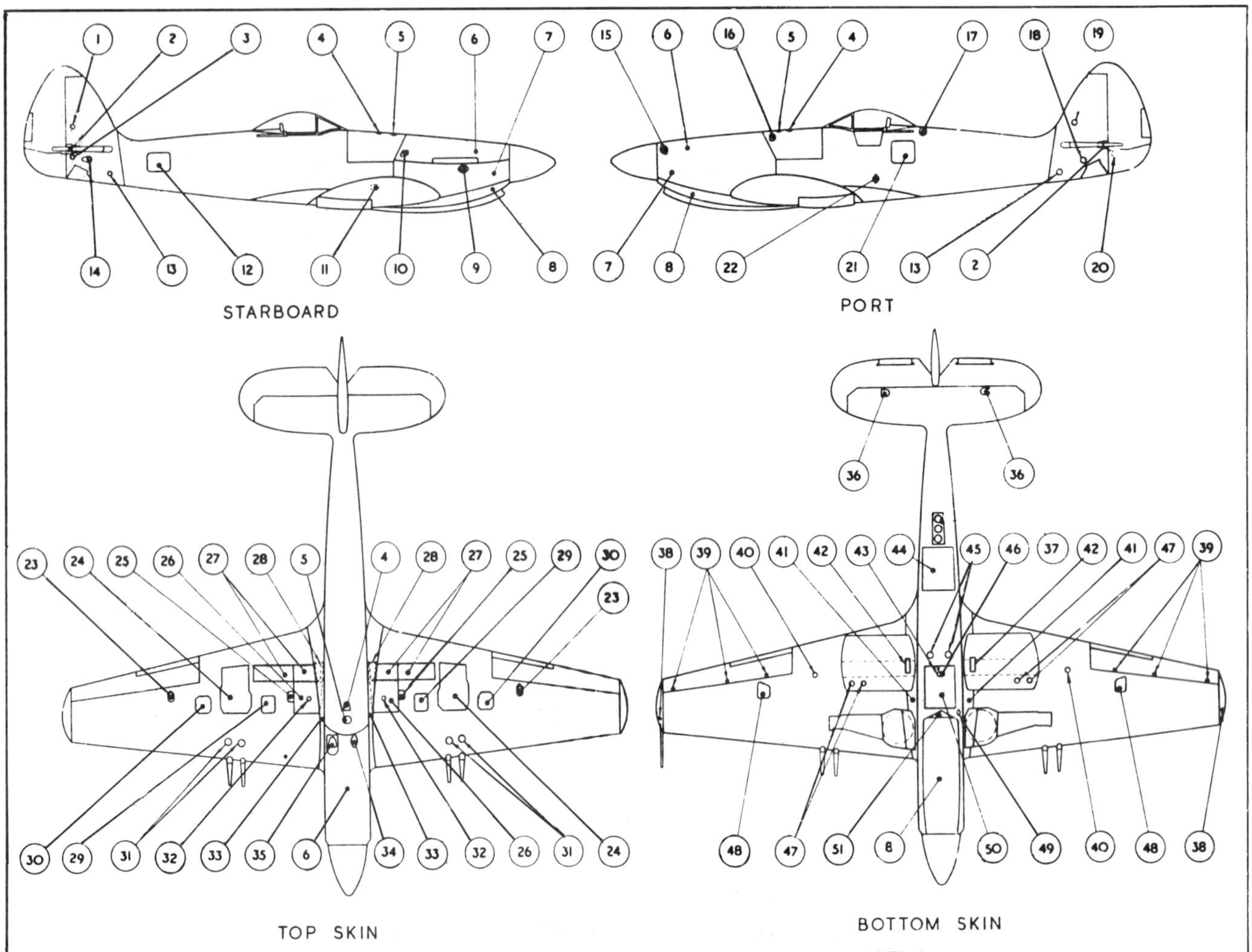

STARBOARD

PORT

TOP SKIN

BOTTOM SKIN

ACCESS DOORS AND INSPECTION PANELS

Key to panel. 1 rudder tab screw jack; 2 elevator gap; 3 elevator trim tab connections; 4 fuel filler cap; 5 oil filter cap; 6 top cowling panel; 7 side cowling panel; 8 bottom cowling panel; 9 engine starter breech; 10 gear box dipstick; 11 field tank connections; 12 DR compass and rear fuselage; 13 flying controls and tailwheel strut; 14 elevator trim tab controls; 15 main coolant header tank; 16 oil filler cap; 17 rear tank filler cap; 18 tailwheel strut; 19 rudder trim tab controls; 20 lower rudder hinge; 21 radio; 22 electrical ground supply socket; 23 aileron actuating rod; 24 guns and aileron controls: 25 radiator flap jack; 26 aileron controls; 27 radiator mounting; 28 electrical connections under fillet; 29 inboard ammunition box; 30 outboard ammunition box; 31 gun gas plugs; 32 wing fuel tank filler cap; 33 wing root connections (top); 34 hydraulic reservoir and air charging valve; 35 intercooler header tank; 36 elevator trim tab screw jacks; 37 identification lamps; 38 wing tip lamp terminal block; 39 aileron hinges; 40 aileron control and flap jack; 41 wing root connections (bottom); 42 radiator drain plugs; 43 cockpit drain; 44 rear fuel tank; 45 saddle tank drain plugs; 46 hydraulic system drain plugs; 47 pipe connections; 48 aileron controls; 49 supercharger drain; 50 main fuel tank; 51 bottom cowling (aft).

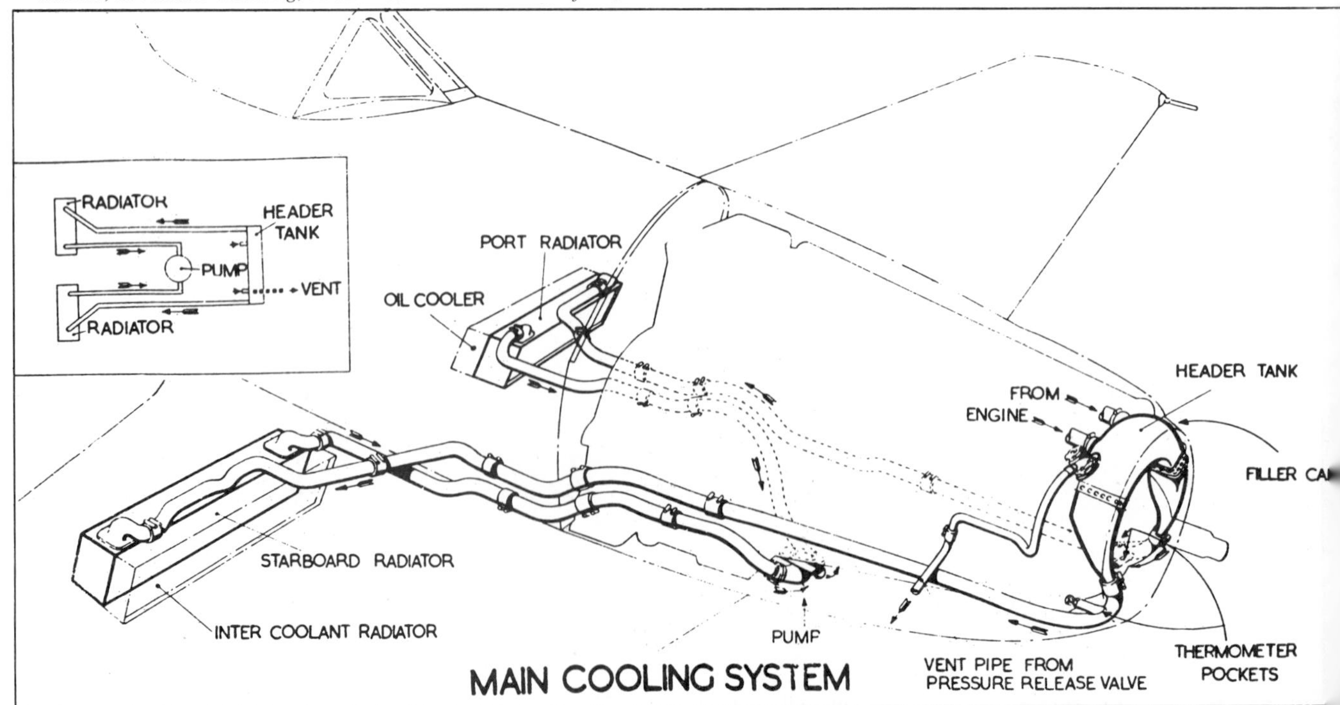

MAIN COOLING SYSTEM

10,165. With a view to providing for full aileron control at the maximum diving speed of 525mph, power operated ailerons were proposed in November 1946 and for this purpose wing strength was investigated on RB516. A control for the power unit was installed in the cockpit to enable the pilot to override it in the event of trouble.

In December 1946 Vickers wrote to MAP about the final total of work completed on the Spiteful/Seafang contract as follows- (A) Complete aircraft to be billed under Contract 1877/C,23(c). Spiteful RB515-525, RB527-531, 16 aircraft. Seafang Mark 31. VG471-479, nine aircraft. (B) Partially completed aircraft to be dealt with under Contract 5757/C.23(c). Spiteful RB535. Seafang Mark 31 VG480; Mark 32 VG481,482,486,488-490. To regularise the position contractually, it is requested that the following serial numbers applicable to partially completed aircraft cancelled by the Department's letter dated 11 July 1946 also be deleted- Spiteful RB533,536,579-581, 5 aircraft. Seafang Mark 32 VG483-485,487,491-493, 7 aircraft.

The final Spiteful variant was the F Mk XVI, only one example of which was built. This was RB518 which had its beginnings in a Supermarine Report dated 7 February 1944. It was entitled Spitfire Type 371 with high powered Griffon engine. Part one investigated the propeller need to absorb the power from the Griffon as developed by 1945. Rotol propellers with five blades of 18.25 inches in width, six blades 16.25 inch and eight blades of 11.5 inch width were suggested. The eight blade unit was assumed to be the better type.

When flown RB518 had a Griffon 101 engine and this was, basically, a two stage Griffon with a three speed supercharger driving a five blade propeller. The aircraft had a faired windscreen and the original Spiteful carburetter nose intake. First propeller tests were with an 11ft.0in diameter model with wide chord NACA 16 section blades, this being tested originally on RB515. Level speed tests were carried out with this and a Rotol five blade double wedge section propeller. These tests were confined to the measurement, over a range of heights, of performance in FS gear. On 6 February 1946 Mike Lithgow was flying RB518 after it had been repaired following minor damage to engine and cowling after a blowback from the carburetter during early flights. At 28,000 feet, during a second run, there was an explosion and the engine failed, only to start again. Lithgow throttled back and turned for base and as he was unable to use the throttle during his landing approach he was forced to cut switches. The fault was found to be a strip of rubber from around the air intake caught up in the throttle valve.

A second propeller was installed, the engine repaired, and trials started once again. These were cut short when the engine failed once more and Lithgow had to make a wheels up landing. Results of the curtailed tests showed that the second propeller, a Rotol double wedge, was the better proposition. It was decided to continue trials with RB518 fitted with a Griffon 121 (Griffon 101 with CR gears) and a Rotol six blade, 11ft diameter contra-prop, the blades having a Clark Y section. Level speed measurements in FS gear were made at heights ranging from 21,000 to 36,000 feet. The trials were again terminated when the Griffon failed and RB518 was damaged beyond repair in a wheels up, forced landing just short of High Post. The contra-prop installation caused a small reduction in level speed at 31,000 feet, and 12mph at 35,000 feet. The Griffon engine with the three stage blower was a complicated unit and prone to failure. The summary of results with RB518 is given in the following table-

S/C gear	height (ft)	rpm	boost lb/sq in	max level speed (mph)
LS	SL	2750	+25	407
LS	10,000+	2750	+25	452
LS	13,300	2750	+19.4	452
MS	13,300	2750	+25	452
MS	20,500+	2750	+25	484
MS	24,500	2750	+20.2	482
FS	24,500	2750	+25	482
FS	27,500	2750	+25	494
FS	35,000	2750	+14.9	478

+ refers to full throttle height

Maximum rate of climb was 4,750ft/min, service ceiling 43,000ft and take off weight 9,070lb. Before RB518 was written off Jeffrey Quill had made several flights with the outer wing sections leading edge modified by introducing a more blunt profile.

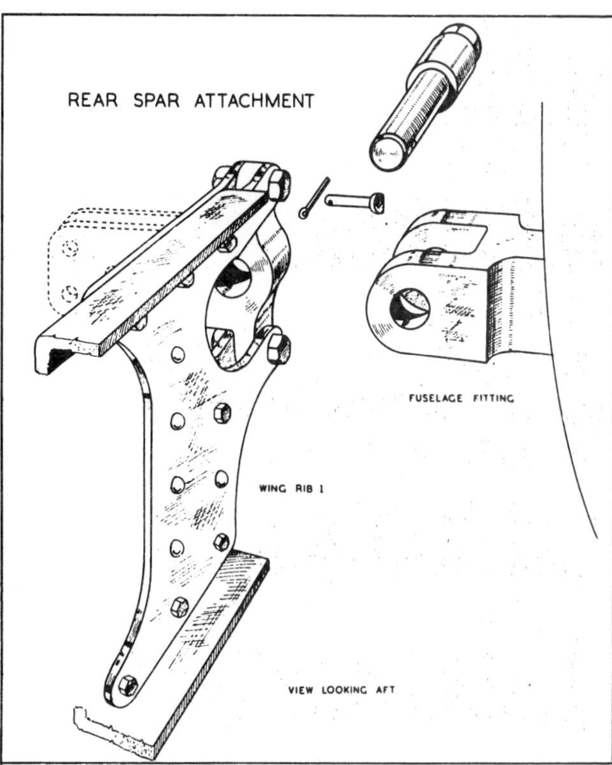

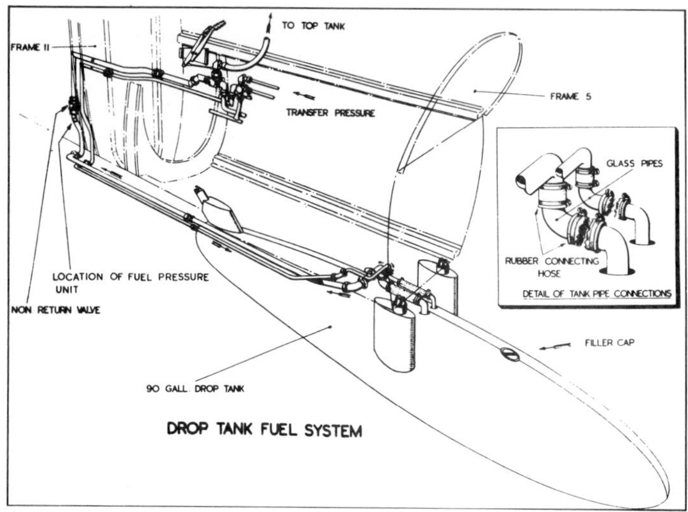

Interest in the Spiteful was now minimal and the revised contract for 650 aeroplanes reduced to 190. Only 17 were completed and the three final examples were not flown but delivered to John Dale for scrap. Mitchell's design had reached the end of its useful life, only the legend remained. There was an abortive attempt to interest the Air Ministry in a jet propelled version in which the Spiteful wing was to be modified and fitted to a new fuselage. Details, below, were published in Supermarine Specification No 477.

SPITEFUL DEVELOPMENT, TYPE 392.

This specification gives particulars of a proposed development of the Spiteful fighter. The wing, chassis and gun installation are Spiteful components which are being put into production at the present time, and represent the firm's latest and most up to date practice both technically and from the production angle. The new tail unit is provided. It may be pointed out that when starting with a completely new design, the fuselage usually takes less time to design and build than the wings and moreover, in production, it is not uncommon to see a row of fuselages waiting for wings. In the case of the present project, therefore, the more difficult half has already been designed and will shortly be in production.

The Spiteful wing should be very suitable for the high speeds obtainable with the turbine engine because it has been designed to improve on the good qualities of the Spitfire wing which is well known to be free from compressibility vices. Engine development has been allowed for and the estimated performance is- maximum speed 579mph at 19,000ft, service ceiling 53,000ft, take off weight 10,250 lb, endurance @ 20,000ft 2.32hr, range 600 miles, rate of climb 4,390 @ SL, 2,760 @ 20,000ft, time to altitude 5.65 min to 20,000ft, take off run 1,066 yds, max diving speed 560mph. The design was referred to as the Jet Spiteful and the aeroplane, in much modified form, finally flew as the Royal Navy's Attacker.

A most startling concept was proposed in the Supermarine Technical Report No 4040 of 26 February 1944. It is reproduced here in its entirety, together with the project drawing. Mitchell would have approved for it was another step forward as had been the F 37/34 all those years ago.

TECHNICAL OFFICE REPORT No 4040 VERTICAL TAKE OFF AND LANDING

The fact that aeroplanes require aerodromes for their operation is often a serious disadvantage, particularly from the military viewpoint. The processes of launching and arresting have been highly developed by the Navy, but are still difficult and hazardous operations, and appear likely to remain so. Machines such as the helicopter and autogyro, which greatly reduce take off and landing problems, are inherently less efficient from the performance point of view and therefore seem unlikely to be military or commercial successes except for a few special purposes.

No attention appears to have been given to the possibility to take off and land using the airscrew thrust to support the weight. Yet a Spitfire could climb vertically if it had a larger airscrew and suitably adjusted engine airscrew gearing (the fuel and oil systems would need some attention, of course). An aeroplane designed to operate on this basis, viz. with vertical take off and landing, is shown on the attached sketches (see right) in comparison with a Spitfire.

With a Griffon engine developing 2,500hp the static thrust of the propeller (19 feet diameter 8-bladed contraprop) is 15,000lb. In order to fly horizontally it needs no more than 100sq ft of wing area (compared with the 230sq ft of the Spitfire), because the wings ae no longer required for landing and also because the large airscrew supplies a considerable amount of lift in level flight.

The normal chassis is eliminated- the machine lands, and stands, on its tail. The resultant saving in structure weight compensates for the increase in airscrew weight, and also for the weight of the two speed airscrew. There is good reason to believe that the performance of the orthodox aeroplane could be bettered.

There are obviously many possible applications, both to military and civil aircraft such as fighters and fast naval types, and there seems to be a distinct possibility of successful application to the small civil aeroplane. It should also be noted that the idea lends itself to the use of the internal combustion turbine. In this case the airscrew would be used for take off and at speeds up to 450mph. Above this speed the blades would be feathered and the exhaust thrust relied upon for propulsion.

In order to design and build such an aircraft, utilising an existing engine, no fundamentally new aerodynamic or engineering problems require to be solved. Moreover the most important step, vertical take off and landing, could be proved by adapting a Spitfire. A. N. Clifton.

The Swiss Air Force displayed an interest in the Spiteful and arrangements were made for a number of its pilots to fly the aircraft. Two were allocated, RB517 and RB523, but they had not been delivered or taken on charge by the RAF. MAP wrote to Supermarine advising them of the situation whereby the official contract prohibited the use of the aircraft for any other purpose than that approved by MAP, and MAP were not prepared to give approval. However, MAP then wrote again to Supermarine with the following proposal- "In the event of total loss of the airframes, engines or other equipment you shall (1) replace the airframes in kind without charge (2) pay the cash value of the engine(s) and equipment. For this purpose the values shall be – engines £2,515, equipment £2,135 for each aircraft". Britain's post war exports had started with a bureaucratic send off.

Wing. Planform equi-tapered leading and trailing edge; section Supermarine high speed 371/I and II; span 35′ 6″; incidence° 1.5 at root; dihedral° 5; aspect ratio 6; area sq ft 210; chord (geometric) mean aerodynamic ft in 5 9.8; ailerons area sq ft 13.16, movement° up and down 16, droop 0; Flaps area sq ft 7.86, movement down° 78; radiator flaps area sq ft 11.34, movement down° 87.5; wing loading lb/sq ft 47.4; power loading 4.19lb hp. Propeller clearance at take off 10in.

Tailplane. Area sq ft 42.56; chord (ma) ft. in 4.1; incidence° root 2 tip; elevators area sq ft 17.39; movement° up 28, down 23; tab, movement° up 20, down 7. Fin area sq ft 9.95, under rudder 2.31; rudder area sq ft 10.55, movement° each way 28; tab, movement° port 9, starbd 13.5.

Engine/s. Griffon RG 4SM 69 2,375hp. Take off 1,520hp/2,750rpm + 12; combat rating (5mins) 2,375hp @ 2,750rpm + 25 @ 1,250ft; 2,035hp @ 2,750rpm + 18 @ 7,000ft; 1,490hp @ 2,600rpm @ 13,500ft + 9 (60mins).

Griffon 90.

Coffman Cartridge starter.

The Supermarine design proposal for a vertical take off and landing fighter, showing a Spitfire for size comparison.

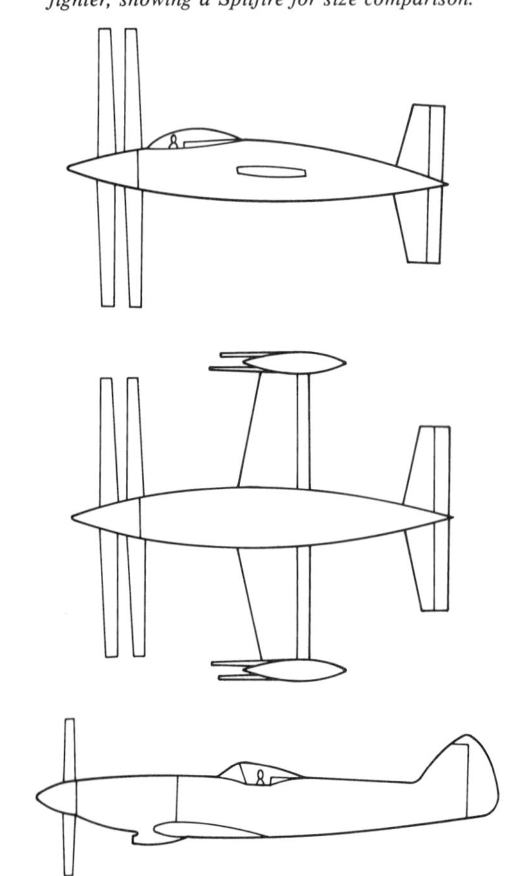

Propeller/s. Rotol R14/5F5/F2 5-blade Dural, left hand tractor 35° pitch range, fine pitch, diameter.

Rotol 6-blade counter rotating.

Coolant. 70% distilled water, 30% Glycol, main system 15½gals, intercooler 3½.

Fuel. 100 octane + 18lb boost, 150 octane + 25lb.

Capacity. Upper fuselage 34½gals, lower 43, rear fuselage 2 x 11¼, 22½, wing inter spar 16. Total 116. later a/c, rear fuselage 62. total 178 gals, plus 90gal or 180 o/ld tanks. Oil 9½ gals.

Armament. 4 x 20mm Hispano Mk V Cannon 16/rpg inboard, 145rpg outboard, total 674. Provision for 2 x 1,000lb bomb; 4 × 300lb RPs.

Performance. (ES) 481mph @ 26,000ft @ 3,000rpm + 18lb; 483mph @ 21,000ft @ 3,000rpm + 25; 436mph @ 11,400ft @ 3,000rpm + 18 (MS); 437mph @ 5,500ft @ 3,000rpm + 25 (MS); 382mph @ SL @ + 18 (MS); 409mph @ SL @ + 25 (MS). Rate of climb (normal auw) 3,106ft min @ 22,000ft (FS) + 18; 3,766ft min @ 17,500ft + 25 (FS); 4,086ft min @ 8,000ft @ + 25 (MS); 4,890ft min @ 2,000ft @ + 25. 3,959ft/min @ SL + 18; 4,828ft/min @ SL @ + 25. Service ceiling (100ft min) 42,000ft. Range (average cruise 240-250mph) normal fuel 564 miles, 5.04mpg; duration @ 20,000ft 2.21 to 2.35 hr; with 180 ferry fuel, speed 240-260mph 1,315 miles, duration 5.09 to 5.47hr. Take off run 840yds, landing 740. Max diving speed 525 mph. Stall 95mph.

F MkXVI Griffon 101.3-speed blower. Max Speed 494mph @ 28,500ft (FS); 483mph @ a 21,000ft (MS); 452mph @ 10,000ft (LS); 408mph @ SL. Max climb 4,760ft min.

Weight. Empty 7,350lb, take off 9,950, max permissible 10,200, max overload 11,400.

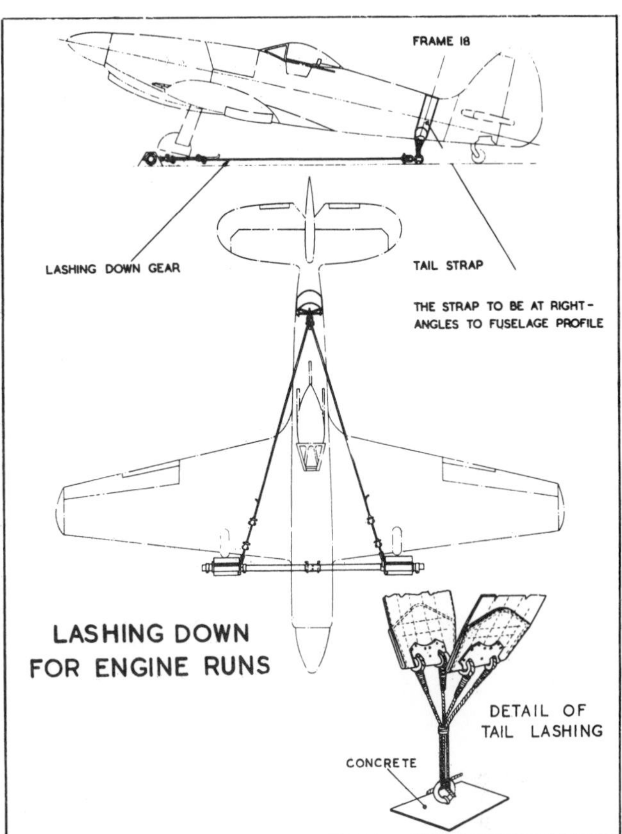

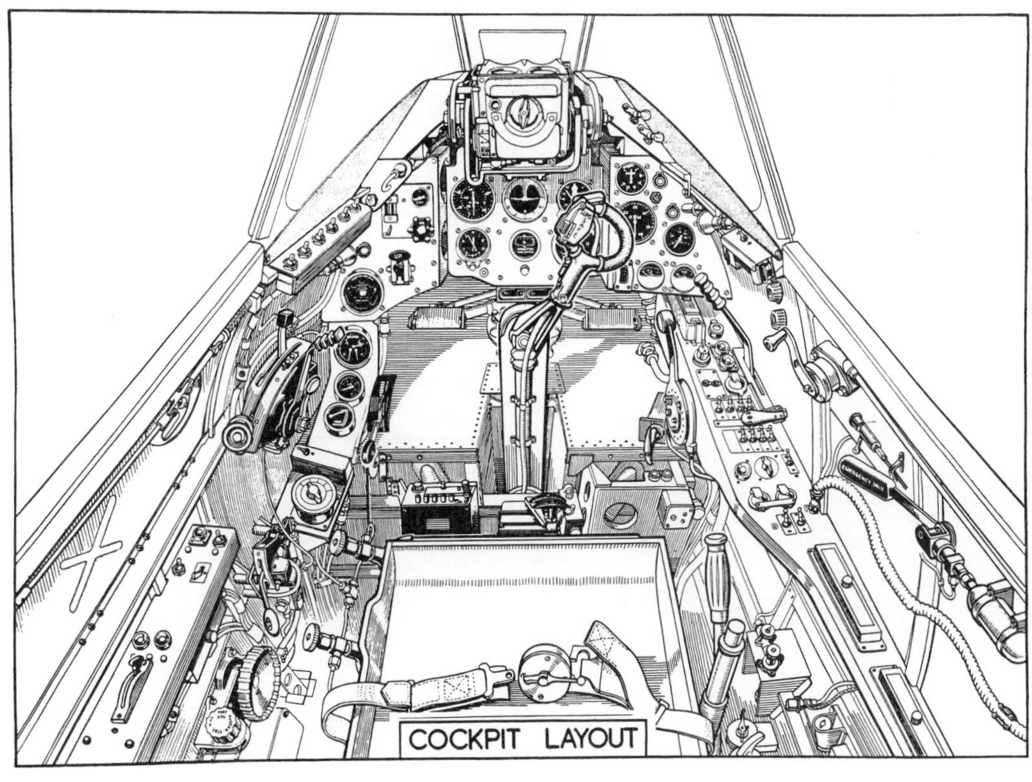

SERIAL NUMBERS

Supermarine Aviation (Vickers) Ltd., Southampton.
Contract No. 1877/C.23(c).
Ninth order for 373 Spitfire Mk21 dated 14 August 1943. Order amended to 373 Spiteful Mk XIV. Nineteen only constructed between March 1945 and January 1947. RB515-525, 527-531, 533-535.
The Original order was for 650 aircraft in the following ranges – NM824-853, 879-906, PM161-168, 184-228, 245-284, 671-676, PS684-725, 739-781, 795-830, RB515-532, 534, 535, 537-557, 571-578, 582-597, 628-669, 683-725, 739-783, 843, 857-898, 912-953, 965-987.
On 12 September 1945 the order was reduced from 650 to 390 aircraft, 280 cancellations – NM824-852, 879-906, PM161-168, 184-228, 245-284, RB841-843, 857-898, 912-953, 965-987. On 12 February 1946 this amended order was also reduced by 310 aircraft – PM671-676, PS684-725, 739-781, 795-830, RB598-615, 628-667, 691-725, 739-783, 796-827, 828-840. On 22 May 1946 it was again amended by a reduction of 58, the order now standing at 22 aircraft – RB526-532, 534, 537-557, 571-578, 582-597, 668, 669-690,. The final amendment was on 16 December 1946 to 16 aircraft – RB515-525, 527-531, 535. Three more aircraft were ordered – RB533, 534 and RT646. These were delivered as dismantled aircraft except for the latter, which was a fuselage only for testing.

RB516 at Boscombe Down for ordnance trials.

RB521, used principally from Farnborough and referred to in their Flight Log as a 'Seafang'.

RB series all Griffon 69 engines

RB515 HPA 31-3-45 CRD makers trials 31-3 FF Quill 2-4 15mins ails 6-4 Farn stall tests emergency w/u ldg bdn 9-4 large root spoilers instal and large tail unit 21-5 trls. Farn 23-5 HPA 23-5 NACA 16 paddle prop instal 11-7 Bdn 23-7 f/ld cd Farn written off 27-9 SOC scr 13-11

RB516 VA HPA 28-2-46 CRD makers trls 6th production a/c 1st to RAF 6MU 6-12 con to FXVI sold J Dale 8-7-48

RB517 VA HPA 30-3-46 CRD makers trls 6MU 27-2-47 sold J Dale 8-7-48

RB518 VA HPA 28-2-45 makers trls CRD AID del report held for CRO G101 instal with 3-stage blower and +25lb boost. This pressure had been tried on the Merlin code name 'Basta'. Con to FXVI 6MU 27-2-47 speeds of over 494mph achieved. Several eng fail and f/ldgs (seven in all). Final ld at Chil u/c oleos forced through wings. 49MU written off 29-3-49 when dropped from salvage crane

RB519 VA HPA 6-9-45 CRD makers trls 6MU 27-2-47 sold J Dale 8-7-48

RB520 VA HPA 22-9-45 CRD makers trls displayed Hendon 2-10 sting hook instal for Seafang trls 6MU 13-1-47 SOC 31-1-47

RB521 VA HPA 27-10-45 CRD makers trls displayed Farn 14-10 Farn 8-4-46 ails trls (the Farn flight log called RB521 'Seafang') Took part in enemy a/c display 29/30-10 6MU 13-3-47 sold J Dale 8-7-48

RB522 await collect SM 25-5-46 took part in Farn display 27-6 HPA test flts 6MU 27-2-47 Farn Jly'48 sold J Dale 8-7-48

RB523 await collect SM 30-3-46 Farn Jne CRD HPA 6MU 11-11 SOC 12-2-47 sold J Dale 8-7-48

RB524 await collect SM 17-8-46 6MU 3-12 49MU 12-2-47 sold J Dale 8-7-48

RB525 await collect SM 17-8-46 6MU 3-12 sold J Dale 8-7-48

RB527 6MU 5-12-46 sold J Dale 8-7-48

RB528 await collect SM 29-6-46 6MU 5-12 sold J Dale 8-7-48

RB529 6MU 3-12-46 sold J Dale 8-7-48

RB530 6MU 5-12-46 sold J Dale 8-7-48

RB531 await collect SM 17-1-47 6MU 17-1 sold J Dale 8-7-48

RB533 never test flown 1 MPRD Cowley Ox dismantled rts sold J Dale 8-7-48

RB534 details as 533

RB535 details as 533

NN660 Spiteful proto FF 30-6-44 JKQ G61 intially then G69. See page for details.

NN664 2nd proto FF June'44 JQ see page 496 for details

NN667 3rd proto. BDn 27-3-46 carbon monoxide cockpit contamination tests; eng and maintenance appraisal 6-6-48. Report concluded a/c to be in poor condition, detail construction criticised in particular numerous anti-crack holes at awkward bends or abrupt changes on section. Twenty-two mods were suggested.

RB517, used for makers' trials until retired in February, 1947

Right: RB518 was converted to a Mk XVI in early 1947.

SEAFIRE

"BETTER THAN NOTHING"

When the Royal Navy went to war in September 1939 it was operating aircraft that were well beyond their prime. The Fleet Air Arm was equipped with the Blackburn Roc four gun turret fighter, the Skua dive bomber and strike aircraft and a small number of Swordfish. Entering service was the Sea Gladiator, a conversion of the land fighter, which the Admiralty had been almost forced to accept as a makeshift until its new fighter, the Fairey Fulmar, reached production status. Although the latter was a great improvement on current naval equipment it was considered by the FAA to be a stop-gap until a high speed fighter became available. It was inferior in speed to its land based contemporaries, the Spitfire and Hurricane, and in addition had to carry the same weight of armament plus a pilot and navigator. Because of the dire need for defence aircraft a number of Sea Gladiators had to be transferred from the Mediterranean to the United Kingdom.

With the exception of the Gladiator all Fleet Air Arm aircraft continued the Navy's pre-war philosophy of having two service personnel to operate it. This philosophy had its roots in the inter-war years when a carrier operated aeroplane, particularly strike aircraft, had to be navigated to its target and back as it was felt that the dual role of pilot/navigator was too much for the pilot. Also, the Admiralty's view was that a carrier borne interceptor would normally be operating beyond the range of land based attacking aircraft, and likely opponents would be strike aircraft similar in performance to their own. The Royal Navy had in the past operated the single seat fighter but they were slow biplanes which seldom operated beyond the visual horizon.

When German forces invaded Norway and the Navy was required to transport troops and supplies to the area and to provide air cover, the lack of a fast, single seat fighter was thrown into sharp relief. The only available aircraft, the Sea Gladiator, was no match for the Bf 109 fighter and when the carrier *HMS Courageous* was attacked by Luftwaffe bombers nothing could prevent it being sunk. A modern, carrier based fighter was urgently needed, and the Admiralty turned to the British aircraft industry to discuss the practicality of producing such an aircraft at extremely short notice.

Why had such a situation arisen? The Sea Lords were aware of the need for a modern interceptor for in November 1933 the Director of Technical Development (Air Ministry) said – "The Fleet has need for fighter aircraft both for operation against enemy reconnaissance and spotter aircraft and for defence against air attack. Due to the peculiar naval conditions the two seat fighter would be the most effective weapon and such an aircraft should have a good all round performance, three hours endurance, w/t and navigational facilities. We would like to have two types- a two seat fighter and a two seat strike reconnaissance". The Director of Naval Air Division (DNAD) agreed with this statement but questioned the value of the fighter – "Assuming that such an aircraft can be designed, then it is confirmed that it can be used on a carrier. But while agreeing there would be occasions when fighter aircraft will be of value to the Fleet, it is considered that the limited aircraft carrying capacity means we cannot devote much of this to have a purely defensive fighter".

A Draft Specification was issued for a compromise aircraft to be ready for trials on *HMS Courageous* in the Spring of 1934. Blackburn Aircraft were to build a prototype which was a two-seat machine, on wheels or floats, capable of catapulting and arresting, for fighter reconnaissance duties. It had to carry a bomb load of a least 500 lbs, be suitable for dive bombing, have an endurance of three hours, auw 6,000 lbs, landing speed 45-50 knots with full load. Armament was one or two fixed forward firing guns, 600 rpg, plus one Lewis with six drums for the navigator/observer. The Admiralty wanted the Air Ministry's view on the possibilities of designing such an aircraft, as production examples were wanted by early 1935, but the reply to the Admiralty's letter of 9 April 1934 was unexpected. It read – "As a general principle it would be unwise to accept such an aircraft. The performance required is not possible for at least four years".

Hawker Aircraft, whose Osprey biplane was to be replaced by the new type, agreed with the Air Ministry view and based upon the aircraft company's conclusions the DTD decided that the Admiralty's requirement could be met by a fighter of 6,000 lb auw with a maximum speed of 200 mph. But, it could not be adapted as a general purpose aircraft. Hawker Aircraft then agreed to submit a sketch design of an Osprey replacement for general purposes.

By October 1934 discussions were taking place on a decision to replace the visual horizon defensive fighter with an offensive fighter and dive bomber, but the question of a new, high performance monoplane fighter with folding wings was to remain in abeyance. NAD 8/34 was to provide for two aircraft types – a landplane and a seaplane for fighter reconnaissance. The Air Ministry thought that a 40 foot wing span might seriously limit performance, but the Admiralty said that storage problems dictated the requirement. DNAD then wrote to the Air Ministry saying that the maximum speed of 193 mph called for in the Specification was too low, for with the ever increasing speeds to be expected from bombers (about the same as present defence equipment) the Fleet would have virtually no defence air fighters at all.

Specification 027/34 produced the Skua and 030/35 Roc from Blackburn, but by late 1937 the Fleet still lacked a suitable fighter. Both the Admiralty and Air Ministry were concerned by this as is evidenced by the Minutes of a meeting held on 22 October that year. It was recorded that all present were aware that the Skua and Roc would be obsolescent by the end of 1939 and that a more advanced design was an absolute necessity. All agreed upon three alternatives which could resolve the problem (1) conversion of an existing Royal Air Force single seat fighter for carrier operation (2) design and build a new type of 6 or 8 gun biplane off the drawing board, an event almost unheard of in those days and (3) to struggle on with existing types until more information was available on the possibilities of converting RAF equipment. Alternative three was out of the question and considered dangerous, although it was recognised that a fighter with fixed, forward firing guns would probably be the final choice. The new Hawker Hurricane was thought to be the obvious aeroplane because of its wide undercarriage, and one Admiral was overheard to say – "Any single seat fighter is better than nothing". It was not a good omen for the future.

By 1938 the situation had not altered to a great degree and the only result of twelve month's deliberations was the formation of the Fleet Air Arm Advisory Committee consisting of Admiralty and Air Ministry officials. It worked in a cumbersome manner; Fleet Air Arm aircraft requirements were formulated by the Admiralty and the information communicated to the Air Ministry, who assessed the feasibility of the requirement. If the Air Ministry approved the requirement DTD and DAMD would consult and recommend what aircraft companies would be invited to tender. AMDP then prepared the official Specification and equipment details. The resultant tenders had to be investigated by both parties and if the Admiralty approved the Air Ministry then placed a contract for mock up and prototypes. An examination of the prototypes was made by the Committee and if approved a production contract was awarded. It was a long and exhausting process.

The Admiralty was by now aware of the possibilities of utilising the Supermarine Spitfire as a ship board fighter, but they wanted to have some control over its production and as a result of this Mr Richard Fairey, of Fairey Aviation, was invited to attend a meeting held at the Admiralty in May ostensibly to discuss the Fulmar prototype and Swordfish production. The Fulmar (08/38) had been ordered the previous February and a contract placed for 127 aircraft at a cost of £1,450,000, deliveries to start in early 1941. AMSO asked Fairey if he could speed up completion of the Fulmar prototype due to appear in October 1940, and he (Fairey) help with Spitfire production as he wanted to get as many of the fighters as possible by March 1940.

If Fairey was surprised at this request he did not show it and replied it was not possible as it would mean producing too many aircraft types in less than a two year period. AMSO countered this by saying that as Fairey had complained at a previous meeting of not receiving sufficient orders to keep his factories busy, he should be in a good position to assist with the Spitfire requirement. Fairey replied that he had meant he was only able to deal with his own designs. AMSO said the Fulmar was really ordered as an insurance against failure of the Blackburn Roc and this event was now fact. Fairey interrupted to say that to produce the 500 Spitfires required by the Admiralty production of most of his current aircraft would have to be abandoned, and the completion date of the Fulmar prototype would be much later than scheduled.

AMSO said that the Spitfire was a small machine and easier to produce than current Fairey types. Fairey was unable to agree with this and said his company was at that moment investigating the position of producing the Spitfire under licence at the Fairey installation in Belgium. AMSO told Fairey it was only fair to realise that there had been difficulties in regard to the Spitfire occasioned by the death of Mr Mitchell and the excessive Supermarine sub contracting in order to meet production dates. However, the problems were being overcome and it was considered the Fairey Company could take the machine in its stride. Fairey agreed with this remark but went on to to say it was a question of time. He then asked if it were really necessary to consider production of the Spitfire, and if it was a question of additional Fulmars could not Spitfire production by Faireys await a decision on these. AMSO squashed this turn of direction by saying no, the supply of Spitfires was urgent and his suggestion had been made with the view to helping Mr Fairey keep his factories busy. AMRD interrupted to say he thought further orders for the Fulmar were bound to be small.

It was a veiled threat which Fairey chose to ignore for he replied that the real difficulty was in doing anything on the Spitfire in the time available. He did not think that an order for 300 Spitfires would be much preferable to 200 Fulmars. AMSO repeated that he had an order he was wanting to place for 500 machines. Fairey said he recoiled from such an order for completion by March 1940. He went on to say – "I would prefer to make suggestions on different propositions which I could put forward involving my own designs. He had not produced anyone else's designs in the last 25 years, and using another company's designs would throw his own design staff out of work." AMSO's final words were that by 24 September 1938 it was thought there would be a gap in the Fairey production lines, but Fairey said he proposed the construction of additional Swordfish. Fairey had taken on his paymasters and emerged the winner. His company's production of the Spitfire would have resulted in the Fleet Air Arm having a sea going variant in service during early 1940. His declining the contract meant the Navy had to wait a long time before the first Supermarine fighter went into battle from a carrier.

The fighter supply situation had deteriorated by September for on 28th of the month the Air Ministry advised the Admiralty to abandon development and production of the Roc fighter. It was being built by Boulton and Paul and the company's facilities were needed to produce the Defiant turret fighter for the RAF. All six prototype Rocs were to be completed and the jigs and tools stored against possible future production requirements. Because of this event the FAA would have no folding wing fighters until the Fulmar came into service several years into the future. Therefore, the Admiralty requested an option of further supplies of the Sea Gladiator, with the Air Ministry bearing cancellation costs of the Roc contract. The Admiralty laid all the stark facts before the Air Ministry – "If", they said, "the Skua also fails there will be no suitable aircraft available for the FAA except for a small number of Sea Gladiators. The Admiralty has always strenuously objected to have to accept converted RAF types but we are deeply committed to this course. The Admiralty is being blown hither and thither for the Air Ministry now have grave doubts about the Skua". The Air Ministry was asked if they would take over the Roc for use as an advanced RAF trainer in order to save money.

The Admiralty then wrote once more to the Air Ministry on 21 November requesting the transfer of 90 Gladiators and also said they needed 150 Fulmars as soon as possible. The DAM issued an adverse aerodynamic report on the Roc in December and this prompted the Admiralty to ask the Air Ministry for a further 100 Gladiators to re-arm *HMS Glorious* by May 1939. Not possible, said the Air Ministry, and offered to supply 47 Skuas they held in store.

The Admiralty turned its attention once again to the Spitfire and requested that one of its test pilots be allowed to fly a series of trials. On 21 November 1939 the Air Ministry sanctioned approval for a Commander Ermen to visit an RAF station for this purpose. After the first flight in a Mk I, R6718, Ermen asked Verney (DTD) on 11 December to investigate the possibility of fitting an arrester hook on the aircraft. Verney said that Joseph Smith, of Supermarine, had been instructed to do so several months ago, and a modified Spitfire had actually flown with an 'A' frame hook on 16 October. A drawing of a hooked Spitfire had also been shown to the FAA on 27 October.

The Admiralty was satisfied with the results of Ermen's test flights and with Supermarine's conversion, and again wrote to Verney requesting he investigate the possibility of folding the Spitfire wing. Verney wrote to Supermarine on 12 December asking about the new modification and for proposals for dinghy stowage. Folded width of the aircraft was not to exceed 18 feet, but the ideal dimension was 13ft 6in. Commander Ermen and Smith met to discuss the full proposals on 18 December and Smith said that accommodation of the dinghy in the existing tail parachute stowage position just ahead of the fin was out of the question, as it would be necessary to cut away the top half of one of the fuselage frames. However, there was room in the port wing root near the trailing edge.

DAM, Fleet Air Arm, then wrote to Smith on 15 December asking if it was possible for 50 Spitfires with folding wings and arrester gear to be produced from scratch in a fairly short period of time. Supermarine replied in a practical manner by submitting a drawing of the folding wing aeroplane, the Type 338 with a Griffon engine on 2 January 1940. The fold was situated just outboard of the main wheel undercarriage well and the wing swiveled back to lay parallel with the fuselage. The aircraft illustrated had a full span of 37ft, fuselage length 29ft 11in, folded width 18ft, folded height 13ft 6in. The height spread was 8ft 2½in. Reduced span flaps were necessary because of the fold. Supermarine said they were able to produce a fixed wing prototype with arrester hook in 13 months from date of order. An alternative was for elimination of the prototype; development of folding wing and hinge of the existing Spitfire wing and the full production. Our drawing shows the proposed arrangement of the swiveling wing. First deliveries of the new aeroplane 11 months from receipt of production order, or

Joseph Smith's proposals for a folding Spitfire for naval service utilised the swiveling wing joint of the N 8/39 which would allow the wing to fold back along the aircraft's fuselage. This drawing of the joint, together with Supermarine Report No 3629 containing complete details of the folding wing Spitfire, was forwarded to the Admiralty.

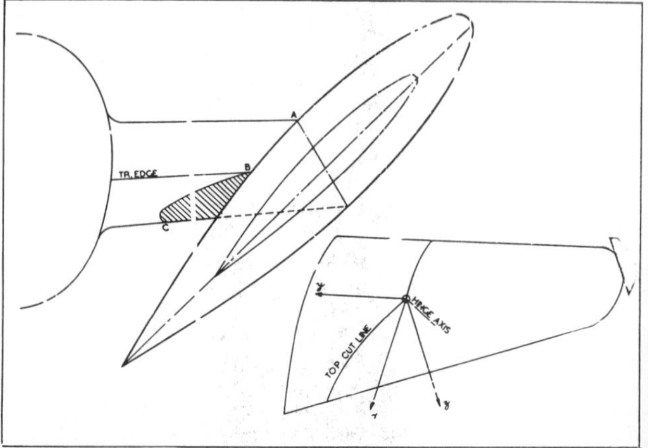

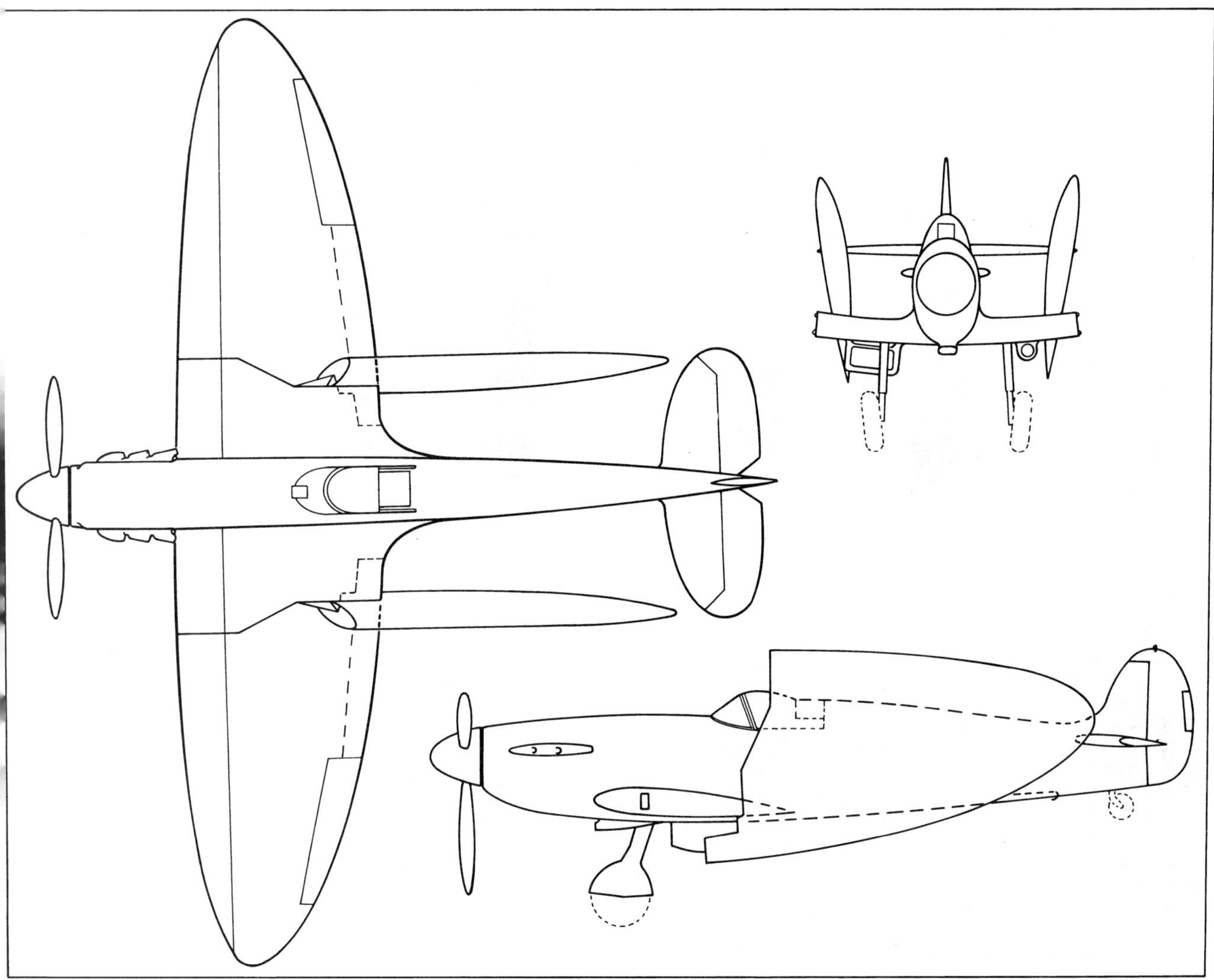

The folding wing Spitfire which Joseph Smith predicted could have been in service with the Royal Navy had the government of the day taken the decision to go ahead with its development.

normal Spitfire complete with folding wing and hook five months from date of order.

It seemed a reasonable development and production schedule, but Verney again wrote to Supermarine on 9 January, via the Director of Aircraft Production, saying: "Please estimate date of delivering 50 Spitfires with folding wings including (1) prototype (2) off drawing board without prototype. If delivery date too far into future estimate time to deliver 25 Spitfires with hook only. And, would these proposals effect deliveries of normal Spitfires to Royal Air Force".

Verney then wrote direct to Supermarine on 16 January: "Use port wing of K9895 and send it to Air Service Training at Hamble for repair and use as a mock-up for folding wing experiments". The wing arrived at AST on 2 February, and on the same day Verney received a memorandum from Supermarine concerning his letter of 9 January, which read: "Folding wing Spitfire –A– (1) prototype delivery five months after instruction to proceed (ITP); two aircraft after 13 months; 14 after 14 months; 32 after 15 months; 50 after 16 months. (2) It is estimated that 50 modified Spitfires could be produced at the expense of 75 Spitfires, normal aircraft. –B– Folding wings without prototype. (1 two aircraft after 11 months; 14 after 12 months; 32 after 13 months and 50 after 14 months). All after ITP".

On 29 February the Admiralty asked the Air Ministry to sanction the building of 50 Spitfires with folding wings and arrester hook, with first deliveries in the following July. The Admiralty said they were willing to soldier on with the Fulmar until the Firefly two-seater became available and they would use the folding wing Spitfire for defence of their naval bases, and for use on carriers where high speed for special operations was needed. AMDP had told the Admiralty that the folding wing Spitfire would take at least as long to bring into production as a complete redesign of the SS Fulmar, and to produce 50 Spitfires (FW) would cost an output of about 200 ordinary Spitfires.

All this time and effort was in vain, however, for Winston Churchill was running the navy and he, apparently, did not want the Spitfire on board his carriers. He had written to Lord Beaverbrook stating that: "I regard it as of very great importance that the production of Fulmars should be kept going". On 29 March 1940 Slattery wrote to Air Marshal Freeman saying: "I received instructions from the 5th Sea Lord last night that the folding wing Spitfire was to be dropped (it was finally cancelled on 16 March) and hasten to let you know what a relief this will be. In order to achieve this I had speak in glowing terms of the Fulmar, and do a little wishful thinking about its performance in years to come with the 100 octane version of the Merlin engine".

This decision was contrary to Churchill's normal character, for he was usually prone to accept any idea which would provide the armed forces with better equipment, and there had to be a reason why he, apparently, opposed adoption of the Spitfire for the navy. The answers are, possibly, to be found in the past and it is worth examining again Admiralty records back to the year 1935. In that year the Admiralty had asked for a single seat, high performance, folding wing monoplane, and investigations were initiated for a two seat and a single seat fighter bomber and fighter. The single seat fighter was to be abandoned but by 1937 the demand was for a similar aircraft with folding wings.

This was followed by a series of specifications beginning with N5/38, which called for a fixed gun, single seat fighter and a two seat, fighter/strike aircraft. Engines specified were the Bristol Hercules or Taurus, and the Rolls-Royce Merlin or Exe. Auw 9,000 lb, maximum permissible overload 10,500; maximum speed 300 knots. A requirement was for either type to be capable of floating for one hour if ditched. Two prototypes were demanded. The next specification was N6/38, the draft of which read: "A two seat, single engined, turret fighter for the Fleet Air Arm to be designed primarily as a deck landing craft and double as a floatplane and be capable of catapulting and assisted take off and arresting. The wings to fold, manually or powered, in a minimal period and the auw not to exceed 9,000 lb." The following figures were relevant: Span not to exceed 46 feet; folded width 13ft 6in; maximum speed at 15,000ft 270 knots; stall 58 knots with full military load; take off into 20 knot wind after a 300 foot run; endurance six hours at 120 knots at 15,000ft, plus ¼hr maximum power at sea level. A four or six gun turret is required, cannon or machine gun. Wing area 350 sq ft; wing loading 28.6 lb/sq ft; fuel 175 gals.

Supermarine were then invited to tender to N8/39 on 19 April 1939. This Specification superseded the two previous specifications and Supermarine submitted their first proposals in Report number 2749.

Two Seat Fleet Fighter to Specification No. N8/39 Points raised in Air Ministry letter dated 10 August 1939 – invitation to tender.

General. The design has been developed from that of the Spitfire and constructional features of it will be retained except where experience has indicated that a change is necessary. Methods have been developed for dealing with quantity production problems inevitably associated with monocoque structures, and works personnel have become accustomed to the use of these methods. In the present circumstances, therefore, the best policy is clearly to develop and simplify a system of construction, the production aspects of which are fully understood and which is highly efficient. A brief description of the proposed construction follows with particular reference to the details in which it differs from the Spitfire.

Wing. Main difference between the Spitfire and N8/39 wing is that the elliptic plan form has been discarded in favour of a form incorporating two straight tapers, which approximates very closely to the elliptic plan and possesses almost identical aerodynamic characteristics. A straight taper is likely to prove a big advantage in the drawing office as well as in the works. Double curvature is avoided and the covering will require no working. A joint is proposed at the junction of the two tapers. Since joints are provided also at the root and at the tip, the wing is divided into small sections for assembly and/or sub contract purposes. The spar is positioned at a constant percentage of the chord and is raked. Spar flanges are parallel extrusions machine tapered and the web is Alclad plate. The raked spar makes it possible to fold the wings without disconnection of the spar flanges, since the hinge axis lies in the plane of the spar web. This avoids a great deal of laborious jigging and represents the simplest possible arrangement. Hinge fittings are simple and robust, and the leading edge lock is of the well proven 'Walrus' type.

The torsion nose in the centre section is being used as a fuel tank as on the B12/36*. The tank shell is of fairly stout gauge and may be armoured at the leading edge. The remainder of the leading edge and outer section between the spars require to be watertight for buoyancy purposes. This is a simple matter since no equipment is housed in that part of the wing. The intermediate section of the wing houses the armament and will be carefully jigged to ensure inter-changeability. Materials used are Alclad sheet and standard drawn section cropped to length. In the event of large quantity production being required, a good many simple pressings could be introduced. Finally, in laying out the housings in the wing for equipment, wheels and cooling, every effort will be made to provide the largest possible clearances between such items and the surrounding structure.

Fuselage. The engine mounting is a slightly modified form of the Rolls-Royce standardised mounting. The accommodation section is semi-monocoque construction and is rectangular with a longeron at each corner. The centre section is recessed into its underside and when bolted in position forms part of the fuselage structure. The top is left open for the installation of equipment and is finally surmounted by the fuel header tank and cabin roof, which closes everything in. Rear fuselage is pure monocoque as on the Spitfire, with a joint provided just ahead of the fin, which is removeable. As on the wing, every effort will be made to provide generous clearance between equipment and structure in order to facilitate assembly.

Tail unit. Is of simple stressed skin construction similar to the main planes in principle, but with lighter scantlings. The fixed control surfaces are covered with Alclad sheet, the moveable surfaces are fabric covered.

The Report then covered in some detail maintenance. Engine was attached to the forward bulkhead by four bolts, auxiliaries and services forming part of the total unit. To remove a wing in the folded position it was necessary to disconnect gun cocking and firing mechanism, aileron and flap controls. A wheeled cradle supported the wing during the operation.

Fuel stowage was interesting for it pre-dated the 'D' wing developed for the Spitfire PR D Type, and it also catered for forward firing guns. A second tank was installed in the fuselage as for the standard Spitfire. This design study was one of the first by Joseph Smith, who recognised the complications of elliptical wing construction, and the wing proposed was based on the NACA 2200 Series designed for the Type 300 to the Supermarine Specification No 425A.

Supermarine Report No 2749 was followed by Report 2799 headed-

AIR STAFF REQUIREMENTS FOR A SINGLE SEATER FRONT GUN FLEET FIGHTER

The Admiralty require for the FAA a single seater, single engined, front gun fighter for operation from Carriers as a ship plane. In addition to air fighting it is to be capable of (a) communications by R/T (b) homing. It is to be designed and equipped for accelerator and assisted take off and for arresting. Quick folding and spreading of both wings together and independently, is to be possible while on the deck of a Carrier in wind speeds up to 35 knots, and the aircraft is to be capable of being hoisted when wings are either folded or spread. The all up weight of the production model is not to exceed 11,000lbs.

Dimensions. The aircraft is to conform to S.I.S. dimensions for carrier-borne aircraft – height 13ft 6in, length 40ft 0in, span 50ft 0in, folded width 13ft 6in (a folded width of 11 feet would be an advantage if this does not prejudice performance).

Performance. Maximum speed to as high as possible for an operational height of 15,000 feet. This would not be less than 350 knots (385mph). The aircraft should have good control and manoeuvrability in the air, both at low and high speed. The stalling speed is to be such that the aircraft will be under full control while making an approach to the deck at 65 knots, using not more than two thirds engine power and carrying full military load (but with only one third of the normal fuel remaining). Take off from the deck of a Carrier is to be possible in a run of 300 feet against a 20 knot wind full military load and fuel as in (endurance). An endurance of four hours at not less than 120 knots at 15,000 feet, plus 10 minutes at maximum power at sea level. Tankage for an additional two hours at the same economical speed is to be provided as an overload, preferably in a separate tank. The designer is to state the endurance with this tankage at maximum cruising speed.

Engine. Any suitably rated British engine. Visual baffles to prevent the pilot being blinded by the exhaust flames when deck landing are required.

View. The pilot is to be given a good view for fighting, deck landing and formation flying.

Armament. Designs are required to allow for two types of armament equipment as follows – (a) Eight fixed forward firing .303 guns (b) four fixed forward firing 20mm guns. In both cases the following conditions are to apply (i) Guns are to be capable of not less than 1° alignment (ground adjustment) movement in all directions, the guns when in mid position being parallel to the rigging datum of the fuselage, a tolerance of ¼° being permitted (ii) Guns are to be situated in the wings outside the propeller disc (iii) The designs should take account of the recoil forces with reference to the effect of these on the trim, in an attempt to keep this effect as small as possible (iv) When the wings are folded, it should be possible to have access to the guns and ammunition containers, and in the folded condition it must be possible to re-arm quickly (v) Provision is to be made for mounting a cine gun in each wing. Ammunition (a) 600 rpg (b) at least 60 rpg.

Equipment. R/T set, homing beacon receiver, A/I, IFF, compasses – one pilot's magnetic, upward firing fixed Very pistol tube, Type C dinghy, pyrotechnics – signals distress marine, 2 in dinghy, smoke floats dinghy distress, 1 in dinghy, cartridges 1½in signal 8, 1½in recognition 6, reconnaissance flares 4.5in in launching tube. Gun heating of approved type, oxygen supply for pilot, sufficient for two hours only. Night flying equipment comprising – standard navigations lights with dimmer, recognition lights comprising standard upward identification light, and the special red, green and white downward recognition lights, blue formation lights.

Buoyancy. Buoyancy is not an essential feature but sufficient enclosed (but not necessarily completely watertight) compartments should be included in the structure to make the aircraft float until these compartments fill.

Securing gear. Hangar securing gear only is required.

Engine changing. Particular attention is to be paid to providing facilities for the rapid changing of the engine. The time required should not exceed two hours. Engine starting is to be by

* *The Supermarine four engined bomber never completed.*

approved electric or cordite multibreech. Electric starting, if fitted, must be self contained and not rely on external power supply, fittings for which, however, should be provided. It must not prejudice the efficiency of the other electrical services in the aircraft.

Protection. Armour protection for the pilot is required against .303 bullets coming from any direction within 15° of right ahead of the aircraft at 200 yards range. Armour protection is also required for pilot against .303 bullets fired at 200 yards range from any direction within 15° of right astern of the aircraft. Self sealing petrol tanks required. Supermarine provided particulars for (a) a Griffon engined and (b) a Sabre engined type, together with a side view drawing of the Type 300 and the following table.

	(a) Griffon engine	(b) Sabre engine
Span (ft/in)	36.10	39.0
Length folded	30.7	31.3
Width folded	11.0	11.0
Wing area (sq ft) gross	242	282
Weight (lb) empty	5485	6170
Weight (lb) gross	8100	9205
Weight (lb) landing	7455	8320
Speed (knots) stall	67.5	66
Speed (mph) engine off	77.5	76
Speed (knots) engine on	59	57.5
Speed (mph) land wt	68	66
Speed @ 15,000ft	344(kts)	370
	396(mph)	428
Take off deck 20 knot wind	300ft	240
Cruise @ 15,000ft	152(kts)	150
	172(mph)	
Endurance @ 150(kts)	4hrs	4

By September 1939 Supermarine were in a position to forward to the Admiralty the Specification No.465, which contained complete details of Supermarine's N 8/39 proposals and drawings of two types, one with the Merlin engine, the other with a Griffon.

TWO SEAT FIGHTER TO AIR MINISTRY SPECIFICATION N8/39

Main features. In the design of this aeroplane to meet the requirements of Air Ministry Specification N 8/39 full use has been made of the extensive Supermarine experience not only of fighters and high speed aircraft, but also of marine aircraft and particularly Fleet Air Arm Machines. Two alternative designs are submitted. These designs are similar structurally and in arrangement, but differ in size; both incorporate liquid cooled engines, the smaller machine having a Rolls-Royce Merlin and the larger a Griffon. The important differences are in folded width and performance, the smaller folding within 11ft, the larger 13ft 6ins. It is understood that the folded width of 11 feet enables five rows to be stored in the carrier, whereas a greater width reduces by one row, or 20%, the number of aircraft which can be carried. While the required performance is exceeded by a reasonable margin on the Merlin aeroplane, the larger Griffon machine is faster by 33 knots at 15,000ft. The relative importance of performance as against numbers of aircraft carried is difficult to assess. Both designs are accordingly submitted.

The main features common to both are – (1) Simple and efficient construction. The monocoque fuselage and single spar metal covered wing as developed by Supermarine over a number of years are well tried and efficient methods of construction, very well suited to high speeds. The fuel tanks contribute to the structural strength and stiffness, thus saving considerable weight. No fabric is used except on control surfaces. The use of smooth Alclad sheet, flush riveted, enables a perfectly smooth and fair surface to be achieved, of good aerodynamic efficiency, easy to keep clean and maintain, and capable of exposure for an indefinite period without deterioration.

(2) Wing folding scheme. The important point about this scheme is that the main spar flanges lie on the hinge line and are, therefore, not disconnected when the wings are folded. One joint only, situated accessibly at the leading edge, is broken in order to fold each outer plane. The arrangement is very robust and straightforward.

(3) Resistance to .303 bullets. The design lends itself very well to armouring. A small amount of armouring is necessary and has been included to protect the top fuel tank and pilot. At the cost of a little additional weight the wing tanks can be protected as well. These are part of the leading edge torsion box and in consequence have a skin of heavy gauge in any case for structural reasons. Protecting these tanks would also automatically provide protection for the bulk of the radiator system and piping, and the chassis and landing flaps and operating gear, which are situated in the wing aft of the main spar. Thus the loss of the machine from .303 fire due either to primary or secondary damage can be rendered very unlikely.

(4) Armament. Alternative provision is made for eight machine guns or four cannons. In either case the guns are grouped just outside the wing folding joint, and access doors are provided aft of the main spar. When the wings are in the folded position these doors are very conveniently situated for re-arming by personnel standing on the centre section plane.

(5) Aerodynamic refinement. Every effort has been made to attain high performance as well as adequate control at low speed. Both these qualities are combined in the Spitfire, from which the present design is developed. The Griffon version in particular has an exceptional performance, superior in every respect to the Spitfire in spite of the handicap imposed by the heavier load and the unavoidable restrictions of carrier usage.

DETAILED DESCRIPTION

Wing. The wing has a single main spar carrying bending loads, and metal covering of heavy gauge forward of the spar carrying torque loads. The metal covering aft of the spar contributes to torsional stiffness on the outer portion of the wing but inboard it carries drag shear loads only due to the necessity for gun access doors, radiator recesses and wheel housings. This type of construction has been developed on Supermarine aircraft over many years, and experience has shown that it is efficient structurally and aerodynamically, and lends itself especially well to modern requirements whereby many important parts are housed in the wing. Reference to the drawings and the model will show that it has also been found most adaptable for wing folding. The hinge line for folding the wing passes through top and bottom spar flanges which thus remain permanently connected. A third attachment conveniently situated at the leading edge is the only point disconnected, and the wing is locked in the folded position by an automatic catch on the trailing edge of the centre section fillet. This arrangement is extremely simple therefore to operate and at the same time is very efficient structurally.

A further advantage is that the wing is easily removed or replaced in the folded condition. All parts concerned are then readily accessible. Apart from the disconnection of aileron controls, etc, it is only necessary to slack back and remove the distance member between the hinge points. The wing can then be lifted off the pintle joints. The nose section of the centre section forms a fuel tank, thus saving weight. Owing to the thick gauge covering necessitated by strength requirements, and the suitable angle of most of this covering, very little armouring would be necessary to render this tank .303 bullet proof. Armouring would render it unnecessary to make the tank detachable, it is considered. It can however be made detachable if required at the cost of a little complication and weight. Slotted flaps are provided over a large percentage of the span.

The main spar flanges are extrusions of moderate length machined to the required section. The wing plan form has straight tapers but approximates to an ellipse. Construction is thereby simplified without loss of aerodynamic efficiency. The shape is good also for lateral control near the stall, which is so important on a deck landing aeroplane. The construction of the wing follows Spitfire lines in general, and in the design of detail components full advantage will be taken of Spitfire production experience. The wing tips are detachable.

Undercarriage. The undercarriage again follows Spitfire experience. Each main wheel is carried by a single cantilever oleo leg mounted upon a robust spigot which is bolted to the main spar. Retraction is by means of hydraulic jacks operated by an engine driven pump. Alternatively a hand pump can be utilised, resulting in a simpler system which has been proved thoroughly reliable. The engine driven pump has obvious operational advantages, and as it is now going into production on Spitfires, will be equally well tried by the time it is incorporated in the present design. With either system a CO_2 bottle is used for emergency lowering.

Armament. Careful consideration has been given to the need for accessibility in the layout of the gun istallations. The alternative.303 and cannon installation are independent in order to simplify the change from one type to the other. The four cannons are mounted independently, two in each wing. A similar installation, but of two cannons, has been carried out on a Spitfire, and firing tests in the air satisfactorily effected.

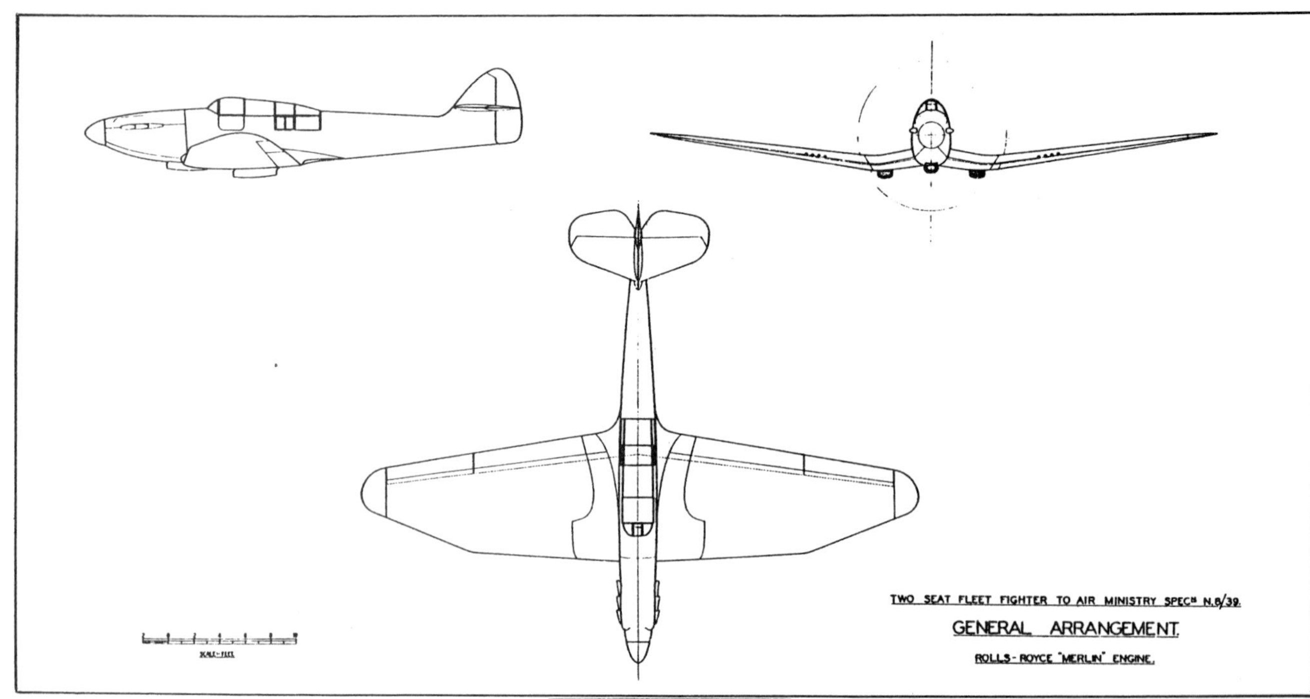

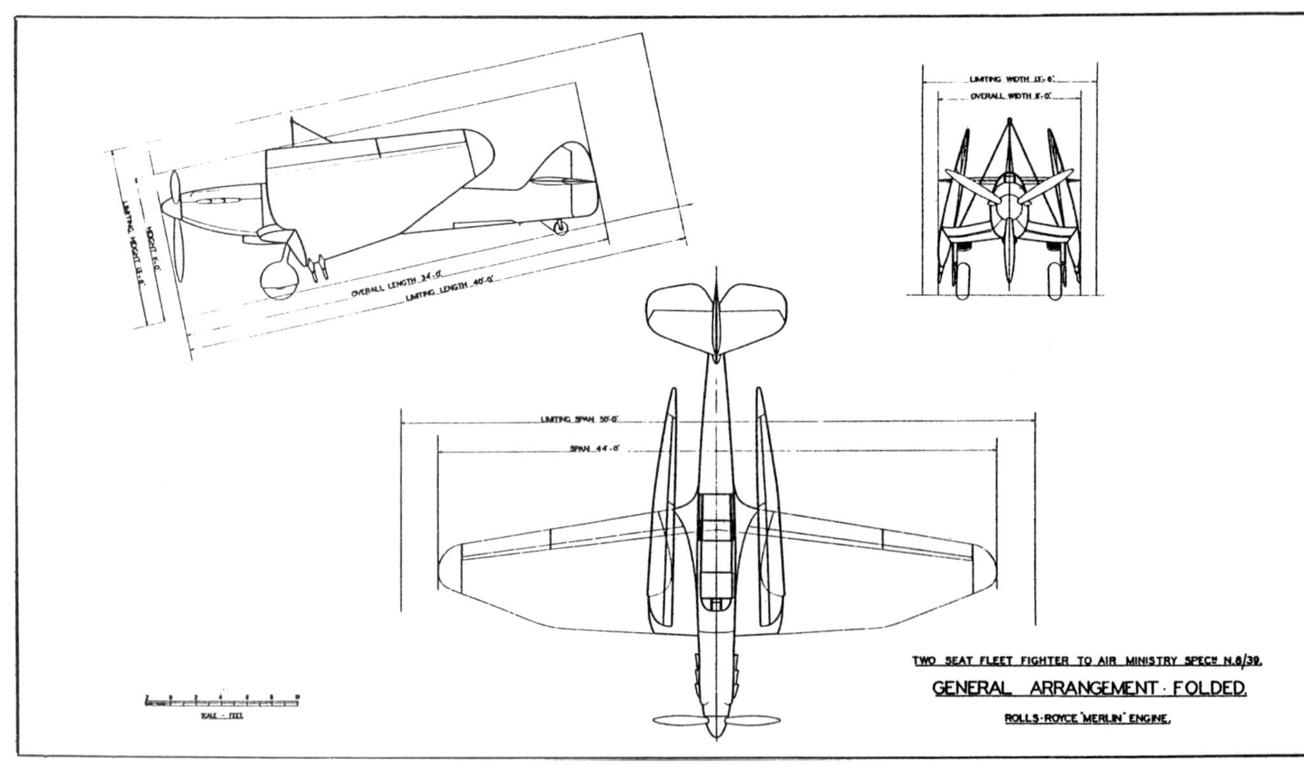

General arrangement of the Supermarine Type 333 to Specification N 8/39. Despite its shape this aeroplane made full use of Spitfire design and development. This version was to be powered by a Rolls-Royce RM 2SM Merlin engine and could be armed with either 8x.303 Browning guns or four 20mm Hispano cannon. Radiator was identical to that of F 37/34 before the Meredith type was adopted.

MAIN DIMENSIONS

	Merlin engine	Griffon engine
Span	44ft	46ft 6in
Length overall (tail on ground)	34ft	36ft
Height overall (tail on g)	11ft	12ft
Wings folded		
Span	11ft	13ft 6in
Length overall (tail on g)	34ft	36ft
Height overall (tail on g)	11ft	12ft
Particulars of wing		
Area (gross)	320 sq ft	360 sq ft
Aspect ratio	6.05	6.0
Type of flap	Slotted	Slotted
% gross area with flap	72%	72%
Flap chord : wing chord	.20	.20
Basic wing section	N.A.C.A. 22 series	N.A.C.A. 22 series

SUMMARY OF WEIGHTS (lbs)
(All figures refer to 20mm gun installation which is 106lb heavier than Browning installation).

	Merlin	Griffon
Weight bare	5634	6405
Fixed Military load and armour	510	510
TARE WEIGHT	6145	6915
Typical Service load 'B'	1425	1425
Fuel (at 7.5lb/gall)	1067	1200
Oil (at 9lb/gall)	108	90
TOTAL WEIGHT	8745	9630
Wing loading lb/sq ft	27.3	26.75

PERFORMANCE

	Merlin	Griffon
All up weight	8745lb	9630lb
Maximum speed at 15000ft	286 knots	319 knots

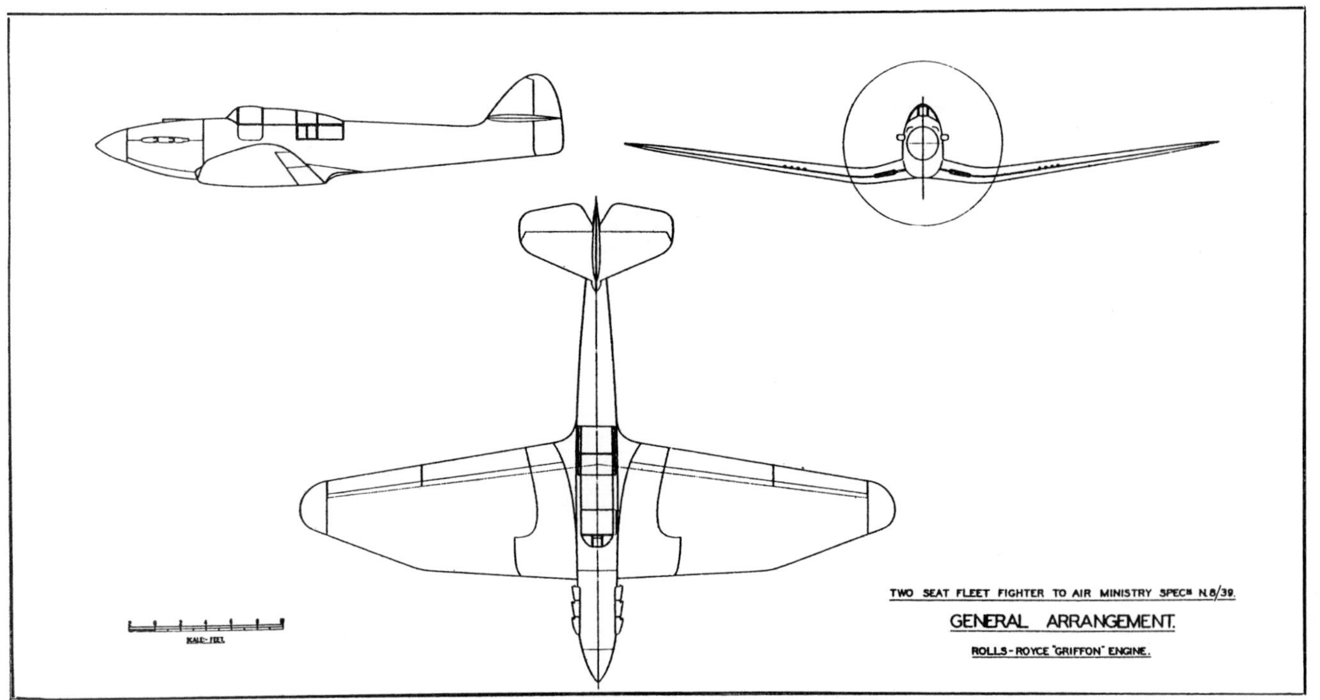

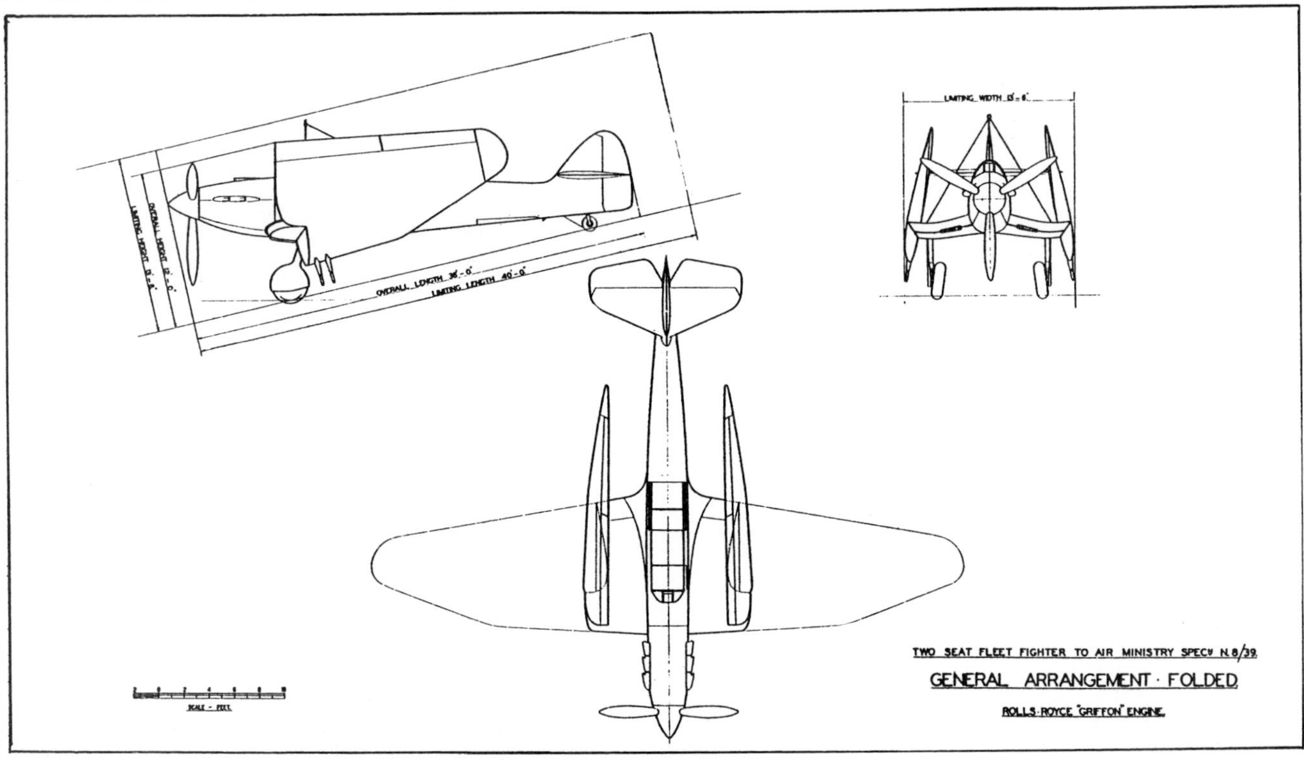

A second version was to be powered by the RG 1SM Griffon and with this engine the three under surface radiators of the Merlin were replaced by intakes buried in the wing leading edge.

N 8/39 was a large aeroplane but its maximum speed was comparable to contemporary fighters.

Maximum speed	297 knots at 18750ft (342mph)	326 knots at 17500ft (375mph)
Time to 15000ft	5.75min	5.0min
Service ceiling	34,700ft	36,900ft
Take off from deck in 20 knot wind	246ft	221ft
Stalling speed, with fuel reduced to 15 gall	57 knots	56 knots

POWER PLANT DATA

Engine		Rolls Royce Merlin RM2SM	Rolls Royce Griffon RC1SM
Rated output	M	1205 BHP 7750ft	1530 BHP 6750ft
	S	1105 BHP 15250ft	1440 BHP 13000ft
Maximum output (without forward intake effect)	M	1225 BHP 9500ft	1560 BHP 8500ft
	S	1120 BHP 16750ft	1445 BHP 15000ft
Take off		1280 BHP	1600 BHP
Weight Dry		1430lb	1650lb
Gear Ratio		0.477:1	0.45:1
Airscrew			
Type		Constant speed 3 Blade	Constant speed 3 Blade
Diam		11 6	12 6
Blades		Wood	Wood

FUEL AND OIL ESTIMATION

	Merlin	Griffon
Gross Weight	8745lb	9630lb
Cruising speed	120 knots	120 knots
Endurance	6hr	6hr
THP required	231	247
Airscrew efficiency	.82	.80
BHP required	282	309
Spec. consumption	.568 pt/BHP/hr	.575 pt/BHP/hr

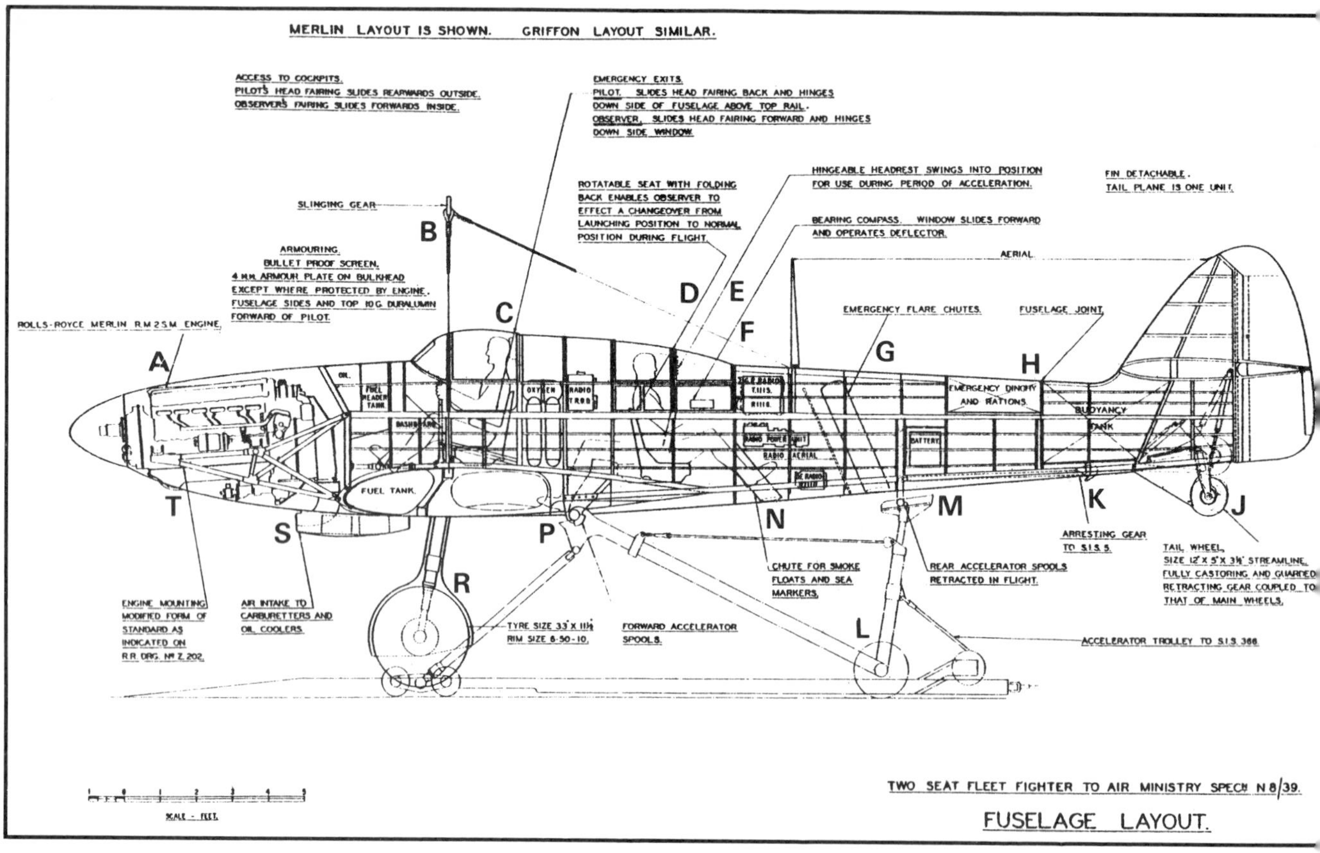

MERLIN LAYOUT IS SHOWN. GRIFFON LAYOUT SIMILAR.

ACCESS TO COCKPITS.
PILOTS HEAD FAIRING SLIDES REARWARDS OUTSIDE.
OBSERVERS FAIRING SLIDES FORWARDS INSIDE.

EMERGENCY EXITS.
PILOT. SLIDES HEAD FAIRING BACK AND HINGES DOWN SIDE OF FUSELAGE ABOVE TOP RAIL.
OBSERVER. SLIDES HEAD FAIRING FORWARD AND HINGES DOWN SIDE WINDOW.

ROTATABLE SEAT WITH FOLDING BACK ENABLES OBSERVER TO EFFECT A CHANGEOVER FROM LAUNCHING POSITION TO NORMAL POSITION DURING FLIGHT.

HINGEABLE HEADREST SWINGS INTO POSITION FOR USE DURING PERIOD OF ACCELERATION.

BEARING COMPASS. WINDOW SLIDES FORWARD AND OPERATES DEFLECTOR.

FIN DETACHABLE. TAIL PLANE IS ONE UNIT.

SLINGING GEAR

ARMOURING. BULLET PROOF SCREEN. 4 MM ARMOUR PLATE ON BULKHEAD EXCEPT WHERE PROTECTED BY ENGINE. FUSELAGE SIDES AND TOP 10G DURALUMIN FORWARD OF PILOT.

ROLLS-ROYCE MERLIN R.M.2S.M. ENGINE.

AERIAL. EMERGENCY FLARE CHUTES. FUSELAGE JOINT. EMERGENCY DINGHY AND RATIONS. BUOYANCY TANK. FUEL TANK. FUEL HEADER TANK. OXYGEN. RADIO. BATTERY.

ENGINE MOUNTING MODIFIED FORM OF STANDARD AS INDICATED ON R.R. DRG. Nº Z.202.

AIR INTAKE TO CARBURETTERS AND OIL COOLERS.

TYRE SIZE 33" X 11½ RIM SIZE 6·50-10.

FORWARD ACCELERATOR SPOOLS.

CHUTE FOR SMOKE FLOATS AND SEA MARKERS.

REAR ACCELERATOR SPOOLS RETRACTED IN FLIGHT.

ARRESTING GEAR TO S.I.S.5.

TAIL WHEEL SIZE 12" X 5" X 3½" STREAMLINE, FULLY CASTORING AND GUARDED. RETRACTING GEAR COUPLED TO THAT OF MAIN WHEELS.

ACCELERATOR TROLLEY TO S.I.S. 388.

SCALE - FEET.

TWO SEAT FLEET FIGHTER TO AIR MINISTRY SPECN N8/39.

FUSELAGE LAYOUT.

A, Rolls-Royce Merllin RM 2SM engine; B, slinging gear; C, emergency exits. Pilot slides head fairing back and hinges down side of fuselage above to rail. Observer slides head fairing forward and hinges down side window; D, rotatable seat with folding back enables observer to effect a changeover from launching position to normal position during flight; E, hingable headrest swings into position for use during period of acceleration; F, bearing compass. Window slides forward and operates deflector; G, emergency flare chutes; H, fuselage joint. Fin detachable, tailplane is one unit; J, tailwheel (size 12 × 5 × 3½in) streamline fully castoring and guarded. Retracts with main wheels; K, arresting gear; L. accelerator trolley; M, rear accelerator spools retaracted in flight; N, chute for smoke floats and sea markers; P, forward accelerator spools; R, tyre size 33 × 11½ in; S, air intake to carburetters and oil coolers; T, engine mounting modified form of Spitfire. Pilot entry to the cockpit was by sliding hood to the rear. The observer hood slid forwards.

Consumption	20.35 gall/hr	22.20 gall/hr
Cruising fuel	122 gall	133 gall
Take off conditions		
Power	1280 BHP	1600 BHP
Consumption	104 gall/hr	136 gall/hr
Fuel for ¼ hour	26 gall	34 gall
Total fuel required	148 gall	167 gall
" "	1067lb	1200lb
Total oil required	12.0 gall	10.0 gall
" "	108.0lb	90.0lb

Wing folding arrangement of N 8/39. Rearming was carried out by crew standing on centre section and loading through wing under surface doors. Close-up is of details of wing fold hinge.

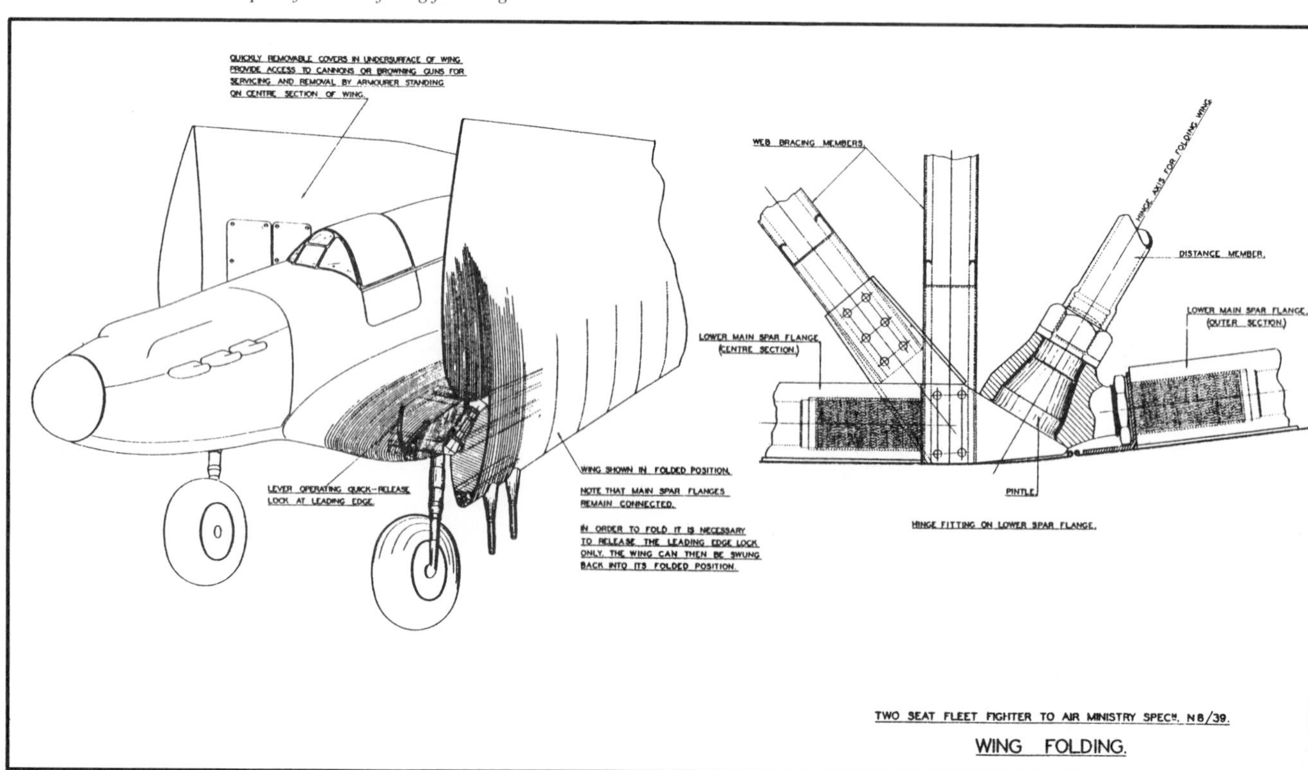
QUICKLY REMOVABLE COVERS IN UNDERSURFACE OF WING PROVIDE ACCESS TO CANNONS OR BROWNING GUNS FOR SERVICING AND REMOVAL BY ARMOURER STANDING ON CENTRE SECTION OF WING.
LEVER OPERATING QUICK-RELEASE LOCK AT LEADING EDGE.
WING SHOWN IN FOLDED POSITION.
NOTE THAT MAIN SPAR FLANGES REMAIN CONNECTED.
IN ORDER TO FOLD IT IS NECESSARY TO RELEASE THE LEADING EDGE LOCK ONLY. THE WING CAN THEN BE SWUNG BACK INTO ITS FOLDED POSITION.
WEB BRACING MEMBERS.
HINGE AXIS FOR FOLDING WING
DISTANCE MEMBER.
LOWER MAIN SPAR FLANGE (OUTER SECTION)
LOWER MAIN SPAR FLANGE (CENTRE SECTION)
PINTLE
HINGE FITTING ON LOWER SPAR FLANGE.
TWO SEAT FLEET FIGHTER TO AIR MINISTRY SPECN. N8/39.
WING FOLDING.

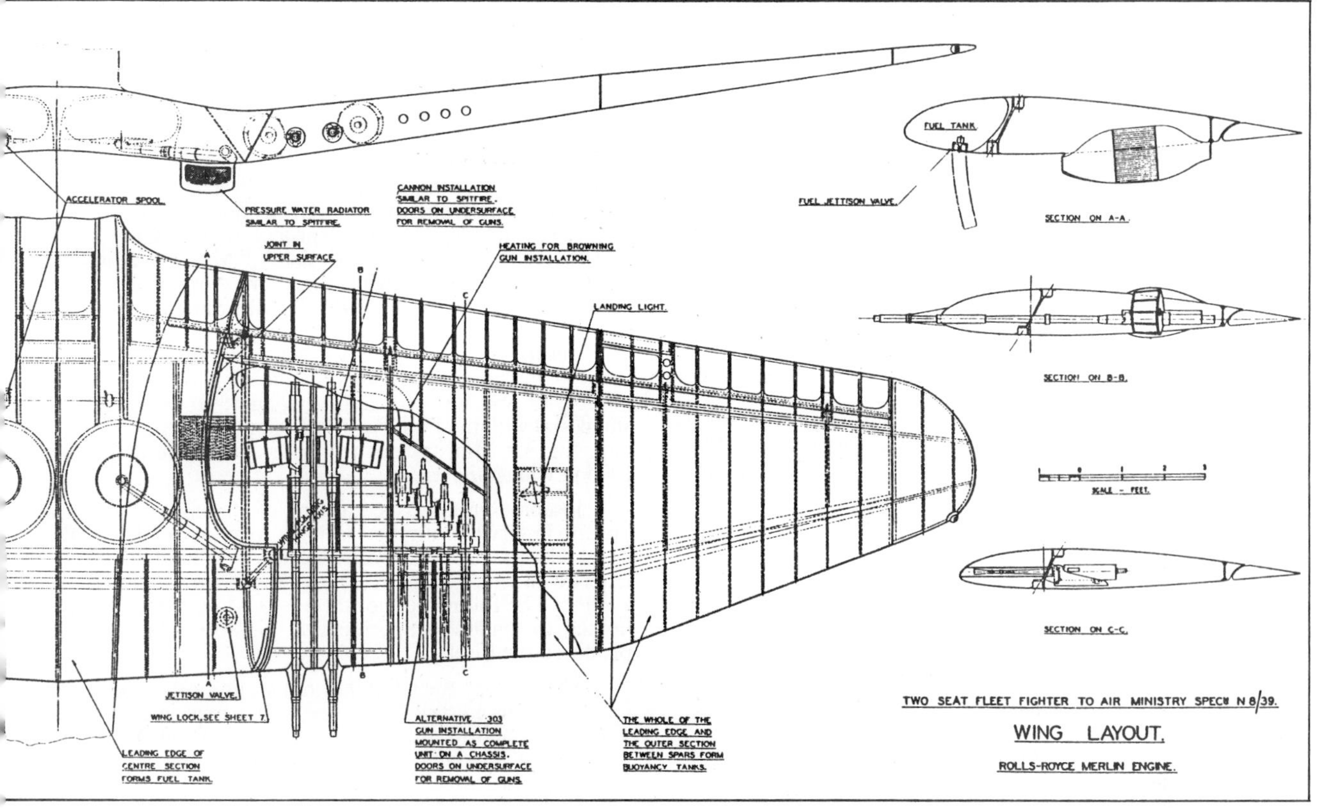

Wing layout reveals gun stations and shows both cannon and Browning locations, although the wing was designed for one type of armament only. Wheels retracted to aircraft C/L.

Martlesham Report M/692C on these tests states "The cannon gun installation, one gun in each wing, was very neat and except for two slight bulges on the upper and lower surfaces of the wing at the rear spar, the standard wing section was maintained. The N 8/39 has a larger wing than the Spitfire and the installation is therefore even neater, the bulges being very slight indeed." The report also states "The effect on the handling of short bursts from the cannon gun was detected but was negligible". In the case of the N 8/39 approximately the same offset of the recoil forces from the CG in terms of tail arm, has been retained.

Four servicing doors are provided and the guns can be removed when the wings are folded by personnel standing on the centre section. Re-arming when stowed between decks therefore presents no difficulty. There is a radiator adjacent to each pair of guns, and should gun heating prove necessary, an adequate supply of warm air is easily provided. The .303 gun installation is arranged outboard of the cannon position. The guns are grouped four in each wing, each set of four being removable as a unit mounted on a chassis. This is a great advantage where re-arming is concerned. As in the case of the cannons, the re-arming operation can be carried out with wings folded, and for heating purposes the radiator ducts are tapped as on the Spitfire.

Fuselage. The fuselage is a shell structure of light alloy Alclad sheet. The main spar and leading edge torsion box of the wing centre section are continuous across the fuselage, which is recessed to receive them. In this way heavy wing joints carrying the maximum spar flange loads are avoided. This arrangement facilitates construction because the portion of the fuselage where the majority of the equipment is installed is open top and bottom during manufacture, being finally closed by the cabin top above and the wing below. If found advantageous the fuselage may be split into port and starboard halves. A joint is provided just forward of the tail unit, however, providing ready access for the installation of equipment in the rear portion of the main part of the fuselage.

Tail unit. The tail unit is of stressed skin construction, with fabric covered control surfaces. Part of the metal skin is attached, as on the Spitfire, by means of wood screws. This method, which has been patented, has been found a great advantage in production and is used wherever the distance between the top and bottom skins is small, or access to internal rivet heads difficult. The fin, above the tail plane, is detachable. The tail plane is in one piece, mounted on top of the lower portion of the fin, which is integral with the tail end of the fuselage. The rather high position of the tail plane is adopted to meet spinning requirements.

Power Plant. Engines. The smaller machine has a Rolls-Royce Merlin engine, and the larger Griffon. Liquid cooled engines are chosen for maximum performance. Mountings. Tubular mountings are employed, with detachable cowling giving ready access to all parts requiring maintenance. Special attention will be given to the elimination of leaks in the cowling joints. Cooling. Twin radiators are mounted in the wing centre section. In the case of the Griffon the ducted radiators are inside the wing, with leading edge intakes and outlets just forward of the slotted flaps. This system has the least cooling drag according to present knowledge. In the case of the Merlin engine, which is designed to an 11ft 0in folded width, restrictions of space do not permit the radiators to be wholly within the wing, and they are recessed instead into the under surfaces. Using water under pressure, tropical requirements are met.

Fuel system. The fuel system is very straightforward. Two tanks are provided. The engine pump is fed from a tank carried in the fuselage just aft of the fireproof bulkhead. This tank in turn is fed by electrical pumps from the second tank which, as already described, forms the wing centre section leading edge. A large overflow pipe leads from the fuselage tank to the wing tank. Jettison valves are provided at the outboard ends of the wing tank well away from the fuselage. The overflow pipe from the fuselage tank is arranged to leave a reserve of fifteen gallons when fuel is jettisoned. The wing is made of thick gauge light alloy and is, therefore, not readily susceptible to damage or leaks. Consequently it is not considered essential to make it detachable, repair in situ being practicable through hand holes. It can be made detachable if desired at the cost of a little complication and weight. The tank in the fuselage is of light alloy also, and follows Spitfire practice.

Oil System. A portion of the fuel header tank is baffled off to provide oil tankage. In the case of the Merlin the cooler is fitted adjacent to the air intake, and is partly housed in the air intake fairing. In the Griffon installation the oil cooler is combined with the radiator matrix. Airscrews. A variable pitch airscrew of constant rpm type with wood blades is preferred.

Accommodation. The pilot is provided with an excellent view, both for fighting and for deck landing. Not only is he seated as far forward as possible, but the low wing with downswept roots further improves his angle of vision of the leading edge. The fuselage is kept as narrow as possible forward of the pilot, and the tilted down engine improves the fighting view. In way of the pilot and observer the fuselage width is increased slightly over the Spitfire so that the extensive equipment can be stowed without cramping the crew.

The observer, who normally faces aft, has a reversible seat in order to face forwards when being accelerated. Ample glazing provides him with a very good all round view. For purposes of taking bearings a sliding window is fitted with a deflector just forward of it. The radio sets to which access is necessary are within reach of the observer, the navigational equipment, such as smoke floats and their chute, is close alongside. A small folding chart board could be fitted if desired. Emergency exits are provided for both crew members.

Bouyancy. Sufficient bouyancy is furnished by structure, mainly in leading edge and outer sections of the wings, to render the use of auxiliary flotation bags unnecessary.

The Air Ministry requested further details of the structure in November, and Supermarine forwarded a copy of Report number 2800, which also contained a list of material requirements. The Supermarine Specification was detailed and contained a number of advanced ideas, such as the possibility of constructing the fuselage in two halves and joining them after installation of services, along the top and bottom fuselage. The concluding sentence of paragraph (3) was wildly optimistic, and the swivelling observer's seat allowing him to face forward during accelerated take of, appeared unnecessary.

On 23 December the Air Ministry decided that the tender designs for N8/39 were not satisfactory and various modifications for the requirement were necessary. These included an auw not to exceed 11,000lb, height 13ft 6in, length 40ft, span 50ft, folded width 13ft 6in. Maximum speed of not less than 330 knots (385mph) at 15,000ft, stall 65 knots on not more than $\frac{2}{3}$ power and carrying a full military load ($\frac{1}{3}$ petrol), take off from deck 300ft in 20 knot wind with full load, r/t set, homing beacon, AI, IFF.

At a conference of Air Ministry and Naval officials, held at the Grand Hotel, Harrogate, on 5 January 1940 the finalised designs for N8/39 were under consideration and there were considerable doubts about the various proposals. Also under consideration was N5/40 to which Blackburn, Fairey, Gloster, Hawker and Vickers had submitted tenders. The Vickers design was considered the cleanest but the small tail raised some doubts about stability. However, it was suggested that it could be regarded as the Spitfire with Griffon engine and, therefore, production would be considerably facilitated. Vickers agreed to redesign the aircraft. Two further points were discussed – one, a suggestion that the Tornado be accepted and built by Cunliffe Owen and two, the Spitfire would be considered only as a compromise.

One of the major reasons for the decision to drop N8/39 was a note from Slattery to the Advisory Committee in which he wrote – "There is some reason to believe that German bombers may use very high altitude blowers to 25,000ft. If this is so the N8/39's speed superiority would disappear. The single seat fighter would have an advantage over the German bomber. Three courses are open to the Admiralty (A) develop an alternative power plant for N8/39 with a 25,000ft blower (B) produce a single seat fighter (C) produce N8/39 and a new single seat fighter. The DAM proposed that (C) be followed and subject to discussion with the Air Ministry a production order should be placed with Blackburn Aircraft for the single seat fighter. This was the N11/40 with Sabre engine and we should place an order for 100 Sabre engines at once. Also, place an order for 200 N5/40 (Firefly) off the board as an intermediate type. Pursue the possibility of obtaining from Air Ministry a number of Spitfires with folding wings*. However, we understand that with the First Sea Lord's approval it has been agreed with the Air Ministry not to proceed with the Spitfires with folding wings and arrester hook."

Joseph Smith was confident of having a folding wing Spitfire in service with the Fleet Air Arm by October 1940 but, as related, the proposal was squashed by Churchill, the official letter confirming this reaching Supermarine on 16 April 1940**. The following month, on 13 May, the company was invited to tender to Specification N5/40F, which eventually produced the Firefly.

The reasons for Churchill not wanting the Spitfire could have been his knowledge of the various specifications in the pipeline, which would have provided the Fleet Air Arm with the aircraft specially suited to its operational requirements. However, due to his intervention the service obtained neither the new aircraft, nor the Spitfire. By early May 1940 France had fallen; Churchill had become Prime Minister of England, leaving the office of First Sea Lord open; the Battle of Britain was about to start and the Air Ministry, in particular Dowding, was in no mood to divert supplies of the precious Spitfire to the Navy. If the procurement system for the Navy had been swifter in its reaction to events; if Churchill had not intervened; if Supermarine had not been so over stretched in production of the RAF Spitfires the Navy might possibly have received the fighter it so desperately needed at the relevant moment in time. Instead, it was two long years before the first converted Spitfires went into service.

**letter to Air Ministry on 29 February.*

***The Air Ministry thought that the invasion of Norway by Germany in April 1940 might have persuaded Churchill to have the Spitfire for carrier defence, but he was adamant in his refusal. He thought the Spitfire had too fast a landing speed for carrier operation.*

"GIVE ME SIX MONTHS"

"I would like to have a word with you in the near future about production of Fleet Air Arm aircraft generally, but wish to bring to your notice the question of the Fulmar. It is already six months late and at the moment the Navy has no eight gun fighter in service. The most modern type is the Skua and this has poor performance (in fact a top speed of only 225mph). I appreciate the urgent need for RAF fighters but learn, however, that FAA aircraft do not appear at all in the priority list sent out to the industry". This was the message from the First Sea Lord to Lord Beaverbrook on 26 May 1940. The war was not going well for France and Britain; the former was on the brink of total collapse following the devastating 'Blitzkreig', while Britain was extricating its forces from Dunkirk. Beaverbrook knew the British aircraft industry could not hope to meet the demands made upon it for all types of aircraft, but he was always the optimist. He replied to Alexander's letter thus – "Give me six months and on 1 July ask what you like of me". Alexander was not to be put off and told Beaverbrook – "After the raid on Scapa Flow on 16 March I need the Spitfire and recommend trials of it so as to replace the Skua. Although the Hurricane is 10mph faster than the Ju88 at 16,000ft, it is barely fast enough".

Despite all the activity by the Fleet Air Arm Advisory Committee, the Navy still lacked its modern, single seat fighter and there were many complaints and accusations being voiced. The DNAD wrote to the Air Ministry at almost the same moment that Alexander had written to Beaverbrook. He said he was most disturbed about the Air Ministry's attitude to procurement of aircraft requirements, and went on – "The whole history of the Fleet Air Arm is a succession of failures to be ready for the event in the shape of having ready and proven a new aircraft type to replace old or unsuccessful ones when the requirement arises, including the Roc, Skua and 'stop-gap' Fulmar" (this could achieve 280mph). Lieutenant J C Cockburn, of No 804 Squadron said – "The Gladiator has insufficient performance to chase and hold the aircraft employed by the enemy. The time between sighting the enemy before he drops his bombs is short, therefore, a high concentration of gunfire is required. Fleet Air Arm fighters should have at least eight guns. These requirements can be complied with by giving us Spitfires".

Admiral of the Fleet C M Forbes, CinC Home Fleet on board *HMS Glorious* agreed – "Our Fleet Air Arm aircraft are hopelessly outclassed by everything that flies and the sooner we get some efficient aircraft the better. We have made a false god of the business of flying on and off a carrier, but now it has been done by four RAF pilots in their first attempt and ten Hurricanes have been flown onto a carrier the matter should be reconsidered". The DNAD then added to his previous letter by telling Beaverbrook – "If the Fleet Air Arm were master of its own house it would do better for it would get its aircraft in half the time it takes at present".

The Fleet Air Arm was in crisis for what it needed was fighters not advice, and Beaverbrook attempted to help by writing to the First Sea Lord – "Thank you for your letter. It appears at first sight that the Miles M20 fighter will be eminently suitable for catapulting from ships for convoy defence and we have already placed an order for twelve. Regarding the Mosquito, Sinclair (Sec of State for Air) thought it would not be suitable as a carrier fighter. A number of M20s will be lost at sea and it might, therefore, be desirable to use an engine less in demand than the Merlin XX".

A list of RAF fighters was drawn up by the Admiralty and among those considered as suitable were the Hurricane, Tornado and Spitfire. Of the Spitfire it was stated "about contemporary with the Fulmar", an odd statement as the list contained performance figures of 300 and 230 Knots maximum speed respectively. 181 Grumman F4Fs, some with folding wings, were to be purchased as a holding exercise until the selected RAF type was ready in sufficient numbers. The Admiralty was also offered 81 ex-French contract, fixed wing Martlets but it was claimed the wings were too wide for the hangar lifts on the *Ark Royal, Illustrious, Formidable* and *Victorious*. Delivery was quoted as being between July and December 1940. Churchill asked if Grumman would make available drawings of the folded wing Martlet so the wings could be produced in England and fitted in place of the fixed wing. The period required to complete this operation was quoted as six months.

The First Sea Lord approved purchase of 1,000 single seat fighters and wanted to place an immediate order with Blackburn for the N11/40 (Firebrand) but Beaverbrook squashed this in a letter saying – "The position is there are only 40 Sabre engines in existence so far and output is not more than three or four per week. Also, the Sabre must first serve the Typhoon". The Admiralty said in view of the urgent need for naval fighters of high performance they were prepared to consider the possibility of adapting the Typhoon as an alternative to the N11/40. Difficulty was, said MAP, echoing Beaverbrook's words, the restricted supply of Sabre engines. Hawker Aircraft clouded the issue by stating – "That while a large proportion of Typhoon parts could be made use of in the 'Sea Typhoon'*, about 75% would be new and this would result in a major redesign of the aircraft. For instance, folded width would be 18 feet and a prototype could not be ready until the Spring of 1942". Beaverbrook agreed with this and said he would proceed with N11/40, adding – "When we find an additional supply of Sabres in America we will make allocation of them for naval aircraft". Churchill wrote to the Air Ministry and said – "The Admiralty will require more and better RAF single seat fighters, either the Hurricane II or the new Spitfire III".

In the same month of October 1941 the Admiralty made another attempt to get its fighters and requested permission to order 1240 aircraft from America under the 'Victory Programme' which would produce the fighters in twelve months from date of order. Monthly output was to begin with 67 machines. Admiral Stark, US Navy, said that war was not far

This Spitfire is thought to be the Mk I, R6718, flown by Commander Ermen on 21 November 1940. Photograph is dated 19 December.

**To Specification N11/40. Project No. P1009.*

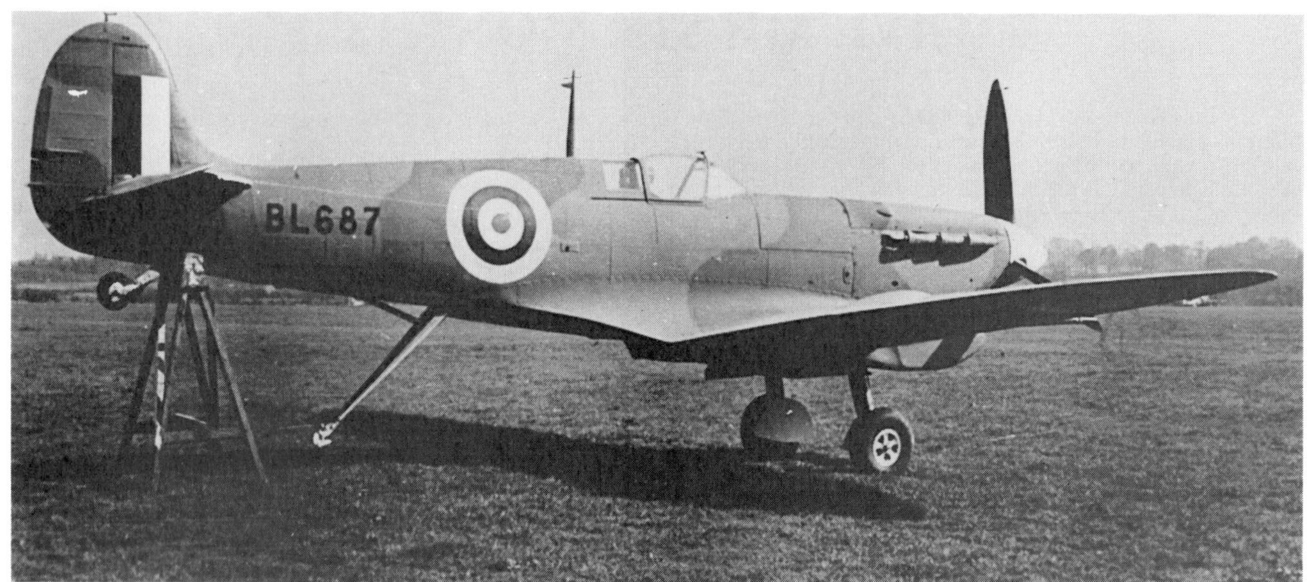

BL687 after an 'A' frame arrester hook had been installed. It was converted from a Spitfire Mk VB and later reserialled MB329. Conversion took place on 10 January 1942.

away in the Pacific and present US output of naval fighters was insufficient for the needs of both navies. The Admiralty wanted to approach President Roosevelt direct, but the War Cabinet vetoed the idea in the interests of preserving the good relationship that had been established between both navies. Grumman Aircraft, in particular, was urged to increase production, but they said total output was limited to 75 aircraft a month until expansion plans were completed. They could only promise deliveries of folding wing Martlets ten months after receipt of order. It was then revealed that there were 18 Brewster Buffalos at Alexandria, Egypt, but they were standard aircraft with fixed wings and, as such, unsuitable for carrier operations. No 103 MU was instructed to design and fit an arrester hook and to have all aircraft ready for operations by January 1941. Nothing came of this instruction.

1940 faded into history and a small number of Sea Hurricanes were in service with the navy. During the opening months of 1941 the Air Ministry was urged to release a number of Spitfires and by the time agreement was reached the latest version then entering service with the RAF was the Mk V. Naturally, the Admiralty asked that they be allowed access to the latest equipment, but the Air Ministry was loath to part with large numbers of the new aircraft. A compromise had to be reached in order that the FAA could have a front line, eight gun fighter, and in the event an offer was made to transfer a number of aging Mk Is, 48 VBs and, later, 200 VCs.

In a visit to Supermarine on 14 October 1941 Commander Grant, Mr Goodwin (RDN2), and Mr Nixon (RAE) discussed with A H Shervell the 'Sea-Spitfire' and said that it did not meet certain of the S.I.S. requirements for aircraft operated from accelerators. The installation of arresting gear appeared to be a straightforward operation and the visitors left Supermarine two Chance Vought drawings of that company's Chesapeake aircraft fitted with similar gear, together with another drawing of the latest type of arrester gear and a drawing of the new RAE arrester hook. Mr P W Howes, of the RTO, wrote to Vickers, High Post, on 19 October and his letter contained these instructions – "The firm are requested to carry out preliminary investigation into the bossibility of using the Spitfire for catapult ATO (assisted take-off), accelerator and deck arresting gear.

Two aircraft, AD371 and AB986, both VBs, were allocated to Worthy Down on 31 October with instructions that AB986 be sent to STU station to enable naval pilots to become familiar with its operation before the naval modifications had been incorporated. For these initial trials the catapult spools and arrester gear were to be fitted. However, AB986 was damaged during the delivery flight and another VB, AB205, was substituted. This Spitfire only made its first flight on 13 December and was issued to CRD at Vickers for the 'A' Frame hook to be installed, following which Jeffrey Quill flight tested it on 6 January 1942. When weighed it had an auw of 6,591lb. It then went to No 778 Squadron for trials. AD371 went to Vickers on 31 December for the hook and spools to be fitted and was weighed at Worthy Down on 15 February 1942 at an

BL676, hooked VB, used for trials aboard HMS Illustrious.

P8537 prepares for take off from the escort carrier.

auw of 6,642lb before going to Farnborough for trials on the 25th as the prototype Seafire Mk IIC. Jeffrey Quill flew AB205, which appeared in his log book as a Mk V, for a series of deck arrester hook trials and he commented – "I think it was purely a trial installation of the 'A' frame hook, and probably went to Farnborough to be taxied into the arrester wires there".

In order to speed trials a third Spitfire VB, BL676, was fitted with an 'A' frame hook by Vickers in October 1941 as a temporary measure and despatched to the Service Trials Unit at RNAS Arbroath. The pilot assigned to flight test the aeroplane was the CO of the Royal Navy Fighter School, Lieutenant Commander H P Bramwell. In November he made a series of practice landings (ADDLS) on the airfield's runway, which had been marked to represent the layout of a carrier's flight deck. The following month he flew BL676 to Scotland and on 10 January 1942 made the first Spitfire landing on *HMS Illustrious*

'Hooked' Spitfire approaches for landing on an escort carrier. The aircraft, P8537, touches down with hook extended. BL676 is then man handled on to the carrier's lift and is finally wheeled out to the hangar deck. Cannon armament had been removed and wing fences fitted over the wheel wells.

anchored in the River Clyde, putting it through a series of deck suitability trials including take-off and catapult launches. His report was, generally, favourable except for poor view forwards during landing.

Commander Stacey Colls and Mr Holroyd visited Supermarine on 5 November 1941 and it was confirmed with Supermarine that AB205 and AD371 would be modified to include (a) slinging gear (for catapult operations) (b) VB wings with two cannon and four Brownings (c) strengthened mountings as required. Production aeroplane should include (a) full tropical equipment (b) overload fuel tankage (40 galls desired) (c) Universal wing (four cannon) (d) immersion oil heater (e) catapult lashing gear (f) hangar lashing gear.

AD371 was now well into its programme at Farnborough and trials with the engine just ticking over, with pilot in the cockpit, were completed on 20 February 1942. On the 26th and 5 to 7 March catapult fly offs were made at a maximum G of 3.5. The Spitfire was despatched to No 778 Squadron at Arbroath; it flew from Macriharush and landed on *HMS Illustrious* for carrier trials. Commander Bramwell carried out a total of five landings and four fly-offs before bursting a tyre. Two ATOs (assisted take off) and landing were made, terminating with a broken tailwheel mounting. Average take-off distance was 336 feet. The trials revealed that the view for landing was inadequate but satisfactory for take-off. The aircraft appeared to disengage from the jaws too early. Also, acceleration characteristics had to be examined further. Churchill had visited *HMS Indomitable* to observe some of the Spitfire trials and as a result he directed that the Air Ministry was to release a number of Spitfires (400 was suggested) to the Navy. He also wrote saying – "It is absolutely necessary to have a comparatively small number of really fast fighter aircraft on our carriers as soon as possible".

BL676 had been returned to Vickers, Worthy Down, for examination and then transferred to Air Service Training Limited for complete conversion to the Admiralty specification. It was received at AST on 10 January 1942 and emerged on 23 March as the Seafire Mk IB. It weighed 5,111lb and with two ballast weights and a 30 gallon overload fuel tank 6,965lb. A tropical filter was fitted; it was repainted in the temperate sea scheme camouflage and was re-serialled as MB328. The name Seafire as suggested by Mrs Freda Clifton, A N Clifton's wife, was adopted by the NAD and this first appeared on Supermarine Report No 3302 of 22 January 1942, which specified Mark IB aircraft (deck arrester gear only) and Mark IIC (deck arrester gear and catapult spools). The table, overleaf, is a copy of the complete specification.

Design hours for the complete conversion were approximately 10,130 and it was not until 15 June 1942 that the first Seafire Mark IB was taken on charge by the Navy. Air Service Training received an order for the conversion of 48 F VB Spitfires to the same specification as BL676 and the designation

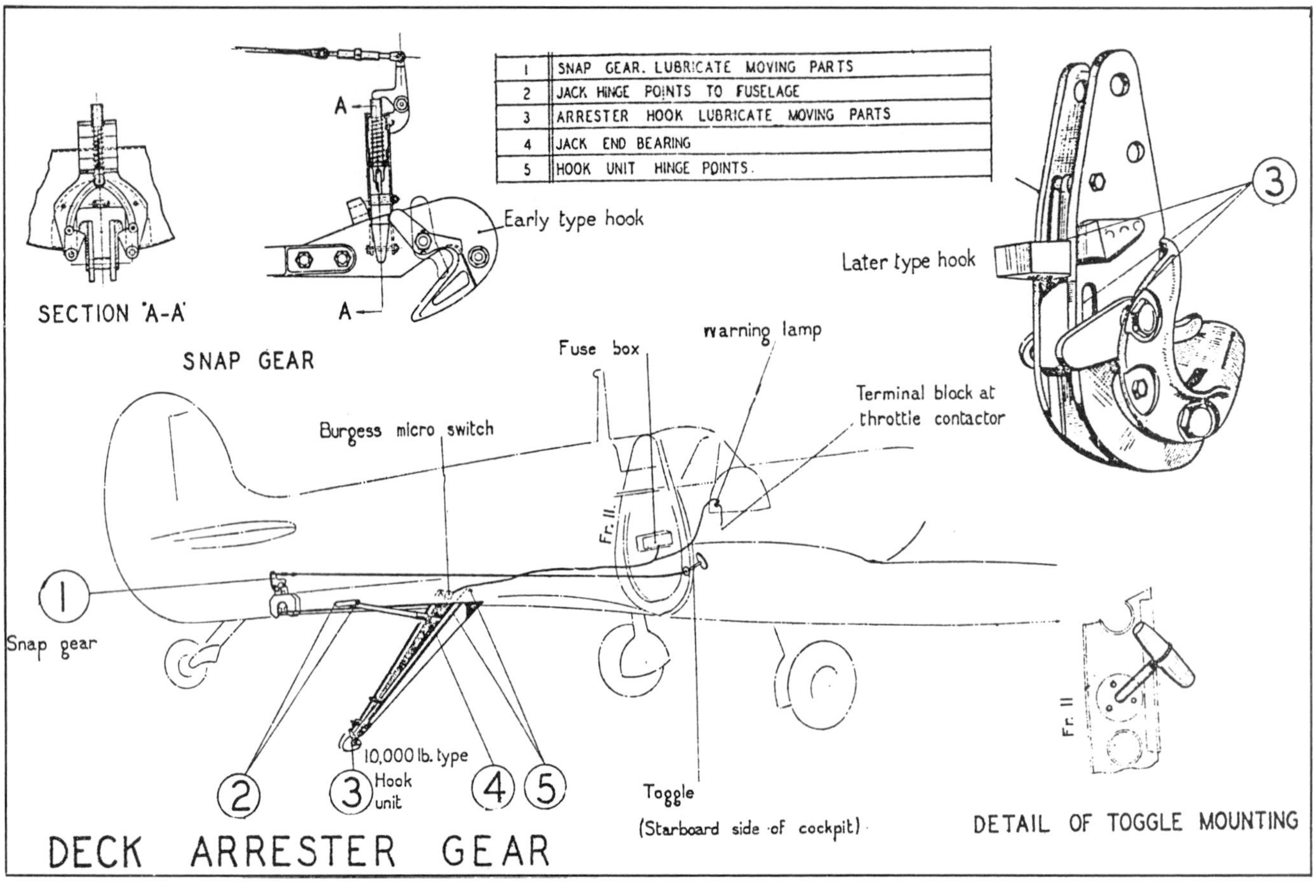

1	SNAP GEAR. LUBRICATE MOVING PARTS
2	JACK HINGE POINTS TO FUSELAGE
3	ARRESTER HOOK LUBRICATE MOVING PARTS
4	JACK END BEARING
5	HOOK UNIT HINGE POINTS.

SECTION 'A-A'

SNAP GEAR

Early type hook

Later type hook

Fuse box

Warning lamp

Terminal block at throttle contactor

Burgess micro switch

Fr. 11.

Snap gear

10,000 lb. type Hook unit

Toggle (Starboard side of cockpit)

DETAIL OF TOGGLE MOUNTING

DECK ARRESTER GEAR

Aircraft mark	IB	IIC	
Condition of armament	2 cannon & 4 Brownings	2 cannon & 4 Brownings	4 cannon
Temperate Seafire loaded			
1. Normal load (lbs)	6565	6825	7055
2. 30gal jet. tank dry	6640	6900	7130
3. 30gal jet tank full	6855	7155	7345
Tropical Spitfire Loaded			
1. Normal load	6610	6870	7100
2. 30gal jet tank dry	6685	6945	7175
3. 30gal jet tank full	6900	7160	7390

Seafire IB adopted. Cunliffe Owen, Southampton, also received an order for 118 examples; a complete list of these aircraft appears at the end of this chapter and details are extremely sparse, before and after conversion, as records have been lost or destroyed. The first 48 Spitfires were not required to have catapult spools and reinforcing of the structure was not needed for this purpose. The 'A' frame hook was attached to the bottom longerons of fuselage frame 15 and was six feet long and hydraulically damped when lowered to project three feet below the tailwheel ground line when picking up the deck wire.

A scissors-type snap gear holding the bill of the hook into the raised position could be released by a Bowden cable operated from the cockpit. The pilot was, obviously, able to lower the hook remotely, but it had to be manually restowed by a deck crew. Because of the additional stresses imposed on the after structure, local strengthening was incorporated on the bottom longerons at the hook and damping jack hinge positions. The complete 'A' frame was faired into the lower fuselage with only the hook's bill protruding into the air flow. Slinging points with local strengthening were also added just behind the engine firewall and behind the cockpit canopy on the central longerons to permit hoisting the aircraft. Three 27lb ballast weights had to be added at the fore end of the port engine bearer and the tail ballast removed in order to bring the CoG back to within reasonable limits.

A second batch of 48 Spitfires (all VCs) were to have been converted and in order to speed up training 54 VBs were transferred to the Navy.

The first Seafire IB was taken on charge by the Navy on 15 June 1942 after a promise by MAP that the first 30 examples would be delivered by the end of May. In the meantime BL676 was being used for a series of sea trials aboard *HMS Victorious* during March and April off the Orkney Islands. The trials were successful and demonstrated that the Spitfire could take off and

NX986 (ex BL434) after trials with explosive 'Cordex' rope charge.

land from a normal carrier deck under accepted service conditions. This information arrived at a particularly vital time for Malta was under seige and desperately needed fighters and other supplies if it was not to be neutralised by the Luftwaffe.

The majority of converted airframes were routed from Air Service Training and Cunliffe Owen to Eastleigh, Nos 38 and 76 MU, Glasgow Docks and then on board a ship.In order to speed up deliveries Supermarine were asked to design a dummy undercarriage for towing the fuselages, without wings, by road. On arrival at the approved destination the wings were fitted, the normal undercarriage lowered and the dummy set returned to Supermarine for further use. The only squadron to be completely equipped with the Mk IB was No 801 which embarked on board *HMS Furious* in October 1942, and they served until October 1944. *Furious* had 'T' shaped lifts and fighters could be stored on the hangar deck. The second squadron to partially equip with the IB was No 842 in the summer of 1943, and this squadron operated from *HMS Fencer*. Several other units did have the variant in small numbers, including Nos 1 and 2 Naval Fighter Schools at Henstridge and Yeovilton, the School of Naval Warfare, St Merryn, the RNAS stations at Lee-on-Solent and Stretton and No 760(r) Squadron at Yeovilton.

AC D
AC C
NX890 in formation with other converted Mk IBs of 736 Squadron. Hole behind exhaust stubs reveals that the gun intensifier tubes have been removed.

HISPANO GUN AMMUNITION BOX
OWNING GUNS AMMUNITION BOXES
·303in BROWNING GUNS
20 MM. HISPANO GUN
RE II - HISPANO GUN AMMUNITION BOX IS BUILT INTO MAIN PLANE STRUCTURE
AMENT INSTALLATION - SEAFIRE MK.II & III

One of the final Mk V conversions, AD567, arrived at Worthy Down on 21 May 1943 for weighing and determination of CoG. Fully loaded it weighed 6,446lb. One Seafire IB was used for tests in March 1944 when it was flying from *HMS Pretoria Castle.* Piloted by Lt. J Underwood it was flown through the carrier's wake, a region of reduced wind velocity with considerable down flow. If the aircraft made too low an approach there was a possibility it could be forced down into the water.

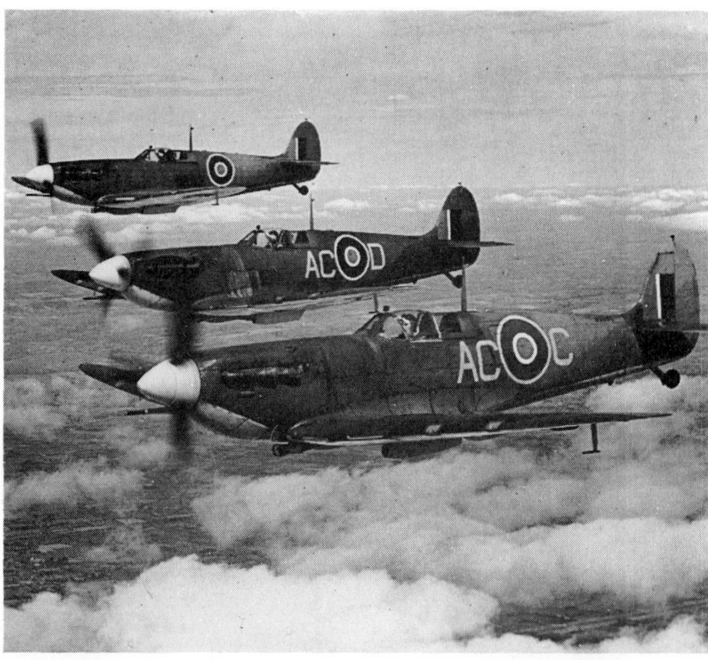

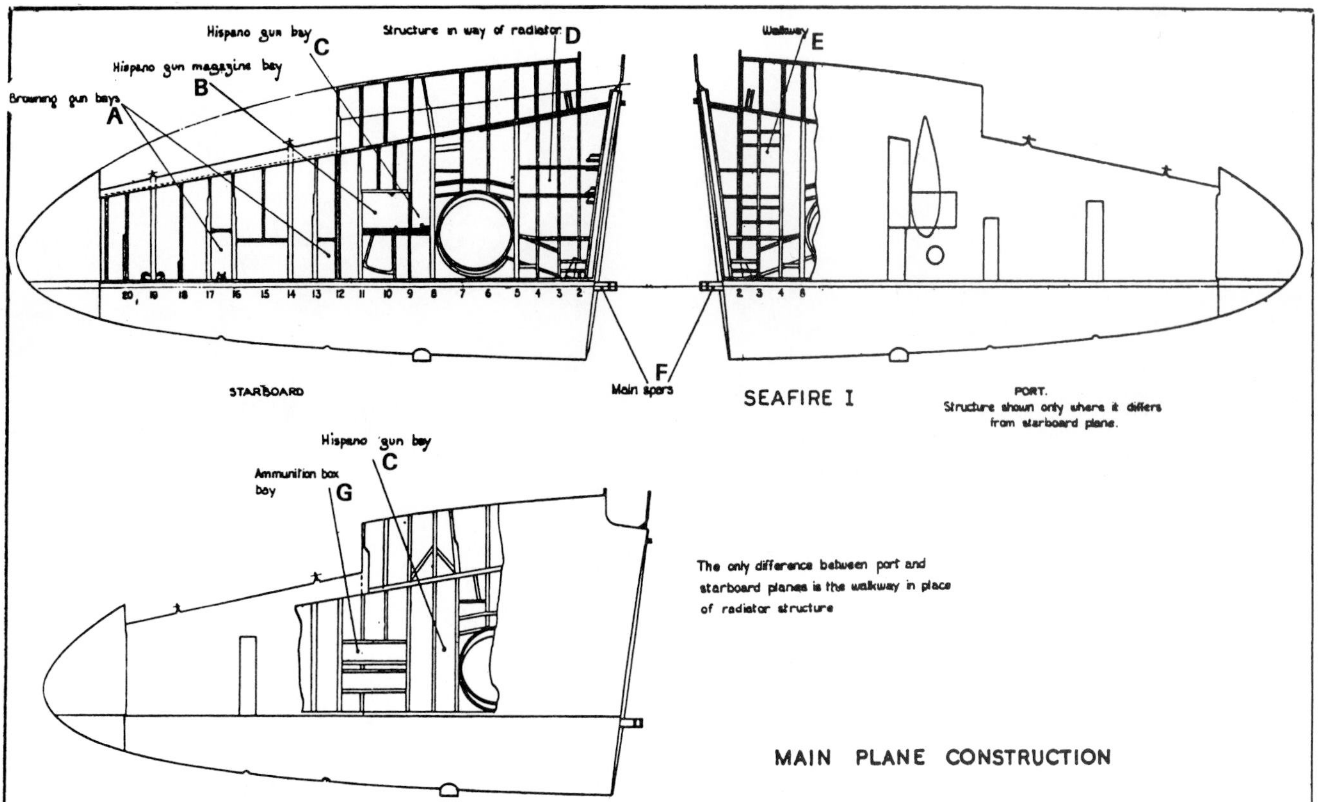

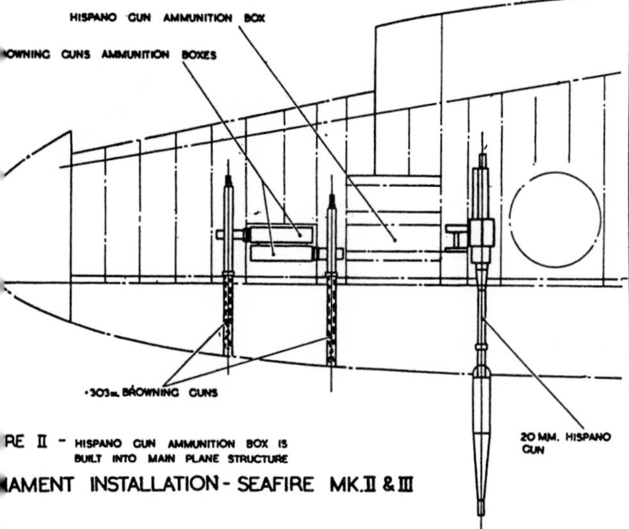

Hispano gun bay C
Structure in way of radiator D
Hispano gun magazine bay B
Browning gun bays A
Walkway E
20 19 18 17 16 15 14 13 12 11 10 9 8 7 6 5 4 3 2
2 3 4 5
STARBOARD
F
Main spars
SEAFIRE I
PORT.
Structure shown only where it differs from starboard plane.
Hispano gun bay C
Ammunition box bay G
The only difference between port and starboard planes is the walkway in place of radiator structure
MAIN PLANE CONSTRUCTION
STARBOARD.
Structure shown only where it differs from Mk I plane
SEAFIRE II

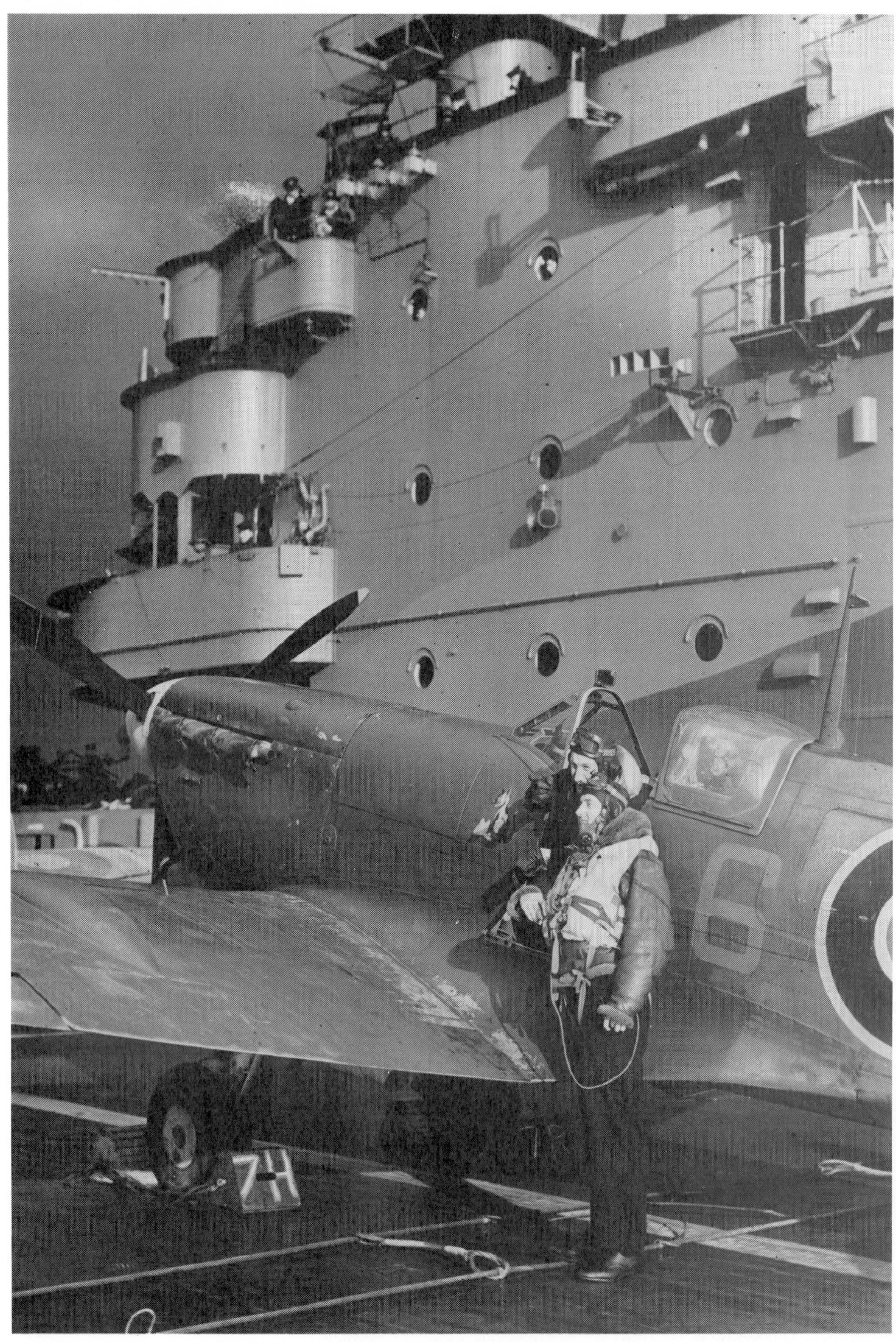

FAA pilots pose with their Hooked Spitfire.

BL676 on board HMS Illustrious.

PA103 in the markings of 736 Squadron. Fulmar in the background.

SERIAL NUMBERS

Spitfire F Mk I loaned to Admiralty as trainer aircraft. N3281, X4331.

Spitfire F Mk I 'A' frame hook X4172, 4997.

Spitfire F Mk II P3716, 7909.

Spitfire F Mk VB W3230, 3235, 3604, 3618, 3756, AD113, 114, 316, 385, 583, AR337, BL253, 383, 421, 483, 489, 512, 537, 562, 567, 582, 613, 756, 776, 778, 891, BM289, 309, 371, 561, 586, 629, 649, EN821, 866, 897, 898, 949, 965, EP130, 174, 180, 686. Total 44

Spitfire F Mk IIB A frame hook. P8537, 8707, 8708.

Spitfire F Mk VB A frame hook W3136, 3522 3769, 3775, 3796, 3846, 3933, 3938, 3941, 3953, AA742, 866, 872, 904, 905, 964, 971, AB190, 205, 213, 273, 845, 857, 899, 913, 929, 940, 967, AD187, 226, 359, 360, 467, 535, 578, 584, AR297, 318, 384, 434, BL252, 366, 419, 443, 628, 759, 818, 858, 895, BM255, 576, EN914, 927, EP170 762. Total 55.

Maintenance airframe MB364 (A350).

Seafire Mk IB Type 340. Converted from Spitfire F Mk VB. Contract B981687/39. Original serial numbers appear in parentheses. Checking these will present complete history of aircraft. All Merlin M45 except where indicated.

MB328(BL676) CB Bondowso. Con AST H 10-1-42 Trop filter, A frame arrester hook and slinging points. VAWD 23-3 BDn 30-3 Hand and fuel syst trls. RNAS Arbr 8-4 Dn. 24-4 Aero Report designated this a/c as a Mk. IIN IFF trls, grd equip instal. Further trls with 30 gal fus o/ld tank. Two × 20mm can, one F24 camera. To compensate for CoG movement after A frame instal 2 × 27lb wghts fitt to eng bearers. 6½lb wght on elev controls. a/c dived to 470mph

MB329(BL687) CB Con AST H 10-1-42 VA Ea 21-4 38MU RNDA 25-4 76MU 15-6 Glas D 7-7

MB330(BL678) CB Con AST H 10-1-42 VA Ea 14-5 38MU RNDA 17-5 76MU 15-6 Glas D 7-7

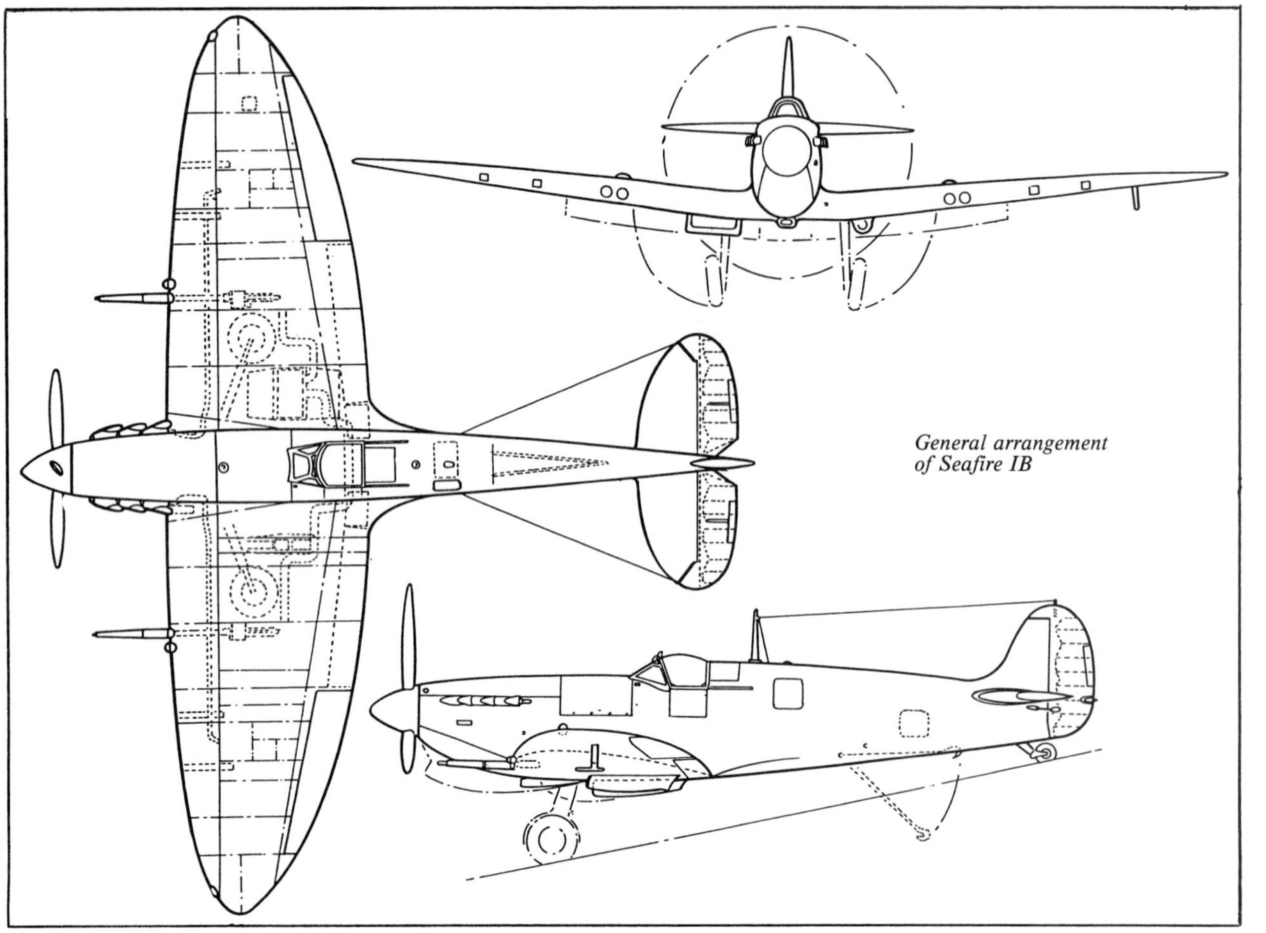

General arrangement of Seafire IB

MB331(BL694) CB Con AST H 26-1-42 VA Ea 30-5 38MU RNDA 3-6 76MU 29-6 Glas D 8-7

MB332(AB416) M46 Con AST H 9-3 VA Ea 26-5 38MU RNDA 30-5 76MU 19-6 Glas D 7-7 93S 30-11

MB333(AB410) Con AST H 9-3-42 VA EA 20-5 38MU RNDA 24-5 HAL 9-6 76MU 27-6 Glas D 8-7

MB334(AB413) Con AST H 9-3-42 VA Ea 8-5 38MU RNDA 16-5 76MU 15-6 Glas D 7-7

MB335(AB408) Con AST H 14-3-42 38MU RNDA 29-5 76MU 25-6 Glas D 8-7

MB336(AB376) Con AST H 13-2-42 VA Ea 30-5 38MU RNDA 4-6 BDn 10-6 radio & communication equip trls. ROS 2-11

MB337(AB261) M61 Con AST H 6-3-42 VA Ea 21-5 38MU RNDA 24-5 76MU 25-6 Glas D 8-7

MB338(AB415) Con AST H 26-4-42 CBAF 3-6 38MU RNDA 12-6 76MU 25-6 Glas D 7-7

MB339(BL679) CB Con AST H 31-1-42 CBAF 2-6 38MU RNDA 6-6 76MU 19-6 Glas D 7-7

MB340(BL689) CB Con AST H 10-1-42 CBAF 1-6 38MU RNDA 4-6 76MU 29-6 Glas D 7-7

MB341(AB414) Con AST H 30-4-42 CBAF 5-6 38MU RNDA 11-6 76MU 8-7 Sth D 20-7 ret to RAF Dec'44

MB342(AB379) Con AST H 6-3-42 CBAF 9-6 38MU RNDA 11-6 76MU 8-7 Sth D 30-7

MB343(AB409) Con AST H 30-4-42 CBAF 16-6 76MU 8-7 Sth D 20-7

MB344(AR444) Con AST H 16-5 CBAF 18-6 P&P 15MU RNDA 23-6 Sth D 20-7

MB345(AR445) Con AST H 17-5 CBAF 21-6 76MU 10-7 Sth D 20-7

MB346(AR446) Con AST H 20-5-42 CBAF 21-6-76MU 10-7 Sth D 20-7

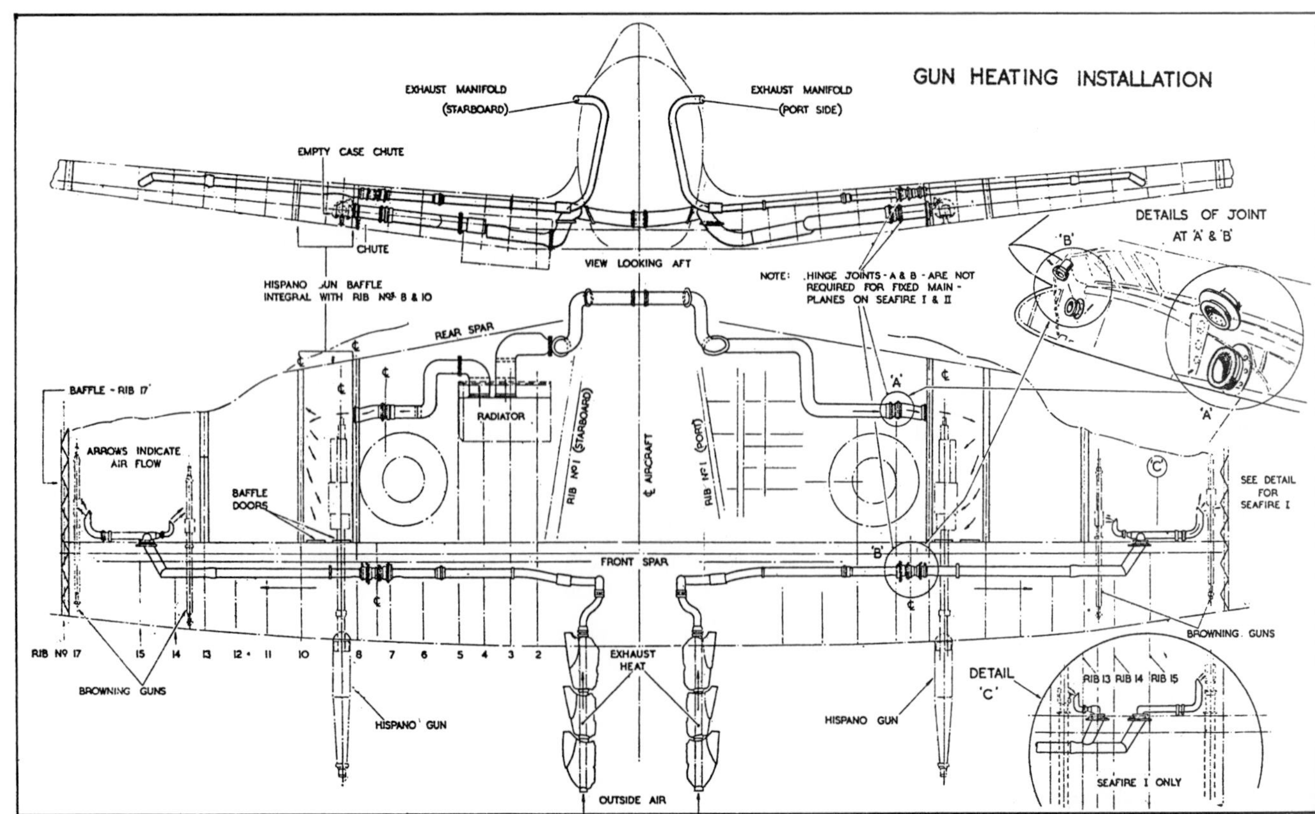

MB347(AR443) Con AST H 17-5-42 VA Ea 20-6 76MU 9-7 Sth D 23-7
MB348(AR549) WAL A/C Contract 124305/40. Con AST H 26-5-42 CBAF 23-6 76MU 10-7 Sth D 20-7
MB349(AR442) Con AST H 20-5-42 CBAF 26-6 15MU RNDA 30-6
MB350(AB404) Con AST H 26-4-42 8MU 4-6 38MU RNAS Doni 6-10 AST 24-1-43
MB351(AB405) Con AST H 26-4-42 CBAF 5-6 38MU RNDA 9-6 AST 7-9 15MU 10-10 ROS 1-4-43
MB352(AB406) Con AST H 26-4-42 CBAF 15-6 RNAS Doni 1-8
MB353(AB407) Con Ast H 30-4-42 CBAF 11-6 RNAS Doni 12-8 ROS 6-4 801S *HMS Furious* sdn by en a/c pilot kld April'44
MB354(AB492) Con AST H 30-4-42 CBAF 11-6 RNDA 17-6 RNAS Doni 1-8 ROS 2-4-43
MB355(AB494) Con AST H new M45 instal. 30-4-42 CBAF 15-6 38MU RNDA 17-6 RNAS Doni 7-8
MB356(EP148) CB AST H Con 29-5-42 Fly Ac F/F CBAF ROS 15MU RNDA 5-7 AST 17-11 ROS 1-4-43
MB357(AR457) Con. 124305/40 WAL Con AST H 18-5-42 CBAF 2-7 RNAS Mach 14-9 Arb 21-10 708S 778S
MB358(AR458) Con. 124305/40. Con AST H 26-5-42 CBAF 4-7 CBAF 4-7 AST 11-9 RNAS Arbroath 15-10
MB359(EP141) Con AST H 30-5-42 CBAF 7-7
MB360(AR460) Con. 124305/40. Con AST H 30-5-42 CBAF 7-7
MB361(AR461) Con. 124305/40. Con AST H 15-6-42 CBAF 21-7 15MU RNDA 4-8 RSO 29-3-43
MB362(EP142) Con AST H 30-5-42 CBAF 8-7 15MU RNDA 12-7 801S *HMS Furious* 1943
MB363(EP144) CB Con AST H 29-5-42 CBAF 7-7 ROS 1-4-43
MB364(EP146) CB AST H Con 29-5-42 CBAF 4-7 ROS 2-4-43 801S *HMS Furious* RN Eng College dbf in fire drill as A350 1957
MB365(EP147) CB Con AST H 30-5-42 CBAF 8-7 15MU RNDA 12-7
MB366(EP291) M46 CB Con AST H 14-6-42 CBAF 21-7 15MU RNDA 4-8 801S *HMS Furious* ROS 2-4-43
MB367(EP293) M46 Con AST H 14-6-42 CBSF 21-7 15MU RNDA 4-8 HAL Farn March'44 assisted t/o trls (RATOG)
MB368(EP294) CB Con AST H 10-6-42 CBAF 11-7 15MU RNDA 21-7 ROS 28-10
MB369(EP295) M46 Con AST H 14-6-42 CBAF 18-7 15MU RNDA 25-7
MB370(EP296) M46 Con AST H 11-6-42 CBAF 15-7 15MU RNDA 21-7 ROS 2903043
MB371(EP299) M46 Con AST H 11-6-42 CBAF 18-7 15MU RNDA 25-7 ROS 2-4-43
MB372(EP301) M46 Con AST H 11-6-42 VA EA 14-7 15MU RNDA 21-7
MB373(EP302) M46 CB Con AST H 11-6-42 CBAF 19-7 15MU RNDA 4-8 ROS 28-11
MB374(EP304) M46 CB Con AST H 10-6-42 CBAF 17-7 15MU RNDA 19-7 Farn Jan'45
MB375(EP308) Con AST H 10-6-42 VA EA 14-7 RNDA 21-7 ROS 2-4-43

NX Series All Merlin M45 unless indicated

NX879(BL635) Salatiga Con AST H 10-2-43 TNAS LoS 20-3
NX880(BL260) Con AST H 10-2-43 RNAS LoS 20-3
NX881(BL521) CB Con AST H 17-2-43 RNAS Stret 30-4
NX882(AD421) CB Con AST H M46 instal 17-2-43 RNAS Stret 18-4
NX883(W3212) Con AST H 17-2-43 RNAS LoSol 5-4 AST mods 16-4
NX884(AD517) P&P SM Con 12-10-42 33MU RNDA 14-2-43 RNAS Stret 22-4 748(T)S
NX885(BL726) CB Con AST H 13-2-43 RNAS Stret 7-4
NX886(BM596) CB Con AST H 15-2-43 RNDA 11-3 RNAS LoS 27-3
NX887(AB933) CB Con AST H 13-2-43 Designated F.IC RNAS LoS 18-4
NX888(BL931) CB 6MU RNDA 1-3-42 RNAS LoSol 7-3 Train a/c for instruction of maint personnel. Ret to RAF 33MU 16-11-42 RNDA 11-3-43 Con AST H RNAS LoS 4-4
NX889(AB902) CB Con AST H 16-2-43 RNDA 11-3 RNAS Stret 30-4-43
NX890(AD582) CB Con AST H 18-2-43 RNAS Stret 7-5 S of AC (736S)
NX891(BL593) CB AST H 19-2-43 RNAS Stret 7-5 Ret to RAF Dec'44
NX892(AB908) CB Con AST H 21-2-43 RNAS Stret 19-4
NX893(BL546) CB Con AST H 1-2-43 RNAS LoS 25-4
NX894(BL529) CB Con AST H 27-2-43 RNAS LoS 15-4
NX895(BL301) RNDA 10-3-43 Con RNAS Stret 19-4
NX896(BL750) CB RNDA 10-3-43 Con RNAS LoS 7-5
NX897(BL373) CB RNDA 21-1-43 AST H Con RNAS Mach 31-5 ROS 13-5
NX898(BL958) 12MU RNDA 14-3-43 Con
NX899(AD387) North Star Con AST H 14-3-43 RNAS Stret 14-5 801S *HMS Furious*
NX900(BM625) CB Con AST 26-11-42 RNDA 13-3-43 RNAS Stret 14-5 794S
NX901(BM377) CB Con AST H 26-11-42 RNDA 11-3-43 RNAS LoS 14-5
NX902(AD358) Con AST H 15-3-43 RNAS Mach 31-5
NX903(BL495) CB COn AST H 17-3-43 RNAS Stret 14-5
NX904(AD579) CB RNDA 12-3-43 Con RNAS Stret 31-5 Ret to RAF Jan'45
NX905(EN825) Con AST H 17-3-43 RNDA RNAS Doni 31-5
NX906(BL493) CB RNDA AST H Con 17-3-43
NX907(BL414) CB RNDA 12-3-43 Con 46MU
NX908(BL986) CB RNDA 16-3-43 Con 715S Ret to RAF Jan'45
NX909(EN890) RNDA 16-3-43 Con RNAS STret 15-5
NX910(BL420) CB Con AST H 21-3-43 RNAS Doni 31-5
NX911(BL983) CB Con AST H 21-3-43 RNAS Doni 11-6
NX912(BL597) CB Con AST H 20-3-43 RNAS Stret 14-5
NX913(BL846) CB Con AST H 20-3-43 RNAS Stret 20-5
NX914(AD580) CB RNDA 8-4-43 Con AST H 11-4 RNAS LoS 20-5
NX915(AD567) CB RNDA 8MU 8-4-43 Con ASTH VAWD 21-5 wghts & CoG load of prod a/c T/o 6446lb. RNAS StMer 31-5 Ret to RAF Dec'44
NX916(AB968) CB RNDA Con AST H 8-4-43 759S
NX918(AB919) CB RNDA Con 8-4-43 RNAS LoS 20-5
NX919(AD365) CB RNDA Con 8-4-43 RNAS LoS 20-5 Ret to RAF Dec'44
NX920(BL855) CB Neils Ebbesen RNDA 22-4-42 Con RNAS LoS 20-5
NX921(BL894) CB Con AST H 23-4-43
NX922(AD556) CB RNDA 15MU 22-4-43 Con RNAS LoS 20-5
NX923 (BM420) CB RNDA 15MU 22-4-43 Con RNAS LoS 20-5
NX924(BM580) Desfd RNDA Con AST H 23-4-43
NX925(EN839) RNDA 23-4-43 Con RNAS StMer 31-5
NX926(BL254) CB Con AST H 9-5-43
NX928(BM634) CB Con AST H 5-5-43 RNDA
NX940(BM632) CB RNDA 5-5-43 Con
NX941(BL522) CB RNDA 5-5-43 Con
NX942(EN763) CB RNDA 5-5-43 Con RNAS StMer 31-5 Ret to RAF Dec'44
NX943(AB181) One For Avee Con AST H 15-5-43 RNDA 17-5
NX944(BL539) Landstorm RNDA 14-5-43 Con AST H 15-5
NX945(BM559) CB RNDA 14-5-43 Con AST H 15-5
NX946(AA750) RNDA 16-5-43 Con
NX947(AD510) CB RNDA 16-5-43 Con
NX948(AB817) RNDA 16-5-43 Con
NX949(AD552) CB RNDA 16-5-43 Con
NX950(BM314) CB Con COAL 26-2-43 Ret to RAF Dec'44 Rivenhall 21-6-45
NX951(AB928) CB Con COAL 1-3-43
NX952(EN851) Lima Challenger Con COAL 17-3-43 RNAS LoS 19-5 ROS VA Ox 26-5
NX953(EN912) Con CoAL 17-3-43 RNAS LoS 19-5
NX954(BL736) Trans to FAA 24-4-43 Con
NX955(BL321) CB Trans to FAA 24-3-43 Con
NX956(AD271) CB RNDA 30-3-43 Con RNAS Stret 9-6
NX957(AD368) Con COAL 31-3-43 RNAS Hens 11-6 700S
NX958(BL570) RNDA 5-5-43 Con COAL 5-5 Farn March'44 with MB307(Seafire IIC) for assisted t/o trls. Shipped ME on *HMS Pret Cast* Jan'45
NX959(BL639) CB Con COAL 5-5-43
NX960(BL901) CB RNDA 5-5-43 Con COAL 5-5
NX961(BM367) CB RNDA5-5-43
NX962(EN864) Con COAL 28-5-43 Ret to RAF Dec'44
NX963(AB809) CB Con COAL 28-5-43
NX964(AB967) cancel
NX965(W3646) cancel
NX966(AD120) CB RNDA 31-5-43 Con COAL 31-5
NX967(BL757) CB Con 899S 13-3-44
NX980(W3372) RNDA 22-5-43
NX981(BL239) CB RNDA 7-3-43 Con AST H 27-5
NX982(AD241) CB Twickenham II Con AST H 27-5-43
NX983(BL930) CB Con AST H 28-5-43 Farn June'44 from AST after conversion for arrester gear drag chain exp. Mod to LR standards by addition of 2 × F.24 vertical and 1 × F.24 oblique cameras in fus. Shipped to ME 4 Ftr Wing Dekhelia Egypt Dec'44
NX984 no record
NX985 no record
NX986(BL434) CB RNDA 31-5-43 Con
NX987 no record
NX988(BM541) CB Con AST H 31-5-43
NX989(BL994) CB RNDA 15MU 31-5-43 Con

PA series All Merlin M45 unless indicated

PA100(BL527) CB COn P&P 14-3-43 RNAS Stret 9-6 842S *HMS Fencer*
PA101(BM570) CB Con P&P 4-3-43
PA102(AD397) CN Con P&P SM 15-10-42, RNAS Stret 29-5-43
PA103(EN770) RNDA 25-1-43 P&P SM Con 28-2 RNAS Stret 3-6 760(T)S Yeovil 736S
PA104(BM626) CB Con P&P 15-3-43 RNAS Stret 2-6
PA105(AD393)CB RNDA 21-1-43 Con RNAS Stret 2-6 761S
PA106(EN764) CB RNDA 21-1-43 Con P&P 9-3 RNAS Stret 2-6
PA107(AD394) CB RNDA 8-1-43 Con RNAS Stret 2-6
PA108(AA932) Con P&P 15-3-43 RNAS Stret 2-6
PA109(AD364) CB RNDA 14-3-43 Con P&P 14-3 RNAS Stret 2-6
PA110(BL695) CB Con P&P 24-9-42 CBAF 18-4-43 748S
PA111(BL492) CB VA EA Con 29-4-43
PA112(AD357) Leicester Division Con Va Ea 29-4-43 790S
PA113(BL770) CBAF Con 19-4-43
PA114(EN790) Con CBAF 18-4-43
PA115(BL586)CB RNDA 8MU 16-5-43 Ret to RAF Dec'44
PA116(BL428) CB RNDA 8MU 20-11-42 Con
PA117(EP166) CBAF Con 31-5-43
PA118(AD184) CBAF Con 16-5-43
PA119(W3371) CBAF Con 7-6-43 39MU RAF 5-9 RNDA 28-9
PA120(BL296)CB RNDA CBAF Con 20-5-43
PA121(BL524) CBAF RNDA Con 23-5-43
PA122(EN910) RNDA CBAF Con 20-5-43 RNAS Doni 5-9
PA123(BL861) RNDA CBAF Con 20-5-43 RNAS Doni 5-9
PA124(BM457) CBAF Con 23-5-43 768S
PA125(BL730) CB Con AST H 14-6-43 RNAS Hens 8-10 33MU 31-10 LoS 22-2-44 (Designated VB Hooked at 33MU)
PA126(BL806) CB Con AST H 14-6-43 33MU RAF 12-8 31 SLG RNDA 27-9 33MU 3-10 RNAS Hens 8-10 (VB Hooked @ 33MU)
PA127(BL904) CBAF Con 6-6-43
PA128(AD252) CB Con AST H 15-6-43
PA129(BL566) CB Con AST H 18-6-43

"THERE ARE ENOUGH SPITFIRES"

Seafire Mk IIC lands on HMS Indomitable.

The Seafire Mk IB was recognised by both the Air Ministry and Admiralty as being an interim type until a production model, the Mk IIC, was available, but supplies of the former were slow in forthcoming. On 4 July 1942 the Admiralty requested the transfer of 500 normal Spitfires and 250 Hurricanes from the Air Ministry to meet its acute shortage of fighters due to the non-delivery of Seafire IBs, the Firefly and Firebrand. The Air Ministry was shocked by this request and told the Admiralty that their demands were unreasonable, and did the Admiralty realise that the Air Ministry was required also to supply 2,400 fighters to Russia during 1942? The Admiralty then agreed to reduce its demands to 267 Spitfires, but by the following September informed the War Cabinet that the minimum number of 'hooked' Spitfires needed was 234 – "If we are to be able to continue the war with a Fleet Air Arm equipped with obsolescent machines". Later the same month the Admiralty asked for an immediate supply of 229 non-folding wing and 143 folding wing Seafires.

The Air Ministry offered to supply 114 Mk VB and 50 Mk I and II without hooks. The MAP said – "There are enough Spitfires in store to meet the Admiralty's needs", and the Admiralty said they were prepared to accept all their fighters without catapult spools but they must have arrester hooks. The Air Ministry explained the Spitfires in store by stating – "It was vital for them to build up stocks of fighters against possible Continental operations in 1943. To meet all of their commitments, and this included delivery of 200 Spitfires per month to Russia, would involve severe rationing of replacements for Fighter Command". They then offered to supply a further 60 Hurricanes by the end of October.

The Admiralty's reply to this was to the point – "The Firefly is still a sick bird and already very late, and the Firebrand seems to have been stillborn. It is still an unknown quantity, the final design is far from being clear and we still have doubts about the Sabre engine. The situation regarding American fighters is rather obscure and deliveries are behind schedule. The Martlet is not really fast and is unable to deal with the Junkers Ju88. We must have more Spitfires, but preferably Seafires. The Fulmar is obsolescent for modern air warfare and the 60 Hurricanes would be purely stop gaps adapted for sea service. Although the Hurricane II has been hooked and operated by *Indomitable*, the wings do not fold and many of those offered took part in the Battle of Britain. The ex-French Martlet Is are a wasting asset as there are insufficient spares to maintain one squadron afloat. The ex-Greek contract Martlets are not equipped for employment on British carriers and will be used for shore duties in the Middle East. I would, therefore, suggest that authority be obtained for a further allocation of Spitfire VCs for the Royal Navy. I consider the position as regards Fleet fighters at the present moment is so grave that authority should be sought at the highest level to allocate another 750 Seafires".

Air Marshall Freeman replied to this letter – "The question of priority for naval aircraft was considered at the meeting of the Defence Committee (Supply) on 9 December last, when it was ruled that the highest priority should be accorded to the production of aircraft necessary for the aircraft carrier. In the course of the discussion you said – 'That it was essential that the aircraft to equip and maintain the aircraft carriers must have priority over everything else. The Minister of Aircraft Production tells me that he has interpreted this as applying not only to naval fighters, but to all types of aircraft required for aircraft carriers. He has, in consequence, given instructions to factories that all aircraft for the Fleet Air Arm must have the highest possible priority. You will see, therefore, that what the First Sea Lord asks for has already been accorded to him".

It was a most unfair assumption by Freeman for he must have been aware of the Admiralty's constant demands for fighters, especially Spitfire/Seafire. Freeman, however, was not finished with his rebuke for his letter continued, twisting the knife as follows – "In your letter on FAA fighters there are certain matters raised which in justice to MAP and its technical staff must be commented on. That the FAA were not in possession of the best carrier-borne fighters in the world at the beginning of this war is the sole responsibility of the Admiralty who, for a number of years, refused to consider speed as an important characteristic of FAA fighters. Speed was deliberately sacrificed for long range and two seats. Those responsible at the Air Ministry for development urged the Admiralty to put a higher value on speed, but to no avail. It was not until Captain Slattery arrived at the Admiralty that this policy was recognised and reversed. Captain Slattery took up his appointment in 1939, and an aeroplane designed in 1939 is not likely to come off the production line until four years later.

"If the word 'modern' is meant to mean 'up-to-date' then the Fulmar was never modern – it was a hotch potch of the P4/34 and was, therefore, five years old when it was redesigned as a FAA fighter. The Admiralty did not consider the Hurricane or Spitfire suitable as a fighter as they still wanted a two-seater. During the last few years the RAF have been fleeced of fighters in order to make up for the previous short sighted policy of the Admiralty. Further, the Hurricanes and Spitfires handed over have to be modified, occupying the time of design staff and of jig and tool makers and upsetting the production line. Not only have the RAF lost the actual aircraft handed over but there has been an adverse effect on the production line itself. It is for AMSO to say whether we can spare another 750 Spitfires and 250 Hurricane IICs, but we must also know how these are to be

MA970 on the catapult rig at Farnborough June 1942. Catapult spools and supporting structure are clearly revealed.

More views of MA970 on a second type of catapult at Farnborough. Close up of overload fuel tank reveals clipped undercarriage fairings to prevent fouling of arrester wires.

matched up with carrier production. When it is realised how seldom the FAA fighters fly off from carriers to attack enemy aircraft, 750 far from being comparatively small, is in fact incomparably large".

It was a hard hitting letter full of histrionic passages, albeit that some comment was valid, for Freeman had overlooked facts that Richard Fairey had bluntly refused to build the Spitfire in preference to the Fulmar before the war had started, and that Joseph Smith had said he could have had a folding wing Spitfire in service at the end of 1940 had the ITP been granted. Churchill, it must be remembered, had killed the Fleet Air Arm Spitfire when he was First Sea Lord, and Freeman's letter was correct on this point.

To make matters worse Churchill, on learning of the exchange, wrote – "In my opinion the Admiralty are themselves largely to blame for the present unsatisfactory condition of the aircraft of the Fleet Air Arm. I should have at any time been ready to help secure deliveries from MAP, but by repeated alterations you (the Admiralty) have crippled yourselves. For nearly two years it has been evident that every aircraft requires, first and foremost, the highest grade fighter aircraft which can be flown on and off a ship". No comment was made on this letter by the Admirals; obviously a Service Chief does not remind his Prime Minister that it was he, as First Sea Lord in 1939, who had ordered cancellation of the folded wing Spitfire.

Alexander, First Sea Lord, thoroughly incensed, wrote to MAP and demanded immediate delivery of 430 Spitfires and a firm promise of 20 more per month to take care of wastage and replacements. The Air Ministry did not comment on the bulk delivery demand, but did offer 10 aircraft per month as from February 1943. They then promised 200 Spitfire Mk VBs complete with FAA modifications for delivery over the next six months, and this would be the maximum number as due to the expansion of the war in the Far East increased numbers of fighters were urgently needed.

A review of Fleet Air Arm aircraft requirements was urgently needed and after it the following opinions emerged. The Firebrand was too heavy and too large to ever make a successful single seat fighter; the Firefly was not the best type as a pure day fighter. There was little doubt in the minds of all concerned that the Seafire represented the answer to the possible single seat fighter for the immediate future and should be adapted as the standard FAA fighter. It was then agreed that (1) large orders should be placed for the Seafire, 110 with Supermarine (2) introduction of a folding wing Seafire as the design was very promising (3) introduce as soon as possible a Seafire converted from the Spitfire F Mk VIII (4) development of the Spitfire Mk IX with a Griffon engine – "May we suggest that Westland Aircraft be devoted to Seafire production

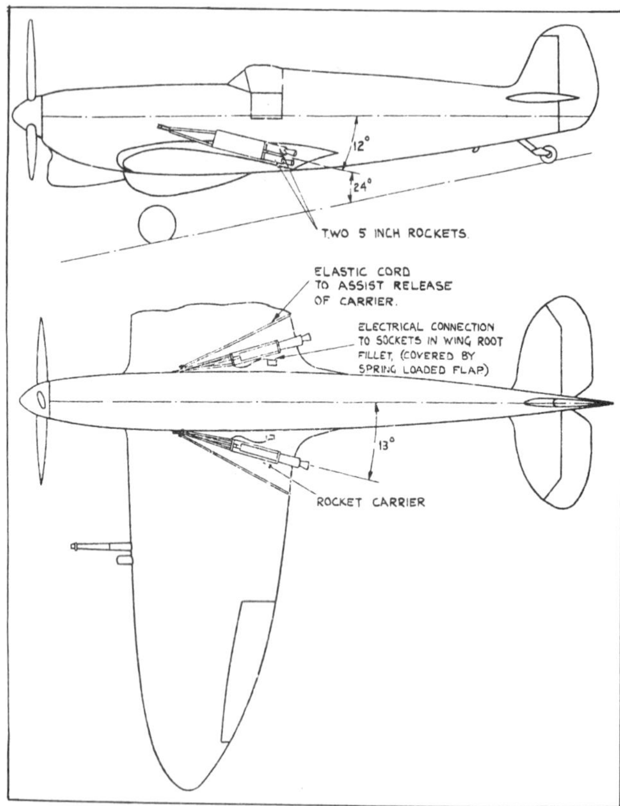

RATOG installation for the Seafire Mk IIC.

Twin 5in diameter RATOG rocket pack and wing fixture installed on MB141 for cartridge accelerated trials at Farnborough. Drawings, above, are of carriers and fittings for service use of RATOG and installation instructions.

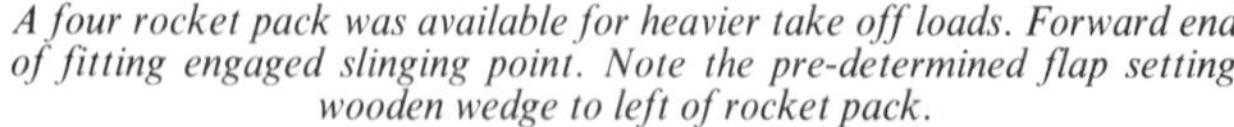

A four rocket pack was available for heavier take off loads. Forward end of fitting engaged slinging point. Note the pre-determined flap setting wooden wedge to left of rocket pack.

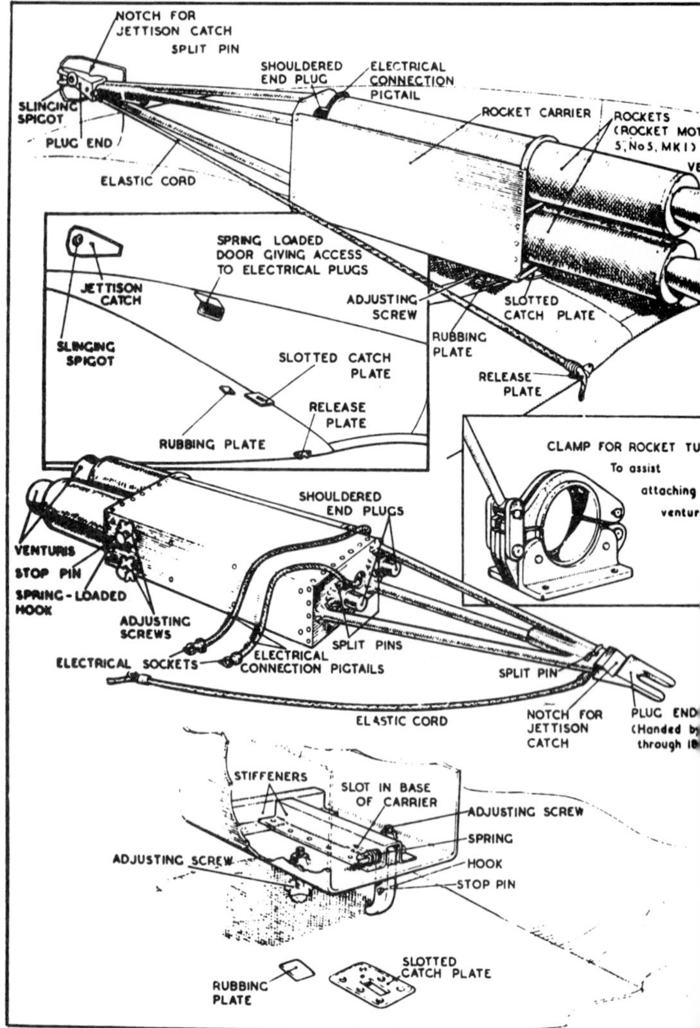

Rockets, carriers and fittings

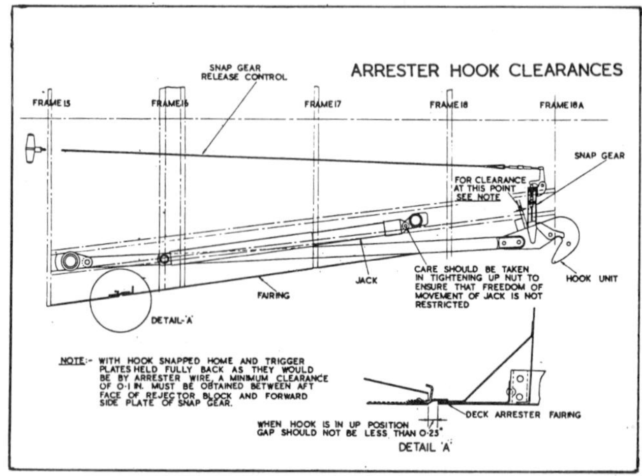

MB307 jettisons its RATOG pack after an assisted catapult take off at Farnborough.

At full bore, RATOG equipped Seafire MB141 leaves the Farnborough runway during trials.

independent of the Air Ministry. The Blackburn factory should also be turned over to the production of the folding wing Spitfires. The advantages are many as the Navy would have the whole of the RAF experience with the Spitfire to draw on, and the Spitfire has already developed into a better fighter than the Firebrand".

Westland Aircraft was the ideal choice as main contractor for the Seafire for both Spitfire production lines at Supermarine and Castle Bromwich had little, or no, room for further expansion; Cunliffe Owen of Southampton had long since repaired the bomb damage to their factory and they became a Westland satellite. Two major contracts were placed – B124305/ 40 with Westland Aircraft, the fourth order to this contract, for 213 Seafire Mk IIC dated March 1942. It was to be completed by January 1944. The second order was to the same contract and was placed with Supermarine as the eighth order for 202 Mk IICs of the same date. This order was completed by April 1943, Supermarine being quicker into production as Westland had to completely re-tool and lay down a production line.

Supermarine had managed to adapt their F VC Spitfire production facility on which to build the new Seafire, and before the first metal was cut on the new order 3,685 design hours had been logged. Jigging and design of the arrester hook fitment bay absorbed 40,000 man hours for the Seafire differed in many ways to the hooked Mk IB. The fuselage was strengthened at the catapult spool positions which were attached to frame sixteen just above and below the bottom, main longerons. Frames 9, 10 and 16 were reinforced and internal strengthening was concentrated on the main fuselage longerons around the radio compartment door. With the Universal 'C' wing, additional 25 lbs of armour plate, wing strengthening to enable external stores to be carried, empty weight of the IIC rose by about 6% over that of the converted IB. As a result the main undercarriage was also strengthened and raked forwards two inches, the latter to prevent the aircraft nosing over. Performance did suffer for the IIC was 15mph slower than the earlier models.

The first prototype IIC was AD371, converted by Supermarine from Mk V, to the Type 357. It flew for the first time in February 1942 and was immediately transferred to RAE Farnborough on 25th of the same month for trials. During the following months it was taken aboard *HMS Illustrious* for deck suitability trials beginning on 5 March. It had an auw of 6,490lb and performed well during normal take off and landing. On the first catapult take off it yawed slightly and the port wheel struck the deck coaming and burst the tyre. On landing AD371 swung and damaged the radiator cowling. The Seafire was returned to Worthy Down for examination after it had completed twenty catapult take offs and slight diagonal buckling was found near the rear fuselage catapult spools. There was also a marked buckle on the starboard side just aft of the tail unit joint at frame 19.

Also, the tailplane had an appreciable list starboard indicating that the spar had been bent. The pilot reported that when flying the Seafire he had to employ full rudder bias, which was in agreement with the tailplane list, so it was decided to

Unpainted Seafire IIC is readied for its first acceptance flight at Worthy Down.

Seafire manufacture at Westland.

reinforce the tailplane spar. The pilot also remarked that the headrest was too far back for catapulting and thought that an adjustable one would be better. A temporary modification added four inches to the front of the rest. Also, the engine tended to cut out during launch but this, too, was soon rectified. Supermarine Report 3592 of November 1942 concluded that the existing strength requirements were inadequate and an increase in strength of at least 50% was needed. AD371 ended up at Arbroath with No 778 squadron.

MA970, the first production Seafire IIC built by Supermarine as the Type 358, made its maiden flight from High Post aerodrome on 28 May 1942 and was weighed at Worthy Down on 9 June. The following figures show the CoG positions for various armament categories and they included a full 30 gal overload fuel tank, tropical air intake, a Merlin 46 engine, nose ballast of 3 × 27lb weights. Thirteen Seafire and seven Spitfire modifications were incorporated.

armament	8 Browning			'B' wing			4 Hispano		
condition of a/c	wght	CoG aft	in. down	wght	CoG aft	in down	wght	CoG aft	in down
	5213	2.9	11.1	5243	2.95	11.1	5243	2.95	11.1
normal load	6665	7.4	9.5	6899	7.0	9.8	7131	7.3	10.2
overload	6949	7.8	10.6	7183	7.4	10.8	7415	7.65	11.1

The Admiralty did want to standardise wing armament as four Hispano cannon but the weight was excessive and it was decided that the 'B' wing of four Brownings and two Hispano would have to suffice. With tropical air intake deleted and 30 gal overload tank in position, the Seafire IIC's CoG was 8.6in aft of the datum, and it could be flown satisfactorily without the nose ballast installed.

Westland Aircraft took longer to make ready its production line and the first Mk IIC rolled off in late December 1942. LR631 was transferred to Vickers, Worth Down, for weighing and CoG determination on 4 January 1943. It had a tare of 5,322lb, normal take off 6,978, and with 30gal overload tank 7,272. It was powered by a Merlin 46 engine driving a three blade Rotol Jablo propeller and a temperate air intake was fitted. It had 18 Seafire and 35 Spitfire modifications. Performance trials revealed a maximum speed of 363mph @ 7,300 feet in MS gear, 398 @ 21,000 feet FS. Rate of climb was 4,900 ft min @ 4,800 feet and 4,050 @ 18,000.

By October 1942 only 50 Seafire IICs had been delivered and four squadrons equipped, but as both production lines accelerated the delivery rate rose. All the early IICs had the Merlin 45 as standard and this operated at its maximum efficiency at 13,000 feet. Naval operations had proved conclusively that most interceptions of enemy aircraft took place at lower altitudes. For the lower altitudes a new engine was needed and when the ubiquitous Mk I Spitfire, L1004, was flight tested with the Merlin 32 engine providing 1,645hp at low altitude in December 1942 the Navy was quick to ask for examples for the Seafire.

The Merlin 32 increased maximum speed of the Seafire at sea level to 316mph and 335 at 6,000 feet. Take off run was reduced and rate of climb increased. It was difficult to obtain Merlin 32s at that time for they were all earmarked for the Fairey Barracuda Mk II strike aircraft, but eventually a number were diverted and when fitted with a four bladed propeller the low level performance of the IIC improved dramatically. With the new engine designation of the Seafire variant was altered to L IIC. There were other advantages with the new;engine; the cropped supercharger blades enabled more power to be provided to the propeller instead of being used to provide more air flow for operation at high altitudes; starting was via a Coffman cartridge which meant that the Seafire would no longer have to rely on having the engine started from a trolley accumulator or a fixed ring main.

To improve maneouvrability at the low operating heights a number of IICs had their wing span reduced by removing the tips in an attempt to increase the rate of roll. As a result of this there was an increase in maximum level speed, but without the additional wing area the service ceiling was cut to about 20,000 feet, take off and landing runs extended and with full military load it was a demanding aircraft under combat conditions. The Seafire, like the Spitfire, originally had no take-off flap setting and in order to resolve the situation the second Spirfire Mk III had carried out a series of trials to overcome this. Full details of W3237 experiments can be found in chapter ten.

The landing run of the clipped wing Seafire caused a number of accidents* and it was decided to fit and test a tail landing parachute. The parachute unit was designed and tested by RAE Farnborough and the S.M.E results showed that the installation withstood a tensile load of 1,200lb, a proof load of 3,020lb, and a maximim load of 4,040lb, the latter at an angle to the axis of the test equipment of 15°. The parachute and housing could be jettisoned in flight and for operations had to be installed before a flight and removed for storage on completion of same. Although the parachute performed to expectations the release hook failed at a cable load of 2,470lbs, and the experiments with both were discontinued.

Final variant of the IIC was the Mk LR IIC for the photo-reconnaissance role. Modification consisted of two F24 cameras, one vertical 20 inch and one oblique 14 inch, and it still retained the full cannon and machine gun armament. The conversion was to MB194 by Heston Aircraft Ltd, in July 1943, who completed all the remaining conversions. Weighing and CoG determination of the prototype took place at Worthy Down on 14 July and the Supermarine report designated the type PR L IIC. It had a tare of 5,310lb, and auw 7,043.

No 807 Squadron was, again, the first to be re-equipped with the LF Mk IIC, but due to extensive demands on the Merlin 32 engine the full complement was not achieved until May 1943. Problems were still being experienced with the Mk IIC's undercarriage and a series of trials was arranged to take place on *HMS Pretoria Castle* on 20 January 1944. Present were Joseph Smith, Jeffery Quill and Furlong from Supermarine and two RAE representatives. Three Mk IIs were made ready for the tests, two with splined oleo legs and one with link and they were fully representative of the normal ship board Seafire.

Supermarine specified that each Seafire be fitted with a cropped propeller and spares to be available. S.M.E Farnborough fitted the necessary accelerometers. A number of landings were made with each of the three aircraft and these were then compared with the results obtained with a fourth. As a result of the test the oleo travel was altered to take care of the landing stresses.

Not all of the Navy's carriers had catapults that could cope with the Seafire's launching spigots and in order to get the heavily laden aircraft off the deck the cartridge initiated (RATOG) take off was a necessity. MB141 and MB307 were modified for the installation of two five inch diameter rockets, each 41 inches long and contained in two carriers. One carrier was fitted to each wing root, and had a total weight of 66lb. Each rocket contained 26lbs of cordite. After the installation had been completed at Worthy Down the Seafires were transferred to Farnborough on 14 January for initial trials. Take off procedure was to open up the Merlin throttle to its maximum and then fire the rockets, which burned for four seconds only. Various combinations of two, four and eight rockets were tested.

MB141 was flown aboard *HMS Chaser* and at the conclusion of one flight the pilot, K. J. Robertson, was killed when he crashed landed on *Chaser's* deck. The second Seafire, MB307, was readied for trials. During early trials at Farnborough with the Seafire in early February 1944 the fabric covering of the rudder and elevators caught fire on three occasions when the rocket's exhaust set the bitumen surface of the runway alight. This was cured by the introduction of flashless powder, but as a temperorary measure the runway was covered with rubber chips and the elevator surface covered with metal in place of the fabric. Trials were then transferred to *HMS Chaser* and both deck and aircrew warned never to fire the rockets when directly over the hangar deck. Trials of the RATOG gear were finally completed aboard *HMS Slinger*. The four rocket cluster resulted in a take off run of 270 feet and the eight cluster 230 feet at an auw of 7,250. Head winds also reduced the run.

The Fleet Air Arm wanted a method by which re-arming on the carrier deck could be speeded up and Supermarine

* *Landing accidents totalled 30% of all Seafire mishaps.*

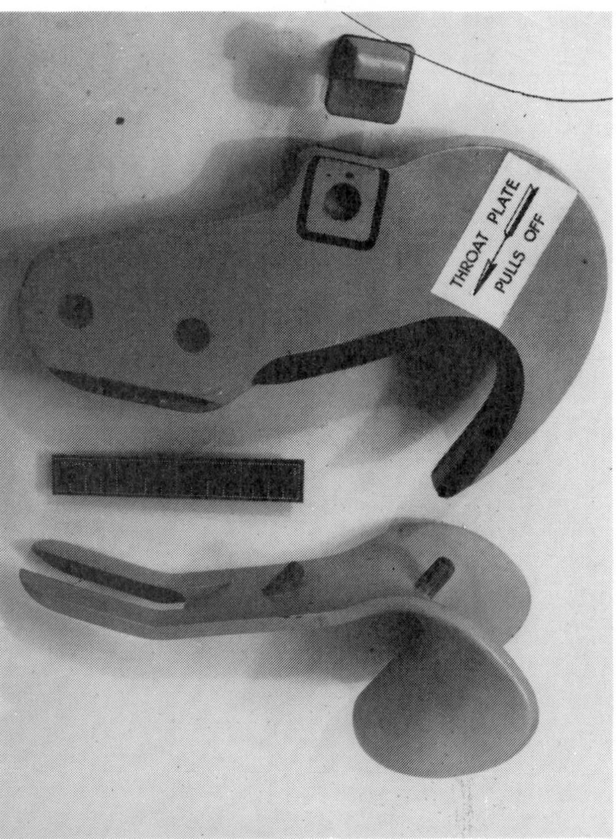

Main components of a forged hook.

Leading edge of wheel fairings were clipped to avoid fouling arrester wires.

A superb Charles E. Brown shot of a flight of Seafire IICs over the Fleet Carrier HMS Indomitable. *From 1943 to 1944,* Indomitable *hosted Nos 801, 807, 809, 880 and 899 Squadrons on various tours, each flying the Mk IIC.*

agreed to construct and test a Seafire wing with a modified undersurface ammunition bay door with quick release buttons and hinges. The modification was not a success for it weakened the structure and had to be abandoned.

The final production Westland-built Seafire IIC, LR764, was at Worthy Down on 18 October 1943 for weighing and CoG determination. It was powered by a Merlin 55 engine with a Rotol five bladed Jablo propeller and had a tare of 5,219lb and an auw of 6,875. It never entered service but was used by many experimental establishments, including Boscombe Down, where it took part in trials with a Seafire Mk III tail unit installed.

During the closing months of 1942 preparations for Operation Torch, the Allied invasion of North Africa, were started and the Admiralty requested the supply of 65 Mk VB Spifires, hooked, but not spooled, for delivery by 15 September. The Air Ministry was also asked to make available 20 old Spitfires without hooks for training purposes by 1 September. If the carrier *HMS Indomitable* was to be used for Torch a further 48 Spitfires would be needed, plus an additional 18 unhooked trainers. All Fulmars were to be replaced by Martlets. During a meeting between the Admiralty and MAP a further 240 Spitfires were demanded but this total was later reduced to 114, 66 of which were to be released by the Air Ministry in the first three months of 1943. "The Fleet Air Arm must have three Seafire squadrons worked up by early 1943. At present No 807 has five aircraft, 801 twelve Mk IB conversions".

The situation was grave and the First Sea Lord wrote to the Secretary of State for Air, Sir Archibald Sinclair, on 22 February as follows- "Dear Archie, We have been examining the effect on the Fleet Air Arm expansion programme of (a) the revised forecast of UK production in 1943 issued by Cripps on 4 January, and (b) the comparative failure of the Lyttleton Mission to obtain additional naval fighter aircraft in 1943 from the USA. It is clear that 1943 is going to be a bad year for us. It will be impractical to form a single alternative armament squadron, and we estimate that even if all our existing shore-based squadrons are disbanded and reserves of all kind reduced to a minimum, there will still be shortages during the year of about 200 single seat fighters. The ACNS (Sir) is in touch with the Air Staff about the possibilities of meeting part of the fighter deficiences, and I shall be most grateful if you can see your way clear to help us in meeting the special requirement for 115 additional cannon-fighter Spitfires for the conversion to Seafire and 30 other Spitfires for training purposes, set out in his letters of 25 and 28 January to Group Captain Irelaw Chapman.

"For 1944 and later, the prospects are in some respects brighter. Cripps is planning to increase production of Seafires by using in addition to Westlands, Cunliffe-Owen at Eastleigh; Folland at Hamble and Saunders-Roe at Weybridge. He hopes to give us 900 Seafires in 1944 and 1,000 in 1945, and on present reckoning this will substantially meet our requirements. I earnestly hope that you will be prepared to agree to this proposal in order to help make good the serious shortages with which Fleet Air Arm is faced both in numbers and quality, of this important type. The Navy's share of the British aircraft industry is a very modest one, and we have suffered the most grievous production setbacks during the last few years". It was also suggested that there should be inter-changeability between Seafire and Spitfire airframes, engines, spares and maintenance and also pilots.

The Seafire Mk IIC provided the bulk of air cover when Operation Avalanche was launched to start the invasion of Italy. Five escort carriers carried between them 106 aircraft, divided between nine squadrons and two separate flights. The action took place in the Bay of Salerno on 9 September 1943 and the squadrons and ships taking part were Nos 879 and 886 on board *HMS Attacker*, 807 and 808, *HMS Battler*, 899 and 834 Flight on *HMS Hunter*, the remainder of 899 Squadron and 833 Flight on *HMS Stalker*, 809, 887 and 897 squadrons on *HMS Unicorn*. Seafires also took part on 10 July previous to the Salerno operation. Attrition was high and more than half the Seafire force was either written off of damaged, due mainly to the calm conditions with little wind across the carrier decks.

SERIAL NUMBERS

Westland Aircraft Ltd
Contract No *B124305/40*
Fourth Order for 213 Seafire Mk IIC dated March 1942. Built as Mks IIC/III between January 1943 and January 1944. The following serials apply to Mk IICs built to this fourth order. LR631 to 667, 680 to 712, 725 to 764.

Supermarine Aviation (Vickers) Ltd
Contract No *B19713/39*
Eighth order for 202 Seafire Mk IIC dated March 1942. Built as Mks IIC between June 1942 and April 1943. The following serials apply to Mk IICs built to this eighth order. MA970 to 999, MB113 to 158; 178 to 222; 235 to 281; 293 to 326.

Twelfth order for 260 Seafire Mk IIC dated 29th July 1942. Built as Seafire Mk IIC between January and March 1943. NM910 to 949; 963 to 982. Total built 372. Westland 110, Supermarine 262.

EN686 to 695, EN710 to 759 (60 A/C) cancelled 12 January 1943.

A/C operationally equipped @ 15MU Wroughton

LR631 M46 First prod a/c. V WD 4-1-43 wts & CG load 15MU 23-1 833S HMS Stal

LR632 M46 15MU 23-1-43 801S *HMS Furious*

LR633 M46 15MU 27-1-43

LR634 M45 15MU 5-2-43 761D S RNAS Hens *HMS Argus* 768S

LR635 M45 15MU 18-2-43

LR636 M45 15MU 15-2-43 AST 1-4

LR637 M45 15MU 7-3-43 759S Yeovil BDn from 899 S RAF Ballyhalmern. Rogue a/c which std at speed and crabbed in flight. Major fault was badly assembled eng cowling.

LR638 M45 15MU 15-3-43 833S *HMS Stal*

LR639 M45 15MU 22-3-43 770S

LR640 M45 15MU 22-3-43 807S *HMS Indom*

LR641 M45 15MU 5-4-43

LR642 M45 15MU 5-4-43 807S *HMS Batt* 1943

LR643, LR644 M45 15MU 5-4-43

LR645 M45 15MU 10-4-43 807S *HMS Indom*

LR646 M50 15MU 17-4-43 RNAS LoS 19-5 con to LF Mk IIC M32 instal

LR647 M50A 15MU 19-4-43 R-RH May/June '43 M32 instal con to LF Mk IIC RNAS Doni

LR648 M50 15MU 19-4-43

LR649 M50 15MU 19-4-43 R-RH May/June '43 M32 instal. RNAS Doni 833S *HMS Stal*

LR650 M50 15MU 27-4-43

LR651 M50 15MU 27-4-43 833S HMS Stal 879S *HMS Attac* Fitt F24 cameras Sept'44. to 1832S RNVR

LR652 M46 15MU 27-4-43 801S Hats

LR653 M50 15MU 27-4-43

LR654 M46 15MU 1-5-43

LR655 M50 15MU 3-5-43 894S *HMS Illus*

LR656, LR657, LR658 M50 15MU 3-5-43

LR659 M50 15MU 3-5-43 894S *HMS Illus*

LR660 M50 15MU 3-5-43

LR661 M50 15MU 17-5-43

LR662 M50 15MU 13-5-43

LR663 M50 15MU 17-5-43

LR664 M50 15MU 20-5-43 759S Yeovil

LR665 M50 15MU 18-5-43 894S *HMS Illus* SOC 12-9

LR666 M50 15MU 18-5-43

LR667 M46 15MU 25-5-43 889S Puttalam, Ceylon

LR680 M45 15MU 25-5-43

LR681 M46 15MU 25-5-43 880S Hatston 761S Hens

LR682 M50 15MU 28-5-43 894S Hens

LR683 M50 15MU 28-5-43

LR684 M45 15MU 31-5-43 con to LF Mk IIC dam ldg

LR685 M45 15MU 31-5-43 894S Hens

LR686, LR687H, LR688 M45 15MU 2-6-43

LR689 M45 15MU 2-6-43

LR690 M50 15MU 3-6-43

LR691 15MU 31-5-43 808S Burscough

LR692 M50 15MU 3-6-43

LR693 M50 15MU 9-6-43 HAL for vibration tests

LR694 M50 To Rotol for prop exp. 11-6-43

LR695 15MU 11-6-43

LR696 15MU 11-6-43 4FW Dekh Egypt

LR697 15MU 11-6-43 880S *HMS Stal*

LR698 15MU 11-6-43

LR699 15MU 18-6-43 889S Puttalam Ceylon

LR700 15MU 19-6-43

LR701 15MU 19-6-43 880S *HMS Stal*

LR702 15MU 25-6-43

LR703 15MU 25-6-43 761S Hens

LR704 15MU 25-6-43 879S *HMS Attac*

LR705 15MU 25-6-43

LR706 15MU 26-6-43

LR707 15MU 30-6-43

LR708 15MU 30-6-43

LR709, LR710, LR711, LR712 15MU 2-7-43

LR725 15MU 3-7-43

LR726 15MU 7-7-43

LR727 15MU 10-7-43

LR728 15MU 10-7-43 FR Mk IIC M32 BDn Mar'44 det of aftmast CoG. Found to be longtitudinally unstable & fitt 6¼lb int wt in elev syst Fitt F.24 cameras, trls with same.

LR729 15MU 10-7-43 787S Witt NAFDU, 879S Nutts Corner.

LR730 15MU 13-7-43

LR731 15MU 16-7-43

LR732 15MU 15-7-43

LR733 15MU 16-7-43

LR734, LR735, LR736 15MU 27-7-43

LR737 15MU 30-7-43 809S *HMS Stal* 11-1-44 RNAS Belfast 16-10 807S *HMS Hunter* dam ldg 3-5-45

LR738 15MU 30-7-43

LR739 15MU 31-7-43 4FW Dekh Egypt

LR740, LR741 15MU 31-7-43

LR742 15MU 6-8-43 4FW Dekh Egypt

LR743, LR744 15MU 6-8-43

LR745 15MU 7-8-43

LR746 15MU 14-8-43 801S *HMS Furious*

LR747 15MU 14-8-43 807S *HMS Hunter*

LR748, LR749 15MU 14-8-43

LR750 15MU 19-8-43

LR751 15MU 21-8-43

LR752 15MU 21-8-43

LR753 15MU 21-8-43 807S *HMS Hunter* April'44

LR754 15MU 27-8-43

LR755 15MU 28-8-43 834S *HMS Battler* 889S Puttalam Ceylon

LR756 15MU 28-8-43

LR757, LR758 15MU 4-9-43

LR759, LR760 15MU 11-9-43

LR761, LR762 15MU 17-9-43

LR763 15MU 25-9-43

LR764 M55 Wd WD Tare 5219 AUW 6875 18-10-43 BDn 30-10-43 hand trls with Seafire Mk III tail unit.

M series. All Merlin M46 unless indicated.

MA970/2972 L.IIC Type 358 M45 HPA FF 23-5-42. First Super L IIC to Navy 19-6 V WD 2-7 VA Winkfield Row 27-7 Farn 19-6 catapult trls RNAS Arb 11-9 for ship's trls CRD HAL 14-9 CRD V WD 17-9 778S 21-9 BDn 13-10 high speed perf trls with and without 30 gal. o/ld tank CRD VA WD 27-10 for con to proto Seafire Mk III. First flight in new configuration 2-11 maker's trls as dev a/c BDn 14-1-43 t/o and land trls of folding wng a/c with normal and clip wngs. Fitt operating mechanism enabling flaps to be preset to 18° for take off (see page 133) Wts and COG load M46 instal with Rotol 4-blade prop. 2nd series trls with normal & clip wng and 4 × 20mm can Hispano Mk II instal. Trans to Farn June'44 for additional trls Max speed in dive 470mph. Fitt both temperate and trop air filter. Coll with Welkin DX282 on t/o and cd It was recorded that during trls the CoG moved aft in high speed dives due, it was thought, to tail unit twisting.

MA971 2999 HPA FF 30-5-42 38MU RNDA 2-6-42 RNAS LoS 7-7 807S *HMS Furious* 8-42

MA972 3008 HPA FF 2-6-42 38MU RNDA 31-5 RNAS LoS 11-7 884S HMS Vict 893S *HMS Illust* 4FW Dekh Egypt ROS 27-10. During its short career this a/c was under rep almost constantly from Oct'42 to Mar'43

MA973 3022 HPA FF 6-6-42 38MU RNDA 8-6 RNAS Arb 9-7

MA974 3032 HPA FF 11-6-42 38MU RNDA 13-6 RNAS LoS 7-7 ROS 17-10 884S *HMS Vict* 801S Hats

MA975 3049 HPA FF 13-6-42 38MU RNDA 15-6 RNAS LoS 8-7 887S *HMS Unic* ROS 24-10-42

MA976 3067 HPA FF 20-6-42 15MU RNDA 25-6-42

MA977 3089 HPA FF 27-6-42 15MU RNDA 29-6 ROS 24-10 748S Farn June'45

MA978 3106 HPA FF 30-6-42 15MU RNDA 2-7-42 AST 7-9 RNAS Mach 19-10 880S *HMS Stal* Italy Sept'43

MA979 3107 HPA FF 20-6-42 RNDA 15MU 2-7 ROS 24-10

From MA980 to the early MB serials the legend on the official movements card read:– "Went from Vickers to AST for completion as Seafire". This suggests that the aircraft were built on the Supermarine production line and completed for entry into service with arrester hook and other fitments by AST, normally at their Hamble plant.

MA980 3126 HPA FF 5-7-42 39MU RNDA 8-7 AST 19-9 RNAS Mach 15-10 FACE 22-3-43

MA981 3216 AST FF 27-7-42 (Con to Spit) AST 5-7 15MU 6-8 AST H 29-9 RNAS LoS 20-11 884S Turn

MA982 HPA 3162 FF 13-7-42 15MU RNDA 14-7 ROS 24-10 AST 3-12 RNAS Doni 20-3-43 884S Turn HMS Argus

MA983 3226 AST (Spit con to F IIC) AST 5-7 FF 3-8 15MU RNDA 6-8 ROS 24-10 884S Turn *HMS Argus* 801S Hats

MA984 3182 HPA FF 20-7-42 15MU 24-7

MA985 3251 AST 19-7-42 FF 13-8 15MU RNDA 20-8 880S *HMS Stal* dam in combat 8-11

MA986 3276 AST (Spit con to F Mk IIC) 21-7-42 FF 16-8 15MU RNDA 20-8 807S *HMS Furious* AST 24-1-43 RNAS Doni 11-4

MA987 3304 AST (Spit con to F Mk IIC) 23-7-42 FF 23-8 15MU RNDA 21-10 AST 21-10 MSFU Speke 11-12

MA988 3316 AST (Spit con to F Mk IIC) 25-7-42 FF 29-8 15MU RNDA 2-9 Farn Dec'42 catapult trls Trans LoS ROS 2-4-43

MA989 3314 AST (Spit con to F Mk IIC) 5-8-42 FF 30-8 15MU RNDA 12-9 South Farn 31-12

MA990 3315 AST (Spit con to F Mk IIC) 7-8-42 FF 31-8 15MU RNDA 2-9

MA991 3305 AST (Spit con to F Mk IIC) 7-8-42 FF 29-8 Con and rep (claimed to have M61 fitt) 15MU RNDA 1-9 AST 7-11 RNAS Arb 3-11

MA992 3335 AST (Spit con to F Mk IIC) 9-8-42 FF 2-9 15MU RNDA 4-9 807S Fabrica

MA993 3334 AST (Spit VC con to F Mk IIC M45 instal) 10-8-42 FF 2-9 15MU RNDA 4-9

MA994 3336 AST (Spit VC con to F Mk IIC) 11-8-42 FF 4-9 15MU RNDA 5-9 ROS 26-2-43

MA995 3337 AST (Spit VC con to F Mk IIC) 14-8-42 FF 4-9 15MU RNDA 5-9 RNAS Doni 27-3-43

MA996 3338 AST (Spit VC con to F Mk IIC) 15-8-42 FF 4-9 15MU RNDA 5-9 RNAS Doni 27-3-43

MA997 3295 HPA FF 26-8-42 15MU RNDA 28-8

MA998 3308 CHA FF 29-8-42 15MU RNDA 30-8 ROS 21-11 880S *HMS Furious* 889S HMS Khedive

MA999 3326 CHA FF 2-9-42 15MU RNDA 4-9 880S *HMS Stal* Sept'43

MB series All F Mk IIC Merlin M46 unless indicated

MB113 3341 HPA FF 1-9-42 15MU RNDA 29-8

MB114 3327 CHA FF 4-9-42 15MU RNDA 5-9 AST 6-11

MB115 3307 HPA FF 29-8-42 15MU RNDA 31-8 894S Mach

MB116 3351 AST (Spit con to F Mk IIC) 25-8-42 FF 6-9 15MU RNDA 8-9 AST 14-11

MB117 3339 HPA FF 1-9-42 15MU RNDA 2-9

MB118 3340 HPA FF 2-9-42 15MU RNDA 4-9

MB119 3345 HPA FF 5-9-42 15MU RNDA 8-9 AST 17-11

MB120 3353 HPA FF 7-9-42 15MU RNDA 9-9

MB121 3354 HPA FF 8-9-42 15MU RNDA 10-9 AST 5-11 884S *HMS Vict*

MB122 3368 HPA FF 10-9-42 15MU RNDA 12-9 884S *HMS Vict* 885S *HMS Form*

MB123 HPA FF 10-9-42 15MU RNDA 12-9

MB124 3376 HPA FF 12-9-42 15MU RNDA 15-9 ROS 2-4-43

MB125 3387 HPA FF 15-9-42 15MU 15-9 AST H Jan'43. Farn Feb C.I. (Cartridge initiated (RATOG) trls Aerodynamic Flight Feb'44 for tailplane stiff trls AST H for mods, May. Farn RATOG accelerator proofing and drag chain arrester gear trls. To FAA for research.

MB126 3392 HPA FF 15-9-42 15MU 16-9

MB127 3397 HPA FF 17-9-42 15MU 18-9 329S Silverstone

MB128 3412 HPA FF 19-9-42 15MU RNDA 24-9

MB129 3413 HPA FF 19-9-42 15MU 21-9

MB130 3427 HPA FF 22-9-42 15MU 23-9 15 Ferry Pl H 23-9

MB131 3428 HPA FF 24-9-42 15MU 24-9

MB132 3429 HPA FF 25-9-42 15MU 26-9 807S *HMS Form* 884S *HMS Vict*

MB133 3430 HPA FF 25-9-42 15MU 27-9 809S *HMS Stal*

MB134 3446 HPA FF 28-9-42 15MU 2-10

MB135 3447 HPA FF 28-9-42 15MU 2-10 Farn Jan'43 from VWD Catapult trls 884S Turn

MB136 3448 HPA FF 29-9-42 15MU 2-10

MB137 3456 HPA FF 31-9-42 15MU 6-10

MB138 3356 CHA LA Mk IIC FF 8-9-42 15MU RNDA 9-9 HAL 24-12 M32 instal con to LA from F IIC. Eng with SU Bendix Stromberg carb. Neg G Farn Jan'43 trls B Dn Feb'43 fuel syst and cons trls with and without 30gal drop tanks Wts and CoG load Max range with full fuel load 820 miles, duration 3.9hrs @ 160mph still air @ 15,000ft. Series of t/o and land trls with o/ld tanks. Wooden wedges set flaps to 16° (see page 526). Trls of VC Univ wng., climb and level speeds with heat ducts for gun bays blanked off. VA WD 22-1-43

MB139 3357 CHA FF 8-9-42 15MU RNDA 9-9 AST 15-11 RNAS Doni 12-3

MB140 3366 CHA FF 10-9-42 15MU RNDA 11-9

MB141 3367 CHA FF 10-9-42 15MU RNDA 11-9 HAL 23-9 for mods South Farn 31-10 from VWD T/o trls CRD VA WD 19-12 Farn 14-1-43 CRD HAL 4-6 instal of RATOG gear. Farn for CI RATOG initial acceleration trls spcl mods. RNAS Crail 5-1-44 *HMS Chaser*. Crash land on *Chaser* Pilot K J Robertson kld a/c i/sea 14-1 HAL for repair, Farn April'44 neg G trls, arrester gear trls. 'G' suffix serial applied after spcl mods by HAL. July'44 assisted t/o trls Gyroscopic gun sight trls with LR766, Seafire Mk III, also with 'G' restriction, applied to the then secret gunsight. FACE Dec'44. (The 3in dia RATOG cartridges originally

MA970 became the prototype Seafire Mk III. It was destroyed at Farnborough in 1944.

tried were unsuccessful. The larger, 5inch cartridge proved satisfactory and was put into prod

MB142 3379 CHA FF 10-9-42 15MU RNDA 13-9
MB143 3381 CHA FF 12-9-42 15MU RNDA 13-9
MB144 3371 CHA FF 11-9-42 15MU RNDA 13-9 884S *HMS Vict*
MB145 3382 CHA FF 12-9-42 15MU RNDA 13-9 AST 31-12 RNAS Yeov 12-4-43 748S 4-43
MB146 3391 CHA FF 15-9-42 15MU 16-9 885S *HMS Form* Aero Naval 167
MB147 3390 CHA FF 15-9-42 15MU 16-9
MB148 3404 CHA FF 19-9-42 15MU 21-9
MB149 3411 CHA FF 20-9-42 15MU 21-9
MB150 3424 CHA LR IIC FF 22-9-42 15MU 24-9 809S *HMS Stal*
MB151 3425 CHA FF 25-9-42 15MU 27-9
MB152 3442 CHA FF 26-9-42 15MU 30-9
MB153 3471 CHA FF 8-10-42 15MU 10-10
MB154 3472 CHA FF 8-10-42 15MU 10-10 7FPP Sherburn in Elmet. Hit bump on land, tried o/s std and dbf CE 31-10
MB155 3487 CHA FF 10-10-42 15MU 12-10
MB156 3488 CHA FF 10-10-42 15MU 12-10 885S *HMS Form*
MB157 3491 CHA FF 12-10-42 15MU 14-10 807S *HMS Furious*
MB158 3500 CHA FF 14-10-42 15MU 18-10 808S Bally
MB178 3362 AST Con to LFIIC 26-8-42. M32 instal with reversible pitch prop. FF 9-9-42 15MU RNDA 11-9 AST 11-11 RNAS Doni 22-2-43 884S Turn
MB179 3370 AST Spit con to Seafire FIIC 27-8-42 FF 10-9 15MU RNDA 12-9 AST 5-11 834S *HMS Batt* RNAS Doni 29-11-43
MB180 3377 AST Spit con to Seafire FIIC 28-8-42 FF 12-9 15MU 15-9
MB181 3352 AST Spit con to Seafire FIIC 30-8-42 FF 7-9 15MU RNDA 8-9
MB182 3378 AST Spit con to Seafire FIIC 3-9-42 FF 8-10 15MU 15-9
MB183 3469 HPA FF 8-10-42 15MU 9-10 AST 28-12 RNAS Yeov 23-1-43 AST 1-4
MB184 3470 HPA FF 8-10-42 15MU 9-10 884S *HMS Vict*
MB185 3489 HPA FF 8-10-42 15MU 13-10 AST 21-1-43 RNAS Doni 15-5 884S *HMS Vict* 761S Hens
MB186 3501 HPA FF 15-10-42 15MU 21-10 884S Turn
MB187 3505 CHA FF 16-10-42 15MU 18-10 ROS 6-4-43
MB188 3510 HPA FF 17-10-42 15MU 18-10
MB189 3533 HPA FF 21-10-42 15MU 24-10
MB190 3532 HPA FF 21-10-42 15MU 24-10 USNAS Patuxent Rover 3-4S
MB191 3508 HPA FF 22-10-42 15MU 24-10 884S Turn ROS 5-1-43
MB192 3541 HPA FF 24-10-42 15MU 25-10 884S *HMS Vict*
MB193 3544 HPA LR Mk IIC FF 24-10-42 15MU 25-10 *HMS Indom* 4FW Dekh Egypt
MB194 3566 HPA FF 28-10-42 15MU 2-11 884S Turn con to PRLII by HAL 14-7-43
MB195 3567 HPA FF 31-10-42 15MU 2-11
MB196 3568 HPA FF 31-10-42 15MU 6-11 809S Perugia
MB197 3569 HPA FF 31-10-42 15MU 2-11
MB198 3592 HPA FF 5-11-42 15MU 9-11
MB199 3593 HPA FF 6-11-42 15MU 9-11 ROS 6-4-43
MB200 3619 HPA FF 14-11-42 15MU 17-11 801S Hatston
MB201 3620 HPA FF 14-11-42 15MU 17-11
MB202 3621 HPA FF 14-11-42 15MU 17-11 ROS 28-3-43
MB203 3626 HPA FF 15-11-42 15MU 17-11 761D S Hens *HMS Argus*
MB204 3644 HPA FF 21-11-42 15MU 22-11
MB205 3645 HPA FF 21-11-42 15MU 22-11 ROS 6-4-43
MB206 3646 HPA FF 21-11-42 15MU 24-11
MB207 3655 HPA FF 22-11-42 15MU 24-11 Farn June'44 Assisted t/o trls
MB208 3658 HPA FF 25-11-42 15MU 28-11
MB209 3659 HPA FF 26-11-42 15MU 28-11 894S Mach
MB210 3680 HPA FF 28-11-42 15MU 30-11
MB211 3681 HPA FF 28-11-42 15MU 30-11 ROS 6-4-43 759S Yeov
MB212 3686 HPA FF 30-11-42 15MU 4-12 894S *HMS Illust*
MB213 3722 HPA FF 8-12-42
MB214 3728 HPA M32 FF 9-12-42 ISMU 9-12 ASTE 1-5-43 RNAS 7-5
MB215 3729 HPA FF 10-12-42 15MU 22-12 894S *HMS Illust* Farn Feb'46 FAA research
MB216 3734 HPA FF 11-12-42 15MU 14-12 AST 1-4-43
MB217 3738 HPA FF 12-12-42 15MU 15-12 894S *HMS Illust* ROS 6-4-43
MB218 3775 HPA M45 FF 21-12-42 15MU 22-12
MB219 3776 HPA M45 FF 21-12-42 15MU 22-12
MB220 3777 HPA M45 FF 22-12-42 15MU 23-12
MB221 3782 HPA FF 23-12-42 15MU RNDA 24-12
MB222 3802 HPA FF 31-12-42 15MU 8-1-43
MB235 3503 CHA FF 14-10-42 15MU 18-10
MB236 3504 CHA FF 16-10-42 15MU 18-10 880S *HMS Stal*
MB237 3513 CHA FF 17-10-42 15MU 19-10 884S Turn 4FW Dekh Egypt
MB238 3521 CHA FF 18-10-42 15MU 25-10 FACB 13-11 ROS RNAS Hats 19-5-43 833S *HMS Stal*
MB239 3537 CHA FF 22-10-42 15MU 24-10 ROS 5-1-43 884S Turn
MB240 3548 CHA FF 24-10-42 15MU 28-10 *HMS Illust*
MB241 3557 CHA FF 27-10-42 15MU 2-11 ROS 22-2-43
MB242 3558 CHA FF 27-10-42 15MU 2-11
MB243 3585 CHA FF 31-10-42 15MU 6-11
MB244 3583 CHA FF 31-10-42 15MU 2-11
MB245 3584 CHA FF 31-10-42 15MU 2-11 809S Fabrica
MB246 3586 CHA LR Mk IIC FF 6-11-42 15MU 7-11 879S *HMS Att*
MB247 3587 CHA FF 6-11-42 15MU 8-11 AST 17-1-43 RNAS LoS 31-3
MB248 3600 CHA FF 7-11-42 15MU 9-11 801S *HMS Furious* 4FW Dekh Egypt
MB249 3609 CHA M61 FF 13-11-42 15MU 17-11 880S *HMS Stal*
MB250 3605 CHA M61 FF 10-11-42 15MU 17-11 880S *HMS Stal*
MB251 3612 CHA M61 FF 13-11-42 15MU 17-11 834S *HMS Batt*
MB252 3628 CHA FF 17-11-42 15MU 20-11-42
MB253 3631 CHA FF 20-11-42 15MU 21-11 880S *HMS Indom* 889S HMS Athe SOC 29-6-44
MB254 3654 CHA FF 22-11-42 15MU 24-11
MB255 3655 CHA FF 24-11-42 15MU 28-11 880S *HMS Indom*
MB256 3656 CHA FF 25-11-42 15MU 25-11 884S Turn
MB257 3657 CHA FF 25-11-42 15MU 2-12 894S *HMS Illust*
MB258 3674 CHA FF 28-11-42 15MU 2-12 ROS VAO 17-1-43 894S *HMS Illust*
MB259 3686 CHA FF 29-11-42 15MU 6-12
MB260 3694 CHA FF 30-11 15MU 2-12
MB261 3695 CHA FF 30-11-42 15MU 11-12 con to FR.IIC M32. B Dn Aprl'44 det of aftmost CoG with and without int/wt
MB262 3696 CHA FF 30-11-42 15MU 2-12
MB263 3707 CHA FF 5-12-42 15MU 6-12 884S Turn
MB264 3723 CHA FF 8-1-2-42 15MU 9-12 884S *HMS Illust* 708S
MB265 3725 FF 10-12-42 15MU 10-12 880S *HMS Indom*
MB266 3726 FF 29-12-42 15MU 10-12
MB267 3732 FF 11-12-42 15MU 15-12
MB268 3731 CHA FF 11-1-2-42 15MU 15-12
MB269 3746 CHA FF 12-12-42 15MU 22-12 894S *HMS Illust* 809S *HMS Stal*
MB270 3749 CHA FF 15-12-42 15MU 20-12 879S *HMS Attac*
MB271 3771 CHA FF 20-12-42 15MU 22-12
MB272 3786 CHA FF 23-12-42 15MU RNDA 2-1-43
MB273 3789 CHA FF 24-12-42 15MU RNDA 3-1-43
MB274 3791 CHA FF 30-12-42 15MU RNDA 2-1-43 FAAC 17-2
MB275 3806 CHA FF 1-1-43 15MU 3-1 880S *HMS Stal*
MB276 3792 CHA FF 30-12-42 15MU 2-1-43
MB277 3805 CHA FF 31-12-42 15MU 3-1-43 894S *HMS Illust*
MB278 3808 CHA FF 2-1-43 15MU 8-1
MB279 3809 CHA FF 2-1-43 15MU 3-1
MB280 3826 CHA FF 8-1-43 15MU 11-1 RNAS Doni 26-8 Arb 15-9 897S 23-10 809S *HMS Stal* 20-2-44 i/sea SOC 15-8
MB281 3827 CHA FF 8-1-43 15MU 15-1 728S
MB293 3633 AST FF 21-11-42 ASTH 8-11 con to LFIIC M32 15MU 29-11 BDn 14-12 Trls with 1x200 or 1x120 lb smoke bomb. Deck t/o trls with same. March'44 trls with Mk III light univ carr with 4x10 lb pract bombs and 4x4½in

Wearing HMS Illustrious *codes, MB240 embarked in October 1942.*

MB293 with trial fuselage bomb racks.

dia recco flares and 4x40 lb. GP bombs. Drag excessive. 879S *HMS Attac*
MB294 AST 3688 FF 23-11-42 15MU 29-11 894S *HMS Illust*
MB295 3669 AST FF 26-11-42 15MU 2-12
MB296 3670 AST FF 28-11-42 15MU 2-12
MB297 3710 AST FF 1-12-42 15MU 10-12 RNAS Hats 19-5-43 880S *HMS Stal*
MB298 3714 AST FF 4-12-42 15MU 11-12
MB299 AST 3743 Contract 1171/ASCRO/C37A FF 12-12-42 15MU 21-12 HAL mods. Farn Feb'43 catapult trls. HAL mods. Farn March'44 trls with drag chain arrester gear. 7-7-44 Trls on elevated P catapult. Trim curve trls on same
MB300 3744 AST contract as 299 FF 12-12-42 15MU 19-12 761S Hens
MB301 3807 AST contract as 299 FF 31-12-42 15MU 5-1-43 807S *HMS Indom HMS Batt*
MB302 3846 AST Contract as 299 FF 9-1-43 15MU 21-12 ROS 2-4-43 808S *HMS Batt* 759S Yeov
MB303 3811 HPA M45 FF 2-1-43 15MU 4-1 894S *HMS Illust*
MB304 3831 HPA LR Mk. IIC FF 8-1-43 15MU 8-1 4FW Dekh Egypt
MB305 3833 HPA FF 8-1-43 15MU 8-1
MB306 3834 HPA FF 8-1-43 15MU 9-1 Farn Feb'44 assist t/o trls in comp with NX958 Seafire LB
MB307 3869 AST M45 FF 13-1-43 15MU 18-1 RNAS LoS 7-5 *HMS Illust* RATOG Trls June'43 Farn Feb'44 RATOG & catapult trls HAL mods Farn assist t/o trls in comp with NX958 759S Yeov
MB308 3873 M45 AST FF 15-1-43 15MU 2-11 Contract as 299 895S 4-43
MB309 3835 HPA M45 FF 9-1-43 15MU 11-1 884S Turn 895S 4-43
MB310 3867 HPA FF 15-1-43 15MU 21-1 M45
MB311 3874 HPA FF 16-1-43 15MU 23-1 M45
MB312 3868 HPA M45 FF 15-1-43 15MU 21-1 808S RNAS Ayr May'44
MB313 3881 HPA FF 17-1-43 15MU 21-1 DeH 5-4-43 807S Fabrica
MB314 3985 HPA FF 21-1-43 15MU 23-1 DeH 5-4
MB315 3896 HPA FF 21-1-43 15MU 21-1
MB316 3902 HPA FF 23-1-43 15MU 27-1 895S 4-43
MB317 3903 HPA M45 FF 23-1-43 15MU 27-1 CRU 31-3 879S *HMS Attac*
MB318 3914 HPA FF 26-1-43 15MU 27-1
MB319 3919 HPA FF 27-1-43 15MU 29-1 895S 4-43
MB320 3924 HPA FF 29-1-43 15MU 3-2 CRU 31-3
MB321 3943 HPA M45 FF 2-2-43 15MU 4-2 807S *HMS Batt*
MB322 3963 HPA FF 6-2-43 15MU 10-2 CRU 31-3 880S *HMS Stal*
MB323 4133 CHA M45 FF 22-3-43 15MU 24-3 761S Hens
MB324 4134 CHA M45 FF 26-3-43 15MU 28-3
MB325 4148 CHA M45 FF 27-3-43 15MU 28-3 759S Yeov
MB326 4176 CHA FF 1-4-43 15MU 8-4 833S *HMS Stal*

NM series all M46 F. Mk IIC unless otherwise indicated
NM910 CHA FF 8-1-43 15MU 13-1
NM911 CHA FF 8-1-43 15MU 11-1 801S Hats
NM912 CGA FF 9-1-43 15MU 11-1 ROS 6-4
NM913 CHA FF 15-1-43 15MU 9-2 801S Hats
NM914 CHA FF 16-1-43 15MU 21-1
NM915 CHA FF 16-1-43 15MU 26-1 894S *HMS Illust*
NM916 CHA FF 20-1-43 15MU 26-1 4FPP Prestwick std final turn to land CE 22-2
NM917 CHA FF 22-1-43 15MU 26-1 887S *HMS Unic*
NM918 CHA FF 25-1-43 15MU 29-1
NM919 CHA M45 FF 2-2-43 15MU 15-2 895S 4-43
NM920 CHA M45 9-2-43 15MU 16-2 CRU 31-3 M32 instal to LF. IIC RNAS LoS 29-4
NM921 CHA FF 11-2-43 15MU 16-2
NM922 CHA M45 FF 11-2-43 15MU 16-2
NM923 CHA M45 FF 15-2-43 15MU 16-2
NM924 CHA M45 FF 16-2-43 15MU 19-3
NM925 CHA FF 16-2-43 15MU 18-2 ROS 29-3
NM926 CHA FF M45 17-2-43 15MU 24-2 ROS 29-3
NM927 CHA FF 17-2-43 15MU 24-2
NM928 CHA FF M45 19-2-43 15MU 24-2
NM929 CHA FF 19-2-43 15MU 26-2
NM930 CHA FF 19-2-43 15MU 26-2
NM931 AST FF M45 23-1-43 15MU 29-1
NM932 AST FF 6-2-43 15MU 14-2 AST 4-4 RNAS LoS 31-5
NM933 AST FF 8-2-43 15MU 18-2 879S *HMS Attack*
NM934 AST FF 24-2-43 15MU 28-2
NM935 AST FF 28-2-43 15MU 9-8
NM936 CHA FF 1-4-43 15MU 8-4
NM937 CHA FF 1-4-43 15MU 8-4
NM938 CB to AST for completion 27-2-43 FF 4-3 15MU 9-3 879S Nutts Crnr
NM939 CB to AST for completion 19-2-43 FF 6-3 15MU 9-3 884S Turn Rotols Stav 21-9-46
NM940 M45 CHA FF 7-4-43 15MU 13-4 886S hit high grnd bad visibility south Isle of Arran 19-6
NM941 M45 CHA M32 instal to LF ICC FF 18-4-43 15MU 13-4 RNAS LoS 18-5
NM942 CHA M50 FF 10-4-43 15MU 13-4 700S
NM943 CHA FF 9-4-43 15MU 16-4 R-RH 8-5 M32 instal to LF IIC RNAS Doni 880S *HMS Stal*
NM994 CHA FF 13-4-43 15MU 18-4 R-RH 8-5 M32 instal to LF IIC RNAS Doni
NM945 M45 CHA FF 15-4-43 15MU 18-4
NM946 CHA FF 15-4-43 15MU 18-4 833S *HMS Stalker*
NM947 CHA FF 17-4-43 15MU 20-4 R-RH 8-5 M32 instal to LF IIC RNAS Doni
NM948 CHA FF 23-4-43 15MU 28-4
NM949 CHA FF 23-4-43 15MU 28-3 RNAS Doni 27-5 884S Turn
NM963 M45 CHA FF 20-2-43 15MU 27-2 759S Yeov
NM964 M45 CHA FF 20-2-43 15MU 26-2
NM965 M45 CHA FF 24-2-43 15MU 26-2
NM966 M45 CHA FF 24-2-43 15MU 28-2
NM967 M45 CHA FF 25-2-43 15MU 28-2
NM968 CHA FF 28-2-43 15MU 2-3 AST 4-4 RNAS LoS 29-5
NM969 CHA FF 26-2-43 15MU 9-3
NM970 CHA FF 27-2-43 15MU 4-3 808S *HMS Batt* 1943
NM971 CHA FF 28-2-43 15MU 9-3
NM972 CHA FF 3-3-43 15MU 9-3
NM973 CHA FF 3-3-43 15MU 9-3 776S
NM974 CHA FF 5-3-43 15MU 9-3 807S *HMS Hunter*
NM975 4069 CHA FF 5-3-43 15MU 9-3 AR Pool Doni 20-5 884S 9-6 834S 17-6 *HMS Hunter* cd/ld 15-7 Airwork Stn 17-8 809S *HMS Stal* cd/ld i/sea 26-1-44
NM976 CHA FF 6-3-43 15MU 10-3 807S *HMS Indom*
NM977 CHA FF 9-3-43 VA WD 11-3 wts & CG load of prod a/c tare 5307, t/o 6963 lb. Airspeed Christch 23-5 ASTH 22-12-47
NM978 CHA FF 10-3-43 15MU 15-3 RNAS Hats 19-5 880S *HMS Stal*
NM979 CHA FF 11-3-43 15MU 15-3
NM980 M45 CHA FF 13-3-43 15MU 15-3 RNAS LoS 19-5
NM981 M45 CHA FF 16-3-43 15MU 18-3 759S Yeov
NM982 M45 CHA FF 23-3-43 15MU 30-3

FOLDING WINGS AND MORE POWER

"Be pleased to inform Their Lordships that I have today witnessed No 899 Squadron carrying out flying practice from *HMS Khedive*. This is the first squadron equipped with Seafires with folding wings to operate from a carrier. I am much impressed with the neat job which has been made of the folding-wing Seafire. Having full knowledge of the difficulties which were encountered in getting a Seafire with folded wings during my tenure of office as 5th Sea Lord, I feel that the Navy owes a great debt of gratitude to Mr Gordon England, of General Aircraft Limited, whose insistence that a Spitfire wing could be folded without appreciably detracting from the performance of the aircraft, was undoubtedly responsible for the fact that we have a folding wing Seafire in service today. If Their Lordships could see their way to conveying their appreciation to Mr Gordon England, I feel sure that this courtesy would be appreciated". A. L. St. G. Lyston, Vice Admiral.

This signal, dated 15 April 1944, from the Flag Officer Carrier Training to the Secretary of the Admiralty, would appear to be a reasonable request for the Fleet Air Arm had waited many years for a folding wing Seafire, and a round of applause for the instigator of the scheme was little enough reward. However, Their Lordships were not amused as was apparent by their signal of 3 May, signed by S Graham Smith 'By Command of Their Lordships'. It read — "The first proposal for folding the wing of Spitfire was worked out between myself (then Director of Air Material) and Mr A Dunbar of the Vickers Company, in November 1939. Reference to Admiralty dockets will show that it was proposed early in 1940 to produce a folding wing Spitfire for use in the Fleet Air Arm, but that the project was dropped at the time on account of the alleged ill effect which it would have had on RAF production of Spitfires. The present means by which the Spitfire's wings have been folded does not differ materially from the original proposals in 1939, though the break is actually made in a slightly different place. I understand that, prior to my return to MAP last year, Messrs General Aircraft, of which Mr Gordon England was Managing Director at that time, had put forward an alternative scheme for folding Spitfires. This scheme was not considered as good as that designed by Messrs Supermarines and, after some work had been done on it, was not proceeded with. There never was any doubt in the minds of Vickers-Supermarines that the Spitfire could be folded; it was solely a question of availability of Spitfires to the Navy. In the circumstances, I am unable to agree with the Flag Officer Carrier Training that Mr Gordon England contributed anything to the successful results which have been obtained. Were such a debt in fact owed, it would be more appropriate to acknowledge it to the Chief Designer and the Chief Engineer of Messrs Supermarines".

The Admiralty signal had got it right, almost, for as will be recalled from chapter 32 the original Supermarine proposal for a folding wing Spitfire was for the wing to fold back to lay neatly alongside the fuselage, the wing twisting to have the leading edge pointing up. The Supermarine/DAM proposal for the double, upward fold was the result of close collaboration between the parties mentioned and General Aircraft. The Supermarine design team, led by Joseph Smith, was aware of the many problems associated with folding wing aeroplanes for a number of promising designs had been proposed, but the thin section Spitfire wing presented a major challenge. The Admiralty pressed for a programme to be initiated, for although the Seafire Mk IIC had been accepted as eminently suitable for carriers and hangar lifts that could cope with the fixed wing of aircraft that could be accommodated at one time. The larger carriers had hangar lifts that could cope with the fixed wing Seafire, but even with this facility storage was a problem on the hangar deck. The smaller carriers presented a much greater problem and when equipped with the Seafire IIC the majority had to be stored on deck, and during rough weather many were damaged, or destroyed, and sea water immersion caused large scale corrosion.

As a result of the Admiralty's request a scheme totally different to the original folded Spitfire wing appeared in the summer of 1942*. A Spitfire Mk I had been seconded to General Aircraft, of Feltham, Middlesex, during April of that year and as a result of close collaboration with Supermarine a wing was produced that had the major fold just outboard of the main undercarriage wheel wells, with a second fold situated at the existing joint between the wing tip and mainplane. General Aircraft did contribute to the development of the folding wing, and although the company deservedly earned commendation for working out production procedures, Supermarine produced the necessary design and development. DAM wanted some of the glory.

As a result of this work MA970, the first production Seafire Mk IIC, was flown to Worthy Down on 2 October 1942 and work commenced to adopt its wing to the double break and folds. It was ready for flying trials on 9 November. Each hinge was formed at the top boom of the front spar and the rear with a locking point at the bottom of the front spar where a tapered bolt was screwed into appropriate lugs. Fairing doors were provided on the upper surface to cover the gaps in the fold line at the hinge. The hinges and main bolt were locked by means of pins operated by a cable from a single lever in each wheel bay.

MA970, the first production Seafire Mk IIC, converted to the prototype Mk III, Boscombe Down.

* *The DTD wrote to Supermarine on 27 March 1942 and as the company was fully stretched with Spitfire production the folding wing requirement was passed to General Aircraft. The mock up was ready on 20 April and approved, and the development passed back to Supermarine.*

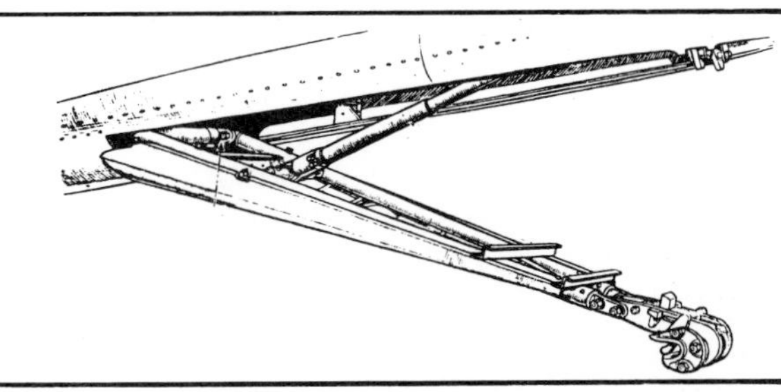

'A' frame deck arrester gear.

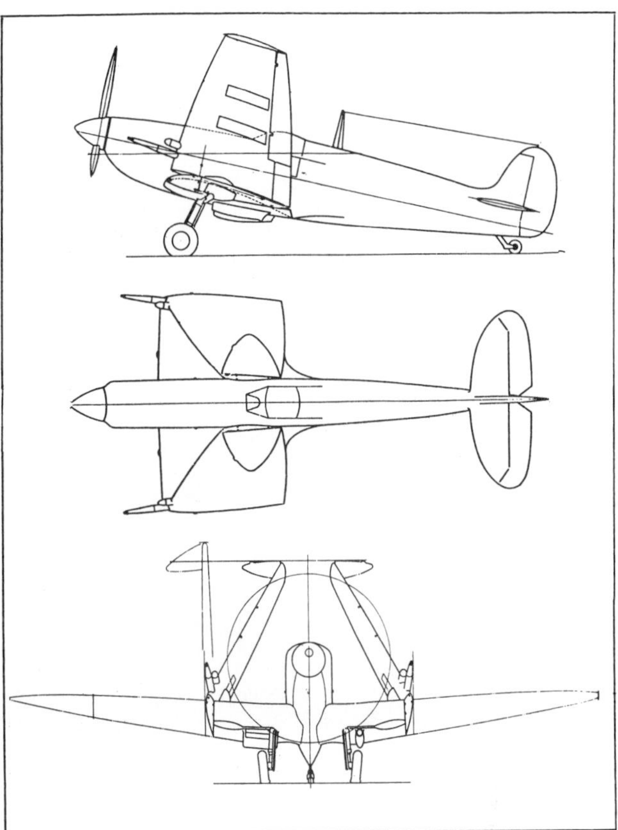

Seafire Mk III, folding wing.

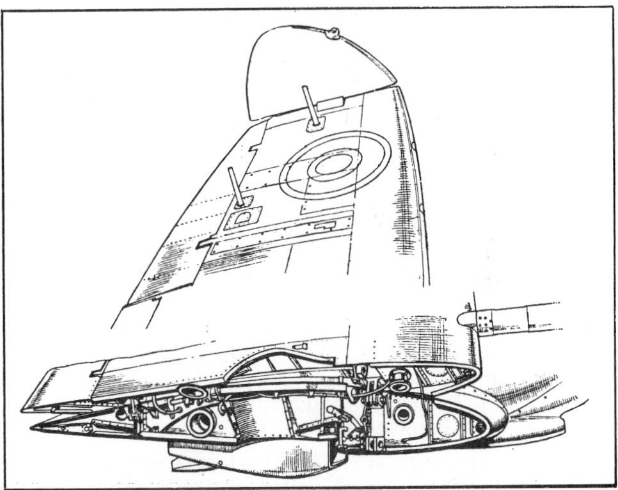

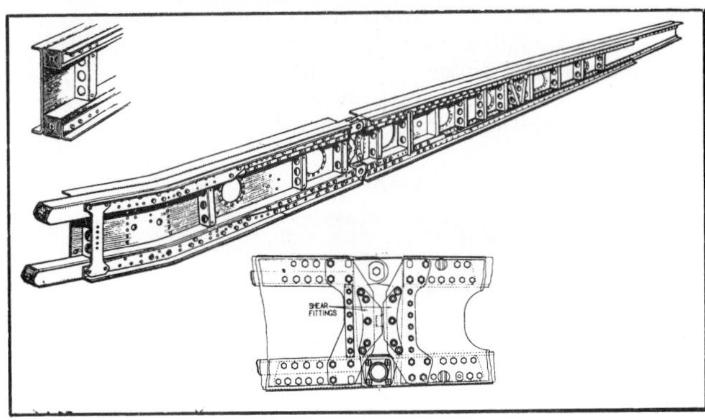

Seafire Mk III main spar and main hinge joint.

Locating spigots were provided in the leading edge, front spar and trailing edge. Gun heating ducts had a felt butt joint at the folds to prevent loss of heat. When folded the wings measured 13ft 4in in width and 13ft 6in in height. It was a good arrangement but it did mean that a party of five ratings were needed to strike it down on landing and also to prepare it for take off.

Power folding was most desirable because of the man power problem, but the weight unacceptable. Manual wing folding took 45 seconds with an experienced team and 50 seconds to spread. Some loss of torsional rigidity had to be accepted but it was maintained at 90% of the wing's designed factor.

When first accepting the Spitfire as the standard fighter the Admiralty had asked for a four cannon wing, but the weight considerations and folding wing mechanism of the new Seafire resulted in the adaptation of the 'C' wing. The outboard cannon bay was deleted and by installing the Martin Baker belt feed the large, wing blister fairings could be replaced with smaller units. A small number of Seafire IICs were retrofitted with this modification, which added five mph to the maximum speed.

The Rolls-Royce Merlin 55 Series engine was specified for the Type 358 Seafire Mk III. It produced the same horse power as the Merlin 45 but had the advantage of automatic boost control with barometic governing. With this the pilot could forget the vital functions of operating the supercharger control as it cut in as the aircraft gained altitude. The 1,470hp was absorbed by a Rotol R12/4F5 4 four bladed propeller, although a small number of early production aircraft had a three bladed type.

Production of the Seafire III was the responsibility of Westland Aircraft as main contractor, with Cunliffe Owen, plus numerous sub-contractors to feed the main production line, but production was delayed because of the waiting involved for delivery of assembled jigs and machine tools. Constructing the folding wing was also a major problem and in order to get the new type into Navy service as soon as possible the first thirty examples from Westland, plus two from Cunliffe Owen, were built as fixed wing airacraft. They were later to be re-designated as F IICs.

The second production Westland aircraft, LR766, was delivered to Worthy Down on 8 June 1943 for contractor's handling trials, and at this period there was a vigourous campaign for the improvement of exterior finish and this Seafire was closely examined. The workmanship was considered to be below standard and a number of sections with serious faults were photographed and copies distributed to other manufacturers as a guide on what to avoid.

A large number of Seafires were being damaged on landing, one of the major problems occurring when the aircraft approached with the hook down. If it did not engage the arrester wire the hook struck the deck and rebounded back into the fuselage. In doing so it struck the block in the snap gear forcibly and the load was then transmitted to the frames, longerons and lower plating. Introduction of more robust stiffeners transmitted the load to the upper shell plating and helped cure the fault.

As related, LR766 was sent to Worthy Down and found to be unstable when the CoG was 8in aft of the datum, the acceptable limit being 9in. It was thought that the aircraft might be a 'rogue', but Boscombe Down had reported a similar situation with LR765, the first production Seafire III, and an investigation was necessary to clear the aircraft for service. With an auw of 7,076lb and three nose ballast weights the CoG was 8.1in aft of datum; at 7,128lb and three tail ballast weights it was 8.9in. The prototype MA970 was also at Boscombe and both it, and LR766, were loaded to 9in aft of datum and tested. MA970 performed in the normal manner but LR766 was still unsuitable. The radio equipment was moved to a different position and the tail ends of both aircraft interchanged with that of the other. Although MA970 was acceptable LR766 became even more unstable. The two stern ends were returned to Supermarine for inspection and as it was required to fly MA970 for further trials a standard Spitfire Mk IX end was installed and the aircraft performed satisfactorily. In order to

LR765, the first production F Mk III, had non-folding wings and was later to be re-designated a Mk IIC.

get LR766 cleared for service a 3½ lb inertia weight was fitted to the elevator circuit.

As the Seafire IIC was also being fitted with the same type of tail unit as the Mk III doubts were raised about the types' stability. The first production IIC from Cunliffe Owen, NN333, was found to be in the same condition as LR766 and it, too, had a 3½ lb inertia weight fitted. It was assumed that perhaps the stern end was at fault but stringent tests revealed the fault lay with airflow over the folding wing joints following tests with an exchange of wings between the IIC and III.

Production of the Mk III was increasing and with it many major modifications were being added on the line. The Hispano Mk II cannons were replaced by the Mk V, a short barrelled and light weight weapon. The wing was also adapted to receive four 25 lb or 60 lb head rockets; two × 250 lb GP bombs; one × 500 lb bomb under the centre section. Complaints began coming in from service pilots over heating of the guns, in particular the ammunition. The first recommendation was to cover the ammunition tanks with asbestos lagging as the hot engine air discharged on to them, and this was followed by installation of a baffle plate. There was no improvement.

The first production Seafire III to leave Cunliffe Owen was NN333 and it was weighed at Worthy Down on 25 October 1943. With a Merlin 55, temperate cowling and nose ballast tare weight was 5,541lb and auw 7,197. The 90th production III from the same factory dispensed with the bulky, tropical air intake and was fitted with the neater, Vokes Aero-Vee unit. Overload fuel tank wing fittings were standard from the 130th aircraft onwards. Undercarriage oleos were still troublesome and a series of trials on board *HMS Pretoria Castle* started on 12 February 1944. Arrangements were also made to test a new device for damping out the still troublesome hook bounce. Both spline and link oleo units were tested with the former performing a little better than the latter. Three propellers were broken during the trials and film record of the fast landings revealed that the Seafire actually gained height after engaging the hook, the aircraft then pitching down on to the nose with full oleo and tyre deflection and broken propeller blades. The new device to prevent hook bounce failed on the first attempt but after modifications worked well.

NF565 from Westland was weighed at High Post on 12 April 1944 with a modified Merlin M55M engine and 97 airframe modifications. Tare was 5,449lb; auw 7,115. LR840 was making its first landing on *HMS Indefatigable* on 24 March and was badly damaged when the port oleo collapsed. Eye witnesses said that the Seafire appeared to have considerable drift to port on landing and upon examination the oleo was found to have collapsed under an inward side load, the vertical load being small. Previous cases of similar incidents had been reported and Seafire modification No 279 was incorporated to cure this defect. Also, the undercarriage had collapsed due to side loads when the ship rolled and so a new locking head lug was designed and installed to eradicate this fault.

It was inevitable that a PR version of the Seafire III would be required and the first aircraft to be converted was MB194. It had one vertical and one oblique F 24 cameras with either 8in (oblique), 5,8 or 14in (vertical) focal lengths, and the final 129 examples of Mk IIIs built by Cunliffe Owen were to this standard. MB194, converted by Heston Aircraft Ltd., was at Worthy Down on 14 July 1943 for weighing and CoG determination with a Merlin 32 engine; Rotol four blade Jablo

Production of Seafire F Mk IIIs at Westland Aircraft.

Seafire III, PR314, was seconded to Boscombe Down in March 1945 and used for ordnance loads handling trials. The aircraft is shown here with 2x200lb Mk II smoke floats, plus 1x45 gallon slipper fuel tank; one Mine A Mk VIII; 12x30lb LC bombs, four under each wing and fuselage on light carriers; 2x250lb bombs B Mk III on the same carriers and 1x500lb AN-M64 bomb on fuselage rack. See also page 538.

propeller; temperate cowling; one F 24 20in vertical and one 14in F24 oblique camera. Tare 5,310lb, auw 7,043.

The next major variant of the Seafire III was the LF and for low altitude performance it was fitted with the Merlin 55M. NF545 went from Westland to High Post on 31 March 1944 with a tare weight of 5,457lb and 7,133 auw for the same conditions. PP986 was weighed on 17 October and in addition to the normal reflector sight it was fitted with the new gyro gun-sight for trials. It weighed 5,449lb tare and had an auw of 7,221. Three LF Mk IIIs from Cunliffe Owen were also weighed at High Post – NN390 had a tare of 5,443lb, auw 7,181; NN409 5,455 and 7,172lb; NN500 5,517 and 7,201lb.

The Seafire Mk III showed a marked improvement in performance over its predecessors and a grand total of 1,220 were produced; 870 by Westland and 350 by Cunliffe Owen. Production began with 103 aircraft with the normal Merlin 55 engine, and these were followed by the L Mk III with the Merlin 55M (cropped surcharger impeller) for low altitude work. The first Mk III was taken on charge by 894 Squadron on 27 November 1943, followed by deliveries of Nos 887,889, 801 and 880 Squadrons. Pilots reported unfavourably on the lateral control characteristics of the III and on excessive changes of lateral trim with speed, heaviness of control and poor rate of roll at high speed. Test showed that the only cure, or improvement, lay in torsional stiffening of the wing. It was planned to plate over the outer machine gun bays and to improve roll by removing the wing tips and fitting balance tabs.

The Mk III saw service with the majority of Fleet Air Arm units, including eight in the Far East, and it flew in most war theatres including the main islands of Japan. After Japan was defeated it remained in service until March 1946 when the last two squadrons, Nos 887 and 894 were disbanded.

On 31 August 1946 an order for 12 Seafire Mk III was signed by the Irish Government and were to be delivered to the Irish Air Corps as numbers 146 to 157 inclusive. All naval attachments were to be removed and the aircraft converted to F Mk VC standards. The first was accepted for delivery at South Marston on 24 January 1947 and the last on 27 September the same year. They were used until 1954/55 when replaced by the Percival Provost T51 and T53. Forty eight were transferred to the French Navy in February 1946 for use with their carrier *Colossus*. Thirteen were transferred from the FAA direct, including RX192, 216, 223, 229, 240, 254, 301, 338, SP150, PR249, 265 and 266, PX951 and 954. Total contract price for the 48 aircraft (plus 18 spare Merlin 55M engines) was £450,000, this to be paid in dollars. Additional airframes would be supplied at a cost of £10,000 each and spare engines also at £10,000.

It was during the period when the Seafire Mk IIC was being introduced and the Mk III was under development that a number of interesting events were taking place. The Seafire was now able to operate at considerable distances from the home carrier as more and more beacon receivers were being installed. This beacon allowed the pilots to home onto their ships and

took some of the strain of navigating. The most startling innovation, however, was proposed by Slattery who said — "Before the war it was policy to carry fighters for fleet defence in ships other than the carrier. This policy was abandoned but it is suggested that it be reverted to. The fleet feels that the need for defence cannot be entirely satisfied by carrier borne aircraft and we should have a carrier cruiser. The new fleet fighters due for delivery will be 40 feet long and 14 feet high when folded and a speed of 400 knots plus. They could be operated from a flight deck of 300 feet and a total 18 fighters could be carried on the carrier cruiser, which might have one lift and eight arrester wires. With such an arrangement 12 non-folding and 18 folded Spitfires could be operated. The take off rate of 40 seconds per aircraft with assisted take off is a reasonable estimate".

A second proposal was also considered — "In order to ascertain how a naval force can best provide for its own fighter aircraft the DNC is to be instructed to prepare various sketch designs of ships to carry fighter aircraft. They are to be called aircraft destroyers; must have a high speed and be capable of dealing with an enemy destroyer in a surface action. They are also to be equipped with torpedoes in order to effect substantial damage to a capital ship". This was not liked by the FAA for only one hangar/flight deck lift was specified; pilots also asked for a completely clear flight deck without a control tower. It was designed to carry 12 Spitfires and had six arrester wires.

Slattery was in favour of the carrier cruiser and said — "Three battle cruisers could carry the same number of fighters as *HMS Illustrious*. As capital ships have proved very vulnerable to air attack without fighter protection a 300 foot flight deck, with hangar deck and side control island, could be incorporated into the design of future capital ships. *Vanguard* is a good example for it could carry 9 to 12 fighters". Drawings of the proposed carrier cruiser and converted capital ship appear on facing page. A scheme was drawn up for the destroyer carrier, but the illustration and details are not available.

In the Spring of 1943 it was realised that the carrier borne fighter was a crucial factor in combined operations and the Admiralty stated — "It is abundantly clear that the mounting of carrier borne operations depend upon adequate production of the best naval fighter — the Seafire. Also, the Admiralty desires to relieve the strain on naval pilots resulting from repeated operations. It is proposed, therefore, to use RAF Spitfire squadrons to replace naval Seafire squadrons suffering casualties or needing rest. In the event of large scale operations it might be necessary to man carriers with RAF fighters to start with. The Air Ministry directions to the Air Staff do not imply that training of RAF pilots for carrier work is to be on a high priority. Futhermore the directions are that a total of 100 pilots only are to be trained".

Sir Charles Portal, for the RAF, said — "I consider it unjustifiable to set aside special fighter squadrons against the possible future requirements of combined operations at a time when both Spitfires and manpower were so strictly limited. It is agreed that we must have ready in advance special equipment such as arrester hooks, and the Air Ministry will arrange for two Spitfire squadrons to be given deck landing training, each pilot to complete a minimum of 30 landings. A number of Mk Vs will be modified with arrester gear". It was suggested that

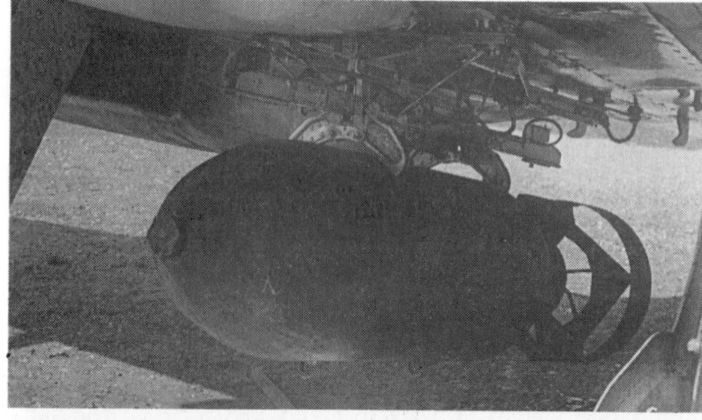

the minimum number of Spitfires to be available at any given time was 532, plus 252 fully trained RAF pilots. The latter to be trained for ADDLs at their home base and then sent to Arbroath for further training before trials on a carrier.

Sir Dudley Pound, Admiral, noted that an RAF squadron had completed preliminary deck landing trials and suggested that if Spitfires were to be used in any combined operations they should take over two days after FAA aircraft had completed the initial stages and withdrawn. The RAF pilots

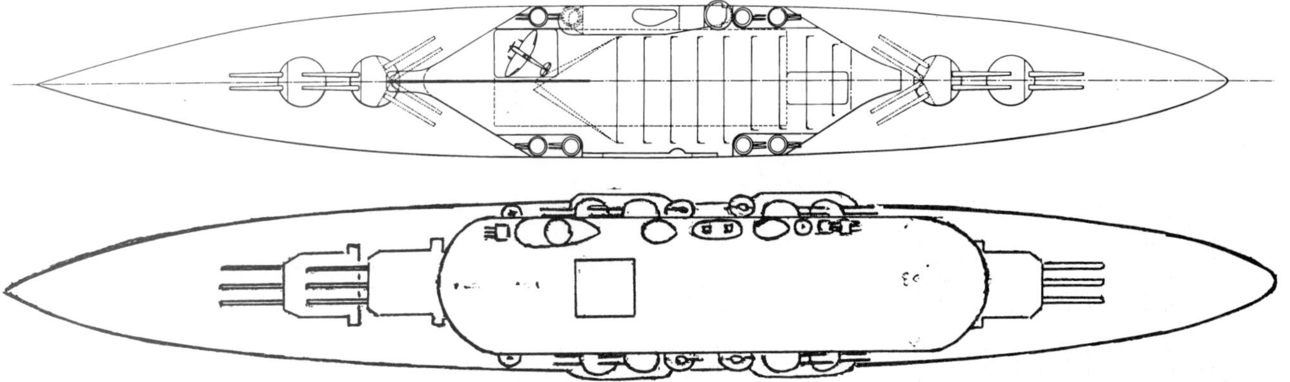

The Spitfire was at one time during 1942 considered as being ordered in quantity to equip specialised Carrier/Cruisers and this plan view reveals shape of the flight deck and main armament. A second proposal to equip every major British battleship with a flight deck in order that it could carry its own defensive fighters is depicted in the second sketch. It was suggested that the Vanguard class could be redesigned to incorporate a flight deck built running from front, main armament to rear. Width of deck 80 feet, length 350 feet with a single lift.

would operate from carriers and in order that sufficient pilots were available a proportion of them on every RAF station should be trained. The initial squadrons selected to begin training were 131, 141, 401, 402, 403, 412, 416 and 64. The majority of pilots tended to land too fast and ignore the batman's direction, but it was considered that 90% of them would be able to operate from carriers in a very short time.

By the end of Summer 1943 the tempo of war was changing and the Admiralty no longer wanted the RAF pilots and Spitfires, and wanted to cancel the training programme. However, Air Marshall Sir Douglas Evill suggested continuation of the scheme as Germany would soon be out of the war and additional squadrons would be available. He wanted to transfer 200 RAF fighters to the Fleet Air Arm from October onwards to help in the war with Japan. In the event the scheme was abandoned as the problems of transporting the RAF fighters was thought to be too difficult.

The Admiralty had also wanted to experiment with other RAF Fighter Command aircraft and had asked for examples of Hawker Tempest and Typhoon for use in carrier trials. They could not have the former for at the time of asking only a prototype was flying. The Typhoon could be converted to serve with the Fleet Air Arm and a proposed design showed it to have many parts in common with the land version. But it needed to have a folding wing of greater area for better take off and landing; it had to be capable of withstanding catapult acceleration loads; have a four hour cruise and six hour endurance capability. Nonetheless the Admiralty wanted to go ahead with the scheme and asked that "a number of aircraft be fitted with a minimum of modifications", adding "although it did not meet naval staff requirements for a single seat fighter it has proved valuable". DAM was introduced to write to the Air Council and ask for the loan of a Tempest and Typhoon, and at the same time enquire of MAP, subject to release of aircraft by the Air Ministry, whether they would be prepared to put the necessary development in hand.

But, the C.-in-C., Home Fleet put a damper on the whole affair — "So long as we continue to obtain advanced marks of Spitfire we would not be outclassed by modern RAF types. It must be remembered, also, that although the Tempest and Typhoon are stronger than the Spitfire, they are cart horses being pulled along by powerful engines, whereas the Spitfire is a racehorse. The RAF consider that the Typhoon, although a very good 'bomber destroyer, (?) it has not the maneouvrability for combat with other fighters". In order to placate the Admirals Typhoon DN419 was released for trials at RNAS Arbroath on 8 February 1943, but it crashed due to engine failure, catching fire on the ground and was destroyed.

At the same period of time the FAA were concerned about pilot fatigue and as a result a Franks flying suit was obtained for tests in August 1943. Seafire pilots wore the suit for as long as six hours and although fatigue due to maneouvres in combat flying was reduced, cockpit agility was severely impaired. Also every pilot wearing the suit had to be helped into his Seafire

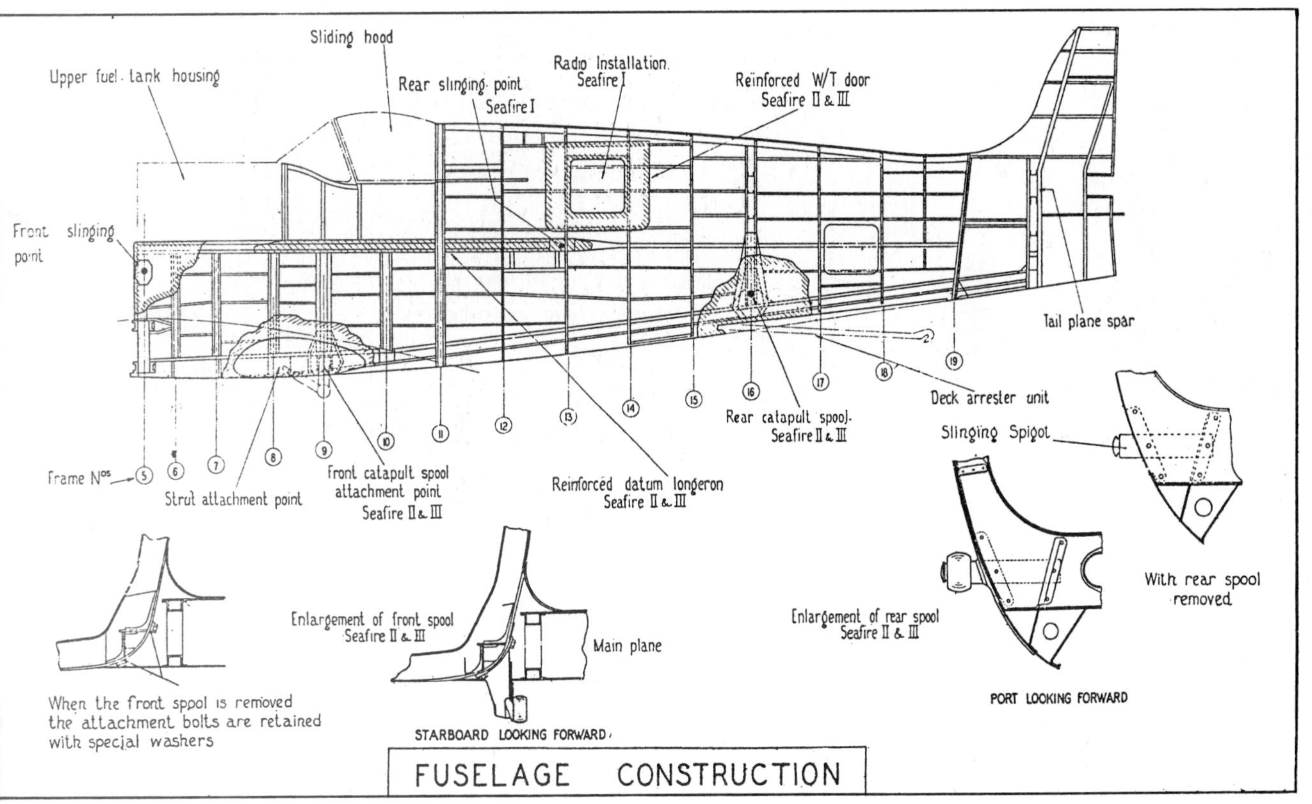

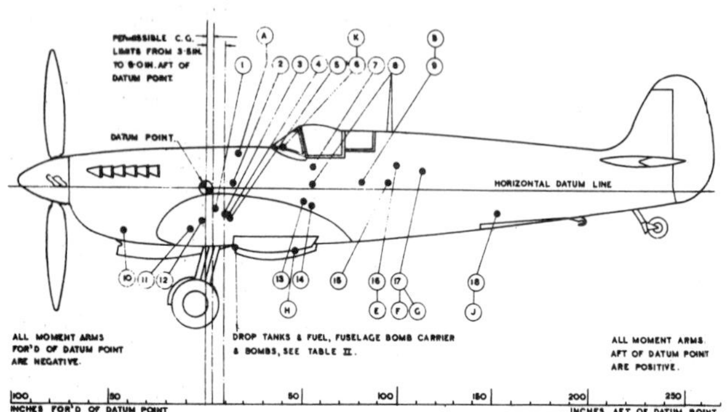

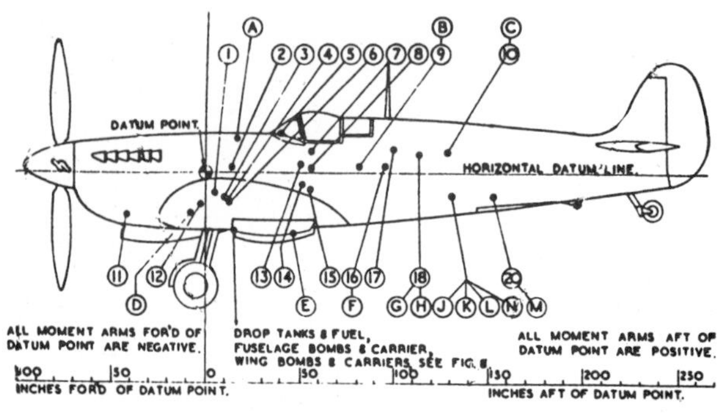

TABLE I.

ITEM NO.	NOTE NO.	TYPICAL REMOVABLE ITEMS OF MILITARY LOAD.	WEIGHT LB.	ARM IN.	MOMENT LB. IN.
4	1	4 BROWNING ·303 IN. GUNS & ACCESSORIES.	112·5	+ 11	+1,238
3		BROWNING AMMUNITION AT 350 RD. PER GUN.	93	+ 9·5	+ 884
12	2	2 HISPANO 20 MM. GUNS & ACCESSORIES.	274·5	- 1	- 275
5		HISPANO AMMUNITION AT 120 RD. PER GUN.	150	+ 12	+1,800
6		REFLECTOR SIGHT MK. II S AND 4 FILAMENT LAMPS TYPE "B".	4·5	+ 40	+ 180
7		1½ LB. INCENDIARY BOMB MK I, CLOCK MK. II, NAVIGATIONAL COMPUTOR MK. III D, & CROWBAR.	4·5	+ 58	+ 261
13		SIGNAL PISTOL NO. 4 MK I AND 14 CARTRIDGES.	8	+ 51	+ 408
11		G 45 CAMERA MK. I, ADAPTOR TYPE 32, FRONT FLANGE, MOUNTING TYPE 27, AND INDICATOR TYPE 45.	8·5	- 8	- 68
9		OXYGEN CYLINDER MK. VC.	17·5	+ 81.5	+1,426
14		DINGHY TYPE "K" IN SEAT PACK TYPE "A", MK. II.	15	+ 55	+ 825
17	5	T.R. 5043 RADIO AND ACCESSORIES.	89.5	+111	+9,935
16		ZB/ARA REMOVABLE RADIO EQUIPMENT.	14·5	+ 95	+1,378
15		R 3067 RECEIVER, DETONATOR NO. D.64 MK I, AND CONTROL UNIT TYPE 1.	35	+ 98	+3,430
18		REAR SLINGING SPIGOTS.	2·5	+ 152·5	+ 381
8		PILOT AND PARACHUTE.	200	+ 55	+11,000
		TOTAL TYPICAL REMOVABLE MILITARY LOAD.	1029·5		+28,803
2		FUEL IN FUSELAGE TANKS: 84 GALL. 100 OCTANE AT 7·2 LB. PER GALL.	605	+ 13·5	+8,168
10	3	OIL IN TANK: 8½ GALL. AT 9 LB. PER GALL.	76·5	- 46	-3,519
1	4	AIRCRAFT IN TARE CONDITION.	5,454		+21,710
		AIRCRAFT IN TYPICAL TAKE-OFF CONDITION.	7,165	+ 8·3	+59,162

TABLE I

NOTE NO.	ITEM NO.	TYPICAL REMOVABLE ITEMS OF MILITARY LOAD.	WEIGHT. LB.	ARM. IN.	MOMENT. LB.IN.
1	4	4 BROWNING ·303 IN. GUNS & ACCESSORIES.	112·5	+ 11	+ 1,238
	3	BROWNING AMMUNITION AT 350 RD. PER GUN.	93	+ 9·5	+ 884
2	12	2 HISPANO 20 MM. GUNS MK. V & ACCESSORIES.	250	+ 2·5	+ 625
	6	HISPANO AMMUNITION AT 120 RD. PER GUN.	150	+ 12	+ 1,800
	5	GYROSCOPIC GUNSIGHT MK. II D & FILAMENT LAMPS.	8·5	+ 43	+ 366
	7	1½ LB. INCENDIARY BOMB, CLOCK, NAVIGATIONAL COMPUTOR & CROWBAR.	4·5	+ 58	+ 261
	14	1½ IN. SIGNAL PISTOL AND 14 CARTRIDGES.	8	+ 51	+ 408
3	10	14 IN. OBLIQUE F.24 CAMERA AND ACCESSORIES.	36·5	+127	+ 4,636
	13	CAMERA CONTROL UNIT TYPE 35	4·5	+ 50	+ 225
	9	OXYGEN CYLINDER MK. VC.	17·5	+ 81·5	+ 1,426
	15	DINGHY TYPE "K" IN SEAT PACK TYPE "A", MK. II.	15	+ 55	+ 825
	20	REAR SLINGING SPIGOTS.	2·5	+ 152·5	+ 381
5	18	T.R. 5043 RADIO AND ACCESSORIES.	89·5	+ 111	+ 9,935
	16	ARI 5307 (ZB/X) REMOVABLE RADIO EQUIPMENT	10·5	+ 95	+ 998
	17	R 3067 RECEIVER, DETONATOR, AND CONTROL UNIT TYPE 1.	35	+ 98	+ 3,430
	8	PILOT AND PARACHUTE	200	+ 55	+ 11,000
		TOTAL TYPICAL REMOVABLE MILITARY LOAD.	1037·5		+ 30,438
	2	FUEL IN FUSELAGE TANKS 84 GALL. 100 OCTANE AT 7·2 LB PER GALL	605	+ 13·5	+ 8,168
6	11	OIL IN TANK 8½ GALL AT 9 LB PER GALL	76·5	- 46	- 3,519
8	1	AIRCRAFT IN TARE CONDITION	5505		+ 27,695
		AIRCRAFT IN TYPICAL TAKE-OFF CONDITION	7224	+ 9·8	+ 70,782

TABLE II

NOTE NO.	ITEM NO.	ADDITIONAL AND ALTERNATIVE ITEMS OF REMOVABLE MILITARY LOAD.	WEIGHT. LB.	ARM. IN.	MOMENT. LB.IN.
3	C	8 IN. OBLIQUE F.24 CAMERA AND ACCESSORIES.	32·5	+127	+ 4,128
4	J	5 IN. VERTICAL F.24 CAMERA AND ACCESSORIES.	34	+132·5	+ 4,505
4	K	8 IN. VERTICAL F.24 CAMERA AND ACCESSORIES.	35·5	+132·5	+ 4,704
4	L	14 IN. VERTICAL F.24 CAMERA AND ACCESSORIES.	38	+131·5	+ 4,997
5	D	G.45 CAMERA AND ACCESSORIES.	8·5	- 8	- 68
4	N	20 IN. VERTICAL F.24 CAMERA AND ACCESSORIES.	42	+131·5	+ 5,523
	B	OXYGEN CYLINDER MK. V."	14·5	+ 81·5	+ 1,182
	A	EXHAUST GLARE SHIELDS & REMOVABLE FITTINGS.	7	+ 16	+ 112
	H	T.R. 1196 RADIO, MOUNTING TRAY & ELECTRIC CONTROL.	39·5	+ 109	+ 4,306
	F	ZB/ARA REMOVABLE RADIO EQUIPMENT.	14·5	+ 95	+ 1,378
	G	RADIO BALLAST: 3 STANDARD WEIGHTS.	52·5	+114	+ 5,985
	E	FRONT CATAPULT SPOOLS.	16·5	+ 45	+ 742
	M	REAR CATAPULT SPOOLS.	4·5	+152·5	+ 686

TABLE II.

DROP FUEL TANKS & FUEL, FUSELAGE BOMB CARRIER & BOMBS.	WEIGHT LB.	ARM IN.	MOMENT Lb. IN.
30 GALL. DROP FUEL TANK, DRY.	68	+ 19·5	+1,326
30 GALL. FUEL IN DROP FUEL TANK	216	+ 16	+3,456
BOMB CARRIER AND ADAPTOR	55	+ 19·5	+ 1,073
250 LB. G.P. OR S.A.P. BOMB.	240	+ 12	+2,880
500 LB. G.P. BOMB.	420	+ 12	+5,040
500 LB. M.C. BOMB.	440	+ 12	+5,280
500 LB. S.A.P. BOMB.	485	+ 12	+5,820

TABLE III

ITEM NO.	NOTE NO.	ADDITIONAL & ALTERNATIVE ITEMS OF REMOVABLE MILITARY LOAD.	WEIGHT LB.	ARM IN	MOMENT LB. IN.
B		OXYGEN CYLINDER MK. V.	14·5	+ 81.5	+1,182
A		EXHAUST GLARE SHIELDS & REMOVABLE FITTINGS.	7	+ 16	+ 112
G		T.R 1196 TRANSMITTER-RECEIVER, MOUNTING TRAY & ELECTRIC CONTROLLER.	39·5	+109	+4,306
E		R.3108 RECEIVER, DETONATOR NO. 39 MK I, AND CONTROL UNIT TYPE 16.	32·5	+ 99	+3,218
K		GYROSCOPIC GUNSIGHT MK. II D. CONTROL UNIT, SELECTOR AND DIMMER.	12	+ 42	+ 504
F		RADIO BALLAST: 3 STANDARD WEIGHTS AT 17·5 LB., EACH.	52·5	+114	+ 5,985
H		FRONT CATAPULT SPOOLS.	16·6	+ 45	+ 742
J		REAR CATAPULT SPOOLS.	4·5	+ 152·5	+ 686

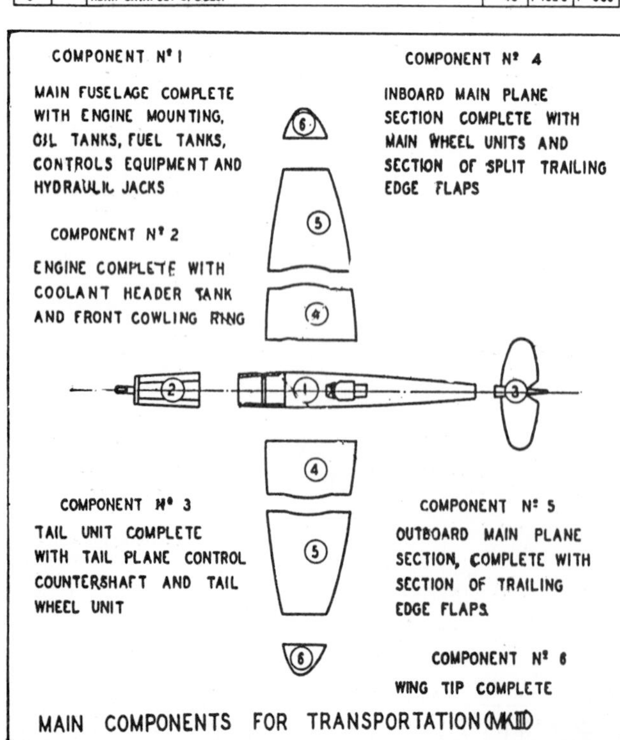

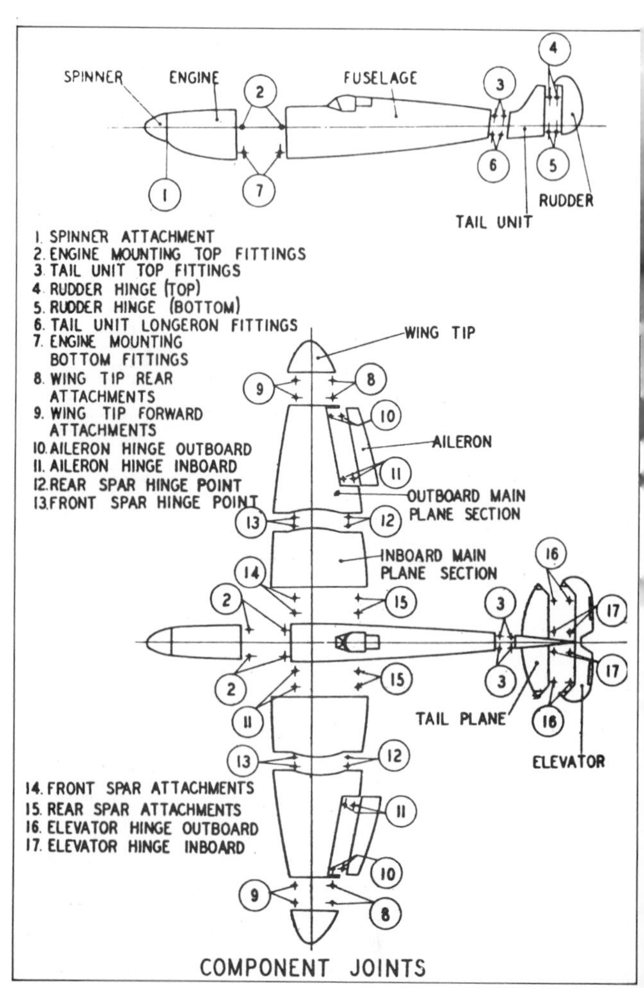

Three views of MA970 after conversion to Seafire Mk III prototype on the RATOG catapult rig at Farnborough. Close-ups show rear catapult spigot and spigot engaged with catapult.

cockpit. Trials were carried out on board *HMS Formidable* by No 807 Squadron, and similar trials took place on *HMS Indomitable*. Take off time with the suit worn resulted in an extra four minutes being added, but pilots did like the suit because when filled with warm water it was most comfortable.

TEST REPORTS FROM SUPERMARINE FLIGHT LOGS

NN380 (Furlong 30-6-44). Loaded to 8ins aft of datum with 3½ lb bob weight. Aileron control and trim considered satisfactory.

NN259 (Morgan 23-7-44). Flown as delivered from Westland. Ailerons impossibly heavy. (Furlong 27-5-44). Now fitted with ailerons from NS493. Aeroplane now considered acceptable. (Morgan 26-7-44). Fitted with ailerons from Seafire Mk XV. Aircraft considered passable.

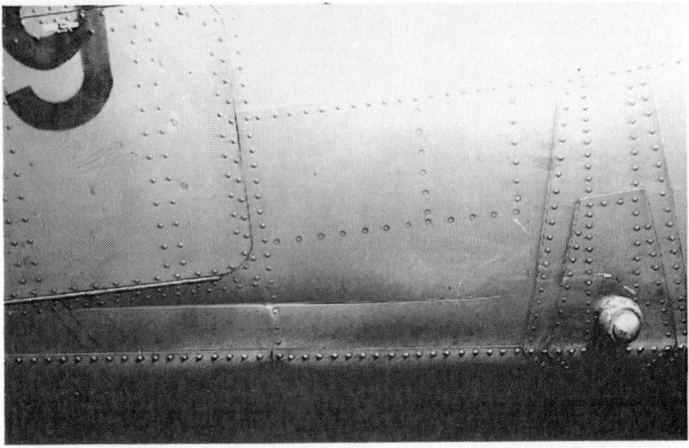

NN267 (Quill 13-8-44). No 'up' lights. Machine quite emphatically left wing low. Difficult to know how it has passed like this. Doors over wing folding joints were blowing half open in flight. (Furlong 17-8-44). It is considered that this aeroplane should not have been allowed to go through production test at Westlands in this condition.

NN409 (Furlong 23-8-44) Cunliffe Owen. Vastly superior to the Westland aeroplane.

NN500 (Shea-S 7-11-44). Determination of carbon monox-

PP975 (Shea-S 3-11-44). Fitted with 500 lb smoke float carried beneath centre section. Given check test before delivery to Boscombe Down and found to be satisfactory. Clearance between the tail fin and the smoke float and ground leaves a small margin over uneven or rough ground when taxying.

PR241 (Quill 29-12-44). Westland metal elevator. Directional stability very bad. On inspection the horn balance of

MA970 sustained damage to the wing trailing edge when undergoing catapult trials at Farnborough in September 1944.

rudder found to be badly constructed. (Quill 31-12).New rudder fitted, directional stability improved but still poor.

PR304 (Shea-S 26-2-45).Westland Investigation of directional stability with modified rudder control system designed to clear rear cameras. Considered to be barely acceptable.

PR314 (Shea-S 17-3-45). Brought over from Boscombe Down and flown with one 250 lb smoke float under each wing and 45 gallon slipper tank under fuselage.

PX921 (Quill 5-4-45). Flown with four R.P. rockets six inch heads. Metal elevator by Cunliffe Owen. Directional stability poor in dive and climb. No doubt due to rocket fins.

PR314 Boscombe Down July 1945. Merlin M55M. Handling with various stores.

French Navy Mk IIIs on board Clemanceau. *One is ex PP932. June 1948.*

Below: PR129 in the fence on HMS Theseus *during May 1946 with No. 794 Squadron.*

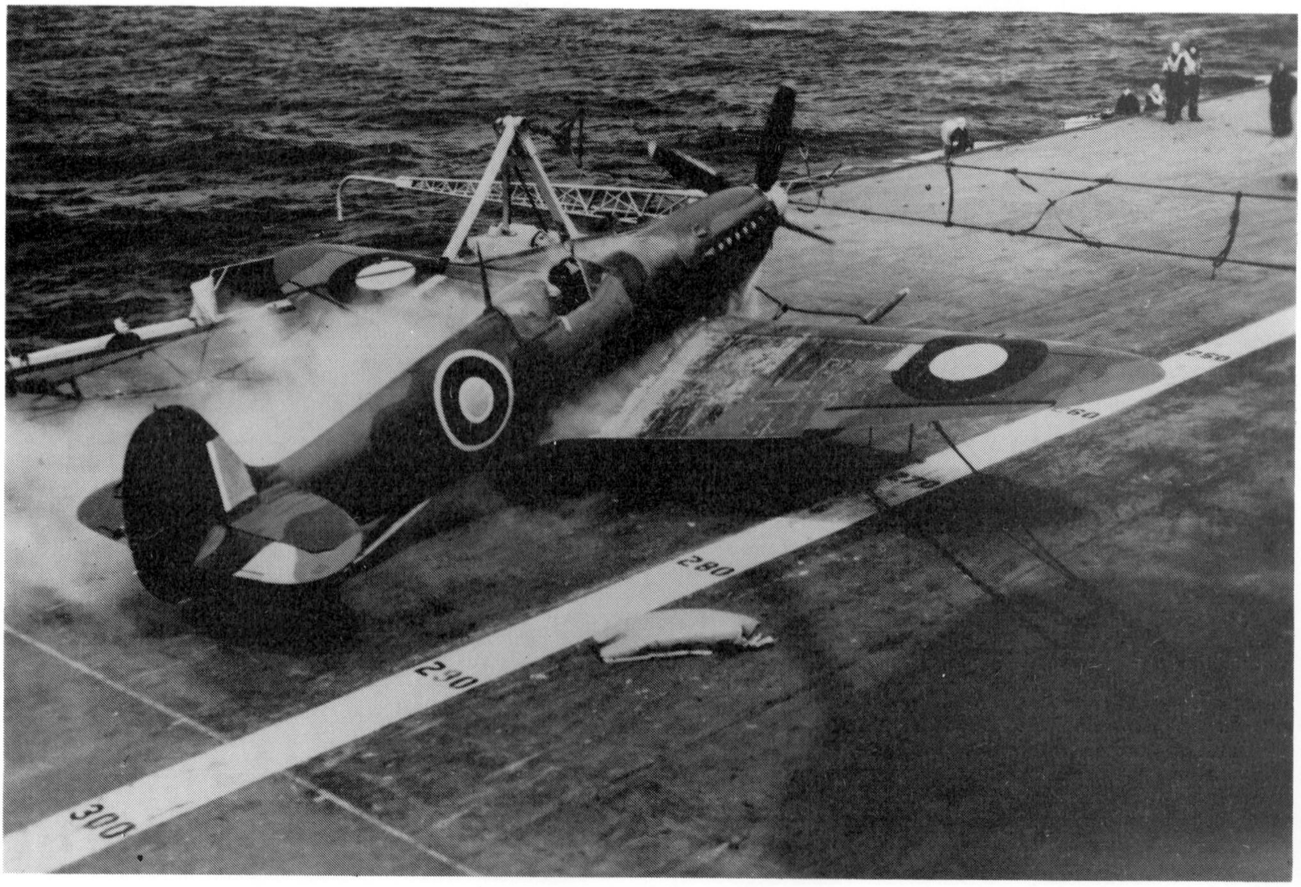

PP921 with rocket projectiles.

SERIAL NUMBERS

First order for 200 Seafire Mk. IIC dated March 1942 from Westland Aircraft under Contract No. B124305/40. Built as Mks. IIC/III between January 1943 and January 1944. The following serials apply to Mk. IIIs built to this first order:

LR765 to 769, LR783 to 820 and LR835 to 881. First 30 with fixed 'C' universal wings.

Second order for 200 Seafire Mk. IIC dated November 1942 from Westland Aircraft under Contract No. A/C 2605/C. 23(c). Built as Mks IIC/III between January and May 1944. The following serials apply to Mk. IIIs built to this second order:

NF418 to 445, 480 to 526, 531 to 570, 575 to 607, 624 to 665.

Third order for 200 Seafire Mk. III dated 5 January 1943 from Westland Aircraft built as Mk. IIIs between April and August 1944:

NM984 to 999, NN112 to 157, 169 to 214, 227 to 270, 283 to 330.

First order for 250 Seafire Mk. III, dated 5 January 1943 from Cunliffe-Owen Aircraft Ltd under Contract No. A/C 2777/C. 23(c). Built as Mk. IIIs between December 1943 and November 1944:

NN333 to 367, 379 to 418, 431 to 476, 488 to 528, 542 to 586, 599 to 641.

Fourth order for 250 Seafire Mk. III dated July 1943 from Westland Aircraft. Built as Mk. IIIs between August and December 1944:

PP921 to 957, 969 to 999, PR115 to 156, 170 to 215, 228 to 271, 285 to 334. (PR175, 210-215 and 228-230(10) cancelled).

Second order for 50 Seafire Mk. III from Cunliffe-Owen under Contract AIR/2777/CB. 23(c). Built as Mk. IIIs between February and March 1945, PX 913-962.

Fifth order for 300 Seafire Mk. III dated January 1944 from Westland Aircraft. Built as Mk. IIIs between December 1944 and July 1945. Part of this contract cancelled, March 1944. See RX 156 to 194, 210 to 256, 268 to 313, 326 to 353.

TOTAL: 32 Mk. IIC (Hybrid) 1,218 Mk. III.

FW indicates fixed wing.

LR765 1st prod Westland-built Seafire III. M50 RNDA 23-4-43 BDn May '43 climb and level speed perf trls. Later re-desig F Mk IIC because of non-folding wings. Nov '43 wts & CG load. Trls with 30gal o/ld tank, 250lb GP or SAP bombs. 3 × 27lb ballast wts fit det of aftmost CG with various loads. 715S St Mer.

LR766 M50 RNDA 29-5-43 VAWD 8-6 Contractor's trls Farn Dec '44 Gyro gun trls with MB141/G Seafire Mk IIC. BDn Nov '44 CG trls with 3½lb int wt in elev cont VAWD 9-6-43 wts & CG load of 1st Westland F III tare 5,500, t/o 7,156lb. 715S

LR767 RNDA 30-6-43
LR768 RNDA 10-7-43 889S *HMS Athel*
LR769 RNDA 30-7-43
LR783, LR784, LR785 RNDA 28-8-43
LR786 RNDA 4-9-43
LR787 RNDA 17-9-43 700S
LR788 RNDA 17-9-43 805S Mach.
LR789, LR790 RNDA 25-9-43
LR791 RNDA 30-9-43 33MU 15-10
LR792 RNDA 30-9-43 889S *HMS Athel*
LR793 RNDA 30-9-43 LoS To French Navy
LR794 RNDA 9-10-43 889S *HMS Athel*
LR795 RNDA 9-10-43 889S *HMS Athel*
LR796 RNDA 9-10-43
LR797 RNDA 15-10-43 889S *HMS Athel*
LR798, LR799 RNDA 16-10-43
LR799 RNDA 16-10-43
LR800 RNDA 20-10-43
LR801, LR802 RNDA 23-10-43
LR802 RNDA 23-10-43
LR803 RNDA 23-10-43 880S *HMS Furious*
LR804 RNDA 28-10-43
LR805, LR806 RNDA 30-10-43

LR807 RNDA 31-10-43 889S *HMS Athel* strk by MB253 29-6-44 over ship's side.

LR808 RNDA 30-10-43 889S *HMS Athel*
LR809 RNDA 31-10-43
LR810 RNDA 31-10-43
LR811 RNDA 4-11-43
LR812 RNDA 11-11-43
LR813 RNDA 6-11-43
LR814 RNDA 11-11-43 880S *HMS Athel*

LR815 RNDA 13-11-43 899S Long Kesh LoS To French Navy

LR816 RNDA 13-11-43 894S *HMS Indef*

LR817 RNDA 13-11-43 887S Skae *HMS Rav* dam on ldg

LR818 RNDA 20-11-43 801S *HMS Furious* 880S *HMS Furious*

LR819, LR820 RNDA 18-11-43
LR835 RNDA 19-11-43 887S Culmhead May '44
LR836 RNDA 27-11-43 880S *HMS Furious*
LR837, LR838 RNDA 26-11-43
LR839 RNDA 27-11-43
LR840 RNDA 27-11-43 *HMS Indef* 24-3-44
LR841 RNDA 27-11-43

LR842, LR843, LR844, LR845, LR846, LR847, LR848, LR849, LR850 RNDA 30-11-43

LR851 RNDA 30-11-43 808S Bally
LR852 RNDA 30-11-43
LR853 RNDA 16-12-43 715S St Mer
LR854 RNDA 11-12-43 880S Hats
LR855 RNDA 11-12-43
LR856 RNDA 24-12-43 887S *HMS Indef*
LR857 RNDA 11-12-43 880S *HMS Furious*
LR858 RNDA 11-12-43 880S Hats
LR859 RNDA 22-12-43 894S *HMS Indef*
LR860 RNDA 15-12-43 880S Hats
LR861 RNDA 18-12-43 880S *HMS Furious*
LR862 RNDA 22-12-43 887S *HMS Indef*
LR863 RNDA 22-12-43
LR864 RNDA 21-12-43
LR865 RNDA 22-12-43

LR866 RNDA 21-12-43 887S *HMS Indef HMS Furious*

LR867 RNDA 22-12-43 880S *HMS Furious*
LR868 RNDA 24-12-43 880S *HMS Furious*
LR869 RNDA 23-12-43
LR870 RNDA 24-12-43
LR871 RNDA 30-12-43
LR872, LR873 RNDA 24-12-43

LR874 RNDA 24-12-43 M55 BDn Feb '44 comp trls with standard & cropped prop. Perf suffered with latter. Replacement for MA970 proto F.III 801S *HMS Furious*

LR875 RNDA 24-12-43 *HMS Indef*
LR876 RNDA 24-12-43 899S Long Kesh
LR877 RNDA 24-12-43
LR878, LR879, LR880, LR881 RNDA 31-12-43

NF418 to NF665 built by Westland Aircraft Co.

NF418 RNDA 31-12-43 FW M55M WAL CRD VAWD 2-1-44

NF419 RNDA 31-12-43 FW 807S *HMS Hunter*
NF420 RNDA 1-1-44 FW
NF421 RNDA 1-1-44 FW 899S *HMS Khed*
NF422 RNDA 8-1-44 FW 899S *HMS Chaser*
NF423, NF424, NF425 RNDA 8-1-44 FW

NF426 RNDA 8-1-44 FW 885S LoS 3NFW *HMS Chaser*

NF427, NF428 RNDA 18-1-44 FW
NF429 RNDA 15-1-44 FW 4FW Dekh Egypt
NF430 RNDA 19-1-44 FW
NF431 RNDA 15-1-44 FW 708S
NF432, NF433 RNDA 19-1-44 FW

NF434 FW WAL 16-1-44 RNDA 19-1 30MU 21-1 899S Belfast RNAS Arb 1-7 809S *HMS Stal* 15-12 cd/ld pushed overbd 1-5-45

NF435 RNDA 21-1-44 FW
NF346, NF347, NF348 RNDA 22-1-44 FW
NF349 RNDA 27-1-44 FW
NF440 RNDA 22-1-44 FW
NF441 RNDA 22-1-44 FW 899S *HMS Khed*
NF442 RNDA 27-1-44 FW
NF443 RNDA 27-1-44 FW
NF444 RNDA 29-1-44 FW
NF445 RNDA 29-1-44 FW 899S *HMS Khed*

NF446, NF447, NF448, NF449, NF450, NF451, NF452, NF453, NF454 RNDA 29-1-44

NF455 RNDA 31-1-44
NF480 RNDA 31-1-44
NF481 RNDA 5-2-44

NF482 RNDA 5-2-44 To French Navy
NF483 NF484, NF485, NF486 RNDA 5-2-44
NF487 RNDA 5-2-44 Farn March'44 trls with cartridge initiated t/o. Land trls with Hawarden arrester gear. RNAS Arb Aug. Continuation of trls with arrester gear.
NF488, NF489 RNDA 5-2-44
NF490 RNDA 5-2-44 Farn March'44. Bdn & VAWD July arrester gear trls.

NF490, serving with No 728 Squadron, from Ta Kali, Malta.

NF491 RNDA 10-2-44 809S *HMS Stal*
NF492, NF493, NF494 RNDA 11-2-44
NF495, NF496, NF497, NF498, NF499, NF500 RNDA 12-2-44
NF501 RNDA 24-2-44 880S Hats *HMS Khed*
NF502 RNDA 19-2-44 760S LoS
NF503 RNDA 19-2-44 715S St Mer
NF504 RNDA 19-2-44 794S Eglington 52 TAG
NF505 RNDA 19-2-44
NF506 RNDA 24-2-44
NF507 RNDA 23-2-44 LoS 5-4 794S Eglington To French Navy 18-9-48
NF508 RNDA 24-2-44
NF509 RNDA 25-2-44 899S *HMS Khed*
NF510 RNDA 25-2-44 *HMS Implac* 7-4-47
NF511 RNDA 26-2-44
NF512 RNDA 26-2-44 718s Hens
NF513, NF514, NF515, NF516,NF517 RNDA 26-2-44
NF518 RNDA 26-2-44 879S *HMS Attac*
NF519, NF520 RNDA 26-2-44
NF521 RNDA 29-2-44 894S *HMS Indef* 728S
NF522, NF523 RNDA 29-2-44
NF524 RNDA 29-2-44 880S Hats
NF525 RNDA 29-2-44 886S LoS des 7-6-44
NF526 RNDA 29-2-44 899S *HMS Khed HMS Chaser*
NF531 RNDA 4-3-44 to A509
NF532, NF533, NF534 RNDA 4-3-44
NF535 RNDA 8-3-44 885S LoS s/dn by Fw190 Normandy 7-6-44 pilot kld
NF536, NF537 RNDA 10-3-44
NF538 RNDA 10-3-44 899S *HMS Khed* 805S Mach
NF539 RNDA 10-3-44 899S Long Kesh 805S Mach
NF540 RNDA 11-3-44
NF541 RNDA 16-3-44
NF542, NF543 RNDA 11-3-44
NF544 RNDA 16-3-44
NF545 RNDA 17-3-44 LF.III M55M BDn 18-8 det of CG with metal elev, 899S Peterhead
NF546 RNDA 17-3-44 899S *HMS Khed*
NF547 RNDA 17-3-44 885S
NF548, NF549, NF550, NF551, NF552, NF553, NF554 RNDA 18-3-44
NF555 RNDA 18-3-44 899S *HMS Khed*
NF556 RNDA 22-3-44
NF557 RNDA 22-3-44 899S Long Kesh
NF558 RNDA 24-3-44 899S Long Kesh

NF545 undertook trials at Boscombe, later served with No. 899 Squadron.

NF559, NF560 RNDA 24-3-44
NF561 RNDA 24-3-44 899S Long Kesh LoS To French Navy
NF562 RNDA 24-3-44 801S *HMS Furious*
NF563, NF564 RNDA 25-3-44 709S
NF565 RNDA 25-3-44 VAHP Wd & CG 12-4
NF566 RNDA 25-3-44 899S *HMS Khed HMS Chaser* cd fus scrp wings to IAC No. 155 Spitfire
NF567 RNDA 31-3-44
NF568 RNDA 25-3-44
NF569 RNDA 29-3-44
NF570 RNDA 30-3-44
NF575 RNDA 31-3-44 899S *HMS Khed HMS Chaser*
NF576 RNDA 30-3-44 to 6428M at Hednesford 8-9-47
NF577 RNDA 29-3-44 885S
NF578, NF579, NF580, NF581 RNDA 31-3-44
NF582 RNDA 31-3-44 801S *HMS Furious*
NF583 RNDA 31-3-44
NF584 RNDA 31-3-44 880S *HMS Furious*
NF585 RNDA 31-3-44
NF586 RNDA 15-4-44 736BS
NF587 RNDA 20-4-44
NF588 RNDA 31-3-44 899S *HMS Chaser*
NF589 RNDA 31-3-44
NF590 RNDA 31-4-44 809S *HMS Stal*
NF591 RNDA 31-3-44
NF592, NF593, NF594 RNDA 7-4-44
NF595 RNDA 7-4-44 879S *HMS Attac* 4FW Dekh
NF596 RNDA 7-4-44 760S LoS 805S Mach
NF597, NF598 RNDA 7-4-44
NF599 RNDA 7-4-44 BDn Jly'45 Car mono cockpit contam tests. Gas present by seeping thro holes just below rails. Trls with NF652 and PX921 (IIIs) and NN263
NF600 RNDA 7-4-44 879S *HMS Attac*
NF601 RNDA 22-4-44 801S *HMS Furious*
NF602 RNDA 7-4-44
NF603, NF604, NF605 RNDA 15-4-44
NF606 RNDA 20-4-44
NF607 RNDA 15-4-44 809S *HMS Stal*
NF624 RNDA 15-4-44 4FW Dekh Egypt
NF625 RNDA 15-4-44
NF626 RNDA 20-4-44 885S 899S *HMS Chaser*
NF627 RNDA 15-4-44
NF628 RNDA 18-4-44 879S *HMS Attac*
NF629 WAL 17-4-44 39MU RNDA 20-4 RNAS Belfast 7-6 768S 9-6 809S *HMS Stal* 10-7 dam e/a pushed into sea 8-10
NF630 RNDA 20-4-44 807S *HMS Hunter* to A2106
NF631 RNDA 20-4-44 879S *HMS Attac*
NF632, NF633 RNDA 20-4-44
NF634 RNDA 20-4-44 718S Hens
NF635 RNDA 20-4-44 718S Hens
NF636 RNDA 20-4-44
NF637 RNDA 20-4-44 899S *HMS Khed*
NF638 RNDA 22-4-44 WAL 22-4 33MU 27-4 RNAS Belfast 7-6 768S 9-6 *HMS Stal* 21-7 Gib 8-9 FTR 7-10
NF639, NF640 RNDA 27-4-44
NF641 RNDA 22-4-44
NF642 RNDA 28-4-44
NF643 RNDA 27-4-44 879S *HMS Attac*
NF644 RNDA 27-4-44 879S *HMS Attac*
NF645 RNDA 28-4-44
NF646 RNDA 28-4-44 718S Hens
NF647 RNDA 28-4-44 718S Hens
NF648 RNDA 28-4-44 801S *HMS Furious*
NF649 RNDA 28-4-44 718S Hens
NF650 RNDA 28-4-44 718S Hens
NF651 RNDA 28-4-44 728S
NF652 RNDA 28-4-44 BDn Jly'45 Trls with NF599, NN263 & PX921 as per NF599
NF653 RNDA 28-4-44 718S Hens
NF654 RNDA 29-4-44 899S Long Kesh
NF655 RNDA 30-4-44

NF656, NF657, NF658, NF659, NF660 RNDA 29-4-44
NF661, NF662 RNDA 30-4-44
NF663 RNDA 5-5-44
NF664 RNDA 5-5-44 879S *HMS Attac*
NF665 RNDA 5-5-44

NM984 to NN330 built by Westland Aircraft Co.

NM984, NM985, NM986, NM987 RNDA 6-5-44
NM988 No record
NM989 RNDA 6-5-44 899S *HMS Khed*
NM990 RNDA 13-5-44
NM991, NM992 RNDA 12-5-44
NM993, NM994 RNDA 13-5-44
NM995 RNDA 13-5-44 807S *HMS Hunter*
NM996 RNDA 13-5-44
NM997 RNDA 13-5-44 899S *HMS Chaser*
NM998 RNDA 9-5-44 899S *HMS Chaser* 899S *HMS Khed*
NM999, NN112, NN113 RNDA 13-5-44

NN114 RNDA 18-5-44 879S *HMS Attac*
NN115, NN116 RNDA 18-5-44
NN117, NN118, NN119, NN120,NN121, NN122, NN123 RNDA 20-5-44 790S
NN124 RNDA 20-5-44 879S *HMS Attac*
NN125, NN126,NN127 RNDA 20-5-44 768S
NN128, NN129, NN130, NN131 RNDA 24-5-44
NN132, NN133 RNDA 25-5-44
NN134 WAL 24-5-44 RNDA 26-5 33MU 768S 9-6 809S HMS Stal FTR 18-10
NN135 RNDA 26-5-44 879S *HMS Attac*
NN136 RNDA 26-5-44 RNAS Belfast 806 879S *HMS Attac* To French Navy 10-4-48
NN137, NN138 RNDA 26-5-44
NN139 RNDA 26-5-44 39MU 1-6 RNAS hens 11-6 LoS for sea shipment preservation 3-10 809S *HMS Stal* 3-5-45 cd into sea 15-7
NN140, NN141 RNDA 26-5-44
NN142 RNDA 26-5-44 899S *HMS Khed*
NN143 RNDA 26-5-44
NN144, NN145,NN146 RNDA 31-5-44
NN147 RNDA 3-6-44 VAHP Wd & CG 8-6
NN148 RNDA 3-6-44
NN149 RNDA 3-6-44 To French Navy
NN150 RNDA 7-6-44 4FW Dekh Egypt
NN151 RNDA 8-6-44
NN152 RNDA 9-6-44
NN153 RNDA 14-6-44 4FW Dekh Egypt 807S *HMS Hunter*
NN154 RNDA 9-6-44
NN155 RNDA 9-6-44
NN156 RNDA 10-6-44 715S St Mer
NN157 RNDA 10-6-44 To French Navy
NN169, NN170, NN171, NN172 RNDA 10-6-44
NN173 RNDA 14-6-44
NN174 RNDA 15-6-44 760S Ayr *HMS Rav*
NN175, NN176, NN177 RNDA 16-6-44
NN178 RNDA 17-6-44
NN179 RNDA 17-6-44 4FW Dekh Egypt
NN180 WAL 16-6-44 RNDA 17-6 33MU 22-6 52MU 4-7 RNARY Coimbatere 9-7 8-9S *HMS Stal* 9-4-45 stk by PP981 on flight deck after ldg SOC ber 7-5
NN181 RNDA 17-6-44 4FW Dekh Egypt
NN182, NN183, NN184 RNDA 17-6-44
NN185 RNDA 21-6-44 887S (flown as MM185)
NN186 RNDA 21-6-44 M55M LF III BDn Sept'44 hand trls with 200lb smoke bomb for ASR duties, plus smoke float
NN187 RNDA 21-6-44
NN188 RNDA 23-6-44 To French Navy
NN189 RNDA 23-6-44 782S
NN190, NN191 RNDA 24-6-44
NN192 RNDA 24-6-44 805S Mach
NN193, NN194, NN195 RNDA 24-6-44

NN196 RNDA 24-6-44 Flown by Flt/Lt Colq to VASM for scr 10-1-49. Trans to VA
NN197 RNDA 24-6-44
NN198, NN199, NN200, NN201, NN202 RNDA 28-6-44
NN203, NN204, NN205, NN206, NN207, NN208, NN209 RNDA 30-6-44
NN210 RNDA 5-7-44
NN211 RNDA 5-7-44 887S *HMS Indef*
NN212 RNDA 6-7-44 887S *HMS Indef*
NN213, Nn214 RNDA 6-7-44
NN227, NN228, NN229, NN230, NN231, NN232 RNDA 8-7-44
NN233, NN234, NN235 RNDA 12-7-44 To French Navy
NN236, NN237, NN238, NN239 RNDA 14-7-44
NN240, NN241 RNDA 18-7-44
NN242, NN243, NN244 RNDA 15-7-44
NN245 RNDA 19-7-44
NN246, NN247 RNDA 22-7-44
NN248, NN249 RNDA 20-7-44
NN250 RNDA 22-7-44
NN251 RNDA 27-7-44
NN252 RNDA 22-7-44
NN253 RNDA 29-7-44
NN254 RNDA 22-7-44
NN255 RNDA 27-7-44
NN256 RNDA 28-7-44
NN257 RNDA 26-7-44
NN258 RNDA 29-7-44
NN259 RNDA 28-7-44 879S Nutts Corner
NN260 RNDA 29-7-44
NN261 RNDA 26-7-44
NN262 RBDA 28-7-44
NN263 RNDA 26-7-44 LF III BDn 9-7-45 Trls with NF599, NF652, PX921. Details as NF599
NN264 RNDA 29-7-44
NN265 RNDA 26-7-44
NN266 RNDA 28-7-44
NN267 RNDA 29-7-44 To French Navy
NN268 RNDA 31-7-44 879S *HMS Attac*
NN269, NN270, NN283 RNDA 28-7-44
NN284 RNDA 31-7-44 887S *HMS Indefat*
NN285, NN286, NN287 RNDA 29-7-44
NN288 RNDA 31-7-44
NN289, NN290 RNDA 3-9-44
NN291, NN292 RNDA 4-9-44
NN293, NN294 RNDA 3-9-44
NN295 RNDA 3-9-44 807S *HMS Hunter*
NN286 RNDA 4-9-44
NN297 RNDA 19-9-44
NN298 RNDA 4-9-44 887S *HMS Indefat*
NN299 RNDA 4-9-44
NN300 RNDA 24-8-44 LF III 807S *HMS Hunter*
NN301 RNDA 19-8-44
NN302 RNDA 24-8-44
NN303 RNDA 19-8-44 899S Long Kesh To French Navy
NN304, NN305, NN306 RNDA 24-8-44
NN307 RNDA 26-8-44
NN308 RNDA 26-8-44 794S Eglington
NN309, NN310, NN311 RNDA 26-8-44
NN312 RNDA 26-8-44 To French Navy
NN313, NN314 RNDA 26-8-44
NN315 RNDA 26-8-44
NN316, NN317, NN318 RNDA 31-8-44
NN319 RNDA 2-9-44
NN320 RNDA 31-8-44
NN321 RNDA Farn 31-8-44 arrester gear trls. Dec, army cooperation trls. To DTD BDn arrester gear trls, Jan'45. March, weather trls. Farn June, in con. arrester gear trls. Jan'46 Hatfield
NN322 RNDA 31-8-44
NN323 RNDA 16-9-44
NN324 RNDA 2-9-44
NN325 RNDA 31-8-44
NN326 L.III RNDA 2-9-44 to A506
NN327, NN328 RNDA 6-9-44
NN329 RNDA 9-9-44
NN330 RNDA 6-9-44

NN333 to NN641 built by Cunliffe-Owen Ltd.

NN333 VAWD Wd & CG 25-10-43 RNDA 1-11 715S St Mer
NN334 RNDA 10-11-43 794S Eglington
NN335 RNDA 31-12-43 794S Eglington
NN336 RNDA 29-1-44 Sch of N.Aw St Mer as A506 Stret April 1950
NN337 RNDA 22-1-44 880S *HMS Furious*
NN338 RNDA 5-2-44
NN339 RNDA 22-2-44 899S *HMS Khed*
NN340 RNDA 25-2-44
NN341 RNDA 29-2-44
NN342 RNDA 9-3-44
NN343 RNDA 20-3-44
NN344 RNDA 25-3-44 899S *HMS Khed*
NN345 RNDA 1-4-44 880S *HMS Furious*
NN346 RNDA 4-4-44
NN347 RNDA 14-4-44
NN348 RNDA 22-4-44 4FW Dekh Egypt
NN349 RNDA 29-4-44
NN350 RNDA 30-4-44 899S *HMS Khed*
NN351 RNDA 6-5-44
NN352 RNDA 9-5-44
NN353 RNDA 11-5-44
NN354 RNDA 13-5-44 4FW Dekh Egypt
NN355 RNDA 26-5-44 4FW Dekh Egypt
NN356 RNDA 20-5-44 4FW Dekh Egpyt
NN357, NN358 RNDA 30-5-44
NN359 RNDA 14-6-44 4FW Dekh Egypt
NN360 RNDA 18-6-44
NN361 RNDA 14-6-44 879S *HMS Attac*
NN362 RNDA 18-6-44 To French Navy
NN363 RNDA 21-6-44 887S *HMS Indef*
NN364 RNDA 18-6-44
NN365 RNDA 24-6-44 4FW Dekh Egypt
NN366 RNDA 19-6-44 Farn Aug'44 879S *HMS Attac* 807S *HMS Hunter*
NN367 RNDA 18-6-44
NN379 RNDA 19-6-44
NN380 RNDA 23-6-44 VAHP Wd & CG 27-6
NN381 RNDA 26-6-44 4FW Dekh Egypt
NN382 RNDA 24-6-44 $FW Dekh Egypt
NN383 RNDA 29-6-44
NN384 RNDA 28-6-44 4FW Dekh Egypt 807S *HMS Hunter*
NN385 RNDA 30-6-44 Farn Jly'44 trls with jett o/ld tanks
NN386 RNDA 30-6-44 794S Eglington
NN387 RNDA 30-6-44
NN388 RNDA 25-7-44 4FW Dekh Egypt
NN389 RNDA 6-7-44
NN390 RNDA 7-7-44 809S *HMS Stal* 879S *HMS Attac*
NN391 RNDA 22-7-44 899S Long Kesh To French Navy
NN392 RNDA 19-7-44
NN393 RNDA 22-7-44
NN394 RNDA 22-7-44 899S *HMS Khed*
NN395 RNDA 27-7-44 807S *HMS Hunter*
NN396 RNDA 28-7-44 879S *HMS Attac* To French Navy
NN397 RNDA 27-7-44
NN398 RNDA 29-7-44 807S *HMS Hunter*
NN399 RNDA 31-7-44
NN400 RNDA RNDA 31-7-44 COAL Stn 31-7 39MU 1-8 RNAS Lossie 23-8 RNAMY Coimbatore stored 16-1-45
NN401 RNDA 29-7-44 *HMS Attac*
NN402, NN403, NN404, NN405, NN406 RNDA 29-7-44
NN407 RNDA 15-8-44 807S *HMS Hunter*
NN408 RNDA 5-8-44 879S *HMS Attac*
NN409 RNDA 18-8-44 VAHP Wd & CG 21-8
NN410 RNDA 15-8-44
NN411 RNDA 16-8-44
NN412 RNDA 16-8-44
NN413 RNDA 12-8-44
NN414 RNDA 18-8-44
NN415 RNDA 23-8-44
NN416 COAL Stn 19-8-44 RNDA 21-8 39MU 23-8 76MU 7-9 RNAS Cochin 8-11 809S *HMS Stal* 17-4-45 pushed overboard by PP944 cd/ld on flt deck May'45.
NN417 RNDA 18-8-44
NN418 RNDA 19-8-44
NN431 RNDA 22-8-44
NN432 RNDA 24-8-44
NN433 RNDA 19-8-44
NN434 RNDA 24-8-44
NN435 RNDA 25-8-44
NN436 RNDA 24-8-44
NN437 RNDA 26-8-44
NN438 RNDA 28-8-44
NN439 RNDA 29-8-44
NN440 RNDA 29-8-44 879S *HMS Attac*
NN441 RNDA 2-9-44
NN442 RNDA 31-8-44 879S *HMS Attac*
NN443 RNDA 2-9-44
NN444 RNDA 31-8-44
NN445 RNDA 11-9-44 879S *HMS Attac*
NN446 RNDA 13-9-44
NN447 RNDA 8-9-44
NN448 RNDA 16-9-44
NN449 RNDA 12-9-44
NN450 RNDA 18-9-44 4FW Dekh Egypt
NN451 RNDA 12-9-44 879S *HMS Attac*
NN452 RNDA 16-9-44
NN453 RNDA 16-9-44 879S *HMS Attac*
NN454 RNDA 14-9-44
NN455 RNDA 20-9-44 879S Nutts Corner
NN456 RNDA 20-9-44 To French Navy
NN457 RNDA 21-9-44 807S *HMS Hunter*
NN458 RNDA 23-9-44
NN459 RNDA 19-9-44
NN460 RNDA 20-9-44
NN461 RNDA 25-9-44
NN462 RNDA 27-9-44
NN463 RNDA 25-9-44
NN464 RNDA 30-9-44
NN465 RNDA 29-9-44
NN466 RNDA 28-9-44
NN467 RNDA 28-9-44 To French Navy
NN468 RNDA 30-9-44
NN469 RNDA 28-9-44
NN470 RNDA 9-3-45
NN471 RNDA 30-9-44
NN472 RNDA 4-10-44
NN473 RNDA 29-9-44 807S *HMS Hunter*
NN474 RNDA 30-9-44 4FW Dekh Egypt
NN475 RNDA 30-9-44
NN476 RNDA 6-10-44
NN488 RNDA 9-10-44
NN489 RNDA 3-10-44
NN490 RNDA 5-10-44 4FW Dekh Egypt
NN491 RNDA 12-10-44
NN492 RNDA 13-10-44 807S *HMS Hunter*
NN493, NN494 RNDA 15-10-44
NN495 RNDA 20-10-44 4FW Dekh Egypt
NN496 RNDA 14-10-44
NN497 RNDA 18-10-44
NN498 RNDA 17-10-44
NN499 RNDA 18-10-44
NN500 RNDA 19-10-44 VAHP Wd & CG 1-11
NN501 RNDA 20-10-44
NN502 RNDA 27-10-44
NN503 RNDA 24-10-44
NN504 RNDA 25-10-44
NN505 RNDA 25-10-44 879S *HMS Attac*
NN506 RNDA 28-10-44
NN507 RNDA 24-10-44 794S Eglington
NN508 RNDA 25-10-44
NN509 RNDA 24-10-44
NN510 RNDA 28-10-44
NN511 RNDA 30-10-44
NN512, RNDA 29-10-44
NN513, NN514, NN515, NN516, NN517, NN518, NN519 RNDA 31-10-44
NN520 RNDA 30-10-44
NN521, NN522 RNDA 31-10-44
NN523 RNDA 7-11-44
NN524 RNDA 22-11-44 794S Eglington
NN525 RNDA 9-11-44
NN526 RNDA 13-11-44
NN527 RNDA 3-11-44
NN528 RNDA 15-11-44 805S Mach
NN542 RNDA 14-11-44
NN543 RNDA 24-11-44
NN544 RNDA 10-11-44
NN545 RNDA 27-11-44
NN546 RNDA 16-11-44 794S Eglington To French Navy
NN547 RNDA 24-11-44
NN548 RNDA 30-11-44
NN549 RNDA 24-11-44
NN550 RNDA 27-11-44
NN551 RNDA 1-12-44
NN552, NN553 RNDA 28-11-44
NN554 RNDA 27-11-44
NN555 RNDA 29-11-44
NN556 RNDA 28-11-44
NN557 RNDA 2-12-44
NN558 RNDA 30-11-44
NN559 RNDA 1-12-44
NN560 RNDA 4-12-44
NN561 RNDA 1-12-44
NN562, NN563, NN564 RNDA 5-12-44
NN565 RNDA 1-12-44
NN566 RNDA 6-12-44
NN567 RNDA 7-12-44
NN568 RNDA 2-12-44 759S 2-46
NN569 RNDA 16-12-44
NN570 RNDA 4-1-45 to A505
NN571 RNDA 19-12-44 759S
NN572 RNDA 5-1-45
NN573 RNDA 9-1-45
NN574 RNDA 4-1-45
NN575 RNDA 11-1-45
NN576 RNDA 8-1-45 759S 2-46
NN577 RNDA 5-1-45
NN578 RNDA 8-1-45
NN579 RNDA 10-1-45
NN580 RNDA 4-1-45
NN581 RNDA 10-1-45
NN582 RNDA 9-1-45 805S Mach
NN583 RNDA 7-1-45 805S Mach
NN584 RNDA 22-1-45 894S *HMS Indef*
NN585 RNDA 25-1-45
NN586 RNDA 12-1-45 805S Mach
NN599 RNDA 18-1-45 899S *HMS Khed*
NN600 RNDA 5-1-45
NN601 RNDA 22-1-45 805S Mach
NN602 RNDA 6-1-45
NN603 RNDA 9-1-45
NN604 RNDA 12-1-45 Store Doni Anthorn 14-1-48 To French Navy 15-1
NN605, NN606 RNDA 18-1-45
NN607 RNDA 17-1-45 805S Mach
NN608 RNDA 17-1-45
NN609 RNDA 23-1-45 To French Navy
NN610 RNDA 19-1-45
NN611 RNDA 22-1-45
NN612 RNDA 23-1-45
NN613 RNDA 6-2-45
NN614 RNDA 29-1-45
NN615 RNDA 1-2-45
NN616 RNDA 9-2-45
NN617 RNDA 7-2-45
NN618 RNDA 1-2-45
NN619 RNDA 8-2-45
NN620 RNDA 9-2-45 To French Navy
NN621 RNDA 7-2-45 880S *HMS Implac*
NN622 RNDA 6-2-45
NN623 RNDA 13-2-45 Doni 10-4 RTP 18-3-48 To French Navy as spares
NN624 RNDA 6-2-45
NN625 RNDA 20-2-45

NN626 RNDA 8-2-45
NN627 RNDA 15-2-45
NN628 RNDA 15-2-45
NN629 RNDA 28-2-45
NN630 RNDA 10-2-45
NN631 RNDA 28-2-45
NN632 RNDA 23-2-45
NN633 RNDA 14-2-45
NN634 RNDA 15-2-45
NN635 RNDA 27-2-45
NN636 RNDA 9-2-45
NN637 RNDA 27-2-45
NN638 RNDA 26-2-45 805S Mach
NN639 RNDA 26-2-45
NN640 RNDA 11-2-45
NN641 RNDA 27-2-45 To French Navy

PP921 to PR334 built by Westland Aircraft Co.

PP921 RNDA 6-9-44 LF III M45M BDn May'45 trls with various stores 8x60lb head PRs on zero length rails & 45gall o/ld tank, PRs on four double tier rails. Type 3 PRs had armoured heads. Trls with heads removed. Car mono cockpit contam test. Attitude measurements with NF599, NF652 & NN263.

PP922, PP923, PP924, PP925, PP926, PP927 RNDA 9-9-44

PP928 RNDA 9-9-44 781S 799S
PP929, PP930, PP931 RNDA 9-9-44 760S
PP932 RNDA 14-9-44
PP933 RNDA 14-9-44
PP934 RNDA 9-9-44
PP935, PP936, PP937, PP938, PP939 RNDA 14-9-44 887S *HMS Indef* cd/ld 20-3-45
PP940, PP941, PP942, PP943 RNDA 16-9-44
PP944 RNDA 16-9-44 WAL 16-9 33MU 25-9 RNAS LoS 23-11 809S *HMS Stal* 6-3-45 DBR by NN416 cd/ld on flt deck pushed overboard 1-5
PP945 RNDA 20-9-44
PP946 RNDA 28-9-44
PP947 RNDA 22-9-44
PP948 RNDA 27-9-44
PP949, PP950 RNDA 22-9-44
PP951 RNDA 23-9-44 899S Long Kesh
PP952, PP953, PP954, PP955, PP956 RNDA 23-9-44
PP957 RNDA 7-10-44
PP969 RNDA 23-9-44
PP970 RNDA 23-9-44
PP971 RNDA 27-9-44
PP972 RNDA 27-9-44 767S To French Navy. Extant Vannes-Mencon France
PP973, PP974 RNDA 27-9-44
PP975 RNDA 28-9-44 LF III M55M BDn 27-11 Trls with 500lb smoke bomb. Deck t/o with bomb on Mk III Univ carr 801S *HMS Implac* FTR over Truk Island 14-6-45
PP976 RNDA 28-9-44
PP977 RNDA 27-9-44
PP978 RNDA 29-9-44
PP979 RNDA 28-9-44 807S *HMS Hunter*
PP980 RNDA 29-9-44
PP981 RNDA 30-9-44 WAL 30-9 39MU 6-10 RNAS LoS storage 17-11 *HMS Hunter* 21-11 809S *HMS Stal* 20-4-45 pushed overboard by NN180 cd/ld on flt deck 7-5
PP982 RNDA 29-9-44
PP983 RNDA 30-9-44
PP984 RNDA 7-10-44 807S *HMS Hunter* i/Irish Sea Spring 1945
PP985 RNDA 7-10-44
PP986 RNDA 7-10-44 VAHP Wd & CG 17-10
PP987, PP988 RNDA 7-10-44
PP989 RNDA 21-10-44
PP990 RNDA 7-10-44 To French Navy
PP991 RNDA 7-10-44 4FW Dekh Egypt
PP992, PP993 RNDA 7-10-44
PP994 RNDA 7-10-44 810S *HMS Implac*
PP995 RNDA 13-10-44
PP996 RNDA 7-10-44
PP997, PP998, PP999 RNDA 14-10-44 759S

PR115, PR116, PR117 RNDA 14-10-44 759S 2-46
PR118 RNDA 27-10-44
PR119, PR120 RNDA 14-10-44
PR121 RNDA 19-10-44
PR122, PR123, PR124 RNDA 14-10-44
PR125 RNDA 31-10-44 *HMS Attac*
PR126 RNDA 20-10-44
PR127 RNDA 21-10-44
PR128 RNDA 26-10-44
PR129 RNDA 20-10-44
PR130 RNDA 21-10-44
PR131 RNDA 26-10-44
PR132 RNDA 9-11-44 AHU Hens 18-1-45 LoS To French Navy 10-4-49
PR133 RNDA 21-10-44
PR134 RNDA 27-10-44
PR135 RNDA 28-10-44 879S *HMS Attac*
PR136, PR137 RNDA 27-10-44
PR138 RNDA 26-10-44
PR139 RNDA 27-10-44
PR140 RNDA 26-10-44
PR141 RNDA 27-10-44 887S *HMS Indefat*
PR142, PR143, PR144 RNDA 28-10-44 'S-129'
PR145 RNDA 28-10-44
PR146 RNDA 28-10-44 899S Long Kesh To French Navy
PR147, PR148, PR149 RNDA 28-10-44
PR150 RNDA 4-11-44
PR151, PR152 RNDA 28-10-44 759S 12-45
PR153 RNDA 31-10-44
PR154, PR155 RNDA 28-10-44
PR156 RNDA 31-10-44
PR170 RNDA 31-10-44 879S *HMS Hunter* To French Navy
PR171 RNDA 31-10-44 FR III 807S *HMS Hunter*
PR172, PR173 RNDA 31-10-44
PR174 RNDA 4-11-44
PR175 cancelled
PR176, PR177 RNDA 9-11-44
PR178 RNDA 18-11-44 Belfast Feb'46 earmarked for French Navy
PR179 RNDA 9-11-44
PR180 RNDA 9-11-44 strk by PX958 Hens 27-8-45
PR181, PR182, PR183 RNDA 9-11-44
PR184 RNDA 9-11-44
PR185 RNDA 9-11-44
PR186, PR187 RNDA 11-11-44
PR188 RNDA 23-11-44
PR189 RNDA 25-11-44
PR190 RNDA 25-11-44
PR191 RNDA 18-11-44
PR192 RNDA 16-11-44
PR193 RNDA 25-11-44
PR194 RNDA 18-11-44
PR195 RNDA 25-11-44
PR196 RNDA 18-11-44
PR197, PR198, PR199 RNDA 25-11-44
PR200 RNDA 18-11-44
PR201 RNDA 22-11-44
PR202 RNDA 25-11-44
PR203, PR204 RNDA 18-11-44
PR205 RNDA 25-11-44
PR206 RNDA 22-11-44 894S *HMS Indefat*
PR207 RNDA 23-11-44
PR208 RNDA 23-11-44
PR209 RNDA 30-11-44 887S *HMS Indefat* PR210 to 215 and 228 to 230 cancelled.
PR231 RNDA 30-11-44
PR232 RNDA 9-12-44
PR233, PR234, PR235 RNDA 30-11-44
PR236 RNDA 30-11-44 M55M VASM refurb to F Mk VC standard. Del IAC as 155 by Sgt Conway to Ballydonnell 29-9-47, withdrawn service 8-8-54 scr 1962. This a/c had wings of NF575 fitted.
PR237, PR238, PR239, PR240 RNDA 30-11-44
PR241 RNDA 9-12-44
PR242, PR243, PR244, PR245, PR246, PR247 RNDA 30-11-44
PR248 RNDA 9-12-44 Belfast Feb'46 earmarked for French Navy
PR249 RNDA 30-11-44 AHU Hens Feb'46 To French Navy
PR250 RNDA 2-12-44
PR251, PR252, PR253 RNDA 9-12-44
PR254 RNDA 9-12-44 887S *HMS Indef*
PR255 RNDA 9-12-44 807S *HMS Hunter*
PR256 RNDA 9-12-44 *HMS Indefat*
PR257 RNDA 9-12-44 AHU Hens Feb'46 earmarked for French Navy
PR258, PR259, PR260 RNDA 9-12-44
PR261 RNDA 16-12-44
PR262 RNDA 9-12-44
PR263 RNDA 16-12-44 894S *HMS Indef* dam com 15-8-45
PR264 RNDA 9-12-44
PR265 RNDA 16-12-44 AHU Hens Feb'46 To French Navy
PR266 RNDA 16-12-44 Abbot Feb'46 To French Navy
PR267, PR268 RNDA 16-12-44
PR269 RNDA 22-12-44
PR270, PR271 RNDA 16-12-44
PR285 RNDA 22-12-44
PR286, PR287 RNDA 16-12-44
PR288 RNDA 16-12-44 To French Navy
PR289 RNDA 31-12-44
PR290, PR291 RNDA 16-12-44
PR292 RNDA 22-12-44 FR II 879S *HMS Attac*
PR293 RNDA 22-12-44 To French Navy
PR294, PR295, PR296, PR297, PR298 RNDA 22-12-44
PR299, PR300 RNDA 31-12-44
PR301 RNDA 22-12-44 879S *HMS Attac*
PR302 RNDA 6-1-45 M45M VASM refurb to F Mk VC standard 1st flown as IAC 146 4-12-46 del IAC 24-1-47 No 1 Sqdn withdrawn service 16-6-54 scr 1962
PR303 RNDA 31-12-44
PR304 RNDA 6-1-45 To French Navy
PR305, PR306 RNDA 30-12-44
PR307 RNDA 31-12-44
PR308 RNDA 30-12-44
PR309 RNDA 31-12-44
PR310 RNDA 6-1-45
PR311, PR312 RNDA 31-12-44
PR313 RNDA 6-1-45
PR314 RNDA 6-1-45 M45M BDn 26-11 hand trls various stores one AN-M64 500lb bomb, one Mk AVIII mine, 12x30lb l/c bombs. T/o & ldg trls with 2x200lb smoke floats & 1x45gall o/ld tank, two 250lb smoke floats, 2x250lb B Mk III bombs & one Mk XI depth charge.
PR315 RNDA 6-1-45 M55M VASM refurb to F Mk VC standard. 1st flown as IAC 147 2-9-46 del IAC 24-1-47 cd SOC 5-9
PR316 RNDA 31-8-44
PR317 RNDA 13-1-45
PR318 RNDA 6-1-45 805S Mach 879S Nutts Corner
PR319 RNDA 6-1-45 805S Mach
PR320 RNDA 13-1-45
PR321 RNDA 6-1-45
PR322 RNDA 6-1-45 To French Navy
PR323, PR324 RNDA 13-1-45
PR325 RNDA 13-1-45 879S *HMS Attac*
PR326, PR327, PR328 RNDA 13-1-45
PR329 RNDA 13-1-45 Belfast Feb'46 earmaked for French Navy
PR330 RNDA 20-1-45
PR331, PR332 RNDA 13-1-45
PR333 RNDA 13-1-45 To French Navy
PR334 RNDA 20-1-45 767S

PX913 to PX962 built by Cunliffe-Owen Ltd, as LF.IIIs.

PX913 RNDA 26-245 794S ld u/c up 23-11-45 Test flt Eglington Dec'45
PX914 RNDA 28-2-45 805S Mach July'45
PX915 RNDA 22-2-45 M55 Test flt SM S/Ldr Morgan 8-8-47 del IAC as 154 27-9 cd 28-5-51
PX916 RNDA 28-2-45 767S Easthaven May'46 ld u/c up 20-2-47 sold French Navy
PX917 RNDA 28-2-45 RNAS Belfast Feb'46 earmarked French Navy
PX918 RNDA 1-3-45 RNAS Belfast Feb'46 earmarked French Navy
PX919 RNDA 1-3-45 sold French Navy
PX920 RNDA 2-3-45 805S Mach July'45 883S Arbroath Oct'48
PX921 RNDA 19-3-45 C Sqdn AAEE BDn 9-4 Trials Mk VIII RP Henstridge 24-1-46
PX922 RNDA 1-3-45 RNAS Belfast Feb'46 earmarked French Navy
PX923 RNDA 28-2-45
PX924 RNDA 1-3-45 M55M flown at VASM 30-47. Refurbished to F Mk VC standard & del to IAC 11-7 by Lt Creham to Ballydonnell. Withdrawn service 19-6-54 scr 1962 IAC number 153
PX925 RNDA 5-3-45
PX926 RNDA 28-2-45 883S Nutts Corner GA ran off peri-track tip onto nose 15-1-46
PX927 RNDA 6-3-45
PX928 RNDA 3-3-45 781S, 769S
PX929 RNDA 3-3-45 VASM to F mk VC standard prod test 6-47 J Derry & del to IAC as 152 by Lt Howard to Ballydonnell 11-7-47. Cd SOC 1-9-49.
PX930 RNDA 28-2-45
PX931 RNDA 5-3-45 Test flt Eglington Dec'46 Sold French Navy 15-6-48
PX932 RNDA 3-3-45 RNAD Belfast Feb'46. Sold French Navy as IF.22 15-6-48
PX933 RNDA 2-3-45 Abbot Feb'46. Sold French Navy as IF.23
PX934 RNDA 3-3-45
PX935 RNDA 6-3-45
PX936 RNDA 5-3-45 M55M VASM refurb to F Mk VC standard. F/F as IAC 156 by Flt/Lt Cole 28-4-47. Del IAC by Capt Johnson 27-9 Withdrwn from service 12-6-54 scr 1962.
PX937 RNDA 26-3-45
PX938 RNDA 6-3-45
PX939, PX940 RNDA 12-3-45
PX941 RNDA 17-3-45 M55M VASM refurb to F Mk VC standard, F/F as IAC 151 15-5-47. Del IAC by Lt O'Connell to Ballydonnell 11-7 Cd SOC 29-6-51
PX942 RNDA 14-3-45
PX943 RNDA 19-3-45
PX944 RNDA 19-3-45 778S Ford i/sea during ldg app *HMS Illust* 25-3-47
PX945 RNDA 26-3-45 Abbot Feb'46 earmarked for French Navy.
PX946 RNDA 19-3-45 Test flt Eglington Feb'47 sold French Navy
PX947 RNDA 31-1-45
PX948 RNDA 26-3-45 M55M VASM, refurb to F Mk VC standard. 1st flt as such 30-12-46. Del IAC as 149 by IAC pilot to Ballydonnell 24-1-47 Withdrawn from service 15-5-54 scr 1962
PX949 RNDA 21-3-45
PX950 RNDA 26-3-45 M55M VASM refurb to F Mk VC standard. 1st flown as VC 3-12-46. Del to IAC as 148 IAC pilot to Ballydonnell 24-1-47. Cd SOC 22-5-53
PX951 RNDA 23-3-45 RNAS Belfast Feb'46 sold French Navy
PX952 RNDA 27-3-45
PX953 RNDA 28-3-45 GA Lyneham during f/f by ATA from 15PP Hamble 19-3. AHN Hens Feb'46 earmarked for French Navy
PX954 RNDA 28-3-45 39MU Cat AR Lulsgate Bottom 31-7 AHU Hens Feb'46 To French Navy
PX955 RNDA 30-3-45 AHU Hens April'45 earmarked for French Navy
PX956 RNDA 31-3-45 test flt Eglington Nov'46
PX957 RNDA 30-3-45 Abbot Feb'46 earmarked for French Navy
PX958 RNDA 30-3-45 761S Hens july'45 strk parked Seafire PR180 27-8
PX959 RNDA 29-3-45 For IAC f/ld on del flt to Supermarine ntu
PX960 RNDA 31-3-45 i/sea stld ldg app *HMS Implac* 15-10-46

Irish Army Air Corps number 149, de-navalised MkIII. Ex. PX948 with M55M engine. Scrapped 1962.

PX961 RNDA 31-3-45
PX962 RNDA 31-3-45 Abbot Feb'46 earmarked for French Navy

RX156 to RX353 built by Westland Aircraft Co.

RX156 RNDA 20-1-45 787S
RX157 RNDA 27-1-45
RX158 RNDA 3-2-45 To French Navy
RX159, RX160, RX161 RNDA 27-1-45
RX162 RNDA 20-1-45794S Eglington
RX163 RNDA 805S Mach Belfast Feb'46 earmarked French Navy
RX164 RNDA 3-2-45
RX165 RNDA 20-1-45 Belfast Feb'46 earmarked for French Navy
RX166 RNDA 10-2-45 To French Navy
RX167 RNDA 3-2-45
RX168 RNDA 20-1-45 M55M VASM refurb to F Mk VC F/F as VC 12-9-47 Del IAC as 157 by Sgt Colland to Ballydonnell 27-9. WFS 27-10-53 sold Dublin Tech Inst 1962 scr 1963
RX169 RNDA 31-1-45
RX170 RNDA 3-2-45
RX171 RNDA 3-2-45
RX172 RNDA 10-2-45 794S Edlington
RX173 RNDA 10-2-45 778S Farn June/July 1946
RX174, RX175, RX176, RX177, RX178, RX178, RX179 RNDA 10-2-45
RX180 RNDA 3-2-45
RX181 RNDA 3-2-45
RX182 RNDa 24-2-45 AHU Hens Feb'46 earmarked for French Navy
RX183 RNDA 10-2-45 To French Navy
RX184 RNDA 10-2-45
RX185 RNDA 3-2-45
RX186 RNDA 10-2-45
RX187 RNDA 10-2-45 794S Eglington
RX188, RX189 RNDA 17-2-45
RX190 RNDA 10-2-45
RX191 RNDA17-2-45
RX192 RNDA24-2-45 AHU Hens Feb'46 To French Navy 1946
RX193 RNDA 17-2-45
RX194 RNDA 24-2-45
RX210 RNDA 24-2-45 VASM refurb to F Mk VC standard F/F as VC 15-4-47 Del IAC as 150 by Capt Ryan to Ballydonnell 11-7 SOC 1955 scr 1962
RX211 RNDA 24-2-45 748S St Mer to A502
RX212 RNDA 24-2-45 741S St Mer Sch NAW
RX213 RNDA 24-2-45 Belfast Feb'46 Earmarked for French Navy
RX214, RX215 RNDA 24-2-45
RX216 RNDA 24-2-45 Belfast Feb'46 To French Navy 16-3-46
RX217 RNDA 24-2-45 748S St Mer to A50
RX218 RNDA 28-2-45
RX219, RX220, RX221, RX222 RNDA 24-2-45
RX223 RNDA 24-2-45 Belfast Feb'46 To French Navy 1946
RX224 RNDA 24-2-45 To France
RX225 RNDA 24-2-45
RX226 RNDA 28-2-45 Abbot Feb'46 Earmarked for French Navy
RX227 RNDA 24-2-45
RX228 RNDA 24-2-45 To France
RX229 RNDA 24-2-45 Belfast Feb'46 To French Navy 1946
RX230 RNDA 24-2-45
RX231 RNDA 24-2-45 76MU 25-3 LoS To French Navy 15-6-48
RX232, RX233 RNDA 24-2-45
RX234 RNDA 23-6-45
RX235 RNDA 24-2-45
RX236 FR LF III RNDA Abbot Feb'46 Earmarked French Navy
RX237, RX238 RNDA 28-2-45
RX239 FR LF III RNDA 18-3-45
RX240 RNDA 28-2-45 Belfast Feb'46 To French Navy 1946
RX241 FR LF III RNDA 12-3-45 794S Eglington To French NAvy
RX242 FR LF III RNDA 12-3-45 Abbot Feb'46 Earmarked French Navy
RX243 FR LF III RNDA 13-3-45
RX244 FR LF III RNDA 24-3-45 Belfast 29-5 LoS to French Navy 10-4-48
RX245 FR LF III RNDA 24-3-45
RX246 FR LF III RNDA 24-3-45
RX247 RNDA 28-3-45 To French Navy
RX248 RNDA 26-3-45 RNAS Doni Sept'46 794S
RX249 RNDA 26-3-45
RX250 RNDA 5-4-45 749S Eglington
RX251 RNDA 29-3-45 Abbot Feb'46 Earmarked for French Navy
RX252 RNDA 4-4-45
RX253 RNDA 28-3-45 Belfast 28-5 To French Navy 15-6-48
RX254 RNDA 28-3-45 Belfast Feb'46 To French Navy 1946
RX255 RNDA 7-4-45 Belfast Feb'46 Earmarked for French Navy
RX256 RNDA 5-4-45
RX268 RNDA 7-4-45
RX269 RNDA 4-4-45
RX270 RNDA 5-4-45
RX271 RNDA 7-4-45 To French Navy
RX272 RNDA 9-4-45
RX273 RNDA 7-4-45
RX274 RNDA 10-4-45
RX275 RNDA 7-4-45
RX276 RNDA 13-4-45
RX277 RNDA 11-4-45
RX278 RNDA 10-4-45 52MU 9-7 LoS To French Navy 10-4-48
RX279 RNDA 10-4-45 52 MU 9-7 LoS To French Navy 10-4-48
RX280 RNDA 11-4-455
RX281 RNDA 12-4-45 To French Navy
RX282 RNDA 17-4-45
RX283 RNDA 13-4-45 To French Navy
RX284, RX285 RNDA 17-4-45
RX286 RNDA 12-4-45 To French Navy
RX287 RNDA 19-4-45
RX288, RX289 RNDA 21-4-45
RX290 RNDA 20-4-45 AHU Hens Feb'46 To French Navy as IF.9
RX291 RNDA 20-4-45
RX292 RNDA 21-4-45 771S
RX293 RNDA 25-4-45 Abbot Feb'46 Earmarked for French Navy
RX294 RNDA 23-4-45
RX295 RNDA 26-4-45
RX296 RNDA 26-4-45 To French Navy
RX297 RNDA 24-4-45
RX298 RNDA 26-4-45 Belfast Feb'46 Earmarked for French Navy
RX299, RX300 RNDA 28-4-45
RX301 RNDA 30-4-45 To French Navy 1946
RX302 RNDA 30-4-45
RX303 RNDA 1-5-45
RX304 RNDA 4-5-45
RX305 RNDA 4-5-45 To French Navy 1946
RX306 RNDA 7-5-45 794S Eglington
RX307 RNDA 11-5-45 To French Navy
RX308 RNDA 10-5-45
RX309 RNDA 10-5-45 AHU Hens Feb'46 Earmarked for French Navy
RX310 RNDA 16-5-45
RX311, RX312 RNDA 15-5-45
RX313 RNDA 18-5-45
RX326 RNDA 24-5-45
RX327 RNDA 24-5-45 52MU 9-7 LoS To French Navy 27-4-48
RX328 RNDA 24-5-45
RX329 RNDA 25-5-45
RX330 RNDA 23-5-45
RX331 RNDA25-5-45
RX332 RNDA 31-5-45
RX333 RNDA 2-6-45 AHU Hens 4-8 LoS to French Navy 27-4-48
RX334, RX335, RX336 RNDA 4-6-45
RX337 RNDA 5-6-45
RX338 RNDA 7-6-45 M55M BDn Sept'45 test of effects of mod metal elev with raised beading on trailing edge. To French Navy. 1946
RX339 RNDA 10-6-45 To France
RX340 RNDA 22-6-45
RX341 RNDA 20-6-45
RX342 RNDA 16-6-45 To French Navy
RX343 RNDA 18-6-45
RX344 RNDA 19-6-45
RX345 RNDA 20-6-45 802S Abbot
RX346 RNDA 20-6-45 802S Abbot 759S 2-46
RX347 RNDA 30-6-45 759S 2-46
RX348 RNDA 25-6-45
RX349 RNDA 28-6-45
RX350 RNDA 30-6-45
RX351 RNDA 30-6-45
RX352 RNDA 9-7-45 794S Eglington
RX353 RNDA 9-7-45

SP136 to SP197 built by Cunliffe-Owen

SP136 RNDA 31-3-45 Abbot Feb'46 Earmarked for French Navy
SP137 RNDA 11-4-45 To French Navy
SP138 RNDA 13-4-45
SP139 RNDA 6-4-45
SP140 RNDA 14-4-45
SP141 RNDA 17-4-45
SP142 RNDA 17-4-45
SP143 RNDA 25-4-45 Abbot Feb'46 Earmarked for French Navy
SP144 RNDA 20-4-45 Abbot Feb'46 Earmarked for French Navy
SP145 RNDA 17-4-45
SP146 RNDA 1-4-45
SP147 RNDA 28-4-45 Abbot Feb'46 Earmarked for French Navy
SP148 RNDA 27-4-45 AHU Hens Feb'46 Earmarked for French Navy
SP149 RNDA 30-4-45
SP150 RNDA 30-4-45 AHU Hens Feb'46 To French Navy 1946
SP151, SP152, SP153, SP154 RNDA 30-4-45
SP155 RNDA 4-5-45
SP156 RNDA 30-4-45
SP157 RNDA 11-5-45
SP158 RNDA 16-5-45
SP159 RNDA 12-5-45
SP160 RNDA 23-5-45
SP161, SP162 RNDA 25-5-45
SP163 RNDA 28-5-45 To French Navy
SP164 RNDA 29-5-45
SP165 RNDA 1-6-45
SP166 RNDA 1-6-45 To French Navy
SP167 RNDA 2-6-45 To French Navy
SP168 RNDA 2-6-45
SP181 RNDA 1-6-45
SP182 RNDA 6-6-45 To French Navy
SP183 RNDA 5-6-45 To French Navy
SP184 RNDA 12-6-45
SP185 RNDA 31-7-45
SP186 RNDA 16-6-45
SP187 RNDA 25-6-45
SP188 RNDA 27-6-45
SP189 RNDA 3-7-45
SP190 RNDA 27-6-45 To French Navy
SP191 RNDA 30-6-45
SP192 RNDA 3-7-45 To French Navy
SP193, SP194 RNDA 3-7-45
SP195 RNDA 12-7-45
SP196 RNDA 20-7-45
SP197 RNDA 24-7-45

THE ADMIRALS TRY AGAIN

Although the Fleet Air Arm had been frustrated in its attempts to obtain a single seat, fixed gun fighter during the late 1930s, and was eventually equipped with the 'hooked' and converted Spitfire and the Seafire IB and IIC, efforts were still being made to obtain an aeroplane specifically designed to its requirements. These efforts received a spur when in early 1939 Rolls-Royce were developing a new engine designed specifically for the Royal Navy. It was the 37 V12 unit, which eventually became known as the Griffon. The Royal Air Force was not interested at that time in the new engine for the Merlin development had only just started and the Griffon was too large to fit the Spitfire airframe without some modification.

But the Admiralty was extremely interested in this most promising engine and they approached Supermarine with a request to produce a Specification for a naval fighter powered by the Griffon and with folding wings. The Supermarine Technical Office Report was dated 16 December 1939 and read as follows –

SINGLE SEAT FLEET FIGHTER NAD 925/39

A rapid investigation has been made of the staff requirements for a single seat Fleet fighter and TWO alternative proposals are submitted.

(a) The Spitfire with Griffon engine and folding wings. Full information of the extensive wireless equipment required is not available but from investigation it appears that this could be accommodated in the standard Spitfire fuselage, and that the required armament can be housed in the Spitfire wing by suitable re-arrangement of mountings.

Flight tests on a Spitfire have been carried out indicating that the stalling speed 'engine on' is 10 mph less than the stalling speed 'engine off'. With its increased flap area the Griffon Spitfire should meet the requirements for approach at 65 knots, and also take off in 300 feet against a 20 knot wind. It has a good margin over the required speed at 15,000ft, and is, therefore, put forward as the most suitable aeroplane which can be put into production at a reasonable time. It is pointed out that the Spitfire has already been flown with a 2,000hp engine and proved to handle quite normally.

(b) A development of the Spitfire with Sabre engine

This utilises certain Spitfire components such as wings, rear portions of fuselage, tail unit, but has a new centre section which incorporates stub wings for increasing the area, and provides an improved view for the pilot. A very high performance is estimated, but the time before production commenced would be longer than proposal (a). Brief weight and performance figures for both proposals are appended.

	Griffon engine	Sabre
Span (ft in)	36.10	39.0
Length (folded)	30.7	31.3
Width (folded)	11.0	11.0
Wing area (gross)	242 sq ft	282 sq ft
Weight empty	5485 lb	6170
Normal take off weight	8100 lb	9205
Landing weight ($\frac{1}{3}$rd fuel)	7455	8320
Stall engine off	7.5	66 knts
Stall engine on	59	57.5
Speed @ 15,000ft	396mph	428
Take off run (20 knt wind)	300ft	240
Cruise @ 15,000	172mph	172
Endurance @ 150 knts	4hrs	4hrs

Another Spitfire converted for Naval operation was not needed by the Admiralty and although both proposals were interesting they were not proceeded with. In an effort to promote adoption of the Griffon engined airframe Supermarine issued Report No 2846 on 15 February 1940 and this summarised details of the folding wing. Final calculations had been completed on a pair of folding wings with an

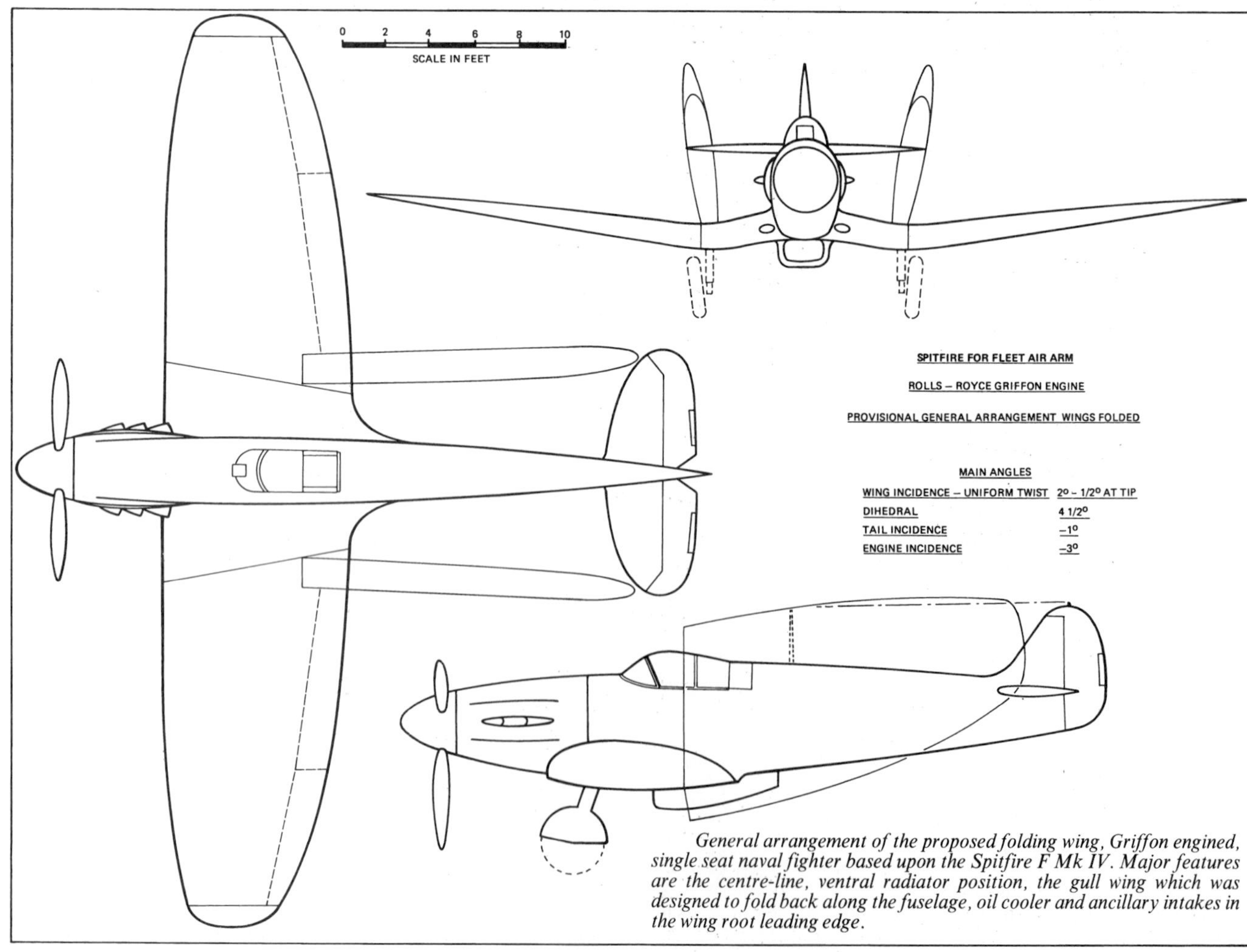

General arrangement of the proposed folding wing, Griffon engined, single seat naval fighter based upon the Spitfire F Mk IV. Major features are the centre-line, ventral radiator position, the gull wing which was designed to fold back along the fuselage, oil cooler and ancillary intakes in the wing root leading edge.

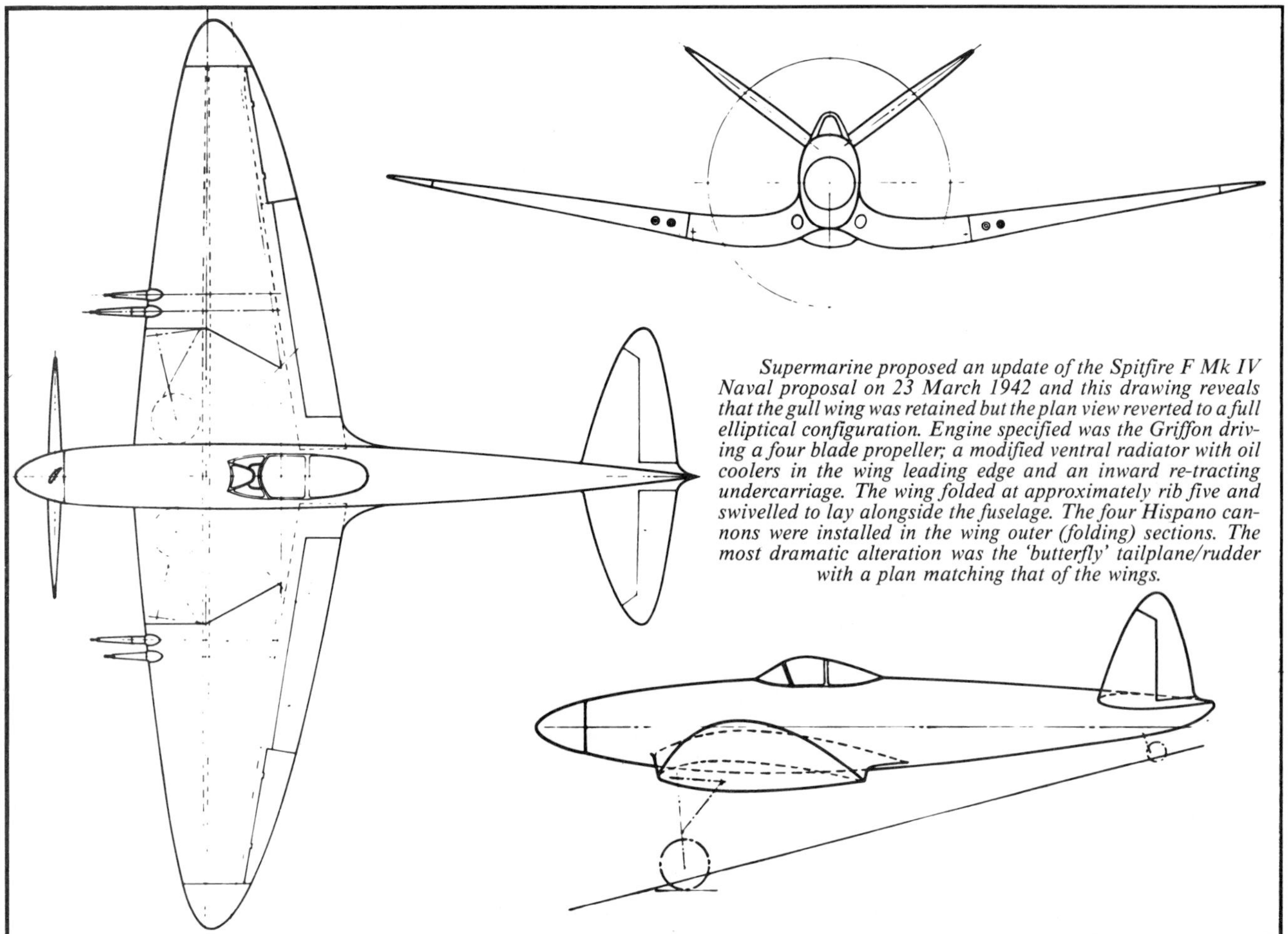

Supermarine proposed an update of the Spitfire F Mk IV Naval proposal on 23 March 1942 and this drawing reveals that the gull wing was retained but the plan view reverted to a full elliptical configuration. Engine specified was the Griffon driving a four blade propeller; a modified ventral radiator with oil coolers in the wing leading edge and an inward re-tracting undercarriage. The wing folded at approximately rib five and swivelled to lay alongside the fuselage. The four Hispano cannons were installed in the wing outer (folding) sections. The most dramatic alteration was the 'butterfly' tailplane/rudder with a plan matching that of the wings.

armament of six 13.2mm Browning guns a total wing weight of 780 lb.

The wing folded at rib five and the additional weight was 241 lb. This assumed an upward fold, but a rotating fold to store the wing alongside the fuselage would have resulted in a rotation of 116° and a folded width of 10ft 4in, well below the maximum of 13ft 6in as specified by the Navy. The folded wing came into contact with the tailplane about eight inches from the tips. One major problem was continuity of the nose torsion box and Supermarine proposed preserving the joint by an attachment on the leading edge. Our drawing shows the general arrangement of the Naval Griffon Spitfire and it will be noted that it is similar to the folded wing Spitfire as illustrated in chapter 30.

By 1941 a prototype of the Spitfire F Mk IV powered by the Griffon engine was flying and the Admiralty's thoughts were again directed to their earlier proposals. With details of the Spitfire F Mk IV as a yardstick the Aero Department at Farnborough was asked to prepare a performance estimate for a naval fighter based upon the new Spitfire and its engine. This estimate appeared in February 1942 and details appear below –

Introduction. At the request of RDN-3 an estimate has been made of the performance of a naval fighter based upon the design of the Spitfire IV with a high altitude Griffon engine. The aeroplane must be capable of operating from an aircraft carrier, or aerodrome, and must be fitted with folding wings, arrester hook and catapult gear. Rough estimate by SME Department give the following weights for the normal Spitfire IV and the naval version with the same wing area (see right).

The additional structure weight is due to the wing folding mechanism and extra flaps in the wings; an increase of weight of deck arrester hook and catapult fixtures in the fuselage and to more severe stressing cases in the undercarriage. Weight of the high altitude Griffon will be roughly 200lb greater than the RG2SM. Increasing wing and tail area will add about 80lb to the structure weight, giving a total of 10,630lb.

Stalling speed. The Specification calls for a minimum safe approach speed of 65 knots with not more than two thirds engine power and carrying full load but with only one hour's fuel. To allow sufficient margin for the pull-out the approach speed should not be less than 1.2Vs. The Specification is,

	Normal Spitfire IV Griffon RG2SM	Naval Spitfire IV Griffon RG2SM
Wings	1400	2100
Fuselage	570	630
Undercarriage	400	450
Tail unit	130	140
Engine mounting	170	170
Controls	95	95
Totals	2765 (29.6%)	3858 (34.5%)
Power unit	3040	3040
Fuel tanks	190	190
Fixed load	670	845
Removable load	1450	1460
Crew	200	200
Fuel, oil	1025	1025
Totals	6575	6760
Take off weight	9340 (lbs)	10,350 (lbs)

therefore, equivalent to a stalling speed of 54 knots with two thirds engine power, or roughly 63 knots engine off. This is more severe than the requirement of 68 knots stalling speed, engine off, in earlier specifications.

The Spitfire IV has a wing area of 249sq ft and a span of 40ft 4in, the plan form being the same as the Spitfire Mk I with the addition of a small extension at the tip. Split flaps are being fitted on the production aeroplane, but slotted flaps have been tried out on the prototype. If the original wing of the Spitfire Mk I is moved outwards and an extra two feet span inserted at the root each side, the area can be increased to 275sq ft with a total span of 41ft 0in. The wing loading is then the same as the Spitfire Mk IV and the strength factors will be unchanged without redesign of the main part of the wing.

The folding mechanism will, in any case, necessitate redesign of the inboard part. Standard ailerons are used and it is assumed that slotted flaps are fitted right up to the fuselage. To meet the specification higher flaps are required, but the position of the rear spar limits the flaps chord to about 23%. Estimated stalling and approach speeds, based on a landing weight of 10,000lb, are compared in the following table:

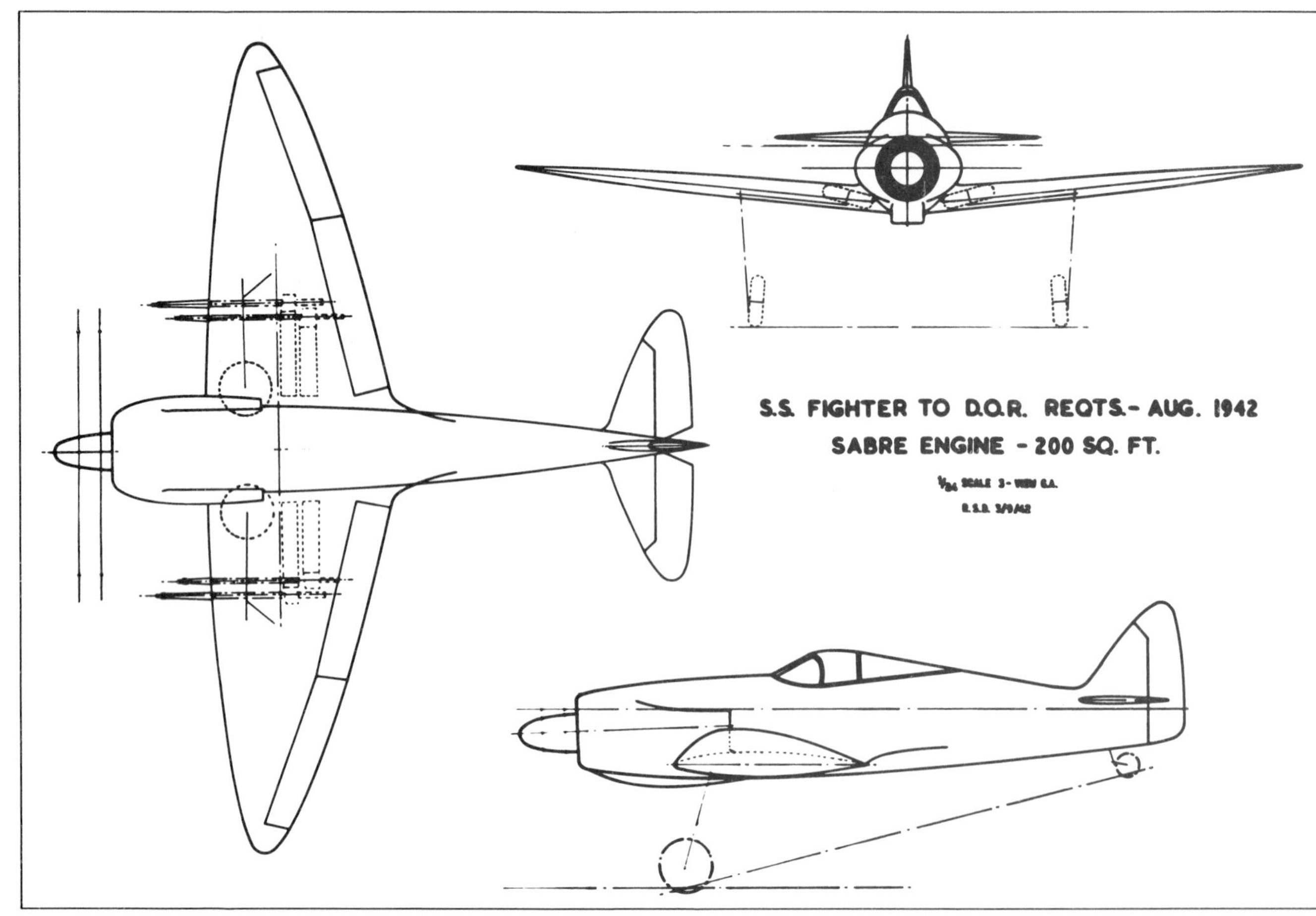

Wing area S sq ft	Wing Span ft	Overall flap span / Wing span	Type of flap	Est CL max. (engine off)	Estimated speed (Knots) Stalling engine off	Stalling engine on	Appch engine on
Specification							65
249	40.4	0.51	23% slotted	1.85	80	69	83
275	41	0.60	" "	1.90	75	64	77
275	41	0.60	23^5 Fowler	2.05	72	62	74
275	41	0.60	35% Fowler or 23^5 Fowler + split flap	2.25	69	59	71

In October 1942 the Admiralty received yet another proposal from Supermarine with modified plan wings and tailplane and folding wings. What Supermarine was proposing was a smaller, lighter aeroplane based broadly on that submitted in the previous March. The folding outer panels were retained but the wings now folded upwards. It had an area of 200 sq. ft. Engine was the Napier Sabre driving a six (2 × 3) bladed contra prop with cooling radiator positioned below the engine cowling. Oil cooler was situated below the engine also and engine exhaust was via ducts at the rear of the engine.

An approach speed of about 70 knots requires a 35% Fowler flap, which is not acceptable without considerable modifications to the wing structure, or a 23% Fowler flap with a small split flap attached to it. Some further increase in CL may be possible by extending the flap underneath the body as on the Firefly.

An increase in tail volume ratio to .42, combined with the greater wing area, requires a tail area of 43 sq ft instead of 33 sq ft. A further increase may be required to give adequate stability at high altitudes and control for landing.

Top Speed. The specification calls for a speed of not less than 360 knots (415 mph) at 23,000 ft. In estimating top speed it has been assumed that the wing area is 275 sq. ft. and the tail area of 43 sq ft. The assumed horsepower, including ejector exhaust and intake drag, for the high altitude Griffon is 1,610 at 23,000 ft and 1,650 at 30,000, the S blower height (allowing for ram effect). With these assumptions the top speed is 344 knots (396 mph) at 23,000 ft and 374 (430) at 30,000.

Endurance. The specifications ask for (1) ¼hr at maximum climbing rpm, ¼hr at maximum power and at least 1½ hours at maximum cruising power in weak mixture at 23,000 ft. (2) Two hours extra with external tanks. To satisfy the specification 170 gallons of fuel is required internally and an additional 135 gallons in external tanks.

Conclusions. The requirement of a minimum approach speed of 65 knots is a severe one and cannot be satisfied without increased wing area and high lift flaps. With the high altitude Griffon engine the top speed of 360 knots should be reached at about 27,000 ft, but not at the specified height of 23,000 ft.

An examination of this estimate and comparison of the proposed Griffon Seafire with folding wing of 1939 shows that the Admiralty and Vickers were correct in their original proposals. However, by this time the Seafire Mk III with folding wings was in the offing. DP845 and DP851, Spitfires with Griffon engines, were undergoing trials and the Admiralty were again forced to await the arrival of the Seafire with Griffon engine, the Mk XV.

"FAR AND AWAY THE BEST INTERCEPTOR"

Ever aware of the need to update Fleet Air Arm equipment the Admiralty was keeping a watching brief on Spitfire development, and following upon the introduction of the Seafire Mk III was looking for its successor. The natural replacement for the III appeared to be the Spitfire F Mk VIII, or Mk IX conversions, trials of the former having started on 8 January when eight aircraft fitted with A frame arrester gear, plus one more aircraft fitted with a sting hook, were undergoing trials at Crail. The Admiralty had asked for trials of a similarly modified Mk IX but the Air Ministry was against such a conversion for it was considered that the next generation Seafire would be used solely for the war against Japan, and as large numbers of Spitfire VIIIs were due to, or in the process of, being despatched to the Middle and Far East war zones, these fighters should be modified at the reception MUs and put immediately into service with the Navy.

Because of this background information the Admiralty requested development of a Seafire equivalent of the Mk XII Spitfire when it was introduced into RAF service, and as a result Supermarine produced Specification No 471 on 29 January 1943 for such an aeroplane. The proposed Seafire variant was an amalgam of several distinct Spitfire/Seafire types, and although utilisation of basic, major components did result in a speeding up of development and production time, it also produced some odd combinations. Engine installation was to be similar to that of the Mk XII complete with a cooling system derived from the F Mk V radiator in the starboard wing and the Mk IX radiator in the port in order to meet all tropical requirements. Fuel systems consisted of an internal capacity of 100 gallons, plus 60 gallons in externally mounted drop tanks. Fuselage was similar to that of the Seafire Mk III and the folding wing was to be based upon that of the F Mk VC with universal armament fittings. The empennage was a modified F Mk VIII, but with a broad chord rudder, rear spar attachment, retractable tailwheel and main chassis of same. F Mk IX Mareng fuel cells were specified for internal wing fuel.

The Griffon specified was the Mk VI (RG 14SM) driving a Rotol R22/4F5/8, four-blade propeller of 10ft 5in diameter. Power output was 1,750 hp which enabled a maximum speed of 383mph to be attained at 13,000 feet. The new aeroplane could climb to 10,000 feet in approximately two minutes. Wing armament consisted of the standard 'B' wing of two 20mm Hispano cannon and four .303 Brownings. It could also carry one 500 lb bomb; rocket projectiles; two 250 lb bombs. Fuel was stowed in four main wing and fuselage tanks, plus combat tanks under the wings. The plumbing was complicated, but it worked.

Following the normal requirement procedure the Air Ministry issued Specification N 4/43 for six prototypes to be built by Supermarine under the Type number 377. Serial numbers were NS487, 490, 493 and PK240, 243 and 245. Designation posed a problem for initially it was known as the Seafire Mk XII. However, it was thought that this would clash with the Spitfire Mk XII and the designation Seafire Mk IV was proposed for the Spitfire IV designation had been dropped in favour of Mk XX. But, the RAF already had in service the Spitfire PR Mk IV and all designations up to, and including , the PR Mk XIII had been allocated; the F Mk XIV reserved for the production model of a Griffon engined Spitfire development of the Griffon powered F Mk VIIIs undergoing trials. So, it had to be the Seafire F Mk XV which was adopted on 15 July. Official reasoning is inexplicable for both the RAF and Fleet Air Arm were operating the Spitfire and Seafire Mk I, II and III, and the explanation was that following the Air Ministry's decision to rationalise variant numbering all future Spitfire/Seafire models would be numbered consecutively to avoid a break in the numerical sequence.

Prototype Seafire XV, NS487, was completed in late November 1943 and weighed in the experimental hangar at Hursley Park on 4 December. It had a tare of 6,013 lb and an auw of 7,861. At this stage the catapult spools had not been fitted. Orders were placed with Westland Aircraft and Cunliffe Owen for 503 examples between July 1943 and March 1944. Production models differed slightly from the prototypes by having a larger oil cooler intake under the port wing, matching that under the starboard; a larger spinner and lengthened engine cowling due to the longer engine.

One Admiral was not at all enthusiastic about yet another Spitfire/Seafire conversion and was to write a scathing report which compared the new model with contemporary American naval fighters. The DAW&FT swiftly replied saying: "Neither the Corsair nor Hellcat can look at the Spitfire Mk IX or XII. It has been decided to produce a naval version of the XII and when we get this, or a modified Mk IX, we shall have far and away the best interceptor in the world, greatly in advance of anything the Americans have now, or as far as we can see, even projected. As it is there is no American fighter, with the exception of the Hellcat, which would be of any use against the best enemy shore-based aircraft. Americans belittle our aircraft and it is a travesty of judgment which can only be written by one so blinded by the Coral Sea and Midway battles". Both viewpoints were extreme but understandable against the backdrop of the sea-air war.

Production started in the Winter of 1944 and first deliveries the following March. The first 384 aircraft, bulk of the production run, still had the original 'A' frame arrester hook of the Mk III. The only difference was a stress requirement of 10,500 lb instead of 7,000. The 'A' frame then gave way to the so-called 'sting', which was installed in the stern of the fuselage

PK240 prototype Seafire XV, minus arrester hook.

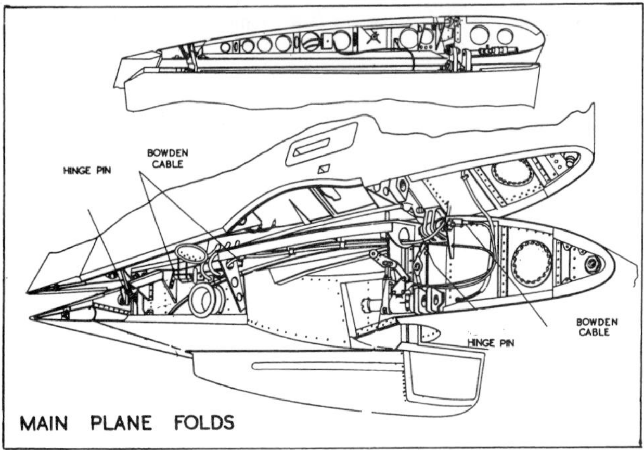

Main plane wing folds.

Sting type hook.

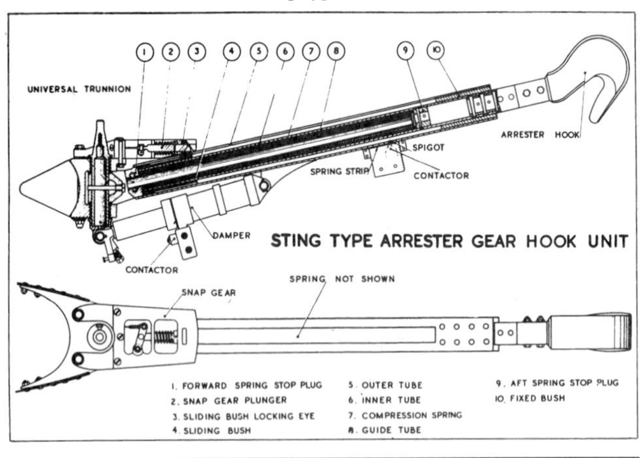

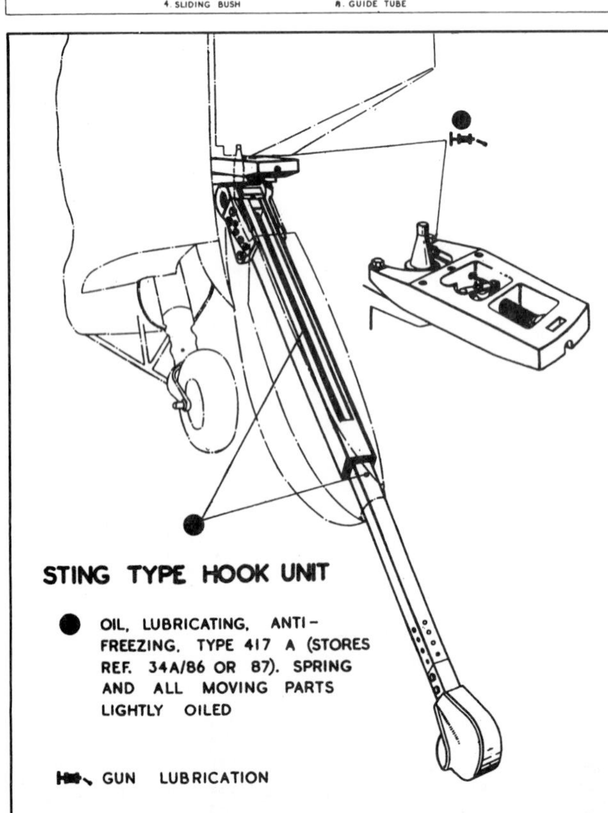

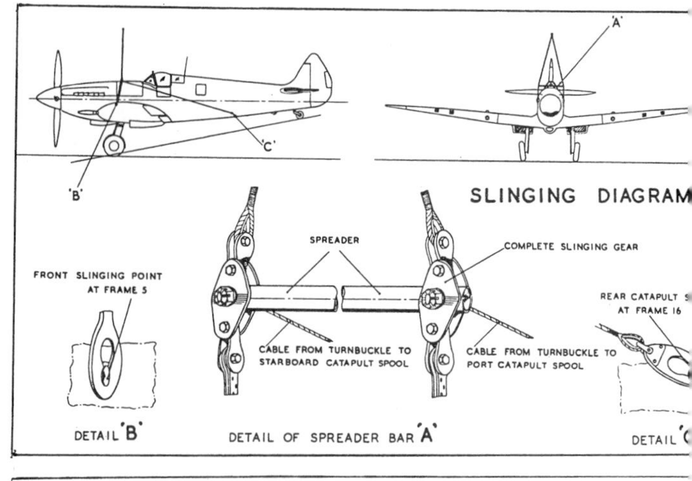

Structure 'A' frame hook.

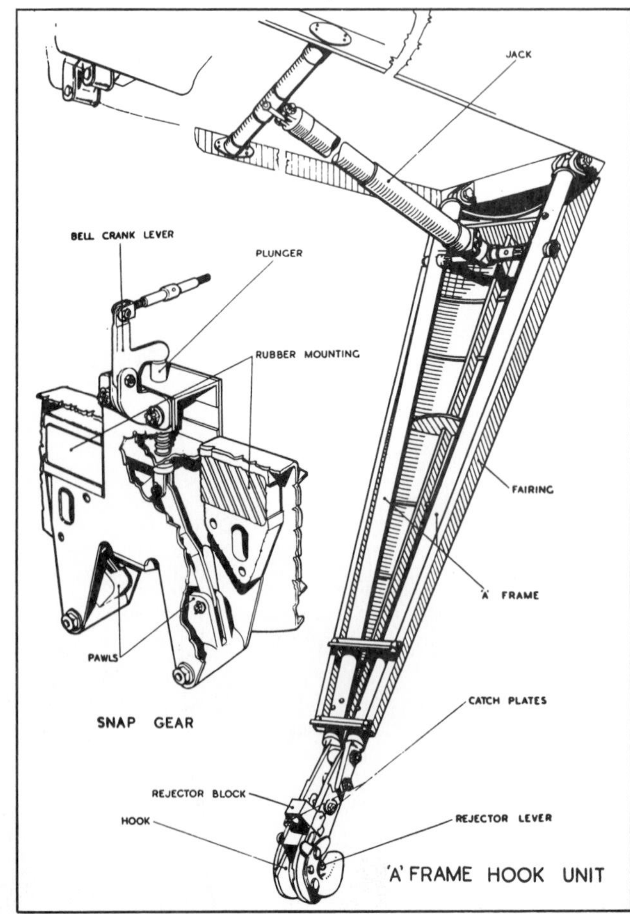

Fly off after missing arrester wires.

Seafire comes to grief after picking up and then dropping wire.

Deck crew manhandle a Mk XV.

Picking up the wire, HMS Pretoria Castle.

at the rudder base. The hook was spring loaded in its housing and when released extended aft about eighteen inches. On release the arm and hook housing were free to drop into the fully lowered position; it could pivot laterally within an included angle of about 30°. To prevent rebound on striking the carrier deck an oleo pneumatic damper was fitted. After landing the hook was stowed in the housing and the latter locked up manually. The sting hook was originally fitted to NS487, and after trials at Boscombe Down and Farnborough the decision was taken to standardise the fitting on all future Seafires.

This decision may appear to have been a mistake for although the rear position of the sting hook helped solve a problem associated with the centre of gravity, the Farnborough and Boscombe Down trials proved conclusively that the 'A' frame was the better proposition. A tailwheel guard was also a necessary fitment with the sting as the wheel tended to foul the arrester wires. This modification was originally installed on late production aircraft fitted with the sting, and retrofitted to earlier machines. In August 1946 all deck landings with the Seafire XV were prohibited, the fault being the Griffon engine. The supercharger clutch slipped at high rpm, and boost settings considered unreliable for carrier operations. Rolls-Royce resolved the problem by supplying a modified clutch which was installed on all aircraft from early 1947.

The Mk XV was capable of catapult launching and RATOG assisted take off, but the Navy wanted something better and needed to have their fighters launched without the preliminaries of loading the catapult or fitting the RATOG rockets. What was suggested was 'tail down acceleration', a forerunner of steam catapult launch. Two cables picking up towing points on each side of the fuselage were attached to a single, central deck hook. Trials took place in September 1943 and were, initially, a failure due to chassis weakness. The problem was passed to Farnborough and on 14 January 1944 they reported that when equipped with link type oleos the Seafire XV was capable of tail down acceleration, provided the initial G could ber held at 2¾. At the same time FAE agreed to flight test the first prototype sting hook.

By June 1944 the RAE was able to report on progress with the accelerating scheme and a Supermarine team went along to Farnborough on the 13th to discuss the situation. Twenty-two launches had been made and they varied from 2.8G to 3.1, with maximum acceleration occurring after four seconds. At an auw of 7,850 lb the Seafire's tyres were fully compressed but there was no evidence of damage. The trials were to continue and the aircraft, NS490, was transferred to RNAS Arbroath. The stern was badly damaged in July and a new unit fitted and Lt. Cmdr Brown began a series of ADDLE trials on the 19th.

The first production aircraft from Westland, SR446, was delivered to High Post on 2 October 1944 for weighing and CoG determination. Tare was 6,274 lb, and auw 8,021. The first Cunliffe Owen Mk XV arrived on 23 March 1945 and weight variation was minor – tare 6,245 lb, auw 8,018. Carrier trials on *HMS Pretoria Castle* began in July using the prototype PK245, which was also to be used for a series of trials in the tail down position. Nine accelerated take offs were made at an auw of 7,980 lb and one with a 50 gallon torpedo tank filled with water.

Supermarine Seafire F Mk XV

Due to a minor accident with the hold back gear PK245 was sent for repair, returning to the carrier on 30 July. A total of 59 take-offs and landings followed, including 14 in the tail down attitude. The trials were considered very satisfactory, particularly as forty five unassisted take offs were made with full ordnance loads.

The various loadings and CoG positions were:

Loads	Weight at T/O	CoG
Normal load (7980 lb) and full 50 gallon o/ld tank	8380	8.1
Normal load, plus 50 gal tank full and two $22\frac{1}{2}$ gal combat tanks empty	8565	8.15
Normal load and 500 lb bomb on carrier	8530	8.1
Normal load, 500 lb bomb and two empty combat tanks	8570	8.1
Normal load and 500 lb bomb combat tanks full	8890	8.0
Normal load and 45 gal blister o/ld tank full	8380	8.05
Normal load combat tanks full	8340	7.75

When the under fuselage drop tanks were full an equivalent amount of petrol was siphoned from the main tanks to preserve the weight balance. RPs could not be carried when wing combat tanks were carried.

The first production aircraft entered service with No 802 Squadron in May 1945 following delivery of SR446 on 26 September the previous year, and by the end of June 1946 the remaining Mk III Seafires were withdrawn from service to be replaced by the newer models. A near fatal accident occurred to SR483 during October when the pilot climbed to 35,000ft and made a slow peel off, setting rpm low and changing to MS gear. Severe buffeting started and he was thrown violently about the cockpit having no control over the aircraft whatsoever. The oscillations were so severe that the harness straps would not remain tight. The pilot blacked out and came to as the aircraft eased out of the dive at 6,000 ft. Tests showed that the aircraft had reached a speed of 310 knots at 30,000, equivalent to a true speed of 531mph (Mach .80) and was subjected to approximately 11G. The bottom pins at wing fold joints had started to shear and the bottom plating just aft of the main spar one foot outside the folding joint had stretched sufficiently to buckle the rivets. The elevator horn had broken off and the stern end of the fuselage showed signs of strain. Laminations of the wooden propeller had opened at the roots. The pilot was extremely fortunate that the Seafire had recovered automatically.

NS487, Seafire MkXV prototype, at Boscombe Down.

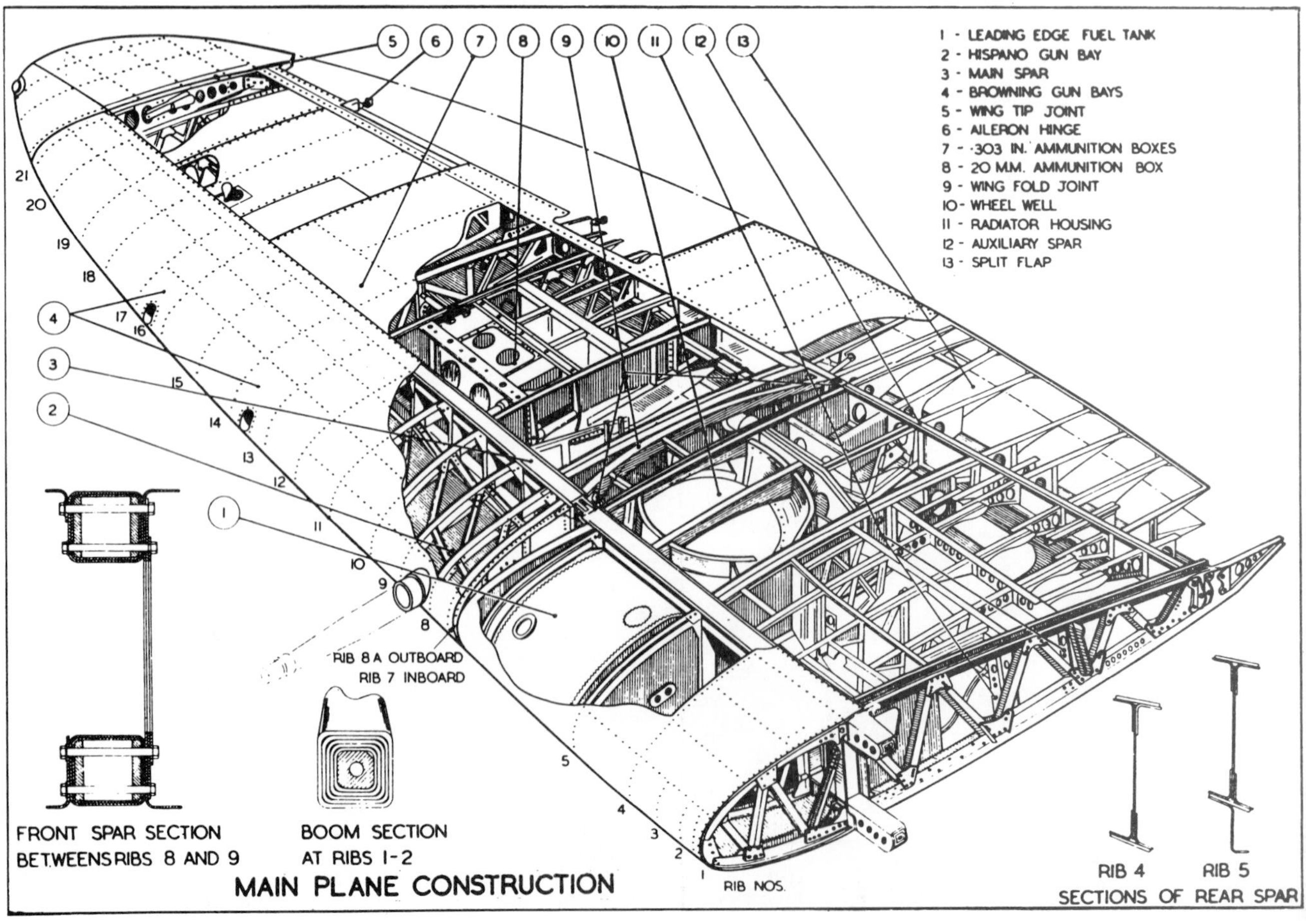

1 - LEADING EDGE FUEL TANK
2 - HISPANO GUN BAY
3 - MAIN SPAR
4 - BROWNING GUN BAYS
5 - WING TIP JOINT
6 - AILERON HINGE
7 - ·303 IN. AMMUNITION BOXES
8 - 20 MM. AMMUNITION BOX
9 - WING FOLD JOINT
10 - WHEEL WELL
11 - RADIATOR HOUSING
12 - AUXILIARY SPAR
13 - SPLIT FLAP

RIB 8 A OUTBOARD
RIB 7 INBOARD

FRONT SPAR SECTION
BETWEEN RIBS 8 AND 9

BOOM SECTION
AT RIBS 1-2

RIB NOS.

RIB 4
RIB 5
SECTIONS OF REAR SPAR

MAIN PLANE CONSTRUCTION

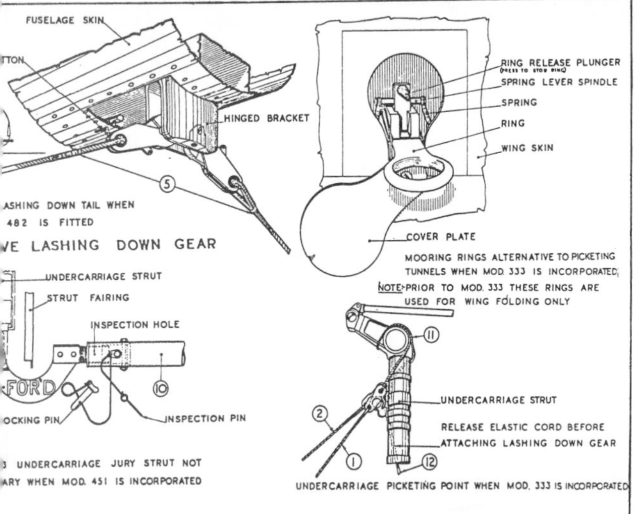

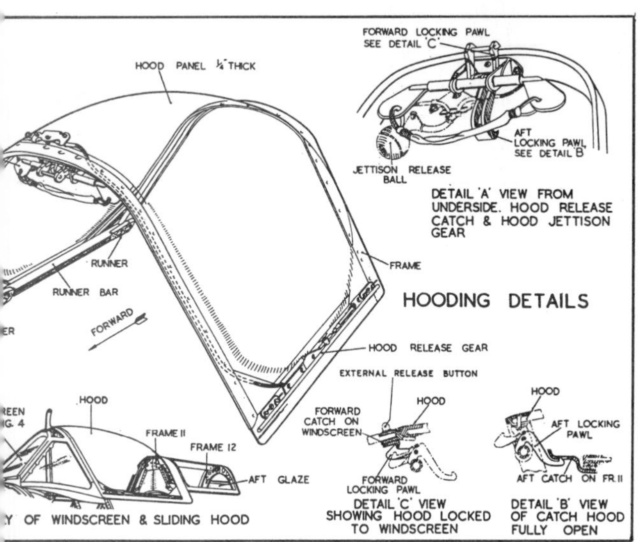

Rebecca was installed in a number of Seafire XVs in 1945; radio controlled target variants were named Sheep and Shepherd.

The Griffon engine had changed the nature of Mitchell's fighter and it was more difficult to fly and control than the original, almost dainty, prototype of 1936. The many pilot's comments of various flights and trials are reproduced here:

NS487 Prototype. (Shea-S 13-12-44). Long chord sting hook type rudder. It is considered the interconnected throttle and propeller would be highly unsatisfactory in Seafire XVs and the decision to introduce them should be seriously reconsidered. (25-8-44). Check of interconnecting throttle and propeller.

NS490 Prototype. (Shea-S 13-12-44). Long chord sting hook type rudder. During this flight the previous impression gained on adequate directional stability and control with the type of rudder fitted was confirmed. (Errington 14-12-44). Check for vibration with new propeller. None found. **(Quill 11-1-45).** Spinning at Boscombe Down with large chord rudder from 29,000ft. (Furlong 6-7-44). Revs and boost check prior to delivery Farnborough. Aircraft on verge of instability and it is considered that the metal elevator should be linked up with the sting type hook. (Quill 18-9-44). Spinning with small rudder. First spin at 20,000ft. Climbed again to 20,000 and after various spins stick put forward. The spin went flat and continued until full engine power applied. This made the spin flatter and faster and there was no chance of recovery and the tail parachute was pulled. This jerked the tail upwards and altered the spin from flat to very steep. **Finally** stopped by use of engine and aileron. The tail parachute broke away at weak link and it is thought that this link may be too weak with a danger of breaking before spin has been stopped. (Shea-S 12-12-44). Investigation of directional stability and control. Large chord sting hook rudder fitted. Effective in all conditions of flight.

NS493 Prototype. (Quill 27-8-44). Tests for A.D.D.L.S. The aircraft is in my opinion a bad proposition as regards a deck landing approach. The fine pitch settings of the propeller are much too coarse and accounts for the low revs and low drag during the approach. It is important that the settings be altered. **(28-8-44). New windscreen fitted, much better than old type.** Propeller pitch still considered to be too coarse. The aircraft floats too much and is not a good deck landing aeroplane. It is not so easy to put down as a Seafire III.

PK240 Prototype. (Shea-S 15-3-45). Runway landings at

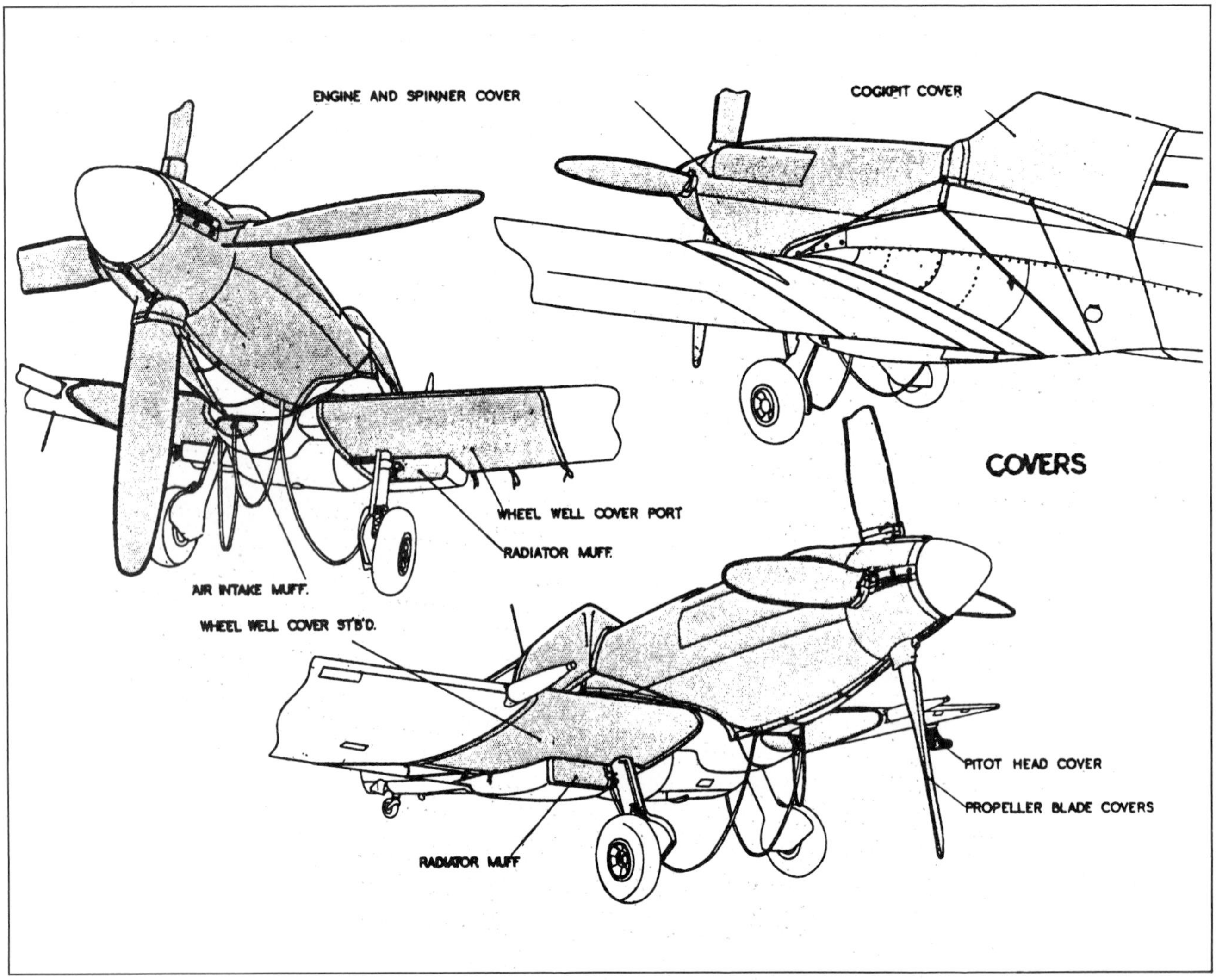

COVERS

ENGINE AND SPINNER COVER
COCKPIT COVER
WHEEL WELL COVER PORT
RADIATOR MUFF
AIR INTAKE MUFF
WHEEL WELL COVER STB'D.
PITOT HEAD COVER
PROPELLER BLADE COVERS
RADIATOR MUFF

Aircraft covers

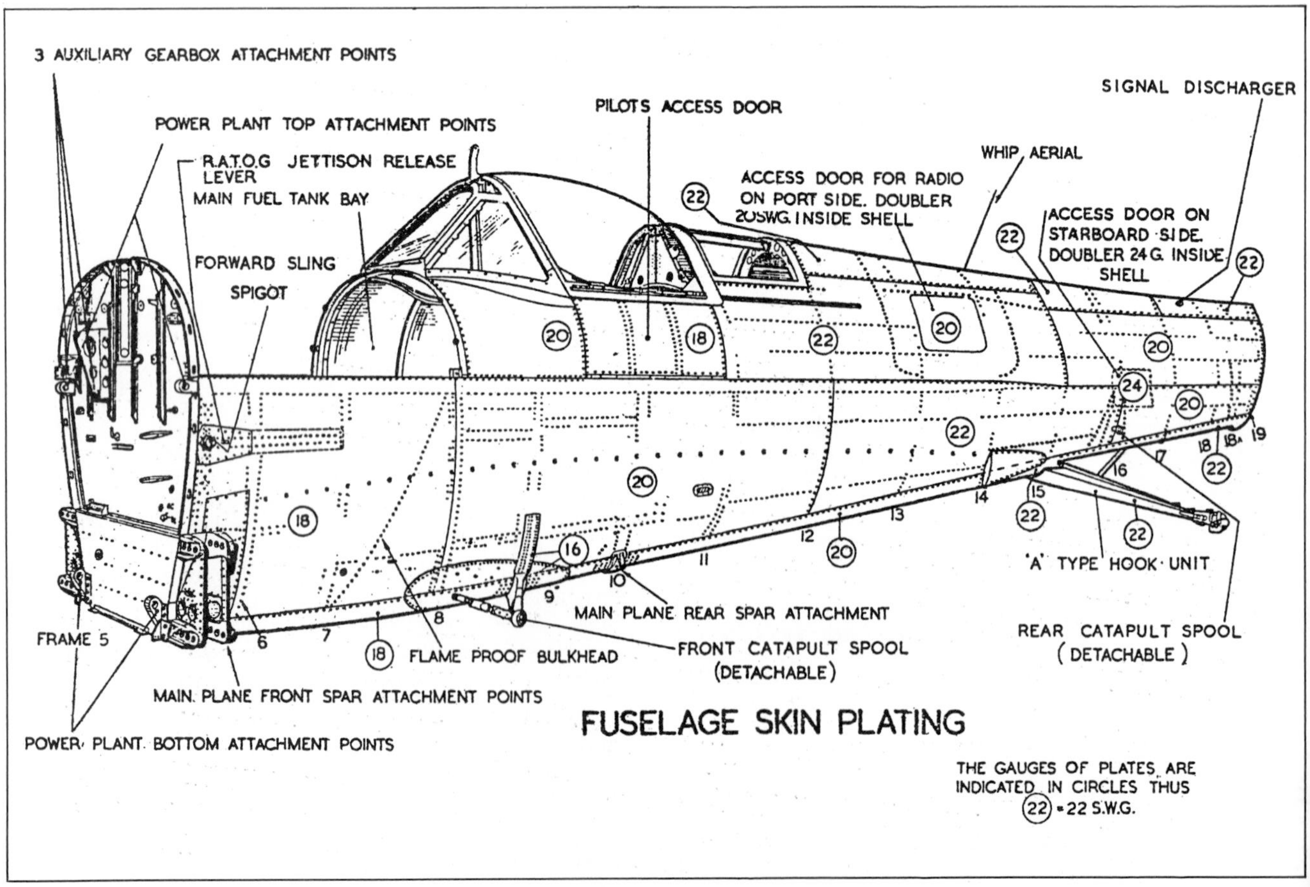

FUSELAGE SKIN PLATING

3 AUXILIARY GEARBOX ATTACHMENT POINTS
POWER PLANT TOP ATTACHMENT POINTS
R.A.T.O.G JETTISON RELEASE LEVER
MAIN FUEL TANK BAY
FORWARD SLING
SPIGOT
PILOTS ACCESS DOOR
ACCESS DOOR FOR RADIO ON PORT SIDE. DOUBLER 20SWG. INSIDE SHELL
WHIP AERIAL
SIGNAL DISCHARGER
ACCESS DOOR ON STARBOARD SIDE. DOUBLER 24G. INSIDE SHELL
'A' TYPE HOOK UNIT
REAR CATAPULT SPOOL (DETACHABLE)
MAIN PLANE REAR SPAR ATTACHMENT
FRONT CATAPULT SPOOL (DETACHABLE)
FLAME PROOF BULKHEAD
FRAME 5
MAIN PLANE FRONT SPAR ATTACHMENT POINTS
POWER PLANT BOTTOM ATTACHMENT POINTS

THE GAUGES OF PLATES ARE INDICATED IN CIRCLES THUS (22) = 22 S.W.G.

Aldermaston and on grass at Gosport and High Post when fitted with modified improved rebound type Port oleo leg. Undercarriage satisfactory. (Morgan 21-3-45). Several landings at Aldermaston. No appreciable difference from normal observed. (Shea-S 5-4-45). Flown with second of two rejected Westland metal elevators. It is still considered to be unacceptable. The stability of aircraft fore and aft is good and elevator light. (Shea-S 5-4-45). Twelve inches of metal beading fitted to trailing edges of elevator. Result is an unbelievable improvement in elevator characteristics. (Shea-S 17-4-45). Fitted with Westland Metal elevator destined for Boscombe Down's use. First flight with elevator as delivered and found unacceptable. Second flight 6 inches beading fitted on trailing edges, unacceptable, particularly at high speeds. Third flight with 12 inches of beading each side. Satisfactory. (Shea-S 18-4-45). Fifteen inches of 5/16th" beading on upper surface of starboard wing tip trailing edge to investigate effect on lateral trim. Some improvement. (Shea-S 19-4-45). Flown with port flap set down approximately 5° by means of a series of wooden blocks fitted along between the trailing edge of flap and wing giving a gap of 1½". Right wing low on the climb and progressively left wing low up to limiting speed. (Shea-S 21-4-45). Wing tips removed for assessing effects on the lateral reversal of trim. Slight improvement and control up to 350 knots. (Shea-S 27-4-45). Flown with original Westland metal elevator with reduced horn area. Improvement at speeds in excess of 220 knots. This elevator is like the F Mk 21 scheme.

PK243 (Quill 7-10-44). Out of trim and the directional gyro not working. Excessive amount of aileron displacement and starboard one floated up 1 to 1½" at medium speeds. (Shea-S 14-10-44). Two short flights for making adjustments to interconnected throttle and propeller control and aileron trim. The aircraft will then be flown north for deck landing trials. (Shea-S 22-2-45). Fitted five blade propeller. Brief handling for stability with new propeller. Three ADDLS carried out and I cannot entertain much hope regarding the alleged increased drag to be obtained from this propeller for deck landings. Starboard aileron floated up excessively in dives to nearly 2" at 380 knots. Considerable reversal of later trim from right to left. (Shea-S 10-3-45). Fitted Westland metal elevator and flown at CG of 8" aft of datum. Unacceptable in all conditions of flight. (Shea-S 11-3-45). Starboard wing incidence decreased by 15 mins. of angle. No effect on lateral control. At 400 knots the port aileron droops ¼" and starboard floats up well over 2". Aircraft so left wing low that both hands are required on the control column to hold wings level. It was noted also that at speeds in excess of 300 knots the starboard wing upper surface on the inboard side of the aileron was panting excessively. The starboard aileron upfloat is verging on being dangerous. (Shea-S 6-5-45). Fittings in trailing edge wing roots giving an increase of 15 mins. to port wing incidence and a decrease of 15 mins. to starboard. Later trim characteristics improved but starboard aileron upfloat still excessive at 1½ to 2". (Shea-S 10-5-45). Flown with starboard aileron tab raised ⅛" on trailing edge. Improvement in lateral trim. (Shea-S 12-6-45). Port wing incidence increased by 25 mins. and starboard decreased by 15. No improvement.

NS490, second Mk XV prototype.

Seafire XV of No.802 (Canadian) Squadron, Arbroath.

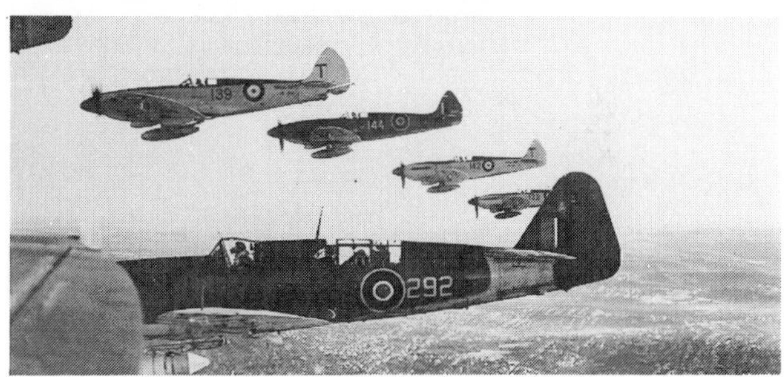

F XVs of No 804 Squadron from HMS Glory out of Sydney Harbour.

PK245 Prototype. (Shea-S 22-2-45). Engine needs adjusting, passed to Rolls-Royce. Aircraft satisfactory. (Shea-S 12-3-45). Wing combat tank fuel transfer check. Transfer time 5½ to 6 min. (Shea-S 16-3-45). Handling with combat tanks full. Aircraft satisfactory. (Shea-S 21-4-45). Fitted with adjustable aileron hinges. (Quill 22-4-45). Port aileron lowered to the extent of .15. At speed to 360 knots no reversal. At 370 both lateral and directional reversal took place, aircraft left wing low and yawing to left simulaneously. Propeller vibration unacceptable. (Quill 2-5-45). Jettision trials of combat tanks. Shea-Simonds flying Boston chase plane for photographs. Both tanks went away cleanly.

PR338. (Quill 22-3-45). Handling with metal elevator. Best

Union of Burma Air Force UB403 wearing B Condition markings G-15-214. It was ex SR642.

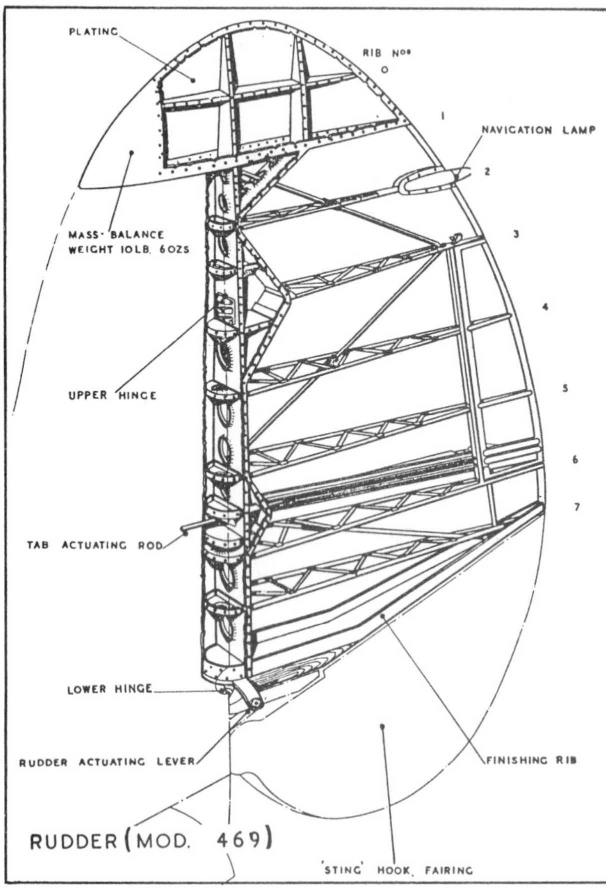

metal elevator I have ever tried and if all were manufactured to this standard things would be a lot better. (Shea-S 26-3-45). Ailerons unsatisfactory. Considerable degree of lateral trim reversal from right to left and starboard aileron was floating up considerably in dives. Port flap door opening at speeds over 370 knots and there seems to be an excessive amount of oxygen tubing in the cockpit.

SR446. 1st production aircraft. (Shea-S 28-9-44). Ailerons not satisfactory. (Shea-S 3-10-44). Flight confirms original impressions of bad directional stability and control. (Quill 6-10-44). 1. Why has this aircraft got the small throttle boss, (2) Why are the shoulder straps too short on all Westland Aircraft, (3) Why is there such a length of oxygen tubing in the cockpit? Directional stability bad. It seems that really the Seafire XV needs the large fin. (Shea-S 18-10-44). Rudder removed and that of PK243 fitted. Directional stability improved. (Morgan 4-10-44). Photography sortie with MAP Hudson. (Shea-S 18-10-44). Stiffer pair of ailerons fitted. (Quill 27-10-44). Flown with Castle Bromwich production metal elevator which was very good. (Shea-S 4-11-44). A.D.D.L.S satisfactory.

SR448 (Shea-S 11-1-45) Flown with mock-up combat tanks in bad weather conditions. Handled well. (Shea-S 17-1-45). Spinning trials at 15,000 and 25,000ft.

SR459 (Shea-S 22-3-45). Westland aircraft due to go to America. Fitted with interconnected throttle and propeller control. This is wrong and Westland should be restrained from continuing the practice. The port rear wing hinge door opened in flight at 300 knots. (Shea-S 23-4-45). Port wing door opened immediately after take-off and remained open throughout the flight. This fault, and others, were reported after I first flew this aeroplane and nothing appears to have been done about them. I WANT TO KNOW WHY. If it were not for the fact that this aircraft is being sent to America with an un-strengthened 'A' frame hook, it would now be possible to land it on a ship without risk to life or limb. Finally, 6" of beading has been fitted to the elevator trailing edge. (Shea-S 24-4-45). I have now reached the conclusion that the possibility of this aircraft ever going to America is more remote. Exactly the same list of snags were recorded during this flight as during my flight yesterday and, in addition, the Coffman Starter Index Control is not working. Sdn Ldr Morgan flew this aeroplane after the snags were again alleged to have been put right. He now reports the tail wheel light is remaining on when the undercarriage has been selected up, the starboard oleo is flat or very much down and the main wheels are out of balance. (Shea-S 26-4-45). Aircraft flown to check work on reported snags. (1) The top cowling is a very bad fit at its trailing edge. (2) The port flap door is still opening (3) The engine is cutting under application of positive G.

General arrangement of Seafire F Mk XV showing 'A' frame and 'sting' hooks.

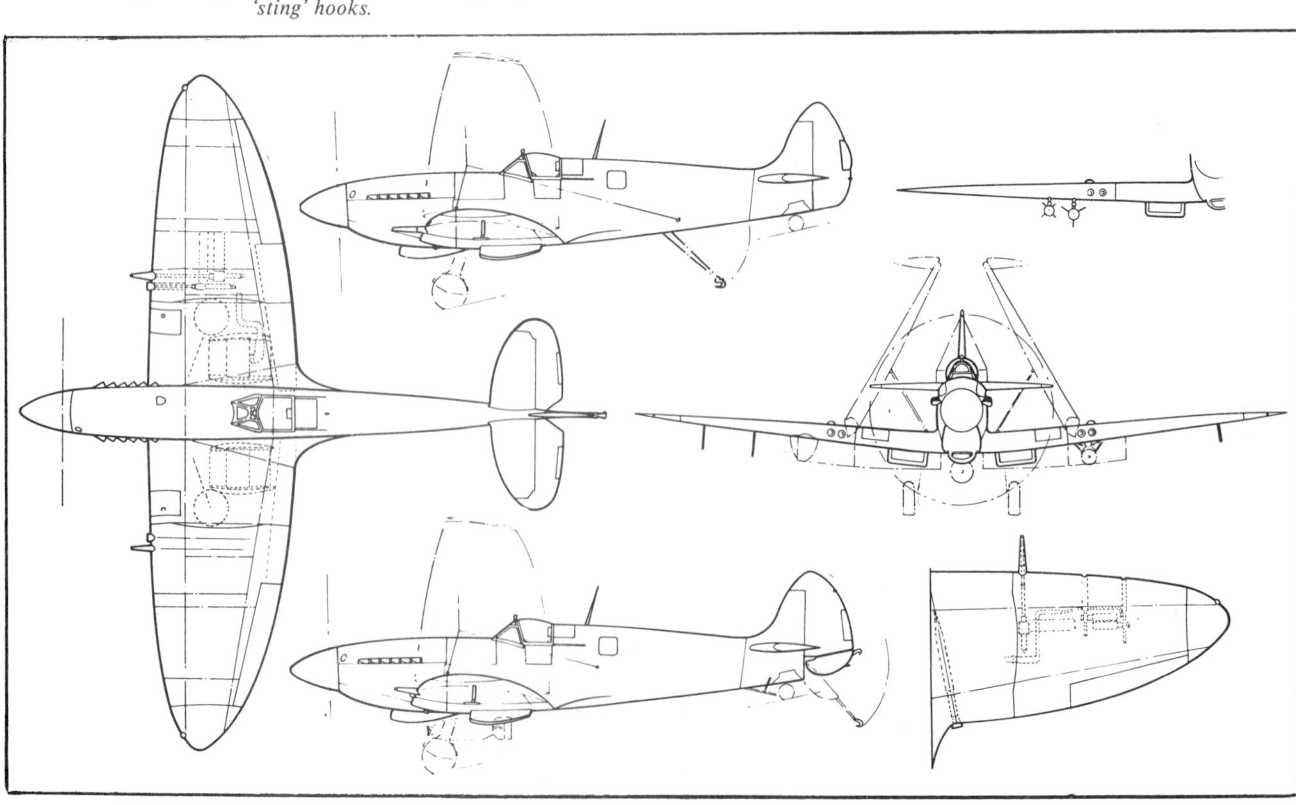

SR460 (Shea-S 22-2-45). Aircraft delivered by Chief Test Pilot Westlands. Aileron upfloat in dives 2 to 2½ inches.

NE490, Farnborough August 1944. Auw 7,850lb. Arrester Gear trials with sting hook installation. A sting hook installation has been designed with a view to decreasing tail rise during arrested landings. Trials required to proof the installation. Brief trials were carried out at RNAS Arbroath on 1 June 1944 and were terminated owing to collapse of tail wheel. Damage also sustained due to arrester rope catching the sting hook fairing. As a result the fairing has been modified and a guard added in front of the wheel.

Trials with the *Illustrious* type arrester gear with a rope span of 80 feet. On 18/19 July taxying runs were made at entry speeds from 37 to 65 knots giving a maximum retardation of 2.49G. Four fly-ins were made successfully on 20th with entry speeds of 65 to 67 knots. Aircraft during arrestment was satisfactory and tail rise moderate.

NS487 fitted sting hook of welded plate and experimental accellerator hooks by R.A.E. NS490 with Vickers sting hook. October 1944. Arrested landing trials *HMS Pretoria Castle* to proof Seafire XV. PK243 and SR448 fitted 'V' hook and snap gear. Twenty nine landings with 'V' hook and 32 with sting hook made during October. Stressed for 1.5G necessitating wind speed over deck of not less than 25 knots. One barrier crash with sting hook aircraft when hook failed to pick up wire on account of tail high attitude after three point touch down. Main undercarriage tyres burst on several landings caused by tyre fouling undercarriage fairing. Aircraft returned to High Post for modifications:- stronger 'A' frames designed for 2G fitted to 'V' frame aircraft and undercarriage fairings cut away. Finer pitch propellers fitted, modified radiator flaps.

November. Trials continued with a further 64 landings with 'V' hooks and 40 with sting. One of 'V' aircraft had a new

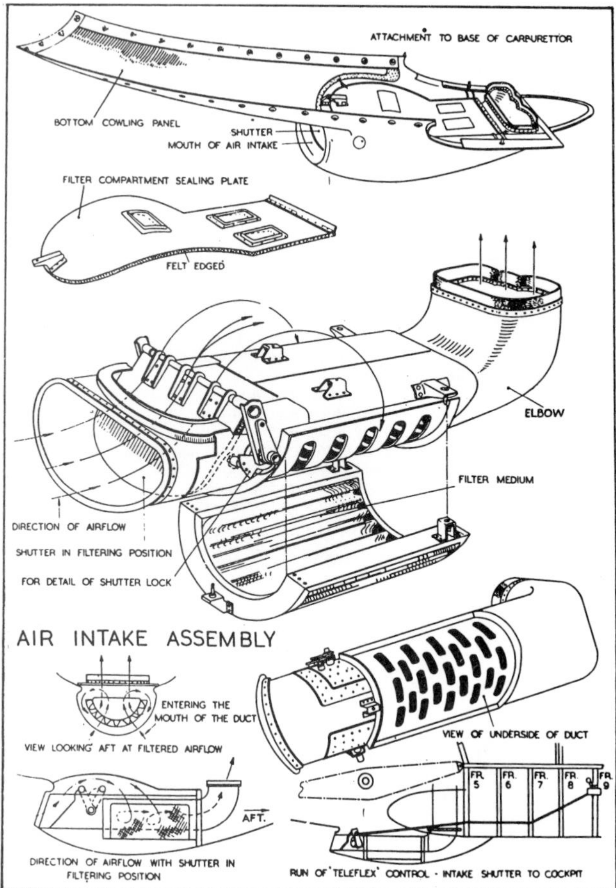

Far East Mk XV comes to grief.

type arrester arm damper and with this the hook returned quickly to the deck and picked up an early wire. One case of undercarriage failure due to leg being forced inwards by excessive side loads. NS487 was landed on *HMS Implacable* for 14 trial landings.

PK245. Tail down launching trials on *HMS Pretoria Castle*, July and August 1945. Investigations to permit launching from type of gear (steam catapult) to be fitted on future British aircraft carriers. The aircraft was fitted with experimental hooks to accommodate the accelerator launching bridles at RAE and satisfactory launches were made from the C.I. (cartridge initiated) accelerator at Farnborough. The acceleration applied by the launching gear was not to exceed the following figures for the various loading conditions:-

Loading condition	auw	maximum applied G
Normal service loading	7985 lb	2.9
Normal plus 30gal blister tank	8258	2.75
Normal plus 2 × 22½gal combat tanks	8347	2.7
Normal plus 45gal blister tank	8389	2.7
Normal plus 50gal torpedo tank	84.0	2.7
Normal plus 500lb bomb	8540	2.6
Normal plus 2 × 22½gal combat tanks & 500lb bomb	8902	2.45

It was agreed that the aircraft should not be landed at an auw exceeding 8,073lb. The tests at RAE were all satisfactory except in two instances when the launching bridle was carried away by the tail wheel. During initial trials on *Pretoria Castle* ten launches were made and on the second the bridle caught the overload tank. The hooks were removed and the 'V' frame hook locked up, the aircraft relying on the sting hook. Three launches were made with the torpedo o/ld tank filled with 50 gals. of fresh water. Tear away patches operated by undercarriage retraction ensured the tank emptying before landing. Two launches were made with the wing combat tanks full and a 500lb bomb fitted. The bomb was dropped and fuel transfer made from wing to main tanks.

The trials showed that the Seafire XV was entirely suitable for tail down launching in all conditions stated and it was intended to test the type from the single track American H.IV.C accelerator fitted to converted escort vessels.

Vickers-Armstrongs. November 1945. Loadings arrangements of Seafire XV (and XVII) under following conditions of take-off, flying and landing:- Normal take-off, RATOG, accelerated take-off, flying, normal landing, arrested landing. (1) Rocket projectiles cannot be fitted when combat tanks are carried, (2) Combination of bombs and rockets are not considered, (3) Any lighter combinations of stores is acceptable, the combinations quoted being maximum, (4) No drop tank can be fitted to fuselage when accelerating under 4-point method (catapult) due to fouling of air intake on 30gal. Seafire tank and of the catapult gear on other tanks, (5) 250 and 500lb bombs cannot be fitted to fuselage station when accelerating under 4-point method. Notes on flying- (1) All forms of flying cleared @ auw of 8,500lbs, but only when combat tanks are fitted, (2) Drop tank is released before fighting or dive bombing.

Supermarine Seafire F Mk XV

PR494 and 499. Fort Nelson, Edmonton, Canada, January 1947. Winter Operations. PR494 sustained damage to undercarriage and propeller through continual landings and take-offs on rough strips. A.D.D.L.S carried out. Cold weather starts difficult but fault was that operator tended to under prime before starting and over prime when engine fired. Throttle advanced by one inch and cold starts satisfactory. Cooling satisfactory with 40% water and 60% glycol. Towing by means of hook. Manhandling on snow or icy surface needed at least 12 men. Mainplane folding with no difficulties. Cockpit heating recommended.

SERIAL NUMBERS

Cunliffe-Owen Aircraft Ltd.
Contract No. A/C 2777/C.23(c).

Second order for 150 Seafire Mk III dated July 1943. Built as Seafire Mk XVs between December 1944 and May 1945. PR338-379, 391-436, 449-479 and 492-522.

Third order for 200 Seafire Mk XV dated February 1944. Built as Seafire Mks XV/XVII between June and December 1945. the following serials apply to Mk. XVs built to this third order; SP136-168 and 181-197.(50)

Westland Aircraft Ltd.
Contract No. B.124305/40.

Fifth order for 140 Seafire Mk XV dated February 1944. Built as Mk XVs between September 1944 and April 1945. SR 446-493, 516-547, 568-611 and 630-645.

Sixth order for 503 Seafire Mk XV dated March 1944, Built as Mk XV/XVII between April and November 1945. The following serials apply to Mk XVs built to this sixth order; SW781828, 844-879 and 896-921. Total 450.

NS487 Proto FXV GVI A frame hook, sting hook later. CRD Contract not to be counted on RAF Returns BDn 25-2-44 proto appraisal eng and maintenance., wts & CG load. Trls with 30 gal slipper tank, also 45 gal. Plus 1 × 250lb & 1 × 500lb bombs. VA HPA Haw arrester gerar instal. Farn Apl'44 catapult & arrester gear trls. Acc during trls. VA WD Aug. RNAS Arb 29-9 accelerator, sting hook, throttle calibration trls Oct.

NS490 Proto FXV GVI A frame hook sting hook later. BDn Aug'44 comp trls with SR448 with two types rud, spins and cooling. Right hand spin more violent than left. Arrester gear trls in comp with SR488. Fitt tailwheel arrester guard, tail para & rud horn guard.

NS493 Proto FXV GVI. Con later by WAL to Seafire FXVII proto June'44 BDn same month level speeds & positional error. Carb mono cock contam tests. Eng & maintenance. Aftmost CoG. Reduced area rear fus, tear drop sliding hood with locking device. No IFF fitted.

PK245 Proto F.XV GVI HPA 22-2-45 test flt Sq Ld Morgan BDn 3-4 fuel function trls with 22½ gal combat tanks under wing (o/ld). Carb mono cock contam tests. HPS maker's trls. Farn 6-5 test flt Lt Cmdr Brown & Quill 16-6 RNAS Arb 28-7 BDn 11-8 con to proto Seafire XVII 777S

PK240 Proto FXV HPA from Haw 24-2-45 test fly Mar'45 to july

PK243 Proto FXV HPA 22-2-45 CHA 10-3 Del by Quill Farn 18-7 *HMS Game* 11-7-49

Seafire Mk XV prototypes., four used for official trials.

PR338 RNDA 21-3-45 HP Sup to Tang 23-3- 33MU 20-4
PR339 RNDA 19-4-45 33MU 20-4 761S
PR340 RNDA 30-4-45 33MU 766S Lossie
PR341 RNDA 1-5-45 805S Mach
PR342 RNDA 3-5-45 805S Mach
PR343 RNDA 7-5-45 805S Mach
PR344 RNDA 30-5-45
PR345 RNDA 31-5-5-45 RNAS Doni 3-6 French Navy 17-6-49
PR346 RNDA 29-5-45 33MU
PR347 RNDA 24-5-45 33MU
PR348 RNDA 30-5-45 33MU
PR349 RNDA 29-5-45 33MU RNAS Doni 23-7 French Navy 17-6-49
PR350 RNDA 8-6-45 VA HPA 33MU 30-6
PR351 RNDA 2-6-45
PR352 RNDA 12-6-45
PR353 RNDA 2-6-45 766S Lossie
PR354 RNDA 15-6-45 805S Masch
PR355 RNDA 11-6-45 to Burma AF as UB406
PR356(RNDA 14-6-45 Farn Apl '46 rate of roll trls
PR357 RNDA 21-6-45
PR358 RNDA 18-6-45
PR359 RNDQ 21-6-45 33MU 766S Lossie
PR360 RNDA 23-6-45 RNAS Doni French Navy 28-6-49
PR361 RNDA 20-6-45 805S Mach
PR362 RNDA 25-6-45 805S Mach
PR363 RNDA 26-6-45 33MU 805S Mach
PR364 RNDA 28-6-45 33MU 767S Lossie to ins A/F A2162
PR365 RNDA 25-6-45 805S Mach
PR366 RNDA 30-6-45 805S Mach
PR367 RNDA 27-6-45 805S Mach
PR368 RNDA 29-6-45 805S Mach 771S in 1951
PR369 RNDA 29-6-45 805S Mach
PR370 RNDA 30-6-45 805S Mach
PR371 RNDA 30-6-45 805S Mach 768S
PR372 RNDA 3-7-45
PR373 RNDA 30-6-45 805S Mach
PR374 RNDA 3-7-45 766S Lossie
PR375 RNDA 2-7-45 805S Mach
PR376 RNDA 30-6-45 805S Mach to Burma as UB409
PR377 RNDA 3-7-45 781S in 1950 FAA ins A/F A2093 Bram June'53
PR378 RNDA 31-7-45
PR379 RNDA 4-7-45
PR391 RNDA 14-7-45 RDU Cul 803S 21-6-47 *HMS Veng* 24-9 to Halfar 11-11 VA EA recon Jan'49
PR392 RNDA 20-7-45
PR393 RNDA 30-7-45
PR394 RNDA 14-9-45 736S RNARY Fleet as A2268 SOC 29-9-56
PR395 RNDA 20-7-45
PR396 RNDA 26-7-45
PR397 RNDA 26-7-45 RNAS Cul 27-7 French Navy 24-6-49
PR398 RNDA 26-7-45
PR399 RNDA 26-7-45 736S
PR400 RNDA 28-8-45 to Burma AF as UB410 (Repaired 5-4-49 at £2,198/11/8d)
PR401 RNDA 21-8-45 (Repaired by 31-1-49 at £1,815/9/6d)
PR402 RNDA 26-7-45 771S
PR403 RNDA 26-7-45 des in fire fight demo SOC 17-3-52
PR404 RNDA 24-8-45
PR405 RNDA 30-7-45 RNAS Cul 31-8 French Navy 17-6-49
PR406 RNDA 27-7-45 767S Lossie to A2176 Bram 1949
PR407 RNDA 24-7-45 to Burma AF as UB418
PR408 RNDA 27-8-45 805S Mach
PR409 RNDA 30-7-45
PR410 RNDA 13-8-45
PR411 RNDA 10-8-45
PR412 RNDA 30-7-45
PR413 RNDA 31-7-45
PR414 RNDA 27-8-45 RNAS Cul 30-8 French Navy 28-6-49
PR415 RNDA 31-8-45 (Repaired by 28-1-49 at £2,246/6/0)
PR416 RNDA 18-9-45 18-9-45
PR417 RNDA 22-9-45 RDU Cul 802S 5-7-47 *HMS Veng* 24-9 Halfar 11-11 VA EA recon Jan'49
PR418 RNDA 5-9-45
PR419 RNDA 14-9-45
PR420 RNDA 27-8-45
PR421 RNDA 30-8-45
PR422 RNDA 6-9-45 to Burma AF as UB415 (Repaired by 2-3-49 at £2,157/7/0d)
PR423 RNDA 5-10-45 805S Mach to Burma AF as UB411
PR424 RNDA 11-1-46 790S
PR425 RNDA 22-9-45
PR426 RNDA 14-9-45
PR427 RNDA 18-10-45
PR428 RNDA 13-9-45
PR429 RNDA 13-9-45 RNAS Cul 15-9 French Navy 28-6-49
PR430 RNDA 24-9-45
PR431 RNDA 16-10-45
PR432 RNDA 12-9-45 Hit high grd Hill of Stake nr Largs Ayrshire 3-2-47
PR433 RNDA 25-9-45 RNAS abr to A2190 Bram 1953 (Repaired 14-7-49 £2,126/17/10d)
PR434 RNDA 26-9-45 to Canadian Navy
PR435 RNDA 11-10-45
PR436 RNDA 26-9-45
PR449 RNDA 4-10-45
PR450 RNDA 28-9-45
PR451 RNDA 4-10-45 to Canadian Navy. Extant Alberta Inst of Tech, Calgary.
PR452 RNDA 6-10-45
PR453 RNDA 26-9-45 RDU Cul 802S *HMS Veng* 2-10-47 Halfar 11-11 VA EA recon 26-6-48 to Burma AF as UB413
PR454 RNDA 29-9-45 to Burma AF as UB410
PR455 RNDA 18-1-46 to Burma AF as UB408
PR456 RNDA 17-10-45 766S Lossie
PR457 RNDA 28-9-45
PR458 RNDA 8-10-45 to Canadian Navy
PR459 RNDA 26-10-45 RDU Cul 802S LoS 22-7-47 802S *HMS Veng* 24-10 Hafar 11-11 VA EA recon 26-6-48
PR460 RNDA 20-10-45
PR461| RNDA 5-10-45 to Canadian Navy
PR462 RNDA 19-10-45 to Burma AF as UB419
PR463 RNDA 19-120-45 to A2178 Bram (Repaired 6-5-49 £2,419/0/3d)
PR464 RNDA 4-10-45 183S in 1947
PR465 RNDA 18-10-45
PR466 RNDA 13-10-45
PR467 RNDA 11-10-45
PR468 RNDA 6-10-45
PR469 RNDA 12-10-45 (Repaired 5-7-49 £1,906/16/9d)
PR470 RNDA 11-10-45 to Canadian Navy
PR471 RNDA 20-10-45
PR472 RNDA 7-11-45
PR473 RNDA 5-11-45
PR474 RNDA 30-10-45
PR475 RNDA 6-11-45 at Stretton 12-10-52
PR476 RNDA 19-11-45
PR477 RNDA 26-11-45
PR478 RNDA 6-11-45
PR479 RNDA 22-11-45 Canadian Navy Dartmouth Nova Scotia VG-AAB
PR492 RNDA 6-11-45 RNAY Fleet 13-9-50 766S Lossie 15-9
PR493 RNDA 10-11-45
PR494 RNDA 30-11-45 GVI to RCAF Res Dept: Edmonton Dec'46 winter trls with PR499 u/c dam during t/o and land from rough air strips. During trls arrester hook release troublesome (Repaired 4-11-49 £1,909/0/2d).
PR495 RNDA 28-11-45 728S
PR496 RNDA 30-11-45
PR497 RNDA 18-1-46 766S
PR498 RNDA 4-12-45 to Canadian Navy
PR499 RNDA 28-11-45 GVI to RCAF Edmonton as per PR494
PR500 RNDA 13-11-45
PR501 RNDA 14-1-46
PR502 RNDA 18-1-46
PR503 RNDA 7-12-45 to Canadian Navy extant Hamilton Ontario Canada as C-GCWK
PR504 RNDA 7-1-46
PR505 RNDA 22-1-46

RCN colours on PR458.

PR461 wearing the later RCN colours. Compare with PR470 below.

PR470 in initial Canadian colours, part of batch of 35 Seafire XVs supplied to the RCN.

PR474 806 Squadron, Kai Tak, Hong Kong, 1946.

PR506 RNDA 9-1-46
PR507.508, 509, 510, 511, 512, 513, 514, 515, 516, 517, 518, 519, 520, 521 and 522 no record.
SP136 RNDA 31-3-45
SP137 RNDA 11-4-45
SP138 RNDA 13-4-45
SP139 RNDA 13-4-45
SP140 RNDA 14-4-45
SP141 SP142 RNDA 17-4-45
SP143 RNDA 25-4-45
SP144 RNDA 20-4-45
SP145 RNDA 17-4-45
SP146 RNDA 21-4-45
SP147 RNDA 28-4-45
SP148 RNDA 27-4-45
SP149 RNDA 30-4-45
SP150 RNDA 30-4-45 to French Navy
SP151, SP152, SP153, SP154 RNDA 30-4-45
SP155 RNDA 4-5-45
SP156 RNDA 11-5-45
SP157 RNDA 11-5-45
SP158 RNDA 16-5-45
SP159 RNDA 12-5-45
SP160 RNDA 23-5-45
SP161 RNDA 25-5-45
SP162 SP163 RNDA 25-5-45
SP164 RNDA 29-5-45
SP165 SP166 RNDA 1-6-45
SP167 SP168 RNDA 2-6-45
SP181 RNDA 12-6-45
SP182 RNDA 6-6-45
SP183 RNDA 5-6-45
SP184 RNDA 12-6-45
SP185 RNDA 31-7-45
SP186 RNDA 16-6-45
SP187 RNDA 25-6-45
SP188 RNDA 27-6-45
SP189 RNDA 3-7-45
SP190 RNDA 27-6-45
SP191 RNDA 30-6-45
SP192 SP193, SP194 RNDA 3-7-45
SP195 RNDA 12-7-45
SP196 RNDA20-7-45
SP197 RNDA 24-7-45

SR446 Griffon VI RNDAA 31-8-44 BDn 27-11 IFF & hand trls. Fined off prop trls Feb'45. Fine pitch settings for deck ldg. Two setting 30 and 28°. difference in these & normal settings insufficient to warrent intro to service a/c. Reason for trls was insufficient drag for deck ldg. T/o trls with SR448 (MkXV) with new prop and NS490 (Mk XV proto). March, det aftmost CoG, carb mono contam tests, metal elev, level speeds& positional error, Comp trls with Mk XI depth charge. Dropping trls June'46. Oil cool & rad suit trls. Fitt 200lb smoke floats for t/o, radio VHF trls & IFF
SR447 RNDA 28-10-44

SR448 GVI SP RNDA 7-10-44 BDn Mar'45 Spin trls. 3rd proto with normal Spit XII type fin & rud. May, radio, level speeds & positional error, comp trls with SR446 & NS490
SR449 RNDA 21-10-44
SR450 RNDA 18-11-44
SR451 RNDA 31-10-44 Airwork Gat refurb to Burma AF as UB4012 (G-15-212)
SR452 RNDA 31-10-44 47MU 24-3-45 33MU 13-5 RNAS Doni 15-5 to French Navy 17-6-49
SR453 RNDA 30-11-44 BDn Feb'45 full gunnery trls revealed 14 panels be removed before re-arming could begin
SR454 RNDA 30-11-44 33MU 7-12
SR455 RNDA 20-1-45 RNAS Doni 10-4 French Navy 17-6-49
SR456 RNDA 20-1-45
SR457 RNDA 22-1-45 S of AS 4-46
SR458 RNDA 29-1-45
SR459 RNDA 3-2-45 USNAS Patuxent River 6-45
SR460 RNDA 8-6-45 RNAS Cul 19-7 French Navy 24-6-49
SR461 RNDA 10-2-45 33MU 1-3
SR462 RNDA 10-2-45 33MU 20-2 to Burma AF as UB414 (G-15-225)
SR463 RNDA 24-2-45 33MU 1-3
SR464 RNDA 10-2-45 33MU 21-2
SR465 RNDA 24-2-45 802S 28-5-47 *HMS Veng* 24-9 Halfar 11-11 ret UK 16-3-48 VA EA recon Jan'49 SOC 28-8-51
SR466 RNDA 31-5-45
SR467 RNDA 21-6-45 FLR Abbott 802S Eglington 21-6-47 *HMS Veng* 24-9 Halfar 16-2-48 ret UK 16-3 VA EA recon Jan'49
SR468 RNDA 24-2-45
SR469 RNDA 12-3-45
SR470 RNDA 28-2-45 to Burma as UB417 (G-15-216) (repaired 13-5-49 £2,148/12/2d)
SR471 RNDA 13-3-45 33MU 14-3 to Burma AF as UB405 (G-15-216)
SR472 RNDA 28-2-45 33MU 7-3
SR473 RNDA 28-2-45 33MU 8-3
SR474 RNDA 12-3-45 33MU 18-3 RNAS Doni 24-3 to French Navy 24-6-40
SR475 RNDA 17-7-45
SR476 RNDA 21-3-45 33MU 22-3
SR477 RNDA 31-8-45
SR478 RNDA 16-3-45 33MU 17-3
SR479 RNDA 26-3-45
SR480 RNDA 30-6-45 767S Lossie
SR481 RNDA 3-4-45
SR482 RNDA 29-5-45
SR483 RNDA 16-3-45 33MU 17-3
SR484 RNDA 21-3-45
SR485 RNDA 20-7-45
SR486 RNDA 16-3-45
SR487 RNDA 20-3-45
SR488 RNDA 4-4-45 33MU 5-4
SR489 RNDA 28-3-45 33MU 29-3
SR490 RNDA 23-3-45 GVI proto. BDn Sept'45 trls to test metal elev
SR491 RNDA 26-3-45 (Rep 19-5-49 £2,017/3/10)
SR492 RNDA 28-3-45 (Rep 27-6-49 £2,131/2/6)
SR493 RNDA 29-3-45
SR516 RNDA 3-4-45 RNAS Doni 18-4 to French Navy 28-6-49
SR517 RNDA 17-4-45 33MU 17-4
SR518 RNDA 12-4-45
SR519 RNDA 9-4-45 33MU 10-4

A deck accident for PR479, RCN

PR498 showing a slight variation on the grey colour scheme.

SR449 Westland-built with 'A' frame hook.

SR475 at Rotterdam, 1945.

SR520 RNDA 6-4-45 33MU 6-4 RNAS Doni 24-4 to French Navy 28-6-49
SR521 RNDA 11-4-45 33MU 12-4
SR522 RNDA 10-4-45 33MU 11-4 RNAS Doni 24-4 to French Navy 17-6 49
SR523 RNDA 12-4-45 33MU 14-4
SR524 RNDA 17-4-45 33MU 18-4
SR525 RNDA 2-6-45 (Rep 5-4-49 £2,033/17/1)
SR526 RNDA 12-4-45 76MU 11-5 to French Navy 28-6-49
SR527 RNDA 16-4-45
SR528 RNDA 17-4-45
SR529 RNDA 23-4-45
SR530 RNDA 31-4-45
SR531 RNDA 18-4-45
SR532 RNDA 18-4-45 33MU 20-4
SR533 RNDA 23-5-45 33MU 24-5
SR534 RNDA 23-4-45 to Burma AF as UB407 (G-15-218)
SR535 RNDA 24-4-45 (Rep 1-4-49 £2,244/7/4)
SR536 RNDA 24-4-45
SR537 RNDA 24-4-45 52MU 27-5-45 8015 Australia *HMS Implacable* Cat A struck SR580 6-1-46 Cat E 18-2 to UK for repair SOC 17-3-50
SR538 RNDA 24-4-45 SR580 6-1-46 Cat E 18-2 to UK for repair SOC 17-3-52
SR539 RNDA 16-7-45
SR540 RNDA 28-4-45
SR541 RNDA 24-7-45
SR542, SR543, SR544 RNDA 30-4-45
SR545 RNDA 23-11-45
SR546 RNDA 11-5-45
SR547 RNDA 3-5-45
SR568 RNDA 11-5-45 VAStn 29-10-48 RDU Anth 5-11 AHU Stret 15-1-50 1832S Cul 22-5 764S Yeov 29-7 799S 18-7-51
SR569, SR570 RNDA 7-5-45
SR571 RNDA 3-5-45
SR572 RNDA 7-5-45
SR573 RNDA 3-5-45
SR574 RNDA 15-5-45
SR575 RNDA 26-4-45 1832S (Rep 31-1-49 £2,279/9/11d)
SR576 RNDA 10-5-45
SR577 RNDA 11-5-45
SR578 RNDA 7-5-45
SR579 RNDA 17-5-45 33MU 18-5
SR580 RNDA 15-5-45 33MU 16-5 struck SR537 *HMS Impalacable* 6/1/46
SR581 RNDA 17-5-45
SR582 RNDA 25-5-45 1831S
SR583 RNDA 15-5-45 33MU 16-5 767S Jly'50 799S
SR584 RNDA 17-5-45 33MU 18-5 26-5-45
SR585 RNDA 26-5-45 33MU 28-5
SR586 RNDA 28-5-45 (Rep 22-2-49 £2,413/8/2d)
SR587 RNDA 29-5-45 1833S
SR588 RNDA 28-5-45 1833S
SR589 RNDA 31-5-45 33MU 2-6
SR590 RNDA 28-5-45 33MU 30-5
SR591 RNDA 31-5-45 33MU 25-5
SR592 RNDA 24-5-45 33MU 25-5
SR593 RNDA 1-6-45 33MU 2-6 767S 780S
SR594 RNDA 24-7-45
SR595 RNDA 7-6-45 33MU 9-6
SR596 RNDA 6-6-45 33MU 9-6
SR597 RNDA 31-5-45 33MU 2-6
SR598, SR599 RNDA 1-6-45
SR600 RNDA 31-4-45
SR601 RNDA 2-6-45
SR602 RNDA 21-7-45 des in fire fight demo Cul Apl'55
SR603 RNDA 25-7-45
SR604 RNDA 14-7-45
SR605, SR606 RNDA 4-6-45
SR607, SR608 RNDA 14-6-45
SR609 RNDA 15-6-45
SR610 RNDA 20-6-45
SR611 RNDA 19-6-45
SR630 RNDA 21-6-45
SR631 RNDA 16-6-45
SR632 RNDA 18-6-45
SR633 RNDA 14-6-45
SR634 RNDA 16-6-45
SR635 RNDA 15-6-45
SR636 RNDA 19-6-45
SR637 RNDA 15-6-45
SR638 RNDA 29-6-45 33MU 30-6 (Rep 13-9-49 £1,594/4/9d)
SR639 RNDA 26-4-45 33MU 27-6
SR640 RNDA 23-6-45 33MU 26-6 700S
SR641 RNDA 18-6-45 GVI VASM RNAS Anth 30-9-48
SR642 RNDA 18-6-45 to Burma AF as UB403 (G-15-212)
SR643 RNDA 27-7-45
SR644 RNDA 20-7-45
SR645 RNDA 30-7-45

SW781 SF RNDA 22-6-45 33MU 26-6
SW782 SF RNDA 26-6-45 33MU 30-6
SW783 SF RNDA 21-7-45
SW784 SF RNDA 2-8-45
SW785 SF RNDA 22-6-45 33MU 26-6
SW786 SF RNDA 22-6-45 33MU 30-6
SW787 SF RNDA 30-7-45
SW788 SF RNDA 28-6-45 33MU 30-6
SW789 SF RNDA 26-7-45
SW790 SF RNDA 27-6-45 33MU 30-6
SW791 SF RNDA 17-7-45 33MU 17-7
SW792 SF RNDA 29-6-45 33MU 30-6
SW793 SF RNDA 30-6-45 GVI BDn Aug'45 trls with R/T Type AN/MPX -1 of American manufacture
SW794 SF RNDA 30-6-45 33MU 3-7 767S
SW795 SF RNDA 29-6-45 33MU 30-6
SW796 SF RNDA 30-6-45 33MU 3-7
SW797 SF RNDA 27-6-45 33MU 3-7
SW798 RNDA 1-7-45 33MU 3-7
SW799 RNDA 6-7-45 33MU 7-7 to Burma AF as UB402 (G-15-213)
SW800 RNDA 30-6-45 33MU 7-7 1831S VAWD June'55 spares to A2256
SW801 RNDA 5-7-45
SW802 RNDA 4-7-45
SW803, 804 RNDA5-7-45
SW805 RNDA 5-7-45 (Rep 5-4-49 £2,342/19/9d)
SW806 RNDA 19-7-45
SW807 RNDA 7-7-45
SW808 RNDA 16-7-45
SW809 RNDA 14-7-45
SW810 RNDA 14-7-45 *HMS Ocean* July 1946
SW811 RNDA 16-7-45
SW812 RNDA 14-7-45
SW813 RNDA 19-7-45 Farn Nov'45 RATOG trls. HPA June. Took part in RAE Display Enemy A/C as RATOG Seafire 27-6-46 A & AEE 2S 28-9-46 (Rep 23-5-49 £1,987/9/9d)
SW814 RNDA 12-7-45
SW815 RNDA 13-7-45
SW816 RNDA 17-7-45
SW817 RNDA 16-7-45 to Burma AF as UB412 (G-15-223)
SW818, SW819 RNDA 16-7-45
SW820 RNDA 16-7-45 1833S Bram (Rep 2-5-49 £2,066/18/9d) SOC 15-10-49
SW821 RNDA 17-7-45
SW822 RNDA 19-7-45 coll with Dominie X7453 Minshull, Vernon Cheshire 11-2-46
SW823 RNDA 16-7-45
SW824 RNDA 18-7-45
SW825 RNDA 17-7-45
SW826 RNDA 19-7-45
SW827 RNDA 17-7-45
SW828 RNDA 20-7-45 (Rep 5-5-49 £2,244/2/11d)
SW844 RNDA 19-7-45 804S
SW845 RNDA 19-7-45 (Rep 4-11-49 £2, 076/15/11d)
SW846 RNDA 24-7-45 1832S Cul 737S SOC 17-3-52
SW847 RNDA 31-7-45
SW848 RNDA 20-7-45
SW849 RNDA 21-7-45
SW850 RNDA 23-7-45
SW851, SW852, RNDA 25-7-45
SW853 RNDA 28-7-45
SW854 RNDA 27-7-45 721S
SW855 RNDA 26-7-45
SW856 RNDA 28-45
SW857 RNDA 31-7-45
SW858, SW859 RNDA 3014-7-45
SW860 RNDA 28-7-45
SW861 RNDA 30-7-45
SW862 RNDA 30-7-45 778S
SW863 RNDA 1-8-45 to Burma AF as UB404 (G-15-215)
SW864 RNDA 31-8-45
SW865 RNDA 25-8-4 728S5
SW866 RNDA 17-8-45 (Rep 6-5-49 £2,626/13/8)
SW867 RNDA 18-8-45 mispainted as A2268
SW868 RNDA 25-8 (Rep 27-1-49 £2,490/8/8d)
SW869 RNDA 2-8-45
SW870 RNDA 1-8-45
SW871 RNDA 18-8-45
SW872 RNDA 30-8-45
SW873 RNDA 14-8-45
SW874, SW875 RNDA 17-8-45
SW876 RNDA 31-8-45
SW877 RNDA 20-8-45
SW878 RNDA 20-8-45
SW879 RNDA 3-10-45 (Rep 2-4-49 (Rep £2,254/0/4d)
SW896 RNDA 21-8-45
SW897 RNDA 22-8-45
SW898 RNDA 24-8-45
SW899 RNDA 24-8-5 to Burma AF as UB420 (G-15-231)
SW900 RNDA 28-8-45
SW901 RNDA 27-8-45
SW902 RNDA 31-8-45 780S
SW903 RNDA 29-8-45
SW904, SW905 RNDA 31-8-45
SW905 RNDA 31-8-45
SW906 RNDA 30-8-45
SW907 RNDA 31-8-45 700S
SW908, SW909, SW910 RNDA 31-8-45
SW911 RNDA 8-9-45
SW912 RNDA 13-9-45
SW913 RNDA 7-9-45
SW914 RNDA 11-9-45
SW915 RNDA 12-9-45
SW916 RNDA 26-9-45 802S Eglington 18-6-47 *HMS Veng* 15-7 Halfar 11-11 ret UK FAA ins a/f A2203 Bram June'51
SW917 RNDA 18-9-45 (Rep 6-9-49 £1,669/15/2d)
SW918 RNDA 12-9-45
SW919 RNDA 19-9-45 1832S Cul
SW920 RNDA 13-9-45
SW921 RNDA 31-10-45 50 TRAG Yeov 6-9-49

MAINTENANCE AIRFRAMES; PR364(A2162, PR377(A2093, PR394(A2268, PR406(A2187), PR433(A2190), PR463(A2178), SW800(A2256), SW867(A2268), SW916(A2203).

CANADIAN NAVY: PR434, PR458, PR461, PR470, and PR479, PR498, PR503.

BURMA AIR FORCE.PR355, PR366, PR400, PR407, PR422, PR423, PR454, PR455, PR462, PR451, PR462, SR451, SR462, SR470, SR471, SR534, SR462, SW799, SW817 and SW863.

LAST OF THE OLD

In June 1944 NS493, the sixth and final Mk XV prototype, was delivered to Westland Aircraft with the instruction to 'modernise' the airframe to bring it into line with the tear drop hood, rear view fuselage F Mk IXs and F Mk XIVs of the Royal Air Force. Westlands followed the styling set by the land fighters, reducing the after fuselage by cutting down the level of the upper longerons and installing the clear view canopy. This major modification tended to produce as many problems as it solved, for most of the rear view Spitfire/Seafire had stability problems, especially when the aft fuselage fuel tanks were used. The modified Seafire, to which the designation Mk XVII had been applied, was then delivered to Boscombe Down for trials. The Seafire was deemed successful and in order to introduce it as quickly as possible into service Westland converted the final 30 airframes on their Mk XV production line to Mk XVII standards.

The many trials conducted with the link and spline types of oleo undercarriage legs resulted in a stronger chassis, which in turn led to the adoption of a strengthened main wing spar to take the increased loadings. The oleo leg stroke had been increased from 4.9ins of the Seafire III to 8 inches. The Mk XVII also had an enlarged fin and rudder, two F24 cameras and (in later production models) a 33 gallon fuel tank in the rear fuselage. A total fuel capacity of 145 gallons was distributed in an upper and lower tank ahead of the pilot and two mareng bags in the wing leading edge. Fuel tank operation was complicated for unless used correctly the centre of gravity could fluctuate violently. On take off the pilot was instructed to use the rear tank and forbidden to make any violent maneouvres until it was empty. He then had to switch over to the main supply. Combat underwing tanks could also be fitted.

The first production Westland built aircraft, SW987, was sent to High Post on 16 May 1945 for weighing and CG determination. With a Griffon VI engine and four blade, wooden Rotol propeller the tare was 6,243lb and auw 8,017. SX232 had preceded it on 3 April and with the same engine/propeller combination it was heavier with a tare of 6,385lb, and auw 8,148. In an attempt to cure cockpit glare when operating at sea the interior of the cockpit was painted matt black, this modification being introduced on 1 June.

SX311 and 314 were sent to conduct a series of assisted take-off and intensive deck landing trials from *HMS Triumph* at the end of June, the main purpose being to test the long stroke undercarriage under typical service conditions. The wheel wells had been modified to accommodate the chassis which had corrected, toe in wheels. 100 deck landings and eight assisted take offs were required and SX311 began the series with seven assisted t/os and 19 arrested landings. It was noted that shock absorption with the new legs was a vast improvement over earlier types and rebound completely eliminated. On several occasions the aircraft were dropped on to the deck without damage. SX311 was damaged during the 19th landing after the pilot had made a low approach resulting in the aircraft striking the round down with hook and port wheel. The aircraft

Ex-prototype Seafire Mk XV NS493 converted to the prototype Mk XVII. It still has the 'A' frame arrester hook and is fitted with the curved windscreen.

SX334 FR XVII with curved windscreen.

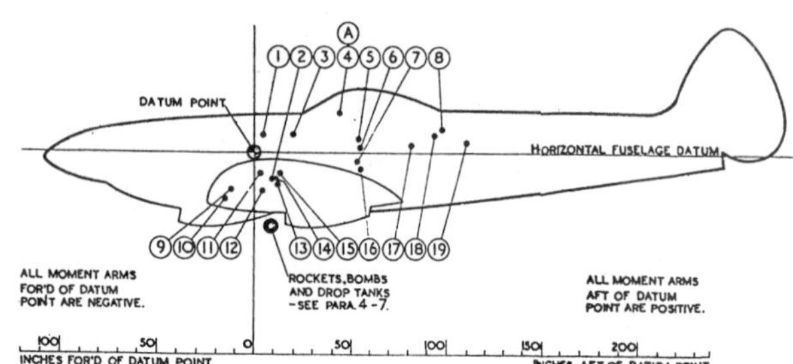

NOTE	ITEM	TYPICAL ITEMS OF REMOVABLE LOAD.	WEIGHT LB.	ARM IN.	MOMENT LB.IN.
1	14	4 BROWNING .303 IN. GUNS AND ACCESSORIES.	112.5	+ 11.1	+ 1,249
2	12	2 HISPANO 20 MM. GUNS AND ACCESSORIES	221	+ 4.0	+ 884
	2	BROWNING .303 IN. AMMUNITION AT 350 ROUNDS PER GUN.	93	+ 9	+ 837
	13	HISPANO 20 MM. AMMUNITION AT 120 ROUNDS PER GUN.	150	+ 12	+ 1,800
	4	GYROSCOPIC GUNSIGHT AND FILAMENT LAMPS.	8.5	+ 44	+ 374
	7	1½ IN. SIGNAL PISTOL AND CARTRIDGES.	5.5	+ 53	+ 292
	5	1¼ LB INCENDIARY BOMB, TORCH AND CLOCK.	3	+ 54	+ 162
	10	G.45 CAMERA, ADAPTOR, FRONT FLANGE AND ADJUSTABLE MOUNTING.	7.5	− 15	− 113
	17	OXYGEN BOTTLE.	17.5	+ 82	+ 1,435
	16	DINGHY AND WATER CUSHION.	23	+ 55	+ 1,265
3	19	T.R. 5043 (S.C.R.522) RADIO AND ACCESSORIES.	79.5	+111	+ 8,825
	8	A.R.I. 5679 (AN/APX-1) RECEIVER, CONTROL UNIT AND DEMOLITION DETONATORS.	30.5	+ 98	+ 2,989
	18	A.R.I. 5307 (ZB/X) RECEIVER, REMOTE CONTROL UNIT AND DYNAMOTOR.	10.5	+ 94	+ 987
	6	PILOT AND PARACHUTE.	200	+ 55	+ 11,000
		TOTAL TYPICAL REMOVABLE LOAD.	962		+ 31,986
	3	FUEL IN UPPER FUSELAGE TANK : 32½ GALL. 100 OCTANE AT 7.2 LB. PER GALL.	234	+ 19.8	+ 4,633
	15	FUEL IN LOWER FUSELAGE TANK : 49 GALL. 100 OCTANE AT 7.2 LB. PER GALL.	353	+ 12.9	+ 4,554
	9	FUEL IN WING TANKS : 19½ GALL. 100 OCTANE AT 7.2 LB. PER GALL.	140.5	− 12.3	− 1,728
4	1	OIL IN TANK: 8 GALL. AT 9 LB. PER GALL.	72	+ 4.5	+ 324
	11	AIRCRAFT IN TARE CONDITION.	6,327.5		+ 25,867
		AIRCRAFT IN TYPICAL TAKE-OFF CONDITION.	8,089	+ 8.1	+ 65,636

NOTE	ITEM	ALTERNATIVE AND ADDITIONAL ITEMS OF REMOVABLE LOAD	WEIGHT LB.	ARM IN.	MOMENT LB.IN.
	A	REFLECTOR GUN SIGHT AND FILAMENT LAMPS.	5	+ 44	+ 220

Loading and CG diagram FR XVII.

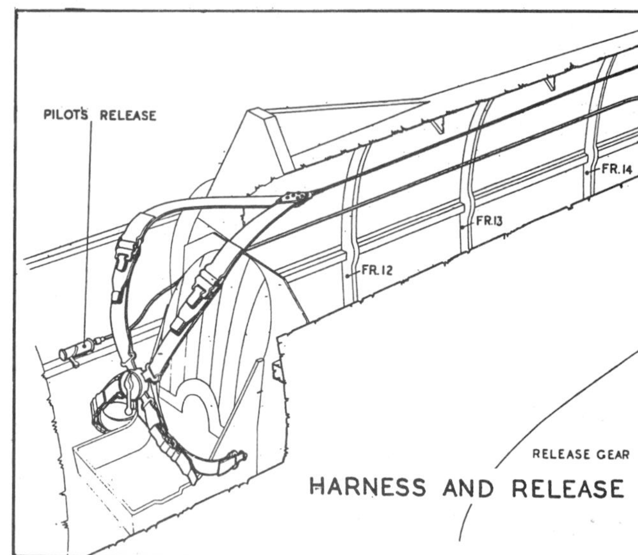

Westland-built Mk XVII has 2862/v scribbled on prop blades.

Loading and CG diagram F Mk XVII.

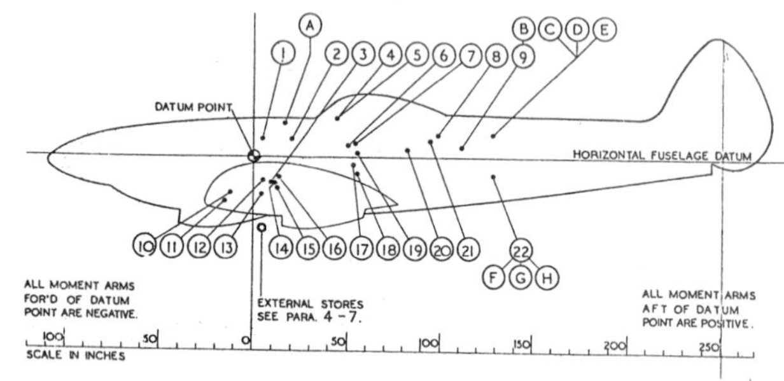

NOTE	ITEM	TYPICAL REMOVABLE ITEMS	WEIGHT LB.	ARM IN.	MOMENT LB.IN.
1	14	4 BROWNING .303 IN. GUNS AND ACCESSORIES.	112.5	+ 11.1	+ 1,249
2	13	2 HISPANO 20 MM. GUNS AND ACCESSORIES.	221	+ 4.0	+ 884
	3	BROWNING .303 IN. AMMUNITION AT 350 ROUNDS PER GUN.	93	+ 9	+ 837
	15	HISPANO 20 MM. AMMUNITION AT 120 ROUNDS PER GUN.	150	+ 12	+ 1,800
	4	GYROSCOPIC GUNSIGHT AND 4 FILAMENT LAMPS.	8.5	+ 44	+ 374
	17	1½ IN. SIGNAL PISTOL AND 8 CARTRIDGES.	5.5	+ 53	+ 292
	7	ELECTRIC TORCH, CLOCK AND NAVIGATIONAL COMPUTOR.	3	+ 54	+ 162
	11	G.45 CAMERA, ADAPTER, FRONT FLANGE AND ADJUSTABLE MOUNTING.	7.5	− 15	− 113
	5	G.G.S. RECORDER, MAGAZINE AND MOUNTING BRACKET.	2	+ 44	+ 88
3	22	20 IN. VERTICAL F.24 CAMERA AND ACCESSORIES.	43	+129	+ 5,547
	6	CAMERA CONTROL UNIT.	4	+ 50	+ 200
	20	OXYGEN BOTTLE.	17.5	+ 82	+ 1,435
	18	DINGHY AND WATER CUSHION.	23	+ 55	+ 1,265
4	9	T.R. 5043 (S.C.R.522) RADIO AND ACCESSORIES.	79.5	+111	+ 8,825
	8	A.R.I. 5679 (AN/APX-1) RECEIVER, CONTROL UNIT AND 6 DEMOLITION DETONATORS.	30.5	+ 98	+ 2,989
	21	A.R.I. 5307 (ZB/X) RECEIVER, REMOTE CONTROL UNIT AND DYNAMOTOR.	10.5	+ 94	+ 987
	19	PILOT AND PARACHUTE.	200	+ 55	+ 11,000
		TOTAL TYPICAL REMOVABLE LOAD.	1,011		+ 37,821
	2	FUEL IN TOP FUSELAGE TANK: 32½ GALL. AT 7.2 LB. PER GALL.	234	+ 19.8	+ 4,633
	16	FUEL IN BOTTOM FUSELAGE TANK: 49 GALL. AT 7.2 LB. PER GALL.	353	+ 12.9	+ 4,554
	10	FUEL IN WING L.E. TANKS: 19½ GALL. AT 7.2 LB. PER GALL.	140.5	− 12.3	− 1,728
6	1	OIL IN TANK: 8 GALL. AT 9 LB. PER GALL.	72	+ 4.5	+ 324
	12	AIRCRAFT IN TARE CONDITION.	6,517.5		+ 33,656
		AIRCRAFT IN TYPICAL TAKE-OFF CONDITION.	8,328	+ 9.5	+ 79,310

NOTE	ITEM	ALTERNATIVE AND ADDITIONAL REMOVABLE ITEMS	WEIGHT LB.	ARM IN.	MOMENT LB.IN.
3	F	14 IN. VERTICAL F.24 CAMERA AND ACCESSORIES.	39	+129	+ 5,031
3	G	8 IN. VERTICAL F.24 CAMERA AND ACCESSORIES.	35	+129	+ 4,515
3	H	5 IN. VERTICAL F.24 CAMERA AND ACCESSORIES.	33	+129	+ 4,257
5	C	14 IN. OBLIQUE F.24 CAMERA AND ACCESSORIES.	38	+129	+ 4,902
5	D	8 IN. OBLIQUE F.24 CAMERA AND ACCESSORIES.	34	+129	+ 4,386
5	E	5 IN. OBLIQUE F.24 CAMERA AND ACCESSORIES.	32	+129	+ 4,128
	A	EXHAUST SHIELDS.	7	+ 16	+ 112
	B	RADIO BALLAST: 3 STANDARD WEIGHTS AT 17½ LB. EACH.	52.5	+114	+ 5,985

SW991, F Mk XVII, has bomb racks under wings but lacks sting hook.

SX277 with gloss paint finish.

slewed sideways and engaged No 5 wire and then struck the port cat walk. The rudder, hook, port wing and radiator and propeller were damaged, but the undercarriage remained intact.

SX334 was weighed at High Post as it incorporated a large number of modifications, including the curved windscreen. Tare was 6,420lb, and auw 8,245. It was one of the Mk XVIIs to be fitted with the twin F24 cameras and as such was designated FR Mk XVII. Little is known about a large number of Mk XVIIs, including SX389, but this aircraft did have a vibrograph control unit mounted on the port side of the cockpit, just forward of the door. It was to record any vibration in the cockpit when the engine was running, and for gun firing the G.45 camera switch operated the mechanism when the guns were fired.

SW987 was flown by Quill and Shea-Simmonds in May and June 1945 respectively. Quill thought that due to reversal of trim the aircraft should never have been passed as satisfactory by the Westland test pilots. Twelve inches of beading was then added to the elevator trailing edge and this improved handling, but Shea-Simonds noted that starboard aileron upfloat was 2½ to 3 inches and it was easier turning to port than starboard.

SX297 was at Boscombe Down in July 1946 for trials of the Mk VIII Type 3A RP installation. It was replaced by SX361 following an accident during a maximum speed full salvo shoot, arriving on 13 November. A total of 104, 60lb heads were fired in pairs and a special G.G.S was fitted with built in guns/RP switch with a different RP graticule. A drop tank was also carried on several of the trials.

The F XVII entered service with No 883 Squadron but the type had a short service life. It spent less than two years as a front line type and was then relegated to Reserve and training squadrons, serving with the latter until late 1954.

It is interesting to note that originally there was no Seafire Mk XVIII designation for it had been agreed that in order to cope with the possibility of more new Spitfire/Seafire marks the land fighter was to continue with those in current use and the Seafire to jump to the mark number 40. The XVII was to be the Mk 41, followed by the 42 (XVIII). The 45, 46, 47 followed at a later date when agreement was reached.

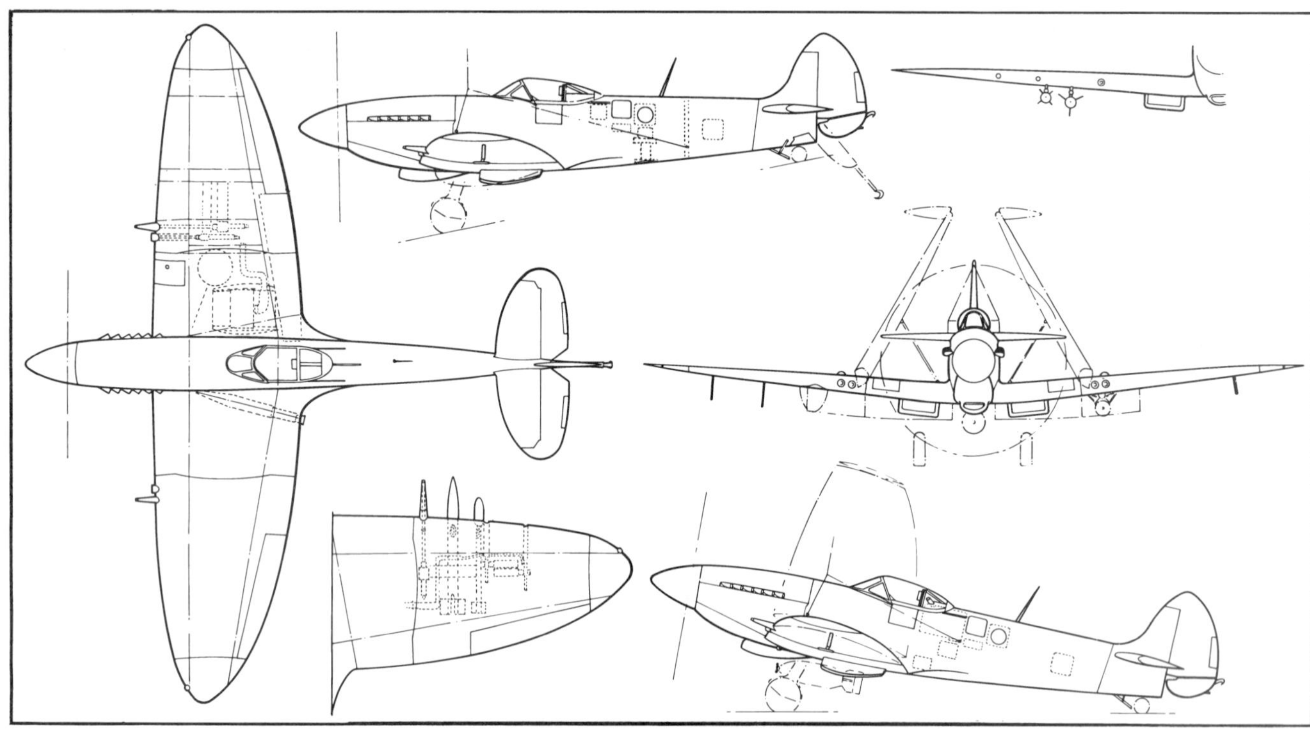

Seafire F Mk XVII and FR. Insets illustrate B wing with two types of rocket projectiles. Slinging points on F differ to those on FR.

SX361 at Boscombe Down, winter of 1946, for trials with Mk VIII Type 3A RP installation. SX297 was first aircraft to be used but it was damaged, to be replaced by SX361. Maximum load 8x60lb heads.

There appears to be no logical explanation for the positioning of wing roundels, SP343 having them painted at wing tips.

SERIAL NUMBERS

Cunliffe-Owen Aircraft Ltd.,
Contract No AIR/2777/C.23(c)
Third for 200 Seafire Mk XV dated February 1944. Amended to 50 Mk XV and 20 Mk XVII. Built as Mk XV and XVII to this third order. The following serials apply to Mk XVIIs built to this order. SP323-327 and 341-355. Cancelled were; SP198-223, 236-279, 293-322, 356-380, 393-438 and 453-461.

Westland Aircraft Ltd.
Contract FNo AIR/3853
Order for 213 Seafire Mk XV dated March 1944. Built as Mk XN/XVII between April and November 1945. The following serials apply to Mk XVIIs built to this sixth order. SW986-993, SX111-139, 152-201, 220-256, 271-316, 332-370 and 387-389. Cancelled were; SX390-432, 451-490 and 503-546.

SP323 to SP355 built by Gunliffe-Owen
SP323 RNDA 22-1-46
SP324 RNDA 27-12-45 BDn Sept to Nov'51. Acc trls with light bomb carrier under fuselage, for practice bombs' 4 × 8½lb; 4 × 10lb; 4 × 11lb; or 4 × 25lb. Trls with 4ft diameter low-drag sleeve & 30ft banner net target drogues were positioned on runway approx 300ft ahead of a/c, facing t/o position, with cable laid as elongated 'S'. Snatch speed was critical. Perf & cooling trls with drogues Farn Nov'51. Launching bridge trls for steam catapult. Towing gear was a bomb slip mounted on an extention fitted to fuselage in place of arrester hook.709S
SP325 RNDA 18-2-46
SP326 RNDA 23-3-46 (Repaired by 28-3-49 at £2,543/15/7)
SP327 RNDA 28-1-46 728S 504/HF Repaired by 15-8-49 at £1,984/18/2
SP341 RNDA 18-2-46
SP342 RNDA 28-2-46
SP343 RNDA 22-1-46 RDU Culham 24-1 FLR Abbot 30-4 WAL mods 1-5-47 RDU Stret 15-8 776S Lossi 22-9 1832S 30-6-49 SOC 2-10-56
SP344 RNDA 22-1-46 Farn Jan to April'48 for trls
SP345 RNDA 6-3-46
SP346 RNDA 28-2-46 RDU Culham 7-3 WAL 13-6 787S 28-5-47 7662S Lossie as LM:109 11-7-48 *HMS Illustrious* cd 4-11 1832S Cul 11-7-49 as CH-122 stored AHU Stret 13-6-50 WOC 2-10-56
SP347 RNDA 22-2-46 RDU Cul 28-2 WAL 20-7 766S Lossie as LM:109 13-10-47 767S Yeovil 26-9-49 Hal Far 11-10-51 728S L-o-S 12-3-52 stored AHU Stret 25-3-52 SOC 2-1-56
SP348 RNDA 27-2-46 RDU Cul 7-3 WAL 3-6 787S West Rayn 9-6-47 Stored Abb 13-1-48 736S St Mer 26-8 737S 31-5-49 Stored AHU Stret SOC 2-10-56
SP349 RNDA 18-3-46 FDU Cul 20-3 WAL 8-4 Helliwells Ltd Walsall for Mods 16-12-47 1831S as ST:108 Stret f/ld Speke Airport 28-5-49 cd/lg 25-6 767S Yeovil cd/ld 22-11-50 stored RDU Stret SOC 3-10-56
SP350 RNDA 14-3-46 RDU Cul 19-3 WAL 8-4 RNARY Doni 21-5 WAL 23-10-47 Anthorn 13-4-48 SOC 2-10-56
SP351 RNDA 26-2-46
SP352 RNDA 18-2-46 Cul 22-2 Abbot 10-10 RNAY Belfast repairs 4-9-48 1833S Bram until 6-6-50 as BR-163 Stored at AHU Stretton 23-7-52 SOC
SP353 RNDA 28-2-46
SP354 RNDA 28-3-46
SP355 RNDA 4-3-46 Stored at AHU Stretton 27-7-55

SW986 RNDA 7-4-45
SW987 RNDA 7-5-45 cd 10-45
SW988 RNDA 18-5-45
SW989 RNDA 20-6-45 RAF Tang 26-6 787S Sept'45 WAL 5-7-46 766S 13-6 RNAY Fleet 23-6-49 coc store 13-3-50 Stored AHU Stretton 27-7-55 WOC 2-10-56
SW990 RNDA 23-6-45 33MU 26-6 RDU Cul 13-7 715S 18-10 736S 12-3-46 WAL mods 31-10-47 703S 29-10-48 1831S 5-4-49 RNAY Fleet recond 8-2-51 SOC 2-10-56
SW991 RNDA 30-7-45
SW992 RNDA 25-8-45
SW993 RNDA 12-7-45 RDU Cul 13-7 715S 18-10 736S 12-3-46 WAL mods 31-10-47 703S 29-10-48 RNAY Fleet 8-2-51 coc store 5-11-51 SOC 2-10-56
SX111 RNDA 25-7-45 RDU Cul 6-7 Helliwells mods May'48 1831S Bram July'50 broke form nr Cul cd nr Abingdon Berks 13-10-51
SX112 RNDA 13-7-45
SX113 RNDA 11-7-45 RDU Ant 4-10-48 *HMS Illust* Mar'49 trls RNAY Fleet 3-7 736S Sept'51 738S July'52 SOC 3-2-54
SX114 RNDA 14-7-45
SX115 RNDA 18-7-45 TOC(RN) 19-7 Doni Sept'45 715S Nov'45 Farn 1946 1832S June'48 1831S July'50 Stret coc store 25-6-55

SX137 before and after going on display at the Fleet Air Arm Museum, Yeovilton.

SX116 RNDA 21-7-45 rep 15-2-49 £2,400/15/2 store AHU Stret 27-7-55
SX117 RNDA 27-7-45
SX118 RNDA 26-7-45
SX119 RNDA 2-8-45 TOC Cul 17-8 RNAY Belfast 20-3-46 WAL mods 5-7 Abbott FLR 25-11-47 SOC 29-10-53
SX120 RNDA 31-7-45 807S Oct'46 1831S 1946 cd nr Stret 19-9-47
SX121 RNDA 20-8-45
SX122 RNDA 24-8-45 TOC(RN) 27-8 AHU Stret 1946 736S July'48 RNAY Fleet 11-7-49 1831S July'51 Stret 25-6-55 coc
SX123 RNDA 23-8-45 Farn Jan'46 HPA
SX124 RNDA 24-8-45
SX125 RNDA 25-8-45 TOC(RN) 27-8 LoS 15-11 766S 22-6-49 728S Halfar Malta 12-2-51 AHU Stret coc store 25-6-55 SOC July'55
SX126 RNDA 28-8-45
SX127 RNDA 27-8-45
SX128 RNDA 10-9-45
SX129 RNDA 30-8-45
SX130 RNDA 3-9-45 AHU Stret 25-6-55 coc store
SX131 RNDA 31-8-45
SX132 RNDA 3-9-45
SX133 RNDA 6-9-45 AHU Stret 25-6-55 coc store
SX134 RNDA 7-9-45 TOC Cul 8-9 736S 5-5-48 799S July'49 1832S Mar'50 RNAY Fleet July'45 Halfar 19-9 AHU Stret 25-6-55 coc store SOC 19-5-56
SX135 RNDA 12-9-45 ETPS Farn 23 May to July 1946 for VHF trials
SX136 RNDA 11-9-45
SX137 RNDA 24-9-45 TOC Cul 25-9 759S 1831S AHU Stret 6-7-54 SOC July'55 Extant RNAS Yeovilton FAA Museum
SX138 RNDA 12-9-45 AHU Stret coc store 27-7-55
SX139 RNDA 21-9-45
SX152 RNDA 20-9-45 AHU Stret coc store 27-7-55
SX153 RNDA 20-9-45 GVI BDn Oct 1945 Handling & fuel functioning trials with 50 gall under fuselage drop tank fitted tear drop canopy Feb 1946 wing tank dropping MJL May 1946 Stored at AHU Stret 27-7-55
SX154 RNDA 5-10-45
SX155 RNDA 22-9-45
SX156 RNDA 22-9-45 TOC Cul 1-10 WAL mods 19-4-48 767S 14-7 AHU Stret 25-6-55 coc SOC 9-5-56
SX157 RNDA 24-9-45 CVI BDn Feb'46 Spinning trials

SX158 RNDA 26-9-45
SX159 RNDA 27-9-45 AHU Stret coc store 25-6-55
SX160 RNDA 28-9-45 778S AHU Stret coc store 27-7-55
SX161 RNDA 28-9-45 781S AHU Stret coc store 27-7-55
SX162 RNDA 27-9-45
SX163 RNDA 28-9-45 737S
SX164 RNDA 28-9-45
SX165 RNDA 6-10-45 AHU Stret coc store 25-6-55
SX166 RNDA 26-9-45
SX167 RNDA 29-9-45
SX168 RNDA 29-9-45 1831S
SX169 RNDA 29-9-45 rep 8-7-49 £2,429
SX170 RNDA 6-10-45 rep 8-7-49 £2,060
SX171 RNDA 5-10-45
SX172 RNDA 11-10-45 AHU Stret coc store 12-10-52
SX173 RNDA 13-10-74
SX174 RNDA 13-10-45
SX175 RNDA 29-10-45 rep 29-4-49 £2,061/4/8d
SX176 RNDA 17-10-45
SX177 RNDA 18-10-45
SX178 RNDA 17-10-45 AHU Stret store 27-7-55
SX179 RNDA 20-10-45
SX180 RNDA 19-10-45 WAL 20-10 RDU Cul 23-10 WAL recond 6-5-46 Stret 26-10-51 SOC 2-10-56
SX181 RNDA 27-10-45
SX182 RNDA 23-10-45 AHU Stret coc store 25-6-55
SX183 RNDA 23-10-45 WAL 23-10 RDU Cul 31-10 WAL mods 19-6-46 Helliwells 8-11-47 AHU Stret coc store 19-3-50 SOC 3-10-56
SX184 RNDA 31-10-45
SX185 RNDA 26-10-45
SX186 RNDA 27-10-45 AHU Stret store 27-7-55
SX187 RNDA 26-10-45
SX188 RNDA 31-10-45
SX189 RNDA 31-10-45 AHU Stret store 27-7-55
SX190 RNDA 14-11-45 AHU Stret store 27-7-55
SX191 RNDA 31-10-45
SX192 RNDA 31-10-45 AHU Stret store 27-7-55
SX193 RNDA 6-11-45
SX194 RNDA 31-10-45 781S 899S *HMS Hunter*
SX195 RNDA 6-11-45
SX196 RNDA 27-12-45
SX197 RNDA 8-11-45
SX198 RNDA 8-11-45
SX199 RNDA 10-11-45

Mk XV11s in use with the base flight at Culham, SX191 nearest.

SX200 RNDA 14-11-45

SX201 RNDA 16-11-45 WAL 14-11 RDU Cul 28-11 807S 24-4-46 WAL mods 18-3-47 1831S Stret 23-8 dam ldg 8-5-49 RNAY Fleet coc 10-1-50 AHU Stret 27-7-55 SOC 2-10-56

SX220 RNDA 10-11-45 WAL 12-11 RDU Cul 13-11 Abbott FLR 17-9-46 WAL mods 24-9 766S 11-9-47 cd 2-5-49 RNAY Fleet 1833S recond 19-7-51 coc 29-6-52 AHU Stret 27-7-55 SOC 2-10-56

SX221 RNDA 14-11-45 WAL 14-11 RDU Cul 16-11 Abbott FLR 27-5-46 WAL 24-6 Helliwells 6-12-47 AHU Stret coc store 16-12-49 SOC 2-10-56

SX222 RNDA 16-11-45

SX223 RNDA 17-11-45 WAL 20-11 RDU Cul 29-11 807S 18-4-46 WAL mods 1833S 21-8-47 VA mods 14-3-49 rep 1-11-49 £2,257 1832S 13-10-50 799S 20-3-52 AHU Stret coc store 2-7 SOC 2-10-56

SX224 RNDA 28-11-45

SX225 RNDA 26-11-45

SX226 RNDA 30-11-45

SX227 SX228 RNDA 26-11-45

SX229 SX230 RNDA 30-11-45 764S

SX231 RNDA 28-11-45

SX232 RNDA 19-1-46 Combat climb & level cooling MJL May '46 767S AHU Stret store 26-12-54

SX233 RNDA 28-11-45 AHU Stret store 27-7-55

SX234 SX235 SX236 SX237 RNDA 30-11-45 736S

SX238 RNDA 7-12-45 782S AHU Stret store 27-7-55

SX239 RNDA 3-12-45

SX240 RNDA 6-12-45 183S

SX241 RNDA 6-12-45

SX242 RNDA 6-12-45 WAL 3-12 RDU Cul 20-12 Abbott 21-5-46 WAL 5-7 1831S Nov '49

SX243 RNDA 6-12-45

SX244 RNDA 7-12-45

SX245 RNDA 14-12-45 AHU Stret store 27-7-55

SX246 RNDA 14-12-45 AHU Stret store 27-7-55

SX247 RNDA 15 5-12-45 AHU Stret store 27-7-55

SX248 RNDA 15-12-45

SX249 RNDA 22-12-45 AHU Stret store 27-7-55

SX250 RNDA 15-12-45 759S AHU Stret store 27-7-55

SX251 RNDA 27-12-45 WAL 27-12 RDU Cul 3-1-46 WAL mods 9-7 1830S 17-4-47 1832S 21-6-49 RNAY Fleet 18-4-51 coc 18-4-51 coc 18-2-52 SOC 25-6-55

SX252 RNDA 22-12-45 Farn June '49 RATOG trials

SX253 RNDA 22-12-45 RDU Cul 1-1-46 WAL mods 22-4 736S 13-11-48 RNAY Fleet 1-10-49 1831S 22-5-50 799S Jan '51d SOC 23-11-54

SX254 RNDA 27-12-45

SX255 RNDA 4-1-45

SX256 RNDA 29-12-45 WAL 29-12 RDU Cul 7-1-46 Abbott FLR 15-5 WAL mods 4-10 *HMS Veng* Halofar 10-11-47 805S 4-2-48 800S *HMS Triumph* 5-8-48 RNAY Fleet 10-1-50 1832S coc 24-11-51 AHU Stret store 27-7-55 SOC 2-10-56

SX271 RNDA 9-1-46 767S

SX272 RNDA 39-12-45 GVI BDn to Farn June '46 IFF trials

SX273 RNDA 12-1-46 741S

SX274 RNDA 31-12-45 rep 2-5-49 £2,443

SX275 RNDA 31-12-45

SX276 RNDA 31-12-45 WAL 8-2-46 RDU Cul 26-4 736S 25-9-47 738S July '50 RNAY Fleet recond 18-9 1831S 29-5-51 AHU Stret coc 13-9 SOC 2-10-56

SX277 RNDA 12-1-46

SX278 RNDA 12-1-46 WAL 12-1 RDU Cul 11-4 CBAF 2-6 766S 4-7-47 RNAY Fleet recond 3-12-49 coc 31-7-50 1831S 18-1-51 1833S 28-9 coc 28-9-51 SC'C 1-10-56

SX279 RNDA 16-1-46 WAL 14-1 RDU Cul 11-4 736S 11-7 VA EA rep 7-9-48 AHU Stret coc 23-3-50

SX280 RNDA 17-1-46

SX281 RNDA 16-1-46 rep 23-2-49 £2,16g

SX282 RNDA 19-1-46

SX283 RNDA 18-1-46 778S

SX284 RNDA 25-1-46 WAL 24-1 RDU Cul 25-4 Helliwells mods 15-11 AHU Stret coc 13-9-50 SOC 3-10

SX285 RNDA 23-1-46 WAL 22-1 RDU Cul 24-4 LoS

SX235, HMS Illustrious, 1950.

31-7 807S 2-8 R-R H 5-9 VA EA rep 7-9-48 rep 5-4-49 £2,283 AHU Stret 17-5-50 coc 1831S 5-1-51 dam taxy ROS 26-4 coc 17-5-52 AHU Stret SOC 1-10-56

SX286 RNDA 15-2-46

SX287 RNDA 26-1-46 AHU Stret store 27-7-55

SX288 RNDA 26-1-46 WAL 24-1 RDU Cul 30-4 WAL mods 17-10-47 1832S 30-9-48 RNAY Fleet 10-5-49 790S

SX289 RNDA 20-2-46 WAL 18-2 RDU Cul 30-4 807S 1-7-47 1831S 11-9 ARA Stret rep 24-6-48 RNAY Fleet 15-9 rep Stret 29-6-51 coc SOC 1-10-56

SX290 RNDA 31-1-46

SX291 RNDA 9-2-46 WAL 8-2 VA HPA 24-4 RDU Abbott rejected 20-5 VA 21-5 WAL mods 2-9 766S 19-6-47 RNAY Fleey recond 16-2-50 1833S 25-10 AHU Stret 24-7-52 coc SOC 1-10-56

SX292 RNDA 16-2-46

SX293 RNDA 15-2-46

SX294 RNDA 23-2-46 WAL 1-3 RDU Cul 1-5 *HMS Veng* Halfar 25-10-47 805S *HMS Ocean* 28-1-48 taxi into barrier struck two Seafires 14-4 728S 14-6 RNAY Fleet recon 11-9-51 AHU Stret 27-8-52 coc SOC 2-10-56

SX295 RNDA 15-2-46

SX296 RNDA 23-2-46 rep 16-11-49 £1,786 Inst of Bramcote June 1951

SX297 RNDA 28-2-46 Handling 4 RPs & 50 gall MJL June 1946

SX298 RNDA 9-3-46 rep 27-5-49 £2,138

SX299 RNDA 28-2-46 rep 7-4-49 £2,109

SX300 RNDA 28-2-46 Inst of Bramcote July 1954 as A205 parts to rebuild SX336 Extant, stored Warwick.

SX301 RNDA 28-2-46 WAL 6-4 RDU Cul 25-6 Helliwells 8-12-47 1832S 17-5-50 LoS rep 26-8 AHU Stret 24-9-52 coc SOC 2-10-56

SX302 RNDA 23-3-46

SX303 RNDA 16-3-46

SX304 RNDA 23-3-46 rep 5-4-49 £2,215

SX305 RNDA 23-3-46 WAL 6-4 RDU Cul 7-5 807S 31-7 778S 12-2-48 73S 11-4-49 RNAY Fleet repairs 7-7 GA 5-4-51 1832S 6-7 759S 24-10 RANY Fleet recon 30-6-52 AHU Stret 6-3-53 coc SOC 1-10-56

SX306 SX307 SX308 RNDA 30-3-46

SX309 RNDA 30-3-46 rep 21-6-49 £1,935 AHU Stret store 6-7-54

SX310 RNDA 6-4-46

SX311 RNDA 6-4-46 WAL 23-4 RDU Cul 15-5 VA HPA 16-5 Farn 23-5 accelerator trls RNAS Ford 17-6 RNAY Fleet rep & recon 8-8 736S 12-3-48 hvy land ROS 5-10-49 1832S 12-1-50 RNAY Fleet recon 18-7 1833S 15-6-51 AHU Stret 23-7-52 SOC 2-10-56

SX312 RNDA 27-4-46 Farn June 1948 trails rep 6-5-49 £2,117

SX313 RNDA 18-4-46 WAL 24-4 RDU Cul 24-4 Helliwells mods 20-1-48 737S 13-10 738S 5-5-50 RNAY Flee recon 10-4-51 AHU Stret 3-1-52 coc SOC 2-10-56

SX314 RNDA 25-4-46 Farn June '46 In RAE display 'Enemy a/c' on the accelerator. RATOG & accelerator trl July. July '47 accelerator equip trls. BDn with Attacker TS41 for RATOG & other trls. LoS Nov '48 land and t/o trls on flexi-deck 778S

SX315 RNDA 25-4-46

SX316 SX332 SX333 RNDA 30-4-46

SX334 FRXVII RNDA 18-5-46 HPA to VASM 30-3-47 fitt curved W/S 800S BDn Aug '47 AHU Stret 26-6-55 store coc

SX335 RNDA 30-4-46

SX336 RNDA 30-4-46 Inst of Bram as A2055 June '53 AHU Stret store 27-7-55 Extant, Twyford.

SX337 RNDA 30-4-46

SX338 RNDA 22-5-46

SX339 RNDA 30-5-46

SX340 RNDA 22-4-46 AHU Stret store 27-7-55

SX341 RNDA 24-5-46 to A727

SX342 RNDA 30-5-46 Farn Oct '48 catapult trls Hatfield Apl '49 fitt dual seal tyres. Farn night fly trls after catapult t/o., arrester gear trls. LoS Aug '49 BDn Farn Sept RATOG trls. Nov, hand, catapult & arrester gear trls., app & land. Weather tests. Replaced the Farn hack R7034 Mk I

SX343 SX344 SX345 800S SX346 RNDA 31-5-46

SX347 RNDA 31-5-46 rep 29-4-49 £2,499 AHU Stret store 27-7-55

SX348 RNDA 18-6-46

SX349 RNDA 21-6-46

SX350 RNDA 24-6-46 800S AHU Stret store 27-7-55

SX351 FXVII RNDA 24-6-46 800S *HMS Triumph*

SX352 RNDA 26-6-46

SX353 RNDA 30-6-46

SX354 RNDA 28-6-46

SX355 SX356 SX357 RNDA 30-6-46

SX358 RNDA 13-7-46 AHU Stret store 27-7-55

SX359 RNDA 13-7-46 799S

SX360 RNDA 20-7-46 Hand 2 wing tanks & 500lb bomb MJL Sept '46. As A2080 at Stret June '55 store 27-7-55

SX361 RNDA 25-7-46

SX362 SX363 RNDA 31-7-46

SX364 RNDA 31-7-46 1831S AHU Stret store 27-7-55

SX365 RNDA 31-7-46 727S

SX366 SX367 RNDA 28-8-46

SX368 RNDA 28-8-46 rep 6-9-49 £1,932

SX369 RNDA 31-8-46

SX370 RNDA 9-9-46

SX386 RNDA 31-8-46

SX387 RNDA 27-9-46

SX388 RNDA 30-9-46

SX389 RNDA 12-10-46 Pattern aircraft for checking spares

SX390-432, 451-490 and 503-546 cancelled.

THE ENIGMA EIGHTEEN

The next Seafire variant was planned as the Type 395 Seafire Mk XVIII for reference was made to it in the minutes of a meeting at Boars Hill on 10 October 1945 between Rolls-Royce and Supermarine representatives. The particular reference read – "Griffon 36. Although prototypes were proceeding there was nothing definite about production airframes and engines. Supermarine undertook to obtain a definite ruling as to when this type was required, and in what quantities, and to inform Rolls-Royce. One Griffon 36 engine has been delivered to Hursley Park".

The design specification indicates it would have been utilised as an armed photo-reconnaissance aircraft with either a Griffon 36 or 37 driving a five bladed propeller. The only other details available are that it was to be similar in appearance to its immediate predecessor with a lengthened fuselage, four .303 Browning machine guns and two 22½ gallon wing combat tanks. The serial allocation for the prototype was RT646 which was later cancelled, as was the designation. The latter was re-allocated to the Spitfire.

The idea of the specialised photo-reconnaissance single seater was being phased out in favour of the FR types and by the time the prototype construction was ready to start Rolls-Royce had produced the Griffon 60 series of engines, and the decision taken to equip the Navy with a navalised version of the Super Spitfire, the F Mk 21. Planning had been in hand for some time for an entry in the Vickers-Supermarine modifications log dated 17 April 1945 read – "To introduce the Seafire 18 (Mk 17 with Griffon 36 engine)."

The only performance figures released on the XVIII applied to endurance. 1.30hrs at normal fuel (101 gallons), combat range 102 miles @ 230mph; 2.02hrs NF + 33gal rear fus tank, CR 189 @ 232; 2.86hrs NF+RT+45 gal wing tip tanks, CR 283 miles @ 230; 2.96hrs NF + RT + 50gal o/ld tank, CR 296 @ 232; 3.60hrs NF + RT + 90 gal o/ld, CR 368 @ 232.

THE SUPER SEAFIRE - STAGE ONE

By the year 1943 the Spitfire/Seafire series of fighters had been in continuous service for over five years, and still the variants appeared. The second prototype Mk IV/20, DP851, and converted Mk VIII, JF319, were fitted with the new Griffon 60 Series engine in that year, the latter also having the lifted, leading edge wing. Supermarine were investigating a new wing and the combination of this and the Griffon had resulted in the Spitfire Mk 21. Large numbers had been ordered for the Royal Air Force, and the Admiralty, after a long delay, said that they wanted evidence of trials results before placing an order for a navalised version.

In a letter to the Air Ministry the 5th Sea Lord wrote:- 'The Seafire Mk XII (MkXV) is well under way and the Seafire counterpart of the Spitfire Mk 21 is under investigation at present and may be regarded as the 1945 fighter. Two types are required: (1) a high class interceptor with minimum petrol in order to have a performance to meet shore-based aircraft and (2) an escort, or long range fighter which must long range endurance to that of a strike force. The latest version of the Spitfire Mk 21, due for production in June 1944, should be accepted without wing fold and minimum of adaptation, i.e. hooks and naval equipment only. We will then have time to investigate the possibility of introducing the more novel variant of the Spitfire 21 known as the Victor, which has laminar flow wings". It was apparent that the Admiralty was again looking for the familiar stop-gap fighter to fullfil its operational needs until the proposed Spitfire (Victor) Mk 23 became available. At the same time Hawker Aircraft was invited to submit a proposal for a navalised Tempest and a schedule for the production of 40 aircraft per month during 1945.

To help events along Supermarine produced Specification No 474 on 5 October 1943 and it was headed- "Seafire Development- Griffon Two-Stage Engine. This specification outlines a development of the Seafire XV incorporating a laminar flow wing and Griffon two stage engine. Details: Wing- Laminar flow aerofoil sections, folding for stowage, wide track chassis. Fuselage- Improved view over nose (8°), and rear view sliding hood. Powerplant- Griffon two stage engine with counter rotating airscrews. Armament- 4 × 20mm cannon with 150rpg. Provision for accelerating and deck arresting. Fuel capacity- fixed tankage 116 gallons; drop tank 45 gallons. Main dimensions- span 35ft 0in; width folded 17ft 0in; height folded 13ft 9in; length overall 32ft 3in; wing area 210 sq ft; airscrew diameter 11ft 0in. Weights- bare weight 6,560lb; fixed military load 395; armour 200; tare weight 7,155lb; typical service load 960; fuel (116gal) 835; oil (9gal) 80; total weight 9,060 lb. Note: Military load is based on Seafire XV except that armament is increased to four cannon with 150rds/cannon and lightened wireless equipment is assumed.

Estimated performance. The following performances are quoted for the Griffon 61 engine (18 lb boost rating). Engine development is proceeding rapidly and increases in boost, improving low altitude performance still further, are certain by the time this aircraft is in production. The dotted lines on the curves are the estimated performances at 25 lb/sq in boost. Maximum speed 424 knots @ 26,000ft; stalling speed full load 88 knots; initial rate of climb 4,900 ft min; service ceiling 41,750ft; take off run from deck, see curve. A hook for the F21 sting arrester with an ultimate strength based on test of 32,500 lb will shortly be supplied by the RAF."

In 1944 Air Ministry Specification N7/44 was issued for the navalised Spitfire Mk 21 and the task of converting the design for naval service was allocated to Cunliffe Owen. Following upon the jump in naval Seafire designations beginning with Mk 41, the designation Mk 45 was allocated to the new Seafire, but the aircraft was to be regarded as an interim type until the new Supermarine wing was ready. Phase two was to produce the Seafire Mk 46 and phase three the Mk 47 in 1945.

The Ministry of Aircraft Production wrote to Vickers on 15 August 1944 and directed them to set aside three F 21 airframes for use as Mk 45 prototypes and allocated the serial numbers TM379, 383 and 389. They were to be delivered from Castle Bromwich to Hursley Park for modification under Contract Aircraft/4425/C.23c. On 24 January 1946 MAP again wrote to Vickers saying that as a result of altered service requirements only two aircraft were needed. TM389 was cancelled.

The converted prototype TM379 was at High Post on 24 October 1944 for weighing and CoG determination.The sting hook fuselage was 33ft 4in in length, slinging points were installed, undercarriage wheel fairings reduced at forward ends to provide clearance over arrester wires and the outboard wheel doors enlarged to compensate for the gap. It had a standard fixed F 21 wing. With a Griffon 61 engine of 2,035hp and a Rotol five blade wooden propeller it weighed (tare) 7,121lb.

It was at Boscombe Down on 4 November the same year for deck suitability trails, where the auw was recorded as 9,410 lb with the CoG 4.9ins aft of datum, undercarriage down. Although a larger rudder had been fitted take off required full left trim. The starboard wing tended to drop on becoming airborne but this was easily corrected by the use of ailerons. In the glide approach, flaps and undercarriage down at 90 knots, controls were light and effective, and lateral stability was good. As the F 21 was considered unacceptable for operations above 25,000 feet, it was recommended that the new Spitfire be restricted to a lower altitude because of the small fin and rudder. Boscombe Down was satisfied with the new aeroplane but the poor directional stability was a cause for concern as a Loose Minute of a meeting between the DCAP and the DAI of 8 February 1945 reveals – "The poor directional stability of the Spitfire F 21 is causing difficulties and Supermarine are investigating. Any changes will amount to minor alterations in the area of the rudder horn balance plus deletion of the balance feature of the tab. Smith has also had some success using the large chord rudder, but I hope we can avoid this for the F 21 Similar work is going on with the Seafire 45 and here the identical solution may apply, but when the CR propeller is introduced a bigger change will be necessary, this taking the form of a forward extension of the fin."

TM379 was returned to Supermarine for the installation of a new Griffon engine modified to drive a Rotol six blade contra-prop. Also, the fin was extended forward on the leading edge. After leaving High Post it was flown for the first time in its new guise by Shea-Simmonds. Naturally Quill, and Shea-Simmonds, flew TM379 and a resume of their flight test reports are reproduced below.

(Quill 27-10-44). Flown for brief handling. Found to be slightly left wing low in the dive, the rudder control with sting hook considered adequate for take off and landing and suitable for deck landing. Directional stability poor. (Quill 27-10). Ailerons heavy, no split armour fitted. The CG, therefore, is somewhat forward of 4.7". (S-S 6-2-45). Fitted Rotol contra propeller. Brief handling flight with aircraft decidedly left wing low. This is my first flight with the contra prop, but directional stability was conspicuous by its absence at all speeds.(Quill 6-2). Very brief flight, extremely left wing low indicating that directional stability was quite unacceptable. (Quill 9-2). Flown with de Havilland contra prop. Fore and aft stability considered better than with the Rotol. However, aircraft unstable and non-acceptable at high altitude both directionally and fore and aft. Considerable vibration from propeller which got worse at high speed. When moving airscrew lever back there is a drop of 10 lbs in oil pressure.

(Shea-S 11-4). During this flight it was noticed that the maximum boost which could be obtained was + 12 lb sq in, the limit being imposed by a wire across the throttle gate. I understand that this control is cleared for 18 lb boost and the wire will be removed. At speeds in excess of 360 knots directional stability and the effects of yaw and pitch in common in F 21 and Seafire 45 aircraft, becomes quite pronounced and neither of these features are considered to be acceptable. It would seem that some benefit may be derived from fitting beading on the rudder trailing edge, and an elevator with rounded horn balance would be an advantage. In my opinion the only real solution for this contra propeller Griffon is the large stern end.

(Quill 11-4). Trailing edge strips had been attached to the rudder to improve directional stability but it is still quite unacceptable.

(Shea-S). This aircraft has an extra 1½in fitted to the rudder horn since its previous flight. In this condition I consider there is some improvement in directional control and stability.

(Quill 16-4). Flown with increased horn depth from 11 to 11½in; trailing edge beading still present. Directional stability regarded as just acceptable. (Quill 17-4). Trailing edge beading removed and replaced by split trailing edge tabs as previously tested on LA213. Little change.

TM379, first prototype Seafire Mk 45, was originally ordered as an F 21 Spitfire. At this time it lacked rudder modification 429 which was the split trim tab. TM379 was modified with the installation of a Rotol contra-prop. The CP installation resulted in a marked fin and rudder modification.

Deck arresting trials with TM379 were carried out on *HMS Pretoria Castle* in late 1944 and early 1945 and Catapult Test Note No 113 contains the full story- "Summary. Trials were carried out at sea on *HMS Pretoria Castle* to proof the navalised Spitfire XXI aircraft for arrested landing on aircraft carriers. They commenced on 21 November. The aircraft TM379 had been proofed for retardations up to 3G by taxying trials into the arrester gear at RAE, Farnborough, on 15 November 1944. A Total of 14 landings was made on the carrier at wind speeds over the deck of 28 to 35 knots. The highest retardation normally recorded was 1.75G with the aircraft at fighter overload weight of 9,400lb. A retardation of 2.55G was recorded on one landing, this high figure presumably being due to a fault in the ship's arrester gear. Damage to the aircraft while landing at a shore base necessitated abandonment of the trials".

TM379 was fitted with a sting hook previously installed on the Seafire XV prototype NS487 but with an S.32 type forged steel hook in place of the welded plate hook. The trials were to determine landing performance of the aircraft at weights up to an overload of 9,400lb, at wind speeds over a deck of 30, 25 and 20 knots, to examine the tendency of pitching during arrest, behaviour of undercarriage and tyres, and the necessity of a tailwheel guard to prevent fouling. Normal entry speed into the arrester wires was 60 knots with a wind average of 30. Approach speeds were between 85 to 90 knots. On the fourth landing the aircraft stalled and the wing dropped, damaging propeller and wing tips.

On 26 February 1945 a letter from MAP arrived at Supermarine with confirmation of the Contract B.981687/39/C.23(c) for 600 N7/44 Spitfire aircraft to be built as the Marks 45/46/47, together with instructions on rate of delivery. As from 1 August five Mk 45s were to be delivered each month until the following November, making a total of twenty. This was to be followed by the production of 200 Mk 46s, deliveries to commence on 1 August 1945 and terminate in June 1946. The Mk47; 150 examples to be delivered from 1 September 1945 and end in December 1946.

The Director of Naval Air Organisation was anxious to obtain examples of the new Seafire mark and wrote to the Admiralty on his hopes for the aircraft. He wrote- "It is considered that the newer marks of Seafire, owing to their exceptional rate of climb and maneouvrability, will be useful as interceptor fighters, particularly against the suicide dive bombers. The Grumman Bearcat will be in large scale production in America some three months before the Seafire Mk 47 and looks like being considerably inferior in performance to the Seafire both as an interceptor, escort fighter or fighter bomber. For at least the past two and a half years efforts have been put into the evolution of a first class, highly bred, British carrier fighter. The Seafire is the answer in its later marks with which we are planning to equip the majority of carriers to fight the Pacific war. However, I do feel some confusion has arisen through the use of the generic term 'Seafire' to cover a number of marks of interceptor fighters which vary in top speed over a range of nearly 100mph".

LA436, a production Mk 45, was flown for maker's trials by Shea-Simonds on 10 and 11 May 1945 and apart from mild criticism of the gun sight obscuring the air speed indicator he thought it performed satisfactory. It was weighed at High Post on 18 May and had a tare of 7,050lb and an auw of 9,358.

Carrier trials of the Seafire 45 continued in July 1945 when the performance of PK245, a Mk XV fitted with tail down launching hooks and wing combat tanks, was compared with two standard production Mk 45s- LA440 and 441. The Mk XV made nine tail down accelerated take offs and arrested landings at an auw of 7,980lb and one at 8,336. The 45s each made ten take offs and landings; on the fifth LA440 damaged its hook and on the eighth the hook pulled out of its mounting and the aircraft crashed into the barrier, becoming a total loss, although the pilot's cockpit remained intact. The Seafire was then returned to High Post. LA441 completed its trials without incident with 15 landings. TM379 then joined the carrier, *HMS Pretoria Castle,* to take part in the trials. Two other Mk 45s LA454 and 480 were flown aboard *Pretoria Castle* the follow-

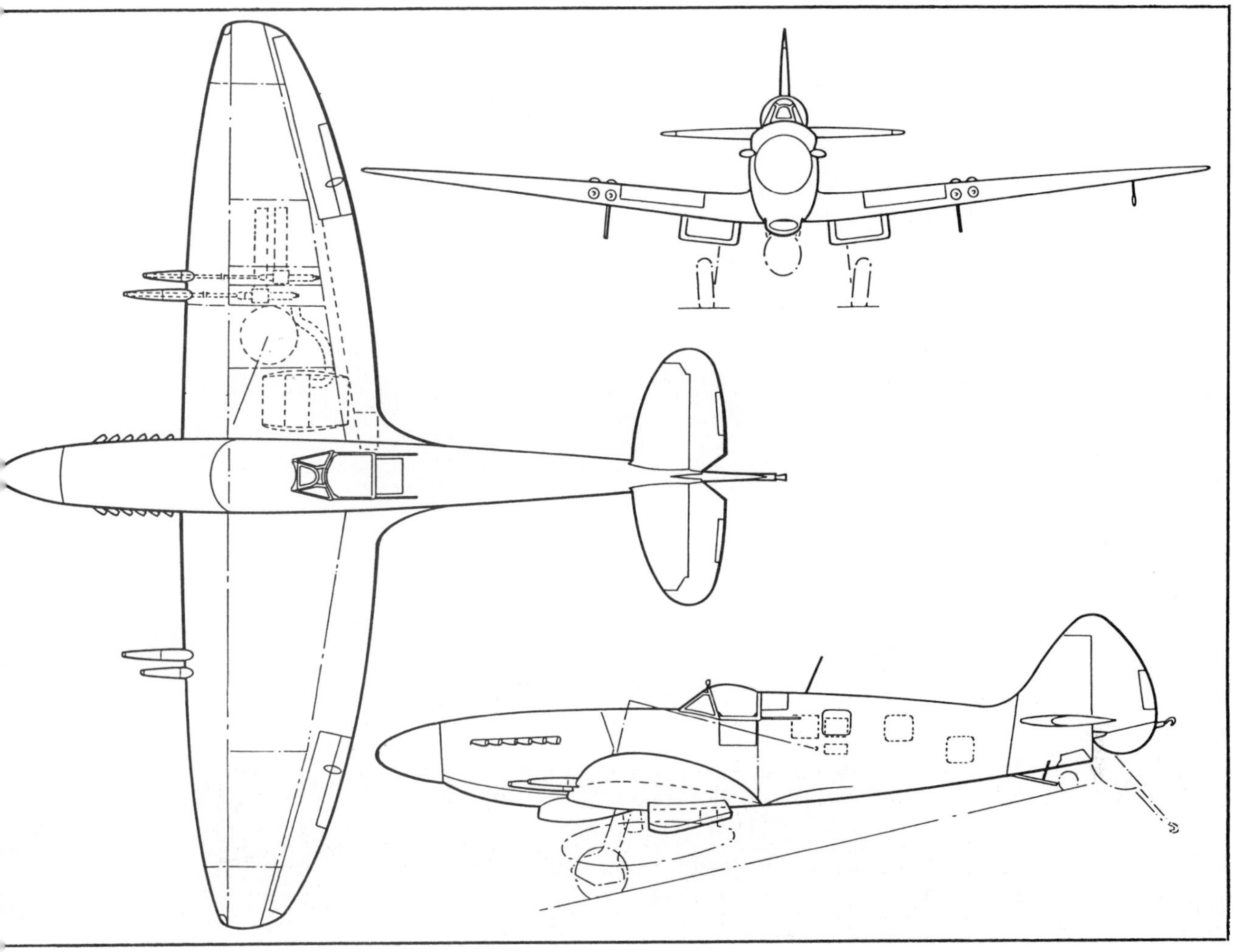

Seafire Mk 45.

.ike the Spitfire F 21 the Seafire 45 needed additional control because of ıe torque from the Rotol five bladed propeller. Initially a small fixed ıngle plate was added above the rudder trim. Modification 429 resulted in a larger plate, plus a split tab.

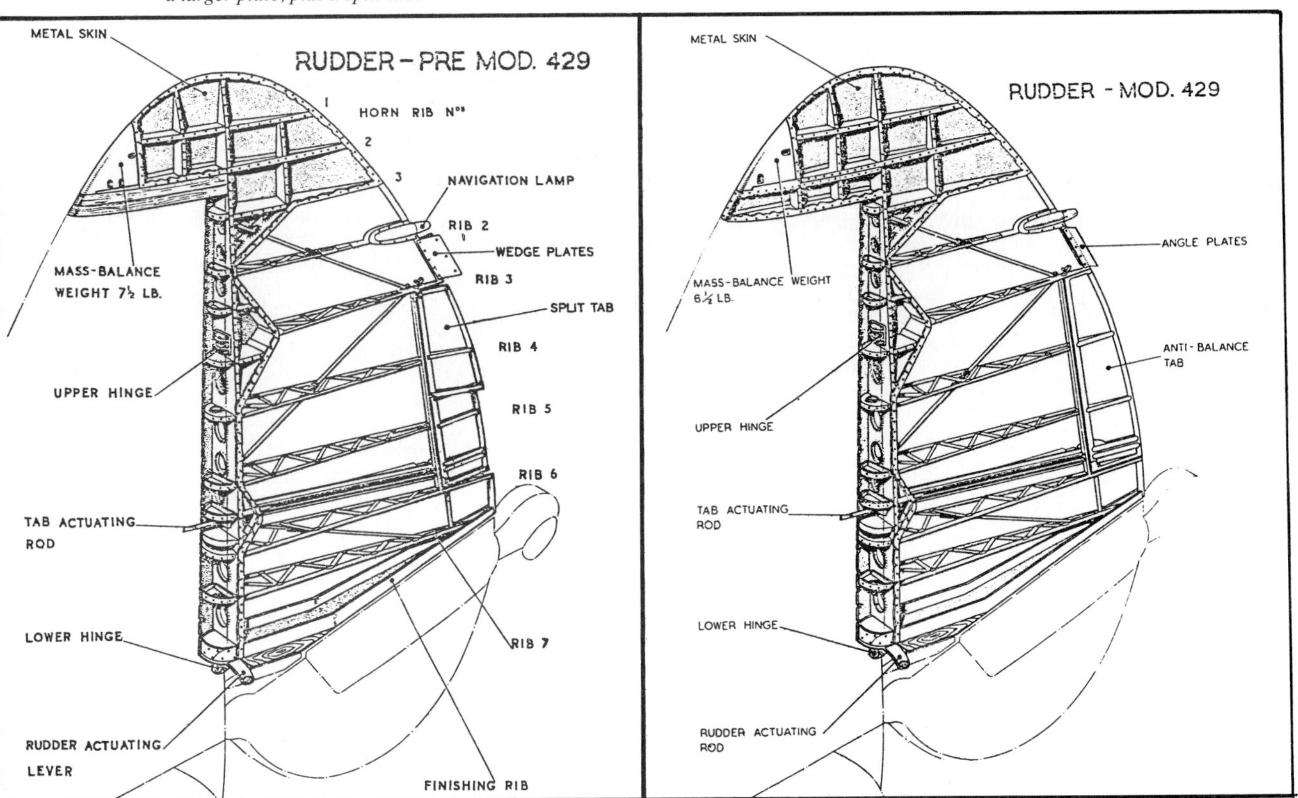

LA446 had its Griffon 61 engine removed and a Griffon 85 contra prop installation fitted in October 1945. It is seen here at Boscombe Down.

ing October to complete a total of 200 deck landings in order to clear the type for service use. The contra prop on TM379 had been changed for a single propeller and it made a brief appearance during the trials. A total of 193 landings were made at an auw of 9,350lb and were considered satisfactory.

Production of the Seafire Mk 45 ran from LA428 to LA499 and a total of 50 were delivered to the Navy. They saw limited service and were soon replaced by the Mks 46 and 47, but their usefulness was not over for a number were used for trials connected with the safety barriers on naval carriers. They were carried out at RAE Meadow Gate with three surplus Mk 45s, LA439, 442 and 450 fitted with contra props during October/November 1951. Auw was 8,400lb and Rotol six blade dural propellers used. LA439 was the first to be launched into the barrier in a tail up position with the engine running at 800rpm. Sixteen 3in rockets pushed the cradled Seafire up to 60 knots, after which the aircraft left the catapult and flew under its own power, pitching onto its nose after the C/Ps engaged the barrier. LA442 was next and apart from the damaged propellers little airframe damage occurred. LA450 followed and it, too, suffered little damage. LA439 was flown for a second trial and after engaging the barrier overturned and LA450 was badly damaged at the conclusion of the final flight.

The trials demonstrated that Wyvern pilots engaging such a barrier would be in no particular danger. A second set of trials using the same rocket catapult at Meadow Gate were initiated using LA448 fitted with a Seafang contra prop for crash landing experiments. The Seafire was launched with undercarriage retracted at a speed of 56 knots on 2 December and travelled 90 feet before the propellers struck the concrete runway. It then skidded 205 feet on the runway, slid across a patch of tarmac for 64 feet and 197ft on the grass surround before coming to rest.

Surplus Seafires were not always that docile when being destroyed for experiments as during one of the Meadow Gate trials a Seafire fitted with crash intertia switches was launched from the catapult for what was supposed to be a 'last' journey of several hundred yards. Watched by an apprehensive group of technicians the Seafire kept going and after several hair raising minutes it crash landed without incident. Another series of trials was concerned with the launch of dead weights from the advanced (steam) catapult then under development. Originally the dead weights were metal tanks loaded to specific values, and in order to make the trials more realistic it was decided to use surplus Seafire 45s. The first aircraft had the outer wing panels from the cannon fold removed and was launched in the tail down position off the Isle of Wight from a carrier. Instead of the Seafire ditching immediately ahead of the carrier it took off and flew in ever decreasing circles around the trials vessel. After five minutes the decision was taken to 'shoot the Seafire down', but before action could be taken the aircraft entered the water to general relief.

LA436 was test flown by Shea-Simmonds on 10 and 11 May 1945 and he reported favourably on the aircraft. It was delivered to High Post on the 18th for weighing and CG determination with a Griffon 61 and Rotol five blade wooden propeller. Tare 7,050lb, auw 9,358. Two main undercarriage failures occurred when the starboard leg of LA454 failed in bending. Trouble was also experienced with hook release after arresting.

The Mk 45 saw limited service and was soon replaced by the Mks 46 and 47.

SERIAL NUMBERS

Vickers Armstrong (Castle Bromwich) Ltd.
Contract No. B981687/39
Seventh order for 300 Spitfire Mk VC dated March 1942. Order cancelled in 1943. Re-established same year for 120 Spitfire Mk 21. Order extended for 92 Seafire Mk 45. First 50 built as Mk 45s at Castle Bromwich 1944 to 1945. The following serials apply to Mk 45s built to this seventh order. LA428 to 457, 480 to 499. Total 50.

600 ordered 12 April 1945 on Seafire 45/46/47 under contract AIR/4424/C.23(c) from Castle Bromwich between VD490 and VE593 as under; VD490-499, 521-568, 582-597, 618-653, 679-696, 714-748, 763-792, 809-856, 869-893, 925-961, 984-999, VE135-162, 176-193, 233-259, 274-296, 328-362, 379-391, 406-447, 462-498, 516-542 and 563-593.

This contract was however cancelled on 1 August.

LA series All Mk 45 Griffon 61 Built at CBAF assembled VASM

LA428 15478 SM 17-1-45 t/flt A Henshaw 20min CRD VA HPA 17-2 Fitt G85 (C/P) Farn May'45 trls. Trans from R Navy to RAF under Admiralty DAE 788/45 HPA-WDn 9-6

LA429 15479 SM 4-2-45 39MU Cole 1-3 G85 (C/P) instal & del to RAF 31-3

LA430 15480 SM 20-2-45 del by Capt Stedall ATA RNDA 39MU Cole 2-3 G85 (C/P) instal and mods tail unit (one of 12 a/c del for RN service)

LA431 15481 SM 24-2-45 RNDA 39MU Cole 28-2 VASM for T.I 20-12 Farn Jan'46 trls VASM 30-4 NAS Cul 15-5

LA432 15482 SM 3-3-45 RNDA del 39MU Cole by F/Capt Ellis ATA 13-3

LA433 15483 SM 11-4-45 RNDA 39MU Cole 4-5

LA434 15484 SM 16-4-45 RNDA 39MU Cole 21-11

LA435 15485 SM 19-4-45 RNDA 39MU Cole 27-4

LA436 15486 SM 27-4-45 HPA 10-5 33MU 21-11

LA437 15487 SM 28-4-45 33MU Lyne 15-5

LA438 15488 SM 11-5-45 RNDA 33MU Lyne 29-5

LA439 15489 SM 15-5-45 RNDA 33MU Lyne 4-6 ret SM 30-5 G85 instal (C/P) 33MU 4-6 Farn Feb'47 surplus to requirements Used for spcl catapult trls with LA422 and 450 Oct '50. See page 574.

LA440 15490 SM 19-5-45 RNDA 39MU Cole 31-5 SM 8-6 re-allot CRD HPA 11-6 Farn 18-6 RNAS Arbroath 27-6 778S

LA441 15491 FF 26-5-45 CRD VA SM 26-5 RNAS Arb 15-6

LA442 15492 CRD VASM 29-5-45 G85 instal (C/P) New tail unit instal. Trls with LA444 Farn Dec'47 surplus del Farn 14-10-50 for spcl rocket catapult trls with LA439 and 450. See page 574.

LA443 15493 SM 2-6-45 RNDA 33MU 9-6 SM for mods 25-6 HPA 30-7 BDn Aug'46 car mon contam tests. Trls with Very pistol door instal. 500lb bomb on Mk III univ carr

LA444 15494 SM 9-6-45 G85 (C/P) instal for serv trls

LA443 went to Boscombe Down in August 1946 for a series of trials, including a number with ordnance loads. Mod 429 has resulted in the addition of the rudder wedge and split trim tab.

LA429 was the second production Mk 45 and as such lacked the rudder wedge and mod 429. New, anti fouling arrester wire wheel fairings are clearly visible.

LA445 15495 SM 13-6-45 CBAF 14-6 SM 21-9 rud trls HPA 17-10

LA446 15496 SM 22-6-45 CBAF 23-6 G85 (C/P) instal BDn Nov'45 trls with new eng

LA447 15497 SM 27-6-45 CBAF 28-6 G85 (C/P) instal

LA448 15498 SM 23-6-45 CBAF 23-6 G85 (C/P) instal Farn Oct'48 for spcl rocket catapult trls. Seafang C/Ps instal.

LA449 15499 SM 26-6-45 CBAF 28-6 G85 instal (C/P)

LA450 15500 SM 29-6-45 CBAF 30-6 G85 (C/P) instal and mods RNAS Ford 10-1-46 778S Farn April'48 surplus for spcl rocket catapult trls with LA439 and 442. See page ????

LA451 15501 SM 29-6-45 CBAF 30-6 RNAS Arb 3-7 SM mods 11-7 RNAS Ford 4-1-46

LA452 15502 SM 29-6-45 CBAF 30-6 RNAS Arb 11-7

LA453 15503 SM 28-7-45 RNAD 33MU 31-7

LA454 15504 SM 10-7-45 RNAD Arb 13-7 HPA 2-8

LA455 15505 SM 24-7-45 RNDA 33MU 31-7 re eng G61 SM RNAS LoS 15-10-48

LA456 15506 SM 27-7-45 COI CFNR 31-9 CBAF for paint 30-9 RNAS LoS 12-8-48

LA457 15507 SM 27-7-45 CBAF for paint 30-7 RNDA 39MU 31-7 CB 1-8 RNAS 3-8

LA480 15508 SM 10-8-45 signal RNAS Anth re alloc CRD CBAF 31-8-45

LA481 15509 SM 6-9-45 allot HPA re allot RNAD Anth 2-9 VA Hen for spcl trls 29-9 SM 3-10 771S 1947

LA482 15510 SM 17-8-45 RNAS Anth 4-9

LA483 15511 SM 22-8-45 RNAS Anth 4-9

LA484 15512 SM 23-8-45 RNAS Anth 4-9

LA485 15513 Sm 24-8-45 allot RNAS re allot RAF Hull for spcl trls 31-8 re eng SM 3-10 RNAS LoS 19-11-48

LA486 15514 SM 29-8-45 RNAS Anth 18-9 SM re eng RNAS LoS 3-9-48 771S

LA487 15515 SM 11-9-45 RNAS Anth 19-10

LA488 15516 SM 14-9-45 RNAS Anth 8-10

LA489 15517 SM 11-10-45 RNAS Anth 30-10- 780S

LA490 15518 SM 15-9-45 CBAF for paint 27-9 SM 4-10 RNAS Anth 10-10

LA491 15519 SM 19-10-45 allot CRD Tang by Admiralty re allot HPA 31-10 RNAS LoS 6-11 for demo

LA492 15520 SM 9-11-45 CRD HPA 26-11

LA493 15521 SM 20-11-45 RAF Hull 21-12 SM 29-12 RNAS Anth RNAS LoS 8-9-48

LA494 15522 SM 17-11-45 CBAF 17-11 allot RNAS Taajmaklosi 787S re allot RAF West Ray 30-11

LA495 15523 SM 26-11-45 RNAS Gosp 14-12

LA496 15524 SM 27-11-45 RNAS Thor Is 14-12 703S

LA497 15525 SM 14-12-45 RNAS Hens 4-1-46

LA498 15526 SM 8-12-45 BDn 29-12 re eng RNAS LoS 22-10-48

LA499 15527 SM 15-12-45 RNAS Anth 2-1-46

TM379 G61 VA HrPK 31-8-44 Farn Nov'44 G87 with Rotol C/Ps instal, plus enlarged fin and rud. COAL Stn 1-9 con to proto Seafire F45 from F21 Spitfire BDN June'45 deck oper suit trls. Two piece non standard rud trim tab. SM 19-12-45 29MU 14-1-46 602S 10-4-47 SOC 3-6-48

SUPER SEAFIRE – STAGES TWO AND THREE

The Seafire Mk 45, 46 and 47 represented the progressive development of the Spitfire Mk 21 to meet naval requirements. The intention was to have a semi-navalised (fixed wing) F 21 in production by January 1945, followed by the fully navalised version in September of that year. Stage Two of navalising the F 21 Super Spitfire was the Seafire Mk 46 and the major differences between it and the Stage One Mk 45 was the Spiteful-type empennage and standardisation of the counter rotating propellers, this arrangement transforming a rather doubtful aeroplane into a pleasant one. However, the wings did not fold making it unsuitable for stowage on some carriers, and of a total of 200 originally ordered only 24 were constructed and delivered. The prototype Mk 46 was TM383, originally scheduled as the third prototype Mk 45, but withdrawn from that contract and delivered to Cunliffe Owen Aircraft for modification.

The new prototype made its maiden flight on 8 September 1944 and by January the following year was well into its test flying programme, this being shared mainly by Quill and Shea-Simmonds. Highlights from these trials are recorded –

(Quill 19-1-45). Check directional stability. During the flight it was noticed that the flaps were opening in the dive with the undercarriage lever in the neutral and up position. An indicator was fitted to the trailing edge of the flap to establish whether the flap was moving or it was movement of the door in the top surface of the skin. Results proved that the flap was moving. Mr Beaumont felt that the flap jack was not at fault and that the trouble was due to flap deflection. It was decided to fit a micro switch to detect flap movement, plus three trailing edge indicators and a camera situated under the aircraft's stern to photograph events.

(Quill) 3-2). Test installations revealed that the flaps moved down when the lever is in neutral and the aircraft moving at 200mph plus. Severe vibrations were felt in the dive.

(Quill 7-2). Handling with sting hook type rudder with extra lamination. Directional stability not acceptable.

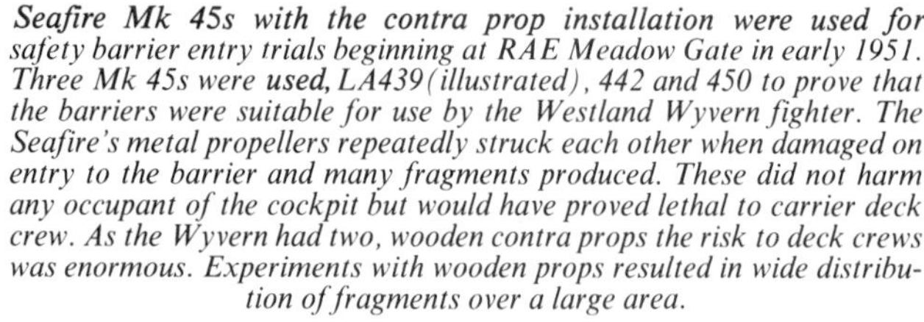

Seafire Mk 45s with the contra prop installation were used for safety barrier entry trials beginning at RAE Meadow Gate in early 1951. Three Mk 45s were used, LA439 (illustrated), 442 and 450 to prove that the barriers were suitable for use by the Westland Wyvern fighter. The Seafire's metal propellers repeatedly struck each other when damaged on entry to the barrier and many fragments produced. These did not harm any occupant of the cockpit but would have proved lethal to carrier deck crew. As the Wyvern had two, wooden contra props the risk to deck crews was enormous. Experiments with wooden props resulted in wide distribution of fragments over a large area.

(Shea-S 12-3). Flown with modified metal elevator with reduced trim tab as fitted to LA211 and 215. Installation unacceptable. Second elevator fitted and flown. Hunting apparent at 250mph.
(Shea-S 3-4). At 420mph the port flap was open at about ½in at trailing edge, with starboard flap door ¼in. The starboard flap was apparently twisting and partially opening at the outboard end. At 525mph and 10,000ft both flap doors open to ¾in at trailing edge. Directional and longitudinal stability shows deterioration.
(Shea-S 8-4). Brief handling flight with thick trailing edge elevator. At 500mph both flap doors opening slightly.
(Quill 12-4). Spinning trials with recovery at 15,000ft. Spins to right uncomfortable and unreliable. In the first spin the aircraft was so rough in its fore and aft and lateral pitching that it virtually threw itself out of the spin after $1\frac{1}{2}$ turns of the spin proper. It is thought that the behaviour of the aircraft in right hand spins is somewhat unpredictable. Aircraft fitted with two separate ASI systems.
(Quill 11-5). Dived in formation with LA436 flown by Shea-Simmonds. At 495 knots LA436 was going steeper and accelerating but vibration on TM383 became such that it was eased out of the dive.
(Quill 24-5). Flown with fabric elevator in place of metal unit on account of vibration in dives. Tests showed vibration was worse and engine suspected as cause. Aircraft smoother with new engine and maximum speed of 510mph attained. After flight it was found that the starboard wheel doors were damaged.
(Quill 13-6). On first flight undercarriage refused to retract so test abandoned. Second flight with four inches of split beading added to rudder trailing edge above the tab. The aircraft as it now stands, whilst not being perfect, is considered good and certainly better than the Seafire Mk XV.

All the 24 Mk 46s had been delivered by March 1947 but none entered carrier service. Most of the airframes were utilised for trial purposes, such as LA 545, 552 and 545, for development of the Seafire FR 47.

SERIAL NUMBERS

Vickers Armstrong (Castle Bromwich) Ltd.

Contract No. B981687/39

The twenty-four F 46s began life as part of the seventh order for 300 Spitfire Mk VC dated March 1942. Contract cancelled in 1943 but re-established as 120 Spitfire Mk 21. Order extended for 92 Seafire Mk 45 and Mk 46 between LA428 and 582. The following serials apply to Mk 46s built to this seventh order. LA541 to 564. Total 24.

LA series A11 Mk 46 Griffon 61, buillt at CBAF, assembled VASM.

LA541 High Post 5-11-45, dives at 450kts, AAEE 21-2-46
LA542 19982 SM High Post 20-12-45, used for hand with wing combat tanks and 9½" RPs
LA543 19986 SM RNAS Anth
LA544 19987 SM FF 13-6-46, RNAS Anth 4-7-46
LA545 First Griffon 88 fitted, FF 26-3-46, CRD 2-5, to Copenhagen 20-6 demo. Fitt spring tab elevator as Spiteful FXIV improvement, fitt Mk47 extended-type intake for comp with standard, standard best
LA546 RNAS Anth 25-3-46
LA547 19991 SM FF 10-5-46, RNAS Anth 4-7
LA548 19992 SM FF 3-6-46, RNAS Anth 4-7
LA549 FF 20-6-46, EPTS Cranfield 3-7
LA550 19995 SM FF 9-7-46, RNAS Anth 9-8
LA551 19998 SM FF 19-7-46, RNAS Anth 9-8, 1832S as '109:CH'
LA552 19999 SM FF 13-8-46, RNAS Anth 10-9
LA553 20001 SM FF 23-8-46, RNAS Anth 10-9
LA554 20005 SM FF 7-9-46, RNAS Anth 19-9
LA555 FF 19-9-46, RNAS Anth 2-10-46
LA556 FF 5-10-46, RNAS Anth 30-10-46
LA557 FF 28-10-46, ETPS Cranfield 18-11
LA558 FF 18-11-46, ETPS Cranfield 2-12
LA559 FF 16-12-46, RNAS Anth 24-1-47
LA560 FF 4-12-46, RNAS Anth 23-1-47
LA561 FF 22-1-47, fitt skid indicator trial instal, RNAS Anth 3-3
LA562 FF 6-2-47, High Post 24-2
LA563 FF 19-3-47, RNAS Anth 29-4
LA564 FF 14-3-46 F/Lt Wigley, CRD High Post 2-5-46. AAEE 14-9, hand trls (Quill) 4 x 100lb RPs, 1 x 500lb bomb, depth charge, 8 x RPs and 50 gall torpedo-shaped drop tank. RNAS Fleet 14-10 rep, RNAS Gosp 9-5-47, RNAS Anth 1-49. 767S 4-50, 738S 7-50, SOC RNAS Anth 29-6-51. Extant, under restoration by Peter Arnold, Newport Pagnell. (One RAF source quotes that this airframe was PV585 produced at CBAF, renumbered, del 27-4-46.)
TM383 prototype, see page 573.

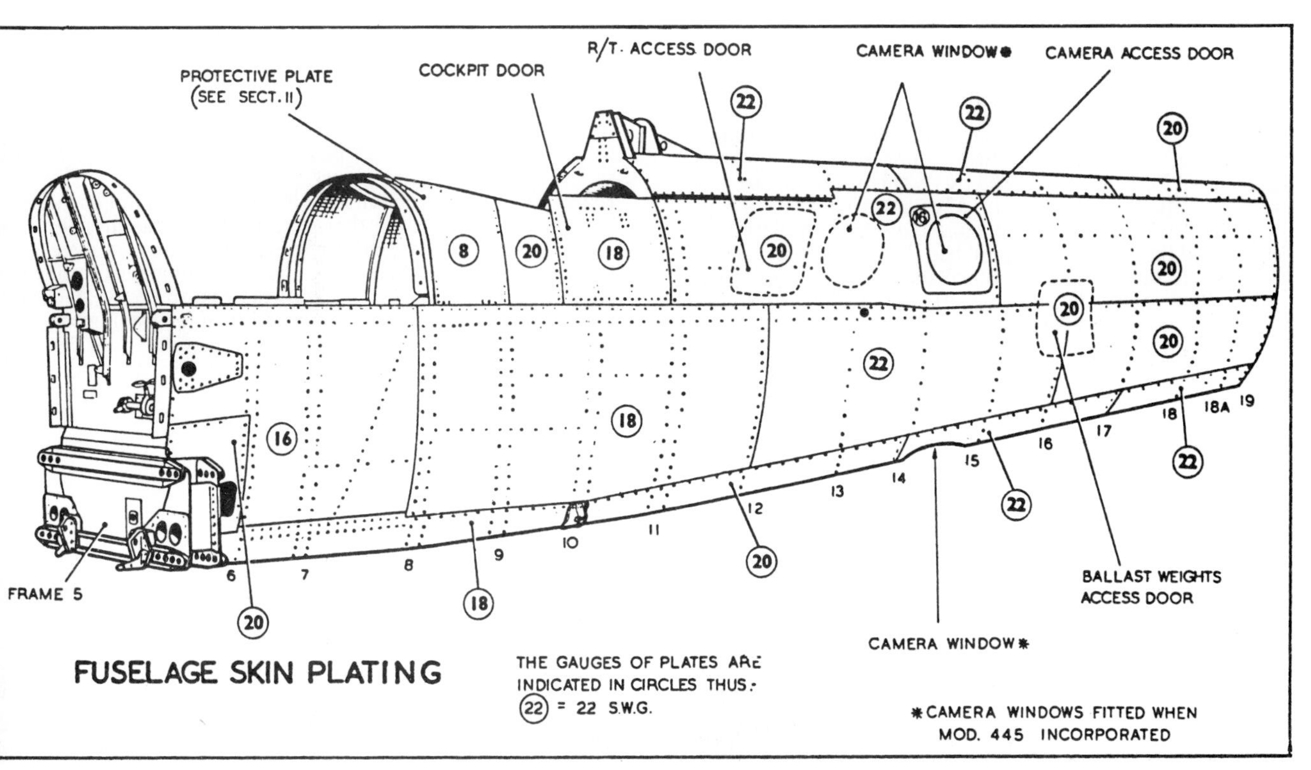

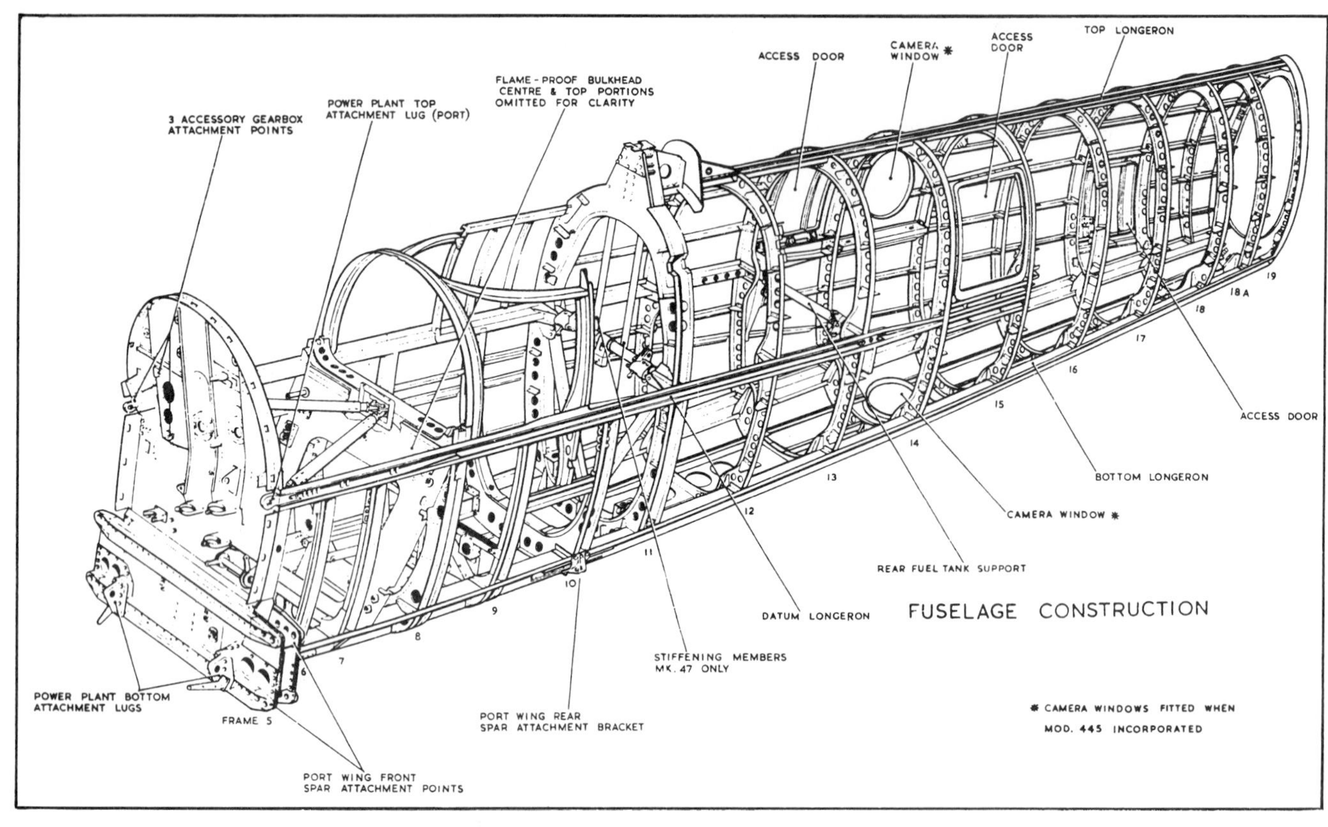

A GOOD AEROPLANE TOO LATE

The ultimate Seafire of the '40' series was the F 21 Stage Three adaption, the F 47, the only one of the series to feature the manual and power folding wing. Outwardly this variant resembled the F 46 but numerous modifications had been incorporated making it the best of the entire Seafire family. The huge Spiteful fin and rudder, extended ram-air supercharger intake installed just behind the spinner and tail down accelerator hooks made it a different aeroplane to its dainty ancestor, the F 37/34. All that remained to identify its ancestry with the 1936 prototype was the outwards retracting chassis. Only 90 examples were built and delivered because of Seafang development with laminar flow wings and also the jet-engined Attacker.

There was no true prototype as such, for much of the trial performance data had been collated using the Mks 45 and 46, the first two production machines, PS944 and 945 serving as trials aircraft. PS944 flew for the first time from South Marston on 25 April 1946, to be followed by PS945 on 12 October. They were both fitted with the Griffon 87 engine driving Rotol contaprops.The following 12 aircraft had the same installation, but VP428,and the next 74 examples, had the Griffon 88 fitted with the Rolls-Royce Mk IIc combined fuel injection and transfer pump, thus enabling the aircraft to be flown under all conditions of 'g' , but 70lb was added to the all up weight. The first of four were fitted with manual folding and spreading and a strut was fitted to secure the wings when folded. PS948 was the first aircraft fitted with hydraulic power folding and spreading, the wing having a single fold just outboard of the cannon bays; with this arrangement no securing strut was required and the time for the complete operation was only 10 seconds. All were fitted with an increased area fin and rudder of 23.08sq ft compared with the 18.345sq ft of the Mk 45, necessary to balance the forward preponderance of the propellers and extra long spinner. Additional area was provided in the tailplane and elevators increasing to 42.56sq ft against the earlier 33.84sq ft.

In November 1946 PS944 was delivered to Boscombe Down for handling and performance trials. Spring tab elevators and a large inertia weight in the system, plus trailing edge beading, improved longitudinal stability and raised the Mach number at which pitching occurred from 0.77 to 0.82. Fuel capacity had also been raised to a total of 287 gallons, including combat and 90 gallon drop tanks. With the huge 170 gallon ferry tank the range became 1,250 miles.

The handling trials at Boscombe Down revealed a feature of the F 47 that did not meet official requirements. This was that under climbing conditions the rudder could not be made to over balance by putting the aircraft into a straight sideslip in which more than $\frac{1}{2}$ to $\frac{3}{4}$ rudder travel was used and a large force was necessary to centralise the rudder. A number of remedies were tried, including various springs fitted to the rudder pedal assembly, a modified trim tab, beading on the trailing edge and increased horn area. They were not successful and the cure was to design and install a dorsal fin extension. This would have

PS944, the prototype folding wing Seafire Mk 47 with Griffon 87 engine. Small fitting under sting hook was the hold back.

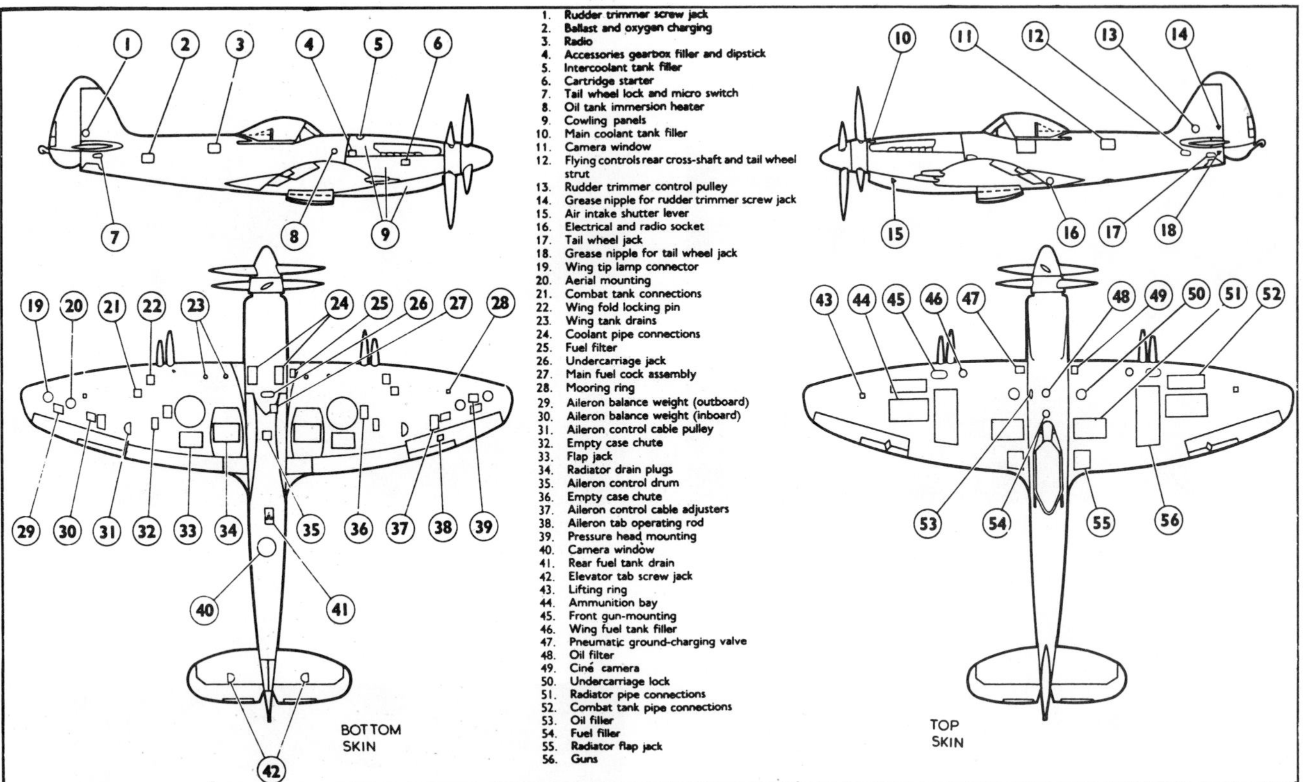

Servicing panels, Mk 47. 1 rudder trimmer screw jack, 2 ballast and oxygen charging, 3 radio, 4 accessories gearbox filler and dipstick, 5 intercoolant tank filler, 6 cartridge starter, 7 tailwheel lock and micro switch, 8 oil tank immersion heater, cowling panels, 10 main coolant tank filler, 11 camera window, 12 flying controls rear crosshaft and tailwheel strut, 13 rudder trimmer control pulley, 14 grease nipple for rudder trimmer screw jack 15, air intake shutter lever, 16 electrical and radio scket, 17 tailwheel jack, 18 grease nipple for tailwheel jack, 19 wing tip lamp connector, 20 aerial mounting, 21 combat tank connections, 22 wing fold locking pin, 23 wing tank drains, 24 coolant pipe connections, 25 fuel filter, 26 undercarriage jack, 27 main fuel cock assembly, 28 mooring ring, 29 aileron balance weight – outboard, 30 – inboard, 31 aileron cable control pulley, 32 empty case chute, 33 flap jack, 34 radiator drain plug, 35 aileron control drum, 36 empty case chute, 37 aileron control cable adjusters, 38 aileron tab operating rod, 39 pressure head mounting, 40 camera window, 41 rear fuel tank drain, 42 elevator tab screw jack, 43 lifting ring, 44 ammunition bay, 45 front gun mounting, 46 wing fuel tank filler, 47 pnuematic ground charging valve, 48 oil filter, 49 cine camera, 50 undercarriage lock, 51 radiator pipe connections, 52 combat tank pipe connections, 53 oil filter, 54 fuel filler, 55 radiator flap jack, 56 guns.

Loading and C.G., Seafire F Mk 45.

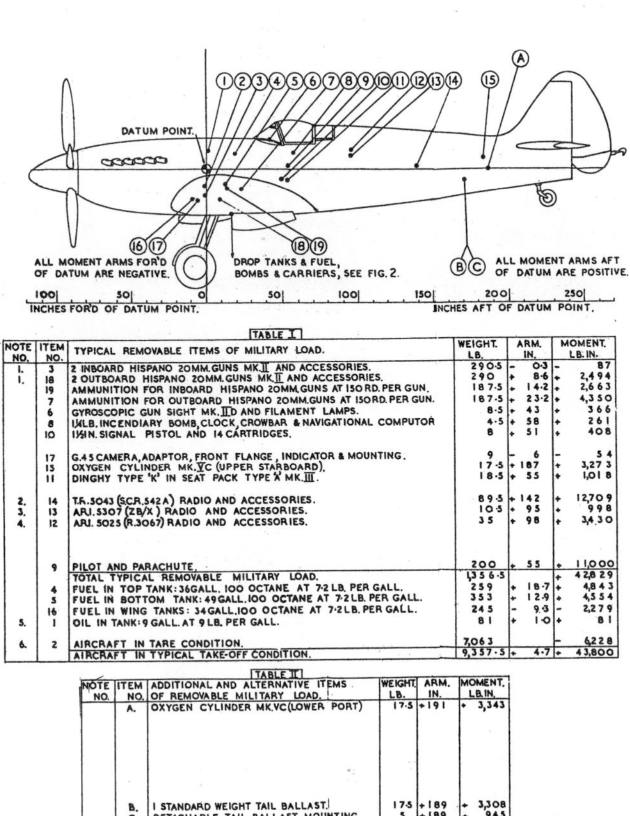

TABLE I

NOTE NO.	ITEM NO.	TYPICAL REMOVABLE ITEMS OF MILITARY LOAD.	WEIGHT. LB.	ARM. IN.	MOMENT. LB. IN.
1.	3	2 INBOARD HISPANO 20MM. GUNS MK.II AND ACCESSORIES.	290·5	– 0·3	– 87
1.	18	2 OUTBOARD HISPANO 20MM. GUNS MK.II AND ACCESSORIES.	290	+ 8·6	+ 2,494
	19	AMMUNITION FOR INBOARD HISPANO 20MM. GUNS AT 150 RD. PER GUN.	187·5	+ 14·2	+ 2,663
	7	AMMUNITION FOR OUTBOARD HISPANO 20MM. GUNS AT 150 RD. PER GUN.	187·5	+ 23·2	+ 4,350
	6	GYROSCOPIC GUN SIGHT MK.IID AND FILAMENT LAMPS.	8·5	+ 43	+ 366
	8	1¼LB. INCENDIARY BOMB, CLOCK, CROWBAR & NAVIGATIONAL COMPUTOR	4·5	+ 58	+ 261
	10	1½IN. SIGNAL PISTOL AND 14 CARTRIDGES.	8	+ 51	+ 408
	17	G.45 CAMERA, ADAPTOR, FRONT FLANGE, INDICATOR & MOUNTING.	9	– 6	– 54
	15	OXYGEN CYLINDER MK.VC (UPPER STARBOARD).	17·5	+ 187	+ 3,273
	11	DINGHY TYPE 'K' IN SEAT PACK TYPE 'A' MK.III.	18·5	+ 55	+ 1,018
2.	14	T.R.5043 (S.C.R.542 A) RADIO AND ACCESSORIES.	89·5	+ 142	+ 12,709
3.	13	A.R.I. 5307 (ZB/X) RADIO AND ACCESSORIES.	10·5	+ 95	+ 998
4.	12	A.R.I. 5025 (R.3067) RADIO AND ACCESSORIES.	35	+ 98	+ 3,430
	9	PILOT AND PARACHUTE.	200	+ 55	+ 11,000
		TOTAL TYPICAL REMOVABLE MILITARY LOAD.	1,356·5		+ 42,829
	4	FUEL IN TOP TANK: 36 GALL. 100 OCTANE AT 7·2 LB. PER GALL.	259	+ 18·7	+ 4,843
	5	FUEL IN BOTTOM TANK: 49 GALL. 100 OCTANE AT 7·2 LB. PER GALL.	353	+ 12·9	+ 4,554
	16	FUEL IN WING TANKS: 34 GALL. 100 OCTANE AT 7·2 LB. PER GALL.	245	– 9·3	– 2,279
5.	1	OIL IN TANK: 9 GALL. AT 9 LB. PER GALL.	81	+ 1·0	+ 81
6.	2	AIRCRAFT IN TARE CONDITION.	7,063		– 6,228
		AIRCRAFT IN TYPICAL TAKE-OFF CONDITION.	9,357·5	+ 4·7	+ 43,800

TABLE II

NOTE NO.	ITEM NO.	ADDITIONAL AND ALTERNATIVE ITEMS OF REMOVABLE MILITARY LOAD.	WEIGHT. LB.	ARM. IN.	MOMENT. LB. IN.
	A.	OXYGEN CYLINDER MK.VC (LOWER PORT)	17·5	+ 191	+ 3,343
	B.	1 STANDARD WEIGHT TAIL BALLAST.	17·5	+ 189	+ 3,308
	C.	DETACHABLE TAIL BALLAST MOUNTING.	5	+ 189	+ 945

Loading and C.G., Seafire Mk 46.

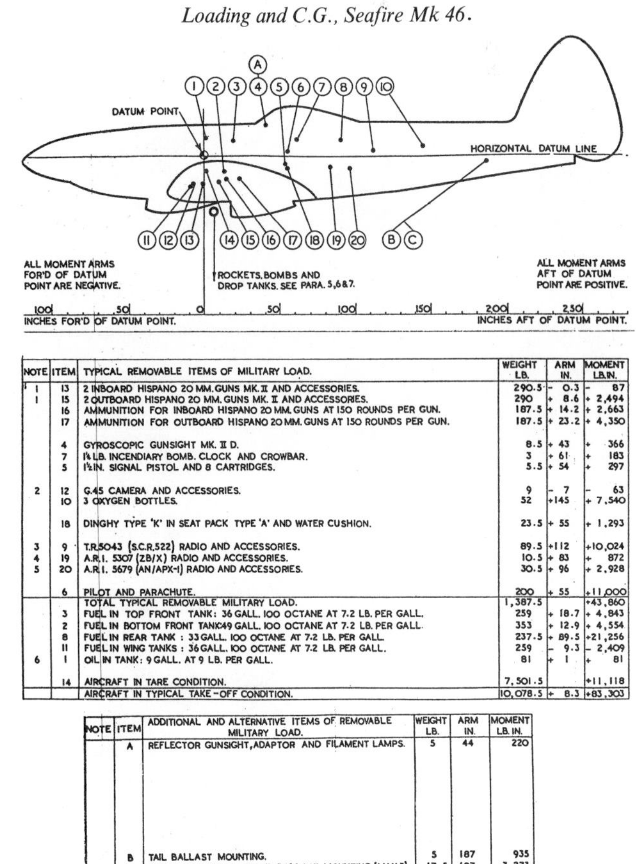

NOTE	ITEM	TYPICAL REMOVABLE ITEMS OF MILITARY LOAD.	WEIGHT LB.	ARM IN.	MOMENT LB. IN.
1	13	2 INBOARD HISPANO 20 MM. GUNS MK. II AND ACCESSORIES.	290.5	– 0.3	– 87
1	15	2 OUTBOARD HISPANO 20 MM. GUNS MK. II AND ACCESSORIES.	290	+ 8.6	+ 2,494
	16	AMMUNITION FOR INBOARD HISPANO 20 MM. GUNS AT 150 ROUNDS PER GUN.	187.5	+ 14.2	+ 2,663
	17	AMMUNITION FOR OUTBOARD HISPANO 20 MM. GUNS AT 150 ROUNDS PER GUN.	187.5	+ 23.2	+ 4,350
	4	GYROSCOPIC GUNSIGHT MK. II D.	8.5	+ 43	+ 366
	7	1¼ LB. INCENDIARY BOMB. CLOCK AND CROWBAR.	3	+ 61	+ 183
	5	1½ IN. SIGNAL PISTOL AND 8 CARTRIDGES.	5.5	+ 54	+ 297
2	12	G.45 CAMERA AND ACCESSORIES.	9	– 7	– 63
	10	3 OXYGEN BOTTLES.	52	+ 145	+ 7,540
	18	DINGHY TYPE 'K' IN SEAT PACK TYPE 'A' AND WATER CUSHION.	23.5	+ 55	+ 1,293
3	9	T.R.5043 (S.C.R.522) RADIO AND ACCESSORIES.	89.5	+ 112	+ 10,024
4	19	A.R.I. 5307 (ZB/X) RADIO AND ACCESSORIES.	10.5	+ 83	+ 872
5	20	A.R.I. 5679 (AN/APX-1) RADIO AND ACCESSORIES.	30.5	+ 96	+ 2,928
	6	PILOT AND PARACHUTE.	200	+ 55	+ 11,000
		TOTAL TYPICAL REMOVABLE MILITARY LOAD.	1,387.5		+ 43,860
	3	FUEL IN TOP FRONT TANK: 36 GALL. 100 OCTANE AT 7.2 LB. PER GALL.	259	+ 18.7	+ 4,843
	2	FUEL IN BOTTOM FRONT TANK: 49 GALL. 100 OCTANE AT 7.2 LB. PER GALL.	353	+ 12.9	+ 4,554
	8	FUEL IN REAR TANK : 33 GALL. 100 OCTANE AT 7.2 LB. PER GALL.	237.5	+ 89.5	+ 21,256
	11	FUEL IN WING TANKS : 36 GALL. 100 OCTANE AT 7.2 LB. PER GALL.	259	– 9.3	– 2,409
6	1	OIL IN TANK: 9 GALL. AT 9 LB. PER GALL.	81	+ 1	+ 81
	14	AIRCRAFT IN TARE CONDITION.	7,501.5		+ 11,118
		AIRCRAFT IN TYPICAL TAKE-OFF CONDITION.	10,078.5	+ 8.3	+ 83,303

NOTE	ITEM	ADDITIONAL AND ALTERNATIVE ITEMS OF REMOVABLE MILITARY LOAD.	WEIGHT LB.	ARM IN.	MOMENT LB. IN.
	A	REFLECTOR GUNSIGHT, ADAPTOR AND FILAMENT LAMPS.	5	44	220
	B	TAIL BALLAST MOUNTING.	5	187	935
	C	STANDARD WEIGHT ON TAIL BALLAST MOUNTING (MAX.3)	17.5	187	3,273

PS948 was at Farnborough during October 1947 for various trials, including tail down acceleration from the steam catapult. In these illustrations can be seen the oblique camera ports in fuselage, combat tanks, zero length RP rails, two × 500 lb GP bomb, 1 × 50 gallon overload tank. Close ups show the forward catapult launch hooks, rear securing hawser on hold back and split rudder from tab and a RATOG tube split after premature firing.

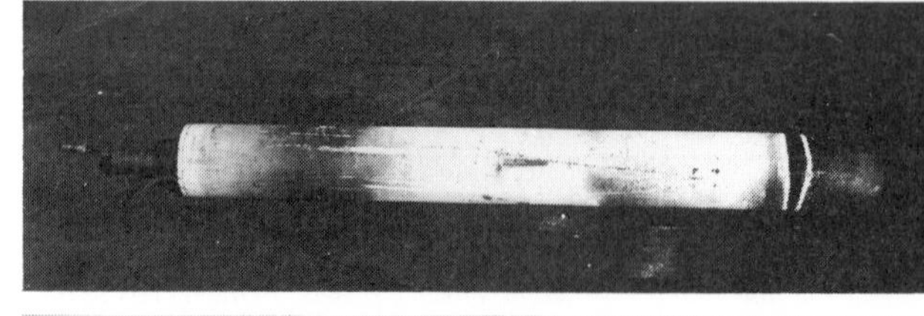

Right: PS948 FR 47 with F 47s in the background.

Below: PS948 in original colour scheme.

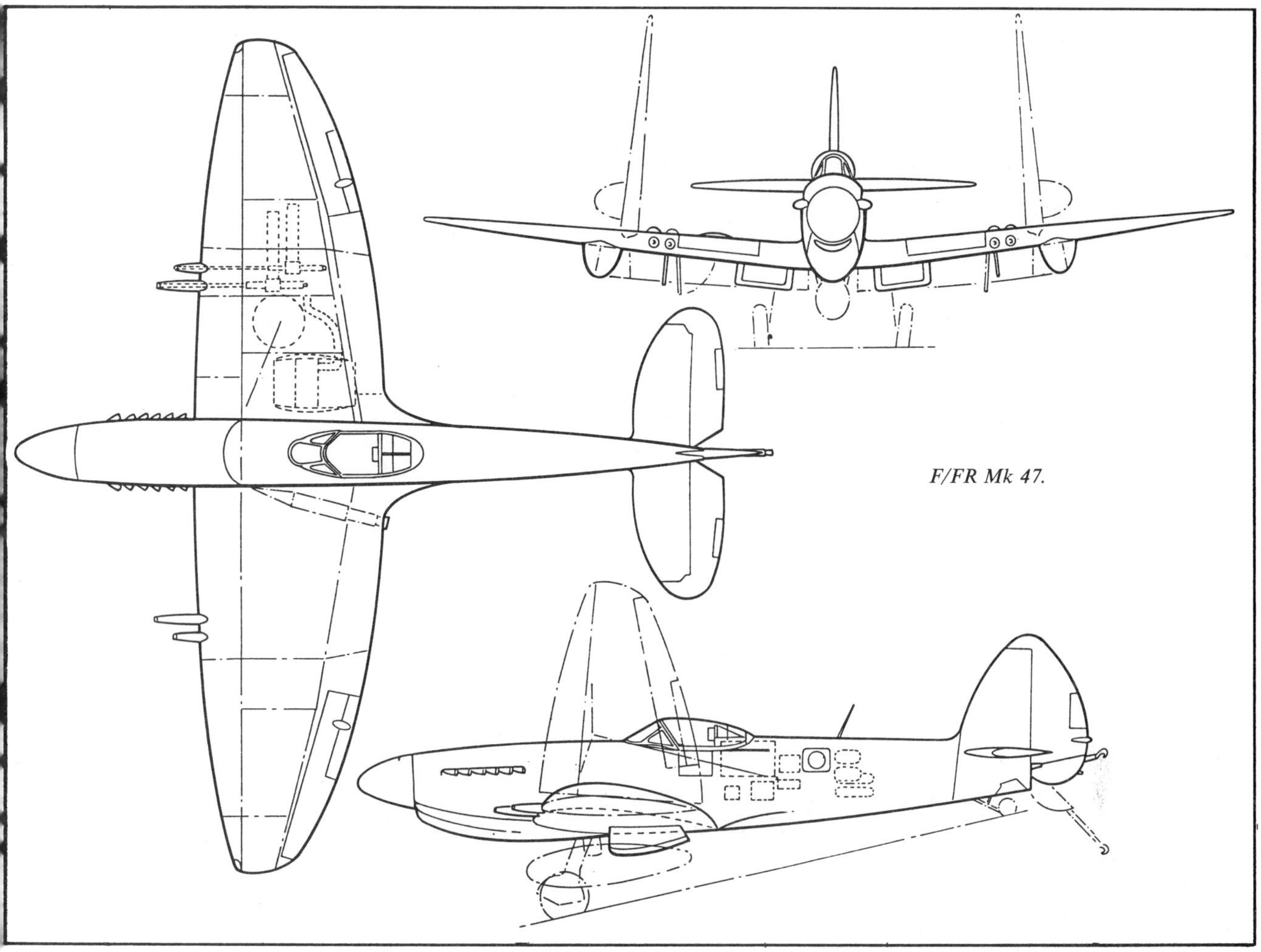

F/FR Mk 47.

been an easy thing to fit to an experimental aeroplane but difficult to introduce on to the production line.

PS945 was used for performance trials, these being compared to those of the F 46. The results indicated that the maximum speed was about 15mph lower than was expected. The comparison F 46s were LA545 and LA552; all three Seafires had a Griffon 87 with Rotol six blade, wooden propellers of 10ft 4in diameter. 545 and 552 had the standard air intake whilst 945 had the new F 47 extended type. This and all production aircraft except PS944 had the curved windscreen, but F 46s had the flattened type. The extended fairing on PS945 on the underside of the engine embraced the air intake filter and brought the opening of the duct right forward to just aft of the propellers. This was supposed to improve the aerodynamic lines along the underside of the aircraft but the comparison trials found the standard intake was superior in all performance aspects. The table on page 580 provides details of PS945 and the two F 46s – LA545 and 552 which were used for the performance comparative trials.

The maximum speed of the prototype Mk 47 was lower than that of either of the Mk 46s and it was thought that the standard Mk 46 air intake was more efficient than that of the Mk 47. Also, during routine maintenance it was discovered that the securing bolts of the air intake ice guard had been ingested by the Griffon's supercharger and so the engine had to be changed. The reasons for the inferior performance of the Mk 47

VP447 with all armament removed.

ARMOUR PROTECTION
BOTTOM OF WINDSCREEN (4MM.)
BULLET-PROOF WINDSCREEN
BACK OF PILOT'S HEAD (6MM.)
EXTRA PROTECTION BEHIND PILOT'S HEAD (6MM.)
BACK OF PILOT'S SEAT (4MM.)
BOTTOM OF PILOT'S SEAT (8 S.W.G.)
FRONT OF FUEL TANK (6MM.)
FUEL TANK COWLING (8 S.W.G.)
FRONT OF PILOT'S SEAT (6MM.)
AMMUNITION BOXES (TOP AND BOTTOM SKIN 10 S.W.G.)
FRONT OF AMMUNITION BOXES (7MM.)
INBOARD
WING FOLD LINE
DETAIL OF AMMUNITION BOX PROTECTION MK.47 ONLY
ARMOUR PLATE.
LIGHT ALLOY.

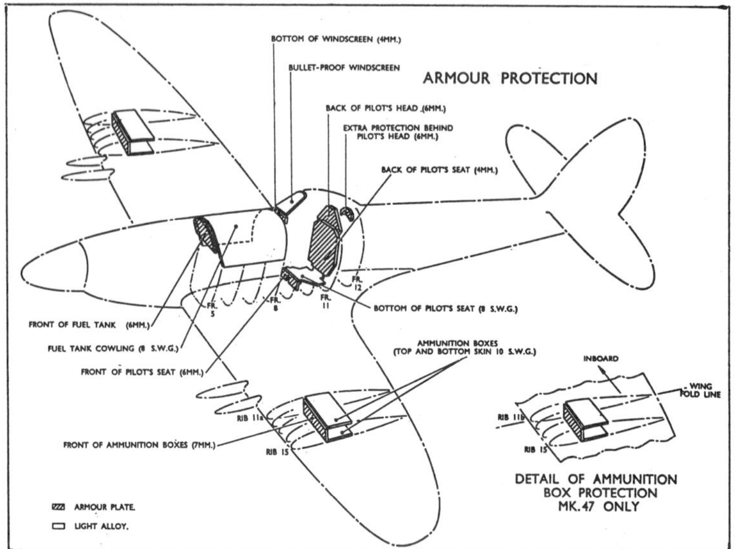

Item	Seafire Mk 47 PS945	Seafire Mk 46 LA552	Seafire Mk 46 LA545
Engine	Griffon 87	Griffon 87	Griffon 87
Propeller (diameter)	Rotol 10ft 4in 6 blade contra	ditto	ditto
Exhaust manifolds	Rolls standard multi ejector type		
Generator duct	Mk 21 (non-exit type)	ditto	ditto
Air intake	Extended type, ice guard & filter fitted.	Spitfire Mk 21 type. Ice guard & filter.	(1) as PS945 (2) as LA552
Windscreen & hood	Rear view narrow hood & faired front to w/screen	rear view hood. Mk 22/24 flat w/screen	As LA552

The following results were obtained:–

Aircraft	2,750rpm + 18lb/sq in boost	Max speed (mph)
PS945	Prototype Mk 47	432.5 at 24,300ft
LA552	Production FR 46	435 at 24,000ft
LA545	Production Mk 46 standard intake	443 at 24,500ft
LA545	With Mk 47 intake	440.5 at 23,900ft

In addition to level speed tests combat climbs were made with LA545 with each of the intakes fitted. Results were:–

2,750rpm + 18lb/sq in boost, radiator flap open

Condition	Standard Mk 46 intake	Standard Mk 47 intake
Max rate of climb MS gear	3,800ft/min at 6,800ft	3,570ft/min at 6,300ft
Max rate of climb FS gear	2,820ft/min at 21,900ft	2,600ft/min at 21,400ft
Service Ceiling	40,700ft	40,300ft

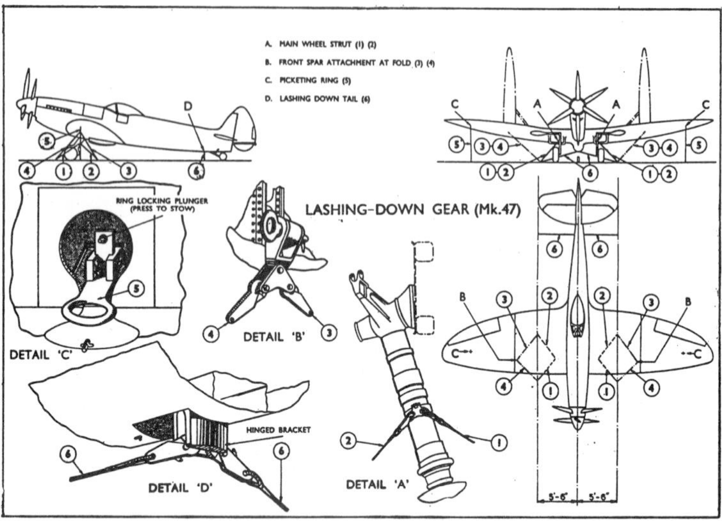

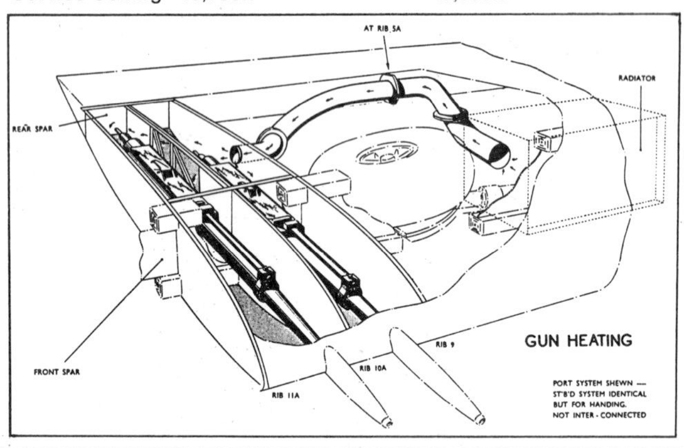

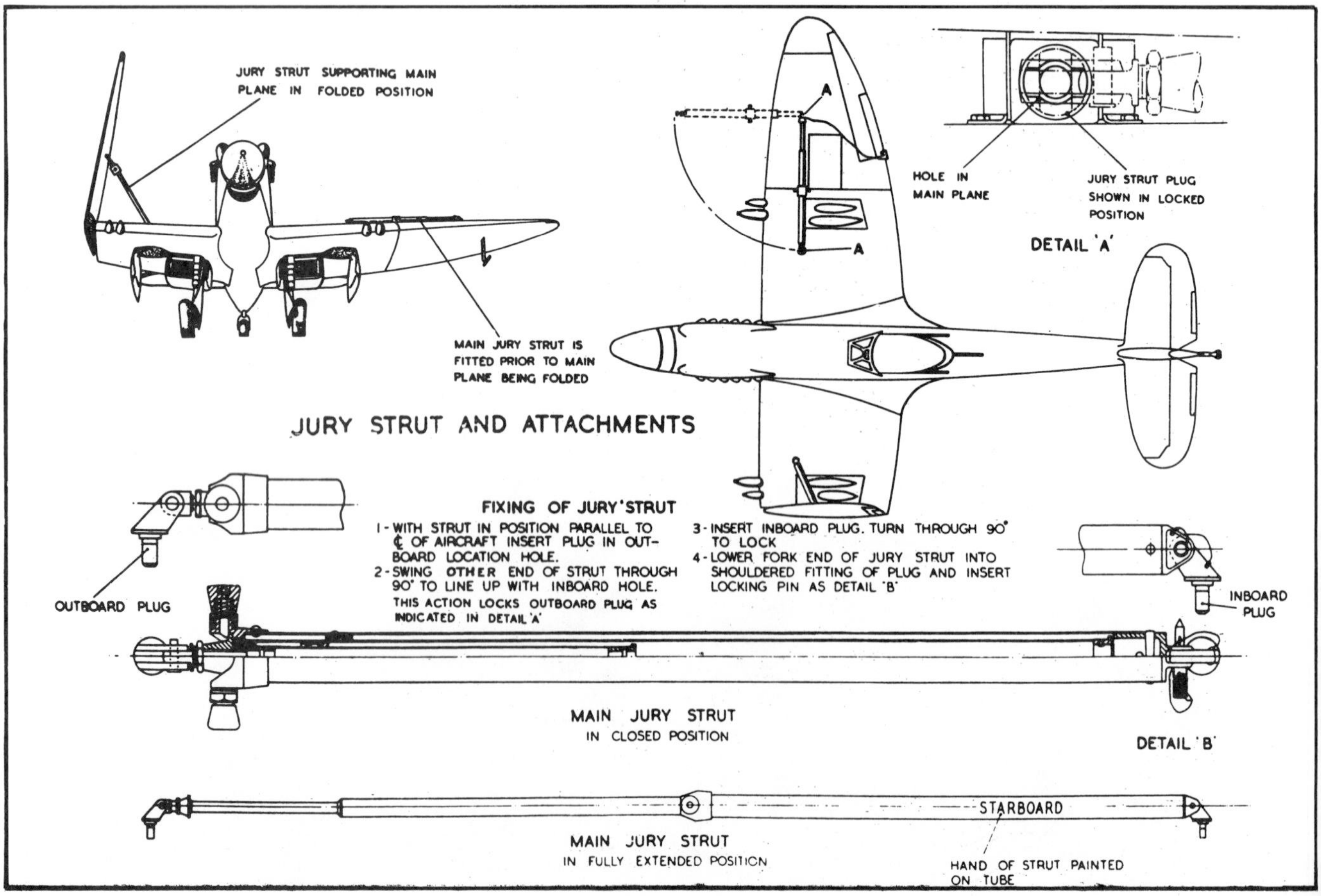

A. MAIN WHEEL STRUT (1) (2)
B. FRONT SPAR ATTACHMENT AT FOLD (3) (4)
C. PICKETING RING (5)
D. LASHING DOWN TAIL (6)
LASHING-DOWN GEAR (Mk.47)
RING LOCKING PLUNGER (PRESS TO STOW)
DETAIL 'C'
DETAIL 'B'
HINGED BRACKET
DETAIL 'D'
DETAIL 'A'
5'-6"
5'-6"

AT RIB 5A
RADIATOR
REAR SPAR
FRONT SPAR
RIB 9
RIB 10A
RIB 11A
GUN HEATING
PORT SYSTEM SHEWN — ST'B'D SYSTEM IDENTICAL BUT FOR HANDING. NOT INTER-CONNECTED

JURY STRUT SUPPORTING MAIN PLANE IN FOLDED POSITION
MAIN JURY STRUT IS FITTED PRIOR TO MAIN PLANE BEING FOLDED
HOLE IN MAIN PLANE
JURY STRUT PLUG SHOWN IN LOCKED POSITION
DETAIL 'A'
JURY STRUT AND ATTACHMENTS
FIXING OF JURY STRUT
1 - WITH STRUT IN POSITION PARALLEL TO ℄ OF AIRCRAFT INSERT PLUG IN OUTBOARD LOCATION HOLE.
2 - SWING OTHER END OF STRUT THROUGH 90° TO LINE UP WITH INBOARD HOLE. THIS ACTION LOCKS OUTBOARD PLUG AS INDICATED IN DETAIL 'A'
3 - INSERT INBOARD PLUG. TURN THROUGH 90° TO LOCK
4 - LOWER FORK END OF JURY STRUT INTO SHOULDERED FITTING OF PLUG AND INSERT LOCKING PIN AS DETAIL 'B'
OUTBOARD PLUG
INBOARD PLUG
MAIN JURY STRUT IN CLOSED POSITION
DETAIL 'B'
STARBOARD
MAIN JURY STRUT IN FULLY EXTENDED POSITION
HAND OF STRUT PAINTED ON TUBE

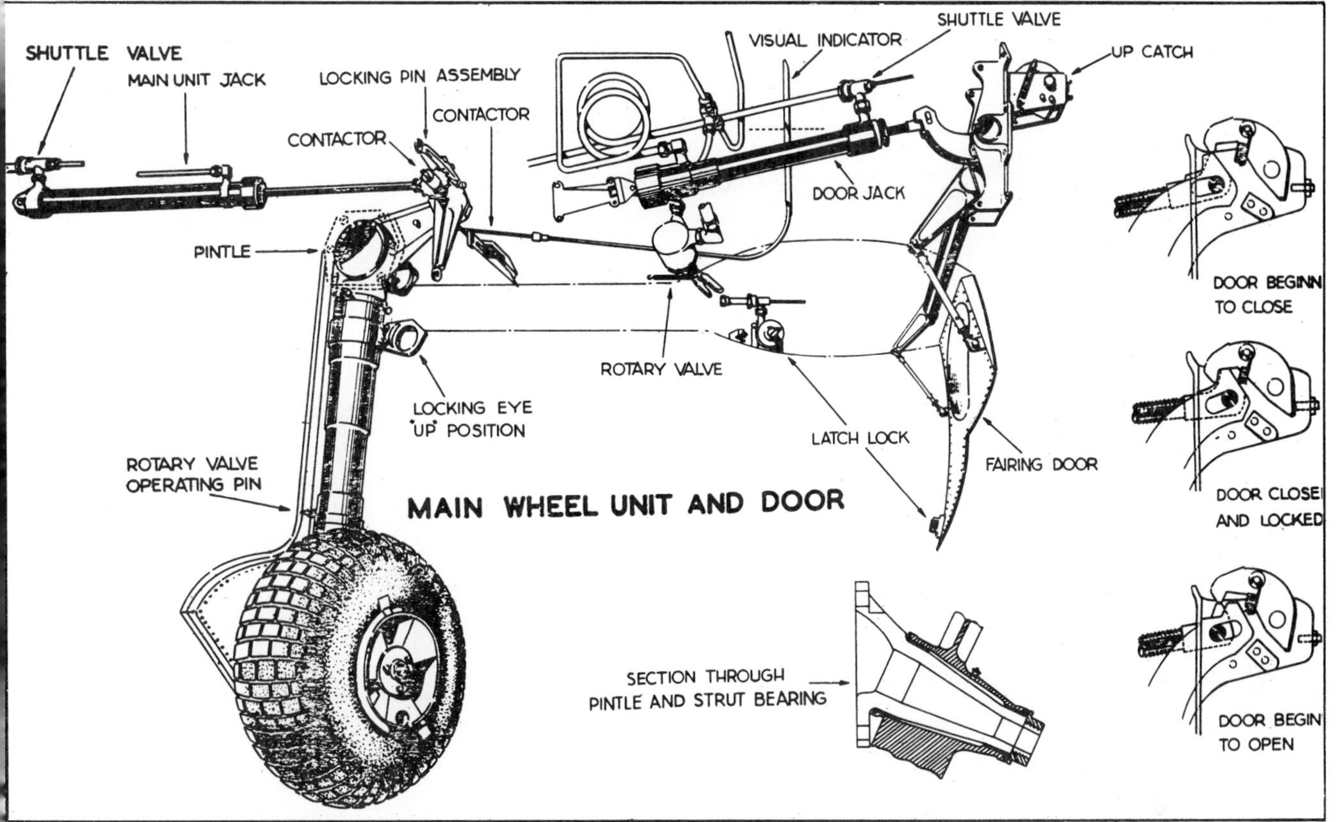

MAIN WHEEL UNIT AND DOOR

when compared to the two Mk 46s were:– (1) the extended Mk 47 air intake was less efficient than that of the Mk 46 due, it was thought to the air flow into the intake caused by the large blade roots of the contra props and the larger wheel well blisters. Tests were also made with the Mk 47 fitted with the Spiteful type air intake.

Cooling trials were next and PS945 was considered free of faults. Longitudinal stability was however troublesome and both PS944 and PS952 were compared for handling after an inertia weight of 15½lb was installed in the elevator circuit. A special valve was fitted to both PS952 and VP464 to improve oil flow.

PS946, an FR Mk 47, was used to investigate range and endurance fitted with a modified Griffon 88 engine which ran at 1,200rpm for cruising. VP463 was used for trials of the Type G ASR container fitted to a bomb carrier under the port wing. The container was dropped in level flight at 150 knots at 4,000ft with the rear end fouling the wing during initial nose down pitch. A modification was introduced to cure this fault. VP463 was then used for jettison trials of the 90 gallon overload tank,

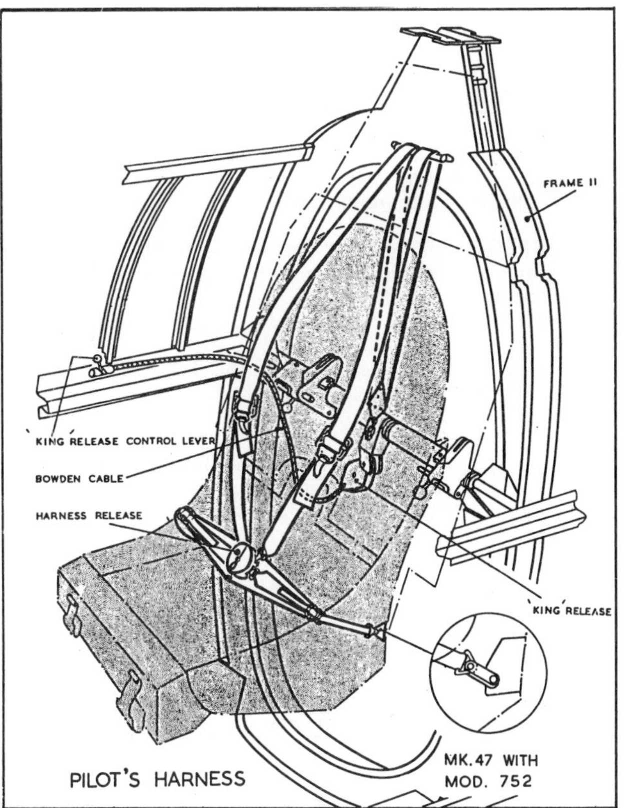

PILOT'S HARNESS

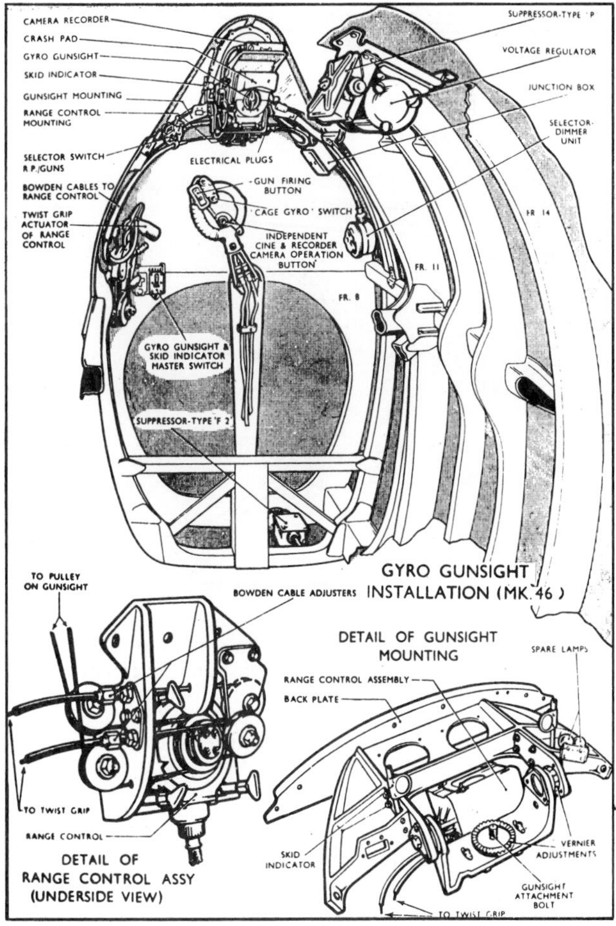

GYRO GUNSIGHT INSTALLATION (MK. 46)

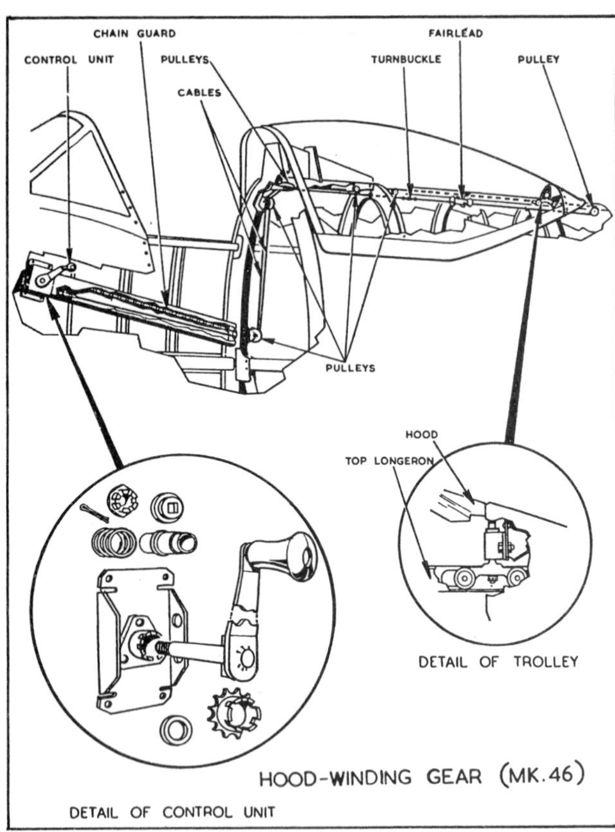

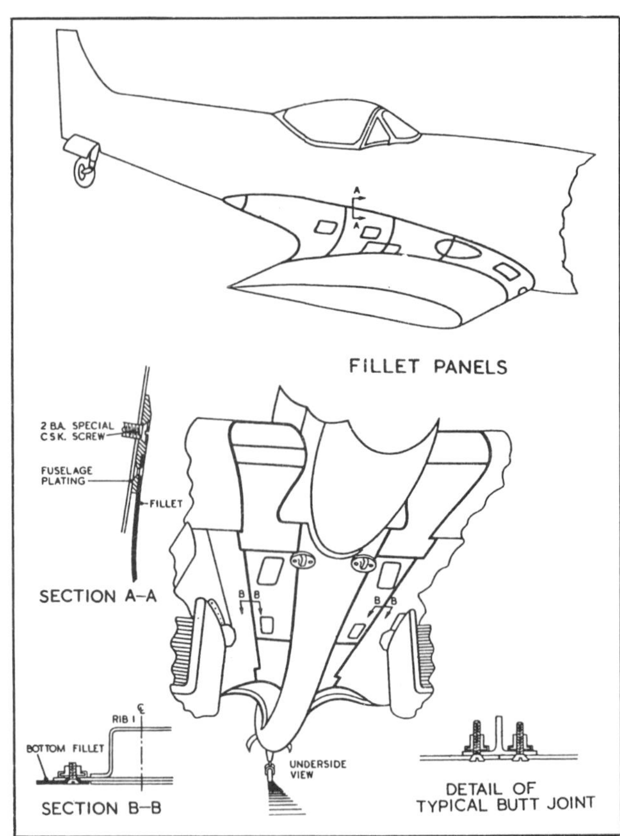

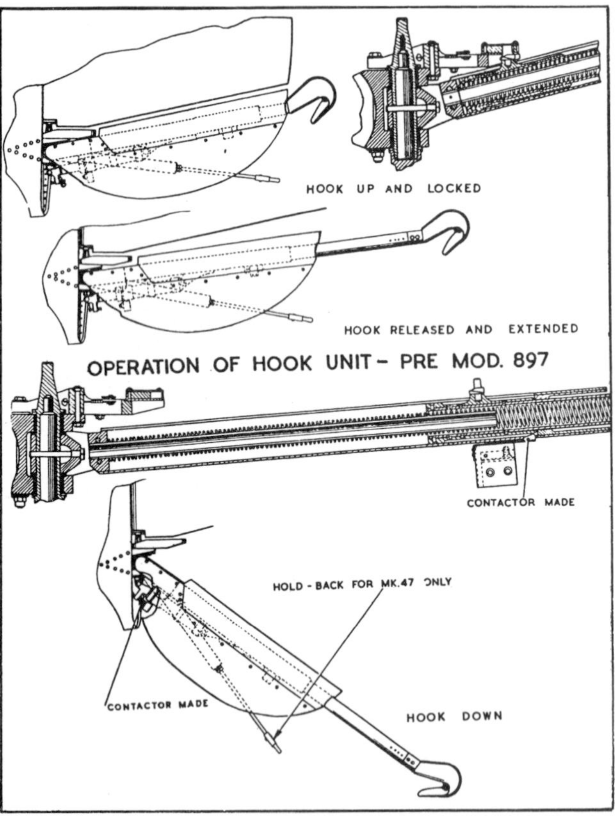

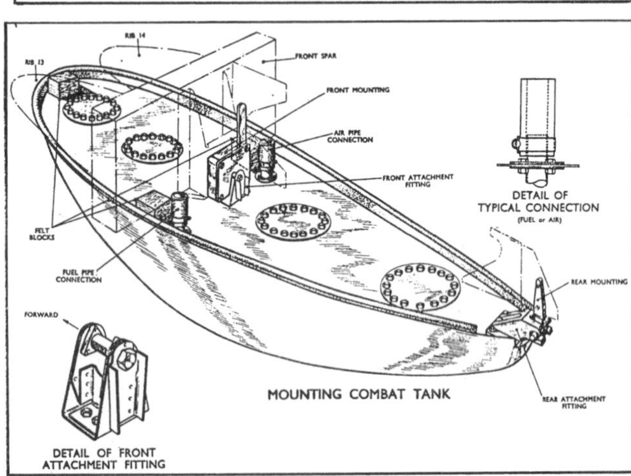

this being released first at the rear, causing the tank to rotate in a tail down direction until clear of the rear support. The tank then fell away cleanly. Examination of cine film showed the tank striking the fuselage, and tests were discontinued to allow a 50 gallon tank to be tried. This tank would not leave the carrier until the latter had been modified. The 90 gallon tank was again tested with a modified tail section and for further development a papier maché one was used. Trials continued with the new tail, which broke off after striking the aircraft's fuselage. The Seafire's under rear fuselage was painted black and the tank white to improve definition on the cine film. VP463 was weighed at Chilbolton 21st June 1948 and had a tare of 8,210lb and an a.u.w. of 10,693lb. At one time VP463 was fitted with:– two Type G A.S.R. containers, two $22\frac{1}{2}$ gallon combat wing tanks and one 50 gallon torpedo overload fuselage tank. With the A.S.R. units fitted the range was reduced by 25%.

Further weights for comparision with the above were:-
PS944 weighed at High Post on 5th June 1946 with a tare of 7,813lb, a.u.w. of 10,121lb.

PS948 weighed at Chilbolton 3rd July 1947 with a tare of 8,225lb, a.u.w. of 10,707lb.

During early service trials of the F 47 several pilots reported that the wing combat tanks had self-jettisoned due, it was found, to excessive clearance between the retaining hooks and the tank catches. VP463 conducted brief handling trials with a larger elevator inertia weight installed and longitudinal handling left much to be desired. The normal $6\frac{1}{2}$lb unit was replaced with a $14\frac{1}{2}$lb unit with the result that this production aircraft then handled as well as the original prototype.

VP463 was transferred to Boscombe Down for handling trials with and without the 90 gallon tank and with the $14\frac{1}{2}$lb inertia weight in the elevator circuit.

Other aircraft included in the trials programme were:-

VP449 used for the Mk 4B gyro gunsight and vibrograph trials.

VP437 to Farnborough 1 July 1949 for accelerating, arresting and RATOG trials. At an a.u.w. of 12,450lb it was tested with two twin rocket carriers with four 5in rockets mounted on each side of the fuselage whilst carrying a full fuel load, plus combat tanks. The 90 gallons overload tank was

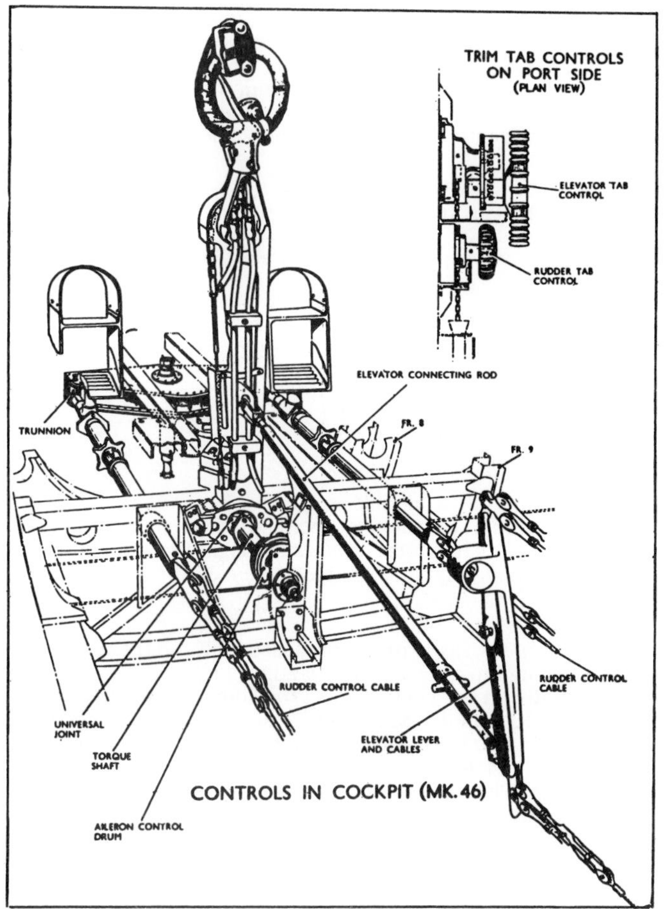

TRIM TAB CONTROLS ON PORT SIDE (PLAN VIEW)
ELEVATOR TAB CONTROL
RUDDER TAB CONTROL
ELEVATOR CONNECTING ROD
TRUNNION
FR. 8
FR. 9
RUDDER CONTROL CABLE
RUDDER CONTROL CABLE
UNIVERSAL JOINT
TORQUE SHAFT
ELEVATOR LEVER AND CABLES
AILERON CONTROL DRUM
CONTROLS IN COCKPIT (MK.46)

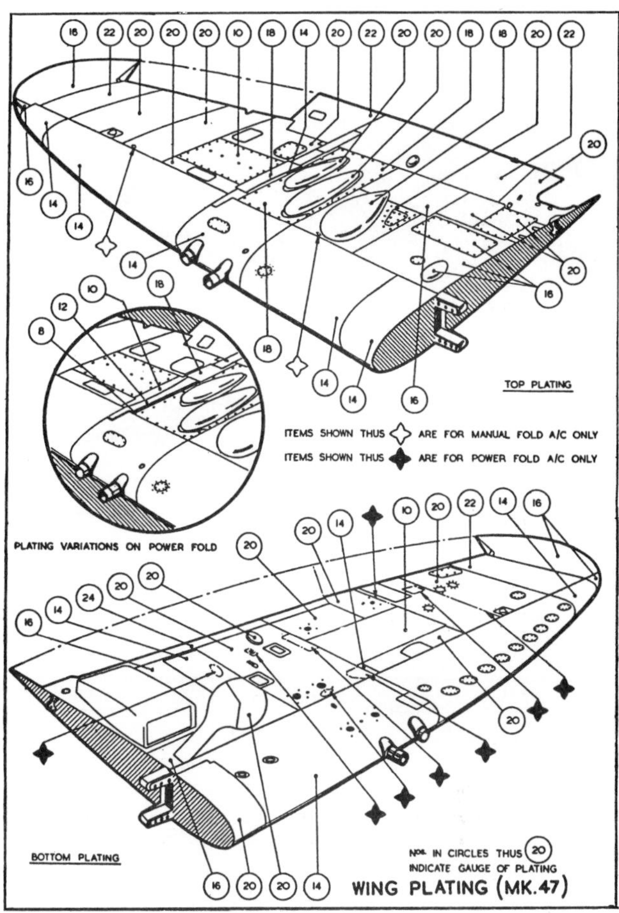

TOP PLATING
ITEMS SHOWN THUS ◇ ARE FOR MANUAL FOLD A/C ONLY
ITEMS SHOWN THUS ◆ ARE FOR POWER FOLD A/C ONLY
PLATING VARIATIONS ON POWER FOLD
BOTTOM PLATING
NOS. IN CIRCLES THUS (20) INDICATE GAUGE OF PLATING
WING PLATING (MK.47)

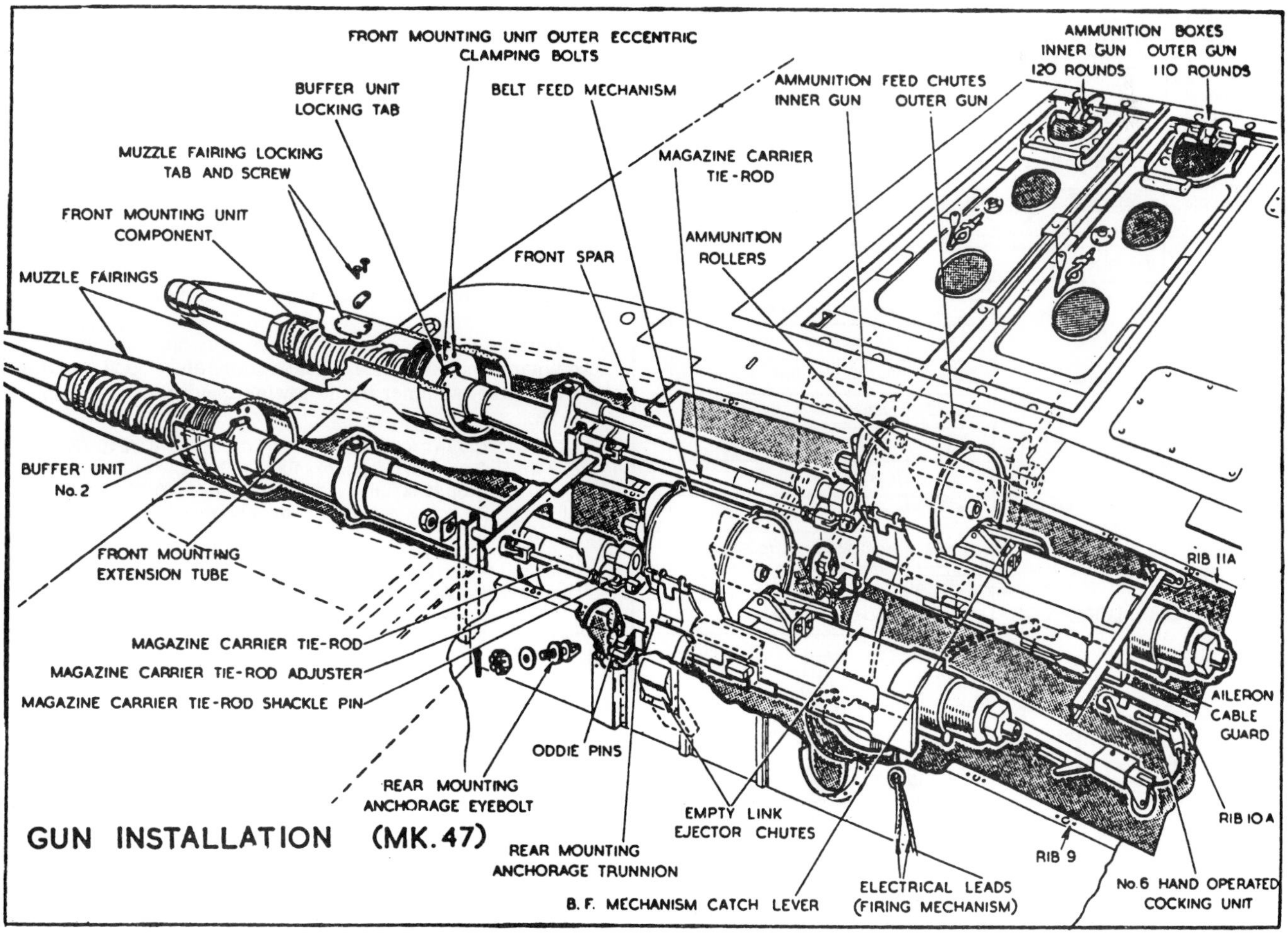

FRONT MOUNTING UNIT OUTER ECCENTRIC CLAMPING BOLTS
AMMUNITION BOXES
INNER GUN 120 ROUNDS
OUTER GUN 110 ROUNDS
BUFFER UNIT LOCKING TAB
BELT FEED MECHANISM
AMMUNITION FEED CHUTES
INNER GUN
OUTER GUN
MUZZLE FAIRING LOCKING TAB AND SCREW
MAGAZINE CARRIER TIE-ROD
FRONT MOUNTING UNIT COMPONENT
AMMUNITION ROLLERS
FRONT SPAR
MUZZLE FAIRINGS
BUFFER UNIT No. 2
FRONT MOUNTING EXTENSION TUBE
RIB 11A
MAGAZINE CARRIER TIE-ROD
MAGAZINE CARRIER TIE-ROD ADJUSTER
MAGAZINE CARRIER TIE-ROD SHACKLE PIN
AILERON CABLE GUARD
ODDIE PINS
REAR MOUNTING ANCHORAGE EYEBOLT
EMPTY LINK EJECTOR CHUTES
RIB 10A
REAR MOUNTING ANCHORAGE TRUNNION
RIB 9
B. F. MECHANISM CATCH LEVER
ELECTRICAL LEADS (FIRING MECHANISM)
No. 6 HAND OPERATED COCKING UNIT
GUN INSTALLATION (MK.47)

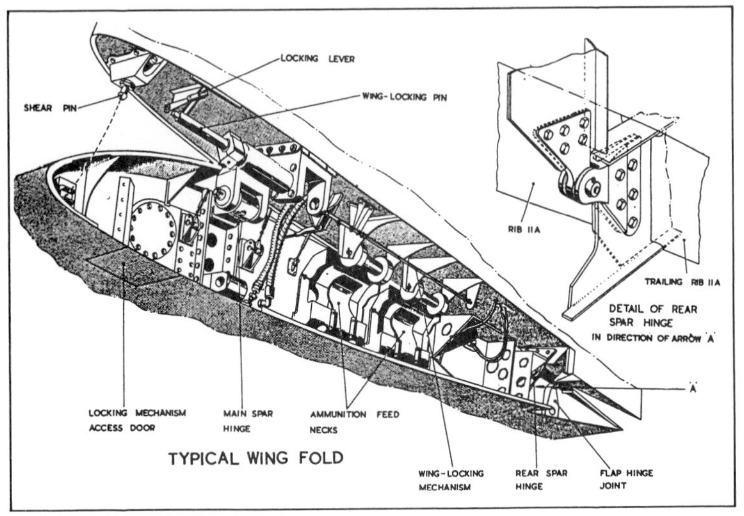

TYPICAL WING FOLD

			PORT WING INBOARD	PORT WING OUTBOARD	ST'B'D WING INBOARD	ST'B'D WING OUTBOARD	REAR FUEL	DROP TANK	FUSELAGE	CAMERAS
EARLY MK.46 AIRCRAFT	PRIOR TO MOD. 445 (F.R. VARIANTS) & MOD. 593 (R.P.)	1	Wing combat tank		Wing combat tank		Top rear tank	50 gall. drop tank	—	—
		2	Wing combat tank		Wing combat tank		Top rear tank	—	Fuselage bomb	—
		3	Wing combat tank		Wing combat tank		Top rear tank	—	Light series bombs	—
LATER MK46 AIRCRAFT	WITH MOD 445 (F.R. VARIANTS)	4	Wing combat tank		Wing combat tank		Top rear tank	50 gall. drop tank	—	F 24 cameras
		5	Wing combat tank		Wing combat tank		Top rear tank	—	Fuselage bomb	F 24 cameras
	WITH MOD.445 (F.R. VARIANTS) & MOD. 593 (R.P.)	6	Wing combat tank		Wing combat tank		Top rear tank	—	Light series bombs	F 24 cameras
		7	Rocket projectiles	Rocket projectiles	Rocket projectiles	Rocket projectiles	Top rear tank	50 gall. drop tank	—	F 24 cameras
MK. 47 AIRCRAFT	WITH MOD.445 (F.R. VARIANTS)	8	Wing combat tank		Wing combat tank		Top rear tank	90 gall. drop tank / 50 gall. drop tank	—	F 24 cameras
		9	Wing bomb / Wing combat tank		Wing bomb / Wing combat tank		Top rear tank	90 gall. drop tank / 50 gall. drop tank	—	F 24 cameras
	WITH MOD.445 (F.R. VARIANTS) & MOD. 594 (R.P.)	10	Light series bombs / Wing combat tank		Light series bombs / Wing combat tank		Top rear tank	90 gall. drop tank / 50 gall. drop tank	—	F 24 cameras
		11	Flares / Wing combat tank		Flares / Wing combat tank		Top rear tank	90 gall. drop tank / 50 gall. drop tank	—	F 24 cameras
		12	Rocket projectiles	Rocket projectiles	Rocket projectiles	Rocket projectiles	Top rear tank	90 gall. drop tank / 50 gall. drop tank	—	F 24 cameras

WING COMBAT TANKS
50 GALL. DROP TANK
90 GALL. DROP TANK
FUSELAGE BOMB UP TO 500 LB
TOP REAR TANK
F 24 CAMERAS
LIGHT SERIES BOMBS
WING BOMB UP TO 500 LB.
FLARES (4 x 4½")
ROCKET PROJECTILES

F.R. MK. 46 (4)

EXTERNAL STORE LOADINGS

F.R. MK. 47 (9)

F.R. MK. 47 (12)

empty, and two 500lb bombs. For tests from the accelerator 18° of flap was necessary for a smooth take off. Three rocket assisted take offs were made on 10/11 March 1949 at 12,450lb. Six launches were made from the B.H. V accelerator with the same load. Eleven runs into the wires were made 15/18 March at entry speeds of 65 to 66.7 knots with no recorded damage.

The various stores carried and a.u.w.s are as follows:-

Loading	Stores	weight(lb)	ins aft of datum u/c down
1	None	10,805	9.0
2	None	10,885	10.2
3	8 × 60lb RPs	10,800	4.9
4	1 × 90 gal drop tank	11,575	9.4
5	1 × 90 gal drop tank 2 × 500lb MC bombs	12,655	8.5
6	1 × 90 gal drop tank 8 × 60lb RPs	12,020	8.0

Maximum permissible weight for take off was 12,900lb and maximum permissible speed without stores but with combat tanks 450 knots. The inertia weight to the elevator had improved handling and was recommended for all production aircraft.

As was the case with the original Seafires so the last Seafire type also had to carry out deck landing and take off trials from an aircraft carrier. These were carried out on *HMS Illustrious* between 13 and 15 May 1947 using three F 47s, PS945, PS948 and PS949, and four pilots, J K Quill, Lt Cdr Carver, Lt Bailey and Lt Baldwin. Their report was that the large area flaps at 66° had achieved their objective, giving an approach speed safety margin greater than on previous marks.

It was all very well designing an aircraft to fly faster, higher and carry more weapons and stores, but if the pilot is unable to see properly then it is all to no avail. This was the case with the rounded windscreen fitted to the production F 47. The 'prototype', PS944, was fitted with the standard Spitfire F 24 type of windscreen and flown by J K Quill and M J Lithgow on 6 Feb 1947. Amongst their comments against the rounded type were; 1. The side panels, being made of ⅞" thick glass mist up on descent from high altitude; this together with the misting of the front panel renders the pilot completely blind except for the small clear space provided by the air blast on the front bullet proof panel. The side panels of the 24 do not mist up. 2. Ordinary vision through the side panels is now very poor. 3. Redesigned shape of windscreen makes curved deck landing approach difficult because of the rear frame. 4. If head moved because of 3. meets an air blast.

Final comment was that reversion to the standard Spitfire 24 windscreen and hood is strongly recommended. It was considered that the operational efficiency of an otherwise excellent machine had been seriously prejudiced.

Handling with external stores was another must for aerodynamic performance considerations and PS952 was flown by M J Lithgow under the following conditions;

1.	23-7-47	Clean - fully loaded	AUW 10,760
2.	25-7-47	2 combat wing tanks full + 50 gall drop tank full	AUW 11,540
3.	7-8-47	As 2 + 2 × 500lb MC bombs (with long tails)	AUW 12,600
4.	12-8-47	2 combat with tanks full + 2 × 500lb MC bombs	AUW 12,190
5.	15-8-47	2 combat wing tanks full + 2 × Mk XI depth charges	AUW 11,740
6.	19-8-47	8 × 100lb RPs (Tier stowages)	AUW 11,580

In all the above tests the aircraft was considered acceptable except in 2 but a change in using fuel from the different tanks was sufficient to make it acceptable.

The Mk 47 saw action with No 800 Squadron in Malaya during the 1949 Emergency and from *HMS Triumph* for strikes against North Korean targets during 1950. The following year, however, all Seafires were withdrawn from front-line Squadrons though the F 24s that remained served with RNVR Squadrons for several more years being gradually phased out of service to become instructional airframes or relegated to scrap categories.

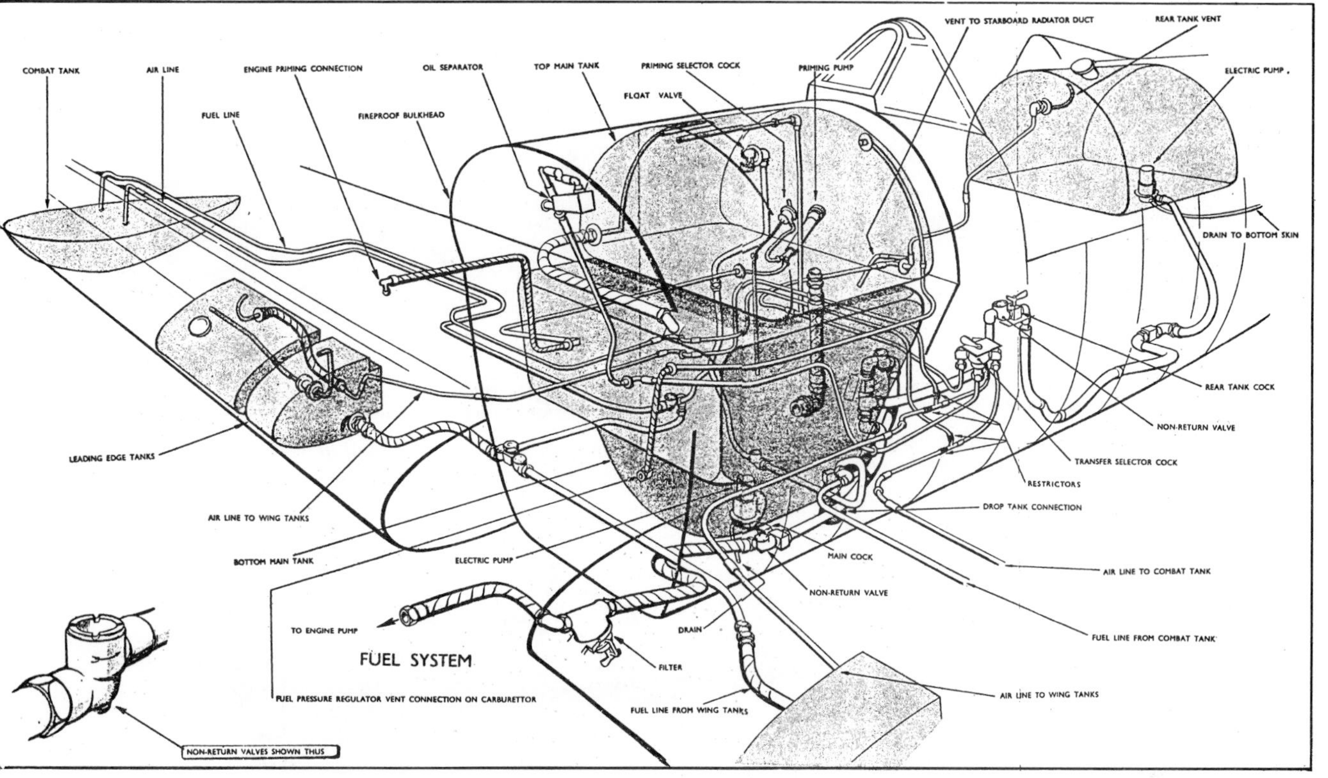
COMBAT TANK
AIR LINE
ENGINE PRIMING CONNECTION
OIL SEPARATOR
TOP MAIN TANK
PRIMING SELECTOR COCK
PRIMING PUMP
VENT TO STARBOARD RADIATOR DUCT
REAR TANK VENT
ELECTRIC PUMP
FUEL LINE
FIREPROOF BULKHEAD
FLOAT VALVE
DRAIN TO BOTTOM SKIN
REAR TANK COCK
NON-RETURN VALVE
TRANSFER SELECTOR COCK
RESTRICTORS
DROP TANK CONNECTION
LEADING EDGE TANKS
AIR LINE TO WING TANKS
BOTTOM MAIN TANK
ELECTRIC PUMP
MAIN COCK
NON-RETURN VALVE
AIR LINE TO COMBAT TANK
FUEL LINE FROM COMBAT TANK
TO ENGINE PUMP
FUEL SYSTEM
DRAIN
FILTER
FUEL PRESSURE REGULATOR VENT CONNECTION ON CARBURETTOR
FUEL LINE FROM WING TANKS
AIR LINE TO WING TANKS
NON-RETURN VALVES SHOWN THUS

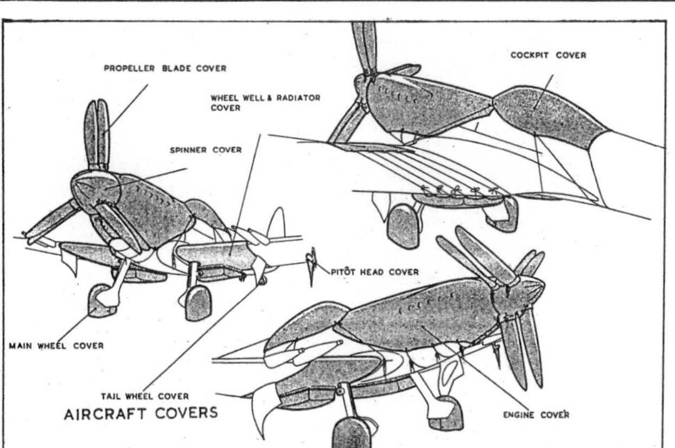
PROPELLER BLADE COVER
COCKPIT COVER
WHEEL WELL & RADIATOR COVER
SPINNER COVER
PITOT HEAD COVER
MAIN WHEEL COVER
TAIL WHEEL COVER
AIRCRAFT COVERS
ENGINE COVER

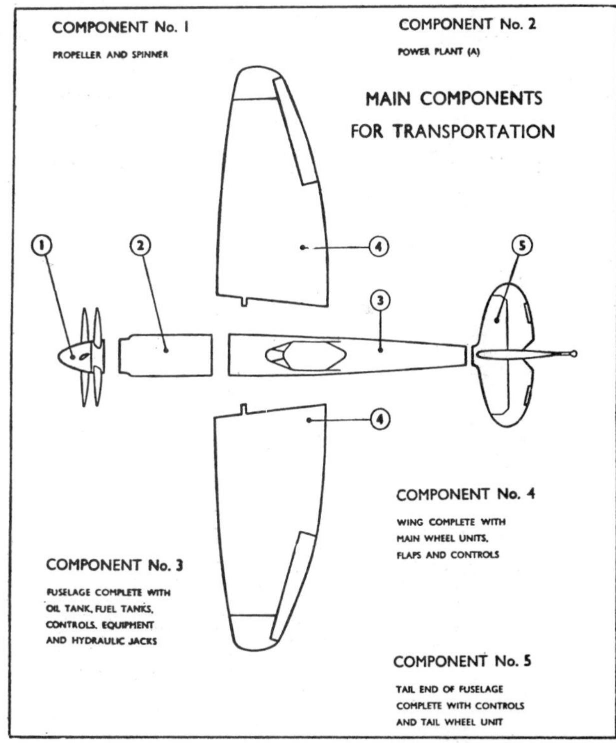
COMPONENT No. 1
PROPELLER AND SPINNER
COMPONENT No. 2
POWER PLANT (A)
MAIN COMPONENTS
FOR TRANSPORTATION
1
2
3
4
5
COMPONENT No. 4
WING COMPLETE WITH
MAIN WHEEL UNITS,
FLAPS AND CONTROLS
COMPONENT No. 3
FUSELAGE COMPLETE WITH
OIL TANK, FUEL TANKS,
CONTROLS, EQUIPMENT
AND HYDRAULIC JACKS
COMPONENT No. 5
TAIL END OF FUSELAGE
COMPLETE WITH CONTROLS
AND TAIL WHEEL UNIT

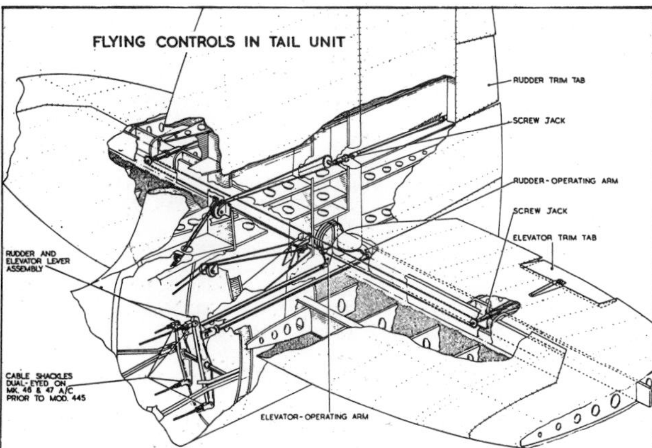
FLYING CONTROLS IN TAIL UNIT
RUDDER TRIM TAB
SCREW JACK
RUDDER-OPERATING ARM
SCREW JACK
ELEVATOR TRIM TAB
RUDDER AND ELEVATOR LEVER ASSEMBLY
CABLE SHACKLES DUAL-EYED ON MK. 46 & 47 A/C PRIOR TO MOD. 445
ELEVATOR-OPERATING ARM

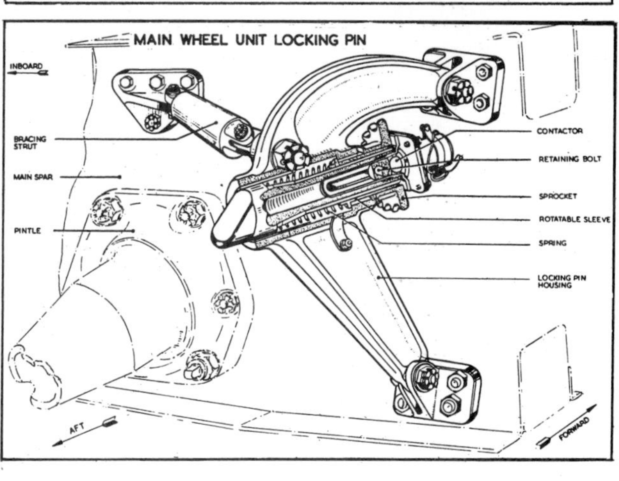
MAIN WHEEL UNIT LOCKING PIN
INBOARD
BRACING STRUT
MAIN SPAR
PINTLE
CONTACTOR
RETAINING BOLT
SPROCKET
ROTATABLE SLEEVE
SPRING
LOCKING PIN HOUSING
AFT
FORWARD

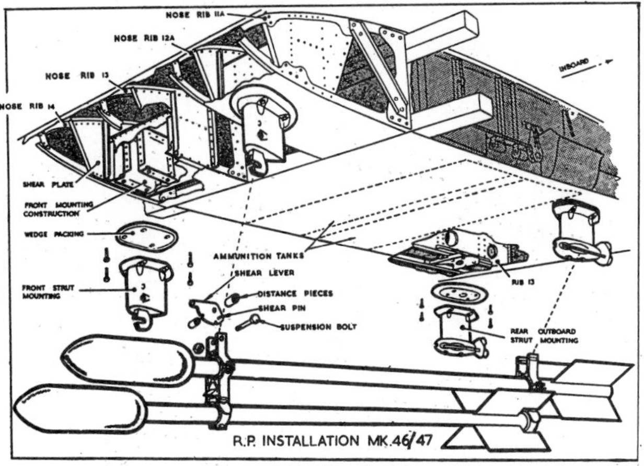
NOSE RIB 11A
NOSE RIB 12A
NOSE RIB 13
NOSE RIB 14
INBOARD
SHEAR PLATE
FRONT MOUNTING CONSTRUCTION
WEDGE PACKING
AMMUNITION TANKS
SHEAR LEVER
DISTANCE PIECES
SHEAR PIN
SUSPENSION BOLT
FRONT STRUT MOUNTING
RIB 13
REAR OUTBOARD STRUT MOUNTING
R.P. INSTALLATION MK.46/47

PS series A11 F.47 Griffon 87.

PS944 Proto F.47 SM 25-4-46 F/F S/Ldr Morgan HPA 2-5 SM mods 2-7 BDN Oct '46 deck land assessment trls & dropping empty & full combat o/ld tanks. Del date to RNAS 9-11 Farn Feb '47 BDn April '47 spin & hand trls Service pilots warned of spin & resultant tail heaviness in dive. Counteracted by addition of 9 inch long angle strips to upper & lower elevator trail edge. At Mach 0.77 the aircraft began a violent, rapid pitching movement. The angle strips raised control up to Mach 0.82 ETPS Farn 26-7-48

PS945 SM 12-10-46 F/F S/Ldr Morgan, Lithgow, Derry HPA RTO 18-11 trim curve HP 30-4-47 Deck land & hand trls on *HMS Illustrious* with PS948 & PS949 13-5 ADDLs 23-5 new trimmer cable fitted in stern 18-6 cooling 4-7 RNDA 6-8 Handling 90 Gall DT J Derry 3-10 Flown to BDn by Derry 10-4-48 Aug assessment trls, cooling & hand with 50 gall torpedo & 90 gall o/ld tanks in comp with LA552 & 545 (F.46s)

PS946 SM24-12-46 F/F S/Ldr Morgan HPA C.O. trls by Lithgow G88 install Flown to BDn by Derry 10-4-47 on loan for one month for full gunnery trials. Fd/ld by J Derry 14-7 Stoppages during neg 'g' manoeuvres. RNDA 6-8 BDn 24-3-48 fuel consumption trials.

PS947 HP-BDn 11-1-47 HP for trils 14-2 RNDA 608 778S

PS948 1st a/c with power fold wings. Farn Feb '47 SM 16-3 test flt Derry Chilbolton to Ford 28-4 Del to RNAS Ford by S/Ldr Morgan for DLTs 6-8 Farn Aug '47 RATOG & catapult trls. Drop tanks & ammo boxes instal before del to BDn 15-4-48 IFOF trls, deck land & hand on *HMS Illustrious* with PS945 & 949 13-5 rep 1949 at £1,550 7s. 8d. VA EA for tests 24-3-50 AHU Stret 6-7-54.

PS949 SM 3-5-47 test flt F/Lt Colquhoun. Deck trls *HMS Illustrious* with PS945 & 948 VA EA 23-7 RNDA 6-8 RNAS Anthorn 4-2-48 778S

PS950 SM 20-8-47 test flt F/Lt Colquhoun RNDA 27-8 RNAS Anthorn 23-9 804S 4-2-48 *HMS Theseus HMS Ocean* to Sembawang 20-5-50 800S *HMS Triumph* 10-5 VA EA 22-1-51 recon 759S 10-9-52 Stret 13-7353 coc SOC 3-10-56

PS951 SM 25-7-47 test flt F/Lt Colquohoun RNDA 27-8 RNAS Anthorn 23-9 rep 1949 at £1,776 4s 4d SM new engine 24-3-50 800S *HMS TRiumph* 736S 1955.

PS952 SM 26-6-47 test flt S/Ldr Derry VA Chil 15-7 G88 instal RNDA 6-8 BDn Sept '47 15½lb inertia wt on elevator system, spring tab stbd elevator, angle strip on upper & lower surface elevator trail edge to raise critical Mach number to 0.84, hand trls with external stores. RDU Anthorn 2-5-50 Stret 1-12 coc SOC 4-10-56

PS953 SM 18-7-47 test flt F/Lt Colquhoun RNDA 31-7 RNAS Anthorn 23-9 LoS 13-11 804S Ford 15-1-48 rep 1949 at £1,863 16s 7d VASM 21-3-50 G88 instal 800S *HMS Triumph* Sept '50

PS954 SM 20-6-47 test flt F/Lt Colquhoun RAF Hand Sqdn Hull 17-7 RNDA 6-8

PS955 SM 28-8-47 testflt S/Ldr Morgan RNDA 29-8 RNAS Anthorn 23-9 Naval Air Fight Unit dev trls

PS956 SM 9-7-47 test flt F/Lt Colquhoun RNDA 31-7 RNAS Anthorn 2-10

PS957 SM 27-9-47 test flt S/Ldr Morgan RNDA 30-9 RNAS Anthorn 16-10 787S

VP series all F.47 Griffon 88.

VP427 G87 RNDA 17-10-47 SM 5-11 test flt F/Lt Colquhoun RNAS Anthorn 21-11

VP428 G87 SM 6-9-47 test flt S/Ldr Derry SBAC Air Show Radlett 8th to 14th SM G88 instal RNAS Anthorn 16-10 RNDA 14-11

VP429 SM 26-11-47 test flt S/Ldr Morgan RNDA 29-11 RNAS LoS 16-12

VP430 SM 25-11-47 test flt FF/Lt Colquhoun RNDA 29-11 RNAS Anthorn 15-12 Stret 25-6-55 coc

VP431 RNDA 11-6-48 RNAS Anthorn 21-6 VA EA 12-7-51 Stret 25-6-55 coc

VP432 RNDA 17-6-48 SM 17-6 RNAS Anthorn 21-6

VP433 RNDA 29-11-47 SM 30-11 test flt S/Ldr Morgan RNAS Anthorn 15-12 VA EA 11-9-51

VP434 SM test flt F/Lt Colquhoun 31-12-47 RNDA 3--1-48 RNAS Anthorn 3-2

VP435 RNDA 3-1-48 RNAS Anthorn 30-1 VAS RP to RNAS Eglington 10-8

VP436 RNDA 28-2-48 SM 28-2 RNAS Anthorn 12-3

VP437 On loan from CSA VA Chil 3--1-48 RNDA 30-1 Farn 25-3 armament trls VA EA 1-7 mods BDn May '50 acceptance trils with wing bomb carrier Em/EF of 100 to 1,000lb loads. Carrier jettisoned by means of toggles on cockpit floor. Farn June '49 RATOG & catapult trls. Naval Air Fight Dev Unit 1950/52. AGT Gatwick 20-4-53 refurb Stret 28-1-54 coc SOC 3-10-56

VP438 SM 21-11-47 test flt S/Ldr Morgan RNDA 29-11 RNAS Anthorn 16-12

VP439 RNDA 25-2-48 SM 3-3 RNAS Anthorn 23-3 Farn 26-5 *HMS Ocean* to Halfar Malta 14-9 804S *HMS Ocean* 14-12

VP440 RNDA 28-2-48 SM 3--11 RNAS Anthorn 22-3 *HMS Ocean* to Halfar Malta 14-9 804 S *HMS Ocean* 30-11 LoS 18-6-49 VA EA 17-5-50 recon Stret 23-5-51 coc SOC 4-10-56

VP441 RNDA 29-11-47 SM 30-11 test flt S/Ldr Morgan RNAS Anthorn 15-12 Squires Gate Sept '71 Ex-tant Confederate Air Force Texas USA as N475F

VP442 SM 10-12-47 test flt S/Ldr Morgan RNDA 19-12 RNAS Anthorn 9-1-48 804S *HMS Ocean* 12-2 Halfar Malta 10-1-49 *HMS Triumph* to Sembawang 25-8 800S *HMS Unicorn* 16-12 Kai Tak 31-5-50 Stret 12-7 coc 1833 S 26-7-52 SOC 4-10-56

VP443 RNDA 22-12-47 RNAS Anthorn 8-1-48 SM 10-1 test flt S/Ldr Morgan VA EA 30-11-51 1833S Bramcote 27-8-52 Stret 25-6-55 coc

VP444 SM 19-12-47 test flt S/Ldr Morgan RNDA 27-12 RNAS Anthorn 9-1-48 804S

VP445 RNDA 28-2-48 SM 28-2 RNAS Anbthorn 22-3 VA EA 22-5-51

VP446 SM 16-1-48 test flt F/Lt Colquhoun RNDA 30-1 RNAS Anthorn 30-1 SM Mi RNAS Eglington 23-7 Stret 25-6-55 coc

VP447 RNDA 27-2-48 SM 27-2 RNAS Anthorn 28-2 800S *HMS Triumph* 1949 Sembawang Singapore used for anti-bandit strikes in Malaya VA EA 18-6-51 Stret coc 25-6-55

VP448 RNDA 30-1-48 RNAS Anthorn 30-1

VP449 RNDA 30-1-48 Test flt F/Lt Colquhoun VA Chil 30-1 G87 instal BDn June '48 trls with Mk 4B GGS VA EA 21-5-51 Stret 25-6-55 coc

VP450 RNDA 25-2-48 RNAS Anthorn 12-3

VP451 SM 25-2-48 RNDA 28-2 RNAS Anthorn 22-3 VA EA 26-4-51 Stret 25-6-55 coc

VP452 RNDA 25-3-48 SM 25-3 RNAS Anthorn 9-4

VP453 RNDA 31-3-48 SM 31-3 RNAS Anthorn 9-4 VA EA 9-7-51 Stret 25-6-55 coc

VP454 RNDA 20-3-48 SM 20-3 RNAS Anthorn 9-4

VP455 RNDA 25-3-48 SM 25-3 RNAS Anthorn 9-4 1833S Bramcote VA EA 19-6-51 Stret 25-6-55 coc

VP456 RNDA 2-4-48 SM 2-4 RNAS Anthorn 12-4

VP457 RNDA 5-4-48 SM 5-4 RNAS Anthorn 16-4 1833S Bramcote VA Ea 1-1-52

VP458 SM 30-3-48 SM 20-4 RNAS Anthorn 22-4

VP459 RNDA 23-4-48 SM 23-4 RNAS Anthorn 7-5 VA EA 17-10-51

VP460 RNDA 30-4-48 SM 30-4 RNAS Anthorn 11-5

VP461 FR Mk 47 RNDA 30-4-48 SM 30-4 800S flew offensive patrols from *HMS Triumph* during Korean War 1950-51

VP462 RNDA 30-4-48 SM 30-4 R-RH 11-5 1833S Bramcote VA EA 17-9-51 Stret 25-6-55 coc

VP463 RNDA 30-4-48 SM 30-4 VA Chil 3-6 G87 instal BDn May'49 wilth airship-type 90 gall o/ld tank. Release speed restricted to 300 kts. comp trls with Sea Fury Mk X. Trls without tank. July'49 trls with 3in dia flare & explosive RPs on zero length underwing rails. Flare heads were unreliable but explosive heads cleared up to a maximum release speed of 300 Kts. G88 re-fitted trls with large inertia wt on elevator system (14½ instead of 6½lb). Trls of dropping 'G' ASR container & 90 gall o/ld tank. Comp trls with Seafire 47 & Sea Fury X Stret 25-6-55 coc

VP464 RNDA 30-4-48 SM 28-5 BDn 22-11 trls of effect of external stores on max speed. VA Chil Nov'48 Q.E.S. radiator instal VA EA 30-10-51 1833S Bramcote AHU Stret 27-7-55 coc

VP465 RNDA 28-5-48 SM 28-5 RNAD Arb 21-6

VP471 RNDA 30-7-48 SM 30-7 RNAS Anthorn 17-8 Stret 25-6-55 coc

VP472 RNDA 23-7-48 SM 30-7 RNAS Anthorn 17-8 Stret 25-6-55 coc

VP473 RNDA 18-6-48 SM 18-6 RNAS Anthorn 22-6

VP474 RNDA 30-6-48 SM 30-6 VA Chil 2-7 1833S Bramcote VA EA 23-8-51 Stret 25-6-55 coc

VP475 RNDA 30-6-48 SM 30-6 RNAS Anthorn 2-7 VA EA 6-6-51 Stret 25-6-55 coc

Production/prototype PS945 at RNAS Ford in November 1953 as maintenance airframe A2186.

Seafire Mk 47 PS947 touches down on a fleet carrier.

VP455, serving with the Volunteer Reserve No 1833 Squadron, from Bramcote.

VP463 with combat tanks and new, post-war colour scheme.

VP474 of No.1833 Squadron during a RATOG take off.

VP476 RNDA 30-6-48 SM 30-6 RNAS Anthorn 18-8 VA EA 30-4-51 Stret 25-6-55 coc

VP477 RNDA 30-6-48 SM 30-6 RNAS Anthorn 8-7 1833S Bramcote VA EA 26-9-51 Stret 25-6-55 coc

VP478 RNDA 30-6-48 SM 30-6 RNAS Anthorn 2-7

VP479 RNDA 30-6-48 SM 30-6 RNAS Anthorn 8-7 VA EA 26-5-51 Stret 25-6-55 coc

VP480 RNDA 30-6-48 SM 30-6 RMAS Anthorn 8-7 Stret 24-2-51

VP481 RNDA 30-7-48 SM 30-7 RNAS Anthorn 21-9

VP482 RNDA 10-9-48 SM 10-9 RNAS Anthorn 21-9 VA EA 30-7-51 Stret 25-6-55 coc

VP483 RNDA 14-9-48 SM 14-9 RNAS Anthorn 21-9 VA EA 27-6-51 Stret 25-6-55 coc

VP484 RNDA 14-9-48 SM 14-9 RNAS Anthorn 24-9 VA EA 10-7-51 1833S Bramcote 25-7-52 Stret 25-6-55 coc

VP485 RNDA 14-9-48 SM 14-9 RNAS Anthorn 24-9 rep 1949 £1,196/2/6 SM 28-2-50 Anthorn 10-3 VA EA 28-7-51 1833S Bramcote 26-7-52 Stret 25-6-55 coc

VP486 RNDA 29-9-48 SM 29-9 Anthorn 1-10

VP487 SM 26-8-48 RNAS Anthorn 24-9 FLR Abbott 1-11 *HMS Triumph* to Halfar Malta 26-3-49 *HMS Unicorn* to Sembawang 28-10 800S *HMS Triumph* 31-5-50 hvy ldg 13-4 ret UK *HMS Unicorn* LoS 19-7 VA EA recon 1-11 Stret 9-10-51 1833S Bramcote 24-7-52 Stret 25-6-55 coc SOC 27-8-56

VP488 RNDA 29-9-48 SM 29-9 RNAS Anthorn 1-10 1833S Bramcote VA EA 30-5-51 AHU Stret 9-7-54

VP489 RNDA 30-9-48 SM 30-9 RNAS Anthorn 6-10

VP490 RNDA 30-9-48 sm 30-9 RNAS Anthorn 8-10 VA EA 26-7-51

VP491 SM 22-10-48 RNDA 30-10 RNAS Anthorn 4-11

VP429 RNDA 22-10-48 SM 23-10 RNAS Anthorn 22-10

VP493 SM 18-10-48 RNDA 30-10 RNAS Anthorn 4-11 FLR Abbott 1-3-49 *HMS Triumph* 26-4-49 to Sembawang 28-9 on *HMS Unicorn* 800S *HMS Triumph* 1-6-50 *HMS Unicorn* ret UK LoS 20-9 VA EA 11-2-51 recon VA EA 9-10-51 759S 25-9-52 AHU Stret 27-5-55 coc SOC 4-10-56

VP494 RNDA 30-10-48 SM 30-10 RNAS Anthorn 17-11

VP495 RNDA 30-10-48 SM 30-10 RNAS Anthorn 17-11

VR961 SM 22-11-48 RNAS Anthorn 5-12 800S Doni *HMS Triumph* to Halfar MAlta 2-6 *HMS Unicorn* to Sembawang 28-9 800S *HMS Triumph* 28-5-50 LoS 12-10 Stret 6-11-51 759S 1-10-52 Stret 25-6-55 coc SOC 4-10-56

VR962 SM 22-11-48 RNAS Anthorn 2-12 FLR Abbott 8-3-49 *HMS Triumph* to Halfar Malta 26-4 *HMS Unicorn* to Sembawang 28-10 800S *HMS Triumph* 7-6-50 VA EA recon 759S 6-10-52 Stret 25-6-55 coc SOC 4-10-56

VR963 SM 30-11-48 RNAS Anthorn 6-12

VR964 SM 30-11-48 RNAS Anthorn 17-12

VR965 SM 31-12-48 RNAS Anthorn 17-12 800S *HMS Triumph*

VR966 SM 31-12-48 RNAS Anthorn 13-1-49 800S Doni 8-7 f/f Halfar 8-7 *HMS Triumph* 27-7 800S LoS 16-1-50 VA EA recon 17-8 1833S Bramcote 11-7-53 Stret 25-6-55 coc SOC 4-10-56

VR967 SM 31-12-48 RNAS Anthorn 11-1-49 800S *HMS Triumph* AHU Stret 27-5-55

VR968 SM 31-12-48 RNAS Anthorn 14-1-49 800S 26-11-51 Stret 25-6-55 coc

VR969 SM 31-12-48 RNAS Anthorn 25-1-49 Stret 25-6-55 coc

VR970 SM 31-1-49 RNAS Anthorn 5-3 VA EA 15-3-51 AHU Stret 7-3-54

VR971 Final F.47 built. SM 28-1-49 VA Chil 18-2 RNAS Anthorn 12-5

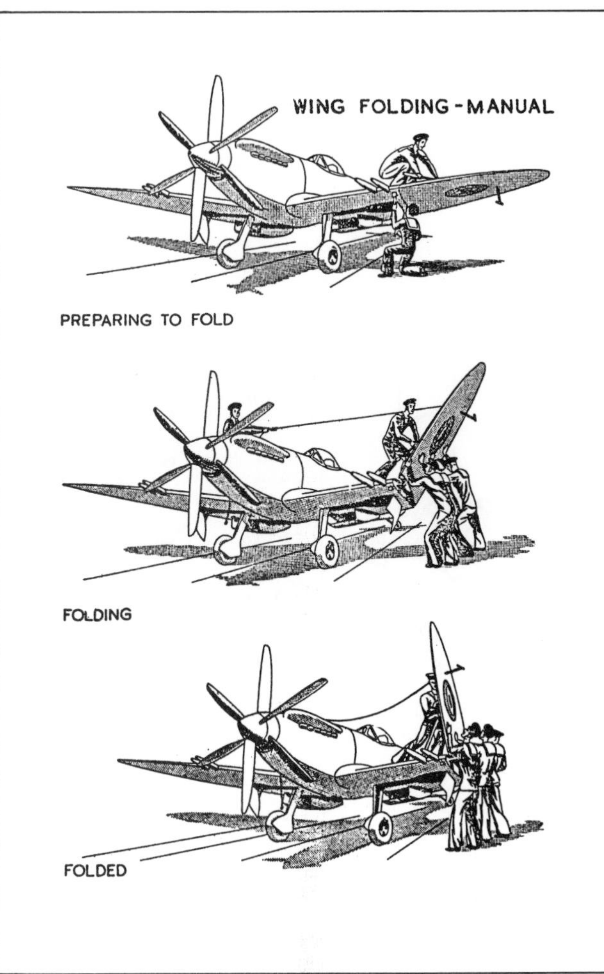

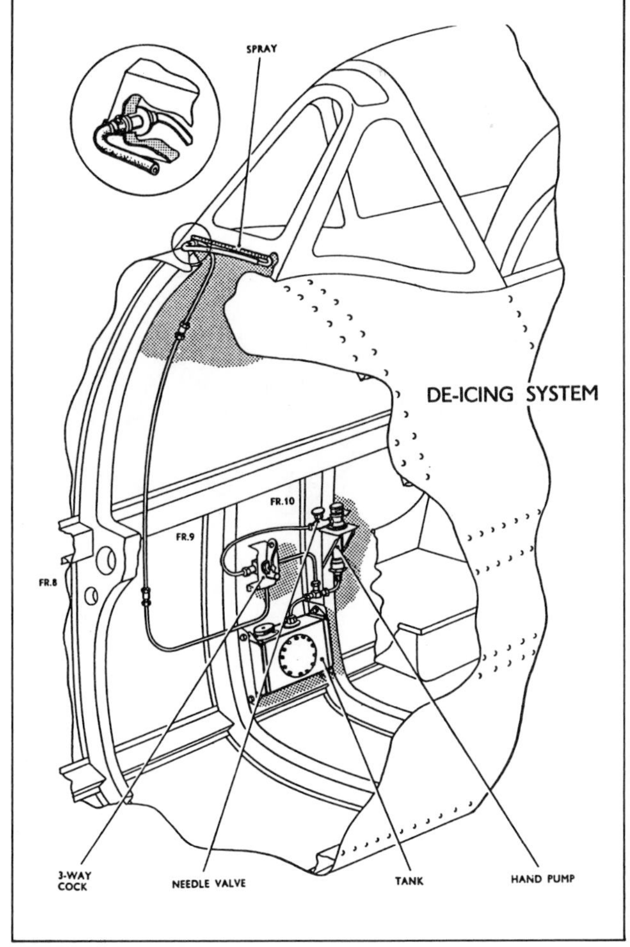

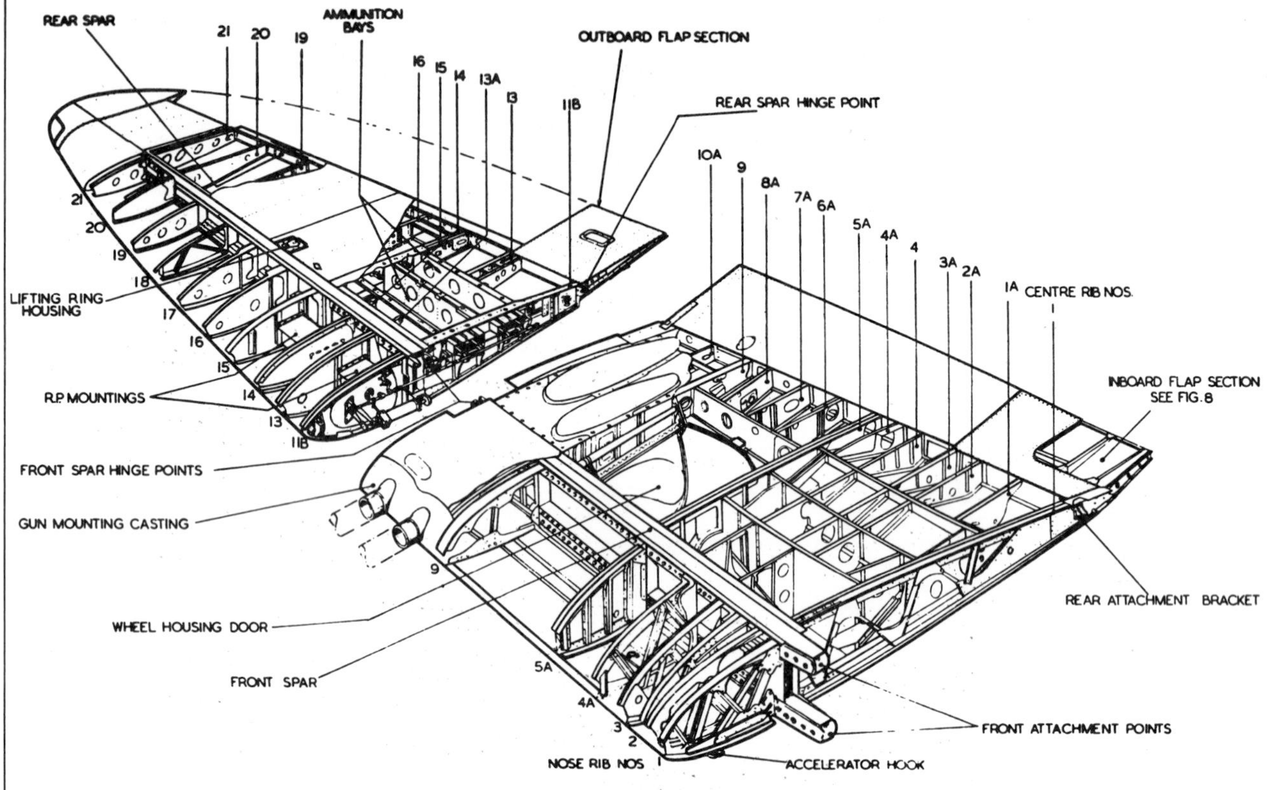

WING CONSTRUCTION (MK.47-MANUAL FOLD)

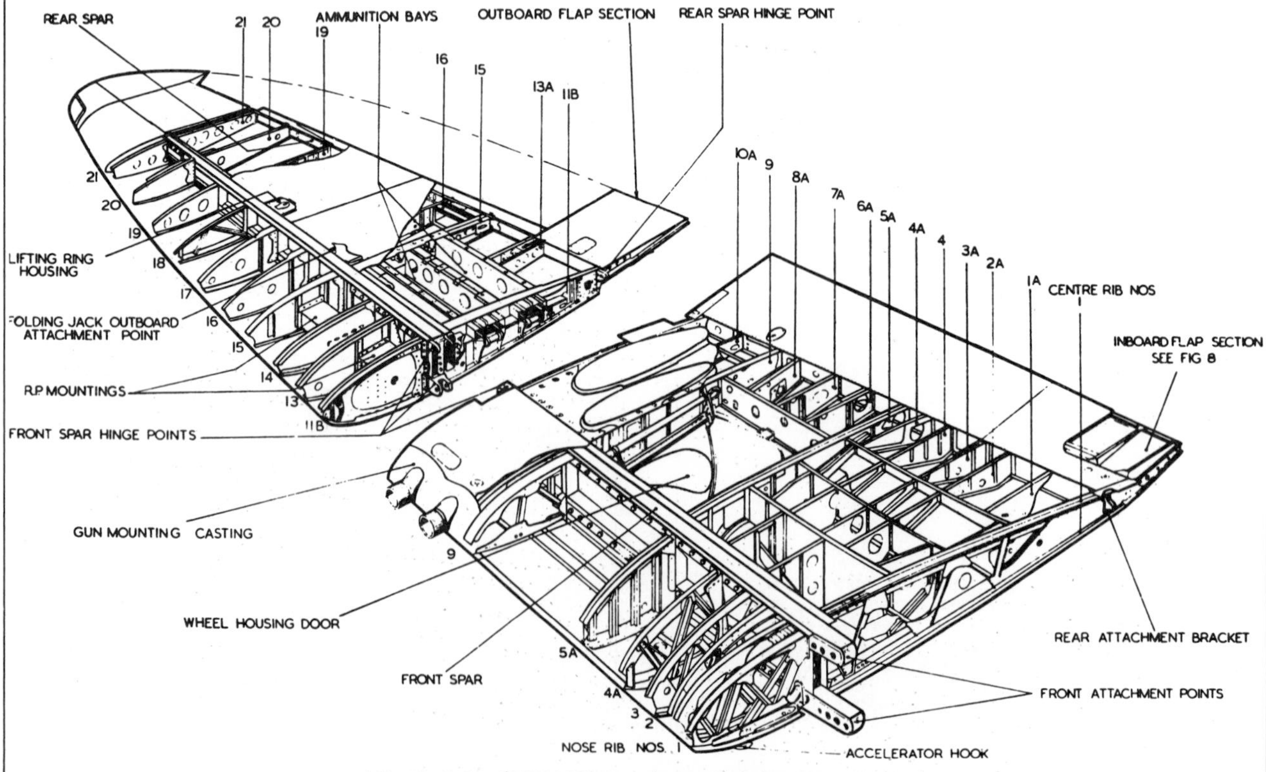

WING CONSTRUCTION (MK.47-POWER FOLD)

THE BITTER END

The Supermarine Type 382 Seafang was a modified Spiteful fitted with a sting hook, folding wings and the other accessories needed for a carrier based fighter. The Spiteful specification had been issued in February 1943 and on 7 October Supermarine Specification 474 for the Type 382 was published to cover an improved development of the Seafire Mk XV with a laminar flow wing and a Griffon 61 engine. A contra-prop installation was a major feature, plus an armament of four 20mm cannon with 150rpg and a fuel capacity of 116 gallons in internal tanks, with provision for a further 45 in an overload tank. Other details were- Span 35ft 0in, folded width 17ft 0in, height folded 13ft 9in, wing area 210sq ft; length 32ft 3in; tare weight 7,155lb; take off 9,030; estimated performance at 26,000ft 424 knots; stalling 88; initial rate of climb 4,900ft min; ceiling 41,750ft.

The complete proposal was submitted to Commander N. S. Slattery of the Royal Navy, Captain Liptrot and N. E. Rowe of MAP, with nil response. Almost two years later the first prototype Spiteful, NN664, made its maiden flight on 8 January 1945, and it was not until 21 April that any move was made to consider a developed aeroplane for the Navy as proposed by Supermarine. On that date the Air Ministry issued Specification N 5/45 for a single seat Fleet Air Arm fighter, and two development aircraft were subsequently ordered bearing the serials VB893 and 895.

Perhaps the Navy's reluctance to order a sea-going version of the Spiteful had been brought about by a letter of 23 March 1945 to the First Sea Lord from MAP- "I have had the attached charts produced so that you may see the development of naval aircraft which is planned for the immediate future. The Seafang is a navalised version of the Spiteful. We shall probably drop this aircraft, as you will notice that its performance is not so good as the Sea Hornet or the Sea Fury, both of which are 1946 aircraft whereas the Seafang is unlikely to appear before 1947. The only value in going on with the design is the possibility of its developing into the Jet Spiteful".

There followed a letter to Supermarine from MAP, dated 7 May. It read- "I am directed to inform you it has been decided to adjust your aircraft orders as follows- Place with you an order for 150 Seafang aircraft. In this connection I am to refer to the department's letter dated 2 May 1945 and to remind you that materials and components rendered surplus by the cancellation of 150 Spiteful aircraft should be absorbed, where practical, in the manufacture of these Seafang aircraft. Serial numbers allotted to the additional aircraft are VG471-505, 540-589, 602-650, 664-679". Vickers had written to MAP the previous 25 April suggesting the same proposal in order to speed delivery of the new Navy aeroplane. A Spiteful F Mk XV, RB520, was chosen as the first, interim prototype, for it had been fitted with a sting arrester hook in early 1945, but after trials at High Post it was still awaiting collection by the services on 22 September. Two years later it was collected and immediately struck off charge.

The Griffon 89 engine had been delivered to Hursley Park by 10 October and eventually installed in VB895, but it was not until the opening weeks of 1946 that the aeroplane made its first flight with the designation Seafang XXXII. It had power operated folding wings and the Griffon drove a wooden contra prop. VB895 was delivered to Farnborough in June, after maker's trials, for deck arresting, during which there were a number of rudder horn failures. The aluminium fitting was replaced with one of high tensile steel, but the rudder failed again, this time on the trailing edge. It was decided to strengthen the entire rudder with an increased gauge skin, plus provision of vertical stiffeners just forward of the trailing edge.

Simulated ADDLS were carried out at Chilbolton and RNAS Ford in June 1947 with flap settings of 76° for landing and 30° for take off. The most suitable landing speed was 95 knots. M. J. Lithgow was the test pilot and at the conclusion of his test reports he wrote:- "In general it is considered that the Seafang is a good deck landing aircraft, mainly owing to the good view and lack of float on cutting the throttle. It is strongly recommended that VB985 be allotted to the STU at Ford, who are extremely keen to do some themselves when the carrier is again available". His last remarks related to a series of deck landing trials on the aircraft carrier *HMS Illustrious* on 21 May.

As with the Spitfire, overseas interest in the Seafang was high and VB895 was flown from Eastleigh to Valkenburg on 19 August 1946 by Lithgow for demonstration to the Dutch Armed Forces. Two days later he repeated the demonstration to American, French and officers of the Royal Netherlands Navy. Despite many enquiries the Seafang was never ordered.

Development of long range fuel tanks went hand in hand with airframe improvements and VB895 was used for a series of trials of an improved release mechanism. When operated it allowed the front of the torpedo shaped tank to drop away first so that the rear pivots supported it before falling clear. Both 90 and 170 gallon tanks were jettisoned up to speeds of 255 knots. The tanks were supported at three points, two forward and one rear and were carried on Ingersoll bomb release slips.

The sixth production Seafang Mk 32, VG471, made its maiden flight before VB895 and was delivered to Farnborough on 15 January 1946 under the designation of Seafang Mk 31. It had a non-folding wing and a five bladed, single rotation propeller of NACA 16 section. Rotols had delivered it to High Post on 19 October 1945 and made a promise to deliver the contra-prop for VB895 after it had completed its second 50 hour test. This was the reason for the delay in flying VB895. Lateral control investigations were carried out with VG474 fitted with standard, slotted tab balanced ailerons, these allowing a rate of roll of 270ft a second at 500mph. A second set of trials were made with Lockheed power assisted ailerons in November 1947. To install the 'Servodyne' controls one of the fuselage 10 gallon fuel tanks had to be removed. The test pilots were impressed with the assisted controls but did not like the

Seafang Mk XXXII, VB895.

Supermarine N5/45 Seafang F31/32

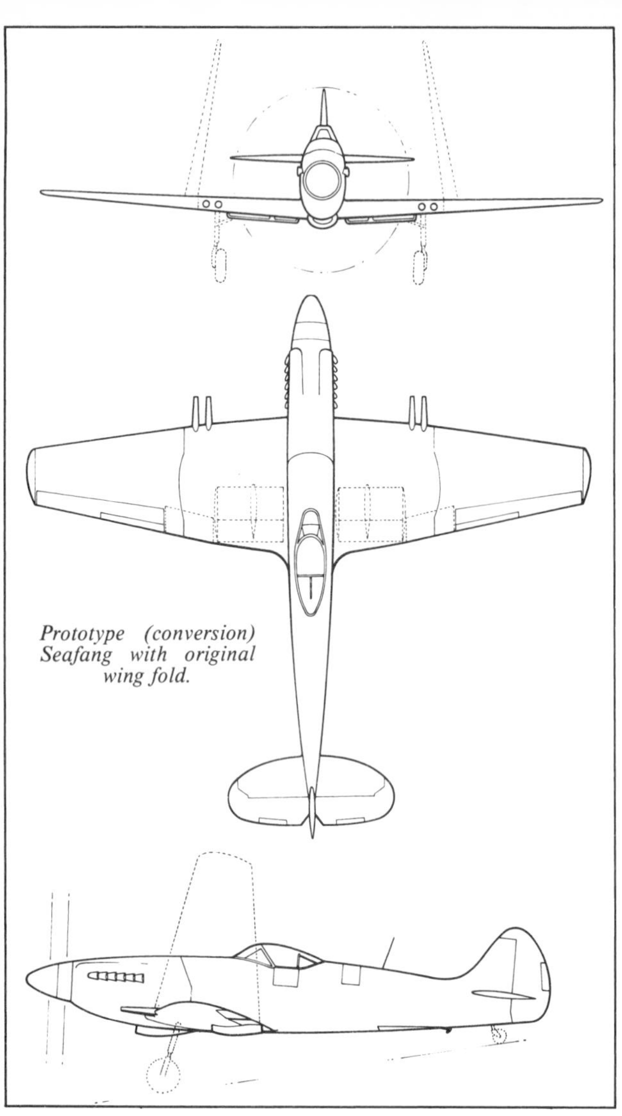

Prototype (conversion) Seafang with original wing fold.

Cannon installation on VB895. To remove guns the aileron control bar was made in two parts, one part of which was lifted for the operation.

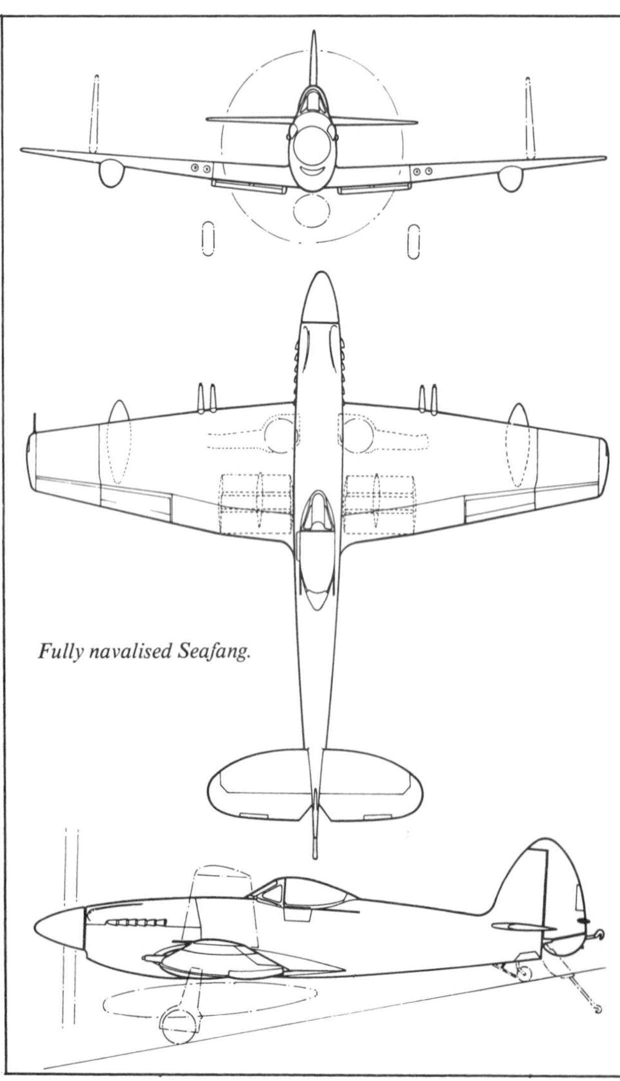

Fully navalised Seafang.

VG471 (above and below) with non folding wing. There was still a hint of the Mitchell Spitfire in the shape.

tendency of the control column to creep from neutral to full travel with only a sharp tap, not a push, on the column.

In order to determine wing profile drag coefficient and the nature of its variation with Mach number, VG475 was fitted with a wake exploration device consisting of a pitot comb on the trailing edge. J. D. Derry flew the aircraft on 23 June 1947 in a series of dives from 24,000 feet reaching a Mach number of .69 and .77. At .75 the aircraft developed a most violent pitching movement, and despite throttling back recovery was not possible due to increasing G loads. On reaching 16,000 feet Derry was able to pull out. The comb was installed between the flaps and ailerons and it was thought that the supporting struts were disturbing airflow over the elevator horn. A smooth fairing was added to the junction of the inner strut and comb support and tests continued. They were abandoned later as the wing contour had to be adjusted to raise the Mach number and this was never done.

In June 1948 VB895 was fitted with a new gun bay ventilation system comprising two intake scoops a side just beneath the wing leading edge and exit pipes on the top surface on the gun bay panels. Service acceptance trials for the Mk V* 20mm cannon had begun at Boscombe Down the previous April and explosions had occurred in the port wing due to ignition of gases which had collected in the gun bays. After the new ventilation system was fitted trials were concluded successfully.

Only nine Seafangs, VG471 to 479, were delivered out of a total of 150 ordered, but seven more were built and delivered in a dismantled condition. An attempt was made to continue the Seafire/Seafang line by a proposal to fit the laminar flow wing to a completely redesigned fuselage using the Rolls-Royce 46H engine. The design had a number of distinctive features including leading edge wing intakes feeding radiators located in the roots, an inward retracting undercarriage with gimballed wheels stored vertically in the fuselage behind the engine, a long engine cowling to accommodate the 46H (Eagle) engine driving contra-props, four cannon and square tipped tailplane and rudder. It was known as the Supermarine Type 391 and the original drawing was issued on 20 June 1944. Estimated maximum speed was in excess of 500mph. The same wing was then proposed for the Supermarine E1/45 Jet Seafang, which eventually was produced as the E.10/44 Type 392 Attacker. A note on the Jet Seafang disagreed with an RAE review of February 1946 which stated- "It should be noted that it is by no means certain that the aircraft will be controllable on the deck because of the inherent ground instability of its tail wheel layout and absence of rudder control at low wing speed".

Supermarine replied- "We disagree strongly with this statement. There does not appear to us any reason why the controllability of this aeroplane on the deck should be in fact worse than any other jet propelled type. Firstly the tail wheel is steerable, and secondly the undercarriage is of wide track with differential braking. The pilot should have full directional control, even in the absence of wind". Mitchell's design went down fighting to the bitter end.

Damage to port wing after explosions in gun bay during static firing trials at Boscombe Down.

Gun bay ventillation was improved after installation of air vents in wing leading edge and upper surface.

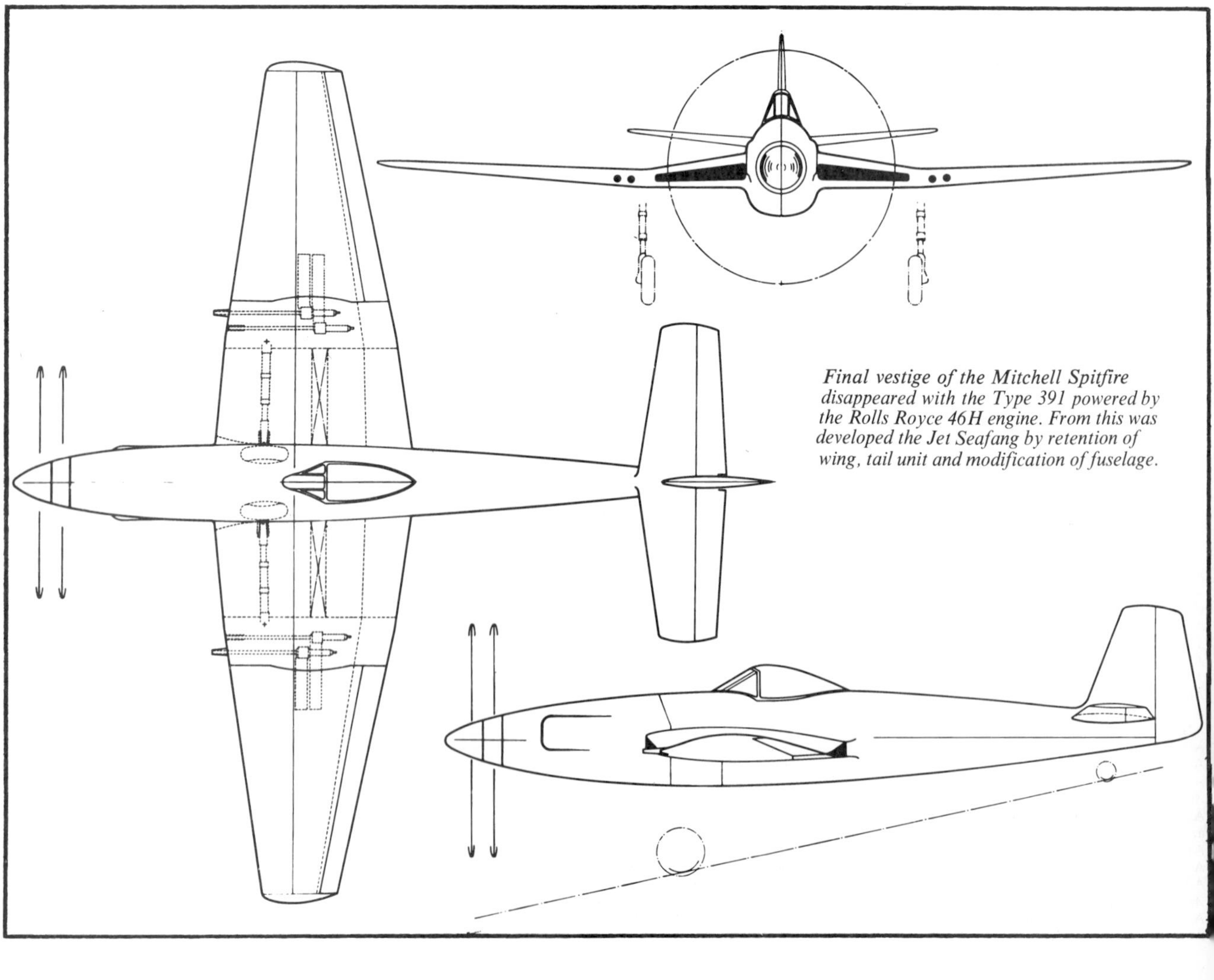

Final vestige of the Mitchell Spitfire disappeared with the Type 391 powered by the Rolls Royce 46H engine. From this was developed the Jet Seafang by retention of wing, tail unit and modification of fuselage.

SUPERMARINE TYPE NUMBERS

Type	Mark Number	Engine	Notes
224	F7/30	Goshawk	K2890 only
300	Spitfire I	Merlin C/II/III	K5054 & production
305	Spitfire	Merlin	Project with two seats and four gun turret
311	F37/34	Merlin E	Design April 1936
312	Spitfire	Merlin	Project with Oerlikon cannon
323	Spitfire N17	Merlin II Special	High Speed Spitfire
329	Spitfire II	Merlin XII	Production CB only
330	Spitfire III	Merlin X	N3297 & W3237 only
331	Spitfire VB	Merlin 45/46	2 Hispano cannon & 4 Browning m/gs
	Spitfire VA	Merlin 45	8 Browning m/gs
332	Spitfire	Merlin	FN gun installation. For Estonia
335	Spitfire I	Merlin II	For Greece. Nil
336	Spitfire I	Merlin II	For Portugal. Nil
337	Spitfire IV	Griffon IIb	DP845
338	Spitfire I	Merlin II	Design, Nov 1939, for FAA
340	Seafire IB	Merlin 45/46	AB205 prototype & production
341	Spitfire I	Merlin II	For Turkey. 15 ordered, 2 delivered
342	Spitfire Floatplane	Merlin II	R6722 on Roc floats
343	Spitfire I	Merlin II	**Long range design, 1940**
344	Spitfire I	—	Supermarine float design
345	Spitfire I	Merlin II	Design with Masden 13.2mm cannon, 1940
346	Spitfire I	Merlin II	C wing, 20mm guns
348	Spitfire III	Merlin XX	W3237 2nd prototype
349	Spitfire VC	Merlin 45/46	Production
350	Spitfire VI	Merlin 47	X4942 prototype & production
351	Spitfire VII	Merlin 61	AB450 prototype & production
352	Spitfire VB(trop)	Merlin 45/46	X4922 prototype & production
353	Spitfire PR IV	Merlin 45/46	F VB converted
354	Spitfire	Merlin 46	Design only, Sept 1941
355	Spitfire V Spl floatplane	Merlin 45	W3760, EP751, EP754
356	Spitfire 21,22,24	Griffon 61	DP851 & production
357	Seafire IIC	Merlin 45/46	AD371 prototype & production
358	Seafire III	**Merlin 55M**	MA970 prototype production Merlin 32/55
359	Spitfire VIII	Merlin 61	JF299 prototype
360	Spitfire VIII	Merlin 61	JG204 & production
361	Spitfire	Merlin 61 (IX) Merlin 266 (XVI)	MH874 prototype & production
362	Spitfire PR X	Merlin 64	MD191 prototype & production
363	Spitfire Trop	Griffon IIB	Design, May 1942
364	Spitfire Trop	Griffon 61	Design, May 1942
365	Spitfire PR XI	Merlin 61	Production
366	Spitfire XII	Griffon III	DP845 & production
367	Spitfire PR XIII	Merlin 32	Production
368	Spitfire VIII	Merlin 61	Heston project. Malinowski wing
369	Spitfire XIV	Griffon 61/65/83	JF316 to 21 F VIII converted
370	Spitfire PR XI Trop	Merlin 61	Design Oct 1943
371	Spiteful	Griffon 61	NN660 prototype
372	Spitfire 23	Griffon 61	JG204 semi-laminar wing
373	Spitfire XIV	Griffon 85	DP851 prototype & production
374	Spitfire PR XI	Merlin 61/63	Mk IX converted
375	Seafire LF IIC	Merlin 32	L1004 prototype & production
376	Spitfire VIII	Merlin 61	Contra-props
377	Seafire XV	Griffon VI	NS487 prototype
378	Spitfire IX Trop	Merlin 61	Design April 1943
379	Spitfire XIV	Griffon 65	Production
382	Seafang 31/32	Griffon 65	VG471 prototype & production
383	Spiteful	Merlin 61	Design, Nov 1943
384	Seafire XVII	Griffon VI	Prototype NS493
385	Spitfire IX Spl Floatplane	Merlin 61	MJ892 prototype
386	Seafire XV	Griffon VI	Fitted rear view hood
387	Spitfire PR X	Merlin 64	Pressure cabin production
388	Seafire 45/46/47	Griffon 61	TM379 prototype & production
389	Spitfire PR XIX	Griffon 65	SW777 prototype
390	Spitfire PR XIX	Griffon 66	Production with pressure cabin
393	Spiteful XIV	Griffon	Production
394	Spitfire F & FR XVIII	Griffon 65/67	Production
395	Seafire XVIII	Griffon 35/36	Production
396	Seafang F32	Griffon 89	Seafire XVII development VB893
501	Spitfire Exp		Power plant development Design, Feb 1946
502	Spitfire T8	Merlin 66	MT818(G-AIDN) prototype
506	Seafire III	Merlin 55	Conversions for Irish Air Corps
509	Spitfire T9	Merlin 66	Conversions (21)
518	Spitfire XVIIIT	Griffon 65/66	None converted

ABBREVIATIONS

Appendix II

List of abbreviations used in this book. Names in italics denotes a ship.

Aban	Abandoned
Abb	Abbotsinch
abort	aborted
Abs	Area Breakdown Scheme
a/c	aircraft
acc	accident
Ack	Acklington
ACSEA	Air Command South East Asia
AD	Aircraft Depot
ADFU	Air Defence Flight Unit
ADGB	Air Defence Great Britain
ADn	Aston Down
Ad S Oc	*Adolph S Ochs*
Ad S Ot	*Adolph S Ottis*
AEAF	Allied Expeditionary Air Force
aero	aerobatics
AF	Airfield
AFDU	Air Fighting Development Unit
Affil	Affiliation
Afghan	*Afghanistan*
AFS	Advanced Flying School
AFHQ	Air Force headquarters
AFTS	Advanced Flying Training School
AGME	Aircraft Gun Mounting Establishment
A&GS	Armament & Gunnery School
AGS	Air Gunnery School
AGS	Aircrew Grading School (post WW2)
AGT	Airwork General Trading
AI	Air Interception
AIEU	Armament & Instrument Experimental Unit
ails	ailerons
Ald	Aldermanston
Ald Park	*Alder Park*
alloc	allocated
allot	allotted/ment
Alph	*Alphard*
ALS	Air Landing School (in India)
alt	Altitude
AM	Air Ministry
AMDP	Air member for Development & Production
Amot E	*Amot Elkerk*
Amstel	*Amelsterk*
Angha	*Anghadive*
ANS	Air Navigation School
Anth	Anthorn
AOC	Air Office Commanding
AOP	Air Observation Post
AOS	Air Observers School
APC(S)	Armament Practice Camp (School)
app	approach
Arb	Arbroath
ArmW	Armstrong Whitworth
arma	armament
ASP	Air Stores Park
Aspha	*Ashphalian*
ASR	Air-Sea Rescue
ASRTU	Air-Sea Rescue Training Unit
ASS	Air Signals School
Assoc	Association/ed
AST	Air Service Training (E-Exeter; H-Hamble; M-Marwell)
ASU	Aircraft Storage Unit
ASWDU	Air-Sea Warfare Development Unit
ATA	Air Transport Auxiliary
ATC	Armament Training Camp
ATCp	Air Training Corps
ATDU	Air Torpedo Development Unit
ATF	Autogiro Training Flight
Atlan City	*Atlantic city*
ATS	Armament Training Squadron
ATU	Armament Training Unit (in India)
Aust Clan	*Australian Clan*
Aust Star	*Australian Star*
Avris	*Avristan*

BABS	Blind Approach Beacon System
BADU	Blind Approach Development Unit
BAF	Belgian Air Force
BAFF	British Air Forces in France
BAFO	British Air Forces of Occupation (post WW2)
Bak	Bakarista
Bal Br	Balado bridge
Bally	Ballyhalbert
BANS	Basic Air Navigation School
Ban Shah	*Bandar Shahpour*
Bar For	*Baron forbes*
Bar Inch	*Baron Inchcape*
BARU	British Airways Repair Unit (in Middle East)
BAS	Blind (later Beam) Approach School
Bas	Basrah
BATDU	Blind Approach Training & Development Unit
BATF	Beam Approach Training Flight
B&P	Boulton and Paul
bboc	brought back on charge
BCBS	Bomber Command Bombing School
BCCF	Bomber Command Communications flight
BCDU	Bomber Command Development Unit
BCWS	Bomber Command Wireless School
BDA	Balloon Development Unit
BD Flt	Bombing Development Flight
BDn	Boscombe Down
BDU	Bombing Development Unit
BEF	British Expeditionary force
Ben	Benson
Ben H H	*Benjamin H Hill*
ber	beyond economic repair
Berr	*Berredch*
BGS	Bombing & Gunnery School
Bham 24	Birmingham 24 (postal district number CBAF)
BHll	Biggin Hill
BNn	Brize Norton
BoB	Battle of Britain
bou	broken up on unit
Boul	Boulmer
BPC	British Purchasing Commission (in USA)
Bom Com	Bomber Command
Br Al	British Aluminium
Bram	Bramcote
Bris Star	*Brisbane Star*
BSDU	Bomber Support Development Unit
BT	Bomber Transport
C2, C3, C5	Categories (damage, etc)
CA	Category A
CAC	Category AC
CA	Coastal Area (pre 1936)
CAACU	Civil Anti-Aircraft Co-operation Unit
CACF	Coastal Artillery Co-operation Flight
CAEU	Casualty Air Evacuation Unit
Cal	Calibration/calibrated
Cal Mon	*Caledonian Monarch*
Cam Leith	*Camarata Leith*
can	cannon
cancel	cancelled
CANS	Civil Air Navigation School
CAR	Category AR
carb	carbon
Card Gib	*Cardinal Gibbons*
Card Grif	*Cardinal Griffin*
Carn Cast	*Carnarvon Castle*
car	carrier
CARRIERS	aircraft, HMS
Athe	*Atheling*
Attac	*Attacker*
Batt	*Battler*
Form	*Formidable*
Game	*Gamecock*
Illus	*Illustrious*
Implac	*Implacable*
Indef	*Indefatigable*
Indom	*Indomitable*
Khed	*Khedive*
P Castle	*Pretoria Castle*
Rav	*Ravager*
Stal	*Stalker*
Unic	*Unicorn*
Veng	*Vengeance*
Vict	*Victorious*
Cat 4R	Category 4 (relaxed)
Cat Comp	Components
CATCS	Central Air Traffic Control School
Catf	Catfoss
Catt	Catterick
CAW	College of Air Warfare
C&C	Crosby & Company
CB	Category B
CBAF	Castle Bromwich Aero Factory
CBE	Central Bomber Establishment
CC	Coastal Command
CCCF	Coastal Command Communications Flight
CCDU	Coastal Command Development Unit
CCGS	Coastal Command Gunnery School
CCP	Coastal Command Pool
CCTDU	Coastal Command Tactical Development Unit
CCU	Check & Conversion Unit (in Middle East)
CD	Coast Defence
cd	crashed
CDCF	Coast Defence Co-operation Flight
CDDF(U)	Coast Defence Development Flight (Unit)
cd/ld	crash landed/ing
CE	Category E
CF	Conversion Flight (after number)
CF(U)	Communications Flight (Unit)
CFE	Central Fighter Establishment
CFS	Central Flying School
CG (CoG)	Centre of Gravity
CHA	Chattis Hill
Chan	*Chanda*
Char Hall	*Charlton Hall*
Chat	*Chatham*
C Hawk	*Cape Hawk*
Chil	Chilbolton
China P	*China Prince*
Chu Fen	Church Fenton
Chu St	Church Stanton
Chu Str	Church Stretton
Chyl	*Chylessa*
CLE	Central Landing Establishment
Clan Camp	*Clan Campbell*
Clan Chat	*Clan Chattan*
Clan Far	*Clan Farquaha*
Clan For	*Clan Forbes*
Clan MacB	*Clan MacBrayne*
Clan MacW	*Clan MacWayne*
Clan MacI	*Clan MacIver*
Clan McC	*Clan Macauley*
Clan McK	*Clan MacKellar*
Clear	*Clearpool*
Clpse	Collapse
Clyde	*Clydebank*
C McBean	*Clan McBean*
CNCS	Central Navigation & Control School
CNS	Central Navigation School
CoAD	*City of Adelaide*
CoAG	*City of Agra*
COAL	Cunliffe Owen Aircraft
C o Ath	*City of Athens*
C o Cal	*City of Calcutta*
C o Chest	*City of Chester*
C o Chy	*City of Chyistian*
C o Der	*City of Derby*
C o East	*City of Eastbourne*
C o Evan	*City of Evansville*
C o Haid	*City of Haides*
C o H K	*City of Hong Kong*
C o Kim	*City of Kimberley*
C o Lanc	*City of Lancaster*
C of Lds	*City of Leeds*
Cole	Colerne
C o Lil	*City of Lille*
C o Lin	*City of Lincoln*
coll	collided/sion
Colleg	*Collegian*
Colq	Colquhoun, Flt Lt L R
C o Lus	*City of Lusaka*
comb	combat
Com Flt	Communication Flight
comp	comparative
con	converted/sion
coc	cocooned
C o New	*City of Newcastle*
Coning	Coningsby
Conak	*Conakrian*
cons	consumption
cont	control/s
contam	contamination
contd	continued/uation
cool	cooling/lant
Copac	*Copacabana*
Corab	*Corabella*
Corn	*Cornwall*
C o Run	*City of Runstone*
C o Shan	*City of Shantoyce*
C o Shir	*City of Shiriotadia*
CPF	Coastal Patrol Flight
Cran	Cranfield
Craw Hon	*Crawford Honey*
Craw W L	*Crawford W Long*
Crew	Crewkerne
CRD	Controller of Research & Development
CRO	Central Repair Organisation
CRU	Contractors(civilian) Repair Unit
CRSP	Contractors Repair Supply Procedure
CRCT	Circuit
CS	Communications Squadron
C/S	Constant Speed
CSE	Central Signals Establishment
Csfd	Cosford
CSU	Central Servicing Unit
CU	Conversion Unit
CUAS	Cambridge University Air Squadron
Cul	Culham
Cycl	*Cyclops*
dam	damaged
D Bank	*Dee Bank*
dbf	destroyed by fire
dbr	damaged (deteriorated) beyond repair
dd	date delivered
Def	*Defender*
Deff	Defford
deH	de Havilland
Dekh	Dekhelia
demo	demonstrated/ion
del	delivery/ed
des	destroyed
det	determined/ation
dev	developed/ment
D Flt	Delivery Flight
DGRD	Director General of Research & Development
Dig	Digby
dis	dispersal
disin	disintegrated
DOD	Director of Development
Doni	Donibristle
DTD	Director of Technical Development
Dung	Dungeness
Dunk	Dunkirk
Dux	Duxford
dvd	dived
dvng	diving
EA	Eastleigh
EAAS	Empire Air Armament School
e/ac	enemy action
EACF	East Africa Communications Flight
e/act	enemy aircraft
EAfr	East Africa
EANS	Empire Air Navigation School
ECFS	Empire Central Flying School
ECU	Experimental Co-operation Unit
Ed Fann	*Edmund Fanning*
EEC	English Electric Company
EFS	Empire Flying School
e/fld	engine failed
EFTS	Elementary Flying Training School
Elanaf	*Elanafaire*
Elamf	*Elamffanc*
elect	electrical
elev	elevator
emergcy	emergency
Emp Arch	*Empire Archer*
Emp Bar	*Empire Barrie*
Emp Cab	*Empire Cabot*
Emp Cam	*Empire Cameron*
Emp Cel	*Empire Celia*
Emp Clan	*Empire Clan*
Emp Clive	*Empire Clive*
Emp Corm	*Empire Cormorant*
Emp Con	*Empire Conrad*
Emp Dar	*Empire Darwin*
Emp Crav	*Empire Craven*
Emp Cuba	*Empire Cuba*
Emp Day	*Empire Day*
Emp Dyn	*Empire Dynasty*
Emp Fran	*Empire Franklin*
Emp Gam	*Empire Gambia*
Emp Gem	*Empire Gem*
Emp Gla	*Empire Glade*
Emp Gran	*Empire Grantham*
Emp Grebe	*Empire Grebe*
Emp Har	*Empire Harlow*
Emp Hav	*Empire Haven*
Emp Hth	*Empire Heath*
Emp Kes	*Empire Kestrel*
Emp King	*Empire Kingsley*
Emp Kum	*Empire Kumasi*
Emp Lib	*Empire Liberty*
Emp Mar	*Empire Marlow*
Emp Mast	*Empire Master*
Emp Mead	*Empire Meadow*
Emp Orch	*Empire Orchid*
Emp Ort	*Empire Ortolan*
Emp Pag	*Empire Pagan*
Emp Par	*Empire Paragon*
Emp Pea	*Empire Peacock*
Emp Prin	*Empire Prince*
Emp Prog	*Empire Progress*
Emp Prow	*Empire Prowess*
Emp Puma	*Empire Puma*
Emp Raj	*Empire Raj*
Emp Ray	*Empire Ray*
Emp Reg	*Empire Regent*
Emp Rhod	*Empire Rhodes*
Emp Stal	*Empire Stalwart*
Emp Sev	*Empire Severn*
Emp Sun	*Empire Sunbeam*
Emp Shack	*Empire Shackleton*
Emp Stren	*Empire Strength*
Emp Tern	*Empire Tern*
Emp Tide	*Empire Tide*
Emp Tow	*Empire Tower*
eng	engine
En R/M	Enfield Rolling Mills
equip	equipped/ment
ERFTS	Elementary & Reserve Flying Training School
ERS	Empire Radio School
Esh	Eshott
E Smelt	Eyre Smelting Co
Ess Trad	*Essex Trader*
ETPS	Empire Test Pilots School
e/tr	enemy territory
Eury	*Eurybates*
EWS	Electrical & Wireless School
exam	examination
exp	experimental
ext	extensive
FA	Fighting Area (pre 1936)
FAA	Fleet Air Arm
FAAC	Flying Accident Category AC
FAC	Flying Accident
FACB	Flying Accident Category B
FACE	Flying Accident Category E
FAF	French Air Force
fail	failure/ed
Fan Hd	*Fanad Head*
Farn	Farnborough
FBFTS	Franco-Belgium Flying Training School
FBTS	Flying Boat Training School

FCCRS	Fighter Command Communications Squadron
FCHA	Fighter Command Handling Squadron
FCPY	Ferry Command Preparation Unit
FEAF	Far East Air Force
Fern	*Fernbank*
FETS	Far East Training Squadron
Ftr F	Fighter Flight
FF	First Flight
f/f	ferry flight
FFAF	Free French Air Force
FFS	Fire Fighting School
FH	Flying Hours
FHH	Fort Hudson Hope
FIS	Flying Instructors School
fin	finish
fitt	fitted
FIU	Fighter Interception Unit
f/ld	force/d landed/ing
Fleet	Fleetlands
fl/o	flown off
FLS	Flight Leaders School
Flt	Flight
F/LT	Flight Lieutenant
fly	flying
F/O	Flight Officer
Folkes	Folkestone
Fond	*Fondadab*
Forad Hd	*Forad Head*
form	formation
Fort Bag	*Fort Bagley*
Fort B	*Fort Boise*
Fort Cam	*Fort Cameousan*
Fort Carn	*Fort Carnousan*
Fort Cham	*Fort Chambly*
Fort Ches	*Fort Chesterfield*
Fort Chur	*Fort Churchill*
Fort Doug	*Fort Douglas*
Fort Ell	*Fort Ellis*
Fort Enter	*Fort Enterprise*
Fort Geo	*Fort George*
Fort Gra	*Fort Graham*
Fort Hew	*Fort Hewan*
Fort Highf	*Fort Highfield*
Fort Highl	*Fort Highland*
Fort Hud	*Fort Hudson*
Fort Hus	*Fort Husam*
Fort Is	*Fort Island*
Fort Jer	*Fort Jersey*
Fort L M	*Fort La Mourne*
Fort Liv	*Fort Livingstone*
Fort Lrd	*Fort Liard*
Fort Mas	*Fort Massac*
Fort Mchst	*Fort Mischisticotia*
Fort McL	*Fort McLeod*
Fort Mich	*Fort Michigan*
Fort MLar	*Fort McLaurie*
Fort Nak	*Fort Nakesley*
Fort Nip	*Fort Nipigon*
Fort Park	*Fort Parkejox*
Fort Per	*Fort Perrot*
Fort Pask	*Fort Paskey*
Fort Phil	*Fort Phillip*
Fort Pt	*Fort Point*
Fort Pos	*Fort Poskoyax*
Fort Rup	*Fort Rupert*
Fort Sal	*Fort Saleesh*
Fort Senn	*Fort Senneville*
Fort Star	*Fort Starchaser*
Fort Stle	*Fort Steele*
Fort Stik	*Fort Stikini*
Fort Thom	*Fort Thompson*
Fort Ver	*Fort Vercheres*
Fort Yuk	*Fort Yukon*
Fowl	Fowlmere
FP	Ferry Pool
FPP	Ferry Pilots Pool
FPU	Ferry Preparation Unit
Fraser	Fraserburgh
FRL	Flight Refueling Ltd
FRS	Flight Refresher School
FRU	Fleet Requirements Unit
FS	Fully Supercharged
FTC	Flying Training Command
FTR	Failed to Return (missing)
Ftr Com	Fighter Command
FTS	Fighter Training School
FTU	Ferry Training School
FTU	Floatplane Training Unit (pre WW2)
FU	Ferry Unit
funct	function/al
Funton	Funington
fus	fuselage
GA	Ground Accident
GAL	General Aircraft Ltd
GAT	Gatwick
GCA	Ground control Approach
CGF	Gunnery Co-operation Flight
GDGS	Ground Defence Gunners School
Ger Don	*Gerrard Don*
Gib	Gibralter
Gib Guido	*Gibralter Guido*
GIS	Glider Instructors School
Glas D	Glasgow Docks
Glenb	Glenbank
gnrl	general
Gosp	Gosport
Gp	Group

GP	General Purpose
GP	George Pickering (only after FF)
GPEU	Glider Pilots Exercise Unit
GPWP	Group Wastage Pool
grd	ground
Gran	Grangemouth
Graves	Gravesend
Grp As	Group Assembly/ies
GRU	General Reconnaissance Unit
GSU	Group Service Unit
GS(U)	Grading School (Unit)
GTS	Glider Training School
GU	Grading Unit
H/A	High Altitude
HAD	Home Defence Depot
HAL	Heston Aircraft Ltd
hand	handling
Hap	Hapmat
Harma	*Harmatorio*
Harmat	*Harmatris*
Harp	*Harpolycus*
Harrow	Harrowbeer
Hasor	*Hasorate*
Hats	Hatston
Haw	Hawarden
Hawk	Hawkinge
HC	High Command
HCCS	Home Command Communications Squadron
HCGC	Home Guard Gliding Centre
HCU	Heavy Conversion Unit
HDU	Helicopter Development Unit
HEA	Supermarine-built (Eastleigh) at dispersal units
heat	heating
Hen	Henley
Hen Jasp	*Henery Jasper*
Hens	Henstridge
Hen Vill	*Henry Villard*
H E	High Ercall
H Farm	*Hope Farm*
HPU	Home Ferry Unit
HGCU	Heavy Glider Conversion Unit
Hibald	Highbaldstow
Hind	*Hindustan*
H Farm	Hope Farm
Horn	Hornchurch
Horor	*Hororata*
Hors	Horsham
HPA	High Post Aerodrome
H Prince	*Highland Prince*
Hr Pk	Hursley Park
HStF	Horsham St Faith
Hull	Hullavington
hvy	heavy
IA	Inland Area
IAF	Indian Air Force
IFF	Identification Friend of Foe
Inch	*Inchanga*
incor	incorporate/ion
Ind	India
Ing	*Ingleton*
inj	injured
Ins AF	Instructional Airframe
instal	installed/ion
Int All	International Alloys
intm	intrim
intns	intensive
int wt	Inertia weight
Inver	*Inverbank*
invest	investigation/s
IoM	Isle of Man
IoW	Isle of Wight
i/grd	Into ground
i/sea	into sea
Isip	*Isipango*
ItAF	Italian Air Force
ITF	Instrument Training flight
ITS	Initial Training School
ITP	Instructions to Proceed
Jap	Japan
jam	jammed
J D Yea	*J D Yeagar*
jett	jettisoned
J G Will	J D Williamson
J J McG	*John J McGraw*
Joy Kil	*Joyce Kilmer*
JWE	Joint Warfare Establishment
Kiam	*Kaimata*
Kal	*Kalrada*
Kar	Karachi
kdn	knocked down
Kee	Keevil
Ken	Kenley
KinL	Kirton in Lindsay
Kit Park	*Kitailana Park*
kld	killed
Knock	Knockholt
Ku Lu	Kuala Lumpur
Laken	Lakenheath
La Pam	*La Pampa*
Lanark	*Lanarkshire*
LAS	Light Aircraft School
ldg(ld)	landing (landed)
Lds City	*Leeds City*
Leer	*Leerdan*
Lecon	Leconsfield
Lea Park	*Leaside Park*
Leuch	Leuchars

lf	low flying
LFS	Lancaster Finishing School
Liber	*Liberian*
Lland	Llandow
Llanb	Llanbedr
LMet	Lawsons Metals
LMS	London Midland Scottish Railway
load	loadings
LoS	Lee on Solent
Lossie	Lossiemouth
LR	Long Range
LRDU	Long Range Development Unit
LUAS	London University Air Squadron
Lft	Luftwaffe
Lyca	*Lycaon*
Lyne	Lyneham
MAAF	Mediterrainean Allied Air Forces
Mach	Machrihanish
Mahad	*Mahadive*
Maids	Maidstone
Maih	*Maihar*
maint	maintenance
MAL	Miles Aircraft Ltd
Malan	*Malancha*
Malt	*Maltyan*
MalWW	Malcolms White Waltham
Man Esc	*Manchester Escort*
Man Prog	*Manchester Progress*
Mans	Manston
MAP	Ministry of Aircraft Production
Mar Cam	Marshall Cambridge
Mars	*Marsdale*
Mars	Marston
Marst	*Marstand*
Mart	*Martaban*
Masir	*Masirah*
max	maximum
ME	Middle East
MEAAF	Middle East Allied Air Forces
MEAF	Mediterranean Air Force
Mearb	*Mearbask*
Meers	*Meerskerk*
Melam	*melampus*
Mel Mob	*Melton Mobray*
Mer	Merlin
Mer Prin	*Merchant Prince*
Met	Meteorological
m/gs	machine guns
MHth	Martlesham Heath
mi	major inspection
minm	minimum
Miss Clu	*Miss Cluston*
miss	missing
Mit Park	*Mitorland Park*
mkrs	makers
Mlfld	Millfield
MMO	Morris Motors Oxford
mods	modification/s
Molot	Molotovsk
mon	monoxide
Mont Bay	*Montgomery Bay*
Mont City	*Montgomery City*
Mount Br	Montford Bridge
mr	major repair
MS	Moderately Supercharged
MU	Maintenance Unit
m/up	mock up
Murm	Murmansk
M Wal	Middle Wallop
NA	North Africa
NAAF	Northwest African Air Force
NAASC	North African Allied Strategic Command
NACAF	Northwest African Coastal Air Force
Nairn	*Nairnbank*
Nanb	*Namballa*
Nanking	*Nanking*
NASAF	Northwest African Strategic Air Force
NATAF	Northwest African Tactical Air Force
Narb	*Narbaba*
NEA	Non Effective Aircraft
neg	negative
NEI	Netherlands East Indies
NES	Non Effective Stock(Scrap)
Newm	Newmarket
Niger	*Nigerstown*
N'land	Northumberland
North	Northolt
nr	near
NTU	Navigation Training Unit
NWA	North West Africa
NWld	North Weald
N Z Star	*New Zealand Star*
OADU	Overseas Aircraft Delivery Unit
OAFU	(Observers) Advanced Flying Unit
Oak	Oakington
OAPU	Overseas Aircraft Preparation Unit
Obs/S	Observation/Squadron
obst	obstacle/struction
Ocean Ch	*Ocean Chata*
Ocean Cour	*Ocean Courage*
Ocean Gal	*Ocean Gallent*
Ocean Load	*Ocean Loader*
Ocean Rid	*Ocean Rider*
Ocean Vac	*Ocean Vacty*
Ocean Ver	*Ocean Verity*
Ocean Ves	*Ocean Vesty*
Ocean Vic	*Ocean Viceroy*

Appendix II

Ocean Vol	*Ocean Volunteer*
Ocean Wan	*Ocean Wanderer*
Ocean War	*Ocean Warden*
OCU	Operational Conversion Unit
OFU	Overseas Ferry Unit
ops (opnl)	operations/ional
Orford	Orfordness
Orient C	*Orient City*
ORTU	Operational & Refresher Training unit
o/s	overshot
o/t	overturned
o/ld	overload
OTU	Operational Training Unit
OUAS	Oxford University Air Squadron
PAFU	(Pilots) Advanced Flying Unit
PAL	Portsmouth Aviation Ltd
Pandor	*Pandorian*
Papan	*Papanuci*
Papar	*Paparnu*
Parib	*Paribonga*
Park Ben	*Park Benjamin*
Par Sea	*Paribonga Sea*
Parn Cast	*Parnell Castle*
PAS(U)	Pilotless Aircraft Section (Unit)
PC	Pressure Cabin
PDU	Photographic Development Unit
Pen Cast	*Penrith Castle*
Pent	*Pentarkete*
perf	performance
Pers	Pershore
Perr	Perranporth
Perth	*Perthshire*
Pet Mer	*Peter Mearsk*
PFF	Pathfinder Force
p/fin	paint finish
(P)FTS	(Polish) Flying Training School
PFU	Parachute Flying Unit
PGp	Pursuit Group
photo	photograph/y
P/O	Pilot Officer
Porow	*Porowydham*
Port Durn	*Port Durnadin*
Port	Portugal
Port Fair	*Port Fairey*
Port Dar	*Port Darwin*
Porth	Porthreath
Port MQ	*Port MacQuarra*
Port Syd	*Port Sydney*
Port Wynd	*Port Wyndham*
(P)OTU	(Polish) Operational Training Unit
PoW	Prisoner of War
PP	Phillips Powis
pract	practice
p/proto	production prototype
Prep Flt	Preparation Flight
prod	production
prog	programme
prop/s	propeller/s
proto	prototype
PRRP	Pilots Reserve & Reinforcement Pool (ME)
PRU	Photographic Reconnaissance Unit
psi	pounds per square inch
PSO/C	Presumed struck off/charge
P Sudan	Port Sudan
pt	paint
pyro	pyrotechnics
QB	Queen Bee
Q Park	*Queens Park*
Queen V	*Queen Victoria*
RAAA	Repaired aircraft awaiting action
RAAF	Royal Australian Air Force
RAAFC	Royal Air Force Flying College
rad	radiator
RAE	Royal Aircraft Establishment
Rad S	Radio School
RAFC	Royal Air Force College
RCAF	Royal Canadian Air Force
RCO	Repair cancelled offer
RDFS	Radio Direction Finding School
REAF	Royal Egyptian Air Force
recat	recatogorised
recond	reconditioned
recco	reconnaissance
refurb	refurbished
Ren	Renfrew
rep	repaired
Res pl	Reserve Pool
ret	returned
RFS	Reserve Flying School
RHAF	Royal Helenic Air Force
RIAF	Royal Indian Air Force
RIM	Rim Rimutaka
riw	repaired in works
RMU	Roving Maintenance Unit
RNDA	Royal Naval Deposit Account
RNeAF	Royal Netherlands Air Force
RNAS	Royal Naval Air Station
RNFS	Royal Navy Fighter Squadron (ME)
RNoAF	Royal Norwegian Air Force
RNZAF	Royal New Zealand Air Force
Roch	Rochford
Rook	Rookley
Ros	Repaired on site/station
RR	Rolls-Royce (H-Hucknall)
R&S	Reid & Sigrist
RSU	Repair & Servicing Unit
R/T	Radio Telephony
rtc	reduced to components
rtga	reduced to Group assemblies
rtp	reduced to produce
RU	Repair Unit
rud	rudder
run	running
RV	Rear View
SAAF	South African Air Force
SAC	School of Army Co-operation
Sai	Saigon
SAL	Scottish Aviation Ltd
Sam A A	*Sameon At Antan*
Saman	*Samannon*
Samarit	*Samaritan*
Samcon	*Samconstantan*
Samer	*Samervan*
Samsae	*Samsaeda*
Samstu	*Samsturdy*
Samtru	*Samtrusty*
Sansu	*Sansuva*
Sansy	*Sansylvan*
Sanny	*Sannythian*
Sap Park	*Sapperton Park*
scr	scrap
SD	Special Duties
SDF	Special Delivery Flight
s/dn	shot down
Sea	Seafire
SEAC	South East Asia Command
Sele	Selector
Ser Flt	Service Flight
Serv	Service
Semb	Sembawang
Ser Sq	Service Squadron
SF	Station Flight
SGT	Sergeant
SHAEF	Supreme Headquarters Allied Expeditionary Force
Shaz	*Shahzada*
Shell	*Shelligate*
Shoe	Shoeburyness
S&H	Short & Harland
Sic	Sicily
Sil Ash	*Silver Ash*
Sil Beech	*Silver Beech*
Sil Lar	*Silver Larch*
Sil Pl	*Silver Pool*
Sil Gu	*Silver Guava*
Sil San	*Silver Sandal*
Sil Will	*Silver Willow*
Skae	Skaebrae
Skeld	*Skeldergate*
Sing	Singapore
S/L	Sea Level
SlFm	Slade Farm
Slnd	Sealand
S/Lt	Sub Lieutenant
SM	South Marston
Snd Fish	*Sound Fisher*
SOC	Struck off charge
SoH	Sutton on Hull
SoTT	School of Technical Training
South	Southend
South	*Southgate*
spcl	special
spin	spin/ning
Spit	Spitfire
S/Ldr	Squadron Leader
SR	Short Range
sscr	sold scrap
stab	stability
Star Fm	Starveall Farm
Sta	St Athan
Stav	Starverton
St Cl	*St Clears*
std	stalled
Sten	*Stentor*
stiff	stiffened
St Mer	St Merryn
St Mw	St Mawgan
Stn	Southampton
stor	store/age
Strad	Stradishall
Stret	Stretton
SU	Support/Storage/Salvage Unit
Super	Supermarine
suit	suitability
Streaf	*Streafkerk*
Stredi	*Samtredi*
Stir Cast	*Stirling Castle*
strk	struck
struct	structure/al
Suff	*Suffolk*
Suss	*Sussex*
Swann	Swannington
Swed	Sweden
swg	Swung
syst	system/s
TAAC	Training Accident Category AC
TAF	Tactical Air Force
Tak	Takoradi
Tang	Tangmere
Tant	*Tantalus*
Taqh	*Taqhadan*
Taran	*Tarantia*
taxy	taxying
TC	Training Command (later Transport Command)
TCDF(U)	Transport Command Development Flight (Unit)
TCU	Transport Conversion Unit
TDU	Torpedo Development Unit
Teak	*Teakoelei*
Tee Park	*Teeside Park*
Tern	Ternhill
Teng	Tengah
TEU	Tactical Exercise Unit
TF	Training Flight
t/fln	test flown
Thom Holt	*Thomas Holt*
Thom Scott	*Thomas Scott*
tip	tipped
TI	Trial Installation
Thorn Is	Thorney Island
t/o	take off
TOC	Taken on Charge
trans	transferred
TRE	Telecommunications Research Establishment
trls	trials
Trng	Trainer/ing
Troil	*Troilus*
Trop(T)	Tropical/ised
TSTU	Transport Support Training Unit
TT	Target Tug (towing)
TTCCF	Technical Training Command Communications Flight
ttl	total
ttl wrk	total wreck
TTU	Torpedo Training Unit
Turk	Turkey
Turkers	*Turkestan*
Turn	Turnhouse
TURP	Training Unit & Reserve Pool (ME)
Tyne	*Tynebank*
UAS	University Air Squadron
u/c	undercarriage
UK	United Kingdom
ULAS	University of London Air Squadron
uninj	uninjured
univ	universal
u/s	undershot
USAAC	United States Army Air Corps
USAAF	United States Air Force
USSR	Soviet Union
VA	Vickers-Armstrong (HP High Post; SM South Marston; O Oxford; WW White Waltham; Hr Pk Hursley Park; WD Worthy Down
WA	Western Area (pre 1936)
WAFR	W Africa
WAL	Westland Aircraft Ltd
Wand	*Wanderer*
Warm	Warmwell
Waro	*Waroonga*
WDCF	Western Desert Communications Flight
WDn	Worthy Down
WDU	Wireless Development Unit
Westh	Westhampnett
WestM	West Malling
West Ray	West Rayham
Well Crt	*Wellington Court*
wire	wireless
Witt	Wittering
Wng	Wing
W/Cdr	Wing Commander
w/o	Write off
Wools	Woolsington
WRGra	*W R Grace*
wrk	wreck
wt	weight
w/u	wheels up
Yeov	Yeovil/ton

AIR MINISTRY SPECIFICATIONS

AIR MINISTRY DIRECTORATE OF TECHNICAL DEVELOPMENT

Specification No. F 7/30
Single Seater Day and Night Fighter*

1 General requirements

(a) The aircraft is to fulfill the duties of "Single Seater Fighter" for day and night flying. A satisfactory fighting view is essential and designers should consider the advantages offered in this respect by the low wing monoplane or pusher.

The main requirements for the aircraft are -

(i) Highest possible rate of climb
(ii) Highest possible speed at 15,000 feet
(iii) Fighting view
(iv) Capability of easy and rapid production in quantity
(v) Ease of maintenance

(b) The aircraft must have a good degree of positive stability about all axes in flight and trimming gear must be fitted so that the tailplane incidence can be adjusted in flight to ensure that the aircraft will fly horizontally at all speeds within the flying range, without requiring attention from the pilot.

(c) When carrying the total load specified in paragraph 3, the aircraft must be fully controllable at all flying speeds, especially near the stall and during a steep dive, when there must be no tendency for the aircraft to hunt.

(d) The aircraft must have a high degree of manoeuvrability. It must answer all controls quickly and must not be tiring to fly. The control must be adequate to stop an incipient spin when the aircraft is stalled.

An approved type of slot control, or other means which will ensure adequate lateral control and stability, at and below stalling speed, is to be embodied.

The design of aileron control is to be such that operation of the ailerons in flight will produce the minimum of adverse yawing effect on the aircraft.

(e) The aircraft is to be designed to accommodate the equipment listed in paragraph 6 and scheduled in detail in the appendix 'A' to this Specification.

(f) The crew, armament and equipment are to be arranged as specified in paragraph 7 of this Specification.

(g) The arrangements for alighting and taking off must be as specified in paragraph 8 of this specification.

(h) The aircraft and all parts thereof are to be designed and constructed in conformity with the requirements of the Director of Technical Development, *Air Ministry.
(*to be known as DTD hereonin).

A 'Type Record' for the aircraft, including all drawings and a complete set of strength calculations and weight estimates must be submitted to the DTD or his authorised representative for acceptance. The constructor, pending acceptance, may proceed with construction if he so desires, but the DTD reserves the right to reject any part or parts so made if subsequently found to be under strength or otherwise unsuitable for H. M. Service.

Two copies of fully-dimensioned General Arrangement drawing to the aircraft as actually built, together with a General Arrangement drawing showing layout of the complete equipment, are to be supplied to the DTD (R D A3) immediately on the completion of the first aircraft. Similarly in the case of any subsequent aircraft if differing from the first.

(i) The aircraft is to be constructed throughout in metal and is to be so constructed and protected to adequately withstand sudden changes in temperature and humidity such as are experienced in semi-tropical climates. Streamline wires, tie-rods and other parts not of stainless steel are to be coated with cadmium or zinc by an approved process. Aluminium and aluminium alloy parts are to be anodically treated.

(j) As soon as possible after the mock-up conference the contractor is to supply to the DTD (R D 4) a General Arrangement Drawing of the engine installation (including fuel, oil and water systems, tankage and engine controls). (See also paragraph 10)

(k) On the completion of the first aircraft off the contract the contractor shall supply to the DTD details of the equipment and its accessories and the detail weights, length and quantities thereof as will enable the Appendix 'A' Schedule of Equipment to be completed.

This information is to be applied by amending a copy of the current Appendix 'A' to agree with the approved aircraft, in conformity with the current master schedule.

Similarly, on the delivery of the last aircraft off the contract, if alterations have been made to the equipment, a suitably amended copy of the current Appendix 'A' is to be supplied to the DTD.

**Much of the wording on any specification of this era is generalised and applicable to a wide variety of types, hence references to 'the crew'.*

(l) All materials used must where possible, be to B.E.S.A. or other standard Specifications as approved by the DTD.

All materials quoted under approved Specifications are to be to the latest issue of the Specification. A list of approved Specifications showing the latest issue may be obtained in writing to the DTD.

Similarly, all A.G.S. parts incorporated in the aircraft are to be to the latest approved issue of the appropriate drawings but the issue number should not be quoted on the aircraft drawing. Where the contractor proposes to use materials for which standard approved Specifications are not available the contractor is required to certify the DTD, in writing, of his intention, and to supply such information and test pieces of the materials proposed as the DTD may decree necessary, to enable adequate tests of the materials to be carried out.

(m) Two copies of rigging and maintenance notes are to be supplied to the DTD (R.T.P.) not later than the date on which the aircraft is delivered to the experimental establishment.

In order to facilitate further reproduction of any diagram contained in the notes, tracings thereof are to be supplied also.

The notes should anticipate any difficulty likely to be encountered by a Service Unit during the development of a new type and are to include –

(i) leading particulars, principal dimensions, and the capacities of fuel and oil tanks in tabular form
(ii) complete and detailed instructions for rigging the aircraft
(iii) any unusual features (including non-standard equipment) from the point of view of maintenance
(iv) lubrication instructions
(v) description of the engine mounting and installation insofar as they are peculiar to the particular aircraft
(vi) three-view general arrangement drawings (showing the horizontal datum line on the side view) and diagrams of the petrol and oil systems
(vii) the approved equipment layout drawings as called for in paragraph 10 (d).

It is to be observed that these notes are required only for a preliminary guide for those who will be responsible for maintaining the aircraft in its early stages and it will suffice if they are written on the lines of a Works instruction.

In the event of the aircraft being adopted for use in the Royal Air Force the contractor will be required to prepare notes and drawings covering the repair of the aircraft by Service Units.

2 Power Unit

(a) Any approved British engine may be used. It is to be noted that, when an engine is in process of development, provision is to be made in the aircraft design for a possible increase in engine weight.

(b) The installation of the engine is to be so arranged that the engine is capable of being rapidly and easily removed from the aircraft.

Supports and footholds are to be provided to facilitate minor repairs and adjustments to the engine installation.

(c) The whole of the cowling is to be designed to facilitate rapid and easy removal and replacement and is to be sufficiently robust to withstand frequent removal and constant handling; wire skewers are not to be used.

(d) The cowling is to be finished in an approved manner so as to give adequate protection against corrosion and to prevent the reflection of light which might betray the presence of the aircraft or dazzle the crew.

(e) Before drawings relating to the engine installation can be accepted the engine, fuel, oil and water systems, and the accessories and piping therefore, must be fitted in the first experimental aircraft and put in proper running order, so that the installation as a whole may be examined and, if satisfactory, approved by the DTD, or his authorised representative.

(f) The airscrew is preferably to be of metal construction, and is to be designed in accordance with the required performance of the aircraft as specified in paragraph 4 of this Specification, but no airscrew will be accepted which allows the maximum permissible r.p.m. to be exceeded in full throttle horizontal flight at the supercharged altitude of the engine, or the normal r.p.m. to be exceeded in full throttle climbing flight at the best rate of climb above this altitude.

A standard engine instruction plate is to be fitted in a portion where it will be clearly visible to the pilot.

2(A) Tankage including gravity tanks to be provided for the endurance specified in paragraph 3.

(a) Adequate air space is to be provide in the oil tank: at least 1 gallon for air-cooled engines and 2 gallons for water-cooled engines

(b) A gravity fuel tank is to be provided sufficient for at least 20 minutes at full throttle at ground level.

(c) The fuel tanks are to be adequately protected from deterioration in a manner approved by the DTD and may be either –

(i) Carried inside the fuselage, or

(ii) Carried inside the main planes. In this case the construction of the portions of the main planes containing the fuel tanks and the installation of the fuel tanks or fuel vapour from a damaged tank spreading to any inflammable portions of the aircraft structure, or

(iii) Carried externally in such a position that if damaged the escaping fuel will be blown clear of all parts of the aircraft structure if in flight.

(d) All tanks are to be provided with readily removable sumps or with approved means for removing all dirt and foreign matter from the interior of the tank.

(e) The delivery from the tank to the piping system is to be so arranged as to prevent as far as is practicable the passage of foreign matter from the tank into the piping system.

Means are to be provided, under the control of a member of the crew, for stopping and restarting the flow from any of the fuel tanks at each outlet from which the fuel would otherwise escape if the pipe line or balance pipe connected therewith were to break.

(f) Arrangements are to be made for the rapid and easy draining of the tanks, and rapid and easy filling with standard filler nozzles.

(g) All tanks are to be designed to be readily removeable from and replaceable in position in the aircraft, with a minimum of disturbance to the aircraft structure and to other installations.

2 (B) **Fuel and Oil Systems**

(a) The fuel and oil systems shall be in general accordance with the requirements of Specification No. 18 (Misc).

(b) All pipe joints are to be of a proved metallic type, and together with all cocks, plugs, etc are to be locked in accordance with A.G.S. Mod 187

(c) The bore of the main fuel pipes must be such that the flow of fuel sufficient to maintain full power on the ground is exceeded by 100% when the carburettor unions are uncoupled and the supply is in the condition of minimum head with the aircraft set at the appropriate angle so defined hereunder in clause (d) (i).

The last section of the delivery pipe to the carburettors is to be of the approved flexible type.

(d) The fuel feed may be either –

(i) by approved pumps from the main tanks direct to the carburettors with a by-pass to a gravity tank, so situated that, when the aircraft is flying, at its maximum climbing angle, or when the aircraft is tail down on the ground, whichever condition gives the greatest inclination of the aircraft axis to the horizontal, the minimum effective head above the jet level of the highest carburettor when the gravity is practically empty is not less than the minimum specified for the type of carburettor used.

In calculating the minimum effective head due allowances must be made for any effect due to acceleration when the aircraft is in motion.

The delivery from the pumps to the carburettor must be via approved release or reducing valve to a distribution cock or cocks so arranged that the following selections can be made.

(1) Pumps to carburettors and gravity tanks.
(2) Pumps to carburettor direct.
(3) Gravity tanks to carburettors.
(4) Off.

Wind driven pumps are not to be used.

An overflow pipe of sufficient bore to deal with all excess fuel must be provided from the gravity tank to the main tank or to some other approved point in the fuel system.

A prismatic float indicator visible to the pilot is to be fitted in the overflow pipes, or

(ii) By gravity tanks alone feeding direct to the carburettor. Such gravity tanks must conform to the requirements laid down in (i) above

(e) A diagram of the fuel system is to be affixed in an approved position in the aircraft.

(f) An approved type of petrol filter is to be fitted so that the whole of the fuel passes through it before reaching the carburettor. The filter must be disposed so that it will be accessible for cleaning.

2 (C) **Cooling System**

(a) Provision is to be made for adequate oil cooling and a thermometer registering in a position visible to the pilot is to be fitted in such a position as to indicate the temperature of the oil supplied to the engine.

In addition, on the first aircraft, an oil thermometer registering in a position visible to the pilot is to be fitted in the return pipe from the engine between the scavenger pump and the oil cooler.

(b) If a water or evaporating engine is used, the cooling system, which is to be installed in accordance with the requirements of DTD, is to be designed to fulfil English summer requirements, with provision for changing to a system fulfilling Tropical summer requirements, with a minimum of alteration. If water radiators are used they are to be fitted with shutters or other approved means of temperature control.

(c) In addition to the thermometer fittings and the thermometers normally required on radiators for production aircraft, the experimental aircraft is to be provided with approved thermometer fittings in the outlet header tanks of each radiator or auxiliary radiator.

2 (D) **Engine Starting and Silencing**

(a) The exhaust manifold of approved type supplied with the engine is to be fitted in such a manner as to provide adequately for silencing, and for flame-damping during night flying.

(b) Provision is to be made on the aircraft by the installation of the requisite approved fittings for the installation of an RAF Mark II Starter and for the rapid and easy attachment of a compressor type engine starter carried on a separate trolley.

(c) Provision is to be made for rapidly warming the engine oil. It must be possible to take off within 2½ minutes from a cold start.

3 **Load to be Carried**

In addition to any stowages and mountings necessitated by the requirements of paragraphs 6 and 7 and by alternative loads, the following load is to be carried during the acceptance trials –

	Removable lb.	Fixed lb.	Total lb.
Crew (1)	180	—	180
Oxygen	15	8	23
R/T Apparatus	46	6	52
Instruments	1	25	26
Electrical equipment	41	17	58
Parachute and belt	20	3	23
Armament			
4 guns and C.C. gear*	120	20	140
Gun sights	—	5	5
2000 rounds S.A.A.	145	—	145
Signal pistol & cartridges	7	1	8
Military load	575	85	660

*This item will be adjusted to the actual gun installation adopted.

Fuel Oil For ½ hour at full throttle at ground level plus 2 hours at full throttle at 15,000 ft
Water If oil – ditto plus 50% excess required
Water – ditto

4 **Contract Performance**

The performance of the aircraft, as ascertained during the official type trials when carrying the total load specified in paragraph 3 and with airscrew satisfying the requirements of paragraph 2(e) shall be –

Horizontal speed at 15,000 ft not less than 195 mph.
Alighting speed not to exceed 60 mph.
Service ceiling not less than 28,000 ft.
Time to 15,000 ft not more than 8½ mins.

The specified alighting speed must not be exceeded, but may be obtained by variable camber or equivalent devices provided that control and manoeuvrability are not adversely affected.

5 **Structural Strength**

(a) The strength of the main structure when carrying the load specified in paragraph 3, plus 100 lb shall not be less than as specified hereunder –

Load factor throughout the structure with the centre of pressure in its most forward position 9.0.

Load factor for wing structure with the centre of pressure in its most backward position in horizontal flight 6.0

Load factor in terminal nose dive 1.75

Inverted Flight

(1) Load factor at incidence corresponding to the inverted stall and with C.P. at 1/3 of chord 4.5

(2) Load factor at incidence appropriate to steady horizontal inverted flight and at the maximum speed of horizontal normal flight 4.5

(b) The alighting gear must be able to withstand an impact at a vertical velocity of 10 feet per second and at this velocity the load on the alighting gear must not exceed three times the fully loaded weight of the aircraft.

(c) When subject to the impact forces on alighting, as specified above, the load factor for the alighting gear must not be less than 1-1/3, and for the remainder of the structure not less than 1-1/2. The load factor for the structure and the attachment fittings of the alighting gear must always be greater than that for the alighting gear itself by the margin indicated above.

(d) The maximum weight per wheel of the aircraft in pounds must not exceed 12 times the product of the wheel and tyre diameters in inches with the aircraft carrying the full load specified above.

(e) The above factors are to be determined by the approved official methods as published by the DTD and the detail requirements given in A.P.970 are also to be satisfied. With a view to minimising the risk of flutter, attention should be given to the recommendations of A.P.1177, particularly as regards the static balance of ailerons.

(f) The wing is to be sufficiently rigid to withstand satisfactorily any torsional or other loads which may be encountered during service operations.

(g) Ribs (both mainplane and tail unit) are required to develop, on test, factors 20% greater than those specified for the aircraft as a whole.

6 Equipment

The equipment as listed hereunder and as scheduled in detail in the Appendix 'A' to this Specification is to be provided for and the contractor will be required to supply and fit all parts necessary for its installation; in the case of R/T panels, etc. the position of all instruments and the identities of plugs and leads must be indicated by fixed labels.

It is to be noted that the weights of various items of fixed equipment listed hereunder and scheduled in detail in the Appendix 'A' but not quoted in paragraph 3, are to be allowed for in design.

Diagrams of the wiring and piping for all equipment installations are to be provided, for carrying in a canvas bag fitted in an approved position on the aircraft.

All equipment is to be installed in accordance with the requirements of the DTD.

(a) **Armament**

Reflector sight (To be installed in accordance with
Ring and bead sight Specification No.G.E.126).
Signal Pistol and 8 cartridges
4 × 20lb bombs
2 × .303in Vickers guns installed in the cockpit under the control of the pilot with C.C gear as necessary.
and either:–
(i) 2 × .303in Vickers guns installed in the cockpit or wing. If in the cockpit and synchronised an additional C.C gear reservoir is to be fitted for them. If in the wings adequate locating arrangements are essential.
or:–
(ii) 2 × .303in Lewis guns installed so that synchronisation is unnecessary. These guns do not require heating. 2,000 rounds of ammunition for the above guns with links or drums as necessary. The minimum supply to be forwarded for any gun is 400 rounds. 400 round drums will be available for Lewis guns.

(b) **Electrical equipment**

Services are to be provided for (To be installed in accordance with Specification G.E. 164).
Navigation and Identification lights
Gun heaters (as necessary for outboard guns)
Wing tip flares (on concealed brackets)
Instrument lighting

(c) **Instruments and General Equipment**

The following instruments of luminous pattern, where available, are to be fitted in the cockpit in accordance with the requirements of the DTD –

1 Air speed indicator
1 Altimeter
1 Revolution indicator
1 Oil pressure guage
Fuel contents guage (1 per main tank)
1 Oil thermometer (An extra oil thermometer is required on the first aircraft)
1 Radiator thermometer (if required). An extra water thermometer is required on the first aircraft)
Boost guage (if required)
1 Watch and holder
1 Pilot's fighting harness (Sutton type)
Oxygen apparatus
1 Map case
1 Turn indicator

(d) **Wireless equipment**

Earth system, bonding and screening in accordance with Specification G.E.125.
R/T apparatus (Two-way)
R/T Box
Fixed aerial

(e) **Parachute equipment**

1 Irving type parachute

7 Disposition of crew, armament and equipment

(a) The pilot's view is to conform as closely as possible to that obtainable in 'pusher' aircraft. The following requirements indicate the ideal view which is considered to be necessary, and the aircraft should be designed to conform as closely to them as is possible in practice.

(b) The pilot must have a clear view forward and upward for formation work and manoeuvring, and particular care is needed to prevent his view of hostile aircraft being blanked out by top planes and centre sections when manoeuvring to attack. Planes should be so disposed as not to obstruct the pilot's view of other aircraft, when his own is pointing within 60° of their direction.

The direction in which obstruction by planes is least serious is in the backward and downward directions.

(c) For landing a good view forward and downward is necessary and the pilot must be able to see within 17° from the vertical over the side when wearing the Sutton harness.

The point on the ground on which the pilot desires to land should not be obstructed by planes during the gliding approach. This applies especially to normal landing manoeuvres such as banked turns and side slips.

The windscreen should be sufficiently high to enable the pilot to have a clear view forward through the screen. When taxying with the tail down the pilot, with the minimum movement of his head, should be able to see directly in front of his aircraft, while with the tail up for taking off he should be able to see the ground 50 feet ahead over the centre line of the aircraft, with his seat in the normal flying position. The top fuselage coaming, on either side of the windscreen, should be as narrow and tapered as possible consistent with adequate protection from the slipstream.

(d) For gun aiming purposes the pilot should have an unobstructed view forward over as wide a cone as possible, the sight being the axis of that cone and his eye the apex.

(e) The pilot is to be provided with 4 guns, and stowage for 2,000 rounds of ammunition as detailed in paragraph 6(a).

Provision is to be made for fitting of a G.3 camera gun complete with firing and cocking controls. The mounting and controls must be quickly removable and must not interfere with the guns and sights in any way. The provision is secondary and must not influence the design of the aircraft in any way.

(f) The pilot is to be provided with a map case, and stowage for knee-type writing pad mounted in a convenient position.

(g) The relative position of the pilot's seat and rudder bar are to be designed to be adjustable both vertically and horizontally to suit pilots of different trunk length and leg reach.

(h) The design of the cockpit must be such as to provide the comfort necessary for the pilot to fulfil his various duties efficiently, and must allow complete freedom of movement, particularly in an emergency that obliges the pilot to take to his parachute.

The cockpit is to be adequately screened from the wind but the windscreen must not interfere with the satisfactory use of sights, one of which should be on the centre line of the aircraft, the sights being interchangeable in position.

The cockpit is to be painted internally with an approved grey-green paint. This instruction does not apply to the instrument board.

The cockpit padding and other upholstery is to be rendered fireproof to the satisfaction of the DTD.

(i) Standard clips are to be provided under the wings for the carrying of one standard bomb rack for 4 × 20lb bombs.

Room is to be provided to enable the bomb release gear for the bombs to be fitted inside on the port side of the cockpit.

The arrangement of the bomb carrier installation must be such that sufficient clearance is provided to enable the bombs to be released even when the aircraft is in a very steep dive.

(j) Arrangements are to be made to provide adequate cockpit heating without resort to electrical appliances.

(k) The dynamo for the electrical equipment is to be stowed internally and driven from the engine. The aircraft designer must agree the details of the drive with the engine designer.

8 **Arrangements for alighting and taking off**

(a) The aircraft is to be designed to pull up quickly on alighting and wheel brakes of an approved type are to be fitted.

The brake controls shall be such that the brakes can be applied together or independently. It is essential that the pilot shall not be obliged to abandon the aircraft or engine controls when applying the brake. Means are to be provided for locking the brakes in the 'on' position so that wheel chocks may be dispensed with if so desired. The whole of the braking system is to be capable of rapid and easy removal when not required.

(b) The aircraft is to be suitable for operation from small, rough-surfaced and enclosed aerodromes.

(c) The alighting gear is to be of oleo or equivalent type in which the use of rubber in tension is eliminated.

(d) The wheel track of the alighting gear must be such as to provide stable taxying conditions in any direction in a wind of 20mph without any tendency for the aircraft to capsize.

(e) The wheels of the alighting gear are to be provided with approved means for lubricating the wheel bearings, which are to be designed so that no wear takes place on the axle.

(f) The design and disposition of the alighting gear are to be such as to allow of the aircraft being readily and securely supported without the use of elaborate jacking, trestling or slinging during and subsequent to the removal of the alighting gear or the wheels of the alighting gear. If necessary, special arrangements are to be made in the design of the aircraft structure to permit of such support being readily given and the points of support so specially provided must be clearly marked on the aircraft.

9 **Miscellaneous**

(a) The aircraft is to be constructed in quickly detachable units for ease of transport and storage.

(b) Means are to be provided for locking the slats in the closed position and maintaining the controls in a central position when the aircraft is left unattended on the ground. The means so provided must preclude the possibility of the pilot attempting to take-off with the slats and/or the controls locked.

(c) Suitable holding-down rings are to be provided under the bottom planes.

(d) The aircraft is to be provided with all necessary hand-grips and other facilities for ease of handling on the ground.

(e) Provision is to be made in the design for the protection of all moving parts against the destructive effects of sand and, as far as may be possible, for their lubrication by grease gun from a central point.

(f) Detachable covers of approved type are to be supplied for the engine and cockpit as a protection against deterioration when the aircraft is pegged down in the open.

(g) The attachment points for the pilot's fighting harness together with those parts of the aircraft to which the belt loads are transmitted are to be capable of withstanding the failing load for the belt or harness.

(h) The design of the structure in the vicinity of the cockpit is to be such as to afford the pilot as much protection as possible in the event of a heavy landing, a crash or overturning.

Such structure should be appreciably stronger than the adjacent parts so that these latter may absorb some of the shock by deformation before the former yields.

(i) The design of the aircraft is to be such that standard Service equipment can be used for ground operations such as fuelling, rigging, manhandling, etc. Particulars of service ground equipment can be obtained on application in writing to the DTD (R.D.A.5).

(j) The design and layout of the aircraft is to be such as to offer every facility for rapid and easy inspection and maintenance in service and, in general, is to permit of maintenance operations being performed with standard service equipment. Special equipment (including tools) shall be provided with the aircraft if an essential supply, but the introduction of non-standard articles is to be avoided whenever possible.

(k) Parts that require to be frequently replaced or inspected are to easily accessible, and fully visible to a mechanic working on them.

(l) Control cables are to be arranged so that deterioration due to wear is a minimum. Means are to provided to facilitate the fitting of new cable and its rapid threading through fairleads. The splicing of cable in place is prohibited.

(m) Positive-locking devices shall be provided for all joints and fastenings; such devices are to be rapidly and easily adjustable.

(n) Adequate facilities are to be provided for inspecting the fuselage interior and working parts, particularly those of the tail skid and tail plane adjusting gear.

(o) Arrangements are to be made for defining the position of the centre of gravity in accordance with Aircraft Design Memorandum No 205.

10 **Provision of Mock-up**

(a) In order that the proposed disposition of the crew, armament etc, may be properly examined and approved by the DTD before construction is commenced the contractor is required to provide a suitable 'mock-up' of the aircraft at his works. The 'mock-up' so provided must include all parts and components which are likely to interfere with the all-round view from the cockpit and must shew the internal arrangements of the cockpit and such details of the engine installation as the arrangements for engine-starting and the positions of cocks, pumps, etc.

(b) The 'mock-up' must be erected full size and must be constructed true to scale and all instruments and equipment must be represented full size.

(c) The 'mock-up' must be capable off being inclined at angles corresponding to the cruising and alighting attitudes of the aircraft and to this end must be constructed to the correct height from the ground.

(d) Within 10 days of the mock-up conference the contractor is to submit to the DTD (R.D.A.4) two copies of provisional drawings of the layout as decided at the mock-up.

Four copies of the layout drawing as finally approved are to supplied to the DTD (R.D.A.4).

These equipment layout drawings are to be to a $\frac{1}{8}$th scale and are to consist of skeleton views of the fuselage and other pertinent structure shewing views of all equipment –

(1) positioned on the starboard side of the aircraft, viewed from the inside;

(2) positioned on the port side, viewed from the inside;

(3) positioned in plan, together with

(4) full views of instrument boards, W/T panels, etc. and

(5) a schedule of equipment indexed to correspond to "Balloon" pointers (a spare column is to be provided for notes or alterations).

Each of the drawings is to show also seats, tanks, controls, etc. appropriate to each view.

In accordance with the procedure laid down in Aircraft Design Memorandum No.135 the contractor is to supply a bare W/T panel as and when required.

11 **Test Specimens**

(a) The Contractor will be required to supply and ordinarily test (see clause (d)) such specimens of parts of the aircraft as the DTD may consider should be tested in order to ensure that the design and construction of the aircraft will be satisfactory.

(b) Tenders for the supply of aircraft in accordance with this specification are to include a Schedule of the specimens and tests considered sufficient to meet the requirements of clause (a) and are to cover the cost of supplying and testing the specimens. Any schedule that is considered by the DTD to be inadequate will be returned to the firm concerned for amendment.

(c) the specimens and tests that will generally be essential are indicated hereunder –

Complete ribs. The specimens are to be tested under the conditions of normal flight and, when appropriate, inverted flight. Metal ribs will be required to undergo, in addition, a vibration test.

Metal spars. The specimens will be submitted to the standard test, if applicable, and otherwise to such test as the DTD may require.

(d) Except as provided for hereafter, the testing shall be done by the Contractor, or he shall arrange for it to be done at some approved Testing Establishment; in either case, due notice of the time and place of the tests shall be given to the DTD so that he may arrange for a representative to witness them; the conditions governing the tests are to be in accordance with the requirements of the DTD and the tests are to be performed to his satisfaction; reports on the tests are to be supplied to the DTD in duplicate. If neither of the aforementioned arrangements is possible, the tests will be done at the Royal Aircraft Establishment, at the Contractor's expense.

(e) The DTD reserves the right to call for specimens and tests additional to those referred to in the Contractor's Schedule, should he at any time after the placing of the contract consider them to be necessary.

(f) No specimen of any part of the aircraft shall be

submitted for testing without it being previously certified by the Inspector-In-Charge at the Contractor's works, that the specimen is typical, as regards materials, dimensions, limits and workmanship of the actual part.

(g) A thin coat of oil or vaseline may be applied to metal specimens to prevent corrosion. Varnish, enamel or similar substances must not be used for this purpose.

12 **Provision of Drawings for a Model**

If at any time the DTD shall so desire, the contractor shall supply the drawings and data necessary for the construction of a true-to-scale model of the complete aircraft suitable for aerodynamic trials in a wind tunnel; such drawings, if required, would form the subject of an amendment to contract.

13 **Publication of Test Results**

The DTD reserves the right to publish data contained in reports of any wind tunnel or other tests relating to the design of the aircraft which may be undertaken on his behalf.

14 **Pre acceptance Test Flights**

(a) Prior to the delivery of the aircraft to the Departmental Establishment at which Type Trials are to take place it shall have been certified to the DTD –

(i) That the aircraft has been subjected by the contractor's pilot to the flight tests referred to in the 'Statement of Special Contract Conditions' accompanying the contract and

(ii) that these tests have shewn that the aircraft is safe to be flown by pilots of the Royal Air Force.

(b) The tests referred to in (a) shall include –

(i) A demonstration that the aircraft may be spun, both to the right and to the left, without undue risk when loaded in accordance with paragraph (3) of the Specification, and with the Centre of Gravity at the aft authorised limit.

For this purpose it is required that the aircraft, after being put into a spin, shall be allowed to complete not less than eight turns before the pilot sets his controls for recovery. The aircraft will be deemed satisfactory as regards its behaviour in a spin if the height loss in recovery does not exceed 1,500 feet. This height loss is to be reckoned from when the pilot sets his controls for recovery until the aircraft 'flattens out' from the landing dive.

(ii) A dive to the terminal velocity.

(iii) A demonstration of satisfactory behaviour during normal aerobatics such as the loop, roll, stalled turns, etc.

Approved by (signed) H. P. Cave
Air Commodore
Director of Technical Development.
Date 1.10.31.

Specification No. F.5/34.
Single Seat Fighter.
Date 16 November 1934.

1 **General**

(a) The speed excess of a modern fighter over that of a contemporary bomber has so reduced the chance of repeated attacks by the same fighter(s) that it becomes essential to obtain decisive results in the short space of time offered for one attack only. This specification is issued, therefore, to govern the production of a day fighter in which speed in overtaking an enemy at 15,000 feet, combined with rapid climb to this height, is of primary importance. The best speed possible must be aimed at for all heights between 5,000 and 15,000 feet. In conjunction with this performance the maximum hitting power must be aimed at, and eight machine guns are considered advisable.

(b) The component parts of this aircraft are to be suitable as regards size, etc, for conveyance by ordinary rail transport or Royal Air Force M.T. vehicles.

(c) The working drawings of component parts of the aircraft are to accord as fully as possible with the requirements stated in Specification No.16 (Miscellaneous) so that if (in the event of the aircraft being adopted for use in the Royal Air Force) parts are required to be manufactured in series, each member of the series will be strictly interchangeable with the original part.

(d) Subject only to the proviso at the end of this clause, the aircraft is to be designed, constructed and equipped in strict accordance with the requirements detailed herein and to the satisfaction of the DTD; is to comply with the requirements notified in all relevant Aircraft Design Memoranda (whether cited herein or not) and is to fulfill the requirements of the Director of Aeronautical Inspection as regards materials and workmanship. The DTD will, if he thinks fit, modify or waive any requirement which the tenderer considers there may be real difficulty in meeting or which might entail serious delay in the production of the aircraft; any representations in these respects should accompany the tender.

(e) It shall be understood as regards any specification, Air Publication, Standard instruction Sheet or Aircraft Design Memorandum cited or referred to herein that the reference is to the current issue thereof.

2 **Pilot's Station**

(a) An enclosed cockpit is admissible, it is to be draught-proof and provided with satisfactory ventilating arrangements.

(b) The arrangement of the cockpit shall provide the comfort and freedom of movement necessary to enable the pilot to perform his duties efficiently. Provision is to be made for warming it with waste heat tapped from the engine exhaust or cooling system.

(c) The pilot's seat and the rudder bar are to be adjustable in flight through a 4-inch range, the former vertically and the latter in the fore-and-aft direction.

(d) the view for searching, fighting and formation flying (whether the aircraft is a leader or otherwise) shall be the best possible. The least important hemisphere is that directly below the pilot. In particular, it is requisite that the pilot, with his harness fastened and the seat at its usual angle, shall have a clear view directly ahead through an angle of 10° down from the horizontal.

(e) the construction of the cockpit and the arrangement of the equipment therein shall permit free movement in an emergency that obliges the pilot to take to his parachute. An emergency exit shall be provided, together with foot and/or hand-holds or equivalent aids to easy and rapid egress from the aircraft in the circumstances referred to above or in the event of it crashing or overturning on the ground.

3 **Armament**

(a) The aircraft is to be equipped with 8 Browning machine guns, adjustable both laterally and vertically for ranging on a target 200 yards away. Electrical or other non-mechanical arrangements for firing are to be incorporated.

(b) The gun installation arrangements should be such that, whilst the drag attributable to them will be minimum, each gun may be removed, replaced, or re-loaded with ammunition easily and expeditiously. The guns should be all be positioned in the wings and outside the airscrew disc.

(c) Stowage for 300 rounds of small arm ammunition per gun is to be provided.

(d) A reflector sight is to be fitted.

(e) Provision is to be made for disposing of the 300 empty cartridges and links in such a way as to ensure that there is no danger of their jamming any mechanism or striking any part of the aircraft.

(f) Provision is to be made so that a camera gun, Type G.22, may be fitted to the aircraft in accordance with Aircraft Design Memorandum No 195.

Specification No. F.37/34.
Experimental High Speed Single Seat Fighter.
(Supermarine Aviation Works).

1 **General**

This specification is intended to cover the design and construction of an experimental high speed single seat fighter substantially as described in Supermarine Specification No.425A and Drawing No.30000 Sheet 13, except that an improvement in the pilot's view is desirable. The aircraft shall conform to all the requirements stated in Specification F7/30 and all corrigenda thereto except as stated hereunder.

2 Power Unit

(a) The engine to be installed is to be a Rolls-Royce PV XIII*.

(b) The airscrew shall be of wooden construction and the provisions of paragraph 2(e) of Specification F 7/30 as regards provision for the effect of a metal airscrew on weight and C.G. movement can be ignored.

(c) The fuel system shall be in accordance with DTD Specification 1004. A duplicate engine driven pump system may be used.

(d) The cooling system is to be of the evaporative cooling type using wing condensers in association with an auxiliary radiator.

(e) Hand starting gear only is to be provided for engine starting.

3 Load to be Carried

The Service load shall be as defined in Specification F7/30, except for departures which may subsequently be agreed between the contractor and the DTD. The fuel load carried is to be 94 gallons with oil appropriate to the endurance by this fuel.

4 Equipment and Miscellaneous

(a) Non-standard navigation lights of a type approved by the DTD may be fitted, and will be supplied by the Contractor.

(b) The requirement of paragraph 8(a) of Specification F 7/30 that the braking system is to be capable of rapid and easy removal is to be deleted.

(c) The reference to handholes or other aids to handling at the wing tips of paragraph 9(d) of Specification F 7/30 is to be altered to read 'Internal provision is to be made for taking holding down guys at the wing tips. Hand holes or grips will not be necessary'.

(d) The requirement of paragraph 6 as regards gun installation is modified. All 4 guns may be installed outside the airscrew disc.

(e) A tail wheel is to be fitted if practicable.

5 Structural Strength

(a) Paragraph 5(b) of Specification F 7/30 is to be altered to read 'The alighting gear must be able to withstand an impact at a vertical velocity of 10 feet per second, and at this velocity the load on the alighting gear must not exceed 4½ times the fully loaded weight of the aircraft'.

(b) Wheels not conforming to paragraph 5(d) of Specification F 7/30 will be accepted, but the actual size and type proposed must be approved by the DTD.

Requirements for Single-Engine Single-Seater Day and Night Fighter (F.10/35).

1 General

The Air Staff require a single-engine single-seater day and night fighter which can fulfil the following conditions–

(a) Have a speed in excess of the contemporary bomber of at least 40mph at 15,000ft.

(b) Have a number of forward firing machine guns that can produce the maximum hitting power possible in the short space of time available for one attack. To attain this object it is proposed to mount as many guns as possible and it is considered that eight guns should be provided. The requirements are given in more detail below.

2 Performance

(a) Speed. The maximum possible and not less than 310mph at 15,000ft at maximum power with the highest speed possible between 5,000 and 15,000ft.

(b) Climb. The best possible to 20,000ft but secondary to speed and hitting power.

(c) Service Ceiling. Not less than 30,000ft is desirable.

(d) Endurance. ¼ hour at maximum power at sea level plus 1 hour at maximum power at which engine can be run continuously at 15,000ft. (This should provide ½ hour at maximum power at which engine can be run continuously, (for climb etc) plus 1 hour at the most economic speed at 15,000ft (for patrol) plus ¼ hour at maximum power at 15,000ft (for attack). To allow for possible increase in engine power during the life of this aircraft, tankage is to be provided to cover ¼ hour at maximum power at sea-level plus 1¼ hours at maximum power at which engine can be run continuously at 15,000ft.

(e) Take-off and landing. The aircraft is to be capable of taking off and landing over a 50ft barrier in a distance of 500 yards.

3 Armament

Not less than 6 guns, but 8 guns are desirable. These should be located outside the airscrew disc. Re-loading in the air is not required and the guns should be fired by electrical or means other than bowden wire.

It is contemplated that some or all of these guns should be mounted to permit of a degree of elevation and traverse with some form of control from the pilot's seat. Though it is not at present possible to give details, it is desirable that designers should be aware of the possibility of this development, which should not, however, be allowed to delay matters at this stage.*

4 Ammunition

300 rounds per gun if eight guns are provided and 400 rounds per gun if only six guns are installed.

5 View

(a) The upper hemisphere must be so far as possible unobstructed to the view of the pilot to facilitate search and attack. A good view for formation flying is required, both for formation leader and flank aircraft and for night landing.

(b) A field of view of about 10° downwards from the horizontal line of sight over the nose is required for locating the target.

6 Handling

(a) A high degree of manoeuvrability at high speeds is not required but good control at slow speeds is essential.

(b) A minimum alteration of trail trim with variations of throttle is required.

(c) The aircraft must be a steady firing platform.

7 Special Features and Equipment

(a) Enclosed cockpit
(b) Cockpit heating
(c) Night flying equipment
(d) R/T
(e) Oxygen for 2½ hours
(f) Guns to be easily accessible on the ground for loading and maintenance
(g) Retractable undercarriage and tailwheel permissible
(h) Wheel brakes
(j) Engine starting – If an electric starter is provided a ground accumulator will be used with a plug-in point on the aircraft, an accumulator for this purpose is not required to be carried in the aircraft. The actual starting must be under control of the pilot. In addition hand turning gear is required.

Specification No. 16/36 Spitfire I Development-Production. Date 28 July 1936.

This covered the first production contract of 310 examples, signed on 3 June 1936. It read – "The aircraft are to be constructed in strict accordance with the drawings and schedules covering the design, construction etc, of the experimental aircraft built to Specification No F 37/34 in the form in which that aircraft, except as modified by other requirements of this Specification or by alterations accepted by the DTD to facilitate production."

Contractual details, similar to those published in F 37/34 followed and it was not until paragraph ten did it specify particulars.

(i) Provision is to be made in the structure for such extra weight as will be entailed, should a Fairey Reed three-blade metal airscrew be fitted in place of the wooden two-blade airscrew
(ii) Two chutes, each 30 inches long × 5¾in diameter, are to be provided to enable the pilot to drop forced landing flares
(iii) The capacity of the lower fuel tank is to be

This refers, obviously, to the Rolls-Royce PV12 and is a typist's error.

**At the time of issue of F.10/35 the traversing gun scheme was under serious consideration. See page 24 for details.*

increased by 9 gallons, and space shall be reserved in one of the wings for an extra tank of 9 to 12 gallons capacity **Verney's thoughts to Sorley concerning additional fuel in K5054 were correct in their assumption that more would be needed rather than less.* Should the extra tank be required, a hand pump will be necessary for feeding its contents to the upper tank, on which a suitable connecting point is to be provided

(iv) Arrangements are to be made for the safe disposal of any petrol which may leak from the tanks

(v) The lower fuel tank is to be provided with a detachable sump

(vi) The stiffness of the wings is to be increased so as to ensure freedom from flutter up to an indicated airspeed of 450mph. In particular, the spar web is to be moved from front to rear of the flange and thicker leading edge sheeting is to be provided

(vii) A tube through which the Very pistol may be fired is to be provided

(viii) Hot and cold air intake pipes of Rolls-Royce type are to be fitted if found suitable

(ix) A locker of dimensions not less than 14" × 10" × 4" is to be provided to hold the pilot's personal belongings

(x) A tail wheel with an electrically conducting tyre is to be fitted

(xi) A curved windscreen is to be fitted in lieu of flat panels if a satisfactory type can be obtained sufficiently early

(xii) The cockpit hood shall be easy to open at all speeds of which the aeroplane is capable

(xiii) A means of regulating the temperature of the cockpit by the admission of cold air thereto is to be provided

(xiv) At those parts of the mainplane or tailplane where riveting of the covering would be particularly difficult to do, the ribs may be made with their lower booms of wood and the covering attached by stainless steel wood screws

(xv) The undercarriage horn is to be modified so as to give a more audible warning

(xvi) The wing tip navigation lamps are to be of standard pattern

(xvii) The gun firing control is to be of Dunlop pneumatic type

(xviii) The pump which actuates the undercarriage retracting mechanism shall be modified so as to increase the speed of raising and lowering the undercarriage

(xix) The mechanical control for rotating the undercarriage lock is to be made specially robust

(xx) If possible, R.A.E. Type G landing lamps shall be fitted

(xxi) Provided no reduction in the performance will be entailed, the hinged flaps on the wheels may be replaced by fixed flaps which, when retracted, will not cover the wing apertures completely

(xxii) The wing tips and the end bay of the fuselage are to be made easily detachable. These components, together with each wing as a whole, shall comply with current interchangeability requirements

(xxiii) The plating for the wings and fuselage may be made of Alclad, which shall be protected by varnish in accordance with the relevant A.D.M.

(xxiv) The spar tubes may be made of Hiduminium, provided all relevant requirements as regards their strength are met

(xxv) Forgings may be of non-stainless steel, protected in accordance with current requirements

(xxvi) The aeroplanes shall be 'camouflaged'. Further instructions in connection with this requirement will be issued at a later date

(xxvii) A simple type of jack, suitable for raising the aeroplane when the undercarriage retracting mechanism has to be tested, is to be provided 'to special order only'

(xxviii) The pilot's instrument board is to be arranged to take the new flying instrument panel

(xxix) The gearing of the elevator trimming tabs is to be reduced, and back-lash at the tabs on both elevator and rudder is to be eliminated, or minimised as far as possible

(xxx) The pipe-lines in the braking system are to be secured to the oleo legs

(xxxi) The fairing over joints in the wing covering is to be such that cracks will not develop therein

(xxxii) The clearance above the pilot's head is to be increased

(xxxiii) The oil cooling is to be improved so that it will be satisfactory for English Summer conditions.

Appendix IV

SERIALS AND BLOCK ALLOCATIONS

Serial numbers and block allocations related to Mark numbers in alphabetical order. Note that some serials are repeated. These were, normally, converted aircraft.

SPITFIRE

K F.I Prototype 5054.

K F.I 9787-9999.

L F.I 1000-1096.

N F.I 3023-3072, 3091-3130, 3160-3203, 3221-3250, 3264-3296 and 3298-3299.

N F.III 3297 prototype.

P F.I 9305-9339, 9360-9399, 9420-9469, 9490-9519, 9540-9550 and 9553-9567.

P F.II 7280-7329, 7350-7389, 7420-7449, 7490-7509, 7520-7569, 7590-7629, 7661-7699, 7730-7759, 7770-7789, 7810-7859, 7880-7929, 7960-7999, 8010-8049, 8070-8099, 8130-8149, 8160-8209, 8230-8279, 8310-8349, 89360-8399, 8420-8449, 8460-8479, 8500-8531, 8533-8536, 8540-8541, 8543-8549, 8561-8563, 8565-8577, 8579-8580, 8582-8584, 8586-8599, 8601-8602, 8605, 8608, 8641-8679, 8690-8698, 8701-8702, 8704-8706 and 8725-8729.

P PR Type D 9551-9552 prototypes.

P F.V 8532, 8537-8539, 8542, 8560-8561, 8564, 8578, 8581, 8585, 8600, 8603-8604, 8606-8607, 8609, 8640, 8699-8700, 8703, 8707-8724, 8740-8759 and 8780-8799.

R F.I 6595-6644, 6683-6722, 6751-6780, 6799-6818, 6829-6840, 6879-6928, 6957-6996, 7015-7028, 7057,7074, 7114-7163, 7192-7206, 7211-7212, 7214-7216, 7250-7252 and 7257.

R F.V 7029-7044, 7055-7056, 7207-7210, 7213, 7217-7231, 7253-7256, 7258-7279, 7290-7309 and 7333-7350.

W F.V 3109-3138, 3168-3187, 3207-3216, 3226-3265, 3305-3334, 3364-3383, 3403-3412, 3422-3461, 3501-3530, 3560-3579, 3599-3608, 3618-3657, 3697-3726, 3756-3775, 3795-3804, 3814-3853, 3893-3902 and 3931-3970.

X F.I 4009-4038, 40951-4070, 4101-4110, 4159-4188, 4231-4280, 4317-4356, 4381-4390, 4409-4428, 4471-4505, 4538-4562, 4585-4624, 4641-4662, 4671-4685, 4708-4722, 4765-4789, 4815-4859, 4896-4945 and 4988-4997.

X F.V 4663-4670.

AA PR.IV 781-815.

AA F.V 718-767, 833-882, 902-946 and 963-982.

AB PR.IV 118-132, 300-319 and 421-430.

AB F.V 133-152, 167-175, 177-199, 201-210, 212-216, 240-284, 320-349, 363-382, 401-420, 450-469, 487-497, 499-502, 504-505, 507-512, 514-515, 517-522, 524-526, 531-532, 535-536, 779-828, 841-875, 892-941 and 960-994.

AB F.VI 176, 200, 211, 498, 503, 506, 513, 516, 523, 527-530 and 533-534.

AD F.I 111-140, 176-210, 225-274, 288-332, 348-397, 411-430, 449-478, 498-517 and 535-584.

AR F.I 212-261.

AR F.V 274-298, 318-347, 362-406, 422-471, 488-532, 546-570 and 592-621.

BL F.V 231-267, 285-304, 311-356, 365-391, 403-450, 461-500, 509-5651, 562-600, 613-647, 655-699, 707-736, 748-789, 801-833, 846-864, 887-909, 918-941 and 956-998.

BM F.V 113-162, 176-221, 227-274, 289-329, 343-386, 399-430, 477-493, 508-543, 556-597 and 624-653.

BP PR.IV 879-892 and 904-937

BP F.V 844-878 and 950-993.

BR PR.IV 410-435 and 641-670.

BR F.V 106-143, 160-161, 163, 165-166, 168-170, 173, 175-177, 179-180, 182-185, 187-188, 190, 192, 194-196, 198-199, 201-204, 226-242, 244-246, 248-249, 251, 253-254, 256, 282-285, 288, 290-296, 299-301, 303-304, 306, 308, 311-313, 315-317, 320-325, 327-328, 344-393, 459-499, 515-549, 562, 564-566, 568, 570, 572-574, 576, 580, 582-584, 586, 589, 591 and 621-640.

BR F.VI 159, 162, 164, 167, 171-172, 174, 178, 181, 186, 189, 191, 193, 197, 200, 205, 243, 247, 250, 252, 255, 286-287, 289, 297-298, 302, 305, 307, 309-310, 314, 318-319, 326, 329-330, 563, 567, 571, 575, 577-579, 585, 587-588, 590, 593, 595, 597-599, 979, 983-984 and 987.

BR F.IX 581, 592, 594, 596, 600-605, 977-978, 980-982 and 985-986.

BS PR.IV 355-367, 489-496, 500 and 503-505.

BS F.V 158, 160-166, 171, 173-175, 178, 181-182, 184, 186-188, 190-191, 193, 197, 199, 201, 218-226, 230-238, 271-291, 293, 295, 298, 300, 305, 335-354 and 530-559.

BS F.VI 106, 108, 111, 114-115, 117, 124, 133-134, 141, 146, 149, 228, 245, 436-437, 442, 448, 453, 460, 465 and 472.

BS F.VII 121, 142, 229, 253 and 427.

BS F.IX 104-105, 107, 109-110, 112-113, 116, 118-120, 122-123, 125-132, 135-140, 143-145, 147-148, 150-152, 157, 159, 167, 170, 172, 176-177, 179-180, 183, 185, 189, 192, 194-196, 198, 200, 202, 227, 239-244, 246-252, 254, 255, 292, 294, 296-297, 299, 301-304, 306-319, 383-411, 428-435, 438-441, 443-447, 449-452, 454-459, 461-464, 466-471, 473-474, 497-499, 501-502 and 506-515.

DP F.XII Type 366. 845 prototype, also F.XX Type 377 845 prototype.

DP F.XIV Type 373 and F.21, F.22 and F.24 Type 356 prototype 851.

EE F.V 600-644, 657-690, 713-753, 766-811 and 834-867.

EF F.V 526-570, 584-616, 629-656, 671-710 and 715-753.

EN PR.IV 153, 155, 262, 264 and 386-389.

EN F.V 112-121, 239-258, 351-370, 515-534, 551-583, 628-637, 763-800, 821-867, 888-932 and 944-981.

EN F.VI 176 and 189.

EN F.VII 178, 192, 285, 297, 310, 457, 465, 470, 474, 477, 494-497, 499, 505-506, 509 and 511-512.

EN F.IX 122-152, 154, 156, 171-175, 177, 179-188, 190-191, 193-207, 259-261, 263, 265-270, 286-296, 298-309, 311-315, 329-337, 339-340, 344-345, 349-350, 390, 392-394, 397-406, 444-456, 458-464, 466-469, 471-473, 475-476, 478-483, 490-493, 498, 500-502, 510 and 513-514.

EN PR.XI 338, 341-343, 346-348, 385, 391, 395-396, 407-430, 503-504, 507-508 and 652-685.

EN F.XII 221-238 and 601-637.

EP F.V 107-152, 164-213, 226-260, 275-316, 327-366, 380-417, 431-473, 485-523, 536-579, 594-614, 636-669, 682-729, 747-795, 812-847, 869-915 and 951-990.

EP887 was not allotted.

ER F.V 114-146, 159-200, 206-229, 245-283, 299-345, 461-510, 524-571, 583-626, 634-679, 695-744, 758-791, 804-834, 846-894, 913-948 and 960-998.

ES F.V 105-154, 168-214, 227-264, 276-318 and 335-369.

JF F.VIII 274-300, 316-336, 392-427, 443-485, 501-508, 557-592, 613-630, 658-676, 692-716, 740-789, 805-850, 869-902 and 926-967.

JG F.V 713-752, 769-810, 835-852, 864-899 and 912-960.

JG F.VIII 104-124, 157-204, 239-275, 312-356, 371-387, 404-432, 465-500, 527-568, 603-624 and 646-695.

Appendix IV

JK F.V 101-145, 159-195, 214-236, 249-285, 303-346, 359-394, 396-408, 425-472, 506-551, 600-610, 612-620, 637-640, 642-649, 651-678, 705-742, 756-769, 771-795, 803-842, 860-880, 885-892, 922-950, 967-979 and 981-992.
JK F.IX 395, 611, 641, 650, 770, 796, 881-884 and 980.
JL F.V 104-133, 139-140, 159-176, 181-188, 208-225, 231-251, 301-338, 346-374, 378-382 and 385-395.
JL F.IX 134-138, 177-180, 226-230, 252-256, 375-377 and 383-384.
LA F.21 187-236, 249-284 and 299-332.
LV F.VIII 643-681 and 726-756.
LZ F.V 807-815, 817-830, 834-835, 844-848, 862-887, 926-946 and 969-988.
LZ F.IX 816, 831-833, 836-843, 861, 888-899, 915-925, 947-956 and 989-998.
MA F.V 261-266, 279-298, 328-368, 383-397, 643-657, 670-682, 684-686, 688, 691-692, 694-704, 850-853,855-859, 861-863, 877, 880-883 and 885-906.
MA F.IX 221-260, 299-315, 369, 398-428, 443-487, 501-546, 559-601, 615-642, 683, 687, 690, 693, 705-713, 726-767, 790-819, 831-849, 854, 860, 878-879 and 884.
MB F.VII 761-769, 806, 808, 820-828, 883-887, 912-916 and 929-935.
MB F.VIII 959-976.
MB F.IX 807.
MB PR.XI 770-793, 888-911 and 936-958.
MB F.VII 794-805, 829-863 and 875-882.
MD F.VII 100-146 and 159-190.
MD F.VIII 214-256, 269-303, 315-356 and 369-403.
MD PR.X 191-199 and 213.
MH F.V 298-311, 564-568, 581-596, 600, 605, 637-646 and 750-755.
MH F.IX 312-336, 349-390, 413-456, 470-512, 526-563, 597-599, 601-604, 606-623, 635-636, 647-678, 691-738, 756-796, 813-856, 869-912, 924-958 and 970-999.
MJ F.IX 114-156, 169-203, 215-258, 271-314, 328-369, 382-428, 441-485, 498-536, 549-555, 557-589, 602-646, 659-698, 712-756, 769-801, 814-858, 870-913, 926-967 and 979-999.
MJ LF.XVI 556.
MK F.IX 112-158, 171-213, 226-268, 280-326, 339-379, 392-428, 440-468, 499-534, 547-590, 602-646, 659-699, 713-756, 769-812, 826-868, 881-926, 939-969 and 981-999.
ML F.IX 112-156, 169-216, 229-277, 291-323, 339-381 and 396-428.
MT F.VIII 502-527, 539-581, 593-635, 648-689, 703-748, 761-802, 815-846, 872-915, 925-969 and 981-999.
MT F.XIV 847-858.
MV F.VIII 112-156, 169-208, 231-245, 321-329, 342-346, 398-441, 456-487 and 499-514.
MV F.XIV 246-273, 286-320 and 347-386.
NH F.IX 148-158, 171-218, 230-276, 289-326, 339-381, 393-438, 450-496, 513-558 and 570-611.
NH F.VIII 614-636.
NH F.XIV 637-661, 685-720, 741-759, 775-813, 831-846, 857-871, 873-875 and 892-929.
NH F.XVIII 847-856 and 872.
NM F.XIV 814-823.
PA F.VIII 952-958.
PA PR.XI 838-871, 884-913, 926-951 and 959-961.
PK F.IX 991-998.
PK F.22 312-356, 369-412, 426-435, 481-525, 539-582, 594-635, 648-677, 680, 684 and 715.
PK F.24 678-679, 681-683, 685-689, 712-714 and 716-726.
PL F.IX 123-169, 185-228, 246-288, 313-356, 369-408, 423-466 and 488-499.
PL PR.XI 758-799, 823-866, 881-925 and 949-998.
PM PR.XI 123-160.
PM PR.XIX 496-519, 536-581, 596-637 and 651-661.
PP F.21 139 prototype.
PS PR.XIX 831-836, 849-893 and 908-935.
PT F.IX 355-380, 395-436, 451-498, 523-567, 582-627, 639-683, 697-738, 752-795, 818-859, 873-915, 929-970 and 986-999.
PV F.IX 115-160, 174-215, 229-270, 283-287, 289-294, 296-306, 308-326, 341-348 and 350-359.
PV LF.XVI 288, 295, 307, 327 and 349.
RB F.XIV 140-189.
RK F.IX 798-819, 835-839, 841, 843-848, 850-858, 860-864, 867, 884-887, 889-890, 894, 898-901, 906-909, 911-912, 914-917, 919-920 and 922-924.
RK LF.XVI 840, 842, 849,859, 865-866, 868, 883, 888, 891-893, 895-897, 902-905, 910, 913, 918, 921 and 925-926.
RM F.XIV 615-625, 648-656, 670-713, 726-770, 783-825, 839-887, 901-943 and 957-999.
RM PR.XIX 626-647.
RN F.XIV 113-160 and 173-221.
RR F.IX 181-211, 228, 231-232, 235, 237-239, 241, 244, 246, 251-254, 258-260, 262, and 264.
RR F.XVI 205, 212-213, 226-227, 229-230, 234, 236, 240, 242-243, 245, 247-250, 255-257, 261, 263 and 265.
RW F.XVI 344-359 and 373-396.
SL F.IX 594-595, 625-635 and 648-665.
SL LF.XVI 541-565, 567-571, 573-579, 596-602, 604-605, 607-611, 613-618, 620-624, 666, 668-676, 678-682, 685, 687-690, 713, 715, 717-721, 724-725, 727-728, 733 and 745.
SM F.IX 135-150, 170-177, 240, 425, 441-463, 486, 504-506, 508-510, 513-515, 517-537, 539-548, 563-597, 610-645, 647, 663, 666 and 668-669.
SM LF.XVI 178-213, 226-239, 241-258, 273-316, 329-369, 383-424, 426-427, 464-485, 487-488, 503, 507, 511-512, 516, 538, 646, 648, 664-665, 667 and 670-671.
SM F.XIV 812-842, 876-899 and 913-938.
SM F.XVIII 843-845, 939-956 and 968-997.
SR PR.X 395-400.
SW PR.XIX 777 prototype.
SX F.22 549 prototype.
TA F.IX 738, 740, 742-758, 760-780, 793-808, 810-840, 844, 850-851, 854-888, 905-948 and 960-999.
TA LF.XVI 739, 741, 759 and 809.
TB F.IX 115-129, 133-135, 142-150, 168-193, 195-197, 213-231, 233-236, 238-243, 249, 251, 253, 393, 413-450, 464-474, 477, 479, 482-491, 499-500, 503, 516, 518, 523-524, 527, 529-548, 563-571, 573, 575-577, 579, 584, 586-587, 638, 640-659, 674, 676-701, 703-708, 710-712, 717-718, 736, 740, 771-808, 824-827, 830, 837-857, 909, 914, 918, 920, 924-925, 938-959, 971-988, 992 and 994.
TB LF.XVI 130-132, 136-141, 232, 237, 244-248, 250, 252, 254-256, 269-308, 326-349, 352-392, 394-396, 476, 478, 480-481, 492-498, 501-502, 515, 517, 519-522, 525-526, 528, 549, 572, 574, 578, 580-583, 585, 588-598, 613-637, 639, 675, 702, 799, 713-716, 733-735, 737-739, 741-759, 828-829, 831-836, 858-868, 883-908, 910-913, 915-917, 919, 921-923, 989-991, 993 and 995-999.
TD F.IX 155, 175, 178-183, 192-213, 287, 290-292, 294-315, 352-368, 370-371, 373-374, 378-379, 395-399, 952-958 and 970-999.
TD LF.XVI 113-154, 156-158, 176-177, 184-191, 229-267, 280-286, 288-289, 293, 316-325, 338-351, 369, 372, 375-377 and 400-408.
TE F.IX 115, 117-118, 121-158, 197, 205, 211-213, 215, 230-234, 236, 238, 289-290, 292-299, 301, 303-309, 312-313, 315, 329, 331, 333, 336-337, 343, 493-535, 549-578.
TE LF.XVI 116, 119-120, 174-196, 198-204, 206-210, 214, 228-229, 235, 237, 239-259, 273-288, 291, 300, 302, 310-311, 314, 328, 330, 332, 334-335, 338-342, 344-359, 375-385, 387-408, 434-471 and 473-480.
TM F.21 379 and 383.
TP F.XIV 236-240 and 256.
TP F.XVIII 195-235, 237-298, 313-350, 363-408 and 423-456.
TX F.XIV 974-998.
TZ F.XIV 102-149, 152-176 and 178-199.
TZ F.XVIII 200-205 and 210-240.
VN F.24 301-334 and 477-496.

SPITEFUL

NN XIV 660, 664 and 667 prototypes.
RB XIV 515-525, 527-531 and 533-535.

SEAFIRE

LA F.45 428-457 and 481-495.
LA F.46 541-564.
LR F.IIC 631-667, 680-712 and 725-764.
LR F.III 765-820 and 835-881.
MA F.IIC 970-999.
MB F.IIC 113-158, 178-222, 235-281 and 293-326.
NF F.III 418-445, 480-526, 531-570, 575-607 and 624-665.
NM F.IIC 910-949 and 963-982.
NM F.III 984-999.
NN F.III 112-157, 169-214, 227-270, 283-330, 333-367, 379-418, 431-476, 488-528, 542-586 and 599-641.
NS F.XV 487 and 490 prototypes.
NS F.XV F.XVII 493 prototype.
PK F.XV 240, 243 and 245 prototypes.
PP F.III 921-957 and 969-999.
PR F.III 115-156, 170-215, 228-271 and 285-334.
PR F.XV 338-379, 391-436, 449-479 and 492-522.
PS F.47 944-957.
PX F.III 913-962.
RX F.III 156-194, 210-256, 268-313 and 326-353.
SP F.XV 136-168 and 181-197.
SP F.XVII 323-327 and 341-355.
SR F.XV 446-493, 516-547, 568-611 and 630-645.
SW F.XV 781-828, 844-879 and 896-921.
SW F.XVII 986-993.
SX F.XVII 111-139, 152-201, 220-256, 271-316, 332-370 and 386-389.
SX F.46 549 prototype.
TM F.45 379 prototype.
TM F.46 383 prototype.
VP F.47 427-465 and 471-495.
VR F.47 961-972.

SEAFANG

RB F.31 520 prototype.
VB F.32 893 and 895 prototypes.
VB F.31 471-480.
VG F.32 481-482, 486 and 488-490.

Appendix V

CONTRACTS

The subject of contracts, production totals and Service serials is a complex one, and in compiling this list the authors had access to the Supermarine Production Records up to December 1943 and to the archives of the Air Historical Branch of the Air Ministry and Vickers-Armstrongs Ltd. Where official information on Service serial allocation is missing, as in the partially cancelled contracts, unconfirmed serials are in italics.

Contractors.
Part One. Supermarine Aviation (Vickers) Ltd., Woolston Works, Southampton. From October 1938, Vickers-Armstrongs (Supermarine) Ltd.

Part Two. Vickers-Armstrongs (Castle Bromwich) Ltd., Birmingham.

Part Three. Westland Aircraft Ltd., Yeovil.

Part Four. Cunliffe-Owen Aircraft Ltd., Eastleigh.

Contracts under review.
Supermarine:- B527113/36., B817241/38., B19713/39., B23634/39., B980385/39., S.B.2415/C.23A., A/c 1877/C.23(c)., C.R.D., Unidentified.

Castle Bromwich:- B981687/39., A/c 5795/C.23(c).

Westland:- B124305/40., A/c 2605/C.23(c).

Cunliffe-Owen:- A/c2777/C.23(c).

The Production Contracts were issued by the Contracts Branch (C.23) of the Air Ministry to the four companies as listed above but, as is evident by the introduction to the Short Histories Headings following each main chapter, these Contracts were sub-divided again and again into orders,often for Mark numbers that differed from that specified in the original Contract. An excellent example of this is Contract No. B197713/39, issued to Supermarine on 9 August 1939. A total of thirteen separate orders was issued and more than fifteen different Marks built, including Seafires, between 9 August 1939 and 18 February 1944. A number of orders were cancelled and amended as Service requirements altered.

Part One

Supermarine Aviation (Vickers) Ltd.
Contract No. B527113/36. To Specification F 16/36, Operational Requirement OR.17.

First Order for 310 Spitfire Mk I
Dated 3 June 1936.
Serial allocations – K9787-9999; L1000-1096
Built at Southampton as Mk I between May 1938 and September 1939. First delivered K9728 19 March 1938; last L1096 7 September 1939. One extra added to production (No. 251) for France as 01 on 12 July 1939. Supermarine production numbers 1-250, 252-311. First 49 aircraft costed at £8783 each; next 26 @ £5782; next 31 @ £5768.10s; remainder @ £5696.

Second Order for 200 Spitfire Mk I
Dated September 1938.
Serial allocations – N3023-3072, N3091-3130, N3160-3203, N3221-3250, N3264-3299. N3297 deleted from contract and built as prototype F Mk III.
Built at Southampton as Mk I between September 1939 and January 1040. First delivered N3023-3026 8 September 1939, last N3293-3295 20 January 1940. Production numbers 312-507. From thereonin these numbers did not run in sequence. 196 Mk I and three pattern aircraft.

Contract No. B817241/38.
Order for one Type 323 Spitfire for an attempt on the World's Landplane Speed Record.
Serial allocation – K9834.
Completed January 1939 and flown in Class B marks N.17.

Contract No. B236634/39.
Order for one Mk III prototype fighter.
Serial allocation – N3297.
Completed in May 1940.

Contract No. B19713/39
First order for 450 Spitfire Mk I
Dated 9 August 1939
Serial allocations – R6595-6644, R6683-6722, R6751-6780, R6799-6818, R6829-6840, R6879-6928, R6957-6996, R7015-7044, R7055-7074, R7114-7163, R7192-7231, R7250-7279, R7290-7309, R7353-7350.
Built as Mk IA/B and Mk VA/B between April 1940 and April 1941. First delivered R6595 9 May 1940, last R7350 24 April 1941. 18 built at Chattis Hill; 482 at Eastleigh. 343 F Mk I; 65 F Mk VA; 24 F Mk VB; 6 PR Mk V C Type; 12 PR Mk IV. One floatplane conversion, R6722.

Second order for 450 Spitfire Mk I
Dated 22 February 1940
Serial allocations – W3109-3138, W3168-3187, W3207-3216, W3226-3265, W3305-3334, W3364-3383, W3403-3412, W3422-3461, W3501-3530, W3560-3579, W3599-3608, W3618-3657, W3697-3726, W3756-3775, W3795-3804, W3814-3853, W3893-3902, W3931-3970.
Built as Mk VA/B between April and October 1941. First delivered W3109 8 May 1941, last W3970 20 October 1941. 272 built at Eastleigh; 79 Chattis Hill; 99 High Post; 25 F Mk VA; 424 F Mk VB; 1 F Mk III; 1 converted floatplane; 3 PR Mk XIII.

Third order for 500 Spitfire Mk I
Dated 9 June 1940.
Serial allocations – X4009-4038, X4051-4070, X4101-4110, X4159-4188, X4231-4280, X4317-4356, X4381-4390, X4409-4428, X4471-4505, X4538-4562, X4585-4624, X4641-4685, X4708-4722, X4765-4789, X4815-4859, X4896-4945, X4988-4997.
Built as Mk IA/B and Mk VA/B between July 1940 and January 1941. First delivered X4011 & 4012 26 July 1940 last X4994 18 March 1941. 9 built at High Post; remainder Eastleigh. 484 F Mk I; 8 PR Mk IV; 4 F Mk VA; 4 Mk VB.

Fourth order for 500 Spitfire Mk I
Dated 19 July 1940.
Serial allocations – AA718-767, AA781-815, AA833-882, AA902-946, AA963-982, AB118-152, AB167-216, AB240-284, AB300-349, AB363-382, AB401-430, AB450-469, AB487-536.
Built as Mk VB/VC/VI/PR Mk IV between August 1941 and February 1942. First delivered AA718 31 August 1941, last AB535 & 536 20 February 1942. 152 built at Eastleigh; 66 High Post; 120 Chattis Hill; 74 HEA; 1 Stockbridge; 3 Henley; 84 not known. 315 FMk VB; 81 PR Mk IV; 87 F Mk VC; 16 F Mk VI; 1 F Mk IX.

Fifth order for 1,100 Spitfire Mk IA/B.
Dated 24 October 1940.
Serial allocations – BP844-892, BP904-937, BP950-993, BR106-143, BR159-205, BR226-256, BR282-330, BR344-393, BR410-435, BR459-499, BR515-549,BR562-605, BR621-670, BR683-721, BR745-772, BR799-831, BR849-877, BR890-935, BR 950-987, BS104-152, BS157-202, BS218-255, BS271-319, BS335-367, BS383-411, BS427-474, BS489-515, BS530-559.
202 aircraft deleted from contract – BR683-721, BR745-772, BR799-831, BR849-877, BR890-935, BR950-976.
Built as PR Mk IV/Mk VB/VC/VI/VII/IX between February and November 1942. First delivered BP844 & 845 4 February 1942, last BS151 & 152 26 August 1942. 213 built at Eastleigh; 132 Chattis Hill; 113 HEA; 100 High Post; 20 Rolls-Royce; 20 not known. 349 F Mk VC; 104 PR Mk IV; 10 F Mk VB; 69 F Mk VI; 3 HF Mk VII; 73 F Mk IX.

Sixth order for 120 Spitfire Mk III
Dated 24 October 1940.
Serial allocations – BS573-618, BS634-659, BS677-724. Contract Air/71.
Order cancelled 27 April 1941.

Seventh order for 500 Spifire Mk VC
Dated 23 August 1941.
Serial allocations – EN112-156, EN171-207, EN221-270, EN285-315, EN329-370, EN385-430, EN444-483, EN490-534, EN551-583, EN601-637, EN652-695, EN710-759.
60 deleted from contract:- EN686-695, EN710-759. Allotted to Seafire Mk IB as NM910-949; NM963-982. 131 built at Eastleigh; 159 Chattis Hill; 113 Rolls-Royce; 34 High Post; 2 HEA. Built as Mk VC/PR Mk IV/VI/VII/IX/XI/XII between November 1942 and August 1943. First delivered EN112 17 November 1942, last EN683-685 15 August 1943. All F Mk IX except 7 PR Mk IV; 19 FMk VII; 81 PR Mk XI; 45 F Mk XII.

Eighth order for 202 Seafire Mk IIC
Dated March 1942.
Conversions of Spitfire VC(T) under contract AIR/1863/CB.23(c) on the production line.
Serial allocations – MA970-999, MB113-158, MB178-222, MB235-281, MB293-326. Built as Seafire Mk IIC between June 1942 and April 1943. First delivered MA971 2 June 1942, last MB326 8 April 1943.

Ninth order for 70 PR Spitfire with Merlin 61 engine
Dated 21 April 1942.
Serial allocations – LV643-681, LV726-756.
Built as LF Mk VIII fighters between November 1943 and January 1944, First delivered LV643 4 November 1943, last LV753 4 June 1944. 15 built at Eastleigh; 31 Chattis Hill; 24HEA. All despatched overseas except LV674. 54 to India; 9 Australia; 6 North Africa.

Tenth order for 426 Spitfire Mk VC
Dated 12 May 1942.
Serial allocations – MB761-808, MB 820-863, MB875-916, MB929-976, MD100-146, MD159-199, MD213-256, MD269-303, MD315-356, MD369-403. Built as Mks VII/VIII/IX/PR Mk X/PR Mk XI/Mk XII between July 1943 and March 1944. Mk XIs MB952-958 were completed to Contract No. A/c 1877/C.23(c).
First delivered MB761 4 July 1943, last MD601 21 February 1944. 179 built at Eastleigh; 141 Chattis Hill; 47 High Post; 50 Keevil; 1 Worthy Down; 8 not known; 115 F Mk VII; 174 LF Mk VIII; 1 F MK IX; 10 PR Mk X; 75 PR Mk XI; 55 F Mk XII.

Eleventh order for 260 Seafire Mk IIC
Dated 29 July 1942.
Serial allocations – MV660-707, MV720-761, MV774-823, MV846-885, MV899-941, MV954-990.
Order cancelled 20 August 1942.

Twelfth order for 60 Seafire Mk IIC
Dated 5 January 1943.
Serial allocations – NM910-949, NM963-982.
Converted from Spitfires Mk VC EN686-695, EN710-759, Seventh order of 23 August 1941.
Built as Seafire Mk IIC between January and March 1943. First delivered NM911 & 912 11 January 1943, last NM982 30 March 1943.

Thirteenth order for 6 Spitfire Mk VII
Dated 18 February 1944.
Serial allocations – SR395-400
Built as PR Mk X in May 1944. 5 built at Southampton; one High Post. Delivered to RAF Benson between 14 and 16 May 1944. SR396 to No. 542 S.

Contract No. B980385/39
Order for 200 Spitfire Mk I
Dated 29 April 1939.
Serial allocations – P9305-9339, P9360-9399, P9420-9469, P9490-9519, P9540-9584.
P9551 & 9552 deleted from contract for completion as PR Mk III. P9553-9567 deleted from contract (9 June 1940) for export to Turkey. Order cancelled and serials re-instated in contract for supply to RAF – P9553-9565. P9568-9584 deleted from contract (9 June 1940) and originally intended for sale to Portugal. Not built. P9544 to Portugal October 1945 – P9566 & 9567 to Portugal as Type 341. Delivered as N.22 and N.23 on 8 and 4 May respectively.
Built as Mk I between January and August 1940. 179 F Mk Is @ £5,120 each. First delivered P9306 2 January 1940; last P9565 31 August 1940. P9547, 9553 to 9561 and 9565 built as Type 341, but converted back to F Mk I on production line.

Contract No. S.B. 2415/C.23A
Order for two Spitfire PR Mk III Type D with Merlin III.
Dated 6 May 1940.
Serial allocations – P9551-9552
Built as PR Type D prototypes August 1940 at £6,500 each. 9551 delivered 21 September 1940, 9552 22 February 1941.

Contract No. Air/1877/C.23(c).
First order for 800 Spitfire Mk VIII
Dated 23 January 1942.
Serial allocations – JF274-300, JF316-364, JF392-427, JF443-485, JF501-528, JF557-592, JF613-630, JF659-676, JF692-716, JF740-789, JF805-850, JF869-902, JF926-967, JG104-124, JG157-204, JF239-275, JG312-356, JG371-387, JG404-432, JG465-500, JG527-569, JG603-624, JG646-695.
Built as Mk VIII between November 1942 and April 1944. JF316, 318-320 built as prototype F Mk XIVs. 495 built at Eastleigh; 229 Chattis Hill; 4 Worthy Down; one Rolls-Royce; 27 High Post; 40 Keevil; one Air Service Training; 3 not known.

Second order for 700 Spitfire Mk VIII
Dated 27 July 1942.
Serial allocations – MT502-527, MT539-581, MT593-635, MT648-689, MT703-748, MT761-802, MT815-858, MT872-915, MT928-969, MT981-999, MV112-156, MV169-208, MV231-273, MV286-329, MV342-386, MV398-441, MV456-487, MV499-514.
Built as Mks VIII & XIV between December 1943 and October 1944. First delivered MT504 23 March 1944, last MV514 22 October 1944. 215 built at Eastleigh; 132 Chattis Hill; 129 Keevil; 23 Aldermaston; one Winchester; 3 Castle Bromwich; 197 not known. 585 F Mk VIII; 115 FR Mk XIV.

Third order for 225 Spitfire Mk VIII
Dated 1 December 1942.
Serial allocations – NH614-661, NH685-720, NH741-759, NH775-813, NH831-875, NH892-929.
Built as Mks VIII/XIV/XVIII between November 1944 and June 1945. First delivered NH614 9 November 1944, last 17 May 1945. 35 built at Chattis Hill; 50 Keevil; 61 Southampton; 45 Aldermaston; 6 Winchester; 2 Castle Bromwich; 6 not known. 23 F Mk VIII; 191 F Mk XIV, 11 FR XVIII.

Fourth order for 144 Spitfire Mk VIII
Dated 29 December 1942
Serial allocations – NM775-832, NM879-906.
Order cancelled and NM776-810 re-allocated to Airspeed Oxfords.
New order for 10 Spitfire Mk XIV, serials NM814-823.
Built as Mk XIVs in March and April 1945. First delivered NM814 31 March, last NM823 24 April.
9 built at Aldermaston; one Chattis Hill.

Fifth order for 100 Spitfire Mk VIII
Dated 9 April 1943.
Serial allocations – PA838-871, PA884-913, PA926-961. Built as PR Mk XI and LF Mk VIII between November 1943 and March 1944. First delivered PA838 3 November 1943, last PA961 24 February 1944. The Mk VIIIs PA952-958 were completed under Contract No. B19713/39 in March 1944. 48 built at Chattis Hill; One Keevil; 2 Aldermaston; 49 not known.

Sixth order for 592 Spitfire Mk VIII
Dated 2 June 1942.
Serial allocations – PL758-799, PL823-866, PL881-925, PL949-998, PM123-160, PM184-228, PM245-288, PM302-347, PM367-404, PM419-462, PM478-519, PM536-581, 596-637, 651-676.
Contract amended several times and finally reduced to 227 PR Mk XI and 124 PR Mk XIX.
Cancelled from contract – PM184-228, PM245-288, PM302-347, PM367-404, PM419-462, PM478-519, PM536-581. PM596-637, PM651-676.
Projected Spiteful production – PM419-462, PM478-495, PM671-676. Cancelled 2 August 1945.
Built as PR XI and PR XIX between February 1944 and May 1946. First delivered PL758 21 February 1944, last PM160 1 March 1945. 13 built at Chattis Hill; 119 Eastleigh; one Hursley Park; 207 Aldermaston; 3 not known.

Seventh order for 200 Spitfire Mk VIII
Dated 17 July 1943.
Serial allocations – PS684-725, PS739-781, PS795-836, PS849-893, PS908-935.
Order amended to 121 Spiteful and 79 PR Mk XIX. Spitefuls cancelled:– PS684-725, PS739-781, PS795-830.
Built as PR XIXs between November 1944 and May 1945. First delivered PS831 27 November 1944, last PS935 18 May 1945. 46 built at Southampton; one Aldermaston; 9 Keevil; 14 Eastleigh; 9 not known.

Eighth order for 50 Spitfire Mk XIV
Dated 14 August 1943.
Serial allocations – RB140-189. (RB140 was duplicated on Kirby Cadet glider). Built as Mk XIV between October 1943 and March 1944. First delivered RB141 12 November 1943, last RB189 3 March 1945. All believed built at Eastleigh.

Ninth order for 373 Spitfire Mk 21 (Victor)
Dated 14 August 1943.
Serial allocations – RB515-557, RB571-615, RB628-669, RB683-725, RB738-783, RB796-843, RB857-898, RB912-953, RB965-987.
Order cancelled and later amended to 373 Spiteful Mk XIV. Deleted from Spiteful contract – RB526 and RB532. Remainder of Spiteful contract from RB536 onwards cancelled during 1947. 19 confirmed built – RB515-525, RB527-531, RB533-535 (See Spiteful contract page 503).

Tenth order for 406 Spitfire Mk XIV
Dated 23 October 1943.
Serial allocations – RM615-656, RM670-713, RM726-770, RM783-825, RM839-887, RM901-943, RM957-999, RN113-160, RN173-221.
Built as Mks XIV and PR Mk XIX between April 1944 and May 1945. First delivered RM615 1 April 1944, last RN220 16 May 1945. 103 built at Chattis Hill; one High Post; 9 Winchester; 67 Keevil; 5 Aldermaston; one Cosford; 132 not known. 22 PR Mk XIX; 384 F Mk XIV.

Eleventh order for 150 Spitfire PR Mk XI
Dated 12 February 1944.
Serial allocations – SM812-845, SM858-899, SM913-956, SM968-997. Deleted from contract SM858-875.
Built as Mks XIV and XVIII between February 1945 and January 1946. First delivered SM813 23 February 1945, last SM997 19 January 1946. 67 built at Keevil; 14 Chattis Hill; 3 Winchester; 2 Eastleigh; 37 Southampton; 2 Aldermaston. 81 F Mk XIV; 51 FR Mk XVIII.

Twelfth order for 300 Spitfire Mk XIV
Dated August 1944.
Serial allocations – TP195-240, TP256-298, TP313-350, TP363-408, TP423-456, TP471-507, TP526-567, TP581-594.
Cancelled from contract – TP471-507, TP526-567, TP581-594.
207 built as Mks XIV and XVIII between December 1945 and February 1946 93 cancelled. First delivered TP196 10 November 1945, last TP456 28 February 1946. 76 built at Keevil; 26 Southampton; 103 Aldermaston; one Eastleigh; one not known; 93 cancelled.

Thirteenth order for 157 Spitfire Mk XIV
Dated 23 February 1945.
Serial allocations – TX974-998, TZ102-149, TZ152-176, TZ178-205, TZ210-240. Built as Mks XIV and XVIII between August 1945 and January 1946. First delivered TX975 13 August 1945, last TZ240 12 January 1946. 9 built at Southampton; 49 Keevil; 98 Aldermaston; one not known. 120 FR Mk XIV; 37 FR Mk XVIII.

Fourteenth order for 100 Spitfire PR Mk XIX
Dated 6 March 1945.
Serial allocations – TZ598-637, TZ658-692, TZ714-738. Last 50 aircraft cancelled 8 June 1945, remainder shortly afterwards.

C.R.D. Contracts for experimental aircraft.
Air/821
Order for two prototypes with Griffon engines to Specification F.4/41.
Dated 26 May 1941. Original designation F Mk IV cancelled.
Serial allocations – DP845 and DP851.
Built 1941

Order for three Spitefuls Mk XIV prototypes
Dated 6 February 1943.
Serial allocations – NN660, 664, 667.
Built 1944

Contract Air/2901/CB.23(c)
Order for three Seafire Mk XV prototypes to Specification N.4/43
Dated 10 March 1943.

Serial allocations – NS487, 490, 493.
Built 1944. NS493 converted to prototype Mk XVII during construction.

Same contract as above.
Order for three Seafire Mk XV prototypes
Dated May 1943.
Serial allocations – PK240, 243, 245
Built 1944. Both contracts at a fixed price of £126,650.

Contract Air/2601/CB.23(c)
Order for one Spitfire Mk 21
Dated June 1943.
Serial allocation – PP139 (clashed with Sunderland Mk III)
Built July 1944 at High Post.

Order for one Seafire Mk XVIII
Dated December 1943.
Serial allocation - RT646, later re-allocated to a prototype Seafang but also cancelled.
Order cancelled

Contract SB.27489
Order for one Spitfire F21 prototype
Dated 27 April 1944
Serial allocation - SW777
Built as PR MkXIX at High Post May 1945

Contract Air/1877
Order for one Spitfire Mk 21 prototype
Dated 27 April 1944
Serial allocation - SX549
Built as F22 by Cunliffe-Owen at Eastleigh 8 November 1944

Contract Air/4425/G.23(c)
Order for three Spitfire Mk 21
Dated 7 May 1944.
Serials allocations TM379, 383, 389.
Ordered from Castle Bromwich and contract amended 15 August for conversion to Navalised F21. LA193 and LA195 were ordered as Seafire F Mk 45 from South Marston and were reserialled TM379 and 383 to become prototype F 45 and F 46 respectively. TM389 was cancelled 9 March 1946.

Contract Air/5176.
Order for two Seafang Mk 32 to specifications N 5/45
Dated 21 April 1945
Serial allocations - VB893 and 895.
First delivered VB895 30 June 1946, last 893 20 December

Unidentified Contracts to Supermarine.
First order for 600 Seafire Mks 45, 46 and 47
Dated 12 April 1945
Serial allocations - VD490-499, VD521-568, VD582-597, VD618-653, VD679-696, VD714-748, VD763-792, VD809-856, VD869-893, VD925-961, VD984-999,VE135-162, VE176-193, VE233-259, VE274-296, VE328-362, VE379-391, VE406-447, VE462-498, VE516-542, VE563-593.
Order cancelled 1 August 1945

Second order for 150 Seafang Mks 31 and 32 to Specification N 4/45.
Dated May 1945.
Serial allocation - VG471-505, VG540-589, VG602-650, VG664-679, 16 built as Mk 31 (VG471-480,10) and Mk32 (VG481, 482, 486, 488-490,6). VG483-485 and 487 deleted, remainder cancelled 1947.

Contract Air/5795/CB.5(c)
Order for 135 Seafire Mks 46 and 47
Dated 15 November 1945.
Serial allocations - VN501-528*, VN542-563*, VN567-598**, VN614-645**, VN653-673**. *F 45 (50), **F 46 (85).
Cancelled 5 December 1945.

Contract Air/5794/CB.5(b)
Order for 64 Seafire Mk 47
Dated 8 April 1946.
Serial allocations - VP427-465, VP471-495.
Built as F 47 between November 1947 and 1948. First delivered VP428 11 November, last VP495 17 November 1948, at a fixed price of £8,900 each. Built at South Marston

Contract 6/Air/636/CB.7(b)
Order for 100 Seafire Mk47
Dated 1 October 1946.
Serial allocations - VR961-999, VS113-158, VS165-199
12 Built as F 47 (VR961-972) between 8 November 1948 and 28 November 1949, at South Marston at a fixed price of £8,900 each.

Part Two

Vickers-Armstrong (Castle Bromwich) Ltd
Contract No.B981687/39/C.23(c)
First order for 1,000 Spitfire Mk II
Dated 12 April 1939
Serial allocations - P7280-7329, P7350-7389, P7420-7449, P7490-7509, P7520-7569, P7590-7629, P7661-7699, P7730-7759, P7770-7789, P7810-7859, P7880-7929, P7960-7999,P8010-8049, P8070-8099, P8130-8149, P8160-8209, P8230-8279, P8310-8349, P8360-8399, P8420-8449, P8460-8479, P8500-8549, P8560-8609, P8640-8679, P8690-8729, P8740-8759, P8790-8799
Built as Mks IIA/IIB/VA/VB between June 1940 and July 1941. First delivered P7280 27 June, last P8799 21 July 1941
921 IIA/B; 79 VA/B

Second order for 500 Spitfire Mk I
Dated 22 June 1940
Serial allocations - AB779-828, AB841-875, AB892-941, AB960-994, AD111-140, AD176-210, AD225-274, AD288-332, AD348-397, AD411-430, AD449-478, AD498-517, AD535-584.
Built as Mk VB between July and November 1941. First delivered AB780 25 July, last AD583 & 584 23 November 1941

Third order for 1,000 Spitfire Mk III
Dated 24 October 1940.
Serial allocations - BL231-267, BL285-304, BL311-356, BL365-391, BL403-450, BL461-500, BL509-551, BL562-600, BL613-647, BL655-699, BL707-736, BL748-789, BL801-833, BL846-864, BL887-909, BL918-941, BL956-998, BM113-162, BM176-211, BM227-274, BM289-329, BM343-386, BM399-430, BM447-483, BM508-543, BM556-597, BM624-653
Built as Mk VB between November 1941 and May 1942. First delivered BL231 23 November 1941, last BM653 16 May 1942

Fourth order for 904 Spitfire Mk V
Dated 23 August 19411.
Serial allocations - EN763-800, EN821-867, EN888-932, EN944-981, EP107-152, EP164-213, EP226-260, EP275-316, EP327-366, EP380-417, EP431-473, EP485-523, EP536-579, EP594-624, EP636-669, EP682-729, EP747-795, EP812-847, EP869-915, EP951-990, ER114-146, ER159-200. EN887 not allocated- error for EP887
Built as Mk VB & VC between April and August 1942. First delivered EN763 26 April 1942, last ER199 4 September 1942.

Fifth order for 750 Spitfire Mk IV
Dated 23 August 1941.
Serial allocations - ER206-229, ER245-283, ER299-345, ER461-510, ER524-571, ER583-626, ER634-679, ER695-744, ER758-791, ER804-834, ER846-894, ER913-948, ER960-998, ES105-154, ES168-214, ES227-264, ES276-318, ES335-369.
Built as Mks VB & VC between August and December 1942. First delivered ER206 29 August 1942, last ES368 28 December

Sixth order for 989 Spitfire Mk VB
Dated 1 January 1942
Serial allocations - JG713-752, JG769-810, JG835-852, JG864-899, JG912-960, JK101-145, JK159-195, JK214-236, JK249-285, JK303-346, JK359-408, JK425-472, JK506-551, JK600-620, JK637-678, JK705-742, JK756-796, JK803-842, JK860-892, JK922-950, JK967-992, JL104-140, JL159-188, JL208-256, JL301-338, JL346-395
Built as Mks VC & IX between December 1942 and April 1943. First delivered JG713 10 December 1942, last JL395 21 April 1943

Seventh order for 300 Spitfire Mk VC. originally ordered from South Marston in 1942 under Contract Air/1941/CB.23(c) but transferred to Castle Bromwich contract on 23 April 1944
Dated March 1942.
Serial allloctions - LA187-236, LA249-284, LA299-346, LA358-395, LA417-457, LA480-519, LA536-582.
Cancelled 1943. Re-established same year for 120 Spitfire Mk 21
Serial allocations:- LA187-236, LA249-284, LA299-332
Built as Mk 21 between July 1944 and December 1945. First delivered LA188 6 September 1944, last LA332 2 January 1946
Order then extended for delivery of 92 Seafire Mk 45 and 46
Serial allocations- LA428-462, LA481-495, LA541-582.
Built as (1st 50) Mk 45 at Castle Bromwich 1944-45; production then transferred to South Marston and LA541-564 completed as Mk 46. Cancelled from contract LA565-582. First delivered LA429 1 March 1945, last LA499 10 January 1946 (F 45).
First delivered LA541 5 November 1945, last LA564 9 May 1947 (F 46)

Eighth order for 680 Spitfire Mk VC
Dated 28 February 1942
Serial allocations:- LZ807-848, LZ861-899, LZ915-956, LZ969-998, MA221-266, MA279-315, MA328-369, MA383-428, MA443-487, MA501-546, MA559-601, MA615-657, MA670-713, MA726-767, MA790-819, MA831-863, MA877-906
Built as Mks VC & IX between March and June 1943. First delivered LZ807 28 March 1943, last MA906 1 July 1943. 300 F Mk V; 380 F Mk IX

Ninth order for 2,190 Spitfire Mk VC
Dated 28 May 1942
Serial allocations:- MH298-336, MH349-390, MH413-456, MH470-512, MH526-568, MH581-623, MH635-678, MH691-738, MH750-796, MH813-856, MH869-912, MH924-958, MH970-999, MJ114-156, MJ169-203, MJ215-258, MJ271-314, MJ328-369, MJ382-428, MJ441-485, MJ498-536, MJ549-589, MJ602-646, MJ659-698, MJ712-756, MJ769-801, MJ814-858, MJ870-913, MJ926-967, MJ979-999, MK112-158, MK171-213, MK226-268, MK280-326, MK339-379, MK392-428, MK440-486, MK499-534, MK547-590, MK602-646, MK659-699, MK713-756, MK769-812, MK862-868, MK881-926, MK939-969, MK981-999, ML112-156, ML169-216, ML229-277, ML291-323, ML339-381, ML396-428
Built as Mk VC/IX/XVI between July 1943 and May 1944. First delivered MH298 1 July 1943, last ML427 29 April 1944. 2144 F Mk IX; 46 F Mk VC

Tenth order for 600 Spitfire Mk IX
Dated 1 December 1942.
Serial allocations:- NG757-798, NG813-856, NG868-916 NG929-968, MG979-999, NH112-158, NH171-218, NH230-276, NH289-326, NH339-381, NH393-438, NH450-496, NH513-558, NH570-611.
First 232 cancelled - 109 NG757-798, NG813-856, NG868-890 15 November 1945; 123 NG891-913, NG926-968, NG979-999. NH112-127 cancelled as F Mk 22s 18 August 1945
368 built as Mk IX between April and June 1944. First delivered NH148 28 April 1944, last NH611 14 June.

Eleventh order for 800 Spitfire Mk IX
Dated 2 June 1943.
Serial allocations:- PK312-356, PK369-412, PK426-468, PK481-525, PK539-582, PK594-635, PK648-689, PK712-754, PK769-811, PK828-868, PK883-926, PK949-998, PL123-169, PL185-228, PL246-288, PL313-356, PL369-408, PL423-466, PL488-499
Built as Mk IX and F 22 between June 1944 and December 1945. Production of F 22 transferred to South Marston. First delivered PK313 16 March 1945, last PL498 1 July 1944.
Cancelled from contract - PK436-468, PK727-754, PK769-811, PK828-868, PK883-926, PK949-990
PK678-679, PK681-683, PK685-689, PK712-714, PK716-726 and completed as F 24 282 F Mk IX: 27 F 24: 260 F 22

Twelfth order for 1,500 Spitfire Mk 21
Dated 6 June 1943.
Serial allocations:- PS938-987, PT103-150, PT163-203, PT220-267, PT281-325, PT338-380, PT395-436, PT451-498, PT523-567, PT582-627, PT639-683, PT697-738, PT752-795, PT818-859, PT873-915, PT929-970, PT986-999, PV115-160, PV174-215, PV229-270, PV283-327, PV341-385, PV399-*441*, *PV452-510*, *PV524-570*, *PV581-628*, *PV638-688*, *PV694*-739, PV752-797, PV820-865, PV879-919, PV934-984, PW112-122, PW134-158, PW173-196, PW221-250
Contract cancelled, later amended to 673 Mk IX
Serial allocations:- PT355-380, PT395-436, PT451-498, PT523-567, PT582-627, PT639-683, PT697-738, PT752-795, PT818-859, PT873-915, PT929-970, PT986-999, PV115-160, PV174-215, PV229-270, PV283-327, PV341-359
Above built as Mk IX and XVI between June and October 1944. First delivered PT335 28 June 1944. 688 F Mk IX: 5 converted to F Mk XVI
Second amendment for 200 Griffon-Seafires (1944)
Serial allocations:- PV734-739, PV752-797, PV820-865, PV879-919, PV934-984, PW112-122. Order cancelled 18 August 1945 before construction started. Third amendment for 14 Seafire Mk 47 (1945). Production transferred to South Marston.
Serial allloctions:- PS944-957
Built as Mk 47 between June 1946 and November 1947

Thirteenth order for 100 Spitfire Mk IX
Dated 25 October 1943.
Serial allocations:- RK798-819, RK835-868, RK883-926
Built as Mks IX and XVI between August and October 1944
First delivered RK799 16 August 1944, last RK925 11 October 1944

Fourteenth order for 73 Spitfire Mk IX
Dated 16 November 1943
Serial allocations:- RR181-213, RR226-265
Built as Mks IX and XVI between August and October 1944. First delivered RR181 17 August 1944, last RR264 18 October. RR233 deleted from contract after collision at Castle Bromwich. 50 F Mk IX; 23 F Mk XVI

Fifteenth order for 700 Spitfire Mk 21
Dated 20 January 1944.
Serial allocations:- RV370-415, *RV431-476*, *RV498-548*, *RV561-608*, *RV628-662*, *RV678-725*, *RV744-789*, *RV800-844*, *RV861*-905, RV918-959, RV971-999, RW113-156, RW168-209, RW225-258, RW273-315, RW328-359, RW373-396
Contract cancelled August 1944
Partially re-instated for 40 Spitfire Mk IX
Serial allocations:- RW344-359, RW373-396
Built as Mk XVI betweeen June and July 1945. First delivered RV345 26 June 1945.

Sixteenth order for 800 Spitfire Mk 21
Dated 1 February 1944
Serial allocation:- SL541-579, SL593-635, SL648-690, SL713-747, SL759-798, SL812-857, SL873-915, SL928-959, SL971-999, SM112-150, SM170-213, SM226-258, SM273-316, SM329-369, SM383-427, SM441-488, SM503-548, SM563-597, SM610-648, SM663-698
Contract cancelled August 1944
Partially re-instated for 558 Spitfire Mk IX
Serial allocations:- SL541-579, SL593-635, SL648-690, SL713-747, SM135-150, SM170-213, SM226-258, SM273-316, SM329-369, SM383-427, SM441-488, SM503-548, SM563-597, SM610-648, SM663-671.
Deleted from contract - SL566, SL572, SL593, SL603, SL606, SL612, SL619, SL667, SL677, SL682-684, SL686, SL714, SL716, SL722-723, SL726, SL729-732, SL734-744, SL746-747
Built as Mks IX and XVI between September and November 1944

Seventeenth order for 1,884 Spitfire Mk IX
Dated 19 April 1944
Serial allocations:-TA738-780, TA793-844, TA850-888, TA905-948, TA960-999, TB115-150, TB168-197, TB213-256, TB269-308, TB326-396, TB413-450, TB464-503, TB515-549, TB563-598, TB613-659, TB674-718, TB733-759, TB771-808, TB824-868, TB883-925, TB971-999, TD113-158, TD175-213,

TD229-267, TD280-325, TD338-379, TD395-428, TD443-490, TD515-546, TD560-*601*, *TD610-659*, *TD668-717*, *TD728-771*, *TD778*-815, TD829-866, TD884-925, TD937-958, TD970-999, TE115-158, TE174-215, TE228-259, TE273-315, TE328-359, TE375-408, TE434-480, TE493-535, TE549-579.
Serials between TD409 and TD951 cancelled on 30 October 1944. Deleted from contract - TA841-843, TA852-853, TB194, TB350, 351,TE386, TE472, TE579.
Built as Mks IX and XVI between December 1944 and June 1945. first delivered TA793 29 November 1944, last TE578 23 June 1945. 850 F Mk IX; 632 F Mk XVI.

Eighteenth order for 276 Spitfire Mk IX
Dated 25 July 1944
Serial allocations:- TL773-815, TL829-870, TL884-916 TL930-967, TL979-999, TM115-136, TM163-205, TM218-251.
Contract cancelled 30 October 1944. TM115 re-instated as Mk XVI and later cancelled August 1945

Nineteenth order for 188 Spitfire Mk XVI
Dated 6 March 1945.
Serial allocations:- TZ747-791, TZ815-843, TZ866-898, TZ921-957, TZ969-998, VA112-125.
Contract cancelled 18 August 1945

Twentieth order for 50 Spitfire Mk 22
Dated 6 March 1945.
Serial allocations:- VA201-250
Contract cancelled 18 August 1945

Contract Air/5795/C.23(c)
Order for 150 Spitfire Mk 22
Dated 15 November 1945.
Serial allocations:- VN301-348, VN364-397, VN413-439, VN456-496.
54 incomplete airframes:- VN301-334, VN477-496 transferred to South Marston for completion as F24 between April 1946 and February 1948. Cancelled from contract VN364-397, VN413-439. First delivered VN301 13 April 1946, last Spitfire to RAF VN496 20 February 1948. 31 built at Keevil; one Southampton; 19 Hursley Park; one South Marston; one not known.

Part Three

Westland Aircraft Ltd.
Contract No.B124305/40
First order for 300 Spitfire Mk I
Dated August 1940
Serial allocations – AR212-261, AR274-298, AR318-347, AR362-406, AR422-471, AR488-532, AR546-570, AR592-621
Built as Mks I/VB/VC between July 1941 and September 1942. First delivered AR212 18 July 1941, last AR620 7 September 1942. 50 F Mk IA; 140 F Mk VB; 110 F Mk VC.

Second order for 200 Spitfire MkV
Dated September 1942.
Serial allocations – EE600-644, EE657-690, EE713-753, EE766-811, EE834-867.
Built as Mk VC between September 1942 and February 1943. First delivered EE601 & 602 21 October 1942.

Third order for 185 Spitfire Mk V
Dated October 1941.
Serial allocations – EF526-570, EF584-616, EF629-656, EF671-710, EF715-753 Built as Mk VC between February and November 1943. First delivered 2 February 1943, last EF753 5 November 1943

Fourth order for 213 Seafire MkIIC
Dated March 1942.
Serial allocations – LR631-667, LR680-712, LR725-764, LR765-820, LR835-881 Built as Mks IIC and III between January 1943 and January 1944. First delivered LR631 & 632 23 January 1943. 110 Mk IIC 103 Mk III.

Contract No.Air/2605/C.23(c)
First order for 200 Seafire Mk IIC
Dated November 1942.
Serial allocations – NF418-455*, NF480-526, NF531-570, NF575-607, NF624-665 Built as Mks IIC and III (*built as Mk III with fixed wings and originally designated LF III(Hybrid) and later LF IIC(Hybrid)).

Second order for 200 Seafire Mk III
Dated 5 January 1943.
Serial allocations – NM984-999, NN112-157, NN169-214, NN227-270, NN283-330
Built as Mk III between April and August 1944. Small number as LF IIC(Hybrid).

Third order for 250 Seafire Mk III
Dated July 1943.
Serial allocations – P921-957, PP969-999, PR115-156, PR170-215, PR228-271, PR285-334
Built as MkIII between August and December 1944. First delivered PP921 6 September 1944, last PR330 & 334 20 January 1945

Fourth order for 300 Seafire Mk III
Dated January 1944.
Serial allocations – RX156-194, RX210-256, RX268-313, RX368-415, RX428-469, RX481-530
160 built (RX156-RX353) between December 1944 and July 1945, remainder cancelled 10 March 1944. First delivered RX156 20 January 1945, last RX353 9 July.

Fifth order for 140 Seafire Mk XV
Dated February 1944.
Serial allocations – SR446-493, SR516-547, SR568-611, SR630-645
Built as Mk XV between August 1944 and April 1945. First delivered SR446 31 August 1944, last SR645 30 June 1945.

Sixth order for 503 Seafire Mk XV
Dated March 1944.
Serial allocations – SW781-828, SW844-879, SW896-939, SW951-993, SX111-139, SX152-201, SX220-256, SX271-316, SX332-370, SX386-432, SX451-490, SX503-546
Cancelled from contract:- SW922-939, SW951-985, SX390-432, SX451-490, SX503-546
Built as Mks XV and XVII between April and November 1945.

Part Four

Cunliffe-Owen Aricraft Ltd.
Contract No. Air/2777/C.23(c)
First Order for 250 Seafire Mk III
Dated 5th January 1943.
Serial allocations – NN333-367, NN379-418, NN431-476, NN488-528, NN452-586, NN599-641
Built as Mk III between December 1943 and November 1944
Second order for 150 Seafire Mk III
Dated July 1943.
Serial allocations – PR338-379, PR391-436, PR449-479, PR492-522
Built as Mk XV between December 1944 and May 1945. First delivered PR338 21 March 1945, last PR505 22 January 1946
Third order for 200 Seafire Mk XV
Dated February 1944.
Serial allocations – Probably ran from SN762-SR369
Contract amended to 50 Mk XV and 20 Mk XVIII
Serial allocations – SP136-168, SP181-197, SP323-327, SP341-355
Built as Mks XV and XVII between June and December 1945

SPITFIRE ENGINES

Appendix VI

Without the Merlin engine the Spitfire would have probably never progressed beyond the design stage for, initially, it had been proposed to install an uprated Goshawk with all the complications of a combined, evaporatively cooled system supplemented by a small retractable radiator. Like the Spitfire, the Merlin was a progressive development which had its roots in the Kestrel series of the mid-1920s. By the end of that decade Rolls-Royce had taken the decision to produce as a private venture an enlarged version of the Kestrel. At almost the same period development work had begun on a second engine which was to influence the design of the Spitfire. The engine was, of course, the Griffon, a development of the 'R' Type racing engine.

The following potted history traces progress of both Merlin and Griffon engines in so far as they influenced the Spitfire/Seafire airframe.

19 March 1932. First design of integral cylinder block and crankcase – Kestrel size – issued. Known as the PV.G, later to be scaled up to the PV.12. PV.G designer was S.F. Pottinger.

26 October 1932. first design scheme of an inverted engine completed, tentatively called 'Merlin'. Design completed at end of April 1933. Detail design not completed but wooden mock-up built. See photographs on page 17.

6 January 1933. First Griffon engine (Mk I), a derivative of Schneider 'R' engine which commenced bench tests. This engine was specified as an alternative to the Goshawk in the F 7/30 – K2890 – to power it in the England to Australia Air Race.

Early 1933. Work commenced in drawing office to scale up the PV.G engine to produce the PV.12. Integral crankcase and cylinder block construction with a detachable 'pancake' cylinder head and double helical reduction gears. The pancake head was superseded later by the ramp type which was retained up to the introduction of the Merlin II. Merlin I production engines (190 units) had the ramp head, and the integral cylinder block and crankcase was discarded before production started. Also, the double helical reduction gears driving the propeller were abandoned in favour of straight spur gears following frequent failure ofthe original gears.

7 April 1933. First detail drawings of the PV.12 engine issued to work shops.

22 April 1933. Sir Henry Royce died.

10 May 1933. Design completed for an epicyclic reduction gear for contra-rotating propellors on PV.12.

31 August 1933. Flight tests started on Hart K2969 with Kestrel VI fitted with rams horn exhaust manifolds of low drag profile and noise and flame suppression. These were specified for the F 7/30 modified design to Supermarine Specification 425. Trials also determined characteristics of high temperature glycol cooling. (See page 15 for drawing of F 7/30 with rams horn exhaust.)

15 October 1933. First bench run of PV.12 development engine. Two built Nos 1 and 2.

July 1934. 100 hours type test completed. International power 790hp @ 2,500rpm @ 12,000ft. Rated boost 2⅝lb, take off power 625hp, dry weight 1,177lb. July to October 1934. Design work on ramp type cylinder head for PV.12 completed and issued to works.

21 January 1935. First design issued for a two speed supercharger for Merlin after completion of 12 months development of two speed blower for Kestrel and Goshawk.

27 February 1935. Bench development started on Merlin 'B' engine, 950hp @ 11,000ft. After 50 hours' running decision made to produce separate crankcase and cylinder blocks owing to casting failures on PV.12 engines.

April 1935. first two Merlin 'C' engines accepted for development tests. These were Merlin 'B' conversions with separate cylinder blocks and separate ramp type head. Also, separate crankcase in which top half was integral with rear half of the reduction gear casing. Dry weight 1,241lb.

12 April 1935. First flight of PV.12 (No 1) in Hart K3036. Original installation composite cooling with a condenser in centre section of top wing, plus a ventral exposed radiator. This composite cooling was originally incorporated into the F37/34 proposal presented to the Air Ministry by Mitchell on 5 December 1934. After eight hours' flying the cooling system was converted to glycol.

May 1935. Attempted civil type test on Merlin 'C'. International rating 955hp @ 2,600rpm @ 11,000ft. Maximum power rating 1,045 @ 3,000rpm @ 12,000ft. 10 October 1935. Acceptance test on first Merlin 'E' engine. This differed from the 'C' in respect of the coolant circulation.

December 1935. 50 hours civil type test on Merlin 'E' completed.

21 December 1935. 50 hours' civil type test on Merlin 'E' completed.

21 December 1935. First flight of Merlin 'C' in Horsley S1436. Rated power 950hp @ 2,600rpm @ 11,000ft. Full throttle power 1,000hp @ 3,000rpm @ 15,000ft.

Appendix VI

Engine	MoS Experimental Nomenclature	Speed 1 = single 2 = two	Supercharger stages 1 = single 2 = two	Propeller reduction gear ratio	Max boost lb sq in	Spit = Spitfire Sea = Seafire	Starting E = electric C = Coffman	Remarks
Merlin II	RM 1S	1	1	.477	+12	Spit I, II	E	100% glycol
Merlin II	RM 1S	1	1	.477	+12	Spit I	E	100% glycol early prod a/c
Merlin V	RM 1S	1	1	.477	+12	Spit I	E	100% glycol converted Merlin III
Merlin X	RM 1SM	2	1	.42	+10		E	
Merlin XII	RM 3S	1	1	.477	+12½	Spit II	C	
Merlin XX	RM 3SM	2	1	.42	+14MS +16FS		E	specified for Spit Mk III
Merlin 32	RM 5M	1	1	.477	+18	Spit PRXIII Sea I, II, III	C	
Merlin 45	RM 5S	1	1	.477	+16	Spit V Sea I, II, III	E	
Merlin 45M	RM 5S	1	1	.477	+18	Spit LF V	E	cropped supercharger rotor
Merlin 46	RM 6S	1	1	.477	+16	Spit V Sea IIC	E	increased dia supercharger impeller
Merlin 47	RM 6S	1	1	.477	+16	Spit VI	E	with cabin blower drive
Merlin 50	RM 5S	1	1	.477	+16	Spit V	E	diaphram controlled fuel feed; deleted later for RAE anti-G
Merlin 50A	RM 6S	1	1	.477	+16	Spit V	E	carb as M50
Merlin 50M	RM 5S	1	1	.477	+18	Spit LF V	E	cropped supercharger rotor
Merlin 55	RM 5S	1	1	.477	+16	Sea I, II, III	E	two piece cylinder block
Merlin 55A	RM 5S	1	1	.477	+16	Spit V	E	modified M50
Merlin 55M	RM 5S	1	1	.477	+18	Spit LF V Sea I, II, III	E	cropped supercharger rotor
Merlin 55MA	RM 5S	1	1	.477	+18	Spit V	E	two piece cylinder blocks
Merlin 56	RM 6S	1	1	.477	+16	Spit VI	E	carb as M50
Merlin 61	RM 8SM	2	2	.42	+15	Spit IX	E	
Merlin 63	RM 8SM	2	2	.477	+18	Spit VIII Spit IX Spit PRXI	E	similar to M61 but no cabin blower
Merlin 63A	RM 8SM	2	2	.477	+18	Spit VIII Spit IX	E	M63 with M64 crankcase & no cabin blower
Merlin 64	RM 8SM	2	2	.477	+18	Spit VII Spit PRX	E	similar M63 plus cabin blower drive
Merlin 66	RM 10SM	2	2	.477	+18	Spit VIII Spit LF IX	E	similar M63 with Bendix Stromberg injection carb & interconnected controls
Merlin 66-68	—	2	2	.477	+18	Spit IX	E	for Turkish Air Force injection carb
Merlin 70	RM 11SM	2	2	.477	+18	Spit VIII Spit HF IX Spit PR XI	E	injection carb & higher supercharger drive gear ratios
Merlin 110	RM 16SM	2	2	.4707	+18	Spit project	E	
Merlin 112	RM 16SM	2	2	.4707	+18	Spit project	E	as M110 with cabin blower
Merlin 266	RM 10SM	2	2	.479	+18	Spit IX Spit XVI	E	Packard-built M66

All Merlin engines were pressure cooled with 70% water, 30% glycol except where defined

MS = medium supercharged

FS = fully supercharged

Fuel 100/140 octane unless defined

A number of Merlin 66 engines for S.O.O. (special order only) converted to +25lb boost (Basta) limited service life

Engine	MoS Experimental Nomenclature	Speed 1 = single 2 = two	Supercharger stages 1 = single 2 = two 3 = three	Propeller reduction gear ratio	Max boost lb sq in	Spit = Spitfire Sea = Seafire Spite = Spiteful Seaf = Seafang	Starting E = electric C = Coffman	Remarks
Griffon 3	RG 2SM	2	1	.451	+12	Spit XII	C	
Griffon 4	RG 2SM	2	1	.51	+12	Spit XII	C	increased ratio prop red. gear
Griffon 6	RG 14SM	2	1	.51	+15	Sea XV Sea XVII Sea XVIII	C	coarse pitch prop controls
Griffon 26	RG 14SM	2	1	.4423	+15	Sea XV Sea XVII project	C	
Griffon 36	RG 23SM	2	1	.51	+18	Sea XV project	C	
Griffon 61	RG 4SM	2	2	.451	+18	Spit 21 Spit 22 Sea 45 Sea 46 Sea 47	C	inter connected prop/ throttle controls
Griffon 62	RG 4SM	2	2	.451	+18@	Sea 46 Spit 21 projects	C C	R-R injection pump +25lb boost
Griffon 64	RG 4SM	2	2	.451	+18@	Spit 21 Spit 22 Sea 46	C	as G62 with Bendix Strom carb
Griffon 65	RG 4SM	2	2	.51	+18@	Spit XIV FR XIV Spit XVIII FR XVIII	C	S.O.O.
Griffon 66	RG 4SM	2	2	.51	+18	Spit PR XIX	C	G65 with cabin blower
Griffon 67	RG 4SM	2	2	.51	+18@	Spit XIV FR XIV Spit XVIII FR SVIII	C	G65 no cabin blower
Griffon 68	RG 4SM	2	2	.51	+18@	Spit PR XIX project	C	G66 with cabin blower drive
Griffon 69	RG 4SM	2	2	.451	+18@	Spite XIV	C	modified G64
Griffon 70	RG 4SM	2	2	.451	+18@	Spite project	C	G69 with R-R injection pump
Griffon 85	RG 4SM	2	2	.4423	+18	Spit XIV Spit 21 Sea 46	C	G65 with contra props
Griffon 86	RG 4SM	2	2	.442	+18	Spit XIV Spit PR 21 project	C	G85 with cabin blower drive
Griffon 87	RG 4SM	2	2	.4423	+18@	Spit XIV Spit 21 Sea 46	C	G85 with +25lb boost
Griffon 88	RG 4SM	2	2	.4423	+18@	Seaf Spit FR XIV Spit 21	C	G87 with R-R injection pump
Griffon 89	RG 4SM	2	2	.4423	+18@	Seaf 31	C	G87
Griffon 90	RG 4SM	2	2	.4423	+18@	Seaf	C	G89 with R-R injection pump
Griffon 101	RG 3SML	2	3	.451	+18@	Spit 21 Sea 46 project Spite XIV	C	basic Griffon with 3-speed supercharger
Griffon 102	RG 3SML	2	3	.45	+18@	Spite PR Spit 21 project	C	G101 with cabin blower no intercon controls
Griffon 105	RG 3SML	2	3	.51	+18@	Spit project	C	G102
Griffon 121	RG 3SML	2	3	.4423	+18@	Spit 21 project	C	G101 with contra props
Griffon 122	RG 3SML	2	3	.442	+18@	Spit PR 21 Sea 46 project	C	G121 with cabin blower drive

@ +25lb boost when using 115/150 octane fuel

S.O.O. = Special order only

27 March 1936. Heinkel He70, Kestrel V, delivered to Rolls-Royce.

3 March 1936. First design issued of one piece flat head with cylinder block for Merlin.

16 July 1936. First flight of Merlin 'F' in Horsley J8611. To Farnborough on 29th for 100 hour flight endurance trials, terminated by engine failure.

25 July 1936. First production Merlin I (RM.1S) .477 reduction gear and 5¾lb boost delivered. Not used in Spitfire.

6 September 1936. 100 hour flight endurance trials of Merlin 'F' at Hucknall started in Horsley S1436. Completed 12 October.

September 1936. Service type test completed on Merlin 'G'.

22 September 1936. Acceptance test on Merlin 'G'. Designation – Merlin II (RM.1S) .477 reduction gear, 12lb boost. Specified for Spitfire Mk I.

November 1936. 100 hours flight endurance trials at Hucknall with Merlin 'G'. Terminated by piston failure on 18th.

November 1936. Service type test completed on Merlin 'F'. 975hp @ 2,600rpm @ 12,500ft.

18 November 1936. 200 hour flight endurance at RAE of Merlin I in Horsley J8611. Completed 13 April 1937. Rated output 970hp @ 2,600rpm @ 12,500ft.

18 November 1936. 200 hour flight endurance at RAE of Merlin I in Horsley J8611. Completed 13 April 1937. Rated output 970hp @ 2,600rpm @ 12,500ft.

June 1937. 400 hour flight endurance at RAE of Merlin II in Horsley J8611. Completed in February 1938.

7 August 1937. Bench development work started on Merlin for short period full throttle running for Speed Spitfire N-17. 2,160hp @ 3,200rpm @ 27lb boost.

10 August 1937. First production Merlin II delivered.

7 September 1937. First flight of Merlin with two speed supercharger in Horsley S1436 at Hucknall. Maximum take off 2,850rpm @ 5⅞lb boost. Rated altitude MS gear 2,000ft, FS gear 11,700ft. Full throttle height MS 5,200ft, FS 16,000ft.

During 1937 the initial flight test and development of a pressurised water cooled Merlin commenced.

1 July 1938. First production Merlin III (RM.1S) delivered. .477 reduction gear, 12lb boost. Specified for late production Spitfire Mk I.

5 December 1938. First production Merlin X (RM.1SM) delivered. .42 reduction gear, 10lb boost. Used in prototype Spitfire Mk III.

1 January 1939. Planning commenced on 37.V12 engine (Griffon II).

24 September 1939. First production Merlin XII (RM.3SM) delivered. .477 reduction gear, 12½lb boost. Specified for Spitfire Mk II.

1 March 1940. Planning commenced on two stage blowers for inter cooler adapted to Merlin. Original work for Merlin 60.

26 June 1940. First bench test of Griffon II (RG.2SM). .451 reduction gear, 12lb boost.

4 July 1940. First Merlin XX (RM.3SM) delivered. .42 reduction gear, 12lb boost. Specified for Spitfire MK III.

14 August 1940. Planning commenced on Bendix-Stromberg carburetter adapted to Merlin XX. Drawings of XX sent to America to form basis of Packard-Merlin 28 engine.

7 January 1941. First bench test of Griffon IIB.

25 April 1941. First bench test of Merlin 60 engine (Merlin XII conversion).

13 January 1941. First production Merlin 45 (RM.5S) delivered. .477 reduction gear, 16lb boost. Specified for Spitfire Mk V.

April 1941. Planning commenced on Griffon 61.

12 July 1941. First flight of inter-cooled Merlin 60 in Wellington Mk VI.

17 August 1941. First bench test of Merlin 61.

19 August 1941. First flight of Merlin 60 in Spitfire Mk III prototype, NS3297.

21 November 1941. First production Merlin 60 delivered.

2 December 1941. First production Merlin 47 delivered.

2 March 1942. First production Merlin 61 delivered.

31 March 1942. First production Griffon II delivered.

25 April 1942. First production Merlin 62 delivered.

17 June 1942. First production Merlin 32 delivered.

'Basta' was the code name for Merlin engines modified by Special Order Only (SOO) to permit operation at 25lb boost. This was to enable the Spitfire to operate at low altitude when chasing the V1 'Doodle-Bug' unmanned flying bomb. With 'Basta' engine life was limited and it could only be used with 150 octane fuel, coloured purple to distinguish it from the normal 100 octane, coloured green.

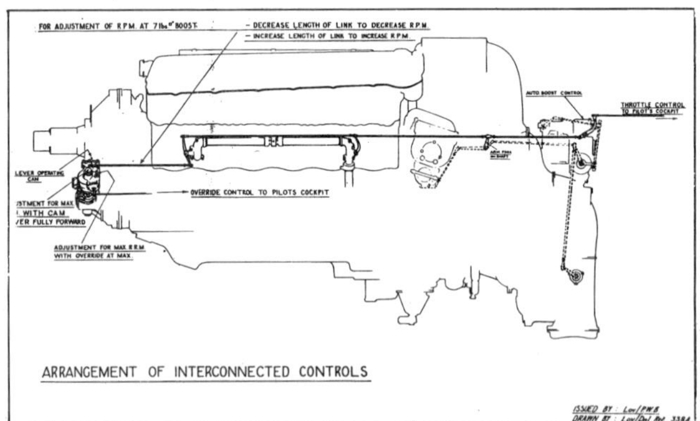

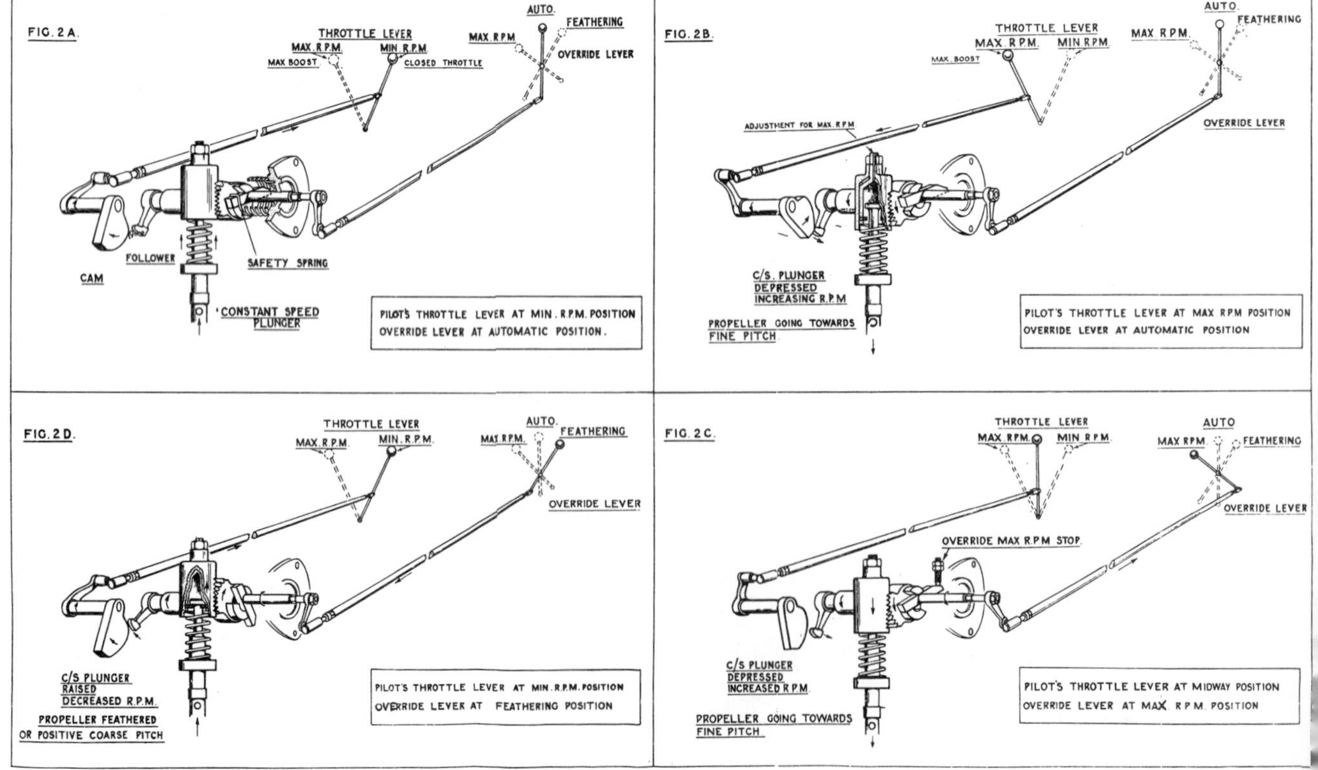

PRODUCTION AND DISPERSAL

When full scale production of the Spitfire finally got under way it was centred on the Supermarine Woolston works, with main assembly and flight testing at Eastleigh Aerodrome. Additional capacity was required and a new factory was erected in 1938 on land re-claimed from the River Itchen. These two factories built complete fuselages and wings and sub-contractors, as mentioned in Chapter One, supplied major components. The persons responsible for planning the sub-contracting scheme were W. Elliot, Works Superintendent, and L.G. Gooch. Gooch had joined Supermarine in November 1935 from the Southern Railway at Eastleigh to work in the Project Office and in December 1939 was appointed Works Engineer. One of his first duties was to plan a local dispersal scheme in the Southampton area, and during the first few months of 1940 his assistant, G. Ilsen, was to organise the production of the Spitfire in small factories and workshops employing people who had not been trained as skilled aircraft fitters.

The Battle of Britain started in July 1940 and Gooch realised it was only a matter of time before the main works were attacked and began moving a number of the vital production units to sequestered buildings in Southampton. The jig and tool department was moved to Sewards Garage on 10 September and wing production transferred to the Hants and Dorset bus garage nine days later. Fuselage and fuel tank jigs went to another garage, Hendys, on the 16th and yet another garage, Lowthers, became a machine shop and toolroom on the 20th. Gooch's insurance plan was seen to be working, and just in time, for the first Lufwaffe raid on the Southampton area took place on 23 August when twelve He111s, flying low, dropped a stick of bombs without damage to the factory.

Eastleigh airfield was dive bombed by six Stukas in late afternoon on 11 September, killing 49 and injuring 92. A direct hit straddled two main shelters but they were empty at the time. Four days later a formation of fifteen Bf 110s attacked Woolston and dropped a total of 23 heavy bombs which missed the factory and badly damaged surrounding property. The factory was slightly damaged by blast. During lunch time on the 24th 17 enemy bombers slipped across the coast before the alert was sounded and attacked both Itchen and Woolston, one bomb hitting a shelter killing a large number of employees. A second attack followed, the main target being Itchen, but damage was confined to neighbouring property.

Two days later the Luftwaffe made a determined effort and two waves of He111s of KG55 raided the Supermarine complexes. The RAF fighters were engaged by the bombers' escort, allowing them to make their run over the factories in perfect formation. Sixty bombs struck Itchen and 80 Woolston, both factories being devastated, resulting in a large number of deaths and injuries. Fighter Command engaged Nos 152, 229, 238, 602 and 609 Squadrons. No 303 Polish Squadron arrived in time to catch the fleeing bombers.

Production of the Mk I Spitfire was halted, but the Mk II was coming into full production at Castle Bromwich. Lord Beaverbrook met the Supermarine executives and as a result a major dispersal scheme consisting of four, separate production lines was initiated. Gooch moved his staff into Polygon Hotel, Southampton, the day after the raid to start planning and the possible areas of production, complete with an airfield for test flying the completed aircraft, were identified as Salisbury, Reading and Trowbridge. High Post, Henley and Keevil airfields coped with final asssembly of airframes and test flying, and at a later date Chattis Hill was converted by the erection of final assembly hangars and an airstrip. Eventually there were 65 units spread over Southern England of which 46 were devoted to production, and the remainder to support units.

The schematic, overleaf, shows (1) the chain of command and (2) the complete dispersal companies. As the listing reveals there were many unlikely candidates chosen to build parts or complete units, including garages, laundries, bus stations, etc. One of the main Southampton units, Hendys, was badly damaged a few days after the major raid on the main works, and the work force had to be dispersed, but three months later it was back in full production. In overall command was Commander James Bird, who was to be appointed General Manager in September 1941, long after the scheme had started, and Gooch was third in the chain.

Attaching the top plating to the tailplane. The wooden strips for attaching the bottom plating by screws are seen clearly.

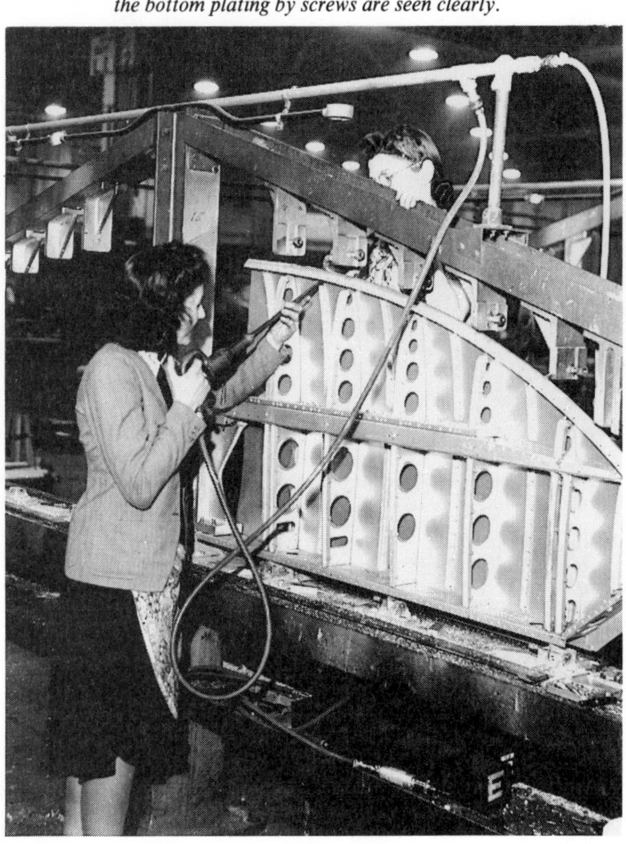

The main wing jig assembly unit. The leading edge rests on felt blocks inside the jig. P7370, a Mk II, went to 74 Squadron at Biggin Hill and was shot down by a Bf109 over Maidstone, Kent, on 20 October 1940. The pilot baled out but died of his wounds later.

Dispersals Organisation

Commander James Bird, General Manager

W Elliot, Works Superintendent

L Gooch, Works Manager

V Hall, Manager, Trowbridge

Forestreet Garage	details & fittings
Rutland Garage	pipes & coppersmiths
Southwick Works	leading edges
Red Triangle Club	canteen
Haverton Cloth Mills	raw material, finished parts stores
Bolton Glove Factory	Westbury area assembly
Hilperton Road Factory	sub assemblies & details
Bradley Road Factory	wings, sub assemblies tool room mould loft
RAF Keevil aerodrome	final assembly & flight test
Curries Garage	completed fuselage store
Moore's Garage	transport dept
Eyken's garage	transport dept

T Barby, Manager, Newbury

Stradling's Garage	detail fittings
Pass Garage	process dept
Nias Garage	toolmakers
Nias Garage	stores
Venture Bus Garage	stores
Mill Lane	sub assemblies
Shaw Works	press & machine shop
Hungerford Garage	machine shop

W Heaver, Manager, Salisbury

Wilts & Dorset Bus garage	wings
Wessex garage	fuselages, tail units, leading edges
Anna Valley garage	tail units, sub assemblies
Chattis Hill Racing Gallops	final assembly & test flight
Chattis Hill airfield	engine overhauls
High Post aerodrome hangar	final assembly, flight test
High Post	experimental & communications flight
High Post Hotel	canteen & accommodation
W H Smith High Street	canteen
Castle Garage	transport
Castle Road No 1 factory	fuselage, engine installation
Castle Road No 2	leading edge, wings
Castle Road No 1	canteen
Castle Road Office	accommodation, admin.

K Scales, Manager, Reading

Vincent's Garage	fuselages, details, sub assemblies
Great Western Garage	wings
Caversham Factory	fuselages, engine installation
Henley Aerodrome	final assembly, flight test
RAF Aldermaston	final assembly, flight test

A Nelson, Manager, Southampton

Holly Brook Stores	stores
Holt House	inspection & AID
Sunlight Laundry	detail & sub assembly
Austin House garage	tank covering & training
Chiswell's garage	press shop & sheet metal details
Short's garage	machine shop
Southend House	accounts
RNAS Worthy Down	final assembly flying & experimental flying
Leigh Road stores	stores
Garratt's garage	transport workshop repairs
Hendy's garage	pre-production
Marwell Hall	finished components
Park Place	WVS rivet sorting
Sholing Store	finished parts stores
Botley Store	finished parts store
Bishops Waltham Store	finished parts store
Sleepy Hollow Barn	accounts records stores
Hants & Dorset garage	wing assembly
Lowther's garage	toolroom
Weston Rolling Mills	tanks & pipes
Newtown Works	woodwork & metal assemblies
Hendy's S'ton	fuselage assembly & tank manufacture
Hursley Road Stores	central stores, raw materials & finished parts
Hursley Park	experimental
Hursley Park House	administration
Wonston Stores	embodiment loan

Fuselages at Eastleigh after painting and application of national markings.

Drilling the leading edge skin before stretching.

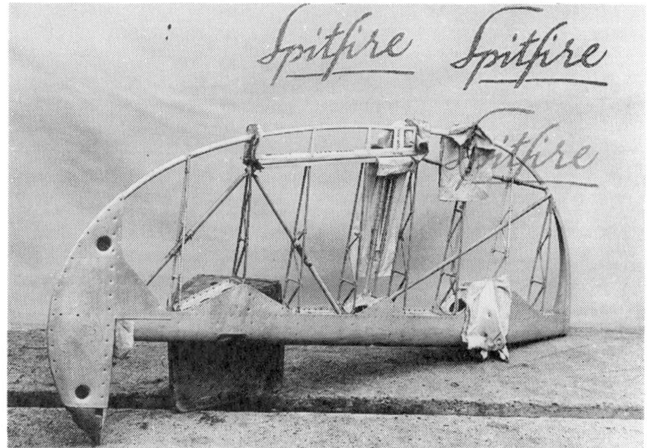

Sewing and doping Spitfire rudders and ailerons.

Engine installation.

The demand for Spitfires was incessant and new variants kept appearing on a regular basis, and to meet this demand it was decided to build new, purpose-built factories. Ten were finally constructed- Hungerford (1). Reading (2). Newbury (2). Salisbury (2). Trowbridge (3). Production engineering and tool design was concentrated on Hursley Park. In order that more efficient use could be made of the dispersal scheme production of the various marks were concentrated into selected areas. Southampton built the V, VI, VIII, IX and XIV. Salisbury handled the V, IX, XII, XIV and the Seafire. Trowbridge boosted Southampton's production with the V, IX, XII, XIV and Reading the IX and XIV, but was also heavily committed to the photo-reconnaissance marks IV, XIX.

A major problem was housing for the dispersed work force, for although local labour in the vicinity of the various units was available, large numbers of trained, key staff had to be found accommodation. All these problems were eventually overcome and a total of 8,000 Spitfires built by the Southampton dispersal scheme. The Castle Bromwich factory had a similar scheme, one that was much smaller than Southampton for the Birmingham plant was much larger and did not need the same volume of support. Test flying for CB Spitfires was from Cosford and Desford.

The Spitfire was not an easy aeroplane to build for it was a mass of ellipses and curves which made for difficulties in large scale production. Had Michell been possessed of foresight he might not have designed the aeroplane with an elliptical wing, but he could have scarcely envisaged in 1935 a production run that eventually totalled over 22,000 units, each requiring many thousands of man hours to build. It is to the credit of Joseph Smith and the many hundreds of design and production staff that this tremendous project was fulfilled.

In addition to production problems was the dispersal programmes, rebuilding bombed factories, the test programme and the continuous modification and production of new variants. All these were overcome to keep the Spitfire in the van of progress.

The fuselage was a monocoque structure built in three major sections (a) engine mounting (b) main fuselage from frame five (firewall) to frame 19 (stern tail unit attachment) and (c) stern section which included the fin. The main fuselage consisted of frames 5 to 19, the first being a solid structure sandwich of aluminium and asbestos to which was attached- at the bottom- stub spars for attachment of the outer wing sections. Aft of this from frames 6 to 10 was the cockpit section produced as a separate unit. Frame 5 and the cockpit unit were then located on a jig together with frames 11 to 19, and the whole built as the basic fuselage skeleton by the positioning of

Out of the wing jigs for internal gear assembly.

Final fuselage assembly at Itchen. At this stage the internal gear was being installed.

View towards the stern depicts oxygen bottles, the control cable runs, main frames, longerons and intercostal stringers.

Plating in the fuselage jigs.

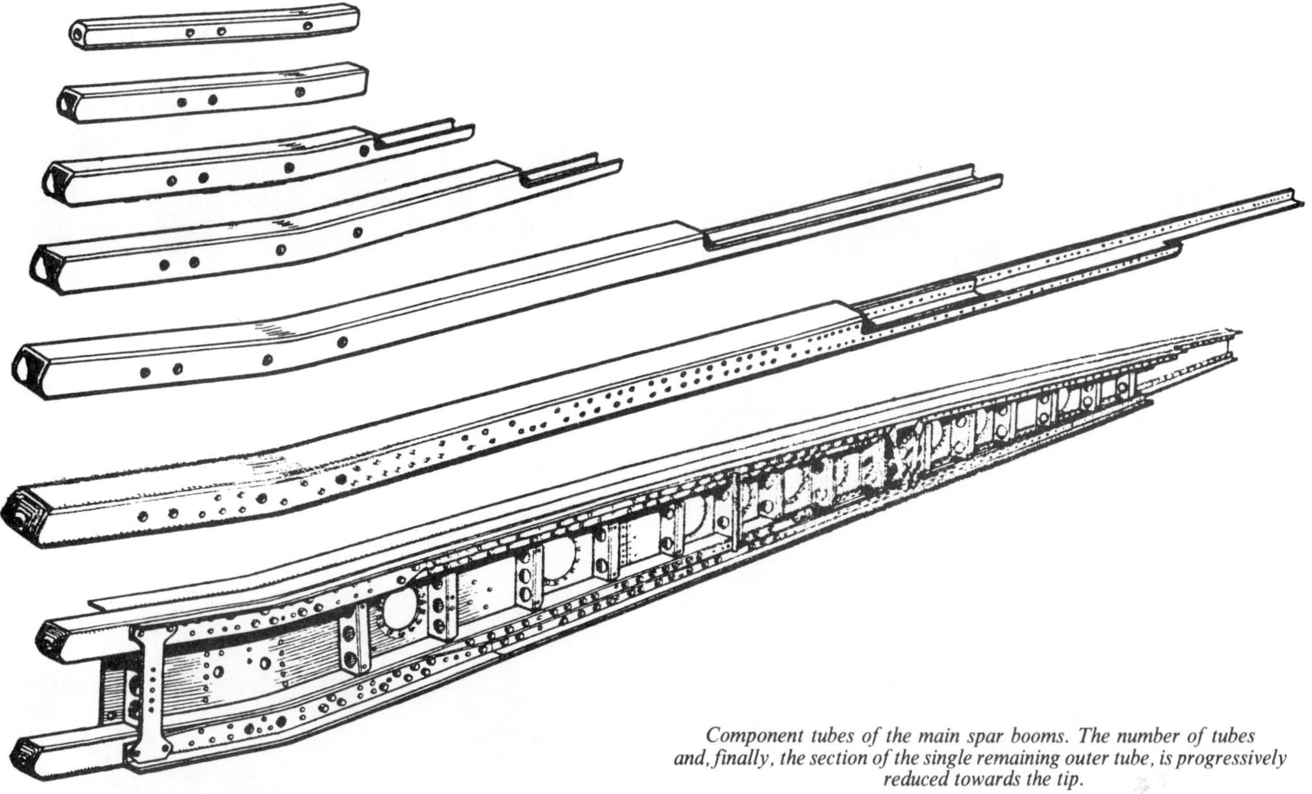

Component tubes of the main spar booms. The number of tubes and, finally, the section of the single remaining outer tube, is progressively reduced towards the tip.

Above: Late production Mk VBs, Castle Bromwich. Below: F Mk 21 and 24s.

Bomb damage after the September raid on Woolston and Itchen.

Bradley Road Works, Trowbridge, undertook fuselage assembly. Mk IXs/XVIs.

Chattis Hill Winchester was used in association with High Post for final assembly and test flying. Under construction are F Mk VBs.

The Itchen Works at Southampton, major unit of the original Supermarine factory complex. In the background Stranraer and Walrus.

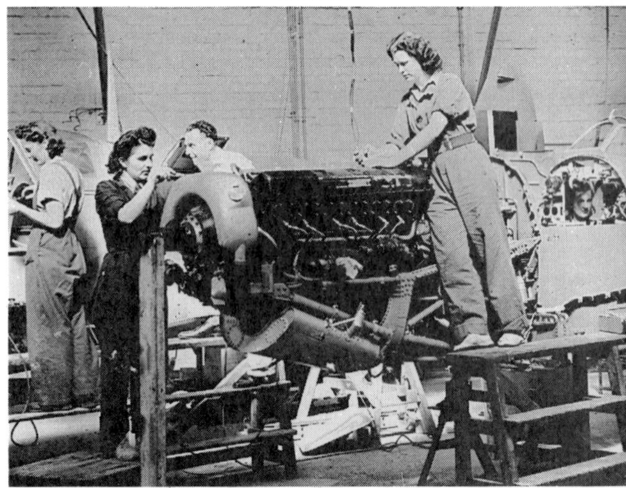

The Castle Road Works in Salisbury where fuselage assembly took place. It is interesting to note that 45% of the work force for the dispersal scheme were women.

Experimental hangar at High Post Aerodrome was typical of the dispersal scheme units.

Aldermaston superceded Henley as a final assembly and flight test facility. View shows the main hangar.

the two bottom V-section main longerons, The top V-section longerons and the side, bowler hat shaped short longerons which ran from frame 5 to frame 14.

The top engine bearer pick-ups were bolted to the ends of the side longerons with the bottom pick-ups bolted to the wing stub spar on the bottom longerons. This skeleton assembly was then located into a main fuselage jig and held rigidly while the intercostal stringers and plating were rivetted into position to complete the monocoque. The plating was 24, 20 and 18 gauge, reducing in that order of thickness towards the stern end. Flush rivetting was specified for the plating from frame 5 to the rear of the cockpit, after which the round, snap head type was used. The points between the skin panels over the same section were joggled so as to present a flush surface, and after the cockpit were lapped.

The monocoque was then removed from the main assembly jig to a second jig where the various holes for wing attachment were reamed and the wing fillets added. It was then cleaned to remove all extraneous material and sent to the paint spraying shops to receive its priming and final coats of Brown and Green camouflage paint, after which it was ready for final assembly.

The rear fuselage also contained the fin. It consisted of frame 19, an L-section former which bolted onto the true frame 19 of the main fuselage structure. Behind this was frame 20, the rearmost and final fuselage frame, and immediately aft of this was the first of three fin posts, frame 21. Frame 22 formed the face of the tail wheel opening and frame 23 was the third and final frame to which the rudder was hung. All the frames were located in a jig and the horizontal fin formers, eight in total, were rivetted to them. Short longerons ran from frame 19 to 20 and the whole was then plated with 22 gauge material.

Singer Motors was the original company to supply the complete Spitfire engine mounting, which was mainly a tubular structure strengthened by a large, rigid frame which formed the central transverse member. The frame was built as a separate sub-assembly, the main bearers consisting of two cranked tubes extending from the front mounting block, through the transverse frame and attaching to the bottom mounting fittings on fuselage frame 5. Assembly was completed in a jig with the mounting in an inverted position.

The tailplane was a straightforward assembly consisting of two spars and a leading edge carrying the sheet metal ribs. Only one side of each rib was flanged for attaching the plating, the other side having wooden strips shaped to the curve of the ribs. When the first side was rivetted the facing side was then screwed to the wooden rib strips. The plating was 24 gauge metal. The finished tailplane and stern sections was then assembled as a unit for final assembly to the fuselage. The elevator and rudder structures were virtually identical, apart from shape and size, for both used similar jigs and manufacturing procedures.

The Spitfire wing was a complicated structure and built around the massive leading edge torsion box. This was a D shaped section based on the front spar which formed, with the leading edge, the major wing unit. The rear spar was a light subsidiary member connecting the trailing portions of the ribs. The main spar was based upon two booms of square section built up from a number of extruded tubes fitting inside each other. At the root the boom was almost solid and was formed of five tubes. The centre tube was filled in with a solid bar 19 inches long, through which was drilled along the length a hole of $\frac{1}{2}$ inch diameter. As the spar progressed towards the tip the inner tubes were terminated, beginning with the innermost. When the tip was reached only the two outer tubes remained and they were cutaway on the upper section to form a channel section, and after another two feet this was reduced to a single section cut away on one side to form a simple angle section. The booms were made to very fine limits by the Reynolds Tubes Company, which supplied the completed boom unit, cranked to give the necessary wing dihedral and ready for assembly. To the rear face of the spar booms was rivetted a single web plate flanged at top and bottom to form a channel section. Angles for the attachment of the leading edge skin were rivetted along the front faces on the booms.

The leading edge skin was made in two sections which were butted together and rivetted to a nosing strip on the inside. Spanwise, the skin was stiffended by intercostal Z section members. Twenty-one nose ribs of lattice and open girder construction provided chordwise support. The leading edge skin was formed on a stretching press from a single blank of 14 gauge duraluminium and when rivetted to the spar booms the rivets were hammered into a counter sunk hole, the heads being removed with a pneumatic chisel. The gun ports were then cut out and following this the leading edge and spar booms were brought together in a jig.

The next operation was fitting the pintle (a large, two diameter pin) for the pivot of the undercarriage leg to the rear of the spar web. The cannon bay structure for the VBs and other cannon armed Spitfires, was built as a separate unit in its own jig and both this, and the leading edge structure, were then transferred to the main wing structure main assembly jig. Two wings, port and starboard, were built at the same time and assembled with the leading edge in the downwards position. Wing ribs numbers one to 21 were located in the jig and the rear spar assembled to them in sections. The trailing edge ribs were rivetted to the rear spar with the rear ends connected by a duralumin trailing edge strip. After the radiator bay and wheel wells had been placed into position and secured the upper surface plating was attached by first drilling through the ribs and rivetting into position. The under surface was more difficult and was sub-divided into a number of sections.

The internal gear including electrical wiring conduits, aileron control cables and compressed air piping for guns, flaps and landing lamp operation, was then installed. Aileron shrouds were next fitted followed by the undercarriage oleos. They were followed by the landing lamp and wing tips and flaps. The machine gun and gun heating tubing of black cellulose acetate were fitted and left loose at the wing root for connecting to the fuselage. All the access doors were fitted before the entire wing was cleaned. The wings were then painted.

Before final assembly all the internal fuselage gear was installed with the fuselage supported on two jacking points in the base of frame 5 point and at the rear, in a cradle, under frame 18. As the unit was nose heavy at this point the tail was held down by a canvas hoop around the fuselage. The engine mounting was bolted into position followed by the cockpit interior, windscreen and hood. All control surfaces were connected to the control column and last of all the pilot's seat. The oil tank was assembled into position and fuel lines connected up. The Merlin engine was next offered into the mounting and supported at four points, followed by the main fuel tanks. Wings were attached, being brought to the fuselage on trolleys on which they were tilted to the approximate dihedral angle. Heating and control systems were connected and the oil, air, hydraulic and electrical systems tested along with undercarriage retraction and lowering. Final item was the propeller after which the completed aeroplane was filled with fuel before final inspection and test flight.

REPAIR CATEGORIES

Large numbers of damaged Spitfires were repaired and returned to service use and the official scale of damage was covered by Air Publications S.154, which prefaced the classifications thus-

REPAIR CATEGORIES FOR AIRCRAFT

(1) The repair categories for aircraft are used to define the degree of repair to be undertaken by service units or contractors in any of the undermentioned circumstances: (a) following an accident, (b) when the condition of an aircraft is such that the repair is considered to be beyond the normal capability of the holding unit, (c) when the aircraft is reported as being surplus to a command's requirements, in accordance with AP3158.

Pre 1941 the categories were- undamaged U; can be repaired on site by unit M(u); repair beyond unit capacity M(c); beyond repair on site, dismantle to repair factory R(B); write-off W; In addition there were prefixes (sometimes shown as suffixes) to indicate cause. FA-n flying accident; FB- operational loss; GA- ground accident; T- technical cause, e.g. engine failure or structural collapse; EA- enemy action. These categories changed slightly between 1941-52- undamaged U; can be repaired by unit A; repair beyond unit capacity AC; beyond repair on site B; to be ground instructional airframe C; write-off E; to components E.1; to scrap E.2; burned out E.3; missing on sortie Em.

From 1952-61 the categories changed once again. Category 1, aircraft undamaged and can remain in service; cat 2 aircraft repairable within second line servicing capacity of the parent of nearest unit; cat 3(Rep) C or cat 3 (Rep) S, aircraft repairable on site but work beyond second line capacity. Aircraft will be repaired by contractor's working party (C) or RSU (S) as decided by Headquarters Maintenance Command; cat 3 (Rep) C Fly or cat 3(Rep) S Fly, aircraft to be flown to contracter's works (C) or suitable service unit (S) if necessary after temporary repair and under restricted flight conditions; cat 3 (Rep) C Fly/Deferred or cat 3 (Rep)S Fly/Deferred; aircraft may be flown under conditions specified by the holding unit until suitable repair date as agreed with HMC; cat 4 (Rep); aircraft not repairable on site because special facilities and/or equipment required. Aircraft in this category will be repaired at contractors works if necessary after temporary repair and under resticted flight conditions; cat 4(Rogue); after technical investigation and air test the parent unit and command headquarters are satisfied that it is a rogue aircraft; cat 5(Components); aircraft beyond economical repair, or is surplus, but is recoverable for breakdown to components, other spares and scrap; cat 5(Scrap), aircraft beyond economical repair, or is surplus and fit only for disposal or scrap; cat 5 (Ground instruction); aircraft beyond economic repair, or surplus, but suitable for ground instruction; cat 5 (Missing), aircraft is missing from flight.

There were many other sub categories and these will be found in the list of serial numbers following each major chapter and in the appendix on abbreviations.

Barnes Bros. Southwick Works built the wing leading edge as part of the Trowbridge scheme.

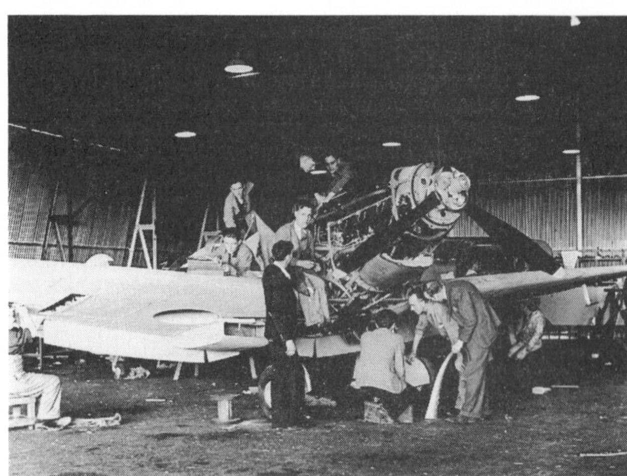

Henley Aerodrome served the Reading Group dispersal and this view shows the final assembly shed.

Outside the experimental flight shed at High Post. Seen are (second from left) a high altitude Spitfire; the two Spitfires to the right of this have five bladed propellers and the new short barrelled Mk V cannon.

Worthy Down was associated with the Winchester area scheme and in this view Jeffrey Quill is seated in a Mk VB fitted with under fuselage slipper fuel tank.

SCHNEIDER TROPHY FLOATPLANES

Although having no direct bearing on the design and development of both F 7/30 and the Type 300 Spitfire, Mitchell drew on his experiences with the Supermarine Schneider Trophy monoplane floatplanes, the requirement for which was to design and construct the smallest airframe consistent with engine power, and to provide enough load capacity for pilot and fuel. This he did with the Supermarine S4, S5, S6 and S6B. This Appendix is concerned only with these four types and the part they played in Mitchell's experience in designing high speed aeroplanes.

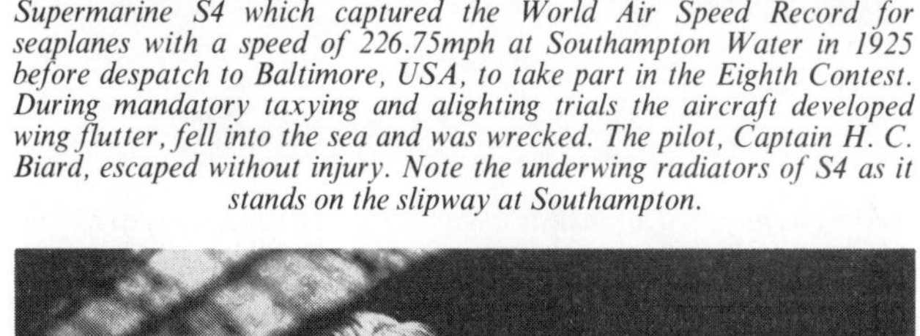

Supermarine S4 which captured the World Air Speed Record for seaplanes with a speed of 226.75mph at Southampton Water in 1925 before despatch to Baltimore, USA, to take part in the Eighth Contest. During mandatory taxying and alighting trials the aircraft developed wing flutter, fell into the sea and was wrecked. The pilot, Captain H. C. Biard, escaped without injury. Note the underwing radiators of S4 as it stands on the slipway at Southampton.

The S4, with Biard in the cockpit, leaving the primitive slipway at Baltimore for trials, during which it crashed.

Henri Biard, Supermarine Chief Test Pilot.

Among those attending the Tenth Contest at Venice was L. Ransome (AID inspector) far left, Major Buchanan (Air Ministry) second left, S. N. Webster (RAF) second from right and R. J. Mitchell, far right.

The S5 was the logical development of the previous aircraft with an all-metal fuselage and wooden wings incorporating the cooling radiators. It was a tiny aeroplane with fuel stored in the starboard float, a practical arrangement providing a bonus in saving space and offsetting the fierce engine torque. Two of the three examples constructed were entered for the race, N219, race number 6 and N220, number 4. The former with a direct drive Napier Lion engine came second at 273.01mph, piloted by Flt/Lt O. E. Worsley; the latter (geared Lion) won the 1927 race at Venice at an average speed of 281.65mph. Pilot was Fly Off S. N. Webster.

The S5 was prepared to make an attempt on the World Air Speed record in March 1928, using the third aircraft N221. The pilot was Kinkead. The tiny cockpit and long engine cowling severely restricted forward view as demonstrated in this photograph.

The record attempt took place on 12 March at Southampton Water and Kinkead is seen stepping into the cockpit of N221 at Calshot ten minutes before making the first run. He was killed soon after take off.

Bearing the race number 5, N219 is towed out for the 1929 race.

The three S6 machines which competed for the 1931 Contest, which took place at Southampton Water. Left to right: S1598 (7); N248 and the eventual winner at 350mph S1595.

The 1931 RAF Team. Left to right: Flt/Lt Hope; Lt Brinton (RN); Flt/Lt Long; Flt/Lt Stainforth; Sqdn Ldr Orlebar; Flt/Lt Bootham who flew the winning aeroplane; Flt Off Snaith and Flt/Lt Dry.

Mitchell and Flt/Lt F. W. Long before the race.

The Schneider Trophy winner and World Air Speed holder S1595 on display at the Motor Show at Olympia in October 1931.

The following table compares general details.

	S4	S5	S6	S6B
Wing span (ft in)	30 7½	26 9	30 0	30 0
Length overall (ft in)	26 7¾	24 3½	26 10	28 10
Length fuselage (ft in)	25 0	22 0½	25 3	25 3
Height (ft in)	11 8½	11 1	12 3	12 3
Wing chord (ft in)	6 0 (root)	5 0	5 8	5 8
	6 3½ (tip)			
Tailplane span (ft in)	8 2	7 9	8 1½	8 1½
Float length (ft in)	18 0	18 6	19 5	24 0
Float track (ft in)	7 6	7 0	7 6	7 6
Wing area (sq ft)	139	115	145	145
Tailplane area (sq ft)	15.8	14	15.8	15
Elevator area (sq ft)	9.5	5.8	6	6
Fin area (sq ft)	5.25	4.50	6	6
Weight (empty) lb	2600	2680	4471	4490
Weight (loaded) lb	3191	3242	5771	6086
Wing loading (lb sq/ft)	23	28	40	41
Power loading (lb hp)	47	36	30.6	26
Maximum speed (mph)	226.75	319.57	357.7	407.5
Landing speed (mph)	85	85	95	95
Fuel (gals)	40	50	106	135
Oil (gals)	5	5	10	15
Water (gals)	10	15	20	25

CAMOUFLAGE AND MARKINGS

The various expansion schemes of the Royal Air Force in the 1930s were far ranging in their broad and detailed requirements, not the least being camouflage colouring, squadron and individual aircraft indentification. The former was designed to make a parked aeroplane less conspicuous; the latter to ease the task of indentifying sister aircraft in the swirl of combat. At the end of World War One Royal Flying Corps aeroplanes were, generally, painted in the drab colours, usually green or khaki, on all upper surfaces, with natural wood or canvas under surfaces. The national markings were on upper and lower wing surfaces with the 'odd' aeroplane painted in the pilot's choice of colours.

By the middle 30s squadron and individual indentification had developed into a complicated system of letters or numbers, squadron heraldry, streamers and other aids. The Air Ministry decided to rationalise and on 31 January 1935 a new system was inaugurated whereby each squadron aeroplane would carry an indentifying letter, which was to be painted in a particular Flight colour, on each side of the fin and rudder. Formation and deputy leaders to have varied shaped and coloured cloth panels on each side of the fuselage in place of the, then, normal wing tip streamers.

The DTD, Verney, wrote to RAE Farnborough on 27 June 1935 asking for trials to test the new system, and he also wrote to the Dunlop Company for the supply of 'Lastex' woven rubber for the fuselage panels. The system was designed to enable a flight, or squadron leader, to transfer his markings to a different aeroplane with the least possible delay if necessary. All undercarriage wheels were to be painted in the Flight colours, these being red, yellow and blue.

RAE were not enamoured with the scheme and suggested that the 'Lastex' panels might prove satisfactory for slow biplanes, but useless for the new, high speed monoplanes then under order in the prototype stage. However, trials were held and the 'Lastex' panels were ripped apart in the aircraft's slipstream. RAE then proposed trials of a new 'temporary paint' (developed at the establishment) which might be more suitable. It was a distemper based material which could be removed by scrubbing with soap and water. It was ready for trials in January 1936 and the problems were immediate. RAF maintenance staff found that although the theory of quickly transferring individual markings by washing of the old with soap and water and painting them on to a second aircraft seemed foolproof, in practice the distemper deteriorated rapidly and had to be continuously renewed; perversely took considerable time and effort to remove; tended to run in heavy rain; added to maintenance and corroded the airframe.

It was back to the laboratory at RAE and by 6 April distemper based material had been abandoned for everything but short term temporary markings, and a permanent cellulose paint developed in collaboration with industry. On 5 March the Spitfire prototype had made its first flight and during modifications that followed it was painted overall in a high gloss grey finish. National markings in the form of Type A red, white and blue roundels of 26 inch diameter appeared on the fuselage, outlined by a circle of white. Fifty inch diameter Type A roundels were applied to upper and lower wing surfaces, while serial numbers were black, eight inch high digits outlined in white on the fuselage and 6 inch on rudder.

By the time K5054 was into its trials programme war appeared to be in the offing and it was decided that all production Royal Air Force fighters would be painted in a disruptive camouflage scheme of Dark Earth and Dark Green on all upper surfaces with sea grey medium under surfaces. A pattern guide in Air Publication 970 specified two schemes know as A and B, the latter a mirror image of A. National markings as specified for K5054 and black serial numbers 48 inches high were to applied under the wings. In the event the large serials were rarely applied to the Spitfire. The date of issue of the new scheme was 20 February 1937 and the first set of official Air Ministry drawings was issued to both Supermarine and Hawker Aircraft by 9 March. Supermarine issued its own camouflage markings scheme to its suppliers on 11 May. A hang over from the washable distemper days appeared on Drawing No 30064, Sheet 17, in the form of an instruction which read – "Indentification markings to be rain proof but easily removable with soap and water". As the drawings did not show the location of squadron code letters, it is to be assumed that the reference

Official Supermarine camouflage and national markings drawing.

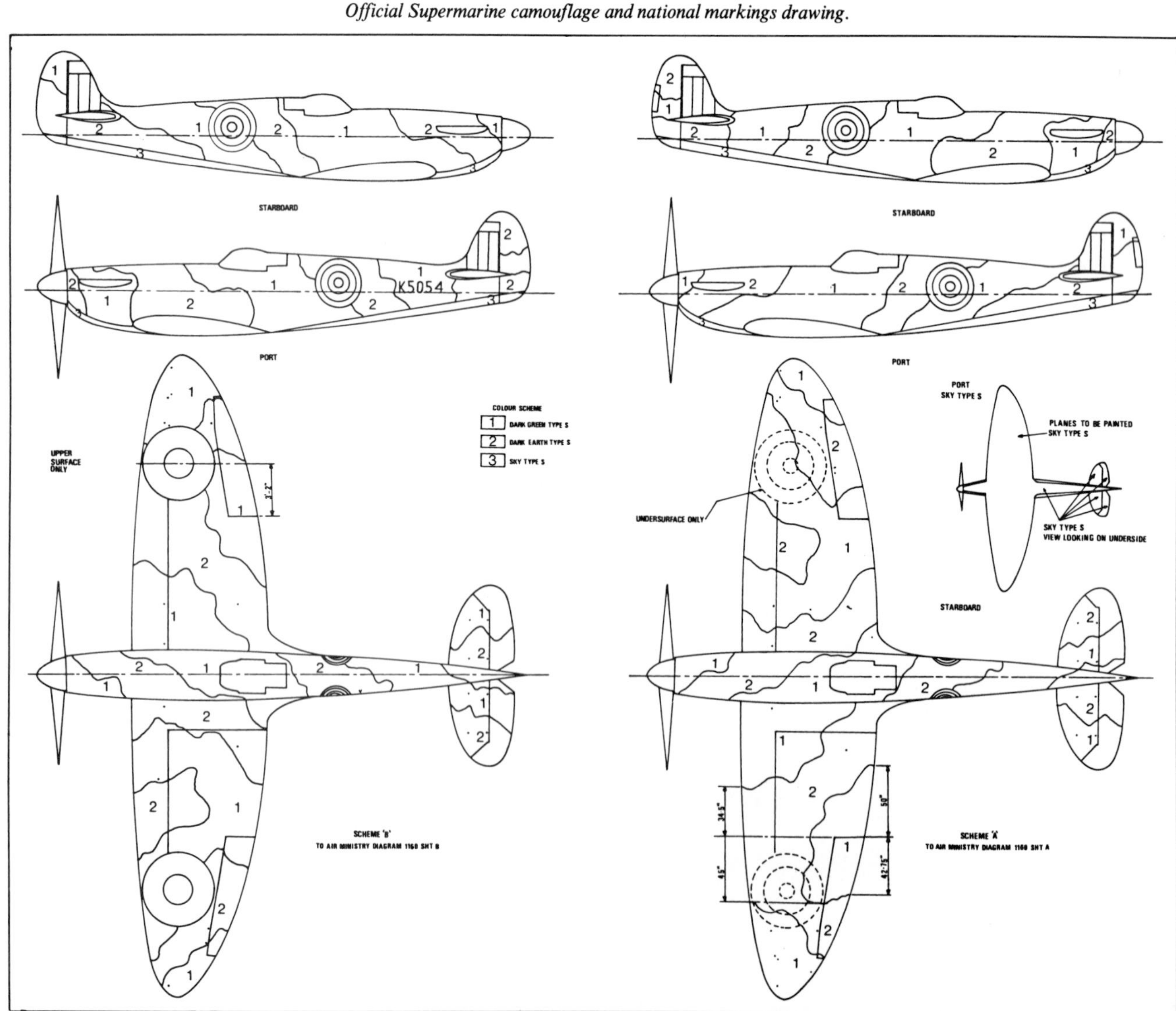

applied to them. Squadron badges were allowed on the fin and the indentification letters had to be applied on each side of the fuselage forward of the national marking, with individual aircraft letters aft. The new paint finish resulted in a reduction of maximum speed by 5mph and Verney asked Boscombe Down for advice on this. The Chemistry Department rubbed a wing smooth and tested it in the wind tunnel, the results showing that a speed increase was possible by treating the complete aeroplane in this manner. For production aircraft the idea was not feasible, but it was never suggested that a glossy paint be used.

While all this effort was being undertaken a letter from Dowding at Headquarters Fighter Command arrived at the Air Ministry. Dated 10 May it was headed "Painting of Fighter Aircraft". It continued – "I have been giving considerable thought to the best colouration of fighter aircraft. I wish to recommend that the underside of one lower plane be finished in silver dope and the other dull black. Against whatever degree of light this arrangement is viewed it will always present a characteristic part-coloured aeroplane.

"As regards upper surfaces I consider that the necessity for aircraft to be inconspicuous on their aerodromes is now of great importance in view of the possibility of their being attacked while refuelling or when dispersed. For this purpose the approved green camouflage scheme should be adopted. The elaborate and conspicuous patterns now painted on fighter aircraft should be abolished". It was agreed to try the silver and black scheme on 28 July.

Not content with voicing his thoughts on camouflage, Dowding wrote again to the Air Ministry on 28 October – "For the time being the indentification numbers should be deleted from lower wing surfaces. I consider that the sides and upper surfaces be finished in green camouflage*. The brown is not suitable for my purposes.

"Squadron markings will be eliminated except for a small crest on the fin and a mechanism devised by which the letter of the day can be continuously transmitted on the downward recognition lights at the will of the pilot." Green camouflage was adopted on 29 December and fighter aircraft were, apparently, to have all green upper surfaces, black and silver under, no code letters and a flashing indentification light.

However, DTD Verney was not at all certain if Dowding wanted the outer wing panels only to be painted in the black and silver scheme, or did it include the centre section. Also, there were many complaints being made against low flying RAF aircraft and indentification serials had to be reinstated. On 9 April 1938 Verney wrote to Dowding asking that he reconsider adoption of the black and silver scheme as it was thought that an enemy could copy it for their fighters. Dowding thought this most unlikely as it would be difficult to differentiate between opposing fighters and it was agreed by all parties to give the scheme a trial.

When the first production Spitfire, K9787, made its first flight on 14 May 1938 it did not conform to what had been agreed between Dowding and the Air Ministry for it was painted in the Dark Earth and Dark Green camouflage on upper surfaces, and aluminium overall under. The standard 25 inch diameter roundel of five inch wide bands was surrounded by an outer ring of yellow five inches wide making a total diameter of 35 inches. The new AI type appeared on both sides of the fuselage, but the wing roundels were Type A of the same coloured rings of 10 inches wide making a total of 50 inches. The underwing, black serial numbers were only 12 inches high.

The Spitfire Mk I entered RAF service with No 19 Squadron on 4 August 1938 when K9789 was received in the A camouflage scheme and by the following October the squadron number-19- appeared on the other machines which had followed it. Most of the numbers were in white, but a number of aircraft had their numbers in red and yellow. The Munich Crisis of the previous September had resulted in all RAF aeroplanes being hastily camouflaged in Dark Earth and Dark Green and many peculiar patterns appeared. The Air Ministry realised that the time had come to rationalise and issued A.M Order A.154/39 dated 27 April 1938. Type B roundels of a red centre and a blue surround were to appear on the upper wing surfaces and fuselage sides and none on under surfaces. Two code letters indicating the Squadron number were to appear forward, or aft, of the fuselage roundel, plus the single letter indicating the individual aircraft on the opposite sides. The letters were to be 48 inches high with 6 inch width strokes and to be grey. Dowding's black (Night) and white (no silver) under surfaces were to be adopted.

The scheme ran into problems at this stage for although the official Order stated – "The lower surface of the starboard plane and half the under surface of the fuselage is to be painted in white. The

Black and white under-surface scheme.

corresponding port side to be painted black", it was misinterpreted by the aircraft manufacturers for they were delivering wings in the appropriate colours which were matched to a fuselage painted silver underneath. This resulted in additional work at the final assembly stage, painting the fuselage black and white to match the wings. Squadron badges were again permitted to be painted on the fin "For purposes of moral", but they were to be painted over in the event of war. A number of Fighter Command Squadrons painted the elevator under surfaces in the opposite colour to the main colour of the wing i.e. black on white wing, etc. The official recommendation was for control surfaces not to be painted as is was not certain if the weight of the paint upset the balance.

Dowding was responsible for the removal of national markings on the under wing surfaces for he thought they broke up the painted surfaces. The Air Ministry, however, were cautious, initially, about this move. "What", they asked, "was the International Geneva Agreement about military aircraft flying without some indication of country of origin". To the surprise of all concerned, except for, perhaps, Dowding, the answer was no such agreement about national markings existed. But Dowding had not won yet. An Air Commodore pedantically quoted King's Regulations, Paragraph 796, referring to under wing markings which had to be applied. Dowding recovered and resisted and the offending Paragraph was ammended to confirm deletion of the roundels. Letters went to Supermarine and other manufacturers that the new scheme was to apply to fighter aircraft as from 17 January 1939, with No 56 Squadron successfully completing trials. War at this time had not been declared, but it was in the ante room.

Number Eleven Group, Fighter Command, was commanded by Keith Park who was enthusiastic about his Chief's new scheme, but posed the question – "How would the Flights reform again into formations after an air battle?" It was almost as if he expected combat to break up at an agreed signal, the opposing forces to form into squadrons and fly home back to base. The following proposal was put forward as worthy of consideration (1) The squadron's basic symbol would be the squadron number positioned immediately aft of the fuselage roundel (the exact opposite of what had been adopted); (2) The A Flight section would have this number painted red for the leading section, the second section would have the top half of the number painted red with the bottom half white; (3) B Flight number would be Blue; (4) C Flight Yellow; (5) D Flight Green. In addition Flight and Section Leaders would have the aircraft spinners painted in the Flight colour. The second section leader would have the rear half of spinner painted in Flight colour with the forward half in white. Incredibly it was agreed to test the scheme and a number of Spitfires and Hurricanes appeared in the complicated scheme. Needless to say it was all scrapped when the hard fighting began. In the whirligig of a dog fight and the aftermath, pilots were only too pleased to keep company with any friendly fighter and head for base.

Dowding's edict that national markings were not to appear on wing under surfaces had to be changed quickly during the first few weeks of war. Aircraft recognition was in its infancy and trigger fingers itchy and during October 1939 a reconnaissance aeroplane was shot

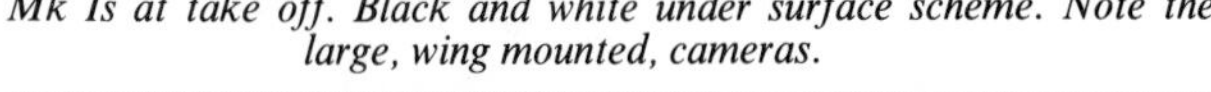

Mk Is at take off. Black and white under surface scheme. Note the large, wing mounted, cameras.

**Dowding mentions this scheme twice and apparently wanted to drop the Brown and Green approved pattern.*

down by RAF fighters. The dull Type B roundels and lack of under wing roundels had blurred the fighter pilot's reactions and it was proved beyond doubt that it was far better for RAF aircraft to be recognisable to both sides than have accidental deaths. A telegram was sent to all RAF units. It, A.949/32, instructed all commands to apply immediately the Type A red, white and blue roundels on upper wing surfaces instead of the Type B. The original telegram was sent on 30 October and was followed by two more on 5 and 10 November which instructed the addition of Type A roundels to all under wing surfaces, except those of fighters and night bombers. There was great confusion and the Air Ministry was forced to send yet another Signal A.M.O A.154 which listed the correct markings to be applied to all classes of aircraft, and the major addition was the introduction of Type A (red, white and blue) roundels to the fuselage sides of all types of aircraft whatever their role. One specific item to go almost unnoticed at that time was the adoption of the colour Sky, to be applied to the under surfaces of Blenheim day bombers only.

The first production Spitfires to incorporate all the new changes appeared after 23 February 1940 and the Type A fuselage roundels had ring widths of 7 inches, larger than the original five inch widths, and following upon the experiences of combat during the French retreat in May 1940 the fuselage roundels were enlarged by the addition of an outer yellow ring. On 16 May a further modification of national markings resulted in addition of fin stripes, three bands of red, white and blue, seven inches wide. On 6 June 1940 the Air Ministry issued instructions that all fighters were to have their under surfaces painted with Sky for contrary to Dowding's views the black and white scheme put the RAF at a disadvantage when battling with enemy aircraft.* Pilots also said that the green and brown upper surface scheme was inferior to the Luftwaffe green splinter scheme at heights of 20,000 feet. The new colour was known by many names, the most popular being "Duck Egg Blue", and this has been quoted in DTD Specification 83A. Supermarine issued its colour scheme drawings on 11 June just before the Battle of Britain.

Under wing roundels appeared on Spitfires once again during the Battle of Britain when the Air Ministry ordered that Type A of 50 inch diameter be applied as from 11 August. By 27 November that year the Air Ministry had ordered that all day fighters were to have their port wings painted black on the under surface, the roundel to be outlined in yellow, the spinner painted Sky and an 18 inch vertical band of Sky was to be painted around the rear fuselage immediately in front of the tailplane. This resulted in some disturbance of fuselage serial numbers and in a few instances the 8 inch digits disappeared to be replaced by smaller numerals and letters painted directly on to the Sky band. On 14 January 1941 the A and B mirror camouflage scheme merged to become A scheme only and by 7 April Fighter Command sent a Signal to all Commands, and the Air Ministry, that all fighters would again revert to the total Sky under surface scheme. The tail was wagging the dog. Type A roundels were also to be adopted.

Aircraft of the PRUs were to be coloured in accordance with operational requirements and the scheme need not conform to the standard system. Special arrangements were to be made for the schemes by HQ Fighter Command**.

It was during the Spring of 1941 that Fighter Command began carrying the offensive to the Luftwaffe in France and it soon became apparent that the green and brown scheme was unsuitable. Trials were initiated on 22 May with Spitfires and Hurricanes at AFDU Duxford painted with a mixture of 50% Sea Grey and Dark Sea Green camouflage on all upper surfaces and Sky under surfaces. A number of Hurricanes were painted in two tones of grey. As a result Boscombe Down received supplies of two shades of paint – Dark Blue and Light Azure. These two shades were applied to Spitfires X4782, P7661 and P8021 for trials. The normal scheme afforded no protection to the Spitfires over the sea. Results proved that the two blues, plus the Sky under surfaces were useless, especially Sky, for the White in the Type A roundel shone brilliantly whenever sunlight struck it. Eventually it was recommended that Ultra Dark Blue be adopted for all upper surfaces with a matt, lighter shade of blue for under surfaces. No roundels to appear on under surfaces.

The Order for this scheme was issued on 11 August 1941 and the new colour was called Deep Sky. In appearance it was a true Royal Blue and when painted in this colour it was claimed an aircraft was almost invisible to the eye at 28,000 feet on a clear day. Boscombe tested one Spitfire with one half of the aircraft painted Sky and the other black. The former glowed a brilliant white at 35,000 feet whilst the latter was not visible. In all instances matt paint was recommended.

Trials at Boscombe continued with schemes for overseas fighters – Dark Earth, Light Earth, Dark Sand, Dark Red Sand***, Tropical Sea paints were Dark Mediterranean Blue, Extra Dark Sea Green. For low altitude photo reconnaissance Spitfires Extra Dark Sea and Dark Green upper surfaces and Mauve under surfaces were tested. Semi permanent and washable distempers were also tried.

After numerous experiments it was decided to paint all fighters in a combination of Dark Green and Ocean Grey upper surfaces and a variation of the Boscombe paint (Deep Sky) Medium Sea Grey under surfaces. The Sky spinner and fuselage band was retained with code and aircraft letters in 24 inch high Sky paint on the fuselage. A totally new feature was a 4 inch wide yellow strip along the outer wing leading edges. This was purely a recognition feature in head on combat. The new scheme was to be introduced as from 15 August 1941.

By early 1942 national markings were altered once again and consisted of a large Dull Red centre surrounded by a broad blue ring with a narrow ring of white as the outer colour. This was known at the Type C and a variant of this, know as the Type CI had a yellow outer ring. Fin flashes were changed at the same time and they were two equal sized outer strips of dull Red and blue with a narrow white centre strip. All RAF aircraft were to have the new markings and these came in three sizes – small, medium and large. The Type C had diameters of 16, 32 and 48 inches, while the Type CI were 18, 36 and 54 inches diameter. On the Spitfire the medium size roundels were used for the fuselage and under wing surfaces. The Type B were retained for under surfaces. Drawings were issued and the roundels used from 21 May.

As the war progressed the surface finish became important as aircraft losses were decreasing and they were in service for longer periods than the early production machines. An indication of how important surface finish was regarded can be ascertained by the

Supermarine drawing of the colour scheme for Seafire F45-47.

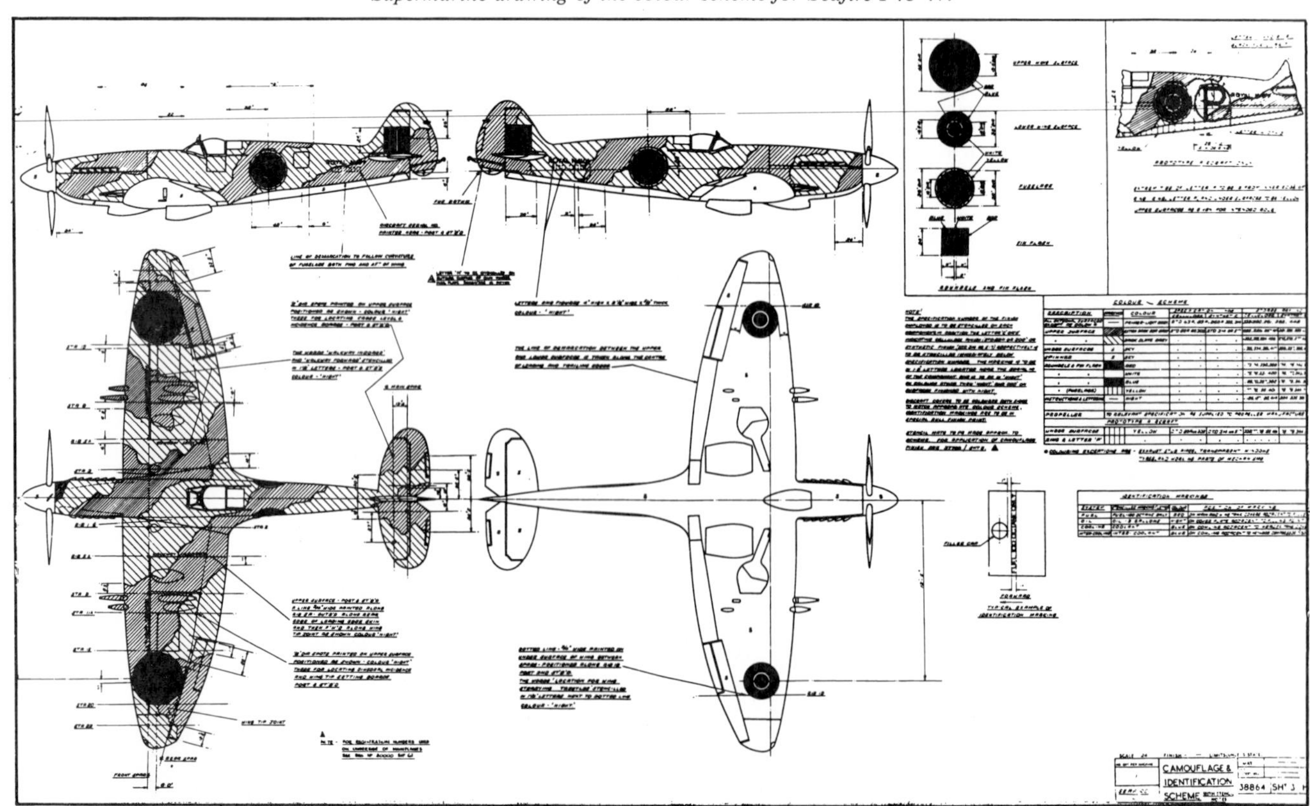

**A note concerning the undersurfaces of fighters issue at this time stated – "The under surfaces of all operational aircraft will be either matt black or duck egg blue and may be either one or the other at the discretion of Commands to meet operational requirements".*

***For PRU Spitfires, Cotton wanted an overall paint scheme of 'duck egg blue'.*

****These colours were specified as 'Tropical Paints'.*

following extract from Supermarine Drawing 37700 Sheet 11 on Seafire camouflage finish. It read – Final aircraft assembly. Dry scuff all over with Hydro-Durexisil abrasive paper, grade 320 (equivalent to one of today's Garnett papers). Having obtained a perfectly smooth contour spray two coats of camouflage colours. Air dry for two hours and lightly rub down. Spray one full coat of varnish and air dry for three hours.

Last operation. Smoothing by abrasive polish. The whole aircraft should be lightly scuffed with Hydro-Durexisil paper, grade 320 or 400 to remove dry spray. Not less than 24 hours, but preferably after flight test, the whole camouflaged surface must be smoothed by a polishing operation using a mixed polish made up of three parts No. 7 polish and one part No. 28 rubbing compound. The leading edges of mainplanes, tailplanes and fins must have special treatment, and hand polishing followed by cleaning with a dry lambswool mop is recommended for these areas. Remember – what you want is smoothness. Don't concentrate on gloss. It is smoothness that make the aircraft go faster.

The Air Sea Rescue Spitfires which entered Fighter Command service during the latter half of 1942 were originally finished in standard day fighter markings, and on 24 January 1943 it was suggested that the grey code letters be changed to Dull red. This colour was also unsatisfactory and the codes were changed to yellow. On 4 February a 12 inch wide yellow band running from rear of the spinner to the tail wheel was adopted as an aid to recognition, and to identify the sqaudrons No 277 was to use barred letter codes; for example T, S, No 276 to have yellow codes only. This was considered to be too complicated and eventually all ASR Spitfires were to have standard day fighter camouflage, yellow code letters and a 12 inch wide black belly stripe from spinner to tail wheel.

The high altitude fighters such as the Spitfire F Mk VII were to be painted with upper wing surfaces in PR Blue and under surfaces in Deep Sky, Type S. Type B roundels of blue and red to appear on the under wing surfaces at the tip and be repeated on the upper surfaces. Fuselage roundels were also Type B plus the normal fin flash. This Order came into effect on 1 December 1942 and on the 9th an Air Ministry warning was issued to all defence units about the new scheme, trials of which began under the code name of 'Complot'. Trials were completed by 17 December and the code name cancelled. PRU aircraft during the same period had an upper colour of Light Grey and PRU Blue under surfaces.

By January 1944 a colour scheme of Dark Grey and Green upper surfaces with Light Grey under surfaces was under test, together with a Sky spinner and rear fuselage band. On 4 June a major alteration was the painting of black and white bands of five inches wide to the wing surfaces six inches inboard of the roundels as an aid to instant recognition during the early days of the Normandy invasion. The fuselage stripes were positioned 18 inches forward of the tailplane. Unit badges were forbidden for use on 24 September and during the same month the black and white 'Invasion' bands were removed from wing upper surfaces to reduce the risk of enemy air attacks when parked. The Sky painted spinner and rear fuselage bands were also removed and the spinner usually repainted black.

On 22 January 1945 all fighter aircraft in the Far East and Pacific areas had to revert to the Type C roundel of red, white and blue on the upper surfaces. The Americans were mistaking the Type B roundel as the Japanese Rising Sun insignia and shooting the other Allied aircraft down. At the same time the outer yellow ring was re-instated. From the end of 1945 Home based fighters were to have the standard camouflage scheme of Dark Sea Grey and Dark Green, while in the Middle East and other overseas theatres a natural aluminium finish was recommended. ASR Spitfires were also to be in natural aluminium. However, bare, untreated metal resulted in corrosion and some protection was necessary. Electro-chemical treatment was tested, as were wax-based coatings, but these tended to become tacky in hot climates and eventually a clear, hard lacquer was developed.

All aircraft of Eastern Air Command were ordered to adopt a 28 inch wide white band on both wings and an 18 inch band on tailplane. From October 1945 all SHAEF and 2nd TAF aircraft were ordered to adopt the natural metal finish, PRU types normal type camouflage, ASR marine camouflage. This order was slightly amended to paint all PRU types silver overall. Coastal Command wanted to retain the old style PRU Blue as they considered silver to be useless, but their request was denied. Coastal Command said that they had painted the Spitfires silver for the PR role, and also their ground staff were most proud of their aircraft's condition in the blue paint. Morale could suffer as a consequence of adopting the all silver finish. The arguments raged for the whole of 1947 until the Air Ministry in a firm note stated – "All day fighters and PRU aircraft must be painted silver overall. There are to be no exceptions". The Spitfire was now being phased out of service and was not greatly affected by the order.

Appendix X

ENTRY INTO SERVICE

Supermarine Spitfire production records were not available, but the entry into RAF service gives an indication of numbers built in any given month.

1938 July K9792, **August** K9790, 9794, **September** K9795, **October** K9796, 9797, 9799, 9800, 9801, 9802, 9803, 9804, 9807, 9808, 9809, 9810, 9812, 9814, **November** K9805, 9806, 9811, 9813, 9815, 9816, 9817, 9818, 9819, **December** K9820 to K9833 (14 aircraft).

1939 January K9835 to 9842 (8 a/c), K9844 to 9851 (8 a/c), K9853, 9888, **February** K9843, K9855 to 9875 (21 a/c), K9889, 9890, 9891, **March** K9876 to 9882 (7 a/c), K9884, 9885, 9886, 9887, 9892, 9893, 9894, 9896 to 9911 (16 a/c), 9913, 9915, 9917, L1040, **April** K9883, 9912, 9914, 9916, 9918 to 9947 (30 a/c), 9949, 9956, 9967, **May** K9854, 9948, 9950 to 9955 (6 a/c), 9957 to 9966 (10 a/c), 9968 to 9992 (25 a/c), **June** K9993 to 9999 (7 a/c), L1000 to 1006 (7 a/c), 1008 to 1029 (22 a/c), 1031, 1032, 1034, 1035, 1036, 1041, **July** L1030, 1033, 1037, 1038, 1039, 1042 to 1059 (18 a/c), 1062 to 1071 (9 a/c), **August** L1072 to 1090 (19 a/c), **September** L1060, 1091, 1092, 1093, 1094, 1096, N3023 to 3050 (29 a/c), **October** L1007, N3051 to 3072 (22 a/c), 3091 to 3117 (27 a/c), **November** N3118 to 3122 (5 a/c), 3124 to 3130 (7 a/c), 3160 to 3180 (21 a/c), 3182, 3183, 3185, 3187, 3188, 3189, **December** N3181, 3184, 3190 to 3195 (6 a/c), 3197 to 3203 (7 a/c), 3221 to 3232 (12 a/c), 3234, 3235, 3236, 3237, 3239, 3240, 3244 to 3249 (6 a/c).

1940 January K9798, N3186, 3196, 3233, 3238, 3241, 3242, 3243, 3264 to 3296 (33 a/c), P9305, 9306, **February** N3123, P9307 to 9319 (13 a/c), 9321 to 9331 (11 a/c), 9337,9339, 9360, 9361, 9363, 9364, 9365, 9367, 9368, **March** N3250, P9332 to 9336 (5 a/c), 9338, 9362, 9366, 9369 to 9385 (17 a/c), 9387 to 9399 (13 a/c), 9420 to 9435 (16 a/c), **April** P9436 to 9443 (8 a/c), 9445, 9446, 9447, 9449 to 9469 (21 a/c), 9490 to 9502 (13 a/c), 9505, 9506, 9507, 9509, 9514, 9515, 9516, 9517, **May** P9386, 9504, 9508, 9510, 9511, 9512, 9513, 9518, 9519, 9540 to 9550 (11 a/c), R6595 to 6642 (48 a/c), 6648, 6686, **June** K9791, P9444, 9448, 9503, 9553 to 9562 (10 a/c), R6685, 6687, 6688, 6690 to 6721 (32 a/c), 6751 to 6780 (30 a/c), 6804 to 6816 (13 a/c), 6829 to 6834 (6 a/c), 6836, 6838, 6839, 6882, 6884, 6902, 6905, 6906, 6907, P7281, 7282, 7284, 7298, 7299, **July** K9875, L1095, P9563, 9564, 9565, R6683, 6799 to 6803 (5 a/c), 6835, 6837, 6840, 6879, 6880, 6881, 6885 to 6893 (9 a/c), 6895 to 6899 (5 a/c), 6901, 6903, 6904, 6910 to 6914 (5 a/c), 6916 to 6928 (13 a/c), 6957 to 6996 (40 a/c), 7015 to 7022 (8 a/c), X4009 to 4031 (23 a/c), 4033, 4035, 4036, 4038, 4051, 4052, 4053, P7283 to 7293 (11 a/c), 7295, 7296, 7297, 7300 to 7308 (9 a/c), **August** X4032, 4034, 4037, 4054 to 4070 (17 a/c), 4101 to 4110 (10 a/c), 4159 to 4175 (17 a/c), 4177 to 4188 (12 a/c), 4231 to 4267 (37 a/c), 4269 to 4271 (3 a/c), 4273 to 4280 (8 a/c), 4317 to 4329 (13 a/c), 4332, 4333, 4335, P7309 to 7329 (21 a/c), 7351, 7352, 7354 to 7360 (7 a/c), 7365, 7366, **September** K9793, P9551, R6894, X4272, 4331, 4336 to 4356 (21 a/c), 4381, 4382, 4384 to 4390 (7 a/c), 4409 to 4428 (20 a/c), 4471 to 4490 (20 a/c), 4493, 4539 to 4560 (22 a/c), 4562, 4585, 4586, 4589, P7253, 7364 to 7389 (26 a/c), 7420 to 7437 (18 a/c), 7439 to 7442 (4 a/c), 7444 to 7448 (5 a/c), **October** K9852, R6900, X4334, 4587, 4588, 4591 to 4621 (31 a/c), 4623, 4624, 4641 to 4646 (6 a/c), 4648 to 4659 (12 a/c), 4680, P7438, 7443, 7449, 7490 to 7494 (5 a/c), 7496 to 7509 (14 a/c), 7520 to 7551 (32 a/c), 7554 to 7562 (9 a/c), 7564, **November** K9834, R6817, X4660, 4661, 4662, 4671 to 4679 (9 a/c), 4681 to 4685 (5 a/c), 4709 to 4722 (14 a/c), 4765 to 4789 (25 a/c), 4815 to 4828 (13 a/c), 4831, P7552, 7553, 7555, 7563, 7565 to 7569 (5 a/c), 7590 to 7617 (28 a/c), 7619 to 7629 (11 a/c), 7661 to 7696 (36 a/c), 7698, 7699, **December** X4383, 4494, 4561, 4647, 4824, 4829, 4830, 4832 to 4845 (14 a/c), 4849 to 4852 (4 a/c), 4855 to 4859 (5 a/c), 4896 to 4907 (12 a/c), 4909, 4910, 4911, P7697, 7730 to 7746 (17 a/c), 7748 to 7753 (6 a/c), 7755 to 7759 (5 a/c), 7770 to 7776 (7 a/c), 7779 to 7789 (11 a/c), 7811 to 7820 (10 a/c), 7822, 7823, 7824, 7825, 7828, 7831.

1941 January R7023, X4496, 4853, 4908, 4912 to 4935 (24 a/c), 4942, 4988, 4989, 4990, P7777, 7778, 7821, 7826, 7827, 7829, 7832 to 7837 (6 a/c), 7839 to 7846 (8 a/c), 7848 to 7851 (4 a/c), 7853, 7854, 7855, 7858, 7859, 7880, 7881, 7886, 7887, 7888, **February** P9552, R6908, 7024 to 7028 (5 a/c), 7058 to 7074 (17 a/c), 7114 to 7144 (31 a/c), 7146 to 7153 (8 a/c), 7158, X4491, 4936 to 4941 (6 a/c), 4943, 4944, 4945, 4991, 4993, 4995, 4996, 4997, P7810, 7830, 7847, 7852, 7856, 7857, 7882 to 7885 (4 a/c), 7889 to 7921 (33 a/c), 7923 to 7929 (7 a/c), 7960 to 7990 (40 a/c), 8010 to 8023 (14 a/c), 8025 to 8034 (10 a/c), 8036 to 8047 (12 a/c), 8049, 8070 to 8076 (7 a/c), 8078, 8079, 8081, 8083, 8085, 8132, 8146, 8232, 8311, **March** R7145, 7154, 7156, 7157, 7159, 7162, 7163, 7192 to 7198 (7 a/c), 7200 to 7206 (7 a/c), 7211, 7212, 7214, 7215, 7216, 7250, 7251, 7252, X4495, 4497, 4498, 4505, 4994, P7922, 8024, 8049, 8077, 8080, 8082, 8084, 8086, 8087, 8089 to 8099 (11 a/c), 8133, 8135, 8136, 8140, 8141, 8142, 8144 to 8149 (6 a/c), 8160 to 8209 (50 a/c), 8230, 8231, 8233, 8234, 8235, 8238 to 8248 (11 a/c), 8250 to 8253 (4 a/c), 8255, **April** R6722, 7160, X4502, 4503, P8131, 8134, 8137, 8138, 8139, 8237, 8345, 8381, 8389, 8390, 8393 to 8399 (7 a/c), 8427 to 8437 (11 a/c), 8440, 8442, 8460, 8503 to 8509 (7 a/c), 8514, 8519 to 8523 (5 a/c), 8525, 8526, 8529, 8533, 8535, 8562, 8563, 8565 to 8569 (5 a/c), 8580, 8583, 8586, 8588, 8594, 8647, 8648, 8650 to 8664 (15 a/c), 8687, 8688, 8689, 8671, 8672, 8673, 8675 to 8679 (5 a/c), 8690, 8691, 8692, 8694, 7029, 7030, 7031, 7265, 7308, 7309, W3109. 3110, 3111, 3113, 3115 to 3119 (5 a/c), 3135 to 3138 (4 a/c), 3168 to 3174 (7 a/c), 3176, 3177, 3178, 3180 to 3187 (8 a/c), 3207 3216 (10 a/c), 3226, 3227, 3238 to 3259 (22 a/c), 3265, 3332, 3364 to 3370 (7 a/c), X4663 to 4670 (8 a/c), **June** K9787, X4499 4848, P8035, 8265, 8441, 8443 to 8449 (7 a/c), 8461 to 8473 (13 a/c), 8478, 8500, 8501, 8502, 8510 to 8513 (4 a/c), 8515 to 8518 (4 a/c), 8540, 8541, 8543 to 8549 (7 a/c), 8571, 8572, 8575 to 8577 (4 a/c), 8579, 8582, 8584, 8587, 8589, 8590, 8591, 8593, 8595 to 8599 (5 a/c), 8601, 8602, 8605, 8608, 8649, 8674, 8693, 8695 to 8698 (4 a/c), 8701, 8706, 8532, 8537, 8538, 8539, 8542, 8560, 8561, 8564, 8578, 8581, 8585, 8600, 8603, 8604, 8607, 8640, 8699, 8707, 8709, 8710, 8741, 8743, 8744, 8745, 8747, 8748, 8750 to 8755 (8 a/c), 8781, R7033, 7034, 7277, 7279, W3114, 3229 to 3226 (8 a/c), 3260 to 3264 (5 a/c), 3305 to 3310 (6 a/c), 3312 to 3325 (14 a/c), 3327 to 3331 (5 a/c), 3333, 3334, 3371 to 3383 (13 a/c), 3403 to 3412 (10 a/c), 3422 to 3430 (9 a/c), 3432 to 3435 (4 a/c), 3439, 3440, 3441, 3443, 3444, 3455, 3501 to 3514 (14 a/c), 3516 to 3523 (8 a/c), 3618, **July** R7199, X4500 AR212, 213, P7280, 8391, 8474 to 8477 (4 a/c), 8479, 8569, 8573, 8574, 8575, 8592, 8702, 8704, 8705, 8707, 8725 to 8729 (5 a/c), 8703, 8708, 8711 to 8724 (14 a/c), 8740, 8742, 8746, 8749, 8756 to 8759 (4 a/c), 8780, 8782 to 8792 (11 a/c), 8794 to 8799 (6 a/c), R7035 to 7041 (7 a/c), 7043, W3326, 3431, 3436, 3437, 3438, 3442, 3445 to 3454 (10 a/c), 3456 to 3461 (6 a/c), 3515, 3524 to 3530 (7 a/c), 3560 to 3576 (26 a/c), 3621, 3629 to 3642 (14 a/c), 3644, 3700, 3775, AB779, 780, 781, 783, 785, 786, 792, 794, 841 to 852 (12 a/c), 854 to 858 (5 a/c), 860, 861, 862, 917, 918, 963, AD240, **August** X4538, AR214 to 218 (5 a/c), R7032, 7042, 7055, 7056, W3577, 3579, 3620, 3622 to 3628 (7 a/c), 3643, 3645 to 3657 (13 a/c), 3697, 3698, 3699, 3701 to 3705 (5 a/c), 3707 to 3726 (20 a/c), 3756 3774 (19 a/c), 3795 to 3804 (10 a/c), 3814 to 3829 (16 a/c), 3831, 3896, AA718, 720, 721, 781 to 784 (7 a/c), 787, 788, 791, 793, 795 to 827 (33 a/c), 853, 859, 863 to 875 (13 a/c), 892 to 901 (10 a/c), 903 to 909 (7 a/c), 912 to 916 (5 a/c), 919 to 937 (19 a/c), 960, 962, 969, 971, 975, 976, 989, 990, 993, 994, AD111 to 115 (5 a/c), 119, 122 to 126 (5 a/c), 128, 130, 133 to 136 (4 a/c), 138, 196, 253. **September** X4503, AR219 to 228 (10 a/c), W3706, 3830, 3832 to 3853 (22 a/c), 3893, 3894, 3895, 3897 to 3902 (6 a/c), 3931 to 3956 (26 a/c), AA719, 722 to 749 (28 a/c), 786 to 800 (15 a/c), 83 to 846 (14 a/c), AB828, 939 to 941 (4 a/c), 961, 964 to 968 (5 a/c), 972, 973, 974, 977 to 985 (9 a/c), 991, AD116, 117, 118, 120, 121, 127, 129, 131, 132, 137, 176, 178 to 181 (4 a/c), 186,187,188, 193, 194, 195, 197 to 210 (14 a/c), 225 to 229 (5 a/c), 231 to 239 (9 a/c), 241 to 252 (12 a/c), 254 to 262 (9 a/c), 264, 265, 267, 268, 270 to 274 (5 a/c), 288 to 294 (7 a/c), 299 to 302 (4 a/c), 304, 305, 309, 310, 312, 314 to 317 (4 a/c), 320, 329, 330, 354, 426, 427, 428, **October** AR229 to 238 (10 a/c), W3957 to 3967 (11 a/c), 3969, 3670, AA750 to 753 (4 a/c), 755 to 767 (13 a/c), 801 to 815 (15 a/c), 847 to 850 (4 a/c), 852 to 869 (18 a/c), 871, 872, 874, 877 to 882 (6 a/c), 902 to 905 (4 a/c), 907, 922, 923, 925 to 928 (4 a/c), 930, 931, 986, 987, 988, 992, AD182 to 185 (4 a/c), 189 to 192 (4 a/c), 263, 266, 269, 295 to 298 (4 a/c), 303, 306, 307, 308, 311, 313, 318, 319, 321 to 324 (4 a/c), 326, 327, 328, 331, 332, 348 to 353 (6 a/c), 355 to 359 (5 a/c), 361 to 367 (7 a/c), 369 to 375 (7 a/c), 377 to 380 (4 a/c), 382 to 392 (11 a/c), 411, 412, 414, 416 to 425 (10 a/c), 429, 430, 457, 461 to 469 (9 a/c), 474, 475, 498 to 507 (10 a/c), 509, 513, 514, 516, 517, 540, 542, 544, 546, 547, 548, 556, 557, 558, 572, 573, 574, **November** AR239 to 252 (14 a/c),

AA851, 906, 908 to 913 (6 a/c), 915 to 921 (7 a/c), 924, 929, 931 to 946 (16 a/c), 963 to 972 (10 a/c), 974, 975, 976, 978 to 982 (5 a/c), **AB**118 to 128 (11 a/c), 130, 133 to 248 (16 a/c), 167, 169, 171 to 175 (5 a/c), 178, 179, 180, 182, 183, 184, 206, 240 to 246 (7 a/c), 300, AD325, 376, 381, 395, 413, 415, 449, 451, 454 to 460 (7 a/c), 470 to 473 (4 a/c), 476, 477 478, 508, 510, 511, 512, 515, 535 to 539 (5 a/c), 541, 543, 545, 549 to 555 (7 a/c), 559, 561, 562, 563, 570, 575 to 584 (10 a/c), **BL**231 to 234 (4 a/c), 236, 238, 239, 240, 248, 249, 251 to 254 (4 a/c), 256 to 261 (6 a/c), 264, 267, 286 to 294 (9 a/c), 298 to 302 (5 a/c), 317 to 328 (12 a/c), 333 to 339 (7 a/c), 341, 343, 344, 349, 351, 352, 353, 355, 356, 365, 366, 368 to 371 (4 a/c), 377 to 386 (10 a/c). 403 to 407 (5 a/c), 410, 411, 412, 425, 431, 488, 581. **December** AB176, AR253 to 260 (8 a/c), 274, 275, AA973, 977, AB129, 131, 149 to 152 (4 a/c), 168, 177, 181, 185 to 192 (8 a/c), 194, 196, 198, 199, 201 to 205 (5 a/c), 210 to 213 (4 a/c), 247 to 259 (13 a/c), 265 to 276 (12 a/c), 278, 279, 283, 284, 301 to 310 (10 a/c), 314 to 316 (3 a/c), 363, 364, 366, 902, AD177, 450 544, 565 to 569 (5 a/c), 571, BL241 to 244 (4 a/c), 247, 250, 255, 295, 314, 316, 330, 331, 332, 340, 342, 345, 346,350, 367, 372 to 376 (5 a/c), 387 to 390 (4 a/c), 408, 409, 413 to 417 (5 a/c), 423, 424, 426 to 430 (5 a/c), 432 to 438 (7 a/c), 444, 448, 449, 450, 461 to 477 (17 a/c), 482 to 487 (6 a/c), 489 to 492 (4 a/c), 497, 499, 500, 509 to 520 (12 a/c), 524, 526 535 (10 a/c), 541 to 547 (7 a/c), 551, 562 to 570 (9 a/c), 576 to 580 (5 a/c), 582, 583, 585, 588, 589, 592, 616, 617.

1942 January AA870, AB132 313, 317 to 319 (3 a/c), 421 to 429 (9 a/c), AB207, 208, 209, 215, 216, 260, 262, 264, 277, 282, 321 to 338 (18 a/c), 341, 343, 365, 367 to 382 (16 a/c), 401 to 412 (12 a/c), 415, 455, 487 to 489 (3 a/c), 491, 493, 495, 496, 497, 503, 508, 509, 790, 911, AD393, 394, 396, 397, 452, 453, 276, 277, AR261, 279 to 284 (6 a/c), 286 to 297 (12 a/c), 318, BL245, 263, 265, 266, 285, 297, 354, 439, 440, 442, 445, 446, 480, 493 to 496 (4 a/c), 521, 522, 523, 525, 536 to 540 (5 a/c), 548, 549, 550, 584, 586, 587, 590, 591, 593, 595 to 600 (6 a/c), 613, 614, 615, 618 to 635 (18 a/c), 637 to 647 (11 a/c), 661 to 674 (14 a/c), 680 to 686 (7 a/c), 688, 690 to 693 (4 a/c), 707, 708, 710, 712, 713, 718 to 724 (7 a/c), 726, 748 to 751 (4 a/c), 753 to 757 (5 a/c), 764, 765, 769, 779, 781, 783, BM631, BP879, 881. **February** X4269, AB170, 211, 263, 339, 340, 342, 345 to 349 (5 a/c), 413, 414, 417 to 420 (4 a/c), 430 451 to 454 (4 a/c) 456, 458 to 468 (11 a/c), 490, 492, 494, 498, 500, 502, 506, 507, 510 to 527 (18 a/c), 531, 532 535, 536, AR285, 298, 319 to 346 (28 a/c), 439, 440, BL235, 262, 296, 303, 304, 311, 312, 313, 315, 329, 347, 419, 420, 421, 447, 478, 572, 655 to 659 (5 a/c), 709, 711, 714, 715, 716, 725, 727 to 736 (10 a/c), 752, 758 to 763 (6 a/c), 766 to 768 (3 a/c), 770 to 778 (9 a/c), 780, 782, 784 to 789 (6 a/c), 801 to 808 (8 a/c), 819 to 833 (15 a/c), 846 to 852 (7 a/c), 854 to 864 (11 a/c), 887 to 909 (23 a/c), 918 to 940 (23 a/c), 956 to 976 (21 a/c), 978 to 982 (5 a/c), 984 to 993 (10 a/c), 995, 996, 998, BM115, 117 to 121 (5 a/c), 123, 125, 127, 140, 143, 144, 146, 148, 149, 152, 153, 162, 191, BP844 to 847 (4 a/c), 849 to 864 (16 a/c), 866, 880, 882 to 892 (11 a/c), 904, 905, BR160, 597. **March** AB214, 469, 528, 530, 534, AR347, 362 to 391 (30 a/c), 389, 391, BL348, 422, 443, 481, 571, 573, 594, 636, 695, 698, 812 to 814 (3 a/c), 853, 941, 994 997, BM113, 114, 117, 122, 124, 126, 128, 134 to 139 (6 a/c), 141, 142, 147, 150, 151, 154 to 161 (8 a/c), 176 to 190 (15 a/c), 192 to 211 (20 a/c), 227 to 267 (41 a/c), 269 to 274 (6 a/c), 289 to 329 (41 a/c), 343 to 360 (18 a/c), 362, 363, 367, 368, 369, 371, 373, 374, 399, 403, 406, 482, 483, BP848, 865, 867 to 878 (12 a/c), 906 to 923 (18 a/c), 950 to 970 (21 a/c), BR106 to 127 (22 a/c), 159, 162 to 172 (11 a/c), 174 to 196 (23 a/c), 198, 199, 201, 226, 229, 230, 231, 245. **April** AB457, 529, 533, AR392 to 406 (15 a/c), 422 to 438 (17 a/c), 441, BL237, 246, 418, 574, 575, 675, 696, 697, 699, 717, 809, 810, 811, 815, 817, 977, BM129 to 133 (5 a/c), 268, 361, 364, 365, 366, 370, 372, 375 to 386 (12 a/c), **BM**400, 401, 402, 404, 405, 407 to 430 (24 a/c), 447, 449 to 477 (26 a/c), 479, 480, 481, 484 to 493 (10 a/c), 508 to 543 (36 a/c), 556 to 561 (6 a/c), 564 to 572 (15 a/c), 574 to 584 (11 a/c), 588, 589, 591 to 597 (7 a/c), 624 to 633 (9 a/c), 640, 642, 643, 644, 647, 648, 924 to 936 (13 a/c), 971 to 993 (23 a/c), BR129 to 138 (10 a/c), 161, 172, 197, 200, 203, 204, 205, 228, 242 to 244 (3 a/c), 246 to 254 (11 a/c), 256, 282 to 286 (5 a/c), 289 to 301 (13 a/c), 303 to 308 (5 a/c), 344 to 350(7 a/c), 352 to 356 (5 a/c), 359, 373 to 379 (7 a/c), 410, 411, 413, 414, EN763 to 766 (4 a/c), 768, 772 to 781 (11 a/c), 786 to 789 (4 a/c), 792, 797, 830, EP181. **May** AB320, 504, 560, AR278, 442 to 459 (18 a/c), 462 to 469 (8 a/c), BL660, 816, 818, BM573, 585, 586, 587, 634 to 639 (6 a/c), 641, 645, 646 to 653 (5 a/c), BP937, BR232, 234, 302, 307, 309 to 330 (22 a/c), 358, 360 to 368 (9 a/c), 380 to 393 (14 a/c), 412, 415 to 430 (16 a/c), 459 to 482 (24 a/c), 562 to 573 (12 a/c), 576, 577, 579, 580, 582, 583, EN767, 769, 770, 782, 784, 785, 791, 793 to 796 (4 a/c), 798, 799, 800, 821 to 829 (9 a/c), 831 to 842 (12 a/c), 844 to 866 (23 a/c), 888 to 910 (23 a/c), 910, 912 to 915 (4 a/c), 917 to 932 (16 a/c), 944 to 947 (4 a/c), 949 to 981 (33 a/c), EP107, 117 to 133 (17 a/c), 135 to 140 (6 a/c), 149, 151, 152, 164 to 170 (7 a/c), 185, 188, 190, 192, 195, 196, 197, 199, 200, 201, 205, 206, 207. **June** AR470, 471, 488 to 513 (26 a/c), BM145, 563, BR139 to 142 (4 a/c), 235 to 239 (5 a/c), 370, 431 to 435 (5 a/c), 482 to 488 (7 a/c), 490 to 499 (10 a/c), 515 to 525 (11 a/c), 527 to 539 (13 a/c), 578, 581, 584 to 596 (13 a/c), 598 to 600 (3 a/c), 602 to 605 (4 a/c), 621, 622, 641, 642, 644 to 649 (6 a/c), 977 to 980 (4 a/c), BS157, 158, 160 to 166 (7 a/c), 168, 169, EN843, 911, 916, 948, EP108 to 116 (9 a/c), 134, 143, 145, 150, 171 to 180 (10 a/c), 182, 183, 184, 186, 187, 189, 191, 193, 194, 198, 202 to 204 (3 a/c), 208 to 213 (6 a/c), 226 to 232 (7 a/c), 234, 235, 237 to 260 (24 a/c), 275 to 283 (9 a/c), 285 to 292 (8 a/c), 297, 298, 300, 303, 305, 306, 307, 309 to 316 (8 a/c), 327 to 354 (28 a/c), 356 to 364 (9 a/c), 366, 380, 381, 384, 385, 389 to 417 (30 a/c), 431 to 444 (13 a/c), 446 to 452 (7 a/c), 454, 455, 457, 458, 460, 462, 463, 466 to 469 (4 a/c), 471, 472, 493 to 500 (7 a/c), 520, 955. **July** AB344, AR514 to 521 (8 a/c), 523 to 532 (10 a/c), 546 to 563 (18 a/c), BR240, 241, 540 to 549 (10 a/c), 601, 623 to 636 (14 a/c), 650 to 663 (14 a/c), 981 to 987 (7 a/c), BS104 to 117 (14 a/c), 119, 120, 122 to 130 (9 a/c), 159, 167, 170, 172 to 197 (26 a/c), 199, 218, 219, 230, 231, EP233, 382, 386, 387, 388, 445, 453, 456, 459, 461, 464, 465, 470, 473, 485 to 492 (8 a/c), 498, 501 to 511 (11 a/c), 513, 517, 518, 519, 521, 522, 536 to 579 (44 a/c), 594 to 604 (11 a/c), 606, 607, 608, 611 to 614 (4 a/c), 616 to 624 (9 a/c), 636 to 653 (18 a/c), 655 to 667 (13 a/c), 669, 682 to 684 (3 a/c), 686 to 701 (16 a/c), 703 to 719 (17 a/c), 721 to 724 (4 a/c), 727, 728, 729, 751, 753, 784, 785, 786, 788, 791. **August** AR565 to 570 (7 a/c), 592 to 616 (25 a/c), BR574, 637 to 640 (4 a/c), 666 to 670 (5 a/c), BS131 to 138 (8 a/c), 140, 141, 144, 145, 146, 148 to 152 (5 a/c), 198, 200 to 202 (4 a/c), 220, 221, 222, 232 to 238 (7 a/c), 271, 272, 273, 275 to 280 (5 a/c), 282, 284, 291 to 309 (19 a/c), 355 to 359 (5 a/c), 427, 428, 429, 431, EP236, 284, 365, 512, 514 to 516 (3 a/c), 605, 609, 610, 668, 685, 702, 720, 725, 726, 747 to 750 (4 a/c), 752, 755 to 783 (29 a/c), 787, 789, 790, 792 to 795 (4 a/c), 812 to 847 (36 a/c), 869 to 877 (9 a/c), 879 to 890 (12 a/c), 892 to 915 (24 a/c), 951 to 954 (4 a/c), 956 to 990 (35 a/c), ER134 to 146 (13 a/c), 159 to 182 (24 a/c), 184 to 187 (4 a/c), 189 to 197 (9 a/c), 200, 215, 216, 217, 219 to 222 (4 a/c), 224, 229, 246, 311. **September** AR617 to 621 (5 a/c), BS121, 142, 223 to 226 (4 a/c), 281, 283, 285 to 290 (6 a/c), 311 to 319 (9 a/c), 335 to 347 (13 a/c), 349, 350, 360 to 364 (5 a/c), 383 to 386 (4 a/c), 388, 430, 432 to 447 (16 a/c), 449 to 452 (4 a/c), 455 to 459 (5 a/c), 461 to 464 (4 a/c), 467, 468, 471, EE600 to 630 (31 a/c), EP878, ER114 to 125 (12 a/c), 127, 128, 129, 132, 133, 183, 188, 198, 199, 208, 214, 218, 223, 225 to 228 (4 a/c), 245, 247 to 268 (22 a/c), 270 to 283 (14 a/c), 299 to 310 (12 a/c), 312 to 346 (35 a/c), 461 to 510 (50 a/c), 524 to 545 (22 a/c), 547 to 562 (16 a/c), 564 to 571 (8 a/c), 583, 585, 588, 589, 600 to 603 (4 a/c), 605 to 609 (5 a/c), 611, 612, 613, 615, 617, 625, 641, 646, 662, 677, 678. **October** BS227, 228, 239 to 253 (15 a/c), 348, 351, 352, 353, 365, 366, 367, 387, 389 to 409 (21 a/c), 448, 453, 460, 465, 466, 469, 470, 472, 473, 474, 489, 490, 491, 507 to 510 (4 a/c), 513, 514, 530 to 538 (9 a/c), 540 to 547 (8 a/c), 552, EE631 to 644 (14 a/c), 657 to 682 (26 a/c), 684, EN124, 767, EP654, ER130, 269, 546, 557, 584, 586, 587, 590, 591, 593, 594, 596 to 599 (4 a/c), 604, 610, 618 to 624 (7 a/c), 626, 634 to 640 (7 a/c), 642 to 645 (4 a/c), 647 to 661 (15 a/c), 663, 664, 665, 667 to 676 (10 a/c), 679, 696 to 709 (14 a/c), 712, 714, 716 to 730 (15 a/c), 732 to 744 (13 a/c), 759 to 762 (4 a/c), 764, 766, 767, 768, 770 to 791 (22 a/c), 804, 805, 807 to 828 (22 a/c), 830 to 834 (5 a/c), 846, 848 to 853 (6 a/c), 855 to 863 (9 a/c), 865 to 874 (10 a/c), 876, 878, 881 to 884 (4 a/c), 892, 984, 919, 929. **November** BR143, 351, 369, BS410, 411, 492 to 497 (6 a/c), 500, 539, 548 to 551 (4 a/c), 553 to 559 (7 a/c), EE683, 685 to 690 (6 a/c), 713 to 739 (27 a/c), 742 to 747 (6 a/c), EN112, 116, 139, 153, 155, 199, 201 to 204 (4 a/c), 206, 207, 223, 224, 225, 240 to 250 (11 a/c), 259 to 262 (4 a/c), 286 to 296 (11 a/c), 298 to 305 (8 a/c), 307, 385, ER131, 595, 616, 666, 711, 715, 731, 758, 769, 780, 806, 829, 854, 864, 875, 877, 879, 880, 885, 887 to 891 (5 a/c), 895, 913 to 918 (7 a/c), 920, 922 to 928 (7 a/c), 930 to 938 (9 a/c), 940 to 948 (9 a/c), 960, 961, 963 to 969 (7 a/c), 971, 972, 973, 975, 977 to 994 (18 a/c), ES108 to 136 (29 a/c), 138, 140 to 147 (8 a/c), 150 to 154 (5 a/c), 168 to 181 (12 a/c), 196 to 201 (6 a/c), 203 to 214 (12 a/c), 227, 228, 229, 231 to 240 (13 a/c), 242, 244 to 255 (12 a/c), 257, 259, 261, 262, 263, 276, 283, 287, 294, 296, 301, 303, 304, 305, 307, 316, 340, JF274, 276. **December** BL479, BR202, BS498, 499, 501, 502, 511, EE740, 741, 748 to 753 (6 a/c), 766 to 786 (21 a/c), 788 to 805 (18 a/c), EN115, 117 to 121 (5 a/c), ES176, 182, 183, 184, 186, 189 to 195 (7 a/c), ES230, 241, 243, 256, 258, 260, 264, 277 to 282 (6 a/c), 286, 288, 289, 290, 292, 293, 295, 297 to 300 (4 a/c), 302, 306, 308, 309, 312 to 315 (4 a/c), 318, 335, 337 to 345 (9 a/c), 347 to 369 (23 a/c), JF277, 279, 281 to 285 (5 a/c), JG713 to 721 (9 a/c), 723 to 731 (9 a/c), 733 to 738 (6 a/c), 740 to 748 (9 a/c), 750, 751, 752, 769 to 772 (4 a/c), 774, 779, 780, 794 to 799 (6 a/c), 801, 803, 804, 805, 807 to 810 (4 a/c), 835, 836, 837, 841, 843, 845 to 849 (5 a/c), 852, 864 to 873 (10 a/c), 875, 877, 879, 880, 881, 883 to 889 (7 a/c), 892 to 896 (5 a/c), 898, 899, 913, 915, 920 to 930 (11 a/c), 934, 935, 939, 944, 946, 947, 951, JK110, 323, 324.

1943 January AB450, BS503, 504, 505, EE787, 806 to 811 (6 a/c), 834 to 844 (11 a/c), 846 to 859 (14 a/c), 861, 862, 863, EN178, 192, 226, 227, 239, 251 to 258 (8 a/c), 263, 264, 265, 267 to 270 (4 a/c), 270, 285, 306, 308 to 315 (8 a/c), 329 to 342 (14 a/c), 351 to 355 (5 a/c), 360, 361, 362, 444 to 450 (7 a/c), 452 to 459 (8 a/c), 461, 464, ER614, 765, ES178, 18, 285, 310, JF286 to 293 (8 a/c), 295, 296, 297, JG732, 739, 773, 775 to 778 (4 a/c), 781 to 788 (8 a/c), 790 to 793 (4 a/c), 800, 802, 806, 838, 839, 840, 844, 850, 851, 874, 878, 890, 891, 897, 912, 914, 916 to 919 (4 a/c), l931, 932, 933, 940 to 943 (4 a/c), 945, 949, 950, 952 to 960 (9 a/c), JK101 to 109 (9 a/c), 111 to 143 (33 a/c), 145, 160 to 165 (6 a/c), 168 to 177 (10 a/c), 180 to 185 (6 a/c), 189, 215, 216, 249, 250, 254, 255, 257, 258, 260, 266, 273, 275, 279, 325 to 334 (10 a/c), 336, 338, 339, 359, 360, 361, 363 to 368 (6 a/c), 508, 511, 512. **February** JK788, BR287, EE846, 860, 864 to 867 (4 a/c), EF526 to 532 (7 a/c), 534 to 560 (27 a/c), 562, 563, 564, EN228, 229, 231, 233, 343 to 350 (8 a/c), 359, 364 to 370 (7 a/c), 390 to 398 (9 a/c), 411, 412, 413, 416, 451, 460, 462, 463, 466 to 469 (4 a/c), 471, 472, 473, 475 to 483 (9 a/c), 515 to 522 (8 a/c), 524, 525, 526, 528, 530, 533, 534, ES107, 291, 336, JF298, 300, 322 to 331 (10 a/c), 333 to 339 (7 a/c), JG749, 842, 882, 937, JK144, 159, 166, 167, 178, 179, 186, 187, 188, 190 to 195 (6 a/c), 214, 217 to 234 (18 a/c), 251, 252, 253, 256, 259, 261 to 269 (9 a/c), 271, 272, 274, 276, 277, 278, 281 to 285 (5 a/c), 303 to 314 (12 a/c), 316 to 322 (7 a/c), 321, 337, 340 to 346 (7 a/c), 370, 371, 373, 374, 383, 384, 385, 387 to 394 (8 a/c), 396 to 404 (9 a/c), 406, 407, 408, 425 to 428 (4 a/c), 430 to 433 (4 a/c), 435 to 462 (28 a/c), 464 to 472 (9 a/c), 506, 507, 509, 510, 513 to 526 (16 a/c), 600 to 610 (11 a/c), 612 to 619 (8 a/c), 637 to 640 (4 a/c), 642 to 649 (8 a/c), 651 to 654 (4 a/c), 656, 657, 658, 660 to 667 (8 a/c), 669 to 675 (7 a/c), 667, 678, 705 to 713 (9 a/c), 715 to 733 (19 a/c), 735 to 741 (7 a/c), 756, 757, 760, 763, 774, 775, 803, to 806 (4 a/c), 809, 810, 814, JL166. **March** BS506, 512, EF565 to 570 l(d6 a/c), 584 to 605 (22 a/c), 607 to 616 (10 a/c), 629 to 637 (9 a/c), EN234 to 238 (5 a/c), 399 to 406 (8 a/c), 414, 415, 417 to 428 (12 a/c), 452, 474, 490 to 493 (4 a/c), 495, 523, 527, 529, 531, 532, 551, 552, 555, 557, 558, 559, 561 to 566 (6 a/c), JF601 to 613 (13 a/c), 332, 340 to 364 (25 a/c), 392 to 403 (12 a/c), JG789, JK235, 280, 375 to 378 (4 a/c), 380, 381, 382, 395, 405, 429, 463, 527, 530 to 534 (5 a/c), 536, 537, 539, 541, 542, 543, 546, 548 to 551 (4 a/c), 611, 620, 659, 668, 676, 734, 742, 758, 759, 761, 762, 764 to 769 (6 a/c), 771, 772, 773, 776 to 796 (21 a/c), 807, 812, 813, 815 to 824 (10 a/c), 826 to 833 (8 a/c), 860 to 872 (13 a/c), 874 to 879 (6 a/c), 881 to 892 (12 a/c), 922 to 939 (18 a/c), 941 to 948 (8 a/c), 950, 967 to 978 (12 a/c), 980 to 983 (4 a/c), 986 to 992 (7 a/c), JL124 to 129 (6 a/c), 131, 133 to 140 (8 a/c), 160, 164, 167, 168, 171, 174, 175, 176, 180, 182, 183, 185, 186, 187, LZ807, 808, 810, 812, 813, MA754. **April** BS354, EF638 to 654 (17 a/c), 656, 671, 672, 673, EN232, 407 to 410 (4 a/c), 429, 430, 496 to l502 (7 a/c), 553, 554, 556, 567, 568, 570, 571, 572, 574, 575, 614 to 627 (14 a/c), JF404 to 411 (8 a/c), 413 to 427 (15 a/c), 443 to 461 (19 a/c), 463, 464, 466, 467, JK236, 369, 538, 540, 641, 770, 825, 834 to 839 (6 a/c), 842, 880, 984, 985, JL104, 105, 112 to 117 (6 a/c), 130, 161, 162, 169, 173, 177, 178, 179, 181, 184, 188, 208 to 216 (9 a/c), 218 to 222 (5 a/c), 224 to 233 (10 a/c), 235 to 238 (4 a/c), 240 to 251 (12 a/c), 253, 254, 256, 346, 347, 348, 350, 352, 355, 357, 358, 360, 362 to 365 (4 a/c), 367, 368, 369, 371, 372, 374 to 384 (11 a/c), 386 to 394 (9 a/c), LZ809, 811, 814, 815, 817 to 827 (11 a/c), 829 to 841 (13 a/c), 844 to 848 (5 a/c), 861 to 873 (13 a/c), 875 to 878 (4 a/c), 880, 881, 885, 928, MA328, 330 to 336 (7 a/c), 888 to 898 (11 a/c), 915 to 925 (11 a/c), 947 to 953 (7 a/c), 956, 992, 997, MB770, 771, 794 to 797 (4 a/c). **May** BS541, EF674 to 689 (16 a/c), EN221, 222, 503, 504, 505, 507 to 514 (8 a/c), 576 to 583 (8 a/c), 628, 629, 630, 632, 653, JF412, 462, 465, 468 to 476 (9 a/c), 478 to 485 (8 a/c), 501 to 515 (15 a/c), 517 to 522 (6 a/c), 578, JK544, 545, 547, 841, JL105, 118 to 123 (6 a/c), 301, 304 to 314 (11 a/c), 316 to 329 (5 a/c), 322, 324 to 330 (7 a/c), 332, 334, 335, 338, LZ874, 879, 881, 882, 884, 886, 887, 899, 926, 927, 929 to 946 (18 a/c), 953, 954, 969 to 991 (23 a/c), MA221 to 232 (12 a/c), 237 to 254 (18 a/c), 256 to 263 (8 a/c), 265, 266, 279 to 289 (11 a/c), 291 to 297 (7 a/c), 299, 300, 301, 304 to 309 (6 a/c), 315, 337 to 355 (19 a/c), 383, 390, 392, 398 to 418 (21 a/c), 467, 468, 477, 481, 483, MB643, 644, 647, 649, 650, 652, 772 to 793 (22 a/c), 800 to 806 (7 a/c), 808, 820, 821, 829 to 846 (18 a/c), 848, 888, 993 to 996 (4 a/c), 998. **June** AB200, EF690 to 701 (12 a/c), 703,704, 705, EN631, 633 to 637 (5 a/c), 652, 655 to 666 (12 a/c), EP615, 891, ER126, 713, ES185, JF523 to 528 (6 a/c), 557 to 577 (21 a/c), 579 to 592 (14 a/c), 613, 628, 629, 659, 700 to 710 (11 a/c), 712 to 716 (5 a/c), 740, 741, 742, JG722, 936, 949, JL132, 159, 172, 302, 303, 321, 323, 331, 333, 336, MA236, 290, 302, 310 to 313 (4 a/c), 356, 358, 359, 360, 363, 366, 367, 368, 385 to 389 (5 a/c), 391, 393, 394, 396, 397, 443, 444, 445, 447 to 466 (20 a/c), 469 to 476 (8 a/c), 478, 479, 480, 482, 484 to 487 (4 a/c), 501 to 505 (5 a/c), 507 to 523 (17 a/c), 523, 525 to 546 (22 a/c), 559 to 586 (28 a/c), 588 to 601 (13 a/c), 615 to 620 (6 a/c), 622 to 627 (6 a/c), 630, 631, 532, 634, 636, 637, 638, 640, 641, 653, 654, 656, 670 to 682 (13 a/c), 684, 685, 686, 688, 689, 691, 692, 694, 695, 700, 701, 703, 706, 707, 708, 711, 730, 739, 807, 851, 852, 853, 855, 857, 898 to 901 (4 a/c), 904, 905, MB822 to 828 (7 a/c), 847, 849 to 854 (6 a/c). **July** AB910, EF702, 706 to 710 (5 a/c), 715, 716, EN569, 573, 667 to 679 (13 a/c), JF516, 614 to 619 (6 a/c), 627, 630, 658, 660 to 676 (17 a/c), 692 to 695 (4 a/c), 697, 698, 699, 711, 743 to 789 (47 a/c), 805 to 810 (6 a/c), 834, 836, JK979, JL106, 163, 165, 223, 337, 372, 373, MA298, 361, 362, 364, 365, 384, 395, 419 to 428 (10 a/c), 524, 621 a/c), 629, 633, 639, 642, 702, 704, 705, 709, 710, 712, 713, 726 to 729 (4 a/c), 731 to 738 (8 a/c), 740 to 751 (12 a/c), 753, 755 to 757 (3 a/c), 759, 761a to 767 (7 a/c), 790 to 819 (30 a/c), 831 to 850 (20 a/c), 856, 858, 859, 861, 863, 877, 880, 881, 882, 885 895 (11 a/c), 902, 906, MB761 to 764 (4 a/c), 855 to 862 (8 a/c), MH298 to 311 (4 a/c), 313 to 316 (4 a/c), 318 to 327 (10 a/c), 329, 334, 335, 336, 349, 352 to 357 (6 a/c), 359, 361, 365, 564, 566, 568, 581 to 585 (5 a/c), 637 to 646 (10 a/c), MJ241, 632. **August** AA875, EF717 to 727 (11 a/c), 729, EN680 to 685 (6 a/c), ES202, JF620 to 626 (7 a/c), 696, 811 to 814 (4 a/c), 816 to 833 (18 a/c), 835, 837 to 850 (14 a/c), 869 to 879 (11 a/c), 900, 901, 902, 926 to 950 (25 a/c), 952, JG119 to 124 (6 a/c), JL110, 111, 234, 239, 351, 353, 354, 370, 395, LZ828, MA369, 506, 628, 683, 687, 690, 698, 698, 699, 758, 854, 860, 863, 878, 883, 896, 897, MB765 to 769 (5 a/c), 863, 875, 876, 877, 889 to 898 (10 a/c), MH328, 330 to 334 (4 a/c), 351, 358, 360, 362, 363, 364, 366 to 390 (25 a/c), 413, 414, 416 to 456 (41 a/c), 470 to 499 (30 a/c), 501 to 512 (12 a/c), 526, 527, 529 to 544 (17 a/c), 547, 548, 550 to 563 (14 a/c), 567, 586 to 600 (15 a/c), 605, 608, 612 to 615 (4 a/c), 621, 622, 647 to 656 (10 a/c), 944, 945, 947 to 955 (9 a/c), 957, 958, 970, 973, 974, 976, 977, 979, 981, 984. **September** EF728, 730, 732 to 739 (8 a/c), 748, 749, 750, JF880 to 886 (7 a/c), 951 , 953 to 967 (16 a/c), JG104 to 118 (15 a/c), 157 to 203 (47 a/c), 239 to 251 (13 a/c), 330 to 334 (5 a/c), JL217, 356, 359, 366, MA693, 760, 879, 884, MB879, 880, 881, 889 to 916 (18 a/c), 936 to 942 (7 a/c), 953, 954, MH500, 528, 545, 549, 602, 604, 607, 609, 611, 618, 619, 620, 623, 635, 636, 657 to 678 (22 a/c), 691 to 724 (34 a/c), 726 to 738 (13 a/c), 750 to 778 (29 a/c), 780 to 796 (17 a/c), 813 to 823 (11 a/c), 825, 826, 828, 829, 830, 833, 834, 838, 849, 888 to 900 (13 a/c), 902, 903, 904, 907, 908, 909, 912, 924, 925, 927, 930 to 937 (8 a/c), 940, 942, 946, 956, 971, 972, 975, 978, 980, 982, 983, 985 to 999 (15 a/c). **October** EF740 to 747 (8 a/c), 751, 752, EN654, JF815, 887, JG251 to 275 (25 a/c), 312, 335 to 337 (3 a/c), 339 to 356 (18 a/c), 371 to 382 (12 a/c), 407, 409 to 412 (4 a/c), 414 to 425 (12 a/c), 427 to 432 (6 a/c), 465 to 476 (12 a/c), 478, 542, JL385, MA329, MB929, 930, 931, 943 to 947 (5 a/c), 949, 950, 951, MH601, 603, 606, 616, 617, 725, 779, 824, 827, 831, 832, 835, 836, 837, 840 to 848 (9 a/c), 850 to 856 (7 a/c), 869 to 873 (5 a/c), 875 to 887 (13 a/c), 901, 906, 910, 911, 926, 938, 939, MJ114 to 156 (44 a/c), 169 to 187 (19 a/c), 189, 191 to 194 (4 a/c), 197 to 203 (6 a/c), 215, 216, 218, 219, 220, 222, 224 to 230 (7 a/c), 232 to 237 (6 a/c), 239, 240, 245 to 248 (4 a/c), 250 to 258 (9 a/c), 271, 272, 274, 275, 277, 278, 280 to 284 (5 a/c), 286 to 293 (8 a/c), 295 to 300 (6 a/c), 302, 303, 304, 306 to 314 (9 a/c), 328 to 336 (9 a/c), 384,

385, 389, 403, RB142, 143. **November** EF753, LV643, LZ816, MB882, 952, 955 to 958 (4 a/c), MD100 to 105 (6 a/c), 221, 223, JF888 to 899 (12 a/c), JG313 to 323 (11 a/c), 325 to 328 (4 a/c), 383 to 387 (5 a/c), 404, 405, 406, 477, 482, 486 to 496 (11 a/c), 498, 499, 500, 531, 532, 538 to 541 (4 a/c), 545, 546, 547, 555, 559 to 563 (5 a/c), 565, 567, 603, 606, 615 to 622 (8 a/c), MH929, MJ188, 195, 196, 202, 242, 243, 244, 249, 276, 279, 285, 301, 305, 337, 339, 340, 342 to 353 (12 a/c), 355 to 358 (4 a/c), 360 to 363 (4 a/c), 366, 382, 383, 386, 387, 388, 390 to 402 (13 a/c), 404 to 428 (25 a/c), 441 to 456 (16 a/c), 458 to 485 (28 a/c), 498 to 521 (24 a/c), 523 to 531 (9 a/c), 533, 534, 575, 576, 578 to 588 (11 a/c), 604, 606, 608 to 614 (7 a/c), 616 to 620 (5 a/c), 624, 629, 630, 633, 643 to 646 (4 a/c), 668, 835 to 845 (11 a/c), PA838 to 842 (5 a/c), 844 to 851 (8 a/c), 860, 863, 865, 867, 892, RB145, 149. **December** JG324, 408, 413, 479, 481, 483, 484, 485, 497, 528, 529, 530, 533 to 537 (5 a/c), 548, 549, 564, 566, 568, 604, 605, 607 to 613 (7 a/c), 623, LV644 to 660 (17 a/c), 732, 733, 740, 741, MD106 to 116 (11 a/c), 118, 119, 120, 217 to 220 (4 a/c), 222 to 245 (24 a/c), MH928, MJ190, 367, 368, 369, 522, 532, 535, 536, 549 to 555 (7 a/c), 558, 560, 562, 564, 566, 567, 569 to 574 (6 a/c), 577, 589, 602, 605, 607, 615, 621, 622, 625 to 628 (4 a/c), 631, 634, 635, 638 to 642 (5 a/c), 659 to 698 (40 a/c), 712 to 733 (41 a/c), 735 to 753 (19 a/c), 756, 769 to 777 (9 a/c), 779 to 797 (18 a/c), 799, 800, 801, 814, 815, 816, 818 to 822 (5 a/c), 827 to 834 (8 a/c), 846 to 858 (13 a/c), 871 to 879 (9 a/c), 881 to 886 (6 a/c), 888, 891, 904, 926, 927, 928, 938 to 942 (5 a/c), 951, MT524, 525, 527, 539, MK226 to 231 (6 a/c), 233, PA852 to 856 (5 a/c), 861, 862, 864, 866, 868 to 871 (4 a/c), 884 to 891 (8 a/c), 895, RB140, 147, 148, 150 to 157 (8 a/c).

1944 January JG480, 527, LV677 to 681 (5 a/c), 727, 734, 735, 737, 738, 739, 742 to 749 (8 a/c), 755, 756, MA752, MB883, 960, MD121 to 128 (8 a/c), 130 to 140 (11 a/c), 142, 214, 215, 216, 246 to 251 (6 a/c), 253, 255, 272 to 281 (10 a/c), 283, 284, 295 to 300 (6 a/c), 302, 303, 315 to 318 (4 a/c), 332, 334, 337, 338, 354, MH610, 941, MJ217, 294, 563, 603, 623, 637, 754, 778, 792, 798, 817, 824, 825, 826, 870, 880, 887, 889, 893 to 897 (5 a/c), 899 to 903 (5 a/c), 905 to 913; (9 a/c), 929 to 933 (5 a/c), 943, 944, 947, 949, 950, 952 to 962 (11 a/c), 964 to 967 (4 a/c), 979, 981 to 999 (19 a/c), MK112 to 127 (16 a/c), 129, 130, 132 to 145 (14 a/c), 147 to 154 (8 a/c), 157, 158, 171 to 176 (6 a/c), 178 to 185 (8 a/c), 187, 189 to 196 (8 a/c), 198, 199, 201, 202, 204 to 209 (6 a/c), 211, 212, 232, 234, 236 to 253 (18 a/c), 255, 256, 280, 281, 282, 285, 287, 292 to 297 (6 a/c), 299 to 302 (4 a/c), 304, 306, 309, 312, 313, 316, 317, 320, 341, 347, 603, 604, 606, 607, MT523, 545, PA857, 858, 893, 894, 896 to 899 (4 a/c), 901 to 907 (7 a/c), 909, 911, 912, 926, 929, 934, RB158 to 164 (7 a/c), 166, 169, 173. **February** JG543, 550, 551, 552, 556, 557, 558, LV726, 736, 750, MB884, 885, 886, 932, 933, 934, 935, MD129, 141, 143 to 146 (4 a/c), 159, 160, 252, 254, 256, 269, 270, 271, 282, 285, 286, 288 to 294 (7 a/c), 319, 320, 324 to 328 (5 a/c), 335, 336, 339 to 342 (4 a/c), 344, 345, 355, 356, 369 to 378 (10 a/c), 389 to 401 (13 a/c), MJ223, 231, 963, MK131, 146, 155, 156, 188, 197, 200, 203, 213, 235, 254, 257 to 268 (12 a/c), 283, 284, 286, 288 to 291 (4 a/c), 298, 303, 305, 307, 308, 310, 311, 314, 315, 318, 319, 321 to 326 (6 a/c), 339, 340, 342 to 346 (5 a/c), 349 to 368 (20 a/c), 370 to 379 (10 a/c), 392 to 428 (37 a/c), 440 to 453 (14 a/c), 456, 458 to 461 (4 a/c), 463, 465 to 468 (4 a/c), 470, 472, 473, 474, 476 to 479 (4 a/c), 483 to 486 (4 a/c), 499 to 505 (7 a/c), 509, 510, 513, 515, 518, 519, 522, 525, 526, 528, 530, 533, 547 to 553 (7 a/c), 555, 556, 605, 608 to 616 (9 a/c), 618 to 630 (13 a/c), 633, 634, 662, 664, 665, 668, 713, 718k, 740, 745, 746, 748, 755, 772, MT526, 541, 543, PA900, 910, 913, 927, 928, 930 to 933 (4 a/c), 935 to 938 (4 a/c), 940 to 950 (10 a/c), 959, 960, 961, PL759, 760, 761, 764, 770, RB165, 172, 174 to 183 (10 a/c), 185 to 188 (4 a/c). **March** JG553, 554, 624, 646 to 653 (8 a/c), 655 to 660 (6 a/c), 664 to 671 (8 a/c), 675 to 686 (12 a/c), JK840, JL107, MA645, 646, 651, 657, MB959, 961 to 966 (6 a/c), 968, MD161 to 174 (14 a/c), 287, 301, 321, 322, 323, 329, 330, 331, 333, 343, 346, 348, 379 to 388 (10 a/c), 403, MJ238, 550, 636, 934, 935, 943, 944, MK177, 454, 457, 462, 464, 469, 471, 475, 480, 481, 482, 506, 507, 508, 511, 512, 514, 516, 517, 521, 523, 524, 527, 531, 532, 534, 554, 557 to 573 (17 a/c), 575, 578, 581 to 586 (6 a/c), 588, 589, 631, 632, 635 to 646 (12 a/c), 659, 663, 666, 667, 669 to 676 (8 a/c), 680, 681, 682, 684, 686, 687, 689 to 696 (8 a/c), 714, 716, 717, 718, 720 to 731 (12 a/c), 733 to 740 (8 a/c), 742, 743, 744, 747, 749 to 752 (4 a/c), 754, 756, 769, 770, 771, 773 to 812 (40 a/c), 826 to 841 (16 a/c), 843 to 849 (7 a/c), 851 to 862 (12 a/c), 867, 868, 881 to 890 (10 a/c), 892 to 898 (7 a/c), 900 to 913 (14 a/c), 916 to 926 (11 a/c), 940, 941, 942, 944, 948, 952, 967, 969, 982, 983, 985 to 993 (9 a/c), 995, ML117 to 143 (27 a/c), 145 to 153 (9 a/c), 170, 171, 179, 192, 194, 202, MT502, 504, 505, 506, 508, 512, 540, 542, 544, PL762, 763, 765 to 769 (5 a/c), 771 to 774 (4 a/c), 776, 777, RB168, 170, 171, 184, 189. **April** EN297, 494, JG614, 661, 662, 663, 672, 687 to 695 (9 a/c), LV728, 729, MB967, 969 to 972 (4 a/c), 974, 975, 976, MD117, 177 to 183 (7 a/c), MJ221, 557, 559, 565, 934, 945, 946, MK348, 529, 574, 577, 579, 580, 587, 660, 661, 677, 678, 679, 683, 685, 688, 698, 699, 864, 891, 899, 914, 915, 939, 943, 945, 946, 947, 949, 950, 951, 953 to 961 (13 a/c), 981, 994, 996, 997, 998, 990, ML112 to 116 (5 a/c), 154, 155, 156, 169, 172 to 178 (7 a/c), 180 to 185 (6 a/c), 187 to 191 (5 a/c), 193, 195 to 201 (7 a/c), 203, 204, 205, 207 to 216 (10 a/c), 229 to 243 (15 a/c), 247 to 262 (16 a/c), 264 to 270 (7 a/c), 272 to 277 (6 a/c), 291 to 300 (10 a/c), 302, 339 to 374 (36 a/c), 376 to 380 (5 a/c), 396 to 404 (9 a/c), 406 to 421 (25 a/c), 423 to 428 (6 a/c), MT503, 507, 509, 510, 511, 516 to 522 (7 a/c), 593 to 613 (21 a/c), 615 to 624 (10 a/c), 626, 627, 628, 632, 648 to 655 (8 a/c), 657, 658, 676, 738, 889, NH148 to 153 (6 a/c), 155 to 158 (4 a/c), 171 to 180 (10 a/c), 182, 339, 341, 393 to 400 (8 a/c), 402 to 411, PL340, 775, 778 to 799 (22 a/c), 824, 828, RM616, 618, 619, 620. **May** LV731, 751, 752, 754, MB973, MD175, 184 to 190 (7 a/c), 349, 350, 352, 353, MJ359, 365, 568, 936, 937, MK617, 697, 842, 866, 968, 984, ML206, 244, 246, 271, 301, 303 to 323 (21 a/c), 375, 381, 405, 422, MT515, 546 to 553 (8 a/c), 625, 627, 629, 630, 631, 633, 634, 635, 656, 659 to 673 (15 a/c), 677, 681, 682, 703, 708, 761, 763, 764, 765, 767 to 789 (23 a/c), 793, 794, MV426, NH181, 183 to 193 (11 a/c), 195 to 218 (24 a/c), 231 to 237 (7 a/c), 239 to 276 (38 a/c), 289 to 308 (20 a/c), 310 to 313 (4 a/c), 315 to 326 (12 a/c), 342 to 345 (4 a/c), 347 to 358 (12 a/c), 360 to 363 (4 a/c), 365, 367, 368, 370, 373, 381, 412 to 427 (16 a/c), 429 to 438 (10 a/c), 450 to 489 (40 a/c), 491 to 496 (6 a/c), 513 to 525 (13 a/c), 527, 529, 530, 531, 533, 534, 535, 540, 543, 544, 546, 550, 552, 554, 570, PL123, 124, 265 to 273 (9 a/c), 275 to 286 (12 a/c), 288, PL823, 825, 826, 829 to 837 (9 a/c), 839, 840, 841, RB167, RM615, 621, 622, 623, 670 to 673 (4 a/c), 676, 677, 708. **June** WE228, JF275, LV753, MJ354, MK369, ML144, MT554 to 565 (12 a/c), 674, 675, 679, 680, 683 to 689 (7 a/c), 704 to 723 (20 a/c), 790, 791, 792, 795 to 802 (8 a/c), 816, 817, 819 to 824 (6 a/c), 892, 928, 929, 930, 932 to 948 (17 a/c), 952, 953, 955, 956, 957, MV458, NH154, 359, 364, 366, 369, 371, 372, 374, 376 to 380 (5 a/c), 401, 427, 490, 526, 528, 532, 536 to 539 (4 a/c), 541, 542, 545, 547, 548, 549, 551, 553, 555 to 558 (4 a/c), 571 to 600 (30 a/c), 602 to 611 (10 a/c), PK992 to 998 (7 a/c), PL125 to 160 (36 a/c), 185 to 228 (44 a/c), 246 to 264 (19 a/c), 287, 313 to 336 (25 a/c), 369 to 408 (40 a/c), 423 to 438 (16 a/c), 440 to 451 (12 a/c), 454, 456 to 460 (5 a/c), 462 to 466 (5 a/c), 488, 489, 492, 494 to 497 (4 a/c), 499, PL838, 842 to 860 (19 a/c), 862, 863, 864, RM624, 625, 648 to 656 (9 a/c), 675, 678 to 688 (11 a/c), 726 to 732 (7 a/c), 734, 735, 739, PT355 to 360 (6 a/c), 360, 363, 373, 374, 379, 380, 395, 397, 403. **July** MK186, MT566 to 580 (15 a/c), 723, 724, 726 to 733 (8 a/c), 762, 815, 825, 826, 827, 829 to 835 (7 a/c), 931, 949, 950, 951, 954, 958 to 969 (12 a/c), 981 to 998(18 a/c), MU112 to 116 (5 a/c), 118 to 121 (4 a/c), 123, 124, 125, 128, 129, 132, 398 to 402 (5 a/c), 404, 405, 407, 408, 409, NH314, PA893, PK991, PL161 to 169 (9 a/c), 337, 339, 341 to 348 (8 a/c), 350 to 356 (7 a/c), 439, 452, 453, 455, 461, 490, 491, 493, 498, PT361, 362, 364 to 372 (9 a/c), 375 to 378 (4 a/c), 396, 398 to 402 (5 a/c), 404 to 412 (9 a/c), 415 to 436 (22 a/c), 451, 453 to 457 (5 a/c), 459, 461 to 468 (8 a/c), 470, 471, 473 to 498 (26 a/c), 582 to 610 (29 a/c), 612, 614 to 627 (14 a/c), 640 to 646 (7 a/c), 648 to 651 (4 a/c), 653 to 658 (6 a/c), 660 to 668 (9 a/c), 671 to 679 (9 a/c), 681 , 682, 698, 699, 701, 710, PL864, 866, 881, 882, 883, 885 to 899 (15 a/c), 901 to 906 (6 a/c), 908, PV116, 117, 118, 120, 121, RM689, 690, 691, 695, 696, 700, 733, 736, 737, 740 to 744 (5 a/c), 746 to 756 (11 a/c), 760, 761. **August** BS310, EN465, MJ457, MK850, 865, MT581, 734 to 737 (4 a/c), 739, 740, 741, 828, 872 to 882 (11 a/c), 999, MV117, 122, 126, 127, 130, 131, 133 to 136 (4 a/c), 138 to 144 (7 a/c), 148, 149, 152, 403, 406, 410 to 424 (15 a/c), 427 to 431 (4 a/c), 433, 434, PA893, 758, 907, 909 to 913 (5 a/c), 915, 916, 917, 919, 920, 921, PT458, 469, 472, 523 to 558 (36 a/c), 560, 563, 566, 567, 611, 639, 652, 659, 670, 680, 683, 697, 700, 702 to 709 (8 a/c), 711 to 738 (28 a/c), 752 to 781 (30 a/c), 784 to 795 (12 a/c), 818 to 837 (20 a/c), 839 to 859 (21 a/c), 873 to 887 (15 a/c), 889 to 915 (27 a/c), 930 to 939 (10 a/c), 941, 943, 945 to 963 (19 a/c), 965 to 970 (6 a/c), 987, 988, 989, 993 to 997 (5 a/c), PV115, 119, 122 to 134 (13 a/c), 136, 137, 138, 142, 146, 148, 149, 152, 154, 193, RK799, RM698, 699, 704, 705, 707, 710, 762 to 765 (4 a/c), 767, 770, 783, 787 to 795 (9 a/c), RR181, 183 to 188 (6 a/c) . **September** MK128, 602, MT742, 743, 744, 748, 766, 883 to 888 (6 a/c), 890, 891, 893 to 897 (5 a/c), 899 to 902 (4 a/c), MV137, 145, 146, 147, 151, 153, 155, 156, 169 to 175 (7 a/c), 182, 194, 321 to 327 (7 a/c), 425, 432, 435 to 441 (7 a/c), 456, 457, 459 to 481 (23 a/c), 483, 485, 486, PA910, 911, 914, 918, 922 to 925 (4 a/c), 950, 951, 953, 954, 955, 957 to 960 (4 a/c), 962, 963, PT559, 561, 562, 564, 565, 783, 838, 929, 940, 942, 964, 990, 991, 992, 998, 999, PV139, 140, 141, 143, 144, 145, 147, 150, 153, 155 to 160 (6 a/c), 174 to 192 (19 a/c), 194 to 201 (8 a/c), 204, 205, 207 to 215 (9 a/c), 229 to 234 (6 a/c), 236, 237, 238, 240 to 270 (31 a/c), 284 to 289 (6 a/c), 291 to 296 (6 a/c), 298 to 302 (5 a/c), 304 to 314 (11 a/c), 316, 317, 318, 320, 322, 324 to 327 (4 a/c), 341, 342, 343, 345, 346, 348 to 356 (9 a/c), RK798, 800 to 819 (20 a/c), 836, 838 to 842 (5 a/c), 847 to 851 (5 a/c), 853, 859, 865, 866, 868, 883, 888, 891, 892, 893, 895, 896, 897, 902 to 905 (4 a/c), 910, 913, 918, 921, 925, 926, RM692, 697, 703, 706, 709, 711, 712, 738, 769, 784, 796, 798, 799, 800, 802, 805 to 814 (10 a/c), 819, 865 to 868 (4 a/c), 871. **October** MT745, 746, 747, 903 to 908 (6 a/c), 910, MV150, 176 to 180 (5 a/c), 183, 184, 186, 187, 189 to 193 (5 a/c), 197, 200, 202, 204, 240 to 245 (6 a/c), 329, 342, 344, 482, 484, 487, 499 to 507 (9 a/c), 509 to 514 (6 a/c), PA952, 956, 961, 964 to 970 (7 a/c), 972 to 978 (7 a/c), 980, 982, 984, 986, PT460, 782, 944, PV135, 288, 295, 303, 307, 315, 319, 321, 327, 344, 349, 357, 358, 359, RK835, 837, 840, 842 to 846 (5 a/c), 849, 852, 854 to 868 (15 a/c), 887 to 926 (41 a/c), RM713, 785, 801, 804, 815, 817, 818, 820 to 825 (6 a/c), 839 to 863 (24 a/c), 869, 870, 872, 873 to 879 (7 a/c), 881 to 884 (4 a/c), 886, 887, 901, 902, 904, 906, 907, RR193, 205 to 213 (10 a/c), 226 to 232 (7 a/c), 234, 235, 236, 238 to 245 (8 a/c), 247, 249 to 262 (14 a/c), 264, 265, SM149, 150, 170 to 184 (14 a/c), 186 to 190 (5 a/c), 192 to 197 (6 a/c), 200, 201, 202, 203, 205 to 211 (7 a/c), 213, 226, 230 to 233 (4 a/c), 236 to 239 (4 a/c), 241 to 253 (13 a/c), 255, 256, 258, 273, 276, 277, 278, 282, 283, 284, 286, 287, 289, 290, 292, 293, 294, 296, 299, 304, 305, 312, 331, 441 to 449 (9 a/c), 451, 453, 455, 456, 522, TA833, 837, 839, 840, 844, 851, 854 to 881 (28 a/c), 883 to 887 (5 a/c), 905 to 909 (5 a/c). **November** JG654, LA201 to 210 (10 a/c), MA255, MD347, MT898, 909, 911, 912, 913, 915, MV181, 185, 188, 195, 196, 198, 199, 206, 207, 208, 231, 233 to 238 (6 a/c), 246, 248, 252, 270, 323, 343, 345, 346, NH614 to 623 (10 a/c), 625, 626, 628, 629, 742, 743, 744, PA981, 985, 987 to 998 (12 a/c), PM123, 124, 125, 128, 129, PS831, RM880, 885, 903, 905, 909 to 920 (12 a/c), 922, 923, 925, 926, 928 to 935 (8 a/c), 937, 939, 940, RN113 to 127 (15 a/c), RR246, SM185, 191, 198, 199, 204, 227, 228, 229, 234, 235, 240, 254, 257, 274, 275, 285, 288, 291, 295, 298, 300 to 303 (4 a/c), 306 to 311 (6 a/c), 313, 314, 315, 329, 339, 333 to 359 (27 a/c), 361 to 369 (9 a/c), 383 to 409 (27 a/c), 412 to 418 (7 a/c), 420 to 424 (5 a/c). 426, 427, 464, 465, 466, 468, 470 to 473 (4 a/c), 475, 476, 477, 479, 481 to 485 (5 a/c), 487, 488, 511, 512, 579, 580 to 583 (4 a/c), 585 to 597 (13 a/c), 611 to 619 (9 a/c), 621, 622, 625, 626, 627, 630, 632, 635, 641, 643, 644, 647, TA882, 888, 910 to 935 (26 a/c), 937, 940, 941, 942, 971 to 974 (4 a/c), 976 to 984 (9 a/c), 986, 987, 990, 991. **December** LA312, MT725, 823, 836, 837, 840, 843, 914, MV203, 205, 232, 249, 251, 254 to 258 (5 a/c), 260, 261, NH624, 627, 630 to 633 (4 a/c), 626, 745, PM126, 127, 130 to 138 (9 a/c), 140, 141, 142, PS832 to 836 (6 a/c), RM864, 924, 936, 938, 940, 942, 943, 957 to 963 (7 a/c), 965 to 971 (7 a/c), 973 to 981 (9 a/c), 984, 988, RN140, RR237, SM360, 419, 467, 474, 480, 507, 516, 538, 486, 523, 536, 565, 568, 574, 584, 610, 620, 623, 624, 628, 629, 631, 633, 634, 636 to 640 (5 a/c), 642, 645, 646, 648, 663 to 671 (9 a/c), TA738, 740 to 758 (19 a/c), 761, 763 to 774 (12 a/c), 776 to 779 (4 a/c), 793 to 804 (12 a/c), 806, 807, 808, 810 to 820 (11 a/c), 936, 938, 939, 943 to 948 (6 a/c), 960 to 965 (6 a/c), 967 to 970 (4 a/c), 975, 985, 988, 989, 992 to 995 (4 a/c), 998, TB116, 118, 119, 124, 130, 168 to 174 (7 a/c), 176 to 184 (9 a/c), 186, 187, 188, 193, 195, 196, 214, 216, 218 to 223 (6 a/c), 225, 230, 232, 235, 239, 242, 243, 248, 249, 254, 255, 256, 282, 414 to 419 (7 a/c), 421, 422, 432, 434 to 442 (9 a/c), 710.

1945 January LA222, MT838, 839, 841, 842, 844, 845, 846, MV201, I253, 264 ato 269 (6 a/c), 271, 272, 358, 360, 361, 364, 365, 366, 378, NH634, 635, PM139, 143 to 152 (10 a/c), 156, PS849 to 852 (4 a/c), 854, 855, 856, RK886, RM693, 964, 972, 982, 986, 987, 989 to 997 (9 a/c), RN128 to 139 (12 a/c), 141 to 150 (10 a/c), 152, 153, 154, 158, 159, 160, SM316, 469, 503, TA760, 762, 805, 995, 996, 997, 999, TB115, 117, 121, 122, 123, 125 to 129 (5 a/c), 131 to 144 (14 a/c), 149, 175, 185, 189 to 192 (4 a/c), 197, 213, 215, 217, 224, 226, 227, 228, 231, 233, 234, 236, 237, 238, 240, 241, 244 to 247 (4 a/c), 250, 251, 253, 269, 270, 272 to 281 (10 a/c), 283 to 297 (15 a/c), 326 to 349 (24 a/c), 352 to 361 (10 a/c), 363, 365 to 373 (9 a/c), 375, 376, 378, 381, 384 to 390 (7 a/c), 393, 394, 395, 420, 423, 424, 425, 493 to 498 (6 a/c), 502, 520, 522, 528, 578, 616, 777, 778, 779, 781, 782, 784, 785, 787, TE193. **February** LA215, 221, 223 to 231 (9 a/c), 234, 235, MT847, 849, 850, 851, 853, 854, 857, 858, MV273, 286 to 289 (4 a/c), 291, 292, 294, 296, 298, 300 to 303 (4 a/c), 306, 359, 363, 367 to 377 (11 a/c), 379 to 386 (8 a/c), NH367, 697, 698, 701, 704, 741, 746 to 750 (5 a/c), 752, 753, 755, 756, 758, 775, 776, 780, PM154, 155, 157, 158, 159, PS857, 861 to 866 (6 a/c), 868, RM786, 816, 983, 985, RN151, 155, 156, 157, 159, 173 to 200 (28 a/c), 202, 203, 205 to 214 (10 a/c), SM212, 812, 813, 816, 817, TA775, 809, 966, TB120, 145 to 148 (4 a/c), 150, 362, 364, 374, 377, 379, 380, 383, 391, 396, 443 to 450 (8 a/c), 464 to 492 (29 a/c), 500, 501, 502, 515, 517, 519, 521, 524, 525, 526, 530 to 533 (4 a/c), 535, 537, 539, 540, 542 to 546 (5 a/c), 548, 549, 564, 565, 567, 568, 569, 571 to 577 (7 a/c), 580 to 598 (18 a/c), 613, 614, 617 to 627 (11 a/c), 629 to 659 (31 a/c), 674 to 692 (19 a/c), 694, 695, 696, 699 to 709 (11 a/c), 711, 712, 714, 715, 717, 718, 733 to 753 (21 a/c), 755, 756, 758, 759, 771, 780, 783, 786, 788 to 808 (21 a/c), 824 to 838 (15 a/c), 846, 847, 858 to 862 (5 a/c), 864, 866, 883, 884, 888, 890 to 896 (7 a/c), 903 to 908 (6 a/c), 910 to 922 (13 a/c), 925, 939 to 942 (4 a/c), 944 to 948 (5 a/c), 950, 984 to 987 (4 a/c), 991, 995. **March** BM160, MJ341, MT848, 852, 855, 856, LA197, 236, 249, 250, 251, 252, MV239, 250, 259, 262, 293, 295, 299, 304, 305, 307 to 317 (11 a/c), 319, 320, NH638 to 659 (22 a/c), 686, 687, 688, 689, 700, 703, 705, 707 to 710 (4 a/c), 713 to 716 (4 a/c), 751, 754, 757, 759, 777 to 779 (3 a/c), 781 to 813 (33 a/c), 892, 895 to 901 (7 a/c), 903, 904, 905, 908, 910, NM814, PT452, PS860, 867, 869 to 885 (17 a/c), 888, RM908, RN204, 215, SM814, 815, 818 to 831 (14 a/c), 833 to 842 (10 a/c), TB298, 518, 570, 615, 628, 693, 698, 713, 716, 754, 839 to 845 (7 a/c), 848 to 857 (10 a/c), 867, 868, 886, 887, 889, 897 to 902 (6 a/c), 909, 914, 915, 923, 924, 938, 943, 949, 951 to 959 (9 a/c), 971, 972, 973, 975 to 980 (6 a/c), 983, 988, 990, 992, 993, 994, 997, 998, 999, TD 113 to 134 (22 a/c), 136 to 154 (19 a/c), 156, 157, 158, 175 to 206 (31 a/c), 229 to 233 (5 a/c), 235, 237 to 242 (6 a/c), 245, 249 to 267 (19 a/c), 280 to 292 (13 a/c), 294 to 315 (22 a/c), 318, 352, 353, 355, 356, 358 to 361 (4 a/c), 366, 367, 952 to 958 (7 a/c), 973, 974, TP256. **April** LA232, 233, 253 to 263 (11 a/c), MV297, 318, 347to 357 (11 a/c), NH660, 661, 685, 689 to 694 (6 a/c), 696, 711, 712, 718, 719, 720, 832, 834 to 841 (8 a/c), 844, 845, 846, 855, 857 to 871 (15 a/c), 873, 874, 875, 893, 894, 902, 906, 907, 909, 911 to 917 (7 a/c), NM815 to 823 (9 a/c), PK314, 316, PS858, 887, 889 to 893 (5 a/c), 908, 909, 910, 913, 915 to 920 (6 a/c), RM627, 628, 757, 759, 766, RN216, 217, SM478, 876, 878 to 888 (11 a/c), TB697, 981, 982, TD207 to 213 (7 a/c), 234, 236, 243, 246, 247, 293, 316, 317, 319 to 325 (7 a/c), 338 to 342 (6 a/c), 345, 347 to 351 (5 a/c), 354, 357, 362 to 365 (4 a/c), 368 to 371 (4 a/c), 373, 374, 375, 377, 378, 379, 395, 398, 399, 970, 971, 975 to 983 (9 a/c), 985 to 991 (7 a/c), 994 to 999 (6 a/c), TE115 to 138 (24 a/c), 140 to 144 (5 a/c), 148, 149, 186 to 189 (4 a/c), 191, 192, 194, 195, 196, 198 to 204 (7 a/c), 206 to 210 (5 a/c), 228, 229, 235, 237, 244, 245, 247, 251, 346, 493, 495, TX986, 988 to 992 (5 a/c), 996. **May** EN470, LA198, 199, 200, 211, 264, 265, 266, 268 to 271 (4 a/c), 273, MV290, NH695, 918 to 929 (12 a/c), PK317, 319, 321, 322, PM496, 500, 501, 504, PS911, PT413, 921 to 925 (5 a/c), 930 to 935 (6 a/c), RM626, 629 to 640 (12 a/c), 643, 644, RN218 to 221 (4 a/c), SM844, 845, 889 to 899 (11 a/c), 913, 914, 916, 917, TA759, TD155, 248, 344, 372, 396, 397, 400 to 407 (8 a/c), TE139, 145, 146, 150 to 158 (9 a/c), 174 to 183 (10 a/c), 185, 197, 205, 211, 212, 215, 216, 230 to 234 (5 a/c), 238 to 243 (6 a/c), 248, 249, 250, 253 to 259 (7 a/c), 274 to 283 (10 a/c), 285, 286, 287, 289, 291, 295, 296, 298, 300, 305, 307, 494, 496, 497, 498, 508 to 511 (4 a/c), 525, 526, 528 to 531 (4 a/c), 533, 534, 535, 549, 550, 552, 553, 554, 556, 557, 560, TP237 to 240 (4 a/c), 257, 258, TX102 to 125 (24 a/c), 127, 184 to 189 (6 a/c). **June** LA272, 274 to 282 (9 a/c), 299, NH843, 847, 848, 849, 851, PK322, 324, 331, 393 to 396 (4 a/c), PM505 to 519 (15 a/c), 536 to 549 (14 a/c), PS886, 926 to 929 (4 a/c), RM641, 642, 645, 646, 647, RW344 to 349 (6 a/c), 374, 376, 379, SL625 to 630 (6 a/c), 632 to 635 (4 a/c), 648, 649, 650, SM916, 918 to 926 (9 a/c), 928, TE190, 252, 284, 290, 292, 293, 294, 297, 299, 301 to 304 (4 a/c), 306, 309 to 315 (6 a/c), 328, 329, 331 to 340 (10 a/c), 342 to 345 (4 a/c), 347 to 354 (8 a/

c), 358, 369, 375, 378, 379, 381, 382, 383, 385, 389, 390, 393 to 400 (8 a/c), 402, 403, 407, 408, 434, 437 to 440 (4 a/c), 443, 446 to 455 (10 a/c), 457 to 461 (5 a/c), 464, 466 to 470 (5 a/c), 473, 512 to 524 (13 a/c), 527, 532, 551, 555, 558, 559, 560, 562, 563, 564, TP259 to 281 (23 a/c), 288, 390 to 398 (9 a/c), 400, TZ126, 128 to 136 (9 a/c), 140, 190 to 198 (9 a/c). **July** LA284, 300 to 306 (7 a/c), NH850, 852, 853, 854, 856, PK325, 327 to 330 (4 a/c), 332, 334 to 339 (6 a/c), 343, 349, 353, 397, 399, PM550 to 555 (6 a/c), 557, 558, 562 to 565 (4 a/c), 567 to 582 (16 a/c), 596, RW350 to 354 (5 a/c), 356, 357, 358, 373, 375, 377, 378, 381, 385, 387, 391, 394, 395, 396, SL542, 545, 546, 548, 549, 550, 552, 555 to 558 (4 a/c), 560, 561, 564, 568, 571, 575 to 579 (5 a/c), 594, 595, 609, 651 to 657 (7 a/c), 660, 662 to 665 (4 a/c), 670, 671, 672, 680, 685, 688, SM927, 929, 932 to 936 (5 a/c), 939 to 949 (11 a/c), TE308, 355, 376, 377, 380, 387, 388, 401, 404, 405, 406, 435, 442, 444, 445, 456, 463, 465, 474, 475, 477, 478, 565 to 578 (14 a/c), TP282 to 287 (6 a/c), 289 to 296 (6 a/c), 298, 313 to 324 (12 a/c), 399, 401 to 408 (8 a/c), 423 to 430 (8 a/c), 432, TZ137, 139, 141 to 149 (9 a/c), 152 to 160 (9 a/c), 162. **August** LA283, 307 to 314 (8 a/c), 316, 317, PK340, 342, 344 to 348 (5 a/c), 350, 351, 352, 354, 355, 356, 370 to 373 (4 a/c), 375, 377 to 383 (7 a/c), 387, 388, 398, 401, 402, 403, 405, 406, 407, 409, 410, 482, 483, 487, 490, PM597 to 602 (6 a/c), 604, 605, RM648, RW355, 359, 384, 389, 390, 392, SL541, 543, 544, 547, 551, 553, 559, 562, 563, 565, 596, 599 to 602 (4 a/c), 608, 610, 611, 613, 614, 616, 618, 620, 622, 623, 624, 658, 659, 661, 666, 668, 669, 673, 675, 676, 678, 687, 689, 690, 713, 717, 718, 719, 721, 724, 727, 728, 733, SM930, 931, 937, 938, 950 to 953 (4 a/c), 968, 969, TE391, 436, 441, 468, TP325, 326, 327, 329, 431, 433, 434, 435, TX974 to 977 (4 a/c), TZ161, 163 to 171 (9 a/c). **September** LA190, 315, 318, 319, 320, PA979, PK341, 369, 374, 376, 385, 386, 389 to 392 (4 a/c), 400, 404, 408, 411, 412, 426 to 429 (4 a/c), 432, 433, 481, 484, 485, 486, 488, 491 to 510 (20 a/c), 512, 513, 514, 516 to 525 (10 a/c), 539, 541, 543, 544, 545, 548, 549, 553, PM603, 606 to 611 (6 a/c), 613, 627, PV290, SL554, 567, 569, 597, 681, 725, SM955, 956, 971 to 974 (4 a/c), TP328, 330, 331, 332, 335, 336, 337, 436, 437, 438, 440, TX978, 979, 981, 982, TZ172, 173, 174. **October** LA189, 214, 219, 220, 321 to 324 (4 a/c), PK430, 431, 434, 435, 511, 540, 542, 546, 550, 551, 552, 554 to 579 (26 a/c), 581, 594, 597, 599, 601, 602, 603, 605, 608 to 613 (6 a/c), 617, 621, 626, 634, PM615, 616, 618, 621, 623 to 626 (4 a/c), 634, SL573, 598, 604, 605, 615, 617, 679, 715, 720, SM975, 976, 978, 980, 982, 983, 984, 985, 987, 988, 989, TP236, 333, 338 to 341 (4 a/c), 343, 344, 345, 347, 348, 349, 363 to 367 (5 a/c), 380, 439, 441 to 444 (4 a/c), TX983, TZ175, 176, 180, 183, 199. **November** LA325 to 329 (5 a/c), PK582, 595, 596, 598, 606, 607, 615, 620, 629, PM612, 622, 628, 629, 630, 632, 633, 635, 651, 652, SM979, 981, 990, 991, 992, TP196, 214, 297, 342, 370, 377, TZ202, 204. **December** LA330, 331, PK600, 616, 619, 622, 624, 625, 628, 630 to 633 (4 a/c), 635, 649, 651 to 660 (10 a/c), 662, 664, 666 to 669 (4 a/c), 671, 672, 674, PM620, 636, 637, 653, TP195, 198 to 201 (4 a/c), 203, 204, 346, 350, 368, 369, 371, 373, 374, 375, 378, 379, 381 to 384 (4 a/c), 387, 388, 389, TZ178, 181, 182, 200, 201, 203, 205, 210, 211, 214, 217, 218, 219, 221 to 228 (8 a/c), 230.

1946 January LA193, 196, 331, PA983, PK384, 580, 614, 618, 648, 650, 661, 663, 670, 673, 676, PM654, SM843, 950, 993 to 996 (4 a/c), TP197, 202, 205, 206, 207, 209, 213, 216, 220, 374, 376, 385, 386, 445 to 448 (4 a/c), TZ212, 213, 215, 216, 220, 229, 231, 232, 234 to 240 (7 a/c). **February** LA191, PK323, 627, 677, 680, 715, SL570, 621, SM977, 997, TE479, TP208, 210, 211, 212, 217, 221 to 227 (7 a/c), 271, 449 to 452 (5 a/c), TR233. **March** RM702, RW380, TP215, 218, 219, 228, 229, 230, 232 to 235 (4 a/c), 455, 456. **April** LA217, PM658, VN301, 304, 317, 308, 309, 314. **May** PM660, VN316, 832. **June** PM661, VN315, 331. **July** VN303, 305, 310, 311, 312, 317, 319 to 323 (5 a/c), 325. **August** PM656, PK326, 682, 683, VN313. **September** PK313, 685, 689, 713, 716, 722, 725, VN327, 328. **October** LA192, PK679, 686, 687, 688, 717 to 720 (4 a/c), 724. **November** PK317, 321, 324, 678, 681, 712, 714, 721, 723, 726, VN326, 330. **December** PM659, TP454.

1947 January PK316, 325, 681, VN333, 334. **March** PK515. **May** PK315. **July** PK320. **August** VN477, 478, 480, 683, 684, 486. **September** VN481, 485, 487. **October** VN482, 489, 491. **December** PK327, VN490, 492, 493.

1948 January VN494, 495. **February** VN318. **May** VN479. **June** VN302. **July** PK333, 547. **August** VN306.

1949 April VN496.

1950 November LA188.

Records of all Seafire models were not available, but a study of the serials and histories attached to every chapter will give an indication of entry into service.

Jeffrey Quill in the Seafang.

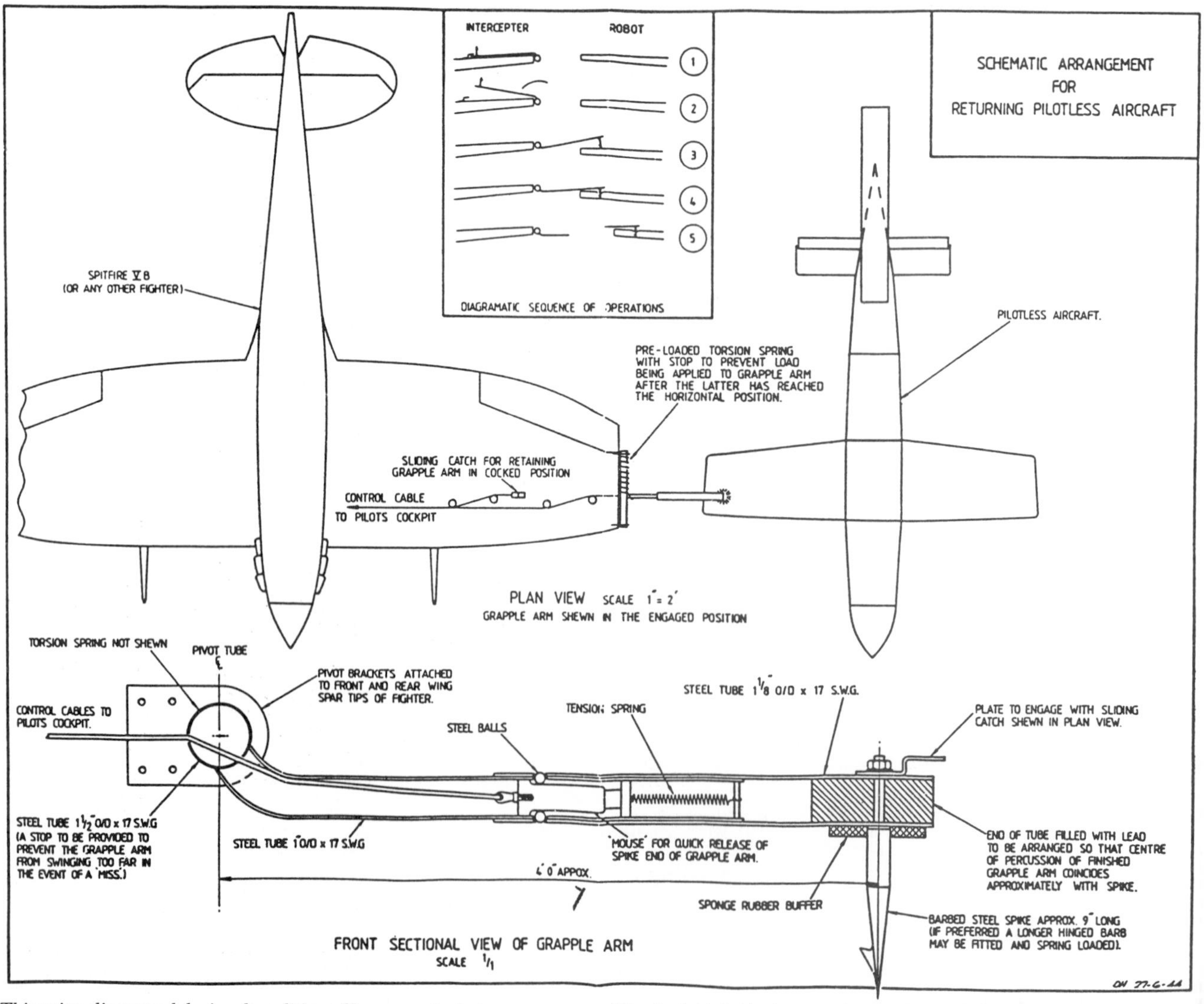

SCHEMATIC ARRANGEMENT FOR RETURNING PILOTLESS AIRCRAFT

INTERCEPTER — ROBOT — 1 2 3 4 5

DIAGRAMATIC SEQUENCE OF OPERATIONS

SPITFIRE V B (OR ANY OTHER FIGHTER)

PILOTLESS AIRCRAFT.

PRE-LOADED TORSION SPRING WITH STOP TO PREVENT LOAD BEING APPLIED TO GRAPPLE ARM AFTER THE LATTER HAS REACHED THE HORIZONTAL POSITION.

SLIDING CATCH FOR RETAINING GRAPPLE ARM IN COCKED POSITION

CONTROL CABLE TO PILOTS COCKPIT

PLAN VIEW SCALE 1" = 2'

GRAPPLE ARM SHEWN IN THE ENGAGED POSITION

TORSION SPRING NOT SHEWN

PIVOT TUBE

PIVOT BRACKETS ATTACHED TO FRONT AND REAR WING SPAR TIPS OF FIGHTER.

STEEL TUBE 1 1/8" O/D x 17 S.W.G.

CONTROL CABLES TO PILOTS COCKPIT.

TENSION SPRING

STEEL BALLS

PLATE TO ENGAGE WITH SLIDING CATCH SHEWN IN PLAN VIEW.

STEEL TUBE 1 1/2" O/D x 17 S.W.G (A STOP TO BE PROVIDED TO PREVENT THE GRAPPLE ARM FROM SWINGING TOO FAR IN THE EVENT OF A 'MISS'.)

STEEL TUBE 1" O/D x 17 S.W.G

'MOUSE' FOR QUICK RELEASE OF SPIKE END OF GRAPPLE ARM.

END OF TUBE FILLED WITH LEAD TO BE ARRANGED SO THAT CENTRE OF PERCUSSION OF FINISHED GRAPPLE ARM COINCIDES APPROXIMATELY WITH SPIKE.

4' 0" APPROX.

SPONGE RUBBER BUFFER

BARBED STEEL SPIKE APPROX. 9" LONG (IF PREFERRED A LONGER HINGED BARB MAY BE FITTED AND SPRING LOADED).

FRONT SECTIONAL VIEW OF GRAPPLE ARM

SCALE 1/1

This print, discovered during demolition of hangars at what was once part of Desford Airfield, shows a plan for fitting Spitfires with a device for capturing V1 flying bombs, turning them round and releasing them in the opposite direction. There is no record of it ever having been attempted.

INDEX

A

B

C

D

E

F

G

H

I

J

K

L

M

N

O

P

Q

R

S

SEAFIRE

T

U

V

W

Y

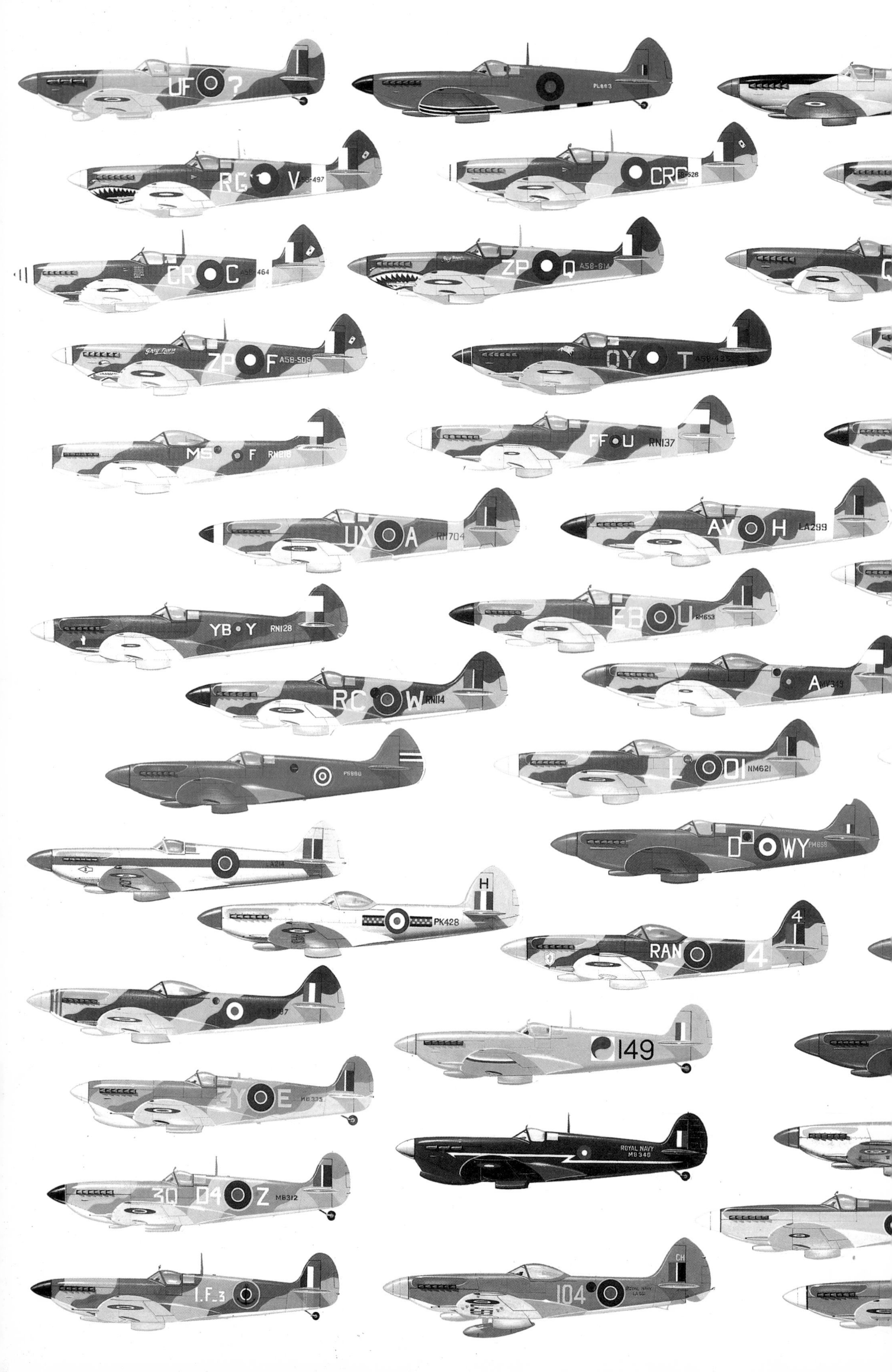